CW00970624

Praise for Travelling to Work

'The best sort of convivial read, like having a gossip with an old friend over a few drinks . . . *Travelling to Work* is a delight. It is a book you find yourself devouring in a great greedy session'   *Sunday Times*

'The life it records is so phenomenally varied . . . How he finds time to update his diary is a mystery. Update it he does though and he does so with fluency, wit, glowing affability and lightning flashes of anger . . . Weaving between observation and introspection, he comes up with a pithy phrase to describe everything from a Suffolk sunset to the end of apartheid but he sparkles most brightly when evoking the speech and the personality of his associates'   *Sunday Express*

'These diaries record an astonishingly successful career . . . Yet he never becomes objectionable; he always keeps that saving touch of everyman, if not quite Mr Pooter, a nobody . . . These diaries are remarkably good company, always dependable, never upsetting: safely enjoyable, page after page. And that's quite a triumph of tone'   *Evening Standard*

'At first you think how lucky Palin is to be living his life. Then, gradually, you see the dark side. He connects with you in a lovely way, which is very calming'   *Spectator*, 'Books of the Year'

'Filled with amusing and revealing anecdotes'   *Observer Food Monthly*

Praise for Volume I of the diaries: The Python Years

'His showbiz observations are so absorbing . . . Palin is an elegant and engaging writer'   *Guardian*

'Accomplished . . . If Palin's comic genius is a given, this is a more rounded portrait of the decade which saw the Pythons become icons. Our favourite TV explorer shows us the workings of an unstoppable machine'   *Daily Express*

'Palin's style is so fluid, and his sincerity so palpable, that it is often easy to underestimate just how talented he is as a comedian, broadcaster and a writer . . . [the diaries] are just too good and he is too modest'
                                                Sunday Express

'Delightful and often extraordinarily funny . . . An entertaining and at times deeply moving read'   *Mail on Sunday*

'If anyone writes a diary purely for the joy of it, it is Michael Palin . . . This combination of niceness, with his natural volubility, creates Palin's expansiveness'   *The Times*

'Palin's steady eye, contemplative bent and instinct for honest appraisal make him the perfect chronicler of a frequently insane period which saw the Monty Python team become the most celebrated comedians in the world'   *Time Out*

'A real delight to read'   *Saga Magazine*

'A slow burn, revealing its pleasures only gradually, and allowing readers the warm glow of hindsight denied its writer . . . This book will make the perfect present for those comedy obsessives of a certain age, who will know exactly what it is long before they have unwrapped it'
                                                Spectator

MICHAEL PALIN is a scriptwriter, comedian, novelist, television presenter, actor and playwright. He established his reputation with *Monty Python's Flying Circus* and *Ripping Yarns*. His work also includes several films with Monty Python, as well as *The Missionary, A Private Function, A Fish Called Wanda, American Friends* and *Fierce Creatures*. His television credits include two films for the BBC's *Great Railway Journeys*, the plays *East of Ipswich* and *Number 27*, and Alan Bleasdale's *GBH*.

In 2006 the first volume of his diaries, *1969–1979: The Python Years*, spent several weeks on the bestseller lists. He has also written books to accompany his eight very successful travel series: *Around the World in 80 Days* (an updated edition of which was published in 2008, twenty years later), *Pole to Pole, Full Circle, Hemingway Adventure, Sahara, Himalaya, New Europe* and *Brazil*. Most have been No 1 bestsellers and *Himalaya* was No 1 for 11 weeks. He is the author of a number of children's stories, the play *The Weekend* and the novels *Hemingway's Chair* and *The Truth*. Visit his website at www.themichaelpalin.com.

MICHAEL PALIN
DIARIES 1988-1998

Travelling to Work

WEIDENFELD & NICOLSON

A W&N PAPERBACK

First published in Great Britain in 2014
by Weidenfeld & Nicolson
This paperback edition published in 2015
by Weidenfeld & Nicolson,
an imprint of Orion Books Ltd,
Carmelite House, 50 Victoria Embankment,
London EC4Y 0DZ

An Hachette UK company

1 3 5 7 9 10 8 6 4 2

A CIP catalogue record for this book
is available from the British Library.

ISBN 978-1-7802-2532-6

Typeset by Input Data Services Ltd,
Bridgwater, Somerset

Printed in Great Britain by Clays Ltd, St Ives plc

The Orion Publishing Group's policy is to use papers that
are natural, renewable and recyclable products and made
from wood grown in sustainable forests. The logging and
manufacturing processes are expected to conform to
the environmental regulations of the country of origin.

www.orionbooks.co.uk

For Helen, Tom, Will and Rachel

*And my much missed
friend Ion Trewin, who
shared the burden of
editing all my diaries
with grace, good humour
and impeccable judgement*

Contents

List of Illustrations

With Dearbhla Molloy, Julia St John and Mike Angelis, Derbyshire, 1990 [8]

Filming *GBH* on location in Bolton, 1990 [8]

With Dan Massey on location in Ulverston, 1990 [8]

Filming *A Class Act* [9]

With Tracey Ullman on location for *A Class Act* [9]

With John Hall and Michael Hepworth at a *Pole to Pole* book-signing, Sheffield [2]

At Longueville Manor near Mallow, Ireland, 1993 [2]

With Freddie Jones, David Blount and the cast and crew of *The Dresser*, 1993 [2]

Section Three:

At the Equator on a research trip to Africa, 1994 [2]

Theatre billboard for *The Weekend*, Strand Theatre, Aldwych, 1994 [2]

With Elena Salvoni at L'Etoile, London [2]

With Lena Rustin at the Cambridge Theatre, London, 1994 [2]

With Travers Reid at the Cambridge Theatre, London, 1994 [2]

Sunday Times photo for *The Weekend,* Yvonne Arnaud Theatre, Guildford, 1993 [10]

Little Diomede Island in the Bering Strait, 1996 [3]

Turquoise lake in the Kamchatka Peninsula, eastern Russia [3]

Joining in with the Kodo drummers, Sado Island, Japan, 1995 [3]

On the Sado Island ferry [3]

Filming in the monsoon at Hue Station, Vietnam, 1995 [3]

With Iban elders, Nanga Sumpa, Sarawak, 1996 [3]

Filming during the tea harvest, Java [3]

Mount Bromo, Java [3]

Helicoptering onto the Cook Glacier, 1996 [3]

In Alcatraz, San Francisco, 1996 [3]

El Tatio geyser field, Calama, Chile [3]

Section Four:

With Robert Lindsay in *Fierce Creatures*, 1995 [2]

With Jamie Lee Curtis in *Fierce Creatures*, 1996 [2]

With Michael Powell at the National Hospital, London, 1996 [11]

The Pythons, 1989 [12]

On-stage with the Pythons at the Aspen Comedy Festival, 1998 [2]
With notebook and pen, 1996 [3]
Party on New Year's Eve, 1998 [2]
Family visit to Greenwich, Christmas 1998 [2]
With Merron and Julian Schlossberg, Nancy Lewis/Jones, Simon Jones
    and Sherrie Levy [2]
With Alan Whicker at the National Television Awards, 1998 [2]
With Spike Milligan at the Talkie Awards, 1998 [2]
With John Cleese [2]

*While every effort has been made to trace copyright holders, if any have
inadvertently been overlooked the publishers will be pleased to acknowledge them in any future editions of this work.*

1 Pankaj Shah
2 From the author's private albums
3 Basil Pao
4 Doug McKenzie
5 Mike Prior
6 David Appleby
7 Nigel Meakin
8 Sophie Baker
9 FremantleMedia
10 Tim Richmond
11 Paul Meyer, The National Brain Appeal
12 Chris Richardson

Acknowledgements

Putting together a volume of diaries is rather like assembling a car from a lot of spare parts. *Travelling to Work* would not have been roadworthy without a great deal of help. Fulsome thanks first of all to Katharine Du Prez who not only transcribed well over a million words from my hand-scribbled notebooks but was an enormous help in the long editing process. Ion Trewin painstakingly and patiently helped me reduce the text to a digestible level. Alan Samson, my editor at Weidenfeld & Nicolson, has been hugely supportive throughout and is probably the only one who knows how all the bits fit together. Paul Bird and Steve Abbott at Mayday have been, as ever, co-ordinators extraordinary. Thank you all.

Who's Who in the Diaries: 1988-1998

FAMILY

Mary Palin, mother, lived at Southwold, Suffolk. Died in 1990. Father died in 1977.
Helen, wife
Children:
  Tom born 1968
  William born 1970
  Rachel born 1975

Angela, sister. Married to **Veryan Herbert** of Chilton Hall, Sudbury, Suffolk. Died in 1987.
Children:
  Jeremy born 1960
  Camilla born 1962
  Marcus born 1963

Helen's family:
Anne Gibbins, mother
Elder sister, **Mary**, married **Edward Burd** in 1964, daughter, **Catherine**, born 1966
Younger sister, **Cathy**

FRIENDS, NEIGHBOURS AND COLLEAGUES

Clare Latimer, neighbour

Terry Jones and **Alison**

Terry Gilliam and **Maggie**

John Cleese, formerly married to **Connie Booth**, one daughter, **Cynthia**, born 1971, married **Barbara Trentham** 1981, one daughter, **Camilla**, married **Alyce Faye Eichelberger** in 1992

Graham Chapman, partner **David Sherlock. John Tomiczek** (adopted).

Eric Idle, married **Tania Kosevich** in 1981

Robert Hewison, contemporary of MP at Brasenose College, Oxford, 1962-5, during which time he persuaded MP to perform and write comedy for first time.

Simon and Phillida Albury. Simon met MP after Oxford in 1965. Television journalist, producer and Gospel music fan.

Ian and Anthea Davidson. Ian met MP at Oxford. Encouraged him to perform in revue and gave him early work at the BBC. A writer and director and occasional Python performer.

Neil and Yvonne Innes. Neil, ex-Bonzo Dog Band. Worked closely with the Pythons especially on their stage appearances. Collaborated with Eric to create the Rutles. Sons: Miles and Luke.

Mel Calman, cartoonist and friend

George Harrison, musician, ex-Beatle. Married to Olivia Arias, son Dhani, born 1978.

Derek and Joan Taylor, Beatles' publicist and wife

Chris Orr, artist and printmaker

Geoffrey Strachan, editor at Methuen who encouraged Python to go into print. Also published the *Ripping Yarns* books.

Tristram and Virginia Powell. Tristram was director/collaborator on *East of Ipswich* and *Number 27* and co-wrote and directed *American Friends.*

André Jacquemin, recording engineer, Python recordist, composer (with Dave Howman) of some Python songs. Founder of Redwood Studios.

Trevor Jones/John Du Prez, musician and composer (Python songs, *The Meaning of Life, A Private Function* and *A Fish Called Wanda*)

Ray Cooper, legendary percussionist who became important go-between and general troubleshooter on all the HandMade films.

FILM REGULARS

Richard Loncraine, film director (*The Missionary, Richard III*). First wife, Judy. Married Felice 1985.

Patrick Cassavetti, co-producer *American Friends*

John Goldstone, producer of Monty Python films – *Holy Grail*, *Life of Brian* and *Meaning of Life*

AT MAYDAY MANAGEMENT/PROMINENT FEATURES

Anne James, management

Steve Abbott, financial management. Film producer (*A Fish Called Wanda, American Friends, Fierce Creatures, Brassed Off*)

Alison Davies, secretary/assistant

Kath James, secretary/assistant

IN AMERICA

Al Levinson, writer, poet, close friend. After wife Eve's death, he married Claudie in 1979. One daughter, Gwenola.

Nancy Lewis, publicist for Python in the USA, deserves much credit for getting them on US TV in the first place. Married actor Simon Jones in 1983. One son, Timothy.

Paul Zimmerman, screenwriter (*King of Comedy*), married to Barbara

Julian Schlossberg, theatrical and film producer, distributor of *American Friends* in the USA

Michael Shamberg, co-producer of *A Fish Called Wanda* and *Fierce Creatures*. Also produced *The Big Chill* and *Pulp Fiction*, among others.

AROUND THE WORLD IN 80 DAYS, POLE TO POLE AND
FULL CIRCLE

Clem Vallance. Devised *Around the World in 80 Days* and *Pole to Pole,*
producer and director on all three series.

Roger Mills, co-director of all three series

Nigel Meakin, cameraman on first half of *80 Days*, and all of *Pole to
Pole* and *Full Circle*

Nigel Walters, cameraman on second half of *80 Days*

Ron Brown and Dave Jewitt, sound recordists on *80 Days*

Fraser Barber, sound recordist on *Pole to Pole* and *Full Circle*

Basil Pao, photographer and fellow traveller

'We're all fag ends in the gutter of life'

Frank Muir, 18 January 1990

Introduction

IN THE last entry of the last published volume of my diaries I was in my bed at home trying to salvage what sleep I could before leaving for nearly twelve weeks away on the most ambitious project I had ever got myself into.

It might well have been a dream then, the semi-wakeful fantasy of a would-be traveller who had reached his mid-forties with no great adventures to show for it. By the time this third volume of Diaries begins, it is no dream. In my first entry I'm just out of bed, washing my smalls, no longer in the comfort of my own home, but in a ship's cabin halfway down the Adriatic Sea. I'm a full four days into a very big adventure which will shape my working life for the next twenty-five years.

This volume charts my attempts to steer an often bumpy course between the emerging potential of the television traveller and the reputation as actor and writer which I'd built up over twenty-odd years of a professional life that had begun in 1965. Even as I'm crossing the oceans filming *Around the World in 80 Days,* I'm hearing snatched messages suggesting that *A Fish Called Wanda* could be the most commercially successful film I'd ever appeared in. As we struggle with the heat and grimness of the streets of Bombay, I hear that my screenplay *Number 27* is pulling in overnight figures of near to eight million on BBC One. Clear signs that this is not the time to give up on the acting and writing. At first, as these diaries reveal, I regard the travels as a diversion from my real work, and no sooner am I returning to London – seventy-nine days and seven hours after setting out in Phileas Fogg's footsteps – than I am hard at work on *American Friends,* the film based on my great-grandfather's diary, in which I was both actor and co-author. Almost simultaneously, I take on the biggest acting challenge of my life, as Jim Nelson in Alan Bleasdale's *GBH*.

The early years of these diaries reveal the roller-coaster ride as I try to hold three careers together. I can't quite believe I took on so much, and many of the entries remind me how the doubts substantially out-weighed the delights. By the mid 1990s my head was above water and I was breathing a little more normally. My confidence, and my bank balance, boosted by good numbers on *Around the World* and *Pole to Pole*, I began to take faltering steps in completely new directions. One was to fulfil a long-standing desire to write a novel, and the other to try and make a go of my stage play, *The Weekend*. The creative chicanes I had to negotiate on both these projects flung me all over the place, and the birth pangs of *The Weekend* in 1994 and *Hemingway's Chair* in 1995 find me confiding my insecurities to the diary more and more. I make no apology for exposing my doubts and fears. After all, as has often been said, you learn more from failure than from success. And diaries can be raw and emotional places, unsanitised by historical perspective.

It became increasingly obvious to me during these years that I was addicted to travel and there was no point in resisting the lure of map and atlas. Not only had the books and programmes been well received, but my tolerant wife didn't try to stop me signing up again. Indeed, rather suspiciously, she encouraged it. Thus, *Full Circle*, the circumnavigation of the Pacific Rim, was born in 1996. It was the longest and most ambitious of the adventures so far, and did not altogether run a smooth course as my wife had to undergo a brain operation whilst I was on the far side of the world. I kept a little of my old life alive playing film comedy again as the head of the insect house in *Fierce Creatures*, John Cleese's long-awaited, long-delayed follow-up to *A Fish Called Wanda*.

As this current volume comes to an end I am still wandering off in all directions: trying my hand at an arts documentary, toying with a second novel, attempting to distil my interest in Hemingway into a book or a film, being seduced, once again, by Hollywood. This is the rough-and-ready, on-the-spot account of a fundamentally wary and conservative soul, drawn to risk like a moth to a flame. Someone who's convinced that his gut instinct is more important than all the advice in the world. Someone grounded and safe who can be tempted into almost anything.

The great journeys which underpin these diaries make me realise, more clearly than ever before, that I don't like to be confined to the main road ahead, that I'm drawn to the backstreets and the side alleys, to the quirky ordinariness of everyday life, to the unexpected and the unexplored. When I'm not travelling I experience something very similar. As soon as life looks predictable, or secure or straightforward, I hop off to one side, lured by whatever it is I've never done before.

All the entries were written at my home in London, unless otherwise indicated.

MICHAEL PALIN
London, 2014

Those looking for full accounts of the three journeys, Around the World in 80 Days, Pole to Pole *and* Full Circle, *which I undertook during the decade covered by these diaries, will find them in the published books of the same name. I shall not attempt to repeat them here. However, in all three of these adventures I kept scribbled notes of more private thoughts, often little more than quick sketches or anxieties mulled over late at night. They're irregular, quite brief, and not all of them have survived, but occasionally their immediacy touches on a raw nerve that reminds me how I really felt as I travelled the world.*

This first selection from these 'private' travel diaries begins four days out of England on Around the World in 80 Days, *as the full impact of what I've embarked on begins to hit home.*

1988

Wednesday, September 28th: Aboard Espresso Egitto *on the Adriatic*

I've just got up, washed two pairs of socks and pants and considered what to wear for the day. As we have shots that are continuity with last night, I have to settle for the trousers I've worn since leaving London on Sunday morning and my second shirt of the voyage.

The sea is calm, my cabin, which is one of the more comfortable, has two beds alongside each other and a shower and loo. A porthole looks onto the deck and a lifeboat hangs above.

The journey has been fast and furious until now. Yesterday we were up and filming at first light in Venice – we left the city yesterday evening.

I still find the nights a problem. Last night I slept six hours, but that was with the help of a pill which I took in a panic about two. I swear not to take them again except in extremis. They do so little anyway.

Occasionally the realisation that this whole project is supported on my shoulders and demands not just my survival but my wit, energy, exuberance and enthusiasm quite terrifies me. It is going to be a supreme test, and now, only onto my fourth day and feeling low on all levels, I just can't contemplate the same continuing for two and a half more months.

But I'm determined to pull this off. Failure is unthinkable.

Thursday, September 29th: Espresso Egitto

It's nearly one o'clock and clear skies outside over the Saronian Gulf. We've just completed the quite dramatic navigational feat of the passage of the Corinth Canal – a man-made gorge it took us an hour to pass through.

Feel in good spirits today after a long sleep.

Phone Helen after breakfast and, despite the crew crouching and filming every word, it is one of our better phone calls and Helen sounds clear and very pleased to hear me – and surprised too. I don't think she'd expected a call from the ship.

These boat journeys will, I think, be a necessary interlude between periods of intense rush and activity.

The crew of the boat are treating us nobly, though I suspect they could turn ugly if they're not enjoying themselves. Today I got up in my *Adriatica* T-shirt, which pleased them – I was promptly given a sailor's hat.

It's hot outside now – the scrub-covered mountains of Greece are all around. Glad of the air-conditioning on the *Egitto*.

Friday, September 30th: Espresso Egitto

This boat trip has been restorative. I'm eager and receptive to places – especially glad I stirred myself from bed this morning to run into Heraklion. I don't suffer, as yet, from seasickness or homesickness.

Fears about my adequacy for the journey persist. I don't think now that I shan't make it, as I did that gloomy first morning on the *Egitto* – my worries now are what I shall make out of it.

My style is friendly, humorous and laid-back. It isn't best suited for revealing things about people – whose right to privacy I respect, as I would want them to respect mine. How much of the time should I be acting?

Saturday, October 1st: Espresso Egitto

Slept fitfully until finally rising at 6.20 to watch us approach Alexandria.

A thorough break with Europe, which I suppose could have been disturbing, but which I find exhilarating and energising. So the day dazzles and everything, all the hard work and the rushing around from location to location and city to city, encourages and stimulates me.

All we need at the end of our first week is sleep. We've filmed well and interestingly on the whole – though it is hard to get people on camera to be as easygoing and informative and anecdotal as they are off.

Sunday, October 2nd: Cairo

Sour taste of tourism at the Pyramids, and back to film two interviews in the bar of the Windsor[1] (where many stars of Egyptian theatre and

1 The Windsor Hotel. Eccentric city-centre hotel. The air-con unit was noisier than the traffic outside. 'I now know why they laughed at me when I'd asked for a quiet room' (*Around the World in 80 Days*).

opera gather!). Conscious of asking easy questions, not probing enough, being almost too respectful. Always after the interview I think of the one question I should have asked.

Monday, October 3rd: Suez

Seven o'clock at the Red Sea Hotel – the silence outside on the straight, empty avenues is quite a shock after Cairo. So is the hot water, even though it's only a shower – no bath since Venice. The room is quite characterless and depressing, as is Suez. Can't wait to get on a boat tomorrow and get moving.

This morning we completed various shots in and around the hotel and I didn't have to go out. As in New York City, one has to be fit and strong to go out into the streets of Cairo, and a two-hour lay-off in the morning to write cards and ring the office was much needed and appreciated. *Wanda* is over 50 million in the States now. [The film *A Fish Called Wanda* had been released in the USA on July 15th.] Terry J starts *Erik the Viking* in Malta on the 19th.

The journey by taxi to Suez was pretty grim. The heat, dust, traffic and fumes of Cairo for the first half-hour were as uncomfortable as anything I've experienced so far on the trip. Once out of Cairo we were in desert – relics of war, barracks and endless rubbish tips.

The hotel is dry and we're all meeting at 7.30 to seek out a place for beer.

Wednesday, October 5th: Aboard the Saudi Moon 2,[1] on the Red Sea

As of today the journey has become quite an adventure. Information reaching us from Jeddah indicates that all our options must be reconsidered. I might have to drive across Arabia – but our visas, we think, confine us to Jeddah. I may be dropped from a container boat to go ashore at Muscat, or we may be in Jeddah for four or five days, losing precious time.

The Arab world was always to be the most difficult, Clem Vallance[2]

---

1 Danish-built ferry. Her sister ship, the *Saudi Moon 1*, ran aground and sank on a reef near Jeddah. The *Saudi Moon 2* caught fire and sank in May 1994 with the loss of nine lives.
2 Deviser and co-director of *Around the World in 80 Days*.

had warned. Even he is now lost for answers. So we move on a rolling sea towards Jeddah and uncertainty on a considerable scale. It will be very hot, we shall have our patience tested to the limits, and we shall have to work a hard and long day.

What's more, we have been eleven travelling and filming days in succession and a day off would be an orgasmic pleasure. None beckons. Add to this poor food on the boat and a delicate situation in my stomach. Still, thanks to Allah – *Insh-Allah!* – it'll be the longest time I've been without alcohol for decades!

Out on deck as I write (10 p.m.) are sleeping, like corpses, hundreds of Egyptian workers, many of whom are leaving everything behind for a year or more.

Friday, October 7th: Red Sea Palace Hotel, Jeddah, Saudi Arabia

Day 13, country number 9. Outside my fourth-floor windows to the left it is a modern cityscape that looks back at me, dual carriageways, roundabouts, traffic moving in plenty of space, tall, featureless concrete high-rise clusters. Move a little to my left, say, to pick up an apple from the complimentary basket, and I look down on a beleaguered, ill-kempt quarter of older houses, four storeys at most with balconies of wood and screens and carved details about the windows.

First thing to be said about Jeddah is that it has been a rest and renewal stop. Our arrival on an uncluttered dockside, even our efficient clearance through customs, thanks to Ahmed and the presence of young Nick from the embassy in Riyadh, was much less of a strain than doing anything in Egypt.

The hotel – affluent, international, but really conforming to American standards of comfort and service – may be nothing to do with the real Saudi Arabia, but it has provided hot water and a bath and space and service and laundry and room to move and gather wits.

Sunday, October 9th: Riyadh

It's 8.30, dazzlingly bright outside and two weeks since I left home on a grey, London autumn morning. Ironically, here in the middle of the Arabian desert, I find myself in surroundings as familiar, comfortable and un-foreign as I've known in those two weeks. English businessmen and English voices downstairs in the lobby of the Al-Khozama, and in the breakfast room croissants and coffee almost as good as any I might have been sharing with Rachel two or three weeks ago.

Perhaps that's why I woke with an unspecifically dissatisfied feeling. Not about the travel, which I'm thoroughly enjoying and responding to, but about this sort of place – it's like America. In my *Arabian Nights*-led imagination it's an exotic, romantic location on the map, but the reality is depressing. Neon bursting out everywhere, buildings everywhere. Commerce and no culture, except the Islamic culture which the West doesn't really seem to want to know about. Cairo was grottier, but it moved me, made me think.

Tuesday, October 11th: InterContinental Hotel, Dubai

Midway through our second day in Dubai. Very hot this morning as we filmed at the dhow-builders – 110 in the sun – sweat poured off us. I took the opportunity for a run this morning, half an hour from 7.45, along the waterfront, past dhows loading, past the small, wood-hulled boats ferrying people to work across the creek, past ancient, wafer-thin old gentlemen in white robes who remind me of my mother.

A pleasant, cosmopolitan scene – Indian, Pakistani faces and Iranians and Syrians, African faces and Semitic faces, fat noses and long, beaky noses. Dull eyes, frightened eyes and calculating eyes.

I've now run three times since we left and would like to have done more, but feel in good shape still and fit for tomorrow's real adventure – the dhow trip.

From tomorrow we have a week in another world, one much simpler and more rugged than our own. Instead of bending them to us (as places like the InterContinental Hotel do), we shall have to bend to them.[1]

1 The journey on the MV *Al Shama*, a dhow carrying goods from Dubai to Bombay, took us seven nights and eight days. We had no radio, radar or GPS and the crew consisted of eighteen Gujaratis, all from the same village in north-west India, only one of whom spoke English. The friendships I struck up with the crew over that agonisingly slow week convinced me that, from then on, it was to be the encounters with ordinary people that I felt most comfortable with and which seemed to produce the best television. A formula that was to hold true through my next seven travel series. In 2008 we returned to India to try and find the crew of *Al Shama*. We found many of them in the dhow-building port of Mandvi in Kutch. We sat down together and watched the journey we made twenty years earlier.

Wednesday, October 19th: Taj Hotel, Bombay

It's late – 11.45. Later, by several hours, than I've been to bed for the last seven days. I feel a slight tiredness in the eyes, an ache, otherwise well. Have eaten today for the first time since my stomach turned on Sunday night. My bags are open and airing, laundry is being done, I'm spread out and reordering my life in this disorderly city after seven days and nights on the dhow.

The experience was unique. Never have I been in a situation where, for so long, I depended upon a group of people quite different from me in wealth, class, race, religion and circumstance. All of us unequivocal in our appreciation of the crew from Gujarat.

How I shall sleep without the stars and the sea remains to be seen.

Thursday, October 20th: Bombay

The end of my first night in Bombay. Post-dhow euphoria dissipated.

I realise in the unblinking light of the morning sunshine that I have days ahead as hard, in their way, as any dhow journey. There's not a day off as we record Bombay, the overnight train and Madras.

I must rise to it all. There's no way one can retreat from the demands of India, no way one can do it on the defensive. Unshaven, unrested and uncomfortable, I must up and face the day and hope I shall pull through. The next five or six days are the most testing of the whole journey.

Friday, October 21st: Bombay

Bombay is the most difficult place to film yet. The people who stare at camera, the dripping humidity, the extraordinary locations – today in amongst grinding poverty watching a mongoose driven to draw blood from a snake. It is wearing us all down. Roger [Mills, one of our two directors] drives us gently, considerately, but persistently on.

Monday, October 24th: Connemara Hotel, Madras

Thirty days have gone. We've been through twelve countries, spent two nights on trains, 13 nights on boats, including seven on an open dhow, and I've slept in 13 different beds since we left London. We've recorded our progress daily, on film, tape and in notebooks. Though there are still 50 days available, I think, on paper, the worst is over. Only six more countries to pass through, and 28 days and nights will be spent at sea.

Hopefully we have more than half of the series already shot. My contribution, I think, will not be precision, analysis and revelation, but honesty, directness, openness and enthusiasm. I hope I reflect the fact that anything can happen on a journey if you allow it to.

Is this enough? I think of seeing all this through Jonathan Miller's and Alan Bennett's and Terry Gilliam's eyes and how much sharper and more original it might all be. But the fact is I have the easy, untroubled character that will, I hope, make me an interesting victim rather than a cool observer.

As of midday on Day 30, at the Connemara in Madras, in my room which was once in the summer palace of the Nawabs of Wallajah, I feel I've achieved something.

Sunday, October 30th: Aboard Susak,[1] *Bay of Bengal*

It's a Sunday and Sundays seem to be the days most susceptible to the stirrings of homesickness. And today aboard the *Susak* I have time on my hands. We've filmed most of our sequences over the last three days of the voyage, so, at the time of writing – 9.20 in the morning – I'm on my bed in the sickroom with the indistinct but mountainous skyline of Great Nicobar Island on the port horizon, nearly a thousand miles from Madras and with two and a half more days' sailing down the busy shipping lanes of the Malacca Strait until we reach Singapore. So, plenty of time to think.

It was a Sunday, too, when I last saw the family, five weeks ago. Five weeks doesn't sound much to me now. Can all that we've done and seen and recorded thus far have taken less than half our scheduled time? All this to go through again and still not be home?

Allied to these thoughts comes the image of Rachel following my progress, pinning up another of my postcards and, I realise, with a guilty and inadequate feeling, that it's Rachel I miss most, because, in a sense, I'm sure she misses me most. All of this quite unfair on Helen, but then

1 The *Susak* was a Yugoslav freighter chartered by Bengal Tiger Lines to transport goods between Calcutta, Madras and Singapore. They could take only two of us, so Nigel went aboard with the camera and I was handed the sound equipment. We were quartered in the ship's hospital.

she's been through it before and she has such a well-organised support system of friends and activities.

What I do know, and what keeps me from ever feeling desperately sorry for myself, is that the journey is, at every stage, remarkable and memorable. I shall never travel like this again, I shall never see so much so quickly, and when I am home and with the family again, I shall miss moments like this, in the hospital bay of a Yugoslav container boat, crossing the Bay of Bengal with the coast of Great Nicobar Island coming closer, and I shall feel sick for travel – as potently as I ever feel sick for home.

Tuesday, November 1st: Susak

It's just after nine in the morning. I sit on deck writing at the table at which we enjoyed the great barbecue party on Sunday. Today the weather is markedly different. Skies are grey and the air is sticky, warm and humid.

Last night was my sixth night in the hospital with Nigel and it was a night of doubts and broken sleep.

Should I be doing this programme? Am I the right man for the job? Should I not be extending my acting and writing skills? Have I not taken a journey round the world as a convenient way of avoiding other career decisions?

As we move slowly by sea, I have plenty of time to think. I'm better when we're on the move, working fast. But I have to face a lot more of this slack-paced travel in the next few weeks and maybe good will come of it … insights will be revealed.

Thursday, November 3rd: Aboard the Neptune Diamond,[1] *South China Sea, Singapore to Hong Kong*

Forty days out of London: quite a landmark. We're currently in 'moderate swell' for the first time since the English Channel, but the wind has grown over the last 24 hours to a Force 7, heading almost straight at us, out of the north, so outside my yellow-carpeted suite with its all-plastic bathroom and yellow flower-pattern chair cover with plaid/gathered fringes, there is a spectacular seascape.

[1] The *Neptune Diamond* was a container ship owned by Neptune Orient Lines.

All of a sudden the sea that has been for so long our firm, friendly, cosseting and encompassing supporter is agitated with ridges of water flying before the wind and smashing against the side of the ship, sending columns of spray high into the sky and waves upturning themselves against the wall and somersaulting backwards to crash back on the next wave, propelling a boiling white wash a hundred yards out to sea.

Sunday, November 6th: Peninsula Hotel, Hong Kong

Yesterday my bag strap broke as I stepped off the *Neptune Diamond* gangplank. Now it's mended, thanks to the Peninsula's expertise. This morning the task I have to set them is to try and plug the holes in my trousers which a parrot made in an unprovoked attack on yesterday's visit to the Bird Market. Well, all right, I had asked the parrot if he knew John Cleese.

Friday, November 11th: Aboard the Jian Zhen[1] between Shanghai and Yokohama

We're four and a half hours out of Shanghai at the mouth of the Yangtze River. The whirlwind week in Hong Kong and China is over, tiredness overcome by the fascination with what I was seeing. A sore throat has been threatening for two or three days.

In my cabin, and sipping the first of my three-day course of Chinese reinvigoration medicine – bought at the shop in Shanghai.

Clem has declared tomorrow a day off.

Saturday, November 12th: On the Jian Zhen

Second day off out of 49. It's welcome, of course, but I'm not terribly good at days off. I catch up with the experiences of the last extraordinary week – notebooks edited and clarified, tapes numbered. I'm glad to rest this niggling sore throat. Treat it to another Disprin gargle after lunch, which relieves, but the air-conditioning's no help.

I have one of the brown parcels of Chinese medicine and, at the time of writing (6.30), feel pretty good. Drew the curtains across and lay

---

1 Once-weekly ferry between Shanghai and Yokohama. A connection we couldn't afford to miss.

and listened to Billy Joel and Pat Metheny and emptied my mind for a couple of hours.

A month tomorrow I'm due home. Light at the end of the tunnel. Will be difficult to keep up the momentum with 19 of the next 31 days on board ship – hard to work feeling the hard work has been done.

Must resist temptation to regard it as over.

Tuesday, November 15th: Tokyo

In bed in the pristine, antiseptic whiteness of the Akasaka Prince Hotel.

Maybe now we're in more controlled, familiar Western environments we'll have to strain harder to find the original material which was all around us in India, Cairo and the Bay of Bengal. (I'm now at the stage where I feel deep pangs of nostalgia for those early days.)

Have made the phone contacts I have to when in the big cities – spoken to Tom who's been sea-cliff climbing in Cornwall, Helen and Ma, whom I got out of the bath.

Thursday, November 17th: On board MV Neptune Garnet,[1] on the Pacific

Safely out of Tokyo Bay at half past eleven. The last night in Tokyo not as bad as I feared. The karaoke bar was very lively and silly and the Japanese there were very courteous. Many autographs were handed out. I think they just accepted I was a television star of some sort, even though they had no clue what I did.

But I sang 'You Are My Sunshine' and it didn't feel embarrassing at the time, though I'm sure it will when I watch it sober. When I finished there was much orchestrated applause from the young Japanese, who chanted 'Eng-land! Eng-land!' just as enthusiastically as they had chanted 'Nip-pon! Nip-pon!' half an hour earlier.

When the chant changed to 'Thatch-er! Thatch-er!' we entered the realms of Grand Surrealism.

---

1 Another container ship, sister to the *Neptune Diamond*. Indian captain and largely Singaporean crew. It took us twelve days to cross the Pacific, but it took Phileas Fogg almost three weeks, so we caught up valuable time on the *Garnet*.

Saturday, November 19th: Neptune Garnet

Back in from a run along the deck. Reckon I covered about 10,000 metres altogether up and down the 250-metre starboard gangway beneath the groaning, screaming and today even trumpeting containers – Pacific swelling beneath me, puffing itself up and heaving our 42,000 tons about with contemptuous ease.

Another squally front is chasing up on us from the south-west, so I'm running between last night's gale and the one that's coming.

Somewhere halfway round the world (for once the cliché is permissible as we approach 170°), William is waking up to his eighteenth birthday. I rang and talked to him from Tokyo and wished him well for his exams, which he takes on the 21st – the day I have twice!

Wish I was at home – either to console or celebrate, as well as to be a sounding board if necessary. Feel I'm somehow missing a vital time in his life. But this is traveller's melodrama, I think.

Sunday, November 20th: Neptune Garnet

Bingo evening. The captain takes these particularly seriously and buys blocks of five tickets (one Singapore Dollar per ticket) each game. This strains the concentration, but between myself and the long-haired, pebble-glassed, slightly manic second cook and steward win five dollars from five cards.

This morning the engines were shut down to repair a leak in a pipe, which gave me a restful lie-in until 9.15. But I could not really relax – the weight of the project still hangs round my neck sometimes, feeling like the albatross that Nigel Walters [cameraman on this second leg of the journey] claims he's seen off the stern, following us.

The storm and an early call (6.30) to film the moment of crossing into the Western Hemisphere is bad enough – but there's also the promise of a wholly unlooked-forward-to 'initiation' ceremony to mark such a crossing. This is said to involve ugly humiliations such as daubing with emulsion paint and drinking some foul liquid. It'll be hard to make it funny, graceful or, really, anything other than humiliating. And as I'm being thus daubed, my son will be taking his Oxford exam!

Monday, November 21st: Neptune Garnet

A first, and probably a last, for the diary. An extra, untitled day. It's not yet the 22nd, but we've already had the 21st, so it's called the 21st again. 'It will be Monday again tomorrow,' as Jason announced solemnly on the PA last night.

Rose about a quarter to eleven and made a cup of coffee and went up to the bridge. The officers were tracing a strange, zigzag course on the map table and only after a while I realised they were marking out a crown for tomorrow's Crossing the Line ceremony. At one point it was tried out on a sheepish electrical engineer. It looked fairly ludicrous against his oily blue overalls.

The wind has shifted to the north today and is cooler, also I think the chief engineer has put on the air-conditioning, after I mentioned to the captain yesterday that it was becoming unbearably fuggy in the cabins. The captain is extraordinarily solicitous and sensitive to our needs. He's lent me his dictionary for Scrabble, and this morning, as we passed a westbound Filipino freighter pitching and taking on water, he ran through the whole of his phone call to the other boat twice, so that we could record it.

Thursday, November 24th: Neptune Garnet

Mid-morning, Day 61, ninth day on the Pacific. Our position is 38.09 N and 138.44 W. Our speed 20.2 knots. A wind from the north-west, Force 6–7, flecks the sea with flying spray.

Everything that could slide about, slid about last night and glasses smashed in the day room. Roger's room developed a squeak he could never track down and our PA Ann's chair broke loose and shot across her cabin with a crash they heard up on the bridge.

I slept badly, as did everyone else. Up a mile one minute and slithering down the next. I would nod off only to be woken by a swingeing change to my centre of gravity, or the sticky heat of the airless cabin, or backache from the awkward, semi-foetal position I'd concertinaed my body into.

But the journey is accelerating. At the time of writing, *Neptune Garnet* is 1,000 miles away from California and 4,000 from Tokyo.

Sunday, November 27th: The Queen Mary, *Long Beach*[1]

After six hours' sleep and the first call home for nearly two weeks, I was up and out with the crew to Venice Beach. A glorious morning. Hockney weather. Our amazing luck with good weather on land and some attractively bad weather at sea continues.

We filmed human robots and Muscle Beach and all the activity against a bright blue sky. I walked beside the Pacific, at the very limit of America, and we were all very happy when we bought some champagne and white wine and set off for the party at Michael Shamberg's [Michael was one of the producers of *A Fish Called Wanda*].

I'd been nervous of this for some time. Its genesis came from a rather abrupt demand from Clem, when I was in my anxious pre-karaoke bar phase in Japan, to 'ring one of your friends in Los Angeles and get them to organise a Thanksgiving party'.

We rolled up Mandeville Canyon in our two hire cars – Nigel W driving myself and Roger.

Guests arrived. All were quite bewildered and no-one seemed quite sure what was going on.

A phone call from London and it's Cleese. I'd not been told that he was being recorded in the next room (the whole thing had been prepared without my knowing), nor did I realise he'd been tipped off I'd be here. So, poor bugger, he and I groped for laughs and wit whilst the light went and Nigel could hardly see my face.

Then, when the light had truly gone, Jamie [Lee Curtis] arrived. Michael kept asking about how much sex I'd had on the journey and the whole thing felt a huge effort. 'Was that an awful strain?' the Professor (aka Roger Mills) asked as we pulled away from the house, soon after five.

I'm now back in the slightly ridiculous environment of the *Queen Mary*. We've had three beers, sitting in the Art Deco bar, with its naughty mural of a cross-section of English society doing a linked-hands dance (by Thomson, 1936), and repair to our staterooms for an early night.

1 Transatlantic liner, former flagship of the Cunard Line. Following her retirement in 1967 she was permanently moored at Long Beach, California as a tourist attraction and hotel.

Saturday, December 3rd: Rensselaer, New York State

It's ten-thirty on a bright, clear morning and our Chicago–New York train is being split between the Boston and the Grand Central sections. Across the River Hudson, about a half a mile away, is the skyline of Albany.

I have just been filmed getting up and have already improvised a jokey feet-washing sequence (Nigel Walters is game for filming anything).

I've been filmed for 68 out of the last 70 days. This time tomorrow we shall, hopefully, be at sea – on the Atlantic, heading for Europe.

Now, as the Good Lord offers a last splendid day to remember America by, I shall watch Albany slide away to the north-west and enjoy the Hudson view. Very content. Not much more to do, so I'm now beginning to worry about what we've done! Suddenly all the talk is of editing.

Tuesday, December 6th: Aboard Leda Maersk[1] on the Atlantic

A good sequence sailing from Newark, past Liberty, Manhattan and out under the Verrazano-Narrows Bridge at dawn on Sunday, and deck shots and a fine Atlantic sunset the same day. We have filmed Lillian cutting my hair and some strange effects of steaming ocean yesterday.

But it's as if we're all, at last, repeating ourselves. Container ship life is much the same, except that it's less of an adventure on the *Maersk* than on the *Garnet*. The weather is grey, damp, but the sea quite restful.

The presence of J. P. Moller, son of the founder of Maersk, hangs balefully over the ship. Jesper [the company rep] speaks of him with reverence, respect and awe. When Jesper says 'he rules with an iron hand' I believe it.

So the more easygoing, down-to-earth atmosphere of the *Garnet* is missing here. The captain is a very jolly seaman and has little time for the bureaucrats, but he too seems inhibited by the head-office presence.

So we wait as the last days slowly and anti-climatically pass. My cold streams out, the sun is gone, *Bonfire of the Vanities*[2] is, at last, a book I want to read and isn't too demanding. I check my diary notes and

---

1 Container ship owned and operated by the Danish company Maersk Lines.
2 Tom Wolfe's best-selling novel set in 1980s New York had been published a year earlier.

drink coffee and contemplate some exercise on deck in an hour or so. I've ironed three shirts and we've had a telex to the effect that all Pacific rushes were excellent.

Friday, December 9th: Leda Maersk

So here I am, almost home and reflecting back. I certainly haven't been through a Gilbert Pinfold ordeal,[1] as in the early, hectic days in the heat of Greece and Cairo I imagined I might. In fact, far from throwing me into a bewildering world of unreality and causing my reason to waver, I think that the journey has, in a way, calmed and settled me. It's been much nearer to sanity than the phone-ringing, celebrity-conscious world I left at home.

As I ran beside the sea today, for the last time, with wind buffeting, albeit gently, and tugging at the tops of the waves, I felt how fond I've become of the sea. I have grown to respect it, and I feel soothed by its motion and its presence. I looked around me for 360°, nothing in sight, a wide horizon – 15 to 20 miles away – only sea and sky.

There was no noise, except for the throb of the engines and the swish of the water and the flapping of the wind. I shall miss that in the car alarm, police siren, drunken singing, car-skidding 'reality' of London at Christmas.

I have had a lot of time to think about myself and wonder how I've measured up.

I know there are people much better at this than I am. I like people and I want to be liked by them, so I have to make an effort to be the inquisitor. I prefer when travelling to take in what's outside by myself, privately, and I respect the same privacy for other people. This makes it difficult to grab people and interrogate them.

Also I find the camera and microphone, even when wielded by considerate and friendly souls like Nigel and Dave and Ron, an embarrassing intrusion. Not always – sometimes people love to talk, can't wait to talk. But to me, confronting someone with a camera crew is like shining a torch on them in the night.

I feel, for better or worse, that the best way I could make a contribution

---

1 *The Ordeal of Gilbert Pinfold* was a 1957 novel by Evelyn Waugh, autobiographical in inspiration, about a Roman Catholic writer who mixes drugs and alcohol and is verging on a nervous breakdown. Much of the narrative is on a sea voyage taken by Pinfold as a cure.

to the project was to be natural throughout – but going around the world with a film crew isn't a natural thing to do and this is where I've come a little unstuck. I try to be me, I try to be as natural as possible, and yet time and again I have to act. Either look happy when I'm bored, or interested when I'm tired, or enthusiastic when I'm feeling ready to quit.

I can act – I can act characters of all sorts till the cows come home – but I can't act me.

Monday, December 12th

Back at home. As I write it's 9.30 in the morning on Tuesday 13th and my 80 days are up. In fact I was at the Reform Club at 4.45 yesterday evening, having completed the journey with 17 hours to spare.

Extraordinary luck with the weather continued, the Channel was calm as a millpond and the sun rose off Felixstowe yesterday in a cloudless sky. But it was a tetchy, awkward last filming day.

We progressed slowly – by container truck to Felixstowe Station, then, after a long wait in a hotel bar full of old ladies with cigarettes and scotch and sodas, to Ipswich.

All too predictable was the British Rail steward's apology for lunch – 'We've got no chef and no food, but we can give you afternoon tea.' So we had afternoon tea and were taken at a commendable rate up to Liverpool Street. We picked our way through the wreckage of the reconstruction and down to the Underground.

All proceeded satisfactorily as far as Tottenham Court Road, where a terse announcement warned us not to alight from the train as there was a 'suspected parcel' and the station had been sealed off. Hurried on to Oxford Circus, and I was filmed on the escalator and way out.

A newspaper seller refused to be filmed and was abusive. The passers-by looked drab and poorly dressed. We moved, filming, down Regent Street. Nearly everyone we asked about filming was obstructive or, at least, defensive, and by the time we reached the Reform Club we were all tired out.

We were not allowed to film in the Reform Club, capping a very bad day for Britain. A meanness and a defensiveness and a fearful surliness marked our return. But our little crew are as good a bunch as you could ever find and we shook hands on the steps outside 104 Pall Mall to seal our achievement.

What do I feel? The usual euphoria of arrival. Reintroducing myself to the once-familiar, rediscovering my old life from a new perspective. I don't feel regret or nostalgia for the great journey – we did it and we'll never forget it.

The house is being painted, or has been painted, inside. The bathroom is being redone. Helen has worked incredibly hard.

My room is full of envelopes, full of the old life, which I shall ease myself into slowly.

Tuesday, December 13th

I think I couldn't have timed my eleven weeks off any better, especially as later, ploughing through two and a half months of press cuttings, it's clear that my profile at home has never been higher. *Wanda* – already at £8 million after eight weeks' release – then the much-publicised and generally admired *Number 27*,[1] TV showings of *And Now, Time Bandits* and *Meaning of Life* and the tenth anniversary of HandMade have had the hacks raking through the Palin files, and my name and photo is all over the place, all spiced by the fact that I couldn't be there because I was filming six documentaries for the BBC.

So I manage to give the impression of being successful, in great demand and, most admirable of all – not available! There's a lesson there somewhere.

Wednesday, December 14th

To Hampstead Heath for first run since the first day of autumn. Wet leaf smell and a chilly edge to the air. Find the hills hard – realise that all my exercise on the journey was generally on the flat – once we passed the Alps there was no mountain scenery until the Rockies.

Much sorting-out of letters and offers. A quartet of interesting documentary prospects. *The Shape of the Earth,* a big Granada spectacular about the people who mapped the world, a 'By-Line' on transport, an examination of a British city. All enticing, but no time left for most of next year.

Then by cab to see Terry Gilliam's *Munchausen*. The cab driver has a sign up saying he's training in Chinese medicine and if any of his

1 My second film for the BBC directed, like *East of Ipswich*, by Tristram Powell, with whom I went on to make *American Friends*.

passengers can spare a minute, he'd like to take their pulse, as he has to have taken 600 pulses at least by the end of the week.

So in Goodge Street, he solemnly gets into the back of the taxi and takes my left- and right-hand pulse. 'You'll live a long time,' he pronounces cheerfully and off I go to the Columbia viewing theatre in Wells Street, passing my likeness in the UIP window on the corner, permed head poking up from a group of fellow *Wanda* stars.

The movie begins like *Time Bandits* – an eighteenth-century city torn apart by war, caught in the middle of chaos. Indeed it reminds me of *Time Bandits* too often. There are cinematic fireworks and magnificent set pieces, but the whole misses the binding of a strong story. There is an emotional involvement lacking.

John Neville is quite superb as Munchausen – old-fashioned acting, with dignity, gravity, humour, charm all portrayed effortlessly.

Thursday, December 15th

Joe, keen Telecom engineer, brings round new telephone receiver, which can be used without picking it up. Very strange feeling, speaking into the air! Will receivers eventually become redundant, like appendixes?

Into the West End for the second time since return. Northern and Victoria Lines to Green Park. Everything still benefiting from the glow of rediscovery.

Meet Tristram [Powell] at Green's Oyster Bar (he chose it as he said I'd probably have had enough 'ethnicity' for a while). We talk over smoked eel, dressed crab and champagne.

American Friends [the film project based on the story of my great-grandparent] has not progressed much further.

Out into Duke Street, St James's, at the sober hour of 3.15. 'It's still light!' exclaims Tristram, with some disappointment. Buy a book of work by Atkinson Grimshaw at Thomas Heneage, where the young assistants jest amongst themselves.

Then back home, reading a film script by Robert Jones on the way. Don't think I want to do it, but flattered I'm still offered parts for men in their 30s.

Call Terry J, but wake him up at about ten o'clock. He films *Erik* until the end of next week.

Friday, December 16th

A few more work offers – including Edgar in Jonathan Miller's *King Lear* – keep coming in.

Had some fresh thoughts on 'AF' as I ran this morning. Centred round making more of the sexuality, and on casting Emma Thompson in it somewhere. I was impressed by her confident and compulsively watchable characters in her series, *Thompson*, last night.

Meet David Rose, head of Film on Four. He is delighted that he has a season coming up next year which will infuriate the Whitehouses – including *Rita, Sue and Bob Too*. He asks if I've seen the article in which Rees-Mogg refers to Michael Grade [Chief Executive of Channel 4] as an ass.

Saturday, December 17th

Swimming with Rachel at Marshall Street Baths. They've been put out to private management since we last went, and the lockers now cost 10p and are just as poky as before. Also the mechanism sticks. The water has been so heavily chlorinated that my eyes sting on contact with it. All in all, a move for the worse.

Sunday, December 18th

Broken night's sleep with Rachel unhappy and raising a temperature and Helen coughing. Wake and lie thinking for a while. All there is to do. Feel the problems of house and home and London life gradually creeping back into the empty spaces left by the 80-day cleansing!

A morning of half-hearted sorting out and planning ahead, Christmas organisation calls, then to Cleese's for lunch. A new lady is by his side, small as Connie, American as both Connie and Babs, but with a hard Southern twang which gives her an odd country-boy edge to the voice. She's called Alyce Faye and she is more like an Australian than an American, direct and funny, and says she knew hardly anything about John's work when they met. I think she vaguely reminds me of Aunt Betty Sheldon [my mother's sister].

The food is rich and plentiful and Montagny or Chablis is served. As usual I hardly have a chance to eat – balancing food, wine and interest in the person you're talking to is not easy.

Talk with Michael Blakemore[1] about work, writing and Maggie Smith. He feels that Maggie comes alive on the stage or when acting; that all the rest of her life is a sort of 'greyness' leading up to the burst of shining brightness when she performs. I like Blakemore. He is a perceptive but modest fellow, full of curiosity about how things are done and why people are the way they are, without offering pat solutions.

Surprise guest standing there as I enter is Nigel Greenwood [my first cousin], who has been brought into the Cleese orbit by Alyce. He is off to the Albert Hall, where Sarah, his sister, is organising some carol do. Talk about 'Uncle Ted' [my father]. Nigel feels he was someone who never really knew what he wanted to be. An eccentric, Nigel thinks. Aunt Katherine [his sister] always regarded him with a certain guarded respect.

Monday, December 19th

I see Steve, the postman, resting his bag on Clare's window sill and sifting our mail. The last few days have been lived under the tension of not knowing whether Will has been successful at BNC,[2] especially as others have heard already.

I can't resist a look through the stack of cards just in case. Nothing very promising. A red herring from the central admissions co-ordinating body at Cheltenham – but second-class and unsealed. Then a thicker letter, white envelope, sealed, addressed to William, postmark Oxford.

It's an extraordinary moment. It is like having my own exam results in my hand.

Should I open it or not? Only one answer and I push my finger under the flap. It takes a moment to focus clearly on the dense page of print, but then it becomes clear that the message is affirmative. He's offered a place. Rachel, who's been languishing on the sofa with a temperature, comes to the kitchen door and I'm thumping the table with joy.

---

1 Michael Blakemore, Australian-born director, who had the previous year worked with Maggie Smith on Peter Shaffer's play *Lettice and Lovage*.
2 Brasenose College, Oxford, where I read history between 1962 and 1965.

Tuesday, December 20th

Write a lot of cards, do some shopping, then off to T2000's[1] Christmas party.

General spirit of optimism. I notice transport issues being discussed in the media as never before. King's Cross fire (incompetence) and the Clapham disaster (also incompetence) have raised questions of safety and, wider than that, how public transport is financed, run and what we expect from it. Things that T2000 has been trying to raise for years.

A mad dash from the glare of Union headquarters in Euston to the more sophisticated, homely and comfortable surroundings of Stockwell Park Crescent for Tristram's Christmas party.

Melvyn Bragg (a suit and tie man, but with the tie knot hanging a button's distance down from an open collar) joins me. Both agree chief physical ordeal of pre-Christmas parties is all the standing. Someone should invent an indoor shooting stick.

Talk of TV. Melvyn, as one would imagine, stoutly defends TV plays and TV documentaries as works of art in themselves, conceding nothing in terms of status or prestige to the theatre, opera or films. 'I'd far rather spend an evening in front of a good TV play than sit in some cramped West End theatre watching second-rate material.'

He tells me about the Cleese interview. Long setting-up process on the day of the interview – JC kept asking if everyone was all right ... much introducing, lot of flattery of Melvyn, then, as they began, he stopped them and suggested that they should first talk to his mother. She was only next door. It would be the work of a moment.

Dr Miller passes by with his son William. He pats me rather fondly on the head. 'Tried to get him for Edgar,' he sighs to Melvyn.

Wednesday, December 21st

A Channel 4 news presenter and his team arrive to interview me about Prominent Features [the film company owned by the Pythons]. Why are they suddenly taking an interest in Prominent? He's quite disarming, says it's Christmas week, there's no news.

---

1 The pressure group Transport 2000 (later Campaign for Better Transport), of which I had been Chair since 1987.

Two and a half hours later a 747 blows up in the sky over a Scottish village called Lockerbie.[1]

Friday, December 23rd: London–Southwold

To the office to leave presents for all, which I bought yesterday. Then head out onto the M25 and eastwards to Suffolk.

Granny [my mother] is still shrinking, it seems. Her arms are bony and she continues to be less steady on her feet. But it's still as good as ever to see her and she's full of the mixture of humour and exaggerated fears and ear-wagging gossip which keeps her going.

Alice Murnane, a friend with whom she had become close – they regularly took Sunday lunch together – has just died, and her funeral was this morning. Mum seems to have taken it all philosophically, or else she's very good at hiding real feelings.

She has some lunch for me. Afterwards I fight against an all-embracing fatigue which is within a whisker of sending me into a deep sleep even as Ma is talking to me. The cure is exercise and about three o'clock I set off across the golf course and down onto the marshes. Hard work against a firm, westerly wind.

In the evening we go to the Crown. Ma insists we walk. The wind has dropped and the air is almost warm. The Christmas lights are on down the peaceful High Street and the Crown is almost empty. Susan serves – full of laughter as usual.

Take a walk to the shore of the North Sea, on which I sailed home eleven days ago. The bright orange lights of the Sizewell B nuclear power construction site sparkle to the south. The lighthouse beam sends out three stabs across the cliffs above me, then revolves away to the north.

Tuesday, December 27th: Southwold

As we are unloading the car outside Sunset House, a tall man with a saucer-shaped face and big ears looms over us. He turns out to be Roger Ward, Kathleen Ward's son. He grasps my mother's hand – what is it about ancient hands that draws the graspers so? – and apologises for having taken his mother away at such short notice. So profoundly

1 A PanAm transatlantic flight was blown up by a terrorist bomb over Lockerbie, Scotland, killing 270 people.

overplayed is his seriousness that Mother gets the wrong end of the stick and assumes Mrs Ward to be dead. Roger's following remarks – about her being 'in a better place' (meaning Perthshire, near their home) – only make things worse.

Once we are safely inside, Mum, who had been wonderfully sympathetic, turns to me in bewilderment. 'Who was that?'

After our sandwiches I walk into the town to check on Daddy's grave. Southwold full of Bank Holidayers.

On the way home, between about 4.20 and 5.15, one of the most spectacular and prolonged sunsets I've ever seen. Far outdoing anything I saw around the world, both in length and intensity. Wide East Anglian skies as the arena, and a collection of various shapes and sizes of cloud, from long, wispy, horizontal to almond-shaped smudges higher, away from the horizon. All catching, reflecting and burning with reds, yellows, dripping golds, pink-salmon reds.

Wednesday, December 28th

To the Tate Gallery to the Hockney retrospective, very full. No-one quite sure what to say in front of the canvases. Botties of men protruding from shower curtains can't be analysed in quite the same way as the light on a Vermeer, or the snow in a Sisley.

Friday, December 30th

I would like to write or read or generally relax, but have to scour the house for Australian things to take to the Guedallas' lunch party.

Decide on the spur of the moment to go as Sir Les Patterson,[1] but can't find anything nasty enough to smear down my shirt. Stick Helen's pillow into shirt and trousers and borrow an awful pair of Dracula teeth from Rachel.

We make our appearances as the Patterson Family and are very well received – I even have a cucumber in my trouser pocket to give the authentic phallic detail.

---

1 One of several personae created by the Australian actor Barry Humphries. The uncouth Sir Les Patterson could hardly be more different from his other creation, Dame Edna Everage. Patterson is overweight, with no social graces and offensive at virtually every utterance.

Talk mainly to the Australians there. All agree that Prime Minister Hawke has quite cleverly dropped the socialism from his Labour programme. Joy [an Australian-born neighbour of ours] tells me how much Sir Les Patterson is detested by Australians!

Saturday, December 31st

Because of the *80 Days* journey, 1988 seems to have come to an end with a rush. A year of travel – eleven and a half weeks on *80 Days* being the longest single period I've spent away from the family, but only half of the 22 weeks I spent out of the country this year.

The winter and spring work done on writing and casting *American Friends* was inconclusive. The script is still not satisfactory. Attempts to float my play *The Weekend* also failed. *Number 27* was, quite successfully, floated, and has added to my reputation as a writer of plays as well as jokes and films.

The summer belonged to *Wanda* and the US publicity tour was made bearable by the growing awareness of how popular the film might be. Now, at the end of the year, it's reached 60 million rentals in the US and is the fourth-biggest movie in GB for 1988.

I seem to be better known than ever now. A mixed blessing. 'He's the famous man' I heard one seven-year-old boy tell his friend solemnly yesterday. But there's also *Bella* magazine ringing to know who I'd most like to do an April Fool on and sounding very aggrieved when I told them I wasn't interested.

The urge to move house, that somehow it's time for a change to the physical parameters of my life, strengthens, then ebbs. At Christmas the house was stretched to capacity, yet it coped and was warm and friendly and characterful and the prospect of uprooting and creating the same cordial feelings elsewhere is frightening. But also tantalising.

I have the feeling that I shall be mooning over the same problem in a year's time from my comfortable workroom in Gospel Oak.

1989

Sunday, January 1st

Mrs B [our cleaner] comes in for a drink and we talk about what Oak Village used to be like. Mrs B bought a pram from a lady who lived here. About that time our house was a 'sort of club' and Mrs B hadn't liked to ask further about it.

Also a wonderful story about the war. There was an air-raid shelter in Lismore Circus and one night a lady came in to find a friend of hers … unfortunately the friend's name was Cass. She couldn't get any response so shouted the length of the shelter for her. 'Cass! Cass!' Mrs B says she never saw such a panic. Half-cooked food went flying as everyone scrambled for their masks.

Tuesday, January 3rd

I read that Harold Nicolson[1] said that a diary should be written for a great-grandson.

So briefly, great-grandson, and just for you, I woke about eight and was at the desk, with the phone off the hook, by ten o'clock, as I began work on the *80 Days* book. I only composed two sentences – but they were the opening two, so psychologically worth a lot.

Wednesday, January 4th

Jonas [Gwangwa, South African musician, ANC stalwart and, briefly, our neighbour] comes round for a drink and to bring back the £200.00 I loaned him.

Pour him some wine and talk about Botswana, which he says is a paradise, but he can never go back there. He was nearly arrested for setting up 'political' entertainment there some years back (i.e. getting

---

1 Harold Nicolson, diplomat and later MP, published three much-praised volumes of political and social diaries covering the mid-1920s to the 1950s.

local blacks together in a band) and chased by South African security people across walls and through gardens.

Thursday, January 5th

Tristram arrives at a quarter to eleven. We discuss the future of *American Friends*.

Upshot of our discussion is that '*AF*' has much going for it, that this year (post-*Wanda*) it should be easier to finance than last, that we can be freer with the casting if we do it through the BBC (Connie Booth[1] rather than Ellen Burstyn, for example), that there are significant improvements to character and plot which have come up today, all of which point in the right direction.

We agree to go ahead. I feel energetic and positive and pleased with the decision. Ring Steve Abbott, who is as enthusiastic as I've heard him and he will go ahead with money-raising plans. Our filming dates will be September and October.

Friday, January 6th

Give an hour's interview to Debbie's nephew Michael,[2] who has set up an arts magazine at the University of East Anglia, which now sells seven or eight hundred copies. It's an un-elitist mag of catholic interests and I like it and him. I think in years to come anything worth really knowing about me will be in magazines like this and not in the publicity handout-fed pages of the daily press.

To dinner deep in the leafy hills above Aylesbury with Liz (née Manning) and Dick Johns. Dick is now an Air Vice-Marshal. (Helen always gets into a tizzy about his rank when sending Christmas cards. Every time she thinks she's got it right, he's promoted.)

Dick and I talk a little about his job. Revealingly, for they've just shot down two Libyan fighters, Dick confesses that he and most of his European colleagues are scared stiff of some of the gung-ho American attitudes.

---

1 Connie Booth, John Cleese's first wife: co-writer of, and played Polly in, *Fawlty Towers*.
2 Debbie Woolard was a dental hygienist who had looked after my complicated mouth for so long that we had become good friends.

Thursday, January 12th: Brussels

Brussels about midday.

My first exposure to the media since *Wanda* work in the UK in September begins with a lunch in the hotel.

Hear a tapping on the glass window of the restaurant and there is Charlie's[1] ruddy face and thatch of silver hair grinning at me. Good to see him and especially Nadine. Charlie anxious to tell me he's going to be very rude about me later on.

More journalists, then at four out of the hotel and down to the Grand Place.

At the florid Town Hall we are shown into the presence of the Director of the Brussels Film Festival, an oldish man with silver-grey hair and a strong, intelligent face. Of Russian parentage. We're introduced to an obsequious character with a red face from the Embassy. I later hear that the British Embassy, having seen *Wanda*, declined to be too closely involved with it – despite the fact that it is one of the country's better export-earners and that it will open a film festival in a country with great respect for British films.

Then we are ushered into the presence of the Mayor of Brussels.

The Mayor is wrapped in a colourful ribbon around his tum, and it's all rather stiff and formal. The room has lots of gilt mouldings and paintings of old Brussels. We're shown these lovely glimpses of how the city must have been without any evident sense of irony. 'There's a pretty square with a small market, is it still there?' 'No, that is now a big insurance building.'

The Mayor reads a carefully written speech, ponderously, but he's reading in English. Charlie, dwarfed by the huge fireplace behind him, leans on his stick and tries to look comfortable.

At the end of this interminable speech Charlie is presented with a medal of the City of Brussels for his work in helping the Resistance – he made a film in 1947 with Simone Signoret on this theme. Charlie briefly replies that on his last trip to Brussels he had a lunch with some army parachutists which began at twelve and finished at twelve the next day. And that's about all.

---

1 Charles Crichton, film director whose long association with Ealing Films (*The Lavender Hill Mob*, *The Titfield Thunderbolt* etc.) led John Cleese to hire him, aged 77, to direct *A Fish Called Wanda*.

Handshakes, farewells to the girl who's shown us the building, then to a rather grim hall of culture where we are to hold a press conference. A translator called Dominique looks even more nervous than Charlie.

Nobody says anything. 'Don't all talk at once,' I try, to break the ice. The ice seems to grow thicker. 'Do you ask us questions, or do we ask you questions?' Still nothing.

The combination of Charlie's incomprehensibility, even to the translator, and the need to pause for regular translation into French makes the whole thing something of an ordeal. Banter, irony and throwaway jokes all die the death.

Eventually we're delivered from this, then three other interviews – press, radio and TV – before being rushed back to the Astoria to rest in the bath (delightful), then don dinner jacket and return to the Palais des Congrès, or whatever the culture hall is called, to be present at the start of *Wanda*.

We're to be interviewed on stage by two presenters, a man and a woman dressed like Christmas presents. Video cameras follow us everywhere, lenses click. Then, flanked by a rather overdone and unnecessary escort of leggy, jolly girls in black, we're led out onto the stage.

I have a plastic fish tank with a mechanical fish in it. Jokes are made, translated, and Charlie flaps his arms and makes a brief speech in French, telling them he hasn't been to Brussels 'il y a quarante ans'.

Then, at last, a break. We're taken to a local restaurant where, without cameras, we meet various Belgian artistic figures, including a cartoonist called Frederic in Corbusier glasses, who is a great Python fan and interesting too. He and his friend have drawn a special cartoon for us to celebrate *Wanda*.

The cartoonists are desperate for more time with me and their patient, hangdog eagerness is much more acceptable than the pushiness of so many of the others, so end up drinking and talking over a bottle of champagne in the bar. They hold London graphic designers in great respect. Belgium a mixture of identities. Much of their surreal tradition comes from this cultural split personality.

Friday, January 13th: Amsterdam

To sleep about 2.15. Wake five hours later, am at Amsterdam Station by five past twelve.

Begin at one o'clock at the Amstel Hotel. Three and a half hours' talking and being photographed. I don't have a lot to say about *A Fish Called Wanda* – the stammer, the character of Ken, all can be dealt with in 15 minutes – so I waffle on, filling in details about John, about how the film was made, what it was intended to say, desperately trying to sound as if I care a damn.

Finish with a TV piece recorded in the Aquarium. Background of huge, plate-sized black and yellow mega-Wandas and an occasionally active pair of sharks. I sit on a high stool in front of the glass and questions are fired at me.

A bright light shines. Faces look at monitors as I speak. I feel as if I'm having a body scan.

Delivered at last from this nightmare and out along the motorways to Schiphol, where I have time to sit with a coffee and cognac and collect my thoughts. I conclude that film publicity becomes harder, not easier, as you become better known and that it is perhaps the most demanding aspect of this whole crazy business.

Monday, January 16th: London–Madrid

I've brought Buñuel's *My Last Breath* to help renew my appetite for a city in which I've never had a bad time. The book, like his films, is a very personal jumble of insights and anecdotes. I'd forgotten that the name of the only porno film he saw when young was *Sister Vaseline* and he had planned to hijack a theatre during a children's matinee, tie up the projectionist and substitute it for whatever was showing.

Madrid is the same temperature as London. Met by an overweight, funny, tragic Argentinian called Inez, who has had enough of Spain after 12 years, finds no emotional support from the increasingly Yuppie, materially obsessed Spaniards. With her is a slim American lady called Chaplin O'Grady.

It's clear both are intelligent and don't take the whole thing too seriously. Ideal companions for Madrid, for, as Inez is depressed with it, Chaplin delights in the things I like about it – bars, restaurants, variety of architecture and richness of decoration.

After six journalists and two TV interviews we reach Restaurante El Landó, where I have to sign a VIP book, just below some gushing praise from Mel Brooks – 'I love your restaurant, I love your food, I love you!'

Saturday, January 21st

To the shops, then with Will to Highbury for Arsenal v Sheffield Wednesday.

It pours with rain. We park about a half-mile from the ground and join the gradually swelling crowd flowing along the terraced streets. The houses are in much better condition than I remember from our previous visits – the dreadful semi-final defeat by Brighton in '82, and the heart-stopping night we nearly beat Arsenal in the Cup in '79. Money has moved into every corner of Highbury.

Good seats on the halfway line. Pitch soggy and pools of water in the goal mouths. Wednesday fourth from bottom and Arsenal heading the League, but of course it doesn't turn out true to form.

Wednesday are lumpen and completely uninspired in attack, but rather solid and consistent in defence – always winning balls in the air. They gradually wear Arsenal down to their level, then midway through the second half audaciously score on the break. Arsenal equalise quite swiftly, but that's as far as they get.

One of the more satisfying features of the game is the presence in the Arsenal half-back line of a lithe black boy called Gus Caesar (presumably Augustus Caesar). He doesn't play well and richly bizarre shouts like 'You're rubbish Caesar!' can be heard.

Wednesday, January 25th: London–Southwold

With Ma by a quarter to twelve. She seems to shrink a little more every time I see her. Eyes bright, but the legs and arms thinner than ever. Her face is heavily dusted with make-up, some of which has rubbed off onto her blue cardigan. She has trouble finding things – bits of paper, envelopes, old magazines lie in piles all over the place. I long to go through them and throw a few things away, but there is a sort of haphazard system to it all.

After lunch I set up my typewriter and enjoy a couple of hours of productive *80 Days* book-writing. It's so good to be away from the distractions of London.

Thursday, January 26th: Southwold–London

Leave Mum waving at the door of Sunset House and head back home. I can feel a little of her disappointment, though she is remarkably free of self-pity and only very occasionally makes me feel guilty at not giving her more time.

Arrive back about three o'clock.

An interview about stammering, for an outfit called 'Link', which I think makes programmes for the handicapped. The director is blind and the interviewer has a stammer. Both are quite tough and unsentimental, with a steady string of subversive one-liners.

Meet Kevin [Kline] and Phoebe and go to see Peter Hall's production of *Orpheus Descending*.[1] Kevin says the British have rediscovered Tennessee Williams – and this is an excellent production. Technically superb – sound, lights, music blend perfectly. Only the melodramatic ending full of screams and gunshots strains my credulity. Maybe it is because a woman behind me keeps hissing 'Oh, God ... Oh, my God, no.'

Friday, January 27th

Up to the shops. The litter caught in the grass and among the scrubby bushes by the new flats on Mansfield Road is thicker and more ugly than ever. The decay of 'socialist' London is painful to watch. The apathy and helplessness of those who live with this filth is utterly depressing. I feel like organising an anti-litter vigilante group – a sort of environmental Guardian Angels[2] – to try and jerk people from this mute acceptance of drabness and mess.

John rings from Heathrow. He's off to the Golden Globes in LA and sounds quite cheerfully resigned to progressing no further than his nomination.

He reels off the latest *Wanda* statistics. A million dollars in a week in Holland, No. 1 in Paris, with three times as many admissions as the next movie, and Italy looking promising.

For the first time since before my world trip, a game of squash with Terry. A good battle which I win 2-1 and am up in the last, gruelling game.

Later in the pub he shows me his half-moon reading glasses. He has had just the same difficulty with small print, bad light, etc. as I have over

---

1 *Orpheus Descending* was the first production of the Peter Hall Company after Hall left the National Theatre in 1988.
2 An international volunteer group set up in New York in 1979 to combat street crime.

the last few months, and nothing makes us feel more middle-aged than sitting with a pint in the Flask taking turns with TJ's specs to read the small print in *Country Life*!

Saturday, January 28th

Helen leaves for skiing holiday in St Anton at half past seven. Her yearly departure almost a routine now. Back to bed, listen to the unfamiliar sound of falling rain. A warm, wet morning.

Simon Albury rings and extols the virtues of the Apple Macintosh. Everything I'm doing at the moment – crossings-out, substitutions, reordering of lines and paragraphs – can be done instantly, he raves, and it only takes 30 minutes to learn. I promise to go round and try it out. But at the moment every writing hour is precious.

Sunday, January 29th

Wake about 7.15.

Try to get back to sleep, but my brain is up early and has a lot to do today. Must work on the book and also work out a speech for the awards tonight. Feel very lethargic and not looking forward to either of these tasks.

Light a fire, for the weather's colder now, not far from freezing. The pressure's so high the barograph needle is almost off the graph.

Work in the garden and, as dusk falls, take a short run, then dress up and get down to the Savoy Hotel to face the photographers, TV cameras and lots of successful people [at the *Evening Standard* Film Awards].

Am sat at the top table! Duchess of Kent, Michael York (wearing make-up, which worries me until I realise he's compering the occasion), Billie Whitelaw, Mrs Charles Dance, Bob Hoskins.

An excellent tableful. If Helen had been there she would have fitted in very well. Billie and Mrs Dance and Mrs Hoskins all, like her, down-to-earth and quite undazzled by it all.

Most people a bit nervous as they're to give speeches, and our table collects three awards – Billie for best actress in *The Dressmaker* and Bob for best actor in *Roger Rabbit* and *Lonely Passion*[1] and I, by proxy, for *Wanda* as best film.

1 Bob Hoskins starred in *Who Framed Roger Rabbit?* and *The Lonely Passion of Judith Hearne*.

Michael York is very nervous and reads his appalling script with difficulty – but after a while rallies and is very charming, even when he can't remember Jack Clayton's name. 'A great British director, one of the foremost names of British cinema for several decades, let's welcome …' then, rather lamely, '… him.'

Charlie, expansive at the microphone collecting the Peter Sellers Award for Comedy. 'People are always saying how much they like working with directors. Well I enjoyed working with actors.' Touching really.

Bob Hoskins is as exuberant as ever and we enact our usual 'When will we work together?' litany. Bob comes up later, fresh from a trip to the loo, with an idea about a plumber who becomes a vampire in modern London. 'That's the one!' he enthuses.

Friday, February 3rd

Drive out to BBC Kensington House for my first glimpse of the rushes of *80 Days*.

Am struck by how much longer interviews seem on film than when you're filming them. That and my walk. Ron Brown was quite right, my feet stick out at 45 degrees when I'm not concentrating, my shoulders fall and I lead off with my stomach. Not a pretty sight. But I'm quite pleased that I never look quite as debilitated as I often felt and that my interviewing is more revealing and energetic than I feared.

Buoyed by what I've seen, I stay on for a quick lunch and a couple of hours more into the afternoon. The two editors have different assessments of what they've seen. The fair-haired, striped-shirted Howard Billingham feels that we are light on material. Dave Thomas [the other editor], on the other hand, says he's 'captivated'. He's been watching solidly for a week and is still caught up in the story. Roger and Clem talk in terms of a possible seven programmes.

It's all quite confusing. All I know is that the seascapes and the shipboard shots lose out on film. Well shot though they are, they mean little out of context. The people and the faces and the land action are the strengths of what I've seen today.

Monday, February 6th

Lunch at Café Flo in Belsize Park with Connie B. I'm not sure how well I sell *American Friends*. It sounds confusing as I tell it, but Connie is interested and my approach is as candid as possible, indicating my doubts over the last two and a half years of the project and for the future as well.

Helen is very angry at supper about the filthy conditions at Gospel Oak School. Some cleaners are off sick. No money for replacements. The headmaster cleans the lavatory himself.

The demoralisation of everything we held dear and cared about in the '60s and '70s is tragic to see. Thatcher has turned us into a selfish, greedy country, supporting and rewarding those who want to make money at the expense of those who are happy to work for nothing more than pride in doing something good.

Perhaps I should be saying this. The trouble is, if I wrote a film about 'everything that's wrong', it would quickly date and I haven't the temperament to maintain anger about anything for very long.

Tuesday, February 7th

Connie calls; she'd been trying to ring me all morning. Says the screenplay is 'beautifully written' and is complimentary about the feel and the 'texture'. She would very much like to do it.

Promise to send her a couple of tapes of my work with Tristram – *Number 27* and *East of Ipswich*.

At 4.30 to William Ellis for Parents' Open Day for the sixth form. Chance to meet Will's teachers. The school does look very run-down. Tragic when you compare the money spent on corporate offices to the lack of money spent on something as vital as education.

My respect for the teachers is increased. Most of them are lucid, helpful and prepared to spend considerable time talking about the children. But it is a rather depressing world and Will's success in the Oxford exams seems all the better considering where it's sprung from.

To Odette's in Primrose Hill for dinner with JC.

He's off to California until mid-April. He wants some time to think, read, clear his mind and decide what to do next. 'I've done everything in comedy, Mickey, there's nothing else I want to do there.'

He tells me of his experience of writing party political broadcasts for the SDP/Alliance. One was all about admitting you've made mistakes. John incorporated some references to Steel's and Owen's differences of opinion on defence.

Owen saw the script and rang John to say he didn't feel that the defence differences should be talked about. JC asked then if there was any other sort of mistake or misjudgement which might be acceptable. Owen, after thinking for a while, said 'I don't think we've made any.' From that moment JC knew he and the SDP/Alliance would never really get on.

Kingsley Amis is at the window table, with three women. When it comes to putting his coat on to leave, he shuffles the length of the restaurant with it half off his shoulder until he can find sufficient room to swing the other shoulder in. One feels he'd rather go half a mile with it like this than have a waiter help him.

Wednesday, February 8th

Dream on and off about the Python meeting that lies ahead. Funny how we met daily, month after month, and now our get-togethers are so infrequent and our reputation so inflated that meetings take on an aura of significance – as if we're somehow affected by our own publicity.

A call from Steve to tell me that the BAFTA nominations have been leaked. *A Fish Called Wanda* has nine, and I have one for best supporting actor alongside David Suchet (*World Apart*), Peter O'Toole (*Last Emperor*) and Joss Ackland (*White Mischief*).

To the Python meeting, held in the echoey downstairs room at Prominent [in Delancey Street, Camden Town]. JC and Graham are there with TG. Graham's appearance strikes me immediately. Apart from looking dreadfully thin, he has red stains across either side of his face, from ear down to the neck, on the left side of which is what appears to be a billiard-ball-sized growth.

'How are you, Gra?' 'I'm fine.' And he goes on to tell me that he has cancer of the throat and is receiving radiation treatment, hence the red flush. He will have completed the treatment by the end of the week and it will, he is confident, have eradicated the growth. But with his pale, drawn face, and spasms of pain as he swallows, he looks very sick indeed. He is quite open about what's wrong and only asks that we do not let it out of the room, for fear of what the press will make of it.

To work and the various 20th anniversary options. No-one cares a great deal about 20th anniversaries, and my suggestion is that we let

Charles Brand and John Lloyd[1] loose on our material to make not only the documentary they pitched for, but also the clip-show which we ourselves are supposed to compile and link. We've all sent in our selection of sketches. 'Isn't it typical of Python,' observes John, 'that's there's no one sketch which all six of us can agree on.' Later he finds that there is one – 'Cheese Shop'!

Then much looking at diaries to decide on next meeting. GC will be in the States from May to August shooting 'Ditto', in which he will be playing the lead. John away until mid-April. TG off round the world. Everyone impossibly committed.

So we all disperse. I go across to the Edinboro Castle for a drink with Graham. He laughs. An ex-alcoholic, homosexual with cancer – he's become the perfect chat show guest. So many shades of the old Graham, dry, funny, wonderfully aware of the absurdities of life that I pray he will look better next time I see him. And an awful, sharp pinprick of doubt somewhere tells me I may not see him again. There is an air of doom about him. TG is characteristically blunt. Gay, alcoholic – he wants to be the first to die as well!

'After today I know we'll never do anything together again,' says TG over a scotch in the Edinboro.

Friday, February 24th

Graham C rings. He has just finished his course of radiation therapy. He sounds much happier and says that he was given a slightly stronger dose of radiation than is usual because his system was deemed strong enough to take it. This he was very proud of, but I suppose it begs the question of why it was necessary to give him more.

But it's now just a question, as GC puts it, of 'collecting up the debris' – meaning possibly minor surgery on glands in his throat. No permanent damage except a few hairs on the nape of the neck. His voice is coming back and he's off to New York at the end of the week to sort out 'Ditto'. Brave man. Find myself quite moved by his straightforwardness and practicality in the face of something as traumatic.

---

1 Charles Brand is a film and TV producer. John Lloyd, who produced *Not the Nine O'Clock News* and devised *QI*, had made a previous documentary on Python.

Monday, March 6th

Into town to meet Terry at George Akers' cutting room – De Lane Lea. Some glimpses of *Erik* on the Steenbeck are impressive. Looks as good as a Gilliam film. In fact, it looks like a Gilliam film (which might possibly be a disadvantage). But strong on design and lighting and camerawork and performance and script (literate) and editing. Looks to be a winner.

TJ and I to Sutherlands.

Good talk about Prominent. TJ thinks it's finished and has virtually told Steve so. Terry will work with the same team that made *Erik* if he does another film. He's starting to work on *The Man Who Could Work Miracles* and we discuss some ideas on that.

The bill is enormous. TJ takes a while to arrive from the table; some rich Americans at the table next door buttonholed him to ask the name of 'the guy who was at the table with you'. They then went into a pane-gyric about my comic talents, which TJ had to listen to, ending up with 'I hope he paid for your meal'.

We laugh a lot at this, as we walk, on a warm, still, multi-odorous evening, down Broadwick Street, which is being recobbled.

Thursday, March 9th

Letter from Al L [Al Levinson, my New York writer friend]. Problems continue. He has a lesion on his liver, only discovered because he specifically asked them to check it out when going in for a hernia operation. It's operable, they say, and he may go into Mount Sinai Hospital. A surprisingly perky letter, though.

Like a driven man, I head on into the Pacific commentary. Enormous difficulty in maintaining enthusiasm and commitment, but haul myself up to the end of Day 57 before a run and then again into town – this time to see Alan Bennett's *Single Spies* with Eric and Tania.

The *Englishman Abroad* is a pale imitation of an almost faultless TV play and its revival on stage doesn't add anything. But the dialogue is always worth listening to. Alan has a Wildean wit and is excellent on observations of his fellow countrymen.

Blunt and Burgess not traitors in the political sense, no deep commitment to Marxism or the Soviet system, just an inability to fit in easily to British life, a feeling of alienation – the Russian connection maintained almost out of spite.

In the second play Prunella S[1] is magnificent as the Queen – this is a performance which transcends mimicry and caricature, it's terrific observation, not only sustained, but growing in substance as the scene goes on.

Friday, March 10th

By Underground to Leicester Square and lunch at Grimes with Tristram. Update on '*AF*'. Tristram is confident we shall make it this year and I think he will push me.

Out to Robert [Hewison] and Erica's.

Good talk, old photos of Oxford. Robert's warning on *American Friends* – I'm not to make it too 'heritage'! He reminds me of the typhoid epidemics in Oxford which almost closed the university at one time.

Monday, March 13th: London–Southwold

Ma says she feels 'very old all of a sudden'. She is undoubtedly thinner, but otherwise there doesn't seem to be much to justify the gloom. She says her feet are now completely flat and one of them is arthritic and making it difficult for her to move.

I usually feel tense and less receptive when I arrive, and unwind over the rest of the day, so I fear I'm not as sympathetic as I should be. I know I've lost a morning's writing and really all I want to do is to get down to it in the afternoon.

Make some progress and enjoy a windy run over to Walberswick. Two herons flap languidly over me as I cross the bailey bridge, long legs swept behind them, parallel to the ground. The gorse is out and the common very bright.

After a bath, a glass of champagne and watch TG [promoting *Munchausen*] on *Wogan*. The audience absolutely silent throughout. Pity, as TG quite engaging, but appears to work hard, and Wogan's only line of enquiry is: are you mad and why spend 43 million on a picture?

1 Prunella Scales, actress and married to actor Timothy West. Basil's wife in *Fawlty Towers*.

Tuesday, March 14th: Southwold

The weather has gradually worsened and when the time comes to take Ma to the Crown for dinner, a fierce, grasping wind is blowing up Godyll Road and bringing slanting gusts of rain with it. Park almost inside the front door and just get Ma in.

A drink in the bar – she a Dubonnet, me a half of Adnams. We're sat in the Parlour Bar, as the main restaurant's fully booked. One other couple and a group of eight, not quite at home here. The women all smoke between courses and the voices are strident, except when they recognise me, when they fall to even more distracting whispers.

I eat haggis and drink a glass of Tyrrell's Flat Red Wine from New South Wales, which is excellent and reminds me that I wrote today to Aunt Betty to congratulate her on becoming a great-grandmother. Notice that Ma had written, in her half of the letter, that there was no sign of her becoming a great-grandmother yet, in or out of wedlock!

Back home, the tempest still blowing. Finish *Jude the Obscure*, which ends in a torrent of tragedy.

Sunday, March 19th

Slow start to the morning. The children go up to Abbotsley for Granny G's birthday lunch, which Helen and I can't make owing to ridiculously early start for BAFTA.

Leave at 4.30, with Helen in a new and very elegant dark blue outfit. She looks in a different league from me! We're there far too early and our driver takes us round Hyde Park for a quarter of an hour. As the car is comfortable and the park about to burst into spring, it's a very relaxing prelude to a long, hot evening.

Masses of photographers as usual and have to stand, grin, turn this way, turn that way, step back a little and eventually, eyes seeing only green spots from the flashbulbs, we're let through.

Bump into Bennett. 'You're the first famous person we've seen,' he says on meeting. *Talking Heads* is up for all sorts, but Alan says he hopes *Tumbledown*[1] will win best play – 'for political reasons' he adds, a bit wickedly.

---

1 *Tumbledown*, drama set during the Falklands War, written by Charles Wood, directed by Richard Eyre, with Colin Firth in the lead.

We're at a table with Jim Higgins[1] and his wife, Charlie and Nadine, a Swedish producer and English wife and Cubby Broccoli[2] and his wife. I think the fact that the evening is mostly dominated by British TV – and fairly radical TV at that – *Very British Coup, Death on the Rock* both winning awards – leaves people of Broccoli's taste rather high and dry.

And I note a sharp and disapproving intake of breath from Jim Higgins' wife when Shawn Slovo, accepting the Best Screenplay Award [for *A World Apart*], said that there was still much injustice in South Africa and a long way to go before a democratic, multiracial society is achieved.

Wanda fails to win Best Screenplay and Best Direction and when Best Actor in a Supporting Role comes up I feel oddly resigned to being part of an evening of disappointments.

Susan Wooldridge reads the awards after some clips of powerful acting from Suchet and the other heavyweights, O'Toole and Ackland. And the winner is 'Mr ...' (Helen says that she knew it was me then) '... Michael Palin'. A genuine moment of great relief and happiness and as I went up to collect it, all I can recall feeling was how wonderful Susan Wooldridge was. All my absurd gratitude for this chunk of credit was personified in her dignified smile and even some clichéd comment she felt she had to make was not enough to break the spell.

Back to the seat, feeling rather hot and trying to be cool. Cleese won Best Actor and gave a long list of people he wanted to thank, including Sir Basil Smallpeice, Ann Haydon-Jones and her husband Pip, and the Tijuana Brass.

Monday, March 20th

Ring Mum early. She says she was so pleased she did a little dance around the room. That I would love to have seen.

Phone off the hook at ten and try to forget the head-swelling events of last night and concentrate on finishing the book. The Atlantic crossing is as anodyne to write about as it was to experience and I find it hard to breathe life into these last days or to say anything new about ships and oceans.

1 James Higgins, head of UIP (United International Pictures) Distributors.
2 Albert (Cubby) Broccoli, American-born film producer, long resident in UK, where he co-produced the James Bond films.

To the Halcyon Hotel in Holland Park to record a short video for Greenpeace, to promote their views in the US. Peter Ustinov flew in from Geneva to record his, Susannah York was in today, and I catch a glimpse of David Byrne's[1] hunted, raccoon-like eyes, looking up as I climb the stairs. He's doing promotion in England anyway and is staying in the hotel, so was roped in to take part. He hurries away before they can ask him to do anything else.

Back home by half past. In between hearing about Rachel's ski holiday, and preparing lamb chop supper, Michael Shamberg calls. He says he has rights to the old Three Stooges scripts, am I interested?

Wednesday, March 22nd

Up to Highgate to a meeting, called by Eric a 'creative meeting', of TJ, TG, himself and me to try and decide on the future of Prominent Features. The usual attitudes. Eric wants to keep Prominent Features and its cache of money ticking over, but only for us to use as and when we want it, for projects in which one of us must be closely involved. TJ agrees.

TG wants Prominent to be involved in the making of other people's pictures without direct involvement from ourselves. His arms begin to flail and he rattles off various mid-European names and multi-million-dollar figures and Ray Cooper[2] and Wendy[3] and George[4] and asks why we don't have people like this running Prominent. 'It should be fun!' he protests.

We meet in the Cromwell Room, one of the oldest rooms at Terry G's Highgate mansion. Every time anyone steps outside, Bryn, the Irish wolfhound which TG used on *Munchausen*, barks in fear. TG mutters gloomily ... 'We had to teach it to bark for the movie, now the fucking thing won't stop.'

Some talk of *American Friends* as the full moon rises into a cold, clear sky. The atmosphere always goes rather chilly when '*AF*' is mentioned. I think I know how they all feel about it, and agree on many of their worries. On the other hand it also brings out the stubborn

---

1 David Byrne, *Talking Heads* front-man until 1991.
2 Ray Cooper, a musician, also a key figure in George Harrison's HandMade Films.
3 Wendy Palmer worked with Ray Cooper on marketing.
4 George Ayoub, also at HandMade Films.

Taurean in me and redoubles my determination to see it through.

A drink with TJ at the Flask. We've drifted apart a little – as happened when TJ was making *Personal Services*.[1] A film is such an all-embracing project that it tends to subsume one's private and personal life, so I understand.

TJ expresses reservations about 'AF' being my *Missionary* role all over again.

Thursday, March 23rd

Maundy Thursday. Day of the washing of feet. The first I hear of it is an eight o'clock news bulletin which reports a terrorist threat to hijack a US airliner over Easter. Rachel will be at Gatwick now, preparing to leave for Florida. Are the chances of her arriving there safely increased or decreased by what I've heard? Better security? Not if the other stories about three youths being able to walk into the cockpit of a jumbo at Heathrow unsearched are true.[2]

Whatever, it's further evidence of the way the great problem-solving developments – cars, aeroplanes, battery farming or whatever – simply produce another set of problems.

To Prominent Studios at half past three. My first look at the new viewing theatre – very neat, and with eight sound speakers on the walls and two more at the screen it is a nice toy.

The Python scripts are being put together for Methuen to publish in the autumn.

Some interesting work coming in for me. The *South Bank Show* want to discuss something for the autumn, *The Times* has offered me a column (which I turn down) and Tim Bevan was asking about my availability to direct a Working Title film in the summer.

Tom goes off to spend the weekend climbing in Devon and Cornwall, Helen to badminton and me to see Alan Rudolph's *The Moderns* [set in 1920s Paris], which I like very much apart from a caricature of Hemingway which didn't feel right. Gertrude Stein terrifying. Keith Carradine excellent.

---

1 *Personal Services*, 1987 film based on the career of Cynthia Payne, suburban 'Madam', written by David Leland and directed by Terry Jones.
2 Only three months after the Lockerbie disaster, three young men were able to board a 747 in Heathrow's maintenance terminal and sit in the cockpit without being challenged.

A BAFTA winner's placard has gone up outside the Plaza, where *Wanda* has been playing since I was on the dhow. Pass the doors of the Reform Club, locked for the Easter holiday.

Friday, March 24th: Good Friday

Normally I'm wary of public holidays – they leave me, like Sundays, a bit listless and aimless and occasionally depressed – but today and the Easter weekend ahead I welcome with open arms. They've arrived at just the right time. The pressure of the book deadline is relieved, but I'm still faced with the quite pleasurable task of reading the whole lot through at the beginning of next week.

I can ease myself into 'AF' rewriting, knowing that every day's work I do on it between now and the end of next week is a bonus I hadn't allowed for.

Write a long letter to Al, who goes in to have surgery for his liver lesion tomorrow.

Dinner with Roger M and Susie. Will Wyatt[1] and wife Jane, who restores pictures, also there.

Roger and Susie have a little house in a low and unpretentious terrace at the back of Shepherd's Bush. They have two bicycles in the hall and four BAFTA awards on the piano.

Roger returns persistently to his theme of the evening – his determination to apply for the job of Head of Religious Broadcasting. He claims to be quite religious – 'I could dispute with the elders' – and a 'smells and bells' man, who would fight against the phasing-out of Latin and the phasing-in of women priests. Helen and Jane take him on quite successfully.

We end up singing hymns at one o'clock in the morning.

Tuesday, March 28th

The Zimmermans arrive at quarter past seven. Paul[2] is now a rewrite man. He says the money's much better, he's good at it, it's less agonising and his Apple Macintosh reduces 12 weeks' work to seven!

1 Will Wyatt, Managing Director, BBC Television.
2 Paul Zimmerman, wrote screenplay for *King of Comedy* and *Consuming Passions*, which he adapted from original Jones and Palin TV play *Secrets*.

After an excellent supper of tomato and mozzarella salad, chicken marinaded in herbs, white wine and garlic we sit by the fire and talk.

A '79 Pauillac delighted Paul Z and he is eloquent without being overpowering. Says interestingly about *Ripping Yarns* that, though he liked them very much, they lacked the 'killer touch', as he puts it. *Fawlty Towers* had that touch, had the sense that the writer had sweated and suffered to get it right. The *Yarns* were gentler and he felt they were written by someone who 'wouldn't die for them'!

I know what he means and it's revealing that the differences of personality, temperament and character between JC and myself should be carried through so clearly into our work.

Paul had not much liked *Wanda*. Thought it hard and cruel and redeemed only by comedy. It doesn't seem to be an East Coast intellectual's film. Which is probably why it made so much money in the States.

Friday, March 31st

A photo on Hampstead Heath for the *Sunday Mirror Magazine* to accompany an interview about the benefits of walking and the problems for pedestrians in London. This is conducted in our garden over a cup of tea. The journalist talks more than I do, which is quite a feat.

Then out to see *The Vortex*.

Full house at the cramped little Garrick, and an excellent performance. Starts mannered and predictable, with Tristram Jellinek doing a Coward take-off. My spirits sink for a while until revived by Maria [Aitken] and Rupert Everett, who are brilliant. Missing nothing – the teasing, the wit and then the awful pathos underneath. The final bedroom scene played at full blast. Best experience in a theatre so far this year.

Sunday, April 9th

Decide not to agonise over work decisions today but let the day pass with as little pressure as possible. Sport helps and play an hour's tennis with Helen in the afternoon.

Kevin K calls from Tacoma, Washington – he begins a movie with Joan Plowright, Tracey Ullman and Larry Kasdan tomorrow [the film was *I Love You to Death*]. Kevin is funny about his Oscar speech. Apparently something about 'Charlie Crichton – one man and his dream' was censored by Hollywood. He'd originally written 'one man and his drink'.

Ring Eric and wish him well on *Nuns on the Run*,[1] which also starts shooting tomorrow. Eric sounds very calm and relaxed about the whole thing … 'It's just acting, Mike, no big deal … I just stand where I'm told to and move to the left and right and work with nice people, take the money and go home.'

Tuesday, April 11th

I drive at a quarter to ten out to Clem V's house in Ealing to look at the 75-minute compilation of episode two of *80 Days* and a 45-minute assembly of the dhow days.

Without music, or explanatory commentary or a sound mix, all of which act as useful cover, my misadventures are laid out nakedly.

Bons mots are equally matched by maux mots, and I am, as I suspected, far too readily agreeable and conciliatory about everything.

But I find the 'long edit' of the dhow quite beguiling. It is increasingly rare to have time for anything on TV. Information must be imparted ever faster to an audience presumed to be easily bored and constantly distracted. The dhow works better for being longer. Its unusualness and charm remain the single strongest impression of the journey and I think that, in order to put this across to an audience as faithfully as possible, we must accord it a fair share of the film. But it may mean seven episodes.

Home and look at the 'Great Railway Journey' to compare my efforts with what I've seen today. There seems little difference except that I've aged a lot. I look preternaturally schoolboyish and unblemished in 1980. Can I have turned into W. H. Auden quite as quickly?

A couple of phone interviews re *Wanda* for Australian video. To bed reading a good poem by Byron about ageing. He considered all his naughty times over at 30!

---

1 *Nuns on the Run*, written and directed by Jonathan Lynn. Idle starred with Robbie Coltrane.

Thursday, April 13th: Southwold

Mum's breathing is alarmingly difficult. Wonder when, and if, she will need oxygen, Dennis Hopper-style,[1] to keep her going.

Take her into the doctor's. As we get out of the car on the High Street she says 'Come again soon … because,' and here she drops all pretence of perkiness, 'I feel very old.'

Beginning to worry about these moments when the effort of keeping going is too much and the defences come down. Compounded by the death of one or two of her closest friends – Alice Murnane, Joan Macpherson – she seems to have less to look forward to.

Back to London and to Prominent Studios. Coded security locks have been put on all the doors and we, who've paid for them, cannot get in because no-one's told us the code.

To a Redwood meeting. [Redwood Recording Studios were a joint project with André Jacquemin, myself and Bob Salmon, an accountant.] The elation and excitement of owning and setting up the studio has been replaced by the sad realisation that it hasn't turned into the butterfly we'd all hoped for. Profit margins are still tiny, so investment, let alone repayment of original loans, is currently impossible.

André seems to have lost some of his vivacity, persistence and urgency and, having never found anyone he'd trust to help him run the place, he's paying the price in overwork and we are reduced to giving half the facility to another company in return for a small guaranteed income.

But he's made a very professional job of the new Sheila Ferguson single 'Misty' and I hope and pray it works for him. Tom leaves his temporary job at the studio tomorrow – not a moment too soon, I fear.

Awful gloomy today. Neither Mum nor Redwood seem as likely to survive as I'd thought.

Saturday, April 15th

Late breakfast. Tennis in the sun at Parliament Hill and back by 4.15. Rachel tells us the news of the awful happening at Hillsborough.[2]

---

1 In David Lynch's film *Blue Velvet*, Dennis Hopper plays Frank Booth, a sinister villain who wears a mask to breathe.
2 Ninety-six spectators died and 766 were injured during the FA Cup semi-final. The police were blamed in two public inquiries for lack of control and for the alteration of evidence.

The story is still breaking and pictures that should have shown a classic struggle between two of the best teams in the League – Liverpool and Forest – show a battlefield of a different kind. Crushed bodies stretched out all over the pitch, small knots of police, supporters, officials, all bearing that stunned, deadened look of anxiousness and disbelief. Ten killed. Fifty killed. Seventy killed. A crowd, out of control, ironically killing itself on the barriers only put there to prevent crowds getting out of control.

The cameras, all there to record happier things, caught filming an appalling disaster as it happens – as if in slow motion. Hillsborough, one of Sheffield's proudest attributes, will never mean the same again.

I haven't felt quite as sick about a tragedy as this, and Britain's been full of them these last few years.

Sunday, April 16th

Helen and I dress up in our black and whites to attend a gala performance of Chaplin's *City Lights* with score arranged and played live for the first time by the irrepressible Carl Davis and orchestra.

The rain is driven hard and cold at us as we struggle down Tottenham Court Road beneath the HandMade umbrella. A bank of photographers flanks either side of the entrance to the Dominion (which I hear some developer wants to remove).

'Michael!' 'Michael?'

A pushy young man demands to know how Chaplin has influenced my work – 'Just the walk, the moustache and the bowler hat, that's all.'

We're all in our seats for quite a while before the royal person – lovely Princess Diana – steps, head bowed, down the aisle to the front row, accompanied, of course, by Sir Dickie. Then a whole troupe of Chaplins – children, grandchildren, great-grandchildren possibly – follow on. They look interesting and all darkly attractive. The strength of the Chaplin gene evident.

A self-indulgent little short in which Chaplin shows off shamelessly for ten minutes is followed by *City Lights*, in which Chaplin shows off, more acceptably, for 90 minutes. The score big and full, but has inexplicable gaps.

However, quite a treat and, considering how comedy dates, a fitting tribute to the little man who was born 100 years ago, along with Hitler, with whom he shared perhaps more than he'd care to admit. An obsessive personality, extraordinary work rate and generally tyrannical attitude to those around him. In the end Chaplin was the one who achieved world domination.

Tuesday, April 18th

Anne James [my manager] rings and I have a long talk about Saturday and the implications of all the Python 20th anniversary stuff. She has told the lawyer negotiating for us in the US that there will be 15 minutes' worth of new material. Without this the network won't touch us. Why the hell are we crawling to the network all of a sudden? Find myself experiencing considerable revulsion for the whole 20th anniversary thing.

With Terry and Al to Langan's Bistro.

Terry still as angry about things as ever. He quotes *Libération*'s judgement on the Hillsborough disaster that it is a symptom of the class war in England. This seems altogether too simple. The success of a team in a city whose morale and pride had received such a buffeting over the last 30 years is responsible. The Liverpudlian passion, channelled into football and ignored, fatally, by the FA and the police. They did not begin to understand what they were dealing with. The aftermath of the tragedy dominates the news and sobers everything. Ninety-five now dead. The impact seems greater than anything since Aberfan.

Wednesday, April 19th

Yesterday morning's 'AF' work hamstrung by demands of my Prince's Trust appearance in the evening. Having agreed to do a quick intro, I now have to do two intros, both almost a minute long. This before a London Palladium well-heeled charity audience, the royals, Chas and Di and, later, an international TV audience.

It's not until midday that I have two links I feel satisfied with.

American Friends writing suffers dreadfully after this. I cannot pull it together. I pace the room; wander downstairs at the slightest excuse and generally experience classic symptoms of writer's block. And always lurking at the back of my mind is the suspicion that no project should be as difficult as this to bring to fruition.

Collected by a car and taken to the Palladium.

We are all assembled in a backstage passageway and sorted into a line, along which royalty will pass. I'm at one end between Kiri Te Kanawa, big and jolly, and Maureen Lipman, thin and less jolly (Jack Rosenthal, her husband, is in hospital having a hip replaced), on the other.

Sean Connery, who is chief host, is brought to the line last. Nigel Havers cracks golf jokes with him.

When we are all, rather gracelessly, marshalled into line, we are moved up to the Cinderella Bar and deployed in a wide semicircle as if about to take part in some strange parlour game. The lights are switched on, the cameramen stand ready, but the royals do not arrive for another 20 minutes. 'Five minutes!' we're told ... 'Three minutes ...' 'They're downstairs ...' 'Here we go,' and Charles is working the line; he looks smaller than Diana, who stands rather imperially – she's definitely becoming the part.

Charles is very good indeed at this sort of thing. Considering he has to move around 40 people – some from pop groups, some from films or telly or stage – and find things to say to all, he is amazingly cool and relaxed. Low-key and informal and appearing genuinely pleased to see people.

He asks Kiri Te Kanawa if she'd seen me in *A Fish Called Wanda*. He'd liked the chips.

Diana is less jokey; her skin quite beautiful – pale, but just tinged with a soft, attractive pink. Though it has to be said that both of them could be impersonators.

Off they go into their box and the show kicks off about eight. My first link, introducing Wet Wet Wet, goes smoothly.

There is now a two-and-a-half-hour wait before my next appearance. There's no Green Room, but we're all directed to Connery's dressing room. Here, in an unattractively furnished and cramped space, said to have been redesigned to Yul Brynner's requirements, I sit with Sean, Marie Helvin, Jerry Hall and Rosanna Arquette, sparkling, squeaky and oddly helpless, who's with Peter Gabriel.

Jerry H fixes me with her big bedroom eyes and reveals, amongst other things, that Mick is a different man in his letters than in real life. To illustrate this she does what I think is rather a cruel impersonation of the great rocker's public utterances, but says his private epistolary utterances are very romantic.

I end up grabbing a snooze in the dressing room. By the time I come to my next link I've relaxed too much and fluff my last line. As I stand out there with my hand mike I'm aware of how vast the Palladium is.

I find the LWT transport service has broken down, so I trudge up Oxford Street, collect a cab and am home, having done my bit for the future king, at half past one, almost eight hours after setting out.

As I make up for a lost supper I remember other moments of the evening. The restless, almost snarling vigour of Sandra Bernhard, and Charles Fleischer, a small, energetic, simian figure with thick curly hair who did the voices for *Roger Rabbit* and who prowled the Cinderella Bar as we lined up, shouting, doing voices and rolling a pair of Chinese balls in his hand.

And Princess Diana frowning a little as she met me and opening with 'Aren't these lines awful?' I told her it was like being back at school again.

Thursday, April 20th

Ready to write, by mid-morning. Better progress than yesterday, but as the notes pile up around me and the aubergine script jostles with the yellow second draft and the blue first draft, I feel myself submerged by the material rather than on top of it.

I think back to all the advice that I've been given about the film but what sticks most in my memory is Helen's observation that the things I write best are written fast – from Python material like 'Blackmail' or 'Spanish Inquisition', which spilled out in an hour or so, through the better parts of the *Ripping Yarns*, like the first half of 'Tomkinson', or the whole of 'Golden Gordon', to the best scenes in *The Missionary* (the butler at Longleat sequence).

Helen's always had a gut feeling for my own gut feelings and this afternoon, as fierce, hailstone-hurling showers appear suddenly out of the east, her words make up my mind. I have no choice but to set *American Friends* aside, possibly indefinitely.

Friday, April 21st

Tristram arrives about eleven. He's clutching a huge and elaborate scroll which he unfolds to reveal a painstaking breakdown of characters and scenes. This doesn't make it any easier to say what I have to say.

Tristram listens sympathetically, but his response is stubborn and tenacious and he will not allow me to let it go. He suggests an alternative approach, which is that he works full-time on it for the next three weeks, relieving me of the pressure of sole responsibility.

By lunchtime he's convinced me that I should not turn my back on it, and shown me that, though the road ahead may not be entirely clear, at least it's not a cul-de-sac.

Then on to see David Pugh[1] in Shaftesbury Avenue.

He likes *The Weekend* and wants to put it on. He has some worries, but his approach is rather like mine when I look it through – much of it is very funny, funnier than most other West End comedies (as Bennett observed a year ago), and it should work.

He asks me some questions which I can't answer as I've forgotten most of it, but I leave at 5.30 agreeing to talk further and for him to organise a read-through. He had the same thought as Colin Brough in suggesting A Bennett as director. I don't think it's likely.

Drive over to Chez Moi restaurant in Addison Avenue to dine with JC (fresh back from LA), Alyce Faye (who adores him) and Steve Martin and Victoria Tennant – his English wife.[2]

John stares round the table at each of us. I think this is something he might have learnt from encounter groups. How do we all look? My hair is mocked – I can't quite see why, but Steve Martin is very complimentary and says I look the way he always wanted to look.

None of the men can read the menu because of failing eyesight, but only Steve (who is nearly three years younger than me) has glasses. He lets me try them – tortoiseshell half-moons.

Victoria is rather good fun. She and I are the two at table who've never been in any form of psychoanalysis.

Saturday, April 22nd

A full Python turnout with Terrys G and J already there with Graham, looking thin, pale, tight-skinned, but much better than a couple of months ago. JC arrives in his great Bentley which can be parked nowhere but in the central courtyard, with Eric ambling in unhurriedly and helping JC to back it very gently into the wall.

John Lloyd and Charles Brand with lots of bits of paper and Martin Hone, their editor.

1 David Pugh, West End producer.
2 Steve Martin and Victoria Tennant married in 1986, two years after they acted together in the film *All of Me*. Her mother was a Russian ballerina, her father a talent agent in London. They divorced in 1994.

First we have a group photo taken, the first for about four or five years. Chris Richardson is the photographer – a recommendation of mine, as was Charles Brand for the compilation.

Then to the screening room and watch about 90 minutes of Python material in three segments. Their choice is interesting, well-linked and -edited and vindicates the idea of having outsiders in, instead of attempting the impossible and making a selection ourselves. Rather heavily leaning on JC, but then he had the pick of the parts in Python and rarely wasted a chance.

It made me laugh a lot and there are one or two scenes, such as the ant salesman in Harrods, which I'd completely forgotten I'd played.

Monday, April 24th

Ma rings me in late afternoon to tell me that the doctor is admitting her to Southwold Hospital tomorrow afternoon, for a week. Then the doctor rings, 'Bill Thom', as he introduces himself. She may have suffered some vertebral collapse, owing to the thinning and brittle state of her bones (due to old age and not eating enough). This isn't quite as distressing as it sounds and may well 'settle down' within a week. She will be able to 'be cosseted and spoilt' in hospital and it will give her the maximum rest and recovery opportunity whilst enabling him to sort out some support for her when she comes out.

All very reassuring, but I can't help feeling that things will never be quite back to normal, that the word 'collapse' is something I'd foreseen as her body shrank and folded and reduced so that it has so little resistance to such an emergency.

Wednesday, April 26th: London–Southwold

At 11.30 I pack my bags and my 'AF' script and set off for Southwold to visit Mum in hospital.

I sit with her in a small day area, nothing much more than an extension of the ward.

A handsome and undoubtedly well-bred lady sits in one corner and receives visitors in plus fours. A cat perches on the wall outside and Granny and I laugh about the view of the graveyard.

Thursday, April 27th: Southwold

Mrs Kiddy [a recommended carer] could be the salvation, as she seems competent and efficient and energetic and will be able to 'take on' Ma when she leaves hospital.

Round to the hospital and find Mum in better control of things, but still holding her aching back. An hour later I leave her and walk into town, laying some of her surplus flowers on Dad's grave.

At six to see Dr Thom, a young man in a tweed three-piece suit. He says the X-ray revealed the least serious of all the possibilities – a vertebra has crumbled and slipped a little; pain for a week, then three weeks' discomfort. Talk about aftercare. He doesn't think she'll need someone all night, so Mrs Kiddy should fit the bill.

Saturday, April 29th

Off to a Python meeting – the follow-up to last week's. A photo for the *Sunday Telegraph Magazine* set up in the shooting studio. Young local photographer called Gered. JC, in his grey Nike tracksuit, is in imperious form. 'Gered? That's much too difficult. We'll call you Norman.' The session is quite brief. Gered patient with our awfully short attention spans.

A quick business meeting and agreement on most of the minor problems.

There is naked enthusiasm for a Soviet Union stage show from JC and Terry, less from myself, Eric and Graham – 'Who's it for, all the English-speaking Russians?' he asks, pointedly.

We split up at 1.30. John to begin the long process of extricating his Bentley, TJ to Cambridge to open, he declares rather mournfully, 'An Arctic Festival. Lots of Eskimos really.'

Tuesday, May 2nd

Warm and summery at last. Sue Summers arrives at 9.30 for an interview re 20 years of Python for the *Sunday Telegraph*. Pontificate on the Python years and become pretentious.

Then a run, then to the BBC for lunch with Colin Cameron – an amiable, solid young Scot who is head of Clem's department. He asks me before we leave to let him know if there's anything else I should like to do in the documentary line.

Wednesday, May 3rd

Down to Tristram's – 50 minutes through knotted traffic, but it's a warm and pleasant day and Tristram's artfully disordered house is looking its best in the sunlight. Whilst Virginia mows the lawn, we work through the script, looking at all the new ideas, new locations, new dialogue.

TJ rings to ask me to lunch but I'm really too deep in the material. He walked out of the *Erik* dub yesterday because he was so frustrated with the slowness and incompetence of the studio. I think he needs cheering up and I feel bad about being too busy.

We work for seven hours, winding up after six o'clock, the resurrection of 'AF' confirmed.

Friday, May 5th

Good, deep sleep takes me into my 47th year. At eight o'clock, as I'm about to attack the pile of presents on the table before Rachel has to leave for school, the telephone rings.

It's Mum to give me birthday greetings for the 46th time, but she sounds unhappy and the celebratory call turns into a problem call. She hasn't been sleeping well and her legs are bad and she has to get up two or three times each night. It sounds depressing and worse since, at a distance, I'm helpless.

Back to breakfast and the presents and cards, when Kay Kiddy rings with her assessment of the last few days. 'Four things you should be aware of. One ...' She's well-meaning, thorough and working superhumanly hard, but I do find her delivery grates.

A lunch meeting with Mary-Anne Page, a potential American source of 'AF' money, and her partner – who make up High St Films.

Mary-Anne P (ex-Yale) is effusive in praise of 'AF' and cannot quite understand why I'm rewriting a script which she found almost perfect. Even if I only believe half of this it's quite a nice birthday present.

Sunday, May 7th: Southwold

Mum, supported by a stick, is waiting upstairs. As is often the case with her, the first impression is worse than the last. Mrs Kiddy has just left, and Mother looks tired and tiny and tense.

The inescapable fact is that she is in considerable pain and cannot find any comfortable position, and until the pain begins to subside she will not be able to eat or sleep well, therefore have less energy for doing all the things she used to do and now can't – like going to church and walking to the shops and running her house her own way.

The rest of the day improves a little. I give her a glass of champagne and we have a talk over things. She says she remembers being taken up to London at the age of five and being asked to strip in a very cold room whilst a doctor examined her back. He diagnosed some inherent weakness and she was ordered to drink lots of milk.

Wednesday, May 17th: London–Cannes

Steve and Patrick Cassavetti, the two bearded ones, come round to the apartment and we walk together along the Croisette.

The first 'pitch' is to Harvey Weinstein[1] of Miramax, who have two of the few films to have created any interest here – *Sex, Lies, and Videotape* and *Scandal*, so is bullish. He works out of a tiny, cluttered room, with three assistants. Patrick greatly approves of this economy.

Surprise myself at how good I make '*AF*' sound after all these years. Real Dale Carnegie stuff. Not a doubt in sight. The new work, largely helped by Tristram, does come out sounding fresh, new and bright. Harvey listens intelligently and asks the right questions. We leave over an hour later with his exhortation not to talk to anybody else!

Thursday, May 18th: Cannes

I'm collected by the beards at half past eight and am surveying other early deal-makers at the Majestic dining room.

At our own power table – with a lady called Sara (specs, Yale-educated) and her assistant Mitch. Problem of pitching at table is that the waiter and his comings and goings become subtly interwoven with the story. It's difficult to pick up the intensity of the film's subtext after a three-minute break to survey the muesli table.

We walk to the Croisette and sit in the sun looking out over a flat, exhausted sea towards Dino de Laurentiis' galleon.

1 Harvey Weinstein backed both films, which marked the debuts of two directors: *Sex, Lies, and Videotape*, written and directed by Steven Soderbergh, and *Scandal*, inspired by the Profumo scandal, directed by Michael Caton-Jones.

Lunch is at the Majestic again and is interrupted not just by waiters and trips to the buffet, but by the regular fly-past of aircraft trailing the Salkinds' latest – *Christopher Columbus* – which drowns out most other deals.

In the afternoon, in room 131 at the Carlton, I tell the story all over again to Donna Gigliotti of Orion Classics, and in the evening to CBS/Fox – Francesca and a young, rather podgy rich boy called Steve.

Activity of this sort demands rest and respite, which comes in the form of a three-and-a-half-hour session at the Petit Carlton with TJ, Anne, Steve and others. Harvey Weinstein appears, shakes my hand very warmly and introduces Michael Caton-Jones, who confuses me by being Scottish. I'm just telling him that no English directors come here anymore when David Leland walks in.

Friday, May 19th: Cannes–London

Walk round to the Cristal, encountering the redoubtable Ingeborg Hansen and her Norwegian sidekick. *Wanda* doing extraordinary business still; she can hardly let go my hand, such is her enthusiasm.

To the sixth-floor restaurant of the Cristal. Terry Glinwood[1] and his wife sit together beside a long table at which Simon Relph,[2] host, arranges myself, an Indian lady financier from Guinness Mahon called Premila, whom I like a lot better than most bankers, Derek Malcolm of the *Guardian*, the Wingates who run the Curzon, Steve A and a couple of others.

Derek M good value. He won a competition at the Carlton for the best recounting of a first sexual experience. 'Mine was the only one that was gay,' he explains. 'I think they gave me marks for bravery.' 'Gay? ...' 'Well, you know, public school, almost bound to be.'

Michael Williams-Jones, head of UIP, enthuses 'It's a real-life drama!' and is so much taken with the existence of my great-grandfather's diaries that he thinks we should publish them a year before to build interest.

The day is bowling along commercially, but then thick, cloggy, humid air begins to drip viscous rain as we thread our way past the building sites to the Virgin office to make a final pitch to Mike Watts.

---

1 Terry Glinwood, producer (*Rentadick, Merry Christmas Mr Lawrence*).
2 Simon Relph, founder and chief executive of British Screen Finance.

Out to the airport and home by 8.30.

The script is waiting – fifth draft of 'AF' on which all my enthusiasm of the last few days is based. Read it through before bed. Find it lean, but too severely pruned. Much of the Palin character of the script lost.

Monday, May 22nd

Another look through the screenplay with Tristram.

We work at a table in Café Flo until nearly five o'clock, as I explain my changes. Discuss what we both feel is the unfinished area of the script – that is the filling-out of the three main characters, especially Miss Hartley, in Oxford. The shape, direction and line now simple and clear, but more flesh I think needed.

We both agree that this is make-or-break time for the project. In two weeks nothing will be quite the same again. We'll be either on a roller-coaster ride to a September start, or back, with tails between our legs, having these convivial and creative lunches.

Back home to devote the rest of the evening to proof-checking of *80 Days* book. A similar exercise to *American Friends*, but with emphasis on cutting rather than adding.

Thursday, May 25th

'AF' corrected screenplay arrives mid-morning. Make some good fresh coffee and set to reading. Pleased with the result. Tight, with a strong, simple structure. All the characters clear and ready to be developed further over the summer and in rehearsal.

Sunday, June 4th

Look through *The Weekend* prior to lunchtime read-through.

With Rachel to Prominent by 12.30.

Then the actors – Edward Hardwicke, Stephanie Cole, who arrived on her bike from Swiss Cottage with a plastic black helmet. Like her immediately. As I offer a glass of champagne to Julia McKenzie, she says with great enthusiasm, 'Wonderful, we can drink to the death of Ayatollah Khomeini' (who snuffed it earlier this morning). Ben Whitrow, who is to read Stephen, arrives later with a worried expression and a suitcase – he's driving on to Sheffield for a Friends of the Earth benefit.

The reading goes very well. Ben Whitrow softer, less bullishly angry than I'd seen the character, but able to sustain well and in the end very funny and moving. Julia McKenzie quite excellent and Stephanie Cole faultless. Rachel [Palin] too is very accurate and funny.

At the end David Pugh says he is now even more keen on putting it on and everyone seems encouraged.

Steve A calls in the evening re *American Friends*. Miramax are interested but they're worried that the lightness and humour of my pitch are not so clearly there in the script. Jim Higgins of UIP thought it very good. Simon Relph and Michael W-Jones should report over the weekend.

Monday, June 5th

Clem V rings with the encouraging news that Colin Cameron liked the *80 Days* rough cuts enough to recommend to Jonathan Powell that the series be extended to seven shows, and Powell's reaction is awaited.

As Will labours through the first of ten days' A Level exams, I embark on an unscheduled rewrite of *The Weekend*, adding a new last scene which works quite pleasingly.

Wednesday, June 7th

Miramax have asked if we would be prepared to look at Sally Field or Diane Keaton instead of Connie. I see no point in such compromise. I know Connie is not a name, but I also know she will give a performance at least as good as either of them and she is here and can write and is a friend and we've worked together – all enormous assets to the film.

Friday, June 9th

Into town, park car and run through the West End to the Wardour Mews offices of Palace Pictures – small, cluttered premises with only some cans of film, VDU screens and Steve Woolley's ponytail to distinguish it from some Dickensian underwriter's office. It looks like *Hard Times*, but with *Scandal* heading for a ten-million gross in the US and even *High Spirits* reviving in Europe, they're bullish. They have David Leland's pic *Big Man* opening in September and they were courting

Roger Pratt[1] as lighting cameraman only today. He's our first choice as well.

Pitch the film, but Nik Powell comes clumping in with his mobile phone, 40 minutes late, in the middle of some vital sentence, so I wouldn't say Steve was riveted. We leave the script and, like brush sales-men, troop out into the street.

Patrick shows me Miramax's seven pages of 'notes'. 'The terrific screenplay caused much discussion.'

Scanning quickly through it I'm depressed by the lack of subtlety (make Ashby more physically comical – a stutter perhaps?), but basic-ally they worry about it being more drama than comedy.

Tuesday, June 13th

Complete typing of commentary, then try to knock off a 1,500-word piece for *Good Housekeeping* on *80 Days* – telling the story through the eyes of my shirt.

Writing seems not to present a great problem at the moment. Maybe I've developed a style at last, or maybe I know my strengths and weak-nesses better, but I find I can turn from commentary to fluent 'feature' piece quite smoothly. And I have to, as there's no time to dawdle.

Helen and I are to go out to dinner with Steve Martin and Martin Short, but only I go as Helen is struck down with some fierce stomach pains which double her up.

To the Hiroko at the Ken Hilton. Not really my idea of somewhere convivial. The service and atmosphere are about as intimate as a refrig-erator. And there is a kind of cultural unease about Steve M. Lingering at table is not his thing – nor indeed an American thing.

Enjoy talking with Victoria T. She took Steve up to see her very county cousins in Yorkshire. It was two days before anyone referred to what Steve did for a living.

Wednesday, June 14th

The hottest day of the year, with the thermometer at 84°, high pollen and very sticky.

1 Roger Pratt shot Terry Gilliam's *Brazil*, later *Fisher King, Twelve Monkeys* and *Harry Potter*.

I have been lumbered with two requests tonight – the first being the publication launch of David Day's book *Eco Wars* at Canada House. TJ originally got me into it and the invitation adds that 'there will be a statement on ecology by Michael Palin and Terry Jones'. Now, this morning, a harassed David Day calls to say that TJ can't be there. So I cobble together a short address and, taking a taxi which edges slowly through thick traffic in St Martin's Lane and Trafalgar Square, arrive at Canada House at about 7.20.

Am introduced, do my bit, leave by taxi for the NFT where JC has asked me to attend a Directors Guild interview after *A Fish Called Wanda*. JC to be interviewed by pink-cheeked Michael Winner, on stage. Not at all sure of my function there, nor is Stephen Frears, whose cheerfully bleak, baggy-eyed face looms up beside me on the way in.

He says that *Dangerous Liaisons* has 'changed my life ... changed my life ... I've got a house in Somerset. I don't have to work all the time'. He looks just the same, like an unmade bed. I can't imagine him ever becoming a country squire.

A very large man emerges from the crowd going to listen to John and, taking him to be Leslie Hardcastle, the Falstaffian figure behind MOMI [the Museum of the Moving Image], I grasp his hand and accept his praise of the film gratefully. Am just about to ask leading questions about his life in theatre admin when I realise that he's not Leslie Hardcastle at all, but Norman Willis, head of the TUC.

Frears and I slip in at the back and I realise I've been remiss when someone asks 'Where were you?' – we 'celebrities' having been introduced at the beginning.

JC in complete command – dauntingly articulate, full of ideas and observations which he expands with the care and authority of a great teacher – a man who feels he has worked it all out.

Norman Willis is asleep after ten minutes. A lot of people fanning their faces. The whole thing, with questions, is over by half past ten and I am not required to take part.

JC leaves with Winner in a big limousine and I walk up onto Waterloo Bridge and take a taxi home.

Thursday, June 15th

It's an almost perfect summer's day and I have to stop at Highgate Ponds to watch a crested grebe, who has nested in open water only a few feet away from a busy path, standing and rearranging her nesting materials before easing herself down onto two white eggs. Also see a heron drifting over the ponds and a rabbit, very fat and comfortable, that doesn't even move out of my way.

To Julie's in Notting Hill for lunch with David Pugh and discussion on *The Weekend*.

We decided that it should go forward – to John Dove[1], to cast a directorial eye over it, and to Denholm Elliott for Stephen.

Saturday, June 17th: London–Southwold

I'm on the road by nine. Heavy traffic, but moving, and I'm not at Sunset House until just before midday. Granny moves quite quickly, and unaided, about the house. She has a loose summer dress and cream cardigan – both symbols of the new regime.

She eats a good lunch and we walk out along the Common later in the afternoon. I find that her hearing is quite a lot worse and that she has suffered a loss of confidence in herself, which it will be very hard to replace. She knows that she is slowing down, she knows that she is less in control, and occasionally I see a look in her eyes which I've never seen in my mother before – it's a look of momentary resignation, as if she has an inkling that things are coming to some sort of conclusion.

So, despite all the sunshine and sitting out on the balcony together watching the cricket, and the love of gossip and the digs at her minders, that's why I leave with a heavy heart.

Tuesday, June 20th

Tristram rings early, just after I've sat down to start a day's work on commentary. He is frustrated with the lack of information, drive, energy and direction in pursuing 'AF'.

This, from a generally calm and tolerant man, galvanises me into calling Patrick. He confirms what I have been left to presume, which is that responses have not been as good as we'd hoped. But as details of any response, good or bad, are valuable, he suggests, and I readily agree, that we should all make time this afternoon to meet and discuss progress. We are eight working days away from our deadline on finance.

1 John Dove, director with long-standing Hampstead Theatre Club connections.

The heat builds up in my room as I sit by the screen. It must be almost as hot as the footage I'm looking at – Dubai shipyard, 100°, about the hottest and most uncomfortable working conditions on the whole *80 Days* trip.

Begin meeting at five. General feeling of disappointment/confusion on part of investors. They liked pitch more than script (honourable exception of Simon Relph). Not antagonism, but bemusement. Also very uncommercial line-up – no stars, except me, new director, etc. etc.

TJ is staying with us tonight. He's mixing at Elstree and, as there is a complete close-down of public transport tomorrow, fears he won't get across London.

TJ has read '*AF*' and before telling me about it says ominously 'I don't want to depress you.' He still feels the film doesn't know what it's about, and that accommodating Miss Hartley and Elinor at the beginning was wrong as it diverted attention from the central figure – Ashby – whom Terry likes.

Friday, June 23rd

Tristram arrives to write at 10.30. Discuss the script again, as he has implemented TJ's suggestion that we lose American scenes at beginning and end.

To Prominent for a hasty meeting with Mark Shivas[1] and Lynda Myles.[2] Not awfully satisfactory – Mark late, Lynda has already seen a copy of the script. 'More passion' she feels is what it needs. I agree.

Have to rush away, eating lunch as I drive, to get to the BBC for the third of my *80 Days* commentary recordings.

At half past two a Xeroxed sheet is delivered warning that the unions have called a strike for three o'clock. About five minutes later another, type-written, sheet announces that the Director-General will talk to the workforce on the internal systems at three o'clock.

No options but to abandon the session and go back to Prominent. As I walk along the corridors of Kensington House, people are either leaving or sitting in groups lounging back in chairs as the monotonous voice of Michael Checkland [Director-General] drones out of the speakers urging negotiation. A scene reminiscent of *1984*.

---

1 Mark Shivas, film and television producer, including *A Private Function*.
2 Lynda Myles, former director of Edinburgh International Film Festival.

Saturday, June 24th: London–Abbotsley

Armed with a thick assortment of 'AF' drafts, I catch the 8.40 local train from King's Cross to St Neots for a final, concentrated assault on the problem script. I have to leave London – the continuing heat is spawning drought talk from the water authorities and disaster from the cereal farmers.

Granny meets me, and I'm at Helen's father's desk by ten o'clock. The garden is rich and full of colour and a thick haze of midsummer smells. The only irritation is the periodic eruption of batches of parachutists from a plane above. They fall, shouting and yipping shrilly and imitatively, whooping with excitement which it's churlish to say is a real fucking nuisance.

I dig away at the Elinor/Ashby relationship, searching for 'more passion' for Lynda Myles and a less perfunctory ending for TG and almost everyone else.

Wednesday, June 28th

Another rail strike, but traffic not too bad as I drive in to Ken House mid-morning to work through fitting commentary for show four with Roger M.

At lunchtime I encounter Colin Cameron, who tells us to go ahead and make the series seven shows.

Thursday, June 29th

At home all day writing commentary for show five, Hong Kong and China. Rather like the journey itself, the commentary gets tougher the further on I go. My eyes ache with the concentration on the small screen, my brain aches with the concentration on *le mot juste*. I feel as if I'm playing some elaborate machine in an amusement arcade.

But I complete by early evening and begin to type it up. Finish at midnight. Reeling.

Sunday, July 2nd

Clear desk and letters in the first half of the morning, after breakfast in the garden. *Monty Python and the Holy Grail* is No. 1 in Athens! *Wanda* still in the Top Tens of Amsterdam, Copenhagen and Stockholm. In Denmark, a doctor died of laughter whilst watching the film.

Drive over to a meeting with Patrick and Steve on this crucial weekend for finance.

The situation is as follows. Nice offers from BSB, CBS/Fox and British Screen; Palace will come in, Virgin deciding. But all the combinations of these offers will not make up the three and a half million needed. However a most unlikely saviour could be LWT [London Weekend Television], who would arrange a cash flow of three million for three UK TV screenings, leaving us to sell the rest.

We still await a definite decision from them and the beards would like me to see Sky TV tomorrow.

Monday, July 3rd

To David Pugh's office to talk about *The Weekend*.

Pugh very keen for me to play Febble and says he can see every reason why it's better to make Febble 55 instead of 65. Then John Dove, a prospective director, arrives. I like him immediately. He talks in sharp bursts, then clutches his face and grins.

He's only read the play once. Finds it 'interesting'. He wants to know a little more of the whys and wherefores, as if he's half suspecting a catch. Why have I written this when I could be making comedy films?

Wednesday, July 5th

Verity Lambert has sent me four scripts from Alan Bleasdale – *GBH* – and she rings to ask if I will play one of the lead roles. Twenty-six weeks' shooting, for Channel 4.

I go to see Rachel's play, *The Godmother*, at Parliament Hill School's 'Drama Space'. She looks to have overcome first-night nerves and plays a difficult part well.

Take the Bleasdale script to bed to start reading. It's a tough part. He's described as early forties, blond, blue-eyed and big. He moves arrogantly and intimidates people unpleasantly. In short, some acting required.

No word all day from anyone involved with *American Friends*! Am now hoping that the whole tortuous process will end, very soon.

Thursday, July 6th

Ring Patrick early.

Nearly two million available from the UK, but it's not enough and Prominent, unlike a Palace or a HandMade, does not have the collateral to borrow a million.

Back to Patrick's office. Feel the oppressiveness of the weather conditioning my views. Feel frustrated and make it clear to the beards that the money must be in place by Friday evening, the 7th of July, or *American Friends* is not made this year. No-one disagrees. Our heads are low enough, and I'm in no shape to take a long call from Margie Simkin re our American casting trip. Who do we want? When do we fly out? It's all squeezing us and we've no room to move or respond.

Home. Read the latest script. It isn't bad. The relationships are richer. It's worth making.

Friday, July 7th

A dense, thick blanket of steam outside. The night temperature fell just below 70°, and a cracking thunderstorm and downpour the only relief.

A run is vital and I leave the house about half past seven. Very atmospheric up on the Heath, which is dripping and steaming. Through the woods it's oddly, unnaturally dark, thick, claustrophobic and unreal. Expect to find strange three-headed beasts or knights in armour battling in glades.

The only people I pass are Frank Bruno[1] and his small, white-haired trainer, walking very slowly up towards Kenwood, deep in conversation, like a pair of dons.

To the BBC to record another commentary. We have done half a dozen cues when a strike is declared and the whole effort has to be abandoned once again.

Monday, July 10th

Simon Relph wants to speak to me. His message is simple. Never has he seen a film that is nearer to being made. We have come so far, done so

---

1 Frank Bruno, British heavyweight boxer, who went five rounds with Mike Tyson in February 1989.

much. Everyone at British Screen wants it to go ahead. We mustn't give up now. He will put his money where his mouth is, etc. etc. The tide of enthusiasm is unstoppable. Within half an hour Patrick and Steve are confirming our US casting trip and *American Friends* is on.

Tuesday, July 11th

Alan Bleasdale calls. He sounds a quiet, intelligent and modestly self-confident man. He pushes nothing and is anxious not to pester me, and this deadly combination, combined with the strength of the scripts, and the fact that I seem to be his personal choice, make for a cordial conversation and I give a firm as possible commitment to making it.

He says that I must read shows three and four, the ones he's really most proud of, which will reveal why he particularly thought of me. Billy Connolly is his choice for Jim Nelson.

Of course, I sit right down, push 'AF' to one side, and begin to read shows three and four. Halfway through three I can stay awake no longer.

Wednesday, July 12th: London–New York

Leave for the airport by car at three o'clock. Flight isn't until seven, but it's another rail-strike Wednesday and we move slowly out to the M4, collecting Patrick on the way.

To the TWA desk. Security tighter. My passport raises queries. 'For what reason were you travelling in an Arab country?' I tell her I was filming for a BBC series … 'Oh, yeah, I saw it,' she replies agreeably, before going on to warn me that the 1-11 we shall be flying to New York on is a Gulf Air plane – 'but completely staffed by TWA.' Did I have any worries?

To the Mayflower Hotel on Central Park West. A short, squat, middle-aged porter with 'Wilson' on his lapel takes me to my suite. 'The world needs comedy,' opines Wilson, and we crack a joke together about 'smoking seats' on aeroplanes. All very New York.

We take a walk round the corner for a couple of beers at a sidewalk café on Columbus Circle.

A good chat, but Tristram and Patrick are beginning to swap names I've never heard of and it is a quarter to five a.m. UK time and we do have 15 girls to see tomorrow.

Thursday, July 13th: New York

Meet Margie Simkin, mid-30s, grey- or perhaps silver-haired daughter of Russian and Polish Jewish grandparents, now one of the leading casting agents in the US (*Beverly Hills Cop*). She is keen to do it all properly and keeps coming up with new names to put on the list for here and LA.

Interviews in my apartment take the form of cheery hellos, comments on the moment – how they got here, where they bought their dress, the time in England, and so on, followed by my telling of the story. As usual I try to do too much to start with and it's drastically pruned by the time I talk to the last girl nine hours later.

The very first girl we talk to, Brigitte Bako, makes a good impression. Few previous films, but Scorsese used her on *New York Stories*. At the end of the day she's co-favourite with Trini Alvarado, pale, dark-haired, curiously prudish about the 'sex scenes', but very appealing, a good height and match for Connie.

Friday, July 14th: New York/Los Angeles

Wake at 3.30 (still jet-lagged) in my room in the Mayflower Hotel knowing, with absolute certainty, that 'AF' is not ready to go ahead.

Yesterday's gruelling ten-hour casting session revealed a lot:

1. After describing the movie ten times I realise that I am telling them what is not yet in the script. So much of the Hartley/Ashby/Elinor relationship is clear only when I describe it, and not in the script.

2. Martha Plimpton, one of the exceedingly bright girls we saw, was describing a movie she'd been in in Germany. 'It wasn't quite right, I could tell that ... but they all said, it'll be OK ... it'll come right on the day. And, of course, it never does.'

3. Another girl asked if it was going to have any present-day element, any character looking back. This, it occurred to me in this early-morning brainstorm, is exactly what 'AF' needs.

4. The long list of girls in LA means that we shall cut even more into our limited rewriting time back home.

Breakfast time: eight o'clock. Called TP and PC together to discuss my concerns. Neither share my worries or seem at all inclined to share them. They listen politely then tell me that the film is certainly not in 'no shape to shoot by September', but quite healthy. Is my time the problem? My part the problem? My clarity of 4 a.m. desperately hard to remember.

We recall four actresses this morning and then prepare to leave for Los Angeles. Jamie L-C's[1] screeching Cockney greeting echoes along the lobby. She's soon embracing me, much to the amazed delight of a party of Mid-Westerners checking in. Full of beans, she goes quickly into an energetic rap about nannies which bewitches Tristram and Patrick.

Saturday, July 15th: Chateau Marmont, Los Angeles

We find a big, round table in the gardens of the Chateau at which to conduct our interviews. Instead of lunch, I take a dip in the pool, which improves things even more and, for the first time since it was mooted that we should go to America this week to audition, I've unwound enough to accept and even enjoy the idea.

We're just going over our choices after a ten-hour session when Helen rings to tell me that Tom has had a nasty accident and has been operated on at the Royal Free after he fell from his bike and got the handlebar stuck in his stomach. He's conscious, no head damage, no bones broken and no word of any interior damage.

Sunday, July 16th: Los Angeles

Eight o'clock in the evening at LAX. Our TWA 747 for London has pushed back two hours late from the jetty. Tristram immersed in 'The Art of the Screenwriter'.

Steve A has flown in from London. We all met in the Ambassador Lounge in late afternoon to discuss the latest financial position on 'AF'. A final solution still seems, frustratingly, to be just out of reach. An abrupt, unsigned fax from LWT appears to have doused any hopes there – cash-flow problems, they say. But we are to keep going as if all was well.

We discuss a further week's postponement of principal photography.

Thursday, July 20th

All going well until a phone call from Patrick. Sounds grave. 'Steve's had no luck in the States,' he tells me.

---

1 Jamie Lee-Curtis, who had appeared in *A Fish Called Wanda*.

Only one shot remains, and that's HandMade – PC and Tristram both agree that we should not accept defeat without at least a call in DO'B's[1] direction. But he's in LA and can't be disturbed until 3.30 UK.

Go up to the hospital to see Tom. He is in a state of constant discomfort and can only get up and walk with extreme difficulty. Some dispute as to when he can come out. An American doctor, whom he describes as 'ruthless', says tomorrow, the staff nurse two or three days. Leave him at 3.30 and return home.

Patrick rings to say that Gary Oldman[2] may be susceptible to the personal approach for Syme. So, just when the film seems to be tottering unsteadily into the 15th round, I find myself talking to an extremely approachable Gary Oldman in New York, where he's making *State of Grace*. Agents get in the way, he agrees, and he does not give a damn about doing leads or not doing leads. If it's a part that intrigues him he'll do it. A script is to be dispatched fast.

Then DO'B rings. He's at the Bel Air, about to rush out to a day of meetings. To his credit, no gloating or 'I told you so's. His last two million presently tied up in the court case with Cannon and is not fluid enough to hold out much hope, but he takes it seriously and asks for scripts, budgets and schedules.

The dreadful uncertainty continues – agonisingly; though now I feel strangely serene and detached from the whole process.

Sunday, July 23rd

A call from Graham C. He's in the Wellington Hospital. His movement became so impaired last week that they brought him in, explored a bit, and found a lesion behind one of his vertebrae. Another outbreak of cancer, in fact. They operated yesterday.

After lunch I go in to see him. He's on his side, but talking quite clearly. Sunday papers scattered around, but no evidence of his having read them. He's puzzled as to why the cancer (which, I note, is the last word he ever uses) should have moved from his neck to his spine. He sounds admirably detached and phlegmatic about it. His colour isn't

---

1 Denis O'Brien, American lawyer and business partner of George Harrison in HandMade Films.

2 Gary Oldman, English actor who played Joe Orton in Stephen Frears' *Prick Up Your Ears*.

bad, but there is still an angry red patch on his left lower jaw, running down his neck.

Monday, July 24th

With TG and Maggie to Peter Hall's *Merchant of Venice* at the Phoenix. Dustin Hoffman is playing Shylock (quite a coup for this unfashionable end of the Charing Cross Road) and has secured the tickets.

TG is not sure what the etiquette is. Hoffman doesn't like to know who's out there on any particular evening, and consequently it's difficult to fix up any rendezvous afterwards. However, TG's booked Orso's and hopes to lure him there.

The heat weighs heavily inside. The 'Phoenix' ironic for conditions tonight. A regular Shakespearian production – difficult to follow until Hoffman comes on. He plays his scenes with an excellent Jessica [acted by Geraldine James], very movingly and completely without displays of pyrotechnics or fussy Method touches. He is Shylock, and now always will be in my mind.

At the end of the show we are led round the back, across the compact little stage, and up to Dustin's compact little dressing room. A line of celebs is being introduced, and just to be in the same room as Mel Brooks and Dustin Hoffman on the night one of them has played the Jewish outcast Shylock is wonderful in many ways.

The Brookses leave and eventually there is only us, Dustin, his admirable lady minder and Geraldine James and a couple of the cast left. It's suggested we go to eat round the corner at a Greek café.

We all squeeze out of a back door to avoid the fans. Terry and I are quite seriously asked by his minder to walk on either side of Dustin just in case. As it is, Charing Cross Road is deserted of all but drifting litter, and our rather pathetic Praetorian Guard act soon evaporates.

The restaurant is way off the *Good Food Guide* circuit – in an unfashionable street opposite Centre Point, but the food is fine and there are only two or three other tables occupied.

Hoffman is enjoying himself tonight. He apologises for not recognising me on the first handshake, and proceeds to enthuse about my performance in *Wanda*. He admits this is the first time he's done Shakespeare and he doesn't understand what the play's all about.

After he's gone, Geraldine J, in a cheap denim jacket with badges, says that he's sensitive to criticism – and that people are constantly arriving backstage to offer suggestions. Connery, and, last weekend, Zeffirelli, who thought the whole production was wrong.

Friday, July 28th

Lunch with Tristram and Patrick.

By the end of the meal we have agreed on a postponement [of *American Friends*], rather than a cancellation, and will try to shoot in March/April next year.

Back home, via the Wellington, where I dropped in to see the doctor [Chapman]. He clearly felt hard hit by not being well enough to attend his mum's funeral two days ago … 'But they gave me Amoxapine in the evening and I thought about her.'

We discuss mothers, childhood (how important it was to value it, remember it, relish it in the way that GC feels Eric nor John ever did), the choosing of partners, exclusion of others, jealousy, etc.

The office has sent him videotapes of classic comedy shows, but the ones which gave him most pleasure were the last six shows of Python. Series 4. His face squeezes into a very contented smile as we discuss these.

He's worried about Terry Gilliam. 'All that energy … he really must try to slow down.'

Tuesday, August 1st

Patrick Cassavetti calls to give me the encouraging news that his rich friend who deals in antiquities (as opposed to antiques) has read 'AF' and likes it enough to offer a half-million. He'd told the story to a group of friends at a dinner party and it had gone down well. It now sounds as though we might have enough equity pledged to secure a bank loan to make the film. Have a slight suspicion that, even at this late stage, the tenacious Cassavetti would like to have a last crack at the autumn dates, but I'm now more convinced than ever that a postponement is the only course.

Friday, August 4th: London–Southwold

Unable to get to Southwold for the last, rushed month, and feeling that show seven commentary is within striking distance of completion, I take the day off to visit Ma.

She walks well, without a stick, and can get up and sit down without pain. Her voice is brisker, crisper, less laden with the weariness of coping.

Sit awhile out on the balcony. The tents of the Boys' Brigade out on the common resemble a World War One scene. The Scripture Union are running children's games, the cricket square, watered day and night, is a lurid green, reminding us of what the countryside was like in the days when it rained.

The sun is still hot when I leave at six. Straight to a party at Julian Charrington's[1] in Parsons Green.

Talk on until 11.30, then drive home. Someone has changed the sign on Gunter Grove to 'Cunt Grove' so well, I nearly drove off the road.

Tuesday, August 8th

Down to South Ken for lunch with Joyce Carey [90-year-old star of *Number 27*]. Impossible to park, such is the prosperity of this part of town, so am late and find TP and Joyce lingering over a Kir at Bibendum.

Joyce – pink hearing aid (with, I swear, an earring in it), mousy brown wig not quite concealing strands of the silvery-grey original beneath, lipstick applied vigorously, but not quite accurately – is delighted with our company. She's convinced I've just walked in from Saudi Arabia and I give up trying to correct the impression. 'Did you like India?' she asks querulously, in a perfect, if unintentional parody of Noël C.

I ask her what her plans are for the rest of the year … 'Staying alive,' she returns, with great amusement. Show her the *Times* review, which she hasn't seen. She slips it in her bag most gratefully, but later I notice her take it out and read it.

She remains absolutely on the ball, matching us in food and drink, and clasping both our hands about three o'clock and declaring that it's time for her to leave us alone.

I drive to the Cromwell Hospital to see GC. He's having radiation treatment on his back. In last week's *Time Out* he told all about his condition. Evidently the *Sun* and *News of the World* were onto him immediately after. He told them the truth as well.

---

1 Julian Charrington. Julian was the camera assistant and stills photographer on the first part of *Around the World in 80 Days*.

Wednesday, August 16th

A taxi to TV Centre to be present at the launch of the BBC Autumn Schedules.

Colin Cameron, head of Doc Features, greets me with a strange left-handed handshake. He is clutching a massive computer printout in his right hand, which is presumably too valuable to let go. He draws my attention, with great enthusiasm, to the figure for the repeat of *Number 27*: 6.7 million, which he thinks very good indeed. As it's nothing to do with his department I am touched.

Then into the studio and escorted by Colin C and Paul Hamann – the other main Doc Features man – to become part of the studio audience for the Jonathan Powell show. Powell sits at a desk with his name on, as if he was an actor in an LE sketch whose partner had failed to turn up.

Clips are shown. The usual unabsorbable mishmash of drama (wife being smashed across the face by drunken husband), documentary (drunken husband being interviewed) and LE (drunken husband jokes).

The hype is greeted with the usual cynicism from the weary hacks, who are given the chance to ask questions of Mr Powell. How much did it all cost, had the strike cancelled programmes and was colour footage of Hitler 'colourised'? It wasn't.

Then the screens are raised to reveal tables groaning with wine and chicken curry. The hacks go for the wine, then fall upon the celebrities. Peter Sissons, looking burlier and more like a Mafioso than I remember, is most popular. Sue Lawley and Esther Rantzen and Anneka Rice and Victoria Wood are the most photographed, and I never have time to eat, nor to talk to any of my fellow thesps.

Thursday, August 17th

To William Ellis to pick up Will's A Level results. I park in the grounds whilst Helen goes in. A boy, white-faced and in shock, wanders trance-like from the school. He sits nearby and buries his head in his hands. A girl comforts him. I've never seen more intense and desperate grief on a face and long to tell him it's not worth it.

Will has three passes, in English, History and Biology.

Friday, August 18th

To the modest home of Tom Phillips, the artist, who is painting the Pythons' portraits. He was described as a 'polymath' in the paper the other day, but is in person not as forbidding as this sounds.

He's done the two Terrys. TJ looks like his mother. He's given them both anagram names – TG is Emily Girlart. Can't think of a female anagram for Eric Idle – but a good male one – Eli Dicer.

He sits me, or rather lets me sit, on an African chieftain's chair. Tom goes off to Africa once a year 'at least' and potters about collecting bits and pieces. He likes the Africans and especially their 'quite open and blatant way of trying to con you'. Also he's impressed by the fact that they are nearly all multilingual. No lingua franca as in India.

The two hours of being examined and painted pass easily. Slightly disappointed that he's not painted me smiling. (Which I've been trying to do, desperately!)

We go for lunch to a magical place in the Walworth Road – unpromising location, but the name – 'Secret Garden' – for once really describes a place. At the back of the Camberwell antiques gallery, along passages and down stairs to what looks like a sort of artists' canteen. There is a wartime feel about it. Nothing spent on decor, but run by women of great friendliness, in a sort of inspired amateurish way. We sit in the garden, overgrown and run-down, but a wide and serene space which is quite remarkable when you consider the drab blandness of the busy road outside.

We talk about pictures, paintings, dealers. He likes Pissarro, who was a good-hearted man and looked after all his friends, whereas Monet would 'whip your wife away from under you'.

Wednesday, August 23rd

Irene[1] rings with encouraging news that Gary Oldman likes the 'AF' script and will do it, if free. With a positive also from Alfred Molina,[2] we're all set for *Prick Up Your American Friends*.[3] I should be delighted

---

1 Irene Lamb, casting director I first worked with on *Time Bandits*.
2 Alfred Molina, actor whose work has ranged from *Raiders of the Lost Ark* to *Prick Up Your Ears*.
3 *Prick Up Your Ears* had been one of the big hits of 1987.

if these two can come in, as this will help the film look different from the Merchant Ivory repertory production line.

Ring Al L – because I feel guilty at not having written for a while. He says I've rung at 'one of the better times'. He is still having treatment for his liver cancer (which Helen says is incurable) and has had trouble walking. Takes water pills. Things don't sound too good and I find myself waffling my way through an apology for not fitting in a trip to the US until December.

With Rachel, Will and Tom to Pizza Express in Dean Street. All my children together again for the first time since the start of July.

Will fell in love with Venice and thinks James Morris's book on it the best thing he read in two months. He says he wants to buy a flat there! This strikes me as absolutely the thing to do, and now is the time to do it!

Thursday, August 24th

Taxi to Tom Phillips, for ten o'clock start on next instalment of the portrait. Today he has a video camera set up on a tripod. In his usual diffident way he affects not to know quite how to use it, and says he's only used it on Lord Scarman[1] so far. Lord Scarman rests on the wall to my right.

Tom thinks Scarman 'a lovely man', but thinks that the government probably got 'the wrong man', as far as they were concerned, to report on Brixton. Scarman a great Africophile and knew and greatly liked black cultures.

At eleven Tom switches on the cricket from the Oval. Great excitement from the commentary box when Concorde flies over, and a moment later we see the beautiful and noisy creature fly past the windows of Talfourd Road.

Friday, August 25th

I'm chasing the Venetian contacts given me by Robert H. One, Jane Rylands, is American and sounds confident and crisp. Property? 'Very expensive here.' About how much was I prepared to spend? Throw a figure out. '200,000 … pounds.' She pauses, only thrown for a moment

---

1 Lord Scarman. Retired judge, who enquired into the Brixton riots of 1981.

and soon her enthusiasm is greatly increased. This would offer no problem. A garden ... did I want a garden? A lovely place in Dorsoduro ... Contact definitely made.

Monday, August 28th

BBC invitation to the Proms at the Albert Hall. This time to see Berlioz' *Damnation of Faust*.

Up to the Council Room, where the rest of quite a large group are assembling.

David Attenborough (is he a 'Sir'? I can't remember) has just returned from Russia looking for the Siberian hamster, 'which I could have bought down the road at Harrods'. He's full of infectious humour and an easy companion amongst all these Arts and Features heavies. He says that when they did find a particularly fine example of the Siberian hamster, his Russian colleague became so excited that he dropped his torch on the creature and killed it.

The performance is magnificent. The Chicago Symphony Orchestra play beautifully and with great assurance, and the massive black-and-white-attired ranks of the Chicago Symphony Chorus are superb. A rich, mellow sound capable of attack as well as the long, gently modulated passages. Quite a wild, romantic story, but everything performed rather decorously, without losing any energy.

Later, the cast come by for a drink. Not the chorus, which numbers 184, but soloists and the conductor, Sir George Solti. Solti, with his well-polished head and an almost yellow complexion, appears and is asked whom he might like to meet. No-one seemed particularly to interest him until he set eyes on me. He rushes up and grasps my hand. 'I have seen *A Fish Called Wanda* three times' – here he holds up three of his priceless digits. He asks me how I got the stammer so well, and so on, and for a while I bask in the envy of the great and good around me.

Thursday, August 31st

Blearily, to Tom Phillips' studio for ten o'clock.

He now has a name for me: I'm Milli Panache – and take my place alongside Emily Girlart and Joy Sterner.

Sunday, September 3rd

At Twickenham Studios by 10.45 [to film the Python 20th anniversary TV piece].

Our Jaguar is met by an awkward, respectful crowd of Python workers, Tiger TV personnel and, always hovering, the documentary crew. Too many people, too much respect.

Terry J, fresh back from holiday, is combative as ever. He says he only read the script on the plane back from Tuscany, and clearly had the same sinking reaction that I experienced. It starts well, but goes on too long, and is not Python. TJ doesn't even like what is Python, and isn't at all happy with the inclusion of 'Hearing Aid Sketch'. His view is that the compilation works very well and anything else that goes in will only reduce it.

JC is the last to arrive before GC. He brings his two daughters, a shy but beautiful Camilla, somewhat upstaged Cynthia ('If you've anything for her in your next film, Mickey, she's not a bad little actress') and Dingbat, as he calls Alyce Faye.

GC arrives about 2.30, about three and a half hours after TG and I got into our schoolboy outfits. He looks very frail and his eyes are staring out of hollowed sockets.

His presence is inspiring, but somehow the sight of him in a blond wig and schoolboy cap sums up the whole misbegotten day.

GC, carried and put into position by two nurses, is tremendous despite weakness. He talks and laughs and, even when squashed in a cupboard with the rest of us at six o'clock, is still uncomplaining.

Monday, September 25th

In the post today two double-page spreads from the *Sun* tell Graham Chapman's own story – the alcoholism (GC's claims for his drinking grow more prodigious each time he tells the story), the homosexuality (which seems to be by implication a sort of disease) and now the cancer. Pictures of him pitifully thin, but back at home. Is talking to the *Sun* and being photographed all over your house really the best thing to do on your first week out of hospital?

Anne rings with an unsettling request. The *Guardian* want me to write an obituary for Graham C. Cannot believe this is the *Guardian* and feel very uncomfortable. Do they know something I don't? Are any other Pythons being asked? Anne confirms it's just me. I cannot go along with it. GC must only be thinking in terms of the future at the moment, and so must I.

Friday, September 29th

To Prominent Studios. TJ not able to make the meeting as this is *Erik* launch day, but JC (wearing glasses, I was relieved to see), Eric and the Gilliam are there. Elaborate and confusing figures are disregarded and Anne, who chairs, asks us directly who is in favour of a move (at the right price), from the studios, and who against? Myself and TJ (whose vote I have) are in favour. JC and Eric against. TG wavering towards our side.

I think the Cantabrigians are surprised. Elaborate my reasons. The place has not developed into a Python film-making community, as idealistically intended; the facilities seem to be administratively cumbersome and financially unpromising; André definitely, and Mayday I think, would welcome the move. I would rather keep my involvement with Redwood than be the landlord of some editing rooms and offices.

'Mikey's bored,' John accurately paraphrases. Eric wavers. If we get a decent price – £2.6 million is suggested as a minimum – how much do we make? It works out that we save, and make, up to £70,000.

TG reiterates the arguments, that it's not fun any more, like Neal's Yard was (Anne's eyebrows up here). JC, who really likes the viewing theatre and being able to park his huge Bentley, refuses to agonise and eventually an agreeable consensus is reached that we should proceed into the projected sale, but should accept no less than 2.7 million.

Tuesday, October 3rd

Time Out is the first journal to sow seeds of doubt in my mind over *80 Days*' appeal. A humourless review which whines about the shame of having to 'pour cold water' over the programme and proceeds to do so with great glee.

Anne rings to say Graham has had a bad night and may go back into hospital. He certainly won't be able to attend the anniversary party tomorrow.

Down to the Holiday Inn Hotel in Mayfair to fulfil a series of interview obligations. First an appearance in a documentary about *Viz*, defending the magazine, then a piece about Python's 20th for Australia's Channel 7. The TV crews are so typical of their countries. The Australians grin a lot, are rather like big schoolboys and seem anxious to get it done and go round the pub.

Then hare off home to a longish chat with CBC – the non-aligned, apologetic, intelligent Canadians.

Establishing shots of me in garden. Squirt what I think is water from one of Helen's garden sprays into my mouth as a joke. Later told it's highly poisonous!

Granny G has arrived for Mary and Edward's 25th wedding anniversary party.

We eat late – it's almost ten by the time we are all assembled at Mon Plaisir, Mary's and Edward's favourite restaurant in courting days, now benefiting from the Covent Garden renaissance and no longer having the rather squashed, cosy, plain and unpretentious French presence it had in the bad old days.

Will rings sounding grave. He's heard from TG, who's heard from Anne, that Graham is seriously ill in hospital. He has secondary cancers all over his body and is not expected to last the night. All this over the noise of popping corks and laughter reminds me of my father dying during the football results. There's precious little dignity around. Ring Terry J. Sal [Terry's daughter] answers. He and Alison have both gone down to the hospital.

Back home. It's half past twelve and been a long evening. There seems no point in my rushing down to Maidstone. I'm legally too drunk to drive anyway. Phone the hospital, but can never get through. Sometime after one I give up and get to bed, expecting to be woken any time.

Wednesday, October 4th

Anne rings at a quarter to eight. Graham has stayed alive through the night. The anniversary party this evening is to be cancelled. I agree. There will be nothing to celebrate.

After breakfast I call David [Graham's partner]. Can't keep back a choke of emotion on the phone and feel rather feeble having to curtail the call, but the moment of regret for Gra suddenly so intense.

Sit for a few minutes in the sunshine on my balcony. The telephone rings. Drag myself back in. It's Alison at the office. She's had a call from JC who has just spoken to Graham's brother, John. Gra has only a few

hours left to live. John is on his way down to the hospital. I um and ah
for a moment. What can I do? Will I be in the way? Consult Helen, who
says I should go. Suddenly the tiredness disappears and, I suppose, a
shot of adrenaline revives the system as I grab whatever I may need,
check the directions and leave for Maidstone.

The traffic is going home all across South London and it takes me
over one and a half hours to get to the hospital. It's set in fields outside
Maidstone, has some bright, post-modernist pavilions at one end, and
a big, heavy Victorian workhouse at the other. Around it a quiet and
spectacular sunset is fading.

Long walk to the Cornwallis Ward. Graham is in a private room at
the end.

At Graham's bedside are John, his brother, heavier, a quite different
shape from the megapodal Graham, and on the other side, holding the
hand above which the bandages conceal a drip feed which is keeping
Gra alive, is John C.

We talk a while, then they go out and I'm left alone with Graham. He
breathes laboriously but regularly.

I'm told that the faculty of sound is known to be the last to go and so I
rattle on about everyday things. About my lousy review in *Time Out*, the
sunset, the fountain being removed from Prominent courtyard.

David comes in, smiling and relaxed. He kisses Graham's head and
smoothes his sallow brow, closes the window a little, tells me that their
house is the next one to the hospital, just across a field. He's happy to
leave me with Gra. David says a room has been cleared where we can go.
I say I'm all right ... 'You Yorkshiremen,' grins David.

I walk round to the window then come back to his right-hand side;
take his cold hand in my hot one and tell him, quite loudly, that we all
love him.

The regularity of his breathing is broken. A long pause, then a long
inhalation. His lower jaw rises, his mouth closes and bares his lower
teeth. I reach for my cup of tea. He breathes heavily. I start to talk again.
A single tear emerges from his right eye and rolls down his cheek. The
mouth is set. The great ridge of Adam's apple is still. There is no more
noise from him. Nothing dramatic, no rattles or chokes or cries. He's
not moving any more.

I don't want to leave him, nor do I want to make any noise or sudden
movement. It's a moment out of time. All I can feel is that I shouldn't be
here, that David and John his brother should be.

There's noise outside. The clatter of patients and visiting friends. I call John and David to go in. They re-emerge a minute or so later. Graham is dead. It's about twenty past seven. John C, David Sherlock and I hug one another together. Tears but not in torrents – just filling the eyes. David S is quite magnificent. He makes it easier for everybody by being genuinely pleased and relieved that Graham's suffering is over.

I drive him back to the house at Barming – ironically the first time I've been there.

David shows me the house. It's unreal to be talking as if it's an ordinary day, but then what should one do? This is his way of celebrating Graham – the rooms he lived in, the chaos of newspapers and magazines.

There was an easel with a rough-and-ready oil painting of the garden gate – did I know Graham had taken up painting? He showed me the pool and the squash court and pulled two Coxes off the apple tree – 'Organic, of course' – for me to eat on the way home.

I left David cutting an Arctic Rose off the tree by the gate to take to Graham – 'His favourite thing in the garden' – and headed back to London. David said as he hugged me goodbye that he felt elated ... 'I know it seems silly.' It doesn't really. I feel something similar as I drive back up the almost deserted A20. Much more tranquil, much more comfortable and at ease than I have been for days. Graham has, after all, been delivered from months of great pain.

I drop in on TJ, who's at home with Al and the children. He's very pleased to see me. He's just heard the news from JC who was lost somewhere near New Cross.

Drink a glass of red.

As I leave, he observes Graham must be the greatest party-pooper in history. I can hear Graham laughing at this all the way down Camberwell Grove.

Switch on the eleven o'clock news. The train of refugees still coming out of East Germany. Odd to know that one is sitting on a headline story which the press still haven't got hold of.

I hardly have time to talk to Helen before the phones start ringing. (In fact as I sat with Graham in the little room he died in, David entered and showed me a name on a piece of paper ... 'Baz Bamigboye[1] rang'.)

---

1 Show business correspondent of the *Daily Mail*.

I don't want to talk to anyone tonight. Rachel has deflected the *Mail*, Helen copes well with the *Mirror*, and, repeatedly, the *Sun*.

To bed about one with both upstairs phones unplugged.

Thursday, October 5th: London–Southwold

The headline in the *Sun* on the day of the 20th anniversary of our first broadcast is 'Python Star Dies'.

The phone is ringing downstairs when Rachel goes to feed the cats at 7.30. Ask no-one to pick it up until I'm up, washed, dressed and fed.

Then to my desk, at 8.30, and open up the shop. The phone calls come without a break. Fifteen times I tell of my reaction, give my assessment of 'Graham Chapman's contribution' either to the phone, or the tape recorder and camera or, later, in the form of two instantly written pieces for the *Guardian* and the *Telegraph*.

Three TV crews visit the house. I've no time to pour boiled milk for a cup of coffee, and it burns away, filling the house with a frightful pong.

The activity subsides about six o'clock. My first interview was with CBS News in New York, my last with CBC in Toronto. I feel emotionally unmoved today. This is a job of work, but I feel I must do it to make sure the right things are said about GC, the introverted extrovert.

I hear, via Anne, that both TJ and Eric have given up and gone to bed. My way of getting away is to leave for Southwold in mid-evening, just as more American interview requests are coming in.

Book a room at the Swan. Am up at Sunset House by a quarter to ten. Mum fit and well, but needs her hair doing. It lies drably across her brow. Nice hour with her, then to the Swan for a drink with Dudley Clarke, the manager, and his staff before bed.

Friday, October 6th

Clear skies as I wash and shave at a quarter to nine. To breakfast and read three obituaries for GC. My *Guardian* piece reads well, but has three glaring mistakes due to hasty dictation. JC has written a short and well-expressed piece in the *Independent* which, thank God, makes up for an appallingly insensitive piece by their own man which ends up revealing why Graham 'was the one who was ultimately dispensable'. My *Telegraph* piece has had the last sentence about 'why we all loved him' removed.

Sunday October 8th

Tom's 21st birthday.

Rachel makes a 1968–1989 poster and Will does some very silly things on the photocopier with Tom's head and other bodies.

Show some early film of Tom which is riotously received. It's almost uncannily appropriate, too, that one of the Super 8 films shot in the very first days of Python shows Tom as a baby at Remenham climbing over a sleeping, supine Cleese and Connie whilst Graham does handstands in the background, and wanders across frame smoking his pipe!

Monday, October 9th

More parties ahead today, but have to rise early for appearance on *Start the Week*.

At BH by 8.30. Melvyn is dapper in a nattily fitting pin-stripe suit, tie and matching handkerchief. Others on the prog are gathering, including Mark Lawson of the *Independent* – one of my favourite journos, funny, informative and enthusiastic. In jest – well, partly in jest – I complain that the paper I've supported since the day of its birth should rap *80 Days* so severely over the knuckles in Saturday's preview, before anyone's had a chance to see it. He asks after the name of the journalist … it was one Stephen Pope … 'Oh, Pope Stephen, as they call him in the office.'

To a viewing theatre at CFS [Colour Film Services] in Portman Close.

People already arriving at the *80 Days* screening. George Harrison, looking on good form with a big, flowing mane of hair, John Cleese, with his mum, and a present of a *Three Men in a Boat* picture, Michael Barnes,[1] looking thinner and more patriarchal than ever. Most of our regular friends there.

I watch it in a sweat of embarrassment, noticing for the first time the dull, intrusive music, the plodding, heavily delivered clichés of commentary, the overlong sequences of Venice and the preparations. Can see quite clearly what the critics are on about and retreat from the applause at the end to grab a cooling glass at the bar.

---

1 Michael Barnes. Director of the Belfast Festival who encouraged me to do my first one-man show there in 1981.

Thursday, October 12th

Mark Lawson is the first critic I read and sure enough he leads with *80 Days*. Beneath the rather unkind headline 'Travel Sickness' is a not unkind review.

He opens with the line 'Is it possible to be too nice to be a television presenter?' This 'niceness' is clearly to be used as a stick to beat me with … What a world. But I like the review for its detail, constructiveness and wit, though I would have liked its conclusions to be a little more favourable. I write him a note and send him a book!

Collect a fat wad of other papers and am quite shocked at the intensity of feeling. *The Times* is a two-line dismissal of all our work, written by Rhoda Koenig, a lady I met in New York some years ago. I remember her as clever but eccentric. (Apparently she dismissed *Miss Saigon* as well.)

The *Express* and the *Mail* both disliked it with a strange vehemence. Nancy Banks-Smith [critic for the *Guardian*] said I'd preserved, into middle age, 'the bright-eyed charm of a baby chipmunk'.

For a couple of minutes my senses smart from the unexpected virulence of these reactions. It's like being spat at in the street. The hurt is quick but does not go deep and my swift surge of anger subsides.

Down to GLR, formerly Radio London. Johnnie Walker is in the chair. An esteemed name from the pirate ships, by way of Radio 1 and now a nicely mellow survivor playing his own eclectic selection of music. Phone lines busy when my presence is announced. One man asks me how drunk I really was in the *Orient Express*. He said he'd been off the booze for a week and really envied me.

A gossipy lunch with TG. He goes on about this last year, which I think has been a blow to his pride – *Munchausen* largely dismissed as an expensive failure; 'Watchmen' never getting off the ground and Prominent Features, his brainchild, in disarray. He variously refers to these misfortunes as a year of doing nothing … a year off … a year out. To the restless TG there can be little advantage to what others might consider a welcome break.

Friday, October 13th

Early call from Granny. Most concerned about Lady Collett's vehement reaction to my denunciation in the *Mail*. Apparently Lady C is wild about this slight to her neighbour's good name and, what's more, is convinced that Alan Whicker wrote the review!

Drive to Shepherd's Bush and meet Verity L, David Jones, her fellow producer, Peter Ansorge, commissioning editor of Drama at Channel 4 and, at last, Alan Bleasdale. They have been in a smoke-filled room for a week, going through every one of the six episodes. Verity is anxious to assure Alan that nothing has been lost that shouldn't have been lost. Bleasdale begs, in a gentlemanly way, to differ. But it's good to see the project still strong.

Bleasdale is talkative, funny and gives off a palpable air of worry and insecurity which is attractive and affecting.

He fortifies himself with very large vodkas and is clearly a fish out of water in London. He's staying at the Kensington Hilton – 'A terrible place.' Has he sampled its restaurant, the Hiroko, the best Japanese in West London? 'I didn't know it existed ... anyway, I've never eaten Japanese.'

GBH is going to be some adventure, and after two hours with these shell-shocked writers and producers I feel a breath of cool, fresh air blowing over the next 12 months.

Saturday, October 14th

I spend the afternoon writing a 1,300-word piece on *80 Days* for Arts and Entertainment's 'TV Guide' in the US before leaving for Helen's surprise birthday evening.

For company, Mary and Edward, Ian and Anthea and Terry and Al, for hospitality, L'Escargot, for entertainment to Ronnie Scott's, where Hugh Masekela is playing.

Ronnie's, especially on a busy night like tonight, has an exciting, sweaty, smoky feel. It's still a triumph of passion over environment, and the hot, densely packed atmosphere is lively and carries a welcome hint of minor decadence in an increasingly 'styled' and designed world.

Masekela begins with a recital of some impressive lists of jazz greats, beginning with the Deep South cotton fields and on up to Chicago and then into South Africa. The music is played with tremendous attack and great virtuosity, especially from the sweat-dampened Masekela and his slim, high-foreheaded, white saxophonist, who hurls the sounds out with seemingly not a bead of perspiration.

Excitement fulfilled and it's a magic hour's set, which none of us wants to end.

Monday, October 16th

Heavy traffic and don't arrive at Tom Phillips' studio until half past ten. 'If you think your reviews are bad, listen to these,' he greets me, with a clutch of cuttings about his recently opened exhibition of 'portrait works' at the National Portrait Gallery.

A man called Richard Dorment in the *Telegraph* is particularly enraged by what he perceives as Tom's overweening ego. 'He even writes his own labels for the pictures.' And why not? I side with Tom.

But it's a cold morning in the studio and I don't feel in sparkling mood. I look at his watercolour of me on the wall behind him, alongside Terry and Terry and now Eric (Di Celeri). I look rather thin and tense.

Only one man he has painted in his studio whom he really disliked – Professor Owen Chadwick, who, on entering, saw a half-finished canvas. 'Ah, painting ugly old women are we?' It was Tom's mum.

Tuesday, October 17th: London–Southwold

A couple of uninterrupted days in my workroom is the least I need, but I have promised to go up to Southwold, where it is no longer as easy for me to work as before.

Ma more demanding now and less flexible, so lunch has to be quickly served up.

Then take her out for a walk, followed by a visit to Lady Collett, to whom I present a copy of *80 Days*. She is delighted. The two of them, both slightly deaf, have oddly unconnecting conversations ... 'How's Mrs Hurran?' 'She fell over.' 'Is she better?' 'You know she fell over?' Lady C gives us sherry at 4.30 and has to draw the curtains across against the piercing bright sunlight. She suggests my mother and she get together to play Scrabble.

Then the best part of the day – a glorious run across the marshes in the still-warm, vaporous haze of a lazy autumn day.

Wednesday, October 18th: Southwold

Described today in the *Independent* as the 'terminally nice Michael Palin'.

Walk across the Common on a day almost as perfect as yesterday. A harassed master struggles to teach Eversley boys outside Ma's window how to play football.

The fact is, she is bored. She has nothing much to do but sit and wait to be fed and walked. She tries to find things she can do on her own, but these all seem to require more and more effort.

Watch the second episode of *80 Days* together. It's the Egyptian and Saudi Arabian section and I feel it all works much better than episode one. Ma nods off as I enter Jeddah.

Thursday, October 19th

After breakfast, round to Ma's by 9.15. Her *Telegraph* bears the headline 'Palin for Prime Minister' on the arts page. I'm now very jumpy about reviews and sure enough this one, with gushing praise suggesting I have all the qualities for getting on with people that Maggie T hasn't, eventually slides into some mild but wearisome stick! Ma has seen no further than the headline and is quite delighted!

Farewells, feeling a little less guilty this time, and into the car.

To Clem's office to sign books for the crews. Roger quite perky about the reviews. 'What they don't realise is that this isn't a serious documentary, it's a stunt.' I don't think Clem likes this. I think all of us waiting for some unequivocally good news. With anything less than this there is the faint smell of blood in the water at Ken House.

Thursday, October 26th

A warm review from Lawson in the *Independent*, recalling his early doubts, but withdrawing them after this third show, which he described as 'high-class'. Also noted that part of my 'charm' was an 'unsneering' way with foreigners.

A message from Stanford's to ask if I could come in early for my book-signing as they have had a surge in orders after last night's programme.

At Stanford's just before twelve, and continue signing until 2.30. They have never experienced anything like it. Trolleyloads of my book wheeled in like piles of bricks. The queue still full an hour after I was due to stop.

Fight my way out of the shop to lunch with Clem at Grimes in Garrick Street, pursued and accosted by locals bearing books or just scraps of paper. Clem confirms that there is now better feeling about the series in the corridors of the Beeb. Oysters and Sancerre and slowly cool down from the excitements of the morning.

I've promised I will go back to Stanford's and sign the rest of the stock. This takes a further one and a half hours, and by the time I fold myself into the back of the taxi I've signed over 650 copies.

Friday, October 27th: London–Stocks House, Hertfordshire

Clem calls with the best news of the *80 Days* transmission thus far – the viewing figures actually built, on the second episode, to 8.6 million.

Back home and into a hectic hour of packing for JC's 50th birthday party. JC's present, a 1939-bottled Armagnac, arrives, as well as his Margaret Thatcher plate. Neat timing in view of Lawson's resignation.[1]

Leave for Stocks at 7.15, arrive at the house less than an hour later. We've been given a room with a waterbed. Already guests gathering in the hall with their obligatory funny hats on.

Jeremy's sheep on my head is easily the biggest and silliest and most inventive. David Hatch later says it's a hat which grew more silly as the evening went on.[2] Every time he looked up and saw me talking earnestly or toying with white wine and smoked salmon, the sheep on my head, wobbling and nodding, gave him more and more pleasure.

The 'entertainment' works extremely well. All my props, especially the parrots and the spangly jacket I found at the last moment, are greatly appreciated, and I read the *This Is Your Life* joke intro smoothly, despite this being the first time I've worn my specs in public. David Frost, John Lloyd, David Hatch (very, very funny in a deadpan BBC way), Stephen Fry ('Some men are born great, some achieve greatness and some have greatness faxed through to them') and Peter Cook – not as good on

1 Nigel Lawson, Chancellor of the Exchequer in Margaret Thatcher's government since 1983, resigned over the role played by Sir Alan Walters, the Prime Minister's economic adviser.
2 David Hatch was an ex-Cambridge Footlight and close friend of John's who rose to become Head of Radio at the BBC. He died in 2007. The upturned sheep on my head was made for me by my nephew Jeremy Herbert.

his feet as he is at table – make the awards, and Shamberg shows some video tributes, including one from Jamie who is seen at home greedily apportioning her *Wanda* money – 'house', 'education', 'divorce'.

It's all a great success and it's a quarter to two before Helen and I climb aboard the waterbed, bringing on distinct memories of the dhow.

Saturday, October 28th: Stocks

Strong winds assault the house and rain is hurled against the windows. We're at breakfast just after Peter and Lin Cook and just before the Frosts. David and Carina are rather a lovable pair. Carina wipes egg from David's lower lip as he rises to pay us a gushingly appreciative goodbye.

We read the papers in the soft-cushioned hall, then walk a while in the sunshine. Then some table tennis. I beat Helen, but lose to Peter C, who is a very large man now. He was the only one who sported fancy dress at the party last night. He came as Demis Roussos.

We all go to lunch at the Bell at Aston Clinton. Feuilleté of mushrooms, stuffed salmon en croute (always too rich and yet I always fall for it) and sweet puddings.

Alyce Faye's birthday evening more subdued than the night before, but some fresh blood – Kevin K, the Hutchisons, M Winner and the lovely Jenny Seagrove. Winner makes a speech in which he says how nice it was to meet everyone at lunch, even if 'the sole topic of conversation was Michael Palin's hat'.

The lights go down mid-meal and we all prepare to sing 'Happy Birthday', but it turns out to be a power cut.

Sunday, October 29th: Stocks House–London

We are down at breakfast at nine.

Peter C arrives, looming, shambolic, cigarette held rather daintily in right hand, hair awry and one trouser leg suspended mid-calf. He says he was woken in horrific circumstances when the electric current came back on in the middle of the night. Apart from the lights, his radio and TV came back at full volume and his hairdryer began to writhe across the floor.

It's a very funny breakfast. At our different tables in this elegant dining room, united by the music of Kenny Rogers on the PA, discussing bribery and smuggling. Peter observes that the first rule of bribery is to bribe the right people. Carter DeHaven, the *Yellowbeard* producer,[1] spent large sums from the budget lavishly entertaining locals in Mexico City who had no influence over anything at all.

Leave a message for JC, who has not yet appeared, and drive down leaf-sodden lanes into a brilliant blustery morning.

Only cloud on an otherwise clear horizon is from my Ma. She says that her back has gone again. Dr Thom who was so excellent in May has gone to Australia. So she's back on painkillers and sounds a bit low.

Saturday, November 4th: Glasgow–London

Wake, at the Caledonian, in much the same state as I awoke last Saturday at Stocks. In a room verging on the vulgar, much bigger than any room at home, with a soft wash of luxury and indulgence about it, and in my mind a clear and clean feeling of work done, of tests survived successfully, of the calm after the storm. All that and the hint of a headache.

To breakfast, then catch the eleven o'clock shuttle south.

Since Monday morning I've signed 3,110 *80 Days* books. BBC Books have authorised a 45,000 reprint, larger than the original first run, and Clem told me last night that a further 300,000 have been added to the viewing figures, taking it up to 8.9 for the bowels and bum episode on the dhow.

Sunday, November 5th

The *Sunday Times* best-seller list is required reading (meaning I have to make a special journey to fetch it and all its concomitants), showing me in there at No. 3 on the Hardback Generals. Any great feelings of literary achievement tempered by the fact that the book above me is the complete *'Allo 'Allo!* scripts. Denis Healey is top.

Long, slow unfolding over breakfast. Thatcher really does seem to be wobbling now. The look in her eyes on last week's Walden show was that of a trapped rat. Today in the *Correspondent* she is, for the first time, equivocal about staying on to lead the party.

---

1 *Yellowbeard* was a 1983 comedy produced and co-written by Graham Chapman. One of the cast, Marty Feldman, died during the filming.

Monday, November 6th

More confirmation of the *80 Days* effect from Anne – Tesco want me to go to various parts of the world to extol their food products, and have offered me £200,000.

In mid-afternoon I go for a run. It's cool today and harder work than expected. Meet Denis King, who is playing at Maureen Lipman's Joyce Grenfell show, *Re: Joyce!* Says it's packed every night.

Now Maureen did ads, and they didn't do her any harm. But somehow it would be such a letdown. Q: What are you doing after *80 Days*? A: A series of commercials for Tesco. Not really on.

Friday, November 10th

Clem calls at 11.30 with the viewing figures for programme four. Good news indeed – a hoick in the audience of 1.3 million to beyond 10 – 10.2. 'We've made it,' says Clem. 'Time for the champagne.'

I don't think I've ever done anything that's pulled in a 10-million audience. For Clem today must be the vindication of all his work. We could fall back, but to have passed 10 on the fourth show represents unequivocal success.

Give an interview to three Arab women – living in England – for a magazine about Muslim affairs. They loved the dhow episode and felt it showed the best of the Muslim way of life – the hospitality, the food, the prayer, the simple values, etc. I was pleased and must write again to Dave Thomas, the editor, who first said the dhow should be an entire episode.

I wash and shower and come down to find a bottle of champagne from Fortnum's and a note from Suzanne Webber to say that my book is No. 1 this week on the best-seller list!

Then TJ rings from Berlin. Almost speechless. *Erik the Viking* opened in Germany on the night they began to pull down the wall. Extraordinary times, he says. The streets full of people in an emotional state. Complete strangers clutching each other. Euphoric happiness.

Tuesday, November 14th: London–Southwold

The fog grew thicker the nearer I came to Southwold. Last few miles very slow. Arrive to find Ma looking like Joan Crawford in her later days, haunting the top of the stairs. 'Oh, Michael! Oh ... I was so wor-ried,' and so on.

Bite my lip – what good would it do to tell her I was driving carefully in fog, that I had said teatime? Anyway, calm and restore her to her chair. But she is not in good shape. The wretched back pain seems to keep her in perpetual discomfort.

As always happens, no moment is guaranteed sacred and the *Mirror* tracks me down to ask some footling questions about Python. As I try to recount 'how we thought of the title', Mum grunts and clutches herself in pain beside me. The room's very hot. She's short of breath.

Eventually we settle to eat supper on our knees. I hate to see her spirit break. She has always been so strong, so stoical, so composed. But humour creeps in ... 'Kiddy came in the other day dressed like the Ayatollah ... some great long thing.' She smiles. She is really most happy watching an episode of *Dad's Army*. This does her more good than any food, drink or drug.

About a quarter to nine, feeling somehow I've failed, I call Kay. Ma wants a painkiller and she wants to go to bed. She can't hear, she can't connect, but her brain knows well that she is in a sad state.

I write all this in the impersonal neutrality of my hotel room, unable to stop making useless comparisons that, at the peak of my own celeb-rity, Mother is at last beginning to give up.

I hope I'm wrong. I hope the pain and indignity will lift with the fog, that we'll all be fresh and everything will seem less bleak in the morning light.

Walk to the sea. Southwold is much quieter now – reverting to its winter ghost-town status. I think about ghosts, about strong and yet insubstantial things. My sense of regret for the days when Will and Tom sat astride the barrels of the cannons in their green duffle coats. Time cannot be held. It slips away, always eluding the grasp.

Wednesday, November 15th: Southwold

To Ma on time. She is uncomfortable, often acutely so, and being with her is like being beside a hospital bed, which is where she would surely be without 'Kiddy'.

A lady reporter rings up and Granny comes back from the loo with such groans and 'Oh, Michaels' and clutchings at the furniture that I have to put the phone down. Then she's quite happy. This technique creates apprehension bordering on panic in those around ('What were you doing? You looked as if you were going to die!') and immediately calms the perpetrator, who then becomes almost sheepishly apologetic.

Thursday, November 16th: Southwold–London

Leave for London at half past ten.

To Dean Street to discuss my involvement in a video to help parents of children who have speech problems – especially stammers. Awfully nice man, middle-aged, called Travers Reid. A stammerer, now almost cured, he remembers 'the day I unlocked my T'. The teacher had gone out and he had taken over and had the class roaring with laughter … 'I've had to tell jokes ever since,' he admits, a little unhappily.

Friday, November 17th

Granny has just rung, sounding clear and confident, to say Dr Hopkins has diagnosed a great recovery. There is almost no sign of the crackle of fluid in her lungs and she went for a walk (in her chair) almost as far as the Harbour Inn today.

The *Independent* has a piece by Peter Kellner on 'The Alternative TV Ratings'. These are the ratings of Audience Appreciation rather than just viewing and result from door-to-door surveys of 3,000 punters. Top of the ratings for the week ending 29th October was … *Around the World in 80 Days* with 85 (anything over 80 he judges 'a clear success').

Audience figures for show five are up to 11.3 million, which makes us bigger than all three other channels put together. This leaves me temporarily disorientated, as if I've just been flung round a spectacular corner on a fairground ride. Exhilarated, a little light-headed and a tiny bit sick.

In the evening I begin to assemble material for the Belfast Festival.

Sunday, November 19th: Belfast

To the Arts Theatre at half past ten.

Over the next hour I sort out an opening, with Michael Barnes as a psychiatrist asking me why I wanted to be a lumberjack and getting me from there into a rap about anniversaries, looking back and then into an autobiographical piece from birth to Python.

Second-half opening and closing worked out. Then to a lunch party at respectable, safe Myrtle Wood Road, where the Troubles seem very far away.

Bath, rehearse new bit in my mind, then, hoping upon hope that I will feel right on the night, I set off up Great Victoria Street, past the latest rash of newly opened restaurants in a city whose revival, as I have seen it over eight years, has been constant, and that despite a continuing emergency.

For a moment in my dressing room I experience a sinking feeling that I am not going to be able to pull off the trick again, but the energy returns, the moment passes and, though the first half has some less successful moments, it is 80 minutes long and I never noticed. Cracking second half and back to dressing room at 10.30, elated and very damp. Glorious moment of relief spreads on into the evening and if I could only bottle this blissful state I'd sip a little each day of my life.

Wednesday, November 22nd

The last of my *80 Days* programmes goes out tonight. Stephen Pope continues his war of attrition to the end – refusing to like it much, but refusing to give up on it, but the other *Independent* preview is wholehearted – 'The last in MP's splendid series. Quite why some have seen his ease in front of camera, professionalism and apparent "niceness" as a handicap is a mystery.' Jeremy Novick joins Mark Lawson on an honourable roll!

Then to Kensington House for champagne with Colin Cameron. Almost two years since his predecessor Will Wyatt first put the idea to me, we have come to the climax of the realisation of the project. Cameron clearly delighted at its success – the figures, etc.

Then on to Angela Elbourne [Production Assistant on *80 Days* and *Pole to Pole*] and Jeremy's small house on 'Chiswick/Acton Borders' to watch the last transmission.

It goes down well. I almost have tears in my eyes at the end.

Thursday, November 23rd

A clutch of final reviews. The *Guardian* is lengthy and quite sensible, selecting the dhow as favourite. *The Times* re-reviews with muted enthusiasm. Peter Paterson of the *Daily Mail* remains grumpily unconverted.

I am asked to do a phone-in to the TV programme *Open Air*, who have never received as many letters for one series. Today all sorts of nice things said. People will miss it ... 'Tears in Dewsbury!' Will Wyatt calls and gushes for nearly 15 minutes. He says 24 calls of support on last night's duty log. Unprecedented.

It's a delicious feeling to have risen above the critics – to feel completely invulnerable. I run, on a cool, bright day, with a wide, stretching peace of mind.

Sunday, November 26th

Read the rewritten first episode of *GBH* and am confirmed in my interest in the part of Michael Murray. Nagging feeling that perhaps the subject of the corruption of socialism in the '70s is not as pertinent as the political changes going on in Europe (and hopefully the UK) at the moment.

Monday, November 27th

Some early Christmas present shopping this a.m.

I feel tired and rather scruffy and am most surprised at the number of people who recognise me until I remember that my on-screen appearance at the end of *80 Days* last week was exactly the same – tired and scruffy and even in the same bomber jacket and trousers. Smiles, hoots from cab drivers and general enthusiasm all round.

Suzanna Zsohar [my publicist from BBC Books] calls to say yet another reprint has been organised, bringing the total number of books in the shops by Christmas to 155,000.

Watch another episode of *Boys from the Blackstuff*. Alan Bleasdale, Alan Bennett, probably the two playwrights whose work moves me most. The chance of working for both is not to be missed.

Tuesday, November 28th

Up and to first appointment, which is at Parliament Hill School. I've offered them a chunk of my ill-gotten gains. Wait in the main hallway – quite pleased to find it clean, painted and friendly.

Judy Base, the head teacher, gives me a list of areas where money might be spent – computer lines to some of the classrooms, carpets in the clattery language classrooms, etc. After yesterday's news on the book reprint, I up my donation to £4,000. Cheque signed then and there. Why do I feel vaguely guilty, seedy, apologetic about bringing out the chequebook and signing? Is it because such behaviour goes against all my parents' attitudes to money – that, like sex, it's something that goes on, but not in public?

Friday, December 1st

To lunch at Odette's with Clem V. Last prog's viewing figures 12.8 million, an increase of one and a half million over last week.

We talk about future plans. Clem assumes that I shall work with him again and that our destinies are now irrevocably entwined. Not unhappy with this, but would like Roger's presence there somewhere. With 'AF' and Bleasdale the front runners for '90, we're talking autumn '91. For the first time Clem comes up with the excellent, almost too obvious suggestion that we should do it independently of the BBC.

Saturday, December 2nd

Call Al L to check it's all right to visit him next Thursday. He has just heard bad news. The tumour on his liver has not responded to the chemotherapy. It's still growing. He has lost 25 lbs with the treatment and they are now taking him off it in order to let his body recover before another course of poison is unleashed on it. More so than I ever knew with Graham, I know this is the end for Al. What a goddamned motherfucker of a year. A beauty and a beast.

Sunday, December 3rd

Drive down to Bart's for Graham's memorial. Rather like arriving at the run-through of a charity show. Groups of people standing about, mikes being tested.

Barry Cryer is to MC. JC has bought himself a leather cap, just when they're going out of fashion in East Germany. Terry J, tanned and fluffy-headed and beseeching, is fresh back from Hong Kong.

Alan Bennett and Jonathan Miller are sat behind us – modestly lurking in overcoats like Russian Secret Service men.

Barry hits the right tone from the beginning – avoiding sententiousness, but not necessarily discouraging it. John is outrageous and does the 'Dead Parrot' sketch. 'Graham Chapman, co-writer of the "Dead Parrot" sketch is no more ...' etc. ... 'He is an ex-Chapman.' It's a fine piece about shock and in praise of Graham's use of it as a weapon. 'I also want to be the first person to say fuck at a memorial service ... (pause) but I daren't.'

No-one puts a foot wrong. There is nothing insincere or not truly felt in the 11 or 12 readings, reminiscences and songs. David is very good – celebrating Graham's giggling and remembering how GC and Cleese were banished from a Trevor Nunn production after an afternoon spent miming climbing a glacier.

I was the last, but my remarks about GC being incorrigibly late were well received. 'I'm sure that Graham is here with us today ... (pause) or at least he will be in about 20 minutes.'

Eric ended with a communal singing of 'Always Look on the Bright Side'. An excellent occasion, managing to be funny, silly and moving at the same time. As the throng began to stand up and move away, John sat for a moment, silently, his eyes full of tears. That I shall remember for a very long time.

Monday, December 4th: London–Southwold

Gather together my slide sheets and speech notes [for an *80 Days* talk], throw overnight clothes in a bag and set off on my travels again. Yesterday morning's fog not repeated and the drive up is uncomplicated and I arrive an hour early, which takes Ma by surprise.

She is sitting with Anne and Kay – a tiny, shrivelled presence in one chair while these two healthy, strong women watch over her, like birds beside a nest.

I walk round to the church hall to sort out the slides and the sound system. All looks efficient. Arrangements have been made to have my mother there – in her wheelchair – along with Mrs Pratt and Lady Collett – combined ages of 250 years!

The hall filled beyond its 200 capacity – at least 240 there. Talk goes well. I have inserted two slides of Mrs Pratt, Granny, Snowy the dog, and Rachel at the door of Victoria Cottage in amongst the dhow sequence – as dreams of home.

It's quite a shock to see someone below the age of 50 come up to the book-signing desk, and especially schoolgirls – three of whom bring up the rear with much blushing and shifting from foot to foot. 'You're a sex symbol at our school,' says one. She is referring to St Felix, the expensive private school where my Aunt Katherine was educated. 'Oh, yes ... the bit where you enter the hot baths in the Rockies, we play that bit and stop the tape, just as you're entering the water.'

Tuesday, December 5th: Southwold–London

It briefly flashes through my mind that the thin little face frowning and waving vaguely from the upper window as I drive away may be the last living image I shall have of my mother. I wish I knew if she was happy or not. Then I would really know whether these lurking feelings of wanting her to be soon delivered from this imprisonment were justified or not. But I'm an optimist and I want her to be there again at the window when I next call – frowning, anxious or not.

Wednesday, December 6th: London–New York

To Heathrow for 10.30 Concorde. Journey uneventful. Usual impressions – the size of the plane compared to the size of the passengers – huge men moving about bent double. The rocket-like acceleration at take-off. The heat of the sun and the friction at 50,000 feet keeps the little tube boiling despite the fierce cold outside.

Nancy [Lewis] has found me a room at the Plaza Athénée. Small, prettily decorated hotel in French Rococo style. My room is spacious. Dark, but quiet, overlooking a blank and characterless New York back wall.

Make calls and walk round to Nancy and Simon. First introduction to Timothy, who favours me with fetching smiles and then joins us at Jean Lafitte for lunch. Nancy hasn't really changed or become overtly maternal and yet she seems a perfect mother – unhurried, unworried and full of the sheer delight of having this new thing in her life. Simon is off to do voice-overs – he is in a suit and hoping to get some Volkswagen business.

Wander the streets getting blown along by the unceasing flow of New York. Buy various things to take up to Sag tomorrow. Call Al. His voice sounds weak. He says I couldn't be coming at a better time, though I'm not sure what this may mean.

Thursday, December 7th: New York–Sag Harbor

Riding out onto Long Island in perfect conditions helps me to set aside some of my apprehensions as to what I shall find at Sag. As it is, I draw up Henry Street feeling optimistic and, as usual, feeling comfortable in and charmed by this good-looking little town.

No-one seems to be about in the house. Then Claudie emerges from the bedroom. She looks well, I'm relieved to see – slim and attractive without make-up and with damp hair. Al is down in the Hold and after some bright pleasantries we go down.

My first reaction on seeing him is one of relief. The fine Levinson head is as strong as ever. He hasn't lost hair and even the marked loss of weight has not distorted his handsome face. But when he speaks the voice is low and does not come clear from his mouth.

He has been asleep. His brow furrows and he reproves himself for falling asleep too easily. 'These drugs … Mike … these drugs.' He tells me later that this has been a bad week. Last night he was awake for hours scratching at his itching skin. The doctor says that the tumour may be pressing against the bile duct and preventing it from emptying properly.

He is overjoyed at the *80 Days* tapes I've brought him and the 'Palin Belfast '89' T-shirt. He and Claudie have loved the *80 Days* book and he relates several times the pleasure he got from being woken by Claudie laughing at a passage she was reading in bed.

He has asked if I will allow a local reporter from the *Sag Harbor Express* to take my picture and do a short interview. Al dons his Breton duffle coat and we drive down to the corner restaurant. His pace reminds me of my father and the occasional confusion is sad to see. But we sit down by the window looking out to the bridge which figures on so many of the cards he sent to me, and the wind-flecked cobalt-blue waters of the bay.

I eat boiled scrod and drink a Boston beer of taste called John Adams. With the sun shining in I notice that Al's eyes look a bilious yellow. He tries to concentrate and occasionally chimes in with a very good line – a flash of the old Al – but mostly he's suffering and trying not to show it.

I like Joe, the reporter – he's an ex-professional musician. Now he paints and does a bit of everything and his jolly, extrovert wife runs a framing business. He takes photos of myself and Al together.

Later I go out to the bank and there is Claudie just getting into her car. She tells me that she is very frightened. That Al was responding so well to the chemotherapy until two weeks ago when the deterioration started. And Al won't accept it's that serious so they can't plan ahead. She wipes the tears from her cheeks and we stare out at the neat, clean tidiness of Main Street and it seems suddenly offensive to me that no-one else seems to care.

I take a walk then go back to Henry Street. Talk to Al down in the Hold. He has high hopes, as I do, of someone from the hospice who is seeing them tomorrow.

Gwenola keeps bobbing her head round the door to get me to come up and open the presents I've brought her (a book of Greek legends and some Christmas socks). She is full of life and shows off and makes up to me and gradually gets closer and sits on my knees. Claudie cooks a meal of chicken and pumpkin pie and we drink some of the champagne I bought this morning in Noyack.

Soon after eight, having embraced Al and kissed Gwen and Claudie, I slide the wide door of the kitchen open and let myself out. As long as Al is there I don't feel sad or deprived. I want him to live only as long as he can see, hear, talk and enjoy himself.

Long drive on a conveyor belt of vehicles west to New York, down into the Midtown tunnel and back into an icy-cold city at half past ten.

Sunday, December 10th: New York

Cold and bright. Brunch and chat with Trini A at a small, check-table-cloth basement. Taking her clothes off in front of a camera is still her big worry. Mum possessive, but she loves her. A good and honest and truthful girl. Definitely the best casting.

Tuesday, December 12th: New York

Have just called Al to thank him for his latest half-written MS 'Match-point' which arrived c/o Federal Express in my room this a.m. He and the family watch an episode of *80 Days* each night before bed. Al cannot get out of his mind the image of old Kasim hugging me at the end of the dhow journey. I'm the same. I can never describe it without tears welling up.

Recorded 12 interviews back-to-back via satellite to Orlando, Kansas,

Dallas, Atlanta, Hartford, etc. Lunch with 'top' TV writers at Villa d'Arte.

Back, as snowflakes drift down, to Associated Press interview. Now to the Rainbow Room for the fourth meal in succession at which I have to sparkle, charm, be poked and prodded, be the star attraction.

Friday, December 15th: Los Angeles

It's five o'clock. I'm writing in the Ambassador Lounge at LAX.

The *80 Days* juggernaut continues to roll. Helen told me yesterday that a further reprint of 15,000 has been authorised, reaching the 200,000 mark, and the Royal Family has ordered a set of tapes for the holiday! And the BBC are to repeat *Ripping Yarns* in January after 12 years of prevarication.

Breakfasted by the pool. The Sunset Marquis is small, low and laid-back. Many Brit guests and quite an assortment of rock musicians still persevering with '70s hairstyles. One band were from Canada and awe-struck to meet me. 'Your tapes, man ... We play 'em all the time ... they keep us going in the tour bus.' Shades of '69/'70 all over again. Python and the rock world's strange compatibility.

This time yesterday I was being exhibited at the Western Show – a vast gathering of 13,000 cable execs. I was doing duty at the Arts and Entertainment booth where people could 'have your photo taken with Michael *A Fish Called Wanda* Palin'. There was an old balloon-painted backdrop and the front of a basket on a raised dais, and here I stood while those who wanted to were given a Polaroid snap of us together.

I looked on it philosophically and tried to do what I had to do in an optimistic frame of mind. It was really no worse than a book-signing without the books. There weren't that many takers – maybe 30 or 40 in the hour – and they were all good-natured and ranged from hot-handed girls to three-stripe military men.

Then out in a limousine, away from Anaheim's convention sprawl, to the more glamorous smog of Burbank and the NBC studios. Arrived an hour and a half before taping at the *Tonight Show*.

I showered; my shirt and jacket were pressed, the questions and Johnny Carson's answers, prepared after yesterday's long and tedious pre-interview over the phone from JFK, were handed to me and I briefly encountered Carson himself down in the gloomy, grubby wardrobe room. He was reciting the 'Parrot Sketch' and I told him how John used it at the memorial service. Later Carson used this as a spontaneous lead-in to the questions, which showed that he's not entirely in thrall to his researchers.

Saturday, December 16th: Los Angeles–London

Manage four or five hours' sleep on the plane, which leaves me in good shape for landfall at Heathrow. The fierce gales forecast do not materialise. The big lady beside me has 'Jesus' in pearls on a brooch prominent on her left breast. She read the Bible during the flight and didn't drink. She smiled a lovely, wide, infectious smile and told me that she'd prayed that the weather would clear up and it had.

All the hostesses have dreadful hairstyles and worn faces. One senior one came up and asked me if I would like them to lay on anything special in London. I assured her I would be fine ... 'You won't be mobbed, or anything?' she asked, in all sincerity!

As the plane bumps down its heavy load onto a wet tarmac, the Bible-reader beams at me and says she will pray for my career.

Wednesday, December 20th

To lunch at Chez Victor. Anne J, David Pugh and John Dove already at table. Time to plan ahead on *The Weekend*. Pugh still very interested. Most of all with me in it. Would I commit to 20-week involvement sometime in '91?

At the moment it sounds tempting. I would enjoy live performing – but is this the best vehicle? Will I really want to do a play I wrote ten years ago for half of a year – when there are bound to be exciting things offered?

Continue trawling through the shops. Rain pours down as I dodge into Hatchards. Am welcomed with open arms. 'Best-seller of the year' I'm told. They've three copies left. As I'm signing them a woman laden with books catches sight of mine and asks eagerly if she can buy one. The assistant manager clasps them protectively – 'These are spoken for, I'm afraid.'

Friday, December 22nd: Southwold

Kay is not prepared to take on day and night supervision of my mother. She tells me of a couple of incidents recently when Mother has been rude to people – she was 'appallingly rude' to Mrs Anstey, and though Kay loves her in a way, she is quite rightly not going to allow her to take over her own life.

I hardly recognise in all this the mother who never let things get on top of her, who was always efficient, hard-working, generous and tolerant – who looked after others impeccably and who can no longer look after herself.

The decay all around seems more real than any of the success. Graham's death and the reduction of Al and my mother to weak, flickering points of light. And my own loss of 100% eyesight, the sudden awareness that I can no longer see everything unaided, brings a whiff of their decay close to me.

Wednesday, December 27th: Abbotsley–London

Up while it's still dark, for we have to return to London and prepare and pack for a ski trip to the Pythonically-named Crap Ner Hotel in the resort of Flims.

Helen and Will sound to have done a sterling job at Southwold. They spent five hours with Granny, on her own. Helen is quite firm with her when she has one of her turns, and I think can deal with them in a more detached way than myself – pulling my own mother's knickers up on the loo doesn't come easy – though how many times do I remember her doing the same for me!

Try and anticipate what will come up over the next few days and call various people. The most difficult call is to Sag Harbor. Gwenola answers, very correctly and confidently, but when she asks if I want to speak to Mummy I momentarily fear the worst. Claudie says Al is eating very little now and finds it very difficult to move from his bed ... 'He's so tired, Michael ...'

But Al does manage to come to the phone. His voice is faint and weary, hardly there at all. I find myself telling him all the things I gushed out to Graham as he lay unconscious in the hospital in Maidstone – that we loved him, and were with him and thinking of him.

Kay Kiddy doesn't think it a good idea to tell Ma that we're going to Switzerland. But I've never lied to her over such things and don't feel at all comfortable starting now. So I ring, with some trepidation. But she sounds fine. Helen's visit had been a great time, she has been off drugs for three days, and is quite well aware of the impending arrival of a

BUPA Home-Care nurse … 'Another creature,' as she puts it, a trifle ominously. I tell her that we shall be away, but keeping in touch, and she seems to take this in without confusion or anxiousness.

Friday, December 29th: Hotel Crap Ner, Flims, Switzerland

I hear the alarm go. It's a quarter to seven in the morning. Still dark of course, but the near, military-moustachioed Crap manager (sorry, I can't resist a bit of that) has advised us to be up the slopes early and to come down early to avoid crowds of day-trippers desperately seeking snow.

I curl up in bed, really feeling rotten, and hear Helen moving around trying to organise all the rest of our party and then deciding she's perhaps started too early. At eight o'clock the bedroom door bangs shut for the last time, the noise of our army on the march recedes and I drift off in and out of sleep until after eleven o'clock.

I take breakfast of a roll, butter and some tea in the Giardino Café, part of this well-scrubbed, fussily decorated but warm little hotel. Don my big Irish overcoat and walk up into the backstreets of Flims to get some idea of what the place is like away from the conveyor belt of a through road.

Quite attractive mixture of town farm buildings – wood-framed, balconied, etc. and a number with cows shedded on the lower floor. If the main road smells of nitrous oxide and carbon monoxide, the parallel 'old road' smells of woodsmoke and farm manure.

To the church, dating from 1517. Nice tall tower and onion dome.

Sit in the sun on the terrace of the Crap, drink a mineral water and a tea and begin to re-read the diaries of Edward Palin, who passed very close to Flims on his Swiss trip of 1859 – 130 years ago. Struck as I read by Tristram's observation that Edward P has much the same attitude to life as myself. He's humorous, given to doing silly things (like bathing naked in rock pools), rather pedantically accurate in things to do with time and topography, clearly enjoys women and their company and often gets carried away with his prose.

1990

Monday, January 1st: Hotel Crap Ner, Flims, Switzerland

What surprises me is how long the eighties have been going. I had not done my first train documentary when they began, nor even *Time Bandits*. What slightly depresses me is how little I've really moved on. I've ended the eighties with another travel documentary and Python and *Yarns* repeats. Nothing very new.

I've survived well, professionally, with clutches of awards, but aside from, I think, learning how to write longer and more sustained drama, there's nothing much I've done in the '80s which I hadn't done better before. Except skiing, of course, and it's this strange and punishing sport which marks the start of the new decade.

Thursday, January 4th

Sitting, pleasantly exhausted by all this day's effort, catching the last of the afternoon sun on our concrete balcony and wondering just where the smell of fresh manure was coming from, when the telephone rings.

It's Kay Kiddy. 'I make no apologies for contacting you by telephone. It is with reference to your mother.' The call reveals little of the nature of the crisis, just enough to make me worry considerably without knowing why. She says she'll ring later after the Doc has been, but it's her opinion that my mother should be in hospital and that I should return at once.

Swissair and the hotel extremely helpful and efficient in reorganising my schedule to catch the midday flight from Zurich tomorrow. Walk up the road to the Cantonal Bank to cash traveller's cheques. The last of the sun has turned the snowless rock face behind the town a golden brown and I feel suddenly quite sad. Sad for my mother, sad to leave Flims and the good times we've had here, sad that things have to come to an end.

Friday, January 5th: Flims–London–Southwold

Arrive soon after five o'clock and go straight to Kay K's. 'I'm sorry you have to see your mother in this state,' Kay keeps repeating, not particularly helpfully. Yesterday morning she had thought her so weak and ill that she feared she wouldn't last until I got back. The current BUPA help is criticised – for smoking, for having a radio with headphones in her room at night and generally ignoring my mother. Dr Hopkins is felt to be another villain of the piece and K suggests I transfer my mother to another, more sympathetic practice.

Approach Sunset House with misgivings, which are quite confounded by what I see. My mother, propped up in her armchair, holds a half-full glass of sherry. On one side of her sits my favourite amongst her friends, Kay Gibson, to whom she is chatting – and a stocky, slightly masculine lady with blonde hair brushed in a parting sits opposite with a paperback.

Saturday, January 6th: Southwold

Am at Sunset House by 9.30. Ma not so good. She can only move now when supported and the question-mark shape of her body is sharply pronounced. The strain on her spine from her bowed back must be considerable. She seems very drowsy and again I notice the slurring of the speech.

I sort out some of her papers and write letters to a number of people who have written to her over the last few months. Time passes slowly in this hot little flat for, whilst Ma can do very little for herself, she dominates the room and one can never relax. She groans, sighs and readjusts her position, then tugs at her dress again. But we get through and by early evening she's more relaxed than I've seen her all day. At 7.30 a big, jolly nurse called Chris arrives, who will look after her for the night.

I leave her about 8.15. Outside the rain is blowing about inhospitably. Dudley, the manager at the Swan, has asked me to dine with him and his fiancée, but I haven't the energy. The day with its constant minute attendance to the fine detail of keeping my Ma interested in life has exhausted me as much as a day on the slopes.

Sunday, January 7th: Southwold

One of the first in the breakfast room. *Sunday Times* best-seller list shows *80 Days* to be the first Non-Fiction No. 1 of the nineties ... 'This book has sold 180,000 copies in two months.'

Feeling vaguely better for this reassurance I walk across the Common to see what I shall find at Sunset House.

There is a note on the table from last night's nurse. 'Your mother had a really good night. She slept through until six o'clock.' Ma is upstairs. The note has raised my hopes, but her appearance is a shock. She looks tired and moves with difficulty. A new face – Sarah, young and spiky blonde hair – is guiding her.

At one point she gives me the look I've seen more than once this weekend – the look of someone who's stuck in the audience at a long, bad play ... 'Oh Michael, let me go,' she mutters at one point.

But the woozy morning gives way to a much happier afternoon. The weather is, by Southwold standards, unusually seductive. Mild, with a sun diluted only by high, white cloud. Kay and Sarah get Granny into her wheelchair and, swathed like a Christmas present, she is pushed off to the sea.

On return she's altogether more alert. She picks up a romantic novel in big writing which Kay Gibson brought her from the library. Out of the blue she asks 'And what is going to happen with your film ... the one about the American girl?' And we discuss it as if the last six months had never happened.

The nurse Anna who arrives at a quarter to eight is slim, soft-spoken and immediately sympathetic. I show her around upstairs and then we sit and talk for a while until Ma dismisses me. She knows I'm staying till tomorrow and is much buoyed by that and she bustles Anna to the stairs and mounts the chairlift, which she controls herself with considerable assurance.

The air is crisp. Fresher than last night as I walk across the Common. I think that the changeover from Kay is not going to be half as bad as I feared. My clothes, packed to last until Saturday night, are drummed into another combination for dinner. I order a glass of champagne and marinated goat's cheese and venison.

Have just finished the goat's cheese and my mouth is watering pleasantly, when a receptionist approaches.

At the hotel door is an agitated Michael Kiddy, Kay's son. ... 'Your mother's collapsed!' He runs with me up the High Street, I cut across the Common. Everyone is upstairs. Mum lies on her left side on her bed, her face drained of colour, her body rigid. Kay is soothing her and comforts Anna, who looks distraught. Apparently she had been bathing my mother, who was in high spirits. Jokes were exchanged and then quite suddenly she collapsed.

Mum's features look set, her eyes are wide and fixed and unseeing. There is no reaction to the pressure of my hand in hers. A Doctor Sanger arrives and examines her.

My mother has had a stroke. A brainstem stroke, which is the most severe. She is unlikely to recover, but could last the night or even for a couple of days. I sit with her and talk on things, knowing that something may be going on inside the shell.

For two hours I sit. Anna has recovered with the help of a couple of cigarettes and she sits and works on some embroidery.

At eleven I leave them to turn Mother onto her right side. Sit downstairs. Thumb through the *Mail on Sunday* – surprised to find a thorough condemnation of the parsimony and unfairness of the government's educational policy.

The kitchen door opens. Anna announces that my mother's dead.

I go upstairs alone. The little body is crouched round like the Tollund Man, but her strong face remains beautiful, though sallow now and silent. I bend and kiss her and thank her for giving me life.

I hear the door shut at the bottom of the stairs. I know Kay and Anna don't want to intrude, but nor do I want to be any longer with a cold shell. I go downstairs. Hug them both.

The rest is practical. The clearing-up. Doctor comes to ascertain time and cause of death: 11.04 p.m. Cerebral thrombosis. The undertaker arrives softly with a friend and a van and asks if we would clear the house whilst the body is removed. Kay, Anna and I walk in the darkness, eased occasionally by a moon scudding between the clouds, down towards Lorne Road, talking between us about the exquisite timing of my mother's death – and how good it was that she had probably been driven to her death by elation rather than fear or agitation. Of course only Anna knows that – and I trust her and it makes her somehow special, this girl who walked into our lives four hours ago and has seen so much.

Kay goes home. I shut off the lights and lock the door. I'm at the Swan at ten past one. The Irish night porter says he'll say a prayer for me.

In all this I forget that Norman Rosten phoned Helen in the afternoon to say that Al Levinson had died the day before Mother. I'd rung Claudie. She sounded strong. As my mother kept saying earlier this evening – 'This is all extraordinary.'

Monday, January 8th: Southwold

Wash, dress, pack and make my way over to Sunset House in order to head off the new girl who will be arriving to look after Granny at eight.

The telephone rings at a quarter to. It's Anna, the nurse from last night. She has done her best to notify the girl who's coming that Ma is dead. As she signs off she asks if she can send me the fish she was embroidering by Granny's bedside. I'm moved to tears and choke for the first time this morning.

Back to the Swan for breakfast. Alone in the big dining room reading of the death of Ian Charleson (of AIDS at 40) and Terry-Thomas (of Parkinson's, alone and penniless at 78). Nice that Mum should have gone at the same time as two others who brought me pleasure.

Then back to the flat to begin a succession of explanatory phone calls, interspersed with the practical business of death – involving undertakers, vicars, doctors and solicitors. Cancelling Mother's newspapers seems the most bathetic moment. She must have received the *Daily Telegraph* every morning for at least 60 years and now I find myself calling Chapman's ... 'I'm ringing on behalf of Mrs Palin ...' 'Oh yes ...' 'She died on Sunday night.' 'Oh dear, I am sorry ...' 'So ... I'd like the papers cancelled from tomorrow.' It doesn't sound final. It doesn't have an apocalyptic ring, but in a way it's definitive.

In the afternoon I have to drive into Lowestoft, to a '60s office building of no charisma, to register Mother's death.

I'm called in by a friendly registrar in early middle age. Help with questions of Granny's provenance, all of which are handwritten onto a form marked 'Death'. My eye strays to files on the window sill marked 'Removal of Bodies Out of England. Deaths at Sea. Bodies Brought Into England. Bodies Never Recovered.'

Armed with legal confirmation that Mother has ceased to be, drive back to Southwold. Now it's getting dark and the flat seems empty and sad.

Some more calls, arrangements for the rest of the week, then drive home. No-one to wave from the window tonight.

Wednesday, January 10th

Morning on letters, 50 or 60 requests for openings of preserved railway lines, woodlands, etc., participation in various forms of agitation.

Lunch with Tristram at Alastair Little.

Talk about deaths. Virginia's mother died in the kitchen, preparing dinner for a friend. Next morning they were all up at the house consoling each other when V asked what had happened to the dinner. It was found, intact, in the oven, so they ate it for lunch.

TP has generous memories of Mother – calls her The Queen of Southwold.

Friday, January 12th

To Central St Martin's School of Art, where British Screen is holding its annual dinner. Just before leaving Steve A calls to say the money is theoretically in place. Believe it or not, LWT has come in with an offer of £500,000, Greg Dyke reportedly liking the script.

Simon Relph welcomes me. He beams like a schoolmaster and promises everything will be all right. Recognise a number of those to whom we went for money and support for 'AF' and who turned us down.

Opposite me is David Hare. He's very gloomy about prospects. 'If you can't get money for your film, who can?'

At the end of the evening talk briefly to Relph. He begins to tell me about his alternative strategy – with the BBC. I've seen Lynda Myles, Mark Shivas and Richard Broke[1] there tonight and none of them have said anything positive about the script, so I have no grounds for hope.

Back home by 11.45. Feel as if some stuffing knocked out of me tonight. A faint air of hostility.

Sunday, January 14th: Southwold

The first January 14th in my lifetime on which my mother will not be around to enjoy her birthday. But her admirable sense of timing last week means that we can still give her a party.

The service goes well. The church itself is a fine setting. TJ was waiting for the coffin to appear and when he saw them raise the casket of ashes he was taken aback ... 'I know she'd shrunk,' he said. I can hear Mother laughing at that.

---

1 Richard Broke. BBC Drama executive in long-time working partnership with Mark Shivas. They produced the Jones and Palin black comedy *Secrets* in 1973.

The choir was out in force and the hymns sung lustily. 'Guide Me, O Thou Great Redeemer', 'The King of Love My Shepherd Is', 'Immortal, Invisible' and 'Morning Has Broken'.

The choice of lesson worked well ... 'There is a time to every purpose under heaven' seemed to suit her departure so well. 'He hath made everything bootiful in his time,' reads Joe Hurran, in unconscious parody of the well-known turkey farmer. I read my address clearly, though received a bit of a shock when I mounted the lectern to find a piece of paper with 'Cleese' written on it. It turned out to be Joe's aid to pronunciation of Ecclesiastes!

Then we repaired to the Swan for a tea – scones, fruit cake, smoked salmon sandwiches. Lizzie [my cousin] and I talked of being Taureans who ate a lot. Lizzie gloomily ... 'As you get older your worst enemy is gravity.'

We were all in good spirits and it's a last tribute to Mother that the tone of the day was as if she had been there herself.

Wednesday, January 17th

To lunch with Eric at L'Aventure. He's sprouting a little moustache for a part as an American homosexual in a 'cult film' he's going out to LA to shoot. How a film can be a cult film before it's made, I'm not sure, but I think it means no money.

Eric, so often the catalyst (I think it was he who really pushed me into writing *American Friends*), comes up with a neat idea which catches precisely my mood at the moment. Telling me that he's just signed our development deal with Universal, giving us each $100,000 to bring films on, he suggests that he should be my producer and commission me to write a modern comedy screenplay. The thought seems so close to what I want to do with the next few weeks that we shake hands on it.

Scribble some thoughts down. An agency which offers culture tours to foreigners, many of them completely specious. Thatcherite Enterprise Britain – screwing the past to keep a business going. Full of enthusiasm.

Call Cleese, just back from the Danube. Did he enjoy the Eastern bloc? 'It'll be fine in five years, when Hilton have built a few decent hotels.'

Thursday, January 18th

To lunch at Langan's Brasserie with Ken Stephinson, his wife Marjorie and Maria Aitken.[1] Maria is wonderfully laid-back and incapable of being dull. Peter Langan had been a house guest of hers in the days before he died. 'Always setting fire to things then ...' He utterly charmed her children, though.

We talk about the problems of telling strangers what you do – especially if one is an actor. Maria was stuck next to someone on a long flight and when the inevitable question came up, for some reason she replied, presumably to shut him up, that she worked in a bakery. He was a baker.

Last call of all is from Patrick Cassavetti. Granada are interested now in '*AF*'. They want to see a budget. I'm afraid I almost howl with frustration and despair. All I feel is another dreadful grating of the mental and emotional gears as we go from reverse into first again. Patrick straight-bats creditably – 'I just don't want to see the last nine months wasted.'

Change into DJ then with Helen to the *Publishing News* Awards Dinner. Am shortlisted, with Newby and Peter Mayle's *A Year in Provence*, for Travel Writer of the Year.

To the Park Lane Hotel, confusingly located in Piccadilly. Hanif Kureishi and Michael Rosen have both come in everyday shirt and sneakers. Frank Muir is affable. 'We're all fag ends in the gutter of life,' he replies cheerfully to my observation that the timing of success is quite unpredictable ... 'One realises that all those things like talent, looks, skill and hard work really don't get you anywhere.'

We, the BBC table, have been sat right across the entrance, probably a fire risk. I am on the main road from the kitchen and am dug in the back endlessly. Quite nice when shapely award-winners squeeze by, but piles of plates not so good.

We are the second award ... and the winner is ... 'Peter Mayle'. Desultory applause which cannot sustain till he gets to the podium. Suzanna Zsohar horrified. I'm a little relieved. Living with the title 'Travel Writer of the Year' in a world of Theroux, Thubrons, Lewises and Newbys would surely be fraudulent. But it's clearly not a popular choice; nor it seems is a creepy Author of the Year Award to Prince Charles for *A Vision of Britain*.

The ceremony, full of missed cues and cheap fanfares, is at moments

1 Maria Aitken, actress, who played John Cleese's wife in *A Fish Called Wanda*.

plain embarrassing, as when P.D. James is silenced in mid-eulogy by a premature fanfare, at others enormously funny – Lord Lichfield discovered taking a quick pull on a fag when the lights are cued early – and only once does it strike an uplifting note, when Robert McCrum of Faber, accepting Publisher of the Year Award, reminds us of the existence of Salman Rushdie for the first time that evening.

Sunday, January 21st

Simon A arrives about four and takes me down to the HQ of Campaign for Quality Television – to brief me before the 'crucial meeting' with David Mellor on Wednesday evening, into which I've been corralled as Rowan Atkinson and John Cleese are both too busy. Not really my cup of tea. I can't get worked up and indignant about something that I know is being fought for perfectly well by others more qualified than myself. Nor is it like transport – a cause that runs deep.

Still, I will help my friend out and it will be another experience. SA even shows the place settings he's already worked out for dinner. 'This is a good place for Terry (meaning TJ) to blow up from, and you'll still have eye contact with the Minister from here.' Then there's an element of subterfuge. 'I can't tell anyone else, but … the ITV companies have all put a considerable sum of money into the campaign, but it's much better if it's assumed we have very little.' This leads to a suggestion that I should be seen to pay for the meal and SA would pay me back.

Tuesday, January 23rd

To Vasco and Piero's[1] (for the first time since Piero's premature death) for lunch with Alan Bennett and Barry Cryer. 'The Three Yorkshiremen' as Barry calls us.

Barry quotes Peter Cook on the Yorkshire Ripper. The police and *Private Eye* became quite thick with each other over the libel case and Peter remembers a policeman recounting one of the killings. Sonia Sutcliffe was obsessively house-proud and her husband wasn't. One night she turned him out of the house for making such a mess of the place, and … 'in the half-hour he was away from the house, he went out and strangled a dwarf'. Peter couldn't apparently contain

---

1 Our favourite family restaurant run by two friends from Umbria.

himself when he heard this. Probably the way the police told it. I asked Alan about corpsing in *Beyond the Fringe*. Apparently Dud went so easily that 'Some nights he'd start before the curtain had gone up.'

Alan sits so low on his back that at times his head is only just above the table top. When he laughs, which he does readily and enthusiastically, he manages with one swift movement to bring hands up to his face, whip his glasses off and then cover his face almost entirely, pushing up his absurdly boyish fringe like a fright-wig impersonation.

Barry sits upright, leaning forward. He occasionally scribbles a key word on his Consulate cigarette packet. 'Peppermill' he wrote after I'd done a bit about Italian restaurants whose status is determined by the length of the peppermill. I remark on the fact that he's smoked Consulate as long as I've known him. 'That's because there's plenty of white on the packet for writing on.'

Wednesday, January 24th

To a party hosted by the editor of the *Correspondent*[1] magazine. This is in an art gallery in Cork Street.

Meet John Brown, the editor of *Viz*. Agreeable, young and unassuming. They were greatly encouraged, at the beginning, he says, by my letter comparing the mag with Python. 'What we all thought, but didn't dare say.' They sell over a million every two months and as it's on 'crap paper' it's incredibly cheap to produce and everyone makes a lot of money.

The champagne flows, the chattering classes greet and kiss and tout for information. I feel it wholly right that I should be going on later to meet the Minister of Broadcasting and do some lobbying of my own.

Our venue is L'Amico restaurant in Horseferry Road – within sound of the division bell.

David Mellor arrives in a blaze of bonhomie. Am struck first of all by his old-fashioned haircut, long and straight like boys at school.

The menu, indeed the restaurant itself, looks a little dusty and depressing, but it is the only restaurant in London where Gorbachev has

---

1 The *Sunday Correspondent* was a national broadsheet. The first edition was on September 17th, 1989, the last on November 25th, 1990. Much missed.

eaten, and in his memory there is a Spaghetti Gorbachev at £5.50. We are in a private room, decorated like a sauna.

Food and wine ordered, Simon gently but firmly begins to put our case: that the granting of a licence for Channels 3 and 5 to the highest bidder, without some positive definition of a commitment to quality programming, will result in a lowering of television standards. After some discussion a concession is granted by the Minister over 'exceptional cases' – whereby a bid of less money, but higher 'quality' might be, and should be, accepted. He says he will do all he can to push this through, but will need all our help to get it past the four or five diehards, who presumably are Thatcher and her ideologues.

Terry J asks why the auction system had been chosen in the first place. Mellor flannels. TJ invokes the Middle Ages ... 'A gift from the King.' We all know that Terry's question is the heart of the matter, and everything else is trimming.

Mellor, who drank red wine, left at eleven, with much cheerful banter. He thought *The Life of Brian* the best thing he'd ever seen and requested a tape to be sent to him.

Thursday, January 25th

Anne J rings. I've been asked to play Gulliver in a film this summer. Script, by Simon Moore of *Traffik*, on its way to me.

Meanwhile, stirrings at *GBH*. I have all the rewritten scripts, but the unavailability of Billy C for the other main part sounds, according to Anne, to have given Bleasdale other ideas about casting.

Saturday, January 27th

To dinner with JC and Alyce Faye at Cibo – an unfussy, new Italian restaurant off Holland Park Road. We go with the Hutchisons. Excellent company – Alan and Sarah are the most natural of JC's friends, quite unaffected by his fame.

Sarah says that the Treasury is awash with money and certainly doesn't need the money from the TV auction. As she points out, it will suddenly start spending at the Budget before the election. So we bleed and suffer for the Tories' survival instinct. Eat lots of wild mushrooms.

Interesting sidelight on *GBH* when JC asks me ... 'What's this I hear about you and Robert Lindsay doing a Bleasdale series ... 26 weeks!'

Monday, January 29th

Talk to Bleasdale, briefly. He says that Connolly has left the project and he now wants me to do 'a straight swap' – Jim Nelson for Michael Murray. 'Jim Nelson, Michael Murray and Jim Nelson are three of the best characters I've ever written.'

I make it clear that I am not asking him to hang onto me at all costs, and if the Connolly/Palin pairing has fallen through then maybe he'll want a fresh start. Robert Lindsay isn't mentioned.

Thursday, February 1st

To Ken Hilton to meet Bleasdale, Verity and David Jones.[1]

Bleasdale, dark-eyed and dark-browed, emerges from the bar looking like a Romanian defector. We talk and by the end of an hour I've agreed to play Jim Nelson, subject to the 'Gulliver' script being less tempting. They all seem to breathe a sigh of relief. Bleasdale reassures me that he's one of the producers and will make sure we have the best people around.

The 'Gulliver' scripts have arrived. A beautiful adaptation by Simon Moore – bringing Gulliver back home at the beginning – to a world which mistrusts and disbelieves him – and keeping his fight for credibility as one of the two stories running in parallel. And I could do Gulliver well.

To bed after twelve – bleary from reading, with sore eyes and confusion about the future.

Friday, February 2nd

News is coming through of de Klerk's liberating speech from Pretoria, unbanning the ANC and the Communists and promising Mandela's release. As Helen says, it's easy to forget, amidst all the paraphernalia of our day-to-day lives, that we are living in momentous times.

Monday, February 5th: London–Lancashire

Have chosen a garlanded venue in the Good Hotel Guide – the Old Vicarage, Witherslack – for rest and relaxation and writing of 'The

---

1 David Jones was Verity Lambert's co-producer.

Twenty-seven days away. Much-needed head
treatment on Chowpatty Beach, Bombay.

With Nigel Meakin, my cameraman. A working partnership that has lasted twenty-five years.

Attack on my trousers in Bird Market, Hong Kong. 'Well, all right, I had asked the parrot if he knew John Cleese' – November 6th, 1988.

Halfway round the world. The crew in Hong Kong harbour. At back: co-director
Clem Vallance with our Hong Kong fixers, MP, and Angela Elbourne, production assistant.
Foreground: Simon Maggs, camera assistant, and Dave Jewitt, sound recordist.

Day 79: Weary warriors on the steps of the Reform Club, having made it round the world
with seventeen hours to spare. Clockwise from back left: MP, Nigel Walters, cameraman on
the second leg, Maggs, Jewitt, co-director Roger Mills, Ann Holland, production assistant.
And they wouldn't let us in.

On Michael Aspel's show with Maureen Lipman (on his left) and Wendy James, founder member of Transvision Vamp.

With Charlie Crichton, my director, collecting a BAFTA for Best Supporting Actor for *A Fish Called Wanda*, March 19th, 1989.

Being silly with
Gilliam. Edinburgh
Film Festival, 1989.

Python's twentieth
anniversary filming
with Steve Martin,
September 23rd, 1989.

Publicising *80 Days* at the Western Show at Anaheim, California. 'Have your photo taken with Michael *A Fish Called Wanda* Palin' – December 15th, 1989.

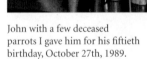

John with a few deceased parrots I gave him for his fiftieth birthday, October 27th, 1989.

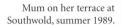

Mum on her terrace at Southwold, summer 1989.

At La Residencia, Deyà, Mallorca, with Helen, daughter Rachel on the right, and her friends Kate and Sylvie Lewis, August, 1990.

With Terry Jones, posing as characters from the *Ripping Yarns* as publicity for a new combined volume of the scripts. January 25th, 1990.

As Reverend Francis Ashby (based on my great-grandfather) in *American Friends*, Oxford, 1990.

Gordon Ottershaw in Barnstoneworth United strip. At *The Complete Ripping Yarns* shoot, January 25th, 1990.

Adventure', named after the restaurant in which Eric and I came up with the idea. The train is remarkably empty and Lancaster Station neat and quiet as a museum. On the way up I complete my reading of *Gulliver's Travels* – which is excellent and intelligent and impassioned to the end. *GBH* remains the one original piece of work I've been offered this summer, but the competition is hotting up.

Collect a white Maestro and sign autograph for Europcar girl and then a 35-minute drive north and then west to Witherslack. My room is in an annexe. Tall and very spacious and only just commissioned. The smell of fresh paint and the tang of polyurethane in the air.

The decoration is a little fussy. Flounced curtains in the bathroom, florid wallpaper with pheasants and a lot of Tiffany lamps. A fire crackles in the hearth, but it's a fire constructed of fireproof materials. Two fireproof logs lie beside it.

Start reading *London Fields* and am reminded how funny Martin Amis is. He's flash and nasty as well, but the constant and dazzling humour (I hate to call it wit) keeps me hooked. Beside the solid soul-searching of Margaret Atwood, it's the cocktail after the long, bracing walk.

Tuesday, February 6th: The Old Vicarage, Witherslack

An orgy of banging and drilling from the next-door room, shortly followed by the screaming roar of low-flying aircraft, makes me feel that this is a sign I should not start on 'The Adventure'. But I persevere, the noise lessens, and by one o'clock I've an opening sequence and some character ideas.

Drive to a recommended local pub – the Mason's Arms, which overlooks the hamlet of Bowland Bridge. This is a small but popular pub, most tables full, over 200 beers available.

For me it's a minor ordeal – heads turning, smiles, stares, whispers. I've lost that most precious commodity, anonymity. Sometimes, as when compliments fly along with the recognition, it's quite exciting, most of the time it's like being the idiot or the leper. Still, worth it for a succulent pint of Thwaites, a roll of thick, fresh-cut ham and a view over the lumpy, hummocky valley that runs north/south from the High Lakes to Morecambe Bay.

Wednesday, February 7th: Witherslack

More crowded tonight. A party of 30-year-olds – 20 years ago everyone in this sort of 'Good Food'/'Good Hotel' Guidey place would be older than me. Now it's almost the opposite.

Also dining tonight, a wonderful couple – she handsome, carefully well-dressed, with a fine string of pearls at the neck, he ancient, craggy, crusty, with thick glasses, a hearing aid, a stammer, a fierce bronchial cough, both somehow communicating throughout and demolishing one and a half bottles of wine and a cocktail between them. County folk, as resilient as the rocks.

Amis continues to make me laugh out loud on every other page. It's all quite shallow, but doesn't half glitter on the surface.

Back in my room, stuffed, I switch on *Newsnight*. In Russia, Communists no longer the single, lone party – they will fight elections like the rest.

Never has history moved so fast in so many directions. Momentous and fascinating. But still treated by the media as Heroes and Villains. Current Heroes, Mandela, de Klerk, Gorbachev. Current Villains, Ceauşescu (obscene on every level now), Stalin, of course.

To bed and sleep by midnight. The wind sighs outside, comfortingly.

Thursday, February 8th: Witherslack

My friends of the first two days have been replaced by another couple from Leeds – he a barrister. Wince a little at the opening gambit at breakfast, 'Ah, good to see another *Independent* reader' (the paper having been going for two years), but we get on well after that.

They talk about books, easily and without pretension, and Salman Rushdie. He knows some of the Pakistani Muslims from the Bradford area who burnt the books. They wanted a little local publicity and were as surprised as he was that the issue assumed such international proportions. One thing clear in the whole issue is that hardly anyone has read the book.

Saturday, February 10th

Call Patrick Cassavetti and listen in disbelief as he tells me that he thinks he has the money for *American Friends*.

I now have to bring the film – and my obligations of conscience to all who have spent time on it – back into the reckoning, just after I've breathed the fresh air of a new screenplay.

Anne is pressing me into 'Gulliver', which sounds so efficient, well-organised and easy. *GBH* dates still unspecified as they bargain for budget with Channel 4.

Give up. Watch Rossellini's *Rome, Open City*. Now there's courageous film-making. 1945 – a cataclysmic year in my lifetime, perhaps to be only rivalled by 1990.

Already, this week, the Russian Communists have yielded a 70-year-old monopoly on power. Enormous arms cuts are proposed. The reunification of East and West Germany could be set in motion within a month and today the momentous news came through that Nelson Mandela will be released tomorrow.

Sunday, February 11th

I settle down with calendars and coloured pens to plot various possible schedules, breaking off to watch the live coverage of the release of Nelson Mandela after 27 years.

If I am to carry out my gents' agreement with Eric to provide a first draft screenplay, *and* do 'AF', then I shall not be able to start *GBH* until August. 'Gulliver', with its 12-week shooting, beginning in June, means I could not start *GBH* until September.

Sunday supper and repeat of the *Murder at Moorstones Manor* Ripping Yarn. Family howl with laughter when the BBC announcer heralds me as 'that awfully nice chap, Michael Palin'. This is becoming quite seriously derogatory.

Monday, February 12th

Patrick Cassavetti here at 9.30 to discuss the feasibility of making the film this year in the light of my commitments.

He says he's worked himself to 'fever pitch' over the last nine months and it shows. He's pale, tired and has a thick cold he can't shake off. Though he personifies all I try to avoid – 'film as suffering' – I respect his dedication greatly, find his constancy to the project moving, and want nothing more than for his energies to be rewarded. 'If I'm not making a film … then I die …' he said. 'I am only in this world to make films.'

Wednesday, February 14th

To lunch with Clem V at Cibo.

In the course of it Clem suggests a future Palin journey. Emerging beneath the North Pole in a nuclear submarine, I would follow the 30° East meridian south across Lapland, past Archangel and down through Leningrad, past Kiev, Odessa, the Black Sea, Turkey, Cyprus, Cairo, down the Nile, the Rift Valley, the length of Africa to Port Elizabeth, then across to Antarctica, where, hopefully, some adventurers or some expedition could be found to take me over an 11,000-foot mountain range to the South Pole. Time wouldn't be such a governing factor, so I could linger in interesting places.

Our plan should be to make it independently, but approach the BBC and A&E for funding.

Buoyed by an excellent meal and a gut feeling that at last I've heard of a viable follow-up to *80 Days*, I drive home to give an interview about my childhood to Ray Connolly of *The Times*.

Ray has good stories from rock 'n' roll's heyday. He was at LSE a year before Mick Jagger and remembers Jagger saying of the group he'd just founded 'All we're short of is a vocalist.'

After supper I call Alan Bleasdale back. The money has been found for *GBH*. A deal has been struck with Channel 4 and it's on. 'I wanted you to be the first to know, after the wife.'

Thursday, February 15th

Now I have the longest, sustained acting role I've ever been offered lying ahead of me in five months' time. It's when I get to worrying about what lies in between that a mild panic lurks around. A draft screenplay to write and a major film to shoot and rewrite. All manner of other small things: offers flood in every day and just sorting through and fighting them off is work enough.

I try to concentrate on 'The Adventure', but I'm half expecting the phone to ring with news of 'AF'. It doesn't.

Saturday, February 17th: London–Southwold

Must visit Southwold today – mainly for diplomatic and social reasons. There isn't a lot to do at the house. It's a mild, damp day. Helen and I leave at 10.15 and reach the house in two and a quarter hours. Fierce wind wrenches at the car doors.

Home, bearing an inkstand which Ma has left to me in her will. It bears an inscription – to 'Edward Palin, from his grateful parishioners at Summertown – 1861'. Now is this a sign that we should do *American Friends*, or not? Its arrival in the house two days before a decision is given is oddly coincidental.

In the *Guardian* Whicker has been stung into public utterance about my interview in which I revealed that he was the first presenter to be offered *Around the World in 80 Days*. He is asked, 'Why did you turn it down?' He calls my journey a seven-hour ego trip, and pleads that in his progs we only see 'the back of my head'. But he's too wise to knock popularity – even if it's a competitor … 'He did do it very well,' he concedes. Between fiercely clenched teeth I should think.

Monday, February 19th

Steve calls at 6.30 to relay the wholly predictable news that another deadline on 'AF' has passed without resolution. Alan Howden at the BBC met with them this morning, together with his reader and their lawyer, and such good progress was made that Steve feels that only two, very small, hurdles remain, and both should be cleared by tomorrow. Extend the deadline yet again.

Thursday, February 22nd

A clear writing day lies ahead. Call Patrick, who still sounds under pressure, but convinced the end, or rather the beginning, is in sight.

I've put the inkstand presented to my ancestor in 1861 in front of me on the desk. Hope this will help.

To dinner at David Attenborough's. Jane cooks a splendid meal – boeuf en croute. Liberal wine. Barry Took, with two of his favourite people, is almost embarrassingly adulatory. 'Why are the two of you so loved by the viewers?' sort of thing. Attenborough brushes it aside in his case and jabs a carving knife towards me … 'And, for him, it's because he's funny.'

After dinner we are shown up to a small library, then up another flight of stairs to a huge open-plan gallery, running the length of the three bays of the house, neatly organised, walls covered with books, beams rising above a semicircular slab of a desk which puts me in mind of mission control somewhere. No word processor, but everything else, including fax, of course. What's more, the books all look as if they are continually used. David very concerned that he couldn't find reference to leaf-eating ants for a whole day – so the system isn't perfect.

Tuesday, February 27th

We begin to get 'AF' back on the road again. Contact made with Irene Lamb, our casting director, who says Colin Firth will do anything for me! She is warmly, spontaneously happy at the end of the conference phone, to hear that we are under way again. Trini is still available.

Into the crowded West End to a sardine-packed theatre to see one of the great hits of the day – *Jeffrey Bernard Is Unwell*.

O'Toole holds sway, just about makes the first half bearable and triumphs in the second. He is a Grand Performer, effortlessly charismatic, a tall, athletic figure in complete control.

Talk to Annabel [Leventon][1] afterwards. They hated him at the beginning of the rehearsal. He only looked after himself and made life very tough for them. Now they would die for him. He leaves the show next week after four months to be replaced by Tom Conti. Brave man.

Sunday, March 4th

To a building in Farringdon Road, which has been acquired by Frontliners – the AIDS organisation run by AIDS sufferers which impressed me so much a couple of years ago. Twice they've been on the verge of buying or leasing premises only to find the sellers panic because of the AIDS association. One of them had to be convinced by a doctor that a building could not catch AIDS, as it's impossible to have sex with one.

Interesting that the patrons nearly all women – the Frontliners themselves nearly all men.

---

1 Annabel Leventon, actress who also appeared in the original London productions of *Hair* and *The Rocky Horror Show*.

Tuesday, March 6th

Slept deeply and it's a quarter to eight when I wake from pleasant dreams. Gird my loins and set off, via King's Cross, for Leeds, where I am to do a piece on homelessness for the ITV charity telethon. Carole Tudor, the Yorkshire TV producer, meets me off the train.

Unfortunately the interview she had lined up with a homeless girl cannot now be done, as the girl killed herself yesterday. She was the third suicide in a week at this hostel. Apparently when one goes, there is often a 'domino' effect.

At the hostel, in the undistinguished Beeston area of West Leeds, I am to interview Ronnie and Les. Many of the other inmates will not be around today for the cameras, as they're wanted by the police.

Ronnie and Les, both in their 60s, are regulars here. They're very well behaved and obliging in the short interview, in fact too much so as they keep interrupting my summary by agreeing with me loudly and making remarks out of the blue like 'We do have a problem, we drink you see.'

Anyway, this is a hard half-hour. The whole set-up resembles a Python sketch. At the end I remark to the excellent trio who run the hostel how agreeable were Ronnie and Les. 'Before they've had a drink,' they warn, chuckling at my eager naivety.

Their point is proved in spectacular fashion when Ronnie returns from the pub within ten minutes, a changed man. No shaking hands and thank yous, he is on the warpath and the enemy is Carole Tudor, who gave him and Les a pound for a drink ... 'What do you think we are?' 'A bloody insult.' 'One pound, for all the money you've got.' Carole seems not much shaken. She has a sort of detachment from it all which I suppose she's learnt from 25 years in television.

Wednesday, March 7th

Down to a studio off Great Portland Street to be beamed live by satellite to a morning show in Melbourne. The security man downstairs asks me if I'm the cab driver they're waiting for. The 'studio' turns out to be an office with a swivel chair set in a wilderness of coffee cups and faxes, with a six-by-four-foot cardboard-mounted colour photo of the Houses of Parliament propped up on a desk behind me. On camera it looks as if I'm in a luxury penthouse 20 storeys above the Thames.

Friday, March 9th

I make my way to Verity's office to meet Robert Young,[1] who will be directing *GBH*. The hallway dominated by the languid bulk of Verity's Great Dane licking his balls into rawness.

A mild-looking middle-aged man, with a soft, just-woken look in the eyes, is at the office doorway. Momentarily take him for a cab driver – it's that sort of week!

Dates are discussed. I find myself almost apologising for '*AF*'s sudden resurrection.

I feel enormously reassured by our brief meeting. Young is friendly and approachable, he says he read it and felt the part could have been written for me. So far no big bad wolves on the project. All the main players nice and uncomplicated.

Friday, March 16th

To the BBC for meetings with Clem and Colin Cameron to make an early pitch for 'Pole to Pole with Palin' as Clem has titled it (embarrassingly as far as I'm concerned). Despite news today of sales of *80 Days* to Russia, Saudi Arabia and about 20 other countries, as well as a Broadcasting Press Guild Award for Best Documentary Series of 1989, Cameron listens coolly and certainly betrays no excess of enthusiasm for the 30° longitude journey.[2] But neither is he hostile.

All in all, we remain knocking at the door, with no more certain chance of admission than anyone else.

Saturday, March 31st

A day of work on '*AF*'.

Knowing that we are to make the film and knowing that we, as good as certain, have Connie and Trini to play the other two main parts, makes these rewrites different, closer, more intense.

On the news, pictures of familiar streets smashed up. There has

---

1 Robert Young, director, who before *GBH* directed five episodes of the Hugh Laurie–Stephen Fry *Jeeves and Wooster* TV series.
2 The 'discipline' of *Pole to Pole* was to try to stick as close as possible to 30° east line of longitude, as we made our way south.

been a poll-tax protest and riots have broken out on the periphery of the demonstration. A sunny, comfortable day ends with ugly scenes of flying truncheons, crowds trampled by police horses, faces contorted with hate, cars set alight in St Martin's Lane.

Pick Rachel up from the Lelands'. David has a cast and crew screening of *The Big Man* tomorrow at the Lumière in St Martin's Lane. 'I just hope there'll be a theatre left.'

Sunday, April 1st

The evidence of yesterday's wanton destruction begins at the top of Shaftesbury Avenue, but is clearest in St Martin's Lane, where nearly every window shows signs of damage, either cracked, partially broken or, in the case of the Renault garage, completely boarded up. A burnt-out Porsche is being examined by passers-by, tall-sided glaziers' vehicles work their way down the street. The Salisbury pub is boarded up.

Into *The Big Man*. Simon Relph is sitting just behind me. He grasps my hand ... 'Now we really are in business.' Feel much perkier and more self-confident now the millstone of doubt and apology for 'AF' is off my neck.

The Big Man starts with images of police and riot shields and the same looks of anger and protest and snarling hatred we saw yesterday filling the street outside. Its central story, of the setting-up and execution of a bare-knuckle fight, very well presented, with strong images and Morricone's music giving it a world-class feel. But underneath this hard film there's a soft and sentimental centre, and the Liam Neeson character hardly changes from beginning to end. One feels these are characters whose destiny is quite predetermined and I felt pleased that 'AF' at least sets out to make its characters change and develop.

Wednesday, April 11th

To supper at Simon A's.

Clive Hollick is also there and the talk is of the possibilities of setting up a TV company to bid at the next round of licence grants, incorporating the values propounded so successfully in the Campaign for Quality Television. TVS [TV South] looks the weakest of the present franchise holders and Simon and Clive have plans, either to buy the majority of shares in the existing company or to make, as they call it, a 'green field' bid, starting from scratch and creating a totally new company. They are keen on pursuing Nigel Walmsley as Chief Executive (my original suggestion) and Roger Laughton as Head of Programmes.[1]

I sense a whiff of the burning rubber of the fast lane, as Clive, clearly, precisely and tantalisingly, sets out the various ways in which TVS, the limping, wounded prey, will be stalked by the new, strong, seemingly unstoppable predator.

The only problem, as far as I am concerned, is my inclusion as an important member of a prospective board, representing the 'values' of CQT.

I could not commit the amount of time required of a serious board member of the new company. In addition I have prog commitments to the BBC (though Simon didn't think this important) and an inclination and a sympathy towards the North, rather than the South.

Hollick very much in cahoots with the Labour Party and tells me that they are going to propose a new high-speed rail link up the spine of England, bypassing London and connecting with the Channel Tunnel. It will be financed, they hope – 'funded' is the word used – by allowing private operators, such as SNCF, to rent out the track.

Thursday, April 12th

At ten Connie here, and a little later Tristram. We work through the script. Connie seems more relaxed and at ease with her part, maybe because she knows it's happening now, and she suggests little line changes which work well and remind me of one reason I wanted her in the first place – because she could write.

I leave this productive and concentrated morning at one o'clock and drive over to Don Pepe in Frampton Street to meet with Clem V and Mirabel [Brook, Location Manager] re *Pole to Pole*. He has worked out a schedule which involves four months' travelling. Suggest a two-week break on the road somewhere, possibly around Luxor or Aswan. Still looks an amazing trip, but the nuclear sub opening beneath the North Pole looks exceedingly problematical and the journey to the South Pole debatable.

Then down to LWT for a Michael Aspel show recording with the Princess Royal as one of the guests.

---

1 Nigel Walmsley was a contemporary at Brasenose and Roger Laughton the executive producer of the *Great Railway Journeys* series.

In my dressing room there is a typewritten protocol sheet which notes that the Princess Royal should be addressed as 'Ma'am' ... 'rhyming with Spam'. Led then to a makeshift 'green room' behind the set and the Princess, shapely and composed, face looking a little older close to, arrives and greets me with extreme affability. 'We passed your dressing room,' she said, 'looking for mine, which we never found.'

She goes on first and astutely refuses to give away family information, except inadvertently ... 'Was there much conversation at dinner when you were young?' 'We weren't allowed down to dinner.' An impression, possibly inaccurate, of a rather tight-lipped, serious lady emerges.

But she is very subversive in her little off-camera asides. A revolving stage, to move us into another position, worries her ... 'I hate these things ... if we go too fast I may well throw up.'

Nigel Kennedy, the extraordinary, Mozart-like genius and wide boy combined, plays Bruch beautifully, spellbindingly, in bandana wrapped around cropped hair, a 1707 Stradivarius clutched to a jacket studded with giant safety pins. He tells a great story of inserting a naughty magazine between the pages of the score of the conductor of the Vienna Philharmonic.

Friday, April 13th: Good Friday

Day at home. Last of our children leaves us. Will is in Portland, Oregon, Tom sleeping rough in the mountains behind Barcelona and at lunchtime Rachel joins her friend for a week in Norfolk.

Ring Alan Bleasdale and fix a couple of days in May to go up and see him and a school for difficult kids and a psychotherapist (at A's suggestion!).

Quiet evening before the box, sobering too, as we watch a programme based on letters home from troops in the Vietnam War – sobering to be reminded that the average age of the 58,000 Americans killed in Vietnam was 19. Those troops, heavily armed and screaming as they raced out of Hueys, were mostly William's age.

Friday, April 27th

Flying back from a short 'AF' writing trip in Ireland. A surveyor in the oil-freight business asks if I will sign his sick bag. He says he has quite a collection of celebrity-signed sick bags. The hostess tells me they don't call them that, they call them cuspidors.

Monday, April 30th

To the launch party for Elena's[1] book at L'Escargot. Elena surrounded by her admirers. She seems to have gracefully put on weight. Her hair looks golden and wonderful. Her husband Aldo hovers, far more nervous than Elena.

A chatter of celebrities – Melvyn there, lock of hair jauntily falling across forehead, looking about twelve. Alan Yentob of course, but John Birt it is who attaches himself to me. We talk about our mutual friend Mick Sadler[2] who has written a radio play with a character who some think, say Birt, is modelled on me, others on him. This is quite disturbing as I've never thought of Birt and me as having anything in common. Success is the common denominator, he reveals, modestly.

He's very chatty and expansive and so is Yentob – realise that I'm a bit of a lucky charm at the moment, as the success of *80 Days* appears to be lasting. My shirt much admired by Yentob and Birt, who is quite a fashionable dresser and not at all as dour as he's made out.

Tuesday, May 1st

Drive down to Hammersmith, to the *AF* production office in Macbeth Road. The offices are located in a big, empty old primary school – Victorian and quite fine, with rows of washbasins only a few feet off the ground.

Out with Irene, Tristram and Patrick to a drink with David Calder, a Pollitt possibility. A dauntingly impressive list of credits, and he is an agreeable and companionable man.

Thursday, May 3rd

I arrive at Cosprop at two for a fitting with our costume designer, Bob Ringwood. He looks a little like Lawrence Durrell and is keen, eager and loves all the scenes we've just removed – the soirée, the cycling

1 Elena Salvoni, long-time manageress at L'Escargot in Greek Street, Soho.
2 Mick Sadler, fellow revue actor and writer at Oxford, now living in Paris.

through the woods and the parting of the ladies at the end.

I'm enormously relieved to see from contemporary photos that dog collars didn't come in until the 1880s and '90s and white neck 'stops' were worn, which look more attractive, less clichéd and take me well away from *The Missionary*. Hair and whiskers were worn in a variety of wild and wonderfully fanciful ways, and I look much more like a Regency figure than a modern clergyman. Bob and his assistant, Graham Churchyard, seem well pleased.

In the evening, with Helen at badminton, I go to the Renoir to catch the last night of *A Short Film About Love* [by Kieslowski]. Compulsively watchable. A careful film, tight shooting and editing and absolutely believable performances.

I come straight home and in the balmy night – warm as 60° outside still – read with care the first of the *GBH* scripts. Look at Jim Nelson as a piece of acting; think how I can make it as successful as the leads in the film I've just seen.

Friday, May 4th

'You've got no pressures any more, have you?' Peter Lewis asked me as I lay upended on his dentist's chair this afternoon. 'I mean, everything's easy now, isn't it?'

Tuesday, May 8th

To lunch in Gloucester Crescent with Colin Haycraft, at Lyn Took's behest. Haycraft, a jolly, bustling, cheerful, donnish man (he loves Oxford and found the name of Edward Palin in a dusty copy of the Oxford Register – 'Honours Degree in Literae Humaniores 1848 ... MA, First Class, one of only 8 awarded that year').

They have one of those charming, rather magically overgrown houses, rather dark inside, but full of atmosphere and a soft, warm comfort, like a patched but favourite dressing gown.

Anna Haycraft, alias Alice Thomas Ellis, is introduced to me. She has big, dark, unavoidable eyes and must have been very beautiful. And still a powerful, heavy-lidded presence. Beryl Bainbridge is there, small-framed, bird-like and amused, a smile always about to happen. A beautiful young son who leaves early to get down to Wandsworth to rehearse Shakespeare.

They all agree Alan Bennett is the best of neighbours, though Hay-craft, whilst being immensely agreeable, fires in brisk controversial shafts, and thinks Alan 'very limited as a writer'! Yes, but who wouldn't die for such limits.

Ostensibly I'm being wined and dined because he regarded my fore-word to Barry Took's autobiography as a work of near-perfection. 'You can write,' he advises me bluntly ... 'It's as simple as that ... some people can, some people can't.'

Beryl leaves to have her verruca attended to yet again. Someone had told her that banana was good for ridding oneself of verrucas, so she'd slept with a banana in her bed feeling rather silly, before being told it was only the skin.

Wednesday, May 9th: London–Liverpool

Catch the 7.50 Merseyside Pullman and, after a breakfast served in leisurely style over one and a half hours, arrive early in the slime-green canyons that lead into Liverpool Lime Street.

Bleasdale, pale suit, floral shirt (a combination he likes), greets me with apologies for the fact that Gerry, his driver, has turned up in a white stretch limousine. 'The Liverpool limousine,' I jest, but realise too late that this is probably true. Gerry remembers driving Maggie Smith and me in the same car during *The Missionary*.

We drive out to the 'Mal-ad' school in Wigan.

The school is residential, with a high teacher-pupil ratio and a sen-sible, tolerant, flexible approach to the children which seems to have paid off, for they are polite and receptive and enthusiastic. In only two of them do I see the lowered brow, intense concentrating eyes and set mouths that suggest something bottled-up.

We sit at lunch tables with them, then afterwards sit in on classes. I play draughts with one boy whilst his friend, a small lad with a crew-cut, offers mad advice and pops any draught removed from the board into his mouth.

One of them asks Alan if he's Engelbert Humperdinck.

Then a beer in a pub, where I meet a tight, lean-faced, charismatic teacher on whom AB has drawn for some of Jim Nelson. His toughness and wry, quick Lancastrian wit put him in a class of his own and remind me further of the task I've taken on.

Then on to see a hypnotherapist called Sam Beacon, who looks Anglo-

Indian. His neat, fragrantly perfumed wife brings us endless small platefuls of fruit and sandwiches whilst Sam shows us a video of him working a lady with an awful fear of supermarkets into a trance.

Alan tries to pin Sam down to what we need to know for Jim Nelson's character and the approach Sam used to treat Alan's own fear of bridges. Alan asks Sam to try his hypnotism technique on me. I just tense up and have to pretend to be affected.

Second time around I decide not to act and so my right arm, which I'm holding in the air and which is supposed to become heavy, never does.

Eventually Sam gives up. 'Well, we've not much time, so I'll put your arm down anyway.'

On the way back in the car Alan and I laugh, wondrously, about it all.

Thursday, May 10th: Liverpool–London

Wake around six. The demands of the part, the scale of my involvement, my inexperience of this kind of drama, all seem heavily negative this morning. I contemplate telling Alan, at breakfast, that I am not the right person to take on this pivotal part, that, all things considered, I will only be a disappointment.

I'm downstairs in the long, bright kitchen at twenty to nine. Radio 2's playing. Bleasdale senior is busy. He smiles, we exchange a greeting and he's off upstairs.

Alan appears apologetically five minutes later. I don't mention any doubts, and doubt I will until it's all over.

Monday, May 14th

This is my first working day on *GBH*: the day I shall meet the actress who is to be my wife and to spend time with Robert Young.

Robert lives on Kew Green, a peaceful and attractive spot, bordered by Jacobean and Regency houses and later terraced houses, spoilt only by an almost continuous squash of traffic heading for the bridge.

Alan is smiling and smoking and a slim, neat woman with short hair cropped at the back of her head is sitting with the two of them tucking into breakfast. She is Dearbhla Molloy, my Laura, and though my first impression is of a possibly severe and serious sort, she has a warmth and above all an easy, unforced, untheatrical naturalness which attracts me.

After a mug of tea we all move into a dining room and sit at a round table with the tallest glass vase I've ever seen stuck in the middle of it, and read through our scenes from the beginning.

Robert is sage, measured and never talks unless he has something to say. He's pleased that I can show anger well – he hadn't expected that. In fact my shortcomings are, ironically, in the humour department: I've not yet found a comfortable way of delivering the Scouse wisecracks that Alan dots generously around for me.

Tuesday, May 15th

At Robert's today are Julia St John, a pretty girl with big eyes who plays Diane Niarchos, and Mike Angelis who plays Martin Niarchos. At the reading Angelis is solid and very funny and his immediate rapport and ease with the material leaves me trailing behind. I can't seem to get the light and shade into Jim yet, though occasionally I hit it and it feels very good.

Meet Robert Lindsay for the first time. He quickly indicates that he knows I was offered Michael Murray first. Daniel Massey, immediately likeable, warm, charming and delightfully silly, is there and Lindsay Duncan who plays Barbara and Julie Walters and the lighting cameraman, also delightful.

The sun shines and it's all very auspicious. Alan smokes, drinks and pads about nervously. He does seem to suffer for his art.

Wednesday, May 16th

Bob Lindsay is reading with me today. He's arrived on a bicycle, with a child seat on the back. He's in quite good shape and I should imagine does some weights. He is reading Murray with writer, director and co-star for the first time – going through what I went through on Monday.

Technically he is good, and his timing is impressive; how he will cope with the introspection of Murray, the personal desolation and inadequacy inside, I don't know.

He asks many and detailed questions which make everything go on a little slowly, but I deliver my final uplifting peroration and we have lunch.

I know that when I hit it – when I am absolutely truthful, I am, as Jim Nelson says, the best. But I need technique to get me there. I fear that the workload (of everything) might just fight against relaxation and ease and enjoyment. In short I have to rediscover the old eagerness – the spirit of the Edinburgh Festival Revue of '64.

Thursday, May 17th

Another fine, warm, dry day. An *American Friends* morning. Blinds down in my workroom and calls to various people. Alfred Molina is back in England. Can he play Syme with a beard and an Icelandic accent? He sounds busy.

I call up Eric and go to lunch with him. This is just what I needed. A break from the twin projects weighing in on me at the moment, a chance to talk with an old friend – and these Python, pre-Prominent relationships seem all the more important now. We have 'The Adventure' to talk about, and Eric is so enthusiastic that he would like to set it up for mid-summer filming next year! We have a long and therapeutic laugh at the thought of playing two ex-RAF types.

Eric's off to France for two weeks, I head towards Camden Town and recycling and some shopping, then home to work on episode two of *GBH*. There is no short cut through Alan's scripts. They are dense and complex and I'm only halfway through the second when I have to shower and change for an evening out with David Frost.

To his house in Carlyle Square, quite a grand London mansion with stripped pine and bare floors adding a touch of character to the dark but carefully chosen decor. Frost has a fetish for photos which proliferate on every surface – all in thin silver frames, and all of himself or famous friends.

His son Miles, who's only about six, asks questions with all the acuity of the master. How much older is my daddy than you? Answer six years. Can interviewing technique be hereditary?

We watch the tape of *How to Irritate People*, in which I took part in 1968. Frost, whose company produced it, wants to put it on sale. It's too long, is appallingly directed and exudes cheapness in sets, titles, etc. However, it has wonderful Cleese/Chapman sketches and some of Graham's most brilliant performances; his Mountie coming backstage for compliments is a wondrous, cringingly painful gem.

Friday, May 18th

A short time working on *GBH* three, then up to Hampstead for dinner with Peter and Lin. Cook and Chung. Peter says he'd very much like to be called Peter Chung. His stomach is huge and pendulous, like Mr Punch's and, when it peeps out from beneath his T-shirt as Peter does some athletic piece of mime, it's like having another person in the room.

Peter is a big, genial presence, but not a solicitous host. Lin gets the food on the table and keeps it all going. Peter eats very little, drinks, but to start with not heavily, and smokes gazing round at everyone inquisitively as if assessing where he should take us all next. 'I'm going to get absolutely plastered, I think,' I hear Peter say to himself as he delves about in the fridge, in the same functional, unsensational tone that one might use if you were going to run a bath.

He sprawls into memories, often very funny, but, like some boozers do, loses sight of us, in absorption in himself. Peter becomes maudlin, sentimental, sharp, bitter, concerned in rapid succession. How cruel he was to Dudley in *Derek and Clive Get the Horn* … He shakes his head, 'I was so cruel.' How he would love to work with Dudley again, but it would have to be on something quite different.

The evening sort of crumbles, but we're not away until 1.30. Find ourselves driving back through agreeably empty streets after second night on the trot with a 50-year-old Cambridge satirist!

Thursday, May 24th

At the *American Friends* production office. David Calder, who's to be Pollitt, comes in this morning and we inch through his scenes together. He tends to RSC dramatics and doesn't quite find a way to cope with the inadequacies, the bufferishness of the character; but his commitment and positive attitude are very encouraging.

After lunch I work with Trini. The 'rehearsal' room is quite accessible – it's just a big, empty, echoing schoolroom, and I suppose Mike the unit driver was not to know that Trini and I were wrestling with one of our more intimate scenes when he walked in with a black plastic bag and began to empty the remains of lunch.

At six o'clock I throw a champagne party for cast, crew, actors and anyone else who can make it. It's at the school and the investors are out in force – two from Virgin, Ceci and Andy Burchill from BSB, Felicity from the BBC and Relph from British Screen. In the plaster-peeling seediness of an old primary school, the final signatures go down and the picture is financed, almost four years after I first thought of the idea.

Sunday, May 27th

Connie comes round to rehearse the restaurant scene which we shoot on Wednesday.

Useful rehearsal. The scene feels as if it has a direction and a purpose and we reduce the 'stodgy historical' dialogue. Then TP and I have a good talk over Ashby. I feel I must play him with less movement and fewer facial mannerisms if he's to avoid being a clone of Fortescue in *The Missionary*. Stillness and seriousness will provide the humour – and this goes for all the potentially 'comic' characters. TP endorses this, and I know that we basically share the same taste.

Trini arrives for supper. I walk with her over the Heath to Kenwood. Her boyfriend Robbie is coming to join her next week, but her mother would disapprove and mustn't know. She looks pale and tired, but so completely Elinor.

Tuesday, May 29th

Picked up at ten and taken to the location at Twickenham. They're filming in Strawberry Hill, Horace Walpole's elaborate and delicately decorated Gothic re-creation, now some sort of educational centre.

At eleven o'clock I witness the first take of *American Friends*. Trini and Connie both looking perfect, wading into the emotionally charged evening before the night-it-all-happens scene, which has been words on the page for so long. Now, today, its realisation on film is work for 50 or 60 people.

Encouraged by what I see. The two rooms which represent the mythical 'Angel Hotel' in Oxford are striking and lightly elaborate, the performances seem assured. Connie and Trini both have trouble with their corsets.

Wednesday, May 30th

My first day as actor on a film set for two and a half years, in a house on Kingston Hill got up to look like an Oxford restaurant of 1861.

My hair is tonged into curls and swept away to one side. I contemplate the state of my face eight years after *The Missionary* and find it wanting. Lines deeply etched on my forehead now rivalled in magnificence by a starburst of creases travelling out from my eyes. I can't remember feeling quite as old and tired for a long time, an almost laughably poor state to begin seven months' acting.

Fred Molina is in today. Fred is full of life and bonhomie and humour and takes a bit of keeping up with. Connie is worried, but then she always is. The set for the restaurant is very effective and with the other diners and the harpist in it feels completely right.

My voice is an octave or two lower than usual – husky through tightness perhaps. I rather like it. The day feels immensely long and there are so many people to be jolly to.

But I manage without incident to do my stuff. I can't say I felt relaxed, though, and I hope this will not show.

Friday, June 1st

Hardly time to register a new month, or look at a paper. Out to Hadley Wood, arriving about seven-twenty. No-one races up with compliments about the rushes so I assume either that they think I don't need them or that there is nothing to say. Suspect the latter. There was nothing extraordinary about my performance.

Work on through the afternoon. Jimmy Jewel,[1] who is very friendly to me but less so to anyone else, smokes almost continually, flicking the lighted end of his cigarette off with swift dexterity just before a take. 'Make your fucking mind up,' he says at one point and I feel Tristram flinch a hundred yards away.

I'm driven to rushes in the Prominent viewing theatre by Steve A.

Champagne is produced by Patrick and Steve afterwards and there is mellowness and relief and, though I have been in these post-first-week euphoria sessions before, I know that this is genuine – for they are a

---

1 Jimmy Jewel, Yorkshire-born comedian, who had a thirty-year partnership with Ben Warris (his cousin); also an actor.

very good crew. I forget in my solipsistic trance that others have been tested this week – especially Tristram, our lighting cameraman Philip Bonham Carter, and Connie too. All have come through with flying colours and everyone is happy for a moment in the damp courtyard below lowering skies at Prominent Studios.

Monday, June 4th

Difficult emotional scene with Trini – in my Oxford room. All much easier and more fun than I'd expected.

Trini grows in confidence and seems able to switch easily to whatever performance is required – apart from earthiness or coarseness. Bryan Pringle is ebullient. Always laughing. Tristram asks delicately if he could take his performance down a bit ... 'Wrong actor!' booms the weather-beaten Welshman and roars with laughter.

Tuesday, June 5th

Awake at six. Up at 6.30. Car at seven. On set at 8.30, hair crimped, calves gaitered, body frock-coated to play my half of the tender, moving scene we embarked on yesterday.

Then into another night-time confrontation. TP very good in his notes to me. It seems I nearly always start too big, and too predictably. He asks me to reduce the level and vary the pace, which is of course the way to a much more interesting performance. This is only my fifth day back down the acting mines and I realise that instinct can only achieve so much.

Finish with Trini in the afternoon and begin the scene with Cable, played by Colin Firth's brother Jonathan. I hadn't expected the pace to be quite as sustained. Another seven o'clock finish. Ten and a half hours on set.

Friday, June 15th

A BSB Film Programme unit have been brought along by our publicity lady, and they keep making incursions into the unit and carrying one or other member away into a far-off part of the garden to be probed.

Apart from the actors, all come back a touch self-conscious, as if they've just had a rather intimate medical examination. Only Connie, of the actors, is terrified of being interviewed. Her self-doubt is so appealing I only hope she never overcomes it!

I'm interviewed after lunch. A swan climbs quite fearlessly out of the water and wanders inquisitively amongst the crew as I talk! My cold seems to be developing nastily as the day wears on. The soft, windless, airless atmosphere doesn't help.

Try some rowing on the river in preparation for tomorrow. Alter some dialogue. How can it be, that after two years of raking over every syllable, Tristram and I are making it up a minute and a half before the take? Beginning to appreciate the organic nature of a film. This one is like cooking some delicate dish. It could be quite ordinary – the ingredients are not exotic – but if they're mixed and added in just the right way it could be unforgettable.

Sunday, June 17th

A delicious prospect of a day when I need feel no guilt at not working, when I can legitimately ease off and give my system a chance to recover. And it's warm and there's some sunshine outside.

Bleasdale rings – they start shooting *GBH* tomorrow. Like us, they're starting in on the emotional hard centre – with Michael Murray, Barbara and Murray's mum.

Try to think of myself as part of them, but it's too remote.

Work in the garden, watch World Cup football and enjoy pork roast for dinner – all of which makes me feel very content.

Tuesday, June 19th

Drive across Central London and down to the old St Thomas's Hospital operating theatre beside Tower Bridge, which is generally open to the public, but which today Prominent Features has hired, to shoot Elinor wandering in to Syme's lecture on dissection.

The character of this old part of London is now quite schizoid. Many fine buildings like the George Inn and the various Wren churches are set amongst attractive, interesting shop and warehouse buildings. All seems to have been well until the late twentieth century and the discovery of the new technologies. Now enormous blunt, anonymous skyscrapers tower over the area – like the huge and unwelcome feet of a giant in a garden.

Watch a couple of shots after lunch, look round the gory museum of old knives, saws, etc. Note that patients in hospital in 1830 were prescribed eight pints of beer a day.

Wednesday, June 20th: London–Oxford

Leave for Oxford at ten to three. Arrive in reasonable shape at the Cotswold Lodge Hotel.

A cup of tea with TP and Alun Armstrong, on for the first time. He's exercised that he's not remembered his father's birthday. TP suggests a telemessage. 'No, they always know you've forgotten them.' I suggest he goes early to the location and finds a card in Oxford. 'What would I find in Oxford for a retired miner?'

In the evening I'm filmed walking up past Brasenose, with the lamps illuminating St Mary's and the Radcliffe Camera: staking claim to a piece of my past in rather a grand way. Reminds me of Charlie Bubbles.[1] The boy made good. Almost 25 years to the day since he finished his full-time education, he returns in a blaze of light!

Patrick and Steve have seen assemblies of the material so far. Patrick voices a slight fear that it may become Bergman in Oxford and emphasises our need to keep the lightness. But apparently the investors are all pleased.

Thursday, June 21st: Oxford

To the location for supper at six, but am not required for first shot (in Merton Street) until it's dark at ten. Much hanging around – but that's what film is. Long periods of waiting, interspersed with nothing to do.

In the library of the building which has become our 'Angel Hotel' a crackly old TV with a blizzard-strewn black and white picture is propped up on a rubbish basket.

We watch England's clumsy toiling against Egypt. Am out in Merton Street, negotiating the awkward cobbled surface and trying to avoid foot contact with Trini's crinoline when an assortment of cries from various ends of the street heralds England's goal, which puts them through into the second round of the World Cup.

1 *Charlie Bubbles* (1968). Albert Finney's only film as a director. He also starred as a self-made man returning to his roots.

Saturday, July 7th

Returned from Oxford at 11.30 last night, having gone to the Rolling Stones 'Urban Jungle' concert at Wembley on the way back. A week of total and time-consuming involvement in the film.

Tuesday the busiest day of all, as we filmed the Lear sequence in the cloisters. First shot at nine, last shot at 9.15. The weather held, which was as well for there were film crews from BBC's 'Film '90' and ABC New York as well as a smattering of freelance journos amongst the visitors.

Wednesday began wet and windy and spirits drooped accordingly. But it was decided to go ahead and use the conditions by shooting the funeral sequence in the rain with umbrellas and all. A long but successful morning, despite choristers at the front running amok and shouting 'Action' in shrill voices – gratified by the Pavlovian response of the rest of us who immediately begin to shuffle forward.

Watch England's semi-final game against Germany with many of the rest of the crew, including boisterous sparks who really do like to sing 'Here We Go!'. England at last hit form and hold the Germans to a 1-1 draw, before being beaten on penalties.

The saddest aspect of the defeat was the sudden puncturing of what was likely to be a hysteria of delight. I really just wanted to see what everyone would do to each other if we won. But it wasn't to be and a complete and deflated silence greeted the successful German kick. After four years and four weeks it was unbelievable to see the stuffing knocked out of people so quickly.

Sunday, July 8th

At four to George Akers' cutting rooms. We watch a couple of assembled sections which TP feels will be a helpful indication of the film's mood and the story development, and how the Swiss stuff can best be played.

See the Oxford section before Switzerland and the Ashby/Elinor night at Oxford. Both delicately and atmospherically shot, certainly a joy to look at. The Syme/Ashby rivalry, the slight mystery about A's hols, but above all the intimation that something is to happen comes out strongly. There is an emotional intensity, and once again it's about the things not said.

This is a great send-off before Switzerland and will help fortify me over the next two hard weeks.

Monday, July 9th: London–Fiesch

Up the Rhône valley, through Sion and Brig, to an archetypally neat Swiss mountain town called Fiesch. (Check in Ed P's diary and find he passed through here in July 1861. He went up the Eggishorn Mountain behind the town and spent two weeks laid up there because of his heel.)

Our hotel, the Christania, is new and clean and family-run. I have an attractive double room under the eaves with a quiet view onto what Tristram calls 'Heidi-like' pastures and the slopes of a mountain.

Not much time to rest as TP, Patrick and I go to the production office, a low-ceilinged old house in the town, to meet the Swiss crew, make some script changes and then drive to the location, the tiny hamlet of Im Feld, which has been transformed over the last two weeks by our construction and art dept into the romantic haven where E and A meet.

Like all Andrew McAlpine's[1] work this is not a chocolate-box set, not glossy or in the slightest twee. It's quite steep too, which adds character. Another great success for location finders and art dept.

Saturday, July 14th: Fiesch

I went up on the cable car to the top of Eggishorn with Bob Ringwood and Armstrong and son. High up, above the tree line, on a worn shelf full of building materials, stands the Jungfrau Hotel, in whose predecessor Ed P spent two weeks 129 summers ago. He noted how thin the partitions were 'which did not suit the honeymoon couples'. At the top of the mountain, snow still lingered and on the north side the Aletsch glacier, grey, crevassed ice, swept round and down to the south-west in a curve of imperceptible motion.

Called for the night shoot. First shot at seven. The last at about ten to five this morning. About 60 extras, much dancing – very muggy and uncomfortable conditions – and finally the kiss. In the middle of all this I signed my *GBH* contract in an upstairs room!

Walked back down from the village as grey dawn turned white, for breakfast in the meadow by the river. Felt like a soldier after battle.

---

1 Andrew McAlpine, New Zealand-born production designer whose films include *The Rachel Papers*, *The Piano*, *The Beach* and *An Education*.

Thursday, July 19th: Fiesch

7.45 a.m. A helicopter comes in to collect cement from the electricity company's cable-car station where I have dressed as Francis Ashby for the last full day's filming.

Later. I had been doing a series of walking shots towards the waterfall. Every couple of minutes the helicopter roared overhead, shattering the calm of a beautiful natural location – bucket either hanging low, or empty, trailing out in the slipstream.

Then there was an odd noise, a sort of irregular and more vehement acceleration of the engine. Did not register any emergency though, and, resting in the generous heat, beneath a bush, I was gently nodding off, whilst the crew moved up to take another shot. Made no connection between my ability to nod off and the absence of the ferrying helicopter.

We hear that the helicopter has crashed – down at our base camp, a few yards from the make-up bus where Connie and Trini are being prepared for later shooting.

But work goes on and soon I'm scampering up warm rocks to the base of the waterfall, pulling down my mid-Victorian underwear and exposing most, if not all, to the camera far below.

As I splash the mountain water over my body I at last understand what could have made Edward Palin pull all his clothes off and plunge into an Alpine pool. The natural basin of rock, the seduction of flowing water, the fields thick with butterflies and the silence from protecting mountains all around.

Walk slowly back down the hill, away from this paradise, quite reluctantly.

First I see Trini and her mother Sylvia sat beneath the trees, Trini working on her crochet, her mother knitting. T's make-up smudged with lines of tears. She had looked out immediately after the impact and seen a man hanging from the helicopter.

Connie B, in dressing gown with hair up, looking every inch the actress, sits reading. I notice she has a glass of red wine beside her – unusual, but probably a reflection on the morning's events. Connie very self-contained, small, bird-like, back straight, never sloppy. I envy that sort of ability to hold things in, to coolly conserve.

Bits of the helicopter rotors scattered all over the landing strip. Holes sliced in the Perspex walls of the cable-car station. A miracle that the make-up bus, or any of our crew, avoided injury.

The day hotting up. Cloudless sky. Must be in the upper 80s. In the p.m. we squash into the electricity co.'s rugged little cable car, and are hauled up to 2,094 metres, nearly 7,000 feet. A bleak, rocky area with tremendous view of the Finsteraarhorn to the north.

The last shot is, most unusually, the last shot of the story – myself and Trini on our honeymoon in Switzerland. Great-grandfather and great-grandmother arm in arm walking across the splendid, dominating landscape of the Alps.

Eventually the sun descends behind the mountain to the west. The light is turned gently but firmly off. Thirty-seven days of filming are complete.

Friday, July 20th: Fiesch–London

In response to requests, I have had the Edward Palin diaries copied and have brought them along, rather like song-sheets, for those who want to take them away.

They are probably all leaving about now – Trini to fly direct to New York, and half of our crew to London via Geneva.

In my bed I turn over in relief at the sudden loosening of the film's grip and relax until half past nine, when I go downstairs for a breakfast of coffee and hot milk, thick honey and fresh brown bread, taken solitarily, apart from a French family.

After a bath I slowly gather together my possessions and am packed by midday.

Then into the Espace and we make for Geneva.

Thursday, August 2nd

To Mister Lighting's new studios out on the A40.

Akers day, we call it, as most of what we're doing has been requested by George Akers. So for a couple of hours, they pick up things in close-up. My Oxford study and then my Swiss chalet room are recreated. Reminds me how much of filming is an industrial process, how little is romantic. Yet there is something romantic about our little band today. A quiet, happy feeling of achievement which cannot be specifically quantified but binds us all together.

Into Central London, to the Royal Academy for a shot of myself and Connie walking away from camera between two rows of statues. At least it's cool in here amongst all the hefty classical figures with arms and penises missing.

Then back into the traffic jams and out to the studios for Connie to change – all for a back-of-head shot in Jimmy Jewel's garden.

And in a small and unpretentious little park in Acton our small and unpretentious film finally comes to an end.

Tomorrow at this time I should be in Majorca with Helen, grabbing whatever holiday time I can.

Eric Idle has become a father again, and there is very good news from Anne on the next big project after *GBH* – the BBC has decided to back our independently produced *Pole to Pole* and we've been given a BBC One transmission slot of January 1993.

Friday, August 3rd: London–Deyà

Up at 7.15. Outside the heat waits, indolently and inevitably, as in some southern city. We leave home at eight o'clock. Newspaper headlines scream Saddam Hussein's promise to 'turn Kuwait into a graveyard' if his invasion is countered with force. For the first time there appears to be an international consensus that his action was unjustified, but ominous silence from the rest of the Arab world.

We are at the hotel in Deyà by three. About half past three I begin the laborious process of hacking away at my Ashby-esque mutton chops with a GII razor, when a cut-throat and a barber's in Jermyn Street are really what's required.

I do shed a year or two as the hair disappears down the basin.

Sunbathe, read deeper into the delightful *Mohawk* by Richard Russo, then out into the village. Look at Robert Graves's grave and marvel once more at the situation of the church and panorama of Deyà coiled below us.

A play is taking place in the open air, there's music in the church and the lizards wait, toes splayed, in the street lamps.

Saturday, August 4th: Deyà

Helen to the sunbeds and me onto our little terrace overlooking roofs and hillsides to read through more of *GBH*.

Richard Branson, who owns the hotel, is about, playing chess with a friend whilst friend's girlfriend watches (later he's on the tennis court with a friend whilst girlfriend watches). He's always engaged in some sort of competitive activity; I never see him sit and read. But then he hasn't got *GBH* or *Mohawk*.

Sunday, August 5th: Deyà

Breakfast at half past nine, as the sun edges up over the mountain rim. I sit outside on the patio and plough on through *GBH* – around me light, sounds and the muted colours of the terracotta tiles and the silvery grey of the olive tree leaves.

See Branson making his way to the pool with a sheaf of files and papers. Later I see him lying in the shade going through them, dropping those he's finished with into a child's blue rubber dinghy.

Finish my latest read-through of *GBH*. My long, final, triumphant speech on socialism prepared in these privileged surroundings.

Tuesday, August 7th

To the Crown viewing theatre for my first look at an assembly of 'AF'. For some reason I feel elated anticipation. Not un-to do with my conversation with Virginia P on the phone last night. She had seen the video of the assembly twice over the weekend. She'd loved the look of it and thought I was 'brilliant'. This has kept me in good spirits most of the day.

There is no doubt that it is an appealing film – the photography, the performances and the story all very watchable and involving. At the end smiles all round. 'Delightful' is the word most often used. 'Everything I hoped it would be,' says Irene Lamb.

Over supper I make a list of Helen's observations. 'Don't make the film any shorter,' she says. It's currently about 100 minutes.

Wednesday, August 8th

Wake to hear the milk van shuffle to a halt and the bottles being collected. It's six o'clock and that means my mind is waking too early.

Try to confuse it, or at least keep it dulled with the most soporific and boring images. But it's no good, it wants action, and it soon finds it in analysing, in the cold, or in this case rather muggy, light of day, my performance in 'AF'.

Find myself wanting. Feel that I am absorbed into the story without dominating and dictating its direction. I do not change enough, or as dramatically, as perhaps I should.

But the day's commitments beckon and at ten minutes to nine I'm at BUPA's new medical centre in Gray's Inn Road.

Usual tests: eyes, ears, blood, lungs, as well as an abdominal X-ray, then the fitness assessment. Though I may feel mentally off-colour, I'm in good physical shape.

I run for nine and three-quarter minutes on the treadmill at seven miles an hour on ever-increasing gradients. This is longer than two years ago when I was filmed having a medical for *80 Days*, so I can assume I'm fitter at 47 than I was at 45. Most memorable moment was Dr Goldin's exclamation as he took his finger out of my bottom – 'You have the prostate of a 21-year-old.'

Autographs and messages for the nurses. I have the sneaking feeling as I leave that to give me any bad news would have so spoilt this morning that they just invented the results.

Sunday, August 12th: London–Abbotsley–Manchester

To Abbotsley for the first time since the Sunday before 'AF'. We walk round the garden – the pond has almost disappeared in the drought – then Rachel hears some of my lines for the week in the little room next to the kitchen, then a bottle of champagne rosé on the lawn and lunch, coffee and loll half asleep on a rug in the sunshine. Then tennis – Rachel and I take a set off Tom and Lisa [Tom's girlfriend] – then some more lines with Rachel and it's time for me to start back home to pack and leave for Manchester.

They're all on the tennis court when I say goodbye, providing the most idyllic tableau. Rachel waves from the drive and at half past four I turn out into the village and head for three or four months of the most challenging work since *80 Days*. Miss them all as I drive the familiar back lanes to the motorway.

Meet Robert Young and Bob Lindsay at the airport. We share a row of three on the Manchester shuttle. The row opposite is entirely taken up by the almost inconceivably massive bulk of Giant Haystacks – the wrestler. He's the largest man I think I've ever seen.

Once at Manchester I'm driven to a meal with Robert Y and Alan B at a restaurant called the Lemon Tree. Alan arrives late, looks harassed.

His play *Having a Ball* goes into the West End next week. It's broken box office records in Liverpool, but he's worried about the London critics. Both men seem pleased with the shoot so far. Julie Walters has been marvellous, they say, quite brilliant.

Monday, August 13th: Manchester

Collected at ten and driven south to the location – an old technical college of some kind being turned into a high-tech modern industrial estate.

All the 'major' actors share a Winnebago. Comfortable, but no privacy. Like a common room. Tom Georgeson, Bob Lindsay, Drew Schofield, Paul Daneman and myself in there as well as Alan B, who occasionally joins us to watch the cricket. The rest of the day's cast – including 30 'assorted lefties' – either sit on the grass beneath warm, cloudy skies, or are squeezed into a grubby, dilapidated double-decker bus.

I meet the selection of Welsh collies which are here to audition for Beulah. The first one is called Spike: an older dog than required in the script, but wonderfully, abjectly, lovable. Head turned up and nuzzling into my crotch. Hard to resist. We run, stop and heel around the gardens. Robert and Alan are summonsed and Spike is unanimously chosen.

After lunch I have my hair cut by Jane then am driven back into Manchester. My time is suddenly my own. A situation I often desperately crave, but now, here, at this odd time, I'm a little frightened of.

Walk down to Sunlight House and the site of 'Herriot's Turkish Baths'. Probably once rather grand, now a health club with impressive tight-shirted exec. girls wearing lots of make-up at the door. Downstairs is a pool of irregular shape into which enamel-tiled columns disappear, giving it the feel of a flooded basement. However, manage 30 lengths and feel better. Keen girl signs me up for fitness assessment tomorrow.

Tuesday, August 14th: Manchester

Leisurely rising, then driven out to Oldham to a drama workshop where most of our children have come from. The head man, David Johnson, is a stern teacher, but produces some impressive performances.

Meet two of those who will be my children. They're lovely – Anna Friel, the confident, attractive 15-year-old daughter of a teacher, and

Edward, with a broader accent, a reassuring face – a 'Just William' lookalike.

Meet David Ross, who is to play scenes with me next week; he's also the lead in *Having a Ball*, which opens to previews in London on Thursday night. A gentlemanly figure, soft-spoken, like a slightly more pert Alan Bennett.

I make my way to Herriot's, where Sharon tries me out 'to find my limits'.

Wednesday, August 15th: Manchester

My first acting day on *GBH*.

Taxi collects me at 7.15. He asks me where the location is, can't find it on his map. It's raining. We drive up motorways towards Bolton, and eventually find ourselves in Lostock; vehicles parked in station yard. I'm taken to the Winnebago.

Because of the rain we first do a scene I haven't even learnt. (As I've been learning manically for the last few days this is quite ironic.) So I bring Jim Nelson to life in a small headmaster's study at Lostock School, Glengarth Drive in Bolton. Phone-answering sequences.

We do a scene at the end of the day almost uninterrupted, with camera on tight long lens following us everywhere. The cut-ins are shot in a businesslike way. Robert Young's vitality and rather patrician control obviously the secret. He looks as if he started yesterday, not eight weeks ago. Alan is there and, I think, pleased by the last scene – when I turn the press hacks away. Because of rain we work until eight.

Thursday, August 16th: Manchester

More rain, so my telephone conversation with Frank Twist is done first. The pickets, and the thugs who will be jumping on the roof, sit mouldering on the bus. The Winnebago is home to five or six speaking actors. Bob complains.

I have the feeling that things are beginning to fall apart a bit. The weather is clearly putting some of the arrangements under pressure and we shall film some of next week's material tomorrow, including one of my important showdown scenes with Murray.

As we're filming in the early hours of Sunday morning it doesn't seem worth my while going home for the weekend. Talk to Will, who's back from France – apparently Tom's new house in Kentish Town is looking very good. Rachel is concerned for me, and how the acting's going, and I miss them.

Friday, August 17th: Manchester

The confrontation scene with Murray seemed to go well, though I did not approach it with sufficient confidence at first. I hope I did it well. I feel I'm too old and too physically slight for Jim. But at six we wrap and my first week is over.

Back at the Portland Hotel. *Newsnight*. War sounds to be closer over Iraq and Kuwait. Sleep while watching most of it. Light out on week, finally, at a quarter to twelve.

Saturday, August 18th: Manchester

Wake about six o'clock. Lie in bed until eleven. Very occasionally I drift into dreams. In one of them, I'm looking out of a corner window, the shutters are opened a crack. I look down as I hear a noise, figures run away, soil and dirt are flung through the shutters and hit my face. I wake sharply, heart beating hard.

I will not succumb to the self-pity of a tired actor alone on a warm, busy day in Manchester, and I take myself off to the Whitworth Art Gallery.

Friendly inside. Much communication with the visitor. Three Camille Pissarros and many Pre-Raphaelites including a voluptuous Rossetti and a weird Millais. Exhibition of landscape painting with good notes relating landscape to the human factor. Generally informative.

Taxi back down the Oxford Road to the health club. Just time for a run on the treadmill. I miss my Hampstead Heath.

At the hotel, I read through all the script for next week. Hard work for me. Two Weller scenes, one with the children and a big one with Murray before I see home again.

Walk down to the Cornerhouse, passing an array of chunky hookers in the streets behind the hotel, cruising along streets lined with chunky buildings and right below the splendid mock-mediaeval façade of the old Law Courts.

Back at the hotel the manager has requested I join him for a drink. He's a nervous, youngish man, and no sooner has he ordered champagne and sat down beside me than the fire alarms sound everywhere. A frightful din and complete confusion. Turns out that the flambé trolley set off the restaurant alarms. 'I'll be skinned alive for this,' mutters the manager, as firemen mingle with guests as if in some sitcom.

He apologises for the absence of his wife who really wanted to meet me. 'She had the vomits.'

Tomorrow morning's pick-up call is four o'clock.

Wednesday, August 22nd: Manchester

Robert Young came into make-up first thing yesterday and said how pleased he was with the confrontation scene in the gymnasium. He talked enthusiastically of 'the strength' in the performance. His word of caution was almost the same as Tristram's, that occasionally I let Michael Palin, with too ready a smile and too expressive an eye movement, through into the performance. Most of the time Jim Nelson dominates and is strong and solid, but I must watch the Palin-isms.

This morning I have a five-and-a-half-page, quite tricky scene with David Ross. David was playing in *Having a Ball* at the Comedy last night, arrived in Manchester at 2.15 a.m. and had four hours' sleep. He's already in make-up being aged, spectacularly well, when I arrive at the Winnebago.

The drizzle means that they are going straight into the common room scene. Robert plans it in one take, running over four minutes. Though tired as we both are, the final result is greeted by all as a success.

As I walk back to lunch, Alan B shouts after me 'That was magnificent.'

Friday, August 24th

Feel cool, calm, relaxed and relieved. Wish I could always be like this. I've appeared as Jim N for nine days now. I know and feel the character; I know that Robert Y is pleased, but the challenge to produce my best in all circumstances is daunting. I simply pray I have the ability to rise to it.

At present, as I experience the pleasure of seeing my house again, and wandering, free from cameras and scripts, into the overgrowing garden on a thick, hot, windless afternoon, I have no fears, and I feel that I have already overcome the darkest worries I had before going up to Manchester.

Tuesday, August 28th: Manchester

Richard picks me up at 7.15 to go once again to the school. Grey drizzle. Morning spent on scene with the children in which I have to entertain them for an end-of-year treat. The mad science experiment. It must be energetic, improvised, and funny. I feel like Jim Nelson's supposed to feel in the script – ground down. Dragging himself/myself to an enormous effort.

It is one of the hardest half-day's filming I've ever done, and at the end of it I feel hot and only half successful. All I want to do in the Winnebago at lunch is to rest and hopefully sleep. But a deputation from the producers – tall, rich-voiced David Jones and large, friendly-faced Caroline Hewitt, the Production Manager, squeeze themselves in and discuss 'problems'.

Evidently Bob L has talked to them about on-set accommodation for actors, co-ordination of calls on set, etc. etc. and it's all been taken very seriously. I make my points and they are concerned and appreciative and say I must always say if anything is wrong. On busy days a second Winnie will be provided.

When Caroline's gone David J lingers. He says the rushes are brilliant. 'I always thought Jim Nelson was an interesting character, but you've made him even more interesting.'

Because I like him and feel that he is approaching this from a writer's point of view, his compliment fell most happily, and, together with Alan's endorsement over the weekend, combined to reinvigorate me in the afternoon.

After wrap go with Lindsay to the gym. I do four and a half miles in 35 minutes on the treadmill and row for five minutes. Then we both overeat at a Japanese restaurant where flamboyant chefs cook at your table and throw eggs in the air.

Friday, August 31st: Manchester–London

Sleep until six o'clock. This is now quite a late awakening for me. Up at 6.45; oh, how hard it is to roll back the bedclothes!

Check out of the Portland; then to Runcorn Bridge with Richard and Julia and Dearbhla. Mike Angelis there too. All day spent on completing the final shot which is really my moment of glory, redemption, self-discovery, the apotheosis of Jim Nelson.

End the day emoting and elating and triumphing and overcoming, with the car parked beneath the viaduct's immense concrete supports surrounded by props men rocking it and local children looking on incredulously. 'I'm alive!' 'Ha-Ha-Ha!' Not my most natural and I can tell from faces of Alan and Robert that it's good. Only good. Robert's cousin Julia seeks me out and looks at me in some admiration. 'You're so patient.'

Home about 9.30. Sit and watch Michael Caine talking about techniques of film-acting. Resolve not to start worrying about next week's work until next week.

Thursday, September 6th: Brockwood Hall, Cumbria

2.50 in the afternoon. In the Winnebago at Brockwood. Dan Massey asleep. His book *Not Prince Hamlet* by Michael Meyer on the table in front of me. Annie Spiers read my Chinese horoscope while making me up … 'A good year, if you do not forget old friends.'

The Winnebago is rocked, as I write, by 50–60 mile-an-hour gusts. The tail end of a hurricane, due to blow into tomorrow. It's continuing the bad run of weather luck which has hit the film from the day I began. Robert Y confesses that we are two and a half days behind. (They were half a day behind when I joined.) This week has progressed untidily.

Began with a strong emotional scene with Dearbhla on Monday to get the juices going, and have also completed the tennis-racket-smashing which I'm glad to be free of. For all the planning and choreographing, in the end I went at it with a frenzied lack of control, which was the only way to do it.

Sunday, September 9th: Trinity House Hotel, Ulverston

It's late afternoon. My shutters are closed against the noise of traffic from the Barrow–Lancaster main road, just outside this uncomplicated, handsome little Georgian rectory.

I am aware that I am running on overdrive. This is a test of stamina as punishing as any since *80 Days*. I knew it would be. My body and mind prepared themselves at the beginning of May. Somehow they keep me together. I learn and remember my lines, I have completed difficult physically and emotionally demanding scenes to what I sense to be general satisfaction.

I wish that I were always on top form. I wish the effort wasn't quite as hard. I wish I could always wake up positive, fresh and vigorous.

I am happy with the crew. There is not a single bad egg amongst them. Robert is everything Robert Lindsay said he would be. Enormously patient, supportive and the complete director.

However wound up I may be at the beginning of the day (and maybe this is just the price of giving a good performance) I relax almost ecstatically at the end and the homecoming drive over the low ragged fells, and the whisky and the bath and the meal, generally with Dearbhla and Julia and Dan Massey, are times of unqualified happiness.

I don't read much outside of the newspapers; I find I can't concentrate. My mind is full of *GBH*, except when I turn off the light and the short but blessed sleep clears my mind of everything.

Monday, September 10th, Ulverston

Think back over a painful but satisfactory night shoot. Rain was to fall throughout the long scene, and I had only thin pyjamas and a pair of Y-fronts against the elements.

The first time we played it the rain was such a surprise to Dan that his voice rose several octaves and he sped through the scene almost halving its time. Robert took him aside afterwards and said he felt he'd missed some nuances. 'You must remember that it's warm spring rain,' tries Robert. 'But it isn't!' says Dan with feeling but not hostility.

A wasps' nest is discovered in the middle of shot and has to be dealt with. A cable burns through, but by six we have the sequence, though one or two cut-aways are abandoned.

The crew applaud Dan and myself after we manage a third long take under the hosepipes!

Up at one o'clock to meet Alan B for lunch at the Bay Horse Inn. A picturesque spot by the Duddon Estuary.

Alan's a great storyteller and we sit out with a light wind taking the edge off a warm day by the mudflats.

He tells us his Princess Margaret story. How she made a beeline for him and Willy Russell at an Everyman Theatre do.[1] How she drank four whiskies in swift succession. How nice she was when Alan spat

1 Opened on Hope Street, Liverpool in 1964. Gave first break to many left-leaning writers and actors.

a piece of vol-au-vent onto her, and how she just wanted to meet actors.

Tuesday, September 11th, Ulverston

Shoot the car chase sequence in our rotten old Volkswagen Variant. Most of the morning taken up with stunt-driving. Andy Bradford, who fell down a mountain as Ashby in Switzerland, now risks his life as Jim Nelson on the back roads of Cumbria.

The commissioning editor for C4 and his assistant are visiting. Alan has to entertain them. A long, very noisy meal.

Remark of Dan's makes me laugh longer and more helplessly than I remember for months. I say that I can control the dog quite easily and it will obey whichever command I give it … 'Come!' or 'Kneel!' … 'Oh, kneel, surely,' says Dan with anxious distaste. For some reason we all collapse.

To bed at one o'clock. Two and a half hours later than I meant to be.

Friday, September 14th, Ulverston

Pick-up at 7.15. The milk and vegetables wait to be collected outside the back door. Travel in with Dan. Pass valleys filled with fluffy white mist. All quiet and untroubled by wind or rain.

Once again to Woodlands, the house Jim and his family have retreated to, bouncing along the field up to the small group of those in the crew who arrive even earlier than ourselves.

Full complement of holidaymaking extras here today – including Anna Ford's father, a very fine, white-bearded gentleman, who looks like an old Boer, and Chris Erwin, whose portrayal of the hero in some performances of *Having a Ball* left audiences gasping … 'Cock like a baby's arm,' was Angelis' description.

Apparently some of the film of the stunt-driving sequences shot on Tuesday has been lost on BR. Depressing news when we're fighting to keep ahead.

Work with horses, dogs and children. Eleven takes of one shot with the dog. But short scene when I burst out onto the balcony with an envelope full of photos screaming for Laura works well. I hit full intensity and dog lady Sue admits to being much moved.

Monday, September 17th, Ulverston

John Cleese on morning TV, hands raised with Paddy Ashdown on Liberal Democrat conference stand! No wonder Alan couldn't get hold of him. Alan wanted to ask John to play the Scottish doctor part, but was very nervous of approaching him.

Shooting more car stuff this morning: a bridge over the river Esk which lies in a most beautiful valley – not spectacular, but low, gentle, wooded and empty. Sellafield Nuclear Power Station is just up the road and the river is, I'm told, seriously polluted, with five times more radiation than anywhere else in the country.

I manage an impressive emergency stop in the roadway, hitting the mark twice. Peter Jessop, the lighting cameraman, most impressed with my stunt-driving.

Tuesday, September 18th, Kirkstanton

To Kirkstanton, a small village on the coast near Haverigg. Featureless apart from a scruffy green, a pub and a farmhouse which is being renovated, expensively and tastelessly.

This is a nuclear neighbourhood – 14,000 are employed in the Trident programme at Barrow and many more reprocessing nuclear waste at Sellafield. A railway line runs close by and every now and then a Plutonium Special rumbles past, the characteristic brown flasks slung on flatbed bogies, full of spent plutonium in rods.

The weather is closing in – gales forecast for tomorrow. So we shoot inside first. Two scenes, one of which is among the most demanding I've done. I have to tell Martin (Mike Angelis) that I'm going mad. When I rehearsed it it moved me to tears, but Robert Y discourages a strong emotional reading.

So, at the last minute, I find my approach changed. I go along with Robert but I feel less sure of myself and the dry joke at the end – about Diane having it off – doesn't play. Robert thinks it does, Alan, whose gut reaction I trust, feels it could be better.

A long, hard scene which takes most of the day, and leaves me sobered.

Sunday, September 23rd

Feel drained of energy. Halfway between worlds. *GBH* on one side and London life on the other. Make an effort to shift myself in some direction. Call TJ and fix some squash and leave message for TG inviting myself round to tea.

In the evening a full house for Sunday dinner. Tom and Will spar like five-year-olds. Tom very funny with his banter about Will at Oxford. 'Have you got your monocle?' etc. etc. He must have taken in more of the Tom Merry world than I'd expected.

A lovely, boisterous dinner, and, through it all, a poignant sense that with Will at Oxford and Tom having left home this month marks quite a sea change in family life. But for tonight – we're the same as we always were.

Sunday, September 30th

The *Sunday Correspondent,* after a brave start, has gone tabloid. *80 Days* book seems to be fading – down to No. 10 in its 45th week. Funny how one is never satisfied. A year ago I'd have been delighted to see it touch the charts at all. Now I shall be very aggrieved if it doesn't hold in there for 52 weeks.

Friday, October 5th

A screening of 'AF' to check out the sound. Terry J there and thought it the most beautiful film he'd ever seen; his laughter helped the atmosphere.

I like the music by Georges Delerue and feel it adds to the quality. Still have misgivings about my playing of Ashby. I think too consistently and persistently severe. Not much burning off him. It's a measure of how good Trini and Connie's performances are that they make my emotional involvement seem convincing.

Wednesday, October 10th: Brookfield Hall, near Buxton, Derbyshire

Alan has agreed to three days of cuts to keep us on schedule. The weather at our location – a house up on the most exposed part of the moor, near Hayfield – has been grey and inhospitable and not at all right for the summer scenes we're shooting. A complicated interior of the four of us took over 20 takes to complete.

Rang Patrick Cassavetti from the house. Stan Fishman of Rank has seen *American Friends* and 'quite' likes it. Will give us the Odeon Haymarket in March or April next year, though. He doesn't think it will do business outside London. Patrick thinks he's wrong. Whatever, I feel badly in need of some unequivocally good news.

Saturday, October 13th

Maggie T used the 'Parrot Sketch' in her speech to the Conservative Party Conference yesterday and I'm rung by the *Correspondent* for a quote.

Patrick says the 50-person 'random' audience research screening of 'AF' went off well on Wednesday. No-one hated the movie and there were one or two excellents!

Sunday, October 14th

Present-opening at the breakfast table. Give Helen a long silver necklace, UB40 tapes, a book on witchcraft in south-west France, and one on Indian cooking, and a big basket of winter-flowering jasmine.

She goes to tennis. I take two signed books up to the William Ellis auction, then back home to find Will has just arrived on his first break from Oxford. Rachel has made a wonderful birthday card, with all Mum's activities and habits noted!

Then we all go off to lunch at Mary and Ed's, after I've spent a very satisfactory hour with Rachel going over the seven big scenes I have next week.

Saturday, October 20th: Brookfield Hall, Derbyshire

One of my most difficult scenes comes up before lunch. It's the Robbie Burns death description – myself and Dearbhla. On the page it's described as enraged – 'tears flow'. I'm aware as I do it, cruelly cold for the crew, that Alan and Robert have reservations.

They take me away to a quiet room – dressed as the children's bedroom with posters of Jason Donovan on the wall – and Robert at some length gives me the wise note that in the retelling of a dreadful experience the emotion is often suppressed and does not need to spill over the surface.

As I walk back to the Winnebago I feel a heavy weight; I'm cross at not having thought of that myself. But maybe I'm the last one to see how I come across.

Dearbhla takes my arm and says I should tell the story in the same way I told her about Angela's death, which she said was calm and matter-of-fact. This helped me enormously – provided the key.

I do several takes with minor script errors – though only Alan spots them. But being a writer myself I know how much accuracy matters, and I'm hugely relieved when, despite the heat and the fatigue, I manage two good and complete takes which they are pleased with.

I walk outside. The light's fading. The line of trucks shields the view on one side, but to the east the wide, bare slopes of the Pennines begin. Alan joins me. He has tears in his eyes. He says there are certain scenes he can't watch without crying.

Fly back to London feeling muted. Less euphoric than seven days ago. It all came harder this week.

Sunday, October 21st

To Simon A at six for a meeting re his idea of getting together a group to bid for one of the new TV franchises.

'Basically, we want you to be a part of it,' says Simon, who claims I am the first person he sounded out, after first hatching his plan in the bath, 'but what role can you play?' Both decide to think about this further, to see if my desire not to become administratively involved or even contractually involved can be reconciled with the desire of him and Clive and Roger Laughton to have me on board.

Monday, October 22nd: London–Derbyshire

Out to see latest version of 'AF' with Patrick, Steve and Tristram at De Lane Lea. Improvements (including dawn shots beneath opening titles) all seem to the good. The music enriches and seems better each time I hear it. Last half-hour almost trouble-free. Some of the middle section still sluggish. I can see extra cuts I would have made but the picture is being neg-cut at the moment so confine my notes to one or two observations about soundtrack which TP will look after later today.

Recycling, checking through latest offers, including a Barclaycard ad – as the new Alan Whicker! (To be directed by John Lloyd, but, that apart, I've not the slightest compunction in turning it down.) Wonderful relief of not having to learn heavy speeches again this weekend. A call from *GBH* to say that they have decided to use myself and Dearbhla tomorrow after all. Could we come up on the late flight?

Thursday, October 25th

Plunged into a silliness over Python's reaction to Thatcher's recital of the 'Parrot Sketch'. 'The Parrot has Twitched' said Paddy Ashdown after Eastbourne and in a sense the by-election slap round the face has made Thatcher look very silly and the Parrot indeed will not be mentioned by her again.[1]

TJ is the only one who still wants to sue her. Anne has come up with a press release reflecting Eric and JC's wish not to sue but to issue a silly statement about Thatcher being 'tired and shagged out after a long squawk'. Too late to sue anyway. Impact lost now I feel. But I have to ring TJ and tell him this. He doesn't push his view and we make amicable arrangements to meet next week.

Friday, October 26th

See an *Evening Standard*. There on the front page is a picture of Derek Hatton being led away by detectives, and the news that he's been arrested in a massive fraud operation involving 300 police.[2] *GBH* is now given another dimension, as the story Alan has written is being played out for real. Extraordinary.

Two small children come trick-or-treating. I tell them to come back on Halloween. They depart, one of them muttering indignantly, 'Going on 'oliday!'

1 Only two weeks after the Liberal Democrats were likened to a 'dead parrot', their candidate David Bellotti overturned a Conservative majority to win the Eastbourne seat, which had become vacant after the death of Ian Gow, who was killed when the Provisional IRA put a bomb under his car.
2 Derek Hatton, unofficial leader of Liverpool City Council when it was controlled by the Trotskyist Militant Tendency, a far-left socialist council grouping.

Sunday, October 28th

Call Alan B. He says that, even more than Hatton's arrest, life has imitated art with the revelation that Wimpey, major contributors to the Conservative Party, are alleged to have funded Militant[1] through Derek Hatton's PR company. Alan is rewriting the ending.

TG comes by. Quite like old times – tea and gossip in the kitchen. He confirms that he loved the look of '*AF*', but felt it was not dramatic enough. Time passed pleasantly, but there were no highs and lows, no 'emotional Alps'.

A long rambling chat leads into Sunday supper – delicately disposing of a chicken whilst Attenborough's *Trials of Life* shows a squad of chimpanzees hunting a luckless monkey and then tearing it apart and eating, as far as I could see, every bit of it.

Monday, November 5th: Manchester

Day 100 on *GBH* goes unremarked. It's the start of another week's work, the 21st in succession, which promises some of the most busy and complex scenes.

Re-meet everyone in the cinder-covered car park of the Taylor Brothers Sports and Social Club in Eccles. There is a high and cloudless sky and it's been a cold night.

Colin Douglas, who has a heavy week as Frank Twist, is in bad shape. He's a big, warm, lovable man you want to hug, but the rewrites of his scenes with me have devastated him.

Colin is 79, his wife died at the start of filming. It had taken him many weeks to learn the lines – he'd write them out time after time – and then suddenly to be presented with a scene, or scenes, demolished and rebuilt had sent him into shock. 'I can't do it ... I've not slept since I got the rewrites.' He shakes his head and it's a desperately unhappy sight to see a big man's pride laid so low. Just like the character he's playing, that's the uncanny thing.

But Robert is sensitive and adapts without fuss, even to the extent of secretly shooting a scene I thought was a rehearsal. This led to Colin giving a fine performance and me drying!

---

1 Hatton was cleared of any impropriety after an eight-week trial.

Tuesday, November 6th, Manchester

Colin is in a dreadful state again. In the Winnie I find myself holding his great shoulders, feeling the heat and stickiness of the sweat through his shirt, as he sheds some tears and says he's not slept and had thought of throwing himself over the banisters at the Britannia Hotel.

I go over the lines as often as he wants, and when we start to shoot Robert end-boards and never shouts 'Action!' Colin rolls easily through the speeches that have been driving him near to banister-hopping, and we complete work scheduled for one and a half days before day one is out.

Thursday, November 8th, Manchester

Jim's apotheosis, and my single most important contribution to this whole nine-hour epic, looms.

Dealing with Colin D, though nerve-racking in a way, has helped me to forget my anxieties. They are exactly the same as Colin's, of course, fear of letting people down, fear of failing to meet the high standards expected of you, fear of physical inability to meet the demands, but Colin's are felt so much more intensely and appear so massive that in comforting him I'm able to put my own fears into proportion.

As the afternoon wears on I pace around the car park trying to keep the lines fresh. It's getting dark by the time I'm asked into the hall. Robert explains to the crowd about the next part of the sequence and then I'm thrown to the wolves.

I do it, and because it is such a strong speech, it fires me and carries me along and after the first minute or so I know I'm launched and that passion and conviction and belief is what I can put across much better than the comedy asides. At the end they applaud spontaneously, and a number of people in crew and crowd come up and congratulate me. John Maskell, the camera operator, says that it's just what people need to hear in politics today. It's not the performance so much as what I was saying that has caught people.

Friday, November 9th, Manchester

We work through the speech again. I run it five times in succession with only minor hiccups.

The day warms up, the hall is hot and smoky under the lights. Robert

L's afternoon, as he plays his breakdown very movingly. Then round onto the reverses of my speech for all the audience reactions. My concentration holds and we finish at seven, with nine minutes of story in the can.

We go to a Pizza Express.

Talk about early sexual experience. Dearbhla reveals she used to put socks in her bra and only whip them out at the last minute. Lindsay Duncan, who has a lovely, rather wistful way of telling a very rude tale, reflects on the number of times she had some sexual encounter with a man 'just to be polite'!

Alan calls late to ask how it went. I'm able to convey the enthusiasm he wants to hear. He's in London, where *Having a Ball* closes tomorrow night. I ask him if he'll be with us next week. I hear ironic laughter, which worries me.

Monday, November 12th, Manchester

Anne James at Mayday tells me that *80 Days* has won four nominations in the American 'ACE' cable awards. Best Doc, Best Editor, Best Script, Best Presenter. The ceremony is on Rachel's 16th birthday – 13th January – and I agree to go over to LA. It will also be my first weekend clear after the end of *GBH*.

Wednesday, November 14th, Manchester

Leave the hotel at 7.40. Collect Colin D from the Britannia for his final day. Once again, deep gloom. And yet this time he cannot blame the rewrites. The Frank Twist phone call scenes he has learnt long ago. But he is as maudlin as ever ... 'I haven't slept since two o'clock the night before last ... I'm leaving the profession after this.'

I can't see much to cheer him up as we drive out to a location somewhere beyond the Manchester Abattoir, a modern concrete complex, unnervingly similar in design to an airport. The bus depot is a bleak and inhospitable place, wind whistles through, though it's still quite mild. As he loves cooking, I've brought Colin a last-day present of one of the glossy Roux Brothers books, but he's in too much distress right now to accept anything other than his fate.

As it is, he once again defies the bogeymen and turns in a big, strong, word-perfect performance.

Saturday, November 17th, Manchester

Day off before Sunday shooting. After breakfast catch up on diary and organise myself before Simon A comes to my hotel room at eleven. He wants to bring me all the latest news on the franchise project.

The trouble is that Simon is much more enthusiastic about the whole thing than I am. He loves the world of wheeling and dealing and fixing. I don't much, except when it relates directly to the fulfilment of a creative project. So I listen and Simon bubbles, as has been the pattern over this matter since it was first mooted. Try as I do, I cannot seem to communicate the real basis of my caution to someone who can see nothing better than to be involved in such a scheme as winning a franchise.

He, Clive and Roger have found a way of involving me, which is that Prominent TV should have shares and a place on the board. Knowing my reservations, he suggests that rather than me (an absentee explorer for much of next year) I should depute someone from Prominent to sit on the board on my behalf.

It's a sunny day outside now, I am still preoccupied and indeed fatigued by *GBH* and I don't really want to waffle on, so I agree to Simon's strategy and about one we break up.

Sunday, November 18th, Manchester

Filming today at the school in Lostock, in which I began my career as Jim Nelson last August.

Feeling of déjà vu as I walk past pickets and slam Michael Murray against the bonnet of his car. Then an assortment of 'on the way to school' shots, which are supposed to be late summer.

Back to the Portland, and settle on the bed and immerse myself in the Sunday papers, all of which are full of Heseltine's bid to oust Thatcher. She comes across, as always, as a friendless person, and if she loses then nemesis will be swift and probably very painful.

Out to eat in the evening with Dearbhla and RL. We wander round deserted streets where everything seems closed and emerge into Albert Square to the bizarre sight of the vast £15,000 inflatable Santa flapping lifelessly against the columns and arches of the Gothic tower of the City Hall. Father Christmas has burst.

Wednesday, November 21st: Brookfield Hall, Derbyshire

The huge St Bernard sprawls in the doorway of the small breakfast room. He buries his head in his paws in a hopeless attempt at invisibility.

The papers are all brimming with the details and speculation surrounding the greatest political upheaval since Thatcher came to power – in the year *Life of Brian* opened. Most of the comment judges her decision last night to fight on and win as being a typical Thatcher knee-jerk reaction. Ill advised, indeed unadvised.

Thursday, November 22nd: Derbyshire–London

Alarm at 6.45. Leave Brookfield at 7.15. There's frost on the car roofs and the climbing sun illuminates the bare Peak hillsides with a pinkish glow. It's going to be a spectacular day.

Work starts at 8.30 with a long walking shot – me talking to Spike. Spike behaves very well and we do two versions and print both takes. Then to the gory sequence in which I discover Robbie Burns (played by Daniel Street-Brown) with left foot melted and bleeding.

Daniel lies, his exposed foot being rigged for pumping blood. A tear or two wells up in his eye as he waits with extraordinary patience. Someone fetches a fan heater.

Then Carl, the second assistant, comes up to me, holding a walkie-talkie to his ear. 'Did you know Margaret Thatcher's resigned?'

The dreadful injuries to the boy are now of only secondary interest to the rest of the crew, as the news filters onto the slopes.

The clouds, and even a light flurry of snow, pass by, and the sun emerges powerfully making the next few hours, until late lunch ('Lunch will be at the end of the day,' as the 1st Assistant puts it), easily enjoyable, with the spreading views dramatically detailed by the low, bright sunlight.

Alan and I shake our heads in disbelief as we sit in our layby near the Lamb Inn eating fish and chips as, on TV, Margaret T enters the Commons. She sits behind Richard Needham so the cameras catch the two faces in juxtaposition. The toppled leader and the minister now renowned for his remark on a car phone that he wished 'the cow would resign'. The drama of the occasion is breathtaking.

Neither of us can believe that the days when daily and nightly we heard her voice dictating to the nation are over. It could be that the theft of the 'Parrot Sketch' precipitated this last slide. Python may, after all, have a greater place in history than we ever imagined.

Rick drives me from the celestial hills of the Peak District on to the murky motorways round Manchester and I catch a delayed 4.30 shuttle back to London.

Rachel and I eat together. She shows me a copy of the *Express Sunday Magazine* – 'Decade of the Nice'. My name there, needless to say!

To bed at 12.30. Thatcher is out. I'm out, about one o'clock. I should be owed hours of sleep, but life, for now, is too exciting.

Friday, November 23rd

The five books I have to read for the Whitbread Book of the Year Award arrive – *Hopeful Monsters*, Nicholas Mosley, *The Buddha of Suburbia* by Hanif Kureishi, *AK* by Peter Dickinson, a biog of A. A. Milne by Ann Thwaite and Paul Durcan's poetry *Daddy, Daddy*. I have to read them, carefully, before January. A lovely task, which demands a break of a week at least. Am toying with Italy.

Tuesday, November 27th

Watching the drama of Thatcher's successor unfolding. John Major two short of absolute victory. Heseltine's quick to make the speech he must have prepared with considerable distaste – a concession that he will never now be Prime Minister. His great bid to lead the party has failed.

Fascinating stuff. Rich in its coincidences and twists of fate.

Wednesday, November 28th

I go to Prominent Studios for a meeting with Simon A, Anne and Roger Laughton re the implications of SA's suggestions about board representation on the franchise. The *Mirror* financial page has got hold, a week late, of the story of my involvement. A picture of myself as the It's Man, dressed in rags and tatters, dominates the page together with the headline 'Mad Mike Wants His Own Show'. Roger L takes this well – in fact he roars with laughter. For me it's all the proof I need of why I shouldn't ever have been involved!

To dinner with Tristram and Virginia down in Stockwell. They have two new kittens they've christened Ashby and Elinor.

Sunday, December 2nd

In mid-afternoon to the Tricycle Theatre to help out at an auction of pictures to raise funds. Mostly very ordinary, but I do buy an original Ken Livingstone watercolour of Thatcher in a coffin with a Struwwelpeter-like Heseltine looming over her. Painted the day she resigned! Outbid someone at £110.00.

Monday, December 10th

Out to dinner at the flat of Julia St John in Chiswick. Dearbhla arrives shortly after, then Alan, big, smiling shyly underneath the single long eyebrow. Too big for the little flat, every time he turns he hits something.

At one point we're talking of Derek Hatton and how close Murray is to him, and Dearbhla observes that Murray is Hatton and Nelson is Alan. Alan shakes his head and smiles … 'Oh no, he's Michael Palin now … that's what's so good … that's what I'm pleased about … It isn't me.'

Tuesday, December 11th

Up at eight to discuss lights in No. 2 with electrician. Then, full of beans, down to Brompton Road to look for presents at Conran.

Two or three ladies come up and are complimentary about the *80 Days* series. One says she wrote me a letter, but that I didn't reply. I apologise, but she says … 'Well, I did say some rather naughty things …'

Patrick reports back on progress of *'AF'* selling in America. There has been no explosion of enthusiasm or rush to buy, but Miramax were very complimentary and are negotiating, though will not pay the advance of 2.7 million dollars that P and S were asking. Atlantic, Avenue, Fox and Paramount still keen. At Warner's the two people sent to see it walked out halfway through.

Wednesday, December 12th

To the Hiroko restaurant for an *'AF'* interview with *Tatler*, personified by Jessica Berens. She doesn't talk about the film much, or gush with praise, but is quite bright and sparky in that confident way that the owning classes have.

We then go on to a photo-session. This takes place in one of the huge, almost Muscovite-scale apartment blocks set in a strange no man's land off the Cromwell Road.

The photographer looks about 18, a tall, pale, rather gawky girl called Arabella. Their flat is what used to be called bohemian. Scattered with objects, paintings, unmatching chairs, all in dark, high-ceilinged rooms.

Ari (as she's called) and her assistant have a little finger puppet for me to play with. Lots of enthusiasm and swirling hyperbole ... 'Oh, you're great ... no, you really ... this is such a joy, to have someone who can just do it.'

They are such a weird lot these rich, young, well born. There's a whiff of decadence about everything, a sort of hint that as soon as the doors close drugs and dressing-up will not be far away.

Finish my session and, feeling old and awkward, am quite glad to leave. Taxi home, then time for a phone call or two before setting out for an evening of parties – John Birt has invited me for drinks at BH, and *Private Eye*, the British Council and Jonathan Cape are all partying tonight.

Off to Broadcasting House. It's really a BBC News and Current Affairs do, so lots of familiar faces of interviewers, newsreaders and politicians and celebrities.

John Birt, like a father figure, welcomes me ... 'Now who would you like to meet? ...' Janet Street-Porter kisses me and carries on talking.

Chat to Ned Sherrin, mention *American Friends* and mishear him when he asks when it's coming out. 'I thought you asked when I was coming out,' I apologise. Ned seems to like this and I promise him he'll be the first to know.

Anna Ford and I chat a while. She would rather be singing and writing than reading the six o'clock news. She's disarming and honest.

Politicos arrive, Cecil Parkinson and Ken Baker especially egregious and smiley. Prof. Carey[1] from Oxford gushes to me about how much his sons love and admire me. Ken Baker smoothly says how rarely anyone ever says that to him. I've had a glass or two. 'Don't worry,' I assure him, 'there must be someone somewhere who loves you.' Have I really said that to the Home Secretary? Am impressed that he remembers the film

---

1 John Carey, Merton Professor of English Literature at Oxford University, also principal book reviewer of *The Sunday Times*.

we saw at the reopening of the Electric Cinema many years ago. *Vertigo*.[1]
New print.

To *Private Eye* in Carlisle Street, but no-one answers the doorbell.

Friday, December 14th

To Hampstead to buy more Christmas cards. Hopeless. Nothing but
boutiques: expensive shops cursed on the area by the accumulation of
wealth nearby. As the rich have got richer so has Hampstead become
poorer – in choice, variety and spirit.

Another working lunch, this time with one Susan Jeffreys from *20/20*
magazine. She had worries about the women in the film. Not knowing
enough about them. She was nice, intelligent and candid. 'I'd have
come out absolutely raving about it, if only I'd been given a little more
background.'

To the Greenwood Theatre to record a Jonathan Ross show – to be
played on New Year's Eve.

We are both dressed in Victorian costume – smoking jackets and
tasselled hats.

Best part of the evening is after the recording when I'm asked if I'd
mind doing some trailers with Jonathan. We ad-lib with props – things
like bananas – which they unaccountably produce. For a few minutes
I taste the pleasure of fooling about in front of an audience again. Jonathan is sharp and funny, but generous too. All in all we make a good
team for a while.

Saturday, December 15th

In the evening to the latest of Jeremy H's[2] productions, this time at the
ICA.

The piece was called *A Few Small Nips* and was devised by J and Renee
Eyre (after their trip to Mexico) as a way of illustrating how a Mexican
artist's work was affected by a dreadful accident on a trolleybus. 'A
copper rail ... entered her abdomen, shattered her spinal column and
exited through her vagina,' as the cheery programme note informed us.

1 A film directed and produced by Alfred Hitchcock in 1958.
2 Jeremy Herbert, my sister Angela and her husband Veryan's oldest child, who was making a name for himself as a theatre designer.

There were four girls and Renee who interpret or recreate in dance and movement the sufferings of the woman. Very graphic, with bare, twisted bodies and a relentless and effective soundtrack (by the man who does music for Derek Jarman, Simon Turner). Moments of calm, then fierce, angry, physical pain. J had done bold work with very limited resources, including a wall that bleeds.

Tuesday, December 18th

A day I am not altogether looking forward to. Taxi at 8.45 to London Bridge and Adelaide House for the first meeting of the franchise bid 'core' group.

I'm early and before going in think I might walk to the middle of London Bridge and see how much has changed since we shot *The Missionary* down at Shad Thames. But there is such a solid body of commuters coming towards me that, rather than try and climb the waterfall, I go with it, into the building.

Both Simon and Roger Laughton emphasise that this is to be a 'lean and mean' exercise. Simon gives a short, inspirational opening speech. A fine and rousing vision whose delivery owes much to SA's fondness for gospel music!

TVS, Television South, is the region we will be going for.

Then Fiona from accountants Coopers & Lybrand analyses all the info we shall need for the bid, which must be made, backed with considerable detail, in about three months' time. Allan McKeown of SelecTV and myself ask a number of questions. McKeown sounds keen and well informed. He looks dangerous though.

Lambie-Nairn, the branding agency founded by Martin Lambie-Nairn, then give us their thoughts on names. A not very impressive shortlist of names are rolled out. The quiet, pale youth from Charles Barker PR almost apologetically suggests what feels to me the best name so far: Meridian. Better than Downland or Southstar or Star TV.

Wednesday, December 19th

To Shepherd's Bush. Meet Roger Mills in the Duke of Edinburgh, a seedy, smoky, unreconstructed working men's dive. Roger, swathed in pipe smoke, sits with the *Daily Telegraph* crossword almost finished on the table in front of him.

Together we traipse up Richmond Way and into Kensington House for Colin Cameron's Documentary Features party. Colin not very happy with the state of things in the department. Cuts in progs and personnel.

Clive James[1] is friendly. He's very keen on Japan. Visits often, is learning Japanese and has just written a novel about London, seen through the eyes of a Japanese man. James works ferociously hard. He looks leaner in the face, more purposeful, more successful, I suppose.

Gerald Scarfe,[2] on the other hand, looks as if he's been living a bit hard. Reminds me, with his boozy bonhomie, of how these sorts of parties used to be before everyone became health-conscious and job-conscious. We are laughing like schoolboys but, as always, one is interrupted by bores and we never finish whatever it is we're laughing at.

Down to Walkden House for the T2000 Christmas party.

New man from BR very different to Grant Woodruff. Soft and rather dreamy ... 'What are the two things you think British Rail should be doing to improve their image?' is his most incisive question. 'Stop killing passengers' is what I want to say, but I waffle politely and don't mention faulty doors and bad signalling.[3]

Friday, December 28th

This time of the year is rather like one long Sunday, a period when the life of the country is in limbo. A limbo of food or television. Few interruptions. I aim to finish *Hopeful Monsters*, which I do, and am much impressed.

Monday, December 31st

Drink to the New Year, which I feel ridiculously optimistic about since reading a letter in the *Independent* which points out that 1991 is a palindrome. 1991. Our year!

Tonight, looking out over the roofs of Gospel Oak on which spills light from a full moon in a cloudless sky, I know that I can still enjoy

---

1 Clive James, writer, presenter, television critic of the *Observer*. His latest novel was called *Brmm! Brmm!*

2 Gerald Scarfe, cartoonist, *The Sunday Times*.

3 Five recent high-profile accidents, including the Clapham Junction crash in December 1988, had resulted in 240 deaths. Signalling problems were a common factor.

myself, express myself and, I hope, look after myself. If I avoided a nervous breakdown in 1990, I think I shall be able to avoid one at any time. A big, busy, bruising year in which I learnt quite a lot about myself.

As for the loss of Mum and Al – I've yet to account for their effect on me. Perhaps the problem is that I never had time to really think about it.

1991

During filming yesterday Robert Y did not seem quite his enthusiastic self. He told me that he had not been able to put out of his mind at Christmas the prospect of an imminent war, and whenever he looked at his daughter Kate, he had been filled with dread at what may be about to happen to the world.

How like 1939 is this? Hussein has clearly all the dangerous mixture of convictions, charisma and cruelty which most dictators enjoy. He has few allies, but the more he can skilfully paint America as the centre of the aggression, the more he will be able to fuse all sorts of blinkered and rabble-rousing 'anti-colonialists' who see hope only in disorder.

The Americans are flexing their muscles, obligingly showing that they are as simple-minded as anyone else. I only hope that beneath the rhetoric there is some diplomatic skill and sophistication at work, otherwise we may well be doomed to see the body bags come home and another celebration of hatred and bigotry.

I must say it puts *GBH* in perspective and Whitbread prizes too.

Monday, January 7th

John Shrapnel, who is to play Dr Jacobs in six scenes with me over the next two days, appears, dressed in black and almost merging with the darkness. I'd expected a rather grand figure, but he is very down-to-earth and untheatrical. Remembers being directed by Eric Idle at Cambridge.

I think he finds the opening scene quite demanding. He has to slide into a Scottish accent almost imperceptibly and also into a working unit who have been together for seven months.

Alan B appears briefly in the passage beside our 'surgery' as we are lining up for the camera. He looks baggy-eyed and bleary and makes gestures of apology before disappearing. Later I hear he's come down with a bug and retired to the Richmond Hill Hotel.

But it is neat that the writer of a scene about a man who always thinks he has something wrong with him should indeed have something wrong with him on the day we film it.

Thursday, January 10th

Talks between Iraq and the US have broken down in Geneva. A photo in the *Guardian* of a handshake between Tariq Aziz and James Baker across the table speaks volumes. Aziz looks almost debonair, faintly smiling, the man in control. Baker looks tense, unhappy and lost.

But first I must clear the final hurdle on *GBH*, which is not an easy one. Almost a page-long speech, of great anger and passion. I suppose one of the most important of Jim's speeches. One of a handful in which Alan's most deeply heartfelt views are articulated. I have to try and resist the party mood and the almost tangible pressure of the prospect of an early finish and rise to the occasion.

Uncharacteristically I make two false starts. Take 2 works well, Alan gives me a thumbs-up, but I feel I have the bit between my teeth, am relaxed and confident with the lines, so I should try once more. I do, and miss the feeling, the rhythm.

On the close-up I'm given, on Robert's instructions, a blow of menthol into the eyeballs to make them water. This feels like another failure. There is a lot going through my head as we finish the scene – mainly centring on my own inability to deliver the speech as powerfully and finely as it deserved.

It's only midday. Robert has suddenly decided not to shoot my reverse and he's making an announcement that this is my last shot and everyone is clapping, and I'm hot and not prepared with words or emotions.

Friday, January 11th

After breakfast begin to tackle the many and various problems that litter my desk, whilst it pours down outside.

Discuss the dates for delivery of book and the eight progs now proposed to make up *Pole to Pole*. Must make sure that I don't fall into the trap of rushing it again. The whole project will tie me up for at least 15 months.

News on 'AF'. Miramax are not offering anywhere near what we wanted for US distribution. Virgin's 'men in suits' are prevaricating over payment in UK and if they have not paid up by January 23rd we may have to sue them and try to get the film back. This would threaten the April opening day. If ever a project was cursed, 'AF' is the one. Its agonising birth was bad enough, now it seems to be unable to walk.

Saturday, January 12th: London–Los Angeles

Arrive at LA in mid-afternoon for the Ace Cable TV Awards. Take a taxi. The driver is a Ghanaian accountant whose home turf is Liberia. He's driving a cab as a temporary job. Doesn't much like LA, but laughs a lot. The day looks fresh and fine.

Quartered at the Mondrian. Noise rising from Sunset Boulevard below, but the hotel's quite fun – a homage to Piet Mondrian, with his colours and motifs and patterns reproduced throughout the building.

All the Arts & Entertainment people are there. Abbe Raven gives me the news that we won none of our three awards yesterday, but they have high hopes for me tomorrow.

Sunday, January 13th: Los Angeles

Run along Sunset then dive down and south towards the green and affluent lawns of Beverly Hills. This litter-less, pristine and orderly grid of long, straight avenues is perfect for running. Traffic's light and the houses present a constant eye-catching variety of styles. The neat manicured lawns all bear the black-on-yellow warning 'Armed Response'.

Relevant indeed as we are within 48 hours of the expiry of the UN deadline when American troops from very much poorer neighbourhoods than this will doubtless be sent into action to fight for capitalism, seen here on Oakhurst, Palm and Hillcrest at its most seductive and potent.

Later, as the limousine takes me to the Wiltern Theater for the ACE Cable TV Awards, I see it's 81 degrees. But I'm in a dinner jacket and won't see much of the rest of the day. Along red carpet and into a big, impressive and wonderfully old theatre. Art Deco at its best.

The Python Showtime special doesn't win and I and others are pipped by Billy Crystal's Moscow film for best writer of an entertainment series.

A&E are not downhearted and continue to be excellent hosts. Nick Davatzes says he's really looking forward to *Pole to Pole*. 'We have a deal!' he enthuses.

Tuesday, January 15th: Los Angeles–Santa Barbara

Sleep through until 8.15. Long, recharging rest. Day of the expiry of the UN deadline. Day of foreboding, but deceptively pleasant here above Sunset Boulevard, probably about as far from Iraq as it's possible to be – until you turn on the TV of course. But I don't – yet.

I take a run round the Armed Response neighbourhood, then back into shoddier West Hollywood. Bathe and breakfast. Hot coffee, granola and berries and an unhurried read of the *LA Times* in the sunshine.

A local newspaper piece tries to explain this feeling of remoteness from the Gulf War fever, as evidence that the real decision-making happens on the East Coast. California may supply the technology that will be decisive in the war, but it remains outside the executive clique.

A stocky man in black T-shirt and worn black-leather jacket approaches. I think for a while it might be Joe Cocker. With a shock of recognition I hear him mention *GBH*. He turns out to be Declan, alias Elvis Costello, who has co-written our music score. He has all the *GBH* tapes and says he thinks my performance is wonderful. He rushes off shouting hopes that we'll see each other again ... 'At the awards,' he laughs.

Long drive down Sunset to the ocean. Temps lower perceptibly and it's quite chilly when I eventually turn onto the Pacific Coast Highway where the wind whips the dust around me.

Reach Santa Barbara at 3.30. The Four Seasons Biltmore is a sprawl of low buildings, carefully landscaped, in the Spanish style. A coach outside with Shriners all standing around in white conical hats.

Walk across the road to the seashore. Firm sand. Lots of joggers, walkers and surfers – though the waves seem modest.

Worry what will happen when the deadline expires – nine o'clock our time. War seems such a ludicrous waste – just for Kuwait – and once it begins how many people and countries and lives will be dragged in? Momentous times.

Wednesday, January 16th: Santa Barbara

At half past three, I switch over to CNN. There is no moving picture, just a map of Iraq and the voice and face of a reporter called John Holliman, but from the sound I know instantly that war has begun.

As Holliman speaks, unhysterically, but with measured excitement, his voice is interrupted by thumping explosions. He is not sure what's going on, but he and his two colleagues are on the ninth floor of a Baghdad hotel. It's 2.30 in the morning, Baghdad time.

So, this incredible situation – of the sounds of war being relayed all over the world from a single microphone hanging out of the window of a hotel in Baghdad, before anyone in the world, bar military commanders, knows the war has started.

Only at four o'clock, when Marlin Fitzwalter[1] is seen hurriedly at the White House to declare 'The liberation of Kuwait has begun', is there official confirmation of what we have heard from Holliman's hotel room.

After an hour and a half I take a walk along the beach. Life goes on. Joggers, surfers, dog-walkers. The mournful sound of a railway siren rings out from the Southern Pacific Line just behind the hotel. Everything seems muted.

This is how it continues – even in the tone of later reports. This doesn't seem to be a jingoistic war. There is none of the jubilation of conflict or the swaggering macho tones of revenge or the triumph of force. It's as if everyone is hoping that perhaps it can be a war unlike other wars; that it can be a short, sharp, technological triumph.

Friday, January 18th: Santa Barbara–London

Scud is the word of the day. Scuds are the missiles which Hussein is still able to fire despite the sophisticated bombing of the last two nights. Scuds are Russian-made and look set to become the equivalent of the Exocets in the Falklands War. Saddam Hussein has Exocets as well.

Walk by the ocean. Clear blue skies, a gentle breeze, a big, bright beauty of a day.

But I have a lunch booked in LA with Eric and Steve Martin, and a plane to catch this evening and a family waiting in London.

It's 1.40 by the time I'm at table with Eric and Steve. I apologise for taking so long. I'd been told it took only 90 minutes from Santa Barbara. 'But you drove on the left,' quipped Martin.

He's currently shooting a two-week appearance in a new Larry Kasdan film.[2] 'A cameo.' We decide two weeks must be more than a cameo. 'A hameo,' Eric suggests.

---

1 White House press secretary to George H. W. Bush and previously to Ronald Reagan.
2 *Grand Canyon*, with Kevin Kline.

At the airport at four. Plane is delayed. There have been two bomb scares at LAX since the war began. A number has been given out on the radio which you can ring to report anyone or anything suspicious.

In the small, box-like room which passes for the Speedwing First Class Lounge, they apologise for the lack of a television, but tell me I can go into Qantas next door … 'They let us use it.'

By rich coincidence I'm prevented from immediately doing this by the arrival of Melvyn Bragg, followed swiftly by Leon Brittan[1] and his little assistant, followed by Steve Morrison of Granada, who is profusely apologetic about turning down 'AF' two and a half years ago, followed by Kenneth Branagh, who's just finished directing a film for Paramount[2] and is flying back because he wants to be with his family.

Melvyn can't understand why there has been so little retaliation by the Iraqis. I think he would like to think that we all panicked and over-estimated their resources. I think SH is lying low, soaking up as much as he can, knowing that unless his people start dying in large numbers, he can gain kudos merely for surviving day by day.

Saturday, January 19th

Young, remarkably young, rosy-faced lads in army uniform holding machine-guns at gates of Heathrow's Terminal 4, and outside, instead of limousines, two army personnel carriers. I see no tanks, but I'm told they're about. Police marksmen can be seen, but unlike the army they keep a much lower profile. It's like Belfast.

Everything reasonably calm at home in this funny little amateur, apologetic, ancestor-obsessed country.

A note from the office tells me that last night's Python repeat was cancelled. Ypres sketch in it. Second casualty of war is comedy.

Monday, January 21st

A BBC car down to Broadcasting House.

Marina Salandy-Brown,[3] whose character is stamped on *Start the*

---

1 Leon Brittan, former Conservative MP and Minister, then a member and Vice-President, European Commission, who died in January 2015.
2 Kenneth Branagh had just completed starring in and directing a thriller, *Dead Again*.
3 Marina Salandy-Brown, Trinidad-born journalist who was editor of BBC Radio 4's *Start the Week*. She returned to Trinidad in 2004.

Week more than Melvyn's, is at the front desk to greet me. An elderly white-haired gentleman who turns out to be Sir George Trevelyan has arrived for the programme a week early.

Melvyn wanders in after we've all sat there, a little awkwardly, for about 20 minutes, and dispenses his ironic smiles and professional bonhomie. 'In view of what we shall be talking about in the programme, I'm going to ask you all a quick question at the beginning, just so listeners know you're there.'

Well, the question Melvyn has chosen for this light-hearted warm-up is, 'Do you think that sexual liberation necessarily follows political liberation?' From that moment I know I am in the wrong place.

Marina warns us not to talk about the war, as the frequency has been split so that Radio 4 on long wave reports only on the war.

Everything this morning, from the spectral presence of Sir George Trevelyan behind the glass, to the instruction not to mention the one thing everyone is talking about, seems designed to create unease and destroy good humour and harmony.

And if none of these is enough, Melvyn has the services of Catherine Bennett, who is brought in, at the raise of an eyebrow or the flick of a wrist, to have a go at the guests.

I notice the bottle of champagne remains unopened on the table as we leave.

Tuesday, January 22nd

Down to Whitbread's Brewery for the Book Prize evening.

We're shown into the chairman's sitting room. Norman Willis appears, bows to Helen and introduces himself as 'Robert Redford'.

Sybille Bedford,[1] who has that manly mutter and skin like some latex compound, announces with ratty indignation that someone on the radio yesterday had said the award was as much about beer as books. 'Absolute nonsense!' she rumbles … 'Who was it said that?' I confess it was me and Sybille is far more put out by her indiscretion than I ever expected and keeps apologising, despite my entreaties.

Shown into a dining room, with a big Sheraton table, writing pads

---

1 Sybille Bedford, German-born writer, long resident in England. Her most recent novel, *Jigsaw*, had been highly praised.

and pens. Here the eleven of us judges sit, myself opposite Gerald Kaufman and beside Jeremy Isaacs. Bill Kellaway, the Awards organiser, relieves us all with the news that there is a clear winner and that is, it turns out, Nicholas Mosley's *Hopeful Monsters*, which five of us chose as the winner, though none chose it as runner-up. Paul Durcan's poetry was second. So my choice conformed with the majority.

We all troop over to dinner (sworn of course to secrecy, even with our wives and friends).

I'm sat next to Penelope Fitzgerald, kind, grey-haired lady who won the Booker Prize in 1979 for *Offshore*. She's very modest and shrugs off my interest in her and how she writes in favour of questions about *80 Days* and Python.

But I persist and am rewarded. She lives with her daughter and son-in-law in what was Arnold Wesker's house in Highgate. 'What happened to Arnold? ...' 'Oh, I think he had a lot of friends ... you know ... he was always very generous ... and I think eventually, over-generous.'

She's quite enjoying writing a thriller. It started as a detective story, but 'it wasn't quite clever enough, so it ended up a thriller'. She is lovely company.

Nicholas Mosley stammers attractively and speaks gently and self-deprecatingly. It's only tonight that I realise he's Oswald Mosley's son. His wife, a pretty blonde, is clearly very fond of him and holds his hand before the vote is announced. I look over in their direction. It's odd knowing what I do.

Wednesday, January 23rd

To the New Connaught Rooms in Great Queen Street, complete with yellow carnation and label announcing that I'm the President of Transport 2000. The occasion is the Best Station Awards.

There can be few awards in which rows of urinals figure as prominently. I think it quite right too, as decent toilets on stations are probably what everyone wants.

Sometimes, as the pictures flick on and off in remorseless succession, I begin to confuse this with some kind of horticultural occasion, such is the emphasis on flower beds and hanging baskets. The eventual winner, Aberdour, looks like a magnificent garden with a railway line just about visible.

To Parliament Hill for Rachel's open day. Rachel is predicted, as a result of her mock exam results, to hit A in every subject except French. All speak highly of her … 'pleasure to teach', etc. etc.

Later, as we have supper together, we talk about school. Rachel says her class not much involved with boys. Whereas Caitlin [Shamberg] had ventured that a third of her classmates in LA had slept with boys, Rachel thinks that probably only one of her class has lost their virginity, but there is a 15-year-old who recently became pregnant by her 24-year-old partner. Rachel very wise and thoughtful about it all and doesn't condemn or endorse.

Wednesday, January 30th

'Happiness stops the moment you know you're happy', or something like that, is how Bonnard, who looked a very morose individual, put it. And today I feel in that delicate state of being, almost totally content with my life.

Considering there is a war on, and that we haven't seen the sun for a week, and that a cold, leaden gloom is settled over the city, my resurgent spirit is very welcome, and I organise myself a day in town.

The smart shops around Covent Garden are full only of assistants. Their windows, no longer stylishly minimalist, are now as desperate as any in the Holloway Road, screaming 'Sale' and 'Reduction' and 'Further Reductions!' Bad times.

Thursday, January 31st

Unmoving weather now for almost two weeks. General sense of stasis – not just as represented by the weather, but in the Gulf War as well.

Casualties on the allied side still low, the impression still of a controlled war in which superior technology is remorselessly stamping out evil chemical facilities and nuclear weapons plants. The tone of most commentaries is to endorse this view and the glowing attention given to the military hardware must be delighting the arms manufacturers whose livelihood had been so threatened by the end of the Cold War.

To the National Gallery for another look at the Impressionism in the Making exhibition – detail worth seeing … sand in the paint of a Monet done at Trouville beach – then walk across the Strand, down past Charing Cross Station which is now capped with a bulky, rather silly Terry Farrell office development.

Going down a blank-faced concrete walkway on the south side of Waterloo Bridge and suddenly I catch my breath in shock. From being alone on a concrete bridge I'm now looking down on a busy world, but one completely different from that on the surface. Of course, it's Cardboard City, home of the homeless. A glimpse of the Third World less than a mile from Parliament, a river's breadth from the Savoy.

It's like a scene from a film. Indeed for a moment I think they may be filming – this must be a set. A series of boxes draped in scraps of various materials. A group of about a dozen are clustered round a fire, hair wild and clothes shabby. Four or five dogs scurry and chase around barking, then return to the fire.

It's quite a shock to the system. A glimpse of a strange and foreign land. I don't dawdle, I don't stare … I feel threatened, morally rather than physically, in my big Donegal tweed coat with my Filofax crammed with credit cards and twenty-pound notes, on my way from the National Gallery to a smart restaurant.

Friday, February 1st

On the one o'clock news, report of de Klerk's speech committing himself and South Africa to the abolition of remaining apartheid laws. Apartheid, like communism, is one of the most emotive political keywords of my lifetime. It looks now as if both will have disappeared by the time I'm 50. Extraordinary and, so recently, unthinkable. And the sun slips through the clouds after many days away.

Monday, February 4th

To TV Centre for a screening of Donald Woods' 'Assignment' prog about his return to South Africa after 12 years.

Donald and Wendy and children there. He smoking and trying not to be nervous.

Donald is the perfect host – from both sides people talk and confide in him. The formidable 'Pik' Botha, bull-like and dangerous, calls apartheid a sin, and Nelson Mandela, gentle and courteous, on being told what Botha has said, smiles minimally and replies … 'Well, that's very nice.'

Lunch with Geoffrey Strachan. Octopus Books – another child of the big-business, acquisitive, 'growth-oriented' '80s – is now faintly shabby.

A book is on show in the foyer with the 'Whitbread Book of the Year' card on it. I think it's meant to be *Hopeful Monsters*, but the cover's missing and the book that's left behind it is John Ardagh's book on modern France.

Geoffrey S very apologetic about the inadvertent printing of my address in the latest editions of the *Holy Grail* book, and is having the unsold 1,700 books doctored accordingly.

Tuesday, February 5th

Virgin have refused to accept *American Friends* as delivered, citing some trivial points, and will take steps to cancel the opening at the Odeon Haymarket.

Steve seems completely baffled and is not able to give me any cogent reason for their behaviour other than that Virgin's owners are in financial trouble.

To my first Russian lesson with Paul Marsh, who lives in Muswell Hill. He has a flat which indicates few luxuries, and is enthusiastic in a clever, self-deprecatory way, peppering the lesson with what I imagine are quite regular gags. But I like him. He's clearly consumed with the subject of Russia and Russian, and I think I shall enjoy his softly authoritative approach and become used to the slightly oily scent of perspiration which pervades the room.

Drive across to the Kensington Hilton where I've fixed a drink with Will Wyatt. He talks of *80 Days* as a great success, largely due to me and my 'faux-naif' approach. Never thought of myself as 'faux-naif'. The Henri Rousseau of the silver screen.

Wednesday, February 6th

Steve rings to say that the bank, supported by six legal opinions, is moving tomorrow to wind up our distribution agreement with Virgin. Steve hopes that we will force Virgin to release the film to us; worst scenario is that they will suddenly find the money and we will be left to pick up the pieces of a distribution plan with a company in whom we have all lost confidence.

The irony is that there should be this great row over money when '*AF*' was made so cheaply.

Thursday, February 7th

Snow lies around, crisp and even. The winters we'd forgotten, the Christmas card winters that seemed to be victims of the greenhouse effect, are back. Sweep paths and clear snow with the same mixture of effort and pleasure as did my father.

To Jeremy Gilkes in Devonshire Street. As I drive through the swirling snow I hear on the radio confused reports of a mortar bomb attack on the Ministry of Defence in Whitehall.

Dr Gilkes looks at what was an irritating and sore spot on my back, pronounces it non-cancerous, gives it a name I can't begin to remember and applies liquid nitrogen – 'This is so cold you'll feel a burning sensation.'

As I leave the snow is thickening and the news is that the mortars were aimed at 10 Downing Street and one has gone off in the garden. Expecting Iraqi terror attacks, it's almost a relief to hear that our old enemy the IRA are being blamed.

The snow gently falls for most of the day and my workroom becomes more like a cocoon as the windows are gradually covered.

The last thing I see before bed is a fax of a piece in *Broadcast* re the Meridian TV bid. There I find myself described as 'former Monty Python star turned film director (*sic*) and actor. A "Mr Nice-Guy" with a high PR profile and a bit of money in the bank.'

My epitaph as at February 7th 1991!

Friday, February 8th

Parliament Hill is a Bruegel snow scene. Several hundred on the crown of the hill sledging, skiing, or just sliding down on old sheets of cardboard. The schools are closed and the North London Line seems rather feebly to have given up the ghost.

Walk beyond range of the sledgers and sliders, down to Highgate Ponds. The Men's Pond completely frozen, but above it on the next pond there is an area of clear water on which Canada geese, ducks, coots and pigeons fight for space. A viciously cold wind.

Tuesday, February 12th

Press launch of the Stammering in Children campaign.

Very well attended. I do TV interviews for BBC, Capital and later LBC. The press conference is filmed. I'm asked to speak and produce quite an articulate volley without notes which I'm pleased about.

The relief at being able to talk about stammering after a childhood spent without mentioning it keeps me going and keeps me articulate and enthusiastic.[1] The two boys who stammer and appear in the film are there. Great boys, full of fun, intelligence and indomitable character.

On way home in taxi put headphones on and practise Russian alphabet.

Ash Wednesday, February 13th

Patrick C rings to tell me the news that Virgin have capitulated and agreed to pay over the money for distribution in full. Should we rejoice? Is a company that's just 'capitulated' the best place to do the best for the film? Is a company that has treated us appallingly badly over the last few months suddenly going to turn sweet? It seems as if we stumbled up the wrong path with Virgin from the very beginning and it would have been better if we'd found our way out and started again.

Thursday, February 14th

Lunch at the Great Nepalese with five members of T2000 staff. The cheerful Gurkha is still there and remembers me. Food is wonderful: delicate and original. Ludicrously cheap too.

General update on T2000 business, and embarrassed request for more money for laptop computers, etc. As T2000 still has so much good sense to impart I agree.

On the way home I have a cab driver who cannot talk – not a stammer, just grunts. Didn't realise at first and he had to write down the word he was trying to say; later I notice a sign, 'Sorry The Driver Cannot Speak'.

Feeling like staying at home and stewing by the fire, but we are asked out to David Frost's for a Valentine's Day dinner.

David answers the door, very charming and welcoming. We're offered

[1] My father stammered for all the time I knew him.

pink champagne and led eventually into a small drawing room with French windows giving onto the snow-covered garden. Present are Tim Rice, the Owens – David and Debbie – and others I don't know.

Debbie Owen is Delia's agent and says Delia has been watching my experience with BBC Books with interest. Debbie says her latest book about Christmas cookery is 'still selling in February!', but that she has no foreign sales at all.

As she's talking her eyes swivel to the latest arrival. People shift positions, men feel their ties. This is obviously quite a guest. Turns out to be the Duchess of York, née Sarah Ferguson, looking rather fine, in good shape, with clear, open features and a striking pile of red hair.

At dinner we are divided onto two tables in two rooms. Helen is spirited away to Carina's room, along with an ex-SDP leader, and I find myself next to the Duchess, with Frost at the head of the table.

Fergie says that she saw me publicising the Stammering campaign and asks how she can become involved. Though her interest is obviously genuine, I feel she is anxious to be taken seriously and to have some moral ammunition to throw back at the press whom she so clearly hates.

She, rather sweetly and awkwardly, asked at one point, with much hesitation ... 'I mean ... may I ask you a question ... do I ... do I appear to you as the same person you've read about in the press?' I mumble something about not reading the papers and embark on a compliment.

She paints a depressing, almost frightening, picture of the royal life. She is monitored and controlled by a group of 'men in brown suits' – the palace staff who, it seems, are forever hauling her over the coals for breaches of protocol.

Friday, February 15th

Apparently the Iraqis have agreed to withdraw from Kuwait. On my way to lunch it's clear that the offer is highly conditional but at least it's the first time in this whole crisis that Iraq has even mentioned the word withdrawal ... and indeed they don't often mention Kuwait.

Lucinda Sturgis, our Production Co-ordinator, made me very worried when she said *American Friends* may be a title we regret in view of the way things are going on in the Gulf (600 civilians killed in a bomb shelter).

Lunch with Jonathan Powell and Colin Cameron, for whose department *Pole to Pole* is being made.

Anne embarks on the hard sell, chiding Jonathan for not agreeing to put out *Pole to Pole* before Christmas 1992. (Powell says it's penned in for January, and always has been – this of course is not good for the book sales, as Anne points out firmly. Powell looks uncomfortable, not sure quite how to assert himself.)

Eventually though we have a good meal and in the end have achieved what I had hoped – an opening of doors, an assertion of our desire to work with the BBC but equally of our desire to be treated as we deserve – as a potentially very successful show.

I switch on the news to hear, I hope, that this morning's Iraqi withdrawal offer may really be the good news we've waited for. Well of course it isn't. Bush has dismissed it out of hand, and the bombing goes on.

A piece in *20/20* – the first of a salvo of '*AF*' articles – depresses me. Susan Jeffreys seems at pains to make the point not only that I don't understand women but that, like most other British male comedy writers, I don't like them.

It told its audience that the film had a serious flaw and suggested I probably did as well. My flaw was being born white, male, middle-class and going to public school and Oxford and never having to suffer.

Monday, February 18th

Drag myself very wearily from bed in time for the eight o'clock news. Reports of explosions at Paddington and Victoria stations. All London main-line stations closed, which sounds a bit drastic.

Fearing dreadful traffic congestion as people travel by other means, I leave plenty of time for journey to Shepherd's Bush for meeting with Virgin Distribution.

We discuss date of release. We might have been discussing the date of a funeral. Virgin's Bill Tennant feels that we are being rushed into a theatre – the Odeon Haymarket – which he feels is too big for us. He would like to open in a 300-seater, not a 600-seater in the West End. The bombs that went off this morning, especially if they indicate a new IRA campaign of disruption, will only make matters worse.

There is to be no TV spend on the film.

Back at home an *Express* photographer is ready, set up in my room. Shots of me on the balcony against a sunset. Though I find these photo-sessions the most unjustifiably time-consuming aspects of publicity, the photographers are usually quite interesting – craftsmen with some of the same characteristics as musicians – streetwise but not boastful. Barry Lewis, today's lensman, knows Spitsbergen well and whetted my appetite for the place where we start the *Pole to Pole* journey. We sit in my room, his assistant, Barry and myself, and drink tea and talk travel.

Tuesday, February 19th

Another interview re *'AF'* – this is the tenth national newspaper piece I've done so far. A bright, tall, upright young man called Andrew Davison.

We talk for an hour and a half. As I tire my mind slips into woolly overdrive. I find it very difficult to stand back and talk about myself and I feel I shall probably be punished in the article for any unguarded slips or intellectual looseness.

By taxi to dinner with JC, Alyce Faye and Len Deighton[1] and his wife. Deighton is a slight man, slim and more donnish than the '60s hard black and white image might suggest. Easy to talk to, unassuming and keen to give and learn information. I thank him for once writing a fan letter to the BBC about *Number 27* … 'Oh, I do things like that,' he said, 'writers need to be told they've done well … otherwise everything on TV's going to be game shows.'

Sunday, February 24th

Switch on my radio as I wobble, blearily, from bed to bathroom prior to a run at nine o'clock, to hear that the allies, or the coalition forces, or the infidels, are deep into Kuwait and even Iraq, having begun their offensive as we were getting into bed early this morning. So far 'the mother of battles' has been without the enormous and dreadful loss of life they predicted and the Iraqis are backing off or surrendering.

Monday, February 25th: London–Glasgow–Dunoon

Up at 6.15. Surprised to see dawn light outside. Winter receding, already. Taxi to Heathrow at a quarter to seven. On the news, buoyant reports

---

1 Len Deighton, writer, whose first novel, *The Ipcress File*, was turned into a film with Michael Caine.

on the progress of the allied advance. Very few casualties, all targets reached well in advance, little resistance.

Yesterday the *Independent on Sunday* carried a brief article by a man describing what it's like to be bombarded or shelled. He drew a graphic picture of the sensory distortion and damage. The sucking-out of ear-drums by the constant changes in air pressure, the adrenaline-filled fear that brings sleeplessness and confusion. The Iraqis have been subjected to the heaviest bombardment since World War One, probably ever. One can realise why they're surrendering.

Flight to Glasgow almost full – no evidence of fear of terrorist attack here. But Hamish MacInnes[1] meets me in Glasgow with the news that all London main-line stations were closed again this morning and a bomb had exploded on a railway line.

Hamish drives me in to the BBC where I record my commentary for *Palin's Progress*.[2]

Back onto the motorway, heading along the south bank of the Clyde, past the massive, and in most cases rusting, cranes of Port Glasgow and Greenock to Gourock and the ferry across to Dunoon, where I've selected a *Good Hotel* entry called the Enmore Hotel to spend two or three days on 'The Adventure'.

Hamish smiled broadly when he heard I was away to Dunoon. 'Oh, y'll get some peace there,' he grinned, 'people only go there to die ...'

My room has a four-poster bed whose posts are wrapped in chiffon and tied with a pink ribbon.

The menu for the evening is rolled up like a scroll and to be found in a silver urn on a tray in the corner of the room. On the bottom of the night's menu the guests' names are printed.

Short but good menu – cheese and herb roulade, carrot soup, a real mother of an Arbroath smokie and plum tart. A glass of Glenfarclas malt and a half-bottle of Sancerre render me pleasantly drowsy.

Tuesday, February 26th: Dunoon

Watch the news as I wash and dress. Saddam Hussein ordering a with-drawal from Kuwait within 24 hours and claiming victory – maybe

---

1 Hamish MacInnes, founder and leader of the Glencoe Mountain Rescue Team.
2 *Palin's Progress*, a film of me and Tom making a father-and-son climb along the Aonach Eagach ridge above Glencoe, shot by Hamish.

this lost something in the translation from Arabic, but it does sound to be an exaggeration, as the faces on thousands of surrendering Iraqi soldiers show only exhaustion, fear and relief at being taken prisoner.

To breakfast, where I first encounter the formidably extrovert Angela, wife of the proprietor. 'And what do you do Mr McLennan?' Her voice rings round the small dining room as she interrogates the only other diner.

Then retreat up to my room to begin work on 'The Adventure', which I haven't touched for ten months.

Watch the news, bathe and down to dinner. Angela in charge tonight. We all learn quickly about herself, her body, her retiring husband and her inability to play squash. Her husband had evidently reproved her for thinking I was a commercial traveller. 'He's the "Fish man",' he'd said. This gave Angela a chance to launch into a further riff ... 'But the fish man only lives in Tarbert ... I couldn't think what he'd be wanting to stay here for ...'

Thursday, February 28th: Dunoon–London

1.15 shuttle to London. Pilot has wonderful dry sense of humour. 'Do sit back and try and relax. This is my first flight ...' pause '... to London.' 'If we can find Manchester we then should find Coventry, then we shall fly into London past Aylesbury and pick up the A41 to Berkhamsted ...' 'For those of you on the right there is a fine view of Welsh clouds, whilst those on the left can see their English equivalent.'

Friday, March 8th

To lunch with JC at L'Aventure.

Little small talk for JC wants to talk seriously about the film – the new film for the *Wanda* team that is.

Film to be about the importance of humour v bigotry and prejudice. He says he probably won't be making it until the early autumn of '92. Not with Charlie. He found it heavy going with Charlie towards the end of *Wanda*, especially, JC says, in the editing stage. Checking out Robert Young. Of course I give him a big recommendation.

We adjourn at a quarter to three. The prospect of having a Cleese-Kline-Jamie Lee collaboration to embark on at the end of *Pole to Pole* is very satisfactory ... 'Give me the occasional lunch between now and when you leave,' JC requests.

Sunday, March 10th

To Camden Town with Helen, Rachel and Will for the cast and crew screening of *American Friends*. Already people are converging on the Parkway Cinema in a practically unbroken stream – as [Helen's sister] Mary said later, 'like people going to church'.

Connie's and Trini's performances are so delicate, so full of precise, carefully controlled meanings. I watch in sheer pleasure, and am often moved.

Rush out at the end. Generous applause from within, at beginning and end of the credits. Then the crowd spills out.

Very strong commendations from Richard Loncraine [director of *The Missionary*], who raved for quite some time, and D Leland, as well as Barry Humphries, who gave me a big hug and pressed me against his smooth, fleshy cheek. All around were heartfelt congratulations. Terry J had 'cried again'. The crew all seemed very happy.

Later Robert Young rings and becomes the third director of the day to rave about the film. He is so fulsome I only wish he were not a film director but a film critic. Nicest remark is that he feels it is such a 'truthful' film. Also a brave film, he says, referring to the uncompromising way in which we've avoided playing the story up, or milking it for comedy.

All this highly satisfactory, even bearing in mind people want to be nice.

Monday, March 11th

Lunch with David Robinson of *The Times*. David is no longer the *Times* film critic. A new young arts editor elbowed him out, and though David does not tell the story accusingly, it sounds as if he's been disgracefully treated.

Geoff Brown is the new critic. 'He's a trasher,' warns David ... 'a good or bad man, nothing in between' and, ominously, 'he doesn't like period stuff'.

Tuesday, March 12th

Two interviews in the morning, including a very good Radio 5 chat with a bright man called Mark Kermode – who notices the dark side of almost any comedy I've been involved in.

Lunch and a chat to Iain Johnstone for *The Sunday Times*. I can answer almost everything except the personal stuff ... 'Are you nice?' 'Of course I'm not.' 'What's the least nice thing about you?' – and there, pathetically, I'm lost for words.

At seven o'clock round to Barry and Lyn Took's. He has Paddy Ashdown[1] and wife Jane to dinner.

Paddy is as one would expect an ex-Marine to be. He is in good physical shape, with a big, ready, eager laugh; he's direct and fires off questions as if he were interrogating one of his men after a reconnaissance raid ... 'How do you sell a film?' 'Who makes the film what it is?' 'At what stage do you know you have a success?'

But we do eventually get on to politics and Ashdown is characteristically candid. He's complimented by Lyn on being honest and not trying to deceive or dissemble in order to get on. Ashdown protests ... 'Look, I am like that at fifteen per cent' – 'Sixteen per cent,' his wife corrects him – 'Fifteen, sixteen ... what the hell ... but if I were up to forty per cent or forty-five per cent I would have to behave very differently.'

He thinks the House of Commons is a dreadful place, but loves being a constituency MP.

Like most politicians I meet they know much less about our business than actors and writers know about politics. They really are in an hermetically sealed world. But I liked them both. He seems enormously sane and sensible ... but he is still only at fifteen per cent. Sorry sixteen.

Tuesday, March 19th

At 12.15 I'm deposited at the Ivy restaurant to await those of the critics and the critics' screening audience who have accepted our invitation to lunch. This is another of many nervous moments in the history of *American Friends*. But there are smiles on the faces of the first arrivals – George Perry and Chris Tookey – and they come bearing warm praise.

Dilys Powell is here; she's unable to move much and sits, bowed over

1 Paddy Ashdown, leader of the Liberal Democrats from 1989 to 1999.

in a chair, reading the press kit. No-one seems to be minding her. I go to talk to her. She turns her sweet, bewitching eyes to me and I feel the same emotional wobble as I did when I met her last at the *Private Function* do.

She tells me that she's followed my career with great pleasure. She had been in trouble at Oxford herself, she said, for being caught climbing back into her college. When she leaves, prodding forward on a stick, I notice she's sporting a pair of scarlet socks and sandals.

About half past two the last critics and friends leave – unhurriedly – Davenport of the *Telegraph* going off to drink with the man from the *Morning Star* – and I can have a rest from two hours' almost non-stop talking.

Time Out carries a full-page colour ad, an article and a review which commends the film as being 'full of small pleasures'. Could be worse.

Out in the evening to Parly Hill to see Rachel's play which she and others in her drama group have written and performed and staged as part of their GCSE. It's a thoughtful, serious piece about a political prisoner – his conscience, etc. Rachel takes quite a dominant role and shows clearly that there is an actress in there. Other plays treat with child abuse, cancer, the Gulf War. Not a lot of laughs.

Wednesday, March 20th

At eight o'clock a car collects me and takes me to TV-am. The interior of Terry Farrell's light, bright, successful building looks sprucer than I remember. There's an air of confidence about the place which may be deceptive. Is this just a conscious effort to appear attractive, knowing that bidders are at the door, eyeing the franchise?

Paul Gambaccini gives the film a robust review and an eight out of ten rating. He also, I notice, does his piece to camera ad-lib, with great confidence. Very unusual.

A half-hour with Michael Parkinson at LBC in Hammersmith. He seems a lonely figure, almost imprisoned in this quiet, soulless, modern ambience. But we have a lively chat. I like him. He's easy to strike up a rapport with (maybe the Yorkshire thing helps) and one feels that he's intelligent and sympathetic.

Away from Parky to St Pancras, and a train ride up to Nottingham.

Here my optimism begins to weaken.

The location of the Showcase Cinema does not seem to be in

Nottingham at all but in an industrial estate a mile or two outside. The Showcase is a multiplex of 13 screens surrounded by a car park. There is a cheerless emptiness to the place.

The Showcase operation is run from America, all decisions on 'events' at the cinema have to be cleared through a lady in Boston. I can't, as I look around the bland, pop-corn dispensary that is the foyer, feel anything other than a sinking feeling that I would rather not be here, and that ironically *American Friends* will not spend much time here either.

Thursday, March 21st

Lie in or read the reviews? Only one answer, so up and buy the *Guardian*. Nice, warm piece from Derek Malcolm, protective of the film 'so gentle it almost hurts to think what will happen to it in Des Moines'.

Call Tristram. Virginia says he's smarting from some cruel mention in *The Times*. Reassure her that blood was expected from the *Times* reviewer after my lunch with David Robinson, whom he replaced.

I pass by a newsagent in Marylebone High Street and pick up likely publications. Best reviews from unexpected sources – a rave in *What's On*. '*Total Recall* it isn't but aren't you glad of that.' Hugo Davenport obliges in the *Daily Telegraph* and even *The Times* is less severe than predicted.

The overall impression is of fondness for the film and respect for its values and qualities, tempered in some reviews with 'buts' ranging from the condescending to the derogatory. Nigel Andrews, who Patrick says 'doesn't like films anyway', concludes a not unpleasant *FT* review with the phrase 'utterly pretty, utterly charming, if also utterly minor'.

Friday, March 22nd

A tonic at breakfast. Rave reviews in *Today* and the *Daily Express* ('better than *Room with a View*'), glowing review from Shaun Usher in the *Mail* and approval and a lot of space on the review page from Kevin Jackson in the *Independent*.

For a time I feel as if I'm on a settled plateau after climbing a difficult mountain. That all the hard work and the gruelling trips to the US and the let-downs from financiers and distributors are worth it.

Saturday, March 23rd

Two unpleasant reviews in the post – one from the *Good Times* opines that 'if one film can bring Michael Palin's career down in rubble this is it'. More abuse, ending by calling the Ashby character 'snivelling'. Another, though less in the category of hate mail, calls it 'so slow as to be almost invisible'. But after yesterday's thick dose of praise these are not enough to rattle me.

What does rattle me far more is a phone call to Patrick at 11.30, an hour before we leave for the airport and a skiing week. Even allowing for Patrick's customary disinclination to exuberance, this is a grim leaving present. Friday night at the Odeon Haymarket was worse than any of us had ever considered. No rush to either of the early performances and only 250, considerably less than half the house, for the main evening perf. Nothing much either of us can say.

I stare out of the window, realising that I'd prepared myself for everything but this. By any standard a first-night failure.

No time to mourn, or even ascertain more information, as we have to organise departure to Heathrow (two taxis) and then flight to Zurich, for seven of us.

Monday, April 1st

Finish unpacking and sorting through letters. Find a lovely, generous review of '*AF*' by Dilys Powell in the latest *Punch* which cheers me considerably.

Alan Bleasdale rings, late. He's under the weather again after weeks of editing and won't be able to make tomorrow's post-synch session. He carefully and dutifully warns me in advance that two scenes of mine have been shortened – neither, he assures me, for acting reasons – the panic attack, now contained in a montage, and fuck, fuck, fuck … which he said just looked as if the writer had kept it all in for no other reason than to hear the character say fuck repeatedly. 'Apart from that,' he rasps, 'I think you're untouched …'

Tuesday, April 2nd

To Adelaide House for a briefing meeting on the present position of the MAI [Mills & Allen International] franchise bid. Quite a shock to see the number of people round the table since our meeting of six weeks ago. The boardroom on the eighth floor is packed. Upwards of 30 people, including Allan McK and his Managing Director, a quiet, neat man called Michael Buckley, who have just flown in from New York.

Roger Laughton seems very relaxed in the chair. Nice to see someone doing the job they really want to do, and he lends the whole enterprise an air of quiet, efficient determination.

As we are introduced I'm described as the man responsible for the choice of the name Meridian, which is not entirely true, though I did champion it very strongly.

Allan McKeown, another man who clearly enjoys his job, pitches the various ideas which he and his clients Marks and Gran and Clement and Le Frenais[1] had come up with at their recent weekend at Chewton Glen. They include a half-hour sitcom for me. Nice of them, but I groan inwardly as I hear my character described as a charming, likeable … etc. etc. It's a two-hander with a cat!

A mythical week's schedule is revealed. Roger rather sweetly admits that the 'In Search of Railways' idea put into peak time on one of the nights is his own.

Meeting winds up after about two and a half hours. The strength and seriousness of the enterprise, what began as a thought in Simon's kitchen one night, is impressive. But I know it's not really my world. The game of winning the bid and running the station doesn't really interest me. I want, as always, to be able to take a step back and observe all this ironically. Yet it could affect thousands of people's jobs and livelihoods.

Wednesday, April 3rd

Letter from Ron Eyre[2] brightens my breakfast time. 'I've just had the best possible evening at *American Friends*' … a film 'straight to the heart and the senses … and your performance showed presence being present rather than acting being acted. A rarity.'

So this morning, with my back niggling and precluding any running, I turn to the problem of 'AF'. Various ideas, thoughts, suggestions flying

---

1 Two writing partnerships: Maurice Gran and Lawrence Marks, best known for *Birds of a Feather* and *The New Statesman*, and Dick Clement and Ian Le Frenais for *The Likely Lads* and *Porridge*.
2 Ron Eyre, director mainly in theatre (*London Assurance* for Royal Shakespeare Company).

around including doing a series of radio ads and if necessary paying for them ourselves. I ring Pete Buckingham from Virgin, and suggest that he and I should meet.

First person I see as I walk into an almost empty Cibo (London is civilised and unrushed this Easter week) is Harold Pinter. He greets me with warm praise for the film, which he had been to see on opening night with Lady Antonia. I know he's a friend of Tristram's but he gushed most gratifyingly. I said I hoped he would proselytise and he recruited the man he was dining with, a small, reddish-brown American who was introduced as Michael Herr,[1] the writer. The three of us bemoaned the macho demands of the box office, much sympathetic head-nodding.

Pete B is very nervous and jumpy, almost his first words are 'You must be having a terrible time', but once he's settled down and had a cigarette and a glass or two of wine (Umbrian by Lungarotti) we have a good sensible conversation. I tell him of the radio ad plan and of course he's enthusiastic.

Home, make calls to Lucinda and decide to go ahead with the radio campaign as soon as possible. To expedite matters the Gumby Corporation, my own company, will produce them. Assemble some good quotes.

To Camden Lock for supper with Rachel, then home and look through Clem's notes on the Egypt–Tanzania leg of the *Pole to Pole* journey.

Sobering schedule shows the filming to be seven weeks longer than *80 Days* – 43 days to Aswan, then 90 to Antarctica and home.

Thursday, April 4th

Tristram has heard very little about the film's performance, but confirms that for many who have seen it the experience was pleasing – including his father, who saw it on video at the weekend. Much taken with Switzerland and the notebooks and all the detail of travel and very complimentary about my performance.

I ask TP if his father has been in demand following Graham Greene's death yesterday. 'Actually it seems to have reinvigorated him,' says Tristram. 'He hasn't been in such good form for a long time.'

---

1 Michael Herr wrote *Dispatches*, one of the major books of the Vietnam War.

Friday, April 5th

To the Haymarket to check the cinema. Very difficult to make out the identity of the film at the Odeon. Small corner frontage – no lettering around the marquee – only bland pink neon stripe. Closer examination: pics of me looking severe and only two quotes, both quite unsensationally placed in cheap Letraset.

Inside, no-one about. Knock on door to box office. A face eventually peers round. 'Yes?' 'I'd like to see the manager.' 'What about?' I point vaguely at my likeness on the big poster opposite, then, apologetically, 'Er … I'm … er … I'm in the film.' Then the penny drops and a few moments later the manager, shirt-sleeved, appears. Youngish man, looking uncomfortable.

Some quick talking to reassure him that I only want to help and I haven't come with any personal bodyguards. He is very sad about the performance, saying that they all like the picture very much, and there's nothing worse than seeing the demise of a film you want to succeed. I query the lack of review-flaunting in the foyer and at the entrance. Suggest having boards made up. He thinks this a good idea and I promise to get the quotes sent round. Ask him about the neon around the marquee instead of the name of the film. He blames this on a previous manager's keenness on the corporate Odeon image!

Monday, April 8th

Drive over to the *Pole to Pole* production office. In Smiley-esque anonymity in the Uxbridge Road looking out over Shepherd's Bush Green. The windows murky with traffic-stirred dust.

This is the first meeting of the '*PTP*' team. I meet Nigel Meakin and his new assistant Patti Musicaro on the road outside. Patti is Italian-American and I think will be a good foil to our Englishness. She's quiet but obviously together and competent.

Roger arrives in a very large coat and immediately the difference between a room with and without Roger is evident. With Roger there's an air of danger, an edge of risk, a hint of provocation. Straight away we're naughtier, riskier and a touch more passionate. He talks about the Eye-ties in Ethiopia and Patti flashes her big dark eyes in disapproval and the place comes to life.

Clem's news of the evening is that there is some hope we shall have a nuclear submarine to take us to the North Pole.

Tuesday, April 9th

It's now two and a half weeks since we received the first good reviews and still the Odeon foyer looks dead as a doornail. A punter is studying the pictures as I walk in.

Down the unlit stairs – light on in the manager's office, can hear him talking. Knock on his door, call 'Hello! It's Michael Palin.' Poor man nearly has heart failure for second time in a week. He says Chris Bailey of Virgin has promised the board and review splash and it should be here today. He brightens on mention of last Saturday... 'had all the feeling of a first night ... very good atmosphere in the bar'.

Tuesday, April 16th

At seven o'clock all the weekend secrecy over our presents from the children is explained. With Rachel and Lisa the ringleaders, they've provided us with 25 separate presents. I'm in my new Margaret Howell flannel suit and Helen's in her new black dress and we both look good and suddenly I'm enjoying the prospect of our 25th anniversary party.

Out in the garden is a silver birch tree which Helen's badminton-playing friend Kathryn Evans delivered by taxi this morning and now the children are all around to watch us open the Great 25 before we leave for L'Escargot. Wonderfully chosen selection – all marked so we open them in the right order.

Begins with the mundane – kitchen foil, refreshers, a bar of Tobler-one, works up through lovely pottery cats and mugs to old prints of the Arctic and Egypt for me, and then little silver pieces – for me a silver bubble-blower, and ending up with a framed set of photographs showing the two of us, and three pictures of each of the children when young.

Terry J, still in Australia, at the Melbourne Comedy Festival, is the only Python missing.

My speech is well received and, I must say, well delivered. Start by pointing out that it is a very special night – the first night (pause) for 13 years (audience a little uneasy) that *Monty Python's Life of Brian* has been shown on network television! Applause, as four of the main cast are here, plus others like McKeown and Neil Innes.

The gathering is always noisy but not loud. Elena, London's greatest maîtresse d', keeps a maternal eye and it's all a great success.

It's five to three by the time we're both in bed – the passing of our 25th year together could hardly have been better marked, or happier.

Friday, April 19th

By three I'm at Paul Marsh's in Muswell Hill. Eleven hours of Russian and I've not much to show for it. Paul is sympathetic and helpful and does not condemn. I'm growing quite fond of him.

He tells me he was Bernie Grant's[1] secretary at Haringey Council during the Broadwater Farm Riots in 1985. Paul is measured, reasonable and not the slightest bit Spart-ish,[2] so the tales he tells have some weight. Winston Silcott's father, a small, inoffensive elderly man, described to Paul the police raid to pick up Silcott. Mr S arrived with the door key just as police were beating on the door and about to use a sledgehammer on it. He told them that he had the key and he'd let them in. They sledgehammered the door anyway.

I asked Paul if he thought Silcott was guilty. He said he wasn't sure but the two who were put away with him were definitely innocent. [All three were acquitted on November 25th 1991.]

Sunday, April 21st

With Will sporting his Wednesday scarf, we set out on the road to Wembley for the final of the Rumbelows Football League Cup. Down Oak Village to Gospel Oak Station, Willesden Junction, change to Wembley Central.

Apart from a flurry of autographs at one point and a longish speech of appreciation for *80 Days* from one of the senior police officers on duty, we get to our seats without much interference soon after two o'clock.

The Wednesday end is already full and the supporters are putting on an impressive display. 'We love Carlton Palmer, he smokes marijuana. Da-Da-Da!' 'Ron's Arm-ee!' 'Ron's Arm-ee!' And 'Always Look on the Bright Side of Life'.

The game itself is not attractive and Manchester United always more

---

1 Bernie Grant, Labour politician, MP for Tottenham.
2 Dave Spart, voice of left-wing activism, was a character created by *Private Eye* magazine.

likely to score. But we keep them out, and then quite unbelievably a speculative crack at goal by Sheridan spins off Sealey's outstretched hands into the net. The Wednesday fans, who have been throwing teddy bears and stuffed toys around the stand and chanting non-stop, deserved this and we are all of us part of a mighty roar of delight.

The second half is 45 minutes of the most exquisite torture. Seldom are so many people in the same place at the same time enjoying the same emotions – whatever their age or sex or background. We are united in our dreadful anxiety, we shout and sing and chant to exorcise the doubt.

The referee suddenly raises his hands, it's the end and we can at last release everything. A shock of collective pride, relief and unequivocal joy.

The Manchester United fans don't stay, but Wednesday's blue and yellow explosion rolls on and is still rolling 15 minutes later when Will and I begin to find our way out.

Man U fans are dead-faced, surly and suddenly scruffy and down-trodden. Wednesday's supporters, yobs and all, can enjoy the victor's role, for the first time at Wembley for 56 years.

Monday, April 22nd

There is a phone call from Patrick C to tell me that the weekend figures on 'AF' are not bad. Despite the misinformation in the *Standard* and the lack of information in the *Ham and High*, we took over £7,000 in London, as good as we ever did at the Odeon with fewer seats. Oxford respectable, Brighton reasonable, only Birmingham hopeless.

Monday, April 29th

Up early – today another connection added to my pre-'*PTP*' physical preparation prog. A regular workout (something I've never done before) suggested by osteopath Andrew Harwich to strengthen my back. So I'm walking past Selfridges at nine o'clock on my way to the Danceworks building in Balderton Street.

The Pilates class is up on the top floor. Small, high room with six or seven people quietly exercising on equipment or on mats. No sounds of sweat, no grunts of effort, and quiet classical music plays, so completely unlike most gyms, which seem to work on a combination of thudding disco and galley-slave atmos.

Tuesday, April 30th

Back home via dry cleaners to find Michael Coveney at my front door. He has come round to tape some impressions, views, info from me for a book on Maggie Smith. Says he's just been to see Alan Bennett who judged Maggie not to be 'the stuff of anecdote'.

Switch on TV. On Channel 2 Ranulph Fiennes struggles to the North Pole, on Channel 4 I'm shouting at Andrew McLachlan in *The Meaning of Life*. *Brian* topped Channel 4's ratings last week at 4.4 million. That was in the 'Banned' season. I think *The Meaning of Life* will offend far more people.

Thursday, May 2nd

Will arrives from Oxford and we go together to the 150th anniversary party of the London Library – neither of us quite knowing what to expect.

They have been given permission to use the gardens in the middle of St James's Square, and two or three marquees have been erected.

Norman Lamont shepherds the Queen Mother around, and we catch glimpses of an erect, pallid and cadaverous Enoch Powell, a neat Jim Callaghan slowly proceeding into the tent with no retinue, only his wife. Thatcher is reported to be there, as is Anthony Powell (though I never see him or Tristram).

Someone in the know tells me some Queen Mother gossip – she apparently did not have much time for Edwina Mountbatten, and when Edwina was eventually buried at sea, the QM, sitting with the family at Windsor, watched dispassionately as her coffin hit the waves. 'Typical Edwina, always did things with a splash.'

A lady with a foreign accent tells me that she has seen and enjoyed 'AF' and leans in confidentially, 'You have a tremendous body.'

Tuesday, May 7th

Take bull by the horns and call Roger Laughton. He is surprisingly agreeable to my suggestion that writing my film script is a more urgent priority than attending tomorrow's Meridian board meeting. 'Of course we'd love to see you, Michael, but we do understand.' Well that's enough for me and I feel relieved to have that off my plate.

My head is muzzy and I'm not on sharpest form. Everything seems to take so long, papers litter my workroom floor, the telephone rings and I find myself shouting at it as the answerphone stands in for me. Radio Kent want to interview me re Meridian – straight away please. Clem wants to know why Anne has not yet signed the BBC contract for 'PTP'. Will comes back from Oxford and needs ideas by tonight for a revue sketch on freshmen.

Thursday, May 9th

Up to Muswell Hill to see Paul. Good session; am learning about Russia as well as Russian.

Though I have a blind spot about being taught things (reaction to my father always telling me what to do?) I feel better for having listened and learnt and I enjoy and revel in the expansion of my knowledge in these hours in Muswell Hill. He's put me on to some Isaac Babel stories. I'm suddenly aware how much there is to read in advance of the Great Journey – now not much more than two months away.

Back home to do letters with Kath. Twelve charities alone in less than a week – Womankind, Oxfam, Film Centre at Sussex University, Linda McCartney for Lynx and Anita Roddick for Amnesty – not to mention the schizophrenics and the Samaritans and the Writers' Trust and Tom Stoppard. To care and be rich – well you're staring into the headlights.

Friday, May 10th: London–Cork

Head out to Heathrow for flight to Chris Orr's show in Cork.

The Crawford Art Gallery is a large, solid building with an excellent space downstairs in what was the old sculpture gallery.

They'd let Chris put a few sculptures around – so there's a figure with a discus and a marble baby at his mother's breast beside the imposing figure of William Crawford on a plinth: 'One of Ireland's worthiest sons – from his youth upwards his heart throbbed for her prosperity.' One or two of Chris's more scatological works have not been hung, including the copulating warthogs.

I'm poured a glass of Murphy's – the local stout. A beautiful colour and somehow its taste and effect are very comforting. Feel myself slipping into Ireland, but remain clear-headed enough to say a few words, with Crawford looming behind me.

Then we're all taken off to some ceilidh dancing in the Metropole Hotel.

About 50 people of all ages taking part. They are rather serious about it (majority of them are women) and the drunken antics of some of our party – among them a bone-thin sculptor who was once a baker in Lincolnshire, who dances on his head – are rather rightly, and indeed literally, looked down on.

Murphy's flows dark as the River Lee outside, which I find myself peering into with Chris at half past one.

Saturday, May 11th: Cork–London

Up at nine and at 9.30 down to breakfast at the 'Clouds' restaurant. Thick clouds seem to have come down over the service.

A shiny-headed, elderly maître d' passes helplessly amongst us like the only doctor at a disaster scene. Eventually, though, I get my muesli and strangely unreal orange juice and brown toast, done for about three seconds. Pick cutlery off other tables.

Read the papers – Frost/Branson almost certainly co-bidders and rivals for TVS – and then walk up South Mall and over various bridges and into a bookshop and then a tailor specialising in Donegal tweed – wonderful cloths at ridiculously low prices. Order a suit that will come out around £250 and buy two coats. The owner/cutter is an Englishman. Says David Puttnam was in recently and bought a whole lot of stuff – 'all loose-fitting'.

Walk round the upper rooms of the gallery. The bone-thin sculptor, more subdued now, sits surrounded by his hideous collection of ceramic hats and straitjackets and plastic dustbin lids, not a single visitor in sight.

Wednesday, May 15th

At half past twelve, half an hour after the deadline, a motorbike rider hands me the Meridian bid document. It comes in a box – rather like a *Reader's Digest* offer.

With Helen to the Ivy for a Meridian dinner. Roger L, dark-eyed from the nights at the bid document, Clive H, very perky and bright, Simon

A and Bill Cotton, Allan McKeown and Tracey Ullman plus some late arrivals – Baroness Flather,[1] Sir Richard Luce and a smattering of local media.

General feeling is that we have prepared an excellent bid. Frost and Branson's company are competitors, as are Carlton (but Carlton will go primarily for Thames). We have done a more thorough job than anyone else – having not only found an HQ site but made an offer and designed a building to go on it.

Thursday, May 16th

Nigel Walmsley rings. His Carlton bid for TVS also went in yesterday. It's somehow neat that the two people I championed as prog heads to Clive and Simon a year ago now face each other as the two heads of the most likely bids. Nigel and Roger have been in amiable contact throughout. Nigel betting Roger an undisclosed sum that he couldn't get the word 'oleaginous' into his bid document and Roger betting Nigel the same about 'mountain greenery'. I haven't looked at the bid doc yet, but the quest for the word 'oleaginous' makes it a much more appealing prospect!

Friday, May 17th: London–Brighton

Read some of the Meridian franchise bid in the taxi to Victoria to meet Simon A for trip to Brighton.

To the Grand Hotel where the first journo arrives. He's an obliging and good-humoured man from the *Argus*. Seems to think that Meridian have done their homework best.

Phone interview then a merciful half-hour to lie down before leaving at 6.45 for the independent cinema in Brighton – the Duke of York. Simon Fanshawe, with the smoothly curved profile of a 1930s toff, joins us together with a comedian called Eddie Izzard who once interviewed me in Sheffield.

Q and A with a full house after *American Friends*.

Fanshawe buttonholes me to go and watch Eddie Izzard. He's transformed from the quiet boy at the dinner to a very funny, un-rabid

1 Baroness Flather, Indian-born lawyer, first Asian woman to receive a peerage. Sat as Conservative in the Lords. Prominent in race-relations work.

stand-up performer, working a large audience well. Nice piece about the people in Hove all being about 80, and how, as a kid growing up there, the youngest person he could find to play with was 76.

Sunday, May 19th

GBH cast and crew screening at 10.30. It's held at BAFTA and consists of episode one, all dubbed, but without the opening titles – 'Being finished in Vienna,' I'm told by David Jones – and some scenes from the end of episode three, including the doctor/Jim scene when the doctor declares he's dying.

It is unquestionably powerful stuff and the audience is dazzled, mesmerised and excited. Nicely, there is a lot of laughter too, at the right places. It works on all the levels it set itself to work at, and I think the vigilance and tenacity of the post-production period has paid off. There is hardly any drop in the tension and the good and bad both come across powerfully.

Alan revealed to Helen that he had ordered up all my work before seeing me and made his mind up on two performances – one, as he said 'in a film I hate', was Jack Lint in *Brazil*, and the other, when I decided to buy the dress in *The Dress*.[1]

It's a lovely feeling to walk out across Piccadilly on a lazy Sunday afternoon with Helen buzzing with suppressed delight at her first look at what took so much out of my life last year!

Sunday, May 26th

At the Hay Literary Festival. Narrow streets full of cars and people.

Am whisked away to be photographed by the *Western Daily Press*. 'They don't want anything literary,' the photographer assures me, without irony. Then back to a hotel 15 minutes' drive away – very posh, English, sorry Welsh, for we are in Powys now, country house converted for rich people with pompous waiters of 17 who come out with lines like 'Half-bottles will be found towards the rear of the wine list, sir.'

Here meet up with TJ, Sue Townsend and, later, Patrick Barlow. In a very spacious and agreeable snooker room with leather armchairs we

1 *The Dress*, a short film with Phyllis Logan directed by Eva Sereny in 1984.

rehearse the 'Aladdin' panto from *Dr Fegg's Encyclopaedia of All World Knowledge.*[1]

Rushed lunch of wild mushroom soup, quails' breasts and other expensive standards, then with Geoffrey Strachan, our publisher, getting increasingly anxious, we're driven back into Hay to be picked up by the local HTV crew stepping out of the car.

Our talk, called 'What's So Funny', is in a tent which is full to overflowing and very hot by the end.

We are then rushed (one is always 'rushed' at things like this) to a book-signing outside. Fegg books by far the most popular and Patrick and Sue very patient.

To remain in my mind above all others as an image of these crazy five hours in Hay is a Lauren Bacall-signed cricket bat! She had been staying at our hotel.

Lovely drive to Oxford for Playhouse talk, along quiet, isolated Border valleys that stretch for miles.

Spot a sign for 'Linton' and pay quick homage to Ed P.[2] No-one about as I walked beneath the gnarled yew tree into the churchyard. In the porch are stills from the film. Fred's bearded Renaissance Syme regards me calculatingly.

Walk round beneath the tower and its soft-red stone spire and wonder if I did the right thing by Edward. Well yes, I decide, I think he would have enjoyed it. Pause a while in the graveyard where he's buried, then continue my journey to Oxford.

At the Playhouse at 8.30. Dressing room is empty. Hear Ned Sherrin being witty over the tannoy and David Kernan singing witty songs and feel rather lonely for a moment, for this isn't quite my thing.

I get to read 'Biggles Goes to See Bruce Springsteen' after about an hour and a half of waiting. Behind me, at a table, are ranged Ned and Victor Spinetti and Sir Ian McKellen and Dame Judi and Michael Williams and other performers.

Miss a few moments but generally read tight and clearly and good laughs – especially from behind me.

Afterwards Ian McKellen, who looks about 22, welcomes me to the

---

1 Palin and Jones comic book published in 1974. Illustrated by Martin Honeysett.
2 My great-grandfather Edward Palin was given the living of Linton in Herefordshire when forced to leave Oxford for marrying Brita.

table and fetches me a glass of wine. Elizabeth Welch[1] finishes the show and is magnificent. Her voice so effortless and her interpretation of the songs immaculate – hitting the right note in every way.

I eventually get away back to the Old Parsonage Hotel – open only four days. Very tasteful and *World of Interiors* at reception, but the taps in the bath have the last laugh today. One completely comes away in my hand and a fountain gushes over me, and later the hotel manager who comes to investigate.

Monday, May 27th

JC has purchased more Burmese cats – he gets them all from Somerset – the latest are no bigger than his hand – as he pursues the search for the meaning of life. He meditates twice a day and one of his current jobs is as writer to the Dalai Lama, whom he met in London. JC says that they didn't exchange a word to start with – they just looked at each other and started to laugh. 'Then I brought Cynthia in and they had a laugh …'

Thursday, May 30th

To Gascogne for lunch with my producer. Eric looking healthy, he's the last Python to need glasses, but he admits the time is getting close.

We talk over 'The Adventure'. EI's view after a quick read this a.m. is that 'it's a good first draft'. Characters are rich and the basic idea of the story works. He feels that the structure and shape of the story now need to be examined and motivations tightened to lose any feelings of arbitrariness.

Useful chat. We agree to sleep on it through June. EI will read it again and make suggestions and we'll meet up in early July to decide on the next step.

Friday, May 31st

Tristram and V and Hermione and Robert Young to dinner.

Earlier this evening Alan and Robert were on *Wogan*. Asked about me, Alan said that I hated, above all else, being called nice … 'but he

1 Elizabeth Welch, American-born singer ('Stormy Weather' and 'Love For Sale'), long resident in London.

is so nice!' he went on and told the story of the only time in the whole of *GBH* when he'd seen me in a sulk, which was when I'd asked for an *Independent* and been delivered a *Guardian*!

Saturday, June 1st: London–Brookfield-on-Longhill

June comes in cool and severe. Determination to follow all the advice to get fit for *'PTP'* pushes me out of bed and down to Marshall Street for a swim.

Home to find my face, lean and ascetic, staring up at me from a fashionably grainy b/w photo in the *Independent Magazine*. Accompanies a pre-*GBH* piece on me by Mark Lawson. Most of it is about my being nice. It's like an actress being only known for the size of her tits.

A podgier Palin photo sloshed across the front of the *Daily Mirror* TV page: 'Bleasdale Blockbuster Turns Two Softies into Boys from the Bash Stuff'. Hilary Kingsley leading off with my pleasure at being able to throw a punch on TV!

Early afternoon departure for Helen and myself, arriving at Brookfield-on-Longhill about 5.30.

Stay in the room I had during *GBH*, with the wide swathe of yellow curtain giving the impression that the sun's shining whatever the weather outside.

Sunday, June 2nd: Brookfield Hall–Sheffield–London

A slow and perfectly served breakfast surrounded by glowing previews for *GBH*.

The Sunday Times talks about it becoming a 'modern classic' – Alan's 'conviction fuelled through two magnificent performances' by Lindsay and Palin. Alan's wide, hairy, smiling visage beams out at me from every paper, as it used to from across this table over half a year ago. Somehow it seems the right time to be here.

Followed, kind of appropriately, by a dip into the more distant past, as I drive Helen over the Snake Pass from Glossop along the Rivelin Valley and via Hagg Lane, Crosspool and Whitworth Road [where I was born] to Graham and Margot's.[1]

---

1 Graham Stuart Harris, a neighbour in Whitworth Road, and a friend since the age of three. Married to Margot.

Memories stirred of bike rides to Ladybower Dam ('Did you really cycle as far as this?' asks Helen), of asking for beer mats in pubs, blackberry-picking with Daddy in the fields beside the Rivelin, of playing football in days as chill and inhospitable as this at Hagg Lane.

In fact it was all as if nothing had changed. Graham stood up a lot and talked loudly and Margot wanted to know what it was like to kiss someone whilst acting.

Monday, June 3rd

At Hammersmith by eight to see Billy Connolly at the Odeon.

Keep thinking of how he would have done Jim Nelson as he starts, a little awkwardly, then warms into two hours of sometimes inspired raconteuring. His ruderies less good when they're direct ... 'I love the word wank!' and much better when they come incidentally and unbidden into his stream of consciousness. 'I don't know where these ideas come from. A wee idea will just come into my mind saying "Use me ... use me".'

Laugh constantly, with breaks; sometimes in tears. Much nostalgia – lots of jokes against modern technology. Lament for the 'on/off' switch. Quite male-oriented, I would think.

Tuesday, June 4th

The glorious fourth of June. It's 5.15. I'm sitting in the garden. Strong sunshine whose heat is moderated by a north-easterly breeze.

On my lap Jonathan Keates' seductive *Italian Journeys*. Below me the lawn I've just mown, beside me a Chambers dictionary to help me with Keates' penchant for the recondite word or phrase.

The commuter trains whine and clatter out of St Pancras and into Belsize tunnel, but I'm here and I don't have to move. A five-minute phone interview re *80 Days*' forthcoming repeat is the only immediate shadow on this very satisfying horizon.

Happiness – a good title for a film and one I was starting on five years ago. Alan Bennett said in an interview that he could only recollect being happy on four occasions. Keates writes of himself – the lonely traveller – 'he finds it so much easier to be wilfully miserable than to acknowledge a genuine happiness'.

I just can't be miserable here on my balcony in Julia Street at this moment, however hard I try. And, as if to add an unexpected extra to my non-misery, the smell of woodsmoke drifts over.

Thursday, June 6th

At nine o'clock, after all the ads, the trailers, the ubiquitous Alan Bleasdale reviews which make my publicity efforts seem positively Trappist, after 18 months of worrying, soul-searching, depression and elation, the first credits entwine – Robert Lindsay and Michael Palin. The second credit is a most enormous red 'in'.

At the end the phone rings like in the old days. First Ron Lendon[1] to say that he understood just what my character was going through – he too had been intimidated at Gospel Oak. Parts, he said, 'moved me to tears'. Tom rang, genuinely and warmly appreciative – perhaps the call that meant most.

Friday, June 14th

A nit-picking *Independent* review of last night's episode – 'the series is becoming more and more Michael Murray's'.

Experience a sudden squeeze of self-pity, which hits the same raw spot – that easily bruised corner of my ego which has so often seen me become a very good second, but never quite a first.

Lunch at Fontana Ambrosia in St John's Wood with JC.

JC asks me what I want, period … my reply 'to know everything' strikes a chord with him. He wants to do a series of comedy films throughout the '90s.

We talk a little about *GBH*. He likes my performance and all the ingredients, but is not quite happy about the way they're put together, wants to know more about why things happen.

We talk for two and a half hours, like friends, and about friends.

Home to deal with letters. Hear from the office that *GBH*'s first episode had cumulative figures of 5.95 million. Doesn't seem quite as much reward for all the pre-publicity as one might have expected, but Channel 4 are very happy.

---

1 Ron Lendon. Charismatic headmaster who guided all our three children through Gospel Oak Primary School.

Sunday, June 16th

The newspapers today are full of Liverpool. The death of Eric Heffer[1] has prompted a vital by-election in Walton on July 4th which will bring out all the Labour divisions. There is a £700 million debt in the city, the binmen are on strike, and Hatton is due to come up for a hearing on embezzlement/corruption charges. The police have requested the *GBH* tapes but Channel 4 has refused to release them.

Alan is in the thick of it again. His uncanny knack of relevancy has worked in a way none of us could have expected. Alan wanted to put the finger on the evils of Thatcherism. She's gone, and his finger is now pointing, with frightening pertinence, at the incompetences of the loony left in Liverpool.

Monday, June 17th

To Cibo to meet Donald Woods for lunch. David Puttnam and Jeremy Thomas[2] sit opposite. Puttnam over a mineral water, Thomas over a wine.

Donald wants to use me 'as bait' (twinkle in the eye here), to try and lure the likes of Paul McCartney and Elton John into providing money for scholarships to help educate black children in S Africa. Of course I'm happy to help. He's quite influenced by American methods, I think, and the idea of a 'star' to draw in the rich and impressionable is one he learnt there, where celebrity is used much more shamelessly than here.

Cleese, also in the restaurant, sends us a half-drunk bottle of mineral water with 'the compliments of Table 1'. I send him back a half-empty salt-dish. Steve Abbott is dining with him. He finished *Blame It on the Bellboy* yesterday and looks harassed. I mention '*AF*' and he promises to check out the latest.

Puttnam, as he leaves, offers me use of his house near Skibbereen, and knocks over the water bottle John has sent us. Donald is too shell-shocked by this rash of celebrities to notice Harold Pinter slip out a moment later.

---

1 Eric Heffer, Labour MP for Liverpool Walton.
2 Jeremy Thomas, film producer of *The Last Emperor*, which won 1987 Academy Award for best picture.

Monday, July 8th

I begin to feel dreadful guilt about my approaching Russian lesson. It's nearly three weeks since my last, rushed, session and I have done no homework. Apply myself as best I can, but can do little but mouth the phrases I learnt in my first three visits.

Paul seems a little disappointed. He is really such a specialist, such a linguistic egghead that it must be of little interest to him to teach at this level. But he's also very decent and polite and doesn't let me know the full extent of his disappointment.

We descend from the heights of grammar to the mundane plain of phrase-book Russian.

Go to car wash on way home. One of the cleaners recognises me as I'm trapped inside whilst the car's being covered in suds from many hands. 'Monty Python ...' he points and screams exultantly to his colleagues ... 'it's the man from Monty Python!' Now, at last, I know what it's like to be a goldfish.

Tuesday, July 9th

A lunch at Fetter Lane with Robert H. He felt moved to ask me, he said, because of his mother's death, less than a month ago. Thoughts of mortality, long journeys and wills came into his mind and he wanted to see me before I disappeared.

He'd bought two plates of smoked salmon salad from what used to be the butcher's downstairs, and I've bought a bottle of Rongopai Sauvignon. We sit, flanked by his leather-bound volumes of Ruskin, in this little room, devoted to writing. It reminds me of Eisenstein's flat in Moscow.

As he is my literary executor he wants to know if I would mind a) having my diaries published and b) edited for publication. No to the second (within reason) and no to the first.

Surprise myself how quickly I reply – it's as if I'd made the decision long ago.

Thursday, July 11th

A session on Russia with Roger Mills. We sit in the garden with glasses of iced water and coffee and talk through Leningrad to Odessa.

Pole to Pole. The last months of the Soviet Union.
With two Lenins in Leningrad, summer 1991.

Comparing pencils with Basil Pao's
daughter Sonia, London, 1990.

With Helen and big friend in
Thailand, 1993.

LEFT: Journey's End. Me and various
poles at the South Pole on the last day
of *Pole to Pole*, December 8th, 1991.

Early selfie. Polaroid taken before the North Pole trip, 1992.

GBH

Dearbhla Molloy, MP, Julia St John and Mike Angelis, Derbyshire, 1990.

Jim Nelson and his school kids, Bolton, August 1990.

Rain acting with Dan Massey. 'The rain was such a surprise to Dan that his voice rose several octaves' – Ulverston, September 10th, 1990.

A Class Act

ABOVE: A chance to extend
my repertoire.

Mr Pilsworth and daughter:
MP and Tracey Ullman.

LEFT: *Pole to Pole* book-signing in Sheffield with John Hall, my geography teacher at Birkdale School, on my left, and Michael Hepworth, the headmaster, on the other side.

RIGHT: Trying out the pipe and slippers, presents from my office on my fiftieth birthday. Longueville Manor near Mallow, Ireland, May 5th, 1993.

BELOW: With Freddie Jones as 'Sir', my director David Blount (behind me) and the cast and crew of *The Dresser*, at the BBC, February 1993.

For me the first half of this *Pole to Pole* journey is dominated by Russia. It's Russia I want to know about, read about, experience, see. Roger feels the same. It is so strange, magnificent, mysterious and flawed. I feel that I may have an uncomfortable time there, but somehow that's what I expect. That's what makes it so unusual and unfamiliar. Russia fascinates me with the same intensity as India did.

Shower, then to meet David Jones for a drink at the Ladbroke Arms.

The full story of the Lindsay/Palin casting. Alan had a photo of Lindsay on the wall as he wrote first draft. Then Lindsay couldn't do because of dates. Billy Connolly charmed the pants off Verity and came in as Nelson. Verity suggested me for Murray and everyone delighted. Then Connolly backed out. Alan goes home and tears up Connolly's photo. Lindsay's plans fall through. He becomes available, but I'm in as Murray and they keep it that way rather than ask me to change. David Jones it was who eventually suggested the swap round and though at first it was resisted, it later became a wonderful idea.

Home and settle in to watch episode six. I thought it so good – a different pace, a quietening of the plot and a tightening of the tension, but the humour and the tragedy constantly, exhilaratingly clashing. All the principals now as confused as the audience.

Rang Alan up afterwards to congratulate him. 'Your ears must be burning,' he said, and with a shy prelude of apology paid me a lovely compliment ... 'You made me proud.'

Head swells, but sinks much too late to the pillow.

Sunday, July 14th

Betty starts being very pleased to see us at about five a.m. She purrs louder and more consistently than at any other time of day – kneads the duvet and stares at us from very close range for signs of life. Then she disappears. There is brief silence and just when you're falling asleep she begins sharpening her claws on the underneath of the bed.

Up to lunch at Gilliam's. Richard Broke and Elaine there.

Richard B says that the effect of *GBH* on the Beeb has been profound, along with ITV's *Darling Buds*, etc. BBC now cancelled £175 million building prog to invest instead in drama!

Monday, July 15th

Books to sign, then some Russian homework.

To the Renoir to see *Andrei Rublev*. It is a long, uncompromising film, using wide sweeping shots and long takes; so it proceeds very differently, say, to the sharply edited modern product like *Thelma and Louise*. But it's a road movie too, with a fine, self-effacing but hypnotically watchable performance by Anatoly Solonitsyn.

'Russia endures' says one character after some spectacular cruelty and devastation has left bodies littered in a burning church. 'Yes, but for how long?' asks Rublev. 'Probably for ever,' replies the other.

Thursday, July 18th

A letter coolly and dispassionately shows the figures for Prominent Facilities' last three months. Costs were about 30,000; income 12,000, deficit 18.

To Pilates.

A fond farewell to Hannah and Sue. I have learnt a lot from them – exercises which I can do as I go, exercises which run completely counter to the punish-yourself theory of British PE drummed into me at school. My back feels stronger and straighter and, as with Alexander Technique, I feel I know my body better, and will from now onwards treat it better.

Meeting at Prominent at five with Terry Gilliam, Bob, Justine and Kevin and Ian. We sit in the viewing theatre, the worst loss-maker of them all. I'm quite wound up and angry, but don't want to direct it at anyone, though I'm generally disappointed that no-one let TG or myself know what was happening. After my work on reorganising the place in February I feel let down.

I've then promised to view *Blame It on the Bellboy* – Steve's latest exec production. Good first half, then a little plodding, but light and agreeable farce. Richard Griffiths on top of Patsy Kensit must be one of the most extraordinary couplings in screen history.

Met Ken Livingstone last night at Vasco and Piero's: 'Michael Murray was too nice to be Derek Hatton,' he told me.

My private notebook for the period 20th July–November 5th, 1991 was lost by Zambian Airways at Lusaka. No personal diary kept again until

December 11th, 1991. The travel diaries I kept were not lost, and form the
bulk of the Pole *to* Pole *book.*

Thursday, December 12th

It's midday. I'm up in my workroom surrounded by piles of letters,
notebooks, films, cassettes, boxes of presents, new books kindly sent
to me. A huge mess. Half of the room taken up by the word processor
Helen has bought and which I know I shall have to learn to use. Try to
view it as a friend and not a baleful technological bore itching to change
my life!

Though I was standing on the South Pole a week ago, I feel that
the whole journey is oddly transitory, almost as if it never happened.
Certainly the enormous effort, the upheavals, the trials and tribulations
and ineffable pleasures have all merged into a sort of homogenous blur.

I suppose that as soon as I have cleared my desk and can start looking
into the diaries and at the photos things will be different. But at the
moment I feel this spatial numbness, as if I'm not quite anywhere. A
temporal limbo.

I've lost about five pounds in weight, largely due to a mixture of unexciting food and an unsettled stomach (possibly affected by the malaria
tablets I've been taking daily for over 12 weeks), and my ribcage continues to be painful after the battering in the Zambezi on 9th November.[1] I
can still only sleep comfortably on my back.

In the evening joined Terry and Al and Basil at Mon Plaisir. It seemed,
once again, as though no time had passed. TJ at one stage, however,
regarded me carefully and said, 'You know, Mikey, I think we're beginning to look grown-up.'

Sunday, December 15th

Spend a couple of hours on the word processor. Not as daunting as I'd
expected. In fact it promises well. Quiet and smooth, an easy keyboard,
no paper to insert, no crossing out or Tippex-ing. At the purely basic
level I can work it, but will just need practice.

Don't much feel like leaving the house tonight, but have promised
Rachel a trip to Vic Reeves' stage show.

---

1 I cracked a rib whilst filming a whitewater rafting sequence.

Audience mainly consists of what Rachel calls 'Channel 4 students'. They are, I'm sure, the natural successors to the Goon Show and Python audiences. Brighter than they like to look, also fairly affluent. It takes a certain confidence and a degree of achievement to laugh at the absurdity of life.

Vic and Bob do their stuff well. They are more original than most.

Wednesday, December 18th

The news on *American Friends* is not as bad as I'd thought. Had virtually written the film off as I heard that post-Venice business in Italy was bad. [The film was shown out of competition at the Venice Film Festival.] I was glad to hear from Steve today that it held on and improved in Italy and may well still be playing. The film opened the Dinard Festival and has been well reviewed in Australia.

Sunday, December 22nd

In the middle of the night I wake up lying comfortably on my right side – the first time I've been able to do so without pain for six weeks. This is exactly the time I was advised it took a rib to heal. Talk to Chas McKeown, who had his ribs crushed whilst filming *Young Indiana Jones* for TJ in the summer. Since then he has had bronchitis, near-pneumonia and a series of debilitating colds. Like many others who've wintered in London, he sounds unhealthy.

Ian MacNaughton, director of the Python TV shows, rings from Germany having just seen episode one of *80 Days*. Apparently I'm now one of his mother-in-law's greatest favourites – along with Pavarotti and Boris Becker! She's 86.

Christmas Day. Wednesday, December 25th

Woke, I must admit, with that unsatisfactory feeling of doubt as to whether I shall psychologically be able to live up to the day. The piles of presents, the tablefuls of food and drink, the bonhomie expected all put demands on a system which really craves a quiet day in the study.

Helen has to get up and start cooking and I'm aware that she is probably as apprehensive as I am. But Rachel comes into bed with us and we open our stockings and this irrational Christmas spirit begins to flutter and grow.

Soon we're up and the house is full of the bright colours of the wrapped presents, and cards cover the kitchen walls and the family silver is on the table and all the weight of tradition and all the happy associations of Christmas begin to work, and then as Granny and Auntie C arrive and, much later, a Palin, Burd, Gibbins, Christmas rolls remorselessly into action.

And it works. We get hot and we eat and drink too much and the present piles are bigger than ever – 'Obscene!' says Helen when she sees them all together.

I am given a Norman Lewis book on India, a marvellous series of old French jigsaw maps, a new watch, a print of 1688 maps of the hemispheres by Tom and Lisa and a CCCP T-shirt from Will, on the day Gorbachev resigned as President and in the week the Soviet Union ceased to exist. Momentous times.

Walk up Parliament Hill in the dark. Long chat with Rachel, who loves the sixth form and is obviously great friends with a group of boys and girls rather than being exclusively with one. I enjoy her company and am proud of her openness and enthusiasm and common sense.

Friday, December 27th

At six go round to the Idles for a drink – first time I've seen my producer since before 'PTP'. His house seems even more *Dallas*-like than I remember, big, empty, warm rooms – the hangings and decorations impressive rather than cosy. Lily is walking now.

As if on cue, Jerry Hall, swathed in a showy scarlet dress, and much larger than I remember her, appears down the stairs. She's pregnant, that's why she's so big. I ascertain she's three weeks away from having Mick's third child. She doesn't look like someone who likes looking like this.

Eric's mother appears. Even Norah glitters expensively, as if she too has just come out of Aladdin's cave. She looks well and sounds strong and I'm pleased to see her.

Then Mick appears – impish, puckish – all the clichés really do apply. He's one of those people with a cheeky face – Eric being another.

Jerry and Mick seem fond of each other. Jerry is dreamily Texan,

Mick quickfire English. He bemoans, insincerely, having three children – and about to have a fourth. 'I'll 'ave to become a house husband ... give up going to work.'

1992

Monday, January 13th

Up in time for the eight o'clock news. Algerian elections cancelled as it seems the Arab fundamentalists will win, and at home politicians trying to talk over each other in macho encounters which leave the listener bewildered and embarrassed.

Rachel is 17 today. We've given her a black-leather school bag, books, a Cure T-shirt and a Mont Blanc fine-point pen. She's still in her room when I start work on the *Pole to Pole* book at nine. I'm pleased I'm here, having been absent for all the three other family birthdays last year.

Back to work. A thorough scan of all the source documents and a very slow start. Rachel and her friends fill the kitchen with the smell of toasted cheese sandwiches.

Tuesday, January 14th

To lunch at Odette's with TG. He's off to Madrid tomorrow and then on to Hollywood for the Golden Globes, for which his latest film *Fisher King* is entered in Comedy and Musicals section!

I tell him that TJ has rung me this a.m. to let me know, amongst other things, that he feels Roger Saunders is unfairly shackled in his Python sales efforts by our refusal to have the programmes dubbed or sold to commercial stations. TJ having been the prime supporter of the anti-dub position – this comes as something of a shock. But he feels the shows have now made their impact on all the people who need to know about them in their pristine form – and it no longer seems worth safeguarding them so jealously. In short, he wants the money, which is fine. TG says he doesn't feel motivated in any direction.

In the evening receive good news re *American Friends* French release. Ring Michel Burstein, our French distributor, to confirm. He says that they are all pleased, the reviews were generally good, but returns in the provinces significantly lower than in Paris.

Wednesday, January 15th

Taxi to Adelaide House for my first Meridian board meeting. Things seem to be going well. TVS messed up their judicial challenge to Meridian, and just before Christmas our licence to broadcast was assured. Meridian bought TVS' studios in Southampton for 13 million, which is considered by those in the know to be a bargain.

Thursday, January 16th

Humiliation at the Post Office today. I have forgotten my glasses and cannot see to fill in a Recorded Delivery slip. Bassant, behind the counter, gently takes it from me. 'I can do that, Michael.'

At eleven o'clock William is packed and ready to be returned to Oxford. Another grey day, but at least his two flatmates are installed already at 35 Jericho Street, so there's someone to welcome him. He sounds more optimistic about this term – resigned to the flat, looking forward to work he enjoys – the Romantics – and determined to get out and involved in more things. I ask him about plans after Oxford. He still seems to like the idea of film school, but travel and writing come in there too.

Tuesday, January 21st

Have jolly chats with Beryl Bainbridge re Polar matters. I ask Beryl if she'd been anywhere near the Pole. 'Oh God, no!' she says ... 'I was once going to spend the night in a tent on the Heath.'

Tuesday, January 28th

To Cleese's for dinner. Things have changed there – the trees outside in the front garden have gone and been replaced by paving. Houses appear to have been knocked together – the swimming pool is operating, paintings plaster the wall.

Talk to JC about *GBH* – 'Fifty-five per cent absolutely marvellous ... and' JC pauses seriously, as if calculating the price of coal ... 'thirty-five per cent rubbish.' But it sounds as if Robert Young is restored to favour as the preferred director of a *Wanda* follow-up.

JC wants me to go and hunt the yeti with him; sometime in spring '93.

Saturday, February 1st

Helen up at the hospital to see her friend Greta who was taken in on Friday morning with serious breathing problems. Helen can only talk about the other occupants of the ward. The man who clears his throat horribly and always concludes his performance with a deeply felt 'Fucking hell!' He's known as Fucking Hell. There's a farting woman opposite, and a lady who isn't quite the full sixpence who takes her clothes off all the time.

Helen goes out to dinner with the badminton group, Rachel to the cinema with her 'posse'. I go to Cibo, to dinner with Michael Barnes. He's asked to go Italian ... 'My left hand isn't all that good at the moment.'

He likes to be early, so at seven o'clock opening time he's ensconced with a scotch and water, and the wine ... 'anything, so long as it's red'. He does seem genuinely relieved, as well as glad, to have me back, and reminds me that there was an element of danger to the journey, there were risks, which I'd become less aware of once we were working. Was Helen worried about me? I've never asked!

Michael's physical condition seems to have deteriorated. He sits heavily and stands with difficulty. His concentration is not as acute as I remember and he is quite alarmingly unsteady when leaving the restaurant and uncoiling himself from the taxi at his hotel in Tottenham Court Road.

One of the problems of going out by cab is that most of the drivers now know me and want to talk. One has caught a glimpse of our sitting room ... 'I thought you must be a brain surgeon with all them books ...'

Tuesday, February 4th

Good writing weather and I do get on, head down on *Pole to Pole* and hoping crises will not intrude. By the time I stop, I'm through Novgorod and heading for Dno! Pile of letters and requests as usual. A fine new book about Shrewsbury School places me (chronologically) as the last on a list of selected Old Salopians, but has my name wrong. So the list begins with Andrew Downes (1549–1628) Regius Professor of Greek at Cambridge, described by contemporaries as 'a walking library', and ends with Michael Edwin (*sic*) Palin (1943–): comedian, actor, writer. I share a column with Ingrams, Rushton and John Peel.

Thursday, February 6th

Lunch with Beryl Bainbridge at Trattoria in Parkway. She chose the place, I set up the lunch. Both of us try and read the menu blackboard they stick in front of you without our glasses, both admit we can't see a thing.

Beryl is very funny, easy, entertaining, gossipy company. She's being rung up by Terry Waite.

He's writing a book on his experience and has approached Beryl for help and guidance. But lately he rang so late that Beryl confesses she had to have a scotch or two to keep up with him. They discussed captivity ... "'Go on Terry,' I said, sort of joking, "you probably really enjoyed it all a bit ... being chained up to the wall"' to which TW had apparently replied that he had found much of the experience beneficial and he was a better man because of it.

She's writing a book about the Crimea at the moment, but has no idea where the Crimea is.[1] 'Up near Leningrad isn't it?' For once I can use the European fold-out map at the back of my diary to good effect ... 'Oh, right down there!'

Letters and calls, then a determined sprint on the writing before going out to dinner with Robert Young. Hugh Laurie and wife Jo and a neighbour, an older man, are there already. Stephen Fry arrives a little later having flown in from Los Angeles that morning. There's talk of doing his book *The Liar* as a film.

Stephen tells me at dinner that *Round the World* has started something called The Palin Effect – actors and comics wanting to do documentaries.

Sunday, February 9th

Watch Colin Thubron on *South Bank* talking about why he travels. Though he's very serious and intense, I like what he says about the urge to travel. It's not escape, it's more about enhancement of your life. Widening horizons, physically and mentally. And the video footage of his entry into Bukhara was magical. A real feeling of a search.

---

1 Beryl Bainbridge's novel was published as *Master Georgie*.

Tuesday, February 11th

Drive across town to the Ladbroke Arms in Notting Hill Gate to meet Roger for a spot of 'beak-dipping' over our pints.

R tells me that Paul Hamann, the new head of current affairs, called the department producers together and announced that they must search for a new Palin, as the current one would obviously be working for Meridian in the future. I'm a little hurt at this. After all, I've announced no public commitment other than to remaining freelance. The fact that no-one at the BBC has ever approached me about a future working relationship is quite odd.

Anyway, the name that came up as the new Palin was ... Ruby Wax.

Thursday, February 13th

Dinner with Alan Bleasdale at the Halcyon Hotel. He's lost weight, after dieting, and looks good. At dinner he tells us, prefaced with 'I don' wan any glass-clinking or anything like that', that *On the Ledge*, the play he's been working on for almost the same time as *GBH*, has been accepted by the National Theatre 'on the sixth rewrite!'[1]

Only Alan could describe so candidly his delight at receiving the fax from Richard Eyre. 'I just wanted to hug someone, to lift them up in the air, but there was no-one there. Not even me dad was in. So I just went round the house doing war-whoops!'

Whilst writing this up, I hear from Kath that I have been nominated for Best Actor at BAFTA, along with Lindsay, John Thaw and Tom Bell – and there's no-one in the house to tell!

Tuesday, March 10th

Started on Sudan writing at nine. Well into flow now. Feel that there is a chance of reaching my goal of Equator by BAFTA.

Receive a nod from LWT, who are broadcasting the proceedings this year, to the effect that if I should win an award I am permitted to make a short speech of thanks. In view of the length of the proceedings they would be obliged if it could be confined to '0.20'.

To a party at Methuen's new HQ in Kendrick Mews, South Ken.

1 *On the Ledge* was eventually first presented at the Nottingham Playhouse in 1993.

Interesting turnout. Michael Frayn, beaming and friendly, Peter Nichols, almost a Frayn lookalike, guarded and not forthcoming. Robert H,
Patrick Barlow, Terry J, David Nobbs, the same as ever. Ivor Cutler,[1]
formidably eccentric – Geoffrey has to find guests to talk to him, rather
like finding meat for an animal. Champagne out of plastic cups. Jolly
nice group of authors, I decide.

Friday, March 13th

An interesting film idea via Angela Elbourne. A proposal that I should
be seen in the US trying to track down Bruce Springsteen; using his
songs as clues and as an excuse to visit various unvisited parts of the
US, viz. Asbury Park. In the end we would meet and exchange whatever.
The idea that intrigued the authors of this proposal is the difference between English public-school, middle-class comedy writer and American
working-class rock idol – or the similarity. Also on my desk, a treatment
called 'Orphans of Empire', a look at the remaining island colonies.

Monday, March 16th

By cab to lunch in Brompton Road with Teddy Warwick and John Peel.
This is one of those events which has taken the best part of ten years to
come to fruition. It's been mentioned so often on our Christmas cards
as to become a joke, but today here we are, gathered together in the almost religiously neat and silent offices of Melody Radio, who are paying
Teddy good money to come out of retirement and help them with some
of his BBC expertise.

I ask about the station. It turns out to be owned by Lord Hanson, very
much as his private plaything. DJs have strict instructions to announce
only the record and the artist – anything more, any statement of opinion or personal prejudice, is spotted by the Lord himself and noted in a
cautionary fax.

J Peel lives in Suffolk most of the time and, beyond his own show,
mixes not at all with fellow DJs. He remembers less about himself at
Shrewsbury than I do, but says he owes an enormous amount to Hugh
Brooke, our housemaster, who appreciated humour and spirit and, in
a way, non-conformity. JP says that Brooke purposely gave him Study

---

1 Ivor Cutler, Scottish poet and songwriter.

13 because it was near the library and it would annoy all those people listening to their classical music.

We talk about Zimbabwean music and his inordinate (this is one of those words he's very fond of using) love for The Four Brothers, who his wife Sheila got along to his 50th birthday as a surprise. We share an inability to dance – crippled by shyness at early dance classes, and a predilection (that's another word he might use) for football.

By the end it feels as if the three of us have had lunch every week for the last ten years. John Peel Ravenscroft – as he was known when we both, briefly, were in the same house at Shrewsbury School – has very clear likes and dislikes (Springsteen is one of the latter, Lonnie Donegan one of the former) and is a storehouse of odd facts about the kitsch of the music biz – e.g. that somewhere in the USA there is Twitty City, dedicated to the life, work and good name of Conway Twitty.[1]

Thursday, March 19th

To Adelaide House for my second Meridian board meeting.

Clive, who clearly doesn't like board meetings and finds them a tiresome necessity, bustles through, but every now and then questions are raised which manage to halt the proceedings.

Lots of figures, and a nice human moment at the end when Shreela Flather persists in pushing her 'help for the community' suggestions. Meridian's execs firmly try to put the lid on this, saying that our duties extend only to making television programmes, but Shreela persists … 'For just £50.00 we could have a minibus to take old people out.' She is so patently sincere, and yet it is so touchingly far from what Clive is in the business for, that I have to smile.

Sunday, March 22nd

I edit the Ethiopian section. It does not excite as it should do. I think I have description fatigue.

Off to BAFTA at 5.45 in an LWT Jaguar. The journey is smooth, but the arrival a mess. In the back way, so we miss the bank of photographers which Helen and I rather look forward to once a year. Instead, as we step out, a ferocious woman shouts at us: 'Picture with the Jaguar, please!'

---

1 Conway Twitty, American country and western singer. Born Harold Lloyd Jenkins.

Then an uncertain researcher leads us to the stage where I'm shown what is required of me as an award presenter.

I begin to pick off a few celebs including Cliff, who is the most extraordinary 50-year-old I have ever seen. Only a trace of tightening skin indicates that he's anything more than 13 years old, and his neat, eager, clean manner all contribute to the feeling I have that he must be kept in a box. That's right, he is like a living doll.

This is a good time to be a nominee, as you can rake in a few congratulations before becoming, most likely, an ignored loser. Stephen Fry cautions me not to leave early as there is a special award which he's presenting which will be of interest. He's looking quite debonair and has lost weight ... 'Not eating, really. Well, I was 17 stone!'

The table is left to right – Helen, who was sat elsewhere but has moved her name-place to be next to me, Beth Worth from Channel 4, then Dan Massey, sporting a hussar's moustache for *Heartbreak House*, and lady friend, Di and Robert Lindsay (hair cut, blow-dried, immaculately styled, beard trimmed), Alan and Julie, Michael Grade and his perky new girlfriend. Alan has his head down already, a bull against the world.

Lindsay Duncan, who I wish had been on our table, is very funny. She'd seen my photograph, she says enticingly, before adding 'at the car wash'. I remember just after Christmas going into my favourite Afro-wash place under St Pancras arches and suffering the embarrassment at having to be photographed for their celebrity board. 'You looked very happy,' says Lindsay.

I'm backstage with Dame Edna and Hale and Pace and a nervous, quite sweet Jason Donovan, when I hear that *Prime Suspect* has taken the Best Drama Serial Award from *GBH*, *Coronation Street* and two others.

We win Best Music and Robert takes the Best Actor so we have our celebrations.

Our director Robert Young had had the best thing happen to him, which was to be given the special award that Stephen Fry so elegantly presented.

Friday, March 27th: Stranraer–London

Returning from Glasgow, after a *Pole to Pole* writing blitz, I find the flight is full and by extraordinary coincidence many of the passengers are people from Channel 4 whom I last saw at BAFTA, six nights ago. Beth Worth brings me up to date on the scandalous goings on over *GBH*'s 'Drama Serial' defeat by *Prime Suspect*.

Knowing that Alan had heard he had won, Michael Grade rang the jurors on Monday morning. Four of them – a majority – confirmed they'd voted for *GBH*. The non-voting chairman of the 8-strong jury was Irene Shubik,[1] an avowed enemy of Verity Lambert. It all sounds absolutely in the spirit of *GBH*.

Thursday, April 2nd

Out to Shepherd's Bush to see the rough cuts of episodes three and four of '*PTP*'.

Disappointed by a 'holiday' programme feel to the start of episode three. The pictures are fine, but it lacks much quirkiness – just endless shots of me walking, travelling, and in the company of conventional characters in surroundings which most people know about anyway. It's the Mediterranean travel brochure world, and doesn't come alive for me until we reach Egypt – after which there is no problem.

But it is the Sudan episode, number four, which will, I think, become a classic; like the dhow, it has the elements of unfamiliarity, danger and improvisation. Nigel's photography on the roof of the Sudanese train is breathtakingly beautiful. Best of all, as someone said afterwards, it needs the minimum of music or commentary, a simple structure holding together a feast of rich material.

Saturday, April 4th

The story of the potential BAFTA scandal over the *GBH* vote is now public since four members of the jury broke the confidentiality rule, claiming that they wrote to the BAFTA chairman saying they had voted for *GBH* and it should therefore have had the majority without any casting vote being needed. An inquiry is under way, but *The Sunday Times* is already calling it Baftagate.

---

1 Irene Shubik, television producer associated with *The Wednesday Play* and *Play for Today*.

Sunday, April 5th

To dinner at TG's invitation with Ray Cooper and Robin Williams at the Caprice.

Robin looks younger and calmer than when I last saw him. His hair has been dyed a sort of light chestnut for his latest film, and I notice he barely drinks. Robin is one minute the earnest, interested conversationalist – a good listener and a good laugher – and the next the demon of improv grabs him and he wrestles in the grasp of what appears to be an elaborate and spontaneous beast of invention.

Sometimes he can extricate himself, but only with considerable effort. Usually he just lets himself go with it – sometimes raising his voice to a shout, but generally not involving anyone other than those immediately around him.

It is a wonderful gift, sometimes eye-streamingly funny, such as his quite magnificent creation of the Indian warrior who rings Kevin Costner about *Dances with Wolves* royalties ...

But generally it makes for an awkward evening. Conversation is possible, but everyone is waiting for the fire to start blazing.

I don't really remember the food.

Monday, April 6th: London–Mountrath

To Dublin, from Heathrow, on the 9.05 flight. Collect my car, and begin to pick my way along the maze of roads to the west of Dublin.

The Irishness of things appeals to me. Ireland may try to look like any other bland and prosperous Western European country, but it is neither. Instead of 'Dual Carriageway Ahead' it has signs saying 'Dual Carriageway Now'.

Turning in the gates of Roundwood House an hour and 40 minutes after leaving the airport.

Carry my bag into a strip-wood-floored hall hung with old portraits, doors on either side and ahead a staircase and a Venetian-style window letting in plenty of light and matching its companion above the front door. A lop-eared middle-aged man with an ironic smile emerges unhurriedly from a side door. 'You're the Cleese man,' he greets me, not at all disagreeably, but I'm a little huffed. 'No, I'm the Palin man.'

No harm done, he shows me upstairs – rooms off a curious criss-cross-balustraded gallery. Big room at the front – yellow, mustard-yellow, chosen in preference to violent-green one on the other side.

They make me a basket full of sandwiches which I eat downstairs in another tall, airy room, with some tea. There are no curtains at Round-wood – all wooden shutters and few soft furnishings – everything is good, old, antique but gone to seed.

But am very happy about my broad Georgian writing desk, which I move across one of the deep-set windows so I can look out onto the lawn, across which ducks potter periodically, to a field with big, oddly pollarded trees, in which three racehorses while away the day.

Down for a drink at a quarter to eight. An English couple – he with Denis Healey flying eyebrows, grey hair, probably late 50s early 60s, both very nice *Good Hotel Guide* types.

A log and peat fire has been lit and I order myself a Bushmills malt and settle down with the curiously cold *Kindness of Women* [by J. G. Ballard]. We are to eat communally, which I must say is something I dread.

A third guest, besides myself, joins us. She's a gnomic little American lady. Quite a bluestocking – possibly even a writer. Even the most inconsequential story delivered in measured, elegant tones and richly ornamented with figures of speech and self-conscious irony. In short, a bit of a pain.

The owner then takes them all off to the pub – but I'm tired and must make a good start at nine tomorrow, and I know that when he says they'll be back at 11.30 he's Irish and doesn't mean it.

Friday, April 10th: Mountrath–London

My week at Mountrath produced a lot of words and I only hope the quality matches the quantity. By one o'clock today I've added nearly 15,000 words to my *Pole to Pole* tally, and am within striking distance of the end. In fact, totting up on the plane on the way back, I have now written over the 93,000 total that I had set myself.

At breakfast, Rosemary, the owner's wife, tells me that my premonition about the election result was right. The Conservatives have won and with a working majority. Major's last-minute appeal to the voters to go with the trend 'in almost every other country in the world' and reject socialism seems to have worked.[1]

---

1 1992 Election result. The Conservatives, led by John Major, retained power with 336 seats against Labour's 229.

On the plane back read Raymond Briggs' *The Man*, which they want me to read for audio cassette. Absolutely marvellous.

Rachel very cut up about the return of the Tories, but Glenda Jackson has taken Hampstead and Frank Dobson, our local man, has not suffered from the lack of my vote – he's in with a five per cent swing.

As if to rattle me back into city life, there is an explosive boom, with an after-boom, from somewhere outside. Helen rushes upstairs. It's reported later as a massive bomb in the City, the biggest ever used on the mainland. A bit of Ireland has returned with me.[1]

Saturday, April 11th

Another distant but frighteningly powerful blast just after we have gone to bed. I make it eight or nine minutes after one o'clock. Switch on the radio for information. Nothing official, but callers, mostly from the Cricklewood, Hendon and Finchley districts, ring in to tell the same story – windows rattled, houses shaken. I'm asleep by the time Helen hears the news that a bomb has exploded under a flyover near the M1 junction with the North Circular.

Thursday, April 16th

To work at nine o'clock, and after an hour I know I shall finish today. Which means that the morning is a little more relaxed than usual. Will, Rachel and Helen are all around. Rachel has drawn us a wonderful wedding anniversary card – my nasal hairs, penchant for pottery shops and dark-brown bread all noted.

I began writing *Pole to Pole* in January – on Rachel's birthday – sharing the book with the rest of my life, trying to fit it in with people, ideas, half-projects, scripts to read, etc. This meant that I never allowed myself time to become absorbed in it, to feel the pace and weight of it, to address the subject matter as anything more than another chore after five months of heavy work.

But since the end of March, and especially through the week at Mountrath, I gave it the priority and the total commitment it needed – and, as I say, I feel on top of the work, and sort of cleaned out; cleansed

---

1 The Baltic Exchange bombing: three people were killed and £800 million worth of damage was done.

by a period of three weeks of, for me, monastic solitariness.

And I know that I never want to go back to the world of trying to satisfy everyone else's demands. I have achieved much of what I want to achieve. Though I don't feel I'm out of the rat race – I no longer believe in it enough to want to win. And that's a start.

At a quarter to four I type 'The End'.

Thursday, April 23rd

An interview with a very bright, chirpy ex-air hostess who now edits the BA staff magazine. One thought-provoking question. If I was able to travel in time would I go for the future or the past? I unhesitatingly plump for the past, which I suppose betrays my literary and artistic preferences over scientific curiosity. Choose Ancient Egypt or Elizabethan England – tempted by the prospect of going to the world premiere of *Hamlet*.

Monday, April 27th

Graphic dream that Helen was having another baby. Couldn't get the midwife, so there was just her and me. (I think I blame *Kindness of Women* for graphic description of something similar.) H lying on a bed with placenta and afterbirth all in amongst the duvet – telling me quite cheerfully that the baby is 'in there somewhere'. I find it but am unable to tell its sex without my glasses on.

Thursday, April 30th

Lunch at Odette's with TG before collecting manuscript. TG good company as ever, but he is working under pressure on the *Quixote*. 'I'm getting boils and my back is going …' he says cheerfully.

He has two offers of finance – 20 mill dollars from Jake Eberts[1] and 23 mill from 'the richest man in France'. Now he's suffering doubts about whether the script will be ready for his projected October shoot and if it is ready, whether it will be any good. He says that J Edgar Hoover would make a wonderful subject for a film. Calls him possibly

---

1 Jake Eberts, Canadian-born film producer, co-founder of Goldcrest with David Puttnam.

the most important and influential figure in post-war America!

He's touchingly keen to do something together again, and promises to send me work so far on the 'Defective Detective' idea, which he says that Richard LaGravenese – his *Fisher King* writer – has not been able to get right.

I feel almost guilty at having completed a book when TG is having such a struggle with his script – but that's the way it goes – we inspire each other and keep each other going forward.

Saturday, May 2nd

Wake Rachel, as instructed, before I go swimming. 'I think I'll give it a miss,' she says, before quite rapidly changing her mind – and we end up with a swim, followed by coffee, orange juice and croissants at Patisserie Val's – first performance of this ritual for a long time.

Then to the bookshops of the Charing Cross Road for Rachel's Shakespeare and trade union books and my Arctic exploration literature. Feel rather pleased to be able to go to Stanford's and ask for maps of the Arctic, when everyone else is scrabbling over the South of France.

May 4th to May 23rd: North Pole journey as described in Pole to Pole. *Unable to shoot this section last summer because of the fragile state of the sea ice.*

Wednesday, May 27th

Have put all other activities on hold – shopping, lunching and cinema-going – until I have completed the Arctic chapter.

I looked into Simon Brett's *Faber Book of Diaries*, and found V Woolf for May 25th 1932 – almost 60 years ago today – in dreadful state of self-doubt. 'What a terrific capacity I possess for feeling with intensity. I'm screwed up into a ball, can't get into step ... see youth, feel old; no, that's not quite it; ... hatred of my own brainlessness and indecision; the old treadmill feeling, of going on and on and on for no reason; contempt for my lack of intellectual power ... reading without understanding ...'

Both these passages were relevant to how I felt and therefore curiously comforting. I even checked on Virginia's dates and found that she too was 49 years old at the time of writing.

Friday, May 29th

Ken Stephinson rings and tries to persuade me to rejoin him for a second *Great Railway Journey*. None of the foreign trips appeal – all too soon after *'PTP'* – but, just as I've decided on a positive negative, Ken mentions Ireland. Now that is tempting. Easy to get to, a country I like and which interests me, a country in which the railway is part of the political drama and a country in which there is no danger at all of a dull interview! By the end of the call I have virtually committed to my first job in 1993.

Thursday, June 4th

I am to spend the day ahead reading Raymond Briggs' latest book, *The Man*, for audio cassette.

To a small studio set back off a side road in Shepherd's Bush. Mike Carrington-Ward is producing the tape. Raymond Briggs is there. He is less assertive and outspoken in the flesh than in his writing. Gentle, really, and immediately likeable.

A small 13-year-old, smaller than 13-year-olds are normally, William Puttock, is there with his mother. He's being taken through his paces by the indefatigably ebullient Mike Ward, and after a coffee the two of us go into a hot little room where we are observed on closed-circuit TV, and rehearse about two-thirds of the story.

Others arrive during the day, including Raymond's long-term publisher, Julia MacRae, whom I liked a lot, and who was very complimentary about the reading, and a marketing lady who had a mock-up of the cassette sleeve with the words 'Read by Michael Palin' across it. William Puttock's mother spotted this straight away and said she hoped William's name would appear alongside mine. The marketing lady looked startled and smiled unconvincingly. She clearly thought the woman was mad.

Friday, June 5th

A programme called *A Stab in the Dark* has put a rather nasty little note through my door, informing me that in 'light-hearted' vein they have not only 'observed' my rubbish but have taken samples to form the basis of a film on their prog tonight. The reason being that I am, according to them, 'an environmentally conscious individual in the public eye', and it is my fate to have my 'commitment' tested.

I ring them up and they cheerfully admit to trespass and say that they won't be using any of my rubbish in the prog. They think they'll have more fun with Sting and Anita Roddick. 'A little squirt of malice' is how the producer put it. I think it just about sums him up.

Sunday, June 7th

Read of the latest lurid details of the Prince of Wales' marriage. Aside from the unhappy, if true, evidence of Diana's suicide attempts, the story seems to be so uncannily close to *Private Eye*'s Mills and Boon spoof of the couple as to further increase the case for the *Eye* being the most prescient and accurate organ of its generation.

Thursday, June 11th

To lunch at San Lorenzo with Robert Fox and David Pugh. Both very good company – we share similar likes and dislikes. They have contacted three directors for *The Weekend*. Mike Ockrent's secretary didn't ask about who or what the play was, just said he's busy for the rest of his life.

Alan Ayckbourn is Fox's front runner and the script will be sent to him. Fox's suggestion for the lead is Nigel Hawthorne, with which I very much concur.

Thursday, June 18th

At midday Steve A comes round, partly as my financial adviser, partly as producer, partly as friend.

Would like to have heard better news on the production side, but the 'AF' story is now so like a long, dull, grey day that the merest break in the cloud is reason for some celebration. Castlehill, the US distribution company, were enthusiastic at Cannes and should be coming up with an offer 'very soon'. Some money has come back from France after a Canal Plus sale, and the Antipodes saw its biggest success.

To Will Wyatt's BBC party for 'writers' at Leighton House. Jimmy Perry[1] looks splendid in cream suit, shirt and tie and shock of reddish-

---

1 Jimmy Perry, deviser with David Croft of *Dad's Army*.

blond hair. He's very complimentary about *GBH* – says that, at the very least, I should have shared the Best Actor Award.

Ken Trodd says he has something for me – 'September ... vicar with a bit on the side?' and Alan Plater wants to propose me for the Writers' Guild. 'Is it a lot of work? ...' 'No, just money.'

Tuesday, June 23rd

I'm due at the Groucho – for an hour with *Me* magazine, and then a 'profile' or 'in-depth' for *She*. The *She* interviewer, Suzie Mackenzie, asks to be alone with me.

Suzie Mackenzie's style most disconcerting. If she wanted to put me on my guard and see my defences go up, she could not have done better.

After an hour and a half of largely uphill work, we adjourn to the bar, and both of us are immediately easier and more comfortable – she less inquisitorial, me less guarded, and for an hour we find ourselves talking about everything. She asks whether I have a sister and what she's doing and she's the first journalist I have told about Angela's suicide. I always want to talk about Angela – and it's women who can talk more openly about it. I can tell she desperately wants to use this in the interview, but I ask her not to.

I'm bumped into by Colin MacCabe,[1] who wheels me back into the Groucho for another glass of champagne and a proposal to write a series of five essays on the films that BFI has in its archives.

Later still, finish Ray Connolly's book about the Beatles' generation and, later still, lie awake worrying about how I could have been so indiscreet with a journalist. Had I been had – by flattery and feminine skills?

Saturday, June 27th

To St Margaret's Hall in Bethnal Green where I am to address the AGM of the Association for Stammerers. (I'd been warned by Travers Reid[2] that I might be there a long time.)

A small hall full of, I assume, stammerers, would be many people's idea of a great comic event. Considering the disabilities they come across with a certain dignity, considerable bravery, and otherwise just like any

1 Colin MacCabe, writer and academic on film.
2 A stammerer himself and President of Action for Stammering Children.

other gathering-together of people to make rather footling rules.

I read a three- or four-minute piece which I hastily assembled last night, then face questions from the floor. Pleased to find that I don't feel at all uncomfortable waiting for the questions to come, nor is there any shortage of them.

To an upper room for a drink (non-alcoholic). Two men I spoke to said that alcohol, far from loosening their tongues, makes their stammer worse. Developing techniques to avoid stammering is what they're all about and that's fascinating. Winston Churchill, one of the great orators of history, had a stammer and his rumbling start to sentences was not an oratorical tool but a stammer-avoidance technique.

Men are about five times more at risk than women.

Thursday, July 2nd

At the cutting rooms by twenty to ten.

We set to work on the commentary for *Pole to Pole* number one. Most of my timings are accurate and the words usually fit, so much of the time is spent examining and dissecting the lines themselves. There is a lot to say in this first episode – route and ground rules to be explained – and a lot of Frozen North to be described owing to lack of the right conditions for recording synch sound.

Mimi O'Grady from the production office appears regularly to take pages back and have them retyped. Then into the recording studio.

The first hour in the hot little box is dreadful. I find it difficult to be as spontaneously lively and involved when I'm surrounded by technical equipment, headphones, green lights, disembodied voices from the control panel – 'He could do that better …' 'Can you get rid of his breath?'

It requires a great effort of stamina, concentration and sheer will-power not to shout 'Do it yourself then!' But I remember this is the way it was before and I know that it is important for every utterance to sound right. That's the pressure, but also the job I'm paid to do. So I drink water and more coffee and get my head down and gradually the effort decreases and the ease increases and we coast quite quickly through the last half.

Finish by a quarter to seven. Nine hours of almost unrelieved concentration leave me quite drained. All I want is a pint somewhere, far away from the hot theatre air.

End up in the Ladbroke Arms with Roger.

Roger is very special – full of life and the wisdom of experience without any of the superiority that might go with it. He's schoolboy and headmaster rolled into one.

Wednesday, July 8th

Trying to crack the commentary for show three. I cannot get the words to fall right; sentences are half formed, a sort of intellectual dyslexia sets in. I know what I want to say but I can't find how to say it.

Some progress. To lunch with JC. First time we've seen each other since his trip down the Nile and mine to the Pole.

I ask him about the therapy. He confesses to being very bored by it now. I decline the yeti film and JC reckons he will not have a *Wanda* follow-up ready now until spring of 1994.

I work on at episode three and suddenly the knack of commentary-writing returns. I remember lightness of touch – thoughts and observations glancing off the films themselves, not trying to compete or over-expand them. This is what will ultimately carry *Pole to Pole* as it did *80 Days*. I've all too often been intimidated by commentary – I've fallen into the trap of reproducing the sort of stuff I used to be so good at parodying.

Sunday, July 12th

Up at Chilton Hall to celebrate Veryan and Valerie's wedding.[1]

Chilly wind. Chilton looking more spruce – and the garden richer and more prodigious – this seems to be Valerie's influence. Derek and Joan Taylor are there, which is all the better for being unexpected.[2] They loved *80 Days*. Derek says George has gone rather serious about Natural Law and things and rather rubbed Derek up by ringing and asking if he was happy with his life and did he want to keep 'floundering around'. 'Not floundering, thank you George,' D had replied a bit testily.

Ann Hollis, wife of the vicar who gave the address, says to me at the end 'This must have been difficult for you.' In all honesty I have to say I haven't thought of it as being difficult. I'm pleased that Veryan is happy

1 Veryan, my brother-in-law, married for the second time to Valerie Stevens, a journalist.
2 Derek was the Beatles' publicist.

and Chilton seems to have lost some of its coldness. Angela never really liked it. Valerie loves it.

Friday, July 17th

Unduly worried about what I said to Suzie Mackenzie, the *She* journalist, about Angela – tried to ring her this week but she's gone on holiday. Talk to the features editor. Not a pleasant encounter. She suggested that nothing is ever 'off the record' with a journalist and irritatingly mentions Lynn Barber as a sort of role model and reference point.

I tell her what I've told Suzie – and my concerns for the Herbert family once it's into the cuttings and the hands of less scrupulous journalists. The features editor won't agree to let me see the copy in advance and puts forward silly objections.

Return a call from Puttnam who wants me to be a judge on the NCR non-fiction panel next year – with Princess Di. I accept. It only means reading four books.

Then by pick-up car down to Chelsea Harbour to be photographed for *She*.

Chelsea Harbour is one of the late-'80s boom developments. Half empty, like Docklands. Isolated and soulless. The Penthouse, on the market at over £3 million, has never been sold.

Monday, July 20th

Rachel leaves for the first day of a week's summer school history course, for which she won a bursary from Camden Council. She is diligent without ever being self-congratulatory or smug; she quietly organises her life (she quite independently has taken out an Amnesty subscription) and I admire her ability to be successful but retain her natural self-deprecating sense of irony. Which is a rather verbose way of saying I'm ever so proud of her.

Will has gone up to Oxford to clear the last remains out of the flat in Jericho Street which I think never brought him great happiness. Tom is working at Redwood Studios while André has two weeks' hols. H is helping restock the sitting room and Martin the painter has moved on to the stairs and hallway – all empty-walled and shrouded in dust sheets by mid-morning.

Work on with lightning flash and thunder rumbling and the rain is still coming down when I finish commentary four at midnight. When we get to bed a half-hour later, both cats are hiding under it.

Wednesday, July 22nd

Collected by car to go to the President's Evening of the RSNC/Wildlife Trusts Partnership.

David Attenborough wrote to me some weeks ago to ask if I would become one of the vice-presidents. The cause of nature conservation and the no-nonsense persuasiveness of David's letter must have combined to catch me on a good day and I said yes – and now I find myself in the only suit I have – a dark-brown wool-worsted quite unsuited to a sticky day like today – being welcomed into this large, marble and chandeliered chamber by Sir David and Lady Att. He's off to the Antarctic soon – but he's never yet been to the Pole.

He says the job of 'high-profile' officers like me, Julian Pettifer and himself is very often to attract and assuage sponsors ... 'And of course – the more they pollute, the more they give us,' he confides with a broad grin. He is quite an operator – able to play the establishment using flattery, humour and enormous charm, yet to hold the credibility of old cynics like myself by his intelligent self-awareness.

Friday, July 24th

Seizing the day, I write a letter resigning from the board of Meridian. Not confrontational or critical in any way – give myself more time to make programmes, which is what I feel I'm really good at.

Awkward, distracting morning in which I try to make a start on show three but find it difficult whilst the Meridian thing remains unresolved. Have to keep going into the garden, where Will is reading *Foucault's Pendulum* in the sun, to find Helen and check with her that I'm doing the right thing.

I never was that interested in running a company, or helping run a company, least of all one in the dull Southern area, or being confined to one particular company. H pinpoints the area that has really prompted my withdrawal – 'You don't want to be bothered with the internal politics.'

Roger Laughton calls back after lunch. To my great relief he is understanding, even humorous about it. He makes no attempt to persuade me to stay, makes a joke about my writing 'the letter we all want to write' and compliments me on expressing my feelings so 'elegantly'. He suggests I send the letter on Monday, by which time he will have been able to prepare Clive [Hollick, the chairman] for the news.

Saturday, July 25th

Read in a weekly TV paper that *GBH*'s repeat audience is just over two million – which surprises me, as did the low figure for the first screenings. I can only conclude that audiences prefer good, clean, escapist fun and have lost their appetite for controversy. TV is sold much more nowadays as a branch of advertising – reflecting its values and techniques. I think that the nineties are for *The Darling Buds of May*, not *GBH*. No-one wants to change the world any more.

Tuesday, July 28th

At St Paul's Covent Garden for Joan Sanderson's[1] memorial service. Glorious summer's day – bright sunshine, cloudless skies, dry air. At St Paul's the vicar is escorting a muttering, grubby man out of the church and trying to be nice to him at the same time. 'Yes ... you wait outside ...'

Quite full, Alan Bennett next to Jo Tewson at the back, Tim West gives an address. Good, rousing, uncomplicated hymns – 'Fight the Good Fight', 'He Who Would Valiant Be'. The batty man remains outside shouting 'Wankers!' at us, occasionally quite loudly.

Suzanne Webber rings to say that, following big orders, the first print run of *Pole to Pole* will be 130,000. (It was 15,000 on *80 Days*.)

Sunday, August 9th

Carol Cleveland rings – very pert and perky. 'I expect you know why I'm ringing.'

... No idea. 'I read about your film "The Adventure" with all the Pythons in it, and I hear it's going ahead, and well ... to be blunt, I hope there'll be a part for me.' Turns out it's some snippet she's read in *TV*

1 Joan Sanderson, imperious actress of comedy, particularly remembered for one *Fawlty Towers* episode. She starred in the *Ripping Yarn* 'Roger of the Raj' and *East of Ipswich*.

Quick giving a lot of completely fabricated information.

Best of the letters: request from Auberon Waugh for me to present the third Literary Review Poetry Award (Alec Guinness and Lucinda Lambton did the first two). 'You are the only people in public life whom the entire staff of *Literary Review* admires'!

Thursday, August 13th

To Liverpool Street by nine to catch the 9.30 to Norwich.

Driven to Richard Clay, the printers, where a machine is churning out sheets of *Pole to Pole*.

Five thousand sheets an hour flop gently onto the stack. Extraordinary to see the fruits of my solitary labour now being processed by half a dozen men, and occupying a million-pound machine 24 hours a day for more than a week.

Then on to Bungay, where Clay's have their HQ.

Satanic Verses was printed here in Bungay. A perfect place to keep it quiet. Apparently they approached the local constabulary to discuss possible security problems, but the threat of Muslim fundamentalists in Bungay was not considered likely.

Friday, August 21st

Drink at lunchtime with Roger M to discuss a Meridian project. Roger Laughton has asked if we could supply four 30-minute documentaries. Over a pint or two at the Ladbroke Arms, with black pudding lunch and sun warming us pleasantly through the open window, I agree to a start date of October '93 – that is presuming we can come up with some ideas drawn from the region.

Tuesday, August 25th

Clem rings early to say that he's just watched programme one with nearly all its bits sewn together and he is very, very pleased. 'It works in the living room,' he enthuses.

Also, have received word that John Hughman[1] is in hospital after a

---

1 John Hughman, actor who was one of the cast of the Jones and Palin *Complete and Utter History of Britain* TV series in 1969.

fall and a serious illness (some sort of blood poisoning) and I go over to see him in the afternoon. He's at St Mary's Paddington in what appears to be a geriatric ward. The premises are run-down and the whole place has a scuffed and demoralised appearance – but the staff are cheerful and patient.

John is lying, in a rather theatrical pose, on top of his bed, with a blanket draped ineffectually across his stomach. He has a clipped white beard, which rather suits him. But there is no disguising the fact that he has, in the year since I last saw him, become sad and old. His eyes wander unless he makes a real effort of concentration – the long, thin hands he was always so proud of twitch at the bedclothes. He's pleased to see me, but he is confused and obsessive about his 'financial problems' – rather like my mother was in the last years of her life.

An old Irish woman has lost her hearing aid and her visitor has to shriek to make her hear. 'No, you're not coming out tomorrow!' Across the way, an elderly man with watery eyes and a bowed head (a head which must have been stoutly handsome and upright once) is being asked by the doctor 'How do you feel about an artificial limb?' – this again in a bellow.

Talk for half an hour. John remembers odd things but mainly looks wistfully unhappy. 'I've lost my zest for life,' he says.

Wednesday, August 26th

Turn my mind to finishing my speech for the *Literary Review* lunch. For some reason I can't crack it as I'd like to.

Down to the wine cellars of the Café Royal – amazing act of trust by the management to allow so many boozy hacks so close to endless racks of wine. Quite dark and rather confusing as a nice American girl introduces me around, apologising that Auberon Waugh, who invited me with flattering letters, has this morning been taken ill – some internal haemorrhage.

After a glass of wine we're all led into a dungeon laid for a banquet.

At various moments during the meal a vivacious and apparently supremely self-confident girl who looks like the young Mia Farrow gets up and announces that she will sing – then goes into Kurt Weill songs.

Richard Ingrams then sets the ball rolling. He is very funny – big and grumpy but neither churlish nor ill-mannered. Tremendous Les Dawson-like delivery. At one point, after mentioning Julie Burchill's name, he shakes his head and mutters darkly and incomprehensibly for almost 15 seconds. Lynn Barber watches adoringly.

Sunday, August 30th: London–Norwich

Gale-force winds blowing as Helen and I leave Oak Village about 10.30 to watch Tom's Hapkido black belt grading in Norwich.

Two others besides Tom are doing black belts, three others 1st Dans. There is a certain formality to the procedure, with bows to the Union Jack and pledges to the flag at the beginning and then much oriental bowing before every stage of the grading.

They must jump over six people and end with a roll, they must break three wooden boards in one movement, break tiles with their feet after jumping up and off a wall, and finally leap over three people and kick-break a breeze block.

It's painful to watch, what with all the time willing Tom to do well and not hurt himself. At intervals a fierce wind shook the building and sent leaves streaming past the window.

Tom was duly awarded his white jacket and black belt.

I watch, like a father in a maternity ward, as the new belts line up for a photograph, all a little awkward apart from Tom, whose great Cheshire Cat smile breaks out and seems to affect everyone.

Friday, September 4th

Kath[1] comes round at five with a fresh supply of work. Lots of letters done. She warns me of the massiveness of the BBC Books publicity campaign. 'You'll need a disguise after this.'

Tell her my idea for a play on the explorer theme. Small expedition, all men, setting out on long and arduous five-month journey together. After three weeks discover one of them is a woman. Kath said they should perhaps all turn out to be women.

Monday, September 7th

Work through the final commentary. I find all sorts of holes in it. It wrote itself quickly and smoothly over the weekend, but in the cold light

1 Kath James, my PA, later Kath Du Prez.

of Monday morning much of it seems slight and insubstantial.

Out with H to dinner with Dan and Laura Patterson[1] in Chalcot Road. Gary Lineker and Michelle and Stephen Fry and his sister Jo the other guests.

Gary L is laid-back, agreeable. His skin is fascinating, very smooth and soft. He's like a young Samburu boy.

He tells the most wonderful stories of the evening – quite late, when everyone's about to go – usually about Gazza. 'He's a 12-year-old, always will be.' He sounds worse than any 12-year-old I've ever met. He would do his business, almost anywhere, often leaving a steaming offering on the bench in the changing room. He would shoot at people with an air-gun, and could be brutally carried away with paint-sprays. His mischief was continuous and, from the sound of it, vacuous – but sometimes horribly funny.

Gary professed great admiration for the player Steve Sedgley, who could fart the tune of 'When the Saints'.

Wednesday, September 9th

Out in the evening to see *Someone Who'll Watch Over Me* – Frank McGuinness' new play transferred to the Vaudeville. David Pugh is greeting his first-night audience.

I ask David P about *Weekend* casting. Denholm Elliott was our new choice, but David tells me that he is dying of AIDS. Can hardly take this in amongst the swirl of well-wishers and starers. The agent who told David this, ever the opportunist, has suggested another client – Ian Richardson.

Thursday, September 10th

On several occasions yesterday I was told by various readers of the *Guardian* that I had been called 'boring' by Lynn Barber (along with Norma Major and Felicity Kendal). I must say I wasn't much concerned – but a letter from Lynn arrives this morning – full of apologies – she'd been misquoted, of course it wasn't true. 'Nice, sane, straightforward' people are not those she can write about without it becoming a bit boring. I'm quite chuffed by the whole episode – and a letter

1 Dan Patterson is a writer and comedy producer who created *Whose Line Is It Anyway?*

from Lynn Barber bearing the words 'Oh God I am sorry' has to be valuable!

Tuesday, September 15th

The next two days are high-profile, Meridian Broadcasting days.

The first production meeting on *A Class Act*.[1] Meet, for the first time, Jo Wright, warm and welcoming, Kim Fuller and director Les Blair, a compact, bearded Mancunian who made *Law and Order*.

The meeting is quite low-key – we all say how we're looking forward to it. There are 12 days to shoot everything, which is tight. Blair, on the other hand, is agreeably loose about the actual shooting.

Then a rehearsal ahead of tomorrow's Meridian advertisers' launch.

Drafts of speeches are read at a podium resembling as closely as possible conditions at BAFTA tomorrow. Notes are given by a pair of women who seem to be in charge. 'Alan, sound as though you mean it …' 'Richard, don't look down' and so on.

Wednesday, September 16th

To BAFTA by eleven o'clock. The Rogers and Richards look tired. This advertising bullshit is not really what they want to be spending their time on. There has been some technical problem with the video inserts.

At 12.45 the first showing – largely for advertising managers of the major companies – Sainsbury's, Weetabix, etc. – gets under way. All goes smoothly except the sales director's speech which is incomprehensible.

The second presentation goes more smoothly. Clive and Sue Hollick very enthusiastic afterwards.

No-one asks about my resignation from the board.

Friday, September 18th: London–Sheffield

Packing and preparing for Sheffield this p.m.

At half past one we set off. The sun disappears and a stickily warm haze of low damp cloud comes down.

To the university – main building. I'm greeted by Professor Blake, the

---

1 *A Class Act*. Meridian TV's first in-house comedy series. A vehicle for the many talents of Tracey Ullman and written by Ian La Frenais and Dick Clement.

Public Orator, who is to commend me for a doctorate, then sidetracked away to the main quadrangle of this tall, classically red-brick university building to be photographed.

Five or six hacks offer me parrots on sticks and Australian bush hats with corks. As I'm wearing the red robe and mortar board of a Doctor of Letters I think they can hardly expect me to hold parrots.

The Vice-Chancellor is a Welshman with a naughty smile who twice played for Manchester City Reserves. He's now a big influence at Sheffield Wednesday, and has been called in to try and improve Trevor Francis's 'man-management' techniques.

At seven o'clock the V-C takes me away to be robed up. Procession very efficiently organised by the Marshal and his assistant, both of whom carry long rods. We wind our way into the Firth Hall – tall, imposing space, well-filled with graduands and their supporters.

I am the first to be installed. I have to stand on the stage whilst a five-minute paean of praise is read out. It's a nicely judged piece, and ends quite touchingly after a quick run through 49 years of my life. Then I'm led to the V-C, who formally installs me as a Doctor of Letters 'in honoris causa'.

I've been grinning manfully and patiently for so long that I now need a few minutes' break. Only get it when I'm in the car, Helen driving, on the misty M1 back to London.

Back home we both agree that it was a very enjoyable occasion – quite undaunting – and the people amazingly friendly. Helen says it's the first time, she thinks, that she's actually been in bed with a Doctor.

Saturday, October 10th

JC rings to ask if he can bring his 93-year-old mother to the *'PTP'* screening on Friday. Also reveals that his latest film idea is based on the old Zoo saga that I wrote with TJ all those years ago – the big animals v the small. Wants to know how I would play the keeper of the insect house!

Friday, October 16th

At half past ten down to the Groucho with a driver who does things like nod at my scraped Mercedes wheel trim and tell me 'You'll have trouble with that later.' He's a member of a caravan club and for some reason wants to haul his caravan up to the North Cape of Norway. I tell him it's not worth it. He seems to have been everywhere but has no idea how to get to Dean Street.

Apparently another batch of mags are out with interviews I did last July; among them is *Me* magazine. Feel rather a fool going into one of the busy little Soho newsagents and asking if they have me.

Home and read the articles. Never feel it's a healthy pastime reading about myself. Do it out of fearful curiosity.

To CFS by seven for *Pole to Pole* cast and crew party – another screening, another evening to try and 'sparkle'.

All the Pythons there. JC prominent in row two. When, in my North Pole camera piece, I say I could go 'that way through Japan ... down that way through India ... but we've chosen the 30-degree line down through Russia and Africa', John lets out an audible 'Oh dear!' – very naughty as it does break everyone up.

But most people seem very satisfied afterwards. JC feels it is a much stronger start than *80 Days* and others say I seem much more relaxed without the pressure of the 80-day deadline.

Saturday, October 17th

Derek Taylor faxes – asking me to turn all my lights off for ten minutes at nine o'clock tomorrow night as a gesture of solidarity with the miners.

Monday, October 19th

Start the Week, on a cold Monday morning.

This morning I have two massive egos to lock horns with – Anthony Burgess and Broadway director Hal Prince. We're to be given 15 minutes each and the thought of Burgess and Prince having to stop what they're doing and listen to me for 15 minutes fills me with something approaching panic.

Delivered to BH at 8.40.

There, the most pleasant thing awaits, a complete surprise.

Burgess, lean with the bloodless skin colour you see on old people in hospitals, and a dry thatch of grey hair, belies his appearance with a bubbling, overflowing delivery, full of enthusiasms.

In little more than a minute he tells me of his admiration for everything I've been involved in, particularly *Life of Brian* – 'a profoundly religious film' – 'You were the centurion weren't you?' interrupts his wife, Liana – small, keen. *GBH* he thought the best thing of all – 'that brought a whole new performance out of you'. And so on.

He had sharp words of criticism for Zeffirelli, with whom he worked on 'The Life of Christ', when Zeffirelli expressed anger that Python should have been allowed to film on the same set as his in Monastir in Tunisia.

Tuesday, October 20th

To lunch at Odette's in Primrose Hill. First, business with Anne, then Roger, fresh-biked from Acton, joins us for a discussion about the documentary commitment to Meridian, provisionally called 'Down South'.

Roger comes up with a very strong idea – which is that I should join four of the region's local papers for a week.

Thursday, October 22nd

Prepare speech for my appearance as T2000 President at launch of Platform – rail users against privatisation – and out into action at eleven o'clock. A sunny morning, less bitter than of late; quite quickly down to the House of Commons. The security guard checks my bag – 'No mosquitoes in here, you know.' This is the first case of post-*Pole to Pole* street banter, which I shall have to get used to.

Walk down the towering, grey, imposing stone passages past groups of schoolchildren and lost foreigners. Rather reassured that in these days of IRA bombs and general twitchiness so many people are still allowed to poke around Parliament.

Up to Committee Room 12. Almost full. Read my piece – part Stephen Joseph's[1] work, part my own gut feelings. A few laughs. Afterwards I'm about to leave when a blind man next to me holds my scarf up – 'I think you forgot this,' he smiles.

Then across to LBC for appearance on Frank Bough's prog. Poor old Frank, now a fallen angel since he admitted visiting a bondage parlour, only a couple of years after admitting drugs and infidelity. He's sporting a ruddy tan though, and seems to have added a few pounds. He reminds

1 Stephen Joseph, executive director Transport 2000, later Campaign for Better Transport.

me for some reason of an old sea captain, weathered by the storms. No longer in charge of the big liners, but quite happy in an old tub.

Sunday, October 25th: London–Norwich

A pile of Sunday newspapers – none of which have much good news for *Pole to Pole*. Only the curmudgeonly opinions of a bored, snapping Jeremy Paxman in the *Mail on Sunday*, a clever, moderately enthusiastic Craig Raine in *The Times*, a tired and bored John Naughton in the *Observer* and finally a fairly savage book review by Adam Nicolson in *The Times* again. He saw glimmers of good writing but felt the whole book had been sacrificed on the altar of TV programming.

Up to Norwich on the train. At the huge Bertrams warehouse within sight of the cathedral I am besieged by booksellers. 530 are attending the open day this year – a record number. Delia Smith, a solid, funny gardener called Geoff Hamilton and myself are the three speakers.

The gathering is treated to lunch and speeches, after which more hysterical signing before just catching the 4.05 back to London. Whingeing and grumpy though the day's reviews may have been, over 800 *Pole to Pole* books have been sold – and most of them signed – today.

Monday, October 26th

Start of the *Class Act* filming week. My first creative obligation to Meridian.

Collected at seven by Art Wilmot, a besuited Jamaican in a powerful BMW 5 Series which he drives fast, crossing from lane to lane as we negotiate the swift dual carriageways running north out of London into affluent, but not very beautiful, Bushey bungalow-land. We turn down a narrow little side road called Titian Avenue and into a red-brick Catholic girls' school which is home for the next two days.

Tracey arrives about the same time. She's refreshingly untheatrical and very funny.

Terry O'Neill is here to take photos of us, which kills some time. Terry a great royalist – and like Tracey and Allan McKeown, two other working-class talents, hates the unions, the miners and especially Arthur Scargill's appearance at the head of a 150,000-strong protest rally in London yesterday.

Home by nine. No-one in, but a message scrawled on a yellow pad on the kitchen table says viewing figures for *'PTP'* one were 8.76 million.

Tuesday, October 27th

With Art to Bushey, leaving Julia Street at the dark and unconscionable hour of 6.15. Bald cap takes an hour to put on. Heavy rain delays shooting; we lose some of the day's scheduled sequences. Les B is attractively laid-back and never even begins to be ruffled by the turn of events. His son tries to teach me some chords of 'Johnny B Goode' before the scene on Thursday.

We soldier on substituting interiors for exteriors and sending a whole crowd of extras and their cars home. Tracey and I rather enjoy playing Jackie and Frank Pillsworth – we call them 'The Pathetics'.

Friday, October 30th

I was walking in the school grounds, learning my lines, dressed as old Frank Pillsworth – bald cap, hair grey and stringy, looking down-at-heel – when a groundsman/gardener shouts across – 'Love your *Pole to Pole* programme.' Then he takes a closer look at me before saying 'You look quite different in real life.'

Later I'm playing a biker in his 30s and I have long, greasy blond hair and tattoos and leathers. We do some improvising – a quarrel between the two of us. Tracey is excellent to play against – she listens, times her line, and always with respect for the partnership.

There's a general feeling that the last two weeks have been happy and productive and that *A Class Act* will be something more than just a fulfilment of an obligation, a rush job between Tracey's court case, over royalties from her work on *The Simpsons*, and her musical with Nick Nolte to which she returns on Monday.

Wednesday, November 4th: Leeds–Edinburgh

7.45: Clinton is the new American President. Despite Peter Snow's manic computer graphics which make me feel ill to look at and which at one time gave Ross Perot several states!

Along traffic-crushed Princes Street to The Caledonian Hotel. Before checking in, I have to be interviewed by the police – give evidence of identification, place and date of birth and details of visit. A Scottish receptionist is trying her best to explain to a Japanese tourist that this is because of the EEC Summit which is to be held in the city in mid-December. As it is believed that the Brighton bomb was planted in Thatcher's hotel weeks before it was activated, and as all the top European leaders will be staying at the Caley, no chances are being taken. The Japanese lady is utterly confused.

Some good news from Anne in London – the viewing figures for 'PTP' episode one have been revised upwards to 9.7 million.

Quite a rush to sign the books, then grab a bath, change and over to the huge, gloomy rooms backstage at the Usher Hall.

They've sold the place out – 2,200 people. Probably the largest single audience I've played to in my life – stacked up in two balconies. Strangely it's less unsettling than talking to a small group of 20 or 30.

Sunday, November 8th

Pole to Pole is my second No. 1 best-seller, having deposed Madonna and held off the challenge of Mr Bean in 3rd place. Once again I'm among the literary giants!

Sweep up leaves in the garden, clear drains and gutters and generally roam the territory!

Monday, November 16th

Very cold and damp, so hardly tempted away from correspondence until it's time to go and meet Rebecca Eaton from Masterpiece Theatre at the Hyde Park Hotel. Read some more of Auberon Waugh's *Will This Do?* on the way, including an account of his being taken for lunch at the Hyde Park Hotel ... 'At every other table in the restaurant there sat a single, rich, obviously unpleasant elderly person of one sex or another, eating alone ...'

This evening the surprisingly unmajestic tea room with its low, oppressive ceiling and curiously anodyne decor is filling rapidly with Japanese. Find Rebecca in a corner. She is a handsome, strong, American woman with regular features and a disconcertingly rambling way of speaking which almost makes me feel she's under some kind of sedation.

Over tea and fruit cake she continues to gently work away at my reluctance to get involved in replacing Alistair Cooke as host of Masterpiece Theatre.

Once Rebecca has accepted that she can't ensnare me, she produces, with appealing candidness, a list of other runners. They range from Stephen Fry and Melvyn Bragg and John Mortimer ('Don't you think he looks funny?') to Mike Nichols ('Not a hair on his body') and Meryl Streep and Peter Ustinov (she turns her nose up) and Tom Stoppard, Alan Bennett and John Cleese.

Going through the list is great fun. I speak highly of John Updike. Rebecca smiles with disapproval … 'He is a terrible flirt, you know … I mean just terrible.' We discuss for a moment whether there might be medical or psychological reasons for such determined skirt-chasing. Maybe it's something to do with his itching and stammering and generally low self-esteem, as described in his book *Self-Consciousness*.

In the end we both plump for Ken Branagh.

Tuesday, November 17th

Schizophrenic weather continues. The rain has cleared and bright sunshine cuts sharply in through the windows.

Rachel looks pale and tired as she sets off for the first of her two Oxford exams.

Third show figures confirmed at 9.7 million for Wednesday night, a jump of almost a million from the Russian episode. Suzanna rings with latest book figures – subscriptions now up to a total of 354,000. Reprints will keep Clay's running at full stretch until December 4th.

Back home and another phone interview, with a US travel magazine. He asks me what my favourite direction is, which is a nice question. After some thought I have to confess it's south and west. Why not north? Feel a direction traitor!

Sunday, November 22nd

Wake up, it must be said, feeling a little surly. A cluster of reasons, I suppose – tired, faced with a day of demands rather than dozing, my social life ill-adjusted after 16 months avoiding friends to concentrate on my work, and so on.

Wrap up a fine-looking book on fairground art for Terry G's birthday and take it up to his surprise party at the Old Hall. Apparently it wasn't a surprise, but I don't think he expected quite such a crowd.

George Harrison has had himself detoxed and now no longer smokes or drinks.

He and I talk about Indian sects and how batty and surreal they can be. George is keen on the Tantric practitioners who can pleasure ten women in one night without coming. He's more intrigued by the fact that they can apparently ingest water, milk and lukewarm drinking chocolate through their penises.

Tuesday, November 24th

To lunch at Zen W3 with Malcolm Mowbray [director of *A Private Function*].

We talk about *An Immaculate Mistake* and Malcolm asks if I would like to play Paul Bailey.[1] I think *Days at the Beach* and *Private Function* are two films of great, quirky character – and I like Malcolm's ability to produce something unusual. He in turn says it's the 'sweet and sour' he likes in a film. Comedy can be tragic and awfully serious moments can be unintentionally and often savagely funny. So I say, yes, let's talk about it when you have a script, and I add it to the intriguing possibilities for next year.

At home an adaptation of *The Dresser* for radio has arrived with a request for me to play Norman opposite Freddie Jones as 'Sir'. I'm intrigued all over again.

Wednesday, November 25th

Run on the Heath and to lunch at the Halcyon Hotel with John C, Cynthia and Iain Johnstone, who is helping JC put the new film together. Iain is deputed to tell me the Zoo story – a large part of which is the old Zoo script Terry and I wrote in the '60s for GC and JC.[2]

I suggest Ken Pile make a brief appearance as an animal rights liberationist who frees a wild animal which promptly eats him. JC sees me as small-mammal keeper, Kevin as a sort of Murdoch maniac who has

---

1 Paul Bailey, writer (*Peter Smart's Confessions* shortlisted for Booker Prize in 1977), whose autobiography *An Immaculate Mistake* was much admired.
2 John was cast as Mr Burster, the man who wanted to keep only the violent animals, and Graham as Mr Megapode, one of the keepers.

come to control the zoo via some conglomerate he's acquired. Jamie would have 'a tougher role' than in *Wanda*.

And so on. The Zoo is a winner, I'm sure of it. So many different strands of current thinking and so many different aspects of twentieth-century life – greed, sentimentality about animals, green politics, marketing, sponsorship of every area of life – can all be covered.

Tuesday, December 1st: Los Angeles

It's a quarter to eight in the morning. I'm writing this in my bed at the Sunset Marquis.

My half-wakeful night was scattered with snatches of a speech I have yet to write and which I will have to deliver twice today at occasions in which I shall be the centre of attraction – a lunch in Los Angeles and a dinner and special screening at the Western Convention in Anaheim.

I feel so much that I need a breather from *Pole to Pole* now. I have lived it, travelled it, written it up, described it in commentary and now for a second successive autumn travelled and talked about it, and I'm pretty close to exhaustion point.

I long to sit all day and read a book, and be at home and share breakfast time with Helen, back in grey, squashed, chilly London.

I can hear the thud and rumble of traffic, unseen beyond the carefully watered screen of trees that rings the pleasant garden here, creating a passable illusion of Eden. It's five past eight. Birds are trilling outside my window (their richness always a bit of a surprise in this city of concrete); I'll have a soothing hot bath, breakfast on the patio, write the speeches that I hope will last me the next week, and later, after the interview with *The Sacramento Bee* is done, maybe I'll snatch a swim and the pleasure of strong sunshine.

Later – half past six in the great wide wastes of my suite at the Anaheim Hilton – a Pentagon of a hotel, flooded at the moment with the 10,000 delegates to the cable convention. I've hauled myself quite successfully through the day.

Thursday, December 10th

Back home, Rachel kisses me goodbye as she leaves for her Brasenose interview at 8.30, but I don't get out of bed until the end of the morning.

News comes in from Anne of our highest overnight viewing figure for the series – 10.2 for number eight. No surge to the dizzy heights of 12.8 as for *80 Days*, but the last three shows have hit a plateau of around 11 million for Wednesday night only.

The announcement of a separation between Charles and Diana delays *'PTP'* by 15 minutes, with a special news bulletin.

Wednesday, December 16th

Arrive at the HQ of NCR in Marylebone Road for the first meeting of the Book Award judges.

To the boardroom with a huge mahogany table, around which 30–35 people could easily be accommodated, leaving room for secretaries. David Puttnam, the chairman, sits himself at the head of this massive piece of furniture. Despite his best efforts, Princess Diana is not going to be on the panel after all. I sit on one side with Diana Rigg.

Opposite me Margaret Jay,[1] tall, dressed in a suit, soberly. She is voluble in her praise of *'PTP'*. Next to her is Richard Hoggart,[2] a markedly accented Yorkshireman, his tie awry, looking benignly from behind glasses – a little bewildered, it seems, but I'm sure this is a front. 'Have we agreed? …' he keeps asking anxiously. Heads nod. 'About what?'

I fought to bring *Fever Pitch* out from the oblivion of the 'Not Recommended' category of readers' reports and now it's on the shortlist.

Finish by eleven. I leave having promised to read 19 books by mid-March!

To Classic FM to be interviewed re the Stammerers. Bomb has gone off in John Lewis and I watch their video screens for signs of the scale of it. Quite small, but Oxford Street closed off.

Thursday, December 17th

Out of the house at 7.15 to London Bridge Station. A minicab with a disagreeable old driver. He began to talk about the IRA – 'The only way to deal with that lot is to line them up and shoot them,' he maintained. For the first time in a long while I was driven to uncontrollable anger and found myself telling this man old enough to be my father that his

---

1 Baroness Jay of Paddington, journalist and politician, daughter of the former Prime Minister James Callaghan.
2 Richard Hoggart, academic and writer, best known for *The Uses of Literacy* (1957).

solution was ridiculous, dangerous and didn't solve anything. 'That's what we used to do in Malaysia,' he went on doggedly, but he didn't really have the courage of his own bigotry and I felt oddly embarrassed, not by what I said, but by showing up what was not aggression so much as ignorance.

This and a long traffic jam on London Bridge, causing us a last-minute sprint to the station, certainly got the morning off to a lively start.

Met the film crew aboard the 7.50 and proceeded to Brighton, Portsmouth and the Isle of Wight, recording interviews with punters as we went – to be used to bind together a 'What's On Meridian' prog for New Year's Day.

Most of them made no distinction between BBC and ITV, many didn't watch much TV and others, when asked about preferences, plumped for comedy and nature programmes. 'More programmes like yours, Michael,' one lady kept saying.

On the hydrofoil to the Isle of Wight, a good group of locals – the further one goes from London the more relaxed people seem to be about talking. But it was not really what I wanted to be doing at the end of a year like this – trying to talk to seven-year-old girls on a double-decker bus from Ryde to Newport and elicit their views on television whilst trying not to look like a molester.

Friday, December 18th

At 6.30 picked up by Naim Attallah's chauffeur in a large Mercedes and driven down to the Mayfair Hotel where I've agreed to draw the raffle and present prizes at Asprey's Christmas Party.

What surprises me first of all is how many people work for Asprey's – there must be 300 there. Sign some books, then draw the raffle, whose prizes seem rather paltry for an outfit like Asprey's – one of them is Naim Attallah's own book, signed, which he presents without embarrassment of any kind.

His generosity, however, evident in the presentation of a beautifully bound leather-backed copy of *Pole to Pole*, decorated and inlaid with a gold design.

Then rush back home, where I'm greeted by Rachel, eyes wide, who says she has had a telephone call from the head of History at BNC, to tell her that they have a place for her, and that her interview in particular had been very good. She'll be receiving written confirmation but he wanted to put an end to her waiting before the weekend.

After so many days of having to appear delighted to see people and interested in everything they're doing, it's an enormous pleasure when real, spontaneous, natural happiness takes you by surprise.

Monday, December 21st: London–Liverpool

Train from Euston to Sean's[1] 50th birthday party in Birkenhead.

A Kenyan-Asian ticket collector on the train is quite bowled over to see me. With a complete lack of self-consciousness or discretion of any kind, he indicates me with a sweep of the hand – 'I can't believe this … on my train! … Michael Palin …' He won't let it lie … 'This is like a dream to me …' By now the other passengers are shifting about and grinning nervously … 'Did you see his programme? … Mm?' Various heads nod sheepishly. He then conducts an impromptu interview … 'Tell me, which place did you like best? You like Kenya? I come from Kenya.'

The upshot of it was that the girl opposite confessed she'd bought my book for her brother, and the man in the seat in front actually produced a copy for me to sign.

Tuesday, December 22nd

A quick and easy journey from Lime Street to Euston, through the largely unspoilt and quintessentially English landscape of rural Cheshire, Staffordshire and the Midlands. Canals, hump-back bridges, low hills, fields and all sorts of trees. Today everything is made hauntingly beautiful by a thick layer of frost, creating a soft, silvery effect, as if the countryside had been artificially preserved. Nothing seems to move. A line of sheep crossing a frozen field towards a trough of hay is about as vigorous as the activity becomes.

Wednesday, December 23rd

There have been no serious explosions over the last few days, but the bombs in John Lewis and yesterday evening in Hampstead Underground

---

1 Sean Duncan, close friend since we were contemporaries at Shrewsbury School. Became a judge.

Station have been enough to keep a jittery, emergency atmosphere alive. My Christmas shopping is conducted to the accompaniment of police sirens and hurtling fire engines.

Most eerie of all was to drive down Gower Street after lunch and to find Malet Street cordoned off. Looking down its broad sweep beyond the blue-and-white plastic police strip was uncomfortable – the cars all in their places, but no-one moving. It's a picture seen so often on TV. It usually preludes an explosion.

This time no explosion, but it did set me thinking that whereas New York, one of the world's most dangerous cities, was wrapped in ribbon for Christmas, dear old Dickensian London is wrapped in police barrier strips.

Monday, December 28th

Take Granny G down to see the Sickert retrospective at the Royal Academy.

On the way home Granny tells me that H used to be known as 'Drip' when she was young – largely because of her vagueness. She got left behind one day when they were all shopping in Cambridge. The rest of the family waited in a tea shop for her and as the door opened shouted with one voice 'Hello Drip!' In walked a clergyman and his family.

Sun reporter rings to inform us (and glean a reaction) that John and Alyce have married in Barbados. Send them a fax saying that the *Sun* let me know, therefore it's obviously not true.

Tuesday, December 29th

Granny G leaves this morning after spending five nights with us. A tall, cloudless sky. The weathervane points ESE and doesn't move much. It's becoming colder by the day.

A Mrs Miller rings from Denville Hall, the care home for actors, to say that John Hughman is very unwell. He has a cancer 'deep down' and the doctor doesn't expect him to live out the week. She sounds a sympathetic woman – she was quite touching when she described the letter of recommendation I'd written for John … 'I'd love someone to write a letter like that about me.' But she knows what I meant and says everyone there has fallen for him!

Wednesday, December 30th

Out to Denville Hall to see John Hughman. It's more accessible than I was led to believe, and looks more like a hotel than a hospital.

His room has a Turkish carpet, attractive curtains, a wing-back armchair, and his Christmas cards, about a dozen of them, are set out on the wall and the table. It's a warm room, in every way; he lies well covered up, his head profiled against clean, soft pillows. It's probably the best home he's had for a long time.

He wakes briefly; displays his familiar smile of welcome and apology and takes in my presence. He then falls back to sleep.

I talk to Mrs Miller over a cup of tea. She has 36 ex-actors, of both sexes, here. There is another home nearby for variety artists. They regard Denville Hall as a bit snobbish. I ask if Joyce Carey is in here. She was here a week ago, evidently, but in her official capacity as one of the council who run the place! Word got around of her presence and she was very soon surrounded by the inmates, who regarded her with great awe and respect.

Back to John. I put a hand on his bony shoulder and tell him what I feel, and what he was probably never told enough ... 'You're a great man, John ... a great man.' His eye flickers open and he startles me with a reply. 'Thank you,' he says quietly, clearly, politely. Before I go we exchange suitable last words. 'Goodbye John.' 'Goodbye,' he whispers, clearly again.

Thursday, December 31st: London–Southampton

H and I set out for Southampton. Along the crowded M3, slowly as fog closes in. Ghost story weather – the mist forming sheer walls of darkness beneath the lamp standards.

Fetch up eventually at the Botley Park Hotel and Country Club. It's an upmarket motel, really – with lots of sports facilities and a sub-Colefax & Fowler-decorated double room called the De Montgomery Suite. Simon and Phillida, both in dressing gowns, join us from the De Wriothesley Suite, which Simon can't pronounce. He apologises for the dressing gown, but wants to put his party clothes on at the very last minute as he's grown rather too big for them!

By taxi through the damp, chilly fog to the TVS studios. Studio 2 has been decorated for the party. A band (live) is playing and black drapes have been slung from the roof giving a tented effect, and little holes cut out to create the illusion of a ceiling of stars.

It's an awkward occasion. To celebrate Meridian's victory would be insensitive as there are many old TVS people who are visibly moved as the last ten minutes of their ten-year reign come up on monitors after a statesmanlike 'healing' message from Lord Hollick.

At midnight a studio show called 'Goodbye to All That' patters to a close and frankly Meridian's opening debut is a great relief. The logo looks good; it's boldly delivered. The first ten minutes flow well and there are some good vox pops. A child says 'I want peace in Yugoslavia and Disneyland in Britain.'

1993

Sunday, January 3rd

Piercing sunlight behind the red blind in my room, the fiercest frost so far makes the grass and rooftops glisten.

After the Sunday papers – one of which observes pithily that 'John Major has all the qualities except leadership, with Margaret Thatcher it was the other way round' – I retire upstairs and begin my NCR reading with Simon Loftus' Puligny-Montrachet.

Watch some of the progs I recorded last night – a piece about Sickert, a man who loved being in the public eye, who sent scribbled instructions to Winston Churchill on how to paint – 'wear old clothes'; then a chilling film about property development in the City of London during the Thatcher years when 96% of all the schemes were approved, resulting, ten years later, in mediocre office space equivalent to 14 Canary Wharf Towers standing empty in the City.

Supper with Rachel and H; a blazing fire and John Betjeman's *Metroland* film to end the day. Better than a cup of Horlicks! Though of the same vintage.

Monday, January 4th

A man arrives to replace our neat, once-efficient, now defunct, BSB squarial with a bigger, less efficient but more commercially successful Sky/Astra replacement. The quality of pictures will never be as good from the Astra satellite, but there we are. Murdoch 1, BSB lost.

Tuesday, January 5th

Restful day in prospect. Weather warms up, bringing rain.

Ring Denville Hall to see how John Hughman is, and am told that he died last night. Mrs Miller rings later to apologise for not calling personally, but it was the day of a big committee meeting. My visit cheered him, she says, but his pain increased and so did his sedation. He died peacefully. It's almost a week since he wished me goodbye.

Wednesday, January 6th

To a studio across the road from Parliament where I do a down-the-line TV piece with an unseen Anne Diamond in Southampton for a show called *TV Weekly* (originally TVS, now made by Meridian). The cameraman tells me that my earpiece has just been used by Virginia Bottomley[1] – 'but it has been washed'. Pity. I was rather excited by this vicarious intimacy. ('I Shared an Earpiece with Virginia Bottomley' – Python reveals.)

Pole to Pole's last episode was seen by 11 million on Wednesday and two million on Saturday's BBC 2 repeat, pipping *80 Days*' highest figure by 200,000.

Thursday, January 7th

To the BBC to record one of the new *Wogan* shows. I'm on with Neil Kinnock[2] and Sheila Hancock.

A grim Green Room in the basement of TV Centre. Kinnock small and wasted, two stone lighter evidently than when he fought the election. He behaves like a bigger man, trying to transmit buoyancy and bonhomie, but it doesn't convince. His world is not showbiz. He tries to talk knowledgeably about it, but cannot remember anyone's name. In short, he's trying hard, but gives all the signs of still being in shock.

Terry W is in make-up at the same time as me. He pats his growing stomach. He exudes a comfortable confidence, based on little more than the fact that he is, unchallengeably, Terry Wogan. He looks like a minor royal uncle, secure and enjoying the good things of life.

I'm first guest on. On the desk in front of him, Terry has a series of cards. On top of the one I can see is printed in large letters 'South Pole – Anti Climax?'

Kinnock comes on and tries hard to be the life and soul.

Politicians need Parliament. They need their club. They seem to think they can manage to move effortlessly into showbiz. Kinnock's performance tonight shows just how difficult it is. 'Showbiz' tightens its ranks, and has its rules, just like politics.

---

1 Virginia Bottomley, Secretary of State for Health since the General Election.
2 Neil Kinnock resigned after Labour's General Election defeat after nine years as leader of the Opposition.

Saturday, January 9th

First dinner party of the New Year. Sepha and David Wood. Sepha Neill grew up with my sister Angela in Sheffield. Haven't asked anyone else because I know shop will be the order of the evening – Angela, Sheffield, etc.

She feels that she and Angela were friends because they were so different from one another. Angela lacked confidence, she remembers, despite being at the top of one class whilst Sepha was bottom of the other. My father was clearly remembered as a strict man – always a stickler for punctuality, imposing times so inflexibly that Angela used to start getting worried half an hour before she had to be home. (I too remember that source of fear.)

Tuesday, January 12th

A dilemma came into my mind as I ran this morning. Someone – was it Clem? – mentioned a Palin journey round the Pacific, and the suggestion was reiterated in a recent letter to the *Radio Times*.

As I fought the south-westerlies to the top of Parliament Hill, I traced in my mind a route starting on the easternmost tip of Russia, looking across the Bering Strait to the westernmost tip of America, and taking on the challenge to get from one to the other the long way round – taking a route down through the Kamchatka Peninsula, Vladivostok, the northernmost islands of Japan, Hokkaido, Korea, China, Vietnam, the islands of Indonesia, New Guinea, the Great Barrier Reef of Australia, New Zealand, across the Pacific to Easter Island, Southern Chile, then up South America through Peru, Ecuador, Colombia, Central America, Mexico, West Coast USA, Canada and Alaska.

The scope of the journey, the pattern of the journey, the newsworthiness of the journey (Hong Kong to China in '97 – earthquake prophecies in California) is attractive, as is the convenient and not entirely arbitrary parameter of the Pacific. It may seem premature, but after a year vowing never to do another mega-journey, I can see 'Palin's Pacific' on the screens in '96.

Wednesday, January 13th

A pale, wet morning. Rachel's eighteenth birthday. A Technics music system was her chief present, which she spent most of yesterday fitting up. There are a lot of time-consuming things to clear up this morning and I get no Whitbread reading done. Will to be packed off to Oxford – he leaves at lunchtime – prior to leaving with TJ for John Hughman's funeral.

To Holy Trinity Church, Northwood, a short distance from Denville Hall, where he died over a week ago. The weather grows wilder by the minute, with terrific winds roaring outside the stout, well-kept little church.

About 15 of us there. The vicar moves us into the front rows to help the singing. The door opens and the wailing winds rise to a screech as the coffin is brought in. Not for the first time, but undoubtedly for the last, I am struck by John's size. It is a long coffin, and maybe it's a tribute to my memory of John that an unbidden comic thought springs to mind – that John's final appearance is like a sketch, a sketch in which a coffin is so long it just keeps going, with no end in sight.

It's laid in front of us, at the end of the nave, and the flowers that Terry and I brought along are placed on top. They are the only flowers.

A short service with two lusty hymns, a fairly half-hearted address from the vicar, who clearly had very little to work with – son of two generations of military men, joined the army in the '30s, never very happy, seconded to the Pay Corps, then a job in the civil service and some difficult times before he started acting in 1968. A life that doesn't lend itself to the usual orations – no roll-call of achievements.

Tuesday, January 19th

To Denholm Elliott's memorial service at St James's Piccadilly.

I squeeze into a row at the very back. The size of the turnout and the lusty singing of 'Praise My Soul, the King of Heaven' are in marked contrast to the funeral of John Hughman six days earlier. Denholm was a very naughty man but marvellous at his job and much loved.

John Mortimer, possibly the most reassuring figure in British public life, spoke elegantly and with feeling through an open letter – 'Dear Denholm ...' Then a marvellous rendition of 'The Owl and the Pussycat' by Leslie Phillips.

On the way out a deep, breathy voice behind me asks how my reading's getting on. It's Diana Rigg. Lionel Bart and Clive Swift are both very friendly. I congratulate Leslie Phillips. 'Quite nervous, you know, with so many of your betters out there.'

More talk with Diana R over the NCR books. *In an Antique Land* by Amitav Ghosh, I suggest, was good. 'Oh, marvellous, but never a winner.' She speaks with such positive authority, such decisiveness, that I can only nod and agree. She turns her impressive attentions to two men who were in a prison camp with Denholm. He once acted Eliza Doolittle whilst chained up, one of them remembers. 'Some of the actors had to wear handcuffs.' Diana hoots with laughter at the recollection.

Friday, January 22nd

An hour on *Dreams of Exile* – the book which H found me so fast asleep over yesterday evening that when the phone woke me I picked up a mug of cold tea and said 'Hello' into it.

Reading it still in the taxi, I go to lunch with Clem.

I tell him that I don't want to do another *80 Days* or *Pole to Pole*. He asks why. I veer between the argument that we did two very successfully, we had luck and good fortune and a third journey of such scale would be tempting fate, and the feeling I have that my career has been successful because I've always moved on – always kept one step ahead of those wanting to typecast me.

We agree to keep thinking and despite all my worries I know we know that somehow, somewhere, we'll travel again.

Tuesday, January 26th

Dinner party – with the Cooks (Peter and Lin) and the Cleeses (even more recently married than the Cooks).

Peter chain-smokes and displays great knowledge of current affairs, scandals and goings-on which befits the owner of the *Eye*! Lin is quieter, but they're both clearly devoted.

JC presents me with a book of some old buffer's reminiscences of Bechuanaland.

Then there is an enormous crash as Peter, on his way upstairs to the loo, tries to walk through the glass door to the hall. He's momentarily stunned as the thick glass smashes, leaving behind an imprint of the great man. Fortunately he's not hurt, apart from a few minor scratches, which are bound up and plastered.

The talk got on to autobiography – Peter dismissed the idea, said he'd only ever got as far as a title. 'Retired and Emotional' was one – 'A Woman in the Body of an Armadillo' was another. I asked him about his ill-fated chat show in the early '70s. The problem was not the guests, but what to say to them. 'They were all my friends you see, or people I'd really wanted to meet like S. J. Perelman, but once they were there I really didn't want to ask them anything.'

Saturday, January 30th

I approach the days of reckoning on *The Dresser*. Called upon to prove myself once again. In at the deep end. The Tom Courtenay replacement.[1] Feel reasonably perky though.

To Broadcasting House for 10.30. Meet Sue MacGregor at the desk as I collect my pass for the day. She asks if Angela was my sister – as she can remember an Angela Palin reading letters on *Woman's Hour* years ago. So I tell her about what happened. She is very responsive, sympathetic, and I should like to have talked longer.

When at last I reach Studio 6A, a large barn of a place, and the only drama studio still in use at BH, I find the cast all sitting around, scripts at the ready. David Blount, his PA Sarah, a half-dozen actors from the Radio Drama Company, another two or three contract actors – 'OAs' (Outside Actors) as they call themselves. Freddie Jones, with his W. C. Fields strawberry nose, rubicund face, a less raddled version of Anthony Burgess – even to the scarf tied round the neck. David introduces us. Freddie is polite but not effusive. I feel like a new boy at school.

Sunday, January 31st

Down to BH. We set to the first half of the play. I find everything unfamiliar – the process of moving around as if acting in a real space, preceded by a studio manager making your noises for you – the difficulty of turning script pages silently – the chummy bonhomie of the radio actors.

1 Tom Courtenay had appeared as Norman in Ronald Harwood's play *The Dresser* in the West End (opposite Freddie Jones) and in the film version (opposite Albert Finney) about a great actor (assumed to be Donald Wolfit [1902–68], actor-manager).

Freddie remains oddly enigmatic. He never joins us for lunch or tea breaks, preferring, as he puts it, 'to go for a cocktail'. He smells of whisky after lunch, but not immoderately so, and his relish of the part is wonderful to behold. He is 'Sir' ... or is 'Sir' Freddie? ...

He lards his conversation with rich theatrical hyperbole. 'My position is quite vile, I realise that,' he says at one point, 'knowing the play, having done the part ... it really is a loathsome position.' He does seem to be genuinely concerned not to seem like the old hand, to play down his seniority and the fact that the play is almost his property.

David Blount takes me into the gallery at six. 'I want to play you something you did really well,' he says ominously. Indeed this prefaces the playing of two or three speeches I did very badly. They have no sense, no unity of delivery; they wander. As he says, radio performance is about concision and precision; no gestures, no grimaces can be used to augment the delivery, the attention and concentration is all in the words – the sense of them is absolutely of paramount importance on radio.

'You know what to say,' concludes David, 'but at the moment it's only coming out at half-cock.'

I take the criticism hard, because I know it's true.

Monday, February 1st

I learnt something from yesterday's playback. I was trying too hard. I was performing Norman rather than letting the part speak for itself. I was starting too high and too violently; the only way was to reduce the initial effort, which, given the size of the part, I couldn't hope to sustain.

All the actors are in this morning – the studio used to the full as we record the Lear scenes. Tympanist, thunder sheets ('Return to Room 608' painted on them), a wind machine, peas rattled in a drum for rain. Actors tell endless stories ... Of one famous name: 'Never knowingly underplayed.' The landlady who apologised to her theatrical lodger after she'd found her being rogered by the milkman on the kitchen table – 'You must think I'm an awful flirt.'

Reminiscences of Wolfit. Asked whether playing Macbeth in the afternoon and Lear in the evening took its toll. 'When I play Macbeth in the afternoon and Lear in the evening ... there is no junket for Ros[1] that night.'

---

1 Rosalind Iden, his third wife.

So it goes on. I just listen. But the day's work is good. Though I don't have a lot of lines, I do them efficiently and I'm aware of a gradually growing confidence as I become familiar with the surroundings and the technique. More positive all round.

Home, at last, in higher spirits. Work till my eyes ache on the speeches and the songs.

Tuesday, February 2nd

To BH by ten o'clock. Set to work straight away. David very pleased at the work we have done on it, and, buoyed by his relief and pleasure, I never really look back. 'You've got it,' he says like a Henry Higgins and he's right. I still have to make every line count, I still have the example of Freddie hitting every intonation, drawing every ounce of emotion and humour from his lines, to aim at, but at least I'm no longer intimidated. I can begin to enjoy myself.

Wednesday, February 3rd

A *Radio Times* survey throws up some unexpected results. Trevor McDonald is considered the television personality most readers would like to see in the Cabinet. Michael Palin tops the poll of those they would most like to see representing Britain at the UN (24%, ahead of Kate Adie at 17%!).

By ten, I'm at Studio 6A for the fifth and final day of *The Dresser*.

In the last section I'm required to break down as 'Sir' dies. We can't leave Freddie on the set as the microphone may pick up his breathing, so I end up emoting to an empty studio chair. From somewhere I find the ability to act grief and tears quite believably.

Freddie comes across from the other side of the studio. 'Marvellous, absolutely marvellous,' he says. Though I have to go through it twice more, this moment of unequivocal praise from Freddie is when I know that I have done the right thing in taking the part.

I've joined the club, as it were. I'm no longer the new boy.

Thursday, February 4th

Hunter Davies, wrapped up like an Iranian spy in black fedora and multi-coloured sweaters, has come to do me for the *Independent*.

Once Hunter has chosen to do you, you have entered his world. There is little I can say which will affect the agenda. His style is to rush at you like a bull at a gate, prodding behind comfortable answers towards the uncomfortable truths he hopes to unearth. The pace is brisk. He doesn't use a tape recorder, he prefers a small red soft-back notebook in which he scribbles every now and then, like a policeman interviewing a witness. His redeeming feature is his twinkling good humour, and his audacity, well cheek really – to which I respond. Despite all my best intentions I'm led into areas I've sworn to avoid – 'niceness', attitudes to critics, and so on. Hunter's juggernaut rolls on.

Wednesday, February 10th

Tom has good news of the rap track. KISS FM 'love it' and are playing it. The video shoot over the last couple of days went well, and there is a lot of interest in using his mini-studio. As usual I ask the clumsy but relevant parental question about money and rewards for all this work. 'That'll happen,' Tom assures me, and I like him so much I don't push.

Thursday, February 11th

Set aside the books and concentrate on writing a speech to match the auspicious occasion of Sheffield's 100th anniversary as a city tomorrow night.

At 6.30 we're collected and driven to the *Publishing News* Book Awards at the Royal Lancaster. A good crowd.

In the gents Roy Hattersley,[1] with whom I'm sharing a bill at Sheffield tomorrow, asks if I'd like tickets to the Wednesday–Southend FA Cup match on Saturday.

The Travel Writer of the Year Award is announced by none other than Peter de la Billière.[2] He makes quite a tension out of it, but then that lovely cathartic moment when I hear my name called, and I'm being clapped and smiled at by 500 people and given a 'Nibby' and I'm embarking on a speech of thanks which I only half expected to have

---

1 Roy Hattersley, former deputy leader of the Labour Party, retired as MP for Sparkbrook at the 1997 General Election.
2 General Sir Peter de la Billière. Retired as Commander-in-Chief, British Forces Middle East in 1991 after serving in the SAS and leading the British forces that retook the Falkland Islands following the Argentinian invasion in 1984.

to give. 'This is almost the greatest moment of my life … the greatest was being offered tickets for the Wednesday v Southend game by Roy Hattersley in the gents.'

Friday, February 12th: London–Sheffield

Wake with a worse than usual headache, probably the result of drinking worse than usual wine.

Onto the three o'clock train and complete the speech somewhere beyond Luton.

In Sheffield on time. Driven to the Cutlers' Hall, which is quite a lot older than the city itself and rather fine, with tall marbled columns and walls hung with portraits of Sheffield worthies – including a Duke of Norfolk looking very sexy in tight white satin hose.

After a drink in the Master's office we're led by a toastmaster in a red coat up the wide, high-Victorian staircase into the Hall itself, via an ante-room where 100 guests who couldn't get tickets are to sit and watch the speeches on closed-circuit. The 'guests' applaud us to our seats with a slightly sinister regular hand clap which I assume is part of the ritual.

It does seem an extraordinary turn of fate, that one who knew Sheffield best as a fairly shy schoolboy, well away from the world of civic power and influence, should, 36 years after leaving Birkdale School, be making the main speech at the 100th anniversary celebration of the city – with a white-haired Derek Dooley (legendary footballer of my youth) sitting a half-dozen yards away from me. Derek Dooley was one of Sheffield Wednesday's most prolific goal-scorers. In February 1953 he was injured in a match. The wound became infected and his leg had to be amputated.

Well, I don't think I let the city down. The time and care I took with the words pay off and, at the end, quite unexpectedly, I receive a standing ovation. This is quite something. Guests along the rows of tables on their feet, turning towards me, beaming and applauding. The Master Cutler grasps my hand, the Mayor too.

Tuesday, February 16th

Hunter Davies' piece in the *Independent* is quite a relief. Good photo – office looks suitably cluttered and I'm not given the searching full close-ups they sometimes deal in. Written in Hunter's staccato, breathless style, it includes a memorable description of the neighbourhood in which I've spent most of my life: 'Gospel Oak, a nowhere place on the wrong side of the Heath.'

By twelve I'm entering the sheltered forecourt of the St Ermin's Hotel in deepest Westminster, for a meeting prior to the Vice-Presidents' lunch for The Royal Society for Nature Conservation.

David Attenborough is deep in conversation with a formidable elderly lady. Her face is deeply lined and wide, strong and healthy at the same time. D introduces her as Miriam Rothschild, Doctor Miriam Rothschild. Daughter of Lord Rothschild.

'I gather we must no longer call you nice,' David teases, referring to my *Independent* interview. I suggest that it's quite a good way of getting things done. Dr Miriam disagrees ... 'I never get anything done by being nice. I swing my battleaxe.'

We adjourn to a small, very warm private room as the other Vice-Presidents assemble, three of whom are Right Honourables – one an Earl, two Lords – and all of whom have either MCs, CBEs or OBEs.

Dr Rothschild takes the lead once we are all sat down. She's shocked by the revelation in the *Observer* that about 250 Sites of Special Scientific Interest are threatened by the new Government Road Building Programme. She demands quick and positive action from the RSNC/Wildlife Trusts. When someone counsels a cautious approach ... 'there could be difficulties' ... she waves them wearily away. 'I don't believe in difficulties.'

Home by 3.30. Start reading Victoria Glendinning's *Trollope* [for the NCR Awards].

Thursday, February 18th

Complete *Trollope*. Victoria G is very interested in T's interest in women – evidenced by the number of women in his novels. Her attempt to get to the bottom (*sic*) of his sexuality is rather exciting. Through Victoria's eyes we look beneath the skirts of mid-nineteenth-century morality.

To BAFTA to see one of the four films from which I and others have to select a Best Adapted Screenplay Award. Odd thing to have to do, because really one should read the work from which the screenplay is adapted to be able to judge.

Sit through *Howards End* and enjoy its lush good taste, and am beguiled by the sets and the costumes and the crisp performances, but my heart is not moved, nor do I wish anything on the Wilcox family but to get them off the screen. I think it's a case of using a work of art to crack a nut.

Sunday, February 21st

John's and Robin Skynner's new book *Life and How to Survive It* has gone straight to the top of the best-sellers, displacing *Pole to Pole*. The two notices I read are not polite.

Ring John to congratulate and abuse him. He is weary. Weary about the reviews, weary about the press generally. 'They will not make any attempt to listen … they are not the slightest bit interested in anyone who appears to be making an effort, however small it might be, to make life a little better.'

We talk for half an hour. Every now and then there is an interruption – a cat walks across the phone, JC coughs scouringly … 'Oh this bloody virus', and, most disconcertingly of all, appears to be taking notes … 'You know that phrase you used earlier, which I've written down …' If only I felt worthy of being a Doctor Johnson.

We've been invited round to Will Wyatt's for lunch. Half expect a respectable, besuited affair, but couldn't be more wrong. Will's house in Chiswick is modest, and pleasantly disordered.

Meet Molly Dineen, who has just received rave reviews for *The Ark*, her self-shot, self-interviewed doc series about London Zoo. She is Irish, bright, quick, restless, and, if she doesn't burn herself out with her own energy, likely to go far. Her stories of the zoo could write 'Death Fish Two' on their own. Gorillas breaking out and attacking chimpanzees; a pony from the children's zoo fed to the wolves. The war between the keepers sounds absolutely plausible!

Tuesday, March 2nd

Cold, bland morning, low cloud, east wind. Opening of the Michael Palin Stammering Centre. Drive down to BH for an appointment with *Today* prog. Am taken straight into the studio. 'John Smith's[1] in there at the moment, and we want a bit of light relief,' confides the PA before apologising '… well, you know what I mean.'

1 John Smith, succeeded Neil Kinnock as Labour leader.

After my remarks on stammering I'm asked to comment on the news of the death of Joyce Carey at 94. Having had no time to prepare I say my bit and then, with some mad rush of blood to the head, go on to make a point about the number of great old actresses who have died this week – mentioning Lillian Gish and, for some reason, instead of Ruby Keeler, Jessye Norman. I'm told later that an apology had to be broadcast after alarm calls from fans of the very much alive and kicking Jessye Norman.

Wednesday, March 3rd

To BAFTA for the meeting of the Best Adapted Screenplay jury.

We sit around a table, wine and snack provided. After the *GBH*/*Prime Suspect* debacle last year, strict new rules apply. No-one must leave the room once discussion has begun; choice of film must be marked by signature. The chairman must keep result confidential.

Our discussion was full but quite enlightening. Peter Nichols was the only one who'd hated *Strictly Ballroom*[1] – 'but I'm like that,' he admitted. Tony Palmer and myself spoke with one voice on most of the films – though he was a trifle more vituperative about *Howards End*.

I think *Strictly Ballroom* is a classic, one of the best adverts for modern film. Rich and complex and far less respectable (*Howards End*), preachy (*JFK*) and introverted (*The Player*) than the others. We vote. There is a clear winner. Charles Wood, our chairman, who naturally, I feel, tends to indiscretion, wants to tell us. It'll be *The Player* or *Strictly B*.

News comes from Howard Schumann of the death of Paul Zimmerman. I hadn't expected him to live, but I still find it hard to accept I shall never see him again. As I tell Terry in a phone call later, I want, above all, to hear Paul tell me his side of the story.

Sunday, March 7th

About ten o'clock Nigel Meakin rings from the BAFTA Craft Awards at Nottingham to tell me he's won the award for best documentary photographer. In view of the fact that the BBC didn't even suggest him as their nomination (he had to be pushed by Clem), this is a tremendous

---

1 *Strictly Ballroom*, 1992 film directed by Baz Luhrmann.

pleasure, relief and so entirely well-deserved a success that I feel I've won something myself.

Tuesday, March 9th

Sunshine again. In my light, bright, glowing workroom (blinds down for first time this year), lose myself in the world of fossils and human origins – Leakey's *Origins Reconsidered*. Realise that we travelled, on *Pole to Pole*, through 'the cradle of mankind', the African Rift Valley, and were hardly aware of it.

After almost two years in which *Pole to Pole* has meant work, I find myself thinking about it with pleasure. Leakey's descriptions of a Kenyan dawn filled me with longing.

Friday, March 12th

Lunch with JC and Iain Johnstone in St John's Wood. Cartoon about JC's book in *Private Eye* … 'Ello Miss, I wish to complain about this book … it has ceased to be interesting.' JC hadn't seen it, and ventured the opinion that *Private Eye* had always treated him well. He'd found Craig Brown's parody of the Skynner/Cleese banter funny. John is definitely less prickly these days.

We have some good discussion on 'Death Fish Zoo'. Must remember to get JC together with Molly Dineen.

A fine spring night. Scent of hyacinths in the cooling midnight air.

Saturday, March 13th: London–Abbotsley

Rake through Waterstones in Hampstead for something to give Granny for her 80th.

Helen back quite late with a dozen helium-filled balloons which we have to try and pack in the car. 'Will they make the car lighter?' a neighbour asks helpfully. Clare [Latimer] brings round the 80th birthday cake. Unfortunately she's spelt Gibbins 'Gibbons', so before we can leave she has to make fresh icing and correct it.

Up at Church Farm, our first glimpse of the marquee. Sits very well in the front garden flanked by Granny's showpiece borders of purple hyacinth, primrose and primula with daffs hurrying forward in the quite unseasonable warmth.

Inside it's lined with flounced yellow nylon. Even the tent poles have been stockinged. Electrically lit sconces add a weird country-house-boudoir touch, and a plastic undersheeting crackles beneath one's feet like some giant incontinence garment.

Thursday, March 18th

The day that ends the reading programme that I've been put through (for £2,500 expenses) for the NCR. Twenty-two books read, about twice my yearly rate, in two and a half months!

At the NCR office by nine o'clock. In addition to the five members of the judging panel, a further four are present. The lady marketing the whole business, two other women, and the literary agent who acts as a sort of court of appeal and whose name I'm never told.

David Puttnam, apologising for his low voice and state of health, deals, with disarming ruthlessness, with the early 'drop-outs'.

The last seven are quite easily arrived at, but from this point on there are two main areas of disagreement. One is over Fred Inglis' *The Cruel Peace*. David stays quiet on this, but I suspect his silence is not one of approval. I am on awkward ground, disliking it for some emotional reason, possibly because Richard Hoggart won't even discuss *his* dislike of *Fever Pitch*, but I cannot be persuaded by Diana Rigg, who found it 'audacious' and Richard H, whose admiration for the work seems to lie uncomfortably close to his admiration for the author. As it's removed from the last four he mutters 'Poor Fred.'

But the nearest we come to blows is over the Iris Murdoch. Once again I'm first to talk about it and I have to put the shaky case for incomprehensibility. Richard Hoggart reveres it, but it's Margaret Jay who puts up the most spirited case. We need a new value system. Never have morals and ethics been so important. Religion has failed us. Age of apathy and uncertainty. New lead needed. Who better than Iris to supply it?

David confesses he was lost with it. Couldn't understand what she was getting at. It was the first book for a long time to remind him that he only got three O Levels. Hoggart cannot conceive of such a major work being set aside. Diana reveals that she thought it very difficult and not fulfilling the criterion of 'available to a wide readership'.

Then up speaks the agent, whose name I must find out. He is respected by all and his words carry weight. 'Iris Murdoch is one of our greatest writers. She has made a living from some of the finest modern novels in the language. If she has written a book which three well-educated, intelligent people at this table cannot understand, then she has perhaps not written a very good book.'

Jay gives in and Hoggart is left muttering and shaking his head as *Fever Pitch* lines up ahead of the Iris Murdoch. But at least I no longer feel quite such a philistine.

At 12.15 *Fever Pitch* (unchallenged except by Hoggart), Wolpert's *Unnatural Nature of Science* (not much liked by Jay), *The English Bible* (not liked by Jay and Hoggart as much as the Trevelyan) and *Never Again* by Peter Hennessy (compromise) are stood up on the table as the four shortlisted books. We have our photos taken with them. I'm given *Fever Pitch* to hold. I think it's understood to be my crusade.

Sunday, March 28th

The IRA have made a lot more enemies after the Warrington bomb killed two young boys out shopping for Mother's Day. Waves of indignation, but the saddest news of all is that in Belfast, where the IRA turn out their terrorists, the Protestants slew five Catholics over the last week, instantly ensuring that the IRA win back sympathy.

Watch Eric being perky on *Aspel*. First evidence of any pre-publicity for *Splitting Heirs*.[1] He's 50 tomorrow. Same age as John Major. Seems unbelievable.

Monday, March 29th: London–New York

Concorde across the Atlantic in 3.27. Listen to *The Dresser*. Unfortunately the noise of this expensive aircraft is such that a lot of the quieter, throwaway lines cannot be heard unless the volume's turned right up. Then Freddie immediately goes into one of his roars, giving the eardrums a terrible battering. Tears in my eyes at the end. I do the last speech well.

Whisked to the Ritz-Carlton by limo. My second rush hour of the day.

TG is in the hotel, two floors down. This seems to be the way New York always is. A great meeting place. Never a dull moment. So I end up

---

1 Written by Eric Idle, directed by Robert Young, starring Eric, Rick Moranis and Catherine Zeta-Jones.

having, as my third meal of the day, a breakfast with TG and Ina. The 1976 Pythons v ABC team.[1] Very jolly.

He goes off to write. I go up to unpack and ring Samantha Dean, Castle Hill's PR lady. She says response continues well, reads me a great review of *American Friends* in *Rolling Stone*.

The sore throat lingers and I have a stomach ache.

Ask at a drug store about vitamin C. A very Jewish pharmacist points straight away to the strongest dose – 1,000 mgs. 'Linus Pauling took *two of these every hour* until he'd squeezed the life out of whatever had gotten into him.' When I take them home I notice it recommends one a day!

Tuesday, March 30th: New York

A call from the Letterman office. I tell them that the story of *American Friends* is not a comedy and that the most interesting thing about the movie is that I play a serious role. 'Well, maybe we have to find a way of saying this from a comedic perspective.'

Saturday, April 3rd: New York

The rain's stopped, there's some sun poking through the clouds. At ten I'm in a taxi to the Met and wandering happily around the Lehman Collection, which includes Vuillards of distinction and some lusty Bonnards too. Then around the American Wing – looking mainly at the paintings – Caleb Bingham's 'Fur Traders' one of my great favourites. Difficult to tear myself away.

Onto the subway to Union Square. Investigate the Quad Cinema where *American Friends* opens in six days' time. A modest, unassuming theatre in a pleasant, unostentatious neighbourhood. Just around the corner is a Gothic Revival church whose tower (erected in 1846) is said to be a replica of Magdalen College, Oxford. I take that as a good omen.

Sunday, April 4th: New York

After breakfast call Julian [Schlossberg, our American distributor]. He's in candid mood. 'If we don't get the *New York Times* we're dead.' The

---

1 Ina Lee Meibach acted for the Pythons in the case against ABC Television.

Times and the *Village Voice* are key to our success in the city, it seems. If either is critical or even lukewarm life will be hard.

Despite all the work of last week, we are still vulnerable. Only hanging onto public awareness by our fingertips.

Thursday, April 8th: New York

Welcome Helen at 10.30. Very happy to see her; it's nice to be on neutral territory, in a comfortable hotel, away from the anticlimactic realities of home.

To add to the pleasure of our reunion, there is an unequivocally fine day, and to celebrate it I've booked a table at the Boathouse Café. Nancy comes along with Timothy. He's very good, but given to standing on his chair and saying 'Excuse me!' very loudly. Simon is stricken with back trouble two nights from opening in *My Fair Lady* out in New Jersey.

At 9.30 I find myself down at one of the halls of NYU for Richard Brown's Film Class. Richard Brown's acolytes prepare me to go on stage. The event, I'm told with pride, is being televised. (It seems nearly everything in America is televised nowadays!) Half an hour on stage. Feel comfortable and relaxed and the adulation helps.

Afterwards give Tristram, Virginia and Archie a ride back to their hotel. On the way we pick up a *New York Times* from a news-stand. Though it's only 10.15, Friday's edition is out. Tristram scans the review page faster than I can. 'It's not good' is all he says.

By the time I've reached Canby's review[1] I have heard enough to know it's very bad. In fact it's the only kind of notice I really am not prepared for – a vicious clubbing to death of the film. There is no quarter given. Every aspect irks him – acting, photography. Well it's impossible to read at one sitting.

Though the Powells must be exhausted, the Canby mugging has roused them sufficiently to suggest we all go for a drink and a bite to eat. We end up at Fiorello's on Broadway – where I seem to remember eating with Patrick and Tristram in the days of doubt about the film three or four years ago.

We can think of no explanation for Canby's virulence. Funnily enough, a few hours earlier at the Cleeses', JC had suggested calling my

1 Vincent Canby, chief film critic of the *New York Times* since 1969.

character Canby – to get back at the critic for his savaging of *A Fish Called Wanda*.

From the heights of praise and approbation at ten o'clock, we're plunged to the depths 20 minutes later; now, at midnight, I walk back along the edge of Central Park, past huddled sleeping figures on benches and in the crooks of walls, feeling curiously light-headed and carefree.

Friday, April 9th: New York

Phone calls to Steve, Patrick, who arrived yesterday, and of course Julian S, who cannot conceal his disappointment. But during the morning word comes in of good reviews in the *News*, the *Post* and *Newsday*.

In the evening I've organised a get-together down in the Village for all friends of *American Friends*. Important not to let it become a wake in the wake of Canby's review, and in fact it works well.

H survives until 11.15; we're the first to leave, apart from Julian S.

A cold wind blowing down 5th Avenue tightens the breath as we walk past the church with its tower modelled on Magdalen College, Oxford, which I had hoped would be a good omen! Not on this Good Friday.

Monday, April 12th: New York

Wake early and, despite myself, fall to worrying about the work that lies ahead – the proximity of, and my unpreparedness for, the Irish *Great Railway Journeys* shoot; the pile of letters that will be awaiting my arrival at home. I wish we could stay in this happy limbo for a while longer, but all too soon it's coming to an end.

Julian calls. He sounds much more cheerful. Says that the *Washington Post* article is coming out this Easter weekend, but not Sunday. Business in both Washington and New York has been sufficiently good to ensure a second week in each. (How we clutch at straws! That this should be good news.)

Run round the Reservoir whilst H goes for a final blast of shopping; in the two weeks I've been in New York, the Park has begun to blossom. Cherry and hawthorn and what looks like magnolia, but the trees generally are still bare.

To Nancy and Simon for a drink and to say goodbye. Simon is on his third or fourth chiropractor and has been assured he will be ready to take his role on Wednesday, but he still stands against walls with the half-startled, half-agonised look of someone preparing to face a firing squad.

On by taxi to 77th and supper with JC.

Talk over thoughts on 'Death Fish Zoo' which have occurred to me over the weekend. Also try out on him my thought on a two-hander. That it should be set in a foreign country, probably in Africa, that we should play diplomats representing the old and the new school thrown together to evacuate the country of Brits in some crisis. JC likes the thought that it should involve the politics of international aid – about which there is much to be said.

Friday, April 16th

Helen has bought me a card, some artificial red roses and a seal cub paperweight for our 27th anniversary. We still get on pretty well, neither of us being confrontational, but both of us being stubborn! As Helen says this morning, it's not been a claustrophobic relationship.

Tom comes round later in the morning. He has been working some 24-hour shifts with Rhythm and Bass, and his studio at Charlton King's Road is in demand. He seems to be finding new confidence – he's playing piano on some of the mixes, and is well on top of the new recording technology.

To a much-put-off lunch with Tony Laryea. After we worked together on *Comic Roots* [1983] he rose fast in the BBC, without compromising his radical tendencies, and was in line for No. 2 at BBC Manchester when he decided to leave and go independent. He has gravitas, but no pomposity.

I chat to him about my vague thoughts on a religious slant to my next project. Been festering in my mind as I found myself becoming more interested in Islam as a result of my travels. Wouldn't such a prog be helpful, as well as giving a new slant to my travels? He was very encouraging. Apparently religion is an area many prog-makers are thinking about now.

Monday, April 19th: London–Derry

Meet Nigel and Julian on flight to Belfast to begin filming our Great Railway Journey. There meet up with rest of the crew at a local hotel. Ken, Hilary, Fraser.

Drive on the pleasantly un-busy roads to Derry, or Londonderry as the Protestant, Unionist, Loyalists call it. A striking city. A little reminiscent of Toledo in its situation on a hill above the river, with the still-solid grey walls built 380 years ago enclosing a tight cluster of roofs and tall spires.

We're the guests at a Lord Mayor's reception. Despite Derry now being 70-30 a Catholic city, the post of Mayor rotates on a power-sharing basis and our host tonight is actually a member of Paisley's DUP.

Lots of city councillors drop in to shake hands. No women, I notice.

Tuesday, April 20th: Derry

Filming delayed from the start by news of a security alert in The Diamond, the central intersection of Old Derry. Where our BBC hoist should be in position.

At Bishop Gate, where armour-plated doors block vehicle access from the Fountain area, there was an explosion at 3.30 a.m. The frighteningly young, smooth-cheeked English squaddie we talk to is philosophical. It was timed to go off at 6.15, he says, when the side door is opened. He observes what it's done to the door, which is completely blown out, and adds 'It was my turn to open the door this morning.'

Thursday, April 22nd: Belfast

This afternoon, as the bright periods diminish and the rain sets steadily in, we visit the Falls and Shankill Road.

I spend a gruelling and uncomfortable afternoon squeezed into the unit Toyota with Ivor Oswald – businessman and guide – in the front, and Nigel and Fraser in the back. The car windows keep steaming up. The steady rain reduces visibility. Ivor drives erratically, but there is no sign of any impatience from other vehicles as we travel up the Falls Road.

At first the surroundings are nothing like as bleak and desolate as I'd expected. Apart from the notorious Divis Flats, there is little high-rise, and a lot of new terraces are under construction mirroring the red-brick Victorian character of the rest of the city. Schools, hospitals, joggers, ice-cream parlours, all the usual trimmings of late-twentieth-century life, not affluent, but by no means uncomfortable or desperate.

The shock is the sight of the police stations and army bases. Façades of concrete and sheet metal garlanded with cameras on infra-red control, from which the eyes of the authorities can observe the seeming normality of streets and gardens. These quasi-military presences must be as much a provocation as a necessity. They represent institutionalised force, embattled and dug in against the outside world. No wonder the men of both sides who attack them have a chance of becoming heroes.

The long streets off the Shankill where Catholic and Protestant communities face each other are uncompromisingly depressing. No amount of neat, brick housing can disguise this awful human mess. For three miles a 'peace line' runs across the city, separating the sides. The price of 'peace' has been the destruction of buildings, the blocking-off of roads, and the erection of more of the big, brutal fortresses which serve to both intimidate and protect.

Even Ivor Oswald, who has good to say for both sides because he 'believes in Belfast', admits that the two will not be reconciled in his lifetime. Ken thinks that being in Europe may hold the key to some sort of readjustment – Catholic Southern Ireland becoming more prosperous – closer links, less isolation. Ian from BBC Belfast newsroom says that as the Catholic birth rate is now so much higher than the Protestant, there could be a majority democratic vote for independence – but that won't be for 20 years at least. In the meantime the emotion and anger of rivalry remains painted on gable ends and written in graffiti. 'No Surrender.' 'Our Day Will Come.'

Tuesday, April 27th: Belfast–Dublin

Take the three o'clock Enterprise train service for Dublin.

The coach is scrubbed and still hung with a hint of disinfectant. The windows all have 'Reserved for the BBC' stickers plumb in the middle, preventing us filming anything until they've been removed.

So out of Northern Ireland, and into the less obsessively neat atmosphere of the Irish countryside. Hedges ramble, fields are lumpy and unused, the dwellings of the poor shabbier than anything seen in the North, but the heart lifts to be away from the video cameras and the steel fences.

Fax from Kath shows 'AF' quietly slipping into oblivion in NYC and Washington.

Wednesday, April 28th: Dublin

The hotel is filling up with football supporters – a big World Cup qualifier with Denmark is being played at Lansdowne Road Stadium, five minutes' walk from the hotel. All around the streets are filled with salesmen, and a live jazz band plays on a traffic island.

We extract ourselves from the seething mass and drive out to Bray Station, south of the city, to film an interview with The Edge[1] of U2. He has requested that it be shot on the DART train service that runs along by the sea, into and across Dublin.

After all our nervousness that he will attract adoring crowds, Edge turns out to be quite mild and unsensational. No dark glasses or army of minders. He emerges from a Citroën BX, diminutive and pale. Been working hard. Six months in the studio completing a new album prior to a tour that begins May 6th.

He says he dreads the thought of touring until it happens, then he just lets it carry him along. Bono is the opposite, he says. Can't wait to get on the road, but discontent sets in as soon as he's on it.

The interview is more like a conversation – he's laid-back, eloquent and modest with a good sense of humour. Likes Ireland, obviously, finds it the best place to live and work and retain a sense of proportion. 'Let's face it, no-one in Ireland can ever be more famous than Gay Byrne.'[2]

He's anxious to avoid getting involved in politics. Perhaps once bitten, twice shy. Ends up ruefully with a send-up of himself – 'It's hard work being an icon, you know.'

Thursday, April 29th: Dublin

A splendid day. We film at the National Library Reading Room, trying to fill out the 'Michael's Irish roots' aspect of the documentary.

Tom Lindert the genealogist has news for me though. At 11.30 last night he heard from his contacts that a copy of the marriage certificate of Edward and Brita Gallagher has been traced. They were married at the British Embassy in Paris by Chaplain Cox on 2nd October 1867. No note of the parentage of either party, which he thinks is odd.

---

1 The Edge played guitar and keyboard in the band.
2 Gay Byrne, Irish broadcaster, famed for his long-running television programme *The Late Show*.

In the afternoon up to Glasnevin Cemetery to walk amongst the graves and talk to a very laid-back American from Orange County who is also looking for his Irish ancestors. He doesn't hold out much hope. His name is Kopnowski.

Tuesday, May 4th: Ardmore–Mallow

We make for Ardmore, down the coast towards Cork. It's a small village on an impressive bay.

Then along the western arm of the bay to interview Molly Keane.[1] She lives in an unpretentious house set on the edge of the cliff, obtained by a long, steep stairway. She is frail and thin and walks slowly with the aid of a stick. All the time I'm there I'm haunted by the thought of her trying to ascend those steps to the road.

Once she's sorted us all out and relaxed a little she begins to show off as only a glamorous 80-year-old can – shamelessly flirting with the men, revelling in her stories of Noël Coward and various raffish horse-owning ancestors.

She cannot really be interviewed fast – her stories stretch out and naturally expand, occasionally she goes hacking off into the undergrowth of some half-remembered episode – usually to re-emerge triumphantly.

Despite sounding quintessentially English, she claims to be Irish. But she despairs of present-day Ireland – all the 'burglaries' and 'break-ins' seem to give her great cause for anxiety. What we shall get from the interview is debatable, but she charmed and bewitched everyone there.

Ken leaves with tears in his eyes. He knew her, through Russell Harty,[2] who was a terrific friend of Molly's, and thinks that may well be the last time he will see her. She calls Ken her 'nephew Ken' and me 'baby Michael' – which is another reason to like her, as I meet her on the last day of my forties!

Train filming takes us through to Mallow and at six o'clock to the handsome Georgian country house overlooking the quiet rural landscape of the Blackwater River – Longueville House.

Surprise arrival of Anne James from London. At midnight Ken orders champagne, and Anne gives me the office present – slippers and a pipe!

1 Molly Keane, Irish novelist, who also wrote under the name M. J. Farrell. Her 1981 novel, *Good Behaviour*, was shortlisted for the Booker Prize.
2 Television presenter of arts and chat shows, who died in 1988.

Wednesday, May 5th: Longueville House, Mallow

Lift my blinds to reveal a gorgeous morning. Still, sunny, mist clearing from the low valley, cows and sheep contentedly grazing right up to the forecourt of the hotel. Magnificent and ancient trees adorn the view (evidently planted in the configuration of British and French troops at the Battle of Waterloo). There could really be nowhere better to raise the spirits on a change of decade.

A busy day's filming, based at the small town of Buttevant, about 20 miles north of Mallow.

Tony O'Neil's bar, which is at the back of his grocery shop, is our base for much of the day, and I salute the passing of my forties, at a quarter to twelve, with a glass of Guinness in his excellent company.

Much filming in graveyards as we search for Gallaghers. It seems that the deeper one goes into all this ancestor-hunting the more opaque the waters become. I really don't know where I am now – caught on slippery ground between fact and fiction.

But the weather stays dreamily warm, the locations are magical and Tony O'Neil is a great host, in a village where everyone is constantly introducing you to someone else.

It's a long day, and made longer when one of our two vehicles runs out of fuel in a dangerous part of a busy main road. At 8.15, I'm directing oncoming vehicles to slow down whilst Fraser leaps around organising relief.

We arrive back at Longueville – quick bath and at last down to order dinner. Sitting in a magnificent room, order myself a glass of champagne. For some reason it takes a while to arrive. Jane, who runs the hotel, tells me that she has a new waitress and she hopes we'll all be understanding. This only increases my impatience. I've earned this drink, for God's sake.

At that moment the tall doors of the drawing room, mysteriously closed, are pulled back to reveal Helen, bearing a tray of champagne glasses. A great coup, in the most theatrical of surroundings. I had already rung Rachel and suppressed a certain irritation on hearing that Mum was at badminton!

A complete and wonderfully welcome surprise. I thanked Fraser for his part in procuring me a woman on this sad day in my life!

Then we eat, splendidly, in the library, a table away from the other guests; presents include an old map of Ireland from Fraser, Nigel and

Julian, a silver container for the 'tooth fairy', a big Guinness jug, and, from Patti, via Nigel, a caricature of the *Pole to Pole* team. Flowers from George H and Olivia too.

To bed on one of the best of days.

Wednesday, May 12th

By bike to the Lansdowne in Primrose Hill. A converted pub, which now resembles a cross between an Amsterdam family bar and a Viennese café. Bare boards, tables scattered about, a blackboard menu strong on aioli-assisted dishes. Music, good wines and small selection of draught beer.

Meet Roger Mills there. A little too trendy for him, I think, but a good pint of Everards settles him down.

The Meridian documentary series I've agreed to do now looks set to be on the Isle of Wight – on video, each episode shot in seven days; intro and outro, no commentary … very different already from the long journeys.

Friday, May 14th

Documentary proposal arrives in the post from the TV Trust for the Environment. Would I host a big series on 'The Aid Game'. All over the world and talk to bankers, politicians, UN people, etc.

Sit on the loo and regard the prospect – hard work but a good chance to make a serious impact on people's thinking. The trouble is that I feel I would be driven in a certain direction – my communicative talents used to someone else's ends. Tempting, but later in the day write and decline.

Saturday, May 15th

Set off for Wembley at 12.45 in a BBC car, supplied by Radio Sport, who have also provided me with three £100 tickets for the Arsenal–Wednesday final. All in return for a live appearance on the Cup programme.

Great anticipation and excitement. Rachel hasn't been to a football match before and I've never been to an FA Cup Final.

Wembley Stadium boasts enormous 'SEGA' sponsorship signs and, like British Airports Authority, seems happy to sell every nut and bolt if there's a company name that can be slapped on them.

Met by BBC PA and led, through the dining (sorry, 'banqueting') room and right up onto the network of metal struts and tubes that holds up the roof. Pick our way across the underside of the roof frame, narrowly avoiding decapitation. I'm quite impressed that anyone gets up here alive.

The sun comes out for the kick-off. Wembley becomes the centre of the whole world, walled-in, caught in a time warp singing 'Abide With Me'– the ghosts of 69 previous finals around.

Wednesday are poor in the first half and lucky to be only one behind, but the recovery of confidence they so desperately need comes in the early second half. Hirst goal – then suddenly we start to play. But never incisive enough. Both teams look tired, short of ideas. Nail-biting goes on into extra time. A draw.

Massive feeling of disappointment, doubtless compounded 80,000 times. To be prepared to give so much, then to be cheated out of the madness, the spontaneous, unfettered joy of victory, leaves an odd numbness.

Fans leaving the stadium are generally quiet, as if they'd seen something they didn't really want to talk about.

Wednesday, May 19th

To the office with the other shortlisted NCR books for final reappraisal. Tonight we shall choose the winner.

Down to the Savoy by seven to meet the rest of the judges. Any hopes I might have still harboured of persuading them round to *Fever Pitch* as winner scotched by Diana Rigg's absence in South Africa, leaving behind a preference order of *Never Again*, Wolpert, Hornby and Christopher Hill.

We repair to the Iolanthe Room, a small, high-ceilinged, timber panelled and pillared side room. Puttnam gives us all a present for being good judges. It's a much more agreeable atmosphere than the boardroom at NCR and there is conciliation and courtesy in the air.

Richard Hoggart says that he has made every effort with *Fever Pitch* – 'I took it to Poland with me'– and whilst he sees qualities he had once closed his eyes to, he wasn't won over. Odd that such a man of the people should find it so hard to support a book that deals so well with a neglected area of popular culture.

Margaret is on good form. She can be formidable – viz. her defence of Iris Murdoch; tonight, with Iris out of the way, she's much more relaxed and professes great enthusiasm for *Fever Pitch*, but seems set on *Never Again*. Still, I say my bit. *Never Again* is a safe bet – another academic work which I find only as good as several other works of historical research we've sidelined. *Fever Pitch* is an original, a book of passion and personality.

Puttnam's enthusiasm for *Fever Pitch* has waned, and I find myself acquiescing in the selection of *Never Again*, reminding myself that I've once more been hijacked by the intellectuals. I lost *My Life as a Dog* to *The Sacrifice* and, though it worried me less, *Strictly Ballroom* to *The Player*.

Thursday, May 20th

Around four a.m. the alarm goes and Helen gets up. She's organised a week's holiday on a Greek island with three friends from her bereavement class. Tickets have to be collected two hours before the flight, etc. etc. I'm barely conscious of her bending towards me in the gloom and planting a farewell kiss and later, when I hear the taxi door slam, I realise that in all the rush and tumble of this week I don't even know which island it is she's going to.

The likelihood of a third travel series comes closer with the writing of a letter from me to Clem expressing my own intentions, in writing, for the first time.

I have suggested a delivery date of October '97, and three filming periods of three months each, out of which we make ten programmes.

Important in my decision is the realisation that the travel series option offers the greatest chance of personal control over a project. The experience of *American Friends* – my own film, yet played at a lot of other people's pace, and to a lot of other tunes – has made me wary of film-making.

Arrive at the Savoy just as Nick Hornby, his fiancée and bevy of publishing ladies also appear. It is an extraordinary coincidence that Arsenal, Nick H's team – the team to which he is so totally, slavishly devoted, the team which caused him to write the book – should be playing Sheffield Wednesday in the FA Cup Final replay at the very moment when the announcement of the NCR Award is going on.

Nip out every now and then to keep an eye on the game. Nick H is sat at a small table near the kitchen, with a bottle of wine and the telly. Some of his minders become a real nuisance, endlessly telling me how lucky we are to have him here tonight. As I'd done so much to get his book into the last four, I felt I didn't need this.

Arsenal go 1-0 up in first half; Wednesday equalise midway through second! Hornby looks hot and distracted. 1-1 at full time.

The meal trails on, video presentations have to be gone through, then as extra time is being played, the judges are at last called up.

My tribute to *Fever Pitch* goes down well. Much laughter and I feel very relieved. Patrick Mill, the NCR man deputed to run the Award, announces Peter Hennessy to be the winner – and Hennessy is lapping up the applause when Mill slips me a piece of paper. Arsenal 2-1.

I think of Rachel out there in the rain, at Wembley for the second time in a week, and I can't, I'm afraid, enjoy any of Hennessy's triumph. I didn't want his book to win, and to see celebration at this time makes me feel oddly as though I'm at the match. A loser amongst winners.

Friday, May 21st

Awful news in the papers; in fact my first reaction when I see a blurred photo in the *Guardian* of the Opera House in Belfast, gashed down the side as if a huge ship had run into it, is that I must be reading some anniversary account of the bombing of 1991. But it happened again yesterday. The IRA left a 1,000lb bomb on a truck at the site where Michael Barnes and I did our interview less than a month ago. Most of the windows of the Europa are broken, the remains of the truck resemble a giant piece of liquorice, and the Opera House has been shattered again.

Later in the morning I call Michael – there's little one can say. He said it was better yesterday when he had to do 17 interviews and there was no time for the full weight of what had happened to sink in. They will not know for a few days how serious the damage is, but the auditorium is intact.

Catherine Bailey, who tried to get me to do a series called 'Orphans of Empire', is now getting different presenters for each one. They've just been to see Alan Bennett. Apparently he liked the idea but was worried that he might be expected to do more than he wanted to – 'I can't be like Michael Palin … I can't talk to people'!

Saturday, May 22nd

A sort of loose schedule has arrived from Clem today which I see bears the title 'Palin's Pacific'. More excitingly for the future, I have a letter from David Pugh which bears the first good news about *The Weekend* since our last 'preferred' actor turned it down. Pugh had sent it on spec to Richard Wilson, whose agent says he likes it very much 'and would be available to do it next February'.

Thursday, May 27th

Compile some thoughts on the Pacific project. Have to think quietly and firmly about my own ability to take it on. The trouble is one forgets very quickly the awkwardnesses and privations of travel. Must be severe with myself – and remember sleepless nights in filthy huts and remorseless early-morning loading of gear and the runs for days on end.

Out to the Royal Academy Annual Dinner. It's all well stage-managed with guardsmen in bearskins sounding a tremendous fanfare to an-nounce arrival of star guest – Mary Robinson, the President of Ireland. She enters, slow, cool and very regal; good-looking but not beautiful, turning a lot of intellectual heads. Her impressively large husband, Nick, walks deferentially behind.

Paul Smith is at our table. He introduces himself saying 'You don't know me but I know you.' To which I'm able to reply 'Of course I know you and I'm wearing your dinner jacket.' Flash the Paul Smith label back at him.

Eric Clapton is also there. I tell him that I'm easing up on commit-ments for the year. 'So am I ... So am I ...' he enthuses. 'I've finally made the decision ... I'm not doing anything at all ... for two months.'

Philip Sutton is opposite. He's an RA [Royal Academician]. They all tend to behave a bit like naughty schoolboys. Leonard McComb sketches faces in the throng and knocks over glasses of wine. A lefty sculptor called Bruce McLean heckles Virginia Bottomley, who gives a dull, school-mistressy speech which is politely received.

Roger de Grey the RA President is cheered to the rafters and halfway through his speech, which he aims cleverly at Peter Brooke, the Heritage Minister, he talks about state aid coming too late to plug the holes in the roof. At that point mock snow falls from on high and sprinkles the top table.

And Tom Phillips RA is sporting a wooden bow tie.

Sunday, May 30th

To Oxford, where Will is only a few days away from his finals.

Will in good form. He shows us two 8-mill films he's made with friends – just larking about, but they remind me of what Terry J used to make at his home in Claygate in 1965.

Will loves the 8-mill camera – without my pushing him towards it – and sounds to have found an aptitude and appetite for making films. 'They listen to me,' he says, with some pride … 'I tell them what to do and they listen to me!' He now wants to be a film director.

Monday, May 31st: London–Llangoed Hall Hotel, near Hay-on-Wye

Looking at the Hay programme I notice that our event is titled 'Poles Apart'. For some reason I'd thought it was only about Antarctic travel, so, wearily, I must readjust the opening as well as finish the thing.

Catch the one o'clock train from Paddington.

Driven into Hay. Meet Daniel Snowman, who could hardly be anything other than an expert on Polar travel, and Beryl Bainbridge, a little nervous. At half past five she orders a large scotch with water – I follow her example.

Freddie Raphael is waiting to give his six o'clock writers' class, but Bernice Rubens bounces in announcing, without seeing him, 'They can't fill up Freddie Raphael's talk for love nor money.' I shush her just in time, but Beryl, bless her, has not noticed and blurts out 'So no-one's going to Freddie Raphael then?'

'Poles Apart' has attracted 900 people, and was the first of all the events to sell out.

We're driven to a tent in the middle of a field. Mud-gouged tracks make our car slither about, but there's a fine view of Hay on its ridge.

The event goes very well. The wind slaps the tent in a very passable imitation of Antarctic conditions, so I feel at home.

Though fearing I would be a lamb slaughtered by wolf-ish experts, I seem to know an awful lot about the place when I put my mind to it.

Wednesday, June 2nd

George H rings ... 'George here ...' he drawls '... Giorgio Armani of Henley.' He tells me that HandMade Films has finally ceased to be. He and Denis O'Brien have had a big falling-out.

George says he theoretically owes £28 million now.

He laughs about it, a little grimly perhaps, but it's clear he's been going through a tough time.

The HandMade Film catalogue – comprising most of our works – is to be put up for sale. He wants to let us know this in advance – just in case, I suppose, we can find the money to buy it. Trouble is our films tend to be the gems of the catalogue and we'd have to buy a lot of dead wood as well, to get at them.

Wednesday, June 9th

Work on my speech to launch Enviroscope tomorrow. Maybe it's the tremendously muggy heat, but I feel quite grumpy at having my time taken up with this Wildlife Trust project. I don't like the name Enviroscope. It looks extraordinarily confused and complicated in practice; I've not been adequately briefed, and Kath is critical of the vast amount of paper this so-called environmental organisation pumps her way.

Thursday, June 10th

Down to the Enviroscope launch. First a photocall in Hyde Park.

A group of well-spoken, healthy-looking schoolchildren from Thame, photographers, and a bevy of reporters. But nothing like the response to the Stammering launch. I think people have been numbed by endless environmental initiatives. Some men in suits from Heinz, who have put money into the production of the Enviroscope pack – which actually looks quite fun – a sort of I-Spy. The youth 'arm' of the Wildlife Trusts Partnership is called, a little sinisterly, 'Watch'.

Most of the time spent signing autographs for the children. I like them, they're bright, but not knowingly clever. At one point the photographer suggests I hoist a young schoolgirl onto my shoulder. Nowadays, of course, this is not at all the correct thing to do. But I do it all the same. Hope she isn't traumatised for life.

Then we troop across to the sombre surroundings of the Royal Geographical Society.

Robert Falcon Scott stares at me from the other end of the room as I take my place at a long table and make one of four speeches. Tell the audience (of 20–30 people) that Enviroscope is not a painful medical instrument. No applause to any of the speeches – but then they are the press.

Back to the office.

Read 'Open Verdict', a script sent to me from Jon Blair. I'm offered the character of a businessman in Hong Kong who sets out to find the reasons behind his 21-year-old daughter's suicide back in England.

Seemed conventional to start with but as I read on I became drawn into the story, largely because it avoided cliché and sensational revelation and generally rang true as a tale of compromises, inadequacies and little mistakes rather than big crises. No underlining of good or bad, hero and villain – but managing to keep the excitement that comes from nothing more than the human predicament.

Decide to think about it over the weekend – the first serious consideration of an acting role since JC decided to begin work on 'Death Fish Zoo'.

Out in the evening to Will Wyatt's BBC Writers' Party, held this evening at the Mall Galleries. From the top of a flight of steps I look down over a sea of hot writers. Will makes a speech. Les Dawson has just died. 'Just my luck,' muses Ian Davidson, when I catch up with him. 'I've just signed a contract for his new series.'

Monday, June 14th

In the evening to the Finnish Embassy in a corner of Belgrave Square for a sauna party to which I was invited, along with Jeremy Paxman (who cancels at the last minute).

Met by a harassed, rather browbeaten Finn, who is head of Public Affairs. He admits me, with many keys and many security locks, to a basement room – table, chairs, massive television screen and two men with the build and slightly seedy worldliness of blue-film actors. One is from a prominent Finnish paper and the other a German from *Die Welt*.

The German is most voluble. I ask him what the German status symbols are nowadays – 'Oh, probably, an abandoned Trabant in the garden.' He is critical of the way Germans travel 'always in groups', and

resorts to speaking Swedish when there are too many of his countrymen around.

We sit and sweat, then drink some beer and take some refreshment,
talk, wrapped in towels, then another session. The beer is weak and the
conversation civilised. It's far from being an orgy.

Out into Belgrave Square about eleven o'clock. Rainer promises to
send me an invitation to his crayfish and vodka party!

Realise how much I've enjoyed being the only Englishman in the
group tonight and how much I enjoy hearing foreigners talk about the
world.

Wednesday, June 16th

To Oxford to attend the Pitt Rivers Museum celebration for Wilfred
Thesiger.

The traffic snarled up right along Westway from the flyover almost to
the Polish War Memorial.

By the time I reach Pitt Rivers the speeches are under way. I'm thrust
into TV interviews beside mammoth skeletons, and photographs with
Thesiger himself.

Thesiger, with his superbly ridged aquiline features, is being pushed
around as well, and the two of us are brought together, blinking in confusion before some display board, beamed at by a gawping crowd. Very
uncomfortable.

Thesiger shows me the goatskin bag in which he kept his camera.
He started with a Leica, went on to a Lutz. The photographs (25,000 of
them) which he has presented to the museum are magnificent. Black
and white, clean, clear, strikingly powerful images. Nothing seems
random – every study is a little work of art in itself.

Then I'm moved on to the President's Lodgings at Magdalen where
Thesiger is staying before returning to Kenya next week.

We're invited upstairs to the Old Library to see maps drawn by T. E.
Lawrence.

Thesiger examines the text through a magnifying glass. We're also
given a glimpse of the oldest handwritten book in existence in Britain –
by William of Malmesbury, 12th century. Someone tries to get a learned
discussion going as to whether a manuscript can be a book.

A chance to talk to Thesiger without the pressures of celebrity. He
doesn't think such a journey as his [across the Empty Quarter of Saudi

Arabia] could be done nowadays – all the Bedouins have pick-up trucks. I ask him about his health on these trips. He claims to have eaten everything put in front of him and drunk from wells and locally filled flasks and never to have suffered any problems.

Thursday, June 17th

To Feltham, to present my *Pole to Pole* talk at what used to be the Borstal there, but is now signposted as the Young Offenders' Institution.

The entrance is newish, red-brick, trying not to be daunting, but by the time you've been through three pairs of security doors – one locked before the other can be opened – and smelt the slightly musty bitterness in the air, you know you are in an institution. Two 15-foot-high fences topped with razor wire and separated by a 'dead area' – treated so that no cover can grow – surround an otherwise quite pleasant, campus-like arrangement of 'houses' and wide stretches of grass. The houses are called after birds – so there are men behind bars in Albatross or Lapwing.

Tea with the Governor, Joe Whitty. He's blunt, opinionated, but basically decent, I think. Reminds me of John Prescott; and in fact both served their time in the Merchant Navy.

Whitty and his deputy have just returned from Kentucky, where he found much to envy. Only 46 maximum in each institution – almost one to one with warders. Here he has 800 (500 on remand, 300 convicted) and 270 warders. In Kentucky they needed no fences or razor wire and, unlike Britain, sentences could be reduced by good behaviour at regular intervals, if there was a prison officer able to speak up for the offender. This gave incentive for the offender to better himself rather than, as Whitty put it, 'sit around all day with dirty books and the television'.

Our English penal system does sound very primitive. Still geared to giving everyone involved a bad time.

Meet some of the inmates. Nearly all working-class, about 50% black. Most were friendly, very little hostility. Confusion, resignation, listlessness.

Overall impression is of waste – waste of human potential – the indescribably depressing feeling of lines of communication being shut off – clanging shut like the barred cell doors they can't disguise here.

As I leave a boy calls out to me from the slit window of his cell. He thrusts a copy of *Pole to Pole* through the bars for me to autograph.

Friday, July 2nd

Lunch with Robert Fox, Pugh and our newest candidate for Stephen Febble – Richard Wilson – now a considerable 'oldie' star from *One Foot in the Grave.*

Wilson is quiet to start with, not over-eager – but I think genuinely likes the work. 'It's a very good first play,' he says, carefully; then realising just what he's said, adds, rather less carefully, 'It's a very good *second* play.'

After a cautious, not altogether comfortable few minutes fencing around his enthusiasm for the script and our enthusiasm for him, Richard appears to have a very difficult thing to say. It turns out that he feels the play is too tough and concentrated a piece to be played more than once a day … 'It's a long journey,' he says – the only bit of luvvie-speak from him all lunchtime.

I'm not quite sure where we are at the end. Does he or doesn't he want to do it?

Taxi to the zoo, where I meet Cleese and Co. in the small mammal house. John is taking Robert Lindsay, Robert Young, Iain Johnstone and various children round the small mammal and insect houses. His hope is that Lindsay will play the small-mammal keeper and I will be, as had always been planned between him and me, in charge of the insects – or invertebrates.

We are allowed into the bat enclosures in the nocturnal areas. A cloud of fruit bats dart and dive around us, full of curiosity, but always just missing contact.

Friday, July 23rd

Down to Waterloo for a day 'auditioning' landladies in the Isle of Wight. My first close look at the new Eurostar platforms – inside a glass-and-steel-sheathed shed designed by Grimshaw. Quite splendid – a stirring piece of design and engineering made attractive without gimmicks. It blends well with the existing Waterloo complex and has a sweep and grandeur which harks back to Barlow's St Pancras. Concrete cut down to a minimum, steel tresses and ribs take the weight.

Meet the indefatigable Robyn, our location manager, and Roger Mills, our director, and onto the 9.32 to Southampton.

First landlady, Miss Wright, is in her 80s, runs the small terraced house without help and clearly is very fussy about whom she likes and doesn't like. She puts on a tape for us in the little back room she calls her 'kennel'. 'Do we like Patsy Cline?'

She then, under Roger's smooth and scalpel-like probing, tells us that her life has been 'marred by tragedy'. The man she was to marry died when both of his lungs collapsed, only days before the wedding. Her father had some problem with a vein in his leg … 'then one day, just after he'd taken my mother some tea, he sat down to tie up his shoelace and his vein burst … you know that blood can drain out of the human body in two minutes'. We sit, fascinated, but appalled… 'My mother had to walk to him, through blood.'

Robyn suggests we go for a different landlady each week, instead of one for the series. The more we talk the better this idea seems.

Last landlady is Wendy – an Islander, wry, bright and down-to-earth. Her place is more isolated but kept immaculately and the single room I would have has a view of the Needles.

It's sunny and warm when we return to Cowes to catch the five o'clock boat back to what they all call 'the Mainland'.

Home soon after eleven, greeted by Rachel with the news that Will has passed out of Oxford with a 2:1 degree. Great relief, tremendous news. All the weariness of the day disappears.

Thursday, August 5th

A recce day in the Isle of Wight.

To lunch with Peter Hurst, the editor of the paper I shall be writing for, the *Isle of Wight County Press*. We meet at a small Georgian house hotel with a view across the bush-bordered, nicely irregular lawns to the River Medina, and on the hill above it the long, hard angles of Parkhurst Prison.

Peter wears a well-cut suit and sports thick, well-groomed silvery-grey hair. The editorship sounds a comfortable and prestigious post which enables him to play golf and be respected and quite powerful in a community of 125,000 people. It's produced from well-equipped new offices in the centre of Ryde by a staff of 90 people.

As one of the biggest stories this week is the charging of 150 people with parking offences, one could be forgiven for thinking that the *Isle of Wight County Press* must be a front for the CIA or possibly some American evangelical group. The image is clean, efficient, and rather dull.

We meet our next landlady in Victoria Street, Sandown. She's likeable, but the place looks like everything my taste – cultural, gastronomic, aesthetic – has fled from. We'll see. Rog, I think, is aware of my disappointment and reminds me, robustly, that it was my idea to go into bedsits.

As I drive back across the island I feel a little better. I must be philosophical about this. If the series is to be different, to have an edge, then it can't just be me sitting around with the *Good Hotel Guide*. I must lie back on the nylon sheets and think of Meridian.

The train back is slow, and has no buffet. Fifteen stops, at one of which a little bevy of BR staff spot an unaccompanied bag. They feel it, squeezing gently. 'Well if it goes bang, it goes bang,' says one of them, which makes us all feel better.

Wednesday, August 18th: London–Isle of Wight

I went to bed quite relaxed about the prospect of *Palin's Column*, but something keeps me awake for much of the night.

Palin's Column is all about personal exposure – in front of camera as actor, with people as interviewer and with the added emphasis on writing as the raison d'être of each programme. So, although it is only the Isle of Wight, my subconscious is readying me – making me alert, forcing me to concentrate, making sure I know that whatever I've done before doesn't make a scrap of difference – from the moment I stand before the camera for the first time today I shall be judged all over again.

A grindingly hard first day – besides getting used to a new place and new crew, we shoot in and around Newport, which is full of holidaymakers all agog. 'Round the Isle of Wight in 80 Days, Michael?' Laughter. On to the next.

Then out to a crowded beach to interview and follow an obsessive fossil collector. Despite the fact that he walks us out across a usually submerged petrified forest off the south-west coast and raves about the tide being further out than at any time this year, I cannot raise much interest in the fossils and the filming in his cluttered council house is a real ordeal.

But energy is still required for 'the arrival at Miss Wright's'. Because our opening day has been so long and because we had to eat on the way home from the south of the island, Roger and I are not delivered to

Seaview until almost 11.30. Miss Wright understandably a bit distressed. And she forbids either of us to have a bath 'at this time of night'!

Saturday, August 21st: Isle of Wight

According to Roger, Miss W calls me Fairy Feet. We are now allowed to call her Dorothy. Yesterday morning we filmed a scene in which I offered to stand her the stake money for a bet – she chose two horses and I went into Ryde and put the bet on.

Halfway through breakfast, with Rog and me weighing up chances of our teams in this afternoon's football, she comes up and gives me a smacking kiss. Her horses came one and two.

Like all old women she's obsessed by money, and throughout the morning she alternates between trying to work out how much she's owed by the bookie and how much I owe her for my two telephone calls. Then it's discovered that a cold tap has been left running and, though it produces hardly more than a steady drip, she says she'll 'kill me'.

At lunchtime we make our way to the Ryde Inshore Rescue HQ in preparation for the Trans-Solent Swim. As it turns out this is another case of something I don't want to do becoming one of the best things I've done. It's well organised, the sun pokes out for quite long spells, and as soon as I see our first swimmer plunge in and come up doing breaststroke I know that perhaps I won't make a fool of myself after all.

My turn comes in what I'm advised is the coldest stretch of the crossing, almost in the middle of the Solent. Our opponents are well ahead, so I don't feel I have to win anything, but the water is getting choppier and there is a lot of traffic building up. In I go (on film) and swim for over 20 minutes.

The only vaguely frightening moment was when my support boat hared off to pick up the last swimmer, leaving me alone, feeling very vulnerable in the face of an advancing hovercraft.

Tuesday, August 24th: Isle of Wight

We rendezvous at the *County Press* office.

The column is handed in and after lunch Peter and I are filmed looking it through.

Wednesday, August 25th: Isle of Wight–London

Into Ryde to interview a police spokesman about black magic, etc. He's not been helpful thus far. But Roger persevered with him and today, in Newport, when I asked him the question 'Who runs the Isle of Wight?', he nodded across the road to the Town Hall. 'Those bozos in there may think they run it, but if you want to see who runs the Isle of Wight, go to the County Club in Newport and the Masonic Lodge in Shanklin.' Free-masonry is strong here, he confirms. Parkhurst is full of 'people the police stitched up'. He's refreshing stuff after the cagey, non-committal editor.

Thursday, August 26th

After breakfast, work through letters, make a phone call to Tom P to ask him if he's interested in writing some music for *Palin's Column*. It's something I'd already discussed with Roger. There is such a tiny amount of money in the budget that we could not afford any established name and would have to have relied on library music. Tom has the equipment, and I hope the ability, without the price. It would be very good experience for him.

Good news from David Pugh – Richard Wilson has signed up for *The Weekend*.

Wednesday, September 1st

Tumble out of bed at 7.20. The dreaded man from Corian kitchen work-tops is our early-morning guest today, and H warns me that he will undoubtedly get some of the way up my nose. She's right, well, quite spectacularly right. He arrives 25 minutes early, before I've had time to break the day in with a cup of tea or a glass of orange juice, and causes immediate disruption.

He is a Python character – usually played by Eric Idle with a nasal voice, a jarring egocentricity and an unerring ability to put backs up. 'Name by name, but not by nature.'

I'm 'Michael', straight away. 'Is this a rest period for you, Michael?'

'Is my little man here to turn the gas off?' I tell him that he will be here at eight. 'Oh, these London boys, they don't know what work is.'

So it goes on ... 'D'you mind if I smoke? A cigarette and a couple of drinks and I'm happy.' Yes, but who else is, I long to say.

Saturday, September 4th

My definition of having time to myself is to be able to pick up a book which I don't have to pick up – to read something which I don't have to read. Simon has sent me his copy of *Borrowed Time* and I'm learning a lot about my teenage hero Bobby D. He chose the name 'Darin' from the faulty neon sign of a Mandarin Chinese restaurant in New York. He doesn't sound an awfully easy man. He had a goal – to be rich and famous and successful by 25 years old. And he achieved it. What is my goal? Did I ever have one? I don't think so. I rarely ever made plans more than two years ahead.

Monday, September 6th

TG persuades me to go to a live reappearance of Pete and Dud, as Derek and Clive, at a Working Men's Club in Kensal Road.

There are photographers clustering round the door of the club in what has always been a rough borderland between Maida Vale and Ladbroke Grove. Upstairs to a crowded room with a stage at one end and camera crews, lights shining like Cyclops, moving about picking off celebrities.

Bodies jostle up against us – Peter, a much slenderer figure than the one who went through our sitting room door. I'm told JC put him onto his private trainer.

Bubbling with good cheer and looking like a couple of naughty schoolboys, Keith Richards and Ronnie Wood greet TG and me with great warmth as if they'd just met lifetime heroes. Very odd. I remember telling Keith he should be Alistair Cooke's replacement on *Letter from America*, but not a lot else.

It's a good, old-fashioned, boozy evening and we all regress to our '60s behaviour. Keith and Ronnie, adept at crowd avoidance, get themselves and select others invited downstairs to the rather plush bar and lounge where the working men sit sipping their beer. Some seem happy with the intrusion, others sit close to their pints whilst Keith and Ronnie chat them up.

Pete and Dud, as far as I could tell, never performed, though Peter did occasionally leave the bar and reappear, claiming they'd done 'another nine and a half seconds'.

Tuesday, September 7th

To the Lingfield at five for squash with Terry J, who leaves in a week for the first of his *Crusades* filming trips.

We part on Rosslyn Hill with a hug – me to the Isle of Wight, Terry to Turkey. Back home I have to pack. The house is still in bandages – the smell of paint hangs in the air. Quick supper as another meeting is still to come.

At nine o'clock David Pugh and Billy and Richard Wilson pick their way over the black plastic sheeting in the hallway. Drink wine and discuss directors. Richard W keeps mentioning my name as a possible – or as a double-act with him, and by the end of the two-hour meeting, when all the other names become a blur (Blakemore not available), it seems to have some sense to it. But no decisions taken.

Wednesday, September 8th: Bembridge, Isle of Wight

Met by Roger and Sally at Fishbourne. Settle ourselves in on the converted Second World War gunboat, which is now painted, bedecked with flowers and sits, the smartest of a line of veteran auxiliary craft quietly rotting on Bembridge Bay.

The top deck is light and airy. My cabin below is tiny and I keep cracking my skull on low beams as I unpack. There is one loo/bathroom amongst us all. The owner is a perky Brummie and it costs £15.00 a night B&B. It's called the Floatel Xoron.

Friday, September 10th: Bembridge

I sleep long and deeply. The creaks of the old timbers don't bother me at all, nor did I hear the rain that apparently fell heavily.

This morning we're taking Dorothy Wright for a coach trip.

We take her on a paddle-steamer trip down the coast. Long walk to the end of Sandown Pier.

I'm trying to remain calm whilst escorting her at a snail's pace and being frequently approached by autograph hunters. I sign rather tight-lipped for one boy, but his mother is very happy – 'Val Doonican was just bloody rude.'

We all eat a cream tea at Godshill, then on to film a spiritualist meeting in Ventnor.

The meeting is another first for me as I've never directly experienced what goes on behind the doors of a spiritualist church. It's a little disappointing. The medium is a popular, cheeky son of the Midlands, an ex-jockey who learnt that he had 'powers' after a serious fall which nearly ended his life. The hall is packed, not with impressionable old ladies but with impressionable people of all ages (there is one family with young daughters) and all walks of life.

Mark the medium sets about introducing people from beyond to people present. Many attempts sounded unconvincing – 'Venice means something to you right? … Vienna? … No, we can't settle for that. Psychics might but we can't (laughter). I see anemones next to you … d'you like them?' Most people try to be helpful and he himself is unfailingly bright and optimistic. Little pain seems to come through and absolutely no recrimination, only reassuring little messages about looking after the garden and eating a balanced diet.

He picks me out at one point. 'I see a little boy called Brian … does the name Brian mean anything to you?'

Monday, September 13th: Bembridge

A wild night, rain and wind. Roger knocks at seven to say my sailing sequence is off.

Lunch at a wonderful café beside Bembridge lifeboat station – multi-coloured Formica table tops and home-made crab sandwiches. *East of Ipswich*, Southwold in the '50s.

The gale blows fiercer as the afternoon goes on, providing a dramatic barrage of sound behind our afternoon interview in the lifeboat shed.

Quick drink afterwards in a pub full of wild, long-haired alternative lifestylers. 'Best marijuana in the island here,' shouts one of them as we leave.

Tuesday, September 14th: Bembridge

Roger knocks at seven. Sailing is on for nine o'clock.

Into *Blue Jay II*, a Bembridge scow – a tough, broad-bottomed, clinker-built sailing boat. The wind is still brisk but has turned from the exposed east to the slightly less exposed north. The rain has stopped.

Well covered against the weather, my instructor Victoria and I bob around. For about half an hour she supervises as I learn to tack and turn. It's impossible to head straight out of the harbour today as the wind is blowing us back in, so manoeuvres are of the essence and, with a quick wind, quick reflexes are necessary.

Roger, filming from a sandy spit, asks if I will now go solo. Apprehensive but unexpectedly carefree, I agree to have a go. Victoria is taken off and I'm on my own. The waves are now quite sharp and after one good turn I fly across the harbour so briskly that I hang on, pulling in the sail tight. The little scow stands almost on its side. Realise that it's filling with water in these unforgiving waves. Pull tighter, lean back, but still it rises as if to capsize. Within a minute there is so much water sloshing about the boat that I'm worried if I shall get out of this. Make another turn, more wind, more tight sail, more water.

At last I give in and call over Vernon, the boat's owner, and Victoria, only just in time to stop it from sinking. Quite a dramatic minute or two as rudder and tiller float away to be picked up by a support craft and the three of us drag the almost helpless (and highly expensive) little boat to shore, and empty out the water.

Roger and the others applaud me; Vernon thought I was deliberately sailing spectacularly, but I feel rather a fool. All of my incompetence, of course, is faithfully captured in sound and vision.

Friday, September 17th

At the house Hamish and the building team are rushing round like headless chickens cleaning up after another week of 'finishing' and before going to Prominent for a party and showing of *Riff-Raff* that I've laid on for them.

Film screening for 22 people. Realise as the film progresses that all of us in there approach it from different ways and I'm not exactly certain whether all the builders enjoy it. Feel doubts suddenly – is Ken Loach, despite his working-class sympathies, still producing a patronising left-wing, middle-class view of the masses? Does anyone want to identify with the exploited – are Clive's boys at all embarrassed at being thought to be working-class? All I can tell is that the ones who laugh most are those who are the most comfortably off.

Leave them all at ten to nine and whizz down to Vasco and Piero's. H and I entertain Julian Schlossberg and his latest flame – a lady called Merron. Rather striking, with long ash-blonde hair and a pale, thin face. Turns out she is a psychic.

He's directing three short plays he's commissioned from Woody Allen, David Mamet and another. Says that I must meet Barbra Streisand – she's good company, unlike her big-screen persona, and anxious to make my acquaintance!

Saturday, September 18th

Begin the first movement of box files from my dusty eyrie to a more permanent, less airy, but hopefully infinitely more capacious area – library and workroom combined. The first file to go up is Python, Series 1, 1969.

JC and Alyce Faye come round, in Alyce Faye's wide Mercedes 230 with the hood down.

JC is about to do a week's filming in *Frankenstein* for Ken Branagh. John claims he's only doing it so he can be stabbed to death by Robert De Niro – I remind him that my death in *Brazil* was also at the superstar's hands!

Alyce Faye has just heard 'Always Look on the Bright Side' being played at a Conservative Party Conference and is rooting around for Eric's phone number so she can leave a message on his machine.

Out to Odette's. John is on one of those diets only he seems to find which allow him to eat almost anything in large quantities. Says he's very close to finishing the first third of the latest 'Death Fish' script, but that my character, Bugsy, fades out a bit and will need to be looked at. He's leaving the UK in the winter, he thinks, and going to California and Hong Kong and points beyond for three months.

Wednesday, September 22nd

'I have Sir David Frost for you,' says a voice on the other end of the phone and after a brief pause the ebullient tones of the Great Man fill the earpiece. David always sounds like a man who's enjoying what he's doing. I haven't detected a moment's self-doubt since that call in the spring of 1969 when a rather anxious Frostie tried to grill me about what he regarded as the defection of JC and Graham from his production company, Paradine, to Python. In short, why were we not doing Python with him?

Sir D wonders if I would be interested in a series of programmes about the parliamentary process which he's putting together next spring. In one of them he would like to have me experience the election process first-hand. Not sure how to say no (as it's quite an idea), but David is sowing the seed, that's all. 'If you fancy running for Parliament just give me a ring,' he bubbles.

Sunday, September 26th

Out to Cibo for their fourth anniversary party. Apparently they give a party at the end of every year to celebrate with and thank their favourite customers. We're on a table already occupied by the Cleeses and Michael Winner and Jenny Seagrove.

Winner has just come back from Dublin, which he loves. (He either loves or loathes things, there seems no in-between.) He and Jenny had lunch at Claridge's, which he loves … 'I was brought up there.' He smoked a big cigar, drank sparingly and was very complimentary about the journeys – 'your walkin' programmes', as he referred to them.

Monday, September 27th

Write a letter to JC to apologise for calling Paddy Ashdown 'meretricious' at dinner last night. Well, not to apologise but to explain why I accepted the words he put in my mouth. I know John cares about these things, but after a long day's entertaining I didn't have much concentration left for political discussions. John, I know, regards me as woolly in this area and I usually try and avoid politics with him, except in the most general terms.

Lunch with Travers Reid at the Overseas League – extremely well-situated club beside the Ritz with gardens bordering St James's Park and a room with bath costing less than £100 a day. Travers, who evidently started the Perfect Pizza chain – country's first takeaway pizza service – wants to know if I will do 'An Evening With' to help Stammering Centre funds. It's become a victim of its own success with 150 families currently waiting for assessment. I promise to help.

Sunday, October 3rd: Ventnor, Isle of Wight

Everywhere we set up the camera people come to talk to me. A simple shot at a telephone box in Ventnor – at nine a.m.! – becomes a distinct effort as I'm besieged by a coach party from Leicester.

All in all, by the time I've driven over to Freshwater Bay to attend a harvest festival at St Agnes Church, I just want to be ignored. Impossible. Little taps on the car window from people asking favours, and a congregation waiting to see me.

At Blackgang Chine a conker festival has been organised. More poking and prodding as I sit waiting in the car. 'You were supposed to be here at eleven ... can you sign to Susan? ... ooh look, he's got his own pen.'

I'm very near breaking point. I'm not in favour of filming the conker championship. I have a sixth sense that it will be a publicity stunt in which I shall be the bait.

Failed miserably to hit my opponent's conker and hoped only that the earth would open up beneath me.

Monday, October 4th: Ventnor

This morning I'm much more on top of things. We drive back to Ventnor to film around the Botanical Gardens – meet Simon Goodenough – the engaging, enthusiastic director who plays Baroque music in the Temperate House because he believes that plants grow better in a conducive atmosphere. He's a feet-on-the-ground dreamer, devoted to his gardens and his plants but with a much wider and non-parochial interest. After a fluent interview, I tell him he ought to do this himself. He's a natural communicator. He could be the Keith Floyd of gardening.

Then suddenly, as a result of five days of Herculean effort, we are finished. I complete my column and read it to Rog over a couple of pints before supper. He's complimentary and I'm relieved. A 2,000-word column and a half-hour programme in five days isn't bad.

Tuesday, October 5th: Isle of Wight–London

Home just after twelve to be told that there is a story on page three of the *Sun* about my cheating at conkers on the Isle of Wight. It seems that the misbegotten episode is not altogether behind me and that Simon Dabell, entrepreneur organiser of the festival and the man who owns a theme park that is slowly slipping into the sea, has manufactured a tale of my disqualification and sent it to the *Sun*.

This prompts a solicitous enquiry from Peter Cook on the answerphone, full of mock concern over the conker story and had I taken leave of my senses? Damage like this not easy to repair – sort of stuff. Within half an hour of my return the *Evening Standard* has picked up the story and rung me for comment.

Friday, October 8th

Ring Eric, he's just packing for a trip to the USA. He and I discuss 'The Adventure'. His view is that I have to set the running by deciding what I want to do with it – and exactly how I want to be part of it. Neither Eric nor myself very keen on directing.

To dinner with Richard Wilson at the latest restaurant on the Keats site. Richard told me it was called Beth's and was run by Fay Maschler's sister (he has an endearing habit of getting names wrong – Downshire Hill becomes Devonshire Hill, Fay Maschler becomes Fay Mailer).

The restaurant is actually called Byron's. They chose the name because of the large, ornate 'B' which hangs outside. 'It had to be a name beginning with B.'

What I could not believe is that Richard has the old script. He has been reading the one without the final scene and without substantial cuts in some of the speeches. Unbelievable. I read him the new last scene at table. He likes it. Richard Eyre is interested in directing – so that decision remains in the balance.

Wednesday, October 13th

Clem arrives to talk about a route for the Pacific project in greater detail. Almost immediately the phone rings – whether it's filing cabinets or alternate cries of help to BT to restore my fax line, or the Miele engineer, or Rab cutting through wires and pipes downstairs, or Nigel scattering paint shavings all over the garden where he thinks we can't see – it is a morning of classic Palin house activity.

Clem sits stoically beside the map and when we do get to talk about the route, the possibilities are beguiling and exciting. It's like planning the world's most wonderful holiday – at this stage anyway. We have five programmes on the western side of the Pacific alone.

To Odette's and lunch and a gossip with Terry G.

'Defective Tec' is, with current rewrites, before the studio heads – with Bill Murray hopefully linked to it. TG thinks JC has been tempted into the Hollywood Butler Syndrome – playing opposite Macaulay Culkin. Hollywood's Joel Silver estimates the casting to be worth 200 million box office and apparently JC will, if he signs, make up to two million! This, TG feels, is real reason why 'Death Fish II' has been postponed.

Thursday, October 14th: London–Isle of Wight

Go over the schedule for our last five hectic days. Tomorrow is perhaps the trickiest day of all – a visit to Parkhurst Prison from which Roger hopes to gather enough material for one half of the show.

To bed, but a broken and disoriented sleep. Never quite sure where I am, or what time of the night it is. Roger's pipe smoke drifts along the carpeted passageway and under my door.

Friday, October 15th: Isle of Wight

At Parkhurst by eight. The Governor, John Marriott, accompanies us round the prison. He is an energetic extrovert, full of expansive hand gestures, jokes, but beneath it all deadly serious about his co-operative rather than coercive approach. A thatch of white hair, a bright red tie, a loud, grunting, braying laugh.

Apart from the IRA prisoners, he allows us to meet, and if the 'inmates' consent, to film, anyone. Indeed we visit the high-security Category A prisoners first. These are murderers, considered to be among the 60 most dangerous men in the kingdom and most of them here for life.

Suddenly I'm in amongst them, in a workshop, and they're shaking my hand and asking me when I'm going to make another of my programmes.

I cannot really comprehend the evil and the violence – because here, now, it's rarely manifest. Only once in the day do I notice a moment of nastiness, and that wasn't much more than a gesture.

At the end of the afternoon I'm 'banged up' in a cell in order to get the feel of the isolation that is twelve and a half hours of every man's 24. Roger and I have planned that I should do a sort of summary of my feelings alone with the video camera – and segue into a summary of my feelings about leaving the IOW after four weeks.

We finish after almost eight hours' continuous filming. All of us rose to the occasion – any tiredness evaporated once we got going. We have shot enough for a whole programme.

In the evening over to Marriott's house in Brightstone for dinner.

It's an old, messy, lived-in, friendly house. Candles, log fire, chaotic family atmosphere, vegetarian food and some extraordinary tales of prison life – the man who changed his name by deed poll to Charles Bronson, the last escape from Parkhurst – Reg Pewter, who got out in the laundry and rang Marriott from Australia.

Tuesday, October 19th

Anne has had a very good meeting with Clem and Paul Hamann this a.m. Paul delighted to receive news that a Pacific project is going ahead. Of course the BBC would like me to start a year earlier. Five years is a long time to wait, they say, between Palin travel spectaculars.

Good news too from D. Pugh. Robin Lefevre[1] – much admired by A Bleasdale and D Molloy – loves *The Weekend* and wants to direct it. So, as one project begins to recede into the past, others are today given strong forward momentum.

Sunday, October 24th

I come to 'Death Fish 2', first draft. Though very funny at times, seems to suffer from the icy hand of good old Cambridge intellectual detachment – people talk and speak because they are the mouthpieces of an argument. My character, Bugsy, could be good, but for my mind there are almost too many keepers.

Monday, October 25th

The news from Northern Ireland is back to its worst – ten people killed in a fish shop in the Shankill Road. Oddly enough I was running through the transmission tape of the railway journey yesterday and there is a brief glimpse of the Shankill Road and Ivor Oswald is talking, drawing up at a pedestrian crossing. Look at my *Independent on Sunday* and there is the crossing on the front page. Right beside it is the blasted remains of the fish shop.

---

1 Robin Lefevre, theatre director, whose work includes the Alan Bleasdale musical *Are You Lonesome Tonight?* (1985).

Sunday, October 31st

A message that Angela Thorne[1] loves the script of 'Weekend' and wants to do it. This is one project that does seem to be leaping ahead.

Tuesday, November 2nd

Meet with Pugh and Lefevre at The Union to discuss the script. David is wonderfully supportive or uncritical – whichever way you look at it. 'I've read the play again, very thoroughly,' he announces, a little ominously … 'and really, all I can say is … it's wonderful.' Robin nods, his dark brow and piercing, intense gaze combining in agreement.

As we work our way through the script Robin has queried only a few minor areas. Scenes that I've broken up should be run on, and there is some work to do on the end of Act 1 and the end of the play.

An harmonious session except for financial implications arising from Richard W's decision not to do matinees and his availability for only eleven weeks in the first West End period.

Friday, November 5th

Sunshine as I run – the beams of low sunlight breaking from behind early cloud to illuminate the delights of autumn leaves, in intense shades of yellow, red and brown. In West Meadow a gentle gust of wind causes leaves to fall from a tree as I run by. They're shed vertically, like a shower, accompanied by a whispering rustle.

Help Will prepare a Bonfire Night party – barbecue and mulled wine for about 20 friends. It's a clear, quite warm night – the temperature almost reached 60 today.

Will's friend Chris works at the Dept of Transport and we talk about the rail privatisation. No single line can ever pay for itself – so any bidder will have to receive government subsidy. So why the expense of changing what's happening already? He can only come out with something rather unconvincing about BR not putting the traveller's needs first.

1 Angela Thorne, actress best known for appearing alongside Peter Bowles and Penelope Keith in the BBC series *To the Manor Born*.

Monday, November 8th

Out, mid-morning, to lunch with my cousin Judy Greenwood apropos of decoration/furniture for the house. Go via Cleese's to have a quick chat about my reactions to 'Death Fish 2' before I go away.

Arrive outside No. 82. Grin manically into the video security camera, largely for Alyce Faye's benefit, only to be screened by a lady with a foreign accent who doesn't think it's funny. The door swings open. No-one there. Wander into the hall, smiling expectantly as one does when about to meet friends.

A blank-faced young man appears from a side room. Is he one of Alyce Faye's children I don't know about? Is he one of John's new writers? No, it turns out that he is going to 'vacuum the driveway'. An invisible presence at the top of the stairs screams down to us 'You wanna Misser Cleese?' Louder, more impatiently ... 'Hello! I up here – you wanna *Misser Cleese!*'

By now thoroughly disoriented, H and I are told (still by someone we can't see) that we must go to No. 84. As we go, the young man, who isn't a new writer or a son-in-law, gestures to me to move my car so he can clear the leaves.

Eventually we are let into No. 84. A vast staircase stretches ahead. I suddenly remember what all this reminds me of – a fairy story – the entry to a giant's castle. I am Russ Tamblyn in Tom Thumb. I thought our houses were now spacious enough, but compared to this we are still living in a matchbox.

JC shows us around – everything is immaculate, not a gap or a piece of bare wall. One room John regards rather bleakly – it's expensively, luxuriously furnished in New York fin-de-siècle taste, but John cannot remember quite what it's for ... 'We thought we'd better give the designer one room he could just go to town on,' he says before closing the door on it, without much regret.

Tuesday, November 9th

A request from Random House Audiobooks that I read Roald Dahl's autobiography for them – but what was very nice was that the Dahl estate had asked me to be the reader.

To Pizza Express with Rachel. Paul Foot, wife and son at next table. The *Mirror*, his old paper – the paper that fired him – has sunk pretty low this week, paying £100,000 to the manager of a gymnasium who had secretly installed cameras to take pics of Princess Di exercising. Pretty depressing – that the *Mirror* should be fighting for press freedom with a tawdry, unnecessary endorsement of blatant dishonesty. Foot says the men who run the paper now are morons.

Monday, December 6th

Whilst running this morning, I conceived a plan to write a novel as soon as possible, certainly over the next year. It would be called 'Uganda' and would be about two men, complete opposites, thrown together by the Foreign Service in some distant but photogenic outpost – Uganda. A framework that could hold comedy, travel, sex and malaria. It's the same sort of idea as I came up with in New York for JC and me.

Somehow feel that this next year would suit the writing of a novel – and the production of *The Weekend* has given me a boost of confidence in my writing.

Saturday, December 11th

A short, sharp dose of flu. I lay in bed for most of Wednesday, Thursday and Friday. There was little question of doing anything else. Either my throat ached (this was the first and worst phase of the illness) or my stomach ached or my head ached. Or else they all ached at the same time.

Was heartened in my misery by hearing that *American Friends* is to make its UK TV debut on Christmas Day on BBC Two. Barry Norman's little piece in the *Radio Times* awards it four stars and calls it 'a gem'.

David Blount calls. *The Dresser* is to be repeated this afternoon. In my present state I feel I can listen to it as part of my recuperation!

He wants to know if I'm interested in playing Mole in a radio version of *Wind in the Willows* (A Bennett's adaptation) to be done for Christmas '94. I have a certain reluctance and don't quite know why. I think he takes that as a yes.

Tuesday, December 14th

To the reopening of the London Transport Museum. Escorted into the old Floral Hall in Covent Garden (whose intricate Gothic ironwork up-stages any of its exhibits) and shown around like royalty. Photographers snap away at me as I sit next to dummy drivers, various people grab interviews as we move around.

Sir Wilfrid Newton and many of the old directors of LT, including Peter Masefield, arrive.

There are quite a lot of bigwigs and my speech must have ruffled a feather or two with its endorsement of Ken Livingstone and the GLC and its lament for the public service ideals which made London Transport great.

Anyway, it goes better than I could ever have hoped. I am very glad that I threw in a few jokes this morning.

More interviews and photo opportunities then at last home, armed with an old Gibson ticket dispenser as a present.

Monday, December 20th

This morning I rang Geoffrey Strachan and enjoyed very much telling him I wanted to write a novel for him. Anne seems excited; she is cautious about how much of an advance I might get – she reckons she could get half a million easily if it were a travel book tied to TV, but for a first novel, even with my name, she estimates Geoffrey's offer to be around £50,000 based on 25,000 sales.

More important is a schedule. I don't want to be pushed into Christmas '94 publication – but want to have the book finished by the end of the year. There will be quite a lot of research, which I feel could be complete by May.

Tuesday, December 28th

Spend most of the afternoon preparing the Roald Dahl autobiographies which I'm reading on Wednesday and Thursday. There are lots of characters. Dahl's boyishly enthusiastic style sometimes palls, but once he's on a roll – usually describing something dreadfully painful – a beating or an accident – the pages come to life. Hope I can achieve that effect tomorrow.

Wednesday, December 29th

Paul is recording technician – a bit lugubrious, but the atmosphere is pleasantly low-key and I'm able to concentrate on the text. A little tight and tense to begin with – feel my voice being scrutinised, I suppose; then it begins to flow and by half past five we have completed *Boy* and the more reflective *My Year*, which I read almost effortlessly.

Thursday, December 30th

Despite feeling in more energetic form today, I make quite a meal of *Going Solo*. Unlike *My Year*, which was largely prose and recollection at peace, *Going Solo* is full of action stories and Dahl's brisk and wide-eyed enthusiasm for everything and everybody. Occasionally it comes to life easily, but at other times becomes a bit bogged down in aircraft names and details.

A man from Random House is present. He seems callow and very young. Why isn't Will doing something like this, I ask myself.

We finish around six. He (the young man) is complimentary, I think. He said he found my voice 'very hypnotic'. I took him into the story. Blame Dahl's writing for that, I say, though I'm pleased he's pleased – I'm always on the lookout for compliments!

1994

Tuesday, January 4th

To Broadcasting House to take part in a 50-minute prog about Terry Gilliam for Scottish BBC radio. 'If you ever want to talk about yourself for 50 minutes, we'd love to do it,' I'm assured by a voice in Edinburgh.

Meet Michael Barnes in the BH foyer and take him to the Regent Hotel beside Marylebone Station for lunch. He seems the ideal companion to share my first glimpse of the grandly restored hotel – largely because he and I appreciate the significance of its origins as the London face of the Great Central Railway. The Great Central was the last of the northern railway links with London to open, and the first to close.

A central courtyard is now an atrium with soaring columns, eight storeys high, supporting a glass roof. The size and scale is a little intimidating, but the lunch is good and we celebrate our reunion with a glass of champagne.

Michael keeps the bad news to the end. On top of the second bomb blast at the Royal Opera House came news from the Arts Council in Northern Ireland that they thought it was time for him to step down. The administrator, a QC of 'nationalist tendencies', did the deed. Michael faced the realisation that targeting the Opera House was perhaps not as arbitrary as was once thought – it is seen as the cultural flagship of Unionism. Not fair, surely, I said. 'What do they expect you to do, put on *The Plough and the Stars* every week?' 'Well, actually, we *are* doing *The Plough and the Stars* next month,' says Michael, rocking with laughter at the irony of it all.

Last year, he says, ended on the most savage note of all with some suggestion that he relinquishes the Festival as well. It seems, in short, that Michael is being pushed out. Some would say, at last, others, after *all* he's done. I have given him a *Great Railway Journeys* book in which I have thanked him for being 'Mr Belfast'.

On a wet, unfriendly day outside the Regent, we make our farewells, which seem poignant. We nearly always have left with something to celebrate.

Wednesday, January 5th

Across Trafalgar Square and into Uganda House. Not much on the walls but a picture of President Museveni. Beaming smiles. I'm assured I will not need a visa to visit the country.

I ask for a copy of Museveni's book *What Is Africa's Problem?* which is modestly advertised on a noticeboard. Whilst I wait for it to be brought down, I sit and read some of the magazines which are in hard covers, chained to the table. Also chained to the table is a brown folder whose contents are scrawled on the front in marker pen. 'Draft Constitution of the Republic of Uganda'.

Friday, January 7th

To Piccadilly to meet Major Grahame, author of *Amin and Uganda*, at the Cavalry and Guards Club. Feel doors opening onto the novel as I climb the steps and into a pillared lobby. A uniformed man looks up unhelpfully.

Iain Grahame emerges from a reading room. He is pleasant enough but radiates caution and unease. As we sit down in the Ladies' Room on the third floor ('only place you can get tea after five'), he fills me in a little about Uganda, about Amin and tribalism and how the madness happened, as he tucks into fruit cake and sandwiches – toasted teacake, his preference, being off. At the end of an hour he politely moves me downstairs. I think he is less suspicious of me than when we started. He encourages me to ring and talk to him again if I want more help.

Saturday, January 22nd

David Pugh signed up the Strand Theatre yesterday, which is very good news, as it seemed to be everyone's favourite choice. Tickets are rapidly selling out for Guildford and there are plans to set up a national tour in the summer whilst Richard W leaves the show to film another series of *One Foot*. All very positive.

I've suggested that Tom P might be able to provide sound effects and Robin seems to like the idea so have put them both in touch. Also rang Attenborough yesterday. He was just back from Africa 'filming plants', but was tickled by his inclusion in *The Weekend* and very happy to rewrite and record the piece of TV commentary.[1]

Called David Blount and turned down *Wind in the Willows*. He says I've been nominated by BBC Drama for a Sony Award for best radio acting perf in *The Dresser*.

Monday, January 24th

Sleep well and happily. The daylight offers less comfort. It is drizzling steadily, but mild for midwinter. Struggle up and into a tracksuit for my last run before Uganda trip. Rachel smiles tragically at me from the top of the stairs. 'It'll be the last time you can take me,' she appeals. She finishes her job at the government health survey on Friday. I fall for this and run her to Belsize Park Underground – damp, dull streets, disagreeable drivers hurrying to work.

Will's new regime has begun. He was apparently up at 7.20, and running on the Heath. He tells me proudly that 'I nearly killed myself, Dad, I nearly *killed* myself.'

Tuesday, January 25th: Entebbe, Uganda

Squeezed on a small bus with a very nice batch of Americans – adventurous, quite elderly. All on a Museum of Natural History tour. Their leader, a tall, lanky man with a prominent chin and a wide, high forehead like an Imax screen, turns out to be John Heminway, who does a lot of travel progs for American TV and Arts and Entertainment.

We're driven round to the Lake Victoria Hotel.

Lots of staff in lots of different coloured uniforms but I still have to wait nearly two hours for a ham sandwich. Don't object. I order a Tusker beer and talk to a man who is selling educational books in Uganda. He says great improvement in last two years, but infrastructure still very poor. The hotel is clean and well kept and my room has everything working.

Martin Hardy, who helped organise some of the African leg of *Pole to Pole*, introduces me to a young Ugandan, neatly dressed in yellow shirt,

---

1 At one point in the play Stephen Febble turns the television off in disgust, as a voice describes insect copulation in some detail. Very sportingly, David agreed to record it himself.

green tie and brown jacket, who is called George and is to be my guide over the next two weeks.

I take a swim in the pool, to wake me up after a short night, and then walk, with George, out onto the streets of Entebbe, ending up at the Botanic Gardens.

It may say at the airport 'Pepsi welcomes you to Uganda', but life is very Hardyesque, lived in fields and side roads where houses have chickens and goats and a few crops like cassava outside.

The Botanic Gardens rather melancholy. Few funds for their upkeep and many of the trees look tired and worn. But little pleasures such as a troop of Colobus monkeys, with their long black and white tufted tails, springing gracefully from tree to tree. The crashing and cackling of hornbills and at the lakeside an abundance of sandpipers and hamerkops and terns.

Wednesday, January 26th: Entebbe–Kampala

A Catalina flying boat will leave Entebbe Airport at 9.30 to fly onto the lake, land and collect the Natural History Museum party; I've become, in less than 24 hours, almost an honorary member of the party, and Pierre, the owner of the Catalina, has suggested I might like to fly the short hop from airport to lake before the main group sets off.

So I find myself, with George, climbing into an A&K Land Cruiser to be driven to the flying boat.

On the way out we pass the old airport building with a burnt-out DC-7 beside it – the scene of the Israeli raid in June 1976. Depends who you talk to here. One local says it was an outrage – 'it felt as if the country had been raped'. Others see it as an embarrassment inflicted upon them by Idi Amin's policies.

Pierre, smoking his pipe, greets me and takes me through to the airstrip where the Catalina stands, blue and red and looking very sharp. Pierre goes round with the Pledge and puts finishing touches to the windows. The plane is 50 years old.

As we take off, pulling into the air at 70 knots, I speculate as to whether the white line along the runway could be the Equator. It must be very close. My Michelin map shows it running slap across the low headland on which the airport is situated.

Exciting few minutes as we bank and turn steeply, almost dizzily around the bay, low over the tree cover and clusters of round, thatched huts and finally smack down on the surface of Lake Victoria. No locals can remember a flying boat landing here since the 1940s so there's a small crowd lining the jetty.

The first lot of Americans climb aboard, with difficulty, from a coast-guard dinghy.

Farewells and photos and I'm taken back to the jetty.

When they're all aboard, the Catalina roars along the water, but seems unable to take off. She kills her engines and aborts. There's no communication between plane and land save through the control tower at Entebbe, so no-one knows quite what's happening.

After an hour or so, and another two attempts at take-off, the dinghy is commandeered again (its two crew have to be woken from sleep) and Martin H goes out to the stricken plane.

Back at the hotel all is confusion. The pilots blame the heat and the strong swell out on the lake. The Americans, all so excited this morning, have been taken off the Catalina before their journey has begun.

Thursday, January 27th: Kampala

Up in my room, begin to make some contacts. British Council man is in Nairobi, back tomorrow. The High Commissioner sounds cautious and a touch severe; he cannot meet me until the day I depart Uganda, which is almost two weeks away.

I walk out into Kampala. The city buzzes vigorously. Crowds fill the broken pavements of Kampala Road. Fine, tall, straight-backed women in the traditional 'Busuti' – long, flamboyantly colourful, frilly-shouldered dresses – pick their way over fallen traffic lights and the empty, twisted remains of parking meters. No-one seems to bother about me as I stand in the shade and make notes – they're all too busy.

The bookshops are a little depressing. They all seem tied to religious organisations and sell much Sunday School stuff and very little about the country.

Back to the hotel where George is quietly, patiently waiting. We go to lunch – tilapia once again, with rice and matoke.[1] Ask George about himself – for as yet he will neither volunteer personal info nor question me. His surname is Byomuhumuza – which looks formidable on the page but when spoken has a mantra-like rhythm to it. He's from Kabale

---

1 Matoke is a starchy plantain banana.

in the deep south-west, on the border with Rwanda. He's 28.

We decide on a seven-day safari to the west, beginning Monday. Then down to the Rhino Bar to have a drink with two American journalists. Talk about the AIDS epidemic here. Government runs condom campaign, Pope, head of the RC Church to which 49% of the population belong, comes here and forbids them.

A chance offer of a flight on a light plane to the wild, remote north-east of the country is gratefully accepted.

Friday, January 28th: Kampala

Lunch with Zahid Alam, an Asian businessman who stayed here throughout the bad years. In 1972 the Asian community was expelled by Amin (still considered by the Ugandans to be about the only good thing he did). There were 70,000 in the country then. Zahid says there are now 12,000 or 13,000.

We eat at the China Palace. As we eat he talks – Amin seems less of an evil in his mind than Milton Obote. In Obote's second term of government it is conservatively estimated that 300,000 were killed, compared to 100,000 who died under Amin. Zahid's father stayed throughout by keeping a low profile. The Nile Hotel, which I can see from my window, was Obote's torture centre; Amin, according to Zahid, dealt with people at the State Research Bureau behind the Kampala Club, which I can also see.

A trip out of town. Down onto the Kampala Road and left opposite the long, colonial façade of the railway station. Turn off the main road and through landscaped estates of large '30s-style suburban villas, some well kept, but most others sadly dilapidated, with windows broken, drainpipes hanging from walls and gardens left to decay.

An indicator points to 'The Source of The Nile' – surely one of the great signs of the world, beaten only by a second sign beside a metal pole barrier which announces 'Source of The Nile. Entrance Fees'. It costs 3,000 for the vehicle and occupants – about £2.00 – then the pole is raised and we drive down a red murram track to a parking area. From here, steps lead down to the site of the Ripon Falls, which Speke was the first white man to look on, in 1862.

A fisherman waits in his old boat in the lee of an island. It does seem incredible that this should be the start of the same river as flows beside the Cairo Sheraton.

Saturday, January 29th: Kampala–Karamoja

Met at the hotel at 7.15 by Samantha Dunn, she of the Emma Thompson eyes and pilot's stripes on the shoulder, and an Irishwoman called Ann Masterson.

Find myself, as last Wednesday morning, being led through the almost deserted airport building and out onto the tarmac. The Catalina which I flew in three days ago is still there, its defunct starboard engine being dismantled prior to replacement.[1]

Sam taxis the Cessna and we take off at nine o'clock.

The gentle green hills of the Lake Victoria littoral gradually give way to great swathes of papyrus swamp on the eastern corner of Lake Kyoga, then to patchy grassland – much of it scarred by burning – and finally into semi-desert. This is Karamoja – an area which has still to be 'subdued' by the government and which the UN still don't consider safe enough to operate in.

The runway is an earth strip with a hut beside it. Even the wind sock has gone. Sam grins. 'Someone's probably wearing it.'

Karamojong youths with a single striped cloth draped over one shoulder stand nearby – holding spears. A group of naked children rush out to watch us disembark. An old man who looks as if he has a cataract shuffles up. He it is who is paid to look after the plane.

Coffee is made then Ann takes me to see a typical manyatta. The Karamojong are a nomadic people – many of the men still walk naked. Central government has never really been able to bring these warlike, cattle-rustling peoples into the administration.

We're shown all the components of the community – an arable area, the ekals, or domestic areas, where families eat and sleep, the area where cattle and calves are kept. When I take notes the children watch fascinatedly.

Women do most of the work here. They build the huts and the fences, they prepare the food and till the ground and sow the seeds. The men seem to sit beneath trees and gossip. They eat meat regularly and don't share it with the women, who eat mainly maize and milk.

It hasn't rained here since last April and water is one of the main topics of any conversation. We visit a borehole nearby and there are tall,

---

1 None of the Natural History Museum party ever got to fly on the Catalina as a new engine had to be brought out from America some weeks later.

graceful men washing and children splashing about and an elder who takes me for someone who knows about water supply. He takes me by the hand to the edge of the borehole drain-off area and bangs on about the hole being in the wrong place.

Sam is anxious to get away before too late. Strong winds are blowing off the mountain and the take-off, as she promises us, is quite hairy. The little plane never reaches more than halfway up the airstrip before winds blow us sideways up and away.

More visual splendours on the way back – not least the long silver Nile, catching the light between grey storm clouds.

Wednesday, February 2nd: Mountains of the Moon Hotel, Fort Portal

Written by torch (between teeth) and candlelight. It's 9.30 at night. I'm on day three of my safari. A mosquito buzzes around.

There is no power in Fort Portal and has not been for three days. This is one of the many colonial hotels fallen on hard times but at least it is operational and the Ugandan flag is raised and lowered every morning.

My candle is burning down – my huge yellow water container waits in the bathroom, there are muted voices and twittering crickets and some noise of cars along a road. Otherwise it's a pleasantly cool night in the tea country at the foothills of the Mountains of the Moon.

Saturday, February 5th: Buhoma Gorilla Camp, Bwindi Impenetrable Forest

It's 6.15 in the evening. I'm writing on the verandah of my tent (set on a firm wooden base) looking out at the steeply forested slopes wherein the gorillas can be found.

For a time it seemed as if our day of gorilla-tracking would be as abortive as the six o'clock game drive at Mweya yesterday morning, when for half an hour we saw only rabbits.

Diana, the Director of the AWF [African Wildlife Fund], found the going very hard, and after two and a half hours we left her with one of the trackers and pressed on, through dense, vine-covered forest floor, hacking our way with a machete until we reached the crown of a hill which our guide said was the line of the Uganda/Zaire border. He found gorilla camp traces just the other side of the border, so they were very probably now in Zaire, and rules say that visitors must stop at the border.

Our guide asks Barbara, one of my fellow guests, myself and Gordon, a local boy, to wait on the ridge while he goes ahead to look for any sign of the group.

After almost half an hour, during which I became a little apprehensive – for we were several kilometres deep in the forest and I had no idea which direction would lead us back to camp – they returned. As they had suspected, the gorilla group was moving into Zaire, but he had located them and they were only 200 metres away. As we had been tracking them for nearly four hours, the decision was taken to stretch the rules and to go after them.

A slippery, awkward, heavily wooded and vined slope fell steeply from the ridge. I could see the silvery reflections off a tin roof in Zaire, beyond the forest. We slithered and slipped awkwardly down. There were blue flowers all around giving off a smell like lavender.

After much crashing and thrashing of leaves and bushes, a serious black face peered up at us from about 50 yards away. Later this same black female climbed a tree obligingly, then leaned on a branch which broke and she fell with it to the ground and that was the last we saw of her.

As we resigned ourselves to returning up the hill, we heard some crashing away to our right and turned in time to get a view of a huge, full-grown Silverback swinging, Tarzan-like, on the branch of a tree. He was suspended there, enormously and quite splendidly, for a few precious seconds, before the huge branch snapped and he, too, fell out of sight.

Sunday, February 6th: Buhoma Gorilla Camp

Around the middle of the night, I'm woken from dreams to find my tent shaking violently. Quickly conscious, I experience a few almost unbelievable moments of not exactly fear but complete disorientation. Have time to grab my torch and shine it at the walls of the tent before the shaking stops.

In the pitch darkness I already feel vulnerable. I think first of all that there are people out there shaking the timber base on which the tent is set. Perhaps they're locals who resent this luxury camp taking over their land. Could it be that the Silverbacks have followed us into camp and are registering their displeasure?

I unzip my tent flap and poke my head out into the night. I hear a zipper go in one of the tents lower down – which is reassuring, and there are voices and lights where the staff are quartered. There is no sign of anyone near my tent.

I switch off my torch and slide into a dozy state. Twice I'm aware of my bed moving; trembling. Is it just me trembling? Are they back?

At 3.10, 35 minutes after the initial shaking, my tent shakes again, violently enough for the mirror to rattle. The sensation lasts maybe five seconds, a lot less than the shuddering which woke me at half past two, but it's enough to get me out of bed, looking rather desperately for a pair of underpants (I shall die in a blazing building one day looking for my underpants!). Pull on trousers, and go out and check underneath the timber base to see if anything could be trapped there. There was nothing. The night was serene.

At breakfast, I was looking forward to having the first line 'Did the earth move for you?' but James, the Kenyan manager of the camp, got in first. There had been an earthquake.

It was a big one too, 6.7, with its epicentre at Fort Portal where we'd stayed four days earlier.

George and I set off soon after eight. Not bad, mountain gorillas and an earthquake in half a day.

Monday, February 7th: Kampala

I have arranged a last meal with George. He told me he'd never eaten Chinese food so I suggested I take him to the Shanghai, at the Kampala Club. He agreed with his funny, slightly dopey smile, 'Oh yes that would-er be good.'

Well the intention is better than the meal, which is rather a disaster. It isn't very good Chinese food – sticky, heavy dumplings and floury spring rolls. I'm tired and quite full, and after catching a chilli in his throat quite early on, George is not happy. So we leave dish after dish.

I give him a copy of *Pole to Pole*, 25,000 shillings in an envelope inside, and a Prominent Features T-shirt which he loves. He also takes the Travel Channel bag, which wasn't really on offer but I'm quite happy.

Thursday, February 10th

A jumble of African images feed through my subconscious during a broken, unrefreshing night and I'm awake long before it's light.

A long session with Kath. We are about to begin when there is an ominous phone call. An *Evening Standard* hack who asks me, politely enough, if I had indeed read several of Dahl's books for Talking Books. I said yes, quite proud of the fact. To which he replied by asking if I knew that there was some problem with Felicity Dahl and they were not being issued. I said I wasn't aware of any such problem, but that if she didn't like the way I read them that would entitle her to a say in this release.

Kath then admitted that they had heard there was a complication. I rang Anne – yes she was going to talk to me about it. I know I've not exactly made myself easily available these past two weeks, but I resented having to learn of this hiccup from the *Evening Standard*.

Walk up to Hampstead in the increasing cold to the Air Studios in Lyndhurst Road for Larry Adler's 80th birthday party.

Made the acquaintance of George Martin, the Beatles' producer, who told me that he didn't think the talked-of Beatles reunion was a good idea. Paul had evidently returned from New York with some Lennon off-cuts given to him by Yoko, which he hoped to mix in with new material. He says Paul wants any new Beatles material to be recorded at his home studio and George wants it to be at Friar Park. Martin suggested dinner sometime and I think I'll take him up on it.

Friday, February 11th

H and I out early to look at a sofa in John Lewis. One or two other errands and home by 10.30, to the news of Mel Calman's[1] death. I can't really believe it. I have a letter in front of me dated 2nd Feb asking me to address his design congress and, better still, to have lunch together. Mel, whom I've known since '*Now*' days – my whole working life – who influenced me to write children's books, who introduced me to Ballymaloe, and Caroline Holden and Pat Huntley and Debbie Moggach – a ladies' man, in the best sense. A wonderfully dry and funny companion. A life force. I really can't believe it. Long talk with Caroline H. Mel died after being taken ill in a cinema. Debbie was with him; which, as far as Caroline was concerned, was the most important thing.

---

1 Mel Calman, cartoonist, best known for his 'little man' character. His work appeared widely in the press, including *The Times*, up until his death.

This and the Dahl piece in the *Standard*, 'Dahling – you weren't wonderful!' and Gwen Watford's[1] death and Harry Nilsson's[2] death, all make me a little depressed.

Monday, February 14th

The Weekend takes a step nearer to reality with the press launch this morning at the Strand Theatre.

Arrive only to find that the black poodle which is to be the focus of the press photos (between myself and Richard) hasn't got there yet.

Richard W takes advantage of the delay to show me the theatre. 'It is very big,' he sighs. 'I saw Dawn French at a dinner last night, and she said she'd lost her voice.' (French and Saunders are in here at the moment.) 'Mind you,' he adds mischievously, 'she did matinees.'

Wednesday, February 16th

By taxi to the first rehearsal of *The Weekend* at Petyt House just along from Carlyle's House, by the Chelsea riverside.

A large crowd of people are gathered, some of whom are the cast. Two others are 'runners' and several others seem to be stage management. A man from the Yvonne Arnaud Theatre confirms that two weeks have already sold out there – before a word is read, this is rather alarming.

'Are you nervous?' asks Richard, straightening the collar of my coat. 'You jolly well ought to be.'

Robin Lefevre, who wears the intensely concentrated look of a man about to free-fall from 15,000 feet, has flown over from Dublin this morning, having opened a play there last night. He was up at 5.30. Richard W looks as if he too might have been up from 5.30 – his expression naturally hangdog, though he's making a big effort to be jolly. Pugh, Stirling[3] and Fox[4] are there to fly the investor/producer's flag.

---

1 Gwen Watford, actress who made her reputation in the theatre, but was widely seen also on television. She won a Society of West End Theatre award in a revival of Noël Coward's *Relatively Speaking* opposite Donald Sinden. She played Tomkinson's mother in the first of the *Ripping Yarns*.
2 Harry Nilsson, American singer-songwriter and very big Python fan.
3 Archie Stirling, married for eight years to Diana Rigg.
4 Robert Fox, producer, youngest brother of the actors Edward and James Fox.

The nerve-racking process gets under way around eleven. Richard is good. He's playing it low and soft as he searches out the character. Marcia Warren as Bridget and Yvonne D'Alpra as Mrs Finlay are spot-on. The rest all groping a bit.

Robin is brisk and businesslike. He plans, he says, to rehearse from 10.30 to 3.00, with a working snack/lunch. No-one demurs.

At three I drive back with Richard. He has a smooth and powerful new BMW – but then almost everything about Richard looks new and quite expensive. He's good company, though tends to whinge a bit about conditions. He had wanted no matinees except for Sunday – which would substitute for the evening – giving us six performances a week and two nights off. Pugh hasn't fallen for this one yet. Richard drives a little distractedly, narrowly avoiding knocking over two pedestrians – on separate zebra crossings.

Saturday, February 19th

A night hovering on the lighter levels of sleep. Have to rise repeatedly, such is the discomfort within.

H suggests a visit to the doc as she fears that it might be the result of some African bug. So, unable to face breakfast, I drive down to the James Wigg practice and sit with a lot of other ill people, reading old copies of the British Museum magazine and *Harpers & Queen*. After 50 minutes I'm seen by Dr Posner, young, neat, with a relaxing surgery manner. Feels my stomach – nothing nasty there. Thinks it may just be gastro-enteritis, suggests some suitable antacid and says that, as a precaution, I should take a stool sample – a 'hot' sample as he graphically describes it – to the Hospital for Tropical Diseases on Monday. Just to be sure there are no parasites at work.

Feeling colder than can be accounted for by the weather, I collect my script and drive down to Chelsea.

Manage to last through rehearsal. Afterwards, as we're all packing up, I mention to Richard and Marcia that I shall have to take my droppings into hospital on Monday and Richard reveals that he has seen many a stool in his time. He was a lab technician once. Looking for tapeworms was the worst. There was no hygienic alternative to just prodding your way through it.

Monday, February 21st

Off to Chelsea via the Accident and Emergency Unit at UCH to drop my dropping. Not as easy as this of course. 'No not here, third floor.' On the third floor, 'No, not here, Microbiology.' I throw a short, gabbled fit and the lady behind the counter relents. 'What is it then?' she asks. I mumble something and she waves the transparent package around as if it's a Christmas bauble and drops it into what looks suspiciously like a rubbish bin. 'That *will* get to Tropical Diseases?' I enquire. 'Oh yes!' I'm assured. 'Leave it with us.'

At rehearsal Angela Thorne reveals that she is 'the world's worst with props', which I hope is thespian hyperbole for her part is almost entirely dependent on them. Richard reveals that he's never done a part of this size on stage before.

But after the first few faltering steps there is a hint of that magical process of transformation which makes this often overrated, over-indulged business so special. Angela begins to play, not just an upper-middle-class woman, but Virginia, wife of Stephen. Richard responds accordingly and with this new-found confidence they begin to enjoy themselves and play the lines, and the lines, having stood up to four days' intense scrutiny last week, still provide laughs and unexpected little satisfactions.

By the time three o'clock comes I'm rather happy – *The Weekend* is not just moving forward but growing as it does so. Now the question is how all this can be nurtured, contained and released at precisely the right strength at the right time.

Saturday, February 26th

Drive Tom and his colleague Sheridan down to Petyt House to meet Robin and play the music they've so far assembled for the play. Fortunately Robin likes the first theme very much, and though he has criticism of the others it's generally because they're incompatible with the tone of the play at a particular time rather than uninspired. He likes the 'wit' and congratulates them both warmly at the end.

Afterwards I take Robin for a drink – he has Guinness, I have Brakspear's, but he refuses to eat anything.

He's an interesting man, self-contained, steely, controlled yet with great reserves of humour. I haven't yet seen the warm side but that's probably because he hates false sentimentality – which makes him so good for the play!

Tuesday, March 1st

This evening I'm going into the Lister to have my bottom looked at and am not allowed to eat or drink for five hours before.

There is something unsatisfactory about going into hospital when you feel not only well, but better than you've felt for several weeks.

I remember being in a room outside the operating theatre and listening with some effort of concentration to a nurse in a green cap telling me how he personally brought in the classical music CDs, one of which was playing in the background as I lay there. In what seemed part of the same conversation an anaesthetist pumped something into my right arm and Mr Scurr, the surgeon, was telling me it had all gone very well.

I was trolleyed upstairs again, into my room, feeling very little pain or discomfort other than the wooziness of the anaesthetic, but a soft-voiced, effete Scottish male nurse was unduly concerned that I should not suffer and jabbed some Pethidine into my left leg. Fell into a peculiar time-disoriented sleep. At times very deep, at others fitful. My legs nearly buckled as I rose to take a pee. This was the one moment in the whole business when I felt frightened.

The night passed slowly. A cup of tea at 6.30, a very good breakfast, *The Times*, and finally, at nine o'clock, Mr Scurr to tell me that the examination had revealed a fissure which had healed itself, two piles which he had injected and nothing further to worry about. I was free to go home.

Thursday, March 3rd

Uncomfortable night, though was rewarded towards dawn with a lovely, satisfying dream of a romance with Jennifer Saunders.

At rehearsal today there is a spat between Julie P[1] and Angela over the brown bread. Angela wants to change some of her moves at the start of the dinner party, Julie immediately defends her own role, digs her heels in. 'Do what you like, so long as I can pass the brown bread!'

---

1 Julie Peasgood, actress who made her name in the television soap *Brookside*.

Friday, March 4th

Another full-cast day. Robin pushes them on through the second act and the dinner party scene to the point where Richard protested quite fiercely. 'Not again!' he muttered, tramping back and forth across the room like a baited animal. But he did it again and did it very well, and watching this big, busy scene play – with props and without books – was exciting.

Lunch with Sally Vincent, a *Sunday Times* journalist, at Bibendum (my choice of venue). She is already at the table. Not a promising sight. She looks very bleary. A woman of my age, smoking and with something resembling a bloody Mary at her right hand.

Her opinions are strong and dismissive. She's not going to ask any stupid questions about my niceness, she wants to talk about sadness and loss. She produces a huge and dusty old tape recorder – the sort that looked neat and compact in pre-Walkman days but now lies on the white linen tablecloth like a sarcophagus.

She asks about Angela, without apology or any false sentimentality – just to find out. I don't think she is playing tricks. I think she is upfront.

She and I put away two bottles of Sauvignon and it's 4.15 before we notice that we've overstayed our welcome. We've talked for three hours – I really can't remember what about but she still wants another session.

Her reaction to the play, which I was pleased she'd read, worried me though. She felt that it all just came round full-circle – things were exactly the same at the end as they were at the beginning. If this is what audiences think then I've got it wrong somewhere.

Saturday, March 5th

When rehearsals finish I invite everyone, including the young stage-management crew – four lads – along to the pub. I tell Michael Medwin[1] he should write his autobiog – or at least have a TV programme made about him. He has wonderful stories – like being introduced to Edith Evans – well, not introduced, but finally noticed by her – 'What's your name, young man?' she asked. 'Michael Medwin.' 'Oh,' she replied, quite impressed, 'any relation to Yehudi Menuhin?'

---

1 Michael Medwin, producer, actor and co-founder with Albert Finney of Memorial Films.

Wednesday, March 9th

Day away from rehearsal. Have to spend a morning on 'long-lead' publicity for *Palin's Column*. Then to St Ermin's Hotel where I'm due to meet Attenborough and others for the Wildlife Trust's Vice-Presidents' lunch.

Three lords, four knights and a minority of commoners, of which I'm the only one without a tie. David A is not here – mix-up with the diary – he's in Costa Rica.

Sit next to Julian Pettifer, at the end of the table. He, like me, is writing a novel this year. He's getting up at five o'clock to work on it. We talk about the BBC and the restricted market for good documentaries. He clearly feels rather miffed that there isn't a place for him in the schedules.

Discussion afterwards. Sir William Wilkinson is kindly and very articulate, only afterwards do I realise he's blind. Lord Cranbrook – 'Gaythorne' to everyone but me – speaks with that utter confidence which comes from being expected to be listened to, and being expected to speak too. Most of them have this gift of confident articulation. The RSNC is really there to preserve more than wildlife – it's also there to preserve these fine old species of British rural aristocracy.

Out to dinner with the Frosts. David's star guest tonight is the Prince of Wales, and we have been previously warned to arrive no later than a quarter to eight.

H and I are at separate tables. I'm in the Carina room, opposite the Prince and between Carina and Linda McCartney.

In the short chats that PC and I had together I was aware very much that he enjoyed laughing and being made to laugh quite as much as he enjoyed having to look grave and serious and dutiful. One or two avenues were firmly closed though. When asked what his reaction was to all the press intrusion, etc. etc. he said quite firmly that he never reads any newspapers any more. I can't quite believe this, but it certainly cut down shared subjects of conversation and reinforced what I'd felt about the royals when I met the Duchess of York at Frost's – that they are being boxed into a corner, and likely to become Howard Hughesian if they go on like this.

As usual, these gatherings feel oddly posed – like those group paintings of famous citizens. Hierarchies are observed and in the end real companionship is stifled by the weight of fame, achievement and significance.

Thursday, March 10th

Today is the first full-length run-through. In fact it is run twice. Looks to be around one hour for the second act and 45 minutes for the first. It seems a mite short to me but I'm assured that a two-hour evening is fine. As Robin says, 'If it's longer than two hours pal, you'd better have a good reason why.'

Home, utterly worn out, to find the baleful presence of Sally Vincent in our kitchen waiting for the second part of our *Sunday Times* interview.

She dismisses most of what was poured into her hefty tape recorder at Bibendum on Monday. 'You're a good listener,' she observes after admitting that most of the tape was taken up with her talking.

She begins to dig. What do I think of prizes? What does feminism mean to me? I was unprepared for the latter and squirmed a) at being asked and b) at the aggression with which it was asked and c) the contempt with which my messy, confused reply was greeted. She became exasperated at her lack of progress – 'I've got nothing on you,' she kept saying … 'I don't know anything about you.' I was rather pleased at this.

Friday, March 11th

Meet Dan Patterson at Groucho's. He rang yesterday to enthuse over 'The Adventure'.

His feeling is that it is very healthy, has a number of well-drawn characters and intriguing situations and comedy locations on which to build. He, like me, sees the end as a confusion to be made sense of, but thinks that this is not a problem – the problem is having too many good ideas, not a lack of them.

In short, it's about the best thing he's read in a long while, he thinks it should be produced as soon as possible and in this country and as a British film – not an American. He wants me to try and rewrite the end, with him as a sounding board and ideas man.

His energy and enthusiasm catch me at an awkward time. I'm delighted by it, but I hear the distant rumble of overwork, rush and hassle in a year which had seemed so clearly devoted to play and novel.

Saturday, March 12th

Drive to rehearsal. For my money, the best run-through so far. Without fail Angela manages to move me. I know it's Stephen's helplessness we focus on mainly, but Angela's unerringly well-recalled and poignant readings of the lines about Driffield and their past always bring tears to my eyes at some point.

So we all break up for the weekend and will reassemble in Guildford, with opening night only three and a half days away. The text and structure have not changed radically since we began. My work has been in detail, and in fighting, in the most productive and discreet way, to get the actors to speak the lines as written.

Buy Paul Durcan's poems inspired by the National Gallery for Doug Adams'[1] 42nd birthday tonight.

It's raining and windy when we arrive at Duncan Terrace soon after half past eight. The invitation said 'Dinner' but not how many people would be there. A cavernous, echoing house with stone-slab floor and not a carpet to be seen. I ask Terry J where Douglas and Jane put all their furniture at a time like this and he says they haven't got any.

Sunday, March 13th

Down to the RAC Club, at Richard W's invitation, to play squash. His regular squash players are all on tour he says.

Yesterday Patsy, Richard's 'voice coach', came to see the run-through and she gave Richard a note which he thought a good one – that Stephen is a man who loves words – because the ability to use words and language is all that he has left. I thought this astute and hopefully it will help cure what I think is Richard's only real fault – a tendency to paraphrase occasionally, to lose precision and clarity. The words are, oddly enough, very carefully chosen!

---

1 Douglas Adams, author best known for creating *The Hitchhiker's Guide to the Galaxy*, which began as a BBC radio series.

Monday, March 14th: London–Guildford

The day is bright, with a low, dazzling sun – put on sunglasses as I drive out west. Long, slow journey. It seems every main road between here and Guildford is being torn apart.

Have to ask a policeman for the theatre, at which I arrive about half past two. It's a compact, mid-sixties building around which the fast-flowing River Wey swirls. It has cafés, restaurants and bars filling almost every available corner. The auditorium is tight, steep and well-raked, rows of red-covered seats with precious little to offer anyone over six foot.

Eileen's set fills the stage. Nothing spectacular, but it feels right except for the problem with gauze back walls to the sitting room. The gauze is there so that rooms in the rest of the house can be lit up when required, but it does mean that when not lit the walls look to be crying out for some kind of ornament.

Tom is there when I arrive, and his music is very much admired – it has class – unobtrusive yet stylish, it helps the transitions no end.

I drive to the hotel.

Tuesday, March 15th: South Lodge, Lower Beeding

The 'invited audience' for the dress rehearsal numbers around 30.

Two sound cues don't work at all, lines are all over the place. To my incredulity, the line after 'sexual drive' – 'depends what sort of car you've got' – proves to be an absolute belter, instead of the intentionally bad joke it's meant to be. The dog shit section at start of Act II is enormously well received, but apart from that it's a ropey old rehearsal.

Rush backstage for notes. Robin rather touches me by telling them – with his customary lack of any sentimentality – 'Do it well for Michael.'

'Full House' sign has been up all day, and will indeed be up for both weeks, so a good buzz inside the auditorium. The audience look like regulars – middle- to old-aged, but decent British types. I fear for the 'fucks'.

Well, all goes well. The laughs are more or less continuous and much to my pleasure, and surprise, they spread right through to the end of the second act. Even the speech about failing to be able to commit suicide has laughs which give the whole play a feeling of unity. It *is* a comedy. It's a comedy about someone who has made a mess of his life. Hancockian, someone said.

Wednesday, March 16th, Lower Beeding

Euphoria a little punctured – or should I say reality restored – by Robin's phone call. Robin goes straight to the point. 'Talked to the lads last night ...' (I only realise a moment or two later that the lads he's referring to are Pugh, Fox and Stirling, with whom he drove home to London.) The end needs to be changed and Robin has a suggestion – that Stephen should not be able to find the tea. Good idea.

More drastic, at first hearing, is Robin's feeling that the first half should be restructured.

As he rehearses the sound levels again and various scene changes I tinker with the script. It all feels like *Saturday Night Live*, or the day of a Python recording. A heightened sense of urgency. We tell the cast of Robin's new ending for the play and try it out.

Thursday, March 17th, Lower Beeding

Watch the performance, as last night, from one of the usherette seats at the back of the circle. Last night a group of women sitting in the café up-stairs congratulated me on writing a play 'from a woman's viewpoint'; tonight at the half a woman watching with elderly parents and husband asks me for an autograph. Someone asks what she thinks of the show ... 'It's just like home,' she says.

I watch couples nudging each other or women casting sidelong glances at their male partners and in those moments I feel a curious sense of power – the power to draw something out of people – without drugs, without a psychology degree – just by showing them someone else's invented experience.

It's a much better show tonight. The dog stays on stage for the first time and, especially in the second act, I feel a consolation, a solid feeling that comes from actors who are no longer scared of whether they will remember their lines.

Friday, March 18th: Lower Beeding–Guildford–London

Watch them rehearse the new order at end of Act One. Everyone seems pleased with it. Robin credits me with its success, though it was he who suggested something was wrong.

These long days at the theatre – nine or ten hours at a stretch – mean that little other work gets done. I have no base, not even a dressing room. I clutch my bag and shuffle around between the theatre auditorium, the café and the offices – I look forward to seeing my own workroom again.

I watch tonight from a single seat at the back of the stalls. There is a dreadful cueing mistake on the newly reordered section, plunging the stage into darkness just as Richard is about to deliver one of the funniest lines of the act. Generally the first half is patchy.

The second works well and there is generous applause at the end. The week has proved that there is much to like in the play. It does hold an audience's attention throughout. But how good does this make it?

I wish sometimes I had the blithe confidence of the convinced. But then I wouldn't want to be Margaret Thatcher or Ian Paisley.

A review, our first, in the *Surrey Advertiser*, calls it 'A good play. Funny and moving.'

Monday, March 21st: Guildford

At half past two leave for Guildford, with Rachel in attendance. Slow journey through the cone fields of Surrey, arrive a few minutes after four.

Show Rachel around backstage. Good to see the new first-half order in place. It's much more effective. Applause at the end of each scene tonight which helps the changes. Second act really settling in well.

Richard is compulsive in the whole section from the herbal cigarette onwards. He keeps the audience with him throughout his descent, and when they've reached the bottom he effortlessly brings them up again.

I'd quite like to be opening in London next week.

Tuesday, March 22nd

Helen has a persistent cough that is wearing her out. Doctor puts her back on antibiotics. But she isn't well enough to accompany me to a meal at the House of Lords with Shreela and Gary Flather and the Alburys.

I have been told to go and meet Shreela in the Peers' Lobby.

No sooner have I been directed to sit on one of the dimpled red-leather benches than I am hissed at to stand up. 'The mace is coming out!' The house has just risen and slowly, solemnly, the uniformed Serjeant at Arms, followed by a man in a suit and spectacles (Leader of the House), emerges from the chamber. I am one of a half-dozen standing, frozen to attention, as a short exchange takes place and the mace-bearer turns and walks past me down the corridor.

We move on eventually to the dining room. Gary points out a slim, stooped, grey-haired figure at the far end of the room, underneath one of the huge portraits of some great man. It is Lord Barber, once plain Anthony Barber,[1] who will always remain in my mind as the first candidate on Python's 'Spot the Loony'. 'Please, don't press your buttons until you've seen all the contestants.'

The food is a mixture – good crab bisque, but lamb so rare some of it remains on my plate like a bloody handkerchief.

After dinner we go on a tour of the building – up the Content, down the Not-Content corridors – the Peers' division areas; into the great chamber with massive murals of Waterloo and Trafalgar.

Beyond the red carpet, where the green carpet of the Commons begins, a growing noise – it's the din from the Commons Bar, loud and raucous as a Millwall pub after a home game.

Friday, March 25th

David Pugh rings to tell me that the head of the agency who does all his publicity saw the show last Wednesday and was so impressed that he wants to redesign the poster to reflect the 'quality' of a play which he had wrongly dismissed as zany comedy. David wants me to think of an ad-line to describe the work – not just a comedy, but, he suggests, 'a comedy of bad manners'. That sounds like asking for trouble from the critics, but I promise to have a think.

Precious little time left to look at 'The Adventure' and decide on my attitude to it as an ongoing project.

Meet Dan Patterson at Groucho's. Dan feels guilty at putting me under pressure. I feel guilty at stringing Dan along then suddenly panicking! What is to be done? Well, I suggest we make it as a TV series! The gallery of characters could then all be kept and developed. I would much rather work closely with Channel 4 or even the BBC than some American-backed film company.

---

1 Anthony Barber, Chancellor of the Exchequer under Edward Heath.

Saturday, March 26th: Guildford

I have said I will go and see both shows at Guildford today – Richard specially urged me to come to the matinee – as it would give him that extra spur to the performance!

During the break I have my photograph taken in Dressing Room 9 for *The Sunday Times*. The photographer has some odd idea of me sitting in a dressing gown and eating Mars Bars. It seems to bear no relation to anything, but in the end the effort of not doing it is much more draining than just getting on with it, so I borrow a dressing gown from Richard and sit and eat Mars Bars.

Whilst they're shooting, two enormous bumble-bees fly around the dressing room and eventually into the huge spotlight, which they hit with a horrible fizzing noise.

The evening is a good show – the laughter and response rolls on. From my vantage point at the back of the stalls I watch the audience. Sometimes they literally rock with laughter, sometimes they howl quite violently (during discovery of the dog mess). I've rarely been in the position of being able to observe the effect a line I've written might have on people. There are moments tonight when I experience, with a very rare directness, the joys of being able to make people laugh!

Sad to be leaving the Yvonne Arnaud – it has been a most pleasant, comfortable and hospitable home.

Drive back, giving a lift to Robin. He thinks that whatever the critics say the play will be around in 200 years' time. Because, he says, there will always be Stephen Febbles. It will be done for the same reason that they still do [Sheridan's] *The Critic* 200 years after it was written. I nod intelligently as the cones flash by on the wounded A3 and make a mental note to read *The Critic*.

We talk about the appeal of Stephen. I admit that there's more of me in him than I might like to think. I can't shoulder all the blame onto my father. We both agree that we hate dogs and dinner parties – in the latter case Robin is almost fanatical. 'I don't do them any more! ...' Dinner parties I presume he means.

Tuesday, March 29th: London–Brighton

Start to read Terry Jones's 'Miracle Man' screenplay, in taxi on way to Victoria, then on the train to Brighton and finally in my hotel room with its fine seaside view filtered through salt-caked windows.

It makes better reading than the *Brighton Argus*, under whose encouraging headline 'Moaning Meldrew passes a tough test' lurks an irritatingly nit-picky review. Mourning the lack of silly walks and funny voices.

The ominous review and the lack of any reports from anyone about the first night have made me a little deflated.

Ring Robin who's also at the hotel. He confirms what I suspected – that last night wasn't so good. According to Robin the cast, over-complacent after a soft and successful time at Guildford, came out playing for their laughs rather than acting the play. He was just off to the theatre to give them notes. He didn't sound conciliatory.

Monday, April 4th

Drive to Wimbledon (rather enjoying *The Weekend* on tour – seeing one's play performed seems a satisfying reason to visit places – especially ones which would normally not be high on the list).

Richard is lying down, masked but awake. The last night at Brighton had been the best so far. Show him the new PM speech; he chuckles. He really is a very decent, patient man. Angela is making up, but very chatty. She has a different style to Richard. If something's wrong it's very wrong for Angela – 'This just *isn't* working,' and so on.

A backstage visit is really a series of diplomatic missions.

Tuesday, April 12th

Eric has sent a long, slightly manic fax trying to sell us a 'Python in Las Vegas' week, which will net us almost a million dollars each. John is back and working with Iain on 'Death Fish 2' – which sounds to be definitely going ahead in summer '95.

Despite the fact that Eric claims John as being the enthusiast for a Python stage show, John reacts rather irritably to the suggestion of such an event happening this Christmas, as he will be on the verge of production; Terry J and Terry G both quite intrigued, so I fax back to Eric offering my services, subject to everyone's agreement, over New Year '95.

Wednesday, April 13th: Crawley

Leave for Crawley – which I estimate will be my eleventh visit to the play in its 30 performances. David tells me that yesterday there was something of a panic – Richard still not there at the quarter – Medwin and Brian Moorehead, his understudy, walking around ashen-white – Angela taking a double dose of beta-blockers! Richard walks in just after the quarter cool as a cucumber. He has a telephone in his car, but every time he tried to ring the theatre all he got was a recorded voice telling him that all tickets for *The Weekend* had been sold!

Robert Fox has flown back from Rome to see it for the first time since Guildford. We're only able to sit right at the back on what they call VIP seats, and just as the lights go down we're evicted from those!

The audience reaction is warm, unequivocally good-humoured, and Richard is now very much on course, making the most of the audience's friendliness. Picking up just about everything.

Thursday, April 14th

To BAFTA where I've arranged to meet Terry G at a special French government-backed screening of Claude Berri's *Germinal*. Others there include Arthur Scargill – who shakes my hand, introduces me to his deputy and speaks admiringly of Ann Clywd, the Labour MP, currently sitting in a coal mine in S. Wales and refusing to come out until its closure notice is reconsidered.

Scargill is less of a ranter than he appears in public. He seems to have a sense of humour, and yet be completely single-minded – about his subject, his theory of working-class struggle, his place in history and his rightness. There just is no other side to the argument – which of course makes him very similar to M Thatcher. Their confrontation was of two bulls locking horns. Both believed they were right.

The screening is addressed by an endearingly scruffy Claude Berri. He makes a funny, self-deprecating intro, but the long three-hour epic that follows lacks, as far as I can remember, one single laugh. It is un-remittingly worthy, epic stuff. *Germinal* as a national monument. I was about as moved as I am at the Royal Tournament.

Bernard Hill,[1] who himself looks a bit Scargill-like, with an obsessive

---

1 Bernard Hill, actor who made his name in Alan Bleasdale's *Boys from the Blackstuff*.

stare, beards me about cars. What can he do about them? I'm very uncomfortable with this role of Mr Anti-Car, so let him know right away that I have a Mercedes.

Saturday, April 16th: Crawley

O'Rourke[1] at the bell again – first to tell me he's washed the pavement in front of my home, removed the weeds, and all I have to do is ring the council and get them to come and fill in the cracks. A moment later the doorbell sounds again and a more agitated O'Rourke tells me that Mr Osifu, his downstairs neighbour, is threatening him with court action for cleaning the street! They are both barmy.

At 5.30 a car collects me and then Robin L and we proceed down to Crawley.

Richard seems to be trying for a lighter, more naturalistic tone, playing much softer than before. Well, it doesn't work. The audience is subdued – well behaved, laughing at the usual places, only without the feeling of celebration which you'd expect from a Saturday night crowd.

The second half is better – it's much more involving anyway – but I'm left at the end with some serious nagging doubts. If Richard can affect the play so much – it doesn't say much for the play itself. The first half, now so used to being played for laughs, is naked and vulnerable without them.

I ask Robin if he thinks Richard will return at Christmas. His reply is ominous and not terribly reassuring – that decision, Robin believes, will be based on 'your reviews, not his'. So back to how good is the play, and how much is it an average piece carried by a very special actor.

First time for a while I've felt negative about *The Weekend*.

Monday, April 18th

More interruptions from O'Rourke, who now accuses Osifu of trying to electrocute him by attaching electric wires to the letterbox.

At the RGS soon after six for the Wilfred Thesiger lecture. A distinguished gathering up in John Hemming's office. David and Jane

---

1 A neighbour with an unfortunate aggressive stance on everything. Lived above Mr Osifu, a Nigerian, in a council house three doors away.

Attenborough, Joanna Lumley and assorted medal wearers, the Duke of Kent and of course Thesiger himself. I don't like to thrust myself at him, so talk to David A (who is worried about having agreed to interview Thesiger for TV. 'I mean ... they all want to know about his homosexuality') and cast sidelong glances at Thesiger's remarkable time-encrusted aquiline features.

Thesiger is compulsively watchable and, being old and very famous, doesn't have to pander to the audience. He bemoans the way cars and oil have broken down the old way of life of his beloved Bedou, he thinks that the amount of guns now available in the country make the prospects for Kenya bleak; he pretends not to be able to either pronounce or understand the word 'ecological' – thus delivering a genteel put-down to an earnest young questioner. He doesn't accept the 'Greatest Living English Explorer' role – indeed he describes it as 'balls'.

Afterwards I'm Hemming's guest at the Geographical Club Dinner, held in an ornate villa off Queen's Gate. As lots of people with drinks fill the room around him, I go across to Thesiger and introduce myself and we have a few words.

Thesiger is only concerned about when we're going to eat. He waves his arm dismissively at the chattering crowds. 'It's always like this,' he grumbles, 'I want my food.'

Looking around I see thick thatches of white hair atop ruddy, regular faces – these are the faces of ageing schoolboys for whom life has been a rum old adventure.

Out of the dinner at 10.30; crowds streaming from the Albert Hall so no cabs to be found. Sir Vivian Fuchs[1] and wife said they'd watched all my *Pole to Pole* episodes!

In the spirit of Fuchs and Thesiger, I crossed Hyde Park by foot and picked up a taxi in Bayswater Road. 'Where've you been then, Michael, flashing in the park?' is my cab driver's opening gambit. I've a feeling Thesiger would have liked that.

Wednesday, April 27th

Richard Wilson has come from the Sony Radio Awards where he had to present Best Radio Performance (Male). I was shortlisted for *The Dresser* but it was won by Richard Griffiths. RW had begun his announcement

---

1 In 1958 Vivian Fuchs led the first team to cross Antarctica via the South Pole.

'And the winner is ... *not* Michael Palin whose play *The Weekend* opens next week ... but ...'

Thursday, April 28th

David rings at least three times during the morning to check on my guests for opening night. Apparently there have been a lot more acceptances than he expected and, as he put it, 'people who started off in the middle of the stalls are now in the upper circle'.

Kath comes round to do letters with me for an hour and a half. Apparently my recent high profile has resulted in a deluge of phone calls asking for my availability – nearly 60 requests in the last two days. Kath says the transport people are the worst – their campaigners will not take no for an answer and seem to find it quite unjustifiable that I do a TV prog about transport and yet won't come and fight for their bypass, rail closure or whatever. I suppose they're a bit fanatical and fanatics are not renowned for taking the wider view.

Much better tonight. Richard playing sharp and hard, Angela wobbly to begin with but honest and effective at the end. Richard takes the audience on an emotional roller-coaster in the second half – with wondrous skill. Silences you could cut with a knife, in between big belly laughs.

Tuesday, May 3rd

Woke early enough to hear our milkman David at the milkbox and the sound of his float clinking off down Oak Village. Stayed awake. So much depends on today – the good name of the play for one – the critical seal of approval which will so affect its future, keep Richard happy and secure a good replacement for the proposed summer tour.

Drive around collecting last presents. Cannot find what I'm really happy with for Robin – settle eventually for a fine malt whisky (after a tasting at Berry Bros and Rudd) and one of the silver, circular whisky flasks – like the one I found so useful on *Pole to Pole*.

Back home and finish wrapping up. Then organise delivery of presents to Pugh and Co. and several bagfuls which I take down to the stage door.

Backstage it's like Christmas – presents stacked everywhere – every dressing room a shrine.

The curtain goes up ten minutes late to a full house. As in all the previews, and unlike all the provincial performances, there is only mild laughter on 'Dear God! No ...' and I hold my breath, but things like Mrs Febble warm up well – good laughter on the Rebecca West line for the first time. Not a bad first half.

Scurry out at the end. David smoking furiously and looking desperately apprehensive. I reassure him. Drink with Jim Wilson, David's genial accountant, at the Waldorf. No-one's raving yet, but the second half is what makes the play.

I slide in after the dinner party is finished and watch with a growing feeling of panic as Richard's light, deft playing hardens up. I turn to find Robin right behind me. Our expressions say it all – he feels what I'm feeling, that Richard is having to work hard. My favourite scene, the one I'm most proud of and which, even in the darkest times, like Bank Holiday Mondays, goes well, is quietly received. I can't watch much more after that, and I turn and slip out. Robin has already left.

I push down the bar on the exit to Catherine Street and walk out into the fresh air. At that moment one of the autograph hunters spots me and they begin to run, pens and books raised, up the street towards me. I turn and shout at them very sharply. I don't want to be bothered, I want time to myself. They stop, clearly alarmed at this loss of affability. Then they slowly retreat back down to the main doors and I walk off around the corner into Tavistock Street.

I cannot control my frustration. I remember kicking at the stone dressing on the back wall of the theatre which hurts my foot quite badly. I feel utterly despondent.

Hear lightish but long applause at the end, then backstage to congratulate everyone. This is where acting experience comes in. Oddly enough they're all very happy, think it went well, etc. Richard, contrary to some nights, has no agonies of self-doubt. Maybe he's just pleased that it's over.

A grand party makes me temporarily forget my regrets and play the role of West End playwright in front of TV cameras and radio and press reporters. Don't see Robin all evening, but Pugh and Billy don't seem to share my doubts any more. For the moment, fuelled by champagne, adrenaline and famous faces, the atmosphere is of unequivocal celebration.

The Waldorf ballroom is a great setting for a first-night party – with its marble terrace surrounding the dance floor and discreet back bar. I've become very fond of the place over the last week.

Ian Hislop particularly complimentary – seemed to have struck something of a chord there.

Home, at a quarter to one on May 4th, knowing my worries are still there and sensing ominous rumbles of dissatisfaction beneath the layers of champagne.

Wednesday, May 4th

Deliberately treat this like any other morning – not reading the papers until I would normally read the papers. H has got to the *Guardian* first though and her grunt and then silence set the ball rolling on a day of almost unremitting critical gloom. 'Python With No Sting' (odd mixed metaphor) is the headline in a Michael Billington piece which is generally condescending and doesn't find Stephen Febble interesting and doesn't feel that we have understood him at all by the end – just 'luxuriated' in his rudeness.

Jack Tinker is destructive but ends with the odd proposition that had my 'name not been on the title page ... the play might well have surfaced to encouraging sounds in far less make-or-break circumstances'.

Today and the *Express* – the only other ones to carry reviews – are much more quotable but by no means raves.

David rings first and advises me not to worry as there are still plenty more to come and they have already made up an ad-ful of good quotes. An hour or so later Richard rings. He sounds lugubrious and though he shrugs off the bad reviews it's clear by now that the balance has tipped quite heavily towards the negative. He mentions the *Standard* as not being good, and this leaves me feeling decidedly uneasy. I'm due at a lunch held by Dewynters – the advertising agency for *The Weekend* – to discuss marketing etc. after the first night.

Take a cab, stopping off at a newsagent to pick up a copy of the *Standard*. It's far worse than I expected. The gist of Nicholas de Jongh's bilious piece is that Richard Wilson is a complete saint who does everything he can to save 'a boring little play' that isn't worth saving.

To Prominent for a meeting together with TG and TJ to think up funny captions for the Ink Group's Python cards. Both Terrys, but especially TJ, are enormously supportive, and my sense of humour returns and takes my mind off everything as we create a calendar with a free extra month called 'Derry and Toms' and featuring mainly rude days, viz. 'Arsehole Day (Tunisia)'. Good childish stuff, but wonderful to wallow in it again.

I'm going down to the theatre, for I feel I must show myself and keep up morale, etc. Park amongst the homeless in Lincoln's Inn Fields and take a quick drink with Robin L and Alan Bleasdale at the Waldorf.

Alan had loved the evening yesterday and roared with laughter. I feel much better for a dose of his warm, emotional, bear-like reassuring presence. Robert Fox has seen the first few minutes next door. Says it's a very good house and all the opening laughs are there.

Thursday, May 5th

Take Rachel to the Gatwick Express en route for her three-week trip to Mexico, with a tour group none of whom she knows. She's trying to put a brave face on it, but I can see that it isn't easy for her. Whilst Helen goes with her onto the platform I buy a couple of papers and look with appalled fascination at the reviews. The *Daily Telegraph* is angrily bad, *The Times* just unenthusiastic.

Drive back home. Pugh rings to wish me a happy birthday, and later faxes through an outrageous quotes page which finds enough from each review to make the play sound like a sure-fire hit! Very creative. Robert Fox also rings – tells me not to worry.

I'm tempted to throw the newspapers straight in the bin – but decide this would be avoiding reality. I carefully cut out the offending articles – which is rather like clearing up dog turds.

Walk over to the theatre – quick chat with each member of the cast. Medwin says John Osborne is in tonight – intrigued by the evocation of his name in Billington's *Guardian* review. He has bought me Osborne's book of essays for my birthday – *Damn You England*. Richard W had sent me some flowers earlier in the day with a note telling me how well the show had gone last night.

Pugh and Billy report good business – £170,000 taken already. No-one is anything other than indomitably cheerful.

To the Marquess of Anglesey then on to Groucho's with TJ. Though he is complimentary about the central characters in the play, his observations otherwise only add to the feeling that has grown in me since reading Wednesday's reviews – or perhaps since kicking the theatre on Tuesday night – that the last few months have been unreal. That what has been said and written about the play this week is the reality. It isn't a strong play. But then I knew that; and I also knew it could be a funny and moving play.

Friday, May 6th

As my cab bounces over the pitted surface of Camden Street, heading south, I reflect on how swiftly the bubble has burst. This time three nights ago I was full of excited expectation, the author of a first play that had virtually sold out its provincial tour and had played to 70% preview business in London.

Now I approach the theatre in a completely different mood. I'm guarded, apologetic, fearful of some fresh shock.

Try to put on a brave face for the cast – the workers at the coal face.

Slip in at the back of the stalls as usual and receive a shock. A dozen rows of empty seats. Up into the circle; lots of empty seats but central block pretty full. I should estimate a 60% house. On a Friday? For a new Richard Wilson play? The conclusion is inescapable – the critics have been listened to.

Saturday, May 7th

Simon A rings and makes the point that with R. Wilson and me on the bill there was an expectation which was perhaps not fulfilled by such a conventional play. He clearly felt the cast were predictable and familiar and would have liked more dangerous casting.

A dreadful and dramatic end to the season for Sheffield United, who are 2-0 up at Chelsea, then 2-2 but need only a draw for another season in the Premiership when, with the last kick of the League season, Chelsea score and United's grip on the parapet is finally loosened.

But to be set against United's relegation and *The Weekend*'s reviews, there's the election of a majority black government in South Africa, the thumping of the Tories in local elections (down to 27% of the vote) and the opening of the Channel Tunnel.

Woken by Rachel ringing from a call box on the main street of Mexico City. Thank God she sounds well and happy and has obviously fallen in with a good party. She's the youngest, and shares a room with a GP who is 30-something but behaves like a 20-year-old. Mexico does sound exciting.

Sunday, May 8th

I turn in cautious fascination to the arts pages of the *Observer* and the *Independent on Sunday*, holding the paper a little away from me, rather as a child might watch a particularly unpleasant scene on television from behind the sofa. Fortunately the reviews of *The Weekend* are confined to brief dismissals at the end of the columns. 'Dire', the *IoS* calls it. 'Dire', the *Observer* calls it.

Later I ring Richard W who seems to have taken it all with a glum jokiness. Apparently in *The Sunday Times* the review is the lead and written in dialogue form. 'You wouldn't want to see it,' is all R can say.

Robert Hewison's view of the savaging of my play was that RW and myself are both seen by the critics to be television people and there's nothing the critics like less than to have stars from another medium, heavily hyped and thrust into their world.

Monday, May 9th

At my desk at 8.30 and ready to grapple with the next big project, which will occupy the rest of 1994, and which should, if all goes according to plan, bring forth a first draft novel.

Realise that, though I've chosen 'Uganda' as the title and Anglo-African relations as a subject, these must never restrict me. The novel could, this morning, be about anything. What I must find is a voice which enables me to speak clearly and honestly and with the humour and understanding that I'm known for, about what really concerns me.

To a drink at the Nell pub opposite the Theatre Royal. David Pugh says he's only just now emerging from a deep and almost incapacitating gloom which affected him at the end of last week. Now, buoyed by the resilience of the booking figures (£10,000 taken just today) and, I suspect, by the backing of Robert and Archie, he is working on an ad campaign, which will concentrate heavily on radio and bringing in the sort of people who packed the Yvonne Arnaud at Guildford and the Hawth at Crawley.

Across Covent Garden and Soho to the Lexington restaurant for a comedy writers' get-together at which I'm sat next to David Renwick.[1]

---

1 David Renwick, creator of *One Foot in the Grave*, in which Richard Wilson appeared as Victor Meldrew.

He is of the view that theatre critics are jealous and unforgiving when confronted by what they see as the alibi of success.

Barry Cryer says it is quite striking how indignant everyone is in my defence. Mind you, he was not happy about the opening night – didn't like the crowds and the hype and he and Terry avoided the party. He thinks that Richard Wilson was not the right casting because it is so similar to Meldrew and therefore will always be Meldrew.

Wednesday, May 11th

Look at the outline of plot of 'Uganda' and spend a moment or two idly wondering what I would come up with if I tried a different approach – i.e. to say serious things through a comic novel rather than comic things through a serious novel.

Well I come up with a title – 'The Man Who Woke Up as Cardinal Richelieu' – and this unleashed quite a little salvo of funny lines and developments. It could be about reincarnation. He could spend a lot of time in France trying to discover more about the man he was, or rather wasn't. And I liked the twist that the more he followed up his alter ego, the more he discovered to his satisfaction that Richelieu was as screwed up as he was, in fact that Richelieu was him.

Have been asked to do an appeal on BBC One for relief aid in Rwanda. For a moment I find myself thinking of saying no because people will say it's opportunism – a sort of instant rehabilitation after bad reviews. Then I'm quite appalled that I should be this worried about what people might think, and agree to do it.

Friday, May 13th

To my car, which is parked as close as I can get to the theatre, among the down and outs in Sardinia Street, off Lincoln's Inn Fields. Two men are beside it, talking. One is leaning against the passenger door. As I let myself in a crust of bread glances off my cheek and onto the ground. The fat mess of a man who has thrown it looks at me with undisguised hostility. The younger man he's been talking to has recognised me and is outraged – ''ere, you just threw bread at him!' He then asks for my autograph.

Saturday, May 14th

All four levels open tonight and R visibly relieved: 'So nice to get a really big laugh.' This sounds really heartfelt, and I'm reminded what he must have been going through these last two weeks. He could not avoid the play as I could. Julie says she feels 'the tide has turned', and it happened on Thursday night. As a result of all this I left the theatre happier than for a long time.

Sunday, May 15th

A very silly idea hatched between myself and TG for writing a comic novel. Take a standard like *Wuthering Heights* and reproduce it virtually in its entirety, except adding another character. Possibly Roger, an insurance salesman who would be glimpsed at a distance, at first, by Cathy or Heathcliff, then would gradually insinuate himself into the action.

Wednesday, May 18th

Long phone chat with Robin.

He says he never expected the critics to turn, as a pack, against me in the way they did. But he instances their recent attacks on Roddy Doyle,[1] previously a golden boy, for his series *Family*. 'They'll allow you so much success and no more.' Robin thinks there's nothing much wrong – reiterates his view that the play will be around in 200 years' time, and recounts a story of Pugh's, that Bill Kenwright[2] had rung him and said that he (Bill) would never have let the show get those reviews. Kenwright evidently wheels, deals, cajoles and usually gets what he wants. According to Robin he would have made sure Nick de Jongh didn't review *The Weekend*.

Saturday, May 21st

Visit Tom who is recording the work of a singer/songwriter called Andrea – from New York, early twenties, strong features, enormous eyes,

---

1 Roddy Doyle won the Booker Prize in 1993 for *Paddy Clarke Ha Ha Ha*.
2 Bill Kenwright, theatrical impresario who put on the long-running hit *Blood Brothers*.

brilliantined hair. Through her, Tom hopes for a lucrative publishing deal.

She says she wants an autograph. I laugh and point to Tom – 'That's who you want. I'm just a has-been.' She shakes her head firmly ... 'You're not a has-been, you're a has-now.' I like that.

Tuesday, May 31st

I woke early and lay awake with various anxieties but as soon as I was up I couldn't wait to get to the novel. All the aimlessness and diffidence that had been making the daily writing sessions such a grind seemed, for now at any rate, to have gone. Maybe the weather had something to do with it. Big clear blue sky. Started with determination, re-read the four thousand-odd words I'd already assembled, edited, elided and, liking the company of my characters, wrote on.

Rachel is all packed up ready for another departure. She doesn't like them and neither do I. Her plane to Greece leaves just before midnight and she will touch down at three a.m. our time. As I drive her through remarkably traffic-free streets to Victoria she says from the heart, 'I don't know how you do this, Dad, I really don't.'

Put her on the Gatwick Express for the second time in less than a month. All part of the learning process, I said as I held her hand at the train window. I'm proud of her.

Collect Richard W and take him out to dinner. I check that it's not one of his alcohol-free days, and he confesses that there haven't been many of those recently. He dresses carefully, taking time to make sure the handkerchief in the top pocket of his blazer is just right, then off we go.

The Ivy is not as riddled with the great and the greedy tonight. We end up bantering with Michael Pennington, just back from a very successful Pinterfest in Dublin, and Alan Rickman, who's just finished filming there and can think of nowhere better to live.

Richard confided to me that he has been offered an OBE and is to accept. He'd obviously agonised – 'Well I don't want to be seen supporting this government, or anything with the word Empire in it,' he explained gloomily. I'm very pleased – and it'll be good for box office!

Thursday, June 2nd

To the Ivy for supper with David P and his colleague Billy. They ask me earnestly whether the bad reviews have put me off playwrighting completely. They visibly perk up when I laugh off the reviews, which I feel I almost can now, pledge myself to giving *The Weekend* the best shot on a tour and affirm that I might indeed write another play. Well, says David, they would love to do another one with me. Jamie Barber is desperate to get it for Guildford and Robert Fox has talked of commissioning me to write something for Maggie Smith.

Opportunists that they are, David and Billy fly the kite of a possible acting role for me in a tour of *84 Charing Cross Road*, opposite Miriam Karlin ... oh, and endless other possibilities. It's nice, an occasion to talk more of the future than the past.

Friday, June 3rd

There is a letter in the columns of the *Ham and High* today headed 'Palin's Play A Pleasure' and is written by a recent visitor to the Strand who had found it a great night out and took exception to the critics stifling, or attempting to stifle, one of the few new West End plays.

Write a short 'Middle Word' for the Python songbook – pure relaxation. Create a rather nice, enthusiastic, chatty, not too bright character called E. F. God – who whinges on a bit about not being appreciated for the effort he put into the Creation, etc. Seven hundred words in an hour – faster than anything in the last month!

Monday, June 6th

A lot of D-Day 50th anniversary mania around. Charles Wheeler's documentary has the authentic ring of passion and despair. Wheeler has a completely unforced presentational style, the ease and naturalness you hear very rarely these days. Articulate without ever being verbose, reflective without ever being sentimental. He showed how rare it is to hear a simple, unaffected, documentary-style delivery.

His film pulled no punches and his observations balanced any sense of triumphalism. It was a hideously bloody offensive, in which we killed thousands of innocent French civilians in order to get at the Germans.

The image of the inflated corpses of dead horses, grossly swollen, teeth bared, by the roadside cut very deep.

Tuesday, June 7th: Birmingham

Quite a decent review of *Palin's Column* in the *Independent* takes up most of the TV columnist's space – Charles Wheeler's infinitely more impressive and important D-Day prog being relegated to a paragraph at the end.

Run in late morning and down to Euston to catch the Birmingham Shuttle to give the keynote speech at the Women's Institute Biennial Conference.

Off at Birmingham International. Sinister hangar-like buildings of enormous size. In one of which are over 10,000 women, of, I'm told, an average age of 55.

I step up onto the platform, feeling like Billy Graham, and launch into my speech after a longish introduction through which I modestly keep my head bowed. I must say that I find myself not the least shy in front of this huge gathering. I've got a good speech (subtext of which is that we need to hear more women's voices in public life), with some successful jokes upfront, and I get quite a kick out of the whole thing. It's probably the most political speech I've ever made, and, as usual, one can't hear people thinking so I don't know how the serious stuff has been received.

Speak for over 30 minutes – great ovation, even though they've been squeezed onto uncomfortable chairs in sardine-like rows for more than two hours. Another interview, a cup of tea and back to London.

The speech took me two and a half days to assemble. Enjoyed delivering it and now feel the delicious calm after the storm.

Wednesday, June 8th

Surveyed the work in progress, then gave an hour's serious thought to an alternative to the novel – a memoir.

I think of all the fragments of childhood memory I've read and enjoyed. Michael J. Arlen's *Exiles* and J. R. Ackerley's *My Father and Myself* are two of my favourites. But then I begin to sway back towards the novel. I feel that I'm being cowardly in leaving it at such an early stage, and I must admit to myself that some of this cowardice is due to the last month's critical battering.

I feel worn out with the effort of not achieving a lot. To bed early with another delightful memoir – Blake Morrison's *And When Did You Last See Your Father?*

Thursday, June 16th

Nothing can really 'rout the drowse' (V. Woolf) today. Have to go up to Hampstead to buy some lunch. Whilst walking back to my car I'm greeted by the amiable grey-bearded figure who runs the Rainbow Alliance – George Weiss. He complains of how difficult it was to get publicity for his recent candidacy in the Euro-elections. In the end he got himself arrested. 'I walked into Hampstead police station with this huge spliff, took a puff and offered it to the sergeant in charge – well, they had to arrest me.' His party are committed to free public transport.

Mr O'Rourke came round this afternoon to tell me that he'd heard my play wasn't doing very well and that I should write a musical comedy. He even offered to find me a backer. A man he'd done some marble-laying for – 'a brilliant dancer, an excellent businessman, Wayne Streep'.

Friday, June 17th

To meet Terry Gilliam for lunch at the Lansdowne.

Terry talks about Hollywood, about his new lawyer, who is one of the three most powerful men in the industry, and his various projects, all of which sound to be dependent on some twist or turn or gamble.

He's full of ideas and images and wilfully refuses to tailor his talent to those he doesn't respect (i.e. most Hollywood studio heads). This makes life difficult for him but on the other hand keeps him fresh and sharp and combative. We bemoan the disappearance of silliness, surrealism, inconsequentiality. Everything now has to deliver, or as they say about movies in Hollywood, it has to 'open'.

At the end of a couple of hours of energetic talk I feel stretched and invigorated and anxious not only to finish my novel but to have something else on the go as well. 'The Adventure'? I worry that creatively I'm a sprinter, whereas someone like JC is a long-distance runner.

Sunday, June 26th, Sussex

Visit to Paul and Linda McCartney. We met them first at Frost's summer party, this time last year. Then again at Frost's dinner and today they've invited us to the depths of Sussex.

We leave at two and turn into the unassuming, unmarked concrete drive that leads to the McCartney farm at about 4.30. There is no gatehouse, radio link-up or fence or, as far as I can see, hidden cameras.

Paul confesses that he is sometimes embarrassed by the disappointment certain visitors try to conceal when they see no mansion or stately home, just a modest, liveable, red-brick, red-tiled house with carefully unmanicured gardens. Paul designed the house – 'first you take a sphere, then you take a triangle', he kept saying.

Paul in good shape. Hair less grey than it used to be; he runs, has done for a few years now. Takes the occasional drink of alcohol but prefers to share a joint with Linda. He's vegetarian, they both are, no meat or fish.

She's warm, open, direct and questioning in the American way – we're talking about Angela's death over the first cup of tea. A son, James, pale face, what looks like red hair, loose sloppy clothes, is introduced. He kisses Helen, rather sweetly, then disappears for most of the time. He goes to the local state school, which for a son of one of the richest men in England is remarkable.

We sit around a kitchen table and talk about anything and everything, but legend always intrudes and Yoko rings while we're there about some letter which John wrote to Paul after Linda had written to John who was, she thought, being beastly to her husband at the time.

We walk round the organic, non-fertilised wild meadow over which Linda is endlessly scattering wildflower seeds. They have a soft spot for animals – giving stable space to horses who are blind or with cleft palates.

About 8.45 we start for home, having left them some Python 'My Brain Hurts' T-shirts, and with a bunch of wondrously aromatic pink roses which were named Paul McCartney by the British Rose Federation or whatever.

I share many of Paul's views about fame, life and success, but am chastened by his work rate; his apparent lack of any wasted moments.

Monday, June 27th

A *Palin's Column* end-of-series party to coincide with the transmission of the last episode this evening. About 20 people. I make them all Pimm's.

I'm afraid there comes a point, when I'm in Parkhurst mouthing some inanity, that I have to get up and walk outside. I feel almost ashamed at my lack of penetration. There are excuses. I was tired – there was the hidden pressure of a column to be written (which was never seen), we were doing a lot on a very tight budget, and so on and so on. But I wasn't very good.

I was lazy. I let Roger create a series around me without ever really sitting down and asking if it was the best we could do. An air of crisis kept us blinkered.

The party in the garden, with excellent food and copious New Zealand white and South African red, lifted me from gloom. Candles lit, both parts of the garden used. Robyn compared the whole scene to a summer evening in Sydney.

Tuesday, June 28th

H and I take a taxi to the Frost garden party. We aim to stay only an hour or so and then go on to see the play nephew Jeremy has designed at the Royal Court Upstairs. However, it is almost impossible for anyone with a modicum of curiosity to sneak away from a Frost summer party. There are so many familiar faces – Kenneth Baker, Lord Tebbit, plus wife in wheelchair, even Lady Thatcher.

What you really need is someone to talk to whom you know awfully well and who won't mind your eyes swivelling and your gaze wandering. The Brooke-Taylors fit the bill perfectly and we work out a very effective reciprocal arrangement allowing us to scan the talent whilst appearing to be talking to each other.

The professional friendship is Frost's speciality. So at various moments I talk with Jane Asher, who is writing a novel, and Gerald Scarfe, who's very happy and content to draw with one hand and hold their baby in the other. John Wells[1] is helpful and funny and kind. He urges me to make *The Weekend* for television, and reassures me

---

1 John Wells, satirist, who created the 'Dear Bill' letters for *Private Eye*.

about the novel, and encourages me to keep my resolve and push on with it.

Alyce Faye appears with Bill Goldman,[1] who gazes around the great chattering throng as if looking into the fires of hell. 'Eight people is my maximum,' he explains.

Largely egged on by the Brooke-Taylors, we've abandoned all plans to see *Thyestes*. It's after nine o'clock and we're among the stragglers. Richard Branson tries to grab our taxi, laughing and offering the driver First Class return tickets to New York if he'll turn us out.

Wednesday, June 29th

Watch Jonathan Dimbleby documentary on Prince Charles. 'Did you have sex with another woman while you were still married?' is one of the questions. Whatever shape the monarchy will survive in after the Queen goes, it is, because of accessibility and availability of this kind, certain that it will be very, very different from before. Charles, though decent, sounded tired and weary, as if almost admitting defeat.

Thursday, June 30th

At the theatre. An appreciative audience in the circle, large enough to warrant the presence of two large St John Ambulance ladies with whom I share the row of seats right at the back.

Hugh Laurie is in Julie Peasgood's dressing room. Tell him about the St John Ambulance ladies and he suggests that they're not the real thing, but people who dress up in the uniform to get in free.

Later, as we walk up Drury Lane looking for a taxi, Richard quite candidly points out that since rehearsals began he's spent 22 weeks on the play, half a year, and doesn't want to see it again for a while. I doubt if he will ever come back, frankly.

Good news is that Hampstead Theatre Club has approached David with a view to co-commissioning a new play from me. Now that's exciting. I have a title floating around in my head since yesterday – 'Love Bites'.

---

1 William Goldman, screenwriter who made his name with *Butch Cassidy and the Sundance Kid* and followed it with *All the President's Men*.

Friday, July 1st

In today's *Guardian* the feisty Suzanne Moore writes a column about the Charles interview. Throughout the 'embarrassing programme' she kept thinking of others who could do the Prince's job better.

'If his job is to be a roving ambassador, to amuse the natives, to conquer the world with reticent English charm, then why isn't Michael Palin king? He is not king because he was born at the wrong time in the wrong place.'

Saturday, July 2nd

Long chat with Derek Taylor – proponent of the triple whammy theory of press treatment. Derek fascinated by the phenomenon, as he saw the Beatles fairy story turn to reality. Once they've decided to go for you, it will be more than once. Well, *Palin's Column* was number two ...

Down to Terry J's for supper. He announces home-made samosas, of four different fillings, seared salmon, guinea fowl cooked in ginger and yoghurt and a selection of Mediterranean and tropical fruits – mangoes and an apricot which TJ bites and cries 'Shit! ... Oh shit ...' We all wait ... What on *earth* is wrong? ... 'This is *wonderful*!'

Saturday, July 9th

With Helen to the last performance of *The Weekend*. A good house, though not full. Three levels open.

The curtain call is, as ever, warm without being delirious. At the end, as we have done so often over the last five months, Robin and myself scuttle out, through the foyer and round the corner to the stage door.

Gather in Richard's dressing room for champagne. He has his god-daughter there – a sweet girl – and also Antony Sher,[1] a soft-spoken, quietly energetic character; he was interested in the autobiographical side of the play. That's another mess I've got myself into in the prelim interviews – giving the impression that Richard's character was my father. Real instance of cart before horse.

---

1 Antony Sher, South African-born actor, writer and artist, who won a Laurence Olivier Award for *Richard III* (Royal Shakespeare Company). On television he made his name in an adaptation of Malcolm Bradbury's *The History Man*.

Marie[1] assures me that there have been 'tears in the wardrobe room'.

I go down to say my goodbyes to the stage staff – Lee and Peter and Trevor and Nicola. They're all busy striking the set. One side of the theatre has been opened up, exposing the Febbles' cottage to the world outside. The driver of a huge pantechnicon is arguing with the police over parking.

I'm sure I shall feel bereft and empty and sad about the ending of this adventure, but for now I just feel relief.

Tuesday, July 12th

There is little difference at the moment between the heat of the day and the heat of the night. A thick, damp, un-British warmth envelops the house.

Julian Schlossberg rings to invite us to his marriage to Merron – 'it'll be at seven p.m. and over by 7.06' – in NYC, July 21st. He feels that we should have a special place at the ceremony as it was with us that they shared their first date. He said he's already had the honeymoon, in Venice. We agreed that it was much more sensible to have the honeymoon before, rather than after the wedding.

Wednesday, July 13th

There seem to be a hundred and one things to do other than write the novel. I try to get to the bottom of this writing malaise – it's hardly writer's block, I can churn the stuff out quite easily – but I'm not sure where the reluctance to concentrate springs from. It is something I've felt before, and something I know I'm prone to: an inability to concentrate on one single area of my life, the ability to be easily distracted by a phone call, a book, maybe something more abstract – an emotion, some obligation remembered, a twinge of remorse or regret at some connection made, but not sustained. I seek inspiration from others, can't find enough of the real, intense stuff inside myself.

Later in the day I wrote a long letter to Michael Barnes, who is himself such a good correspondent and who wrote me possibly the most comforting, certainly most elegant, letter on the demise of *The Weekend*.

---

1 Marie Harper, wardrobe mistress.

Writing back made me aware of what a heavy, subversive weight the last five months have been.

In writing to Michael I feel the first lifting of this weight. I can begin to feel and say what I want. There is no longer in the back of my mind that fear of an audience not turning up, or another critic chewing up my work. I feel a little released.

Thursday, July 14th

Meeting up with Suzanna Zsohar at a restaurant off the Fulham Road called Aubergine. That part of the world doesn't half sparkle with the comforts of life. Antique shops, galleries, posh interiors shaded from the sun by wide blinds, everything in mint condition. Would I rather live here? Well on a summer's day it has a seductive quality but to really enjoy all this would cost a lot of money, and you would be surrounded by those with a lot of money to spend – and by and large they've never been my favourite income group.

Gazpacho in a coffee cup, little pieces of fish, superbly fresh and presented with such care and attention and colour and beauty and delicately patterned sauces that it's like eating a stained-glass window.

Good discussion with Suzanna, she understands my wish to avoid press publicity for a while (well, for ever, to be honest) and thinks that one trade occasion, plus a couple of signings, would do more good.

Taxi down to Camberwell, where the walls are decorated with graffiti rather than frescoes. 'Stop Graffiti' would be a wonderful piece of graffiti.

To Terry J's, to be interviewed for a *Guardian* Python 25th anniversary piece.

Talk, sitting under the shade of the trees, about how we met and how we wrote. 'Is it too early for a glass of wine?' Terry miaows invitingly at about ten past five, and soon a bottle of rosé nestling in an ice bucket appears beside the wrought-iron table and the reminiscences grow broader and more vivid, though not necessarily more accurate.

As so much of Python was born in or looking out over TJ's garden, I feel a sort of completeness, a rounding of the circle to be here talking about it.

Friday, July 15th

Meet Robin L at the Lansdowne.

We cover the usual ground and there is little he has to add to what he said before. Look at the pedigree of the people who read the play, liked the play and backed the play ... 'I don't do bad plays' was the closest he got to admitting his own status ... Given that these were experienced folk going into it with their eyes open, then I must understand that the extent of the critical clobbering was totally unexpected.

Not a lot of help, but it means I can accept the seductive theory that I suffered not because the play was bad, but because so much I had done in the past was so good!

Saturday, July 16th

Out to Maidenhead to the Flathers' 'At Home'.

Most of the guests seem to be Indian and there is a faintly post-colonial feel to the occasion. The Indians, being sensible, stand in small groups beneath the trees on the periphery of the lawn – the pink Brits, of which there are only half a dozen, tend to gravitate to the sun.

I'm introduced to the Indian High Commissioner – a dapper, erect man of middle age who looks as if he might well drink his own urine, and who, having been told who I am, directs me, somewhat regally, to a patch of shade and addresses me (this is the only description of his donnish technique) on the subject of two ideas he has for programmes about India. One quite good – all about the story-telling that's so much a part of Indian culture.

Ben Okri[1] was there with a tall, red-haired English lady called Rosemary. Okri is gently spoken, with big, round, slow, soft eyes. He talks earnestly but lightly. A big enthusiast of my work, recognises special qualities of naturalness and ease which he finds affecting.

We talked about writing. Don't feel self-conscious at the first-draft stage, he advised – write on, keep moving, write to explore and discover. It all may be rejected in a second draft anyway. 'Don't lose your natural playfulness,' he advises. Though I would imagine I'm 20 years older than him, I feel like the father-son role reversed.

1 Ben Okri, Nigerian-born novelist and poet, winner of the Booker Prize in 1991 for his novel *The Famished Road*.

Monday, July 18th

Look at two possible work places for August to the end of the year. A basement and first floor in Gloucester Crescent is just too big for one, largely absentee writer.

Even in the short time I was in the street I caught sight of Clare Tomalin pottering out to the letter box. Word of my arrival would spread like wildfire amongst the Frayns, the Millers, the Haycrafts, the Bainbridge and the Bennett.

On to 54 Delancey Street, not far away in Camden Town, which is much more like it. Top-floor flat in grubby state and a blue plaque on the front of the building announcing that Dylan Thomas lived here!

Wednesday, August 3rd

Returning home from a break down in the Lot Valley. Two thousand miles of French roads without cone or contraflow. On the 60-mile journey up from Portsmouth, three of the latter and many thousands of the former. Compensation is the surprisingly beautiful Hampshire landscape – a soothing and attractive balance of hills and trees and fields – through which the road curves and turns. There is a light, woolly mist around and, for a while, a good feeling of being up and about before the race begins.

With the energy of the recently re-returned I clear the desk and set to on piles of letters. Midway through the afternoon have something of a revelation.

Maybe it was provoked by the news that *East of Ipswich* is to be repeated a month today, but I found myself reaching for the 'Tea with Hemingway' file. Work done five to six years ago for Jack Rosenthal's 'Article For Sale' series and abandoned in favour of last rewrites on *American Friends*. I remember that I abandoned it reluctantly – and remember that Tristram was a great supporter of the story. Could it form the basis of a novel?

Quick read-through suggests yes. Plot and characters far more advanced than 'Uganda', and the territory, English small-town, much more familiar to me.

What was worrying me about 'Uganda' was its scale, its presumption. A novel about colonialism set in a country in which I have spent three weeks. I could see myself being shot down for choosing a big subject but producing a small book.

Thursday, August 4th

At ten I'm ready for my first day in the newly rented 'novel-only' apartment in Delancey Street.

Have to confront the consequences of my new thinking on the novel. This afternoon have a meeting booked with Geoffrey [Strachan] to discuss blurb and a book jacket design – for 'Uganda'.

Write down arguments against 'Uganda' and in favour of Hemingway and vice-versa. It boils down to the fact that 'Uganda' was a concept, never really a story, whereas Hemingway is a story, and the way through it much clearer.

By the time Geoffrey arrives, I've made my mind up. I shall write *Hemingway's Chair*.

Geoffrey is commendably unshocked, or appears to be; he gauges my mood and feelings and, being the gentleman that he is, refrains from a sarcasm that would be quite in order.

A couple of hours later the worst part of my volte-face is over. We talk more in two hours about the Hemingway idea than we have in three months on 'Uganda'.

Monday, August 8th

New regime.

Settle myself in at 54 Delancey, check the marmalade and white cat is in position on the top of Dylan Thomas's green caravan down in the garden below – it is. Soon after 9.30 set about *Hemingway's Chair*.

TG, who has been doing Python 25th anniversary interviews at the Studios, comes by, claiming to be a Dylan Thomas fan. I tell him to fuck off (through the intercom and in Welsh) and we walk down to the Delancey Café for lunch.

He says, gloomily, that he's the greatest living non-film-making director. Claims to have encouraged Tarantino to make *Reservoir Dogs*.

Friday, August 12th

To Southwold today to research small-town east-coast post offices for the novel. Leave at a quarter to seven. Roads going out quite smooth, traffic pouring in as there is another rail strike today. After Ipswich slow to a crawl behind caravans and hay lorries, but reach Southwold Common in almost exactly two hours.

Chris Richardson runs the post office, which he has bought, as a business, and it's dwarfed by an emporium of toys, stationery, books and sweets which extends at the back, converted from an old sorting shed.

My angle in the story seems instinctively right – modernisation is proceeding fast in the post office, hurting a lot of employees and confusing others. Everything now is about making money – the Post Office provides a business service which the government would like to put in competition with banks, building societies etc. Customers must be dealt with swiftly and a 'proactive selling policy' is encouraged to make them buy more than they want every time they come to the counter.

A fascinating glimpse of how much a centre of community life is being changed.

To the church to look at the gravestone of Mum and Dad – surrounded by wild daisies. A strange woman brushing up another grave claims to remember me, when I was 'so high, taking the best red apple from the front of Bumstead's window, with your school cap on and your socks rolled down by your ankles'. She must be a bit mad, though I'm quite happy to be mistaken for Just William.

On the way home make two visits – one to see my mother's old and trusty neighbour, Mrs Pratt; she's sitting in her glassed-in porch and can hardly see anything any more, but once she has recognised me, and I've taken her arm, she proves to be quite on the ball and delighted I've called in. Sit and talk with her for a while. We have a look over the fence to Croft Cottage, and when it's time to go her eyes have watered a little.

I've known her nearly 30 years. She doesn't want to go into a home. Won't even have a home help. Independence of a countrywoman.

Friday, August 19th

On Wednesday I sent the first two chapters – over 10,000 words – to Geoffrey S and received a fax next day which sounded happy with the characters, the way things were going and endorsing the decision to step aside from 'Uganda'.

This morning the character of Nick Marshall came to life – not just a symbol of modern, thrusting business, but something more manic and idiosyncratic.

In the afternoon I start on the American intellectual – she's now to be called Ruth – introduce her via a letter back to the US which I really enjoy writing.

A very clear idea of the potential of the characters and the course of the story comes to me. Almost feel I could go ahead and write the whole thing in a fortnight.

Tuesday, August 23rd

Cycle to Delancey Street, buy milk at the Portuguese shop on the corner; ease into the book and begin to get stuck into some of the conflict scenes.

Rang both Robin L and Alan Bleasdale to wish them well in shooting *Jake's Progress*, which they begin in Ireland next week for 26 weeks solid. Alan is being transported out there in a specially blacked-out Winnebago so he won't be able to see the motorway ahead.

He's been to another hypnotherapist who counselled him to think of something very good, when he had visions of something very bad. 'You know what? I thought of sex,' he admitted, bashfully, 'and I've been thinking about sex ever since.'

Alan is one of the few people I know who never forgets I keep a diary and at one point chuckled a lot at some gossip, but said he couldn't tell me because I'd write it down.

Wednesday, August 24th

Another early run sets me up for an excellent morning's writing. At one Tristram arrives. Inspects and approves the premises, especially the top room with its low, angled ceilings. 'I love properties, as you know.'

TP had actually met Hemingway on two occasions at the home of a wealthy American, Bill Davis, who kept a splendid house in Malaga which he liked to fill with, preferably literary, celebrities.

Remembers seeing Hem swimming – head bobbing up and down like a terrier. Legs were extraordinary. Knotted and gnarled like tree trunks.

Best story is of Tristram arriving back at the house after a long, incautious day in the sun. He was very burnt. Hem took him in hand and said he should rub vinegar all over the burnt area, soak in a hot bath and then rub some more on. TP said it worked.

Tuesday, August 30th

Cannot think how to go forward. Feel that what's gone before is just a whole bunch of words. Why would anyone want to put this inside book covers? I pace the room desperately. Sometimes on the verge of tears. There seems not only no way forward, but no reason for going forward.

Feeling awfully low I decide on an early lunch. Over my ham and salad sandwich from the corner shop I read some of Carlos Baker on Hem.[1] At the start of the chapter on *The Sun Also Rises* there is a quote from Hem to Scott Fitzg, which could have been spoken across the table to me. 'There is only one thing to do with a novel, and that is to go straight on through to the end of the damned thing.'

Which is what I do, and by the end of the afternoon I've put in a respectable day – with another thousand words added. I feel a little shaky but I just mustn't care. What I must do, however scrappily, is get to the end of the damned thing.

Wednesday, August 31st

The complete cessation of IRA activities to begin at midnight. It's a piece of news which could lead to something as momentous as the black majority rule in South Africa, the collapse of communism in Europe, etc. etc.

John Hume[2] has worked wonders. The Sinn Fein leadership – Morrison and Adams – looks fresh, comparatively young and acceptably intelligent. The Unionists look old and bitter – their voices sound shrill and bigoted and there is a complete refusal amongst them to accept any degree of Unionist culpability in the last 25 horrible years.

1 Carlos Baker's scholarly biography of Hemingway was published in 1969.
2 John Hume, founder of the Irish Social Democratic and Labour Party, who shared the Nobel Peace Prize with Ulster Unionist politician David Trimble.

Tuesday, September 6th

Finding it easier to pick up and run with the story than I have for some time. Reading Hemingway has helped, which is rather neat and fortuitous. I respond well to his best writing – when it's clean and uncluttered and direct and robust and he's taught me not to agonise over being clever – searching for the adjective or adverb no-one will have heard of is not necessary – 'good' and 'fine' and 'big' and all those simple, strong words can be sufficient.

The first draft script of 'Wanda 2' is sent round and I start to read it as soon as I can. It is tremendously reassuring. The story moves on briskly, there is potential in all the characters and above all it is very funny. Good to see JC still on form.

Thursday, September 8th

To tea with Alan Bennett, who is awaiting the publication of a collection of his diaries and writings in early October.[1] *The Madness of George III* has just been filmed[2] but he didn't spend much time on location; there was a first-time director and Alan thought his job would be difficult enough without having the writer hanging around.

He makes some tea. I've bought two custard tarts from Ferreira (the Portuguese on the corner) which have welded together in my pannier. Alan sits at his desk and scoffs his enthusiastically. He still plays with his tie – today it's a knitted one in a rather lurid green. It seems he's as comfortable with a tie as I am without one.

Talk about how we write. Alan says he finds it difficult to work in complete isolation. At his house in Settle he watches people go by outside and it helps. I ask him if he's ever written a novel. 'Ooh no,' he says. 'I couldn't do that. I can hear what people say, I can see how they speak, but I don't know how they think. I don't know enough.'

Ramble through the latest doings of old friends. AB asks if I've read the Kenneth Williams diaries. 'Terribly depressing,' he says, 'if you think you're having a miserable time you should read these.' And he gives me a taste ... 'Came home, ironed sweater. And that would be all!'

---

1 The collection was called *Writing Home*.
2 *The Madness of King George* was directed by Nick Hytner and won a BAFTA for Best British Film.

He commiserates with me over *The Weekend* (which he never saw). He remembers them having a go at him over – what was it called, *Enjoy*? – so he's not entirely critic-proof.

Friday, September 9th

To Ladbroke Road for a meeting on 'Death Fish II'. JC, Iain J, Roger Murray-Leach, the art director, Robert Young, Hugh Laurie, Michael Shamberg. We sit round the boardroom table, with Lucy Willis' wonderful oil painting of a drawing class at some West Country prison mirroring our efforts.

John has prepared questionnaires for us all with headings such as 'What Doesn't Work?' 'What Needs More Work?' 'What Would You Cut?' 'How Would You Restructure?' and space below them for us to write in our opinions. And this is what we are asked to do for half an hour. Like schoolboys at exams (Hugh shields his paper with his forearm), we toil away trying not to take it too seriously, but anxious to be seen to be helpful, clear and concise.

Lucy Willis, artist of the prison picture, sketches us at work.

To Oakley Square in Camden Town to look at a possible flat for William. Big sturdy houses looking out over an un-exotic public garden studded with big chestnut trees. The 2-storey flat is big enough for two or even three. A new conversion. Reminds me of the way Sunset House was when first converted. Carpets down, all electrics provided; virtually ready to move into. A definite contender. Within walking distance of three main-line stations!

Saturday, September 10th

Come home to an urgent message to phone Denise Parry-Jones, Dizzy, Nigel's wife, Terry's sister-in-law. At last get hold of her, only to hear that Nigel died this morning of some stomach illness. Al is away in Italy. Diz doesn't know where Terry is in the US. I eventually track him down to the Sunset Marquis in LA. It's the middle of the night but I have to wake him and tell him to ring Diz. Can't give him the news myself. He rings back later. 'He had such a rotten life,' says TJ.

Friday, September 16th

Yesterday I took down 'A Bit of a Break', the novel I wrote in eleven weeks in 1977. (I think the title is awful and would like to rechristen it 'Nobody Here'.) It's much better than I thought in the sense that the writing is in parts authoritative and the central character a little more proactive than our Martin. Set it aside feeling gloomy on two counts – one that my writing style seems no better, and possibly worse than it was 17 years ago, and the other that 'Bit of a Break' seemed to ride the balance of humour and seriousness more satisfactorily than *Hem's Chair*.

The sun comes through. The two fat ginger cats spread themselves out on the wall of one of the gardens below and for a while it's like summer again.

Tuesday, September 20th

We leave about 9.45 to get down to Nailsea for Nigel's funeral. I have an imperfect image of Nailsea being this side of Bristol. In fact it's south and west of Bristol, off the M5 and near the coast of the Severn Estuary. We stop-start in the heavy traffic out of London.

It becomes clear as we make our way as fast as possible up a busy M5 that Nailsea is unattainable by midday – when the funeral starts.

Lightning stop at a filling station, off the motorway, then up to 120 mph on a curving gradient out of Avonmouth. Then into country roads, with solid elderly drivers who are not in a hurry and take great exception to others who are. Everything thrown in our way, but we reach the church only ten minutes late.

It's a neat old stone church with a tower. Almost full inside. Terry is on his feet giving a round-up of Nige's life – he waves us into the front row! opposite Diz and the children. Terry is energetic, restless, lots to say, but not much of a voice left to say it in.

Two local Labour Party men speak, one complete with red tie and red buttonhole. I speak, then Geoff Burgon, who wrote music for *Brideshead* and *Life of Brian*, speaks and plays 'Ain't Misbehavin' on the trumpet – very smoothly and mellifluously. Lady priest does prayers, we sing a hymn, 'Breathe through the heats' etc. then process down a lane to the graveyard. Despite the foul weather in London it is bright, with white scudding clouds, and the sun shines as Nigel is buried.

Then to the pub close by. Good chat and many memories. Some of the people in the local Labour Party didn't even know Terry was Nige's brother, so good was he at concealing his background.

Wednesday, September 28th

The novel has much greater momentum now. H asked me the other morning 'Is it funny?' and when I said 'No, not really' she said 'That's what you're good at.' Not judgementally or anything, but I think she's right and I must not forget there will be an expectation for me to provide laughs.

Meet Clem V for lunch.

There has been an awful ferry accident in the Baltic in the middle of the night. An Estonian ship keeled over and 800 feared drowned. Clem is concerned about safety in the transport services of the old Soviet Union. Planes are crashing with frightening regularity because there is no money for parts, or inspections or proper maintenance.

But, like me, he's looking forward to our third great journey together. Can hardly believe, as we sit congenially sipping American Sauvignon blanc and tucking into wild mushroom risotto, what we shall be putting ourselves through in the years to come.

Thursday, September 29th

Down to the RAC for a game of squash with Terry.

Afterwards we walk to the Chandos at the bottom of St Martin's Lane to have a pint before going on to the premiere of Ken Loach's *Ladybird, Ladybird*. In the pub, a young chap – regular features, well spoken, smart but unostentatious – comes up and shakes my hand. 'Congratulations,' he says, 'you keep many of us fighter pilots alive.' He's based in Coltishall in Norfolk. Apparently they give themselves 'hours' for their favourite comedy programmes. One hundred hours of *Blackadder* is pretty good, but he says there are people who've done 1,000 hours of Python!

Big crush at the Lumière. Ken, mild and retiring, shelters near the men's loo. He looks like a train-spotter, but his films are wonderfully powerful and this one, like the others, has the knack of showing you poverty and violence, but making you feel at the end of it that you understand these people more and pity them less.

Sunday, October 2nd

At 7.15 H and I arrive at the Dorchester for the Writers' Guild Awards in a Berryhurst car driven by a sinister, taciturn young man with a slight Central European accent, all in black with golden blond hair.

Welcoming committees of rather anxious, full-bodied, bespectacled women, but among them the reassuring presence of Alan Plater and his deputy chairman David Nobbs.

We are between Susannah York (co-host with Jimmy Perry) and the cartoonist Richard Wilson on one side and Honor Blackman, looking well-groomed, smart and still devastatingly attractive, on the other.

Susannah looks a bit nervous. We talk about how difficult it is in our business to remember the names of all those we've worked with and how we both fear these sorts of occasions for that reason.

Jimmy Perry, passing around us at the time, pats Susannah on the shoulder. 'It's lovely you could do this for us, Joanna.'

Colin Dexter, writer of *Morse*, is at our table. He's small, like a very old baby with a mischievous, gnome-like presence. In the gents before the awards begin he is confiding. The girl he's with is very excited to be on the same table as me – she's an ex-policewoman from Oxford. Dexter goes into rhapsodies hearing that Rachel is to go to Brasenose. Most of *Morse* filming is done there.

I see Richard Curtis and Emma Freud there and tell R that I'm presenting in his category and that I hope he wins, though I know I shouldn't say that. Well, he said, just read out my name whatever happens.

My piece goes well and Richard C is the winner for *Four Weddings*.

Monday, October 3rd

Rachel's first day at Oxford.

Lines of cars outside Brasenose, also unloading. Rachel in determinedly bouncy form. First good news is her room – number 5 on staircase 7.

If ever there was a room in which I might say my career began it's this one. The low beam, the window seat, the step down into a bedroom. This is where Robert Hewison and I wrote and planned our cabarets; where we ate Polish sausage and I learnt to love endive salad!

She's unpacked and the shabbily decorated room has taken on some of her life. We leave about 5.30. There are parents hugging their children all over the place. The men get a peremptory shoulder to shoulder, the girls something more lingering.

Monday, October 10th

The warm, settled days continue. On the very last lap of *'Hem's Chair'*, so in to work soon after nine. The final, apocalyptic sequence falls into place nicely and I race to the finish, spewing forth nearly 3,000 words in four hours flat.

Type 'The End' at ten minutes to two. No great traumas, but I shed tears for Martin as I write him off. Well, not so much Martin as the others left behind.

Then I have to start at the beginning again and work my way through. Corrections on every page and some quite substantial rewrites which I have spotted at early read-throughs.

H asks the uncomfortable question – 'Is it the sort of book you would want to read?'

Tuesday, October 25th

Have set myself up again at 54 Delancey, after eleven days away, re-reading the novel in the Hemingway locations of the Basque country.

Geoffrey, big in many layers of brown, arrives a little after ten. First of all we talk general points. Geoffrey, to his credit, is businesslike, thorough and doesn't attempt to disguise the fact that he feels there is work to be done. He finds the main characters interesting, contrasting and wants to know more about them. He feels the townsfolk should be better and more fully rounded. He is of the opinion that more cuts are necessary rather than extensive rewriting and that the book will take it, as it's at a good length.

I push as far as I can, without sounding alarmist or defeatist, my doubts about the weight and consequence of the book. Geoffrey plays a straight bat, refusing to supply false enthusiasms or countenance any convenient despondency. He reiterates its strengths – 'You've written some good scenes, and there is an effective story ...' and so on.

Back at the flat he fetches out his copy of the text which is peppered with pencil marks and we sit at the table together and begin a much more intense and fraught process than this morning's amiable chat.

The light goes and we huddle together around one lamp.

Wednesday, October 26th

The novel continues its relentless progress. We go to Michelin House to meet Angela Martin, slim, open and friendly Publicity Director, and Simon Westcott, conspicuously young Marketing Director.

There is a tremendous demand for this as yet unfinished work. Smiths want to give me a Hero Promotion – star of the month as it were, and sponsor a signing and reading tour in March. Both Angela, whom I like more and more as we go on, and Simon are expecting a bigger campaign than any I've done so far. Angela accepts my preference for provincial rather than metropolitan venues, and I'm able to steer Simon away, I hope, from cult-of-personality promotion. I'm mindful of the fate of *The Weekend* and want to make quite sure I get up as few noses as possible.

Friday, October 28th

The *Ham and High* runs a feature on Gospel Oak, trailed on the front page as 'Gospel Coke. Gospel Oak, a classic London village, home of Michael Palin ... and a cocaine and heroin problem as bad as anywhere in the capital.' Inside is a story of classic urban decay rather than classic villages. Whether it is worse now than it ever was I don't know. Drugs are more widely available, jobs and money less widely available, Camden, the great protector, is now rate-capped and reduced, so yes, it's hardly surprising it is worse.

I tell Helen that it's probably wiped ten thousand off the house prices at a stroke, but she thinks it all rather exciting! At least we live somewhere where something is going on.

To 54 and await Geoffrey. He says that he's just finished reading through to the end for a second time, and 'you know,' rubs beard ... 'it's very good'.

Monday, October 31st: London–Manchester

Off to Euston for the Manchester train.

Waterstones is busy. Joseph Heller is to give a talk and reading downstairs. Into a basement room where Heller is already at work, signing, surrounded by piles of his latest, *Closing Time*. Head down and writing his name time after time as books are thrust at him, he looks less the great author and more the toiling galley slave.

Our cab driver, with a Liverpudlian Irish accent, tells us that he too has written a book. He wrote it in prison. For the first ten years, he tells us, he wrote nothing, but he decided it was time to tell the story of how he ended up with a twelve-year sentence.

Good old Suzanna goes straight to the point. 'Excuse me, but what were you in prison for?' she calls through the grille. 'If I tell you,' he replies as if he's been asked the question many times, 'it mustn't go outside this taxi.' We all agree. He pauses, effectively. 'Murder.'

Tuesday, November 1st: Manchester–London

Joseph Heller and his wife Valerie are travelling on the same train with us. We stop and talk on our way to breakfast. She is slim and dark and a good twenty years younger than him I would think. He has broad, almost Geronimo-esque features and his complexion is pink and fresh and glowing. He looks healthy but confesses to demolishing much of a bottle of scotch during the signing and talk last night.

I compliment him on *Something Happened* and he says a lot of people are 'coming round to liking' the book. Published in 1961, it was the follow-up to *Catch 22*. He is in London for a week then to Oxford to be interviewed at the Union. Staying at Claridge's. He insists on the morning and most of the afternoon off. He was interviewed by Terry at Hay Festival. He'd caught a Python retrospective in the States and thought Terry looked better as a woman.

Tuesday, November 15th

To a PEN-organised reception at the slightly run-down Royal Society of Literature in Hyde Park Gate. A bevy of authors promised and punters pay £25.00 to come and mingle.

Ronnie Harwood describes the awful privations of writers in prison for what they have written and one thinks facetious thoughts about how many writers in this country you might like to see in prison for what they've written.

A very nice moment after the speeches end. Ronnie Harwood pushes his way through the throng towards me, grasps my hand and congratulates me on *The Dresser*. He had so many letters, he said, all mentioning the strength of my performance. He is wonderfully fulsome and to be congratulated thus by the author swells my pride in the best way. He asks if I would like to do it on stage. I waver. Am I too old? No, he says, two men in their 80s recently played it.

Renew acquaintance with La O'Brien – Edna,[1] who greets me with a soft brush of lips on cheek and a slow, enveloping stateliness which feels like being gently smothered by some naughty aunt. Tell her about the novel. 'What's the title?' she asks with breathy urgency. 'Good title.' Then she asks me how it begins. I start out on an explanation and she interrupts. 'No, no, I mean what is the first line?' She talks with loving intensity of the importance of 'first lines', and I rather pathetically cannot remember a word of mine.

Sunday, November 20th

JC has invited H and me round for a quiet evening. He's had a bad week. Film writing to do but also lots of tasks that took time without giving satisfaction – like talking about parking spaces on the filming! Jamie has decided to take on a film in early spring which has disrupted dates. Kevin has become concerned about whether he should play two roles.

Tuesday, November 29th

Must complete my second draft rewrite today, and do so.

To the *Literary Review* 15th anniversary party at Simpson's.

I think the *Lit Review* is more of a club than a magazine – perhaps even more a state of mind. Or a symbol. It loses money, has a modest circulation yet is something of a cause. Bron Waugh's helmsmanship and the generally constructive and generous tone of its contributions (viz. Beryl B's lovely review of *Pole to Pole*) attracts young and old writers. It's fashionable, a little exclusive.

Not that that word's the one that springs to mind as I climb the wide-carpeted stairs of Simpson's in the Strand.

The rooms smell of old gravy and the diners look, from a brief glimpse, like good territory for a George Grosz.

There is a competition, hosted by Bron, for the worst sex in a novel award. Last year it was won by Melvyn for *A Time to Dance*, and apparently he sportingly arrived to collect it. Award presented by Marianne Faithfull.

---

1 Edna O'Brien, Irish novelist who made her name with her first book *The Country Girls*.

A flame-haired temptress asks me how P. J. O'Rourke was when I interviewed him on Saturday. She feels very foolish when I tell her that it was Melvyn Bragg who interviewed P. J. O'Rourke. 'Of course, you're Michael Palin! I much prefer you to Melvyn Bragg!'

I get a kiss from Marianne Faithfull, who says, before I can say the same thing to her, 'I feel as if I've known you all my life'!

Home by 9.15. More wine. H out. Realise I am drunk. Drink lots of water and crash out early.

Later H says she knew I must have been enjoying lavish hospitality as she could hear me snoring from downstairs.

Thursday, December 8th

This is the 13th consecutive day I have worked on the novel. Generally I have begun between 9.30 and ten in the morning, always at the Dylan house, except for last Sunday at home. Here I work until about two hours after it gets dark, i.e. about six o'clock. Drive home, have supper and put in two or three more hours before bed, usually at midnight.

There are notes in the margin about almost every character involved – 'let reader know more'; 'who is this, what is he/she wearing'. This aspect has been the hardest work, but I think Geoffrey right to pin me down to detail and precision. I've always had a lazy streak. 'Lines of Least Resistance' is my favourite autobiography title.

Friday, December 9th

If there were ever a time when I could say the novel is finished, this is it. Though Geoffrey will trawl through it with an even finer toothcomb next week, what I deliver today is essentially what *Hemingway's Chair* will be.

Began August 8th. Finished December 9th. Four months. Not enough. But what would be enough?

Thursday, December 15th

Dreamt about a land covered in white frost and my dream comes true this morning. Sun slowly pulling itself above the stagnant polluted air, but it's still a beautiful winter morning.

To 54 Delancey as Mary O'Donovan arrives at 10.30. Mary is the copy-editor at Methuen. She's brisk and efficient and confident in her judgements, though I should think she's not much older than Tom.

Have to go through the entire novel, page by page, one more time.

Home and, despite great weariness and the enormous attraction of an early night and a sleep of more than five and a half hours, we have to get ready to go out to George H's Christmas party.

George looks more like the garden gnome than the slim, fine-featured executive these days. He's wearing, he says, his 'Tibetan Book of the Dead Boots', which he last wore at the White House when George Bush was President.

Ade Edmondson wandering about clutching a beer and looking gently bemused. Very keen to know what I'm doing. I realise that I can't stop them treating me with respect, however much I want to pay it back to them. Harry Enfield calls me Mr Palin and I feel instantly like one of his Cholmondley-Warner characters. Feel more at ease with the Neil Innes and the Ray Coopers – my coevals rather than my admirers.

Sit next to Derek and Joan Taylor. Many laughs. Derek disappears to smoke a joint and comes back very bright-eyed.

The McCartneys' chauffeur-driven Mercedes limo is idling outside the front porch as we slip by and, feeling very good and comfortable, head back to town.

Monday, December 19th

To Portobello Road for a drink and view of the exhibition at Tristram's new gallery/shop up in the less trendy, but possibly emerging, fringes of Golborne. Trellick Tower looms a half-mile away. TP's gallery reminds me of a little Irish bar. The walls decorated with a sort of sponged yellow wash. A round green garden table and a red-leather bench give a car-nival contrast to the lines of halogen lamps on wires which illuminate the works. It's quite chic, a mixture of high and low tech as Tristram says.

George Melly[1] is sitting comfortably at the table. He says we've met somewhere recently. I can't remember, and as I seem to have been the victim of mistaken identity cases so often recently – but I venture the *Passionate Woman* premiere – Melly doesn't think so. He says he never goes to the theatre – can't hear. Went to *Liaisons Dangereuses* and could

1 George Melly, writer, jazz singer, film and TV critic for the *Observer*, died in 2007.

hear the man's voice, because the pitch was right, but the woman's not at all.

Unload my heavy coat – for the weather has turned wintry at last – and my accumulation of shopping. TP shows me round. He's got a nice little office at the back, which has windows onto a yard and for some reason reminds me of the time-keeper's office at a factory.

Jonathan Miller arrives with his wife Rachel. He's having two days off between operas. Describes someone he's met in New York as having so diluted his Jewishness that he refers to him as having had a Jewdectomy.

Miller rants on about the critics. I mention my experience with *The Weekend*. 'I was away for that,' he adds hastily.

Monday, December 26th

Read slim Boxing Day papers. I detect a sense of national embarrassment over the royals and their revelations. Embarrassment and shame. As if we have allowed some unpleasantly prurient and titillating side of ourselves to be publicly exploited. I think there is a revulsion from the whole thing now.

Saturday, December 31st

Morning at various shops. London streets still quiet.

Drop in at No. 54 on the way back. The room in which I wrote *Hemingway's Chair* is much as it was as I worked there. Two big felt pin-boards on the walls in front of me and to my left, index cards of the chapters.

Onwards, after a last lingering look at the modest, unspectacular premises, overlooking Dylan Thomas' caravan, where so much of my year was spent, to familiar haunts – the Persian dry cleaners, the Indian stationers, Renata and Rafael at Giacobazzi's Delicatessen.

Renata doesn't like the passing of a year. It generally makes her sad and regretful. I look forward so much to a new year that I never grieve for the old one, I say. 'I don't like change,' she says. This I can sympathise with too. But I'm a nostalgic with a fascination for the future.

Helen has cooked an Indian meal for our New Year's Eve party tonight. Everyone arrives about 8.30.

The old year slips away and 1995 is ushered in by Dame Vera Lynn on BBC One.

1995

Sunday, January 1st

Without really meaning to I find myself at my desk, with some Gene Vincent[1] playing, beginning to turn the pages of *Hemingway's Chair* yet again.

A rare and welcome feeling of optimism takes me. Maybe it's because I'm not yet again reading the book in rigorous silence, fearing doorbells and telephones, or in haste, aware of all the other things I should be doing. I'm reading for once because I want to read it.

The music seems to give life to the writing and the energy of the writing blends with the energy of the music. I keep replaying some of my loudest CDs, alternating Vincent with Southside Johnny and the Asbury Jukes.

Turn off the deck at midnight – after 'All Night Long' fades for the umpteenth time, and I feel at that moment that I have nothing to be ashamed of.

Tuesday, January 3rd

Rachel toils away upstairs, working as hard, now Christmas is over, as she ever did last term at Oxford, Tom is in a studio somewhere recording the work of a rapper called The Darkman and Will is enjoying the life of Riley on skis at Val d'Isère.

The roads are quiet. Drive across Hyde Park and down to the Michelin Building with unusual swiftness.

Simon and his assistant Jo at Reed Books are bright and helpful, but they have been conditioned into behaving and thinking in a straitjacket – determined by targets and flow charts. Dreams, hopes, inspirations must not be indulged in during office hours.

I ask them not to call it a 'brilliant' new novel, which they think very odd – but I feel that's for others to say, not ourselves. (The real reason for my reluctance is that I don't think they will!)

---

1 Gene Vincent, pioneer rock-'n'-roller, introduced to me by John Peel when we were both at Shrewsbury School together in 1957.

Sunday, January 8th

I wake quite soon after I first drift off. Was the sound of breaking glass the tail end of a dream or the first indication of wakefulness? Nothing to be seen outside the window. Back to bed.

Woken again by sound of letter box rattling. Then hear footsteps passing beneath the window – sounds like a man and a woman. No evidence of anything being put through door. Feel a little uneasy. Back to bed after checking the time. It's 4.15.

A few minutes later footsteps, faster and heavier, stop on our corner. Then I hear letter box shutter rattling again and subdued voices. Someone is trying the front door. Letter box rattles again. Tiptoe downstairs. Voices outside the door, though I can't hear what they're saying.

Clear view of two young lads – late teens – beneath the telegraph pole talking and glancing again at the house. What strikes me first is their appearance. Their shabby, ill-fitting clothes, the dirt on the face of one of them makes a classic picture of poverty. They look like they're from the very bottom of the heap.

One of them, a skinny, dark-haired boy with cadaverous features, is swaying on his feet. His eyes look slow and dead. Then the other one, a fairer, fleshier-faced lad, turns, holding what looks like a metal tape measure, open a foot or so, and they both come straight towards the window from which I'm observing them.

Tiptoe upstairs and ask H to ring the police. Can hear the metal being inserted between the window frames. Panto-esque farce now takes over as I move about the landing and into my room looking for paper and pencil to write down a clear description of the two. Don't want to risk switching light on or making any noise. Of all the pens and pencils I emerge with I choose the white one; back again, produce a biro that won't write.

Meanwhile the two would-be intruders continue testing the window. Then the phone rings. H grabs it quickly. It's the police. Probably because of their altered state the sound of the phone fails to deter the lads, and they are duly caught outside the house by a police van and four support cars.

Around 10.30 two Detective Inspectors arrive to take statements.

Would I be prepared to testify in court if the case ever got that far? I say yes.

The fingerprint lady arrives. She's number three in the Met, I was told by the Detective, in clear-up rate success. She does a thorough job, dabbing her brush at the window as H and I sit inside, giving statements at separate tables. Only at the end does her professional detachment waver. 'Could you sign my job sheet?' she asks.

Monday, January 9th

Lin Cook rings to tell us that Peter is dead. She can hardly speak. Once again that awful, palpable sense of loss, a feeling of time being called – but in Peter's case, called too early.

The news comes through about 10.15. Just after eleven I'm on Radio 5 Live with a hastily cobbled-together tribute.

The phone rings as soon as I've put it down; it's the *Standard* wanting my thoughts, then my nephew Marcus rings from *Newsnight* to see if I would come in and do a tribute. I feel that others knew him better, could say more about his professional career and that it might be presumptuous of me to turn up.

Helen goes up to see Lin. She is very distressed.

The death of anyone you know produces a kind of heightened introspection, and when it's someone you know and have become close to – and recently, driving them home late-night from parties, I feel we have become close to Lin and Peter – it's a momentary feeling of vulnerability, of the cold hand of the reaper coming very close indeed.

Meet Michael Barnes at Two Brydges.

Michael has not heard the news about Peter. He sits, long legs and long hands elegantly stretching across the sofa before the artificial flames of the fire, smoking and drinking a whisky. He is a thin version of Peter I think – what I mean of course is that he is an incorrigible and unrepentant smoker and drinker.

Michael then tells me two recent experiences – one, when he fainted in an Italian restaurant in Belfast and was taken to the City Hospital where, perhaps because of the way he looked, five days of tests were done. Brain scans and heart-rate monitors, etc. all revealed nothing.

Then just after Christmas he had a blackout whilst walking home, and remembers nothing of a fall which left him with head wounds that needed six stitches and an overnight stay in the City Hospital. He later discovered he had fallen.

I'm not sure why he tells me these stories at such length, but despite the underlying theme of basic good health, I think there is fear that something may happen again at any time. I notice that he put away two whiskies, a half-bottle of Côtes du Rhône and three measures of Armagnac before attempting the narrow, lethal stairs of Two Brydges.

We part in the street and I cannot help but feel as I press my arm around his bony shoulders that I fear for Michael's survival as urgently as I sometimes used to fear for Peter's.

Tuesday, January 10th

Work at home on various bits and pieces. *Observer* rings to ask if I would contribute a 700-word piece about Peter C for Sunday. Say yes.

Catch first episode of TJ's *Crusades*. A bit breathless and busy, but Terry is wonderful. He doesn't really seem to mind what he looks like.

Wednesday, January 11th

Outraged by news that John Marriott – the Governor of Parkhurst who so impressed me when we filmed there – has been sacked as a scapegoat for the Parkhurst escape.[1] I set my thoughts down in a letter to the *Independent*.

Wrestle with the Peter Cook obit. Very much aware that this is something I must get right. Temptation to assume I know all about his life – of course I don't.

Monday, January 16th

Feeling twitchily anxious about my *Tatler* phone interview re *Hemingway's Chair* this morning. The first proofs of the book have gone out to long-lead journalists and, I presume, to the *Omnibus* people, and this will be one of the first outside, upmarket reactions.

Their interviewer is Cressida Connolly, daughter of Cyril.[2]

---

1 John Marriott was sacked by the Home Secretary, Michael Howard, following the escape from Parkhurst of three prisoners. He had been Governor of the Isle of Wight prison since 1990.

2 Cyril Connolly, influential literary critic remembered for his 1938 autobiography *Enemies of Promise*. His daughter, Cressida, is a writer and novelist, whose collection of short stories, *The Happiest Days*, won the PEN/Macmillan prize in 2000.

'Your novel,' she begins, and follows this with a long silence. My heart sinks, and a drowsy numbness ... She sounds kind, polite, not at all lofty, but I can't get any signals as to approval or disapproval.

Only at the very end of our amicable and sympathetic chat does she reveal that she liked the novel. Found it funny and also full of pathos and how nice it was not to have a relentlessly comic style.

She also revealed that Cyril was terribly pleased by the Pythons' reference to him at the end of 'Eric the Half a Bee' – 'Cy-ril Con-oll-ee?' 'Who?' 'Cyril Connolly'. They had the record and replayed it hungrily!

Tuesday, January 17th

Some interesting work offers, including playing Ratty to A Bennett's Mole in an animated version of *Wind in the Willows* being done for Carlton. The two other main characters to be played by Rik Mayall and Michael Gambon. Really can't resist. It's one and a half days and I'd do it for the lunch-break company alone!

Wednesday, January 18th

Lunch at Groucho's with Dan P. Catch up on things. In theory, I turn 'The Adventure' over to him now, knowing that I shall have no time until the end of 1997 to look at it in any concentrated way.

On the way out, I see Anna Haycraft talking earnestly to Jeffrey Bernard[1] who sits, white as a corpse, in a wheelchair beside the bar. I like the fact that the wheelchair is by the bar and in the main thoroughfare. No chance of anyone missing him, or vice-versa.

George H rings. He's back from India. He's most concerned that his postcard from the Udaipur Lake Palace hasn't arrived, but tells me what it says. 'There we were, hundred of us, living in't palace in't middle of lake. We 'ad to get up in't morning – lick palace clean wi'our tongues ...' Then he says 'I hear you've been seeing the bass player from our band.' Takes me a while before I realise he means McCartney. George has a good sense of silliness. Better able to send it all up than Paul.

---

1 Jeffrey Bernard, writer of the 'Low Life' column in the *Spectator*, who was immortalised in Keith Waterhouse's play *Jeffrey Bernard Is Unwell*.

Tuesday, January 31st

A letter from the BBC Radio Drama department. It's from one Duncan Minshull, Chief Producer, Readings, who has received an advance copy of *Hemingway's Chair* and thinks it would make 'a terrific and topical addition to *Book at Bedtime*, a real summer treat'. He proposes my recording it in ten 15-minute episodes, which would coincide with publication.

I spend the evening preparing for my debut as 'Ratty' in *Wind in the Willows* tomorrow.

Wednesday, February 1st

I am determined to walk to work – the recordings are being made at George Martin's 'Air' Studios. Step out with my umbrella. There just before nine.

Alan Bennett, who's playing Mole, is already in the studio sitting in splendid isolation at one of two long tables, each covered with a white, embroidered tablecloth, creating an effect (with all the hi-tech equipment) halfway between an operating theatre and a tea-shop. Actually the place is a converted church, and beyond the expensive shell of the recording studio are tall arched windows with stained-glass rose patterns at the top.

Alan and I try to gossip in between takes, but it's not easy with a half-dozen people in the box listening to our every word.

He'd recently been contacted by Dudley Moore's biographer, and thought it most peculiar that Dudley had clearly put about the story that he was a poor and put-upon working-class boy who had suffered a harsh, almost Dickensian upbringing.

And talking of Dickens, A tells story of David Hockney, who had been to see the musical *Oliver* and was disappointed that the homosexual nature of the relationship between Fagin and Dodger had not been brought out enough. 'Well, I mean,' says Alan, Mole-ishly, 'there's no sex in Dickens at all.'

By 12.15 we've completed all we had to do and A decides to go home for lunch.

Back up the hill again for two o'clock and Michael Gambon, as Badger, is already at the table. Big, crumpled, lived-in look. He's soft-spoken and affable, with no apparent actor's tricks or psychoses.

He and Alan B fall to talking about Michael Bryant (who played Ratty in the first National production of Alan's adaptation). Alan confesses that he was terrified of Michael Bryant the only time he'd worked with him, and Gambon confirmed that he is a hard man on stage. 'Tells you to "fuck off" as soon as you come on.'

George Martin makes a paternal appearance. (I don't have the cheek to ask him if he'd seen himself described in a magazine article recently as 'the Michael Palin of rock'!) He says the studio conversion cost about £15 million. 'Half the money was Japanese, so I feel I'd done my bit to pay them back for the Burma Railway,' he says, elegantly.

Thursday, February 2nd

The call has been delayed until eleven, so no great rush this morning. There is some very pale light outside at a quarter to eight now, which shows the winter slowly waning.

There is quite a chunk left for Alan and myself to do, which rather pleases me as I'm enjoying working opposite him. Slightly hysterical end-of-term atmosphere today.

Alan has, at one point, to do some wild-track 'fighting' noises. He screws up his face with effort – a sort of squeak comes out and he collapses into fits of laughter. 'Oh dear,' he laments, trying desperately to gather his concentration for another effort, 'this is why I never wanted to be an actor!'

All of us, I think even Alan, a little regretful to be told that it's all done.

Rik M has arrived for some publicity photos, and Gambon too. Rik is currently in a new Simon Gray play with Stephen Fry.[1] Gray is on a bottle of champagne a day, Rik says. 'I don't know if he drinks it all. He just likes to have it there.'

Monday, February 6th

The *Daily Mail* calls and asks if I would write them a piece about my feelings on the current state of the Labour Party. When I tell them I'm

---

1 Stephen Fry disappeared to Belgium while appearing in the London production of Gray's play, *Cell Mates*.

too busy they suggest me putting my name to a 'ghosted' piece. Tell them no, more vigorously.

Ring Alan Bennett to check if he is coming with H and myself to see Maggie Smith in Albee's *Three Tall Women* on Friday. When I ask if he'd like to bring someone, he says he hasn't anyone to bring. He laughs when I make sympathetic noises, and says it's not so much that he hasn't got anyone, but that there are very few people he would risk bringing along to meet, as he calls her fondly, 'the flame-thrower'. 'They'd have to wear asbestos suits,' he says, making himself laugh a lot.

Tuesday, February 7th

Down to Bush House to take part in an hour-long phone-in for National Public Radio.

Bush House, soaring skywards and grandly dominating the long, southward perspective of Kingsway, has still one of the finest exteriors in London, and the fact that it preludes a building devoted to nation speaking peace unto nation nicely combines the spirit and appearance of the place.

A slim young girl whose second name is Haybill takes me up and out and round the back and down an iron fire escape and eventually to a quite roomy studio from which I shall be able to talk to the American nation. That's precisely what does happen – the smooth, almost purring voice of interlocutor Carl Suarez oozes through from Washington and introduces me to all sorts of people from Tallahassee, Florida, to Seattle, who all want to talk to me about the current running of *80 Days* on PBS.

Ms Haybill sits with me and occasionally fiddles with the controls. It's a very intimate situation. Just the two of us and the whole of America.

Wednesday, February 8th

To Harley Street to have a combined insurance medical for 'Palin's Pacific' and 'Death Fish 2'. Dr Forecast doesn't quite convince as a doctor. The whole process over without me even having to take shirt or shoes or socks off. Rather wearily, he hands me a small plastic container. 'Could you do a urine sample? For the BBC.'

Friday, February 10th

To *Three Tall Women*. Wyndham's Theatre packed. Maggie's pulling power. In the first act she looks a bit like the Thatcher dummy in *Spitting Image*, tight and sharp and malevolent. But it's not she who is the unsympathetic character in the play, whatever Albee might have intended. It's the young, hard lawyer. So Maggie gets the laughs and carries us cheerfully on to the half. Second act better but still not a good play.

Backstage and into Maggie's presence. Again, the disarming, purring lower register of the voice. She hugs Alan – his raincoat flies everywhere. It's like a scene on a station in the '50s. Then, with less abandon, she gives me a hug.

Then on to the Ivy. At one point Alan, who was voted Most Popular Author of the Year at the Nibbies last night, professed that he rarely had phone calls – 'I sometimes pick the receiver up just to see if it's working.'

Tuesday, March 7th

My first glimpse of the hardback of *Hemingway's Chair* – the finished work.

Turn it over and read a little. I keep doing this at various points during the day. It gives me pleasure. Something about the artefact itself – the confidence of the design, the printing, the binding, the price even – seems to elevate the text, endow it with some distinction, some significance. Never have the words felt less arbitrary.

Wednesday, March 8th

Angela Martin and Kath round to discuss 'HC' tour and publicity. Try to avoid exposing myself to too many of the 'big' celebrity articles which I find it so difficult to deal with, and at the other end of the scale avoid 'My First Kitchen' sort of stuff.

There are two photos in *Bookcase*, the W. H. Smith's free mag. One on the cover makes me look like a younger Warren Beatty – lashed in make-up on a beach, inside an extraordinary combination of quiffy, swept-back, wind-blown hair and someone else's sweater (I should be aware by now that if I wear someone else's clothes I look like someone else).

Research trip to Africa for my never-completed novel *Uganda*. At the Equator with my guide, George Byomhumuza, February 1994.

One of the two good reviews of *The Weekend*. And we made the most of it.
Strand Theatre, Aldwych, May 4th, 1994.

Enjoying a Drink

LEFT: With Elena Salvoni, my all-time favourite maître d', at Elena's L'Etoile.

BELOW LEFT: With Lena Rustin, the speech therapist whose work on stammering in children inspired the Michael Palin Centre; and (BELOW RIGHT) Travers Reid, who got me involved, at *An Evening with Michael Palin* at the Cambridge Theatre, London, April 17th, 1994.

RIGHT: *Sunday Times* photo for *The Weekend*. 'The photographer has some odd idea of me sitting in a dressing room and eating Mars Bars. The effort of not doing it is so much more draining than just getting on with it, so I borrow a dressing gown . . . and sit and eat Mars Bars.' Yvonne Arnaud Theatre, Guildford, March 26th, 1994.

Full Circle

Little Diomede Island in the Bering Strait. Where we started our journey round the Pacific Rim on August 28th, 1995, and ended it on August 14th, 1996.

Spectacular, almost unreal turquoise lake in the caldera of one of the many volcanoes in the Kamchatka Peninsula, eastern Russia.

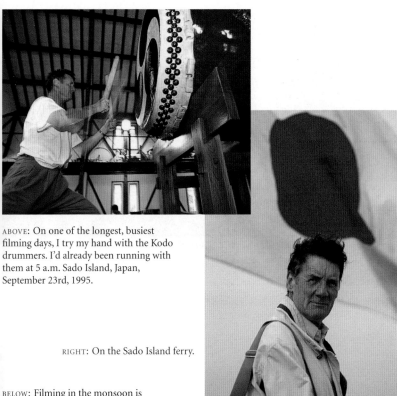

ABOVE: On one of the longest, busiest filming days, I try my hand with the Kodo drummers. I'd already been running with them at 5 a.m. Sado Island, Japan, September 23rd, 1995.

RIGHT: On the Sado Island ferry.

BELOW: Filming in the monsoon is not to be recommended. Hue Station, Vietnam, November 23rd, 1995.

With Iban elders (and one-time head-hunters) in a communal longhouse, Nanga Sumpa, Sarawak, January 1996.

Getting in the way of the tea harvest, Java.

ABOVE RIGHT: The one and only time I've looked down into an active volcano – Mount Bromo, Java.

RIGHT: Helicoptering onto the Cook Glacier at the end of our long voyage down the western rim of the Pacific, March 1996.

My morning in Alcatraz – with two men who'd spent a lot longer than that here. Now they take guided tours. 'A day described as "almost flawless" by Fraser at dinner'– San Francisco, August 2nd, 1996.

El Tatio geyser field. Spectacular steam effects at 4,500 metres. Calama, Chile.

According to Angela Martin, Adrian Edmondson said I looked like k.d. lang.

Saturday, March 18th

Car collects me at 12.15 to go to my first official *Hemingway's Chair* function. Held at an anonymous modern pile of a hotel called Copthorne Tara, as if after the heroine of a tacky novel.

About 350 booksellers, currently in the middle of a conference, crowd in for this Reed Books-hosted event.

It's much more successful than it seemed likely to be. The food is good, and the four author speakers – Paula Danziger, the children's author, Dr Stefan Someone[1] (the obligatory gardening expert that every publisher likes to trundle out), Michel Roux and myself – are each allotted a course, rather than all kept until the end.

I'm the final speaker, accompanying the coffee, but sandwiched very close against the start of the England-Scotland rugby match.

I feel on top of my brief, as it were – the speech is very well received, mainly, I think, because I've talked less of myself and more about booksellers and bookselling. Know your audience. It pays off.

Brian the driver, who has had them all in the back of his car – 'John Cleese – he's much better now', Peter Ackroyd – 'well, he's a gay alcoholic isn't he' – drives me back via Museum Street in Bloomsbury so I can look for a J. B. Priestley first edition for Barry Cryer's 60th tomorrow. 'Boydy loves this street. I often have to bring him here' (Will Boydy, that is).

I've a feeling that I could find out a lot from Brian, who is genially, amiably indiscreet. I now know that Boydy, and Mrs Boydy, have a 'château' south of Bordeaux. Brian gives a grunt of wondering appreciation as if thinking of the Temple of Solomon.

Tuesday, March 21st

To the National Portrait Gallery, to which I have been invited for the private view/launch of the Richard Avedon show. A mass of photographers beehive around the entrance. No way of getting in except dodging through the traffic on Charing Cross Road.

1 Dr Stefan Buczacki.

Once in, herded upstairs to a 'reception'. Not allowed into the Avedon yet as Princess Di is paying a visit first.

Eventually we're allowed downstairs. Doors open, men with walkie-talkies push a way (unnecessarily) through our ranks and Lady Di, talking to, and towering over, little Dick A, walks past us. Does she double-take on seeing me? I had the distinct feeling she did; it made the whole shambles worthwhile.

Later I collar Avedon; he's very charming and remembers me. Our photo (the naked Pythons) is in the catalogue but not in the exhibition. Avedon, who looks like a little golden-haired doll, smiles apologetically – 'You're much more used to all this than I am.' Nice to have made contact. Twenty years on. Then some loud, proprietorial voice summons him. 'Richard! Over here!' No question of apologising for breaking into our conversation. It's not that sort of occasion.

Friday, March 24th

Into Holland Park to be interviewed on a bench by Frank Delaney.

Delaney, like a sort of Irish Ned Sherrin, burbles on, most agreeably. Feel he should be in a periwig for the bons mots and the little observations fall lightly and profusely. He does tell a very good story of Michael Winner banging on the door of a Portaloo and shouting to his lighting cameraman that he wanted him on set. The cameraman shouts back, 'I'm sorry, Michael, I can't deal with two shits at once.'

Brian drives me home. Is indiscreet about Ranulph Fiennes and Sir John Harvey-Jones. 'He likes to have two pints before every interview'!

Monday, March 27th

Interview with Andrew Duncan for *Radio Times* about my involvement in the launch of BBC's Mental Health Week (which I record on Wednesday). Offer information about Angela. Am amazed how fast journalists move in once you've volunteered some very personal information. No holding back. 'Does it worry you that you are now the same age as your sister was when she died?'

Friday, March 31st: London–Edinburgh

To the Caledonian Hotel, which I always feel is some sort of 'lucky' hotel. It was here that I heard that *Pole to Pole* had gone to No. 1 two and a half years ago, and here that I finished that extraordinary week when *80 Days* became a hit, and the book entered the charts, for the first time.

Tonight it came up trumps again – though in a more unexpected way. The Suzie Mackenzie piece appeared today in the *Evening Standard*. Apart from the awful headline 'How I Forgave My Father's Sins', it was a strong, moving piece.

Angela's 'gassing' of herself came up in the first arresting paragraph – but it was a good, fair piece, related to '*HC*', which she called 'a marvellous first novel', and which pieced together all sorts of small revelations about my relationship with my father accurately and with real sympathy. I read it twice, and with tears in my eyes both times.

Monday, April 3rd

Publication day.

To *Start the Week* studio. Talk to Tom Stoppard, big and slim and hardly a sign of conventional ageing on complexion or in the dense blackness of his thick, Byronic locks.

Melanie Phillips kicks the programme off with five minutes on hypocrisy – hardly designed to start the 25th anniversary edition with a bang. We all have to chip in. Nerve-racking really.

Then I have a few minutes on *Hemingway's Chair*. Melvyn murmured to me before we went in 'If I say the name Amis came to mind – Kingsley Amis – I hope you wouldn't take it amiss (*sic*)'. That's as close as he got to praise, but he's quite pleasant, jovial and indulgent with it on air.

Stoppard is like Martin, the hero of my book, something of a Hemingway addict. He says he's now weaned himself off the worst of the effects – buying every first edition he could lay his hands on, etc. 'You should have come to see me,' he advises afterwards. 'I could have saved you all that research.'

To the Victoria Station signing. It turns out to be the best attendance so far. For a solid hour there is a queue.

One man gives me his *Standard* to sign. 'Put "Roxy Music" at the bottom,' he orders. When I ask what on earth for he looks pained. 'You're

Bryan Ferry, aren't you?' Much laughter from Angela. When I say no he looks cross, as if I've deceived him.

Tuesday, April 11th: Nottingham–Sheffield–Manchester

With breakfast comes a *Guardian* review of '*HC*'. I brace myself. It's another man – why do they nearly always give the book to men to review?

The inevitable mixture – praise and punishment. But at least the praise rather warm and unexpected. He was very complimentary about my ability to write a sex scene and thought that the book was essentially a love story. No-one has seen it quite like that before.

It's a day of continuous, if not absolutely clear sunshine. Sheffield sprawls over the hills. We sign books at Blackwells – a lovely manager, keen staff, but hard hit by the removal of Sheffield's shopping centre to Meadowhall. Then out to Meadowhall.

It's the first time I've seen this legendarily successful complex that covers the site of Hadfield's East Hecla steelworks. Nearby are the remains of Edgar Allen's.[1] One long, black-sided shed still bears the name, but next to it just an empty, cleared area where the trackwork department used to be. The foundry's gone too – now part of the approaches to the shopping centre.

I'm just glad that I still have memories of pre-Meadowhall Tinsley, indeed of pre-viaduct Tinsley, memories of the grandeur and grime and the days when Vulcan really was the god of Sheffield.

Meadowhall is shopping as theme park. Spanish villages sprout for no particular reason – and it's quite in keeping with the whole surreal logic of the place that I have to be presented to the shoppers in a huge circular central hall, thick with the smell of burgers and chips, where crowds are eating.

Not only this but I'm interviewed as they eat. A smooth, alarmingly controlled man, who betrays not the slightest apparent awareness of the absurdity of what we're doing, asks me questions about Hemingway which I can barely hear above the noise of the throng. Our conversation is relayed onto a huge multi-panelled, closed-circuit TV screen above our heads. It is an awesomely pointless exercise and I take pleasure in

---

1 The Edgar Allen company where my father worked as Export Manager until his retirement in 1965.

imagining the least likely writers to be put through this ordeal. Anita Brookner? Nabokov?

Tuesday, April 18th

Breakfast, shower and at five to nine Graham Fordham, my driver for the next 16 weeks of *Fierce Creatures*, rings the doorbell.

Into Pinewood at twenty to ten. Meeting in the boardroom – English manorial library with real books behind latticed doors. So many old friends – Maria Aitken, Robert Lindsay, Robert Young, John, Cynthia, his daughter, Jonathan Benson[1] – a copious reunion. Neither Kevin nor Jamie is here yet.

A read-through begins.

As we read it occurs to me that this is Basil Fawlty time – John has created for himself a character more flexible, less tight and angry than Basil, but able to mine the same rich seams of physical comedy, outrage, double-take, double entendre. It is a return to the JC we know and love and roar with laughter at.

We read again, then lunch and there is a general feeling of satisfaction and indeed quiet excitement. It works. We trudge off to see the animals – ring-tailed lemurs – camply draping themselves in their Newcastle United-coloured tails, coatimundi – with long, ceaselessly enquiring noses. I try my tarantula, Terry. Soft, weightless and hairy. I like him.

Wednesday, April 19th

Collected at nine. In the boardroom all morning. John rather fond of statements like 'I think that all the problems occur in the following scenes' – so we are manoeuvred, skilfully but indulgently, towards certain group scenes at the end.

We're taken onto the site where the zoo will be, and with JCBs grinding past and lorries and dump-trucks and drills and hammers drowning out John's voice, he tries to explain to us all where we shall be on a set that hasn't yet been built. I applaud the generosity of his enthusiasm in taking us there but question the practical usefulness of the exercise.

Then back indoors and more reading and discussion of the end scenes.

1 Jonathan Benson, First Assistant Director, *Life of Brian*, *A Fish Called Wanda* and *The Meaning of Life*.

Much of Bugsy's role is not even written – the continuous chattering and ear-bending has all to be filled in. So I feel a bit out of it. The loner that Bugsy is seems to have become me.

To the Bush to see *Trainspotting* with Will. A squeeze, as the place is absolutely packed.

Very exciting – from the start the performance of Ewen Bremner as Mark rivets the attention. He speaks fast, broad Scots but with a range and clarity which is both soft and sometimes quite ferocious. His skinny body twists, turns and contorts into El Greco-esque attitudes, seemingly changing from foetal to stretched and staring heavenwards.

Two and a half hours of the most exciting theatre I've seen for a long time. Makes me very thankful that the little Bush theatre, above the pub, is able to present this uncompromising kind of work and proud to see my name as one of its 15 gold patrons.

Sunday, April 23rd

Run, feeling hearteningly agile. A keen, cool, south-westerly refreshes, but dies quite soon after I get home and the morning mellows into hazy warmth.

In mid-afternoon up to Helen's tennis club in Wood Vale to watch her play in a ladies' tournament.

Terry Turner, tennis coach, a man who if drawn would have been created by Raymond Briggs, is welcoming. He talks very seriously of Helen. 'She's a class player now,' he says, with an almost fierce pride.

At home ring TG in LA, where, I'd just heard, he had been kicked about the face by a horse. 'He isn't even arguing with anyone, that's what worries me,' says Maggie.

The fall, whilst out riding on his day off, sounds nasty, with hooves thudding into his face, and, more alarmingly, the back of his head. He said it was like being attacked with two baseball bats at the same time. Stitches back and front, and back on set the next day.

He is clearly driven mad by the stars on *Twelve Monkeys*. They seem to treat schedules and calls with disdain – ambling onto the set when they're ready. He sounds like someone who can't wait to get home – but film shoots are like that – however good, however happy or unhappy, you're always looking for that light at the end of the tunnel.

Wednesday, April 26th

At Hatchards' Author of the Year Reception.

I'm introduced to Laurie Lee. He is a solid man, an inch or so smaller than me, but a considerable presence in his heavy coat. His face is strong, quite fleshy, and his stance bold and confident, though I realise that he is holding a rather upmarket white stick, and must be blind.

Any feeling of awkwardness or embarrassment dissipated by the presence of Clare Francis, holding onto his left arm, and by Laurie Lee's reaction to being told who he's speaking to. He grasps my hand and tells me how wonderful my work is and how much pleasure I've given him and how he hates me because my books sell in such vast quantities!

All this is relayed with considerable humour and with such intense directness that I find myself seriously questioning his blindness. At last I manage to blurt out some corny compliment about *As I Walked Out One Midsummer Morning* being one of my favourite books, and one of my favourite journeys. Laurie Lee, without any malice, says 'You got the title right.'

Ben Okri is there, in a striking, elegant white suit, all flashing eyes and big smiles; Edwina Currie[1] too, behaving just like politicians do behave – treating everyone with professional attention as though we are either constituents or would-be voters.

End up sharing a cab home with Rob Newman,[2] who is going to Leverton Street. We get on very well. He's a fan, but we talk about comedy and performance and about how difficult it is to always, effortlessly, hit form.

Thursday, April 27th

Helen asks if I'd had a lot to drink last night. Apparently she had come to bed to find my E. M. Delafield lying on the duvet and me, fast asleep, with my glasses on. When she'd removed the glasses I'd woken with a start. 'Thank you very much indeed,' I'd apparently said.

To work at Pinewood. JC is there but declares he's infectious and

---

1 Edwina Currie, Conservative politician who lost her seat at the 1997 election. Her published diaries revealed a four-year affair with John Major.
2 Rob Newman, comedian who made his name alongside David Baddiel in the BBC series *The Mary Whitehouse Experience*.

urges everyone to keep their distance. Within an hour he and I and Carey Lowell[1] are rehearsing what's known as 'The Farce Sequence' and John is sitting on my head with his hand over my mouth – having completely forgotten about the spread of his disease.

In the afternoon, at last, Hazel Pethig[2] and I decide on Bugsy's 'look'. The all-black, loner figure doesn't suit the words, so he's now looking more like an assistant BBC sound man, merged with a minor trade union leader. Sports jackets and cardigans – but long hair.

Monday, May 1st

Peter Cook's funeral. When we eventually reach Hampstead Parish Church, there are few people outside apart from Dudley Moore and legions of lenses. They form a thick gauntlet right up to the front door.

Once inside we're ushered right to the front by John's assistant Garry. Climb into the pew in front of John, who looks like the forbidding priest in *Fanny and Alexander* – all in black, tightly buttoned and black-tied. I hear him mutter something like 'no tie, I see,' as I squeeze past Alan Bennett, also in a suit, and into place alongside Michael Winner (blue suit, white shirt, no tie). In front of us are Peter's daughters, all in black. Everyone looks very serious, and I'm quite surprised. This doesn't seem true to Peter's spirit at all.

Various addresses and readings – Alan B funny and honest and free of sentiment. His line that 'as a young man, Peter's only regret was that he'd once saved David Frost from drowning' almost brings the church down. David Frost is behind me, in the pew with John and Alyce Faye and Dudley. He takes it admirably.

John's composed a poem and manages to deliver it, but only just. Both Peter's daughters dab their eyes profusely at this point. A short poem, read beautifully and directly by Eleanor Bron, brings the tears to my eyes, unexpectedly – and largely because it's really about Lin and the love Peter had for her.

Dudley, dressed dark in a musician's way and moving with that strange American-style power-walk which I observed in Kevin and Michael Shamberg – cool, apparently preoccupied with higher things,

---

1 Carey Lowell, American actress who played a Bond girl in *Licence to Kill* in 1989. Married Richard Gere in 2002.

2 Hazel Pethig, costume designer on all the Python TV shows and films.

humbly aware of one's exalted status – plays 'Goodbye' at the end of one
and a half hours, during which we've listened to Radley College Choir
sing 'Love Me Tender' and a tape of Peter as E. L. Wisty.

An unexpectedly successful balance between the solemnity of the
church and the sharpness of Peter's humour. Not nearly as relaxed and
ribald as Graham's memorial, but affecting in a different way.

Friday, May 5th

Out to Pinewood and more rehearsals on the grass. Everyone seems
to know it's my birthday and I'm given cards and presents by the three
assistant keepers, Kim, Julie and Choy-Ling, who call themselves my
Zoo-ettes! Choy-Ling, who, according to Julie, has three nipples, has
given me a box containing two chocolate nipples.

At the end of the rehearsals I've ordered some bottles of Taittinger
and the caterers have done a good job of keeping them iced. So the party goes on, under the trees and beside the rudd-filled lake (into which
people occasionally toss slabs of French bread just to see the enormous
numbers of fish who flock to eat it). It's a midsummer atmosphere.
Everyone very happy and friendly.

Will rings from Venice where he has secured an internship at the
Guggenheim. He's found an apartment, on the Campo San Margherita,
and moves in there tomorrow.

To supper with Mary and Ed at the Ivy.

At the end of the meal Will Carling and Julia and Hugh Laurie and
Jo come by on their way out. Carling jests that he could be out of a
job tomorrow, having been heard on television calling the board of the
Rugby Football Union 57 old farts.

Tell Hugh how well 'Death Fish 2' is going, which has the desired
effect of making him dreadfully apologetic about pulling out.

Saturday, May 6th

Will Carling has been sacked as England captain.

Tuesday, May 9th

John has bounced back from the drawn anxiousness of the first two
weeks of rehearsal and is looking well prepared for the start of filming

next week. Kevin still away in the US. Jamie not yet comfortable with Willa; she falters, uncharacteristically, in scenes with the keepers. Must be daunting for her, confronted with a line of all-British actors. She is deep into *Hemingway's Chair*, and displays an almost childlike enthusiasm and relish for it. She advises that I must make a movie of it.

I feel sadly aware that there is not as much fun in Bugsy as there was in Ken. The work is largely ensemble, almost chorus, work about which I just can't get as excited.

Wednesday, May 10th

Richard Loncraine and Felice to supper. They arrive bearing that heightened sense of drama that always attends anything R is involved in. He has heard, literally on the way over here, that *Richard III* – or Richard 3-D, as a friend of his daughter described it – is to go ahead.

His reaction is similar to that of Terry J who heard, also this week, that *Wind in the Willows* is to go ahead – a sudden rush of doubt. In Terry's case whether the script is right (I read it over last weekend and though I don't think it's that strong, it has charm. The Americanisation of the story for Disney hasn't helped). In Richard's case it's a question he thinks of 'whether I can make Ian (McKellen) a star'.

Richard has pursued it without let-up. When Angelica Houston backed out at the last minute, he rang Warren Beatty (who'd called Richard after *The Missionary*, to say how much he'd liked it) and within a week had Annette Bening as Houston's replacement.

Thursday, May 11th

To Pinewood. A publicity blitz has been organised, which JC hopes will assuage the journalists and keep them off our backs through the shoot.

Some shots of the four of us recreating the *Wanda* poster – only with Jamie holding a wallaby instead of a goldfish. John gasps with pleasure at the strapline 'They're Older, They're Richer, They're Fatter and They're Back!'

Then we're led before the photographers of the world. It's almost royal baby time – a semicircle of lensmen, with video-camera crews prowling around the periphery trying to pick off any or all of us. It's easy to feel like an animal. Jamie cannot resist taking on the press. She strides up to them like a confident stripper to an audience of lager louts. Of course, they love it.

The movie is from today officially called *Fierce Creatures* – John has had his way – and oddly enough, as the day goes on and I hear more and more of the press mention the new title, the more acceptable it sounds.

Then a Japanese press conference. About 25 Japanese journalists applaud us as we come in, listen politely, laugh at the most bizarre moments. When JC, through the interpreter, is asked if there is any country in the world which does not know about Monty Python he says 'Papua New Guinea' and they all fall about.

After lunch we're put before the European press – some 70 of them – and then installed in hastily sound-baffled cubicles in four corners of a big room whilst the journalists are circulated, for four minutes only, to each of us. At the end the journalist is given a cassette of the recording, like a child being given a sweet after a visit to the doctor.

Friday, May 12th

Have contacted Hannah at Pilates again.

Hannah, who reckons she last saw me in February 1992, is as effusive as ever. She admits that she'd now like to get out of Pilates. 'If I have to say "pull your stomach in" much more, I may well scream.'

Anyway, I'm very glad to have gone back. My muscles are stiff and awkward in certain positions but on the whole I feel in good shape. Hannah is very encouraging and I book a series of sessions to help prepare me for the Pacific journey, on which we embark in less than four months' time!

Monday, May 15th

An easy start to the shoot, as I'm not called until midday.

Not too many thesps there – and some of my favourites – Maria Aitken, Carey Lowell, Michael Percival – so atmosphere becomes quickly like a good garden party. Occasionally, people come back from the set in the big, black Mercedes, looking a little shell-shocked. But mainly we talk and laugh and devise uses for some of the strange attachments I have in my coat of many pockets.

An orange rubber tube particularly excites Maria, who thinks I might use it to threaten M. Percival with an enema. So lots of 'Sleeping with the Enema', 'The Enema Within' jokes.

Midway into the afternoon comes the familiar news that they probably won't get to our scene today after all.

Tuesday, May 16th

Good news from Kentish Town Police that we shall not have to go to court over our attempted burglary. They've pleaded guilty, as one of the accused has just received eight months for another break-in whilst out on bail. I hear from various people who ring, during the a.m., that an account of the incident has appeared in several of today's papers. On my way out to shops I pick up a *Telegraph* and there I am: 'Michael Palin Foils Fumbling Burglars'.

Wednesday, May 17th

Out in the street Murphy's men are raising the paving slabs to lay the cable container pipes. Another Irishman is helping Mr Brown paint his house. 'You wouldn't think he'd painted the Sistine Chapel, now, would you?' says Mr Brown to Helen. The other man, young, thick-set, dark hair, florid face, protests from the top of the ladder. 'Paint it? I built it.'

Monday, May 22nd

My first big day on *Fierce Creatures*. The spider sequence in John's office.

Most of the morning spent, anti-climactically, waiting for re-shoots of last week's material, then giving lines off as John's close-ups are covered. Instead of getting on to me after lunch, the schedule is changed to film a quite different sequence.

All the extra keepers have arrived. A crowded, noisy afternoon in the rich, overgrown gardens of the house. At least I get a line and a close-up and everyone seems happy.

Wrapped by 6.30. Graham drives me to Bond Street for the Fine Art Society's Christopher Wood and Summer Show preview. A clutch of Sickerts – including a version of 'Ennui', which is one of my favourites.

Whilst I'm sipping a white wine and poking around the small and ill-attended Christopher Wood exhibition encounter Nigel, my cousin. After warning me about the Sickert – 'too clean' – he suggested we move on up Bond Street, as there seems to be a general open evening in the galleries.

Into Wildenstein's. Judge Tumim[1] is there peering, muttering and being generally jovial.

Ask Tumim about John Marriott at Parkhurst. He liked the man but believed he had no option but to take responsibility for the lax security. He also agreed that there was no way to run a long-term offenders prison without giving the inmates some autonomy.

Back home, as I clean my teeth, I listen to the first of the 'Book at Bedtime' *Hemingway's Chair* readings. Funny to hear myself filling the Radio 4 airwaves at this intimate time.

What is everyone doing while I tell them a story?

Tuesday, May 23rd: London–Lainston House, Hampshire

Out to Breakspear House and to my 'Prowler' caravan/trailer, with its slightly disconcerting sticker on the window advising that it's made of Trichloroethane, 'a substance which harms public health and the environment'.

Shoot my reverses on the spider sequence.

Unlike on *Wanda*, we have instant colour, sound video playback of every shot. This is alarming in some ways – an extra element of pressure – not just the cameraman watching but as many as can crowd around the monitor.

Home, pack my things, make some last phone calls and leave for Hampshire.

At about 8.15 arrive at the Lainston House Hotel.

Shown to a room called 'Walnut'. Woody, manor-house style inside. Big armchair, sofa. Four-poster with barley-sugar uprights. Plenty of space.

Ronnie Corbett is the next one to arrive. We meet for a drink in the libraried bar.

Order a Lagavulin – a rich, peaty, tarry malt. Sip it out on a terrace which overlooks a garden of tall, mature trees and a long grass strip which descends towards an avenue of limes – some of which they say are 250 years old. There is not a breath of wind. Everything seems frozen, in a state of suspension.

1 Judge Stephen Tumim, Chief Inspector of Prisons for England and Wales since 1987.

Wednesday, May 24th: Lainston House

Breakfast rather graciously, with Ronnie. Still no sign of anyone else. Twenty-minute drive to Marwell Zoo. It's set amongst thick woodland (as is everything in this part of Hampshire). Plenty of animals – cheetahs, hippos, tigers – everything we tracked for so long across the South African savannah to see on *Pole to Pole* – here for the price of a ticket. And looking in much better shape than most of the animals in Africa.

Jamie's first day on the picture. She's shaken everyone up with her firecracker, no-holds-barred directness. She noticed my haircut and said 'That's a great haircut, it looks like a tarantula.' Then, after a pause, 'Mine looks like a vagina.' Now the dust has settled and she's ready for action.

Nothing very demanding. I'm wrapped at five.

To my woody room and write and learn my 'ad-libs' for tomorrow! Bugsy's spiel has to be long enough to fill the space required, but this does involve a lot more learning.

Over a drink in the lounge – she white wine, me Lagavulin – Jamie is subdued and serious. Serious about acting, which she loves. Talk about technique – different directors' styles – till all the others arrive.

Thursday, May 25th: Marwell Zoo

There are so many people working today – Steve Abbott [Producer on *Fierce Creatures* as he had been on *Wanda*] has counted 200 people on the week's payroll, and that's not including our own actors.

Jonathan Benson and Robert keep a good pace going despite casts of thousands – human and animal – and the constant presence of the public, as the zoo could not be closed whilst we work.

Otherwise the big story on the unit is that Cynthia and Lisa Hogan, two of our cast of keepers, apparently came across a couple making love on a grave in Winchester Cathedral's grounds, around midnight. The couple had not only not stopped, but on being seen had redoubled their efforts.

As I sit on the lawns at Marwell with hard bright sunshine alternating with chilly shadows as the clouds scud across, Steve A mutters darkly of major problems coming to the boil at a meeting tonight.

The construction team will not have the Pinewood zoo ready on time.

They are now weeks behind and there will have to be serious changes made in script and/or schedule.

Friday, May 26th

Arrive at the opening of Camden's newest library for seven o'clock ceremony.

Phil Turner, bloke-ish Head of Arts in Camden, speaks.

Turner is a politician. Perfectly nice, but still comes out with ... 'Well, we'll have a new government soon.' This is the smug face of Camden Labour – the complacent cant that caused so much chaos, inefficiency and waste over the last 20 years ... 'Well ... it's the government's fault.' Bollocks, you lazy sod, I think, but smile sweetly and take my leave.

Sunday, May 28th

Another seven hours of sleep – alarm wakes me at a quarter to seven. Phone BA. Hear that the Boston flight, bearing Violet Gwangwa,[1] our one-time neighbour from South Africa, is on time. Dress, grab some orange juice and set off for the airport. It's raining.

Violet doesn't appear until nine. She'd waited one and a half hours to clear immigration. She's as stoic as ever though, and with her soft, intelligent voice chatters on about the women's group she's travelled to the States with, to learn how they can teach the poorest women to learn to help themselves, rather than rely on state handouts.

We eat lunch in the garden together as the clouds bluster about, illuminating us at intervals, like a lantern show. Jonas, her husband, doesn't make much money as a musician, though he's called upon all the time – V says it's unfair, but as one of the ANC brothers he's expected to give his services for nothing.

V says illegal immigration is one of the new and most potent problems. Three million crossed the border illegally since independence, attracted by the wealth and job prospects. If they're repatriated they come back again. The aching problems of Africa seem quite insoluble – by our criteria anyway.

1 Violet, married to Jonas Gwangwa. Both ANC stalwarts during the apartheid years.

Tuesday, May 30th

Wake, just after seven, with a sudden, tightening feeling of comprehensive anxiety. For a while I feel quite immobilised.

This weight does not lift until after I've washed, dressed, exercised (without enthusiasm), breakfasted and left for Prominent Studios to meet Bobby Birchall, the designer we've chosen for the 'Palin's Pacific' book.

I have committed to a nine-part travel series, and a book to go with it, both of which have already paid me an advance. I have two people, well three, with Kath, waiting to hear what I have to say about book, design, working together. I have two options – one, to run screaming from the room, the other to run the meeting.

I run the meeting.

Sunday, June 11th

To the RAC at eleven for squash with TJ. Despite his increasing girth, which, together with recently Toad-shaved head, gives him more than a hint of Mr Creosote, he wins three games on the run.

They have put back *Wind in the Willows* for two weeks, and he's no further on with the cast. Nothing heard from Connery or Tim Roth. Turned down by Hugh Grant. TJ is going to offer Rat to Eric. He's asked me to record the voice of the sun!

Thursday, June 15th: Marwell Zoo

I can never remember such long hours and such hard work doing so little. I begin to allow myself some self-pity – feeling that, whereas I was intrinsic to *Wanda*, I'm marginalised on this one. Kevin slips in and out of character. Jamie paces like a cat – occasionally purring – more often than not hissing and showing her claws.

The crew seem tired. They watch it all, but I wouldn't say there was a close feeling of involvement. There is an uncomfortable whiff of elitism about the place.

Maybe I'm feeling jaundiced because I'm tired – maybe I'm tired because I'm feeling jaundiced.

The flamingos and ducks are brought along today – to make the lake seem idyllic – for a reputed £3,000 per day. The schedule slips and my day off tomorrow, Friday, is more likely to be a half-day after all.

Friday, June 16th: Marwell Zoo

Onto the grassy knoll, now worn thin by five days of movement, by nine o'clock.

John has a lot to do, concentrates hard, but also is clearly feeling on top of things – and these are some of his most difficult scenes. He sits beside me. We talk about my plans for the Pacific Rim. Earlier this week he told me of yet another film plan of his – not the sex comedy with he and me and Maria A, but a film of Peter Shaffer's *Black Comedy*, in which all the characters behave as if they're in the dark. This is the one he now wants to make – 'very simply – one stage at Twickenham – pretty soon after I've finished this'. My schedule will not release me until two years from now, at very earliest. John ruminates, sympathises and nods ruefully. 'Well, it looks as if I shall have to do it without you, little plum.'

When I think of *American Friends*, *The Weekend* and even *Hemingway's Chair*, I cannot avoid a feeling of having stumbled over the past few years. I wish I could say I had an irrepressible self-confidence, but I haven't. And this encounter just dampens the fire a little more.

Wednesday, June 21st

Talk to Robert Lindsay in his dressing room before the day's work begins. Says that he checked his part in the script which was sent out at the end of last year, and had 185 lines; he's now got 32.

John does his shots most of the morning. We talk a bit today. He asks for my advice on performance. Just relax, is all I can say. Avoid it becoming one-note.

Alyce Faye picks her way onto the set. She wears a new and expensive designer outfit every day – indeed one of the small pleasures of the filming is the arrival of AF – for not only is the outfit always different, she has in tow different celebrities – today Nicole Farhi and Eduardo Paolozzi,[1] big, thick, dark, with a massive face and built like a tree. His voice is deep like it's come from way underground.

John's new masseuse, a bespectacled lady called Wendy, gives my upper back half an hour's attention. Her fingers are extraordinarily strong and seem to pierce through to the deepest tissue. 'Deep-tissue' massage is what she's really about. She talks of 'opening people up'.

1 Scottish sculptor and artist, knighted in 1988.

I can barely stop from crying out – and make feeble small talk about the trees to cover my pain. Later, I hear everyone feels the same. Maria A says she could hardly walk for a couple of days.

Friday, June 23rd

We're shooting in the Pinewood zoo today for the first time, and will have lions, tigers and leopards working with us.

Enlivened by arrival on set of Charlie Crichton and Nadine. Charlie, his strong, long, handsome face well tanned, looks very little different from the way he was eight years ago. Nadine, however, seems much more frail.

Charlie is set down in front of the leopard's cage, and various members of the old *Wanda* team are ushered into or a trifle shyly approach his presence, as if he were ancient royalty – a revered icon. Amanda, John's assistant, brings him a large scotch in a small, chunky glass tumbler which he takes in his badly shaking hands. He's still the same slightly prickly, mischievous self, though. His face breaks easily into a smile, and he grips his walking stick with reassuring strength.

Monday, June 26th

A shot is being set up when Robert Y, today sporting a very British panama hat, marches up and says very loudly and emphatically that he is going to widen the shot 'because that's what Michael Shamberg wants!'. This was not meant to be funny. This was anger, exasperation and impatience combined.

Jamie has a copy of Janet Leigh's first novel. It's called *The Dream Factory*. She laughs about the sex scenes ... 'I just can't take all that you know ... I keep wanting to ask – was this how I was conceived?' She finds one of the offending scenes and is about to read it but breaks into giggles and asks me to do it. So I sit and read Jamie a very bad sex scene written by her mother.

Friday, June 30th

In at nine. Not called onto the set until a quarter to one. Have just avoided having to read the other character in a dreadful man-woman confrontation scene which Carey Lowell wants to tape as an audition for her next film. Sample line – Her: 'I'm a lesbian.' Him: 'How am I supposed to take that? I have a penis you know.' Her: 'I sure do. I've had it in my mouth enough times.' And Carey was about to have me record this with her in a studio full of carpenters making scenery!

Am wearing long johns and a vest, as part of my inside-the-tiger-skin costume, and this attracts whistles as I walk down to the zoo. A whole crowd of people around the camera; much admiration of my underwear. Then someone turns me round to be introduced. 'Here's someone you may know.' Find myself looking down at the screwed-up-against-the-sun expression of the Duchess of York. Much laughter at our predicament. She takes it in her stride (probably quite used to meeting men in their underwear) and introduces me to her daughters – all prettily attired in bows and pigtails.

Saturday, July 1st

First shot is on Robert L and myself, and Bille Brown.[1] No-one else there – no featured keepers, 'B' keepers, 'C' keepers. In the chill grey of the morning we get the sequence together, quietly and thoroughly, and JC seems well pleased.

About midday we're in our stride when the set-up we have prepared has to be struck so that a jogging shot of Jamie can be covered before lunch. For some reason this causes another flare-up amongst the ruling body and I hear Jamie having a go at John; she's pouring out her indignation. JC fights back. Those of us near this drama tuck our heads deeper into our crosswords, and listen.

Sunday, July 2nd

To the RAC to play squash with Richard Wilson. He wins 3-1, though the games are close. The RAC is like a vast, elaborately decorated morgue this Sunday morning. RW suggests coffee.

The newspapers are laid out on a long, heavy oak table. On the front of them 'Divine' – the hooker in the Hugh Grant case – thrusts her body seductively off a bar stool. She's naked save for a 'censored' sticker

1 Bille Brown, Australian writer and actor. He died in 2013.

across the genitalia. She's also sprawled across the *News of the World*, to whom she has sold her story of 'the incident'. Hugh Grant's manhood, we're told, was 'cute'. 'We're not going to read that are we,' says Richard severely, and we don't.

Monday, July 10th

Enjoy acting at last! Instead of a-line-a-day stuff – an actual exchange or two to get stuck into – and with Lindsay as well, so it's back to *GBH* confrontation time. One of the most enjoyable morning's work since shooting began. For once, I was completely surprised by the lunch break.

Tuesday, July 11th

Hot and sticky, especially in the small bar in which we're filming. Michael Shamberg's driver has head-butted another driver in an argument at the turn-in to the location.

Wednesday, July 12th

Up at 6.30, to ring Rose before I go to work. She says that my Aunt Betty, who died last night, had motor neurone disease and would not have lasted more than six months. When Rose had to go into her mother's end of the house and look for details of the funeral, she found an underlined instruction – '*No* female celebrant.' We both screamed with laughter at that. So typical.

Michael Shamberg announces to me that the poster is to be shot on Saturday August 19th – thus knocking out any real hope of a feet-up, sun-and-sand break before setting off for the Pacific.

Saturday, July 15th

Sleep well – up quite late. At 10.30 still at breakfast and the papers. Grim news from Bosnia as Srebrenica is 'cleansed'. Always uncomfortable to be reminded that our fellow human beings, the great brotherhood of man, are still capable of deliberate, brutal, callous cruelty, in the name, presumably, of some greater good. Feel v. pissed off with J. Chirac, latest in a long line of French poseurs, who is windbagging about action from the elegant comfort of the Elysée Palace. Still, after two weeks of Hugh Grant the newspapers seem to have realised it's time for some bad news.

JC rings. A rapid response to my fax of yesterday evening re my week off. Promises to sort something out. He's having a big scheduling meeting tomorrow. Can I wait? Touched by his concern. We talk a little about the film. Both of us felt last week was good.

Tuesday, July 18th

JC is very solicitous these days – doubtless aware of some tensions among the actors. So John takes time to tell me that things took longer today than expected – 'Kevin has to have time' – and that after a quick 'Tiger Terror' scene tomorrow a.m. we would get on to the 'Rollo's New Office' sequence – 'and knowing you and me, Mickey, we should have that knocked on the head pretty quickly'.

Wednesday, July 19th

It's around 5.30 when we begin the New Office rehearsals proper. By this time the air has grown hotter and heavier. It's a lumpy, lethargic atmosphere. Robert has decided to shoot the bulk of my lines – in effect a short monologue – in one single movement, without cut-ins, so I have to get it right. JC, with whom I practised it for the first time this afternoon, has suggested amendments which I have to try and remember. I'm suddenly having to call on reserves of energy and concentration that are by now dangerously thin.

We make several takes. 'Three in a row,' JC is fond of saying. Lots of heads nod sagely around the video screens, but JC and I both know that it could be easier, more relaxed.

Eventually, after two takes are aborted because of me, JC, who is being fanned down between takes with squares of cardboard, suggests we look at the best of them and if we think we can do better return fresh first thing tomorrow.

Leave the set disconsolately – though JC v. supportive. Brighten up as soon as I get home. After all, what am I doing but asking for time. Everyone else does. As JC says – if this had been a quick TV sketch show several of the takes would have worked just fine, but 'if it's going to be around in ten years' time we might as well get it right'.

Friday, July 21st

At lunchtime an assembly of 15 minutes' edited material is shown on the big rushes screen. It is impressive. The performances hold up and, though it is funny, it's also quite a lot of other things. Dramatic, touching, tense.

JC's scene with the animals in the loo, indeed all his stuff, is much better judged than I expected. The intensity he puts into the character is right, proper and very effective. In fact all the leading characters have an edge to them which is not just quick and cheap and phoney – it's based on truth and should sustain throughout the story. As I said to JC afterwards, even if the rest of the hour and a half's material is lousy, he's still got a great movie.

John Du Prez v. complimentary. Says I make tedium hilarious.

Tuesday, August 1st

Organise my unexpected day off – first down to Covent Garden, where I visit YMCA Adventure shop for things like mosquito nets, sleeping bags, bath plugs and waterproof leggings.

Then home and spend afternoon on Pacific preparation – checking supplies; reading; writing a sort of preface, a 'why' for the journey.

Thursday, August 3rd

To the set at Pinewood, which is wide and spread out and resembles the layout of a small school sports field. It's almost two weeks since I last saw everyone, and yet it seems as if they are all doing just the same things as they were when I left. It's like returning to a party that's been running for hours.

Jamie prowls, looking sharp, ironic, restless and edgy. 'There are just three words you need to know about this place,' she says through clenched teeth, 'Wasp! Wasp! Wasp!'

Friday, August 4th

Another morning of low-grade acting. A crowd growing ever smaller behind Kevin who is in his element – playing a big, bold, unequivocally central role – full of physical attack and extemporaneous embellishments.

In marked contrast to the rest of the sunburnt unit K has preserved an almost deathly pallor. He is followed around the location by his stand-in, Joshua Andrews, son of Anthony, bearing an umbrella like some punkah-wallah. K drives himself around in one of the buggies.

Jamie regards it all with ill-concealed impatience.

We talk more today – Jamie and me. I improvise some great 'Ifs' of history – If Joan of Arc had been deaf, If Hitler had been nice, If Shakespeare had been dyslexic, that sort of thing. Jamie insists that I call my agent 'within the hour' to sell the idea.

Some of the others are trying on their animal costumes for Monday. 'I'm giving my beaver,' shouts Robert L.

Monday, August 7th

So the panda cage scene gets under way. Find the morning hard work. It's one of those scenes that Robert seems to want to shoot every which way, and as the costumes are hot and quite uncomfortable, the process seems to go on for ever. Lines repeated endlessly in a variety of shots – and off screen for a variety of different actors.

Ronnie points out, without malice, that the scene is virtually a monologue for Kevin, with occasional interruptions from ourselves. Mind you, Ronnie, dressed as a sea lion, has as good a chance as anybody of stealing the scene.

John spends much of the day imprisoned in a kangaroo suit – but at least the hard tail serves as a sort of natural shooting stick and he sits back on it gesturing at people and making serious points about the filming with his short, shapely front legs.

Finish after seven o'clock. Graham drops me off at the Brackenbury for dinner and a chat with Roger and Clem about the Pacific Rim. This is the first meeting we've had together since they've come back from their various recces.

We have 50,000 miles to travel and 25 countries to pass through, in nine programmes. We will have to work hard to prevent it being rushed and sketchy.

All of us agree that the sit-down, set-up celeb interviews should be jettisoned in favour of the nuts and bolts of travel. Roger has already moved to cancel General Giap and Imelda Marcos!

Wednesday, August 9th

As ever, the end of the main shoot comes suddenly – and all those of us who at many points couldn't wait for it to end are now suffering the sharp emotional tugs of departure.

At the end of the afternoon I insist that they try a shot of me running towards camera, with Robert L in the tiger skin on my back, to intercut with the funny stuff they've shot running away.

Robert is hoisted onto my shoulders – or rather I lift him up as others take his weight. As soon as 'action' is given, there is a ten-second delay because a pile of cans is visible in shot behind me. Then I move forward. Realise this is very different from the rehearsal. This skin is much heavier. Robert has heavy boots pressing into my ribs. I need to run but know I can't. Stagger two or three paces then feel this huge weight pulling forward on my back and I subside and fall to my knees.

Feel very foolish, but enough has been seen on camera for JC to feel, as I do, that the sequence really needs it. But I equally well know my limits and I know that I cannot carry this weight at the speed which will make it work.

Thursday, August 10th

Watch rushes. The short, pre-collapse footage of myself and RL on my back is good. Shamberg asks if I would give it another go with a lighter skin. I agree and he goes off to fix it.

Next attempt is much better – actually reach the camera. However the tiger skin had fallen down and obscured my face – thus counteracting the one real reason for doing it myself. A third attempt is even better, but on the playback one of the assistants holding Robert didn't clear fast enough.

JC thinks they have enough. Only Shamberg is sufficiently unhappy with it to ask me for one last go.

Well, despite assurances, I know he is right. A good, long, clean five to six seconds would be better – the more of the run the funnier the sequence – it's as simple as that. I agree to a last attempt. It works perfectly. As I lower Robert one of the stuntmen pats me on the shoulder. 'That is not easy,' he says.

Friday, August 11th

The mild elation of the morning must be the left-overs from the last shot of yesterday. Whatever it was, it helped my confidence, and I began a rehearsal of the bugging of the Churchill Suite about 8.15, feeling steady and competent.

JC, seeing 16 pages to be shot by next Thursday, several of them involving motion control, is anxious to complete what he calls 'our stuff' as quickly as possible. It is planned to shoot the two long bugging scenes in simple, single set-ups.

The outcome of the morning exceeds my wildest expectations. By one o'clock we have shot almost four pages' worth, including both my long dialogue scenes, and everyone is very happy.

In the afternoon we consolidate, with cut-ins and the first of the true farce moments with John and myself – then J, myself and Carey L, racing from door to door and so on. This very satisfactory day's work comes to an end at half past five when we break for the poster shoot.

I'm very hot – my shirt sticking to my back – as I descend the stairs from the set to the floor of the shooting stage where a BBC doctor – young and keen and wide-eyed – awaits with a serum of anti-tick encephalitis vaccine which I shall need for travel in Siberia. 'Was that John Cleese's voice I heard, by any chance?' he asks, in fascination.

Friday, August 18th

At the studio things are quite tense – though no-one puts direct pressure on, it's clear that they want to have the insect house finished by twelve so that the crew can pack up for the 24-hour trip to Jersey.

Except that the ants haven't yet made their appearance. They arrived the night before from Arizona via San Francisco – in a jar, accompanied by an ant wrangler on a Virgin Upper-Class ticket. There are 65 of them. By no means striking in size or behaviour: about three-quarters of an inch. Why we can't find British ants to do the job, I'll never know.

I have to be ready in tight close-up to start my speech as soon as the ants are in the right place – and they are there only very occasionally, when a sugar-water trail is marked out.

So I poise, the tongue-twister lines on the tip of my tongue – knowing that I have to be as cool and calm as at any time on the picture. It eventually works. Robert v. complimentary to me. Says my bottle held very well. 'But it usually does,' he adds.

Tuesday, August 22nd

The curly, bug-like hair-do and the thin, apologetic sliver of moustache applied, hopefully for the last time.

I end up, first as top-half of the character only, then, and finally, as the eyes alone. Bugsy fades like the Cheshire Cat and disappears at 1.20 on the 76th day of shooting.

I'm officially counted out with an announcement from John. 'You'll probably be delighted and deeply relieved to hear that this is Mickey Palin's last day of shooting.' Applause.

Sunday, August 27th: Anchorage, Alaska

So here I am, five days after finishing four months on *Fierce Creatures*, in another hotel room in another strange place, about to embark on a year's journey around the Pacific.

I know the alternatives. I know that I have made myself enough money – I know I could spend most of my life at home in London – eating and drinking well, reading, meeting friends, taking the Eurostar to France and beyond for the occasional long weekend.

But then I also realise that it's all relative: without the challenges, without the effort expended, peace and quiet and tranquillity don't seem as sweet or as intense. I am, whether I would admit it or not, doing just what I often criticise others for – I am being competitive, I am playing my part in the endless, and especially Western drama of punishing self-advancement.

I kept a personal diary on Pole to Pole, *but it was lost in that dark and destructive last week in Zambia, in the days after Mpulungu and Dr Baela. I shall try again to keep a few notes of my own on this Pacific journey. Not to record everything I see – that's all noted elsewhere, on tapes and in my black travel notebooks – but what I'm feeling inside – how I'm bearing up.*

Tuesday, August 29th: Nome Nugget Inn, Nome, Alaska

The waters of the Bering Strait are lapping onto the sea defences 50 yards from where I write.

Yesterday the sun shone and a normally very cautious helicopter pilot decided it was clear to go out to Diomede Island. The weather improved during the day – we got all the shots we wanted; I coped with a long, semi-scripted to-camera piece on a hill overlooking the village and only a mile away from the International Date Line.

Last night jet lag settled and I slept pretty deep and pretty long. This morning a big interview piece done – my humour and nerve intact. I'm enjoying myself – and find Nome agreeable and friendly. I'm recognised everywhere – even on Diomede I was a 'star'! Bad for the romance, but helps with the people.

So, we're off and running. Only 50,000 miles to go!

Sunday, September 3rd: Westmark Hotel, Kodiak, Alaska

About to leave for the bears/camping sequence. Possibly, apart from the Nome beach sequence on Friday, this is the worst thing I could be doing at the moment. Stomach unstable after Ex-Lax last night and in the middle of a foul and fierce cold.

What I need is a day in bed. What I get is another plane flight, some more butch filming, standing in rivers and sleeping, at the end of it all, in a shared tent. Only good news is that where we're going, Camp Island on Karluk Lake, it's too cold for mosquitoes.

Wednesday, September 6th: Westmark Hotel, Kodiak

Returned from Karluk Lake, not one night later, but three nights later, owing to a shutdown of all air services out of Kodiak for two and a half days (fog). Considering how awful I felt when I last spent a night in this unprepossessing hotel, with smells, stains, slow service and fine views, I'm now remarkably well.

Camp Island was basic in some ways – no elec or running water, sleeping in tents (I shared with Basil) – but comfortable in others – very good, home-cooked meals, fresh air, a grand location, and, owing to the weather, enforced relaxation.

Apart from a dreadful night on Sunday (Nigel's 50th birthday) I slept extremely well. Only the occasional growl of a bear and the sound of the wind off the lake and the occasional patter of rain on the roof of the tent.

Tuesday, September 12th: Olga's, Yelizovo, Petropavlovsk, Kamchatka Peninsula, Siberia

Everything about Russia is difficult – the simplest arrangements and transactions are made complex. Olga's is, in itself, the sort of place that one feels could only exist in Russia – a big, quite handsome wooden house, built on traditional lines only two years ago – but lights, hot water, heating all quite mercurial. It's only September but I sleep now dressed like a paratrooper – socks, sweatshirt, tracksuit bottoms. Whatever cold there is the house seems to trap it.

But fortune shone on us yesterday – the weather was good, the light clear and we made an extraordinary journey in a big, grimy Mi-8 helicopter north to the Kronotsky Reserve – we circled the rim of volcanoes, we walked amongst hot springs in calderas and looked at plant life which has adapted itself to living in streams and waterholes at 90°C. We bathed in a filthy hot stream by a woodman's hut – we saw geysers erupt from a dozen holes in a cliffside. It was one of the greatest accumulations of natural wonders I've ever seen – and we concentrated it successfully into a day, and filmed it.

I'm gradually adapting, like the plant in the 90° stream, to the Russian way. It requires much more tolerance, patience and personal initiative than is ever asked of us in the pampered West.

Thursday, September 14th: Ocean Hotel, Magadan

Arrive back gloriously tired after three and a half hours' solid and concentrated filming in and around one of the last visible slave labour camps established in this remote and forbidding Kolyma region in the Stalin years.

Magadan is generally infuriating – full of dour and desperate Russian rules, gloomy corridors, curtains that don't draw, etc. Here in the Ocean Hotel there was a hint – or more than that – a manifestation of heavy, drunken violence in the dining room (after wonderful Magadan crab which Basil had encouraged Igor, our Russian guide, to buy in the market – the largest, spikiest crab I ever saw).

But this is a grim place, no two ways about it; the ugliest city I think I've ever seen – no, correction, the most featureless – and yet Ivan the prison camp survivor was wonderful and live on my TV at the moment Moscow Spartak are beating Blackburn Rovers 1-0, at Blackburn.

Another given in Russia – as the curtains don't fit the windows, so the sheets don't fit the bed.

Sunday, September 17th: Vladivostok

Tomorrow is the big end of prog one scene in which I dress as a sailor and sing with one of the finest choirs in Russia – the Pacific Fleet Ensemble. Roger tends to set me these tasks because they require a real stroke of inspiration and panache to bring off. Not easy, but unforgettable if they work.

The Russian diet is a bit of a plod. Breakfasts always uninspired. Only eggs, eggs, eggs. Have never eaten so many in my life. Miss cereals and fruit and the occasional sweet pudding.

Feel a bit out of touch with home – haven't spoken to H since Anchorage ten days ago.

Still, all in all, with my ivory walrus from Diomede as my talisman, this has been a good, strong start.

Have drunk more than I meant to these last few days – but drinking with the crew is a quick, effective way of rewarding ourselves.

Tuesday, September 19th: Vladivostok

Sunny, settled morning. Yesterday we completed the Alaska/Russian programme in some style – the song and the choir generally regarded as a great success; so I am much relieved.

Sixty-eight rolls of film, 3,000 miles, three weeks.

Friday, September 22nd: Mano Town, Sado Island, Japan

Writing this in bed at Pension Nagakura, beneath fearsomely bright coiled strip light, at 9.10 on a Friday night. We shall be leaving here at five tomorrow morning to start one of the busiest days of this second programme's filming. Running with the Kodo drummers and working right through until seven or eight at night.

I took Basil's advice and tried a preparatory run before supper. Up into the wooded hills behind our hotel – gardens, women with straw bonnets held close in place by headscarves, working in the fields until the light begins to fade, harvesting the rice. When they've gone they're replaced by scarecrow likenesses of themselves. Smells were good – woodsmoke, drying rice stalks on racks, earthy, pungent, grassy odours.

Came back with all systems intact. A snort of grappa from the flask Graham Fordham gave me and sink beneath lurid green and purple smudged flower-designed blanket. Tomorrow an initiation for all of us.

Saturday, September 23rd: *The House of the Red Pear, Ogi, Sado Island*

Ten p.m: On my futon, on the tatami. As tired as I have ever felt on the trip. Was running with the Kodo drummers at twenty past five. Have been filmed eating breakfast with the apprentices, conducting interviews and hitting the big drum, now, fourteen hours after first sequence, still filming, this time dinner. Everything new to me – the ryokan quite unfamiliar – no chairs or bed in room, all washing communally downstairs. This is what has really exhausted me – being tired in somewhere unfamiliar, without understandable procedures and regular comforters to fall back on.

The film crew is noisy – the walls are thin – I've run out of good humour, tolerance and patience – I just want the world to shut the fuck up and let me sleep.

The pressure of work meant no further personal notes were kept as we travelled through Japan and into Korea over the next month.

Friday, October 20th

Back home.

Cleese rings, pretending to be a reporter from Aberdeen; he says the first of nine reels of the 'Death Fish' film look strong and he's very happy. He assures me that my performance is 'super'.

Out to *Wind in the Willows* wrap party down by the Thames at Westminster Boat House.

I don't immediately recognise the man with Alison. Only after I've greeted her effusively do I realise it's Terry. Eyebrow-less, almost hairless and his face an almost puffy yellow. He finished shooting as Mr Toad on the day we finished in Korea.

On the way out run into Steve Coogan on his way in. Shaggy head of curly dark ringlets confuses me for a moment but I'm glad to be able to rave a little over Alan Partridge. He raves in return. Says he used to record *Ripping Yarns* dialogue by pointing a mike at the telly. He'd then play it back to people, acting out the visuals as he did so.

To bed at 11.30 when the travel fatigue hits.

Saturday, October 21st

A beguiling, sunny autumn day outside and, without much of a plan, I drive into the West End to do some shopping.

Certainly there is a pattern to returning home – in my case anyway. First of all elation at being back – sometimes quite manic. This is accompanied by a fierce, potent energetic desire to catch up – on family, letters, work, people, the house. This lasts for most of my first day.

The day after there is an almost inevitable reaction. The extrovert, exhausted, collapses into the introvert. The feelings that all problems can and will be solved in a single day are ridiculed by cold reality.

Perhaps there are those, and I envy them, who never experience this emotional roller-coaster. Maybe their lives are uncomplicated, their minds, like their desks, uncluttered. Today, as the day wears on, I experience the ambiguousness of my feelings towards the work I do. The kick, the excitement, the richness of my working life is replaced by a formless, patternless arbitrary world in which nothing is exactly as I want it to be. Faces of friends neglected pressing against the window.

Friday, October 27th

After two months' solid involvement in the series and many early mornings spent musing on it, I still have reservations about 'Palin's Pacific' as a title. It's not *my* Pacific. But there never seems to be an alternative. As I'm bemoaning this, a sudden, quite clear image of what it should be comes to me. It should be simply 'Pacific' – 'with Michael Palin' or whatever as subtitle, but keep Pacific clear and strong. The problem with all the alternative versions – 'A Year in the Pacific', 'Pacific Circle', 'Pacific Progress' – is that the additional words belittle and reduce the only word that matters – Pacific.

Anne is taken with it and Kath too. I think, at last, and quite undeliberately, I've cracked it.

Monday, October 30th

Lots of traffic heading into town. One dirty, smoke-belching van makes me so angry that if I'd been alongside I think I would have had a go at the driver. I'd rather see pollution wardens than parking wardens but I suppose there's no money in pollution prevention.

Successful at last in finding some decent shoes. I was looking in the window of Paul Smith when Paul himself appeared, tall, birdlike, Notts accent still intact. He has the engaging, slightly old-fashioned look of a Midlands comedian. He's just come back from Japan – where he now has 150 outlets. Layers are in, he tells me. Not shirt and jacket so much, as T-shirts augmented with shirts, then if necessary a waistcoat or even a cardigan. Layers popular in Japan because of the Japanese aversion to perspiration, he says. He escorts me round the store, opening the shoe department especially early, just for me.

Thursday, November 2nd

To Gray's Inn Road at nine for my first BUPA check-up for over two years. The consulting rooms are cold and could do with a refit, but nurse very jolly as I go through tests. Always in the back of my mind is a determination to prove I am not on the decline.

Work terribly hard – blowing into tubes until I cough like an old man, straining to hear the faint sounds in the audio test, bending forward to an agonising stretch position – 'very good, above average' – oh, the magic words!

Weight a fraction up on last time but negligibly so. My appearance clearly pleases the doctor. 'Believe me,' he says, warming to his theme, 'a lot of 52-year-olds I see look more like 72. They're bald, overweight and …' I almost think he's going to say something like 'detestable', so enflamed has he become at health standards. He looks immaculate, needless to say. Not a nostril hair out of place.

Friday, November 3rd

I have accepted Simon Albury's invitation to visit him at the Grayshott Hall Health Club where he's spending this week.

Taxi to Waterloo, then train to Haslemere.

Simon meets me at the station. Drive to Grayshott – a big house, probably Edwardian, set around what could be a much older stone keep. Uneasy combination of country house hotel and sanatorium. Guests are in flannelled dressing gowns.

Lunch is definitely more of the sanatorium than the hotel. Food is buffet with calories marked on each dish, ranging from 'Spinach quiche, 250 calories' to 'Endive salad. Negligible'.

Harry Enfield is there. He's been down for a week trying to give up smoking again. 'But I knew,' he says with his ethereal smile, 'that all I want when I get back to London is a glass of wine and a fag.' Simon, who had not recognised Harry, now denounces him fiercely as the one who sets a furious pace on the Fitness Walk.

True enough, as Simon and I assemble for the walk after a copious low-calorie lunch, it is Harry who sets off like a rocket round the flower beds and down across the lawn to the woods. Simon, who has brought some leather boots in which he could climb Everest, keeps up with him for a while before falling back. Our instructor has to keep shouting directions to the fast-disappearing figure of Harry whilst at the same time dealing with a couple of stragglers.

The skies have cleared and are now as intense a blue as you'll get in November. All's well with the world, except that we're lost. Simon thinks he knows the way out and shouts into the woods behind him 'Hallo! We're going *up*!' and up the hill we go.

An hour later we cut, dangerously it seems to me, across a golf course and back to the house.

Harry, who seems to have barely broken sweat, is changed and leaving for London with a young blonde.

Monday, November 6th

Another fine, sunny morning after cold night. Brilliant sunshine bathes house and garden. TG calls during the morning and we meet at Odette's for lunch.

Twelve Monkeys is within two weeks of completion. Studio excited despite only OK test screenings. As TG says, with Brad Pitt and Bruce Willis they're guaranteed a good opening weekend and after that … who knows.

Terry is already planning ahead to 'The Hunchback of Notre Dame' with Depardieu.

Back home to turn my thoughts to 'Pacific', the book. JC calls. Salutes my work on the film in less than hyperbolic terms … 'I really have to say, Mickey, that I can see absolutely nothing wrong with it.'

Rachel works away at her essay on the Civil Rights Movement. A bookish quiet descends on the house.

Thursday, November 9th

To the David Hockney drawings exhibition at the Royal Academy.

Hockney there in the midst of them, chatting and signing for an endless stream of fans with great ease and apparent enjoyment. No sign of the tortured artist there.

Only as I was about to leave did I pass by the great man, resolving to shake a hand at least.

Hockney caught my eye and recognised me, which always helps. He came across, detaching himself from a hovering group hanging on his every word, and we shook hands. Talked about Salts Mill and the gallery project he supports there. He said he was going up to Bridlington to see his mother, but he could never stay long away from Los Angeles because of his dogs. Then he grabbed my arm and drew me to him and whispered close into my ear 'Bridlington's wonderful. Hasn't changed since 1953!'

Friday, November 10th

Rang Alan Bennett to get Hockney's address. I told him of Hockney's aside about Bridlington not having changed since the '50s. Alan is scornful. 'It could do with a bit of change, Bridlington. It's a terrible place.'

Out in the evening to Ronnie Scott's. I'd promised Graham and Maggie Fordham an evening out, as we never had time after the end of *Fierce Creatures* – also I thought it would be good to take Kath and John Du Prez to celebrate their engagement.

Welcomed like an old friend by the disparate group of large, slightly shambolic men who guard the door at Ronnie's. They look like fugitives from a jazz band themselves.

A Cuban group called Los Van Van. There are 16 of them, clustered on the confined stage, trombonists just about finding space for their slides, violinists for their bows, and charismatic straw-hatted lead singer containing an unstoppable dancing shuffle on a piece of floor the size of a sixpence.

Saturday, November 11th

For a haircut at ten. A playfully camp light-black boy called Alfie. Somewhat disconcertingly his hands shake and at one point, going for a razor, he cuts himself. He grins apologetically. 'I'm always doing that,' he says.

Feel I'm reliving the 'Barber Shop' sketch, except that Alfie doesn't appear to be shaking from fear – more likely from too much happiness the night before. He talks to me in the mirror. 'I love cutting hair,' he says. 'I love the feeling of power it gives me to know that I can ruin someone's sex life for the next six weeks.'

Monday, November 13th

After ten minutes of repeated re-ringing I get through to my doctor and book an emergency appointment to check out my gravelly chest.

At the surgery a young, good-looking man in dark glasses, coat collar pulled up, twitches and paces nervously. Two younger boys, early teens, who look as if they might be Arabs, with thick, curly hair, shout and jump about, apparently oblivious to everyone else around them. A mother tries ineffectually to stop a small, hyperactive five-year-old from ripping pages from one of the magazines. A big Indian or Bangladeshi woman, swaddled in scarves and coats, sways up to reception. Her eyes look dead, vacant, unconnecting. She communicates by nods and grunts. Her little girl is pretty and lively. A wild-haired man stares at the floor and mutters.

The staff are saintly – presumably achieving many small satisfactions in a day of intolerable pressures.

Out in the evening to a screening of *Fierce Creatures*. This is the first time I've seen all that summer work assembled. Eighty invited guests at Planet Hollywood's screening room. Very comfortable. John pacing around outside the theatre wearing his Cockney fruit-seller outfit. Cap pulled down low, big warm windcheater, jeans and trainers.

No shortage of laughter, and it was good and consistent too, right through the first 50 minutes of the movie. Then it began to sag as the plot became more convoluted and just about everything to do with Kevin's Vince McCain character failed – especially exposing himself to the tiger. But there were good moments, well received, right up to the end.

So everyone involved visibly relieved. Not least me, as Bugsy makes an impact. I get laughs and, apart from in the dreadful scenes with the keepers by the lake, I'm happy with my performance. That it took four months of my life is, on the other hand, barely believable from the amount of time on screen.

Flew back east after a month's break at home. The China shoot was postponed till next year for various reasons so we picked up the journey in Vietnam, continuing on to the Philippines before returning home for Christmas.

Saturday, November 18th: Saigon Hotel, Hanoi

Woke this morning at eleven. Slept nearly 12 hours after 36 hours' virtually sleepless travel from London via Hong Kong.

A cacophony of horns and children's voices rises from the street below, incessant except in the smallest hours of the night.

Hanoi is one of the most evocative place names. In the '60s and '70s it was more than just the name of a city, it was also a description of the enemy (if you were American), a state of mind – dour, hard-line, intransigent, severe but indomitable.

Well, from what I've seen last night – as our eight hired cyclos made their elegantly seedy way up the elegantly seedy boulevard to a rooftop restaurant – and what I'm hearing four floors below as I wake after my long restorative sleep, it is anything but severe.

There is a liveliness here, a tolerant and tolerable crush.

And in a couple of hours, after lunch, we shall be in the middle of it, beginning work on episode four of 'Pacific'.

Thursday, November 23rd: Century Riverside Inn, Hue

The rain which began as persistent drizzle this morning is now coming down in a series of increasingly heavy downpours. The silhouetted figures, hunched beneath capes, riding bicycles and scooters and pedalling cyclos, look like the stragglers of some retreating army.

The room is fairly shabby and small and has no bath or river view, but the bed's comfortable and I rather like its cell-like intimacy.

Vietnam is the most demanding country we've yet filmed. Though there are signs of accelerating modernisation and change it is still a modestly equipped Third World economy.

Beggars wait at all tourist pick-up points, extending bony, withered hands, or shuffling legless torsos towards the steps of the bus. Wherever we go where tourists are seen, there is a nudging at the elbow and an imploring look. Children, often beautiful and irresistibly bright-eyed, hold out their open palms, or demand pens or chewing gum. Along most of the inner-city streets there are open drains, and in Hanoi many ponds and canals clogged thick with rubbish and human waste.

One of the advantages of the raw, unpolished, Third World feel of Vietnam is that almost everything you point the camera at is interesting – and Roger has found a good number of English-speaking Vietnamese to be my companions.

This is good, purposeful travelling. Rough and ready, unpredictable, demanding but full of character and incident.

Saturday, December 2nd: Baguio City, Luzon, Philippines

Come on Michael, get a grip. There will be more times like this, when you've had to wake before six, travel for two or three hours, shoot, travel, arrive exhausted at another new town that's beginning to look the same as all the rest, be given an official tour of said town when all you want is sleep, soap and hot bath. Arrive at hotel to find yourself in dimly lit room, close to main road, next door to an aviary of very vocal caged birds, with no bath, and not even a towel.

Travel fatigue is insidious. Once it digs in you find that you concentrate with difficulty, operate automatically, move sluggishly and consequently feel you have not done your best – this leads to negativity, which itself adds to potential fatigue – and so it goes round again.

Well this is what I must snap out of. Must not let any vicious circles form around me. Here we go again.

Because the helicopter could not reach the Banaue rice terraces owing to poor visibility, a series of great strokes of luck gave us a spontaneous sequence involving landing on sports fields in the middle of a game, hailing Jeepneys, driving up past landslips and mudslides to the terraces – and finding the cloud so thick that I improvised a piece to camera in which I read about what they couldn't see from the guidebook.

We had pulled a sequence out of nowhere – and everyone felt duly elated. This was travelling and filming at its best. Emergency becoming the mother of invention.

So, apart from lack of quality sleep, a bright light and a bath, I really should not have much to grumble about. And indeed, after pouring all this out to my diary I feel I have begun to make sense of all this madness, to order my priorities, and that there is no reason why I should succumb, fall behind or cease to operate. I must, shall and want to go on.

Wednesday, December 6th: Pearl Farm Resort, Davao, Philippines

I'm sitting writing in a small, curved-back wicker chair beside a wicker table with a hard laminated top. I'm drinking water, humouring my digestive system which has been unpredictable since Baguio, and have beside me John Berendt's *Midnight in the Garden of Good and Evil*, which I have just laid down after reading the opening chapters and being quite seduced by it. His early descriptions of Savannah seem to catch my mood at the moment, relaxed, curious, aware with pleasure of what I'm doing and where I am. In short, happy and comfortable.

Outside, only a patch of light caught by the hull of a small bobbing white boat indicates the gentle black expanse of water that laps up to and underneath my nipa-thatched, bamboo home on stilts.

I learnt the rudiments of scuba-diving in a sequence yesterday – in the swimming pool and in the sea.

I went into the water at about 11.30. A little awry to start with, I began to settle down. The coral was beautiful, lush and succulent and of wonderful extravagant designs. On it grew sexy purple plants moving like hair tossed in the wind.

I became more confident. Learnt to rely more on my own breathing.

Filling lungs and holding breath to rise, breathing firmly and constantly to fall.

Suddenly, like learning to ride a bicycle, I could feel myself at ease beneath the water.

I think the turning point came at the end of the morning session, when at a depth of about 35 to 40 feet I had difficulty drawing my breath. The gulps got shorter and shorter. I gave my instructor Louie the wobbly hand 'something wrong' signal and he quickly checked my gauge, swapped my regulator for his spare, led me to the surface and changed my tank which was almost out of air.

The fact that I was able to cope, on my first real dive, with an emergency of this kind says a lot for Louie and his training yesterday, but also made me pleasantly aware that I was basically comfortable in an unfamiliar world.

Thursday, December 14th

Descend through a thick-ish bank of clouds into a damp, cold, pre-dawn London.

Graham Fordham meets me again. This time he's researched the breakfast situation and drives me only as far as the Hilton Hotel, the big, white, glass and steel rectangle next to Terminal 4. The interior is crisp and clean and modern and stylish – the breakfast isn't bad either.

Catch up on gossip. *Fierce Creatures* is in the States being test-screened over this week and the coming weekend. Word is that Universal are very happy with it.

Long, slow journey home.

Unpack and then work through piles of letters. Nothing nasty in the woodshed – and one very pleasant note from Richard Briers, who praised *The Dresser* and said that he'd listened to the tape three times!

I feel great pleasure at seeing my room again and being back in my own home.

Sunday, December 24th

Have to be strong-willed to get myself out and running this cold morning, but I'm rewarded with bright blue winter skies and virtually empty fields and meadows. As I run past Kenwood House there is not a soul about. For a minute or two I can almost feel that the place is mine.

After breakfast out to Camden Lock. At the bric-a-brac stall I buy a small, hand-painted bowl with a rather glamorous picture of Cardinal Wolsey on it. The man apologises for not recognising me straight away – 'You look so much younger. Have you stopped working or something?'

Wednesday, December 27th

Take Granny back soon after one. She is very concerned about the state of the roads and as we go north the fog lights are flashing, though the fog itself lurks no closer than halfway across the fields we pass. But it gives a grey, inhospitable aspect to the countryside and the ice is frozen hard onto Blacksmith's Lane as I pull into Church Farm.

A walk through the house brings on memories of past Christmases. Happy memories of being woken on cold, silent mornings by the children, barely able to contain their excitement. Sad, because things will never be quite like that again. Is it their innocence I'm missing? Is it that that's irreplaceable?

Must remember that there were all sorts of problems, crises, emotional ups and downs in those Christmases I'm so busy romanticising. But for a moment I stand in the bedroom upstairs and the smell and the look of it are so unchanged and evocative.

Sunday, December 31st

At three o'clock in the morning O'Rourke, probably in some sort of protest against a noisy party in the students' house between us, turns up his Caruso operatic collection to full-blast. The sound must have woken anyone who wasn't already partying and has absolutely no effect on the students, whose thumping beat goes on – though not nearly as loudly as O'Rourke's blasting opera. So 1996 is borne in on a note of hysteria.

I look out across the roofs of Elaine Grove. The fog that closed in last night hems in the day. It's a flat, lifeless aspect outside and in a way it reflects my own mood at the moment. I feel in abeyance. Coasting. Not consciously, but somewhere inside. I'm already beginning to prepare myself for another departure.

1996

Monday, January 1st

O'Rourke claims to have seen a friend of mine ... 'MC'. 'Name mean anything?' 'Michael Caine. I met him down at the Harbour.' I ask O'R how he knows Caine. 'I doubled once for him in a film. I've got eyes just like his you see. It was only in long-shot, of course.' I really wonder where he gets it from.

Thursday, January 4th

Out to shops – Clem called and reminded me of how wet it is likely to be from Borneo to North Australia, so buy myself a cape and some waterproof trousers.

Then drive over to Whitechapel, where I eventually find the Art Gallery – very handsome Art Nouveau stone façade – and take in Emil Nolde exhibition. His painting is big, vigorous, using very deep, strong colours.

Terrific thick oily seas and good too at the effect of clouds and smoke. Don't much like his grotesque, fantasy works – but the exhibition is an eye-opener.

As is a stroll around this part of East London. Spitalfields is nearby. Some early-eighteenth-century terraced houses in reddish-brown brick – many very well looked after. They cluster around Hawksmoor's cathedral-sized Christ Church – like Nolde, H believed in adding a bit more. Neither man given to restraint. And around all this is a Bangladeshi community which adds a rich but disconcerting element to the mix.

I lapped it all up. More and more I find great pleasure in the city – in all its nooks and crannies. London gets better. I must try to always organise myself and my work so that I have time for it.

John C rings. This is the first time I've spoken to him since I returned, and since he had the US screenings.

What he tells me is quite startling, though John makes it all sound businesslike and rather unremarkable. After three screenings in the US the problem areas have come out clearly as being at the very beginning and the ending.

Almost all the last 20 minutes of the movie is to be jettisoned, thrown away. 'They hate Vince being killed.' So the rhino goes, the tiger skin, the scene by the lake we rehearsed till it died. All go.

The re-shoot will take two weeks, it will be done in LA and JC estimates I shall be needed for no more than two of those days – 'three possibly, say four at most'.

On Friday, January 5th, myself and the film crew flew from Heathrow to Manila and resumed our Pacific journey at Zamboanga in the southern Philippines, and from there by ferry to Sabah on the island of Borneo. Two weeks later we had reached Sarawak on the western coast of Borneo. On our return from filming in the interior some very bad news was waiting.

Saturday, January 20th: Kuching, Sarawak

On Thursday 18th, around a quarter to five in the afternoon, we arrived back at the Holiday Inn from the longhouse up in the Ulu Ai. Three days and nights there had been more comfortable than I expected. The weather had been largely dry. Apart from a frustrating day stuck in a boat being, at times literally, pushed upriver, we filmed copiously and successfully and even Nigel reckons we have a ten-minute sequence.

On the bus on the way back from Batang Ai Dam I slept, dictated snippets into the records, read *Captain Corelli's Mandolin* and arrived back soothed, calm, clear-headed and even rested.

A fax was handed to me as we re-checked in. It was short and chillingly to the point. Please contact Helen as soon as you arrive as she needs to talk to you urgently.

My stomach tightened straight away. All the trivial little delays – in being processed, signing forms, waiting for the room card to be issued (mine was the last) – became barely tolerable. I rushed to the phone as soon as I had let myself into the room.

H had hardly begun to tell me that there was nothing to worry about – when the doorbell tinkled and I had to lay down the phone to let in an elderly bellhop who unloaded my bags unhurriedly and seemed a little disappointed at my brusque return to the phone.

So I learnt about her tumour, the cause of the splittingly painful headaches which had been at their worst whilst I was in the jungle. I learnt about the loss of control and feeling in the arm. I learnt that she had been unable to bear it and at her sister Mary's insistence had consulted a specialist at the National Hospital for Nervous Diseases, that he had given her an examination and found a sebaceous cyst called a meningioma between skull and brain, and that he had arranged for her to have it removed on Monday 22nd by one of the top surgeons, a Mr Powell.

She kept emphasising the word 'benign'. This sort of tumour is, evidently, always benign. It is not in the brain, but pressing on it. The operation is orthodox and straightforward and relatively common (though her particular condition is found in only one in 100,000 people).

The story of Helen's tumour is covered in the book Full Circle. *At risk of repetition I shall not tell the tale again in detail. The operation was indeed straightforward, but I never stopped worrying until it was over.*

Tuesday, January 23rd: Hotel Natour Garuda, Yogyakarta, Indonesia

12.45 a.m: To bed happy. I have heard from the hospital in Queens Square that Helen came out of the theatre at four UK, eleven Indonesian time, on the 22nd, that it was a 'textbook operation', the tumour is out and, although she still has a problem with movement in her left hand, she was conscious enough to send me her love and say she was fine.

Have rung Rachel and Tom (Will is at work) and will ring the surgeon this evening.

Wednesday, January 24th: Yogyakarta, Indonesia

Back at the hotel, mid-afternoon. Ring H again. She's recovering well, but I can tell by the fact that she's so pleased I've rung that the difficult time for her may just be beginning. She will not be able to go back to life as it was for quite a while and once the euphoria of having been rid of the tumour is over, the realities of tiredness, not to mention residual shock, will sink in.

Tomorrow I shall have to be up at six for a seven o'clock departure and another long drive on the stressful roads across to film Mount Bromo from the rim – a volcano up close.

But Helen is always in the forefront of my mind and I already find myself worrying that the hotel in Bromo (which even Clem thinks is rough!) will not have the easy telephone communication that has seen me through this extraordinary time. I shall ring again before I go to bed – after I've packed yet again. I can't quite take in that a week ago today I didn't even know she had a problem.

Friday, January 26th: Hyatt Hotel, Surabaya, Java

Fortune and the gods smiled at us this morning, and the superhuman effort of filming a complex sequence at a quite extraordinary location – an active volcano – almost entirely before 6.30 a.m. was blessed with good weather and clear visibility, and the very real possibility of having to stay another day there was avoided.

The last leg of the journey was completed by 1.30. Eko gave us a few last hair-raising moments as he raced back from Bromo to Surabaya. The road journey has dominated the week and much of it was hellish. To have it over is a huge and wonderful relief.

Have rung Helen and she sounds much stronger. She is having the 'staples' out later today, but the surgeon is so pleased he says there is nothing to stop her going home when she wants, and he added that when she does get home she's not to treat herself as an invalid!

Monday, February 5th: BA Flight 005, Heathrow–Tokyo

A catch-up on the last few days. Leaving the crew to take a temporary break in Bali, I reached home on the last day of January.

Graham dropped me at the house at half past seven and I made my way stealthily upstairs – feeling like a burglar in my desire not to wake anyone. So I had my first glimpse of H's shaved patch – gleaming, I swear, and giving her head the lopsided look of a monk whose tonsure has slipped.

At breakfast I note the scar, more than six inches long, which runs from the back right-hand side of her skull across the top and curves a little to the right again before it ends. Evidence, which H proudly points out, of the hole at one end of the scar through which a tube was inserted to draw off any bleeding after the op. I'm relieved at her colour, the normalness of her face. She doesn't even look tired. She shows me the scan pictures. The size of the tumour quite frightening.

Thursday, the 1st of February, is bright again, but there's a hard frost.

Tidy up the garden, make phone calls, shop. My sore throat continues and wears me down.

Helen feels a little better and stronger each day. It's ironic that, having come all this way to look after her, I find myself croaking and snuffling wretchedly and H having to look after me.

Then a bombshell. A fax from Simon to tell me what he fears he would not be able to tell me in a phone call – that Derek Taylor has stomach cancer. He's been advised that it is malignant and inoperable. What timing – Derek heard the news on the same day that his son Dominic had his first big starring role on TV.

Did letters with Kath who told me Alison Davies[1] is getting married Saturday morning – the next day – at only 24 hours' notice. Find myself bitterly resenting the world's unwillingness to stand still when I want it to.

Slept well again on my third night home and had energy enough to buy a present (a double magnum of Château Talbot) with a card and tie some ribbon round the neck, and get myself to Sadler's Wells Theatre by 10.30 for the reception.

I have to give a father-of-the-bride speech and read telegrams from JC and Eric – 'I thought she was gay.'

Home, rather pleased with myself, only to find H seething. A *Mail on Sunday* reporter had doorstepped her whilst I was out, asking persistently about my return, the operation, etc. etc. He had a photographer with him and asked H if she wanted her picture taken. At first she didn't twig that he was a reporter – thought he was from the Residents' Association.

The combination of being duped and asked such personal questions left her angry and quite hurt. The latter made me take up the case. I put together a fax which I sent to the editor of the *Mail on Sunday*. It took two or three hours of precious time but within half an hour of transmission I received one back from the Editor, Jonathan Holborow – apologetic and concerned.

On the whole, though, the mercy dash home worked. I was glad I had been able to see Helen so close to the operation – see her cropped head and her scar and feel the little bristles growing on her scalp and our togetherness over the four days was important, though often low-key.

1 Alison Davies, for years my assistant at the Mayday office, and before that assistant to the Pythons.

She's happy to let me go back, though I wish I could have had a couple more days. She still seemed, beneath the solid, straight-bat, manage-anything veneer, to be a little dazed as I left.

Now, just after nine o'clock in the morning, I'm gazing down on Japan. Like seeing an old friend again – though the mountain ranges of central Honshu look more dense and impressive than I remember.

We shan't be long in Japan, maybe an hour and a half, if the flight to Darwin leaves on time.

We approach over an odd landscape of desiccated straw-yellow golf courses and small forested hillocks. Japanese – neat, precise, carefully arranged. A bonsai landscape.

Reunited with the crew in Darwin, we resumed filming with a north to south crossing of Australia, via Alice Springs.

Saturday, February 10th: Hilton Hotel, Adelaide

Roger this morning had heard on the news of an IRA bomb in London. Sinking feeling turned to something much more uncomfortable when I heard that the bomb went off at Canary Wharf, where Will works, and at night, which is when he works. There are many injuries apparently but no news of fatalities.

For a moment my senses reel, stagger, and I have to shut down for a minute or two, as I did when I received the fax to ring Helen from Kuching.

But there were no further details. I'd tried ringing H twice this morning and had received no reply.

From feeling vaguely pleased that she was well enough to have gone out, I went to the other extreme, imagining all sorts of sinister implications in her absence. Will hurt in wreckage, H at hospital or bedside.

Monday, February 12th: Flight AN93 Adelaide–Alice Springs

I rang Helen before I left. Bleary, unfamiliar voice of recently deeply sleeping wife tells me that it was Will's day off anyway, and he is fine.

The *Australian* has the only thorough report of the Canary Wharf bombing I've seen this weekend. It's now the South Quay Plaza bombing – and the big tower where Will works not affected.

We're in the last segment of a demanding run of filming days. We've worked and travelled on every one of the last eight days and now we're on the road again – squeezed aboard an Ansett flight to Alice and Ayers Rock. Prospect of long drive and more filming this afternoon followed by a night sleeping rough and one of the toughest days of all, at the camel muster tomorrow.

Our shadow races ahead of us as the 737 pulls off the tarmac and out over the jade-green surface of Gulf St Vincent. We've all got our heads down – knowing there's hard work ahead – but Australia has so far been generous in material and comfortable in the living. And not much time to think of anything but work.

Wednesday, February 14th: Alice Springs

Evening after one of our most memorable day's filming – the camel muster. Wind strengthening from the south-east and the 300-foot escarpment wall that rises a half-mile from my hotel window is in shadow.

This time yesterday I was in the overland vehicle to Alice, tired, grubby, bruised and bleeding after the camel mustering, one of the most extraordinary of filming days.

I haven't been worked as physically hard for many years. Nigel and Steve were working both cameras during the day – every sequence was well covered, none of them were mere duplications. It was a tough day, but should produce one of the great sequences, and last night I felt a tremendous sense of satisfaction and achievement. And quite a lot of pain.

Wednesday, February 21st: Sydney Airport

Confusing mixture of feelings as we prepare to leave Australia.

Various concerns nag away at my peace of mind. None of them has much to do with work, which has progressed well here. I thought the central desert area quite magical and we have plenty of material.

I've been most affected by the news from back home. For almost a week Helen has had a particularly virulent form of flu which has laid her very low indeed. When I rang she was either in bed or resting and her voice sounded tired and flat. I felt for her even more than during her brain operation, for this was a cruel blow just as she was recovering, and you don't get sympathy twice – and flu is less spectacular and frightening to people than head surgery.

Equally depressing is the resumption of the bombing of London by the IRA. Perhaps we shouldn't have taken the ceasefire for granted, but the return of pictures of bloodied faces, broken bodies, twisted, shattered property in places where I've walked and worked and know so well fills me, especially this morning, with another kind of helplessness. The awareness of how little we can do, for all our apparent sophistication and applied intelligence, to stop people killing their fellow human beings.

I shouldn't be surprised. The Provisional IRA have their own brutal, effective programme and little that has been said and done by John Major in the last 18 months can really have assuaged them. They don't kill as lightly and cynically as people like to make out – they kill out of an intensity, a fierceness, a dogged, deep, unshakeable belief, as people have done throughout history.

I'm beginning to think, like Vita and Harold Nicolson[1] in their letters on the outbreak of the Second War, that evil is gaining the upper hand. That goodness and decency are threatened. Added to that I felt a sudden closeness to my country. A protectiveness. As if, like Helen, it is suffering from an outbreak of illness, and I should be there.

Tuesday, February 27th: Kaikoura, New Zealand

It's a quarter to five in the afternoon; roughly twelve hours ago I got out of bed to begin the day's work, now, with the work well done, I sit sipping a cup of tea I've made myself at the Norfolk Pine Motor Inn, looking out from my room across a quiet-ish road, a line of robust Norfolk pines, complete with chunky, long-fingered leaves, a short beach to the sea. I'm a hundred yards from the Pacific Ocean (on which I spent most of this morning whale-watching).

The Norfolk Pine is run by Glenys and John – a lovely middle-aged couple of courteous, straightforward kindliness.

So refreshing, after many days of impersonal, system-designed, businessman-led accommodation, to encounter a place that expresses the taste and personality of the owners, that's unpretentious, and by the side of the ocean. I feel as warm towards it as I did towards the Nome Nugget Inn in Alaska, all those months ago.

News from home better. No more bombs. Helen making progress each day.

1 Vita Sackville-West, novelist, and her husband Harold Nicolson, politician and diarist.

Wednesday, March 6th: Christchurch–Auckland, Air NZ

Highlight of the week was not Shotover-jetting or walking up through the natural beech forest above Paradise, it was a wonderful and quite unexpected adventure with Louisa Patterson and her husband and her helicopter which filled the middle hours of this departure day.

Louisa P one of the many NZ-ers who recognised me (in a café in Dunedin), but the only one with a private helicopter business and a confident, provocative free-spiritedness which combined to provide a glorious view and a most surreal lunch.

Our neat, black, fly-nosed Hughes helicopter deftly settled on a pinnacle of the Remarkable Mountains overlooking Queenstown and the snow-capped ranges beyond. A picnic hamper spread – ham, Brie, sliced tomato and avocado, kipper pâté, salami, fresh, thick, soft brown bread, fruit and a bottle of Bollinger champagne nestling in a bucket in the lee of one of the horizontal slabs of crumbly schist that stack up to the summit of the ridge.

Louisa disappears behind a rock and emerges triumphantly at the same moment as the strains of some crackly 1940s Hawaiian guitar. It comes from a wind-up gramophone, and is soon followed by a selection of some of the other 78s which had been thrown in as a job lot when she bought the gramophone.

So 'The Ballad of Davy Crockett' fills the silence at the top of the mountain, as our long journey south from Alaska comes to an end. Now we have to turn north again. Up the American coast, back to little Diomede Island to complete the circle.

Thursday, March 7th

Through a thin layer of cloud from brightness into gloom – fields, hedgerows, roads and rivers of Buckinghamshire drained of colour. My journey has lasted 27 hours or so. Only in the last four or five did I become impatient, fidgety and almost literally itching to be home, skin drying in the merciless air-con, sore throat and proto-cold beginning to dig in.

H comes to the door looking fine and pretty with blue beret at jaunty angle (to hide the patch where the surgeons went in).

Tom is there, having just taken H to M&S, and her Colombian friend Epi comes to visit. Main change in H's life is caused by her forced inability to drive for a year. Now people have to come and see her.

My room, my books, my house, the garden, my interest in everything around me renewed by absence. This little world suddenly special, no longer commonplace ... something to relish. It's a remarkable feeling and one which I count as paradoxically one of the great pleasures of travel. The almost sensuous delight in the ordinary and commonplace.

Friday, March 8th

JC's re-shoot seems to be in trouble. Kevin cannot make April or May and Jamie won't film in August. The location is now to be back in London, as Universal have found it too expensive to shoot in LA.

Tuesday, March 12th

Phillida rings to say that the news on Derek Taylor is not good. Chemotherapy not an option. Derek's days are numbered, but in what measure no-one can tell.

JC calls. He is still re-writing with Iain Johnstone; he has found this whole business of the re-shoot frustrating. When Shamberg suggested that if I couldn't make it in July, they shoot it without me, he finally said enough was enough and now they are working on late August, early September dates.

John sounds calm, composed, in control before letting slip that 'no-one liked the keepers, that's the problem'. First I've heard. 'In America?' 'No, no in England as well.'

What sort of revisionism is going on I dread to think – but if the opening scenes with Jamie and Kevin didn't work and 20 minutes of the ending didn't work, and they didn't like the keepers, what is left?

Thursday, March 14th

Drive H to the National Hospital for post-op check-up with her surgeon, Michael Powell. Queens Square is a long rectangle, quiet; as restful a thoroughfare as you'll find right in the centre of town. A most suitable site for a hospital for nervous diseases.

Mr Powell, tall, bony, Lenin-bald with a prominent skull with a distinct bump in the back as if a heavy object might once have fallen across it. Beard, cheap shirt, loose at the collar. His movements seem ever so slightly unco-ordinated. His eyes are soft and humorous, he behaves like a very physical man trying to be gentle.

This is the man who, a little over seven weeks ago, carved a side out of my wife's skull, removed a tumour, scraped, cleaned – 'sanded' as he put it with a smile – the piece of skull and replaced it. Hard to imagine such trauma being inflicted when I look at H sitting there serene and healthy – having been twice to the gym in the last few days.

Not that Mr Powell thinks this unusual. He avoids any sense of mystique or any air of superiority. He might have just sold her a new kettle or be offering an estimate for some kitchen work from the way he talks to her.

I want to tell him that his attitude, his reassurances, his refusal to dramatise or pontificate about the operation helped both of us cope with it better than we could ever have expected, but there isn't really a moment.

All he wants from me is the chance to dress up as a Gumby and pose with me outside the hospital. 'All neurosurgeons I know are enormous Python fans.'

Friday, March 15th

When I arrive at John's, Iain Johnstone and Amanda greet me warmly. Despite what JC later refers to as 'cash flow' problems, his little army of faithful retainers still seems to be in place. The court of Cleese still looks and sounds impressive.

JC appears, he looks tired and tense. With typical psychotherapeutic directness, he explains why he is indeed feeling a little tired and tense. He's just heard that his younger daughter Camilla has fallen from a horse in Chicago. She's not badly hurt but she's in hospital having tests.

He turns his attention to my trousers. 'Did you make them yourself?' I tell him later that they're rather expensive, from Armani, and I've got three pairs. JC looks down at them. 'Are you wearing them all at once?'

We walk across Holland Park Avenue, heading for a quiet lunch at the Halcyon.

The restaurant not full, but Simon Gray and Patrick Barlow were at one corner table and Prince Edward and two men at another. Edward looked across and smiled and on my way to the loo I stopped and chatted. He's the least regal of the royals I know, the least imperious.

He seems pleased to see me. He looks the same age as I remember him at the Royal Knockout – eight years ago? Very young and choirboy-like.

Whereas Simon Gray looks like a wicked choirmaster. Eyes flicking about the restaurant, features red and choleric.

Wednesday, March 20th

Talk to our Executive Producer Eddie Mirzoeff and tell him that I've decided on 'Palin's Pacific' as a title. He agrees with the same smooth and immediate readiness with which he greeted the news that I didn't want to call it 'Palin's Pacific'.

Friday, March 22nd

Papers full of the potentially appalling consequences of the BSE, mad cow affair, after scientists have gone public with their strong suspicion that BSE has leapt a species and infected humans who have eaten beef. No hard facts or advice. Everyone frightened.

As H says, the CJD disease takes ten years to incubate, and so our children, who ate beef in the late '80s, could, like us, be very much at risk if there is an epidemic. Apocalyptic news which vies with details of a huge increase in airborne tuberculosis, which is already on its way to becoming a new, life-threatening epidemic. There'll be some reading of the Book of Revelation tonight.

Sunday, March 24th

Reacquaint myself with *Hem's Chair* in advance of two busy days of paperback publicity. Made a list of reviews under Good, Equivocal and Bad. About 15 each under Good and Equivocal and only four under Bad, so feel less defensive about it all.

Monday, March 25th

Two television interviews at Carlton in late afternoon.

Carlton now inhabits the South Bank tower that used to belong to LWT and it is a great shock to see how completely the old television world has been broken down. Camera operators are young and nervous.

They also have to act as sound operators – checking mikes, etc. The position of my lapel mike – not a complicated business – is changed three or four times in a minute.

The programmes are loose, rough, amateurish. The frothy waffle of the content is quite depressing, the ignorance and lack of pride in the job quite unbelievable. It's as if all the qualified people had just been killed in an air crash, leaving the programmes to be made by a skeleton staff of students.

Tuesday, March 26th

Valerie Grove arrives to interview me.

The interview seems to fly off at various tangents – mainly because she is bright and curious and extrovert and we share many of the same concerns – about London lacking a central authority – even a mayor – about the shabby state of Camden, about the delights of the Heath. She does seem genuinely approving of *Hem's Chair* – being particularly complimentary about Ruth.

Wednesday, March 27th

Will round early evening. He has been offered a permanent staff job with the Mirror Group – £21,000 a year. He's pleased that it will offer him a chance to plan his employment, holidays, etc. for some months ahead. More security, but he doesn't think he will stay there for more than a year.

To dinner with JC at Alastair Little's new restaurant off Ladbroke Grove. Minimalist decor, minimal ambience – fierce eschewing of the candlelit, tablecloth kind of atmos. John, big green Bentley spread out along the kerb in front of the restaurant – 'I can keep an eye on it' – is in reflective mood.

He once again expresses desire to make a walk-on appearance on the Pacific doc – preferably in some quite out-of-the-way place like La Paz. Says he'd do it for the price of an air ticket.

Wednesday, April 24th

To lunch with Will at Café Flo. A good catch-up with his news and his plans. He's coping well with the unsociable working hours at Mirror

Group (where his official title is sub-editor). But he admits that he's restless, that he wants to keep on the move – doesn't want to be confined to one job or even living in the flat he has at the moment. He loves books and words too much to want to spend the rest of his life in front of a computer screen.

I see much of myself in Will – a need for constant change and stimulation grafted onto a deeply conservative sense of solidity and responsibility.

Sunday, April 28th

Epi, H's Colombian friend – full of warmth and infectious enthusiasm – comes round with husband and son for tea and a talk about Colombia, which is coming up on our itinerary. She has family contacts there. Brings coffee-table books which favour the great and strikingly beautiful interiors of some of the old houses.

Alongside this there is 'Narco' Colombia. A country where a drug baron wanting to strike a deal could offer the government the money to wipe out its national debt at one go. She describes the complete lack of political morality – the insidiousness of corruption running through every aspect of public life. But she still manages to make it sound unmissable.

Monday, April 29th

H and I spend several minutes trying to record a new message for the answerphone. It keeps recording things like 'Press this!' 'No, no, press that ...' followed by laughter and failed attempts to be serious. Like a pair of schoolchildren. Still.

To Groucho's to meet Dan Patterson and Ian Brown [his writing partner], who have some ideas and questions to ask on 'The Adventure'. Never feel altogether comfortable in Groucho's. To do the place properly you have to act a bit. You have to decide what role you're going to play before you go in. Generally quite ordinary people but occasionally someone larger than life looms up and you feel you should grasp their hand, then you remember this is Groucho's and it wouldn't be cool. Then you overcompensate and cut people dead. I muttered most unsatisfactorily at Clement Freud as we passed.

Monday, May 6th

To lunch with JC at Poons in Whiteleys (at his suggestion).

Much of the meal taken up with JC's renewed interest in the sex comedy. 'Small budget – ten at most, no American stars, shoot in Ireland, good for tax, you and me, maybe Julie Christie as your wife. What's not to like.'

Wednesday, May 8th

Over to Prominent for the first full Python business meeting since, according to Kath, 1989. I'm upstairs talking to her when I hear Terry G's boisterous arrival, bronchial laughter in return from Cleese and some squeaky sighs and groans from Terry J.

We all squeeze around the glass-topped table in the tiny meeting room. Eric is summoned up by phone from LA where it's eight in the morning. The phone call lasts three and a half hours, which is the time it takes for us to deal with the backlog of work.

The reorganisation of the Python companies is dealt with constructively. Clarifications necessary. Jokes keep diverting attention. Eric suggests that the 'B' shares be called Half-a-Bee shares. John adds an 'Eric' to this – so they will now be known as Eric the Half-Bee shares.

A lot of it is to do with who controls Python in the event of our deaths. After debate it is felt that only Pythons should have control over their companies – even down to the last one alive.

The only real contentious area is the dreaded Prominent Features. Terry G is greatly exercised about the way it's been left to run quite vaguely. John has taken 69,000 dollars of his money out, as has Eric, on projects which are manifestly not to be Prominent Features. Can they, should they do that?

I'm in favour, at a push, of keeping Prominent Features. It has a name, it has back product. But later, over a Japanese meal with the two Terrys, I feel Acrimony Films may be a better name.

On May 15th we left London for the last and longest of our Pacific filming legs. This one, from Cape Horn in the south to the Bering Strait in the north, took us away from home for three months.

Saturday, May 18th: Hotel Cabo de Hornos, Punta Arenas, Chile

It's half past five on a day at the end of a southern autumn, and it's almost too dark now to see the statue of Magellan, borne on the backs of Indians, which stands at the centre of the Plaza de Armas, seven floors below me.

Four years and a few months ago, on my way to Antarctica in the middle of a Southern summer, I kissed the bronze toe of one of those Indians, which traditionally means that you will return to Punta Arenas. I did return, safely, a few days later, after reaching the South Pole.

Now I've returned a second time, and I'm sure I shall have to kiss the lucky toe again, as we set out on the long journey to Alaska.

This is almost the first private time since our hurtling progress to the Americas began at Heathrow last Tuesday night. We reached Santiago early on Wednesday morning, and within three hours were flying Air Patagonia to Punta.

We didn't stop there, but piled our 800 kgs of equipment and baggage into a twin-engined Otter and took off for Puerto Williams – a further hour's flying time to the south. Groggily unloaded onto a 130-foot Chilean navy patrol boat, the *Isaza*, where I spent my first night in South America, grinding out towards Cape Horn.

Barely rested, we had to take advantage of the weather to film our approach to and landing on Cape Horn.

Our second day of filming was along the Beagle Channel, taking advantage of generally clear weather and spectacular locations, then another night aboard the *Isaza*, tight and cramped and convivial, but no private space.

Now the wind howls outside my window, but for the time being we are home and dry; the last leg, which will seem endless at times, has begun with a severe test of stamina. The reward has been a chance to see lands very few will ever see, and enter a lonely, hard world which must look virtually unaltered since Darwin described it in his diary over 160 years ago.

Monday, May 20th: Costa Australis Hotel, Puerto Natales, Chile

Almost everyone else in the crew seems to switch the television on as soon as they get in their room. I like the time to think.

I think about the journey, what I've learnt and what I've seen and once that's in perspective – a mundane task of checking the tape-recorded notes and tidying up my notebook entries – I let my mind go and settle where it wants.

Called Helen last night and heard that our cat Betty was dead, her lungs had collapsed and the vet had drawn off ten millilitres of pus from them. Helen had tried to give her a healing pill but Betty had bitten her hard, leaving three deep incisions in her finger. Betty's legacy, as H put it.

It's only quite late in our conversation that I can tell her that I've been to Cape Horn, and stood on it too. What I want to exult about and share doesn't sound exciting any more. Betty's death sort of subsumes everything.

Sunday, May 26th: Chiloé Island, Chile

Have been awake for a long time. Outside the gale continues to blow, rattling the roofs and slapping rain against the windows. This is very bad weather indeed and we have a long, hard day's filming ahead. Now, just after my alarm goes, I find that there is no electricity. I want to curl up in bed and put the sheets over my head.

I can summon up nothing but resignation at the thought of cooking with the locals all morning, then having to listen to music and songs I don't understand for the rest of the afternoon. And, worst of all, having to look as if I'm enjoying it. All my systems – my mental and psychological systems – are at full stretch. Something will get me through, but after this – another two and a half months still to go.

Tuesday, June 4th: Calama, Chile

Dawn breaking at the El Tatio geyser field. Apart from being the highest place on which I've ever set foot, it was good to film, wondrous to behold, and the warmth of the steam and the sun slowly conquered the Arctic cold – it was minus 12 when we reached the geysers at seven o'clock. Roger's dire warnings of the headaches and nosebleeds that he and Vanessa had experienced on their recce were not fulfilled. Apart from flatulence, I suffered no effects of being, at one point, only 250 feet short of 15,000.

Fraser had the sound of the fumaroles to record, Nigel had pre-dawn, drifting steam and, after sunrise, brilliantly back-lit steam – in between huge swathes of mountainside turning a rich pink-brown.

I'd begun to get gloomy, thinking to myself that this last American section was a mistake.

Then along come days like today in El Tatio, and though I'm sore-eyed with tiredness after two very early starts and with the prospect of a long, late work and travel day tomorrow, I feel good enough to want to write up the diary. This is a most beautiful country. Press on.

Friday, June 28th: Hotel Sol del Oriente, Pucallpa, Peru

Bolivia and Peru have been more demanding. The altitude made everything hard work – I slept, and dreamt, in shallow breathless bursts, so was always quite tired.

Cuzco a brief and beautiful breather, then the long, nine-day hike to the Urubamba, and seven of those days and nights under canvas. Tents fine, slept extraordinarily well, but life at the horizontal, and sand accumulating in everything, and shitting supported on sand-fly-bitten hands over a small hole full of other people's mess took its toll and we are all immensely happy to be through all that in one piece.

Monday will be the first day of July and (according to Nigel, who keeps these scores assiduously) the exact halfway point of our three months in the Americas.

Across the street professional letter-writers sit beneath colourful umbrellas waiting for business. Occasional blaring loudspeaker announcements announce the presence of a circus in town.

The food in Peru has been dull and generally unexciting. I miss good breakfasts particularly. Ask for coffee, even in this, the best hotel in Pucallpa, and you will be brought hot water, a spoon and an old, rusty-lidded tin of Nescafé.

My reading time has been prescribed by the pressure of the work and the nature of the places we've stayed recently, but I have finished Leigh Fermor's *Letters from the Andes* and launched into Hemming's *Conquest of the Incas* and Llosa's autobiography, but am currently caught by the great García Márquez – *Chronicle of a Death Foretold*.

Shaved for the first time in ten days. I'm ready for work tomorrow – Day 200 on the road.

Friday, July 5th: Hotel El Dorado, Iquitos, Peru

We are in limbo land at the moment, killing time very slowly as we wait for a boat to take us down the Amazon.

The crew, as Fraser put it, feels 'uncomfortable' when it's not working.

But this town has a charm and an atmosphere which Pucallpa lacked, and I enjoy walking the grid-plan streets – up Próspero, down Morona and onto the recently completed esplanade looking over the Amazon – which at this dry season looks less like a mighty river and more like a plain of flooded fields. The town has a colonial past, stretching back over two hundred years and culminating in the great rubber boom of the late nineteenth and early twentieth centuries. This has left behind a legacy of interesting, well-decorated town houses, with tall, arched French windows giving out onto classically pilastered balconies, and some eye-catching Azulejo tiling.

I've rung home and all goes on quite happily without me. I can almost hear Helen trying to scour her memory for some remarkable detail to feed me with when I ring from the back of beyond.

El Comercio is spread out on my bed; in it the news that Charles has offered 30 million to Diana as a divorce settlement.

Thursday, July 11th: Victoria Regia Hotel, Bogotá, Colombia

I feel as happy and contented and comfortable as at any time on this long, sometimes apparently endless journey. It's a euphoria which is bound at some point to pass away and return me to uncomfortable reality, but for now – 3.15 in Room 810 at the Victoria Regia – it's worth recording that I feel very happy indeed.

For what reasons? Firstly and mainly that 24 hours ago we reached the nadir of discomfort – on the *El Arca* where lights, water and air-con all ceased to function, leaving us, on the sweaty banks of the Amazon, trapped in a night of suffocating heat and rampant mosquitoes.

Crossing into Colombia at the small frontier town of Leticia, we discovered that our main sequence there – the coca plantation – was impossible to film owing to recent action by the DEA, the American Drug Enforcement Agency, and the Colombian government.

Decision taken to leave Leticia and fly straight to Bogotá. No-one complains. We are all pretty desperate to get out of the jungle.

So, at two this morning, to the Hotel Victoria Regia, a small, elegantly furnished, comprehensively efficient town-house hotel.

There is abundant hot water, dispensed from brass taps into bath tubs big enough for two. Lights work; hangers are unbroken, there are desks and tables with comfortable chairs to match.

Breakfast is a feast and there are luxuries like fresh milk, almost unheard of in Peru.

Awful things may lurk elsewhere in the city, but Oma Libros – a bookstore with English-language books, newspapers and a café – was a complete realisation of fantasies in which I had been indulging since we left Chile.

At the reception desk, the first four draft scripts of a sitcom by Roy Clarke which Geoffrey Perkins at the BBC wants me to do – and which Anne thinks the best thing she's read for me in ages.

Friday, August 2nd: Fairmont Hotel, San Francisco

It's nearly midnight. Have just closed the curtains on a magnificent view of the city skyline as seen from my room on the Fairmont Tower's 22nd floor. I'm a lucky boy. Only two more weeks to go; we have worked a day described as 'almost flawless' by Fraser at dinner tonight (we shot in Alcatraz and the Castro).

Steve Robinson and I had a good natter tonight about art and architecture. It began with him mentioning the Saltash Bridge and me saying that the victory of George Stephenson over Isambard Brunel was a significant portent of the way Britain was going to go. Opportunism and profit defeating style, flair, care and craftsmanship.

Friday, August 9th: Crest Motor Inn, Prince Rupert, Canada

Bands of light rain and wet mist drift across the fine, wide view of water and forested headland.

I can hear voices from the piers down below and occasionally a white float-plane will fly low out of the sound. Chunky, solid-hulled little fishing boats have been busy going in and out all day long.

Quite suddenly, it seems, the greatest journey I have ever undertaken, and probably ever will undertake, in my life, is coming to an end.

As I write, I'm aware in the back of my mind of that little nodule of apprehension that troubles me from time to time. We still have a lot of travelling left – several thousand miles and some potentially inhospitable locations – and many human elements leave margins for error.

Hanging over all arrangements is the start of *Fierce Creatures* re-shoots a week today, which will require my energy and concentration for 14 days on the run.

The script, in a black folder, is beside me on the neat, bottle-green upholstered cushions of my alcove seat. There's a lot of new material to learn – 'Anywhere where you can see that Bugsy can talk more – just talk more' – John's written. It's clear that Fred Schepisi,[1] the new direc-tor, likes the Bugsy character, which is why I have so much work ahead. I approach it with greater confidence than before.

Tiredness has been the enemy since we left San Francisco. I was sorely tested by a long, damp day at the logging competition near Vancouver.

I performed, like a performing bear, doing what was expected, being a sport and deep down hating most of what I had to do and how I had to do it. And finally I fell in the water whilst running across a log and the ritual sacrifice was duly delivered and everyone was happy – though I showed my happiness in a howl of heartfelt indignation. Right in front of the camera, sodden and weary and trapped in the ring, I beat my hands on the grass and gave up. 'I want to go home!' was all I could shout, over and over again. I felt utterly, truly, completely broken. Everyone was delighted.

Monday, August 19th

After an unexpectedly sprightly three days, almost unaffected by jet lag, I find myself waking sluggishly on this fourth morning home.

To Pinewood for hair, make-up checks and to meet Fred Schepisi.

He's informal, no-nonsense, and any fears that working for a new master might be uncomfortable are quickly dispelled. He says simply that if Bugsy is to be funny because of his monomaniac verbal persist-ence, then he has to talk almost all the time. He could see from the footage that Bugsy's part was underwritten – as were John's and Jamie's – hence his encouragement to John to beef up Bugsy, and the reason why I am on call for all but two of the 20 shooting days ahead.

I always felt it a weakness that Bugsy was not more intimately

---

1 Fred Schepisi, Australian director of *Last Orders* and *Six Degrees of Separation*.

involved in the denouement. In the new script I am the *deus ex machina*, and have a much more complete role. So now it's up to me to make something of it.

Wednesday, August 21st

A good, brisk productive morning's work. Actually enjoy doing my close-ups and my delivery relaxes and Fred is pleased. Best of all, I did a professional job, and added to it that unparalleled feeling of having done something the best way it could be done – a feeling I rarely experienced on the last shoot.

What has helped me is that John no longer feels the need to direct, to whip up the cast's enthusiasm with his exhortations, songs, chants and the whole act he put on to make up for what he thought were others' shortcomings. Now John concentrates on his acting and Fred, with his mixture of ribaldry and Aussie bonhomie, runs the show and sets the tone. Ironic that Aussies should be brought in to save a film whose villains are Aussies.

Friday, August 23rd

Into the bee costume for the first time. I shall be wearing it for most of next week. Because of the weather we remain indoors and set to a short but complicated little scene involving Kevin being discovered stuffing a body in the freezer. Kevin and Jamie are both more relaxed and I'm pleased to have rediscovered the good working and non-working relationship we all had on *Wanda*.

Kevin wildly, richly, grandly inventive. Jamie told me yesterday that she'd been sitting out on the set minding her own business when she saw a penis appear from beneath the shorts of one of the crew. 'He just waggled it about a bit and stuck it back,' she claimed. Later, as I was outside on my way to work and she was returning to her dressing room, I asked her if she'd had any more visions. 'You better believe it,' she said, and as she added 'goodnight Michael' she swiftly pulled down her top and revealed her right breast.

It was only after she'd passed that I realised that one of the drivers was beside me, shammying the window of his Range Rover. 'Did you see that?' he said, adding regretfully, 'Trouble is, if I tell anyone about it, they wouldn't believe me.'

Monday, August 26th

They've decided to move calls an hour earlier. To maximise daylight, I'm told. So I'm awake at five and picked up at 5.30.

Lines around the lemur cage at beginning and end of John and Jamie's first 'love' scene. Fred using Steadicam again. He gives me a couple of new thoughts for lines – just before the take. 'Keep talking,' he says. A challenge to be confronted then and there. And I must say I find that I do like working this way.

John thinks I should have a separate credit – 'endless additional dialogue by Michael Palin'.

Tuesday, August 27th

The morning taken up with a quick-fire, quite long dialogue scene between, largely, me and Kevin. We barely had an exchange in the original script. Now Bugsy's unstoppable drone has a chance to drive both Vince and McCain mad, with fatal consequences in the latter case.

Home to find a note from H to say that Jonathan Margolis has been commissioned to write a biography of me. He has already done one on John, which John asked us all not to co-operate on. My immediate reaction is one of indignation. I don't want him to write a biog of me and I resent the assumed confidence that I will co-operate.

Wednesday, August 28th

Kevin is high as a kite today – soaring off into sweeping voices, extravagant gestures, keeping himself going at a level of barely controlled manic intensity. He rarely comes down to earth. It's dazzling and exhausting.

'Anything you need Kev?' one of the crew asks routinely.

'Oh, a night's sleep, perhaps,' Kevin bats back tersely, only just joking.

Saturday, September 7th

As the various last shots are cleared up, the atmosphere becomes increasingly like that of a school on the last day of term. I wander the emptying studios, prompting Roger Murray-Leach to liken me to a boy whose parents have failed to turn up to collect him.

Jamie, who has given me as a parting gift a Paul Smith fish keyring, is drinking strawberry vodka from the bottle as I get made up around six.

There is red wine sloshing about the make-up area – a joyful reaction to a no-alcohol-on-duty clause in the employment contract. Bille Brown is bade farewell in the traditional manner – called to the stage, although still in his underpants, to receive our applause, hugs, etc.

Then it's Kevin's turn. Fred makes a short farewell speech calling Kevin 'a great talent and a pleasure to work with'. No-one would disagree with the first part, but like all great talents Kevin sometimes loses sight of the contribution of lesser talents. It becomes a solitary world when you're that talented – but he is still a kind, thoughtful, highly intelligent, serious man. I'd like to lark about with him though, one day.

Fifteen and a half months since the first scene of *Fierce Creatures*, John and myself are the only two left.

I know everyone wants to be done, but I still have three quite tricky little speeches to deliver, with the camera tight on my head and shoulders.

The clock is moving towards eight o'clock. Everyone is blearily staggering towards the tape, but I have to be clear and concentrated and remember that what I do now on this echoing, emptying stage will potentially fill screens all over the world.

All of which is my own self-congratulatory way of saying that my nerve held and I didn't slip a word on three takes. 'Check the gate.' And it's over.

Sunday, September 8th

It's a pleasure to lie and luxuriate in bed – until Elsie and Edith spring up onto the duvet and attack my radio during *Letter from America*. It's bizarrely like Alistair Cooke Being Attacked by a Duck (Python 1971) as the urbane 88-year-old purrs on whilst Edith chews the aerial and Elsie tugs the radio across the bed.

We lunch with John and Michael Shamberg and families at La Famiglia, off the King's Road. Michael S, heartened by the last three weeks, is more like the Shamberg I used to know on *Wanda*. He says he now has to go back to the States and 'start selling' the film. He does not anticipate much trouble – in fact he thinks the trailers that have been appearing over the last year might help.

John thinks I've been a 'really good stick' for working so hard so soon after my return. All is sweetness and light.

Monday, September 9th

After some debate with H I agree not to try and start work on the Pacific book at six in the morning (my thinking being that I have become so used to rising early over the last year that it would come naturally).

Look at the schedules again – estimate words to be done, time allowed. All of my books have, from necessity, been confined to a season – a spring or an autumn generally. Once again, I'm tight up against dates set by expectant publishers, and of course, in this case, expectant editors, directors and producers. Fourteen weeks is the time I have to complete a first and, virtually, last draft.

Friday, September 13th

Will comes by. We go down together to visit Tom at Whitfield Studios, where he, John and George are producing two tracks for a girl duo called Akin.

Tom and the boys look very much at home with the long, winking beds of equipment – the screens, digital controls and so on. Brockpocket, as he and his two partners call themselves, have a certain gentle swagger now.

Though Tom has not yet hit the jackpot, he clearly has style and substance. Next year will be their make or break year he reckons, with most of the work they've stockpiled coming onto the market. Tom has a good, straightforward, sensible attitude to it all. He's philosophical. He has H's calm centre.

Tuesday, September 17th

To BH to record my *Week's Good Cause* for the Prison Reform Trust. I wasn't much impressed by the original script, but the cause is a good one, and I spent time rewriting it so that it sounded more genuine and natural and less clichéd. No point in doing something like this unless you can do it with feeling.

To the South Bank for a private view of a new exhibition of Mel Calman's work at the National. Arrive early so get the cab to put me down on Waterloo Bridge and walk the rest. The underbelly of the South Bank Centre darker and more hellish than ever. The Royal Festival Hall has a presentation of Richard Rogers' plan for redesigning the area. It looks striking – great waves of polysomething or other will cover and unite the place.

Barely a day goes by now without some architectural muscle-flexing. Foster's Millennium Tower revealed at the weekend; the new British Library our entry for the Architectural Biennale in Venice. With the help of lottery money and the increasing wealth of rich patrons, architects are enjoying a sort of renaissance.

Thursday, September 19th

Good story in Alec Guinness' *Book of the Week* reading of his gloriously underplayed diaries. Coral Browne on stage when asked if the wig was bothering her replied 'Darling, I feel as if I'm looking out of a yak's arse.'

Monday, September 23rd

Anne rings. She has been talking to Clem, who says he can do nothing more about graphics until he has a title. So must confront this one. Sometimes I sink back to the ease and convenience of 'Palin's Pacific'. If I wanted to please everyone this would be the one. But my own objections still stick. It's not *my* Pacific.

Monday, October 7th

Leave at ten o'clock for Oxford. Car loaded to the gunwales. It's a grey morning in London but the sky brightens as we reach Oxford. Usual combination of emotions. Oxford, more than anywhere else, and certainly more than London, reminds me of the ageing process. I mourn a little for my time here – which seems, at a distance, to have been full of promise and opportunity, freshness and self-discovery, a sort of golden time where everything was ahead of me.

At the same time I see Rachel's golden time (or so I presumptuously assume it to be) also fading. This is her last year. Already, the day I found her room in the Library Staircase was Robert's old room seems far away – lost for ever. So I sense the poignancy of both our lives either passing, or having long passed, important formative stages.

Rachel is swept away by her friends – her room is big, with en suite shower and bathroom, quite recently renovated and high, on New

Staircase overlooking the quad and close to a big owl's head gargoyle. Desk before wide mullioned window.

At 12.45 arrive at St Edmund Hall to have lunch with Stephen Tumim, who asked me to drop in and see him if I were passing.

Stephen, whose first week this is as Principal, is like a child with a new toy. He greets everyone cordially, especially the lower members of staff, and is anxious that I should meet as many dons as possible. He's so enthusiastic about his various new jobs – including Fine Arts Admissions Tutor at the Ruskin. 'I'm hoping to get one of my ex-prisoners in. He's a lifer; rather good painter, I must say.'

He has old-fashioned ways and an old-fashioned appearance – half-moon specs and bow ties – but is lively, full of jokes, many at his own expense, and as bright and sharp as a 20-year-old. Except most of the 20-year-olds, struggling into their new rooms at the start of a new term, look far from bright.

Wednesday, October 9th

Need a suit for tonight's BAFTA 50th so, at last possible minute, drive to Grey Flannel in Chiltern Street.

Suit having been altered, trouser bottoms taken up, etc. – all in space of an hour – H and I are into a cab heading for Piccadilly.

This is a royal occasion, so there is much standing around and waiting and keeping spaces clear and announcements like 'the royal party will be arriving here in approximately eight minutes'.

Jim Acheson[1] and Julia and Helen and myself find ourselves in the row directly behind the Queen and the Duke. Their seats are marked by two fudge-coloured antimacassars. Jim has a plan to remove one of them at the end, and have me sign it to Julia's mother Valerie in New Zealand!

It turns out to be the one on the seat of the monarch herself. Not that the Queen leans back much. She sits bolt upright like a perched bird – as though at some horse trials.

Two Fellowships are awarded – one to Freddie Young,[2] the camera-

1 Jim Acheson, costume and production designer. Worked on *Brazil* and *Time Bandits*. Won three Costume Design Oscars for *Restoration*, *Dangerous Liaisons* and *The Last Emperor*.
2 Freddie Young, cinematographer, long-time associate of David Lean on his films *Lawrence of Arabia*, *Doctor Zhivago* and *Ryan's Daughter*, all of which won Academy Awards.

man, who is 94 today and can barely move without help. He makes it to the microphone and between slow, laboured, emphysemic breaths gives brief thanks then, holding the audience spellbound with his breathing difficulties, he adds 'If you ... want ... to ... see ... any ... more ... of me ... (long pause) I'm on *This Is Your Life* on Friday.'

Then a four and a half minute round-up of 100 years of British cinema in which I made the screen three times – *Private Function*, *Grail* and *Life of Brian* – and *Wanda* was in there too.

After the presentation, the Queen and Prince Philip leave for a private room and Jim Acheson swiftly pockets Her Majesty's antimacassar.

We're fetched to meet the Queen, who is showing admirable stamina. Her Majesty is turned in my direction and somewhat to my disappointment her face registers a complete blank. Eddie Mirzoeff prompts her about my recent travels.

I'm determined to get some reaction from her, and when I say that we were allowed home from filming for brief periods – 'to save our marriages and get our washing done' – her well-dusted face breaks into genuine jolly laughter.

Later, George Perry says that the only things she really enjoyed in the Best of British compilation were appearances by Sid James.

Tuesday, October 15th

Near-despair strikes mid-morning as, after cruising confidently along with the book, I accidentally press some odd combination of keys and the entire third section disappears.

For a half-hour or more I am utterly desolate. Helen's out, so I can't seek help and consolation. Will is very encouraging. He comes round, despite having been on night shift at the *Mirror*, and calms me down, says he's had whole essays disappear and that once he has resigned himself to rewriting – says the rewrite almost always an improvement.

So, keep the phone unplugged and get my head down. What makes it hardest at first is knowing that the 4,000 words or more that I've lost felt so clear and easy to write.

But by six I have completed over 3,000 of them and in most cases with greater fluency than when I first wrote them.

Sunday, October 20th

To Leicester Square Empire at 9.30 for screening of Steve A's *Brassed Off*.[1]

A heaving crowd, through which members of the Grimethorpe Colliery Works Band are dragging heavy instruments – kettledrums and euphoniums – for a pre-film recital. In the film they play the Grimley Colliery Band which, at the climax of the picture, wins the National Championships at the Albert Hall. Last night the real Grimethorpe band came second, by one point!

The film is well made and funny and quite gripping despite some spongily sentimental material when the goodies behave as too good to be true and the baddies as too bad. Reminds me of a *Ripping Yarn* sometimes. A good credit for Prominent.

Late start and finish because of the crowds. Back home as swiftly as possible, pick up H and out to Henley for lunch with Peter Luff.[2]

Fortunately, John Lloyd and wife Sarah are also late, coming from the other side of Oxfordshire. John reminds me of Lytton Strachey, or some eminent Victorian now his hair has receded and his face has lost its youthful glow. He is good company – intelligent, curious and infectiously world-weary. He shrugs off his achievements – *Not the Nine O'Clock* and *Blackadder* – and claims to have done nothing he's particularly proud of for several years. 'I make my money doing commercials with John Cleese.'

Big flag-floor kitchen and roast lamb around a refectory table. Feels like one of John's commercials. Lloydey, as they call him, says wistfully to me that 'I would like to meet whoever wrote the script of your life.'

Cross the road to drop in on George H. The spindly wrought-iron gates open and we roll up the green and gloomy drive with its trees so big on all sides it's like opening a door into British Columbia.

I always feel that what you see of George's house is just the tip of the iceberg – indeed there probably is an iceberg somewhere – but I do feel that he seems very small at the middle of it all, and yes, probably quite exhausted. He says he rarely comes up to town now – though Olivia likes to shop and meet friends.

---

1 *Brassed Off* was produced by Steve Abbott and directed by Mark Herman: the same team that made *Blame It on the Bellboy*.
2 Producer of the first Amnesty International Charity Show *The Secret Policeman's Ball*.

Dhani is what one might call a fine boy. He's slim, good-looking, articulate and confident, without being a pain at the same time. He's one of the best coxes around and recently joined the Leander Club.

George is thinking of going to India 'to get healthy again', and then have a long holiday. I envy him that, but not all the rest of his life. As he is tucking himself away, I'm just enjoying getting back to people.

Wednesday, October 23rd

To lunch with Donald Woods. He's given up smoking but not drinking. 'I may be a fat drunk, but at least I'm not smoking.'

Donald is using me again to get money for his various Eastern Cape projects and particularly for his scheme to teach black journalists. 'I have to teach them to be confident enough to be critical,' he says. 'Critical of their own people.'

Thursday, October 24th

Sid, who suffers from vertigo, comes to clean the windows. He tells H later that he is also an alcoholic. H asks if he is undergoing any treatment. He says there is an alcoholism unit at the Royal Free but he can't go to it because it's on the tenth floor.

Sunday, October 27th

To the 'BBC 60 Gala' at TV Centre. The Centre itself is lit with coloured floodlights and revolving spots and a makeshift doorway has been erected leading across the circular forecourt where Ariel stands on tiptoe, forlornly looking out over a fountain that never works.

A glut of celebs step out of rain-sodden taxis onto red carpet – BBC clearly aiming for Oscars feel. Charlie[1] from *Casualty* (H most excited here) then Robin Day and Alan Whicker – both nominated, like me, in Favourite Presenter section. 'We're in competition,' shouts Robin Day, who obviously takes the whole thing quite seriously.

I'm to give the first award for Favourite Sitcom Performer. My envelope contains the name of David Jason. Give him the rather skinny,

1 Charlie Fairhead, played by Derek Thompson.

skimpy likeness of Ariel and a hug for old times' sake. Next year will be the thirtieth anniversary of *Do Not Adjust*.[1]

Other winners, chosen by the public in a telephone poll, show that, generally speaking, it's the shows they remember most recently that win. So *Men Behaving Badly* collects the award for Favourite Situation Comedy Ever on the BBC – beating *Fawlty Towers*, *Porridge*, *Hancock* and *Steptoe* – and making a farce of the whole thing.

Des Lynam wins Best Presenter Ever, beating out Richard Dimbleby's challenge with the first report from Belsen in 1945.

Attenborough loses out to Des Lynam. Python to Victoria Wood.

Friday, November 1st

News of *Fierce Creatures*. Word is that the Monday screening and 'focus group' out on Long Island didn't go well. Only 58% returned the good to very good. Fred [Schepisi] then edited out ten minutes that weren't working and scores went up by 15% on the Wednesday screening.

So, after all these years of time, energy, money and hard graft, *'FC'* looks likely to be a 90-minute quickie, its shape and content decided eventually by 20 people in Long Island. JC's 'message' scenes – all his in-dignation at the system, his invective against the modern management style – have virtually disappeared.

Saturday, November 2nd: London–Edinburgh

To King's Cross to catch the twelve o'clock.

Strong winds in Edinburgh. Walk from Waverley to the Caledonian through Princes Street Gardens, quite an effort against Force-8 gale, but worth it just to take in the big, bold, jagged shapes of the city.

To the Scottish National Gallery of Modern Art in a very fine, august, black-granite classical building on Bedford Road.

The Anne Redpath Exhibition, to which I've loaned two works, is wonderfully rich – shows what a versatile, determined and talented woman she was. My 'Menton' has found two friends – both painted during the same visit in 1949 – and the much-admired 'Blue Tablecloth' is next to one in similar ice-blue style. Feel rather like a proud parent at

1 David Jason was one of the cast of *Do Not Adjust Your Set* (1967-9) along with Terry Jones, Eric Idle, Denise Coffey and me.

speech day as I eavesdrop on people pausing in front of my paintings.

Meet Eleanor Yule and Mhairi McNeill from BBC Scotland who want me to present a half-hour film on Redpath. Our feelings much the same about treatment – so agree to go next June.

Sunday, November 3rd: Edinburgh–London

Read the papers and look out over the grey slate roofs and stern stone walls of the city, and beyond them the scudding waters of the Firth of Forth. The view is bathed in sharp sunshine one minute, the roofs and walls black and oily with rain the next.

To the gallery at eleven. Philip Long, the young man whom I've dealt with on the exhibition, is there to show me round before it opens to the public. A more restful way to see the Redpaths – and in natural light as well. Philip says she was greatly influenced by the early Renaissance painters she saw in Florence, then later by Van Gogh, Vuillard and Bonnard.

Upstairs there is a fine, small selection of Picassos and good Scots Colourists like Peploe and Fergusson and the smoothly elegant Cadell.

A journalist from the *Scotsman*, a New Zealander called Susan Nick-alls, arrives to ask me some questions about the pictures and Palin and art. She drives me to a café to talk. It is set on a cobbled hill near some of the most expensive property in Edinburgh. Sitting at the window with fresh flowers on the table and a stone wall and leafy patch of lawn outside, I feel we would fit into a painting rather well.

Tuesday, November 5th

BT ring to try and get me to do an advertising film – one of a pair – Whoopi Goldberg 'pretty certain' to be doing the other. Say no. Anne says that this same man rings almost every year to try and interest me in becoming a BT salesman.

Wednesday, November 6th

To the Royal Television Society Gala – dread word again – to mark 60 years of television.

Alan Whicker is one of the first people we see. After greeting each other, Alan stretches out a hand and tucks my errant collar down beneath my jacket. Somehow it was a touching gesture. Paternal really – as if I were his offspring and he was in some way responsible for me – which in a way is all quite true.[1]

Thursday, November 7th

Into the West End to have my photograph taken with Helen's surgeon, Michael Powell, at the National Hospital. Both of us, at his request, to be dressed as per his favourite Python sketch – the Gumby brain surgeons.

He's brought along what Gumby kit he can muster, in a carrier bag. So find myself in a most surreal situation; dressed in gumboots, knotted handkerchief and brandishing a surgical steel bradawl above the head of one of Britain's leading brain surgeons.

After it's done we remove our gumboots and hankies and he offers to show me the theatre in which H had her op. We go through into a small, narrow room, when he breaks off – 'Oh dear, there's someone in here.' We both peer round the door and there is indeed someone in there, shrouded in hospital green, laid at a 45° angle with a surgeon working in their spotlit head. Powell is quite unfazed; exchanges some boisterous greetings, which are returned from one of the masked figures around the body.

Sunday, November 17th: Suffolk

By 9.30, when we leave for Suffolk, the rain has begun. Progress is smooth and we are at Sudbury by eleven. Find Derek Taylor's turn-off, through low-lying meadowland on the road to Long Melford.

An old, weather-boarded Suffolk mill house, full of character, and with a tributary of the Stour running nearby. Today in the rain, with ducks ruffing and puffing and standing on their heads in the water, it seems almost to be floating. Comfortable rooms full of engaging bits of bric-a-brac as well as some good Clarice Cliff[2] pieces.

Derek is a little thinner maybe, but his complexion is ruddy and he does not look like someone who has inoperable stomach cancer. Of course they did operate and apparently his stomach is, as a result, up

---

1 Alan Whicker was the first to be approached to present *Around the World in 80 Days*. He turned it down.
2 Clarice Cliff (1899-1972) was one of the best-known Art Deco ceramics designers.

near his heart, but he had no chemotherapy, or further 'killer' surgery. Despite the Beatles offering him the best that money could buy, Derek ended up with the surgeon at the West Suffolk Hospital whom he liked and trusted.

The quality of his life, he thinks, is immeasurably better now than if he had had further, expensive chemical treatment. His wit isn't dimmed, but he is noticeably more frail.

He has several stacks of videotapes – many containing snippets of old news broadcasts or documentary programmes like *Yesterday's Men*, which with great prescience he recorded and kept.

He's still working on Beatle projects – setting up interviews with the Fab Three.

Monday, November 18th

A totally unsolicited catalogue from a coin dealer. I ring and complain that I have never bought coins and don't want any more catalogues from them. A bored man at the other end is quite unapologetic. 'We've recently rented some names from an outside agency,' he tells me, chillingly.

Friday, November 22nd

A rush of sorts in the evening as the lookalike BAFTA award which Helen's friend has made as our present is not ready until 20 minutes before the cab comes to take us off to Roger Mills' 60th birthday.

First person I see as I pass Roger his mock award is Eddie Mirzoeff, Chairman of BAFTA.

Peter Bazalgette,[1] a life-and-soul-looking fellow with a colourful waistcoat, has arranged a *This Is Your Life* for Rog and would like me to take part. 'I'll point to you,' he organises, 'and then you can tell a few stories about Roger. That's all there is to it.'

I begin my contribution with Roger's immortal words – '"Michael, I wouldn't ask you to do anything I wouldn't do myself" (pause). Which is why I've been dressed in drag, rubber, Maori loincloths …' Roger roars with laughter throughout – he is his own best audience.

---

1 Peter Bazalgette, television producer, led the successful independent company Endemol, which produced *Big Brother*. Appointed Chair of the Arts Council in 2013.

Thursday, November 28th

Shoulder pain wakens me again, in the night. Hunted feel – the end of a month looms – the *Full Circle* book is well behind targets.

Run, with difficulty. After the schoolboys shouting 'Knees up, Grandad' last week, I have an elderly passing stranger remarking 'Old feet getting flatter aren't they?'

Want to kill him, but can't stop.

Friday, December 6th

Evening out at Vasco and Piero's with Mary and Edward.

There are still some diners there from lunchtime. One, halfway through a stumbling phone call on his mobile, holds the phone up to me. 'Here!' he slurs. 'Say something to the wife!'

I lean into the phone and say 'You'd better come and get your husband, he's making an awful fool of himself.'

Friday, December 20th

To Pinewood in pouring rain. In Theatre 7 for a sound editors' final screening of *Fierce Creatures*. Wonderful way to see it for the first time. Big screen, empty theatre.

Jerry Goldsmith's music gives an immediate big-movie buzz. It isn't great music or anything, it just has a bustling, Dolby-filling confidence about it.

It's a short film now – 93 minutes – stripped of all pretensions, and generally honed to comedy scenes that deliver good farce and well-hit one-liners. It's a solid, aggressive piece of work. Kevin and Jamie attack; John defends well; and I'm quite sidelined, stuck amongst the keepers. The keepers collective in *Fierce Creatures* fulfils the same sort of role as Ken Pile in *Wanda*.

Sunday, December 22nd

JC calls from Santa Barbara. Opinions of the film seem good. In fact he says the French distributor has predicted that it could do even better there than *Wanda* because it's broader comedy. There has been a review in a US magazine which calls it, not a sequel, but in every way an equal of *Wanda*, so JC feeling cautiously relaxed about it.

Out to dinner being given for Julian and Merron at the house of a friend. Turns out to be a very big house in Maida Vale. The host is a smooth, well-preserved American called John Knight, who is 56 and just back from a trek up Kilimanjaro, and his wife, Donna, attractive in a friendly, un-intimidating way. She has co-produced plays with Julian.

Tom Courtenay and his wife there. We touch briefly on the radio production of *The Dresser*, but it was clear that Courtenay found more satisfaction working with Albert Finney[1] than Freddie Jones.

Feel a sort of kinship to Courtenay. He, like me, prefers the quieter, more understated roles. He's not a shouter and prancer. I'm stunned to learn that he's 59. He has such a boyish, mischievous quality, I've always had him down as a closer contemporary.

---

1 Albert Finney was chosen to play 'Sir' in the film version of *The Dresser*.

1997

Wednesday, January 1st

Was preparing for another Far Eastern departure this time a year ago, and have hardly stopped since then; can look back on five episodes filmed and many thousands of miles covered, a three-week re-shoot of *Fierce Creatures* and over 100,000 words of a new book completed.

It's maybe too early to tell if it's permanent, but I have felt different after completing a year's Pacific filming. A great wave of relief came over me after that.

I have felt a real sense of freedom, and a sense that I am much more in control of things – or perhaps it's just that I'm happy with my life – I'm happy to be what I am and spend much less time on what I want to be.

Saturday, January 4th

The next worry doesn't take long to present itself. It slides into my bed, insinuates itself as I have my head still on the pillow – both H and myself confined to the house, our tennis and running cut short by the hard, unyielding winter weather.

It's the 'Palin's Pacific' problem that will not go away. I cannot reconcile myself to it as a title – just possibly for a TV series, though certainly not for a book – and I know that I must face my worries this weekend, and come to a conclusion, for after Monday I shall be off round the world on *Fierce Creatures* business and will have little time or opportunity to affect matters here. This is my last chance to put up or shut up.

I ring Roger. He is aware of my reluctance to go with 'Palin's Pacific'. Strangely, it was something he said when I called him at the end of the year which started this whole train of thought running again. Roger's mother hadn't liked the title at all. 'It sounds as if he owns it,' she'd said.

'Does Pacific have to be in the title?' he replies to my suggestion of 'Pacific Circle'. 'If it doesn't then we could go back to *Full Circle*.' This strikes an immediate chord, for some reason it sounds and feels right, even though it was Clem's original suggestion and had long been abandoned.

Sunday, January 5th

Wake with acute indecision in early hours of the morning. *Full Circle* can't be right, it's not strong enough, and has no notion of where we are. 'Pacific' has to be in there.

I now know exactly what is meant by an agony of indecision, for I suffered physical manifestations of my tortured internal debate. At one point actually got out of bed again and walked into the bathroom, silently moaning.

Pester H about the title. She advises me to stand firm on *Full Circle*. Doesn't like the compromise – 'Pacific Circle'. 'Too difficult to say.'

At a Twelfth Night drinks party, someone asks if I've heard this morning's *Desert Island Discs*. John has chosen me as his 'luxury object'. Feel vaguely disreputable.

Tom comes round. Without asking him I notice he looks at the two possible new titles which I've printed up and stuck on my wall. '*Full Circle*, I like that,' he says with gratifying and unsolicited enthusiasm.

So the day of doubt comes to an end, with family having the prime say in the matter.

Tuesday, January 7th: New York

Call Anne. *Full Circle* has met with varying degrees of approval – from the editing rooms who were unimpressed, through Eddie who liked it, through Paul Hamann, Head of Documentaries, who wasn't so keen right up to Michael Jackson, Controller of BBC One, who liked it most of all. He wants it, as it is, without a subtitle, which was what I had hoped.

Wednesday, January 8th: New York

Across the park by taxi to Julian Schlossberg's apartment in the San Remo building on Central Park West. Marbled reception area of serious munificence – like a dream of old New York wealth. Approach to apartment poky, but opens onto big, wide rooms which are prevented from being grand and impersonal by careful use of big pieces of antique furniture. A massive refectory table stands laid like an altar with candles already burning.

A young man, who I'm much surprised to hear is 50, engages me in that sort of sharp, slightly gruffly humorous way affected by well and privately educated East Coast Americans. It turns out he's squiring Elaine May.[1]

Talk to Elaine M about many things. She remembers *The Missionary* fondly – says that people should make movies like that which have the author's stamp and not the producer's. Not impressed by the *Fierce Creatures* subway campaign. 'The subway's for blacks and Englishmen.'

Thursday, January 9th: New York

At 11.30 Jean Glass from BBC Worldwide Americas and her Vice-President of Public Relations, disconcertingly called Joe Kennedy, come to the hotel to meet up before we all go to see St Martin's Press, who will be handling the *Full Circle* book in the US.

We taxi down to St Martin's to meet Thomas Dunne. He has an office in the Flatiron Building – right on the apex of the triangle. Exciting view of New York to the north and across to the Hudson. Views of the old wood-cladded water tanks on a vista of roofs gives this aspect of New York a nineteenth-century feel.

Tom is middle-aged, ruddy-complexioned and approaches with an amused, ironic expression on his face. Young men from surrounding offices have clustered in to meet me. 'We never had this with Joan Collins,' cracks Dunne, who looks a joker.

Friday, January 10th: New York

Picked up by car and travel with John C, huge, bearded, capped and wrapped in a great cloak like Nanook of the North. To the once very familiar 50th Street entrance of NBC in Rockefeller Center. We are to be guests on *Saturday Night Live*.

Up to the studio where rehearsals are under way. Bobby the floor manager is still there and lean, grey-haired, dour Phil on lights is now white-haired, dour Phil. Otherwise the writers are the usual preppy bunch of amiable twenty-somethings. The same cue-card technique still used. Kevin Spacey is the host.

Sit next to JC at a desk and rehearse through a longish cold opening

---

1 Elaine May, American actress, writer and director best known for her comedy partnership with Mike Nichols.

which features JC, myself as anchorman with Lorne Michaels, explaining new censorship rules for TV. We're required later to rehearse the 'Dead Parrot Sketch'.

A small group of people, including Lorne and Spacey, gather around the set with something uncomfortably close to reverence on their faces as they watch us work it through. It is still funny and we do play it well so I leave fairly happy that we shall cope tomorrow night, despite a heavy day on *Fierce Creatures* publicity.

Saturday, January 11th: New York

Car pick-up from my hotel at 8.15. Snow has fallen again – maybe only an inch or so, but enough to make Central Park look tempting. But I only see it from a window high in the Essex House.

Jamie didn't much like the film when she saw it in LA but this morning she concedes that 'people' will like it. As usual she paces like a lion, squawks like a mynah and exudes a terrific, irrepressible bubbling combativity. She wants something, or someone, to take on.

We are all taken to our separate rooms (marketing, being the science it now is, has learnt that group interviews are costly and wasteful). In my room are two high chairs, two video cameras, the top of my bee costume, a big lemur photo, a poster of the movie and an illuminated tableau of stuffed lemurs.

In addition to the two camera operators there is a tape operator and a studio manager who explains the rules – six minutes only – and times each encounter.

The word is only good. The media saw the movie last night and, from what I can tell, all of them enjoyed it. So the questioning is curious but not hostile and by the end of a further 25 interviews I'm beginning to think, like the journalists, that we are a 'special group' – that there is 'a chemistry' between us.

At 6.15 back at the hotel. H has been shopping and spending the afternoon with Nancy and Tim. Only have half an hour with her before yet another limo pick-up and transported to *Saturday Night Live*.

At 11.30 we settle behind our desks, the red camera light shines and I start the edition of '*SNL*' for January 11th 1997 rolling with the words – 'Hello I'm Michael Palin. Please don't applaud, we're short on time.'

'Dead Parrot' duly executed about 12.40 a.m. The parrot bounces off the counter and falls on the floor when JC throws it up. This unsettles him and for a line or two he loses the rhythm. There isn't a lot of audience response, but we are performing it with our backs to them.

Head hits pillow at two a.m.

Helen's best memory is of walking out through the crowds of 20 or 30 autograph hunters, and hearing one of them turn gleefully away. 'I've got Michael Palin's autograph!' To which his friend says 'What about John Cleese?'

'Which one's he?'

'The tall one with the hat.'

Sunday, January 26th

Straight into the West End for the cast and crew screening of *Fierce Creatures* at the Empire Leicester Square.

Lots of people to clap arms around and celebrate with. It's only when I talk to Alyce Faye on the stairs that I hear the worst. The takings on the first night in the US were low. It sounds as if the unthinkable might have happened, and that the *Wanda* magic has not struck twice.

I accompany JC and Alyce to the Ivy for brunch. Everything seems suddenly sour. The Ivy is not serving for another hour, says a man at the door. JC says that an appointment had specially been made on his behalf. The man asks, 'Well, who are you?'

Inside eventually, we sit and hear the melancholy news. *Variety*, the *New York Times*, four and a half thumbs-up from Ebert, and a clutch of other good reviews did not seem to make much of an impression on Middle America, where awareness levels of the film amongst the young remained low despite TV campaigns, etc. So – good in San Francisco, bad in Detroit and Dallas.

Thursday, January 30th

Glum, grey weather. Torpid winter morning. Ugly smell to the air. At 8.45 off to London Zoo to be photographed for a *Daily Mirror* piece.

Warm, damp atmosphere at the insect house. Am photographed with a cricket-eating spider, smaller than Terry the Tarantula. Dave, in typical keeper fashion, tells me that tarantula is a word 'only those Americans' use. The spider I worked with in the film was a bird-eating spider.

Promised the insect man (sorry, the Invertebrate Conservation

Officer) that if I made any money from this film I would put some of it towards expansion of the insect, sorry, invertebrate quarters.

Monday, February 3rd

I set to work on the commentary for the first episode of *Full Circle*. For a moment I'm immobilised, unable to face the first few frames, frozen by the significance of it all. What I write in these next couple of hours will probably be the most quoted commentary of the series. Critics usually watch first episodes only.

Saturday, February 8th

JC rings from Santa Barbara.

There is not much good news. Exit polls only average. He seemed surprised by the big drop in Australia – as though he might not have known about it. JC will not take a tax year out, but will sell Ladbroke Road and live, quite comfortably, he suggests, off the proceeds. He sounds almost relieved. He says there has rarely been a morning in the last two years when he has woken up looking forward to working on the film.

Thursday, February 20th

Bouncing out of my *Fierce Creatures* interview with Michael Owen in the *Evening Standard* has come an over-dramatised, much-embellished account of Helen's illness a year ago. It has now become, by turns, 'life-threatening' and I 'rushed to her bedside'. Michael O just about drew the conclusion that I would not be doing any more travelling because of H's illness.

The *Daily Mail* wants to put a reporter on to do a serious 'H tells the world' piece. H is not keen and wants to forget about it.

Friday, February 21st

Meet two UIP reps who tell me that *Fierce Creatures* has not done half badly here, taking 1.13 million in first week. All the bad reviews seem confined to the papers I read!

Thursday, February 27th

To the editing rooms to view prog five with Clem. He has a tape of some of the map sequences. My first impression of the opening swoop is that, in their primary-colour stylisation of the earth's surface, Australia comes out, perversely, as bright green. If ever there were a case for red, brown or even yellow, surely this was it.

Another problem has to be faced – the vexed question of an extra show to fit in all the wonderful material from South America.

We stay until nearly eight o'clock to look at programme eight in a rough 64-minute assembly. It is strong – Cuzco, train journeys, Machu Picchu – but only takes us to the other side of the Pongo Rapids and first sight of the Amazon. Logically this should mean that the next and last episode – nine – would go from Peru to Alaska, which is obviously ridiculous.

I suggest contacting the BBC as soon as possible to tell them that it does now look as if we have the material for another programme. I know Michael Jackson, Controller of One, will be at *Showcase* next week and though this might be a time to mention it, it might be best to ask Paul Hamann to sound him out first.

Friday, February 28th

At the editing rooms find Roger out of sorts. He's had a cold for three weeks and last night put his back out. Discuss the extra prog issue in the light of what I saw last night. Decide to call Paul H. Asks various questions and then agrees to have a word with Michael Jackson. Rings back a couple of hours later to say that Jackson would be prepared to find a ten-prog slot in return for a joke about me to use in his intro at BBC *Showcase* on Monday night!

Meanwhile, Eddie, whom we've called but has been out all morning, rings. Eddie is 'pissed off' that he was not consulted before we spoke to Paul. What a nightmare it is entering the minefield of an hierarchical organisation like the BBC.

Wednesday, March 5th

At 12.30 I'm picked up on a Limobike – a luxury motorbike taxi which has to take me swiftly through London traffic to the Park Lane Hotel to collect a special Python award from *Empire*, the film magazine. An outrider bike has a photographer snapping away as we wend our way round Cavendish Square and down Bond Street.

Elton John gives us an award for 'inspiration'. John and Eric on video from California. JC particularly good. Gives medical info on us all. TG already dead – being represented here today by his Mexican twin. Terry J has had series of massive heart attacks and has come here on one of his last days alive. I'm still around but have you seen these, he asks, and holds up what he claims are my latest chest X-rays. He taps a detail on the photo – 'This is not good.'

Thursday, March 13th

With H to see Mr Powell for a year's check-up at the National Hospital. There is a hole where the tumour used to be which is now full of water. Powell says it was definitely orange-size. 'Won the award for best meningioma of '96,' he added cheerily.

Having reassured Helen that he wouldn't need to see her for another five years he gets down to the real business, which is having me sign some of the photographs of him and me as Gumbys in one of the operating theatres.

Sunday, March 16th

To the Barbican to see 'Modern Art in Britain 1910–1915' exhibition. A small collection of greats by Cézanne, Van Gogh, Gauguin, Picasso and Matisse, Derain, Vuillard, Bonnard and others is the bedrock of an exhibition which shows how English painting of the period was influenced.

It does make the English response to the outpourings of great work from Europe seem inadequate, mean, spinsterly stuff. Vanessa Bell and Duncan Grant do their best. Roger Fry is more homage than talent. Sickert comes out well – at least you felt a great unqualified appetite for life there – but no-one else seems to match Matisse's and Picasso's lusty enthusiasm and celebratory sensuousness, or Van Gogh or Derain's way with colour.

Basil arrives with the layout of *Full Circle – The Photographs* which he takes to the BBC tomorrow. It's a crisp, clean, cool book with photos of cloud formations which I fear will have BBC sales reps' hearts plunging.

Monday, March 24th

Out to supper at the Caprice with Richard Loncraine and Felice.

Unpleasant end to evening. Our taxi smashed into outside the restaurant by a van driven by a young peroxide-blond man with bare feet. Slammed quite hard into side of us, crushing driver's door and pushing us across Arlington Street. Then a strange and surreal slow-motion scene – or so it seemed – as one of the clutch of photographers outside the restaurant came across, stuck his camera up at the window and started taking flash photographs of a shocked Helen and myself, sitting in the back.

Then the photographer came round the other side, snapped happily away at the two of us – dazzling and further disorientating us. He then grinned at me and said in what sounded like a Spanish or Portuguese accent: 'Scare?' I'm afraid I let him have a piece of quite sustained verbal. Told him he should go and do something useful. He whined on about 'only doing a job' before retreating back to his pack.

Monday, March 31st

At 8.15 I climb up my spiral staircase and onto the gravelled roof and there, as H suggested, is the Hale-Bopp comet in the north-western sky. Quite clearly visible to the naked eye. The surprise is just how large it is – the tail, especially, is much fuller than I had expected. Put the binoculars onto it. Can see the nucleus – white and round and tiny compared to the billowing tail around and behind it – not long and slim but thick and chunky. I think this is the first time in my life I've seen a comet. It is as close to Earth as it comes – around 125 million miles away – and will not be seen again for 4,000 years.

Monday, April 7th

Weekend spent working on commentary for seven. This is one process which can never be hurried. However fresh, bright and rested I may be, it is still a plod. Odd and perverse bits of editing trip me up and stall any momentum. Facts must be checked again. Maux mots turned into bons. And so on.

Rachel, revising modern British politics, came to 1979, the year Thatcher was first elected. The year of the last Labour government. She asked me what I remembered of it. I looked it up in my diary, found May 3rd, day of the election. Not a mention!

Tuesday, April 8th

Eddie calls to say he has spoken to Paul Hamann and *Full Circle* is now officially a ten-part series.

Friday, April 11th

To lunch with TG. Nick Cage, after being difficult for so long, is happy to do 'Defective Detective' next spring and in the UK as TG wanted. This left a gap this summer, but this appears to have been fortuitously filled for him by the firing of Alex Cox from *Fear and Loathing in Las Vegas*. Ralph Steadman and others have asked TG to step in and take over at the last minute – Johnny Depp is in place, they have money. TG off to the States to set it up – says it's just what he needs now – an injection of good, bubbling, last-minute adrenaline.

Tuesday, April 22nd

Mhairi and Eleanor, the two feisty ladies from BBC Scotland who want me to present a documentary about Anne Redpath, come round. They love the house and I can see (and hear) them occasionally slip into professional talk about lights, angles, etc. in that rather detached way, like doctors discussing a patient in bed.

Eleanor sounds a sharp director and Mhairi has excellent observation – noticing things in my paintings that I never have.

To Parkin's in Motcomb Street for Stephen Tumim's private view of paintings by prisoners. People spilling out onto the pavement. Looming above most of them is Patrick Procktor. He extends a long, bony hand and introduces me to some bewildered Asians standing beside him – 'This is our star explorer.'

Push my way into the throng. A familiar-looking man, tall, less elegant than Procktor, turns out not to be familiar at all. He's an ex-con who did four years for drug-dealing and learnt to paint in prison.

I ask which he's painted. One is a big, bold, red Bacon-like piece of three men and a door, called 'Bouncers'. It's a 'must-buy', and I struggle through the wonderful mixed crowd of Belgravians and crop-headed ex-prisoners and secure it for £1,100. Later Stephen goes round telling people I've bought the best picture in the place.

Wednesday, April 23rd

Family tree sent by relative shows Scots great-grandparents on Mum's side. Her grandfather, a Chapman, invented the lighthouse reflector.

Saturday, April 26th

In the evening we go round to the Tooks' for dinner with David Attenborough. His daughter Susan is there. Unmarried, very pleasant company – education consultant. Susan talks about inheriting and having to make sense of all the work that Jane used to do in running David's affairs.[1] He hasn't and never has had an agent.

David and I talk about making programmes – putting people at their ease, making contact, etc. D thinks that sex is a universal reference point. There is a bit of the schoolboy about him, which alongside his perception, intelligence and articulacy could be seen as a bit of a character flaw, but makes for an attractive mix.

On our way out David pauses to enthuse over the marble panels by the front door of the mansion block. 'Look at those!' he cries, jabbing a finger at fossil shapes by the doorbell and running off a number of unpronounceable names. 'Four hundred and fifty million years old!' he declares. 'Isn't that the age of the Earth?' 'No, no ... that's billion – four and a half billion.'

That's the difference between Attenborough and me. He knows it. I'm always learning.

Tuesday, April 29th

Prepare myself for the BAFTAs. I have agreed to present an award but not stay for the meal.

At the Albert Hall by 5.45.

Once inside shown to a hot, airless room below the ground where celebrity presenters gather. Richard Wilson is there. Beneath his

1 David's wife Jane died earlier in the year.

jacket he has a fat Labour rosette which he is plotting to reveal on the podium.

Michael Caine, with Shakira, looms over everybody except Stephen Fry. Michael says it's a great time to be in England – 'snooker, cricket, football and the election, all on the same day'.

Frost and Clive James work the room briskly. Helen Mirren loves to give and receive attention. Eddie Izzard arrives, wearing nothing under his dinner jacket. His arrival animates almost everybody. They love him, especially Helen M.

I'm out fourth. My winner (for Best Comedy) is *Only Fools and Horses*. John Sullivan in a dreadful state of nerves, despite this being his third BAFTA for the series.

Thursday, May 1st

The six-week election campaign is over. The *Today* programme is completely devoid of any political stories and the result is rather eerie. Everything and everyone we've heard virtually non-stop for the past one and a half months has been silenced.

To the polling station at Gospel Oak. Almost everyone going in and out at this time of day is elderly. They greet me with great friendliness. It's like giving blood. We're all doing our duty and feeling virtuous. Consider Lib-Dems. I believe them to be the most honest and least divided of all the parties, but tactically as much as anything put my X opposite Glenda Jackson's name.[1]

Work on until the polls close at ten, then settle to watch the results. It's pretty clear from exit polls that the Conservatives have been walloped, and that I shall be witnessing something I haven't seen since I was 31 years old, the election of a Labour government.

The scale of the victory gradually unfolds. It's almost exactly as the polls had been predicting, for months and years. Still, the hours between one o'clock and Michael Portillo's demise around three are breathless and dramatic. Stories which would one by one have occupied the headlines for two or three days now come concentrated in a deluge of less than two hours.

Malcolm Rifkind and Portillo and Sir Marcus Fox, three faces representing the solid, confident leadership of the country, are all forced to

1 She won the Hampstead and Highgate seat with 57 per cent of the vote.

eat humble pie[1] – not for once allowed the security of their own people, their own slogans, their own lighting, their own spin doctors; they are tonight, as near as possible, naked before the people. Reduced, in shabby public halls, to standing beside men dressed as chickens and other no-hopers who reckon the deposit will have been worth it just to stand on the stage behind a famous man.

Shy, almost apologetic little smiles are the order of the day. It's as if the game is up. They've been caught. They needed to throw a six to win but they could muster only a one.

Cecil Parkinson very funny. Asked if there will now be much squabbling amongst the Conservatives replies 'I don't think we've got enough people for a squabble.'

By the time my head hits the pillow my countrymen have elected the youngest Prime Minister this century. The once-groggy and near-dormant Labour Party, reeling after repeated blows from the electorate, has bounced back to reduce the Conservatives to their smallest number since, I'm told, the days of Lord Liverpool.

No wonder I can't sleep for a while.

Friday, May 2nd

John Major announces his resignation and goes off to watch cricket at the Oval, and little Blair, for whom the chipmunk comparison is quite the most accurate, goes to kiss the Queen's hand. A student of kissing would have had a field day watching the body language up and down the country last night. Cherie, awkward, feeling she had to be seen to be overwhelmed with a physical desire to merge with her husband. Would Kenneth Clarke kiss his wife? It seemed inconceivable and was. The Kinnocks were the best public kissers.

Thursday, May 8th

We fit commentary ten on the Avid.[2] It's much faster in one way, no reel changes, footage adjustments, unspooling to fit leader tape or rearrange

---

1 Malcolm Rifkind, Michael Portillo, Sir Marcus Fox, Conservative grandees, all of whom lost their seats as Labour under Tony Blair ended eighteen years of Conservative government, gaining a majority of 179.

2 Avid, developed in America in 1989, is a computerised, non-linear editing system. This was the first time we'd used it.

a sequence, but at the same time the material seems less precious and unique – just a series of random images on an electronic machine.

The 'frame' is no longer as important as 'the look'. I, being a Romantic where technology is concerned, miss working surrounded by the comforting background of celluloid strips, the outward and visible evidence of our work.

Sunday, May 11th

Up for a run at eight. In West Meadow a harmless-looking beige Labrador lollops towards me and delivers a sharp nip to the back of my left leg. I'm not moving fast, there's no question of shock or surprise, or even aggression on the dog's part; he just came over and bit me. His owner is a lean, quite elderly man I frequently see. He doesn't seem much put out. 'I'll give him a good hiding,' he says, with a grin.

Run on. Lloyd Dorfman[1] is walking up Lime Avenue. He's most concerned by the news, says I should go to hospital and have a tetanus jab. Run on for quite a way in nervous apprehension of my body suddenly freezing in mid-motion, before I remember that I'm covered for tetanus until 1998.

Thursday, May 15th

To supper with JC. I remembered, at the last minute, that it was exactly two years ago today that *Fierce Creatures* began shooting. John gave an ironic smile. 'Oh God, that film!' he said, affecting pain at the memory.

He's comfortable. He doesn't need anything else. He's finally shaken off material things and seems on the verge of what he's always wanted – time to learn and listen.

I've heard this many times and know that John's ability to cut himself off from the world is about as likely as Tony Blair retiring from politics. But I do know what he's struggling to get away from – which is dealing with people of average intelligence and ability. JC is a thoroughbred and if he can't win, he'll pretend winning doesn't matter. He wants to do 'some trips' with me. 'Go on a few jaunts.'

---

1 Lloyd Dorfman, founder of Travelex, the foreign exchange business.

Friday, May 16th

Call from Will to say that he has been offered a place at the Courtauld on their History of Architecture course. This despite an interview on Tuesday at which he admitted he did not shine. But they seem to have seen through his nervousness and he has achieved what he's been after for almost two years.

I receive a letter from the Royal Geographical Society inviting me to participate in some daunting seminar about the future role of Geography ... 'As you hold a key position in our national life.' Could this be me they were referring to? I've never felt less like someone occupying a key position in anything.

To celebrate Will's news at V and P.

Vasco is quietly chuffed about the election victory. I tell him that there could be a New Year's Honour on the way. He says John Cunningham has been in three times since the election. 'And he is the Minister for fish,' V points out, 'and that he comes here for his fish, makes me feel very good.'

Tuesday, May 20th

Ring Eric to check on time of arrival at Cliveden for the Python summit tomorrow. I have a glimpse of what to expect when I tell him that I met JC last week and didn't think he sounded keen on the new film project. 'Well he can write to *Time* magazine and explain why he thought it was such a good idea two months ago.' E clearly cross that JC had gone public to *Time* mag over E's film idea.[1]

Later out to launch of new publishing venture started by the *Modern Painters* people.

I fall into a chat with David Bowie, who is there as one of the co-financiers of the venture.

He is very comfortable and relaxed, adept, I suppose, at creating around him an oasis of ordinary, everyday life, whilst being the goldfish at the centre of the bowl. Talk about Sickert. Bowie thinks his later work – like the graphic, inspired high-kicking chorus line, or the 'Camden Town Murders' – v. impressive. 'I mean, who would do

---

1 Eric had suggested a possible updating of *The Holy Grail* using the same knights twenty years older, embarking on a crusade.

that nowadays without howls of outrage from the newspapers?'

He looks good. Hair dyed carrot-orange and spiky, wearing a woolly purple polo-neck jersey – blithely confident that it doesn't matter what the hell he wears. He is the man. He sets the style.

He now lives in New York. He used to be in Switzerland. His wife Iman says that the beautiful thing about Somalia, where she comes from, is the people not the landscape. In Switzerland, she says, it's the opposite.

Wednesday, May 21st: London–Cliveden

Pack and drive up to Cliveden for the Python get-together. Terry G, hair drawn tight back in grey ponytail, is there with Eric and Terry J in the vast hall of this immodest house.

Eric draws up an agenda and we discuss the film idea first. Four of us clearly interested in proceeding, cautiously, with the 'Last Crusade' idea. John yawns a lot and at one point actually nods off. For half an hour the ideas pour out. Not always very good, but there is much of the old Python energy and mischief still there, and, amongst the four of us, a real comic empathy.

The stage show in Las Vegas is talked about on JC's return. I am the least keen on this one; everyone else, bar Terry G, moderately enthusiastic. I'd rather put our energy and efforts into new material which acknowledges that things have changed.

Nothing decided. JC has thawed out a little and four of us go on a walk down to the river and round the estate.

We stroll along past the red Victorian boathouses and gamekeepers' cottages where Profumo strolled with Christine Keeler. Terry J then goes for a swim, I go up to my room – the Prince of Wales Suite.

Have a bath in most wonderfully deep enamel, grey-marble-topped tub, and feel gloriously lucky and spoilt.

Can't remember much of the meal.

The usual mutterings about the accounts. TJ especially critical of the amount spent on management, which is almost a third of total profit.

John goes to bed and the rest of us seek out the snooker room and Eric and I take on the Terrys. They are even worse than Eric and myself, who are coasting home to victory when TJ is suddenly transformed into Steve Davis and pots almost everything that's left.

Friday, May 23rd

Anne comes round and we share a taxi down to the Ritz to meet Tom Dunne of St Martin's Press.

Tom is good company, congenial, a little mischievous but enthusiastic. He compliments Anne on the impression she made on everyone at St Martin's when she went to NY two weeks ago, buys us martinis, and is grateful for all our help on publicity, delighted that the PBS schedule has been fixed, delighted to hear that we now have an extra episode and concerned only as to whether he has enough books.

He asks me if I'm ever going to write a novel. I tell him I'll send him a copy of *Hemingway's Chair* to read on the plane back to NYC.

Saturday, May 24th

This is what I have been looking forward to. A plateau of peace and quiet after a week scrambling over rough, unknown terrain.

Ring JC and get Alyce Faye. She's wonderfully indiscreet and seems to say just what comes into her mind.

According to Alyce, John had driven down to the Cliveden meeting 'like thunder'. He hadn't wanted to go and was very worried that we should force him to do things he didn't want to do. He came back, evidently, much happier.

JC attempts to explain his 'contradictory' position. 'If someone like Robin Williams offers me three weeks' work with practically no lines, I'm happy to do it. I just don't think I'm up to another long shoot with all the work that has to go with it.' I point out that the advantage of the Pythons is that we are a group, we have a director, a designer, and several writers with whom he can share the load. And anyway we're not talking about a film till '99.

Tuesday, May 27th

My morning is cheered by a report in the *Guardian* of a man who fell a hundred feet down a hillside trying to avoid a 'bouncing 8lb Double Gloucester cheese'. Actually, his injuries sound quite severe, so I shouldn't really have smiled so much.

Receive a fax from Tom Dunne – handwritten, which is his style – to say that he has read *Hemingway's Chair*. 'Good clean fun' is his three-word assessment. He would like to publish it in the US next spring.

Friday, May 30th: Chilton

Leave home around quarter to ten and stop at Stoke-by-Nayland after an hour and a half. Hottest day of this present high, dry, sunny period.

Sit on a grassy bank in the churchyard, beneath the 120-foot, four-stage tower, and read up my Pevsner. It's been so long since I've done something like this. I suppose my father's constant 'churching' could have put me off, but quite the opposite – it's an appetite of his which I happily share – and have passed on to Will as well.

But this is not a complete, drift-where-you-want day off. I have to check my watch as I stand before the 500-year-old tomb of Anne Windsor, as I'm due at Chilton for lunch.

Oddly enough, I hadn't decided to come here because of the tenth anniversary, yesterday, of Angela's death, but now I'm here, it seems right. I'm not too good at remembering people on special days – my memories of Angela come, unbidden, at pretty regular intervals, and with varying degrees of intensity.

Valerie opens some wine and we eat salmon and new potatoes and raspberries from the garden. More and more of the land surrounding Chilton is being sold off to the burgeoning industrial estate.

Walk round the garden and then go, on my own, across the field to St Mary's Church, which stands, solid and red-bricked, at the very edge of the sea of development. But the approach from the house is still countrified and soothing, and the old church retains its dignity, despite some doors and windows having been boarded up.

Realise, with a shock, that this is probably the first time in ten years that I've seen Angela's grave. A solid, small stone with her name and the name of Mum and Dad on it.

A few minutes later, drive along the pot-holed track to Brundon Mill to see Derek T.

He's in blue-denim shirt and trousers, has lost weight since I last saw him, but his head and mane of well-cut grey hair still striking and not at all bowed by what must be considerable pain. He has his legs on a stool in front of him, and leans back on a pointed cushion which he calls the V-sign. 'Two relatives have already died on it,' he points out. The Taylor smile still firmly intact – eyes and mouth very much alive.

He's listening to a selection of Eric Coates's music. The strains of 'In Town Tonight' and 'Music While You Work' – immortal memories lightly fill the room and outside the sun shines hard on the grass and the surface of the water as it spills over the weir.

After a bit we sit outside. Derek selects a panama hat for me. In the garden he stretches out on a slightly lopsided plastic recliner. He says that now he has to realise that he could be at the top of a steady downward spiral. The cancer is still there – though a couple of recent operations have relieved some of the pain.

His regrets are clearly expressed – emotion well held in check. 'Why me?' is, he says, 'the ignoble thought that does occur'.

But we laugh a lot. Talk about the flashers of our youth. 'Go into any air-raid shelter in West Kirby,' Derek remembers, 'and you'd find a 30-year-old man with an erection.'

Tuesday, June 10th

Redpath documentary filming at the house.

George Bruce, an 88-year-old who made a film on Redpath in 1961, arrives to be interviewed. He is an unstoppable talker. A lively man, great self-dramatist, working poet, Python fan – he genuinely came near to hysterics when I recited 'Parrot Sketch' as we sat out on the benches in the garden.

Eleanor Yule, the director, who has a good, inventive, imaginative way of shooting, was finding it hard work with all the reflecting glass surfaces. And the phone kept ringing.

Friday, June 13th: Cap Ferrat, French Riviera

Today we get to see what lies behind the high stone walls of the Château St Jean, which was the Château Gloria at which Anne Redpath's husband worked as an architect in the 1920s and '30s for an American carburettor millionaire called Thomson. There is a sign on the great timber gates reading 'Chien Très Méchant'.

But the Dubai Ambassador who currently owns it is only here for a month or so and we have been allowed to film in and around it. Two Finnish people act as housekeepers and there is a gardener and a huge, black Great Dane.

The house is more like a pavilion. It's full of objets d'art. Many of the Rococo or Louis Quinze style. Dripping gilt.

Saturday, June 14th: Roquebrussanne

Drive west to the Var. Into green, wooded countryside; wide, flat plains ringed by low forested ridges.

Spend the afternoon filming up at a Carthusian monastery. Father Bruno, one of 14 middle-aged men who live at the monastery, proves to be a hermit of the Python kind. Immensely voluble, humorous, gregarious and apparently worldly. He gives us permission to film inside the monastery itself. It's a celibate order so the producer and director have to wait behind in the 'public' tower at one end of the complex.

Father Bruno laughs heartily as the doors close – 'Now you won't have to obey the ladies for a while.'

Sunday, June 15th: Roquebrussanne–London

Wind rustles the leaves and sets my shutters creaking and banging. Up at eight. Bright morning of clear Provençal sunshine. Breakfast, then set off for Nice Airport.

Full flight arrives back at Heathrow just after lunch. Into taxi, complete with *Sunday Times* which runs the 'Relative Values' piece showing Tom and myself, apparently fused together, growing out of Primrose Hill like Anne Redpath's houses grow out of the hills of Spain, Corsica and the Canary Islands.

Not a bad piece – nothing that makes my heart stop or my face blush. The writer has put words into our mouths and inscribed her own demotic on us. I refer at one point to Tom having been 'such a timid kid'. Eurgh. I'd never say 'kid' like that. But names, details and the general summing-up is accurate and sympathetic.

Monday, June 16th: Edinburgh

A series of shots in and around the New Town – starting in London Street, where Anne came to live at the end of her life (funnily enough, I find myself uncomfortable saying 'Anne'. I have the feeling that she was the sort of person from whom you would have to earn the right to such familiarity). Pass Johnston Terrace and the Castle Arms. It's now

As Bugsy in *Fierce Creatures*. With Robert Lindsay
and our tiger, August 9th, 1995.

Me as a bee with Jamie Lee, on the *Fierce Creatures* re-shoots, August 23rd, 1996.

Gumby brain surgeons. One of them really *is* a brain surgeon. With Michael Powell, the man who saved my wife, National Hospital, London, November 7th, 1996.

With my indispensable travelling companions: leather and canvas bag
with lots of pockets, notebook and pen. *Full Circle*, 1996.

Friends United

ABOVE LEFT: Palin's New Year Party team wearing a selection of my travel hats. Left to right: Phillida Albury, Ian Davidson, Anthea Davidson, Ranji Veling, Mary Burd, MP, Helen P, Simon Albury (where's his hat?) and Edward Burd. New Year's Eve, 1998.

LEFT: Family visit to Greenwich, Christmas 1998. Back row: Will, Tom. Middle row: Helen, Rachel, MP, brother-in-law Edward. Front row: Helen's mother, Anne Gibbins, and two sisters, Cathy and Mary.

ABOVE: New York pals. Left to right: Merron and Julian Schlossberg, Nancy Lewis/Jones, MP, Simon Jones, Sherrie Levy.

RIGHT: Alan Whicker presents me with Best Documentary Award for *Full Circle* at the National Television Awards: '. . . that Whicker should have to present me with the award does sort of bring things, well, full circle' – October 27th, 1998.

Pointing out my hero. With Spike Milligan at the Talkie Awards. The Goon shows were an inspiration and he was given a special award for *The Last Goon Show of All*, November 6th, 1998.

With my tall, funny friend. Almost anywhere – 1988–1998.

32 years since we met Eric Idle of the Footlights for a drink there during the Edinburgh Festival. End up in Newington, a stylish but less flashy end of Edinburgh, where David Michie, Anne R's son, lives.

David Michie paints and I talk to him. With the Digibeta[1] silently working away we can record for 40 minutes without a break, and without the sound man ever having to complain about camera noise.

He's an imposing man with a fine, handsome, strong face. A respectable man of Scottish arts, OBE and wary of any indiscretions. But wheedle out a few good stories and quite a moving last admission about the funeral, and the mistake that he and his brothers might have made in keeping it so plain and simple that no-one even spoke in his mother's honour.

Tuesday, June 17th: Edinburgh–London

An interview with Eileen Michie, who sat for many of Anne's pictures. She says she's always depicted reading a book – which she did because she was so bored. A very lively, intelligent woman, quite a high-powered scientist in the field of hormone research. Born in Hawick, like AR, and married David, her second cousin. They're a busy, aware, alert, rather loving couple. Absolute salt of the earth.

Interview, and my last shot of the film, complete around 1.30.

It has been a pleasure. As good as I hoped. Eleanor, Mhairi and the crew excellent company – Eleanor with a good, fresh eye for the material, a refreshing lack of bullshit and an admirable tenacity in getting what she wants. I think she will do very well.

Wednesday, June 25th

Monster book on 'Success' by Martyn Lewis arrives, via the office. No wonder it wouldn't slip through the letter box, it's a great, fat tome that looks rather like those big sex surveys (Hite, Masters and Johnson) that the Americans were fond of producing in the '70s.

At the start of my interview contribution I resolutely express my unease with the whole premise of the book, but am still accorded 20

---

1 Digibeta short for Digital Betacam, a cassette video camera developed in 1993. Film cameras, which we used for our travel programmes, could only shoot ten minutes of material before changing magazines, but were thought to produce better-quality images.

pages – more than most of the illustrious, rather worthy, mostly male contributors.

Friday, June 27th

Helen is to collect Rachel's things from Oxford this a.m. I'm off to record more commentary.

Then hear just before eight o'clock news that the M40 to Oxford is closed in both directions as a power cable has come down.

Ring H immediately on the mobile, but as I'm doing so, am followed into my parking spot opposite Dillons by police van with flashing blue light. A police lady gets out and, quite pleasantly but firmly, informs me that I'm to be booked for using a mobile while driving (a very new offence, of which I heartily approve).

Into the van as the rain patters down on the roof. Particulars taken. When she asks me to spell my name, the two young policemen with her (v. fresh from cadet school I would think) apologise that 'she's not a Python fan'. As she gets out to check my number plate they apologise again. She's very zealous. Had two people already this morning. They'd have let me off, they assure me!

Monday, June 30th

Basil rings from Hong Kong, ten minutes before the handover. I've been watching solemn Chris Patten, puzzled Prince Charles and inscrutable Tony Blair on the podium for a half hour or so. Rain sheeting down on the outgoing Brits.

Basil is on Cheung Chau and has a crowd of people there for a handover party. 'What you drinkin' Mike?' Bas demands to know. 'Tea,' I lie. I'm not drinking anything. I'm working. He persuades me to fill a glass at this great moment and then, as the National Anthem is played for the last time and the Union Jack descends after 156 years at the top of the Hong Kong masts, to stand up. 'We're all standing up here, Mike.'

Só, half stood up at my desk with a glass of grappa, I salute the end of British rule in Hong Kong. Feel no great tugs of emotion, despite the bands and the *Britannia* and the kilts. I wish the PLA didn't goose-step, and I wish I felt the slightest sympathy for or compatibility with the Chinese who have taken over. But I don't understand them and I feel no real sense of common purpose either.

Change into DJ and out to the Hatchards 200th anniversary party. Suppose I should draw some comfort from the fact that a bookshop has lasted longer than the British in Hong Kong.

A motley collection. Melvyn and Salman move around with the world-weary ironic smile of senior prefects. I'm introduced by Roger Katz, the manager, to Princess Margaret (who, he says admiringly, still comes into the shop to buy her books 'during open hours'). Big wide eyes, an element of flirtatiousness in her responses. A very large tumbler of whisky and water is produced for her.

Find myself thrust into line as she leaves, alongside John Major, who has been eyeing the shelves in a distracted way, frequently alone save for a big girl who is his private secretary. She seizes my hand and introduces me, for the first time in my life, to the ex-PM. His handshake is cool, his face pale and he affects a rather debating society defensiveness – trading cool, patronising quips as though he perceives me as a threat of some sort.

Perhaps he would have thawed out if we'd had more time together, but that is the nature of these events. They are useful for networking, or for making and keeping up superficial acquaintance. Not much more.

Thursday, July 3rd

Low, scummy skies. Clem here at nine just after arrival of rented palm and bamboo plants which he's ordered, in some megalomanic burst of inspiration, for background in one of the video introductions we are to shoot today. He says Eddie Mirzoeff was a changed man after seeing prog nine. Almost sentimental about the series and lyrical about its pleasures – even enquiring as to whether we might do another!

Two of the three introductions are completed quite swiftly – though I do make a Freudian slip – referring at one point to 'only 25,000 meals' instead of miles, to go. This leads to some rapid calculations and the conclusion that Nige and I ate around 850 meals together on this journey.

So quite possibly my last filming with Nige is completed, eight years and ten months since he first filmed me in Stanford's, at the start of *80 Days*.[1]

---

1 We were to do five more series together.

Wednesday, July 16th

Invited to lunch by Geoffrey Strachan at Frederick's in Camden Passage.

Geoffrey keen to pin me down on my writing intentions for next year. Talk over ideas – a possible memoir instead of a fully-fledged novel. Possibly even an 'In Search of Hemingway' travel book.

Heard this morning that Rachel gained a 2:1.

Tuesday, July 22nd

Have promised the day to *Time Out*, who have an idea of doing 'Around the World in 18 Hours' – a tour of all the different cultures in London.

So a big Land Rover arrives for me at ten – with photographer and Scots girl called Elaine Paterson who is Features Editor and reporter on this assignment.

Down to Brixton Market – which is impeccably well kept, clean, attractive and very friendly. If this is what a good riot brings then one wonders why there aren't more of them.[1]

Such delights as The Souls of Black Folk bookshop – a West Indian second-hand bookshop where I pick up a '30s English novel called *Black* and a copy of Charlie Mingus' autobiography which made such an impression on me 25 years ago.

Armenian church in Kensington – and talk to the Archbishop. Incense and Gulbenkian money. Lunch at an Iranian restaurant opposite Cibo. Then to huge Japanese supermarket on the Edgware Road, where Elaine and I play automated electronic downhill ski-racing, eat sushi and drink Kirin beer. Then to the wonderfully elaborate Hindu temple in Neasden. Fantastic building skills opposite the crummiest houses of north-west London.

To the Polish Hearth Club, where the pre-*80 Days* departure dinner was filmed.

High-ceilinged rooms, waitresses with blonde hair and high cheek-bones, slouching men – an air of prosperous negligence.

Then out into the hot and steamy West End. Eat fish, sweet potato and plantain at the Africa Centre – as true to my memories of Africa as the Japanese supermarket was for Japan.

Then out of Africa, and drag our tired limbs to Shaftesbury Avenue

1 There had been major racial disturbances in Brixton in 1981 and again in 1985.

and a salsa club, down below street level. A dancing partner is provided for me. This is like *Full Circle* all over again and I have the same mixture of exhaustion and relief when we have done our final duty and climbed the stairs.

Home by 11.30. Have earned my publicity today.

Saturday, July 26th: Sunset Marquis, Los Angeles

To the Villa Pool and there is Michael (official designation: Villa Pool Butler) who shakes my hand warmly, shows me the three-week-old kittens who have made their home beneath a palm tree and tells me that the old rock and roll bands are using the hotel again. The Eagles are checking in later. 'They're quiet as church mice now,' he adds.

Call Eric and arrange to see him after lunch.

Eric's house looks even bigger on second sight. But big in a sort of disordered, profligate way – rooms spread, sprout and extend all over the place. Dogs yap at my heels. Eric's daughter Lily romps around after them.

Eric is limping – he shrugs off my enquiry. Sit out by the pool. The Connollys call. Billy is a neighbour.

We talk about the film. John remains against it, what do I feel? I still think it offers the best prospect for a Python reunion.

We decide that instead of making the next movie we should spend the money on an ad campaign and trailers only. 'I want you to write some more jailers,' Eric says with feeling.

Sunday, July 27th: Los Angeles

The Ritz Carlton Pasadena is a chillingly well-ordered place – a sort of luxury penitentiary on which the outside world seems hardly to impinge. Thick carpets, lush but characterless gardens, an attempt at French classical style for no real reason.

Then the centrepiece of the day, and my raison d'être for the trip – the *Full Circle* presentation. I'm on stage before 60 or 70 journalists who have been through three weeks of such presentations. Kathy Quattrone, Chief Exec of PBS, tall, in powder-blue suit, introduces me as a 'Renaissance man' in a long, droning preamble which means I have ground to recover right from the start. But we get some laughs and they applaud at the end, which I'm told happens very rarely.

A party out on the terrace at which I meet an ebullient black man with chest and stomach vying with each other to see which can burst out of his clothing first. His job is to check the tapes received by PBS for any sign of naughty bits, in particular white men's willies.

He it was, he said, who was alerted to the sight of a full-frontal Michael Palin in the Odessa mud baths sequence in *Pole to Pole*. He had to re-run the tape to see if my member 'wobbled about at all'. 'Movement is what they don't like,' he assures me. Having judged it to be indeed moving, he proudly tells me that he became 'the man who pixelated Michael Palin's pee-pee'.

Wednesday, July 30th

Will picks up H and myself at 9.30 and we drive down to Spitalfields to see the house he so enthused about last week.

The house, in Hanbury Street, is on what the current owner describes as 'the Front Line' between old Spitalfields and the rest of the world. Bare brick walls, wooden-board floors. Much of the building has lasted since it came into existence in 1717.

A dank, earthy, unconverted basement, some sizeable rooms on ground and first floor. Big, tall bedroom windows look out over the tiny backyard and on top of the house is the old silk weaver's attic with long glass lights on either side. These are the special feature of the area – originally settled by the Huguenots.

Across the other side of Hanbury Street is the ugly brick and steel roof of Truman's Brewery, extended in the '70s at the expense of a row of Georgian houses. Spital Square had already fallen. In the seventies – that infamous decade for London architecture – John Betjeman and others squatted what remained of the old houses and that is the only reason they're here now.

By the time we've walked the area and are taking coffee in Commercial Road Market even H has come round to the qualities of the place. When I get home I call the agent and register a cash offer, ten grand short of what they asked.

Thursday, July 31st

Am at my desk taking care of business when the estate agent rings about my offer for the house in Hanbury Street. He ums and aahs and generally suggests that they might take it off the market if they don't get what they want. Other people in the running, etc. etc.

It sounds like the estate agent mess I don't want to be part of, so I ask him the question straight – 'What would clinch it?' 'Three-oh-five,' he says … 'perhaps.' I don't want to wait or mess about so I offer 305 and he will call them later.

H back at 11.45. It's still raining. She is not at all pleased by the news on the house. The jump of 15,000 she sees as a complete con.

Perhaps she's right. I'm too positive, too easy to please, too eager. Perhaps I've made a terrible mistake.

Friday, August 1st

I'm on the point of ringing the estate agents to reduce my offer – but when I do get through they tell me straight away that the offer has been accepted.

Saturday, August 2nd

In the evening to Simon and Phillida's for a barbecue. Ben Okri and Rosemary there.

Talk of America. Ben says he feels uncomfortable there – especially in New York – and thinks colour is still a significant issue. After all the political advances in our lifetime the blacks in America have more rights – but they remain different, uneasily integrated. He much prefers London, where there is a cosmopolitan feeling which derives much more from celebrating differences than fearing them.

I like Ben, but he's canny too.

On our way down Kilburn High Road we talk about writing. He thinks knowledge of the area you want to write about is most import-ant. Know your subject – want to write about it. In two days I shall be in France, with time to think about what I might want to write about next.

Monday, August 4th: London–Prayssac

The terrifically clammy air clears by evening; we swim, lie on bed in declining sunlight and doze as if we'd crossed half the globe to get here. Unwinding it's called. All will not be complete relaxation. Edward has a brochure for the Cinéma Louis Malle announcing a 'soirée exceptionnelle' tomorrow night with Michael Palin, in person, 'parmi nous lors de séance de *Creatures Féroces*'.

Tuesday, August 5th: Prayssac

Outside the theatre is a big *Fierce Creatures* poster and two good French reviews, plus an inked notice announcing my presence tonight. Michel Legrand, the theatre manager, is a likeable man with neat, greying hair, round specs in metal frames and a lazy, attractive smile. He suggests I turn up at the cinema at 8.30 for a drink and a few words before the film. He says he has a 'traducteur', but I tell him I'm happy to give a short speech in French.

Down to the Cinéma Louis Malle by 8.30. The small foyer is hung with all sorts of MP-related posters, including one very rare one for the French version of *Private Function* – *Porc Royal*. Marcel tells me there is a strong market in pig posters.

The audience seems mainly British on holiday or with homes here. Young girls with names like Olympia and Romilly gather round for autographs.

Despite early misgivings there is a half-full theatre for me to address at nine. Michel makes admiring opening speech. I give my two-minute oration, regretting that the film has 'pas de frites dans le nez, pas de chiens morts et, malheureusement pour moi, pas de baisées avec Jamie Lee'. (Use of word 'baisées' carefully checked beforehand as Edward says it may mean to 'go down on someone'.) They show a trailer for *Brazil* and then the Prayssac premiere of *Fierce Creatures*.

Wednesday, August 6th: Prayssac

By chance, have bought *Le Figaro* and there is yours truly standing, bag on shoulder, beneath a shaft of sunlight in an Istanbul bazaar, and above it a long review of *Pole to Pole* – *D'un Pole à L'autre* – which begins a 16-part run on Arte this evening. It calls it an 'excellent' series and notes approvingly that I do not make judgements or condescend, and that I let people speak for themselves. Best of all (which I ask to be read several times), it likens me to such travellers as Lord Byron!

This is a great tonic at the breakfast table as we look out over the dripping woods and hills, on whose higher slopes still trail patches of mist.

Thursday, August 21st

Lunch at the invitation of Karen Wright of *Modern Painters*. She has commissioned a cover from Tracey Emin. 'The first cover we've ever commissioned,' she says proudly. Unfortunately Tracey's contribution is an embroidered square reading 'Fuck Modern Painting'. Karen is distraught. Her husband says he'll leave her if she puts it on the cover. W. H. Smith will refuse to stock it. I really can't understand her pusillanimity. If you commission from Tracey Emin, this is what you get. Anyway, it's rather colourful and sweet and quite a good joke.

Tuesday, August 26th

My upturned face stares out at me from the cover of the *Radio Times*, under the massive headline 'Palin's Pacific'! Serialisation of the book covers four pages inside – there are endless details of books to be bought and tapes to be won – a whole MP industry blossoming ahead of next Sunday's premiere.

Sunday, August 31st

Preparing for a run, I put on the radio about ten to nine and am aware at once that something is wrong. Instead of the laid-back semi-news or charity appeals that usually fill this time on a Sunday I hear Jeff Banks talking of someone who has clearly passed away – a woman, a Royal, someone of style.

My immediate reaction is that it must be a special edition marking the death of the Queen Mum. Just my luck, I feel ruefully, on the day we've waited for for two years, we're upstaged by the Royal Family. How utterly unfair.

Then at the end of the interview – Banks is hustled off – I hear the quite paralysing news that Princess Diana and Dodi Al-Fayed have been killed in a car crash in Paris. I can't move for a moment. Half dressed, I stand there by the basin, staring down at the radio as if it might have developed some technical fault. The words coming out couldn't surely refer to real life.

Then I realise it's true and this is one of those 'Where were you?' moments – like in the tiny dark back room at 24 Parker Street, Oxford, where I heard about the Kennedy assassination, or on Gospel Oak

Station when Holly Jones told me of Lennon's death.

The radio coverage repeats the news like a mantra, as if only constant repetition will make it a reality.

I wonder whether I should run – whether or not anything less than sitting stunned and sombre will match the ugliness of the moment. I decide to go, of course, but hope there won't be too many people I know, because in a way I feel embarrassed to have heard what I've heard.

It's a grey, characterless day – not much light in the sky.

People pottering about on Parliament Hill, walking their dogs as if nothing had happened. Perhaps, I think, they don't know what I know.

Up to Maersh, our newsagent. Collect some of the papers.

Late editions carry the news of her death, though it was not confirmed until three or four in the morning; the *News of the World* headline reports her injured – the *Independent on Sunday* does not even have mention of the accident.

Paparazzi are blamed for causing the high-speed chase which sent her car out of control. It all seems appallingly likely. The photographers chased her to death. And apparently some of them stood and took the final photographs. There's an awful primal feel to the whole thing – mixed in with Greek myth – with the beautiful and the damned.

At about 12.30 Will Wyatt rings to give me details of how the extraordinary events of the day will affect the launch of *Full Circle*. The BBC has decided to keep BBC One clear throughout the evening for Diana news. *Full Circle* episode one will still premiere at eight o'clock, but on BBC Two. The whole series will begin again on BBC One, from the top, next Sunday.

Monday, September 1st

The Diana story dominates. There is, at the moment, no other news.

I feel, in one way, cheated of our moment, our launch, our chance to make a bold start and the strongest possible impact after two and a half years of preparation. On the other hand I feel less affected by that tightening apprehension that always follows a big launch. We'll be lucky to be reviewed at all.

Over to Mayday for a meeting re our will, finances, etc. We're joined by a tax-planner from Ernst and Young.

No sooner has our man begun to explain the intricacies of forward tax-planning than the phone rings with the first overnight ratings, hot from Eddie M. We pulled in an average of 4.5 million, a little more than the Jonathan Dimbleby Diana fest, for which we were cleared from BBC One. *Heartbeat* on ITV scored thirteen and a half million.

Wednesday, September 3rd

Rung by a lady from the *Daily Mail*. Slight foreign accent, delivery tired and lacklustre as though her heart isn't in it. 'We're asking famous celebrities (*sic*) where they were when they heard the news about Diana.'

I tell her I was in the bathroom.

'Were you in the bath?' she asks tentatively.

I can only be honest. 'No, I was halfway between the basin and the door.'

This is becoming wonderfully surreal. But she's not giving up. She's under orders, clearly.

'And what did you do when you heard, ring friends? Switch on the television?'

'I went running.' Also the truth.

'What were you thinking about when you were running?'

I couldn't take any more of this and gave a quick, probably rather clipped summary of my feelings and the call ended.

Frightening. Maybe I'll hear from the Compassion Police if I don't conform to the required State of Grief.

Saturday, September 6th: London–New York

It's the day of the Princess of Wales' funeral. Crowds have turned out in greater numbers than any day since the end of the war. This may be right or wrong, but considering the press coverage, which has effectively accepted a week of mourning, and a mounting mood of public adoration (and by implication, condemnation of the cold-hearted Queen for remaining at Balmoral), it's not surprising. Whatever it is that Diana is seen to represent, it's something more unequivocally good in death than it ever was in her life.

There are strong letters in the *Guardian* and the *Independent* bemoaning this sentimental selectivity but they are drowned out.

I can't help getting caught up in it. Diana's coffin, draped by the Royal Standard (was this a concession by the Queen?), is making its way on the back of a horse-drawn carriage with mounted Hussars and scarlet-tunicked guardsmen with black busbies walking along beside.

And the huge crowd is quiet. If you close your eyes you could think that, apart from the Hussars' horses and the occasional sound of sobbing, there was no-one else there.

The most unexpectedly moving moment for me (I didn't shed a tear until Spencer's address) was the commentator's observation, as the hearse finally reached the gates of Althorp Park, that 'this is the last any of us will see of Diana, Princess of Wales', and in through the gates went the car. Ridiculous really, it's not as if we can see her anyway, but after this extraordinary week which has rendered almost all other national and international events unimportant – Mother Teresa died yesterday and Jeffrey Bernard too, and Georg Solti this morning – this marks the end of it all. A finality.

Fly out to New York. Concorde is full of American luminaries who must have attended the funeral. Dr Kissinger and his beanpole wife towering over him are in the second row, behind Rupert Murdoch and his son. Anna Wintour is tucked up under a blanket in the back row of the front cabin.

I shall not easily forget standing beside Kissinger and Murdoch (surely two of the most demonised figures of our generation) at the baggage retrieval in JFK on the day Princess Di finally disappeared.

Monday, September 8th: New York

Lunch with Tom Dunne in the Post House. We talk of how utterly Mother Teresa's death has been eclipsed by Diana. Christopher Hitchens[1] – 'he's a naughty boy, and I like naughty boys' – is a friend of Tom's and two years back was excoriated in some circles for writing a damning article about Mother T – her refusal to support the Indian government's birth control measures, her willingness to take money from dictators like Duvalier and other insalubrious characters. From the brief coverage of her demise it's clear that she was admired more than loved.

The morning's news – a phone call from Helen to tell me that Derek Taylor has died. Apparently he had had enough of the pain and turned over one last time and that was that. The family all with him. There's a funeral on Friday which, sadly, I shan't be able to make. Write a letter, then and there, to Joan.

1 Christopher Hitchens, British-born polemicist, long resident in the United States.

Tuesday, September 9th: New York

Slept uncomfortably. Diana didn't pervade my dreams but Derek's death did. I lay there, awake from the still dark hours, thinking about this latest loss – another light out of our lives. Knew that I must do my best to try to get to the funeral.

There isn't a lot for me to do on Friday which can't be done on the phone from the UK. By the time my first interview rolls up, just before eleven, I've booked myself on the 9.25 Virgin flight out of Newark on Thursday night, and feel much better for it.

Meet Mike Myers who tells me that despite the Diana week of grief his comedy *Austin Powers* has done well in England – but not before every print was first recalled to have a reference to the break-up of the Royal Family removed.

Wednesday, September 10th: New York

To Fox Television for *Vicki Lawrence Show*. Willie Nelson and someone who's written a book about him, and Chuck, a big, all-American hunk and game show host – *The Dating Scene*, *Love Connections*.

Chuck delivered a most eloquent and generous tribute to my shows and Willie Nelson held up a copy of *Full Circle* to camera and then began to slowly open the pages! This American legend, with a face half ravaged by a full life and as noble as an Indian chief, managed to carry this off with dignity – all I could do was fall to the studio floor and bow a few times before him.

Friday, September 12th: Newark–London

Slept, though all my joints seem to ache from the effort, until woken for breakfast about an hour out of London.

We're 45 minutes late touching down – but the weather is good, and the bags are through swiftly. The office have done a good job and found me Brian, a friend of Graham F's, to drive me to Sudbury and back. We're out of the airport with two hours still to go.

Everything fine until the M25 eastbound fills, slows and finally comes to a halt.

Brian stays cool, finds a turning off and we cut through the rural lanes of Hertfordshire.

St George's Sudbury is very fine – perpendicular with wide side aisles and fine tombs and brass plaques and a delicately painted ceiling in the chancel.

As Derek's body is brought in, a soft patter of rain strikes the roof; the shower intensifies into a small storm, with accompanying thunder, as the service goes on and stops as the coffin leaves.

Derek, apparently, planned the service carefully, chose the readings and the music and the guests. Some Kathleen Ferrier, 'Danny Boy' by Phil Coulter and James Galway – Stéphane Grappelli as a recessional.

It's a good service – as Derek would have wanted it – literate, eclectic, dignified.

Back to the Mill. Jonathan Clyde asks if I would like to say anything.

But there's not much left to say when I get to my feet. I point to the irony of having to choose between publicity and Derek, the supreme publicist, to get here.

Wonderful tributes from the likes of Brian Wilson and Van Dyke Parks are read out – showing how much this very English man was loved in the USA.

But for me the star was Derek's brother, reminiscing about how Derek once kissed him – for reassurance – on his first day at prep school. His tone, his wit and his timing all eerily echo Derek's.

It's almost 6.30 when we're shown out of the side gate by Dominic to find Brian waiting patiently in the Jaguar. He said he'd heard the piano being played. I said that it was Jools Holland, who remembered Derek saying that the best way to clear a room was to start playing the piano.

Saturday, September 13th

It seems at last that O'Rourke has gone. The windows on which he stuck his defiant notes of protest against the council have been sealed with dark, vaguely sinister metal frames, and the lavatory bowl in which he grew flowers is dumped at the kerbside awaiting collection.

Monday, September 15th

Overnight figures for the Japan/Korea episode were 6.4 and 25% of the audience. *Heartbeat* strides away with 14.4 and 56%. The highly praised Hawking and the long-awaited Alan Clark *History of the Tory Party* cobble about 2.5 million between them.

Eddie confirmed that we have removed the Diana reference in programme four.

Wednesday, September 17th

To Charlbury with H to see Geoffrey and Susan S. We decide to take the train.

Charlbury is a tiny, immaculate station with one of the old Great Western wooden signs – big, bold, bulky brown lettering – and a goldfish pond maintained by the Women's Institute.

GS and I talk about the prospects of a book from me next year.

Geoffrey is keen on a comic novel. I don't think he wants me to be too introspective. I tell him of 'Glasgow y Valencia' – the drain-cover salesman idea. He likes that.[1] Also my thoughts on some sort of Hemingway book – in time for Hem's centenary in '99.

Friday, September 19th

Anglia Trains have been pressing me for some time to agree to have one of their trains (not locomotives sadly) named after me. I agreed a while ago and now, on this drizzly mid-September morning, my bluff has been called.

At Darsham Station – so full of private memories. Television crews, radio reporters, pressmen all waiting for me where once there was only my little mother.

Drizzle abates long enough for a speech of welcome from Andy Cooper of Anglia. Then I reply and, uttering the immortal words 'I name this train Michael Palin', pull a curtain cord to reveal my likeness, or rather a shadowy outline of my likeness – made up of lots of white and black dots. ('It looks really good from 100 yards away,' Andy reassures me.) Beneath this spectral depiction is my name. The whole lot is stuck on the side of a one-coach unit.[2]

Still, my mother and father would have been proud and they keep coming to mind, especially poignantly when Andy presents me with

1 The idea came to me as I was sitting outside a café in Segovia in Spain. In front of me I noticed a drain cover with the words 'McNaughton and Sons, Glasgow y Valencia'.
2 The class was named after famous East Anglians. I've quite often found myself sitting on 'Delia Smith'.

two framed photographs of Darsham Station over the last 100 years. In both of the sepia snaps it's virtually deserted, which is how I remember it.

We're rocketing home through the eastern suburbs of London when someone whispers in Andy Cooper's ear and he heaves a sigh and turns to me – 'Smidgeon of bad news ... there's been a train crash outside Paddington.' He adds, 'It affects all of us, a thing like that, we know how it feels.'

Tune in to six o'clock news. A high-speed train is spread all over the line at Southall, coaches entangled with a line of yellow goods wagons. Eight people reported killed, 170 wounded. Overhead wires dangling. Words like 'carnage' bandied about. It's described as the worst rail accident since Clapham, in December 1988.

Feel sorry for Anglia – they worked hard and could not have treated me better today. They went all-out for publicity for themselves, the East Suffolk Line and the railways. Now all that publicity has been negated.

Tuesday, September 23rd

To the Soho House for a long interview for the *Daily Telegraph*.

At the end of a reasonably agreeable, non-invasive interrogation a photographer arrives and we go out into Romilly Street for some snaps against a garage door. Norman Balon, notorious landlord of the Coach and Horses,[1] ambles up the road.

He casts a dyspeptic eye in my direction and wheezes out a half-cough, half-laugh. 'What are they photographing you for, eh? You're so fucking ugly.'

I'm chuffed that he even recognises me, let alone feels me worthy of abuse.

Saturday, September 27th

Driven down to the LWT Tower on the South Bank for an interview with Clive Anderson.

Shown to a tiny, dim dressing room. Just relax, I'm told, yet when I

---

1 The Coach and Horses pub was the long-time venue for *Private Eye*'s fortnightly lunches, and the setting for the play *Jeffrey Bernard Is Unwell*.

try to I'm subjected to a constant series of knocks on the door; the last of which is quite bizarre. Standing in the passageway is Chris Eubank, the boxer, clad only in white underpants and holding up a pair of trousers. 'I'm going to show the world a new Chrith Eubank tonight,' he promises and asks if I know where the wardrobe lady has gone.

Friday, October 10th

To TV Centre, where I'm to appear on *Blue Peter*.

All goes well, except that during the 'make', as they call the 'now here's something you can make at home', I used 'God!' as an expletive and was apparently caught on camera sniffing the glue pot.

Friday, October 17th

Paul Lambeth, clean-limbed, well-dressed lawyer dealing with the Paragon litigation,[1] comes to see me, as he needs some details before preparing my deposition – i.e. my statement to the court.

I like him, and have no trouble in backing up with facts and personal experience those things he would like me to say. The case has been set for March 9th 1998. There seems no way in which Paragon can win, but 'points of law' could be enough to prevent us from winning.

Friday, November 14th: *The Grand Hyatt, Hong Kong*

Bas and I talk about future travel. Cuba seems a must in the spring. Bas has printed out a proposal for an Islands series. I enlarge on the type of shorter-distance, stay-longer travel that I see as a new direction after the mega trips. Suggest calling each one 'Living In' (as in 'Living In Calcutta', 'Living in Ouagadougou', 'Living in Bahia'). I would stay in a place for six weeks, living with a local family.

We take a couple of martinis to celebrate the past, the present and the future of Palin and Pao as night falls and the sheer sides of the buildings around us are transformed into jewelled columns of light.

---

1 A company called Paragon claimed worldwide rights to *Life of Brian* after they bought the HandMade Films back catalogue. Python went to court to win these rights back.

Sunday, November 23rd: London–Salisbury

H and I leave the house at 10.45 for lunch with Sir Edward Heath at his house in Salisbury. Curious to know why I've been invited and what sort of occasion it is. We've been sent a guest list which looks rather grand – Kenneth Clarke the last Chancellor and some 'Excellencies'.

Arrive a bit early and draw into a service station for some petrol. The Indian cashier's eyes are shining and, as he hands me a receipt, he blurts out 'Kenneth Clarke was just here!'

Arundells is a handsome Georgian house, long windows, solid, square and built of stone with a columned portico projecting from the front door.

The door is opened by Sir Edward himself. He resembles a great big soft toy. Face pink and wide, hair white and neat, eyes alert and very bright. Disarmingly reassuring.

We are offered Dom Perignon in a small sitting room, walls hung with Chinese watercolours.

Meet the other guests. The Clarkes, Richard Webber, a wild-haired academic, I think. Very easygoing, down-to-earth – reminds me of Richard Hoggart. Heath's secretary – young, dark, attractive in a tomboyish way – and her 'young man', a surveyor. The American Ambassador and his wife are announced.

We move into a dining room, a well-proportioned room, quite tall, not grand. Food exquisitely served – butter in silver-lidded dishes, cut glass, etc. Cabinets of fine china on one wall – watercolours (he has two in the hall by Winston Churchill – not very good).

The American Ambassador, Philip Lader,[1] is keen to get to know the country (he's never been ambassador anywhere else). Asks direct questions to the table, in most un-British manner, like 'May I ask all of you what you feel has been the greatest change in Britain over the last ten years?' Some say food, I suggest the growing awareness of being a multiracial community.

Heath, who likes to speak in well-judged, weighty sentences, feels that it is the deference to the consumer. 'Everything must be available for the consumer. The consumer is king.' He enlarges on the point that excellence has suffered. If 'the people' do not understand something it

1 Before becoming US Ambassador to London, Philip Lader, a lawyer, held various posts in President Bill Clinton's administrations.

can't be done. Mr Webber concurs. He feels the last ten years have seen a 'dumbing-down'.

Ken Clarke, a gourmet, says that, whereas you used to have Chinese restaurants and Indian restaurants, taste now has become so sophisticated that people demand to know if it's Cantonese or Szechuan, or South Indian or Rajasthani.

Every now and then Sir Edward rings a small glass bell and a fresh course is produced.

His house reflects a real interest in the rest of the world – which is why perhaps he invited me. In front of everyone he praised the series for opening minds and extending horizons and says that he was very sorry to hear me say that I was doing no more.

I hear him telling the American Ambassador that he was once asked by Mao Tse-Tung what he thought of Kissinger. 'Well I told him,' Heath begins in typical anecdotal style, 'I thought he served his government well. That he was a man of intelligence with a good grasp of affairs and a devotion to his work.'

'He was shaking when he came to meet me,' Mao replied.

'Coe-niac?' asks Sir Edward as we assemble, efficiently, in another room – this one filled with photographs, stood in serried ranks upon every flat surface like gravestones. He doesn't push his experiences, nor his contacts, except in a quietly startling way – viz. handing round the cigars from a polished wooden box he's clearly very proud of, 'They're all Havanas, Castro sends them to me every Christmas.' The American Ambassador's eyes are out on stalks.

I feel a growing awareness that being a world leader makes you eligible for a special club – the World Leaders' Club – with its free gifts, discounts and fraternal Christmas greetings. Tory or Communist, it doesn't really matter, as long as you've been a Leader.

I'm slipped a message asking if I would kindly look in at the kitchen before I leave, as some of the domestic staff would like their books signed. Sure enough there are eight *Full Circles* laid out on the kitchen table.

Sir Edward bids us goodbye at a few minutes after four. We're the last to leave. Across the gravel drive and out through the wrought-iron gates, at which stands a tall blonde with a machine-gun. 'I 'ope you signed my book for me!' she calls after us as we walk into the Cathedral Close.

Saturday, November 29th

Last day of my out-of-London signings. A week in which I estimate,
conservatively, that I've signed five and a half thousand books, and in
which we hit the No. 1 slot on the *Sunday Times* list in some style, with
figures of 31,700, 11,000 more than Bryson in second place and considerably more than even the big Christmas paperbacks – Pratchett and
Francis and *Bridget Jones's Diary*.

Wednesday, December 3rd

Talk to Cleese.

He says, triumphantly, and with a great wheeze of anticipatory laughter, 'I bet you can't guess who I'm having lunch with on Sunday.' When
I say Edward Heath, he's quite chastened.

Wednesday, December 10th

To the RGS to give a lecture on Peru.

Try not to look at the front row – apart from Hemming, the great
Peruvian scholar and South American expert, there is the author and
travel writer Redmond O'Hanlon, Tim Renton the old Arts Minister
and his wife, and the Peruvian Ambassador at the Court of St James's.

I drew the sting by saying that for me to be addressing myself to things
Peruvian in such company was like the Spice Girls giving advice to the
Royal Opera House – laugh – mind you, I think they'd take advice from
anyone these days – not a great line, but an even bigger laugh!

The talk lasts just about an hour – then I take questions, and eventually I'm extracted from the throng and driven back to John Hemming's
for dinner.

Small, pretty house in Edwardes Square off Kensington High Street.
Upstairs are the distinguished guests – the Rentons, the cadaverously
elegant Sir Anthony Acland, Provost of Eton (his wife tells me Princess
Anne is a great fan of the journeys!), O'Hanlon, John Hatt of Eland
Books, John Julius Norwich and wife Mollie.

There's also Princess Alexandra and Angus Ogilvy – both of whom
apologise profusely to me for not having been able to attend the lecture.

Acland's wife talks about a book she's reading in a weary way – 'Why
do they always have to deal with, well ... what I'd call the sordid things

of life. I mean the books seems to me to consist of,' she touches her finger as she rattles off each word – 'menstruation, masturbation, motherhood and murder.'

I ask Princess Alexandra what's the most dangerous thing she's ever done. 'Oh, that's a *very* difficult one.'

Tuesday, December 16th

In the evening of an undemanding day I go round with Will to Hanbury Street – first time I've seen it since it became my property – or Will's to be legally accurate – seven weeks ago.

Walk right up to the top. There's no light in the weaver's attic, and there are glimpses of a broody, ash-coloured winter sky between the rafters. Out of the northern window rises the industrial skyline of the old brewery – great tubes and vents and piping running above the roof levels, a striking Gilliam-esque silhouette; on the southern side are the gardens and back walls of the old Princelet Street houses, and to the west the emphatic stone spire of Christ Church looms over what remains of old Spitalfields – a curious mixture of benevolence and malice – or have I been too affected by Ackroyd's *Hawksmoor*?

At a quarter to ten Brick Lane is buzzing. Like a Martin Amis novel come to life this is London raw and nervy. Bright lights like an Eastern bazaar, narrow, crowded streets along which a big Mercedes noses through.

It's a heady atmosphere down here. I'm muddled and confused and enthralled by it.

Wednesday, December 17th

To the Ivy for one of TG's 'celebrity in town' evenings. Tonight it's Johnny Depp who is over here looping *Fear and Loathing*. Ray Cooper makes up a foursome.

Depp is an interesting, quietly attractive character. Like Kevin Spacey, whom I met on *Saturday Night Live* at the beginning of the year, Depp is physically undemonstrative, soft-spoken, but his whole manner, and the way he will snap into someone else's voice to make a point, suggests that there is a lot there. Contained energy.

He's a Python fan, needless to say, born in Kentucky – and he seems to have a touch of that attractive Southern politeness.

He, like Simon Albury, was present at Allen Ginsberg's memorial service. He'd seen Ginsberg a couple of weeks before he died (Ginsberg must have loved him – a successful, competent, vulnerable, pretty boy). He told Depp he was looking forward to meeting the Grim Reaper 'and getting in his pants'.

Thursday, December 18th

Out to supper with JC at the Halcyon. It's really a catch-up opportunity. John rang me yesterday to tell me that Alyce Faye has gone to America ahead of him and that he has invited along a female companion – 'tall, blonde, American,' he sighs 'inevitably'. He's happy to supply a 'blind date' for me, he says solicitously.

So I meet up with Caroline Langrishe,[1] who played a scene with John in the latest Michael Winner film.

'Langrishe Go Down' I found myself saying, without thinking it other than a cleverish literary reference.

'Yes, I'm afraid that's something I have to live with,' she replies.

Almost a year ago exactly I saw the final cut of *Fierce Creatures* for the first time, out at Pinewood. 'We made 45 million,' says John, tonight. 'Not bad.'

JC off to California on Saturday. He brings up the subject of the Python film – and despite seeming to be the black person in the woodpile last May, has obviously been thinking about it. He gives an alarmingly precise rundown of the character he seems to now want to play in it – organiser of a women's crusade. It's very funny and just confirms in my mind that John, like the rest of us, and possibly more so than the rest of us, doesn't really know what he wants.

Wednesday, December 24th

Once again we have our Christmas Eve party. Over 40 people from the neighbourhood plus some of Helen's and Rachel's friends.

Richard Lindley asks if I'm going to become one of 'the great and the good'. 'Some form of acknowledgement is well overdue I would have thought.' I tell him that I'm not really interested in all that – committees,

---

1 Caroline Langrishe, actress well known for appearances in series such as *Lovejoy* and *Sharpe's Regiment*. *Langrishe Go Down* was the first novel by Irish writer Aidan Higgins.

charities, patronships, university degrees. They're all on offer, but I prefer to stay free of these ties. I don't want to live my life to someone else's agenda. I tell him I was never head boy, or head prefect – I never took things seriously enough.

Tuesday, December 30th

Fall to reading the Jonathan Margolis biography for the first time.

He has a significant observation about an aspect of my 'development' which still puzzles me, namely, how I managed to perform so confidently at Oxford. Though this confidence in front of an audience was there – I'd won the Bentley Elocution Prize at Shrewsbury (one of many things he missed in a dismissive chapter) and acted regularly with the B & C Players on my 'gap year' in Sheffield – he notes 'Where the remnants of Michael Palin's shyness disappeared to in the autumn of 1962 was anybody's guess, perhaps it had never really been anything other than a childish trait exacerbated by his father's crushing lack of encouragement for all but the most humdrum of ambitions.'

Much skimping (Shrewsbury very thin), some inaccuracies of detail and over-emphasis on trying to compare the origins of my career with those of JC. But generally his instinct leads him to the right places.

Wednesday, December 31st

The year ends very quietly. Almost too much so. For the first time in many weeks I find myself waking earlier than usual and staying awake. It's part of a process I know well enough now. Hard work – like the production and marketing of *Full Circle* which has dominated my year – fills all one's working hours, leaving little room for idle thoughts – for the mind to wander. Decisions have to be taken swiftly, and they're limited to and conditioned by the task in hand.

Once the pressure's off, as it has been since my last book-signing in Manchester, there is a period of sheer and wonderful elation, the incomparable pleasure of not having to work hard. This quite quickly replaced by the often unsettling speculation about what lies ahead.

One thing is clear after *Full Circle* – that I could make travel programmes like this until I die. I've carved out a piece of the market that is now unquestionably my own – as much as Monty Python was to the six of us who made it.

So, should I accept that this is what I'm best suited for, and stop trying to be an arts presenter, or a novelist, and just get on with bringing
people the sort of pleasure they derived from *Full Circle* – the sort of
pleasure that no-one else seems quite able to purvey? I don't know. All
I can say as '98 strikes, is that I shall continue to need to provoke and
possibly punish myself into not resting on any laurels; *Full Circle* was a
considerable achievement, but it's over. That was last year.

1998

Monday, January 5th

What the newspaper calls 'a family of deep depressions' continues to produce spectacular weather. This morning starts grey and mouldering, another morning which gives hibernation a good name. Then the weathervane swings round to the east and much colder air tugs the temperature quite rapidly down, before finally settling in the north-north-west from which comes a most dramatic deluge; this eventually passes, leaving a short respite before semi-night returns again – accompanied by rumblings of thunder and hailstones scattering onto the garden table.

Drive over to Islington to meet Mike Slee and Martha Wailes of Principal Films who want me to make a film about Cuba with them.

Mike Slee is a slim, neat man with tight, well-cut greying hair – not far off my age I wouldn't have thought. Martha is younger. The pair of them look very English.

I have to hedge my enthusiasm for Cuba with reservations about time, availability and the fact that so far I have not made any plans beyond the novel this year (and even this is not contracted).

Wednesday, January 7th

Have been asked to lunch at Anna Haycraft's. She has a project she wants to talk to me about.

To Gloucester Crescent. Normally casual garden gate replaced by large cell-block door with remote control lock. Anna, small, pearly-white skin, big TV screen spectacles emphasising rather than disguising the tragic look in her eyes, apologises. 'We've had lots of burglars, I'm afraid. A big Rastafarian just walked in and took the television!'

She shows me Henry Mayhew's book on London.

I give her some advice – suggest that if it is done as television, it should be shot in the style of the current fly-on-the-wall docs – impressionistically, quick fades in and out.

Anna says she refuses to go on programmes like *Start the Week*, or anywhere where she can't say fuck. She's most interested in the death of a lady who was struck by a falling lamp-post in Cavendish Square during the weekend's gales. Darkness, literal and metaphoric, seems to cheer her up enormously.

About eight we drive down to Tower Hill to see Fiona Shaw's *Wasteland*, which she's performed nightly over the last few weeks at the unheated, barely lit shell of Wilton's Music Hall on the corner of Cable Street and Ensign Street. Have invited Ray Cooper and Dearbhla Molloy along.

Tall chamber, with barleycorn cast-iron columns, freshly painted in gold, supporting the gallery. Narrow stage. Like Sickert's music hall paintings come to life.

She speaks the difficult poem very well. Clear, strong and, although I miss most of the references, I feel she understands what she's saying completely. Her confidence carries the evening.

Dearbhla is on good form and looks very well – her red hair well cut and shining almost gold. Ray rubs his bare scalp and tells wonderful stories about acupuncture. He had needles in his forehead when the acupuncturist stuck one in a tender part of Ray's anatomy, causing Ray to cry out in pain and involuntarily slap his hand to his brow – driving the needles already there deeper into his skull.

Tuesday, January 13th

Letters, phone calls, then set to work to implement changes to end of *Hemingway's Chair* for Tom Dunne. He has asked if I would rewrite the ending to make it clear my hero hadn't perished. I enjoy doing it. I have no feeling that the end is sacrosanct; rather the opposite, I relish the chance to play around with the words again. It was always ambiguous and ambiguity is quite bad for a writer, I think.

I look forward to concentrated writing again. The offers of television documentaries – the ideas about religions, Cuba, Hemingway, railways – have come in such a flood that it is almost impossible to select one from the other. It feels increasingly sensible to say no to the whole lot – this would reduce the agonising at a stroke.

Sunday, January 18th

Out in the evening to what promises to be a dauntingly intellec-tual evening. We've been asked by Sarah Hawkins to 'meet' Steven

Pinker – the American with big, wild, 1970s hair who's just written a much-publicised book on language called *How the Mind Works*. Doris Lessing, Richard Eyre and academics Colin Blakemore and Steve Jones are promised as light relief.

As it turns out Pinker is very polite, un-stuffy and not at all pompous. More like a very clever kid than a professor. Colin Blakemore had cancelled earlier in the day – last night his windows were smashed by animal rights activists who have been giving him and his family a hard time since he made some public statement of support for tests on animals.

Doris Lessing is the greatest surprise. I had her down in my mind as a severe woman (the weathered face, hair pulled back from her forehead), rigorously intellectual and somewhat ascetic in her approach to life.

'We all know you,' she said as we were introduced, as if her own strong features weren't iconic. She's modest and realistic and though she was always very much against the arrogance of white Africans, accepts that the blacks have made mistakes 'of a quite different kind'.

Talk to Pinker about stammering. He thinks that there is a genetic cause – it's something that's passed on through families. I tell him that I know of no other stammerer in my father's family, before or since.

Tuesday, January 20th

A chance to read *You've Got Mail* – the new Hanks movie, their first together since *Sleepless in Seattle* – in which there is a part they want me to do. It's quite a bright, cool, witty, up-to-date script – v. middle-class, A-B readership, and my character William Spurgeon is clearly based on Thomas Pynchon (reclusive novelist). Three scenes; quite fun. Seriously tempted to break my rule on cameos.

Thursday, January 22nd

To Camberwell for squash with Terry J. Best game for a long time. Hold on at 2-2, then fall apart in the last game. Traditional ritual of a beer, and then a meal.

He's enmeshed in a number of projects which aren't making him any money and says he's been quite badly affected by the hold-up of Python monies – which are currently being used to finance the case against Paragon.

Friday, January 23rd

Anne rings to say that the new dates for *You've Got Mail* seem clear. She's also managed to up my fee from an initial offer of 50G to 100G. As usual, I feel a frisson of nervous indecision here. Normal, retiring MP would settle for 50G and not rock the boat, but another part of me knows that everyone else will be trying to negotiate up. That's what I pay Anne for, I suppose, to be all the things I'm not.

Saturday, January 24th

Read some of the depositions on the Paragon case and speak to Terry G. He has heard rumours that Jon Slan and Paragon – the chief villains of the affair – may both be taken over by another company – a week or so before the hearing. How does that affect us? Why can't this all be settled out of court?

Monday, January 26th

Make calls, including one to Nora Ephron, co-writer and director of *You've Got Mail*. She repeats her, and everyone else's, delight at my acceptance of the Spurgeon role. 'When I called Tom (Hanks) and said, well, guess who we've got for Spurgeon? "Bill Clinton" was the first name he came up with.' (Spurgeon makes a pass at Meg Ryan's Kathleen.)

I in turn tell her I'm glad to play a character with no redeeming moral virtues.

Rachel is back from France for a few days. She's going to sort out future plans then return to do casual work and attend a French conversation class for two weeks.

Wednesday, January 28th

To Lincoln's Inn by a quarter to nine. The same quiet quadrangle that featured in *Wanda*. A meeting has been called by Anne and Paul Lambeth, our solicitor, with Mr Munby, who will be our counsel at the hearing in March on the Paragon case. He's a short, smiling, welcoming man in an ordinary sort of suit. Looks like he'd be very good company.

He thinks that we have an above-average chance of winning on all counts. He has one area of doubt however. This concerns the presence of a side-letter between Denis O'Brien's company EuroAtlantic and Python relating to but separate from the two main contracts on which he will base most of our case. Only in the side-letter is there a mention of forfeiture – of the film returning to the Pythons in case of breach of contract.

Munby feels that there may be a problem in proving that Paragon ever saw the side-letter. So, though we may be able to prove breach, we should not necessarily get the film back.

Over weak coffee and biscuits, in a very small room, he goes over the case. If any Python is called it will be me – attendance by any of us at the hearing would be appreciated as proof of our interest/seriousness in the case.

To see Kevin Kline at the Dorchester, where he is to promote *In & Out*, a comedy with Frank Oz directing.

Upstairs to his palatial suite and we have a half-hour or so to talk. He has an interesting observation about *Fierce Creatures* – that the problem was that John is at his best when creating awful people (Fawlty, Otto, etc.) and least convincing when trying to write warm, friendly, decent ones (his own character as Archie in *Wanda* an exception). I think he's right. John is happiest when he's on the attack. And funniest too.

Thursday, February 5th

Into the DJ and off to the Hilton for the *Publishing News* Awards. I'm one of the four nominees for Book of the Year.

There is a reception upstairs for celebrity guests which turns out to be a slightly deceitful way of putting us all to work. Champagne is handed out and just as you see a friend you'd like to talk to – Benedict Allen, Jane Asher, Jilly Cooper or whoever – you're hauled away, made to stand in front of a microphone and camera.

Some good questions – some completely silly. 'What's your favourite word in English?' 'Carpathian,' I say – the interviewer looks quite lost and rather put out. 'And the worst?' 'Stub.' 'Why is that?' There's no scintilla of humour behind it all.

Then to the tables. Whenever there's a quiet break for conversation, disco music blasts out over the 900 guests.

Ned Sherrin explodes into his monologue. It's all delivered at a desperate and relentless pace. For some reason the name of Leni Riefenstahl comes to mind as the music, the flashing lights, the manic exhortations from the man on stage are all piled together to create a sort of crowd hysteria.

Book of the Year, presented by Jane Asher, goes to Helen Fielding for *Bridget Jones's Diary*. It has been a phenomenon, and though issued only in paperback, has sold 700,000 copies.

Not winning always makes these sorts of evenings seem even more pointless, but, as usual, met some good people. Helen Fielding, a quite solid, northern lady, says she wished I'd presented her with the award as she'd always been 'insanely jealous' of me. By the time I asked why, someone had come up and badgered me with an autograph book.

Kathy Lette[1] wondrously, almost crusadingly, physical. She wraps herself around me and announces that she'd like to put her hand on my bottom. I'm about halfway through telling her a hand-on-bottom story when John Mortimer approaches. Kathy transfers her sinuous embrace to Mortimer as briskly as in the 'ladies' excuse-me' dances that were popular in my teenage days!

Sunday, February 8th

Only thing of real interest from the outside world are faxes from Anne and Steve which suggest that Paragon are at last realising that their own legal action could do them a great deal of harm. As from last Friday, they have made 'without prejudice' suggestions of a settlement. They have offered us their share of the rights in *Life of Brian* for £500,000. We would still have to pay our legal costs as well.

I call Steve. He, like me, agrees that this is pretty outrageous but if taken as the first position in a compromise, not as bad as it looks. If they reduce the purchase price to say £150,000 he thinks it will be worth serious consideration.

Thursday, February 12th

Down to Rathbone Place to record some introductions and promos for a Python weekend that a small cable channel, Paramount Comedy, are planning for April.

I was struck again by the number of people around the crew; there seems little change from the great days of BBC over-staffing, though in

---

1 Kathy Lette, Australian-born writer, married to lawyer Geoffrey Robertson.

this case the superfluous staff are young and probably quite badly paid, whereas the BBC was over-staffed with the middle-aged and well paid.

They have all sorts of bright ideas for serving up the Python episodes, films, etc. The new electronic capability has greatly increased the potential for deconstructing Python.

Then lunch with Paul Hamann and Peter Salmon.

I end up saying all I want to say – that I am not contemplating any 'big' TV involvement for 18 months at least, that I am happy working with the BBC, that I have no wish to become a pet presenter for them or anybody else (I've turned down hosting both BAFTA ceremonies this year) – that when I do do something it must be special, it must involve adventure.

Hamann plugs away at the MP-J.Cleese co-travel prog, but I'm wary. Sometimes two presenters can seem a bit cosy, and run the risk of cutting out the audience.

Friday, February 13th

There has been no response from Paragon to our rejection of their settlement proposal, and it looks as if we are now committed to spending another slice of money – £70,000 or so – in preparing briefs.

Thursday, February 19th

Out to dinner with Suzanna Zsohar and Michael Ignatieff. Salman Rushdie, wife Elizabeth and baby Milan are there.

Salman talks a little about his situation. The fatwa has been reasserted, nine years after it was imposed – and he is bitter that New Labour has promised so much – a meeting with Robin Cook[1] – but delivered so little. He says united international action is required but the French and Germans don't want to rock the boat with Iran.

At the end of the evening after vodka, and borscht and thick pasta and cabbage and plenty of wine and even some fierce brandy, we get up to leave and suddenly there are two young men with us.

Only later does H tell me that they had been there all evening, eating in the bedroom. They are, of course, Salman's police protection team. Young, strong, polite, well turned-out.

1 Robin Cook, Labour MP, Foreign Secretary since the General Election.

Elizabeth, Salman's wife, pretty in a sober way, with pale skin, goes off with the baby. Salman moves quickly downstairs (quite contrary to his discursive, rambling style in the flat) and into one of the two cars parked in the almost empty Clare Street. The two cars, keeping close to each other to avoid any interception, move away as if there is a magnet between them.

We're going the same way – up to Islington. They wait at a set of lights in Goswell Road and let us pass. And I feel a little guilty – well more than a little guilty – as I speed on over the hill and down towards the spires of St Pancras – that, as a fellow writer, I've done so little to help him. Because Salman is so full of life – so obviously delighted to be the focus of attention – and such a performer – I tend to forget his predicament.

Friday, February 20th

Head for the sun and light of the Bonnard exhibition at the Hayward Gallery.

For an hour I concentrate on the canvases. The effect of a brace of Bonnards is to bring time to a standstill. His is an unhurried world – a listless, languid, slow pattern of relentlessly repeated events, actions and scenes. It creates an almost palpable sense of a quiet, shuffling world, broken only by the sound of soft splashing bath water and the occasional sigh of wind in the trees.

Everything about it is *sotto voce* – nothing violent, swift or sudden intrudes. I never was aware of this before, but today the feeling is strong and gives me the sort of satisfaction I drew from a film like the *Quince Tree Sun*.[1] Understated, closely observed, diurnal detail.

Tuesday, February 24th

Out to a dinner at Daphne's in Draycott Avenue hosted by Michael Bloomberg, whose name is all over the place now on financial and other news services.

He's a shortish, trim man in mid-50s, tanned and professionally healthy. He has a much taller girlfriend – Mary-Jane, with big, red, Pre-Raphaelite hair but an almost gawky manner which is appealing but lessens the impact of her striking looks.

---

1 Released in 1991, about the painter Antonio López. Directed by Victor Erice.

She's marvellously indiscreet. The picture she painted of her inamorata – 'Do you work with him?' I open the conversation. 'Oh no,' she gives a slightly cackling laugh … 'I just sleep with him' – is of a hard, sharp, clever businessman – 20 years with Salomon Brothers – who has quite hawkish economic views. And later, I hear, aspirations to be Mayor of NYC.

She seems obsessed by the backwardness of Europe – 'All these guys thinking all they have to do is a 30-hour week?' she asks incredulously.

Thursday, February 26th

To do my duty for the Prince's Trust – this involves hosting a fundraising lunch with successful businessmen and women.

Tom Shebbeare, who runs the Trust, hails me in the street. He's busy lashing his bicycle to a lamp-post, which is too thick to take his locking clamp. I help him secure it higher up where it hangs like a tutu.

I've evidently pulled in a star guest – Elisabeth Murdoch, daughter of the Dirty Digger and second in command at Sky-BSB.

Murdoch is slim and seems serious. She has what looks like natural blonde hair and a bone structure and complexion which is as prominent as it is delicate. When the host retells my story of how Kevin Kline's character in *Fierce Creatures* was moved to New Zealand and officially modelled on Sam Chisholm to avoid offending Murdoch, she seems to take it, if not with a laugh, with a quite unoffended ease – as if she hears stories about her father every day.

I make a short speech at the start of the meal – without notes, I've decided – and it's the right decision as notes would have looked rather over-formal. A good discussion about helping young people find work, begin businesses, etc.

The whole event takes about two and a half hours of my lunchtime, and they all seem to think it's been a success. Tom stares in fascinated appreciation of my phrase 'children are born enterprising'. He loves that.

Saturday, February 28th

Call Basil. He's suddenly being offered good Hong Kong work – ironic, as he's on the point of moving out. Tourist board want him and, more excitingly for him, so does the new airport company.

In the course of our usual mix of business and banter he suggests that a possible way out of the Hemingway for 1999 impasse would be for him to do a photo-book of all the places Hemingway worked and lived in, and I would only have to come up with the text. This sounds a marvellous idea. A real breakthrough.

Immediately plunge into research on Hemingway places. This keeps me occupied until supper.

Rachel arrives back from Paris at six, with two bulky suitcases, her five-month study time there now finally over. Half an hour later I have to run her to Belsize Park, on her way to a party.

Monday, March 2nd

Wake early. I wonder if I've not been too impulsive in my reaction to the Hemingway idea. After all, it's less than 48 hours since Bas floated it and from my reaction he would be right to presume that it will all soon be sorted out and going ahead.

How much do I really want this? Hem's 100th anniversary is next year. We shall have to move fast.

Paul Hamann rings to follow up on things talked about at our lunch in mid-February. Wants me to float the idea of a Python evening on the BBC (which followed on from my enthusiasm about Paramount's weekend of Python), and after some tentative probing suggests that I might like them to commission a researcher to go and do some preliminary work on the Sahara idea!

Wednesday, March 4th

Anne collects me by cab and takes me for a catch-up lunch at Damien Hirst's Pharmacy in Notting Hill Gate.

It's a wonderful joke – only because it's carried through so completely. The windows that flank the entrance are full of carefully displayed preparations (true or false I don't know) and the reception desk is a counter attended by young men in white pharmacists' jackets. The downstairs bar looks and smells like a dispensary and must be a pretty awful place for a drink – but earnest unsmiling couples sitting with champagne buckets beside them seem to take it seriously enough. I like the obsessive detail and the carrying-through of the idea. As I say to Anne this is the first restaurant that's really made me laugh.

Upstairs the chemist motif is more diluted – but the walls are papered with pharmacological charts and there is a small picture on the menu of a pill being dropped out of a bottle and proffered on the hand. The generous bright sun is screened by white blinds.

Tell Anne of the Hem idea. She is of the opinion that the photo-book on Hemingway Trail/Places/Travels is a substitute for the obvious idea which is a TV series, of which the book would be the spin-off. She observes that I talk about Hem's places with such enthusiasm that it feels to her a much stronger bet than the novel.

Her other piece of news is that I may be called to court after the Python reunion at Aspen.[1] Life seems to be getting complicated.

Friday, March 6th: Aspen, Colorado

In the afternoon the first meeting with all the people involved in our show – which is around a dozen people apart from ourselves.

First surprise is when we're handed a 30-page 'script' of our spontaneous appearance, with pink cover. On the whole it's cordial, but TJ the most uncomfortable with prepared links and set pieces.

Earlier in the day we bumped into Eddie Izzard – who has a show here. It's suggested he be the mystery skier who comes on stage with us when we're first introduced.

I think much will be sorted when we rehearse at the theatre tomorrow. 'Rehearse?' says Terry with indignation. I fear there will be tears before showtime. Terry G has already run into flak after asking if the journo Giles Smith, who is travelling with him for a *New Yorker* article, can attend the planning meeting. Eric is not happy. 'We don't want bloody Boswells in here.'

Terry G has asked if I'll come to Hunter Thompson's ranch with him this evening. The idea appeals in a kind of diary-filling way but my head tells my heart that I'm short of sleep already and tomorrow will be a long day.

End up going to see three short Steve Martin sketches and an Alan Zweibel playlet down at the Jerome (the only really interesting hotel in Aspen). Amused to see that Eddie Izzard also has a *New Yorker* scribe in attendance. Such is Eddie's stature these days that he gets John Lahr.

1 The surviving five Pythons had been asked to the Aspen Comedy Arts Festival for an on-stage interview and to receive an American Film Industry Award.

Saturday, March 7th: Aspen

Breakfast with TG and the Joneses. Al's off skiing for the second day running and I envy her. Seems ridiculous to be in one of the great ski resorts of the world and confined to corporate hotels and meeting rooms.

Meet beside the Terrace Restaurant in a completely unexceptional private room. The five of us plus our new manager Roger Saunders.

In a couple of hours some positive decisions are taken. To investigate syndication (i.e. cutting the shows into 65 22-minute chunks, with our consultation) and to use the 30th anniversary of Python – October next year – as a commercial springboard.

JC proposes a stage tour for the 30th anniversary. Six weeks, end in Vegas, clean up, etc. etc. He's got the time to spare to organise it – 'with a committee of us' he suggests airily.

So, remorselessly, the stage show '99 seems a front runner. Terry G, who wasn't back from Hunter T's until two this morning, hunches into his seat, fiddles with his ponytail and does his best to be non-committal in the face of John's persistence. Terry is hoping to get 'Defective Detective' up and running by then. I voice my worries – lack of GC bad enough, but without TG involvement, disastrous.

Nothing is allowed to slow the process of a Python relaunch, and by the time we pack up it's even suggested we announce the show during the taping tonight.

On to the Wheeler Opera House for a run-through. It's an unusual and quite beautiful interior with a roof painted night-time blue and dotted with golden stars. Seating for 350–400 in well-kept maroon velour seats. A curved balcony and boxes – occupied by the cameras.

The set is good – a series of overlapping panels covered in bold Python images, the foot, various TG faces, all give colour and depth to the stage. There is old-fashioned English country house furniture around, tea and biscuits on a trolley – upholstered Edwardian-style chairs.

Eddie Izzard there to rehearse the opening. We decide it's better if he doesn't wear a ski outfit, just appears as himself, and it's only as he begins to answer the first question about how we got together that we become aware of him and drive him off the stage. Robert Klein, the moderator, asks anxiously if someone is at least going to mention Eddie's name. 'No, fuck him!' is the general response – which Eddie thoroughly enjoys. Klein can't quite see the joke. 'You're hard men,' he mutters.

All seats sold, a video-feed set up to the foyer – all seats sold there, another video-feed to 1,200 people in an adjacent hotel.

To the theatre. Hair, make-up, Lahr shadowing Izzard, Giles Smith hovering around Gilliam. John sits bolt upright in his dressing room, an oxygen mask clamped over his face and two cylinders beside him. A frightening sight. Although it's a quite acceptable way of dealing with the altitude, it nevertheless looks like some chilling glimpse of mortality.

The show begins recording a little after 9.15. All goes well with the clips, the entry and Eddie's moment. Then Robert K, who doesn't look at all at ease, asks some quite unanswerable question about what it is 'in your gut' that makes you want to do comedy. I mumble something, Terry J bravely launches into a school reminiscence. TG, with consummate timing, kicks over the urn with Graham's ashes in. From then on, we're invincible.

After it's over, there is mayhem on stage. The press have been given half an hour to get their stories and the camera crews from CNN and *Entertainment Today* and NBC News and God knows what jostle with the *Aspen Times* and students with tape recorders and an incongruous middle-aged public school man from the *Daily Telegraph* and people like Ted Danson and Kelsey Grammer from *Cheers*. Those who come up to me have evidently heard that the stage show is happening – though we didn't mention it on the recording.

Eric wasn't surprised by the rush to confirm the stage show. He says John told the press last Thursday.

Sunday, March 8th: Aspen

Should have slept the sleep of hard work rewarded – in fact, at first light I'm lying awake consumed by an indignation that both causes, and grows with, my wakefulness. John should never have told the press that we were doing a 30th anniversary tour when we had barely considered the details and problems.

He had done exactly what he would have violently and vociferously objected to in anyone else – he'd steamrollered us into a course of action purely because it suited him, then created a fait accompli by announcing it publicly.

Rang H and let off steam, then I cheer Rachel up when I tell her I'm hoping to go skiing with Eddie Izzard later in the day.

Later I call Eric who talks me down in his best and most persuasive style. No harm is done, he says, by announcing the tour – it gives a focus to the enormous enthusiasm for and appreciation of Python as evidenced by last night's event.

We should take advantage of JC's positive mood.

I talk to John, briefly. He's the only Python staying in Aspen tonight so I shall have dinner with him and hopefully have time to at least register the criticism.

Then hire ski gear and climb on the bus to Buttermilk Mountain. Can't be sure I'll remember how to ski (it must be about six years since our last holiday in Switzerland).

Eddie arrives a little late, gesticulating wildly to someone at the other end of his mobile phone. Have a beer together then up the chair lift.

Some good runs down – long, wide, safe slopes. Eddie on his snowboard – or sometimes skidding flat on his face. As he says, with snowboarding there is no halfway point between looking good and a complete idiot.

We ski until the light begins to go and the black shadows become dangerous and, like a pair of happy, slightly battered schoolboys, catch the bus back to Aspen.

Have a half-hour massage, which is a wonderful complement to the skiing, and, by now thoroughly relaxed, leave for supper with JC and Eddie.

I can't really in the circumstances give full vent to the anger I woke with this morning, but as we pick our way carefully across the road and down the slippery sidewalks I voice my doubts as to the wisdom of announcing a stage show we don't know we can do.

John shrugs off the problem, says that it's not fixed, but it's worth letting people know we're keen; he says that clearly he wouldn't want to do it without everyone's involvement. He himself is prepared to work hard on co-ordinating it.

To a smart, cramped little restaurant called The Renaissance.

Eddie says that women seem more, rather than less, attracted to him when he's dressed in women's clothes; John's fascinated. Eddie suggests he might start gently, say, by wearing some eye-liner.

Tuesday, March 10th: Aspen–London

The purser has to shake me quite violently before I wake. Have slept five deep hours over the Atlantic and we are an hour from Heathrow.

Have breakfast and return to Hem's *The Dangerous Summer*, which has only strengthened the resolve I made as I lay in bed in Aspen on Friday morning to do something on film for next year's Hemingway anniversary. His writing still hits home and without too much artifice, just concentrates and engages the mind and the senses.

So, dropping into London once again – Python revived at Aspen, a new direction for the year ahead, and an awards ceremony at the Grosvenor House in four hours' time.

Awards ceremony organised by TRIC – Television and Radio Industries Club – 960 people squeezed into the Great Room.

I pick up BBC Personality of the Year Award, and have to stay as we're also nominated for BBC Series of the Year which is the last award. It's announced, to my complete surprise, by Baroness Thatcher, who is roared to the rostrum by the suits.

'And the winner is,' I hear her voice intoning, '*Full Circle with Michael Parlin*.' Is this 'Parlin' a joke – or, like JC's 'Pallin', a way of having a dig? Gasps and laughter from all around. I urge the directors and Anne to get up and help me, but they are nowhere to be seen as I move through the tables and up into the presence of Baroness T.

Thatcher is small, bony, her face white and waxy, her handshake cool but a little damp at the same time. 'The only programme to win the double,' she says to me, quite pleasantly, with a touch of the schoolmistress in the tone and sentiment.

After referring to my award announcement as 'probably the shortest speech Baroness Thatcher ever made – but, as far as I'm concerned, absolutely the best' – I begin to tell the story of the old ladies in the Amazon village and the saliva-spiked cocktail, only to become aware of Mrs T standing close beside me and breathing 'Steady!' every time I mentioned the words 'old lady' and 'cocktail'.

I struggle on with the story as the audience begins to warm to our double act. I steal a look to one side and her gaze bores into me. 'I can see why she stayed in power for ten years,' I confide to the audience, who love it. I take another look at Thatcher. Still staring, with almost primal intensity. 'Steady!'

Somehow I got to the end of the story. I understood then what had happened. Baroness T thought the story had to be about her – relating, probably, to her well-known appreciation of a glass or two. But she didn't seem to know what exactly was going on any more than I did, and I felt confusion, rather than anger, emanating from her as we had our photos taken by a barrage of cameramen on the side of the stage. Me with my arm round Baroness Thatcher.

Thursday, March 12th

To Court 18 at the Royal Courts of Justice which manages to feel very large and very cramped at the same time. Most of the volume is in the height.

Squashed along narrow benches, one behind the other, are about 20 people. On our bench is the genial, wise-cracking Norman Horowitz, our main witness. John Goldstone is up in the witness box, which is on the same height as the judge, who is called, memorably, Justice Rattee.

The court rises, but the tape-recording doesn't work, so the court adjourns whilst the machine is fixed. Modern technology including tapes and computers has been unceremoniously stuck onto G. E. Street's Victorian Gothic woodwork – lengths of black cable secured to delicately carved cornices and architraves with gaffer tape.

Just when I think I'm set for the afternoon session I'm called up.

The Channel 4[1] lawyer speaks in soft, insidious tones – far worse than being shouted at. He leads me into defending *Life of Brian* despite the censorship and Church disapproval, then smoothly turns my far too helpful reply into some sort of judgement that *'LOB'* may now be less successful because it is no longer controversial.

As I had had no preparation for any of this I felt quite helpless and afterwards realised I'd been tricked into saying all sorts of unhelpful things.

But I'm away after lunch. General feeling being that they don't have much of a case and that the judge is very impatient of the time they're taking with witnesses.

Friday, March 13th

Rachel off to work at At-It Productions – could this possibly be the first day of a television career?

To TV Centre to see Peter Salmon, the new Controller of BBC One, and pitch 'The Hemingway Travels'.

For the first time in any of my 33-year dealings with the BBC top brass

1 Channel 4 with Paragon were co-defendants.

I feel I'm treated, unequivocally, as an asset. We talk for three-quarters of an hour. Peter makes little notes about H as I go along. 'Four wives eh?' – he scribbles something down. 'Lust for life,' he mutters approvingly at one point.

There is some distraction in the back of his mind – I know that. I know I'm sharing his time, but he's remarkably positive and likes the idea of four 50-minute progs – Palin on Hemingway – for autumn 1999. BBC One.

Leave the BBC at three. Home. Should be feeling elated but I've been through all this before and part of me is heavy with the awareness that this will mean being tried in front of a television audience again, rather than enjoying the quieter pleasures of novel-writing.

Sunday, March 22nd

Today apply myself to Hemingway. Put together a 'sales pitch' for the series – as much to convince myself as anyone else. Take down the Pacific map that's dominated my wall since the summer of 1995, and replace it with 'The Ernest Hemingway Adventure Map of the World'.

There are many ifs and buts to the series. I'm no further on with decision on director, or whether to go for old friends or new blood.

Monday, March 23rd

Feeling unsettled this morning. Spring equinox has brought thick, low cloud cover and a cool day – which doesn't help raise optimism. So many issues unresolved, from Python's stage show proposal with Tom Hoberman[1] to my insecurity over the Hem series.

I was on the verge of offering Roger Mills the Hemingway job this a.m. His knowledge of Cuba seemed important. But Paul Hamann calls to suggest I contact David Turnbull, whose work on the Jonathan Meades[2] series I saw and greatly admired last year.

Turnbull rings and, though I waffle a lot, I hope I give some impression as to how and why I came to this project and how I want to

---

1 Tom Hoberman, Eric's lawyer in the States, was putting together a deal for the stage show.
2 Jonathan Meades is a writer, broadcaster, actor and critic, who specialises in polemical, cultural documentaries.

proceed. He's soft-spoken, makes erudite quips, but I know there is a keen intelligence there. We agree to talk at the weekend when he returns from filming Meades in Birmingham.

This cheers me up somewhat. At least it's a positive lead in the 'new broom' direction.

Terry J's response to Hoberman's proposal is a bouncy, enthusiastic account of how he's dreamt the opening sequence of the new stage show and is now v. enthusiastic towards it. At the same time he reckons it probably isn't possible without TG – which to me means it probably isn't possible, period.

Thursday, March 26th

Meet Roger at the Yorkshire Grey – a pub-brewery close to ITN where he's editing his film on Yeltsin.

A chance to talk and catch up over a few pints. He's been offered a series on cricket with Mick Jagger which may or may not happen. Alex Richardson, our editor, is soon to be busy on a new Jeremy Mills 'docu-soap'.

So I don't feel so bad telling them of my plans for the Hemingway series. As I say to Roger, 'I've taken the advice you gave me before *Full Circle* and gone for a completely new team.' But, as a sop, I suppose, I can't help speculating about the next travel series – beyond Hemingway – 'Sahara 2000?'

Friday, March 27th

Martha Wailes,[1] who has also worked with Jonathan Meades, is next to come by. She has a quiet, understated determination. I liked the feeling that she has for Hemingway – think I could work well with her, and it may be very good to have a female perspective.

To a room in the bowels of the Law Society in Chancery Lane for a Python meeting to discuss all the moves since Aspen. Eric is, once again, on the phone in the middle of the table.

JC, I felt, had cooled on Eric's Hollywoodish pressure and come closer to my more cautious view of what we should commit to. He's

---

1 Martha Wailes, producer of *Hemingway Adventure*, who had also previously worked with James Burke.

also adamant that he would feel most uncomfortable doing it without Terry G.

After preliminary chat amongst ourselves an agreement is reached on enquiring further into a three-city, nine-week maximum, less than 2,000-seater auditorium deal. TG's involvement not to be taken for granted.

The discussion is amicable and concentrated and businesslike. Eric brings up Las Vegas because he says so much more money can be made there (in return for a very short engagement). I'm not keen. 'Not for a million?' Eric comes back. I should have said no, not for a million, but that would be selfish!

Tuesday, March 31st: London–New York

Ten-thirty Concorde slips out of Heathrow on time. Met at JFK by 'service and greeting' staff and briskly out to a car and into my second metropolitan rush hour of the day.

In Central Manhattan 15 minutes early for my *You've Got Mail* fitting.

To a costumier called Grace in the theatre district. Met by Albert Wolsky, short, balding, civilised and very sweet. 'Everyone's so excited you're here,' he keeps saying, without affectation.

Takes an hour or more to refine the look Albert has planned for me into something I'm comfortable with. Do I have enough energy left to go over to the set? I do, and at the hottest part of the day I find myself on the corner of Columbus and W69th. Cables, cranes, makeshift shelters, trailers, girls with headphones and mouthpieces carrying coffees across a side street littered with chairs.

I find Nora only after she's pointed out. She doesn't look like or come across as an archetypal director. She's short, physically slight, with an intelligent face framed by dark hair and dark glasses. Nice and easy – possibly a little tortured round the edges – more like an academic than a filmic.

'We're all so excited that you're here,' I hear again. I meet Meg Ryan – slim, quite delicate, though her face in some odd way gives off light – a friendly, uncomplicated first impression.

A wearying process as I try to select the right glasses to wear. This involves some hanging about, waiting for Nora to come and approve.

She and I talk a little while about the character. She doesn't want Spurgeon to be American; she thinks people shouldn't be forced into unfamiliar accents and she rightly observes that if it's not spot-on, an American audience will notice and it will distract from the comedy.

Go away relieved.

Thursday, April 2nd: New York

To Nora E's trailer where we are to read my two scenes (it's the second, more complex one we shall start later tonight). Meet Delia, Nora's sister and co-writer. She's gentle, likeable, undemonstrative. Defers to her sister but I suspect is influential. Meg is there and Greg Kinnear, good-looking young actor who was in *As Good As It Gets* – nominated I'm told later.

Always find read-throughs demanding. They're absolutely unimportant to the final result, but absolutely important at the same time. This is the first moment Spurgeon comes to life – and these early stirrings have to feel right.

I'm not yet absolutely comfortable with the lines as written or the level at which to pitch Spurgeon, so the response is muted. Maybe a dose of reality after all the expectations.

Not ready to work until 9.30 – by the time the rain machines have all been tested and the lights set. Opening of the scene – 'loitering, lurking, skulking, stalking' are my first lines.

A little uneasy to start with but good notes from Nora enable me to gradually focus the character and capture a vanity and a detachment – cocooned in self-belief – which feels right. Meg Ryan is solid, dependable, she has the ease which comes from having been with the team and the project from the beginning. Thoroughly professional.

Despite eye-aching fatigue I manage to keep my own professional standards up. I have the words tight, and make the right moves at the right time and hold the umbrella in the precise best way – and see to all the mass of other concentrational details that make up a film performance.

At midnight I'm released.

Friday, April 3rd: New York

Good news as I arrive at the set at five o'clock this afternoon. The dailies have been seen and liked and Nora is already hatching plans to extend my first appearance in the scene in the shop.

It's exciting in a way I've never experienced before. Being on a big film, outside my own country, the only non-American in the cast, working under the cranes and gantries on the busy streets of New York. Life goes on around us – restaurants and cafés are Friday night full. Clusters of people stop at the end of the street, rubbernecking.

As the night wears on, only serious night owls are still out and about. At half past three I walk down to the other end of W69th, onto Broadway where the yellow cabs are flying by and look back up the street we've taken over, a whole row of brownstones lit for my close-up, and as I walk slowly back up I can see Meg, wrapped in a big, black jacket, coming towards me for the next shot, and I think to myself that only New York and Paris have this legendary quality – this alchemy about them – that ability to transform ordinary life into something infinitely more dramatic.

At four o'clock I'm through. The rest of my scenes to be shot in a month's time. Fond farewells, back to the Lowell and pack and set the alarm for 9.30, which, as I turn the light out, is four and a half hours away.

Tuesday, April 7th

Anne round for a Hemingway series meeting. We go over the crewing plans. Turnbull, obviously, but Martha as producer. Eddie Mirzoeff already installed as BBC Executive Producer. I spoke to Nigel last night and he is very keen to shoot it. Still necessary for the various parties to meet and check each other out.

Thursday, April 9th

Rang Michael Katakis, the Hemingway rights manager, in Montana. V. positive. He has already spoken to Patrick Hemingway – eldest son who will be 70 this year – and they are happy to bless the project and help where possible.

Katakis sounds serious, sensible and sympathetic. He is a writer himself and photographer, his wife an anthropologist and they are currently working on their own documentary. He clearly doesn't like New York, and is very keen for me to come out to Montana and do some fly-fishing and meet Patrick and talk.

He is at pains to point out that he is not keen on mythologising

Hemingway and feels that what I do or write myself about Hem should not be censored by the family.

Friday, April 10th

Have the rolling news on in my workroom at 5.35 when news of an agreement in the Ulster peace talks comes through and the unfamiliar sound of concord, however temporary, is heard around the table as each of the chief participants sums up and is applauded.[1] I wonder, though, if what was undoubtedly made possible by George Mitchell's skill as chairman, and the last-minute efforts of Blair, Ahern and Clinton, can be sustained when they are all gone.

Tuesday, April 21st

To studios near the Westway to film my contribution to an ad for the new BBC digital service. It will use various 'friends' of the Beeb, from Stephen Fry to Alan Partridge to Harry Enfield, to extol the virtues of digital TV. I have the pay-off line, the last appearance in the commercial, pushing my way up to camera through the jungle.

The jungle that's been assembled for me in Olaf Street W11 is more convincing on camera than the one we filmed in by the Urubamba in Peru. And it has no bugs and is temperature-controlled.

Thursday, April 23rd

Supper at the Commonwealth Club as guests of Peter Luff. Paddy Ashdown is amongst the fellow guests.

He tells stories about Northern Ireland (where he is from and where, in 1977, he was commanding a force of Marines) with superb renditions of the Irish accent. He thinks Prescott and Blair a good team and was impressed by how bright Prescott was.

There is a general feeling that New Labour has been, over the last year, a good government. Paddy recalls Blair telling him early on just how much they wanted to do. But he adds that the 'openness' is a misapprehension. He says he has known no government 'more secretive'.

1 This was to become known as the Good Friday Agreement.

The service is quite bizarre. All of us who order liver are brought quail and my cheese has custard on. What part of the Commonwealth are the staff from, I ask Peter. He seems to find this hugely funny – 'Spain!'

Saturday, May 2nd

Various local chores – to the recycling depot. Bill Oddie's there. Draw his attention to a new bin for 'Spectacles'. He said one for 'Scripts' would do well round here.

Monday, May 4th: London–New York

Arrive on time to a JFK shrouded in warm, low mist and semi-dark at half past six. Into the terminal behind a jet-load from Haiti – thin old men in white suits and blue trilby hats, children in bright dresses and ribboned pigtails. Make us look so boring.

To the Inn on Irving Place by a quarter to eight. Mine is top-floor room of this three-storey brownstone, converted and full of tasteful nineteenth-century pieces of furniture. I'm in 'Edith Wharton' and have three windows which look down on Irving Place – which has restaurants, greengrocers and a bustle that is quite different from that outside the Lowell. Rarely a suit in sight.

There are new pages for my scene on Friday – just completed by Delia E – and quite difficult too – plus a letter from her saying that she's half-way through *Hemingway's Chair* and 'loving it'. So, back into the warm bosom of the Ephrons.

Tuesday, May 5th: New York

Woken periodically by constant street noise three floors below me. Cars, cabs collecting diners from the clutch of restaurants along Irving Place, then dustcarts crunching up the waste, street cleaners swishing slowly along the kerb, then delivery trucks and vans starting the whole process going again.

Breakfast in the tastefully furnished parlour downstairs. Good, fresh orange juice, strong coffee and croissants.

Work on the new lines and make arrangements with Michael Katakis to visit Montana if and when I'm released from *You've Got Mail* next Tuesday morning. He's just come back from Cuba – says Gregorio Fuentes, Hemingway's boatman, is 101 and still going strong!

Wednesday, May 6th: New York

Filming over on the Upper West Side. Myself and Greg Kinnear – as he tails me out of the subway, etc. Skies overcast, which is helpful as this is supposed to be Fall. Occasionally whole trees in autumn colours can be seen being hauled across intersections.

In the afternoon we move to a big sports store on Broadway. Here, to my complete surprise, I'm presented with a cake and the crew stand around the displays of sportswear and sing 'Happy Birthday'.

Thursday, May 7th: New York

The new lines from Delia E are a gratifying show of confidence, but as they're meant to be bad poetry they're hideously difficult to learn. Run through them as I pump the treadmill at the Equinox gym on Broadway.

Across town to the Chelsea Piers, a massive complex built around the renovated White Star Line jetties – where, amongst other things, the *Carpathia* arrived in April 1912 bearing the survivors of the *Titanic*.

My trailer is in the car park beside the murky waters of the Hudson. Onto the set of the bookshop. Meet up with Meg again. She's very interested to hear I may be going to Bozeman next week, as she and Dennis [Quaid] have a house there.

Rehearse. Without light or costume and the crew hanging around, but it's still a performance and these first impressions, so deceptively casual, are very important.

They release me, after one more rehearsal and block, around seven o'clock.

Sunday, May 10th: New York

Collected at 7.15 for what I hope will be my last day on *You've Got Mail*. At our location, just off Wall Street, in a quarter of an hour.

We have a subway train and three stations at our disposal to shoot the scene in which I make my first appearance. Complicated by need for 30 or 40 extras to be deployed, plus awkwardness of wielding the camera in confined space as the train moves.

Shuttle our way between Fulton and Broad Street covering the scene thoroughly.

I'm finished by two in the afternoon. Traditional movie farewell – 'That is Mr Palin's last shot' (of what I reckoned must be my 14th film).

Up into the rain again, distribute presents. John Linley, the DP, even offers his services should I need some emergency shooting done on *Hem's Chair*. He's an exceptionally nice man who looks like Aubrey Beardsley.

Back to the hotel. The few days I've spent on the picture have been hard, concentrated work, made more difficult by a long lay-off from movie acting, over 18 months, a strong character who needed to be played forcefully, and, of course, a completely new group of people to work with. All tremendously helpful and friendly – but the prize goes, I think, to Albert, the costume designer and the first member of the crew I dealt with when I arrived at the beginning of April. A sweet and good man. I gave him a book and signed it with feeling!

Tuesday, May 12th: New York–Bozeman, Montana

An uneventful flight to Denver – whose brand-new airport stands on the plains, waiting, it seems, for some enormous influx of non-existent passengers to materialise. Thoroughly modern, everything matching, lots of space – even a copy of *Hemingway's Chair* in the bookstore.

The flight north to Bozeman is a twin-engined turbo-prop Dornier and reminds me, with its enormous engine filling the frame of the window beside me, of the flight to the North Pole.

Bozeman on a wide plain, surrounded on every side by snow-capped ranges. Michael K is waiting for me. He's a big man with a gently bulging midriff, a greying moustache and dark, intense eyes which remind me of another Greek, Michael Angelis.

His house is unremarkable. A recently built grey clapboard bungalow in what we would call a close, at the end of a newly built road. Inside it's light and spacious and I can see from the copper skillets and the gleaming stainless steel pans that they're serious about food.

This is borne out by a fine meal preceded by smoked salmon with peppercorns and a glass of Laphroaig.

Last thing I remember is Michael telling me the sensational news that there is a new Hemingway book coming out – an African memoir – written in mid '50s – edited by Patrick H. Material never seen before.

Wednesday, May 13th: Bozeman, Montana

Aware of much moving around – and am not surprised to hear that Michael gets up and runs a mile and a half at five-thirty, then either he or Kris takes their insatiably energetic black retriever, Angus, across the golf course.

Breakfast – slices of Ogen melon, cafetière coffee and National Public Radio. Michael likes to talk and talk seriously. Conversation (which he claims is hard to find amongst his American friends) is to him like water in the desert.

Thursday, May 14th: Bozeman, Montana

We spend a very productive morning at the solid old wooden table discussing the Hemingway project in depth. With a little trepidation, I give Michael my first synopsis to read. He's complimentary and approving. As far as he's concerned this is the best Hemingway proposal he's seen. Neither over-adulatory nor cynical – and as he sees it the key to it is that it is Hemingway seen through my eyes – the eyes of another traveller, and not an American.

In the afternoon Michael drives me up to Buffalo Jump, a section of rocky escarpment over which the Indians, sorry Native Americans, used to drive herds of buffalo, who were then finished off and cut up for food, pelts, etc.

We climb to the top. Magnificent views; huge spaces. Big, wide plains, the presence of snow-capped peaks evoking the altiplano of the Andes. The weather, ever changeable, dumping rain here and there, alternating cloud and sun in glorious light patterns.

Well whipped by the wind and rain we return to Bozeman for a couple of beers at Boodles. Useful input from Michael on the best dates for shooting. He thinks we should do the Gulf Stream and Cuba soon – preferably in September. He rings a friend in Key West – 'Have you had your martini yet, Fitz? When's the Gulf Stream colour at its best?'

He enthuses about Michigan – is so glad I'm doing that because many people under-rate that early part of Hemingway's life. Plays me a tape of Hemingway reading his work.

Friday, May 15th: Bozeman–Chicago

News of Frank Sinatra's death on the radio. Eighty-two. Somehow one thought people like that immortal.

To the airport and onto the two o'clock flight – with Michael and Kris watching me onto the plane. Michael is an unusual man. Shy but successful – son of a Greek immigrant who made good in Chicago property, a musician good enough to be the solo act for Tina Turner and Joan Armatrading in his touring days. A vulnerable man who has done tough deals for the Hemingways. He and I could almost have an Al Levinson/MP relationship, I feel. He likes writing letters in fountain pen, he warns me.

Saturday, May 23rd: Oxford

Rachel's graduation.

Installed in the Sheldonian by 10.50 – there's a fight for places on the hard wooden tiered seating. We clamber up to the very top row and settle in an alcove with a good, if precipitous, view of the open arena beneath and the tall oak doors through which the graduates will enter in their new robes.

We enjoy the various deans who have to introduce their prospective candidates in Latin; some have it memorised and deliver it confidently, smoothly, co-ordinating the bows and turns to the Vice-Chancellor and Proctors, others have to read part of it. One of them, an elderly man with flowing white hair, reads each announcement from a card stuck in the centre of his mortar board.

Rachel is the first of her group so has to hold the hand of the silver-haired, rather natty Dean of Aen Nas, The Brazen Nose.

About one o'clock it's all over and we mill outside. Make our way to college.

Rachel, now with the white fur trim of a BA on the neck of her gown, sits at High Table.

I have someone opposite who used to live in Belfast and much of the talk is of the imminent disclosure of the referendum result in Ireland.[1]

Actually, I first hear it in the car on the way home, and the news

---

1 Two referendums were held in Northern Ireland and in the Republic to gauge support for the Good Friday Agreement.

is good – 71.12% 'Yes' in Northern Ireland and 96% 'Yes' in the South. More importantly, it's estimated 55% of Prods have voted yes.

Sunday, May 24th: London–New York

Across the Atlantic for the fourth time this year.

Welcomed, quite touchingly, at the Inn and I must say my room – my Edith Wharton – looks fabulous with the late-afternoon sun angling through my three street-side windows.

There are four boxes of *Hemingway's Chair* books to sign – which I set to after unpacking.

Read my review in the *New York Times* – 'Not the Full Monty' – 'MP's latest novel owes more to Kingsley Amis than John Cleese'. It's a prominent review taking up most of the page next to that of John Irving's latest novel – so I can't complain of not being taken seriously.

By odd coincidence, one of the few other books extensively reviewed is a new biog of Gerald and Sara Murphy.[1] All being well I shall be meeting up with their daughter Honoria tomorrow at twelve. As ever – things happen in New York.

Monday, May 25th: New York

Honoria Donnelly Murphy is a striking woman – over 80 with patrician white hair and a nose that is hooked like a Roman. Her face is heavily powdered and she wears elegant black. Her daughter, Laura, is 30-something, perky. A single mother by the sound of things.

She has brought photos and slides of Hemingway, and two or three letters (copied) – one the very moving letter he wrote to Patrick Murphy when he knew the boy had little chance of recovering from his second bout of TB. 'No-one you love is ever dead.'

'Everyone sought his approval,' she said, 'he was that kind of man.' Once she remembers pulling her hair in a bun and securing it with 56 different pins. When she asked Hem what he thought he nodded – 'Too many pins.'

Honoria moves quite slowly, but purposefully, with the aid of a stick, along to the Blue Water Grill in Union Square where we eat well.

1 Gerald and Sara Murphy were Scott Fitzgerald's models for Dick and Nicole Diver in *Tender Is the Night*. Their biography was called *Everybody Was So Young*.

She has liver cancer but is in remission, which makes me very sad for she's a warm, friendly and easy companion.

A good day, in which the most remarkable piece of information was possibly that this exquisite repository of Victorian taste called the Inn at Irving Place was a Rasta flophouse 15 years ago.

Saturday, June 13th

Note death of John Marriott, the energetic, friendly and liberal Governor of Parkhurst, who entertained us with such generosity when we filmed *Palin's Column*. He was 51. I wrote a letter to the paper protesting against his dismissal from Parkhurst after the break-out. Can't help feeling another life force snuffed out whilst meaner, lesser men survive.

A fan has sent me a copy of the *Dandy* – in which I'm now immortalised as Michael Railin – Famous World Traveller, complete with notebook, pencil and shoulder bag. The family especially like the way my nose is drawn. I just like appearing in the same comic as Desperate Dan. One of those magic, not quite believable connections with my childhood. On a par with hearing Elvis Presley loved Monty Python.

Sunday, June 14th

I've had an odd, hovering sense of dislocation over the last few days, maybe even weeks.

I'm sort of echoing what Michael Katakis was trying to say when we talked in Montana. Where is home? This is not a question that troubled me, but recently it's been on my mind – as I stare out of aircraft windows at the world below.

Perhaps it's partly to do with my reconnection with America – well, the USA. This year's work – on Hemingway, on the Ephron film, on the Hemingway book tour – has put me back in touch with the American way of doing things. The enthusiasm they have shown for my work – and my work with Python too – is infectious and rather gratifying. The likes of Norah, Sherrie, Michael K and Nancy have reminded me how bright and stimulating the Yanks can be.

Then back to England, and its fields and neat old rural patterns seem oppressive; the city, as usual, a little frustrating. Car alarms, more graffitied scribbles, wanton destruction and Tube strikes threatened.

And, oddly, and though it irritates me to have even noticed it, let alone allow myself to be pricked by it, there is the latest Honours List. June Whitfield, John Peel, etc. all given some sort of recognition. What services does one have to give to be recognised? I can only assume that the Pythons are on some sort of blacklist, otherwise the group's work would have been recognised as having as universal an effect on TV comedy as the Beatles did on music.

I spend a couple of hours in the afternoon composing three letters to the Travellers Club, who have, after Frank Herrmann's promptings, finally elected me as a member.[1] I was prepared to accept, if only for access to one of the most beautiful buildings in London, but how much time do I want to spend with a body of men who regularly vote against the presence of women, except on sufferance and on the peripheries of the club?

Monday, June 15th

I hear that Anne has had an offer accepted for premises in Tavistock Street in Covent Garden. She's not certain when she will move the Mayday office there. Eleanor and Gloria – mainstays of my financial management – are both leaving. This succession of bombshells (not all unexpected) leaves me dazed and confused.

Worried too as to where Tom will find work. Talks of picking up with Sheridan again – his working life, as he comes up to 30, increasingly resembles a record that's stuck.

Rachel is only on the payroll of At-It for another ten days. Will is working to finish his thesis for his MA by the end of the week.

Thursday, June 18th

A proposal from Hoberman about the Python tour and marketing in the US has come through on the fax. I scan it quickly and am not encouraged by what I see – 54-show, nine-week tour in the US alone – some of the theatres well above the 2,000-seat capacity we preferred.

To dinner at Robert Young's. John Mortimer and his wife Penny among the other guests. Mortimer, who has become Sir John Mortimer

1 Frank Herrmann, retired publisher, influential member of the Travellers Club.

in the latest Honours List, lies back in a chair with a stick alongside him and apologises for not being able to get up. He'd had a fall and twisted his ankle.

He and I were both at Brasenose. He was there with Archbishop Runcie, and recounts with some amusement a mention of himself in Runcie's autobiography. Runcie, who has apparently seen Mortimer with girls 'at the bus stop' on frequent occasions, refers to Mortimer's 'irrepressible member'.

Asked John about writing. He does all his work longhand on a legal pad. 'I never learnt to type.'

Good food, immaculate decoration. Mortimer drank well and ate little and we all packed up around midnight.

Sunday, June 21st

Call Marianne, wife of John Marriott, ex-Governor of Parkhurst who died last week. I ask if he'd been ill. She says, sounding shockingly cheerful, that he'd been upstairs, on a rowing machine, had come down, walked round the garden and 'fell dead at my feet'.

What with news of Tumim leaving Teddy Hall after only two years as Principal (difference of opinion with unpleasant bursar) I feel that my two Great White Hopes for a sensible attitude to prisons and prisoners have suffered from the forces of reaction.

Marianne says that John was on verge of a breakdown after his Parkhurst dismissal. 'Look at that footage you shot,' she advises, still with a chuckle, 'in the recreation area there's a whole group of prisoners saying what a good bloke the Governor is – well at least two or three of them went over the wall that night.'

Thursday, June 25th

Spend much of the morning reading through Justice Rattee's judgement on the Paragon/Channel 4 case. It's 92 pages long and, like many of the best novels, it demands early concentration and repays it with great drama later on.

Rattee is clearly appalled by the behaviour of Paragon and Jon Slan – 'a thoroughly unreliable witness' – and singularly unimpressed with their solicitor – 'evidence extremely unsatisfactory ... impulsive carelessness'.

Channel 4 hardly come out of it well. They have still not exercised their right to appeal – only 24 more hours to do so.

Saturday, June 27th

This morning I put my mind to the Gospel Oak tree-planting. Should I rely on off-the-cuff or write down my thoughts on the inspirational nature of the event?

The public garden – about 80 feet by 20 feet – where the oak is to be planted is little more than a strip, but it has been carefully and painstakingly prepared.

A bossy, blonde lady with 'Steward' written on a yellow badge secured to her left breast stands up and addresses the small crowd, then asks me to plant the tree. She's taken half the words out of my mouth already and does not seem to consider it worth asking me to say a few words.

So once the oak is planted (and it is a sapling descended from the oak tree at Hatfield House under which Princess Elizabeth was sitting when told she was to be Queen Elizabeth I) I uncharacteristically have to ask to speak.

The bossy blonde bemoans the 'negativity' of the local residents, but I wonder if she ever gives them a chance. I suggest, obliquely, that gardens like this, places where people can get together and meet naturally – pubs, cafés, libraries – are more important than people going round banging on doors and asking people to join this or that.

Tuesday, June 30th

As England's next 'hour of destiny' arrives in France[1] I make my way up to a lecture hall behind the Royal Free Hospital, with the running order of my slide show rolled up and tucked away in my inside pocket.

Helen Marcus of the Friends of Hampstead Town Hall is looking worried – a lot of people have called in to say they'll send the cheque, but they have to stay and watch the football.

A small handful of punters fill the first few rows of the hall. But I do my best for them.

When I finally walk back down an eerily quiet Agincourt Road and

1 England v Argentina in the World Cup.

past the flats, the game's obviously entered extra time for there is a telly on in nearly every house I pass.

Golden goal period. David Beckham off. England only have ten men but are holding the Argentinians. They hold on until penalties. Enormous relief, impossible tension. A's second goal saved, then Ince saved. Neither side looks that comfortable.

There's only H on the sofa and me, just arrived, in the hall, when Batty's poor shot is saved and he joins Waddle and Southgate in the growing group of those who have had the final word in another – glorious – English failure.

Thursday, July 2nd

A conference call to discuss reactions to the Python tour proposals.

A BT voice comes on and links us up one by one – first me, then TJ in Wales, 'from where I'm talking I can see a sheep', then Eric in Venice, at the Cipriani, and finally JC, sounding already a wee bit testy, in Montreal where he's filming with Bette Midler. TG can't be found. He's gone to Italy but I relay his general unwillingness to the rest. No-one thinks his lack of performing is completely disabling, provided he's involved in other ways.

Over a period of 40 minutes we agree on certain specific requirements with which Hoberman's people should go back to the producers. Nine weeks max; six shows a week; four different venues all in the USA; average size around 2,500 people.

Eric is happy to do it on a rock concert basis – big side-screens enabling us to play enormous halls. JC and myself most keen on performing in a pleasant atmosphere where we have some control over the audience.

Monday, July 13th

A phone call over the weekend from Robert Agnew asking me to come to Belfast for the festival. At a time when the news is all of people leaving the province as the Drumcree siege[1] persists, his invitation has a certain perverse attraction and I agree in principle to a one-nighter.

I ask about Michael Barnes. He's been in hospital and is now at a

---

1 The 1998 Drumcree siege was inflated by a decision from the new Parades Commission to ban the traditional route of the march. Three children died in the protests that followed.

nursing home. His short-term memory has almost gone. I think of him this morning and feel a short, sharp choke of despair at the ruthlessness of ageing. Sometimes you want time to stop and people to be always as you want to remember them.

Wednesday, July 15th

At eleven I drive to the Stammering Centre for a photocall with children for a magazine article.

I never really mind coming to the Centre. Not only is the welcome enthusiastic but the atmosphere is always upbeat and positive, and it's good to meet the parents and the children who've benefited. A mixed bag today, articulate, confident private-school boy from Chelmsford (without parents), and a local father with cropped haircut and stitches down his forehead with wife and, equally articulate, son.

Roger M, my *Daily Telegraph* correspondent, has rung to tell me that there is a review of last night's Mike Wood programme on Alexander the Great headed 'In the Steps of Palin the Great'. One of *Full Circle*'s best reviews, he says. A year late.

Thursday, July 16th

Ann Jefferson[1] arrived just after I left this morning. She's very easy to chat to, and we eat in and listen to her horror stories of life in Wilton, Connecticut. She was diagnosed as having Lyme's Disease just before she flew over. From deer ticks. It's what Kevin had at the start of *Fierce Creatures* filming. Seems particularly prevalent at the top end of the property market.

Makes me quite relieved that I live in a city. 'Much healthier than the countryside.' 'Oh, much!' says Ann with feeling.

Monday, July 20th

Good news from the Law Courts. Damages have been discussed today and as Paragon are in receivership we're pursuing Channel 4 for most of the money. They claimed today that as not all points against them were proven they were prepared to give no more than 50% maximum. The

1 Ann Jefferson, one of Helen's oldest friends, who was living in America.

court considered this and ordered them to pay 80%. Very good news for us – and prospect of something like two-thirds of our £500,000 costs being reclaimed is not a distant one.

Tuesday, July 21st

A list in this morning's *Independent* of the 100 books of the century chosen by the editorial board of Modern Library, a division of Random House. In the opinion of Gore Vidal, A. Schlesinger Jnr, W. Styron, A. S. Byatt, John Richardson and others, Hem's Nobel Prize-winner *The Old Man and the Sea* doesn't rate. In fact EH barely scrapes into the top 50 (*The Sun Also Rises* is at 45). He would doubtless have whizzed round in his grave to have seen Scott Fitzgerald at 2 (*Great Gatsby*) and 28 (*Tender Is the Night*).

Watch *42 Up* – remarkable continuation of the *7 Up* series begun in 1963 by Michael Apted. The most odious of the seven-year-olds has grown up to be the most successful – a QC now so prominent that he would not appear in the programme.

All the encounters had an intense and revealing power. There was nowhere for the interviewees to hide, one felt, because we know them too well. A dozen plays there.

Sunday, July 26th

To Henley with H to see George H.

George is in amongst his recently planted trees – he's put in 150 in the last couple of months. He emerges from beneath an arch made from old tree stumps – a wonderful, elaborate, fantastical construction. He's looking good. Trim figure. Hair shortish.

On the broad, green, sloping curve of grass, as we shuffle about trying to find patches of sunlight coming through the trees, he launches into a long description of what he calls with a rueful smile 'my little brush with cancer'.

He tells, quite matter-of-factly and unemotionally, the story of connections and revelations – discovery of a spot on the lower inside surface of the mouth leading to discovery of a spot on the upper part of one lung. Most of it happened in the last year, and though the lung treatment (removal of what did turn out to be a malignant spot) was done at the Mayo Clinic in America, the six weeks of acutely uncomfortable laser therapy on his neck and throat was done at the Royal Marsden in Sutton, Surrey.

George drove himself every day, five days a week, for six weeks out along the M4 and the M25 to have his 30-second zapping.

George leavens all this with his Indian wisdoms about the transience of this bodily life – 'We have always been here and always will be here' – and praises the Self-Realisation Fellowship for their help and prayers.

We move on up to the house for tea. The little front room, where Olivia keeps her glasses in a silver metal case like my own, with a label reading 'Kitchen' stuck on it.

It seems every corner and every detail of Friar Park is preoccupying them. George admits that the Matterhorn's not in great shape and the Rockery is a wilderness. But he's had carpenters build a small Russian 'dacha' complete with onion dome and cross, and a ring of stones he calls Friarhenge.

We end the evening sitting near Friarhenge, whilst George stokes a campfire.

It's extraordinary in a way – this restless, creative, inventive multi-millionaire ending up, happy as Larry, sitting round a fire of twigs and branches.

It begins to rain. We're shielded for a while by the trees but around 10.30 we strike camp and begin to start back.

Tuesday, August 4th

Call Terry J and put to him my views on the Python tour. I'm as frustrated as everyone else by the lack of hard detail on the offers – or realistic detail anyway – and suggest that we scale down the whole project, and instead of nine weeks on the road, play one week (say five shows) on one stage with making of film or TV deal added on.

This way we could make some money without committing to the slog and complication of a tour, and try out a show that could be exciting but not have enough time to become boring in the playing. We could always then play it elsewhere in 2000. TJ adds that under this shorter arrangement TG may become fully involved.

The house is quiet as I pack once again, for a Hemingway recce in Havana. I feel a touch of loneliness. A reminder of how much fun I have with the family, and the prospect of leaving home yet again at 4.45

tomorrow morning on a project which I know will keep me away from them for much of another year.

Then I realise that I've been through all this before – on Python films, *Ripping Yarns, 80 Days*, etc. etc. It's part of my life and probably always will be.

Saturday, August 8th: Ambos Mundos Hotel, Havana

It is ten to ten in the morning as I write, here in the building, indeed on the very floor, in which Hemingway was turning the Spanish Civil War into *For Whom the Bell Tolls*, 60 years ago.

Notes before leaving Ambos Mundos, and Havana, for cooler climates on the Great Lakes. The great sweaty heat reducing all human movement to a slouch or a stroll. The weight of the humidity bowing the shoulders. Only one street away from Obispo and O'Reilly, both prepared for tourists, are potholed road surfaces, torn wiring, houses that look abandoned but are lived in – bicycles and tricycles, thin, almost emaciated old women – the smell of human effluent.

Street traders, people waiting, squatting, crouching. Awful prison of language – not knowing enough Spanish to really respond to these people. Are they all trying to sell me something, or is it just a natural openness which I've mistaken for hassle?

Hemingway never wrote about life in Havana – he always wrote about one country whilst in another.

Monday, August 10th: Petoskey, Michigan

Petoskey itself is a comfortable, well-behaved, well-looked-after town. Last night David [Turnbull] and I found a micro-brewery and drank wheat beer – tonight we're booked in at a restaurant called Andante – which, ominously, promises 'eclectic gourmet dining'. The word gourmet frightens me enough – God knows what the eclectic will involve.

Tuesday, August 11th: Petoskey

Am quite shattered by the concentration of a one-hour Python conference call prompted by reaction to my last week's proposal for one week in Vegas. More later, must pack now – but it was one of the more bitter Python altercations. I've made a dent in the nine-week option, and won a few days' breathing space to consider a less Hollywood-driven alternative. JC also off the nine-week option, but only because it won't raise him enough money.

Cloud thickening out over Little Traverse Bay. Temperature down. Time for a coffee on the terrace which looks across to where the railway station once stood and from which EH drew inspiration for a story or two. What an unlikely place to be deciding Python's destiny!

Monday, August 17th

Run for first time since my morning plod by the shores of Little Traverse Bay, followed by the Python conference call in which the relentless forward momentum to a megabucks, money-at-all-cost Python tour was checked. Today, it's followed by a meeting of the British Pythons – Terry J, John, myself and Terry G – at Nico Central to discuss a possible new direction.

The meal is rather bad. Terry J has taken against the place from the start and becomes especially heated when they can't find him a toothpick.

Gilliam is a little subdued. He says he's 'numb', but it's good to have him back in the group discussion. JC clearly doesn't fancy a long tour and in the end we agree on two weeks' preparation and rehearsal, and two weeks at Las Vegas.

Over in Washington President Clinton goes on TV to admit his fling with Monica Lewinsky.

Wednesday, August 19th

Terry J calls. Eric has sent an email reply after hearing news of the meeting. As we both agree, not a friendly response and certainly not an understanding one.

So, for a moment, the process is stalled. EI suggests we pay off the lawyers and forget the whole thing. The first seems something devoutly to be wished.

Stay at home all day and, despite mugginess inside, and tempting sunshine outside, I try to focus down on an order of filming for the Hemingway series. A script and a structure for the USA and Cuba.

Thursday, August 20th

Finish up my Cuba notes and put it all together for a production meeting.

David arrives at 12.30 – wearing a music biz T-shirt and carrying his Hem papers in a plastic bag and bearing the news that Clive James is about to film one of his 'postcard' series in Havana. They'll be there from mid-September.

When Martha arrives clutching a vast amount of paperwork, I make them sandwiches and we sit down to examine all the various problems of time, location, budget, etc.

It's a good session. After two and a half hours I feel that we have come further than in all our previous discussions.

No fancy special effects – we don't have time; will attempt to shoot Cuba for the marlin-fishing tournament and before Clive James, then have a rest back here for two clear weeks before going to USA. Return to Idaho for Sun Valley/Ketchum ending to the series at end of the filming.

The clearing of the air on 'HT' and a conciliatory fax from EI agreeing to the two-week Las Vegas proposal has lifted my mood from sluggish pessimism to real enthusiasm for the task ahead.

Clinton, in whom I'm afraid I've lost much faith after Monday's weasely Lewinsky performance, is in front of the American people again – telling them with the same firm jaw and steely gaze why he has ordered air strikes on Sudan and Afghanistan without consulting the United Nations.

He's now punching some foreigners – only this, we all know, will affect our lives far more than his devious dismissal of Lewinsky.

Friday, August 21st

Have arranged Damien Hirst's Pharmacy for a boys' night out with TG and Ray. The Medical Council challenged the name Pharmacy and it has been changed by anagram to Aram Cyph.

Ray becomes very vociferous about the destruction of the old East End and predicts that the Millennium Dome will be the ruination of Greenwich. TG has been approached by the Dome Fillers. It's clearly a big corporate clean-up in there and what TG would like to do (a version of his Human Body fairground ride) would be in far too poor taste for any big sponsor – so that's that.

Sign the bill with a pen shaped like a hypodermic. Pick our way through packed crowd of young who are now dancing downstairs amongst the pill cabinets, past the wannabes clustering round the entrance and then a long natter by the car in Ladbroke Terrace. So long that TG has to go into a neighbouring garden to relieve himself behind the hedge.

Thursday, August 27th

Drive to TJ's for squash. He looks even more harassed than me and has evidently had a very similar day of phone calls, demands, etc.

The game is probably therapeutic. Forty minutes devoted to one subject only. I'm unable to overcome my serving shortcomings and lose yet again – my last victory seems to recede into the mists of time.

Home at eight. Am reading A. E. Hotchner's memoir *Papa Hemingway* at exactly the point where he recounts a long, rambling, bitter phone call from Hemingway about the intolerable demands of celebrity – the photographers, the requests for interviews; the impossibility of getting any work done. Fax the page to Terry.

Saturday, August 29th

To Covent Garden to augment wardrobe for the filming ahead. Entering the Emporio Armani at 10.30 on a Saturday is a pretty intimidating experience. The 'assistants' (perhaps storm troopers would be a better description) are ranged across the threshold; unsmiling, dressed in black, like some sort of personal army (Giorgio's of course) of cool. Very fascist and thoroughly unpleasant, until you actually talk to Giorgio's soldiers and realise they're rather nervous and from South Shields.

Monday, August 31st

A year ago Princess Diana died and *Full Circle* went before the public for the first time. Feel as if I haven't done much that's new since then.

Publicity, publicity, publicity – revisiting work of the past – Python revisited in Aspen, *Hemingway's Chair* revisited in the USA in May and June.

Tuesday, September 1st

Work on the Chicago/Michigan ideas. David T arrives. I make sandwiches for lunch and we talk through material. Halfway through our
discussions the phone rings – it's Nora Ephron. Pleasantly but efficiently
she lets me know that my contribution to *You've Got Mail* is on the cutting room floor.

Apologies – it was too long, impossible to cut – 'we tried triage', look
forward to working together again. I'm no wiser by the end. Except that
I had doomy feelings about the character even while we were shooting.
He seemed a clever idea but rather an alienating character. I think I was
too heavy. 'Everyone loved having you around.' Well that's something.
Maybe I could just visit film sets in the future.

On to André's studio. Record 80 limericks to coincide with reissue of
my 1985 collection. Cassette should be ready by November.

Wednesday, September 23rd

Taxi down to Covent Garden. Walk over to the Orion HQ in St Martin's
Lane.

Michael Dover, the editor/publisher of Weidenfeld Illustrated Books
– which is the imprint bidding for 'Hem's Travels' – is a smooth operator – tall, blond hair falling onto forehead, upper-crust accent.

We talk. They show me some of their books, which are certainly no
better than the BBC, but they do sound to be a highly focused company,
with books as their priority and a good international network. Dover is
a friend of Tom Dunne's which helps, and I have a feeling that they will
be much less fazed by Basil's input than the BBC.

At the end of an hour together I meet Anthony Cheetham, who is the
head of the company. He beams, listens and tells me 'I just wanted to
shake your hand before you left the building.'

As we walk back Anne and I talk through the pros and cons. We
stop for a coffee at the Seattle Coffee Company on Long Acre. Both
of us have some reservations over Dover's manner – the soft words of
encouragement sounded oddly abrupt and businesslike – but we liked
the feel of the company. I think that the Basil factor is important – more
than ever if he's designer – and I remember how irritated he always was
with procedures at the BBC.

I like Cheetham and I think, because of the money they're prepared to spend, that they will sell it well. Anne confirmed that they have no options on any future books of mine.

By the time we're back at Tavistock Street I've made my mind up to try Orion/Weidenfeld for 'Hemingway's Travels'.

New director, new producer – why not new publisher. Only way to learn.

Home for lunch. Halfway through afternoon Rachel rings to say she's been offered a job at Choice, on the new BBC Digital service which began this morning.

Saturday, September 26th

Good news that Will has got a job at the Georgian Group for three days a week. Their remit is to protect and preserve Georgian architecture. Like Rachel with the BBC, there is the feeling of being on the first rung of ladders that both of them want to climb.

Thursday, October 1st

To Tavistock Street for a long letter session. Among the many requests is one asking me to join the Millennium Dome experience. I've been rather dreading some approach from them, but this one is couched in such obscure millenno-babble that I have no difficulty in saying no. 'We feel your talents would be best suited to The Mobility Zone'!

Friday, October 2nd

A letter from Alan Bleasdale begins 'You wrote to me on New Year's Day' and ends by offering me the part of Brownlow in his adaptation of *Oliver Twist*.

He says 'there has been something stopping me from writing to you, until I'd written for you'. Filming will be Feb–June next year. I hope my dates might fit.

Saturday, October 3rd

Work hard to clear as much of my desk backlog as possible, and set to packing for US. A small celebration of Tom's upcoming 30th which will fall when I'm in Petoskey next week.

I'm very proud of him – he's come through 30 years as well as any son of a celebrity. He's his own man – quite stubborn, but persistent and hard-working. Of course I often think I should have pushed him more in this, that or the other direction, but he doesn't strike me as angry or frustrated with where he is now. Precious little angst in the boy. Possibly too little. He's much more of H's temperament than mine.

Tuesday, October 27th

By car to the Savoy – an invitation to a celebratory lunch for Schuyler 'Skye' Jones's[1] CBE, with which he has been invested this morning.

A wonderful mix of guests – Wilfred Thesiger, David Attenborough and a large tribe of Skye's in-laws.

Attenborough is on good form. He asks me, in mock horror, about the news that I am leaving BBC Books. He left them years ago, except as salesman. He is so baffled, as I am, by the new management terminology at BBC Worldwide that he actually shows me his notebook in which he has written down his editor's new title – full of words like 'genre' and 'global', and no mention of the word books.

The jolly party breaks up around four o'clock. Time to get back home and dress up for the National TV Awards at the Albert Hall.

About halfway through the long event the documentary award comes up and out comes Alan Whicker, tiptoeing gingerly through the silver gossamer set to announce and present.

'And the winner is' – professional pause – '*Full Circle with Michael Palin.*' I am so convinced that this will follow the BAFTA pattern that I'm already clapping for the camera trained upon me, in case I should look churlish. Takes a moment or two to sink in that I'm actually applauding myself.

Complete surprise, but this voted for by the viewers rather than the secretive, insider committees of BAFTA. And that Whicker should have to present me with the award does sort of bring things, well, full circle.

1 Schuyler Jones, curator of Oxford's Pitt Rivers Museum while teaching cultural anthropology at the university.

Friday, October 30th

Talk with David Turnbull and Martha Wailes before Martha goes to Milan, Sunday, to begin two-week recce in Italy.

I feel now that I know the dynamics between the three of us a little better. I had been cautious with David, not wanting to stifle his own thoughts and his independent perspective on the series. Now I think that he has said probably all he wants to say about basic approach, i.e. avoid anything that smacks of conventional arts biography, and is happy to sit back and be led by my enthusiasm – which he regards as less suspect than Martha's enthusiasm.

Martha still straitjacketed by her careful, linear approach to H's life – but she seems to have relaxed and accepted that what comes out will generally be my preferences and perceptions.

To Tristram and Virginia's for supper. Georgia there with new baby Hope. Tristram cooks veal knuckle.

Talk turns to diaries. Tristram confesses to keeping one in his teens. 'Deeply, deeply embarrassing,' he says. 'Everything was either "pleasant" or "boring".'

A pleasant evening. Not at all boring.

Monday, November 2nd

To a reception for BBC 'performers' and 'contributors' up on the 6th floor of TV Centre.

Think of Rachel and wonder how her first day at BBC Choice is going.

At the reception I encounter Peter Salmon, who's talking to Richard Wilson. Peter talks of the continued agonies of supporting Burnley – 'I'm getting really tired of failure.'

Frost appears – we talk about his family – all the boys are going to Eton. I ask him if he knew Diana as well as he knows Charles. He says that he and Carina used to see her for a while then she would disappear from their life for long periods. She was godmother to their youngest child, though. Now she's been replaced by David Seaman![1]

Peter makes a short speech, the main drift of which is to announce, in awed tones, that in just over a year's time the BBC will be embarking

---

1 David Seaman, England and Arsenal goalkeeper. Frost himself was a pretty good goalkeeper.

on its greatest single programme ever. The Millennium. Oh God. Thirty-six hours of continuous presentation. Oh God. And many presenters will be needed.

Much muttering and looking away from the assembled Frosts, Deaytons and Attenboroughs. What does this forebode – MP on a Pacific island?

Leave around a quarter to eight. Rachel back at home an hour later. A good first day. Her team all women.

Tuesday, November 3rd

Alan Bleasdale rings. 'Brownlow's getting bigger and bigger,' he confides. All of which is quite painful as I shall have to squeeze even more time out of tight 'HT' schedule. 'You get to do a pistol-whipping in episode six,' AB tells me, as if this might really sway it.

To Orion, to first meeting with Michael Dover since the decision to go with Weidenfeld & Nic's for 'Hem's Travels'.

It's 3.30 and prematurely dark outside. The red neon lights from the St Martin's Theatre across the road stand out like a slash of lipstick.

Talk through thoughts on the book so far. Dover is hoping to meet up with Basil in New York in early December. There has been a lot of foreign interest since Frankfurt and he clearly wants to try and get as much of the book blocked out a.s.a.p. so the foreign translations can be given time to produce the books in Hem anniversary year.

As we discuss dates there clearly is a problem. I undertake to write the Cuba section by mid-December, but cannot concentrate on the rest until March 22nd. Eyebrows raise. I had hoped to be available for Bleasdale's *Oliver Twist* during that period. Eyebrows bounce off ceiling. I know now that I'm not destined to play Brownlow.

Thursday, November 5th

Ring Alan B and tell him I can't do *Oliver Twist*. He says he lost me and Robert Lindsay in half an hour and now he's slipped a disc.

JC calls; he's in London to make a series of commercials for Sainsbury's at Christmas campaign – then he returns to US.

We talk a little about the Vegas stage show. Roger Saunders told me that it is still being prosecuted and the MGM Grand, with capacity reduced to 2,900 seats, may be the best.

'I'm not going to cry myself to sleep if it *doesn't* happen,' says John.

Friday, November 6th

To the Landmark Hotel for second award ceremony since return from filming in Montana. These are The Talkies – awards for the spoken word. I'm at Table 2, right in front of the stage, with various BBC Worldwide luminaries and next to me Mary K – Alan Bennett's long-time producer. She says Alan is getting a lifetime achievement award but will not be coming along. There has been some development 'in his illness' as Mary K puts it.

But Spike Milligan has come along and I'm put next to him for most of the meal. He comes in, with his manager Norma Farnes in attendance, looking very frail.

A female acquaintance comes across to pay homage. She squats down beside his chair. Spike turns to her. 'You used to be much taller.' To a cheery greeting from radio producer Jonathan James-Moore, Spike replies with an equally cheery 'I've been looking for your name in the obituaries for the last five years.'

I'm up for Best TV or Film Spoken Word Tape for *Full Circle* and win the category jointly with the doyen of all readers, Martin Jarvis.

A few awards later, Spike is named winner of the comedy award for *The Last Goon Show of All*. He receives an instant and unanimous standing ovation and when he steps down and returns to the table Norma tells him he should have said something. Spike shook his head and said softly, his eyes still wide, but a little moist as well now ... 'I was overcome.'

Later, I ask him what he reads – 'Biographies, autobiographies. Anything about the war.'

'Why are you so interested in the war?' I ask him.

'Well, I was in it, wasn't I.'

Thursday, November 12th

Sort through correspondence; think about my Belfast Festival performance tomorrow night. Had planned a first half of *Full Circle* slides and second half of readings and chat, but feel this wrong for the occasion and settle on an hour of reading and biographical reminiscence (I've given them the title '30 Years Without a Proper Job').

Friday, November 13th: London–Belfast

Seventeen years on from my first appearance at the Festival, the city feels very different. No longer a gauntlet of vehicle checks and security inspections. Very little sign now of a city under siege.

The Hilton is the latest state-of-the-art hotel. Prada-style black uniforms look a little odd on chunky Ulster bodies, but my suite on the eighth floor is comfortable, bright and has everything working.

Then across to the Whitla Hall at Queen's. This is from the old Belfast and is a big institutional hall designed for exhortations and degree ceremonies rather than intimate comedy.

I'm on, eventually, at 8.15. The theatre is sold out – 1,200 people. Bad start as the radio mike begins to crackle. The sound man, who seems to have been expecting the worst, brings another up to the front of the stage. Change the mike. The second one seems to be better but then it too begins to hiss and screech and I abandon both, to loud applause from the audience.

Saturday, November 14th: Belfast–London

To East Belfast to a gallery called The Engine Room, part of an old mill building. There is a Bill Viola installation. A baby being born on one side, a man dying on the other.

At one moment the newborn baby (apparently Viola's grandchild) and the dying, skeletal man (his father) seem both to share the same expression of patient suffering with this thing called life which neither of them ever demanded.

I'm driven out to the south of the city to see Michael Barnes. Modern, gabled bungalow accommodation for elderly people who have lost or partially lost their minds.

Michael is at a table with a couple of elderly ladies.

His beard has gone and he looks a little hunched, but he recognises and embraces me and smiles his generous smile and begins to laugh.

I've been advised to ask him if I can see his room – this gets him away and into some privacy. So we sit on his bed and look through books on trains and old photos of Armagh and so long as he sticks to the present he's fine. He laughs, and we make each other laugh, just the way we used to, but any attempts at personal reminiscence just peter out. He waves his long elegant hands dismissively ... 'Oh well, never mind.'

I didn't see doctors and couldn't ask whether things might change, because if this is premature senility, then it's come awfully early. He's not yet 70.

Monday, November 30th

Try and decide which of my dwindling supply of 'lounge suits' I should wear for the John Birt dinner this evening.

When I'm shown into the upper room at Broadcasting House where the drinks are being served, he shakes my hand warmly – and checks the suit. He is encased in some very modern black number which looks like something archdeacons wear – with no opening visible down the front at all.

A few guests already there including Germaine Greer, looking wild and woolly – grey hair erupting around her fine, strong head and with little metal glasses on she looks, for a brief moment, like John Cleese in drag.

I break the ice by, first of all, kissing her warmly, which she doesn't seem at all prepared for, and remembering the days on *Twice a Fortnight* when I carried her through Kenwood. 'Carried Germaine?' picks up Birt, with rather unflattering incredulity.

We're joined by a man called Charlie Whelan, an amiable, law-unto-himself presence – with a roguish, teasing line in banter, an ever-present mobile phone. He's Gordon Brown's adviser.

When all 20 of us are present we're sat at a long table and the lights are dimmed very low. Birt stands up and hits a glass for silence and assures everyone that this is not a seminar or a chance to talk about the inner workings of the European television code of practice – we should enjoy ourselves. He does add something about being a chance to thank some of the BBC's most successful contributors – and mentions myself and David Croft by name.

Talk travel for most of the meal to Jane Birt. John is deep in conversation with Lord Falconer – a minister of state – whom I later see chatting intensely to Anthea Turner, who has one long leg stretched out across a row of chairs.

Bill Oddie gives me a ride home, confesses that he doesn't really like things like this – always feels like a naughty schoolboy and finds no-one ever talks about the things he enjoys – music and, well, Bill, I suppose.

Home around midnight.

Tuesday, December 1st

John C calls from America about the Python stage show.

He signals that ten nights in a 2,000-seater at Las Vegas doesn't look as if it will provide enough capital to make up for the time spent preparing the show which he estimates as three weeks. So, he's backing off. Asks me my opinion of the alternative – big audiences, relying on TV screens to see us. I'm not keen and neither is he.

Thursday, December 3rd

A note from St Martin's, congratulating me on *Hemingway's Chair*'s appearance on the *New York Times* list of the Year's Notable Books.

Friday, December 4th

Ten years ago today I was leaving New York on a container ship, a week away from the end of my *80 Days* journey.

Today I'm up at 7.30 and down to the Tottenham Court Road to film another Clem Vallance travel epic. Only this time my involvement should be a maximum of 80 minutes. Have agreed to start a Comic Relief relay which will take a videotape through Africa, filling it on the way with images of Comic Relief work, messages from Mandela, etc. I'm to be filmed collecting the tape from a humble Tottenham Court Road hi-fi shop and setting up the next step, which is to take it to Rolf Harris, who will design the cover.

Because what we're doing is fundamentally so easy, it takes for ever.

Eventually complete the shot, and later a trailer for Comic Relief night in March. Farewell to Clem – who's on very benign, good-humoured form. I feel gently regretful that we aren't planning anything else together. Still, ten years is a neat, comprehensive period. Time to move on.

Sunday, December 6th

Largely working day. Pushing on to complete 8,000 words on Cuba.

Monday, December 7th

In that half-hour or so before I get up, the unsatisfactory Python stage show business pushes itself, once again, into the front of my mind. Try to push it back as I have done many times recently, but this morning it is dogged and demands to be taken seriously before it will go away.

Talk to H about it at breakfast. 'It' being my continued concern about the creation of a completely new show. Who will organise it and will it work? Eric and John are both over in California, Terry J, whom I spoke to recently, is busy rewriting 'Mirrorman' yet again and TG doesn't care.

Nothing seems to be happening between us.

So I must seize this beast and I know I shan't be able to settle to any other work until I have. Spend the morning composing a fax to send out to all the Pythons explaining my worries about the sort of thing we are planning and suggesting we do a much less formal 'Evening With' show or shows in New York or LA. In other words, stating the position I've always held but have twice compromised under pressure from the others.

Oddly enough, when I ring Roger Saunders to check if he's heard much from the others (which he hasn't) an offer of six days at the Beacon Theater in New York has just come in.

This sounds a lot better than the Millennium Dome which JC mentions a lot.

Wednesday, December 9th

To the Overseas Club in St James's Place in time for the Declaration Dinner, being organised by the Medical Foundation for Victims of Torture to announce fund-raising plans for a new centre.

I am sat next to Brian Keenan,[1] whose head is shaped like Enoch Powell's and who has a look of Enoch in the intense, slightly fierce, set of the eyes. Talk about their days of imprisonment. He calls them 'our

---

1 Irish Republican who, with John McCarthy, was held hostage in Beirut from April 1986 to August 1990. McCarthy was not released until a year later.

holidays' – 'when we were on our holidays' etc. He didn't take the offer of psychiatric help after their release – 'I felt if there was something that needed to be done, I'd better do it myself' – and he is sceptical of the good it did.

He says his captors thought America was the Great Satan, yet they wore bandanas to make them look like Sly Stallone in action.

He's disgusted by the level of violence in entertainment. Also pretty disgusted by David Trimble – 'Oh don't get him onto Trimble,' says John McCarthy. He thinks that in an Ireland united the Protestants would probably be more secure and successful than they are in the divided Ireland they're so anxious to promote.

Thursday, December 10th

Python developments – a fax from John via Roger. He feels that there isn't enough 'energy' in the group for a stage show. Terry G doesn't want to do it – 'Eric is on the sidelines' – Terry J will go along with whatever anyone else wants to do, and my new proposal ('for a rehash of the old show' as he puts it) doesn't interest him at all.

So, as John goes on his travels, all bets seem to be off. I feel unhappy and uncomfortable about my role in all this, yet ultimately I think I was right to sound continued warnings. I could, and indeed hope to be persuaded that we should do some sort of reappearance together, but the way things are at the moment, as John rightly recognises, there is no central driving force trying to make the show happen.

Thursday, December 17th

More cards, send first slice of the 'Hemingway's Travels' book to Michael Dover, and into town for lunch at Neal Street Restaurant.

Antonio Carluccio looms up, gives me a big bear hug and tells me that he's been to ITV to set up a series of travels. 'Like you do, only with food.' He mutters dark criticism of BBC Books. He has left them and will work for Hodder Headline until 2003.

He tells us all a joke about the Mafia – little Mafia boy writes to baby Jesus – 'if you ever want to see your mother again' – and goes off to do his Christmas shopping.

News of bombing raids in Iraq, and postponement, by two days, of impeachment vote on Clinton.

Friday, December 18th

Talk to Michael Ignatieff, who has been travelling with Richard Holbrooke, the US special envoy who brokered peace in Bosnia and has been currently struggling to hold the Wye Agreement (aptly named) between Israel and Palestine together. Michael, who is writing a piece about him for the *New Yorker*, asked how he approaches his task. Holbrooke apparently quoted the haggling scene from *Life of Brian* as his inspiration!

Will tell Eric this when I reply to his email, which has a severe go at me for changing my mind on the stage show and suggests therapy.

My morale improved by a complimentary fax from Michael Dover who says he wouldn't change a word of my text (this bodes well for the rest).

Monday, December 28th

Day of the post-Christmas river trip, so no long lie-in. Rewarded by quiet streets and have time to show Granny our new office location in Tavistock Street and Waterloo and Blackfriars Bridge views before gathering with the others for the 10.30 boat from Embankment Pier to Greenwich.

Full family turnout. Eleven in all. Onto a barge with chairs and a plastic hood. It's a quarter full, almost entirely of foreigners, as we turn under Charing Cross railway bridge and head downstream.

A Cockney commentary, full of jokes of the corniest sort and not even told with any charm, just routine taxi-driver sort of prejudices. Edward and especially Catherine Burd, both architects, made apoplectic by references to the National Theatre – 'thought by most architects to be the worst building in London'. Piers Gough's Cascade Towers – 'they say they were designed to look like a boat under full sail. Well all I can say is he's obviously never been on a boat in his life', and the Millennium Dome – 'biggest waste of taxpayers' money this country's ever seen'.

In a way I prefer this batty bigotry to a recorded message, but that's quite a perverse view to take.

An hour to Greenwich and the changes along both banks are considerable. Housing runs in a broken line on the south bank and an almost continuous line on the north, all the way to Greenwich. Canary Wharf is expanding again, after its dodgy hiatus in the late '80s and the bombing in the '90s. London's eastward spread looks inevitable and unstoppable now.

The Dome, a strange new shape, a blister amongst the strips of housing and the fingers of the tower blocks, looms beyond Greenwich's elegant seventeenth- and eighteenth-century façades.

We climb up the hill to the Observatory, following an ant-trail of visitors. There is a space on the wall below Flamsteed's Wren-designed building where the zero line of longitude runs. It's covered in graffiti.

Tuesday, December 29th

Low cloud, grey dawn. I think of Cleese in Barbados, or Eric in his pool in LA. What am I doing stuck here in this grubby, graffitied corner of dour, cold England, when I could be in the sun too?

This is much too complicated a line of enquiry to unravel, and anyway, it just makes me depressed lying there, playing the where-could-I-be-now? game.

Complete U-turn in mood as I switch over to hear Darren Gough's last over of the Fourth Test in Melbourne. Australia defeated!

Thursday, December 31st

If last year was a big one (*Full Circle* completion and transmission), this was its much-reduced younger brother. *Full Circle* echoed through until March, when Aspen revived Python (only for it to be put back in its box), and stimulated me into the Hemingway project. Sidetracked, and ultimately sidelined, by *You've Got Mail* (currently No. 1 in US). Surprised, very pleasantly, by the success of *Hemingway's Chair* in America.

A sputtering firework of a year. I hope that it will lead to a better display to end this millennium.

Extracts from
Michael Palin's Diaries, 1999

1999

Friday, January 1st

We both hope it's the shape of things to come, for the grey clouds of Christmas have rolled away and it's a scintillating start to '99. A great calm has descended after the efforts and the visitings of the past week and I feel wonderfully relaxed and rested, and also in one of those receptive and responsive moods in which everything around me looks its best – the house, the vase of flowers and the bowl of fruit catching the light on the oak table, with Anne Redpath's seductively colourful 'Old Town, Menton' looming above them.

My room, my books – everything that was under siege a week ago is now looking right.

So I spoil myself with a fleshy Patisserie Val croissant at breakfast, then divide the day between my room, a few letters and phone calls (Jeremy H rings – says I've come top of some Radio 5 poll on whom people would most like to see open the Millennium Dome – apparently Peter Stringfellow came last!).

Saturday, January 2nd

A long, full sleep would seem to have been the logical consequence of a serene and restorative New Year's Day, but once again that worry about being really good at anything (even sleeping) seems to have risen from somewhere, and I slept quite lightly, waking often, listening to the wind as another low-pressure system blows in from the west.

A lie-in and slow start to the morning. No real reason to leave the house today. Make a start on more Hemingway book material.

Ken Cranham and Fiona come round. Ken was recently lined up for a new TV series – it was written for him, but Peter Salmon judged him to be too old. 'Just as well, really,' says Ken, 'there was an awful lot of sex in it.'

TG rings to try and fix a lunch next week. He's been for a Gilliam family reunion in Dorset over New Year and raves about it. 'It was the

Madding Crowd all over again. I had to be Bathsheba and all the rest of the family were Terence Stamp.'

Watch *Bulworth* (another contender for my Oscar vote) later. A brief and flickering pain as I see Shuler Donner's producer credit. She produced *You've Got Mail*, and we got on well.

It reminds me that I *do* care a little that I've heard no explanation for my excision from the film, indeed no word at all from any of those people who were my friends back in New York in April. At the same time I console myself with the fact that I care much less about these little ego dents than I used to.

Sunday, January 3rd

Blustery wind and showers racing across as the airstream moves to the north. I assault Parliament Hill in a cold, whipping rain, but it eases as I run and there are breaks in the cloud when I make my final sprint up Oak Village.

To two local drinks parties – one with Susan Wood, the music teacher, who's just come back from walking in Sicily. Armageddon, in the shape of our neighbour Richard Drake's worst fears for the Y2K outcome (the Millennium Bug that may bring all our computing systems crashing when 2000 starts), is discussed. Bruce Robertson, who looks like a benevolent cartoon character, believes quite simply that, if it's in people's interest to sort it out, it will be sorted out. So, in the absence of any exact and precise information, the issue divides into two camps – optimists and pessimists. Which seems to be how most people are approaching the Millennium as a whole.

Monday, January 4th

To the Travel Clinic in Harley Street. Voluble Irish doctor/pathologist has lined up all the jabs I need. Typhoid and tetanus and meningitis. 'It's the meningitis season in Uganda,' she assures me. (And in Yorkshire too if the news is anything to go by – two students in Rotherham died of the disease over New Year.) I'm also given a booster of polio vaccine on a lump of sugar – more uncomfortable than any of the jabs, which are now administered with such fine needles that you hardly feel the penetration.

I'm to be off games for 48 hours, drink a lot (not, of course, alcohol), rest.

Various tasks completed at home, I look over plans of things to come and begin some work on the next section of the *Hemingway Adventure* book. The office is back in action. Feel quite depressed by current state of Python, and as there is no-one taking a leading role in organising us I imagine things will drift on.

Watch *Lolita* – Adrian Lyne's film with J. Irons. Not bad, not bad at all, though they've cheated a little by making Irons look almost younger than the nymphet.

Wednesday, January 6th

Picked up by cab to go down to the Royal Academy. I've been asked to record an appreciation of one of the pics in upcoming Monet in the 20th Century exhibition, for a series of one-minute progs on BBC 1.

My cab driver is a soft-spoken Afro-Caribbean who rather shyly asks if I wouldn't mind him asking me a question. There is an odd pause before he begins, which, as it turns out, is what the story is all about. Both he and his wife stammer. His nine-year-old son has now developed such a bad stammer he can hardly speak and his four-year-old daughter, with no previous problems at all, lively and outspoken, has suddenly begun to stammer too. He'd seen me talking about it on television and wonders if I have any helpful advice.

His lack of self-pity despite his obvious pain at what is happening to his children is very moving; I forget all about the painting and just what I'm going to say about it, and make sure that he has the number of the Stammering Centre and knows where it is.

In the RA forecourt temporary covered space is being put up to cope with the crowds – 100,000 tickets have already been sold, and it will all be on a regimented, time-controlled basis. The PR lady in attendance reckons it will be their biggest exhibition of the century.

I'm led upstairs to a gallery with only one painting on display – the one painting I'm to talk about – a view of the Thames from the Savoy – begun in 1899, completed in his studio in the next century.

Around me the rest of the Monets, 80 of them, are all still crated, just arrived from Boston. Apparently they have to stand for 48 hours in the new environment before they can be opened.

So, water-lily ponds, Rouen Cathedrals, Waterloo Bridges, all of enormous value, lean casually against the wall.

An extraordinary thing to behold. The backstage work of an

exhibition. The paintings are not yet in costume and make-up; they're fine paintings, but not yet stars.

So I feel privileged to witness all this, as I record my short interview and try my best to say what *I* like about the picture and not what the producer is trying to push me into saying. She wants me to angle it towards travel, I want to talk about the sky. 'Lots of enthusiasm,' she urges. 'Remember, it's BBC 1!'

Friday, January 8th

Clear skies. To Harmood Street, where, at No. 104, a delightfully enthusiastic lady called Josie, married to a Kurd, takes a mould for the Michael Palin mask we need for the Venice Carnival sequence. Have to lie flat and have my hair and all superfluous areas covered in cling-wrap, a couple of straws for breathing inserted in my nose, and a soft, cold mud of dental plaster layered onto my face.

The next twenty days were spent filming for the Hemingway Adventure *series in Africa. Hemingway, always accident-prone, had been involved in two plane crashes in 36 hours. We had something of a scoop when we reached the small town of Butiaba in Uganda, where his second crash took place. A local man, who had never been interviewed before, had not only witnessed the Dragon Rapide bursting into flames on take-off but had picked up some of the remains of the plane, one piece of which he insisted I keep. I found myself returning to London with a certain amount of apprehension. What would be the security implications if they found aeroplane wreckage in my bags?*

Monday, January 25th

Slept around nine hours, which must have recharged the batteries. Just as well, for a busy day ahead.

Preliminary discussion with Luke Jeans over tomorrow's shoot for the Stammering Centre video. Grab time for a short run, during which the heavens open. Return home drenched, but out a few minutes later to the first of the day's meetings – with Basil, who's designing the *Hem Adventure* book, to show Michael Dover and Orion's art director the pages he's put together so far.

All laid out on Michael's desk. He purrs happily – only demurring over a one-and-a-half-page spread of a wall. 'What is happening here?' he asks politely. 'Nothing's happening, it's a wall,' says Basil. 'One of Basil's little indulgences,' murmurs the art director.

To the office for meeting with the 'HT' production team. Italy and France both imminent and have to be discussed as virtually one continuous stretch of filming. Unlike Africa, which was largely retracing, in quite a linear fashion, we have to be more creative in Italy, and there are several contrived 'comedy' sequences in both Italy and France which will have to be tried before we know if they work and are at all necessary. So, a touch of the unknown.

The masks are ready. Hemingway's good – MP less so. Which I think confirms my impression of the two of us side by side in the book. He does make me look very ordinary.

Then out with Bas to Number One Aldwych for a martini – a sort of celebration for a good first reaction to the book. We conclude, once again, that we're lucky, jammy bastards.

Tuesday, January 26th

Woke, as if still on East African time, in the dark hours. Mental safari in my head, so I'm exhausted by the time I get up. Car over to the Stammering Centre. Normally, a bevy of children and therapists overwhelm me as soon as I set foot in the place, but today Diana de G keeps it low-key, so only one autograph and three therapists.

Luke Jeans is good. Able, efficient and knows what he wants. I have to introduce the film and back-reference it and ask for money etc. at the end. Quite a lot to say and I just have to concentrate and say it and mean it.

He wants to do a longer documentary piece about the Centre. Would I be prepared to do a voice-over? Of course I say yes – this is one cause which I always make a priority.

Up to Moro in Exmouth Market where I have arranged to meet Basil for a Bunter-ish lunch.

At a round table by the door is Nick Elliott, head of drama commissioning at ITV, and with him Prince Edward, who still seems absurdly young. He rises to shake my hand and I congratulate him on his engagement.

Nick, very much the old warhorse, greets me with a poignant cry of 'Brownlow!' Of course it's his people who are financing the Bleasdale

Oliver Twist. I'm slightly thrown as everyone round the table seems to be quite familiar with the intricacies of my involvement, or *non*-involvement, in the project.

But I do try out my idea of post-cooking programmes – eating programmes. 'Eat the World', which was my friend Michael Katakis' idea. Much laughter – Prince Edward, a paragon of politeness, remains standing and listening attentively.

Time, then, to catch up with myself – begin to select a wardrobe for Italy, make some calls.

Alone in the evening (H at badminton, Rachel at a film), I drive down to the Renoir to see *The Apple* – an Iranian film made by an 18-year-old female director. It was an austere, slow film, but the performances and the sense of claustrophobia in the house involved and the extraordinary ordinariness of the world outside very well conveyed. But by this time I'm a prey to sleep deprivation and only the uncomfortable cinema seat (it's easy to be on the edge of it) keeps me conscious in the slower passages.

Wednesday, January 27th

Shopping, visit to office – only Mirabel there, as Laura and Martha are both on the Italy shoot and out gathering last-minute items – cloaks etc. – for Carnival. Pick up schedule. Italy seems overly extended for what we have to collect (20 minutes max on estimates), but there is a lot of to-ing and fro-ing from Veneto to Milan and back. It will be hard work.

San Siro Stadium has refused permission for us to shoot the Red Cross stretcher sequence. [At the age of 17 Hemingway had volunteered as an ambulance driver in Italy in the First World War and my director, David Turnbull, wanted to recapture a sense of this by having me join a Red Cross team at one of the big Milan games.]

Letters with Annie, tax returns to be signed, then, with Basil, up to a meeting with Michael Dover, and two of his cohorts, on the book. All rather a rush of decisions – by three o'clock I'm in the YHA shop for last-minute weatherproof accessories, and up to the gym for a workout.

In the evening, after packing my bags, H and I go out to supper with Basil at the Royal China's new branch in Baker Street. Basil extols the pork belly.

I sleep very badly – not just PFT, pre-filming tension: there is another element to my continued wakefulness. It's as if I'm wired; tingling with consciousness at 3 a.m.

Then I hit upon a possible explanation – Basil has often described the effects of too much MSG in Chinese cooking, and this eye-stretched alertness seems to fit the bill.

Up at seven. It's a gloomy, wet morning.

Friday, January 29th: Venice

At our hotel close by the Rialto. This morning we came into the city from Caorle, where Hemingway used to go on duck shoots – and wrote about it in one of his worst books, *Across the River and into the Trees*; wild, windswept lagoon scenery. Mid-morning to the Palazzo Tron to meet Alberto Franchetti, from one of Venice's most famous families. His dad took EH shooting and composed operas in his spare time. Alberto, a chain-smoker, talks to us on a balcony looking down over the Grand Canal. Quite stunning location. But it doesn't seem to make him particularly happy. The increase in outboard motors on the Canal has made life in what would seem to me to be a paradise almost intolerable.

'My mother was the last of the family to sleep on the Grand Canal – now it's impossible.'

He asks if all went well in Africa (apparently an Italian guide had just been robbed and killed in Kenya and people are saying it's not safe any more). He remembers EH in Venice. He didn't seem like a happy man, he says. Nor did he seem much interested in La Serenissima. 'He sat in his room in the Gritti Palace and drank.'

I bring up the slightly awkward subject of how the book – *Across the River* – was received by the locals.

He smiles fleetingly. 'The truth is that nobody read it.'

Index

MICHAEL PALIN is a scriptwriter, comedian, novelist, television presenter, actor and playwright. He established his reputation with *Monty Python's Flying Circus* and *Ripping Yarns*. His work also includes several films with Monty Python, as well as *The Missionary, A Private Function, A Fish Called Wanda, American Friends* and *Fierce Creatures*. His television credits include two films for the BBC's *Great Railway Journeys*, the plays *East of Ipswich* and *Number 27*, and Alan Bleasdale's *GBH*.

In 2006 the first volume of his diaries, *1969–1979: The Python Years*, spent several weeks on the bestseller lists. He has also written books to accompany his seven very successful travel series: *Around the World in 80 Days* (an updated edition of which was published in 2008, twenty years later), *Pole to Pole, Full Circle, Hemingway Adventure, Sahara, Himalaya* and *New Europe*. Most have been No 1 bestsellers and *Himalaya* was No 1 for 11 weeks. He is the author of a number of children's stories, the play *The Weekend* and the novel *Hemingway's Chair*. Visit his website at www.palinstravels.co.uk.

MICHAEL PALIN
DIARIES 1980-1988

Halfway to Hollywood

WEIDENFELD & NICOLSON

A W&N PAPERBACK

First published in Great Britain in 2009
by Weidenfeld & Nicolson
This paperback edition published in 2014
by Weidenfeld & Nicolson,
an imprint of Orion Books Ltd,
Carmelite House, 50 Victoria Embankment,
London EC4Y 0DZ

An Hachette UK Company

5 7 9 10 8 6 4

A CIP catalogue record for this book is available
from the British Library.

ISBN: 978-1-7802-2902-7

Typeset by Input Data Services Ltd,
Bridgwater, Somerset

Printed in Great Britain by Clays Ltd, St Ives plc

The Orion Publishing Group's policy is to use papers that
are natural, renewable and recyclable products and
made from wood grown in sustainable forests. The logging
and manufacturing processes are expected to conform to
the environmental regulations of the country of origin.

www.orionbooks.co.uk

For Angela

Contents

List of illustrations

MP with stand-in Gerry Paris[2]
MP with Kevin Kline[2]
John Cleese trying to get information from MP[13]
Ken Pile. Fan photo[13]
Jamie Lee Curtis and MP embrace[13]

The family with Granny outside Sunset House, Southwold 1987[2]
MP on location with Joyce Carey, *Number 27*, June 1988[2]

1 Brian Moody
2 Author's Collection
3 HandMade Films Partnership
4 Sam Emerson
5 Pic Photos
6 Trevor Jeal
7 Andy Hanson
8 Chris Richardson
9 David Appleby
10 Mark Mullen
11 David Farrell
12 Erik Heinila
13 David James

While every effort has been made to trace copyright holders, if any have inadvertently been overlooked the publishers will be pleased to acknowledge them in any future editions of this work.

Acknowledgements

As with the first volume, *1969–1979: The Python Years*, I have had to reduce over a million words of diary entries to something nearer a quarter of a million. In this task I have, as before, been sagely advised and supervised by Ion Trewin. Michael Dover at Weidenfeld & Nicolson has been a constant encouragement in the completion and collation of the edit, and Steve Abbott and Paul Bird at my office have been, as ever, hugely supportive.

Once again, I must reserve my most special thanks for Katharine Du Prez for her patience and persistence in the Herculean labour of transcribing the contents of twenty-four close-packed, handwritten notebooks.

Who's Who in the Diaries 1980–1988

FAMILY

Mary Palin, mother, living at Reydon, Southwold, Suffolk. Father died in 1977.
Helen, wife
Children:
Tom born 1968
William born 1970
Rachel born 1975

Angela, sister. Married to **Veryan Herbert** and living at Chilton, Sudbury, Suffolk. Died 1987.
Children:
Jeremy born 1960
Camilla born 1962
Marcus born 1963

Helen's family:
Anne Gibbins, mother
Elder sister, **Mary**, married **Edward Burd** in 1964
Daughter, **Catherine**, born 1966
Younger sister, **Cathy**

FRIENDS, NEIGHBOURS AND COLLEAGUES

Richard and Christine Guedalla, and daughters Louise and Helen, neighbours

Clare Latimer, neighbour

Terry Jones and **Alison**

Terry Gilliam and **Maggie**

John Cleese, formerly married to **Connie Booth**, one daughter, **Cynthia**, born 1971, married **Barbara Trentham** 1981, separated 1987

Graham Chapman, partner **David Sherlock**. **John Tomiczek** (adopted)

Eric Idle, married **Tania Kosevich** 1981

Robert Hewison. Contemporary of MP at Brasenose College, Oxford 1962–5, during which time he persuaded MP to perform and write comedy for first time.

Simon and Phillida Albury. Simon met MP after Oxford in 1965. Television journalist, producer and Gospel music fan.

Ian and Anthea Davidson. Met MP at Oxford. Encouraged him to perform in revue and gave him early work at the BBC. A writer and director and occasional Python performer.

Chris Miller and Bill Stotesbury. Chris looked after Eric's son Carey during *Life of Brian*. Bill is a designer and banjo player.

Neil and Yvonne Innes. Neil, Ex-Bonzo Dog Band. Worked closely with the Pythons especially on their stage appearances. Collaborated with Eric to create the Rutles. Sons: Miles and Luke.

Mel Calman, cartoonist and friend

George Harrison. Musician, ex-Beatle. Married to Olivia Arias, son Dhani born 1978.

Derek and Joan Taylor, Beatles' publicist and wife

Chris Orr, artist and printmaker

Charles McKeown, actor, writer and performer in many MP films and TV shows

Geoffrey Strachan. Editor at Methuen who encouraged Python to go into print. Also published the *Ripping Yarns* books.

Tristram and Virginia Powell. Tristram was director/collaborator on *East of Ipswich, Number 27* and worked on development of *American Friends.*

André Jacquemin. Recording engineer, Python recordist, composer (with Dave Howman) of some Python songs. Founder of Redwood Studios.

Trevor Jones/John Du Prez, musician and composer (Python songs and *A Fish Called Wanda*)

Ray Cooper, legendary percussionist who became important go-between and general troubleshooter on all the HandMade films

OFFICE

At Mayday Management/Prominent Features:

Anne James, formerly Henshaw, manager. Married to Jonathan James, a barrister.

Steve Abbott, accountant/management, also film producer (*A Fish Called Wanda*)

Alison Davies

At EuroAtlantic/HandMade:

Denis O'Brien, Chief Executive, Executive Producer (*Time Bandits, The Missionary, A Private Function*)

Mark Vere Nicoll, legal expert

FILM REGULARS

Richard Loncraine, Director. First wife Judy. Married Felice 1985.

Neville Thompson, Producer

Mark Shivas, Producer

Julian Doyle. Editor, cameraman, who could turn his hand to any part of the film-making process. Indispensable part of both Python and Gilliam films.

John Goldstone, Producer of Monty Python films – *Holy Grail, Life of Brian* and *Meaning of Life*

Sandy Lieberson, Producer and sounding board for many projects, including Terry Gilliam's *Jabberwocky*

Patrick Cassavetti, Producer

IN AMERICA

Al Levinson. After wife Eve's death, married Claudie Calvez in 1979. Gwenola is their daughter.

Nancy Lewis. Publicist for Python in the USA, deserves much credit for getting them on US TV in the first place. Married actor Simon Jones in 1983.

The Films:

MONTY PYTHON LIVE AT THE HOLLYWOOD BOWL

Directors:	Terry Hughes (concert sequences)
	Ian MacNaughton (filmed sequences)
Producers:	Denis O'Brien – Executive Producer
	James Rich Jr – Concert Film Co-producer
	George Harrison – Executive Producer

Cast:	Graham Chapman
	John Cleese
	Terry Gilliam
	Eric Idle
	Terry Jones
	Michael Palin
	Neil Innes
	Carol Cleveland
Writers:	GC, JC, TG, EI, MP, TJ
Additional material:	Tim Brooke-Taylor
	Marty Feldman
	Angus James
	David Lipscomb
Editors:	Julian Doyle (post-production director and editor)
	Jimmy B. Frazier (editor: concert film)

TIME BANDITS

Director:	Terry Gilliam
Producer:	Terry Gilliam
Executive Producers:	George Harrison
	Denis O'Brien
Associate Producer:	Neville C. Thompson
Cast:	John Cleese
	Sean Connery
	Shelley Duvall
	Katherine Helmond
	Ian Holm
	Michael Palin
	Ralph Richardson
	Peter Vaughan
	David Rappaport
	Kenny Baker
	Malcolm Dixon
	Mike Edmonds
	Jack Purvis
	Tiny Ross
	Craig Warnock

Screenplay:	Michael Palin
	Terry Gilliam
Music:	George Harrison
Editor:	Julian Doyle

THE MISSIONARY

Director:	Richard Loncraine
Producers:	Michael Palin
	Neville C. Thompson
Executive Producers:	George Harrison
	Denis O'Brien
Cast:	Michael Palin
	Maggie Smith
	Trevor Howard
	Denholm Elliott
	Michael Hordern
	Phoebe Nicholls
Screenplay:	Michael Palin
Music:	Mike Moran
Editor:	Paul Green

MONTY PYTHON'S THE MEANING OF LIFE

Directors:	Terry Jones
	Terry Gilliam (segment 'The Crimson Permanent Assurance')
Producer:	John Goldstone
Cast:	Graham Chapman
	John Cleese
	Terry Gilliam
	Eric Idle
	Terry Jones
	Michael Palin
	Carol Cleveland
	Simon Jones
	Patricia Quinn
Screenplay:	GC, JC, TG, EI, TJ, MP
Editor:	Julian Doyle

BRAZIL

Director:	Terry Gilliam
Producers:	Patrick Cassavetti (co-producer)
	Arnon Milchan
Cast:	Jonathan Pryce
	Robert De Niro
	Katherine Helmond
	Ian Holm
	Bob Hoskins
	Michael Palin
	Ian Richardson
	Peter Vaughan
Screenplay:	Terry Gilliam
	Tom Stoppard
	Charles McKeown
Editor:	Julian Doyle

A PRIVATE FUNCTION

Director:	Malcolm Mowbray
Producer:	Mark Shivas
Executive Producers:	George Harrison
	Denis O'Brien
Cast:	Michael Palin
	Maggie Smith
	Denholm Elliott
	Richard Griffiths
	Tony Haygarth
	John Normington
	Bill Paterson
	Liz Smith
Screenplay:	Alan Bennett
Original story:	Alan Bennett and Malcolm Mowbray
Music:	John Du Prez
Editor:	Barrie Vince

A FISH CALLED WANDA

Director:	Charles Crichton
Producer:	Michael Shamberg
Executive Producers:	Steve Abbott
	John Cleese
Cast:	John Cleese
	Jamie Lee Curtis
	Kevin Kline
	Michael Palin
	Maria Aitken
	Tom Georgeson
	Patricia Hayes
Screenplay:	John Cleese
Story by:	John Cleese and Charles Crichton
Music:	John Du Prez
Editor:	John Jympson

Timeline

Main work projects during the period January 1980–September 1988

1980:
Writing and acting in *Time Bandits*
Filming 'Confessions of a Trainspotter', one-hour episode for BBC *Great Railway Journeys* series
Acting and filming *Monty Python Live at the Hollywood Bowl*.

1981:
Writing *The Missionary* and *Monty Python's The Meaning of Life*
Time Bandits released
First One-Man Show at Belfast Festival

1982:
Writing and acting in *The Missionary* and *The Meaning of Life*
The Missionary released in USA

1983:
The Missionary released in UK and Australia
The Meaning of Life released in US and UK. Wins Special Jury Prize at Cannes Film Festival
Film *Comic Roots*, one-hour autobiographical documentary for BBC
Second Belfast Festival Show
Begin filming *Brazil*

1984:
Complete *Brazil* filming
Filming *A Private Function*
Shoot short film *The Dress*
A Private Function has Royal Premiere in London and opens in UK

1985:
A Private Function opens in USA

British Film Year
Dr Fegg's Encyclopeadia of <u>All</u> World Knowledge published
Write *East of Ipswich* film screenplay for BBC
Third Belfast Festival Show
Limericks published

1986:
Become Chair of Transport 2000
Brazil released.
East of Ipswich filmed in Southwold, Suffolk
Begin writing 'The Victorian screenplay' (later to become *American Friends*)
The Mirrorstone published
Ripping Yarns premieres on US TV

1987:
East of Ipswich shown on BBC2
Start filming 'Troubles' for LWT (cancelled after one week due to union dispute)
Write *American Friends*, first draft
Write *Number 27* film screenplay for BBC
Filming as Ken Pile in *A Fish Called Wanda*
First discussions for *Around the World in 80 Days*
Fourth Belfast Festival Show
Resign Chair of Transport 2000

1988:
Rewriting, financing and casting trips for *American Friends*
Filming of *Number 27*
A Fish Called Wanda opens in America
Begin London filming on *Around the World in 80 Days*
Leave London to circumnavigate the world

Introduction

These diaries cover a period of my life when, briefly, the prospect of international stardom shimmered on the horizon. As the decade began the Monty Python brand was resurgent. *The Life of Brian* was causing a stir, our stage show was about to be revived at the Hollywood Bowl and there was unprecedented financial interest in any new film we cared to write. By the time these extracts end it was all very different. Python, after many premature obituaries, had, in effect, ceased to be. So, to all intents and purposes, had my chances of a Hollywood career. The last entry records my anxiety, not about films, but about an eighty-day journey around the world.

It wasn't that I hadn't given a film career a try. Between 1980 and 1988 I either wrote, or appeared in, seven movies. In varying degrees, all of them received support and interest from the major studios. Universal picked up *Monty Python's The Meaning of Life* and, together with 20th Century Fox, picked up Terry Gilliam's *Brazil*, Columbia took *The Missionary*, *A Fish Called Wanda* was made for MGM. The doors of Hollywood were open. Nor was I reluctant to look inside. As the diaries show, I was spending more time on the West Coast than the East. I was hobnobbing with studio executives and being flown by Concorde to casting sessions. And yet, in the end, my feet remained firmly on this side of the Atlantic.

I still can't quite work out why all this happened the way it did, and I re-read the diaries with a mixture of curiosity and disbelief. The overall impression is of a kaleidoscope of characters and events, clarity and confusion, of great strides forward and long and rambling cul-de-sacs, from which a pattern emerges, but only briefly, like the moon between clouds on a stormy night. I'm in my late thirties when this volume begins and my mid-forties when it ends, so one might imagine that the course of my life and career would be settling down. But the inescapable conclusion from reading these entries is that this is a man who still doesn't really know what he wants to do, or what he's particularly qualified to do.

If this were a history, or an autobiography written in the future looking back, I feel sure the temptation would be to impose order and reason and logic on this period of my life, to detect themes and trends that led in one direction, in other words to make sense of it all.

But diaries don't allow such luxuries. The events of everyday life are by their nature unpredictable, not at all at ease with the order that we crave as we grow older. Meaning changes, slips, adjusts, evolves. Narrative exists only in its most basic sense.

Which is why I like diaries. The map may be constantly changing, the steering wheel may be spinning all over the place, but diaries are the sound of an engine running, day in and day out.

MICHAEL PALIN
London, April 2009

'I did, I think, nothing'
Evelyn Waugh's diary, *26th June 1924*

1980

As a new decade began I was enmeshed in two new projects. One was collaborating on the screenplay of a children's fantasy dreamt up by Terry Gilliam, and the other a proper serious documentary, on railways, for the BBC. Both of these were off my normal patch, which was exciting in a way but a little less predictable than I'd have liked. The bedrock of the family was being quietly and unsensationally strengthened; Helen and I had been married nearly fourteen years. Tom was eleven and Will was nine and Rachel coming up to five. Which meant a lot more responsibilities than the same time ten years earlier. And I still had no regular job. I was an intuitively stable character living in a state of almost permanent flux. Quite a balancing act.

Keeping a diary had, after tentative beginnings in 1969 and 1970, become an ingrained habit, and a discipline too. Like the running I'd recently taken up, it was something consistent, a necessary complement to the mercurial world of work. Something to keep me grounded.

I continued to write up the diary most mornings, aware as ever how selective I had to be and how little time I ever had for honing and shaping. But I kept the story going. Just about.

Unless otherwise indicated, the entries are written in my house in Oak Village in North London.

Sunday, January 6th

With the social and gastronomic excesses of Christmas and New Year over, life this weekend has returned, after many weeks, to something approaching calm. I find I can easily cope with eight hours' sleep a night. I find I enjoy having time to sort my books out or take the children out or sit in front of the fire. I feel my body and my mind adjusting to a new pace and a new rhythm. I've hardly used the car in the last week. I haven't been into town, or shopping, or having business meetings. And I feel the benefits of this pause, this time to take stock of the present instead of endless worryings over the future or the past.

I've become a little self-sufficient, too. Though Gilliam is a regular visitor – like a mother hen having to keep returning to the nest to make sure the eggs are still all right – I'm responsible for the writing pace at the moment. I know that just over the horizon is the full swirl of a dozen different projects, meetings, responsibilities, considerations and demands, but for now the sea is calm.

Monday, January 7th

Denis [O'Brien] was back from the States today. According to TG he has no backers for the film [*Time Bandits*], but intends to go ahead and do it himself – just to 'spite them all'. I think this leaves me feeling as uncomfortable as it does Terry. But I read him some of the opening scenes, which cheer him up.

Pat Casey[1] rings to know my availability. She has a movie part which was written for Dudley Moore. He's now charging one and a half million dollars a picture and wants to do some serious acting, so Pat is asking me if I would be interested in the part. I have to turn it down as I'm occupied this year.

Wednesday, January 9th

At Redwood [Studios] at four. Eric, moderately well laid-back, occasionally strumming guitar. Trevor Jones[2] bustling. André[3] looking tired, but working faithfully. Graham [Chapman], who is getting £5,000 a month from Python as co-producer of this album [*Monty Python's Contractual Obligation*], sits contentedly, with John [Tomiczek] in attendance. He seems, as usual, not quite in tune with what's going on around him. I record the Headmaster's speech and that's about all.

Up to the Crown at Seven Dials for a drink with Terry Gilliam and Roger Pratt.[4] This is more like the real world for me. I can believe in the three of us and the place and the people around us far more than I can in what's going on at Redwood. Clearly TG feels the same. He's a bit

1 Patricia Casey produced Monty Python's first film *And Now For Something Completely Different* in 1970.
2 Trevor Jones, composer. To avoid confusion with the film composer of the same name he is now known as John Du Prez. Wrote the music for a number of Python songs as well as the film *A Fish Called Wanda* and, with Eric Idle, the musical *Spamalot*.
3 André Jacquemin, long-time Python sound recordist and composer.
4 Roger Pratt, camera operator on *Time Bandits*, later, lighting cameraman on *Brazil* and, more recently, two of the *Harry Potter* films.

confused by Denis's attitude to his film – on the one hand he is supportive and confident in TG – the next he's suggesting stars and names with almost frantic indiscrimination.

Thursday, January 10th

Rachel's first day at Gospel Oak School. It's a rather glum, hard, cold day with weather from the east. I don't see Rachel leave as I'm at the Mornington Foot Clinic. Mr Owen natters and reminisces as he slices at my foot – removing not only the corn but valuable minutes of screenwriting!

Home by ten. Rachel seems to have taken to school without any traumas. In fact Helen seems to have been affected more by the experience.

Unplug the phone and get down to the knotty problems of making an adventure serious and funny. Jim Franklin[1] rings to offer me a part in the Goodies and Pat Casey to try and induce me yet again to take a Dudley Moore cast-off.

Friday, January 11th

Up and running early this morning. The temperature is just on freezing and the grass on top of Parliament Hill is covered with frost. Feel immensely refreshed and thoroughly awoken.

Arrive at T Gilliam's just after 10.30.

Progress is steady but not spectacular, though TG is very amused by the Robin Hood sequence.

To Denis O'B's for a meeting at two. Denis looks weary. He was up working on 'structures' for TG's film until 2.30 yesterday morning. But he seems to be as bright and tenaciously thorough about all my affairs as he ever was.

Home by six. Feel encouraged after our meeting. Denis has talked of an India project – and self-financing of it, rather like TG's film – but basically my encouragement stems from the knowledge that with Denis we are in a different league. For the first time we are being offered the prospect of quite considerable financial rewards. Denis clearly identifies

1 Jim Franklin directed four of the *Ripping Yarns*.

money with power – although in our case our 'power', in terms of reputation, was established and created without vast rewards. Now Denis wants the rewards for us and through us for himself.

At the moment he seems to have admirable goals, but I have this nagging feeling that our 'freedom' to do whatever we want may be threatened if Denis is able to build up this juggernaut of Python earning power and influence. A few of the most interesting projects may be rolled flat.

Monday, January 14th

To Anne's [James] for a Python meeting with Denis. JC, fresh returned from Barbados, stands there shivering. Anne, as thoughtful as ever, has provided some lunch. Meeting is basically to discuss Denis's two offers for the next [Monty Python] movie – from Warners and Paramount. Warners want a screenplay before going ahead, Paramount just a treatment. Denis is asking for 6.4 million dollars.

Time is of the essence, as Paramount, who are offering a better financial deal, do require the movie for summer 1981 release. This, I feel, puts pressures on the group which we would rather not have – and thankfully no-one feels any different. But JC suggests that we go along with Paramount at the moment and just see if, after the seven-week March/April writing period, we have enough to give them a treatment – 'In which case we could all go ahead and make a lot of money very quickly.'

Though we all feel the Paramount deal for the next movie is the one to pursue, Denis is proposing to try and place *Grail*, now released from Cinema 5, with Warners, so they can do a *Life of Brian/Holy Grail* re-release in the US next summer. There is no great enthusiasm for selling the Bavaria film as a Python Olympic Special to the US networks in summer of this year. Eric reckons there will be no Olympics anyway. Certainly the Russian invasion of Afghanistan has shaken things up.

TG comes round and we talk over Denis and the movie. But I'm feeling very unsettled about my role in it at the moment. The script is clogged and I've lost a day's writing today. There seems suddenly so much to do and I refuse to give up my railway project [contributing to the BBC's *Great Railway Journeys*], despite reportedly 'generous' financial inducements from Denis to prolong my work on the TG movie.

André arrives very late, bringing a quite beautiful tape of Trevor Jones's arrangement for 'Decomposing Composers'. How the hell I'll sing it, I don't know.

Thursday, January 17th

Go with Tom and Helen to a 'parents' view' at Acland Burghley Comprehensive, one of the three local schools which Tom will have to be selected for, and where he will be well ensconced by this time next year.

A modern school, presenting a forbidding aspect, cloaked as it is in heavy grey concrete. The doors and passageways give the immediate impression of a hard, unpretty, pragmatist mind at work. But the library/reading room, where about 20 of us parents assemble, is warm and bright, the shelves are well-filled. I noticed *Soviet Weekly* alongside *The Economist*.

We were shown into a biology room and given glowing prospects of the future of this school. However I couldn't help noticing a large piece of paper on the front of a cupboard low on the ground near our feet, which bore the simple legend 'Whoever reads this is a cunt'.

Friday, January 18th

The world seems to have started 1980 so badly that I have on occasions this past week questioned the wisdom of working myself to a standstill when all the elements for the start of another global war crowd the newspapers for headline space. Ultimatums are flying around and ultimatums, to me, are synonymous with the outbreak of World War II.

It may in a few years sound rather laughable that Jimmy Carter threatened Russia that he will pull America out of the Olympics if the Russians haven't withdrawn their forces from Afghanistan by mid-February, but combined as this pronouncement is with the volatility of unsettled Iran and the much more threatening stances being taken up in preparation for President Tito's imminent death in Yugoslavia, the potential flashpoints seem sure to light something.

But it all ultimately is unreal and either you panic and sell everything you've got to buy gold, or you just sit down and have breakfast, presuming it won't be the last one. And of course it isn't.

Saturday, January 19th

Denis O'B rings. His proposal for my work on the T Gilliam film is that I be made a partner, along with Terry G, in the production company, so I will be able to share with TG the depreciation on capital which will be worth £60,000 in tax advantages. Don't ask me why, but this is clearly a generous move on the part of George [Harrison] and Denis O'B, who are the providers of the money.

And I can go ahead with the railway documentary – 'If you really want to,' says Denis, unhappily, knowing that there's precious little he can do to squeeze more than £2,400 out of the BBC for what's ostensibly 12 weeks' work!

In the afternoon a two and a half hour visit to Haverstock School. A lived-in, scuffed and battered collection of buildings. Impressed by the straightforwardness of the teachers. Impressed by the lack of waffle about tradition, Latin and prayers and the emphasis on the future and helping all the children of whatever ability equally.

An impossible ideal, some may say, but at least these teachers are confronting the most basic problems of an educational system with great energy and cheeriness. I was encouraged.

Monday, January 21st

The world situation seems to have cooled down, though I see in my *Times* that Paul McCartney is still in jail in Japan after being caught at the airport with naughty substances. How silly. Eric reckons it's a put-up job – part of John Lennon's price, which he's exacting from Paul for being rude to Yoko.

At five I brave the skyscraper-induced blasts of icy wind that whip round the Euston Tower and find myself in Capital Radio, being asked questions on, and reading extracts from, *Decline and Fall*. I find I'm never as lucid when the tape's rolling as I am over a glass of wine at home an hour later and in the course of an hour I get tongue-tied and fail to say even what I meant to say – let alone whether that was worth saying or not. I'm in august company – Denis Norden and Melvyn Bragg are the other two pundits on this particular book. JC has already said his piece about *Twelfth Night* (from which Shakespeare didn't emerge very favourably) and TJ is soon to do *The Spire* by William Golding.

Wednesday, January 23rd

The fine weather's back again. Tito's recovering and the steel strike is still faced with government intransigence. I have either pulled, twisted or bruised some muscle below and to the right of my kneecap, so I rest from running today, despite ideal, dry, cool, bright conditions out there.

Work on with TG script. The end is in sight, but is this writing to order – 6lbs assorted jokes, half a hundredweight of nutty characters and 20 yards of filler dialogue – really going to stand up? I'm encouraged when I think of the general level of movie dialogue – but this movie has to be judged by exceptional, not general level.

Write myself to a standstill by four and drive into the West End to see *Apocalypse Now*. Impressive – there is no other word for it – and the action sequences of the war are rivetingly watchable.

But the last half-hour – the meat, one feels, of Coppola/Milius' message – is a huge con. The action slows, the dialogue and performance become heavy with significance, sluggish with style.

Thursday, January 24th

Stop work at one. A couple of phone calls, then drive down to Neal's Yard for the Grand Unveiling Ceremony of the 14/15 Neal's Yard sign [designed by Terry G]. On one side red lurid lips and teeth bear the legend 'Neal's Yd. Abattoir' (to correct the present unwholesome imbalance in favour of the wholefooders who have proliferated all over the yard) and on the other side 'The British Film Industry Ltd'.

When I arrive it is made clear to me that a few choice words will have to be spoken and yours truly is the man to speak them. So we troop down into the yard and there, on this perfect sunny day, I bewilder all those queuing for non-meat lunches at the bakery by giving a few loud, but brief words, then smashing a champagne bottle against the building. 'God bless her and all who work in her.' It breaks the second time.

Friday, January 25th

To Terry Gilliam's at 10.15 for session on the film. TG likes the Ogre and the Old Ladies scene, but I think feels that the Evil Genius is too much on one level of cod hysteria. I agree, but we still have time to go over the characters again and invest them with a few more quirks.

We go to lunch at the Pizza Express and talk over the more serious problem of the 'content' of the script – the attitude to the characters, to Kevin's adventures – the message which gives the depth to a superficial story of chase and adventure. Really I feel the depth is there anyway, it's a question of how obvious to make it.

Leave for Dr Kieser's[1] surgery, where I have a cut and cover job on one of my front upper teeth – so my dental surgery is in its third decade. At one moment, as he works on the gum and bone, it begins to hurt. 'Is that pressure or pain you're feeling?' asks Kieser urgently. God ... how on earth do I tell?

Friday, February 1st

A rush for the tape. Began reassembling and rewriting the section from the Spider Women to the end at ten. Lunch at the desk.

TG arrives about 7.30 and I stumble to the 'End' by eight. He will get all this mass of stuck-up, crossed-out, type-and-longhand-jumbled sheets to Alison [Davies, at the office] this weekend. All should be returned by Sunday a.m., so I can then read through and learn the awful truth about this amazingly speedy piece of writing.

I go to bed at midnight with the satisfaction of having completed my self-set task of a TG script in the month of January. It would be marvellous if the script were of a high standard, worked and immeasurably increased the confidence of all working on the project. Or was the rush just at the expense of quality, an exercise in the lowest form of writing to a deadline?

I shall see. For now, I'm just very happy with a job (almost) done.

Saturday, February 2nd

In the afternoon the sky clouded and heavy rain set in. Took William, Rachel and the Mini down to the Natural History Museum, whilst Tom P and his friend Tom Owen went 'tracking' on the Heath. Rachel is doing dinosaurs at school and met one or two of her friends there. The central area was very full, but as soon as we ventured into the further recesses of the building there was plenty of space amongst endless glassily-staring models and half-dissected bodies.

1 Bernard Kieser, periodontal surgeon extraordinaire, carried on the fight to keep my teeth in my mouth, with increasing success.

Willy went off on his own to, among other things, the human biology section. He is very keen on biology, having just begun talking about it at school. To her great credit, his teacher started straight in with human reproduction, etc, rather than frogs or bees. So Willy now knows all the practical details of procreation, whereas Tom, who affects to know, still calls sexual intercourse 'sexual interchange'.

Sunday, February 3rd

Read papers in the morning. Polls taken in January indicate that more people are expecting World War III to break out now than at any time since Korea. Probably a meaningless statistic, but it makes Python's next film subject gruesomely relevant. Actually the sabre-rattling of the Americans over Afghanistan has died down a little, but they still frighten me more than the Russians.

Terry G brings round the script of the movie, fresh from Alison the typist, and after supper I begin to read. I finish late – it's nearly one. My first reaction is that it's paced wrongly – the individual scenes are in some cases too long themselves, or appear too long when placed next to another, fairly static scene. I missed being gripped by the story, too.

Lay in bed remembering points and scribbling down. Tomorrow I've given a day to Terry G that should be spent on railway research, so that we can talk right through the screenplay.

Monday, February 4th

Up to Terry's. The heavens open and it pours for the rest of the day. Against this gloomy background we slog through. TG liked the script more than I did, I think, and is greatly pleased that Irene Lamb, the casting director, for whom TG has much respect, also likes what she has seen so far and feels there will be little problem in getting good actors interested.

It's clear that there is one more day of writing needed to flesh out the end, especially the hastily-written character of the bureaucratic Supreme Being. So I'll have to restructure the week accordingly. Everything else will have to be squeezed.

Still have no title for the TG epic other than 'The Film That Dares Not Speak Its Name'.

Tuesday, February 5th

Talk over scripts for the new Python film with TJ. We read through and apportion who would be responsible for what.

TJ and I have a game of squash, then a pint of Brakspear's at the Nag's Head in Hampstead. TJ, though bemoaning the fact that he hasn't written anything new for months, is suddenly, and healthily, I think, full of ideas and projects of his own – including the possibility of making a film of *Hitchhiker's Guide to the Galaxy* with Douglas Adams.

Terry goes off to meet Douglas. I drive to a rather swish and un-Pythonlike function at Les Ambassadeurs Club. We are invited here by Warner Brothers Chairman Frank Wells – the man who, TG tells me later, did more than anyone else to try and block the *Life of Brian* deal. He was tall, fit, with those peculiar American spectacles that make a man's face look slightly effeminate; mid-forties, or early fifties, with a firm handshake.

Spread out in the scarlet-panelled, sumptuously-carpeted lower room at the Ambassadeurs was a host of men in grey. An impeccably-manicured host too – hardly a hair out of place on any of them. These were the agents and studio heads and accountants – the businessmen of showbiz.

A cameraman was in attendance, which always indicates that the gathering is a little more than just a thank you from Warners. I was photographed with Eric and with Frank Wells and Jarvis Astaire.[1] I was pleased to see Sandy [Lieberson] and his missus, because Sandy was at least not wearing a grey suit and Birgit was one of the only women there.

Gilliam is wonderfully scruffy, I'm pleased to say.

Leave at 8.15. Avoid getting run over by the sea of chauffeur-driven Rolls Royces and Jags and Mercedes littering Hamilton Place.

Wednesday, February 6th

Work through the last few scenes of the TG film until after lunch, then drive to Denis O'B's. Try to be absolutely clear with him that what I want for Redwood is to keep Bob[2] and André. Denis worries that Bob is 'driving

---

1 Wells was President of Warner Brothers, and later of the Walt Disney Company. He died in a helicopter accident whilst on a heli-skiing trip in 1994.

Jarvis Astaire, businessman and influential sports event promoter. Co-produced the film *Agatha* in 1978.

2 Bob Salmon was André Jacquemin's accountant and helped to set up Redwood Studios.

a wedge' between myself and André. Really he is accusing Bob of all the things that Bob is accusing Denis of doing. Denis will not hear a good word said for Bob – but I've made my decision. I'm not prepared to lose André, and if Bob goes, André goes. So Denis talks business and I talk people and that's that.

Drive back in a rain-sodden rush-hour to Abraxas [sports club in Belsize Park gardens]. Am soundly beaten by Richard [Guedalla, my neighbour] at squash. Makes me very depressed. But recover over a bottle of champagne, which I open to mark my last day on, or delivery of, the TG film script. Read TG the new Supreme Being scenes, which he likes.

Tom arrives back from another disco. Not just 'slow dancing' this time, but girls sitting on boys' laps. Reminds me of Eric's wonderful song for the *Contractual Obligation* album, 'Sit On My Face and Tell Me that You Love Me'.

Monday, February 18th

Springlike weather, with daytime temperatures around 50°F, now into its second week. I cycle up to Terry G's in sunshine. From 9.30 till lunchtime we work through the script – still tentatively, but not very enthusiastically, called 'The Time Bandits'. Fortunately we both agree on the major area for cuts and every little rewrite helps. TG is very unhappy about the vast amounts of money the crew are demanding – inflated by commercials. It doesn't help the 'British' film industry at all.

Down to Redwood Studios, where Eric, TJ and myself record 'Shopping Sketch' and 'All Things Dull and Ugly', plus one or two other snippets for the album.

From Redwood round to Anne J's to take in some more Python scripts from last autumn's writing session to be typed up in preparation for Wednesday's meeting. What is rapidly becoming apparent about *Brian* is that Denis's forecast of earnings from it in 1980 was drastically over-optimistic. The £250,000 figure he mentioned in November now looks likely to be nearer £40,000.

Although the distributor's gross in the US was over nine million dollars, over four million was spent on publicity and advertising – and this was where Warners were weakest. Their posters and their slogans were constantly changed and we never approved any of them – now they present a bill for this fiasco which is equal to the entire production budget of the film. It is a scandal, but there seems to be nothing Denis can do. They won't even supply him with figures.

The upshot is that not only will there be not a penny profit from America from a movie which was one of the top 40 grossers of the year in the US, but the earnings will hardly cover half the production cost. So the chance of making any more money – beyond our £72,000 fee for writing and acting – depends on the rest of the world. Fortunately the UK is looking very strong, Australia is holding up well and France and Germany remain to be seen.

Wednesday, February 20th

Python enters the 80's! Pick up Eric on the way to JC's. Arrive at 10.30. Everyone there and chortling over the latest and looniest batch of selected press cuttings about *Brian*. It's noted that Swansea has banned the film totally. Four hundred people in Watford are petitioning because the local council have recommended the film be an 'X'.

Coffees are poured and we settle round JC's ex-prison table, which now seems to be Python's favourite writing venue. Our ages are checked around the table. I'm still the youngest. No-one wants to spend time on business, we all want to write and make each other laugh, but business has to be done, so it's decided that we will make a clean sweep of it today. So Anne stays with us and Denis is summoned at three.

The disillusion with Hollywood and all things to do with Warners and *Brian* lead us into thinking how nice it would be to do a small-budget film just for the fun of it – keeping our own control and making money in the way *Grail*, with its modest budget, did, and *Brian*, with its Hollywood campaign, didn't. Denis is anxious to set up all sorts of production and syndication deals in the US, and he's talked to CBS about two Python TV specials, for which we would be paid 700,000 dollars each.

No-one wants to do specials for the US, but there is still the German material. Suddenly it all gels. We will use the German material, plus some old sketches, plus anything we wrote in October/November and reshoot as a quick, cheap movie. The mood of the group is unanimous. Fuck Hollywood. Fuck CBS. Let's do something we enjoy in the way we want to do it – and so economically that no-one gets their fingers burned if a Hollywood major *does* turn it down.

DO'B seems unable to respond at our level and talks business jargon for a while. I like Denis, and I think he likes us, but he is only in the early stages of finding out what everyone who's ever dealt with Python has eventually found out – that there is no logic or consistency or even realism behind much of our behaviour. No patterns can be imposed on the group from outside. Or at least they can, but they never stick; they crack up and the internal resolutions of Python are the only ones that last.

From international film business to the waiting room of the Mornington Foot Clinic. Mr Owen uses a 'coagulator' on my corn today. I have to have injections around my little toe, which are rather painful, then a sharp, electrified needle burns up the capillaries. All this counterpointed by Mr Owen's extraordinary views about the evils of the world and socialism in particular. I'm getting worried – I think that he is a character I've invented.

Monday, February 25th

Spent much of the weekend, unsuccessfully, trying to finish *Smiley's People*. Also trying to find time to organise the house, spend time with the children and other worthy hopes doomed to failure!

Rachel pottered around me with her Junior Doctor's Kit, taking my blood, giving me blood, thrusting toy thermometers in my mouth, whilst I tried, hopelessly, to assimilate the mass of opinions, facts, thoughts, figures and ramblings which make up the insidiously attractive substitute for experience that is the Sunday papers.

Collected Eric from Carlton Hill and we drove on to JC's. A talk through material. Eric and John have searched the archives, Terry J has been away, GC doesn't appear to have done much, but I saved my bacon by writing an extension to 'Penis Apology',[1] which produced an outstandingly good reaction. Near hysteria. I think Python is definitely working out all the repressions of childhood – and loving it!

Lunch with the French translator of *Holy Grail* and *Brian* at the Trattoo. A wonderful-looking Frenchman with a very special face which could not belong to any other nation. White hair, eyes droopy with a sort of permanent look of apology, a long, curved nose which never goes far from his face at any point. A lovely, squashed, humorous, used feel to the face like a Gauloise butt in an ashtray.

1 'Penis Apology' was a very long-drawn-out health advisory at the beginning of the film warning the audience that there may be a penis in shot later on. The apology became longer and more complex, including discussions from Bishops for the Church's view etc. It was never used.

Home by six. Have promised TG that I will read the new, shorter version of 'Time Bandits/The Film That Dares Not Speak Its Name', so I spend most of the evening on that. Poor Terry is being given a hard ride by the doubters and the pessimists. On reading I feel that the movie, which is, after all, an act of faith in TG, is, on balance, do-able by May. But only just!

Tuesday, February 26th

The weather has sharpened a little, but most of February has now gone, with no weather that wouldn't have graced an average April. In short, no winter at all here. But I don't feel any benefits. Wake up feeling like a piece of chewed rag. I have a sore throat, a mild coolness of the blood and a general enervation. There are so many loose ends to be tied up. I feel old for a few minutes.

Some work after breakfast, then round to Eric's. That's very cheering – mainly because all of us are happy to be together at the moment and the tapes that André's prepared of the sketches and songs for the LP assembled by Eric, with a certain amount of gentle bullying over the last two months, are a great boost.

To lunch at a nearby French, where Eric chides Graham for not being totally opposed to nuclear power. Eric deals only in certainties. His views, like his lifestyle at any one time, are very positive.

The talk veers to desultory discussion of bizarre sexual exploits. GC caps all, as he puffs at his pipe and declares that he once had an Indian in an aeroplane. JC is quite skittish too and suggests that perhaps the Pythons should set each other a sexual task. I agree to try and seduce the Queen!

I have a brief script chat with T Gilliam (cheering him up, I hope). Then I drive both of us round to a rendezvous with J Cleese, who was given TG's script and wants to, or 'is prepared to', talk to us about it. John is looking after Cynthia at the moment, on his own as far as I can tell, since Connie's in New York for 11 days.

Cynthia answers the door. With her long blonde hair, tastefully ribboned back, and her neat school uniform she looks, at nine years old, like an Estée Lauder model. Very New York, somehow. She chats confidently and behaves quite like a young lady 10 or 15 years older than she is, but she's humorous with it, which keeps her on this side of precociousness.

She comes out to eat with us. No room at the Japanese, so we go on to

Mama San – a clean, smart, soulless Chinese in Holland Park Avenue. Cynthia won't really let John get a word in, but after half an hour she settles to sleep beside an unoccupied table and the three of us talk about the script.

JC speaks with a slight, elder statesman of comedy air, as if he really *does* know how, why and when comedy will work, and we feel a little like naughty boys being told what's good for us. But this is rather unfair to John. I think he went out of the way to try *not* to sound too paternal, and he did give us some sound, unselfish advice, much of which will help in the rewrites. But I couldn't accept his final judgement – that we should postpone the movie on the basis that one day it could be a marvellous film, but if we rush it and go on the present script, it will be just a good-natured mess,

Mind you, JC had a piece of gossip that rather undermined his chances of 'stopping' the movie. He'd heard that Sean Connery was interested and Denis O'B has flown to California to see him!

Friday, February 29th

To Gospel Oak School to see Ron Lendon [the headmaster] about Tom's future.

Ron's report is glowing. Tom, it seems, is regarded very highly indeed. He is in Verbal Reasoning Group 1 – which is the comprehensive system's acknowledgement that abilities have to be tested at some point. There is less chance of him going to William Ellis [school in Highgate Road] if he's Group 1 – the idea is to spread them around the local schools. But Lendon, whose manner is chatty, informal, direct and quite unpatronising, feels that William Ellis is the best place for Tom. His closest friends – Lendon makes much reference to 'peer' groups – will be going there, he's keen on music and Lendon admits that he thinks the academic standards are higher at William E.

An interesting sign of the times is that Tom is one of only three boys amongst 15 in his class who does not come from a broken home.

So we come out greatly heartened and I feel once again the great relief that our children – all of them – will have started out at a school as caring and sympathetic as Gospel Oak.

Work on Python material for a couple of hours, then meet TJ at the Pizza Express in Hampstead. TJ has written something which he cheerfully acknowledges as the ultimate in bad taste – it's all about people throwing up – very childish, but rather well controlled, dare I say – it had me in as prolonged and hysterical a bout of laughter as I can remember.

Saturday, March 1st

Always feel that March is the end of the winter, but this year there has been no winter to speak of and this mild, orderly March morning is only different from much of January and February because the sun isn't shining.

Have to go and talk over script details with TG. The advantage of living within walking distance of your collaborator. Stroll up with my script over the Heath. Up to Terry's mighty attic. Listen to a couple of tracks of the new Elvis Costello.

The good news is that Ian Holm wants to be our Napoleon and loves the script. No further news from Denis who is, much to TG's irritation, still star-searching in Hollywood.

Walk back at 8.15, past South End Green where *Life of Brian* is in '5th Fantastic Week' at the Classic.

Sunday, March 2nd

A most relaxed and happy day. Sun shone – a very springlike Sunday. I cleared my desk prior to beginning the railway script.

Found lots of excuses to talk, drink coffee and generally indulge in what's called a writer's 'negative capability', but eventually was ready to start. Notes assembled, clean sheet of foolscap in the typewriter (I still use a typewriter for the serious stuff!). Then a strange tension gripped me – a tightening of the stomach, a light sweating of the palms just as if I were about to go on stage.

Do all writers, or any writers, suffer this 'typewriter fright', or is it just because I'm a writer/actor and I know that anything I put down now I will have to enact at some future time? Anyway, it's a very difficult task to start the documentary. To actually set this huge and daunting mass of facts and accumulated knowledge in motion.

Monday, March 3rd

Woken by bright sunshine. Rachel unhappy about school. I take her. She tries to be very brave, but bolts back towards the house when we get to the end of Oak Village, and I have to carry her most of the rest of the way. When we arrive at the school, her class are already sitting quietly, waiting for the register.

On the way back up Oak Village, an old lady leans out of her window. She looks distraught. Her gas supply has failed, and she's had no tea or heating. She's asked the gas people to come round, but she's concerned that they're not here. This all takes my mind off Rachel's predicament as I go home, phone up the gas, and Helen goes round to see her and make her tea and fill her hot water bottle.

Set to writing Python stuff. Rachel arrives back from school, a lot happier than when she went, but she *did* cry – 'Only one big tear,' she told me.

Tuesday, March 4th

Another sparkling day. Clear blue skies and a brisk chill giving an edge of freshness to the air. Write more Python material – it's flowing easily and I'm enjoying the chance to write some fairly direct satirical stuff again. Jury vetting was on the list today. And the courts generally.

From two until half past three, TJ and I read. TJ has a good idea for the RAF Pipe-Smokers – extending into wives. I've written huge amounts, as usual, but this time it seems to stand up – and almost nil failure rate over the last two days, which is encouraging. See what the others think on Thursday.

TG has been hearing from Denis O'B in Los Angeles.

Denis, who had sent me a telegram saying the script was 'sensational', is voicing doubts over the quality of writing – especially in the 'Napoleon' and 'Robin Hood' scenes. He even suggested to TG that they could 'get some writers in'. He still hurls out casting suggestions which bear all the hallmarks of a man more desperate about a bank loan than about anything to do with quality of script or trust of the writers – Burt Reynolds for the Evil Genius, Art Carney for the Ogre. All the qualities these actors have are blinded for me by Denis's heavy-handed Hollywood approach. It's killing T Gilliam and may kill the film.

I go to bed trying to put it all out of my mind. But a nagging corner can't be forgotten – I *did* write the script in a month. Denis is right – it *could* be better. Am I just now beginning to get some inklings that I really made a wrong decision to get involved in this project at all? Wrong not because I couldn't do it, but because I couldn't do my best.

I know I'm funnier writing unrestricted Python material. I know I could contribute more as a writer if it had been a 'Ripping Yarn' sort of story. But it wasn't. Will it ever be what everyone wants it to be? Or just a jumble of different ideas and preconceptions? Is it comedy or adventure? Why should it have to be either?

Because that's how Hollywood wants it to be, and Denis wants Hollywood.

Wednesday, March 5th

No brooding today. Up at eight. Buy *The Times* and read of Mugabe's victory in Rhodesia. The Brits have been patting themselves on the back for organising such an orderly election – in best British fashion – so they can hardly grumble at a Marxist getting 62% of the vote. It seems one of the most hopeful transitions from white to black power. But it's taken a guerrilla war to make the point and that must give great heart to guerrilla movements in other countries.

Thursday, March 6th

Rain, most of the day. To Eric's for a Python read-through. Neil [Innes] is staying there. He looks cheery and already his new life in the Suffolk countryside seems to have made him physically different. As though the land has moulded our ex-Lewisham lad. He's rounder. His hair, arranged in a neat coronal around his bald pate, is much fuller and frizzier than I remember before. He looks . . . He looks rather like a Hulme Beaman[1] creation.

Terry J looks tired and harassed and throughout the day there are odd phone calls for him which give one the feeling that his life is a box which is far too full. John C is grumbling about his health again – doing a perfect imitation of the Ogre in *Time Bandits* which he didn't like!

Eric is being very friendly, warm and accommodating. Terry Gilliam isn't there (which provokes some rumblings of discontent from Eric, who, I think, being unaligned to either of the main writing groups, feels that TG's absence deprives him of an ally). GC is as avuncular and benign as ever. And arrives easily last. Eric is trying to get GC to stop smoking his pipe so much. He's the only Python who still smokes.

---

1 S.G. Hulme Beaman created the Toytown stories, some of the earliest children's books and radio programmes I remember.

JC reads out an outrageously funny schoolmaster sex demonstration sketch. Our stuff doesn't go quite as well as expected this morning. Eric has a chilling ending for the film, when the outbreak of nuclear war is announced. He's been reading about the dangers of, and plans in the event of, nuclear war happening.

We talk for a while on this subject, which is so macabre and disturbing because the weapons for our destruction exist – they're pointing at us now – and our response is to build more.

Friday, March 7th

Tried to write a startlingly new and original, brilliantly funny and thought-provoking piece for Python. Did this by staring out of the window, playing with paper clips and shutting my eyes for long periods.

Monday, March 10th

Pressing on. Endless days of writing. They seem to have been going on forever and are stretching on forever. Not that I mind *that* much. I quite enjoy not having to drive across London, not having to go down rain-spattered motorways to locations, not having to make meetings and business lunches, not going out to dinners or buying clothes.

Yes, I'm afraid this monastic existence suits me rather well. I shall keep it up this week, hoping for a breakthrough on Python and a completion of the railway script – then I shall take Concorde to New York at the expense of NBC and 'party' for 24 hours.

Work on Python until it's dark outside, then break and work on the railways until midnight. Impossible. I'm beginning to sink under a mass of names, lines, distances, facts, details, anecdotes, diversions, sidings . . .

Tuesday, March 11th

Denis O'B rings – he's returned from the States and positively glowing with enthusiasm for the TG/MP movie. He has Sean Connery absolutely 'mentally committed' (which means he hasn't enough money for him) and George H, who at first was not at all sure why Denis O'B was putting his money into it, has now re-read the script twice, feels it has great potential and is trying to hustle Jack Nicholson into letting us have his name on the credits!

Paramount have agreed a distribution deal with Denis in the US and are seeing it as a new *Wizard of Oz*! However, they are very keen to get the hottest name in Hollywood – Gilda Radner – onto the credits too. Denis, who knows nothing of Gilda, has promptly turned several circles and is now homing in on Gilda as the Ogre's Wife instead of Ruth Gordon. 'Apparently she does a really good old lady on *Saturday Night Live*.'

I have to puncture Denis's epic enthusiasm here. She may do a great old lady, but Ruth Gordon *is* a great old lady, and would easily be my choice (if we need names) for the part.

Wednesday, March 12th

Schizophrenic weather. Today almost continuous rain – yesterday bright sunshine.

To Eric's for a Python meeting.

Over lunch we discuss the general balance of material, which seems to fall into School, War/Army and North-West Frontier. Lists are made in the p.m. and a putative running order worked out. This is the stage when there is much talk of 'What is the film about?' and how we can relate the various themes – whether we should start conventionally or with an apology for what's to be seen. Quite good progress.

Thursday, March 13th

Revision of the railway script proceeds rather slowly. I think one reason is that I have become so steeped in the material over the last three or four weeks that I've lost a lot of the initial enthusiasm. Also concerned about how funny to make the start. In short, I don't think I've found the right tone yet.

Run off my uncertainties at lunchtime. Back to a phone call from Denis. He has just received a mortal blow to his pride from Edna Jones at BBC Contracts. Denis, international financier and deal-maker extraordinary, cannot get the BBC to budge from a max of £2,400 plus £1,800 once and for all foreign sales on the railway programme. Denis, who believes in the success ethic even more than the work ethic, says he's contemplating throwing himself off his balcony!

Saturday, March 15th: London and New York

A dull morning, but no rain, fog or snow to threaten departure. With only a couple of light bags, a book – *Moviola* by Garson Kanin – and a *Time Bandits* script for Ruth Gordon (Garson Kanin's wife!), drive the Mini to Heathrow and park it, as I'm only away for one night.

Board the 11.15 Concorde, a few minutes late – some problem with the earlier flight. But we're airborne, with thunderous noise, by twelve, and there are no more problems. I'm VIP listed and this means it's impossible to quietly stew in a mixture of champagne, relief and a good book without being hauled out to sign an autograph for the crew and visit the flight deck.

The pilot and co-pilot seem more anxious to ask me about Python than to tell me about Concorde, but I do ascertain that they use five tons of fuel every hour and that the fastest Atlantic crossing so far has been two hours 56 minutes.

Well, they catch up half an hour and I'm at Kennedy and through customs and into bright sunshine and crisp snow cover just after 10.30 NY time.

Arrive at NBC at four. Rehearse the moves cold. See Lorne,[1] the cast, Belushi, who is back to do a special appearance. Of *1941* he says 'I was bad, the film was bad', but he's very pleased with the state of the *Blues Brothers* – his soon to be released picture with Aykroyd.

As usual Belushi's presence does not please everybody. He's very rude about the present state of '*SNL*' – and seems disgruntled that he's come back to do so little. Both points are understandable. The material on this 100th show reflects age rather than quality and Belushi isn't given much funny stuff. He's smarting because he's been cut out of 'Update' to accommodate one of the 'star guests', Ralph Nader.

After an hour of reacquainting myself with everybody and rehearsing in a darkened set, a dull, persistent headache has set in. So I take an hour off before the dress rehearsal, go back to the Berkshire Place and lie down. Don't sleep, but at least I'm not working or talking.

Shower and leave the hotel at seven, US time – which means it's midnight UK time. I have somehow to try and pace myself to perform live in front of the watching millions at what will be, for me, about 5.30 in the morning at the end of a very crowded day.

---

1 Lorne Michaels produced the ground-breaking, talent-spinning NBS *Saturday Night Live* show. And still does.

When 11.30 finally arrived and the signature tune blared out I knew that I would be alright as the adrenaline started working to clear my befuddled system of the combined effects of too much food, alcohol and fatigue.

The sketch went better than ever and I got a gratifying round of recognition applause when the audience saw me for the first time. I also over-acted happily and shamelessly. John Cleese would have been proud of the way I killed the tarantula.

Thursday, March 20th

Spring starts either today or tomorrow, I'm never sure. The rain's stopped, but there was a frost last night. It's cold, clear and clean.

At a quarter to ten Helen, Tom and I drive up in the Mini to William Ellis School for our interview with Mr Perry [the headmaster]. Talk to one of the senior boys – wearing a gown. Will they still keep gowns in the comprehensive era? He was very well-spoken and presentable and surprised me by saying, quite undefensively, that he wanted to become an accountant.

Into Mr Perry's bland but unintimidating study. Tom is asked most of the questions. What he likes about Gospel Oak – Tom, seriously, 'Well, it's very spacious, but quite small.' His hobbies, interests, friends, preferences (Tom declared for science). Tom answered quite unprecociously and at greater length than I expected. Mr Perry said that it was almost an accepted fact that children from Gospel Oak were more articulate than the norm.

Drive over to EuroAtlantic for a meeting with Denis and T Gilliam. Main subject is whether or not we think J Cleese is right for the Evil Genius. Apparently Denis took the bull by the horns and met the disgruntled Cleese, who's not so far forgiven Denis for promising us a quarter of a million pounds each for *Brian*.

Denis has so successfully charmed JC with soft words and capital allowance schemes, that JC can now see the advantage of being in TG's movie after all – as a partner. Denis is keen, but both TG and I are unconvinced. Other names hang in the air. Connery still isn't fixed. Ruth Gordon neither. Denis is disappointed that John cannot be easily fitted in.

Watch the BAFTA awards at 9.30 with a glimmer of hope, but little more than that. The Light Entertainment Award is the first. Bruce Forsyth comes on to present it and does an annoyingly unnecessary and lengthy preamble, whilst Anna Ford, Edward Fox and Princess Anne watch lugubriously.

My first pleasure is to hear the laughter in the hall as they show the shooting scene from 'Roger of the Raj', but I can't believe it when Forsyth announces 'The winner is . . . the winners are: Alan Bell and Jim Franklin for . . . *Ripping Yarns*.' I just leap up and give a few lusty yells. It's like Wednesday scoring twice against Everton in the '66 Cup Final.

The boys come downstairs and stare at me.

Monday, March 24th

TG and I drive down to the King's Road in pouring rain to dine with executives from Paramount and Denis O'B at the Casserole Restaurant.

There were three Paramount people. A young, bright little man, with a combative heckling approach which settled down as one got to know him. He was called Jeffrey Katzenberg, was 29 years old and admitted that he was paid a lot because it was a very high-risk job – the turnover of Hollywood execs is spectacularly fast. His bluffer, less devious, funnier friend was also younger than TG or I and was called David.

They joked heavily as we arrived. Probably to cover their embarrassment at the fact that an hour earlier Paramount HQ had telexed Denis O'B to say that if he stalls on the next Python deal (which he has) then they will stall on the *Time Bandits*. So Paramount in LA are playing Denis's game.

But these two were at pains to deny any close association with their colleagues. These two were interested purely in talent and were keen to know more about the *Time Bandits*. They particularly wanted to be reassured about the dwarves (I mean, just how odd would they look?).

Wednesday, March 26th

At my desk at 9.30 to confront the formidable task of rewriting two scenes for the *Time Bandits* before leaving for the Python promotion in Paris at 3.30. But the muse is helpful and by one I have rewritten the 'Future' and, even more satisfactorily, I hope, the 'Titanic' scene.

Leave for the airport at a quarter past three. Onto an Airbus for Paris. Packed solid – must be two or three hundred people. Read my book on the Greeks by H D F Kitto. Most inspirational. In the air only briefly, but on the plane for over an hour.

Python Sacré Graal is in its 71st week of its third reissue in Paris! So clearly there is a cult here, and it's based on only one movie.

A rather dreadful evening at a Sofitel in the 15th Arrondissement. Up to a bleak room on the 16th floor of this French Holiday Inn, where we ate. No-one knew why we were here, or who all the guests were, but it turned out to be some sort of special viewing for Avis, who are renting us the cars for the three days.

Python spirit was high, despite this debacle, though, and much enjoyment was derived from trying to find how many things on the table we could assemble around John before he noticed. Huge numbers of plates, glasses, bread baskets and even an ornamental bowl of flowers were discreetly manoeuvred in front of him, but he never noticed.

Thursday, March 27th: Paris

Interviews – for *Le Figaro*, *La Revue de Cinéma* and finally a cartoonist called Gottlib, who has a Gumby fascination and gets me to enunciate clearly and slowly the *exact* words for 'Gumby Flower Arranging' into a small tape recorder. The more seriously I try to oblige, the more ridiculous the situation becomes. Eric doesn't help by constantly cracking up and when I finally make it through to the moment of flower arranging the doors of the room open to reveal an enormous bunch of flowers being carried through. The interviews draw to a close by seven. Terry J and I go off to eat at La Coupole. I have ears and tail – and TJ is most impressed. We talk, for the first time, about the *Time Bandits* script, which TJ has half-read. He wasn't impressed with it until the Greek scene!

Saturday, March 29th: Paris and London

Woken from a very deep sleep in the Hotel Lotti by the soft clinking of a breakfast tray. It's half past seven. Pull myself out of bed and wander across to meet the breakfast, wearing only my underpants, when I'm suddenly aware of the nervous, twitching, apologetic presence of the Very Naughty Valet in my room.

Terry had warned me that there was a man who very lasciviously enquired whether he wanted his shoes cleaned, and here he was, in my room, having caught me with literally everything, apart from my pants, down! He wasn't at all fazed by my appearance, but came on in and started to arrange my chair for breakfast in a most epicene manner.

Finally I fled to the bathroom and made loud and hopefully quite unromantic sounds of ablution until I knew he'd gone. Then I crept out again and got to grips with two fried eggs, coffee out of a swimming pool cup and croissants which were pale imitations of Patisserie Valerie's.

The door I never heard open. But I was aware of the presence of the lustful valet even before he said 'I have something for you, sir ...'. With virgin-like caution I extended my hand to his and he dropped two small bars of soap into it as if they were ripe grapes.

Sunday, March 30th

No work – for the first time in many weeks. The weather back in London is crisp, with high white clouds and breaks of sunshine – and the city looks a lot less grey than Paris.

William and I go for a lunch picnic in St James's Park and walk up the traffic-free Mall. Gentle Sunday strolling in the heart of the city. We eat our lunch on the deckchairs, then improvise a quick game of cricket. Afterwards we drive on to the London Dungeon – William is doing the plague at school, so this *can* be called an educational visit.

This evening Helen – who has bought a £150 dress for the occasion! – and I dine out at Leith's with Denis and Inge [Denis's wife], Terry G, Maggie, George H and Sean Connery – our latest casting coup for *Time Bandits*. Connery is as he seems on screen – big, physically powerful, humorous, relaxed and very attentive to women. He talks with the unaffected ease of a man who is used to having an audience. His main love is clearly golf, but he has some good and sensible suggestions to make on his part as King Agamemnon.

Thursday, April 3rd

Arrive at JC's by ten.

Some progress, but nothing sweeps the gathering off its feet. JC reaches a peak of frustration. 'Nine weeks of writing,' he practically sobs in anguish, 'and we haven't got a *film*.'

But we make lists and from the best elements – mainly 'Kashmir' – I suggest that we play six members of a family – a sort of Python saga, set in the *Ripping Yarns* period of 1900–1930. The idea of telling the story of a family seems to appeal and quite suddenly unblocks the sticky cul-de-sac we appeared to have written ourselves into. It suits me, a *Yarns* film with all the team in it – something I've often been attracted to.

So, quite unexpectedly, the day turns around. At the eleventh hour we have a style, a subject and a framework for the new film.

Ride back with Eric, who becomes very angry when I tell him that John Cleese is doing something in the TG film. He feels this is a plot on Denis's part to make TG's into a new Python film. Eric seems to be able to take *Ripping Yarns* and *Fawlty Towers*, but Gilliam's extra-Python work he has no tolerance for, feeling that it just copies Python and isn't original.

A half-hour phone call with a researcher from the *Dick Cavett Show*, who's doing a pre-interview interview. He says he thought my remark about showbiz being 'a branch of American patriotism' was brilliant, but I can never remember saying it.

Friday, April 4th: Good Friday

The sheer pleasure of having a morning to myself – even though I have to spend it reading the *Time Bandits* latest revised script – is incredibly healing to my creaking system. Clear the desk, write the diary, pull down the blinds against the strong sunlight, brew up strong coffee, and settle down to reading.

To my relief, the *Time Bandits*, as of April 4th, is not in bad shape at all, and most of last week's rapid rewrites, though in many cases the result of writer's cowardice, do seem to improve the shape and pace of the story. So by the time I've completed a thorough read-through I'm feeling very positive.

Up to T Gilliam's to discuss with him. Find him in a house of illness. Amy puffy with mumps, Maggie, newly pregnant, looking very tired, and TG crumpled and dressing-gowned. His temperature returned to 101 last night and he was thrown into a sweating turmoil after a phone call from Denis O'B in Los Angeles. TG thinks he has 'brain fever'.

We talk through for four hours. And by the end I'm exhausted by the effort of keeping concentration and a sense of proportion and not succumbing to Gilliam's periodic moments of eyeball-widening realisation ... 'We only have seven *weeks* ... ' 'I haven't even ... ', etc, etc.

Look forward with glorious anticipation of relief relaxation to my two days off in Southwold this weekend with Rachel.

Sunday, April 6th: Southwold, Easter Sunday

Slept a welcome eight hours. Woken by chirpy Rachel at eight and up and eating croissants on Easter morning by 8.30.

Brian appears to have had some effect on Granny – she confessed that she didn't go to church on Good Friday . . . 'Thinking of you and your film, I just couldn't.' Has it shaken her faith constructively or destructively? She *did* say she couldn't take Pontius Pilate seriously any more!

Tuesday, April 8th

Drive over to Eric's for a Python meeting about the next album, which we have to deliver under the terms of our Arista/Charisma contract.

Eric suggests we call the album 'Monty Python's Legal Obligation Album' and I suggest that we have it introduced by some legal man explaining why we have to deliver it and the penalties if we don't. This replaces the tentative 'Scratch and Sniff' title.

So we are all going back to our notebooks to cull material and have it typed up, and we reassemble on my 37th birthday to record.

Thursday, April 17th

Gilliam has had positive chats with Jonathan Pryce to play the Evil Genius. Pryce is apparently tremendous in *Hamlet* at the Royal Court and if we get him I think it will add to the extraordinarily confusing richness of the cast.

Bike up to Belsize Park then spend an hour sorting out mounds of unanswered fan mail (well, about 40 letters!) to give to the Python office to dispose of. This is quite a milestone as up till now I've always replied myself – even short, scruffy notes – but such is the amount of work behind and before me that I really can't manage the time any more.

Tuesday, April 22nd

A fine drizzle as I cycle round to Mr Owen the Feet at a quarter to nine. Start of Rachel's second term at Gospel Oak today and she doesn't show any sign of nerves.

Mr Owen talks for 40 minutes and cuts away at my corn for five. 'I would have been a professional violinist if it hadn't been for the war . . . '. A cat wanders through the surgery.

Thursday, April 24th

Jonathan Pryce cannot do *Time Bandits* – he's holding out for a part in
the new Steven Spielberg – so we discuss alternatives. David Warner top
of the list. Denis O'B still wreaking awful havoc with TG's peace of mind.
Airily suggesting we try to get [Peter] Sellers to play the Supreme Being.
TG sounds tired and heavily pressured.

Friday, April 25th

Train to Manchester. Although I spend most of the journey bent over my
books, I can't help overhearing that there has been some sort of US raid
on Iran during the night. About one man in the whole restaurant car
seems to have heard the early morning news – and says that the Americans
launched an Entebbe-style commando attack in Iran which ended with
two US aircraft smashing into each other in the dark and killing eight
men.

It really does sound like a most perilous affair and makes me aware of
that where-I-was-when-I-heard-the-news sort of feeling – here I am
speeding towards Manchester on the day the war broke out!

Arrive at twenty to twelve. Met by Roger Laughton, Ken Stephinson's
boss at BBC Features.[1] He's a chattery, eloquent, rather macho head of
department, who went to Birkdale School, supports Sheffield Wednesday
and also went briefly to the same Crusader class[2] as myself! 'Then why
weren't we best friends?' he asked, jokingly but quite significantly.

He drives me out of Manchester to Ken's quite extraordinary converted
station cottage at Saddleworth. Extraordinary, not just because expresses
thunder past not ten feet from his windows, but because the stretch of
railway line is magnificent – coming from the south over Saddleworth
Viaduct then curving in an impressive long bend to disappear then
reappear in the shadow of massive slabs of moorland.

Marjorie cooks us a very tasty, delicate meal, which we eat in the Ladies'
Waiting Room, whilst listening solemnly to President Carter's live
message to the US people at one o'clock our time, seven o'clock a.m. their

---

1 Ken Stephinson, BBC Manchester producer who recruited me to present an episode of
Great Railway Journeys.
2 The Crusaders' Union was an evangelical Bible Class for boys and girls.

time – describing, quite straightforwardly, his own personal responsibility for the immense cock-up.

Monday, April 28th

At Park Square West to meet Ron Devillier,[1] who is on his way back to the US after a TV sales fair in France. Ron is anxious to market the Python TV shows in the US and, in view of his pioneering work in awakening the US to MPFC [*Monty Python's Flying Circus*], we listen to him with interest.

Cleese, who had not met Ron before, clearly warmed to him and at the end of an hour's discussion (Ron emphasising the extraordinary audience ratings which Python still picks up whenever it's shown in the US), John proposed that we should meet in a week's time, when all of us reassemble for the recording of *Python's Contractual Obligation Album*, and we should agree to approach Ron formally and ask him to set out his terms for distributing Python tapes.

Denis is quite actively pursuing a company called Telepictures Inc, who he hopes can be persuaded to handle *all* Python product (in and out of the series).

Again the big business approach of Denis confronts and seems to conflict with the decentralised Python plans, which are born of mistrust of big American companies and trust in individuals whom we like instead. I foresee the Telepictures v Ron Devillier situation becoming a head-on battle between Denis's 'philosophy' and our own.

Tuesday, April 29th

As I drive from Wardour Street up to TG's I'm quite forcibly struck by the inadequacy of the title *Time Bandits*. It just won't create much of a stir on the hoardings, marquees and billboards. My favourite new title is 'Terry Gilliam's Greed'.

1   Ron Devillier ran Dallas Public Broadcasting station, the first place in America to show a series of Monty Python uncut and in its entirety, back in 1972.

Saturday, May 3rd

The post brings a very cheering letter from the headmaster of William Ellis to say that Tom has a place at the school from next September. So do most of his best friends, so this is good news indeed, especially as Willy will now automatically be offered a sibling's place.

As a reward I take Tom out for lunch and a trip to the South Ken museums. But the reward turns into quite an effort – for I take Louise and Helen [Guedalla], Rachel and Willy as well as Tom.

Buy the children McDonald's fast food, then drive on down to the Geology Museum. Have to detour as Kensington Gore is cordoned off because of the Iranian Embassy siege at Prince's Gate. Now in its fourth day – and deadlines and threats have passed. There is massive police presence, but a remarkable calm now as the siege becomes a London institution.

Rachel and Helen haul me round the various exhibits and we in fact visit three museums. My mind is a mass of surrealist images from a score of exhibition stands and I am quite exhausted by the time we get home at six.

Wednesday, May 7th

After a poor night's sleep, up in good time and down to Euston by 9.30. Myself and the film crew catch the 9.55 to Manchester. I'm supposed to be an ordinary traveller in an ordinary second-class coach, but will viewers think it entirely coincidental that the only other occupants of the 9.55 today seem to be Orthodox Rabbis?

Monday, May 12th: Grosmont, North Yorkshire

We drive over to Grosmont to interview Kim Mallion about restoring railway engines. It's a strange process trying to appear natural whilst having to do unnatural things like stand in an unusual relationship in order to keep the interviewee's face to camera, having to cut him off in mid-sentence because we have to move casually to another pre-set position and at the same time trying to mentally edit his remarks and your questions, knowing that this whole encounter will probably take up no more than one minute's film. I began to realise why TV interviewers and presenters develop their aggressive pushiness. They're doing their job. Well, I'm glad I'm in comedy.

Tuesday, May 13th: Grosmont

Woke at four to the silence of the countryside.

For a moment or two, lying there in the pre-dawn in the isolation of this tiny North Yorkshire village, I was seized with a crisis of confidence. What I was doing all seemed so unreal. I am not a documentary presenter – I have no special knowledge or authority to talk about railways, or even a special skill in getting people to talk. I have been chosen mainly because of what I have done in the past, which has made me into a reasonably well-known TV figure, but more precisely I've been chosen because Ken senses in my personality something which the viewer will like and identify with.

So there I am, lying, listening to a cuckoo which has just started up in a nearby wood as the grey gives way to the gold creeping light of another hot day, trying to bring into sharp and positive focus this ephemeral 'personality' of mine, which is my chief qualification for this job. How I wish I were dealing in something much more finite – like the skill of an engine driver or a cameraman. Something which you can see, feel, touch, switch on and off. But no, for an hour on national TV I am to be everyone's friend – the traveller that millions are happy to travel with.

Up at a quarter to eight, resolved to treat my predicament in the classic existentialist way – not to worry, just to do. The weather is perfect for our idyllic shots of Egton Station and the Esk Valley Line. I lie in the grass by the track reading Paul Theroux's terrible adventures in La Paz [in *The Old Patagonian Express*] and thinking myself in paradise here, with the hot sun shining from a cloudless sky and wind in the thin line of pines above my head.

Wednesday, May 14th: Teesside

Interviewed a man who knew some details of Stockton-Darlington, the world's first public passenger railway. Only after the interview do I find out that his son had been crushed to death six weeks before owing to the negligence of the nearby factory where he was an apprentice. It would have been his 18th birthday today, the man told me – on the verge of tears. He'd had a lot of personal problems – the break-up of a marriage, etc – and this was the last straw. He apologised for not being able to remember all the details for me, but the doctors had put him on a drug after his nervous breakdown and it left him irritatingly cloudy on

memories, he said. He'd half-built a model train. Just an ordinary
bloke.

Thursday, May 15th: Newcastle

On to the 125 at Darlington and various shots of The Traveller looking
around him. I've long since run out of delightfully informal, spontaneous
and casual gestures and am now concentrating on trying not to appear
too idiotically interested every time I look out of the window.

My rosy-spectacled view of Newcastle provoked a nice comment from
a local. I was raving about the wonderful easiness of the Cumberland pub
in the working-class district of the Byker and someone quipped, 'Oh, yes,
the Cumberland. They say there's one bar full of locals and one bar full
of playgroup leaders.'

Friday, May 16th: Newcastle–Edinburgh

Wake to sunshine and clear skies and the chorus of squeaks, rumbles and
soft hissing of diesel exhausts from the station below. Outside a panorama
of cars and trains crossing bridges. Tyneside coming to work.

We board an HST for Edinburgh which is half an hour late. I haven't
been on a single punctual train this week.

Between Berwick and Edinburgh, as the train staggers home with an
out-of-action rear power car (what a bad day for this to happen to British
Rail), I sit with three randomly selected 'members of the public' and we're
filmed chatting. Maybe the age of television is conditioning us all, but
they speak with the easy assurance of people who are interviewed daily.

My last memories of elegant Edinburgh, as serenely unflawed in its
beauty as ever, are of a group of very drunken chartered surveyors milling
around in the lounge of the North British at midnight, tipping each other
in and out of a wheelchair. If they'd been punks they'd have been out in
the gutter, but they were Chartered Surveyors of this Fine City and were
in dinner jackets and had paid well for their tickets, so no-one stopped
them behaving like the worst sort of hooligans. My last image was of
them falling on top of each other and knocking back Napoleon brandy
from the bottle.

Saturday, May 17th: Kyle of Lochalsh

Up and across the Central Highlands – shot of me reading, etc. On time at Inverness's crabbed and disappointing little station. Inverness full of yobbos, drunks and ladies with twinsets and pearls doing their Saturday shopping. We have time off. I make for the castle, but in front of it are three fairly incapable teenage Scots. One turns and spits long and high into the air. To my astonished horror another runs forward, tries to catch the gob in his own mouth and fails.

The other thing that I notice in Inverness this sunny Saturday afternoon are the number of churches. Severe, pencil-thin towers – the grey pointed fingers of disapproval. Enough to drive you to drink.

So begins the memorable nightmare of the journey to Kyle. The train has an observation car on the end, a special old coach with free-standing armchairs and tables.

Ken's idea is to fill the special coach with travellers whom I casually chat to, plus one or two specially researched guests. One of whom is a Mrs Mackenzie, a 99-year-old who I'm told remembers the railway on the day it opened in 1896. She's a wonderful, bright old lady, but not soft of hearing, and my first question – a tortuously-phrased effort to elicit information as to how old she was – is received with a stony silence. A pleasant smile, but a stony silence. I try it again, then again even louder. The crew and the rest of the compartment must be either splitting their sides or squirming in embarrassment.

For a full ten minutes I persevere, trying everything, but, like a man with an enormous fishing net and six harpoons trying to catch two small fish, I end up with very little for a lot of work. It leaves me exhausted, though still in admiration of old Mrs Mackenzie.

Tuesday, May 20th: Mallaig

At 10.30 I'm filmed boarding the Skye ferry to Kyleakin. The cameras are staying on the mainland to film exteriors from the Kyle train. I'm free until after lunch and, as I have no option but to go on to Skye, I decide on a morning's walking to compensate for much eating and drinking over the last few days.

I stride on out of town, having left my case at the Caledonian MacBrayne [ferry] office. I stop at a hotel which is a country house – red-grey stone and tall pitched roofs – set in very lush gardens with brilliantly deep pink rhododendrons and a settled air of detachment and solid comfort.

But as soon as I step inside my stomach tightens with the identification of a very early feeling of my childhood of a claustrophobia, a fear of being stifled in dark rooms with well-polished doors, in which old ladies move in the shadows.

Mallaig, which we reach in the evening, is even bleaker than Kyle of Lochalsh, a fairly wretched spot to be faced with the prospect of a night in – after a day like today. But I have a room overlooking the Atlantic and the sharp points of Rum and the volcanic spur of Eigg and there is a sunset after all and it looks quite idyllic with a score of fishing boats heading for the harbour.

After the ritual of an evening meal together ('Are the "Melon Cubes" out of a tin?' one of our number enquires ingenuously. 'Oh, *yes*...' the waitress assures him quickly), Ken and I go to visit the engine driver whom we will be filming tomorrow, as his wife has called and asked us over.

They're rather a special family – with three children roughly the age of my own, and yet Ronnie McClellan must be over 20 years older then me. He married late to a very bright and articulate district nurse. Their children come down in dressing gowns to meet us (it's 9.45) and shake hands solemnly and politely. They don't have television, but they have dogs, cats and, I think, some animals in the croft. The children kiss their father obediently but warmly. I should imagine he's quite a strict and traditional father.

Back at the empty vastness of the West Highland, the two men who were drinking half and halfs (Scotch and Heavy) at six o'clock are still drinking half and halfs at twelve. Ken beats me three times at pool. Go to bed feeling inadequate.

Nylon sheets and a colour scheme which looks as though an animal's been slaughtered in the room. Read Michael Arlen's *The Green Hat* and enjoy the utter incongruity. It gives me great comfort to know that Cannes and Mallaig exist on the same planet.

Wednesday, May 21st: Mallaig–Glenfinnan

Fresh Mallaig kippers for breakfast. Later I'm told that there's no such thing as a Mallaig kipper as there's a ban on herring fishing. So it was probably a Canadian herring – which may have been kippered in Mallaig. Anyway, I ate two of them.

An especially beautiful journey down along the coast – made more civilised by the presence of a buffet bar and a couple of glasses of wine. I have to be filmed in the said buffet bar with two Danish students and a flavour chemist from Chicago who is over here on a cycling tour of Scotland. He's a great Python fan and he's honestly called Constantine Apostle.

Our hotel here – the Glenfinnan House – is situated in an almost unbeatable Highland surrounding. Pictures of Bonnie Prince Charlie's heroic failures (it was here at Glenfinnan he gathered his forces in the summer of 1745), a set of bagpipes, pieces of igneous rocks on a dark-stained mantelpiece in a passable imitation of a baronial hall.

The house is set beside a lawn surrounded by broadleaved trees and running down to Loch Shiel. Beside a wooden jetty, a couple of rowing boats bob on the water. Walk down to the jetty and look down the length of Loch Shiel, at the sheer magnificence of the spurs of epic mountainside tumbling down to the lakeside.

As we unload, a cool-looking kid of ten or eleven skids up on his bike. 'Do you live here?' I ask ... The boy, in a particularly businesslike way, nods and adds, quite naturally, 'D'you think I'm lucky?'

To bed around midnight. It seems almost a crime to close the curtains against such a view.

Monday, May 26th

A Bank Holiday again. Surfaced mid-morning. Regular phone calls and door bells ringing – mostly for the children, who have the next week off school. There was lots I wanted to do and a big pile of mail. Most of all I wanted to do nothing – to be at no-one's beck and call for a bit.

Terry Gilliam comes round soon after six. The first week of *Time Bandits* is now complete, but the shoot in Morocco was gruelling even by TG's standards. Moroccans less good at organisation than Tunisians, which didn't help, but they managed 97 slates – some in locations only accessible by mule.

After one week in Morocco he'd come back feeling like he did after ten weeks of *Brian*. Rushes on Wednesday will show whether this almighty opening effort will spur everyone on, or be the start of the collapse.

Thursday, May 29th

A heavy day ahead. The sky is grey and lowering, but still no rain. Prepare for the arrival of the BBC unit to film outside and inside the house. Also today we're expecting Al and Claudie[1] to stay, so No. 2 has to be prepared.

As it turns out we have a most successful shoot. We block off Julia Street with a 60-foot hoist to shoot an epic 'leaving home' scene. Helen and the three children all have to do their acting bit and acquit themselves very well on all four takes. Really it's an elaborate reconstruction for the viewing public of what happens every time I leave home for filming away. Rachel, last out, hands me my toothbrush with an easy self-confidence which I hadn't expected at all.

Friday, May 30th

Helen goes out to badminton and Al, Claudie and I make a rambling feast out of quite a simple selection of soup and cold meats, ending with a liqueur tasting – Al determined to try all the bottles he brought over from Brittany. Their Jacques Brel tape played loudly – Al enthusing, as only he can, over each track. 'One of the greatest people of this century' is Al's verdict on Brel.

Claudie comes to life more when the subject turns to France, but her English is now much more confident. But I wish she would eat more and smoke less. Al wants to have a baby – they want a girl and they have a name, 'Chantelle'.

A warm and woozy evening. Much laughter.

Tuesday, June 3rd

Listen to the Python *Contractual Obligation Album*. I'm afraid it does sound rather ordinary. One or two of the songs stand out and there are some conventional sketches of Cleese and Chapman's (man enters shop, etc) which are saved by good performances. Twenty-five percent padding, fifty percent quite acceptable, twenty-five percent good new Python.

---

1 Al Levinson, an American I'd met in the seventies, and some of whose writing I'd published. His second marriage was to Claudie, a young Bretonne.

Saturday, June 7th

Drive up to T Gilliam's for a meeting. Terry is very deflated. He looks and sounds quite pummelled by the pressures of this creature he's brought into life. Filming all week, meetings with actors in the evening, all weekend looking at locations.

Now Amy wants his attention and he wants to give me his attention. So we work on rewrites and additions for next week whilst Amy piles me up with teddy bears and races round the room with a manic energy, shouting, tumbling, grimacing. The only way we can work is by me reading the script corrections as a story to one of Amy's teddies. A bizarre session.

Monday, June 9th

Work and run in the morning. Talk to a fan from Indiana on the telephone at lunchtime – she was visiting England, had seen *Grail* 17 times and *Brian* nine times and loved everything we did.

To Denis's office at two. Meet Peter Cook there. He has a very silly hat, but we have a few laughs, mainly about a pop group Peter had seen in Los Angeles called Bees Attack Victor Mature. Peter rambles on a while, then wanders off – a little concerned as to how he'll find his way out of the EuroAtlantic fortress. Denis has just done a deal for GC's *Yellowbeard* screenplay, provided that the screenplay is rewritten. So Peter Cook, whom Denis was much impressed by at Amnesty, is to rewrite the script with GC – and they have a six-million-dollar production budget. Denis does want to see us all happy.

What Denis doesn't know is that E. Idle has probably slipped the O'Brien net. A very positive letter from him in France – the 'Pirates of Penzance' now looks more likely to happen. Gary Weiss [Eric's director] is a very 'hot' property and he wants to do it. Eric now has a direct phone line in Cotignac, but asks me to promise not to give it to Denis, under threat of setting fire to my stereo.

I leave, having told Denis that the next thing I want to do is a film on my own – probably to shoot next summer.

Watch last hour of the Test Match v West Indies on the box, then Helen and I, suitably tarted up in DJs and long dresses, drive down to Kensington for the reception at the Royal Geographical Society to commemorate their founding 150 years ago.

The Queen and Prince Philip and the Duke of Kent are to be there. We've joked about going and not going, but tell Helen it's my duty as a diarist if nothing else.

Sir John and Lady Hunt are receiving the guests. He's quite frail now and totally white-haired. Lady Hunt seems very bright and on the ball.

I meet the daughter of Lord Curzon, on whose land the RGS HQ was built, and the sparkling wine with strawberries in it is going to my head quite pleasantly when we are asked to move away from the gravel terrace. Quite amiably, but firmly. Around us some people are being lined up as if for some military manoeuvre – not in a long line, but in a number of short ranks, like football teams.

Helen and I are enmeshed with a world authority on gibbons, who also happens to be an enormous *Ripping Yarns* fan and slightly more pissed than we are.

The Duke was, at one point, just beside my right shoulder and sounded to be having quite a jolly time, but entourages always deter chance encounters, so I didn't spring forward. About 10.30 he and Queenie disappeared inside.

Helen and I, quite mellow, but hungry, left about 15 minutes later, but, as we prepared to cross Kensington Gore, there was a shout from a policeman who was standing only 100 yards away from the SAS siege building – 'Stay in the middle!'[1] We froze on the traffic island in the middle of Kensington Gore and realised that the Queen had not yet left.

In fact at this moment her Daimler, with the swollen rear windows for better visibility, was sweeping away from the RGS. The light was on inside so the Queen and the Duke could be seen, and for a moment in time we on our little traffic island and the Head of the British Empire came into eyeball to eyeball contact. Helen waved. The Queen automatically waved back, the Duke grinned and the black limousine curved left and right into Hyde Park and was gone.

Thursday, June 12th: London–Llanwern

To Paddington to catch the 1.15 to Newport. There is a long wait, blamed first on signal failure, then, with what sounded like a stroke of inspiration

---

1 Just over a month earlier the SAS had spectacularly stormed the Iranian Embassy in Prince's Gate, ending a five-day siege by Iranian separatists. Five of the gunmen and one hostage were killed.

from a tired guard, on a bomb scare. But it enables me to complete the 'Robin Hood' rewrites, losing the 'Future' sequence.

Finally arrive at the Gateway Hotel, Llanwern, at about four o'clock. Various members of *Time Bandits* crew are surfacing after the second of their week of night shoots at nearby Raglan Castle. Last night a lady on stilts 'lost her bottle', as Ian Holm put it, but the crew seem to be in good spirits.

TG and I discuss the rewrites. Then I go to my room and watch some of the England v Belgium match – some promising football and one of the great international goals by Wilkins, then fighting on the terraces and the Italian police react fiercely with riot police and tear gas.

TG's fictional recreation of the sack of Castiglione is not unlike the actual scenes I've just witnessed on the terraces in Turin. Both take place in North Italy and in each smoke is drifting everywhere and bodies are falling. But TG's pictures are much more impressive and I'm tantalised by the brief amount I've seen of this strange film that is slowly and painstakingly taking shape in the rain at a nearby castle.

Tuesday, June 24th

Midsummer's Day. And, as it turns out, the first day in the last three weeks when it hasn't rained on the *Time Bandits*.

Out in the mosquito-ridden beauty of the Epping Forest, with the pollarded trees striking wonderfully Gilliamesque poses, with lumps and gnarls and strange growths, Shelley [Duvall who's playing Pansy, one of the star-crossed lovers] and I and the mammoth unit enjoy a dry day. Not 20 miles away, there were fierce storms with hailstones scattering the players at Wimbledon and Lord's.

Wednesday, June 25th

After more shots with the dwarves passing us, Shelley and I get on to the rain sequences. I can't complain. I wrote the dreaded word 'rain', and here it is in all its dispiriting glory, courtesy of the Essex Fire Brigade. Not a terribly good take and the next 40 minutes are spent under a hair-dryer, preparing my wig for a re-take. But then it's lunch and I have to go to the pub with a plastic bag over my head.

Afterwards a fairly horrendous experience in the second rain scene, when Shelley and I are down to our mediaeval underwear. The elements of the developing shot are so various that it takes six takes before we have a satisfactory conclusion. And on each one we have hoses directed on us for about a minute and a half.

Shelley seems much more tolerant of the ordeal than any actress has a right to be. But, as she says in the car on the way home, it's better than having to cry every day for seven months with Kubrick! Nicholson had to take a six-month break after the movie [*The Shining*] was finished to get himself straight again.

Thursday, June 26th

Drive to Pentonville Road, where, on the hill from which the great Victorian painting of St Pancras was made, I find myself in the BUPA medical centre for a screening. No particular reason, I just thought I should have a complete medical check-up and where better than under the personal eye of one of the BUPA centre's leading lights – Alan Bailey.[1]

Alan reassures me on one point: that Parkinson's Disease isn't hereditary. Then he examines me, pokes, prods and fingers my genitals, after which we have a talk about houses, education, the possible break-up of ILEA [Inner London Education Authority], and he offers me a drink from his metal cupboard full of Scotch and other drugs. I have a beer and meet the doctor who is, as Alan cheerfully informs me, 'in charge of the clap clinic here'.

The clap man is neat, less of a character, and we talk about beta-blockers – pills which reduce the heartbeat. He thinks them a quite brilliant advance, and yet could talk only of the dangers of their misuse.

Alan is quite keen to show off the body scanner in the basement and the instant computer details of each patient. So far, all the results of my tests show no danger areas. I'm four pounds lighter than I was when I came seven years ago at eleven stone seven, and I'm five foot eleven inches – which is news to me and means I'm officially taller than I thought I was! Sight and hearing are 100% apart from one frequency of hearing – that of telephone bells and gunshots!

---

1 Alan was one of Graham Chapman's closest friends. They had met as medical students at Bart's Hospital.

Monday, June 30th

I have something of a record in the make-up line today – four layers – my own tightly-cropped hair, a bald bladder on top of that, a wig stuck onto the sides of that and, to top the lot, a toupee. The make-up takes a couple of hours, but Elaine [Carew, my make-up artist] and I now get on so well that I hardly notice the time passing. I can't blame anyone but myself for any inconvenience either, as I wrote it.

Katherine Helmond, of *Soap* fame, who is Ruth Gordon's replacement, is on the set for fittings, etc, together with Peter Vaughan, who plays her Ogre husband. She's delightful, Vaughan strong and quite quiet with his foxy little eyes and mouth easily cracking into a smile.

Shelley and I work all day on an impressive set of the 'Titanic'. Final shot is uncomfortable and involves me losing my toupee and causing a lot of damage. They like it on the third take and we wrap at 7.30.

Tuesday, July 1st

A stormy night as a depression, pushed by cold north winds, crosses over us. The blind flaps and bangs and it's as cold as November. Up at seven and drive through the rain to the studios [at Wembley] by eight.

Into mediaeval outfit this time. A steady morning's work on the coach interiors (Shelley and I sitting in a coach resting on inner tubes of lorry tyres – four men waving trees above our heads).

In the afternoon, as we prepare to shoot the dwarves dropping on Pansy [one of the two star-crossed lovers, played by Shelley] and myself, the director hurtles through the air towards us, strikes Shelley sharply on the left temple and knocks her almost senseless. Gilliam spends the next half-hour comforting a very shaken Shelley. Turns out he was demonstrating to one of the dwarves how safe it was to fall.

I work in my dressing room, waiting for the final call. Rain and wind outside. Quite cosy. Stodgy food and assistant director constantly coming round to ask if there's anything I want. Stardom means eating too much. After eight, Neville Thompson, the associate producer, arrives in my 'suite' to tell me that they will not be getting around to Shelley and myself this evening. The shot has been cancelled, as this was Shelley's last day on the picture.

Wednesday, July 2nd

To Park Square West by ten for a Python meeting. Eric is already there, playing the piano. I've no idea how today's meeting is going to turn out – all I know is that John has told Terry G that he's never felt less like writing Python and yet officially we have this month set aside for just such an enterprise ...

Terry J arrives next, looking mournful – with reason, for he has his arm in a sling. Apparently he threw himself on the ground at a charity cricket match last Sunday and has a hairline fracture of a bone called the humerus.

John arrives – he's growing his Shakespearian beard back again, I think. He claims it went down very well with the ladies and shaving it off (which he did for the *Time Bandits*) only revealed what a tiny mouth he has. I advise John to have his mouth widened. He says he is considering another hair transplant.

We talk briefly about Python's general biz. Denis's call for a business meeting and a meeting to discuss his exciting new proposals for a distribution network of our own are met with almost universal lack of interest. 'Tell him we went off to sleep,' John advises Anne when she is desperately asking what reaction she should relay to DO'B about his proposals.

Then to lunch at Odin's. Cliff Richard at the next table looks permanently off the beach at Barbados. Apart from Eric, the Pythons are white, apart from TJ who's grey. After a long wait, and some white wine, I lead off perhaps provocatively by asking who wants to write the new Python film this month. Then it all comes out.

JC wants a month of leisurely talk and discussion and does not want to face the 'slog' of nine-to-five writing. I suggest that we don't yet have a very clear and positive area or identity for the subject matter of the film and that we should only write when we are really 'hungry' to write. But it's Graham who quite blandly drops the real bombshell – he's working for the next few days on a *Yellowbeard* rewrite and then he hopes to film it in Australia during the winter. This straight pinch from previously discussed Python plans is a real stunner and the well-controlled indignation of Eric and Terry J rises to the surface.

I have the increasing feeling that we are going through a period similar to the post-*Grail* days in '75, '76, when individual Pythons want to stretch their legs. Terry G led the field with *Time Bandits*, I've done the *Yarns* and the 'Railway' documentary. So I'm not too worried about proving myself.

I don't know about Eric, but he was clearly amazed when John suggested we didn't meet together till next Wednesday. At Eric's surprise JC dropped all pretences – he hung his head in his hands and became cross. 'I'm tired . . . I've done six weeks of . . . ' and so on.

This lunch and the discussions were all part of the painful process of preserving Python. We don't fit into any easy patterns, we ask each other to make enormous compromises, adjustments and U-turns, but we do produce the best comedy in the country.

Not much rest at home, for at 6.30 I'm collected by Graham in his Mercedes and we drive one and a half hours out to Associated Book Publishers in Andover for a sales-force-meet-authors binge. It all seems quite a tiresome waste of time, except that Christopher Isherwood is there, which saves the evening for me. He's 76 and looks fit and neat. His skin is weathered like an elephant's leg, in contrast to the softer, tanned brown of his friend Don Bachardy. Bachardy has bright eyes and looks terribly healthy. He's almost a carbon copy of Isherwood. Isherwood talks to Graham about a supermarket they both share in Brentwood, Los Angeles.

Isherwood talks fluently – like a man used to talking and being listened to (GC tells me his voice has become quite 'stentorian' since doing lecture tours). I would love to spend more time with him and Don – they seem such a bright, lively pair in this drab and colourless sales conference world.

Wednesday, July 9th

To Gospel Oak School for the Infant Concert. Rachel is a sheep. She wears her clean, Persil-white T-shirt and petticoat and a cardboard mask which makes it difficult for her to see, and the sheep bang into each other. Rachel's class less imaginative than the others, but her rather morose teacher did wear black fishnet tights.

Monday, July 14th

Hurry through the rain to 2 Park Square West and a Python meeting. Eric and Denis are already there. I'm wearing a 'Leica' disposable jacket and hood which I acquired [whilst filming] at the Rainhill Trials at the end of May. Eric says I look like a red sperm.

All Pythons present except, of course, Gilliam. Denis has greatly looked forward to this meeting, for this is the first time he has aired his latest proposal to the group as a whole. The proposal is that Python should become involved in the setting-up of an independent UK film distribution company – HandMade Films.

Denis rides all interruptions as he slowly and impressively reveals his plans. But he is not a good judge of people – and of English people especially – and instead of being received with wide-eyed gratitude, his proposals are subjected to a barrage of strong scepticism.

Eric wants to know how much it all will cost us and then queries whether or not we need it, as it will mean yet another source of interminable business meetings. John C queries Denis's assumption that there will be eight 'Python-based' films at least in the next five years. He certainly isn't going to do one, and neither is Eric. Also the assumption that *Time Bandits* and *Yellowbeard* will each make at least £650,000 in the UK is received without conviction.

Denis's worst enemy is his own ingenuous enthusiasm in the face of five very complex, quite sophisticated minds, four at least of which distrust one thing more than anything else – uncritical enthusiasm. So it's left undecided.

Denis rather rapidly runs through the rest of the agenda, but he's lost us. The more he enthuses over terms, deals, percentages, controls, etc, the more John turns his mind to doing anagrams on his agenda (he had a good one for Michael Palin – i.e. Phallic Man).

To lunch at Odin's. Terry suggests the group should spend three days in Cherbourg, writing. John thinks we should do a film about the Iliad. Denis looks bewildered.

Wednesday, July 16th

Children are prepared for school – with the right clothes, shoes, music, forms for teachers, etc. At ten to nine Sam Jarvis arrives to work on painting the outside of the house and settles first of all for his cup of tea. Letters are sorted, diaries written and banks visited on the way to Cleese's for a Python session.

Only John is there at the appointed time. He's thumbing through his address book for someone to take to dinner ... 'Come on, Michael, you must know some ravishing creature ... ' and so on. He grins happily when I half-jest about the demise of Python. Eric is still unwell, TG's off

... 'I think we should disband this rapidly-crumbling comedy group for at least a year.' John grins ...

At seven leave for Tom's orchestral concert at Gospel Oak. Tom plays a clarinet solo, piano solo and a duet with Holly [Jones] and is one of the two or three stars of the show. I feel very proud, especially as his clarinet piece is quite difficult. Both Helen and I dreadfully nervous in the audience.

Sunday, July 20th

After breakfast and Sunday papers, I retire to workroom (most reluctantly) to prepare for tonight's Save the Whales concert. Various tiresome little props and costume details to sort out, but Anne H is a great help and locates such things as Gumby glasses and the like. I write a new piece – a short monologue about Saving the Plankton.

I complete my plankton piece, gather props and cossies into a big suitcase and, in a state of numbed resignation, set off under grey skies for the Venue in Victoria. I forget Gumby flowers, vase and mallet and have to drive all the way back from Regent's Park.

The Venue is a cabaret-type theatre, with audience at tables eating and drinking, so they don't seem to mind us starting nearly an hour late. From then on I begin to enjoy it. All the lethargy of a Sunday disappears and is replaced by the sharpness of performing adrenaline. 'Plankton' goes especially well and is received all the better for being obviously specially-written material.

Second half the audience are in very good form. 'Save the leopards!' someone shouts as I come on in my leopard-skin coat as the spangly compère of 'Shouting'. I reassure the audience that it *is* artificial, whereupon the rejoinder comes smartly back 'Save the artificial leopards!'

Home with huge feeling of relief and satisfaction – 100% different from the way I felt on leaving seven hours ago. Am I a manic depressive?

Monday, July 21st

Anne rings early to say that Python has been offered four days at the Hollywood Bowl at the end of September. Two weeks in LA in late September, all together, would, I feel, do our writing chances and the group's general commitment to working together so much good that we should decide to go ahead with it as soon as possible.

Wednesday, July 23rd

TJ comes up after lunch. It's actually too hot to work upstairs at No. 4 – sticky, with bright, shining sun unremitting – so we decamp to No. 2, to the leaky double bedroom. TJ rather content here. Says it reminds him of Belsize Park![1] There complete 'Sperm Song'.

In the evening (we work on until 6.30), I ring John C to find him very disappointed with his writing progress. He claims not to have been really well since last Friday and says that he and GC have not written much and he doesn't like the family idea and could we not postpone the entire film for six months?

Thursday, July 24th

Blue skies and high summer again – the fine weather is persisting despite all forecasts. So a fresh buoyancy to my step as I come back from Mansfield Road with the papers – abruptly slowed down by the news that Peter Sellers died last night. Though not as sudden and unexpected as the news seen in a French paper on holiday in 1977 that 'Elvis est Mort!', it affected me in the same way. Sellers and Milligan were to the humour of my pre- and teenage days as Elvis was to the music.

Friday, July 25th

Duly arrive at J Cleese's at ten – bringing Eric. It's a hot day. John is upstairs recovering from taking Cynthia for an early-morning swim. We meet out in John's garden – this prospect of unbroken sunshine is so rare this last month that the sun-worshippers in the group (everyone except TJ) feel unable to ignore it.

JC proposes a moratorium on the film – period unspecified. This rather deflating proposal is perhaps made more acceptable by a general welcoming of the Hollywood Bowl show. This, after brief discussion, is received most constructively. It makes the film postponement seem less like a positive break, more of a long interruption of work in progress. We shall be together for two or three weeks in LA in late September, we will do four nights at the Bowl and it is agreed that it shall be videotaped for sale to US TV.

---

1 When Helen and I married in 1966 we lived in a flat at 82 Belsize Park Gardens.

Our 'break-through' writing of yesterday and the days before is not even read out. John seems happy to let things drift. There's a listless feeling. EI says July is a rotten month to write anything.

No-one has yet really decided how long this 'interruption' should be. Six months is the minimum and any attempt to compromise on this meets very strong objections from John. But six months merely means an almost impossibly short period for the resolution of any alternative plans, so a year is proposed. And reluctantly accepted, as if acknowledging a measure of defeat.

We shall meet again to write the movie in September 1981.

Wednesday, July 30th

Catch the 8.55 Euston–Manchester train to see the first assembly of my 'Great Railway Journey'.

At the BBC we watch the 62-minute first cut on a Steenbeck. My impression is of endless pretty railway trains disappearing behind trees – clichés of this sort of documentary. There is little evidence of my own impact on the journey ... but more disappointingly a very ordinary, flat feeling to the camerawork and strangely the editing as well.

It was a depressing viewing – depressing because I value Ken's friendship and the working relationship between us, depressing because I had hoped that his unconventional choice of presenter indicated his intention of trying some exciting and experimental approach to the programme. Depressing because I had to fight Denis O'B so hard to come up with something so dull. I think Ken is well aware of my feelings, and there is a conspicuous lack of over-enthusiasm.

So when I dash off to catch the Manchester Pullman back to town, I know I have a job of work on – much more than I expected to do at this stage of the programme, but there is hope and I have always in the back of my mind the memory of my first reaction to the initial cut of 'Roger of the Raj'.[1]

---

1 A *Ripping Yarn* which I at first thought hadn't worked at all, but has since become one of my favourites, not least for Richard Vernon and Joan Sanderson's wonderfully played dining room scenes.

Thursday, July 31st

To the foot man at 9.30. He's running very late. I sit in his little surgery in Mornington Road, with a nun and a sad, rather dim, shuffling old Irishman, and write my Python album notes.

Then to EuroAtlantic for what is supposed to be a couple of hours of business and a couple of hours of thought on the content of the stage show. It turns out to be four hours of business and hardly a thought for the content.

Once again Denis pushes us towards the Telepictures video deal and the distribution company. All of us weaken on Telepictures, apart from Eric, who maintains that we should not give video rights for seven years to a company we know nothing about. At one point Eric suggests directly to Denis that he is in some way an interested party on Telepictures' side. Denis denies this. Eric will not be moved, though, and vetoes the agreement until he's thought about it more.

Monday, August 18th

Meet Ken Stephinson for lunch and we have a very productive chat about the documentary. He feels as I do that it's bland and rather dull at the moment, but we hatch plans to revive, restore and enliven it. The only thing that worries me is that I calculate I have a maximum of 12 clear writing days before Hollywood.

Thursday, August 21st: Copenhagen and Malmö

Caught British Airways' 9.25 flight to Copenhagen [for *Life of Brian* publicity] with Terry J and Anne Bennett (of CIC, our distributors) from a marvellously uncrowded Heathrow.

We lost an hour in the air and landed at Copenhagen at 12.05. A Cadillac limousine (looking very out of place) swept us and our Danish hosts through the neat, clean streets of suburban Copenhagen, with row upon row of apartment blocks, but mainly of brick, with pitched roofs and in small units, usually angled to avoid a wilderness of long concrete vistas.

From this neat, clean, modest little capital we took a neat, clean hydrofoil across to Malmö in Sweden.

I hear from TJ (confirmed by Anne Bennett) that Python has not begun too well in Germany. Strong religious anti-reaction in Stuttgart –

elsewhere sluggish. So Brianity is perhaps not to be the new world religion after all.

As we leave Malmö for the University of Lund the wind has freshened. Not much impression of Sweden on the way. An extension of Lincolnshire perhaps.

About a quarter past eight we are introduced and go into a question and answer session. Most of the questions seem to come from Englishmen or Americans. Round about nine TJ is getting rather restless and asks the audience (numbering 300 or so) if he can ask *them* a question. Much eager nodding. 'How many of you want to go to the lavatory?' Our hosts take the hint and wind up the session. For some reason we sing them the 'Lumberjack Song' and that's it. Both of us quite tired by now.

We're driven to the Students' Union and eventually find ourselves in a small, circular room where a table is laid. We each have a glass of rather weak beer – they are not allowed to serve full-strength beer to students – and nothing is happening. Outside the wind is strong and gusting and rain is lashing the panes.

Finally a large plate of Swedish crayfish arrives. They've been marinaded in beer and dill (very popular in Sweden) and are quite tasty. Then bottles of aquavit, which are drunk to the accompaniment of rather hard drinking songs. A lady called Lotta Love, said to be Sweden's foremost groupie, also comes in from somewhere.

Terry J is strongly resisting Anne's and my attempts to get us all onto the last hydrofoil to Copenhagen. I know that we must get back. We have to start early tomorrow and the drinking – already producing a noisy and rather belligerent atmosphere – will only accelerate.

With great difficulty we get TJ up and mutter our apologies. We just manage to get downstairs and into our waiting limousine, which then drives like hell into Malmö. The wind buffets the car on the motorway, causing it to veer dangerously at high speed, but we *do* reach the quay in time and to my intense relief the hydrofoil is still running, despite the storm. We are in Denmark again by one.

Friday, August 22nd: Copenhagen

Terry is terribly thankful that we didn't let him stay in Malmö, and he goes off for a walk whilst I bathe, do my morning exercise and gently test my body and brain for any damage caused by Sweden yesterday.

Outside the life of Copenhagen goes on, very unhurried, like model life in a model village. Even the workmen are clean and I don't believe that they really have the work to do anyway. They must be Play People. Eventually decide that the men engaged in raising and replacing paving stones opposite the hotel are in fact now reduced to cleaning the underneath of the Copenhagen streets.

At about ten o'clock we start interviews in our room, followed by a press conference downstairs, after which we are to give a TV interview. A Danish actor is portraying a Norwegian. The Danes and Swedes both find the Norwegians a Scandinavian joke – slow-witted, thick-headed, humourless fishing folk – and they send them up unmercifully. The fact that Python's *Life of Brian* has been banned in Norway causes our hosts great glee and the Swedes have a poster tagging the film 'So Funny it was Banned in Norway'.

We are then taken to the Tivoli Gardens for lunch and more filming. By now my head is clear, but my stomach is distinctly off-balance. I drink mineral water, eat more ham and eggs, but find to my horror after lunch that we are to be interviewed on the Big Wheel. I'm now feeling very queasy and not at all far from the point of uncontainable nausea.

Here I am, quite likely to be sick even if I just stand still, being loaded onto a big wheel compartment opposite a grinning interviewer, a cameraman and a sound man. The wheel moves up, we hang over Copenhagen then swing down, round, up again, going faster. Only desperate laughter at my plight and Terry's touching concern and huge gulps of cool air as we swing up keep my stomach contents from being vividly reproduced on Danish television.

At last the living hell comes to an end and I'm quite proud to have survived. But the interviewer hasn't finished, he wants more. High over the city we go – I really can't answer any more. Even TJ is going groggy. 'Alright,' is all I can shout. 'I give up! I give up!' At the end of the torture I'm white and wobbling, something's churning away inside. At last I can pause ... No I can't ... We're led away to be photographed doing funny things with the Danish comedian.

Then into the limousine, to be driven, with the dubious aid of stomach-lurching power-assisted brakes, to Danish radio. At last our Danish hosts seem to have got the message that I'm unwell, so I'm escorted carefully from the limousine and the first request is a 'toiletten' for Mr Palin.

Monday, August 25th

Work on the 'Railway' programme – looking through the video cassette and running and re-running. I'm very much encouraged, and there is enough in there to give a high-quality look to the programme – now all we need is a cohesive element of typical Palin stuff. I need to inject into the documentary what I can do best – which is not, clearly, being a straight documentary presenter.

Go out for a pizza in Hampstead, full of Bank Holiday revellers. We talk over '*TB*'. Terry is as positive about it as I've heard him since May. Highly excited by the battle scenes at the end.

I feel much encouraged by today – both on '*GRJ*' and '*TB*'. At one time I was feeling that I have fallen between so many stools this year that I can only have done myself harm, but now it looks as though all the hard work and hassle may just have been worth it.

Monday, September 1st

School starts again – Rachel and Willy to Gospel Oak today, Tom to William Ellis tomorrow. Tom has tried on his blazer, matching shirt, dark trousers, dark shoes and hates them. I must say it's a little sad to see him suddenly restricted by a uniform. Some loss of innocence somewhere.

Before I start work I have to go through the unnerving and slightly distasteful business of giving myself an enema – to clear out my bowels in preparation for a visit to the botty doctor this afternoon.

After squeezing the phosphate mixture in, I realise I'm unsure what an enema is quite supposed to do. Should I retain the fluid for a certain time? I'm downstairs looking up 'enema' in the *Shorter Oxford Dictionary* when events overtake me and I just reach the lavatory for ten or fifteen minutes' worth of quite uncomfortable straining, with nothing to read but an article on the state of the economy.

Then to the Medical Centre. Talk with Alan Bailey, then meet Mr Baker, the botty doctor. He takes various particulars, then I'm led to a room next door with various contraptions lying about. My eye flicks over them, wanting – and at the same time, not wanting – to see the sort of thing which will be going up my bum.

The doctor enters, formally, from another doorway. I'm laid down, naked and with my legs up in my chest, and the ordeal begins. His first probings are, after penetration, not too bad, quite bearable, but the higher he gets (and I can feel this tubing peering and turning and twisting and thrusting up into my stomach) the more severe the pain.

I'm told to take deep breaths and I grasp the nurse's hand tightly as he squeezes air and water into my bowels to enlarge them so he can see better. For some moments the pain is acute. I can feel sweat dripping off me. The worst thing is not knowing how long it will last.

Finally the pain eases and he begins to withdraw his instrument. Never have I been so glad to have an examination over. It turns out he's been using a sigmoidoscope and 50 centimetres of thick, black tube. 'Wonderful view,' he says, disarmingly ... 'Maybe you ought to do a postcard series,' I suggest, but he doesn't laugh.

Thursday, September 4th

Complete a rough draft of the new 'Railway' commentary by lunchtime. Then run on the Heath – it's almost a year to the day that I began regular running.

I've kept at it, apart from two or three weeks on the 'Railway' documentary and a week in Cyprus. I've run in Central Park and across Fisher's Island and pounded the lanes of Suffolk and the long hills between Abbotsley[1] and Waresley and I've run in rain and snow and 80° sunshine. In darkness and on Christmas Day.

I do always feel better after a run. It's as simple as that. And the physical well-being is very rapidly transformed into a feeling of mental well-being. Running makes me feel relaxed and gives me all the complex satisfaction of a test successfully completed, a feeling of achievement. I hope I shall still be at it in a year's time.

Then I write some extra lines for David Warner in ' TB'. Manage to get the word 'sigmoidoscope' into the script.

Saturday, September 6th

So full of the joys of spring today that I ring George H and invite myself over for the afternoon.

Have lunch in the garden, scan The Times, then leave, taking Tom and Willy and open-roofed Mini. In Henley an hour later. George is mending an electric hedge-cutter which cut through its own flex. As George tinkers

1 Abbotsley, a small village near St Neots in Cambridgeshire, is where Helen's mother lives.

in homely fashion with his garden equipment ('I *was* an electrical apprentice,' he assured me. 'For three weeks.') the boys and I swim in the buff in his swimming pool, surrounded by lifelike voyeuristic models of monks and nuns.

Then George took us in a flat-bottomed boat around the lake and at one point into water-filled caves. George told me that Crisp[1] modelled one of the caves on the Blue Grotto on Capri and we went on to talk about Gracie Fields and how King Farouk [of Egypt] had been a great admirer and had come to Capri to live with her, but all his secret servicemen and bodyguards filled the swimming pool all the time and she eventually had to turn him out.

As we stood on the bridge surveying the lakes and the towers and turrets of the extraordinary house, George told me that he really wanted more space. He doesn't want to have people anywhere near him. The other weekend he'd rung up Knight, Frank and Rip-Off,[2] as he calls them in friendly fashion, to enquire about a 1,600-acre farm in Gloucestershire next door to his old friend Steve Winwood. 'Do you want *all* of it ... ?' the man had enquired incredulously.

Thursday, September 11th

Basil Pao[3] comes round for a sort of farewell meal together before he returns to his native Hong Kong for a long stay – perhaps permanent. I like Basil and feel warmth and trust and friendship easily reciprocated. Basil tells how he was known as 'Slits' for five years at his English public school and the reason he was sent to the school was because at the age of twelve he was a heroin runner for the Triads!

He outlines his novel, which is epic and sounds very commercial. Put him into a taxi about 12.45. Sad to see him go, but lots of good intentions to visit.

1 Sir Frank Crisp (1843–1919), a successful and eccentric solicitor, created the gardens, when he bought Friar Park in 1895.
2 The estate agents Knight, Frank & Rutley.
3 Basil, a Hong Kong-born designer and photographer, was introduced to me by Eric Idle in 1978, when he brought him in to work on the *Life of Brian* book.

Friday, September 19th: Los Angeles

It's ten minutes to five in the morning. I'm sitting at my desk in my suite at L'Ermitage Hotel on Burton Way in Los Angeles – Beverly Hills to be strictly accurate.

I try to sleep, but my mouth is dry from the air conditioning, so I get up and pour myself water – drink and settle down to sleep again. But my mind refuses to surrender – I notice the refrigerator as it rumbles suddenly into one of its recharging fits. It's huge, much bigger than the one we have at home for our family of five, but only contains four bottles at the moment. And I can't turn it off so I resolve not to worry about that – it's something I must learn to live with, for Suite 411 at L'Ermitage will be home for the next 15 or 16 nights.

I must also learn to live with the air conditioning, which also boosts itself noisily every 45 minutes or so. And I must learn to live with the occasional hiss of water from an invisible tap somewhere near my head, and the metallic clangs and roar of igniting truck engines from the depot outside my window.

It's a desolate time to be awake, the middle of the night. Even in America. I suppose I could watch television, but the thought of yielding to a very bad movie is worse than lying there trying to sleep.

Pour myself a glass of Calistoga mineral water – one of the four bottles in my massive refrigerator department. I tidy the room and try and improve my attitude towards it – to try to get to know it a little better.

The almost obligatory reproduction antique furniture of these hotels gives the place a sort of spray-on 'Europeanism'. It's called a Hotel de Grande Classe (which is an American phrase, not a French one, neatly translated by Neil Innes as 'a hotel of big class') and the place is carefully littered with books of matches and ashtrays. A table before the window has a basket of fruit, courtesy of the management, on it, a bowl of sweets which would set the children's eyes popping, and a rose in a thin vase, which came up with my breakfast yesterday. There are reproductions of European artworks on the wall – I have the 'Night Watch' by Rembrandt behind me as I write.

Saturday morning, September 20th: Los Angeles

At 10.30 we all assembled in the lobby of the hotel and gradually trickled in the direction of our rehearsal room for a first look at the script.

Rehearsal room is a vast hangar of a place, ten minutes' walk from the hotel.

In this bleak great shed, full of Fleetwood Mac equipment in boxes with little wheels, we sit and talk through the show. A couple of short songs from the album are to go in – 'Sit On My Face' at the start of Part II and Terry's 'Never Be Rude to an Arab' (though Terry does very much want to do his Scottish poem about the otter – this doesn't impress over-much, though he auditions it courageously). John and Eric are doing 'Pope and Michelangelo' instead of 'Secret Service' and one of TG's animations – 'History of Flight' – may be cut.

Afternoon spent running words – and making ourselves laugh as we renew acquaintance with the show and material we haven't done together for over four years. In particular 'Salvation Fuzz' – perhaps the most anarchic and unruly and disorderly of all the sketches – gets us going. A very heartening afternoon.

Back to the hotel at five. Sit in the jacuzzi, talk with Neil and Richard Branson of Virgin Records, who is rather pleased with himself having this day sold off Virgin's loss-making US offshoot. Apparently no-one was interested until he doubled the price, then they came right in.

Monday, September 22nd: Los Angeles

To rehearsal at 10.30. André is there, and also Mollie Kirkland – the very efficient stage manager, who worked on the City Center[1] show. Both welcome and reassuring faces. Denis O'B looms in, beaming in such a characteristic Denisian way that we have all started doing it. He gives us all a copy of [Peter Nichols' play] *Privates on Parade*, but is mysterious as to exact reasons why.

Apart from two thoroughly enjoyable run-throughs in our rehearsal cavern, there seems to be little really good news about the shows. Ticket sales are only at 50% so far. The costs are beginning to increase and Roger Hancock is threatening to pull Neil out of the show because of haggling from Denis.

We are all trying to avoid being dragged into all this peripheral activity and are concentrating on tightening, sharpening and adding to the show. And in this we have been successful – our approach and our spirit is much less tense than it was in New York.

---

1 *Monty Python Live at City Center*. New York, 1976.

After the afternoon rehearsal, out to Universal City to see Paul Simon in concert at the Universal Amphitheatre. It's a spotless clean place, staffed not by bouncers, heavies, ex-army PT instructors and the general run of London concert toughs, but by endless numbers of bright-eyed college kids with red blazers.

The concert was clean and crisp too. Under a full moon with the almost unreal shadowy line of the Santa Monica Mountains in the background, Paul did his unspectacular but endearing thing, backed by a superb group of top session musicians playing with a disarming lack of big presentation.

The Jesse Dixon Singers came on and quite dwarfed Simon for a while with their polished, pumping Gospel songs. At one point I thought Paul had been literally swallowed up by one of the massive black ladies with whom he was duetting.

We ate, all of us, afterwards, and at two o'clock TJ swam.

Tuesday, September 23rd: Los Angeles

Wake at eight-ish ... snooze, worry vaguely about voice and the Bowl, then up at nine for a lounge in the jacuzzi under the cloudy morning skies.

I feel time hanging so slowly at the moment.

John said he doubted whether the group could ever agree on anything again and reiterated that he himself no longer enjoyed writing in the group and had never wanted to repeat the 13 weeks of what he considers non-productivity on the script this year. It was history repeating itself. 1972 all over again.

A mood of determined resolution not to be brought down by John's despondency grows. TG, away from so much of the Python meetings this year, is here, and Graham joins us too and we reaffirm a basic aspect of our work together, which JC and Denis O'B and others sometimes tend to cloud, which is that it's fun.

To the Hollywood Bowl. Much standing around here and a photo-session distinguished by marked lack of enthusiasm amongst the Pythons. How old will we have to be to finally stop putting our heads through chairs, eating each other's legs and rolling our eyes? Saw an obviously posed picture of the Three Stooges going through the same ordeal the other day – and they looked about 70.

Wednesday, September 24th: Los Angeles

The air is officially described as 'unhealthful' today.

I lunch with Denis O'B. He's taking all of us away for little chats, but I think it's a sign of the good health of the group that everyone reports back to the others.

He talks of the 'family'. This is his concept of the group. A family in which we all do little creative tasks for each other. I know that he is moving around as he says this, prodding away, waiting for the opening to spring out – yet again – '*Yellowbeard*'! Yes, here it comes. I give a categoric no again. DO'B retreats.

Actually we have a good and open chat over things and he doesn't talk high finance and he restrains his bouts of Denisian 'glee' to a little outburst about all the Warner executives who are coming to the show. 'I tell you, Michael ... there is so *much* interest ...'

Drive myself up to the Bowl. Still the rig has not been finished. Neither of the 20-foot-high eidophor screens are up, but otherwise, with drapes now hung, the acting area is beginning to feel and look quite intimate.

We work on until midnight, then back to the hotel for a small party given for us by Martin Scorsese, who has a 'condominium' above us at the hotel. Delightful food, cooked by his chef, Dan; Dom Perignon and Korbel champagne, and Scorsese, who speaks so fast that at a recent film festival he had to have someone to repeat his English to the translator, before the translator even began.

Tells stories of *Raging Bull*, which is the picture he's just done with De Niro – who at one point had to put on 60 lbs.

Friday, September 26th: Los Angeles

Drive down to Musso and Franks for a pre-show meal. TJ declares sensationally that this is the first time he's ever eaten before a show. I remind him of last night. 'Oh ... yes ... apart from last night.'

Back at the Bowl, five thousand paying customers. Denis has had to drop the lowest price from ten dollars to seven to try and fill up the extra seats. So there are about five and a half thousand folk out there for opening night.

The show goes well. The audience is reassuringly noisy, familiar, ecstatic as they hear their favourite sketches announced – and it's as if we

had never been away. A continuation of the best of our City Center shows.
Thanks to the radio mikes my voice holds up.

Afterwards an extraordinary clutch of people in the hospitality room.
I'm grabbed, buttonholed, introduced, re-introduced, in a swirl of faces
and briefly held handshakes and abruptly-ending conversations. There's:
'I'm Joseph Kendall's nephew ... ' 'I'm Micky Dolenz's ex-wife ... ' 'We
made the T-shirts you got in 1978 ... ' 'Do you remember me ... ?' 'Great
show ... Could you sign this for the guy in the wheelchair?'

Finally we free ourselves of the throng and into the big, black-
windowed Batcar, signing as we go, then smoothly speed off to a party,
given for us by Steve Martin in Beverly Hills. His house turns out to
be an art gallery. Every wall is white, furniture is minimal. The rooms
are doorless and quite severe in shape and design. There's a soft pile
carpet and it's all quiet and rather lean and hungry. In fact just like its
owner.

Martin is very courteous and straight and loves the show. He isn't
trying to be funny and we don't have to respond by trying to be funny.
But his girlfriend does have a tiny – as Terry J described it – 'sanforized'
poodle called Rocco, which pees with both legs in the air.

This is the comedy high spot of the evening.

Sunday, September 28th: Los Angeles

Have booked back four days earlier than I'd expected – on the Tuesday
night flight. Back in London on the first day of October – all being well.
Helen tells me Rachel cried herself to sleep after talking on the phone to
me last Sunday, and asked for a photo of me to put beside her bed!

I don't think I will go to Hugh Hefner's tonight. Graham says it's like
getting into Fort Knox, but there's no gold when you get in ...

GC's book *Autobiography of a Liar* [in fact it was called *A Liar's
Autobiography*] has been one of the features of this trip. Coming out at
the same time as Roger Wilmut's 'History of Python' – which is straight
and competent and almost depressingly like an early obituary – GC's is
a sharp, funny, chaotic, wild, touching and extraordinary book. Written
in great style, very lively, it's already got TJ very angry about
misrepresentation and JC greatly relieved, for some reason, that it doesn't
say unpleasant things about him.

Feel very much sharper and better prepared for the show tonight.
Probably to do with being less tired. It was a good audience once again.

Afterwards one of the scene boys said how much nicer we were to work for than pop groups!

Monday, September 29th: Los Angeles

Drive up to Hollywood Boulevard to buy toys, clothes, T-shirts, etc as presents. Everything's there, including the names of stars like Sir Cedric Hardwicke embedded in the sidewalk outside a shop selling erotic lingerie. A sign reads 'It's not expensive to look chic, but it's chic to look expensive'. Another LA motto.

Anne reckons our total BO take over the four nights will be 350,000 dollars – the total possible being 450,000. Not a crashing success, but we'll cover costs. Any revenue will come from the TV sales, which Denis says will only fetch 300,000 dollars. There are, however, the invisible earnings that it's impossible to quantify – record sales, movie re-run attendances, and just keeping the Python name up front there.

Tonight we have a film and a video camera backstage and the audience lights keep going up at strange times. But the audience stay with us and at the end a large section of them won't leave. They wait up to half an hour for an encore we don't have. There'll be outraged letters in *Rolling Stone* about that.

Behind stage, in our small and ill-appointed dressing room beneath the Bowl, we entertain G Harrison, who looks rather shell-shocked after a trip to Montreal to see a Grand Prix, then a drive across the border to New York to avoid a Canadian air-controllers' strike. It's very good to see how he lights up with the satisfaction of seeing us all performing.

Anne has organised bottles for our dressers and drinks behind stage for our rather dour American crew, of whom only a handful have tried to make any contact with us at all – my favourite being a dwarf, who carted huge weights around, generally behaved like a roadie and had an easy, warm, approachable manner.

Eventually I was driven away from the Bowl to a party flung our way by H Nilsson, who lives in a house of modern, airy design, atop a ridge of mountain above Bel Air.

Harry Nilsson, so big, all-embracing, soppily friendly and sporting a complete and refreshing lack of the obligatory LA tan, moves around with his young son on his shoulder. Not drinking, either, as far as I could see. He's terribly happy that George H has surprised him by turning up.

Saturday, October 4th

Today I'm up and out to buy the croissants and the papers. But London disappoints with its shabbiness, with the endless unswept, litter-strewn pavements and the lack of anything new and bright and lively.

A pint and a half of IPA at lunchtime with GC and John Tomiczek at the Freemasons. The remarkable thing about our meeting was that Graham had given up smoking. His most familiar landmark – the pipe with its attendant paraphernalia – proggers, matches, ashtrays and lumps of half-burnt tobacco – have, if he's to be believed, been discarded for ever . . .

He says he's not *quite* sure about what he's done, but it was an impulse when he arrived at LA Airport last Wednesday evening and was confronted with some of the worst smog he'd ever seen in the city – so he'd decided not to add to it. So he hasn't used this prop . . . that he'd had since the age of 14 . . . for almost 72 hours. 'Mind you, I've had to hit the Valium rather hard to make up for it.'

Tuesday, October 7th

Helen and I and parents and all the kids of Gospel Oak packed into All Hallows Church to give thanks for the harvest.

Rachel's class sang a 'Potato' song to Mr Muxworthy's guitar and babies cried as the vicar tried to defy the appalling acoustics of this strange Gothic Revival interior. Talked with Father Coogan afterwards – 'Very Hampsteady food,' he observed, looking down on a font with smoked salmon peeping out from behind Yugoslavian crispbreads.

Have instituted a 'read-a-Shakespeare-play-a-day' regime. More realistically, I've subtitled it 'Read Shakespeare's plays by Christmas and his sonnets by New Year'. Decide to read them through chronologically, as they were written, and completed *Love's Labour's Lost* today. Plenty of laughs and relentless wisecracking. A real Marx Brothers screenplay.

Wednesday, October 8th

Tom is twelve today. He says that 'I only woke up at 5.30 . . . that's not bad . . .' But he is now a fully-fledged adult as far as air travel goes, as I find out when booking a half-term holiday for us all in Ireland at the end of the month.

A depressing foray to Tottenham Court Road/Oxford Street to buy a new 8 mill film to show at Tom's party. Depressing because of the domination in that corner of London of the awful, blinking, hypnotising spell of video ... There is video equipment everywhere – video films, video games – and it's like a giant amusement arcade providing a sort of temporary electronic alternative to listlessness. Lights flash and disembodied voices bark out of electronic chess games and football games. There doesn't seem to be much joy around here.

Rather staid interview with the BBC at Broadcasting House. TJ does it with me.

The IBA ban on TV or radio advertising of *Monty Python's Contractual Obligation* provides the main gist of the chat.

'Do *you* think it's filth?' she asks us.

'Oh, yes,' we reply hopefully ... and I add 'and worse than that, puerile filth ... '

The nice lady interviewer doesn't know quite what to make of a comedy album called *Monty Python's Contractual Obligation* and neither do we. But all parties try hard.

After the interview TJ and I go to eat at the Gay Hussar in Greek Street. I have quite delicious quenelles of carp and then partridge and lentils. We knock back a couple of bottles of Hungarian wine and admit to each other that neither of us really thinks the album we've just been plugging is much good.

After the meal we walk through Soho to the very hub of its wheel of naughtiness – to Raymond's Revue Bar in Walker's Court. Here there is a small auditorium called the Boulevard Theatre, where a new comedy club called the Comic Strip has just opened. For a long time after the Establishment folded there have been no such clubs in London, but recently the Comedy Store opened and now this. White and Goldstone[1] are involved and this was the second night.

As we wait to collect our guest tickets, a demure voice announces 'The second part of the Festival of Erotica is starting now ... members of the audience may take drinks into the auditorium if they so desire ...' Sober-

---

1 Michael White, a theatre producer, had courageously put money into *Monty Python and the Holy Grail*. It was produced by John Goldstone, who also later produced *Life of Brian* and *The Meaning of Life*.

suited businessmen down drinks and shuffle off to the Festival of Erotica, whilst the rather scruffier, long-Mac brigade troop into the Comic Strip.

In a small, low room with a stage and seating for about 150, only the front two or three rows are full. There are about six or seven acts, including guests. One duo, calling themselves Twentieth Century Coyote, were excellent, with one superb performer. Targets seem to be the new establishment of the left – feminists, alternative society jargon, social workers.

In the intermission buy drinks in the bar and the Comic Strip trendies mingle with the Festival of Erotica straights, whilst two ladies rub and lick each other on a video film projected above the bar. TJ kept wanting to 'just pop in' to the Festival of Erotica, but we stay with the comics and talk to them afterwards. All very young. I wish them well … but the Twentieth Century Coyotes were the only ones I would really keep my eye on.

Tuesday, October 14th

Into town to see the two and a half hour first assembly of *Time Bandits*.

The effect of the wall sliding back in the room and the first fall into the time hole are stunning, then a series of very funny sequences – Napoleon, Robin Hood, Vincent and Pansy, David Warner and the Court of Eric and the Ogres – lift the film and involve me totally.

It really is the most exciting piece of filming I have seen in ages. I want to be cautious and I want to see all the problems and not be carried away, but the sum total of my impressions leaves me only with heady enthusiasm.

Wednesday, October 15th

Graham Chapman on *Parkinson* (the first Python to be there, I think). Quiet, pipe-less, subdued, but, as an ex-alcoholic homosexual, steals the show.

Thursday, October 23rd

J Goldstone rings to say that the *Life of Brian* appears to be making great progress in Barcelona. Starting slowly, it got good reviews and after two or three days audiences began to pour in. Now didn't I always say I liked the Spaniards?

Write letters and babysit in evening as H goes off to badminton. Watch John C in *Taming of the Shrew*. John gives an excellent performance. Controlled and clear, as you'd expect, and the quiet moments work as well as the screaming. Better, in fact.

He's still not one of those actors who seem to start each new character from scratch, but he did make one listen to every word and as such did a much greater service to Shakespeare – and to J Miller, the director – than most of the other actors.

Friday, October 24th

The weather continues various. Today is bright sunshine, which makes a lunchtime visit to Shepperton all the more agreeable.[1]

First we visit the *Ragtime* lot, which has been built on the triangle of green fields below the reservoir, hired from the Thames Water Board. It's been used sensationally. There are two long New York streets of the 1900's, intersecting halfway. The J P Morgan Library and the brownstones look so solid and substantial and the cobbled streets and paved sidewalks and lampposts so painstakingly reconstructed, that after a few minutes in the middle of all this the only unreality seems to be the Friesian cows munching contentedly in the sunshine behind Madison Avenue.

Then to the newly refurbished canteen and catering block, open now for two weeks. I feel quite elated at what has been achieved after three years of constant nagging, reaching desperation point so often that I almost gave up hope. But today what was so often a running sore on Shepperton's reputation is now bright and gleaming and freshly painted as a set for an ad. The kitchen, through which birds used to fly and, for all I know, nest, is now compact, clean and full of new equipment.

In the bar I meet Iain Johnstone,[2] who is very surprised to hear of my directorship of Shepperton. Iain nodded to the restaurant. 'The *Gandhi* mob are here.' Richard Attenborough is indeed here, for a planning meeting for his forthcoming film on the great man.

---

1 I had been on the board of Shepperton Studios in south-west London since making *Jabberwocky* there in 1976.
2 Journalist, critic and TV producer.

Monday, October 27th: Ballymaloe House, Ireland

It's raining at a quarter to seven when I'm woken by Rachel talking to herself. At eight we go down to breakfast – table with bright blue and white check cloth beside a long window of gracious Georgian proportions. Free-range eggs and bacon like it used to taste before it was sealed and suffocated in cellophane packets, and home-made bread and toast too thick and generously cut to fit in any toaster. This sets us up well for the day and, to improve matters, the rain sputters to a standstill about ten.

We play a word game, trying not to listen to the party nearby talking about operations, diets and how many times they've been on the verge of death (the next morning Helen hears the same woman, pen poised over postcard, asking at the desk how to spell 'anaesthetic').

Thursday, October 30th: Ballymaloe House

On Tuesday afternoon, with the wet weather cleared away and sunlight filling the house, Mel [Calman] idly suggested that he and I collaborate on a children's story. I started work on *Small Harry and the Toothache Pills* that afternoon and completed it and another shorter tale, *Cyril and the Dinner Party*, by Wednesday evening.

I've called them both 'Ballymaloe Stories' and given the scribbled pages (snatched from Rachel's drawing pad) to Mel to think about. Mel says that he isn't the right illustrator for the longer story, but will have a go on Cyril. So that's all rather exciting.

Otherwise I have done very little. I've read a rather fine little book on the history of Ireland by Sean O'Faolain, published in 1943, which makes me stop and think. The English have done some dreadful things to this country in the last four centuries. Greed, adventure, religious conviction or plain bullying have all played a part and even in this quite restrained and tolerant account there is an awful lot to shame England and the English.

I shall hate Irish jokes even more. The lovely thing about the Irish and the way the jokes arise, is their literalness. They seem not to be a guileful people, they're straight, direct, gentle, and yet very good at conversation, at describing beauty and at making strangers feel at their ease.

Our room is full of kids for most of the day, including the ubiquitous Cullin – he of the chunky thighs, who follows Rachel and is rather rough and Irish and makes her alternately excited – 'Can you see what colour my knickers are?' – and prudish – 'Go away, I hate you ... I *do*.'

Friday, October 31st: Ballymaloe, Cork and London

Last night Mrs Allen chatted to us for a while and said goodbye, as she wouldn't be seeing us this morning. Mel tells me that when working on *The Ballymaloe Cookbook* with her, he found that she kept a little card about guests' vagaries. Some are not welcome again. Against one man she'd written 'Free with his hands in the evening'. Which all makes her sound a rather censorious, stern lady, but she's far from it. She's hardworking, capable, but very tolerant and entertaining. An excellent hostess.

I think we're probably all ready to return to England. My run last night was quite a battle after another lunch, following another solid breakfast, following a fairly unrestrained dinner.

We reach Cork about 9.30, getting lost in the traditional manner. When there are signposts at junctions they invariably have only one arm and one destination (usually where you've come from).

TG rings. Paramount are not interested in *Time Bandits*. Last Monday there was a viewing for Filmways and apparently it went amazingly well. The Filmways head of production was jumping up and down at the end, grabbing TG and calling the film all kinds of success.

The next morning Denis rang TG to say that the Filmways board has rejected it. Too long, too British. TG said he was absolutely stunned at the news after the reaction at the viewing. Denis is now fighting (which he enjoys), but is getting twitchy about his money and the long interest rate on which he's borrowed it.

Sunday, November 2nd

At 3.30 I drive down to BH for appearance with TJ on a chat programme. It's ostensibly about the new *Ripping Yarns* book [*More Ripping Yarns*] and then is to be widened into a whole exploration of the technique, limitations, causes, effects and everything else to do with 'humour'. The sort of thing I dread. A knitting machine operative from Oldham is to be on hand to ask searching questions and a man is on a telephone in Plymouth for further interrogation.

In the event the man in Plymouth never speaks and the poor man from Oldham is tongue-tied with nerves. So Jones and I rattle on and afterwards I have a glass of wine, sign some autographs and meet Kate Adie – a rather dynamic lady who tells me that she was with Princess Anne unveiling something in Darlington. It turned out to be a particularly unprepossessing plaque to 'The Spirit of New Darlington' and, as everyone applauded, Princess Anne leaned over to Kate Adie and muttered a heartfelt 'Fuck me'.

Monday, November 3rd

Attempt to go to Python writing meeting at Anne's on my bike, but the pump decides to treat me badly and sucks air *out* of the tyre. Abandon cycle for the Mini which decides, equally unhelpfully, not to start without much coaxing. So eventually arrive at this first meeting of Pythons Without John for Further Work on the New Film in an unrelaxed rush.

Anne has, I gather on Eric's instigation, kitted out the downstairs room of 2 Park Square West as a Python writing place. We have a table and our own coffee machine and some flowers thoughtfully laid out on top of a filing cabinet.

Tuesday, November 4th

The weather seems to have London in an East European grip.

Still not enough to deter me from cycling to the 'office'. There to find two bits of good news – *Life of Brian*, which, after much censorship to-ing and fro-ing, finally opened in Norway last week and has taken 100,000 dollars in the first three days. And in Australia the album has sold 25,000 copies in a couple of weeks and is now officially a gold album there.

Whether any of these pieces of good news actually strengthen our resolve to persevere with the new movie or not is debatable. But certainly our little room with its fresh flowers, fresh newspapers, fresh coffee and a ping-pong table is the nearest we've come to the Python clubhouse. But I don't remember a great deal of work being done in clubs.

I watch the Carter and Reagan election. It's very obvious that Reagan is going to win. I must confess I've never known why Carter has been so disliked in the US. Also I find it interesting how Reagan, whose initial candidacy was greeted with jeers and sniggers, is already being accepted as a sane and sensible leader of the Western World. No-one on the ITV panel really had the guts to say what they were saying about Reagan before he won. Now it's all smiles.

Tuesday, November 11th

Tonight I go to see *Babylon*, a hard, uncompromising British film set in Brixton.[1] The setting of the film and its subject make me feel very soft as a writer dealing with the Raj and with Robin Hood and railway trains. There is so much energy in the black music – so many good performances from the black actors that their repression should be seen at worst as a scandal – demanding more movies like *Babylon* – and at best a pointless waste of a national asset. For even in their most hysterical moment of frustrated rage against the white neighbours who tell them to shut up and go back to their own country, Trevor Laird yells 'This *is* my fucking country.' They're here. We need them and we need their creative energy far more than we need the energy expended in hate against them.

As I leave there's a black boy with a coloured knitted hat leaving up the stairs with me. Bouncing up with the arrogant, easy stride of the kids in the film. And I wanted to just make contact – say something about what the film had done to me. And I just didn't know how to do or say it. I smiled and that was all.

Sunday, November 16th

To lunch with John and Linda Goldstone. A couple of actors from *Shock Treatment* – the follow-up to the *Rocky Horror* film – are there. One is an actress called Jessica Harper, who is in *Stardust Memories*. When John's next guest – a bubbly, middle-ageing American who talks much about jet-lag – arrives, there occurs the following conversation:

'This is Jessica Harper.'
Man: 'Oh, I *loved* your new movie.'
Man's girlfriend: 'I loved your new movie too.'
Jessica H: 'I'm so glad you loved the movie.'
Man's girlfriend: 'Oh, we really loved the movie.'
Man: 'And you were great.'
Man and friend: 'Oh we *loved* the movie.'

1 The story of a young rapper/musician (Brinsley Forde) seeking success in the alienated black community of South London. Directed by Franco Rosso and shot by Chris Menges.

The man was Henry Jaglom, who's got a movie called *Sitting Ducks* at the London Film Festival. He was very funny in a Jewish, improvisatory sort of way. I liked him a lot. His girlfriend, Patrice, was later seen by Helen taking 12 of the largest pills Helen had ever seen. Jessica Harper was a sweet, light, gentle lady who ate no meat and was of such a slight build she looked like a little doll.

And there was an actor called Cliff de Ville (or some such) who had seen us at the Hollywood Bowl and who, sadly for him, spoke and looked just like Jack Nicholson.

Thursday, November 20th

With trepidation to Owen the Feet, having vowed never to return to his shabby little Mornington Foot Clinic, with its fighting dogs in the waiting room and 100-year-old chair.

Today he seems more eccentric than usual and I wonder if he will extract some sort of vengeance upon me for shutting him up rather firmly last time. He injects my toe and gives me the electric needle cauterisation treatment. I was glad to be out of there with the toe still on. He told me that if it was painful in the next week to bear it.

Hobble into the Python meeting at 10.30.

At 12.30 J Cleese arrives to play with the Space Invaders game and watch the 60-minute video of the Hollywood Bowl stage show – which JC has been in charge of editing. All of us feel the sense of occasion is lacking. It is, after all, *Python Live at the Hollywood Bowl* and at the moment it's just Python Live Against Black Drapes. TJ's initial worry that it would look boring is borne out. I'm afraid it doesn't excite any of us.

Should there be a possible 83-minute version for theatrical viewing? TJ and EI feel emphatically no, the rest of us would like to see one assembled. I feel that if the material is well done (and performances at the Bowl weren't bad) and the cartoon film sequences are fresh, we could quite honourably sell it in France, Scandinavia, Australia and possibly Canada at least.

Tuesday, November 25th

To EuroAtlantic.

Denis is in – having just arrived from the West Coast. Without a *Time Bandits* deal. So obviously he's subdued. He asks me what we thought of the video of the Bowl. I said no-one was that elated by it, and there were very strong feelings in the group that we should not even *attempt* to make a movie version.

Travel-crumpled Denis went off to have a haircut (saying he had to look tidy tomorrow because he's going to ask someone to lend him £2 million).

Wednesday, November 26th

Can actually feel the warmth of direct sunlight on my face this morning as I toil over post-synch lines for *Time Bandits*. Rachel sits beside me reading – she's home with a sore throat and suspected flu.

Fortunately I'm in quite good creative flow at the moment and the lines come quite easily. I even find a couple of slogans (which I'm usually rather bad at). '*Time Bandits* – it's all the dreams you've ever had. And not just the bad ones.' (This is changed after I try it out on Tom, who immediately suggests 'not just the good ones'!)

Reading *The Wheels of Chance* by H G Wells, which Jan Francis's husband, a writer called Thomas Ellice, has sent me, hoping that I might be interested in the part of Hoopdriver.

I read the story in about three hours and liked it a lot. H G Wells is a good comic writer – well in the Jerome K Jerome class and even better when he brings in the political angle – the Hampstead women with their New Way of life – and Hoopdriver becomes a full and rounded character, a nonentity who becomes a hero. I love leading characters who are introduced: 'If you had noticed anything about him, it would have been chiefly to notice how little he was noticeable.'

Thursday, November 27th

I visit the eccentric chiropodist, Owen, at 9.30. He launches into a stream of consciousness about prices, his son-in-law, the Jewish mafia who run London Zoo.

He puts on some paste to further kill the beast straddling my toe, assures me it will hurt, tells me not to run for a week and, with a gloomy nod of the head, suggests that there are chiropodists about who wouldn't have touched it at all.

George H rings. He had seen an assembly of '*TB*' and been very worried by some of the 'amateurish' stuff between the boy and the bandits – at the end especially. He felt the film should be a lot shorter and had advised Denis not to hawk it around in its present state. All of which depressed me somewhat.

At nine my episode of the *Great Railway Journeys* is aired. I was relieved how well the programme held together. Most of the potentially embarrassing spots had either been ironed out or well-padded with music and sound effects.

I expect this will not be enough for the critics. But it was enough for me – and Barry Cryer and Angela and my mother – who thought it was the best of the series, 'and not just because I'm your mother'.

Friday, November 28th

Pesky reviews. *Telegraph* generously lukewarm, *Guardian* crustily lukewarm, *Mail* happy. All stop short of personal vilification, all mention the pre-opening credits 'confession' piece as a good sign of comic delights to come and all register various degrees of disappointment that they didn't materialise.

Drive down to Coram's Fields to be present at the launching of a new 'play kit' ('kit' being a radical/progressive word for what used to be called in car showrooms 'literature'). It's being launched by Fair Play for Children, of whom I am a vice-president, to try and help teachers and play leaders with the problems of getting multi-racial kids to play together.

Neil Kinnock MP is there. He's the Labour spokesman on education and carries with him a little notebook, pages scrawled with figures and notes. Gleefully he unearths some figures he'd given to Paul Foot about Heinz beans' current ad campaign – buy Heinz products, collect the labels and you can exchange them for new equipment for your school. For 86,000 labels you can buy a video recorder and camera set. Kinnock did some quick sums, searched in his little book and came up with the triumphant result 'That's £21,000 for a video set-up.'

Glenda Jackson was also there – nice, friendly, open and quite unaffected. There's a small video film made by the organisation, which typifies all their problems. Full of good intentions, but hopelessly over-serious in presentation. Not a smile in it. Just a dose of current sociological jargon. And this is all about play. I said I would be prepared to help their next video presentation. Glenda J agreed too – so they could have quite a cast!

Had to rush away at 12.30 to get to a Python meeting.

A successful read-through. Eric has written a classic – 'The Liberal Family'. GC has made some progress and Terry is very anxious to show Graham his penis. It has some deficiency which he is worried about.

Tuesday, December 2nd

Today we sit and stare at the board on the wall on which cards bearing the names of sketches have been hopefully pinned. Graham muses rather distantly and Terry and I sputter on. But around lunchtime it dies. We only have a working lunch – sandwiches on the table – and afterwards Eric, who has been in one of his silent spells, suddenly galvanises us all into working out a story.

The end of the world, 6,000 A D, the bomber with the Ultimate Weapon, all disappear and we build on the one constant of the month – the working-class family sketch of mine, a fabric of a story about – guess what? – three brothers of the Forbes-Bayter family and the rise to fame, wealth and power of Trevor from obscure working-class origins to become Prime Minister just as the final nuclear war breaks out.

It's all in place by five o'clock, but I feel quite drained of energy as the room empties. I can hardly believe that after all this work and discussion we have come around to a 'Ripping Yarn' which Terry and I could have written in a fortnight on our own.

I find curious solace in talking to a reporter from a Boston, US, radio station. Anne revives me with a scotch and I quite enjoy answering questions from this perky little guy like 'Do you think Britain's really finished?'

Wednesday, December 3rd

I have to say as we meet that I do think the family story we worked out yesterday was a soft option and that the End of the World and the 90-minute countdown remains for me a much more striking idea and a more thoughtful subject altogether. There is no disagreement here and for a while it seems that we have two films. A 'Yarn' and an 'Apocalypse'. Terry J loves the idea of making two films at the same time and showing them at cinemas on alternate nights – Monty Python's two new films.

Friday, December 5th

To EuroAtlantic for the six o'clock Python meeting. Denis O'B has stage-managed the encounter quite carefully. There is an air of calculated informality and there are delicious Indian titbits to disarm us to start with – 'No meat in *any* of them,' Denis assures us, with a significant look at Eric.

Then one by one the various members of the EuroAtlantic team give us a report – which sounds less like a report and more like a justification, at times as blatant as a sales pitch, of their own usefulness. Even though John Cleese isn't present they still sound intimidated and there is an unrelaxed air to the proceedings until Steve Abbott[1] punctures it well.

The atmosphere is very different from the unalloyed enthusiasm of the New Dawn of Python beside the swimming pool at Fisher's Island 14 months ago.

I drive Anne back at the end of the meeting and she is fuming.

I watch *Points of View* which says glowing and wonderful things about the railway programme – 'The finest programme ever' – and flatters me wonderfully. I really seem to have tapped the ageing, middle-class audience.

Saturday, December 6th

I take William over to Upton Park – not more than a 40-minute drive – to watch Sheffield Wednesday versus West Ham. The usual 10–15 minute walk from car to ground, but two tickets are waiting for us – £3.50 comps – left by the Sheffield trainer. And inside it's perfect. A cold, but dry afternoon with a wintry sun lighting up the East Stand opposite us. There's a crowd of 30,000 and an anticipation of good things to come. All the images with which the press have fed us over the last weeks and months of the danger and alienation of the football grounds are absent. I feel quite elated to be there with William and our thermos of hot chocolate and a brass band playing marching stuff over the loudspeakers and an Uncle Mac-type announcer advising the crowd to enjoy themselves judiciously – 'Let's keep the fences away from Upton Park'. And I notice for the first time the absence of the now increasingly common steel barriers to fence in the crowd.

1 A bright young Bradford-born accountant, not long down from Cambridge and recently employed by Denis O'Brien's company, EuroAtlantic, in Cadogan Square, Knightsbridge.

Tuesday, December 9th: Southwold

At Gospel Oak Station by a quarter to nine to combine a visit to Southwold with my first opportunity to thoroughly revise the *Time Bandits* script for publication at Easter.

It's a dull and nondescript morning – the shabby, greying clouds have warmed the place up a bit, but that's all. I reach the station in good time. Holly Jones is waiting for her train to school, having just missed the one in front with all her friends on. It's she who tells me that over in New York John Lennon has been shot dead.

A plunge into unreality, or at least into the area of where comprehension slips and the world seems an orderless swirl of disconnected, arbitrary events. How does such a thing happen? How do I, on this grubby station platform in north-west London, begin to comprehend the killing of one of the Beatles? The Rolling Stones were always on the knife-edge of life and death and sudden tragedy was part of their lives, but the Beatles seemed the mortal immortals, the legend that would live and grow old with us. But now, this ordinary December morning, I learn from a schoolgirl that one of my heroes has been shot dead.

My feelings are of indefinable but deeply-felt anger at America. This is, after all, the sort of random slaying of a charismatic, much-loved figure in which America has specialised in the last two decades.

Once I get to Southwold I ring George. And leave a message, because he's not answering.

I work through for a five-hour stretch and we have a drink together by the fire and watch tributes to John Lennon, clumsily put together by newsroom staff who know a good story better than they know good music. And Paul McCartney just says 'It's a drag' and, creditably I think, refuses to emote for the cameras.

What a black day for music. The killer was apparently a fan. The dark side of Beatlemania. The curse that stalks all modern heroes, but is almost unchecked in America – land of the free and the armed and the crazy.

Wednesday, December 10th

Arrive a couple of minutes early at Liverpool Street, enabling me to catch the five to six North London Line. Solemn rush hour travellers, preoccupied in themselves, until a man gets on with a watch which plays a 'digital' version of 'The Yellow Rose of Texas'. This makes many more people than I'd expect start giggling. Which is heartening.

At home pick up car and race out to a meeting with Denis O'B at EuroAtlantic. All routine stuff, until Denis makes me a convoluted offer of 180,000 dollars to go to Sri Lanka (he shows me most alluring pictures) and take Helen and the kids for a while, early next year. I'm a little lost as to why, then suddenly the penny drops. He's trying to get me to rewrite *Yellowbeard* again!

All I commit to Denis is that I shall have a first draft script of my own movie ready by the end of June, 1981. And that's that. Denis does tell me, which I must say I find a bit surprising, that TJ has agreed to the Sri Lanka bait and will be working on *Yellowbeard*. I won't believe this till I see Terry.

Tuesday, December 16th

Watched Ken Loach's *The Gamekeeper* on TV. His lack of sensationalism and his delicate and seemingly effortless portrayal of real life amongst those people generally ignored by the commercial writers and directors is really admirable. He is, I think, the most consistently rewarding director working in Britain. But his marvellously observed celebrations of English working-class life will, it seems, never be as popular as the escapist gloss of *Dallas*. Which is a sad thing. Write 17 letters in reply to some of the 40 or 50 I've had as a result of the 'Railway Journey'. Quite a different audience from the Pythons. Mostly 70 and retired, I think. Is this the Silent Majority?

Wednesday, December 17th

At one I leave for a Shepperton Board Meeting. Fortunately *Ragtime* are about six weeks behind, keeping the studio well-used over Christmas and into January.

One of the few things on offer in early '81 is *Yellowbeard*. I'm not surprised to hear from Charles Gregson [a fellow director of the studio] that he was told that *Yellowbeard* was a Python film and that I was in it.

Thursday, December 18th

My foot is alarmingly red and a little swollen and Helen has looked in her books and is bandying words like 'toxaemia' around. I have two tickets at the Screen on the Hill for the first night of Woody Allen's *Stardust Memories*. I hope that people will mistake me for an aged, but legendary film director as I drag myself, arm round Helen's shoulder, up Haverstock Hill. Actually I feel more like a Lourdes pilgrim fighting off disease and imminent death just to reach the shrine of comedy.

The cinema is full and I like the movie very much indeed. But I can see that my appreciation of some of the scenes depicting horrific excesses of fan worship comes from having experienced this sort of thing and viewed from the other side, this could be seen as Allen kicking people in the teeth.

Though my foot still throbs angrily, I feel the worst is over. I have been cured by a Woody Allen movie!

Saturday, December 20th

The Irish hunger strikers have called off their action within 24 hours of the first expected death. This is the good news for Christmas – though how I abhor the naivety and dangerously ill-informed sensationalism of the *New Standard* billboards in Soho yesterday – 'Total Surrender'. The demise of London evening papers over the last five years is terrible to watch.

1981

Sunday, January 4th

Amongst the snippets of information buried away in the Sunday papers under endless travel articles and ads, is one that really made me feel that we live in special times – industrial output in the 1970's in the UK rose by 3%, the only decade when it hasn't reached 10% since 1810. Will this be the decade then that future historians see as the end of the Industrial Revolution?

Tom roller-skates up and down deserted streets outside. It's a chill, dull day. Willy and [his friend] Nathan do experiments – making cork tops fly out under pressure of a murky vinegar and yeast mixture and other Just Williamish pursuits.

Denis O'B calls. Says he's taken a New Year resolution not to mention *Yellowbeard* and probes a little as to my intentions. He can't really operate satisfactorily, I don't think, unless he can have all his clients neatly filed and buttonholed under 'a project'. I am trying – and intending – to be unbuttonholeable for as long as I can.

Wednesday, January 7th

To Owen the Feet at half past nine. Still having difficulty vanquishing the bugger and he re-dresses it, though I expressly forbid any of the acid which nearly burned my foot off just before Christmas. But he's quite gentle and efficient and we get on much better now that our 'political' limits have been drawn up. I learn he was a Mayfair foot man before. He is the society chiropodist I wrote into *The Weekend*.[1]

On to Wardour Street for a viewing of *The Long Good Friday*, which looks like being HandMade Distributors' first product. It's a story about gangland violence and organised crime in London.

Yes, it does glamorise violence, but any violence is glamorous to certain people and you would be irresponsible to only make films about 'nice'

---

1 A play which I'd completed at the end of 1979. It was eventually put on in the West End in 1994 with Richard Wilson in the lead. Michael Medwin played the Foot-Man.

subjects. And Bob Hoskins' portrayal is excellent – and the whole film justifies itself by being a well-written and quite thought-provoking piece. I put it after *Babylon* and *Bloody Kids*[1] in a top ten of recent socially provocative, English-made pictures which all deserve support and a wider audience.

Thursday, January 8th

Jim Beach[2] rings. He wants me to write a 'Biggles' film script. Apparently they have commissioned one which was strong on adventure, but lacking in humour. Just like the 'Biggles' stories, I pointed out. Jim laughed, a little unconvincingly. 'I hear you're unbribable,' he cajoles. Depends what the bribe is, say I. 'Oh, there is a lot of money' – he mentions in rapid succession Robert Stigwood and Disney and director Lewis Gilbert, who was ecstatic when he heard I was being approached. Eric Idle had told Beryl Vertue in Barbados that Michael was *the* world's best 'Biggles' writer.

I weathered all these names and these flatteries and came out with my own individual project intact. Still free. Indeed, strengthened in my determination by these blandishments.

Bought *David O. Selznick's Hollywood*, plus a tin of praline for G Chapman's 40th birthday. We go round to Graham's for a party.

The house reflects the change in GC's living habits. Instead of boxes full of gin and tonic bottles, a rather medically-oriented bookcase. No tobacco wads lying around – the place clean, spotless almost. Graham has a flashing bow tie and is tanned from a sun machine.

Meet Ray Cooper, soft-spoken, rather spare and wispy musician who is Denis's latest client and who will be in charge of the difficult task of coordinating and arranging George H's music for *Time Bandits*. He's a very unassuming, instantly likeable guy, with a bright Greek wife. Has a house in Wapping. In Narrow Street.

As Ray and wife and Helen and I talked on, we realised that most of the heterosexuals had left. Went upstairs to see Kenny Everett, who was sitting in David's room on cushions, with lights low and three or four young lads in attendance.

---

1 *Bloody Kids*, made for TV in 1979, was directed by Stephen Frears, written by Stephen Poliakoff, produced by Barry Hanson and shot, as was *Babylon*, by Chris Menges.
2 Occasional legal adviser-turned-producer. Later became manager of Queen.

Everett was a little drunk. Liked the railways, said he hated television. We had a rather stilted conversation, then he asked me for lunch. I think 1981 could be the year of a thousand lunches.

Friday, January 9th

A year and a fortnight ago it seemed that the world was coming perilously close to a global punch-up when the Russians invaded Afghanistan. But it turned out that it was microphones rather than sabres which were being rattled and everything went off the boil. Looking at *The Times* and *Mirror* headlines this week, I fear we are little further forward, in fact, probably many steps back. Poland, so directly involved in the start of one world war, is, we learn, in danger of being occupied again. Reports resurface in the papers, rather randomly, to the effect that the recent activity of the 'free trade union' movement, Solidarity, is about to goad the Russians into another New Year invasion.

So the pressure is kept on to stand ready to defend ourselves against the still creeping tide of international communism. (This is when our own capitalist alternative is unable to give three million people in this country anything to do.)

This brings me to the heart of the fears which, in my uncharacteristically pessimistic moments, tightened my stomach one morning this week. Dr Kissinger. He's loose again. Talking about the need for more US military involvement in the Middle East and waving away the European peace initiatives. Here is the 'diplomat' of the '70's – the has-been who believes the world must be run by brute force – and it surely cannot be coincidence that his latest iron-fisted threats come only five days before Ronald Reagan becomes President.

Saturday, January 10th

Up at half past eight and taking William down to Hamley's to spend the £7.00 token he's been given by Simon A.[1]

Regent Street is delightfully free of punters. The crescents and stars of the Christmas lights looking naked and forlorn in the sunlight. We wander around, dazzled with choice, in this grubby and overrated toyshop. Willy can't decide what to buy.

1 Simon Albury. Old friend and William's godfather.

But I'm less reticent. On an impulse I fork out £59.25 for my first ever electric train set – a Hornby layout with a Coronation Class Pacific. I've waited 28 years for this moment since I used to watch Anthony Jonas in Whitworth Road play with his layout – and occasionally be allowed to put a derailed cattle wagon back on the line.

So begins my 'lost weekend'. Can't wait to get the LMS set home and set it up. In the afternoon the two boys and I make a pilgrimage to Beatties of Holborn and stock up on more track and some rolling stock that's in the sales. Back home again and from then on I resent any interruption.

Monday, January 12th

Decide to make some positive moves on the *Small Harry* story. Go in to see Geoffrey Strachan as a cloudburst of hail hits London. Geoffrey's honesty is something greatly to be valued and I keep forgetting he's the Managing Director of a publisher, so openly does he dispense it.

I left him with the story.

Build a new railway layout.

Tuesday, January 13th

This morning I waited half an hour at the Mornington Foot Clinic for Mr Owen to finish talking to the lady before me. Every word can be heard out in the 'waiting area' and I caught one memorable phrase . . . 'If there's one thing I *don't* like, it's an unshaven man.' Much agreement from the lady patient.

Wednesday, January 21st

A few thousand miles south, the American hostages[1] are flying into Algiers Airport and a few thousand miles west, Reagan is being sworn in as President. Now the enormous humiliation of the hostages is over will Reagan extract some vengeance – just how will he practically live up to his big talk of a Great, Respected America? Watch half in excitement, half in real fear.

---

1 In November 1979, Iranian militants had taken American Embassy staff in Tehran hostage and held them for 444 days, releasing them only after Jimmy Carter's presidency ended.

Friday, January 23rd

After lunch I drive down to Wapping to see Chris Orr. Wapping High Street is the most unlikely high street left in Britain. Some fine houses remain, but mostly it's corrugated iron and mud and warehouses turned into wine stores.

To Chris's room at New Crane Wharf. I look at his latest etchings. The humour and the style and skill and originality are all there. Now, instead of illustrating prose he's putting words as commentary onto prints.

We walk downstairs and along cobbled streets past warehouses which other artists have moved into, but not greatly changed. Reminds me of Covent Garden just after the fruit market left. To a red-brick building opposite the Prospect of Whitby pub which announces that it was built in 1890 for The London Hydraulic Power Company.

I'm shown around by a young man and an older character, who is quite marvellous and would be a superb TV presenter – a working man's Kenneth Clark. Very articulate, tells a good story, is never lost for words, ideas and references – all presented in a light and original fashion. He tells me about the use of hydraulic power in central London, pumped around a network of ten-inch cast-iron pipes below the ground which would now cost a fortune to lay. When the Hydraulic Power Co finally closed down – only four years ago – it had 3,000 subscribers, controlling the rise and fall of theatre safety curtains, lifts, the vacuum cleaners in the Savoy Hotel and, its star client, Tower Bridge.

Home to hear that *Parkinson* want me to do their show on Wednesday. I've never felt any great loss at not being on Parky – in fact Python as a group refused the dubious honour twice – but the guests with me are to be Sir Peter Parker[1] and Robert de Niro. These two, representing the best of railways and acting, are both men I admire, and out of sheer joie de vivre I accept.

I have to ring Ken Stephinson about something too and I tell him with jovial innocence that he's been scooped by *Parkinson*. There follows a chill of disappointment from the Manchester end of the phone.

I, of course, have completely and clumsily underestimated the office politics of the BBC (not being one who normally experiences such things). I had agreed to go on *Russell Harty* at the end of February and,

---

1 Popular, accessible Chairman of the British Railways Board from 1976 to 1983, and the only one to have a locomotive named after him. He died in 2002.

from what Ken says, the impact of such an appearance would be lessened if I were to turn up on *Parkinson* less than a month before. The rivalry obviously matters deeply, so I retract and ring the *Parkinson* office and decline to appear.

A rather irritating little episode. All I feel is that, on looking back on it, everyone's reactions will seem ridiculously over-done and quite unnecessary. Including mine. That's enough of that molehill anyway.

Sunday, January 25th

Fine, dry, mild day. Confined to No. 2 for most of the time, varnishing the table for the railway. But the great outdoors beckoned and I felt in such a relaxed and unrushed state that on the spur of the moment, having read the Sundays and discovered what a 'structuralist' was, I decided to take Willy and Rachel into town.

We ended up at the practically deserted Tate Gallery. Both Willy and Rachel excellent company. Willy remarked on how few women artists were represented (a quite amazing disproportion – could only find Gwen John) and, as if by telepathy, just after I had the distinct feeling that the Rothko room reminded me of Stonehenge, Willy said it reminded him of a circle of stones – Stonehenge, he said. Rachel thought all the bums and titties a bit rude, but we all three had a thoroughly enjoyable time – without getting bored or feeling that we were appreciating art out of duty.

Monday, January 26th

Work on the railway again – and try and solve the sidings problem. I find I become so involved in trying to unravel the complexities of it all that it's hard to tolerate any interference. Which tonight comes in the shape of T Gilliam, who brings round some tapes of the sort of music Denis wants George to put into the film. It's average to good George Harrison quavery trillings, with some fine guitar, but seems to be quite at odds with the rather crisp, brittle, neurotic pace of the movie. Well, tomorrow we shall have all this out at a viewing and later chat with George.

I lure TG (quite easily) into playing trains.

Tuesday, January 27th

The days have become so warm, what with this balmy, recycled Florida weather washing over us, that wasps are waking up and flying into my workroom. The garden is coming alive too, eager shoots poking out in trepidation then, sensing it's spring, pushing boldly on. They're probably going to have a terrible time in February.

To Wardour Street for the *Time Bandits* viewing.

I'm very pleased with the way the film looks. The sound effects have revived my enthusiasm, which had waned a little over the last two viewings. Felt today like I did the first time I saw it – that between us we have put together an adventure story full of curiosities.

Still more music to go on, however, and afterwards I go with Terry to Ray Cooper's flat in Wapping to discuss this very matter.

24 Narrow Street, Wapping. Quite an address. We walk across the threshold and into another world. From poverty and desolation to wealth and taste. There is bare brick everywhere – much of it, I gather, the original wall sand-blasted. The brick is of mellow, autumnal gold and very restful and elegant.

Up in the lift two floors and step into a breathtaking open-plan room, with three big windows giving onto a balcony and then the Thames. Wide and impressive at this point, on the base of the U-curve between the Tower of London and the Isle of Dogs.

Everything has its place and the room is carefully and orderly set out, with coffee table books on the coffee table and a round dining table full of salads and delicately set platefuls of taramasalata and things. Crowning the whole a magnum of Château Ducru-Beaucaillou '69.

George arrives (in brand new Porsche), having driven from Cadogan Square in about 15 minutes. He brings Derek Taylor, whom I'm most pleased to see. Derek thrives on chat and good relaxed company and we're never at our best in the artificial world of meetings.

George gives, either coincidentally, but I think actually quite deliberately, the current Denis O'Brien line on *Time Bandits* – that it should be 90 minutes. There's rather a lot George doesn't like about it and I wonder if he really is the best person to be doing the music. But he seems to want to do it, though he does reveal a little petulance over the fact that Denis is constantly asking him to dip in to finance films.

'What the hell, it's only a tax-loss picture,' says George at one point. He laughs. But the laughter must grate on TG.

Wednesday, January 28th

Try to reach Richard Loncraine[1] to explain my decision not to do *Brimstone and Treacle*. Can't reach him.

To Methuen to see Marilyn Malin, the children's editor. I feel on very safe ground with her. She has the Methuen caution. Like Geoffrey. But it transpires that she really does like *Small Harry* and wants to publish it and is happy with Caroline [Holden] as designer.

It all seems to fall into place. I promise to push through the contract with minimum fuss (if terms are reasonable). Methuen undertake to print at least 15,000 copies. So I do feel rather pleased with myself as I walk out and up Holborn to the shops. Thanks to Mel Calman and Ballymaloe!

Home. Reach Loncraine. He's very disappointed, he says kindly. Fox were very interested and both Ken Trodd and Potter himself had been in favour of the casting. But it must be third on my list this year – after my film and my word to Thomas Ellice about 'Wheels of Chance'. To go to the top of my list it would have to have been something that was totally and unequivocally unmissable. And it wasn't that.

Thursday, February 5th

To Charing Cross Station to catch the 10.45 to Hastings to have my portrait painted by John Bratby. I'm looking forward to it, in an intrigued sort of way.

We clatter through the labyrinth of South London. There are no non-stop trains to Hastings, which is perhaps the most indicative clue to the nature of the town itself. A seaside place without the style of Brighton or the industrial and economic usefulness of Southampton or the travelling status of Folkestone or Dover. The train approaches it with an ever-increasing number of stops. As if reluctant to ever get there.

There aren't many getting off this February morning. As I walk down the steps to the booking office and what they nowadays like to call 'the concourse', I catch sight of two figures, peering like co-conspirators in an

---

1 A commercials director and inventor. I'd tried, without success, to get him to direct some of the *Ripping Yarns*. He in turn had asked me if I'd be in his film of Dennis Potter's 1976 TV play *Brimstone and Treacle*, to be produced by Ken Trodd. It was filmed in 1982 with Sting in the starring role.

English 'B' movie of the '50's from behind the window of the refreshment room. They collude, then start to move out.

Bratby is round, small and beaming shyly. He reminds me of Raymond Briggs's Father Christmas. He doesn't say anything or shake hands, but not in an unfriendly way. Dark-haired, dark-skinned wife with good-humoured eyes. She indicates an ordinary, untidy, red station wagon. Of English make, I think. We drive through Hastings, I making my cheerful, mundane observations about the place, their reactions not quite pre-dictable. She doesn't like Hastings.

Their house comes up sooner than I'd expected. A rambling Georgian mansion with a tower on top linked to the house by a glass conservatory in the sky. It's set in quite unpretentious surroundings overlooking the town of Hastings and the sea.

She lets me out then discreetly drives the red car away and John Bratby takes over, showing me the way along a scruffy passage into a studio. Dominating is a big oil painting of Paul McCartney, dated 1967. Paul looks like a sad little waif – and it seems very much at odds with the capable, super-businessman I hear he is. Maybe that's why he left his portrait here.

Bratby, who seems more at ease now he's in his studio, points me to the chair where I must sit. It's like visiting the doctor's. The same relationship between myself, the object, and the professional. On my left side a window, not very clean, on my right a spotlight turned towards me. A big paraffin heater of modern design considerately set for me.

For the first half-hour he doesn't touch the three foot by two foot canvas on a stand in front of him. He compliments me on my healthiness; he is amazed that I'm 37. I find as we talk that he is much concerned with death and ageing. He is also glad to hear that I don't take life too seriously. Only when he reached the age of 50, he said, did he realise that life didn't have to be taken seriously and he wishes he'd discovered this earlier! He is quite ready to laugh and laughs rather well. He amused me too when we both were comparing notes about the fascist tendencies of Kenwood House attendants. Once they accused Bratby of having added a daub of paint to Rembrandt's nose in the self-portrait there.

Patti, his wife, keeps us well filled with coffee. He drinks it in vast mugfuls, as he squeezes more and more tubes of oil paint on to an already thick, full palette. Occasionally he stops talking, which I find disconcerting until I realise that he is concentrating so hard that he has ceased to regard me in the conventional dialogue relationship.

He likes to work in England. He loses his identity when he travels. He works very solidly. He prefers to work in his studio. He is much impressed by people like myself whom he regards as 'the last people' – individuals who stand out from the herd. He's concerned by creeping Bennite egalitarianism, stamping out all quality in life – all the odd ones who by their own great talents stand out ... again this slightly alarming elitist theorising.

After about three and a half hours he asks if I want to see it. And there, amazingly, it is. The canvas is full, with short, thick streaks of oil paint – dozens of colours and shades – and there is me as Bratby sees me. It is done. I have to admire it, because he seems to have achieved so much with such apparent lack of effort. His painting is a complex process, yet he's achieved quite a simple image. He says that while I'm there it's difficult to let the painting speak for itself, but it will, he says, over the next week.

And then the car is ready outside and we're back into the 'B' movie. Patti drives me away to the station and onto the train back to Charing Cross.

Sunday, February 8th: Church Farm, Abbotsley

Wake, most reinvigorated. Breakfast at half past nine. Scan the *Observer*. A really encouraging report that the Minister of Transport, Norman Fowler, is giving his support to a sensible investment plan for the railways – sensible because it plans to inject twice as much government money over six years or so as it does at the moment. Sounds bold. Could all the ads and the publicity skills of P Parker, and even our series of railway documentaries have helped?

On either side of a succulent roast beef lunch I and the boys clear round the pond. Heavy, muddy, but satisfying work. Willy dredges out all sorts of old bits of rubbish – roller skates, tennis balls and bits of old pram – with his usual uncontrollable glee. He falls in eventually.

G. Chapman rings. Obviously pushed by Denis, he rather quickly blurts out that he wants me to be in *Yellowbeard*. Just as quickly I repeat my rejection of the offer. Then he talks about Telepictures. What is my attitude? Against, I say. 'Oh dear,' says the doctor, 'it's going to be a bad week for Denis.'

Monday, February 9th

To Cadogan Square to meet Denis O'B. I tell him that I'm against any Telepictures deal which involves decimation of the Python shows. This causes Denis some concern, as he says we have made a deal in good faith (though Telepictures have been granted the good faith rather than Python) and he's extremely worried about going back on his word. My suggestion is that we let Telepictures have Python product on the stipulation it isn't cut at all – and see if they want us badly enough to be able to accommodate such a demand.

Feeling I've been consistently negative thus far (in D's terms), I agree in principle to flying to Atlanta in May to speak on the *Time Bandits* book's behalf at the big publishing sales convention.

As five o'clock and my departure time closes, Denis finally gets around to *Yellowbeard* again. No, Denis, I'm not budging. It's not worth discussing. 'Wait a minute,' says Denis, 'hear me out.' So he tries to rush headfirst at the brick wall again – except from a slightly different angle this time. All he wants is one week of my writing time ... no more ... just one ... and (as I stand up) ...

'Michael ...'

'I listened to you.'

'... And what's more –' but at that point the Great Salesman is cut short in mid-pitch by a sharp and silly series of knocks on the door and George Harrison's head appears, beaming leerily.

George carries a sheaf of company reports and, oblivious to the urgency of D's business with me, he sits down chattily and shows me one of them – 'Sing Song Ltd' – which has a net loss of £34.

We listen to some of GH's new songs. 'All Those Years Ago' is my favourite of a number of very good tracks.

Sunday, February 15th

Take the children swimming to the Holiday Inn at Swiss Cottage. We practically have the pool to ourselves. After I've come back and am settling down to cold roast pork, the phone rings. It's 9.30 and the *Sun* newspaper wants to know if there's any truth in the rumour that John Cleese has been married today in New York. I tell the hackette that I know nothing, but think it extremely unlikely, what with John being gay and all that.

She persists in her intrusion, I persist in my fantasy – and she eventually gives up. Silly world.

Monday, February 16th

Eight-fifteen, start to drive down to London Sessions House for two weeks of jury service.

The Sessions House is a solid, impressive, neo-classical building started in 1914. It's been added to and there are now 19 courts within its 'grounds'. Park my car at a meter, then join a mass of some 200 new jurors, who are herded into Court Number 1 – a classic of the TV and film sort, full of wood panelling with a vaguely Baroque flourish. Here we sit and await a preliminary chat. A peculiar feeling – a roomful of 200 people, none of whom knows each other. Early banter tails off, and within five minutes all 200 of us are sitting in a tantalisingly breakable collective silence.

Then we're reduced to groups of 20 as our names are called and the groups are led off to one of the other courts; it's all rather like school.

My fellow jurors seem to be drawn mostly from the working classes, with a sprinkling of woolly-minded liberals like myself. There seems to be a notable absence of anyone looking rich and successful. I suppose you don't have time to do jury service and become rich and successful.

Sit for over an hour in a smoke-filled room. I try to read Sir Walter Scott's *Waverley*, but his convoluted prose and circumlocutory embellishments are not ideal for such a situation. I hear a loud voice beside me … 'Yeah, there's a TV personality on one of the juries. Mate of mine saw him this morning … Can't remember his name.'

Then, just as the day seems irretrievably lost, our room is called, again, and we are led upstairs. This time I'm called onto the jury. There are no challenges and we actually begin my first 'live' case as a juror. It's not one to enter the annals of Great British Trials, but there are satisfyingly comic complications involved.

The two accused are Indians, two young men with fashionable Western moustaches and pudgy faces, who have six charges against them arising from a fight they are said to have started in a pub in Clapton, E5, on an August Sunday in 1979. (There are very few cases ever heard here that have been waiting less than a year to be called.)

We are now actually belonging to a case – we have a purpose and, for the next two or three days, this judge, the three barristers, the clerks of the court and the two moustachioed Punjabi bandits in the dock will all be locked together in a curiously reassuring intimacy.

Wednesday, February 18th

Drive down to Newington Causeway for more life with the Singhs. Publican and two assistants gave evidence, as did an enormous policeman. Medical evidence was read out as to the seriousness of the eye injury caused by a thrown bottle to an apparently innocent old Indian watching. There is permanent damage to the eye and he has to wear contact lenses. So this is the most serious aspect of the case.

Back at home, Terry Gilliam rings. He has been on the phone to Denis in LA for one and a half hours, discussing *Time Bandits*. After their chat today, in which TG took Denis through the film cut by cut, demolishing nearly all his suggested edits, TG reported Denis to be sounding very unspirited, not to say low, not to say depressed.

I think the process of learning how difficult we all are is more painful than Denis ever in his worst dreams expected.

Thursday, February 19th

At times today as I was locked in an unmoving line of traffic on the approaches to Russell Square, I felt a surge of panic at the thought of keeping His Honour Justice Bruce Campbell QC and his entire court waiting.

But I was there on time and, after a further half-hour of Judge's summing up, our moment of glory arrived, and they had to wait for us whilst we were locked in our windowless little room to try and reach a verdict. Without much dissension we decided to acquit him of the first charge of actual bodily harm, as it was a case of one man's word against his.

The court reassembled, our foreman gave our verdicts, then the antecedents of the accused were read. Both had been in trouble with the police before. Onkar has three children and one about to be born; he's only 23, has not got much of a future either, but has just recently been taken on as a bus driver. Despite the heart-rending pleas of the counsel, our kindly, humorous judge stuck his chin out firmly and became the stern voice of punishment. Onkar Singh was to be jailed for three months, his brother three months, but suspended. And that was that.

Friday, February 20th

Split into a new jury group and assigned to Court 7.

Observed a Jamaican being sent down for eight months for illegally importing and probably dealing in cannabis. I suppose there is a danger that cannabis-dealing leads on to dealing harder drugs – but this was certainly not proven here. The man's girlfriend and mother of his two children had just gone into hospital with a blood clot on the brain, but the judge disregarded all this. Disturbing, especially when I think of the vast number of people – respectable and rich included – who smoke and trade in cannabis freely.

Then a frightened, wide-eyed black kid comes into the dock. He took a knife and threatened a shopkeeper and stole £40.00. He is sent to Borstal, despite this being his first offence and despite strong recommendations in his favour from Lambeth Borough Council, whose representative was present in court.

Monday, February 23rd

I asked at the Bailiff's Office about my chances of avoiding a long case on Thursday (my *Russell Harty* night) and they were most understanding and decided that the safest way was to discharge me from a second week's jury service altogether. This took a moment to sink in, then a great feeling of relief at this unexpected freedom. I had to wait an hour to collect my expenses, so sat in a café opposite the courts and read the paper and mulled over what to do with this free week.

Walked across Waterloo Bridge – something I hardly ever do – stopped and looked in the church of St Mary-Le-Strand, which I never, ever do, being usually far too busy roaring round it in a car. Peace and quiet and Baroque extravagance in the middle of one of London's busiest one-way traffic systems. Noted that the church was built by order of Parliament from money raised by a tax on coal!

Friday, March 6th

This morning – a march against unemployment. Can I come? But despite feeling personally more scornful of Thatcher and her solutions – Surrey Power, as I call it – I still have this aversion to making a lot of noise in a public place in direct support of any political force. Mainly because I don't easily believe in political solutions.

I think you have to work and communicate on a much more basic level than behind banners or tub-thumping on platforms – this is the showbiz side of politics. I personally feel much happier encouraging tolerance and understanding on a man to man level, or through my humour rather than telling people something which I don't believe – i.e. if you follow this leader, or endorse this system, everything will be alright.

Sunday, March 8th

Complete *Waverley* (which works on me like Hardy – demanding much loyalty and dogged persistence to begin with, but finally rewarding perseverance with a good tale and leaving an after-taste of affection towards the worlds he's described and the characters he's filled them with).

This very evening, begin to read Proust's *À La Recherche* ... Feeling limbered up after *Waverley* and *Romola* and spurred on by the purchase, for £50, of a new and much-praised edition by Kilmartin.

Monday, March 9th

Unexpectedly I wake with a hint of tension, usually experienced in more extreme forms when I have to go filming, write a debate speech or appear on *Just a Minute*. But today it's anticipation of my own self-imposed project – the film script, which (in tandem with Proust) I begin today.

Sit at my desk at a quarter past nine, comfortably cocooned against steady, unbroken rain outside, and realise that, despite two months of intended mental refreshment and stimulation, I'm still as riddled with incompatible alternatives for stories as I ever was.

Nothing springs instantly to my pen – no characters so all-consumingly important that I have to write about them. It's a shame really – all those people out there with burning convictions and desperate messages to the world which they can never make anyone listen to and here am I, pen poised to create entertainment for the world and not knowing what I want to say.

Wednesday, March 11th

Go up to William Ellis in the evening to hear about the curriculum, etc. Headmaster clearly pleased with progress so far on the transition from grammar to comprehensive. He does sound as though he loves his work.

Turnout of parents almost all middle-class – others seem to leave the school to get on with it. (Trouble with democracy these days?)

Eric rings later to fix up a Palins/Idles theatre trip next Monday. Tells me that Graham has just been on the phone to ask him to be in *Yellowbeard*. But surely ... ? No, says Eric, *Yellowbeard* is not dead. GC has nine million dollars of Australian money and is planning to film it off the Queensland coast. Eric is worried about how best he can say no yet again.

Thursday, March 12th

Classic writing morning. Up to the desk, clear space and open notebook at about five to ten. Estimate when I should finish. Two-thirty seems reasonable. Yawn. Stretch. Yawn. Look blankly through all I've written this week, trying desperately to summon up any belief in the purpose of these arbitrary scribblings and character snippings. Long for coffee, but it's an hour away.

The hour passes with hardly a line written. It's like insomnia, in reverse. My mind refuses to wake up.

I take the opportunity (rare this week) of a dry spell and run. As I pound up the path to Parliament Hill, a title occurs to me – 'The Missionary Position'.

Maybe, though, that's too whacky, too leading, so I settle for 'The Missionary' and the subject matter of the film swims into clear focus. An idealist, a tortured idealist in the last days of the British Empire – the missionary work would be interpreted as widely as possible, and the title has a nice touch of irony. Come back 45 minutes later muddy but feeling that I've made a breakthrough.

Cook Toulouse sausages with apples for Robert H[ewison].

Over dinner he makes what he calls, with characteristic modesty, a brilliant discovery – that the six Time Bandits are the six Pythons. He's awfully pleased at making this connection and seems quite unmoved by my own denial of any such parallel. For the record, anyway, our casting was: Randall – Cleese, Vermin – Gilliam, Og – Graham, Fidgit – Terry J, Strutter – Eric, Wally – me.

Friday, March 13th

Had a vivid dream this morning. It was set in Halifax. Very positively Halifax.

It was hazy – a mixture of Lowry and Hieronymus Bosch – but on top of the hill the walls were of rich, red stone and I walked through col-onnades and arcades built in seventeenth-century classical style and met young students who told me what a wonderful place Halifax was.

At the writing desk by ten. I pursued the idea of *The Missionary*, which began to fall very nicely into place. By lunchtime I had actually sketched out a synopsis – with a beginning, middle and end – which I dared to become quite excited about. In the afternoon I tightened and typed this up. So by four, at the end of the first week's writing, I have a story. I feel, as I say, warily confident. Will see how it survives the weekend.

Tuesday, March 17th

A mighty clap of thunder as a short and violent storm passes overhead as I settle into a piece for the *New York Times* – Howard Goldberg having sent me a telegram asking for a piece on Prince Charles and Lady D. Have completed it by seven.

Ring HG in New York. He's frightfully worried that I will not, as he puts it, 'keep it clean'. 'I'm hired by Calvinists,' he explains. Dictate through to the *Times* later in the evening.

Wednesday, March 18th

Take Tom P (who's been off school today with a cold) up to St Anne's Church, Highgate, for the first night of the William Ellis opera 'Death of Baldur'. This has been the big musical event of the year for the school. It's an English premiere and the composer, David Bedford, is there with short, well-cut grey hair, looking like a natty parent. Tom is in the 'off-stage' choir and is tonight stuffed to the gills with throat sweets, etc, to help his voice.

I cannot understand a word that's being sung throughout the hour, but it's evidently to do with revenge, blindness, the gods and other gloomy Nordic specialities. Not a laugh in it. The orchestra is good, but the church swallows up voices and makes it very difficult to stage.

Very effective integration of pebble-banging – with the 'pebble-choir' ringing the church behind the audience and setting up a wave of staccato sound which had the effect of swirling stereophonic sound.

Home to hear from Howard Goldberg that he had loved my piece for the *NYT* on Prince Charles and was planning to run it on Sunday. He kept going into fits of giggles over the phone whilst checking spellings, etc. Most encouraging.

Thursday, March 19th

Estimated by lunchtime – and ten mornings' work – that I have 20 minutes of good material to start *The Missionary*, and another five or six quite strong.

Friday, March 20th

Driven out to Friar Park in stately fashion in the back of Ray Cooper's elegant and comfortable 26-year-old Bentley – all wooden panelling and a good smell of leather.

On the way Ray tells me that George had a phone call two weeks ago from some anonymous American telling George he had a gun and an air ticket to England. It all sounded like a horrible hoax, but the FBI found that a man in Baltimore had been seen in a bar making just such threats and bragging about his air ticket. George H's place was ringed by police for a week – and he had a bodyguard with him at all times. Considering all this, George met us in very relaxed style. He was up on the slopes of his Matterhorn, with the builders who are busy restoring this fine piece of eccentric garden landscaping.

Saturday, March 28th

Willy and I drive off to go to see Wednesday play at [Leyton] Orient.

It's a warm day, the ground at Brisbane Road is small, neat and feels far more of a local family atmosphere than any others we've been to this season.

It seems that a Wednesday goal has to come, but instead a scuffle at the far end and Orient have scored on one of their rare visits to the Wednesday area.

This stings Wednesday – crowd and players – into some strong retaliatory measures, but within minutes Orient have scored again and it's over – as is probably Wednesday's chance for promotion.

A satisfying incident as we walk to the car. In the long line of cars moving up to the main road are three lads, one of whom leans out of the window and shouts in delight at me ... 'Heh! It's Eric Idle!' I smile, but weakly, I expect, and walk on as they noisily discuss who I'm not.

About 15 yards further on their car approaches and they pass up the road with a chant of 'We know who you are!' This is followed almost immediately by a crunch of colliding metal and a crackle of shattering tail-light as their car thuds into the one in front and pushes that one into the one in front of him.

Monday, March 30th

Drive down to the first of a week's Python meetings at 2 Park Square West.

We appear to be very much in accord over our exasperation, frustration and consternation about Denis's role in our affairs. In Anne's pains-takingly-assembled report on life with EuroAtlantic, she suggested that she and Steve [Abbott] could run our day-to-day affairs from 2 PSW.

A remarkable degree of unanimity within the group that now is the time to sort out this whole question.

To dinner with Clare [Latimer].[1] Excellent food, plenty of drink and jolly company. A vicar from St John's Wood who tells me he took 50 of his most fervent worshippers to see *Life of Brian* last Good Friday – instead of moping about church 'mourning'.

Wednesday, April 1st

A dry, warm day with soft, high cloud. Everyone in a good mood. Eric suggests we all of us make a list of the pros and cons of DO'B. The lists turn out to be remarkably similar. Tax planning and tax structures are commended, but all the pro lists are much shorter than the cons – which include over-secrecy, inability to listen to or understand things he doesn't want to hear, and use of word 'philosophy'.

At lunch – Anne makes us delicious asparagus tart – we get fairly silly. Decide that the Pythons should purchase our own nuclear deterrent. We put a small ad in *The Times* – 'Nuclear Missile wanted, with warhead, London area'.

---

1 Caterer and next-door neighbour for many years.

Friday, April 3rd

Denis is pleased that we have decided to go ahead with theatrical release of *Hollywood Bowl*. Which we now decide to call, simply, *Monty Python at the Hollywood Bowl*. But try as we can to drill into him that he should go for smaller distributors with more time to listen, the more Denis retreats back to the majors whom he knows.

He claims that the small distributors only handle 'exploitation' pics (violent or sexy or blatantly both, which are so bad that money is only made by a quick, sharp killing in selected theatres). His feeling is that all distributors are idiots, but he will try and find us the most benevolent idiot.

Sunday, April 5th

Denis calls me. He asks me to try and patch up the Gilliam/Harrison relationship. Not that TG has done any more than express reservations about George's music, and the last song in particular, but GH has taken it badly and feels that he no longer cares – and if TG wants to write the music he can write it himself.

I try to defend TG's position by saying that the use of GH's music was rather forced on him. Denis returns to the financial argument (does Terry realise how much money the film is costing?) which is slightly unfair. Anyway, as Denis memorably puts it, 'You just don't treat Beatles this way.'

Monday, April 6th

Collect Rachel from school, then ring George. He isn't angry in the conventional sense – I mean, no shouting or swearing – but he just is sad and a bit fed up. 'I was just a fan,' he puts it, 'who wanted to help you do things because I liked what you all did.'

But after all this comes out, we get down to discussing the end song. I tell him we both like it musically, but we've now got some new lyrics which change only the verses. Let him listen to them and sling them out if he doesn't like them. But of course he does quite like them – and is happy to do them and will send a demo later in the week. I hope all is healed, temporarily at least.

Dash off to the Python meeting.

It's quite obvious that the group as a whole trust Anne more than Denis (JC wanted it to go on record that he mistrusted Denis less than the rest of us) and Eric was the only one who signed the letter to Denis with his surname. 'Denis is the sort of person I want to be on surname terms with,' was the way he put it – and I promised to write that in my diary.

Tuesday, April 7th

To Eric's by car about seven o'clock. He has now assembled enough material for six TV programmes to be made by his company – Rutland Weekend Television – and sold to England, the US, Australia, Canada, etc. They're comedy sketch shows, basically – with music animation special effects and all set in the legendary Rutland Isles, where anything can happen.

Anyway, Eric wants me to come and play one of the three stars, along with himself and possibly Carrie Fisher. Filming would, he thinks, not take more than eight weeks and would be done in the winter on a lovely tropical island.

I'm drawn by the immediacy of doing a TV series on video and by Eric's unportentous, let's-just-get-on-with-it attitude and refusal to treat it as the most important thing ever. But it's a month, at least, accounted for and at that time I may be in pre-production of *The Missionary*.

Saturday, April 11th

Family outing to *Popeye*.[1] We ate excellent hamburgers in Covent Garden and the sun came out and shone on us as we walked through the Garden, past the escapologist, through St Paul's churchyard, where trees have been planted in memory of actors buried there. One rather undernourished little shrub was ironically plaqued 'In memory of Hattie Jacques'.

Home to hear that there was burning and looting going on in Brixton as we had wandered through the quiet bustle of the West End on this sunny Saturday afternoon.

1 Film version of the comic-strip. Robin Williams was Popeye and Shelley Duvall Olive Oyl. Robert Altman directed. Jules Feiffer wrote the screenplay and Harry Nilsson the songs.

Monday, April 13th

Help prepare for dinner with Steve Abbott and friend Laurie.

Part of my reason for asking him round is to find out more about his feelings about Denis and Euro. Basically he is concerned about divided loyalties. He cannot carry on working for the Pythons and doing what is best for the Pythons within the EuroAtlantic framework because he feels the decisions taken for the benefit of EuroAtlantic are very often contrary to the benefit of the Pythons.

Both Steve and Laurie are politically to the left, Laurie enough to have changed her bank account from Barclays (naughty South African connections) to the Co-op. Only to find that the Co-op use Barclays as their clearing bank!

Steve is I think a man of good, basic, honest convictions and if for this reason he's leaving EuroAtlantic, it makes me listen very carefully.

Tuesday, April 14th

Dry and cool. Drive down to Crawford Street to have hair cut by Don [Abaka, our family hairdresser for many years]. We talk about the Brixton riot and that Don who is, I should imagine, a very easy-going and law-abiding black – a part of the establishment if you like – still can say, as if a little surprised, 'I've not been in any trouble with the police, but I really feel worried sometimes that if there's trouble in a street they'll pick me out.'

Home to work on *The Missionary*, but for some reason, as the clouds clear and the sun shines from a blue sky, I find myself surrendering to the pleasantness of the day. Sit in the garden seat in the sun and read Bernard Levin's infectious raves about three of his favourite restaurants in Switzerland. Makes my mind drift to thoughts of holidays and sun-soaked balconies in small French towns and poplars motionless above sparkling streams and good wine and company and celebrating.

Watch the space shuttle land most skilfully. Feel, more than I ever did with the moonwalks, that the success of this first reusable spacecraft is the real start of what an American astronaut rather chillingly called 'the exploitation of space'.

Thursday, April 16th

Hardly see Helen, on this our 15th wedding anniversary morning. Am woken by Rachel at a quarter to seven, standing by my bedside, dressed and ready to go. She wakes William by tickling his feet (the only way, he claims, he can be woken up) and the three of us make for the quarter to nine North London Line train to Broad Street.

Uneventful journey to Darsham, though we found ourselves in the breakfast car next to an assured, rich-voiced, late middle-aged Englishman with half-moon glasses, sitting with a fortyish, mousy-blonde lady, with the large, bony, open features of an English upper-class gel.

He began to make notes about some speech he was to make ... 'The recent clashes in Brixton, foreseen by Mr Enoch Powell over fifteen years ago –' His eligible companion interrupts ... '"Clashes"? Do you think "clashes" is a strong enough word?' 'No, no, perhaps you're right ... Battle? ... Mm ...'.

We left them, still composing, at Ipswich. Met by Mother at Darsham. She looked a little wearier than of late and drives a little slower and a little nearer the centre of the road.

Sunday, April 19th: Southwold, Easter Sunday

In the afternoon I read through Robert H's manuscript of the Python censorship book, which he wants me to check before I go to Crete. It's well-researched, thorough, lightly, but not uncritically, biased in our favour. The word I've written in my notes to sum up his endeavour is 'scrupulous'. Unsensational in presentation, but not necessarily in concept – it's really everything I hoped it would be.

Tuesday, April 21st

Over lunch spend a couple of hours with Steve talking about EuroAtlantic, my finances and the possible transfer of our immediate financial affairs to a Steve and Anne-run office.

Steve reveals fresh facets of his straightforward, unassuming but very independent nature. He declines a coffee because it's the Passover and he's eating only Kosher food for a week. He almost apologetically explains that he's not even a born Jew. He just began to take an interest four or five years ago, learnt Hebrew and another Judaic language and set himself certain standards of observation which he readily admits are somewhat inconsistent, but one of them is to eat nothing but Kosher food throughout the Passover period.

Saturday, May 2nd: London to The Chewton Glen Hotel

Drive down to Hampshire for the Python weekend. Collect Gilliam at 7.45, then Eric at eight and, despite some build-up of holiday weekend traffic, we are driving through the New Forest by half past nine and to the hotel, set in a rather nondescript conurbation near New Milton.

The Chewton Glen Hotel is unashamedly expensive – a soft, enveloping atmosphere of thick carpets, armchairs, soft voices, chandeliers. From the BMWs and Jaguars in the car park to the miniature of sherry with the manager's compliments, everything reflects money. Like a padded cell for the very rich. But it suits our purposes – we're here, after all, to concentrate our minds on one of the most important decisions Python has yet made.

There is remarkably little dissension from JC's opening assessment that we should tell Denis that we no longer feel we need a manager. That there should, in the interests of economy and efficiency, be one Python office to administrate the companies, and that future relationships with Denis should be on an ad hoc basis.

Within a couple of hours we've reached a heartening degree of agreement and JC is left to compose a letter. I go to the billiard room with TG for a game on a marvellous full-size table. The balls feel like lead weights after the half-size table at home. Then to lunch. The food is good – delicate and lots of things like lobster and snails and shallots.

Then a game of snooker, a game of squash with Terry J and back for more snooker and dinner. Quite like old times, with Graham leaving early to go to a gay club in Bournemouth (for the second night running, I'm told) – but even better than the old days because GC doesn't get pissed and can drive himself.

Talk, over the champagne and cream of Jerusalem artichoke soup, of Bobby Sands and his hunger strike. Eric and John think it's something you should be able to laugh at – and they do. TJ, and I agree with him, feels that the laughter must come from recognising and sensing a basic truth in what you're laughing at and you can't laugh at something you feel is dishonest – and I think it's dishonest to think of Sands as a worthless villain. And dangerous too.

To bed before midnight. How easily the 'historic' decision has been made. It's not often Python so clearly and unanimously sees the rightness of a decision and it's such a relief that it's happened like that today. It now remains to be seen how DO'B reacts. I hope he will not see it as a stab in the back, but a stab in the front. He should have seen it coming and it shouldn't prove fatal.

Sunday, May 3rd

At eight, feeling good and refreshed and bright, I walk down the drive of the Chewton Glen, taking care not to trip over the floodlighting bar which points up at the pine trees, and, taking the sign for Barton-on-Sea, make for the English Channel cliffs.

I can see the Isle of Wight in the distance. It's a dull morning with the sun only a faint lemon glow in a thickly-padded off-white sky. There are women walking poodles called Pippa and empty seaside hotels and a ravaged and collapsing shoreline which has no drama, excitement or visual splendour. Gardening and Walking the Dog Land 1981.

We assemble about 10.15. There's a re-reading of the letter to Denis and some corrections made. JC is so anxious to emphasise our inconstancy that there's a danger the cold reality of the message may not get through.

Then follows a chat about the next film – and one of the remarkable displays of the collective Python mind doing what it does best, best. Ideas, jokes, themes pour out from everyone round the table so fast that no-one wants to stop and write any of them down for fear of losing this glorious impetus. The court framework for the next movie comes up – the idea of us all being hanged for producing a film that is only a tax-dodge. It's all rich and funny and complex and very satisfying.

Tuesday, May 5th

Starts well, my 38th, with a clear and cloudless morning – the sort of day May ought to be, but hasn't been so far.

Work on the script – slowly but surely. Anne comes round at lunchtime with the letter to Denis to sign. JC has put back some of the wordiness that Eric and I took out, but it seems to be clear and bending over backwards to give us the blame!

I hear Denis will not be back until the weekend and wants a meeting with us next Monday. There's a sort of inexorability about it, like watching someone walk very, very slowly towards a concealed hole you've dug.

Wednesday, May 6th

First thing this morning, am putting out milk bottles when I encounter Peggy from No. 1 Julia Street. She's very sad because a week ago her case against her landlords was dismissed. She's got to move and No. 1 will be sold. Ring Steve and instruct him to try and buy it for me.

My *New Yorker* piece on Cinderella comes back with a rejection. Like A Coren's rejection note from *Punch* some years ago, the worst thing is the profuse apology – almost tangible embarrassment of the contact at the magazine. He's right, of course. He likes the incidental jokes which I like best and feels the whole a little too dull and conventional. A warning sign for all my writing.

Thursday, May 7th

My Bratby portrait has arrived. I hang it, not altogether seriously, but mainly to frighten Helen, above the piano. I don't like his interpretation of me particularly, but his technique of thick oil paint applied with short knife strokes in dozens of colours does make the picture very exciting. It certainly stands out, as an original should, in our houseful of rather restrained repros and prints. Quite ebullient and bright.

Friday, May 8th

Despite many comings and goings in the house (window cleaners to give estimates, recently-robbed neighbours to look at our burglar alarm system), I have the best writing morning of a bad week.

I write a sequence this morning that I know will be funny (the lost butler) and at least breaks a week in the wilderness.

Looking forward to a lazy evening in, when Denis rings. He's back and he has evidently seen the Chewton Glen letter.

He sounded calm, and in a realistic frame of mind. He was not entirely clear about what the letter proposed – could I elucidate? I elucidated as best I could, with kids clamouring for supper and Helen washing up beside me. We wanted DO'B to be an ad hoc, independent figure who we could come to for the major things he'd proved himself good at. Our essential aim was to simplify our business affairs.

DO'B was silent for a moment, but seemed to accept all this.

He talked about his 'upside' and his 'downside' and rather lost me here, but the long and the short of the call was that we should have a meeting as quickly as possible – and it needn't be a long one, he said. I promised I would ring Anne and ask her to set one up for Monday. Throughout Denis's tone was only a little injured and defensive and mainly practical and realistic – and quite friendly.

I talk to Eric later. He sounds unhelpful over the DO'B situation. He doesn't want to meet him and absolutely refuses to give DO'B any sort of preferential option on the next film at this stage. I bit my lip, and nearly my desk as well, at this.

Monday, May 11th

I drove down to BUPA to present Dr Gilkes with a long-running Palin saga – the Great Verruca, or Corn, as it once was.

He examined it and, as it has changed its shape and become less spread out, with more of a peak on it, he reckoned he could cut it out. And without much more ado, this is what he did. Using an instantaneously-acting local anaesthetic, he cut and chopped and sliced – sometimes with such great effort that I could scarcely believe it was my little toe and not some thick oak tree he was working on. Then he cauterised the edges, bandaged it all up and I hobbled out. But at least my verruca, which has been with me for nearly two years, was now in the dustbin.

I'd made Gilkes happy – 'It's been a jolly good day for the knife,' he assured me when we'd agreed on surgery. 'Some days I hardly use it at all,' he added regretfully.

I was to go straight from my verruca operation to a meeting with Denis O'B. It all seemed rather symbolic.

I hobbled in, the last to arrive (apart from Eric, who was just then landing in New York). Anne had thoughtfully provided white wine and some canapes. Denis sat looking a little careworn, but raised a smile. He had a notepad full of appointments and projects which he flipped through – films he was hoping to bring in through HandMade Distributors.

At about 7.20, after we'd been talking for an hour, John had to leave because he was taking someone to the theatre. So it was left to the four of us to decide on the next move with Denis. If we wanted to terminate – as 'I think the letter says' – Denis wanted to do it as quickly as possible.

Was there an alternative to complete and final termination? Terry J asked. Some way in which he could run a financial structure with us and liaise with the office at Park Square West? Denis didn't like this. It was all or nothing. He wanted to be free to concentrate on all the other areas EuroAtlantic could go in. He might, he said, get out of films altogether.

Graham asked if there were any 'offshore structure' which could be kept going. No, again Denis was adamant. Steve could not run a structure such as the one Denis had set up and which he still today talked about with loving pride.

So at about eight o'clock, as a dull evening was drawing to a close outside, we had to take a decision. Should we terminate? It really was the only answer. It was what the letter, signed by us all on May 5th, had said anyway. And so it was agreed and Denis left to begin to take down the structure and prepare for us a list of proposals for the ending of our relationship.

I couldn't believe it. My verruca and manager out, all within four hours.

Wednesday, May 13th

Manage the first full morning's writing this week and feel much better for it. Recently-gouged right toe is preventing me from running, so after lunch go down to Beatties and buy some LNER '30's imported teak rolling stock with the ten quid Ma gave me for my 38th. It crosses my mind that I'm 38 and still sneaking off to toyshops.

Down to Camberwell for dinner with the Joneses and, as it turns out, a rather boozed Richard Boston.[1]

He really doesn't look in good shape, which is a pity as he's such a mine of wondrous information – and knows such gems of political history as the fact that a gorilla once raped a French president's wife in the Elysée Palace, which is, of course, next to the zoo, and for many years afterwards the president was paranoid about gorillas.

And all this on the night the Pope was shot and Tom helped William

---

1 One of the first journalists to 'get' Monty Python, he was also a vigorous campaigner who, with Terry J, started an environmental magazine called the *Vole*. He gave his interests as 'soothsaying, shelling peas and embroidery'.

Ellis swim to a 20 point victory in the schools swimming gala. And another hunger striker died in the Maze.

Saturday, May 16th

Angela and I head for Linton – our great-grandfather's parish from 1865 to 1904. I'm intrigued by Edward Palin – the man of great promise who in his early 30's was senior tutor and bursar of St John's College, Oxford, and who gave up the chance of great things to marry Brita, an Irish orphan girl – herself the subject of a great rags-to-riches story – and settle at this tiny Herefordshire village and raise seven children.

There is the grave in the churchyard where he is buried together with two of his sons who pre-deceased him – one who died at Shrewsbury aged 18, another killed in the trenches of the Somme. Next to his grave and upstaging it is the grave of Caroline Watson, the American who found Brita the orphan and brought her up.

Determined, as a result of this weekend trip, to follow up some leads on the Palins – St John's College being one of them.

Friday, May 22nd

This is the day appointed for the changeover of Python affairs from EuroAtlantic at 26 Cadogan Square back to the more leisurely Nash terraces of Regent's Park. From today Steve and Lena [Granstedt, his assistant] work for Python and not EA.

I remember my embarrassment at having to tell people Python was with EuroAtlantic Ltd – an ugly name really, but I have had very good service from them. I rang Corinna [Soar – EA Company Secretary] – she was very touched by my letter and we had a quite unrecriminatory chat. She says it will be better when the changeover has actually happened. It's the transition process that's painful. I want to say to her how concerned I am about our future – that we don't see our move as a solution, just an inevitable part of the continuing development of Python, but I can't get into all that. I suggest we have lunch. Coward.

Wednesday, May 27th

Drive down to Wardour Street for a *Time Bandits* viewing.

George's single is No. 14 in the US charts and now he's under pressure to release follow-up singles – and we're under pressure to put another George song at the top of *Time Bandits*, as a potential US single. George admits with a smile that 'You grumble at them (the public) like hell when you're *not* in the charts, and then when you are in the charts you grumble at them for putting you there for the wrong reasons' (the aftermath of the Lennon shooting).

I don't like these viewings, especially when I know the room is full of people who have tried desperately to have many sections of the film cut. For the first half-hour everything seems wrong.

The laughs come for the first time on Cleese's 'Robin Hood' scene. From then on the 'audience' loosens up and I relax and George's big, bright arrangement of 'Oh Rye In Aye Ay' caps the film perfectly. At least we can talk to each other at the end. Even George, a harsh critic up to now, thinks the film is almost there, but hates the opening credits.

I must say, after today, I have a chilling feeling that we have fallen between too many stools. Not enough sustained comedy for the Python audience to be satisfied and too much adult content ('Titanic' references, etc) for the children's audience. We could just have created a dodo.

Friday, May 29th

Helen comes up to tell me that a 'For Sale' board is going up on No. 1 Julia Street. Steve A contacts Stickley and Kent, the agents. They are asking £37,500. Steve says he will get the keys.

Look at 1 Julia Street with Steve (financial) and Edward [Burd] (architectural). Damp, crumbling and filthy inside. Steve cannot believe that people were living here only a week ago and can believe even less that anyone should hope to get £37,500 for it. Edward thinks that the external walls, beneath their cracked and powdery rendering, may be stronger than they look. He reckons it would cost £30–£36,000 to renovate, and if we were able to buy the place for £25,000, despite its present state of extreme decay, it would be good value. Ed is going to find out more about the agent's hopes for the house and Steve says he can't wait to start working out how best we can pay for it!

Steve's business sense is as eager as Denis's, but his style utterly different. Denis is real estate and yachts, Steve is going to the March for Jobs rally at the weekend, three-day cricket and Springsteen.

Saturday, May 30th

Watch a clean, efficient, rather soporific goalless draw between Wales and Russia. It does one's perceptions good every now and then to see Russia – the enemy, the nation whose existence justifies enormous expenditure by Estaings, Thatchers, Carters and Reagans on weapons of destruction, the iron threat to Poland and Afghanistan, the home of Philbys and Burgesses, the cruel oppressor of Jewish minorities and cultural dissidents – playing a World Cup game at Wrexham.

Monday, June 1st

Wake to streaming, unequivocal sunshine, which looks set in for the day. Make all sorts of resolutions for the month as I sit down at my desk at a quarter to ten. I am determined to finish the first draft of *The Missionary*.

At half past six the results of my latest foray into consumerism are brought round to the house. A Sony Walkman II – an amazing miniaturised stereo set, with thin, light headphones and a cassette-sized playing machine. If they can make such sound reproduction quality so small now, what of the next ten years? A button perhaps? A pill you swallow which recreates the 8-track wonders of Beethoven's Ninth from *inside* your body?

Also I'm now the proud owner of a small colour telly with a six-inch screen which fits on the kitchen shelf and will also undoubtedly revolutionise my life, until, in due course, the wonder of these marvellous technological advances wears down into acceptance.

Moral of the tale – do not rest hopes and enjoyments on Sony products. Man cannot live by machinery alone. All technological advances bring built-in dissatisfaction.

Wednesday, June 3rd

A late, light lunch, a few minutes in the sunshine, then back up to the workroom again. But the combination of heaviness from a persistent head cold and some rumbling guts ache knocks me out and, drained of energy, I skip supper and take to my bed about the same time as Rachel.

Just stay awake long enough to catch Terry J's first programme as presenter of *Paperbacks*. Helped on by a sympathetic and very well-mixed selection of guests, Terry came across as Terry at his best – serious, but good fun, mainly sensible, but occasionally enthusiastically carried away, positive but gentle. All in all, I thought, an excellent debut and such a change from the smooth old hands of TV presentation.

And I did take in an awful lot of what was said about the books – it reminded me of how much more I took in of Shakespeare when I watched John Cleese in *Taming of the Shrew*.

And his guest, J L Carr – an ex-schoolmaster who publishes little 35p books from his home in Kettering – was a wonderful find. He is the compiler of such indispensable volumes as *Carr's Dictionary of Extraordinary English Cricketers* and *Carr's Dictionary of English Queens, King's Wives, Celebrated Paramours, Handfast Spouses and Royal Changelings.*

Friday, June 5th

A week after first being alerted to Stickley and Kent's board at 1 Julia Street, I ring Stickley's with my £25,000 cash offer. An Irish female most curtly receives the offer and, with hardly any elaboration, tells me crisply that it will not be enough, but she'll take my name. Twenty-five thousand pounds in cash for that dump and she almost puts the phone down on me. Irrational – or perhaps this time rational – anger wells up. Write a letter confirming my offer and refuse to increase it at this stage.

To lunch at Mon Plaisir with TG.

TG and I have a very good, convivial natter and excellent meal. It's as if the major pressures on the *Time Bandits* are now lessening. Our collaboration has perhaps been one of the more successful aspects of the film. There are rumours that Denis is having some success with his '*TB*' viewings in America.

Then I go off to a viewing of the film again.

There is a constant, steady level of appreciation from quite a small audience and at the end I feel so elated, so completely risen from the gloom of the showing nine days ago, that I can hardly run fast enough through sunlit Soho streets back to Neal's Yard.

Terry is upstairs, alone in the big room looking over the yard with an editola in one hand and film in the other, still trimming. 'Sensational' is the only word I can use. At last I feel that *Time Bandits* has lived up to all the work that's gone into it.

Drive up to 2 Park Square West for a Python meeting.

There is a long agenda and yet we spend the first half-hour talking about possible changes to the Hollywood Bowl film. John is quite despairing. He buries his head in his hands and summons up what appear to be his very last resources of patience. 'I crave order,' he groans, looking at the remnants of the agenda, whilst Terry J suggests we put Neil in the film and possibly a bit more animation, and JC moans inwardly that he only wants to do this 'bloody thing' to make some money (I rather agree) and Eric it is who puts the frustrating but incontrovertible arguments for protecting our reputation by putting out only what we think is the best.

Sunday, June 7th

Another eight-hour sleep – too rare these days. The swirling south-westerly winds have died down, but the sky is overcast.

As if to suit the mood of the weather, Angela rings. She says she is in a depression and has been for the last two weeks. She's decided to drop her social worker job and is looking for something 'exciting'. She keeps talking of her low self-esteem. She's not easily consolable either, but puts on a brave and cheerful front. I can offer sympathy but nothing very practical.

I wonder if she finished this Whit Sunday watching, as I did, Cassavetes' *A Woman Under the Influence*. It was about madness and was rivetingly well-played, hard, depressing, uncompromising, but it aired a lot of problems and was ultimately optimistic.

I go to bed sober . . . sobered, anyway.

Monday, June 8th

A day of deck-clearing before an all-out assault on *The Missionary* script's last few scenes, which I hope to complete up in Southwold, with Suffolk countryside for inspiration and no telephones to distract.

Stickley and Kent call to tell me that my offer of £25,000 for No. 1 Julia hasn't been accepted, so I have to work out the next step. I want to make a £30,000 offer to put them on the spot, but after talking to Steve I revise this downward to £28,500 to allow bargaining room up to 30.

Wednesday, June 10th: Southwold

Wake to rich sunshine and birds chattering everywhere. Excellent con-ditions for a solid morning's writing at the desk presented to my grandfather from 'His grateful patients in Great and Little Ryburgh and Testerton',[1] fifty years ago this November.

Great strides made in the plot and this writing break has already justified itself completely. No phone calls, no doorbells, no carpet-layers, cleaners, carpenters, painters or television engineers, just my Silvine 'Students' Note Book – Ref 142 – Punched for filing', Grandfather's desk and the soothing, wholesome view – pheasants scurrying through a broad field of new-sown peas and a chaffinch strutting and posing on the telegraph wires outside.

Later, watch Terry J being hypnotised on *Paperbacks*. He says very little and eventually breaks into tears. Rather disturbing, I thought, for the tears don't look like tears of joy but of fear and uncertainty and loss.

Saturday, June 13th

Prepare for our sideshow(s) at the Gospel Oak School Fayre. The Palin contingent (minus H who is at badminton) troop along to the school at 1.15, armed with 'Escalado', blackboard, notices and a bottle of sweets which the nearest number guess can win. Congratulate Ron Lendon, the head, on the MBE he acquired in the honours lists published today.

For three and a half hours solid I take money and start races. 'Escalado' proves to be a compulsive hit. The races are as often as I can physically take the money, pay the winnings and start again. A cluster of a dozen kids keep coming back – addicted. We make 10p per race and by a quarter to six, when I'm hoarse and staggering to start the last race, we've taken about £19.20, which means nearly 200 races.

The whole fete, in warm, dry, sunny, celebratory weather, seems to have done well. Even Willy, who looked very miserable earlier on as he tried to tout custom for his 'guess the sweet' attraction, had taken over £7 by the end and had brightened considerably.

Monday, June 15th

Denis O'B rings from Los Angeles. He doesn't seem to have any ulterior motive than to be reassured that I'm still there and writing a script for

---

1 Edward Watson Palin was a doctor who lived at Fakenham in Norfolk. I still correspond with a retired policeman who remembers Dr Palin taking tonsils out for free in his kitchen after church on Sundays.

him. He doesn't attempt to put pressure on in any direction. He sounds very vulnerable suddenly, as if he genuinely cannot understand how it could possibly be that five majors have already passed on *Time Bandits*.

I feel very sorry for him and if he was deliberately trying to soften me up then he succeeded. Any doubts I may have had about giving him first option on *The Missionary* faded as I put the phone down and left him to Universal.

Tuesday, June 16th

At seven o'clock, despite a last-minute volley of phone calls, I wrote the magic words 'The End' on my film – approximately two and a half working months from that run in mid-March when the title and subject suddenly clarified in my mind.

How good it is I really don't know. A cluster of scenes please me – the rest could go either way. I now have ten days of typing during which I shall tighten it up.

Thursday, June 18th

To Neal's Yard for more '*TB*' publicity – this time an interview for Granada TV's *Clapperboard*. For a simple interview on film there must be about ten people – production secretary, producer, publicity ladies, crew, etc, quite apart from Chris Kelly, who's asking the questions, TG and myself.

Terry has only just embarked on the first serious answer when he dislodges a huge can of film, which crashes to the floor noisily and spectacularly. Granada are very pleased.

Sunday, June 21st

Took Rachel to the zoo. Much activity in the bright sunshine. Baboons copulating, polar bears flat out on their backs with legs immodestly spread, scratching their belly hair slowly – like something out of Tennessee Williams, tigers crapping and penguins looking very dry and unhappy.

This evening we have to decide on how George H's song 'That Which I Have Lost' is accommodated in the opening titles. Neither Ray nor Terry feel satisfied with the song there at all. George, pushed by Denis, has done his best to make a version that works. But it was the wrong song in the first place and no-one has the courage to see that, so tonight we agree on a compromise. Part of the song under the opening names, but keep it clear of the thudding, impressive impact of TG's titles.

Wednesday, June 24th

The only event of any great significance in an otherwise unworkmanlike day is a call from Gilliam halfway through *News at Ten* to tell me that Denis has finally given up hope of selling *Time Bandits* in Hollywood. Disney, who apparently were closest to a deal, finally gave him the thumbs down. Apparently it was a case of the old guard at the top overruling the newer, younger, less conventional execs below.

Perhaps, TG and I feel, it would have been a lot better if Denis had organised a preview – like the *Brian* preview in LA which so impressed Warners. He has only tried to sell it at the top. And failed.

To bed resignedly. I feel sorry for TG. So much now depends on a big success in England. If it does badly here, or even only quite well, there is a real chance of the movie sinking without trace.

Friday, June 26th

Buy *Screen International*. The British film industry does not seem very healthy. Rank have just announced plans to cut 29 cinemas. The head of Fox (*not* an Englishman) in London gives a glib, gloomy, heartless prognosis that sounds like Dr Beeching – cinemas will only survive in about 20 major cities. The British don't go out any more. Video recorder sales are booming. Unfortunately I think he's right. It's going to be hard, if not impossible, to reverse this trend away from theatrical visits.

Wednesday, July 1st

To Gospel Oak Open Day to look at Willy and Rachel's work. Place full of doting, involved Gospel Oak parents. Impressive exhibition in the hall. Willy's dissatisfaction with his teacher this year doesn't seem to be reciprocated – she has given him a very good end of term report. But I can't imagine many circumstances in which Gospel Oak kids would receive bad reports – unless they were mass murderers, possibly. Rachel is as good as gold, I'm told by her nice teacher, Miss Evans.

Work until eleven, when I watch very good (possibly the best) edition of *Paperbacks*. TJ enthusing, as only he can, about Rupert Bear with

Alfred Bestall, 86-year-old chief artist of the stories, there in the studio, complete with loose false teeth.

Monday, July 6th: London–Edinburgh

Helen takes me down to King's Cross to catch the 'Flying Scotsman' to Edinburgh to read the 'Biggles' stories [for BBC AudioBooks]. Full of Americans being roughly treated by a particularly cheeky set of waiters who execute all their tasks with a barely-controlled violence just this side of politeness. What a change from the Liverpool Street lot.

All confirms my feelings that it's the differences between human beings themselves which account for all our economic, social and political injust-ices and not the other way round. In short, there are plenty of shits in the world and unless we can find some wonder drug to cure them or neu-tralise them, I think we have to live with the fact that they will always cause trouble.

At Edinburgh by a quarter to three. Meet the team and the adaptor, George Hearten – possibly the complete antithesis of his hero, Captain W E Johns. Ex-Fleet Air Arm, so he knows how to pronounce 'altimeter', he turns out to be a reggae expert and, when we do discuss who we would all like to have been, reckons he's the Glaswegian Albert Camus.

The concentration required on the readings is quite exhausting. We do two stories and Marilyn [Ireland, the producer] sounds pleased.

Then back for story number three. This is harder and towards the end I find myself unable to say 'thousands of splinters flew' and, though we finish it, Marilyn rightly suggests that we stop for the day.

Tuesday, July 7th: Edinburgh

After breakfast walk down to the BBC and, at about eleven, we start one of the most gruelling, physically and mentally demanding day's work I can remember. Again the concentration required is greater than anything I'm prepared for, with preliminary read-throughs of each episode included. I have to speak continuously for two and a half hours, in six or seven different voices. My eyes swim out of focus when I stand up – my brain has rarely been required to work so fast – to process and redigest so much information, all the time knowing that this will be judged as a performance. We plough through five episodes by five o'clock, leaving two for tomorrow.

I feel drained – 'Biggled', I think must be the word, well and truly Biggled – as I lie back in my bath at the North British with a Carlsberg Special as a reward.

Wednesday, July 8th: Edinburgh–London

Up to meet John Gibson of the *Edinburgh Evening News* at breakfast at nine. We talk for almost an hour. He's easy company, and a dutiful journalist – he makes sure he scribbles something down about all my activities. This is primarily a *Time Bandits* piece.

From talking to him I am reinforced in this feeling that's been coming over me lately – that my reputation follows about three or four years behind what I do. Somehow, though none of the individual projects were treated with respect or reverence at the time, the cumulative effect of Python and *Ripping Yarns* and the *Life of Brian* and the 'Great Train Journey' seems to have been to raise my stock to the extent that I am now not only good copy everywhere, but also I sense a sort of respectfulness, as if I'm now an experienced hand and a permanent addition to a gallery of famous British people. It's all very worrying and offers me little comfort, for I know I am still the same bullshitter I always was.

A quick walk through Prince's Gardens – where everyone is lying out in the sun like extras in a documentary about nuclear war. Up the Mound to a restored National Trust house in the Royal Mile. Fascinating, but as soon as I enter it there is quite a stir amongst the nice, middle-class family who run it.

I'm followed from room to room by a breathless young man who finally confronts me in a bedchamber – 'Excuse me, but you are Eric Idle from Monty Python ... ?'

Friday, July 10th

More rioting on TV tonight.[1] It's replaced sport as the summer's most talked about activity. The scenes are frightening. One can only hope lessons will be learnt fast. Whitelaw and Thatcher go out of their way to support the police, but bad policing and the effects of unemployment vie with each other as the two most oft-quoted reasons for what's happening.

1 One of the most serious in a summer of urban riots took place at Toxteth in Liverpool. A thousand police were injured and many properties destroyed.

Tuesday, July 14th

Settle down to read *The Missionary*, which arrived today from Alison –
the first really smart copy. It read far better than I expected. It seems tight,
the religious atmosphere is strong, the story and the characters develop
well and, all in all, it's just what I had hoped – a strong, convincing,
authentic sense of place, mood, period and a dramatic narrative providing
a firm base for some very silly comedy.

I finish reading at half past eleven and, though I write these words with
great trepidation, I feel the film is over 70% right – maybe even more.
Now names of actors, directors, keep coming into my head.

But the chiefest decision of all is how to play Denis. I must show it to
him, or I think be prepared for a final breakdown argument with him.
The situation is full of uncertainties and dangers. My prestige is such that
I could show it to any number of producers and get a sympathetic hearing.
But I have told DO'B that I will offer it first to HandMade – so there's
the rub.

Wednesday, July 15th

I call Denis in Fisher's Island [his home near New York]. It's half past
eight in the morning there and Denis sounds subdued, a little cautious
at first, but when he realises it isn't bad news, he begins to wind up and
by the end we are both beginning to celebrate.

He asks if I have a director in mind. I mention Richard Loncraine, who
I haven't spoken to for a few months, and could still be a long shot.
I mention spring of '82 for shooting and he says 'We would have no
problem' – 'we' being, I presume, he, EuroAtlantic, Trade Development
Bank and George.

Feel relieved that I've taken a positive step forward. It would remove
endless complications if Denis accepted the script. Should hear something
by the weekend.

To Rachel's end of term concert at Gospel Oak. A rather flat affair. All
the children look as though they're acting under orders. Rachel plays a
lettuce.

A call from Loncraine. Good news – for me – is that the *Brimstone and
Treacle* film has collapsed – Bowie having let them down very much at
the last minute. He has two film projects he wants to do, but claims to be
very keen to work with me, and wants to see the script as soon as possible.

Thursday, July 16th

Out of the house at a quarter to eight. Stuck in rush-hour traffic, ironically trying to get to Marylebone High Street for Radio London's live programme called *Rush Hour*.

Talk to Jackie Collins, who's also a guest. She's doing the circuits for her new book, *Chances*, which my Radio London interviewer confides to me is 'the filthiest book I've ever read'.

Out in Marylebone High Street by nine o'clock. [*Time Bandits* opened in London yesterday.] Buy all the papers and treat myself to a reviving plate of bacon and eggs and a cup of coffee at a local caff. Read the *Guardian* – 'British, if not best'. Plenty of praise, but all qualified. In the *New Statesman* our friend and *Jabberwocky* fan John Coleman said many things, but concluded that the taste left by the film at the end was not just bad, it was sour. Cheered up by an unequivocal rave in *New Musical Express*. Nothing else.

Drove on down to Terry J's. Terry is on good form. *Paperbacks* has finished and we natter happily over various things. Realise that I'm enjoying writing with an immediate sounding board again. In fact I have rather a good day and add to the 'Catholic Family' sketch rather satisfactorily, whilst Terry deals genially with a mass of phone callers.

Home soon after six. Bad review on Capital. Much praise for the film, but he blatantly calls it the new Monty Python film. If I had more time and energy I'd sue him.

Friday, July 17th

In early evening an important call – the first professional opinion on *The Missionary* – from Richard Loncraine. He liked it up to page ten, then not again until page sixty, from whence he felt it picked up.

But I was hopeful from our short chat for two reasons. One that he doesn't dislike it enough to not want to do it, and the other that all he said about the script and intentions about how to film it I felt very much in agreement with.

Now Denis and Terry J are to report! They're the only others who have copies.

Saturday, July 18th

After lunch a party of ten of us go to see *Time Bandits* at the Plaza.

The audience is responsive, consistent and picks up the jokes, but I find that, at one or two points, we stretch their goodwill by over-extending on a moment that's already been effective. The Giant is on for too long and the trolls don't add much. Heresy I know to agree on this, but the acts *do* hold up Napoleon and *don't* get a positive reaction. And, though I don't object to the parents blowing up at the end, we hold the moments afterwards for too long, as if making a significant statement, and, in doing so, overloading the gloom and killing the black humour.

So I came away feeling a little numbed. Despite three or four people seeking me out to tell me how much they'd enjoyed it, I was disappointed that I'd seen faults in it and that there wasn't a greater sense of excitement amongst the departing audience.

TG rings later. He feels this sense of doom as well.

Sunday, July 19th

Woke to yet another day of concern. I have to learn my 'Plankton' speech for a Save the Whales rally in Hyde Park. Then there's the Sunday papers – how will *Time Bandits* fare today?

A marvellous selection of qualified raves. But somehow the qualifications seem to be significant rather than the raves. I read Alan Brien, who starts wonderfully and then qualifies. Philip French in the *Observer* chunders on at length for a column and a half before one word of doubt. But then it comes in, like a trip wire 20 yards from the tape at the end of a mile race.

As I describe them to Gilliam later – they're the worst set of rave notices I've ever seen.

I feel Alan Brien's observation is the most perceptive thing anyone's said about the film – 'Where it falls below earlier Python movies, or Gilliam's own *Jabberwocky*, is in the sense it gives that once the basic idea was established the makers thought everything else would be easy.'

Still, no time to mope, as I have to take myself and rapidly-learnt script down to Hyde Park to address the Save the Whales rally – which was allowed to go ahead by [Police Commissioner] McNee despite a month-long ban on London marches following the riots, because it was termed 'educational'.

Monday, July 20th

Start of a Python writing fortnight. We tried such a session a year ago and it was not successful. Today, a year later, things feel very different.

Time Bandits is complete, so TG is back with the group. Eric is relaxed and well after France. Terry J has got *Paperbacks* out of the way and is keen to get directing again. Graham, with *Yellowbeard*, and myself, with *The Missionary*, both have projects which look like being completed by summer '82.

We decided, without any bickering or grudging, that we should now work separately until the end of the week. Everyone agreed that this film should not be extended indefinitely and if it was to become a reality it had to be next year.

So, after lunch and an amiable chat, we disperse to our separate writes.

About ten o'clock DO'B rings from Fisher's Island. He's just finished reading *The Missionary*. As I expected, the last thing he wants to do is give any artistic judgement on the script. He talks of it purely from a business point of view. He sounds to have no doubts that it's a commercial reality and he's treating it accordingly.

DO'B reckons it's an eight- or nine-week shoot, 65% studio, and will cost about one and a half million. We are looking at a March, April, early May '82 shoot.

Thursday, July 23rd

Drive over to Richard Loncraine's office in Clarendon Cross. How neat, well-preserved, paved and bollarded this little corner of Notting Hill has become. Charming, I should think is the word. Richard bounds down to answer the door, and is soon showing me his latest gadgets (he runs a toy factory employing 200 people making ridiculous things like eggs with biros in the end), pouring me some wine, raving about *Time Bandits*, which he thought absolutely wonderful, calling *Chariots of Fire* 'Chariots of Bore' and generally bubbling and enthusing like an English version of Gilliam.

Richard is going to do it and will commit to it. He repeats that he wants to work with me and he's doing it largely out of faith in what I can achieve, which is flattering and exciting at the same time, and because, although there is much in the script he thinks doesn't yet work, he thinks there's more that does.

The next step is to bring DO'B and Loncraine together next week. But I think I can say that *The Missionary* became a reality tonight.

Sunday, July 26th

Richard rings to suggest Maggie Smith for Lady Ames, which shows he's been thinking positively about it.

Monday, July 27th

To a Python meeting at 2 Park Square West, giving T Gilliam a lift. A successful day, everyone participating. John tending to chair in a bar-risterish way, but it's all good Python trough work. We re-read the 'bank-ers'. They nearly all survive and, by half past three when TJ has to go, we have a solid 50 minutes, with viable links and a sort of coherence.

Ring Terry J to find out if he has read *The Missionary*. He has, and finds it all 'unbelievable'. Not an encouraging reaction. Set off to [Euro-Atlantic in] Cadogan Square. Denis, tall, tanned and looking as con-fidently turned out as ever, meets me and we walk through the balmy evening to the Chelsea Rendezvous.

I start by telling Denis that all three people who have read *The Missionary* haven't liked it. A little provocative, I suppose, but it's the way I read the reactions. Terry J's, strangely enough, doesn't trouble me as much as I thought. Maybe, as TJ and I just improvised over the phone this evening, it would be better for Welles to be given a mission in England – possibly the saving of fallen women. But talking to Denis I feel, obstinately perhaps, that my instincts are right and that my choice of director is right and that the film can work. Denis is not at all dis-couraging. Quite the opposite.

Tuesday, July 28th

I wake in the early hours in general discomfort – head and tooth aching and very hot. Just not ready for sleep, so walk about a bit. Then, from three a.m. until half past four I sit and scribble some dialogue for a new scene in *The Missionary* – trying to take the story in a different direction, as I discussed with TJ over the phone.

Drain my cup of tea and look up finally from deep absorption in the work, to see the sky has lightened to a dark, pre-dawn blue. Feel much better. Feel I've defeated the aches and pains! Back to bed.

Later take Granny and the Herberts to *Time Bandits*.

Afterwards we all walk down Regent Street into a Mall thronged with pre-wedding [of Charles to Diana] crowds. A feeling of celebration and slightly noisy camaraderie, as if the revolution had just happened. Of course, quite the opposite; everyone here tonight was celebrating the longevity and resilience of the Establishment.

There was a mass of sleeping bags and plastic all along the edge of the pavement – rarely much class or style, except that under the trees outside the ICA a long table had been set with candles and four men in full dinner jackets and bow ties were sitting down to a meal and wine.

Saturday, August 1st

Time Bandits biz in second week is down, as Denis said, by about 20%, but then so is everyone's except James Bond and *Clash of the Titans*. We move up to No. 3 in London above *Excalibur*, now in its fourth week, and the fading *Cannonball Run*.

Marvellous review by Gavin Millar in the *Listener*. I wonder if TG had time to see it before he went off to France yesterday. The *Ham and High* [the *Hampstead and Highgate Express* – our local paper] and many of the rest of England papers turn in good reviews too, so that all cheers me up. But the bad news is that the figures for week one in Bristol are, by any standards, very disappointing. Cardiff is better, but certainly no signs of it being anything but an average performer outside London.

Sunday, August 2nd: Southwold

An early lunch (cheese and an apple) and drive back through Suffolk villages and down the M11, listening to another tense Test Match. Cloudless sky when I arrive in Oak Village. Australia nearly 100 with only 50 to go and seven wickets standing. But by the time I've unpacked, oiled myself and settled down for a sunbathe on the balcony they have collapsed and within an hour Botham has wiped them out and England have won.

Wednesday, August 5th

I drive into town for lunch with Neville Thompson at Mon Plaisir.

Neville is the third of the main strands of *The Missionary* project. Denis is supplying the money, Loncraine the direction and Neville could be the producer.

Like everyone else he has qualifications about the script, but has faith in the project. I try to give him as many 'outs' as possible, but he clearly feels that there is some rich vein to be tapped wherever Pythons are involved – even if he can't immediately see it in *The Missionary* as it stands. I feel a little like the Missionary myself at the moment, trying to convert the waverers to the joys and virtues of this bloody film.

Loncraine rings. He's back from New York, where he's been to see Sting – of 'Police' – for part in *Brimstone and Treacle*.

Thursday, August 6th

Over to Loncraine's for further talks on *The Missionary*. Richard has read it again and sees certain problem areas. Richard talks from the hip a bit, firing ideas out fast and in a not particularly disciplined way. Tendency to broader jokes, but, on the credit side, we come up with three very good visual additions to the script which I can immediately incorporate in the rewrites. Another heavy storm breaks – starting with an apocalyptic clap of thunder – 'Didn't like that idea, did he?' says Richard, looking out of the window respectfully.

Reagan has dismissed 13,000 of his air traffic controllers for going on an illegal strike, but Sheila [Condit, who was organising our US holiday trip] has checked with LA Airport and international flights are coming in 95% on time.

Friday, August 7th

In the evening Helen goes to badminton. I stay in to watch the news. Whilst Reagan pursues his hard line against the air traffic controllers, European air traffic controllers are quoted as advising against flying to the US. Disturbing stuff – 25 near misses reported in US air space since the strike began, the new military controllers plus non-striking controllers are working longer hours and 'safety is being endangered'. American government says rubbish, and the airlines flying to the States say so too. But not a very comforting way to have to start the holiday. I feel that, if the BA pilots are still prepared to fly with the new controllers then I'm happy – but don't go to bed elated.

We flew to California on August 9th for a family holiday, having rented a house at Point Dume, near Malibu.

Wednesday, September 2nd

Denis met with Loncraine and got on well and is anxious to sign him up. *Time Bandits* is still No. 3 in London. It will not be the blockbuster they were predicting. They'd been looking for a distributor's gross of a million, but have revised this downwards to half a million. But he has done a deal in America. Avco Embassy are to release the *Time Bandits* on November 6th with four million dollars committed to prints and advertising. Modest, by today's standards, and Avco Embassy are guaranteed against loss by Denis and George.

Thursday, September 3rd

To my desk to wrestle with the most immediate problems. One of the first calls on our return, Tuesday, was from a humbled Stickley and Kent asking if my offer of £28,500 for No. 1 Julia Street still stood. Apparently they have had some difficulty selling at £37,750. As my offer had been so summarily dismissed, I told them I would think about it.

Helen is not really keen and sees No. 1 as a lot of hard work, but on the other hand she does see the advantage of having control over the site. Edward keen to take on the job and will supervise, so on balance I stick to my first instinct and renew my interest – at the same time twisting the knife a little and giving my cash offer as £26,500. We shall see.[1]

On to viewing of *Hollywood Bowl* on screen for first time. Sixty-five minutes it runs. Sketches well performed and quite well filmed – the rest a wretched disappointment.

Back at Neal's Yard, those Pythons who saw the film – Terry J, John, Graham and myself (TG and Eric being in France) – all agree it isn't right. Main criticisms – links, atmosphere, shapelessness.

I felt very proud of our little group today. In the face of much pressure to put the '*Bowl*' film out as soon as possible, to recoup our money and to have done with it, we held out for quality control first.

---

1 We never did buy No. 1, but snapped up No. 3 years later!

Tuesday, September 8th

Drive into town to join the London Library and take out, at last, some books on African missionaries – *Winning over a Primitive People*, etc – to read as background on the film.

Evening of phone calls, latest of which is Denis O'B ringing from New York. I tell him all is well, except that both Richard Loncraine and Neville Thompson think that the budget will be nearer £2 million than £1 million.

Turns out that he has sold *The Missionary* project to George on the basis of a £1.2 million cost.

Thursday, September 10th: Southwold

I watch a programme about the colossal, massive, virtually incredible madness of our world in 1981 – the designing, building and deployment of weapons of self-destruction.

It worries me that we accept now that we have to live with bombs which could kill two million people with one blast. That somewhere in the world there are men designing and manufacturing and loading and aiming and controlling and making serious considerations of policy based on the use of such weapons. Meanwhile we pay for such collective madness with unemployment, a crumbling health service, a polluted planet. It seems we know that we shall destroy ourselves somehow and the multi-megaton bombs are like the cyanide pills which will put us out of our misery instantly.

Wednesday, September 16th

A solid morning's work on *The Missionary*. Few distractions and I fall into a good rhythm.

To the airport to collect Al and Claudie. Wet roads. Repairs close the motorways, London seems empty, ghostly. At the airport soon after ten – find them waiting, the plane was early. Best flight ever, opines the bronzed and ageless poet, pulling eagerly on a cigar as they had sat in non-smoking. Claudie, just a gently convex stomach showing discreetly, looked very well and in good colour.

Friday, September 18th

Up to Burgh House at 6.00 for the Grand Launch [of Al's book of poems, called *Travelogs*]. Robert laid out a display of Signford's[1] wares on the piano of the Music Room and hardly anybody turned up. More and more I had the feel that I was in one of Richmal Crompton's 'William' situations. Involved in one of his 'grate skeems' which never quite work.

But there were enough there for me to rise to my feet and embark on the speech. No sooner had I begun than a dozen latecomers arrived in the next one and a half minutes, so the speech wasn't helped, but the party was. And in the end it was quite difficult to move everyone out.

Then out to Vasco and Piero's [Pavilion Restaurant] with Al, who had been quaffing malts during the afternoon, then much champagne at the party, but was in a big, expansive bear-like mood of delight, Claudie, and Mike Henshaw[2] and his excellent new 'companion' Penny. We all had a wonderful time and Mike paid.

For Mike and me it was a reconciliation. Having been good and close friends for 13 years, accountancy got in the way and we have not spoken or seen each other for two years. We picked up as if nothing had happened.

Wednesday, September 23rd

In mid-afternoon take advantage of dry, still, bright weather for a run across the Heath, then down to Eyre Methuen to discuss with Geoffrey S and Terry J a new edition of Fegg which we agree to call *Dr Fegg's Nasty Book*. We look through the artwork of the old – now seven years past – up in Methuen's boardroom, sipping white wine and looking out over a panorama of city buildings turning reddish-gold in the waning sunlight.

Thursday, September 24th

Work delayed this morning by arrival of TG, fresh from Hollywood, bearing such gems as a market research survey on *Time Bandits* – a wonderfully thorough and conscientious document analysing test

1 Signford was an off-the-shelf name for a small publishing company I had set up, with Robert Hewison's help. Its first book was by the artist Chris Orr.
2 Michael Henshaw, my first accountant, had been married to Anne, who had become my manager, and the Pythons' manager. She had re-married, to Jonathan James, a barrister.

screenings and reactions to all the various elements of the film in that earnest American way which reduces all things to 'product'. They confirm that the film is not for Fresno, but it could well be for bigger, more 'sophisticated' city audiences.

Interesting thing it *did* reveal is that the audience at Sherman Oaks went to the movies on average ten times a month, and in Fresno seven. Which shows the health of movies in the US is still good, whereas here the admissions level is still dropping to all-time lows.

Work on the Fermoy scene, but got involved in helping Tom with his geography homework. Then drive down to the Long Room at the Oval cricket ground for Pavilion Books launching party.

Soon was in the middle of a swirling throng – past the literary editor of the *Express*, Peter Grosvenor, on to a very persistent Scottish lady publisher who wants to have lunch and discuss some project involving Miriam Stoppard, Tom Stoppard and sex, grabbed by Molly Parkin, who's very oncoming – she says I always was her favourite – and meet Max Boyce. 'Oh I love being in a corner with two comedians,' she soothed, as we had photos taken together.

Then Bob Geldof in green lurex jacket, black skin-tight trousers and mediaeval floppy boots approached and we hailed each other like old friends, though I don't know him that well. After a brief exchange of mutual abuse, we talked about school and missionaries and he swore blind that he had been at a missionary school in Ireland where the French master was mainlining quinine, Irish was compulsory and, even if you got seven or eight 'O' Levels, none of them counted if you failed Irish.

Friday, September 25th

Drink in the Nag's Head. Aggressive podgy Cockney looms up.

'Are you Eric Idle?'

'No …'

'You're Eric Idle.'

'No, I'm not …'

'Well, it's a very good impression,' he mutters and wanders back to his mates.

Saturday, September 26th

After lunch out with the family to visit Uncle Leon in Hampton Wick, in the tiny, neat, long and narrow cottage which Leon moved into only two weeks before Helen's Aunt Peggy, wife of 38 years, died early this year. He took a long time to recover and said he couldn't bear being alone in the house in the evening. He confessed very touchingly that he's often found himself turning to talk to someone who isn't there.

A big tea with scones and home-made jam, then home under angry skies ranging from slate grey to pitch black, through the well-kept roads of Hampton and Twickenham. Perfect example of Tory middle-class orderliness. No rows of council flats with rubbish flapping around them, or grandiose public works schemes left half undone through lack of funds. This is the tidy, thrifty world of private planning, from which the poor and the underpaid seem absent. But at least personal enterprise is allowed and encouraged to flourish here, when the grey blocks of Camden seem only to have extinguished it.

Back home I watch quite brilliant first film of Bill Douglas trilogy,[1] *My Childhood*.

Tuesday, September 29th

Came near to giving up this morning. For a full hour I sat and stared. Every word I wrote seemed dull and wooden. The last three weeks of fairly solid application (well, two and a half, anyway) seemed to have produced just sludge. And tomorrow was the last day of September, when I had once optimistically estimated I would be finished with the [*Missionary*] rewrites.

But abandoning now would seem so feeble. I had to carry it through. Besides, I'd burnt my boats – turning down every other piece of work. So it was that in the hour and a half before lunch I buckled down and ideas began to flow and in fact I was well into my stride when the door bell rang at 2.30 to herald the arrival of a BBC crew to film me giving testimony in a programme about giving up smoking.

---

1 Made in 1972, it tells the story of a boy born into poverty in Scotland and his relationship with a German POW. Douglas made only four films, all autobiographical; bleak but brilliantly observed.

Sunday, October 4th: Southwold

Woke at 8.30. The boys already downstairs and breakfasted. Outside a steady drizzle, which increased to heavy rain, and the children and I took Mrs Pratt [my mother's neighbour] to morning service at Reydon.

We leave her and drive into Southwold for more secular activities. Despite all my doubts and rational resistance to the dogma of the church, I still feel a powerful guilt at taking the children to the amusement arcade on the end of Southwold Pier on a Sunday morning. You don't notice the presence of the church in London, as you do in Southwold.

Wednesday, October 7th

To the Escargot in Greek Street for meal with Terry and Al. Terry has just returned from his *Fairy Tales* promotion trip to Birmingham (which he hated) and Manchester (which he found well-heeled) and Liverpool (sad tales of the decline of the Adelphi).[1] Give the manager one of my complimentary tickets to Mel Brooks's *History of the World*, which is having a glossy preview at 11.30.

Find myself sitting next to Harold Evans, Editor of the *Times*. He seems to be very anxious to please – asking me what I'm doing, as if he knows me. Make some jokes about the SDP, then he admits that he does think they are a very sensible lot. This, together with a propensity to do the right thing by clapping whenever Mel Brooks appears on screen, makes me suspect him. Surely *Times* editors should be made of harder stuff?

The film is dreadful. Having dispensed early on with any claim to historical accuracy or authenticity and any exceptional attention to visual detail, the whole thing depends on the quality of the gags. And the quality is poor. It's like a huge, expensive, grotesquely-inflated stand-up act. A night club act with elephantiasis.

Thursday, October 8th

Tom becomes a teenager. Just writing those words makes me abruptly aware of time passing. He has lots of books about aircraft and Helen

---

1 A once-glamorous hotel for transatlantic liner passengers. Helen is convinced our daughter Rachel was conceived there on the night of my friend Sean Duncan's wedding in 1974.

and I are to buy him a new clarinet. He goes off to school very happy.

I take him and three friends out to Century City in Mayfair – a new hamburger place, all silver-sprayed 'hi-tech' décor. Only open three weeks, but looking decidedly run down. Still, the food was good and we all sat inside a dome painted silver. At one point Alex Robertson declares, almost proudly, 'Gosh, my mum and dad wouldn't have been able to afford *this*.' Echoes from all round the table.

Saturday, October 10th

Buy presents for the evening's celebrations to mark EuroAtlantic's tenth anniversary. The celebration is to be held, somehow appropriately, aboard a boat called the *Silver Barracuda*.

Mark Vere Nicoll [EuroAtlantic's legal wiz] makes a speech and presents Denis with a leather-covered photo album which is also a music box. Denis gives a long speech in reply. Quite fluent and informal. But he does at one point pay tribute to Peter Sellers – adding, somewhat unnecessarily, 'Who can't be with us tonight.' George, ever in touch with the other world, shouts back, 'Don't be so sure, Denis.'

Wednesday, October 14th

Helen is 39. But looks a lot younger.

Mary, Edward and Catherine Gib arrive at 8.00 and I take them all out for what turns out to be a very successful Mystery Evening. First to the Gay Hussar – good food and efficient, old-fashioned service. Then on to Ronnie Scott's to see Panama Francis and the Savoy Sultans – a Harlem Thirties jazz and swing band. Beautiful to listen to, presented stylishly and with the added poignancy that they are a dying breed. In ten years many of them won't be left. But the two hours we spent there in their soothing, infectious company were rare magic.

Thursday, October 22nd

Just after five o'clock I suddenly found myself at the end of *The Missionary* rewrites.

I've spent about five and a half solid working weeks on the rewrite and there are only about a dozen pages left intact from the 121-page first version. So I have virtually written a second film in about half the time it took to write the first.

But for the moment, at the end of this crisp and invigorating day, the feeling is just one of an onrush of freedom – of time to spare – the emergence from isolation.

Monday, October 26th: Ballymaloe House, Ireland

We landed at Cork at ten o'clock, our VW minibus was waiting and we drove without incident to Ballymaloe. The bright sunshine of London was replaced by rain in Ireland. By early evening it's clear enough for me to go for a run – up past barking dogs and along a narrow road which grows more and more wild and directionless – giving rise in the dark corners of my mind to California-like fears of sudden mindless violence. (I was not to know that about one hour before, in the London we had just left, a bomb had exploded in a Wimpy bar in Oxford Street[1] – the IRA claimed credit.)

Thursday, October 29th: Ballymaloe

Woke about 8.00 to hear Rachel colouring industriously across the other side of the room. Then to breakfast – which now stretches from nine till ten. I love our little tableful and it's a joy and complete relaxation to sit, after children have gone, with a dependably tasty cup of coffee and gaze out of the long Georgian windows at the damp autumn countryside.

We have a packed lunch today and, on advice from an Irishman staying here, drive to Cobh and Fota Island.

Cobh, an old fishing town and fadedly elegant resort, is approached across a causeway, past an old blockhouse or pill-box on which are daubed the words 'Cobh supports the hunger strikers'. Then there are a number of small black flags on short makeshift flagpoles nailed up to telegraph poles.

Unlike anywhere else we've been in Southern Ireland, this year or last, there is a definite frisson of hostility in Cobh. It's clearly official municipal policy to support the IRA – although these initials are never mentioned. It's always 'our boys' or 'our countrymen'. Beside the station, now a fish-unloading yard, posters are stuck on the wall – clenched fists surmounted

---

1 Killing the man who was trying to defuse it.

with the words 'Stand Up To Britain' and an incongruous picture of Maggie Thatcher with the words beneath 'Wanted. For The Torture Of Irish Prisoners'.

The memorial to those who died in the *Lusitania* has been turned into an IRA memorial, with placards hung round the necks of the 1915 sailors giving the names of the hunger strikers. Like so much in Ireland it is a rough and ready gesture – there's no style or care particularly taken. It's functional, rather ugly and very depressing.

Mary [Burd] gets fish lobbed in her direction by the unloaders and there's some laughing and sending-up. My final image of this potentially rather attractive Georgian town is of a grimy 40-foot trailer being driven at violent, shaking speed along crowded streets, blood pouring out of the back and onto the road.

Wednesday, November 4th: New York

The car horns start to blare and I know I'm in Manhattan [for the opening of *Time Bandits*]. A fine 27th storey view out over Central Park. The trees in full autumn colours, mustards, russets, yellows. Very fine, a stretch of calm on this restless island.

General atmosphere of cautious excitement improved by continuing news of fresh enthusiastic reviews. Jack Lyons [Avco-Embassy's publicity man] says he has nearly all the majors covered, but so far his spies in the *NY Times* have not been any help with leaks about the Canby review.[1] Canby's review will be out on Friday, but, if all else fails, Jack says he'll get a leak from one of the compositors on Thursday afternoon!

In the evening we have a Gala Premiere and I drink an awful lot of champagne. Jack has arranged for me to escort Eleanor Mondale, a rather classically good-looking 21-year-old blonde, who resembles, especially, with her hair-do and use of knickerbockers, a chunky Princess Diana.[2] She is quite used to the bright lights and walks with a serene sort of Scandinavian poise through all the ballyhoo. And there *is* ballyhoo.

We are driven to the theatre in limousines and disgorged before a small waiting crowd gathered good-humouredly rather than ecstatically behind

---

1 Chief film critic of the *New York Times*. He died in 2000.
2 Walter Mondale was Jimmy Carter's Vice-President from 1976 to 1981. Eleanor, a radio presenter, was diagnosed with a brain tumour in 2005, but seems to have successfully fought it.

wooden barriers. Then we go inside and meet the good people who have been invited along. Meet Frank Capra Jnr, the new head of Avco-Embassy, whom I quite like. James Taylor, looking like the earnest maths master in a prep school, comes up and re-introduces himself.

After the movie begins, Terry G, Nancy, Eleanor Mondale and I take off to a ceilinged, fashionable but un-chic restaurant down on 18th called Joanne's. Shelley [Duvall] joins us later with news of a complete fiasco at the Gala Premiere. It was held in a twin cinema complex and apparently the sound was very bad in the first one for ten minutes, and in the second the picture came on upside down after the first couple of reels.

Thursday, November 5th: New York

Driven by a talkative chauffeur – they don't call them chauffeurs over here, I notice, but 'drivers'. This one goes into a monologue about 'celebrities'. 'I do like celebrities. They're very nice people.' He tells me how, as a cabbie, he gave a ride to Frank Sinatra and then rushed home and rang his mother at three in the morning to tell her the news. He also has taken Gilda Radner to the dentist and tells me all sorts of intimate details about her bridge work.

I notice that the driver is totally grey – cap, trousers, jacket, shoes, hair and face. Amazing. To the mid-West Side in sight of the big liner bays, for the *Dick Cavett Show*.

The programme progresses in uneasy fencing between comedy and seriousness. Cavett doesn't want to look like the dullard, so he indulges my subversive silliness instead of bringing it under a tight rein. The result is that some comedy works and there is nothing to fall back on when it doesn't.

The limousine takes us on to NBC and the *Robert Klein Hour*. This is a radio show I have come to enjoy greatly. Klein is relaxed, sharp, funny and good at guiding a disparate guest list – which includes Meat Loaf and Loudon Wainwright III – who remembers straight away that we met last in a massage parlour.

End up eating at Elaine's. Shelley is along with us for a while. Good Italian food, nice busy atmosphere.

TG gets his first sight of the Vincent Canby review. I'll never forget his face as he studies it, at the table beside Woody Allen and Mia Farrow, with the waiters pushing by. 'Studies' is far too mild a word for the extraordinary intensity of Terry's expression. His eyes stare fearfully like some Walter Crane drawing of an Arthurian knight confronting the face of Evil. Two years of solid commitment can be rendered quite spare in one review. At the end he lays the paper down ... 'Yes ... it's good ...'

Monday, November 9th

'*The Missionary* Mark II' arrives from the typist's, and I fall on it and read it through eagerly. It reads very well and I'm happy with the last-minute cuts and readjustments. And I laughed more, much more, than at Mk I.

Send the script round by cabs to Neville and Richard L. Watch some television. Can't keep my mind on writing. I'm half hoping the phone will ring before I go to bed and bring some breathless enthusiasm from one or other of them for the new script. This is what I need now.

At 11.30 the phone does ring. It's Rita from Los Angeles. Though it's only lunchtime Monday in LA, she tells me (in strictest confidence, she says) that *Time Bandits* took 6.2 million dollars over three days of its first weekend. This is bigger than any film ever handled by Avco (including *The Graduate*).

I'd still rather have had a phone call about *The Missionary*.

Tuesday, November 10th

Halfway through the morning Neville Thompson rings. My heart sinks utterly as he tells me that he wants to see the original script, because he feels I've lost a lot in the rewrites. I'm sure he doesn't realise what a dashing blow this is after two months' rewriting. Anything but wild enthusiasm is a dashing blow!

Denis calls in the afternoon and brightens me up with the news that *Time Bandits* has taken (officially) 6.5 million dollars in its first three days in the US. He estimates it will overtake *Life of Brian*'s total US take in two and a half weeks. Incredible news, almost as incredible as Neville not liking the new script.

Wednesday, November 11th: Belfast

Still no word from Richard L. Off to Heathrow at 11.00 to take the 12.30 shuttle to Belfast. Bag searched very thoroughly and wrapped in a cellophane cover before loading. Flight half full. Land at Aldergrove at a quarter to two.[1]

Belfast is not unlike Manchester or Liverpool. A once proud and thriving city centre suffering from the scars of industrial decline. Fine, red-brick warehouses empty. New office blocks – featureless and undistinguished. The university and its surrounding streets quite elegant; Georgian and early Victorian Gothic.

The Europa Hotel is screened at the front by a ten-foot-high mesh wire and everyone has to enter through a small hut, where my bag was searched again and my name checked on the hotel list. Then into the hotel, with its thick carpets and Madison Suites. No-one seems to find it remarkable any more that such a smart façade should be upstaged by a makeshift hut and barbed wire. Will they make the hut permanent one day? Will it be landscaped – or would that spell victory for the forces of disorder?

I have a pleasant two-room suite with an 8th floor view. Michael Barnes, tall, with long hair and sweeping beard, is very charming. 'I know we'll get on,' he said, 'because you write such good letters.' And vice-versa, I should have said, for it was something about his first approach to me by letter that brought me here.

Michael B told me that I was the second Festival attraction to sell out – two days after Yehudi Menuhin and two days ahead of Max Boyce! Anyway it was quite restorative for my ego to see a long queue of people waiting to get into the Arts Theatre.

Up tatty stairs to a small dressing room with light bulbs missing. Sort out my false noses, moustaches and at a quarter to eight I go on. The first part of the programme is what I've written and cobbled together since returning from New York. It goes well, but, after what seems an interminable and gruelling length of time, I glance at my watch between changes and, to my astonishment and despair, it's still only eight o'clock.

In fact it's just after 8.30 when I finish 'Fish in Comedy' – and I'm very hot and sweaty. For a moment the question and answer session seems doomed. Then all of a sudden it begins to happen. A steady stream of well-phrased, fairly sensible enquiries give me ample scope to talk about and enact scenes from all the favourite Python topics – censorship, the Muggeridge/Southwark interviews, etc.

1 I had been asked by Michael Barnes, director of the Belfast Festival, to go over and give a performance. It was my first one-man show. I was to do more, but only ever at Belfast. The Troubles were at their height.

There are some very enterprising audience suggestions – 'Did you know, Mr Palin, that it is a tradition for solo performers who visit the Arts Theatre, Belfast, to run round the auditorium from one side of the theatre to the other? The record is held by Groucho Marx at 45 seconds.' So I peeled off my jacket, paced out the course and went off like a rocket. 38 seconds. Whoever he was, I should have thanked him.

So I rambled on until ten to ten, just over two hours on the stage. Thoroughly enjoyable. Michael Barnes very pleased backstage.

Friday, November 13th

Gemma, a helper at the Festival and English girl, says that the worst thing about living in Northern Ireland is the way people have become used to the violence. They hardly turn a hair when a bomb goes off. Her father, who has worked here for years, will return to England when he retires. Resignation and survival rather than hope or rebuilding seem to be the watchwords.

I leave on the 10.30 shuttle. We take 55 minutes, with the help of a north-westerly tailwind, to reach Heathrow, where it's dry and sunny.

At half past two Neville Thompson arrived to talk about *The Missionary*. His doubts, which had worried me so much earlier in the week, seemed less substantial as we talked and I think I was able to persuade him that there were very funny things in the script. He in turn gave me a thought about Fortescue's character which clarified something very constructively – that Fortescue should enjoy sex. A simple, but clear observation, which gives greater point, irony and tension throughout.

Saturday, November 14th

This is one of those mornings when it's worth buying *Variety*. 'Bandits Abscond With 69G in St Lou', 'Boston's Ambitious Bandits Bag 269G', 'Bandits' Larcenous 45G in KC', 'Bandits Looting LA. Hot 368G'. Lovely breakfast reading.

Sunday, November 15th

Work in the afternoon, watch Miles Kington's 'Great Railway Journey', which makes me want to start travelling again. But the best news of the week is that Loncraine rings with a very positive reaction to the new script. He thinks it's an easier read and much funnier. Eight out of ten, he thinks, rather than six for the first one.

Monday, November 16th

I had to bestir myself and turn out, on an evening I dreadfully wanted to be in, to run the auction for Westfield College in Hampstead. Predictably chaotic student organisation, but on the whole very nice people. They gave me a list of nearly 100 items to be individually auctioned.

The slave auction at the end *was* fun. Boys offering their services to do anything for 24 hours. Girls offering massage. I won that myself – with a bid of £23.00. Finally I had to auction my own face, on to which anyone could push a custard pie. Not once, but five times. Collected nearly 30 quid for this alone. All the pies were delivered by girls, and the last two gave me kisses through the foam!

Thursday, November 19th

At six o'clock take Willy and Tom to the Circus World Championships on a common in Parsons Green. This is a Simon Albury trip – his present to Willy on his 11th birthday.

It's mainly a TV event with cameras all over the place and a wonderful BBC floor manager squashed into a very tight-fitting evening dress with white socks on and an arse so prominent it looks like a caricature of Max Wall. Simon has secured us seats right by the ring – so we can see the sweaty armpits, the toupees and the torn tights that the viewers at home will miss.

The things I like least about circuses are animals and clowns and there are neither tonight. Instead about a dozen different varieties of balancing act. Russians holding ladies doing headstands on top of a 20-foot pole balanced on their forehead, petite Chinese ladies who throw (and catch) coffee tables from one to another with their feet. A Bulgarian boy who jumps backwards off a springboard and lands on the shoulders of a man, who is in turn on the shoulders of three other men.

The virtuosity on display is dazzling. One Polish woman can do a double backward somersault off a pole and land on the pole again. Dangerous area for punning.

In the middle of it all Willy has the evening made for him by being called out by the ringmaster as a birthday boy. There in the middle of the ring in the middle of the Circus World Championships, Willy publicly declares his support for Sheffield Wednesday! We don't get back until 11.00. Boys tired and happy and I hungry.

Saturday, November 21st

Time Bandits is No. 1 grossing film in the US almost exactly two years after *Brian* held the top spot. I still can't get over a sense of awed surprise. US new releases are falling like nine-pins. The brightest successes, apart from *Time Bandits*, are *Chariots of Fire*, still only on limited release, and *The French Lieutenant's Woman*, which is going well, but not spectacularly. Three English movies setting the pace.

George rings. He's got my *Missionary* script – but said he'd do the film just from the letter I sent with it! What *did* I say? He does express a worry as to whether *The Missionary* will interfere with the Python film and says he doesn't want to be the cause of any split in Python. As I told TG later, this didn't sound like a spontaneous George H concern. I mustn't get paranoid, but it suggested to me that someone somewhere was trying to shut down *The Missionary* for unspecified reasons.

Monday, November 23rd

Richard Loncraine rings early. He just wants to talk and make sure we are still happy. I give my usual reassurances, though I must admit I haven't had time to read the script for a week! RL's main concern seems to be making a movie that will be noticed – especially in the States. I tell him that, with *Time Bandits*, *Chariots of Fire* and *The French Lieutenant's Woman* doing good business over there, they are just ready for a beautifully photographed, sensitive portrayal of Edwardian period life, full of belters.

I hope he's convinced. I know it will be better when people are signed and the movie is an established fact, but at the moment I feel the strain of dealing with bigger egos than I became used to at the BBC – where people were just falling over themselves to get near a 'Ripping Yarn'!

Wednesday, November 25th

To Park Square West for Python writing. Very cold today. The house in which Python has been through so much now has a beleaguered air. As

Anne and family have moved out to Dulwich it's now just an office, and a temporary one at that. But we are well looked after. Jackie [Parker] scurries about making us coffee, setting out biscuits and nuts and putting Tabs for Graham and Perrier for the rest of us in the fridge. The result is that we ingest steadily. Anne even ensures that a plate of sweets – Glacier mints, chewing gum and Polos – is on the table after our quiche and salad lunch.

Usual desultory chat – about *Brideshead*[1] on TV again – generally agreed it's overblown. TJ wants to talk about sex or get angry about the way Thorn-EMI have put *Brian* onto video, cropping it for TV. John will suddenly call me over: 'Mickey. Tell me what books you've read in the last four months.' Today I give him Al Levinson's *Travelogs* to read. It sends him quite apoplectic. He cannot understand how people can write modern poetry. 'It makes me quite Fawltyish,' he cries.

We proceed well on a general pattern and order of sketches. But at one point the Oxford/Cambridge split, avoided most successfully for the rest of this week, suddenly gapes. The point on which we argue is not a major one, but John rationalises his obstinacy as being the result of his grasp of 'the structure'. It's hard work, but in the end he wins his point.

I find myself telling TJ that I shall be mightily relieved when this next Python film is done and out of the way and we don't have to write together for another four years.

Monday, November 30th

Full of Monday hope and optimism, I launch into Python writing. Feel much less rushed, muddled and negative than on Friday.

To Covent Garden for a special tenth anniversary meal given by Geoffrey and Eyre Methuen for the Pythons.

All of us are there, as well as wives, except Alison Jones (who is out planning a campaign of action against school cuts). Anne and Jonathan, Nancy Lewis [our Python manager in America] and several Eyre Methuen types. A beautiful Gumby cake and indoor fireworks adorn the table in our own dining room.

Eric is in a suit, and myself too – otherwise all the Pythons look exactly

1 An 11-part adaptation of Evelyn Waugh's book had begun on Granada Television in October, and proved hugely popular. Jeremy Irons was Charles, Anthony Andrews Sebastian and Diana Quick Julia. Charles Sturridge directed.

the same as they always did. Graham [Sherlock] is there with David, and I sit next to John's new wife, Barbara. She says she desperately wants to take him back to LA for a few months, but he won't go as it gives him the creeps.

Tuesday, December 1st

Into Python meeting at 10.30. I read the large chunk that TJ and I have put together right from the start to beyond 'Middle of the Film' and into the 'randy' sequence – which goes exceptionally well. The whole lot is very well received and even applauded.

JC and GC have written some first-class stuff about an Ayatollah, but then one or two of their later scenes – especially a torture sequence – drags on and becomes a bore. Eric has written a couple of nice things and plays us a song he's recorded – 'Christmas in Heaven'.

We discuss which of the Pythons has talked the most in group activities since we began 13 years ago. John will have it that I'm the outright winner, but I think he greatly underestimates himself and, of course, Terry J. Graham happily accepts the Trappist sixth position, and when JC wants to know whether he or TJ talk most I have to say it's absolutely equal, because whatever statement one of them makes is almost automatically contradicted by the other.

Then much talk of where we go to write in January. GC wants to go to Rio for naughty reasons. I suggest a mountain chalet in cool, clear Alpine air. But swimming and associated aquatic releases are considered important. No conclusion. Except that we don't go to Rio.

Watch *Brideshead*. Halfway through, when Charles is just about to crack Julia, the doorbell rings and we're brought down to mundane earth with the news that the sun-roof on the Mini has been slashed open and the cassette/tuner has been ripped out. The police seem wholly unconcerned with the possibility of apprehending anyone. 'Be round in the next couple of days,' is their reaction.

Wednesday, December 2nd

TJ arrives at 1.30. Unfortunately only a small part of the section I'm rather proud of makes TJ laugh, so we ditch most of it and, in the two and a half hours remaining, cobble together a possible penultimate sequence, starting with the Ayatollah breaking into the sex lecture and the firing squad of menstruating women. It's mainly TJ's work.

Neville rings with the best news so far on *The Missionary*. Irene Lamb, the casting director who was so good on *Time Bandits*, has read the script and likes it 'immensely'. Clearly she's had a most positive effect on Neville. Tonight he says 'You know, Michael, I think that *very* little needs changing.' John Gielgud is available, and Irene has already made the best suggestion so far on the knotty problem of Lady Ames – Anne Bancroft.

Saturday, December 5th

Buy *Variety*, *Screen International* and croissants. All are nice. *Time Bandits* still No. 1 in the US after three weeks, with *Raiders of the Lost Ark* chasing behind.

I drive over to Notting Hill for meeting on *Missionary*.

Some very good ideas come from our session and I find RL's suggestions – especially for setting each scene somewhere interesting, trains, etc – very encouraging and exciting.

At half past five Denis O'B arrives, and we have our first meeting together – DO'B, RL, Neville and myself. I've brought a bottle of champagne with which we christen the film.

Then some thoughts on casting. RL floats Laurence Olivier, with whose wife he's working at the moment. Denis throws up his eyebrows in horror. 'He's a sick man!' This rattles RL a bit and nothing is solved.

I drive Hollywood's currently most successful executive producer back to Hyde Park Corner, in my Mini with the slashed roof lining hanging down above his head.

Sunday, December 6th

Time for quick breakfast. Drive rapidly, for it's a Sunday morning, over to Clarendon Cross.

Richard is already in his office with his business partner Peter Broxton. They're looking at Loncraine-Broxton toy ideas for 1982. Boiled sweets in a box which is a moulded resin mock-up of a boiled sweet wrapper.

We begin, or rather continue, our work on the *Missionary* script at half past nine and work, very thoroughly, without interruption, until midday. Careful concentration and analysis. This is the least funny, but very necessary stage of the script. Does it convince? Do the characters fulfil a function? Is there a moral? Is the story clearly told? And so on.

Monday, December 7th

Write a grovelling letter to Sir Alec Guinness, accompanying a script, then to meeting with Denis O'B. I'm there for nearly three hours. I try to keep our thoughts on *The Missionary*, to impress upon Denis that I think he has been over-optimistic in only allowing £1.6 million budget. He in turn tells me that it is the most expensive of the three films HandMade Productions are planning for 1982. Mai Zetterling's *Scrubbers* is £525,000 and *Privates on Parade* (with J Cleese) is £1.2 million. But he won't give me final cut in the contract – says only Python get that and Gilliam didn't on *Time Bandits*.

The dynamic and shifty-eyed duo of Jeff Katzenberg and Don Simpson[1] are back in town. But this time, over a drink and inexhaustible servings of nuts amongst the green fronds of the Inn on the Park lobby, they pitch to all of us, bar John Cleese.

Basically they don't want to lose out again as they did on *Brian* and *Time Bandits*. They want us badly and sugar this with rather unjustifiable statements of the 'You're better now than you ever were' variety. Unfortunately I have to leave at 8.30 before the 'nitty-gritty' is discussed, but I can feel the incorrigibly plausible double act beginning to soften the Pythons' notorious antipathy to Hollywood majors.

Tuesday, December 8th

All quiet. Everywhere. Even at eight o'clock. Helen the first to notice the snow. Everywhere. Not a sprinkling fast turning to slush, but a 14-carat four-inch-thick blanket of snow, which is still being quietly augmented from a low, heavy, colourless sky. Lovely to see Rachel at the window of the sitting room in her long nightie, unable to take her eyes off the wonder of it all.

Wednesday, December 9th

To a viewing theatre to see *Elephant Man*. A private showing, organised by Neville so we could see the most recent performance of Anne Bancroft.

---

1 In 1982, Simpson was superseded as head of production at Paramount by Katzenberg. He nevertheless went on to co-produce successes like *Beverly Hills Cop* and *Top Gun*. He lived hard and died of a drug overdose in 1996.

A very fine film. Admirable in its unsensational, underplaying treatment of the man. Some weird and wonderful images of London mark David Lynch out as a most original director. Almost unbearably moving for an hour, then somehow the attitudes became so clean – liberals versus working-class louts and drunks – that I lost some of the intensity of involvement which I had when [John] Hurt was a piteous, grunting creature being treated kindly for the first time.

I think Anne Bancroft could be too old and maybe too strongly dramatic. Lady A must have a skittishness ... a light, naughty side, of which, I think, youth may be a not inconsiderable part.

Friday, December 11th: Southwold

A cold grey morning. Helen rings to warn us of more heavy snowfalls in London, at least double what came down on Tuesday and it's still falling. Four people have been killed in a train accident in thick snow in Buckinghamshire and Ipswich Station has closed. So I decide to stay put.

Denis rings. He has given Loncraine the fee and percentage he asked for, but wants to defer L's last £5,000 until he's brought the picture in on budget. Loncraine refuses and won't even meet Denis until the deferment is sorted out. DO'B wants to be tough – walk away and let RL come running back to him – but fears that this will have a deleterious effect on relationships. I agree with this. I also think the money being fought over is so paltry in view of Loncraine's value to the project. So Denis reluctantly backs down.

All this over a crackly line from London, whilst next door, in my little writing room overlooking the snowswept fields, with the tiny two-bar electric fire, is my script and my scribbles, on which nearly £2 million-worth of expenditure depends.

Sunday, December 13th

As I write (7 p.m.), wind is flicking snow against my writing room windows, there are reports that blizzards have hit the South-West and the electricity has failed there too. A bomb has gone off in a car in Connaught Square, killing two, and there is a news blanket over the army take-over in Poland.

An almost apocalyptically gloomy day. The sort of day to make one question the point of writing comedy – or writing anything. Actually it also makes me feel, so far, comfortable, cosy and rather anxious to get on with work. But then I have money to afford light and heat and food and drink in abundance, and I have four other bright, lively, busy people in the house with me. I *am* one of the fortunate ones, this bleak, snowswept, wind-howling evening.

Monday, December 14th

Disappointment on the faces of the children as the snow has been whittled down to brown slushy piles. I have a clear work day at home. Neville rings – says he has budgeted *Missionary*, and it comes out at £2.5 million overall – £1.3 million beyond Denis's first figure and 0.5 million beyond the Loncraine estimate. But Neville very level-headed about it, says there are trims that can be made, but this is what he will present Denis with.

Wednesday, December 16th

Below freezing again – making this Day Nine of the very cold wintry spell. But clear skies. Work well on script in the morning.

To bed at 12.30. George H rang earlier in the evening. He was anxious that I would have to give up some of my *Time Bandits* money as a result of possible renegotiations and he didn't think I ought to. He was very flattering about my role in keeping the thing together. Very touched.

Monday, December 21st

The forecasted thaw in nearly two weeks of freezing weather did not materialise and we wake to thick, swirling snow, two to three inches deep, which has once again caught everyone by surprise.

Go to see *Chariots of Fire*, as I'm dining with Puttnam tomorrow. A very fine and noble film – like a sophisticated advert for the British Way of Life. Some marvellous, memorable sequences and a riveting performance by Ben Cross as Harold Abrahams. I came out feeling as I used to when we saw films like *Dambusters* 25 years ago.

Found disturbingly similar sequences in *Chariots* and *The Missionary*, and also began to get colly-wobbles about *Missionary* casting. Ian Holm and John Gielgud merely will emphasise how similar we are to other British films. But then we haven't got Ian Holm or Gielgud yet.

Tuesday, December 22nd

Very cold and gloomy with swirls of snow. Ice in Julia Street for a fortnight now.

Have lunch appointment with David Puttnam. Just about to brave the elements when Neville rings with the news that Gielgud has turned down the Lord Ames part. What stings me more is that there was no particular reason given – he just didn't want to do it.

I gave up the attempt to drive to Odin's and slithered down traffic-packed side streets. Puttnam about 20 minutes late. He's immediately friendly, open, and he does seem to know everybody, especially amongst the 'establishment' of TV and films – Alasdair Milne, Huw Wheldon. He meets them on all his committees. Nice story that Huw Wheldon was to have been in *Chariots of Fire*, but couldn't do it and was deputised at the last minute by Lindsay Anderson.

Puttnam talks at a clipped, brisk pace, as if there's so much to say and so little time to say it. I think he's proud of his success and his work rate – a revealing cliché about being 'just a boy from a grammar school . . .' He's complimentary about *Ripping Yarns* – thinks the toast scene in 'Roger of the Raj' one of the funniest things he's ever seen.

He's keen, almost over-keen, to talk business, and writes down the names of a couple of books I mention to him as filmable (*Good Man in Africa* and *Silver City*). He says Goldcrest Productions have a lot of money and promises to get one of the bosses to ring me re the financing of the next Python movie. He also sounds quite positive about *Greystoke*, with its £1 million forest set, coming to Shepperton.

Friday, December 25th: Christmas Day

And it is a White Christmas. The snow is not fresh, deep, crisp and even, but it's only a couple of days old and soon the clouds clear and give it a sparkling brightness – of the sort that is always depicted but never happens.

Tom opens his stocking at 2.30 and goes to sleep again, but we don't get jumped on until eight o'clock. A bedful of all the Palins (except Granny) as Helen and I undo our stockings.

Tuesday, December 29th

At one I have to drive into town for lunch with Ray Cooper to discuss his doing the part of the Bishop. Ray has laid on a lunch at Duke's Hotel, in a Dickensian side street off St James's and opposite 'The house from which Frédéric Chopin left to make his last public appearance at the Guildhall'.

Small, expensive, immaculately tasteful little dining room – rather in the Denis class of spending, though. A bottle of Corton Charlemagne, oeuf en gelée (rather tasteless) and some very delicious fegato alla Veneziana. We talk about casting of *The Missionary*. Ray's choices for Lady A would be Helen Mirren or Faye Dunaway – both strong on projecting sexuality. And he knows Dunaway.

Wonderful table-talk from the only other occupied table – 'I have a little Bulgarian.' 'There's quite a lot of jewellery Brenda doesn't wear all the time.' And things like this.

Up into Soho to meet Eric for a drink at the French Pub. The French is full of weird people, who seem already drunk when they come in. One man is kneeling on the bar trying to pull up the barmaid's skirt. It's all rather like being in a Chris Orr print.

Eric and I, in quite playful mood after the champagne, drive over to Claridge's where we are to meet Sherry Lansing, the studio head of Twentieth Century Fox, and the most powerful woman in American movies.

What Sherry Lansing offers us in Claridge's is much more straightforward and uncluttered by looks, whispers and double-talk than what Paramount offered us at the Inn on the Park. Twentieth Century Fox want the next Python movie and they are prepared to finance it and distribute it however and wherever we want. The board would give us complete control over its production unless they thought the script totally worthless. Tim Hampton would be Fox's representative and could be used as little or as much as we wanted. It was as clear and as positive as that. We told her she was making a big mistake and she laughed. I liked her very much. We said we didn't like *History of the World Part One* and she didn't seem to mind.

At 8.00, with a kiss on both cheeks, she left us and I took Eric back in my grubby little Mini and we decided that we should get drunk together more often.

Thursday, December 31st

Rather a miserable day on which to end the year. I feel quite a few degrees below good health. Nothing very dramatic, just aches and lethargy. This deterioration could not have come at a worse time, as I have Neville chasing me and Richard Loncraine returning from Wales, doubtless vital and restored by Christmas, to read with great anticipation the new script that I have put together. The final, very important twists and turns must be written today and tomorrow.

I set to, but lose quite a bit of time talking with Denis (from Switzerland) and Neville (about casting – he's suddenly strong on Ann-Margret).

I think I'm probably cleaning my teeth when 1982 begins. Helen and I see the New Year in without fuss – on fruit juice and Disprins, not champagne, for me. I hope the way I feel is not an augury for 1982, when, if all goes to plan, I shall need every scrap of energy.

1982

Sunday, January 3rd

Up at ten feeling fully restored and unbearably bouncy for a while. I take Rachel up to the playground on Parliament Hill. The sun's shining and it's very warm for early January. Lots of the attractions in the playground are empty or broken. It's a sadly declined place. This gentle, unambitious meandering walk up to the swings is something I haven't done much in the last three or four years, and it used to be de rigueur every weekend we spent in London, when the children were small. I forget that Rachel still is small.

We have a lovely time together, pottering, nattering, playing at trains in the Adventure Playground. It makes me sad and nostalgic – and this makes me cross, because I know I'm regretting being older – or getting older, anyway.

Monday, January 4th

To see Phoebe Nicholls, who was Cordelia in *Brideshead*, and who I'm recommended as a Deborah. Meet her in Langan's Brasserie. She's much slighter than I'd expected, with ringlets of curly dark hair, and big dark eyes, in a narrow little oval face.

I embark on a laborious explanation of the story and she watches in politely rapt attention. 'Oh, but it's lovely,' she says, as though it's a living thing. A baby or a new puppy. I instinctively feel that she will be interesting. She has a certain delicateness about her which I think will help convince the audience that she really *can* think Fallen Women are women who've hurt their knees.

Tuesday, January 5th

To EuroAtlantic Towers at 10.00 for a casting meeting re *Missionary*. Gielgud's rejection has left us with two less adequate possibilities of replacement – Donald Pleasance and Trevor Howard.

Perhaps our strongest advance in this morning's session was to eliminate any spectacular, but possibly dumb, beauties in favour of Maggie Smith – attractive, striking, skilful actress. Parts too, we hope, for Ronnie Barker and Ian Holm.

Friday, January 8th

Ominously quiet outside as we wake. Another heavy snowfall – the third already this winter and the papers are full of articles about The New Ice Age and the Frozen Eighties. It's thin powdery stuff blown all over the place by a bitter north-east wind. It's coming through the cracks in my study window and has covered Tom's homework books with a thin layer of snow.

We struggle up to William Ellis School at midday with William, for his interview with the headmaster. Have to sit in the corridor for 15 to 20 minutes with boys thundering by between lessons. Quite liked the atmosphere there. Am in my worst old jeans, sneakers and a windcheater – my father would never have entered the headmaster's study in less than a suit and spit-and-polished shoes.

Saturday, January 9th

Drive car out through snowdrifts and slither down into an agreeably empty London for a viewing of the *Hollywood Bowl* film – the first since Julian [Doyle] spent weeks trying to lick it into shape in LA. And it is greatly improved – linked far more smoothly and the sense of live occasion much stronger now there are better-chosen cut-backs to audience, etc. In short, a film which we now feel we will not be ashamed of. Performances very strong, particularly Eric.

Home by two o'clock. It really is so cold that all my systems seem to seize up. An hour in a catatonic trance before the sitting room fire improves things and I then set to with all the last-minute *Missionary* calls – to Richard and Denis (who has rung John Calley[1] in the US to ask whether he thinks Maggie Smith or Anne Bancroft would be the bigger box-office name. Calley told him neither meant a thing!) He says, as he puts it, I can have my head over Maggie Smith and he won't stand in my way.

---

1 Calley, a friend of Denis's, is one of the most successful producers in the film industry. He headed Warners and was later CEO of Sony Pictures, owners of Columbia.

Call George in Henley at nine o'clock. After a few rather terse exchanges he says 'You're obviously not a *Dallas* fan, then' and I realise I've interrupted a favourite viewing.

It had been decided that, as with The Life of Brian *and Barbados, we needed somewhere exotic to finalise the new film script; Jamaica had been chosen.*

Sunday, January 10th: Jamaica

Touch down in Montego Bay about 8.30. Soft, stifling blanket of hot, humid air takes me by surprise.

A large black limousine is backed up outside and Brian, our driver (why is there always a Brian wherever Python goes?), squeezes us all and luggage in.

About an hour's cramped and uncomfortable drive through the night along the north coast of the island. We turn into the drive of a long, low, unadorned rectangular mansion, called 'Unity', some time after ten o'clock. A youngish black man, Winford, and a middle-aged, beaming black lady, Beryl, come out to settle us in.

Our main problem is the selection of bedrooms. Four of the rooms, all off a long passageway/landing on the first floor, are splendid – spacious and well-furnished and one has a full tester four-poster. But there are three other rather small rooms, less well-furnished and clearly intended as children's rooms, annexed on to the main bedrooms.

So we sit in the grand downstairs sitting room, with a fine selection of polished wooden cabinets and Persian carpets, and wing-backed armchairs and some attractive maritime oil paintings, and draw our bedrooms out of the hat. J Cleese has been very crafty and claims there is only one bed which he, being so tall, can fit in, and that so happens to be in one of the 'master' bedrooms, so he isn't included.

Terry G and I pick the two sub-bedrooms. At least they all look across the lawn to the sea (about 100 yards away) and mine has a bathroom. A heavily stained bathroom with rotting lino and no hot water, but a bathroom all the same – though I share it with Mr Cleese, who has the big double bedroom of which mine is the 'attachment'.

Winford advises us not to swim tonight as there are barracuda which come in from behind the reef at night-time. This puts a stop to any midnight high-jinks, though Terry J goes and sits in the sea. But it's a lovely night with a big full moon and, apart from the inequality of rooms, I think Unity will serve us well.

GC is quietly puffing away as we sit outside. He looks like any trustworthy GP. But his pipe is well-stocked with Brian's ganja.

Monday, January 11th: Unity, Runaway Bay, Jamaica

I sleep very little. Possibly three and a half to four hours. Doze and listen to the sea. I sit up, turn on the light and read our script at 5 a.m. It's light just before seven and I walk outside, having unlocked my room door and the heavy iron doors at the top of the stairs and then the iron and wood double doors out to the garden. Clearly this property is a target.

The house is right beside the sea, only a lawn and a few trees between us and the Caribbean – and the trees are healthy-looking and have leaves of many and rich colours. The house is kept spotless, and already the leaf-scratcher is removing the six or seven leaves that have fallen on the patio overnight. The house is not so grand as Heron Bay [the villa in Barbados where we worked on *Life of Brian*] – there are no soaring Palladian columns. Its simple shape and plain limestone construction dates, they say, two or three hundred years back, when it was the chief house on the Runaway Bay plantation. The mountains rise up behind the house and across to the west.

I sit at the table and read my script. There are one or two young black boys hanging around the beach. One of them comes over and sits down and introduces himself as Junior and offers me ganja and a trip to see Bob Marley's grave. He says he's 19 and he grows his own pot up in the mountains.

Run up the beach as far as the Runaway Bay Hotel and back. Nearly a mile. Then a swim in the limpid, lukewarm waters of the Caribbean.

Breakfast is good coffee, fresh grapefruit and eggs and bacon and toast from very boring sliced bread.

Everyone's reactions to the script are then discussed. All of us, to some extent, feel disappointed. I think the material is still very static. It could still be a radio show. The rain seems set in for the day as we sit around for a long afternoon discussion session.

It's agreed that we should proceed from the material we have and create a strong story or framework to contain it. Some silly moments in this free and fairly relaxed session – including a title from TG, 'Jesus's Revenge'. But though everyone occasionally flashes and sparkles nothing ignites.

Supper is early – about 6.30. We've bought in some wine from the supermarket across the road and we have a delicious starter of fish mixed with akee fruit – a little black, olive-like fruit off one of the garden trees.

Then a group of us go up to the Club Caribbean next door. A black lady pinches Graham's bottom and GC altruistically turns her over to TJ. It turns out she is a hooker. She looks a nice, open, smiley lady, and keeps dropping her price in a determined effort to interest any of us. As TJ finally leaves, empty-handed, she asks him for two dollars.

Wednesday, January 13th: Jamaica

An early breakfast, and splitting into groups by 9.30. Terry J and Terry G, Eric and JC, myself and Graham.

GC and I, however, soon find ourselves in one of the most bizarre and distracted writing sessions of all time. Beryl, the cook, was under the impression that someone would take her up to the market, eight miles away, for all the provisions she will need for the Jamaican food we've asked her to produce. So GC and I decide to take her and work on the way.

It starts quite well as we drive up winding mountain roads for a half-hour and emerge into a busy little township with a stout stone Anglican church set in the middle of it. GC and I make a quick shopping sortie for shoes and swimming trunks then back to the car. Vegetables in the back, but no Beryl.

Still talking over our idea for a John Buchan-type story framework, we have a Red Stripe beer in a small bar. Beryl comes back and deposits fish, but then has to sally back into the market for yams.

Halfway down the perfectly named Orange Valley, beside stone walls and almost classic English parkland, is an akee-seller. We skid to a halt. When we proceed again we not only have akees, but also two black boys who want a lift. Stop at the supermarket for bully beef, and our writing session finally turns into the gates of Unity two and a half hours after we set out.

I ring Rachel and wish her a happy seventh birthday in still-frozen London.

After lunch we sit and present our ideas. I present GC's and mine. A breathtaking, marvellously choreographed musical overture all about fish – with us in spectacular fishy costumes. Then into an exciting Buchan mystery tale, involving strange disappearances, unexplained deaths, all pointing to Kashmir. The hero would have to unravel the story by various clues, which bring in our existing sketches.

John and Eric have taken the view that the film is primarily about sex and they've reinstated the Janine/girls' paradise idea that I'd gone off a year ago. Even less response to this idea.

TG and TJ have gone back to first Python principles to link it – a rag-bag of non-sequiturs and complex connections. It's full and frantic and, when TJ's finished describing it, there is silence. It's as if no-one can really cope with any more 'solutions'. As if this is the moment that this material – the best of three years' writing – finally defeated us.

I take Eric's advice and we walk up to the Runaway Bay Hotel and sit on the terrace there and have three very strong rum punches and get very silly and laugh a lot and devise the idea of a Yorkshire Heaven, in which Yorkshiremen are revealed to have been the chosen people.

Thursday, January 14th: Jamaica

Wake to sunshine and a feeling that today is make-or-break for the film. We certainly cannot continue stumbling into the darkness as we did yesterday.

TJ says that, from the timings of the sketches we all like alone, we have over 100 minutes of material. This seems to spur people into another effort. TJ suggests a trilogy. The idea of a rather pretentious Three Ages of Man comes up and a title 'Monty Python's Meaning of Life', to which Eric adds the sub-head 'See it now! Before it's out of date'.

We decide to group the material together into phoney pseudo-scientific headings – 'Birth', 'Fighting Each Other' and 'Death'. Suddenly ideas come spilling out and within an hour there seems to be a remarkable change in the film's fortunes.

Friday, January 15th: Jamaica

Writing has definitely taken a turn for the better. Eric, TJ and I in the big room make some encouraging progress on linking the 'War'/'Fighting Each Other' section. TG stands on a sea-urchin just before lunch. He's in some agony for a bit and has about nine or ten black quills in his heel. Doc Chapman ministers to him. Neville T rings from London to say the

[*Missionary*] script is probably two hours long. When I tell the Pythons that Sir Laurence Olivier has never heard of us, he is heaped with abuse.

Out to dinner with Jonathan and Shelagh Routh.[1] This involves a convoy into Ocho Rios and beyond.

Rather characterful house, very different from the mansion of Unity. It's a collection of wood-framed cottages, set on the edge of a low cliff down to the sea. Foliage everywhere. About 20 people amongst the foliage. An Australian diplomat – who, at 25, seems to run their High Commission – his Texan wife, who seems bored with Australian diplomacy. There's an English artist called Graham, tall and rather aristocratic, a French/Australian who writes novels and tells me that Jamaica is a very restless society and not what it seems on the surface. Much resentment of whites.

On my way from the Rouths' a man in khaki tries to hitch a lift, but I speed on. Only later do I realise I've driven straight through an army roadblock.

Saturday, January 16th: Jamaica

Snooze a little, watch Eric doing Tai Chi on the lawn, then breakfast at 9.00, and set to with Eric and TJ to put the last section of *The Meaning of Life* into shape. Not very inspired work and we get rather bogged down on the 'Christmas in Heaven' song.

At 4.30 everyone returns from various postcard-writing, T-shirt-buying trips to read through work assembled over the last three days. JC and GC and TG have come up with a tremendously good, strong opening set in a hospital during the birth of a child, and there is only one section of the film about which people have doubts.

The *Meaning of Life* theme and structure does seem to have saved the film and justified our being here. There are now tightenings and improvements to be done and songs to be written and these will occupy us for our four remaining writing days. Tomorrow we have off.

A beautiful 'zebra' butterfly flutters around us as we read. A good omen, perhaps.

---

1 Jonathan Routh introduced and presented the enormously popular *Candid Camera* TV series in the 1960's. He died in 2008.

Monday, January 18th: Jamaica

GC announces at breakfast, after one of his regular and interminable phone calls to London, that he is going to sue Denis O'B. This causes a few dropped jaws over the toast and marmalade. Apparently GC, having enlisted the help of Oscar Beuselinck[1] to try and buy back the *Yellowbeard* rights from Denis, who keeps increasing his demands and conditions, has just heard that Beuselinck has found enough ground for negligence in Denis, and Anne, to proceed with a lawsuit. As GC says, the shit has hit the fan in London.

All of us are concerned that Anne should not be hauled over the coals – especially as she has been doing everything to try and improve GC's financial position over the last few months by getting the rest of us to withhold payments, etc. But GC lights his pipe in determined fashion and sounds terse and unmoving.

Late lunch, and at 4.30 Jonathan and Shelagh Routh arrive to collect and lead us to a place called Round Hill, where a friend of theirs is laying on a beach party for us.

Pleasant, countrified drive, avoiding mongooses which are apt to suddenly scuttle across the road. When JC returned from his trip to Kingston and said he'd passed four dead dogs and a calf, GC speculated that journey distances in Jamaica could be categorised quite usefully as a 'two dead dog journey' or a 'three dog, one pig journey'.

Round Hill turns out to be an estate of luxurious holiday homes set on a headland with very beautiful views. We are taken to a little house higher up the hill, set amongst the trees, for a party given by 'a prominent Washington horsewoman'. She welcomes us with a bright, quick, sympathetic smile and sincere handshake. Her long blonde hair is swept up on top of her head most dramatically, but giving the physical impression that her face has somehow been swept up as well and is pinned painfully somewhere in the scalp. She wears a long white dress. I am in running shorts – thinking only that we were coming to a beach party.

JC lies flat on his back on the grass at one point, worrying the hostess who thinks he's passed out drunk. He is in a wicked mood and clearly hates these sorts of people.

---

1 Prominent and flamboyant entertainment lawyer, whom Python had consulted after Bernard Delfont and EMI had pulled out of *Life of Brian* at the last minute.

Tuesday, January 19th: Jamaica

In the afternoon we read what has been done so far. JC and GC's 'Death' sequence is not in the same class as their marvellous 'Birth' opener of last week, so everyone becomes disconsolate again. It's too late in the afternoon to whip up much enthusiasm, so a rather important day peters out.

The two Terries and I accept Winford's invitation to go to a local birthday party celebration.

We walk about half a mile up to Bent's Bar. It's 8.30 and a four-piece Jamaican band – rhumba box (home-made and very effective), a thumping banjo, a guitar and a high-pitched, effective little singer. He looks well-stoned by 8.30 and, as the evening goes on, he becomes progressively more incoherent until he ends up clearing the tables whilst some imitator takes his place in front of the band.

The birthday is of Mr Bent, a large, paternal-looking black with greying frizzy hair, who introduces himself to Terry with a broad smile, a firm handshake, and the words 'Hello, I'm Bent'. He, like most others we've met, either has been to England or has relations there. I note that not even the most courteous Jamaicans have said anything about their relatives enjoying England.

Wednesday, January 20th: Jamaica

There isn't a lot to do but type up. It's decided to meet in London for three days in mid-February and then to take a final decision on whether to go ahead.

No-one, I think, feels we have a *Brian* on our hands, but there is a hope that we have something which we all feel we could film in the summer.

And so to bed, for the last time, in my 'servant's' quarters.

Sunday, January 24th

Late afternoon settle to read *The Missionary*. It is indeed a hefty script – 149 pages, and closely written, too. Glad to find that my own notes for cuts correspond by and large with Neville's and those suggestions of Penny Eyles[1] who timed the script. Neville rings, anxious to know when I can produce the 30-minute shorter version.

---

1 One of the most sought-after script supervisors in the UK. She'd worked with me on Stephen Frears' *Three Men in a Boat* and on *Monty Python and The Holy Grail*.

Tuesday, January 26th

There has been good news this morning – Maggie Smith likes the script and wants to meet. Apparently her comment was 'The fellers get the best lines, so I want the best frocks.'

Opening of Eric's *Pass the Butler* at the Globe. Crowd of celebrities and celebrity-spotters throng the cramped foyer as this is first night. Meet Lauren Hutton, model, actress and, as it turns out, world traveller. 'Ask me about any island,' she challenges. I catch her out with the Maldives. But she does seem to have been everywhere and is going to give us some information on Sierra Leone [which we'd chosen for a family winter break]. She advises us to have every possible injection there is.

Wednesday, January 27th

Down to the Cavendish early for the rest of my inoculations. Young male doctor this time, with vaguely jokey patter. He arranged in a line all the various syringes, then went to work. Tetanus followed typhoid and cholera into my upper left arm, then he stuck gamma globulin in my left buttock and waggled it about (the buttock, not the gamma globulin).

Back home for another two hours' work on the script, then down to the London Library. There is a two-day rail strike on as train drivers battle against BR Management's latest 'modernisation' plans. Park in St James's Square, and select some books on East African missionaries amongst the labyrinthine passageways and dark back rooms of this eccentric library. I get lost in the Topography section and can't find Uganda.

Come away at half past five armed with such gems as *In the Heart of Savagedom*.

I'm outside the Berkeley Hotel, where we're to meet Maggie Smith, a quarter of an hour early.

I realise that this meeting with Maggie Smith is one of the most crucial on *The Missionary* so far. She is the first 'name' we seem to have a chance of securing, and her part is the most crucial in the film apart from my own. She knows nothing about me, yet is expected to help create with me the complex relationship that is at the heart of the story.

She arrives about ten minutes late. Reminds me of Angela somehow – with her neat, almost elfin features. She is dressed expensively and with a hint of flamboyance and her red hair looks as though it's just been done. Which leads me to wonder, just for a moment, if she had taken all this trouble for the meeting.

I congratulate her on her *Evening Standard* Actress of the Year Award [for *Virginia*], which she won last night. She looks rather weary but she has an instantly likeable naturalness and there is no difficulty in feeling that one's known her for ages.

She was very cross that the 'fellers get the lines, I want the frocks' line had been quoted to us, and claims she never said that. She was a mite worried about Olivier as Lord Ames – and in a polite but unambiguous way made it clear she regards him as having a 'very odd' sense of humour (i.e. none).

Richard arrived, bubbling like an excited schoolboy. His keenness seemed like over-enthusiasm at times, especially contrasted with Maggie Smith's languor. She drank vodka and tonic and we drank Löwenbräus. I settled into the sofa, also affected by her calm. She had no problems, she said, about the script, and when we left, after an hour together, she kissed me warmly and her face lit up again and she congratulated me once more on the script and was gone.

Thursday, January 28th

Take an hour and a half for a run. The Heath chilly, muddy and grey. Then down to Broadcasting House, to which I have been invited to celebrate forty years of *Desert Island Discs*.

I arrive in the Council Chamber, a semi-circular room above the main entrance, just as a group photo is being taken. About 20 cameramen, and television video cameras photographing little dapper Roy Plomley, who sold the series to the BBC the year before I was born.

Clustering around him I can see the Beverley Sisters – all dressed alike – Michael Parkinson, not a hair out of place, Frankie Howerd, Lord Hill.[1] It's like being at Madame Tussaud's. I'm hustled into the far corner of the crowd, next to the tall, slightly shambling figure of Roald Dahl. 'Let's just hope they've got wide-angle lenses,' he observes unenthusiastically.

I have to go and sign a book to be presented to Mr Plomley. I see Roald Dahl sitting quite happily on his own, so I go and introduce myself and

1 Best known as the BBC's Radio Doctor during the Second World War, he became Chairman of the BBC, retiring in 1972. He died in 1989.

bother him with praise. He confides that a good 'standard' popular kids' book is the way to make money. A successful children's author will do a lot better in the long run than Graham Greene. We talk about children being over-protected by authors, and he tells me that he has received many letters of complaint about his books from teachers, and *Danny* [*Champion of the World*] is banned in Denmark because it 'teaches children to cheat'.

We're having a jolly conversation and have only been photographed once, when Dr Jonathan Miller looms up, being frightfully energetic and effervescent and solicitously enquiring after my future plans because he does want to get Pythons back on stage – not doing Python, but Shakespeare or whatever. (Interesting that J Cleese had come up with the idea in Jamaica of the Pythons doing a Shakespeare play together.)

Friday, January 29th

Drive up to Bishop's Stortford to talk to the school sixth form.

Questions routine and orderly until one boy rose and asked 'How difficult is it to get into the BBC if you're not gay?' I couldn't quite meet this with cool equanimity, but I got my best laugh of the afternoon by telling the boy that I was sure he'd have no problem getting in. 'That naughty boy Robertson,' as I heard him referred to quite endearingly in the staff room afterwards.

Neville rang to tell me Olivier has asked for a million dollars to play Lord Ames. Which makes a decision very easy. Not Olivier.

Thursday, February 11th

Down to the London Library to procure books on prostitutes. They are all filed under 'S' for 'Sex' and I can't for the life of me find the 'Sex' section. End up abjectly having to ask a girl attendant. 'I'm looking for Sex,' is all I can say.

In the evening Helen plays badminton. I go out to see *Arthur*. Dudley very funny – manages to make all his jokes and gags have that attractive quality of spontaneous asides. That rare thing – a comedy with laughs all the way through *and* a happy ending. Sets me to thinking about the *Missionary* ending.

Friday, February 12th

Drive down to Methuen to look over Caroline Holden's artwork for *Small Harry*. It's bright and full of life and though on occasion her attention to detail lapses and she loses a face or an expression, I'm really very pleased. Take her for a drink at the Printer's Devil in Fetter Lane. She finished the book up at her parents' house – Mum and Dad helping out. Caroline still poor and having to work in a pub to make ends meet. I do hope the book does well for her sake.

Monday, February 15th

Drive over to Clarendon Cross, arriving there at ten. Spend the day with Richard and Irene seeing 24 young ladies at 15-minute intervals to select from amongst them our Fallen Women. By 6.00 we've talked, laughed and explained ourselves almost to a standstill.

Home. Talk to Denis, who rings to find out how we got on with the prostitutes. (George H terribly keen to be there during auditions.) Terry G rings spluttering with uncontrollable laughter. He had just finished reading 'Mr Creosote' and had to tell someone how near to jelly it had reduced him.

Wednesday, February 17th

We see about 20 more actresses. A half-dozen are good enough for speaking parts – and the results of Monday's work and today's are very encouraging. But other clouds on the horizon – mainly financial. Richard thinks that the Art Department budget is impracticably small and both Richard and Neville told me yesterday that there is no way the present script can be shot in nine weeks. It'll need ten at the minimum.

All those things to think of as I drive to Anne's for an afternoon Python session. A strange feeling to sit at the table listening to other people's offerings without having had time to provide anything myself. JC/GC have put together a quite funny Grim Reaper piece. Eric has written a new opening song and a very short but effective visual before the 'Penis Apology'. Terry J has also been prolific.

At the very end of the meeting, just as I'm off to see Denis O'B, Anne tells us that Graham would like us to meet Oscar Beuselinck, the lawyer, tomorrow. Why Graham couldn't tell us I don't know. It's another bombshell from Chapman – who evidently is still going to sue Denis and wants us all to meet Oscar tomorrow and hear the whys and wherefores. All more than a little irritating.

Thursday, February 18th

Decide I shouldn't go to Graham's meeting with Oscar Beuselinck. Lawyers on the warpath are a dangerous breed and I am concerned that attending a meeting called specifically to point out all the bad points of Denis O'B may not be the best thing to do when I'm currently trying to get an extra £500,000 out of him. And Oscar would be only too keen to say he'd 'met with the Pythons'.

I have an hour or so of the afternoon left for writing before TJ arrives. We compare notes, then he goes off to the GC meeting, whilst I carry on extending the 'Hotel Sketch'.

A meeting with Denis. DO'B clearly won't accept Neville's latest budget figure of £2.5 million, but on the other hand he is not asking us to reduce, nor even stick at £2 million. He's now talking of £2.2 million. Our whole discussion is helped by the fact that Trevor Howard has accepted the part of Lord Ames. (Neville said he was especially keen to do it when he heard *I* was in it!)

Round to Clarendon Cross and then on to Julie's [Restaurant] for supper. We go through the script – take out the dockside sequence, which has some jokes but is very expensive, and also one or two short exteriors, and we find that we can still make cuts without irreparably damaging the film. Indeed, we have one very positive new idea, which is to open on a school honours board with the name being painted out.

Tuesday, March 2nd

Best news of last week is that Michael Hordern, who was reported to have turned down the part of Slatterthwaite, has now had second thoughts, likes the script, finds it 'immensely funny' and has been signed up. So Moretonhampstead, with Maggie Smith, Trevor Howard and Michael Hordern, is looking like a quality household.

Wednesday, March 3rd

Assailed with information (Irene), opinions (Richard) and warnings (Neville) on all sides as we attempt to cast the medium and small parts. Any featured (i.e. speaking) actor has, under a new Equity agreement, to be 'bought out' – i.e. given enough pay to make up for the actor relinquishing rights on future TV, video and other sales. It boils down to a minimum of about £157.00 per day for a 'cast' actor. So the morning is one of continuous small compromises to cut down the use of such actors – a process which surely wouldn't please Equity if they saw it.

There are still some major roles unfilled. Graham Crowden has had a hip operation and may not be well enough to play the Bishop.[1] Richard suggests Denholm Elliott, other front-runners are Nigel Hawthorne and Ian Richardson. Elliott will be twice as expensive.

Ray Cooper comes over at lunch and meets Richard for the first time. They got on well, as I knew they would. Both are artists, and indeed Ray C endears himself to Richard by remembering him as a sculptor. Ray is to be Music Co-ordinator for *The Missionary*, which fills me with great confidence.

Bombshell of lunchtime, as far as Richard is concerned, anyway, is that Freddie Jones, for whom Richard was prepared to move heaven and earth to accommodate in the picture, now says he doesn't want to do it anyway. This has plunged Richard into a bad mood performance and he rails on about faithless actors and how shitty the entire thespian profession is. I blame his diet.

Friday, March 5th

Through exceptionally slow-moving traffic to Holland Park, to talk with Ken Lintott, who made my *Brian* beard and who is head of make-up on *The Missionary*. I've lost a lot of weight, he says. He wants me to try growing a moustache again.

---

1 In the end he took the part of the Reverend Fitzbanks, Fortescue's prospective father-in-law.

Wednesday, March 10th

Neville says we've no more money left. Everything is accounted for. There's no spare. But the cast we're assembling is most encouraging. Even Celia Johnson may be on again. She likes the script, but wants the name of her character changed, as one of her greatest friends is Lady Fermoy! Denholm Elliott, Graham Crowden and Peter Vaughan look certain. Fulton Mackay less so, as he has been offered five weeks by Puttnam on a new Bill Forsyth picture.

Richard rings. Denis will not agree to the test viewing clauses RL wants in his director's contract. In America it is standard in Screen Directors' Guild contracts that, should the producer want to alter the director's delivered cut, the director has the right to insist on there being two test screenings before audiences of not less than 500 people. Anyway Denis now says that this is out of the question. It's not really my problem, but I assure RL that I'll support him. He talks of leaving the picture, which I don't think is all that likely.

Thursday, March 11th

Work and run in the morning, then to Bermans to meet Trevor Howard. Find the great man in a first-floor dressing room, standing in stockinged feet half in and half out of a hound's-tooth tweed hunting outfit, surrounded by dressers and costume designers. To my surprise Howard strikes me as a diminutive figure. His full head of fine, carroty red hair stands out.

He gives me a rich, warm smile and shakes my hand as if he's really been wanting to meet me for ages. He talks sleepily and when after the fitting we suggest taking him out for a drink he brightens visibly. Though his breath already smells of alcohol, he says emphatically, 'Yes, why not! I've been on the wagon for three weeks and I feel *so* tired.' We take him down to Odin's. He has a gin and tonic, RL and I a bottle of Muscadet.

He keeps repeating how much he's looking forward to doing the part, though curiously, in the midst of all this enthusiasm, he expresses great concern over the brief little bedroom scene between Ames and the butler. He's very unhappy about any hint of homosexuality. We agree to talk about this later, and he leaves to collect his passport for a trip to China he's making for a British film week there.

Back to Bermans at 4.30 to meet Michael Hordern. He looks older and his face redder and veinier than I'd expected. He has a straggly beard – better advanced than my moustache – which he's growing for the BBC's *King Lear*. Quite eccentric in his delivery, and sentences tend to end abruptly and be completed with a sort of distinctive hand gesture. He says he can understand about Trevor Howard – worried about a 'machismo image' as Hordern puts it. The two of them worked together on *Heart of the Matter*, but Hordern is characteristically vague about the details.

Whilst at Bermans, Neville rings and asks to meet me as urgently as possible, as a problem has arisen over the credits. It transpires that Denholm Elliott wants star billing alongside Maggie S and Trevor H. I have no objection – I always tend to think that the problems start when people read the script and *don't* want a credit. But Denis won't have it.

Neville, who is in charge of negotiations with the artists, wants me to intercede with DO'B, who is skiing in Colorado at the moment.

Home for delayed supper at eleven o'clock, followed by three-quarters of an hour on the phone to DO'B in Colorado. The process of trying to change Denis's mind is like opening doors with a battering ram. Eventually they'll give, but one has to be prepared to patiently, insistently, repeatedly run at them from exactly the same direction each time.

Saturday, March 13th

It's a very bright, clear, sunny morning. Work in the garden, then take the children down to the London Dungeon. All three love it there – the frisson of fear is very cleverly maintained throughout, yet the place is not insidious or unpleasant. The victims of the rack and the murdered Thomas à Becket and the plague rats (live) all co-exist in a rather friendly, reassuring way.

Certainly all these dreadful horrors put all the children in a very good humour and we drive back across London Bridge to see the Barbican Centre, opened last week. It's a 'culture complex' within the Barbican estate. Approach, across a piazza, as they describe cold, windswept open spaces these days, to buildings that house the theatre, cinema, library and conference hall. In front of them is another 'piazza', with fountains and lots of captive water, which looks very green and stagnant and has napkins which have blown from the outdoor restaurant soggily drifting in it.

The place is full of lost people, and men with walkie-talkies looking anxious. The children love running up and down the stairs with mirrored ceilings or sitting in the comfortable new cinema. But at the moment it feels like a giant Ideal Home Exhibit, new and half-unwrapped and not at all integrated with the rest of the Barbican estate – on which one sees nobody. But then those who can afford flats in the Barbican can probably also afford second homes for the weekend.

To the BBC by 6.30 [for an appearance on *Parkinson*]. In a hospitality suite I talk to Parky and he runs through the questions. Researcher Alex accompanies me everywhere – even to the toilets. At 7.30 the recording begins. Jimmy Savile is on first, then there's a brief chat from Andrew Lloyd Webber and a song from Marti Webb, then I stand listening to my introduction on the filthy piece of backstage carpet which leads – cue applause – to the spotless piece of carpet the viewers see and a seat next to Parky.

Parky is much easier to talk to than Russell Harty – he's more relaxed and seems content to find out rather than turn fine phrases. I feel comfortable and am able to be natural – hence probably my best performance on a chat show yet.

Donald Sinden comes on third and when, in his rich, plummy RADA voice, he refers, with some pride, to meeting Lord Alfred Douglas, Jimmy Savile says "oo?". Sinden doesn't seem to mind being interrupted that much, but Parkinson affects mock-headmasterly gravity and banishes Savile and me to 'sit with the girls' [the backing singers for the band]. Probably to his surprise, and certainly to the surprise of most of the cameras and the floor manager, we do just that. We so upstage Sinden's interview that he is asked back on again next Wednesday.

Afterwards I chat to Andrew Lloyd Webber, who gives me his phone number as he lives right beside Highclere House, where we're filming the Fermoy scenes. He also asks if I write lyrics! Savile drops the information that he is paid more to do his ads for the railways than Sir Peter Parker is for running them.

Sunday, March 14th

Up to Abbotsley for Granny G's 69th birthday. I take Granny a life-size cardboard replica of Margaret Thatcher (whom she hates), some flowers and a bottle of Vosne Romanee '64.

Grand football match on the back lawn by the barn. Rachel, Auntie Catherine and me v the two boys. We lose on penalties. Rachel quite fearless in the tackle. Leave for home at 6.00.

Monday, March 15th

To BUPA House to have a pile injected. A not very painful, but strangely uncomfortable sensation. As I lay curled up, proffering my bum, I remembered that this was the first day of the *Romans in Britain* High Court trial.[1] How suitable.

Wednesday, March 17th

Donald Sinden appears for the second time on the *Parkinson* show, armed with blunderbuss and whip. Parky seeks to make light of Saturday's 'incidents' and Sinden says that his children thought Saturday's programme very funny – and a 'classic Parkinson'. The whole episode has achieved some notoriety, as if Jimmy Savile and I had broken some unwritten rule, that no-one should enjoy themselves on *Parkinson* when someone else is plugging their latest product.

Friday, March 19th

To Dorney Reach near Maidenhead, to look at the rectory.

Much readjusting of thoughts, but, again, after a prolonged, concentrated and wearing debate, we settle on the exact shots. Neville dictates rather tersely into his pocket recorder as RL orders lighting towers and mock walls, etc. I admire RL for his endless enthusiasm for filling frames and his refusal to scale down *his* vision of the film. Neville hints darkly that Monday, when the heads of departments put their bills in, could be a day of reckoning.

Back from Dorney to buildings around St Pancras and King's Cross. A rooftop on some condemned flats will be the Mission roof.[2] Wonderful period panoramas of Industrial Revolution Britain, but not too easy to enjoy them as steady drizzle comes down, putting a fine twist of unpleasantness on an already cold and prematurely dark evening. After recceing brothels and walking shots, we pack up about a quarter to seven.

1 Howard Brenton's play, produced by the National Theatre in 1980, contained scenes of simulated anal rape. Mary Whitehouse, the morality campaigner, brought a private prosecution against the production. She later withdrew from the case.
2 Culross Buildings stood defiantly until the summer of 2008, when they were destroyed for the King's Cross redevelopment.

Monday, March 22nd

A long Python film meeting.

The apportionment of parts, which took us a couple of very good-humoured hours after lunch, is such an important moment in the creation of the film; we've been writing for three and a half years, and yet the impact of the movie for audiences is probably far more affected by what happened in the 75 minutes at Park Square West this afternoon.

I don't think there are any rank sores or festering injustices, though TJ thinks Eric may have wanted to do the end song, which has gone to Graham – doing a Tony Bennett impersonation!

Universal have few qualms about giving us the money – three million dollars up front, assuring us each of over £150,000 by the end of the year, well before the movie goes out. Python has never had better terms.

Tuesday, March 23rd

Parkinson programme calls up to ask if I will present an engraved shovel to Parky at a special surprise party to mark the end of his last BBC series next Wednesday. [He's a great fan of the shovel-owning Eric Olthwaite from *Ripping Yarns.*] I must have been rehabilitated!

Wednesday, March 24th

To Upper Wimpole Street to see a specialist about the ache in my ear. He rather throws me by asking if I've come about my nose. I feel myself falling into a Python sketch . . .

'My nose . . . No.'

'It's just bent to the right, that's all . . .'

'Really?'

'Oh yes, but nothing serious. Let's talk about the ear . . . '

(Pause)

'You don't have any trouble with the nose . . . ?'

'No.'

'Well, I should leave it then.'

With Laurel and Hardy in the garden. I bought them off a market stall on Canal Street, New York. Hardy's neck broke in the plane's luggage locker.

'Take Rachel on a mystery tour. By lucky chance there is a raising of the bridge as we are there. Watch from an abandoned little jetty upstream from the Tower' October 27 1984

Tom with Denis the cat.

The eternal dream. By a pool, with a book, somewhere hot. Kenyan holiday, January 1983

'I've got to have fruit!' Tied to a tree with Shelley Duvall, as Vincent and Pansy in *Time Bandits*, 1981

Shooting the *Time Bandits'* Giant on the roof of Wembley Studios. Among those looking bored, Maggie Gilliam and Julian Doyle on camera.

Pythons in Hollywood. MP, Terry J, Eric I, Graham C, Terry G and John C. Behind us, the Bowl. September 1980

On the set of *Time Bandits*. (left to right) Neville C Thompson, Associate Producer, John Cleese (Robin Hood), George Harrison and Denis O'Brien, Executive Producers. Summer 1980

Monty Python Live at The Hollywood Bowl, September 1980

John rehearses his Silly Walk.

Dead Parrot sketch always went down well. Never more so than with the performers.

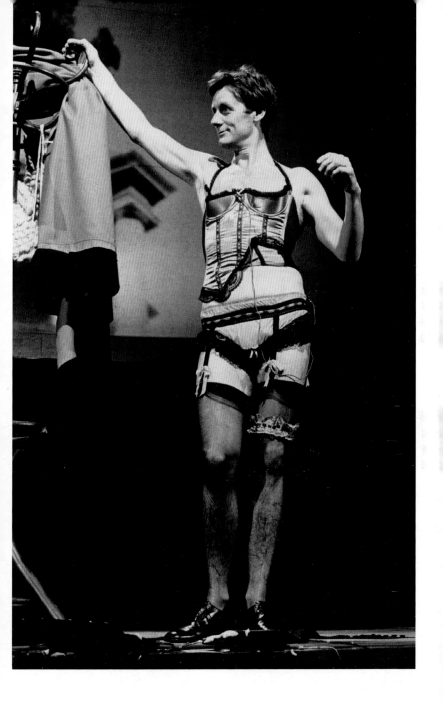

Disrobing after the judge's summing up.

The Missionary, 1982

Fortescue and his women. Caught between fiancée Deborah Fitzbanks (Phoebe Nicholls, left) and Lady Ames, benefactress, (Maggie Smith, right)

Nepotism at work. Rachel Palin, (centre), on the set at Finsbury Circus, April 24 1982

'No people, no sun-oil, no deck-chairs, no poolside bars selling over-priced drinks'. Bathing in the waterfall at Shava Lodge after the Kenya shoot, June 13 1982

'As I wait for the clouds to clear the sun,
I see our two Executive Producers emerging
from the orchard'. Richard Loncraine, director,
George H and Denis O'Brien on location,
May 1 1982

John Kelleher of HandMade (centre)
and I collect our most cherished, and
only, award, from the French town of
Chamrousse. 'I check in the atlas.
It does exist' March 26 1985

Charles Fortescue,
man with a Mission.

Missionary publicity. Judging, and participating in, a custard pie throwing contest at the Southern Methodist University, Dallas, Texas, October 7 1982

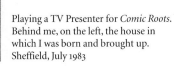

Playing a TV Presenter for *Comic Roots*. Behind me, on the left, the house in which I was born and brought up. Sheffield, July 1983

Thursday, March 25th

Only the continuing gorgeous weather keeps me going. After yet another all too brief night's sleep, I'm up to grab some breakfast and leave for a recce to Longleat[1] at eight o'clock. Somewhere on the way to look in the car I collect a large evil lump of sticky, smelly dogshit on my shoes, and I've transferred it all over the house. I resign myself with ill grace to missing breakfast and set to to clean it up, but can find no disinfectant.

At this point I crack and fly into a helpless state of rage, banging the dressing table in the bedroom so hard that Helen wakes up thinking World War III's started, tearing my shoe off and generally behaving quite hysterically. It's a combination of the pressure of work – burning the candle at both ends – and the lack of time I've had to talk to Helen about everything that's happening. But it passes, I'm collected by Brian, H forgives me before I go and I feel a storm centre has passed.

Richard drives me on to Longleat and we work and talk on the way. Arrive at midday. Take the guided tour, then meet with Christopher Thynne, the second son, who runs the house. Knows me from one of Eric Idle's parties, he says.

He came with Georgie Fame who broke a table.

He shows us wonderful passages. Bedrooms that are workable but a little small (all country house bedrooms it seems are a lot smaller than one would think). He shows us into Lord Weymouth's part of the house where garish paintings of all sorts of sexual endeavour cover the walls. He shows us the first printed book in England, a collection of Adolf Hitler's signed watercolours, plus a paper which has Adolf's signed approval of one of three designs for the Swastika symbol.

Sunday, March 28th

Leave for Abbotsley around 11.00. Sun shining in London, but mist is still thick as we drive up into Hertfordshire. Arrive at Church Farm at 12.30 – and I go for a last run for many weeks.

As I pound up the hill beside silent ploughed fields with the mist clinging around me like a cool refreshing blanket, I feel ready for *The Missionary* and ready for Python. I know in a sense that I'm entering a

---

1 Longleat House, an Elizabethan stately home which has been in the same family, the Thynnes, for over four hundred years. The head of the family is the Marquess of Bath.

tunnel from which I shall not emerge until October, at least.

I hit out at the air with my fists like a boxer, feeling ready.

Back to Abbotsley for lunch. The sun comes out. The boys play football. I teach Rachel to ride her bike, on the same stretch of road up to Pitsdean Hill on which I taught Willy, in the teeth of a storm, a few years ago.

Today in the still sunshine, Rachel's little triumph seemed to have greater significance. I sensed one of those special moments between us. We both felt so proud.

Monday, March 29th

Brian [Brookner] drives me in his red Mercedes to the National Liberal Club off Whitehall. First glimpse of the reality of *The Missionary* is a string of Lee Electric trucks parked in this quiet street. On the other side of the road Richard's Winnebago. Cables run across the pavement into the wide lobby of this once grand, marble-floored Victorian club.

The first time I appear as Charles Fortescue is in this lobby and, by almost eerie coincidence, the character is born beside a huge contemporary oil painting of Gladstone's first Cabinet, in the centre of which sits one C. Fortescue – a youngish man, not at all unlike the missionary I'm playing.

The conversion of the National Liberal Club's billiard room into a gymnasium has been stunningly successful. Opening shot is ready by ten, but the generator goes on the blink and we don't complete my entrance to the club until eleven.

As the slow pattern of waiting established itself, I nodded off twice. My cold continues to tumble out, but didn't seem to affect my mood or performance. Now that filming has begun I know I shall survive, but now it's a question of keeping standards high – and producing something better than anything I've done before (apart from the Fish Slapping Dance, of course).

Tuesday, March 30th

Lunch is a meeting with Geoffrey S, Richard, the stills photographer and myself, to discuss the book [of *The Missionary*]. Eat up in one of the vast, dusty galleries at the top of the building.

RL clearly feels GS is too cautious and GS does not react well to RL's expensive ideas for the book. I find having to conciliate the most tiring work of the day. It means no relaxation at lunch either and I have to rush down to do close-ups in the first real dialogue scene with Denholm.

Feel a surge of nerves as I wait to go on. I look round at this huge room, filled, just for me, with 30 period gymnasts. I look round at the 40 or so faces of the crew, all watching, waiting to see what I do. As if this isn't enough, I catch sight of Angela, Jeremy and Veryan up in the balcony, looking down.

I start to wobble. I have to go into this scene clutching briefcase, hat and full cup of tea. I'm convinced the tea-cup will rattle so much that I'll be asked to do it again – and that'll make it worse – and what am I doing here anyway? We do the shot, and I control the cup and the moment of blind panic passes, and I feel settled and refreshed and the rest of the day seems light and easy.

Up to Lee Studios to look at the first rushes. They look marvellous. [Peter] Hannan's lighting is of the very best – I've hardly ever seen my stuff looking so good. The various textures of the wood and tiles come across strongly and clearly. It looks interesting and gives everything in the frame a particular quality and to the whole an atmosphere you can almost smell and touch.

As to the performance – although Denholm does not do the Bishop as Graham Crowden would have done, he nevertheless comes over strongly on screen, and manages the mixture of comedy and seriousness very effectively.

I leave Lee's in great euphoria and raring to get on with the film.

Wednesday, March 31st

Picked up at the relatively civilised hour of 7.45. To Culross Buildings behind King's Cross and St Pancras. Marvellous location for trainspotters. The sky is grey and it's cold, but we start shooting without much ado amidst the flapping washing. First scenes with our prostitutes.

I have a small and rather tatty caravan, with a basin, but no running water, and a seat which shatters immediately I sit down. Denholm a little more together on his words today than yesterday at the club, but, like any actor, is bucked up tremendously by praise of any kind – and it helps him that I can enthuse so much over the rushes.

All goes ahead well until after lunch when the sun comes out, which makes the roof of the tenement buildings a much more agreeable place to be, but impossible to work on because of the light change. Go down to my caravan and sleep for an hour. After a two- or three-hour wait, RL decides to abandon shooting for the rest of the day on account of the sunshine. Denholm and I run tomorrow's scenes through.

Then off to rushes at Lee's and home for an hour before taking a taxi down to the Main Squeeze Club in King's Road, where M Parkinson's 'surprise' end of series party is to take place. I've rehearsed a little speech as Eric Olthwaite.

Arrive to find small, rather empty basement club. No-one I know. Parky arrives and is cheered, moderately, and at about 11.15 I'm asked to make the presentation. I'm shown onto a small stage, on which I'm blocked to view for half the people there. Then the microphone feeds back – whines and whistles – and I find myself having to make ad-libs with the likes of Kenny Lynch, Jimmy Tarbuck, Spike and Billy Connolly only feet away.

I survive, just, and there are laughs at the right places. Present the shovel to Michael Parkinson as 'The Second Most Boring Man in Yorkshire'.

Stay on at the club for about an hour. Talked to Michael Caine – about Maggie S mostly. 'She's brilliant,' he said, 'but watch her.' Told me I'd have to work hard to keep in the scene with her.

Then a hatchet-faced 'adviser' signalled discreetly to Caine that he should be moving on. I left soon too.

To bed about a quarter to one. Duty done. Slept like a log.

Thursday, April 1st

This morning it's raining. So for a couple of hours I sit in my caravan in Battle Bridge Road and catch up on work – e.g. reading page-proofs of *Small Harry and the Toothache Pills*.

At eleven it clears and we work steadily through the scene, finishing by six. Denholm takes a long while on his close-ups; his daughter's come to watch him. 'Amazing how difficult it is to act with one's family around,' Denholm confides, and, for a man who has made 73 films, he certainly doesn't seem to have the secret of instant relaxation.

After filming, which ends at 7.30 with a beautiful street shot with a background of the St Pancras gasholders silhouetted against a rosy dusk sky, and Peter H personally wetting the cobblestones to catch the evening light, I go with Irene in the Winnebago to talk over casting as we drive to rushes. The Winnebago has been dreadfully ill-fated this week, breaking down everywhere. And tonight is no exception. Richard curses modern technology roundly as we lumber up the Marylebone Road with the handbrake stuck on.

To rushes at Rank's executive viewing theatre in Hill Street, Mayfair. First glimpse of my relationship with the girls. It looks relaxed and unforced. Fingers crossed we've seen nothing bad so far.

Denis claims to have finalised a deal with Columbia for *The Missionary* and the latest news is that they are preparing a 1,000 print release in the US for late October. This is exhilarating, rather terrifying news.

Friday, April 2nd

Leave home at 7.30. We are filming at the Royal Mint in Tower Hill. Abandoned ten years ago, it has a fine classical main building (used in *Elephant Man*) and workshop outbuildings. A very satisfactory set up for my scene with McEvoy (Peter Vaughan) as we can use three levels and drive a Chapman Hoist into the interior courtyard and follow the actors down. It is our Healed Leper shot, really, one long developing shot.[1] Only here it is more satisfying and better used, as the various elements of the bottling factory are introduced as we walk. It ends with us passing a fully practical steam engine – driving three belt-drive machines, and a loading bay with period vehicle, as well as a horse and cart glimpsed out in the yard.

Peter and I walk through the scene at 8.15, but the first take is not until 3.50 in the afternoon.

It is very hard work for an actor to come in for one day and shine as expected, under great pressure of time. But Peter's performance is always word perfect and, though a little tighter and tenser than I'd hoped, he's still excellent and solid. After seven takes all sides are satisfied and we finish work at seven.

To the West End for dinner with Maggie Smith. Maggie is funny, much less made-up and more attractive than when I last saw her, and quite obviously looking forward to the thing immensely. She brushes aside any apologetic concerns RL and I have for the shooting schedule – which involves her first of all appearing at 5.45 a.m. on Monday up to her knees in mud on Wapping Flats.

---

1 Most of the 'Healed Leper' scene in *Life of Brian* was played in one shot, with camera operator John Stanier, a Steadi-Cam strapped to his body, walking backwards through 'the streets of Jerusalem' for some three minutes.

We go off, arms linked, past crowds clustering round a police-raided night club, the best of chums.

Saturday, April 3rd

I'm losing a sense of time already. I wake to my alarm and obediently swing my legs off the bed and make for the bathroom, like a battery hen. Shave, clean teeth, go downstairs to do exercises, dress up in the bedroom.

Brian [Brookner] arrives today at 7.50, and carts me away. Must, however awful I may feel, arrive in a jolly mood at the location – co-producer, actor and writer can't be seen to weaken. Actually, once up and about I feel fine and the only frustration of today is the length of time filming takes.

I'm at Ada's brothel, situated in the old Fish Office on the Railway Lands. From the brothel window, as I stand ready to be Charles Fortescue, I can see the trains slipping in and out of St Pancras.

A long wait whilst Peter H lights Ada's room. It has no outside light source, so he has to create this impression from scratch. Listen to the Grand National, in which a horse called Monty Python keeps up courageously before refusing at Becher's the second time around. Much more sensible than falling, I think.

At tea Angela, Veryan and Jeremy arrive. Tea in RL's Winnebago. Richard is one of the few directors who, after six consecutive, very full days of filming, can still bother to make tea for his star's family.

Sunday, April 4th

Breakfast in the garden and read, with a certain disbelief, the news that we are virtually at war with Argentina over the Falkland Islands. It seems a situation better suited to the days of *The Missionary* than 1982. It may feel unreal, but papers like the *News of the World* are howling for vengeance and Ardiles was booed every time he touched the ball for Tottenham yesterday.

Took Rachel and Louise to the swimming pool at Swiss Cottage and was just sitting down to evening 'Sunday lunch' of roast lamb and a bottle of Château Bellac, when the door bell rang and TG appeared, breathless for information on the first week of *The Missionary*. He wanted to know what had gone wrong and how far we were behind! Children behaved abominably (with the exception of Tom) at the meal as TG rabbited on.

Later Willy explained that he had founded a Get Rid of Guests Club.

TG is waiting for Stoppard to finish his involvements with Solidarity before beginning work on *Brazil*, for which TG has now signed a deal with an Israeli super-financier.

Monday, April 5th

Arrive at location in Wapping at 5.15.

God is very definitely with us this morning. The sun rises into an almost clear sky – with just a hint of cloud, to add contrast and perspective. There is a little wind and the Thames has a strip of still, reflecting water across it, ruffled into the softest ripples on either side. It is a perfect dawn and, as the sun and the river rise, we film hard for three hours and a half – from 6.15 until nearly ten, when our last reaction shot of the little boy – 'Will it be a mission?' – is shot with water lapping around the camera legs.

This was Maggie Smith's first day. She uncomplainingly began work on *The Missionary* standing in a foot of muddy Thames water, pulling a ship's wheel out of the slime, and managed to smile winningly and help us push the barrow over wet and slippery rocks in take after take.

Then on to the Mission – in Lant Street, Southwark, and another tremendous boost for morale. The set – of the girls' dormitory – was quite superb. When I first walked into it, I was quite moved. Something about the pathos of the simple beds with their few possessions beside them, grafted on to a bleak industrial interior.

Lunch with Maggie S and Richard in the Winnebago. All amicable and quite easy, though I still find Maggie S and the long experience of acting she represents quite a daunting prospect.

Tuesday, April 6th

Down to the Mission in pouring rain. If our dawn shot had been today it would have been disastrous. As it is we are inside all the time, completing the scene in which Maggie leaves the Mission. I find it hard work to start with. Maggie is smooth, efficient and professional – consummately skilled at timing and delivery. Keeping up to her standard, particularly when we don't yet know each other that well, and when the fatigue of eight days' hard filming in the last nine takes the edge off one's energies, is not easy. But I survive.

I fluff a line on a take, which annoys me, as I'm usually pretty efficient at lines myself. Then Maggie mistimes a move on a later take, which makes me feel much better. Eventually the complicated master shot is in the can and I feel much relief.

Terry G comes down to watch the shooting. He's impressed by the Mission set and says of Maggie, in some surprise, 'She's really funny . . .'

A journalist called Chris Auty – jeans, leather jacket and matching tape recorder – is here from *City Limits*. I waffle between takes. Must try and work out in my own mind what this film is about – instead of relying on visiting journalists to make up my mind for me.

Thursday, April 8th

I have a more luxurious caravan today. Richard approves. Maggie S is still in one of the poky little ones. 'You could hang meat in it,' she drawls elegantly, referring to the spectacular lack of heating.

Maggie and I work on the scene where she finds me in bed with the girls – Maggie being released about five. RL thinks something was lacking in her performance today.

Then to look at rushes. Helen comes along – her first glimpse of anything to do with the film. She hasn't even read the script!

Much relieved and pleased that the first major scene between Maggie and myself makes people laugh. It looks fine and beautiful – *every*thing looks fine and beautiful, but it's good to hear naked, unadorned laughter and especially as these are the last rushes before Denis returns.

Friday, April 9th: Good Friday

Feel good and virtuous and only a little cross at having to speak to a Danish journalist on the phone from Copenhagen about my 'Railway Journey', which goes out there next week. Had to explain trainspotting to him. He told me *Time Bandits* was a great success in his country, where it isn't shown to under-15s because of 'the violence'. It's also called, quite shamelessly, 'Monty Python's Time Bandits'.

Sunday, April 11th: Southwold, Easter Sunday

Strongish north wind throwing showery rain against the house. Take Ma to Southwold Church for the Easter service.

Before the service, conducted by the same vicar with the same permanent grin of redemption that he wore when Dad was put in the ground almost five years ago, we go to see the grave. It's in a small plot with several other crematees. As Mum happens upon it, she raises her voice in horror, 'They're all *dead*!'

She means the flowers.

I don't feel I can take communion with her – I just don't believe securely enough. So after the main service of rousing Easter hymns, I walk along to the front, in the teeth of a wrinkling north wind, past some of the old haunts, counting the years Southwold has been part of my life – about 25.

Home, for Granny's stew, then venture out in a still-inhospitable afternoon, though there is no rain. We walk along the beach, throw stones, push each other about, chase and generally have a very happy time.

Tuesday, April 13th

The news which dampens all our spirits is that Denis O'B, back from the States, has seen the assembly thus far and word, via Neville and Ray, is that he found the sound very difficult to hear and the pictures too dark. I suppose, because we were all so euphoric about the results, we took this news much more heavily than perhaps it was intended. But his reaction undoubtedly casts a pall over the proceedings.

Thursday, April 15th

Our first day at the Ezra Street location, where controversial amounts of the construction budget have been spent to improve the look of this East End neighbourhood. Something like £100,000, I think. Ezra Street itself has been resurrected, with a 50-yard frontage of mock houses, so well made that an old lady pointed one out as the house where she was born and another asked the council if she could be moved into it.

There are practical steam engines, piles of cobble-stones, and huge letters have transformed the local school into a Missions to Seamen Home. There are four complete streets we can use – over a quarter of a mile in all. It's the most impressive build I've seen on a film since the 'Ribat' [at Monastir for the *Life of Brian*] – and I think tops even that.

Friday, April 16th

Our day is plagued by the presence of a *Nationwide* film crew, who trap me in my caravan and suggest that I play all the locals when they interview them. I quickly abort that idea and send them off to talk to the *real* locals ... 'Oh, yes, that's quite an idea.'

A *Daily Express* lady, quite unfazed, sticks stolidly to her questions as I change in my caravan. I'm in and out of costume and make-up changes all morning, which leaves me with few reserves of patience and, when at last lunch comes and my poached trout is being borne to my caravan, the very last thing I need is an interview with *Nationwide*. But that's the moment they've chosen. The result is a very bad interview and considerable irritation. 'Oh, you were in the *Life of Brian*, were you?' asks the interviewer at one point.

In the afternoon Maggie S hides in her caravan to avoid having to talk to *Nationwide*, the *Daily Express* lady quietly and doggedly continues with her questions and I concentrate on trying to preserve sanity and remember what the hell I'm doing in Whitechapel, dressed as a clergyman.

Saturday, April 17th

Lunch with Denis to discuss my personal stuff – contracts and the like. I still do not have a signed contract, nor have I accepted any payment for *Missionary*. We walk from Cadogan Square to a pleasant, almost empty Chinese restaurant in a basement off Knightsbridge.

Denis tells me more about the Columbia deal, which, as far as I'm concerned, is the most unbelievable part of the *Missionary* saga. That we should have completed three weeks of shooting, only 13 months after the first word was written, is fantastical enough, but that we should be going out with the finished product in a thousand theatres across the US after 19 months is almost terrifying. But our little film is, give or take settlement of details, Columbia's big film for October/November.

Denis was in conciliatory mood – anxious to talk about the good things in the film. He's pleased with Richard, he was very impressed by Ezra Street and he thinks my performance has 'captured all the nuances'.

Back home I was just nodding off after lunchtime wine when TJ dropped in, having walked across the Heath. We sat in the sun and drank coffee. He had seen the assembly yesterday – chiefly to look at Peter

Hannan's work with a view to using him on *Meaning of Life*. It was enormously encouraging to hear that he had liked it so much he'd kept forgetting to look at the camerawork. Not only looks was he complimentary about, but also the humour.

Thursday, April 22nd

Work out at Dorney in the morning and then nearby to a beautiful avenue of trees down by the river for a shot to out-Tess *Tess*. This is the first longish dialogue scene between myself and Phoebe. Phoebe a little apprehensive. I've written her one of my 'jargon' parts – a lot of detail about filing systems which she has to learn parrot-fashion.

I keep correcting her when she says 'Pacific sub-sections' instead of 'specific sub-sections', but it turns out she's virtually dyslexic on this particular word. A huge shire horse drawing a plough clatters past at the start of each take.

The waving green wheatfields shine in the late evening sun. Phoebe looks slim and delicate in her wasp-waisted long dress, and the jets from Heathrow bank steeply to left and right above us.

Saturday, April 24th

Up at seven. I take Rachel with me this morning, to be part of the crowd in a 'busy London street' shot, which we're shooting in Finsbury Circus. Ninety extras and a dozen vehicles, including two horse-drawn buses. Signs of our own making cover up banks and travel agencies. A big scene.

Lunch in Richard's Winnebago with a journalist lady and Maggie S. Maggie very solicitous of Rachel, who sits with unusually well-behaved taciturnity, nibbling a cheese sandwich. We chat to the journalist. Maggie S clearly not enamoured of the press and resists attempts to be photographed by the *Sunday Mirror*.

Home, collecting a McDonald's for Rachel on the way, about a quarter to eight. Ring George H, who is just back from Los Angeles. He's jet-lagged and watching the Eurovision Song Contest. I just want to communicate to him some of the end-of-the-week elation I'm feeling. He promises to come and see us next week.

Monday, April 26th

Picked up by Brian at seven. Graham Crowden in car as well. Very genial and avuncular. As we drive into Oxfordshire, on a disappointingly grey, though still dry morning, he describes how he was shot by his own Sergeant-Major during arms drill in Scotland in 1943. He said that when the rifle went off there was none of the usual histrionics that actors and writers usually put into such tragedies, just a dawning realisation and a desire to be as polite as possible about it. 'I think you've shot me, Sergeant,' was all he could say – and the Sergeant's reply was 'What is it *now*, Crowden?'

Thursday, April 29th

This ridiculous confrontation with Argentina looks more and more like sliding from bluster and bluff into killing. But the government's popularity has risen 10% overnight since the re-taking of South Georgia and Murdoch's *Sun* is writing about 'blasting the Argies out of the sky'. This episode shows the true face of the nasties. Crimson, angry, twisted, bitter faces.

Saturday, May 1st

Not used during the morning as a series of sharp and hostile showers passed over. Some hail. Whilst they filmed Deborah and the photography scene I remained in the caravan, completing various tasks like thank you letters to the actors, and writing a new introductory narration for *Jabberwocky*, which I heard from TG yesterday is to be re-released in the US during the summer. He's very excited by the improvements made by Julian in re-editing.

Give lunch in my caravan to the 'Repertory Company' – Graham, Phoebe, Tim [Spall], Anne-Marie [Marriott]. Open champagne to celebrate good work done and, sadly, our last day all together. Quite a smutty lunch with RL's description of Long Don Silver, a man with a huge dong and varicose veins, who used to be featured in a club on Sunset Strip – hung upside down.

In one of the afternoon's sunny spells we grab a shot of myself in a horse and trap arriving home. As I wait for the clouds to clear the sun I see our two executive producers emerging from the orchard. George looks like Denis's son. His hair has reverted to Hamburg style, swept backwards off the forehead. He hands me a magnum of Dom Perignon with a pink ribbon tied round the neck. I embrace him warmly, then the cue comes through and I'm swept away round the corner.

They stay around for the next shot – a small, hot bedroom scene between Deborah and myself. George squashes himself into a corner of the room behind the lights, but only a yard or so from Phoebe. She's quite clearly made nervous by his presence and her face and neck flush and we do three very unrelaxed takes. Then George gets uncomfortable and moves off and we finish the scene.

Sunday, May 2nd

J Cleese rings to hear how things are going – having read his *Sunday Times* and been reminded it's my birthday on Wednesday. He starts *Privates on Parade* a week Monday. Says he can't remember what he's been doing for the past few weeks, but his pet project at the moment is the book with his psychiatrist. We wish each other well and he offers his services as a critic at the first fine cut stage of *The Missionary* in June.

T Gilliam arrives before lunch and we actually find ourselves writing together again – on the intro to *Jabberwocky*. He points out that I could be 'starring' in three separate movies in the US this summer: '*Bowl*' opens in late June, *Jabberwocky* in July and *Missionary* in October.

After he's gone, Tom beats me at snooker, I drink a beer I didn't really want and am suddenly faced with a lot of learning for the Fermoy scene and a 'surprise' party ahead of my pre-39th birthday tonight. I am at my worst – grumpy, resentful and unhelpful.

About half past eight Terry G and Maggie and the Joneses arrive and I cheer up with some champagne. Nancy [Lewis] and Ron [Devillier] are a surprise, as are Ian and Anthea [Davidson] – who I haven't seen for ages. Also the Walmsleys,[2] Ray Cooper – who brings me lead

1 Peter Nichols' stage play about a British Army theatrical troupe in Malaysia in 1947 would be Denis O'Brien's next HandMade production, directed by Michael Blakemore and starring John Cleese.
2 Nigel and Jane Walmsley. Nigel Walmsley was at Oxford with Terry Jones and myself. He went on to run, among other things, Capital Radio, Carlton TV and the television ratings organisation BARB. Jane was a journalist and TV presenter.

soldiers and a bottle of Roederer Cristal champagne. Robert H and Jackie – six months pregnant. Chris Miller and Bill are there and the Alburys. Twenty people in all. The Inneses are the only ones who couldn't make it.

It's a lovely party and I don't deserve it after being so surly in the p.m.

I drift – no, I plummet to sleep, thinking how nice it is to have a birthday party and wake up the next day, the same age.

Monday, May 3rd

To the Odeon Leicester Square for showing of rough assembly of *Missionary* – mainly for George H and Denis.

The projectionists are very slovenly with the focussing and as each cut comes up there is a long wait until it's sharpened up – only to go again on the next cut. But the laughter comes – especially from Denis – and the gymnasium scene (which had worried RL and myself) goes extremely well. At the end George turns and shakes my hand. Denis has been oohing and aahing at the beauty of shots and is quite genuinely and spontaneously pleased by it all.

This is just the boost we needed before starting on the last lap of the film – in Longleat and Scotland. But it pleases me most that George likes it, for it's his enthusiasm and love of the *Yarns* and the work I've done in Python that really made it all possible.

He tells me that there may soon be a settlement in the Apple business. 'Twenty years and we're just starting to get royalties for *Please, Please Me*.' As we go down in the lift he assures me that there will be no problem financing this film ... 'Denis wants to keep everything tight ... but ... the money's there, you know ... if you want it.'

Tuesday, May 4th

Leave home at 6.20 and drive, with Brian and Rosamund Greenwood, up the M4 to Highclere in Hampshire. The crisp, clean beauty of the countryside making the news that we have torpedoed an Argentinian battleship off the Falkland Islands seem even more unreal.

Arrive at Highclere just before eight o'clock. Already in the car I've been reassured and relieved to hear Rosamund Greenwood read the scene, with a gentle touch, but drawing every bit of comedy from it. When we 'line-up' at half past eight, I'm doubly happy to hear Roland Culver, who at 82 has an excellent combination of good acting and sparkle in the eyes. His sole line, 'Hello', brings the library down.

It's a very gruelling day, learning and retaining these long speeches, but we work on until eight o'clock, leaving three close-ups still to be done and a forbidding amount of work for tomorrow. Brian drives me to the salubrious Ladbroke Mercury Motor Inn at Aldermaston Roundabout.

A message from Terry J to ring him. As I do so, at 9.30, he's watching the news, which has just come in, of the sinking of a British destroyer in the 'non-war'. The first British casualties. How crazy. Talk about TJ's rewrites on 'Every Sperm is Sacred'. He's elaborated on the sequence quite considerably.

Wednesday, May 5th: Highclere House

In the papers, 'HMS Sheffield Sunk' on the front page. It's been a cold night. Light frost on the cars outside the Mercury Motor Inn.

Drive up with Neville to the location, arrive at Highclere at eight. Quickly into close-ups of the death scene, which we complete by mid-morning. Everyone who came down on the coach this morning knows it's my birthday – they announced it on the radio!

Lord Carnarvon potters amongst us with good-humoured nods and bits of chat to the ladies. He looks like every American's idea of a belted earl – down to his velvet carpet slippers with the interlinked 'C' monogram embroidered on them.

With hard and concentrated work we finish at eight o'clock in the great hall at Highclere. It's goodbye to Phoebe, Graham Crowden (a lovely man, but a terrible worrier about his acting. As Ray C says, Crowden raises worry to an art form) and Rosamund Greenwood.

One of our unit drivers has left the picture without telling anyone, so I find myself driving in Richard's Winnebago in a pelting rainstorm past Stonehenge at half past ten. It's a stormy pitch-black night. We stop at a lay-by and RL makes toasted sandwiches for my birthday dinner.

Sunday, May 9th: Longleat House

On location by 7.45.

After a day and a half languishing unhappily at her hotel, Maggie is here, but looking rather frail. After an early shot in the hall, Michael [Hordern] is allowed off for a day's fishing, and Maggie, RL and myself rehearse lines and moves, alone, in the Chinese bedroom. The scene plays very neatly and both Maggie and I find it very funny to do. Feel quite pleased with myself – as a writer this time.

A long lighting set-up.

Maggie and I make a start on the scene, but it's late in the afternoon and jolly tiring to act on the peak of form then. The very funny run-through in the morning, before the cameras were in, now seems utterly remote. We wrap at six o'clock and Neville, in the midst of his gloom, has to laugh when he tells me the news that Trevor Howard has arrived, but passed out in the lounge of the hotel, which he thought was his bedroom.

We talk for 45 minutes – Neville, Richard and myself – while the rest of the unit stream up the road to the birthday party I'm giving for them at the Bath Arms. Neville estimates a budget overage of nearly £200,000 if we go two days over at Longleat. It's the confrontation with EuroAtlantic which he is trying desperately to avoid for he knows that once they start interfering his job will quickly become impossible.

Monday, May 10th

Quite cloudless sky today, as we drive through leafy lanes up to Longleat. I discuss with Neville my thoughts early this morning – for cuts and reschedulings to help us through the week.

In mid-morning word goes round the unit that 'Trevor is on his way'. Trevor duly arrives and is guided to his caravan. When I go to see him he grins glazedly, but welcomingly, like a great bear just hit by a tranquillising dart. We eat lunch together, then I give him script changes and he is loaded back into his car and driven off to the hotel.

Back up in the Chinese room, Maggie and I finally get into bed. The scene seems to play well and when we wrap at seven we only have two shots left to do. A showing of assembled material for all the crew has to be cancelled as we all sit expectantly in the library and the projector fails.

Tuesday, May 11th

All wait with rather bated breath, but Trevor is fine. Fortunately he's seated at a desk, writing to *The Times*, so he can virtually read his lines, which he does, writing them out carefully, with shaky hand, on the paper in front of him.

Meanwhile I wait around, unused to the inactivity. Every now and then a shout from Michael Hordern as he bangs his head yet again on some projecting part of his caravan. His head is now covered in wounds.

Wednesday, May 12th

Outside the weather is gorgeous, inside it's hot, difficult work as I do one of my few dialogue pieces with Trevor. He is sitting there trying to survive. We collect the lines on the most basic level – if he can put the words in the right order, that's a good take. I find it a strain and cannot act with any ease or comfort. Richard feels impatient and the crew have to break the brisk momentum they're into whilst lines are rehearsed.

Maggie's cool and competent delivery picks up the pace again in the afternoon and we remain on schedule when we wrap at seven.

Thursday, May 13th

Met at the location today by news from Bobby Wright, second assistant – known affectionately by Maggie as Bobby Wrong. 'Bad news, Michael. There's a neg. scratch across the bedroom scene.' Maggie and I had joked about this on Tuesday when we'd completed the scene in a fast, efficient, very hard day. But then I hear from Richard it's only on two easy shots.

Finish the sitting room scene. Trevor much better today.

At lunch we're invaded again. RL's bank manager, two children, two secretaries, as well as the 'NatWest House Magazine' photographer *and* Richard's mother and her two friends descend. There is no real relaxing over lunch today. 'When you're acting,' asks one of the secretaries of me, 'how do you know when to do all those expressions?'

Friday, May 14th

RL is shooting the entire dining room sequence on a master – dwelling longer on Maggie and myself and Hordern than on Trevor, who sits in splendid isolation at the far end of the table, a good ten yards from Maggie and myself.

About three o'clock we enter the hot, airless dining room and start to work on the scene, which has a soup-pouring slapstick joke in the middle of it, which requires quite a bit of working out. We do seven takes. RL enthusiastic about the last two. We manage close-ups on all three of us, though one long speech (six lines) defeats Trevor utterly and we have to abandon it, in close-up, anyway.

General elation at completing dead on seven o'clock. Drinks with Lord Christopher and wife, who have been very kind and accommodating, and at eight Neville, Brian Brookner and myself are in the car heading east to London.

Suddenly we are within two weeks of completion.

Sunday, May 16th

TJ rings. He says he reckons doing *Meaning of Life* will be a doddle. I gather Peter Hannan has been sent a script and is first choice for cameraman.

Open house for the rest of the day – variety of children and friends in and out. The boys, much more independent now, up to the Lido with friends. Helen and Rachel together playing some all-embracing, mysterious game. How could I want to leave all this? I do value it so much and sometimes wish I had a freeze-frame mechanism which could seal me in this present sense of contentment. But it is a fragment and soon the time comes for me to move on, collecting other fragments.

Monday, May 17th: London–Aviemore, Scotland

Wake in a Simenon novel – three in the morning, train stationary in a sodium-lamplit marshalling yard. We must be somewhere near Glasgow, where the train splits, half for Fort William, half for Inverness. To sleep again, lulled Lethe-wards by the friendly clatter of wheel on steel. Arrive at Aviemore a few minutes late at twenty past seven. We drive the 45 minutes to Ardverikie House.

Work progresses slowly as it always does with a new location and new people. We have period vehicles, including an 1899 Daimler, which prove temperamental, and the weather alternates unhelpfully between sun and cloud.

I have a room in the house, which is far less preferable to a caravan. It's like being entombed in this cold, grey temple to deer slaughter. I start the day with rowing shots and wet feet as I clamber from Loch Laggan and run towards the house. Smoke guns in the birch groves on the opposite bank complicate (but improve) the shot, and Neville is already twitchy enough by lunchtime to confer with Richard and myself about the Scottish schedule. Richard is bristly and will not compromise on rowing shots. Uneasy peace.

We are staying 45 minutes' drive away from the location in the ghetto of the Aviemore Centre. A bleak and inhospitable attempt to create a 'leisure complex' of the late '60's style, which proves once again that the more impressive the surrounding landscape, the less impressive are the powers of human design and imagination. I have a suite, but it overlooks the car park.

Go to bed feeling a bit surly, after ordering trout and champagne on room service, which arrives quite efficiently, with a flurry of autograph books.

Tuesday, May 18th: Aviemore

Drive to Ardverikie – on the way pick up a hitch-hiker with a dog, who turns out to be one of our extras, who's missed the bus. A young man with a weather-beaten face, he's a casual labourer with a wife and child. They sound like gentle people, ingenuous and idealistic. The £15 a day they are getting to do our 'Chariots of Fire' joke has, he says, 'made all the difference'.

I know Richard is uneasy about this whole section. He says he's not sure how to direct it. Both of us know it's on the thin red line between us and 'Two Ronnies'/'Carry-On'-style mannerism.

'You're glum,' says Maggie to me, in some surprise. 'You never look glum.'

After lunch we set up for a grand shot of the procession leaving the house. Two cameras, a crane, lovely sunshine between the clouds, but both the old cars refuse to function properly and we have to abandon the shot. I climb in through a window, and that's that for the day.

Back at the hotel, I eat with Maggie. Salmon is good and we sit and talk on until the place is long-empty. She does worry and things do get her down. She reminds me of Angela, bright, but brittle.

Wednesday, May 19th: Aviemore

Looming clouds after much rain in the night. Lighting and planning the interiors takes time and I feel weary and unenergetic. Still can't set my mind to anything else. Have hardly read a book since *The Missionary* began.

We work on the extra hour, until eight. Like yesterday I am only needed in the last shot – to be squashed behind a door. For various reasons the scene between Corbett [David Suchet] and Lady A does not play right, and Maggie is uncomfortable. We wrap at 8.15, but, though the scene was satisfactory, neither Richard nor I felt it was exceptional, which is why we employ Maggie.

Back at the hotel after shooting, ring home, ring Ma, and settle down to watch a Ken Loach film set in Sheffield. Have ordered a halibut and champagne from room service. But Neville comes to see me, and another crisis has to be faced. The need to re-shoot the scene with Maggie and D Suchet tonight has really only confirmed Neville's fears that we will not collect the Scottish stuff in eight days.

I have looked as clearly and constructively as I can at script and cuts, but I think back to the *Ripping Yarns* and how we always left the 'adventure' finales to the end of shooting and almost inevitably compromised. So we must get this one right.

Halfway through our gloomy discussion, the halibut arrives, ushered in by the maître d'hotel himself and two flunkeys, like some life-support machine. It's already been delivered to Maggie Smith by mistake.

Thursday, May 20th: Aviemore

Not called early today, but cannot sleep very soundly after noisy departure of unit vehicles at seven. Feel very low for various reasons. Lack of central involvement with what's going on is primary. Ring home and talk to Rachel and Helen, who says TG rang and raved about the look of what he'd seen of *Missionary*. Somewhat cheered, set out at nine for the first day on the moors location.

After parking car am driven up a steep and rutted track, along which two bridges have been built by P Verard and the construction team. On the side of a broad slope our caravans are perched, and a motley collection of minibuses, Land and Range Rovers, Weasels, Sno-Cats and other vehicles. This is base camp.

Half a mile away the picnic scene is being set up in a very picturesque bend of a stream. The champagne and the strawberries and the cut-glass set out on a table perched on a cart (a good idea of Richard's) look wonderful.

Richard maintains he doesn't ever want to direct sequences like this again. He wants to work on films of the scale of *The Last Detail* – with small locations and small casts.

George Perry of the *Sunday Times* is in attendance. He's rather well-read and has wide terms of reference and I feel very dull and boring as I talk to him about *The Missionary* in my caravan.

Afterwards we wander down to the picnic location and it's quite pleasantly warm and sunny as the unit lounges on the grass. I'm used for one shot about five o'clock, then come back to my caravan with George.

I gather that further down the track there have been ructions with Maggie as she does the last shot of the day. Can't find out what's gone on, but as she walks back to base camp she looks grim.

Friday, May 21st: Aviemore

At base camp by eleven. Most of the actors wandering around in an unused state. Apparently no shots have been done yet as the Sno-Cat, go-anywhere, do-anything Arctic exploration vehicle has stuck halfway to the location, and toppled most of the camera equipment out.

Very slowly the unit straggles across the mountainside to the butts. Maggie in full Edwardian costume and wig looks very bizarre in the creeping caterpillar vehicles. I talk to her about yesterday. 'How *is* Richard?' she asks drily. She cannot understand his rapid changes from gloom to manic enthusiasm. It was this that threw her, she claims.

By midday our little army has been moved to the location, even as rumours are confirmed that we have landed again on the Falkland Islands. I note that the 'conflict', as they are still calling the Falkland confrontation, has been running almost exactly as long as our filming. Both seem to be reaching crisis point at about the same time!

After a Perrier and pork chop lunch, I walk over the hill to the location, accompanied by Bobby Wright, who occasionally screams into his walkie-talkie. 'They want to know how many blacks Richard wants in the crowd at Liverpool? ... No, *blacks* ... Five percent? ... Chinese? ... Alright, no blacks, but five percent Chinese ... ' And so on ... It all drifts away into the silent vastness of the Scottish hills.

Sunday, May 23rd: Aviemore

The Scottish *Daily Mail* has hysterical headlines about our 5,000 heroes – the men who yesterday went ashore in the first official re-invasion of the Falkland Islands. Even the *Times* is full of diagrams with graphic explosions and heroically-sweeping arrows. It's real war out there now and the implication in all the reports is that it will escalate and many lives will be lost before anyone can stop it.

Drive Maggie to Ardverikie House, where we are invited to late lunch with Richard in the Winnebago. RL, with his restless energy, wants us to go and eat on the island in the middle of the loch. Maggie, with her equally strong determination not to be impressed by such mad suggestions, demurs. In the end we compromise and RL takes us out onto the loch in his little dinghy. It pours with rain – a prolonged, cold shower – we've nowhere to shelter and the only wine he's brought is a rich Sauternes.

Arrive back drenched and Richard gives us a complete change of clothes. Maggie looks lost in a huge pair of his trousers. But it's jollied us along. Peter Hannan arrives and helps barbecue the steaks – with oregano and tarragon. Very nice. The showers pass and there's a period of beautiful early evening sunshine.

Tuesday, May 25th: Aviemore

We have an important scene to play this morning – Maggie's 'dying words' in the cart. Our first scene of real, unadorned affection for each other.

The wind blows as violently as yesterday, but it's warmer and our real problem today is too much sunshine. We have to play the scene whenever a cloud comes over, and it takes two or three hours. But it plays easily and naturally, without great dramatics, which I'm sure is the right way. Maggie happier today, which helps. I fool around a bit and try to keep morale up. But the relentless battering from the wind eventually gets through to me, as we push ourselves into a series of wide shots as the sun goes down and the wind takes on a bitter, unfriendly edge. But at least the rain holds off and we finish all we need on the grouse moor.

Back to the hotel. Glorious hot bath. Then have to summon up shred of strength from somewhere to attend a unit party downstairs in the Post House. Second wind and end up dancing and talking until four o'clock. Need to let off steam.

Friday, May 28th

Wake quite early and doze. Rachel comes into our bed about 7.15 to cuddle up with me. Bright sunshine and the papers full of the Pope's first visit to Britain. Brief, illusory feeling that we have finished. Buy the paper for the first time in weeks, eat breakfast at my own table – other delusions of freedom.

Down to Tite Street in Chelsea with Brian. London looking marvellous in perfect May sunshine. We are shooting in a wonderfully cluttered old studio – a marvellous, characterful, eccentric house in a street full of marvellous, characterful, eccentric houses, mostly studios dating from the 1890s and decorated in early Art Nouveau style.

When we *do* shoot, Trevor takes a long time and has to have his words on an idiot board. Maggie says she should have seen the warning lights this morning when Trevor arrived in Tite Street with a broad smile at a quarter past ten, looked at his watch and said 'Open in a quarter of an hour.'

Tuesday, June 1st: London–Aviemore, Scotland

Awake most of the night – not troubled, just very hot and sticky and aware that I have only till 5.35 to sleep. Brian calls for me at 6.15. We pick up RL and catch the 7.40 Inverness flight from Heathrow, with the 39 others in our reduced unit.

Drive to Ardverikie House. 'Decathlon acting' this afternoon – riding horses, leaping and running onto carts and finally endless rowing shots back and forth across Loch Laggan.

Even after the sun had sunk behind Creag Meagoidh there was a soft pink glow in the sky over the loch, whilst the sharp outlines of the mountains behind us were slowly concealed by a soft mist. The water was still, the mosquitoes frequent, and it was very, very beautiful. I was still out there – a madly rowing vicar – at 9.30.

Wednesday, June 2nd: Aviemore

Work in the afternoon – running up stairs and along corridors.

RL has organised a party after shooting – there are two lambs roasted on the spit, a bonfire, candles in the trees, sangria and beers to drink.

A 'band' arrives, comprising two rather sullen young Scotsmen, who sit, slumped, on the side of the specially erected stage beside the shore, with drooping cigarettes, murdering popular ballads, and being saved only by a bagpiper and Ken Lintott and Ramon singing 'Sit On My Face'.

Towards ten o'clock RL prepared for his illuminated spoon-playing performance. As part of his 'light show', he ignited explosive on his hat, which shot a blast into the sky and made a much appreciated smoke ring eddy over the gathering before anyone realised that Richard had quite severely burnt his hand. He was taken off to a local doctor.

Thursday, June 3rd: Aviemore

For an hour or so this morning the bedroom scene, in which I try to dissuade Maggie from killing Lord A, became rather heavy work. First it lay rather flat, then RL wanted me to be more assertive, which led to me being louder and stronger, but making the lines sound suddenly melodramatic.

The scene clicked when we played it softly, listening to what each other was saying and responding accordingly – which sounds obvious, but is actually a difficult effect to achieve in a film, with marks, tight, precise movements and a clutter of camera, mikes and semi-slumbering members of the crew all around.

Saturday, June 5th: Aviemore

Another clear, still, sunny morning. Yesterday was the hottest of the year in Scotland and today seems set to cap it. Am soon put to work on ride-through shots up in the woods beside the loch. Shafts of sunlight through the trees and hordes of midges.

Rest of the day doing interiors – running up twisting staircases à la *Jabberwocky* and hanging off battlements. All in my hat and long black coat, which is very uncomfortable today.

In the garden a man plays with his children. It's all hot, still, unmoving and vaguely unreal. Reminds me of the *Grande Meaulnes* or *Picnic at Hanging Rock*. A feeling of melancholy in the back of my mind as I look out. Regret and some sadness.

Of course, it's the last day of main shooting. These people who've helped me and been a daily part of my life for the last ten weeks will be strangers again tomorrow.

About 6.30 I do my last shot up in the turret room. There's a smattering of applause. Maggie dashes off because she can't bear goodbyes. I leave the crew filming a stunt man on the battlements and head back to Aviemore. On the way I stop at Maggie's hotel to drop something off for Ramon. Meet Maggie on the way out. Her eyes start to fill with tears. Find a lovely note from her back at the Post House.

Bathe, collect some champagne and sandwiches and catch the 9.34 sleeper to Euston. A party in my compartment with the camera crew, Chuck Finch and Ken Lintott. No chance for further melancholy.

A much-reduced unit then moved out to Africa, to shoot Fortescue's days as a missionary.

Wednesday, June 9th: Samburu Lodge, Kenya

A good night's sleep, but woken by the accumulating cacophony of birdsongs and screeches and baboon roars. At breakfast hornbills and yellow weaver birds fly to the table-side and a vervet monkey makes a sudden lightning dash and removes Peter Hannan's toast. A moment or two later a vervet disappears up the tree with a sugar bowl. The waiters throw rocks after the monkeys in desultory fashion, but I should think deep down they rather enjoy the guests being made a monkey of.

About eight we set out to see the mud-walled Mission hut which Peter Verard and Norman Garwood have been here for a week constructing. It looks marvellous. Beside it is my tent – with portable writing table – and three mud huts made by Samburu ladies.

At the local school we are treated as VIPs as we arrive to listen to 'Greenland's Icy Mountains' sung in English by the Samburu kids. Proudly their teacher, Leonard, conducts them, and solemnly the children sing. A little flat in parts, but the words ring out clearly from a score of serious little black faces – 'The heathen in his wisdom bows down to wood and stone.'

Thursday, June 10th: Kenya

My first day of *Missionary* work in Africa. Alarm goes at half past five. Shave and dress and it's still dark outside. Assemble, cups of coffee and tea, and out to the location, nearby in the park, ready to cycle at first light. Pass an angry bull elephant, impala, gerenuk (the deer that never drinks) and the little black drongo bird.

At 6.30 punctually the sun comes up – so fast that there is little time for red skies and orange light – it's almost straight into a soft yellowy-green. On 'Action!' I set our vintage cycle in motion, but the pedal snaps.

Later, I'm walking past some camels with my umbrella up, when the sound camera breaks down. Lunchtime crisis. The camera, with all its sophisticated technological bowels spread open, lies on the bulrush benches in the little mud chapel. It's pronounced dead and all sorts of gloom descends. Urgent messages to London, but the nearest telephone contact is 40 miles away in Nanyuki.

We carry on with a mute Arriflex.

Friday, June 11th: Kenya

We are ready to start filming in front of the Mission hut at six o'clock. Me writing a letter home beside a roaring fire. There's a brisk wind and sometimes the flames threaten to engulf my writing desk.

We take a two-and-a-half-hour break in the middle of the day. Walk with RL (who never stops) amongst the trees and scrub, looking for insects. He finds mainly dung and scarab beetles and puts them in his jar.

Just after lunch the village kills a cow. It's a ritual slaughter carried out by the morani. The women of the village are not allowed to be a party to it, so the ceremony takes place beyond the thorn branches which mark the limits of the manyatta.

After being cruelly manhandled out of the truck, the cow is killed with a warrior's spear driven quickly and neatly into the back of the head to sever the spinal cord. I remember now the repeated dull crack of metal on bone as the spear was driven home. Then the twitching cow is laid on its side and a cup is carefully made from the loose skin on the throat. This is filled with blood, and the elders of the tribe are the first ones to stoop and drink the blood.

As I watch from the discreet shade of a thorn tree, the chief calls to me, 'Hey, Padre!' and beckons to the makeshift cup of blood. I mutter something apologetically about having to get back to acting and hurry off to the manyatta.

The other unlikely event of the afternoon was the arrival of Neville Thompson with a new synch sound camera. The message had reached him at 5.30 on Thursday evening and, with commendably quick thinking, N was in Nairobi with new equipment at nine Friday morning. Neville, white and rather haggard, appeared briefly in amongst the huts as I was trying to put together an ad-libbed argument with an aged Samburu. Then he was gone.

Saturday, June 12th: Kenya

This is the morning when we do Fortescue walking past wild animal shots.

When we sighted elephants after 30 minutes of driving, engines were cut and I walked out and past the beasts whilst Bagaboi – a Samburu ranger – covered me with a loaded rifle from behind a hedge. They all thought I was very brave. 'Hasn't he ever seen anyone trampled to death by an elephant?' Bagaboi asked, and of course that was absolutely the point. I hadn't. What appeared to them as courage was just massive ignorance.

Unsuccessfully tried to get near giraffe and crested cranes. I was told to walk slowly and deliberately through the grass 'because of the snakes'.

We shot the choir in the Mission hut in the afternoon. They had managed to learn three more verses of Bishop Heber's convoluted prose in the last two days and we were very pleased and applauded them.

Sunday, June 13th: Kenya

Today the reward of safari with no filming. Derek Barnes [our Kenya location manager] is taking myself, RL, Shuna [Harwood, costume designer], Gary White [first assistant director] and Peter Hannan to Shava Park, near to the Samburu but, he says, much quieter. So we assemble once again around the bougainvillea-clad entrance to the lodge, just as the sun is rising. Baboons scurry after the trailer taking rubbish to the tip, like dealers at a jumble sale.

After two and a half hours we drive up to Shava Lodge. The sun shines in shafts of light through the foliage and gives the whole place a Garden of Eden-like quality. And they are well-equipped too. A full English breakfast – bacon, sausage, the lot – is cooked for us on a barbecue and served with thick-cut marmalade and toast. On an impulse I suggest Buck's Fizz and, extraordinarily enough, they have a bottle of champagne chilled.

Oohs and aahs of quiet pleasure, added to by the gentle hurrying of streams which flow from a diverted river down through the lodge gardens to the river.

Derek, armed with a panga, cuts a route down to the base of the waterfall and Hannan, Gary and myself strip off and walk beneath the waterfall itself. The hard, cooling water thuds down on us. Afterwards we sunbathe naked on a rock by the river. It's quite perfect and I could easily stay there until the end of the day – no people, no sun-oil, no deck-chairs, no pool-side bars selling over-priced drinks – just sun and water and solitude.

Out to the airport. At ten to twelve, with RL supine on a customs counter, the camera crew, Norman Garwood and myself partook of our last Tusker beers at the airport bar.

A rather crumbling, tired little group we were – with the results of our three days' intensive filming in brown boxes in an airport trolley. As someone said, this really was the end of picture party.

Thursday, June 17th

Drive up to Lee's for a viewing of the latest rough assembly of *Missionary*. Present are a half-dozen besuited young executives from Huttons [HandMade's advertising agency].

Denis is there, looking very cheery, because even *Scrubbers* seems to be going the right way now.

We see about one and a half hours of the film. Start is sticky as usual, but once it gets going, largely helped by DO'B's infectious laughter, it works well and smoothly. No standing ovation at the end, but people clearly impressed.

Interesting reaction from Huttons was that it took them by surprise. It was nothing they had expected from either the synopsis or from previous work of mine. They all talked very positively about it – shook my hand and congratulated me.

Have to leave early to go to a Python wig-fitting.

Monday, June 21st

Halfway through one of the most hectic years of my life. That in itself is encouraging. I'm still alive and healthy. A few grey hairs showing since *The Missionary*, but I feel quite trim (11.1) and just about on top of things.

Take Rachel to school. Apparently her teacher says she has been much better this last week. I think she needs her dad and I feel very relieved that my five weeks' absence on *The Missionary* is over (longer, I suppose, if one counts the weekends and the early starts and late finishes we worked even when we were in London).

A showing of the film so far at four.

There is much good laughter and the Slatterthwaite sequence goes so well that it's impossible to follow in terms of audience reaction.

The Scottish sequence is disappointing to me in terms of performance. The last 15 minutes become very serious and very quiet and I don't enjoy them at all in the present company. I know they're wishing Michael Hordern would come on again (says he paranoically).

RL is very anxious for me to work with him on the next two weeks' editing – for we have to present a fine cut at the end of that time.

He wants me to cancel my trip to Columbia in LA. I feel it's essential to meet these faceless people before I go into Python confinement, so we compromise. I will go to the States for two days instead of three, returning Friday lunchtime and working with Richard right through the weekend.

Tuesday, June 22nd

At 9.20 a car collects me and takes me down to the US Embassy to collect my passport. There is a tube strike so the roads are packed. It's raining heavily. Into the dreadful world of visa applications – rows of faces looking anxiously to a row of faceless clerks behind desks. No-one wants to be there. I collect my passport – have to sign that I'm not a communist or a Nazi, and several pieces of paper for fans who work in the Passport Office.

Then out to Heathrow, where I arrive at eleven. The delights of travelling First Class then take over. I have only hand baggage so check quickly through and into the BA Executive Lounge for some coffee and another long call to RL. I feel we should not show Columbia the end of *The Missionary* until it's right, but Denis has a video with everything we saw yesterday on it – so we'll have to do a re-editing job, and erase some of the tape. Get Rose Mary Woods[1] in as adviser!

The flight leaves a half-hour late. DO'B travelled Club Class with his two daughters. I visited them occasionally – taking them smoked salmon and other First Class delights. Denis's daughters sat, very well-behaved, and read and coloured books whilst DO'B immersed himself in columns of figures. Most of his deals, he says proudly, were worked out at 35,000 feet.

---

1 At the Watergate hearings in 1973 the hapless Rose Mary Woods, President Nixon's secretary, claimed she'd 'pressed the wrong button' on her tape recorder, accidentally erasing four and a half minutes of what could have been incriminating testimony.

Wednesday, June 23rd: Beverly Wilshire Hotel, Los Angeles

Denis calls about nine o'clock to tell me that their reactions to the three video segments of the movie which they've already seen have been excellent. Everyone from Antonowsky (he's the President of Marketing) downwards filled with enthusiasm. That's a good start.

Am picked up by Denis and Inge at ten. He rents a brand new Mercedes, and we drive out to his office at Burbank. There meet Dan Polier – a thin, slowly-precise talking, late-middle-aged man with neat silver-grey hair – and David Knopf his chunky junior partner. They are Denis's sidekicks on film distribution.

'Just been working with a fan of yours,' says Polier. 'Steven Spielberg.' That doesn't spoil the morning either. Apparently they are working on *ET*, which looks set to be the biggest box-office picture ever.

At midday we walk over to Columbia Pics.

Long, low, modern office. Softly and thickly carpeted. Tall, gaunt figure of Marvin Antonowsky looming over them all. He stands like a great bird, eyes flicking around, his lean frame held back almost apologetically. He welcomes me into his office with some kind words about what he's seen, then a group of about eight or nine Columbia hacks are brought in. All seem very quiet and respectable and deferential. Young – mostly my age or less. Ken Blancato, the creative publicity head, is neat and trim and looks like a hairdresser. They don't immediately strike me as an intimidatingly forceful team. Very well-behaved in the presence of their president, behind whose desk is a shelf full of maybe 40 screenplays. I notice *Scrubbers* is there, alongside *The Missionary*.

Antonowsky and Blancato are very confident that they have some wonderful campaign ideas and, without much ado, an artist reveals six of the most crass and dreadful drawings I've seen in my life. If I had set down on paper my worst fears of what they might produce, these would be they. A grinning, Animal House-like caricature of myself with girls dressed in 1960's Playboy Bunny-style outfits, with tits and thighs emphasised at the expense of period, beauty, truth, honesty and everything else. I have to say I find them a little obvious. 'Oh, yeah, well that's why we have another version . . .'

Ah, the subtle one. The subtle one consists of me kneeling at a long bed, with a dozen 1950's beauties lined up on either side of me in a parody of the Last Supper. I sit there, with all these expectant faces looking towards me, and I wish the floor would open and swallow me up – or swallow them up, anyway. If ever there was a moment when I wanted a Los Angeles earthquake, this was it.

But the moment passed and they proved to be not at all unadaptable. It was not a terribly easy session, though. They revealed, with a sparkling air of revelation, their slogan: 'He gave his body to save their souls.' Denis sat there remarkably unmoved and I couldn't leap up and down with excitement.

Thursday, June 24th: Los Angeles

Some more writing of blurb for ads, then Denis collects me at ten. Drive to his office at Warners and I show him, Knopf and Polier my suggested ad lines and synopses. They are instantly typed up, to be presented to Columbia at our 11.30 meeting.

Also sketch out an idea for a trailer – very quick, short one-liners showing Fortescue becoming progressively more trapped. DO'B loves this and, when we file into the even more gaunt and haggard Antonowsky's office, DO'B cheerfully announces that I've solved everything – we have radio, TV and trailer advertising all sewn up. His faith in me is embarrassing, as I fumble with pieces of paper to try and bear out this hyperbolic introduction.

I read them some of the ad lines – quite a few chuckles. Outline the trailer idea, which is also met with approval. 'He had a lover, a fiancée and 28 fallen women. And he said yes to all of them' sounds the favourite, though they still cling to their 'He gave his body to save their souls' line. But Antonowsky reacts well, directs them to work on the lines I've proposed and, unless he is just flannelling me, I feel that we have progressed by leaps and bounds since yesterday – and hopefully my work yesterday evening and this morning has given me the initiative.

Taken to Hamptons – a big, noisy hamburger restaurant just beside Warners' Burbank studio – by Polier, Knopf and Denis O'B. Then a return visit to Columbia, in which I am wheeled into a conference room where about 15 PR people sit round a table. Ed Roginski, a rather calm, soft-spoken and intelligent head of publicity, chairs the meeting and all those around the table introduce themselves to me – name and position.

They ask me things like whether I have any special needs I would like catered for when I go on promotion. They are (thankfully) against a three-week cross-country whistle-stop tour (which TG underwent for *Time Bandits*). They suggest instead a week and a weekend in New York –

including a 'Junket Day', when they bring key out-of-town press and radio into the city, all expenses paid, and throw me and, they hope, Maggie to them.

Polier and Knopf feel that the sooner exhibitors can see *The Missionary* the better for choice of cinemas, etc. Columbia is going through a bad time with *Annie*[1] – despite enormous amounts of publicity effort it has not brought the house down on its nationwide launch – and there really isn't any picture they can get excited about (apart from *Python Live at the Hollywood Bowl*, which opens tomorrow) until *Missionary* comes along.

A limousine picks me up at 4.30 and I'm driven back to the airport. Onto the 6.30 flight.

Sleep through *On Golden Pond* for the second time in three weeks.

Monday, June 28th

The start of Python rehearsals and writing for *Meaning of Life* coincides with the first national rail strike for 27 years and a London tube and partial bus stoppage. I drive quite easily to Regent's Park, and by great good fortune, find a parking space right outside the new office, and arrive only just after JC. He, too, is sporting a moustache. He grins delightedly at me and says I look *quite* different. Not sure how to take this.

Python Live at the Hollywood Bowl opened at 60–70 cinemas in NYC and Philadelphia to overwhelming apathy. Various reasons put forward – first weekend of excellent weather in NYC; very strong opposition from Spielberg, *Star Wars* and *Rocky*; opening too wide with too little publicity. EI very strongly blames *Secret Policeman's Ball*, which GC advertised on American TV evidently.

After a half-hour discussion it's clear that no-one has an answer. The movie collected good reviews in both the big NYC papers.

Eric wins 'The Meaning of Life' song with no declared supporters for TJ's version apart from myself and TG, and neither of us felt Eric's version deserving of any stick. But on 'Every Sperm is Sacred', on which TJ has done – *had* to do – so much work, there is quite a strong split. Eric takes up the position that his version is much better, musically and in every other way, than TJ's. GC bears him out quite vehemently. TJ says that his version is better, musically and in every other way, than Eric's.

---

1 A big-budget movie based on the cartoon strip Little Orphan Annie, starring Albert Finney and Carol Burnett and directed by John Huston.

Once we start discussion it's clearly crucial that JC comes down firmly in favour of TJ's version.

Tuesday, June 29th

Sandwiches at lunch and talk over the ending. Eric feels that we have cheated the audience by not having come to grips with our title. I see our title as being a statement in itself. There is no way we can tell anyone the meaning of life – it's a cliché and we are using it ironically to show how irrelevant we can be when faced with such a pretentious subject. John sees fish as the answer to our problem.

Eventually I ad-lib, with Eric's help, a very short and dismissive lady presenter winding up the film and reading the meaning of life from an envelope – this fed on from a nice idea of a Hollywood awards-type ceremony where we asked a glittery compere to come on and reveal the meaning of life. He opens a gold envelope and reads . . . 'And the meaning of life is . . . Colin Welland!' I think this was the best laugh of the day.[1]

We broke up about 3.30. I had a cab driver who at one point came out with the line 'Do you know how long I spent in the shower last night . . . ? One and a half hours . . . Mind you, I felt better at the end of it.'

Saturday, July 3rd

Bowl returns even worse than Denis had led me to believe at the beginning of the week – we were 'gasping' in Philadelphia to a gross less than that of a *Bambi* reissue the week before and in NYC only managed 125,000 dollars at 58 sites! Dreadful.

If the cliché 'you've seen one, you've seen them all' applies to any sphere of human activity, it must be school fairs – or 'fayres' as they're wont to call them. As with the Gospel Oak Fayre two weeks ago, the William Ellis version was the usual collection of bric-a-brac, shabby clothes and grubby books for sale. A few gallant sideshows run by the boys. Two tombolas run with steely-eyed efficiency by the sort of parents who like running things. Some rather wet chicken tikka out in the car park, and not much else.

Helen had put together a hamper and she sat for nearly three hours

---

1 At the 1982 Academy Awards Welland had famously brandished the Oscar for *Chariots of Fire* and shouted 'The British Are Coming!'

beside it for about £17.00. Tom played in the wind band in the main hall at four, which was a very pleasant addition to the usual format. Took the girls back via a toyshop and bookshop in Kentish Town (I bought Mary Kingsley's *Travels in West Africa*), then home.

Am I getting more like my father in old age? I've noticed definite signs of easily roused impatience and intolerance since *The Missionary*. I put it down to the fact that co-producing, writing and acting was a giant public relations job in which I had to be all things to all men every day for eleven weeks, and the thing I need the rest from most is not acting or writing, but people.

Saturday, July 4th

Take the children for a swim. Re-read W L Warren's book about my favourite English king – John. Discover Angevins had violent tempers. Also that the twelfth century was the best-documented in English mediaeval history.

Monday, July 5th

To Python rehearsal, to find that Neil Simon had been on the phone and wants to meet me – he has some film project.

After a costume fitting I drive up to Britannia Row Studios in Islington to record 'Every Sperm' track. Ring Neil Simon. He professes himself to be a fan, says he is halfway through 'one of the best things I've written' and there's a part in it for me. Arrange to meet him on Wednesday.

The recording session is delayed while they find a piano tuner, so I sit in the big and comfortable games room and watch England start their vital match with Spain. They must win and by two goals to be certain of going into the semi-finals. Our defence is unshakeable, mid-field quite fast and controlling most of the game, but we can't score. 0–0 at half-time.

In between play I've been singing 'Sperm Song' to Trevor Jones's rather solid beat. Eventually we find a combination of takes we're comfortable with and I drive home to watch the second half. England fail to score and slide out of the World Cup. It's a hot evening.

Tuesday, July 6th

Third day of another rail strike. NUR gave in rather pathetically last week. Now it's ASLEF's turn [ASLEF was the train-drivers' union]. Reprehensible Thatcher statements likening ASLEF to the Argentinians we defeated 'so gloriously' in the Falklands.

Drive in at ten and we rehearse three or four sketches, on sofas doubling as First World War trenches, with our scripts in hand. Fizzles out about one. Costume fitting for me as a schoolboy.

Home for a run, do some work, then I have to change, bathe and go down to meet Marvin Antonowsky at Odin's. I've arranged the meal at his instigation, and he says he's very pleased that it's only the two of us, as he would just like us to get to know each other a little better.

He seems to be rather ill at ease with the food and the ordering, but talks quite fluently about his early days in advertising, his admiration for Frank Price – the President of Columbia – his stint as head of programmes at NBC, during which he claimed credit for starting *Saturday Night Live*; his move to ABC and eventual elevation to marketing head at Columbia.

He compliments me, with a sort of little head on one side smile, 'You're a good little actor ... you come over well on screen.' He clearly wants to work together again and assures me that Columbia would like to do the next thing I come up with. When I tell him I'm meeting Neil Simon to discuss a part he gets very excited. Like all Californians he uses hyperbole quite undiscriminatingly, starting with 'wonderful' for people whose guts he probably hates and working up through 'amazing' and 'marvellous' to 'absolutely incredible' human beings. Neil is 'absolutely incredible' and 'a great friend'.

Wednesday, July 7th

Over to Inn on the Park to meet Neil Simon. A man of about my height with a warm, friendly manner answers the door. He apologises for walking with a lean, but five days ago he slipped a disc, after watching Wimbledon (at Wimbledon – he's a tennis freak). Apparently he went into spasm one morning as room service called and he retold, with comedy writer's relish, how he pulled himself across the room and collapsed at the open door as he let in his breakfast. He couldn't be moved from the doorway for two hours – body half out in the passage as curious guests walked by.

After some talk and some morale-boosting admiration of my 'natural and likeable' acting persona, he told me of his project – a half-written play with a part just right for me. Apologising for being unable to précis the idea, he asked if I had time enough to read the 60 pages of his typed first draft. I agreed readily. He gave me the script, then went discreetly into his bedroom with the two *Ripping Yarns* books I'd brought as a present for him.

I recall the play was called 'Heaven and Hell' and began, with a disconcerting resemblance to *Arthur*, on a scene between an elderly butler and a very rich young man who is a miser. He's bashed on the head in a carefully organised collision in his car and taken by a gang to a warehouse which has been got up as heaven.

It looks so like the heaven that this character has come to know from the 1940's movies he always watches, that he believes in it, and when they tell him he has three days to go back to earth and raise enough money to avoid them sending him to hell, he falls for it. Some very funny lines, but a disappointingly one-dimensional character.

I find my attention wandering as I read to what I'm going to say to this most famous of all American comedy writers when I've finished. Fortunately he makes it very easy for me and we talk about the character and I can express some of my feelings about him being real and under-standable and Simon agrees and says he will put in more at the beginning explaining the young man's miserliness. I have to say that I can't make up my mind, that I'm very flattered, etc, etc, but being a writer myself I will probably want to write something of my own after *Missionary*.

Truth be told, I found the play lightweight in the two areas I enjoy so much – character and detail. I'm very tickled to see he has a rather insignificant character in his play called 'Antonowsky'.

Thursday, July 8th

To Claridge's to meet Ken Blancato – Columbia's VP of publicity [to organise a shoot for their poster]. Am not allowed into the cocktail lounge, as I have no tie or jacket. 'Rather silly in this weather, I know, sir . . . ' agrees the porter in thick overcoat who escorts us out.

Sit in the lobby and have a couple of beers. Blancato is a New Yorker and worked in Madison Avenue. He's also a frustrated writer. When I reiterate my reservations about the roof-top shots with the girls, etc, he grins rather wearily. I feel I'm just making a nuisance of myself.

I go on from Claridge's to Neal's Yard, to try another recording of

'Every Sperm', as Monday's didn't sound entirely satisfactory. André and
Trevor have rather different views of how to approach my vocal, and it's
not a particularly successful session, as I'm in a rush anyway.

On to Mon Plaisir for a meal with TG. He says he'd rather like to be a
monk. We talk some business. We've seen figures that show 17 million
dollars returned to [Avco] Embassy [from *Time Bandits*] and none of
that is owed to either of us.

Friday, July 9th

Car picks me up at 8.30 and drives me down to the Great Northern Hotel.
King's Cross and St Pancras silent and deserted at the end of the first
week of the rail strike.

Onto the rooftop – another hot, slightly hazy morning. Richard is there
with son Joe, a bit subdued. Also he doesn't like what David Alexander
[the photographer] and Camille – the bored, drawling, world-weary
Columbia lady who is Blancato's number two – are doing. He's very quiet
as Alexander sets up the shot and fires off reels of film like there's no
tomorrow.

At lunchtime we're finished and down the contraceptive-scattered
stairwells into cars and on to Lant Street, where Norman Garwood and
co have rebuilt my Mission bedroom.

I have to work rather hard leaping up and down and presenting endless
expressions to seemingly endless rolls of film, whilst the photographer
urges me on with shouts ranging from '*Won*derful,' which means very
ordinary, to 'Just the best!' when I'm trying a bit.

At one point Camille, who looks dreadfully out of place in her Beverly
Hills straw hat and white strides, steps in to change a shot in which three
Mission girls are in bed, and I'm below. We're not allowed to show any
rude bit, or suggestion of a rude bit, so I've made sure that the girls are
well-wrapped in sheets (quite unlike the way they appear in the film).
But this is not enough for Camille, who fears that the very suggestion
that the girls might be nude *under* the sheets could result in the ad
running into trouble in the Deep South.

At this my fatigue – that intolerable fatigue of working hard on a job
in which you have no confidence – causes me to crack and we have a
heated exchange on the subject of *The Missionary* and the Deep South.
'It's not me . . . ' she keeps pleading, which makes it worse, because I want
to know who it is who wants to do this to our film. That there are more

than averagely narrow-minded people in the Deep South I don't doubt, but what are we all doing here today, working our asses off to try and reach down to their level?

Monday, July 12th

Slept unsatisfactorily – woke at intervals from four o'clock onwards. The adrenaline is beginning to flow – the surge of nervous energy that I will need in the next ten weeks has to come from somewhere and the last two weeks since *Missionary* 'finished' have not really been enough to get right away from one film and into the other.

To the Royal Masonic School in Bushey, a largely red-brick amalgam of all the old public school architectural clichés. A few flying buttresses here, a clock tower and some cloisters there.

JC asks me about ASLEF and the implications of and background to their strike. I think he might be sending me up, but he's quite serious. I was quoted, somewhat misleadingly, in the *Mirror* on Saturday as saying I supported ASLEF. It's just that I can't stand to hear this self-righteous government trying to pretend it's more of a friend to the railways than the proud, independent, much-maligned and bullied train drivers' union. If the government really had the good of the railways at heart this present action would never have happened.

We're starting with a scene involving Cleese and myself and an entire chapelful of boys and masters. I play a chaplain and the similarities to March 29th continue as I don a dog collar and have my hair swept back. I even keep my *Missionary* moustache.

Thursday, July 15th

To the Masonic School again. Feeling of despondency as Brian drives me into the gates. I feel no emotional attachment to this location, as I did to those on *The Missionary*. It's a place of work. The weather doesn't help – it's overcast and looks like rain. Caravans are a good walk away from the location – so nowhere really to rest during the day.

EI cheers me up. He's in good form and we sit and make each other laugh whilst waiting for lighting set-ups in the classroom. I've brought him Signford's two Chris Orr books, which he wants for David Bowie, who has much admired Eric's Orr collection.

Keep in touch with *Missionary*, where Maggie S is patiently waiting for me to come in and post-synch with her. But have to keep giving them increasingly pessimistic estimates and in the end the session is abandoned and I find myself still being a schoolboy in Bushey at seven o'clock.

Sunday, July 18th

Leave at eight and drive out to Twickenham. I enjoy the sunshine and the emptiness of the roads and the little courtyard at Twickenham Studios, with flower tubs everywhere, is convivial and friendly. Richard has arrived on his bike, which he describes disarmingly, as 'Probably the best that money can buy' – and then proceeds to tell stories about how he fell off it and rode into parked cars.

Post-synch the entire 'Bottling Factory'[1] scene and we finish at one o'clock.

As I arrive back at Julia Street I find a group of kids around a cat lying in the gutter – obviously barely alive after being hit by a car. I ring the local RSPCA and they ask if I could bring the cat in. Am just loading it into the hamper I won about 30 years ago in a Fry's Chocolate competition when the Browns – the Irish family on the corner opposite – return from their Sunday lunchtime trip to the pub. Mrs Brown becomes very tearful when she identifies the cat I'm bundling rather unceremoniously into my hamper as once belonging to her granddaughter Deborah, who died tragically of appendicitis after a doctor's mix-up.

I drive to Seven Sisters Road. RSPCA man thinks there's a fair chance of its survival, which I wouldn't have expected. Cats' broken pelvises do heal quite successfully usually.

Home to the Browns to bear them this welcome news. Mr Brown, who calls me 'Palin' or 'Young Palin', insists that I stay and have a drink. A Scotch is all that's on offer – served in what looks like an Austrian wine glass. But it's very pleasant – like walking into the snug bar of a very convivial pub. No introductions or all the delicate, defensive small talk which the middle classes are plagued with – the Scotch warms me physically and mentally and I have a lovely half-hour. Mr Brown very Irish, with lilting voice, soft and very articulate, and always a quiet smile in

---

1 This scene, in which Fortescue goes to ask for money for his Mission, was shot, rather grandly, at the old Royal Mint on Tower Hill. Sadly, it held up the story and never made the final cut.

everything he says. They couldn't be more different from the sobbing group I left half an hour before. They celebrate their happiness just as enthusiastically and openly as their grief.

Friday, July 23rd

My twelfth early start, and twelfth working day on the trot. At least this morning I am spurred on by the sight of light at the end of the tunnel – by the prospect of not only a weekend off, but then seven filming days in which I'm not involved.

But today is no easy downhill slope. For a start Eric and I have a long dialogue scene [in the hotel sequence] – four and a half minutes or so. TG has a wonderfully complex and grotesque make-up as the Arab Porter. Then there is much re-lighting and building of rostrums after TJ decides to shoot the whole scene in one. So Eric and I walk through at 8.30, then wait, in make-up and costume, until a quarter to one before they are ready.

We do two or three takes at about 1.30, and in two of them I forget my lines and have to stop – which is unusual enough for me to make me rather cross and depressed when lunchtime comes. I really feel the accumulated fatigue of an eleven-week shoot and then these last twelve working days. Fortunately after lunch with EI and the strangely attired Gilliam, I feel better and, although I have to push myself physically hard, I find that I'm actually enjoying the piece.

TG, with his blind eye (as used in *Holy Grail*), nose too big for him and the wheel on his false hand broken, has created for himself his own peculiar nightmare, and he will be trapped in it again on Monday.

Sunday, July 25th

A party at Barry Cryer's in Hatch End. Roomful of comedians. R Barker, R Corbett, Eric Morecambe, Frankie Howerd, Peter Cook prominent.

Chat with Ronnie C. With a relieving sense of self-mockery, he reveals his customary interest in Python's financial affairs, business arrangements, etc. RB looks around gloomily. 'Too many comedians here,' he says. 'Not so good for character actors.' He too is obsessed with Python's wealth. 'All millionaires now?' he asks, not wholly unseriously.

Peter Cook, who wasn't exactly invited, is more forthcoming and entertaining. He's come straight from Vic Lownes's[1] house and somehow found himself at Barry's. He's very pleased with the video version of his Derek and Clive second LP. He says it's going to be shot in 2-D. He asks me in what part of Africa *The Missionary* was shot. Turns out his father was a DC in Nigeria. Cookie, in a rare moment of sentiment, clearly felt quite an admiration for his father – 'People ask me about influences on me – the Goons, Waugh, etc, etc – but in the end the person who influenced me most was my father.'

One of the King Brothers – Michael, I think – tells of a very funny stage act he used to work with – a man who wore a German First World War helmet and threw a cartwheel in the air and caught it on it as the climax of his act. The audience loved it. Only the rest of the cast (who used to flock into the wings whenever he was on) could see the acute expression of pain on his face every time he did it.

Monday, July 26th

With the lighting already up and the Hendy hotel room piece already played through, I'm ready for my close-ups by a quarter to nine and have done the scene by 9.30. I feel looser and funnier and much more on top of the scene than last Friday and almost wish we could do the whole thing again.

But Eric is much quieter today. He apparently suffered a 24-hour 'flu yesterday, with hallucinations and temperature. His voice is huskier than Friday and he is clearly not happy with the performance. But he improves as we go on, and cheers up too. His son Carey comes to the set, a small, bright-eyed, scrawny little lad clutching a copy of *Rolling Stone* containing an interview with his hero – Sylvester Stallone – in *Rocky III*.

Leave the studio at two. Six shooting days off – feels like a school half-term, saying goodbye to everyone. Home for a wonderfully normal, unrushed evening with family and a BBC programme on the chances of survival for Londoners in a nuclear attack.

Death from a nuclear blast would be short, sharp and sudden. Especially, the programme suggests, if you're living in Kentish Town!

To bed, very content.

---

1 Victor Lownes III was the London head of the Playboy organisation and had been the driving force behind Monty Python's first film *And Now For Something Completely Different* (1970).

Thursday, July 29th

I go up to CTS Music for the second day of *Missionary* music recording. I've never seen film music recorded before, so to enter this spacious modern studio, with its control room like a mighty ship's bridge, from which the eye is drawn downwards to a 60-strong orchestra, and beyond them to a screen high on the wall on which my antics appear, is stirring and a little frightening.

Everyone seems so competent and capable, from John [Richards] the mixer at his 36-track desk, to Mike Moran with his enormous score sheets, to Harry Rabinowitz (old acquaintance from *Frost on Sundays*!) looking not a day older, with headphones on and baton raised, to the orchestra of session men, who are probably from the London Symphony or the Philharmonic, but today are in jeans and T-shirts and reading newspapers in between cues. It's an epic undertaking and, when the Scottish themes thunder from the speakers to fill the control room, it's very moving.

RL and I have been discussing for the last few days an alternative photo idea for the print-ads – of Fortescue under a lamppost in the street, where normally only whores would stand. The contrast would be funny, there are three or four whores in the background to add any of the titillatory element Columbia might want. So it's resolved that there is no other way but for me to go to Denis this evening and heave some more money out of him.

Surprisingly, he accepts my point that we could do a better job here, and he likes the idea of the lamppost and the prostitutes. He will ring Columbia and tell them we want to shoot an alternative. The onus is now all on us to come up, in quite a rush, with something that lives up to our confident stand.

Tuesday, August 3rd

See assembly of 'Mr Creosote' at lunchtime (instead of lunch). Evidently 9,000 gallons of vomit were made for the sketch, which took four days to film. It's been edited rather loosely at a poor pace and dwelling too much on TJ's actual vomiting, but the costume is marvellous in its enormous surreal bulk, and Mr C's explosion is quite awful and splendid.

Wednesday, August 4th

The sticky heat continues. Oppressive, sluggish, still heaviness.

I feel quite tense from fatigue today and find myself at midday facing a long close-up take with my heart suddenly thudding, my voice thickening and my head swirling. Not a good sign of my condition, I feel. I just want to get away from films, film people and the whole process. But I am firmly stuck in it for the next few months.

As if to underline this, no sooner have I finished at Elstree than I have to go down to the Tower Hotel to prepare for an evening's shoot on the new poster. Peter Hannan comes along to help supervise the lighting of the street, we have four prostitutes and Angus Forbes is the photographer.

It's warm and still in Shad Thames where we're shooting, which helps to keep everybody happy and patient as the clock moves on to midnight, when we finish and drive back over Tower Bridge to the hotel to change. Find myself, dressed as a vicar, with Tricia George dressed as a most comely whore, in the lift with two American tourists. As they disembark at the ninth floor I gently remind them that 'London still swings'. 'Right!' was their nervous parting shot!

I'm home at 1.15.

Thursday, August 5th

Collected at 8.30 by Brian. I have a one-hour make-up as Debbie Katzenburg. Feel testy and rather low. For some reason the continuing news of the Israeli bombardment of West Beirut sickens me and I can't read the paper.

Eric, TJ and myself in drag, Cleese the Reaper, Chapman and TG the men. One of the few sketches involving all the Pythons.

The afternoon's work is slow – things like JC's beckoning bony finger taking up a lot of time, as special effects, animals and children always do.

TJ suggests we eat out together. Neither of us notice the irony that, although we've spent the whole day on a sketch in which a dinner party is poisoned by salmon mousse, I start with a delicious salmon mousse.

Friday, August 6th

A long morning around the table in a hot studio in drag. Simon Jones is playing the sixth member of the dinner party. He's a very good man with a quiet wit, well able to stand up for himself. In one morning he learnt the Python lesson in survival – over-act in your close-up, it's your only chance. Actually he did his piece modestly and very well.

Long afternoon as we have to dress in cottage walls every time we move round to do close-ups. GC and I are the last to be done. Then more special effects as we die. Eric and I blow out the candles then collapse, motionless on the table for 40 seconds. Cynthia Cleese hiccups during one of these long silences and sets us all off.

The day stretches on into evening and we sit and play games. JC hears that EI is dining out with David Bailey and, when EI has gone, expresses great incredulity that anyone should want to have dinner with David Bailey. Then he suggests we play a game – 'Not Michael, because he's far too nice about people' – to list our worst-ever dinner party.

After JC has been hauled back for yet another close-up of the Grim Reaper, Eric asides to me that it can't be much fun having dinner with John Cleese.

Saturday, August 7th

Tonight at six and eight are the first two public showings of *The Missionary* in America. Keep remembering this at odd times during the day. Moments of pleasurable anticipation.

Wolf a croissant, then up to Elstree for a tiger-skin fitting, only to find that my other half of the skin is in a pink suit doing the 'Galaxy Song' on Stage 3. Yet another breakdown in communication. Round to Stage 4 where mighty office buildings are being erected for TG's £100,000 'Accountancy/Pirate' epic.

Tucked in a corner is a tiny Yorkshire '30's cottage, filled with children who are rehearsing 'Every Sperm' for Monday. Little Arlene Phillips, with her bright, open face and pink and maroon matching hair and tracksuit, is taking the kids through the number. We work out some movements for me to do, and then I read the build-up lines – all about 'little rubber things on the end of me cock' – some kids snigger, the younger ones smile up at me innocently.

Home – and a relaxing evening in, broken only at one point by a huge series of explosions to the north. It's not the Israelis bombing possible PLO meeting houses in Kentish Town, or the IRA – the huge cracks and flashes lighting up this stodgy August evening are for the 1812 Overture, being played at Kenwood [open-air concert].

To bed after watching (and staying awake for) Hitchcock's *Notorious*. Superb performance by Ingrid Bergman. Very sexy. Put the phone right beside me in case I should get word from LA ...

Sunday, August 8th

Richard L rings about half past two. The news is not good. He says he's confused and disappointed and just wishes I'd been at the viewings with him. He felt the audience was unsuitable – general age between 16 and 23, predominantly male – the *Stripes* and *Porky's* sort of audience. All subtitles and understated scenes went by in silence. Howls of appreciation and whoops when Maggie (or rather, Maggie's stand-in) goes down on me under the bed-clothes and the whores hop into bed.

But the figures – considering the nature of the audience – are not as discouraging when I think about them: 2% excellent, 30% very good, would recommend to friends, 40% average, quite enjoyed it, 19% only fair, and 9% thought it the worst movie they'd ever seen.

RL rings later in the evening. Says he's spoken with Denis O'B, who was, so I hear, not downhearted. They have come up with a list of proposed cuts which they want to make next week and show at a sneak preview in NYC on Saturday the 14th. Could I come? Concorde both ways. I have to say no, as Python is away on location in Scotland and Yorkshire.

Tuesday, August 10th

Arrive at Elstree 9.15. Wide shots first, with all the kids in. Mothers in attendance.

TJ is worried that there may be a walk-out if we say either my line – 'Little rubber thing on the end of my cock' – or one of the kids' lines – 'Couldn't you have your balls cut off?' – so we plan a subterfuge. I will say 'sock' instead of 'cock' (taking care not to over-emphasise the initial letter) and then the dastardly substitution will take place in the dubbing theatre. The boy's interruption will be of a quite harmless variety – 'Couldn't you sell Mother for scrap?' – when everyone is present, but we'll record the real line separately when everyone's gone.

The afternoon is very hard work. I have to go through the opening speeches, song and routine over and over and the room is warming up, and the kids, though well-behaved, have to be continually instructed and calmed down, which gets tiring. They all call me Dad, off the set.

Finish with the children (as we have to by law) at 5.30 and for a moment Ray Corbett [first assistant director], Hannan, Terry, Dewi[1] and myself slump onto chairs in the little room amongst the discarded toys – like shattered parents at the end of a two-day children's party. Nobody has the strength to say anything for a while. Then, with a supreme effort, we gird our loins and complete my tight close-ups. I end the day wild-tracking the phrase 'Little rubber thing on the end of my cock' ... 'over the end of my cock', and so on.

Thursday, August 12th: Glasgow

Leave the hotel at 8.30. Drive half an hour out to the north of the city, past more flattened slums, rows of shops with boards and metal frames over the windows. Then through wooded, pleasant suburbs to Strath-blane, where we are quartered.

Some hanging around, talking to local press, crossword-puzzling and finally making up with mutton-chop whiskers and moustache, and squeezing into custom-made leather boots and the rather handsome navy blue uniform of a major in the Warwickshires of 1879.

Then we're driven a mile to the location – a five-minute walk up a hillside, where a British encampment has been constructed beneath a bare rock cliff, which I later gather is known in the area as Jennie's Lump.

Sudden drenching squalls of rain and cold wind cause us to abandon the planned shots and spend the day on weather-cover, with scenes inside the tent originally planned for Elstree. But it isn't only the unsettled weather which is forcing us to use weather-cover. Rumour reaches us during the morning that nearly 100 of our carefully selected and measured Glaswegian extras have walked out after a misunderstanding over costume in the local village hall.

A small group of very vocal Africans became angry when they were shown how to tie loin cloths by Jim Acheson (on the stage).[2] They had

---

1 Dewi Humphreys, camera operator, went on to become a successful TV director (*Vicar of Dibley*, *Absolutely Fabulous* and many more).

2 Acheson later won three Oscars for Costume Design: *The Last Emperor* (1987), *Dangerous Liaisons* (1988) and *Restoration* (1995).

been misled, they shouted. They thought they would be wearing suits. Poor Jim and his excellent wardrobe team faced a 1982 Zulu Uprising, as a group of two or three blacks shouted about being degraded, tricked ... dishonoured, etc, etc ... And 100 of them were taken back in buses to Glasgow.

We went on shooting – oblivious to all this – and completed most of the tent interiors by six o'clock. Back to the Albany. Bathe and change, looking out of my eighth-floor window across the wet streets to the grand, two-storey classical facade of Currie and Co, Building Trade Merchants. A fine, confident, assertive building, now in disrepair and white with bird shit. It looks as out of place amongst the new Glasgow horrors as a piece of Chippendale in a Wimpy Bar.

Dine with John Cleese and Simon Jones in the Albany restaurant. TJ restless at a nearby table with a dour Danish journalist. Simon Jones is relaxed, talkative and amusing. It turns out that he, like me, can't roll his 'r's.

Friday, August 13th: Glasgow

Cleesey very unwell this morning. We think it was the crayfish last night. At the hotel in Strathblane he looks awfully wan and up on the mountainside, as we prepare for the first Zulu attack, he is farting and belching, and at one stage actually throwing up against the barricades.

We have had to recruit white Glaswegians and brown them up as Zulus. I must say they are very patient and charge at the encampment ten times. It's a long day, heavy on extras and blood and smoke, and light on lines for the officers.

Newspapers – local and national – carry the story of the Zulus yesterday. Some very funny reports, especially in the *Glasgow Herald*. The nationals such as *The Times*, which refers to today's cast as predominantly 'unemployed youths' – note the use of the word 'youth', always pejorative – are less accurate. Still, all excellent publicity.

Try to contact Richard in New York, eventually get a rather fraught line from Strathblane to the Algonquin. Shout my instructions to some American receptionist and feel very abstracted from it all until I leave my name and the receptionist quickly returns 'As in *Ripping Yarns* ... ?' The Atlantic shrinks suddenly. But I never get to talk to Richard.

Back to the Albany. The bar is jostling with film technicians demanding of the hard-pressed barladies things like 'Two vodka tonics, two Guinness, two dry martinis, a soda water and take your knickers off.' An extra day's shooting tomorrow.

Sunday, August 15th: Bradford

To Bradford, where we eventually find the Norfolk Gardens Hotel – part of the atrocities which replaced a lot of Bradford's sturdy stone town centre with stained pre-stressed concrete. 110 of the 118 rooms are taken by our crew.

To bed 11.30. Walls wafer thin and I can hear every word from a TV blaring next door. Read half a page of Nabokov then drop off.

Woken at 2.30 by a call from RL to say that the New York preview went very well indeed with over 80% of the cards putting the film in the top three categories.

Monday, August 16th: Bradford and Malham, Yorkshire

Sixth week of Python filming – 17th week of filming since the end of March – begins with the pips from my calculator alarm slicing gently into my semi-consciousness at 6.45 a.m. It looks wet and uninviting outside.

Drive out to the location with Simon Jones, who points out to me the theatre in Bradford where Henry Irving [the great actor] collapsed, and the Midland Hotel, in whose foyer he died shortly afterwards, neglected by the hall porter who thought him a passing drunk. Sad end.

An hour and a half's drive into fine, rugged scenery up on Malham Moors.

Eric, Simon Jones and I wrap ourselves in blankets and wait in an upper room at the hostel. It's an old hunting lodge, which is now a centre for school sixth forms to come for field studies. A lot of walkers tramping around downstairs. They irritate me for some reason. Maybe it's their smug, self-satisfied preparation for all weathers.

Eric and I get into our make-up base for our Cocktail Party Ladies; outside the wind howls and the rain lashes at the windows. God knows what it must be like for Cleese, out on the moors as the Grim Reaper. Amazingly enough, in the midst of the tempest, we find that the TV set gives an excellently clear picture of a tranquil scene at Lord's, where England are fighting to save the Second Test Match v Pakistan.

JC arrives back at midday, absolutely soaked through, but in surprisingly high spirits. He takes great heart from the fact that TJ thought the shot they'd just done was second only to a day of seasickness in the Newhaven lifeboat as the most uncomfortable filming of his life.

Our appearance on the moor is put off well into the afternoon. I organise a subversive but, I feel, necessary trip to the pub in Malham at lunchtime. As I buy pints of Theakston's, I feel I have to explain to the lady at the bar why I'm in false eyelashes and full ladies' make-up. I tell her I'm in a film. She says apologetically, 'Oh, I never see films, I'm afraid. If anyone comes in here hoping to be recognised I'm afraid I can't help.' Eric, Tania [Eric's wife], Simon J and Graham C (with young friend) laugh a lot at this.

At a quarter to six I'm officially wrapped for the day, and England lose the Test Match by ten wickets. Back down to Malham Tarn Centre to frighten (or excite) the first batch of hearty walkers who've just filled the hallway after a 17-mile hike.

Thursday, August 19th: London–Bradford

At Twickenham I at last see the cut of *The Missionary* which they viewed in New York last weekend. It looks very beautiful. The relationship between Maggie and myself seems to come over well and is just as much what the film is about as the comedy.

Arrive at 8.55 at Leeds/Bradford Airport after leaving Twickenham at 7.15. Eat in my room and settle down to a long phone call with Denis O'B in Fisher's Island.

DO'B says Columbia are rapidly losing confidence in the movie, mainly because there weren't enough 'excellents' on the movie cards. He says they wanted to put it off till January and release it only in a couple of cities even then. He says he has pulled them back from this, what he considers suicidal, course, and reminded them that they are legally obligated to open the picture on the 22nd of October. But they've reduced the print now to between 400 and 600.

At last I feel we have some genuine response from Columbia – even if it is panic. My adrenaline is already flowing and I'm ready to fight for the film – to prove to Columbia not just what a good thing they've got, but why it's a good thing (because it's *different from*, not the *same as Porky's* and *Stripes* and *Arthur*), and to prove to Denis that I know better than he what works in a comedy film. It's difficult to do all this from a hotel room in Bradford, but I suddenly feel determined. This next week is crucial.

Friday, August 20th: Bradford

I'm driven out to Skipton at 7.30. A cold wind, occasional rain.

Terry has to ask some householders with strange, lop-sided faces if he could throw mud on the walls of their house. 'So long as you don't come *in*side,' they reply fiercely.

My shots are completed by midday. Buy a superb pork pie – North of England pies are a much underrated local delicacy. Am driven back to the Norfolk Gardens Hotel in Bradford, where I consume the pie with the remains of last night's bottle of Mercurey, then turn my room overlooking the bus station into an office for the afternoon.

Ring Marvin Antonowsky at Columbia – decide to put my head in the lion's mouth. He's brisk but amiable. Wants to have dinner with me in London on September 5th, will test our poster alongside their own and, in response to my queries about his reactions to the film, he says whilst not being 'ecstatic' about the results of the viewing, they are still behind the film nationwide on October 22nd. How many prints, I ask? 300–400, says Antonowsky. Going down!

Wednesday, August 25th

Because of poor weather this week, the 'Tiger Skin' scene has been postponed and we are doing the 'Hospital' today. Nice to see little Valerie Whittington and Judy Loe again. Valerie has all day with her legs apart as the Mother, Judy is the Nurse. I'm the Hospital Administrator. Suddenly occurs to me as I see them there that I've been to bed with both of them, on screen.[1]

A tedious day as I have a part which is not involved in the whole scene, but just important enough to keep me there all day.

I don't finish doing very little until after six and only just get down to the Preview One viewing theatre in time for the seven o'clock *Missionary* viewing.

DO'B has been on the whole quite long-suffering on *The Missionary* – has supplied the money when it's really come to the crunch and not interfered too much with the script. Tonight he sounds defensive and says things like 'Even if it's not commercial, I'm glad I've done it.'

---

1 With Valerie Whittington in *The Missionary* and Judy Loe in the *Ripping Yarn* 'Curse of the Claw'.

Taxi home – back by midnight. Cab driven by a 'Silly Walks' fan. He calls it 'Crazy Walks'. Very weary.

Friday, August 27th

We attempt the 'Jungle' scene, so I have two parts to play – Pakenham-Walsh and the Rear End of the Tiger.

JC complains about performing against bright lights – quite rightly. It does reduce facial mobility by about fifty percent. JC mutters bitterly, and not for the first time, about pretty pictures at the expense of performances.

TG, who desperately wants to get this over with, so he can get back to his 'Pirate/Business' epic on Stage 4, is laboriously encased in a complete latex mould of a Zulu. Then the sun goes in, and does not reappear, except for a brief glimpse, when we try the shot. But TG, who's been inside the costume for an hour, has sweated so much that one side of the Zulu sticks to him.

The 'Tiger' is eventually abandoned and instead we shoot the tracking shot of the approach through the forest. Endless takes. Constant calls over the walkie-talkie for the Test Match score.

Saturday, August 28th

Today is perhaps the most crucial in the whole history of *The Missionary* so far. We will have two showings of 60 people each – one a general audience, the other my friends and sternest critics. There can be no excuses. If the response tonight is half-hearted there really isn't much we can do.

TJ and Simon are both there and I take them round to the Ship to talk about it. Both of them thought it had worked very well, but equally both felt that the reason for my journey to Scotland was not well enough explained. After a quick Pils, I'm back to Film House.

Cleese and Gilliam and Chapman have all come along. A full house. JC asks me to sit next to him and Barbara.

Good response to the painting-out of the name pre-title sequence (which DO'B would prefer to cut) and plenty of laughter from then on. Feel more comfortable with larger numbers and there are fewer embarrassing moments. Applause at the end. Close friends all seem to have enjoyed it. John Goldstone especially happy. Cleese, surprisingly, liked it a lot.

Go to eat at Bianchi's with John and Barbara, Terry G, Helen and Ray Cooper. Over the meal JC surprisingly candid about things. He says he regards *Yellowbeard* as 'a dreadful script', but is doing it mainly because GC came to him 'and actually used the word "plead"' to try and persuade JC to come in.

JC repeats what he once told Humphrey Barclay[1] about his writing relationship with GC. 'Some days I write as much as 75%. But most days it's 95%.'

Barbara very nice. She reckons *The Missionary* could have more success in the US than *Privates on Parade* as it's a more general, less specifically British theme and it's optimistic and leaves a warm feeling in the audience.

No-one, however, felt it would be a blockbuster. A nice, likeable, gentle film.

Wednesday, September 1st

Fakenham Press Ltd, who, to my pleasure, were responsible for *Small Harry*, have been closed down by their parent company. Three hundred out of work. Very sad. Fakenham being Father's childhood home, it seemed neat and appropriate that my first children's book should be made there.

Friday, September 3rd

The joy of not having to get up and go filming soon evaporated by the awareness that the last days of *The Missionary* are running out. It must be in final form by the end of the weekend.

Spend a couple of hours this morning agonising over how to alter the narration to accommodate various people's criticisms of plot and story confusion. Sort out the end quite satisfactorily, but it's in the middle of the last half, where TJ – backed up by Simon Albury – was vehement about making it clear that 'some inexplicable force' drew Fortescue to Scotland, that I have the trouble. Cleese, normally a great hunter and destroyer of woolly plots, had no trouble following the story or understanding why he went to Scotland as he did. Lynsey de Paul[2] went further and asked if those who couldn't follow the plot were mentally deficient.

---

1 TV producer and colleague of JC's from Cambridge Footlights.
2 Lynsey, singer and songwriter, was, for some time, a neighbour of ours.

Saturday, September 4th

See from *Variety* that *Monsignor*, a film starring Chris Reeve as a priest, is opening on the same day as *Missionary* in the US. Seeing the advertising reminds me painfully of the area we haven't yet sorted out – posters, etc. The image of *The Missionary*.

Take Willy and his friend Nicky to the Valley to see Sheffield Wednesday's second game of the season – against Charlton. Perfect afternoon for football. Sun, not a breath of wind and the pitch verdant and springy. Wednesday have a glorious and unequivocally deserved 3–0 victory.

Usual police presence outside – motorcycles, Alsatian dogs at the ready. The ever-present tension not relieved by their presence.

Up the main road, off which our car is parked, a crowd suddenly starts to run. There are shouts, ugly faces contorted with rage, bricks and bottles thrown. The police seem to do nothing.

I see a bottle tossed at the window of a house, another hurled from a van full of supporters, which lands and smashes beside a baby in a pram at a corner shop. Quite why the cruelty and hate behind the fighting can be so easily fanned, I don't know. And the urge to destroy and damage is strong. It's almost entirely the work of boys from 13–18, with one or two sinister older ones stirring it up.

Wednesday, September 8th

To Elstree at lunchtime to be Debbie yet again.

Jonathan Benson is the new first assistant and keeps us all cheered with his special Bensonian brand of dry wit, which comes out, just as does the dry ice, at the beginning of each take.

We are eventually free soon after 7.15. A quick transformation from Debbie to a freshly-scrubbed actor, then home and into a suit to become Michael Palin for the *Brimstone and Treacle* opening at the Classic, Haymarket.

Afterwards to a party given by Naim Attallah, described today in *Private Eye* as 'The Palestinian Millionaire'. He had red shoes, that's all I remember.

Not a bad party. Pursued Selina Scott, the lovely newsreader, and was about to introduce her to Sting as Selina Sutcliffe, realising only just in time that I was getting muddled up with the Yorkshire Ripper's wife.

Saturday, September 11th

With almost indecent haste, the day has arrived when I complete my second major feature in five and a half months. People tell me I look inordinately well – I blame the sunshine of April and May – and, apart from waking up some nights in cold sweats, or not even sleeping, I have just remained sane and I think I've given some good work. I do feel tired, but have been carried along on the energy of elation – occasionally dented by a poor day's work, or an average viewing. On the whole, I must say, I feel wonderful.

Today all the Pythons are together to be fish and, as this is probably the last time we shall be gathered in one place until February next, there is an added note of almost hysterical urgency around. Iain Johnstone's[1] BBC crew are filming the ABC '20–20' film crew filming us trying on our fish harnesses. I'm a goldfish, Graham a grayling, the two Terries perches and John is a carp.

It's a very weird and effective make-up, making us all look like John Tenniel's *Alice* pictures – semi-anthropomorphised.

'Shit, it's Mr Creosote' are the memorable last words of the day, nine weeks after John and I had begun the film in the chapel of the Royal Masonic School.

As if to bring everything full circle, RL rushes into the dressing room as lashings of solvent are being applied to my hair to remove the glue, with Polaroids of the day's poster session.

On the way home in the car TG and I discuss it and TG feels it's too solemn and stylish and too busy. He feels that we should be looking for a much simpler, more direct approach. Even something as corny as lipstick on a dog-collar, he says.

Sunday, September 12th

As I lie awake, some time around nine o'clock, I feel with great certainty that Richard's second attempt to produce an alternative to the Columbia poster is still not right. It lacks a sharp and clear indication that *The Missionary* is comedy – it's fun, something to be enjoyed.

1 Iain was a producer and presenter of BBC's *Film Night*. He was also an author and later worked with John Cleese on the book of *A Fish Called Wanda* and the screenplay of *Fierce Creatures*.

TG's aside about a dog-collar with lipstick on comes into my mind. It's clear, neat and simple. As soon as she's conscious I tell H about it and she enthuses.

Tuesday, September 14th

Run in the morning. The Heath is filling up again as if summer had returned unexpectedly. Pass a group of ladies with easels in a line and five straw hats and five cotton skirts all painting next to each other.

Sit out after my run and soak up the sun – read on with Nabokov, write some letters, then collect my *Missionary* outfit from Bermans for another and final attempt to crack the poster.

Drive down – roof open, a balmy evening – to W8, to yet another photographer's studio.

As it gets dark I clamber once again into my *Missionary* robes, Sandra [Exelby – make-up] plants a thick, rich red kiss on the dog-collar – we try various angles of kiss – then I'm out in the street, where one should be on such a warm and beckoning evening, trying the silly expressions.

About nine o'clock I'm called in to take a very urgent message from Helen. She had heard from Mark Vere Nicoll, who had in turn just been rung by Antonowsky with the alarmingly sudden news that if *The Missionary* is not delivered to Columbia by this Friday they will pull out of the deal.

I call Antonowsky to try and find an explanation. He's out at lunch. Could I call back in 45 minutes?

Finally get through to Antonowsky. I ask him what's going on over the delivery dates. MA goes straight into some story about Richard Pryor involving Columbia in a damaging lawsuit because the final, fully edited version had not been shown to the blind bidding states. MA cannot let this happen over *Missionary*. 'It's us who have to pay, not you,' he garbles on. The movie must be ready to be shown within a week of this Friday or they're stuck.

'Can we deliver it by Monday?' I ask – any delay will help us.

'I'm only the middle man,' Marvin, President of Marketing and Distribution, pleads.

Tom McCarthy is the man to talk to about delivery.

At 12.30 a.m. I get through to DO'B at the Carlyle Hotel. He is in a fighting mood. MA had called him this morning and said that the movie was off, there was no deal. DO'B had argued with him for an hour and left MA in no doubt that if he pulled out he would have a major lawsuit on his hands. Anyway, DO'B has now declared war on the man who [he] said only a week ago was decent and straight. Any communications with Columbia must be noted down word for word and any agreements struck must be passed on to Denis so vital evidence is in writing.

I sense that Columbia still have some hope for the picture, but Denis firmly believes that they are now trying desperately to extract themselves. But then this is probably de rigueur in Hollywood, I comfort myself as I drive back home.

Wednesday, September 15th

Good news is that Columbia have not renewed attempts to cancel the film. Tom McCarthy is being helpful and we hang on by the skin of our teeth. But it was Richard who suddenly brought me down to earth by reminding me that the movie opens in the States five weeks from tomorrow. No wonder they are desperate for delivery.

Thursday, September 16th

Indian summer continues. Balmy, sultry sunshine – more like the South of France than South of England. Work at desk in the morning, lunch with Kathy Sykes [producer's assistant], a treat for all her hard work. Eccentric restaurant in Richmond called the Refectory, beside the church, run by a rather fine-looking man with a weathered, baggy-eyed face.

I have to let myself dwell for a moment on the vagaries of chance which end up with my sitting at lunch with Eric Sykes's daughter nearly 30 years after Graham and I sat and watched his programmes on the telly in Sheffield and dreamed of nothing finer to do than be Eric Sykes. Now I find Kathy telling me that Eric wants a part in my next film.

Saturday, September 18th

The roads of London are so empty at 5.15 on a Saturday morning that any other vehicle glimpsed in the rear-view mirror appears as a threat.

Pick up Loncraine, who groans unhappily as we head out onto the A40. Still pitch dark when we reach Rank Labs at Denham, and their long, low modern buildings and general Hollywood aspect only increase the dreamlike quality of the experience.

To the viewing theatre to see a checkprint taken from the interpositive that leaves for the States this very day. Although there are only a handful of people watching, most of whom have seen the movie endlessly, I feel tight-stomached at the lack of reaction, until someone else enters and starts to laugh most encouragingly.

The laughing man turns out to be Mike Levy – one of the top men at Rank. 'Lovely movie,' he says and then starts to take his own lab apart for not projecting the print with the correct light intensity. Once that is corrected we can see, to our relief, that there is nothing wrong with the print itself. Peter Hannan is very unhappy about the grading in two or three places and will be going out to the States on Wednesday to make the changes in LA. This is our last line of hope.

A sour-looking man brings any further discussion to an end by pointing out that he has to take the film to the States today. So I leave Denham at eight o'clock with the sun already hot and my film being loaded into the back of a Cortina Estate.

RL and I have breakfast with Hannan at a South Ken café. We are preoccupied with what's wrong with the film, rather than what's right. What a long way we've come from the euphoria of the early rushes, five and a half months ago.

Wednesday, September 22nd

Drive down to Knightsbridge for lunch with David Puttnam. Large numbers of police are about, closing off roads in preparation for the TUC Day of Action march. Down an almost empty Pall Mall with policemen lining my route. Can't help thinking how many police witnesses I would have if there were an accident. Probably two or three hundred.

Puttnam is already at a table in Mr Chow's – eager, voluble, enthusiastic, but a listener as well as a talker. He's been at a government-run committee this morning and is off to give a speech to Channel 4 this afternoon. *Local Hero* is coming along wonderfully and he thinks it may have as big an impact as *Chariots of Fire*. He has projects involving Rowan Atkinson, he's bought the rights to *Another Country*, he's produced a Channel 4 series, *First Love*, and has a new movie which starts shooting in Dallas in October.

We moan together about lack of time to read, be with the family (he's 41 and has a 20-year-old daughter). He asks me how I manage. I say it's quite simple, I just act as my own safety-valve. I don't have a secretary and an office set-up as he has; I take on as much as I can myself cope with, which is generally too much, but not half as much as the indefatigable Puttnam.

I hardly remember what we ate. I drank Perrier, he a bloody Mary. He told me of plans for filming the complete works of Dickens. He'd come up with the idea on holiday when, it seems, he'd read several of the books and a biography of Dickens himself. He's costed it at £50 million and is keen to find out whether Shepperton has the space for a brand new Dickensian back lot. If the project happened on the scale Puttnam was talking of today it would be a rich prize for any studio.

He's very pleased to know that I'm proposing an across-the-board percentage share-out for the crew on *Missionary*, as he did on *Chariots* and *Local Hero*. He gives me some useful advice on how to set it up. He estimates that on *Chariots* the crew will each get £1,500! His secretary, who is on something like half a percentage point, will get £75,000!

He doesn't seem anxious to get away and we chatter on for a couple of hours – about a mill he's bought in Malmesbury, where the mill-race will be used to generate electricity, about Jacqueline du Pré, in a wheelchair at a nearby table – and about the possibility of working together. He wants me to write one of the *First Love* films.

Return call to Ken Blancato in LA. They 'love the concept' of our latest poster and will be testing it at the weekend, but definitely using it for some of their smaller ads.

Friday, September 24th

Spend the afternoon reading the six children's books I have to review for the *Ham and High*. Very English all of them – and all printed in Italy. Alternate between moods of determination to criticise quite severely and general easy-going bonhomie. Hardest thing to write is the opening paragraph – my attitude to children's books. Am stuck on this when the time comes for us to brave a prolonged downpour and drive down to the Aldwych to see some Indian classical dancing from our ex-babysitter Asha Tanha.

Asha dances her Arangetram – a solo display of various classical South Indian dances. She's on stage for an hour and a half – and to see quiet, slight, soft, retiring little Asha dancing, miming and holding an audience of 150 for that long is a real eye-opener. She dances very gracefully and it's a difficult combination of rhythm, balance, expressions and story-telling. Very beautifully done.

I feel the frenetic pressures of London life very satisfactorily loosening and, although the music is not easy for the Western ear, I felt very much better when we left at ten than when I came in at half past seven, rushing out of the rain and the lines of stopped traffic on the approach to Waterloo Bridge.

Saturday, September 25th

Changeable, tempestuous weather. Helen collects a kitten, which we call Denis.

Sunday, September 26th

I scribble a few notes for a speech at today's cast and crew viewing of '*The Mish*'.

Conventional, but not over-enthusiastic applause. I suppose many of them have seen it before, or are looking at their own work. I can't see why I should have expected this to be the best audience so far.

But almost before the 'HandMade' title has faded, Denholm is leaning over my seat, enthusing rapturously. He thinks it's 'marvellous, a little classic', and both he and his wife go on for some time in this encouraging vein. Helen still loves it and Tom, who was there with his friend Jasper, is very pleased with it too. No rush of hand-shaking fans, but a solid majority of those who think it successful.

Stay talking until five o'clock, then home. Have not eaten and feel very lumpen with the wine. Tom and Jasper are thumping out jazz improvisations on the piano, Rachel and Willy are encouraging our new cat, Denis, to hurl his little body round the kitchen, so I take to bed for a half-hour, then sit rather sleepily and read the papers.

Down to LBC for a ten o'clock programme on which I am to be the Mystery Guest. Evidently one caller susses me out within two minutes, but they don't put him through until 10.30. Meanwhile, I've been guessed as Danny La Rue, Larry Grayson, Melvyn Hayes and Kenneth Williams.

Watch *Roseland*,[1] and enjoy Denis going crazy. So nice to have another Denis in my life.

---

1 1977 movie about the Roseland Ballroom in New York City. Not a commercial hit but very touching.

Wednesday, September 29th

Columbia are postponing the opening of *Missionary* to November 6th. Reason given is that there are now four other 'major' movies opening on October 22nd.

Linda Barker from Columbia calls, presuming I'm coming out for the three weeks to October 22nd anyway. What's the point of doing promotion which climaxes two weeks prior to the film opening? She reacts like she'd never thought of this one before and promises to talk to her bosses.

Conference call around ten from Antonowsky and Roginski. MA starts by saying that all my TV appearances can be taped and used later – when I protest that I'm not going to work my ass off on a publicity tour which doesn't include the last two weeks before the movie opens. Compromise suggested – I do the college circuit as planned, starting next Monday, then return to the UK for two weeks and then come back for one week LA, one week NYC.

To bed a little grumpily with the TG/Stoppard script of *Brazil* to read.

Thursday, September 30th

Driven to Elstree. Work on some last-minute rewrites of the 'Middle of the Film'. Then into a wonderful, off-the-shoulder, 1950's style costume, supplied at the last minute by Vanessa Hopkins, which brings back all those images of my sister and *Heiress* magazine and her first smart grownup posed photograph.

Work very solidly in a concentrated spell from eleven until two, without, I think, even leaving my armchair. As I give my final speech, I really do feel that at last it's over.

Saturday, October 2nd

TG comes round and we talk about *Brazil*. I feel that the story of Jill and Lowry takes forever to get off the ground and there is more observation of the tatty world of the future than plot development. Some repetition of good ideas, too. TG feels that Stoppard has softened it a bit, and I think he may be right. The characters talk without any edge. Their behaviour is observed with amused detachment rather than commitment. And the scale of *Brazil* is such that it cannot just be a gentle story like *The Missionary*. TG films for much higher stakes. Still, many good moments, effects, surreal dream sequences, which will work.

Sunday, October 3rd: London–Washington DC

Gather together my things for the first week of *Missionary* promotion, including sketches, bits of old speeches – anything that may help. Remember that Graham Chapman used to begin his US college appearances by asking the audience to shout abuse at him.

Landed in Washington in early evening. Dulles Airport, set in mellowing, wooded Virginia countryside, was unexpectedly quiet. I was paged at customs and given VIP treatment, rushed through and out into a waiting limousine by a girl called Sherry.

As we drove into Washington she showed me some of the 'merchandising'. T-shirts with 'The Missionary University Tour' unexceptionally written on them. A polo-neck with 'The Missionary' and the words 'Give Your Body To Save My Soul' on.

At eight o'clock – one o'clock a.m. my time – I go into a press conference for college students. There are about 20 people there and Marvin Antonowsky sits in as well. Many of them have seen the movie and I'm told they laughed a lot at the showing, but one black student I spoke to didn't think it would mean much to a black college audience.

Marvin seems well pleased, though, and likes what he calls 'all the additions'. Over dinner – soft-shell crabs – he fishes for what I'm doing next. Suggests a re-make of *Kind Hearts and Coronets*. Confirmed that he didn't like *Privates on Parade*. Says he finds Nichols' work too black and cynical. But we have another of our easy, friendly, convivial meals. We never seem to be at a loss for things to chat about.

Monday, October 4th: Washington DC–Toronto

An idea occurred to me for the start of my proposed University of Maryland speech. Owing perhaps a little to memories of Edna Everage's showmanship, it was that I should compose some lines of rather bad poetry in honour of the University of Maryland.

At 9.30 Sherry arrives to take me downstairs to talk to a reporter from a month-old daily newspaper *USA Today*. We have breakfast in Les Beaux Champs – 'A French restaurant self-assured enough to serve American wines'. Grapefruit, scrambled eggs and bacon, ignore the 'Bakehouse Basket'.

The reporter saw the movie at the Washington showing last Friday. He himself liked it but did not enthuse, and he *was* worried by the big launch, multi-print treatment. He felt that Columbia will drop it like a hot potato if it doesn't perform commercially.

To the campus of Maryland University.

The students take me round back passages and up fire escapes to a theatre where I am billed to speak. 'Meet Michael Palin. Free.' say the posters.

Inside the theatre are TV crews, photographers, a stage, a dais and a full house of 750 students (with some turned away, I hear). Seeing a brown paper bag I grab it, empty out its contents and enter the auditorium with it over my head. Two besuited young students say nice things in introduction and I'm given a scroll for making the world laugh and then a floppy, big soft toy turtle.

Wednesday, October 6th: Chicago

To Northwestern University, north of Chicago on the lakeside.

A picturesque, leafy campus looking out over Lake Michigan. I am to talk to a class on ... 'Acting Problems in Style-Comedy' at the Theater and Interpretation Center. It sounds pretentious, but the people involved, particularly the professor – Bud Beyer – are very warm and friendly. All nervous and sweating in the 80° humidity. Many good words about my film and the 'Great Railway Journey', which has already been shown on PBS here more times than on the Beeb in England.

The University Chaplain makes a very funny and complimentary speech about myself and the '*Mish*' and presents me with a stuffed wildcat. I read my poem and say goodbye.

To Columbia Pictures headquarters in a faceless office building in a half-completed plaza beside O'Hare Airport. I'm photographed with the girls and do my Prince Charles bit, shaking hands with everybody. I learn that they are very pleased with the exhibitor's reaction in Chicago, Minneapolis and Milwaukee. '*Mish*' will open in 14 theatres in the Chicago area – including two prime sites. Everyone seems very keen and hopeful.

Thursday, October 7th: Dallas

Alarm call at 7.15, but I've been awake since seven, trying out lines for today's poem. Southern Methodist University is not easy to rhyme.

A crowd of maybe 200 kids are gathered in the open air around a makeshift stage. I'm presented with a plaque for being 'A Missionary for British Humor in the US'. Poor PA is a curse, but my poem in response goes down well. I feel like an old-style politician at the hustings – talking off the back of a truck. The audience is receptive and appreciative and after I have finished there follows a custard pie throwing contest, which I am to judge. Taken quite seriously by beefy male students (no women contestants), including one who delivers a custard pie on a motorbike, à la mediaeval tournament.

Friday, October 8th: San Francisco

My first appointment of the day – a live interview at Station KQAK, the Quake. As I entered the limousine, Melanie [my publicity lady] chilled me to the marrow with the news that 'Really crazy things are happening down there. Robin Williams has been there since six o'clock with some other improv comics and it's just really crazy!'

Oh, God . . . Dear God, do I have to?

There was a bustle of excitement, then I was shown into the studio itself, which was densely packed with fans. They had nowhere to sit and clearly no provision had been made for their presence at all, but there they all were, like the crowd at one of Jesus's miracles, squashed into this hot and airless room, gazing at their heroes – in this case Alex Bennett, a gentle, bespectacled DJ, Robin Williams, red-faced and driven with comic improvisation like a man exorcising some spirits, and a local comic, who had a neat moustache and was also working hard, though no match for Robin.

I was cheered on entry and shown to a place midway between these high-pressure comics and two microphones. 'This is worse than the Queen's bedroom,' quipped I, helplessly . . . looking round at the sea of faces. Suddenly everyone, I realised, was staring at me, waiting for me to be witty, marvellous and funny. It was a nightmare come true – like some massive overdose of shyness aversion therapy.

Robin Williams was in his element, switching with incredible speed and dexterity into an ad-libbed playlet. Never at a loss for words, and remarkably consistent. He held the show together. Jeremy, with the moustache, and myself, shared a microphone – there was no point in my sharing Robin's. The humour was West Coast – brittle, topical, cruel, mocking, black, but with some wonderful flashes of fantasy. RW took the new film *Road Warrior* and turned it into 'Rhodes Warrior', the tale of a rogue Rhodes Scholar left alive on earth after the holocaust – 'Tough, educated, he read his way through trouble'.

The worst moment was when I was asked to describe *The Missionary*. It sounded so leaden and mundane in the midst of all this sharp, hip humour – as if it were coming from another world. I was left helplessly asserting, in the silence that followed my dull little description, 'It *is* funny . . .'

But the biggest test of the day is yet to come. My visit to the campus of San Francisco State, where Columbia, I'm later to learn, have been working very hard on my behalf.

To everyone's relief, there is a crowd – estimated at over 1,000 – clustered in the bright sunshine around a makeshift stage. It's San Francisco, though, and my 'award' this time is not to be presented by a nervous student or a well-meaning chaplain, but by – what else in SF – a comic.

My 'introducer' is Jane Dornacker, a big, busty lady, who wears her 'Give Your Body To Save My Soul' T-shirt quite spectacularly. But she does like to talk. It's a fierce, competitive world, the world of improv, and once you're up there and it's going well, you stay. She is getting quite raunchy by now, with jokes about haemorrhoids being a pain in the ass and masturbation in San Quentin. I can see the organisers are getting twitchy because there are innumerable TV crews covering the event and there is precious little material they'll be able to use. In fact one has given up altogether. Eventually Dornacker draws to a close and has to give me my award for 'moral virtue'.

Read my poem, heavy on royal family jokes, which they love out here. Thank God for Michael Fagan.[1]

Monday, October 18th

J Goldstone had rung to tell me of a private screening of *My Favourite Year* – the Peter O'Toole film comedy which has received such good

---

1 Fagan, an Irishman, had twice broken into Buckingham Palace. In July 1982 he got as far as the Queen's bedroom and talked to her for ten minutes before being apprehended.

reviews in the US. I went along to the EMI Theatre in Wardour Street where, a few weeks ago, I was biting my fingernails showing *Missionary* to my friends.

Before I left I spoke to Sue Barton in New York, who cheered me no end with the news that *Cosmopolitan* had written a very good review of *The Missionary*. So it's two against one so far. (*Newsweek* good, *Time* not so good.) Not a bad start.

My Favourite Year was a lovely little film. A light piece of nostalgia for the 1950's, based on Mel Brooks's experience as a writer for Sid Caesar. For anyone who's hosted *Saturday Night Live*, it had extra significance, being shot at NBC in 30 Rockefeller Plaza and being all about the problems of star guests on live shows.

It felt much the same weight as *The Missionary*. Gentle humour, laced with slapstick, enjoyment of characters as much as plot, and shot through with moments of pathos (beautifully handled by Peter O'Toole). Seeing it, and bearing in mind its early success in the high-energy world of US comedy, gave me as much hope for *The Missionary* as the news about *Cosmopolitan*. I left the cinema with the feeling that I hope people will have after *The Missionary*.

Tuesday, October 19th: Southwold

Up to Suffolk. Ma meets me in the new Metro. She doesn't use first gear, as it's rather difficult, and at the moment mistrusts most of the gearbox, but seems a lot safer than in the ageing 1100.

It's warm and dry enough to sit out in the garden before lunch, and in the afternoon take Ma for a walk, in a friendly wind, out onto the cliffs beyond Covehithe.

Saturday, October 23rd

Columbia call and ask if I could find out from Maggie S if she will come to the States at any time. Not really my job, but Maggie has a way of making things difficult for anyone to get decisions out of her.

Ring Maggie. She won't say 'yes', but she does know that it helps the movie to appear in person and I think that for me she will do a couple of days in New York.

Home to start packing when TG arrives. He wants to talk about '*MOL*'. He saw it at an excellent showing (he says) on Tuesday. He felt weak points were 'Hendys' (too long, but liked) and the tiger skin exchanges and Eric's Waiter and Arthur Jarrett. But his real worry is his own piece. It will be 15 minutes at least and he wants to know my feelings about its inclusion or not in the main body of the film.

All this in our bedroom, with me in underpants checking how many pairs of socks I might need and Helen in curlers about to change.

We go off to see 'A Star is Torn' – a one-woman show by an Aussie lady called Robyn Archer, which is playing to packed houses at the Wyndhams. She sweeps briskly through a repertoire of impersonations of great popular lady singers of the twentieth century, many of whose qualification for inclusion in her act seem to be that they died of drug abuse round about the age of 40. I'm sure this cheers up my 40-year-old wife no end.

Sunday, October 24th: London–Seattle

A strange feeling of unreality as I go back to *The Missionary* and its American opening. I'm sure I shall fall into the swim of things, but at the moment I just feel a deadening sense of weariness.

My scalp itches and I've forgotten to pack any toothpaste. My little kitchen and my family come to mind in sharp contrast to the world I shall inhabit for two weeks, and I know that I am coming near the end of my ability to lift up, inspire, charm, enthuse and everything else that has had to take me away from home so much this year.

Our 747 dips below Mount Rainier, tallest peak in the 'contiguous' USA, impressive and Paramount-like out of the southern windows, and we are on the ground in Seattle nearly an hour and a half late at about 3.30. The reward is a smooth, efficient, clean, empty terminal and the quickest entry ever into the US.

Monday, October 25th: Seattle–Los Angeles

At 8.30 we leave for my first appointment – an appearance on a local morning TV show – *Northwest AM*.

Back to the hotel to talk to a Jewish girl from New Jersey. Her quick, nervous speech and voluble hand gestures are definitely un-Seattlian. Talk for a half-hour over coffee, then I'm led downstairs to a group of six, mostly young and studentish scribblers, waiting for a brunch interview.

We take off an hour late and run into a heavy concentration of rain clouds.

Wonderful dialogue behind. A fat woman with a dog in a basket.

'Oh, my ears feel funny,' she exclaims as we descend into LA.

'Hold your nose and blow,' suggests a helpful neighbour.

'Blow what?' she cries, mystified.

We are bundled off briskly in LA. Almost a couple of hours late, but through the airport, or rather the half-rebuilt shell of it, in about 20 minutes. Outside a shambles of pick-up vehicles, including my enormous length of grey limousine, which is accompanied by a dapper little matching grey driver, who takes me direct to the Academy of Film and TV Arts.

At the Academy I meet Ed Roginski and Marvin, and other Columbia folk, as cocktails are being served before the showing to what seems to be a large and impressive audience, full of critics and film folk.

Grit my teeth over the sound in the pre-title sequence – how I want that hymn sound to crescendo! – and the grubby darkness of the boat sequence (one of the less successful in the movie), but the audience respond well and pick up most of the possible laugh moments, applauding occasionally. Marvin, next to me, disconcertingly keeps checking his watch.

The Longleat sequence is clearly going to become a classic, with Hordern's performance beyond criticism.

Marvin takes myself and Linda Barker, head of talent relations (!), to a meal at Trumps – all white walls and very chic. I think I ate some bass. Best news is that we have picked up another good review in *New York Magazine*.

Tuesday, October 26th: Los Angeles

A brief meeting with Marvin A and Randy Wicks to show me two alternatives for the newspaper ads – one has 'Michael Palin', the other 'Monty Python's Michael Palin'. I am against the 'Monty Python' mention and Marvin gives in to me, though he would rather use it. The small print ads are using the lipstick on the collar picture – so all that extra work was worth it.

Four interviews in my quite small suite fill the afternoon, then off to *The Merv Griffin Show*. These are the appearances I look forward to least. The movie is sacrificed to the ego and image of the host – which is what these shows are all about. Merv just makes money and grins egregiously. He has not seen the movie.

I wait in a green room, with no sign of a decent drink, together with two 'nutritionists' whose book *Life Extension* is a national best-seller in this land of instant cures. They remind me of the old quacks of the Wild West selling patent medicines. They are an extraordinary pair. He talks incessantly, she, small and wiry, shows me her arm muscles.

As I'm leaving the studio Jack Lemmon passes, with a crowd of guests. A publicist asks me if I want to meet Lemmon and before I know it I'm shaking hands with the great man, who turns out to be a Python fan – as are all his family, he says.

I tell him that he and Peter Sellers are my favourite comic actors of all time. As if he's been on chat shows so often, Lemmon quickly cues into an anecdote about Sellers writing a whole set of false reviews of a Lemmon film which completely fooled him. But he looked baggy-eyed and unfit, and a slight slurring of the words and blurring of the gaze suggested he'd been at the old liquor. But at least I'd told him how wonderful I thought he was.

I've survived the day pretty well on adrenaline, but as I relax over a meal with Polier and Knopf and their wives at the Mandarin in Beverly Hills, I begin to wilt.

I glean from them that Columbia are confident enough in *The Missionary* to have increased the prints to 500, that Polier and Knopf reckon three million dollars for the first weekend would be what they would hope for, and that they share my view that outside the big cities the film could be slow.

Thursday, October 28th: Los Angeles–New York

Alarm call at 6.30. Down to the limousine at seven. The sun is still not up as we start towards the airport. Tom, the driver, is a Romanian, and this accounts for his strange, very correct English. He works for a firm whose boss was once Elvis Presley's bodyguard and who specially asked him to tell me what a total fan of Monty Python Elvis was!

I'm at LA Airport and checked in by 7.45. 'Vicky' is our stewardess for the flight. As she goes through the ritual of checking our names, she comes to the seat next to me – a rather overweight, middle-aged American announces his name is Boyer. 'Oh, that's pretty,' she returns automatically.

Delivered about six to the Sherry Netherland. Two windows look straight down 5th Avenue into the forest of skyscrapers and the others look the length of Central Park South and out to the Hudson and the New Jersey shoreline.

Monday, November 1st: New York–Boston

Collect magazines, as this is the first day of public reviews.

Anson of *Newsweek*, we already know, liked it. *Time*, we suspected, didn't, and mercifully their totally dismissive review is short – though top of a column in which three movies are contemptuously tossed aside under the heading 'Rushes'. I find myself in company with Sean Connery and Fred Zimmerman's *Three Days Last Summer*, and the almost universally mocked *Monsignor*, with Reeve and co, as victims of Richard Schickel's contempt.

But *New York Magazine*'s David Denby runs it as his major movie story of the week, with a photo and the subhead '*The Missionary* is a satirical and naughty film – an aesthetically pleasing object that's also very funny.' Columbia's rep is very pleased and now feels we have enough to launch the movie on Friday *with* reviews.

At three Stuart from Columbia arrives with a middle-aged reporter from the *New York Post*. The trend of the *Post*'s questions reflects the newspaper. Why do we always go for religion? Do I expect shocked reactions? Surely the sight of a priest in bed with three women at *once* is going to cause some problems? (Smacking of reporter's lips.) When I point out that I am never seen in bed with three women he seems genuinely perplexed and shakes his head in disbelief. 'Well I'm *sure* I saw you in bed with three women.'

Into the traffic on what has become a hot and sultry evening, as I head out to La Guardia and catch the Eastern shuttle to Boston.

I'm no sooner there than a local TV station is clipping mikes to my shirt and sitting me down in the foyer beside the popcorn with a light glaring in my face and an earnest lady reporter who hasn't seen the movie. She asks me questions like 'Do you believe in God?' and 'Your children are very important to you, right? How are you structuring *their* future?' She actually runs out of tape on the question 'What do you believe in?'

After the session, at which I'm encouraged by this predominantly young audience's applause when I mention the names of Maggie Smith and Trevor Howard, I'm taken out to eat with Michael Bodin, the critic of the *Boston Globe*.

He thought *The Missionary* was a good film, but could have been a great one. Interestingly enough, he used the Magna Carta line in Africa as an example of the promise of greatness which he felt the first five minutes of the movie held out. This line was inserted at the very last minute of the very last dub.

We talked about movies until the waiters began to put chairs on tables at a quarter past twelve. (He it was who told me of the latest piece of linguistic butchery at the hands of the anti-sexists – in nearby Cambridge, Mass, the term 'waitress' is out, replaced by 'waitrons'.)

Tuesday, November 2nd: New York

I'm beginning to develop a phobia about American make-up artists. With very little grace they just slap on layer after layer of base and powder until I resemble Michael Palin about as much as the Madame Tussaud's waxworks resemble real people. Today a large black lady in a curiously confusing blonde wig works me over. 'I saw you on *Good Morning America* ... you looked awful ... all white ... what was the trouble?'

'Make-up,' I replied with pleasure.

Wednesday, November 3rd: New York

As the release day comes nearer, I feel myself wanting the pace to accelerate.

Variety calls the movie 'congenial but commercially uncertain'. It's a mixed review, complimenting me on my acting, liking the film, finding some 'wonderful moments' and 'exquisite photography', but managing to sound quite negative in conclusion. The script could have gone into more detail on three of the sub-plots, it said.

The doubts sown by *Variety* are encouragingly countered by *Hollywood Reporter*, which thinks the film an artistic and box-office winner for Columbia. This is the only review so far to suggest we might make money, and coming out of such a hard-nosed journal as the *Reporter* makes it doubly welcome.

Thursday, November 4th: New York

I go on to *The Letterman Show* in the last half-hour. I bring a grubby cellophane bag of things to present to Letterman but refuse to open up. He never tries to get into the act much and just lets me go on. I overact and fool about shamelessly. But he shows a clip and reaffirms that the reviews have been good and I get some laughs and applause and at 6.30 another show is over.

Back to the hotel, wash, change, then drive downtown, collecting Richard Loncraine on the way, to talk to a film class. Disconcertingly, they take a straw poll (before I've been revealed to be there) in which 40% of his audience say they didn't like the film. One woman who did like it, says 'I hate Michael Palin, but I loved this movie.' Richard nearly died at this.

We drive in search of tomorrow's *New York Times*. The excitement mounts as we find ourselves a half-hour early at the newsstands, so we head for the steamy rear of the *New York Times* building.

We wait in the car as Stu [Zakin, from Columbia] disappears into the night. He races back. Our pulses race with him. 'It's there!' he cries. 'It's there!'

'Well bring it, for God's sake ...'

'I need *change*,' Stu shouts, in a rare show of excitement. We have a rushed whip-round and he disappears again.

At about 10.10 he reappears with two copies of tomorrow's *Times*. I read one. Richard and Stu the other. I start from the top. Stu, much more practised, flips through to the end. He is the first to discover it's a good review. We have the most important critic in New York, and another daily paper to boot. That's two out of three, whatever else happens. Relief and joy.

Back on my own in the Sherry Netherland at 1.15. I spread out the *New York Times* lovingly. Better than Canby's review is the big ad for *The Missionary* which contains quotes from four good reviews, including one from *US Magazine*'s Steven Schaefer, which I didn't even know we had. 'Don't Miss The Missionary – a delight from beginning to its marvellous end.' 'Hilarious – Michael Palin is smashing' – *Cosmopolitan*. 'Michael Palin has finally left his mark' – even *Newsweek*'s backhanded compliment looks stirringly impressive in big print.

How on earth can I sleep? Who can I ring? They won't be up in England, so I try and sleep and will ring early.

There can have been few better moments when I've laid my head on the pillow than at the Sherry Netherland Hotel, New York City, as the rain finally breaks the late heatwave.

Friday, November 5th: New York

And the news continues to be optimistic. Rex Reed has given us a glowing review, which makes a clean sweep of all three New York daily papers.

Over to WCBS and Independent News Network to meet Jeff Lyons. At the end of the radio interview he asks if I will put my voice on tape for his home answering machine. Apparently he asks everyone he interviews to do this and now has an unrivalled collection of phone answerers, including David Niven, Peter Ustinov and Max von Sydow.

Then round to the crowded, noisy, dark security of the Oak Room at the Plaza for a drink with Nancy and Bruce Williamson – the *Playboy* film critic. Bruce is very good company, a droll but not pushy teller of stories and a lover of trains to boot.

During the afternoon the gilt has been slightly skimmed off the top of the critical gingerbread. I picked up a copy of the *Washington Post*, to find myself judged very harshly by one Gary Arnold, who seems to have felt the film was an unmitigated disaster for which I was almost entirely to blame.

Saturday, November 6th: New York–London

Helen and I have been apart for nearly four months this year, and when I called her yesterday, full of excitement at the news from NYC, she sounded so glum that I changed plans to leave on Sunday and decided to go back as soon as possible. I've been sustained over the past few weeks by interviews and the anticipation of reaction. Now the first wave of reaction has come and gone I want to get away from limousines and hotel rooms and do things for myself again.

On to Concorde, which leaves on time at 9.30. Only famous face I recognise is Rupert Murdoch, spectacles low down on his nose, looking like a don putting finishing touches to a thesis.

We cross the Atlantic in three hours and 15 minutes and I'm home at Julia Street six hours after leaving the Sherry Netherland. Lovely to see them all again.

I ring Neville, Maggie Smith, Norman Garwood [our art director] and Peter Hannan in a mood of great elation. Thank God it's over.

Sunday, November 7th

Denis rings from Dallas in mid-afternoon. We have apparently done well in New York and Los Angeles, but not well outside the major cities. He gives me some fairly wretched figures: 800 dollars for the first night in Boulder, Colorado; equally unimpressive in Las Vegas – just over 1,000 dollars; Phoenix 1,500 for the first night.

Denis saw a rave review in Dallas last night, but it isn't doing any business in the south as a whole. Denis's projection for the first weekend is 1.8 million dollars – a long way from Knopf and Polier's estimate given to me as we sauntered down Rodeo Drive, licking ice-creams, ten days ago.

Monday, November 8th

I decide to call Polier and Knopf in LA direct. The weekend has been by no means the failure Denis suggested. Whilst not looking like a block-buster, the figures for three days are 'highly respectable' (Dan's quote). They are likely to reach 1.86 million for the weekend, not 1.3. But isn't this considerably short of the three million estimate? 'Oh, no, our three million forecast was for the *week*.'

'This is no hit and run picture,' is how Dan put it. Still awaiting Columbia's verdict. They won't be ecstatic, says David, but there's a fair chance they'll get behind it.

Tuesday, November 9th

A fine, clear morning. Helen says I should stay in bed, but I do enjoy breakfast time with the family. I like to wake up with them.

Cleese rings mid-morning. He asks me if I will write a letter to the Press Council supporting him in his case against the *Sun*, which published an account of the Zulus in Glasgow story quoting JC as saying to the black extras 'Which one of you bastards did a rain dance?' JC is very cross at the total inaccuracy and will not let the matter rest. The *Sun* have not been helpful. He wants TJ, myself and Ray Corbett [the first assistant director] to help out as witnesses.

Thursday, November 11th

Spent the early part of the morning writing a thank you letter to Anton-owsky – something he probably doesn't receive very often, but I *do* feel that Columbia ran the campaign very competently.

Then drive down to the South Bank for the first film of the London Film Festival – *Scrubbers*.

Scrubbers turns out to be a well-made film with superb and convincing performances from the girls. Mai Zetterling has succeeded in giving flesh and blood to characters who are normally regarded as 'beyond society'.

The only problem I had is that the depiction of prison life has been done so often and so well recently in a series of documentaries. So, in *Scrubbers* there were many moments when I felt myself caught up in cliché – the stock psychiatrist, the hard governor, the keys in locks, the clang of doors. But the girls were Mai Zetterling originals, and were the heart and soul of the bleak, gloomy, violent picture.

Friday, November 12th

RL has rung to say that Warren Beatty had called from Hollywood to say how much he had enjoyed the movie (these are the little unexpected bonuses which are as much a part of the satisfaction of making a movie as any grosses).

Out for dinner to Judy Greenwood's[1] in Fulham Road. She lives in a comfortable, homely clutter above her own antique shop with a dog, a daughter and a builder husband called Eddie who has an earring and had just broken his toe. Judy is forthright, easy company – with striking Palin looks.

I defend comprehensive education and the NHS rather limply to Eddie, who has no scruples about buying a better education or buying himself out of pain ... And why not? I wonder gloomily – arguing out of form more than conviction.

Saturday, November 13th

Write to Al Levinson after reading his short story 'Nobody's Fool' – a piece of real-life drama thinly fictionalised and very revealing and moving. Al

1 Judy is my cousin. Youngest daughter of my father's sister Katherine.

is so near to being a good writer, but just fails, sometimes – as in 'Millwork' – by the very tip of his fingernails. So I write back encouragingly, but cannot offer more concrete support – like an unqualified rave or an offer to publish. I still have most of *Travelogs* unsold.

Denis rings at six o'clock. As soon as I hear 'unfortunately', I know that *Missionary* has not made a solid commercial showing across the States. New York he hasn't heard from, but Chicago, even after the TV ads extolling its virtues through the reviews, is 33% down. San Francisco 27% down, Denver 31%. Even Los Angeles – where Denis says all word is that *The Missionary* is a resounding success – is 10% down.

The final overall figures will continue to be 'mediocre' and 'so-so' until Columbia pull out from 'between the mountains'. If we had opened only in NYC and LA *The Missionary* would have been hailed as a triumph. *That's* what irks me tonight.

Sunday, November 14th

A day for sitting at home with the Sunday papers and a lot of wine at lunchtime.

But I have agreed to go to the Oxford Children's Book Fair, and at half past eleven I leave, with somewhat sinking spirits, to drive out along the splashy A40.

At Oxford it's bitterly cold. I park by the new Law Library. An elderly man in a blue overcoat passes me; on his left breast a string of medals, tinkling softly. Of course, it's Remembrance Sunday – poppies and war veterans, with the added immediacy of the Falklands War this year.

Nearly all the grimy façades of my day have been cleaned, resurfaced and repointed. Oxford seems generally more opulent. The Randolph Hotel, where the Book Fair is taking place, full of well-heeled diners.

Up to the Ballroom. My presence is announced over a forbidding PA system and I'm given a chair, a table and a pile of books to sit beside. By four o'clock I've sold about ten copies of the book [*Small Harry and the Toothache Pills*]. David Ross [from Methuen] and the organiser from Blackwell's Children's Shop seem very pleased, though my presence seemed to me something of a waste of time.

Nice, silly evening at home, all of us playing a game after supper and being noisy. Then, after the children go to bed mercifully early, H and I sit by the first fire of the winter.

Monday, November 15th

Called Polier and Knopf at one o'clock and their news rather took the stuffing out of this gentle, easy day. *Missionary* is down 25–30% everywhere, including the NY and LA areas, in its second weekend. The take for the weekend was 1.4 million, as opposed to 1.86 the first weekend.

The 'good news', as Knopf puts it, is that Columbia are still supporting the movie with TV (in NYC) and press in the big cities. It's doing well in Toronto and Vancouver. Not holding up on Broadway/Times Square, where they have now sussed that it's not a sex movie! All the quality areas of cities are still reporting good figures – but David says rather ominously that the picture 'may not be long for this world'.

Thursday, November 18th

S Albury rings. He would like to do an Eric Olthwaite series for Granada, with someone like Charles Sturridge directing and himself producing. Everything about the idea, apart from being Eric Olthwaite for a year, appeals to me.

Friday, November 19th

Twelve years ago, when William was born, I was in the middle of shooting my first film *And Now For Something Completely Different*. Today my seventh film, *The Missionary*, is at No. 2 in the list of Top Grossing Films in the US.

The appearance of *The Missionary* above *ET* and the rest (for one glorious week!) was the high point of this crowded day.

Went down to the Python office and signed things and saw Lena, Steve's Swedish book-keeper, celebrate her last day at the office. Apparently she's always leaving packets of tampons around, so they presented her with a smart little case with a special plaque on it engraved with her name and the word 'Tampons' in very large letters.

Then, via shops, home to prepare for William's ambitious disco party, which is to be held tonight at No. 2.

The party runs from seven until half past ten. About 18 invited. The boys arrive earlier than the girls, but the girls, when they do appear, virtually take over the music and dancing. Some of them, in black berets with short skirts and black fishnet stockings, look about 23. The boys look younger, less self-assured, and spend most of the early party throwing and squirting things up the far end of the room. My heart sinks for a while. The girls talk, all at once and at the top of their voices, about clothes.

But gradually everyone thaws out. By the end I actually have a few boys dancing with the girls (they've been scared stiff of them for most of the evening). We have a joke-telling competition which is quite successful, and at 10.15 most of them seem unhappy to leave. Several of the girls give me a kiss for working the disco as they disappear into the night. Nobody smoked and nobody drank (probably their last year of innocence).

Tuesday, November 23rd

Halfway through the evening David Knopf returns my call. The third weekend is much as expected. Sadly no miracles have been performed. *The Missionary* has slipped 32%, below a million dollars for the weekend, and may lose up to 100 prints, which Knopf is not too unhappy about, though he is trying to persuade Columbia to keep as many prints working over the big Thanksgiving holiday weekend as possible.

'What do they feel about *The Missionary*?' I ask David, full of innocent curiosity. 'They've forgotten it,' returns David with admirable bluntness.

Wednesday, November 24th

Writing a speech for tonight's Young Publishers' meeting. Meeting takes place at the Cora Hotel in Tavistock Place, a stone's throw from Gandhi's statue. Not that anyone would want to throw stones at Gandhi's statue.

A full room – maybe 70 or 80 present. Behind the table are, left to right, Geoffrey Strachan, Sue Townsend, whose *Secret Life of Adrian Mole* has made her Methuen's newest best-seller, a very nice girl from the SPCK who is chairing the meeting, myself and Nigel Rees.

Tonight's theme is Humorous Publishing. Geoffrey is serious and efficiently informative. Sue Townsend is endearingly and honestly confused. 'I can't talk, that's why I write,' was the way she began her speech. Nigel Rees was smooth and seemingly nerveless, as befits a BBC radio personality.

I spoke last and the speech made people laugh very well for the first five minutes, then slightly less so as I warmed to the theme of 'Geoffrey Strachan – The Man Whose Life Was Changed by Humorous Publishing'.

A productive hour of question and answer. One lady who asked the quite reasonable question as to whether or not men preferred Python was told very sharply by another woman in the audience that the question was quite irrelevant! At the Spaghetti House in Sicilian Avenue I sat next to Sue Townsend, who I thought would be the most fun. She lives in Leicester and is quite happy about it. Especially as she is within stone-throwing distance of the house in which Joe Orton was born. Not that anyone ... (That's enough – ed.).

Thursday, November 25th

To Cambridge Gate for a financial discussion with Steve and Anne. For over an hour they briefed me on the appalling problems of trying to give some of my money away – in this case five percentage points of my *Missionary* royalties to be divided amongst the crew. Because I was not the company which hired the crew in the first place I'm almost totally unable to make any agreement to reward them in a way in which I shall not be severely fiscally penalised. Infuriating and frustrating.

Saturday, November 27th

Up, earlier than I would have wished, to take Willy to William Ellis to play rugby. He says he's doing it to be the first Palin to actually play in a W Ellis school match (Tom was often selected but always avoided playing). As I left him outside the school gates on Highgate Hill at a quarter to nine on this very cold, foggy morning, I could only feel sorry for him.

Drove down to Old Compton Street. Snatched a quick look at *Variety* before driving off and saw, to my surprise and pleasure, that *Missionary* is No. 3 in the US in its second week and holding quite respectably at over 6,000 dollars per screen.

Time Bandits is No. 4 on re-issue, so yours truly is the proud author of two films out of the American top four. If only I could feel that it meant something.

Sunday, November 28th

Missionary showing at the London Film Festival. The performance is sold out. I'm taking both grannies, as well as Angela, Veryan, Camilla and friend Deirdre from Strathblane (scene of Python's 'Zulu' episode) and Marcus.

A good feeling to see everyone hurrying out of the cold night into the QEH to see my film. 1,250 people inside and throughout there is regular laughter and prolonged applause at the end. Fulsome praise from Geoffrey Strachan and family and Barry Took and family and others who I don't know. Mother bears up really well, revelling in the pleasure of not just meeting Barry Took, but hearing such praise of her son from him.

Neville had reservations, when we all went for a meal afterwards, of the production-value-swamps-the-comedy nature. He felt I could have made it funnier and more robust if I'd been let off the hook. Terry J, who loves much of it, had similar reservations and told me to stop playing such dull characters!

Tuesday, November 30th: Southwold and London

The weather has settled over the weekend into a stable coolness. Last night it was two degrees below freezing. Leave home at 9.45 with Granny and reach Croft Cottage two and a half hours later. Suffolk is beautiful today in the bright, crystal-clear sunlight. Walk up the road past the sugar-beet collectors at work in the fields.

Cheered up by news from David Knopf that *The Missionary* take was up 15% at Thanksgiving weekend. The picture has now gathered in six and a half million dollars, but the best news of all is that Columbia now consider it 'playable'. (Paul Mazursky's *The Tempest* was evidently *not* playable.)

Dinner at Odin's with Marvin Antonowsky. Marvin still thinks a select-ive release would have worked better, but he admits that you can prove almost anything with hindsight.

He says emphatically that it has established me as a performer and advises me to get an agent for the US. I told him that my primary interest was in writing a movie – 'That's fine,' chomps Marvin, drooling walnut and lettuce salad. 'Next time write it present day and not too British.'

He will play *The Missionary* until Christmas then take it off and re-play it again in February, with press, in selected markets. 'The one thing *The Missionary* has done,' affirms Marvin, 'is established your creditability outside of the group ... I shouldn't say this to you, but you are now established as a *very* good light comedy actor!'

I buy Marvin the meal and we part, with a bear hug, in Devonshire Street, soon after eleven.

Thursday, December 2nd

Largely spent assembling speech for the Society of Bookmen tonight.

Leave for the Savile Club at six o'clock. Walk across Christmas-crowded Oxford Street and arrive by 6.30. The dark-panelled lobby of the unexceptional house in Brook Street is no preparation for the prettiness of the upstairs rooms in which the Society are holding their Christmas dinner. Beautiful walls and ceilings, the dining room picked out in eggshell blue and evidently based on a room in the Nymphenburg Palace at Munich (a nice link with Python!)[1] and the anterior room equally delicate, but in autumnal colours.

No-one recognises me at first and they all look frightfully impressive, reminding me of university dons – not exactly smart and well groomed, but rather academic and a few very distinguished manes of white hair.

I've based the first part of my speech on the fact that Sir Hugh Walpole, the founder of the Society, is not mentioned in the *Oxford Dictionary of Quotations*. But very few of the assembled gathering seem to know or care much about their founder – so the first minute or so is received politely. Realise that they are going to be a difficult audience. Clearly they aren't going to laugh uproariously. Nothing so uncontrolled. But I persevere and adapt my pace and the level of delivery and salvage some respectable applause.

Then some questions. One particularly granite-faced old man asked me who my three favourite humorous writers were. Why three, particularly, I don't know. 'Nabokov,' I began. He clearly didn't regard this as serious, so to annoy him further I followed it up with Spike Milligan. 'Oh, he's a bore!' says this most interesting of men.

Then a squarely-built, rather rabbinical-looking figure rose momentously and I felt I was about to be publicly denounced. But instead he suggested that, as my speech had been probably the best he'd ever heard at the Savile, the restrictions on reporting be lifted, allowing the *Bookseller* to reproduce my magnificent words in full. Only a few people supported this particular line, however, and I was left with the curious sensation of

1 We filmed there for Python's German show in 1971.

having simultaneously delivered an excellent speech to half the room and a dreadful one to the rest.

The man who had so fulsomely praised me turned out to be one Tom Rosenthal, Chairman of Secker and Warburg and Heinemann. He later asked me, most respectfully, to sign his menu.

Friday, December 3rd

Collected *Variety* and saw that *The Missionary* was still in touch with the leaders in its third week – at No. 6. New York seems to be saving *The Missionary* almost single-handed.

As I draw up outside the shop in Old Compton Street to buy the paper, I hear on a newsflash that Marty Feldman has died after finishing *Yellowbeard* in Mexico [he was 47]. The *Mail* rings later for some quotes. My best memory of Marty is that he was the first person to talk to me at my first ever *Frost Report* meeting back in 1966.

Take Helen and her friend Kathryn Evans to the Lyric Theatre to see Spike Milligan's one-man show, which opened last night. Only half full, I would estimate. Rather tattily put together, with a lot of lighting and sound botch-ups.

He obviously knew I was in because he kept shouting for me ... 'Is Michael Palin here, and has he paid?' Then in the second half he read a poem for me.

Monday, December 6th

In the evening we go out to dinner at David Puttnam's mews 'empire' in Queen's Gate, Kensington. Beautifully furnished and full of fine things, but also a lovely mixture of irregular spaces, large kitchen and small bedrooms off passageways, and a spacious upstairs sitting room with an unlikely roaring wood fire. A country farmhouse on three floors.

He's off to the States on Thursday to show the first cut of *Local Hero* to Warners. Compared to Columbia, his approach to marketing *Local Hero* in the States is very sophisticated – involving the enlistment of ecology groups and other special interest groups that can be identified and given preview showings, etc.

Puttnam confesses to loving working out grosses – sitting up long into the night with his calculator.

The Oscar for *Chariots of Fire* – Best Film 1981 – is almost casually standing on an open bookshelf. A heavy, solid, rather satisfying object. Has a Hollywood star ever been clubbed to death with an Oscar? It feels in the hand like an ideal offensive weapon.

Wednesday, December 8th

Richard has received a letter from Denis O' B, thanking him again for his work on '*The Mish*' and offering him five more percentage points on the film. 'Now I know it's officially a flop,' was RL's reaction.

Thursday, December 9th

A drunk in charge of a Volvo banged into me in Camden High Street. I tried to borrow a pen from passers-by, but they were all drunk too. It was like a dream.

James Ferman, the film censor, had seen '*Mish*' today, given it an 'AA' and said he thought it marvellous, one of the best comedies he's seen. Now why can't we put that on the poster instead of 'AA'?

Saturday, December 11th

Up through Covent Garden to Leicester Square to see *ET.*

The theatre is, of course, packed solid, and the lady next to me starts crying quite early on. It *is* a magical film, affecting and fresh and surprising and delightful despite all the prolonged build-up. I would think it almost impossible not to enjoy it if you have any sense of magic and imagination. It's pitched perfectly and, though many of the moments and situations are on the verge of being at least clichéd, at worst corny and sentimental, the picture succeeds all along with its supremely confident story-telling. Rachel is the only one of our party who comes out in tears, though I have been brought, pleasurably, to the brink on half a dozen occasions.

Later that evening Spike Milligan, in conversation on BBC2, names me as one of the few people (Norman Gunstone and Tommy Cooper are two others) who make him laugh.

Tuesday, December 14th

Set off, in a mad rush caused by a rash of ringing telephones, to meet my fellow dignitaries by Kentish Town Station.

We gather beneath a brightly painted canopy, salvaged with great imagination by a couple of local architects, BR and Camden Council from the remains of Elstree Station. Camden School for Girls sing carols behind the red ribbon, and a member of Camden's planning department struggles to make himself heard over the dual roar of Kentish Town traffic above and British Rail's trains beneath whilst being totally upstaged by an eccentric-looking old lady, with what appears to be a laundry bag, on the dais behind him.

My celebratory ode goes down extremely well and as soon as I've finished there is an instant demand for copies. I'm posed for silly photos and asked by one passer-by if I do this sort of thing professionally.

To Nigel G's[1] gallery, where I meet him and Glen Baxter, a cartoonist with Python-like tendencies, whom I greatly admire. Baxter has a thick tweed overcoat and a podgy, easily smiling face below a knitted tall hat. He looks like a sort of Yorkshire Rastafarian.

We talk over how best Nigel and Glen B could get a film about Baxter together. He's avoiding doing too many more of his *Impending Gleam*-type pictures as he feels he's almost saturated his own market. It's not just that there are a spate of bad Baxter imitations, but what hurts him more is that some people think the worst of them are done by him.

Call David Knopf. The bottom seems to have completely fallen out of *The Missionary* on its sixth weekend. A meagre 248,000 dollars. Knopf again strongly recommends collaboration on a film with John Cleese. 'Comedy team of the '80's,' says he.

Sunday, December 26th: Abbotsley–London

Early lunch and, at 1.30, a rather hasty and precipitous departure for London, as I have to be at a Python film viewing at three o'clock. Only an hour from Abbotsley to Gospel Oak. Roads very empty until we get into London. Lots of people taking Boxing Day constitutionals on the Heath. Drop the family off, unpack the car, then down to Wardour Street.

The Bijou is packed and hot and smoky. All sorts of familiar faces there – Arlene Phillips (who's just been turned down as choreographer for the new Travolta film, she tells me), Jim Acheson (still full of

---

1 My cousin Nigel Greenwood, elder brother of Judy, was much respected in the art world as a dealer and gallery owner. He spotted Gilbert and George early and Glen Baxter too. He died in April 2004.

excitement about the New York Marathon – he says I *must* go next year) and old acquaintances rarely seen these days like John Sims [the photographer] and C Alverson [writer and collaborator with Terry Gilliam on *Jabberwocky*]. Eric I conspicuously absent.

The film seems to go very quiet about a third of the way through, but ends very well, with 'Creosote' the high point. Afterwards I find that most people felt the first half worked very satisfactorily and if there *were* any longueurs they were either in the 'Pirate/Accountant' sequence or towards the end. But most people seemed to be quite bowled over by it.

This time five out of six Pythons have seen the film. There are no drastic differences of opinion. Everyone feels that TG's 'Pirate/Accountant' section should be in the film, not as a separate little feature on its own. And everyone feels it should be quite heavily pruned. I suggest it should be ten minutes at the most, Terry J about eight, Graham, quite firmly, seven. GC gets a round of applause from the meeting for his performance as Mr Blackitt, and TG for his 'Death' animation.

Thom Mount from Universal, who has come over to discuss release dates, etc, breaks in to announce that he thinks the film is wonderful and he would hardly change a single moment. As he's quite liked and respected by us all, this does visibly change the mood of the discussion.

Universal want some previews in the US as soon as possible to test reaction. They want to attempt a first ad campaign too.

All of which puts considerable pressure on my Indian travelling companion Mr Gilliam, who must cut his 'Pirate' piece, complete his animation and discuss ads, all before he meets me in Delhi on the 23rd of January.

1983

I was about to take on a mini world tour. A combination of a family holiday in Kenya (organised by Monty Ruben, who had sorted out our Missionary shoot in Africa), publicity for The Missionary *in Australia and a long-awaited tourist visit to India, where I was to meet up with Terry Gilliam. The quickest way from Kenya to Australia was via South Africa, where apartheid was still in place.*

Sunday, January 9th: Nairobi–Johannesburg

Aware, as I write the heading, of the ludicrous ease of world travel today. Here I am imagining myself in the steps of Marco Polos and Vasco da Gamas and Livingstones and Stanleys – or any one of a dozen Victorian lady missionaries – and yet between 9.30 and 12.30 this morning I passed Mount Kilimanjaro and the Ngorongoro Crater, crossed the Zambezi in flood, flew over the Limpopo and reached the Transvaal – and all this with no greater discomfort than waiting for the next Buck's Fizz to arrive.

Land 20 minutes early at Jan Smuts Airport in Johannesburg. The ambivalence of the world's attitude to South Africa is apparent straight away. Here is a smart, expensive, efficient international airport and yet there are not enough airliners using it to justify the installation of jetties.

Most conspicuous absence of course is the American airlines. And one can understand it – America, for all her faults, has confronted all the problems of an open, free, multiracial society and taken its share of riots, marches and protests. South Africa has tried to avoid the issue.

My driver is a black and, as we drive in through neat and tidy suburbs, past white congregations filing out of church, it all looks so peaceful and contented and comfortable that I'm forced to ask him a few journalist's questions. His replies are not voluble, or emotional, but it's clear that he does not see things with quite such rose-tinted spectacles. 'In England it is better, I think.'

He doesn't say much for a while, but just as we are turning towards the hotel he says 'I have dignity . . . just like anyone else . . . This is what they won't let you have here . . . dignity.'

My hotel turns out to be a characterless Holiday Inn amongst a lot of equally characterless buildings that comprise the characterless centre of Jo'burg. There is a station which is about 100 years old, red brick and vaults and marble columns and elephant's head motifs and a frieze depicting, I presume, the Great Trek.

In the middle of all this I find the Blue Room Restaurant. Tables set out with solid Sheffield stainless steel, plates bearing the emblem of South African Railways on substantial wooden tables set beside polished marble pillars. Whatever the food, I have to have my lunch in the middle of this faded splendour. The meal is one of faded splendour too. I choose an Afrikaans dish, Kabeljou, which turns out to be a rather chewy piece of battered fish, which reminds one how far Johannesburg is from the sea.

Afterwards I walk into the station beneath a 'Whites Only' sign. Make my way down to the platform and, like a good trainspotter, walk up to the sunlit end where the big locomotives wait.

As I return I find myself, for convenience sake, taking the nearest stairwell, and the fact that there's a long line of blacks going up it too doesn't occur to me as at all odd until I come out at the top of the stairwell into a completely different Johannesburg from anything I've seen so far. Broken cans, discarded bottles, dirt, blowing paper, and, though it's full of people, none of them is white.

I realise, with a momentary mixture of fear and embarrassment, that I am indeed in a 'Blacks Only' world. There is no hostility, though – the blacks are just busy talking, meeting, napping, lolling – they're in their own world. What I object to most of all is that I should have been made to feel some guilt about being amongst these people.

It's this feeling of a shadow nation of blacks, which just isn't acknowledged, which is the most disturbing impression of SA.

Monday, January 10th: Johannesburg–Perth

In the First Class cabin is a family who are emigrating from SA to Australia. The father is a solicitor and avocado farmer – parents English, he was born and bred in SA. But now he's taking his family out. He points to them. 'There's no way I shall let them die fighting for an indefensible cause.'

He talks bitterly of the arrogance and inflexibility of the Afrikaans National Party. The English are treated almost as badly as the blacks by them, he said. Although he had a prosperous farm, he had no clout in politics at all. The Afrikaners are a small, self-perpetuating elite –

repressive, intolerant and dogmatic – and it's they who have driven him away.

Arrive at Perth at 2.30 a.m. Met by Doug O'Brien of GUO Film Distributors, a big, friendly, gentle man, to whom I take an immediate liking. Into Perth to the Hilton Parmelia – a big, new hotel, one class up from the President Holiday Inn, Jo'burg. Now I'm a film star and I have a suite on the eighth floor. All I can see outside are swirling freeways and lights on hills.

I've never been further from home.

Tuesday, January 11th: Perth, Western Australia

To lunch at a restaurant with a fine, indeed stunning, view over the waterfront. Arthur, the owner of an 18-cinema chain in Perth and area, and Norman, GUO's theatre owner in the city, were dining with us.

Arthur has a fine line in Aussie swearing, specially effective because the phrases come out quite naturally and without affectation from this fairly elderly gentleman. Describing a local millionaire called Bond – 'Of course, he stuck his cock in a cash register' (i.e. he married into money). A Sydney Indian restaurant is recommended with the warning that it used to be known as 'The Blazing Arsehole'.

Back to the hotel afterwards. Not welcome in the restaurant as I have no jacket. The receptionist immediately takes the side of the restaurant. 'One of the waiters had a heart attack tonight, so they may be a little tense in there' – pure Fawlty.

Friday, January 14th: Adelaide and Sydney

To ABC Adelaide for two very pleasant and easy BBC-style chats with programme hosts who were both very complimentary about '*The Mish*'. Another station at which a man called Carl phones in and goes into a swingeing attack on me for being sacrilegious, etc. At one point he throws in Pamela Stephenson's name, blaming me even for her – and calling her a 'wicked Jezebel'.

At Sydney we are met by John Hartman, Managing Director of GUO.

To my room at the Regent – a 30-storey brand new hotel, from one of whose 19th-floor rooms I have a breathtakingly impressive panoramic view of the harbour, the bridge, the Opera House and the shores of North Sydney.

A surprise phone call from Basil Pao, who is in Sydney after three years' 'exile' in Hong Kong. He says he has just received a call from John Goldstone asking if he will design a *Meaning of Life* poster.

No sooner have I put the phone down than Goldstone himself rings to confirm a rumour I heard that Universal want the *Meaning of Life* to open in America at Easter.

Saturday, January 15th: Sydney

Meet Basil in North Bondi. He's at the home of a small, pretty, quite tough lady called Lydia, who is the agent of Jim Sherman [a playwright] and Philip Noyce, the director of *Newsfront*.

We drink champagne looking out over North Bondi Beach, and the scene reminds me, again with great poignancy, of my holidays at Southwold – brown, barefoot people coming home to little bungalows for supper, the toilets and bus shelters at the edge of the cliff, the sun and salt-tarnished paintwork and, above all, the feeling of lazy days. Quite, quite different from Africa *and* America. It's all so terribly ... terribly English.

We eat at a nearby restaurant – really good food, not posh or pretentious, just very well cooked. Meet Bruce Chatwin there – he is rather sneery about things in a slightly aggressive, camp way which I don't awfully take to. There's almost an edge of cruelty somewhere there. Anyway, we bravely persevere in eating out in a force 5 gale, whilst being visited every now and then by drunken naval officers who recognise me and bring us complimentary glasses of port.

Then into the Rocks area again, where we go to see a group Basil knows. As they finish playing the room empties, leaving a lot of men without women and a crush of empty Fosters cans just dropped on the floor. 'This is the fall of Australian heterosexuality,' says Lydia.

Sunday, January 16th: Sydney

Wake about 10.30 with a cracking headache. Am extremely delicate for the rest of the morning. Bathe gingerly. Walk up to the corner of George Street to meet John Hartman, who is taking me for a drive up the coast to – I hardly dare contemplate the word – lunch.

It's a hot day – about 25 Celsius – and I'm picked up in the white Mercedes by a chauffeur complete with grey suit and peaked cap. I'm driven north along suburban roads that eventually blend into a déjà-vu Essex. I have to avoid sharp movements of the head, so when John Hartman in the back faithfully points out the (very few) objects of interest, I move like a man in an invisible neck brace.

I must be acting the interested passenger quite convincingly, as he appears determined to show me the local beaches. We stop at one and Vince, the chauffeur, parks our white Merc right up by the sand dunes and we have to pile out and walk around like a brace of property developers. How much I would rather be just lying out in the sun like everyone else. 'You've got a lot of clothes on for the beach,' comments a passing girl bather.

I'm mistaken for Eric Idle – only this time by someone who met Eric only last week, an Englishman who manages four of the England cricket team, who are now losing one-day games with the same consistency that they lost the Test Matches. He says they'll be in Sydney on Wednesday, so I promise I'll arrange seats for them at Wednesday's '*Mish*' preview.

Sunday, January 23rd: Delhi

Very quickly through the airport. I'm in the queue behind a Yorkshireman from Keighley who's just come in from Taiwan. I push my luggage trolley up a short, drab, ill-lit passageway and out – into India.

Huddled shapes spring towards me out of the darkness – men with scarves tied round their heads, as used in comic strips to denote sufferers from toothache. 'Taxi, sir?' I look vainly round for some sort of 'authorised' sign, determined to avoid falling into the clutches of the unlicensed, but I have made the fatal mistake – momentary hesitation – and within seconds my cases have been wrested from me and bundled into the back of a taxi.

There are six Indians already in the cab. The owner turns them out with much arguing and shouting and ushers me into the back. We start the engine, we stop, we argue, the boot is opened, more shadows appear from the dark, and suddenly my cabbie is gone, replaced in the driving seat by a young, unshaven desperado with an oily cloth tied bandanna-fashion round his head. He is joined in the passenger seat by another wild and mad-eyed individual. They look like archetypally dangerous men, but they drive off and out of the airport and strangely I feel quite safe and reasonably confident.

Eventually (though they miss the entrance once) we find the Imperial

Hotel in Janpath. Not impressive, but at least familiar – there are even American Express signs about. A message from TG in my cubby-hole, welcoming me to India. My bags are carried up to my room.

A succession of Indians in white cotton uniforms appear, elaborately bowing and scraping, turning the bed back, turning lights on and generally doing lots of things I don't really want them to do. Then the chief bed-turner waits and asks me if there is anything I want. Because he is there, I ask for a beer, and he arrives many minutes later with a bottle of something by the name of Jasmine Parrot, which tastes sweet and is quite undrinkable.

At eight I am in the breakfast room, which is full of waiters, but not of guests. TG arrives about five minutes later. The rendezvous has worked. It had seemed quite unlikely when we parted four weeks ago, agreeing to 'See you for breakfast in Delhi'.

TG and I take an auto-rickshaw and our lives into our hands, and head towards Old Delhi.

We are dropped near the entrance to the Old City. The street is full of people, animals and every kind of activity – men being shaved on little wooden platforms, dogs with awful sores lying peacefully beneath huge cauldrons of some steaming dal, children, cows, cyclists, an old man turning a makeshift Ferris wheel made of biscuit tins or petrol cans. It's Gilliam's world completely – just what he tried to recreate in *Jabberwocky.*

We visit a Jain temple. Off with our shoes and socks. Rich smell of incense mingled with sweaty feet. The strict Jains believe that all life is sacred, even bugs and flies. On our way to the temple we passed an elderly, quite chubby, entirely naked man being led through the streets. In any other country, I suppose, the little group around him would probably be police ushering him into the nearest paddy-wagon. Here in India he's a holy man.

Continually seeing things which nothing, except fiction, has ever prepared me for. For instance, outside the Red Fort is a man selling false beards – and TG has a picture to prove it.

Monday, January 24th: Delhi and Agra

Alarm goes at six. Pack in the sepulchral gloom of my room and set off with TG into the mist of a slowly-emerging Delhi dawn. A shadowy world of hooded, cloaked shapes.

Onto the Taj Express bound for Agra. We are in First Class Air-Conditioned.

We pull out on time, through this strange, atmospheric, blanketing morning mist which gradually clears to reveal the much read-about sight of Indians crouching in waste ground by the railway line and donating their night-soil. Little botties catching the morning light.

We are offered breakfast by a waiter in white cotton denims – stained and dirty. We order omelette. It arrives, accompanied by a banana, two pieces of toast and a battered Thermos of tea. The omelette is cold, thin and pinched.

For me one of the great beauties of the Taj Mahal is its setting. Not so much the well-known line of fountains which approaches from the front, but the Jumna river which flows along the back of the Taj. I sit out on the marble terrace with the shimmering iceberg-like bulk of the Taj Mahal on one side, and look out over the wide river bed, mostly dry, with its two or three bridges and, in the haze a mile away, the impressive long line of the battlements of the Agra Fort.

At the Mughal Room Restaurant. Not very good curry served whilst an impassive Indian quartet played 'My Way'.

Tuesday, January 25th: Agra–Jaipur

Refreshed and ready for the fray again. Book a taxi to Fatehpur Sikri and back.

Our taxi driver leaves us at the gates to the great palace, built during our Elizabethan period by the Emperor Akbar as the capital of the Moghul Empire, and then for some reason abandoned in favour of Agra. Towers and cupolas and columns all please the eye and lead from one to the other both literally and visually. And it's on a ridge, so there are views from the pretty turrets across the quiet landscape of green fields.

TG and I cannot believe that tourist groups are given one hour only to visit this wonderful complex. We even found a complete 'bath-house wing' which no-one else was being shown. Cool vaulted chambers, a hypocaust and several rooms all linked – presumably for the various temperatures.

We are taken then to Agra Fort Station. No 'Air-Conditioned Firsts' for us this time. We are in Hard Plastic First. An Indian gentleman, whom we come to know as our guardian angel, warns us, before he alights at the first stop, to bolt the door after him or else 'the students will try to get in'. He doesn't elaborate on this, but we follow his advice.

After a few minutes of pleasant rattling along through the outskirts of Agra the door handle rattles, then the door is banged, then the handle is wrenched more persistently. It is 'the students'.

At the next stop faces appear outside the window. 'Why will you not open the door?' TG holds them at bay through the bars, trying to explain the First Class ticket system. 'You are not right-thinking!' they shout back. Then the train starts off again and they resort to more heavy banging, laughter and jeers and then, rather more disconcertingly, leaning out of the window next to our compartment and staring in. It all helps to pass the time and after an hour or so they get bored.

We arrive in Jaipur at a quarter to eleven. Outside the station the rush of rickshaw and auto-rickshaw drivers is broken up and dispersed by bearded men with batons and sticks. There seem to be 30 or 40 auto-rickshaws lined up and no trade, so TG has little trouble in beating some poor local down from ten to four Rupees (about 75p to 20p). Our driver hurtles us through the streets of Jaipur like a man demented, his cloak billowing out in the cool night breeze.

We are staying at our first Palace hotel – Maharajahs' homes so enormous that they have been recycled as hotels. This one is called the Rambagh Palace. A long drive approach and impressively sizeable floodlit walls. TG is very rude about it and blames me for wanting such First Class travel!

To bring us even more rudely back to civilisation, there is a film crew here. They're shooting *The Far Pavilions* and have just had a party on the front lawn of the hotel. TG is recognised by the props man, who worked on *Time Bandits* with him.

Wednesday, January 26th: Jaipur

Breakfast in a cavernous dining room of immense size, furnished in a sort of European hybrid manner – a cross between Disneyland and Versailles, as my travelling companion describes it.

About nine we leave for the town. Outside the hotel Omar Sharif is learning his lines beside a row of parked cars.

We walk through the back streets of Jaipur. The Indians, unlike the Africans, don't seem to mind a bit having their photographs taken – in fact they arrange themselves in rather decorative poses and leave their names and addresses with you afterwards if it's been a particularly good one.

We return to the Rambagh Palace, who confirm that we have no rooms for the night. Indian Airlines' flights to Udaipur are booked and there is no chance of us getting on the overnight train because it comes from Delhi and is bound to be full.

We are recognised. The [*Far Pavilions*] director turns out to be Peter Duffel. He's a softer Lindsay Anderson lookalike. Amy Irving, his leading lady, asks to be introduced, though it turns out I'd met her briefly at Lee Studios when she was filming *Yentl*. She hears of TG's and my plight and offers one of the spare beds in her room for the night should we be desperate!

Then Vishnu comes into our lives. Vishnu is older and looks a little wiser than the average run of motor-rickshaw drivers and he it is who takes us to the bus station to try and book on the overnight 'de-luxe' bus.

After watching their heads shake negatively for ten minutes I begin to give up, but eventually Vishnu is summoned into a dark corner and within minutes he's back, trying to restrain a proud little smile. Money exchanges hands and we are on the de-luxe bus to Udaipur.

When we see the de-luxe bus, we are somewhat taken aback. Our seats are right at the front with a partition little more than two foot six inches in front of us. The seats don't recline and the journey time is nine hours.

Thursday, January 27th: Udaipur

Stop at 3.30. Realise, as we pile out into the clear and pleasant night air, that I'm rather enjoying the journey – it's not an ordeal at all. There's something very calming about being in India. They don't fight and fluster and bite their nails and moan and complain and it makes for a very unstressful atmosphere. No toilets at this stop – so just a pee in the darkness and a cup of sweet tea. Enjoy the understated feeling of camaraderie amongst the passengers, of which we are the only two whites.

It's a clear, bright day and after breakfast TG and I are off up to the City Palace. Another enormous labyrinth of rooms, stairs and temples. It was lived in not long ago and has a rather sad museum with old Rolls Royces, mangy stuffed bears, many beautiful paintings of tiger and elephant hunts and life-sized cardboard cut-outs of the Maharajahs, which are quite a shock.

Sit in my room with a Herbert's lager and watch the light fading on the shore and feel very peaceful. TG and I eat at the hotel, then have a last drink out beside the pool in the courtyard which is all lit up. We're the only ones to use it.

Friday, January 28th: Udaipur–Delhi

I'm at the airport even before the staff... they're just unlocking the doors. So I'm first at the check-in counter. A small, rotund, self-important little man eventually surveys my ticket and pushes it aside. 'Only OK passengers now, please.' My jaw must have dropped visibly, for he continues 'You are only wait-listed, please wait until the aircraft comes in.'

Suddenly I feel how far Udaipur is from anywhere else. Times, figures, estimates click round in my head, but no comforting alternative presents itself. But hope brightens as the plane is obviously emptier than I've expected and at last, with as little emotion as he'd turned me away, he takes my ticket, scribbles across it, and hands me a boarding card.

Arrive at the Imperial, to find a telegram giving the first weekend's *Missionary* figures. Sydney outstanding, Melbourne disappointing and Adelaide very good! Late lunch at the Imperial. For the sake of *Ripping Yarns* and *The Missionary*, in which characters were always eating it, I choose a plate of kedgeree, which is superb, and a bottle of Golden Eagle beer.

Tuesday, February 1st

Up at 8.15. The children rush upstairs to tell us, as we are dressing briskly in freezing bedroom, that John Cleese is on TV in his pyjamas. It's true. He's the star showbiz guest on this, the first programme of TV-AM – another new TV company started by David Frost and the second supplier of breakfast programmes to have started this year.

TJ rings. He's just back from a lightning Concorde trip to the US for *Meaning of Life* previews. Two showings in Yonkers went so badly that TJ and JG didn't even bother to look at the cards. An audience of young (15–22) cinema-goers predominantly. Eighty walk-outs.

TJ's spirits restored by a showing in Manhattan which was very well received. As often happens under pressure, some sensible cuts have been made quite quickly – 'Luther' is gone and much of the 'Hendys' too. The film sounds trimmer. Universal, as a result of these last showings, are definitely going ahead on March 25th, but with a limited release – probably even less than *The Missionary*.

At 12.30 call John Hartman in Sydney – *The Missionary* is evidently No. 3 in the country. The good news is that attendances were up everywhere in the second week.

Friday, February 4th: Southwold

On the way to Ipswich I complete the last few pages of '*Anna K*' – the book that has been my friend and guardian throughout Kenya, South Africa, Australia and India. Find the last few chapters – Levin discovers The Meaning of Life – rather comforting. I resolve to live my life better and not get angry with people any more.

Tuesday, February 8th

Very cold still – getting up is not fun. But I sleep on this morning very easily, feeling that only now have I readjusted and caught up on my sleep after the World Tour. The builders arrive and start digging foundations for the extension to No. 2.

As Cleese is coming to dinner tonight, I feel I must see *Privates on Parade*, my HandMade stablemate. It's on at the Classic Hampstead, so I go to the 3.35 showing. The 'conversion' of the Classic to a three-screen complex has been so brutal that the Screen One has been set on a new level halfway up the old auditorium. Even the old wall decorations have been left, severed, as a reminder of the modest but homely theatre it once was. A long, flat, empty space extends between audience, who number 15 this afternoon, and screen. But it's in focus and the sound is clear, so I have to be thankful for that.

The concert party numbers are well done and, as they were at the core of the stage success, are performed with panache and attractive skill by Denis Quilley and S Jones and others. Cleese and Michael Elphick are impressive at first, but gradually the film is dragged down. Relationships are hinted at, briefly consummated, then dropped just as they might have been getting interesting and Cleesey becomes saddled with the unenviable task of providing comedy as a palliative for all the floundering 'serious' realities of war at the end.

He ends up with a desperate silly walk in the closing credits – as if finally confirming that the film is supposed to be a comedy, despite the balls being shot off, etc, etc.

Thursday, February 10th

To Duke's Hotel to meet Mike Ewin – HandMade's distribution man since December. Short, stocky, homely figure with a respectable suit. He does come up with one or two classic remarks for a film distributor, particularly his cheerful admission that he hasn't seen the film ... 'But, you know, Michael, I don't think it's really necessary to see a film to know what sort of film it is.'

Walk through St James's Square and into the Haymarket to look at our launch theatre and meet the manager.

The manager, Brian Rami, is quite a character. Youngish, aggressive, Greek Cypriot I should imagine. He is a theatre success story – taking tickets in Hackney two or three years ago, he's won Classic's Manager of the Year award. He briskly goes into the attack with Ray [Cooper] and myself, asking where our posters are and where the trailer and photo displays are, as he could have been playing them for the last week. 'Good man,' I say, in response to his enthusiasm. 'Don't "good man" me,' he replies sharply, '... just give me the goods.'

Snow is beginning to fall quite thickly as Ray and I enter the scarlet and black world of The Hutton Company, but, as the *Sun* might say, we were soon seeing red of a different kind. The complications with the poster's artwork, combined with the time it will take London Transport to hang them, make it now likely that the posters will not appear until the 1st of March, two days before the film opens.

I am quite unable to control my anger and frustration. Colin MacGregor [who's in charge of our campaign], in his languid public-school manner, tries his best to calm things down, but I'm afraid there's no stopping me. Silence and heads hung everywhere.

Friday, February 11th

Today Colin MacGregor informs me that London Transport have agreed to start displaying posters on Underground and buses from February 18th – two weeks earlier than yesterday's date – and that with a bit of luck they can arrange to have poster artwork completed by the weekend. I hate to say it, but violence does seem to work – even if it's only the violence of my opinion.

Monday, February 14th

To Mel Calman's gallery at 12.30. We talk of ads, posters and the lack of good design. More positively we talk over the idea of opening a cinema in Covent Garden. It's something I've heard mentioned elsewhere, but somehow, this being a Monday lunchtime and the start of a week, Mel imbues me with great enthusiasm for the idea and, as I walk back to the car, I feel all the elation of one who has just acquired a cinema in Covent Garden.

To Bertorelli's, where a researcher for the Time Rice (Freudian slip), Tim Rice Show on Wednesday is taking me to lunch. Pre-interview interviews seem to be all the rage now. It's a very bad habit imported from America. So I talk for an hour or so to this keen, rather aggressive Scots girl, who asks me dreadful questions like 'Does comedy have a comic significance?' 'Is comedy a moral force on the world stage?' I get very twitchy about three o'clock, when she still has ten questions left to ask.

Sunday, February 20th

I drive over to Lime Grove at seven o'clock for an appearance on *Sunday Night*. Into the quaintly termed 'hospitality room', where I'm offered some wine from a bottle they keep on the window sill outside.

We record about a quarter to eight. Eric Robson, who did one of the 'Great Railway Journeys', is the presenter – a solid, dependable, likeable man. As the credits roll and the contents of the show reveal filmed reports on how Christianity is coping in the poverty-stricken conditions of South America, *The Missionary* seems embarrassingly frivolous.

The Dean of St Paul's, another interviewee, smiles a little uncertainly at me, as the story of the film is being explained by their resident reviewer – himself a clergyman. His review of the film is not awfully good. He thinks it 'a 50-minute television programme blown up to 90 minutes', 'not very serious', 'an adolescent fantasy', etc, etc. 'My fantasies are much more grown-up,' he ends. They do drop themselves in it, these people.

The trouble is, as this is a religious programme, *The Missionary* is treated, out of perspective I think, as a carefully thought-out comment on the church. When he accuses the satire of being rather limp and safe, I counter by saying that the church gets the satire it deserves. Feel a few frissons cross the studio as I say this and hope the Dean of St Paul's doesn't mind.

Monday, February 21st

Bad news comes in early evening when Ray rings to say that the trailer has hit fresh, and quite unexpected, snags in the shape of the film censor, who has refused to grant our trailers anything less than an 'X' unless we remove mention of the word 'prostitutes' and cut a sequence in which I say 'I was just telling Emmeline how relatively unimportant sex is', despite the fact that he has given both these lines clearance for any audience over 15. The ridiculous thing is that he will allow us to replace 'prostitutes' with 'fallen women'. The mind boggles.

Thursday, February 24th

Good news of the day is that Maggie Smith has agreed to come to the press screening and may even appear on *Terry Wogan*.

But the day's excitements are not over. At home, as Helen is getting ready for another evening's badminton and the spaghetti's boiling away on the hob, Mel Calman calls to tell me that à propos our St Valentine's Day enthusiasms for a cinema in Covent Garden, he has heard of a building for sale in Neal's Yard! It's No. 2, has a salad bar on the ground floor, room for a gallery and coffee bar on the first, an acupuncturist on the second and a self-contained flat on the top. Cost £275,000. I'm very keen. Keen to buy in such a special spot as Neal's Yard and keen to help Mel C and the Workshop. Watch this space!

Stay up until 1.15 to watch the Bermondsey by-election, the culmination of a particularly vicious and intolerant campaign against Peter Tatchell. The Alliance Party are crowing. Labour *do* seem to be in quite serious trouble.

Saturday, February 26th

Arrive at TV-AM's still-unfinished studios in Camden Town. Bright, light, high-tech building decorated in the Very Silly Style, with representations of pagodas and African jungles. It's like one huge Breakfast TV set.

I'm on talking about *The Missionary*. Parky likes it. Calls it 'an important film', too, and shows a clip. They give a number on which viewers can call me with any questions. Over 200 questions come in, and they're all very excited at TV-AM as it's the largest number of phone calls for anyone they've ever had. I wish George Harrison 'Happy Birthday' on air – even though he's incommunicado in Hawaii. But I am wearing the Missoni sweater he gave me and at least ten of the calls are about this.

William and I stay for breakfast with Parky and Mrs Parky – a nice Yorkshire couple – in a rather narrow and cramped canteen which Parkinson complains about. He seems to be quite brisk with his working colleagues. I shouldn't think he suffers fools gladly.

Monday, February 28th

Off to the Classic Haymarket. The press show has run for about 75 minutes. Brian Rami is very enthusiastic about the whole thing. There is applause at the end (very rare in critics' screenings), but only he and I know that it was Rami who started it!

Walk down across Pall Mall to the Turf Club. At least it's a dry, quite pleasant day. Upstairs at the Turf, in two elegant, high-ceilinged rooms, there is a good crowd of pressmen, plus one or two of the Fallen Women and Phoebe.

Maggie S herself arrives about half past twelve. She still hasn't seen the film and I feel that she will probably continue to avoid it, as is her habit. But she looks very bright and attractive and sparkles for the press she dreads so much.

Mr Chandler, the rather icily elegant major-domo, is all smiles and very obliging today. 'All the gentlemen of the press seemed to have enjoyed the film ...'

As I'm about to go, Mr Chandler appears up the stairs once more ... 'Do you know Medwin?' And sure enough, Michael Medwin, looking very perky in what looks like an oleander-pink scarf, comes bounding up behind him and I find myself drinking a further couple of glasses of champagne with him at the bar downstairs.

Mr Chandler keeps saying 'He'll have to become a member, you know,' in a generous fashion. And Medwin promises to propose me and says that 'Chalky' White[1] and Albert Finney will second me. We talk over the

---

1 Our colloquial name for Michael White, the celebrated producer and major investor in *Holy Grail*.

film industry. He seems quite sanguine about 'going into the city' and getting money and most hurt that *Memoirs of a Survivor*[1] (much praised) did not receive the commercial attention it deserved.

Tuesday, March 1st

To the City University to be the 'guinea pig' at one of Bob Jones's press conferences at the Department of Journalism. After an hour of this, drink with some of the tutors there. I'm listened to with far too much respect these days. I suppose it must have changed me somehow. I no longer have to look for an audience. They gather around me – even quite intelligent people – and wait for the oracle to utter.

Home to anonymity and abuse from children.

Thursday, March 3rd

Missionary opening day.

An equivocal review in the very influential *Time Out*, specifically criticising my role as being inadequate to support the film, is followed by a short, but very negative piece in *City Limits*. In the *Guardian*, Derek Malcolm has me casting the paper aside in disgust and sitting head in hands in that deep, sudden desolation that only a bad crit can bring. But when I read him again, I realise it's quite a praiseworthy review, but rather obscurely written.

Terry J rings and suggests squash and lunch, which I eagerly accept. TJ has been at Technicolor labs doing last-minute work on the *Meaning of Life* print. It's now a time panic as bad as anything that happened on *The Missionary*.

I'd forgotten about the *Standard*. Have a quick scan through Alexander Walker and it is very good – for me and the film. A big photo, lead story, headline 'Mission Accomplished', phrases like 'The *Missionary* is very, very funny' and a comprehensive relishing of the finer points of the movie which almost makes the piece look like an extension of our own advertising. This puts a new spring in my step and a quite different complexion on the day.

Drive into the West End to the Classic Haymarket. The acting manager,

1 1981 film written & directed by David Gladwell from a Doris Lessing book. It starred Julie Christie. Michael Medwin was the producer.

Ken Peacock, is in the bar. He's very pleased and reckons it could take £2,000 at the end of the day. The best Thursday for ages, he says.

Up to the projection room to say hello. My handiwork slowly unwinds from the longest spool I've ever seen. Rather exciting seeing it all through the small windows.

Friday, March 4th

A rave review of *Missionary* in the *Mirror* and the *Daily Mail* and the *Daily Express*. I only come down to earth a little with *The Times* – but even that headlines its film column 'Great Comic Acting' and only attacks the script for not being better.

Helen returns with the *Financial Times*, which also says many positive things, but in the end wanted 'a bit less caution, a little more anarchy', whereas Coleman in the *New Statesman* called *The Missionary* 'unfashionably well-written', which I don't understand but like very much.

Then after lunch there is quite suddenly a great anti-climax. The film is out and running. The radio and television shows will be looking for new celebrities and different shows next week.

At this very moment I have nothing to do – no problem to solve, no crisis to defuse, no-one to hustle . . . just a grey, wet day coming to an end and some writing which I can't settle down to. This evening Helen and three of her badminton chums are going to see my film. I shall stay at home.

Have supper with the boys and, feeling very weary, go to bed early.

Sunday, March 6th

A marvellous *Sunday Times* piece by David Hughes ending 'Here is a serious humorist trying his comedy for size. Not yet finding a visionary focus. Lacking edge. But your bones tell you that he will soon make a real beauty of a film, as exciting in achievement as this lark is in promise.'

The *Telegraph*, the *Mail on Sunday*, the *Express* and the *News of the World* are all highly complimentary. Castell in the *Sunday Telegraph* concludes 'Beautifully tailored and consistently funny, *The Missionary* is bound to convert you.'

We should publicise these reviews as quickly as possible. No time for faint hearts. We have stolen a week's march on *Local Hero*, which will be shouting about its success very soon, but it will be a similar sort of critical response and I want as many people as possible to know that *The Missionary* was there first.

Take Helen and the children to La Cirque Imaginaire, a lovely, gentle, funny circus-style entertainment performed by Victoria Chaplin, her husband and their two children. A real family circus with no animals more dangerous than a rabbit, a toucan and two ducks.

Wednesday, March 9th

To L'Escargot to meet Mike Fentiman and Robin Denselow's girlfriend Jadzia to discuss my making a half-hour documentary in their *Comic Roots* series. I liked him and they warmed to my ideas and it looks like we have ourselves a show. In June, probably.

I aim to start work on a new screenplay in April and May, break in June for *Comic Roots*, and complete at quite a leisurely pace during July and August. Rewrites in September and October, by which time ready either to begin setting up filming or to write something with TJ.

Drive down to the Classic. Traffic at a standstill in St Martin's Lane as the teachers and students are marching in protest against education cuts. Eventually reach the bottom of the Haymarket. My silly vicar looks quite striking above the marquee.

Thursday, March 10th

Nikki [from HandMade] calls to tell me that Cannon Classic will be taking an ad in *Screen International* to announce that *Missionary* has broken the house record! And a projectionist at the Barking Odeon has been arrested by the police for taking a print of *The Missionary* home with him in the boot of his car – with intent to tape it!

Tuesday, March 15th

To the Odeon Haymarket to see *Local Hero*. Apart from reservations over the Houston interiors – where both design and direction seemed less sure and the jokes, about American psychiatrists, more familiar – the film quite captivates me. Forsyth is remarkable in his ability to recreate on screen the accidental quality of humour – the way things that make you happy happen so quickly, spontaneously, that try as you can you never quite remember afterwards.

Princess Margaret is coming to see *The Missionary* at the Classic Haymarket tonight. Brian Rami is in an advanced state of excitement. 'She is one of your greatest fans,' Brian relays to me, and urges me to come down if I can.

I speed down to the West End, arriving with about five minutes to spare. Brian R is, of course, immaculate, and looks my faded jeans and windcheater up and down with alarm. In the end Princess Margaret arrives with such speedy precision that I don't have a chance to see her as she moves quickly, but hastelessly, up the stairs behind a phalanx of very tall people. She *does* want to meet me, Brian confirms, so could I come back at a quarter to nine.

At a quarter to nine I stand clutching my signed copy of the '*Mish*' – should I have written to '*Your* Royal Highness Princess Margaret' in it? – waiting for the performance to end. Martin, the projectionist tonight, is very excited, as are the predominantly Asian and African sales staff.

Down the stairs comes the little lady, almost gnomic in the relative size of head to body, and clad in black. She shakes my hand easily and talks without formality. I can't remember much apart from apologising that I should be there at all at the end of the film – waylaying cinemagoers! But she says she thoroughly enjoyed it and asks about the Scottish location, so I am able to tell her that it [Ardverikie House] was nearly the Royal Residence once. We chat quite easily and she introduces me to her very tall friends and they all laugh and endorse her opinion. Then she is taken out and past the queue – clutching my signed book.

Brian R and I drink a coffee afterwards. This film has already given him much pleasure, but tonight surpassed anything.

Tuesday, March 22nd

The telephone goes. It's Richard L. Richard has left home.

'Where shall I go? What should I do?' As if I know. Nothing in my experience quite prepares me for this. The enormity of the split he's now admitted clearly frightens him. I tell him if he needs help, or a bed, or company, that I shall be here.

Write letters and prepare stew for supper. Then, just as I've served, Richard arrives. His normal behaviour is so near to hysteria that it's difficult to tell how abnormal he is at the moment.

He eats the stew (later, when I'm trying to explain to Rachel that Richard's behaviour is because he's very, very unhappy, she philosophises 'Well, at least you got rid of the stew'). When I come downstairs from reading *The Secret Garden* to Rachel, he's asleep on our sofa.

There's not much more I can do and, feeling quite weary myself, I go to bed and to sleep at eleven.

Sunday, March 27th

A wet, dull Sunday. Helen [back from skiing in Austria] unpacks and very gradually begins to readjust to life at sea-level.

Potter around at home, unburying No. 2 from the builders' dust and debris of the last six weeks. It's quite exciting – like a new house emerging from hibernation. Tom P will move in here after Easter.

Watch and delight in *Betjeman* – the final episode. Full of gems – he's such a warm, kindly, generous but cheeky presence. On top of a cliff in Cornwall he's wheeled into shot clad in a black bomber jacket with a 'Guinness' tag inexplicably obvious over the left breast. His mouth senile and droopy from the effects of Parkinson's (that I know so well), but his eyes alive, alert and mischievous.

He's asked if there's anything in his life he really regrets . . . He considers a moment, the Cornish clifftop wind untidying his hair and making him look such a little, isolated, vulnerable figure . . . 'Yes . . . I didn't have enough sex . . .'

Monday, March 28th

We have used up most of our £80,000 launch budget, but Denis has agreed to about £5,000 extra to continue support over the upcoming Easter weekend. I hear from Ray that Stanley Kubrick wrote to Denis congratulating him on the *Missionary* campaign, which he had noticed, admired and envied. For an apparent recluse he keeps in touch, it seems.

To lunch at L'Escargot. Colin Webb of Pavilion Books is at another table. He tells me that the *Time* critic, Richard Schickel, who has given '*MOL*' such a good (and important) review, really *did* like *The Missionary*, despite his dismissive piece. He had been in a 'very depressed state' when he wrote it and has since seen it again and thinks it 'a gem of its kind'.

Home about six. The phone rings instantly. It's Tim Brooke-Taylor conveying to me an offer to direct a new Gounod opera at the Buxton

Festival. We have quite a long chat and he tries his best to persuade me to do something that both of us agree is tantalisingly out of the ordinary. But I end up turning it down and inviting Tim and Christine to dinner.

Terry Gilliam appears. He looks rather careworn. America was awful, he says. He was unable to sell *Brazil* to Paramount or Universal and is extremely bitter about Hollywood studios all over again.

Tuesday, March 29th: London–New York

Exactly one year since I began filming *The Missionary* I leave the house to catch the 10.30 Concorde to New York. The flight (all £1,190 of it) to New York is being paid for by Universal Pictures for my work on behalf of the second film I made last year – *The Meaning of Life*.

A limousine takes me into New York, past the burnt-out tenements of Harlem to the discreetly comfortable Westbury Hotel at 69th and Madison. It's a fine, clear, cool day – the buildings stand out sharp against piercing blue skies.

Visit Al and Claudie on my way to the first interview. They have been through a bad four weeks – awful journey back from Paris and Claudie recently very ill and worried at one point that her bronchitis was cancer. Also a new property company have taken the block and want to make Al an offer to sell his lease, so they may contemplate a complete move to Sag Harbor in the early summer. Their little daughter Gwenola delightful, smiling, full of beans.

Drive back uptown to a bar/restaurant in the theatre district for a drink with Richard Schickel, his wife and daughter. He officially rescinds his review of *The Missionary*, saying quite sportingly that he shouldn't have dismissed it and anyway his wife had disagreed with his views right from the start. So that made me feel better and we now have quite a good relationship.

Off to Broadway Video, at Lorne's invitation. It's all looking very smart now. In a basement studio in the Brill Building Simon and Garfunkel are working on a new album, which has taken one and a half years already. They're listening to a drummer, Eddie Gatt, doing over-dubs.

Paul greets me effusively (or as effusively as Paul ever could be), then goes back to careful concentration on the track. Art Garfunkel sits behind him and nods his great beaky head every now and then – 'That's good' – but Simon is really in control. Art passes some coke on the end of a penknife. I decline, much to Lorne's comic disapproval.

Friday, April 1st: New York–London

Down to another ABC studio to record an interview with a man whose extravagant name – Regis Philbin – denies his very regular appearance. We do ten very successful minutes. The producer of this new show is Bob Shanks – the man who six years ago was responsible for the butchering of the six Python TV shows which took us to court and eventually won us custody of the shows. He looks older and more unkempt. Quite shockingly different from the trim, smooth executive with nary a hair out of place whom we fought at the Federal Court House.

He jokes about it as we shake hands. 'We met in court … '. Really he's done us a lot of good in the end and it's a curious coincidence that less than 12 hours before meeting Shanks again, I heard from Ron Devillier that we have sold the Python TV shows to PBS for a fee of at least a million dollars for two years.

Sunday, April 3rd: Easter Sunday

Helen has not slept much and is groaning in pain at eight o'clock on this Easter morning.

Throughout the morning she is in great pain and discomfort. Cheerful Doctor Rea arrives at midday, quips about my appearance on the back of buses, examines Helen and takes a sample. He has no bottles, so I have to run downstairs and fetch one of Helen's marmalade jars.

The doctor takes a quick look at Helen's specimen, holds it up to the light for all Oak Village to see and pronounces it like 'a rich Madeira'. He says Helen has all the symptoms of pyelitis – an infection of the tubes leading from the kidneys to the urinary tract. He prescribes some pills, which I rush out to Belsize Park to fetch from a Welsh chemist, who's also seen me on the back of the buses.

Sunday, April 10th

Collect the Sunday papers and try to put off further rehearsal for the Stop Sizewell 'B' concert as long as possible.[1] I feel an enormous disinclination to appear on stage tonight. A wave of weariness which I feel sure is mental

1 Sizewell 'B' was a nuclear power plant planned for the Suffolk coast. It was built between 1988 and 1995.

more than physical. I have been so much in the public eye over the last year or so – and each day, with very few exceptions, I've been required to smile brightly, chat optimistically and generally project constantly, when all I really want to do is to disappear from sight for a while.

Dinner at Mary's is a welcome break – very jolly, with Granny G declaring that she has grown cannabis in her garden ... 'And I'm growing more this year' – but I have to leave after an hour and drive down to the Apollo Victoria for the call at 3.30. The theatre is huge and it takes me half an hour to work out a way through the labyrinth of tunnels to our dressing room, which TJ and I are sharing with Neil Innes and Pete Capaldi (one of the stars of *Local Hero*).

At four o'clock the cast is summonsed to the foyer to hear the running order. Various bands – Darts, UB40, Madness – and a strong selection of comedy groups – Rik Mayall and the Young Ones, National Theatre of Brent, as well as Neil and Julie Covington and Pamela Stephenson. TJ is told that they couldn't do an explosion, so he decided to cut 'Never Be Rude to an Arab'.

Then a long, long wait whilst UB40 monopolise the stage, which is filled with a vast and forbidding array of speakers, amps, wires, leads, plugs and sockets which make Sizewell 'B' look as dangerous as the Faraway Tree. Backstage is a no-man's land of bewilderment and confusion.

Jeanette Charles – the Queen's lookalike – arrives in our dressing room about seven to add yet another bizarre element to an already lunatic situation.

The curtain doesn't go up at 7.30 as the bands are still rehearsing. Jeanette C, now totally transformed physically and mentally into the Royal Person, protests vigorously at the delay – 'I have to go to a Bar-Mitzvah ... ' she announces imperiously to some desperate and confused dis-organiser. 'When quarter to eight comes I must go like a bat out of hell to Chigwell.' Very Joe Orton.

Monday, April 18th

Begin writing new screenplay. Rather than spend days or weeks on elaborate research or agonising over a subject, I decide to ride straight in on the 'Explorers' idea which came to me about four months ago.

To dinner with Graham and David. Was supposed to be with TJ as well, but he rang this morning, having had Creosotic eruptions during the night, to cancel. Take GC to Langan's Brasserie. He's half an hour late. Still, I enjoy sipping a malt whisky at the bar and watching caricatures of rich people entering. Feel like I'm watching a parade of the people George Grosz used to draw.

GC looks a bit drawn and haggard and, as always, has the slightly distracted air of, as TJ put it, 'someone who wants to be somewhere else'. Great praise for Peter Cook for keeping everyone happy in Mexico and Eric for being 'divine' (according to David). GC goes back to the US for *Yellowbeard* sneak previews this week. He has reached the stage of not knowing whether anything is working any more.

Friday, April 22nd

To the BBC to discuss further my *Comic Roots* piece with Tony Laryea, my director.

The headquarters of *Open Door* is, ironically, almost impossible to find. I drive past it several times and in the end have to ask directions at Lime Grove.

Talk to Tony in an office full of clutter and overflowing out-trays. Very John le Carré. I tell him my thoughts about the structure of the piece. He is a little taken aback when I suggest David Frost as someone to interview. But he was seminal to the Palin career. It's taking further shape and looks like being a very rich programme. At least an hour's worth at the moment.

Talk to a Dutch journalist for an hour. He has 38 questions.

John Goldstone makes one further attempt to persuade me to go to Cannes – using a free ticket for Helen as bait. I can't, I'm going to Newcastle. Suggest Helen goes with one of the others!

Sunday, April 24th

I embark on mass picture-hanging and clearing up in the garden until Gilliam arrives and we talk about the state of the world for an hour and a half. He *is* going to Cannes, but isn't going to wear a dinner jacket for the special evening showing. Says he'll only go if the dinner jacket very obviously has vomit all over it.

He says that he misses working in the flexible Python way and that Tom Stoppard is much more of a professional writer, wanting to be sure he's being paid before doing rewrites … and 'Stoppard's stuff is so hard to rewrite'. But they are at the casting and location-hunting stage.

Monday, April 25th

J Cleese rings to ask us to dinner. He says he's writing his own thing and would I play a man with a stutter?

At 2.15 two young men, Edward Whitley and another whose name I forget, come to interview me for a book on Oxford. They were meant to come last Friday, but their car had broken down. They're quite pleasant, rather plummy-voiced Oxfordians. I expect from the more comfortably-off classes.

But their interviewing is less comfortable. They are aggressive and rather impatient (nothing new with students), but with an added and more sinister tone – it is as if they have made their mind up about Oxford and what it was like in my time, and nothing I say would really change what they want to think. Whitley, especially, is a clumsy, gauche questioner.

In short, what I had hoped would be a pleasant chance to recall what Oxford was to me, turns into an inquisition. I pour them coffee and try to cope with all their questions, but there is such a humourless, sour feeling emanating from Whitley that it isn't easy.

I know I have another one-hour interview to go to at 3.15, as do they, and when, at 3.20, they turn their probing eye on to *The Missionary* and begin, in rather measured, well-rounded tones, to pull it to pieces, I quite simply run out of patience with their hostile cleverness and leave the house.

On to a Python '*MOL*' meeting with the two Terrys and John G and Anne. TJ and I put together a nice little 40-second radio ad and it's quite a jolly session. Goldstone says '*MOL*' is over 10 million gross in the US, but we need 40 million gross to start making money.

Tuesday, April 26th: London–Oslo

Out to Heathrow about one o'clock. Time for a coffee, then onto a Super One-Eleven to Oslo. At three o'clock UK time, four o'clock Norwegian, we're over the mainland of Norway and flying across a chill and desolate snowscape of forests and frozen lakes and finally into Oslo itself.

A man comes out to welcome the flight on a bicycle. We leave the plane and down to the terminal through holes in the tarmac. John Jacobsen,[1]

---

1 John Jacobsen, a writer and general fixer, was Norway's greatest Python fan.

thin, bearded, with his odd, ironic gaze, meets me and drives me into the centre of town and the Continental Hotel. Pleasant, local feel to it and a large room overlooking the main street of the town.

Don my suit and tie and am taken at eight o'clock to the Continental Hotel dining room (the best restaurant in Oslo, I'm told). Here I meet my hosts for tonight, the two who run all the cinemas of Oslo – for, like alcohol retailing, cinema exhibition is here a municipal monopoly. The dark lady with a sad, Munch-like face is Ingeborg. The middle-aged, friendly, unassuming man is Eivind. 'You are not so high ... ' begins the dark and Garbo-esque Ingeborg, 'as on the screen.'

Wednesday, April 27th: Oslo

To a restaurant overlooking the city for a late lunch with Jahn Teigen, the Norwegian comedian/singer/composer, who became even more of a national hero when he returned from the Eurovision Song Contest two years ago without a single point.

He's a tremendous Python fan, but a very intelligent one too and I like him enormously. Having a lunch together is a real relaxation from the usual round of slightly forced politenesses which these trips are all about. He's making a film about King Olaf, the tenth-century Norwegian hero. His concerts sell out all over the country and he's clearly the biggest fish in this quite lucrative pond.

Thursday, May 5th

Forty years old. Feel tempted to write some pertinent remarks about The Meaning Of It All – a mid-life, half-term report on Michael P. But there isn't much to say except I feel I'm still going – and going very hard and quite fast – and the pace of life and experience doesn't seem to show any sign of flagging.

I feel that I've entered, and am now firmly embarked on, a third 18-year 'section'. The first 18 were my childhood, the next 18 my preparation and apprenticeship and now, for better or worse, I *am* established. If I died tomorrow I would have an obituary and all those things.

The very fact that Rachel should creep round the door of our room at eight o'clock, full of excitement, to tell me that my birthday was announced, over my picture, on BBC Breakfast TV, shows what status I have had thrust upon me. I have the feeling that, as far as the public is concerned, I am now their Michael Palin and they are quite happy for me to remain their Michael Palin for the rest of my (and their) life.

So here I am. Healthy and wealthy and quite wise, but I can stay and sit comfortably or I can move on and undertake more risks as a writer and performer. Of course I *shall* go on, but, as another day of writing my 'new film' recedes and disappears, I realise that it won't be easy. And I should perhaps stop expecting it to be.

Friday, May 6th

Running on the Heath this morning, pounding away the effects of a poor, anxious night's sleep, my mind clears as my body relaxes and I resolve to extricate myself from some of the many commitments in which I have become entangled over the years.

This morning Clive Landa rang from Shepperton. Clive tells me that Lee Brothers have made a £2 million offer for the studio and two property companies are also anxious to buy it (and knock it down, of course). I feel that all my efforts over the years have counted for very little – and, to be honest, I haven't been asked to contribute a great deal of time and effort anyway. So I think I shall proffer my resignation as soon as possible.[1]

The crucial problem over the next months is whether or not I shall have time to write a screenplay by August. It's clear that *Comic Roots* will take up at least four weeks and the ever-increasing demands of publicity will devour much of the rest. Unthinkable though it might seem, I feel strongly that I must extract myself from *Comic Roots*. I shouldn't be spending four weeks on my past, when I'd rather be spending it on my future.

Saturday, May 7th

I open the Camden Institute Playgroup Fete.

I spend three-quarters of an hour 'being a celebrity' and trying to avoid a persistent mad camerawoman who wants me to do something 'goofy' for the *Camden Journal*. And all the time I'm doing this public smiling I'm inwardly trying to prepare myself for my next confrontation – with Tony Laryea over *Comic Roots*.

1 Clive Landa was Managing Director of Shepperton Studios. In view of the amount of work I was doing elsewhere I sent in my letter of resignation on June 2nd after nearly seven years as a director.

We talk upstairs in my workroom. I put to him, unequivocally, all the problems I foresee and ask if there is any way I can get out of doing the programme. Tony uses no moral blackmail, nor emotional entreaties either; he says that if we don't do it now we will never do it and, although there was theoretically time to find a replacement for me, he obviously doesn't want to. He is understanding of my problem and we end up going through the schedule cutting my time spent to its finest.

Sunday, May 8th: Cannes

Am met at Nice Côte d'Azur Airport by Duncan Clark, CIC's head of publicity. I feel in good shape and the Mediterranean sunshine only improves things. As we drive through the neat and tidy streets of the outskirts of Nice and on to the road to Cannes and Monaco, I begin to feel a distinct whiff of the Scott Fitzgeralds. Terry J arrived yesterday and has already taken all his clothes off and run into the sea for a TV crew.

Our car draws up outside the Carlton, where I'm staying. One or two confused photographers put their cameras up, but it's hardly a star arrival and I notice one of them still has the lens cap on.

Meet up with the others on the terrace at the Carlton at half past eight after a bath. Graham and John T, John G and the two Terrys and wives. With them is Henry Jaglom (whose *Sitting Ducks* I enjoyed so much), so we have time for a short exchange of compliments over a beer. His new film is being shown out of competition on Wednesday evening – the same time as *The Missionary*.

Monday, May 9th: Cannes

This is Python day at Cannes. We are officially announced – each one introduced – and our answers instantly translated into French. Neither the questions nor the instant translation process make for an easy exchange of information and certainly they don't help our jokes. One woman claims to have been physically ill during 'Creosote'.

I am asked about Sheffield and I end up telling the world's press that Sheffield girls have bigger breasts because they walk up a lot of hills.

Then we are taken up on to the roof and given a photo-grilling of Charles and Di-like proportions, with cameramen fighting each other to get dull pictures of us. I've never, ever been the subject of such concentrated Nikon-ic attention. It's all very silly and years ago we would all have been persuaded to be much more outrageous.

Then, suddenly, we're free. The Terrys, Graham and Eric go back to the hotel to prepare for the splendours of the Gala Presentation of '*MOL*' tonight, and me to return to England en route for Dublin. But as long as we are here we're good publicity fodder and, as GC and I walk along the Croisette, some keen young photographer asks earnestly that we come to be photographed with Jerry Hall – 'She's on the beach, just there . . . ' he pleads.

After Missionary *promotion in Dublin and Newcastle, I took a short film-writing break in Canonbie, north of Carlisle.*

Friday, May 13th: The Riverside Inn, Canonbie

Awake at eight. On the radio the news is all of pre-election sparring. Margaret Thatcher's transformation into Winston Churchill becomes increasingly evident as she singles out defence (i.e. wars and the Falklands) as the main issue of the election.

Down to the wondrous Riverside Inn breakfast. I'm offered a duck's egg. Very large and tasty and rather nice as I can see the duck that laid it from my window as I write. It's white. Called Persil, they tell me.

Short walk, then up to my room, with its disconcertingly sloping floor, to wrestle with the problems of a nymphomaniac drug addict accused of the ritual murder of a well-known Scottish footballer. The rain comes down gently and steadily, with sudden enormous surges – unlike my writing. I cannot reconcile myself to the 'Explorers' tale completely. There isn't enough that is new, original, different and exciting about the characters and I feel that the Polar icecap will look great for five minutes, then lose its grip on your average audience hungry for laughs.

Saturday, May 14th

TG comes round. He came back from Cannes last night. He now has his money for *Brazil* – a Universal deal for US, and Fox worldwide. Very pleased. Asks me if I'm available to play Jack Lint. I say no, of course not, but he knows I am.

Monday, May 16th

Tackle backlog of desk-work from last week. Talk to Mike Ewin who tells me that we are actually *up* by £120 in our eleventh week at the Classic H. He's also pleased with good, but not sensational, provincial figures thus far. 'The trade is pleasantly surprised,' as he puts it. And we have a second week at Weston-super-Mare, which he considers a considerable triumph!

Less good news from David Knopf, whom I phone in LA. The re-release of the '*Mish*' ran only three weeks in LA and has just opened at the Sutton in New York to little enthusiasm, leading him to rate the chances of a complete national re-issue unlikely.

And Python's '*MOL*' is fading. It did well in each area for about three weeks and that was that. It now looks as if it will take less in the US than *Brian* (nine million as against eleven).

Wednesday, May 18th

Feel rather dejected this morning. Even the news that Buckingham Palace has requested a 35 mill print of *The Missionary* to be taken aboard the Royal Yacht can't lift me from a very black gloom. Anger at everyone around, myself most of all. Feel frustrated by lack of time to write and not even sure if I want to write what I'm writing.

Watch Chas McKeown's prog on TV,[1] his first series for BBC TV. Some good jokes, nice lines, spoilt by heavy LE mugging. There ought to be something that you could put in the tea at the Beeb canteen to stop quite reasonable actors going at comedy like a bull at a gate.

Thursday, May 19th

John Goldstone phones at 8 a.m. to tell me that *Meaning of Life* has won second prize at Cannes – the Special Jury Prize.

Write up and type out my *Comic Roots* basic script. My writing time for the 'Explorers' first draft is now narrowed to six weeks, but I try hard not to think about this.

I collect the boys from the William Ellis swimming gala at Swiss Cottage. Tom has come second in two of his races and both he and

---

1 It was called *Pinkerton's Progress*. Set in a school, it was written by Charles and directed by Gareth Gwenlan.

William have been members of successful relay teams, so they're both in very good spirits.

Sunday, May 22nd

Read all the papers in the hope of some blinding revelation as to who to support at the election. Cannot stomach Thatcher and feel that her faceless, obedient Tebbits and Parkinsons are about to inherit the party. Labour is the only likely alternative, but they are hamstrung with doctrinaire stuff about quitting the EEC and abolishing the House of Lords and far too vulnerable to the boring constituency committee people and the intolerant, grumpy unions. I suppose I shall vote Labour in the hope of giving Thatcher as big a shock as possible.

Monday, May 23rd

I take a taxi down to Piccadilly – to the Royal Academy Dinner at Burlington House. The great mystery of the evening – which is why I was unable to turn down the invite – is why I am there. Who is my friend amongst the luminaries of the Royal Academy? After all, I haven't set foot in there for over a year.

Inside my coat is checked and I ascend the staircase between lofty marble pillars towards a circular chamber from which come the pleasant, rich strains of a small orchestra.

I am announced by a man in a scarlet jacket and received by Sir Hugh Casson, a diminutive, rather cheeky-looking man resembling a perky cockatoo. He is very charming, considering he doesn't know me from Adam, and he in turn introduces me to a pair of be-medalled, beaming buffers.

Then I am in amongst the central rooms of the Academy, offered what I think is champagne, but which turns out to be rather ordinary Spanish sparkling. I look at all the pictures – all ready for the Summer Exhibition – and I look at all the worthy academicians who are gathering and I suddenly think – suppose I meet no-one all evening who knows me.

I am sat next to a lady called Meg Buckenham. She has a direct, unaffected good nature which makes me glad of my luck. She made up even for the presence of Kasmin, the gallery owner, on my other side. Small, tanned and noisy. He regales everyone who will listen with stories of himself and seems very sure that he is the most desirable sexual object in the room.

Across from me is Ruskin Spear – a man who looks exactly like Father Christmas. He speaks in a deep, richly-textured, gravelly voice and seems to be gently mocking everything around him. He calls me 'Palin' in an amused schoolmasterly tone. 'I'm bored, Palin . . . ' he will suddenly say.

We have speeches from Princess Alexandra. Beautifully poised, regal and smiling winningly, but it doesn't make up for a terrible line in royally-delivered cliché. Sir Hugh Casson, sprite-like, is up and down between each speaker, jollying everyone along. It's his 73rd birthday and he's presented with a huge cake in the shape of the leaves of an opened book.

Lord Gowrie speaks for the government. He's in the Northern Ireland office. He has a thick head of hair and looks fashionably attractive in the Yves St Laurent mould, but again his looks belie his speech-making capabilities and he turns in a smooth, but vapid performance.

Sir Hugh is up again eagerly and he hands over to Lord Goodman, who replies to Sir Hugh's toast on behalf of the guests. I've never seen the notorious Lord Goodman in the flesh – only in *Private Eye* caricatures, where he is portrayed always as some vast lump topped with an elephant-like head. Although Goodman isn't quite as gargantuan as they make out, he is an extraordinary-looking creature and the prominent ears, with their dark, hairy inner recesses, are riveting. But he has the gift of the gab and scuttles through a quite unprepared speech very mellifluously. I warm to him. He is not malicious, nor cheap. He speaks intelligently and quite wittily.

Sir Hugh makes the final speech – one last attempt to butter us all up. Apparently I am present at 'one of the great banquets of the year'.

After all these toasts and some belligerent shouts of 'Rot! Absolute rot!' from Kasmin beside me, we are free to leave and mingle and take brandy from the trays carried through.

By this time several of the RA's are becoming tired and emotional and the limping figure of Ian Dury and the academician Peter Blake have joined our little group, and I'm being asked by Peter Blake to accompany him over to the Caprice for a 'nightcap'. Say farewell to Sir Hugh on the stairs. He gives Meg B a long hug. I feel like the errant young suitor in the presence of a father-in-law.

Across to the Caprice, walking slowly so Dury can keep up. He's very jokey and good value and keeps calling me Eric. At the Caprice a rather drunk young blond cruises round the tables and ends up in deep discussion with him. This is Jasper Conran. As usual on these occasions nobody really knows why anyone else is there, and it's very bad form to ask.

Sunday, May 29th

Helen packs in preparation for Newcastle trip with the children. Play snooker and try my hand at capitals of the world on the new BBC computer. I really can't wait for everyone to be gone, so I can set to work on 'Explorers' (I have a tantalisingly clear week ahead).

Another hour of halting progress brought to a rude conclusion by the appearance of TG. He's just back from working with Charles McKeown – the two of them are rewriting Tom Stoppard's script for *Brazil*. He's already setting up *Baron Munchausen* as his next film, in case *Brazil* really doesn't work! American majors have forked out 12 million dollars for rights to distribute – only thing they don't like about *Brazil* is the title.

Home to bed, in silent, empty house, by midnight.

Monday, May 30th

I make a clear start on opening scenes. But still the whole project seems arbitrary. My heart is just not in it. Staying here whilst the family is away to avoid distractions, I find myself waiting quite eagerly for distractions.

Tuesday, May 31st

Michael White's office ring – the Turf Club is still pursuing my membership and wants details of birthdate, place of education, interests. Think of lying and putting down 'horse-racing' (Alison D suggests 'horse-spotting', which I like), but settle for the dignified restraint of 'writing and travel'.

Monday, June 6th

With not very worthy feelings of guilt, reluctance and resentment, I acknowledge the fact that I could and probably should have spent more time on the '*MOL*' radio commercials which we're recording this morning.

Drive into town at 9.15, new Phil Everly tape blaring, roof open. André's just back from two weeks in California looking more successful every time I see him. JC arrives, GC doesn't.

John looks very hairy with beard and long black hair. He is in quite a skittish mood and wants to do lots of silly voices. He does an excellent Kierkegaard. He's just finished work on a book with his psychiatrist – 'Seven or eight weeks solid . . . I just haven't had a moment.' Fall to talking about autobiographies. John wants to call his '24 Hours From Normal'. And for a Python biog we both like the title 'Where's Graham?'

Friday, June 10th: Southwold

After breakfast accompany Ma into Southwold. 'This is my son Michael – you've probably seen him on the television.' And if that doesn't work, it's followed by the blatant – 'He's in Monty Python, you know . . . !'

Saturday, June 11th

Up at eight. Preoccupied with the NBC piece [for a new show called *The News Is The News*], and the problems of learning three and a half minutes of straight-to-camera material by half past ten. A very lordly Daimler arrives to collect me at ten. The driver wears thin and expensive-looking leather gloves.

By the time we reach Whitehall I have almost learnt the piece, though haven't been able to go right through without a fluff. The Queen is Trooping the Colour in the Mall and there are crowds everywhere. With the boldness of the blissfully ignorant, my Daimler turns into Downing Street at half past ten – third or fourth in a line of similar limousines, except that they all carry ambassadors or diplomats on their way to fawn to the recently re-elected Leaderene.

Of course I'm turned back, having been given no clearance by NBC, and my driver dumps me unceremoniously in busy Whitehall.

A guardsman on duty asks me to sign the inside of his peaked cap. ('It's all I've got,' he says apologetically.) A rather attractive lady PC grins at me.

Producer and cameraman appear.

We retire to the pub opposite to kill the half-hour before the No. 10 Press Officer arrives. At midday it's decided that valour is the better part of discretion and all three of us march up to the police barrier. The particular constable on duty this time recognises me as no threat to the

PM and we're in and walking up the narrow street – one of the most famous, if not *the* most famous, narrow streets in the world.

The camera is set up, alongside a permanent display of three or four video cameras and a group of pressmen drinking cans of Harp lager and not looking at all respectful of the hallowed ground they're on. Behind me the rather dull façade of No. 10. I notice all the net curtains are dirty.

With little fuss and bother we start shooting. After a while the press hacks stop talking to each other and come to listen (this in itself is very disconcerting). Some of them I can see falling about with laughter and this encourages me through to the end of an almost perfect take.

And not a moment too soon. A very senior PC looms up and looks very cross. The photographers seem delighted and snap away at him telling us off. We're asked to leave. As we do so, reporters cluster around asking if I'm the new Home Secretary, etc, etc.

Thursday, June 16th

Pick up Ray Cooper and he and I set off for a day at Henley.

George is waiting for us before the recently scrubbed walls of Friar Park. He wears a shaggy old sports jacket which he claims has been threaded through with dental floss.

Transfer from Ray's hired black Range Rover to George's black Porsche. George drives us to Marlow as if he is at Silverstone. We dine at The Compleat Angler. It's superbly sited beside the broad weir at Marlow, looking out over a view which is the very epitome of nature tamed.

George, as usual in such places, is extremely ill at ease to start with. He resents the 'posh' service and feels that, considering he can afford to buy the restaurant several times over, the staff are unnecessarily snotty. But he loosens up over a bottle of champagne. Some excellent smoked salmon, and trout, and a second bottle – this time of Aloxe Corton '69.

We laugh a lot and talk about films and not being able to write them. I think George thinks that I've come to see him to ask for money, and offers it eagerly and generously. But when he finds out that all I have to tell him is that I can't write a film by August he sympathises and loosens up. 'I've been trying to retire for half my life,' he mourns.

Back at Friar Park, George runs through whole scenes of *The Producers* word for word – acting the parts out extremely well. Olivia has some American girlfriends who have 'dropped in' whilst touring Europe. When they've gone, Ray opens some pink Dom Perignon, which is very rare and must have cost the earth, and we sit in the little kitchen and talk about Python and things in an easy, effortlessly friendly way.

George gives me a souvenir as I leave – a baton belonging to the Chief Constable of Liverpool, which GH took off him at the Liverpool premiere of *A Hard Day's Night*!

Saturday, June 18th

The general ease and pleasure of the day added to by the fact that we only have to walk ten yards or so for our dinner tonight. To the Brazilians who are renting No. 24. Elias, who is the husband, a psychoanalyst, cooks. He is an intellectual in the Continental sense of the word – critical, left-wing, multi-lingual, serious, a little intimidating. She is voluble, full of laughter, from a massively populous peasant family.

They are not a grumbling pair, but do criticise the English reserve – the long faces of neighbours.

He has come to study because the best of the German Jewish psychoanalysts came here before the war and it is, as a result, the best country in the world for the study of psychoanalysis. But the British immigration people are very difficult and always give him a hard time when he returns to the country. They're never violent, they never confront you with any direct accusations, he says, they just make you feel bad.

Tuesday, June 21st

Leave for Ealing at one [for *Comic Roots* filming]. The set, to represent No. 26 Whitworth Road [my birthplace in Sheffield], is at Tony Laryea's brother's house and looks quite effective.

At 2.15 Spike M arrives. As usual with him there is a brittle air of tension and unpredictability, but he and I sit down and natter for a half-hour about the Goons – the coining of words like 'sponned' [as in 'I been sponned!']. He raves about 'Eric Olthwaite'. I rave about Eccles.[1] By the time the second camera is up and ready to shoot he seems to have relaxed.

An aeroplane thunders low overhead as soon as we start. His answers to my questions about the Goons are almost identical to the answers I always give when asked about the Pythons – we did it to make ourselves

---

1 At one point in the interview I told Spike how I'd only seen Peter Sellers once. 'I passed him in the corridor at Wembley Studios.' To which Spike replied crisply, 'Very painful.'

laugh, to laugh at authority, we always had a love/hate relationship with the BBC, etc. Even the name 'The Goon Show' was their own and only reluctantly accepted by the BBC, who wanted 'The Crazy People Show'.

Then Spike has to leave and my mother arrives. She is very nervous, as one would expect of someone making their TV debut at the age of 79, but soon gets over it as we sit together on the couch and in the end she is utterly professional and quite unflapped. She tells her stories smoothly and says delightfully disarming things such as (of *The Meaning of Life*) '... Of course it's very rude ... but I like that.'

Friday, June 24th

Rush away at midday to Gerry Donovan to have the temporary dental bridge he put in four years ago checked. He reminds me that 'It usually comes out about this time of year.' Last year when I ate a call-sheet on the way back from '*Mish*' filming in Liverpool and the year before in some pleasant Cretan village as I tucked into freshly spit-roasted lamb. But this year, touch wood, it remains.

Monday, July 11th

Out in the evening to a screening of *Bullshot* at the Fox Theatre. George H is there and Ray and Norman Garwood and David Wimbury [the associate producer] and various others. Twenty or thirty in all. Find the first ten minutes very ordinary, and the overplayed style rather off-putting, but the film gradually wins me over, by its sheer panache and good nature.

George opts to drive with me from Soho Square to Knightsbridge, but when I can't find where I've left my car, I feel he wishes he hadn't. A bit like an animal caught in a searchlight is our George when out on the streets and I can see him getting a little twitchy as he and I – a Beatle and a Python – parade up and down before the diners on the pavements of Charlotte Street, looking for my car.

Of course no-one notices and eventually I get George into the Mini and across London. He gives me a breakdown of one or two of the Indian cults currently in this country – Rajneesh I should be especially careful about. No inner discipline required – just fuck as many people as you can. Sounds interesting.

Our Chinese meal gets quite boisterous owing to the presence of a dark, slightly tubby Jewish girl who does 'improv' at the Comic Strip. I find these American 'improv' people the most difficult of companions. Most of them are perfectly nice, decent, reasonable company until they start performing – which is about every ten minutes – and you are expected to join in some whacky improv.

But we outstay most other people in the restaurant and become very noisy and jolly and all drink out of one huge glass and muck around with the straws and end up on the quiet streets of Knightsbridge being appallingly loud at a quarter to one.

Thursday, July 14th

Have been offered the part of Mother Goose in the Shaw Theatre panto and also the lead in a new Howard Brenton play – rehearsing in August. Torn on this one, it sounds the sort of heavy, non-comedic role that might be quite exciting and unusual for me. But August is hols and September/October is writing with Terry J.

Spend the afternoon being photographed by Terry O'Neill for *TV Cable Week*. Terry is a Londoner with an insatiable curiosity about every-thing that's going on – the Test Match, jazz (when he finds out that Tom is learning the saxophone), films (he's directing his first picture in the autumn – *Duet for One* – Faye Dunaway, his wife, in the lead). Very much one of the lads – I can remember playing football with him ten years ago. He was a good winger. He's down-to-earth and unpretentious and probably keen to be the best at everything he does.

Photos everywhere – with railway, at desk and with family. All self-conscious to some degree, except Rachel, who loves being photographed!

Sunday, July 17th

At seven, after cooking baked beans and toast for the children's supper and leaving Thomas in charge again, we drive out to Olivia's party at Friar Park.

Arrive there about 8.25 and cannot make contact through the intercom on the locked gates, so we drive round to the back gate and press more buttons. A passing horsewoman suggests we try again – 'Probably got the music on rather loud,' she explains.

When we do gain admittance, there is a very restrained group of people standing politely sipping champagne, and listening to nothing louder than a harp, in a tent at the end of the lawn. Friar Park, pristine and floodlit, looks like the venue for a *son et lumière*, up on the rise behind us.

Joe Brown arrives. Calling everyone 'gal' or 'old gal', he proceeds to rave about 'Golden Gordon', repeating all the moments – but unlike Spike getting them word for word right. He has been able to get over here because the promoter of his concert was hit by a sock filled with billiard balls and is temporarily out of business.

The champagne flows liberally and people wander about the house. In his studio George demonstrates a machine which will make any sound into music electronically.

We meet Nelson Piquet, the Brazilian driver who came second at Silverstone yesterday, and John Watson is here too.[1] Piquet a little, perky, pleasantly ambitious Brazilian. He loves his work. No doubts, no fears, from what he says.

The evening cools and the setting is quite perfect. Derek [Taylor] tells me the code used to avoid mentioning drugs specifically. 'I've got all the Charles Aznavour albums to play tonight' means an evening of the naughtiest, most illicit substances, whilst a Charles Aznavour EP may just be some cocaine . . .

And so, on this high note, we drive out of this dreamland, down the M4 back to reality.

Wednesday, July 20th: Southwold

Catch the train at Gospel Oak. Breakfast on the 8.30 from Liverpool Street. Mum collects me and drives me in her blue Metro back to Croft Cottage.

Have to do some PR with her new neighbours. At one point he takes my arm and leads me to one side . . . He apologises, hopes he's not speaking 'out of turn', but my mother is . . . 'well . . . no longer a young woman', so have I 'any contingency plans'?

---

1 Piquet was the Formula One champion that year, as he was in 1981 and 1987. John Watson, from Northern Ireland, had won the British Grand Prix in 1981.

Thursday, July 21st: Southwold

A restorative nine-hour sleep. Outside the best of English summer days – a clear sunlight sharply delineating the trees and cornfields. Sparrows already at dustbaths in the garden below.

Sort out some of Daddy's old papers – finally commit to the Lothingland Sanitary Department many of the school bills, school insurance bills, etc, which he had painstakingly kept. Learn from the family record that my grandfather – a Norfolk doctor – was also a very keen photographer and had exhibited in London. He was a gardener of repute and a Freemason. He and his wife sound a fiercely competent couple. Founding the local Red Cross, etc.

Home for lateish ham supper. Helen tells me about her BUPA medical screening today and of the dashing doctor Ballantine who picked her leg up and waggled it about!

The evening almost spent (and both of us weary) when Alan Bennett rings and, with much umming and aahing, asks if I would like to read a part in a new screenplay he's written. It's about a chiropodist, he says ... oh, and pigs as well. Of course I fall eagerly on the chance and a neat man called Malcolm Mowbray – fashionably turned out – brings the script around.

Read it there and then – such is my curiosity. Slightly disappointed that the part of Gilbert Chilvers is not a) bigger, b) more difficult or different from things I've done. But he does have his moments and it's a very funny and well-observed period piece (set in 1947).

Decide to sleep on it.

Saturday, July 23rd

To the seven o'clock performance of *King of Comedy* at the Screen on the Hill. Very enjoyable – one of the less dark of Scorsese's modern parables, with much wit and many laughs and another extraordinary and skilful and concentrated and successful performance by De Niro. Jerry Lewis (one of my childhood heroes) excellent too.

Come home and, over a cold plateful and glasses of wine, think about the Bennett play. Decide that it is not a difficult or special enough part to drop either my writing with TJ, Belfast Festival commitments or semi-commitment to TG. Ring Alan in Yorkshire, but cannot get him.

Sunday, July 24th

Up to Abbotsley – driving through heavy, but very localised storms and arriving in time for a tennis knock-up before lunch. The air is heavy and damp and the sunshine breaks through only occasionally.

Hang the hammock and play more tennis – pursuits that mark the summer and for which I have literally had no time for two years. A lovely afternoon.

Alan Bennett is up in North Yorkshire and he says the lights have all just gone out. I tell him of my liking for the *Private Function* script, but of my problem with commitments until the end of the year. 'Oh, it won't be till May at least,' counters Alan. 'That's the earliest Maggie's available.' [He wants Maggie Smith to play my wife.] So there seems no point in saying I've decided over the weekend not to do it.

Sunday, August 7th

Rave preview by Jennifer Selway of the *Observer* for Friday's *Comic Roots* – Michael Palin's 'brilliant' half-hour. I can't remember this adjective ever being applied to my work *before* it's been seen – only on rare occasions many years after when affection has distorted the memory.

Sunday dinner together – watch a Scottish/Canadian writer [Robertson Davies] on the excellent series *Writers and Places*. Feel a great appetite for all things written and described. Maybe it's the relaxing break of ten days in France which has finally cleared my immediate work problems away and let other aspects of life come to the front of my mind and imagination.

Thursday, August 11th

Tom and his friend Paul Forbes leave at seven to cycle to Brighton. Helen says she can't help being worried about them.

Drop the Mini at the garage to be serviced, then Helen drops me at Alan Bennett's house on the corner of Gloucester Crescent. A camper van with what looks like carpet covering it is parked in front of the front door. Alan opens it – a little hesitant, a touch of awkwardness and an instant warmth as he shows me in to the crepuscular gloom of a sitting room which seems to have been very carefully protected against daylight. Mark Shivas and Malcolm Mowbray are on a couch against the far wall. Alan offers me a comfortable old chair and disappears to make coffee.

I long to have a good look round, but am aware of Shivas and Mowbray wanting to talk and set us all at ease. My overriding impression of the place is of elegant dusty clutter – rather like the set for Aubrey's *Brief Lives*.

Alan reappears. We talk politely of France … holidays … then Shivas asks me about my availability. Well, I can't go back on what I'd said to Alan … I *do* like the piece and well … they are all watching me … yes, I'd love to do it.

From then on we discuss finance generally and I realise that Shivas wants someone to bankroll the entire project and so far has no definite bites. In answer to his questions about HandMade I cannot but recommend he try them – though it somewhat complicates my position, as the Bennett film will be taking away time from my own project for HandMade.

After an hour there doesn't seem much more to say. Slight feeling of reserve, which does not emanate from Alan, but more likely from Shivas. I suddenly miss Richard. Everything's a little too polite and circumspect. Walk home.

Tom rings from Brighton at 11.30. He got there in four hours. They're coming back by train.

Spend the rest of the morning writing my obit tribute to Luis Buñuel for *Rolling Stone*.

Saturday, August 13th

In the *Telegraph*, a *Comic Roots* review under the nice heading 'Chortling beamish boy', I learn 'there is something roundly Victorian about Michael Palin's face, a durable cheerfulness not to be found among other members of Monty Python's Flying Circus … alone of the Python team he can deflate cant without venom', but cautions 'John Cleese's angry logic is missing from his humour'.

At five o'clock Felice[1] and Richard cycle up here. RL has a film to direct now, and is into top gear, with that bristling, bubbling, provocative self-confidence which he adopts to paper over the doubts beneath.

---

1 Felice Fallon, an American writer, became Richard Loncraine's second wife in September 1985.

Sunday, August 14th

To Angela and Veryan's 'Jubilation Party' at Chilton. It's to celebrate, or mark the occasion of, Angela's 50th birthday, V & A's 25th wedding anniversary, Jeremy's 22nd and his top 2nd in Politics at York. It's all been organised by the family as the caterers went bust a week ago.

So we are parked in a field by Marcus and a nice, bright-eyed girlfriend of Camilla's from Oxford, with whom she is going to Mexico and the Yucatán this holiday. I'm green with envy.

As the early cloud clears a perfect day develops. Not unpleasantly hot, but hot enough to make the ample shade from the big copper beech and lime trees on the lawn seem very welcome.

The moat is filled, now the bridge has been repaired, and is covered in a solid green veneer of duck-weed. New-born ducks skid around as on the surface of a billiard table.

Lots of Herbert relatives, and the slightly disturbing presence of Sir Dingle Foot's widow, Lady Dorothy. She used to be engaged to Daddy, and he called it off when she wouldn't agree to drop her political affiliations with the Liberals. Now I feel she regards Angela and me as the children she never had. 'Can't go too near people – I fall over so easily,' she warns. She invites Helen and me to one of her parties ... 'I do enjoy a good party.'

Angela in a '50's-looking dress which could have been one of the earliest she wore. And that's meant as a compliment. Can she really be 50?

Monday, August 22nd: Glasgow

To the ABC cinema complex at Sauchiehall Street. Met by the manager – neat moustachioed war veteran with Royal Signals tie. Up to one of their many 'lounges' where a 'spread' is laid out for the hungry and thirsty press at present sitting watching my film.

So I move into fifth gear and smile a lot and am completely helpful and co-operative and remember names and show a polite and hopefully completely straight face, even when a little old lady from the *Jewish Echo* asks me why I called the film *The Missionary*. Actually it is not as daft a question as it sounds, her point being that the title might put people off, which is something I've heard before, and which troubles me because I'm sure it's true.

Then en-taxi to the Woodside Health Centre, where it has been arranged for me to have the second part of a typhoid vaccination. The Health Centre is set amongst a jumble of modern blocks of flats, which have largely replaced the solidly stone-built red sandstone tenements which look rather good wherever they've been renovated.

The doctor writes on my form '*The* Michael Palin', and sends me off to the Treatment Room. Can't help reflecting on the glamour of showbiz as I sit in this little roomful of the ill amongst modern tower blocks with litter blowing all around. Eventually I'm seen by a stout, warm, friendly nurse and jabbed.

Tuesday, August 23rd: Edinburgh

At breakfast in the rather appealingly dilapidated, unmodernised, Scots-Gothic country house that is the Braid Hills, the ceiling starts to leak and champagne buckets and washing-up bowls are requisitioned with great good humour by the staff.

At midday I take a taxi to the Dominion Theatre, where *The Missionary* will open on Tuesday. It's an independent cinema in the smart Morningside area of the city, run by the genial Derek Cameron with an attentiveness which befits one whose father built the place (in 1938). The bar and restaurant are run and designed as places to linger and they have a busy clientele of all ages, who come here, some of them, just to eat and meet.

Local Hero is in its 17th week and *Gregory's Girl* for a third year. Bill Forsyth's favourite cinema? I ask Derek C. Oh yes, he says, when he comes here he just raises his hands to heaven ...

I cannot think of a pleasanter place for *The Missionary* to have its Scottish premiere.

Saturday, September 3rd

After breakfast TG drops in. I haven't even finished reading his *Brazil* and was hoping I'd have this morning to complete it, so can't give any very knowledgeable criticisms. But I like the part of Jack Lint and TG says he has kept it away from De Niro – just for me! So it's agreed that I'll do it. Filming probably some time in December.

Later in the morning Terry takes me up to the Old Hall in Highgate – his new £300,000 acquisition. Horrible things have been done to it inside, but its garden bordering on Highgate cemetery and the panorama of

London from its plentiful windows are almost priceless. Of course it's enormous and rambling, but still just a town house, not a country manor. And TG needs the challenge of the space like a drug. I find the damp old smell of the wretched conversions make the house depressing, but TG says it has quite the opposite effect on him because he knows what he can do with it.

Read *Water*, the latest DO'B project from Dick Clement and Ian La Frenais, who are his latest blue-eyed boys. DO'B would like me to play the part of Baxter. First 16 pages are wonderfully funny, but it all falls apart and there isn't a laugh after that. No characters are developed, new characters are thrust in instead and the jokes become stretched and laboured.

Sunday, September 4th

Dick Clement rings re *Water*. I'm honest about my feelings and, indeed, it's refreshing to talk to someone like Dick who is intelligent and tactful and is, after all, a TV writer with an impressive record – *Likely Lads*, etc. We can understand each other's language. He professes his liking for naturalistic comedy, and yet sees *Water* as an international film. I tell him that I think 'international' comedy a very dangerous concept.

I find Dick's choice of Billy Connolly to play the black revolutionary a real commercial cop-out . . . 'Well, he'll be sort of brown,' Dick reassures.

Monday, September 5th

Hear to my great disappointment that the '*Mish*' has not opened well in Scotland. And despite my great welcome by Derek Cameron at the Dominion, and his great hopes for the picture, I hear from Mike Ewin that he's pulling it off after three weeks to put in *Tootsie* – again.

Python, on the other hand, had its best provincial figures anywhere in the UK at Edinburgh. Nearly £10,000 taken in the first week of the Festival. And '*MOL*' continues strong in the West End, where it's out-performed *Superman III* easily.

Tuesday, September 6th

Today Tom and William start the new school year. This is for Tom the start of serious work – the run-up to 'O' Levels.

Helen says Tom is just like her at school, scatty, easily distracted and not really happy being taught maths and French and things. But neither of us should draw too much satisfaction from seeing neat parallels between our children's efforts and our own. They are not us, after all, they're them.

I go on down to TJ's and we read each other our starts. Both quite respectable, both start in space. Jim Henson rings, anxious for TJ to commit to directing a piece called 'Labyrinth'.

Tuesday, September 20th

I am tempted by a phone call from Ray Cooper to attend the first of a two-night concert in aid of Multiple Sclerosis, in which many great rock stars of the '60's, all friends of Ronnie Lane who has MS, will be appearing, including Ray C.

As if starved of live performance for so long, Ray tucks into the opportunity with gusto. I've never seen him live before, only heard the legendary tales. And he is a revelation. Impeccable timing and precise movements combined with a sense of high theatrical style which just avoids being camp or purely exhibitionist, is wondrous to behold.

But even Ray is upstaged by the extraordinary appearance of Jimmy Page, who weaves his way around the stage like a man who has been frozen in the last stages of drunkenness, before actually falling over. He sways, reels, totters, bends, but still manages to play superbly. The others look on anxiously and Ray tells me at the end that Page isn't well ... 'And he lives in Aleister Crowley's house.'

But the coup of the evening is the appearance of Ronnie Lane himself. Led, painfully slowly, onto the stage by Ray (who is everywhere) and Harvey Goldsmith, he is strong enough to sing two numbers. Very moving.

And Ray, going at his gong like the demented anti-hero of some nineteenth-century Russian drama, hits it so hard that it breaks and falls clean out of its frame.

Thursday, September 22nd

Another good morning's work on 'The Man Who Was Loved'.[1] Really

---

1 Like a number of other film-writing ideas around this time, this was a Jones/Palin screenplay that remained on the drawing board.

solid writing, not stop and start stuff, and few interruptions. Let letters pile up and just get on with it.

Terry comes up at two and we have a read-through. He has opened out the Viking saga (with a good song) and he likes what I've done on the modern, slightly more serious story. It does look as though we could have two films! Some discussion, then we swap scripts again and work on until after five o'clock. A good and productive working day – like old times.

Then TJ goes off to sign copies of *Erik the Viking* at the Royal Festival Hall and Helen and I go down to the Methuen Authors Party at Apothecaries Hall in Blackfriars.

As we go in, Frank Muir is on the way out. Some hail and farewell chat. I remember *The Complete and Utter Histories* – and his courage in putting them on. He remembers our piece about the waves of invaders in ninth- and tenth-century England being controlled by a man with a megaphone.

Only later in the evening do I find out that Frank's latest book for Methuen is called *The Complete and Utter My Word Collection*!

David Nobbs is anxious that I should read his latest novel because it's set in Sheffield. I'm afraid it's on a pile with dozens of things people have sent me to read. Even just acknowledging that they've sent them cuts my reading time down to about a book a month at the moment. This is another area of my life I must sort out.

Friday, September 23rd

Alison rings with the latest offers. BBC Bristol are doing a heritage series about Britain – would I write the one on transport? *Omnibus* want me on a programme about taste. Yet another video magazine seems to have begun, just to annoy me. Interview about *Missionary* and *Ripping Yarns*? And at last, at the grand old age of 40, the first offer to play Hamlet – at the Crucible, Sheffield.

In the evening we go down to Terry's for a meal with Ron Devillier. TJ cooks marvellous Soupe Bonne Femme, herring and roast pork, with lots of salads and bits and pieces.

TJ plays his accordion and the dog, Mitch, sings. However, Mitch will shut up instantly if anyone laughs.

Wednesday, September 28th

I read perceptive E M Forster remarks about his own fame. He says it made him idle. People were just happy for him to be who he was – to be what he had done, and there was no need for him to sully an already impeccable reputation by doing anything new.

To Shaftesbury Avenue to see *Yellowbeard*. On the plus side are likeable performances from Eric and Nigel Planer and Marty and Peter Boyle and a neat, classy cameo from Cleese, good costumes and some fine Caribbean scenery and excellent music. Against this a very disjointed piece of direction – no-one seems to know what they are doing or why – some dreadful hamming by the likes of James Mason and Cheech and Chong[1] which kills the few good lines stone dead.

Thursday, September 29th

Nancy L rings and after weeks of dithering I say yes to the *Saturday Night Live* date for January 21st. I don't really want to do the show again, but it does make a good focal point for my mother's trip to America.

Monday, October 3rd

Am offered the lead in 'Cinders' at the Fortune Theatre when Denis Lawson leaves in January. Turn it down on grounds of incompetence – I can't sing very well and certainly can't dance.

At 12.30 Helen and I leave for Kew Gardens, to attend a launching party for Bill Stotesbury's Tarot-designed book on structural engineering. Turns out to be a marvellous relief from the traditional wine and gossip launches. For a start we go by train, round the backs of North London. Pleasant walk to the gardens at Kew, except for the deafening noise of incoming aircraft – which means all conversations have to have Nixonian gaps in them. Helen insists on filling my pockets with conkers.

We are shown coffee and bananas (which used to be sent straight to the Queen, but aren't any longer) and a palm dating from 1775 and propped up like John Silver on long steel crutches. And trees that are now extinct, called cycads, which dinosaurs used to feed on.

1 Richard 'Cheech' Marin and Tommy Chong were an American stand-up comedy duo. Their material drew on hippies, free-love and the drug culture generally.

Tuesday, October 4th

A very dull day. I sit in front of the Viking saga all morning with hardly more than a page filled. The trouble is not that I can't think of anything to write, but that I can't think of anything *new* to write. The historical setting with the contemporary characters has been so well explored in *Grail* and *Brian*, and when I start to write on with TJ's adventures in boats I'm into *Time Bandits* territory. The law of diminishing returns.

Wednesday, October 5th

Into black-tie for the BFI 50th Anniversary Banquet at the Guildhall. Find I'm the only Python invited – though, among the 700 guests there are many whose contribution to British films is far less obvious than TJ or TG or any of the rest of the team.

As at the Royal Academy Banquet, I am next to a lady who is excellent company – in this case Christine Oestreicher, who made a short called *A Shocking Accident*. She is funny and quite good to have a giggle with at all the pomp and circumstance around.

'Trust you to have a girl next to you,' says John Howard Davies.[1] He is rather cross, having read somewhere that there were to be no more *Ripping Yarns* because the BBC couldn't afford them. I say I thought it was the main reason and he rather curtly agrees with me, but mumbles about there being others.

There are speeches and presentations of gold medals to Marcel Carné, Orson Welles, Powell and Pressburger[2] and David Lean.

Prince Charles makes a neat, effortless speech. Surveying the gathering he says it resembled an extraordinary general meeting of Equity. Harold Wilson has to go to the lavatory during the royal speech. Orson Welles re-tells stories about John Gielgud and gets massive applause, then we all 'retire to the library' for drinks.

Barry Took is very agitated about *The Meaning of Life*. He hated it, his

1 John, a child actor who played the lead in David Lean's 1948 film of Oliver Twist, directed many top BBC shows including the first series of *Fawlty Towers* and the first four shows of *Monty Python's Flying Circus*. He was Head of Comedy at the BBC in the late 1970's, when the last of the *Ripping Yarns* were made.
2 Michael Powell and Emeric Pressburger produced, wrote and directed some of the most stylish and inventive British films, including *A Matter of Life and Death* (1946) and *Red Shoes* (1948).

daughter hated it – 'she even preferred *Yellowbeard*' – and 'the daughter of one of the richest men in Hong Kong hated it'. His attack is rambling but persistent. He won't leave the thing alone. Badly shot, disgustingly unfunny – back to 'the urine-drinking' aspect of Python, he thundered. All in all, from an old friend, a strange and manic performance. But then Barry is strange, and there are more chips on his shoulder than you'd find on a Saturday night at Harry Ramsden's.

Sir Dickie Att and Tony Smith are working overtime, shovelling celebrities in front of Prince Charles, who is still here, wandering around. As I am telling Ray of the vehemence of Barry T's outburst, Prince Charles catches my eye. A moment later he steps across to me . . .

'I loved your film,' are the first words of the heir to the throne to me. Not a bad start. He was speaking of *The Missionary* . . . he loved the locations, especially Longleat. I ask him where he saw the film – 'Balmoral,' he admits, lowering his voice. Princess Margaret had recommended it, evidently.

Attenborough is a little concerned that the Prince's unscheduled chat with me is going on rather a long time. He begins to move him away. The Prince calls to me . . . 'I hope you'll make another one.' 'Yes, I will . . . if you've got any ideas.' At this the Prince returns . . . 'As a matter of fact I have got an idea.' Attenborough's face, already red with effort, goes puce and his eyes dart from side to side.

So Prince Charles tells me his idea, which is from a press cutting he'd seen about a home on the South Coast for people suffering from phobias. Every sort of phobia was catered for. He says he told Spike Milligan and he loved the idea. 'I'll write it and you can be in it,' is my parting shot. To which he responds well. A nice man, and easy to talk to.

I go to say goodbye to Sir Dickie, as most people seem to be drifting away, and he clutches my arm emotionally – 'Have you seen Orson?' I haven't seen Orson. 'You must see Orson . . . '. He finds a lackey . . . 'Take him to see Orson.' I'm not really desperate, but Sir Dickie insists. 'He's in a little room, outside on the left.'

And sure enough the Great Man (in every sense of the word) is sitting at a table in this very small, plain side-room, which looks like an interview room in a police station.

Orson comes to the end of a story, at which the adoring group of four or five young and glamorous guests laugh keenly. Then I am brought forward. 'Michael Palin from the Monty Python team.' Orson rises, massively, like the sun in India, and grasps my hand. He is clearly confused, but smiles politely. His head is very beautiful and he has a fine, full head of hair. I congratulate him on his speech.

His eyes flick to one side as another visitor is ushered into his presence, one of the Samuelsons,[1] who is telling Orson of the wonderful collection of film memorabilia he has. Orson is responding with polite interest again.

Sunday, October 9th

Take the Levinsons, who are staying with us, to the zoo. I enjoy the visit, especially seeing the delight in Gwenola's (21-month-old) eyes as she watches the prowling tigers and calls out 'Charlie!' – the name of the cat next door in Sag Harbor.

From the zoo down to Covent Garden. Take them into St Paul's – the actors' church. There on the wall of the church is an elegantly simple plaque to Noël Coward – and this the day after I read in his diaries his version of the Bible story – 'A monumental balls-up.'

We watch *Comic Roots*. Then, over Calvados, talk about the state of the world – and the soggy, comfortable, stifling affluence of the late '70's and '80's, as a contrast from the '60's, when it was exciting to write and new things *were* being said. Tell Al that I no longer feel the burning urge to write another film. I want to go to Rangoon.

Friday, October 14th

Ring Anne and express my total lack of interest in a proposal from a BBC producer to do a series called 'Monty's Boys'. Documentaries all about 'the greatest comedy group ... etc, etc ...' We really must avoid being embalmed by the media. If the BBC think we are so wonderful, marvellous, legendary, etc, why did they only repeat 13 shows in nine years?

To a fitting for *Brazil* at Morris Angel's with Jim Acheson and Gilly Hebden. Jim a bit jolly after a lunch with Robert De Niro who has agreed to do the part of Tuttle. Feel quite tangible sensation of excitement and pride at the prospect of sharing the billing with such a hero of mine. Jim says that all the talk of *Brazil* being awash with money is quite misleading. Says he hasn't much more than for *Bullshot*.

---

1 Sydney (later Sir Sydney) Samuelson started one of the most successful film service companies in the UK. He also was one of the leading lights behind the founding of BAFTA.

Saturday, October 15th

Tom off to play rugby at Edgware. A wild day outside – the barograph plummets and as I write up in my room there are gale-force gusts which threaten to take the whole room away. And it pours. A great day to be at the work desk, but I have to leave at 12.30 to have lunch with Denis and Ray.

We talk of the 'Pig' film, as DO'B calls the Alan Bennett piece. I feel DO'B is unhappy about the Bennett/Mowbray/Shivas group. He senses that there could be another *Privates on Parade*, whose demise he now largely ascribes to arrogance on the part of Simon Relph [the producer] and Blakemore. Again I mistrust DO'B's view of history – surely he wasn't forced into doing *Privates*, it was his scheme. Also I sense that DO'B doesn't have a great sympathy for what I really like in the script – the sense of location, period detail and atmosphere.

Home and begin reading TG's latest *Brazil* script. Nod off. TG drops by. My fee demand is the big talking point. It came as quite a shock to them.

Monday, October 17th: Southwold

DO'B calls. He has had a very good meeting with Mark Shivas and is all set to go ahead in April on the 'Pig' film!

Thursday, October 20th

Anne J rings to report *Brazil*'s 'final' offer in reply to my/her request for £85,000 for my services. They've offered £33,000 and reduced the time by a day. Anne is not at all pleased. I abhor such negotiations. It's all silly money, but I find their attitude typical. Lots of bragging about the money available, then suddenly a complete tightening of the belt as reality strikes. And in a film like *Brazil* the priority is clearly being given to the sets, props and special effects. But we play the game a little – if only to establish our resentment at the treatment. So for today I'm not doing it for a penny less than £50,000!

After dinner Anne rings with the result of the day's progress on *Brazil*. They have not shifted on the £33,000, but have agreed to a percentage.

Saturday, October 22nd

To Belfast. The British Airways shuttle has improved its service no end, as a result of serious competition from British Midland, and the flight, though full, is on time and well run.

Past the roadblocks, but apart from a couple of green flak-jacketed UDR men patrolling, no overt signs of the troubles. Lunch at BBC Broadcasting House. Double security on the doors.

On the programme with me is a Belfast boxer called Barry McGuigan. He's fighting for the European middle-weight title in four weeks' time and goes to Bangor Sands to train. No sex for four weeks, he tells me. He's a completely unaffected, straightforward man. He pronounces 'guy' as 'gay', which makes for interesting complications, and refers to God as 'the Big Man'.

He and I face a panel of Belfast teenagers, some of whom look quite terrifying with either Mohican hairstyles or completely shaved heads. But the questions come easily. The best one they ask me is 'Now you've made all this money, do you still want to make people laugh?' The questioner perhaps doesn't realise what a raw nerve he's touched.

Wednesday, October 26th

To the Turf Club at lunchtime. Peter Chandler introduces me to Jimmy and Brian the barman and Edward on the door. Have a glass of champagne in the snooker room and a toasted sandwich. Rather like being back at Oxford – notice-boards and people older than me calling me 'sir'. Ask Chandler about the horse-racing connections.

The club has many owners and trainers, but, he continues without a trace of unpleasantness, 'isn't open to jockeys'.

After supper go to see a Michael Powell film, *The Small Back Room*. A war story, set in spring 1943, full of psychological insights, shadows and claustrophobia, as well as much comedy and a bomb disposal thriller ending. The theatre is disappointingly empty, but three rows in front of me are Harold Pinter and Lady Antonia.

Thursday, October 27th

At 6.30 I go to Rail House at Euston to the launch of a book on Britain's railway heritage.

Cornered by two reps from Michael Joseph. Talk turns to the US invasion of Grenada. One of them feels we shouldn't let ourselves be pushed around all the time.

I get rather irritated with his mindless jingoism and say quite bluntly that I thought us wrong to go to war over the Falklands. He reels backwards with a strangled cry and our relationship isn't the same afterwards.

Monday, October 31st

Cleese rings. Brief tirade against *Private Eye*, who call him Sir Jonathan Lymeswold – he thinks that Ingrams is motivated largely by envy, in that he wanted to be an actor at one time. Ask JC how his time off to read books is going. Nothing has changed. JC isn't reading books all day long but deeply involved as ever with Video Arts – which swells with success daily, engulfing John's free time like a great unstoppable creature. But I ask him to lunch at the Turf next week – a chat for old times' sake – and he's pleased about that.

Wednesday, November 2nd

My writing progress reflects the weather conditions. Dull and Soggy. But as I run at lunchtime an idea breaks through the mists.

The Heath is eerily atmospheric. Closed in, the mist adding a touch of menace, making the front of Kenwood look shadowy and insubstantial. The solution to the predicament of the businessman who is lost on his way to work is that he has died. He is in Hell. Hell as the basis for the film – very strong. A clear image and one which you could describe in one sentence, but not one which in any way restricts our flights of fancy.

Ring TJ when I get back. He's enthusiastic. I feel wonderfully encouraged by this breakthrough and the more I think about it, the more levels it can work on. But no time to pursue it now, as I have to do domestic business such as buying fireworks for Saturday's party.

Then in the evening meet Michael Barnes for a chat. We meet at the Turf, but aren't able to eat there as there is some stag night. Hoyle, the night porter, is very nice to us as we are ejected … 'We *do* have an arrangement with the Institute of Directors, sir, I'm sure they'd be pleased to see you.' I wish I had his confidence.

Friday, November 4th

Nick Lander of L'Escargot confirms that he will do my Ma's 80th birthday party lunch – even though it means opening the restaurant specially.

Have cleared a number of calls, etc, by eleven and start to elaborate on the 'Hell' idea. Become very bogged down. It could go in so many directions – can't decide which, so write very little.

Ma rings, because she's just seen the news and wanted cheering up after seeing the bucket in which Dennis Nilsen boiled boys' heads.

Monday, November 7th

To Crimpers in Hampstead for my *Brazil* hair cut – a strange-looking affair which makes me look like Alexander Walker.

Out into milky afternoon sunshine and near 60's temperatures, feeling conspicuous in my new head, to Alan Bennett's for a chat with him and Mowbray over 'The Pig Film'. They haven't a final [Pork Royale was still in the running] title yet. Make some suggestions about seeing Gilbert and Joyce arrive at the town at the beginning and one or two other comments which Alan writes down. My strongest crit with a much-improved script is the way Gilbert fades away at the end.

As we leave I notice that there is someone living in the Dormobile parked tight in his front garden. 'She's watching television,' whispers Alan ... 'She?' 'Oh ... I'll tell you all about it next time,' he promises ... And I leave Malcolm, Alan and the old lady watching TV in his garden.

Thursday, November 10th

Lie in bed casting anxious thoughts about *Brazil* out of my mind. Like seeing James Fox on TV last night and realising what a finely-controlled actor he is. Why wasn't he Jack Lint? Like worrying that I should be worrying so much about something I know I can do.

At nine o'clock Jonathan [Pryce] and Terry G arrive for our read-through. Jonathan is low-key, halting and rather unconfident about the lines. Old actors' ploy – on the day he will be firing on all cylinders and I shall have to work hard to stay on the screen. Terry G would like me to smoke a pipe. I ask him to get me one, so I can practise in Ireland.

At twelve we go our separate ways – Jonathan to Hampstead to have yet more hair off, and me to lunch with John C at Duke's Hotel.

JC is delighted with Duke's and views with amused admiration this 'new side' of my life – as he calls my recently-developed St James's/Turf Club axis. We have an effortlessly pleasant wander around various subjects near and dear to our hearts.

JC shows off with a few names of the more esoteric Spanish painters. Professes an enjoyment of art galleries and a desire to go on a journey with me somewhere.

We both enjoy our lunch so much we decide to make it a regular feature. Or this is the last shouted intention as we part company in the still warm, but declining November sunshine in St James's.

Saturday, November 12th

Help Helen prepare a meal for Elias and Elizabeth – the Brazilian psychiatrists from next door. Helen makes a wonderful meal – tomato and tarragon soup, followed by gravadlax and chicken in a creamy sauce, apple pie, cheeses – Beaume de Venise.

Elias gives me a short, revealing history lesson about Brazil. A totally exploited country (by Britain and Portugal) until the late nineteenth century. Books forbidden there until 1832. No university until 1932. Didn't realise that Brazil's independent history was so short.

Elizabeth is great fun, but both are hopeless Francophiles – France is beyond criticism as far as they're concerned. To go to France or Italy, they say, after England is to go into the outside world! They think the English press are the worst in the world when it comes to analysis of foreign news.

I returned to Belfast for a second stint at the Festival. This time my one-man show was more ambitious and played for four nights at the Arts Theatre. With my debut in Brazil *imminent, it probably wasn't the wisest thing to have done.*

Sunday, November 20th: Belfast–London

A very cultured shuttle flight back, with musicians, singers and actors all anxious to be on the first plane to Heathrow. I sit next to Lizzie Spender, a publicist and part-time actress who's well connected. She is to play my wife in *Brazil* and we meet quite by coincidence.

Home by a quarter to one. Feel a desperate need for air and space before *Brazil* envelops me, so I take a Sunday run (usually something

I avoid as the Heath gets busy). Feel well-stretched, but cannot run easily as have pulled a muscle in my side in last night's record-breaking round the auditorium bid. (10.07 seconds!)

Set off, with Terry G, to Wembley for a run-through on the set of our Big Scene tomorrow. The studio is bitterly cold inside, but the set's very exciting. Jonathan arrives. I always feel he is rather taut – as though something inside is finely tuned, wound up with precision to be released at just the right moments – when he's acting.

We work through the scene and I try the various props such as electronic temple-massagers – American barbershops, 1950's. We're there for about three hours, then gratefully home again for a Sunday dinner – only the second meal I've had at home in ten days.

Monday, November 21st

On the set there is the well-behaved unfamiliarity of the first day on a new picture – and a big new picture, scheduled for 25 weeks. But there are many *Missionary* faces, and my progress to the set is constantly interrupted with handshakes and reintroductions. I feel it must be making Jonathan rather fed up. It helps me, though, and the early part of the day is as agreeable and jolly filming as I can remember. TG on good form, and the camera and sound crew are excellent company.

But the character of Jack Lint is still vague in my mind and after lunch, when I'm into the three or four fast speeches of jargon, I fluff more than once.

I realise that I should have spent much more care and thought in preparing for the part – thinking more about the character, spending more time with Jonathan and more time learning difficult lines, and not going to bed so late in Belfast. But we get through it, and I'm not sure how the effect of my uneasiness will show. At the end of the day TG says he has never seen me as nervous before.

Tuesday, November 22nd

Collected at 7.15. A very cold, crisp morning. Ice on the car windows.

We start shooting in Jack's office a couple of hours later. Take the scene through to the end on my close-ups. Then we work back through it on Jonathan. We have completed the scene – eight pages of close-packed dialogue – by four o'clock.

By then the race is on to complete two other short scenes, scheduled for the day before. One involves me packing a case, fitting my bullet-proof vest, taking my jacket and leaving the office whilst talking rapidly to Jonathan. Two or three times I come completely unstuck on the lines – 'sabotaged adjacent central service systems, as a matter of fact in your block'. We complete the scene, but it's a jolt to my pride and confidence that I was not more in control.

Home to prepare supper for the children, as Helen is in UCH Private Patients' Wing, having the growth on the end of her finger removed under general anaesthetic. I have a day off tomorrow and can look forward, at last, to a night's sleep without anxiety about filming.

Friday, November 25th

I suppose I should have smelt a rat when my call was set for ten. Far too generous a call for anyone who is going to be used during the day. But I take some work in.

In between whiles walk up to the set, which is dominated by a massive 30-foot-high piece of totalitarian architecture. The lobby of the Ministry of Information. Very impressive and rich in bits of comic detail. Nuns looking with approval at little displays of military weapons.

TG has hit upon a very striking style by mixing the gadgetry of *Star Wars* with a 1940's world. He's avoided the space suit, high-tech look which everyone has done to death and replaced it with the infinitely more sinister effect of modern TV surveillance techniques being used amongst McCarthyite, G-Man figures and costumes.

Highly apologetic second and third assistants inform me that I shall not be needed for the second day running – which is a pity as I've two or three times felt just like doing it.

Saturday, November 26th

Helen, Oak Village police snoop, rang her 'Crime Prevention Officer' today to report a shady man at old Miss Clutton's house and was told, after a long delay, 'I'm sorry, your Crime Prevention Officer doesn't work weekends.'

Denis O'B calls. He's trying again with *Water*. But having re-read the script I know it's going to be only a slightly more exciting version of *Yellowbeard* and *Bullshot*.

At the same time I reassert my inclination to do Bennett's film. He sounds as though he has not yet decided on this. Was he waiting to see if I bit on *Water*? They have John Cleese already, he says. Why has John said yes? It's another ordinary, mediocre part which he will be able to do with his eyes shut ... But he's old enough to decide for himself. Or has he said 'I'll do it if Mike will do it'? I have always said no to *Water* and have said 'no' again today. It's not my thing.

Tuesday, November 29th

Collected by [my unit driver] Roy on a cold, dark morning at 7.10.

No waiting around today. A concentrated morning's work on the first encounter between Sam and Jack. I start tense – projecting and acting. But, gaining confidence from repeated successful takes, I'm able to deliver a genuine, easy-going Jack – not the college boy pin-up that TG perhaps had in mind, but an unforced, easy naturalness that I never had last week.

TG looks battered. Unshaven, dark-rimmed eyes, one of which is bloodshot. But he's clearly in seventh heaven – doing exactly what he enjoys best.

Wednesday, November 30th

Back to the TJ/MP script today after a three-week lay-off.

TJ sounds unusually relaxed about it ... he admits he no longer feels the desperate pressure to make a film as soon as possible. Our reputation is such that we must maintain a very high standard – and if this takes a while, then we are lucky to have the time to spend getting it right.

Back home, see Julian Hough[1] wandering about in Oak Village. A strange, slightly disconcerting presence. He himself admits he's spent four sessions 'inside' (a mental hospital) in the last few years, and is now putting together a one-man show, having left Patrick Barlow and the National Theatre of Brent. He has a cup of tea and, having talked of his plans, he leaves, ambling off in an amused, unrushed gangle down Oak Village.

Nancy [Lewis] rings to ask if I will speak at the wedding, as her father can't be there. I'm honoured.

---

1 Julian Hough was a strange, tormented and talented actor who appeared in one of the *Ripping Yarns* and who had hugely impressed Terry Jones and myself when he appeared with Patrick Barlow in the *Messiah*, the first production of the eccentric and funny National Theatre of Brent.

Friday, December 2nd

Car picks me up at eight. To the studio where, to my amazement, I am finished and done with by eleven o'clock. The scene in which I leave the office, take the lift and leave Info Retrieval, talking to Jonathan the while, is at last complete and the bulk of my work on *Brazil* is over.

Saturday, December 3rd

To St Paul's, Covent Garden, for Nancy and Simon's wedding.

A heavily bearded Eric Idle slips into the row next to me. What an extraordinary place for a Python reunion. A year after making our second 'blasphemous' comedy, we're in a church singing 'Love Divine All Loves Excelling'.

Cleese, alone, is two rows in front. He keeps making Dick Vosburgh laugh by singing with great emphasis words like 'next', long after everyone else has stopped. Gilliam, with family, is in the front. Terry has his duvet-like coat and, with his new, short haircut, Eric says he looks like an 'inflated monk'. Jones, also with family, has a Mac that makes him look like Jones of the Yard and, entirely suitably, Graham is late!

Someone has alerted the press and there is a barrage of photographers, who try to get all the Pythons to link arms with the bride and groom. John and Graham totally ignore them. But eventually, after persuasive lines like 'Two minutes and we'll leave you alone', we are snapped and can go back to reacquainting ourselves with those we haven't seen for far too long.

Then Helen and I take a taxi down to Glaziers Hall, beneath London Bridge. A man in a red coat is announcing. We give our names as 'Mr and Mrs Figgis'. The sight of Nancy in white looking like an 18-year-old in her first dress already brought tears to the eyes at St Paul's. Simon looks ineffable and timeless, but Nancy does seem to have leapt back 20 years.

Simon's best man, Philip, small, with a short beard, has asked if he can break the rules and speak before me, as he is the only non-professional to speak. Turns out he's a barrister and in fact the *only* professional to speak. A very clever, witty, slightly long speech, with hardly a glance at his notes.

I have my usual copious sheaves of longhand, but, despite sherry and champagne, I manage to read them quite spiritedly and everyone seems

This photo call at a
Python video launch
seems to contradict my
diary entry, 'we all come to
the conclusion that zaniness
after 40 isn't possible'.
The Pythons, sans Eric,
and Carol Cleveland,
London September 3 1985

Sheepish of Gospel Oak.
Supporting our local
City Farm, 1984

The Meaning Of Life, 1982

Dad in 'Every Sperm Is Sacred'.

Christmas in Heaven. (left to right) Idle, Palin, Jones and friends in foreground. Chapman, Simon Jones and Jonathan Benson look on.

Telling the children the facts of life. 'I will say "sock" instead of "cock"…and the dastardly substitution will take place in the dubbing theatre' Elstree Studios, August 10 1982

Jones, Gilliam, Palin, Cleese, Idle and Chapman emerge from the jungle. 'Endless takes. Constant calls over the walkie-talkie for the Test Match score' August 27 1982

Brazil, 1983-84

Jack Lint. The nastiest character I've ever played. Sadly.

Rehearsing with Terry G and Jonathan P in the lobby of Information Retrieval

Using my heavy duty massager when Sam Lowry (Jonathan Pryce) bursts in unexpectedly. 'At the end of the day TG says he's never seen me as nervous before' November 21 1983

Gilliam the director with Ray Cooper, actor, musical director, gourmet, percussionist extraordinaire and all-round good bloke.

My mother crosses the Atlantic for the first and only time in her life, at the age of 80 years and 2 days. New York City January 1984

Mum, with Angela, at the *Saturday Night Live* after-show party. 'There is no question of Granny not wanting to go – in fact she stays there until four a.m.' January 21 1984

With my sister Angela, Nancy Lewis and Mum in Central Park.

East of Ipswich. Tristram Powell, director, in cap and Innes Lloyd, producer, worry about the weather, Southwold, Suffolk, June 1986

Wearing my Biff T-shirt at the *East of Ipswich* wrap party at the Crown Hotel, Southwold

MP, Gilliam, David Robinson of *The Times*, John Cartwright of the British Council, and our Russian escort Elena, on Jabberwocky visit to Moscow and Leningrad, November 1986

My mother and her neighbour,
Lily Pratt, outside Croft Cottage,
near Southwold, Suffolk.

Launching a rebuilt steam-engine
at the Bluebell Railway.

Mahendra 'Mash' Patel, our newsagent.
Such reserves of patience and good
humour that our family name for him
is Mr Nice Man.

'Sam Jarvis has arrived to start decorating
and is extremely worried about the
whereabouts of his tea bags'

pleased afterwards. Jones (Terry) says they were the two best wedding speeches he'd heard.

Monday, December 5th

The morning starts at Julia Street, with an influx of kitchen-fitters, electricity meter-readers. Sam Jarvis has arrived to start decorating and is extremely worried about the whereabouts of his tea-bags.

Ring TJ, who has spent all morning on the phone and had no time to work. Put finishing touches to a peace speech, then drive down to Camberwell, via the picture-framers in Islington. Brief glimpse of the nightmare world of bottled-up traffic on the way through London. Unmoving lines of huge lorries in the drizzle. Dark, enormous, steaming, hissing, hostile and hugely out of scale with the buildings and streets they clog.

Anyway, though we didn't expect such a thing to happen, we both become fired with enthusiasm over the Viking musical idea.

We shall now go away and read about the Vikings, and not try to do a pastiche of bad Hollywood films about Vikings, but work from an informed base – as with *Missionary*, *Brian*, etc. Ideas should come from the reading.

Then I drive up to Camden Institute where I deliver my five-minute piece on peace to open Peace Week there. A small but appreciative audience of middle-aged, grey-haired intellectuals, students, slightly dog-eared supporters of the cause and people who look a little mad.

Tuesday, December 6th

Very content sitting in the sunshine reading tales of Harald 'Blue Tooth' Gormson and others. Vaguely aware of the presence of London out there – of friends to be called, lunches to be shared, books bought, projects discussed, cards sent to faraway places, but otherwise little to disturb my peace and contentment.

DO'B calls with a gloomy forecast for the survival of the 'Pig' film. His 'people' don't think it will be commercial. Very difficult to sell. Still a TV film basically, and so on and so on.

DO'B calls again at 4.30 to tell me he's had the meeting with Shivas and the project is definitely going ahead. 'The Yorkshire Mafia', as he calls Bennett and Mowbray (with Shivas an honorary member), will actually be opening an account with HandMade this week. DO'B chides me over *Water*. 'Why don't you do commercial films for once, Michael!' I want to say 'Why don't *you* do commercial films for once, Denis.'

Later in the evening I call George in Henley. Tells me that at the 'Beatle Summit' last week affairs and problems that had been dragging on unresolved were sorted in a day. Yoko had been (pause) 'very nice' (this followed by a chuckle) and the only problem had been Paul's defensiveness for the first hour until he realised that the others weren't ganging up on him after all.

André rings to tell me the good news that our *Meaning of Life* commercials have won Best Use of Comedy on a Commercial and Best Entertainment at the Radio Awards. The entire series of commercials received a commendation. André very chuffed as we beat Rhys Jones/Mel Smith's Philips ads. When I think that we threw together the scripts almost on the spot, it's even more remarkable.

Saturday, December 10th

TG arrives. Evidently Arnon Milchan has already done a 30 million dollar deal for TG's next two pictures. They are to be *Baron Munchausen* parts I and II. And Twentieth Century Fox are *very* keen. So TG's future looks very rosy. Quite rightly he has at last been appreciated as a film-maker of rare talent and accordingly he must be offered as much work as possible. I feel as I talk to Terry G that Terry J and I should both be in this same position, but we are, with the best will in the world, holding each other back.

Watch the latest American 'sensation' – *The Day After*. A TV film about the effects of nuclear war on the American Midwest.

In the hour after it finishes, Robert Kee, solemn and Solomonic, gravely adjudicates a discussion.

Most depressing of all is that, of all the David Owens, Denis Healeys and Robert McNamaras, no-one makes the simple promise that nuclear war is unthinkable and utterly appalling and therefore everything and anything that *can* be done to prevent it happening must be done and with all speed.

Go to bed profoundly depressed.

Tuesday, December 13th: Southwold

Finish [J. G. Farrell's] *Troubles* on the train, as we wait at a signal check this side of Manningtree. Excellent book. It has really caught my imagination and involved me. Reminds me of Paul Scott, but a little less heavy on the history and stronger on the symbolism. Farrell, the author, died at 46. Tragically young, as they say.

Wednesday, December 14th

Morning at the desk. No word from TJ, so after phone calls and writing of a few more cards, I have time to sit and work out strategy for the next projects. Time for some hard-headed realistic forward-planning of the sort that cheers up a neat, anally-retentive little list-keeper like myself no end.

Decide to go further with [my play] *The Weekend* – and have asked Douglas Rae[1] if he will give me an opinion. I think I know what he'll say, but I'd like a mainstream West End management opinion to see whether it's worth bestirring myself on this one.

In the evening we go round to drinks with the Goldstones.

Tracey Ullman is introduced to me by Ruby Wax – whom I met at RL's on Thanksgiving. I like Tracey U – she's funny and quite sensible and, thank God, isn't always manically funny. The TV companies wanted her to do sitcom, but she turned her nose up at that and felt she wanted to do film half-hours – 'like female *Ripping Yarns*', she says to me.

Peter Cook lurches in. His shirt tails pulled out from his trousers, his tie loosened and harbouring a neat deposit of cigarette ash on the top of the knot.

Once he has got a bead on me he teases me about my appearance on the front of the *Ham and High* this week (a report of my Peace Week opening speech at Camden Institute ten days ago, complete with rather smug photo of myself next to a peace banner). 'Wassallthis bloody peace yeronnerabout?' is directed at me from close spittle-throwing range.

My last glimpse of him is out in the street, a shambolic shaggy figure shouting after me 'Well, if you ever get fed up with peace ... !'

---

1 Urbane, experienced theatrical agent and friend of Denis O'Brien.

Saturday, December 17th

Book-signing at the Paperback Bookshop in Oxford.

At 3.15 I can thankfully cease to be on public display and walk slowly down to the station with Geoffrey S, who's come up to escort me. We catch the 4.25 back to London. On the way I talk an awful lot about our films and specially about Paul Zimmerman's Hitler film.[1] Geoffrey is such a good sounding board.

I drive him up to Highbury and on the way back up a clogged and unfriendly Holloway Road I hear on the car radio of the news that a bomb has gone off amongst Christmas shoppers. It was outside Harrods and nine people are reported dead, scores injured.

The awful thing about such attacks is the increasing deadening, demoralising fact that there are people who take pride and pleasure in killing indiscriminately and there is nothing that can totally be done to prevent them achieving their ends. Grim stuff to come back to.

Sunday, December 18th

Leave the house at 10.15 for a Python group meeting – the first for over a year.

The meeting is good-natured. Arthur Young, McClelland Moores' accounts are not only accepted and the accountants reappointed but, at TG's suggestion, a motion is passed that a singing telegram should be sent round to tell them so.

Graham asks if he can vote by proxy and if so can he be his own proxy. John Cleese reveals that he may be Jewish. He also says his father had a nanny who had been kissed by Napoleon. I tell them that my ancestor had hidden Prince Charles in the oak tree after the battle of Worcester. To which EI came up with the 'O' Level maths question 'How many royalists does it require to hide a king in an oak tree?' Graham says he's discovered family links with George Eliot. I am complimented on my

1 Paul's basic premise was that Hitler had survived the war and was living in a place called The Thousand Year Ranch in Paraguay. He contacts some American agencies to see if they might arrange a tour of the USA when he would tell his story and atone for everything. The only person who'll even consider taking him on is a New York agent desperately down on his luck. He is, of course, Jewish. Hitler becomes his client and the story rolls on – Hitler becoming a huge hit on US television. No surprise then that, in real life, no American studio was interested.

speech at the Lewis/Jones wedding and Eric is complimented on his outstandingly bushy beard.

Monday, December 19th

Although a morning of recovery would have been a good thing, our house today promises to be invaded by Sam (paint), Ted (windows), Ricky (lights), Helena (vacuum cleaner), a window cleaner and Stuart (burglar alarm). Any large-scale invasion of our intimate little property always makes me twitchy – they take over, making me feel like an odd and eccentric man in the attic, who sits on a swivel chair all day booking restaurants and thoughtlessly going to the lavatory just when they're working in it, on it or around it.

Into Covent Garden to meet Eric and Tania at a pub in Drury Lane. Eric reveals that [his play] *Pass the Butler* is doing marvellous business in Stockholm, like Python. Eric and I try to analyse this phenomenon and decide it can only be that the Swedes have no sense of humour of their own and have to import it.

Tuesday, December 20th

Watch marvellous piece by Alan Plater about Orwell's visits to the Isle of Jura and his battle to complete *1984* against the advance of TB. Ronald Pickup's performance quite excellent. How he managed to keep the catarrhal rattle in the back of his throat I don't know. It was as complete a portrait of another man as any actor could hope to achieve. Comparable with Ben Kingsley's 'Gandhi'.

Sunday, December 25th: Christmas Day

Breakfast about 10.15 – can hear church bells ringing in Lismore Circus. Helen has to cook potatoes for the lunch at Mary's. As we prepare to leave at 12.45, run into John Sergeant (Anne Alison's brother and Oxford revue acquaintance), who is BBC Radio correspondent at Westminster.

He reckons that Willie Whitelaw's wonderful 'Willie-ism' over Northern Ireland – 'We must not pre-judge the past' – ranks as a great unconscious profundity, and says that Margaret Thatcher loves publicity and is becoming smoother and smoother and more frighteningly competent at it. To the press after the Harrods bombing a week ago:

'Where would you like me?' 'Would I look better here?' 'How will you be editing this?' Etc, etc. Maybe that is in fact the only way to deal with the press, but Sergeant's point is that Maggie is now becoming unduly preoccupied with presentation rather than substance.

Friday, December 30th

To the Hayward Gallery.

Dufy's work a celebration of light, colour and movement. Sea and sky and sporting ritual – regattas and race-courses figure large. Cumulative effect of his work is like opening a window onto the Mediterranean on a perfect summer's day. His fabric designs are an eye-opener – all done 50 years ago, but seem absolutely up to date.

Drop in at the Portal Gallery and see Eric Lister. Like most of Bond Street, he's empty of punters, but instantly into stories and showing me objets drôles as if we'd never stopped looking from the last time I came in. He shows me a device which incorporates a minimally inflated balloon which can be clipped onto the underneath of the shoe to give an impersonation of squeaky shoes.

Just before I leave, his friend, who has sat quietly at his desk, demonstrates a watch he's been given for Christmas, whose face can unclip from the wrist and from which arms and legs can be extended, making it into a little stubby figure which can stand on the bedside table at night.

1984

Wednesday, January 4th

Up, before Helen, and let Sam J in (he's now decorating No. 2), then go running – so feel quite perky by the time Roy arrives to take me to the studio. Am having my hair cut when De Niro appears – hot off the overnight plane from NYC, to prepare for his scene tomorrow in which he shoots me. He's very quiet and, as is the way with people you admire inordinately, there's very little to say.

De Niro goes away to practise abseiling.

The afternoon goes by and stretches into evening before I'm used. Go to the editing room and look at the first reel. My performance in the lobby is not good. Ian Holm and Jonathan impressive. Depressed for a while.

Thursday, January 5th

Quite quick run down through light, early-morning traffic to Croydon Power Station (built, I'm told by Robert De Niro later in the day, in 1948 and closed in 1980).

The Mercedes turns in off a works slip road and into a service road between 220-foot-tall cooling towers. Beside one of them stands the crane from which is suspended the steel cage from which Tuttle's raiding party will descend.

For the first hour there is coffee and nothing to do but settle in our caravans.

After an hour of desultory chatter we are called up to the set and for the first time and probably the last few times of my life, I enter a cooling tower. It's like being at the bottom of the barrel of some giant cannon.

A long, narrow walkway leads from the side to a 15-foot-diameter platform in the centre of the tower. Rehearse and work out how I shall die, so that my stunt double knows what to do.

Lunch – in my caravan. TG, Bobbie De N, Jonathan and me. TG cross at lack of progress, mutters that it should have been done with models all along. Talk turns to lavatory stories. TG recounts how he was peeing in the toilet of a smart little restaurant in France when he noticed a turd on the floor beside the bowl. Just at that moment there is a knock on the door – a queue has formed. How does our hero avoid being mistaken for the ill-aimed turd-dropper? Poor TG has no alternative but to come out looking as unconcerned as possible.

Am driven to the Selsdon Park Hotel, about 15 minutes away, where TG is overnighting as well.

Have a bath, then wander downstairs to wait for TG. The public rooms are furnished rather fussily, with heavy patterns, copper ornaments, much recent old-wood panelling – like endless Agatha Christie stage sets. Everything is expensive. My little single room (with good bathroom) is £51, a half-bottle of champagne is £10.25. And this is Croydon.

To bed at 11.30. Have fallen into a deep sleep almost as soon as I switch the light off when I'm woken by the incessant, jarring screech of a fire alarm. My room is almost vibrating with the noise.

A few minutes later the horrendous noise dies. With thudding heart I settle down to try and sleep, only to be woken by a telephone call reassuring me that it *was* a mistake. I wonder if they mean staying here in the first place.

Friday, January 6th

We progress, slowly. None of TG's camera moves are easy. A lot of high angles or low angles and complex little movements. The chill gets through to the bones, slowly but surely. There is some light drizzle after lunch which makes the narrow platform suddenly lethal and I skid twice towards the edge on one of the takes.

The day ends with my 'death' scene. A specially-prepared, remote-controlled bullet hole is fired out of my baby face mask, splashing so much blood on the camera that they can't see anything else and it has to be re-shot.

Three times I spin round to a special mark, wrench my mask off as the camera closes in and finally spin round to Jonathan, alone in his torture chair, and, grasping helplessly at him as I fall, collapse via knees to the floor.

A glass of red wine in the make-up caravan in the middle of this awesome palace of pre-stressed concrete is one of the best things of the day. One of the others was the visit of Ray Cooper, bringing a touch of style to the cooling tower. He is very excited about the Bennett film – but confirms that George H still hates the script.

Sunday, January 8th

Watch a 1973 film biog of Noël Coward on TV this afternoon. Never realised quite how prolific he was. At the age of 26 he had three or four shows running simultaneously in London – he had made a name as actor, writer and lyricist. He continued throughout his life to turn out new work with what sounds like extraordinary facility. He says in interview that he wrote *Private Lives* in four days – 'And . . .' long pause ' . . . not one word of it was changed.'

Blithe Spirit wrote itself in a week and one of his most famous songs was written in 20 minutes in a taxi stuck in a jam.

Tuesday, January 10th

Down to Devonshire Street for lunch at Langan's Bistro with David Puttnam (his invitation).

He starts straight in by offering me a *First Love*.[1] Either as writer or director, which is very nice as it's a very prestigious, well-produced series, which has been sold to the US for theatrical release. Jonathan Benson, who has now given up assistant directing, has written one of them. Puttnam says that when he asked Jonathan why he was giving up, JB told him that it was because he wanted to be able to have a shit whenever he wanted, instead of having to go through day after day holding it in until there was a long enough break.

Wednesday, January 11th

Low cloud, persistent drizzle. Glad to have a day at the desk. Become very enthusiastic about doing a *First Love* for Puttnam. The more I think of the tale of meeting Helen, Southwold, etc, the more comic possibilities I see, and also some clear ideas on locations, characters. Very liberating it is when an idea strikes and appeals so completely. Ring Puttnam immediately, but he's in a meeting, of course.

---

1 This was a generic title for a series of films on a theme. Not to be confused with the US TV series of the same name.

Read through Dr Fegg's work prior to meeting with Geoffrey Strachan this afternoon re re-publication.[1] In the densely-packed American edition some very funny stuff lies well concealed. Definitely worth a re-publication, for much of the book would be new in the UK anyway.

TJ has had the same reaction to the 'Fegg' material as myself, only more so. He says, without any sign of a boast, that he was in tears of laughter reading it.

General agreement on progress and some useful suggestions for what is right and wrong for the book. I suggest that it should be *Dr Fegg's Nasty Book – A Family Guide to All The World's Knowledge* – and that we should put a 'Keep Away From Children' sticker on it. TJ suggests better wording: 'Keep Out of Reach of Children'.

Thursday, January 12th

By taxi to Westminster and Dean Stanley Street, hard by the Victoria Tower in the mixture of very attractive Queen Anne terraces.

Into one of these I have to go to do a 45-minute chat about self and work for the British Forces Network. I feel a much closer identification with an audience than I usually do on these shows. Whatever I feel about our army being in the Falklands or Belize or Beirut, I have experienced home-sickness and I should think these radio shows are like manna from heaven to their audience.

Finish at one and wander amongst the attractive little streets like Lord North Street and the late classical flashiness of St John's, Smith Square. Then across into the Victoria Gardens. How well the Houses of Parliament and the Abbey and St Margaret's, Westminster go together. They are all inspiring, imaginative buildings in their way – built largely for the eye of the beholder. Turn 180 degrees and the heart sinks at the sight of the accountants' buildings marching grimly along from Vauxhall.

Saturday, January 14th

Prepare the house for likely visitors this afternoon. Wrap presents and write cards for Mother, who is 80 today and somewhere between Chilton Hall and Gospel Oak.

---

1 *Bert Fegg's Nasty Book for Boys and Girls* was written by Terry J and myself and originally published in 1974. We had plans for an edition with new material.

She arrives with Angela at eleven, looking quite spry and dressed in a neat claret purple two-piece with a touch of flamboyance in a ruff-like frill at the neck. She really looks excellent, as well as I've seen her at any time in the last few years. Angela too, with her hair done nicely and well cut, looks fine.

L'Escargot, which has especially opened for us, has set a buffet in the upper room, which is a perfect size for the 26 of us and full of light and airiness.

I give a short speech and mention that air travel was only three weeks old when Granny was born – the longest flight had been for 120 yards. Tomorrow she will be taken from London to New York in the time it would take my father to park the car – this is well greeted, but allows me to wish that Father were here today to laugh at it himself.

Sunday, January 15th: London–New York

Sleep well. Up with the alarm at 7.45. Leave with Ma and Angela in a taxi at 8.45, just as a light snow is falling.

At the Concorde check-in I spy Steven Spielberg, Sir Lew Grade, with his white, pasty, sepulchrally-blanched head, and Tom Conti. The whole flight passes so smoothly that I don't think Mother or Angela really sense that we have crossed the Atlantic, or exchanged continents at all. Ma takes to it as easily as she might the train to Ipswich.

After unpacking and resting, we walk, along dangerously icy sidewalks, up to Avenue of the Americas, then taxi to the Tavern on the Green. Nancy has managed to book us a table in the richly-kitsch Crystal Room, only by mentioning that it was part of my mother's 80th birthday present. We are right by the window and the sun is dazzling. Outside is Central Park in the snow with a mixture of skaters, skiers, joggers, walkers and sledders passing by as a sort of continuous background entertainment.

Around the Plaza is a great throng of police – the Chinese Premier is staying there. One of the policemen on duty hails me, 'Hey! Michael', takes off his glove and shakes my hand – something no policeman in England would do with such unaffected directness. This impresses the relatives.

Then round to Nancy and Simon's for their American wedding party – or rather the party to offer a chance for their rich NYC friends to give them presents, as Simon puts it to me. I'm getting increasingly tired and find a party of all my NYC friends rather hard work on the smile button – on the first day here.

Find Granny and Angela chatting to Jeremy Irons – whose performance in Stoppard's *The Real Thing* has just been hailed as a major Broadway success. Introduce myself and we talk about all sorts of mundane things. Irons claims not to be interested in the razzmatazz and public image of a Broadway star, though he doesn't altogether convince me.

It's ten o'clock, nearly ten-thirty, when I finally get Mother away and taxi back to the hotel. To round the day off – a Python repeat ('Trim Jeans', etc) on PBS. They're still awake and laughing and enjoying it at eleven – four, UK time. Amazing.

Monday, January 16th: New York

Meet with [*Saturday Night Live* team] Dick Ebersol, Bob Tischler and a lady called Pam, whose function isn't clear. This is a sort of introductory meeting before I go to meet the rest of the writers. Ebersol, who is a big man, was mugged after the show on Saturday night at 4.30. Two black eyes and two broken ribs – and on Central Park South ...

After an hour's chat we go over to the Rock and I meet, or in some cases renew acquaintance with, the writers.

Then I'm given my office – which is in fact Eddie Murphy's office and contains stacks of unopened fan mail as well as one or two opened letters – one from a fan (white), who wants to 'ride on your star'. The various writers in their various combinations come along and talk and try out tentative ideas on me. Without Lorne there the whole process is rather businesslike – less pleasant, lazy chat, more of an organised schedule, but this suits me well, as I have Angela and Granny waiting at the hotel.

And they're raring to go again.

Tuesday, January 17th: New York

I spend the morning in my room writing up a couple of ideas for the show. The monologue fits together neatly and is written within an hour. It involves Ma – it's too good to miss the opportunity of using her when she's in New York.

At midday she and Angela return – spirits indomitable after a hot morning at Macy's – we eat a quick snack in my room – and Ma doesn't seem too averse to appearing in the monologue. Indeed, at one o'clock when a limousine and a photographer arrive to collect us all at the hotel for the *Saturday Night Live* photo-session, Mother is carefully dressed and coiffured and ready for anything.

Then I go to the '*SNL*' office. Sell the monologue idea without much difficulty – in fact Dick Ebersol is so enthusiastic that he calls in the new publicity lady for the show and tells her to release the story that Michael is co-hosting '*SNL*' with his mother. She will not only be the first mother to co-host, but, he thinks, the oldest host ever on the show.

Wednesday, January 18th: New York

To the Rockefeller Center – snow now driving and quite thick – it looks wonderful swirling past the windows of the 17th floor.

Dick Ebersol warns me 'You're in the first nine sketches'; it also turns out I'm in the next nine. No time for shyness, just get up and throw myself into them as best I can – most of them sight unseen. It's rather enjoyable – like auditions for a college smoker.

I'm free at six and meet Angela and Granny at a recommended restaurant in the Theater District, called The Palatine. Have to crunch over a few snow-caked sidewalks to get to it, but once there I can tell I shall enjoy it. It's calm and relaxed and this marks it out as something of an oasis in New York terms.

Towards the end of the meal Father Jake, the Catholic priest who runs the restaurant, visits us at table. He sprays cards around like a computer salesman and bemoans the problems with the Vatican, who don't, he says, take kindly to a priest with a liquor licence. I am moved to write in a brand new visitors' book they've been given by a guest from Texas, 'Why shouldn't God be a gourmet?'

We leave with much bowing and scraping from the priest, who has been told who I am by a waiter. One final curiosity is that the hat-check woman apparently used to run the restaurant.

Thursday, January 19th: New York

At 12.30 I walk across Fifth Avenue and into Rockefeller Plaza for a rehearsal on the 17th floor. At 2.30 down to the studio to record some promotional spots – with Mum. Any worries I've had about her performance in front of camera disappear when I see with what confidence and aplomb she mounts the stage and delivers her little rejoinders to me.

She makes everyone in the gallery laugh when, after one take of the first promo, she asks, rather loudly, on camera, 'Well, what's next?'

Saturday, January 21st: New York

Mum has been given Eddie Murphy's dressing room for the day.

Dress rehearsal offers a foretaste of the sort of reception she is to get from the audience. Much greater than I had expected. She can do no wrong.

The music crescendos and at 11.35, a week after reaching 80, Mum leads me out in front of the cameras. Apart from forgetting to grab my arm at the first cue, everything she does is exactly right. She remains herself, natural and dignified, and yet displaying a winning sparkle of humour in the eyes which absolutely wins the audience over.

So Mother and I, in what must surely be one of our finest hours, are eventually taken, full of compliments, down through the lobby of 30 Rock – where Granny signs an autograph – into a waiting limousine and down to Joanna's [Restaurant on Madison Avenue] for the party. There is no question of Granny not wanting to go – in fact she stays there until four a.m., when the main lights are switched on in an attempt to flush out the most persistent revellers!

Monday, January 23rd

Mercifully, I have a day clear before *Brazil* tomorrow. And just as well. I sleep for ten hours and don't surface until 10.30.

Granny still looking well. It's as if she has gone into a sort of physical and mental overdrive in the last year. When she should have been descending the age spiral – in terms of ability, mobility, health and general comprehension – she is in fact coasting along extremely confidently and competently, as if all the excitements of *Comic Roots* and *Saturday Night Live* have actually had a rejuvenating effect.

Angela, according to Helen, is as relaxed and easy as she has seen her for a long time. Of course, what I forget is that Angela and I have hardly spent as much as a week together since I was a small boy.

Angela goes off to lunch with Veryan and at 12.15 the car I've hired to take Granny back to Southwold arrives. Momentary panic when I ask him whether he knows the route and he nods confidently and says 'It's right after Gloucester, isn't it? Sorry, sorry, *Ipswich* ...' With some misgivings I wave goodbye to my co-star.

Tuesday, January 24th

The children are all at home as ILEA teachers are marching today in support of their employers, and against government plans to get rid of them. All the children are desperate for snow, but it seems we are the only corner of England and Scotland to escape unscathed.

TG tells me that the De Niro scene aged everyone. A minimum of twenty takes on each shot. He was nervous (of his reputation, I suppose) and forgot lines and missed business, and all this after more rehearsal time than any other actor in the film. Pryce tells me that one day De Niro just threw everything down in frustration and stomped off to lunch. I feel rather reassured – clearly geniuses are not immune from the strangely disturbing effects of the film.

Tuesday, January 31st

Ring Mark Shivas re *Private Function* [as 'the Pig Film' is now known]. As far as he's concerned it's all going ahead, but at the slightly later time of April 30th (with a week's rehearsal before). Only problem is a tight budget. DO'B at one point had even questioned the need to go to Yorkshire to film Yorkshire. Ian Holm and Ian Richardson are both being touted.

I feel completely lacking in energy and confused about plans. Not in the right mood to take decisions at all. Pick up the Noël Coward diaries and scan some entries for '50 and '51. Camp old theatrical that he was, there is an energy and a delight in his own work which rather encourages me. One has to put out in order to get anything back. Rush, stress, pressure is one side of the coin. Success, recognition, approval and the giving and receiving of pleasure is the other.

I look again at my start on *First Love* yesterday and realise that I can't simply put a line under it and say – 'next year maybe'. Strike while the iron's hot.

Work through until about seven, steadily and quite satisfactorily. Watch Gavin Millar's 'Secrets' – second of the *First Love* tapes Puttnam sent me. Very strong, original, well sustained. A lovely oddity.

Read some of Orwell's life. I don't like him very much so far. Must always remember he went to Eton, his best teenage friends were called Jacintha and Prosper and he had a caterpillar called Savonarola.

Ring Mum. She's had a prolapse and didn't really want to tell me.

Nothing serious, but it involves going to a gynaecologist in Gorleston ...
'I've *never* been to Gorleston,' she says disapprovingly.

Thursday, February 2nd

For the first time for nearly ten years we don't have to take the children
to school. Or, to put it more sentimentally, we've taken Rachel to school
for the last time. As from two weeks ago she now goes off on her own.
One thing the children have in common is a desire to get to school as
early as possible. Tom is usually away whilst we're still dressing ('I'm
going now, right?'), Willy, after tormenting Denis, goes at about 8.30, and
Rachel is straining at the leash to leave as soon as the road-crossing man
arrives, which is just before nine.

Drive to Oxford to give a talk to the Brasenose Arts Society. Have
nothing prepared – will have to throw myself at their mercy and encourage
questions. Plenty of time to think as I sit in traffic jams on the way out to
the M40.

At BNC by 7.30. Met by a small welcoming committee.

I think how nice it would be to talk about my work to this very nice,
bright group of six BNC undergraduates – get down to some depth,
think more carefully about things, accept more probing criticism, encourage more controversial questions. As it turns out this is not to be, and my
talk to the BNC Arts Society is a public performance in front of 290
people packed into the JCR. I'm ready for it and do enjoy it and we do
cover quite serious matters – censorship, religious and political convictions, etc. But really they want me to make them laugh.

Their next speaker is William Golding OB, who apparently is donating
his Nobel Prize medal to the college.

Friday, February 3rd

Take the *First Love* tale on for an hour, then am rudely interrupted by the
arrival of a director of SieMatic. He has a black BMW (no harm in that,
of course), a sheepskin suede coat, a beer gut and a pushy aggression
mixed, uncomfortably, with a chummy and affected sycophancy of the
'Hello, Michael' variety. 'I'm at Michael Palin's house,' he says, loudly and
pointedly, when ringing his office.

He blames all the damage to the kitchen units on John Lewis and proof
of the depths of his bovine insensitivity is that he does not bat an eyelid

when he turns to me and says 'You don't mind if I get our PR people to come and talk to you, do you? I mean, if we can get some publicity and you're agreeable . . . '. It's like Cunard ringing me to do a voice-over, the day after my family drowned on the *Titanic*.

Then the Complaints Manager of John Lewis appears. Neat, slim and at least having the good grace to look apologetic. Both parties try to shift the blame to each other whilst we stand rather uncomfortably in between. 'Have you seen any of John Cleese's training films, Michael? They're *very* funny . . .'

Saturday, February 4th

TG has come to tell me of his decision to re-shoot the central Jack/Sam scene which I did so badly in November. He has just seen an assembly and it is one of two scenes he thinks don't work. It's not entirely my fault. TG says it's overwritten and much of the info it puts out has been superseded by scenes they've shot since. Sam's character isn't consistent either. In all he admits it was a very silly scene to shoot first. I'm relieved and pleased that we shall have another stab at it.

Tuesday, February 7th

Work on 'Fegg'. In the middle of a sea of odd ideas when someone rings asking to speak to the late Michael Palin. It's Spike. He says there's no point in asking for people who are living any more. Then he unfurls a stream of consciousness for about ten minutes – which turns out to be the outline for a play which he and [John] Antrobus are putting together for the autumn.

Set in the last war, in a vast government prune warehouse, scientists convert prunes into gas, Rudolph Hess arrives in Scotland, *The Desert Song* slowly and inexorably takes over the play, etc, etc. He compliments me at the end of these wild ramblings by saying he wants someone of 'wit and élan' to play an officer. I think he means me.

Tuesday, February 14th

Rachel very disappointed that I didn't get any Valentine cards, so she makes me one at breakfast.

At lunchtime Mr Alberts, Complaints Manager from John Lewis, arrives with a bottle of Krug champagne and a plastic display bowl of flowers which looks frighteningly like a graveside ornament.

Friday, February 17th

Work on the 'Vikings' until TJ arrives mid-morning. We read through what we have after this first week of concentrated film-writing. Very encouraging it is too. TJ has pushed on with the story and written a very macho song called 'We Don't Talk About Babies', which is marvellous. I've filled in a few holes and created a nice group of women at a devastated village.

But the best feeling of all is one of genuine and productive partnership. Both of us are contributing good material, but also both of us are enlarging and expanding on each other's ideas. Five good, forward-looking, confident days (largely because both of us were able to put in full working days without much interruption) and I now feel even more certain that we shall make this film.

Tuesday, February 21st

To Lee Studios at half past eight. Some of the numbing, negative feelings return. Why didn't the scene work in the first place? Why am I still so unsure of this character, which I was so enthusiastic to play in the first place? What am I supposed to feel – bringing the crew back onto the scene, having the set rebuilt? Was it mostly my fault? And, worst of all – will it go any better?

On the first couple of opening takes this tension – this wanting to do it exactly how I know I can do it, but having to concentrate too much on moves and props – produces the same tight, unrelaxed performance as I felt myself helplessly giving three months ago to the day. Then, as I get used to the props and the lines, I suddenly hit the note I know is right.

TG too is delighted. One take is perfect. Everything eases up, and I'm raring to go. But of course that take wasn't *technically* quite right, so we have to go again.

Holly Gilliam[1] loosens up the atmosphere and is really very good

---

1 Terry had rewritten the scene we'd shot on the first day's filming in November 1983 and among the changes had written in his daughter Holly, three at the time, to make nasty Jack Lint seem more of a family man.

indeed – both in behaviour and her lines. She makes all our business together seem very natural.

Friday, February 24th

At the studio they are trying to shoot reverses on Holly G, who is not playing very well today. When I arrive only Terry G (operating the camera), Maggie and Holly are on the set. Every now and then TG emerges and stalks up and down rather crossly before returning for 'one last go'. Then it's time to shoot all the reverses on Jonathan. I get into costume, but not make-up and spend most of my time trying to avoid being crushed by the dollying camera, whilst Jonathan uses the lens hood as his eyeline anyway.

This is the last day of principal photography and everyone seems to think it very suitable that I should be here on the last day and the first day. We have a merry lunch and I do enjoy myself, but I see what was shot on Tuesday and, though it's better than the first attempt, I still seem to fit the part of Jack Lint like a round peg in a square hole. An odd experience. I don't think I've ever seen myself so uncertain of who I'm playing.

Saturday, February 25th

Buy Leopoldo Alas's *La Regenta*, which I've decided will be my post-Orwell literary experience. It's much bigger than I thought.

Crick's book has won me round to a great liking for Orwell – not of everything he says or the way he says it, and I'm sure I too would find the Old Shag he smoked as unpleasant as everyone else, but he thrust himself into things with an uncompromising relish for life and sustained himself with a strange mixture of anger and admiration about how this country was run and organised with which I constantly felt sympathetic. He was on the right side.

Sunday, February 26th

Sexagesima. Now there's a film title for you. Begins at seven when Helen wakes up and leaps out of bed with unusual celerity. Her alarm has been set too late and the cab is due in 15 minutes. Make the pre-skiing cup of tea and Willy, Rachel and I kiss her goodbye and wave the cab off into a dull, wet, cold morning.

William and Rachel play together, Tom finishes his homework – writing a ballad with rather a lot of help from Dad – and we end up playing Totopoly. I cook scrambled eggs which are rather hard and they all laugh. But they go to bed without any sign at all of missing Mum.

Monday, February 27th

TJ here by eleven. The preparations for the 'Erik' voyage and the start of the voyage itself are rather superficial and sound to me too like *Yellowbeard.* We've lost the contact with the reality of life in Viking times from which our early material was drawn.

TJ reads his bio-rhythms on my calculator and finds that he is going through a bad period for intellectual effort! He then goes into a mental decline for the rest of the day, constantly wandering off for a pee or some decaffeinated coffee. But we assemble the first half-hour's material and send it off to Alison to type.

I then have to drive into town to see two films [up for awards] at BAFTA – *Another Time, Another Place* for Phyllis Logan and *Sophie's Choice* for Kevin Kline.

Ben Kingsley and Don Sharp – two of my co-jurors – are there. Ben Kingsley makes rather dramatic gestures such as 'Kevin Kline!' followed by a sharp blow with his fist to his balding forehead – which I think is meant to convey a superlative. I think power has made him mad, but he's quite affable.

Wednesday, February 29th

After breakfast TJ rings. He thinks we should talk as he is not sure where to take the story on. So clean up here and drive down to Camberwell.

We have reached a sticky stage. Terry's 'What's it all about ... really?' stage. It is very important because, although I would go on writing funny scenes and characters till the cows come home, TJ cannot write until he really knows what the story and the leading characters are about.

To Lower Regent Street for a party given by the Hogarth Press to launch a new range of imprints. Meet Miles Kington, Tariq Ali – who I haven't talked to since Oxford; he says his eleven-year-old daughter is a terrific fan of mine! – and a man called Ian Hislop asks Tariq to introduce him to me. He's a round, small man with a squidgy, reassuring face. He's assistant editor of the *Eye,* writer for the new puppet show, *Spitting Image,* and I recently read and liked his *Listener* column. He says *Spitting Image* found it difficult to make a Maggie Thatcher doll unattractive enough, as she is such a wretchedly fine-looking woman!

Friday, March 2nd

Drive to Greenpeace HQ in a nondescript industrial street in Islington for a presentation ceremony. TJ and I have both donated £1,000 to help Greenpeace pay the fine they incurred whilst monitoring the nuclear pollution from Sellafield/Windscale. Spike Milligan was to have presented us with the framed certificates of shares in the Greenpeace boat, but Pamela Stephenson stands in for him – 'Spike told me to apologise, but he's got radiation sickness and shouldn't touch anybody.'

Bruce Kent of CND is there. He says the food is much better than at his office. It's all vegetarian. Outside there's a photo-call and one of the photographers calls out to Monsignor Kent 'Could you put your arm round Pamela, please?' Kent, to his credit, twinkles back at them but refuses to go along with the suggestion.

Change (Clark Kent-like) into my dinner jacket in the Python office and taxi to King's Cross and join a long and winding queue for the 3.30 Newcastle train. I'm in Durham, about 20 minutes late, to second the motion that 'This is the Age of the Train' [at a university debate].

A meal, which far surpasses anything we got at the Oxford Union. I don't really enjoy such celebrations *before* the debate as much as I would after and I have to do some polite talking and listening to the wife of one of my opposers on one side, and Tony Ridley, head of LT (trains), on the other. Ray Buckton [leader of the engine drivers' union] is making them all laugh down the other end.

Ray is the only one of us who has not observed the request to wear a dinner jacket, and he is here with one of his advisers, a nice, quiet man who lives in Savernake Road. In a very earnest tone he tells me how much like 'The Missionary' is Michael Meacher MP, his new boss-to-be. 'A cross between Michael Palin and Joyce Grenfell,' he says.

Buckton speaks largely without notes. His speech is a mixture of astute and skilful attack and a lot of revivalist, preacher-like waffle. But he has a natural warmth and humour that is very much the stock image of the trade union leader. He can laugh at himself. He suggested before the debate began that, as we were all enjoying the port after the meal so much, he should cancel the debate by calling the speakers out on strike.

Monday, March 19th

Despite feeling a degree or two under manage to write another satisfying scene for 'The Vikings', when Thangbrand becomes maudlin and sentimental with Stovold, and also invent a seer who is not good at the immediate future, but can foretell that a Viking will win Wimbledon. No-one knows what he's talking about, of course.

I am enjoying writing again and, like fresh-struck oil, the jokes, characters and dialogue are now beginning to flow freely – for the first time since we started writing in February.

TJ comes up at lunch. He hasn't hit a similar writing streak for the last couple of weeks, but is pleased with the way it's heading and we have a constructive afternoon session, despite the fact that TJ only had three hours' sleep last night. Terry did shake his head rather ruefully as he arrived and say 'Oh, *when* will I grow up?'

Wednesday, March 21st

At 3.30 Malcolm M, Mark Shivas and Alan Bennett call for me in a small Volkswagen and we head out to Broxbourne to look at the pigs. They are quartered in amongst a very sad collection of buildings, animals and 'attractions' called Paradise Park.

The pigs are very friendly and bouncy and have been hand-reared since birth, about four months ago. We all remark on their little pink, naked provocative botties. Hope the crew will not get over-excited. We're shown a Vietnamese Black Pig – a mournful creature who was in a film with John Cleese – a crow which has been on TV-AM and a lion which once worked for the Post Office.

Thursday, March 29th

Make or break day on 'The Vikings'. Down to Terry's by 9.30 and we begin to work through the script. I sit at one desk and read through and whenever we come to a character who needs a name, or a line that's superfluous or a joke that doesn't work or a plot-line that's inconsistent, we stop and go back over it. We deliberately try and avoid major rewrites, but we're continuously changing and correcting. With few interruptions we work through until 7.45.

One of the interruptions is David Frost ringing – in buoyant mood –

to ask if I will appear on an April Fools' Day programme and announce some new pressure group or lobby group – he suggests 'height-watchers'. It's all to be done very straight. Ken Livingstone will be on, frightening people with plans to make Londoners drive on the right-hand side of the road.

Thursday, April 12th

Camden Council are sweeping the roads an awful lot these days. One thing Thatcher has done by introducing legal restraints on both the GLC (abolition) and Camden (rate-capping) is to stimulate both authorities into an orgy of PR. Nary a day goes by without a petition to be signed, or a new sticker to be stuck up, or a fresh slogan – Camden vehicles now carry: 'A Camden Service', 'Too Good to Lose'. Suddenly they're all on their best behaviour.

To Baker Street for a chiropody lesson in preparation for playing Gilbert Chilvers. Malcolm is there as well as a man called Graham, who is the 'chiropodial' adviser. He shows me the kit I shall have and we discuss various finer points, such as would I spread the patient's toes aside for examination (or, in Malcolm's case, a better shot!) and are the feet erogenous? The adviser is a bit cagey on this one, as if he doesn't want to commit himself.

Then we sit in on a consultation by another chiropodist, Nigel Tewkesbury. Tewkesbury anxious to show, quite convincingly, how a good chiropodist should relate to feet, by holding and touching and grasping them firmly, which gives the patient confidence. I leave with my consultant's bag – to practise at home.

Wednesday, April 18th

Have a long, slow breakfast and read (quite thoroughly for me) a *Guardian* page about the various ways in which government and police can snoop on us. I should think that my £1,000 donation to Greenpeace has not gone unnoticed.

At four o'clock to Fortnum's to have tea at the invitation of Amanda Schiff, who is Sandy Lieberson's deputy at Goldcrest.

Amanda – 'I don't eat meat and I don't eat fish' – tells me of the Goldcrest/Samuel Goldwyn scheme to make a series of small-budget contemporary comedies for a ceiling of £800,000 each in England, with

British writers and stars, which will hopefully be made on a continuous and regular basis like the Ealing comedies. I like the idea.

After tea back into the real world. Jermyn Street is silent, many of the shops closed, sealed off to all cars. Policemen stand at the corners diverting the pedestrians. I want to buy some shaving cream from Ivan's the barber's, but he's shut. A few feet from his door a blue polythene sheet is stretched from a rough scaffolding frame over the entrance to the street leading to St James's Square where the Libyan Embassy is under siege after yesterday's killing of a policewoman.

At the bottom of Lower Regent Street the Great British Public crowds around hoping to see some action. The police, who seem to be the only government-supported agency with money to burn these days, are everywhere. Behind the polythene sheets are the tense faces of flak-jacketed marksmen – a far cry from the jolly, helmeted presence on Jermyn Street.

Thursday, April 19th

At a quarter to eleven I'm away down to see Maggie S in West Sussex. Through Frimley, Farnborough and Aldershot. Army and car parks. Then through Hindhead and Haslemere, in narrow, claustrophobic little valleys past houses that all have names – 'Uplands', 'Nutcombe' and the like – and a forest of Conservative local election stickers in the window. I wouldn't have thought they'd need to advertise.

We start by sitting outside sipping champagne. Toby, Maggie's second son, is there. He's been buying weights and muscle-building equipment. Maggie is a little alarmed because, as she puts it, 'their father was rather interested in that sort of thing for a while'.

I've brought Maggie and Bev[1] a pretty white vase that looks a little like a hospital specimen jar, with some blue and white everlasting flowers from Neal Street East and a pot of Gospel Oak marmalade. All the flowers have the price on them. Maggie removes the tags with great speed, skill and discretion.

She's cooked tagliatelle con carne and there's fresh bread and white wine and we have a really easy, delightful lunch.

They've just returned from holiday in Ischia with Sir Larry and Joan Plowright. Sir Larry ga-ga much of the time, says Bev. Had a habit of

---

1 Beverley Cross, a writer and librettist, married Maggie Smith in 1975.

asking about who someone was, very loudly, right in front of them. Maggie and Joan were spotted by paparazzi in a steam bath.

Maggie throughout looks lovely. Her red hair suffuses a softly-tanned face with a glow of health and attraction. But, as ever, I feel that sometimes she is going through the motions of life – there is always a part of her – the passionate, instinctive part which makes her a great actress – which is in abeyance or being held in reserve – somewhere in there, private from us all.

At a quarter to four, after some chat about the hotels in Yorkshire (this aspect of filming always concerns Maggie) and the script itself – neither of us think the ending satisfactory – I say my goodbyes.

When I get home, I practise chiropody on Helen.

Monday, April 23rd

At ten minutes to midday we all set off for Henley for a lunch party in Aunt Betty's honour.

Richard O[1] makes a short and effective little speech reminding us that tonight Aunt Betty and Mother will be sleeping in their old home together for the first time for 53 years. Aunt Betty looks a little frailer than Ma, with a fine head of vividly white hair. Mum, in her 80th birthday dress, looks in good colour and full of life. Together they look like two china figures from a set; absolutely alike and quite different from anyone else there.

After lunch there is croquet and a lot of photos are taken. Clare, my goddaughter, is a great joy. She tells me with disgust how her headmistress had forbidden a videotape of *The Missionary* to be shown at the school club. I suppose I must have the attraction of the notorious.

Tuesday, April 24th

Sleep well and wake about half past seven. The sun shining from a brilliant blue sky as I gulp half a cup of tea and, armed with script and chiropody kit, set off for my first working day on 'Pork Royale' [as *Private Function* had become, for a while].

Go via the Body Centre, where I have an hour's massage – from an ex-actor who worked on Alan Bennett's *Forty Years On*.

---

1 Richard Ovey, first cousin on my mother's side, inherited the family estate at Hernes where both my mother and her sister and Richard's father, Dick, were brought up.

He does come out with rather disturbing observations, viz my right leg is shorter than my left and this can 'put my whole body out'. I have small, hard deposits of crystallised fatty substances on some of my nerve ends, which are not being properly disposed of owing to tensions. I question him about this and he reveals that everyone has these deposits, adding, quite ingenuously, 'except, of course, enlightened beings'.

Arrive at St Helen's Church Hall, quite a grand and spacious place. Maggie and Liz Smith and Bill Paterson and Rachel Davies, who plays Mrs Forbes, and Richard Griffiths are there, as well as make-up, wardrobe and sundry others.

Alan gives a short intro to the effect that all this will work best if played absolutely seriously. Malcolm concentrates on the scenes between Maggie, Liz and myself. Malcolm is not keen on exaggerated Yorkshire accents; 'a hint of Yorkshire' is the order of the day for us. So into rehearsal. Alan watches some of it and occasionally guffaws loudly, but mostly sits discreetly at the other side of the hall, reading his paper.

I voice some of my worries about the ending, but Malcolm is gently firm and Alan doesn't bite, so we're left with it.

Wednesday, April 25th

Mark Shivas rings to warn me that there is some fighting over the budget. HandMade want £1.3 to become £1.2. Mark says they can't and, should DO'B call me about it, could I emphasise how much we're getting for so little.

Rehearse with the Smiths again, and find Gilbert much easier to play with less effort. Malcolm thinks he should be 'a bit dull'. Certainly playing him softer and gentler and more naturally seems to work. I feel much calmer after today's rehearsal. Maggie says she didn't sleep well last night – worries about the accent and, as she says, 'them all thinking what a terrible mistake they've made'.

A curious week. Adjusting to being an actor again is proving quite a roller-coaster for the nervous system. Sometimes I feel surges of nervous apprehension bordering on panic, at others I feel the delicious sense of really looking forward to showing how well I can do something. Confidence is all-important and mine veers sometimes.

Friday, April 27th

Today I have to do Alison Steadman's feet. Not an ordeal at all, and Malcolm is quite pleased by my show of professional chiropodic skill! Real progress in the characterisation of Gilbert in the Church Hall this afternoon. Malcolm is quiet, but persistent and, on the whole, accurate in his criticisms and suggestions.

Denholm is with us for the first time today. I congratulate him on his BAFTA award. He straightaway goes into a story of how he once walked out of BAFTA with Dirk Bogarde, when Denholm had won his first Oscar. Bogarde said to him as they left, 'So you've got your little piece of tin, eh?' 'Well,' says Denholm, eyebrows twisting and folding as only he knows how, 'what a ponce, I mean!'

The afternoon wears on. Maggie tries on her costumes and is instantly transformed into a thin, slight, mousy woman. I'm sure such a transformation can't please her any more than having to say the line 'I'm 38', as she looks at her reflection in the polished car.

Saturday, April 28th

Drive down to South Ken to Le Suquet Restaurant to lunch at DO'B's invitation to meet his new lady, Noelle. We have an enormous platter full of all manner of shellfish, which takes almost two and a half hours to crack, crunch, split, lick and prise our way through.

DO'B, Helen thinks, is anxious to find out about the film from me. It's as if he wants to be excited but finds an almost impenetrable barrier between him and the Mark/Malcolm/Alan triumvirate. This irks him.

We get back home about a quarter to five, just in time for the most exciting news from the BBC's teleprinter in recent memory. Sheffield Wednesday have beaten Crystal Palace 1–0 and are to be in the First Division for the first time since before William was born.

Take Helen down to the Dominion Cinema to see René Clair's *The Italian Straw Hat*, which is being performed for one night only with a full orchestra. The occasion a little better than the film. At the end of the performance, René Clair's wife, a very sprightly lady, makes a short, well-received speech of thanks in perfect English.

Monday, April 30th

Wake, by quarter-hours from six o'clock, to first day of filming on 'Pork Royale'. Roy awaits with his sparkling Mercedes, a neat, trim, RSM-like figure, on the corner of Elaine Grove.

At the location by eight o'clock. It's a 1900–20's house at the top of the hill in Ealing – a cross between mock-Tudor and Arts and Crafts.

Shown up to a bare upstairs room with so few amenities that, had it not been such a warm, outdoors day, could have ruffled the start of the shoot. Denholm Elliott, Richard Griffiths, John Normington are all in one bare room. I'm put in solitary splendour next door.

First shot is under way briskly and consists of me cycling along a hedge looking up at the house.

Then a series of shots of the three 'plotters' round the table, which takes up the bulk of the rest of the day. Talk to Alan, who tells a good story of a lady friend of his mother's who shared the same chiropodist. Having to let Mrs Bennett know of a changed appointment, but not finding her in, she'd scribbled a note and slipped it through the door: 'Foot Lady, Friday, 5.30'. Alan's father, a butcher, finding the note couldn't fathom it out and eventually decided it must be a hot tip for a horse race.

Tuesday, May 1st

Out to Ealing, for the second day of what is now officially re-christened *A Private Function.*

Denholm and his cronies work on the invitation scene and I have to find things to do to pass the time. This production cannot afford caravans to protect stars' privacy, so I sit in the patch of front garden on my chair with my name on it. I may feel the need of somewhere to hide away when the pressure goes on in Yorkshire. But by then Maggie will be with us and she won't settle for chairs in the garden!

Alan is always on hand for a chat. In reply to my asking him why he doesn't do more acting, he just says, rather forlornly, that no-one ever asks him. He kept getting offered vicars, he says. His relationship with Mowbray arose because he liked [Malcolm's] 'Days at the Beach' so much he wrote to him. Mowbray wrote and thanked and expressed admiration for A's work and later brought him the idea for the 'Pig' script. Nice when things happen organically like that. It's like doing things at university.

Thursday, May 3rd

Collected at 10.30.

Roy, stocky, bronzed from a sun-lamp, turns out to be a Buddhist chanter. Says he was introduced to it by Bill Weston, the stunt man, who always looks slightly out to lunch, but is a chanter too. I've brought an Otis Redding tape in with me today, but it seems rather insensitive to have it blaring whilst Roy is telling me how the chants have 'made things happen' and 'given me a more positive outlook on life'.

So in the end he puts on a cassette of Buddhist chants, as the Mercedes swings past Lee Studios and through Wembley to some woodland behind Perivale.

The first noise I hear as I approach the sylvan glade is the squealing of a fractious pig.

I'm used just before lunch, but the pig is very soporific and we have to try the scene again afterwards.

I have to lure the pig quite a few yards, along a plotted path with a sharp right-angled turn. No rope or halter, just with bread. The first take is slow and the pig goes off at a tangent, but it gets better and the second take is almost perfect. Suddenly realise it isn't as difficult as everyone thought it would be. Provided I brandish the bread near enough to the pig, it follows quite obediently and I can regulate its pace. This is a great relief to all.

Leave the location in very good spirits, especially as I have two days off before the four six-day weeks of continuous working in Yorkshire. Pleased with myself at having passably succeeded at chiropody and pig-stealing.

Friday, May 4th

Up to the Rosslyn deli to buy food for lunch here with Anne J. We talk over business and dates and projects. Say no to the lead in the re-make of *Italian Straw Hat*, but yes to a limerick book. Scripts have arrived of 'Stovold the Viking'. Looks short.

Go through correspondence and play squash with TJ at five. Our first game for several weeks. I win. Afterwards a familiar pint at the Flask. TJ seems much more excited by his script for 'Labyrinth' than by 'Stovold the Viking', and from various things he says I get the feeling that he's decided his strength lies in fantasy and that our paths are more rather than less likely to divide over the next years over this difference in subject matter.

Tom is having a 'gathering' at No. 2. Constant comings and goings through the kitchen. Generally very polite and considerate, though they consume gargantuan amounts of tobacco and rifle the fridge for beer, which I don't approve of. Nor am I very pleased to spend my last hours as a 40-year-old sweeping cigarette stubs, half-eaten chicken legs and crisps off the floor of No. 2.

Saturday, May 5th

My mother rings at nine. I'm still in bed. She's sent me £50 – an unheard-of sum for a present from her. She says it's after 'all the things you've done for me'.

Helen has given me a six-foot-long giant pencil – beautifully reproduced and a very silly, but satisfying and striking piece of decoration. An AA guide to hotels and restaurants from the children gives no mention of the Troutbeck in Ilkley – which is to be my home for the next month.

Tuesday, May 8th: Ilkley, Yorkshire

Feel remarkably together and well prepared for the day. Alan is at breakfast and hadn't gone to sleep until two as he had the room over the bar. 'It was like Christmas down there,' he says, rather morosely.

He goes and I'm alone in this recently-refurbished, rather ornate dining room with 'Adam' pretensions and a giggly waitress who reports loudly my every word back to the kitchen.

I'm driven down solid, leafy roads to a cul-de-sac in Ben Rhydding and up to Briargarth, which is my home for the film. A long, detached, stone house of (probably) Edwardian vintage, with a porch and gables. Carpenters, painters, sparks swarm over it. Loud banging, shouts, and, amidst it all, actors – myself, Maggie and Liz – wandering gingerly, waiting to take possession.

Gradually the first scene creaks into action. Round the table, eating Spam. We reach around for our characters, absorbing all the clues and helps and hindrances of this brand new place in which we must act as if it were all too familiar.

Maggie, brittle and tense so often in non-acting moments, gives so much out when she plays the scene that it's exhilarating to be with her.

A hot bath and a lager. Then walk down into Ilkley – clean, ordered, respectable, with oriel windows above the shops, glass-canopied arcades and ornamental flower beds. It's like the Garden of Eden after Gospel Oak. Choose Chez François – a wine bar – for a solitary meal.

Read of Buñuel and the Surrealists in Paris in the late '20's and '30's. Similarities with Pythons. Bourgeois against the bourgeoisie. Buñuel sounds rather like TJ. Very interested in sex and the Middle Ages and blamed the media for all the world's ills.

Wednesday, May 9th: Ilkley

Drive my hired Ford Orion into Ilkley to look for a birthday present for Alan, who is 50 today. Buy him a card with a pig nestling provocatively, and a pair of nail clippers.

I've also booked a table at the Box Tree Cottage for tonight as an extra present.

Have pre-ordered a bottle of champagne and this helps Alan over his initial awe of the establishment – 'I've only walked past it' – and we have a very jolly time. The Mary Whitehouse lookalike who explains the dishes to us remembers me from Python days.

Alan and Maggie are all ears and eyes for what's happening at the other tables and there are some good characters. I think all three of us are easily moved to laughter at the most inconvenient times.

Mark S joins us. The food is original and very good, with the timbale de fraises outstanding. It's based around their home-made rose-water ice-cream and is delicate, light, aromatic and quite superb. But quite a large shard of glass in my cucumber and onions throws the Mary White-house into near panic. She offers to re-cook all our meals, bring us free liqueurs, some more wine – anything short of giving us the meal free which, on reflection, would have been the only thing for a place like the Box Tree to do.

A bottle of Bollinger is thrust into my hand as we leave. And Alan, I think, was truly touched. He said he'd never been taken out to dinner on his birthday before.

Thursday, May 10th: Ilkley

We scan the papers for latest news of Honeybun, the pet rabbit of the British Ambassador in Libya, which he left behind when the embassy was closed, much to the horror of the animal-loving British public. The *Mail on Sunday* arranged to have the rabbit flown back. The *Guardian* produced a quote from the ambassador's wife to the effect that she loathed the rabbit – 'I wish we'd eaten it before we left'. The *Mail* reporter was then caught by customs at Gatwick bringing a live animal back in the passenger section and his paper now stung for about £2,000 quarantine charges. The story has kept us going all week.

The pig is brought in and for half an hour we are all banned from the surgery whilst it gets used to its paper. 'Pig's business' appears on the call sheet, but there is no need for the prop stuff as Betty trundles about depositing dark grey turds with the regularity of a train timetable every eight minutes or so.

The situation seems very bleak for a while then, with judicious use of sardine oil smeared on the floor and on the toes of my shoes, the pig turns in a series of excellent performances as the room becomes progressively smellier.

Friday, May 11th: Ilkley

Another good night's sleep and down to breakfast at ten to eight. Malcolm sounds very pleased with rushes and Alan, who comes down later, says that he found my performance 'touching', which is unexpected and rather touching.

Sunday, May 13th: Ilkley

They get round to my five-second cycling shot at five to eight at night – nearly eight hours after my call. Malcolm apologises with great concern. Alan and Maggie tell him how angry I've been about the whole thing and Maggie says she heard my caravan shaking with sobs. For a moment Malcolm believes them.

At the Troutbeck, Alan buys the meal for Maggie, Malcolm, myself and Don Estelle. We are the only diners and the food is so consistently devoid of flavour that one suspects certain special anti-cooking skills. But we laugh a lot. Alan digs gently at Malcolm, 'Buñuel would never have kept an artist waiting eight hours', and Malcolm plays up to it gracefully. But the emptiness of the dining room and the distant sound of jollity from the folk club don't raise the spirits.

Tuesday, May 15th: Ilkley

Maggie, Mark S and myself are dawdling in the car park at Ben Rhydding Station after lunch, remarking on how many trains seem to be coming through this archetypal country station which miraculously escaped the Beeching axe, when Alan B steps out of one of them. Though he never told us himself, we know that he's been up to London to collect yet another award for *Englishman Abroad*, so we greet him with a round of applause. Alan goes very pink and is delightfully embarrassed.

He says it was an awful occasion. They'd been sat next to the band, he says. He squirms as he tells us of the discomfiture he feels at having to make speeches at these occasions ... 'I feel such a twerp ... the microphone's always the wrong height ... and your voice suddenly booms out saying something quite fatuous. I haven't been given anything since 1971 ... then all this ...'. He shakes his head with bewilderment.

More slow progress in the afternoon as we wait for the pig to be coaxed up and down the stairs. The day trails away. I sit at the top of the stairs in my long underwear, kitchen knife at the ready, whilst shouts of 'Shit-bucket!' rise from below.

Thursday, May 17th: Ilkley

Today I avoid hotel breakfast and lie in bed until a quarter to eight. With Roy to the location at 8.20. Not much for me to do again. A crowded living room scene. Black drapes shroud the lower half of the house. La Nuit Américaine. Pete Postlethwaite and Jim Carter do amazing magic tricks – probably born from years of standing around at rehearsals or waiting to go on.

Denholm chain-smokes – as do most of them. Only Jim and myself of the actors don't smoke. Alan B says he has a cigarette every now and then. He says when he's trying to think of a plot – which he finds very difficult – he has a Consulate. The actors assure him that they're the worst.

The pig goes from strength to strength and received a round of applause after her first performance this morning. Maggie still very worried about her piano-playing. She scratched herself on the brass antlers of the cocktail decanter whilst rehearsing this morning and rather ruefully mutters that she'd hoped it had been worse and she'd have had an excuse for getting out of the piano-playing altogether.

They talk about their favourite Shakespeare plays. I feel dreadfully dull when the talk turns to theatre and aware of how different my world is from the rest of these thespians. Maggie dislikes *Merchant of Venice* – 'All Portia does is tell Larissa to close the curtains.' She doesn't have much time for *Taming of the Shrew* either.

Monday, May 21st: Ilkley

Up just before eight, with news on Radio 4. The miners' strike still dominates,[1] as the Falklands War did throughout *Missionary*. Local 'Day of Action' in Yorkshire has stopped mainline trains, local bus services, etc. But not the slow, steady progress of the filming.

In one of the re-shoots the pig suddenly went off ginger biscuits. Denholm said he'd noticed the precise moment the attraction of the biscuits palled ... 'Amazing,' he ruminated, 'like a Pauline conversion.'

Tuesday, May 22nd: Ilkley

After lunch a freshly killed pig is delivered – supplied and chaperoned by a ruddy-faced little rock of a man in overalls. Everywhere there is earnest talk of where a pig is stuck in order to kill it, how long it takes to bleed it, etc, etc. We have to carry it upstairs and it feels very strange – as if still just alive.

At one point I go upstairs to the loo only to find my way barred by a huddle of people around the pig's carcass. There is a flash of staple gun from one of the chippies, a sharp click and the brown detective's hat is stapled to the pig's head. Quite the most sinister thing I've seen in a long while.

Finish Buñuel [*My Last Breath*] – a delight of a book, especially the chapter on his likes and dislikes. He lived and worked most of his life in Mexico and Spain, but had a yearning to live in Sweden or Russia. Buñuel feels like Rembrandt – a warm, direct, flawed, life-enriching character. Reading the book makes you very glad to be alive – which is what I need as the seemingly endless day draws on in Briargarth.

1 The strike of 1984–5 was prompted by the threat of job losses and pit closures. Arthur Scargill's NUM (National Union of Mineworkers) confronted Margaret Thatcher's Tory government for almost a year.

Wednesday, May 23rd: Ilkley

We're on the Bolton Abbey estate in very beautiful countryside up the Wharfe Valley. The drive here this morning left everyone speechless with appreciation – the road winds through woods and undulates gently beside the river. A carpet of bluebells in amongst the trees adds the icing to a rich and almost perfect English pastoral scene.

I, alone of the thespians, have a caravan – a mousey, small affair, parked right next to the props van where the drivers gather and talk loudly about fucking. I, prissy little bourgeois, trapped in the mind-improving expectations of my class, try to read more of *La Regenta*.

Walk some way along the road. Out of sight of the vehicles all is peace and tranquillity. A soft heat. Shirts off day. Walk up into some fields on the edge of the moor.

A herd of Friesian heifers takes a liking to me. They walk – first one, then the others – slowly after me as I cross a meadow. Then they break into a run and I have to make a rushed scramble up and over the high stone wall.

Thursday, May 24th: Ilkley

Arrive at the location just about the same time as the St John Ambulance lady. I tell her that we've got the wounded lined up against the wall, but she doesn't have much of a sense of humour.

Nor, I think, does the lady who brings the 1947 Riley. She provides Alan and me with enormous pleasure as she corners Denholm Elliott with her autograph book. The book seems to consist almost entirely of Conservative politicians, a massive haul which she got from the party conference. She points them out proudly to Denholm, who is utterly bored ... 'John Nott ... he's quite famous ... ' 'Yeees ... ' 'Selwyn Gummer, of course he's very famous now ... ' 'Yeees ...'

The weather is hot and balmy, a BBC unit from Leeds come out to film us filming and pick Alan and me off in separate interviews. They completely ignore the likes of Bill Paterson, who is likely to be very famous indeed after *Comfort and Joy*, but then these after-six programmes are never very good at spotting trends, only following them.

After a morning of what Gerry Paris [my stand-in] and I call 'we might' shots – 'Michael, we might see you in this shot' – I have a steady succession of scenes to do in the afternoon.

I do always enjoy myself when there's some playing involved, some eyeball-to-eyeball acting – some exchange of mental energies instead of cycling, waving and reacting to people who've left three hours before.

Friday, May 25th: Ilkley and Bolton Abbey Estate

Alan B shows us all a cheque from the BBC, for sales of *Englishman Abroad* in Sweden, Denmark, Norway and Belgium. £8.50!

It's time to grovel in the pig sty. The pig mixes a few long, grey turds and a pee or two with the manure that lines the stall. Myself, Tony H, Preston and Tony P-R and Derek all squashed in there.[1] Have to grab Betty's back leg, which takes some strength as she shakes it violently. But she is immensely long-suffering as I grab her in take after take, and never becomes vicious.

Annie Wingate [production manager] is hovering anxiously about the sty as we edge towards 6.30 and still three shots indoors to do. Malcolm's technique when she asks him to hurry is superb. He nods very sympathetically as she describes the situation, thinks hard and then manages to say, without a hint of sarcasm, 'But . . . if we don't shoot this properly . . . ' (long pause) ' . . . it won't work.'

But at 6.30 it's done. Wash off the shit and into the waiting Orion. At Doncaster by eight. There is a restaurant car on the train which makes the longish journey time – two hours 22 minutes – to London very bearable. A scotch, celery soup, roast lamb and cheese and a bottle of red wine as we head south, stopping everywhere. Sleep from Stevenage into London and have to be woken at King's Cross.

Sunday, May 27th: Barnoldswick

12.30: In a spacious caravan in the car park of the Civic Hall, Barnoldswick – pronounced 'Barnswick' or 'Barnslick'. The rain rattles on the roof. It's very cold. Have done some cycling and parades shots this morning, which we got in before the worst of the rain.

This town has a Rolls-Royce engine works, but from the look of the people and the number of shops 'Closing Down', it seems far from prosperous, and certainly has none of the confident comfort of Ilkley. The 'B' in RB-211 stands for Barnoldswick.

1 Tony Haygarth played the farmer, Preston was the name of his son. Tony Pierce-Roberts was director of photography and Derek Suter was the clapper/loader.

At lunch most of the unit find a local café. A lady emerges from the rain-sodden throng and corners Alan. 'I just want to shake your hand, Mr Blezzard.'

Thursday, May 31st: Ilkley

It's Denholm's birthday today and he's having a lovely chin-wag with the ex-Lord Mayor of Bradford – a lady – who is a very strong, competent, articulate lady and is playing the Lord Mayor in the film.

AB has been unable to wriggle out of a proposed *South Bank Show* profile on him. He says he just can't bear the thought of shots of him driving along moorland roads with his thoughts over. But whereas on Wednesday he announced firmly that he wasn't going to do it, he's now been persuaded by personal intervention from the young producer who flew up to see him. 'Oh, I'm *such* a coward,' he admits despondently.

Today Alan has an acting role in the film. He has the part of Man Coming Out of Toilet and looks like Robert Redford as Jay Gatsby in his evening dress, and blond hair brushed back.

We are rushed into the final dance sequence, as Richard (Allardyce) has to leave first thing tomorrow to play the lead in 'Volp' (as he calls *Volpone*) over the weekend.

We go on late and, after a day of heat and crowds, the band strikes up and everyone sings 'Happy Birthday' and 'For He's a Jolly Good Fellow' to Denholm when we wrap about 9.15. Very moving as he stands in the middle of the floor acknowledging the applause.

In the car on the way back D and I fall to discussing how much time we need to get up in the morning when filming. I say 20 minutes. Denholm needs an hour. 'I have to have at least five cups of tea and I *do* like to read.' I say that all I really have to have is a good shit, but D says he can't possibly shit in the morning – he's far too nervous.

Sunday, June 3rd: Ilkley

Teeming rain this morning. Alan is in a very gloomy state about the cuts and foresees that one of today's scenes – the businessmen talking in the function room – could go in addition to the others already under sentence. No jokes from him today, just an atmosphere of near-desperation.

Malcolm elides shots and scenes in order to save time. My crucial 'blow-up' scene has to be done in one take, which is a pity, but inevitable,

I suppose. Not until about five do we even get onto what was first on the schedule this morning. I stay in my caravan or sit in the sun in the car park listening to Van Morrison on my Sony – anything to avoid the gloom indoors.

Maggie and I work hard in the first part of the day. She smiles at my attempt at sarcasm over the slow progress. 'It just doesn't suit you,' and adds 'Take a tip from the acid queen.'

After five the pace suddenly speeds up and the work goes on until 11.30. Everything bar one shot (the toilet) is completed.[1] But will the crew survive late nights all week? And even if they can, will the scenes that are constantly being put on one side ever be caught up?

More time and money is still needed.

Tuesday, June 5th: Ilkley

Maggie in a very sore mood for some reason. She's tense, terse and seems to take every suggestion Malcolm makes as a personal insult. Very difficult, as her attitude affects the whole unit by degrees.

Unexpectedly, who should arrive on the lunchtime train at Ben Rhydding, but Ray Cooper, in spotty grey suit and black brogues.

Ray asks me to dinner at the Devonshire Arms at Bolton Abbey and I ask Maggie along. She accepts, to my surprise, and, apart from being very worried that she's dressed only in jeans, is sweetness and light and charm and naturalness all evening. Ray, of course, treats her well with great courtesy and flattering respect. He remembers her from when he was at the National.

We talk of film acting versus theatre acting. Talk of *Way of the World*, which she's doing at Chichester. I say that the reward of all the work must come when she steps out on stage in front of an audience. 'Oh no, I can't be bothered with that, rehearsing's the only bit I like. Getting it right, working it out.'

At eleven drive Maggie back to the hotel we've today been shunted into – the Post House at Bramhope. There is Bill Paterson in the bar. He's

---

1 It had been difficult to find the location for the scene in which Gilbert Chilvers is confronted by the local business mafia at a urinal. Then one morning in Betty's Tea Rooms in Ilkley, Alan B appeared, full of excitement. 'We've found a toilet', he enthused, 'near Paddington Station, and it'll take ten!' Only as heads turned and the noise level dropped did we realise what this must have sounded like to the middle-aged, respectable, and largely female clientele at Betty's.

now like a ghost, doomed to wander round Yorkshire waiting to be used. Very bad scheduling, but he is so tolerant.

Wednesday, June 6th: Bramhope, Yorkshire

Up at eight. Papers and radio all full of D-Day's 40th anniversary. Once more the noble art of war celebrated and minds taken for a while off present discontents. Reagan the film actor is here and the D-Day remembrance is ideally suited for his and Thatcher's particular brand of ham.

This is positively our last day at Gilbert's House. On the original Hugely Optimistic Schedule this was to have been May 22nd.

I run upstairs in my underwear pursuing the pig with a knife, then a halting unsatisfactory day of much waiting and very short bursts of activity. Around me the house is being cleared away and by the evening it has become rather sad and lifeless.

I leave the house and my dressing room with the half-peeled wallpaper hanging in strips and the little rooms we got to know so well and the book called *Instantaneous Personal Magnetism*, with only a twinge of sadness. I expect I shall miss it more as time goes on.

It's 11.15 after a dour drizzly day, the location caterer's moussaka was very strange and I had to secrete it in a black bag, and there's an extended day tomorrow. Being an optimist I'm sure it will come out all right, but I feel at the moment something is wrong in the mixture, something quite important – the ingredient of space – scale and sense of location – may be lost in this continual concertina-ing process.

Thursday, June 7th: Bramhope

It's with resignation rather than eager anticipation that I finally prepare to lead the pig into the car. The car is a meticulously preserved Wolseley Hornet. The owner, fortunately as it turns out, isn't present, but his father, an Arnold Ridley lookalike, is.

The attempt to film a single take of me leading Betty down through the groves of wild garlic and into the Wolseley founders, as Betty can in no way be persuaded to enter the car. Various methods are tried as time ebbs away and the pressure begins to rise. Huge insects, drawn by the arc lights in the woods, thud into the reflectors.

The two cameras are moved, we try again. Then suddenly the pig is in the car and, not only that, she's nuzzling at the windscreen, sitting up in the front seat. I get into the car and, moving Betty's massive bulk, am able to switch on the headlights, release the brake and slip out of shot.

But in all the attendant confusion, the first assistant has been caught in a reflection and we have to set it up again. On the next take Betty panics and lunges desperately for the driver's window. Her trotter is bearing down on my genitals and her underbelly is slimy with something or other and the smell of fresh pig shit has replaced the pleasant woody-leathery aroma of the car's interior.

I'm released and Betty's released, but the car is a pig sty – shit on the back seats mingles with old food and scraps of apple and pig saliva smears the inside of the elegant windscreen. Says our car owner ruefully: 'I could have written this better – I'd have written it without a pig in.' He indicates Alan – 'He's no Ibsen, is he?'

Roy drives me back over the dark, silent moors. I'm back at the Post House just after half past one. I tell the receptionist I've been trying to get a pig in a car. She obviously thinks I'm completely drunk. But I have witnesses.

Monday, June 11th

A depressingly run-down location in Exmouth Street, across the road from Mount Pleasant Sorting Office.

My dressing room is the small bedroom of the assistant barman of the Exmouth Arms who's away for the week. Racing cars, John Player Grand Prix of the World racetrack passes, *Sun* and 'Daily Starbird' calendars, and other pictures of sexless blondes bearing mammarial mounds as if displaying the latest racing car accessories.

'Who's in it then?' I hear asked with imperious Cockney sensitivity just behind me as I await the cue to start the scene . . .

'Michael Palin, Maggie Smith, Denholm Elliott . . .'

'Oh, no-one we've ever 'eard of then?'

Alan arrives with a crisp new paperback edition of Carlyle's selected writings (he'd found Vol. 3 of Carlyle's *Frederick the Great* in a set-dressed bookshelf in Ilkley and was quite hooked). Looking through the intro Alan finds to his concern that Carlyle had, in later life, been author of a pamphlet on 'The Nigger Problem' and, even more disconcertingly, one of Carlyle's books was discovered in Hitler's bunker.

End the day carrying a half-carcass of pork downstairs.

Tuesday, June 12th

My last chiropody scene – and the most jolly, Sue Pollett being a very good subject. Alan arrives on his bike.

He tells me that the old lady who lives in the Transit Van in the driveway of his house considers herself to have equal rights over the entire property. She complained about Alan playing his music too loud, so he tends to listen on headphones. He admits that he does sometimes sing along with the music in his phones, which must sound odd, but was not prepared to be told by her that she had heard strange sounds coming from the house, as from someone under the influence of drink!

A long day and the meat is beginning to smell. An old actor called Don Eccles, who was once directed by Bertolt Brecht and W H Auden (they hated each other), joins us. We sit on chairs in the street.

Farewells. Rather sad to leave them all. I like the crew better as we get to know each other. It does say a lot for working with a repertory of actors and crew – as Python and Woody Allen have found to their advantage.

Friday, June 15th

Cleese rings. I put to him thoughts on 'Vikings'. He isn't anxious to become involved in any more films besides a Michael Frayn script (JC as headmaster) he's been sent and the film he's been writing for many months with Charles Crichton.

About one o'clock Helen hears something in the street outside. Look out to see two men, one with black gloves, going down the street trying car doors. Helen rings police. Just slipping to sleep when police knock on door. Helen goes down – tall, dark, handsome PC to say they caught the pair. They were let off with a caution, having pleaded that they were very pissed off after seeing *Friday 13th Part II*, which they regarded as a complete waste of money.

Sunday, June 17th

TG rings to ask if I'm going to Pam Stephenson's party. I'm in that 'I will if you will' mood. So we find ourselves, at nine-fifteen, driving along unlikely back streets of Hammersmith looking for a house described as No. $1\frac{1}{2}$ The Fish Factory.

Pam wears a dress made of a facsimile copy of *The Times* for March

19th '84 (when their much-publicised baby was born) and people bring her outrageous presents. The Pope's double waits at the door, a man dressed as Tarzan serves the drinks, dressed only in a loincloth and holding a plastic club with difficulty. A fully-turbaned Indian sings 'Living Doll' and other classics in front of a live band.

There is neat, trim, smiling and genuinely good-humoured Dick Lester, belligerently entertaining Peter McDougall, setting his moustache alight regularly as he fires his roll-your-own cigarettes.[1]

Talk to Billy [Connolly] as we're leaving. He's lost so much weight he looks physically much less substantial than his brawling, extrovert comedy style suggests. We talk of *Water*. He has one more week to go and is driving down to Devon for the filming after the party. I notice he's not drinking.

Saturday, June 23rd

I have a long-standing commitment at the Bluebell Railway to re-launch the only North London Line steam loco existing anywhere.

Met at the station by David Ryder and the team who have restored 58830 to service. Mostly much younger than myself. All with other jobs – electronic engineers, British Caledonian ground staff, etc.

At 2.30 the loco is steamed up the platform. Give my short speech, which is upstaged by a loud railway announcement, followed by the sweep in of the preceding train, which obliterates three-quarters of my audience. Raise three cheers for the team who worked on the loco, then I'm given a ride on the footplate up the five miles to Horsted Keynes and back, through classic English arable landscape, looking well in the sun.

There can't be many industries in which you can, or even would want to, return to your old trade well into your 80's as some of them do here. A mucky, dirty enterprise full of happy, fulfilled workers.

Wednesday, July 4th

To Don's for 9.15 haircut appointment. The extraordinary mixture of *Brazil* and *Private Function* has left my head looking like a hairstyle

---

1 Lester directed, among other things, the Beatles' films *Hard Day's Night* and *Help*. McDougall, a gritty Scots playwright who wrote for BBC's *Play For Today* and was always on the verge of delivering a screenplay for HandMade.

exhibition site. Don notices the silvery threads. I'm going grey, gently but alas irreversibly.

This evening I go to catch my first glimpse of a *Brazil* cut at the Baronet viewing theatre – a full house with 30 or so people crammed into a very small space.

The film is two and a half hours long. As expected, each frame an oil painting. A garden of visual delights. Dream sequences puzzling but unfinished.

Jonathan's central performance is masterly. He holds all the disparate pieces together. Manages to react 600 different ways to the same sort of situations and carries you along, explaining by expressions what we are required to think and feel.

Detail as usual of design, costume, props, etc, marvellous. Definitely a film for two or three viewings. Doesn't have the naive charm of *Time Bandits* – in fact has no charm at all – but is a spirited, inventive, enormously intriguing work of imagination made celluloid.

Thursday, July 5th

Jonathan Pryce rings to borrow a video machine. He still has some flying shots to complete. *Brazil* will have been a year of his life. He goes to New York in October to do *Accidental Death of an Anarchist* on Broadway, for a nine-month contract. He says he now can't open the script without depression setting in. On the page it seems to be so awkward and yet he knows that everything happens in the performance.

He hopes to get a film part – opposite Meryl Streep – in David Hare's *Plenty*. This is why he needs the video – to copy some of the *Brazil* tapes to show the director. 'It's always the way,' he says dolefully, 'these sort of directors never really know who I am.' In his way he is as powerful as Brando or De Niro. But you have to be in the right sort of movies and you usually have to be American to be that big.

Tuesday, July 10th

To Waterloo on the Underground for a trip to the Methuen reps' conference at Andover.[1] Since yesterday LT have banned smoking on all

---

1 Jones and Palin's *Bert Fegg's Encyclopeadia (sic) of All World Knowledge* was one of their top titles for the autumn of 1984.

their Underground trains. A great step forward. Smoking should only be allowed in large country houses after dinner.

Later out with Helen to see Erice's *The South*[1] – a superb, hauntingly beautiful film. Perfectly controlled and paced and shot to focus our attention on the simple elements of a very sad and touching tale. Goes above *The Servant* in my Top Ten instantly. And as a writer I am impressed again by how few histrionics are needed to make it work, how few epic visuals, grand locations and characters. It is precise and precisely satisfying.

And Helen is quite tearful afterwards as well as during. Wonderful.

Thursday, July 12th

A rather important day ahead. My first sight of *Private Function* – my life for seven weeks in May and June.

I quite enjoy Gilbert and find myself wanting to see more of him and his wife and ma-in-law. Lots of good things in '*PF*'. Performances – especially Denholm E (best thing he's done) and Richard – are all strong and watchable. Much laughter.

Only drawbacks – too much sub-plot detail in the middle of the first half and a pervasive depressing feeling about most of the characters, their relationships and the world they inhabit, which makes it rather an inward-looking piece. That's where Gilbert is important – he's honest, if plodding, and one of the only characters with whom Bennett really allows the audience to develop sympathy.

No music yet, or pig effects.

To L'Escargot with Ray and Malc and Mark and Annie.

I only have time for a smoked haddock starter before I have to rush back to [Roger] Cherrill's to post-synch 'screams and gurgles' for *Brazil*. I die horribly three or four times, then back to L'Escargot for the rest of the meal.

Friday, July 13th

Steve [Abbott] has just come back from a week in Russia. Though it didn't radically change his views about Russians, it did make him more anti-American. So much in what he saw and did contradicted the American-

---

1 *El Sur* (*The South*), by Spanish director Victor Erice, was released in 1983.

instigated anti-Russian propaganda. He was free to wander, he found a synagogue where Jews were free to practise their religion. He found the great buildings of the past preserved carefully and beautifully. He found an underground system in Moscow superbly clean and free of ads and litter.

Wednesday, July 18th

I pack ready for three days up in Southwold. On the way I go to a screening of *Private Function*.

The film has lost ten minutes and now runs 94. Denis looks like being proved right, for most of the trims and tucks are beneficial.

'I see you've lost me then,' says Alan in mock umbrage, referring to the ending-up on cutting-room floor of 'Man Coming Out of Lavatory'.

Saturday, July 21st: Croft Cottage

As I write this, ten has just struck downstairs on the carriage clock I had restored for Mum. It's a Saturday morning. Birds sing almost constantly from various vantage points around the house. Heavy low cloud flattens out the landscape. It's cool.

Outside the window in front of me is a telegraph pole and a makeshift scarecrow of yellow polythene in a field of potatoes and clover. There is no other sign of human habitation.

The extraordinary appeal of Croft Cottage – and one that I feel sure I shall not be able to enjoy for much longer – is this momentary time-lessness, this feeling of being settled in a warm and comfortable armchair from which one can survey the past easily, the present comfortably and the future hardly at all.

Sunday, July 22nd

We play a lot of tennis, for the first time this year.

Suddenly aware of time passing when Helen and I are struggling to beat Tom and William. They're both potentially very good. Tom has a fierce serve, but doesn't concentrate hard enough to produce it with consistency. William is the eye-opener. He has a very quick eye, can't serve overarm well, but always seems to be in the right place at the right time (if you're playing *with* him) or the wrong time (if you're against him). Helen and I just hold our own, but very soon we'll be out of their league.

Monday, July 23rd

A run – as I feel I need all the exercise I can get before the holiday indulgences begin on Wednesday. It's very hot and humid and the going isn't very comfortable. I note from the *Sunday Times* that Jim Fixx, whose book was the greatest single influence on my decision to start regular running five years ago, has died of a heart attack aged 52, whilst ... running.

Halfway across Kenwood Meadow I meet Warren Mitchell. He says he's breaking in a new hip and talks of a return to Alf Garnett with Dandy Nichols in a wheelchair.

To the Zanzibar to meet Sam Goldwyn. Sam is tall, clear-eyed, silver-haired, strong-jawed. He could be an evangelist or a Republican politician or the owner of a million fast food restaurants. In fact he's a rather gentle, concerned, almost avuncular figure who has a strong liking for British comedy of the gentler kind. He's nice about what he's seen of *A Private Function* and thinks we have 'a real winner there'!

We discuss a possible remake of the 1974 TV play [*Secrets*] TJ and I wrote (coincidentally enough, with Warren Mitchell playing the lead), which Sam G likes in script form, but feels that there should be a rewrite developing a more sympathetic character.

The second idea, and more constructive still, is that if TJ and I don't feel it's fresh enough to be our next writing project, then is there anyone else we could trust? Both TJ and I quite independently suggest David Leland. Good on structure, taut and spare in his writing, convincing on the big business detail.

Tuesday, July 24th

To West Hampstead for lunch with JC. The restaurant is completely empty when I get there. I walk in, mildly put out at not even being able to find a waiter, when John's head pops up from beneath one of the tables and squeaks, mouse-like, making my heart stop momentarily.

We are almost the only diners. The waiter is a complete Manuel clone. We talk of friends and eventually of the whole area of behaviour, relationships, etc – the subject nearest to JC's heart at the moment. He does

seem to spend an inordinate amount of his time thinking about himself –
trying to get to the bottom of why he is what he is and is there anything
he can do about it?

It's a very warm, humid afternoon. Neither of us is in a great hurry
and JC drives me, at a stately pace, back to Julia Street in his Rolls. He
makes strange faces as we ring the doorbell, aiming to surprise Helen,
but surprises instead Sam Jarvis the painter – whose reaction as he opens
the door is something well worth seeing.

Wednesday, August 8th

Ring Eric to thank him for our weekend [at his house in France]. The
difference between us, I thought pithily as I plodded up to Kenwood
today, is that I'm a natural agree-er and Eric is a natural disagree-er. But
we are in harmony over the likely enjoyment of another collaboration –
Python or Python without John. Eric says he'd been thinking of a 'Brian
2', when Bowie, with whom he was lunching, suggested we do the 'Old
Testament' ... 'We could be so rude about the Jews.'

The idea of 'Python's Old Testament' attracts me more than I'd
expected. I feel as though we've done the hard bit of the Bible, now we
can do the fun bit – special effects, loopy characters, invasion, sacrifice,
empire-building and so on. The usual Python territory, in fact. I promise
I will mention it to TJ and that we should keep in touch by letter.

Thursday, August 9th

Taxi to King's Cross at half past twelve to travel with Terry J to York, for
my first look at Terry's 'Chaucer' talk.[1] I'm only going as curious travelling
companion and am not expected to do anything myself, so it's almost
another holiday excursion for me.

We eat on the train – some power-failure in the buffet results in the
bizarre plight of the steward advising us that 'anything in the fridge will
be warm'.

Tell TJ of the 'Old Testament' idea. He isn't as keen as I was. He feels
that the 'Old Testament' is so much about the Jews and their history that
goyim like ourselves are not the best-qualified people to write about it.

1 Terry, fascinated by Chaucer since university days, had written the book *Chaucer's Knight*,
published in 1980.

He prefers Greek classics as a possible base. We talk about the rest of the year's work. I feel 'The Vikings' should be put in abeyance and I think TJ does too.

Two hundred or more members of the New Chaucer Society assemble to hear Terry. Derek Brewer, Master of Emmanuel, introduces TJ as 'the twentieth-century embodiment of Geoffrey Chaucer' and mentions that he and I are currently at work on a Viking musical. This raises tremendous laughter from the assembled academics, who are obviously anticipating some entertainment tonight.

Terry doesn't disappoint them. With chest bared and hair in disordered profusion, he cracks off at a pace too fast and a pitch too high for most people to immediately comprehend. But for an hour and a half he keeps me completely involved in twenty lines of 'The Knight's Tale'. Told, part as performance, with throwaways, jokey slides and well-chosen anachronisms, and part as a detective story, it's compelling stuff and throughout TJ's energy and enthusiasm keep it on a superior level of interest to most academic arguments.

Monday, August 13th

In the evening we go round to the Pryces' in Queen's Crescent. Jonathan determined to offer us the best, so we have Kir, then a bottle of Cahors they brought back from staying at T Gilliam's in France, and *then* ... a bottle of 1963 port given them by Roger Pratt. Much talk of how to open it. JP goes next door to borrow a decanter from Frank Delaney. 'Of which sort?' is Delaney's admirable reply.

I chatter on, rather enjoying myself, until after twelve. Both Jonathan and Kate look exhausted and Helen has long since stopped listening and is gazing into the decanter stopper.

Wednesday, August 15th

In the afternoon the fluffy heat turns to darkening skies and occasional rain. Enervating weather, but drag myself into town to buy office files and to take back my running shoes. At Cobra they tell me I suffer from excessive pronation as I run and they prescribe some wonderful and expensive new Nike shoes which come with a small booklet explaining everything they do for the excessively pronating runner.

As I leave the shop clutching the most sophisticated trainers I've ever bought in my life, an assistant comes up to tell me that 'rumour has it' John Cleese just visited the Westbourne Grove branch and bought exactly the same pair. Two excessive pronators in one comedy team?

Saturday, August 18th

To Friar Park. George greets me, neat and wiry in his white cotton trousers and a 'Welcome to LA' T-shirt with a comical graphic of twisted, knotted freeways.

We sit and talk and soon I mention, *have* to mention, what I've heard of his reaction to *A Private Function*. He is indeed almost completely negative about it. He hasn't been able to read more than 11 pages of the script, he doesn't think it is a story or a world that will appeal to many people. He doesn't like the pig and also says, in a kindly enough way, that it is the first thing I've done when I haven't made him laugh.

Then we walk out into the gardens, which look wonderful in the still soft, very warm sunshine. He shows me the impressive work of one Keith West – a New Zealand botanical illustrator whom George is using to illustrate another edition of his songs. Beautiful detail and precision, rich colours. Occasionally mistily mystical, but so are many of the songs he's asked to illustrate. GH says he's written over 140 songs. 'Quite a lot, really.'

Later he takes me up to the studio and rather coyly plays me a song he's written for a musical about a one-legged tap dancer (the subject came up after he and Ringo went to see *42nd Street*).

About 7.15 I start to go, but GH is buzzing with ideas for a musical. 'Hawaii ... you could use Hawaii, there's a volcano with an ash cone in the centre bigger than Centre Point.' He comes to life as it's time to go. He desperately wants to create or be involved in creation – to, as he puts it, 'blow all my money on myself for once'.

Monday, September 3rd

Today is the fifth anniversary of my decision to try and make running a habit. I don't celebrate it in great style. I have an either bruised or cracked rib (post wind-surfing), which nudges me painfully as I run. A still-unsettled stomach and rather sore Achilles tendons.

I trot rather gently round my Heath course. The grass is turning brown from lack of rain, the place cries out for a dowsing. Cloud is building up as is a strongish warm wind. The fifth anniversary run is an effort, but, as ever, having finished I'm rewarded with a glowing feeling of satisfaction.

Tuesday, September 4th

A phone call from producer Clare Downs. She prefaces a request by saying that David Puttnam had told her I quite wanted to do more serious parts. I must have sounded guarded at this, for she laughs brightly.

What she wants me to do is a short film which Paramount and the NFFC [National Film Finance Corporation] have suddenly produced the money for, with a view to having it made and screened by the end of December to qualify for the awards. It sounds an above-average number, but what really swings my interest is that Phyllis Logan has already agreed to do it. I would be her husband.

The script is sent round. It's called *The Dress*. It's quite a meaty role, lots of sexual jealousy and desire and all that, but neatly written and definitely quality. A week's filming in October. Could fit it in, I suppose.

Wednesday, September 5th

I've come to regard September as the start of the working year. New projects ahead, the pleasant, reviving, drifting summer behind.

In the spirit of such feelings, begin a new 'country house' comedy completely from scratch. Quite where it goes I'm not sure. I do like the title 'The Man Who Averted World War II'.

David Leland shares my double ticket for a preview screening of *Spinal Tap*.

Very skilful, accurate parody of musicians on tour, observed to accentuate the humour, but never at the expense of a controlled authenticity which makes it very satisfying recognition viewing. Christopher Guest and Mike McKean uncannily good as English heavy metal stars.

To dinner afterwards. Twenty-five people squashed up at table. Sit opposite Stephen Frears and beside the producer of *Spinal Tap*, a lovely, bright New York lady, who I would gladly have produce anything I do!

Drive Leland back to Highgate and he gives me the first 40 pages of his new script about Cynthia [Payne] to read. He wants some feedback before he goes on.

Thursday, September 6th

Look at The Novel ['A Bit of A Break', written in 1977] again. Frustrated by lack of progress on the film, I decide to contact John Curtis at Weidenfeld, who showed interest in reading it five years ago. He is still there and still very interested.

Ring Cleese to fix a lunch, as I am the Python appointed to try and interest him in the proposed meeting about whether we ever make a film again which Eric is trying to set up in mid-October. JC is quite brisk on the phone and with more than usual exasperation explains that he's just put his neck out, 'and a man's waiting upstairs to put it back in again'.

Friday, September 7th

To meet Clare Downs and the director, Eva Sereny, to talk about *The Dress*. They are highly embarrassed about offering me only £2,400 for the work, but this is out of a total budget of £100,000 and, as I say, I'm not doing it for the money. I hope I shan't disappoint them.

Eva Sereny I like immediately. Hungarian, married to an Italian and based in Rome, 'but never in the same bed two nights running' is how she describes her life as a photographer of international repute. This is her first venture as director. She describes the overall sepia look she wants, with the red of the dress standing out.

Sunday, September 9th

Up at half past nine. Read the Sundays and come across an interview by George Perry with *Spinal Tap* people. They liked Goons and Monty Python and saw JC and MP as 'comic geniuses'. This cheers me up, especially after a week in which the comic genius has been particularly elusive, but it nudges me suddenly in a certain positive direction – one, to write something for myself which will make people laugh rather than just smile, and two, to perhaps explore the biography – the 'life of', or the documentary.

Monday, September 10th

Lunch with Cleesie. He's waiting for me at Odin's with an incipient growth of beard. 'I hate saying I'm growing it for a film, in case people think I'm an actor,' he says, quite sincerely. He's playing an English sheriff in a Lawrence Kasdan film to be shot in Arizona. 'Two weeks' work, Mikey ... in a *lovely* part of America ...'

He is very anxious to hear about everything I'm doing, but claims to be well ahead of me in days off this year. When I tell him I've had an unproductive week, he proffers some advice – that, in the same way, he says, that the creation of Basil Fawlty had been a bringing-out of Fawlty-esque frustrations in John himself, so I should try and create a character which brings something out of me, something which I feel very strongly about.

I broach Python, as prelim to asking John to October meetings, but there is nothing there.

Sunday, September 16th

Worried about my stools. The currently fashionable indication of good health is that your stools float. Mine sink like so many *Titanic*s.

Screen International reveals that British cinema attendance has plum-meted – like my stools – yet again this year. It comes home to me that there is no longer a commercial prospect in making films that will only be understood in my own country. Video deals and early TV sales could, I suppose, save a very small budget. But no room for anything ambitious. Depressing. And renders me even less consumed with energy for a new *Missionary*.

Watch the first of the *Great River Journeys*. Very good stuff from Michael Wood on the journey up the Congo to the interior of Africa. Helen worried about his theme of utter solitude and man against Africa, knowing there was a six- to eight-man production crew, but I suspend disbelief.

Tuesday, September 18th

[On my way back from a literary festival in Ilkley.] Geoffrey Boycott boards the train at Wakefield. Sunburnt face with hardly a line, he sits, chewing and reading his paper, with an enviable Zen-like detachment. He wears a lightweight pale brown windcheater with the legend 'Pierre Cardin' prominently displayed.

I am honestly too nervous to go up and introduce myself. I'm like a schoolboy again and, as a schoolboy, I always had to rely on those braver than myself to break the ice in a situation like this. At the point when I've almost plucked up courage and am right beside him, a passing middle-aged lady suddenly pulls up beside me and stares – 'Michael *Palin!*' The moment is lost.

Thursday, September 20th

It's 18 months since I sat down to write a *Missionary* follow-up.

The film script has become like a mountain. I can't yet find the best way up. Have tried three or four paths, but none lead to the top. And behind all that is my ever-returning doubt as to whether the mountain is worth climbing at all.

A run on a splashy Heath. The black paint flung across Kenwood House has now been there since Monday. 'Support the Miners' and 'No Pit Closures' scrawled across the pristine south façade. It's an ugly sight. Dispiriting in every way.

Wednesday, September 26th

Steve tells me the good news – that as from this month *Jabberwocky* is in profit. After eight years my percentage is suddenly worth something – £1.20 to be precise. But I also have an unexpected bonus of £1,500 which I evidently deferred at the time.

TG arrives hot from the *Brazil* cutting rooms. 'How can I spend so much time there without the film getting any better?'

Friday, September 28th

At ten o'clock a taxi takes me to Alwyne Road, a pretty, shady little backwater in Canonbury. No. 33 is to be the location for our house in *The Dress*. It's about to be sold, or just has been, for over £300,000. Full of conspicuous luxury – jacuzzi, double bath, sauna, electrically opening bedroom curtains and so on. The small garden borders the canal. It's a very harmonious little area, not a house or a leaf out of place.

Enjoy this morning's rehearsal. Phyllis and I try the final scene for the first time. We've discussed with Eva whether this encounter should be sexual passion or more tenderness. Decide that the latter should predominate. This morning we try an embrace or two. Eva seems very happy with the result.

Friday, October 5th

A bathroom mirror shot and I'm shocked at how puffy and grey-eyed I look. Only five weeks ago I was in peak of post-Sardinia condition, now I look as if I haven't slept for weeks. Perhaps it's the cold. Phyllis and I in bed beside an open window, half-naked. Outside the skies darken and the heavens open. Very heavy rain and flashes of lightning and splitting cracks of thunder. Then a long wait for Phyllis to change make-up.

Lunch in the pub nearby, as the rain and the turbulence continues.

Phyllis (two dark rum and peppermints) and I (one and a half pints of Young's Bitter) splash back through the rain to 33 Alwyne Road.

Another wait for make-up, then from four o'clock until about nine a period of intense and concentrated work. All the energetic après-party scene to be done, as well as the delicate and vital transition from anger to love in the bedroom.

Eva seems especially happy with one of my takes, on which I feel I bring out something a bit different, something unusual for me – without eyes and teeth – just interior feelings. Phyllis is very impressive. There seems to be nothing she can't do. She has an instinctive feel for the exactly right level at which to pitch a performance, which makes even Maggie S seem laggardly. Feel I'm seeing a very good actress indeed – all she needs now are the great parts.

Our love scene together – our lyrical, camera-twirling moment of intimacy – turns out, of course, to be as workmanlike a process as putting handles on car doors. A hot and sweaty Robin Vigeon bending around us with a hand-held Arriflex, Phyllis worried about when to get out of her shoes and how to get her dress to fall at the right moment. Me tripping over her shoes at the end [of] one lyrical, sensitive, romantic take.

To bed at midnight again. Cold still flowing copiously.

Saturday, October 6th

Rachel is to play my daughter. Asked to bring toys, she refuses to bring any Sindy dolls or other paraphernalia at first, then relents and brings one doll.

Camera, on a crane, is setting up for the final sequence of the dress falling to the ground after floating away from the window. The famous dress, which neither Phyllis nor I like very much, is flapping down from an invisible wire over Alwyne Road. All this takes a long time and then there are more than two hours to kill in the cold house.

Once acting, Rachel is fine; her shyness disappears as she takes on the character. Stephen, the chatty confident boy, on the other hand, clams up when asked to act.

But about half past five, in a blacked-out taxi, we finish the shooting. Champagne is produced. Eva says thank you – she's quite drained and obviously can hardly believe that it's done – and Clare says 'It's been an easy week'. 'Easy *fucking* week!' shouts Phyllis and everyone roars with laughter in relief and sympathy.

For me it's been everything I'd hoped – an exercise in acting and in becoming involved with new and talented and pleasant people. I'm not sure about my part, the script, and how it will all eventually look, but it's been a tough and concentrated and satisfying piece of work. A kick up the arse. Rachel much complimented so we end the day a lot happier than we started. And she's £25.00 better off.

After completing The Dress *and before Fegg publicity began I visited friends in America, particularly Al and Claudie in Sag Harbor. Al had had cancer treatment quite recently.*

Friday, October 12th: New York/Sag Harbor

Amongst the rest of the news in my *Times* at breakfast today – besides the Bush/Ferraro debate and the subway fires – is a small paragraph reporting a bomb in a hotel in Brighton, where Margaret Thatcher was staying for the Conservative Party Conference.

For the next two days I devote myself to Al L. At eleven a.m. am at the *New York Times* office, to see one Ed McDowell, a writer on the world of books and publishing, whom Norman Rosten[1] has put me in touch with.

In a small room which could have been an interrogation room in a police station, I'm granted an audience with McDowell, who turns out to be much less daunting than I'd been prepared for by Norman. In fact he becomes quite intrigued by the story of my involvement with Al. Thinks my loyalty is almost unbelievable – the very fact that I've come over to see this unknown writer strikes him as very ripe.

Encouraged by this I take a cab back uptown to collect a car for the journey to Sag. A silver Buick Regal from Avis on 34th.

1 New York-born poet, playwright and novelist. He wrote a memoir of his friendship with Marilyn Monroe, and from 1979 to his death in 1995 held the title of Poet Laureate of Brooklyn.

Al and Gwenola are at the house. Claudie is working as a lunchtime waitress. Al looks stronger and fitter and less changed for the worse than I expected. In fact the loss of 15 lbs of weight improves him. He smokes his pipe, drinks his drink and is very mobile, though obviously not able to bend, stretch, lift and carry as before. Gwenola full of energy in his stead. And interest too. 'Have you got balls?' she queries as I change my trousers upstairs.

We drive out to Mecox Beach. The sea is big. I'd forgotten how impressive and monumental is the size of the Atlantic. After several hols in the Med one gets used to a tame sea. This is ocean. The wide, straight beach is deserted, left to the big, spray-clouded waves that steam in. Gwenola and I paddle and run up and down. I feel light and airy and happy to be out of New York for a while.

Saturday, October 13th: Sag Harbor

Wake occasionally in the night to the gratifying sound of a rising wind in the powerful Norwegian maple tree outside. Go for a walk around the neat and pretty streets by the house. It's a blustery, overcast morning, despite the forecast of sun. Generally low, timber-framed, weather-boarded houses, most detached with garden space generously distributed and many of them well over 100 years old. No-one else is walking at nine o'clock, though. Everyone slides by in their quiet, powerful cars.

Al talks quite openly and often about his new artificial defecatory system. Shows me all the bags and the tubes and seems quite happy now about having no working asshole any more. He also talks about the hospital – the horrors and the humours of which will doubtless come out in a new book.

Friday, October 19th

Wake to rain and blustery wind. A few calls, then down to Fox viewing theatre in the West End for my second look at *Brazil*. Some cuts, especially towards the end, make it easier to follow and maintain the tension well. The bombing sequences with people being pulled from the wreckage, indeed the whole terrorist/paramilitary security force there suddenly very relevant after the Brighton bombing and growing controversy over police methods in the miners' strike.

At the end Terry is surrounded by besuited distribution and marketing men. Clearly they are excited. Pass on one or two of my thoughts, then TG is swept upstairs to a distributors' 'working lunch'. Leave him to it and grab a couple of pork pies and a cup of tea and eat them as I walk back through the rain to the car park.

Wednesday, October 24th

To a launch for 'The Young Ones' book *Bachelor Boys*. It's at Ronnie Scott's and the place is already packed.

Ben Elton signs a book for me (to Rachel) and Rik Mayall (the only one of the cast there) hangs around like me at the stairs that lead into the main part of the club, largely because there's hardly an inch of open space through which to move further.

A Sphere Books rep rather anxiously asks Rik if he's going to mingle. 'Well I'm sort of mingling here,' he indicates vaguely. He's going to the National to play in *The Government Inspector*, but first is doing a tour with Ben Elton. I ask where I can see it, and he says Slough would probably be the nearest.

They're not doing any more *Young Ones*, apparently. The bus over the cliff at the end of the last episode was meant to be a final statement. There's something serious about the way he refers to this that restrains me from saying that it was only in the last series that I'd really got to know and want to see more of the dreadful characters, and that surely they shouldn't quit now.

Out into the rain and back home for Rachel's open day. Neat, very thorough work. Lots of ticks and 'excellents', but still a tendency to invert letter order in the more difficult words. But her teacher Miss Kendall is lovely and full of humour. Rachel can't wait to leave for school these mornings and can't wait to come back and play schools in the evening. But she definitely wants to be an actress.

Romaine Hart rang.[1] She raved about *Private Function*. Was only concerned that from her meetings with HandMade she caught the feeling that they were not prepared to push it as hard as she thinks it deserves.

She also said that it was the first film at the London Film Festival to sell out and has been six times over-subscribed!

---

1 Romaine founded the very successful chain of 'Screen' cinemas in and around London.

Saturday, October 27th

I wake with a slowly developing near-panic at the thought of an unplanned Saturday ahead. Why should this be? Outside the sun shines from a clear sky, which unsettles me. Makes me feel I should be in the country, or somewhere with a garden into which the sun reaches for more than six months of the year.

Read in the newspaper of screenwriters meeting at the NFT for a weekend to discuss their problems. Problems I share and with which I sympathise. But I'm not there – I'm here at home, feeling aimless. I read of the CND march in Barrow to protest against the building of four submarines, each of which will carry warheads capable of delivering 7,200 times the force of the Hiroshima bomb. And I'm here at home, sitting upstairs basking in the sunshine.

I feel inadequate because I can't teach my children any practical crafts and skills, because I know so few. I feel inadequate that I have no plans to take them to see this and that in London – concerts or walks or museums. But, having enjoyed a life of not having to go out at weekends amongst the crowds, I've become spoilt.

There's work to do, of course – limericks to write, film scripts to be looked at and ahead a massive programme of signings and interviews – but where to start, where to begin, what to do?

Force myself away from this slippery slope and decide to take Rachel on a mystery tour. She loves the idea and we set off after lunch. First to Tower Bridge, where, for the first time, we climb the towers and walk along the linking crossways, with views out over the city and the river down to Greenwich.

By lucky chance there is a raising of the bridge as we are there. We watch it from some abandoned jetty a little upstream from the Tower. We find ourselves beside the 'William Curtis Ecological Park', an old lorry park which two years ago was filled with soil and boulders and is now a sort of controlled wasteland.

Rachel and I talk with a girl who is working there. It will only last for two more years – that's as long as developers can keep their hands off the site – but she shows us other places in London where similar conservation experiments are going on. It's the accidental, surprise nature of this little patch with its view of the Tower of London across the river which makes both of us respond so eagerly to it.

Wednesday, October 31st

I'm at Lime Grove Studios by 6.15.

Dr Fegg's dummy has arrived and is sitting vacuously in the studio on one of the sofas. In a crowded make-up room, re-introduce myself to Frank Bough and learn for the first time that there is hot news about. Just over an hour ago word came from Delhi that Mrs Gandhi has been shot.

Apologise for being here to do something as frivolous as 'Fegg' publicity on such a day, but Bough grins reassuringly. 'I'm damn glad you're here . . . we'll need some light relief.'

Frank, ear doubtless buzzing with unconfirmed rumours that the ruler of India is dead, manfully reads 'Sawing a Lady in Half' and 'Daffodils go Ping and Oink'! Even he seems to run out of patience at the end and sums up with a broad smile 'And we're expected to buy this rubbish this Christmas?'

It's not until 7.45 that the 'unconfirmed' becomes 'confirmed' and the BBC newsmen rub their hands in glee. All systems go. Interviews, race for the first obituary, phone links with Delhi.

Meanwhile in a small back room are gathered Terry, myself, Rick Wakeman, Johnny Cash, Stan Orme MP, Ray Buckton of the TUC, two asthmatics, a man with a pumpkin and the author of a book on haunted Britain.

Cash nods courteously and introduces himself to everybody. 'Hi! John Cash.' We bask in modest glow of pride as the Great Man tells of his visit to the Python show at City Center, New York. Says he loved it. Oh God . . . I can't cope. Elvis Presley a fan, now Johnny Cash . . . Is nothing sacred?

Rick Wakeman is relentlessly cheery and invites us – 'if you're in the Camberley area on Thursday' – to his stag night, at which a pornographic Punch and Judy show will be the highlight. 'The crocodile does *amazing* things,' Rick enthuses.

Unexpected reaction from Weidenfeld's John Curtis – he likes the novel and wants to publish!

In the evening I drive Tom and friend to King's Cross, from where he embarks for his sixteenth birthday present – a parachute drop, after two days' training near Peterborough.

Monday, November 5th

Catch the North London train from Gospel Oak at a quarter to eight. Still feeling rather grumpy and not happy at the prospect of three more days Fegging. Encounter TJ in the bookstall at Liverpool Street. His nose is red and slightly swollen, the end of it covered in scabs and scratches. I ask him what happened. 'A woman bit it,' he explains. For some reason, I'm not as surprised as I should be.

TJ lost his temper with a difficult boy at a firework display and sharply ticked him off. Some time later a man knocked on his door and asked 'Are you the man who beat up my son?' Terry, now quite reasonable, denied that he'd 'beaten up' anybody. The man repeated his question. TJ, again sweet reasonableness, was about to ask him in to discuss the whole question, when out of the darkness sprang a woman, teeth bared, who bit Terry on the end of the nose and wouldn't let go. In her fury she tore at his hair and yelled and screamed and eventually TJ could only force her off by poking her in the eye (a form of attack much used by JC in Python sketches).

One British Rail breakfast later, he's feeling much better and quite relieved to have an excuse to be out of London. Norwich is reached at a quarter to eleven, we're met at the station. Terry is asked about his nose by the rep. We are taken straightaway to Radio Norfolk, where Terry is asked about his nose again.

Talk to local journalists, sign some stock copies, explain about TJ's nose, then we are unleashed on the public. The public are unfortunately not unleashed on us, and they come through in a very thin trickle – lots of buck-passing from shop to rep to sales department, but it's clear that a midday Monday in Norwich is not a peak book-buying time.

On 'Look East' the big story of our visit is of course ... Terry's nose. With close-ups and everything. The nasal damage is worth more than any Fegg dummy.

The pleasantest part of the day is a half-hour break when TJ and I saunter round the cathedral. We walk the cloisters talking about the Lollards.

Tuesday, November 6th: Manchester

To the 'Stuart Hall Radio Show'. Stuart Hall is not of this world as I know it. I just can't work him out. At no point in our talk, or our interview, is there the slightest evidence that he's heard, or understood anything we're saying. He's not rude, he's not loud or aggressive, he just doesn't seem to be quite there. Only when he is talking about himself as a collector and showing us watches or magnifying glasses does he really seem to come alive. Quite curious really.

Wednesday, November 7th: Leeds

After breakfast – and confirmation that Reagan has won every state but two[1] – we begin our day's work at Radio Aire. I feel rather perky today. Is it because I know it's the last day? Is it perhaps because the Radio Aire interviewer is very grateful to me for speaking to him during *Private Function* in Bradford, when no-one else in the cast would? But it helps me through the day and I don't feel as imbecile and facetiously trivial as on previous days.

Thursday, November 8th

Time for a run this morning before a busy day of *Private Function* publicity.

The questions are friendly and generally concern the pig, though I'm asked whether or not it was difficult to play a part so obviously suited to Alan Bennett with Alan Bennett present. I'd never really thought of it like that.

On to L'Escargot for dinner with Robert H and Erica.

Robert vehement that I should not let Weidenfeld have my novel. He says that Lord W is trying to sell the company, that its heyday is over, that it's going to get terribly stung over the Jagger biog and that they are 'celebrity' publishers who will publish more because of who you are than what you've done. He's very fierce. And John Curtis is his publisher.

Home after midnight.

---

1 In fact, Reagan won every state except for DC and Minnesota, the home state of his Democratic challenger Walter Mondale. Reagan took 58.8% of the total vote, Mondale 40.6%.

Saturday, November 10th

As I eat breakfast I hear on the radio of the Lord Mayor's Procession and, lured by the sun, I suggest that Rachel and I go down to see it. The procession is jolly, but full of floats it's very hard to cheer – the National Clearing Banks, the Solicitors' Society, Tate and Lyle Sugar, the Stock Exchange, British Telecom, British Airways. An uneasy mixture of rich modern companies in a curiously eighteenth-century-style procession.

'Rule Britannia' precedes the Lord Mayor's coach. This is pure panto – a baroque gold-leaved extravaganza from which the Lord Mayor leans, beaming and waving as if just about to go into a song.

To cap our morning out we pass by Sir John Soane's house on our way back. It is open, so I am able to introduce Rachel to this wonderful treasure trove, with so much more atmosphere than a modern museum. The sense of the continuity of the place with its maker suffuses the house quite magically.

A McDonald's at Warren Street, then home. Make myself a smoked salmon sandwich and, with a glass of Puligny-Montrachet, settle up in my workroom to catch the last of the sunshine.

Don't respond awfully well at first to the arrival of Julian Hough. He's clearly on some downward self-destructive curve. He says he finds familiar places very comforting in his present state and claims to have visited Buckingham Palace twice already today. He fairly rapidly drinks two glasses of Puligny-Montrachet '73, then, with that strange walk of his, arms by his sides hardly moving, he launches off into the outside world again. It's like seeing someone in great pain and being powerless to help.

Monday, November 12th

Taxi to Wardour Street at nine, for post-synch on *The Dress*. Waiting at the lift in Film House when Phyllis hurries in. She looks rushed and a bit tired. She's come down from Glasgow on the sleeper.

A concentrated three and a half hours' work, ending up with re-voicing (and re-noising!) our love scene most unromantically. Kissing with one eye on the screen. Passion to picture.

Eva, Clare D, Phyllis and I have lunch at the Golden Horn – a Turkish establishment with lots of unpronounceable dishes, one of which is translated as 'brain salad'. *The Dress* is to be premiered on the last day of the London Film Festival, after Louis Malle's new film.

Tuesday, November 13th

Drive down to Camberwell for our first day's work on *Secrets*[1] with Paul Zimmerman. A long and ugly drive down in clogged traffic and as my feelings for the project itself are equivocal, I'm in rather a negative mood when Paul Z opens the door to me at five past ten.

Nor is there any chance of acclimatisation with Paul. He works from the moment he opens the door with a constant patter of quick Jewish patois. He's very funny and very sharp, but in the end the remorselessness of the stream of asides, ideas, self-deprecations, is rather like facing an endless stream of ace serves. I'm constantly retrieving balls from the back of the court.

From this frenetic display of words very few constructive ideas appear. I worry that whatever Paul does to *Secrets* he won't be able to make it English. He acknowledges this and expects that he will 'sort out the structure ... put the whole thing together', then leave us to Anglicise it.

Thursday, November 15th

I leave for Terry's at ten to nine. The fog lifts by the Thames and sunlight sparkles off St Paul's dome and the river and from a thousand windows. Ahead South London is still mist-blanketed. The contrast is very beautiful.

On the way down I hear a vintage piece of phone-iniana. Peter Stringfellow, the Sheffield steelworker's son turned millionaire London club owner, talks some good, homely nonsense but occasionally reveals alarming gaps in the otherwise almost cosmic scale of his knowledge. 'Can I ask Mr Stringfellow for his views on vivisection?' A pause, then, boldly and sincerely, 'Well, I'm not against the operation, but I certainly wouldn't like it done to me, only to find I meet a girl two weeks later who I fall in love with and want to start a family.'

1 *Secrets*, originally broadcast in August 1973 as Jones and Palin's contribution to a Mark Shivas/Richard Broke BBC series called *Black and Blue*, now began a second life as a possible movie, spurred on by Sam Goldwyn Jr. It becomes, variously, 'Consuming Passions', 'The Chocolate Film', 'Chocolates' and 'The Chocolate Project'. And eventually it does become a movie, *Consuming Passions*, 1988, directed by Giles Foster.

After what seems like forever, Sarah Ward intervenes and sorts out the misunderstanding. There is much laughter and the questioner (who does not laugh) puts his question again ... 'Mr Stringfellow ... what *do* you feel about vivisection?' There is quite a long pause, then, finally, 'Well, what is it for a start?'

Monday, November 19th

William 14; we buy him a Toshiba head-set with radio and cassette, plus pens, pencils, a diary and all the stationery stuff he likes. Jolly breakfast.

To lunch at Sheekey's with John Curtis and Victoria Petrie-Hay, of Weidenfeld, to hear the first publisher's reaction to my novel. Curtis is, as I'd expected, middle-aged, with a roundish, ruddy face coming to a point at the chin. He looks neat and rather old-fashioned – more like a prosperous farmer than a publisher.

He runs the lunch whilst deferring to Victoria – a younger woman with dark hair and dark-rimmed eyes and a big, defiant face – on all matters of literary criticism. She is neither sycophantic nor tentative. She feels that the first third of the book is one of the best pieces of comic writing she's come across and is not in doubt that such writing could stand on its own and I need not be defensive or bashful about it. She doesn't like the Suffolk scenes and gives quite pithy reasons why not – too melodramatic, too many deaths, another change of scene, loss of good early characters, loss of early comic tone. I agree with her.

Having come along to the lunch feeling that I must be strong with myself and hold out for a completely new book (using this one as experience), I am swayed enough by her criticisms (echoed by Al and others) to consider the advantages of rewriting two-thirds of the book and carrying on with the character of Avery, who I've become quite fond of.

John wants something signed – would a contract help? I say no. Just good to know they're very keen, and I also say I can't be pushed into a date for further work, what with 'First Love' looming, but that I will come back to them first. 'You can write,' says the dark-eyed lady with great enthusiasm, and that is the best part of the lunch.

Tuesday, November 20th

Cab down to Theatre Royal, Haymarket. 'Panto rehearsal, is it?' asks the driver solicitously. I tell him it's a press reception for a new film. He sounds vaguely disappointed ... 'Ah, well ... so long as you're busy, that's the main thing.'

At the portals of the Theatre Royal by 12.30; the daily press film critics have just seen the film. Denholm is there, with Liz Smith (faithful troopers), and the three of us are photographed with the poster – which looks very strong, perhaps Malcolm won his case after all.

Maggie arrives later, setting up a flurry of cameras and notebooks. Indicating the extraordinarily close proximity of the boxes at stage level, she says 'Olivier was there last night. A bit disconcerting. He has to be as close as possible, poor dear. Deaf as a post.' [Maggie was currently appearing at the Theatre Royal as Millamant in *The Way of the World.*]

The high point of the occasion is having Dilys Powell introduced to me. She's small and frail and moves with difficulty, but I've rarely been opposite a face with such a combination of keenness, charity and warmth. Her big eyes sparkle with life and interest and awareness and make the noise and bustle all around seem tiresome.

Wednesday, November 21st

Both the grannies now assembled in the kitchen.

At 6.40 our taxi arrives. The weather has turned against us after a very tolerable day and it's raining hard as we draw up outside the Odeon Haymarket [for the Royal Premiere of *A Private Function*].

Talk to various friends before having to go up on stage at 7.35 for that part of the evening described forbiddingly in the programme as 'Michael Palin entertains'.

After about ten or fifteen minutes I still haven't received the signal that the Royal Person has arrived, but I've run out of things to say so I thank everyone and am shepherded back up the auditorium to await with my fellow thespians. Denholm has gone to Marrakesh, Maggie and Alan are both acting, so the line consists of Liz Smith, Alison S, John Normington, Bill P, Richard Griffiths and myself.

The Princess walks down from 'Foyer 1', where she's met Malcolm and Val, his wife, and is introduced to us. I have quite a long chat about the film, acting with pigs and future plans.

Then we follow her into the auditorium of the Odeon. I don't think I shall ever make such an entry to a cinema again. Distant memories of slinking furtively into the grubby darkness of the Palace Union Street nearly 30 years ago come into my mind, but tonight I am entering the Odeon Haymarket behind Princess Anne to the sound of a fanfare.

Well-combed, expensively coiffured heads turn as we file into Row T. Princess Anne's place is denoted by a lone antimacassar carefully laid over the back of the seat. The National Anthem is played and I feel terribly important. Just in front and to the right my little mother cranes round for a better view. Poor Princess Anne has to sit with a programme and a bouquet of flowers on her lap throughout.

The film looks and sounds very good and there is plenty of laughter, though the various royal references – 'My wife has two topics of conversation – one is the Royal Family, the other is her bowels' – take on a new frisson of significance.

At the end Princess Anne, with Helen, myself and the Mowbrays dutifully following, file out in a silent line. Then she is gone and we soon follow – to a reception at Maxim's.

As the two grannies, Angela, Veryan, Helen and myself struggle past the Comedy Theatre (scene of my first London acting appearance 20 years ago) in the wind and rain, the photographers suddenly surge forward and, pushing us to one side, direct a salvo of flashes at a long, sleek, black limousine, from which emerge Ringo Starr and Barbara Bach and Olivia Harrison.

Once the Princess has gone we move to a sit-down supper. Goulash is very ordinary and my bridge comes out in it. Neither Malcolm nor Maggie show up, which I find remarkable, but the rest of us enjoy ourselves.

Thursday, November 29th

A wonderful review in the *Guardian* – 'nothing would give me greater pleasure than to see this film in the top box-office earners next week' – but the expected dampener from *Time Out*. Richard Rayner takes the same view as the *Melody Maker* – the acting is fine, but the film is a mess. A Bennett taken to task for not facing 'the realities' of the rationing period. It's a slipshod review, praising, in the cast, one 'Richardson', which shows how accurately they have faced up to the realities of the film.

Work on 'First Love' in the morning and limericks in the afternoon.

Tea-time greatly improved by a rave Alexander Walker review in the *Standard*. 'I'm glad I lived long enough to see it!'

Ring Mother who sounds a bit low. She's 'coping', but I'm a little worried. Probably suffering post-Royal Premiere depression.

Friday, November 30th

To lunch with Richard Loncraine at L'Étoile. Tells a good story of actor Lou Gossett, with whom RL worked, for a while, on *Enemy Mine*. RL once asked him, in one of their rare moments of philosophical intimacy, what was the one thing Lou really enjoyed. 'I'll tell you, Richard – it's fucking and sushi.' 'That's two, Lou,' suggested RL ... 'Hell, it's the same thing to me,' replied the megastar cryptically.

A night at home. Evening ends with me becoming rather hooked on a snooker semi-final between Higgins and Thorburn – both of whom have a marvellous, battered, dissolute charisma which is so much more refreshing than the boring, bland healthiness of the Coes and Steve Davises, the Torvills and Deans. Long live Alex Higgins and his fags and beer. Though, the way he goes on, he probably won't!

Sunday, December 2nd

In the Sundays – 'Fegg's' first appearance in the best-seller lists, at No. 6 on the 'General' chart, and a nice review of 'Fegg' by Russell Davies in the *Observer*, opposite the Philip French rave for *Private Function*. A nice feeling for a Sunday morning. The brief, illusory satisfaction of being wanted.

Then down to the Lumiere for the world premiere of *The Dress*. Lumiere full – six to seven hundred people. A Louis Malle film, *Crackers*, on first, and before that Derek Malcolm 'informally' introduces Eva S, Phyllis and myself to the throng.

I really don't like going to the cinema like this. Miss the dark anonymity – here are Phyllis and I now, marked men and women. *Crackers* is not very good. Heavily played comedy. Louis Malle crying out for a Woody Allen to show him how to direct a comedy of charm and wit.

Then it's over and almost without pause we're into *The Dress*. I think that this is a mistake, and does not help distance *The Dress* from comedy, which, with me in it, the audience clearly expects. They begin to titter early on.

I found my performance difficult to judge as I was not required to play for laughs – so none of my conventional yardsticks of success applied. 'Serious' acting of the sort I do in *The Dress* seems to be dangerously easy to do and my feeling at the end is one of confusion. I sense that in Helen who thought it very funny to be watching me being so serious.

Wednesday, December 5th: London–Southwold

At Liverpool Street the big expensive, automatic destination board is still only half-working. The lead story in my newspaper is of another fatal rail accident – the sixth in as many months. It looks to me as if the railway system is very near breaking point.

I take deep breaths and try to control my bitter feelings about what Margaret Thatcher's war against organised labour is costing this country. I feel these are darker days even than in the early '70's when Heath took on the miners. This time people are paying for 'strong government' with their lives.

But all these awfulnesses seem less immediate as I reach Suffolk and eventually step off the train at Darsham to find my exiguous mater, stooped and thinner in the legs, scouring the incoming train with a frown.

The field behind the house is full of potato-pickers. They're aided by a mechanical plough, a tractor-trailer and a fork-lift truck, but the picking of the potatoes from the cloggy earth is done by hand. There are a dozen figures, well wrapped in thick coats, scrabbling the potatoes into old fertiliser bags. Bent over the job. Old-fashioned, unskilled agricultural labour in the wind and the rain, a hundred yards away from where I sit at my desk trying to pick the right words out of the equally cloggy soil of my imagination.

Thursday, December 6th: Southwold

Wake at half past eight. Low cloud and rain. No potato-pickers. Work until one. Weather clears and temperature drops sharply without cloud cover.

Mother said quite categorically that she doesn't like driving the car any more, and, as nearly categorically as she's ever been, that she can't foresee another winter at Croft Cottage.

Reckon I've spent about ten hours this week on *East of Ipswich* (as I'm provisionally calling 'First Love') – the progress has all been forward and quite exciting.

Sunday, December 9th

At the London Palladium for something in the nature of a good turn to J Cleese, who was committed but is filming in the US. We're supporting the Oncology Club – oncology being the study of tumours – and it's a big house to fill.

Terry and I look like the oldest members of the cast – which I realise with a shock we probably are. Neil [Innes] is there to cheer us up. He's given up smoking, on his 40th birthday.

I open the show – almost on time at 7.30 – with the 'Politician's Speech', which goes well, but not ecstatically.

Alexei Sayle begins the assault on the audience with a display of manic energy and lots of 'fucking' and 'cunting'. Chris Langham has a lot of wanking jokes and Rik Mayall does a piece about an elephant giving someone a blow-job in an Italian restaurant. This last marvellous.

It's over by 10.30 and we go to a small party at which Neil is given a birthday cake in the shape of a piano. All the foul-mouthed 'alternative' comedians sit quietly with their wives or girlfriends.

Wednesday, December 12th

Am settling down to watch *Oxbridge Blues* when the door bell rings and there is the red face and sad apologetic smile of Julian Hough. He spent last night in the cells, he claims. He's no money and has resorted to stealing – rather proud of the fact that he took a bottle of white wine and a jar of caviar from a shop in Hampstead – and then went back for some carrots.

Sunday, December 16th

M Mowbray tells me that Mr Gorbachev – the Soviet No. 2[1] visiting the UK at the moment – has requested a print of *A Private Function* to be delivered to the Soviet Embassy! Alan apparently very pleased.

1 Konstantin Chernenko was the President of the USSR until his death in March 1985 when Gorbachev succeeded him.

Monday, December 17th

To Duke's Hotel for a Python meal.

GC and EI discuss the relative merits of cocaine – 'A killer ... keep off it,' counsels Eric fiercely – and acid, which both agree taken in the right circumstances with the right people can be marvellous. Graham says he played snooker under acid and 'couldn't do anything wrong. Potted every one'.

EI has been doing Lampoon's '*Vacation* II'. He said that at least he was keeping up his record of having appeared 'only in flops' apart from the Python films.

At the end of a very good meal, I, a little playfully, ask of the gathering when we might all work together again.

A Python History of America emerges as front runner. A totally fabricated history using facts as and when we want them – rather on the lines of GC's *Liar's Autobiography*.

Best feeling about our little reunion was the reaffirmation that when we are all in accord there is no more satisfying group to work with. The shorthand that exists between us all cannot be replicated outside. This bond is stronger than it ever was – a bond of people of roughly the same age who have shared a unique experience. I hope we can be something more than a luncheon club.

Wednesday, December 19th

Across the West End to St James's Park on my way to a lunch given by the Chancellor of the Duchy of Lancaster *and* Minister of the Arts, Lord Gowrie.

I approach behind a seedy figure in a dull brown overcoat who turns out to be Alan Bennett. So pleased to see him I give him a big hug. The security man has my name in the book, but not Alan's. 'Oh well, up you go anyway,' he says to him.

Room 622 is the office of Lord Gowrie. A small collection of mixed artistes – Ronnie Scott is sitting already talking, there's Cleo Laine and Melvyn Bragg and Stephen Frears. Why are we all here? seems to be the general theme of most of the conversations.

Bob Geldof, definitely the man of the moment for writing and organising the Band Aid Christmas record for Ethiopia, arrives bristling over the government's decision to collect VAT money on the record –

which everyone had made for nothing. The Minister of Arts, sensing this, seems to spend a lot of time grinning at whatever the unshaven Boomtown Rat says.

Jeremy Isaacs – who has done an excellent job with Channel 4, I feel – comes across to tell me that the IBA have refused clearance to put the *Life of Brian* on TV – even at 11.15 at night. It might offend 'Christian sensibilities' they say. Isaacs is hopping mad and looking forward to a fight.

Monday, December 31st

Visited Beatties [the model railway shop]. Collected various accessories, including trees and a lot of people – 'army personnel', 'commuters', etc – all in little bags. Ian Davidson later suggests they should have little models of well-known people – like 'Sir Harold Nicolson'.

On the way back I stopped at Alan Alan's Magic Shop in Southampton Row, where I was served by a small, neat, be-suited gentleman with an arrow through his head. Quickly and efficiently he demonstrated an extraordinary variety of bangs, squirts, farts and electric shocks as if he were selling nothing more exciting than a coal scuttle. Little children watched in awe as their fathers idly toyed with a pack of sexy playing cards only to receive a sharp electric shock from the pack. I bought a variety of revolving and lighting-up bow ties, an exploding pen, dribbling glass, etc, etc, to give as presents at our New Year's Eve party.

For me a curious year. *Private Function* the unexpected highlight. *Brazil*, hard and salutary experience, looks like distinguishing itself in 1985. But I'd not found in 1984 a new and successful vein of creative writing. The limericks are slight, the 'Vikings' unsatisfactory, 'Fegg' fun and frivolity.

Best moment of the year is in the picture beside me as I write. Mother, hardly bigger than the railings behind her, standing, with a broad smile, on the snowy sidewalk of Brooklyn Heights, with the buildings of Southern Manhattan mushrooming behind her. Journey of the year, undoubtedly.

1985

Thursday, January 3rd

The papers are full of news of the *Life of Brian* ban by the IBA. *Guardian* reports/describes the film as 'parodying the life of Christ'. This misrepresentation irritates me and I spend the first working hour composing a letter to the paper.

Turn down four days' work on a P&O Ferries ad and a training film for a company called Interlink. Wash the Mini, take our old video recorder round to Alison Davies and meet her dog called Burglar. She says she does find calling him in at night quite silly.

Monday, January 7th

In the evening Rachel and I go to BAFTA for a special screening of *The Dress*. An overflowing house, with more than a dozen standing at the back.

Flurries of laughter at moments when I feel the film is taking itself too seriously, but apart from those and the fact that my shirt collar doesn't look as though it fits properly, I quite like the piece, or at least I don't cringe with embarrassment as I did at the Lumiere showing.

Rachel is quite pleased with herself too, and probably will never be as excited again by seeing her name on the credits.

Eva tells me that it will be going out in this country with *Beverly Hills Cop*, the Eddie Murphy film which is currently one of the biggest successes ever in the US.

David Leland rings with words of praise. 'Is there another side of Michael Palin I don't know about?' he'd asked himself. He thinks 'reaction' acting is the hardest of all to do. I still think it's the easiest.

Saturday, January 12th

After early shopping, take Rachel on a little birthday trip to the Bethnal Green Museum.

Then I take her to Islington to pick up a key for the Art Deco clock

I bought for TG's birthday, then lunch together at the Pizza Express there. We do enjoy ourselves and, on Rachel's last day in single figures, I can't help but feel glad that I'm enjoying her growing up – that I don't have a romantic, nostalgic, escapist longing for her to be five or six again.

A rather ordinary evening, enlivened a little by Tom arriving home about ten with 'some friends', five out of six of whom are women. They process through the house to No. 2. I feel like one of the exhibits at the Bethnal Green Museum, sitting by the fire reading my *New Statesman* as they peer curiously through the glass door at me.

Sunday, January 13th

Watch a very impressive programme on Alan Bleasdale. I envy his street wit, and his delight in writing and, in Bleasdale's case, the seriousness and urgency and fluency with which he seems to be able to write about now. Working-class writers seem to have much more to say about the present state of things. But will he be hoicked up by his talents into a sort of honorary middle-class writer? Watching the programme made me want to buckle down to my own writing. To produce something with some edge, some guts ...

Wednesday, January 16th

No fresh snow, but bitter cold. I hear that this is likely to be the coldest day in London for 20 years. Wrap up well, in double-sweater order, and once again get to grips with *East of Ipswich*. Pleased with the morning's progress. Am very strict about not answering the phone until one o'clock and it helps.

Phone my mother, who is resigned to her 'imprisonment', and re-plan my visit to Southwold for next Tuesday. Angela phones – Chilton without water despite being surrounded by a moat, which is frozen enough to skate on.

Some masochistic streak in me has me pulling on my tracksuit at two and off for a run. I've met most conditions in the five years I've been a Heath regular, but never cold as intense as this, and I feel I have to try it – one, because I feel I need exercise, and two, because it's there.

Monday, January 21st

Afternoon curtailed by an interview at the Python office with Michael Owen of the *Standard*. He's a card. A wry, gossipy, ruddy-faced little man. Sardonic and quite bitchy. He'd seen *Brazil* (although he doesn't admit so to start with) and couldn't make head or tail of it. I say I'm glad he isn't the cinema critic and ask where Mr Walker is these days ... 'Oh, in Hong Kong,' says Owen, 'doing something or other for the CIA.' Alexander Walker and the CIA, that's a new one.

Our chat, based on his viewing of *The Dress*, which he liked, is a little defensive – testing each other's tolerance towards teasing. He is one of the few journalists whom Maggie S gets on with. He describes her as a very rare and delicate thoroughbred, but admits that this is not the kind of thing he could say to her face ... 'You make me sound like a bloody horse,' he mimics, quite accurately.

Maggie is to get the *Standard* award for Millamant, he confides, indiscreetly.

Thursday, January 24th: Southwold

Put Mother's house once again on estate agents' lists, but this time with the serious intention of moving her within the year. The man I speak to says he has a house on the Common which is being converted into four flats. It sounds interesting. He suggests I move as quickly as possible as they are under offer already.

A light snow-shower swirls round the Common as we look at the architect's plans for the ironically-named Sunset House. The rooms look of reasonable size and, though the two ground-floor flats are already gone (to single, elderly ladies), there are two more, on the first and second floors, with two bedrooms. One of these is already being chased.

Home in good spirits, but no Helen, the fire won't light and the first stage BAFTA awards show nominations for *Private Function* as Best Film and in most categories except Best Actor. For an hour this hits me very hard, but looking at those who have been nominated (including, of course, the obligatory pair for *Killing Fields*), I realise how little chance an easy, natural, light comedy performance stands.

Monday, January 28th

To Odette's to meet Jonathan P.

He tells me that Liz Smith went all the way up to Leeds for the *Private Function* premiere last Thursday, a week early. He's getting quite a steady flow of job offers, including eight weeks in Samoa and Australia playing Robert Louis Stevenson. 'If only it weren't so bloody far away,' he mutters, rather gloomily.

Tuesday, January 29th

Best news of the day comes from John Kelleher at HandMade. *The Missionary* has finally been sold to a French distributor. They've had good reactions to their screenings and are spending 200,000 Francs on the launch!!! Les peanuts, mais c'est quelque chose.

Kelleher also tells me that *Private Function* is to open the LA Film Festival – Filmex – in March (as I think *Holy Grail* did about ten years ago). And *Private Function* has been selected for the Un Certain Regard category of the Cannes Film Festival – 'the second most prestigious category' as JK describes it.

See Maggie collect an *Evening Standard* award for Best Theatre Actress of '84. Maggie accepts it nervously and yet still has time to complain about the lack of heating in the Haymarket dressing rooms.

Monday, February 4th

I take a taxi to the Inn on the Park to meet Marvin Antonowsky, who called me yesterday. He hugs me to his bosom and then we have a drink and a chat.

He loves *Brazil* and likes to see himself as Terry's supporter against Sid Sheinberg. Sid S wants to cut the picture with Terry. Marvin thinks Terry should cut it without Sid, make ten minutes' difference, and then Sid S would be happy. Trouble stems from the contractual requirement to supply a 125-minute film, no more. TG has supplied a 140-minute film.

To Fitzroy Square to meet Tony Ross, who is to illustrate the limericks. He is a boyish, middle-aged man. He's soft-spoken, enthusiastic and went to art school with John Lennon. At one time he knew more guitar chords than John and claims to be the only man who was asked to join the Beatles but turned it down!

Wednesday, February 13th

Richard Benjamin[1] has rung Anne re a film part he wants me to do (via Spielberg's Amblin Entertainment). He's in town and would like to meet. The script is sent over. It's called *The Money Pit* (heart falls at the title) and it's by David Giler. There are hundreds of relentlessly funny New York Jewish one-liners, but the whole lacks any real warmth, depth of character or indeed charm of any kind.

I am to play the part of a successful, sexually irresistible orchestra conductor. Well ... I ask you.

Sunday, March 10th

To collect papers at ten. Mr Nice Man[2] has been attacked in his shop. Three days ago at four o'clock a boy of 15 or 16, wearing a mask and holding a gun, came into the shop with a bag which he laid on the counter and asked Mr N to fill with the money. He struck Mr N and as he fell down behind the counter he grabbed at something beneath it to break his fall. The 'gunboy' thought he was going to a weapon or an alarm and rushed off.

What can this intelligent, polite, hard-working Asian make of this country? I notice a greater contrast than usual between the US and the UK on my return [from *Private Function* publicity in New York & LA]. There seems to be a weariness here, a lack of direction, a lack of unity, a low national morale (the defeat of the miners is only seen as a great victory by the Thatcherites) and a feeling, quite unlike the States, that the bad news can only get worse.

Monday, March 11th

To the family dentist – Mr Lewis – in Camden Town. I no longer have enough confidence in Gerry Donovan to replace the constantly ejecting bridge. Quite a break, after 20 years with Gerry, whom I liked very much, except as a dentist.

---

1 Actor (*Goodbye Columbus*, 1969), producer and director. *The Money Pit* was eventually made with Tom Hanks, Shelley Long and Alexander Godunov in the lead roles and released in 1986.
2 Our family name for Mahendra 'Mash' Patel, who ran, and still runs, our local newsagents. He has a wonderful temperament and apparently limitless reserves of patience and tolerance.

Lewis's surgery is busy, unglamorous and informal. He is a very direct, no-nonsense Northerner, and impressed by the state of my mouth. 'Quite a battlefield in there,' he mutters in some awe. But he sounds much more businesslike than Gerry and clearly relishes sorting it all out.

I ring Susan Richards [at Enigma] for her reaction to *East of Ipswich*. She likes it and, more encouragingly, says she feels it is much nearer a finished product than a first draft. Puttnam and Goldcrest sound like parting company over the *First Love* series, which hasn't been a financial success, and Susan R has a Machiavellian plan to try and get them to drop *East of Ipswich* so it can then be taken to Anglia TV, who she thinks will absolutely leap at it.

Saturday, March 16th

Helen's taxi arrives at 4.30, which must be a record for early starts.[1] She looks almost unfairly bright and breezy considering the hour. Bid her goodbye from the top of the stairs, then back to bed and sleep through without difficulty for another three and a half hours.

I go up to Pizza Express with the Pryces. JP very funny about the 'celebrity' screening of *Brazil* at which no-one recognised him. He didn't mind so much before the film, but when, after two hours 22 minutes constantly on the screen, very often in searing close-up, the first person to come up to him afterwards said 'Are you Patrick?' he could take it no longer.

Tuesday, March 19th

Trying to keep up my resolution to catch up on movies while Helen is away, I drive down to Cinecenta to see *1984*. It impresses me a lot, though I can see why [Michael] Radford got annoyed with the grafting on of the Eurythmics soundtrack. He keeps very tight control of the picture and it's only when the modern music comes in that it begins to sound like a pop video.

Struck by the similarities with *Brazil*. The police state, the dreadful grubbiness of the city, the love story which is at the heart of the action, the tiling in the torturer's cell, the design of [Richard] Burton's office,

---

1 She was leaving for what had become annual skiing excursions with friends from her badminton class. This one was to Val d'Isère.

even the chair in Room 101 itself and the eventual destruction of the central character. It's all there in both films.

But whereas Radford keeps his nasty tale tightly under control, TG fires off in all directions. Difference between the two people, I suppose. But Radford's careful, wordy approach to his adaptation of the Orwell tale produces considerable yawns and restlessness, which I've never heard in a *Brazil* screening. Mind you, you can never hear anything in a *Brazil* screening apart from the film.

Monday, March 25th

To see Mr Lewis for preparation work on my new bridge.

Lewis is the complete renaissance dentist. He rambles on – no, ramble is not the word to describe his delivery, it's more abrasive, views expressed challengingly, inviting confrontation, which it's hard to provide with a mouth half full of mould-making gunge. Anyway, in an hour and a half he covers a wide ground from dentistry (which he loves), psychoanalysts (whom he doesn't like), nineteenth-century English watercolourists (who he not only likes, but collects and knows a lot about), to Russian drama (which he goes to see regularly with his wife, who is a Russian) and to holidays in a camper in Southern Turkey. Turkey he likes very much because it is as he remembered Greece (now spoilt) 25 years ago.

He enjoys playing to a captive audience, but does his job skilfully and carefully and with a pride in the result which dear Gerry never seemed to convey.

Tuesday, March 26th

The Missionary has won top prize at a festival of 'humorous films' at the French Alpine town of Chamrousse (which I check in the atlas. It *does* exist; it's near Grenoble).

A Private Function increased its take in NYC this weekend and went up in its second week in Boston. In the UK it will have grossed a million pounds by the end of the month and hopefully one and a half million pounds by mid-May. So over a third of the initial production cost could be cleared in the UK alone.

Wednesday, March 27th

Shivas sends over Canby's latest from the *New York Times*. He has written a long piece criticising the tendency to 'cynical' comedy – the Hollywood genre of *Ghostbusters, Porky's, Risky Business,* etc – and contrasting with 'sceptical' comedies exemplified by *Purple Rose of Cairo* and 'the delightful new British import *A Private Function*'. 'Performed with dazzling assurance by Miss Smith, Mr Palin, Denholm Elliott . . . *A Private Function* is a comedy of the first order . . .'.

To lunch at Odette's with Walmsley to give him the Glen Baxter entitled 'Walmsley seemed to be experiencing some difficulty with the seafood salad' – at which our waiter laughs so much he is unable to describe the vegetables and another, more serious waiter has to come and replace him.

Monday, April 1st: Glasgow

To Glasgow for *Private Function* publicity. A photo with the Lord Provost and two pigs in a pen outside the Odeon. The Lord Provost is a game little Scotsman who reluctantly enters the pen where two hairy pigs – one of which I'm assured is a boar – snuffle violently for food in a bucket, which I hold. The photographers shout at him as if he were some witless object – 'Lord Provost! Look up!'

Then into the theatre to talk to the audience after the screening. The film seems to have been appreciated. Sign autographs and generally receive good feedback from the young in the audience.

Then more photos with the pigs and the Lord Provost outside in the street. One of the pigs is snapping greedily – just like the photographers – and despite my warning that the food has run out they keep me in there until it bites my finger quite sharply, draws blood and at last they believe me.

Thursday, April 4th

Up to Hampstead to address the Hampstead Gay Community. The organiser apologised in advance for some recent poor attendances. He said that a well-known writer 'who shall be nameless' refused to speak until ten people arrived. They never did and he somewhat reluctantly spoke to nine. Last time they had an MP – Matthew Parris – who gave a complete, self-contained party political speech and no-one knew what to say afterwards.

So I am flattered to find 30 people at the Citizens' Advice Bureau – none of them looking anything other than completely respectable and demonstrating the shallowness of the archetypal 'gay' look. I respond to their general laughter and appreciation and thoroughly enjoy talking and answering questions for an hour and a half.

Friday, April 5th

After breakfast and settling and clearing my desk of immediate business, I settle down to read Paul Zimmerman's 'A Consuming Passion' as *Secrets* has now become. Full of expectations. But after a bright, but roughly-written opening, it gets stuck for page after page on a broad exploration of all the jokes about collecting human bodies, making it a heavy black farce rather than the sharp satire I'd hoped it could be.

At four I go to the Body Centre to play squash with TJ. We discuss our reactions. They're both the same. Disappointment.

Saturday, April 6th

Talk to Paul Z. He says TJ called him last night whilst 'well oiled' and was therefore able to be very frank. PZ sounds resilient, but clearly unhappy at our reaction. But Goldcrest and Goldwyn have reacted well and he (Paul) is so pleased with it, that he makes me feel rather a spoilsport. 'The ball's in your court now,' is Paul's view. 'Tell me what you want me to do.'

Tuesday, April 9th

A harassed Mr Jones arrives at half past ten. Settle down with a cup of tea. Then we begin to compare notes on the Zimmerman script, prior to meeting Paul at lunchtime.

As we talk it's clear that Terry and myself are in general agreement that what is wrong is that Paul has gone for a much too stylised, full-frontal, 'schlock' approach, emphasising the acquisition of meat and the procurement of human bodies much too directly. The tension of the concealment attempt has gone and the believability which to me seemed the raison d'être of the whole piece is shot to pieces.

It's clear that we cannot expect Paul to rewrite it on the lines we want, nor can we co-write it with Paul. Either we find a new writer altogether, or we abandon the project or Terry and I take it on.

Now, whether it's the effect of a beautiful spring morning, or sheer relief that there is a solution, or a real burst of new thoughts stimulated by Paul's work, or a combination of all three, Terry and I have not only decided that we shall write the next draft ourselves, but we've also set aside the rest of this week and dates in May and June to work on it.

Paul arrives here at one. He's as nervous as we are about 'the confrontation', but over lunch at a chic but quite deserted Belsize Village restaurant called The Orchard, all three of us discuss quite amicably and agreeably the proposed solution. Paul would like not to be 'dismissed from the case' completely, but to be there to advise and criticise. 'Use me, I'm quite good really.'

Sunday, April 14th

The *Sunday Times* echoes the prevalent optimism about London with a colour supplement devoted to the revival of the city. Periodically London is rediscovered, it blossoms then fades back into its elusive ordinariness whilst somewhere else is discovered. But if the '60's were Swinging London, the mid-'80's are Smart London. The 'revival' is based on money. On the ability of businessmen to do business with the Far East in the morning and New York in the afternoon of the same day. Thank God for the Greenwich Meridian.

Monday, April 15th

Cannot find the right book to read at the moment and feel very exercised about this. Decide on Arnold Bennett – because he describes 'ordinary people interestingly', it says on the blurb.

Saturday, May 18th: Southwold

A long night's sleep enlivened by some wonderful dreams, including Maggie Smith singing a song called 'Lobster Time'. A fine morning.

After breakfast we go to view progress at Sunset House. Shape of the rooms now clear, so we can make some early decisions about furniture, etc, which is really why Angela and I are up here together. One thing which slightly disappoints is the height of the bay window, which is such that when you sit you lose most of the view.

Monday, May 20th

I go to the French pub and there are Bernard McKenna and writer Colin Bostock-Smith, sharing a bottle of wine after the successful read-through of one of their scripts. Bernard has severed relations with GC after *Yellowbeard* disagreements. We retell good tales of Tunisia, including the time Bernard and Andrew MacLachlan got an entire Arab crowd to chant 'Scotland!' (when GC walked on as Biggus Dickus).

Wednesday, May 22nd

Woken by a loud crash outside the window. It's five a.m. In deepest sleep the sound seemed almost unreal, a jarring, violent impact with a high, almost metallic top note. Helen it is who discovers a pane of the down-stairs window smashed, apparently with the end of a stout, five-foot-long wooden post which lies outside the window. No sign of an attempt to break in. Back to bed after clearing it up. Slightly shaken, but I feel that it's one of those random, irrational acts of destruction which occasionally occur round here – plants pulled up, aerials bent. Neither of us can think of any reason someone would do it on purpose. Back to sleep. Helen dreams of massive disasters.

Thursday, May 23rd

At BAFTA at four to meet Tristram Powell, to talk about *East of Ipswich*. He is a lean, open-faced, relaxed man, anywhere between three and ten years older than me I would think.

He, it turns out, is a director, not a producer as I'd assumed, and I think would make a very good job of it. I feel quite a bond with him by the end of our chat. And I have a feeling he's Anthony Powell's son, but I never dared ask because it would have involved me having to admit I never made much headway with *Music of Time* Vol I. Now I'm determined to try again.

It would be very neat if all worked out and *East of Ipswich* could be made by Powell some time next year. Certainly our meeting today seems to have solved the major problem of director.

Collect Granny's clock from Camerer Cuss – always struck with curiosity as to how the clock expert there manages to reconcile such precision work with his very shaky hands.

Friday, May 24th

To Mayfair to meet TJ and then Sam Goldwyn re the 'Chocolate Project'. Meet TJ at a pub in Shepherd's Market. He's on good form – having just had a 'breakthrough' over the ending of *Erik the Viking*.

To Sam Goldwyn's flat in nearby Hertford Street. Shepherd's Market feels very much like Soho is always thought to be but never is. Here there are still ladies in doorways who say 'Hello' as you pass. Sam settles us both down with voluminous scotches and watches us talk about the film.

At one point find his wife standing at the open window of the bedroom and smoking out of it. When I asked her for the loo, she spun round like a 'B' movie actress playing guilt.

After a morale-boosting chat we share a taxi back to Cavendish Square, feeling rather jolly. The sky has cleared and left London looking fresh and sparkling.

Tuesday, May 28th: Abbotsley–London

Tom Maschler [of Jonathan Cape] rings in ebullient, heavy-sell mood to ask if I will write a children's story for a new book which will be 'a very big seller indeed'. He won't tell me why, but eventually he makes the secret sound so attractive to himself that he has to tell me. Holography is the key. A new process which can apply holographs to the illustrated page – he compares it to the pop-up book, or Kit Williams' *Masquerade* in potential appeal. Maschler exudes self-confidence, power, excitement, fame, success, but basically it's all a sales pitch. As Michael Foreman is the artist and as it only has 2,000 words, I express interest in a meeting later in June.

Wednesday, May 29th

Write to Al L and settle to watch the much looked-forward-to European Cup Final.[1] Instead find myself watching sickeningly familiar scenes of drunken fans fighting. This time, though, it is even worse – a wall has collapsed, killing 25. No-one seems to know what is going on. Fans are throwing missiles at each other; police with riot shields seem to wander about the ground to no particular plan or purpose, occasionally hitting people as hard as they can. The fences look flimsy, the barriers between the rival sets of supporters virtually non-existent. What were they expecting?

The death toll from the wall collapse mounts, but the crowd, on the verge of hysteria anyway, are not told. Jimmy Hill and Terry Venables trade solutions – national service (Venables), withdrawal of passports, more Thatcherite toughness (Hill), and Bobby Charlton chips in with a plea for the restoration of corporal punishment.

But it is the lack of any controlling hand over the activities at the stadium that is most frightening. Fortunately most of the crowd wait patiently and sensibly, but the 'minority' still hurl anything they can lay their hands on. At one end a group of Italian boys posture and swagger with sticks and iron piping, whilst the Brussels police just watch.

Thursday, May 30th

To the Royal Academy to look at the Summer Exhibition. Somewhere inside me I just want to enjoy the good things of Britain after the awful shame of Brussels. The events last night were a national humiliation and there's a sense of sobering shock today, mixed with an almost eerie frisson of fear. I think the actuality TV coverage has made the difference, causing millions of people to experience the violence as if they were actually there.

Crowds mill around the elegant rooms of Burlington House. See one small painting I fancy for £200, but it is snapped up just ahead of me. Come away with only a confused swirl of images in my mind – landscapes, Bonnard-esque views from interiors out through windows, occasional nudes and comfortable portraits of successful middle-aged men.

1 The match, between Juventus and Liverpool, took place at Heysel Stadium in Brussels. Thirty-six Juventus supporters died when Liverpool fans charged at them and a wall collapsed. The game went ahead, Juventus winning 1–0. English clubs were banned from all European football competitions for the next five years.

Some shopping, then home by cab.

Julian Hough has dropped in. He's just out of the Scrubs, and Helen says he went on about how nice they all were inside, reading Camus and Shakespeare.

Friday, May 31st: Hull

To King's Cross to catch the train up to Hull for my 'celebrity lecture'. [Part of a series of appearances outside London, which I, and others, had agreed to give for British Film Year.]

No seats are booked in a crowded Edinburgh express and one of the HST cars fails, so we arrive at Doncaster 40 minutes late and have to take a taxi on to Hull. We arrive at the party to launch the Hull Film Festival somewhat rushed. I'm shown straight to the Disabled toilet.

Then into a room full of local worthies. Have to remember that the *Life of Brian* is still banned in Hull! Some sweet German wine, a bite at a buffet and a chat with two very nice people who won a competition for seats at the lecture (which sold out two weeks ago) by answering questions such as 'What was the name of the leading pig in *Animal Farm*?'

Who should then stroll onto the scene but J Cleese, who begins work on a Frayn script, *Clockwise*, in Hull on Sunday.

John had hoped to get into the lecture unannounced and ask rude questions from the back. As it is, I find him all too near – in the second row, just below the stage on which Iain [Johnstone] and myself recline in rather grand, high-backed winged armchairs.

Q and A with the audience is successful and we go on for 90 minutes before Iain asks John if he has any words to sum up Michael Palin. Poor JC. He tells the audience that I am the most genuinely silly person he knows. 'He doesn't have to work at it. It's straight from the heart.' I counter by thanking JC for teaching me everything I know.

Discuss mothers with JC, who says with feeling 'My mother is dreadfully stupid, completely neurotic, but I do like her.' Later JC thaws out enough to say 'You know, the other day I suddenly thought how nice it would be to do another Python TV series.' Here he pauses, very effectively. 'I thought that for about six hours.'

Saturday, June 1st: Hull

Driven by the organiser of the Festival, together with two friends, out to
Beverley, a very attractive little town. The Minster dominates the skyline
rather like the church at Haarlem in seventeenth-century Dutch landscapes. Honey-coloured stonework, very beautiful decoration around the
west front, a fine building.

A thriving market place in which stands our destination – the Playhouse Theatre. Built as the Corn Exchange, it has been a cinema for over
50 years. Now run by a largely volunteer force and saved from closure by
a fire-eater and his wife. It doesn't make much money, but they count
Private Function as a great success – an average of 99 a night, says the
manager.

Up a ladder through the projection room to the manager's office, where
I am treated to some of his grapefruit wine. More photographs. Local
paper not there, which seems a poor piece of organisation.

From the Picture Playhouse to a Sam Smith's pub known colloquially
as 'Nellies' – run until a few years ago by two 80-year-olds who insisted it
should not be substantially altered. So, aside from bare wood everywhere,
there is also gas light and in the evenings a folk band plays by candlelight.

Back to Hull, pausing to look at 29 Victoria Avenue, where the parents
lived in 1932/33. A small, characterful Edwardian semi, with a big mock-
Tudor gable and some quite elegant stained glass. It stands in a modest,
leafy avenue, built as part of a 'development' with wholly surprising
baroque fountains at two of the crossroads.

Home by four. Helen in the garden. Join her and am quite lazy until
it's time to go next door to Eliz and Elias' for dinner. Five psychoanalysts
there. Two Americans, two Brazilians, two Argentinians. The conversation tends to the serious and there is much post-mortemising of the
Brussels riots.

Elias thinks that part of the problem is that the English bottle their
feelings and passions up – there isn't much on-street or café debate and
discussion. Emotions too are kept tightly under control, so that when
they snap they snap more fiercely and a lot more repression is poured
out than in Brazil. The Argentine thinks that the British lack of volatility
does have its advantages.

Wednesday, June 5th

Michael Barnes rings at breakfast time to discuss Belfast Festival dates.

More thunder forecast today. As I run over Parliament Hill I look out over London and it lies swathed in a soggy mist, as if it's raining upwards from the ground.

Tom is in school doing his second exam paper of the day – 'O' Level French – William is off school for four days during this fortnight because of teachers' 'industrial action'.

Some more writing, then drive into London, park at the Chinatown car park – near whose entrance gather a group of winos, who sit amongst the litter, occasionally hugging each other, their red blotchy faces the doors they've shut against the rest of the world. If they were rich they'd be in clinics in Hertfordshire.

Tuesday, June 11th

Osborne of Adnams rings to tell me that a new offer of £44,000 for Croft Cottage has been received from the single lady, Mrs Marshall. Should he go back to the couple? I made it clear that I and Ma and Angela all would like the house to go to someone who will live there. This apparently counts out the couple, who want it as a second home, until their retirement. So after some to-ing and fro-ing I agree on Ma's behalf to start negotiations for the sale of the house for £44,000.

Wednesday, June 12th

I work through the work I've done in the last two weeks on 'Chocolates'. Then at 12.30 down to TJ's. He has been suffering a 'low-grade headache' for the past two weeks and this finally laid him low over the weekend.

He does perk up, though, enough to get angry about Mary White-house's remarks re the Brussels tragedy in the *Guardian*. She sees it as an indictment of the permissive liberalism of the last 30 years!

Despite his low state of health he comes up with some good and incisive comments. I leave my notebook with him and at 4.30 set off to drive across London to the TV Centre.

Arrive at White City about five minutes late for a meeting with Innes Lloyd and Tristram P re *East of Ipswich*. Innes Lloyd [Alan Bennett's favourite producer] has the reassuring look of a much-loved schoolmaster and the bearing of a naval commander. Tall, upright, of good colour and gentlemanly amiability, I find it hard to immediately connect him with Alan's caustic Northern observations, but easy to like and trust him.

He says he loved the script and we talk for less than half an hour before deciding that it should be approached primarily as a TV film – and who better to do it than the Beeb? Innes L will put it to [Peter] Goodchild, who's head of drama. Leave the BBC feeling very hopeful. Like Ma's house, this project seems to be fitting together suspiciously easily.

Sunday, June 16th

About to rush to squash with Richard when George H calls from Australia. He's in a Sydney hotel room (it's 2.30) and for some reason announces himself as Jane Asher. He sounds at first rather sleepy and, as the call goes on, rather drunk. I'm reminded of GC's inexplicable midnight calls, except there is no invective here, just a rather sad GH reflecting on the joys of chewing 'Nicorette' gum, and anxious to tell me that he's given up smoking, and drugs, and his only vice is Carlton Lager, three of which he's just consumed. He wants to know if I will come to China with him and his acupuncturist next year.

Monday, June 24th

At six I am at Tom Maschler's office at Jonathan Cape. A huge, at present characterless room, dominated by a carefully restored Adam ceiling (all Robert Adam's specifications, including choice of colour, were found in the British Museum).

Tom, lean and brown and smoking roll-ups, presides over a cautious little group, including Mike Foreman and a man whose name I never really catch. He is the hologram expert, a big man with the look of an early 1970's rock drummer.

The book, as Maschler assured me, could make us all *very* rich, and the early 1970's rock drummer [Richard Seymour] emphasises that it must be of the finest quality, using holograms integrated into the text and into M Foreman's illustrations. It sounds exciting and, as they all turn and look at me hopefully, I say yes and promise to write a new, two- to three-thousand-word children's ghost story by the time we leave for the Seychelles (about five weeks away).

Back home I hear from Tristram Powell that Peter Goodchild likes *East of Ipswich* very much and wants to go ahead with it – probably next April.

Sunday, June 30th: Southwold

Helen drives me down to Liverpool Street. They have begun work on the demolition of Broad Street, which is a sad sight – its façade is one of the finest and most unusual of all London's main terminals.

At Ipswich Station, I'm buying a cup of coffee when a 'youth' on roller skates rockets into the station, grabs hold of me to steady himself and shouts 'Get the police'. He's followed by a very thin, weedy, unhealthy-looking man who proceeds to attack the roller-skater and heap curses at him. Then a very angry lady arrives and screams abuse – 'You fucking pervert', that sort of thing. A burly American keeps them apart and does a fine job, but the ferocity of the woman's anger – 'You insulted my father-in-law last night ... you faggot!' – takes quite a while to subside.

Saturday, July 13th

To the desk for an hour, lunch and flop out again, periodically watching the Live Aid concert and the Test Match. First quite upstages the second. Wembley packed and from the air looking like an open sardine can, but no menace in the presence of this huge crowd (well, I suppose they've all paid £25 minimum). It looks like a day out for the white and well-off. But the music is good, the spontaneity of a live event exciting and, because it is a Giant Global Good Deed, everyone feels united in a most unusual way. If I were a rock promoter I'd feel vaguely uneasy about the happiness which is engendered when people know that no-one is making a profit.

Thursday, July 18th

At two o'clock I'm at BUPA for a screening (medical, that is). Two years since I was last here and feel that I should keep up regular inspections. Everything seems to be fine. On the computer questionnaire I print in that my libido has decreased – mainly because I'm bored with my own lack of any interesting medical history but the doctor doesn't seem interested. My favourite this time is 'Have your stools changed colour recently?'

With my body well serviced, I return home, make some calls, then go to put on my DJ for a black-tie invitation to *The Life and Death of Colonel Blimp* at the Screen on the Hill, in celebration of 50 years of the National Film Archive. No DJ. Remember Ed B borrowed it for Glyndebourne. Race round to Albert Street with half an hour to spare and collect it. Then find that I can't remember how to tie my bow properly. Eventually it comes back to me, after a fashion.

Arrive at the cinema with 15 minutes to spare. Have my photo taken with Romaine and then TG and Maggie arrive. Both TG and myself have made an attempt at black-tie. Jonathan Miller and Jack Gold and Gavin Millar have neither tie nor black.

Michael Powell and Pressburger come onto the stage at the beginning. Powell, arms stiffly at his sides, looking like a well-disciplined doorman in his plum-coloured tuxedo, beams wickedly. Emeric Pressburger is close by his side, but is old and can't move much and looks a bit like Powell's dummy.

Powell starts by telling us what a very British film this is – 'Shot by a Frenchman, produced by a Hungarian, designed by a Prussian, scored by a Czech …' He reflects a moment, then continues, 'In fact about fifty percent of the crew were enemy aliens at the time.' He gently but firmly debunks the notion of film-makers making a grand decision to work for a particular country – films were made 'where they fell'.

Pressburger comments rather acidly on the need for an intermission because the projection at the Screen isn't able to show 160 minutes non-stop. 'I was quite pleased when I heard that there was an intermission, as it showed that 1940's film-making was ahead of 1980's technology.'

Then they trot off and the epic begins. As a piece of comedy it has its ups and downs – some gross over-playing in minor roles (of the Germans, of course), and some long, laboured comedy scenes – but always surprises – the beauty of the sets, the superb colour, the lovely performances, especially of Anton Walbrook. In the end a feeling of having seen a warts and all tribute to Britishness – its heroism, naivety, bumbling incompetence, luck and charm.

Friday, July 19th

Lunch with Puttnam.

The Mission is responsible for him losing a stone in weight. The food in Colombia was dreadful. They're now on their way (by overland convoy) to Argentina to finish shooting. He's confident it will work, but is tight-lipped about 'Revolution', which he says has been very badly organised and is four million over on below the line costs.

He says straightaway that he's happy for me to take *East of Ipswich* to the BBC. But 'get in there quick', he confides and advises that I keep foreign rights and access to negative (to blow it up from 16 to 35 if necessary) and outtakes. Try a 50/50 split with the Beeb on all foreign proceeds.

Now he's lost some fleshiness around his face, his big eyes look out through his trim beard, at which he tugs when he's not running his fingers along the inside of his collar.

As usual I am drawn by his liveliness, good sense and charm to overlook the relentlessness of the hustle, the continual selling and the breathless pace of the man's life. But as a gossip, he's second to none. The Royal Family detest Thatcher, but Prince Charles has a lot of time for Ken Livingstone – as does his mother!

Monday, July 22nd

At midday begin the ghost story [for the hologram book]. I don't feel in a very good frame of mind about it. I feel that I've accepted an unnecessary pressure – to come up with a story merely so that Maschler can sell it at Frankfurt. Would it not be better to take time to find the *best* story, then sell it?

Perhaps sensing a mixed enthusiasm, my system rebels and I find myself with the worst sort of literary lassitude.

Despite the hostile weather outside – fierce gusting winds bringing dark clouds over low and fast from the west – I decide running is the only way to break out of this slumberland. Hard to stand at the top of Parliament Hill, so strong is the westerly gale, but after that it improves and at one point I'm running in sunshine and looking out over a thin, black-clouded belt of rain drifting right across Central London.

Once back I find myself much fresher and sharper and, carrying on through the evening until 10.45, I complete a ghost story. Not, I feel, *the* ghost story, but at least something to show I've tried.

Thursday, July 25th

Only with meticulous plans and copious lists will I be able to survive today. So many projects have to be attended to, cosseted, completed and confronted, as tomorrow I intend to put up the shutters until September.

Various calls to bring the Croft Cottage/Sunset House situation up to date. Brian D [Duncan, builder] promises me that September 30th will be a sensible date to aim to have moved in by. Ring Ma. She worries, despite all my assurances. 'I've never done anything quite like this in my life,' she tells me. There's a first time for everything, even at 81, and I try and set her mind at rest and give a generally reassuring morale boost. She's trying so hard not to be a burden, but has to reiterate how she finds it such a lot of money and almost implying she's not worth it. She has the good, solid Christian virtues that money and wealth mean not a thing – but spends all her life worrying about them.

Monday, August 12th

To a meeting re 'A Consuming Passion' at Goldcrest.

The sumptuous luxury of their new Wardour Street HQ is something of an irony in view of their recent, well-publicised financial troubles and boardroom struggles. But at the moment they're still in business and, in amongst the carpets, the mirrors, the high-tech decor and internal gardens, we set to discussing our low-budget comedy!

Goldwyn is there, Amanda [Schiff] and Sandy [Lieberson], who joins us later. Goldwyn is the most concerned. He doesn't like Watney killing Rose, Kingsley and Irons. He feels that this will be a shock for the audience. Terry J accepts this, but thinks that the audience need to be shocked. Well, we're not prepared, says Sam, for a character we've grown very fond of to kill another character we've grown very fond of. Both TJ and myself are unable to press home our disagreement with total conviction, as neither of us have read the script for two weeks.

Sandy L breezes in. He's been trout-fishing with Puttnam in Wiltshire. He takes a back seat to Sam when discussing the script. Various suggestions for adopting, adapting and improving come up and TJ and myself agree to rewrite in mid-September. Sam G is trying to push the film in November, which is clearly going to be a rush, but reveals that he doesn't consider his criticisms basic enough to hold up the making of the picture.

Talk turns to directors. TJ won't say he can't do it, so that door is still left ajar. Loncraine's name comes up. Sam G roots for Malcolm M.

We break up about six, with rough agreement on rewrites, no decision

on director or shooting date and no further meetings planned until
September.

Wednesday, August 14th

TG appears.

The *Brazil* battle is hotting up. Arnon [Milchan], who TG says now
has the bit between his teeth, is showing the uncut print to as many
influential people as he can in New York. Alan Hirschfield [at Twentieth
Century Fox] rang Sid Sheinberg and offered to buy the film. Universal
declined and are threatening legal action to stop Arnon showing the
original version to critics, etc.

TG leaves after doing a very funny mime of chimpanzees mating,
which he saw on some TV nature film.

Friday, August 16th: Oslo–Haugesund, Norway

[On a train across Norway, on way to British Film event.] The driver is
called John, he's younger than me and wears a constant half-smile.

As we pass placid, glassy-calm lakes I mutter the usual appreciations.
Not for a moment relaxing his quiet smile, he reminds me that there is
'no life' in these picturesque lakes, thanks to pollution from Britain and,
to a lesser extent, Germany and Poland. The Norwegians are not at all
happy about the British attitude (which is to do bugger all and stop others
from doing anything) and I cannot defend it and am quite embarrassed.
He's proud, though not crowingly so, that Norway has the second highest
standard of living in Europe and the second lowest unemployment rate
(in both cases after Switzerland). But there are only four million of them.

No restaurant car at all on this six and a half hour journey and on the
trolley only rolls and no alcohol, except for a special low-strength beer,
which has all the adverse effects of making you flatulent with none of the
benefits of either taste or mild euphoria.

The Norwegians control alcohol sales very carefully. Only government
monopoly shops can sell liquor at all and then only at certain times of
day. Consequently, JJ [John Jacobsen, my host] confirms, there is a lot of
drunkenness and moonshining.

We climb to a summit of 4,300 feet above the tree line and above the
cloud into a brightly-lit no-man's-land of grey rocks and dirty snow.

We reach Bergen at 2.05 and walk rather aimlessly from the station towards the quayside – the Brygge – where are the tall, thin houses of the Hanseatic merchants, before queuing for the hydrofoil in rapidly-deteriorating weather.

A three-hour journey. Both of us sleep for a time and I read some of A Powell, which feels very incongruous. We stop four or five times at various islands and reach Haugesund about five minutes late.

JJ is quite anxious by now, evidently hotel bookings have been confused and we are expected by the Mayor at dinner within ten minutes. Both of us change in my room.

I can't find the bathroom light or get the key out of the door. JJ can't find the lavatory flush. Fifteen minutes of pure Keystone Cops before we emerge, only slightly less crumpled than before, but at least be-suited.

A long table, set with British flags amongst the flower arrangements. Myself and JJ, whose attitude to things I quite like, are sat at the end like naughty schoolboys. In the middle are the likes of Roger Moore, Liv Ullman and the Mayor and British Ambassador.

Speeches at the end. The Mayor of Haugesund is very smooth and fluent and uses references to Andy Capp – 'We're passing one of the oldest pubs in London. Capp: Why?' – and manages to be politely flattering about the James Bond movie *View to a Kill*, with which the festival has just opened.

The British Ambassador murmurs a vague and wet 'Hello' as he passes. Clearly not the slightest clue who I am. JJ feels that we've been upstaged by Bond. Frankly I was much happier at the naughty boys' end of the table.

Saturday, August 17th: Haugesund, Norway

We visit the world's largest herring table, which stretches for a couple of hundred yards up the main street in an attempt to break the Guinness world record for serving the greatest variety of herrings! Pickled herring in pineapple – that sort of thing.

The *Private Function* press conference has been moved from the hotel to the YMCA. Here, in a gloomy, inhospitable hall, about 30 journalists gather. A quick and nervous man takes it upon himself to introduce me and act as interlocutor. To add to the absurdity, two heavy mikes are on the desk top in front of us.

This overkill produces one of the most uninformative and pointless press conferences I've ever attended. But I have to maintain calm and composure through silly photos outside and two more interviews, even though I'm hot, tousled, sweaty and smell of crab and shrimp.

Nor is there any let-up. Before I can go back to the hotel I have to go to rehearsals for the Amanda Awards, Norway's first ever film and TV awards ceremony. I have the unlikely honour of presenting the first Amanda of all time.

Norway's leading theatre actress introduces herself enthusiastically to me. She's called Winky and as far as I can tell the show's producer is called Bent.

Leave the hotel at 9.45 for the awards. These go off quite well and I just about get away with my Norwegian pronunciation. At the end all the presenters have to reassemble on stage and simulate the spontaneous joy, happiness, warmth and wonderfulness of the occasion. It's during this ordeal that friendly Liv Ullman shakes my hand and introduces herself and says she hopes I'm going to the party afterwards. We all stand there with bunches of carnations whilst the press snap away.

At last, when it's time to go, Roger Moore suggests I come with him and his party back to the Park Hotel – he hints mysteriously at the chance of crayfish. But I have to find JJ and hope I'll get a chance to talk to Liv Ullman so, unlike Roger M, I give the official party a try.

Crowds of people, but no Liv Ullman.

When at last I reach the Park Hotel it must be around three o'clock. Whom should I encounter on entering, but Roger Moore. 'Michael! You *missed* the crayfish!'

He welcomes me profusely, and brings from his room a bottle of Chivas Regal and a bottle of Glenfiddich and sets them on the table.

He really wants to say how much he wants to work with us, how he loved everything I'd ever done and watched me on the *Cavett Show* (why this comes up particularly, I don't know) and so on. He is especially keen to know what Gilliam is like to work with.

At one point a hotel guest comes up to Moore for his autograph. As he signs, Moore points at me and asks the poor petitioner if he knows who I am. The man nods and reveals that he saw *Private Function* this morning. 'Did you like it?' asks Moore. He nods. 'Which did you like most, his film or mine?' Bravely the man considers, then, with a shriek from Roger Moore, indicates me.

As we set off for bed, Moore reiterates his desire to do something – indeed anything – with the Pythons. 'I work cheap.'

It is a quarter to five.

Tuesday, August 20th

Lunch with Basil and Pat [Pao].

Basil spent two weeks in Cotignac working on 'The Rutland Isles' script with EI. Basil suggested a change in approach which was evidently too drastic for Eric, so the collaboration sounds only fifty percent successful. He seems now much more certain that he will get the job of assistant art director on the Bertolucci China movie [*The Last Emperor*] if and when the finance is finalised.

Into Covent Garden for some shopping, to Peter Lewis in Parkway for a check on my new bridges. He took his family in a minivan up the east coast, then up through Lancashire. 'Depressed towns really interest me.' He went to Rochdale, on his holiday.

Thursday, August 22nd: Southwold

Outside it begins to rain heavily and I hear the clock strike one downstairs well before I slip off to sleep. I wake about six hours later and lie for a while wondering why I was able to sleep for nine hours night after night in the Seychelles. I conclude that I am suffering from a condition which expands even small anxieties into a general level of tension which it's hard to evade at night and which awaits me first thing in the morning. Not that today threatens any major worries, but maybe Tom's imminent 'O' Level results are there at the back of it all.

Hear Mother coughing. She 'wakes' me at 8.15. There's been another air crash, she says, pushing aside the curtains to reveal the clear blue sky of a perfect East Anglia morning, something at Manchester . . .

Phone rings at ten. It's Tom. He sounds worried, says Mother, holding out the phone and looking thoroughly confused. Talk to him. He's passed in six out of seven subjects so far, with chemistry a disaster and English still to come. This is right at the top end of his (and my) expectations and I'm terribly pleased for him.

Talk on the phone to Tom Maschler. Bad news, he says, Michael Foreman has decided he hasn't time to be involved. 'He's probably heading for a nervous breakdown,' confides Tom. Maschler, I fear, is one of those manically energetic souls who never get nervous breakdowns, only give them to others.

Monday, September 2nd

Lunch with Geoffrey Strachan. We meet at 1.15 in Fleet Street Rugantino's and talk about GS's idea for a Palin travel book. Decide that it should take the form of a diary, should be unashamedly personal and subjective and based on my notes taken over the years, as well as trips to come. GS likes my plain title 'Going Abroad', and I quite like 'Travelling to Work'. Agree it should be a project for at least two years hence. Both of us become very enthusiastic.

After lunch I walk to the Turf Club for my annual visit.

The club is open, but deserted. I sit myself at one of the dull, brown leather armchairs on the dull, green carpet beside the huge windows overlooking the dull drizzle over St James's Park.

On the way out I at last hear sounds of life from the billiard room, but on looking in find the barman playing on his own. By the door there is a neatly-typed notice reminding members that denim jeans are not considered permissible apparel. I leave and cross the road in the rain. Looking back I have the melancholy feeling I've just visited a benevolent old uncle in hospital. And he hasn't long to live.

Tuesday, September 3rd

TG comes round and we proceed together to the BBC for a photo-session and lunch/reception to mark the release of the Python videos.

On the way TG brings me up to date with the *Brazil* saga. Sheinberg is refusing to make up his mind, but has it put about that he will not be releasing the picture this year, and that there is still work to do on it.

But Arnon M has artfully revealed to an LA journalist that several of the national critics, including Bruce Williamson and Joel Segal, have seen the film in its original version and raved about it. The story, published in an LA paper recently, has added fuel to the controversy and hopefully will force Sheinberg into a more positive attitude. A decision is expected this weekend.

We assemble in a bunker-like room beneath the BBC in Langham Place. Terry J is back from France and looks slightly dazed. Graham, rather pale and thin-faced, is benign, amused and, as always, not quite there, and John, sporting a blue pin-stripe suit with dead parrot tie, is his usual lordly self. Eric is not present.

We have our photos taken with rather dog-eared cut-outs of Michelangelo's 'David' in a small garden in Cavendish Place. It's all rather low-key, as none of us can think of anything interesting to do, and we all come to the conclusion that zaniness after 40 isn't possible.

Back to the basement, where food has been laid out (including dressed crab, which is definitely a step up in BBC's catering style) and a Python video replays 'Piranha Brothers' and 'The Spanish Inquisition' in the background.

After what seems like an hour of talking, one of the organisers notices I haven't had a spare breath for any food. Gulp down some crab and pâté and then am dragged back to answering why the Pythons don't get together any more, when all I want to do is get together with the other Pythons.

Wednesday, September 4th: London–Southwold

Talk with Richard Seymour – the hologram man. They now have secured the services of Alan Lee to replace Mike Foreman. According to Seymour he is the finest illustrator working in the country today – as was Mike Foreman, when he was on the project.

I feel more and more like the world-weary, worldly-wise old owl these days.

As the rain and wind spread yet again from the west, I go to bed with *Adrian Mole*, which I'm discovering for the first time, and find it makes me laugh very much and, I think, for all the right reasons.

Friday, September 6th: Southwold

Sleep well and wake in good spirits to a bright, cloudless sky. To work by 9.30 after a bloater breakfast. Quite a successful morning on 'Cyril', considering this is my first day devoted entirely to the new project. *Cyril and the House of Commons* comes together quite nicely.

After lunch I concentrate on the clearing of Croft Cottage. Already we've filled a black bag with old bills and accounts and other minutiae which my father would never throw away. Go through a lot of photographs from the halcyon days of my father's life. Full of smiles on the liner *Arcania* coming back from the USA in the mid-twenties. Lots of pictures of him dressing up and fooling about, then some more suave portraits. His nose and prominent, rather sensuous eyes and lips remind me closely of Tom P. He was a very pretty boy and doubtless had to fight off a few at Shrewsbury!

The clearing is at once a revelation and an irksome, rather depressing job. My mother keeps finding fresh bags of letters, or old ties, or other objects, which appear, unannounced, on my bed, on the desk where I'm working, or in the middle of a room we've just cleared.

In late afternoon I revisit Sunset House and find two or three things still to be done. Drop in on Brian Duncan who is, as usual, gaily reassuring about everything.

Back to Croft Cottage for what I suppose may be my last run along these lanes.

It couldn't be a more perfect evening to remember them by. A big, burning, golden sun slowly descending behind Reydon Church, brushing the deep golden brown of the corn with a tinge of red. A harvester, with visored driver, is cutting the corner field.

Sunday, September 8th

In mid-afternoon I drive down to the V&A to see the watercolours of Bonington, Prout and others of the early nineteenth century. This at the behest of Lewis the Dentist, who collects nineteenth-century water-colours.

Find an artist called William Wyld, who excites greater admiration than either the neat, methodical Prout or the elusive, but exceptional, Bonington.

Then up to the top floor of the Harvey Cole Wing to look at the Constables – very appropriate as I did homage to Dedham Vale yesterday. Realise for the first time that the A12 dual carriageway runs clean across the middle of Constable's favourite view.

Monday, September 9th

Back to 'A Consuming Passion'. TJ reads me, over the phone, a letter from Paul Z – 'Seriously, I hope you won't fault me if this letter doesn't overflow with enthusiasm for a draft that virtually obliterates my previous work.' His letter is like Paul – funny, articulate and bracing. But his reaction, together with Amanda's two-page critique, combine to reduce our energy and enthusiasm. Suddenly it's an uphill task again.

After lunch TJ suggests we avoid Grove Park for working as they have a pneumatic drill in action. So we go instead to his boat in St Katharine's Dock. Here, two huge cranes swing round on a nearby building site, helicopters rattle overhead every 15 minutes and there's the constant distraction of various other members of the boat-owning community arriving back unsteadily from lunches.

The dock should be a charming, attractive haven, but I feel uneasy there. Uneasy at the scale of development, building and demolition which marks the 'regeneration' of Dockland. It's being largely undertaken by the big construction companies and will, I fear, come out as a grotesque parody of Olde London – neither excitingly modern nor convincingly historic. I think it'll be buggered up in the way the City of London has buggered up its Thames shoreline (though perhaps nothing could be as bad as that).

Wednesday, September 11th

Have been dipping into V Woolf's extraordinary diaries over the last few days and found a neat phrase – to 'rout the drowse'. Sounds like street talk, in fact it describes what a good walk does for her creative energy. So, as I feel increasingly addled, I eventually go for a run, which routs the drowse most successfully.

We seem unable to clinch a screenplay and I think it's because we have different preferences which it's hard to reconcile – TJ for fantasy and more overt moralising, myself for the fine detail of life, without necessarily having to make a judgement. TJ wants to be engaged in the issues. He wants to tackle injustice, incompetence, bigotry or whatever head on. I am more the spectator. More detached, therefore perhaps more able to go in close without getting stung.

TJ carries an emotional involvement into everything he does, finding it difficult not to say everything he wants to say about the world in each script, which is why he isn't so good on characters. He won't stand back and allow them to have a life of their own.

Friday, September 13th

Feel somewhat lethargic and lacking in clear-headed energy for today's vital decisions on 'A Consuming Passion'.

Clearly TJ doesn't want to have anything more to do with the rewrites as he has pressing problems of his own – 'Erik' and 'Nicobobinus' [his children's story] foremost – so I suggest that I write a third draft, aiming to complete in relatively unrushed time – by Christmas or late November if possible. This decision lightens both our minds. The only factor which could affect it is quite a surprise – Amanda Schiff rings to say she's being made redundant by Goldcrest. Sandy L will ring. Where all this leaves us I don't know.

Tuesday, September 17th

Meet Sandy L at the Flask. The meeting becomes like a Python sketch when a very chatty young man in a suit becomes irrevocably involved in our discussions after recognising me and then TJ.

So, whilst Sandy explains, lengthily and frankly, the politics at Goldcrest which have led to his resignation, he has occasionally to answer questions like 'What do you do?', 'What *is* a producer?', and so on. Sandy is marvellous and plays it most courteously and unpatronisingly and patiently. But it is rather like having one of our own creations – a Pither or a Charlie Legs – incarnated before our very eyes.

Wednesday, September 18th

To Chelsea by cab to be witnesses at Richard and Felice's nuptials.

The Chelsea Register Office is decorated rather like one of those 'no questions asked' hotels where you go when you're not married. There's a lot of Indian restaurant flock wallpaper and cheap chandeliers. As far as I can see there are no fresh flowers. You probably have to order those yourself. The short speech from the Registrar binds Richard and Felice to eternal faithfulness, which Richard thinks is 'a bit much'.

We drive back to their house and kill time for a couple of hours, which is an odd way to carry on on a precious weekday working morning, but a rather satisfactory change of pace. Time to take in all the wonders of Richard's interior decoration – his kettle which makes the noise of an American train whistle when it boils, his compact disc set-up, his several thousand pounds' worth of bicycle. He asks me if I'll come on a cycling and railway trip through Java in November. Apart from my Belfast commitments, I think I wouldn't know how to work his bicycles.

Thursday, September 19th

At eight walk up to William Ellis for a meeting to hear the local MP for the school, Geoffrey Finsberg, talk about the eight-month-old dispute between teachers and Sir Keith Joseph. Finsberg talks for a half-hour with the soulless precision of a politician who has been too well briefed. He concentrates almost entirely on the teachers' rejection of a new pay and promotion package three days ago and their refusal to go to arbitration.

No-one makes the pithy point that if this package is so wonderful, why wasn't it offered eight months ago? The questions from the floor come, for the first half-hour, from articulate, organised opposition, whether Labour Party members or teachers, and Finsberg quite happily deals with them. They're his own breed after all.

Driven by fear that he will go away with the impression (that he so wants to go away with) that we parents are being innocently led to the slaughter by a militant, unionised minority, I stand up at the end and ask him why he thinks Sir Keith Joseph is so generally and universally disliked and mistrusted by teachers of all shades of opinion. He slips out of the question as smoothly as he slips out of the meeting five minutes later.

Saturday, September 28th: Southwold

The day of the Great Move. Everything is on schedule. Angela has been up there for a day already.

The weather has made everything much more like a celebration, less like a departure. The sun is warm and bright and generous and makes the spreading panorama from the windows of Flat 2, Sunset House, a very adequate replacement for the cosier, more reassuring cornfields on either side of Croft Cottage.

The Herberts moon about until about half past eight or nine, then Veryan, who has been hanging mirrors, screwing in toilet rolls and coat hooks, Marcus, who's been telling me all about his recent trip to Burma and Thailand and Malaysia, as I stack books and shelves, and Camilla all embark for Sudbury, after we've christened the neat home with Mumm Cordon Rouge.

After Ma goes to bed I walk out for a bit to get a feel of the location of the new home. The night air is moist and still and vaporous. I follow a bright arc light and the sound of rhythmic thuds to a wall bordering the Common. Sounds like night filming. I peer over a flint wall to see, beyond a smouldering bonfire, a group playing floodlit croquet on a trimly-kept lawn. A good enough image on which to retire.

Retrace my steps through the wet grass to my mother's new home. Angela and I share a room. She reads. I fall asleep.

Sunday, September 29th: Sunset House, Southwold

Sleep very soundly – a good omen for the future. Wake about 8.30. Find Granny downstairs amidst the debris of the half-unpacked kitchen. Apart from her early morning coughs, she seems remarkably unruffled by the whole thing – she's faring much better than her children.

Spend the morning unpacking and positioning furniture. Mrs Haythornthwaite asks us across the landing to No. 3 for a drink. Despite a plummy accent and the confident bearing of one long used to the company of 'professional' people, she is bright and amusing and down-to-earth and very long-suffering, but without a trace of self-pity.

Married three years ago, for the second time, to an old soldier turned farmer who suddenly had a stroke and is at present confined to chair and stick and moves stiffly.

But he is alert and funny and likes a midday drink – legacy of the army, she says. Mother becomes quite flirty with the old man, despite being about 15 years his senior.

Angela and I drive over to Croft Cottage. The wine has wrought its usual havoc upon my energies and vacuuming the whole house is quite a push.

After an hour or so of cleaning, we leave Croft Cottage for the last time. I still cannot feel sentimental about it – but it was only the second house my mother lived in, in nearly 50 years. It looks good today, I feel we're passing on something quite special, not really losing it.

Thursday, October 3rd

Up to Highgate for lunch with Graham C. He and David and John T and Towser and Harry[1] are all moving down to Maidstone next week to a new house in the country. It's a seventeenth-century house with additions including an indoor swimming pool. Graham seems continually

---

1 Towser and Harry were their two dogs. Harry was named after Graham and David's great friend, musician Harry Nilsson.

hard-up and paying out huge bills to builders – but he does drive Aston Martins and likes his house to have a pool and a gym.

Graham is a bit twitchy and unrelaxed to start with, but expands during the meal. We talk diet. He's very keen on the low-cholesterol, low-fat diet, and takes it far more seriously than me – with regular blood tests, etc. I suppose this is the price you pay for being a doctor and knowing so much more about what's happening inside you.

He seems to have no immediate work lined up. Still looking for alternative funds for [his film project] 'Ditto' after Paramount backed out.

Bid goodbye to GC and to his association with Highgate, the Angel pub, dinner parties with amazing food and eccentric service, the house where I first met Ray Cooper, and so on . . .

Sunday, October 6th

Packed up both cars, then up to Abbotsley for lunch.

Its conker time and I went with Rachel into the church graveyard and we soon filled a small bag full. Sign of the times is that the boys, who used to love to collect conkers, hardly appeared all afternoon. Both were working away at homework.

Looked into St Margaret's Church which had been decorated for the harvest festival. On the altar was a loaf of bread, a glass of water and a pint of red-top. The Redundant Churches Fund, who saved this church from rotting the last ten years, have done a very careful job of preservation and restoration. Took Rachel in and for once I could show her what the church almost looked like when we were married. If it decayed so rapidly in the 15 years after our wedding, how on earth has it survived since the thirteenth century?

Tuesday, October 8th

Sam Goldwyn rings to find out what's going on with 'A Consuming Passion'. I have to trot out the same tale of disillusion which I've already given Sandy (twice) and Amanda Schiff, but no-one seems to tell anybody else, which leads me to have some fears over who is actually claiming the project.

Sam G is very keen. He would fly over tomorrow if it would help strengthen our resolve. He reiterates his point about the dearth of good comedy. I tell him that we'll decide one way or other by the end of October.

Wednesday, October 9th

A day (almost) to myself. Run at lunchtime and then complete my second 'Cyril' story, in the process of which I come up with a nice idea of a man whose moustache has a life of its own.

Thursday, October 10th

Wake at twenty past five. Feel quite rested, despite less than five hours' sleep. Arrive at the BBC about an hour later. Usual disorienting walk along anonymous and labyrinthine corridors. Last time I was here Mrs Gandhi died. This morning it's Yul Brynner (and will, later in the day, be Orson Welles), whose demise doesn't disrupt the programme as drastically as the late Indira.

Frank Bough reads limericks to a bleary audience at seven o'clock, and reads them very well. I make various appearances throughout, the last being with Lance Percival and the man who runs Battersea Dogs' Home (either he or one of his dogs farts silently but fiercely on air while sitting next to me) and Tony Ross, who is doing some on-the-spot illustrations. I can't think how Bough survives – I feel I've done a day's work by 9.15.

Friday, October 11th: Birmingham and Leeds

To Pebble Mill. A 25-minute radio interview, then preparation for the one o'clock TV show.

I appear first of all in a kilt with my foot in a bucket, reciting a limerick about [Bob] Langley [the presenter]. Ben Kingsley is the other main guest – hot from *Othello* at Stratford. I sign a book for his son Edmund – 'as in Kean'.

Then to Leeds.

Appear live on *Calendar*. The autocue has one of my limericks printed up wrong – instead of a lady from Louth with a lisp they've put up 'A lady from Louth with a limp'.

On to the Hyde Park Picture House – the characterful little pre-First War cinema on the corner which is running a Michael Palin week. *The*

Missionary and *The Dress* tonight, as well as two personal appearances by me. Jeff Thompson, the manager, who runs the place for love rather than money, says he could have sold the house three times over tonight, which is good for the ego.

Saturday, October 19th: Shrewsbury

To Shrewsbury and park near the Kingsland Bridge (now a 5p toll) beside St Chad's and walk into the Quarry and look up at the schools sat on the hill. The long, red-brick rectangle in early Victorian workhouse style unchanged, as is the steep slope below it whose zig-zag path I know so well from rowing days.

I go to see Rigg's Hall. Much of the freedom which I had to wait until university for is now available here – single-occupancy study/bedrooms for the sixth-formers, girl visitors, a much more tolerant attitude to the school dress.

I walk upstairs, on my own, and look into the bedroom I first occupied in May 1957. The room is almost the same, the iron bed-frame is almost certainly the same. Duvets are the only sign of the times. Try to remember the complicated feelings I had in that same room on my fourteenth birthday – my third or fourth day at Shrewsbury. Pride and loneliness, anticipation and expectation and aching home-sickness. A formative room, and now enshrined in *East of Ipswich*! The power of the writer! Or perhaps the scourge of the writer – to have to remember, to have to note and identify and record every damn thing.

At 5.15 I pay a last call to the school buildings, say my farewells and walk out of the Moss gates. It's beginning to get dark and there is a still, misty mustiness over the site. It was on evenings like these that I would, in my last term, October '61, make my way to a secluded spot and there light up a Capstan and feel, at last, truly grown up.

Wednesday, October 23rd

To a meal at the Gay Hussar with Barry Cryer and Alan Bennett. A sort of 'Three Yorkshiremen' sketch. We're an oddly-matched little trio, but the effect of three keen senses of humour keeps us going. A lot of BBC reminiscences, at which Barry excels.

He always attributes the source of a story most generously. He tells of Dennis Main Wilson once rounding on John Wells in the BBC bar, pint of beer clutched in the crook of his arm, and firing at him 'Christianity ... bum steer?'

Alan is acting in a Nigel Williams play for the BBC. I ask him about the part ... 'Oh, the usual,' he says. 'I went in for a costume fitting and they took one look at what I was wearing and said "That'll do".'

I drive Barry C back to Finchley Road Tube. He thinks Graham Chapman has become duller since he gave up strong drink.

Friday, October 25th

Clean the house in preparation for Sandy Lieberson and the Gilliams.

TG has only just returned from the US, where his battle with Sid Sheinberg is coming along nicely. He was invited to show *Brazil* (in the UK, European version) at USC [University of Southern California], but Sheinberg himself phoned USC to put pressure on them not to show the film, and in the end only clips could be used. A great rabble-rousing speech from Terry won over the students, but the Dean remained unmoving and refused to let the film be shown! DO'B, for the record, thinks that TG can never win and is doomed as far as any future work in Hollywood goes.

Sandy is a great supporter. I tell him that I want to direct. He seems to think this is a very good idea, but suggests I should do some small film or at least some directing exercise before taking on a major film. He will put me in contact with Colin Young at the National Film School.

Saturday, October 26th

Cast around for a 46th birthday present for John. But the magic shop's closed, so I give him a bottle of '61 Lynch Bages and a copy of *Rogue Herries* in memory of the 'Cheese Shop'.[1]

At 7.30 to Rue St Jacques in Charlotte Street. JC, looking as relaxed and expansive in company as I've ever seen him, greets me. He's tieless and this is the first time I've out-formalised him!

About 20 guests. Peter Cook is not drinking and very funny, but still

---

1 John as Mr Mousebender: 'Good morning, I was sitting in the public library in Thurmond Street just now, skimming through *Rogue Herries* by Horace (sic) Walpole, when I came over all peckish.'

one of those people who like to take the floor when they talk. His eyes have a way of moving fractionally slower than his head.

Saturday, November 2nd

We are invited to a party before the Primrose Hill firework display. We cram into Clare's shop and drink the first mulled wine of the winter, then up to Primrose Hill, where there is a spectacular gathering – reminiscent, in heads silhouetted against bright light, of the closing scenes of *Close Encounters*.

At the top of the hill is a bonfire which sends huge sheets of flame swirling upwards. As that begins to die down, heads turn to the bottom of the hill where the firework display begins. The Telecom Tower winks in the background, like a giant firework which won't go off. 'Oohs' and 'Aahhs' and orgasmic shrieks of delight fill the air.

Everyone in very good spirits, hot dogs are sold, but it's the sheer size of the crowd which is impressive – 20,000 at least, I should imagine.

Back to Clare's shop, where Mary and myself fall into conversation with the cookery editor of *Options*, who happens to be one of James Ferman's team of film assessors (she won't use the word 'censor'). She says that they have had to enrol new staff to deal with all the videos – especially the Indian videos, which cannot show a kiss, but are incredibly violent. I ask her why Python TV shows and *Ripping Yarns* are both '15'. She promises to find out. 'Is there a "fuck"?' she asks.

Sunday, November 3rd

The sun, low, clear and brilliant, encourages me out of the house again, this time to take Rachel to the zoo. The tigers pace disturbingly and continually. The ostriches and emus and cassowaries are in poor housing and look rather seedy. The penguins remain my favourite entertainment.

Then we walk up Primrose Hill together. Though it is very cold, the leaves are still on the trees and the great glowing gold sun picks out the fading colours with breathtaking richness. We pause at the top of the hill and marvel. With Rachel beside me, in her fashionable and elegant navy blue coat, it's one of those moments when you wish you could freeze time.

Wednesday, November 6th

Read Malcolm Mowbray's long synopsis of 'Watching the Detectives' – a very 'Private Functionesque' tale set in '30's Exeter. Small-town hypocrisy and deceit, but this time for sex rather than meat.

Mowbray, rather like Terry G, counsels me against trying to 'learn directing'. He says Colin Young will not be able to give much help and that the best preparation for directing is just the 'burning desire' to direct. A good lighting cameraman will do the rest.

Friday, November 15th

Sleep fitfully. Apprehensive on waking of how I will cope with a foodless day. [A 24-hour fast for an Oxfam publicity campaign.] Answer is to get to work and a brisk morning follows of Belfast [Festival] preparation.

To the Old Hall at one to borrow some moustaches from Maggie. At the moment the interior puts me in mind of some mediaeval ducal palace with a half-dozen workmen (at least) going about their business – carpenting, sawing, joining, painting. The top floor is beginning to take impressive shape. Terry G has such flair for design and an enviable knowledge of how to achieve the effects he's after. It's all quality stuff, too, and must be costing a fortune. I could never spend money this way. Not that I wouldn't want to, but I just wouldn't know how to. I would have panicked long ago.

Lunch and its temptations past, I drive to Bedford Square for a meeting at Jonathan Cape. Present are Richard Seymour, 'Gauleiter' of the project, Alan Lee, quiet, intense illustrator, and four people from Cape. Maschler apparently threw a wobbly some weeks ago and has been 'resting'.

On the table is a typed schedule which tells me the book is called 'Toby' and that I have to have the finished text by the 29th of November. As this is the first positive information about the project I've had since early September, I'm not immediately helpful. But am disarmed by Alan Lee's gentleness, enthusiasm and the beauty of his drawings and the first of the holograms (of the boy looking in the mirror), which is exciting.

Try to avoid the kitchen. Drive up to the Everyman and a new print of Clouzot's *Wages of Fear* gets me through the evening. By the time I'm home it's 11.15. No visions, no heightened senses, just weakness.

At two minutes past twelve I tuck into broccoli and cheese. The whole exercise a bit of a fraud. I think that to know real hunger is to not know where your next meal might come from.

Tuesday, November 19th: London–Belfast

Had forgotten how far Gate 47 – the Belfast gate at Heathrow – is from everything else. Sort of symbolic of the UK's arm's-length attitude to the 'province'. The Hillsborough Agreement between Thatcher and Garret FitzGerald [the Irish Prime Minister], signed last Friday, has resulted in cries of outrage from the Prots and much-increased security at Gate 47. Intensive searches, unpacking my bag item by item. Clusters of police behind uniformed security staff and, even after one's been through this, I notice a parked car at the bottom of the aircraft steps, watching us all as we embark.

Wednesday, November 20th: Belfast

An 'Ulster breakfast' in the Carriage Room. Can't quite see what is so quintessentially Ulsterish about bacon, egg and sausage, but there is some fried soda bread lurking. Break all my dietary rules and tuck into the lot.

At 6.15 we begin a run-through. Topping and tailing and only just time to try the changes. We don't finish until a quarter to eight.

By 8.05 I am ready for action. But news gradually filters backstage that there are problems. In fact the sound system has completely broken down. There's no sound 'box' at the Arts. It's all done from an old-fashioned tape-recorder on some packing crates. Someone in the audience complained that they couldn't see for the tape-recorder, and nice, helpful David took one of the packing crates away.

We have to take quick, alternative action and I decide to do the second half (Q and A) first. At least I have something to talk to the audience about. So I go out 15 minutes late and the audience response is so immediate, responsive and fulsome that I really begin to enjoy myself. From somewhere come a host of ideas, improvisations, one-liners, bits of repartee, that I'm sure I should never think of in 'real life'.

Thursday, November 21st: Belfast

Wake feeling quite pleased with myself after last night. Take my time and get to breakfast just after ten. The Ulster breakfast, I am informed, stopped at ten. But I could have an Ulster grill. This turns out to be exactly the same as the Ulster breakfast.

Friday, November 22nd: Belfast

Bobby Charlton is sat at one of the tables at breakfast. Freddie Starr at another. Freddie asks me to join him, but I've just scanned through an irritating review in the *Irish News* and want to have another look at it.

'Frequently not funny' is the phrase that really sticks. There is lots of credit for the way I carried on on Wednesday, but he makes it sound as if the material was weak. Funny how stupid things like that can cut through – despite the raves in the *Telegraph* and in the *Newsletter*.

I'm rung just before I leave for the theatre by the BBC to ask if I'll appear as a 'guest celebrity' on a Children in Need appeal which is to be done as an inter-Britain link-up.

So I find myself at midnight, halfway through my first square meal of the day, locked in interview with Sean Rafferty and a man who calls himself Fearless Frank (though Sean calls him Fearless Fred for a while), who once hung upside down for a record time to raise money for charity.

Saturday, November 23rd: Belfast

To a book-signing at eleven. The shop looks as dead as the city centre. Not my fault – it's all because of the rally called by Paisley and Co to protest against the Anglo-Irish Agreement. Within two or three days of the Agreement being signed, the city was covered with 'Ulster Says No' stickers. Still, our cultural oasis – the University Bookshop – moves about 100 books of *Limericks* in one and a half hours.

Then I'm whisked away to a school fund-raising to present prizes. But this again is in the centre and is half-empty. The master in charge is very sad. They've made several thousand pounds less because of Paisley's action and he thinks the Unionists should make up the difference! But the children who are there are the usual bright, lively, cheeky, alert kids who give the lie to the idea of a city gripped by depression and apathy. I enjoy meeting them. Sign autographs.

On my way back to the Forum I find my path blocked. The police don't recommend me trying to get through. An army of marchers is heading straight for me. Group after group, band after band, fifes, drums (struck very loudly), red and white and blue uniforms, bowler hats, sashes. A solemn and quite impressive sight, until you look at the faces. Unattractive most of them – hard, blotchily red, unsmiling.

Wait for a while, then notice some children joining the procession and nip smartly in amongst them. A few steps later, having been briefly part of the biggest Protestant rally in Belfast since 1912, I'm across the road and into the Forum.

Tuesday, November 26th: London to Dulverton

At last, a completely selfish journey.

Rush around getting my things together. Can't decide between Proust and *La Regenta*, so take both. These two, plus a *Good Food, Good Hotel* and *AA Road Guide*, make the case weigh a ton.

At Paddington board what they call 'The Torbay Express'. It's full of Southwoldy people. Well spoken, elderly and quite eccentric. 'They used to start the train with a great whistle from the engine and now they just glide orf without you hardly knowing,' says a very old, white-bearded character behind me, ruminatively.

We leave late, but catch up time and as we reach Taunton the sun comes out. Collect my car.

Drive to Dulverton, which is a neat, quite charming little village of no great architectural merit, enclosed by steep, wooded slopes. The Ashwick Country House Hotel is a couple of miles outside the town, almost on the edge of the moor.

Lots of calligraphed signs around. One says that the wallpaper in the hall is a 1901 William Morris original. Another announces, as I enter my large bedroom, 'Complimentary drink'. I sip it, it's French vermouth. A card reads 'Welcome to Ashwick House – Mr Pabin'.

Inside, the hotel is almost as silent as outside. As I go down to dinner I notice for the first time that my room is called 'Larch'! The other two guests are in Chestnut.

Wednesday, November 27th: Dulverton

Eat sausage and bacon in solitary splendour looking out at the lawn, the tall fir trees and the ponds.

Into Dulverton to buy a newspaper and a waterproof. Then, rather than drive a long way, I go as far as Tam Steps and head off up the valley of the River Barle.

The path is difficult. Slippery, muddy and winding a contorted route through woods and over roots ready to take advantage of any lapse of concentration. So it's a bit of a scramble, beside a river alternately calm, clear and stately and then rushing over stones. The clouds thicken and I'm caught in a couple of hail showers.

All goes well for a while, but with hills to climb and rivers to ford and bog to extricate myself from, I'm still walking as darkness is falling. As I wait on the Dulverton Road for a flock of sheep to pass by, a motorist offers me a lift. Takes me to the Tarr Steps turn-off, so I've another 25 minutes' half-running, half-walking, past a group of farmers outside an EHS – an Experimental Husbandry Station. Men in paramilitary green jackets and Land Rovers – snorting with laughter at something.

Very relieved to be back at Ashwick. Estimate I must have covered 16 miles or thereabouts today. That's about 20 with yesterday. One other couple at dinner.

They take some pride in what's called their 'Presidential Suite', which can be completely separate from the rest of the hotel – own cooking, own bar, own entrance. Mr S [the proprietor], a gentle, kindly man, says there *are* people who want this service – but not what sort of people they are. The mystery thickens – especially as in amongst all the delightfully calligraphed notes on the hotel is one reading 'We regret we are unable to accommodate armed security guards on the premises'!

Friday, December 6th

Waiting for the hologram story, which I've decided to call *The Mirror-stone*, to come back from Alison.

She likes it more than the first draft, which is always a good sign. Feels it's more direct, less obscure, aimed more clearly at a younger age group. I check it through and make various alterations and edits, which Alison puts onto the processor, and copies should reach Alan L and Richard S by the weekend.

About five, as I have just finished the story, Michael Owen from the *Standard* rings and, in his flat, almost sinister tones, tells me that the judging panel for the '85 awards have given me the Peter Sellers Comedy Award for *Private Function*. Now there's a nice thing. The awards will be doled out, at the Savoy, on the 26th of January, which is the date I've held in my diary for more than a year as the New York Critics' Circle awards.

I'd promised to present. But in this case, as I say to Michael O, it's better to receive than to give.

Sunday, December 8th

Read *The Mirrorstone*. I'm quite pleased, but there are moments when the story content seems perilously arbitrary and I wouldn't say that this project is one which fits me like a glove.

In my prescient moments I do worry that, such will be the fuss made of the book, there will be little chance of my avoiding responsibility, so I should be sure not to make it something I'll be embarrassed about. But then it isn't a project with any precedent – not in my experience. A story to fit a technique.

Meal with Terry J. He's casting away on *Personal Services*, which he keeps referring to as 'Personal Functions'.

Monday, December 9th

To Richard Seymour's studio in Fulham.

They read the new draft then and there. On the whole they seem pleased, but not ecstatic. The discussion then becomes wider, with Richard S having a number of proposals and Alan, much more quietly but equally persistently, putting in his criticism as well. Our talks last for nearly four hours.

For some reason Jonathan Miller's son is there to take photographs of the three of us for the publishers. Is this some legal precaution on their part? Why waste valuable time taking publicity photos when we still don't have the book?

Am not home until 9.15 and I know that I'm now under pressure. I have tomorrow to co-ordinate all the new ideas into a third draft. Will have to cancel my National Film School visit.

Tuesday, December 10th

At 1.15 I scribble the last lines, but am not at our rendezvous – the Pontevecchio Restaurant in Old Brompton Road – until ten to two. Apologies, then read through the new material as best I can with waiters interjecting things like 'Spinach?', 'Who is the gamberetti?' and so on.

Wednesday, December 11th

At 8.30 I'm at my desk looking over *Mirrorstone* again. Final, final amendments, then it's off to Valerie Kettley at Cape by lunchtime.

I celebrate my relief at the work accomplished by sitting and reading Al L's 'Roommates' at one go. Though I feel dozy and below par, my condition is as nothing to the awfulness Al describes in this 'novelised' account of his cancer op.

At one point he finds Python on hospital TV and gratefully switches over to his favourite show, only to find it's the 'Brutal Hospital' sequence – with TJ staggering towards him, blood pouring from his stomach. Al, for perhaps the first time in his life, can't take Python and flicks the switch.

Thursday, December 12th

Lunch at the Gay Hussar with Richard Faulkner, the man I met by chance at Leeds Station whilst on the rounds with *Limericks*, and a lady called Susan Hoyle, from Islington. A brisk, earnest, forceful but not overbearing woman.

They ask me to become Chairman of Transport 2000. This I am completely unprepared for, but they are persistent and persuasive. An architect was Chairman, but he now wants to move on. I should need to attend a monthly board meeting, write occasional letters and make appearances occasionally on TV and radio. Susan H would supply me with the facts and figures.

I leave the Gay Hussar and cross Soho Square with my mind racing. At last a chance to become involved on more than just a nominal level with one of the issues I feel most strongly about.

Friday, December 13th

In to my copy-editing appointment at Cape.

Flat, moist, drab, very mild weather as I drive down there. Valerie [Kettley], very motherly, and deceptively soft, then begins to go through their suggestions for improving grammar, etc. This is on a much more comprehensive scale than I've ever been used to before. I'm just inordinately glad that the text is only 4,000 words.

Before I leave I'm shown into Tom M's office. He's lost weight and looks rather wild-eyed and jumpy. Not a man who is completely better.

He refers to the 'time off' and admits that he'd reached the stage where he could no longer read a simple letter. Here he motions to his desk, which looks as chaotic and disordered as Tom himself. 'Well, I'd been working 18 hours a day for 25 years' and so on.

I feel a bit sorry for him. This huge, high-ceilinged office suddenly feels like a mausoleum and I have the feeling that Tom knows and everyone else in Cape knows that his best days are over. That he is now almost a revered relic in the company he's done so much for.

Sunday, December 15th

Yesterday the LA critics chose *Brazil* as their Best Film of the year, TG as Best Director and the script as Best Screenplay. This, over *Color Purple* and *Out of Africa*, was an enormous surprise to everybody, but now puts *Brazil* in as a potential Oscar-winner. And it's not yet been shown.

TG and Arnon are off to the States in the next couple of days to try and negotiate the requisite one week's playing time it will need, before December 31st, to be eligible for the '86 Oscars. In ten days the NY critics will be selecting their winners and *Brazil* is now bound to be taken a lot more seriously. Amazing scenes, as they say.

Dinner with the Alburys. SA's octopus soup sensational. Then osso bucco. Talk to him about the Transport 2000 proposal. He advises acceptance.

Tuesday, December 17th

Drive over to J Goldstone's Christmas cocktail party. Not that there are cocktails. No-one in our line seems to offer them.

Al Clarke [the editor and film producer] confesses that he has nominated me for a best supporting performance award for *Brazil*. He says he's quite concerned as to where such a convincing streak of nastiness lies hidden! Ruby Wax says she spent three years trying to learn how to pronounce my name.

Outside as we leave the rain pelts down. Makes for a difficult drive on to our next venue – the Elton John concert (featuring Ray Cooper) at Wembley Arena. Ushered by walkie-talkie-wielding promoter's men to the 'guest enclosure'.

All we can see is the back of Elton's head.

Ray gets an enormous ovation when Elton introduces the band. I can see why Elton may be nervous of having him there. He is so much more charismatic than dear old Elton – described so well by John Peel in the *Observer* as giving the impression of not so much a rock singer, more an amiable mini-cab driver.

Afterwards Elton, who seems very aware that we are Ray's pals and that Ray is very highly thought of, is almost defensive to start with. Shakes hands with his left hand and seems to only want to talk about the *Meaning of Life* and the 'Grim Reaper' scene, which he regards as a work of pure genius.

We talk of Watford and Sheffield Wednesday and he says the football chairmen and managers who run the FA are, en masse, a depressing bunch.

Friday, December 20th

A wet and miserable morning. Low, gloomy, damp skies. To Euston to catch the 9.35 to Birmingham with Hettie, who's organising *Limericks* publicity. We talk about Transport 2000, on which I still haven't taken a decision. I feel myself that if I had really thought it the right thing to do, I would have said yes a week ago. This indecision, I sense, is a way of saying no. Hettie sensibly makes the point that whatever decision I take I'll regret at some time.

The buffet crew are in a mellow, pre-Christmas mood and strains of 'Always Look on the Bright Side of Life' fill the train – hummed, rather badly, over the intercom!

Monday, December 23rd

Valerie Kettley of Cape calls to hear my reactions to their latest changes. It takes more than an hour to talk through the latest draft.

Tom M wants the front part reduced even further. Valerie is paid to do Tom's bidding and tries desperately to make every line, every word cut she can. We end up friends, though, after I bridle to begin with.

The unusually inviting weather lures me to a run after we've finished our exhaustive talk. As I run I talk through with myself the Transport 2000 offer. I feel that I must make up my mind and resolve to do it as soon as I get home.

For two or three miles most of my thoughts are negative. I'm an entertainer, a comedian – I've no business launching into things I know so little about. I haven't the time, I shall be dragged into all sorts of activities above and beyond running meetings – and I may not be able to do that anyway.

Against this is a feeling that here is a rare chance to do something sensible. To help a good cause. Is it not my public duty to become involved, if it will help them? The public and private sectors of my life are locked in struggle.

I really cannot make a decision. But as I run down from Parliament Hill I'm pretty much decided to say no. When, after a bath, I pick up the phone to Sue Hoyle, I'm pretty much decided to say no. When she answers I say yes. On the condition that it's a year only.

Wednesday, December 25th: Christmas Day

Wake at nine from a deep sleep. Children already dressed. All of them clamber on our bed as we undo our stockings. All I hear from Rachel is 'Dad! You've left the price on!' A very good feeling of being together, sharing the day.

I read out bits of *A Christmas Carol*, as I do whenever we have Christmas here. Note the use of the word 'good' eight times in one sentence and think of Tom Maschler's endless notes on my *Mirrorstone* copy – 'repetition'! He'd have had a field day with Dickens.

Sunday, December 29th

Most of the day I have that restless, slightly unfulfilled feeling which hits on a Sunday. I suppose I miss religion – which throughout childhood used to take care of most of the day. In its most negative form – a guilt about doing anything too weekday-ish – its effect is still with me.

Watch a review of '85. Full of ugly images. Football hooligans, South African police, striking miners and police striking back. And the West, like the weather today, in the frozen grip of the forces of conservatism. Not a year I shall miss.

Tuesday, December 31st

A little nervously up to the Royal Free at 9.15 for an appointment with Morgan, the urologist. Freudenberg has suggested I see him after passing blood a few weeks ago – and once before in Sierra Leone.

Nearly all the ancillary staff seem to be West Indians, rather in the way that most of those who keep Heathrow Airport clean are Indians – it can't be just coincidence. I'm carrying with me a sample of urine in a jar that once contained apple sauce.

I see Dr Morgan at a quarter to ten. A man of about my age. He asks me a lot of questions, then examines me. After this he tells me he would like to run some tests, just to 'eliminate possibilities', though he hints that it could be something minor and quite safe, like a blood vessel in the bladder temporarily rupturing.

I am to have my blood tested and to come in for an X-ray on Thursday morning. He would then like to do a cystoscopy – which is a bladder examination up the urinal tract. He thinks he can get me in on Thursday afternoon. This is all rather sudden (and causes a part of my mind to entertain paranoid imaginings).

I set off on a late run across the Heath.

Of course there's probably nothing much wrong, but clearly the tests will be looking for signs of cancer and I feel a twinge of panic, which isn't helped by the encroaching darkness and the sound of a bell being dolefully rung outside Kenwood House by one of the park staff.

1986

Friday, January 3rd: Royal Free Hospital, Hampstead

Read some of Ackroyd's *Hawksmoor* until at 8.30 two nurses arrive with my pre-med. This is injected in the bum and is called Omnipon. Delightful feeling of drowsiness without fatigue.

Listen to Haydn's string quartets and some of Bruce Springsteen. Try to read, but the lines roll in front of my eyes. They're running late on the op before me, I'm told, so I have another three hours on Omnipon.

Then it's time to take a journey to the theatre which exactly recreates the speed, the door-banging, but not the discourtesy of the start of *Meaning of Life*. I'm asked for my autograph at the end of the journey. Someone says 'No, not now', but I find myself surprised that I can still write.

In the ante-room I'm in the middle of telling some story to the anaesthetist, who is pumping something into the back of my left hand, and then I'm in a recovery room and hear my nurses saying 'He looks better than when he went in'. I'm so pleased to see them all I just start talking again. I think I'm the only one in the recovery room who's conscious.

I doze on and off, but am reading a book within three hours of the op. Helen comes in at about 3.30 and says that Morgan has rung up to tell her everything was OK. I knew it would be.

I have a disconcerting and painful pee. Burning sensation, then blood – quite thick – and a sort of urinary cough – air spluttering out through the penis.

Sunday, January 5th

Not sure whether or why the two-day exploration of my urinary system should be responsible, but I have a good night of qualitatively quite different dreams than usual. Clear physical images, some nice erotic moments. Maybe something still lingering in the system.

Down to the South Bank. Rachel comes along with me. The 'Ten Day Wonder' event is a GLC booking, so I have to sign an assurance that

I won't perform in South Africa or Namibia. I resent this – it's as if I can't be trusted to make my own moral decisions.

I go on at 2.30. The house is about two-thirds full and there are a lot of under-sixes.

Small Harry and *Cyril* read the best, *Limericks* the worst. Not much response to Belloc or A A Milne, or Just William. End up making up limericks on the spot. Find I've done one and a half hours without a break – no wonder I feel a surge of weariness.

Tuesday, January 7th

By taxi to Golden Square for a showing of JC's new film, *Clockwise*. Starts promisingly, even though many of the jokes are sub-Fawlty – including, amazingly enough, kicking and hitting a car that won't go.

Eventually the level of laughs begins to drop as the situation becomes more familiar and some LE [Light Entertainment] casting, music and direction fail to lift it to the level that JC's performance merits. He comes in well ahead of the field with Frayn second and [Christopher] Morahan [the director] plodding along way back. Too safe by half.

Sit with Eric and Tania and Terry J and Steve and Iain Johnstone. John is relaxed and eventually sits with us and we have the sort of chat which shows the best side of the Pythons. Sensible, generous, but critical. John, far from being put off, listens intently and agrees wholeheartedly that the ending does peter out – with no satisfactory resolution.

Just before I leave, JC takes me on one side and asks, almost apologetically, if I mind him writing a part for me in his next film. He says it's a four-hander. Me, Kevin Kline, John, Jamie Lee Curtis!

Wednesday, January 8th

A dark, gloomy morning. To work, but phone calls dominate the morning. *The Mirrorstone* comes back from J Cape with lots of 'as's' and 'buts' queried, but basically almost there. Read through and ring Valerie K back and by early afternoon the copy is agreed, finished and I can forget that for a while.

To the dentist at five. Kieser opens a bottle of champagne afterwards to celebrate New Year – funny drinking with five other people all in white coats.

Thursday, January 9th

I'm rung by the British Council to ask if I will go to Czechoslovakia with *Private Function* at the end of the month. I'm very keen to see Prague – one of the few European capitals I still haven't visited, so say yes, providing it can be a weekend.

TJ says EMI have today withdrawn their offer for foreign rights to *Personal Services*. Michael Hordern turned down the part of the Wing Commander who, at one point, TJ admits, does have to be masturbated by one of the ladies. Apparently Alec McCowen is happy to do it.

Monday, January 13th

Into taxi for one of the more important meetings of my life – the Transport 2000 introductory party and board meeting at which the fate of my chairmanship will be sealed. No turning back after today.

The organisation's offices are in a drab, low, sixties building beside Euston Station. They're the HQ of TSSA, the railway white-collar union. (I am moving into a world riddled with initials.)

Susan Hoyle, who is humorous in a rather deadpan, busy way, takes me across the Euston Road, pointing out one of the most dangerous pedestrian crossings in London, to meet Jimmy Knapp and Ray Buckton[1] at the NUR HQ. This is an '80's block and more like Madison Avenue or a TV company than a railway union. But amongst all the smoked glass and tastefully-designed wooden furniture, there is a tell-tale British touch. On the desk at reception is a ledger headed in scribbled biro 'Air Conditioning Complaints'.

Up in the lift to a floor where all is soft carpet and silence. No-one seems to have much work to do. After a short wait, Susan and I are shown into a spacious, smart, though not intimidating office.

Jimmy Knapp, taller than I expected, a big, genial man with an almost albino-pink complexion and a jolly thatch of white curls which spill down onto his upper cheek, rises to meet me. Ray Buckton is on the other side of the table.

Knapp is easy, friendly, unforced. He flicks through my CV, but clearly

1 These were the two most powerful men in the railway unions. Jimmy Knapp was General Secretary of the NUR (National Union of Railwaymen) and Ray Buckton was General Secretary of ASLEF (Associated Society of Locomotive Engineers and Firemen).

knows nothing of my past work (perhaps a good thing).

Buckton just goes on about my speech at Durham. Flatteringly, he seems to have remembered more of it than I ever could. He says it was one of the best he's ever heard.

After 20 minutes or so, we take our leave. Jimmy Knapp assures me that if we ever want any help or support from him or Ray B it will be forthcoming.

Back perilously across the Euston Road and by this time about a dozen people are in Richard Faulkner's office for the buffet lunch to meet Michael Palin. The older members – representing Wales and Devon, for instance – are very gentlemanly and courteous.

A number of people arrive by bike, and the big, bearded, Northern CAMRA Mafiosi – who, I am to find out, virtually run the board meetings – are a little guarded, perhaps feeling their power threatened. I don't know.

Harley Sherlock, the outgoing Chairman, is enormously nice. Affable, straightforward and competent, with lashings of the best sort of disarming charm.

I have prepared a short statement of my qualifications and disqualifications – emphasising that I don't regard my appointment to the chair as a fait accompli – and until it's put to the vote later this afternoon Harley is still Chairman. He's obviously held in great affection and I am most envious of his fluency and patience and diplomacy.

At 4.15 I make my apologies and, with a well-received 'May the best man win', I leave them to the 'election'. Out in the windy streets I seek out a 24 bus to take me home in preference to a taxi. Symbolic gesture!

An hour or so later Susan H phones me at home to tell me that I have been unanimously elected Chairman of Transport 2000.

Tuesday, January 14th

Ring Ma on her 82nd birthday. (If I live as long as her I'll see 2025!)

At quarter to twelve drive out, through a fierce hailstorm and some fine celestial lighting, to the Film and TV School at Beaconsfield. I have an appointment with Colin Young – the head of the school.

Colour photos, well taken and expressive, of all the students and teachers are stuck on a notice-board and this companionable feeling – of an enlightened university campus – is quickly evident.

After showing me two studios, Colin gets hold of a lean, intense man with big eyes and high cheekbones called Paul. He is the No. 2 here and Colin asks him to lunch with us. We talk, Paul and I, for a while about what has to be learnt about directing.

Colin takes us into 'New' Beaconsfield to an almost deserted Chinese restaurant of very good quality, where he orders authoritatively. 'The only thing you need to be a director is confidence,' he asserts confidently.

Then they ask me about my film (the one that I want to direct). I feel apologetic and faintly embarrassed as I take up their time waffling about my inability to start writing.

At the end of the meal, as we sit in the car, Colin (like Jimmy Knapp yesterday) insists that I should call him if there are any problems and that I should consider coming for a one-week session at the school in the summer, but the last thing he says, of my desire to direct, is 'We do think you should do it'. Well, this is the year of trying new things, I think, as I head out onto the M40.

Thursday, January 16th: Southwold

Fancy the Crown for an evening meal, but Ma is quite shocked by the £10 price for a three-course meal and dismisses it.

A diplomatic call upon the Haythornthwaites, mainly to thank her for all her work on the hallway. Have a scotch and a chat.

He was in the Parachute Regiment. She is the daughter of a Jewish father who worked in the film business for a while. She went to work on *Vogue* – hence the good taste of the decorations. Very complimentary about my mother, 'Very game', 'Out in all weathers'.

Wednesday, January 22nd

To the T2000 office. Meet Susan H.

Over a very good Indian meal, we talk a bit about each other and backgrounds. She's twice married, a first in PPE from Somerville, has a son called Tom who's a year younger than Tom. She's persuasive, talkative, sharp, restless and enjoys gossip. I like her. I feel rather dull and soggy but hope it doesn't show.

On to transport business. Do we want to supply a judge for *Motor Transport*'s awards for the most environmentally-sound lorry? We shouldn't be endorsing lorries at all, but we should be aiding any belated recognition that they damage the environment. Susan is in favour of agreeing.

Then she talks at length about personalities in the office. I still feel like a prospective fiancé coming to meet his new family, so I listen and avoid too much judgement.

Home via Belsize Park with a feeling of slight unreality. Can I really fulfil all the functions (to quote the Bank Manager in 'Eric Olthwaite')? I know here and now that I shall not be able to take on the workload when I'm making/selling the next film. Next year something will have to change.

Friday, January 24th

David Leland calls and offers me the part of Eric in *Heartbreakers*, which he's directing for Channel 4 in the autumn. Eric is a 'totally charmless' character and David L is interested to see how I could do something which doesn't rely on charm.

He also says something about wanting to push my acting a bit further out. I know what he means. Take a few risks. Well, again, it all fits in with Putting Myself on the Line Year. Agree to read the script.

Sunday, January 26th

Not since *Private Function*'s Royal Premiere 14 months ago have we dressed up together like this. [For the *Evening Standard* Film Awards.] After one unsuccessful attempt and a whole day's shopping last week, Helen has assembled a very stylish, elegant outfit. She's bought long earrings to go with it at Camden Lock today, and new evening bag, shoes, etc.

Arrive at the 'river entrance' of the Savoy Hotel about seven.

There are only about eight awards. Alan and Malcolm win the first – Best Screenplay for *Private Function*. Alan's speech is short and to the point – 'It just shows you can't go wrong with incontinence.' Norman Garwood wins the next award – Technical Achievement for *Brazil*.

Joanna Lumley gives a very generous, clear and humorous intro to my award, which is number four.

Stephen Frears collects the Best Film award for *My Beautiful Laun-derette* from Rod Steiger, who looks as if he is in a catatonic trance. But his ringing inspirational clichés bring a nice touch of Hollywood to this rather low-key, 'British' evening.

George, exceedingly nervous, and Denis, even more so, go up to collect the last award of the evening, one given to HandMade Films by the Duchess of Kent. George describes her as 'Your Majesty', inadvertently. She counters that that is 'one or two up from me', to which George, quick as a flash, replies 'Nothing's too good for you, ma'am.'

Monday, January 27th

Arrive at TV-AM just after dawn. A more comfortable, relaxed, expansive feeling to the place now it's comfortably ahead of BBC's *Breakfast Time* and expanding its advertising revenue. Roy Hattersley and Nicholas Ridley are sitting in the foyer. Not talking to each other.

I chat to Hattersley briefly about Sheffield. He asks me where I am from. When I say 'Ranmoor/Crosspool borders' he gestures with his forefinger under his nose ... 'Oh, the posh end.'

He goes in and scraps with Ridley over the upcoming Commons emergency debate on the Westland leaks.[1] Ridley is dismissive, patronising, and can't have done himself any good.

Nick Owen, one of the presenters, reveals that I was his house captain of football. He was at Shrewsbury for one term with me, and I had written about him in the house football annals. All this poured out onto a million breakfast tables.

Also Jimmy Greaves, quite out of the blue, declares his love of *Ripping Yarns* and especially 'Golden Gordon'.

Home and an interrupted morning's work. Phone calls from Maggie S ('Darling, you looked about 12, as usual') and an interesting job offer from *Jackanory* to read *Charlie and the Chocolate Factory*.

Evening at home, fairly quietly, with the TV. Thatcher chews up Kinnock. She sounds like some prehistoric bird swooping, shrieking about her nest. News item of the day – 'The remains of a Polish tax-collector have been found in two suitcases.'

---

1 Two weeks earlier, Michael Heseltine, the Defence Secretary, walked out of the Cabinet after his plan to save Westland, the British helicopter company, by merging it with European companies was overruled by Thatcher. She questioned the MOD's independence and insisted Westland be merged with the American company Sikorsky.

Tuesday, January 28th

At seven Angela comes round for supper and a natter. It's a pity so much of her brightness and energy is unexploited. She is still quite brittle and castigates herself for everything. She feels she hasn't lived and has had her eyes tested today and been told that she'll have to wear glasses when driving. All this depresses her more than if she were a placid, easy-going type like her brother.

Wednesday, January 29th

Terry seems remarkably unruffled by the fact that Zenith have now withdrawn their money from *Personal Services* and the project looks doomed. Most backers can't see the humour, only see the outspoken sex.

Mum rings to say Mr Haythornthwaite across the way has died. I liked him, glad I knew him.

Read Kundera's *Joke* for most of the evening – as a sort of preparation for Czechoslovakia, where the book and the author are banned.

Friday, January 31st: Prague

Not much to see of Czechoslovakia until we break out of the clouds and head in over one of the most enormous factories I've ever seen. Note from my reading that it was a Czech (Čapek) who coined the word 'robot'.

At Praha Airport are planes from China, Cuba and Algeria. We are the only capitalist airline. Met by a slightly harassed, chatty, humorous Englishman called John Green. He's the cultural attaché and looks like Alec Guinness playing Alec Guinness. He wears a sheepskin coat which has seen better days and looks less smart than most of the Czechs.

He moves me briskly through the formalities ('You never get much trouble if you come in from the West, it's the East Europeans they give a rotten time to'). John Green is the first of many people over the weekend who emphasises that the Czechs do not think of themselves as East Europeans, but as Central Europeans (we are, after all, further west than Vienna). They hate the Russians (in common with nearly every other Soviet satellite). They were the fifth most prosperous economy in Europe before WW2 and had close cultural links with Great Britain.

To Wenceslas Square, which is in fact a gently-sloping rectangle, with wide road and sidewalks. Hotel Jalta, in heavy National Socialist style, but comfortable inside with mini-bar, bathroom and radio and TV. The breakfast menu offers 'grey bread – any chosen sort'.

Much waiting around whilst the various delegations sort out my future. Am introduced to my interpreter Irena, a slightly nervous, greying-haired lady in mid-50's with a sensitive and kind face. When we are out walking she emphasises 'everything I say is only my own point of view and shouldn't go further'.

On to a special showing of the film [*A Private Function*] for university and embassy people. I introduce the film in English. As soon as it begins I go off on my own for a walk into the old town, across the Charles Bridge. Quite magical.

Back at the screening, I'm buttonholed by a red-eyed English teacher from the university. He warns me darkly against getting too involved with the 'embassy crowd' and that 'You'll never meet any real Czechs, 'cos they don't know any'. I arrange to meet him tomorrow.

Irena and her husband Dick take me to eat. Dumplings and red meat seem to be a Czech speciality. Then I'm taken to a 'Theatre of Small Spaces' – in effect an intimate cabaret-style club. A group called Ypsilon sit about on stage . . . loosely structured, talk, discussion, maybe leading to a sketch. Place is packed. In the second half I'm called up on stage. Perform a little and then sit there grinning idiotically whilst the Czech banter swirls around me.

They know all about irony and apparently they put across a lot of criticism, cleverly veiled so the authorities won't see it. A sort of intellectual second economy.

Saturday, February 1st: Prague

Sleep seven hours despite great heat from air conditioning. As I sit on the lav wrestling with the unperforated toilet paper, I try to sort out a few thoughts for my various public appearances today. Scrambled egg, good strong coffee, then meet Dick, who is going to walk me round this morning.

His wife and two children wanted to visit friends in York in 1977, but she had to apply to the Ministry for permission and was at first given the stock reply 'apply again in seven years'. But she knew the wife of a top official and the whole process was speeded up. As Dick tells me such things he drops his voice – as if the streets themselves might be bugged.

From habit probably. I shouldn't think he is aware of how odd this behaviour looks to me.

We pass Kafka's house. He shrugs and smiles a little bleakly when I ask if Kafka is still read in Czechoslovakia ... 'Oh, he's read ... but he's not published.'

He takes me into a wine bar – a Vinerana – a small, smoky, whitewashed room, with plain wooden tables and counters. We have a couple of glasses of excellent, fruity Moravian white. He tells me that Jan Schmidt of Ypsilon apologised after the show last night for not talking to me more on stage, but as the house lights went up to welcome me he noticed two men from the Ministry of the Interior sitting at the back. These are the shadowy government 'cultural officials' who can close their show at any time, so he decided to play safe.

We talk about Britain. Dick says that the Czechs think of Britain as a golden land of freedom and cannot believe things are bad there. The football riots made the worst impression, everything else bad they regard as government propaganda and discount it. Dick says that the Czechs are very racially prejudiced and would agree with Enoch Powell.

Then we walk up the hill to the splendidly-sited British Embassy, to which Her Britannic Majesty's ambassador has summoned us for lunch. Very formal, lots of servants and polite introductions to a number of Czech theatrical folk who have been rounded up to meet me.

Then whisked away to a screening of *Private Function*.

Another speech, translated this time, more flowers, champagne, and, at last, driven back to the Jalta by Mr Green. By now it's six and within ten minutes the phone rings to announce the arrival of my teacher friend and his colleague – studying Czech, from Lancaster University. Both fairly classic types. Anti-London, anti-privilege, beer-drinking in quantity. But not lost for a word and soon we are in a long, old, vaulted room, simply, almost austerely, appointed, full of all manner of Czechs – man, woman and child – drinking beer.

Then up the hill to another pub – this is the Black Cat. Some Czech ladies at the table next to us in a merry state. Czechs have very bright, humorous eyes when they want to use them. Have long since forgotten what the teachers and myself have been earnestly talking about, but we agree to repair to the hotel as all the pubs have, quite sensibly, closed.

Sunday, February 2nd: Prague

Wake after eleven o'clock. Feel a heavy pain in my right hand. Head not too bad, stomach queasy. Lie there as if hit by a bulldozer, then ease myself out of bed, cursing myself for missing my looked-forward-to morning walk round Prague, and a little concerned that I've probably missed breakfast and within an hour I shall have to get myself across town to Sunday lunch with my interpreter.

Only then do I become aware that things are not too good. There is a line of bloodstains on the pillow and sheet and duvet. My hand is quite grossly misshapen and, though I have no usual feelings of hangover, my face is uncommonly sallow. I wash and shave and clean my teeth with difficulty. Usual exercises out of the question. Just getting dressed is an athletic feat. But with my hair washed and a fresh shirt and a set of clothes on, I feel that I can at least venture out. A cup of coffee and a glass of fruit juice washed down with mineral water, then out into the town. I vaguely remember trying to have a bath, falling ... but not much else ... Oh, dear ...

After my lunch I find myself in the southern part of town, pushing open a door of a grubby apartment block and walking into a lobby which smells of old meat. Upstairs to the flat above the butcher where the cultural attaché and his wife lives.

They were burgled two days ago and the police could not have been more thorough until they suddenly broke off the inquiry, leading Green to suspect an inside job. But he's like the best and worst of the English ... quite stoical and unemotional about the whole thing. Takes it with a pinch of humour. At one point he leans forward, and without a change in his tone of voice, warns breezily ... 'By the way, this place is almost certainly bugged ... I don't know if they're listening at the moment, but it's best not to mention any Czech names of people you've met.'

After supper we go into the centre to a concert in a grand, excellently-restored, neo-classical hall. The government gives an awful lot of money to the arts ... but of course they must be officially approved.

We end up drinking Czech liqueur and talking about the various celebs who've passed through Prague. The actors he liked, the musicians, especially orchestras, he found rather loud and apt to behave in Millwall-ish fashion at airports.

Monday, February 3rd: Prague

To lunch with two men from the Czech film organisation. Officials, probably Party members. The older man asks me to describe Margaret Thatcher's policy. Monetary control, tight legal restraints on opponents, intolerance of debate and discussion, strong defence capability ... as Irena says afterwards, I could have been describing the Czech Communist Party.

She puts me on the 4.45 plane home. I give her a four-day-old *Guardian* and any other English literature I can find – a *Listener*, a copy of Larkin's 'Whit Sunday' poems and Anita Brookner's *Hotel Du Lac*. She slips them quickly, discreetly, into a brown cotton bag.

Tuesday, February 4th

Up to the Royal Free by 10.45 to see Mr Morgan. A Lowryesque collection of the old, infirm, squat, bent and shuffling gather around the desk at Clinic 4. A man next to me talks of his brother-in-law ... 'We put him away last Friday. He was a great racing man, lived for the horses, so you know that bit of the funeral service where they throw earth on top of the coffin? Well, I threw in a betting slip, along with the earth.'

After a wait of 40 minutes or so I am called in. Today Mr Morgan is surrounded by seven or eight students. He grasps my hand effusively and I let out a yelp of pain. He looks at my still-swollen right hand and I tell him what happened in the bathroom in Prague (grins from the reverential students) and he says he will get someone to look at it right away.

Within a half-hour I'm down at Orthopaedic, signing an autograph for a porter, chatting to a boy who'd broken his leg acting, and being shown into Mr Wilson's room. He looks, squeezes, has me X-rayed (long chat with radiographer about *Brazil*), and then shows me that I did indeed cause myself more than a bruise in Prague. I can see clearly a fracture in a bone on the side of my hand – the metacarpal, he tells me. He puts the side of my right hand and little finger in an aluminium-backed splint, which I shall have to wear for three weeks. It will be six weeks before it completely heals.

Feel on remarkably good form, but writing isn't easy and I shall have to take to the typewriter. Ah, well, it all fits in with this year of doing things I've never done before. Like breaking a bone.

Sunday, February 9th

On returning from the Mansfield Road grocery store with a bottle of milk
in either hand, I hurried across Elaine Grove to avoid an oncoming car
and felt my trusty 15 quid shoes, which have been my mainstay for seven
or eight years, slipping on the hard-packed snow and I was upended.

Instinct made me protect my be-splinted right hand, which threw me
off-balance, and I ended up lying on the ground with the broken glass of
a milk bottle sticking from the base of my left thumb. (The other bottle,
I'm pleased to say, was safe and sound in the three fingers of my broken
right hand.) I remember staring for far too long at the chunk of glass
which had inserted itself into my flesh like a wafer stuck into soft ice-
cream. Then I picked the glass out, and I was aware quite coolly that
I had hurt myself rather badly. Still managing to carry the other bottle,
I squeezed my hand over the wound and walked home. The driver of the
car rolled down his window. 'You alright?' 'No,' I said. He grinned and
drove on.

I was then driven to the Royal Free. Even as queasy as I was, I did
appreciate the regularity of my visits there so far this year. I was stitched
up and Diana [wife of my friend Sean Duncan, and a doctor] stayed with
me for the hour and a half I was in there. Apart from the 'freezing'
injection into the wounds before they were stitched, I felt remarkably
little pain, nor had I lost much blood, nor, thankfully, and according to
Diana very luckily, had I cut any tendons.

Monday, February 10th

At Walkden House [T2000 office] I begin the first of many explanations.
Susan H thinks the sight [of two bandaged hands] almost uncontrollably
funny. A lot of gasps and 'Oh, no's'.

We walk across Melton Street to the grey marble slab of Rail House
[British Rail headquarters]. Up to the meeting, which is in Room 101 –
though no-one alludes to the significance. Grant Woodruff, British Rail's
Director of Public Affairs – grey-haired with a young face – opens the
meeting briskly.

We have a briefing on the Channel Tunnel[1] and we're asked to

1 The Bill to approve its construction had just been given a third reading. It became law in
July.

help put pressure on the customs and excise to make checks on trains which they at present refuse to do, and to cause a fuss over Section 8 (grants for freight transport) at the DTP [Department of Transport].

Lunch is up on the seventh floor. There are about 15 of us altogether, including three out of the four past executive directors of T2000. I feel that the BR attitude throughout is brisk, a little patronising, as if we're seen quite clearly as a bunch of weirdos, as you get in all societies of the world, and are really only there to make good, honest businessmen's work that much harder. They're the do-ers, we're the talkers.

Wednesday, February 12th

The side-effects of my two accidents seem almost entirely beneficial. I'm improving the speed of my typing, I get washed in the bath by Helen and I've slept long and well for the last three nights.

Thursday, February 13th

At half past twelve a brown, plain-clothes police car, grubby inside and smelling of stale cigarette smoke, picks me up to take me to Kentish Town nick, where I (with my Curse of the Mummy's Tomb hands) am to be guest of honour at a lunch. The topics of conversation are predictable. Camdenspeak – the name given to the attempts by our council to purge the language of any words with sexual or racial connotations – is high on the list. So onto the scrapheap of progress go such words as 'chairman', 'ladies', 'midget' and, of course, 'black'. Officers are completely bemused that Accident Black Spots cannot be called that any longer.

All present, and there must be 20 senior detectives in the annexe room with brick wallpaper, agree that things are 'getting worse'. Nearly all are against the decision to put armed police into Heathrow ... indeed every one is against arming the police force any more than at present. They don't like political duties – either in Nottinghamshire or Wapping. There are few obvious heavies, but equally few who can make intelligent conversation. An air of benevolent philistinism.

One stands head and shoulders above the rest – a man called Blair, who has written a seminal (dare one use the word in this context?)

textbook on rape and is sharp, soft-spoken and acute. Either he will rise like a rocket or else he'll resign.[1]

About three and a half hours later I'm driven in an official police Rover through Kentish Town. 'What a dump,' says the driver. 'I wouldn't bring kids of mine up here.'

Friday, February 14th

Yet another visit to the doctor's starts the day. This time to have my wound looked at. Nurse says it's healed well and removes the stitches. Back home to write copy for the *Limericks* book, then take Rachel by Underground to County Hall, where she is to receive a prize for being one of the six winners out of 10,000 entries in an ILEA poetry competition.

County Hall is enormous – built with such pretension and high expect-ation, and now beleaguered and rather sad, a cross between a school, a hospital and a parliament house in the Third World. No colour, no pictures on the walls – it feels like something that has been stripped to its bare essentials, robbed of any respect it might once have had. Across the river from its windows can be seen the Gothic pretensions of the Houses of Parliament, where the fate of County Hall was sealed last year [when the Greater London Council was abolished].

Rachel and the five other winners read their poems bravely in front of the barrage of photographers and TV lights, and tears fill my eyes as Rachel finishes her poem about Tom. A moment of real pride.

Wednesday, February 26th

A check through my speech in the taxi and a long, slow journey to St Katharine's Dock. With some difficulty I find my way to the *Jock*, a stout, broad-beamed sailing barge. A small, quiet handful of journalists. Harley Sherlock looming above them all; the thin, heroic Gallic face is Pierre Bermond – Chairman of Transport 2000 International, who has come over for the press conference [called to introduce me to the media].

I start well with a couple of ad-libs, then dig into my speech, which I deliver as well as I could have hoped, but it seems to fall into a vacuum. I have some ringing phrases, which receive no reaction, and some jokes,

---

1 In 2003 the 'man called Blair' became Sir Ian Blair and two years later Commissioner of the Metropolitan Police. He resigned in 2008.

which receive no reaction. Maybe it's like this at press conferences. To someone brought up on the need for audience response it is a little disconcerting. I introduce Pierre Bermond, who also is received in this polite vacuum.

A cycling magazine want a picture of me on my bike, an anti-road-widening campaigner wants me to come to the first day of a public inquiry. *The Civic Engineer* wants to take me to lunch and Capital Radio interview me on the round bed in the captain's cabin. The owner of the *Jock* is a very smooth fish, who clearly thinks that my involvement with such people is quite inexplicable.

From there by cab to *London Plus*, the BBC's evening programme. Stuck in the worst traffic jam for years, and arrive breathless and am rushed straight onto the show. At least I have first-hand experience of the problems T2000 wants tackled. Home by cab at nine.

Phone rings immediately – it's BBC *Breakfast Time* wanting me for tomorrow.

Monday, March 3rd

A fine day and sniff of a change to more generous weather in the air. To the Television Centre for 10.30. There are about 20 people in the studio involved in putting [my reading of] *Charlie and the Chocolate Factory* on the air.

For an hour and a half they check captions and I sit reading in make-up beside a make-up lady who looks exhausted, hardly exchanges a word with me and occasionally slumps forward onto the worktop, all in.

I'm aware, during the day, of the sad fact that for many people in the studio this is a dull job. The girl at the teleprompter reads her Ken Follett paperback at every available moment. A caption man, whose job is to put five caption cards in order every two hours, falls fast asleep as we begin to record.

The work required from so many people is so minimal, so unfulfilling, that I see with the force of a blinding clear light that any new technology which could replace some of these jobs would be relieving people not of noble struggle but of extreme monotony and boredom.

Tuesday, March 4th

To the BBC for the third day running, this time to meet Innes Lloyd and mark the 'official' existence of *East of Ipswich*. Nat Crosby seems still to be the main choice of cameraman. Innes is extremely helpful and responsive over casting – and accepts that Tristram and myself are thinking away from big names.

Meet 'the girls', as Innes refers to the three ladies of varying ages who are the basis of the team – Thelma Hornsby, who was on *Three Men in a Boat*, is one of them. They seem very efficient and I have a confident feeling that the production will be well looked after. It will need to be. The shooting schedule is now only 23 days.

Friday, March 7th

Up to Hampstead for lunch at La Cage Imaginaire with a reporter and photographer of *New Civil Engineer*.

Then to Julia Street to be photographed with a bike giving views on cycling in London. Cannot pose with my own bike as the saddle's missing. Halfway through the photo-session Mrs Brown on the corner arrives back boisterously drunk and insists on being snapped with me. Later she confides 'We've just been to a funeral.'

Thursday, March 20th

For some unknown reason Denis [our cat, not our producer] has chosen one of the busiest days of the week to pee on the sitting room sofa – for no apparent reason. Scrub down the offending parts of sofa, then out into a grey and wet street for the paper, only to find our bag of litter upturned. Stuff all that back, collect the *Guardian*, find that a dog has evacuated right outside the front door.

By taxi to Kensington Town Hall for a conference organised by T2000 with some money from the GLC.

I creep into the room, expecting a handful of keenies, but find that the place is full – 70 or 80 people – with their little tables and writing pads in front of them.

Listen to two platform speeches. Both much more critical than my own. Mayer Hillman of the Policy Research Institute is uncompromisingly in favour of immediate legislation to regulate private motoring.

I take the stage at two o'clock and feel loose and in control as soon as I get going. Deliver another mixture of laughs and, hopefully, serious scoring points. Over in about ten minutes, apologies and leave.

Have the feeling I may have rather overdone the ham.

Monday, March 24th

John explains to me his new film 'A Goldfish Called Wanda'. I am to play a man with a stammer who kills Kevin Kline by running him over with a steamroller. John bemoans the fact that he's written himself another 'boring, uptight authority figure', but otherwise sounds very enthusiastic and is anxious to plan ahead so it can fit in with my dates.

My 'dates' depend on a conclusion to 'Explorers', to which I attend later this morning, for the first time in several weeks. Can make little headway. Suddenly free from weeks of tight deadlines, I'm momentarily lost, and cannot work out my priorities.

At seven I drive into London for a 'reception' at the Reform Club given by Richard Faulkner and Will Camp.[1] (Faulkner's 40th birthday, Camp's 60th.) The Reform Club seems to embody the twilight of Empire better than any building I've been in. Apart from telex machines, there is little inside this time capsule to suggest that the Boer War is not still in progress. Huge Corinthian columns dominate the interior spaces, which are grand and dusty and faded. Leather armchairs, a few people scattered about drinking and talking.

Upstairs and round a gallery to the immense and gloomy library. Here, a gathering of about 100–150 is swallowed up in the vastnesses of shelves ten stories high, more Corinthian columns and a soothing old brown ceiling with panels and stucco.

And quite a gathering – Michael Foot, Peter Shore and one or two less well-known Labour front-benchers. Bob Hughes and Prescott and others. Norman Lamont and a smattering of Tories. I feel like a new boy at school. People keep asking me who I want to meet. I really just want to meet someone who isn't powerful or famous, just good company. But these gatherings are clearly lobbying occasions.

I talk to Peter Snape, MP for West Bromwich and an ex-railwayman.

---

1 Will Camp knew everyone in the political world. In one of his obituaries in 2002 he was described as 'Writer and corporate and political adviser'. In 1999, Richard Faulkner was made a Labour peer, Baron Faulkner of Worcester.

He's concerned about the effect on railways of the abolition of the Metropolitan Counties who gave much help to local lines. Bob Reid of BR is there, a thin, aquiline, rather interesting man physically. He would look just right in a monk's cowl or on a cross.

Wednesday, March 26th

Sitting at the desk a fresh approach to the new film occurs to me, forcefully and with the instant attraction of having solved an increasingly encumbrous problem – where to go with 'Explorers'. A simple two-hander, a love story, a sort of 'Long Encounter'.

A curious week, thus far. Charitably it's part of a recovery and re-stocking after the last few hectic weeks, at its worst a reaffirmation that I really don't know what to say next.

Down to the Python office to move this impasse momentarily with a T2000 interview. Michael Williams from *Fleet News* – a freight-oriented periodical – waits patiently, as from the room where the interview is to take place comes Arnon Milchan. Warm embraces, face against his stubbly chin – his shrewd, playful eyes close into a smile. Commiserations over lack of Hollywood Oscars, agree to meet for lunch in London soon, then back to *Fleet News*. Wonderful collision of two worlds.

Watch the *20/20* TV programme about *Brazil* – Terry as the little man who took on Hollywood ... and won. Now officially enshrined in US mythology. Terry's supporters (especially amongst journalists) are impressive. The programme, aired two weeks ago, apparently added 20% to the box-office.

Tuesday, April 1st

No more GLC.[1] As much as anything about their passing, I shall miss their radical and stimulating attempt to shift the centres of power and influence in this country from big institutions run by middle-class, public-school-educated men to everybody else normally excluded from power. And they've been open and extrovert and consultative.

I see from yesterday's *Telegraph* that the lorry ban is to be ended immediately on 69 miles of road which the DTP has now taken over.

1 The Greater London Council, London's administrative body since 1965, the year I came to live in the capital.

Sensitivity, tolerance, understanding and conciliation – it's a spirit utterly alien to the Thatcher-inspired politics of the '80's. Irony is that it should take a woman to combine all the worst of the new male middle-class attitudes.

Some brighter news is the arrival in the post of Caroline H's two 'Cyril' covers, which look bright and eye-catching and colourful. My hope is that they'll be taken for Adrian Mole books and sell millions! These two, combined with the first sight of Alan Lee's *Mirrorstone* cover, bode quite well for next Christmas and make me feel I've done some work after all!

Sunday, April 6th

Up and across the Heath just after nine. A cold east wind, but good for running. Pad past Michael Foot, who lurches from side to side as he walks, like a rather overloaded cart. He occasionally shouts for Diz [his dog, Disraeli].

Home for a long, leisurely levée. Ring TJ to wish him well for tomorrow's start of *Personal Services*.

Down to the Shaftesbury Theatre. Rory Bremner, encountering me at yet another charity show, asks me if I work professionally any more.

I'm on at the end of the first hour, reading 'Biggles'.[1] At the difficult stage of knowing it just well enough to look away from the book long enough to lose my place. So one or two fluffs, which irritate me. Neil Kinnock and Glenys are down there in the front row.

Our 'Custard Pie' routine[2] does not disgrace us, but Graham ballses up the lines on a couple of occasions – and, as TG points out, 'He's the one with the script!' All of us aware that it's timid stuff compared to the quite frenetic energy of the Mayalls and Henrys and Edmondsons.

We're all behind Geldof at about 11.30 singing 'Feed the World' and the show ends just on the four-hour mark.

Collect our carrier bags as Rik packs up his dead chicken, which he'd previously stuffed down his trousers, Frank Bruno, who's been playing Juliet to Lenny Henry's Romeo, removes his mediaeval bodice, and we all repair to the Marlboro' Crest Hotel, where a party is provided.

---

1 A piece written in the style of Captain W E Johns, about Biggles, Algy and Ginger trying to get tickets for a Bruce Springsteen concert.
2 An academic lecture on slapstick comedy.

Ade Edmondson tells the awful tale of how Bob Geldof, who had been playing the Cliff Richard part in the Young Ones hit, took it upon himself to smash Edmondson's guitar live on stage, presumably thinking it was a prop. It was in fact a Fender something-or-other, Edmondson's most prized possession.

Rik, talking of his disgusting act, says he was very worried about his parents seeing it, but his father had quite approved – 'Just how they used to talk in the navy!'

Monday, April 7th

Lunch with Tristram and Innes. Innes, in his bluff and hearty way, is quite a canny operator. He's always nibbling away at the script in an effort to cut down on cost and time. The word 'crowd' in a script still terrifies the BBC.

Tuesday, April 8th

Lunch with JC at Cage Imaginaire.

John looms in from Flask Walk looking like one of the steelworkers from *The Deer Hunter*, in a woolly hat and a chunky, inelegant wind-cheater. When he's taken off his jacket he still has several layers of sports jackets and sweaters underneath.

He's had bad 'flu for about a week, he says, and over the last few days it's induced 'the sort of depression I haven't felt for ten years'. The root of the depression is the recurring Cleese bogey of feeling trapped – trapped by success, by work responsibilities like Video Arts, trapped even by the film he's writing for me, Kevin Kline and Jamie Lee Curtis, with Charles Crichton ... 'Quite honestly, Mikey, if Charlie Crichton dropped dead tomorrow I probably would abandon it.'

What he does want to do ... 'I've reached a time in my life ... ' is learn, read, travel and not have any work responsibilities at all unless, for instance, 'Louis Malle asks me to go to Greece for a few weeks'.

Thursday, April 10th

Taxi to the BBC for the first auditions at 10.15. Then finalise script with Tristram and spend the afternoon dictating the corrections to Innes's secretary.

The office opposite is occupied by Ken Trodd – an intense and slightly disconcerting presence. His office is full of junk. His clothes are everywhere and in the middle of it all a TV shows DBS programmes from Ted Turner's US channel.[1]

To outward appearance there is an air of precarious improvisation, but undoubtedly this shabbily-appointed fifth floor at TV Centre is where the British Film Industry exists. Chris Morahan, Gavin Millar, Alan Clarke, all have current projects under discussion. Richard Eyre is in production. Fifteen or so films are made here in a year, on a rolling programme which the 'Wardour Street' film industry never seems able to achieve.

Monday, April 14th

Talk to Tom about his continuing inability to concentrate on his 'A' Level maths course. I just want to keep the lines of communication open with him. His friends are largely a street crowd and in many cases his academic inferiors, but he has a strong loyalty to them, which sometimes gets in the way of his work. I feel it's very hard for me to advise him not to spend so much time with these people.

Tuesday, April 15th

Feeling in one of my late-afternoon lethargies, I walk for a while around Covent Garden, looking for a present suitable for tomorrow's 20th wedding anniversary. Eventually settle on a book called *Fatigue and How to Beat It* – mainly because I'm too tired to keep looking.

Simon and Phillida round. We go out to *After Aida* at the Old Vic. A rather heavy piece to start with, but the second half is especially effective – with light and energetic playing from Ian Charleson and big Arnold Bennett-*Clayhanger*-like prickly authority from Richard Griffiths.

The restoration of the Old Vic is magnificent. One of the finest theatre interiors in town since 'Honest' Ed Mirvish spent two million quid on it. Pity it is only half-full. Later go backstage. Actors in their underpants – always a bit of magic destroyed.

RG berates us for being the worst audience they've had.

---

1 Direct Broadcast Satellite. Satellite TV was not yet available in private homes.

Wednesday, April 16th

The day after Reagan bombed Tripoli, and after the shock the gradual realisation that not only has Reagan set in train the dreadful prospect of more and more warlike actions, of further reprisals by Libyan fanatics in Europe, and of a generally much less safe world, but that 90% of Americans are behind him! My feelings of revulsion against this dark side of America – the clumsy, ugly face of power without intelligence, the world bully – have quite put me off going over there next week.

Happily 70% of Brits polled oppose Thatcher's decision to let our bases be used, but that's about the only good news.

Write a nice piece called 'Biggles and the Groupies' which gives me more pleasure than I've had at the typewriter in a long while.

Friday, April 18th: Sheffield

Gather myself together for my third transport meeting in two days – this one up in Sheffield.

At Midland Station I meet Jo Guiver, the Buswatch co-ordinator, who turns out to be a bright, likeable, jolly sort with a huge backpack, as if she's walking the country. Hint of difficulties ahead when I'm introduced to Layna, who is of Polish stock, with a punky haircut and a Vegan.

I rise to speak, a little despondently, to about 30 faces. Susan follows me, then a smooth, but quite plausible man from the South Yorkshire Passenger Transport Executive.

Then Layna's two friends, one called Jesus and the other Mark, speak inaudibly, though quite sensibly, from the back, but it is clear that they are not at all grateful for having had three years of the lowest fares in the country and instead want to have a go about travelcards, etc.

We close about 9.35 with my rather waffly summing-up. Must learn to do this better. A hotel has been booked for Jo, Susan and myself, but we have to be in by 10.30. Susan hasn't eaten since three, so this is out of the question and we ring the hotel to ask for dispensation. No-one answers.

Thanks to a friendly member of the audience we are driven to the hotel. The door is locked and no-one answers the bell. Our driver sees people in one of the rooms apparently watching TV. After much banging on the window, one of them is persuaded to open the door for us. A card beside a bell reads 'Reception and Emergencies'. We ring the bell but no-one appears. The guest shrugs, 'They live in the basement.'

We leave after ringing the bell yet again and I end up buying all three of us rooms at the much more pricey Rutland Hotel nearby.

Sunday, April 20th: Southwold

Mum meets me at the door, anxious, no doubt, that I wasn't here earlier. Quite sharply aware of her frailty. She's thinner than ever – especially her arms and legs – and moves with greater difficulty than usual. Quite a change and for a while it worries me.

I've brought lunch and afterwards I'm just happy to sit and talk. Her alertness and humour and liveliness are unimpaired, I'm glad to say. Julie next door has had a man in all night. 'It *could* be her brother. Of course, it's no business of mine,' and she rounds it off with a laugh at herself.

After supper we watch *Heimat*.[1] My first view of it and I'm very impressed. Late night walk and contemplate writing a Palin-style British *Heimat* – extended version of the memoir-style of *East of Ipswich*.

Wednesday April 30th: Paris–London

The plane arrives in London three hours late after a further fault is found as we taxi out for take-off. So tempers are already frayed when we arrive at Terminal 4 (recently opened and subject of a big ad campaign and much media attention).

One man checking all UK and EEC passports. A very angry and vocal little Scotsman, who turns out to be an MP (wearing his House of Commons tie!), finally approaches one of the officials and indignantly puts the case for more than 400 travellers who are in the middle of the nightmare. The official, without a word, gets up and walks away.

The MP turns to us and, arm upraised in the manner of Lenin or Robespierre, shouts 'Come on, everybody through! Everybody through!' Some reluctance, then a few start to move. The officials turn in horror and make to apprehend one of the passengers but they're simply brushed aside. The frightened look that so quickly replaced the smug look of power will remain imprinted on my mind. Not to put too fine a point on it, I saw through power for a moment.

1 An 11-part German series directed and co-written by Edgar Reitz, which follows the fortunes of a family in a Rhineland village from 1919 to 1982. There were two further series in the 1990's and the 2000's.

Thursday, May 1st

In the evening go to the William Ellis summer concert. The headmaster is waiting anxiously on the steps bemoaning the lack of parental interest – 'Where *are* they all?'

Inside there is some excellent music and the attendance does swell quite quickly. Tom plays both saxophone and clarinet. He still does his Cheshire Cat grin a lot and looks bashful, but plays well.

Talk to Rachel's headmaster – Nicholas Harris – afterwards. Teachers starting industrial action again and Rachel likely to lose her school journey for the second year running. The effects of the government's attitude to public-sector schools continue to worsen.

The hope that I had for state education has dwindled to the point where I'm beginning to seriously question whether we made the right decision for our children. The answer certainly is that we did, at the time, but should we not take another decision now – to remove them from state education before the whole thing collapses? I feel that we must keep the faith. The ideal of equal opportunity in education cannot be seen to fail. Maybe I should be more vocal. Maybe I should organise a school journey together with other parents.

But, being the lazy non-activist I am, I end up at home watching the *Heimat* episodes I missed whilst away.

Friday, May 2nd

A balmy warm smell rises up to my room as I sit with a solicitor and answer his various questions on the origins of the 'Lumberjack Song', what it means and why it's sufficiently important to us to want to proceed against United Biscuits and their agents for using it as the basis for a commercial.

Silly situation, really. 'Lumberjack Song' is just a bit of nonsense, but in order to establish the principle that we've been wronged, we have to pretend it's of great significance – a piece of modern culture. But I do resent the way it's been used without permission, especially as I would have given an emphatic 'no' if we had been asked.

Friday, May 9th

I read David Leland's *Heartbreakers* script. The character of Eric tantalises me. He's a marked difference from the characters I usually play. I talk a lot about my freedom to do 'what I want', and yet my acting roles in recent years have been very similar and, with the exception of *Brazil* and *The Dress*, nice and safe. Eric is neither nice nor safe and the part is better than *Brazil* or *The Dress*. So I'm tempted, despite the fact it looks like cutting into my writing time.

To the office and an interview with *Labour Herald* about T2000.

Of course they're all very elated by last night's local government and by-election results in which the Tories were roundly trounced. In Camden, depicted by Thatcher and the government as wasteful, over-spending and dangerously left-wing, there are now even more Labour councillors.

Go on from the office to see the Jamie Lee Curtis film *Love Letters*. A low-budget, serious and quite strong US picture. Jamie is good. It's interesting to see her playing a woman not a glamour girl. The small Cannon Theatre is cramped and full of smoke. Not a great environment to see a movie.

Monday, May 12th

Read a deposition on the 'Lumberjack Song' from a solicitor, based on our talk last week. Very rough, ungrammatical and badly phrased – and rather depressing. Trying to assert 'rightness' seems to involve entering a world where patience, stamina and self-belief have first to be tested by irritation and frustration. And it rains outside. A filthy May thus far.

To Chalk Farm Station, thence to Euston – litter, pervading shabbiness – and to the Great Nepalese Restaurant in Eversholt Street – inviting, comfortable, spacious, friendly. There to meet and talk with Susan and Jo Guiver prior to the board meeting.

'The Future of Transport 2000' comes up about four and clearly cannot be fully debated in this meeting. Peter Horton [one of our local group representatives] stokes the fire a bit here, 'Important document', 'We put it off last time', etc, etc. Quite unhelpful, but maintains his own position as guardian of the heart and soul of Transport against the wily and untrustworthy Londoners.

Massive relief at another board meeting completed. I have a worrying feeling that I didn't enjoy it as much as the first. Is this the familiar Palin pattern? Attracted by something new, accepting an unusual challenge and then, once the challenge is overcome, being rapidly disillusioned by the usualness.

Tuesday, May 13th

Walk across into Tavistock Square. Sit beside Gandhi and the tulips, as a brisk cool breeze dilutes the warmth of a, so far, clear, sunny morning.

Try to focus my mind for the next hour on *Mirrorstone*, for I have to jolly along the Cape sales conference on the same subject within half an hour. I remember so little about it, except Cape's prodigious editorial interference. Look at Gandhi for inspiration, a hunched bronze figure over there in the centre of the flower bed. He doesn't look at all like Ben Kingsley.

Summoning up all my powers of positiveness, I head for the conference venue at the Drury Lane Hotel. A modern, concrete infill hotel, which doesn't improve the north end of Drury Lane. Silent foyers, signs, conference suites. Up to the fourth floor. Am on the phone to the office when Tom M emerges, greets me warmly and says 'You're on!'

Without further ado I'm ushered into a room packed with expectant people. Most of them sit round a table which must be thirty yards long, but many others sit behind them. It's like an over-stocked peace conference. I'm told Roald Dahl is to be there later in the morning. God knows what that rather shy and reclusive author will make of it.

Tom announces me and I waffle on as best I can for a few minutes. Jokes go well, general good reception, but occasionally I catch the hardened, cynical faces who recognise a Maschler hype when they see one. Tom says a quick word, leads me out, cries 'Thank you, you were wonderful!' and shuts the door. I'm left quite alone in a small ante-room. Search for my coat and leave.

Taxi takes me across to Acton, to the BBC Rehearsal Room for the *East of Ipswich* read-through.

John Nettleton and Pat Heywood are wonderful as the Burrells. Nettleton misses not a single line or a single moment of humour. I don't think I've heard anything of mine read as well first time.

After playing Mrs Wilbraham in the read-through and seeing the crew and cast together, I begin to feel broody for acting.

Thursday, May 15th

This morning a letter from someone who had never forgotten the image of me having breakfast in the Lochalsh Hotel looking out over Skye and had eventually made a pilgrimage to the same breakfast table. Not only was it all he'd ever hoped, but he took a friend and they fell in love and 'have been in love ever since'.

Gilliam rings. We talk over *Munchausen*. He's off to LA next week, though, to talk to Fox about the production. Once again he chides me about not being able to write any more – about being busy with everything but the main thing, and so on.

Friday, May 16th

To Martin Lewis's party.[1]

Ever since reading the Rachel Roberts book [*No Bells On Sunday*, published 1984][2] I've thought of Lindsay Anderson and how I could use some of his acute and down-to-earth good sense. But I couldn't really think of any reason why our paths might cross again. And there, on the lawn outside Martin's basement flat off the Finchley Road, is the man himself. A little larger in the belly than I remember, but his fine hawk nose still the distinctive feature.

I am so pleased to see him, I don't have time to think what to say, so out comes my spontaneous pleasure. We have a very good, too short, natter. Lindsay, who stands so close that I feel myself being edged into a flower bed, is, he says, going to start a campaign against the use of the words 'rather', 'slightly' and 'quite'. He would cut this diary at a stroke.

He hasn't yet seen *Private Function*. He confesses that he thinks he might not like it, but clearly doesn't like himself much for saying so. And he couldn't go to *Room With a View* because he's fed up with films 'in which Maggie Smith and Denholm Elliott are *so good*!'.

He also is the first person I've come across who didn't like *Englishman Abroad*. His brow creases painfully at the mention. 'Oh, too facile . . . all

1 Martin is a comedy entrepreneur and party-giver, now living in the USA. He had worked on some of the Amnesty shows and was a friend of Lindsay Anderson.
2 Rachel Roberts won a BAFTA for her performance in *This Sporting Life*, directed by Lindsay Anderson in 1963. Married to Rex Harrison from 1962 to 1971, she died in 1980.

those *camp* Englishmen.' The only film he's liked recently is *Crazy Family*.[1] 'The violence is so *productive*'!

Then across London to dinner with Richard Seymour and his wife at his little terraced cottage on the main road at Richmond. The smell of the trees and the countryside and the glimpse of the river's bend are wonderful and remind me how rough our part of north London is.

Look through the *Mirrorstone* dummy – see most of Alan's drawings for the first time. The holograms are much smaller than I expected and not really as comprehensive a part of the book as I'd imagined.

Foresee the dangers of the Maschler approach. He has so sold the book on the new techniques that I think there is a distinct danger that the hype could rebound on him.

Saturday, May 17th

A sour, gusty morning of continuous rain. Shop for food, read the papers, then across the road to the Oak Village residents' 'Spring Lunch'.

I meet the new people from No. 1 Julia Street. He's called Denis, which must have given him a few uncomfortable moments when Helen's been out at night shouting for the cat!

Tuesday, May 20th: Southwold

Find the [*East of Ipswich*] unit in Walberswick rehearsing the gents scene, with the car. Tendency of John Nettleton to huff and puff in comic fashion. Suggest to Tristram that John deliver the line with less effort. This he does on the third take and it sounds much better.

A local, with rich, upper-class accent, cycles by – 'Out of the way, you *bloody* people!'

Thursday, May 22nd: Southwold

I am at the location, right in front of Glan-Y-Don,[2] at eight o'clock.

Elinor [our production manager] and her local team are deploying

---

1 A Japanese film, released in 1984. Directed and co-scripted by Sogo Ishii.
2 The guest-house on the corner of Pier Avenue and North Parade where my parents and I stayed on our summer holidays from 1959 to 1964, and on which 'Tregarron' in *East of Ipswich* was based.

extras along the beach. Occasionally they have to be moved back as the tide reaches its height. But someone seems to have boobed and the tide, which is supposed to turn at nine, rises remorselessly and seems to delight in hurling the odd wave at any extra we place, and at every camera position we set up.

We keep retreating, then re-setting, and the sea calms, then out of nowhere a line of salt-white foam hurtles across the beach, forcing everyone to leap out of the way – with varying degrees of success.

Saturday, May 24th: Southwold–London

Various shots around the house with Edward Rawle-Hicks – who is daily becoming more secure and solid in the part. Rather a poignant moment as I pass Glan-Y-Don this morning on my way to its film equivalent and there are the Palins of the 1980's having breakfast.

Send a Stanley Spencer postcard of Southwold beach 50 years ago to Puttnam to tell him that our lunch plans of two and a half years ago are becoming film!

The catering truck is parked behind the toilets at the far side of the pier – one of the least salubrious spots in all of Southwold. Here the unit spreads itself beside the dog-shit, the oil and the remains of scattered dry bread crusts which even the seagulls ignore.

At home William greets me with news of 94% in his chemistry mocks – best in the year – and Rachel has one of the leads in the Gospel Oak fourth-year play. Tom has been learning how to defend himself with a short stick and is covered in bruises.

Open one or two of my pile of letters. Someone wants me to do *The Missionary* as a stage musical.

Wednesday, May 28th: Southwold

After lunch, in an upstairs room amongst the narrow bedrooms of the Crown [Hotel], Ken Pearce [the editor] shows the first rushes I've seen. Very encouraging. Every beach shot is highlighted for me by the wind, which blows at the hair and the ladies' dresses and tugs at the windbreak and seems to epitomise east-coast holidays.

Sunday, June 8th: London–Southwold

Bundle things together and set off about midday. I feel tired and not particularly happy, as if some dark cloud is temporarily settled over me. Very curious feeling. Vestiges of shyness. Or is it just that a film unit is a potent and demanding entity and you're either part of it completely or just a visitor? I'm uneasily in between.

They're at The Mount.

Inside 'Tregarron', the combined efforts of Sally's design team, the costume, actors and actions are very satisfying to behold. It's the 'white soups' scene, with the room silent save for the joyless scraping of soup bowls. We've put one of the ladies – Miss Chatty or Miss Oliphant – in a neck brace, after seeing so many of them around Southwold.

Tuesday, June 10th: Southwold

To the location early.

Innes is quietly putting pressure on me to write 'another version' of Graham Crowden's sex-talk speech, omitting words like 'penis' and 'vagina'. He is worried about 'losing some of our audience too early on'. I refuse to write an alternative because, as I say to Innes, 'I know that's the one you'll use'.

Quick look at rushes. Leave Tristram to go to Aldeburgh for Dame Janet Baker and dress and drive out to Tinker Patterson's house on the marshes. Tinker, Norman Parkinson's favourite male model, had encountered me in The Mount, which he now owns, grasped my hand warmly and said how delighted he was to find another Old Salopian and would I come round to dinner so he could tell me stories of School House in 1944?

Margot, Tinker's dynamic German wife, has just returned from the Continent – stealing menus for her new patisserie/coffee house on North Parade. An act of purest optimism, but she says there are a number of new, young professional people coming to Southwold who will patronise it.

Tinker tells me of a prep school master who used to come around and check the boys' hand positions before they went to bed. 'Hands Up North' he would say, which meant that they should point their hands palm upward and lay them on the pillow. 'Hands Down South' meant only depravity.

We have a simple supper – 'You're talking about school, so I'm afraid it's school food,' says Margot, modestly.

Tinker gets out school photos and tells me of boys like Spurway and Cameron and how he'd once been asked to eat food off the floor. He clearly loved his Salopian days and wants to know how much it had changed in the 13 years between his leaving and my arriving.

Then we get on to talking about East and West Germany and how the Baltic Coast is like Suffolk and how soap-powder is still considered a luxury item for Margot's cousins in the East. Tinker tells how Margot's father – a Stuka pilot in the war – wore an Iron Cross at a recent posh dinner at Fishmongers' Hall – much to Tinker's amusement.

A beautiful and tranquil sky as I leave.

Saturday, June 14th: Southwold

We finish at 6.35 beside the lighthouse in Stradbroke Road. Nineteen days and four nights, 23 shooting days altogether.

Celebrate the end in the Sole Bay Inn with a pint of Adnams with Nat [Crosby, the cameraman] and Innes and Tristram and others. A moment to savour. The relief, the feeling of achievement and the sympathetic surroundings, the bond of the team, all combine in a low-key but incredibly satisfying moment. Eventually Tristram and I are left talking as everyone leaves, as if in a curtain call at the theatre.

I have my reservations still about some of the sequences, one or two moments of performance and amount of cover left un-shot, but, all in all, I've never felt something done as close to the way I wanted it done as this.

At eight we repair – Tristram to the Crown, myself to Sunset House – for a bath and brush-up before the end-of-filming party at nine.

We're in the Upper Room [at the Crown Hotel] and music is already blaring out – 50's hits. Innes makes a short speech and thanks me for 'introducing us all to Southwold'. Granny sits happily in the midst of it all, attracting, as if by some perverse magic, all the tallest men in the room, who have to bend double or sometimes even treble to listen.

Monday, June 16th

Go to see the latest possible Python property purchase. This is a collection of buildings off Delancey Street in Camden Town.

The layout of the odd assortment of buildings around a central 'court-yard' feels just right for our purposes. There's a very good space for André, promising surroundings for Anne and Steve and the office, as well as small, low buildings ideal for viewing theatres, production offices and editing rooms.

TG scrambles, burrows, prowls, plans, elaborates. He responds so unfailingly positively to life that all I can do is watch and marvel. TJ has a black eye. He went to the help of a black man who had been nearly run down by a car in South London and was punched in the eye by one of the assailants – who were white.

We have tea and citron pressés in the Delancey Street Café and discuss next moves. Very positive feelings all round, but the asking price of £420,000 is considered excessive. TJ counsels an offer of £300,000. Anne feels she can start no lower than £360,000.

Have officially left Barclays Bank after 25 years. First Coutts cheque signed today.

Friday, June 20th

Start the day with a huge surge of optimism for the great-grandfather, Brita Gallagher story, encouraged by a *Listener* book review of *The Tender Passion*, a survey of Victorian attitudes to love, sex, attraction, infatuation, etc.

For an hour or so I'm convinced that at last this is the answer to screenplay problems. But, as I run in late morning in order to think over the idea, various difficulties cloud my previous optimism. Chiefest of these is that, were I to play the main man, I should be casting myself as a straightforward, sexually-involved clergyman, and that has a familiar ring to it. So I return, dripping sweat in this high humidity, with only the frustration of another clear path ahead blocked.

Anne rings to discuss how she should approach purchase of the Delancey Street complex. She thinks the seller will definitely *not* budge below £400,000 (he's shifted already from 420G, I point out). The more I think about the place, the more positive I become. It *is* right, somehow, and I would hate to lose it. Anne decides to go back (she feels much as I do), with a 'final' of £380,000.

Saturday, June 21st

Our offer for 68a Delancey Street (£395,000) has been accepted!

Chilly, windy, overcast morning for the tenth Oak Village Street Party. Miss the lunch as I have to go to Harrods for a book-signing. Read some limericks to a polite, but bewildered group of shoppers in the children's book department, then sign for an hour and a half and shift 120 books.

Last week someone sold seven in two hours, so I feel I've earned my champagne and smoked salmon sandwiches in an office looking out over Knightsbridge. Harrods, like the transatlantic airlines, has suffered considerably from Americans' fear of Europe since the Libyan bombing.

Back to the street party. Dance, flinging myself into some R&R with Helen. To bed at half past two for the second night running, after enjoying late-night chat with Mr Brown on the corner, who told me that I 'should have been born an Irishman'. High compliment indeed!

Monday, June 23rd

The morning not a good one. As time drifts by, I resort to all the writer's time-wasting devices – walking downstairs, making phone calls that aren't vital, pottering, reading snippets of other works – and all the time hoping that, like Maradona's 'Hand of God' last night,[1] something would strike and show me the future.

I read some of *The Tender Passion* and also some more of great-grandfather's notebooks (he did mention young women, or just women, an awful lot), but by the time one o'clock comes I am not much further on with a decision.

Relieved to be temporarily released from my frustration, I go to Odette's for lunch with Eric I. He gives me some encouragement, partly by telling me that he's been writing very badly recently, and partly by a very sympathetic response to the Victorian idea.

By 6.30 I'm at the Commons to meet David Mitchell, the Transport Minister (Railways). He takes me to the Commons Bar. No-one else I know there except Roy Jenkins at a table by the window. Amidst the

---

1 Maradona's disputed first goal, in which he appeared to put the ball in the net with his hand, was the first of two he scored for Argentina in the quarter-finals to put England out of the Mexico World Cup 2–1.

almost suffocating leather and oak panelling, have a beer – the Minister a tomato juice.

He advises me to feel free at any time to ask him or his department for any help with facts and figures and he assures me that he keeps telling the DTP that we are not 'dangerous'.

Tuesday, June 24th

Drive over to the Riverside Studios by Hammersmith Bridge to see Max Wall (now 78) in *Krapp's Last Tape* with TG, Helen and Maggie. Max is marvellous. He moves carefully and precisely, his timing and eye for detail are exact and delightful. Maybe it's because, as TG says later, Max *is* Krapp. Audience predominantly young.

Afterwards we stay for a drink with him. It's as if no years have passed since Pembroke Castle and the rain in summer '76. Max still drinks a pint of Guinness, slowly. He remembers *Jabberwocky* line for line and we talk nostalgically of John Le Mesurier and others he remembers with generous enjoyment, and how he used to keep his teeth in a little bag at his belt. He talks quite cheerfully about his various 'conditions'. 'Fallen arsehole,' he confides, out of the girls' earshot.

Wednesday, June 25th

JC rings from a hospital bed where he's having a cartilage operation. The goldfish film seems set for May/June '87.

Robert H comes round for dinner. Talk over Robert's plans for various theatre groups he's trying to help, but I resist his pressure to commit Gumby funds. It's not so much the money as the fact that I have too many fingers in too many pies. I must reduce my involvements or they will at worst swamp me and at best become a blur of half-participation.

Tell him about the Victorian film. His advice is that I should write the Edward Palin character for another actor than myself, someone physically different – only then will I break away from the good old *Missionary* types.

Thursday, June 26th

At 2.30 to Rachel's classroom for the last progress report on any of our children at Gospel Oak. Mrs Deadman says Rachel combines the best of

Tom and William, that she has great potential – she was one of two girls who did not drop a point in her maths test – she is sensitive and easily bruised, but has developed a toughness and determination which will carry her through.

The girls run the class, says Mrs Deadman, and Rachel's table are far and away the most talented. And – some of them – very difficult. Rachel's problem is that everyone wants to be friends with her, and she is nice to them all. If she was able to be as sharp to them as some of them are to her she'd be less hassled.

Monday, June 30th

Hot night, morning starts cloudy. Am reading *Tender Passion* and making notes when it occurs to me that what I need is some up-front money to tide me through the period of research – in short, I need what I've avoided taking on my 'new film' for years: a good, old-fashioned commission.

Look at the calendar and apportion time for three projects up to the end of '87 – the Victorian film, a short film, possibly to be done at the National Film School as a prelude to directing the Victorian film, and some time in summer next year provisionally set aside for JC's film.

An evening phone call from D Leland awakens my interest in the part of Eric in *Heartbreakers*. It would ruin all the plans made earlier today, but would give me a new direction in acting, to complement the 'new direction' in writing to which I've now committed myself. Can I do both?

Wednesday, July 2nd

To the House of Commons with T2000 team.

Searching procedures at the door take a while. A man is trying to hand in a small gift-wrapped box with a ribbon around it, which he says is a present for the visiting German Chancellor. The lady at security wants to know what's in it. He doesn't know.

We pass through and into the Gothic world of Parliament, winding up back stairs to what could be the maids' quarters or the room of some demented sister who's not talked about, but turns out to be Committee Room 17. Inside a panel of ten MPs sit in a semi-circle around a secretary who takes shorthand of the proceedings. Opposite the semi-circle is a table at which currently are sitting four men from the Transport Users' Consultative Committee. They're all Major-Generals and look most impressive from behind. We slip in at the back, where a half-dozen people are listening.

I, who have been quite looking forward to the experience, find it one of the least pleasant of my T2000 outings thus far. The courtroom atmosphere, the ritual, the respectful 'grown-up' procedure, the 'sirs' and the 'I beg, Mr Chairman' – in fact all the quasi-legalistic panoply – make me uncomfortable. I feel as if I want to speak but can't. Or is it just that I don't know what they're talking about?

Monday, July 7th

Rachel is having her tea today when she asks 'Are you unemployed?' Expostulate as I do, there is a grain of truth in her question which rankles. Of course I have hardly a spare moment, but much of the time is spent holding on – to friends, obligations, duties such as T2000 – and comparatively little, at the moment, in the creation of new work.

Tuesday, July 15th

Taxi to L' Escargot and lunch with Sandy L. I had this morning sent round to Sandy the Victorian film idea, merely for reference. He thinks it has great potential, feels I should go to someone like the National Film Development Fund for first-stage writing money and that I should make up my mind whether to direct or act. More or less decide then to direct. It seems such a short and logical step on from writing and anything that might prevent me playing a sympathetic clergyman again must be a good thing.

To St James's Square. Slowly because of the heat. All the flowers around the 'shrine' for the policewoman shot by the Libyans are dried up and dead as I cross the square and into the time-warp that is the London Library.

Nervous, bookish, soft-spoken assistants with mad clothing direct you to the various areas of human experience. 'Domestic Servants, next to Dogs.' Takes a while to familiarise myself with the layout, but soon I'm getting into the swim of turning the lights on and off and encountering strange figures in between Ireland and the Gambia.

Leave with seven books, taxi back home. Driver's a great fan and I have to talk a lot and sign his book.

Not much time to unpack before Angela H arrives in preparation for

Rachel's appearance in the Gospel Oak musical 'Carrots' tonight. Give her a glass of champagne. Helen rushing in and out, house not very restful.

To the school.

Rachel gives her cheeky Cockney character – Carrots – a hint of timidity and uncertainty which she shouldn't really have. But she delivers her lines with good expression, clarity and assurance, and once she's free of the stageful of unmoving people and into one-to-one acting she's excellent. She sings two solos falteringly and a third very promisingly and robustly.

Wednesday, July 16th

A very sultry night, through which I sleep with considerable ease, until eight. At 9.15 I am at Acland Burghley School to discuss Tom's progress with Mr Trafford, his D&T [Design and Technology] teacher.

We talk for almost an hour about the poor funding of the course. Officially he has about £12 allotted per pupil per year for equipment! He manages to augment this ludicrous amount by various devious means – but fund-raising and PR are taking up far too much of his teaching time. Without whingeing, he paints a sad picture of neglect and obstinacy in the education system. He's not against some form of assessment, but first of all wages and resources need to be improved – morale is very low.

Thursday, July 17th

A cool and refreshing day – sun without the sweat. Reach my goal of four hours' research and reading. Helen rushes around all day buying food for the Gospel Oak school leavers' party which we go along to in the evening.

Rachel and a few friends produced an end of term magazine today which seems to sum up all the creative brightness of Gospel Oak School. All the children have been happy there and have made good friends. I shall miss it.

Wednesday, July 23rd

The Royal Wedding [of Prince Andrew to Sarah Ferguson] is everywhere. Thirty-one countries have pulled out of the Commonwealth Games. Reagan has outdone Thatcher in trying to clothe economic expediency in moral respectability, calling sanctions against South Africa 'repugnant'.

Saturday, July 26th

A leisurely start to the day, then embark on a clear-up of my workroom, sorting out the piles of books, letters, scripts, papers, many of them sparking flashes of guilt at work not dealt with, an opinion unexpressed, a cause unaided, but I have done so little work of my own these past few weeks that I really cannot feel any great qualms over my inability to respond to everyone else's demands.

Lie awake and talk to Helen, which I don't do often enough, of my worries about the Victorian film (am I desperately chasing a red herring?), about T2000 and my doubts which are fast developing into certainties – I'm not an institutional man, a committee man, a board man. I'm a writer, an actor, an occasional visitor – a flea who can sting and bite occasionally. I'm not cut out for Head of House.

Thursday, July 31st

To the Zanzibar to meet Michael Barnes, who is taking me as his guest to the Bolshoi Ballet at the Royal Opera House. As I've seen neither, this is a double first.

Before the opening of the ballet an announcement is made to try and forestall those 'who may try to use this occasion to make some sort of protest'. In a very English way the manager asks them not to disrupt the performance but to come and have a word with him at the interval. Obviously he's referring to those already protesting across the road, outside Bow Street Police Station, on behalf of Soviet Jewry.

The ballet is *The Golden Age*, and an unlikely, but entertainingly odd piece. Not grand or historical, it takes place, almost in the present day, at a seaside resort on the Black Sea and involves healthy undefiled workers' co-ops and a 'sleazy', but rather attractive night club called the Golden Age, where, dressed in dramatic blacks and golds, the bourgeois dance the tango.

Indeed, and most bizarrely, there's, at the start of the second act, a marvellous Shostakovich arrangement of 'Tea for Two'. Lots of echoes of American musicals – including *West Side Story* and *Sweet Charity*. I begin to be carried away and from then on the sheer skill, energy and excitement of the music and dancing are completely riveting.

Friday, August 8th

Drive to Oxford by ten and into St John's. Through two quiet, dignified quads to the library. I arrive at the same time as a bearded American scholar who is there to look at a thirteenth-century illuminated manuscript. Am reminded of the quiet wealth of the colleges – not in their buildings, beautiful though they are, but in cellars, archives, cupboards and chests.

I easily pass three hours at a desk with copies of the Oxford Calendar for 1843–62, and make copies of a number of pages and also of some good contemporary sources. Up above me is a marvellous long chamber with plaster and wood vaulted roof and Archbishop Laud's bust.

By the time I leave Oxford seems to have woken up and the spell is broken. The college buildings swarm with beefy Americans in Bermuda shorts, all here for some summer study course. One thing these colleges are getting very good at is making money.

Back to London by five.

Just enough time to say hello to Al L who arrived from Brittany yesterday, then off to an hour's tennis coaching.

Saturday, August 9th

Take Al to the bookstores of Charing Cross Road to satisfy his craving for Stevie Smith. Am struck by how rich London now is in bookshops. Despite the cinema revival, four-channel TV, cable, video, booming theatre, a lot more people seem to have a lot more time to read.

Have a half of bitter at the Crown in Seven Dials. Al so full of fears and worries – mainly centring on Gwenola and the effect on her when he goes. He has had two scares over the last two or three years and precious little has gone right, apart from the fact that he has survived, where many wouldn't, and Claudie, with her plain, philosophical Breton good sense, has been a tower of strength.

I take him on an 'East London' tour. To satisfy both our curiosities. First to Leadenhall Street to see the Lloyds Building. I like it more this time, perhaps because Al's so enthusiastic. For him it's a work of genius. I appreciate today the way it fits in and complements the buildings around. It's big but light and its lines continuously broken, giving vistas through, across and round it, so at times it gives the impression of translucence – not a quality associated usually with the intimidating and imperious City buildings.

We drive on to the east and find ourselves amongst the glossy, high-tech of the renewed, revived Isle of Dogs, where enormous investment has transformed Docklands, to the benefit of businessmen and to the detriment of the local people who have found themselves largely unwanted, their neighbourhood swiftly, comprehensively, unapolo-getically re-ordered by outsiders.

Wednesday, August 13th

On the Victorian film news is that all goes ahead well. Steve has met with Sandy L and got on well. We decide not to go for an advance from the Film Development Fund. It's not money I need, and the submission will require synopsis and waiting for processing, all of which will take time away from my vital priority – to produce a script or other evidence by the end of October that we are not all barking up the wrong tree.

Back to Camden Town for a visit to Peter Lewis. He pronounces my teeth in good shape and talks about his Prussian grandfather who broke two ribs putting up a deck chair. Hear on the radio that 63% of callers in an LBC poll want British troops out of Ulster.

Monday, September 1st

Begin work on the Victorian screenplay.

Unsure about the sound of the dialogue – the period flavour – the detail – Latin verse, etc – but once I'm going it doesn't hold me up and I experience the pleasure of creating characters, lives, incidents; enough this morning to leave me optimistic.

Rachel has gone off for her first day at Parliament Hill, with her new Cahors black satchel, black earrings, white shirt and black skirt.

Ring Ma and Angela. Angela says she's in the middle of quite a serious depression. She's decided to be forthright about it and not cover up. Is there anything genetically responsible, she wonders. Perhaps Daddy suffered from depression as well. He certainly took things very seriously, was underpaid and had a stammer, but could this be genetically trans-mitted?

Cleese calls to say his script is finished. Tony Jay evidently approved greatly – which John is cross about as he'd hoped Tony would suggest the

20-minute cut it needs. I suggest John sends the script to someone he knows really hates his stuff. John finds this very funny. Top of his list is Richard Ingrams, with Peter Ackroyd a close second.

Wednesday, September 3rd

To the Python office to have my photo taken – to help out a student who's doing a portfolio of writers 'because they're most likely to be at home'. Can't get used to the intrusion of the lens poking towards me. Then an hour's chat with two very young, keen Python fans, who run a mysterious magazine which, they assure me, comes out about every four years.

After a couple of hours of being famous and unpaid, I meet with Anne and Steve. Their latest reservations concern the extra money needed – over and above buying studio equipment and the freehold to the buildings – for the creation of Redwood Delancey. Costs now up from 48 to 101G.

Rather a gloomy chat. I have the money, but it clearly irks Steve to advance yet more of my money to the project – interest-free. These are nervous times for Redwood. I think we have no option but to be bold and resolute and hope that in ten years' time (for it won't be before) it's all been an amazing success and a nest-egg for old age.

Thursday, September 4th

Angela and Veryan round in the evening for Angela's birthday present – a home-cooked meal. Champagne, tomato soup, chicken and mango, cheese, fresh berries and '79 claret, all very nicely cooked and served and Angela cheerful for most of the time. She responds to our house like someone warming themselves at a fire.

Friday, September 5th

To lunch at Odette's with TG. Voluble, boisterous, endlessly full of ideas and opinions. He wants to create some sort of 'corporate identity' to embrace Python and post-Python and ex-Python solo efforts. He's so restless – like a rubber band has been wound up in his formative years and has now been let go.

From Gilliam to the quieter dynamism of Richard Faulkner. I'd hoped to mention my feelings about retirement. More and more I'm becoming convinced that chairing is not me, but as soon as I bring it up Richard skilfully side-steps it, referring to my 'leave of absence' next year. It will be more permanent than that, and one of these days I shall have to tell him and he'll have to listen.

Back home – ring Tristram. London Film Festival have passed on *East of Ipswich*. Snobs. Bias against comedy? I just feel it's a backward push after both '*Mish*' and *Private Function* were at the Festival.

Sunday, September 7th

A sunny day in prospect. Late rising. Read Sundays. Martin Amis in the *Observer* reviewing *Speed* is fairly certain that being a nice guy is a positive disadvantage to a writer. This puts the wind up me. Perhaps I recognise a truth. My main problem is that I'm a lazy writer. Line of least resistance. There's another title for my autobiography: 'Lines of Least Resistance'!

Sit out in the unbroken sunshine over lunchtime and Helen and I work our way through stacks of old photos – ordering, albuming and ditching. They do present a view of a placid, gregarious, well-travelled, spirited and close-knit family of which I'm proud and for which I'm grateful. Dare I say a family with less than its fair share of troubles.

Tuesday, September 9th

Steady, but unspectacular morning on the Victorian film, which I would like to call *American Friends*, though the Wim Wenders *The American Friend* niggles.

Reading a *Guardian* article on Eton College's shabby treatment of their properties in London, when a very clear idea for a TV play occurs to me. The efforts to move a rather dignified and well-bred old lady from a house which the powers of commerce want to develop. Plenty of scope for little ironies, social comment and on a subject dear to my heart – greed versus dignity, coercion against consideration. Spend an hour writing the first couple of scenes, which flow easily.

The prospect of writing two new scripts before Christmas becomes a reality and an attractive one at that. After all the hopes and half-starts and *Limericks* and *Mirrorstones* and *Cyrils* of the last 18 months, I feel now solidly employed, stretching myself and enjoying a simple and satisfying return of writing appetite.

Thursday, September 11th

Tom is back from school and by his face and general uncommunicativeness I can tell all is not well. We talk for some time about his aversion to maths, his feeling of inferiority compared to the others in his class, and it's obvious by the intensity of his feeling that he is finding it difficult. Is this because he's faced with the realities of very hard mental study and concentration for the first time, or is it that he's genuinely unable to understand the work? I think the former.

Out to have dinner with Jonathan and Kate, prior to his disappearing up to Stratford for *Macbeth*.

We eat at Zen in Hampstead, or Zen W3 as it's cleverly called. The décor is chic black and white. It could be Beverly Hills or New York. An incredibly noisy table of Chinese businessmen passing Chivas Regal round the table with the speed of a Catherine wheel, turn out to be the management and owners.

No wonder they're celebrating – the place is packed. It's so self-consciously designed to attract the young, rich and successful that it's acted like a magnet to the new Hampstead money – not money which lives in the village, but, I suspect, in the new villas of Finchley Road and Golders Green.

There are no traditional materials, London brick or timber. The wood has been removed and replaced by a giant weeping fig tree which stands two floors high. The food is delicate, beautiful and incredibly tasty; unlike the atmosphere.

Late to bed after we ask for the bill from six different waiters.

Friday, September 12th

Receive photos from Mick Powell taken a week or so ago. I think I may be in for a W H Auden face – or at best a Michael Parkinson. A lot of lines appearing. The sight of them mentally ages me several years. Have noticed other signs recently – I hardly listen to pop music on the radio now – it's talk or classical.

To Clare Latimer's 35th birthday party at her shop in Chalcot Road. Slip over as I'm going in and crack my hip on the pavement. Not too seriously, but feel very foolish as a group of lads are passing the shop and mockingly surveying the noisy, middle-class guests clutching wine glasses within.

But there are some pleasant ladies there – always a much better prospect for small talk than men – and excellent food. I thaw out, but feel old and leave with the elderly and those who have babies.

Tuesday, September 16th: Southwold

I apply myself to the Victorian film, which has become *American Friends*. Writing, sometimes a little meanderingly, but writing all the same, and quite pleased with progress.

After lunch some letters and another short spell on the film, then across the Common for a run.

When I return a notice has been stuck across the windscreen of my Sierra – 'Please move your car so we can park outside our house. Public car parks are provided.'

A visit to Julie Haythornthwaite (such a spectacularly different neighbour from Mrs Pratt). She pours me a scotch and ice and we talk. She's most concerned about Angela, who was in to see her recently, and was, she thought, not at all well. We discuss some whys and wherefores and as Angela obviously finds it easier to open up to Julie than to Mother, then I don't feel I'm betraying anyone. Julie has a number of friends in the same boat.

Wednesday, September 17th: Southwold

For no reason at all, other than there being no reason at all, I find myself unable to sleep, despite being too sleepy to read.

I'm at the desk by nine, though. There then follows a sort of re-run of the previous night, except that instead of sleep eluding me, this time it's a story eluding me. Sense of the same helplessness, close to despair, as the minutes turn into hours and nothing comes. The little room and the cramped table, which once seemed so friendly, now conspire against me, as does the east wind moaning around the roofs and wires outside.

But I persevere with my four hours. Nothing to show at the end of it except frustration at the impasse into which I've led the characters.

Back to some letters and then my great stand-by – a run. Running can never be anything but positive – that's the joy of it.

Thursday, September 18th

Down to Bedford Square to collect *The Mirrorstone* from Tom Maschler. My first sight of the finished work. Tom gushes uncontrollably, unstoppably about its brilliance and genius and beauty and I grope around, like someone having a very bright light shone in their face, to try and find the source of this dazzling hyperbole.

Momentarily a squeezing of the stomach. The holograms are tiny and none of them work in the dull early evening light. Tom rushes to put on his old Habitat standard lamp. It doesn't work at first. Then, with the help of the spotlights, some of the holograms come quite impressively out of the book.

I flip the pages. All sorts of negative thoughts. Brilliant draughtsmanship but blank faces. The whole book takes itself too seriously.

Thursday, September 25th

Complete four hours of good, steady progress on *American Friends*. Then a run and some calls – including one from the British Council asking me if I would like to go with TG, David Robinson of *The Times* and John Cartwright of the Council to the Moscow Film Festival. *Jabberwocky*, *Brazil* and *Private Function* are all represented. Very excited – another November possibility, if I can clear the book publicity dates.

To Visconti's *Ossessione* at the Renoir. Few people there and, as it shakes into black and white life with dramatic music and the title large across the screen, I hear a voice behind observe in some surprise – 'Oh, it's Italian.'

Saturday, September 27th: London–Southwold–Norwich

I'm away by ten and, after a slow slog along busy roads, at Granny's by one.

She potters out to see where I'm parked. I've brought lunch – some smoked salmon and peaches. Conscious of having to make an effort every time I hear 'Are you looking for something, dear?' when I open a drawer or cupboard.

All I want to do after lunch is sleep in an armchair over the newspapers. I settle instead for sitting outside on the balcony. The light breeze and the grunts and imprecations of rugby players on the Common keep me awake. The sun is soothing and we have a natter over all Granny's worries – damp patches in the bedroom, bathroom window opening, income tax – nothing too serious.

It's almost a year since she moved from Reydon, and as I kiss her goodbye at four and leave her waving from between the parked cars that concern her so, I feel very relieved with the way she has coped with the whole upheaval. And proud of her too.

To Norwich.

I'm welcomed by Kingsley Canham – slight, bearded administrator of the regional film theatre, Cinema City.

Even before a cup of tea or an introduction, I'm being talked at by two 'young people' from a group called Snowball. They want to use law against the bomb. Their aim is to get so many people to commit the 'minimum' crime at a nuclear base – cutting a strand of wire, etc – that they will clog the courts and eventually their view that a small crime committed to prevent a bigger crime is not illegal will be examined. The boy tells me proudly he's been inside for 40 days. 'But the police are getting wise – they're not arresting us any more ... we have to go and give ourselves up.' Promise I'll read their literature.

Tuesday, September 30th

Collect Eric I and Tania by cab at Carlton Hill and we are deposited at the Royal Court Theatre at a quarter to eight. An audience of quality packs every seat for Bennett's *Kafka's Dick*. One feels that there are at least six reserve casts amongst us.

The play is based on the rather neat premise of a writer (Kafka) being magicked forward in time to the house of one of his greatest fans (an A. Bennett household complete with Alison Steadman as the unfulfilled, sexy wife, and an old father who is about to be put in a home – Alan plagiarising *Private Function* surprisingly shamelessly). A lot said about the artist's right to privacy and the grasping, twisting manipulation of money-grabbing agents, publishers and other lesser talents.

'Woody Alan Bennett' is how Eric sums up our views of the evening.

Tuesday, October 7th

Like the mild and gentle weather, my writing goes on mildly and gently and my days fall into a settled and unchanging pattern.

A run, and then shopping for Tom's birthday present. A couple of hours around Jermyn and Sackville Street. Buy him a rather fine razor, slim, black and beautifully weighted. When I get home I find it's been used and I kick the cat and generally throw a fit, seeing as it comes from Oggetti and was not cheap. But it's hard to complain to these new and fashionable 'gift' shops. Like their goods they feel themselves out of reach of the general public.

Taxi down to the Coliseum to see Eric in *The Mikado*. A splendid theatre inside, voluminous and impressive, with marbled columns and huge, gilded statues of lions and charging horses. A full house and curtain goes up on an imaginative and striking set – which has the effect of making the characters look like the occupants of a decaying white dolls' house.

Very unsatisfied by the staging of the first half. Why is it in the '30's and why is so much of the comedy played like the Marx Bros? Eric keeps his end up well, but comes into his own in the second half and steals the show from under the noses of the fine, trained singers, because he, almost alone, is able to exploit the comic potential.

Wednesday, October 8th

At work by half past seven. Quite a good morning. Tom is 18. We give him £84 towards a 'boogie box' (ghetto-blaster, Brixton briefcase) and a desk tidy (hopefully), his razor and a Chris Bonington climbing book.

Tom's lifestyle and his expectations are so different from mine at 18 that I find it hard to empathise with him as he sits at the breakfast table surrounded by his cards and gifts. But the famous Tom grin is much in evidence, so I feel perhaps all's well and we ease off our pressure on him to be a bit more like us.

His martial arts training shows in a fit, good-looking, lean body. Reading and writing don't seem to appeal.

Meeting with Steve. He wants to tell me about the latest plans to protect all the other Pythons from the effects of Graham C's impending bankruptcy. (Having said that, it's been impending for at least a year.)

Anne and Steve propose a buy-out of GC's share of Python – his directorships and everything else. Then, if he does go under, we shall not have his advisers on our boards, nor his liabilities either. It seems a more significant emotional moment (the first Python to go under, the first 'legal' break-up of the group) than financial.

Friday, October 10th

Am conscious of letting the average slip back this week. The less time I spend, the less easy it is to maintain my commitment. Have lost sight of the whole work this week in a mad dash for the end. Now I am relying heavily on my three days in Yorkshire next week to get back in touch with the script, leaving me two weeks to trim, edit, order and make it presentable for November typing.

Monday, October 20th

To the Fox preview theatre in Soho Square to meet John C, and for the first time the various people involved in 'Goldfish Called Wanda'. Charles Crichton does seem to have some difficulty with speech and movement, but has a wicked smile and I get to like him more and more as the evening goes on.

We're seeing an American film called *Ruthless People*[1] which has taken a lot of money out there.

It's a West Coast film and I suppose is as far from the intelligent, perceptive, graceful world of Woody Allen as it's possible to be. But the fact that it has been so successful accords with my reading in the paper that 40% of students in a poll at the California State University hadn't heard of Mikhail Gorbachev.

On afterwards to a meal at the White Tower. Jonathan Benson, who is now with Shirley Russell,[2] immensely good company and it's so good to see him again. Later Kevin Kline and Phoebe Cates arrive, though no sign as yet of Jamie Lee.

Kevin K, quite unmaliciously, recounts tales of Sir Dickie calling African extras 'Darling' to their obvious bewilderment. They've been filming 'Biko' [later, *Cry Freedom*] in Harare, which he found incredibly dull and uninteresting and says he feels they got out just in time.

---

1 Released in 1986, it was directed by Jim Abrahams and David Zucker and starred Bette Midler and Danny de Vito.
2 Shirley Russell, costume designer, ex-wife of film director Ken. She designed costumes for most of his hits, including *Women in Love*, *Tommy* and *The Boy Friend*.

Wednesday, October 22nd

To the Great Western Hotel for lunch with David Mitchell.

The Minister, plus two private secretaries, arrives at one. The three of them immediately go to the toilet.

A pleasantry or two. He was at the House until 4.31 this morning. Then I begin by mentioning the topic that cannot be ignored – the report in the papers of this very morning that the government is to cut BR's grant by 25% next year.

He tries to lecture me (agreeably enough) on the link between funding and performance, on not solving a problem by 'throwing money at it'. I declare my readiness, as a taxpayer, to see my taxes used for the creation of the best possible rail system, and so we go on.

He seems almost frustrated by BRB's [British Railways Board – the management] willingness to accept these cuts. He suggests that they don't need to. If they feel unable to keep up quality of service on the money they are getting, then they should say so.

Friday, October 24th

We leave at eight for JC's birthday party at 82 Ladbroke Grove, whose interior glitters and drips pictures and opulence. It's been once again redesigned, and has a lush, soft, rich creamy feel to it.

Michael Frayn is there – nice, ironic, soft-spoken with a gentle, permanently amused look. Reminds me of his contemporary, Bennett, in his undemonstrative self-possession.

Talk to JC's mother, who sits in a corner and talks quite cheerfully about how she's been stuck in the corner. Keeps saying 'John would think I'm silly' or 'John would tell me to stop being a nuisance'. She's 87 and seems extraordinarily fit. Am able to tell her how the recent *Fawlty* repeats keep my mother from total gloom!

Sunday, October 26th

Jonathan P calls by with [his son] Patrick. Hear about Jonathan's battle with the sponsors. He refused to play Macbeth (the day before rehearsals began) when he saw that Barclays Bank [who had invested heavily in South Africa's apartheid regime] were sponsoring. Barclays' £60,000 was returned and JP kept on. But he's been suffering from considerable criticism, especially from the theatre staff, who resent his interference. He says he's had notes stuck under the windscreen wiper of his Mercedes giving last year's Mercedes sales figures in South Africa. But he's weathering the storm. His hair is growing long and his beard looks more like Lear than Macbeth.

Monday, October 27th

A Russian visa application arrives by motorbike. William has to be taken to an architect's practice in Camden Town where he is starting a week's 'job experience'.

To King's Cross and the sigmoidoscopy clinic. There are seats outside it now where you can wait. An elderly man next to me reads his M M Kaye whilst from within there are some stomach-chilling shrieks of pain.

Friday, October 31st

At my desk at 9.30. Down to page-numbering, but still noticing bad lines, overwritten, unnecessary dialogue and plot discrepancies. Change as much as I can, and by half past twelve the completed screenplay – eight weeks, roughly 300 hours of writing – is ready for its first delivery. Only as far as Alison and the word processor this time, but it feels satisfyingly weighty and, whatever its deficiencies may be, I feel a sense of relief that I have persevered and have completed the process. If I'd left it half done, or even three-quarters done, feel it might have joined many other uncompleted screenplays in the 'One Day Perhaps' file.

Monday, November 3rd

Drive down to the Imperial War Museum for a party to launch Spike's latest and last volume of war memoirs.

Spike is in a three-piece striped suit, the suit he uses, so he says, to visit his bank manager. At his most benevolent and easy. I tell him how I read an extract to a fourth-year class at William Ellis of his *Hitler – My Part* and suddenly found myself describing the 'semen-stained underpants' of Sergeant Harris. Spike thinks my discomfiture hilarious. I leave him to his various admirers. He sits down for most of the party and people come to him.

Tuesday, November 4th

To Ealing for a look at *East of Ipswich*. My first sight of it for three months and first sight of the finished product (give or take some grading adjustments). Enormously pleased. George Fenton's music adds a touch of class and life to the piece wherever its pace slackens. The sound-mixing is confident and all in all it seems to work most gratifyingly. The comedy and the pathos, the atmosphere and the oddness all seem to balance and Edward R-H's performance grows in stature every time I see it.

Afterwards have a drink with Tristram P in the Fuller's pub across the road where we so often used to end Python filming days. It's half past five, dark already, but clear and cold and I feel an unequivocal glow of achievement as I drive home.

Friday, November 7th

1.30 Python lunch. I'm the first there. Eric, with a little trilby hat on which reminds me of his unforgettable portrayal of the Duke of Kent, steps down from a taxi. Sign a *Life of Python* book for his mum, then Terry J, Terry G (encased in thick Donegal tweed coat) and Anne and Steve all arrive. Terry J has got everyone kissing everyone else these days, but I pass on TG and Steve.

TG is soon to announce *Munchausen* and would like to announce a sort of post-Python production company, based in Delancey, etc, like Enigma or HandMade. Eric suggests Enema – motto 'bums on seats'.

At five o'clock to squash with TJ. I just win the battle of the business lunch.

Then I have to hurry across a wet and windswept London to 82 Ladbroke for a reading of 'Goldfish Called Wanda'. My first acquaintance with this project, which is already as far as having chosen the caterers.

Inside the warm, soft-pile comfort of JC's home, Jamie Lee Curtis awaits. Physically much more delicate and waif-like than one expects from her screen presence and her face somehow darker and slimmer. She has a softness guarded by a sharp-eyed, defiant exterior. Kevin Kline arrives half an hour later, from almost his last day on 'Biko'.

After Chinese take-away supper, we settle, around an artificially roaring log fire, and the windows slightly open as it is such a warm night, to read the 'Goldfish'. We don't finish until twenty to twelve, and this is the problem. This quick-fire farce should have been over in half the time, but

Kevin finds it difficult to sort out his various voices and the Anglicanisms such as 'loot' and 'doing the job'. John has to explain the stage directions at some length, so it all drags on a bit.

I enjoy playing Ken and see potential for a much more eccentric, physical and unusual character than I usually play. JC is quite straight. There just aren't enough laughs. Maybe they are all there, but this evening compares unfavourably to the readings of Cleese/Chapman sketches which were nearly always a treat.

Sunday, November 16th

Jolted to hear that Angela has been no longer able to cope with her depression and has been taken into the West Suffolk Hospital for two weeks. This hits me hard.

Wednesday, November 19th: Moscow

It's half past four, USSR time, as we touch down. A queue at the passport control. Another Englishman next to me warns of at least one and a half hours of queuing, here and at baggage control. Gloom descends, which isn't helped by standing for four or five minutes in the glow of a prison-search-style striplight, with an angled mirror beyond so they can check the back of my head. But I'm cleared through.

A very reassuring British figure steps forward to meet me. 'Are you Mr Battersby?' Then I'm alone again. Notice a pretty, be-furred Russian lady eyeing me. She introduces herself as Helen and hands me a business card on which her name is printed as 'Elena'. Call her Elena from then on.

She whisks me briskly through baggage clearance. A huge Seagull (Chaika) black limousine is waiting. Looks like a '50's Chevrolet. Russian pop music blares out. Elena asks the driver to turn it down, but the control isn't working. Eventually he tugs at some connection and the whole system gives up.

Cannot take in much of what we're passing as we speed along a broad, straight, featureless, empty road towards the centre of Moscow. I am to be driven directly to the Archive Theatre, where *Jabberwocky* is to be shown at seven o'clock.

Enormously wide, straight roads, bulky solid buildings, wide, empty spaces, soaring walls. Feel like Tom Thumb.

The Archive Theatre has Russian and British flags up outside and heads turn as I emerge from the Seagull. Hands are shaken and I'm taken into a back room where coffee cups are laid out, alongside cakes, pastries and orange and mineral water. No sign of a vodka anywhere. (Apparently Gorbachev has decided to try and confront the problem of drunkenness and officially frowned upon alcoholic entertainment. No public places are allowed to serve alcohol until after two o'clock.)

Terry and John Cartwright of the British Council and David Robinson of *The Times* arrive.

Terry G comes in, rumbling in American and with his video camera turning. He even takes it into the auditorium, where 300 Muscovites are assembled to watch the film we made together ten years ago. As part of his speech he turns the camera onto the audience. Most laugh. Some do their hair.

We're presented with carnations and the film begins. Watch 15 minutes or so. Rather depressing reminder of how much my face has aged in ten years.

Then I'm driven to the Sovietskaya Hotel to wash and brush up before catching the 11.45 night train to Leningrad. (I later hear it on good authority that most Intourist trains run at night so that foreigners won't be able to see 'sensitive' installations.)

Talk for a while. David Robinson tells of the way Murdoch bussed his journalists into Wapping.[1] He had certain phone numbers to ring to find out where the bus would be leaving from, and always an Australian voice answered! His review of *Rosa Luxemburg* was criticised for taking up too much space when there was an English film also on release. 'We are a Conservative paper,' he was told.

Thursday, November 20th: Leningrad

Outside all is grey sub-light. A line of tanker wagons silhouette against the sky as we move slowly into Leningrad.

Magnificent view of the Neva from my dispiriting little room.

---

1 Rupert Murdoch, with the support of the Thatcher government, had moved production of his newspapers (*The Times*, the *Sunday Times*, the *Sun*) out to custom-built non-unionised premises in Wapping. After a vicious dispute lasting almost a year the power of the print unions was broken in the same way that union power in the mining industry had been broken two years previously.

Everything functional – one tiny picture, three empty beer cans in a cupboard, water too dirty to drink, bedside light switch doesn't work.

Monday, November 24th: Moscow–London

When the pilot announced we were leaving Russian air space there was a ghoulish cheer from Americans on board but one American student I just spoke to claimed his Moscow trip had been the 'high-point of my year'.

Like the American I found the visit an extraordinary and unusual one. A glimpse into a world about which we talk so often and yet know so little. The beauty of Moscow was a surprise – the number of churches on the Kremlin, with their twirly domes quite the antithesis of the monumental architecture I'd expected. The warmth and friendliness of most of those we met was reassuring and surprising.

The early comfort-shocks – poor lighting, poor food, absence of small restaurants and bars, joinery that didn't join, almost empty shop counters, cheap and grubby curtain and furnishing materials, exasperatingly impenetrable bureaucracy, compounded by the gloomy weather and gloomy faces – were depressing and almost frightening after the West.

However, as the days went by I adjusted. I no longer kept making comparisons with what I'd left, but with what was there, and though my material expectations may have lowered, I was able to enjoy and appreciate other values – an absence of the bombardment of advertising, a lack of anger, violence and pressure, the pleasure of discussing basic issues of freedom, responsibility, social organisation and the like in a country where all these issues really matter.

The knowledge that the Workers' Revolution has only produced a different kind of privileged elite who *can* travel abroad, who *can* book tables in restaurants and who *do* get food from private sources without having to queue, gives one the impression that this is not a particularly happy country. But the genuine warmth and emotion from Elena when we kissed goodbye today at the airport makes it impossible for me not to want to return.

My last memories are of the airport building, which was clean, spacious and almost empty. And TG and his four-hour video film of delegates to the first British film week for seven years, slung round his shoulder as he scuttled off to the flight to Rome and discussions with the *Munchausen* designer.

Tuesday, November 25th

Wake at six, i.e. nine Moscow, then sleep for two more hours – filled with Muscovite dreams of wide streets, looming buildings and silent, slow-moving lines of people.

Talk with Steve about *American Friends*. A cautious, even faintly embarrassed reaction. I really must finish reading it and see what's wrong!

Then by Underground to Stockwell to present certificates to local school children who've drawn variations on the 'Red Bus' theme for a local public transport pressure group. The children's pictures are marvellous. Bright and imaginative and full of little jokes and bits of detail, and all very different. Nearly all the winners are either West Indian or Asian.

To the Bijou for the cast and crew screening of *East of Ipswich*. All four 'juveniles' there. Three of them currently have no acting work at all.

I love the film. Nothing I've done gives me as much unqualified pleasure. So glad to be able to transmit my elation to those responsible, especially Edward, John, Oona and Pippa[1] – with whom I end up drinking in the Intrepid Fox. 'You weren't in *Crossroads*, were you?' asks an aggressive gay at the bar.

Thursday, November 27th

To the T2000 office for a pre-AGM briefing with Susan H. None of them seem to be lit up at the thought of, as Susan puts it, 'spending what looks like the last good weekend of the year in the Oldway Centre at Paignton'.

Spend two more hours on my speech, then set to my other task for the week, reading both *Erik the Viking* and finishing *American Friends*.

A very bright sunlight glows around my workroom as I begin to read Terry's jokey adventure of sunless Iceland. Some dynamism missing at the centre of the film and also the balance between anachronistic comedy and gritty Norse/Bergmanesque realism not struck quite right. By comparison *American Friends* is wordy, but I'm encouraged by its richness and the potential of all the characters.

Leave for squash at four feeling very optimistic and quite excited that

1 Edward Rawle-Hicks, John Wagland, Oona Kirsch and Pippa Hinchley were the four main younger-generation actors in *East of Ipswich*.

we have two Prominent Features here.[1] Find myself quite eloquent about *Erik the Viking* – and hopefully offer Terry some good advice. He seems very happy at my reactions, and in turn I'm going to make some instant changes to *American Friends* and let him read it whilst I'm away.

Saturday, November 29th: Paignton

Walk to the Oldway Mansion, a huge house, built on the proceeds of sewing machine sales by the Singer family and set incongruously amid the nylon and print semis and just up the road from the ex-cinema. It is completely out of character for T2000, but Cyril Perry, our organiser, fixer, and member of the NUR Executive Committee, has set us up in the ballroom, and orchestral music plays over speakers in the marbled hall.

I'm a little thrown by the scale but, before I can settle, a squat, mediaeval-looking figure is introduced to me as the Mayor's assistant. Cyril Perry has evidently secured the services of his worship to open our proceedings.

I am marched away by the Beadle – and addressed familiarly from the start as 'Mike' – to meet the Mayor.

The Beadle treats the Mayor like a dog or a ventriloquist's dummy. 'At 9.30 sharp we proceed around the gallery, and I bring the Mayor into the ballroom. Everyone stands. We go to the podium, you will say a few words of introduction, his worship will declare the conference open, you may reply, then I have to take him out again.'

Sunday, November 30th: Paignton–London

The morning session begins at 9.30. Kerry Hamilton, who made a TV series called *Losing Track* – one of the few to have something to say about public transport – is a guarded feminist, with a hard and daunting Irish exterior, which melts away somewhat when she's not under threat. She says that when Channel 4 first commissioned her series they repeatedly insisted it must be 'controversial'. When it was finished and done (with a five million viewing slot for one of the programmes), their judgement was that it was too controversial! She shows excerpts, which liven up the talk.

1 Prominent Features was the name of our new Python-based film production company. A name dreamt up, as I remember it, by Alison Davies at the Python office.

Will and Eric in France. Summer 1984. I'd had a Geoffrey Boycott T-shirt made for Eric as we were both slightly obsessed with the Greatest Living Yorkshireman.

My friend Al Levinson (left) with Norman Rosten, poet laureate of Brooklyn, and like me, a champion of Al's work.

A Private Function, 1984

ABOVE *A Private Function* was the last of five films I made with George Harrison and Denis O'Brien as Executive Producers. The HandMade logo was a Gilliam design.

ABOVE RIGHT Advertising bicycle clips with Alan Bennett, North Yorkshire, May 1984

RIGHT 'Kill it, Gilbert!'. MP, Betty and Maggie Smith.

BELOW With Maggie, enjoying a break from porcicide in the garden at Briargarth, May 1984

With Alan and Maggie
and the foot from my
chiropodist's surgery,
on the set of the dance
sequence after the
Mayor's dinner, June 1984

Anne Gibbins, Helen's mother,
with my mother and Helen at the
Private Function Royal Premiere,
November 21st 1984

Toilet of the Stars. (left to right) Denholm Elliott, Jim Carter, MP, Pete Postlethwaite,
John Normington and Richard Griffiths in the gents at The Great Western Hotel
Paddington, June 1984

Will, Tom, Rachel and Helen on holiday in Majorca, August 1986

'Photographed with a bike giving views on cycling in London. Cannot pose with my own bike as the saddle's missing' March 7 1986

12 Feb 1987

Dear Michael

Thank you again for appearing on my show.
I'm so sorry for the delay, but I just today
received the enclosed photograph back from the
corner drugstore. (Unfortunately, it was the
corner drugstore in Fairbanks, Alaska.)

I hope you'll think of this photograph as
a remembrance of your appearance. Let it also
serve as a small token of my appreciation.

XPPP Joan

thankyou, god.

All-American look for the Joan
Rivers show. She was the only
American host who ever wrote
me a thank-you letter.

A Fish Called Wanda, 1988

Comrades in arms.
(Clockwise from top left): With Charles Crichton, director; Gerry Paris (the best stand-in in the world); Kevin Kline, chip abuser and friend.

John C (Archie Leach) trying some unsuccessful information retrieval.

Ken Pile. Fan Photo.

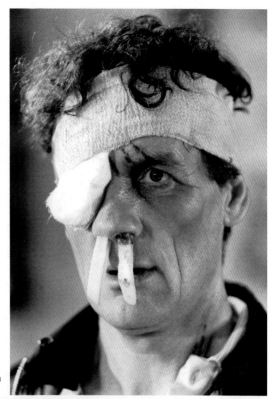

'Start the day being kissed repeatedly by Jamie on the bathroom floor. Very pleasant form of acting' July 17 1987

Tom, Will, Helen, Granny and Rachel brave an east coast gale outside Sunset House, Southwold. 1987

With 90 year-old Joyce Carey, friend and muse of Nöel Coward, on the set of *Number 27* 'Apparently her skirt fell down as she stood in the rose garden. "Normally I would have laughed, but this time I was a little cross," she commented' June 23 1988

At midday I wind up the conference, final speeches of thanks abound, and I'm quite touched when John Gregg – the white-haired, kindly Devonian member, who has spent the entire proceedings with a hand cupped behind his ear – rises to propose a vote of thanks to me. He calls my chairing 'genial'. They all seem very happy and content and, though I was steering blind through much of the weekend, I think that I found my way through all the pitfalls, kept control and maybe managed to stamp some of my character on the proceedings.

All back together in the train – and a jolly crowd we are. In fact my hope that the experience of the AGM would be the final straw that made up my mind to resign, is unfounded. Still, no time to reflect now, as I have to unpack, repack and set off on my travels again tomorrow to promote *Ripping Yarns* in America.

Tuesday, December 2nd: New York

Live at Five call to say that owing to the President's announcement of the appointment of a special prosecutor,[1] there won't be room for me on the show. They need a seven-minute 'window'. As I was set for a ten-minute interview, this is quite a blow for the CBS/Fox machine.

Feeling unadventurous and low on energy I remain in my room, occasionally going to the window to watch fierce rain lashing the home-going crowds ten floors below. I watch extensive coverage of the Iran arms deal crisis. Call some friends, then order supper. Drink a half-bottle of red wine and then have to fight against sleep. So in a most unsatisfactory state when Judi Marie and the limousine call at 9.15 to take me to a live TV interview.

The interview is quite hard work. Get through it on nervous hysteria. Thick greasy coating of make-up and nothing to drink but cold coffee, whilst all around, like flies, the crew do their Python impersonations. I'm afraid I'm just not in synch with them tonight.

---

1 The announcement that Lawrence Walsh was to be appointed as a special independent counsel marked the latest step in the murky Iran-Contra affair, the biggest scandal of Reagan's presidency. The US was accused of illegally selling arms to Iran in order to raise funds to help anti-Communist 'Contras' overthrow Nicaragua's left-wing Sandinista government.

Wednesday, December 3rd: New York

Paul [Wagner, in charge of publicity for CBS/Fox] rang and was quietly and politely critical of my CNN interview last night. He felt that I let the interviewer guide me and didn't push *Ripping Yarns* enough.

Then on to a very badly-run new TV show called *Made in New York*. The make-up man hasn't turned up and I'm made-up by the other 'guest' – a lovely, pregnant singer.

To the *Letterman* show. Julia Child on before me, cooking hamburger. Her electric ring doesn't work, and she improvises marvellously. Lovely, big, slightly shambolic lady who looks like John in drag and is a wonderful breath of fresh air after the coiffured Leona Helmsley clones of the past two days.

Swept away from NBC to drive uptown for another TV chat show – *Nightlife*, with David Brenner. Water has flooded their control room after recent storms and recording is delayed by an hour. I never feel at my best between four and six anyway, and after the day and *Letterman* I have to work very hard at being happy to be there. Brenner is a good host, if a little less playful than Letterman. I'm on for half an hour.

Still no let-up as Paul wants me to 'work the room a little' at a big video dinner-dance at the Marriott Marquis.

On the stage a man called Ken Kai is exhorting free enterprise on to further challenges. Hardly a word he says can be understood owing to a thick Oriental accent, but at one point I plainly hear him say 'Get up off your asses!'

Thursday, December 4th: New York–Los Angeles

Breakfast arrives late, packing and bill-paying all in a rush, then sit in slow traffic through the mid-town tunnel, arriving at JFK 45 minutes before the American Airlines flight to the West Coast.

I'm driven to the 'Carson' studios. Someone called Jay Leno is hosting.[1]

Am shown a dark and wretched dressing room with my name on it and a tray of food in the middle of the floor. All eaten. Lot of hanging around, omens not good. But as air-time nears things brighten up.

1 *The Tonight Show*, an American institution, had been hosted by Johnny Carson since 1962. This particular night he handed it over to a comedian called Jay Leno. Six years later, when Carson retired, Leno took over *The Tonight Show* full-time.

Amy Irving is one of the guests. A bevy of 'friends' cluster round her in the make-up room, but she remembers very well our encounter in India nearly four years ago, when she and a friend offered Terry G and me use of their room at the Rambagh Palace, and we chose the overnight bus to Udaipur!

Am last on. Amy I is lovely – a little nervous and formal, but very beautiful. Eva Marie Saint – older, and more relaxed – looking back on working with Brando, etc. Dignified and very funny.

Then me last. For some reason the scales fall from my lips and I'm blessed with the gift of tongues, going into a very silly improv about my mother being a sword-swallower, being the oldest high-wire act in England – the wire having to be 18 inches wide – and my father having a dental comedy act. Taking his teeth out and impersonating great world leaders (the Yalta Conference comes to me from somewhere).

Could not have done this with Carson. I think everyone feels the difference – Leno is much more like Letterman.

Thursday, December 11th: New York

Meet Paul Zimmerman at the very Jewish Carnegie Deli.

Already at midday every table is taken – everyone squashes in next to everyone else. It's friendly and fast. Businessmen on one side, mother and child on the other.

My pastrami sandwich is ridiculous. About 25 layers of pastrami strain the rye to breaking point. A wooden nail pierces the whole lot in a vain attempt to hold it together. I ask Paul why on earth they make anything this big. 'Guilt,' he says. 'It's an expiation of 2,000 years of history, a desperate attempt to make up for everything that's gone wrong.'

Paul's fortunes are improving. He's been paid – or promised – 100 G's for writing a film called 'Digby' for Denis O'Brien.

Makes up for a complete falling-out with Goldwyn over 'A Consuming Passion'. This is now being rewritten by one Andrew Davies. I get an odd feeling when I hear this. A twinge of jealousy? Like hearing that one's ex-wife has yet another new man!

It begins to snow; quite pretty for a while, then it turns to rain. I buy a copy of *Mirrorstone* at B. Dalton's for the Zimmerman family. Paul insists the assistant knows that I'm the author of the book. She takes some convincing. 'They like to know things like that,' Paul assures me as we spill out into the crowds.

Friday, December 12th: New York–Dayton, Ohio

Land on time at Dayton – at a quarter past one [to see Simon Jones in a touring production of *My Fair Lady*]. Clean, clear, still, a complete change from the freneticism of New York.

To the theatre. Simon's dressing room is more like a service closet. Pipes across the ceiling, a very small mirror and worktop and that's about all. Various people have signed the wall, including Steve Lawrence,[1] who has signed 'I'll be right out' on the door of the lavatory.

They've sold out. 2,800 seats. Apparently Richard Harris came here with *Camelot* and sold out a week, making 380,000 dollars, of which Harris took 10%. Now I understand why people do these gruelling US tours.

Have never seen the stage version of *My Fair Lady*, and am impressed by the literacy of it all, and the part of Higgins especially is full of wonderful lines. Simon plays him at a brisk, belting, no-nonsense level – projecting at a volume well above most of the others. The part is admirably suited to Simon's skill at the testy, quizzical and dryly down-putting. And he sings with confidence too.

Saturday, December 13th: Dayton–Sag Harbor

Breakfast together with Nancy and Simon (who sounds seriously croaky). We drive to a Dr Feelgood who has been suggested to Simon for his vocal problem. Leave him in a smart surgery at a spotless, low-slung, modern building among a lot of similar, comfortably affluent erections in a road called Corporate Way. The doctor is called Boyles.

Nancy then takes me to the airport.

At La Guardia I pick up a Buick Skylark – with digital display panel – and, with only one brief wrong turning, find myself in three full lanes of moving traffic along the LI Expressway, passing turn-offs to Babylon and Jericho.

Al is cooking when I bang the glass of the sliding door on his porch. Embraces, greetings (the pattern of the last week). He looks thinner and moves more slowly. Yes, he has aged. Tea and a bagel as a late lunch.

Presents are exchanged and opened. Then I take a short walk along the darkened streets – Division, Madison, Rogers and Jermain. The houses

1 American singer, born Sidney Liebowitz, best known for duets with wife, Eydie Gormé

all different, all interesting, yet something missing – I think it's people.

After a delicious fish stew (cooked by Al) and cheese and Far Breton [a prune flan] and a lot of wine and calvados, Al and I walk together down to Main Street.

Al sounds discouraged. Morale low. He writes, he says, but with great difficulty and . . . who for? Sometimes he says he feels like a 'bull elephant, just waiting for the end'.

To bed soon after eleven, on a put-you-up in the sitting room. It's so cold I have to sleep in my sweater.

I get up to pee. It's 1.30. Al is in the kitchen reading E F Benson. He raises his big, impressive head and gives me one of his most heavy-lidded looks. In a tone of great weariness he says 'I'm waiting for the irrigation system to work.'

I bid him not to strain his eyes, and return to the sitting room. I'm quickly asleep.

Sunday, December 14th: Sag Harbor–New York

The sun streams in. The comforting sound of a home coming to life. Occasional patter of feet, a pause. I'm being looked at. Then back to the kitchen, footsteps slapping on the exposed floorboards. Sound of shushing.

About a quarter to nine I give up further sleep. I've had seven hours on this makeshift bed. Feel on good form. Al, in dressing-gown and *Missionary* sweatshirt, is at his 'irrigation' again. He's also begun reading *American Friends*.

We talk about the screenplay. I know as I descend the steep steps into his writing bunker that the news will not be good. And for some reason it all seems to fit Al's mood at the moment. There's hardly a glimmer of light in the picture. His criticism is pretty comprehensive. There seems nothing, at first, that he likes about it.

We go for a walk, round a wildlife reserve which is deserted by all wildlife on this bitterly cold morning, except for black-headed chickadees tame enough to take crumbs from the hands of three parka-ed humans.

After the gloom of the 'hold', we talk constructively. I realise where I've gone wrong. It's too wordy (I knew that), too much reported speech, and the 'incidents', such as death of his mother, blackmail, Symes's seduction, are perhaps too strong, too dangerously melodramatic. A simpler telling of the tale seems the solution.

At two I leave for New York. For the first few miles drive in a melancholy mood. But I put the radio on and soon the patter of music, ads and the endless traffic flow anaesthetises all but the most basic senses.

Thursday, December 18th

TJ tells me he's read *American Friends*. 'Tell me the worst' is my (post-Levinson) reaction, but it turns out most gratifyingly that he enjoyed most of it, and once or twice was moved to tears. He has criticisms, such as predictability, therefore tediousness, in the early setting-up of the stuffiness/priggishness of Ashby, but he is the first who's started his criticism by saying he liked it.

We repair to the Flask. Squally showers whip across Rosslyn Hill as we walk up past a well-advertised *Mirrorstone* window at the High Hill. Heard from Don at the Belsize Bookshop that he had sold all his copies – 'And we took a lot' – so something is happening.

Over a pint we talk further on *American Friends*, then turn to *Erik*. TJ now feels that there is nothing much in the way of making the picture. Lisa Henson and Warners are very keen and quite anxious to close a deal.

Talk about casting, and to my honest surprise TJ names me as one of the two or three names for Erik. The others being Harrison Ford and Michael York. But, as TJ is very keen for the film to be primarily a comedy, it does suddenly seem very plausible that I should play the lead.

Encouraged by TJ's comments I'm resolved to treat *American Friends* as a working project, but there are rewrites to be done and there is a time problem in shooting the Alps in summer, when I'm officially committed to John's *Wanda* project. So it seems quite attractive to set aside autumn and winter '87 for *Erik* and have my film ready to roll in early summer of 1988. If JC's works out too – a nice continuity of work.

Saturday, December 20th

By taxi to Harrods. Meet Richard Seymour and Rachel Kerr, Jonathan Cape publicist, in the book department. There follows a disappointing *Mirrorstone* signing session from twelve until 1.30. If the Harrods staff hadn't rallied round it would have been near disaster.

Then home and almost straight out, despite misgivings, to a misbegotten Camden Council cock-up called 'Citizen Cane's Christmas

Cracker'. This involves me standing in Father Christmas outfit in a cold, draughty, empty warehouse as it is getting dark, rattling my money box and trying to solicit funds for homeless children from charity-battered punters. Abused by most people – 'Where's your beard?' (it was worn this morning by Ken Livingstone, but wouldn't fit me).

I am one of a number of 'celebrity' Santas. Monsignor Bruce Kent is to do a stint after me. There is no publicity as to who the Santas are, or a hint that there might be anything special about them. In fact the whole occasion makes one's heart bleed for our borough – and for substantial amounts of our money – that both should be in the hands of such basically decent, incompetent folk.

Thursday, December 25th: Abbotsley, Christmas Day

At nine o'clock Cathy G, Granny P and myself drive round to Abbotsley Church for the Christmas Service. We would have walked, but for the problem of getting Granny P over the stile. The service is held in the chancel only. A number of rough-looking lads seem to be officiating, together with a myopic organist with Brylcreemed hair combed sparingly away from a low brow. The priest is of that waxy-hued, rather baby-faced complexion – as if he'd been brought out of cotton wool only very recently.

But there are 35 souls there, and I feel it a very satisfying continuity with the past to be standing next to my mother. She complains about the modern language in the service.

Full of virtue we file out, after taking communion, at a quarter to ten. I tell the waxy-faced vicar that I was married in this same church 20 years ago ... and am still married ... 'To the same woman,' I add, which Cath thinks very funny.

Friday, December 26th: Abbotsley

I have an idea to take Tom P for a driving practice to Ely, with a visit to the cathedral my reward for sitting with him. The idea spreads rapidly and is soon a full-fledged expedition, involving all of us except Rachel, who watches *Chitty Chitty Bang Bang* on her own.

Veryan rings. Angela is back in hospital. She took an overdose of pills, but is now back and her condition is satisfactory. Veryan tentatively suggests that perhaps the hospital was irresponsible in sending her home at the most dangerous time of the year. They sound to me almost sue-ably negligent. But it's a measure of how desperate she is.

Sunday, December 28th: Southwold

Enjoy the drive across to Stowmarket, very easy on the eye. Then onto the new, improved A45 to Bury and find myself tensing in preparation for what I will find at the West Suffolk Hospital. Long, low, modern building, quite carefully and thoughtfully landscaped.

Park and walk in through the main entrance to find myself completely alone. No-one at Enquiries, no-one anywhere, and no plan of the hospital or indication of where I can find Ward F8. Eventually, at a chocolate slot-machine beside an AIDS warning display, I find another visitor who knows the hospital better than me. She directs me upstairs.

Ward F8 is the medical ward where Angela has been put temporarily after her overdose on Friday. This afternoon she is to be moved back to the psychiatric ward, where she has spent most of the last five weeks. I'm directed vaguely and find Angela, a slight slip of a figure, apparently asleep in a chair beside her bed. The bed has been stripped and on the mattress is her case.

Angela isn't deeply asleep and opens her eyes quite quickly. Her hands are hot, her eyes dead and limpid. She talks slowly in a monotone. At first it's as bad as I feared, but gradually she revives and the blanket covering of negativity lifts every now and then. She knows that hospitals don't particularly like 'overdosers' – thinking of them as people who abuse drugs – but the nurses and staff seem kind and cheerful enough. She's brought some lunch whilst I'm there, which she eats with enthusiasm.

I stay for an hour or more. Have never hugged my sister as much as I do in the ten minutes or so before I leave. But my reward is to see her smile, make some quite bright small talk about my coat, etcetera, ask about my plans.

I leave her, a frail figure waving at the end of a hospital corridor. Have to walk very slowly to let my emotions sort themselves out. When I do start back for London, I drive straight back without stopping for lunch. As I drive I feel sure I did some good to Angela, feel encouraged by the spark still glowing at the back of a fire that at times seems to have completely gone out, guilty that I didn't stay longer and determined to do all I can to get her away from the hospital.

Monday, December 29th

I decide to call Richard F and Susan H together before the year's out, hopefully, and tell them that I cannot continue as Chairman for much longer.

The chairmanship of T2000 was good and worthwhile as an experiment, and an experiment which could only take place in the deliberately time-marking, low-profile two years I've just been through. There really is no place for these experiments if I am to make films as well. And one thing I am sure of, after tasting various alternatives in the last couple of years, is that I want to make films.

1987

Within 15 minutes of arriving at Sunset House I have rung Angela at the hospital and arranged visiting times.

An hour and ten minutes' drive; the hospital car park is packed, but then public transport is almost completely absent in Suffolk. Am parking when we see Angela waving vigorously from a ground-floor room opposite, a completely different person from the drowsy, slurred, almost helpless figure I left here eight days ago.

She meets us at reception and writes her name in chalk on a board – 'Angela Herbert – out with family'. Hers is the most elegant and controlled script.

Then we walk to the car, drive into Bury, walk some way to a wholefood coffee shop, where we have tea and a talk. Be positive, don't raise anything complicated, keep cheerful, burble on.

But with Angela today it is hardly necessary. She is much more aware and alert. She has had four ECT sessions this week and they seem to have pulled her sharply out of the depression in a way in which the drugs never did. She laughs quite easily. But I can see that the limits of her composure are still narrow.

She tells me, when Granny is in the loo, of how she nearly killed herself twice. Her tone is alarming – it's almost one of pride, as if to say 'Now, that's something I *can* do.'

But she is responsive and good company throughout. A cold walk down to the car, dropping in at an antique shop on the way she notes down details of some library steps for Veryan. Her hand is steady, but her memory has suffered. She doesn't remember me going to see her last Sunday week at all. And I was there for one and a quarter hours.

We drive back, Mother and me, twisting along the friendly 1120. I'm optimistic in the short term, very concerned in the long term. Mum just feels that we must get her out of 'that place' as soon as possible.

Wednesday, January 7th

The snow, ice and chaos forecast have not materialised. A cold, but benign morning with weak sunshine. I'm offered the lead in *Bulldog Drummond* – a new Stephen Fry treatment for Chichester, and *Me and My Girl* in the West End . . . !

To lunch at Langan's Bistro to tell Susan and Richard that I can't continue as Chairman of Transport 2000.

Richard shrugs off the problem and immediately suggests that we should appoint another Vice-Chairman, besides himself, possibly Harley Sherlock, and that the two of them should run things for a year until I can come back.

He and Susan both feel a departure would do unnecessary damage to T2000 at the moment and that the members are so pleased to have me as Chairman that they would rather do anything than see me resign.

Thursday, January 8th

Up at eight and after breakfast begin work on a transport article. Susan Hoyle rings to tell me that she has been shortlisted for a new job, and would I be prepared to give references? Pleased for her, but can't help feeling that this news hard on the heels of yesterday's pleading for me to stay cannot be coincidental. They must have both been aware of the considerable extra pressure which will have to be borne by a Chairman when the Executive Director resigns. Feel a distant twinge of righteous anger.

To Cambridge Gate. Meeting re Prominent Features. John C is happy to put his film through PF, but doesn't want to be a director or have anything to do with the running of the company. Eric is brisk, organising, and pays for this by being voted Chairman. Terry J is uncharacteristically quiet, TG the most visionary.

Many questions raised. How big should we be? How big should the launch be? Who should we employ? How will the launch be run?

Monday, January 12th

Off by taxi to Walkden House. Today is the first of our new, extended board meeting days – another measure of the extra work the organisation has taken upon itself in the last twelve months.

Steer them as best I can towards finance, etc, but have to end at 12.30 for our 'celebrity lunch'.

A big, amiable-looking man with very fair hair and pinkish skin stands awkwardly in our little office. This is John Palmer, Deputy Secretary at the Department of Transport and our first 'informal' lunch guest. First impressions lead me to think we have chosen well, but once we have collected our sandwiches and our glasses (I stick to orange juice) and begun talking I realise otherwise.

He maintains, I think, an almost scornfully Mandarin vagueness which I feel is an insult to the generally good and balanced questions that come from our members. He talks slowly (maybe this is deliberate) and everything is approached with a caution that could be taken for ignorance, except that he has been the man in charge of surface transport planning at the Department for ten years.

Back to our board meeting at 2.20 after seeing Mr Palmer off. 'Do you want any more of our chaps?' he asked.

Thursday, January 15th

The 'Winter of Misery' (LBC this morning) is into its fifth day. Snow remains uncleared in Oak Village and there is no rubbish collection again.

Don the gloves and woolly hat and run into the bitter wind. Plenty of children on Parliament Hill sledging on everything from proper sledges (very rare) to plastic red and white striped barriers pinched from road-works abandoned during the bad weather. Arrive home glowing.

Monday, January 19th

Rendezvous with our T2000 delegation. Susan has been unsuccessful in her application for a new job, but is taking it philosophically. We walk through Euston to the new British Rail HQ in Eversholt Street. Two of our members manage to lose themselves in the Euston concourse for five minutes.

Small, plain meeting room. No concession to art or decoration. Chris Green from Network South-East is our first speaker. Greying hair growing tight across the head, a broad head, like a ram or a rugby player, which puts me in mind of Al. Like his head, his approach is solid, factual, no nonsense, no frills, no rhetoric. He is forcefully impressive. A touch of impatience establishes his superiority comfortably. He knows the facts, we don't. He runs railways, whilst we talk about it, sort of attitude.

Bluntly honest that he has a problem with staff recruitment. Many of his drivers (the majority) are over 50 and it takes five years to train them. Blunt about the unions, overmanning – messianic about one-man operations. But he does talk more than just containment – he talks of expansion, he talks of new lines – to London Airport, to Stansted – and hints at the prospect of a new NE SW Underground line for London.

Up to the Forth Room for a lunch of tough meat, but some good talk. Will Camp is there in lieu of Richard Faulkner. He has a wonderful nineteenth-century face, with twinkling eyes and a fuzz of dark hair garlanding his baldness. He has a languid manner – talks softly, but persistently.

He reminds me that the Labour government's attitude to railways, in the days when Tony Crosland was in charge, was unhelpful. They regarded railway users as pampered and subsidised and Conservatives were much more pro-rail. Quite glad to hear this, as I have just written in my 'On the Move' article that we should not presume that a change of government will put things right automatically.

Thursday, January 22nd

Veryan rings to say that the pipes are leaking at Chilton, but that Angela is out of hospital and could she come to us at the weekend?

Angela comes on and my heart falls. She sounds very low – quite different to her perky self of two weeks ago. The hospital didn't work out well, but she has taken the blame for that herself – 'a failed patient'.

I am shaken and affected in a way which surprises me. I think it's because I have been confronted with the fact that Angela is not cured, that the hospital has been ineffectual. And, with Angela in the state she sounds to be in at the moment, I fear that anything we can do will be ineffectual too.

I keep my worst fears from Mother, when she calls, and Helen when she gets back, and when we eventually do talk about it together it is constructively and reassuringly. Angela will be with us on Sunday.

Friday, January 23rd

Into a rush of a day. To BAFTA to be present at the press show for *East of Ipswich*.

Arrive a little late owing to inane cab driver. 'Not your lucky day, is it?' he remarks cheerfully as he takes me on some unerringly disastrous detour. Then, out of the blue ... 'Did you know diesel fuel isn't inflammable?' He is full of observations on the nature of diesel fuel ... 'If you inhale diesel ...' (pause) '... it makes you violently sick.'

I scurry away from him, across Piccadilly and up the gloomy stairs to BAFTA.

I tell Tristram the outline of 'No. 27', the story of the lady being evicted by Eton College.

Home by 5.30. Adrenaline buzzing. The prospect of completing 'No. 27' after the second draft of *American Friends* suddenly seems the best option for the rest of the year. Less well paid, but infinitely more rewarding in other ways than doing a 'cameo' for some American film.

We are about to go to bed when the telephone rings. It's 11.25. The rather apologetic, frightened voice at the other end is from the *Daily Mail* and wants me to give him Terry Jones's number. Of course I refuse. But that is not the end of it. The hack calls again, fifteen minutes past midnight. This time he asks if I will ring Terry Jones and ask him to call them. I refuse with a little more asperity.

Saturday, January 24th

On the *Sun*'s front cover ... beside the bold, black headline 'TV Python Comic At Sex Orgies' is a rather camp photo of my writing partner and bosom friend of 22 years! 'Jones, 44, is said ... ' (wait for it) 'to have chatted to ... Cynthia Payne – who faces charges ... at the foot of the stairs.'

It is an astonishing piece of comedy come true. The sort of headline Python and *Private Eye* have been making fun of for years. Now, as ever, the paper has the last word. The full report of the police 'stool-pigeon's evidence is within. And very high-farce it is too, with tattooed ladies from Leamington Spa and transvestite bottoms being pinched.

To Chipping Barnet for André J's wedding. An old church, Victorianised.

Terry J slips into our pew with Alison at the last minute. I think it's quite something to know someone who's appeared on the front cover of the *Sun*. To have shared a pew in church with them on the same day is beyond the realms of the hoped-for.

Much standing around outside. Trevor Jones, alias John Du Prez, cheerfully refers to TJ as the Sex Beast, and Terry, who seems to have taken it all with equanimity, is resigned to the fact that nothing he can say will make any difference to what they print. He is now resigned to trial by innuendo. (I must say, it does seem a bit weedy, Anne and Steve being quoted as saying he went to the sex parties for 'research'.)

Sunday, January 25th

Another anonymous day of cloudy skies. A windless, unshifting Eastern European blankness. Grim stories of Wapping riots. Both sides blaming the other for violence.

Thatcher will not talk, listen, understand or concern herself in any way with those individuals who do not entirely submit to her way of regenerating Britain. In the end, if their protests continue, they are 'marginalised' (vogue word of the mid-80's) by her, her ministers and most of all by her greedy, subservient press, and then, quite simply, roughed up.

Jeremy delivers Angela about five. She looks well; slim figure and well-cut, thick, dark hair, and a woollen two-piece tracksuit sort of thing.

We watch *Screen 2* on the BBC. A very funny Simon Gray play, 'After Pilkington', but – good old BBC – it ends up with a disturbing portrayal of a mad woman who sticks scissors into men's necks. Just when we wanted something uncomplicated and jolly.

As she goes to bed, Angela voices the desperation that is frighteningly close to the surface. 'What's it all *for*?' The unanswerable question. Leaves Helen and me to go to bed in a sober mood.

Monday, January 26th

Pleasant evening – supper with Rachel and Angela, then a game of Trivial Pursuit by the fire. Angela as bright and convivial as I remember her at the best of times.

The evening, though, ends splendidly, with me reading some of Wordsworth's *Prelude* and Angela really appreciating it – whereas the family always disappear when I start to recite. Quite spontaneous silliness – I put on an accompanying record of train noises and read John Betjeman, then Angela reads Joan Hunter Dunn and we all go to bed.

Tuesday, January 27th

Bad news of the Maudsley Hospital is the only cloud on the horizon. Mrs W, whom Angela was seeing last year, will not be able to see her until next week and Veryan, ringing this morning, could not improve on this. Rather a nuisance, as renewal of contact with the Maudsley was to be the focal point and purpose of this week.

There follows a gloomy lunch and repeated declarations of worthlessness. Physical manifestations like shaking and sweating make both of us alarmed. Helen goes off to her piano lesson, I determine to talk to someone on Angela's behalf and try and break this deadlock of inaction. She desperately wants to be taken into the Maudsley.

I arrive ten minutes late at squash and TJ says I look white. I suppose it is shock.

Wednesday, January 28th

Collected by car at six to go to the *Wogan Show*. Jeffrey Archer is just being ushered in as I arrive. The black-uniformed commissionaires greet him effusively, then turn to me looking blank. I explain who I am and why I'm here. They look confused. Whilst they're ringing for clearance, Wogan, looking relaxed and tanned, appears, greets us both warmly. Archer, like a sort of gusher of ingratiating enthusiasm, grasps both our hands and lays into the familiarity straight away.

As we walk upstairs he tells us how he'd been seeing 'Alasdair' (Milne) only this morning and noticed the letter E was missing from the words 'Director General' on his door, and 'D'you know what?' (pause to allow audience to appreciate story-telling technique), 'I went straight round to the nearest Woolworth's and bought him one of those awful, mock silver letters you see on the front of people's houses, and sent it round to him!'

Archer is awfully pleased with the story. We pass Donald Soper, modest in his cassock and looking quite incongruous in this company; Jeffrey cannot but be the first to grasp the great Methodist's hand.

Pass into make-up, then up to the Green Room. Jeffrey Archer is re-telling his Alasdair Milne's door story.

Soper is on first and is, as usual, fluent, balanced, articulate and provocative.

Archer is next and straight away there is bristle and drama. Wogan nudges him into a remark about 'the scandal'.[1] Archer, to his great credit, doesn't side-step. But he begins to warm up and soon is clearly displeasing our Terry by embarking on long, hectoring monologues about the virtues of free enterprise and the Western way.

Archer, to be fair, plays the game well. I talk about Mr Heeley's[2] sex talks and Lord Soper has the impeccable last word when he says that when he was given a sex talk at the age of 14 he had the distinct impression that he knew more about the subject than did his teacher.

Wogan, amiable as ever, is the only host who seems to actually want to stay and have a drink with his guests afterwards. While he and I are talking about TJ and Cynthia Payne, Jeffrey Archer comes up and tells us both the Alasdair Milne story again!

Back home. Am about to settle down to stew and dumplings with Angela when Charles Sturridge calls. I suppose it wouldn't be too dramatic to say that it's the call I've been hoping for, but virtually given up expecting, ever since I knew that he had taken over the *Troubles* screenplay, or, indeed, ever since I read the book during my second stint at Belfast in 1983.

Over a long phone call it transpires that he has always had me in mind as a possible Major, but the crucial factor is now the age of the actress to play Sarah. After six months of auditioning Irish actresses he has only two front runners. One is 27, the other ... 'Well, I hardly dare tell you how old she is.' Fifteen, coming on 16, but like a young Helen Mirren.

So, Charles is not yet decided which way to go; if it's the 27-year-old then I could be the Major, if it's the 16-year-old the age gap would be too obvious. Would I like to see the script? It is sent round to me within the hour. Two fat two-hour episodes.

With Denis [the cat] and shots of Armagnac for company, I sit down and read the entire four-hour adaptation, finishing by 2.30.

---

1 Archer had been accused by two newspapers of paying hush-up money to a prostitute called Monica Coghlan, with whom the *Daily Star* alleged he had had 'relations'. Archer successfully sued the *Star*, and though he was cleared of charges, the scandal forced him to resign as Deputy Chairman of the Conservative Party. He was found guilty of perjury in 2001.

2 Howard Heeley was the Headmaster of my prep school in Sheffield. Boys about to leave the school, mostly aged 12 or 13, were required to attend one of his 'sex talks' which took place in his study and involved desk items, such as paper-clips and ink-pots, as props. Most of us came away deeply confused.

Thursday, January 29th

Up in time for the eight o'clock news. Still don't feel tired. Too much going on. *Time Out* has a very favourable piece on *East of Ipswich* – 'a considerable delight'.

I sit down and write captions for *Happy Holidays*.[1] In the middle of dictating to Alison, Sturridge rings on the other line. Maybe *because* the call is so important, I press the wrong button and Alison stays, but Sturridge disappears and I have no number for him.

Sit there feeling foolish for about three minutes. Then he rings back, I tell him that I have liked the adaptation and, subject to a few date difficulties, am happy to do it. I warn him I can't play the piano or dance, and he laughs. Says he is delighted and, though he's still cautious, he sounds genuinely pleased – or is it relieved? He has to see the actresses again, though, and will ring me tomorrow to talk further about the part.

Friday, January 30th

To Kenwood with Angela. Pleasant walk inside and outside. Put it to her as gently as I can that she should find somewhere else to stay from next weekend. She understands. But she is still enclosed and tense – even at a time like this when place and company should be congenial and conducive to unwinding.

Later in the afternoon she packs, then drives the car down to Veryan's office (no mean achievement for someone feeling terminally depressed). She is to spend the weekend at Chilton.

Sandy L rings from Atlanta. His reaction to *American Friends* is one of wary admiration for my bravery in going for a story and treatment so far away from what he'd expected from me. On detail he wants Brita to be warmer and more sympathetic and Ashby to be less one-dimensional. I know that both will be in the playing, but it obviously isn't coming across from this script.

---

1 Encouraged by Colin Webb at Pavilion Books, I'd written text for a collection of vintage British railway posters. It was published in 1987 under the title *Happy Holidays*. It was one of the most enjoyable things I ever did.

Sunday, February 1st

Leave for TJ's – Rachel, Helen and myself – at eleven. As ever, 9 Grove Park is already full of people. There's always a foreigner or two, and twice as many children as Al and Terry have. TJ breathlessly scurries about, muttering genially about the number of people expected vis-à-vis amount of food available. Somewhere a telephone is always ringing.

A meal appears. Sancerre flows. TJ goes round the table embracing. He introduces Jill Tweedie as the woman 'whose book changed my life'.[1] There is so much noise, chatter, occasional howlings of attacked children that I'm almost relieved when 3.30 comes round and I have to hurry back for a four o'clock meeting with Charles Sturridge.

Charles arrives in dirt-encrusted black Citroën as we are unloading. I make coffee for both of us and we adjourn to my workroom. Two hours of discussion later, as the sun sets and I reluctantly switch on the light, anxious not to interrupt a cogitative atmosphere, it's clear that I have the part of Major Archer in 'Troubles' if I want it.

What a commitment – on both our parts. I hope I can deliver his high expectations.

Monday, February 2nd

[*East of Ipswich*] Reviews ranging from complete ecstasy (the *Daily Mail*, invoking Wilde and Noël Coward as my peers!) to virtual dismissal – Nancy Banks-Smith.

Angela arrives back from Chilton in seemingly good form, but I have little time to chat as have to get myself down to Transport 2000.

We walk over to Unity House to meet (after many cancellations) Jimmy Knapp to talk over salaries. Jimmy remarks on *East of Ipswich*. Yes they both watched it and 'it was greatly appreciated by my wife'. Nuff said.

We have a good session. There is no chance of getting the full amount we have asked for, but we come away with half and a few other promised benefits. I think he is straight and he's certainly convivial enough today. We shall see if he can deliver.

---

1 The book was *In the Name of Love*, published in 1979, and later described in the *Guardian* (for whom Jill Tweedie wrote her columns) as 'a dazzling set of observations about love, sex, men and women'.

At home brief time to talk with Angela. She seems very much more positive.

Tuesday, February 3rd

Lunch at Grimes in Garrick Street with Charles Sturridge, Michael Colgan and James Mitchell – the lawyer who I wrote to three years ago to express my interest in 'Troubles'.

I put my point about dates and don't get much sympathy back from the producers, but Charles is concerned and will try and do some readjustments to save perhaps a couple of days of my Mürren [family skiing] trip. I so much want to see Mürren again, but it seems unlikely.

The producers asked me, as a writer, if I was happy with the title. They are worried that the Americans will not understand it. But so far their only suggested alternative is 'The Major and the Fisheater'!

Wednesday, February 4th

Michael Colgan from 'Troubles' rings. He's the amiable, artistic one of the production duo, I sense. Apologising for 'being a bad producer by telling you this', he goes on to say how delighted the three of them were after our lunch at Grimes yesterday. I *was* the Major, he says, and they were 'walking on air' after meeting me. Then he alludes to the unsavoury business of the contract and how they had asked LWT to go to the limit. Also bad news on the skiing holiday, which doesn't seem negotiable.

Thursday, February 5th

Nothing is heard from 'Troubles', so I continue in this limbo-land, unable to confirm, cancel or plan anything from March to May.

Clear my room and spend an excellent evening with Angela at the Caravanserai Afghan restaurant in Marylebone and then at the screen on Baker Street seeing *Heavenly Pursuits*. Angela is well disposed to her Maudsley lady and prefers her technique of P and M to a full-blooded Freudian analysis. P is for pleasure and M for something not necessarily pleasurable but achieved – hence the M for mastery. Angela has to keep a weekly record of P and M moments.

This evening definitely P.

Friday, February 6th

Angela leaves at five. Her two weeks' stay with us is over and I'm quite sad in a way. When on form she's very good company. I know she depended on us and was warm in her appreciation of what we did for her. I hope she'll be able to continue moving forward as she has done over the last few days.

About half past five Anne rings with the final terms of 'Troubles'. They're acceptable. Now I have no longer any reason not to do it. The die is cast. I'm spoken for until the end of May.

Michael Colgan rings. He assures me that he will try his best to make sure the little things are provided for me – such as somewhere to write. Then Charles rings. It's been a long week since our talk in the gathering twilight last Sunday when my destiny began to be firmly linked to his.

So by seven o'clock all is done. Barring some dreadful accident I am to embark on the longest and largest single acting job I've ever done.

Wednesday, February 11th

Start the day with a reassuringly approving bunch of letters re *East of Ipswich*, sent over from the BBC. Tristram rings to say that we had a viewing figure of 6.5 million and were top of BBC2 for the week. For a programme starting after ten on a Sunday evening this is considered good.

Thursday, February 12th

Talk with Anne over contract details on 'Troubles'. LWT are not being helpful. Their contracts lady prefaces most of her calls to Anne with the advice that she's worked there 23 years.

But there are certain specific conditions which will make my life more pleasant over the next 14 weeks, like sole use of room or caravan to work in, a car in the morning which doesn't cruise the whole neighbourhood picking up the rest of the cast, and some policy on stand-ins. The more I think of them during the day, the more I'm convinced they're not petty details.

Saturday, February 14th: Southwold

Up by nine. The rain from the west hangs low and mistily over the Common. An odd 'friend' of Ma's rings to say how much she hated *East of Ipswich*. She tells her that she loved God, she loved her (my mother) and she (had) loved my father, but she hated the film. It was the sex again that was the problem. And this from someone who has had five husbands! Ma takes it all very well, but is clearly quite shaken. Fortunately I have brought up a sheaf of letters and reviews from people who thought otherwise.

Mr Hurran (Ma's protector) comes in as I'm reading a story in the *Daily Telegraph* about a cricket team which is destroying all its boxes because of fear of AIDS. He takes the Sierra and has the cassette-player mended.

I have promised Angela I shall drop in at Chilton on the way back, even though it adds well over an hour to the journey. She and Veryan are there. Angela reading 'Troubles' with one of the cats pinning her down to the kitchen chair. She seems enormously better. At the edges there are glimpses of frustration and fear and sometimes she is almost too bright (as if making a great effort), but a transformation from the Angela who came to us at the end of January.

Monday, February 16th

I sleep well and take a cold, early morning run before my car arrives at a quarter to ten to drive me to the read-through. My driver, John, is young and has a habit of blowing air out in a sort of silent laugh.

We cross the river and head ever further into the wastelands of Rotherhithe. It's rather as if I'm being purposely disoriented. We could be in Novosibirsk. At an ill-converted, light industrial building we find one of LWT's 'colonies' and I'm led through into a smoky room with protective grilles on all the windows, rather as I imagine border police stations in Ireland.

I'm taken round by Charles to meet the cast. Rosamund Greenwood, Rachel Kempson, with a glowing, handsome face and a bright slash of lipstick. Patience Collier, who has a special reclining chair and sits amidst us all most incongruously. Gwen Nelson, who's 86 and reads her script with a huge magnifying glass.

Ian Richardson, I note with some dismay, is a smoker. He looks surprisingly rubicund, an agricultural tan. Colin Blakely is suffering the effects of some skin disease which has left him completely bald and his skin looks pale, exposed and very fragile. He smiles and shakes my hand with such open warmth that I know I shall like him. Same too for Tim Spall.

I'm introduced to Fiona Victory. High cheekbones, defiant eyes, long, dark hair – she was aptly described by Charles as an Irish Charlotte Rampling.

After all the introductions, Charles makes a short speech and the read-through begins. I suppose, to be honest, I am not quite comfortable; as my first line (which somehow seems the real psychological moment of commitment!) approaches, I feel my heart thumping more than it should and my body tensing up in preparation. But quite quickly the moment is over and I've not made a complete fool of myself.

The rest of the read-through is easier, though strange to be reading such intimate scenes in public with a Sarah I can't even see beyond the cluster of heads. I think the scenes with Ian and myself will be fine. We read until after one o'clock. Tomorrow Charles will split us up for rehearsal.

Good phone chat with Eric I, who loved *East of Ipswich* and also has some very pithy remarks about *American Friends*. He says it reminded him of a Hardy story and when he read the script he felt that it must have been adapted from a novel! Both agree that speeches in Latin will be hard to sell to Hollywood.

Tuesday, February 17th

Taxi to Grimes Restaurant, this time to meet with Ian R, Fiona and Charles. Warm to Ian. He is very actorish in delivery and self-dramatising style, but regards it quite unashamedly as his trade. He says, without any immodesty, that he's a very easy person to work with, but then catches my arm and adds 'But I'm very easily hurt.'

Fiona and Charles and I are driven to London Weekend, here to rehearse in a long, narrow, un-cared-for office with an absolutely wonderful view out across the river.

Someone is editing *South Bank Show* theme music interminably from next door, which makes it difficult for us to maintain the intensity of concentration that listening to Charles demands.

About 5.30 Charles has to go to a production meeting. Both Mitchell and Colgan look nervous. Clearly things are still in a very restless state.

I walk over Waterloo Bridge, because I like doing it, but a north-easterly wind makes the cold as intense and unbearable as any this winter. En-taxi for a private view of Virginia Powell's paintings and pastels in Motcomb Street.

Introduced to Harold Pinter ... 'Do you know the population of China?' he asks. (He has a suave blue coat and neat tie.) Evidently it's over one billion now. But my evening is made when I at last manage to tell him that I did McCann in *The Birthday Party* at Oxford and it was the high point of my Oxford acting career! To which Pinter replies 'Oh, I *know* all about that ... I know all about your McCann.'

Off into the Belgravian night, fortified by a glass of white wine, feeling marvellously relaxed and comfortable. Home to a glass of champagne, some salmon and a steak. Watch a man having an artificial hip fitted (on TV).

Wednesday, February 18th

At 5.30 I'm taken to Penge to the Peggy Spencer Dance School [for 'Troubles'] to relive the horrors of dancing class which I had tried to exorcise in *East of Ipswich*. I have to learn the rudiments of a foxtrot with the twins.

Peggy Spencer is a tall, erect, but kindly lady. I jab her once or twice with my feet, which she says do stick out. But the hour-long session, watched with irreverent amusement by the drivers, is not as hair-raising as I expected, in fact it's quite successful. The twins are wonderful. Very natural and un-actorish.

Thursday, February 19th

To Morris Angel by ten for fittings. These take an hour and a half and the suit looks very dapper. Then, clutching two pairs of leather shoes which I have to 'break-in' by Monday, I find a cab.

To the Great Nepalese for a lunch with Susan. Amongst our general chat we touch on (or rather, I force into the conversation!) my worries about the future of my chairmanship. Even before 'Troubles' the prospect of JC's film and my own seemed to preclude my continuing; now I shall have to miss the next two or three meetings.

I suggest some sort of honorary or presidential (how the word jars) role and by the time we finish our mughlais I realise I've as good as resigned.

From the Great Nepalese I'm swept away in [my driver] Billy's Mercedes for a haircut. Christine, a close-cropped peroxide-blonde Scot who will be 'looking after me', does the job well and without fuss. The process of Majoring goes on, and I'm taken to an upper room to practise playing, or looking convincingly as if I *am* playing, 'Eine Kleine Nacht Musik' with Fiona.

Friday, February 20th

Meet Tristram for lunch. Have chosen La Bastide in Greek Street. Its chintzy, bourgeois, salon-style interior is at first disturbingly, then refreshingly un-designed. Naff in fact. But the food is excellent. I have boudin and apple and it tastes authentically Froggie.

Tristram helps the atmosphere with a marvellously positive reaction to *American Friends*.

If I don't direct *American Friends*, I promise Tristram (on the corner of Greek and Old Compton) that he shall be top of my list. Definitely the best reaction thus far. The only one that made me want to rush straight back and read the thing.

Steve has positive news of the JC film. It looks like a July 13th start and some ridiculous amount like 300,000 dollars in the kitty – per person. None of the stars to get more than any other (which is kind to me, I think).

Home by 11.30. If I had wanted just one restful day this last week of 'freedom', this wasn't it.

Helen packing and preparing for Switzerland [the family skiing holiday I'm missing because of 'Troubles'] means we don't get to sleep until half past one.

Saturday, February 21st

The withdrawal of all the human sights and sounds and feelings seems to strip the house bare for a moment. It's as if the carpets had gone or the water had been cut off. Something essential has disappeared. Despite a shortage of sleep, I don my tracksuit and head for Parliament Hill and Kenwood. My solution to everything!

Back at nine and breakfast and organise myself for an overnight to

Southwold. Thank goodness for my mother and for a lovely and appreciative card re *East of Ipswich* from Maggie Smith.

Have just relaxed pleasantly by the time I reach Sunset House, when Ma imparts the news that Angela has rung only an hour before to say that things are 'so dreary' at Chilton that she's coming over to stay the night.

Sunday, February 22nd: Southwold

Lunch together then time to go. Angela tests me on my lines.

I head back to all the whopping challenges of the next 14 weeks at a quarter to three. Home by five. It's cold and empty and darkness is falling at 4 Julia Street and Denis is waiting for me.

So is another Denis – for within ten minutes of my arrival the telephone rings and the cheery voice of Denis's namesake resounds. DO'B has, he claims, been trying to contact me all weekend to say how much he liked *American Friends*. His reaction even caps that of Tristram. DO'B gives a complete, unqualified rave and concludes that there may be two weeks of rewriting, but that's all. Wary of his praise as of his criticism, but there is no doubt that this is heartfelt and what is more exciting is that he can and will finance it next year. He says as much.

Practise piano and tying ties and putting on collars.

Monday, February 23rd

It should be a very significant sort of day. Lightning and thunder and some stirring music should accompany its dawn, for this is the First Day of Filming.

Actually, it's A First Day of Filming. I reckon it's my tenth – if you include *Three Men in a Boat*, but not *Time Bandits*. The tenth time I've been through all this. But it's two years and four months since I spent much time in front of a film camera and that's the most significant.

That's why I've lain awake most of the night – my body ready much too early. The signals hurtling from the brain to the four corners, waking nerve ends that should have been left to curl up and relax.

Into the Mercedes and down to the Isaac Newton Junior School off Portobello Road, where the vehicles are drawn up. It's a cold, bright morning. Good conditions to start anything.

Charles S is a careful, quiet, but thorough director. I feel he's watching everything and he won't let me be loose or lazy. As I want this to be an exceptionally good and consistent performance I'm pleased, but when my confidence in my ability and stamina sags I find his persistence hard to cope with. But the day's work is done. And by 4.30 at that.

I feel rather like someone who, for the last two weeks, has been running alongside a rapidly-moving vehicle and not really able to get on board. I think I'm aboard now, but I'm pretty breathless still.

Tuesday, February 24th

We have moved today to the Linley Sambourne House in Stafford Terrace, behind Kensington High Street. Sambourne was a *Punch* cartoonist and the house is now preserved as a museum of late-Victorian interior design and decoration. Dark and gloomy with heavy drapes, some intricate but rather well-hidden William Morris wallpaper, stuffed animals in glass cases and every inch of wall covered with an eclectic selection of his cartoons, and various etchings on all sorts of subjects – classical, French eighteenth-century stories, and so on. Presumably various leaves from books he'd illustrated.

My first scene with Rachel Kempson plays quite sweetly. Rachel is a lovely, very easy-going partner and I think Charles is quite pleased.

I realise that this is to be unlike anything else I've done. There can be no question of getting by on the first couple of takes with an accurate caricature, as we do so often in comedy – Sturridge is very fussy, very concerned to get things right and quite happy to go to seven or eight takes if necessary – and it always seems to be necessary.

Poor Rachel K hopes to have finished with our bedroom scene by lunchtime, for her 'stays' are killing her. She eats little at the catering van and tells me that the worst thing about the costume is that it encourages strange wind effects in her stomach.

We complete the scene and I make use of the Michael Palin Room (supplied as per contract) at the top of the house. Alan Polly, of props, is most solicitous and has provided me with Perrier and even a Thermos of coffee. So I sit squashed into a springless armchair, coat pulled round me against the cold, and a pile of books about Victorian life, which I thumb through, an eye open for suitable information for *American Friends*.

Thursday, February 26th

A difficult day ahead – perhaps the most difficult of the week. First scenes with Sarah, including our piano duet and some more emotional stuff around the fireside.

Charles takes me to one side and swells my confidence with genuine enthusiasm for my performance. The scene that made him feel so 'buoyant' was the Major's bedroom scene with Rachel, which he says was very moving and suggested the sort of depth which he was hoping for in choosing me for the Major.

The afternoon spent largely on a very complicated lighting for the 'war reminiscences' scene. By the time we get to do our bit, it's nearly 5.30.

But it is done. There are eleven or twelve takes. I try to imagine I'm seeing the horrors of war, when in fact I'm seeing 25 people, all standing ten feet away, directing all sorts of equipment at me. Fiona is easy to work with. A serious girl, but with an attractive Irish sense of madness just below the carefully controlled, non-smoking, non-drinking, body-exercising exterior.

The last scene set for the day has to be abandoned. This is the first time we've fallen behind. But I'm quite elated at the work done and pleased that I've survived a tough couple of days.

Friday, February 27th

Collected at 7.30 and down to Banstead to a sprawling, but handsome collection of Victorian buildings which comprised, until only a few months ago, Banstead Mental Hospital. Today it is to be a hospital again – of 1918 vintage – and I am recovering from a gas attack.

Complete change of temperature after the tightness of the first few days – it's now almost balmy. Breakfasts are sorely tempting. Black pudding has been my downfall this week and with it scrambled eggs – fresh and irresistible – and two rashers of bacon. It helps to pass the time, I suppose.

Talk to CS at one point. It's as difficult to get things out of him as it was with Frears; it just isn't his nature to gush or headline his feelings. But he has two problems. Colin Blakely, who is undergoing chemotherapy, and still appearing in the West End, has collapsed and will at the very least be unavailable for his first appearance on Monday.

More serious is that some of the scenes we shot earlier in the week may be unusable. I can't elicit exactly where the blame lies, but it seems the lighting is not everything that CS wants. Something to do with exposure. CS, however, refuses to see the setback as a negative thing, and hopes to win something out of it – more time, presumably.

This is less than good news in view of the effort put in this week, but you have to be prepared for everything and this is just another frustration to be absorbed.

The bed scene is not shot until quite late. We all wait around with our variously gruesome facial injuries. I listen to the *True Stories* soundtrack on the headphones.

Then a mad rush to shoot the last sequence of the week – the bathroom. All I have to do is sit in a hot bath with my eyes bandaged and not play with myself. Finish, with much shouting and wafting of steam, at seven o'clock.

Saturday, February 28th

Sunshine spills into the garden and it's generous and unseasonable enough for me to be able to sit outside and read the papers and feel its warmth. My feeling of well-being is augmented by the lack of phone calls, the ability to potter round the house, the pleasurable anticipation of seeing the family again, and a quite different attitude to the 13 weeks' work ahead than I had last weekend. Quite a lot of my uncertainty and anxiety has been laid to rest and replaced by glimmerings of control and confidence. And, dare I say, enjoyment.

Cleese rings and we talk a little about the part of Ken. I swallow for the moment my reservations about the film itself – well, I can't say I don't like it, that I find it everything I wouldn't write myself: hard, uncompassionate, leering. I have a feeling this is the one I shall do for money, rather than love.

All the family back about 7.30. No fierce tans, but all looking well and full of praise for Mürren. For a moment I feel rather like Helen must do when I come home. My neat world invaded. How different from this time last week when I missed them all so much!

Sunday, March 1st

Buy two magnums of '62 Leoville Lascases for Barry and Terry Cryer, whose 25th wedding anniversary we are invited to tonight.

Just as we are about to leave, Charles S calls. 'Good news and bad news,' he begins, with characteristic enigmatism. The good news is that all the heads of London Weekend's various departments who've seen the film think my performance is wonderful. The bad news is that it's so difficult to see the performance that they are suspending filming for a week.

Helen and I reflect on this stunning news as we drive out to nice, ordinary, uncomplicated Hatch End. A wonderful reunion evening with Ronnie Barker, Tim [Brooke-Taylor], Graham C, Eric, David Nobbs, Roy Castle, Kenny Everett and others.

Barry's speech involves going round the room and thanking us all individually. Quite a brave feat. Once you've set out there's no going back. But his 'speech' is capped by a very funny and composed series of one-liners from his 13-year-old son, Bob.

Not much time to talk to Barry, whose hair resembles more and more that of a Regency footman. Ronnie Barker, in striped blazer as if he's just come off the beach, helps hustle me away after midnight from the clutches of a well-oiled K Everett.

Monday, March 2nd

Examine possibilities of a three-day break in the latter half of the week, if I'm really not required. Narrow down possibilities to Venice (most exotic, but familiar), Paris, the Lake District (have been enjoying W's *Prelude* and fancy some contemplation).

See the evening off by a log fire, trying to make up my mind about early casting possibilities on *American Friends*. Anne Bancroft seems way ahead as Miss H; Brita has to be a new 'star'. Ian Holm or Bob Hoskins would make a splendid Weeks, and D Day Lewis is quite a possibility for Syme. Difficult not to put Denholm or Maggie in as a matter of course.

To sleep easily. An hour later a mad lady bangs at the door and rings the bell. I panic. Helen quite sensibly calls the police.

Tuesday, March 3rd

Charles rings as I'm at my desk, about ten. The news on 'Troubles' is that there is likely to be a fight between union and management.

Apparently management are strongly and unanimously on our side and Nick Elliott [LWT's Head of Drama] has very forcibly warned the union about the consequences of trying to force their own lighting cameraman back. As CS puts it, a dance now has to be played out with its own elaborate moves. The union will meet today and decide, on principle, to back their man. Later the management will, in response, cancel the project. Then the union's employees who stand to lose a great amount of money from such a step will put pressure on and by Friday a compromise will have been reached.[1]

Apparently John Birt[2] is in fighting mood and not mincing words. If the union prevails it will be the end of filming at LWT, so he says. Words, threats, poses – it's all going to be very sour and probably quite childish. Equity are not supporting the ACTT.

CS didn't think it a good idea for me to go as far as Venice, so I book up a Lake District hotel.

At 6.40, in my DJ, set out to address the Chelsea Clinical Society at the Berkeley Hotel. For various reasons, mainly 'Troubles', I have not had time to write them one of my prepared speeches, and, with unusually blithe confidence, haven't worried.

Met by Stanley Rivlin, enthusiastic, very Jewish, like an unkempt bear. I'm told he only does one operation, that's varicose veins, and he's made a fortune. In even lower voice I'm told he did Mrs Thatcher.

Talk about my film career, de-glamorise, pig stories, etc. Amazed that these high-powered professionals not only listen but listen most appreciatively.

But the day is not over. After midnight Michael Colgan rings to tell me that 'Troubles' is now officially cancelled. John Birt gave his decision at eight o'clock.

Unlike CS this morning, Colgan is emotional and far less positive about a satisfactory outcome with LWT. He reiterates ('It's been said behind your back and now it should be said to your face') that everyone is delighted with my performance, but his tone about the affair is quite different to Charles, more on the lines of 'I want you to know that whenever this gets done you'll be our Major ...'

Colgan sounds weary both in the short and long term. He sounds like a man who wants to get as far away as possible from LWT and to make a fresh start with 'Troubles' as an independent feature.

---

1 In short, we were caught in a variation of the many employer versus union struggles of the 80's. LWT were taking on an in-house, unionised labour force.
2 Director of Programmes at London Weekend Television since 1982. He left to join the BBC as Deputy Director General in 1987.

Friday, March 6th: Applethwaite, Keswick

Breakfast at 8.30, and drive east and south along Ullswater. Start walking at 10.15, along Martindale, realising that I've unthinkingly chosen a path straight into the wind, which flaps and tears at me in gusty assaults, threatening to remove the hat I bought this morning in Keswick.

After 15 minutes come to a small church, really just a simple rectangular building without tower or arches or any adornment – just grey stone walls and a slate roof. Set by the river, with a farmhouse a hundred yards away, otherwise quite isolated. Go inside and find an interior of such simplicity and dignity that it brings tears to the eyes. A plain stone floor, with some wooden movable pews, an ancient stone font, a table as an altar, and at the back a pulpit, carved, seventeenth-century. Nothing unnecessary, no show, no spiritual fireworks, but very affecting, especially as the wind batters at it. To me a much more profound and successful religious building than St Peter's in Rome.

Walk along the road up the dale. A collection of deserted farm buildings, substantial stone constructions with broken roofs and holes in the walls. But all carpeted with snowdrops – in and out of the buildings.

Pass through farms full of free-range animals – chickens clucking, cockerels patting about with self-satisfaction, bulls in straw-floored stone barns. Good smells. Then the road ends and a track pulls up towards the ridge. The rain turns to sleet, which then turns to snow. A horse on its own, black and slightly-built, shelters behind a wall and yet comes out to walk with me for a while, as if pleased to see a friend.

I push on up, the snow gets heavier, the wind now blows all the time and drives the sleety-snow stinging onto my face. I'm not quite sure where I am, except that below me the gently protective dale recedes and a sweeping amphitheatre of rock curves away to the south.

At the top at last, I feel now completely alone and cut off from the world. The snow here is six inches deep at least and conditions seem to be worsening. Turn right and walk along the ridge between Martindale and Boredale. But the constant fierce presence of the wind persuades me that I must abandon the path and, in a long, controlled sideways slip, I descend into Boredale, sending a deer darting away round the edge of the hillside.

Sunday, March 8th

Papers full of horrific details of the ferry that capsized outside Zeebrugge, *Herald of Free Enterprise*. It sounds much more like the victim of free enterprise. All sorts of safety corners cut in order to be 'competitive'.

It looks very much as if the 'suspension' of filming is going into a second week. LWT and the unions are locked in their own internal struggle, which involves issues far greater than just this programme. Meanwhile, in order to have some alternative to this stasis, Mitchell is beavering away to try and set up some independent deal. Decision will have to be taken by the end of this week.

Monday, March 9th

So begins my second week in limbo. Like a soldier who has seen action briefly, been superficially wounded and then unexpectedly withdrawn from the lines, I don't quite fit in anywhere. What makes it worse is that I spend much of the time, on the phone, having to explain to people why I'm not away at war, after I'd kissed them all goodbye.

Angela comes by for tea and to collect the two tickets for *King Lear* that I had thought I should never be able to use, but now of course could. She seems much more confident and in control of things. Did we over-react that first week she was here?

Tuesday, March 10th

Anne has been talking to Colgan; a re-start date of March 30th is mentioned. Quick calculation suggests this is impossible, as it would not free me until the end of the first week in July, a week before *Wanda* and no time for rehearsal.

Terry J arrives. He is not happy with lack of progress on 'Erik'. Eleven Hollywood studios have passed. Orion are the only hope and they want young American stars in it. TJ wants more ingenuity from John G and Prominent Features in suggesting alternatives. So he is in a sort of limbo himself.

Susan Hoyle rings to report on yesterday's [T2000] board meeting. The idea of elevating me to a presidential position has been well received, and so long as I can stay on as Chairman to the end of this year, will be implemented. Relief.

Wednesday, March 11th

In the afternoon Colgan rings and spins me a wonderful Irish yarn about the 'Troubles' reserve package, involving clandestine support from London Weekend management, who have already gone to the lengths of 'smuggling' scenery out of the building at 4 a.m. to get it out of the union's hands. The union has threatened to burn any sets already made if it goes ahead without them.

The cancellation cost to LWT will be £1.16 million, but they can get some of that back if the new 'Troubles' production can use sets, costumes, drawings, etc, already acquired. Equity is being completely co-operative, a designer from *Out of Africa* will come in to help – even Hugh Leonard, who wrote a screenplay for 'Troubles' which wasn't used, has sent them a good luck telegram.

Colgan slips into romanticism ... 'They all want to see this little Irish company taking on the big boys ... and showing they can win.'

I promise to find out the exact end dates from *Wanda* to see what my availability in the autumn might be. JC's approach to the *Wanda* film is the exact opposite to 'Troubles' – careful, considered, full of dates and detail supplied almost a year in advance.

So I shuttle between the hysteria of 'Troubles' and the icy calm of *Wanda*. The best I [can] do is to offer myself to 'Troubles' immediately after *Wanda* and right up to my pre-production period on *American Friends*. This gives him October to February. Not the best filming dates.

As I explain all this I feel I am talking myself out of the Major, probably permanently.

Thursday, March 12th

The phone is ringing as I get back – it's Michael Colgan. He puts the problem to me quite starkly – either they go in late March and re-cast, or they postpone until the autumn and hope to keep me. Could I meet them to discuss this second alternative? Fix a meeting at the Python office (before we meet, Colgan asks me not to reveal to anyone, even Charles, that the bulk of the 'rescue' money is coming from LWT).

The meeting hovers between dream and reality. They seem very anxious to do all they can to accommodate me, but the *Wanda* schedule spreads itself, languorously, over the summer, and Anne thinks that my contract will demand an extra two weeks on top of the ten I'm already booked for.

They will investigate the feasibility of postponement until the autumn, I will do my best to reduce the *Wanda* 'insurance weeks' in September.

Home, feeling much better about things. A real chance of saving my part. Touched also by their loyalty to me.

Friday, March 13th

My Major's moustache is five weeks and two days old. Helen said I ought to shave it off, but somehow I still pathetically hold out hope. Shaving it off severs my last, fragile hold on the character of Brendan Archer!

Nancy [Lewis] calls, at eight o'clock, thinking she'll get me before I start on the last day of my third week of filming. I have to pour out the story all over again. (The *London Daily News* seems to have been the only paper to run the story, with three reports, each progressively more accurate.)

Nancy has a five-week film part with Bill Cosby, in San Francisco from April 13th, for me. Just to complicate matters.

Saturday, March 14th

Night's sleep broken by awareness of Helen's early departure. She's gone by a quarter to eight, off to Saas Fee.

A fine, dry, sunny day. Shopping, and at one o'clock over to Islington to have a drink with Ken [Cranham] and Fiona [Victory]. Airy first and second floor of a handsome, though externally grubby, villa in Thornhill Road. Well-polished bare boards, big hand-made carpets, a chunky, rough-hewn table which probably cost an earth or two. Ken, hair all swept back, has aged interestingly. Curious mixture of naughty boy and careworn middle-aged man. Both flash across his features in seconds.

We walk down past well-kept, gentrified town houses, which remind me of what Gospel Oak might have been but for the comprehensive redevelopment plan. Thornhill Road, Islington, is the sort of place where people who devise comprehensive redevelopment plans live.

To a pub called the Albion. Ken is a great teller of theatrical tales – he really has acted with almost anybody. Tells a touching story of playing Beckett with Max Wall. Wall, very tired before they went on, rested his head on Ken's shoulders in the wings, Ken gently massaged his co-star's temples. Max after a while perked up enough to say gloomily ... 'That's the trouble with this business, you're only as good as your last performance.' Then, just as the lights came up and they made their entrance ... 'Like marriage, really.'

Fiona laughs at my thought that filming in Ireland would be less complicated than dealing with LWT unions and their persistent demands ... 'You don't know Ireland,' she chuckles.

Sunday, March 15th

After breakfast William and Rachel express interest in a trip out. Rachel has become interested in the Great Fire, so I suggest we go to where the fire began and look for Fish Street and Pudding Lane and Farina's the baker where it actually started.

The City is now littered with awful, unimaginative, dispiriting modern buildings. The complete boringness of the tallest of them – the NatWest Tower – seems to have set the tone. And the site of the Royal Bakers where the fire began has suffered particularly ignominiously, with a long, low, concrete façade (for Lloyds Bank), which makes a Second World War bunker look sensitive.

Rachel takes some photos. At least the Monument can't be redeveloped for offices. There is a solid wedge of traffic through the heart of the City and across London Bridge. Into the middle of it all comes a stream of beautifully-kept Morris Minors with anxious owners consulting bits of paper. A vintage rally gone hopelessly wrong.

Monday, March 16th

The script of the Bill Cosby film arrives; read it in the cab on the way to a *Wanda* get-together at the Meridiana Restaurant.

At least with Python we had an eccentric, understated surrealism which kept things fresh and unpredictable; here the sledge-hammer of zaniness has been wielded mercilessly. It's cruel, corny, clumsy stuff, and I feel that I'm not yet ready to do *any*thing for money – even be Bill Cosby's butler, with some good lines.

At the Meridiana are gathered Charlie Crichton, Roger Murray Leach [the art director], Greg Dark, Jonathan Benson, Sophie [Clarke-Jervoise, John's assistant], Steve and JC. A pleasant group, and I begin to feel very warm towards this film, which up till now I've rather underestimated.

The bungling incompetence of 'Troubles' has increased my admiration for *Wanda*'s single-minded efficiency. JC makes much of the relaxed, wonderful, easy time we're going to have.

Thursday, March 19th

Anne has spoken to Michael Colgan and all seems set for an October 5th start on the new, improved 'Troubles'. Only myself and Ian Richardson know this, according to Anne. Until I hear more I can't quite be sure, but it's the best possible solution.

Wednesday, March 25th

I have been invited to an Author of the Year reception by Hatchards. The reception is on the top floor of New Zealand House, from which there is a fantastic panorama of London.

I see Roald Dahl across the room with Jane Asher and Gerald Scarfe and realise that I'm too shy to barge in there. I still have the mentality of an outsider looking in. I don't share their lifestyle, I don't easily have their apparent cool poise and urbanity – well, not in these circles. They circulate because they know people will want to speak to them.

Anyway, Bob Geldof brings me out of my shell, hailing me warmly. He's just come from doing a commercial for shaving which he's rather pleased with. I hint at disapproval and he snaps at the bait. 'My morality is absolutely clear. I just want to make lots and lots of money' – classic Cleesian position.

Friday, March 27th

A morning of desk-clearing is eclipsed by trouble at 'Troubles'. Anne rings with report of negotiations. The money being offered for the new 'Troubles' is not much more than the old. She spent three hours with Colgan even to get this far. Colgan wants me to sign a letter today committing myself to the part in October, for 16 weeks and almost all in Ireland. As he has not yet got Charles's signature, this seems like putting the cart before the horse, but when Colgan calls a few minutes later I agree to his request for a meeting and hie myself to the neutral Mountbatten Hotel.

Ferociously strong gusts of late-March wind strike from time to time, reminding us comfortable city-dwellers how fragile a place we live in. For a moment a whole street goes out of control. People, caught unawares, stagger at the force of it, lose their belongings. People help others retrieve their hats, wild newspaper spreads spiral high over buildings to dive-bomb the innocent in neighbouring streets.

At the Mountbatten all is calm. They even serve herbal tea ... orange flavour. Colgan is a teetotaller, which he says is almost unacceptable in Ireland. The only way he can not drink and maintain a shred of respect is to say he's on the wagon. That at least conjures up feats of heroic consumption at some time in the past.

The gist of our hour-long armchair discussion is that there is money available to re-mount the film. 'Don't ask me who it is ... I can't tell anybody. I haven't *even* told my wife.' (Helen, when I tell her this after-wards, is the first to mention the IRA.) The money needs written com-mitments – signatures. Evidently he is asking for mine and Ian Richardson's. These will satisfy them.

But what of Charles – who seems to be the artistic driving force?

Colgan, who is a humane, tolerant and sensitive man, looks pained as he describes Charles's reaction to the autumn re-start. Evidently Charles felt that this was a chance for a whole 'new' look at the way they might do it. This could involve a different sort of location, and he is very keen to get Peter O'Toole as Edward. Colgan is an admirer of O'Toole, but says he is impossible to tie down and will be a destabilising factor. Colgan, in short, has run out of patience with Charles and wants a deal to be struck which would then be presented to Charles. October 5th or not at all.

I am most concerned not to stitch up the one person who involved me in the project, nor am I willing to sign my autumn and winter away to another director.

Tuesday, March 31st

Gallop on with 'No. 27' [as the play about property developers had become]. The flow seems so easy that I worry it will all be junk when I put it together, but it's a wonderful feeling, wanting to write.

With Helen to the 'Gala Preview' of *Personal Services*. A red carpet has been laid across the pavement in Jermyn Street, but the only illustrious names I see are Jones, Leland and Gilliam. Then Cynthia is amongst us and we are all roped in for a photo. Cynthia sparkles, figuratively and literally, in a tight-fitting diamante sort of number. 'One, two, three se

... x!' she choruses for the cameras. There's a big red lipstick mark on her left cheek.

Afterwards to a 'reception'. Wine is free, but Helen has to pay £2.00 for a non-alcoholic drink. I meet Bert Kwouk, so I feel I achieve something.

Thursday, April 2nd

My invitation to attend a special preview of LWT's *Scoop* arrives in the post. In the form of a mock telegram, it talks of 'delightful LWT onlaying drinks'. It just stirs in my mind a now-receding, but still potent resentment of the company, none of whose representatives have given me one word of solace, or explanation, let alone apology, since cancelling 'Troubles' five weeks ago.

Work through the afternoon, trying hard to keep to one side the desperate cries from various charities that have come in today's post. People *are* starving in Mozambique, young children *do* have cystic fibrosis, AIDS *is* dreadful, and all these causes lie balefully staring out at me from my letter tray. Cover them up with a request to write an introduction to another railway book!

Monday, April 6th

Lunch at Odette's with Steve and Michael Shamberg [*Wanda*'s American co-producer]. Shamberg looks and sounds East Coast, in fact he's from Chicago and now works in LA. He has an aristocratic drawl and a pleasant, laid-back approach, which is easy, quite intelligible and relaxing.

Shamberg thinks we should have a theme song for *Wanda*. Suggests someone like Phil Collins, who is popular in the US but British. Groans from Steve. Apparently it was suggested to JC, who didn't know who Phil Collins was. Mind you, he also thought Sting was called String, and Boy George George Boy, so not much hope of guidance there.

Write a letter to the Bishop of Birmingham re chairmanship of T2000. Checking a hunch, I find from Robert Hewison's *Python – The Case Against* that he was indeed one of the bishops who spoke out against *The Life of Brian*.

Tuesday, April 7th

Start the day with a lot of energy. Organise a family party here for Granny next week. This involves ringing Angela at Chilton. A small, unhappy voice answers. She's feeling awful again. At least she doesn't disguise it with me. She feels guilty about Granny – not seeing her enough, not being able to tell her what she's going through. She's doing her tap-dancing and working at the Quay Theatre [in Sudbury], etc, but she says they're only temporary diversions and 'the blackness', as she calls it, always returns.

Monday, April 13th

Wake to a dull morning. Am to launch a public transport initiative called 'Freeway' in Trafalgar Square mid-morning, only to hear that the launch has been cancelled, as the special bus broke down.

Good news on the transport front is a letter from Hugh Montefiore, ex-bishop, confirming his interest in the T2000 chairmanship, and requesting me to phone him after Easter.

Take Ma, by taxi, to the Clore Turner gallery [at the Tate]. She manages well, despite a swell of visitors. I manoeuvre her tiny, increasingly gnome-like bulk into gaps beside pictures wherever we can find them.

Then to the restaurant for lunch. Hard to hear each other and the waitress calls Granny 'the young lady with you'. But Mum has a wonderful way of filtering out angst in such situations. I quite envy her cheerful smile.

Home and help prepare for a big night at Julia Street – the arrival of all the Herberts for a family dinner. Angela has driven down from Chilton. She arrives first at a quarter to seven. She tries to be cheerful and on top of it all, but clearly is not comfortable.

A noisy and merry occasion, except for Angela's unease. 'Find me a job with witty people' is her last (despairing) attempt at a smile and a lifting of the spirits.

Tuesday, April 14th

To an un-looked-forward-to task at Highbury Magistrates' Court, to which I'm called as a witness in the case of the owner of the cab that hit our car last November.

No-one either welcomes me or even tells me what to do or where to go. Ian, big Scot from across the road, who took the cab's number, is already waiting. We sit for half an hour completely unattended.

Then a police officer, there to give evidence, recognises me. He moans about the Crown Prosecution Service, which is only a few months old, and replaces the police's own prosecution service.

A little later, after we've been sat there for 50 minutes, another helpful policeman comes to tell us that the case is on at the moment, but has just been adjourned owing to non-appearance of a witness.

He suggests we sit in the back of the court and wait to talk to the prosecutor. We do so, and are eventually told that the witness who didn't appear was Mr Palin. At which point I spring up and tell them I've been outside for the past hour. Magistrates full of apologies and very pissed off with a hopelessly confused, overworked prosecutor, who hasn't even looked our way, let alone consulted with us.

Thursday, April 16th

Twenty-first wedding anniversary. A very warm day in prospect.

A call from the production office of a film which Chris Menges is directing.[1] Would I come out for a week in June to Zimbabwe to play 'the nicest man in the world'? Unfortunately it's the second week of *Wanda* rehearsals. Also a call from *Animals' Roadshow* – would I like to be interviewed, with Denis, by Desmond Morris?

From the ridiculous to the sublime!

Back at home catching up with the diary before going out yet again when a call is put through to me by Rachel. A voice, of no particular class or distinction, says 'Prince Edward here'. I play my reactions cautiously, my mind flicking at double-speed through a card-index of possible Prince Edward impersonators, but it transpires it really is Prince Edward.

He wants me to join a giant *It's a Knockout* competition to be held for charity at Alton Towers in ... of course, June. It's on the day we're rehearsing, and the day when I would like to be in Zimbabwe with Chris Menges. Explain my problems, but he deals with the first one by saying that JC will take part if all the *Wanda* cast agree.

---

1 *A World Apart.* It won the Jury Prize at the Cannes Film Festival in 1987 and BAFTA Best Screenplay in 1988. The 'nicest man in the world' was played by Jeroen Krabbé.

At seven by cab to the Latchmere to see Bernard Padden's potato plays. Padden rang earlier in the week to make sure I came along. Have roped in Terry as well.

The theatre is casually run by very tall, wafer-thin, young students. 'Are you unemployed?' TJ and I are asked at the ticket office ... We joke – something about only for tonight. This cuts no ice at all with the young man who rather curtly elaborates, as if talking to very stupid people, 'Are you currently in acting work?'

Friday, April 17th: Good Friday

Call Alan Bennett to pass on my favourable reaction to last night's Padden play. He will try to go to it. He confesses that the heavily gay ambience would worry him. I tell him to take a butch friend with him – 'a hulking heterosexual' as Alan puts it.

He's trying to write another stage play – 'I'm always trying to write a stage play, but I just can't come up with the plots.' He says he has no difficulty writing the monologues currently being made by Innes for the Beeb.

Then I call Cleese, who disarms me with very generous observations about *East of Ipswich*, which he has at last got around to seeing. He's the third to mention it this morning.

He and I laugh as loudly as I have for a long while over John's revelation that the first thing he knew of the recent discoveries about the Queen Mother's relations was a headline on Teletext 'Three more Royal relations found in Surrey mental home'. It was the 'more' which really broke him up.

Sunday, April 19th: Easter Sunday

Up to Church Farm by lunchtime. Tom drives some of the way and Rachel shows me her diary. She gives days marks out of ten. Hasn't had less than six and a half this year!

Do some garden clearing and weeding for Granny. Often think I would make a good gardener. Solitary, contemplative, open-air sort of life has an attraction for me. Yesterday, skimming the papers for hints of places to go for a break at the end of May, I lighted with interest upon an article about Mount Athos. You can spend 96 hours with the monks evidently – living very simply in a splendid location – olives and bread and hard beds. Strikes me as perhaps the sort of 'new' experience I should be looking to sample.

Wednesday, April 22nd

To the Minister of Transport. His office is located in the HQ of the Department of the Environment in Marsham Street. It is one of the drabbest, shabbiest, most utterly dispiriting of all the drab, shabby, dispiriting buildings put up in the 1960's and '70's. The fact that it houses the ministry responsible for the environment is richly ironic.

Three men sit ranged at one side of the table; the Minister at one end, his private secretary, who transcribes all we say, in laborious longhand, into a big book – rather like the old Boots' scribbling pads. We are not encouraged to shake hands with the advisers – two on buses, one on rail tunnel – and they sit there, either frozen with fear or with boredom.

Mitchell is very welcoming and easy, though, and only gets at all disturbed when revealing that he has been sent a broadsheet from the GLC in Exile along with our [magazine] *Transport Retort*. He cannot disguise his distaste for the GLC in Exile and becomes quite headmasterly, as if warning a boy from associating with 'townies'. They are '*intensely* political' he warns us.

Thursday, April 23rd

Fine spring morning. Amongst other things, a script arrives from Susie Figgis on behalf of Chris Menges, bearing a short, but memorable note on the part offered – 'it is in fact Joe Slovo, who is one of the most important figures in the struggle for the liberation of South Africa ... '. It certainly makes a change from the camp butler or the zany transvestite English hairdresser.

Read it through, sitting in copious bright sunshine. Very moving. It's written by Shawn Slovo, who is, I assume, son of Joe. [Shawn is, in fact, his daughter.] Straight to the heart of a family directly affected by the cruelty of the SA regime. Makes all the stuff we're doing here seem suddenly trivial – window-dressing. This is spare, tightly-written, unsophisticated but enormously inspiring. It's literally about life and death.

So ring back and express my enthusiasm. They will not be able to get back to me until Monday – so Prince Edward will have to wait!

Friday, April 24th

JC has committed us to the Prince Edward charity weekend (good publicity for the film, he's been told) and so it looks as if I shall be wearing huge mouse masks and falling into water rather than playing one of the most important figures in the struggle for South African liberation.

By Underground to a lunchtime meeting with Nick Elliott and James Mitchell at L'Etoile.

Elliott says that LWT are definitely intending to go ahead on October 5th. They see no problem with the unions as IBA are to stipulate that in future 25% of programme content must be independent. Their 'Irish' agreement will ensure that 'Troubles' comes under this category. They do not want to make many changes from the previous set-up, but will have to look for another director, as Charles S wanted 'too many new conditions – including reappraisal of the part of Edward'.

No pressure is put on me to sign on the dotted line, and we leave on good terms at a little after half past two.

Wednesday, April 29th

TG rings. He's somewhere between Rome and Spain. He calls with criticism of 'No. 27' – very similar to TJ's thoughts. He feels, as I do, that it could be expanded, but is still basically a TV film.

He offers me the part of the Prime Minister in *Munchausen*, and has Max Wall in mind for the Sea Captain. He is now after Peter O'Toole again for Munchausen himself.

Then a whole series of calls. The Menges film must start on the 15th of June and won't change its dates for me. So I have to ring the royal office and accept, rather equivocally, the *Knockout* invitation.

(TG and I speculated earlier that it is an indication of the way things are that knighthoods, CBEs and the like are more likely now to be won by wearing ten-foot-high rabbit heads on the fields of Alton Towers, than in little boats squeezed between the North-West Passage, or for heroic encounters with the French fleet!)

Friday, May 1st

A delightful evening, apart from calls to Granny and Angela, which give a depressing picture of some of Angela's visit last week. Angela had been quite open with Granny about her state of mind. Angela says she sees in Granny all that lies ahead for her – loneliness and confusion. I point out that Granny is 83 and remarkably bright and undemanding compared to many much younger mothers and mothers-in-law. But through Angela's desperately distorted view of life, everything around her can be interpreted at its worst.

But then the delightful bit – Rachel cooks, serves and clears away a meal for Helen and myself. It's for our anniversary.

Wednesday, May 6th

Up at a quarter to eight for a few minutes of what, at present, I laughingly call 'meditation'. It is quite a soothing bridge between night and day, but as soon as I close my eyes Gospel Oak sounds like an international traffic hub.

To Tony Stratton-Smith's[1] memorial service at St Martin-in-the-Fields. Keith Emerson plays a somewhat laboured piano piece, 'Lament to Tony Stratton-Smith' (sic), which sounds like a prolonged Elton John intro. Michael Wale talks from the enormously high pulpit about Stratt's fondness for public houses, though, of course, no-one mentions that it was 'the lotion' (as I heard Robbie Coltrane put it on TV later) that did him in.

Graham does a rather perfunctory introduction to 'Always Look on the Bright Side'. They play the whole lot – even the verse about life being a piece of shit and always looking on the bright side of death. But, as they say, Tony would have approved. I am the only other Python representative there and very glad I went as we have three wonderfully stirring old-fashioned hymns – including 'Jerusalem'.

Graham and I walk back to the Marquee, where some hospitality is laid on. GC doesn't seem very relaxed, but then he never has since he gave up the lotion. He's been working very hard, doing his lecture tour of the US, and is now rewriting 'Ditto' yet again.

At six o'clock Helen and I set out in the blue Mini for Buckingham Palace.

---

1 Tony Stratton-Smith, a successful indie music manager, started Charisma Records, for whom most of the Python albums were made, along with those of Genesis and John Betjeman. He also helped finance *Monty Python and the Holy Grail*. Tony owned a racehorse called Monty Python, somewhat less successful than the comedy group of the same name.

There is something quietly satisfying about driving up the Mall knowing that, unlike everyone else, you are going into the house at the end. Smiling policemen direct us past the camera-wielding public, across an outer courtyard and through an arch between two scarlet-coated guardsmen.

There is a rather gloomy courtyard at the back which could do with some greenery. Have to open the bonnet and boot of the Mini, and the underneath is searched with a mirror.

Then in through the porte-cochère, familiar from Royal Weddings, into a hallway, with a raised area straight ahead. We are shown by the ubiquitous footmen up a red-carpeted, silent staircase and eventually, to the accompaniment of a low and respectful hum of conversation, we find ourselves in a long room with a curved glass ceiling. This is the Picture Gallery.

Prince Edward, all informality, comes across and talks to us quite chattily. He's got this thing together himself, and I feel quite touched by his ingenuous resolve and complete innocence in the face of many hardened fund-raising wheeler-dealers, some of whom are represented here.

The Prince makes a short speech and attempts to explain the proceedings on June 15th. It sounds either like a complete nightmare of embarrassment and potential humiliation or a surreal experience of hallucinatory bizarreness, according to how much you've had to drink.

Monday, May 25th: Southwold

I get my head down over 'AF' at nine, emerge for an hour's lunch at one, then a more or less uninterrupted run-through until half past six.

By evening the curious east-coast micro-climate has produced low, sweeping trails of mist, only as high as the water-tower some of them, which reduce Southwold to a shrouded silence, like something out of the 'Ancient Mariner'. Potter forth with my little mother into the vaporous evening. Welcome at the Crown almost better than the food, which is oddly tasteless tonight.

Celebrity for the evening is Maureen Lipman, looking wonderful and expensive in a big black and white patterned number with nice, crumpled hubby Jack Rosenthal and two children in tow.

Maureen's *Wonderful Town* has finished (early, I would think), but she says the pleasures of being thrown in the air by six Brazilians every night were finite – especially when two or three didn't turn up.

Tuesday, May 26th

To dinner with Barry Cryer and Alan Bennett. Organised by Barry again – and at the same venue, the Gay Hussar. Alan arrives clutching his back and front bike lights, which he secretes beneath the table. He drinks only Perrier; Barry and I have wine.

We catch up on the news. Alan waxes lyrical about *My Life as a Dog*.[1]

Barry has become friends with Ben Elton. He says Elton commented once on how much Barry smiled. 'None of our lot smile much,' he'd said. Elton thinks that we've lost the art of story-telling – this clearly is why he likes Barry!

Alan is still in trouble with his plots, he tells us, as he unchains his bike from the railings before cycling back to Camden Town.

I'm home by half past eleven. Angela is staying with us until the end of the week. Notice that her hair is greyer than I remember, but she looks as neat and petite and tidy as ever. Tomorrow she has some work at the BBC.

Wednesday, May 27th

Angela left for the BBC this morning in quite a funk, but survived in the Duty Office until half past seven. But she doesn't think that she is confident and composed enough to work there yet.

Thursday, May 28th

Helen and Angela go to play tennis at Parliament Hill. When they get back I hear from an admiringly disbelieving Helen that Angela has defeated her. She ran everywhere and quite took Helen, who has been getting cocky recently, down a peg.

By seven o'clock I have assembled the new '*AF*' script. What it needs now is another dispassionate read-through. But cannot do any more good to it tonight, so let it be and have stew with Angela, Rachel and Will and then out to see a film with Angela.

To the Classic Tottenham Court Road to see *Desert Bloom*.[2] I like it a

---

1 A touching and at times very funny Swedish film, directed by Lasse Hallstrom and released in 1985.
2 Released in August 1986, it was directed by Eugene Corr and starred Annabeth Gish, Jon Voight, JoBeth Williams and Ellen Barkin.

lot. A family saga of quality and sensitivity with an attractive re-creation of Las Vegas in 1950. It is about madness, fear and families, but the happy ending makes me feel less anxious about Angela's reaction.

She enjoys it too.

Friday, May 29th

I am up at seven o'clock. A lovely morning helps. Sun rising visibly and generously. Have read the new '*AF*' through yet again and found a couple of scenes to take out; so a very productive last read-through. By half past ten my two years of writing are over and the year of acting lies ahead.

Then say goodbye to Angela, who disappears up the street in her hired Volvo about 11.15. She never seems well in the morning and, once again, before she leaves, makes it clear that we can never understand how awful she feels.

Helen tells me that she sounded an even more chilling warning than usual and, as I drive down to some shopping and the Python office, a real fear passes through me. Still, she is on the way to her psychiatrist and she has shown a remarkable ability to function perfectly well this week. I like having her to stay, though she does have to be pushed away from a tendency to want to just 'lie and curl up'.

To Holloway Road to find some clothes for Ken Pile [my character in *Wanda*]. A wonderful Jewish men's outfitter called Garman. The manager and owner serves in the shop and chews a cigar. It's all very Broadway. Quite like old times with Hazel [Pethig] – very jokey and relaxed.

Am in my study making my lists when Helen calls me downstairs. It's between 9.30 and a quarter to ten. 'It's Angela ... she's done it,' is all I need to hear. Then I speak on the phone to Veryan, who confirms that Angela has killed herself. She went to the psychiatrist, then saw Veryan at lunchtime, and seemed on good form, telling him all about her week with us. She returned to Chilton, and there, at about the time Terry and I were chasing around a squash court, decided to go to the garage and asphyxiate herself.

Helen, very composed, though her eyes stare helplessly. I ask her to ring my mother. I've never asked her to do anything as important in the whole of our life together and she copes with it unquestioningly. I decide that I must go to Southwold straight away. As I leave, all I ask for is a couple of the green apples that I like to see me through the journey. But Helen had given Angela the last two.

I am up at Sunset House by ten past twelve. As I drove I was not taking much in. I knew I didn't want music or to hear anyone else's happy world still going on. I suppose I wanted to be sorry and that's what I was doing.

Ma in very good shape, considering. A little shaken, but it seems not to have caught her emotionally. She had seen it coming too. There is not much to be done tonight. I ring Aunt Betty in Australia. Hear myself saying (because there is a real danger using equivocation to an aged lady 18,000 miles away) 'Angela is dead. She took her own life this afternoon.'

As I settle into bed soon after one o'clock, in the same air of unreality, I pick up the bedside book – a collection of *Spectator* competition pieces selected by Joanna Lumley. Inside it reads 'To my brother Michael from sister Angela, Happy Birthday 1986'.

Saturday, May 30th: Southwold

After a broken, unrefreshing night's sleep, am up at 8.30 to face the practicalities of the day which will, I'm sure, keep all of us from digesting the full impact of what has happened. Mum seems still to be in complete control. The tendency to incomprehension which Angela found so irritating in her, is in fact a strength. I don't think it is lack of comprehension anyway. I think it is an ordering of priorities which comes from an instinctive awareness that survival is the most important thing. No wonder Angela could not respond.

Phone calls come in and the vicar calls. A short, well-meaning little man with a seraphic smile and an arrangement of very fragrant white flowers, cut by his wife.

He brings his particular brand of soft-spoken solace which seems quite at odds with the business-as-usual atmosphere of the flat. He holds my mother's hand solicitously (she won't even let *me* do that for long) and stares at a photo of Angela.

After this well-intentioned little charade is over, I get on with the more painful part of the day – to ring Veryan and then to break the news to various relations – Hernes, the Greenwoods. The task is made easier by the fact that everyone knew she was ill, so there is no sudden complete shock to confront.

Lunch with Ma and at two o'clock I leave her. She does not want to change her life or routine. Sticking to it is her best way of managing.

And the old ladies downstairs have both been assiduous in offering her company and sympathy. In fact she's been completely dry-eyed about the whole thing.

Then the journey I'm really not looking forward to – from Southwold to Sudbury. It's a beautiful afternoon, softly warm, and the Suffolk fields and woods and ochre-washed houses look their best.

First to greet me at Chilton is Camilla, then the two boys. All of us on the edge of tears, but controlling them. Great comfort in being with people who you know are feeling the loss as intensely as you are. Veryan is mowing the lawn. Tomorrow there was to be a local walk, meeting for refreshment at Chilton. They have decided not to postpone it.

The children make some tea and we sit in the small yard at the back of the kitchen and for two hours chat about everything but Angela. Jeremy's Jane arrives. I think it helps them all having outsiders there to distract from their grief. I feel very close to them, which is a warm and satisfying feeling, an unexpected bonus of the tragedy.

Drive back to London, still numbed, and by the time I'm home am able to sit and talk about it, over a glass of wine, matter-of-factly.

Nor do I feel any need to cancel our dinner with Terry and Al. Quite the opposite. I want to see people. I want to talk about Angela. I don't want to sweep it aside or under any carpets. And of course Terry is just the right person to be with.

We eat at 192 – a bright, trendy, new place in Notting Hill. TJ anxious and full of touching sympathy, but articulate and sensitive. Al too, though at one point she breaks into the sort of tears I've kept at bay all day. An excellent evening altogether, and I shall never be as grateful for the Joneses' company as I am tonight. And for Helen's strength and common sense, too.

Refuse to accept complete desolation. As she was unable to.

Sunday, May 31st

Still some more phone calls to be made. Betsy-Ann [cousin on my mother's side] says, apologising in advance for saying it, that she thought it 'a very brave thing' that Angela had done.

After the phone calls, another side of me cries out for satisfaction, for a dose of revitalising normality. The day at Abbotsley proves to be just that.

And what a day – warm in a gentle way, soft and summery – the garden full. The hammock is slung, football and cricket and rounders played. Gardening done and a copious lunch. The best of days.

Tuesday, June 9th

At Chilton for lunchtime. Helen, I think, more tense than I am. This is the first time she's been to Chilton since Angela's death, and she and Angela had become much closer in the last few months – talking in the kitchen, shopping at M&S, tennis, etc. I think Helen saw herself as a lifeline and in a way she feels more affected by Angela's death than I do.

Piers [Veryan's brother, a barrister] is there, with stories of his chaotic but busy life. His three-piece-suit – originally well chosen and quite stylish, is turned up at the edges and a little creased from over-use.

We set out for Colchester Crematorium – Marcus, Veryan and, in our car, Piers, Helen and myself. The crematorium is within shouting distance of Colchester Barracks, where, in the autumn of '82, I was screaming at a squad of recruits and actors for *The Meaning of Life.*

The innocuous collection of buildings where the cremation is to take place make no special impression. Somehow I don't want to remember the place. One or two other people – I remember a woman in a flowery hat – walk by, otherwise we are left very much alone.

The efficient and discreet funeral director, who seems to have one eye missing, checks we are all ready and then we make our way to the door.

At that moment, Angela's coffin, on the shoulders of four men in dark raincoats, is carried past us.

We then form up behind the coffin and make our way into a small chapel, whilst pre-recorded organ music sounds, tastefully, from some-where. It's all quite strange and disorienting to think it's used all the time – rewound and used again. It's like sleeping in someone else's sheets.

The presence of Peter Hollis, a priest and friend of the family, a sane and sensible man of no pomposity and a tough CND pedigree, makes the whole tawdry occasion special. He asks us to be silent for a while and remember Angela in our own ways. Then he reads some simple prayers – never over-sentimental or over-emotional, but one felt he shared with us all something of Angela.

Then, with the words, 'She is at rest', the curtains draw across (I find myself fascinated by who causes this to happen – someone listening somewhere pressing a button – are they automatically triggered in some way?) and the coffin slides away. I am dry-eyed, mainly because I don't look at the coffin, nor do I want to let my grief out in such an anonymous place.

We shake hands with Peter Hollis and then an awkward moment of not much to say in the car park before Helen and I leave for London.

We talked there and back about Angela.

Wednesday, June 10th

Park by the Serpentine Gallery and walk down to the Polish Club in Exhibition Road.

Always struck at this time of year by the sheer weight of greenery – the thickness of the crowns on the trees, the lushness of bushes and shrubs, the deep, thick pile of grass cover. It's June, it's raining, and England puts on its own impression of a Continental rainforest.

At the Polish Club I sit with a Perrier and wait for Tristram. Dark, smiling eyes of the girls at the bar – friendly, curious. It is like being in a very benevolent foreign country.

Hardly anyone else dining there, except for a few very smart, grey-suited Polish men, well preserved, with interestingly aged faces. Tristram tells me that they're the Polish Government in Exile.

Excellent borscht and then dumplings/meatballs and sauerkraut. Some good talk on 'No. 27' and *American Friends*.

In the evening to a PEN club function at the Zoo restaurant. Myself and Charles Sturridge and Dorothy Tutin have been invited as special guests to thank us for our help in last year's fund-raising effort 'The Sentence is Silence'.

I find myself temporarily next to a fierce lady called Sybille Bedford. Neither she nor most of her friends know who I am.

Unfortunately, once Michael Holroyd makes his opening speech welcoming self, and others, I make a grab for the bottle of red wine on the table, magnanimously and enthusiastically offering it to all the old ladies. A chorus of disapproval and very odd looks. Sybille protectively clutches the bottle. It turns out to be her own and not, as I thought, a complimentary. Many apologies. My confusion compounded by the fact that I'm discovered to be on the wrong table – I should be at high table, next to Dorothy Tutin.

Thursday, June 11th

Wake to rain. Election day.

Vote, and spend most of the late evening watching the results come in. The exit polls are complete spoilsports, quashing any real chance of surprise. Like reading the last page of a thriller first.

Nod off in my chair and finally to bed at two with the Tories well set for a third term. A depressing sense of inevitability and, to be honest, a hint of relief. The opposition just don't seem to have got themselves together yet.[1]

Sunday, June 14th

Drive, unhurriedly, across Derbyshire to the Peveril of the Peak Hotel, where Helen and I are staying in company with many other celebs [for 'It's A Royal Knockout']. An unpretentious, low group of buildings set amidst trees and fields.

Time to sit downstairs and read the papers and have coffee before setting out in a bus for Alton Towers.

At Alton Towers the security operation is elaborate, with police, private security and young PAs all armed with radios. We're taken to see the set – a wooden sixteenth-century castle-cum-manor house façade facing the slightly less real ruin of Alton Towers across the lake.

After a talk from Prince Edward, who seems to be completely in his element, we are all settled in the stands to watch a run-through of all the games by a special squad – who, we find out later, are largely from the army. Then to try on costumes, and eventually back in a bus to the hotel.

Assemble for a coach to the dinner at Alton Towers, at which four royals will be present. They are all staying at the Izaak Walton Hotel and I'm told no four royals have ever stayed together in one hotel before. Hence the security.

Our coach is late leaving because Princess Anne (created Princess Royal yesterday) is late arriving. We are jammed in. As we sit waiting we are treated to the sight of security men in a field chasing cows away from Nigel Mansell's helicopter.

Eventually we move off, and all the way from the hotel to Alton Towers

1 The Conservatives won with a majority of 102. It was Margaret Thatcher's third consecutive victory. Labour, whose share of the vote increased by 1%, was led by Neil Kinnock.

the route is lined with police and, on the odd occasions when we pass a house, by waving citizens. We pass regally through the town of Ashbourne, then out, up and over the quiet hills, and ride into Alton Towers between cheering – well, waving – crowds until we're drawn up outside Bagshaw's Restaurant. The weather is still fickle and umbrellas are provided for us as we scurry into the hostelry.

First glimpse of the 'other' royals. Andrew, thick-set, with a wide neck and big, piercing eyes. Fergie, eyes always looking about, smaller and slighter than I thought.

We're at tables. Next door but one to me is Margot Kidder, less irrepressible than usual, as she is jet-lagged and flu-ey, but still great company. Beside her, looking distinctly unhappy, is Nick Lowe, her current man. He turns out to be a kindred soul, articulate and full of the same sort of childhood memories I have. We get on well, though later Margot tells me this is exceptional, as Nick is not happy at this sort of do and fears for his street cred.

Prince Edward makes a speech, peppered with well-told jokes. I congratulate him on the one about the Scottish lady discovered in the snow by a relief helicopter which yells down 'Red Cross!', to which she shouts back 'No thanks, I've given already.'

Prince Andrew and Fergie are by this time throwing bread rolls about and as we leave we all have to crunch over a layer of sugar crystals which Andrew emptied over Michael Brandon's head.

Then back into the coach and off into the night. All the staff of the restaurant watching us, noses pressed against the window.

Monday, June 15th: Peveril of the Peak Hotel, Derbyshire

Into our costumes for a dress rehearsal. The rain stops, but it's dreadfully muddy underfoot. Still, Python filming and pop festivals prepared me for all this. I'm in the first game, which involves winding a cannon uphill on a capstan and having to jump over the taut rope at every revolution. We're dressed in four-foot-wide rubber rings with skirts hanging round them. It's absolutely killing.

Then I have to try the 'Mini-Marathon', which involves attempting to cross a revolving pole whilst having food thrown at me by Viv Richards. I fall in twice. George [Layton] is very good and John Travolta refuses to take part in two of the games in case he gets his hair wet.

At lunch the indefatigable Pamela Stephenson, who doesn't seem to be living if she isn't performing, coaches her team in a chant and we decide to call ourselves the Pandas.

After quite a wait, Prince Andrew appears to give us a team talk. Normally he would be considered intolerably bossy, but as he's third in line to the throne, it seems excusable. Then we're all sent off to change.

At four o'clock, after team photos, we line up behind our various royals and their banners. I'm at the back of our team and next to Fergie. She it is who starts the chorus of 'Why Are We Waiting'.

The crowd fills the stands, whipped by a cool, but mercifully dry wind, as we parade in after the fanfare.

First game is disastrous for us. Working savagely hard, we are in the lead when Gary Lineker and George Lazenby catch their skirts in the coiled rope. Not only do we come third, but Lineker has to suffer the indignity of being pulled out of his skirt by the Duke of York and others.

My turn on the pole in the Mini-Marathon ends in predictable ignominy as I join Mel Smith, Sunil Gavaskar, Barry McGuigan and others unable to make the crossing. Lazenby once again distinguishes himself and wins three points for us.

We don't come to the final game until nearly seven o'clock.

At the end Andrew becomes the army officer again and barks 'Everyone on the stage!' at us. 'Sounds as though he's won it,' I mutter to Princess Anne (who indeed *has* won). 'Oh, no,' she says, in that wonderfully lugubrious tone she uses to great effect, 'he's always like that.'

We have come second, which, after our early failures, is quite a relief. Everyone begins to peel off their mediaeval frocks and goodbyes are fondly exchanged. Prince Edward thanks every one of us and presents us with a Wedgwood commemorative bowl. I shake Andrew's hand and say goodbye.

At the hotel, goodbyes to such as Steve Cram, quiet, self-contained, and Meat Loaf, who tells me with some embarrassment that Fergie has taken to calling him 'Meaty' and says she wants to visit him in New York.

At last into our car and back to being the Normals. No police escort, but cordial waves from the detectives as we pull away from the Peveril of the Peak. It's as though all of us know that we have been part of a very peculiar, but almost magical occasion, the like of which will never be seen again.

Tuesday, June 16th

Scan the papers – the more popular of which carry a story about Prince Edward swearing at the press at a post-event press conference. His question as to whether they'd enjoyed themselves had been met by stony silence from the hacks – none of whom had been allowed in the arena or near the contestants.

In fact Edward had done wonderfully well in keeping them away and undoubtedly making the whole occasion relaxed and informal and enjoyable – 30 hours out of real life.

To JC's for the first day's rehearsal on *Wanda*. Jamie opens the door and gives me a big hug and a kiss, which is not a bad way to start the film. We spend most of the day reading through. The clash of styles – Cleese/Palin revue-based instinctive efficiency, Kevin Kline's New York method and Jamie Lee's West Coast directness – makes for an interesting day.

Kline is up and about with the script, touching, grabbing, shouting, always exploring every bit of the part. He has a disconcerting habit of dropping into the double lotus position with the same ease with which I would bend down.

Michael Shamberg is there, his sigh and mournful tone very recognisable. He makes up an American threesome; Charlie Crichton makes the third of the Brits.

There are many cultural clashes. The Americans can swear and motherfucker this and that, but are squeamish about a word like 'penetration'. They like things to be worked out, explained through in a way which makes even John seem wildly spontaneous.

But there is strength there – in technique and in physical presence and in sheer control and range with Kevin, in a bright and lively physicality from Jamie L. The scenes between John and Jamie are well played and very moving, JC having early on echoed Alan B's remarks at the first rehearsal of *Private Function* – make the characters real and the comedy will follow.

By the end of the day we are not even through the script. Hazel arrives and we try costumes, etc. Mine is approved of. Throughout John has been alert and guiding and never once irascible. The sun shines on and off in the garden outside and the house is comfortable, though the chairs are almost too big, like small rooms.

Wednesday, June 17th

We carry on reading through. Kevin prowls and pounces, but always with a strange softness of touch, which makes his behaviour entertaining and stimulating rather than dominating. JC hisses and wheezes with laughter and occasionally thumps the table and breaks into uncontrollable coughing. Charlie C listens wryly, interspersing intelligent observations, always with a twinkle in the eye and a generally well-calculated aggrieved air about the way John treats him.

Jamie is straight off a movie (which she hadn't much enjoyed) and into this set-up, with three people of whom she clearly is in some awe, and all of whom have quite different approaches to the acting.

We have a much freer approach than she has been used to and she is beginning to expand into it. At the moment she is as jerky and brittle as Kevin is broad and relaxed.

Friday, June 19th

Down to Park Lane to test drive a Mercedes 190 which I am toying with as a replacement for the Sierra.

We splash through the rain, which allows the salesman to show off the 86-degree wiper action and deliver some predictable abuse towards a march which has been holding up the traffic. There are red banners, Arabic writing and students, and he goes into a 'why do we allow them in the country' bit, but back-pedals like a true salesman when I respond with some liberal waffle about freedom to protest being better than revolution.

I shouldn't imagine Mercedes drivers are a left-wing bunch, and herein lies my concern about becoming one. Like it or not, it does rub people's noses in it. It is an expensive thing and, like travelling First Class, you are *seen* to afford it. On the other hand it is silent, strong and feels safer and much more strain-resistant than most cars I've ever driven.

To Upper Brook Street and Le Gavroche. JC, whose generosity has been well displayed this week, is hosting a dinner, ostensibly for Cynthia's end of exams, but with Shamberg, Kevin, Jamie and husband Chris, Helen and a girlfriend of JC's all there as well.

Occasionally JC looks paternally over to Kevin and myself as we talk, and he beams broadly and mutters some aside to Helen. He gets on well with Helen and at one point asks me across the table 'Is she as rude to everyone as she is to me?' I tell John he's privileged.

Saturday, June 20th

Rehearsal at JC's. The Americans have problems with the beginning – over how Otto is discovered, how their relationship is established, etc, etc. Kevin does most of the asking, but Jamie, who went running in Battersea Park at a quarter to seven this morning, takes a dynamic lead in suggesting answers.

JC is tired and not taking it in too well. I concur with Charlie C that there is no good reason for jettisoning the start we have, and that it should be made to work better with the injection of some of the ideas that Jamie has come up with.

Jamie makes us all a salad lunch and the atmosphere remains friendly and cordial, but for the first time I sense that JC's patience is being sorely tried by Kevin – for whom the present opening was written after they were in Jamaica together.

I haven't been home long when JC rings to apologise to me for what he feels might have been a bit of a wasted day for me. But I can honestly say it wasn't. The time we're spending together being very useful and instructive.

Later in the evening our new neighbour [Jonas Gwangwa] comes to our house after he's locked himself out. He's a tubby South African black with a kindly, well-used face and it turns out he's currently musical director of the 'Biko' film, in which Kevin has a lead role. The other musical director is George Fenton, who wrote the *East of Ipswich* score.

Tuesday, June 23rd

I have had the bright idea of having my character's hair curly, and Barry the hairdresser goes over my scalp with the curling tongs. Much too hot to start with, and a puff of smoke and violent smell of burning hair don't exactly bode well. But Barry has 'done' Ann-Margret and others, so not to worry. The result is quite effective. It certainly changes my usual 'boyish' look and the usual line of my haircut too. Show it to John, Charlie and others and, apart from Kevin, who reacts against instant decisions anyway, it finds general approval.

Wednesday, June 24th

We rehearse the various sequences that will occupy me for all but a day of the first two weeks. John tends to concentrate on the performances, whilst Charlie, walking-stick in hand, looks for the shots.

At lunchtime JC disappears to his office for a salad and a lie-down. Charlie adjourns to the bar, reminding me as he does so that the genesis of *Wanda* came from JC telling him what a good stutter I could do.

Kevin has now settled for a small, black cap, which tapers the top of his head, making him look a little ridiculous, sinister and fashionable at the same time. He wears a flowing black coat with blue stripes and the stagey flamboyance reminds me of Marlon Brando's outlandish outfit in *Missouri Breaks*.[1]

Thursday, June 25th

Into rehearsal. Jamie, projecting energy at an almost reckless rate, stares, frowns, worries, opines, suggests. At one point she comes up to me a little awkwardly and kisses me juicily on the lips. She apologises, but says she did it because she's going to have to do it in the scene coming up. Wonderful, but very American.

Lunch with Kevin and Donald Woods, whom Kevin plays in 'Biko'. Woods is a very lively, instantly warm man with a twinkle in his eye. We talk about the 'Biko' film. He says how careful they had to be in the script and in the making of the film to give 'equal air time' to all the various African resistance groups.

He also tells of how our new neighbour Jonas and George did the final music section. Apparently Jonas came into the session completely arseholed and played every single instrument to great effect. For a news-paperman Woods is infectiously indiscreet.

Friday, June 26th

JC is playing and re-playing what he calls the 'renunciation' scene with Jamie. Iain Johnstone is prowling around, recce-ing for a film about the

---

1 1976 movie, directed by Arthur Penn and starring Marlon Brando, Jack Nicholson and Randy Quaid.

filming. Jamie is very cross that she cannot seem to play the scene the way JC wrote it.

Then we have a read-through. Problem seems to be that it's still too long. Despite her glumness, Jamie still comes in with acute suggestions for cuts. Later in the afternoon we're talking and she tells me that the only way her father [Tony Curtis] could get a date with her mother [Janet Leigh] was by pretending to be Cary Grant.

'Biko' has been completed today and I go for a couple of lagers with Donald Woods and his wife Wendy in the bar. They live now in Surbiton. They seem to detect no irony in ending up in Surbiton after such an exciting and dangerous life, wading across the Zambezi, etc.

Monday, June 29th

Board the 8.55 to Birmingham International, where we begin the first day's filming on the 'Eco' programme on Transport 2000.

A small crew and an efficient day's filming. We start almost the moment I arrive, in the airport, then on the MAGLEV, and later at the main entrance to the National Exhibition Centre.

The end of the day's filming is of my returning, as the 'ideal' business traveller, to be met by a loving wife at home. Hazel, the lady they have secured to play the loving wife, is quite a surprise. She sits sipping wine in the garden. She is the complete antithesis of a wife. Her whole appearance, from the bouffant, tinted hair to the ankle bracelet, via the voracious pink lipstick, is of one who threatens the whole institution of marriage.

On the third take, when the director has suggested that we hold 'a beat longer' on the kiss, her tongue is exploring my mouth (which is quite taken aback) in no time.

Being devoured by Hazel on a Solihull housing estate on a tropical June day is, I have to admit, the least expected perk of chairing an environmental organisation.

Saturday, July 4th

We arrive at Chilton at 11.15.

I walk Mother slowly along the path to Chilton Church, across the fields, where the ripening corn is half her height. We move slowly, meeting people on the way – their first reaction is to smile at the fineness of the day. It's extrovert weather. At one point, looking behind me, I see my own family following along behind, surrounded by cornstalks.

A wait at the church before everyone is in – and Peter Hollis starts the service at 12.15. Beside me is Granny, then Helen, Rachel, Will and Tom. In front of me is Veryan and then the children. An organ plays. Across the aisle and through the vestry I catch a glimpse of golden sunshine and green grass framed in a doorway.

The first hymn is 'Breathe on Me, Breath of God'. Chris Bell[1] gives a short address and, as he says later, 'I only just got through it'. Very brief, unflowery, and he sums the tragedy of my poor sister up so well when he says 'If only she could have seen herself as we all saw her'. I read a lesson from One Corinthians – 'Faith, Hope ... Love' (not charity). I would have preferred something more immediately relevant, but it's beautiful language, though I still don't understand quite what I was saying.

At the end of the service we walk to the tiny graveyard where a hole has been dug to receive Angela's ashes, which stood on the altar during the service.

A short prayer by the admirable Peter Hollis at the graveside and then, for a moment, all the grief flows out. Every one of her children lets the tears come, and I embrace each one of them.

From this moment on Angela's life and the memory of her will recede slowly but gently into the past and into memory. The tears will flow less easily (though they are pouring down my face as I write) and the lives of those she knew so well will readjust to being without her. But in the middle of this hot summer day, amongst the fields beneath which lie old Chilton Village, the precise moment of loss is marked amongst us all.

Then, as happens, real life resumes. There's Terry J and Al to be welcomed. Everyone to be talked to. I walk back with Derek Taylor.

There is Pimm's and orange juice at a table beneath the copper beech, as we walk over the bridge. A wonderful party develops – full of memories of the last one here.

Everyone who had seen her recently seems almost to have expected what happened to happen. Everyone thinks it an awful, tragic waste. As Sepha points out, Angela looked ten years younger than most of her contemporaries here today.[2] She was so good at bringing the family together, says Joan Herbert, Veryan's cousin.

This last thought leaves me with the only real sadness at the end of an

---

1 He and his wife Carys were long-time friends of the family.
2 Sepha Wood is one of Angela's closest friends from Sheffield days.

afternoon far, far happier than I'd expected, and that is whether such an occasion will ever happen again. Angela was the common friend of all these people. Now, as her memory fades, will we all see each other again?

Wednesday, July 8th

Drive over to Hackney. At the Assembly Room I find a crowd of maybe 100–130 people listening to Dinah Morley – a local politician. Dave Wetzel, transport head of the GLC and in my book a Good Man, speaks before me. Very disappointing – list of all the good things the GLC did, then, rather than apply the lessons to the current subject – which is transport in Hackney – he ends with a long Labour rant. Purely political and quite unconstructive, especially as the Tories have just been voted in by a resounding majority for the third time.

Before I speak, the Mayor of Hackney, who is chairing, has to announce some business, but at the same time a large black lady is announcing something at the back of the audience. The Mayor plods doggedly on, the lady's voice rises, people's tolerance for their brothers and sisters begins to wear thin and she's asked to shut up. '*You* shut up!' she returns lustily, and continues barracking.

The Mayor seems unable to control her and she's still ranting on when I'm introduced. I stop and sit down until she subsides, but when I do go on it isn't very comfortable.

At the end a distracted middle-aged lady with wild hair comes up to me, 'You don't mind me asking, do you, but are you left-wing?' 'Moderately so, yes,' I reply judiciously. 'Oh, thank you. In that case could you sign my book?'

Thursday, July 9th

Taken down to Daniel Galvin in George Street to have my hair permed. This is the most drastic change to my appearance I ever let myself in for. As it was my suggestion to play Ken curly, I've only myself to blame. The process of perming is all quite soothing. It's a nice place and I'm fussed over. Some foul lotion, smelling of ammonia (it is in fact sulphur), is poured over my curlers.

My first real test of the new head is, incongruously enough, at a small party given by Sir Robert Reid of BR to his 'good friends'. So the first time I actually get to meet the most powerful man in the railways is six hours after I've had my hair permed.

Friday, July 10th

Picked up at nine and to the studio for rehearsal.

My dressing room is quite spacious. It's separated from Kevin's by a sliding wall. Kevin has an extraordinary quality of making himself look big and impressive, when he isn't a lot taller than me, in fact. His room is full of costumes, back-exercising equipment, books, etc. Mine is almost empty.

The day's rehearsal ends at six. In the course of which dogs are auditioned. One of the terriers has to resist. 'The Resisting Dog', it becomes known as, and will as such go down in my list of possible public house names.

Saturday, July 11th

To Harrow Driving Centre at half past ten for a second session of motorbike tuition. It doesn't all come back to me at first and I become dispirited. But I persevere and, with the patient help of Phil, improve and by the end am able to drive with a passenger on the back and manoeuvre through a slalom of cones without knocking any over. Like learning any skill one has to pass through the barrier of complete clumsiness.

Monday, July 13th

The usual, slightly over-hearty buzz of a first day's filming. Whilst I am in make-up Cleese arrives and as a present gives me a poster from the LMS in 1954, which announces the re-opening of the refurbished Gospel Oak Station – complete with wonderfully idealised picture!

Kevin gives me a gay book by one Phil Andros, published by the Perineum Press, called *My Brother Myself*. In it he's written 'Dear Michael, Happy Wanda. I love working with you. Herewith a book I found which could be developed into a project for the two of us.'

I am alone with the goldfish in the first shot – 'Hello Wanda' – and it's disposed of quickly and efficiently and we then embark on a roughly chronological sequence of scenes in George's flat. The speed of Alan Hume's crew and the understanding between us after two weeks of rehearsal, combined with John's unflagging enthusiasm and advice and delight in what he's seeing, make for a very productive morning.

Wednesday, July 15th

Experience the first real hints of how unsettling it can be acting a scene with Kevin. We're playing the scene in which I discover him on the lavatory (or pretending to be on the lavatory). The first barrier to sharing the scene is that Kevin is retreating into himself to discover whatever he can bring out of the lines and the action. I feel, perhaps wrongly, that this is not a process to whose depths I can be admitted. I feel a little like the magician's assistant.

Then, as we run it through, I'm aware of Kevin's reaction against direction, against marks, against restriction of any kind. Like a pacing lion he has to work out his own parameters. Charles Crichton tells of how when he worked with Alec Guinness they could never be seen to use marks. One evening he and the camera had plotted out where the great man should stand and a mark had been, inadvertently, left there.

When Guinness saw it in the morning he deliberately ignored it and played with his move for an hour before eventually coming to rest on exactly the same position as the mark.

By the end of the day, even JC is getting a little impatient with Kevin's habitual look at the end of every take, which is deep gloom.

Our last scene together for the day – his proposition to me on the stairs – feels very good. JC applauds generously at the end of a particular take and says that I won't do anything much better than that ever again!

Thursday, July 16th

Up at 6.45. Pick-up at 7.15. Complete the scene on the stairs with Kevin, then a long hiatus as they shoot Tom Georgeson and the police arresting him.

There is no sunshine about either – just a melancholy-inducing low cloud. At last, in mid-afternoon, I'm required, and work on, concentratedly, until six. Then a look at the rushes.

After they're over, Charlie, who is congenitally averse to showbiz hype, wobbles a bit and casts his soft, dog-like eyes up at me . . . 'You're bloody marvellous, you really are.' I'm quite taken aback and hopelessly unable to handle the thoroughness of his compliment, but it sends me home mentally beaming from ear to ear and I hardly remember the soggy, lethargic evening, and the long lines of blocked traffic almost every way we turn.

Friday, July 17th

Start the day being kissed repeatedly by Jamie on the bathroom floor. Very pleasant form of acting. We move on very fast and I'm in nearly all the set-ups, and in a variety of different make-ups, combinations of bandages and cuts and bruises.

Am immensely relieved and rather proud of the fact that I have been the heaviest used of all the characters this week, and that I've not just survived, but flourished, despite fatigue. I think performance has always brought me to life, and I feel more confident, more quickly in Ken's persona than I ever thought I would.

Life's little ironies, No. 32: Christopher Morahan is at the studios, casting for 'Troubles'!

Monday, July 20th

Begin work on the fish-eating sequence, for which I have my head bandaged, one eye covered, a bruise and scratches, and am tied to a most uncomfortable chair. Later I have chips inserted into my nose by Kevin. Not difficult to show expression of distress, and Charlie's decision for me to play the scene (and the rest of the film) with one eye covered doesn't seem to affect the degree of laughter from the crew.

The day wears on, as filming days do; all the days, weeks, months, even years of preparation for a scene are finally whittled down into a few hours. It's all businesslike. Charlie bangs his stick and laughs at himself . . . 'I can't remember what the hell's going on.'

Kevin spends most of the day racked by doubt – even when he's done the most brilliantly inventive take he stands, shrugs, and looks like a man who's just been given a tin of contaminated beef.

Tuesday, July 21st

More of the fish-torture scene. Good word on the rushes of yesterday. I am subdued during the morning – the part is so uncomfortable – but in the afternoon we begin the slapstick, stammering scene with myself and JC.

John, who has found even his generous policy of praise and encouragement is not always a match for Kevin's mood of gloomy reappraisal, beams with real happiness as we start to play the scene together. By the end of the afternoon he is corpsing regularly and suggesting we write a film together.

Finish at six. A physically very hard day for me – perhaps the most demanding so far – but on the rushes I can see that my one-eyed reactions are funny and, as Dave drives me home about seven, I feel, despite a 12-hour day, that I am really enjoying this return to uninhibited comedy. A chance to expand and experiment – a world away from the 'heroes' of '*Mish*' and *Private Function*.

Wednesday, July 22nd

Shamberg feels that there should be closer footage of the fish being eaten by Kevin. Charlie stoutly resists, saying that any more specific shots would spoil the 'beauty' of the piece and make it 'vulgar and coarse'.

I carry on after lunch and it's not until half past four that I'm released from eight successive days of heavy filming. Say my farewells until late Friday.

JC rings about 8.30 to tell me he thinks that the shot of me with the chips up my nose and the pear in my mouth – still desperately berating Kevin – is the funniest thing he's ever seen me do.

Thursday, July 23rd

The office phones. Someone who has seen me in *The Dress* wants me to play in Pinter's *Betrayal* at the New End Theatre – a 'major' actress is lined up to play opposite me. More tempting is increased interest from Steve Woolley and Nik Powell at Palace in my availability for a new Neil Jordan film. They will send the script to me.

Looking with half interest at what the Everyman may offer for a night out, I see that Charlie's *Lavender Hill Mob* is on at six. This must be a sign. I drive up there. Unfortunately the accumulated fatigue of the last two weeks decides to hit me as the film begins. Almost as soon as a succession of nostalgic images – the old censor's certificate, the Rank gong and the leaves of Ealing Studios' logo have come and gone – I'm fighting against a fierce desire for unconsciousness.

The film is a delight – played with great humour by basically rather nice characters. Its strengths are amiability and a good pace. I hope that Charlie will be able to inject the same into JC's film.

Friday, July 24th

Read Neil Jordan's *High Spirits* halfway through and am considerably intrigued. It's Irish-American hokum, but my part is quite interestingly manic and as I run over the Heath I feel a great surge of enthusiasm for the project.

My head clears, too, on *American Friends*. Decide to confirm Tristram as director, with the possibility of the now freelance Nat Crosby as photographer, and to try and make it as cheaply as possible. So the *Missionary* gloss would go and we should concentrate on the characters rather than the crowds of costumed extras. Ingenuity will be the key.

The second half of *High Spirits* is a bit of a come-down. The comedy becomes more desperate and the laughs cruder and the last page is dreadful. In fact the script bears all the hallmarks of Hollywood's corrosive influence. Suddenly, it doesn't seem like a good idea.

Wednesday, July 29th

Heavy rain as we start the day's filming. I am bent double in the back of a van with wet, sticky, grubby floor, trying to control a Doberman with a pair of pink knickers in its collar.

Back in my caravan I try to cat-nap. Overhead a gigantic flash of lightning and almost simultaneous clap of thunder.

Dog shots in the early afternoon and I end up back in the van with the Doberman, which is a very amiable, if somewhat confused, dog clearly not given to the level of ferocity required. 'Give his bollocks a squeeze,' someone suggests. Then he becomes realistically angry. His eyes stare and strain, his teeth are bared and I'm damn glad there's a muzzle. I'm dismissed at a quarter to six.

Back home, Neil Jordan calls from LA and before he can do any extra persuasion, I tell him I've decided, for time reasons, not to do *High Spirits* ... well, it's almost true. Unlike producers, he doesn't put up much of a fight and seems resigned.

Thursday, July 30th

After lunch I experience the odd sensation of nervousness and uncertainty as I approach a fairly simple shot. Despite rave notices from all sides for my work in the film so far, I still have only myself and my own gut feelings to trust and to deal with.

In the scene I have to discover that not only has a dog been killed, but that Mrs Coady has died of a heart attack. Gloom and remorse must turn to smiles and laughter. I do it, but formularistically, with tight representation of laughter, instead of laughing because I want to. Charlie is very happy, though, and moves quickly on to the next shot.

For the first time I feel rushed and confused. I felt critical of my performance, even if he didn't. I talk to Charlie. 'If ever you want to do it again, you just have to say,' he replies magnanimously, before adding 'and I'll say "*Bloody* actors"!'

Friday, July 31st

A frenetic day. A new location by Clerkenwell Green.

Two filming crews filming us being filmed, or, worse still, filming us off-camera, 'relaxing'. Feel like a caged animal being prodded through the bars to be animated, amusing – to do tricks – when really all I want to do is sit as quietly as possible and harness my energies to complete the day.

Charles Althorp[1] interviews me for NBC's *Today* programme. I manage to be lively, but unimaginative. He is quite sensible, softly-spoken and easy to talk to. Then the prying eyes of Iain Johnstone's crew pick me up and I improvise with John and everyone laughs, till we run dry.

Jamie is back with us. She's edgy and, as I'm beginning to realise, covers her edginess with a manic display of extrovert energy. As John is in the middle of being interviewed by NBC, interminably, Jamie grabs a policeman and leads him to arrest John. It works very well and the policeman goes all pink.

But when Jamie does the same thing on Kevin, who is giving an equally interminable interview to Iain Johnstone, it backfires; Kevin is not much amused, and poor Jamie sits down again, deflated. She is like a bright

1 Princess Diana's brother. He became 9th Earl Spencer after his father's death in 1992.

child, very up or very down. Open, eager, energetic, but always demanding a response; thriving on attention, but frequently finding it's the wrong sort.

The afternoon is even more like a circus. We are crowded into narrow streets, hemmed in by dour old council housing, filming a car exchange on a getaway (the police obligingly tell us that this location has been used for just this purpose by real crooks, twice in the last six months).

Jamie is practising the line 'Shut up!' when a group of Scots winos stagger past. One turns on her – 'You fuckin' shut up!'

David Byrne, whose *True Stories* was one of the most interesting films this year, and whose 'People Like Us' tape has brightened many journeys to Southwold, appears with Michael Shamberg (who carries his mobile phone like a sinister black detonator). A thin man, with big, soft, dark eyes, hair in a pony-tail and a rather nervous, apologetic manner, which is belied by sudden bursts of lusty laughter.

The motorbike has to be ridden for the first time. I have to ride it whilst holding the black bag of clothes, which is something I never practised. Charlie decides on no rehearsal. 'Either he'll do it, or he won't.'

As it happens I do it, and they're happy with the take, and the Lowryesque crowd begins to disperse as the unit moves off for the last shot. For me it's the end of week three, the end of my 13th full filming day out of the first 15.

Wednesday, August 5th

We're up early – seven o'clock – to see William off on his cycling trip to Holland; he's going with friend Nathan for two weeks. Everything squashed into two pannier bags on his new Muddy Fox mountain bike. Brightly-coloured Bermuda shorts and his recently-acquired Pizza Express baseball cap give him quite a jaunty look as he heads off up Elaine Grove, on a soft, quite cool, autumnal morning.

To the Curzon Mayfair to catch the first performance of the highly-praised *Jean de Florette*.[1]

Enjoy the film – my attention constantly engaged by absorbing wide-screen photography and a small group of characters giving riveting performances.

---

1 Directed by Claude Berri and starring Gérard Depardieu, Yves Montand and Daniel Auteuil.

Turn it over in my mind as I drive north, to see if I can winkle out any lessons for *American Friends*. Keep it simple, is as far as I get.

Monday, August 10th

Today we are filming at one of the maintenance areas at Heathrow.

British Airways have, extraordinarily, given us a 747 to play with for the week and it's tugged into position at the back of our shot. Only the tyres are of human scale – the rest towers above us, comparable only to some huge cathedral or fortress.

Special effects are responsible for the false concrete with which the area is being surfaced, and into which Kevin must fall and die. It's made from a base of porridge and Camp coffee, and smells a bit like pig swill.

I have a steamroller to drive, which looks formidable and belches out black diesel smoke. Quite easy to operate, though not for racing, and I enjoy bearing down on Kevin very, very slowly.

Wednesday, August 12th

A stunt man is squashed into the porridge first thing, as Brian (special effects) drives the front wheel of the roller over him. All executed with skill and admirable lack of fuss and bother; everyone applauds.

More steamroller-driving in the afternoon takes us almost to the end of the sequence, a day early. My last lines are screamed out above the noise of steel on porridge.

A pleasant, but humid evening. Tom enthuses to me about climbing, in which he clearly finds success and confidence.

Thursday, August 13th

At the airport soon after eight. A low, damp morning with drifting drizzle. Melvin [the second assistant director] greets me with the news that they have reversed the day's shooting and will first be doing the final sequence inside the Jumbo.

So, a morning in the caravan. Dip into a 1920's travel book about 'Undiscovered France', which Jonathan Benson has brought in for me. Jonathan loves France and all things French, and is very interested in my imminent departure for our summer visit to the Lot. He remembers reading a card stuck up amongst others offering 'Cane-chair saleslady' and 'French lessons', which read simply 'Phone 487 3294 for the Lot'.

Friday, August 14th

A mild and benevolent morning, and there is a cautious air of celebration about the unit. Can't be just the sunshine, or because it's Friday, I think that a general air of confidence is seeping into us all. This is the end of five weeks' filming, in which there has not been one day which hasn't produced something remarkable, and Michael Shamberg's only worry is that it may be too long.

Jamie, to whom I have given a copy of *American Friends* earlier this morning, retired to her trailer and read it all at a sitting. She is tremendously enthusiastic. 'I get so many scripts, I have to tell you, if something like that came along I would ring my agent and say "Get me the job" ...'

Saturday, August 22nd

David [Dodd] and Andaye and sons Alex and Jehan are round at Simon Albury's. We talk about the '60's, about the change that has happened since then, and the Conservative '80's. Nothing in the US has really changed deep down, Andaye feels. Reagan has managed to divert attention away from the problems of hunger, poverty and prejudice by concentrating his time and his efforts on those who are successful, tough, patriotic.

We are deep in a conservative cycle, I wonder if when there is a return to restlessness, and questioning, radical attitudes, the conditions for their dissemination will be the same. In '68 quite a lot of people, journalists, editors, media folk, went along with the celebration of change; now, as the Murdochs tighten a stranglehold on the press and international money markets are so sophisticated that a crisis of confidence in a radical government could be quite quickly implemented, one wonders how open or democratic any display of dissatisfaction will be.

Back home at four to see Patrick Cassavetti[1] as the next stage in pulling

---

1 Among other things, he'd produced *Mona Lisa* for HandMade, co-produced Terry Gilliam's *Brazil*, been associate producer on *Made in Britain*, David Leland's powerful TV series about the state of modern education, and location manager on Gilliam's *Time Bandits*.

'*AF*' together. We talk for an hour. Patrick impresses with his seriousness, his knowledge of what's going on in films, attitude to the crew and the team and lack of interest in big money film-making. Leave him with the script. If he says he wants to produce, then I shall be flattered and encouraged.

Monday, August 31st

Work through letters in the morning. Jo Lustig,[1] an amiable and even historic figure of our times, calls to tell me that Anne Bancroft would love to hear from me on '*AF*'. Al L sits in No. 2 and reads 'No. 27'. A lovely day, warm and sunny and breezy. Lunch together in the garden.

Later I run and afterwards ring Anne B. Response is heartening. She begins by gushing her praises for my work and the Pythons – though what she's seen of my solo efforts I cannot establish. She is admirably direct and funny and sounds quite irresistible.

She says she's touched that I've written a part for her and yet doesn't waffle or flood the phone with insincerity. Our brief contact is very exciting and hopeful. But will the script justify the approach?

Wednesday, September 2nd

The location is a church school hall in Roehampton, which is doubling as a prison visiting room.

Kevin, Jamie and Tom Georgeson are playing a scene. Phoebe, Kevin's trim, dark-haired lady, looks on. She chuckles ... 'Kevin will always try to steal the scene some way or other.' I am able to grin agreement. 'Did he do his zipper up in that last take?' she asks.

Kevin and Jamie are finished by lunchtime. Lunch with JC, who has reduced his waist by four inches since he started his pre-film diet, Robin Skynner, his straight-backed psychiatrist and fellow author, and two comedy writers – Renwick and Marshall. Having been one of a comedy duo, I recognise the identification problems. One automatically thinks they're one interchangeable entity. Renshall and Marwick. They seem very amiable.

---

1 Press agent and manager whose clients included John Cassavetes and Jack Kerouac. In 1986 he co-produced the film *84 Charing Cross Road* with Anthony Hopkins and Anne Bancroft.

After lunch a couple of scenes with Tom Georgeson. At one point he seems very troubled by how to deliver the line 'Un-be-fucking-lievable!'

At that point Charlie gives one of his occasional extraordinary performances which reveal a natural clown, or ham, whichever way you want it. He leaps up, flings his sticks to one side and bellows the line at top volume and with ferocious energy. Spontaneous applause breaks out in our smoky, crepuscular hall. Tom admits he can't follow that.

Thursday, September 3rd

For most of the afternoon I'm in black – balaclava and tracksuit and shoes – robbing safes of jewels. The set has an end-of-term feel to it, marooned as it is in the almost empty Studio 3.

Kevin arrives later, to see the rushes. He says he would like to direct. My view is that I wouldn't like to perform and direct. Kevin says that's what Laurence Olivier did, to which Charlie replies that Olivier could do it because he was a dictator on set.

Home, but not much time to relax, for Al is bubbling after reading *The Weekend*, which he thinks is absolutely marvellous, and does cause me to re-examine it. He also gives me a half-hour's wisdom on 'No. 27', which he feels has more errors.

To Vasco and Piero's for another splendid meal and a more gentle and thorough continuation of all we've talked about during the week. What is so agreeable about Al's company is that he does care about people and how they are and how we depict them and, well, the struggle of the artist to find the truth, and all this makes me so glad to be with him rather than at the table across the gangway where they seem to manage to talk about the Spanish air controllers' strike throughout a three-course meal.

Friday, September 4th

To 68a Delancey Street which, from September 1st, is now the Python, Mayday, Prominent address. It is Prominent Studios.

Amongst all the plaster and sawdust and stacks of gypsum board, and pipes and the sound of generators, hammers and drills, can be found various office staff – already quite cosily installed, though the walls need painting and the stairs are still under construction.

New additions to the staff include Liz Lehmans, Steve's assistant, and John Roebuck, who looks even less like an accountant than Steve or Ian.

I've brought them a plant in a rather handsome glazed pot. Just to add to the chaos.

Saturday, September 5th

At last, after two or three days of lines crossing, make contact with Patrick Cassavetti. He has read 'AF'. Felt the first half rather laboured – 'stodgy' is the word he uses – but as he read on he became involved and, finally, moved. As we talk it is clear that he is interested, would like to work on it with me, but is carefully and strategically hedging his bets.

He sees difficulties in attracting finance, as the film is not easy to target at an audience. I agree. It's an act of faith, in a way. If we believe enough we'll make it work. He is heavily committed at the moment to a David Hare film, which if it goes will keep him solidly involved until after Christmas. We agree to consult in three or four weeks. So . . . no producer yet.

Dinner with Jonathan B and Shirley at Strand on the Green. The approach to their house – or rather their complex, for it contains Shirley's frock business as well – is very spectacular. An alleyway leads off the mundane side street to reveal the river and a darkly wooded island in the middle, the lights of Kew Bridge off to the right, a newly-painted iron railway bridge to the left, and towers and chimneys standing in sharp silhouette against a honey-coloured evening sky. Inside, wide, open-plan rooms.

Jonathan reveals that he shouted at Charlie yesterday for only the second time on the picture. Charlie then became extremely docile and repentant, leading Jonathan to think perhaps he'd over-reacted. 'God, the man can drink though.' Jonathan recounts that during the half-hour they spent together in the pub after Friday's filming, Charlie downed eight scotches. 'He's like a pickled walnut,' Jonathan declares, but agrees that he has survived amazingly well on a long shoot.

Monday, September 7th

Ring Camden over the rubbish levels in God-forsaken Lismore Circus. Then write a long letter to Anne Bancroft.

To Seven Dials Restaurant in Covent Garden for lunch with Terry J.

The restaurant is, surprisingly, half-empty. Thierry, the maître d', who used to be at Mon Plaisir, runs it now and greets me warmly. TJ is

celebrating not only *Personal Services*' first prize at a Swiss comedy festival! but also *Nicobobinus* being No. l in children's paperbacks. He has
had a 'marvellous' hols in Corsica and admits that he is feeling much
more confident these days.

TJ's lack of confidence may not have been evident, cloaked as it was
by Welsh directness, bonhomie and strong opinions. But I think TJ
means creatively and here we tangle a bit. We talk about collaboration –
or rather Terry talks about collaboration, for I have nothing to offer at
the moment. Whether he wants me to rewrite or addend *Erik the
Viking* or not, I don't know. Anyway, the discussion turns into quite a
minefield.

TJ telling me how he felt *The Missionary* should have been written.
Fortescue as a very highly-sexed man – not a man avoiding sex. I *do*
accept TJ's point and think he's right, but TJ plants yet another mine,
very close to where I might tread, suggesting that the 'wrong' course the
film took was the result of my personal approach to life.

Whether I like it or not, I do regard TJ as a bit of a conscience and this
hits home. Perhaps I am too tight, controlled, careful.

As usual we drink too much, and end up being treated to 1942 Armagnac by Thierry, who's having his dinner on the other side of the restaurant.
I leave with a vague sense of dissatisfaction. We haven't quarrelled, but
we've bristled at each other.

I have a two-hour briefing with Susan H at the T2000 office. Find it
very hard to keep awake. But cups of tea help and am much sobered when
the time comes to drive to the BBC.

Will Wyatt, head of documentaries, looks like an airline pilot, as do
the other two whom he calls in to talk to me. Their offer is for me to write
and present a recreation of Phileas Fogg's journey *Around the World in 80
Days* for the BBC. Would try and travel round the world, on surface
transport only, in the allotted time, accompanied by two film crews – one
filming me, the other everything around me. Six 50-minute programmes
would come out of it (hopefully). Drink Perrier and play it very cool.
Must put my own film first, but as an autumn/winter '88 job it's very
tempting.

Tuesday, September 8th

Woken at 7.15 by a phone call from the London *Evening News* to say they
have a news item that Jonathan Ross is planning the first all-nude chat

show and that myself and Simon Callow would be stripping off. Could I comment?

Thursday, September 10th

Drive down to Marylebone Road to Radio London for another interview re the AIDS show.

With me on the interview is a young man called Nick who has AIDS. Like Princess Di I shake his hand and feel no threat. He has been a PWA (Person With AIDS), as they like to call themselves, since June. He doesn't look ill. He is pink-skinned, short-haired and very sensible and straightforward. Almost impossible to fully comprehend that he will die soon.

Buy some gifts for people on *Wanda* – including some old travel maps of France which I've decided to give to Jonathan B because I can't think of anyone – myself included – who'll get more out of them.

Friday, September 11th

Alarm at 6.15. At 6.45 collected, with Hazel.

Chin-wag as we proceed across London heading for a pet cemetery in Cobham.

My last 'official' day of filming is in amongst graves with marble tablets beneath which lie 'Spotty', 'Susie, Naughty But Nice' and, ironically, the one I have as my opening mark, 'Monty, 1970–1981'!

Charlie says 'As this is your last day, I'm going to show you how to act' and he clambers over the gravestones with complete disregard for their occupants and the little plastic fencing that surrounds them.

My last shot is me looking terribly unhappy behind a tree. In fact, apart from a nagging feeling of inadequate sleep, I feel the opposite. The crew give me a little round of applause, Charlie says, with quite palpable sincerity, 'I think you're quite a good actor'. Joe Steeples interviews me for the *Sunday Times*, who take photos of me, scratched and bandaged, amongst the graves, various of the crew want autographs and, to cap it all, Iain Johnstone's camera crew hover for a last interview.

Jonathan Benson is very delighted with his maps, but apprehensive of his invitation tomorrow to Kevin and Shamberg's – when 'charades' are to be performed. JB hates charades. 'That's what we spend the whole week doing,' he mutters, rather grumpily.

Sunday, September 13th

At half past five I leave for a charity show for Frontliners at the Piccadilly.[1] A cluster of thin, ill-looking men determined to be brave sit in the front seats at rehearsal. Drag queens abound. Funny that homosexual men should go to such lengths to imitate the female – like vegetarians making cutlets, I suppose. In the line-up Liz Smith, Graham Chapman and Sheila Steafel and Paul Gambaccini.

I'm first on. I read 'Biggles'. Audience receptive, but not ecstatic. In the second half I do the 'Martyrdom of Brian', which goes well and I do smoothly. We all sing 'You'll Never Walk Alone' at the end. Sea of male faces in the front rows lighting up with pleasure at being part of it all. Really quite moving.

Wednesday, September 16th

Back at my desk – call comes from Colin Brough of Akela Productions, who has read *The Weekend,* as have his two assistants. They all like it very much and feel that, apart from some updating, it is in very good shape and they would like to produce it. I agree to look through and make immediate changes and meet them at the beginning of October.

Thursday, September 17th

Go for a run, and reflect on work. One thing does clearly stand out in my mind, and that is that the *80 Days* documentary would be a chance of a lifetime. It will give me a combination of acting and writing and could be fitted in with *American Friends* if they were prepared to shoot late in '88. By the time I pad sweatily (for there's high humidity) through the traffic on Mansfield Road, I have 90% made up my mind to say yes to the project.

Sunday, September 20th

Terry G calls from Highgate. He starts filming tomorrow on *Munchausen.* A first week of night shoots! Bill Paterson is in the cast. Terry is delighted

1 Frontliners was a pioneering self-help organisation for HIV/AIDS sufferers. It was disbanded in 1991 following fraud and nepotism investigations by the Charity Commissioners.

with him. Sean Connery is to play the King of the Moon, and I, as Prime Minister, shall therefore be working with him in December. Max Wall has turned down the part of the Sea Captain.

The film is already suffering bizarre strokes of fate. The Italian stunt co-ordinator died, of old age. The horses they had specially trained cannot be used on the Spanish locations owing to some African Horse Disease, and the two performing dogs have a rare liver condition.

Monday, September 21st

At last! Word from Anne Bancroft. A spirited note, but judiciously worded to give no assumption of commitment to 'AF'. She says my accompanying note was 'spot on' and diagnosed 'the weakness of the screenplay'. She urges me to start re-writing straight away, 'don't wait for October or November', 'then send it to me'. 'It would be wonderful to work together.'

Tuesday, September 22nd

By 7.30, when I get up, the skies are clear and it's a strikingly good day for positively the last of *Wanda*.

My first scene is a shortened version of the bathroom scene in which Jamie seduces me. Jamie has an idea for it, JC has an idea and I have an idea. Jamie's is the best. She envelops my mouth in mid-catatonic stammer with such a generous kiss that afterwards, almost in a trance, I give her the information as if healed of my stammer.

So Jamie kisses me about eleven times (including rehearsal and close-ups). Then she is applauded, for it's her last shot. She cries as a huge bouquet of flowers is presented.

Jamie and Kevin both write me fulsome and emotional notes which just underline how undemonstrative we Brits are. Jamie gives something to *every* member of the crew.

Amidst all the present-giving there is still work to do and, as JC and I prepare for a shortener for the 'stammering scene' – or at least the slapstick part of it – Charlie makes an announcement. 'I'm very happy to be able to tell you that this is the *last* acting shot.' Fun to be doing it with JC.

More applause at the end. My last shot of all, ten weeks and a day after my first, is a close-up of me writing 'Cathcart Towers'.

Linda in make-up and Claire the nurse tell me I've been voted by the women on the crew as the man on the crew that they'd most like to spend a weekend in Paris with. Jonathan Benson is second, and very put out. He mutters about 'the euphemism – a weekend in Paris'!

Out to the Meridiana in Fulham Road.

Jamie very emotional again. Her high spirits are so fierce, in a way, that the sheer effort of keeping up with her own enthusiasms must tire her out. JC is presented, by Shamberg, with the Emmy he's just won in the US for his appearance on *Cheers*.

Some bond has been forged between us all, but I'm not yet sure how strong it really is, after the hype. Maybe much stronger than I think.

Saturday, September 26th

Take Rachel down to Marshall Street Baths in Soho for a swim. She loves swimming and doesn't do enough of it and I'm very much happier with a weekend if I work some exercise into it.

The baths are impressive. Custom-built – maybe 50 or 60 years ago. Stone fittings and marble surrounds to the pool. A sort of Art Deco curved ceiling, restored in the last year, and a good-size, almost empty expanse of water – and all this within spitting distance of the London Palladium. I think we may have made a find here.

On the way home drop off at 68a Delancey Street to find an army of builders spending my money. The building is now moving forward at a reassuring pace. Talk to a contract painter down from Wolverhampton – 'They won't work weekends in London.'

Monday, September 28th

Dying to begin work on the '*AF*' rewrite, but T2000 still hangs onto me and my time. The process of parting company with them is a slow and lingering one, and though I took the decision to resign in the 'Troubled' days of February, I still find myself, not writing my film, but taking the Underground to Euston for another BRB [British Railways Board] meeting.

Then we are treated to a most depressingly impenetrable hour's dis-quisition on railway marketing, scattered with American business jargon rather proudly, as if the dynamism of the words will somehow miracu-lously interact with the business itself to make it as efficient. As it is, the words are a smokescreen, and we learn almost nothing, except how to make an interesting and very relevant subject deeply boring.

Wednesday, September 30th

To TV-AM to record a story for Children's Book Week. I read the last chapter of Spike Milligan's *Badjelly the Witch*. Rather pleased with myself, as no fluffs and plenty of spirit – 'We didn't expect *acting*,' says the floor manager afterwards.

To lunch at Odette's with Clem Vallance[1] – for the next step towards my *80 Days* project. He has a background in travel and anthropological ventures – he once took Gavin Young to do a programme on the Marsh Arabs.

We get on well together, but the most dramatic thing about the lunch, apart from getting on well together, is that a date for departure is fixed – September 13th 1988. Almost a year from now, at the tender age of 45, providing Michael Grade [Controller, BBC1] likes the idea and I have no second thoughts, I shall be embarking on the longest journey of my life.

Friday, October 2nd

In Oxford with Tristram. We travel up to John's together to talk to Dr Boyce, the Bursar, about the possibility of using the college for filming next summer.

Boyce is a pleasant, approachable man, anxious to know that we shan't be 'lampooning the college' or giving it 'the "Brideshead" treatment'. He walks us around. We leave him a script and assurances that we are interested in a serious re-creation of the college life in the 1860's. He smiles, not altogether convinced, I feel. Maybe it's my haircut.

To lunch at Brown's in St Giles. A 'fern restaurant' as Tristram advises me such places are called, owing to the profusion of rather dull, potted Filices.

Home to be de-Kenned by Don. My curls, or most of them, removed after two months and three weeks of looking like Gaddafi, Malcolm McLaren, Simon Rattle and 'a thin Dylan Thomas' (TJ).

---

1 Clem came up with the original idea of the television series *Around the World in 80 Days* and asked for me as presenter, after Alan Whicker and Clive James declined. I later learned that journalist Miles Kington and Noel Edmonds had also been offered the job by the BBC.

Monday, October 5th

By Underground to Leicester Square and a short walk to the austere and temporary-looking suite of rooms above St Martin's Lane that pass for Akela's offices. Colin Brough has almost nothing to say about the rewrites of *The Weekend*. He's more enthusiastic about the clutch of new titles I've slung together on the train between Chalk Farm and Leicester Square.

He, and I, quite like 'Listen', but I also have a fondness for 'Putting the Cat Out, and Other Things to Do at the Weekend'. Brough looks horrified at this – do I realise how much it will cost in small ads?

He has some interesting ideas on casting and direction (I notice a very elegant rejection slip from Michael Caine on a side-table) and seems to want to expedite the project by sending a copy ASAP to Paul Scofield. It would be ironic if he accepted, for he was Angela's idol when she was a teenager, and we used to tease her about him! On directors he suggests Alan Bennett and Ron Eyre. Both excellent choices and a reassuring indication that he's thinking in the right sort of direction.

Thursday, October 8th

To a six o'clock drink with Robert to mark the publication of his new book – 'Now this one you *must* read,'[1] Robert insists, and I feel guilty. It's quite slim, but a little polemical for my leisurely tastes – about our museum policy and how we live in the past too much.

Geoffrey Strachan is there. He looks wary as he tells me of the imminent likelihood of the disappearance of Methuen London. The Thomson group, ex-owners of *The Times*, have bought Associated Book Publishers, but are not interested in keeping on general books or Methuen Children's Books. Geoffrey and co-directors think they can raise ten million for a management buy-out, but, gloomily, he reckons Thomson's could hold out for £20 million.

Whatever happens, things will never be quite the same again and Geoffrey and Methuen – our greatest publishing friends for the last 15 years or more – may be parted in the next few months.

---

1 This, Robert Hewison's fifth book, was *The Heritage Industry*, published by Methuen, with illustrations by Chris Orr and photos by Allan Titmuss. It argued that 'instead of manufacturing goods, we are manufacturing *heritage*, a commodity which nobody seems able to define'. As it happens, I have read it and it holds up very well.

Friday, October 9th

Clem Vallance rings from the BBC, much aggrieved that Will Wyatt has told him he cannot direct *80 Days*. A director, Richard Denton, will accompany me round the world, and Vallance will do all the setting-up. He is most indignant, especially as Denton has no particular qualifications for 'travel' filming, which is Vallance's speciality. The first reversal for what seemed like such a simple, effective idea.

Wednesday, October 14th

Still no word from A Bancroft on availability in LA in November. Getting a little tight as I have to book my Round the World First Class Apex at least two weeks before leaving.

Business to do in the morning. What do we want our credit to be on *Consuming Passions* [aka 'The Chocolate Project' etc] and do we want a credit at all? Decide that to take our names off completely sounds very significant – and I'm not sure what it would be significant of. They want 'From a story by ... ', but TJ and I prefer the accuracy and greater detachment of 'Based on the television play *Secrets* by ...' I'm sure this will involve Anne in much faxing with the West Coast!

To a wet and windy Soho for another Spike Milligan book launch, in an upper room at Kettners.

Michael Foot and his wife pass on the way out. 'Spike's looking awfully smart these days,' observes Footie, in his surprisingly strong and ringing tones.

I leave at eight and, hurrying through the rain, holding aloft the purple umbrella which Angela bought for us, make my way along the pitted pavements of Greek Street to the Gay Hussar, where JC is waiting for me.

A good meal and a comfortable and loquacious session – mainly about *Wanda*. JC surprised that within five days of finishing the film he'd totally forgotten it. He doesn't want to direct (actually, he's like me – he'd quite like to, but is worried about the technical side) and is 'quite honestly' not desperate to do another film. 'The difference between us, Mikey, is that you seem to be able to enjoy things.'

I think he'd rather be a philosopher – if only it paid better.

Thursday, October 15th

I watch *84 Charing Cross Road*, Anne Bancroft's latest film. One or two thoughts go through my head. The only negative one is whether or not she's too old for the character I'm writing (Connie Booth appears briefly in the movie and I'm struck by how good she might be as a 'younger' Miss Hartley).

But Bancroft's superb ability to fill characters with life without becoming fussy or exasperatingly hyperactive, and her ability to move me (to tears by the end of the movie) are breathtaking. She is a strong, big, major actress and would give '*AF*' an enormously firm centre.

Friday, October 16th

In the depths of the night we're woken by the telephone. Not ringing, but dying. Lights flash and strange, helpless gurgling sounds emit from the receiver. Then it falls silent. Notice that the light outside the bathroom has gone out.

Downstairs to the hall to fix the trip-switch and at last pin down what is odd – the house is in complete darkness only because the street is also in complete darkness. Up to my workroom. A tempest is raging and bits and pieces of leaves and twigs and God-knows what rubbish are being forced under the glass and scattering over my desk. No lights anywhere, except for the stairwells of the flats and the reassuring yellow ring at the top of the Post Office Tower.

Back to bed. It's by now about 4.25. Helen decides she's hungry and gets up. The unusualness of a power-cut makes me switch on the radio, but can pick up neither LBC nor BBC, only the emergency services – police, ambulance, etc.

The lines crackle out stories of 'Trees blocking the eastbound carriageway of the A12', 'Lorry and trailer blown over blocking the M20', 'Borough Surveyor urgently requested to go to Erskine Road W12 where four-storey block of flats in state of partial collapse', and the most dramatic thing about it all is the calmness of the voices, the ordered, efficient lack of emotion in lines like 'There has been a major power failure'. Exciting stuff.

Try to go back to sleep, then snapped into wakefulness by the sound of some heavy metal object cracking against walls and cars.

Power is restored to us by 7.30, but still news is coming in of continued blackouts. Winds of 94 miles an hour were measured on the ground and a gust of 110 mph on the Post Office Tower, after which the gauge broke.

The phones ring – grannies are both safe. Up at Lismore Circus a huge tree has fallen and several smaller ones are leaning crazily. Boughs and leaves and branches provide an unbroken carpet around the shops. Mr Nice Man and his papers are there – except for the *Independent*. Everyone's talking to each other, as if it's the war.

I have an appointment with press cameras at the zoo at eleven, to publicise Oxfam's Fast Week.

I'm the only one of the 'celebrities' who've made it. Tom Baker and the manager of QPR have cried off and a lady from *Eastenders* will be late. The press are consulted and word comes back that they will probably only print a picture of me and the *Eastenders* lady together, or possibly just the *Eastenders* lady, but certainly not me alone!

Later in the afternoon I go for a run. The sun has gone and been replaced by a very cold, light rain.

Six or seven huge trees are flattened, with disks of earth and roots measuring 20 feet by 15 feet suddenly wrenched up and standing where the tree itself used to be.

In the grounds of Kenwood House, there is devastation. Paths are almost impassable and an avenue of limes which forms one picturesque approach to the terrace in front of Kenwood has been almost totally uprooted. There is no-one else around now, and being in the middle of this dreadful damage is quite eerie. One thing's for certain – the reassuring landscape I've run through for eight years has been drastically changed. It'll never be the same again.

On the news I hear that Kew Gardens have suffered enormous losses, which cannot be made good within a lifetime.

To dinner at Terry J's. The impressive avenue of Camberwell Grove is a shambles, with two cars completely crushed.

The assembled company is somewhat muted, almost as if a party is indecent after what has happened. Ken Branagh and Emma Thompson are there. Emma, with her short, cropped, red hair, looks so different from her *Fortunes of War* character that, despite having stared at her for 50 minutes last Sunday night, Helen still doesn't recognise her!

She is of the Phyllis Logan school, easy, well adjusted, direct, funny, unaffected and great company. Ken is nice, modest, similarly approachable and unshowbizzy. They are obviously very fond of each other, and a couple, though not living together.

Terry has salmon and crudités and bags of Sancerre and four mighty crabs which just happened to have caught his eye, and then the confit de canard, with lots of red wine.

Terry is like a man with a starting-handle, working with enormous energy, emotional and physical, to give us a really happy, 'different' evening, and then, I sense, vaguely disappointed that the vehicle he's started hasn't gone forward as fast as he'd like. Personally, it's one of the nicest, happiest, jolliest, least Dinner-Party-ish evenings I've spent for ages.

Home, past the remainders of what the radio is at long last admitting was a hurricane. Britain's worst since 1703.

Friday, October 23rd

Will Wyatt from the BBC wants to come and put his (i.e. the BBC's) view of the Vallance affair to me next week. Now this is one of those times when I can gauge how exalted I have become, when the BBC Head of Documentaries is prepared to come to me.

Drive in state to JC's 48th birthday do. Peter Cook is there this year and we spend a lot of time on talk. JC still intrigued at why Ingrams hates him so much. He thinks it's envy. Peter thinks not. Definitely not. Peter will not hear a word against Hislop or Ingrams.

Peter seems very easy-going at the moment, happy writing bits and pieces for *Private Eye*, doing an HBO special [Home Box Office, founded 1972, the pioneer of cable television]. At one point he asks me if I find it hard to 'do' any more. Meaning write and perform comedy. We both agree that we miss the quick turnover to write and perform. Long, slow-burn projects like *American Friends* are all very well, but they lack opportunities for what I think Peter and I can do well, which is rabbit endlessly on and make people roar with laughter while doing same.

Talk with Jack Rosenthal, who is sitting next to Helen. He is a very amiable and sympathetic fellow and his high praise for *East of Ipswich* means a lot, for he is one of the finest practitioners of recollective comedy.

Monday, October 26th

My first sight of *Wanda*, cut together.

And very good it is too. As I had expected, uncluttered, competent direction, no artistic gimmicks, and a pretty tight edit by John Jympson.

John C has made Archie work completely – his best all-round per-formance since Basil Fawlty. Kevin and Jamie are immaculate.

I find myself a little disappointed with myself. God knows why – maybe it's just because so many people have built up what I've done: 'star of the film' nonsense. I think it's not that I do what I do badly, it's just that I'm not really called on to do much more than react to other people's bullying. What I can do best of all is the subtler shading of character and perhaps that's what I missed in Ken, except for a few lovely moments – two of the best being those I did on the very last day of filming.

Afterwards John has us all in for a session of thoughts and reactions. Thorough to the end.

Wednesday, October 28th

Decide that I can wait no longer for messages from Jo Lustig, and I ring Anne Bancroft direct. Once again I find her good sense and clarity very attractive. She suggests I get the script to her via Mel (Brooks, her husband), who is travelling to the US on Concorde on Friday. She will read it as quickly as possible and will call the office – Anne or Alison – early next week with a reaction.

She thinks that the only reason for not wanting to talk in LA would be if there was *nothing* constructive she had to say. Even if she had criticisms, suggestions, etc, would it be worth my while coming? Yes, I agree readily.

Thursday, October 29th

With Anne to a screening of *Consuming Passions*. Perhaps because our expectations had been so low, we both react with relief to the first few scenes which are well played by Tyler Butterworth and full of well-exe-cuted slapstick jokes.

After that Jonathan Pryce and Freddie Jones and Vanessa Redgrave show that they had been given free rein and that it had worked. Though it all goes rather adrift at the end – 'pantomimey' as TJ put it – it is hugely enjoyable along the way. A real curiosity.

Back at Prominent Studios I have my first piece of luck for the day – Mel Brooks is at his hotel, before leaving for a dinner. Yes, of course he will take the script. 'Love your work,' he barks, by way of signing off.

Home by eight. Send off the script and at last I can afford to spend time thinking seriously about going round the world. [To see Thailand with Simon Albury, then home via Los Angeles and Anne Bancroft.]

Friday, October 30th: London–Bangkok

I set to reading *American Friends* with greater care than yesterday's enforced rush. This time I have 13 hours and 45 minutes' flying time ahead of me. I can luxuriate over every full-stop and comma.

At the end of my read I have to admit that it begs as many questions as it answers. Structurally it's more confident and it has an interesting shape now that it's seen through Miss W's eyes. And yet expanding the Bancroft role has also put the spotlight on the other two main parts. It's become a little more of a psychodrama than a nice, period, comedy-adventure drama and, now I have embarked on the course of examining the leading characters in more depth, I think I have gone forward, but into uncharted territory.

So I cannot lie back and enjoy the hoped-for luxury of knowing I had cracked *American Friends*. It will remain to nag me, to pull at the fringes of my attention all the time.

My night on the plane begins too early, and is interrupted with a stop at Bahrain, so I do not sleep, and by the time we ease down over the rice fields of Southern Thailand I've been awake for 22 hours.

Tuesday, November 10th: Bangkok–Los Angeles

4.25 a.m: Am about to shave, ready for a five o'clock departure to the airport and on to LA, when Anne J calls. Bancroft has rung. She has not been well – laryngitis or something worse. She does not see much interest in the character. Anne's feeling is that she doesn't want to do it.

Standing naked in a Bangkok hotel bathroom I receive the news philosophically. I shall have to speak to Bancroft at some stage. I am booked on a plane that leaves in two and a half hours and I have very little chance at this time of the morning to check out alternatives.

Financially I might, with a quick withdrawal to London, save on a few US hotel bills, but I would have cancellation fees and the possibility of no flights to London today and extra expense in Bangkok. Keep going forward, I feel.

At 5.45 in Bangkok Airport. When I ask if there is a First Class lounge, the girl replies 'In February'.

Midnight, and we're approaching the Bay Area. Have crossed over the Date Line, so it's Tuesday again, and it's already nine o'clock in the morning. Can see the Golden Gate Bridge and can understand why Americans like coming home.

7.20: At the Beverly Wilshire.

The year of Living Dangerously continues: after 'Troubles', it's clear that '*AF*' will not go. Talked to Anne Bancroft, who sounds nicer and more sympathetic each time we speak. She says she doesn't think I've yet made my mind up what it's about. The latest draft showed I could write – the writing even better than the second draft. But it's like a fine suit of clothes, without 'the nakedness', as she describes it, beneath. She says she's a perfectionist, but it's that sort of criticism which is worthwhile.

Read in the *LA Times* that TG's *Munchausen* has stopped filming for two weeks and the completion guarantors want to replace TG. Will my December *Munchausen* work fall through as well?

Wednesday, November 11th: Los Angeles

Woken about 9.30, by a dreadful banging on the door, which turns out to be the air-conditioning having a trauma. Outside a very bright, clear, perfect day, a real advert for life in the Pacific South-west. Warm, dry air blowing out from the desert. Skies a deep blue, no smog.

Walk up Beverly Hills Drive, buy a paper, breakfast at Il Fornaio. The girl at reception is a 'big fan'.

Ease slowly, luxuriating in this glorious weather, temperatures in the upper 80's, back to the Beverly Wilshire. I take some sunshine, swim, then Michael Shamberg sends a slim young Virginian called Karen to collect and take me to Fox Studios.

Note: LA people always sit *by* the pool. Only foreigners seem to go in!

Shamberg looks mournfully delighted to see me. Takes me to lunch at the commissary.

First person we meet is Mel Brooks. Chunky, rack-like, barrel chest, with a firm, no-nonsense light paunch, he grabs my hand a lot – shakes it probably five or six times. 'I forgive you guys everything . . . I want you to know . . . you're so good, I forgive you for all those ideas you used.' Is he joking? 'Spanish Inquisition?' He digs me knowingly. Not sure what's going on.

(Chris Guest[1] later tells me that Brooks has an almost pathological inability to accept competition – it's all a reduction of his own world. Apparently he said, after seeing one of Allen's early movies, 'When Woody Allen was born, I died'.)

Saturday, November 14th

T Gilliam rings.

He's home for a weekend before returning to Rome to take up the cudgels again. He thought two days ago that it was all over and he would walk away from it, but apparently Charles [McKeown] pulled him round and gave him a talking to and together they came up with a formula for cutting the script which could ensure survival. McK is in Rome rewriting at the moment.

Jake Eberts[2] has emerged as TG's latest hero. He has moved mountains to keep the film alive and apparently told TG that 'Whatever happens, let me do your next two films'. So there are silver linings, but TG is not looking forward to returning. Whatever happens, he says gloomily, the next 12 weeks will be hell.

The personal postscript to all this is that it looks as if my part will be a victim of the cuts. Terry says he will have to give me something else – he can't have a Gilliam film without me – but he sounds as though this is just another addition to his growing multitude of problems.

Sunday, November 15th

Stay homebound. JC calls in the evening. The film is down to 117 minutes. Larry Kasdan, 'one of the brightest Americans I know', saw it last week and raved – so JC is very pleased about that.

I ask him how *he* is. 'I'll tell you something that'll really make you laugh,' is the way he leads into it . . . 'Are you ready for a laugh? I've moved

1 Chris Guest, Jamie Lee Curtis' husband. Actor, writer, musician – *This is Spinal Tap* (1984), and later director too – *Best in Show* (2000), *A Mighty Wind* (2003) and others. In 1996 he inherited his father's title and became 5th Baron Haden-Guest.
2 Eberts, a Canadian film financier and producer, was, with David Puttnam, the founder of Goldcrest, the most successful British film production company of the 1980's. They made the successful *Chariots of Fire*, *The Killing Fields* and *Local Hero*, and the less successful *Revolution* and *The Mission*. Eberts left Goldcrest and set up another British-based film company, Allied Filmmakers, in 1985.

out.' He says it hasn't been working for two years, and he's only leaving now because he feels confident enough of his relationship with his daughter that she'll 'understand that I'm not sleeping there, but can still see her each day'.

Thursday, November 19th

The King's Cross Tube disaster is another nail in a dreadful year for the country.[1] *Herald of Free Enterprise* tragedy, the storm of October 16th, a series of fatal motorway pile-ups – quite a battering.

Friday, November 20th

Down to the T2000 office.

Susan has been much in demand by the media over the last 36 hours. She bemoans the fact that it takes a major accident for the press to show any interest in transport. Jonathan [Roberts] has been the man of the hour, for he issued a report on the Underground for some users' group after the Oxford Circus fire of '85. Full of suggestions for safety improvements (which were not taken up) and prophetic words about only luck that there has not been a major disaster ' ... and luck has a habit of running out'.

We talk over tomorrow's AGM, at which I will officially step down as Chair after 21 months – or 22 if you count my pre-press-launch work.

Saturday, November 21st

To Brixton for the AGM and conference of T2000 – my last day as Chairman. The *Independent* has front-page coverage of Earl's Court Underground – damning photos of rubbish, inflammable grease, empty fire-buckets, and fire equipment locked in cupboards.

The Brixton Recreation Centre is a brand new building which looks committee-designed. A cluttered interior with escalators, lifts and staircases everywhere. Impossible to find one's way around. Eventually, having asked a cleaner, I'm directed to the 'Social Rooms'.

The AGM goes briskly along, with no problems, unlike last year. I am

1 A fire which began in uncleared rubbish at the bottom of a wooden escalator left 31 dead and 60 injured.

presented with *Jane's Urban Transport Systems* by John Gregg, who makes a short and kind speech, referring specifically to the fact that throughout my chairmanship meetings ended on time!

Then Hugh [Bishop Montefiore] makes a crisp, funny speech – wondering at one point whether he had been chosen for his knowledge of 'vertical rather than horizontal transport'. I reply.

As I reach the climax of my speech – and one of the few serious bits – a booming metallic voice comes over the Tannoy: 'Julian to the poolside please ... Julian to the poolside.' A fitting climax to my two odd years as Chairman!

The rest of the day is taken up with a T2000-organised conference on disability and transport.

A blind, or partially-blind, man from Sheffield – John Roberts – is quite excellent. Funny, clear and compelling. He it is who makes a plea for the Swedish attitude to public transport – that it should be designed and run so that it is accessible to everybody, including the ten percent of all travellers who are, in effect, disabled. He wants no special buses, specially-adapted trains – just the awareness in the first stages of design that 99.9% of the country's travellers must be able to use transport, not 90%.

Sunday, November 22nd

Terry G rings from Rome to confirm that my part as Prime Minister of the Moon is no more, but offers me the consolation part of a man who is discovered in a corner singing a mournful song, prior to falling dead from his seat. 'It was going to be my part,' he admits. Being a great admirer of Terry's parts and conscious of the fact that De Niro wanted Jack Lint and TG stuck by me, I assure him that I'm happy to sit this one out.

Wednesday, November 25th: London–Belfast

Tom has had his injured finger diagnosed as a fracture (a Hap-Ki-Do injury) and the surgeon wants to put a pin in it. He's booked Tom into the Royal Free today. So Helen and Tom are preoccupied with getting him to the hospital and I'm preoccupied with packing for Belfast. Three bulging bags – T-shirts, costumes and my own stuff.

Leave home at midday.

In the Arts meet Jimmy and Paddy again – my faithful stage staff.

Paddy has lost weight and seems to be very short of breath. We all look older. It's getting dark now and I notice people lined up at the windows looking down into the street. There's rumour of a security scare.

I carry on running through the sound cues with Joe, who is a new man. Young. He apologetically tells me that he broke his arm three weeks ago and still isn't quite himself. He is in charge of all the lighting and sound cues! Very Irish.

Malcolm, the general-technical manager, comes up to us. 'We've been asked to leave the theatre.'

Outside in the street a couple of the grim, colourless army Land Rovers are parked. White ribbon is being unwound across the pavement and Malcolm hurries us as far away as possible. We walk to College Gardens and wait at the office. I desperately need some rehearsal time tonight, but it becomes clear that I'm unlikely to be going back.

The general impression from reports and rumours is that the whole of central Belfast has been sealed off. Then we hear that the M1 motorway has been closed.

The Europa Hotel is evacuated. Michael [Barnes] reacts calmly, puffing a little more fiercely on his cigarette and forgetting that he has one already smouldering in the ashtray. It looks as if the security alert is a big one, though there are no reports of any explosions.

Michael has to take some decisions and cancels the Lyric's production of *The Hypochondriac* [Molière's *Malade Imaginaire*] – 'A lot of money wasted there,' he shakes his head resignedly, rather than angrily. He then opens a bottle of champagne and we begin to get a little drunk.

The Europa will not be cleared until two o'clock. There have been so many alerts all over Belfast that the bomb disposal teams cannot cope.

I end up being offered a bed on the floor at Robert Agnew's house.[1] Thus I find myself in the unreal calm of a suburban house in Myrtlewood Road, finally getting my head down in Robert's front room at a quarter to one.

Thursday, November 26th: Belfast

I wake in the middle of the night. Not immediately sure where I am. I look up and there, staring down at me, is Rowan Atkinson. The walls of the room are covered with Opera House playbills.

1 Robert was the business manager of the Belfast Festival.

Doze some more, then lie awake thinking of my own show. Completely unrehearsed, yet by the time this day is over it will have played to 500 people, and possibly been telerecorded. The script isn't even complete. Try to go to sleep and forget about it. Only partially successful.

Last night 21 different bombs and suspect vehicles were dotted around the city by the IRA in an attempt to show they still have formidable ability to stretch the Security Forces. Two vehicles were detonated and the rest were hi-jacked vehicles with no bombs in them.

At the theatre Ulster TV cameras are installing themselves. They are anxious not to disrupt at all, and they won't need extra lighting, but I feel exposed suddenly. The show has always been so private.

We go up at 8.10. I'm discovered standing on the podium for the 'Olympic' opening and rewarded with a good round of applause. Everything hangs together. I'm pleased with my delivery. Most of the cues work. Very few laughs dropped.

Tuesday, December 1st

To Goodge Street and Heal's Restaurant, where I am to meet Clem Vallance (at his invitation).

Clem V tells me of an embarrassing lunch that the BBC laid on a year ago to try and tempt Alan Whicker to be the presenter of *80 Days*. As soon as Whicker heard that not only could he not bring 'the little woman' along, but that he might have to spend several days and nights on an Arab dhow, not much more was heard.

Clem says I was always top of *his* list, with Clive James second. He floats the possibility of approaching Michael Grade to make it independently,[1] but really there is little we can do until the BBC make the next move.

Wednesday, December 2nd

Denis is in very bad shape. Apparently he started shaking this morning and Helen took him again to the vet. But now he's breathing only with difficulty and in short, gravelly intakes. Every now and then he retches violently, bringing up very little but bile, but clearly causing himself great

---

1 He had just joined Channel 4 as the new Chief Executive.

discomfort. Helen is out. I ring the emergency vet, who counsels me to keep him warm.

Thursday, December 3rd

Denis is at the top of the stairs, but very weak, still breathing in dry, rasping gasps occasionally accompanied by fierce twitching of the head. I drive him to the vet at Islington with Helen. I wait in Cross Street, noting a run-down but elegant Georgian terrace of town houses opposite me.

We drive home. The vet will call us again at five o'clock with news. A day of phone calls clouded by the chance that one of them may announce the end of our Denis.

Friday, December 4th

A script by Jonny Lynn called *Nuns on the Run* has arrived with Eric's blessing.

Then by taxi to Soho to do an LBC interview with Michael Aspel re the Python album. I like Aspel. He's straight and amiable and likes a laugh and our piece is as relaxed and comfortable as any I've done for a while.

The day begins to gather momentum as Helen prepares not only for a dinner party tonight, but also for a TV interview she's to do for the BBC on 'Motherhood'. I take out the car and go to collect fuel, booze, food, etc.

When I get back at about half past three, Helen greets me with the news that Denis is dead. The vet and Helen took the decision about ten minutes before she had to go into the interview. Sally Doganis, producer, seems pleased by the piece. 'There won't be a dry eye in the house after they've heard Helen,' she tells me. I imagine that it must all be to do with the loss of Denis, but in fact she is referring to Helen's contributions on motherhood.

Not only is the news of Denis's death communicated to me before an entire BBC film crew, but as they are clearing up, the children arrive back and have to be told. With Rachel it's unbearable. She's at the front door having said goodbye to her friends. I'm unloading logs. I call to her. She turns and pre-empts the careful phrases ... 'Is Denis dead?'

Tears well up in both of us and I put my arm round her. If only the film had been on 'Loss' or 'Grief' they'd have had a real scoop.

Sunday, December 6th

After breakfast Rachel and Helen go off to Islington to collect Denis's basket from the vet and I am hoovering the stair-carpet an hour or so later when they return, with another cat peeping out like a rejuvenated Denis. Rachel was so taken with this five-month-old tabby which the vet had been looking after for some time that she and Helen decided then and there that they should bring her home. She's a spayed female. No name. Helen will look out for a neutered male to be company for her.

I must say at first I am a little shocked by the speed of the arrival of the replacement for Denis. I feel I haven't had enough time to accept his absence. But she is a perky, curious, friendly little cat. Permanently wide-eyed of course, especially at the to-ing and fro-ing in our house, the glass, lights, mirrors and so on.

A very good roast beef Sunday dinner and we debate names for the cat. Nancy, Lucy, but Tom finally cracks it with Betty. So Betty, with her colouring which is, as Will says, a negative of Denis – smoky black where Denis was white – comes to be part of Julia St life.

Wednesday, December 9th

Steve A arrives. An update on all our activities.

He tells me of the *Wanda* screening in NYC. Seventy-eight percent of the cards filled in (243) put the movie in the top two of five categories.

Anyway, MGM are now pleased, though by mutual agreement they and the producers will alter certain things which the screening seemed to tell them. The audience didn't like to see blood when the dog's crushed, and felt the fish torture too hard to take. And these are the audiences that flocked to the cheerful slaughter of *Beverly Hills Cop*.

Ring Camilla to find out if her friend saw the Belfast show and catch her in a tearful state. She's been dealing with a suicide at work and had been affected by the news of the churchman who committed suicide yesterday in a fume-filled car in a garage, and just had no-one to talk to. So we have a long talk about Angela.

Camilla finds that the men in the family don't talk easily. Friends just don't mention it. I feel the same and it's a great relief to both of us to break the silence.

Thursday, December 10th

At lunchtime to Twickenham – a near-two-hour journey to re-dub one line. Charlie is there, as benignly grumpy as ever ... 'I don't like *people* very much, you see,' he confides cheerfully as we go upstairs to the dubbing theatre. He also tells me that the audiences in New York liked me very much, and that's why he's had to cut the torture scene!

Sunday, December 13th

When I return home I find another cat there. This is Albert, a male tabby – younger than Betty by three or four months. I can't see much of him as he won't come out of his basket, from which he blinks at me without moving.

Betty's first reaction is not reassuring. When not actually hissing at Albert, she growls and hisses at the basket.

Against the background of this delicate relationship, and indeed of their relationship with us and our house, the afternoon passes with occasional glimpses at the paper, lots of phone calls and some Christmas card writing.

Tuesday, December 15th

Jonathan Ross calls to tell me that the 'nude chat show' idea is off for Friday. None of the women would agree to do it, except for Janet Street-Porter.

To the new Waterstone's in Hampstead. Wonderful. A New York-style bookstore within walking distance of my house!

Wednesday, December 16th

Hassled by a phone call from the 'organisers' of the King's Cross Disaster Fund photo-call which I've agreed to attend, suddenly making it all sound far more elaborate – with carols to sing and Dickensian costumes, etc.

I drive to Chalk Farm. Announcements on the platform of delays due to shortage of staff – if only there were video information screens at station entrances, one could decide on bus, foot or an alternative before being stuck on the platform.

To Leicester Square Theatre at which a selection of notables is assembling.

Most of us have baulked at being asked to wear Dickensian outfits. Carols are sung, we all do 'Hark the Herald', then photos are taken, from which peripheral celebrities are ruthlessly excluded – 'Mr Davenport, could you step out, please!' 'Good expressions, now!' TJ quite amused and thinks this could be a new, instant form of directing. 'King Lear ... look sad ... this way please ... good!'

Bill Paterson appears, as he often does, from nowhere. He's late for the call, but no-one knows who he is anyway. We go for a coffee – myself, TJ, Bill, Marcia Warren and Anna Carteret. On the way I'm buttonholed by the Thames TV crew. 'Michael, could you give us a piece straight from the heart, all right?'

Friday, December 18th

Am collected for the Jonathan Ross *Last Resort* show at seven.

The show is all set up as a beach party and I'm given some long shorts, a loud shirt, sweater and '50's sunglasses.

Janet Street-Porter is on the show and doesn't impress. She evidently rates herself rather highly – arrives at the last minute, cars collect her immediately afterwards – but what really pisses me off is that she eats in her dressing room, then puts the half-eaten, mucky trayful of mutilated food out in the corridor. She then pushes it along to my door. 'I can't stand having trays outside my dressing room.'

A run-through. I'm to appear on a donkey. Seems to work well. At the end everyone is delighted. 'If in doubt, get in a Python,' Jonathan enthuses.

Saturday, December 19th

First inkling that the Ross interview might not have been as riotous as it had seemed, comes from Rachel's very muted response. 'You were very silly, Dad,' is about all she will say as we drive into Soho for our Saturday morning swim.

Sunday, December 20th

Up the road to a lunchtime drinks party with a new resident. I feel all should be done to keep the reality of the community spirit to which we all pay lip-service. In a very small room full of women (mainly), I meet a paediatrician in Kentish Town – a New Zealand lady, both voluble and opinionated, who writes children's books – and [long-time residents] Miss Clutton and Miss Goodman.

Little old Miss Goodman greets me with 'How did you like China?'

Impressed that she even knew I was travelling at all, I correct her good-naturedly ... 'Thailand'.

'The china I gave Mrs Palin.'

Miss Clutton is on excellent form. Wafer-thin and neat to the point of severity, she has great spirit. The extrovert New Zealander talks about what hell it's been having her house converted and being without a bathroom. Miss Clutton grins cheerfully, 'I'm *still* waiting for mine.' This slightly throws the conversation off its middle-class path, bringing it to a total stop when she adds 'I haven't had a bath for 75 years.'

Tuesday, December 22nd

Some local shopping – am told to 'Piss off' by a grubby shopkeeper with a Mediterranean accent, just because I want to buy one clementine and one lychee for Helen's stocking. And I was in such a good mood.

Back home, find a *huge* hamper of fruit from George Harrison.

Out to dinner at ZenW3 with Terry G and Maggie, during Terry's brief break from *Munchausen*. 'What's the latest?' I ask him, adding hastily '*briefly*'. 'Thirty-six million dollars,' is his reply. He wants to talk about doing a different sort of film, a small, funny film made with people he likes. He's fed up with being called 'Maestro' and having all these sycophantic and highly-paid Italians with incredibly fragile temperaments waiting on his every word. He saw an hour's footage this afternoon. 'The money just isn't on the screen ... it's OK, but no way should that have cost 20 million.'

Because it's been so long since I last heard it, even his grumbling seems fresh. Maggie is to have another baby. God knows when he had time for that.

Friday, December 25th: Christmas Day

Granny sits on the sofa listening to Lord Denning's *With Great Pleasure* (Denning has a way of sounding exactly as one would expect a wise old lawyer to have spoken 500 years ago). Helen is peeling potatoes and watching *White Christmas* on TV in the kitchen. Tom and Will are ringing friends. Rachel's piling the presents into bags. We've been blessed with a sunny morning.

Round to 100 Albert Street.

Christmas lunch never fails to be jolly and the presents then virtually swamp the upstairs room, leading Edward to mutter that the house is too small. An aircraft hangar would probably be too small to accommodate a Full Gibbins Christmas.

Granny Burd, the oldest of the grannies present, sits erect as ever, and at one point leans over to Catherine B to ask if she knows she has a bit of silver on the side of her nose. As Catherine had her nose pierced about two years ago, this produces some mirth. Granny B thought it was a Christmas decoration.

1988

Sunday, January 3rd

Wild, wet weather for most of the morning. No temptation to do much outside. Clear my room in preparation for a re-start on '*AF*' tomorrow. Write to Sepha and Chris and Carys Bell to invite them to some sort of get-together, because I feel Angela is in danger of becoming a non-person, the memory of the good times in her life trapped by the nature of her death.

Monday, January 4th

Violet, Jonas's wife, is round from next door to ask Helen's advice on schools. She doesn't think she can go back to her home in Botswana, let alone South Africa. I cannot conceive of what threat someone like Violet poses to prompt the South Africans to bomb her house, which they did in Botswana, sending bits of Jonas's piano flying everywhere.

I ask her if they feel safe here. Violet nods her head emphatically ... 'Oh, yes ...'

Tuesday, January 5th

Carys Bell responds immediately to my letter about Angela. She's also at her writing desk, putting finishing touches to her second Welsh-language novel. Even on the phone the memories spill out. Angela was very practical. Yes, I'd forgotten that.

Ring Alan [Bennett], whom I feel I must now approach head-on over *The Weekend*. Just before Christmas Brough called to say he had had a rejection from Scofield. His second preference is to approach Alan B as director. I don't think Alan would be interested. The play isn't delicate or oblique enough, too clumsy I think he'll think. Arrange to go and see him on Friday. For tea. He's not a lunch person. Quite ascetic that way.

Wednesday, January 6th

Lunch with Peter Luff.[1] He is an enthusiastic European. I didn't know his mother was Belgian. He sees 1992, the end of customs barriers in Europe, as a Great Day, and is working for a movement to raise the awareness of the Brits in advance of the changes in '92. Thatcher is aggressively anti-Europe, which doesn't help.

Watch a 100-minute tape assembly of material for [a documentary called] *From Fringe to Flying Circus*. There is a revealing moment in an interview with Jonathan [Miller] and Alan [Bennett] in which they're asked about satire.

Jonathan feels that, apart from Alan, none of them were particularly concerned about attacking anything.

Thursday, January 7th

In the afternoon begin work transcribing Edward Palin's diaries. Much of it is slow and lacking in great eventfulness, but I find his handwritten, notebook descriptions very compelling, even when he's off on one of his obsessions, such as the state of Catholic churches.

Perhaps because I know so few people have ever seen these notes, perhaps because I feel close to the spirit of them, being a notebook-er myself, the words seem very direct, the communication immediate, as if he'd been in Ragaz only last week and, what's more, that I'd been with him. He does sound a cheery, uncomplicated, gregarious character. This slightly complicates my decision on how to present him in the film.

Friday, January 8th

Using the breakdown of scenes I worked out late last night, I transfer *American Friends* to cards, *Saturday Night Live*/Lorne Michaels style, which I pin up on the board in my room beneath the framed brass title-plate of *The Missionary*.

Phone off the hook, I sit and talk myself through the scenes, making adjustments here and there and scribbling thoughts in a notebook. A

1 Peter had produced 'The Secret Policeman's Ball', the first of the Amnesty fund-raising concerts back in 1976. He had also proposed me (successfully) for Fellowship of the Royal Geographical Society.

growing feeling of exhilaration as the storyline becomes clearer and the characters sharper.

The odd tension I've felt all week lifts and, although I would like to sit down and write my way through the whole film here and now, I am due at Alan Bennett's for tea.

Alan makes a mug of Earl Grey. 'I write all the time,' he confesses, waving his hand helplessly towards a pile of papers ... 'I'm like Tolstoy, but I just don't know what to do with it all.'

Alan, as ever, gives the air of being unambitious, unplanned, unstructured, but of course that's not the reality. He's clearly quite buoyed by his appearance in *Fortunes of War*[1] and admits he'd like to do more acting.

I explain to Alan about *The Weekend*. When I tell him about Paul Scofield, he laughs – 'Every one of my plays has been sent to Paul Scofield.'

Alan gives me the latest bulletin on his van-lady. 'If you see a red light on, don't worry ... it's her rheumatism light.' I ask what a rheumatism light is. 'I don't know ... she exposes herself to it.'

Monday, January 11th

An hour's drive out to Twickenham Studios for some more *Wanda* post-synching, much of it in an attempt to make my reactions in the fish-torturing scene less pained and more aggressive.

Up on the screen, on relentless loops of film, are shards of my performance – a performance into which an enormous amount of pain, effort and energy was poured. Now, quite clinically, on a chilly January evening, we're banging a few nails in, shoring it up there, making good here and leaving it to the sound mixer to paint over the cracks.

To an acting purist the process must look like sacrilege, but it's all part of making a product, part of the composite mish-mash to which all individual egos and identities have to bow. Next month the TV version is to be recorded, a shaming little exercise in which all 'rude' words from 'bastard' upwards must be removed.

---

1 Seven-part BBC TV adaptation of Olivia Manning's novels set in Bucharest at the time of the Second World War. Kenneth Branagh and Emma Thompson starred. Alan Bennett played Lord Pinkrose.

Wednesday, January 13th

Woken by Rachel coming into our room to open her birthday presents.
A mini-Christmas.

To work at nine and a very productive day follows – all sorts of surprises
as I try to get Ashby, Brita (as I've decided to call her again) and Miss
Hartley more involved with each other. They *all* have much more to say
for each other now. They're fuller characters and I like being with them.

I work through until five o'clock when it's time to light the candles on
Rachel's cake and, with Helen [Guedalla] as her sole guest, sing 'Happy
Birthday' at her party.

It's raining persistently, but not heavily, as I park the Mini in Bedford
Square at a quarter to seven and cross briskly, via Tottenham Court Road
and Oxford Street, to Wardour Street and another screening of *Wanda*.

John has asked along a 'panel' of friends, so we are going to have
one of those 'think-tank' sessions afterwards. Charlie C abhors them,
preferring to rely on professional instinct.

The trouble is we are being asked to judge why an imperfect film
(the sound unmixed, lines and music missing) might offend certain
Americans. It's all wallowingly hypothetical and, though clever souls like
Jonathan Benson and André slope off afterwards, I am lured into a session
at a table at Groucho's.

I experience a form of intellectual claustrophobia. My mental processes
will not apply themselves to the problems of *Wanda* in the way John
expects. John, as usually, dissects the film with the icy and impressive
precision of a Mercedes mechanic stripping an engine. Fay Weldon comes
across with an opinion which sounds confident and starts the ball rolling.

Michael Frayn has some good 'farceurs' ideas, but they involve bringing
in another character at the end, which seems quite wrong to me. I think
the best suggestion for beefing up the ending is that Otto should appear,
cement-clad, at the window after the plane's taken off. That's my idea, so
perhaps that's why I like it.

Friday, January 15th

Though tantalisingly close to the end of my rewrite, I shall do no more
this week as I have agreed to go to Wakefield to 'unveil' a 130-foot-long
sculpture on the station.

The taxi doesn't turn up, so Helen, who is on her way to take Albert to be castrated, gives me a lift on to King's Cross. I end up running for the train.

We are about ten minutes late in Wakefield, having lost the southern fog somewhere north of Newark, and a crowd of photographers, reporters and at least two television crews converge on me as soon as I step off the train.

A defunct siding has been attractively converted to take the sculpture, which consists of five fan-like constructions of painted timbers, arranged in a graceful rise and fall effect, which Susan Hoyle rather unfairly described as looking like a fence that had been recently blown over.

A short speech and I unveil a plaque, at the end of which is my name. For some reason seeing my name up there on a plaque fills me with intimations of mortality.

To the town hall for a reception. Speeches from the Chairman of Leisure Services – an unrepentant leftist. When he hears that Wakefield Station is to be restored in its old colours, he cannot resist some dire remark about hoping it isn't blue, for Wakefield has always and *will* always be red! This flourish seems to embarrass most people.

Tuesday, January 19th

Letter from JC with his various proposals for rewrites on *Wanda*.

Phone Sophie with my reactions, only to hear that the great man, far from hanging on the end of the line for my pearls of wisdom, is in Kent for three days shooting a 30-second commercial. 'He's being paid billions,' says Sophie, reassuringly.

Outside the cloud is thick and the light dim, but it's still not cold, as I put finishing touches to the fourth draft of '*AF*'. By eleven it's done. The last two and a half weeks have been the fastest, most concentrated and most satisfying work I've done for a long time. If it is a good omen that the script has had a happy birth, then the chances of this one surviving are very high.

Alan B rings, he sounds to have 'flu ... 'I'm in bed ... I'm reduced to watching a programme on the beaches of Rimini.' We agree to put off our *Weekend* meeting this evening.

A friendly-sounding man rings from LA. He is producing David Leland's film and wants to give him a surprise on first day of shooting by having the entire crew turn up in long shorts of the sort worn by David in [the *Ripping Yarn*] 'Golden Gordon'. Wants to know a bit of dialogue to have embroidered on the shorts. Suggest 'Shorts don't matter, it's what's inside them that counts.' I feel a warm breeze from the past.

Friday, January 22nd

Prepare for Chris and Carys Bell, who are coming to dinner in response to my letter about Angela, and keeping memories of her alive, as it were.

Talking to them, I become aware of how little I knew about Angela's history of depression and how far back it stretched. Chris says that Veryan virtually brought up Jeremy for the first few months.

Carys goes back even further, to when Angela was in Brownies, and tells of a friend who knew Angela then and who said that when she took over from someone in a Brownies play, having understudied her proudly, she 'went to bits', as Carys put it.

I've a lot to learn about my family. It seems that they have to die before I can really find anything out.

Saturday, January 23rd

Drive to Gloucester Crescent around five. The 'rheumatism light' is on in the caravan as I open the gate, but is switched off by the time I'm at the front door.

We fall to talking of *The Weekend*. Alan seems very positive. He read it three times. He has some helpful thoughts about the end and we laugh a lot. Halfway through our chat the phone rings. 'Oh, how nice of you ... oh ... well, writers don't usually get noticed ... ' and so on. He is clearly being praised.

Muttering that he'll get a pencil, he mouths to me in mock horror 'Ian *McKellen*!' McKellen has heard that Alan is to be given an award for *Prick Up Your Ears* at the *Evening Standard* bash tomorrow and wants Alan to mention the 'homosexual' Clause 28 which the government are trying to introduce in the Local Government Bill, making it illegal to 'promote homosexuality ... in a pretended family relationship'. Terry J wrote a good, outraged piece in the *Guardian* on Wednesday.

He advises me to send the play to Ron Eyre.

Sunday, January 24th

To the *Evening Standard* Awards at the Savoy.

There is a royal in attendance – the Duchess of Kent – and Helen and I are taken from anonymity in a jolly throng of film celebs to a brightly-lit corner of the room, where we stand rather awkwardly with other 'royal fodder', such as Bob Hoskins and wife and Jane Asher and Gerald Scarfe and Deborah Kerr. The latter seems frail and rather confused by the whole thing. A crush of cameramen accompany the royal personage, elbowing anyone else out of the way.

At last it's our turn and the whole circus focusses on the three of us – Helen, me and the Duchess of Kent. The Duchess (and, as with Princess Anne, I can't help noticing how enviably cool and unflustered she remains) goes immediately into a soothing routine which does not betray for a moment whether she likes my work or not, whether she's actually seen it or not, or indeed if she knows who I am or not. After a warm wash with the royal lather, I throw in a few observations of my own on life, work and writing comedy and immediately wish I hadn't.

Then the camera crowd and their royal leader move on and we are left in the no-man's land of après royalty.

The awards go smoothly. Alan B very effectively alludes to Clause 28 as requested – he talks of the thin line between 'promoting' and portraying homosexuality.

Monday, January 25th

A day largely taken up with writing a piece on 'something I feel strongly about' for *Family Circle* magazine. Try to marshal all my indignation about poor transport provision into a cogent argument and bore myself stiff in the process.

Terry G calls me in the evening to offer me the part of the King of the Moon. The *Sunday Times* was right yesterday – Connery has turned the part down.

The dates on which TG would like me are the 22nd to 26th February. Exactly the weeks of our skiing holiday. It seems I'm doomed never to ski at Mürren. But I tell him categorically that I have to take the holiday, especially as it may well be my last chance for a while, if '*AF*' goes ahead. He'll make sure the script is sent to me tomorrow.

Wednesday, January 27th

TG rings from Rome. The latest is that I cannot be the King of the Moon as I am not bankable enough. Film Finances have drawn up a list of Connery substitutes and my name isn't on it. Gene Wilder is the current favourite and then Walter Matthau.

Thursday, January 28th

At seven o'clock by cab to Gloucester Crescent to pick up Alan, with whom I am to see *Lettice and Lovage*.[1] News that the appeal on behalf of the Birmingham pub bombers has been flatly turned down worries Alan.[2] He feels it's not just that it's been turned down, but that the uncompromising and complete rejection of any fresh evidence sounds like a show-trial.

Maggie is effortlessly brilliant and keeps me smiling – sometimes weeping with laughter – throughout the first act. Alan has doubts at the interval. 'What do you think the play would be like without her?' He says that the lines in *The Weekend* are much funnier than those he's heard tonight.

The second act leaves Maggie on hold and brings Margaret Tyzack to the fore. She's a good actress, but the role is full of tired old lines and attitudes and her conversion to Maggie's theatrical games doesn't begin to convince. Both of us are rather silent in the third act and, as we get up at the curtain to go backstage, Alan breathes 'This is where the acting comes in.'

Saturday, January 30th

Jonas Gwangwa comes in for a glass of wine. Talk over things in South Africa. Jonas says morale of the black people is very high. Hints at strikes against foreign company bases in South Africa. On a lighter note he says

1 A play by Peter Shaffer, who also wrote *Equus*. Maggie Smith won a Tony for Best Actress in 1990 for her role as Lettice Douffet.
2 In November 1974 bombs exploded in two Birmingham pubs: 21 people were killed and 182 injured. The Provisional IRA were blamed and in 1975 six Irishmen were found guilty and sentenced to life imprisonment. After a campaign led by the MP Chris Mullin, their sentences were overthrown by the Court of Appeal. In 1991, after spending sixteen years in prison the 'Birmingham Six' were declared innocent and released.

that the one thing the government can't understand about the ANC and the African resistance is that they laugh a lot.

Jonas says that some of the apartheid laws are so silly they should be laughed at. Blacks and whites can marry in some places, but they cannot live together in the same township. But there are one or two de-segregated coaches on the railways now. The only place that those enjoying a mixed marriage can actually procreate is in certain coaches on the 7.15 to Johannesburg!

Monday, February 1st

Up at eight. Tired. Dragging myself into another important week. Fierce weather outside. Wind, sometimes very strong, and occasional deluges. Look again at 'AF' in light of Tristram's recent comments. Bolstered by a call from Irene Lamb, who finds the script delightful. She thinks Ellen Burstyn a good choice and will send videos over.

Will Wyatt calls with 'the good news'. All is to go ahead on the *80 Days* trip. I must disappoint him with my reaction, for he asks 'Do I detect a note of caution, or is this your natural state?'

Thursday, February 4th

To an Eric Clapton concert at the Albert Hall, for which Ray has secured us [tickets]. He has two spares, so Will and his friend Raffi, who cannot believe their luck, come along too.

The concert is well received. Ray, of course, mesmerising. He doesn't just play, he performs; an extraordinary ritualistic, stylised, eye-catching performance it is too. Just a tap on a bongo drum from Ray is a piece of consummate showmanship.

After the concert, a wallow, in the Elgar Room, with the celebs.

Bob Hoskins says he would love to do a film with 'you lot', as he calls us.

Phil Collins also very keen. Says that after doing *Buster* his appetite for acting came right back.

William and Raffi, having shaken the hands of the likes of Clapton, Starr, Collins and Bill Wyman, say they're going to cut their hands off and keep them.

Friday, February 5th

Put down some ideas for my appearance on a Comic Relief eight-hour bonanza this evening. Think I'll play my Manager – chance to re-do Dino Vercotti.[1] As I write I have the feeling that Dino's world-view is quite a good vein of humour. Rather like Edna Everage – once the character is there the material is inexhaustible.

My head is thick, my nose streams, but I take a couple of Honduran lagers and a taxi to the BBC.

Then upstairs to the sixth-floor hospitality, where the new men of the BBC – Jonathan Powell and John Birt – are hosting a night-long 'reception'. Yentob of Two is there, and much the jolliest and most approachable of the three wise men.

Talk to Jennifer Saunders and Dawn French and Adrian Edmondson, and I can't help noticing how nicely they're treated by the BBC, these enfants terribles of alternative comedy. They stand comfortably and confidently at the centre of things, the new establishment. Still, there could be much worse establishments.

In the 'Most Popular Sketch' section, 'Parrot Shop' is voted No. 1 and 'Lumberjack' No. 3. So not a bad night for an ailing comedian.

Monday, February 8th: Southwold

Irene comes back with the first intelligence on Ellen Burstyn (born Ena May Gilooly!).[2] She's free in the summer. But she's with heavy agents CAA. A fellow casting director in New York gives her bad word of mouth – not much sense of humour, self-centred, fussy. Irene dismisses all this as the sort of talk which always surrounds very good actors or actresses who are difficult when doing run-of-the-mill work because they want to make it right. We decide to send her the script ASAP.

---

1 Dino Vercotti and his brother (played by myself and Terry Jones) were two hopeless Italian Mafiosi who appeared in Monty Python offering 'protection' to the British Army (played by Graham Chapman).

2 Best known, probably, for her performance in *Alice Doesn't Live Here Anymore* (1974), she is a prolific stage and screen actor and the first woman President of American Actors' Equity.

Wednesday, February 10th

Meet with Ron Eyre to discuss his thoughts on *The Weekend*. He lives up the modest end of Ladbroke Road, if there is a modest end, in a sensibly-sized terraced family house. Ron has no family and has just let off various flats in the house.

Our hour or so ends inconclusively with Ron saying that there's not much to do, but there's a lot, and hedging further on whether he would be interested in directing it. He reminds me that he turned down the chance to direct the early Michael Frayns *and* the early Ayckbourns. Is this to demonstrate the frailty of his own taste or just to let me down gently? But I leave with a clutch of very good suggestions for further work to be done.

To lunch at Hilaire to meet the putative second director of *80 Days*, Roger Mills.[1] I like him and feel comfortable with him straight away. Maybe it's because he is drinking gin, which he then spills over the menu, but he reminds me, in spirit, of Ian MacNaughton.

He further endears himself to me by telling me that *East of Ipswich* has won a BAFTA nomination for Best Single Drama. This couldn't have come at a better time for the Palin-Powell partnership.

We discuss attitudes to the journey, the programme and the BBC and reach near-unanimity on all of them. I do feel we have to be seen to take the rough with the smooth in this – the days in dingy hotels in Djibouti will add immeasurably to the audience's cathartic appreciation of the Taj in Bombay.

Out to dinner at Meridiana with John C, Jamie and Kevin.

Paul Simon arrives; Kevin has asked him along. He glides softly to the table, he smiles softly, he speaks softly; a well-modulated man. Easy and amusing company, though one feels that there is part of him kept carefully hidden.

Later Kevin is very complimentary about my performance – 'In the scene with me I was watching *you*,' he admits incredulously.

---

1 He was one of the most successful and experienced of BBC documentary producer/directors. He had created the *Forty Minutes* format, which won him two BAFTA Awards for Best Documentary series. Rather than take a job as Executive in charge of BBC1 documentaries, he had opted to go out on the road. *80 Days* was his first job as a freelance.

Thursday, February 11th

Patrick C [Cassavetti] arrives at nine. He has some reservations about the script, but they don't seem substantial. His feeling for the spirit of the piece is much the same as mine. I like his enthusiasm for film and he has a distinct preference for the tightly-budgeted quality picture than for anything big and expensive.

He still has *Paris by Night* to see through post-production and is still not sure if he can commit to '*AF*'. Rather as with Ron Eyre yesterday morning, I'm left with the impression of cordiality and sympathy and evasion.

Car collects me at 2.30 to go down to Roger Cherrill for some more *Wanda* post-synch. This time it's for the US TV version! I have to say 'flaming' instead of 'fucking', but draw the line at 'bashing' instead of 'buggering' and change it to 'brutalising', which still has some bite to it. Kevin K has re-voiced about 40 lines! John is there. I thank him for his uncontrollable hospitality in funding meals for us all. He gives me the old twinkle. 'You should do commercials, Mickey.'

To the Bush Theatre to see Dervla Kirwan's play [Dervla was Charles Sturridge's recommendation for Brita in *American Friends*].

Dervla is nervous. I hope I've not made her so. She's intriguing. A face that it's impossible to sum up in a word. She can look different from every angle. She has long, dark hair and would be perfect in period costume. I find her interesting and appealing and she reveals clearly in this play that she's a natural actress. At times her maturity shows well beyond her 16 years.

We shake hands afterwards. She's obliging, friendly and with just enough shyness. Don't stay long as have a full day tomorrow and shall be meeting her again. But am excited and know that we're on to something good.

Monday, February 15th

Begin the morning in good heart, but gradually the lack of reaction to '*AF*' grinds me down. The last call I had from Steve's office was on Friday late afternoon to tell me that none of the MGM heads would be in London or New York in the next few weeks. So to see them I must go to LA. *The Weekend* – silence on all fronts, apart from a good chat with Irene Lamb, who has been enthusiastic throughout.

I try to tinker with the script. But I feel I am working in a vacuum and inspiration dries to a thin trickle. Worse still, because I'm expecting 'significant' phone calls, every one that comes in and isn't about the film hits a raw nerve of expectation and jars it into irritation.

Thursday, February 18th

Hear from Steve that he's read in the trades that Burstyn is on the Berlin Film Festival jury which is sitting at the moment. The fact that her agents (CAA) allowed us to go ahead and courier the script to her in LA has inexplicably lost us at least a week.

To a BAFTA screening of Tarkovsky's *The Sacrifice*. It's one of the four nominations for Best Foreign Film and I've agreed to be on the judging panel.

A scattered audience of about a dozen people, none of whom I know. They all look frightfully serious, knowledgeable and intellectual. Bump into Mark Shivas in the lavatory. He's very pleased to hear I'm a juror – 'Brighten it up a bit.'

The Sacrifice is not a bright film. It's a carefully-paced, Bergmanesque piece about a man who's so intelligent he has nowhere to go but insane. Solemn and serious, full of marvellous images and brilliant lighting by [Sven] Nykvist, but ultimately I find it a rather tiresome muddle. It ends, suitably I think, with two men in white coats coming to carry off Erland Josephson, who's taken two and a half hours to go barking mad.

Taking advantage of a Wanda *screening there, I had decided to go to LA and try and drum up interest in* American Friends. *Alan Ladd Jr, CEO of MGM, who had made* Wanda, *had shown interest in my project.*

Sunday, February 28th: London–Los Angeles

Wake and worry about the LA trip. The film can no longer be just 'a project', a chance to prove myself or any indulgence like that. I shall be going to sell it. I shall be looking for a commitment. Is it really, absolutely, what I want to do? I lie there and occasionally the scale of it all washes me with fear.

Steve and JC are at the new TWA check-in, being brown-nosed by the VIP staff. Lots of jokes, broad smiles and we're even taken from the lounge to the gate on a sort of motorised golf buggy. Whilst seated on this silly vehicle, JC solemnly gives an interview to a lone press hack, whilst three cameramen snap him from all angles. 'Yes ... the separation is amicable'[1] and so on.

Monday, February 29th: Westwood Marquis Hotel, Los Angeles

About one o'clock a minor triumph – I actually prise out of the agent Burstyn's number in Paris and at last we talk. She likes the script – finds it 'very well written' and 'charming' – but feels that she and I should meet 'before you cast me'. This is the call I had hoped would come before I left London, but at least it's encouraging.

To an enormous new polished marble skyscraper to meet our lawyer who is doing the MGM deal – David Nochimson. His law firm also represents clients such as Michael Jackson.

On our way in we meet a short, combative man called Tom Hoberman, who is Eric's lawyer. He talks to us for a while in his office, which is fashionably anti-corporate. For such as Tom – men at the top – informality is the order of the day and the office is full of old wood high-backed chairs, Persian carpets and a general anti-institutional arts and crafty feel. I'm reminded of how we used to decorate our studies at school.

Hoberman clearly loves all the competition, the fight, the struggle, the deal (America's fastest-selling book at the moment is called *Making the Deal* by Donald Trump, the property billionaire from NYC). When he hears of Ellen Burstyn his reaction brings all our delusions down to earth ... 'She is a good actress, but she wouldn't open up a picture any more ... you could pull her in for around 300 (thousand dollars) ... '.

Back to the hotel and dinner with JC, Michael Shamberg and his wife Megan. JC, fresh from his masseuse, is sharp, funny and marvellous on things like American inability to appreciate cricket, 'or any game not directly based on greed'.

Tuesday, March 1st: Los Angeles

Steve and I repair in our little Toyota Tercel to Island Pics, to meet Russell Schwarz. He indicates that there are changes afoot in the financing of

1 This was from his second wife Barbara.

Island Pictures[1] and makes it fairly clear that we would not be in their price range.

Back to the hotel for calls to England. Also speak to Ellen B in Paris. I will take her to dinner, at the Pharamond, Friday night and Tristram will fly over on Saturday to talk. If decision taken, Steve can do the deal with her agent before he leaves the US.

A half-hour massage and a swim before leaving for the MGM meeting.

Our meeting is with Alan Ladd Jr. Small, erect, striped blue shirt and hair, which needs a trim at the back, brushed tight down over his skull. Dark hair and dark eyes. He also favours traditional wooden furniture in his office, quite at odds with the modernity of the building. Big, squishy, comfortable armchairs and sofas.

I like Ladd but, as we leave, I honestly cannot gauge what might be the prospects for a pick-up of *American Friends*. But I don't think Steve and I could have put our case better. The formal submission will be made next week.

Drive back to the Westwood. Charlie [Crichton] arrives in the bar after his flight from London. When he wants a drink he hoists his walking-stick in the air.

Wednesday, March 2nd: Los Angeles

Down below me white-clad Hispanics are already attending to the pool area at which white-bodied Caucasians will later lounge. In Beverly Hills other dark people will be out clipping the lawns around the 'Armed Response' signs.

To breakfast with Steve – coffee, fruit, two eggs, bacon, hash browns and a croissant. Usual sprinkling of film people. Shirley MacLaine scuttles out of the elevator looking serious.

We have run out of meetings for a while, so have time to sit in my room and catch up. Then walk out to the shops in Westwood. A beautiful warmth in the air, the neat beds of pansies outside the hotel sparkle.

The unlikely figure of Charlie Crichton approaches, preceded by the walking-stick. He's perspiring slightly but has already walked up through the Botanical Gardens and halfway round the UCLA campus from what I can tell.

---

1 Island Pictures had released *A Private Function* in America.

Talk of Sandy – Alexander Mackendrick[1] – who lives in LA but not for much longer, according to Charlie. He is anxious to get JC and Mackendrick together while there's still time.

A white limousine transfers JC, Charlie C, myself and Steve to Lorimar (the old MGM studio) for a screening of the latest version of *Wanda*.

Watching the pic in the US for the first time I notice how much easier they are with Kevin than in the UK. He brings out laughs easily. The JC/Jamie rewrites at the end are smoother, but just compound the immorality, rather than solving it, and Kevin reappearing at the window seems a crude mistake. But enormous buzz of appreciation at the end. Frank Oz[2] shakes his head in admiring disbelief – notes with pleasure the intensity of the performances.

Friday, March 4th: London–Paris

Take the 2.30 flight to Paris. Am staying at L'Hôtel. It used to be the Hôtel D'Alsace and Oscar Wilde died here in 1900. The year my father was born.

Inside everything is very small – rooms, lifts tightly packed in a curve around a central gallery which runs uninterrupted to the top of the building. It's like being in an extremely chic lighthouse.

My first sight of Ellen B is of a shadowy figure in the back of a taxi which slides up outside the hotel about 20 minutes later. I launch into brisk and well-rehearsed instructions, in French, for the cab driver, after which Ellen touches my arm gently and advises . . . 'It's alright, he's from Cambodia.'

The driver is indeed Cambodian, came over to Paris in 1975 and has never heard of his family since. This starts our evening off in a fairly serious vein, and when we are installed at Le Pharamond she continues to talk rather intensely about her worries for the world – especially what's happening in Israel at the moment.

In between apologising for the cold blasts of air from the street which send shivers along our row of tables every time someone opens the

---

1 Along with Charlie Crichton (*The Lavender Hill Mob*), Mackendrick had directed some of the classic Ealing comedies of the 1950's and early '60s including *The Ladykillers* and *The Man in the White Suit*. Since emigrating to Hollywood he had made, among others, *The Sweet Smell of Success* with Burt Lancaster. He died in 1993.
2 Frank Oz, puppeteer, actor, director, created and voiced many of the famous Muppets before moving on to direct feature films, including *Dark Crystal* and *The Little Shop of Horrors* (1986).

door, and trying to be attentive and concerned when I really wish the conversation were on a less demanding level, I'm aware that she has a broad face with a pretty mouth, soft skin and a good complexion, a slightly bloodshot eye, and she brushes golden hair back with a hand in plaster after a fall from a horse in LA two and a half weeks ago.

She has her idiosyncrasies, some of which are a little worrying, such as the fact that D H Lawrence came to her in a dream and she's now reading his poems – in public.

Halfway through our meal I had a little twinge of fear that we were barking up the wrong tree, but as we taxi home I'm a little more reassured. Maybe I'm too tired to think.

Drop her off, then, despite not having a coat suitable for the sharply cool weather, I walk, for an hour and a half, around the Left Bank, stopping at a couple of bars, enjoying what only certain great cities can provide – a marvellous set against which to invent and play your part. Like Venice, Paris dramatises everything.

Saturday, March 5th: Paris–London

Tristram arrives from London at 12.15. Cannot raise Ellen B – her phone is always engaged. TP and I set off to walk to her apartment, but when we arrive there is no name on the bell.

As a last resort, perhaps thinking what a Truffaut hero would do under similar circumstances, I try a loud, crisp shout of 'Ellen!', which echoes between the high walls of the narrow street. Sure enough shutters open several floors above us and the day is saved. It could turn out to be one of the more significant shouts of my life, for she had not known her phone was out of order and was feeling rejected and finally rather cross.

All is put to right over an expensive but delicious lunch at La Perouse – an ornate, old-fashioned restaurant on the Quai des Grands Augustins. Snow flurries sweep over the Seine. We sip champagne (her suggestion) and Meursault and eat angler fish and wild mushrooms and are about the last to leave (though no-one hurries us).

Ellen much more relaxed and afterwards Tristram remarks on how much humour she has – more than he'd expected. He finds her more soft, attractive and vulnerable than he'd seen Miss Hartley.

Wednesday, March 9th

Ring Ellen B, as have heard the good news this morning that a deal has been done with her agent. She must have insisted on a quick settlement, because he evidently agreed to our price – 300,000 plus 40,000 deferment and ten percentage points. She sounds happy and anxious to meet, so I have to arrange a visit this week which will fit in with my plans and her language lessons. We go for Friday morning.

Then to BAFTA for the jury deliberations on Best Foreign Film. Clear from the start that Nigel Andrews, Carole Myer and Philip Strick all regard Tarkovsky as God, and I think they're just trying to be polite to the rest of us in not being completely dismissive of the alternatives.

No-one fights for *Jean de Florette* or *Manon*, but Peter Greenaway's film editor – John Wilson – and I put up persistent arguments for *My Life as a Dog*. The trouble is that we are up against those who feel that even a difficult, confused, occasionally very dull film with a risible ending is, if it's by Tarkovsky, intrinsically more worthwhile than an accessible, moving, entirely successful picture by someone else.

In fact, the more we say we like *My Life as a Dog*, the more the Intellectuals seem to shift impatiently. It's not about enjoyment, it's not about accessibility. The more people who like a film, they seem to be saying, the more suspect must be its artistic credentials. We lose.

Thursday, March 10th

Tristram here about half past ten. He went to see *Handful of Stars*[1] – Dervla's play – last night, and did not like her much.

Over to the BBC to have a drink and chat with Clem, Roger Mills and Will Wyatt. All is amicable and in fact this is the best *80 Days* meeting so far.

It's decided that we shall make the journey in January 1989. Much clearer for everybody. Also I'm quite articulate on my feelings about the style of the programme. The rough with the smooth – a documentary unlike any other ...

---

1 A play by Billy Roche. One of his Wexford Trilogy.

Friday, March 11th: Paris

Walk around, past the ever-present security forces along the Rue de Varennes to Ellen's apartment. Arrive there at nine o'clock – give or take a few minutes – to find that she has breakfast neatly set out and coffee brewing.

She has a view of the Eiffel Tower and over the wall into Rodin's Garden, with a group of burghers in a permanent huddle just below the wall. She also overlooks a small hotel with cobbled courtyard. An elegant and discreetly quiet corner of Paris. Her flat is small, brightly decorated and full of light.

During our conversation about the script, Ellen comes up with a very pertinent suggestion about her relationship to Brita – basically that she should at first be encouraging Brita towards Ashby, then she falls herself. Several nice ideas for new scenes or for adding to existing scenes stem from this. An excellent and productive session.

I leave her about half past eleven, as she prepares for her afternoon classes. She says she's making very little headway with the French language. I find we talk very easily and that she has an attractive wit and modesty – she is very concerned to know the dates of filming – 'I need a month before to lose weight . . . I tend to expand between work.'

To Charles de Gaulle. A South African team of some sort – speaking Afrikaans – are waiting for our flight – they 'can't wait to get back to Jo'burg and the sun'. A tough-looking lot with vacant red faces. One is so hirsute that his chest hair erupts from beneath his collar and tie and emerges as a kind of jet-black ruff around his neck.

Briefly touch base at home, then to the Bijou Theatre to see *Temptation of Eileen Hughes* – Tristram's latest film for the BBC. Bijou projection doesn't help what is a gloomy, unhappy little tale which I don't much warm to.

Afterwards talk to Nigel Walters, the lighting cameraman. He has been approached to go round the world with me and is most enthusiastic. He tells me the original *80 Days* idea was to be on video, with live reports and with Noel Edmonds as the traveller.

Saturday, March 12th

In late afternoon go with Rachel and Tom to Latchmere Leisure Centre, where Tom is taking part in a Martial Arts Display.

He and his class, under Gavin, are the best item on the programme. Well drilled and presented, they take us through from simple exercises to routines, throws, fights and leaps, to Gavin breaking six roofing tiles with one blow of his forehead. Tom, the youngest of his group, is very lithe and crisp in his movements. Rachel and I are both impressed. At the moment he is a Green Belt, second rung on the ten-rung ladder to Black Belt, but he clearly will do well, and fast, if he sticks to it.

Monday, March 14th

Lousy weather, cold and wet. Donald Woods calls – just for a chat. Reception of *Cry Freedom* not as good as hoped in the US, but excellent in Europe. He's been travelling everywhere with it, even Iceland. Says he nearly phoned me from Portland, Oregon, where he found himself in the house of friends for whom Python was the greatest show ever aired. Donald wanted to show off that he knew me!

Tristram here at 10.30. Work on through the script. Had been to M&S to buy sandwiches for our lunch, but the shelves were bare – no delivery yet. Writers with withdrawal symptoms looked dazed and disbelieving – saw Denis Norden heading helplessly for the chicken tikka.

A meeting re Prominent Studios, with Anne, Steve, the trustee in a suit and tie who's rather nice, Eric I, Ian [Miles, our accountant] and Terry G, is not as fraught as expected. We are only £175,000 over the estimate of £1.2 million which we were given in January last year. But, as Anne says, at one time it was to cost £200,000 to refit. Malcolm Ballisat, the 'outside' trustee, is very reassuring – we have a wonderful building and it's a credit to our pension funds.

The next step, however, is to equip the viewing theatre, sound transfer and editing rooms as best we can. So far they are shells. If we want them we must find £300,000 more.

Tom [currently on the staff] is back at Redwood at midnight to lock up. They are working him savage hours at the moment and he shows signs of demoralisation.

Friday, March 18th

Steve rings to tell me that MGM do not want to do *American Friends*. This is a bit more of a blow than I had expected. For a couple of hours I have to work very hard to be cheerful.

Decide must take the bull by the horns and ring Burstyn, Tristram and Irene with the news. When all this is over and I am about to settle to work, Terry J rings, so I have to tell him the saga.

Find it very hard to concentrate on the rewrites. The sun shines happily outside, but in my room I am assailed with doubts – why continue writing a film that will never be done? Has my bluff finally been called? Is this the beginning of the end for '*AF*'? Has reality intervened? And so on.

In the absence of any word of hope from Steve on '*AF*', I call Ray and begin the delicate process of re-opening links with Denis O'B. Ray promises to call him ASAP.

Saturday, March 19th

No time for brooding – to Marshall Street for a swim, which sets the world to rights, then home for breakfast and at midday a call from Ray Cooper. He's contacted Denis. Denis is very happy to look at the script, but he sounded one or two dark words of warning about hawking it around, disinclination to co-production and so on.

I feel that the approach to Denis is necessary, but regrettable in a way. Steve will surely suffer in some way, but I checked with him yesterday on the HandMade initiative and he agreed it should be made.

Sunday, March 20th

It's raining as Helen and I, in our 'awards' gear – Helen in her very sexy purple sequinned top and black skirt – step into a taxi for the Grosvenor House and BAFTA. Park Lane is a sodden jam as taxis and limousines disgorge some of the 1,000 or more guests.

We talk to Jonas and Violet – Jonas here for the *Cry Freedom* score. Peter Sissons is chatty – his Channel 4 news by far the best thing on TV. Ben Elton is much confused at walking down the grand staircase to the accompaniment of a fanfare from Royal Marine trumpeters.

The fate of *East of Ipswich* is over very quickly. *Lifestory* wins in that category – music, applause, one minute of glory for the producer/director, then on to ... the best adapted children's documentary in a foreign language. End of our, admittedly slim, hopes.

Johnny Goodman reads a hugely verbose tribute to Bergman off autocue and at the end of the massive build-up fluffs his name – Iggimar Bergman. Ennio Morricone provides widespread unintentional laughter by referring to Princess Anne as 'His Royal Highness'. His award – for the *Untouchables* music – is extraordinary, when Jonas was overlooked. Was Sean Connery really the best actor of the year in *Name of the Rose*? Was David Jason really better than the incomparable Coltrane as TV actor?

Jean de Florette was outvoted as Best Foreign Film, but voted Best Film.

Thursday, March 24th

To Prominent Studios for a meeting with Tristram and a reading with Dervla.

We read three scenes with Dervla in the eight-track studio at Redwood. She still imbues everything with this odd and precocious air of sophistication. What is beneath it, I don't know. TP clearly thinks very little. So it's inconclusive, and I leave to play squash with TJ feeling that we have no Brita and, as yet, no film.

We talk of '*AF*' and it's clear that TJ didn't much like the January rewrite. I thought I'd solved it, TJ thinks I've lost sight of what the story essentially was.

I've deliberately tried to widen it – to make it less like *The Missionary*, to give the three main characters equal weight – as TJ says, I've approached it like a novel. I still think this is the way to go, but TJ gives enough good criticism for me to walk back down Hampstead High Street to my car, with mind almost made up to accept a postponement and to concentrate on a 'No. 27' and *80 Days* year.

Friday, March 25th

Wake early. About half past six. Doze and mull over the matter of '*AF*'. From every way I look at it, the case for a postponement seems solid. The recent work on the script only emphasises how far it is from being just right (as Helen said last night, the best things you do are clear in your head before you start).

TJ's words of last night echo Anne Bancroft's of last December: 'Why do you want to do the film?'

By eight o'clock, when Rachel brings Betty up to snuggle down beside Helen in the bed, my mind is virtually made up. But first this newest draft must be completed, and I do this in a couple of hours. Talk to Tristram and Patrick, who both feel I'm being sensible.

Sunday, March 27th: Southwold

Wake about eight, still tired. Take Ma to church. It's Palm Sunday. We have to leave in plenty of time so she can ensure her usual pew. We have almost the entire nave to choose from when we get there.

Her friends gather, generally single ladies, who I assume have outlasted husbands. They all have something wrong with them. Every snippet of talk is of 'bad nights' and people being '*much* worse'.

A last walk to the sea and, as the sun spills out of the mess of rain clouds, I leave for London, and am in Covent Garden by a quarter to seven.

To the Albery Theatre for an ILEA support concert. To raise money for a parents' ballot before the government can destroy ILEA. Rachel told me only last week of the effects that the cutbacks on education in the wake of ILEA dismemberment are having – larger classes, some subjects withdrawn.

Helen tells me that yesterday she had the *News of the World* and the *Sunday People* checking on a story that Graham C might have AIDS. They were preparing this solely on the basis of how he looked at BAFTA. GC had already been contacted and had told them, with his customary reticence on such matters, that he had not indulged in penetrative sex for ten years! What more could I have said?

Friday, April 1st

Settle into a long evening's TV with the first part of *The Sorrow and the Pity*. Absorbing and provocative. How much history is propaganda? How many of the contemporary images we have of the period are distorted by bias? Ophuls' film is an attempt to look at German-occupied France in as truthful and balanced a way as possible.

As Paris is falling the phone rings twice in rapid succession. First it's Ellen B's agent, Todd Smith. I tell him I've been trying to contact her all week. All he wants to know is that we'll come back to Ellen first next year. All I really want is the chance to speak personally to her, thank her and assure her that this is so.

In a couple of minutes I'm in the Burstyn position, fielding a proposition from Frank Oz that I should co-star as a smooth English conman, with Steve Martin as an incompetent American conman, in a film he's making on the Riviera this summer. Says he's keen and Steve's keen to have me.

Tuesday, April 5th

My copy of 'King of the Mountain', the Steve Martin/Frank Oz film, has arrived from Mike Medavoy's[1] office. I read it at one go before we leave for dinner. Though the part is written for an American, it reads quite well as an elegant Englishman, and, though there is dancing and water-skiing with one arm to cope with, I read the part with mounting interest.

Different for me – I'm not the victim, or the shopkeeper, but the dominant instigator of most of the events – and a meaty role which would place considerable demands on my acting, but that is what I need.

A message from the office to tell me that Innes Lloyd has a definite go-ahead on 'No. 27', shooting in June. Suddenly I'm in demand and the year looks like being acting, writing and documentary.

How fitting that this Dies Mirabilis should end with Granny G's 73rd birthday party at L'Escargot – Mary, Ed, Cathy, Helen and I – and that Princess Diana should be at the table next door.

She holds her head and shoulders in a hunched, protective curve, as if not wanting to draw attention to herself. Her generally downcast, but big and beautiful eyes and pink cheeks very attractive. What she can be making of the bulbous man next to her, shouting about 'lesbian co-operatives in the Balls Pond Road' and other jeering anti-leftist clichés, I can't imagine.

We all get up around the same time to leave. She drives off, herself at the wheel, from a car parked right outside. Elena, of course, has dealt with the whole thing *most* discreetly.[2]

Wednesday, April 6th

Various phone calls re 'King of the Mountain'. Steve reveals JC turned down the part, but most reluctantly apparently.

Drive to Twickenham to make noises of myself sliding down a baggage chute. Charlie and John Jympson tell of a rather unpleasant meeting in LA after I'd left with a music supremo called Newman who was very rude about everything and asked John C if he'd ever done comedy before. I *do* laugh at this.

---

1 Mike Medavoy was the co-founder of Orion Pictures Corporation.
2 Elena Salvoni, legendary maîtresse d', at Bianchi's and then L'Escargot in Soho, and now at L'Etoile in Charlotte Street. In 2005 she celebrated 60 years in the business.

Frank Oz rings. He admits to being very embarrassed. Another actor is involved who had been sent the script and who had not responded and who suddenly wants to do it. I'm about to reassure Frank that I know who the actor is, when he tells me it's Richard Dreyfuss.

Just as well I do not have a great ego over these things. Yet my part in 'King of the Mountain' is someone with a huge ego, so I'm assertive for half an hour. Oz very sympathetic, says it's not entirely his decision. Producers, money boys, etc.

Work on the script until half past eleven. Only in bed do I allow myself to ride a wave or two of self-pity. It feels as though I'm doomed not to act again – already this year *Munchausen*, *American Friends* and now this have slipped from me. Add all these to 'Troubles' and a pattern emerges that could be attractive to a paranoiac.

Mind you, I sleep much better than when I thought I *had* the part.

Tuesday, April 12th

Frank Oz calls. Dreyfuss read for my character, Lawrence, and couldn't get it. Too much energy, he couldn't play the laid-back characters, he wanted to be Freddy. So I'm back on the list and he would like me to fly over to New York before the end of the week.

He calls back at ten minutes to midnight to ask if I can fly on Concorde on Friday.

Wednesday, April 13th

Up at 8.30, and by ten heading off with William towards Winchester. He wants to see the cathedral and the library in pursuit of his Malory enthusiasm.[1]

Winchester, an hour and a half from home down the M3, is a good-looking, well-kept little city. A pleasure to walk around.

On the way back we discuss Thatcher and what's happening in the country. For the first time I feel that sense of helplessness before the weight of the Thatcher machine. It's changing everything that I've believed in

---

1 A collection of stories and legends about King Arthur was collated by Sir Thomas Malory under the title *Le Morte D'Arthur* and published by William Caxton in 1485. An earlier version known as the Winchester Manuscript was discovered in Winchester College Library in 1934. It's now in the British Library.

in the years since I left Shrewsbury, and there seems no way of stopping it. I feel too old to change things, but William understands what's happening and knows it's up to him and his generation to carry the torch of concern, compassion, co-operation and conscience. (That's enough alliteration – Ed.)

Friday, April 15th: London–New York

I'm bouncing in a limousine through the shattered landscape of 2nd Avenue, Harlem. Buildings either burnt-out, bricked up or covered from head to foot in graffiti. Here in Harlem the security is quite overt, bent iron grilles, padlocks hanging onto rusty metal.

Then into the nineties and regeneration begins. Instead of decay there is cautious conversion. Once into the eighties we're among some of the most expensive apartments in the world. It's all New York. Like an eccentric friend – it's impossible to understand but has to be constantly talked about.

I set my bags down at the Parker Meridien. I notice my computer-printed check-in slip is headed 'Star of Monty Python's Flying Circus'. If this gets me a room with a view then it's fine.

I'm 31 floors up and looking out towards the greening park and amongst the towers around me is the famous Essex House, or Excess House, as it would be renamed in my autobiography. From here I can appreciate how gigantic the letters are atop the hotel and I should imagine in a storm there must be considerable likelihood of being struck by a falling 'S', 'E' or 'X', or possibly all three at the same time.

At a quarter to twelve US time, a quarter to five my own bodily time, I'm deposited at 50 Riverside Drive on the West Side, where Frank Oz's apartment is located. Steve is already there.

We talk, have coffee. I sense that Steve has been through this before. I can't help being affected by the knowledge that I am a name on a list. Not *the* name. We read some scenes. Frank O shows me photos of the villa where they're shooting. He's anxious that I should have as much material as possible on which to base the character.

Well, I find I'm not giving Frank quite what he wants. He wants it light and debonair and elegant and stylish and I am not delivering. I'm suddenly tight, heavy, plodding and predictable. I have to face it that I'm out of practice and it isn't coming nearly as easy as I expected.

After an hour and a half we go for lunch at a Japanese round the corner.

Across the road Irving Berlin lived as a recluse for many years; at the corner is a hookers' hotel. There's a welfare hostel across the street from one of the most expensive private schools in the city.

At lunch I learn more about the film. They've changed the title to 'Dirty Rotten Criminals'.[1] When I also hear that the mystery writer is Dale Launer, who wrote the ugly *Ruthless People*, I begin to feel that my lustreless reading earlier may have saved me.

Walk back across Central Park. Magnolia, azaleas and hawthorn in blossom, but at the same time the number of odd, mad and sinister and threatening individuals wandering by seems to have increased and I feel a little jumpy. Brought out of my reverie as a woman passes, stops, turns back and gasps ... 'Oh God, I have just passed a myth.'

Monday, April 18th

Cannot shake off persistent feeling of the blues this morning, and a nagging feeling of slipping backwards, of projects aborting left, right and centre.

All this tinged with a common enough gloom ingredient – am I doing the right things with my life? Should I have stayed in grubby Gospel Oak? Should the children have gone to beleaguered local state schools, instead of gaining the enviable confidence that private school children seem to have?

These last considerations all come under the heading of envy, which I know to be one of the Deadly Sins, and one which would be present at any level, so I refuse to take them too seriously. But they niggle, as a lot of other things niggle, this morning.

Friday, April 22nd

Happily listening to 'How to Write a Screenplay' on *Kaleidoscope* when Oz calls, 'just to keep you in the picture'. Now Dreyfuss is re-interested and also onto the scene has strolled M Caine; 'It's between you three,' a rather harassed-sounding Oz assures me.

More and more I don't want to do it, but, just as much, I *do* want to be chosen. I think Caine is probably the nearest he will get in an English actor to the effortless charisma of Niven.

---

1 And it was to be changed again to *Dirty Rotten Scoundrels*.

Tuesday, April 26th

Am bought lunch by Hilary Neville-Towle of BBC Books. Rather of the class and style of most publishing ladies, but very nice, un-pushy and interesting.

She reawakens my enthusiasm for the *80 Days* trip and I try to forget that the contract cannot be signed because of the ridiculously low fee which the BBC have offered. Good progress on the book, which *must* look more exciting than the *Great River Journeys* she brought along. Poor photos, dull format.

With Helen, to dinner at the Garrick with Mel [Calman] and Debbie [Moggach, a novelist and Mel's partner]. Like all these old clubs it's on a grand scale – with huge windows and high ceilings – but everything, from the armchairs to the doorman, is slightly shabby.

This is an element of the English way of doing things that the Americans just couldn't understand. They would make everything shiny. A coat of paint, unless applied with a liberal mixture of dust, would ruin this place.

Wednesday, April 27th

I check through my *Number 27* rewrites as they come hot off the presses. Tristram rings to say he has found the complete Miss Barwick – Joyce Carey, who actually *is* 90!

William arrives back from a week's biology swotting in Pembrokeshire full of heroic tales of William Ellis's effortless superiority over the other schools. He hears later in the evening that his 'A' Level history teacher has just quit, on the verge of a nervous breakdown. Will thought him a good teacher who knew his subject; still, no match for the Thatcher/Baker steamroller under which all London teachers are being squashed.

Sunday, May 1st

A significant coincidence. As the first part of 'Troubles' begins on LWT, Frank Oz rings to tell me that they've decided to go with Michael Caine!

The latter doesn't hurt nearly as much as the former.

In fact, now I can contemplate a more leisurely summer, richer in everything, I hope, except, of course, money!

Wednesday, May 4th

Set off for a poetry-reading at the Chelsea Arts Club in honour of Robert Graves. The Club is in an odd and characterful white building on Old Church Street; the bell must be pressed before you can enter (so the sound of the bell ringing marks the entire evening).

As I arrive, a very elderly lady is being assisted towards the low Beatrix Potter-like doorway.

I have a pint of beer. Out in the garden, which is very green and airy and protected, George Melly sits alone.

Spike is late, so the poetry-reading is postponed for an hour. I'm taken to meet the old lady I held the door open for. She is Ros Hooper, Robert Graves's sister, and she's 94. Quite easy to talk to once one ceases to be apologetic and sycophantic and behaves naturally. She clutches a book of Georgian poetry. She's clear-eyed and says she can still read quite unaided. She also hears and digests info in the middle of this noisy throng with great ease.

She's most concerned about the food and she enquires of every admirer who is brought to meet her when the food may be provided.

Spike arrives, looking very well, smooth of complexion and with a ruddy pink glow, either from fresh scrubbing or from the country life he now enjoys in Kent. He was quite a friend of Robert Graves and talks to Ros for a while.

Spike and I have an exchange of jokes. 'Why are you so nice to me?' he suddenly asks. 'Because I like you.' When Spike is on good form I can hardly imagine anyone better to be with – the combination of silliness, huge generosity and emotion makes him at times irresistible.

Eventually the delayed homage to Graves takes place.

Laurie Lee reads so well that I and the audience hang on every syllable and I'm made aware of how important it is to read poetry aloud. Ros Hooper reads beautifully too.

I shake a few hands and slip away from this sardine-like dining room and into the street. It's a cool, but pleasant evening. The whole thing quite surreal and dreamlike. But somehow suitable that I should be there to remember a writer whose *Goodbye to All That* was one of the seminal books of my early teens, turning me towards other war writings.

Friday, May 6th

'AF' is such an elusive number. Every time I read it, questions arise. Now why didn't I ask them earlier? I feel like someone trying desperately to fill a suitcase, from which bits keep popping out. Even when it's shut there are lumps which you know you must sort out before you go anywhere. But I feel as I read through today that I am at least editing from strength.

To Delancey Street for a meeting about 'AF' with Patrick C, Tristram and Steve A. I take the initiative and suggest that we tuck our horns in a little, trim the budget and head for UK or European money first, largely because of my gut feeling that this will be a difficult one to sell to the US and that MGM's reluctance will likely be matched elsewhere.

Saturday, May 21st

To William Ellis to see their production of *Midsummer Night's Dream*. A great success. That one could spend three hours on those small, hard chairs, in that acoustically suspect hall and hardly notice physical discomfort says a lot for them. Always good to hear Shakespeare interpreted by good people discovering it for the first time. Will Palin, as he is in the programme, did the lighting, and I am proud of him.

Sunday, May 29th

Wake about seven. Cannot forget that Angela took her life a year ago. Everyone seems to have coped with it, though my hopes of talking about her, her life and death and the whys and wherefores with the family haven't materialised.

Though it doesn't haunt my life, when I stop and think of Angela, I cannot believe she isn't there, and that's when the pain begins.

Wednesday, June 1st

To Eaton Place, where Joyce [Carey] lives in a ground-floor flat. She has warned us that there is some building work going on nearby, and would we mind drinks instead of tea.

An erect and handsome woman with slow-moving eyes comes to the door. She behaves towards me like a 16-year-old, flattering and flirting quite shamelessly. Is the chair comfortable enough? Would I like some taramasalata with my whisky?

She's effusively complimentary about the script. Tristram uses a phrase of Jonathan Miller's to describe the process – 'a Niagara of praise'. She tells stories of Noël [Coward] and has several photographs of him – in fact those days, presumably between the wars, seem to have been her happiest.

At one point she asks Tristram if he's a bully.

We leave after an hour or so, leaving her in her tiny room, with her dark Maitland oils of London parks and her Corot miniature, and her signed photos of Noël – he wasn't a bully, but 'he knew what he wanted'.

Monday, June 6th

Take Ma to the Hayward Gallery, where 85 pictures from the Phillips Collection in Washington are on show. Mum astute enough to loathe the grim, concrete approaches to the gallery and the extraordinary two-floor gap between one half of the exhibition and the other, but the pictures are all interesting and some are amongst the best of that particular artist's work – notably an atmospheric empty city and railway tunnel of Edward Hopper, the complete contrast of Renoir's party after the regatta, a big Bonnard panorama, and Van Gogh's entrance to the gardens at Arles.

How they can put a coffee shop at the top of the Hayward Gallery and build windows too high to see out over the river is just another on a quite limitless list of questions I should like to put to Denys Lasdun on behalf of the despairing punter.

We walk by the river. Notice a new passenger boat service in operation – the Thames Line, sponsored, as most endeavours in the country are nowadays. This time it's Barclays Bank who get their ugly logo across the stern. Lovely walk, high, puffy white clouds. A Dufy day over London.

Saturday, June 11th

Decide only to do the 'Politician's Speech' at Wembley. The concert [Free Nelson Mandela] has already attracted controversy – the South African government condemning the BBC for televising it at all – but there it is on my TV at midday, the stadium packed out and nothing heavily political besides a large backcloth showing Mandela behind bars which says everything that needs to be said.

My car arrives for me at three. It's been arranged for me to bring William and three friends, but the driver will not take more than four people, so Tom brings Will in the brown Mini, trailing us through the back streets of Harlesden.

A dark, cavernous hospitality/reception area is filled with the sound of the music and there are monitors and a huge screen to accompany the pounding beat. And nowhere to get away from it.

On the whole it's run unintimidatingly, with much of the work being done by smiling young women. Rather as one might imagine behind the lines in the First War.

All of a sudden I'm buttonholed and led up towards the stage. Catch my first glimpse of the 70,000 crowd. Mainly young and white, whereas backstage was mainly middle-aged and black.

They want me on early as Stevie Wonder's organ has been stolen and everything is being rearranged. Then they ask if I can do more than I've planned. Say three minutes – as long as possible. It's been bad enough being dressed as a Tory MP throughout the afternoon, and now to be asked to incorporate another piece. Decide on 'Plankton', though I don't have the gear.

Miriam Makeba is coming to the end of her set on the big stage. I am to be on immediately she finishes. Rehearse the words and think of links furiously. Makeba finishes. I am poised. Makeba begins again. Finishes. Jubilation. On I go ... Makeba launches into one more number.

Not only has Wonder's equipment gone missing, Lenny Henry's mike has gone down, so I will not be introduced. Irony that I, who have come here to make an introduction, miss the honour myself.

Walk out. It's very strange. A feeling of slow motion, as if performing to a drunk. The huge crowd swings slowly, heaving, rippling and lurching, in my direction. A strange lack of connection between us.

Decide that I'd best just plunge in, hoping I have the attention of a few thousand.

Monday, June 13th

To the Everyman with TG to see *La Grande Bouffe*. This is rarely revived and I am interested to see if it is as good as I remember it.

Despite it being a very scratched print, and a little too long, it is. The audacity and outrageousness of it, with the sexy and the scatological so stylishly combined, are an object lesson.

Bad taste served up with good taste. Ugo's death, being spoonfed till he's stuffed at one end and gently masturbated by a schoolteacher at the other, is one of the greatest and most bizarre deaths in cinema – closely followed by Piccoli experiencing a terminal fart.

We eat a small amount afterwards at the Pizza Express.

Friday, June 17th

An urgent message to call JC reveals that MGM have changed the release date for *Wanda* yet again. It's now to open in selected theatres in New York, LA and Toronto to gather word of mouth in time for the big release two weeks later. My dates are all now in upheaval.

To lunch with Tristram. 'I need rather a lot of wine,' he confesses. We laugh a lot.

Maybe our laughter is just pre-filming hysteria. I know that there will be more problems with this than with *East of Ipswich*, and the finished product will not be as special or as much loved. Awful to feel that way.

But for now on, with slightly hysterical cheerfulness, we talk about the British attitude to sex and 'all that sort of thing', as his mother puts it. According to Tristram his father has become much more outspoken on the subject than he used to be. Apparently he's now quite likely to refer to someone as a 'silly cunt'.

Home about six, then out to a hap-ki-do demonstration with Tom's class, in a Catholic premises behind the Royal Free. Odd to see them breaking breeze-blocks with their hands beneath a huge mural of Christ displaying juicy stigmata.

Thursday, June 23rd

To the Disabled Ex-Servicemen's home in Ealing, where 'No. 27' is filming. There have been problems since Monday. Five hairs in the gate – an unforeseeable chance at any time, but all this afternoon and all involving Joyce, whose first day it is. They have fallen behind despite working until nearly ten o'clock last night.

But the sunlight, filtered through the trees, is very pleasant and the location comfortable, if one can get used to the presence of limbless servicemen in wheelchairs dotted about.

I am able to make a few suggestions and entertain Joyce – who does seem to have taken quite a shine to me. Apparently her skirt fell down as she stood in a rose garden earlier. 'Normally I would have laughed, but this time I was a little cross,' she confesses.

Tuesday, June 28th

Drive to Epsom College which has become Melford School for the day. A slow journey – one and a half hours for about 20 miles. Cool and drizzling when I arrive on the site which is spacious and well endowed with cricket nets, fives and tennis courts and various pitches.

Afternoon spent in the still rather horrible conditions, shooting the scene we nearly cut – the aborted royal arrival at the end. Three hundred boys in suits and the school band. It looks impressive and is completed by 4.15. Early wrap, so everyone euphoric.

I had to be available to sign autographs (apparently they got a cheaper filming rate because of this!). About 120 boys availed themselves of the offer. I wrote a different message every time, knowing they'd compare them. Humour very strained by the end.

Back home, crossing the river at the fourth attempt – all usual routes blocked – I have a message to ring Shamberg. I know it bodes ill, and it does. Shamberg, not even deigning to break his monotone in sympathy, tells me that there are 'awareness problems' with the picture and that the release date has been changed again.

Wednesday, June 29th: Southwold

Whilst running an idea occurs to me for the 'Articles for Sale' drama series to which I have been asked to contribute by Jack Rosenthal. It's to do with Hemingway – the object being a seat which one fits to the deck of a boat for deep-sea fishing – as in the famous photo of Hemingway. From this I work out a story involving a post office clerk and Hemingway fantasies.

Back at Sunset House scribble my ideas down while waiting to cool down. The lines, characters and odd ideas spill out quite fluently.

Thursday, June 30th

As I leave Granny sounds rather a pathetic note, saying that she feels so 'bereft' when I'm away. I'm afraid I scold her a bit for using such emotional blackmail, but it does show that she is not as composed as she appears.

Money matters of all kinds are a perennial source of anxiety and I drive myself to the limits of frustration reassuring her that she need have no worries.

Park my car near Blackhorse Road Station and a very easy Victoria/Piccadilly Line ride to Knightsbridge. At Wheelers 'Carafe' restaurant in Lowndes Street almost exactly five minutes late for my lunch date with Joyce C.

She is sitting amongst a sea of empty tables, down in the basement. Her neat appearance, erect bearing and eyes with their characteristic imploring look. She's wearing a very well-chosen azure blue dress with a pattern of white flower petals. She advises me to have the sole. 'Dover, of course, not lemon.' She chooses gravadlax to start with. 'Very sustaining.'

She politely asks me a little about myself, but I hurry on to talk about her and all her experiences. She confesses 'I'm a bit of a mixed bag, you know. My father was Jewish, but he didn't know he was Jewish for quite a while ... he'd say terrible things about Jew boys and then suddenly remember ...'.

Talk turns to Noël. Her mother – Lilian Braithwaite – was in Noël's very first play – *The Vortex* at Hampstead Everyman. She tells me, with some hesitation, of something Noël said to her once in a taxi – the gist of which was that he liked Joyce because 'Though you're the most feminine of women, you have the code of a man.' 'Well, I think it just meant I wasn't silly,' she says modestly. But it says a lot about her, and about Coward.

She was with him in Portmeirion and discussed *Blithe Spirit*, which he then went off and wrote in five days. For a time she and Noël C used to, as Coward put it, 'mystify people' at parties. They did a sort of improvisation based on characters suggested by the audience and 'many people tried to make a fool out of him, but no-one ever succeeded'.

The beans arrive, 'Fashionably undercooked,' comments Joyce with a twinkle. Rather as with my mother this morning, the only thing that ruffles Joyce's composure is the financing. She asks several times if she's paid the bill (she insists on taking *me* out) and the Oriental waiter smiles very tolerantly and reassures her gently.

I walk her back to her flat in Eaton Place, slowly, crossing many roads. She shows me a garden she likes on the way. At the flat she insists on giving me a brandy and then shows me some more of her pictures – including a graphically very bold painting of Coward's, of a Jamaican standing amidst palm leaves with the blue mountains and dark skies behind. She's very proud, too, of the portrait of her mother. A pre-Raphaelite beauty.

Saturday, July 2nd

At 12.30 I go to Camden Lock to cut a cake celebrating 40 years of the NHS. Frank Dobson, our local MP, is one of the other participants and I'm quite keen to meet him as he's one of the livelier and more effective Labour performers. Meet him in a café opposite the tatty, run-down Camden Labour Party HQ. He's a very jolly, hustling figure, full of jokes about poofters in the Durham Labour Party.

We walk to our spot, which turns out to be a small trestle table which is the Labour Party presence at the Lock. Frank has a megaphone with which he harangues the largely apathetic shoppers. Lots of ill-looking people come by – old with shrunken faces and eyes cast down, their faces dull and many resentful of our being in the way.

Frank is heckled by a surly and humourless cluster of *Socialist Worker* and other left-wing pamphlet-sellers, who are virtually falling over each other in Inverness Street today. I only hope they have better luck with the proletariat than we do.

Sunday, July 3rd

Bathe and shave and then talk over the phone to Benedict Nightingale, who's writing a piece for the *NY Times* on *Wanda*. He was at Cambridge with JC and remembers him as a quiet, rather self-effacing figure.

TJ then rings. Nicolas Cage sounds like a possible Erik and TJ is going to NYC tomorrow to talk to him. By coincidence staying at the Parker Meridien, as am I.

On the 6.30 news we hear of an Iranian airliner shot down by the Americans by mistake. Nearly 300 killed. Talk of reprisals will hardly reassure my mother!

Monday, July 4th: London–New York

Buy M Shamberg's cigars and have a glass of orange before boarding Concorde. I've become blasé about travelling supersonic now, which is sad. It used to give me such pleasure. Now it's like a commuter service. Full of Americans who came over for the Wimbledon final, which was rained off yesterday. 'If the rain stays like this, we could be home in time to catch it live on TV.' None of them mentions the shooting down of the Iranian airliner.

We leave London in rain and low cloud and land in hot sunshine in NYC.

My cab driver, a thin-faced, sallow-skinned, unhealthy-looking white man, talks compulsively – repeating endlessly a story of blacks at Penn Station who've taken to robbing car drivers ... 'There's a fucking precinct house two blocks away! I tell you, if this was New Orleans they'd have sorted those guys out. They'd have broken their fuckin' legs by now.'

Tuesday, July 5th: New York

Call Al L only to hear that he has some problem with his spinal nerve and can hardly walk. He can't come to the screening on Thursday. I suggest that I could go to see him on my return from LA, but his sister has 'decided to choose that weekend to get married again'. He is mortified and convinced that 'the big foot', as he calls it, is coming lower.

Picked up at 12.15 by Sue Barton, whom I remember with pleasure from the *Missionary* publicity days. She tells me Ed Roginski, who was Antonowsky's right hand and a very good man indeed, is dying of AIDS. She was in California with him yesterday.

Wednesday, July 6th: New York

It concerns me that I have trouble focussing in on small print. Taking out the diary this morning at the Parker Meridien, reading the menu last night at the Museum Café, remind me that my eyesight is becoming fallible. Also the odd crackle (the only way I can describe it) on the left side of my chest has had me wildly fearing that my system is about to seriously rebel against the demands put on it.

Picked up by limousine and taken down to the Gramercy Park end of town for a series of satellite interviews ahead of the *Wanda* opening. These consist of myself and Jamie on a sofa, John in a leather wing-backed armchair, with some funereal flower arrangement on a table in front of us, being interviewed about the movie by largely invisible interrogators, whose name and destination we only know from cards stuck across the bottom of the camera – e.g. 'Wilmington, Harry Brubaker', then 'Des Moines, Jack Phibbs'. We sometimes hear their voices in our ear-pieces before the interview begins. 'Michael *who*?' I hear from Linda in Washington.

Out to see *Much Ado* in the Park. Our limousine intrudes us almost up to the auditorium itself. We disembark in the middle of a wide-eyed mill of 'ordinary people' and for the rest of the evening are on display.

Being one who prefers to watch rather than be watched, I find it all faintly uncomfortable. John cruises along with it, but then he never really does notice people. Jamie is a little brittle, on edge, wanting the fame, because she's American, but feeling uneasy with it because she's intelligent.

I've never been to the Free Theater before. No-one pays, except for refreshment, so it's a much less formal, more relaxed crowd than you usually find in a West End or Broadway theatre.

A marvellous production. Full of life and energy and humour. Kevin [Kline] is on great form as Benedick and Blythe Danner matches him. As night falls, the stage and the lights of the village set focus our attention more clearly, as the play is drawing us in at the same time.

Thursday, July 7th: New York

My lunchtime radio interviewer has postponed until tomorrow as her husband was held up at gunpoint by two kids in Brooklyn and forced to drive around for much of the night before being robbed.

New York seems a lot crazier than I remember it. Perhaps it's the heat. Temperatures are up into the low 90's and it's humid and cloudy. Thanks to the wonders of air-conditioning I don't notice the extreme weather – except for the occasional soft blast of air between lobby and limousine.

Friday, July 8th: New York

To the Bay Hotel (formerly the Taft), where we are to talk to the out-of-town press. It's a most luxuriously appointed hotel on Broadway and 61st. Absurdly expensive touches such as a small silver display tree with a truffle chocolate perched on the edge of each branch.

JC arrives with advance copies of the *People Magazine* review. It's a rave – especially for John, but nice words for everybody. I'm called a 'deadpan delight'.

Then we are all distributed to various rooms, and there, like whores in Amsterdam, we sit waiting to be talked to.

Saturday, July 9th: New York–Los Angeles

We are travelling (Shamberg, Cleese and myself) on MGM Grand Air to Los Angeles. Small, luxuriously appointed airliners (727s) with a convenient and rather cosy little terminal building. The plane itself is decorated like Caesar's Palace; thick pile carpets, velour seats, deep, artificial and violently unmatched colours, mirrors, frills of one kind and another.

To the Four Seasons Hotel. Both of us so pleased to see unequivocal sunshine after the hazy mugginess of the East Coast that we repair straight away to the pool, which is crowded with rather uncommunicative LA types.

As we sit there, JC opines that he would rather like to do a Python stage show – provided we could do 'Cheese Shop'. I'm of the opinion that if we do it we should do it in a smaller theatre – 1,000 seat max and well equipped. JC would most like to do it in LA. I favour Sydney.

Talk about GC. John thinks that Marty F[eldman]'s opinion that GC was in love with JC is not far off the mark.

We swim and sunbathe and then both feel the effects of the NYC week and collapse rather in the evening.

Sunday, July 10th: Los Angeles

Breakfast at the Sidewalk Café. My first cooked breakfast of a disciplined week. A bookshop adjoins the very busy restaurant and there I buy two or three more Hemingways – so impressed was I by *The Garden of Eden*, and encouraged too by a favourable reaction from Shamberg and Cleese when I told them of the 'Tea and Hemingway' script yesterday.

Gilliam is with us. He and Cleese haven't met for months. Here in the relaxed, neutral and unthreatening territory of Venice Beach, they both unwind. JC chides TG for having to have an enemy, be it a Denis O'Brien or a Sid Sheinberg.

TJ is still looking for an Erik. He sounds dispirited.

I sit by the pool for an hour with JC, who is very chatty. We swim and JC puts down some intense psychology work with a very boring title and poaches my Hemingway, *The Sun Also Rises*.

TJ and Carrie Fisher pick me up to drive down to the Ivy at the Shore

Restaurant, where are gathered Jamie, Rob Reiner[1] and Cleese.

Jamie and Carrie immediately fall into conversation – their lives are so similar. Both offspring of star parents, beautiful mothers and promiscuous fathers. Both hardly knew their fathers, both of whom later became dependent on drugs. Both mothers too went through difficult periods. The thought of Debbie Reynolds too stoned to work is, to my 1950's British view of her, quite unthinkable. Now these two tough children have reversed the roles. They are looking after parents who seem driven to childishness.

Friday, July 15th: San Francisco–Los Angeles

Not an easy start for the day. I am at Alex Bennett's radio show on – with live studio audience. Alex I like – he's benign, amusing, with a long moustache, a long history and an engaging, elder-statesmanlike aura – but this early exposure to the fans is gruelling. Grins, handshakes, autographs, how-dees, how-are-yers, how-you-doin's and inane replies to inane questions take their toll, and by the time I'm at the mike in a studio filled with the faithful I'm feeling the pressure.

But Alex seems entirely happy with my presence and schedules me for a further half-hour. 'When guys like Michael Palin come along, I just want to say hang the news, but we have to have it ... so let's make it quick ...'

Back to the Portman for breakfast and the reviews. The first shock is that Canby, such a loyal friend in the past, hates it. But Sheila Benson in the *LA Times* gives a much more comprehensive and better-written rave. Still, Canby rankles and stands as a stern warning against over-confidence.

Saturday, July 16th: Los Angeles

To breakfast with Tom Jacobson and John Hughes to talk over the 'Larry Meister' project.[2] I like them. Jacobson is quiet, trim-bearded and soft-spoken. He's from Kansas. Hughes is chubbier, pale-faced, bespectacled,

---

1 Reiner had directed *Princess Bride* and *Stand by Me* but was perhaps best known for directing, and appearing as the director, in the seminally wonderful *This is Spinal Tap*.
2 Tom Jacobson was a producer and John Hughes a writer, producer and director (*National Lampoon's Vacation*, 1983, *Ferris Bueller's Day Off*, 1986, *Planes, Trains and Automobiles* with Steve Martin, 1987). They had sent me a script to consider called 'Larry Meister Late for Life'. It was, as far as I know, never made.

like the clever boy in the class. Articulate, humorous. They're both younger than I expected. As so often happens, they know my work more thoroughly than I know theirs.

John C comes down to breakfast, sits at the other side of the dining room and starts to make 'yak-yak' gestures out of their view, but not out of mine. Later he is stricken by one of his lung-wrenching bronchial spasms, which usually result from him finding something incredibly funny. In this case it turns out to be the Vincent Canby *New York Times* review. Introductions are made. Jacobson cannot quite get over the fact that we get on so well after twenty years together.

Tuesday, July 19th: New York

Over to NBC to appear with Jamie and John and Kevin on Phil Donahue's show. Donahue, an agreeable man of the people, is a show for Middle America, but has big ratings and it is a great coup that he should be spending a whole hour with *A Fish Called Wanda*.

Kevin, whose vanity did not go unremarked in the *New Yorker*, is already in make-up. He's careful and attentive and gives them advice as to how to darken his moustache. Jamie and John are live by satellite from Los Angeles. Jamie, with her fringe and glasses making her look like someone deliberately not wanting to look attractive (and failing), looks wan beside John, who's clearly been at the poolside a bit more, so much so that when he smiles he looks like one of the Black and White Minstrels.

Facing Kevin and me on the platform is an audience of some 200 New Yorkers. They ask questions like . . . 'I really like you and are you married?' 'You look great with hair like that, will you keep it that way?' Nothing profound and the average IQ of the entire audience would probably equal that of A J Ayer's earlobe, but it's a nice, genial show.

Monday, July 25th

First off today is an *80 Days* meeting with Clem, Angela [Elbourne – production manager] and Anne J at Ken House.[1] They now have a bigger office and one wall is covered with a whiteboard chart. Only the first day is filled: 'September 25 – 11.00 Depart Victoria, Orient Express'.

---

1 Kensington House in Shepherd's Bush was the hub of the dynamic BBC Documentary Features output. It's now been turned into a chic hotel called K West.

It's undoubtedly exciting to be in the office now the project is official, contracted and under way. They are putting onto the bare bones of the route the flesh of actual trains and vessels. The Orient Express and Venice will be an exotic start. From Singapore to Hong Kong they have us aboard *Ben Avon* – one of the three largest ships afloat.

A drink in the bar, then drive over to Brecknock Primary School in York Way to present books to the leavers. The school is on the run-down border of Camden and Islington, on an island of houses and shops, triangled by busy roads. Old, stout building of pre-First World War vintage. Inside a good spirit. It's full of children's work and drawings and clutter.

As the rest of the school sing a couple of songs the leavers, all of 11 years old, wait maturely and with a right sense of responsibility to collect a book each and shake my hand. After which I'm required to say a few words on the subject of 'moving on'. Produce a sheaf of notes, then tell them I can't read my writing and throw it away. This seems to cheer them up.

Wednesday, August 10th

Breakfast enlivened by some San Francisco cuttings re *Wanda* sent, generously, by Don Novello.[1] I have already heard via Steve at the weekend that John was extremely concerned as to how I had engineered such a rave review for myself in the *San Francisco Chronicle* – what sexual favours had I granted the critic? How much money had changed hands? It is rather a gushing piece – 'The comic performance of a lifetime. He's up there with Sellers, Guinness and Mastroianni'! And that's even before he's mentioned John.

To White City to see 'No. 27' on the Steenbeck. My first glimpse of any cut footage.

First impression of great pleasure in the lighting and art direction – both nice and carried off with a sure touch, as is most of Tristram's interesting direction. Seems a little slow at the start, but strong

---

1 I had worked with Don on *Saturday Night Live* in the 1970's. His best-loved character was Father Guido Sarducci, a Vatican spokesman. In 1977 he produced a very funny book of fake letters by a creation of his called Lazlo Toth, and their genuine replies from politicians and others in authority. *The Lazlo Letters* were the inspiration (unacknowledged) for *The Henry Root Letters* by William Donaldson, published in the UK in 1980.

performances, especially from Alun A and Robin Bailey, draw one in and the story-telling is quite exciting.

Really very pleased, and apparently Goodchild is too.

Thursday, August 11th

I finally see Hemingway's life through to its double-barrelled conclusion. Lynn's book leaves a bad taste.[1] Why was Lynn's work as highly praised as the cover quotes imply? A word-processor job with a few theories about Hem's mother nailed in there. All seems, like his subject's life, to have been ended in a hurry.

Friday, August 12th

To a Redwood meeting with Bob and André. Profits around 25,000 this year. Next year a bigger rent and rates bill and we shall need to increase turnover by about 30% just to break even. At the moment it seems alarmingly quiet.

Chris Pearce [the Manager of Delancey Studios] is so prickly – forever shouting at people, even arguing with clients – that Bob and André at one time seriously thought of moving to get away from him. Apparently Tom P burnt some toast this morning and set the fire alarm off. Chris went off as well and began shouting and screaming. I'm glad to hear that TP shouted and screamed back.

Tracey Ullman rings halfway through the meeting. She very much wants me to be on the show. As she puts it, 'I've got four lovely Jewish writers who are just waiting for me to get some English man on the programme.'

Finish our meeting. It's agreed Tom will be asked to stay on for a second year, which is a relief. André says he's very good at picking up information, but *as* good at forgetting it the next morning.

Saturday, August 13th

Wake Rachel about nine and together we go down to the Marshall Street Baths. The baths, run at present by Westminster Council, are to be taken

---

1 My own view, of course. *The New York Review of Books* called Kenneth S. Lynn's *Hemingway* (1987) 'One of the most brilliant and provocative literary biographies in recent memory'.

over by an outfit called Civic Leisure from August 28th. Present staff will have to go. Socialism rolled back a little bit more.

At the end of the evening Helen and I are flopped in the kitchen when the doorbell goes. Helen urges me to look very carefully through the spyhole before opening it. I look through the spyhole. There, beside the scaffolding, clutching an envelope, is one of the Beatles. It's George, with the Wilburys' sleeve notes he wants me to have a look at.[1] Dhani and Olivia are in the car and Dominic Taylor [son of Derek and Joan] and his girlfriend.

I invite them all in. After all the years of embarrassment about inviting George and him not being able to come at the last minute, this spontaneous visitation is a wonderful relief – despite the fact that the house is in a dreadful mess. But Dhani loves it all and wanders around, occasionally checking with me about details of Python shows. He specially likes the foot on top of the TV [which Denis O'B had given me after *A Private Function*].

Turns out it's Dominic's 21st, so we open a bottle of champagne.

Tuesday, August 16th: Southwold

Sleep well. Woken by the sound of St Edmund's clock striking eight. A perfect summer morning, sunshine in profusion, hardly a breath of wind and the outline of the horizon on the North Sea razor-sharp.

After breakfast sally forth to the town – buy home-cured smoked haddock and fresh-dressed crabs and brown bread – called a cobbler – home-baked at the back of the shop.

Return, ready for half a morning's work, only to find Ma ready to go out to the vicarage coffee morning and surprisingly adamant that I should accompany her. So I do, and it's worth it. Mum quite a celebrity and much twittered over by various local ladies. 'We look after her, you know,' they proclaim over her head, as if talking about a prize vegetable.

Delicious crab for lunch. Sit out on the balcony. Some desultory sports training is going on below us on the Common.

---

1 A couple of months earlier George had asked Eric Idle, David Leland and myself if we'd help make a spoof publicity film for a group consisting of himself, Tom Petty, Roy Orbison, Bob Dylan and Jeff Lynne. They called themselves The Travelling Wilburys. We never made the film but I wrote sleeve notes for the first of their two classic albums. And I'm quite proud of that.

Mum tells me more openly than she ever has before of the circumstances of my conception. She remembers the day exactly, she says. For some reason she knew that she had to do the deed. After years of vacillation Daddy would do nothing. She remembers it well, the summer day in 1942. 'The vicar and his wife had been round for tea – we'd had tea on the back lawn.'

That night, as if, she hints, at some divine bidding, she tricked Daddy into impregnating her by leaving out her pessaries. There is no doubt in her mind that that was the night and that she knew what she was doing; she remembers every detail of the event, she says, even what was on top of the cupboard! She also knew I would be a boy, though Daddy, to the bitter end, thought otherwise and already had me down as Elaine!

Wednesday, August 17th: Southwold

At breakfast Ma says she feels 'unsettled'. I ask her about what and she dithers a while, as if worried that she has already over-dramatised her feelings. 'Well, everything, you know ... Southwold just isn't the same ...' Not quite sure if she's trying to say more. I can't read the signal.

But she seems happy enough and her sangfroid recovers as I carry my bags down to the car. A letter has been delivered by hand, addressed to me. Quite unsolicited, from the local Tory councillor, quite ingratiating and asking me if I will be the 'Famous International Celebrity' they've promised will judge some photo competition. I realise that the days of quiet inconspicuousness at Southwold are numbered and I resent that.

Thursday, August 18th

To Notting Hill, then Holland Park and lunch with John, just back from the US. He's relishing having his house back – Barbara having now moved out to a place nearby. Inside there are empty walls (Barbara's huge canvases having gone) and dusty rings on the carpet where pots and vases have been removed. He drives me the short distance to the Hiroko in his new Bentley. 'It's not *new!*' he insists.

A light, clean Japanese lunch with gossip and the latest figures. They are estimating a 50 million gross and this, together with 20 mill for TV rights and a conservative forecast for non-US rentals, should make my points worth 350,000 dollars.

Our lunch is awfully pleasant and friendly and relaxed and we gently remind each other of the things that have made us laugh together. I am able to tell him that Helen and Rachel saw *Wanda* on Tuesday and raved.

Back home via shops for two more interviews – the first is with Anthea Hewison. She's interviewing me for *Here's Health*, but has just trapped her sciatic nerve and has to conduct the entire interview from a prone position.

Tuesday, August 30th

To the BBC for an *80 Days* meeting with Clem and Roger and Anne and Angela. Roger makes one or two suggestions with his stolid, commonsensical approach, symbolised by his pipe. He is worried that we may be top-heavy in the early interviews and that some of them may bite the dust. He also has an idea for me to check out garbage disposal whilst in Venice! (Apparently it's quite spectacular and certainly a different view of the canal life.)

Then to the London Library, where I enrol Will as a member and show him the quiet, woody time-warp of the Reading Room where he will write his extended essay.

In a burst of opportunism, I end up buying, in Jermyn Street, a bag which I hope will be sufficient to take my things round the world. It's made of a strong canvas and leather and when I get it home Helen's immediate reaction is that it's too small. Well, I shall have to practise with it. It's certainly easy to carry about on the shoulder – as Clem advised.

Sunday, September 4th

The *Sunday Times* carries a piece headed 'The Wonder of Wanda', an apparently unsolicited gem of a story about how successful the film is in the US.

Spend much of the morning working through the *80 Days* schedule. Play tennis with Helen later in the afternoon, and win rather competently. Back home for gardening and family phone calls to Ma and the Herberts. We plan on a get-together in London before I leave for my circumnavigation.

Tuesday, September 6th

Reassuringly good night's sleep and feel quite calm as the first day proper of the project that is to occupy almost my entire next year comes round.

Taxi to Stanford's, where I meet my *80* Days film crew. Nigel Meakin, cameraman, short, friendly, straight, agreeable and unpeculiar.

Ron Brown, the sound man, is tubby. He seems most concerned about the plans for accommodation in the boats and the hotels and who's sharing with whom. But he does listen and in between the banter is a considerate and deceptively gentle character.

As we prepare to shoot, a phone call comes through for Ron – 'The Pope wants you for Friday'. He has indeed been asked to Rome, for he is the Pope's favourite sound man and has accompanied the great man on many travels.

What with Roger Mills having just returned from Vietnam and Ron Brown talking of the cookery programme they've just completed in Hanoi, I'm made clearly aware of my own parochialism. Documentaries are like a club, travel documentaries a club within that club.

Thursday, September 8th

Ring Joyce C early to confirm our lunch arrangement for tomorrow. I tell her that I'm enjoying the sunshine. 'Yes, it's a great comfort, isn't it?' she replies with the impeccable delivery of a great tragic actress.

Friday, September 9th

Tristram P arrives to talk over the future of *American Friends*. Innes has read it and, as he puts it, wants to 'pick it up and run with it', which sounds encouraging.

We take Joyce to lunch at Bibendum. I help her up about 20 stairs to the restaurant only to find out there's a lift. The restaurant itself is of striking design. Very big windows, two of them stained glass. Conran furniture – clean, crisp and fairly soulless.

Rex Harrison is dining at another table. He looks like an old dog, his head nodding slightly forwards, food and drink held close to his eyes. An aged man. Ask Joyce if she knows him and she does. In fact she's been to see his show in London – *The Admirable Crichton* – at the Haymarket.

We effect an introduction between Rex and Joyce and as soon as he's with people he animates and transforms from being merely an old man to a charming, humorous and enormously attractive old man.

His wife, a Swiss woman, younger by far than him, is brisk but friendly ... 'Come on, Harrison!' she orders. 'They're just about to order their lunch.' 'We're just holding hands,' says he, gazing down at Joyce, who leans back, smiling up at him. He shakes hands with Tristram and me. 'This is the writer,' says the umpteenth Mrs Harrison. Rex smiles at me warmly. 'She enjoyed it so much, you know.'

Joyce reveals that Rex H was in the American production of her play *Sweet Aloes* and it was a disaster. She wrote under the pseudonym Jay Mallory – professionally it was better to be androgynous at that time. A reviewer in Scotland said of the play ... 'Mr Mallory is a most impertinent young man'. She enjoyed that.

Tuesday, September 13th

Drive to BUPA HQ, where I'm to be filmed having a medical check-up.

The crew have to sit amongst men in dressing gowns and I sense mutiny rumbling. Ron keeps asking why we're filming so much pre-journey material, and especially why we're talking to Alan Whicker.

I'm whisked off into a dressing gown and given the tests. Results similar to last time, except that vision in my right eye is less good. The dread word 'optician' is mentioned – and for the first time in my life not in a sketch!

Friday, September 16th

Out of bed about ten past eight. Feel more relaxed about things now the filming's begun, though big questions like how good will I be at the job, how will we all get on together, and how long will three months seem, remain.

By 10.30 I'm at the Royal Geographical Society in Kensington. It's a pleasant late-summer day and the park looks quietly green and tempting from the windows of the Society.

John Hemming is very welcoming and helpful and enthusiastic. He has been on expeditions to Brazil and has been among the first men ever to make contact with primitive Amazon tribes. He's lost many friends – ironically more killed in road accidents than by man-eating tigers or poison darts.

We film in the library, which is wonderful, well stocked and makes me feel colossally under-prepared. Leave with a big book on Oman under my arm.[1]

Rest of the afternoon at the Health Centre, receiving jabs. Then to the producer Jackie Stoller's fine, eighteenth-century office in Bedford Square, for a get-together with the writers of 'Article For Sale'.

Alan Bennett and Posy Simmonds and Jack R are already there. Alan, with white-socked Hockney-like legs thrust characteristically straight out in front of him. Jack is looking strained and poorly and not surprisingly, as he is going into hospital within a month for a hip replacement.

Carla Lane arrives. She talks about a pigeon she's befriended and about meeting in the vet a man who had brought along his snails.

Posy, slim, white, in a simple black top, is instantly disarming and tells me how when she was a bridesmaid at a wedding at the age of ten she put a tortoise on her head and it peed all over her.

We ask, over smoked salmon and cucumber sandwiches, about things like deadlines and special requirements. 'Will rogering be allowed?' asks Posy, in the tone of a Jane Austen heroine.

Monday, September 19th

To a house in Hambledon, near Marlow, a quite beautifully situated Thames Valley village, enclosed by wooded hills and bordered by misty green meadows. Here I am to do an interview, along with George H, for a programme on ten years of HandMade Films.

The house, largely shuttered, belongs to Harry Hambledon, who owns the village.

George is not at ease and feels that it would have been much better for me to be interviewed alone, then I could say what I really feel about HandMade. This is DO'B's idea and George evidently likes it no more than having to wear black-tie at next Friday's party.

When at last we're through, George tries to persuade me to come over to Friar Park. I tell him I can't as I'm meeting Alan and Barry C for one of our 'Three Yorkshiremen' meals. George tells me to bring them all up

---

1 Oman was to be a key location in *Around the World in 80 Days*. It was to be the place we picked up a dhow to cross the Arabian Sea to India. In the event all plans fell through in Saudi Arabia, and we ended up having to make a considerably longer dhow journey from Dubai.

to Friar Park ... 'We'll get drunk together'. For a moment the idea of adding George and Friar Park to our threesome is tantalisingly bizarre.

Am whisked back to Vasco and Piero's rapidly enough for me to be first there.

Noël Coward is talked of. Alan recalls Coward commenting at a party at which Dudley [Moore] had had the temerity to play the piano ... 'Oh, how clever, he uses the black notes as well.' But Alan found Coward very helpful and charming. They first met when Coward came backstage after *Beyond the Fringe* in New York.

Alan drives us all home in his new Audi. At a traffic light in Kentish Town, a fussy little middle-aged man comes up to the car and demands a lift to Highgate. Alan, momentarily confused, but, ever the good Samaritan, agrees to take him part of the way.

So in gets this red-faced, rather truculent man, who sits there like a character in a bad play or, more to the point, a Python sketch. His presence rather silences our bonhomie and, when Alan drops me at Lamble Street and I see him drive away with Barry and the man in the raincoat sat in the back, I laugh all the way to the front door.

Tuesday, September 20th

A day of considerable pressure on the *80 Days* front.

More gruelling London traffic, then into Lloyd's of London for an interview with the man who, among other things, writes the names of all the shipwrecks in the book. The building is like a huge toy, with the escalators looking like a clockwork motor up the centre. No-one that I talk to likes it very much.

The human inhabitants are at first glance all men, all comfortably covered and impeccably dressed. 2,000 of the well-off classes beavering away. It's like a giant public school at prep.

The analogy is confirmed by a steady stream of bits of paper darts, pellets and rubber-band catapults that drop from the galleries during the interview. 'Oh, you've got off lightly ... it's usually much worse than this,' says my interviewee.

Wednesday, September 21st

To interview Alan Whicker at the Dorchester Hotel. Will life on the voyage be as hectic as this? I hope not.

Whicker's room is approached through a series of valets and PR persons. One would think we were visiting royalty. There is a positive, almost religious, build-up of reverence as we approach the door of his suite. In the first of many coups de théâtre the door is actually only leading to a flight of stairs, off which there is another door at which the great man, greyer in moustache than I expected, welcomes us.

Whicker is fascinated with *Wanda*'s earnings and, by extraordinary coincidence, CNN-TV, which rabbits on from a corner of the room, suddenly shows a familiar face. It's me and my perm, illustrating the movie charts of the week – which show *Wanda* still number three in America.

All this serves to keep my end up, which is what you feel you have to do with Whicker. He is very much the Godfather. The way he tells his stories, knowing he's keeping everyone waiting, indicates that he's used to having things his own way. The suite, with the view over the park, must be one of the most expensive in London, and it's coming off our production budget.

Whicker is sharp, alert, dapper – competitive – generous with advice and with his time. Oozing charm as we leave. Before we go he talks about Roger M – 'a strange man', 'a man of ferocious intellect'. Whicker's tie and blazer are as important to him as Roger's lack of them are to Roger.

Thursday, September 22nd: Southwold

Listen to the BBC's 'Get By in Italian' tapes in the car. Whicker was quite adamant about what to do in an emergency – 'Don't try and speak the language, you probably won't be able to anyway. I just use Britishness, it never fails.'

Feel weighed down by all the work I've to do and after lunch set myself up at the kitchen table with the telephone. The oppressiveness of the phone calls and the interviews for 'No. 27' and so on seem worse as I see my mother looking very much frailer than before.

She cannot sit up on a dining chair for long as her coccyx aches. She says the doctor does nothing. I ask her what she wants to be done – 'Oh, you can't *do* anything ... it's arthritis.' The skin on her thin little arms hangs down in folds. I suppose I've never seen anyone of nearly 85 so closely before, but her body, bowed over by her spinal curve, seems to be so inadequate for the job. But she remains cheerful and is determined to be good company and she potters around and cooks and reads and looks at the photos I've brought.

After supper I have to work again – honing the HandMade speech.

Later walk through deserted Southwold to the North Sea. I shall have been on such an unimaginable adventure by the time I next see it again. Walk to the edge of the waves, which are building up noisily in anticipation of a windy night.

Friday, September 23rd: Southwold–London

I feel happier and more confident about Ma's condition as we eat our lunch. She has rationalised my absence on the trip and there is no longer a hint of a moan. As we part she says 'It's a school term, that's all . . . just a school term.'

The still-blustery wind keeps her from coming into the street to say goodbye. She waves from the door. Make a mental note that at some time I shall have to get angry with the builder over the door and the rapidly crumbling window sill.

So little Ma recedes and I set myself to the hurdles that remain today. To the doctor's for a double gamma globulin jab and home at five.

Then back to the speech. Feel hot and rushed – the paraphernalia of the journey lies on the floor of my room. Lists of things to do lie accusingly on the desk. A scotch and ice calms the racing system and at seven I'm at last finished with the speech.

The dinner [celebrating ten years of HandMade films] is at the Old House at Shepperton and is like a much jollier, friendlier version of the BAFTA Awards.

I find myself on the programme under Master of Ceremonies, and beside 'Music: Carl Perkins and his band'.

Just before I go up, Michael White cautions 'Take it slowly'. The opening jokes about this being HandMade's latest film are well received – the talk of Denis not being able to do co-production because the lift at Cadogan Square is too small, hits home, and from then on I know I shall have a good ride.

At the end everyone is very complimentary. Denis tells a long and only moderately funny dirty joke in reply and George heckles him unmercifully.

George presents me with a gift for mastering the ceremonies – it's one of his old Oscars with my name scribbled on a luggage label and stuck across the base.

Much fun later on and a lot of jawing. Had meant to get home early, but it's four o'clock before head hits pillow.

Saturday, September 24th

A wet, warm day – straggly low storm cloud and strong winds. In *Variety Wanda* is the No. 1 grosser for the first time.

Gradually assemble a workroom full of bits and pieces needed on voyage. Find, after all the preparation, that I've forgotten simple things like toothpaste.

Mary, Ed, Helen and I escape to L'Escargot for a last meal.

Lots of last minute hitches, including the small accompanying bag being rather small and it has to be substituted, but considering I have less to set off with for 80 days round the world than I normally take for two weeks in the States, I'm quite pleased.

To bed about two o'clock and to sleep an hour or so before dawn. There's no turning back now.

Index

'This is an entertaining and at times deeply moving read. With nearly two decades of recent diaries still untapped, we may confidently sit back and wait for more. And not, I hope, for something completely different'
Mail on Sunday

'Palin's style is so fluid, and his sincerity so palpable, that it is often easy to underestimate just how talented he is as a comedian, a broadcaster and a writer ... [the diaries] are just too good and he is too modest'
Sunday Express

'If anyone writes a diary purely for the joy of it, it is Michael Palin ... This combination of niceness, with his natural volubility, creates Palin's expansiveness'
David Baddiel, *The Times*

'His showbiz observations are so absorbing ... Palin is an elegant and engaging writer'
Guardian

'Palin describes the uncertain birth and astonishing success of the Python phenomenon, alongside his own revealing observations on success, love, the death of his father and the joys of family life'
Daily Mail

'Palin's steady eye, contemplative bent and instinct for honest appraisal make him the perfect chronicler of a frequently insane period which saw the Monty Python team become the most celebrated comedians in the world'
Time Out

'A real delight to read'
Saga Magazine

'A slow burn, revealing its pleasures only gradually, and allowing readers the warm glow of hindsight denied its writer ... This book will make the perfect present for those comedy obsessives of a certain age, who will know exactly what it is long before they have unwrapped it'
Spectator

'A wealth of fascinating stuff about Monty Python'
Independent

'Accomplished ... If Palin's comic genius is a given, this is a more rounded portrait of the decade which saw the Pythons become icons. Our favourite TV explorer shows us the workings of an unstoppable machine'
Daily Express

MICHAEL PALIN is a scriptwriter, comedian, novelist, television presenter, actor and playwright. He established his reputation with *Monty Python's Flying Circus* and *Ripping Yarns*. His work also includes several films with Monty Python, as well as *The Missionary*, *A Private Function*, *A Fish Called Wanda*, *American Friends* and *Fierce Creatures*. His television credits include two films for the BBC's *Great Railway Journeys*, the plays *East of Ipswich* and *Number 27*, and Alan Bleasdale's *GBH*.

In 2006 the first volume of his diaries, *1969–1979: The Python Years,* spent several weeks on the bestseller lists. He has also written books to accompany his seven very successful travel series: *Around the World in 80 Days* (an updated edition of which was published in 2008, twenty years later), *Pole to Pole*, *Full Circle*, *Hemingway Adventure*, *Sahara*, *Himalaya* and *New Europe*. Most have been No. 1 bestsellers and *Himalaya* was No. 1 for 11 weeks. He is the author of a number of children's stories, the play *The Weekend* and the novel *Hemingway's Chair*. Visit his website at www.palinstravels.co.uk.

MICHAEL PALIN
DIARIES 1969-1979

The Python Years

WEIDENFELD & NICOLSON

A W&N PAPERBACK

First published in Great Britain in 2006
by Weidenfeld & Nicholson
This paperback edition published in 2007
by Weidenfeld & Nicolson,
an imprint of Orion Books Ltd,
Orion House, 5 Upper St Martin's Lane,
London WC2H 9EA

An Hachette UK company

5 7 9 10 8 6 4

A CIP catalogue record for this book
is available from the British Library.

ISBN: 978-1-7802-2901-0

Typeset by Input Data Services Ltd,
Bridgwater, Somerset

Printed in Great Britain by Clays Ltd, St Ives plc

The Orion Publishing Group's policy is to use papers that
are natural, renewable and recyclable products and
made from wood grown in sustainable forests. The logging
and manufacturing processes are expected to conform to
the environmental regulations of the country of origin.

www.orionbooks.co.uk

For my mother and father

Contents

List of illustrations

On pages xx and xxiii of the preliminary pages:

As Ethelred the Unready in *Complete and Utter History of Britain*, 1969 [1]
MP in Hampstead pub [1]

Section One:

Edward Palin, MP's great-grandfather [1]
Edward Palin, MP's father [1]
Edward 'Ted' and Mary Palin [1]
With Ian Davidson at a Python rehearsal, 1970 [2]
At a charity football match, 1970 [2]
The Pythons in Germany, 1971 [1]
With Hazel Pethig and Eric Idle at Norwich Castle, 1971 [1]
With Eric Idle, 1972 [1]
With Ian MacNaughton, Windsor, 1972 [1]
Anne Gibbins with William and Tom Palin, 1972 [1]
Cathy Gibbins with Tarquin, Abbotsley [1]
With Helen at a local fete, 1972 [1]
With Tom at home, 1973 [1]
Edward and Mary Palin, 1975 [1]
'Dead Parrot' sketch with John Cleese, 1973 [1]
Front cover of the *Radio Times*, August 14th, 1973 [1]
With Eric Idle and Mark Forstater on location for *The Holy Grail*, 1974 [3]
Cast and crew of Holy Grail on location for *The Holy Grail*, 1974 [3]
The Pythons on location for *The Holy Grail*, 1974 [3]
With Graham Chapman, Terry Gilliam and Terry Jones on stage, 1975 [2]
With Terry Jones, 1975 [1]

1 From the author's private albums
2 John Ferro Sims
3 Drew Mara
4 Carl Samrock
5 Camera Press (Lionel Cherrvault)
6 Edie Baskin

Who's Who in the Diaries 1969–1979

Certain names recur at various points during the diaries. Here is a rough list of those who make regular appearances.

FAMILY

Edward (Ted) Palin born July 1900
Mary Palin (née Ovey) born January 1904
Retired from Sheffield to Reydon, near Southwold, Suffolk in December 1966
Children:
    Angela born 1934, died 1987
    Michael born 1943

Angela married Veryan Herbert in 1958
Children:
    Jeremy, born 1960
    Camilla, born 1962
    Marcus, born 1963

Michael married Helen Gibbins, born 1942, on April 16th, 1966
Children:
    Thomas (Tom), born 1968
    William, born 1970
    Rachel, born 1975

Helen's family:
Father, **Dearman Gibbins**, died 1963
Mother, **Anne Gibbins**, born 1913
Elder sister, **Mary**, born 1940. Married **Edward Burd** in 1964.
    Daughter, **Catherine**.
Younger sister, **Cathy**, born 1945

FRIENDS AND COLLEAGUES

The Stuart-Harris family. Lived next door to the Palins in Sheffield. Father, Charles, was a doctor and became Professor of Medicine at Sheffield University. Mother, Marjorie. Graham, the eldest son, married to Margot, and MP's oldest friend. Daughter Susan is a psychologist and younger son, Robin, also a doctor. Married to Barbara, a New Zealander.

Robert Hewison. Contemporary of MP at Brasenose College Oxford, 1962-5. Fellow cabaret performer and writer. Author of a series of books on modern cultural history, expert on John Ruskin.

Terry Jones. Met MP at Oxford in 1963. First performed together in the Oxford Revue, Edinburgh Festival 1964. Wrote together for television on *The Frost Report*, 1966. Married Alison Telfer, 1969. Children: Sally and Bill.

John Cleese, married to Connie Booth. Separated in mid-1970s.

Eric Idle, married to Lyn Ashley. Separated in mid-1970s.

Terry Gilliam, married to Python make-up supremo Maggie Weston.

Graham Chapman, lived with David Sherlock, later adopted John Tomiczek.

Ian and Anthea Davidson. Met MP at Oxford. Encouraged him to perform in revue and gave him early work at the BBC. A writer and director and occasional Python performer.

Ranji and Rolf Veling. Ranji is a friend from Helen Palin's teaching days. She is Sri Lankan, he is Dutch.

Simon and Phillida Albury. Simon met MP after Oxford in 1965. Television journalist, producer and gospel music fan.

Graeme Garden. Contemporary of Eric Idle at Cambridge. Writer-performer who worked with MP on *Twice a Fortnight* (1967) and *Broaden Your Mind* (1968). First wife Liz and daughter Sally were frequent visitors.

Bill Oddie. Cambridge contemporary of Eric's. Lived nearby. Also worked with MP on *Twice a Fortnight*. Regular source of football tickets.

Tim Brooke-Taylor. Friend and provider of work for MP on *Broaden Your Mind.*

PYTHON'S EXTENDED FAMILY

Ian MacNaughton. Director of TV series and first film *And Now for Something Completely Different.*

Eke Ott. Became the second Mrs MacNaughton.

André Jacquemin. Recording engineer with whom MP went into business as Redwood Studios. Besides being official Python sound genius, André, with partner Dave Howman, wrote and recorded songs for Python and *Ripping Yarns.*

Michael Henshaw. MP's first accountant, from 1966 to 1974.

Anne Henshaw. Michael's wife, who took over Python affairs as de facto manager in 1974.

Barry Took. Marty Feldman's co-writer and the man who helped push Python to the BBC.

Carol Cleveland. Started as glamour girl casting but her talent for well-played, well-timed comedy made her Python's favourite real woman. She appeared in the films and stage shows as well as the TV series.

Neil Innes. Musician. First worked with MP, TJ and Eric I. on *Do Not Adjust Your Set.* Indispensable to the Python stage shows. Neil also appeared in *Monty Python and the Holy Grail* and *Monty Python's Life of Brian* as well as helping Idle create the Rutles.

Hazel Pethig. Costume designer from episode one of the Monty Python TV series through to *Monty Python and the Meaning of Life,* thirteen years later.

Julian Doyle. Editor, cameraman, who could turn his hand to any part of the film-making process. Indispensable part of both Python and Gilliam films.

Geoffrey Strachan. Hugely supportive editor at Methuen who encouraged Python to go into print. Also published the *Ripping Yarn* books.

Tony Stratton-Smith. What Geoffrey Strachan was to Python books, Tony Stratton-Smith was to Python records. Endlessly encouraging founder/proprietor of Charisma Records, who enthusiastically indulged most of Python's whims and even named a racehorse of his 'Monty Python'.

Jill Foster. MP and TJ's agent at Fraser & Dunlop.

John Gledhill. Agent at the Roger Hancock office who looked after Python affairs until 1974.

Mark Forstater. Producer of *Monty Python and the Holy Grail.*

John Goldstone. Producer of *Monty Python and the Holy Grail* and *Monty Python's Life of Brian.*

AT THE BBC

John Howard Davies. Child actor who played Oliver Twist at the age of nine, director of three earliest episodes of *Monty Python*, then Head of Comedy during the later *Ripping Yarns.*

James (Jimmy) Gilbert. Producer/director of *The Frost Report* – MP and TJ's first TV writing break. Head of Comedy in the latter days of Python, then Head of Light Entertainment Department at the time of *Ripping Yarns.*

Duncan Wood. Head of Comedy during first three Python series.

Bill Cotton Jnr. Head of Light Entertainment.

Terry Hughes. Director of the hugely popular Ronnie Barker and Ronnie Corbett series. Producer/director of first three *Ripping Yarns*, until elevated to Head of Variety.

Jim Franklin. Special effects expert on *The Frost Report* who took over the production and direction of the next four *Ripping Yarns* after Terry Hughes was promoted.

Alan J.W. Bell. Produced and directed last two *Ripping Yarns* – 'Golden Gordon' and 'Whinfrey's Last Case'.

Mark Shivas and Richard Broke. Drama producers who backed TJ and MP and encouraged them to write *Secrets* (1973).

IN AMERICA

Nancy Lewis. Publicist for Buddah Records who almost single-handedly fought to get Python accepted in America, and became their US manager.

Ina Lee Meibach. Lawyer in New York who organised Python's battle against ABC TV in 1975.

Al Levinson. Writer, teacher and dramaturge for American Public Theatre who became MP's good friend and regular correspondent in the late 1970s. Lived in New York and Sag Harbor, with his wife Eve.

Lorne Michaels. Producer of *Saturday Night Live.*

Acknowledgements

I must thank my editor Ion Trewin for reducing mountains to molehills, and Michael Dover at Weidenfeld & Nicolson for his unfailing encouragement. Steve Abbott, my agent, has been a model of sympathy and naked commercial brutality and my wife and family, lured on by curiosity perhaps, have been trusting, realistic and supportive.

The Monty Python team fills these pages and reading through the material made me realise how intricately our lives intertwined. Our differences are not glossed over here but neither is the very close bond of friendship that links, or in Graham Chapman's case, linked us all together.

Last, but certainly not least, I owe enormous thanks to Kath Du Prez who typed up over a million words and not only lived to tell the tale, but more than anyone, convinced me that this might be a tale worth telling.

MP

As Ethelred the *Unready, Complete and Utter History of Britain, 1969.* 'Well you won't be doing any more of those,' John predicted, accurately as it turned out.

Introduction

I HAVE KEPT A DIARY, more or less continuously, since April 1969. I was twenty-five years old then, married for three years and with a six-month-old son. I had been writing comedy with Terry Jones since leaving university in 1965 and, in addition to contributing material to *The Frost Report, Marty Feldman, The Two Ronnies* and anyone else who'd take us, we had written and performed two series of *Do Not Adjust Your Set* (with Eric Idle, David Jason and Denise Coffey) and six episodes of *The Complete and Utter History of Britain*. After the last one went out in early 1969, John Cleese rang me.

'Well, you won't be doing any more of those,' he predicted, accurately as it turned out, 'so why don't we think of something new?'

So it was that, quite coincidentally, Monty Python came into my life, only a month or so after the diary.

This was far from my first stab at keeping a regular account of how I spent my time. At the age of eleven I resolved to record each day of the year, and kept it up until the 18th of July. The style was staccato, and looking back now, quite surreal.

Letts Schoolboy's Diary, January, 1955
Tuesday, 18th. Big blow-up in prayers. Had easy prep. Listened to Goon Show. Got sore hand.
Monday 24th. Had fight with (form) VR. Got hit on nose. Did two sets of prep. Jolly hard! Cabbage for lunch. Watched TV.

At regular intervals I tried to resume the habit, but as I grew older keeping a diary seemed an irksome duty, like writing to one's parents, and anyway, there was far too much going on in my teens and early twenties to have either the time or the inclination to write it all down. Yet there remained a nagging feeling that it was a small failure to let life go by without in some way documenting it. The feeling persisted as I grew older. All I lacked was the will-power.

Then, one night, after a meal at the house with my wife Helen and Terry Gilliam, who happened to have dropped by, I found I'd run out of cigarettes (at the time I had a twenty-a-day habit). I looked for a half-crown piece for the slot machine up the road, but could find nothing. I rifled through drawers, flung open cupboards and slid my hand down the back of sofas with increasing desperation.

'You're an addict,' warned Terry.

I smiled wanly. 'I'm not an addict, I would quite like one last cigarette before bed, that's all.'

'Look at you,' Terry persisted, as I began rummaging in ever more unlikely sources, in the laundry basket and amongst the marmalade, 'you need your fix!'

'Look,' I hissed, tipping up the shoe-cleaning box and forensically scrutinising the contents, 'I don't have to have a cigarette. I never have to have a cigarette, it's just a small pleasure, all right?'

'Not if you can't sleep without one.'

The only way to face down these taunts was to deny myself the single thing I wanted most, a nice firm pull on a freshly lit, deliriously soothing, pungently bracing tube of tightly packed tobacco coaxed from a brand-new packet of Piccadilly Tipped. And that's where the will-power came in. For the first time in many years I went to bed without a cigarette.

Not only did I survive without the second most satisfying smoke of the day, next morning I survived without the first most satisfying smoke of the day and I never bought a packet of cigarettes again.

So cocky was I that I looked around for other giants to wrestle. As it happened I had, for the first time in years, some free time on my hands. My writing partner Terry Jones was away and I had arranged to travel to Switzerland for a few days with Helen and the baby. Why not have another crack at the diary? It would keep my newly liberated fingers occupied and writing about my post-nicotine lifestyle could only strengthen my resolve to keep it that way. I bought a Ryman's reporter's notepad, smoothed down the front page, wrote the day's date across the top and underlined it. And I've been doing the same thing most mornings of my life for the past thirty-seven years.

There are times when I've resented the whole process, when I've felt lumpen, dull and inarticulate, when detail has slipped away and the whole exercise has seemed completely pointless. But the longer I've kept the diary the more inconceivable it has been to abandon it. It's become an effective and tenacious parasite, mutating over the years into something as germane to my life as an arm or a leg.

The motivation for keeping the diaries remains the same as it always was, to keep a record of how I fill the days. Nothing more complicated than that. Though this inevitably involves emotional reactions, I've never treated the diary as a confessional. Once I've noted the day's events, usually the next morning, there's little time left for soul-searching.

The perfect, well-crafted, impeccably balanced entry persistently eludes me. Prejudices bob to the surface, anger crackles, judgements fall over each other, huffing and puffing. Opinions and interpretations are impulsive, inconsistent and frequently contradictory. But I'm not sure if that matters. After all that's where a daily diary differs from autobiography or memoir. It is an antidote to hindsight.

It seals the present moment and preserves it from the tidying process of context, perspective, analysis and balance. It becomes history, but quite unselfcon-

'A nice firm pull on a freshly lit, deliriously soothing, pungently bracing tube of tightly packed tobacco, coaxed from a brand-new packet of Piccadilly Tipped.'

sciously. What proves to be important over a long period is not always what a diarist will identify at the time. For the historians' sake I should probably have noted every detail of the birth of Monty Python, but it seemed far more important to me to record the emergence of my new family than the faltering steps of a comedy series that would probably last no more than two years. And that, I feel, is as it should be. Legends are not created by diaries, though they can be destroyed by them.

This selection is culled from thirty-eight hand-written secretarial notebooks amounting to some five times the volume of material reproduced here. The early entries sit a little awkwardly as I search for a voice and a style that relies on more than lists of events. My reward for perseverance, often in the face of tempting discouragement, is to see the diary bed itself in and slowly begin to tell a story, with regular characters, a narrative, and a sense of continuity.

In the course of these diaries I grow up, my family grows up and Monty Python grows up. It was a great time to be alive.

MICHAEL PALIN
London, January 2006

Michael Palin is not just one of Britain's foremost comedy character actors, whose inventive genius and astonishing versatility were vividly demonstrated in his widely acclaimed *Ripping Yarns* series; he also talks a lot.
Yap, yap, yap, he goes, all day long *and* through the night, twenty-three to the dozen, the ground littered with the hind legs of donkeys, till you believe it is not possible, simply not possible for him to go on any longer, but he *does*. He must be the worst man in the world to take on a commando raid. You might as well take a large radiogram with the volume turned up. On and on, hour after hour, tiring the sun with talking and sending him down the sky, Michael chats, quips, fantasises, reminisces, commiserates, encourages, plans, discusses and elaborates. Then, some nights, when everyone else has gone to bed, he goes home and *writes up a diary*.

JOHN CLEESE
Publicity biography for Life of Brian, *1979*

1969

Though the first entry of all was April 17th, 1969, I've opened the diary on the first day of Python filming. All the entries were written at my house in Oak Village, north London, except where otherwise noted.

Tuesday, July 8th

Today Bunn Wackett Buzzard Stubble and Boot[1] came into being, with about five minutes of film shot around Ham House. It was exhilarating to wake up to the first day's filming of a new show, especially as the sun was streaming down the village and, despite it being only 7.00, I decided to travel to the BBC on the bus and tube. Sure enough, the clouds came up as I put my foot outside the door, and this April-like weather pattern of showers and sunshine was repeated during the day. We arrived at Ham House about 9.30.

It is a Jacobean house, of pleasing proportions, very restrained, but in a more homely and welcoming way than a classical building. A line of Greco/Roman busts in oval niches along the line of walls leading up to the house give you something to remember it by. We were filming Queen Victoria's slapstick film with Gladstone, and the beautifully kept lawn and flower beds at the back of the house provided just the right kind of formality to play off against.

In the afternoon the changes in light from sudden brightness to dullness caused us to slow down a little, but by 6.00 we had quite a chunk of 'Queen Victoria and Her Gardener' and 'Bicycle Repairman' done, and it had been a very good and encouraging first day's shooting.

---

1 The name of a fictional forward line from a John Cleese soccer monologue, and the current name for what was later to become *Monty Python's Flying Circus*. Among other titles we tried unsuccessfully to get past the BBC were 'Whither Canada?', 'Ow! It's Colin Plint', 'A Horse, a Spoon and a Bucket', 'The Toad Elevating Moment', 'The Algy Banging Hour' and 'Owl Stretching Time'. Increasingly irritated, the BBC suggested the Flying Circus bit and we eventually compromised by adding the name Monty Python.

Wednesday, July 9th

Arrived at TV Centre by 10.00, and was driven in a BBC car, together with John [Cleese], Graham [Chapman] and Terry [Jones], out beyond Windsor and Eton to a tiny church at Boveney. Dressed to the hilt as a young Scottish nobleman of the Walter Scott era, I was able to cash a cheque at a bank in the Uxbridge Road, without the cashier batting an eyelid.

Thursday, July 10th, Bournemouth

Up at 7.15; Graham C called for me in a mini-cab; we got to Waterloo in plenty of time to catch the 8.30 to Bournemouth. We had breakfast on the train. At Bournemouth we were met by a mini-van and driven to the Durley Dean Hotel, where we were to stay that night. I don't think words can fully convey the depression that swept over me as I entered the Durley Dean. From outside it was bad enough – a five storey red-brick block of indeterminate date, but I should guess 1920s – it looked completely ordinary, if anything institutional. Inside there was firstly a dimness, secondly a pervading smell of gravy and thirdly a total lack of any colour – in the carpets, the lino in the passages, the paintwork in the rooms – everywhere the management had opted for the colour most like stale vomit.

One saw a few guests, mostly elderly, about half of them crippled, wandering about, as if looking for someone to tell them what to do. What with the grey weather, the lack of much to do (it was mainly Terry's 'Changing on the Beach' film) and the gradual realisation that all Bournemouth was as drab and colourless as the Durley Dean, I felt very low all morning.

After lunch we filmed on, collecting crowds of people watching Terry take his trousers down. Graham and I, finishing early, went back to the Durley Dean. The depression I had felt in the morning was lifted slightly by the sun shining into my room, and plenty of hot water for my bath. After that Graham and I drank at the hotel bar until the rest of the unit returned. I made the mistake of telling the barman that Graham was a doctor, and soon he was telling Graham about his insomnia and his sweating and his bad feet.

John C arrived from London and, together with Graham, a lady designer, a lady extra, a focus puller and one or two others, we sampled the nightlife of Bournemouth. We ended up in the Highcliffe Hotel night-club where, for 7/6 each we enjoyed 45 minutes sitting in dimness with a drink, whilst the band had their break. When they arrived back (three middle-aged men, looking like failed Sam Costa,[1] who played 'Fly Me to the Moon' in quite a forgettable way), Graham asked them to play 'Happy Birthday' for John Cleese (it wasn't his birthday at all). But the amplification was so bad that we couldn't hear the announcement and the point of the joke was lost.

Friday, July 11th, Bournemouth

Drive over to Shell Bay, beyond Poole, along a flag-lined route – the Queen is visiting Poole today.

In the afternoon filmed some very bizarre pieces, including the death of Genghis Khan, and two men carrying a donkey past a Butlins redcoat, who later gets hit on the head with a raw chicken by a man from the previous sketch, who borrowed the chicken from a man in a suit of armour. All this we filmed in the 80° sunshine, with a small crowd of holiday-makers watching.

We finished at tea-time and were driven to take our leave of Durley Dean and catch the 5.56 train back to London. On account of an unofficial signalmen's strike, the train took two and a half hours to get to London and left Bournemouth half an hour late. But John, Graham, Terry and myself took a First Class compartment and talked about Shows 4 and 5 and decided that we really had an excellent week filming. Ian Mac[2] is marvellous – the best director to work for and, with a fellow Scots cameraman, Jimmy Balfour, he really gets on with it.

Back in London 9.00 – taxi from Waterloo, end of one of the great days.

Wednesday, July 16th

Filming today in Barnes. The weather continues to be excellent – if anything a little too hot – 80°+ all day.

After lunch we watched Apollo 11 blastoff, on its trip to the moon.

Ended up the afternoon prancing about in mouse-skins for a

1 Sam Costa was a heavily moustachioed TV presenter, actor, singer and DJ.
2 Ian MacNaughton produced and directed all the Python TV shows, apart from the first three studio recordings and a few days of film, which were directed by John Howard Davies.

documentary about people who like to dress up as mice. That really made the sweat pour down the chest.

To the many life-changing experiences around this time – fatherhood, quitting smoking, keeping a diary – must be added the alarming discovery that teeth I'd always thought of as glowingly healthy were found to be precariously attached to considerably less healthy gums – a legacy of poor care and too many sweeties in my misspent youth. Treatment involved a series of surgical procedures in which the gum was opened, cleaned up and stitched together again. These were undertaken by Mr Robin Powell, a robust Australian periodontist who once likened it to working on his rockery at home.

Saturday, July 19th

Up early to go to Mr Powell for the fourth and last of my dental operations. I was at his surgery by 9.10. He hadn't arrived, but the nurse sat me down and gave me her *Daily Telegraph* to read. He arrived about ten minutes later, cheerfully announcing that he'd had a late night and a lot of drinks, however he said his hand was steady. It needed to be, for this was the most difficult of all the operations. One tooth was obviously more badly infected than he had expected. I even had to go into the next-door surgery during the operation so that he could use the extra-high-speed drill there. He also took out one of the roots of the tooth, and also a nerve, which gave quite a lot of pain. Mr Powell kept apologising, but I felt at least that I was getting my money's worth. I was finally patched up at 10.10 and drove off to the TV Centre to have a look at the week's rushes

After the rushes, made the final organisational decisions about the Great Picnic, which Gilliam had suggested a couple of days ago and which was now becoming reality. Helen, Thomas[1] and myself, Graham and David,[2] John and Connie, Terry G and his girlfriend and Alison and Terry J set out in our various cars for Henley – loaded with food and wine. It was a very cloudy day, but warm, and along the motorway a patch of sun made us seem less foolish. We drove out to Remenham church, which I had chosen from pot-luck as being a convenient place for an idyllic river-

1 Our son, born in October 1968, so nine months old. The only Python child at the time.
2 David Sherlock, Graham's partner. They'd met in Ibiza in 1966.

side picnic. Everything could at this moment have gone hopelessly wrong – the sky was glowering, it was 2.30 and everyone was getting hungry – but Remenham proved to be just the right kind of place – through a gate and we were walking along a flat bank of pastureland with the Thames flowing beside us. We picnicked opposite Temple Island – ham off the bone, paté, salad, several kinds of cheeses, cherries, apples and strawberries, beer sausage, smoked pork, red and white wine and coffee – it was a wonderful spread. Thomas scavenged amongst the food, and was to be seen eating vast chunks of French bread on and off for about an hour. Everyone, Gilliam especially, became infected by picnic madness and there was a hopping relay race and a lot of fighting. The generous doses of wine numbed any possible after-effects of my gingivectomy.

Thomas stood without holding on today.

Monday, July 21st

At 3.00 this morning I woke Helen, and we both watched as the first live television pictures from the moon showed us a rather indistinct piece of ladder, then a large boot, and finally, at 3.56, Neil Armstrong became the first man to set foot on the lunar surface. He said the ground beneath his feet (I almost wrote 'the earth beneath his feet') was composed mainly of dust – for a moment one felt he was in danger of falling into a kind of quicksand – but soon he was reassuringly prancing about and telling us that the one-sixth gravity conditions were less hazardous than in simulation.

The extraordinary thing about the evening was that, until 3.56 a.m. when Armstrong clambered out of the spaceship and activated the keyhole camera, we had seen no space pictures at all, and yet ITV had somehow contrived to fill ten hours with a programme devoted to the landing.

To bed at 5.00, with the image in my mind of men in spacesuits doing kangaroo hops and long, loping walks on the moon, in front of a strange spidery object, just like the images in my mind after reading Dan Dare in the old *Eagle* comics – only this time it's true. A lot of science fiction is suddenly science fact.

Thursday, July 24th

Met with Ian and the two Terrys at the BBC. We listened to some possible title music – finally selected Sousa's march 'The Liberty Bell' from a

Grenadier Guards LP. There's something about brass band music that appeals to me very strongly. Probably it's all to do with my subliminal desire to march along whistling national songs. It's very difficult to associate brass band music with any class of people. Most enthusiasts perhaps come from north of the Trent working class, but then of course it has high patrician status and support from its part in ceremonial. So in the end it is a brass band march which we've chosen – because it creates such immediate atmosphere and rapport, without it being calculated or satirical or 'fashionable'.

An hour is spent from 5.30–6.30 watching colour pictures of Apollo 11's return to earth. Again how old-fashioned a) the landing (they landed upside down), b) the scrubbing of the spacecraft and the space-suits, in case they are carrying deadly lunar germs, c) the whole business of helicopter rescues, appears. One is almost conscious of the laughter and amazement of viewers in thirty years' time, as they watch film of the first men on the moon returning home.

Friday, August 1st

The days seem to merge one into another without particular distinction. It's tending to feel like that with the writing at the moment. We have four shows completed, but apart from the two weeks' filming in July, there has been no feeling yet of concerted effort on behalf of the show (now, incidentally, renamed *Monty Python's Flying Circus*). Partly because John and Graham have fingers in a lot of other pies – especially their film, *The Rise and Rise of Michael Rimmer*.[1] However, it seems that the next two weeks will be much harder work. At least, there is some kind of urgency. August 30th is our first recording date and we have another week's filming starting on the 18th. Time is getting shorter. But at least it's nothing like the hectic pace which we were starting on this time last year with the first *Frost on Sundays*. Accordingly, I've had much more time at home and, as I write this, I'm in the sitting room with Helen sewing and Thomas being fascinated by the sewing machine.

Terry took Helen and myself and Quick and Ken, Philip John,

[1] Directed by Kevin Billington, executive producer David Frost, it came out in 1970. Surely the only comedy in which Peter Cook and Harold Pinter appear in the acting credits?

Gerald[1] and a girl from Germany whom Terry and Al had met on holiday in Crete, to the Hiroko Japanese restaurant in Wigmore Street.

Before entering our room we had to remove our shoes. Here Ken and myself made what I expected to be the first of many faux pas. After taking our shoes off, we noticed some oriental style slippers nearby and presumed that we ought to put these on in true Japanese style. Grumbling that they were all too small, we eventually selected two pairs and were tottering to our room when one of the Japanese 'attendants' – it wouldn't be quite right to call them 'waitresses' – stopped us excitedly and told us to take off the shoes. Then we realised the awful truth – that they belonged to people already eating there.

Sunday, August 3rd

John C rang up in the morning to ask if I felt like working in the afternoon, so I ended up in Knightsbridge about 3.00. It's funny, but when one has written in partnership almost exclusively for the last three years, as Terry and I have done, and I suppose John and Graham as well, it requires quite an adjustment to write with somebody different. Terry and I know each other's way of working so well now – exactly what each one does best, what each one thinks, what makes each of us laugh – that when I sat down to write with John there was a moment's awkwardness, slight embarrassment, but it soon loosened up as we embarked on a saga about Hitler (Hilter), Von Ribbentrop (Ron Vibbentrop) and Himmler (Bimmler) being found in a seaside guest house. We do tend to laugh at the same things – and working with John is not difficult – but there are still differences in our respective ways of thinking, not about comedy necessarily, which mean perhaps that the interchange of ideas was a little more cautious than it is with Terry. However, by the time I left, at 7.15, we had almost four minutes' worth of sketch written.

Tuesday, August 5th

Another workday at Eric's.[2] A good morning, but then a rather winey lunch at Pontevecchio in Brompton Road. That is the trouble with

1 Diana Quick and Ken Cranham – actors, friends, neighbours of Terry J, and, at the time, an item. Philip John was a work colleague of TJ's botanist girlfriend Alison Telfer. Gerald was a friend of theirs.
2 Eric Idle.

working at John or Eric's – both are surrounded by a very good selection of restaurants, temptingly easy to go to, especially after a good morning's work, but debilitating and expensive.

Wednesday, August 6th

A thought struck me as I saw a man in an open-necked shirt walking up Oak Village – and that was that, for at least twelve successive years, the first half of August has meant Palin family holidays – either at Sheringham in Norfolk or, later, at Southwold.

I have some wonderful memories of those holidays. Of sitting in the lee of the hill above Sheringham where the golf course was and watching the steam train pulling away towards Weybourne. Of enormous games of tennis on the beach with the Sanders family, of plastic macs and wet days (they do seem to be predominant), of sitting excitedly in the back of the Austin 10 (which we inherited when Granny Ovey[1] died in 1951) and the yearly thrill of seeing a pebble-house, and of seeing the sea for the first time.

Now August 6th has no special significance, it's another working day – but it's a token of the enormous difference between my life and that of my father or most people in the country. I have no fixed timetable. I may go away any time of the year, for any length of time, at little more than two weeks' notice. This degree of unpredictability is beyond the sphere of most people – it is an awful thought how regular people's lives contrive to be.

On this August 6th 1969 I am at home. Terry and I are determined to make this a really productive day, to make up for the semi-productive, rather frustrating Monday and Tuesday. We work on till 8.00, finishing our big 'Them' saga. An 85% success day. Very satisfying – and we really worked well together.

Thursday, August 7th

Drove down to Camberwell Grove (where Terry was living) at lunchtime. Lunched with Terry and D Quick, who has a week's break from filming *Christ Recrucified* for BBC2. In the afternoon we worked rather slowly –

1 My grandmother, Rachel Ovey, from whom we inherited our first fridge as well as our first car.

lots of diversions, e.g. Terry's telescope, which he has bought for his father's birthday, a film which Terry bought that morning, and finally a walk. It seems at last, after almost a year of waiting, that Terry and Alison may have got the house they made an offer for in Grove Park, Camberwell. We walked past it – tall, solidly suburban, in a quiet road on top of the first hill you come to going south from Westminster.

In 1966 my parents (Edward 'Ted' Palin and Mary Palin, née Ovey) retired to the village of Reydon, just outside Southwold in Suffolk. Southwold had already played a big part in my life, for it was on the beach here in 1959 that I first summoned up the courage to talk to a tall, slim, mischievous-looking girl called Helen Gibbins. This led to a holiday romance, which led to marriage, in 1966, and birth of son Thomas (now known to everyone as Tom). The different names I use for my father show, I suppose, how my relationship with him changed as I grew older and the children came along. In these early entries he is, as often as not, 'Daddy', as he had been throughout my childhood, but I was also trying out the more formal (and grown-up) 'Father', and later, seeing him through my children's eyes, he was to become 'Grandfather'.

Sunday, August 10th, Southwold

The weather again very fine and warm, and the lunchtime bathe was once more an enjoyment rather than a challenge. In the afternoon, Daddy and I walked from Potter's Bridge, on the Lowestoft Road, across uncharted fields to the sea at Easton Bavents – the seaward limit of Reydon Smear. Here I bathed again. The sun was shining down, undiluted by any wind, as we walked back through the barley fields to the car, the road smelling of melting tar. In the evening D went to sing his second anthem of the day at S'wold Church – his activities as a chorister seem to be about the only outside activity he can partake in. He can't swim, or pull the bells, or even ride his bicycle. Suddenly, from being very active, he is a spectator. Since his coronary in 1964 he has had confirmed Parkinson's Disease (for which a possible cure, L-Dopa, was mentioned in the *Sunday Times* today), back ailments, etc, etc, and has aged very rapidly.

We ate salmon and drank a bottle of white wine for supper, and afterwards Helen and I walked along the sea front. For the record, it is ten years, almost to the day, that we first met here.

Monday, August 18th

Started off for the TV Centre in some trepidation, for this was the first day's filming, and, in fact, the first day's working, with John Howard Davies, our producer for the first three shows. However, as it turned out, the day could hardly have gone better.

John has an unfortunate manner at first – rather severe and school-prefectish – but he really means very well. He consulted us all the way along the line and took our suggestions and used nearly all of them. He also worked fast and by the end of the day we had done the entire 'Confuse-a-Cat' film, a very complicated item, and we had also finished the 'Superman' film. All this was helped by an excellent location – a back garden in a neat, tidy, completely and utterly 'tamed' piece of the Surrey countryside – Edenfield Gardens, Worcester Park.

Wednesday, August 20th, Southwold

At 8.30, John and Terry, in the Rover, and Eric and myself, in Eric's Alfa Romeo, set off for sun, fun and filming in Suffolk.

Terry and I went round to the Lord Nelson, a pub almost on the cliffs. A step down took us into a warm, low-ceilinged room, which seemed to be mainly full of locals. The barman recognised us from 'Do Not Adjust', so we felt even more at home there. Ended up drinking about three and a half pints each and leaving at ten past eleven in the traditional convivial manner.

Back at the Craighurst (Hotel), Terry giggled so long and loud that Heather, the production secretary, thought I had a woman in my room.

Thursday, August 21st, Southwold

A very plentiful, well-cooked breakfast at the Craighurst, and then out to Covehithe, where we filmed for most of the day. The cliffs are steep and crumbling there and the constant movement of BBC personnel up and down probably speeded coastal erosion by a good few years.

Mother and Father turned up during the morning and appeared as crowd in one of the shots.

In the afternoon heavy dark clouds came up and made filming a little slower. We ended up pushing a dummy newsreader off the harbour wall, and I had to swim out and rescue this drifting newsreader, so it could be used for another shot.

Saturday, August 23rd

Mr Powell looked at my teeth and was very pleased with their progress. In the afternoon I went over to the TV Centre for a dubbing session. Everyone was there, including Terry Gilliam, who has animated some great titles – really encouraging and just right – and Ian MacNaughton, short-haired and violent. He seems now to have dropped all diplomatic approval of John H-D, and is privately cursing him to the skies for not shooting all the film he was supposed to. I think this sounds a little harsh, as the weather was twice as bad with John as with Ian.

Thursday, August 28th

This morning rehearsed in front of the technical boys. Not an encouraging experience. I particularly felt rather too tense whilst going through it.

Watched the final edited film for the first show. A most depressing viewing. The Queen Victoria music was completely wrong, and the Lochinvar film[1] was wrong in almost every respect – editing and shooting most of all.

Terry and I both felt extremely low, but John Howard Davies, relishing, I think, the role of saviour, promised to do all he could to change the music on 'Victoria'. We went off to the bar and who better to meet there than John Bird, in an unusually expansive mood. He greeted us as warmly as when we were doing *A Series of Birds*[2] two years ago. He is somehow so untarnished by clique or cliché or any conditioned reaction, that talking to him can only be entertaining. But one doesn't say much as his *knowledge is infinite.*

---

1 John C dressed as Rob Roy is seen galloping urgently towards a church where a beautiful girl is about to be married. Cleese arrives in the nick of time – ignores the girl and carries off the bridegroom.
2 A John Bird, John Fortune series, directed by Denis Main Wilson, on to which Terry and myself had been drafted as script editors.

Saturday, August 30th

The first recording day. Fortunately Friday's fears did not show themselves, so acutely. From the start of the first run the crew were laughing heartily – the first really good reaction we've had all week. The sets were good, John kept us moving through at a brisk pace and our fears of Thursday night proved unfounded when 'Lochinvar' got a very loud laugh from the crew. In the afternoon we had two full dress runthroughs, and still had half an hour left of studio time.

As the time got nearer for the show, I had a pint up in the bar and by the time the 'guests' began arriving at 7.30, I felt as relaxed as I have done for days. Tim Brooke-Taylor noted that we seemed very unruffled.

Barry Took[1] won the audience over with his warm-up and, at 8.10, *Monty Python's Flying Circus* was first launched on a small slice of the British public in Studio 6 at the Television Centre. The reception from the start was very good indeed, and everybody rose to it – the performances being the best ever. The stream-of-consciousness links worked well and when, at the end, John and I had to re-do a small section of two Frenchmen talking rubbish, it went even better.

Afterwards there was the usual stifling crush in the bar, the genuine congratulations and the polite congratulations and the significant silences. Our agent, Kenneth Ewing, did not appear to like it – but then he's probably waiting to see what other people think.

About sixteen of us finished the evening at the Palio de Siena in Earl's Court Road, in festive mood. Full of relief.

Sunday, August 31st

The end of August, it feels like the end of the summer, with the weather cool and changeable, the garden looking waterlogged again.

On the Isle of Wight, 150,000 people gathered to hear Bob Dylan – the gutter press are having their work cut out to track down smut in a gathering which seems to be happy and peaceful. 150,000 people and all the violence that the *Mirror* could rake-up was a man getting his head cut on a bottle. It shows how evil papers like the *News of the World* and,

1 Co-writer of many shows including *Round the Horne*. Father figure of Python. He pushed our series forward, and lent it an air of respectability at the BBC.

I'm afraid, the *Daily Mirror* are. They have chosen to pick out isolated incidents – a couple making love in a bath of foam, a girl dancing naked – and make them seem like crimes. They are trying their best to indict a young generation, who seem to be setting a triumphant example to the older generation – an example of how to enjoy oneself, something which most Englishmen don't seem really capable of, especially the cynical pressmen of the *News of the World*. It's all very sad.

Saturday, September 6th

Today was the final of the Gillette Cup between Yorkshire and Derbyshire – so for a Sheffielder and a Yorkshireman it was quite an afternoon. As I hurried along St John's Wood Road I wondered to myself whether it would be all over and how empty it would be (brainwashed, perhaps, by the *Daily Mirror*, which had already billed it as an 'undistinguished' contest). But Lord's was actually full. There were, apparently, about 25,000 people there – 3,000 less than at Highbury a couple of hours earlier, but many more than when I went to see the Test Match v the West Indies. Derbyshire were in retreat. 136 for 7 against Yorkshire's 216, with 15 or 20 overs left. But they lasted for an hour, until, shortly before 7.00, the last Derbyshire batsman was caught and the pitch was immediately invaded by happy, beer-filled Yorkshiremen, young boys, vicars and a very few women. Speeches and presentations were made and the MCC Establishment was heartily jeered, and Colin Cowdrey was happily booed as he came forward to present the Man of the Match award. But it was Yorkshire's evening at Lord's, and around the Tavern were gathered those nightmarish faces. Sweaty, splenetic and sour. Not pleasant really.

The diary almost buckles here under the weight of writing, filming and recording as well as learning to be a good father to my son and a good son to my ailing father. My resolve weakens and the 1960s slip away without another entry. How could I miss the creation of the Spanish Inquisition and 'Silly Walks'? To be honest, because at the time neither I, nor any of us, I think, saw Python as a living legend, pushing back the barriers of comedy. We were lightly paid writer-performers trying to make a living in a world where Morecambe and Wise, Steptoe and Son *and* Till Death Us Do Part *were the comedy giants.* Monty Python's Flying Circus *was a fringe show, shouting from the sidelines. It was another job, exhilarating at times, but in the great scheme of things not more or less important than changing nappies or hoping for a lucrative radio voice-over. When I pick up the diary again, we're into the 1970s and times are beginning to change.*

1970

Wednesday, January 14th

Since the last entry, just over four months ago, we have completed the first series – 13 episodes of *Monty Python's Flying Circus*. The press were unanimously in praise of the show – Milton Shulman wrote a major article on it after the BBC mysteriously dropped it for two weeks after the fourth show, Jimmy Thomas of the *Daily Express* attacked *Frost on Sunday* for not realising that Monty Python had changed humour and brought it forward when Frost was trying to put it back, we were favourably compared with *Broaden Your Mind* in the *Telegraph*, have had an article in the *New York Times* and, two days ago, received the final accolade: an appearance on *Late-Night Line-Up*[1]!!

Otherwise reaction has been less uniformly euphoric. Doctor Stuart-Harris – now Sir Charles Stuart-Harris since the New Year's Honours[2] – loves it, and a lot of people say it is the only thing worth watching on television. Ian MacNaughton's mother sits through it in stony silence. Letters of congratulation came from Spike Milligan,[3] Humphrey Burton,[4] to name but two.

Viewing figures averaged out at three million, not bad for 11.10 on Sundays. Practical results are promises of another series, repeats of this series at a popular time, an entry for Montreux, and a possibility of a 90 minute cinema film of the best of the series for showing in the States. This last is the pet project of Victor Lownes, London head of Playboy, who raves about the show and is, at this moment, in Chicago selling it to his boss, Hugh Hefner.

The most gratifying feature of the show's success is the way in which it has created a new viewing habit – the Sunday night late-show. A lot of people have said how they rush home to see it – in Bart's Hospital the large television room is packed – almost as if they are members of a club. The repeats – at popular time – will show us how big the club is!

1 Serious BBC2 arts programme, fronted by, among others, Joan Bakewell.
2 Father of Graham, my childhood friend from Sheffield.
3 Spike's 1969 series *Q5* had been an inspiration to us. It had been directed by Ian MacNaughton.
4 Head of Arts Programmes at BBC.

Yesterday we went further into negotiations about forming Python Productions Ltd – which now seems to be decided – and next week we will set to work producing a film script for Victor Lownes.

In the morning I took Helen to the Tate's exhibition of Elizabethan portrait painting – called the Elizabethan Image. There were some fine portraits – particularly by Hans Eworth, William Larkin and Nicholas Hilliard – but the subjects were usually titled persons, formally posed, and one longed to see a painter who recorded Elizabethan life on a rather more broad pattern. Two interesting paintings were by Henry VIII's court painters and were blatant and virulent anti-Papal propaganda. One of them showed the Pope being beaten to death by the four apostles, with all his trappings – the rosary, the tray of indulgences, etc – on the ground beside him.

Tuesday, January 20th

The houses around Lismore Circus are fast disappearing – Gospel Oak is being laid waste. I get the feeling that Oak Village is like a trendies' ghetto, hanging on for dear life, until the mighty storm of 'civic redevelopment' is over and we can walk once again in a neighbourhood free of noise and mud and lorries and corrugated iron and intimate little rooms with pink flowered wallpaper suddenly exposed by the bulldozer.[1] It will probably be another two years before there is any semblance of order from all this chaos – by then I'll be 28 and Helen will be 29 and Thomas will be three and going to nursery school.

Monday, February 16th

Terry and I have completed two films for Marty's[2] special – written in reluctance, conceived in duty, they are based on ideas of Marty himself. They're long, but that's about all. Somehow, since Monty Python, it has become difficult to write comedy material for more conventional shows.

1 Camden Council had a ten-stage plan for the redevelopment of Gospel Oak. This involved knocking everything down and starting again. Oak Village was stage ten, and because of resolute opposition from residents and media was able to stem the tide. A compulsory purchase order had been dropped in 1968, though hovered as a threat until the early '70s.
2 Marty Feldman, one of the *At Last the* 1948 *Show* team, and co-writer, with Barry Took, of much radio comedy. He was now a star in his own right.

Monty Python spoilt us in so far as mad flights of fancy, ludicrous changes of direction, absurd premises and the complete illogicality of writing were the rule rather than the exception. Now we jealously guard this freedom, and writing for anyone else becomes quite oppressive. The compilation of all the last series, plus new links, into the film script 'And Now For Something Completely Different' has been completed and the script should be with Roger Hancock.[1] No further news from Victor Lownes III, under whose patronage the work was done.

The third of our more concrete achievements since the end of Monty Python – now six weeks away – was to write a 10–15 minute script for a trade film for Intertel. We got the job via Graeme Garden and Bill Oddie (veterans in the world of commercials), who were too busy to waste time on it. As a means of income during the lean season it had the advantage of being quick and fairly easy to write, no further obligations, except some acting in it if we wrote ourselves in, and no chance of it clashing with Monty Python.

As we await the final schedule for this Intertel film, Terry is writing his novel, which he won't tell me about because he says it will stop him writing, John is in Dar es Salaam for two weeks, and I am about to start writing Monty Python II, for, as Eric reminded me on the phone today, there are only eleven weeks until we go filming in May, and we are seriously intending to have eleven shows written by then.

The weather recently has been clear, crisp and sunny. Snow fell about four days ago and remains still. We have at last got a fire for the sitting room.

Thomas is as energetic as ever. He helps around the house with devastating results.

Thursday, February 19th, Southwold

At the cottage Thomas was much taken with his new mattress with animals on, but yelled when left to go to sleep. My mother quite obviously thought he ought to be left and that he was just being obtuse, but in fact he merely wanted to see what was at the bottom of the stairs – and once he'd had a look, he went quietly back to sleep. A triumph of reason over discipline.

3 Tony Hancock's brother, ran an agency which represented, among others, Eric Idle and Bill Oddie.

Friday, February 20th, Southwold

In the morning we shopped in Southwold, where everyone was going along bent against the wind. But one felt it was a clean, scouring wind, blowing away a winter full of damp and grey and drizzle. Mainly in celebration of this weather, Dad and I decided to go further afield for our afternoon walk. We drove to Minsmere, which is south of Dunwich and renowned for its bird reserve. We parked on the cliffs, for which privilege one normally has to pay 2/-, for these are National Trust cliffs, and have been bought for the nation. But not paid for, apparently.

We walked for almost two hours, with the wind too violent for any conversation – along the beach, where we were protected by the cliffs and there was no wind, only sunshine – and beside the tall bank of reeds that fringes Minsmere Reserve. But we saw not a single bird. The largest feature on the landscape is man-made, and that is the extravagant bulk of Sizewell Nuclear Power Station. But it is obtrusive only because of its sheer size. There is no smoke, no noise, no busy air of the factory about it. It is a silent, brooding presence, totally out of proportion to anything around it.

Friday, March 6th

Began as an ego-boosting day of sorts (two fan letters and a request for autographed photos!) and ended as definitely ego-damaging.

In the afternoon, full of joie de vivre, and encouraged by the warm sunshine, I parked my car in Montpelier Square, and went in search of Benton & Bowles Advertising Agency, where I had been asked to go in order to 'meet a man' about a Maxwell House commercial. I felt fairly buoyant, especially as they had previously asked me to do something, but had been unable to afford my fee (only a miserable £50), and also because Jill[1] had specified that it was not an audition. So I felt good as I crossed the Brompton Road and walked for about 100 yards up Knightsbridge.

Upstairs in the thickly carpeted reception area, the girl at the reception desk is talking to a friend – a Knightsbridge and South Ken trait. She asks me my name and I have to repeat it three times. 'Is Miss Sconce expecting you?' This is my first rebuff. I'm not important

1 Jill Foster, our agent. She worked for Kenneth Ewing at Fraser & Dunlop.

enough for reception to have been given my name in advance. 'Go down to the Lower Ground Floor,' says the girl, 'and Casting Department is on your left.' That's all and back to her friend.

Downstairs I go. No evidence of Jane Sconce or anybody. Through a door I hear the sound of recorded playbacks of voices saying 'Maxwell House – the most exciting sound in coffee today.' I hear another voice from another room: 'All we need is just any out of work actor.' The awfulness of the place and the awfulness of the people make me decide to leave, forget it all, forget this ghastly basement with closed doors. But for some reason I stayed and I found Jane Sconce's office, and she was ever so nice, but really *so* busy, and she took me into this room, and there was a trestle table, two jars of Maxwell House on it, and at one end of the room were four men and a girl, and a camera and a monitor. It was an audition. I tried not to listen as the patronising 'director', or whatever, bombarded me with instructions as to how to deliver my lines, my head swam with that awful feeling of being on the panto stage at the age of seven and how I hoped I wouldn't wet myself. But try as I could, I was unable to avoid reading the script. That was the nadir of this whole sorry enterprise. 'Shake a bottle of powdery coffee and what do you hear? Nothing. But shake a bottle of new Maxwell House and you have the most exciting sound in coffee today.'

I did it quickly and sent it up at the end. The 'director' sharply reproved me for sending it up. At this I attacked for the only time in the afternoon. 'I can't really take it seriously – this is the kind of stuff I spend days writing sketches about.'

But I *did* do it seriously, and I did hurry out without offending any of them, without telling any of them how incredibly cheap and nasty I found the whole set-up.

Sunday, March 8th

I walked over the Heath, which was still snow-covered. The sky was a light grey, but the sun filtered softly through and on the north side of Parliament Hill there were two or three hundred tobogganists and spectators. The spectators ranged across the skyline – like the start of an Indian charge. Sledges were everywhere and half-way up the hill was an ambulance. I walked on to Kenwood House. It never ceases to fill me with some gratitude that at the half-way point of a walk across open grassland and woodland not 20 minutes from the centre of London, one can walk amongst Joshua Reynolds, Gainsboroughs, Romneys, a Turner and a Rembrandt self-portrait.

We watched David Frost 'hosting' the Institute of Television and Film Arts awards at the London Palladium. *Monty Python* was nominated for four awards and won two. A special award for the writing, production and performance of the show, and a Craft Guild award to Terry Gilliam for graphics. But somehow the brusqueness of the programme, and its complete shifting of emphasis away from television and towards Frost and film stars, made the winning of the award quite unexciting.

None of us was invited to the awards ceremony, as the girl who was organising it 'didn't know the names of the writers' of *Monty Python*.

Tuesday, March 10th

At 9.45 I found myself in Mount Place, Mayfair, ringing the bell of Joseph Shaftel, a film producer. The reason for this heavy start to the day was a phone-call from Fraser and Dunlop the night before, asking me to go and meet a casting director for a new Denis Norden-scripted comedy film to be shot in Rome. Apparently my name had been put forward together with those of Graham Chapman and John Cleese; however, still smarting from my experiences at Benton & Bowles, I arrived prepared to be humiliated a little.

But no, all was sweetness and light. I was ushered into a small 'conference' room where sits Denis Norden,[1] who shook my hand and fixed me with his extraordinarily kindly eyes, which made me feel considerably happier about the meeting. He introduced me to a small, shaven-headed American director, who proceeded to send himself up in a most frightening way, and a sleek, immaculate Italian, who I presumed was a co-director.

The conversation turned on a 'Sheffield Wednesday' badge I happened to be wearing, and it suddenly felt as though no one quite knew what they were all there for. Perhaps they were sizing me up. However, it seemed to be taken as read that I was going to do the part – that of a detective's assistant who happens to be an art expert as well – and all the meeting was for was to sound out my availability. Five days' filming in Rome and a day in Florence really made it sound spectacularly attrac-

[1] In partnership with Frank Muir he had written some of the best radio comedy including *Take It From Here*, one of the few programmes to bring my mother, father and myself together round the wireless.

tive, but it seemed as though May would be the filming date – and by then I would be in the middle of Monty Python filming.

Graham, who had been in before me, was waiting, and we crossed Berkeley Square and went into a coffee house. After coffee, and poached eggs on toast for Graham, we were walking back when I found I'd lost my car keys. The day came to an irritating halt as I scoured Berkeley Square and district staring hard at the pavements and gutters. No luck, I had to go back to Joseph Shaftel's apartment. What must they have thought – Michael Palin back again, with some trumped-up story about losing keys. He must want the part pretty badly.

However, they leapt up and down and were most concerned. The dynamic director, who had previously been doing a passable impression of an imbecile, now surpassed himself, suggesting I look in my pocket. The Italian was quite distraught and was turning the room upside down; only Denis seemed to preserve some sense of proportion. I backed out thanking them profusely, and for all I know they're still looking.

Friday, March 13th

Drove Graham down to Terry's for our first major script meeting for the next Monty Python series. At the moment we have no contract, as we are holding out for a bigger programme budget. The BBC are obviously not used to artists stipulating total budget, but it is something we feel very strongly about, and a stiff letter from Jill Foster was followed by a prompt BBC offer of £4,500 per show plus £25 extra for the writers – a total increase of over £1,000 per show over the last series. (But £4,500 only makes us equal with e.g. *World in Ferment, Charley's Grant.*) We are holding out for £5,000.

We spent most of the day reading through. Terry and I had written by far the most and I think this may have niggled John a little. We punctuated the day with an enormous Chinese taken-away lunch. Utter over-indulgence. Large quantities of king-size prawns, sweet and sour pork, beef slices, etc, left at the end. Work-rate cut by half. With one possible exception, the sketches read *before* lunch fared much better than those read after.

Drove up to Abbotsley[1] for the weekend, arriving about 10.00.

1 Abbotsley, near St Neots in Cambridgeshire, home of Helen's mother, Anne Gibbins. Helen's father, a farmer, died in 1963 at the age of 53, from heart complications that would now be dealt with by routine surgery.

Saturday, March 14th, Abbotsley

In the afternoon we went into Cambridge, and whilst Catherine[1] and Helen went to look for clothes, I pushed Thomas in his pram across Trinity Hall Bridge, a quick look at King's College from the Backs, and then we walked along in the direction of Trinity and St John's. The wrought-iron gates of both colleges carried signs banning push-chairs from their grounds, but we eventually found a way in. Thomas was very good as I pushed him past the front of Trinity, alongside garden beds with no spring flowers yet showing, up to the Wren Library, which is half-way through external restoration, and looks like a half-unwrapped present. Coming out of the back door of Trinity was none other than Christopher Isherwood, ex-Cambridge, now living in California. It seemed entirely right that he should be there, and I almost went up and spoke to him. About eight or nine years ago, when I was waiting to go up to Oxford, I read most of his novels, and especially those more obviously autobiographical – *Lions and Shadows, The World in the Evening*, I liked a great deal. I think I found his sensitive, vulnerable and ingenuous hero rather sympathetic.

However, I couldn't remember all this, and the great novelist, the man whose life I felt I had shared those years ago, walked away towards the Backs, and Thomas and I looked at the ducks on the Cam.

Sunday, March 22nd

Today began with a mammoth walk across the Heath in order to tire Thomas out. We took some bread for the ducks, but, alas, another lady was there before us with the same intent, and she lured them all away – so Thomas and I were left throwing large amounts of succulent white bread to a bald-headed coot. On the way back Thomas made the acquaintance of a dark brown cocker spaniel, and I made the acquaintance of its owner, a dark brown Englishman with a Viva Zapata moustache, shades and elegantly effortless brown sweater and trousers. In short, the kind of person who makes one feel slightly overweight and a little shabby. He was a fashion designer, with a journalist wife and two kids, Justin and Sean. Justin was about five, and had a gun with which, he said, 'I'm going to shoot babies.'

1 Helen's niece, then four years old.

An afternoon party at Eric's. There, surprisingly enough, Thomas was in his element. For two hours we hardly saw him – he cried only when Marty Feldman a) trod on his hand and b) knocked him over, and for the rest of the time he pottered about, and was seen to be dancing, pinching the book from a serene little girl who sat reading, and thumbing through a book of erotic postcards. A good little party. Black and Tan to drink and I renewed acquaintance with D Jason, H Barclay[1] and Rodney Slater, ex of the Bonzo Dog Band, now a child welfare officer in Modbury Street, Kentish Town.

Tuesday, April 14th

At the BBC there was nowhere to park – the excuse being 'Apollo 13'. In explanation of why 'Apollo 13' should be responsible for filling the BBC car park, Vic, the one-armed gateman, just said 'Apollo 13', in a way which brooked no argument.

In fact it was early this morning that Apollo 13, having just passed the point of no return, had an explosion in one of the oxygen tanks, and this put the Command Module's engine out of action. So this is the first Apollo mission to have gone seriously wrong in space, after a launch which made no headlines because people were just getting used to the smoothness and precision of these first moon missions.

On the way to the BBC I saw a poster for the film *Marooned*[2] – which is a very believable tale about three astronauts stuck in space and the rescue operation to get them back to earth.

The main difference between fiction and fact is that, in the film, another rocket, carrying a never-fully-tested module, is fired to send someone up to save them. There has been not the slightest mention of a possibility of any rescue craft getting to Apollo 13. And this seems to be the most dangerous aspect of the whole, so far glorious, moon landing programme. The Americans have gone all out to get men on the moon as fast as they can, without perhaps consolidating the situation nearer home – e.g. by building space laboratories outside earth's orbit, or by working on a less expensive form of rocket fuel. The result is that, when

1 David Jason had been one of the cast of *Do Not Adjust Your Set*, produced by Humphrey Barclay, yet another of the Cambridge comedy mafia, who also produced *The Complete and Utter History of Britain* for Terry and myself in 1968–9.
2 1969 film, directed by John Sturges, starring Gregory Peck and Gene Hackman.

the Apollo astronauts go up, they are out on a limb – if they cannot get back to earth there is no possibility of fetching them.

Back at TV Centre, while Roy Jenkins [Labour Chancellor of the Exchequer] was presenting his fourth Budget to the House of Commons in optimistic circumstances, we were having an equally optimistic meeting with Ian M. He was sober, confident and relaxed. We talked about the BBC's idea of making an album of the best of the first series, the budget for the new series, and ended up with a very convivial drink at the Club.

We all felt very much happier as we drove home. Summer was in the air, and the Budget was fairly harmless, making nothing more expensive and nothing cheaper, but at least I read that the country's trade balance was the most favourable since 1822. Now that does knock the myth of Victorian imperial prosperity on the head. Walked up to the library and back over the Heath.

Thursday, April 16th

At 10.00, cars arrived to take us to the Lyceum Ballroom off the Strand to be presented with our *Weekend* TV awards. We were rushed into the stage door, where a few girls with autograph books obviously thought we were somebody, but none of them were quite sure who. Inside the stage door, steps led down an inhospitable brick staircase to a small room, which was probably a Green Room, full of slightly shabby celebrities and their hangers-on. From the inside of the Lyceum came a heavy, noisy beat and periodic PA announcements for 'Arnold Ridley'.

It was all rather nightmarish, grinning faces loomed up, people pushed through, Eric Morecambe looked cheerful, a dinner-jacketed young man with a vacant expression and an autograph book asked me if I was famous. I said no, I wasn't, but Terry Gilliam was. Gilliam signed Michael Mills'[1] name, the twit then gave the book to me saying, 'Well, could I have yours anyway?' So I signed 'Michael Mills' as well. We all signed 'Michael Mills' throughout the evening.

1 Michael Mills, Head of Comedy at the BBC, was the man who green-lighted Python in the summer of 1969. Despite a disastrous meeting at which we could give no satisfactory answers to any of his questions, he came out with the memorable words, 'All right, I'll give you thirteen shows, but that's all!'

Monday, April 20th

Down at Terry's to put together the fifth show of the new series. A mid-morning disappointment – the Rome filming trip, which had always seemed to me too good to be true, has almost collapsed. Virna Lisi, the leading lady, is ill and the schedule is now in disarray. A slim chance that I may be needed before my Monty Python deadline, but I am inclined to write it off. Bad scene. Loss of suntan and at least £300, not to mention experience.

The other four of us, or should I say three and the hovering Chapman (no, that's unkind, and this is a kind diary), the other four of us worked on until 6.45, and completed and read through what I think is one of the best shows to date.

Tuesday, April 21st

An interesting and hard-worked morning giving my voluntary performing services for the Labour Party. Easily the most decisive political act of my life, and almost the only one – though previously I had once voted Labour in the GLC elections. I suppose voting for and supporting Labour is just another painless way of appeasing my social conscience. But it's not much, I cannot see how anyone with a social conscience could vote Conservative. The film which I was doing today had been written by John Cleese, who is now what you might call a committed Labour celebrity – and I mean that in a good sense – somebody who is prepared to *do* something to keep the Conservatives out. At present Labour is increasingly successful in the polls. Two opinion polls out this week actually gave Labour a lead over the Tories for the first time for three years and, in the GLC elections last week, Labour won thirteen seats, their biggest electoral success since they came to power.

Friday, April 24th

Down at Terry's in the morning and for lunch, and from there to the BBC, where we all gathered to watch the playback of two of the last Monty Python series, which were being shown to an American named Dick Senior, who is interested in syndicating them in the States, and an American girl by the name of Pat Casey, who is to be in some way connected with the production of our Playboy-sponsored Python film to be made later in the year.

The first one we were shown was Show 11, and it was painfully slow – the 'Undertakers' and the 'World of History' were two ideas ground underfoot by heavy-handed shooting and editing and also performance. It made us look very amateur and our face was only partly saved by Show 12 – a much better looking show with 'Hilter' and 'Upper Class Twits' providing two of the most remembered items of the series.

Dick Senior seemed a little taken aback, but he was a very intelligent man and could obviously see that there was a cumulative attraction in Monty Python, which an isolated showing could not necessarily convey. Nevertheless, Show 11 is not one to use for sales purposes.

At 5.00 Terry and I arrived at Pinewood Studios to talk to Betty Box and Ralph Thomas about our rewriting *Percy*.[1] After walking for many yards along corridors and up stairs, which one was never sure were entirely real, we arrived at the office which they share. Both of them younger than I imagined. Ralph Thomas seemed the more genuine and pleasant of the two, Betty Box being kind, but hinting at a hard edge beneath. For about one and a half hours we talked and I got the feeling that they were impressed by our criticisms of the screenplay of *Percy*, and anxious for us to rewrite as much as we can in the time. (They start shooting in June and we are filming from May 11th onwards.)

Saturday, May 2nd

By 10.00 was at the Camden Theatre for the recording of a Monty Python LP. The original impetus for this had come from the unaptly named BBC Enterprises, producers of LPs such as *Salute to Steam* and *Keep Fit with Eileen Fowler*.

Straightaway the pattern of the day was established. The record, we were told, was to be done extremely cheaply, we were not going to have it in stereo, we could not afford to pay any copyright for the use of our invaluable music links – so it was all done on an organ, which reduced everything to the level of tatty amateur dramatics.

Spent the morning in the rather attractive Camden Theatre – a fairly

---

1 Screenplay about a penis transplant, eventually filmed, starring Denholm Elliott, Hywel Bennett, Britt Ekland and others. Betty Box, producer, and Ralph Thomas, director, were responsible for a string of Pinewood Studios hits, including *Doctor in the House*.

small theatre, with Atlases supporting enormous mock columns, and a rather luxurious intimacy about the atmosphere – reading through the scripts, briefing the sound effects men. Somehow, one felt, this should have been done sooner.

Helped by Graham Chapman's bottle of scotch, the actual recording, at 4.30 in the afternoon, was really quite enjoyable. Not having cameras to play to, one could judge one's audience, and one's effect on the audience, much more easily. However, the audience was small, most of the sound effects were inaudible and we had never had time to rehearse side two, so there were many things which got little or no response – 'Hilter', 'Nudge-Nudge' and 'Soft Fruit' were especial casualties.

Tuesday, May 5th

My 27th birthday – I bought *The Times Atlas* as my major present – with £3 from Southwold.

Helen bought me a garden chair, which was immediately put to use. This is real garden weather, our patch has been transformed from the quagmire of April, to a firm little lawn with tulips, pansies, wallflowers filling the border, and the clematis and Virginia creeper suddenly springing to life.

A hot 27th birthday – as my mother wrote in her letter, it was a very hot day twenty-seven years ago.

Monday, May 11th, Torquay

Left home around 10 o'clock in the Triumph and, collecting Graham on the way, set out for Torquay and our first two-week filming stretch away from home.

Our hotel, the Gleneagles, was a little out of Torquay, overlooking a beautiful little cove with plenty of trees around. Eric, Lyn[1] and John were already there, sitting beside the pool. The decor was bright and clean and the rooms looked efficient – and there were colours about, instead of the normal standard hotel faded reddish brown.

However, Mr Sinclair, the proprietor, seemed to view us from the start as a colossal inconvenience, and when we arrived back from Brixham, at 12.30, having watched the night filming, he just stood and

1 Lyn Ashley, Eric Idle's wife.

looked at us with a look of self-righteous resentment, of tacit accusation, that I had not seen since my father waited up for me fifteen years ago. Graham tentatively asked for a brandy – the idea was dismissed, and that night, our first in Torquay, we decided to move out of the Gleneagles.[1]

Tuesday, May 12th, Torquay

At 8.00 I walked down to Anstey's Cove below the hotel. It was a dry, fine morning, the sun was in and out, it promised to be a better day. Down by the sea, surrounded by high basalt cliffs, it was tremendously peaceful. The calm of the sea affected me, made me feel relaxed and gave me a great sense of well-being. The sea, waves gently turning over on the shore, is so tranquil compared to the antics of the people who want to get near it – the amusement arcades, the 6d telescopes, the hotels with greasy food, the guest houses with sharp-tongued landladies, the trousers rolled up, the windbreaks, the beach-trays, the sand-filled picnics, the real Devon cream ices, the traffic jams at Exeter, the slacks, the sun oil – all of this endured in order to get near the sea. Two-thirds of the world's surface is water, why should seaside resorts always seem to have so little room?

Back at Gleneagles, I avoided breakfast and Graham, Terry and I asked Mr Sinclair for the bill. He did not seem unduly ruffled, but Mrs Sinclair made our stay even more memorable, by threatening us with a bill for two weeks, even tho' we hadn't stayed.

We checked in for the night at the Osborne, a four-star hotel which is really a converted Georgian terrace overlooking the sea. They were so conditioned to middle-aged and elderly guests that, when I asked at reception for vacancies, she looked at me with some uncertainty and said 'Staff?'

That afternoon we filmed 'Derby Council v. The All Blacks', at Torquay rugby ground, and then in the evening some night-time election sequences at a vast neo-classical mansion in Paignton, which used to belong to the sewing machine millionaire, Singer, who married Isadora Duncan.

Here we filmed until midnight, and arrived wearily back at the

1 Eric and John decided to stay. In John's case a lucrative decision as he later based *Fawlty Towers* on Gleneagles.

darkened Osborne, for sandwiches and late-night drinks and a discussion, later very heated, with Graham about the worth or worthlessness of keeping a diary.

The diary withstood all pressures to end its life. In bed at 3.00.

Wednesday, May 13th, Torquay

After breakfast Terry went off to film at a rubbish dump a piece of Jean-Luc Godard ciné verité involving an exploding lettuce.

It was another hot day and Graham and I, in leisurely fashion, paid our bill and drove round to the Imperial. Here we spent what must rate as one of the most luxurious and effortlessly pleasant mornings of my life. We lay in the sun beside a beautiful heated sea-water pool, and had gin and tonics brought to us.

After a swim and drinks and sunshine, we went into the restaurant, where we ate a most excellent meal, accompanied by a half-bottle of Meursault. After that, we drank Grand Marnier and I smoked a cigar in the lounge.

I hope I never get used to that way of life, I hope I can always enjoy self-indulgence as much as I enjoyed it, that first, sunny perfect morning, at the Imperial.

We drove out to the location and spent the rest of the afternoon playing football dressed as gynaecologists.

Tuesday, May 19th, Torquay

A day on the beach. We start filming 'Scott of the Sahara', an epic film/sketch scheduled for three days. I play Scott, a sort of Kirk Douglas figure swathed in an enormous fur coat with perpetual cigar, looking more like George Burns. John plays the drunken Scottish director James McRettin, Terry plays Oates, Mike, a coloured ex-van-driver with a disconcerting Devonshire accent, plays Bowers and Carol[1] plays Miss Evans. An absurd looking bunch, we set up on Goodrington Sands, a stretch of rather stony sand south of Paignton. Signs saying 'Deck Chairs', 'Beach Trays', 'Ices' abound – this particular stretch of sand has been mercilessly tamed by the holidaymaker.

1 Carol Cleveland, who understood the Python style so well she became almost the seventh member of the team.

It's remarkable how our evening entertainment revolves mainly around food and meals, whereas two or three years ago, when on location for, say, *The Frost Report* at Littlehampton, or *Twice a Fortnight* at Minehead, the first thing we did was see what was on at the pictures. I suspect it's largely the Chapman hedonistic influence, which is also partly to blame for us wasting money at the Imperial.

But then, we are a lot richer than three years ago.

Wednesday, May 20th, Torquay

In the evening, another session with Terry J on *Percy*. Again slow work, stymied by the sheer amount of rewriting needed to make the vacuous last scene work. One good thing about the evening – we discovered the Apollo, a Greek restaurant in the centre of Torquay. The TV is always on, and the kebabs and hummus were excellent. As soon as we ordered kebabs, the proprietor, a large Greek, asked us if we were from London. He said, sadly, that no one from Torquay ever seemed to eat the Greek food – it was always the sausages, chips and peas.

Friday, May 22nd, Torquay

Our last day in Torquay. By a mighty effort of work, from 8.30 to 11.30 on Thursday evening, Terry and I had typed out three-quarters of our *Percy* rewrites (running to twenty-four pages of foolscap) and sent them off to Betty Box.

Today's filming, consisting mainly of short bits and pieces with the milk-float ('Psychiatrists' Dairies') had very much the end-of-term flavour and, by 6.30, John, Connie,[1] Eric, Lyn, Graham and both the make-up girls had started back to London. Terry and I shared a room at the Links Hotel for our last night in Torquay. The Links is where we should have stayed all along – the cost of living there is about 60% lower than the Imperial, but the bed was more comfortable, it's open all night, the bar does not charge extortionate prices, and just in one evening we got to know the manager and his wife and many of the guests, including two hard-drinking Catholic priests.

---

2 Connie Booth, actress and co-writer of *Fawlty Towers*, married to John Cleese.

Saturday, May 23rd

4.00 a.m. A soft light in the sky, fresh smells, and the far-off sound of a car, then silence again. Shown out of the back door of the Links by a night porter, a quick cup of black coffee and one of last night's sandwiches, then into the car and off to London. Even at 4.30, the roads coming south were very busy, but the Devonshire countryside at 5.00 looked so beautiful that I kept wanting to stop.

Hardly any traffic going my way, but plenty going west as I tore over the Salisbury Plain. Stopped at a lay-by overlooking Stonehenge, and drank more black coffee and ate the remainder of the sandwiches. By 7.45 I was on the outskirts of London. By 8.45, 270 minutes and 214 miles later, I was back home. Thomas was standing on the bathroom stool cleaning his teeth, with no trouser bottoms on. I just cried, I was so pleased to see him.

Sunday, June 7th

Terry and I had to spend the morning working on another of our small-earning sidelines. This time it was a rewrite of a film called 'How to Use a Cheque Book' for the Midland Bank.

Thursday, June 18th

General election day. Ideal polling weather, dry with warm sunshine. Every public opinion poll in the last two months had put Labour clearly ahead – the only possible shadow on the horizon was a 1½% swing to the Tories published in the latest opinion poll – taken *after* the publication of the worst trade figures for over a year, and Britain's exit from the World Cup last Sunday. Nevertheless, everything looked rosy for Labour when I left Julia St at 10.00 to go down to Camberwell.

The morning's work interrupted by the delivery of a large amount of dung. We were sitting writing at Terry's marble-topped table under a tree sheltering us from the sun. All rather Mediterranean. Suddenly the dung-carriers appeared. Fat, ruddy-faced, highly conversational and relentlessly cheerful, they carried their steaming goodies and deposited them at the far end of Terry's garden. As they passed I gleaned that they had come from Reading, that they had started loading at 5 p.m., that one of them was about to go on holiday to

Selsey Bill – his first holiday for seven years. After about twenty-five tubfuls they were gone, but at least they left a sketch behind.[1]

When I turned on the election I heard that in two results there was already a confirmed swing to the Conservatives. I watched until about 2.30, when it was obvious that the opinion polls were wildly wrong – the country had swung markedly to the right. Edward Heath, perhaps more consistently written-off than any Opposition leader since the war, consistently way behind Wilson in popularity, was the new Prime Minister.

My feelings are mixed. What I fear is a shift to the right in the national psyche; there are many good and honest and progressive Conservatives, but there are many, many more who will feel that this election has confirmed their rightness in opposing change, student demonstrations, radicalism of any kind. There are also those who will take the Tory victory as an encouragement to ban immigration (Enoch Powell doubled his majority), bring back hanging, arm the police force, etc, etc.

The Labour government was courageous and humane in abolishing hanging, legalising abortion, reforming the laws against homosexuals, making the legal process of divorce less unpleasant, and banning the sale of arms to South Africa. I am very sad that they are out of power, especially as I fear that it is on this record of progressive reform that they have been ousted.

To bed at 3.00. A long, hot day.

Friday, June 26th

Yesterday we recorded the first of the new Monty Python series. Although there was only about 15 minutes of studio material to record, it had gone remarkably smoothly. There were small problems during the day, but generally there was an optimistic air about the show. None of us had all that much to do, so there was perhaps less tension than usual. We even managed a complete dress run-through, which is almost a luxury compared to some of our hectic recordings in the last series.

The audience was full and, even in our completely straight red-herring opening – the start of a corny pirate film which went on for nearly five minutes – there was a good deal of laughter, just in anticipation. Then John's 'Hungarian Phrase Book' sketch, with exactly the right amount of lunacy and scatology, received a very good reaction.

1 'Book of the Month Club Dung', which found its way into Show 6 of the second series.

Out to the Old Oak Common Club for a rehearsal of Show 3.

A most strange atmosphere at the rehearsal. Ian seemed a good deal less happy than last night; everyone seemed rather quiet and unenthusiastic. Perhaps it's the structure of this particular show, which consists mainly of myself as Cardinal Ximenez and Terry J and Terry G as the two other Cardinals, so the other three members of the cast have comparatively little to do. Perhaps it's also this very dull, oppressive weather. The near-80s temperature of the last month is still here, and the weather is generally overcast and muggy.

Sunday, June 28th

In the morning I pushed Thomas across the Heath to Kenwood House. He loves being taken through the woods and now points excitedly at the trees, and gives bread to the squirrels, who will come right up to the push-chair.

After lunch I went down to the St Pancras Town Hall to rehearse our short Monty Python contribution to a show called 'Oh Hampstead'. The title is, to say the least, equivocal – as it is a charity show, directed by John Neville[1] in order to raise funds for Ben Whitaker, the Labour MP for Hampstead up till ten days ago.

John and I rehearsed 'Pet Shop/Parrot', and Graham and Terry were to do the Minister whose legs fall off. Struck by how very friendly people are when there is the feeling of a cause about. The stage manager and the lady who offered us cups of tea were so matey that it made up for John Neville's slightly detached theatricality.

As we waited to go and perform, we were all taken with unaccustomed nerves. It was live theatre now – no microphones, no retakes, and it brought us up with a jolt. But the audience knew we were giving our services free for the Labour Party – and they'd paid from £2 10s to £10 to watch, so they must have been pretty strong Labourites. Anyway, it went well.

Decided to take up our invitation to Ben Whitaker's after the show party. He lives in a sensibly, modestly furnished Victorian house backing on to Primrose Hill.

I think the party may have been rather foisted on him – he seemed to be opening bottles of white wine with the somewhat pained expression

1 Classically-trained Shakespearean actor and director.

of a man who cannot reconcile the joviality around him, or, indeed, the money he'd spent on the wine, with the fact that he had ten days earlier lost his seat in Parliament, his job as a junior minister, and his chance of political advancement for at least ten years. It would be fairly appalling to be told one could do no more shows for four years and yet for a man of any ambition that's what it must be like. How ungrateful Hampstead has been to Ben Whitaker, I thought, as I shook his limp hand and left his limp party at about 1.00.

Saturday, July 11th

My consumption of food and drink is increasing in direct relation to a) the money I earn and b) the amount of time spent with Graham Chapman, the high priest of hedonism. Terry Gilliam recently gave what seemed a good clue to Graham's attitudes. Terry suggested that Graham, having once made the big decision – and it must have been greater than the decisions most people are called on to make – to profess himself a homosexual, is no longer concerned with making important decisions. He is now concerned with his homosexual relationships and in perpetu-ating the atmosphere of well-being which good food and drink bring, and in which the relationships thrive. He doesn't want to think too much about himself now, and above all he does not want to have to struggle. He seems to feel that having stated his position he now deserves the good life.

Helen's elder sister Mary, and her husband, Edward, had recently become third-part owners of Roques, a collection of dilapidated farm buildings among the wooded hills of the Lot Valley in France. This was the first of what were to become almost annual summer pilgrimages.

Saturday, August 1st, Roques

I write this by the light of the Lumogaz lamp on the round wooden table in the barn at Roques. Outside the barn it is a still, dark night, behind us a wooded hill rises steeply and, above the trees, the stars, many more than one sees in England. The crickets make a continuous background noise, like an electric fence, small insects land on the paper and have to be pushed away. It is 9.30, Mary and Helen, looking quite preggy now [she had become pregnant again in February], are cooking pork chops over an open fire.

We have been officially on holiday for a week. The last recording was Show 6 on July 23rd. Eric was the first to go, he flew to the south of France on the 24th. On that day the rest of us met Roger Hancock for lunch and formed Monty Python Productions Ltd, on the corner of Dean St and Shaftesbury Avenue, after a convivial, but expensive and badly served meal at Quo Vadis restaurant – where you eat surrounded by photos of the stars, taken at the restaurant. Each photo seems to have caught the victim unawares.

Graham flew to Corfu on the Saturday morning, secure in the knowledge that his extraordinary gamble in trying to write Monty Python and thirteen Ronnie Corbett shows at the same time had been successful, for the simple reason that everyone had done the work for him on Monty Python. In fact on Monday, when John went off to Rome for two days' filming prior to a holiday in Rhodes, Terry and I were, as usual, left to pick up the pieces, tie up the loose ends and make sure that Ian was happy from the writing point of view before we *all* vanished.

We left home in the Austin to drive the 600 miles to Roques. Apart from taking a wrong turn at Tonbridge, which caused our first momentary panic, we arrived at Lydd, on the tip of that monotonous V of reclaimed land which contains Camber Sands and Pontins Holiday Camp, Dungeness Atomic Power Station and its spider's web of power lines, and Lydd Ferry Port.

The buildings of the Ferry Port rather unconvincingly carry the traditional airport jargon – Departure Lounge, Departure Bay, etc, etc – but, when you come to move to the plane, you leave a pleasant English tea room to find that only five cars and eight people are on your flight. A rather old and battered nose-loading plane, proudly bearing the title 'City of Aberdeen', stood on the tarmac. Thomas was fascinated, as he has recently taken to pointing at planes quite vociferously, and to see one at such close range, and then to get on it, and then to take off, was all too much. He kept pointing out of the window at the wing and saying 'Plane?'.

Down below, the last sight of England I remember was a field next to Lydd Airport, which we passed just after take-off, littered with dismembered aircraft.

A delightful journey. The plane never seemed to go above 5,000 feet, it was a clear sunny day and the Palin family made up one third of the total personnel. Very homely – and only 25 minutes before we were flying over the lush dunes and neat holiday houses of Le Touquet.

Le Touquet Airport perpetuated the Trips Round the Bay atmosphere which characterised the whole flight. For some reason or another we didn't have the green insurance card which indemnifies one against third party accidents on the Continent, so, within thirty yards of where we first set foot in France, I parted with 70 Francs (about £5 10s), an auspicious start.

With very little trouble about driving on the right-hand side – at Le Touquet they break you in easily – we drove off towards Rouen, lunched in a field near Crécy, and arrived for the evening at L'Aigle, a town in southern Normandy, where Edward had recommended we stay at the Hotel Dauphin.

On Thursday morning, we had croissants and coffee in bed and left at 9.00 for what we hoped was a straight 350-mile drive through the Loire and Perigord to the Lot.

But things have a way of happening unexpectedly, and we were not fifty yards from the hotel when the exhaust pipe broke in two. The sun was already high in the sky, and my French was not very confident as yet, and it was therefore a most frustrating two hours whilst we waited for a garage to repair the exhaust, gazing imploringly at small enigmatic Frenchmen, watching for the slightest trace of sympathy or urgency.

Eventually it was mended and we left L'Aigle at 11.15. Soon a warning light on the dashboard frightened us enough to turn off the engine and cruise downhill to another garage. We found that this light meant that our oil filter needed to be changed in the next 300 miles, but this was little consolation as we ground our way to the town of Montoire, where we bought bread and lunched in a hot and insect-ridden field. This was the nadir of our journey. We were only about 100 miles from L'Aigle, the car seemed to be cracking up, and the heat was making things even worse. But after lunch Thomas slept for about two and a half hours and we made good time, crossing the Loire at Amboise and reaching La Trémouille, well into Limousin, before stopping for tea. I decided that we might as well press on and try to reach Roques that night.

Roques is an old farmhouse made primarily of local limestone, and looks solid and attractive, with plain wooden roofs and floors. Downstairs there is a kitchen cum eating cum sleeping cum reception room with a large fireplace. Off this is the main bedroom. Stairs ascend to a long room, one half uninhabited, and the other half now inhabited by the Palins. It's rather like a loft, with a dusty wooden floor, but a newly improved roof. Below the ground floor is the washing/bathing room. Again a long room, of which one half is tiled in local red tiles, with a recessed circular shower area and a double basin. At present they are awaiting the attentions of a M. Prunier to connect up the cold water, but hot water is as yet provided either by boiling or by the Baby Burco.

Eating and cooking during this hot, dry weather take place in the barn, which is open on one side and is swathed in early morning sun, which makes breakfast a great meal.

All in all, Roques is solid and simple. One is a long way from telephones and television, there is no water, but there *is* electricity. The silence is frightening, but the satisfaction of the solitariness after London is worth everything.

We eat well here and drink the local wine – and by local, I mean grown one mile away by the small farmer who used to own Roques, M. Lapouge.

Thursday, August 6th, Roques

The hot weather continues. It's now a week since we left London and, apart from one stormy evening, it has been sun and clear skies.

Today I decided to go and visit the local médecin. This was mainly a result of Helen's prompting, and by the continuance of the discomfort which I've been getting every time I pee.

I arrived at his house about 10.00 and his son was lolling about the garden. No sooner had I asked where the doctor was, than the youth motioned me to follow him and leapt on his motorbike. With him and his friend giving me a motorcycle escort, I proceeded in triumph for the 200 yards to the doctor's surgery in the Boulevard Gambetta. Here I waited for nearly an hour and a half until the doctor called me in. His surgery was filled with cigar smoke. I reeled off my carefully prepared speech and all was well until *he* started to question *me*. 'Quand vous *pee-pee*,' he kept insisting, and there was I referring proudly to 'la urine'. He was rather aggressive in the face of my blank incomprehension, and when I came away I had a number of incredibly complicated instructions, which I did not understand, and a consultation fee of 16 Francs – about 25/-.

It was 11.45 and I had with me a sample bottle which I was to fill and take to the chemist. As I drove home, angry at thus wasting a morning, I remembered that the chemist closed at 12.00 for about two hours, so that it would be much better for me to deal with it all before 12.00 than to have to return after lunch. This caused me to take the side road in an attempt to find a quiet, private place to fill my tiny bottle. But the houses were much more prolific than I had hoped and I ended up shielding myself against the car and, with some difficulty, directing my urine into the bottle, the remainder trickling over my hand. This was the end of stage two of my morning of bitter frustration. Stage three began when I found that the medicines prescribed for me at the chemist's totalled 146 Francs, and included four large phials of intramuscular injections – which I had to take to the hospital on the next four days for injection dans 'la fesse' – in the buttock.

The day at last picked up. We'd decided on a sightseeing trip. The drive was pleasant, we were in no hurry, and I was laughing quite happily at my experiences with le médecin. Then fresh trouble broke. Just as we were about to drive up to Domme, the bastide town, there were frightening grating noises from the gearbox. It had finally packed up in three gears. The noise was like a football rattle. I'm sure that the accumulation of tribulations had produced a numbing effect on me, for I felt only a moment's bitter anger, then passed quickly to the state of resignation. We drank an aperitif whilst waiting for a garage to confirm what we already knew. The gearbox, which showed signs of collapse at the beginning of the year, had chosen the small, rather unattractive town of Cenac, 600 miles away from home, for its final death rattles.

Tuesday, August 11th, Roques

At lunchtime Cathy Gib[1] innocently queried whether or not Thomas was on Helen's passport as well as my own, for Helen is taking him back to England. Of course, he was only on my passport. Swift action demanded a phone call to the nearest British Consulate – in this case Bordeaux.

The British Consulate was perturbed at the lack of time to fill in the various forms, so Edward, Mary and myself set off in the Triumph for a totally unscheduled trip to Bordeaux – a 150-mile journey.

1 Cathy Gibbins, Helen's younger sister.

At La Rede, about one hour from Bordeaux, it became obvious that we wouldn't arrive before the Consulate closed at 5.00, so I made another phone call and, after becoming slightly eloquent with a woman who suggested we come along tomorrow morning instead, I eventually received an assurance that someone would be there till 6.00.

So began the last breathless lap. Edward drove manfully and, with the help of a brand-new autoroute just before Bordeaux, we reached the city at 6.00. Directing from the Michelin *Red Guide*, I frantically guided Edward through the Bordeaux rush hour until, at 6.10, we reached the Cours de Verdun. I leapt out, clutching passports, and arrived, dishevelled and breathless, at the Consulate.

There, all was calm. An official, and he was, in every sense of the word, an official, had happily stayed on and, in an atmosphere rather like that of a benevolent but uninspired English master's study after school, I signed the various forms. He proudly produced a number of impressive stamps and, over all this, the last great emergency of a holiday full of emergencies, the Queen gazed down impassively on her tousled subject.

On the way back we ate in Verdelais, just across the wide Garonne from Langan. It was an excellent meal of fish soup (in which I committed the most risible faux pas – tucking in to the red-hot anchovy sauce, which I'd mistaken for the soup itself).

Was heavily bitten in the night and slept badly – only one really good night in twelve.

Sunday, August 23rd

The last week has been spent filming in or around London, ending up at our traditional location – Walton-on-Thames – on Friday. It was less hot this time than in the past – I noticed this because for the last shot of the day I had to stand beside a fairly busy road clad in the It's Man[1] beard and moustache and a bikini. Next to me was John Cleese, also in a bikini.

---

1 The It's Man was a cross I'd made for myself, by suggesting that at the start of each show a haggard, wild-eyed old man should stagger out of incredibly uncomfortable situations, lurch to camera and with his last breath squeeze out the word 'It's'. I was unanimously chosen to play the part, one of the most consistently uncomfortable in Python.

Saturday, September 19th

Our running feud with the BBC Planners has come to a head, for not only is the new series going out at a time – 10.00 Tuesday – which is also the regional opt-out slot, so Wales, Scotland, Ireland, the Midlands and the South don't *see* M Python, but there is to be a break after three episodes when Python will be replaced by 'Horse of the Year Show'.

Our only positive reaction in this matter was to write a very gently worded letter to Paul Fox[1] expressing our disappointment. Last Wednesday we were visited at rehearsal by Huw Wheldon, managing director of BBC TV. It was obviously a peacemaking mission – an attempt to cheer up the lads on the shop floor – an exercise in labour relations. But in his favour it must be said that he *did* come, he avoided being patronising or pompous, he *had* arranged for us to see Paul Fox next week, and he *had* rung the *Radio Times* editor to ensure some more publicity.

We were all extremely deferential, but the visit made us all feel a little better – I suppose we were disarmed by the mere fact of such a deity deigning to notice us, let alone enthuse over the programme, and it does make us feel in quite a strong position for next week's meeting with Paul Fox.

Sunday, 20th September

Terry arrived at 1.00, and together we went up to Graham Chapman's to prepare our material for a charity show – in which we are doing 30 minutes. It's in aid of Medical Aid for Vietnam – which J Cleese refers to as 'Grenades … er … Elastoplast for the Vietcong'. But officially the proceeds from this evening's show will go to providing medical aid for those civilians involved in the war in Vietnam, who do not receive US aid. I think this is a very humane cause, and I believe that the Vietnam war is an international tragedy, in which one can no longer talk of the right side or the wrong side, or the right solution or the wrong solution, but one can at the very least help *all* the thousands of civilians who are dying or injured. If I really thought that the money I helped to raise was being spent on killing people, I would not have done the show, but I trust Hanoi – certainly as much as I trust the Americans, if not more.

1 Controller, BBC1.

We ate an excellent roast beef and Yorkshire lunch at Graham's, rehearsed rather frantically – we are still looking for scripts to learn the words *from* – and set off in Terry's car along the gleaming new Westway to the Questors Theatre at Ealing.

The feeling, as we worked through the lighting plot with Ray Jenkins, a TV writer who asked us to take part, was very much like the Etceteras' Sunday revues, which I produced at Oxford in 1964 and 1965. 'Light stage left, light stage right', 'cross-fade', 'blackout', etc, etc. The adrenaline was flowing healthily as we waited to go on for our first spot at the start of the show.

But the first we knew about the show having started was a hissed urgent voice on the intercom, 'Monty Python – you are two minutes late on, we are waiting for you.'

One or two people were starting a slow handclap as we reached the wings. We launched into the familiar 'Tide',[1] then the interview with the Minister whose leg drops off, a monologue called 'Co-Ed' and finally 'Working Class Culture'. By the time we'd finished we had won the audience back, but immediately all the good was undone, as the group who were to follow us – 'Humblebums'[2] – did not know they were supposed to be on, and were obviously going to take some time to set up their amplifiers, speakers, etc. There was no compere to explain to the audience, just an awkward silence. We eventually leapt into the breach, did a few silly walks and whatever quickies we could remember.

The Humblebums were from Glasgow – and played rather gentle, attractive songs, there was an African group beating out some ethnic melodies which came nearest of everything to taking the roof off the place, and top of the bill was the classical guitarist John Williams – who was not only a fantastic guitarist, but a beaut guy. He was, I must add, a Monty Python fan, so there was a good deal of mutual admiration.

We taxied home at 11.30 feeling very happy and pleased we had done the evening and, who knows, we might have helped someone somewhere to put a rifle ... er ... bandage on ...

1 A sketch from the Oxford days, which involved an enthusiastic foreign salesman extolling the virtues of Tide, apparently unaware that it's a washing powder. He eventually pours some into a bowl, produces a spoon and, with a big smile, eats it. Horrible to perform as, for some reason, I never got round to substituting the washing powder for something edible.
2 A Scottish folk-singing duo, one of whom was Gerry Rafferty and the other, Billy Connolly.

Thursday, September 24th

At 6.30 we all trooped up to the sixth floor for our meeting with Paul Fox, Controller of Programmes, BBC1. A slightly comic entrance. We knocked tentatively at his door and went in, nobody was in the ante-office, everything was tidied up and deserted. We had been standing some moments in the outer office feeling a little disorientated when Paul Fox's door opened and this bulky man with a generous nose and large ears appeared, Paul Fox, no less. He was clearly more nervous than we were – but then he was in a fairly indefensible position, and there *were* six of us.

Inside he poured us drinks and there was the usual difficulty over seats – offices just aren't built to accommodate the Monty Python team.

Fox started by explaining why MP went out at 10.10 on a Tuesday night. Two things I felt were wrong here. One was his premise that it wasn't a pre-nine o'clock show, although I would reckon 8.30 would be its ideal time, judging from the reactions of my ten-year-old nephew Jeremy, his six-year-old brother Marcus,[1] and the large teenage section of the audience at the shows.

But Fox was conciliatory throughout. He sugared the pill with promises of a repeat of eight episodes of Series 1 immediately following our present series and, next year, a total repeat of Series 2 at a national time. He clearly realised that he had underestimated Monty Python, but his apologetic manner did encourage us to talk freely with him about some of our other complaints, e.g. lack of any BBC publicity for the new series, the removal of our invaluable researcher, the budget (which he hotly defended as being above average for LE [Light Entertainment]: moot point) and the two-week break in our transmission after the first three shows. Obviously we could not get him to change his mind, but we came away from his office after one and a half hours and several drinks feeling optimistic that we had at least said everything we wanted to say, he had been friendly and one hopes he was also receptive.

Back home in a cab.

1 Jeremy, Marcus and Camilla, the children of my sister Angela and her husband, Veryan Herbert.

Sunday, September 27th

No papers for the last week owing to some strike by the delivery people
– but this morning I felt the need for some Sunday reading, so I drove
down to Fleet Street and bought an *Observer* and *Times* from a man in
Ludgate Circus. A lot of people milling about in Fleet Street – looking
out for lone newspaper sellers, or calling at the *Daily Express* building –
the only paper which seemed to have a stock of copies at its office.

4.15. Visited National Film Theatre with Simon Albury to see *Arthur
Penn 1922* - a documentary about the director of *Left-Handed Gun,
Bonnie and Clyde, The Chase, Little Big Man* and a great number of
Broadway theatre successes, especially *The Miracle Worker.*

The first film, about and starring Vladimir Nabokov, was a small gem
– mainly because Nabokov himself is such a character. He manages to get
away with an opinionated arrogance, partly because he is obviously not
taking himself too seriously, but mainly because of his facility with words
– which in the film he denies, saying that he failed to inherit his father's
gifts of description and fluency – he has a beautifully dry humour, wonderful pieces of observation, and an overriding good nature which quite
make up for his pedantry. I once read many of his books, the film made
me want to read more – especially his autobiography *Speak, Memory.*

Sunday, October 18th, Abbotsley

After breakfast Thomas and I go on a long walk around the village. In
the field opposite Manor Farm, the two great carthorses have just been
fed. The man who feeds them tells me he has worked the land at
Abbotsley since 1926. Then tractors cost £120, now they're £1,120, but the
carthorses' days are over. What it took a single-furrow horse-drawn
plough to do in a fortnight, a five- or ten-furrow tractor can now do in a
day. He doesn't seem to have regrets, but he loves the horses – he says
that when you had an eager team of horses, they kept at the plough from
seven o'clock till three, with no lunch, until they got tired.

Monday, October 19th, Southwold

Left Abbotsley at 11.00 and drove over to Southwold, leaving Helen and
Thomas to stay at Church Farm. The Suffolk countryside seems to be at
its best in autumn, and the drive was beautiful. We ate lunch together,

and then Father and I drove into Southwold and walked along the sea front. It was cool and sunny, and practically deserted – the season seems well-finished. Saw welcome additions to the Southwold scene – two Adnams drays, with big dray-horses. They have only just been introduced – to deal with local deliveries, apparently to save the money on lorries. I must say they add to Southwold's atmosphere – it's a town that absorbs progress and innovation in only very limited amounts and this technologically retrogressive step is quite in character.

Tuesday, October 20th, Southwold

During this afternoon the weather turned suddenly and dramatically from the reflective, gentle calm of a sunny autumn morning, to an angry sky, N.W. wind and driving rain. At the harbour, the sea was as high as I've seen it, with breakers crashing against the harbour wall. As I write this diary in bed, the wind is still strong outside, but the heavy rain has stopped.

Tonight we ate liver and kidneys, with a bottle of St Estèphe, and watched Monty Python. One of my favourite shows – with the bishop film and the poet-reader, the Gumby announcements and the strange chemist's sketch. Went to sleep with the comforting sound of the wind buffeting the windows.

Wednesday, October 21st

The *Punch*[1] lunch, to which we had been invited by Miles Kington (a friend of Terry's at Oxford, and mine as well in London), is a traditional affair. Originally it consisted of the contributors only, who met, once a week, to discuss subjects for the political cartoon. It is carried on now as a meeting-place for journalists, humorists and writers generally, who may be regulars on *Punch*, or prospective contributors.

We assembled with the other guests for pre-lunch drinks – names I have known so well for so long became faces – Norman Mansbridge, E H Shepherd, the appallingly unfunny David Langdon. I met the editor, William Davis, an economics journalist, probably late thirties, possibly describable as a 'whizz-kid'. His humour I find very ponderous – he nearly

1 A quintessentially British humorous and satirical magazine which first came out in 1841 and ran for 150 years. With readership declining from a peak of 175,000 to some 8,000, it was finally closed in 2002.

always has a serious political or topical point to put over, and yet, because he is editing *Punch*, it is given an ill-fitting and tenuous humorous context. When Davis attempts politics and humour, humour loses – unlike Norman Shrapnel of *The Guardian* or, to a lesser extent, Alan Watkins of the *New Statesman*, who seem to mix the two well.

We were shown in to lunch. About twenty or twenty-five of us around a large table; on the walls of this dining cum conference room were framed covers of old *Punches*, photographs of the staff past and present, famous framed cartoons, etc, etc. I sat next to Miles on my right and Vincent Mulchrone on my left. Mulchrone is a well-known feature writer on the *Daily Mail*. A very amiable man, with a North Country accent (I really expected him to be Irish), he was exceedingly self-effacing and seemed more keen to talk about moving house than his journalistic adventures.

At the end of the meal, as we drank coffee and brandy and smoked cigars, Davis hammered on the table and the traditional scavenging of ideas began. It was very reminiscent of *Frost Report* conferences four years ago. It was ironic that the man who provided most of the ideas for *Punch*'s Christmas edition was John Wells – a regular contributor and ex-editor of *Private Eye*, the magazine which has probably done more harm to *Punch*'s circulation than any other. Terry and I also suggested quite a number of ideas, as did B.A. 'Freddie' Young – *Punch* contributor and theatre critic of the *Financial Times*. But he was the only one of the 'older' generation who seemed to be on the wavelength of most of the suggestions. Others, including *Punch*'s film critic, Richard Mallett, who must be the only living critic older than the medium he writes about, nodded rather wearily and drank their brandy.

Thursday, October 22nd

Took a taxi to the Playboy Club in Park Lane, for a party to celebrate starting production on the film.

Inside, the Playboy Club is a taste wilderness. The bunny girls are a real affront to style, desire, everything. They stand around in these ugly costumes which press their breasts out and grasp their buttocks – so that they look like Michelin Men. The bare shoulders are quite pleasant, but the costume's brutal and unsexy and the bunnies seem to have been drained of character, they are either sickly sweet or rather brusquely military.

The evening was not unpleasant – spoke for a while to Dudley Moore, and even Eric Sykes patted me on the arm and said how much he enjoyed the show. I left at 9.00 and by 12.00 I was back in Southwold, having caught the 9.30 train to Ipswich and driven on from there. To go from the Playboy Club to the east Suffolk coast in four hours is as big a change of environment as you're likely to get in England.

Monday, October 26th

Today we started filming *And Now For Something Completely Different*. I got up at 7.00, after having woken at intervals during the night. It was pitch dark outside. It brought back memories of *The Complete and Utter History* filming – almost exactly two years ago. But instead of having to drive out to a location in my own car, I was picked up in an enormously comfortable black Humber Imperial and driven, in the company of Graham and Terry, to our location in Holloway. It was a school gymnasium where we were filming the 'Soft Fruit' sketch, but when we reached the location I felt a sudden, nervous tightening of the stomach, as I saw a line of caravans parked by the side of the road – and opposite them a large white caterer's lorry and lighting generator.

Terry and I were sharing a caravan. It was very spacious and comfortable, with a dressing room and a kitchen in it. We all sat around the table before filming began, joking about this new luxury, like schoolboys in a new form room.

We were on the set by 8.30, changed and ready to film. The 35mm camera was another impressive sign that this was a film, as were the many people whose sole job seemed to be to look after us, give us calls when we were required, fetch us coffee if we wanted it, and generally keep us sweet. But our mirth was great when we saw a man struggling to stick an 'Eric Idle' sign on the back of a picnic chair. Did we really all have chairs with our name on? Yes we really did and, by the end of an eleven and a half hour-day, with only a half-hour break at lunch, I realised that the caravan, the chairs and the ever-helpful production assistants were there to help us work harder, and they were vital. To have a place to relax in after a take, without having to worry about finding out what is happening next, is a luxury we never had on television filming.

The crew seem, without exception, to be kind, friendly and efficient. Ian seems happy and confident; in short, it is a very enjoyable and impressive first day. We have finished the 'Soft Fruit' sketch[1] – which is about four minutes of film.

Finally, to sink back into a car and be driven home is a wonderful load off one's mind.

Saturday, October 31st

We have finished a week's filming now. In retrospect, Monday was our best day in terms of output, but we filmed at a steady rate throughout the week. On Wednesday we started a week's location shooting at Black Park – an expanse of pine forest, silver-birch copses, open grassland and beech-covered lakeside, which happens to be just next door to Pinewood Studios. By Friday we had shot the 'Lumberjack Song', the 'How Not to be Seen' opening and most of the 'Joke' film. Morale in the unit is very high.

Tuesday, November 3rd

In the evening Helen and I went down to the Open Space Theatre in Tottenham Court Road, to see The Scaffold show.[2] The Open Space is what its name implies, and very little else. We were late and just outside the entrance doors we met [Roger] McGough and Mike McGear dressed in neo-Gestapo uniforms waiting to go on. Brief handshake, but the feeling that we'd cheated by meeting them.

As it turned out the show was about love and sex and permissiveness – a variety of sketches apparently about the danger of a sexual revolution – when sex becomes an order, when permissiveness is not only approved of but essential, but without feeling and without emotion – destroying both the romantic young lover and the mackintosh-clad old man.

It is quite a common statement nowadays that sex kills love, and it is often put forward by the wrong people for the wrong reasons, but I felt a sympathy for McGough's writing – I don't particularly like aggressive sexual attitudes, the Danish porno fairs, the *Oh! Calcutta* celebrations of

1 In which John plays a crazed RSM teaching a bunch of squaddies how to defend themselves against bananas and various other forms of soft fruit.
2 A group, formed in 1963 in Liverpool, performing sketches, poems and songs and comprising John Gorman, Roger McGough and Mike McCartney, Paul's brother, who appeared under the pseudonym Mike McGear.

the sexual act, the 'frank, outspoken article' and the 'frank, outspoken interview' with the latest 'sexologist'. But all this seems to me infinitely preferable to repression of sex and illiberal or intolerant attitudes being accepted as 'morally correct'. The public discussion of sex must, I feel, help more than hinder, encourage rather than depress – and I'm not sure whether McGough would ultimately agree with this.

Saturday, November 7th

Slight scare this evening. After spending the late afternoon painting Thomas's room, Helen had quite severe contraction pains. We were due to eat out at Paul Collins' that evening, picking up Simon and Jenny Hawkesworth[1] on the way. At 7.45 there was panic. I was finishing the painting, Helen was worrying about imminent childbirth and Simon and Jenny were waiting for us to collect them. However, Helen was reassured by a phone call to Dr Graham Chapman, and we bundled Thomas into the car and arrived at Paul's house in Barnes about 8.45.

Helen did *not* have a baby.

Sunday, November 8th

I do seem to play a lot of seedy, unsuccessful and unhygienic little men. After washing my hair and shaving at 7.00 in the morning I am driven to work and immediately my hair is caked down with grease and my face given a week's growth of beard.

Ken Shabby[2] was especially revolting, with an awful open sore just below the nose. But Terry J (who has seen the rushes) is worried that it was shot with too much emphasis on Shabby and not enough wide shots to create the joke – which is the relationship of this ghastly suppurating apparition to the elegant and tasteful surroundings.

---

1 All three were friends from Oxford. Paul and Simon were both barristers and Jenny, née Lewis, a singer and poet.
2 Shabby, a disgusting man with a pet goat, who appeals to the father of a beautiful upper-class girl (Connie Booth) for her hand in marriage, but spoils his chances by, among other things, gobbing on the carpet.

Monday, November 9th

We are filming now at the empty, recently sold A1 Dairy in Whetstone High Street. The immediate significance of filming in Whetstone is that, for once, it favours those who live in North London – i.e. G Chapman and myself – who have long since had to leave earlier than anyone else to reach locations in Ealing, Walton-on-Thames and points south. Now we reap an additional benefit of Hampstead living – half an hour extra in bed – and when I am being collected at 7.30 each day, in darkness, the half hour is very welcome.

The dairy premises are so far excellent for our sketches – for they have the same rather dreary atmosphere of failure which characters like Scribbler and Mr Anchovy and the marriage guidance man are born from.

It takes a long time to set up the lights and to lay the track for the first shot. My hair is greased heavily and parted in the middle. It lies clamped to my head like a bathing hat.

Once the first shot is done, progress becomes faster. From the performance point of view, I enjoy the security of being able to do a performance several times and, with the sketch actually done in sections, one is not so worried about remembering words. I enjoyed one take particularly – I felt I was working hard on it and my concentration never dropped.

Thursday, November 12th

Shooting at a pet shop in the Caledonian Road. It's a grey, wet, messy day and this particular part of the Caledonian Road is a grey, wet, messy part of the world. In the pet shop there is scarcely room to move, but the angel fish and the guppies and the parrots and the kittens and the guinea pigs seem to be unconcerned by the barrage of light – and the continuous discordant voices. The shop is still open as we rehearse. One poor customer is afraid to come in, and stands at the door, asking rather nervously for two pounds of Fido. 'Two pounds of Fido,' the cry goes up, and the message is passed by raucous shouts to the lady proprietor. 'That's 15/-,' she says. '15/-,' everyone starts to shout.

We're finished by 5.30. Outside the shop is a little boy whose father, he tells us, is coming out of the nick soon.

'What'll you do when he comes out?'

'Kill him.'

'Why?'

'I hate him.'

'Why do you hate him?'

'He's a ponce.'

All this cheerfully, as if discussing what kind of fish fingers he likes best. As I walk back to the caravan a battered-looking couple argue viciously in a doorway.

Home for a bath and a change of clothes, and then out for the evening to the Warner Rendezvous – a new theatre opening with *The Rise and Rise of Michael Rimmer*, which was written by Peter Cook, John Cleese, Graham Chapman and Kevin Billington, the director. Graham, David and I walked round the back of the crowd into the foyer. It was full of people – not obvious first-nighters, and not an inordinate amount of stars. Peter Cook and Denholm Elliott were standing with their ladies, flashing smiles. As we walked down into the lower foyer, Peter looked up towards us and said in a funny voice, 'Oh, they're all here.'

The seats in the cinema were certainly comfortable, and there were little surprises, like Lord George-Brown[1] and his wife arriving, which reminded us that it was no ordinary night at the movies, but a premiere – Sparkle! Sparkle!

Rimmer with its built-in topical appeal, very funny moments, good performances, is still a second-rate movie – ephemeral enjoyment which makes no special impression and says nothing new, apart perhaps from one very memorable scene when the Prime Minister goes on a prestige visit to Washington for personal talks, and takes his place at the end of a long corridor full of potentates, including the Pope, who each move up one place as the President sees them.

After the film we went with Graham to a party at Les Ambassadeurs, a club in Park Lane. Lord George-Brown came in and stood with his wife rather gloomily until Graham and Terry went over to talk to them. Terry afterwards said that Lady Brown was very bitter about politics and was bemoaning what it did to people.

Terry Gilliam and I collected some food and talked for a while to Arthur Lowe[2] and his wife. Arthur Lowe's performance was about the best in the

1 Labour Foreign Secretary in 1966. Resigned in 1968 after differences with the Prime Minister, Harold Wilson. Liked a drink.

2 Later the legendary Captain Mainwaring in *Dad's Army*.

film, and it had been rather scandalously cut down. Beside Peter Cook's wooden smoothness, perhaps Lowe's performance was too good.

I ended the evening with an ominous feeling of impending drunkenness. I remember walking unsteadily up the stairs from Les Ambassadeurs, to be treated by the doorman to phrases such as the over-solicitous 'I'll get your coat, sir', and the downright abusive 'Not *driving*, are we sir?'

Friday, November 13th

After a busy day filming the remains of 'Upper Class Twit of the Year' in fine, sunny weather, arrived home with Terry and together we joined the rest of Monty Python at Chez Victor restaurant in Wardour Street at 8.30, for a paid meal – i.e. we had been hired by an ad agency to have some ideas about a new Guinness commercial.

My first impression was surprise at the number of advertising people present. A representative of the film production company, a director of commercials, an agency man, a product representative and two or three more.

We drank – I carefully, for my stomach was still recovering from Thursday night at Les Ambassadeurs – and, at about 9.00, sat down to our meal. There were various sinister preparations which tended to make me withdraw into silence, e.g. tape recorders and microphones hung around, a type-written sheet with their basic idea for the commercial, and muttered messages between the admen about how best to let us all have our say. Added to which, Messrs Jones and Gilliam led off with ideas of such enthusiastic vehemence that I retreated even more deeply into my shell. After some quiche lorraine and halfway through my liver, I began to lose this feeling of silent panic, and, as the ideas got away from the rather restricting basis which the agency had imposed, I found myself enjoying the whole business much more. Graham C, however, who isn't particularly talkative or assertive, found it all too much and, with a brief word in my ear, departed at about 10.00.

Thursday, November 19th

At 6.00 I was awakened from a deep and satiated slumber – Helen said she felt stronger contractions, but was unsure whether to ring the hospital. Went to sleep again.

At 6.30 woke to hear Helen expressing dissatisfaction with the telephone – it was out of order and she was trying to ring the hospital; the contractions were stronger than ever.

Thomas was crying and outside the rain was beating down the village in heavy waves. I felt grim – but got up, dressed, went over to Edward and Jayne's[1] and got them out of bed to use their phone. When I got back Helen's contractions were quite severe – she was in favour of getting an ambulance – but I bundled her and Thomas into the car and set off through the rain for UCH [University College Hospital]. Arrived there at 7.00. No porter in reception, didn't know where the labour ward was, and Helen was leaning against a trolley in considerable pain. Eventually a porter appeared and all he could do was reprimand me for parking on an ambulance place. Left Helen in the lift with him and went back to the car. Drove Thomas over to Camden Town and left him at Mary's, then arrived back at the hospital at about 7.45. Fortunately it was a day in which I only had one shot to film. At 8.00 I rang the location, and was able to get out of that one shot so, by incredible coincidence, I had the day off.

I settled down in the waiting room and snoozed. At 8.45 I began to feel very hungry – I'd been up for two and a half hours. I found a nurse and, with breakfast in mind, asked her what state Mrs Palin was in. The nurse giggled a little and said 'She's delivered.' A little boy – 6lb 12oz.

There Helen was – in a very modern delivery room – looking for all the world as if she'd just been to the shops and back. Hair neat and unsweaty, face a healthy, unruffled pink. Apparently she had given birth in the admissions room just after 8.00 – she had been bathed and was being put in a wheelchair to go up to the delivery room, when she had to tell them that the baby's head was sticking out. The doctor was off having breakfast, so two nurses delivered the child.

After tea at Mary's I visited Helen at 6.30. William, or Matthew as he then was, was small, wrinkled and wizened. When I touched him his face creased into a look of bitter discomfort and annoyance, but I really loved him.

Friday, November 20th

Back to filming. Unsettled, mainly wet weather set the schedule back, but I enjoyed the day – it was somehow less bewildering than yesterday.

1 Edward and Jayne Arnott, neighbours.

At lunchtime I bought ten bottles of wine and we all celebrated William's birth. Eric was appalled by the name William and felt Matthew much less boring. Terry was the opposite.

It's funny, but I have doubts about Matthew – as Terry said, it's 'Hampstead children with page-boy haircuts'. Happy with William.

Monday, December 7th

As I lay, half-awake, watching William being fed, the lights all went out. It was the first power-cut I can remember since the days we lived in Sheffield, caused this time by a work-to-rule of the electricity supply workers. Our lights were out for two hours. Apparently they were switching off selected areas in rotation. The work-to-rule is now three days old, and we have had five power-cuts, the longest being three hours yesterday afternoon.

Tuesday, December 8th

A Python cast lunch at fashionable Parkes restaurant in Beauchamp Place.

At our luncheon – I had lamb which was mainly very expensive – we talked about the future. It seems that all of us are prepared to start work on another TV series next November, except for John. He claims to want a year off to read and absorb knowledge, and possibly travel, and generally improve his mind, and yet he has accepted a commission to write at least six of a new series of *Doctor in Love* for London Weekend, a series which has apparently plumbed new depths of ordinariness. So, I have a feeling that John will be only too keen to write another series of Monty Python in twelve months' time.

Graham will be writing some more shows for Ronnie Corbett. Eric is quite keen to work on the screenplay of a film idea suggested by Ian – about bank-robbers marooned on Skye – but I fear I may have dampened his spirits rather heavily, by showing less than enthusiasm for it as a Python idea.

Terry Gilliam is writing cartoons for Marty, and then, we hope, directing a half-hour script on which Terry and I started work this morning.

Wednesday, December 9th

I wasn't required on the last day of shooting, but a car collected me in the evening and took me down to Greenwich for the end-of-film party at the Admiral Hardy.

Everyone was smiling, embracing, promising, exaggerating, confessing and forgetting in the manner of business parties – and show business parties especially. It had been a happy film, because each day made people laugh, but if it had been made in a time of full employment, when producers and production managers had to pay a crew well to keep it, our film would have been in trouble, for the relationships between the cheese-paring producers and the hard-working crew were at times near breaking point – only the precarious employment situation in the film industry kept some of the men at work.

This evening the power-cut in the Hampstead area caught us in the sauna at the squash club. Total darkness descended as I was about to leave the shower, clutching my towel. Candles were soon provided, but I dread to think how some of the members might have taken advantage of the total darkness.

Thursday, December 10th

Rung by the BBC and asked if I would like a three-day trip to Munich with Ian at the beginning of next week – to discuss possibility of a co-production between Monty Python and fellow funsters from Bavarian TV.

This evening I repaired to Devonshire Place to have some more dental surgery – the first for almost a year, at the hands of Mr Powell. It was only one tooth which required treatment, and Mr Powell's new surgery is so comfortable that it's a pleasure to lie there. Whilst he was working on it, he called in a colleague who was most impressed by my condition. 'I've never seen that before,' he told Powell, gazing at my mouth – I felt a surge of pride in these rotten old teeth, and am fully expecting to be visited at home by reporters from *Dental World*.

Was seized with desire to sit in a cinema and, after a quick meal, went up to the Haverstock Hill Odeon to see John Boorman's *Leo the Last*. However, some 30 minutes into the film, at a point when it looked as though it could suddenly become interesting, the lights failed. The dreaded power-cuts, which had only yesterday left me blind and naked in the sauna baths, had struck again.

Tuesday, December 15th

In the evening we go round to Graham Chapman's for food, drink and
Monty Python No. 12. It is the first time that Helen and I and William
have been out in the evening since W's birth. Plenty of time to reflect on
this, as I carry William up five flights of bare concrete stairs to the
Chapman penthouse.

It was really an evening for Python authors and their wives/lovers –
and it worked very well; there was a happy and relaxed atmosphere.
However, for some reason John was unable to come. Graham was
obviously very disappointed – but it is difficult to tell what he is thinking on evenings like this. He is so busy in the kitchen preparing food. We
eventually eat, ravenous, at 10.45, after which he seems to pace about
in a most unsettled way. It is strange that someone who takes so much
pride and care in producing such excellent food has absolutely no idea
how to serve it. The delicious meal of lamb, stuffed with salmon, was
served with all the style and elegance of an army kitchen. But the
company was good and the drink was abundant, and the show – which
was the first one of this new series that we recorded – had edited
together well, and was especially good because of the diversity of ideas:
the false 'Black Eagle' pirate opening, the dirty phrase book, the paintings going on strike in the National Gallery. Terry Gilliam's 2001-style
animations, the Ypres sketch with its false starts, the over-acting hospital, were just a few of them. By general consent, one of the best shows
we've done.

Sunday, December 20th

I got ready for the third successive drinking evening – this time it was
the BBC Light Entertainment Group who were the hosts.

The only remarkable thing about an evening which is really only
any night in the BBC Club – with slightly better food – was the attitude
of the Programme Controllers. An article in *The Times* on December
16th had detailed, fairly prominently, the continuing saga of
Python's mistreatment by the BBC Programme Planners. Stanley
Reynolds was the author, Terry Jones his chief informant, and about
80% of his article was correct and true (which is high by journalistic
standards).

David Attenborough, who is, I believe, Assistant Controller of

Programmes,[1] edged his way over to me quite early in the evening and began some rather nervously jocose banter. 'I feel I ought to come and talk to you – being one of those responsible for the repression of Monty Python.' But he made the point that the programme had done extremely well as a result of the BBC's treatment – which is an argument one cannot deny, and any altruistic feelings for the viewer in regions that don't get Python, must always be tempered with the knowledge that it's because of them we get assured repeats, and the extra loot which accompanies them.

Paul Fox, on the other hand, seemed genuinely aggrieved – not that he questioned our grounds for complaint, he seemed chiefly appalled that Stanley Reynolds had got the story. 'That drunken, etc, etc,' muttered Fox, standing in the middle of the hospitality suite, like a great wounded bear.

Monday, December 21st

In the afternoon collected the new car – a Simca 1100 GLS. A five-door estate in the best functional French tradition. At least, when I picked it up at the garage, it was clean and sparkling and looked absolutely brand new. When I bought the Austin Countryman three and a half years ago, it looked as though it had been standing in the rain for several weeks. So this, at least, was a good start to the justification of my decision to buy French rather than English.

Thursday, December 31st

1970 drew to a close in bitterly cold weather. Apart from some dubbing still to do on the film, Monty Python is finished – we spent almost a year on one thirteen-week series and six weeks making a film – now it remains to be discussed as to whether or when we do another series. In December Terry and I have almost completed a 30-minute TV show for Terry Gilliam to direct but, apart from this, and the possibility of more Python, the future is tantalisingly empty. John, Eric and Graham all seem to have gone back to writing for other people – Marty, Ronnie Barker, in John's case *Doctor at Large* – all of which is sad, for we have achieved a big success with our own show and yet only Terry and I seem

1 In fact, he was Director of Programmes.

to be progressing on from Python, rather than helping other shows to emulate it, and we are earning less money for our troubles.

We spent the last hours of 1970 down at Camberwell, where Terry and Alison served up a truly epic meal – antipasta, salmon, pheasant, delicious chocolate mousse, cheese, two kinds of wine and a menu!

So 1970 went out with a well-satisfied belch.

1971

Friday, January 8th, Glasgow

Caught the 10.05 'Royal Scot' express at Euston. Terry, Alison and I were travelling to Glasgow to see the production of our 'Aladdin' pantomime at the Citizens Theatre. It was a dull, rather misty day as we tore through the Midlands towards Crewe.

Eating a meal on a train is one of the great pleasures of life. How else could you have soup with Wigan all around you, steak and kidney pie as the expanse of the Irish Sea approached nearly to the window, and coffee with the fells and crags of the desolate Lake District on either side?

Our rooms had been booked in the Central Hotel, which adjoins the station. It is a railway hotel, built in monumentally impressive proportions in the great age of railway expansion. The walls were about three foot thick, with about fifteen foot width to play with on each step of the mighty staircase. After leaving our bags, we decided to walk in the direction of the Citizens Theatre.

We never did reach the Citizens, but we did find a bar, with very old brown, varnished tables and a wooden floor, and we did meet three shabby men, one of whom told us at great length why he was an alcoholic, and then asked for one of our empty whisky glasses. With elaborate furtiveness the rather sad-eyed, younger man of the three took the glass towards his flies, unbuttoning his coat at the same time. I watched amazed, and then a little relieved, as he produced a surreptitious bottle of what looked like sherry and filled the alcoholic's glass with it.

We walked back to the hotel, bathed, and took a taxi across the river to the Citizens Theatre where *Aladdin* by Michael Palin and Terry Jones was the first pantomime the Gorbals had seen for years.

The theatre is a neat size, with a circle and a balcony. We were met at the door, and ushered into the Manager's office. The Artistic Director, Giles Havergal,[1] we learnt, was in Tangier. After seeing the pantomime, we understood why. None of the cast seemed to be able to act too well – they certainly didn't seem to be enjoying it – and, despite the enthusiastic

1 Who first commissioned the panto for the Palace Theatre, Watford.

support of the kids, they hurtled through it. What few gems of wit there are in the script were lost for ever, and the creation of atmosphere, which is perhaps something the script does best, was spoilt by the speed and incomprehension of the line delivery. The principal boy had been taken ill and the girl playing her looked marvellous, but acted like a Canadian redwood. The love scene with the princess was one of the most embarrassing things I've ever witnessed – combining, as it did, her extraordinary lack of acting ability and the princess's extraordinary lack of charm.

Afterwards we met Phil McCall, the Widow Twankey of the pantomime. He regarded us cautiously at first, as though he felt rather guilty about the way the pantomime had been done – but when he realised that we didn't hate every minute of it, he became quite friendly, and we went next door, to the Close Theatre Club – a student-run club with a bar and home-made food. We ate plates of chilli and drank a bottle of scotch, which Phil McCall produced, surreptitiously, from his coat. We parted on very convivial terms, and walked back across the bridge to our hotel.

In one of the huge high-ceilinged rooms, we watched the Marx brothers film *Duck Soup* on TV.

Sank, happily, into bed at about 1.00.

Around this time Python morphed into a stage show. Tentatively at first, but it was the start of something that was to snowball from the West End to Broadway and eventually to the Hollywood Bowl.

Sunday, January 31st, Coventry

As Terry and I walked through the deserted, rain-soaked streets of Coventry at 11.45 at night, for the first ever Python stage show, it was amazing, exciting and rather frightening to turn the corner and see the Belgrade Theatre seething with people like bees round a honeypot. Here in this silent, sleeping city was a busy, bustling theatreful of people – nearly 1,000 of them. From behind stage one could hear just how enthusiastic they were – there was shouting and cheering before anything had happened. There were ten men dressed as 'Gumbies' in the front row of the circle.

When, at 12.00, the house lights faded, John entered as the Spanish

narrator in the 'Llama sketch', and there was a mighty cheer and prolonged applause. As soon as Gumby came on for 'Flower Arrangement',
the show ground to a halt again with almost hysterical cheering greeting
each line (a good example of the 'primitive' style in comedy). For the
first half of the show there was a vocal majority killing lines, laughs and
all attempts at timing. After a while they seemed to tire themselves out,
and one had the satisfaction of hearing people laugh at jokes and words,
rather than cheering each character who came on, at random
throughout the sketch.

We finished at about 1.30 a.m. but the audience refused to leave –
even after the auditorium lights had been on for some time. If any of us
so much as put a head around the curtain there was wild applause. After
two or three minutes of this, John went out and spoke to them like the
good headmaster he is – thanking them for being a wonderful audience
and adding savagely 'Now will you *please* go home.' This they enjoyed
even more – and it must have been over five minutes after the end that
they at last stopped applauding.

It was a strange kind of hysteria for a comedy show to create – one
can't imagine it happening to previous 'cult' shows like *Beyond the
Fringe* or *TW3* – perhaps it is because Monty Python itself is less controlled and contrived than these shows. We have created characters
which we ourselves find hysterical, why should we then be surprised that
an audience reacts in the same way?

We walked back to the hotel at 2.30 a.m. – with half a dozen grown
men with knotted handkerchiefs over their heads disappearing down
the road in front of us.

Monday, February 1st, Coventry

After breakfast at a café across from the hotel – called, believe it or not,
'The Gay Gannet' – Terry and I drove off in the Simca to revisit my old
school at Shrewsbury.

Terry is such a good companion – his insatiable sense of wonder and
discovery added immeasurably to the enjoyment of seeing the school
again. I showed Terry the studies, stone passages and stark bedrooms,
which had virtually been my life for five so-called 'formative' years. They
hadn't changed much, except that the studies seemed to have no restrictions on decoration – every *one* seemed to be decorated with rich curtains, colours, and huge photos of Mick Jagger. The only really sensuous

study in my time was John Ravenscroft's (now John Peel, the Radio One intellectual). On the notice board was a rule about women in studies – *women in studies!* An unthinkable sacrilege ten years ago.

In the school buildings there was even more exciting evidence that sacrilege had been, and was being committed throughout the school. On every landing, and on seemingly every spare piece of wall, in what had been dull passages and dark corridors, there were paintings done by the boys. One of them, on the same dour landing I must have passed thousands of times, on my way to the History Library, breathlessly late, on this same landing was a large canvas depicting a clothed youth on a bed, with three ladies around him, wearing only black stockings, suspenders and pants, revealing their crotches provocatively. Presumably it was intended to represent the schoolboy's dream – but to hang this dream in the school buildings seemed to be the best thing that had happened to Shrewsbury since Philip Sidney.[1]

Wednesday, February 3rd, Southwold

Father is now on L-Dopa, a new breakthrough in the treatment of Parkinson's Disease. It is still very expensive (each pill costs about 18/-), but his shaking seems very much better. His movements, and especially his grasp, are becoming more impaired, Mummy now has to help with things like tying shoelaces and buttoning awkward buttons. He takes about three-quarters of an hour to get up, shave and dress.

We went for a walk along Southwold front, in the gathering dusk. There was an exceptionally beautiful sunset – so many shades, from rich deep red to delicate pale pink. We drove on to the Common for a while and watched it.

Wednesday, February 10th

We lunched today at the BBC, Kensington House, and talked with the producers of *The Car versus the People*, a documentary in which we have sadly become involved. The lunch was quite pleasant – little was decided, though much was said, but we did meet Bill Tidy, one of the funniest cartoonists in the country. In fact, it is very, very rarely that a

1 1554–86. Complete Renaissance man and along with Charles Darwin and the founders of *Private Eye*, among the most famous old boys.

Tidy cartoon doesn't raise at least a titter in me. He's a Yorkshireman, beer-drinking and unaffectedly open and straightforward. He carries around with him the convivial atmosphere of a local pub on a Friday night – evident in the way he leans back in his chair and the way he tells stories. He seems to be getting enormous pleasure out of life. He has, it turns out, a child who is either ill or handicapped, and one is enormously glad for the child's sake that it has him as a father.

After our lunch grinds to an inconclusive halt at 3.00, we make our way over to TV Centre to appear on *Ask Aspel* – a show, compered by clean-shaven, charming, man for all seasons Michael Aspel. The idea is to play clips from BBC programmes which children have requested. Apparently they have a request for some Monty Python clip almost every week – giving the lie perhaps to Paul Fox's confident assertion that Monty Python would never work in a pre-nine o'clock slot.

Monday, February 15th

Decimal Day. Today, not only our old currency, but a small portion of our everyday language dies for ever and is replaced. In looking back, this day will perhaps appear as just another step away from the archaic obstinacies that set Britain apart from other countries of the world, and a step which should have been taken much earlier.

Funnily enough, I find myself resenting the new decimal coinage far less than the postal codes (which I fear will one day replace towns with numbers – and after towns streets, and after streets …?), or the all-figure telephone numbers which dealt one mighty blow to local feeling in London and, in the process, made it practically impossible to remember phone numbers.[1]

But the decimal coinage system seems to clarify, rather than confuse. I have no sentimental regrets at the passing of the threepenny bit, or the half-crown, only slight irritation that the sixpence – an old coin – should be incorporated into this new system, even temporarily, and also that for some inexplicable reason a number of smaller shops are still working in pounds, shillings and pence.

1 Our own area code changed from GULliver to the soulless 485.

Wednesday, February 17th

At 3.00 I arrive at the studios of Advision to do a voice-over for a Chesswood creamed mushroom commercial. It is the first of about half a dozen voice-over offers which has come to anything – which is pleasing because, of all the pride-swallowing things one does for money, voice-overs are the least painful. They generally take up only an hour or so of one's time, your face does not appear to link you with any product and the money is useful but modest enough to allay any guilt feelings about selling out.

There was the usual gaggle of advertising men present and, judging by the subtlety and intellectual complexity of the advert, six reasonably intelligent wombats could have done the job just as well.

Sunday, February 28th

I had been feeling guilty for some weeks that I had made no effort to follow up my decision to have William christened at St Martin's, the local church standing amongst the rubble of the Gospel Oak rebuilding scheme. And today I took the snap decision to go. I was literally summoned by bells. It was a strange feeling going into a church I did not know for a service that I did not really believe in, but once inside I couldn't help a feeling of warmth and security. Outside there were wars and road accidents and murders, striptease clubs and battered babies and frayed tempers and unhappy marriages and people contemplating suicide and bad jokes and *The Golden Shot*, but once in St Martin's there was peace. Surely people go to church not to involve themselves in the world's problems but to escape from them. And surprisingly also, here in the middle of devastated Kentish Town, was a large, unusually designed stone building, with polished pews and shining brass and a vicar and faithful people gathered. Though rationally I would find it difficult to justify my participation, I nevertheless was glad I went. In a funny way, I was really moved by the faith of the fifteen old ladies, four men, a choir (black and white) who were there with me. But seeing the vicar afterwards I felt a fraud.

Friday, March 5th

In the evening, a sneak preview of *And Now For Something Completely Different*. It is on at the Granada, Harrow, with [Gore Vidal's] *Myra*

Breckinridge. The manager is there to meet us when we arrive at the cinema. We are led upstairs and seated on the left-hand side of the circle, about six rows from the front. The whole idea of showing us ceremoniously to these seats is rather ludicrous, as the place is virtually empty.

Then the curtains draw back and there is our film. I found it dragged heavily and parts of it were downright dull. But my judgement is probably coloured by seeing most of it before – several times. I still feel sad that we didn't write more original material.

Sunday, March 14th

Python's success has resulted in a number of offers – e.g. a Python Christmas book (Methuen), three separate record contracts (Decca, Tony Stratton-Smith[1] and good old BBC Enterprises, who despite themselves appear to have sold over 10,000 of our first LP), merchandising T-shirts, West End shows for Bernard Delfont, etc, etc.

Terry and I and T Gilliam feel very much that we are in danger of losing sight of the wood for the trees. Python is a half-hour TV show and cannot easily be anything else. Any transformation of this show onto record, or onto the stage, will inevitably lose something from the original. The alternatives are therefore to put out these weaker substitute Pythons and make money from very little work, or else to work hard to make everything Python is involved in new, original, critical and silly. This requires a great deal of effort and, as all of us are at the moment employed on other pressing projects, no one seems willing to expend it. So we stumble on, with no great sense of direction. Like the record and the film, we have already stumbled into unsatisfactory compromises. I think there are a great many ahead.

We now have John Gledhill – of the Roger Hancock office – acting as the organiser and agent for Python Productions. It is going to be a hell of a job. Today we talked about notepaper!!

Some kind of sanity has prevailed, in that John C, after being reluctant to do any more TV Pythons, is gradually becoming one of the staunchest advocates of a new series, to be made in the autumn.

---

1 Racehorse owner, John Betjeman fan and general bon vivant, Tony started Charisma Records. He died, much missed by all, in 1987.

Monday, March 29th

Today, more filming for the May Day show,[1] including one gag involving John and myself – in the Grimsby Fish-Slapping dance – which ends up with my being knocked about eight feet into the cold, green, insalubrious waters of the Thames. However, once the waiting is over, this kind of stunt is quite pleasurable – it should almost certainly look funny and you are immediately fished out, undressed and given brandy, which is better treatment than most people who fall in the river could expect. Also you experience this pleasant feeling that, just by jumping into the river, you have justified your existence for that day, and can relax into a state of quiet euphoria.

Friday, April 23rd, St Andrews

The rain poured down all day. Terry rang and said that he and Alison had decided to go up to St Andrews (for our cabaret with John)[2] at lunchtime. As I had to wait until six o'clock for a dubbing session, I booked myself on to the flight to Edinburgh.

I was met by a cab driver who was to take me to St Andrews. We drove north, over the Forth Road Bridge and up to Kinross on the motorway. This then petered out, and the roads were narrower, more silent, with occasional holes, filled with deep puddles. What with the driving rain, the wind and the increasing remoteness of the area, it was, as the cab driver remarked, 'real Dracula weather'.

We arrived at St Andrews at 2.30. The hotel was beside the sea and, although I couldn't see the waves, their noise was quite deafening. I paid the cab driver £10, and he set off back to Edinburgh.

In the hotel I had the following conversation with an obliging night porter:

Night Porter: 'Would you like a cup of tea?'
Traveller: 'Well, that would be nice – but have you anything stronger?'
Porter: 'No, no, can't do that, sorry, not now.'

1 An attempt to produce a Euro-comedy link-up to mark May Day. We were chosen to provide the British segment, for which we created a number of very silly traditional dances.
2 John was always getting offered cabaret engagements, and he preferred to do them with Terry and myself than on his own. They paid quite well. He gave them up after being savagely heckled by London University medical students.

Traveller:	'Oh, dear.'
Porter:	'Would you like a glass of beer?'
Traveller:	'Yes, that would be fine.'
Porter:	'Righto.'
Traveller:	'There's not the slightest chance of a drop of scotch?'
Porter:	'A beer and a scotch?'
Traveller:	'Yes, please.'
Porter:	'Righto.'

Saturday, April 24th, St Andrews

My eight o'clock alarm call with newspapers arrived at 7.30, without newspapers. I drank a cup of tea and read a little, then lounged in the bath and pondered rather gloomily on the amount of work that lay ahead today.

At 2.30 we turned up at the Younger Hall, whose interior was as cold and inhospitable as the exterior. The most obvious problem we were going to have to face was the acoustics. One's voice simply died about half-way into the auditorium, unless we spoke at full blast. With long sketches such as 'World Forum', 'Lumberjack Song', 'I Don't Go Out Much Nowadays' monologue,[1] 'Gambolputty', 'Pet Shop' and gross and noisy ones like 'Shabby' and 'Gumby Flower Arranging' to do, this didn't bode well for two performances.

There was no time to eat, and hardly any to drink, before the first show. As usual the house was packed and the audience consistently appreciative. But it isn't a performance *I* shall remember with much pride. In the back of my mind throughout was the spectre of a second performance, and the gradual deterioration of my voice as I strained and shouted my way through. The 'Lumberjack Song' was a disaster. John, as the Colonel, came on and stopped it once, and we all trailed off and then had another bash – only slightly less distinguished than the first. My long monologue, 'I Don't Go Out Much', was delivered badly and without much confidence.

From the very start of the second performance it was obvious that they were a noisier, more appreciative audience – many of them little

---

1 A monologue I wrote for the 1965 Oxford Revue at Edinburgh. I always preferred to write and create characters rather than jokes *per se*, and this depended very much on performance.

short of ecstatic. I know I used them disgracefully, with shouting, grins, nods, ad-libs, etc. But it was amazing how much more impact every item had. For about 80 minutes it was almost five laughs a minute – 'I Don't Go Out Much' went down as successfully as it used to in Edinburgh – thus justifying Terry's faith in it (I don't think *I* would have put it in the show). All in all, this was one of the great performances. I especially enjoyed corpsing John (he maintains I got him five times).

Wednesday, May 12th

Terry and I have been working fairly solidly together – firstly finishing our eight-sketch commitment for *The Two Ronnies*, which has turned out to be the most unrewarding task financially and artistically. The sketches are drawn from us with lavish praise and unrestrained enthusiasm – and yet when we see them on TV they have been changed and coarsened and we are not happy.

But secondly we have been writing our Munich show,[1] which has been like old times, with lots of wild ideas developing.

On May 5th I was 28, and on May 6th at lunchtime we heard that we had come second at the Montreux Festival – winning The Silver Rose. The winner was an Austrian show, which everyone said was exactly like Python and I must say the title – 'Peter Lodynski's Flea-Market Company' – is not entirely dissimilar. But the lesson of Montreux is why did a Python copy defeat a Python original? The answer I fear is that their production and presentation was slick, whereas ours was unforgivably sloppy.

Saturday, May 15th

This morning we were woken by William at 7.15, then, for a short while, peace, until Thomas gets out of his cot about eight o'clock and is to be heard banging around the house in a very busy way.

Eventually he arrives outside our door, and there is some prolonged heavy breathing. He does not, for some reason of his own rather than ours, like to come in before we ask him, and so it depends on how tired

1 The brainchild of German producer and Python fan Alfred Biolek, this was to be a show written by and starring the Pythons, speaking German. It was duly recorded at Bavaria Studios in Munich in early July 1971. At least I can now sing 'Lumberjack Song' in German – a great way of clearing crowded ski slopes.

we are as to how much we take advantage of this uncharacteristic docility. But as soon as he is in the bedroom he rapidly starts to organise a book to be read, despite our half-hearted attempts to persuade him that an extra half-hour's sleep would do him the world of good.

Once we have all got up – now seldom later than 8.45 – and had breakfast, I normally take Thomas for a walk, or on Sundays for a more ambitious outing – last week we went on the North London Line to Kew Gardens. This morning Thomas wanted above all else to try the paddling pool in Parliament Hill playground. He was blissfully happy there for about an hour – and we then went on to feed the ducks on Highgate Ponds, returning home via the café for an ice-cream. Thomas is good company now and chats quite fluently. William sleeps the whole way.

Friday, May 21st

Eric is busy on the Monty Python book, but Terry Gilliam is fighting his way through, and perhaps out of, a lucrative 'Marty' [Feldman series] contract. The American TV people will not let Terry use any nudes, or even see the cleavage at the top of a pair of buttocks, and his Christmas card film, which went out in England in a children's programme on Christmas afternoon,[1] has been banned altogether from American TV. Such is television in the land of the free.

Sunday, June 20th

The first day of recording on our second LP in the Marquee studios. It was a good feeling to be working on Sunday in the middle of Soho – and the session is run almost entirely by and for ourselves. Unlike our previous BBC record there is no audience, and we are able to do several takes on each sketch to try and improve on it. This is very beneficial in one way, but I shall be interested to hear whether we need the impetus of a live audience – whether in fact we subconsciously concentrate harder and bring the better performances out of ourselves if we have an immediate soundboard for our antics. There is one very amenable young engineer, and Terry J is producing.

1 On *Do Not Adjust Your Set*.

Monday, June 21st

Another day spent in the recording studio in Dean Street. We worked hard, but my doubts about the record began to grow. Firstly, because it contains fewer bankers (i.e. strong, memorable sketches) than the first record. This is partly explained by the fact that the more conventional verbal sketches translate easily onto record, whereas the more complicated, tortuously interwoven sketches of the second series lose more away from their visual context. I am still worried by the lack of a reaction to our recording – but I put this down as much to my own weakness of judgement as anything. More seriously, I wish that everyone had been prepared to put some work into the writing of the record.

Thursday, June 24th

Leaving the studio at 3.15, Terry and I had about two hours to buy assorted props and costumes for a cabaret at the University of East Anglia in the evening. It was a hot day and, to my added frustration, the shops around Camden Town and Hampstead were all closed. I was looking for old coats, berets, scarves, etc, for Ken Shabby – and there is little worse than driving in a hurry on a hot day round closed shops to try and find torn old clothes. However, the Simon Community in Malden Road was open, and proved to be just what was wanted – but there was hardly time to throw the things in a suitcase, with toothbrush and black velvet suit, before the taxi arrived and we were taken off to Liverpool St.

There were thousands more people equally hot and equally hurried, and we only just managed to get seats in the restaurant car. John and Connie arrived with about 20 seconds to go, complete with cage and stuffed parrot.

We rehearsed the cabaret – it was about 50 minutes' worth – and arrived at the ball by about 10.00. We were shown to a cabaret room and a succession of the usual, rather anxious, slight, dishevelled officials came to tell us what was going on.

The University of E. Anglia, like many of the newer English universities, has had a fair amount of publicity for its sit-ins, protests, marches and other symptoms of left-wing radicalism. I was surprised, therefore, that this element seemed to be quite absent from the ball. They appeared to be an audience of exactly the same people who Robert [Hewison] and I performed to at Oxford about seven years ago.

Wednesday, August 4th

Meeting this morning between Charisma Records and John Gledhill, Terry Gilliam and myself to discuss the record cover. Our suggestion was not the easiest thing to sell. A classical record, with everything crossed out rather crudely and 'Another Monty Python record' scribbled in at the top. On the back a 97% authentic spiel about Beethoven and about the finer points of his Second Symphony – but, for those who can bear to read it through, it is gradually infiltrated by tennis references.

Charisma seem almost an ideal record company – or indeed company of any kind. Their offices in Brewer Street are functional, rather than plush, set on three floors above a dirty bookshop. Tony Stratton-Smith, who founded the company, has a tiny office at the top, with two hard wooden benches (giving the little room a rather ecclesiastical feel), a desk, a table, and an interesting selection of moderniana on the walls. They do not seem to have any fixed attitudes to their products, they seem to take decisions with the minimum of fuss and, what's more, they agreed to our record cover – which is quite a risk for any company.

Thursday, August 5th, Southwold

Caught the 8.00 train from Gospel Oak to Broad St. Thomas stood at the door to wave goodbye in his pyjama top – he was very good until I had almost reached the end of the village, when I heard a beseeching shout of 'Kiss! Daddy. Kiss! Kiss!' as I turned the corner.

From Broad Street I walked down to Liverpool Street Station, which, at 9.15 in the morning, is like swimming against a very fierce current – such is the surge of people pouring up the approach that in a momentary flash of panic I wondered if I would ever make it to the station. It was a rather frightening sight – this sea of faces. It was like some clever documentary maker's piece of film illustrating the increasing conformity of people's lives.

Ate breakfast on the train and was met at Darsham Station at 11.30.

Daddy and I walked across the common to the Harbour Inn. The L-Dopa tablets seem to have completely stopped his Parkinsonian trembling – but they cannot disguise his increasing vagueness and the difficulties of keeping up with what is happening around him.

In the evening I walked up the lane towards Frostenden. It was a clear evening and the sun shone on the gold fields of corn through the trees which side the road and straggle the landscape rather haphazardly, not in neat copses or woods like in chalk country. The effect was warm and secure and reassuring. At the same time, in London, Richard Neville[1] was being sentenced to fifteen months' imprisonment for publishing the Schoolkids issue of *Oz*. I can't help feeling that he would have appreciated this countryside for the same reasons that I do – and yet the only way society has of dealing with his imagination and intelligence is to put him away for over a year.

Wednesday, August 11th

Drove down the A3 through the Surrey Green Belt to visit one of Helen's friends from teacher training college – it was looking very green today, and the woodland, with patches of rough heathland emerging from the trees, dispelled the usual feelings of claustrophobia I have when driving through England's most middle-class county.

After lunch I left the women and children and drove the five miles or so into Guildford, a town with many more old and fine buildings than I remember before. I went to what must be one of the largest, and certainly the most haphazard second-hand bookshop in the country – Thorp's. It took me nearly one and a half hours to cast a very cursory glance over about 70% of their stock – shelved in a variety of different little rooms and one big timber-roofed chamber, in such a way that makes one suspect that the disorder is all part of a careful filing system, which takes years to appreciate fully.

I bought a handsome volume of Bulldog Drummond stories. I felt I ought to have an example of this unique genre – the public school, ultra-xenophobic spy story. It makes great reading – everyone is always 'fixing' each other 'with piercing stares'.

At supper I got into conversation with our hosts about the *Oz* sentences. Clearly, and rather disturbingly, their minds were made up – *Oz* and its editors were evils that had been judged guilty, and let it be a lesson to all others who are threatening the moral fibre of our society, and the most alarming thing was that they did not have a clue as to what *Oz* Schoolkids issue was. They automatically thought it was a collection

---

1 The editor of *Oz* magazine asked for teenage schoolkids to put together an edition. The 'schoolkids' produced an issue which put Neville and others in the dock at the Old Bailey, accused of corrupting morals and intending to 'arouse and implant in the minds of those young people lustful and perverted desires'. His long hair was ordered to be forcibly cut.

of obscene material which the editors had written to try and corrupt schoolchildren. They were quite taken aback when I told them that the issue had been written by schoolkids – and that the jury had acquitted them of the charge of corrupting children's morals. They had complete misconceptions about hippies – J said he wouldn't dare get into an argument in case they set on him. They talked about 'London' as a descriptive term for all rather suspect, critical, left-wing, un-British opinions, and implied that it was here in Surrey that the 'English way of life' would be defended to the bitter end.

The four-month gap at this point is the result of that diarist's nightmare, the loss of an almost complete notebook. According to family folklore it was dumped in the rubbish bin by my son William who, at the age of one, had developed a great interest in putting things inside other things. Whatever happened, it never reappeared. Momentarily bereft, I felt like giving up the diary altogether but the loss made me realise that it had become such a part of my life, that it was inconceivable to jettison it. If anything, I compensated by writing more.

Friday, December 24th

Yesterday I found a smart gallery in Crawford Street and ended up spending £45 on a primitive of two cows painted by someone called Beazley in 1881. Actually I didn't know it was a primitive – the cows looked perfectly normal to me – but it's a very in-word in art circles at the moment, and I think it means that commercially I'm onto a good thing. Be that as it may, I'm glad to have the painting, because at last I've found something that I really enjoy looking at – and the serenity of the two cows is quite infectious. In my quest for pictures I went into another art gallery in Crawford Street and spent an uncomfortable few minutes looking round under the baleful eye of a drunk proprietor – and I mean really drunk, full of self-pity, with red, streaming eyes and almost unable to utter a word – whilst across the table sat a young man gazing impassively at him. As I left the owner tried to get me to have a drink with him. I declined and his face dropped as if he had been bitterly hurt.

Saturday, December 25th

A rather fine, sunny morning, and for the first time in our marriage we woke on Christmas morning in our own home.

Thomas saw James across the road, and then they both saw Louise looking out of her window, and soon there was an impromptu gathering of little children comparing presents on the pavement outside our house. The quiet of the day, the sunny morning and the neighbours all talking made me feel very glad – about staying in London, and about living in Oak Village. If it doesn't sound too pedantic, I felt that this was how city life should be.

Monday, December 27th

In the evening I was part of a rather curious function at the Abraxas Squash Club. This took the form of a fancy-dress squash match between Monty Python and the Abraxas staff, with John, Terry and myself representing Python.

Terry was dressed in oversized trousers, John as a ballerina in a tutu, and I had borrowed the wasp's outfit from Hazel [Pethig]. Playing as a wasp may have looked spectacular, but it was in fact rather difficult, as part of the costume consisted of two extra legs, to the end of which – on Helen's suggestion – I had tied two extra pairs of gym shoes. However, when I tried to make a shot, these spare legs would swing round and nudge my aim. In consequence I lost all three games to a man dressed as a savage.

Tuesday, December 28th

To the Odeon Kensington to meet my mother, Angela, Veryan and the three kids and take them to see our film *And Now For Something Completely Different*. It lasted eleven weeks at the Columbia and took nearly £50,000 at that cinema alone (over two thirds of the cost of making the picture). Its one week at Oxford ran into four weeks as a result of the demand, and it was held over for an extra week in Leicester and Liverpool. All of which bodes well for a film which Terry and I thought would be received with jeers.

We all sat in almost solitary state in the 80p seats at the front of the circle. It was a strange feeling – here I was sitting next to my mother, who had only come to films with me as a rare treat when I was young, watching me on the big screen. Unfortunately the tedious repetition of old material in the film hardly swelled my mind with pride.

Friday, December 31st

Harold Nicolson used to sum up his year on December 31st with a few pithy words. It's a sort of diary writer's reward for all those dull July 17ths and October 3rds. (Will I still be keeping my diary on Dec. 31st 1999? Now that's the kind of thought which gives survival a new urgency.)

1971 was my fifth full year in television and certainly on the face of it we have achieved a lot. A TV series, which has reached the sort of national notoriety of *TW3*. 'Monty Python', 'Silly Walks', 'And Now For Something Completely Different', etc, have become household words. The TV series has won several awards during the year, including the Silver Rose of Montreux. The second Monty Python album has sold over 20,000 copies since release in October, and *Monty Python's Big Red Book* completely sold out of both printings within two weeks. It has sold 55,000 copies, and 20,000 more are being printed for February. In London it was top of the bestseller lists. And finally the film which we made a year ago and were so unhappy about, looks like being equally successful.

From all this no one can deny that Monty Python has been the most talked about TV show of 1971 – and here is the supreme irony, for we have not, until this month, recorded any new shows since October 1970.

The split between John and Eric and the rest of us has grown a little recently. It doesn't prevent us all from sharing – and enjoying sharing – most of our attitudes, except for attitudes to work. It's the usual story – John and Eric see Monty Python as a means to an end – money to buy freedom from work. Terry J is completely the opposite and feels that Python is an end in itself – i.e. work which he enjoys doing and which keeps him from the dangerous world of leisure. In between are Graham and myself.

1972

Sunday, January 2nd

In the morning, Rolf, Ranji [Veling] and I went for a long walk on the Heath and talked about Rolf's pet subject – how to simplify life. He feels that the problems of pollution or increasing crime or mental illness are the result of us all wanting and being offered too much.

I'm glad that there are cars and planes and television and washing machines, and I think we cannot suddenly pretend that they have not been invented – but I feel we must control their use, and that they should be used not to dictate but to stimulate. Any urban planning should include an open play area at least twice the size of the car park, instead of the opposite; there should be severe restrictions on cars in central London – but above all, in every area there should be greater encouragements for people to meet and talk – not in official meetings or on two nights a week, but all the time. There should be space indoors and outdoors, where people would want to stop and gather. At the base of every block of flats there should be a big, well-furnished well-equipped coffee shop or restaurant, a big foyer with papers, magazines, books on sale – and even a few fairground attractions. It would mean a radical redirection of funds available for housing, but one quarter of the vast wealth in the hands of private property developers would, I think, help to equalise a system which at present is doomed – the colossal difference in living conditions which is being widened every day as new council estates are built on the cheap – and with them is built boredom, jealousy, repression, anger ...

Helen and I drove over to Simon Albury's flat in Ladbroke Grove. Simon was fairly high when we got there, as were David and Stan. Unstoned were most of the wives, David's sister Rosemary, and ourselves. Source of the stuff was R.[1] I drank bourbon and smoked occasionally, and heard riotous tales from Rosemary Dodd about her Cordon Bleu cooking

---

1 Drugs were a source of great interest at the time. It was quite respectable to have experienced them in some shape or form. Simon had worked on a research paper on drug use for the Home Office.

for the nobility. She had worked with the Queen's cousins for some time, and apparently they drank so much that at one meal there was a special footman detailed to stand behind the hostess and hoist her politely up every time she sank beneath the table.

R, as lithe and big-eyed and diffident as ever, suddenly becomes animated. He is smoking his third or fourth joint of the evening (no passing around here – it's R's joint) and telling me of his poetry writings. After a long and serious build-up I was expecting *The Waste Land* at least, but what I got was 'Zim, Zam, Zap, the Zimbabwe is going to Zap you man' – as Simon A remarked, 'Pot never helped anyone.'

Tuesday, January 4th

At Terry's when Amin – a Pakistani from Alison's Botany Department – returned from Pakistan. He was out there throughout the brief India–Pakistan war – in which East Pakistan was finally taken by the Indians on behalf of the Bengalis who live there. It was a short, sharp war, which has resulted in the setting up of the independent state of Bangla-Desh. Amin was bitter about the Pakistani surrender, and his primary reaction seemed to be emotional – hurt national pride, and a desire for revenge – but as he talked it was clear that he also had a secondary, more realistic reaction, which was relief that the war had ended, and the hope that India and Pakistan would now live together. It was a strange sensation, sitting in a comfortable south London sitting room, hearing from someone who only a month before had been living through air-raids, in a country where the old and infirm had come down from the mountains to the 100° desert to fight – clad in furs and skins.

Friday, January 7th

Back into our routine again – a week of dubbing, writing, rehearsing, and recording.

Today there are two major sketches – one with Graham C as Biggles, using generally abusive language, dictating a letter to King Haakon thanking him for the eels, and finding out Algy was a homosexual – the other was a parrot shop type of sketch with John as a customer in a cheese shop, and myself as an obliging assistant, who has none of the cheeses the customer asks for – and John goes through about fifty, before shooting me. Typical of the difference in writing since the first series, is that, no longer content to just write in a cheese shop as the setting, there are throughout the sketch two city gents dancing to balalaika music in a corner of the shop. Our style of humour is becoming more *Goon Show* than revue – we have finally thrown off the formal shackles of the *Frost Report* (where we all cut our teeth), and we now miss very few chances to be illogical and confusing.

Tuesday, January 11th

This evening, in order to cheer ourselves up after a day in which it rained solidly, Helen and I went to see Woody Allen's film *Bananas*, and another comedy *Where's Poppa*[1] at the Essoldo, Maida Vale. Both the films made us hoot and roar with laughter – though neither added up to much – there were just delicious moments of comedy. *Bananas* was rather like a Python show, with the same kind of feverish pace and welter of jokes and joke situations. *Where's Poppa* was another very funny Brooklyn Jewish comedy.

Came back feeling very much better. Read more of Charlie Mingus' autobiography *Beneath the Underdog* – amazed at the speed of the book and the great turns of phrase and styles of speech which Mingus and his Watts friends speak. Conditions may have been bad and Whitey may have been a continuous oppressive force, but they knew how to have a good time – and there's much more spontaneity and honesty and good, plain communication in Mingus' world than there is in our own.

Saturday, January 15th

At home doing odd-jobs for most of the day. In the afternoon a giggly phone-call, and a girl from Roedean, one Lulu Ogley, rang from a phone box with some of her friends. They wanted to know what I was really like!

Lulu spoke rather like Princess Anne, but asked fairly sensible questions, whereas her friend was unable to bring herself to ask whether or not I was married. Last night John Gledhill gave me a phone number from an anonymous girl who wanted to contact me, and a few days back

---

1 Directed by Carl Reiner (Rob, his son, and director of *Spinal Tap*, appears in a minor role). It starred George Segal and Ruth Gordon.

I received a rather sultry photo from a girl of seventeen. Altogether most disturbing.

Monday, January 31st

At lunchtime I went for a run across the Heath, and had that rare and pleasurable sensation of running in a snowstorm – the snow silencing everything, emphasising isolation, but cooling and soothing at the same time.

The papers and news today are full of Bernadette Devlin's physical attack on Mr Maudling in the Commons.[1] The shooting of thirteen Irish Catholics in Londonderry yesterday has made England the most reviled country in the world. For almost the first time in the whole of their impossible task in Ireland, the troops seem to have been guilty of a serious misjudgement. Now Bernadette shouts loudly and viciously for revenge. It all seems a most unpleasant and violent spiral, but surely now the British government must start to take the Catholics seriously.

Tuesday, February 1st

In the evening we met Terry and Al for a drink at the Lamb in Lamb's Conduit Street, and afterwards they took us out for a meal to a hitherto untried restaurant, La Napoule in North Audley Street.

Terry became very excited and emotional about Ireland and the Londonderry march. He totally blamed the government – on the grounds that they are the ones who hold the position of power, and they are the ones who should be held responsible for any trouble. I argued realistically rather than instinctively that, as the government had rightly or wrongly taken the decision to ban marches, this decision had to be enforced, hence the presence of troops. The marchers must have expected some trouble for they are quite well aware that any march attracts groups of people who want a fight and will do anything they can to provoke one. The soldiers must have panicked and fired at random, but the explosive situation was caused by the stubbornness of the government and the anger of the Catholics.

2 As Reginald Maudling, the Home Secretary, tried to defend the British Army's killing of thirteen civilians on what became known as Bloody Sunday, the MP Bernadette Devlin, 21 years old and the youngest woman ever to be elected to Parliament, crossed the floor of the Commons and punched him in the face.

I am very cautious of people who are absolutely right, especially when they are vehemently so – but the inaction of the government and especially Maudling's statement last night that any yielding to Catholic pressure would be 'surrender', smacks of Lyndon Johnson and Vietnam and makes me angry and frustrated with Heath's unpleasant government.

Thursday, February 3rd

After a morning's work at Camberwell, we drove over to John's for lunch and a chat about possible new additions to the cabaret at Nottingham University. We decided to put in 'Argument' sketch – a quick-fire Cleese/Chapman piece from the new series, and one or two smaller additions such as the 'Silly Ministers' and the 'Time-Check' – 'It's five past nine and nearly time for six past nine. Later on this evening it will be ten o'clock and at 10.30 we join BBC2 in time for 10.33. And don't forget tomorrow, when it'll be 9.20,' etc, etc.

We caught the 4.50 St Pancras to Nottingham train – spread ourselves over a First Class compartment and rehearsed.

Apparently the demand for tickets had been so great that we had been asked to do an extra performance, with about 700 students at each. They were a very good audience, not drunk, intelligent and appreciative. Our performances were a little edgy, as we were doing new material for the first time, but the second house, at 9.15, was much better. We did about 40 minutes each time, and were paid a little less than £200 each for the evening. In between shows we were visited by interviewers from student papers, rag magazines, Radio Nottingham and the revue group – all of whom were ushered into our presence in a carefully supervised way, making one feel like a visiting Head of State. We then travelled the thirty-odd miles to Lincoln, where we were to do our third cabaret of the evening, at the Aquarius Club.

A little side door next to Woolworths led us into this charmless little club, where two of the first people we saw were police, and the other two were bouncers. There seemed to be a general air of anxiety and unease about the management of the club, but I suppose this was their natural manner, in the best Vercotti[1] traditions. We were led upstairs through a very small room so thick with smoke that it felt as though they were

1 Luigi and Dino Vercotti, two hugely ineffective Mafiosi, created by Terry J and myself.

doing laboratory tests to see how much humans could take before passing out. As the time for the cabaret drew nearer, we became quite fatalistic about it and decided to tell them from the start that we were unarmed. A minor scuffle broke out nearby, the basins in the gents were full of vomit and there was a general brooding feeling of squalor and suppressed violence. Imagine our great and pleasant surprise when we started the cabaret and, apart from two girls in the very front, they not only listened quietly, but also roared with laughter.

Sunday, February 6th, Southwold

Arrived at Croft Cottage at 9.45. Both parents looked well. It was a dull and rainy day and not one to lure us outside, but I did cycle to Wangford before lunch and afterwards we walked along the sea front at Southwold. It was a heavy sea, with a strong on-shore wind piling up big breakers. We heard later that one man had been drowned and three others miraculously saved when their fishing boat upturned off this very beach a few hours earlier.

At home in the warmth of Croft Cottage, we shut out the miserable day and ate, drank, watched television and talked. The march of civil rights protesters at Newry this afternoon turned out to be entirely peaceful, which was a tremendous relief after last week's shootings in Londonderry. In the news pictures from Newry one could see cameras – still, film and TV – everywhere, waiting for the violence that caught the media unprepared in Londonderry.

Still Mr Heath and this complacent, indolent, arrogant and unfeeling Tory government refuse to try and ease the situation. Talk in the papers of troops being brought in to deal with the miners' strike – altogether I feel disgusted and depressed by the heartlessness of this government towards the underprivileged. From now on I am a fervent socialist. (This could change within a week – ed.)

Thursday, February 10th

Assembled for an all-Python writing meeting at Terry's at 10.00. John sends word that he is ill. Extraordinarily sceptical response. However we work on, and for a laugh decide to write a truly communal sketch. Accordingly all four of us are given a blank sheet of paper and we start to write about two exchanges each before passing on the paper. After

an hour and a half we have four sketches – with some very funny characters and ideas in them. They may all work if interlocked into a four-
sketch mixture. Eric suggested that we all be very naughty and go to
see *Diamonds are Forever*, the latest of the James Bond films at the
Kensington Odeon. After brief and unconvincing heart-searching, we
drive over to Kensington – but, alas, have not been in the cinema for
more than 20 minutes when the film runs down. After a few minutes
there is much clearing of throat, a small light appears in front of the
stage and a manager appears to tell us that we are the victims of a
power cut (this being the first day of cuts following four weeks of government intractability in the face of the miners' claim). For half an
hour there is a brief, British moment of solidarity amongst the beleaguered cinemagoers, but, as we were shirking work anyway, it looked
like a shaft of reprobation from the Great Writer in the sky.

Friday, February 11th

So serious is the emergency that there are now certain areas which three
or four times a week will be designated 'high risk' and liable to up to
eight hours power loss per day. Camberwell must have been one of
them, for we worked by oil lamp-light from 10–12, and from 3 until 5. At
5.00 drove in to Python Prods. offices to meet Alfred Biolek, here on a
five-day flying visit. He told us that the show we made in Germany had
been shown with generally favourable reactions and he wanted us to fly
over for a weekend and discuss plans for a second German-made programme in September.

   Home by 7.00 to a darkened house, so I reckon I have spent eleven of
my working hours without electricity today. The news is exceptionally
gloomy. The miners have refused to break and the emergency will last for
at least another two weeks. A nauseating Heath speech on TV and the
awful complacency of Lord Stokes[1] on *Any Questions* moves me to send
£50 to the miners.

Sunday, February 13th

General feeling of utter gloom from reading the papers – the power
emergency, the civil war in Ireland, the imprisonment of anti-Smith

1 Donald Stokes, Chairman of British Leyland Motor Company.

people in Rhodesia, all rather unpleasant. Shinwell,[1] a politician of sixty years' standing, was on the radio saying that this emergency was worse than the General Strike of 1926, because the feeling in the country was more bitter, and it does seem that Heath and the Conservative government – who pledged themselves to 'unite the country' when they were elected – have, by their non-government, succeeded in polarising it more than ever.

Monday, February 14th

Drove down to Terry's and we worked at putting a show together. Driving home has become quite an adventure now, for with the power-cuts I never know which traffic lights will be working and which won't. Street lights have generally been turned off, and when there is a blackout as well it becomes quite eerie. Driving at rush hour round the darkened Elephant and Castle, with hundreds of cars and as much light as a Suffolk lane is a disconcerting experience. But in a way it seems to take some of the urgency and aggression out of driving.

Tuesday, February 15th

At 10.30 Eric arrives and we work together rewriting three film pieces of Eric's for the next six shows. (Terry is having a day at home.) Our next power-cut comes at 3.00, and we carry on working by candlelight, waiting until 6.00 to do our typing. I must confess to quite enjoying this enforced disruption of routine. It appeals also to that yearning, deep in the back of one's subconscious, to be controlled by the elements – it's a form of security against all-powerful technology. The security of having to stop certain activities when the sun fades and the light goes. After all, only three generations of Palins have known electric light – before that stretch back the influences of many, many ancestors who lived in a permanent power-cut.

Saturday, February 19th

The coal strike is over. Yesterday the Wilberforce Court of Enquiry recommended 20% pay-rises for the miners on the grounds that they were

1 Emanuel 'Manny' Shinwell (1884–1986), socialist peer, the longest-lived politician of his times.

a special deserving case. The miners didn't accept immediately and in late-night bargaining with Mr Heath, secured even more concessions. The picketing was called off at 1.00 this morning, and the miners, after a ballot next week, should be back at work at the weekend. They will have been out for eight weeks – and the country, we are constantly told, is losing millions of pounds due to industrial power-cuts. It seems to me that the Wilberforce report has shown the government to be completely and utterly responsible. The miners 'special case' is not something which Wilberforce himself has discovered – it was clear to anyone before the strike started – but the government, faced with either admitting that their incomes policy was unjust, or trying to break the miners, as they did the electricity workers last year, chose to try and break the miners. In the end the miners won – and the weeks of reduced pay and unemployment which they had added to their already unpleasant working conditions, were made worthwhile. I regard my £50 as well spent!

An interesting sidelight to the strike has been the almost uninterrupted rise of the Stock Exchange during the weeks of crisis.

Monday, February 21st

Took a day off from writing to sort out various dull items of household management and run on Hampstead Heath in the drizzle. In the evening Graham Chapman and David and Barry Cryer[1] and his wife Terry came round for a meal. Graham arrived rather drunk and sullen after a bad day's work, and was rather bellicose to start with. At one point he started into a violent tirade against carpets, and how much he hated them. Barry Cryer remains the same – funny, considerate, straightforward and modest, a winning combination, which has been absolutely consistent since he first introduced himself to me at my first *Frost Report* meeting six years ago. He is the perfect antidote to the introverted unpredictability of Graham, and we all had a splendid evening.

Tuesday, February 22nd

The weather is still grey and dismal. At 2.30 the news comes through of an IRA bombing at Aldershot. An officers' mess has been blown up in

1 Barry and Marty Feldman were the two writers who welcomed me when I arrived for the first script meeting on *The Frost Report*. Barry and I and Terry J later wrote and performed for *Late-Night Line-Up*, from which we were eventually sacked.

retaliation for the killings in 'Derry. But the casualties are five cleaning ladies, one military vicar and one civilian.

Wednesday, March 15th

At Bart's Hospital sports ground at Chislehurst we spent the day filming Pasolini's version of the Third Test Match – complete with a nude couple making love during the bowler's run-up. Two extras actually obliged with a fully naked embrace – which must be a Python 'first'. The filming went smoothly, as it has done all this week. John C hasn't been with us, as he dislikes filming so much that he had a special three-day limit written into his contract.

This evening Helen went out to her pottery classes, and Terry J, Terry G and Viv Stanshall came round for a meeting. The reason for this particular combination was that Viv Stanshall (whom we last worked with on *Do Not Adjust Your Set* – and who has since been doing some very weird and imaginative and original pieces for radio, as well as occasional gigs) had been in touch with Terry G to enlist his co-operation in a musical cartoon – ideas by Viv Stanshall, pictures by Terry G.

However, at the moment Gilliam is going through a spell of disillusionment with animations. He no longer enjoys doing them, and claims his ideas have dried up as well. He is much more keen on directing or writing live action, and this he wants to do in collaboration with Terry J and myself. Gilliam felt that the injection of non-Python ideas from Viv might actually get us going on something, instead of just talking. We all got on well, we ate Helen's fantastic pâté, frankfurters and sauerkraut, and drank several bottles of Sancerre.

In the general mood of confidence and optimism which the Loire had generated, we decided to try and find backing for a 90-minute, feature-length film involving the four of us. Watch this column for further exciting developments.

Thursday, March 16th

Another good day's filming, ending with a marvellously chaotic situation at a flyover building site at Denham on the A40. I was narrator in front of the camera, describing how work was going on a new eighteen-level motorway being built by characters from 'Paradise Lost'. So behind me were angels, devils, Adam and Eve, etc, etc. All around us was the deafening noise of huge bulldozers. We were trying to time the take to the moment when the largest of these mighty earth-movers came into shot. So amidst all the dirt and mud and noise you would hear Ian shouting 'Here he comes!' Rick the camera operator shouting 'Move your harp to the left, Graham!' George dashing to take Adam and Eve's dressing gowns off, then the earth-mover would stop and plunge off in another direction, and all the efforts were reversed.

Thursday, April 6th

Almost two years and nine months to the day since we shot our first feet of Python TV film at Ham, we were at Windsor to shoot what is probably our last. On July 8th 1969 we started with Terry dressed as Queen Victoria, and today we finished with myself dressed as an Elizabethan.

Tuesday, April 11th

Terry and I meet Bill Borrows of the ACTT – the film technicians' union – to ask about joining as directors (for our summer film). The union, which five years ago was all powerful, and held the crippling ITV strike in 1968, which got London Weekend off to such a disastrous start, is now on its uppers. There are few films being made in England (only eleven this year) and the union has 70% of its members unemployed. Along with many other unions it has refused to register under the government's Industrial Relations Bill, and it may go under.

So Bill Borrows was indeed pleased to see Python people. *And Now For Something Completely Different* was, after all, a very successful British film – it's breaking box-office records at a cinema in Canada even now. We were given forms to fill in, and it looks as though there will be no trouble.

Saturday, April 15th

Cool, but often sunny – this was the nearest to a spring day we have had since the middle of March. In celebration of it, we went 'en famille' on the train to Kew Gardens.

At the station we have to wait for an hour, as a woman has trapped herself underneath a train. I presume it was a suicide attempt. People go and stare at her, but the ambulance is a long time coming, and the railway officials are in a complete panic. No one knows where the key to the first-aid cupboard is, for instance. Classic English characters emerge in such a situation – a lady, laden with parcels, tells Helen almost regretfully 'I didn't see any blood across the line or anything – I don't think she'd cut her wrists or anything. Why do people do it, that's what I wonder.'

We were on the station for an hour – which says a lot for Thomas and William's patience. Home by 6.30, and Helen and I spent the evening watching the box. I finished E L Doctorow's *Book of Daniel* – a novel about the Rosenbergs (who were executed for treason in the early 1950s anti-commie atmosphere in the US). Written through the eyes of their son Daniel, it is good because it shows how complicated are the various reactions of family and friends to what now seems just a monstrously unfair case. It's full of atmosphere – the Bronx in the 1950s, for instance – and yet another novel which makes me want to go to America. Here I am, nearly 29, and never outside Europe.[1]

Sunday, April 16th

Our sixth wedding anniversary.

We have reached a kind of material plateau at the moment – a house, two cars, two babies. Now we have more time to think about ourselves, and avoid becoming complacent lumps. We go out by ourselves once a week if possible, to a cinema and a meal, and can always go to the country at the weekends if we become really cheesed off. But we're no longer the young savers, or the young home-hunters. We have a lot – the question now is, what are we going to do with it?

I'm fond of Oak Village – with its relative peace from the motor car, and its scale, which enables you to see your neighbours often. Today I sat in the garden and read about rising house prices in the *Sunday Times*. This place is now probably worth £20,000, which is a 70% increase in four years. We are well-off by most people's standards – but we don't really want to move from here, we don't really want a bigger car. Our biggest luxuries are food and drink.

---

1 Rectified two months later, when Terry J and I made our first trip to America for three weeks of sightseeing from New York to New Orleans, the Grand Canyon and San Francisco.

Saturday, April 22nd

Simon Albury turned up unexpectedly in the evening. We've missed his schemes and stories over the last couple of months – but he made a great comeback this evening, firing me once again with great enthusiasm to go to the States. I must say all the omens seem right at the moment. I have the money and the time in the summer, and I only have one year to go until I'm 30 – which, rightly or wrongly, I regard as a psychological turning-point beyond which one can no longer lay claim to youthful enthusiasm. Also Simon will be in New York making three films for *Man Alive* – the BBC programme he now works for. And of course it's convention time in June, when the American election year really starts to hot up. I've always been fascinated by American politics, and I find the idea of attending a convention exciting in itself, as well as giving a point to going to the States.

Thursday, April 27th, Southwold

I lunched on the train to Ipswich. Excellent railway-made steak and kidney pie, washed down with a bottle of Liebfraumilch. The weather began to clear, as I got on to the little diesel train from Ipswich to Darsham, and, by the time it arrived at Darsham at 3.30, the sun was shining on the fresh, clean Suffolk countryside.

My father met me and drove me to Southwold. He seems as slow as usual, but one can't help feeling that he still has a lot of untapped potential for enjoying life. For instance, he had been on a choir outing to see 'The Black and White Minstrel Show' in Norwich, but he and the Vicar left the main party, and went to see *The Go-Between*[1] instead. Ostensibly not the kind of film my father would like at all, but he enjoyed it so much that he wants to see it again. This was very encouraging – and I can't help feeling that, as his old irascibility decreases, and he is forced to take things more slowly, he does enjoy diversion more.

Unfortunately he is still no conversationalist, and, although still interesting and jokey in his own stories, he finds it impossible to follow anyone else's. This is clearly very difficult to live with, and my mother has become sharp and rather quick to reprove him. I can't blame her.

1 Directed by Joseph Losey, script by Harold Pinter. Set in East Anglia, close to Fakenham where my father was born and brought up.

Her mind works so fast and she has for so long lived with someone who shares hardly any of her interests. The sad thing is that both of them suppress each other's potential instead of developing it. My visits are a sort of escape valve for both of them.

Sunday, April 30th

In between showers, I took Thomas and Willy out to the Zoo. The new monkey house is being feverishly finished off in preparation for the Duke of Edinburghal opening on Thursday. It is not completely satisfactory as the glass fronts of the cages tend to reflect the faces of the crowd. Perhaps it's a subtly intended reversal. The gorillas, orang-utans and chimps bask in rather aseptic glory in their new premises. The sea lions were the only animals who really gave us value for our 80p – and the wild boar had new babies, which gave her a bit more box-office appeal. Thomas was most interested in the dead mice in the owls' cages. In fact he seems preoccupied at the moment with dead things. Any animal not actually moving encourages Thomas to ask 'Is it killed?'

Friday, May 5th

Awoke aged 29. It was sad that the early May sunshine had vanished – to be replaced with grey drizzle. I broke my dietary controls on breakfast and ate eggs and bacon and toast.

We drove on to rehearsal at the new BBC Rehearsal Rooms in North Acton. Although in a drably industrial area – with a view from the window as depressing as that from the old London Weekend Rehearsal Rooms in Stonebridge Park – the block is well equipped and still smart. There are all your favourite telly faces Dr Who, John Paul from *Doomwatch*, Harry Worth, etc, etc. For the footballers amongst us, there is a spacious, soft-rubber covered floor, ideal for indoor footy. Eric is going to buy a ball.

Saturday, May 6th, Abbotsley

A quick lunch, and then to Winhills Junior School in St Neots. At 3.00 I had to be one of the judges in the May Queen contest. Helen, her mother, and three parents, Thomas, William and myself sat at a long table in the playground, whilst no less than fifty-seven entrants for the

May Queen competition paraded before us at the top of some steps. It was not a very pleasant experience seeing these 8–11-year-old girls reduced to such nervous wrecks by the combination of the booming PA system and our appraising stares. Also it took a great deal of time, and the wind was now cool and strong. In addition, William kept climbing up the steps towards the girls, and playing to the audience quite appallingly. However, in the end, a girl was selected. Not my particular choice, but she was a bonny, cheerful-looking redhead, with an English-Rose-like honesty about her. It was rather a revelation to be told by a little girl next to me, 'I don't know why you chose 'er – she swears all the time!'

Sunday, May 7th

Got to talking politics with Helen's mother – she is equally shy of arrogant Conservatives and doctrinaire socialists – and she sees the worst of both on her committees.[1] She says how sad it is that party politics mean so much in local government. There are even fewer chances of an independent like herself being elected when the new areas come into force next year.

Thursday, May 25th

The last Python TV recording for at least eighteen months. Our last show contains the 'wee-wee' wine-taster, 'Tudor Jobs' – with a long bit for myself – both sketches which John doesn't like at all, so there is a slight tenseness in the air. It's a very busy last show, with plenty for everyone to do, and only a small amount of film. A fairly smooth day's rehearsal, but it was unusual to see Duncan Wood [Head of Comedy] and Bill Cotton at our final run-through. Apparently they later told Ian that there would have to be cuts in the show. This is the first time they've ever suggested any censorship – in what has been quite an outspoken series. The recording was chequered. Graham was in a very nervous state – he had been worried by his pulse rate, which he said was 108 before the recording – and was drinking as he hasn't done since December and January's recordings, so in one sketch he skidded to a halt, and it was about eight retakes

1 Helen's mother was on the Huntingdon and Cambridgeshire county council as an Independent, specialising in education.

and ten minutes of recording time later that the sketch was eventually completed.

After the show there was hardly time to feel relief or regret, as Python was cleared away for maybe the last time ever. After a drink in the club, we went on to a Python party at the Kalamaris Tavern in Queensway. We crammed into the basement with cameramen, vision mixers, make-up girls, Python people and their hangers-on

Saturday, May 27th

In an attempt to get most of our Python work out of the way before the summer recess at the beginning of June, we worked all yesterday on material for the German show, and this morning there was still no time off, as I had to gather scripts, props, train times, etc for our first foray into mass cabaret – at the Lincoln Pop Festival tomorrow. It is a frustrating business trying to buy simple things like vases to smash. People are so keen to sell you the unbreakable one. I hadn't the heart to tell the man who sold me on the many virtues of plastic flowers – 'they can be cleaned when they get dirty' – that all I wanted them for was to smash them with a wooden mallet.

Sunday, May 28th, Lincoln

Dawned cloudy and grey yet again. But at least the high winds of the past two days have gone. It's still not good weather for open-air pop festivals, and the Sunday papers are full of reports of mud, and tents blowing down and general bad times from Bardney. We took the 10.15 from King's Cross to Lincoln and British Rail did little to dispel the gloom of the morning by keeping the buffet car locked, and not even a cup of coffee available for the whole journey. We read the papers and rehearsed.

At about 4.00 we set out for Bardney, about ten miles east of Lincoln, and the Open-air Pop Festival [the first to be staged in England since the Isle of Wight in 1971].

In many ways this festival is being used as a test case. There is a great deal of opposition from property owners and Tories generally to the festivals – which they see as insanitary occasions catering for insanitary people who want to take all kinds of drugs, fornicate en masse in England's green and pleasant land, and listen to noisy and discordant music. Locals will be terrorised, property laid waste and traditional English rights generally interfered with. So this festival has only been allowed to go on on condition that if there has been unreasonable nuisance caused, its organisers, Stanley Baker[1] and Lord Harlech, are liable to prison sentences.

The first evidence of this mighty gathering, estimated at 50,000 people, was a long traffic jam stretching from the village of Bardney. People later confirmed that the jams were caused by sightseers who had come to 'look at the festival'. Most of the audience clearly couldn't afford cars, and there to prove it was a constant stream of kids walking beside the road making for the site.

The weather had been really bad for the start of the festival, with gales blowing two marquees down on the Friday night. The marquees could not be salvaged as fans had torn them up and used them as protection from the elements. Real Duke of Edinburgh's Award stuff.

It was about 9.15 when we eventually got through the village. As we were supposed to be on at 9.55, and traffic was at a standstill, we walked. Terry especially was becoming most agitated, and in the end we asked a policeman if there was any chance of a police escort or a police car to take us the remaining mile or so up to the site. He managed to get us a lift with two plain-clothes CID officers. The first thing they wanted was our autographs, and then they embarked on as vicious a piece of driving as I've ever seen. Speeding up the side of the column of cars, they drove maliciously hard at the straggling groups of long-haired pedestrians, blaring their horns and giving 'V' signs.

Once at the site we were taken by John Martin, the organiser, to Stanley Baker's caravan to have a drink and last-minute rehearsal. In Baker's caravan there was iced champagne, and Mike Love and Al Jardine of the Beach Boys (who were appearing after us) sitting around. Slade were over-running – we weren't likely to be on until 10.30. I had a second glass of champagne. We seemed to have cleared everyone out of the caravan. Baker looked in occasionally, smiled rather a strained smile, and disappeared into the night.

At last we were called on. It was about 10.45 when we embarked on what was certainly the most spectacular cabaret I've ever done. The whole occasion seemed to be only comprehensible in terms of

1 Rugged Welsh actor who was also a shrewd businessman and founder member, with Lord Harlech (former British ambassador to Washington), of Harlech TV.

comparisons. For instance, here I was doing 'Tide' to 50,000 people, when I first did it nine years ago to about thirty in the Union Cellars at Oxford. Dennis Wilson of the Beach Boys came up to me and shook my hand and congratulated me, when only seven years ago I was packed in the Odeon Hammersmith trying to catch a glimpse of him.

They started with our signature tune, and there was a roar of recognition from the audience. The lights were very bright, so one couldn't really see the audience, and it was difficult to judge the laughs, which came as a distant rumble – like the beginning of an avalanche. There seemed to be more people on the stage behind us than the entire audience we usually get at cabarets. I had the feeling that we had a certain interest above those of the other groups because revue has never really been attempted on this scale before. On either side of the stage were 60 x 40 foot Eidiphor[1] screens with TV pictures of our faces, and the sound was very good. We tried some new material from the third series – and one of the sketches, the Proust competition, lay there. Otherwise the response was pretty good and 'Pet Shop' went tremendously well – with great surges of laughter. At the end we did seem to get a mighty ovation, and there were shouts for more long after John Peel's announcement.

Before we left Bardney, I felt that I really ought to correct my lingering impression of the day as being one big traffic jam, so we went out into the press enclosure to watch the Beach Boys. The stage itself was high above the crowd – the angle of it giving the same sort of impression as the terrace in the Kremlin from which Soviet leaders are always seen saluting. The figures, even from where I was, were tiny, but the huge screens and the sheer power of the sound, made them seem gigantic.

We were driven back to London in a mini-bus, drinking brandy and eating chicken sandwiches, as the first light of dawn appeared over the Hertfordshire hills.

Wednesday, August 2nd

John Gledhill phones with news of the advent of Python in the States. The first commercial manifestation has been the recent release by Buddah Records of our second LP, *Another Monty Python Record*. Already Buddah seem to have scored a minor coup by getting extracts

1 Large-screen television projector devised by Dr Fritz Fischer. Last used in 2000. From the Greek *eido*: image and *phor*: phosphor/light-bearer.

from the LP onto the stereo-sound selection of Pan Am's transatlantic flights. They have also got the 'Spam' song onto *Current*, the first issue of an audio magazine – an LP consisting of interviews with Presley, Manson, Ted Kennedy and other significant Americans. It's only in the experimental stage at the moment, but full marks to Buddah. I think that the curiosity value of this strange LP – coming out of nowhere – might work well for it in the States.

Thursday, August 3rd

My new black Mini was delivered this morning. Don Salvage, who personally brought the car round, has such an unfortunate manner about him when describing the car that I almost assumed it must have been stolen. Especially as when I rang him about buying a Mini automatic, he first of all told me it would take at least three to six months. Then next day he rang to say he could find one immediately.

Monday, August 7th

Visited Mr Powell's surgery at 10.45 for a session with the hygienist. She turned out to be the girl who had been Mr Powell's nurse during my early batch of gingivectomies, so she must have known my mouth as intimately as only a dentist can. I was given a short, but severe introductory talk about the generally poor state of hygiene in my mouth – and the dangers it presented – whilst at the same time being given the sop that I cleaned my teeth 99% more thoroughly than the rest of the filthy British public. But this wasn't enough, as a vivid red mouthwash indicated. It contained some ingredient which showed red wherever there was a bacteria-carrying layer on my teeth. She rubbed my face in it by showing me the offending red patches in a mirror – complete with epicene red lips. I was cleaned up and given two toothbrushes, a reel of dental floss, and red tablets to show whether my cleaning was getting better. Left at 11.30 feeling quite inspired, and determined to fight this battle for dental survival, against all odds.

Saturday, August 12th, Southwold

Sun shone in the morning and tempted us down to the beach. We took the windbreak and an axe, which is Grandfather's traditional instrument for knocking the windbreak into the sand. It may save him money on a mallet, but one does feel rather sinister taking a wife, two small children and an axe down to the beach.

Sunday, August 20th

Mid-morning, Bill Oddie rang to know if I would like a lift to Clapton for another Monty Python XI fixture. The pretence of the Monty Python XI becomes more and more flimsy – in this match we are only represented by Terry and myself. On the way to the ground, Bill tells me how he and the other two 'Goodies' switched on the lights at Morecambe (a quite considerable showbiz accolade). Bill was unashamedly delighted by the fan-worship – especially the drive in an open car along Morecambe front. It's interesting that no one in Python – even John in one of his most philanthropic moods – would ever have agreed to switch on the lights at Morecambe.

At Clapton Orient (once a league team) there was a 2,000 crowd, mainly of young kids. Our XI consisted of Terry, myself and Bill from TV plus Frank Lampard and Harry Cripps (both West Ham professionals) and a Millwall player. Jimmy Hill[1] led the opposition.

Sunday, September 3rd

Today I was to play cricket for the first time for about twelve years, in a village match organised by Alan Hutchison, John [Cleese]'s ex-Reuters friend. Drove Tim Brooke-Taylor and John down to Bordon in Hampshire, about one and three-quarter hours from London. My romantic image of village cricket was punctured slightly when we arrived. There was no rough and tufty village green, surrounded by neat cottages and a welcoming pub. Bordon is an army village, and we had to drive through the camp to get to the ground.

We found ourselves beside a remarkably professional-looking pitch – almost a Test Match wicket. The opposition, Blackmoor Village, were mostly young men in their twenties and early thirties, and looked to have most of the benefits of regular practice. There was no pub, but a pavilion (I think reserved for the officers), which served drinks all

---

1 Footballer (Brentford, Fulham), administrator (credited with invention of 3 points for a win system) and panellist (*Match of the Day*).

afternoon. Our side, plus hangers on, was clearly Oxbridge-based – there were elegant, sharp-featured, well-kept ladies, and clean-cut, straight-backed men.

We fielded first, and their first wicket pair put on about 80 before we got one of them out. Fielding, once one has got over the stark fear of a very heavy little ball travelling straight towards one, can be a most relaxing business. I bowled an over with two wides, two very good length balls, one of which was hit hard at me, and I made the mistake of pretending to catch it. The ball hit me hard on the little finger, on its way towards the boundary, but I prevented a run because, as the ball hit my finger, it dislodged a flesh-coloured piece of plaster, which fell to the ground, rooting the batsman to his crease in horror.

Tim bowled two overs, which were both very silly – on occasional balls John would run in front of him up to the wicket, then peel off just before Tim bowled. One of the Blackmoor team was out to a blatant throw – but they had us by the short and curlies anyway – so they accepted the comedy with good grace.

Enjoyed seeing Tim again – and it is refreshing to talk to someone of our age and background, outside the Python group. Tim will take on almost any work, and seems untroubled by the search for quality. This means he gets less frustrated, and more money, than we do.

Monday, September 4th

Python reassembled at Terry's after three months off. Everyone seemed happy to be starting again. Eric had had a recurrence of his liver trouble, and was not drinking, and Graham was one and a half hours late.

A cautionary visit from John Gledhill in the late afternoon. He brought us the latest figures for the film – which most of us had been conditioned into thinking was one of the box-office successes of the year. But up to about five months of its release, the net take (after Columbia had creamed off their share) was only $227,000. We do not start to make a penny until it has passed $500,000 and even if it took $1 million, we would still only stand to make £2,000 each. So the film, which John G reckoned had made us into world stars, has still only brought us £1,000 each. This had an amazing effect on the Python group. Suddenly everyone wanted to work. Within half an hour we had agreed on a third LP for the Christmas market, another book for next year, and a film script as soon as possible. No talk of holidays this time.

Thursday, September 14th

A week of great activity. In five days we have assembled a third Python LP to be in the shops for Christmas. Over half the 50–60 minutes' worth of material is new, and, unlike the second LP, everyone has contributed to the writing. Among the new ideas for the record were a 'B' side consisting of four concentric tracks, all starting at different places on the first groove, so that the listener could get any one of four different versions of the 'B' side; also there was an idea for an extra large record cover, two foot square; a 'free' 'Teach Yourself Heath' record included in the LP, which would use actual Heath speeches to analyse his voice, and teach people the best way of reproducing it. The title we settled on was 'A Previous Monty Python Record'.

We met for lunch and a final read-through of material and, at 5.30, André,[1] the engineer who is doing our new LP, came round and we spent a couple of hours going through the script for sound effects and music cues. Fred Tomlinson and his singers[2] and Neil Innes, ex of the Bonzos, had to be contacted about music – but by 8.00 last night the material was in typeable shape and ready to be sent off to John Gledhill.

I took half an hour off for a run on the Heath – a last futile attempt to prepare my system for the onslaught of German hospitality – and then took Helen out for a meal. She had worked hard looking after six writers and two children during the day, as well as ironing and sorting out my clothes for three weeks in Munich.[3] We ate at Abbots in Blenheim Place, St John's Wood – a small restaurant with a large and interesting menu (red mullet, pigeon, etc), but full of a party of visiting American businessmen, and English people on a 'smart' night out. But it did us both good to leave the house for a while, and made it a very happy last evening.

1 André Jacquemin had engineered several sessions with me, going back to 1966. His committed, efficient, no-nonsense skills impressed me and he became Python's engineer of choice.
2 The Fred Tomlinson singers had played, among other things, the original Mounties in 'Lumberjack Song' and the original Vikings singing 'Spam! Wonderful Spam!'
3 Where we were to be based for the second of two Python specials made for Bavarian TV.

Friday, September 15th, Munich

Apart from Graham feeling a little sorry for himself, the six Pythons all seemed on good form on the plane. At the airport we were thoroughly frisked for weapons and the plane had to delay take-off for half an hour whilst the baggage was searched. All these extra precautions were a result of the shootings of the Israeli athletes and the Palestinian guerrillas at the Munich Olympics last week.

As we expected, this year was more businesslike – we spent the afternoon in costume fittings, and it wasn't until the evening that we had time to relax. Alfred [Biolek, our German producer] and Ian had fallen out for some reason, which is not a good start, and Ian and Eke[1] didn't join us for a meal. After the meal, the inevitable Why Not? Club [well-known from our previous Munich filming]. It had been enlarged and repainted, and we were treated to some classic examples of the Why Not's 'see and be seen' philosophy.

Edith, the proprietress, looking even more like a model out of a very high-class shop window, was soon working hard to mix a powerful concoction of celebrities. After a while the words 'Swiss fashion photographer', 'model from Berlin', 'Austrian TV writer', all sounded the same, as the music of Gilbert O'Sullivan blasted out, and one mouthed greetings to shadowy faces in the gloom. Highlight of the evening was when Alfred appeared at my side, in a state of high excitement, to announce that Christine Kaufmann, Germany's leading actress, and ex-wife of Tony Curtis, was not only here tonight, but, and here Alfred became almost uncontrollable, she *loved* Monty Python!! Soon she was brought to our table, and the meeting of the greats took place. She wore her black hair long and unstyled, wore a simple dress, and her face was thin, fine-boned and un-made-up. I liked her at once, but conversation was made doubly difficult by the music, and by her boyfriend, a German disc-jockey, who chattered about the wonders of Python without even a break for commercials. He was clearly the kind of person who was used to being listened to, rather than listening, had an annoying habit of referring to Python as being very popular with 'all the intellectuals'.

After their whirlwind visit, their places were taken by yet another model – this time a real head-turner, with carefully arranged red hair,

---

1 Eke Ott was the sister of Max, who designed the German shows. Ian MacNaughton fell in love with her and she became his second wife.

a rich suntan, and a thin cotton shirt unbuttoned to the waist. Apparently, Thomas[1] assured me, she had been in *Playboy* magazine. I drank the last remains of my white wine. Miss Playboy's photographer escort, meanwhile, had ordered a magnum of Calvados.

Outside it was 1.30 and raining. I walked home with John – wet, shabby, tired, but still just celebrities.

Wednesday, September 20th, Hohenschwangau

Filming in Neuschwanstein Castle. A clear and sunny day. In the distance the sun picks out the snow on the mountains of the Austrian Alps. It's a perfect day for throwing a dummy of John Cleese from the 100ft tower of the castle to the courtyard below. The tourists watch with great interest – an English couple and their young brother-in-law can't believe their luck that they've found Python in Germany. We finish filming by 11.00 and now have a break until 6.00 for we are night-shooting inside the castle. (Apparently we are lucky to have received permission – for the last crew to film here was Visconti's film of King Ludwig, and apparently they had messed the place up a bit, and urinated in the fine Wagnerian interiors, and were generally unlikely to be asked back.)

I was playing Prince Walter, described in the script as 'rather thin and weedy with a long pointed nose, spots, and nasty unpolished plywood teeth'. The make-up man, George, made a superb job of personifying this creature. My own hair was laboriously curled with hot tongs into a silly little fringe, which made me look like an underfed Henry V, and it took almost two hours before I was ready with my long turned-up nose and spots, to leave the Hotel Müller and be driven up to the castle.

A perfect Gothic horror evening – a cool breeze, and a full moon, glimpsed through the trees and occasionally blotted out by scudding clouds. As we drove through the silent and deserted stone archways of the castle, there was but a single light shining high in the dark walls. Ludicrously clad, wearing a silly false nose and carrying a crate of beer for the unit's supper, I was led through echoing passages and through stone-vaulted halls towards the filming.

2 Thomas Woitkewitsch, translator of the Python German shows.

Thursday, September 21st, Hohenschwangau

Another fine, sunny day. Into Prince Walter outfit. Sat around outside the hotel thus attired, read Raymond Chandler, wrote postcards and confused the tourists – who start to appear in droves at about 11.30, are everywhere like insects, and like them, disappear in the cool of the evening. Filmed beside a lake. Eric played his guitar, the crate of beer was kept warm in the water of the lake, and Connie Cleese raped me (on film). What more could a man want of the day?

Friday, September 29th, Munich

Only last night did I learn for certain that today we were to do the most complicated sketch of all – the 'Hearing-Aid' sketch – an old *1948 Show* sketch in which I was given joint billing with John. We could only use the shop to do it in after 8.00, so it was a most uneven and awkward day. As we rehearsed Ian took a phone call from his P.A. in England. She had received a note from Duncan Wood in which he ordered another round of cuts in the current *Python* series.

Terry J sees it as part of a plot to keep the BBC out of any major controversies until the charter has been renewed in 1974. Ian MacNaughton feels that he will be out soon anyway, as the LE bosses hardly talk to him now, and he is prepared to fight with us against this decision. Maybe we cannot win, but I feel it is as important as anything not to lie down and accept this censorship. John C, for the record, wants to avoid any confrontation with Bill Cotton and Duncan Wood, he wants a chat over dinner, and a bit of gentle bargaining.

Thomas came in later on in the rehearsal and added to our increasing feeling of paranoia by telling us that Hans Gottchild, the enormous, Hemingway-bearded head of Bavaria TV had been most displeased with the Python rushes, calling them 'dilettante'.

By the time we had filmed as coal miners at the full-scale model of a coalface in the Deutsches Museum, I felt quite exhausted. All I wanted was a sleep, and all I was going to get was an under-rehearsed, complicated five-hour sketch.

As it turned out the evening was not too bad. We worked in long takes, which required great concentration, but made the whole process seem faster. It was about 10.45 that John and I ended the sketch by hurling ourselves out of a very expensive Munich optician's, on to a pile of rugs and cushions.

Saturday, September 30th, Munich

Caught an S-Bahn train to Starnberg, where we are all expected for food and drink at Eke's father's lakeside house.

John C was there, myself, Eric, Terry G, Graham, Roger Last,[1] Terry and Alison. Everyone was in mellow, gentle moods – perhaps just suffering from tiredness. There were no confrontations, explosions, truth games or any other games. Eke had cooked bean soup and delicious pork and garlic, and we mostly sat in the kitchen swapping stories and drinking wine.

Arrived back at the hotel about 12.45, dog-tired, to find that I had been moved out of my room as two time-honoured guests had arrived late in the evening. I was greeted by the manageress and her effusive assistant, who were both a little worried about my reaction – especially as they had done all the moving. I wasn't unduly concerned where I slept, so they must have been quite relieved at my reaction, but then I found that I had been quartered, not in a separate room, but in a small bed in John Cleese's room. This did niggle me, partly because John's room smelt of stale cigarette smoke, and I was feeling quite fragile in the abdominal area, and also because of the attitude of the lady who had arrived for my room. There was no word of apology – she was merely concerned to let me know what an inconvenient day she'd had. I went to bed ruffled. John arrived in a mellow mood about 1.15 and offered me brandy. I remember reacting to this with a slight feeling of nausea.

Sunday, October 1st

Woke at 7.00. Splitting stomach ache, violent diarrhoea. I would have to be in John's room. Tried to make diarrhoea as quiet as possible. Only the evening before we had been laughing over the fantasy of a 'Hotel Noisy', where a high standard of noise was maintained throughout, and here I was, up at sparrow's fart, rocking John's lavatory. John sportingly maintained he heard nothing.

1 Python production assistant. A lovely, soft-spoken man with an interest in Norfolk churches. When we filmed a football match between a team of gynaecologists and Long John Silver impersonators, Roger was the one whom Graham persuaded, in the interests of medical authenticity, to go out and buy eleven vaginal speculums.

Monday, October 2nd

Arrived back after rushes at about 7.45. There was a call waiting for Terry from Midhurst – it was Nigel[1] to say that their mother had been taken to hospital. Terry was immediately on to BEA to book a plane back to England. He was in a rush and a hurry, but seemed to be in control. Al came upstairs and broke down and cried for just a moment – there was no flight back to London tonight from anywhere in Germany.

Thomas [Woitkewitsch] was fortunately here to help, and he started to ring charter flights and private air-hire firms. The irony of the situation was that we had all been invited to Alfred's to watch an Anglo-Dutch comedy show which Thomas had produced. As Terry phoned Chichester Hospital from Alfred's bedroom, the strident shouts from the telly grew louder and more disconcerting. I sat and talked to Graham in the neutral room. He had spoken to the ward sister and she had told both Graham and Terry that her chances of recovery were minimal. Graham argued clearly and reasonably, and yet still sympathetically, that it was not worth Terry's while trying to charter a plane to London in order to see his unconscious mother.

It was about 10.00 when I saw Terry in his room. He was sitting in a wicker chair, he seemed composed, reflective and rather distant. I clasped him around the shoulders. He said he was happy just to 'sit and think about her'. Graham and I left, and went next door to the Klosterl, for a meal with Alfred, Thomas and Justus [our cameraman]. Not a great meal. Back to the hotel at about 11.30.

A note from Al was stuck in my door. 'Terry's mother died at 9.20. He has gone to sleep with the aid of a sleeping pill.'

For a moment I felt a strange stifling surge of sadness. My eyes welled with tears and for a few moments the news hit me really hard.[2]

Wednesday, October 4th, Munich

In the hotel I was waylaid by Madame, offering me a bottle of brandy as recompense for being thrown out of my room last Saturday. I didn't

1 Terry Jones' elder brother. A journalist.
2 I had got to know Terry's mum well in the days when I visited the family home in Claygate, Surrey. She was an endearing lady and we were very fond of each other. Some of Terry's drag roles on Python were uncannily like her, though absolutely *not* Mandy in *The Life of Brian*.

accept it, but did drink a couple of schnapps with her, and listened to her problems – which seem infinite, ranging from lack of sleep to lack of guests. She seems an unhappy lady intent on making herself more unhappy.

Little time for a bath and a dollop of Yardley's Black Label Talc, before being collected by my driver for the last time, and taken to the end-of-filming party at the Alter Wirt Gasthaus in Grunwald. He was in a sharp suit and seemed to be positively sparkling with anticipated pleasure.

NB: An important clue to the somewhat enigmatic character, whose driving has so often filled me with fear – he and his wife perform in blue films. Felt less afraid of him when I heard this.

Thursday, October 5th, Munich

A clear, crisp, cold clinical day. Paid my £40 phone bill. The lady at the hotel shared with Monika[1] this impression of distant suffering – both had an air of melancholy about them. I wonder if this is to do with the German past. Ostensibly, and materially, more people in Germany seem to enjoy better conditions than in England – the economic recovery from the war has been massively successful. I should imagine that the psychological scars must run deeper.

Must read more German novels – for here if anywhere is a chance to try and prove Solzhenitsyn's point that art and literature are the only spiritual ambassadors between countries. Will re-read Gunter Grass's *Tin Drum*.

Flew back to London with John and Eric. John is a good travelling companion in so far as he is nearly always recognised by stewards and stewardesses who pamper him blatantly; and Eric and I were able to catch a little of this reflected blandishment.

Monday, October 9th

Today I am about to earn £850. This is more than Helen earned in a whole year as a professional teacher.

For this £850 I am required to perform two 15-second commercials for Hunky Chunks. The make-up is poor, the studios of TV

1 Our German wardrobe mistress.

International in Whitfield Street are shabby – so why this money? Well firstly because Quaker Oats, the client, make so much profit from selling their foods that they can afford to throw away £850, and secondly because the bait has to be very tempting to make self-respecting human beings, let alone actors, talk about 'The moist, meaty dog-food that contains more concentrated nourishment than canned dog-food.'

So I sold my soul for £850, and was made to squirm for it. The first ad was done outside in the street with me, a crate of dog-food and a camera. Who should come along as I was recording, but David Jason who lives nearby. He and John Cleese (who was working on the same Hunky Chunks series) hid in a doorway and peered out at me in the middle of a take.

Sunday, October 15th

Thomas and I and William returned from a walk on the Heath to find hordes of policemen in about half a dozen assorted vehicles, milling around Richard and Christine's house on the corner of Oak Village. In the middle of the blue helmets was Helen, obviously the centre of some attention. For an awful moment I thought that she was being arrested – an unimaginable irony in view of her obsessionally law-abiding behaviour. However, it turned out that Helen had been alerted by Muriel of the house opposite to a man climbing over the wall of the Guedallas' with a colour TV set *and* stand. It gradually dawned on Helen that the Guedallas were away and also that TV repair men didn't work on Sundays, and anyway they usually tried the front door first before climbing over the back garden wall.

So Helen and Muriel's husband Bob went looking for this character, and took themselves by surprise when they rounded a corner and literally bumped into him. Helen – quite courageously, considering he had an Alsatian dog with him – asked him what he was doing in the Guedallas' house. Declining explanations, he made a run for it and Helen, *not* Bob, made a grab for him. He easily pushed her away and ran off. Bob shouted valiantly after him, 'We've got your identification.' And he was gone.

Helen had already rung the police. They soon descended in droves – local fuzz and Scotland Yard. The unfortunate telly-snatcher didn't stand a chance. He was picked up almost immediately and so were the

TV and the stand. Helen was quite the local hero, and very pleased with herself.

Saturday, October 21st

Dinner across the road with the recently moved-in neighbours, Rod and Ann. Ann (we found out) is the sister of John Sergeant, who was in revue at Oxford two years after me, and with whom I once did some sketch writing about four or five years ago. He acted in the Alan Bennett series *On the Margin* as Bennett's straight man[1] and then left comedy for news – worked at Reuters and now with the BBC as a sound reporter.

Tonight we were reunited. We spent a very enjoyable evening, and I was especially interested in his stories of reporting from Vietnam and Belfast. Vietnam is badly beaten up, but not such a totally flattened country as people make out – the on-the-spot action news film, which the American networks put out as reports from the battlefield, are all taken by South Vietnamese cameramen. In Ireland everyone reads the papers avidly. The IRA leaders are available at all times to talk to newsmen if you know the right number to ring. John was hijacked in his car once by an IRA man who threatened to blow his brains out if he tried to resist.

Monday, October 23rd

At 8.00 I went out to a Gospel Oak meeting. There are quite a number of consultative meetings held in and around Oak Village, as the whole area is being subjected to such massive redevelopment. In 1951 the first redevelopment in Gospel Oak was Barrington Court – by Powell and Moya. It's a long, ten-storey block, but is as good as many present-day functional designs, and better than most. The West Kentish Town development followed in the 1950s – it's not picturesque, but it is low-rise and friendly.

Then a progressive deterioration of architectural standards, which reached its nadir in the appalling block which borders Mansfield Road and is known locally as the Barracks. It is without charm,

1 I auditioned for this series myself, but John was judged to be funnier and got the job. Quite rightly. He later, of course, became ITN's political correspondent.

without style, without any beauty whatsoever – it is essentially a mathematical achievement, a result of juggling a lot of people with a little money, stymied as the Camden planners are now by the general abandonment of high-rise blocks.

Some of the new occupants were at the St Martin's Church Hall tonight to hear proposals for Lismore Circus renovation and for the next part of the Gospel Oak scheme.

The meeting was entirely staffed by stereotypes. If one had written a play with these characters in it would have been called facile and uninventive. Mr and Mrs Brick of Kiln Place – a physically formidable pair and both with plenty to say forcibly and clearly. The populist vicar, who couldn't resist occasional semantic jokes; the hard-line Marxist, in a nondescript coat but with a fine, strong, lean face, worn hard and lined in struggles for the proletariat. The woolly-headed liberals, the gentle, embarrassed architect, and even the local hippy, a squatter who berated the platform from the back of the room for being cynical and hypocritical in even having this meeting at all.

Notes that stuck in my mind – a small Andy Capp-like figure telling the platform with a feeling of frustrated sadness, 'Living round here is bloody terrible.' The soft-voiced, inoffensive, architect taking on the wrath of the gathering as well as its repartee. He was talking of how, even when the builders were working, 'Lismore Circus retained its trees, its flowers, even squirrels ...'- 'and rats' came a voice from the audience. The lack of enthusiasm for the plans from the audience was understandable, but very, very sad. For here was an enlightened borough, with a good and humane record, selling something that people didn't want in the most democratic way possible.

Friday, October 27th

An eventful day. Began with a Python meeting at John's to discuss future long-term plans. An interesting thing happened. I had originally told Charisma that we did not want individual writing credits for the two sides of the single ('Eric the Half-Bee' by Eric and John and 'Yangtse Song' by myself and Terry) on the grounds that Python had never before singled out writers' specific contributions. But Eric had told Jim that he wanted his name on the single. So this was the first awkward point that I brought up with John and Eric this morning. Predictably Eric bristled, but with a bitterness that I didn't expect. He wanted his name on the record because he was going to write more songs and this would help him. He lashed out bitterly at what he thought was merely a weak-kneed way of protecting Graham. John, however, agreed with me – that the principle of Python's 'collective responsibility' was more important. Eric went quiet, John went out to make coffee. I felt bad vibrations and tried to think of a compromise. But as suddenly as the storm broke it was over. Eric apologised, said I was absolutely right and that he was being stupid about it – but all this came out in such a way that I felt a warm flood of friendship as well as considerable relief.

After the meeting we all drove over to the BBC to see Duncan Wood and discuss the cuts he proposed in our new series. These cuts involved the excision of whole sketches about a French wine-taster who serves his clients only wee-wee, and an awful City cocktail bar where upper-class twits ask for strange cocktails – one of which, a mallard fizz, involves cutting the head off a live duck. Other cuts included the word 'masturbating' (a contestant in a quiz game gives his hobbies as 'golf, strangling animals and masturbating'), the phrase 'I'm getting pissed tonight' and most of two sketches, one about a Dirty Vicar and the other about the Oscar Wilde Café Royal set, who run short of repartee and at one point liken King Edward VII to a stream of bat's piss. But we were protesting mainly about the volume of the cuts, not particular instances – tho' Terry crusaded violently on behalf of masturbating, launching off at a Kinseyian tangent about the benefits of masturbation. 'I masturbate, you masturbate, we all masturbate!' he enthused. Duncan crossed his legs and pulled hard on his cigarette. Our point was basically why, if we are going out at 10.15 – well after children and family peak viewing – are we suddenly being so heavily censored?

Duncan Wood at first protested that we weren't being heavily censored, that four cuts in the first nine shows wasn't bad (I must say in the first of the series we got away with the line from a judge, 'Screw the Bible, I've got a gay lib meeting at 6.00,' which certainly couldn't be spoken on any other TV service in the world). So he has clearly relented over certain of the cuts he wanted Ian to make. He promised to review Shows 12 and 13 again, with us, so that we could all see what we were talking about.

After the sting had been taken out of the meeting we got to talking about censorship generally – and why the BBC seemed to be suddenly more frightened of causing offence. Genial Duncan chain-smoked and talked in a vague and roundabout way of 'pressures from outside' causing a temporary tighten-up in censorship. Who and what these pressures were was never revealed. There seemed no evidence that there was popular support for BBC censorship – quite the opposite – the most outspoken of BBC progs, *Till Death Us Do Part*, has an audience of nearly 20 million, and Python itself has higher viewing figures than ever (round about 10 million for the first show of the latest series). Duncan was either stalling or genuinely didn't know, but there was a sinister 'I am only obeying orders' tone to his whole attitude.

We parted amicably – he was happy because he had said nothing and got away with it – as Eric said it was like arguing with a piece of wet cod.

Saturday, November 4th

I travel down on the 24 bus – I really prefer public transport these days: it's more restful, cheaper and wonderful entertainment along the way. Bonuses like an early-morning walk through Soho – one of the areas London ought to be proud of for the quality and quantity of its delights. It is, for instance, a much more honest place of enjoyment than Mayfair, with its Rolls-Royces, expensive shops, poor and snobbish restaurants and red lights. This Saturday morning Soho Square was free of cars, people were washing down the pavements outside their restaurants, there was a quiet and leisurely feeling of waking up, and I felt very happy to be in London.

Spent three hours with André, editing and tightening the B side of the new album until it was in a very strong and satisfying shape, then, with Terry and André, walked across Regent Street and into Savile Row, where the Apple Studios are situated in a well-preserved row of Georgian town houses. They seem to be the only place that has the technology to cut our multiple B side.

Down the stairs to the basement. Into a foyer with heavy carpets, two soft sofas and felt covered walls, all in a rather dark, restful plum colour. A big glass-topped coffee table, designed for only the best coffee table books, was littered with copies of the *Daily Mirror*. A flamboyant stainless steel strip was sunk into one wall. Immediate impression on entering the cutting room of being in a Harley Street dentist's consulting room.

At one point, about 7.00, I had just come back into the studios after having a drink when a slight, thin figure walked towards me. The face was familiar, but, before I could register anything, a look of recognition crossed George Harrison's face, and he shook my hand, and went into a paean of praise for Monty Python – with the same exaggerated enthusiasm that I would have lavished on the Beatles had I met them five years ago. He said he couldn't wait to see Python on 35mm, big screen.

Finally left Apple about 8.00 – the cutter, John, promised to have more attempts at the cut over the weekend, but the chances of producing this highly original B side don't seem too rosy.

Tuesday, November 7th

Heard during the afternoon that Apple were unable to cut the three-track B side. Terry took the tapes round to EMI for them to have a go, so we can only cross our fingers. Tonight is American election night, and I invited Simon Albury and his brother Robert round to hear the results and watch the telly special from 12 till 2.00.

Sadly McGovern got wiped out, almost totally, carrying the District of Columbia's three electoral votes, and Massachusetts – who probably voted because of Kennedy anyway. He has been dogged by misfortune in his campaign – mainly the Eagleton affair, but also because Nixon played a crafty, quiet campaign. It was not until this last week that people have really begun to lay into Nixon's record – he was somehow let off the hook by the press, not because they praised, but because they failed to criticise him until too late.

To bed about 2.45.

Wednesday, November 8th

At last an, as yet, uninterrupted day's writing ahead of me, a luxury which hasn't happened for a long time. Thomas leaves for his playgroup at 9.55. Helen takes William out to the shops. All is quiet for a bit – the sun shines in onto my desk, and I feel all's well with the world. But the phone soon starts ringing – EMI cannot do the cut, what shall we do?

Almost an hour is spent ringing round the Pythons to get them to a meeting on Thursday to listen to the record. We decide to cut the B side in mono, which apparently will allow the three-track cut to work. So Apple now have the job again.

Looked at a book of Yoga exercises.

Friday, November 10th

In the evening a pleasant meal with Robert [Hewison]. Delicious beef olives cooked by the maestro. As usual I was impressed and injected with academic enthusiasm by the neat order of Robert's little flat – with its shelfful of Goncourt journals in French, the latest books on Coleridge – of course his great Ruskin collection (Robert is now a B.Litt.).

Monday, November 20th

Arrived back in London after a long weekend in Southwold with Helen, Thomas and William.

Brought two family portraits back home – one of my great-grand-father, Edward Palin, Vicar of Linton, drawn almost a hundred years ago, I guess – a fine looking man – and the other of his wife Brita née Gallagher – she by contrast looks hunched and rather wizened. I should imagine that was drawn nearer the turn of the century. Amazing to think that I have physical genetic links with these remote figures.

I had this wrong. The older lady was not Brita, my great-grandmother, but Caroline Watson, a rich American lady who had adopted Brita when she arrived on a coffin ship in New York in the 1840s, an orphan from the Irish potato famine. I was to discover fuller details from a cousin of my father's (entry for September 30th 1977). It was such a remarkable story that in 1990 Tristram Powell and I made it into a film called American Friends.

Wednesday, November 22nd

Success with Mark Shivas!

Terry and I talked our way into a commission for an hour-long 'Black and Blue' play – with an improvised verbal synopsis which he appeared to be quite pleased with. It required quite a gamble on his part, and we both felt greatly encouraged by his confidence.

Impressed by his modesty and the almost Spartan simplicity of his office. As producer of the highly successful *Six Wives of Henry VIII* series, he must be one of the most sought-after producers in TV and yet he remains in an anonymous, nondescript, austere office in TV Centre. Such are the artistic attractions of working for an organisation such as the Beeb that they tend to cancel out other *dis*-advantages. After seeing Shivas, we visited Ian MacNaughty and then Terry Hughes to whom we delivered a *Two Ronnies* script. Ian MacN – with Eke always at his side like a prowling lion to encourage, goad, solace, and generally keep him healthy – was in his office, but he didn't know for how long. He wants to go freelance next spring, presumably to do another Python film, for we have never made it clear we will be directing it ourselves.

I think perhaps we should now come clean and let him know that there is not much more work for him with Python. He is a much happier man now than he used to be. So any final break will be that bit more difficult.

Monday, December 4th

A very successful Python meeting at John's. Everyone was remarkably direct about future plans and there was a remarkable freedom of pressure on anyone to fit in with others' plans. The basic factor in the future life of Python is that John has had enough of Python TV shows – he doesn't enjoy writing or performing them – the thought of doing any more makes his stomach tighten, so he said. He is the oldest of us, he has done more TV than any of us, and had done twenty-six *Frost Reports* before any of us really started performing. So he's ahead of us in the disillusionment stakes – tho' I cannot agree with him at all about the drudgery of doing TV shows. I find them hard, but exhilarating experiences and I'm still at the stage of appreciating how fantastically lucky I am to have the opportunity to write and perform my own material, on TV, almost free of restrictions. Still, John does not share this view – and will not commit himself to any more Python work after the film next summer.

The next major factor was that Eric and Graham especially were concerned about making some money next year – so far, making a film is the least lucrative thing we've done. To solve this we decided to try and fix up a two- or three-week university tour in April, on the lines of our successful Coventry Festival show a couple of years ago.

Later in the evening, Eric rang me up – still a little worried about where work, therefore loot, was to come from in the next year. I had mentioned my keenness to do some more TV next Christmas and Eric was ringing to lend support to this. Has today seen the first seeds of a new post-Python TV series, without John and possibly without Graham, or will we, as I forecast, find ourselves all together again next December?

It rained all day. I gave up [John Barth's] *The Sot-Weed Factor* on page 440 and started to read Laurie Lee's *Cider with Rosie*, by the fire.

Tuesday, December 5th

Drove to Harrods to see around their own chocolate factory – the first breakthrough in our protracted attempts to gain some first-hand experience of a chocolate factory for our 'Black and Blue' script. Harrods was like an ocean liner in the dark, rainy, wild evening. A Mr Jackson from the confectionery department, white-haired, but probably no more than 50, with a knowing smile and a rather self-deprecating manner, took us into Harrods underground travel network via a Colditz-style entrance behind the butchery department. We walked under Knightsbridge, feeling even more as tho' we were in an ocean liner – only this time in the engine room.

The chocolate factory was small and personal. None of the machines was enormous, and the whole process seemed to be on a human scale. We saw Harrods exclusive after-dinner mints being stuffed into their little bags by middle-aged working-class ladies; presumably to be elegantly extracted by rich and well-perfumed hands in some Kensington salon. Also I was amused to see how the delicate marking was placed on top of each Harrods 'Opera' chocolate. A matronly cockney lady dipped into the liquid chocolate mixture and inscribed these magnificent chocolates with a deft flick of her nose-picking finger. This was the 'hand' in the 'hand-marked' chocolates.

Thursday, December 7th

In the morning I worked up at home, writing on a little further with the 'Black and Blue' script. Terry was returning this morning from Liverpool, where he had been chairing a meeting about 'cooking and cholesterol', so I was on my own.

At 12.30 arrived at TV Centre to see a playback of our controversial Shows 12 and 13, which Duncan Wood and Bill Cotton have told us must be amalgamated into one, on the grounds of their (to them) offensive tastelessness. Today was our last chance to change this decision, for rather than accept their judgement and trim the shows, we had asked at least if we could see again what we were being accused of, and we had asked that Paul Fox might view the shows as well.

This he was doing in an upper room of the BBC at the same time as we were seeing them in a lower room. Both shows had generally scatological themes, but in nearly every case the naughty material was hardly worth making a fuss about, and most of it was less questionable than some of the material in the first two series (viz. the mother-eating sketch). Neither show was our best, but I certainly could see no earthly reason for combining the two and wasting an entire show.

That evening I was very glad to hear from Ian that Fox had felt this way too, and had insisted on far fewer cuts than Wood and Cotton – which goes to prove that either prurience or cowardice, or a mixture of both, are important factors in LE's official judgement. This was the first time we have ever divided the BBC hierarchy – and the appeal to Fox has this time come out to our advantage. I shall be able to approach him in a new light at the BBC LE binge in a couple of weeks.

Tuesday, December 12th

Terry and I are now well into a writing routine and we're making solid progress.

Rosemary rang from the BBC to say they had received a can of real Devon cream addressed to Mr Pither[1] from a dairy in Bovey Tracey!

Drove home via the BBC to collect my cream – it contained a note from the owner of the dairy thanking us for the free publicity for Bovey Tracey in the 'Pither' show, correcting our pronunciation from Bôvey to Burvey Tracey and ending up 'I think you are all mad'.

Sunday, December 17th

Woke up feeling very depressed. I faced yet another Sunday spent working on the script – and I've had hardly any time at home for about two weeks. The Atticus article on Python in the *Sunday Times* transformed depression into mute despair. A terrible photo, and a worthless column, written in pseudo-joke style – all I dreaded – and, what's worse,

---

1 Reg Pither was the bobble-hatted cyclist on a tour of the West Country whom I played in the 'Cycling Tour' episode of Python.

wrongly attributing nearly all the quotes – and I was unlucky enough to be given Graham's! Thus, the remarks I felt least necessary when we gave the interview – like 'Where is John Cleese, anyway?' and 'Make sure you say that John Cleese is the middle-aged one'- were faithfully reported as spoken by me! Also my name at the beginning was spelt Pallin.

Drove down to Terry's to work; he didn't seem to be particularly worried by the article. Graham rang during the morning. Helen told him I was upset, which I don't think I'd have bothered to do. He and I rang John – John appeared to think it was quite humorous.

Arrived about 10.00 at the BBC party – which is very much an establishment affair, and Python have always regarded it with some suspicion. However, with the notable exception of John, Eric and Terry G, we decided to go along this year. In fact Terry was even wearing his black tie. General feeling of warmth and well-being about this year's binge – the food was more imaginative too with ambitious failures like moussaka. Graham C was stalking through the throng, heavily dosed with drink – presumably to cope with the evening – he was wearing a Bill Oddie T-shirt, spelt Bill Addie, and John Tomiczek[1] was wearing one spelt Bill Oddle (sic). 'Who would you like me to insult?' Graham asked unsteadily. Bill Cotton Jnr occasionally looked anxiously in Graham's direction, but I think that most people present had learnt what to expect from past experience, and poor old Gra was unable to pick a fight.

Half-way through the evening Bill Cotton made a farewell speech to David Attenborough. He delivered his paean holding his cigarette behind his back, like someone who wasn't meant to be smoking, but who certainly wasn't going to waste a good cigarette. Attenborough accepted, to rapturous applause, what looked like a BBC litter bin.

Towards the end of the evening Terry and I plucked up enough courage to approach some of the greats – Milligan, the elder statesman, who has had a remarkably successful year, first his autobiography, *Hitler – My Part in his Downfall*, then a mini-*Goon Show* revival – with a special last *Goon Show* recorded in October for the BBC's fifty years anniversary – and patronised by royalty. He remained sitting through most of the evening, with no shortage of visitors and well-wishers and sycophants like ourselves coming over to see him. He walked very obviously in front of Bill Cotton, just as Bill was selling David Attenborough, and was heard to shout irreverently during the speech. Eric Morecambe

1 A young Liverpudlian who Graham and David adopted.

is another one who never dropped his comic persona all evening. If one talked to him, or if one heard him talking to anyone else, he was always doing a routine. He has a very disconcerting habit of suddenly shouting at the top of his voice at someone only a foot away.

Almost exactly true to the pattern of two years ago, one of the last people I spoke to was Eric Sykes, who has a series on Thursday nights,[1] two hours before us, which gets about the same rating. He's very much easier to talk to than someone like Milligan or Morecambe, because he's a gentler character altogether – even when performing. He was very impressed with the 'Pither Cycling Tour', and was generally flattering about my performances.

So at 12.00 the band of Light Entertainment workers disbanded. I was struck by how young we still are compared to most of the people there. Apart from the Goodies and ourselves, nearly all the performers and writers there are in their forties or even fifties.

Wednesday, December 20th

An interesting piece of work could come our way. This morning I was rung by Memorial Enterprises – who have made films like *Charlie Bubbles*, *If* and *Gumshoe* – in short, some of the best British films of the last few years. Michael Medwin wanted to speak to me. I was quite excited, but it turned out that he wanted to talk over the question of our writing a 20-minute promotional film for the States to put out as advance publicity for *O Lucky Man*, the latest Lindsay Anderson film, with Alan Price and Malcolm McDowell. Alan had suggested that I might have some better ideas for a promo film than Warner Bros' own publicity men.

I met them at the editing rooms of De Lane Lea in Wardour Street. The film was likely to be very prestigious, and clearly they are gambling on a big commercial success. It has been edited down to three and a quarter hours, and is due to be first screened as the official British entry at Cannes. They are a very pleasant group of people – Lindsay, serious and mock-serious by turns, the kind of person who seems to invite you to make jokes about him, Alan, as self-deprecatingly gloomy as ever, and Medwin, very like the cheerful Cockneys he used to play in 1950s British war films – though much less over the top. He was pleased to hear that

1 Called simply 'Sykes'.

Helen and I enjoyed *Charlie Bubbles*,[1] he said we were members of a select club – not of those who enjoyed it, but of those who saw it, for somehow it never found favour with the big distributors.

1 Directed by Albert Finney, and starring himself as a hugely successful Mancunian return-ing to his roots. Co-starred Liza Minnelli. It was written by Shelagh Delaney.

1973

Monday, January 1st

A good start to the New Year – Python has won the Critics' Circle award as the best comedy show of the year; beat Terry at squash; and at 3.00 we had a meeting with Mark Shivas and Richard Broke to hear their verdict on our 'Black and Blue' script, which was favourable. I think they were surprised how over-cautious we were about our ability to write anything longer than sketches. It restores my faith in myself as a writer – not just someone who left university seven years ago, with no real qualifications and a lot of lucky breaks. Terry's eyes are really on direction – it is this urgent desire for complete technical control that is for him the most important aspect of creation, whereas for me the personal satisfaction of having written or performed something well is usually enough – for then my ambition tends to lead away from the editing room and the dubbing theatre to travel abroad, to reading, to being with my family.

Friday, January 5th

9.30 – arrived at De Lane Lea editing rooms in Dean St to see the 3¼ hour version of Lindsay Anderson's new film *O Lucky Man*. It still needed some editing and dubbing to be done, but it was a very impressive film – and tho' some sequences worked better than others, nearly all of it was of a very high standard – in performance and photography and direction and conception, and there were many moments when I felt a very strong and complete sense of involvement.

At the end, as the lights went up in the little viewing theatre, Lindsay appeared through the door of the theatre with Alan. He laughed and said he'd been spying on us from the projection room. I mumbled my appreciation – but had hardly time to get my thoughts together, and felt rather inhibited about saying anything in the presence of so many people intimately concerned with the film.

Terry and I drove over to the Medical Centre in Pentonville Road, for a complete physical check-up in modern computerised conditions – which normally costs £30, but had been given to us free by Alan

Bailey.[1] The relevance of the film suddenly seemed uncannily close. Only an hour ago we had been watching a film which took horrific looks at scientific medicine, and in which the charming smile and the 'Would you come this way please sir?' were usually a prelude to something most sinister. Now here we were, in the clean, aseptic atmosphere of a rich man's clinic, being shown into a small cubicle and asked to strip off down to shoes, socks and pants. Alan fortified us beforehand with a large whisky – he really is the most wonderfully cheerful and reassuring man. The tests included a blood test, a urine test, a very thorough Question and Answer sequence, which worked by pressing buttons, and looking at a screen, the answers being fed straight into a computer. I found the alternative answers fascinating – from 'I have never coughed blood', 'I have coughed blood, but not in the last year', to the appalling and inevitable 'I have coughed blood often in the last year'.

Tuesday, January 9th

Reading my *Daily Mirror*, my eyes fall on an item 'Monty Python Axed'. The story ran that the BBC were stopping Monty Python and were not making any more. It also ran the story of two sketches being cut from the last show, as if to imply that the show had been cut by the Beeb on grounds of indecency. The inaccuracy of the headline, and the fact that it appeared in a paper which boasts on its front page 'Largest European Sale', moved me to ring the *Mirror*. The TV man who had instigated the story was very pally and 'Hello Michael' with me, but I think a little taken aback that I attacked a small news item so bitterly. It was, he said, part of a much longer article which he had written, and the headline had not been composed by him.

However, Jill Foster did ring the BBC and Bill Cotton did send out a press release denying the story. But the *Evening Standard* rang up during the day to say that they noticed some confusion between the *Mirror* story and a Philip Purser interview with me in the *Daily Mail* (implying that Python would go on) and Radio Sheffield sent round a man to do an interview about Python's plans. So I became a minor celebrity for a day – and lost a lot of work time too.

---

1 Graham Chapman's close friend. They'd both studied medicine at Bart's, but Alan went on to practise.

Thursday, January 25th

Met Tony Smith[1] – the man who is probably going to land the first ever Python road tour.

He was a surprise. Longish hair, unkempt, shirt pulled over what must be a beer-belly – a friendly open face, and a total absence of traditional promoter's accoutrements – cigars, sharp suits and big talk. He was quietly confident that a Python tour would be a sell-out. Bannister Promotions have offered us a guarantee of £17,500, but Tony Smith reckons that we could make 21 or 22 grand – on a percentage split with him. I must put this to the rest of the team. Smith has fairly impressive credentials, including recent sell-out tours with The Who and Led Zeppelin.

At 1.15 gave an interview to a Belgian journalist for a radio programme which is featuring the new Python record on one of its shows – which is more than they do here, and the record isn't even for sale in Belgium! I said Mr Heath ought to take his trousers off once a year. The Belgian evidently felt this was quite a risible Eurojoke.

Saturday, January 27th

Winter this year is being very unfriendly to romantics. No snow, let alone a blizzard, winds moderate, weather warm, and now, to cap it all, bright sunshine. At 2.00 we had a Python meeting at John's. We decide to do the Python tour with Tony Smith. We talk about details of performance and dates and places. I find it extraordinary that John can undertake such a violent month of really hard work repeating basically old material – and yet will not countenance doing another series of Python. I suppose it's all a question of time and money. My God, we're getting so mercenary. Eric is almost totally involved in ads. He has been the most successful of us – with his 'Nudge-Nudge' selling Breakaway chocolate, and another ad in the offing. This afternoon he rang me to say that Gibbs toothpaste had approached him to ask if he could set up a five-minute film for their sales conference. It had to be made quickly and fairly cheaply. Eric proposed that we set it up as a package, with the two of us and Terry. It sounded like good experience – it wasn't for general commercial purposes, and it could be rude. What's more, it's work. I accepted on behalf of us both.

1 Not to be confused with Tony Stratton-Smith, whose Charisma label put out our albums.

Thursday, February 1st

To Portman Square for presentation of the Gibbs film script. Waiting outside the office was Rita Allen, of Selling and Sellers Ltd, who is a conference organiser and valiantly trying to appear relevant to this project. She is mid-thirties, with tired eyes, skilfully concealed in a well-made-up face.

In the office Colin Hessian deferentially introduces me to his boss, a Mr Finn. We sit round a rather silly table, and I read the script through – Gumby voices and all. It goes down surprisingly well. Hessian roars with laughter. Finn is clearly worried that we all like it so much, and after some discussion we make some simple changes – in order to give it a happy ending.

There is controversy over the vox-pop 'I only like toothpaste with crab or hake in it'. Finn doesn't like this. Hessian, being a good deal more independent than I would have expected, stands up for it strongly. What a silly discussion – it puts me in mind of Terry and Duncan Wood arguing the virtues of 'masturbating'. Anyway, they accepted the script happily.

Thursday, February 8th

Up at 6.30. Terry is here by 6.45. It's just beginning to get light, but it looks an unpromising day. Heavy drizzle and dark, dull, low clouds. We are hoping to film the entire Elida-Gibbs salesman film today – some six or seven minutes of script. Fortunately we start early, up amongst the faceless 1930s shopping arcades of Colindale, and by 9.20 a longish sound sequence is completed.

We finish shooting about 6.00, with thirty-seven set-ups in the can. During the course of the day, I have been a filthy, coughing tramp, thrown out of a shop, a salesman in glittering white suit who leaps out of the roofs of cars over shop counters and, right at the end of the day, the most difficult thing, a straight-to-camera hard-sell tongue-twister on the virtues of Close-up Green toothpaste. But I think everybody enjoyed the hard work – tho' it was cold and wet, there is no stronger feeling amongst a crew than when each person in it knows that the other person is working flat out. Terry was excellent – but does have a tendency to get over-excited, which is not so good when others are getting over-excited as well. This is just the time for icy calm.

Friday, February 9th

Arrived at Rules [restaurant] about 1.00. In an upstairs room the Pythons, and several people from Methuen, who had worked on the book [*Monty Python's Big Red*]. On the table were individual sugar Gumbies, and a large chocolate 'Spiny Norman',[1] and menus on which each dish was followed by an appropriate review of the *Big Red Book* – trout followed by 'flat, thin and silly', etc. The meal was to celebrate sales of over 100,000 paperbacks. Couldn't get excited or impressed about it, though – it only added to my feelings of guilt. Here we were, being given an enormous and expensive free meal, in honour of us earning large amounts of money. Also I can't help feeling that Python is better employed creating than celebrating. However, it was a chance to overeat.

From the Methuen lunch – feeling full of cigars and brandy, which ought to be Rules' coat of arms – walked back through sunlit Covent Garden. Knowing that the whole area will be redeveloped (keeping odd buildings of 'historical merit'), it's rather like one imagines walking through London in the Blitz. You know what's happening is not going to do the city any good, but you're powerless (almost) to stop it. However, pressure groups of all opinions seem to be more successful now – Piccadilly and Covent Garden have both had big development plans changed by community action and protest. The sad thing is that the basic thinking behind these redevelopment schemes never changes. Blocks (of offices mainly) dominate. Where there was once a gentle elegance and a human scale, there is now concrete and soaring glass. The City of London is rapidly getting to look like a Manhattan skyline, which doesn't worry me so much – but the blocks creeping into the West End are more sinister, for they are forcing a primarily residential area into acres more of hotels, offices and widened roads, and the scale of London's buildings – which are, by and large, reasonably small, friendly and non-monolithic – is every day being lost.

Tuesday, February 13th, Southwold

Took a day and a half's break in Southwold – having time off from immediate commitments. On the train at Liverpool Street – a late start,

1 Mr Gumby wore knotted handkerchiefs on his head and shouted very loudly. Spiny Norman was the giant hedgehog which the gangster Dinsdale Pirhana was convinced was watching him.

but the train tore through Essex to make up time. I ate breakfast and read the paper. Peace, perfect peace.

Met by Mother and Father in the car. Now he doesn't drive long distances. A few weeks ago he had a skid on the way home, and it clearly worries him greatly. He is also very worried about being left at home alone. Apparently he watched a TV programme about Parkinson's Disease, and at the end was almost in tears, and kept telling Ma how lucky he was to have her.

He is now definitely thinking of himself as an invalid, the times when he tries to make out how incredibly active and busy he is are getting fewer. I think he knows now that taking an hour to dress is a long time for an active man. He is aware of his mind and his concentration drifting. He cannot grasp any concept, statement, idea, argument that isn't utterly straightforward.

My mother looked well, I think she is almost happier now that she knows that all she can do for him is just to look after him. When he was fit and well, it must have been more difficult for her to accept that there was hardly any sympathetic contact between them; now he is more an invalid, their relationship is at least clear-cut.

Thursday, March 1st

In the afternoon we went to see Mark Shivas at the BBC. He hopes to have either James Cellan Jones or Ted Kotcheff to direct our 'Black and Blue' script. Talking of the future, he showed considerable interest in the Pythons' second film – and suggested a man called David Puttnam[1] as a source of money. Terry afterwards thought Shivas himself might have been interested in the producer's job. He seems very confident in us – when we mentioned to him about the waiter script which we have been working on, he said he could almost certainly get a 'Play for Today' slot for it – which is the kind of talk we're not yet used to.

Saturday, March 3rd

I went out shopping in Queen's Crescent market before lunch. In many ways it's a sad place – you notice especially old, shuffling ladies,

1 Produced *Chariots of Fire, The Killing Fields* and *Local Hero,* but his only major credit at this time was *That'll Be the Day* with David Essex.

poorly dressed, with twitching mouths. You hardly ever see them in Hampstead or Belsize Park. These are people who make a complete and utter mockery of 'democracy' and 'equality' – they're the casualties of the primitive rules of competition which run our society, and the welfare state just keeps them alive. That's all.

Take Thomas and William on to Parliament Hill. It's the English cross-country championships, quite a sight. Over 1,000 runners streaming round the Heath. It was like a *Boy's Own* story. David Bedford – the hero who failed at Munich – was leading the field, as he ran lightly down the hill a foot or so away from us.

Behind Bedford trailed hundreds of runners with no hope. Men whose chins were already flecked with white dried spittle, small, bespectacled balding men with shoulders smartly back, lank, long-haired boys striding down the hill like Daddy-Long-Legs. We moved up to the top of the hill to watch the second lap, and Thomas was running all over the place in his little green duffel coat, trying to emulate the runners. The sun came out as they ran around the second time, and the Heath suddenly seemed small as the long line of multi-coloured vests stretched as far as the eye could see. Bedford was pipped in the second lap by a New Zealander. It was an exhilarating feeling to have been present at a big national sporting event, without having to pay any money, squeeze through any turnstiles and sit where one's told.

Sunday, March 4th

My parents have been married forty-two years. I wonder how many of those were happy.

Sitting writing my diary up in the afternoon when there is a noise outside. A parade with banners passes up Lamble Street towards the new blocks at Lismore Circus – a loudspeaker van follows up. It urges non-payment of the extra 85p a week rent, made necessary by the government's Fair Rent Act. Camden was one of the last boroughs in the country to give in to this act. It's good to see someone still fighting – but like a protective hen, I became all at once aware of feeling alarmed at this civil commotion – a momentary fear that these are the voices of the have-nots, and they somehow threaten us, the haves.

Rung up this evening by a girl who is organising a pageant of Labour. A re-affirmation of socialist ideals – largely sponsored by actors such as

Anthony Hopkins, Vanessa Redgrave and others. Heartening to know so many of one's favourite actors are anti-establishment, but I react against her rather vague left-wing patter, and her presumption that so long as anything was anti-Tory it was good. I go along with her most of the way on this – but in the end, rather than argue, or ask her to explain any more, I agree to send £25. All she seemed to want was money. Money to bring coachloads of workers down from the north.

Monday, March 5th

A Python meeting at Terry's. The first time since the third LP in September that we have all contributed to a creative enterprise – in this case the second Python film. It was in many ways like a typical Python working day. Graham arrived late, and Terry made the coffee – and there was the usual indecision over whether to have a small lunch in, or a blow-out at one of Camberwell's few restaurants – we even played touch football on the lawn, for the weather is mild and sunny – a sort of Indian summer at the wrong end of the year. But for me, the most heartening thing of all was the quality and quantity of the writing that Python has done over the last week. John and Graham, writing together apparently untraumatically for once, had produced some very funny material. Eric had a richer selection of ideas – which sparked off a lot of other ideas, and Terry and I had a rag-bag of sketches – more than anyone else, as usual, but with a pretty high acceptance rate. Today we proved that Python can still be as fresh as three years ago, and more prolific.

Thursday, March 8th

Worked at home – as there was a rail strike, and reports of enormous traffic jams. Outside they're pulling down the line of old houses remaining in Lamble Street. There's something compelling about destruction – as tho' it's really more in our nature than building. I decided to make a photographic record of the rebuilding of Lamble Street from start to finish – all on a single three-minute piece of film.

I heard on the lunchtime news that a bomb had been found in a parked car near Scotland Yard – and it was believed to be connected with the Ulster border referendum being held today. It wasn't until the early evening news that I heard that there had been two big explosions in London. A bomb had gone off outside the Old Bailey – over 200 people were injured and one man killed – another had gone off in Whitehall. The impact on the media was tremendous – 'Outrage', 'Belfast comes to London', etc, etc.

Friday, March 9th

Left for Terry's at 11.15, after a good couple of hours' work. London is under siege, or so it feels. Traffic solid around Tottenham Court Rd – partly because of limited rail service owing to the prolonged go-slow and yesterday's total stoppage, and partly (as I discovered as I tried to take a short cut through Fitzroy Square) due to bomb scares. The area around the Post Office Tower had been totally cleared and cordoned off after a caller had said a bomb would go off at 11.30. Nothing went off. Neither did it at Thomas's play school in Kentish Town, which was also evacuated after a scare.

Sunday, March 11th, Abbotsley

Stricken, during the night, with a strange malaise of the bowels. Spent from about ten to three until six o'clock on the lavatory reading much of Norman Collins' *London Belongs to Me*. Spend the morning in bed with the Sunday papers and no breakfast or lunch. Thomas is fascinated and keeps coming up to see if I'm alright – bringing me Lego and finding some medicine for me – and talking ever so sweetly and politely. Gradually the visits become more frequent. He brings Willy along with him. A plateful of four thin pieces of toast (all I wanted for lunch) has only two left on it by the time Thomas has brought it upstairs. Around two o'clock both he and William ended up in my sickbed listening to stories, so I decided that it was no longer worth being ill and got up around three.

Friday, March 23rd

It has been a glorious week of sunny weather. We have been working for three days on the Python film script with maximum productivity. Ideas have been pouring out, and we have had very concentrated, but quite tiring writing sessions. Today at Terry's we sat outside in the sunshine to write, and for the first day this year I caught the sun. Al fresco lunch with wine and a Chapman salad. John busy writing biographies for the press – 'Despite what Michael thinks, he is not good company.'

Thursday, March 29th

At 5.30 we met Mark Shivas at the BBC and went to meet James Cellan Jones, who is to be the director of *Secrets*, our play for the 'Black and Blue' series. We took bets on what he would be like as we drove along the A40. I envisaged him as a rather burly, stocky man, with a loud voice. I was right, except I may have over-emphasised the loudness of his voice, and I didn't know that he'd have no socks on. He may be brilliant, but I didn't feel an awful lot of sympathy for our play, nor an awful lot of knowledge of it and, when Terry asked about writers attending editing, he closed up like a shell. But as we will be on the Monty Python tour when it's rehearsed, filmed and recorded, there is little we can do, so we might as well leave him the play, and see what comes out the other end. I can see embarrassment and disillusionment somewhere along the line, I'm sure.

Friday, March 30th

Mark Shivas rang early to apologise for what he called J C-Jones' 'scratchy' behaviour towards us. Had we not thought he was being like a prima donna? I said it hadn't worried us, but there were one or two points when we felt that he had the wrong end of the stick, and Shivas promised to talk to him. I feel Shivas is on our side rather than his, but this is probably the feeling he gives everyone, which is why he's such a good producer.

Monday, April 16th

Our seventh wedding anniversary, and fourth year of the diary. Over to B&C Records to talk about promotional work for the tour. On the steps of B&C met the beaming and effusive Tony Stratton-Smith – one of those few people who cheers me up whenever I see him. He was especially full of himself today for he has, almost single-handedly, secured Python's first TV foothold in the US – a deal with the Eastern Educational Network to put out the shows, uncut and unabridged. It's not a lucrative deal, but it's a great breakthrough. Tony now has to get two sponsors for the show and has high hopes of Apple, the Beatles' company – George H is very interested.[1]

Back home to write some programme copy for the stage tour. Helen had a good suggestion yesterday. All its pages will be on one big sheet, which can be folded up into a programme, or kept as a poster. Good Python thinking.

Easter Monday, April 23rd

The first official day of the 'First Farewell Tour', but Terry G, Terry J and myself have been working hard on it for about two weeks, collecting the film, writing and creating the programme, making slides, organising the sound tape with André. The much looked forward to holiday, which Helen and I were to take last week, evaporated under intense pressure of work. We left for Abbotsley at lunchtime on Good Friday. Took some champagne to celebrate Helen's mother's election to the new county council[2] as an Independent.

Rehearsals started at 9.30 at the Rainbow Theatre in Finsbury Park. It's a mammoth 3,500-seater theatre, with wildly flamboyant interior. The huge ceiling is studded with twinkling stars and above the proscenium and along the side walls are passageways, alcoves, balconies, in Spanish-Oriental style, with lights in as if for the start of a massive Shakespearean production. It's a magnificent folly – and it seems an obvious target for developers. However, it continues in being as a rock concert theatre – probably helped by the decision of the Albert Hall not to stage any more rock concerts.

Friday, April 27th, Southampton

Woke about 7.00. Slept fitfully until 8.15. Feet sweating, but fairly calm. A bath and breakfast. It was a fine, sunny morning, so we walked to the theatre. In the distance we could see the enormous liners in the docks, and some way ahead, the steel letters on a grid high above the surrounding buildings read 'Gaumont'. Altogether rather an epic place to start the tour. There was an almost tropical feeling – as if we had come 700, not

1 In the end, Dusty Springfield made an on-air introduction to Python's first appearance on New York's Channel 13.
2 Due to Boundary Commission recommendations, Huntingdon ceased to be a county and

70 miles south from London. I became aware of blossoms everywhere, of lush chestnuts in bloom, and a warmth in the air, with a healthy sea edge to it.

The sound is clearly going to be a difficult problem, for, in addition to music and sound f/x on tape (now being worked by André), we have film and animation sound from the projector, voice-overs from two off-stage mikes and six radio mikes, all to be mixed and controlled by Dave Jacobs, a short, dark, grey-eyed young guy, who has had about six hours' sleep in the last three days. In fact everyone looks tired, but the adrenaline of an imminent first night keeps everyone going.

Graham was using more than adrenaline to keep him going. He arrived at 10.00, already a little bleary from drink, and violently angry that he had not been told where to meet us. Gradually he calmed down, but unfortunately the damage was done – what everyone feared might happen, but hoped that for once it wouldn't, *did* happen. By 6.00 Graham was very drunk. We finished a dress run-through at 5.15, with many imperfections still not sorted out, and some difficult costume changes keeping us all tense.

The first house was just over half-full and was happy, rather than ecstatic. But it certainly couldn't be compared with the reception we'd had at Coventry. Perhaps most amazingly of all, 'Silly Walks' went by with an almost embarrassing lack of response, and there were many cases of mikes not being switched up, etc, etc. There was only half an hour before the next house, so there was only time for a cup of tea and a sandwich before we gathered on stage for 'Llamas'. John, Eric, Terry G, Terry J and Neil resplendent in their Spanish gear, Carol in her sequinned leotard, and me in an old mac with 'Eat More Pork' written on the back, and my Gumby gear underneath.

As soon as the curtain went up for the second house, the atmosphere was one of wild enthusiasm. Favourite characters – John in the Llama sketch, Gumby, Terry and Graham as Pepperpots, Eric as Nudge-Nudge, and Graham's Colonel and Ken Shabby – were given rounds of applause, and 'Pet Shop' at the end was as self-indulgent in performance, and as hugely popular in reception as it has ever been.

But Graham was far gone. He had missed his entrance in 'Argument' twice, made 'Custard Pie' a dull shadow of its former self, and slowed down many a sketch. Only his own 'Wrestling' had been done really well.

Upstairs in the restaurant of the Dolphin, Graham and Eric reached a point of explosion and Eric threw down his napkin with a rather impetuous flourish and left the restaurant. Later Graham, Eric and John had 'full and frank discussions', in which John told Graham straight out that he had performed very badly in both shows and if he went on like this every night there was no point in him continuing on the tour. For my own part, I feel that Graham's condition was the result of a colossal over-compensation for first-night nerves. He had clearly gone too far in his attempt to relax – maybe now the first night is over he will no longer feel as afraid.

Saturday, April 28th, Brighton

At 10.00 we left Southampton and moved along the south coast to Brighton.

The first house was not brilliant – there were severe sound problems, late cues and sketches which went on too long.

The second house was better, with a big audience response, but again difficulties with sound and film. Helen was there to see it, so was Maggie,[1] Barry Cryer, Ronnie Corbett, etc. Very few congratulations flying around – a sort of tacit approval at best, at worst a positive awkwardness. As I waited outside the theatre after the show, waiting for John G to sort out which cars should take us home, I felt very depressed. I feel that my contribution to the show is not as great as it could be. I feel that we are marking time – regurgitating old material, milking the public in a way Python never has done quite as blatantly. But as Helen, and Carol's hubby Peter, who travelled back with us, said, the audience loved it, and with a few changes it has the makings of a great show. We have already made some cuts – 'Half-a-Bee' song didn't even last two performances – but there are others.

Saturday, May 5th, Birmingham

The tour is now in its second week, and we have done eleven shows already. My voice is getting a little husky and I hope that if I treat it carefully it will last tonight's show at the Hippodrome and three shows in Bristol before two days off in London. And I am, almost as I write, 30 years old. Thirty years old in this Post House, a colourful, but colourless hotel, which could be anywhere in any country. Thirty years old and enjoying all the benefits of standardisation.

1 Maggie Weston, ace make-up artist who became Mrs Gilliam.

Most of the people who stay in these places are businessmen, and that's what I feel is the difference between my being 30 in Birmingham and 20 at Brasenose, and ten at Birkdale[1] – now, for better or worse, I am a part of this standardisation – a money-earning, rate-paying, mortgage-owning man of business. For Python is business – it's no longer an unpredictable, up one year, down the next kind of existence. Python has the magic ingredient, 'market potential', and our books and our records are only on the verge of making as much money as we could want. And yet some of the spontaneity and the excitement has gone as security has crept in and, although I am in a job which still allows me to wear knotted handkerchiefs over my head and have 2,500 people pay to see me do it, I still feel that I am a 30-year-old businessman.

The show went well, tho' my lack of voice is becoming a slight and annoying restriction. At the end of 'Pet Shop' I did the usual 15-second approach to John and, feeling the end of the show only thankful seconds away, said 'D'you want to come back to my place?' Conscious of the laugh being less ecstatic than when my voice was working. But worse was to come. John turned to me and said 'No'. It didn't get much reaction and a combination of disappointment at this rather poor ad-lib and consuming fatigue made me just remain silent, look suitably disappointed and wait for the curtains to close. I really was in no mood for witty extemporisation. But I suddenly became aware that Eric, in a compere's spangly jacket, had come forward to the front of the stage and was talking to the audience. 'Ladies and gentlemen, this evening is a very special evening for one of us here tonight …' then it became clear … 'for tonight Michael Palin is 30 years old.' The audience cheered, my mind started racing as I began to go through my options … Eric was going on … 'And tonight we've brought along one of Michael's very great friends …' faces of John and Terry looking at me grinning … 'one of his most favourite personalities in the world of showbiz … Mrs Mary Whitehouse!' Neil plays a few chords, and on comes Eric's mother – the spitting image of the good Mrs Whitehouse,[2] bearing a cake with candles. Everyone is looking at me, grins have become grins of anticipation – what will I do? How will I react? Carol Cleveland brought me a bunch of chrysanthemums – and there was the get-out. I found

1 Birkdale Primary School, Sheffield, which I attended from 1948 to 1957.
2 Mary Whitehouse, concerned at the decline in public morals, started the Clean-Up Television Campaign, which became the National Viewers' and Listeners' Association. She never directly attacked Python, but saw the BBC as a den of impropriety.

myself saying 'Ladies and gentlemen, I would like to say how pleased and proud I am to have received this cake from that great shit Mary Whitehouse (cheap, but desperate and it got a good laugh) and all I can say at this moving moment is ... (relapse into Gumby voice) ... ARRANGE THEM ... IN THE CAKE!' And plunge the lovely chrysanthemums into the lovely cake.

I had got out of it, and the audience were clapping and laughing and singing 'Happy Birthday'. I felt not only relief, but great pleasure and thanks that my birthday had actually been made remarkable – as I said to Eric, 'At last there's something to write in my diary.'

I had organised a birthday meal for everyone at Lorenzo's, an Italian restaurant. Food passable, wine and champagne. Sat next to Robert [Hewison], who ten years ago almost single-handedly pushed me into revue performing.

Back at the hotel I remember Neil helping me to my room, where I stripped off and collapsed into bed. Neil, Terry, Eric, Carol and I can't remember who else crowded into the room. We read poems from the *Oxford Book of Twentieth Century Verse*. Neil insisted on spilling wine over my carpet. The last I remember is Neil offering me a joint, which I declined – for my system had had a big enough battering for one day. An enormous card had arrived from André and Dave, someone was eating my chocolates and, about 3.30, my thirtieth birthday ended, and I lay back, utterly exhausted and very, very happy. Thank you Birmingham.

Sunday, May 6th, Bristol

Left for Bristol at midday with our driver, Bill; Eric and John in the other limousine with Sid driving.

As we drove out of Birmingham, we ran into a violent cloudburst on the motorway out of the Midlands. Bill confided to us that he was staying behind Sid because Sid's car wasn't working too well and the brakes were in a very dangerous state. Nevertheless, we were having some trouble keeping up with him. I looked at the clock. We were touching 100. In front Sid was swaying his limousine around like a raft in a storm. I buried my head in Evelyn Waugh's diaries in *The Observer*, or else tried to sleep. I felt doubly glad I was with Bill – but uncomfortably aware that the window was misting over, and yet Bill was blaming the poor visibility on the intensity of the rain. Terry J, behind, suggested he use the demister. Bill didn't know where it was, and Terry and I had to show him.

When we reached Bristol we had to stop and ask some passers-by where the Dragonara Hotel was. Shortly, as we approached a roundabout, there was this brand new brick pile with a huge sign, 'Dragonara', crowning it. I could scarcely believe my eyes as Sid turned into the roundabout and, inches from the sign itself, sped away and off to the left, up a hill and out towards the docks. Bill, after turning on the dual carriageway, drove past both entrances of the hotel and off to the roundabout *to follow Sid*.

Thursday, May 17th, Edinburgh

One of the most vocal and enthusiastic audiences we've had. The usual knot of twenty or thirty autograph hunters outside, and one of them asked me to come and have a coffee and a drink with them. Foolishly I indicated our fat Daimler, and muttered something about the Queen Mother waiting; but then had to sit in the car for a full 15 minutes for John to finish signing. A couple of belligerent Scots looked resentfully at the car, and I thought we were going to have a repetition of Birmingham, where someone spat on the windscreen.

Even when we eventually left, Sid took us steadfastly the wrong way. I have never been on a journey with him when he has gone directly from point A to point B. We drove out along the road to Peebles tonight – and we made the mistake of thinking that it was so clearly *not* the right road that Sid must be at any moment about to turn off. But it was not until I shouted to him 'Is this the Glasgow road, Sid?' that he took action and we veered off to the right. We were now in the middle of a housing estate, with our enormous limousine squeezing its way into a cul-de-sac, some ten miles from our hotel.

The consistency with which Sid goes wrong is such that, as Neil said, the law of averages ceases to apply.

Friday, May 18th, Edinburgh

Neil and Eric very pissed tonight on stage. The unusual spectacle of Eric not quite in control. The difference in his timing showed how crucial timing is. Both his long travel agent monologue and 'Nudge-Nudge', which usually provoke enormous reaction, went by almost unnoticed. Neil was falling about behind stage, in high spirits, and his 'Idiot Song' was wonderfully bad – full of wrong notes. A show to remember, but not necessarily for the right reasons.

Saturday, May 19th, Edinburgh

Did not enjoy the first house particularly. They were not a very voluble audience, and I was anxious about my voice as usual.

The second house much noisier, and managed to get through it – with the voice standing up surprisingly well. Back at the hotel, tired and hungry, to be confronted with 'night service'. Could we have a bottle of champagne, please? Much conferring with manager and his lackeys – then a very smartly dressed young man came to tell us that we could only have drinks available in the 'night store' – this included a selection of dishes limited in quality and quantity, as only the British know how. Of the six items available, four were not available. I ended up with a gin and tonic, a large brandy and a roll and cheese.

Went to bed. Could not get to sleep owing to presence of David Bowie and his acolytes in the hotel. Bowie is currently the hottest touring property in Britain, having recently played to 18,000 in Earl's Court. Tonight Bowie was in Edinburgh – and staying about a couple of doors down on the same floor as myself. They weren't exactly noisy, there were just so many of them. From 2.00 to 3.00 and beyond it was like trying to sleep through the invasion of Poland.

Sunday, May 20th, Edinburgh

At 12.00 sauntered down to the lobby – which was filled with the Bowie party's gear, and Bowie attendants. What a relief from roomfuls of grey suits – this morning it was almost as though squatters had moved in. Tall, gangling men in worn denim moved through the throng like a dozen Jesuses, sharply dressed chicks sat around smoking – everyone wore a relaxed air of confidence – they were, after all, part of the hottest road show in Britain. With our Sunday papers and our conspicuous lack of hangers-on we looked very dull and anonymous.

Outside the hotel was Bowie's splendid personal conveyance, a chunky black and white Dodge Van, which looked like nothing I had ever seen – it was an armoured car, in effect – with thick steel sides and black windows. A stylish version of a Black Maria.

The second house at Glasgow earlier in the day, was, I think, the best performance of the tour so far.

Even the police had come in to watch us. Five or six of them, including two policewomen, sat behind stage and watched the second show, and one of them came on and jumped around during the Idiotting sequence. They managed to find a bottle of whisky for Graham from nowhere.[1] In fact, as they left, they asked us if we wanted 'anything else'.

Monday, May 21st, Leeds

Two more full houses and great enthusiasm again.

Back at the hotel a strange little group was gathered in the lobby, in the middle of which was David Hemmings, a sort of sub-Frostian whizz-kid, who made a whole lot of films after *Blow-up* and became Hollywood material. Also he built up a business called Hemdale, which I suspect is now linked with Frost in some way, who is of course now linked with Slater-Walker, who have just joined with Hambros Bank, and who, as *Private Eye* put it this week, are soon to make a bid for England.

Anyway, David Hemmings was heavily drunk, and Graham Chapman, also heavily drunk, was having quite a verbal battle with our Dave. Graham was lurching about telling Hemmings that he wasn't going to go to bed with him. Around Hemmings were various ladies and battered-looking men, who, it turned out, were all from Yorkshire TV. A feeling of confrontation and combat in the air. As of rival gangs circling each other. Python sitting rather aloof, Hemmings being loud and organising little trials of strength – like picking matchboxes off the floor with your teeth, whilst leaning over an armchair. Eventually the gangs came together, and Hemmings got us involved in a game of American football; he tried one run with the cushion we were using as a ball, and crashed down over a whole tableful of drinks – broken glass everywhere – and it was only after this that the night porter, a man of extreme tolerance, came and cooled things down. Whilst the others were deciding whether to carry on the game outside, I went to bed. It must have been 3.30. Outside a good Yorkshire mist was closing in.

Wednesday, May 23rd

After Leeds a long run down to Norwich, which was our thirty-fourth performance since we started at the Gaumont, Southampton, twenty-seven days before. My parents came to see the show. It was good to see

1 At that time Glasgow was a dry city on Sundays.

my father there. I didn't think he was up to going to the theatre, but it was his own decision.

The first Python stage appearances abroad were on an eccentric tour of Canada. All the team were there, augmented by Neil Innes and Carol Cleveland.

Sunday, June 3rd, Toronto

In Toronto, a small crowd, maybe 150 in all, were waiting outside the customs and, as we came out of the customs hall, there was quite a lot of cheering and shouting. (Apparently our TV show had been out the night before and CBC had added an announcement that we would be at the airport at 6.00.) They were a cheerful rather than a violent crowd. Signed a few autographs and climbed on to an old British bus with an open upper deck, which had been provided for us. CBC had also provided a four-page illustrated news-sheet called 'The Flying Python' and were wearing Gumby T-shirts. There was a lot of effort involved, but somehow the welcome seemed anti-climactic – the fans were not quite vociferous enough, and there was a lot of time spent sitting on top of the bus feeling rather conspicuously spare, before we moved off.

The trip into Toronto was soon cut short when a policeman flagged down the bus and turned us off the motorway for travelling too slowly.

This morning I woke at about 4.30 with a feeling of complete disorientation – it took me some moments to remember that I was in a hotel room, and it was quite a shock to remember that the hotel room was in Toronto. A heavy wave of homesickness came over me – the room was colourless and unfriendly, the hotel was massive and impersonal, and I was going to be away from home in rooms like this for the next three weeks. I switched on TV. In a chintzy set with potted palms, a very well made-up, expensively gowned, 35–40-year-old actress was talking to Kathryn Kuhlman, a frizzy-haired, rather wild looking mother/confessor figure. The actress was telling of how she gave up her life of sleeping pills, and came to know Christ. At moments she tried to cry, but couldn't – it was a grotesque, but quite compulsive exercise in hard-core bad taste. As Kathryn Kuhlman turned to camera to make her final message on God's behalf, piped music soared in, and, as the credits rolled over this programme that had been about giving all up to join Christ, I caught the title 'Miss Kuhlman's gowns by Profil du Monde'. An extraordinary programme – a kind of coffee-table Christianity.

Tuesday, June 5th, Toronto

I switched on the Watergate hearings – and here was instant courtroom drama – the characters seemed to be characters I'd seen before – the Edmund O'Brien figure of Sam Erwin, the chairman, the film star smoothness of Senator Howard Baker, and the star today – Sally Harmony – a somewhat overawed, but quite pretty divorcee, who was trying to explain away her involvement in the bugging. The whole Watergate case has taken up more press and broadcasting time than any other cause célèbre I can remember. The Americans watch it with fascination and they are given all the hearings all day on three channels. There are signs that the coverage is beginning to slacken, however. I think the initial shocks have all been absorbed by now, and unless Nixon is found to be directly involved in the bugging or cover-up of Watergate, the story will not pick up its impetus of two or three weeks ago.

Meanwhile there was Sally Harmony, sweating lightly on her upper lip, being cross-questioned in front of millions. It's so like fiction that there could be a danger that it will become fiction in people's minds.

Wednesday, June 6th, Toronto

After about five hours' sleep last night, I was called at 6.30 to go for an early show interview with CTV – the main alternative channel to CBC. Terry J and Terry G were the only other two whom Tony [Smith] could persuade to do it, and the four of us left the Royal York Hotel at 7.00 in a cab. It was a grey morning, our route took us out of the city centre, and along an expressway with huge apartment blocks on either side. Enormous numbers of new apartments must have been built in the last ten years, and it was all residential – I could see no factories, or even shops, just acres of instant neighbourhoods.

Our interviewer was called Percy. He was a young and fit-looking 50-ish, with a very open friendly face, but we didn't know how serious he would be. As he was in a single shot doing an introduction to camera about how brilliantly zany we all were, I pointed my finger at his speaking mouth, and he bit the end of it. From then on, he almost took over the show. We talked seriously for a moment, then anarchy would break loose, and at one point Percy stood up and flung his coffee mug on to the studio floor, where it shattered. He rugby-tackled Terry Gilliam as we upturned the table on set.

They all seemed to be in the spirit of things by now, and, as the programme neared its end, suggested we do anything we wanted to whilst the girl and the other link man were signing off. So we leapt on the girl in the middle of her final announcement and the show ended with a chase.

Friday, June 8th, Montreal

The performance tonight, at the vast impressive Place des Arts, was nearly sold out – almost 2,500 people there, which I think is the biggest crowd we've played to on the tour. Mind you, we need them – for with the expenses of hotels, etc, we stand to make little more than £1,000 each for this whole Canadian effort. (John G had once estimated it as high as £3,000 each.) However, a good audience and, with the help of a neck mike, my voice is in fair trim for our two shows in Ottawa tomorrow. Two very good reviews of our show last night – one from a heavy, bearded, youngish critic who told me that he thought Python was better on mescalin.

Sunday, June 10th, Ottawa

Talked over the subject of the moment – whether or not to extend our tour to make TV appearances in the States. This was first mooted in Montreal by Nancy Lewis, from Buddah Records in New York, who have been responsible for a great deal of Python promotion in the States and who, apart from the record, are also trying to persuade Columbia to take the wraps off our film. Nancy, who is a very kind, gentle girl, has absolute faith in Monty Python's saleability in the States, and she has fixed up a series of TV interviews – including the *Johnny Carson Show*, and the *Midnight Show*, and film showings and radio interviews. But these will involve staying on in North America for about five days longer. John C and I are very much against this. I know how disappointed Helen would feel, and I desperately want to get back home anyway – having been away, apart from odd days, for nearly two months.

We decide on a compromise decision – i.e. that those who want to go to the States – Graham, Terry and Terry G – should appear on behalf of Python on the TV shows, and John and I would go to San Francisco and leave on the 24th. But during the course of yesterday evening it became clear that only John and I were happy with this arrangement, and the two Terrys especially felt that it was all or none.

As I thought about it, and as I talked to Nancy, who has almost put her job in jeopardy on our behalf (for Buddah are to pay all expenses), the more I realised that I ought to go, for Python's work is not down to one person, and if a majority of the group feel strongly enough that the American publicity is necessary to sell the work we have all done together, then the minority has a strong responsibility. So I agreed to go, and called Helen today and told her the sad news that we would not be returning until the 28th. She took it very well, but it is so difficult to explain satisfactorily when one is four and a half thousand miles away.

John C is vociferously against going. He regards it as an exercise by PR people for PR people – he strongly objects to being forced to do it, and last night, in the bar of the hotel, said straight out to Terry G that he enjoyed the industrial relations films he has been doing, much to our scorn, as being more worthwhile than Python. This saddened me, but at least John was saying what he felt.

That evening we were taken to a British High Commission-sponsored party at an apartment block. Some classic English stereotypes, including a man with a red face and a bow tie who asked me rather peremptorily if I could find him some ginger ale, and then spent the rest of the evening apologising that he hadn't recognised me. He kept coming up and remembering things I had done in the show and how marvellous they were.

Monday, June 11th, Ottawa–Calgary

A long travelling day. Owing to the selective strikes, we didn't leave Ottawa airport until about 12.00, and then had to fly to Toronto to transfer to a plane to Calgary.

On the journey I started talking about Python, the States and the group itself to Graham, and it suddenly became very clear to us that if we all, apart from John, wanted to do another Python series, then we should do one. The reaction in Britain and Canada showed that there was a great demand for a new series, and John had stated his position vis-à-vis Python very clearly on Saturday night at the Chateau Laurier in

Ottawa. Maybe a fourth Python series was born as we flew over the wheatlands of Saskatchewan.

Thursday, June 14th, Calgary–Edmonton

Up at 9.30 to travel to Edmonton. Should be exhausted, but couldn't summon up the energy.

On the plane sat next to John C, and had a good long chat. He is still very anti our trip to the States – now saying that it will be a loss financially, despite Buddah Records taking care of the hotel bills. He hates chat shows, and feels that in doing them Python is going against all its principles.

We landed at Edmonton out of grey skies. Before even going to the hotel, Terry J, Eric, Carol and myself are whisked off to the Edmonton Press Club. When we arrived there, about thirty people were sitting around tables in a dark basement, drinking.

Slowly but surely, it became obvious that we could not get away without some sort of cabaret. Eric and Terry first took the microphone and, after some opening banter, asked for questions. A silence, then one wag chanced his arm. 'I'd like to ask, as there are two of you up there, could one of you get me a Carlsberg.' Laughter. Then Terry and Eric grabbed this unfortunate pressman, pulled him indelicately across the dance floor and poured beer over him. It's quite amazing what Python has become.

Friday, June 15th, Regina, Saskatchewan

We have already cancelled our appearance in Saskatoon, owing to heavy travel costs and very low advance bookings. So we are here in Regina – Ordinary Town Canada, with its wheatmarket and its oil refineries and its RCMP headquarters, for two days, with almost no chance of making a profit.

Slept for two hours in the morning, a sleep broken only by a Tony Smith phone call, after I had been off for ten minutes, asking if I would appear on a lunchtime chat show, being recorded NOW. I told him I wanted my name right at the bottom of the list and, as I was the first person he'd rung, he was able to apply more heavily persuasive methods on the others. After I woke up, I had a shower, and ordered up some hot hors-d'oeuvres and a half-bottle of Chianti and a jug of coffee, watched Terry J, Terry G, and Graham on TV. Terry G very funny, slowly tying his mike lead around himself until he finished the interview totally trussed up and then died.

Saturday, June 16th, Regina, Saskatchewan

Terry and I had a lunchtime drink at the Red Lion Beverage Room, and played shuffleboard together, and then with a local. Canadians, as a whole, are about the most open, friendly people I know. There are none of the guarded, reserved, slightly resentful looks one sometimes receives when trying to meet the English. After lunch I lay on my bed, looked out over Saskatchewan and read *Jane Eyre*. I don't think I have ever felt so rested on the whole tour.

In the evening, a rather poor meal at a dimly lit restaurant called Golfs – it was trying its hardest to be exclusive and smart, and personified the worst aspects of North American snobbishness: 'Would you care to be seated for a cocktail?' Or, when we wanted to eat, 'Oh, indeed, sir, the hostess will come and seek you out.' And, when we were sat at table, 'This is your table for the evening, your waiter will be Randy.' At least that got Graham interested.

Despite the gloomy fears of Tony Smith, the ticket sales at Regina had increased greatly in the last two days, and we had a very respectable 60% house.

Wednesday, June 20th, Vancouver

At last the end of term has arrived. Tonight, in this well-appointed but fairly unexciting town, surrounded by pine-clad mountains, 8,000 miles from England on the edge of the Pacific, we perform *Monty Python's First Farewell Tour* for the forty-ninth and last time. Vancouver has treated us well, with the most extensive publicity coverage so far in Canada, plus more than the usual parties and receptions – and, in a 3,000 seat theatre, one 70% house on Monday, over 80% on Tuesday (when we broke a fifteen-year record at the Queen Elizabeth Theatre – taking $3,000 on the door) and tonight a complete sell-out, with people turned away.

Thursday, June 21st, San Francisco

We caught the 4.00 United Airlines flight to San Francisco via Seattle. The American Customs and Immigration at Vancouver Airport were less than welcoming, and we left Canada, this warm, friendly, straightforward, happily unexciting country, in a morass of red-tape, form-filling and an indefinable feeling of mistrust.

Arrived in San Francisco in the evening. As we drove from the airport it was dull and rather cool, and the cloud hung low over the mountains around the town like duvets hanging out to dry. Our hotel was called the Miyako. The hotel is designed in Japanese style, both inside and out, but this turns out to be compromised in many ways. Only a minority of the rooms are what I'm told is authentically Japanese – i.e. beds which are just light mattresses on the floor – the lobby is run with traditional American Western hotel efficiency – so much so that I witnessed the peculiar sight of a Japanese man trying to check into this Japanese hotel, and being unable to make himself understood.

Saturday, June 23rd, San Francisco

Nancy, Terry J, Neil and I and Eric are driving today down the coast road from SF to LA. We hired a couple of cars, which Buddah paid for, and at 7.00 or thereabouts, made our first stop at Monterey. With my susceptibility to romantic names, I felt we had to see Monterey, but it was rather anti-climactic. The harbour is a good deal less attractive than Brixham, and there was little hint of the magic of the place in the jettyful of seafood parlours, amusement arcades, rotten gift-shops, which sold ashtrays and books by Steinbeck. We drank a beer and set off towards the even more romantic names like Big Sur and Barbary Shore. A pilgrimage from Steinbeck, through Miller and Kerouac to Chandler.

We reach the mountains of Big Sur around 8.00. They are very beautiful – ridge after ridge ending in steep cliffs into the sea. Forested and wooded slopes with strong, clean smells on the edge of the Pacific. But it's slow driving round the promontories, down steeply into the valleys and up round the mountains again, and there are few hotels or restaurants – it being a national park.

We stop about 8.30 at the Big Sur Inn – a remote, low, cottagey building which wouldn't have been out of place in a Beatrix Potter illustration. I went in to ask if we could have a room for the night – and found myself in a comfortable, cheerful pair of dining rooms. Antiques and old furniture were everywhere, but not in a set-up, stylised, decorative way, but just as a haphazard collection, like a crowded Victorian sitting room. They had no rooms or reservations for dinner.

At 1.00 we stopped at the Holiday Inn in Santa Monica. They were full, but told us of a motel which might have vacancies. Suddenly, after resigning ourselves to sleeping en masse in any room we could find, we had five rooms booked at the Vandenburg Motel in Santa Maria.

In the dimly lit bar an ageing lady was playing the piano, spurring on a small and equally ageing group of residents to sing 'Frère Jacques'. The response was patchy. We sat at a table and ordered brandy and white wine. After a while the pianiste signed off with a sad, slightly drunk, speech to the effect that this was her last night here for a while (God knows where she was going to next), and she was looking forward to coming back and entertaining them all again. This received little encouragement from the ten or fifteen people left. I went to bed about 2.00, and put a quarter in the Magic Fingers.[1]

Sunday, June 24th, Los Angeles

In no other city have I seen such enormous hoardings advertising groups and their LPs. Grinning faces of Jack Carson, Andy Williams, John Denver and Diana Ross, a hundred times larger than life, look down on the strip. We passed Dean Martin's restaurant, and, not much further on (across the road from a huge hoarding advertising Led Zeppelin's latest LP *Houses of the Holy* with a strange picture of naked children climbing over what looked like the Giant's Causeway), we found our hotel, the Hyatt Continental. On the side of the marquee it read 'Buddah Records Welcomes Monty Python's Flying Circus'. We were in Hollywood.

Monday, June 25th, Los Angeles

At 2.30 three of the production team of the *Midnight Special* arrived to talk over our spot in the show tomorrow night. They were very American, all slightly paunchy, and wisecracking a lot – but genially. We talked over our prepared programme, which included animation, 'Gumby Flower Arranging', a clip from the 'Silly Olympics' film, 'Nudge-Nudge', 'Children's Story', 'Wrestling' and Neil's 'Big Boots'. (This

1 The Magic Fingers Bed Relaxation System was a way of vibrating your bed to lull you comfortably to sleep. A quarter of a dollar would wobble you gently for about five minutes. It always worked for me, until it stopped, whereupon I woke abruptly.

programme, like that for *The Tonight Show*, had to be without John, who flew back to England last Friday.) After going through the details of the show, we had to put on what felt like an audition. A run-through, cold, for these three TV men. Fortunately they laughed a lot, objected to nothing, and we felt greatly encouraged. At one point we asked them what would happen if there was no such laughter from the studio audience. He dismissed our worries lightly. 'We can always sugar it,' he said.

Tuesday, June 26th, Los Angeles

At 5.00 we arrived at NBC Burbank Studios to record our eight-minute slot for the *Midnight Special*. This is a relatively new rock show, which has built up a strong following and goes out at 1.00-2.30 in the morning every week. It's primarily a music show and is taped in gigantic sessions starting at 8.00 in the morning and going on until midnight. There is an informal live audience, who sit around on cushions, and look modish – a cross between campus and St Tropez. When we arrive at the studio Al Green's group are just playing, there's also an English band called 'Foghat', who seem very pleased to see us. It seems like bedlam, with groups wandering around, getting mixed up with other groups.

Sitting in the dressing room, we drink white wine from the store across the road (for there is no bar at NBC) and at 8.00 they are ready to tape us. For some reason there are no monitors in the studio, so the audience cannot see our animation or film clips. A friendly, but not ecstatic reaction.

Wednesday, June 27th, Los Angeles

At 11.00, up to the pool for an hour and a half. Graham's entourage has now swelled to five or six. We have hardly seen him in the last four days. He has been looking for a beach house to rent for a holiday after we've finished here. He found one in Laguna. Graham was an eye-opener in Canada. He drank far less, was much less aggressive and his performing was sure and confident – the best I've ever seen it. Perhaps it was because he was on his own. As soon as he is faced with the extraordinary complexity of his private life it seems to sap his energies totally. His worst performances on the English tour were when John Tomiczek's family were sitting morosely in his dressing room.

A lunchtime meeting in Nancy's room with a man from the *Los Angeles Free Press*, a sort of West Coast Village Voice with a fair smattering of extraordinary small ads – 'Your Penis Longer in 30 Days or Money Back'. 'Men – learn to wrestle with two nude ladies at the Institute of Sexual Intercourse.' We ordered up hors-d'oeuvres and Graham, Terry G, Terry J and I talked about ourselves to a tape recorder once again. Terry J's heart was clearly not in it, and he ended up back in my room watching the Watergate hearings – which he has been following avidly.

At 2.30 we once again drove out on the Hollywood Freeway to the NBC Studios. Whereas the *Midnight Special* has an audience more likely to appreciate Python, the *Tonight Show* is an all-American institution. At one go, Python will be seen by the few aficionados in New York and San Francisco, and also by the Mormons in Salt Lake City, the tobacco farmers of Louisiana and the potato growers of Idaho, the blacks in Harlem and Watts, and possibly even John Dean, President Nixon and Senator Fulbright.

To make things more nerve-racking, it was to be recorded as a live show, with no stops or retakes, for the tape had to be ready an hour or so after recording to be flown to the various parts of the States for transmission the next evening.

A great air of unreality. Here was Python going out to its greatest single audience ever, and to us it was no more than a hastily organised cabaret. We were totally unknown to the audience, and felt like new boys at school. At 6.00 the recording started. This week Joey Bishop, one of F Sinatra's and D Martin's buddies, was hosting the show as regular host Johnny Carson was on holiday. Bishop was on good form, fluent and funny. When it came to our spot he produced our two latest LPs and tried, quite amusingly, to explain the crossed-out Beethoven cover. All good publicity. The sketches went smoothly – tho' our starter, the two Pepperpots[1] talking about soiled budgies, was totally lost.

Friday, June 29th

Arrived home about 10.30. Thomas had stayed away from school to meet me, and we spent the morning unpacking and discovering things like the fact that my two Indian canoes from Banff wouldn't float, or

1 Pepperpots was the generic name for the screechy ladies in *Monty Python*. John and Graham coined the name because of their shape.

even rest for a moment on the surface of the water. As Thomas pointed out – the Indians weren't really very good at making canoes.

We spent much of July on holiday near Castiglione della Pescaia in Italy with our friends Ian and Anthea Davidson, their daughter Clemency and a lot of very tiny, very vicious sandflies called serafini.

Friday, August 10th

It's now about two and a half weeks since we flew back from Italy and, during that time, although I've succeeded in avoiding any major work commitments, we seem to have been busier than ever, renewing friendships that have lapsed since April and enjoying, with a sort of revived energy, living in London.

Like yesterday, walking through Bloomsbury, south of the Museum, a neat, compact village of Victorian terraced houses with bookshops and magic shops and an atmosphere of small-time human activity, a well-worn, lived-in feeling. The sun had come out and was shining from a clear sky, suffusing the buildings with a golden glow. Of course, I need hardly say that there are plans to knock this down.

Two weeks ago today, I drove up to Southwold and took the old man to Cambridge for a reunion dinner. I looked after him as carefully as I could, carrying his bag into the college lodge, as if he were a freshman. It was quite a curious reversal of the roles – for his reunion was for all those who had left Cambridge in 1921/22, so around the lodge of Clare's new buildings had gathered a group comprised entirely of 73-year-old men, all a little rusty and unfamiliar with the proceedings, exactly reliving their first days at the college over fifty years ago.

I showed the old man to his room, which was in a far corner of the quad. He was in a room opposite his slightly fitter friend Clive Bemrose, who had undertaken to 'keep an eye on him', though I had noticed that even Clive Bemrose couldn't remember to do his flies up after a pee. I felt very out of place, with my long hair and baggy denims.

In the quad a floppy, fattish, rather shambling man, with a case as tatty as my father's, and a head as bald, asked us the way to Thirkell Quad. My father double-took in surprise, 'Well I never, if it isn't my old best man, Bags Cave.'

Recognition spread less spontaneously across Bags' face, but at last it came. 'Good Lord,' he said to my father, 'Hugh St John Gordon! ... Palin,' he corrected himself. My father didn't seem to notice anything untoward, so pleased was he to encounter Bags. It was Silence and Shallow.

'How are you, old boy?'

'Oh, wilting a little, old boy,' said Bags, sadly, and started talking about hospitals.

Being back in Cambridge transformed and inspired my father in such a way that I could visibly see it doing him some good. He was suddenly in control – he knew where he wanted to walk to, and he remembered Cambridge well. I noticed afterwards that the only time he was a little restless was when we walked around the new buildings at St John's. The joy of Cambridge for him, at his age, is in its lack of change. It doesn't disorientate him as other cities do, for he can still see many, if not all, of his old haunts. We walked around the colleges, drinking in the privileged atmosphere, on a perfect, calm, sunny evening. I think we both felt great enjoyment during the one and a half hour walk, and it left no question in my mind as to whether it was worth bringing him or not.

Two days later, on the 29th of July, it was Angela's 40th and Jeremy's 13th birthday and we went down to Dulwich for lunch. The sun came out for us, and we lay in the garden and drank sherry and I tried to take a few photos, as it was one of the very rare occasions on which the family was all together.

It occurred to me what a polite lot we all are. I can remember Angela's childhood being punctuated with violent rows and shouting matches, I can remember many occasions when I hated my father for his intolerant, irrational rule-making, and his surliness to my friends, but now, with age, we've all mellowed. More optimistically, there doesn't seem to be any repetition in Angela's or my family of the lack of contact between father and children which we experienced.

In the garden after tea, Grandfather[1] sat in a deck chair, increasingly concerned with his lack of bowel movements. Granny, getting a little tired, tried to ignore him, and sat talking to Helen. Jeremy, Marcus and Camilla took Thomas and myself on at football. Veryan was cross at the mess we'd made to the lawn. Angela's chief present was an almost new

1 Daddy, Dad, Pa, Father, 'the old man' has, as Thomas and William grow older, morphed into 'Grandfather'.

Citroen 6. The first time she's had a car of her own. (Later in the week it was rammed up the back at some traffic lights.)

Next day I took Grandfather down to the West End and dropped him in the Mall, collecting him later from the dark recesses of 'his club', the Institute of Mechanical Engineers. He appeared to be at a low ebb. He didn't feel like shopping for the coat he had wanted, and said that his wretched condition was definitely slowing him down. With some misgivings I took him to the Barque and Bite, on the Regent's Canal. It was conveniently un-full, and, as it turned out, we ate a really excellent meal. He had melon and a very generous Dover sole, I succumbed to salmon and asparagus quiche and guinea fowl, he drank beer, I had a half-carafe of house wine. He liked the situation and he relaxed a lot during the meal. We had a good chat and I even told him that Helen and I were possibly going to have another baby – something which I wouldn't dare tell any other member of the family.[1] It didn't sink in at all, but it felt good to be in confidence-sharing mood with him. He livened up a lot after lunch, and I took him, Thomas and William to Syon Park for the afternoon.

As I drove out along the M4, I became aware that all three of them were asleep – all nodding gently. After a moment Grandfather woke up and said, à propos of nothing, 'There's a plane.' He kept on about planes and the airport and in the end I asked him directly if he'd rather go to the airport. He jumped at this and, in the heat of mid-afternoon, we found ourselves on top of the Terminal 3 car park, watching the activity. After 20 minutes or so, he said he'd had enough, so we started back. We never did get to Syon.

The next morning, I took him to catch the 11.30 train back to Suffolk. He looked rather tired and had little bounce left, and it was as well he was going back. But I think the four days had in fact done him a great deal of good, in taking his mind off his ailments, real and imagined, and giving him things to do – the trip to Cambridge, the airport, the Barque and Bite, which showed him that he is not yet an invalid. In fact, his capacity to enjoy himself is very strong, but he needs pushing.

On Tuesday, Terry and I played squash in the afternoon, and then went on to the BBC for a meeting with Cotton and Duncan Wood about the future of Python. Cotton restated his position that if we were to do a show without John it should not be called Monty Python – it should try

1 And which didn't materialise for another eighteen months!

and be something different, and it should be tried out in an on-air pilot, with a possible series next year. We in turn had bristled at the idea of having to prove ourselves in a pilot, and so it devolved on John C. How involved is he prepared to be in a new series? If he is adamantly against any involvement when Bill rings him, then we shall have to think about alternatives.

Tuesday, August 14th

This evening at 10.05, the first TV play written by Terry and myself went out on BBC2. *Secrets* had been given a blaze of pre-publicity of the sort normally reserved for the Cup Final. Mainly, I think, because it was the first of a new series, with a prestige star, Warren Mitchell, and a prestige producer, Mark Shivas, and a prestige director, James Cellan Jones. But also because it was at last something new in the midsummer wilderness of repeats. Anyway, we had the *Radio Times* cover, several trailers, and nearly every critic wrote it up as the main thing to watch this evening.

Helen and I took the children down to Terry's and watched there. As the show started I felt a tingling nervous expectancy, and, although it was all recorded long ago, I watched it as if it were live, willing the actors on to say the line faster or slower, hiding my head during a grossly over-played scene, laughing with tremendous relief when we all laughed. Many things were too cod and too heavily played, but I felt it looked very professional. Graham rang to say he'd enjoyed it and, about 12.00, Barry Cryer was the only other caller. He liked it, but, I think, with reservations. Whatever happens, I don't think after the enormous publicity build-up the critics will ignore it.

Wednesday, August 15th

I opened the *Daily Mirror* to find the headline on the TV page 'Choc Drop Flop'. I groaned, but reading on was worse. It was a violently unfavourable criticism, savagely attacking the writers but, 'as a favour', not mentioning our names. *The Guardian* had nothing.

I bought the other papers, and the situation seemed worse. Both Peter Black in the *Mail* and Richard Last in the *Telegraph* felt that it was the writers who were at fault. Last compared us with Evelyn Waugh, unfavourably of course, and Black felt we hadn't been very clever. Mind you, as a critic, he can hardly have any credence when he caps his review by saying 'if only Graeme Garden, as the Major in the Monty Python series … could have stopped it'.

James Thomas in the *Express* thought it fell flat and it was not until I read *The Times* that there was any crumb of comfort. At least he thought it was hilarious. For two or so hours, I felt like a hunted man. I didn't even ring Terry, I didn't really want to go out.

About 11.00 Simon A rang. He had seen it with his brother and a friend and they had all found it very funny. His objections were the same as mine – that more realism would have helped, that the overplaying of the slapstick made the tale seem more trivial than it was meant to be – but it hadn't spoilt it for them. His call cheered me up a lot, and from then on the day began to improve – Terry G had liked it, with reservations, Ann across the road had enjoyed it without reservations.

In mid-afternoon Mark Shivas rang. He sounded briskly efficient as he expressed his satisfaction with the way the play had been received. People he had come into contact with all seemed to like it. He said that Peter Black and James Thomas had both arrived ten minutes late for the press showing, and that all the good reviews were from people who had not seen it at the press showing – *The Times* and the *Evening News* and the *Evening Standard* (both of whom liked the play a great deal). Shivas was highly pleased, and to reaffirm his confidence in us, he fixed up a lunch date next week, to talk about our writing another play.

John Junkin[1] rang in the evening, just to thank us for making him fall off his chair.

Wednesday, August 22nd

To Sound Developments Studios in Gloucester Avenue. John and I are doing commercials for Corona lemonade (they must have been some of the first commercials to be made for Capital Radio, the new London commercial radio station, which doesn't start broadcasting for another few weeks). Quite a jolly hour – tried different voices – two very modest and unaggressive ad people.

We drank coffee and stood outside in the sun. John is clearly determined to remain uninvolved in any major Python TV project. He says he is writing with Connie, which is something he always wanted to do, and which gives him the afternoons free! In addition he is doing voice-overs

1 Comedy actor and writer. Linked closely with Marty Feldman.

like this one to make quick money. I presume, tho' he doesn't talk about it, that he must be working on his films for industry as well. He was keen on doing another record and on being involved in the next Python film.

When I mentioned rewrites of the film, John hesitated for a moment, then cryptically hinted that he would try and make himself available for this. As the film was written by all of us for all of us, I was a little concerned at his attitude, but it turns out that he is hoping to spend three months in Africa from January to March. This made me inwardly very angry, because he knew the film was around, and he must have realised that there would be more work to do on the script. But that is John all over, he can be incredibly self-centred, and, if he wasn't so charming with it, I would have told him so.

Later in the morning I took a bus down to Whitehall and visited the Inigo Jones exhibition at the Banqueting House. The Banqueting House is one of my favourite London buildings – stylish, elegant and civilised, totally unlike the heavy, neo-classical façades of the Home and Foreign Office across the road. I suppose the key is that Inigo Jones was a Sean Kenny[1] figure – a theatrical designer who spent more time designing fantasy buildings than real ones, and this is perhaps why the Banqueting House has a lightness of style, with ornamentation that looks as tho' it's meant to create exuberance. The Foreign Office and the Home Office were built and designed by Victorian engineers. They are solemn and full of a sense of their own importance.

Graham rang, still very worried about the future. It's all a bit of a bore, but I eventually said I would ring Bill Cotton, and find out whether the series was on or off. Bill, who was quite pleasant, couldn't see why we were all so scornful of a pilot. His diagnosis was that there was pride on both sides, and why didn't we stop being so stiff-necked? Bill said he would talk to Duncan and ring back tomorrow.

Thursday, August 23rd

A shopping trip with Helen. Based in the King's Road area. A very good lunch at the Casserole. Robert used to take me there when we were doing *Hang Down Your Head and Die*[2] in 1964. It was one of the first

---

1 Sean Kenny, one of the cool young stage designers of the 1960s, died in 1973, aged 41.
2 *Hang Down Your Head and Die*, an Oxford University theatre show about capital punishment. Terry J, Robert and I were in the cast. It came to the Comedy Theatre, London, in 1964, produced by Michael Codron.

London restaurants I went to – one of my first encounters with Sophistication. So it was appropriate that one of the first people I saw on entering was William Donaldson, Esq.,[1] blacklisted theatrical agent and the man who paid me my first ever wages after I left Oxford (£50 for working on *The Love Show*).[2]

Willie looked a little hunted, but was as urbane as ever. 'I was going to say how much I enjoyed your play, Palin' (which he pronounced Par-lin, as always) 'but I thought it would be a little unctuous.'

Helen and I hardly talked, just listened to the table next door where two aggressive ladies from the world of PR were meeting with an Australian publicity man.

'Is he camp?'

'Well … er … yes, yes, but not in the way …'

'He's incredibly religious.'

'Oh, I would so love to go to India.'

Just getting off to sleep when Graham rings (11.20) in his vehement shouting mood to tell me that Marty had had a slight nervous breakdown, and other things which don't interest me at all, especially when I'm standing naked in my office getting my balls cold. But they clearly do mean a lot to Graham, and I am hamstrung by an ever-conciliatory nature. It's at times like that that I wish I was forceful, opinionated and rude.

Friday, August 24th

Took Thomas by bus and train down to Greenwich. We walked around the Cutty Sark for half an hour. Interesting to see the tiny, short bunks which they slept in. The sailors can't all have been four foot long. Then up the river in leisurely style to Westminster. Journey of nearly three-quarters of an hour, tho' skirt-flapping hovercrafts do it in about ten minutes. A gentle and unusual way to see London. Sad to see the rows of wharfs. Free Trade Wharf, Metropolitan Wharf etc – all empty now, as so much of the loading and unloading is done at Tilbury and further down river.

Now it's all a rather eerie, dead world, until you reach Tower Bridge

1 He later wrote *The Henry Root Letters*, amongst other things.
2 *The Love Show* was a theatrical documentary about attitudes to sex through the ages. Brainchild of Willie D, who brought in Terry J to write it. Never produced.

and the first of the big new developments, which will eventually change the whole emphasis of this part of the river from trade to housing and leisure. Hotels, marinas, all these things are promised.

Wednesday, August 29th

To Ingmar Bergman's *Cries and Whispers*. A superb piece of film-making – not just technically flawless, but enriched by technique. The acting, as usual with Bergman, was strong, precise and utterly convincing. The placing of the camera, the movement of the camera, the lighting and the extraordinary colours of scarlet, black and white, created the mood and made a not unconventional script and situation into a film of total involvement and great beauty. Both Helen and I were stunned. As we stepped out into the brashness of the Tottenham Court Road, it seemed an unreal, trivial world. Very powerful. If I could make one film like that in my life I would be quite happy to retire.

Saturday, September 1st

Bill Oddie offered me one of his season tickets for Chelsea this afternoon. They were playing Sheffield United, and, although they were unlikely to be classy opponents, at least I could see my team in action.

It was a game which brought bowed heads, groans of despair and mute helplessness to the Chelsea supporters around me. Chelsea, with players of real flair like Hudson and Osgood, after a first 15-minute burst, could do nothing right. Sheffield United, a messy and undynamic side to start with, were made to look like quite classy.

Bill grumbled throughout, in his rather endearing way – the only thing he doesn't seem unhappy about is birdwatching. He's energetic and involved in his work, rather like Terry, he seems thoughtful and very aware. I always think the Goodies must be growing more sophisticated, but then he tells me that they're off to Weymouth to shoot a Goodies and the Beanstalk special.

Monday, September 10th

In the evening I spent nearly an hour on the phone with J Cleese.

We talked over everything – but I feel John wants to get completely out of all Python involvement. What a long way we've come since John's phone calls four and a half years ago when he was trying to set up Python. So much has changed in John. V. interesting. We talk about it all the time.

Tuesday, September 11th

Thomas's first day at school. He was dressed by 8.15 and quite clearly full of excitement. At 9.30 he walked off down the road with Helen, holding his envelope with 48p dinner money in it.

At lunch dropped in at the Monarch in Chalk Farm Road, as today was the last for Nick and Mum, the two who ran the Monarch and made it such a relaxed and friendly pub. A small literary coterie had gathered to pay their last respects. There was Graham, Barry Cryer, Bernard McKenna,[1] Tim Brooke-Taylor, an incredibly effusive John Junkin and myself. I've never been in a group which has taken over a pub as they did today. We sang 'Irish Eyes Are Smiling' at full blast, several times. Tim had a nice story. He said to John C at the radio show on Sunday, 'I hear you're dithering about Python.'

'Er … not really,' said John.

Thursday, September 13th

The news is of fresh bombings in London yesterday, of the overthrow of the first democratically elected communist government of South America in Chile, of Mr Heath's rosy optimism in the face of an enormous trade deficit.

In the afternoon Terry came here. He thought of 'The Monty Python Matching Tie and Handkerchief' as a title for the new LP. We played squash at 4.30. Just for name-dropping purposes, Al Alvarez[2] was there, extolling the beauties of his villa near Lucca in Italy. I felt like a holiday all over again.

In the evening I gave Graham, John and David and Nancy a lift down to Terry's, where we spent a jolly evening watching old Python shows. I must say, I can't share Terry's enthusiasm for re-viewing of the shows. They seem far too ephemeral to me. Interesting imperfections.

---

1 Comedy writer ('Doctor' series), actor, terrific fan of modern jazz and bullfighting.
2 Al Alvarez (b. 1929) is a poet, critic and poker player. He was a keen squash player too, and most of our conversations took place half-naked in the changing rooms.

Optimistic developments today – it's rumoured that the BBC will offer us seven Python shows next year.

Wednesday, September 19th

Lunchtime meeting at Methuen's to discuss promotion of the *Brand New Bok*. Interesting social differences between the publishing crowd and the B&C Charisma Record crowd. Publishing is white wine and lunches at Rules – Charisma is beer and shorts at the Nellie Dean and afterwards at the Penthouse Club. Today it was all white wine, sandwiches and smiles in the office of David Ross, a small, sharp-faced Scot, who is in charge of their publicity. Advance sales have already totalled 105,000 and the book isn't out until Nov. 1st. There were copies there for all of us. I was pleased with the way it looked – once again the artefact had exalted the material, and I was relieved that the vast amount of sexual content in the writing was arranged so that the book didn't appear totally one-track minded.

One of the great satisfactions of the book was the success of the lifelike dirty fingerprints printed on every dust-jacket. Our publisher Geoffrey Strachan told the story of an elderly lady bookseller from Newbury who refused to believe the fingerprints were put there deliberately. 'In that case I shall sell the books without their jackets,' she said and slammed the phone down so quickly that Geoffrey was unable to warn her that beneath each dust-cover was a mock soft-core magazine, featuring lots of barebottomed ladies beneath the title: 'Tits and Bums, A Weekly Look at Church Architecture'.

Saturday, September 22nd

Out early to buy breakfast for Pythons. A sunny morning, a crisp autumnal edge to the air in South End Green. It's funny how autumn seems to have started so punctually. 9.30, Eric arrives – the first time I've seen him since we parted company at Los Angeles Airport on June 28th.

John's here, all smiles – and in fact everyone except Terry G. Orange juice, hot croissants and coffee, then a big read through of material for the new album. A sketch which Graham and I collaborated on yesterday has John and Eric in stitches. But still nothing very exciting. One section of a 'Phone-In' type sketch, which Terry and I wrote, is about the only piece that has everyone rolling about.

Tensions flare at the end of the meeting when Terry, in passing, mentions that Mark Forstater will be fulfilling a kind of producer's function on the film – John reacts strongly, 'Who is this Mark Forstater?' etc, etc.[1] John has a way of making it sound like a headmaster being crossed by a junior pupil, rather than equal partners in a business disagreeing. Terry quite shaken and retires to the kitchen to avoid exploding.

Around 1.30 everyone leaves except Eric, who is in a cheery mood and anxious to find out about future of the group who met this morning. He and I drive down to Camden Town, and buy a kebab at Andy's, then come back here and talk. Eric in a much more obliging and co-operative frame of mind than he has been in the past. He says he is living on no money, and I believe that from anyone who comes from Earl's Court to Gospel Oak by bus at 9.30 in the morning.

Wednesday, September 26th

Terry and I went up to the Flask in Hampstead and had a good air-clearing talk about the future. We both feel now (c.f. flight to Calgary three months ago) that another series of Python for the BBC – with John writing a regulation three and a half minutes per show – is not worth doing, certainly at present, if at all. I was not encouraged enough by the material we wrote for the record to believe that Python has vast untapped resources. I think we may be straining to keep up our standards and, without John, the strain could be too great. On the other hand, Terry and I do have another direction to go in, with a play in commission and another on the stocks. We work fast and economically, and still pretty successfully together. Python it seems is being forced to continue, rather than continuing from the genuine enthusiasm and excitement of the six people who created it.

Monday, October 1st

Sunny and warm. Took Thomas to school. Now he doesn't even need me to come into the playground with him. We cross the road, past the lollipop man, and then Thomas asks me to stay on the corner and runs the

---

1 Mark Forstater, an American film producer living in London, originally introduced to us by Terry Gilliam.

last twenty yards up to the school gate on his own – with his blanket and his apple.

One of my earliest memories is of the school hall at Birkdale, with my mother saying goodbye and leaving me standing there with my shoe-bag, bitterly unhappy. I must have been Thomas's age, just five. 1948.

Drove up to André's to listen to the tapes of the LP. Some sounded very flat. Terry G, Terry J and myself discuss possibility of an extraneous sound effect running throughout the record (e.g. Indian attacks or a cleaning lady using carpet sweeper, etc) – which could be faded up to enliven some of the less exciting sketches.

Wednesday, October 3rd

A Parents' Meeting at Gospel Oak School. Went in with Christine,[1] met Jean Oddie on the door, she introduced me to Adrian Mitchell and wife.[2] They were all in a long line outside enjoying an illicit cigarette before the meeting began. Meeting attended by 150 or so parents. Headmaster says this is remarkable attendance. He has been asking around other schools and finds that most have less than ten parents along to meetings like this. But Gospel Oak does demonstrate what tremendous differences there can be between schools within the state system.

This school has a nucleus, or perhaps even a majority, of enlightened, liberal, *Guardian*-reading parents, who are concerned about their children and the way they're brought up, to the point of obsession. They not only read books and articles about education, they also write them. It must be one of the most literate, articulate parent groups in the country. The school functions better through this interest – more time can be spent teaching the kids than disciplining them, and everyone seems to benefit all round. But the disparity between Gospel Oak and other schools the Head Teacher mentioned is disturbing – for when people talk of state education as providing equal opportunity for all kids, they are in cloud cuckoo land. I'm just glad Thomas is at Gospel Oak where opportunities are more equal.

1 Christine, a neighbour and the wife of Richard Guedalla, my occasional squash partner.
2 Adrian is a poet, playwright and novelist. His wife Celia started the Ripping Yarns second-hand bookshop, a treasure trove on the Archway Road, north London.

We elect a Parent Manager for the ILEA Manager's board, and then are shown a 20-minute film about child molesters. Quite well-made, I would like Tom to see it. A discussion on the merits of the film afterwards. Lots of articulate women. There must have been upwards of 100 psychiatrists among them.

Monday, October 8th

On Saturday afternoon Thomas's fifth birthday party. Twelve kids altogether.

Sunday spent playing with Thomas's new toys and reading about the Arab-Israeli War, which had broken out that morning with all the inevitability of the sun rising. Took Thomas and Willy up onto Parliament Hill to try and fly his new kite. Heard someone describing to a group of friends some of the jokes from our second German show, which had gone out on BBC2 the night before. Couldn't fly the kite. Packed it up, and walked home ignominiously.

In the evening Hazel and Andrew,[1] Roger Last and Simon Albury round. We watched the start of a new *Frost Programme* series – it was about private education. It started such an animated discussion in the room that we soon ignored the telly and turned it off. Conversation at last killing the art of television.

First day of legal commercial radio. Very dull. Newsreader couldn't read news properly.

Tuesday, October 23rd

At 5.00 into a quite eventful Python meeting. Everybody is present, tho' Graham's about half an hour late. This is the second of our 'chase Gledhill' meetings. Gledhill looks more relaxed and cooler than when I saw him at his Barbican flat a week ago. Then I thought he would crack up within a day or two. Now he seems more confident. He takes control from the start, and offers for discussion a number of fairly unimportant points. Do we want to appear on the *Russell Harty Show*? Everyone says no, apart from Graham. We are into royalties on the second record! £19 each. And who wants to go to Denmark for a two-day publicity trip?

Having cleared these out of the way there is discussion about the

1 Hazel Pethig, Python costume designer; Andrew was her partner at the time.

[Michael] Codron[1] offer of six weeks, starting at Christmas, in the Comedy Theatre. Eric and John are very keen. Terry G less keen, myself very anti. For some reason I find myself in the rare position of being out on my own (tho' Terry J, I think, feels the same, but is keeping tactfully quiet to avoid accusations of a block vote). Briefly, I see it as six more weeks of a show which I find very dull, and here we are going to the West End, forsaking our Rainbow/pop following – which, John says, 'scares the shit out of me' – for the £2.50 circle and front stalls audience, with a show that seems to me full of old material – some of it done in the West End before. What has become of Python the innovator? Are we at the end of our creative careers, at the tender ages of 30–32?

Graham arrives, I think a little fortified, and from the stage show the talk goes on to accounts. Graham is the first to attack fiercely. He says we have asked for the accounts for long enough, and John has done nothing – but John G produces an envelope and, with a triumphant smile, reveals – six copies of the company accounts. A breathing space, everyone feels better, Graham looks discomfited. John G follows this up with optimistic details of payments to come within the month. Such is the success of this move, that he manages to get away with the extraordinary revelation that Tony Stratton-Smith does not have the money for the film. Tony's offer, we had been constantly assured, was the one cert. in a changing world. Then I notice the beautifully presented accounts are only for the year up to October 1971! They are two years behind.

At last the attack develops. Gilliam rants and raves and expresses his frustration very forcibly, banging the chair. Eric is very quiet. John C wades in, tho' not ruthlessly. I try to tell John G why we are dissatisfied – that he has for too long been giving us definite optimistic pronouncements which turn out to mean nothing. Graham gets angry again, and John G reacts – cleverly, in retrospect – with injured aggression. He fights back. 'Then why not get yourself another Python manager?' he says, sweeping his glasses off with a flourish. You could have heard a pin drop in Waterloo Place this uncommonly mild October afternoon. John G, unconfronted by a barrage of protests, moves quickly on, but into an area where, for the first time, he commits himself too far – 'Frankly, as far as I am concerned, Python may not be here next year, and I've got

1 Successful West End producer for, among others, Michael Frayn, Harold Pinter, Simon Gray and Alan Ayckbourn. Gave me my first and last West End break in the Oxford Experimental Theatre production of *Hang Down Your Head and Die*, in 1964 when I was 21.

other eggs in the basket which I have to develop as well …' Still no reaction. He retracts and returns to safer ground, 'In any case, I think this is the only area where I may not have produced the goods.' Here followed the most damning silence of all. We'll see what develops.

I left the meeting feeling pleased with myself for not giving in over the stage show, but with the unhappy feeling that somehow we must do something for the sake of the group. As Terry G says, there is a danger that we should become too purist, and in rejecting everything because it isn't *quite* right, we end up with nothing but principles.

Thursday, October 25th

To the office of Michael White in Duke St, St James's. A successful and fairly prestigious young impresario – *Sleuth*, *Oh Calcutta!* and many other well-known titles on the framed playbills around his office. Pleasant, disarming, unpretentious feel to the offices.

John Goldstone[1] was there and Mark [Forstater], and we started to chat after White had offered us a drink. He and Goldstone seemed to share many of our feelings about what the film should be like. White talked of the 'really good comedy film' which has yet to be made. What he meant was, I think, that our film should not depend on TV for anything more than a sales impetus, it should be a film of merit in itself. Such intelligent interest in our film we haven't encountered before. All in all it was an amicable meeting – but then John Cleese in Cambridge Circus was one of White's prized talents 12 years ago, and Terry has also been in a revue which White backed.

Tuesday, October 30th

Tonight a long phone call from John Cleese. He proposed asking John Goldstone to our Python meeting on Thursday to explain the deal and tell us where and if he thought Mark would fit in. In the end we agreed to ask Mark along first, just to give him a hearing – but even then I was made to feel I had wrung a major concession from John.

---

1 John Goldstone was a film producer brought in by Michael White. I'd first met him at Barry Took's in the days before Python.

Wednesday, October 31st

John Gledhill rang this evening. The clash comes nearer. I told him we were meeting Mark tomorrow. He was taken aback, but recovered. 'He's no negotiator, anyway,' says John. Finally he says, of course, whatever Mark's function, he, Gledhill, will do all the deals. I ring Mark later. Mark wants to do all the deals because he says that Gledhill is very bad at it – and was embarrassing at a meeting with Goldstone recently. So, the collision may come earlier than I thought – perhaps tomorrow. Co-operation, as an option, seems to be receding. It's all a long way from being out there filming and I find it depressing to have to get into this personal tangle. Especially as there is no villain of the piece, no easy target whom we can slander and malign. Both Gledhill and Mark are nice people.

Evening a little brightened by the extraordinary latest news from Washington. Two of the most vital tapes, which Nixon has finally agreed to hand over, do not exist. On a vital John Dean conversation – the machine wasn't working!! The Nixon/Gledhill situations do have a number of parallels. In either case there is a central figure who has far more work and far greater responsibilities than he can cope with, and yet is determined to fight, by some very devious means, rather than relinquish any of this work or any of these responsibilities.

Thursday, November 1st

Surprise, surprise. A cordial, relaxed, totally constructive meeting at John's. All of us present, and Mark as well. Mark explained the film deal, thoroughly and efficiently, and also gave us a run-down on how he would hope to be involved in the film, and how much of a cut he would like.

At 6.00, a party at Methuen's to launch the *Brand New Bok*. No famous names, instead representatives of the printers, blockmakers, binders, etc, who had ʰeen involved in actually making the book. During the party Gledhill had very good news about the NFFC,[1] who were only too keen to go ahead with Python, White, Goldstone. John had with him a sheet of Heads of Proposals, which towards the end of

1 National Film Finance Corporation, government-sponsored agency with money to invest in British films.

the party he was getting people to sign. I couldn't take much of it in at that time, but seeing other signatures, and presuming it was merely a contract for story development in order to get the £6,000 front money, I, too, signed.

Monday, November 5th

Another Python meeting chez Cleese. When I arrived there at 1.00 John Gledhill was sitting on the arm of a sofa looking wide-eyed and uncomfortable. Also there were Mark, John C, Eric and Graham. No one seemed to be talking to each other. It was like a morgue. Then Terry J and Gilliam arrived, and we walked up to Tethers for lunch and a chat.

Once in Tethers, Terry J asked Mark to outline his criticisms of the contract which John G had asked us to sign at the book launching party last Thursday night. As Mark ran through the clauses, it was increasingly clear that we were being asked to sign away our copyright on the film – which is tantamount to signing away every bargaining counter Python ever had. Mark will draft a new agreement, with his solicitor, and we will present it to Goldstone later in the week.

Wednesday, November 7th

Met Irene Handl[1] at Studio G today where we were both to do a voice-over. A lovely lady who immediately talks to you as tho' you've been friends for years. If Bill Tidy is the spirit of the Snug Bar personified, then Irene Handl personifies the warmest, most comfortable armchair by the fire.

Monday, November 12th

Esther Rantzen has rung to ask if I will do an interview about the *Brand New Monty Python Bok* on her prog, *Late Night Esther*. I agreed, and found myself leaving home at 11.00 p.m. to go down to the studio. Nervous, I'm afraid, despite many interviews, etc. I still find projecting myself less easy than it used to be – maybe I'm just more self-conscious now. Sit in an ante-room clutching my 'Bok'. The Producer,

1 British character actress and author of two bestselling novels, *The Sioux* and *The Gold-Tipped Pfizer*. I'd grown up with her wonderfully distinctive voice on the radio.

small, bearded, bespectacled, appears. He doesn't look like the kind to take risks, so (with some difficulty) I select a fairly inoffensive passage about what to do on meeting the Royal Family.

On the air about 11.45. A dull old prog with lots of stock BBC muzak to put everyone to sleep. Esther doing her bit very well, with great energy considering she had done a radio prog at 9.00 in the morning as well. We have a rather unimpressive chat. Esther reads the extract from the 'Bok' rather badly (afterwards I find this is mainly because the bearded, bespectacled little Producer keeps screaming through her earphones to tell her to stop before she reads anything compromising).

Tuesday, November 13th

Met with Jimmy Gilbert at BBC in the morning.[1] Jimmy very genial, welcoming – very much the feeling of a nostalgic reunion, for all of us, except Gilliam, had helped to keep Jimmy in material for two series of *Frost Reports*. He had only inherited Duncan Wood's office the week before, and it was still in the process of changeover. The walls were bare, a disembowelled record-playing unit lay against one wall, and Jimmy looked far from at home in it.

I'm not sure if he really grasped what we wanted – which was, in effect, a new series of Python, without John, and different in style from the others by being unified, organic half hours, and not just bric-a-brac, loosely slung together. He is going to see Alasdair Milne[2] next week and will put the programme suggestion to him. Quite a substantial part of our future is now in genial Jimmy's hands.

Thursday, November 15th, Southwold

I went up to Southwold on the train to see how the parents were. Found Mother looking fairly chirpy and less tired than when I saw her last. Daddy is slower and less capable each time I see him. However, he still responds to my visits in much the same way – it's obvious that he enjoys them and that he's pleased to see me. But his mind wanders and he is easily distracted, which is making Mother very irritable. I always remember him as an irritable man easily moved to the sharp reproof, happier with the sarcastic

1 He'd just been promoted to Head of Comedy.
2 Managing Director, Television.

put-down, embarrassed by the open compliment. Now, unable to marshal his thoughts and actions very clearly, the tables are turned and he is the victim of another's bottled-up bitterness and impatience.

While I was there we went for a long walk in the cool bracing sea air at Minsmere, with a big red sun sinking behind the bird sanctuary as we walked. He has had more hallucinations recently. He talks about 'When that man was in the kitchen ...' and so on. Recently he locked the door in the evening, in case 'those men' got in. He knows by their accents that they are quite cultured, and they are apparently friendly, but it is frightening that they should be so real to him.

Saturday, November 17th

Ate breakfast on the Ipswich–London train, and read some of Ivan Illich's book *Tools for Conviviality*. In the words of the old cliché, a most thought-provoking book, and very depressing – for he so clearly and radically tackles the problems of 'progress' and social organisation that I was left with a feeling of profound dissatisfaction and yet at the same time helplessness.

His diagnosis – that we have gone too far, too fast, that we are the slaves, not the masters of technology, in short that the contribution an individual can make to society has become so limited and so insignificant – is very clear, but where do we begin to change things? How can we eventually start renouncing what we have in order to go back to a less complicated society but one with greater respect and freedom for the individual? Suddenly I am aware that aggression and greed are not vices which suddenly spring up and are crushed in a war, they are institutionalised in the system we live in.

Back home to complete and utter disorientation. There are men on my roof erecting a corrugated iron temporary roof atop some scaffolding. This new structure towers over our house only marginally less conspicuously than the hand of God actually pointing at the front door. I suppose I felt like the soldier returning from leave in the war only to find his house had gone, except in this case it had grown.

Monday, November 19th

William is three today. The day when he was born now seems so remote. Those were the days when everyone seemed to be having kids. Now everyone seems to have mellowed and settled. After all the excitement we've all calmed down a little. There are not so many babies, there are more little people now.

I took Tom to school, then down to Terry's for another meeting on the film. Some good stuff from Eric – and some of the pieces I'd written at S'wold went down well, which was encouraging. At lunchtime Terry had a shouting match with John which blew up from nowhere, and the intensity of T's outburst took even John by surprise. It was all about T feeling oppressed by John's rather dismissive handling of any suggestion of Terry's. In fact John is trying to be fairly accommodating, but he does tend to dominate the group more than he used to.

In the afternoon he suddenly had to leave and Terry Gilliam had to leave in order to drive John and Graham in to the Centre. Eric went off to see a film, and Terry and I were left with the fag-end of the afternoon and the dirty coffee cups.

Saturday, November 24th

Drove up to Abbotsley at 50 mph as the government had requested. Most people appeared to be observing the unofficial limit.[1] It was rather like being in a slow-motion film.

Tuesday, November 27th

Worked at Terry's in the morning. A very poor session. We both wrote 75% tripe, and seemed unable to summon up excitement or concentration about the film. The most I could manage was a sketch about Galahad having smelly breath.[2] This was the level. But after a lunch of cold spring greens and beans, we decided to call it a day, and went through our mutual morale-boosting act about bad days and good days and the amount we'd done last week, etc, etc. Terry didn't cheer up much until I dragged him into London.

We parked in Leicester Square, then took in one hour of Pasolini's *Canterbury Tales* which Terry G had recommended. Superb recreation of mediaeval England – the kind of style and quality of shooting that we

1 The result of petrol shortages after the Arab-Israeli war.
2 Prompted by my reading out a sketch about a knight using coconuts instead of a horse, we agreed around this time to investigate the King Arthur story as a basis for the new film.

must get in our film, to stop it being just another *Carry On King Arthur.*

Wednesday, November 28th

Met at TG's later. He has been reading various fine-looking books on mediaeval warfare, and found that much of the absurd stuff that has already been written for the *Holy Grail* film has healthy precedents (e.g. taunting one's opponents and, as a last resort, firing dead animals at them during a siege – both quoted as mediaeval tactics by Montgomery). Then over to John's for a script meeting.

Mark F was there. The film deal is still not finalised. Apparently our Fairy Godmother, Michael White, is being quite businesslike with us – his cohort, John Goldstone, wants 12½% and a fee for a job whose function we cannot quite pin down, and Michael White wants his name prominently on the credits, plus various controls and final word on appointment of crew, production staff, editing, etc. So Mark has not signed yet. At the same time, Tony Stratton-Smith has come up with an offer of £45,000 from Pink Floyd, so there are alternative sources giving us a stronger hand against White.

Thursday, November 29th, Bradford

Woken by alarm at 7.00. Collected Graham from Belsize Park, and we got down to King's Cross by 7.30. Joined the rest of the Methuen party for a trip to a literary lunch in Bradford – where we were expected to give some sort of speech, along with Denis Norden, Gyles Brandreth and Leslie Thomas. Breakfast on the train. Jilly Cooper, of the low breasts and alluring smile, was also there.

At Leeds we were met by a coach which took us on to Bradford – a puzzling piece of planning this, as the train went on to Bradford anyway. We drove past a tripe works and into the grey centre of the city, spattered with a light covering of snow. Even since we were last in Bradford for Python filming three years ago, the demolishers have started to attack and replace some of the finest Victorian buildings. The stylish glass and steel curved roof of Victoria Station is going, a marvellous, grimy, black Baroque hall in the centre of the town is being knocked down, and so is an old, fine, stone-walled market. They are being replaced by the usual faceless crap. Four-lane highways and insurance company offices, with no style, or beauty, or sympathy. Our literary lunch was held in one of these new and faceless blocks – the Norfolk Gardens Hotel.

We disembarked from our coach (a funny thought, somehow – a coachload of writers) and were taken into a carpeted ante-room leading to the dining room, where we were given drinks whilst the guests assembled. Mostly ladies, but a number of younger ones who didn't look quite like the hangers and floggers we'd expected.

We started our communal Python speech with Graham doing 'Thank you very much and now some readings from the "Bok"' as a very prolonged mime. Then I got up and read some 'Biggles' in Swedish and then out of the book. Quite rude stuff, I suppose, but no one seemed to worry unduly. Terry read the 'Horace' poem and John finished up by reading a rather disappointingly unfunny piece from the 'Fairy Story'.

Then we sat outside in the ante-room and signed endless copies of the 'Bok'. Jilly Cooper was sitting next to us and, as she wasn't signing as many as we were, Terry passed one lady's Python book to Jilly to sign. The woman grabbed the book back, saying 'I don't want her to sign ... I don't agree with her.'

Too rushed to keep a daily diary for the next month, I rounded up the salient events after Christmas.

Friday, December 28th

It's a still, grey, anonymous afternoon.

At the beginning of December I had been working with Terry J down in Camberwell [on the script of what was to become *Monty Python and the Holy Grail*] and had a wearying week travelling as much as possible by public transport, owing to the 'oil crisis' – the 30% cut in Arab supplies to the West which has resulted in near-panic this week at the petrol stations. Many only open for two or three hours a day, and police have had to sort out traffic-jamming queues at many garages. London Transport, with a 30–35% undermanning problem, is no longer as efficient as it used to be, and it's quite common to wait 10 or 15 minutes for an Underground train, on a dusty, dirty platform (Victoria Line excluded). However, I arrived only about 15 minutes late at Tony Stratton-Smith's office. Tony, smiling and benignly jokey as ever, opened a bottle of sparkling wine and detailed his proposals for raising £75,000. £25,000 was to come from Led Zeppelin and £20,000 from Pink Floyd. Tony Stratton himself would make up the last £25,000, and small investors like Michael Wale[1] wanted to put in £2,000. Tony asked one or two routine questions, but altogether his offer seemed a lot more attractive than White–Goldstone. All he wanted for supplying finance was 5% – but Mark, a steady negotiator to the end, got him down to 4½%.

Both Led Zeppelin and Floyd were prepared to write or play theme music for us – an additional bonus, which could boost our chances in the States.

In the second week of December the weather improved – we had long sunny spells and clear skies. The oil panic passed its worst stage, but it was clear that the Arabs, by the simple expedient of controlling the exploitation of their own oil, had at one stroke brought the era of unquestioned expansion to an end. The very suddenness of the effects of the oil cutbacks is amazing. Only a month ago Anthony Barber [Chancellor of the Exchequer] and Heath were telling us that Britain was at last heading for sustained economic growth, and if we all pulled together, an era of prosperity and boom would be on us by the end of '74. On December 12th I was at Belsize Park Post Office collecting petrol rationing coupons – old-fashioned Suez coupons, still bearing the authority of the Minister of Power!

The government of expansion and progress has introduced an Emergency Powers Bill, which bans all display lighting, enveloping London in pre-Christmas gloom. Railways and coal, both despised and run down in the last fifteen years, are now being talked of, together with North Sea oil, as Britain's hope for the future.

The film script was completed on Friday 14th – but still without enough group work on the links and plot scenes. But some very funny writing from all sources – Graham and John in particular were back on form.

On Christmas Eve collected Grandfather and took him to an afternoon carol service at Westminster Abbey. On the way he talks some complete nonsense. Strange non sequiturs, as his mind gropes from subject to subject, forgetting where he began and what he was trying to say. But it clearly is a great source of pleasure to him to sit in the Abbey for an hour. I left him there and drove around Westminster.

1 Journalist and co-writer of *Now!*, the TV pop show produced by TWW in Bristol, on which I spent six months as a presenter in 1965–6.

London was quiet and empty. The lack of public display lighting (except for the Norwegian Christmas tree in Trafalgar Square, which has been given a dispensation for today and Christmas Day), the feeling of impending industrial crisis, only temporarily stemmed by Christmas, the various IRA bomb explosions in the last two weeks, all couldn't help but create a melancholy atmosphere.

I rather liked it actually. I drove into Soho, and drank a coffee and bought the last croissants before Christmas at a little French bakery, and it seemed that people were more ready to smile – were a little more aware of each other, rather than the headlong rush to buy, sell, display, offer, wrap, fill. But I could just be over-romanticising.

Python has been directly hit by the new emergency fuel-saving powers. TV has been ordered to close down at 10.30 and our repeats, scheduled at 11.25, are now presumed cancelled.

1973 is the year which saw the break-up of the Python group. I was unable to accept that it was happening – indeed there were possibly more combined projects in 1973 than in 1972. The *Brand New Bok*, the *First Farewell Tour* from April to June, the *Matching Tie and Handkerchief* LP, the film script. But all these projects were, to a certain extent, Python cashing in on a comfortably receptive market, rather than breaking new ground. The only project of '73 requiring new creative effort was the film – and although much good new material came up, there was nothing like the unified enthusiasm of the first two series. A freshness has gone, and 1974 will see just how we pick up the threads again.

1974

Friday, January 4th

The industrial trouble with the mines and railwaymen has now eclipsed the oil crisis. The government decided on an all-out confrontation with the miners and the railwaymen. Mr Heath's bluff with the three-day week has been called. Now both sides are sweating it out, while the country gets darker and colder.

Met with Graham and John Gledhill at lunchtime. Graham is going to assemble a trial script for Jimmy Gilbert at the BBC to satisfy their need to see what Python may be like without John. A humiliating experience to start the year with. John Gledhill has at last some money from the Canadian tour – £350 each, but JG has managed to get us assurances of £1,500 each for a week at the Theatre Royal, Drury Lane in February.

Left JG's in a hurry to get back home to collect Thomas and take him to the Mermaid to see *Treasure Island*. I wanted to have a pee, but decided to wait till I got home. I must have underestimated the urgency of the situation, because no sooner in the car than I wanted to go desperately. Every traffic light was agony. I drove my Mini like a stunt driver, passing whole traffic jams, overtaking on the inside, outside and middle in my agony to get back. But I made it, rushed in and hung over the lavatory in a cold sweat, eventually being forced to lie on the bathroom floor, still in my long black coat. Thomas was sympathetic. I told him I had a stomach ache and he patted my doubled-up shoulders with kindly consideration and said that he gets stomach aches as well.

We set off at 2.00 and arrived about five minutes late at the Mermaid. An action-packed version of *Treasure Island* played for all it was worth. Enormous explosions, violently realistic stage fights – in one of which young innocent Jim Hawkins knees an evil pirate in the balls – much to the kids' delight.

Tuesday, January 8th

Met Eric and Terry for lunch at Pontevecchio in Old Brompton Road. Eric ordered a bottle of champagne and orange juice and we sipped this whilst waiting for T to arrive. Outside a really angry day, with heavy rain lashed against the windows by gale-force winds. The grimness of the weather rather matched my mood.

Left with the feeling that our futures are distinctly unsettled. Lots of offers, but few which seem to have much sense of direction. We haven't done a new series for eighteen months, and the current repeats are the last time we will have a series of Python on BBC TV, unless Jimmy Gilbert can get the go-ahead for a non-Cleese show. The film is a development, and certainly the best thing we have around, but so far no final word on finance. To spread further despondency, all I needed was a call from J Cleese.

It came in the evening. There had been the suggestion, from his very own lips, when we put the film together in December, that we should spend a week on it in mid-January. Tonight, when I ask him about availability, he tells me that he can only make one and a half days' meetings during January and none at all until the first two weeks of February. This bombshell is dropped quite unapologetically. I swallowed for air and within a moment or two my reaction came – but it wasn't as I expected. It was a reaction of relief rather than anger, a sudden welcome burst of indifference about John and his future and his work. He may come in with us, he may not, but as from this evening I couldn't care less.

Friday, January 11th

Down to Joseph's for a haircut at 1.00. He has just bought his own electricity generator – for unlike food stores, restaurants, cinemas and TV stations, hairdressers are not exempt from the emergency electricity restrictions and can only work half-days. All the lights were switched off, but J was taking advantage of an anomaly in the law which allowed him power to dry the hair of people who had been washed in the morning shift.

Small hints of emergency life around. The *Radio* and *TV Times* are now very slim, with only a couple of pages devoted to indirect programme information. Cardboard boxes and, indeed, packaging of all kinds, are increasingly short. In shops now tins, etc, are packed on a slim cardboard base with polythene wrapped around them.

In the evening Helen and I went to see Marco Ferreri's *La Grande Bouffe* at the Curzon. A stylish, revolting, very funny and very sad film about four men[1] who decide to eat themselves to death. Some of those

1 Played by Marcello Mastroianni, Michel Piccoli, Philippe Noiret and Ugo Tognazzi.

heavy, over-rich meals at restaurants taken to ultimate, absurd lengths. Outrageous but never offensive, never heartless, never cheap. Sad to think that it can't even be given a national certificate and has to be restricted to London viewing.

Monday, January 14th, Southwold

Mother looked encouragingly well on her 70th birthday. She is living testimony to the fact that people can thrive on a difficult life. Her face may have aged, her stoop increased a degree in the thirty years I've known her, but her energy, mental and physical, is barely diminished. It's great that at 70 she seems as likely to survive the next twenty years as myself or Thomas or Willy. There is no hint of age withering her.

I took them out to the Crown Hotel in Framlingham for a celebration lunch. The hotel was warmed by a blazing log fire, the food was good and simple and the main hall of the hotel had as extensive and fine a selection of Tudor beams and timbers as I've seen. Very gemütlich. Afterwards we walked along the battlements of Framlingham Castle. It was a cloudy, but bright and mild day, and the expedition was quite a success.

I left Southwold to get back to London at about 5.00. Heard on the car radio that the latest and maybe the last attempts at conciliation between government and TUC had broken down, and there was to be a full rail strike tomorrow.

Tuesday, January 15th, London

Python meeting at T Gilliam's. We decide to do two weeks at Drury Lane, tho' I have a feeling in my bones that we would have done better to concentrate on one smash-hit week and leave people wanting more, rather than expose ourselves and our material to the spotlight for two weeks.

There was some fairly bitter debate over timing of the film and rewriting. In the end, after the personal differences had been aired, we got down to some fast and efficient business, dates were agreed and there was a very useful hour's discussion of the film. An idea I had for the gradual and increasing involvement of the present day in this otherwise historical film was adopted as a new and better way of ending it, so I felt that I had done a bit of useful work over the last hectic month.

We decide to call our Drury Lane show *Monty Python's First Farewell Tour (repeat)* and overprint it with the words 'NOT CANCELLED'.

Thursday, January 17th

At lunchtime, met Tony Smith, John Gledhill, Terry J, Terry G and André at Drury Lane to have a first look at the theatre in which we will be spending two weeks at the end of February. A gloomy first encounter. In the dark foyer, flanked by dusty, heavy pillars and classical columns, the eye is immediately drawn to a war memorial – to the fallen in two wars.

The approach to the auditorium, the passageways and halls, are furnished and decorated in the grand classical style. Doric columns, porticoes, domes, balustrades and statues of great actors in niches. On the walls flanking the wide and impressive staircases are huge oil paintings. It somehow feels as likely and as suitable a venue for Python as a power station. The size of the auditorium would a year ago have made me laugh and run out straightaway to return Tony's contract, but having rehearsed in the Rainbow, and played the Wilfred Pelletier Theatre in Montreal, both of which hold over 3,000 seats, the wide open spaces of the Theatre Royal (2,200 seats) no longer hold quite the same terror. Nevertheless, the sight of three balconies and innumerable lavishly decorated boxes, and a general air of London opulence and tradition, tightened my stomach a little.

Friday, January 18th

GC and I, at GC's suggestion, went to the BBC to talk to Jimmy, who is vacillating still over a BBC series. Frightfully welcoming and anxiously effusive. He took us to lunch and straightaway brought up the subject of the series. He wanted to check one or two details – just so he could make a clear suggestion to his superiors, he said. From then on he talked as if the series was in the bag.

It seemed as tho' some decision had been made in the Beeb to treat us nicely again, and Graham and I completed a tidy half-day's work on behalf of Python by collecting a list of seven studio recording dates from Jimmy G, which, being in November, would fit in well with our year's schedule.

Suddenly it seems that 1974 could be our busiest and most creative since '71.

JG told us that to date *The Brand New Monty Python Bok* has sold 161,000 copies, and the new record is selling faster than any of the previous ones. Less hopefully, he showed us a decidedly gloomy letter from BBC sales people in New York; despite all Nancy is doing, they do not seem any closer to a US TV sale of the series.

Indeed, one station in New York had, apparently, 'indicated a positive distaste for the program'. But the sales people, who are part of Time-Life Films, have evidently been affected by something like the same masochistic enthusiasm for the programme that Nancy has. At the end of the letter they did say that, for them, selling the programme was becoming rather like a crusade.

Sunday, January 20th

Took the kids for a short walk up to Lismore Circus with Sean[1] (Thomas's godfather) and Simon (Willy's godfather). They rode their bikes for about ten minutes, when a window in Bacton (the tall tower block in the Circus) opened and a vehement old lady shrieked at them to 'go away and play where you live'. I've always felt sorry for old ladies in high-rise blocks of flats, up till now.

Tuesday, January 22nd

The national situation looks depressing. No deal with the miners or with the railwaymen. The restrictions on lighting, TV and the Government's SOS (Switch Off Something) campaign, have now become quite accepted aspects of national life. The three-day week is still in operation.

Thursday, January 24th

I was still talking to the man from Coverite Asphalters on the roof at 11.30 when I remembered I should have been at the Theatre Royal, Drury Lane, for a press party to launch our two-week 'season' at the end of February.

Eventually reached Theatre Royal by cab at 11.55. Monty Python, not over-announced, on the outside. At least we have our name on paper, if not in lights. (When will anyone ever have their name in lights again?) Inside, a box-office without a queue. Up the wide staircase to the Circle

1 Sean Duncan, now a judge in Liverpool. We'd been at Shrewsbury and Oxford together.

bar, which is of the proportions of Adam's library at Kenwood House, with four huge Corinthian columns dwarfing a motley collection of about thirty press folk.

Nicholas de Jongh of *The Guardian*, looking tubby and rather windswept, moved amongst us with an uncertain, rather indulgent smile and a notebook, asking us for witty things to say. At least Eric had something reasonable (which appeared next morning in the paper). He was feeding his son Carey at the time, and replied 'It was all right for Oscar Wilde, being gay. He didn't have to feed babies, he had both arms free for being witty.' N de J: 'But Oscar Wilde had children.' EI: 'Trust *The Guardian* to know that.'

Sunday, January 27th, Abbotsley

Today, a pleasant lazy day. Thomas and I made a bonfire, we sawed some wood and played football and went off on an archaeological trip around Abbotsley. Thomas had uncovered pieces of old china in the garden, and pursued this new interest quite keenly during the day. A joint of beef and Yorkshire pud for lunch. I don't think I've ever not enjoyed a Sunday at Abbotsley – it's one of those unchanging, unexceptional, but unfailingly satisfying institutions, when the whole pace of life slows to a comfortable, convivial saunter.

Home at 8.30 to find the plasterer, Bill Berry, at work. Bill Berry is quite a character. He's a tiling man by trade, and is at present relaying a marble floor at London Airport's Terminal One. He's done Buckingham Palace and the National Gallery as well, he told me.

He's always coming out with strange non sequiturs. You'll be talking to him about terrazza tiles and he'll suddenly say 'Croup,' with an air of great finality. You look around bewildered. 'Croup,' he repeats, even more positively, and points at Thomas, 'That's what he's got.'

Friday, February 1st

Drive into town for a meeting with *New Musical Express*, who want us to review the week's new singles for them. Their offices in Long Acre are securely locked, but after much bell-ringing, tall, rangy features editor T Tyler leads me through deserted corridors up to an eyrie high in the building, where various members of *NME* staff sit in candlelit gloom.

They are all fairly cock-a-hoop over press reaction to their Marianne

Faithfull interview, published yesterday, in which Marianne said quite quotable little things about how she'd slept with three of the Stones to find out which one she liked best.

In the evening Helen and I and Mary and Edward went to see Truffaut's *Day for Night* – a film about filming, which left me with the kind of happy escapist pleasure that old Hollywood comedies used to. Afterwards we ate at Rugantino's, where I had brains for the first time. They tasted like roe, soft and spongy. It's funny, one can happily eat a cow's liver or a sheep's kidney, but eating brains seems to encroach on dangerous, mystical and spiritual areas. Like eating roast mind.

Friday, February 8th

An election has been announced for February 28th – depressing news, for the Tories will probably win and they don't deserve to. Heath has been stubborn to the extreme with the miners, who are now to start on a full strike. He was elected on a pledge to create 'one nation' – and he's now whipping up Tory middle-class anti-worker feeling as hard as he can. One of the points of the Tory manifesto is that the government should not pay security benefits to strikers' families. It is as near as Heath has yet gone to outlawing strikes, and is indicative of an across-the-board tightening of controls on personal freedom, which is becoming very sinister. We may not have a 1984 like George Orwell's, but if the Tories have their way we will be a very carefully controlled society indeed. All very sad, especially as Labour and the left are muddle-headed and ideologically dogmatic.

For me it's just head down and keep working. The three-day week does not so far seem to have damaged the country too much. The only real shortage is toilet rolls! But the foreign press make out we are almost in the state we were in in 1940, on the verge of collapse. Heath's propaganda seems to be every bit as effective as Hitler's was.

Monday, February 11th

Into London with Terry J to a meeting with Geoffrey Strachan at Methuen. He had read and liked our material for the *Fegg* book,[1]

---

1 This became *Bert Fegg's Nasty Book for Boys and Girls* (Methuen, 1974), later revised and improved as *Dr Fegg's Encyclopaedia of All World Knowledge* (Methuen, 1984).

would like to commission it – and started talking about size of the book, paper, art director, etc. Drank a Kronenbourg at the Printer's Devil to celebrate the birth of Bert Fegg.

Friday, February 15th

Today Geoffrey rang to say that a board meeting of Methuen had officially approved our book project and he was going to go ahead and commission it. Meanwhile we have had meetings with a cartoonist called Martin Honeysett, who has in the last year drawn some very funny, Python-like cartoons for *Punch* and *Private Eye*. Terry was especially keen for Honeysett to be involved, as he had met him at a *Punch* party and taken a great liking to him. However, it turned out that Martin Honeysett had never met Terry in his life and was pleased, but a little bewildered, to get such an enthusiastic phone call from him. Terry had, in fact, met quite a different cartoonist.

Sunday, March 3rd

We have now completed seven shows at Drury Lane – ending last week with a grand flourish of two shows on Friday and two shows on Saturday. I am chewing pastilles and gargling with honey and lemon three times a day as a result.

The gilded, glittering Drury Lane must have been amazed by the scruffiness of the audience on the first night. Kean and other great British actors of the past would have turned in their graves if they could have seen the front row full of Gumby-knotted handkerchiefs on the opening night on Tuesday.

The reviews have been surprisingly extensive – it takes a second-hand collection of old TV material for critics to start taking Python really seriously. Harold Hobson was greatly impressed and called us true Popular Theatre – and Milton Shulman, perhaps our first critical friend of the TV series, was equally enthusiastic. Despite the fact that it's an old show, already toured in the provinces and Canada, London critics have devoted enormous space to analysing it, even in the grudging *Observer* review (which described Terry and myself as 'virtually indistinguishable' and tending 'to screech a lot').

We're in the fortunate position of not having to rely on reviews to sell our seats. Despite the fact that Drury Lane holds 2,200 people, we are booked solid for two weeks, we have extended our run to four weeks, and at every performance there are apparently touts out the front selling tickets for £5–£10.

Whilst we were Gumbying at Drury Lane, there was an election – one of the most exciting for years, in which Heath failed to frighten the country into massive anti-union protest and came out with fewer seats than Labour. Heath has not yet resigned and, as I write, is busy haggling with the Liberals and others to try and form a coalition. Suddenly British politics have become alive, volatile and exciting.

Monday, March 4th

Into our second week at Drury Lane, and a lot of business to do during the day.

Meet with the Henshaws[1] and Nancy L and Ina [Lee Meibach].[2] There were some sandwiches and white wine. Under discussion was Nancy's official future with Python. At a recent meeting we decided to put Nancy in charge of our new music publishing company, Kay-Gee-Bee Music Ltd, and also to give her control of records and recordings and all future contracts.

Ina waxed lyrical about the future of Python in the States – and rather frightened everyone by talking of a 15% fee for Nancy's work. We still see our roots as an English TV comedy show, and I think we are all wary of the American monster, where everything can be so BIG and success can be so ENORMOUS and so on and so on.

The live show has been a must for pop personalities. Mick Jagger and Bowie have shared a box – rather off-putting, actually, they were right beside the stage – and Ringo has twice been to see it.

Tuesday, March 5th

The Tories finally gave up trying to form an anti-Labour coalition and Wilson is PM again. A great appointment is [Michael] Foot, as Minister of Employment.

1 Michael Henshaw had been my accountant since 1966. His wife Anne was helping sort out Python's affairs.
2 Nancy's lawyer in New York.

Friday, March 8th

In the throes of a heavy cold – woke up after a night of sneezing and running nose with an incipient sore throat. And two shows tonight. I really felt low, and very worried that my voice would not survive especially as we do not have another night off until next Tuesday. Rang for an appointment with Doc Freudenberg [my GP], but he was fully booked. I was advised to go along and wait. Rang Terry and cancelled our work plans for the day. Got to the new health centre in Kentish Town and waited there for two hours before seeing Freudenberg. He prescribed penicillin for the sore throat, but was really more interested in how the show was going!

Eventually got home and went to bed about 2.00. Very low ebb. Slept on and off and listened to the radio. Feeling a helpless lump. Down to the theatre at 7.00. Drank lots of hot lemon and was helped by a throat spray. Strangely enough, although it seemed unimaginable to perform two shows when I was lying sneezing in bed this afternoon, once at the theatre it became a job which had to be done. For four hours I almost forgot about the cold, and the combination of theatre lights, leaping about on stage and having to concentrate the mind on acting probably did me more good than a day off.

Friday, March 15th

An easier week, this third one. Tonight is our last show of the week, and we also had Tuesday off. Also the two-shows-an-evening dates are all behind us, so the pressure of the first two weeks has eased considerably. My cold is a lot better and the voice is bearing up well. We have at last completed the Python film script. Terry and I, as usual, did most of the rewriting. It took us a week and a half of very solid work, and today we completed that by deciding formally to cut the 'King Brian the Wild' sequence – the film is now shorter and has more shape.

This morning we met at Terry Gilliam's at 10.30 to read through our rewrites. The BBC had a sound team there. They are anxious to do an *Omnibus* programme on Python. None of us is particularly keen to be subjected to the sort of documentary which we're always sending up, so we were all a bit lukewarm towards the slightly pushy producer who was present at our meeting. A concentrated three-hour session on the film. Little argument, except over the 'Anthrax' sequence, and at 2.00 we had agreed on a final script. All of us, bar John, went to a Chinese restaurant in Belsize Park to celebrate.

Saturday, March 16th

Angela had said that two weeks ago, when she went up to Southwold, Grandfather had deteriorated rapidly.

He was seen last night by a psychiatrist from St Audry's Hospital in Woodbridge, and his condition was serious enough for him to be taken in first thing this morning. He didn't go by ambulance – he went in the car with my mother and a nurse, but it sounds as tho' his brain is now so affected by the Parkinson's that he may never see Croft Cottage again.

I rang my mother this evening. She sounds relieved that he's at last being properly looked after – but even so said she misses him.

Friday, March 22nd

Tonight there are some shouters in, and a drunken group up in a box. The week's audiences have been capacity, apart from Monday and Tuesday, and, rather than become jaded, the show has brightened up a bit, and we're enjoying it more than ever. John has added little embellishments to 'Silly Walks' in order to corpse me. Terry and Graham, as the two Pepperpots, have a continuing battle with each other centring around lipstick and names. Graham's lipstick tonight stretched round his mouth, up and over the top of his nose; Terry had a phone number written in lipstick across his chest. They also have fun with names – starting by calling each other comparatively simple medical names (Mrs Scrotum, Mrs Orgasm), they have now become wonderfully obscure – Mrs Vas Deferens – and tonight's masterpiece from Graham was Madame Émission Nocturnelle.

In the 'Custard Pie', when I have to shout 'Hey Fred!' at Terry G, I have varied the names a lot – but none with greater success than 'Hey Onan!'. That was a week ago, and I haven't had so many people laughing on stage since. Tonight, however, I could tell that John C was reacting to the noisy crowd as he usually does, by tensing up, and 'Pet Shop', normally a corpser's delight, was rushed through at quite a lick.

Saturday, March 23rd

Last night tonight.

This was the show that Tony Stratton-Smith was recording, and yet responses to such great favourites as 'Silly Walks' were the worst ever.

Graham was very fuddled through 'Four Yorkshiremen' and in the 'Election' sketch, John forgot a fairly important line and 'Parrot' ended prematurely after I replied 'Yes' instead of 'No' to John's query about the slug, 'Does it talk?' He chased me off the stage claiming afterwards he was too tired for ad-libs.

Champagne and scotch on stage for the company and friends. The stage hands were in sentimental mood and genuinely seemed to have enjoyed the four weeks. By an extraordinary coincidence there is a man who works front of house in the Theatre Royal called Mr Gumby. He was small and middle-aged and looked a bit like what I imagine Richard Goolden looks like as Mole in Toad of Toad Hall. He kept insisting that I call him Leslie, and I realised I was repeatedly calling him Mr Gumby, just to relish the name. Anyway, I got the cast to sign my Gumby handkerchief for him, which will surely confuse him even more.

Tuesday, March 26th, Southwold

Up to Southwold on the train. Met at 11.30 at Darsham by Mother. From Darsham we drove into Wickham Market and had lunch at the White Hart, then drove on to St Audry's Hospital near Bury St Edmunds.

Up anonymous institutional corridors smelling of disinfectant, until we reached the Kenton Ward on the second floor. It was a long room, bigger than I had expected, with high walls. About twenty beds neatly set out. In the first part of the ward the TV was on and about fifteen or sixteen men were slumped in chairs around it. I didn't notice them at first because they didn't react at all as we entered the ward, whilst the three or four nurses and two male attendants sitting at a table beyond a glass partition turned immediately. There was little sign of life from the inmates.

Then I saw my father sitting on the side of his bed. Here was the man who played football with me, who ran along the towpath at Shrewsbury when I rowed in Bumpers, who used to try and teach me to overcome my fear of the sea at Sheringham. He was now sitting on his bed with his head bent, muttering to himself, and picking with helpless hands at the cord of his pyjamas, which were open, exposing his white stomach. He didn't look up as I approached him – he didn't hear as I talked to him. When eventually one of the male nurses came across and, like dealing with a child, firmly but pleasantly did up his pyjamas and put on his dressing gown, he at last looked up. His eyes were heavy and dull, with a film of moisture across them and a rim of white along the lower lids.

George helped him round to a chair and we sat down to talk. 'George,' Daddy explained, was a man 'whose instructions it was best to ignore.' We later found out that 'George' was really called John and clearly he depended on him – but his old cantankerous nature had not wilted entirely. As we sat, he talked almost non-stop. He would start long descriptions about what had happened that morning and the story would wander into flashbacks of the past with an undetectable deftness that many film directors would envy. He was talking about how he had been on the lavatory that morning – and suddenly said that he finished on the loo at 10.47.

'10.47?' we asked.

'Yes, that was the train to Shrewsbury', he went on, 'which they used to drag me on to kicking and screaming.'

He had some strange Pythonesque fantasies in his mind too. Apparently the hospital was run by the Japanese, and last night one of the patients had sat on a 'beautiful' marmalade cat, which had had surgery this morning.

After talking for an hour or so, we were asked down to see Dr Hyde, who is dealing with the case. On the way to his office we passed a line of old padded cells – they looked like stables with strong wooden doors, with a spyhole in each. They were going to be knocked down any time now, said the doctor. He was a tall, thin, wispy-haired 40ish man – the kind of brainy boffin who moves rather nervously, and throws his body around in a slightly uncoordinated fashion. Eminently accessible, he seemed to want to answer all our questions. I guessed afterwards that he was trying to be optimistic. I don't think he holds out much hope for my dad. He has cerebral arterial sclerosis, like having a prolonged stroke, and, although he has made progress since entering St Audry's, the general pattern from now on will be downhill. But how much does my father still know about where he is, and who we are? How seriously should we take his desire to come home? It would be awful if his perception was much clearer than we thought, that it was just his body which had failed him. The doctor was noncommittal, but did say that we should try, in any way, to give him some hope, something to look forward to – perhaps in a week or so we could take him out in the grounds in a wheelchair. He didn't hold out much hope of him ever coming home again.

Wednesday, March 27th, Southwold

The paper full of the Budget details. The *Daily Telegraph* came out in its true colours, saying that this, Healey's first Budget, would hit the managerial classes. I weep for the managerial classes. May they be spared the worst – to sell their second car, to have to change the BMW for an Austin because it uses less petrol. To have to have one instead of two gin and tonics when they get home after a hard day's managing. Grudgingly the *Telegraph* mentions the rise in pensions for old people – the £500m subsidies for basic foodstuffs like bread and milk and meat and fish, the reductions in National Insurance contributions and in income tax for those earning less than £3,000 a year. It sounds to me to be a good, fair, just Budget – an attempt to solve inflation *and* help people who suffer most from it – i.e. those who can't afford one car let alone two, and those who can't afford one gin and tonic, let alone two. Mind you, it's easy to say this from the lofty heights of one who could afford an entire quart of gin every evening.

We got to the hospital at about 6.45. The inmates of the ward were queuing up for a milk drink. The nurses were talking amongst themselves – they obviously try not to mollycoddle the patients too much. My father was on his bed again, away from the others. He was agitated about something and tried straightaway to tell us about it – but his stammer was too bad. His lips couldn't form any sound, they just opened and shut like a fish. We got him up and he walked, with a stick and unaided, around to the chair where we had sat yesterday. Like yesterday, once he was in the chair, he talked a little more fluently. Today his mind was on some sort of meeting there had been in the ward – a man had spoken for three-quarters of an hour – it was some sort of Farmers' Union meeting.

He didn't seem to take a lot in, until we discussed our chat with the doctor yesterday. Then he appeared to know that Easter was in a fortnight, and when I said we would take him out for a drive then, or in a chair around the grounds, he looked up and said quite clearly and emphatically, 'But I want to come home.'

Saturday, April 6th

Ten past seven in the evening, writing the diary out in the garden. In the last week everyone's been coming out of doors again, in the wake of an early blast of summer. Hyacinths, providing a delicate whiff every now and then, are just about on the turn, but they've been out in profusion. Wallflowers of deep yellow and deep red and a single small white daffodil are out at the moment.

After lunch today Eric and Graham came round for what was to have been a Python (less John) meeting re the new TV series.

We have to decide whether or not the VTR dates which Jimmy provided in February are still practical. Things look bleak. The dates were fixed at a time when we were only doing two weeks at Drury Lane instead of four, and we have enormously underestimated the amount of time which the two Terrys will have to spend on the film. They will neither of them be able to concentrate for any length of time on a new TV series until late August – which is when Ian wants all the scripts in. So either Graham, Eric and I write all the scripts, which I think is out of the question, or we make an awkward compromise and start to film one month later, or we put the whole thing off until the spring. Eric, who has a small TV series of his own planned for January '75, is keen to leave the series till the spring of next year.

After our meeting in the sunshine, Eric stayed on here to bath (for his bathroom has been half-demolished by a gas explosion last week! Firemen and police rushed round. Eric said it was rather like a sketch – with firemen drinking cups of tea in the sitting room!) – Helen and I took our relentlessly energetic boys for a long overdue walk to the Heath. Thomas kept finding pieces of china in the huge piles of earth dug up where they're enlarging Parliament Hill running track. Promised to start a museum for him when we got home.

Sunday, April 7th

Rang Terry J. He was of the opinion that it would be impolitic to alienate the BBC by refusing at this stage to do a series it had taken so long to set up. As Terry's attitude was a rather key factor (for he will have to work incredibly hard if he is to contribute much to the series *and* edit the Python film) I was quite heartened. Certainly the most comfortable solution would be to do the series on the dates offered. Terry was more worried about finding a new direction and positive and strong ideas for the series, so I left him to have a think and call me back later. Eric was basically quite easy-going and adaptable, provided he could safeguard his three months in France during the summer.

Monday, April 8th

Tony Stratton-Smith rang in the evening – he had been listening to the *Python Live at Drury Lane* tapes and was enthusing as only Strat can. He wanted to release a live album in June, as the high point of a Python month – a big promotional push to boost sales of all our LPs. Tony reckons this Python month could shift another 80,000 or 90,000 of our records, which, as he says, would keep us off the breadline during the summer! A lucky coup is that *NME* [*New Musical Express*] want to issue 400,000 Python flimsies as a give-away with their paper in late May.

Thursday, April 11th, Southwold

Helen, Angela, Granny and I arrived at St Audry's Hospital at about 4.00. Grandfather was sitting watching TV. He got up when he saw us and seemed to recognise the four of us and be genuinely pleased to see us. He was in day clothes for the first time, and looked 100% better, tho' still a little stooped and his eyes were moist.

Fortunately, due to his much improved state, I was able to talk quite matter-of-factly to him about the problems of getting out. He wants to come back straightaway – he lives in a half real, half fantasy world of telegrams from Granny to say he's coming out, recommendations from the doctor – everything he says is geared to his release from this 'Institution' as he calls it. He has tried to get out twice, and has been discovered by nurses half-way down the stairs. One nurse was treated to a volley of abuse, so she says, when she tried to stop him.

But today he was negotiating tenaciously with me, like an ageing politician trying to strike one last bargain, pull off one last coup.

Easter Sunday, April 14th, Southwold

Drove over to St Audry's after breakfast to bring Grandfather home for the day. (It's nearly a month since he went into hospital.)

Took him some clothes and a box of chocolates for the nurses. They dressed him behind some screens, while I spoke to Mr Smy, the charge nurse. We were talking fairly softly, but when I mentioned to Mr Smy that Grandfather recently had been very confused there was a shout from behind the screen – '*I'm* not confused.'

Sun shining as we drove back to Southwold – the sharp cool wind at least had blown fogs and hazes away and the countryside looked fresh and green. A great day for colours, heavy dark shadows on the pine trees, and a vivid, almost luminous green on some of the fields.

We had a chicken casserole for lunch and he drank a glass of Alsace wine. Afterwards he pottered around the house, looking in all the rooms, trying to make helpful comments, but they generally came out as grumbles. His life is very much geared to his current obsessions, and these obsessions are nearly always anxieties and problems. There seems to be nothing that makes him happy any more. He told me he dislikes all the nurses, and clearly he is finding it very difficult to be told what to do by people who, as he says, 'have an inferiority complex' (a social inferi-. ority complex, he means), which they take out on him. He even said they mutter about Mummy after she's gone because 'she's well-dressed and well-spoken'.

At 6.30, Granny and I drove him back to the hospital.

Monday, April 15th, Southwold

After lunch, built a new piece of fence for Granny, whilst she and Helen sorted through an old chestful of Grandfather's papers. Letters from Shrewsbury home to his parents, old school reports, Indian Railway timetables, dance cards from Poona, with the names of his partners for the evening marked.[1] A fascinating collection – in the Shrewsbury and India days much evidence that he was quite a charac-ter, enjoyed life and was sociable: 'always looks as though he has done something wicked, but never has' – school report from Shrewsbury.

His later letters to the head of Edgar Allen's,[2] for instance, complaining that the £1,600 salary he was receiving in 1960 was hardly sufficient for a 'public school-educated, university graduate', have a much more hopeless air about them.

But Thomas and Willy love his old bundles of cheques and Thomas has taken to playing 'bank managers'.

---

1 In the 1920s, soon after qualifying as an engineer, my father spent five years in India on various public works projects including the Sukkur Barrage across the River Indus in what is now Pakistan. He was always very proud of that.
2 The Sheffield steelmaker for whom he spent many years as Export Manager.

Tuesday, April 16th, Southwold

Woke feeling refreshed, then suddenly my heart sank to my stomach as the full weight of work about to descend, the number of small problems, things to be done, things to avoid being done, hit me. A silly reaction, to be so bowled over. It will disappear when I am up and doing things, but the pleasure of being in Suffolk, remote from all phone calls, deals, confrontations, etc, etc, is just beginning to sink in, and I think the sudden realisation that the brief rest was over and that tonight I would be back among the pressures, hit me harder than usual this morning.

We had a superb little lunch, it being our eighth wedding anniversary, with a half-bottle of Bollinger, and delicious freshly caught cod with mushroom sauce.

Drove home via St Audry's where we stopped off to see Grandfather. As I took him back after a short walk to the car park, he mounted the stairs to the ward with a heavy sigh and murmured, 'Here we are ... the via dolorosa,' and he stood at the window, waving, trying to smile as Thomas (unconcerned of course by the fate of his grandfather) and I walked away in the late afternoon sun to our car. It could have been heart-rending, but I am trying to keep the whole thing in proportion, and not become too emotional about his condition. It may seem heartless, but it's the only way, I'm sure.

Monday, April 29th, Ballachulish, Scotland

Sitting down to write this overlooking the broad sweep of Loch Leven. Below me cars are queuing for the Ballachulish ferry, across the water the sun shines through a break in the cloud, pinpointing a small whitewashed group of cottages and emphasising the green of the fields running down to the water's edge. Beyond them the mountains rise into the mist. A tranquil sort of morning. We have been in Scotland a little over twenty-four hours. On Saturday night I said goodbye to Helen and the boys in the usual unsatisfactory way – a rushed meal together – a 'Quick, can you sew on this?' and 'Have you seen my that?' sort of leave-taking. I won't see them again until May 25th. Still, Scotland has been very welcoming, and I feel relaxed and comfortable and invigorated here, after the busy two weeks since we left Southwold.

During that time we rehearsed the film [*Monty Python and the Holy Grail*], inevitably rewrote some of the scenes as we did so. But it came to life during rehearsal – we began to laugh at each other's performances again, and from being rather an albatross of worry round our necks (finance, script, etc, etc) the film became enjoyable and fun.

I'm trying to think how I can begin to chronicle all that happens on this film. Will try a kind of shorthand and see if it works.

Tuesday, April 30th, Ballachulish

First day of filming. Woken at 6.45. Sunshine streaming through the curtains. Into chainmail and red-cross tabard. A difficult day today – the Bridge of Death scene where Eric and I die and Lancelot is arrested by the police. Dangerous too – from what I hear. Difficult decision over Galahad's blond wig. Instead of noble and youthful, I look like I should be serving in a supermarket. End of Galahad as a blond.

Such is the economy on this film that not only do the actors have a mini-bus rather than cars to go to the location, but they also have to drive it.

John (Lancelot) and I (Galahad) driving up through Glencoe in a Budget Rent-a-Van in full chainmail.

Scrambled up to the Gorge of Eternal Peril – this took about 15 minutes of hard climbing.

Camera broke midway through first shot.

The day is hastily rearranged and, from having been busy, but organised, it was now busy and disorganised. The sun disappeared. John Horton's smoke bombs and flames worked superbly. Graham as King Arthur got vertigo and couldn't go across the bridge. He spent the day rather unhappily cold and shaking. Eric and I and John sat around listening to stories from the Mountain Rescue boys about how many people perish on these spectacular mountains each year. Five or six deaths usually.

Terry J comes up to me in the afternoon and says he's 'a bit worried about Terry G's priorities in choice of shots'[1] – we run two and a quarter hours overtime, until nearly 8.00. Everyone in the young unit seems happy enough.

Enjoyed the sight of Hamish MacInnes, head of Mountain Rescue in Glencoe, flinging rubber corpses of knights into the gorge. More terrifying ledges to climb round on tomorrow. I hope Gra's OK.

Back at hotel at 8.30 for large Bell's and a bath. Couldn't really face

1 *Monty Python and the Holy Grail* was directed by both Terry Jones and Terry Gilliam.

the four-course hotel meal, so sat in the bar with Eric, drinking scotch and watching card tricks.

But Sunday night was the *most* eventful, when I giggled a great deal over the menu after some very high-quality grass of Eric's, and Graham ended up being seduced by an Aberdeen gentleman on a fishing holiday. Graham resisted evidently, but was well pissed and woke me about 1.00 banging on my door saying he was Ethel de Keyser.[1]

On Monday night he woke me *again* just after I'd dropped off, when I heard him in his room saying 'Betty Marsden!' rather loudly in a variety of silly ways.

Tuesday night, however, he was kind enough to be content with putting a note under my door with 'Best wishes, Betty Marsden'[2] written on it.

Wednesday, May 1st, Ballachulish

At lunchtime still no word that we were needed. Eric and I sit in the quiet, well-kept garden beside the hotel, thinking we're rather like officers at the Craiglockhart Hospital,[3] sitting waiting to recover before being sent back to the Front. Eric says he's Sassoon, and I'm Wilfred Owen – who had 'a bit of a stocky body'.

Lunch with Mark, Eric and John, who is trying to read a book of philosophy and is constantly rather cross – but quite fun. He continually goes on about the 'bovine incompetence' of the waitresses – who are certainly no Einsteins, but good-hearted Scottish mums.

After lunch the unreality continues. Eric and I go round to Ballachulish House to play croquet in the sunshine. Ridiculously idyllic. The Lady of the Manor, a tweedy, rather sharp Englishwoman, appears with an enormously impressive, kilted, very red-faced Scottish laird, who leaves in a large old Lagonda. All too Dr Finlay for words. Eric idly fantasises we may have caught them 'in flagrante'.

After the croquet and a few words with the Lady of Ballachulish, more sitting in the disabled officers' garden. At about 3.30 the call comes. Sir Robin and Sir Lancelot drive their Budget Rent-a-Van up to

1 Ethel de Keyser (1926–2004), South African anti-apartheid campaigner.
2 Betty Marsden (1919–98). Actress on *Round the Horne* and in *Carry On* films. Why Graham chose her name I don't know. She had once expressed a wish to die with a glass of gin in her hand, so maybe that was it.
3 A Victorian pile in Edinburgh where officers were sent for treatment of shell-shock during the First World War.

Glencoe, complete with a message from the producer to say we must stop by 6.00. At about 6.00 we are hanging onto the ledge above the gorge waiting for a long shot of the Bridge of Death. Terry J directs Terry G to get some more dirt on his legs (as the Soothsayer).

Then suddenly John Horton's effects go off, a few flares, firecrackers, smoke bombs, then, surprising everybody, huge mortar blasts which send scorching barrels of fire high into the air – the grass and trees are burning. No one (except John H) knows where the next blast will come from. Gerry Harrison shouts, TJ shouts. John's stand-in races across the bridge with suicidal courage, only to be told to get back again as the camera can't see anything through the smoke.

I think we may have a few more days of difficulty before the film gets together. TG was very unhappy as he sat on the top of the mountain. And Galahad drove the van back.

Rather sad notices around Ballachulish today asking for volunteers to join an army for a scene tomorrow. They're only getting £2 and I think even the Scots will baulk at that.

Cocktail bar – 8.45. Neil [Innes] arrives from London via train, bus and foot. Great rejoicing. Within an hour he's on the piano, spurred on by Eric, and a bearded left-handed Scots accordion player and a guitarist materialise from somewhere and the Ballachulish Hotel resounds with rather raucous sing-along.

Thursday, May 2nd, Ballachulish

Woken by whine of my tape recorder about 1.00. Woken again by Neil plus guitar coming in to sleep in the spare bed in my room about 2.00. Finally woken by loud sneeze at 10.00.

Eric and I have another lazy day at the rest home for officers, while Graham and Terry are finding the Castle Aaargh! We go to the location about 2.00, and they still haven't had a lunch break.

Graham is getting shit poured all over him. He's taking a great deal of punishment in these first few days of filming.

Wonderful chaos round about 4.00. Out on the island the motor boat which drove the wondrous ship in which Arthur and Bedevere reached the Castle Aaargh! broke down and Terry J was left drifting across Loch Leven with the radio communication set. Terry G, in great Errol Flynn style, leapt into another dinghy, pushed it out with a flourish, but failed to make the engine work and was left also drifting about twenty yards out to sea. The whole scene, enacted in front of a motley army of extras, was great entertainment value – and cheered everyone up enormously.

Finally, frenetically, the army shot was completed, and, going into heavy overtime yet again, the day finished about 6.20. Or rather didn't finish, because we then had to drive to Killin on Loch Tay, our next location. Graham and I in the Mini, driving over the most forbidding, lonely landscape in Britain as night fell – rain, mountains on either side, huge black clouds hanging on their summits.

Friday, May 3rd, Killin

At last a chance to see the scenery we drove through last night. We are filming in a cave three or four miles beyond Ardeonaig, and the road winds rather prettily along the side of Loch Tay. From where we are filming – a rather tough ten-minute climb from the road – you can look down the length of Loch Tay and across the other side to the mountains, tipped by Ben Lawers (nearly 4,000 feet). A spectacular location, but soon filled with the flotsam and jetsam of filming – boxes of equipment, tea urns, Land Rovers churning up and down the hill with lights, and wood for the construction team.

A slow day's filming, it seems. Rather a lot of worried faces when we run into overtime again. Hazel especially has hardly had a moment to organise herself and her costumes, and looks completely shattered.

Julian [Doyle] took me aside after filming today as we walked down the hillside and said he was worried that the way things were being shot this week was putting a big strain on the budget (almost the entire £1,000 allowed for overtime was spent in this first week) and there would have to be some compromises by the Terrys somewhere along the line.

So we had a meeting at the Killin Hotel tonight in among the costumes, and the production/direction points of view were put forward. I think Terry G accepted that they would have to simplify the shooting script and perhaps compromise on some of the locations. Terry J was less compromising, but in the end everyone decided that we should postpone final decisions on Hadrian's Wall, etc, for a week, to see if we could catch up. It was also decided not to move to Doune until Monday.[1]

1 Hadrian's Wall was dropped later as being too far away. The Scottish National Trust had vetoed most of our castle locations, deeming the script 'not consistent with the dignity of the fabric of the buildings'. Doune was a privately owned castle.

Saturday, May 4th, Killin

A good day's filming at last. Even John and Eric aren't grumbling, even tho' we go into overtime again. John Horton's rabbit effects are superb. A really vicious white rabbit, which bites Sir Bors' head off. Much of the ground lost over the week is made up. We listen to the Cup Final in between fighting the rabbit – Liverpool beat Newcastle 3–0.

More good rushes in the evening. The boat that takes them across to the Castle Aaargh! looks really magical. It will give the film just the right kind of atmosphere and build-up to make the non-ending work. Terry Bedford's[1] effects, especially his fondness for diffusing the light, work superbly.

I bought drinks for everyone at dinner as it's my birthday tomorrow, then had a couple of smokes with Neil, went for a walk and shouted abuse at a Celtic supporter on a bicycle. Utterly collapsed about 11.00.

Sunday, May 5th, Killin

Thirty-one. A birthday on the road again. Slept until 10 or 11 – at half past eleven a knock on the door. It was Neil, complete with a birthday present – three ducks, a yo-yo and a junior doctor's kit! Downstairs about 12.00. The foyer of the hotel was littered with Python gear. Hazel was working on costumes and the other half of the hotel foyer was full of Make-up's wig boxes. Neil and I decided that it would be best to avoid the Killin Hotel for the day. Drove up into the Ben Lawers National Park. We walked for nearly three hours in total solitude, and managed at last to reach a patch of snow – about 2,600 feet up.

We drove back around Loch Tay – passing on our way the town of Dull – which was exactly as its name suggests. We couldn't even find a shop to buy a postcard with 'Greetings from Dull' – so we stopped for tea at Weem. Tea and scones served by a Scottish lady with a soft, high-pitched voice, in a reverential atmosphere rather more like a funeral parlour than a hotel. Bought Neil a meal at Ardeonaig – where we found Eric, who had been spending the weekend there, away from the rest of the unit. He sent me a silly birthday message on a meringue, which was delivered to the table, and also bought me a bottle of champagne. I was nearly tempted to stay at the Hotel Anthrax, so lulled was I by the meal

1 Director of Photography.

and the wine and the attentions of one of the ladies – but fortunately my 31st birthday passed celibately and Neil and I drove home about 11.30.

Monday, May 6th, Killin

Eric and I dressed as monks (gear that really rather suits us) toiling up to the cave at 8.30. Very clear sky and the sun is already hot. Quite a long piece for me today as the monk who reads the instructions about the Holy Hand Grenade. As the sun is so bright, all the camera angles have to be changed, and the actors, so much fodder in the process of film-making, find themselves standing on a steep slope, precariously perched barefoot on rather slippery mud. All the knights are in the stream down below. Terry J gives me a good piece of direction which makes my perf. more silly and lively. But it is a hard morning's work for everybody. For the first time we see the pages – they are weighed down with very heavy packs and their first movements have to be uphill over rather difficult terrain. Everyone very near the end of their tether – Graham shaking and quivering with suppressed neurotic rage – when lunch break is called at 2.30.

I'm not needed in the afternoon, so go back to the hotel and decide to go off early to Doune. Rang home first, and spoke to Tom, who burst into tears, and all I could hear was his sad pleas that he wanted his Daddy back home. Quite disconcerting and left me feeling very depressed. Then the car wouldn't start. But John C (to whom I had promised a lift) helped me to push it up the main street of Killin to a garage, where a Scottish Jimmy Cagney promised me he would 'charge it for a wee while', as the battery was flat.

JC and I sat on the rocks on the Falls of Killin – those same falls of which Helen had sent me a postcard in 1962, which put us back in touch after a year and turned our little Southwold romance into an Oxford romance as well. Oh, how soppy.

John and I talked about life. I sympathise quite a lot with his urge to be free of the obligations and responsibilities of the Python group – but I feel that John is still tense and unrelaxed with people, which compounds his problems. He has more defences than Fort Knox.

But he was very enjoyable company and, after we collected the car from Mr Cagney, we drove into Doune, stopping at Callander to have a leisurely meal at a sixteenth-century hunting lodge turned into a hotel – full of antiques, old prints, a rather delicate atmosphere. John and I talked about psychoanalysis – John is going to a new man, who he reckons has changed him greatly – told John to try harder to do things which he enjoyed, and not to accept work he didn't enjoy. Hence JC went to Kenya for two months and says he has never since felt the psychosomatic symptoms which he always used to get while working.

And so to Doune at 10.00. This is to be our home for the next two weeks.

Tuesday, May 7th

Up at 7.15, after a rather uncomfortable night. The walls of the room are paper-thin and, tho' I have a spacious double bed, I was continually woken by strange sounds from the pipes and the plumbing – including an irregular dripping noise – rather like a Chinese water torture, which went on all night, and which I could never track down. John and Eric equally disaffected with the Woodside and later today they move out to a hotel in Dunblane which apparently has sauna baths and a swimming pool. But the Woodside has a rather friendly, welcoming atmosphere downstairs which I would be sad to miss. So I decide to stay.

Today we shoot the Camelot musical sequence. A long and busy day for 50 seconds' worth of film. Dancers dressed as knights wrecking Camelot. In the middle of the day Mark has arranged a press call, but as the two Terrys are busy directing, the brunt falls on Eric, Neil, John and myself. The usual questions: who is Monty Python? How did you all get together? Obvious questions maybe, but they drive us potty. Lots of photos – can you all put your heads round the shields? Etc. Eric and Neil try to escape, Colditz style, by walking out of the gate when Mark isn't looking, talking terribly urgently to each other – they made it back to the hotel before being recaptured.

We pass the afternoon with a game of football. Despite the chainmail, some quite good moves. Bill Hagerty of the *Daily Mirror* stays around with a photographer – he is apparently doing a big centre page spread on us. He has a better technique than most journalists. The indirect approach. He just stays around, chats and gets to know us – and only occasionally jots in his notebook. I told him the story of Graham shouting 'Betty Marsden' – which will probably end up on ten million kitchen tables!

Wednesday, May 8th

The first of two and a half days on the Castle Anthrax scene.

Spent the morning being drenched by the Perth and Kinross Fire Brigade. Next time I shall think twice about writing a scene in a raging storm. I start behind camera, and before 'Action!' I am solemnly wetted down by Tommy Raeburn of Props, with a little greenhouse watering can. I then rush up through rain provided by a fireman from behind a bush, to a castle made of cardboard.

Thursday, May 9th

Amazing how much eating one does on filming. If you get up at 7.15 it is nice to have a cup of coffee at least before going over to the Doune Rural Hall (headquarters of the WI) and, with a full breakfast menu available, I am quite often tempted to a kipper or even a piece of toast. Then, at 10.30 on set, there is more coffee and soft, delicious bap rolls with sausages and scrambled egg. Ron Hellard supplies a gargantuan lunch with much pastry and potato, which is also hard to resist. At around 4.00 tea/coffee and cakes (v. good home-made currant buns) and, after a drink back at the hall at the end of the day, and a look at rushes (shown, extraordinarily enough, in the Silver Chalice Bar!), there is a four-course set meal at the hotel. Consumption is about double what one eats at home.

This was the second day on Castle Anthrax. Doune Castle's severe granite halls are now filled with about twenty girls in diaphanous white gowns, shivering against the cold. John C, Eric and I are sitting with Neil on an old bench in the Great Hall, singing old Adam Faith/Cliff Richard hits, in a desperate attempt to combat boredom. The bathing scene takes two hours to set up – the girls giggle a lot, and generally it's about as sexy as a British Legion parade.

We shoot on late – until 7.30 or so – utterly shattered – but Carol C stood up to it remarkably well and was v. funny. Like Neil, she is an honorary Python, and has very little trouble in clicking into our way of doing things.

Friday, May 10th

9.30: In Anthrax Castle again, with Tommy poised with watering can.

'Michael, can you fall about six inches to your left?' after I have crashed onto the stone floor for three rehearsals already.

11.00: Still waiting for the shot. Terry J, who tends to become very Ian MacN-like sometimes – 'Come on, now *quick*, we must get this shot in before 11.25, we really *must*!' Terry G is working away more quietly with the camera crew, checking the shot, putting a candle in foreground here and there. Gerry Harrison, the first assistant director, for all his some-times alienating head prefect manner, is always very accessible and can get a cup of coffee for shivering actors.

Out in the main courtyard of the castle, a BBC crew from *Film Night* are interviewing Graham C. Quite glad to avoid that sort of thing, really.

'Alright, the generator's been refilled with petrol!'

'Let's go.'

'Come on, we must get this shot in by 12.25!'

We finish Anthrax with a last v. good take, especially from Carol, and that sequence is now finished, and we go out to the front of the castle.

The BBC doggedly film the filming. Cardboard battlements have to be added on to the castle before John does his taunting. 'John! Don't lean too heavily on the battlements, you can see them bending.'

At about 4.30 there are a few distant claps of thunder, the sky turns a fine deep grey – which Terry Bedford is very pleased about – and we get one shot in with this background before an enormous cloudburst empties the field in front of the castle.

The cry of 'It's a wrap!' goes up, and Tommy Props leaps out into the still pouring rain with a look of great exultation and starts to clear up. He particularly has had a fiercely busy week, and no one wants to work late tonight.

Back to the Women's Institute to change, then to the hotel for a drink and rushes. The table I'm sitting on in the Silver Chalice Bar splits right across, and the manager, Mr Ross, is left rather pathetically holding this broken half table when some non-Python guests arrive to check in.

Saturday, May 11th

A rather grey day, with intermittent rain. At the gates of Doune Castle Philip Jenkinson is standing with the *Film Night* crew.

I haven't been chatting with him for long before we have been imper-ceptibly shuffled into an interviewing position beside a car, and I find myself being filmed at about 11.00 in the morning, the dullness of my replies matching the dullness of the day! After that they move over to a well in the courtyard and interview Graham, who at least managed to get some silly lines in – he deliberately mishears Phil Jenkinson's rather facetious remark about an 'insanity' clause being built into the contract – 'There is an insanitary clause, yes.' Funnily enough, Phil Jenkinson is besotted by Eric Idle's take-offs of him and constantly refers to them.

John is doing the Taunter on some artificial battlements at the back of the castle. He's getting very irritated by TG's direction of his acting. TG tends to communicate by instinct, gesture and feeling, whereas John prefers precise verbal instructions. So TJ has to take over and soothe John down.

Then the shot where live ducks and chickens, as well as dead rabbits, badgers, etc, are flying over the battlements. Small boys are recruited to help catch the chickens as they're flung over. 'Those spotted roosters are fast,' warns Tommy.

A rather jolly day, with much corpsing from John, Eric and myself when Brian McNulty, third assistant director, in rich Glaswegian, reads in John's Taunter's lines for us to react to. How can you react without laughing to a broad Glaswegian saying 'Of course I'm French, why do you think I'm using this outrageous accent?'

Monday, May 13th

The day of the Mud-Eater. Clad in rags, crawling through filthy mud repeatedly and doggedly, in a scene which makes the flagellation scene from *Seventh Seal* look like *Breakfast at Tiffany's*. Extras all supposed to have plague – boils and pustules everywhere. People really do look wretched and, after two hours wallowing in the mud, because the plague village is such a convincing set, reality becomes fantasy and fantasy becomes reality. The camera crew, the scrubbed and well-dressed line of faces looking at us and occasionally turning a big black machine towards us, seems quite unreal, a horrible dream.

At the end of the day I have to eat mud. John Horton prepares a mixture of currants, chocolate instant whip, pieces of fruit cake and cocoa, and pours it out onto a patch of soil from which it is indistinguishable.

That night at dinner the menu began with 'Various effluents' – and I asked Mr Ross rather gruffly what this meant, then saw the rest of the menu – 'Mud cocktail', 'Fillet of sole à la slime', etc, etc. A complete mud menu.

Later in the meal I was presented with a bowl of mud which I dutifully tasted. It turned out to be solid cooking fat coated with chocolate. So the Mud-Eater seems to have passed into the folklore of the film.

Thursday, May 16th

The last three days have been like the start of shooting in Ballachulish. Phoney filming. Sitting waiting to be called. Tranquil mornings at the Woodside. There has been work to do, but none of it very taxing. Twice Graham and I have worked our lines through for the opening scene, and twice it has been postponed. From the end of this week onwards I am going to be in practically every scene, and the only advantage of these lazy days has been a chance to enjoy the sunshine and to keep the journal up to date.

News coverage has been extensive – the *Mirror* had a front page picture of John, and a big double-page centre-spread with a large picture of us all in knights' gear, posed as a football team. A very good 'entertainment' piece by Bill Hagerty. The *Express* had a large, much less interesting, half-page, which made the early editions until they found the *Mirror* had scooped them and was later withdrawn. *Newsweek* had a whole-page feature on Python (tho' mainly John – 'an ex-*Newsweek* staffer'). The *Times* Diary had a short unpleasant piece of gossip – about John hating filming.

Weston Taylor of the *News of the World*, a rather dog-eared, but quite amiable sort of chap, has been hanging around. Eric was very rude to him, mistaking, I think, one individual for a newspaper's policy. But then Eric was also very rude to Andrew Tyler of *NME* who arrived in Killin on May 4th, and tried to interview Eric on the mountainside, with very little success. Perhaps 'very rude' isn't quite fair, but Eric gave him a rather sharp little homily. 'Most of my friends who I know and like have done interviews, and I don't recognise them in the interviews,' he said.

Anyway it turns out that Tyler's one-week sojourn with us turned out to be a largely accurate, amusing, exhaustive and informative account of Python filming. (Copies of the 'Python' issue of *NME* with Mr Gumby plastered on the front and the flimsy record of extracts from *Live at Drury Lane* and the big interview arrived on the set when I was doing the Prince's Room scene. Greeted with much interest by the make-up girls – whom he described as 'sour-faced'. Much mirth from everyone.)

Saturday, May 18th

End of third week's filming. I've had the second longest single speech in the film to do today. A large crowd scene with lots of mutilated extras. Must have done the speech at least fifteen times.

There's a party tonight organised by the camera crew – so I've had a bath – gratefully washing away two days in wig, beard, moustache and heavy make-up, and I'm thinking how much longer I can delay having a drink!

Downstairs – Met one of the crew waiting to go to the party. He looks serious. 'Mike,' he says. 'We work bloody hard out there, and I think we deserve it.'

I'm a little puzzled. 'Deserve ... what, Ron?'

'Women.'

He looks me in the eye like a man who thinks I can give him medical treatment. 'Women ... Mike ... that's what we need.'

Monday, May 20th

Spent a day in the hills above Callander doing a great deal of silly riding.

Strange surreal moment: a wooden cut-out of Camelot, which stood on the top of the hill, and looked utterly three-dimensional and realistic, suddenly blew away.

12.00 midnight: whilst soaking in my bath I hear a distant shout. 'I'm going to bed, but I don't necessarily have to go to bed alo-o-one.' It's Dr Chapman in the passage. He repeats the line three times, like someone selling scrap iron and it recedes along the corridor.

Friday, May 24th

In the hotel room catching up on the diary whilst they film the Historian. A very heavy week for me – with two long speaking parts on Wednesday and Thursday. I am not sure, but I don't feel quite on top of the performances. Something tightens up inside me during a take – the relaxation and control of a rehearsal is lost. Mind you, filming is an appalling process for reducing an actor to the role of machine.

In the Knights of Ni, for instance, I was to do close-ups first. Directly in front of me are a group of anoraked people squatting down, far more preoccupied with their equipment than with me. Someone reads the lines off in a flat voice, which gives you little encouragement. An eyeline keeps you looking at no one at all. Two huge white polystyrene reflectors enclose me on either side – it feels like acting in a sandwich. Then you are about to start and the sound isn't right – and then the sun comes out and that isn't right, as the camera focus has to be adjusted – and during this so much of one's spontaneity and relaxation just drain away.

Yesterday a long day as the Father – for the second day running a part involving heavy make-up, beard, moustache, etc. A great sense of relief when it was finished. Have not done such sustained and exhausting acting as I have this week since the last Python series. Creating new characters suddenly seems an enormous effort.

A little disappointment at the rushes tonight – saw my first appearance as the Father in the wedding scene, and didn't feel I was quite funny enough – but again, all the early close-ups of my speech to the crowd were done cold, without the crowd there, to some arbitrary mark, and it was Terry J's very good idea to make me do another take in close-up right at the end of the day. That, I think, is quite funny.

Monday, May 27th

Helen and the children come up from London. Helen, who is probably pregnant again, is feeling worse in the evening than the morning. The boys stayed up to watch the rushes and see their dad in a lot of strange guises.

Rather pleased to share with Helen and the kids the silly things I've been doing over the last four weeks. It was the Knights of Ni, which people seemed to like quite well.

Tuesday, May 28th

A rather fraught morning. Today we are to shoot Robin and the Singers' encounter with the Three-Headed Knight. But Graham, who is one of the three heads – the other two being myself and Terry – is not back from London. It's a complicated piece of learning, which needs all of us to rehearse it properly, and in the last week or so Graham has lost all his early confidence over lines and can hardly remember even one-line speeches.

Graham, Terry and I huddle into the cab of the camera van to learn the words. (One thing we MUST have on future filming is a caravan or, even better, a Dormobile, which is purely for the actors to use. When there is nowhere to sit, nowhere to relax while they spend one and a half hours setting up the shot, one can get very ratty.)

Anyway, we huddle in the camera van, a magazine of film sticking into my back, a battered little jackdaw beside me in its box (John Welland, the camera operator, found it and is trying to nurse it back to health on Ron Hellard's scrambled egg). I wasn't enjoying myself at all. Graham couldn't get it right.

Finally we are strapped into our Three-Headed Knight costume at about 5.00. All my apprehensions about it were unfulfilled. Graham, with just a little prompting, was fluent and funny, and Terry J was the one who seemed to be physically suffering in the uncomfortable costume. We were released about 6.30!

Wednesday, May 29th

John, dressed as a magician, spent much of the morning on the narrow top of an extremely impressive pinnacle of slate, across the quarry from us.

Twice the cameras turned. Twice John, towering above the green and pleasant vistas of the Trossachs, gave the signal to summon forth mighty explosions. Twice the explosions failed, and John was left on this striking, but lonely, pinnacle. He kept in good form, reciting his old cabaret monologues across the quarry, but it was a hard start to the day for him – and he was cold and subdued by the time he came back.

Once again it was a day where visual effects took the major amount of time, leaving John's quite long passages of dialogue to the later part of the afternoon. John's performance was good, but he had passed the point when it might have become inspired. But then you never know on film.

Thursday, May 30th

God appeared to us in the morning – with the help of John Horton's fireworks. Tom came down to the location and was quite impressed to see my now rather shabby Galahad gear – especially the sword. He and Willy played around with the other kids on the mound leading up to the castle.

Finally called to do the opening sequence of the film at the end of the day. Usual difficulty with 'swirling mist', as it was a totally unmisty day. But beautiful views all around from the castle battlements – rolling green hills stretching into the distance, tranquillity, peace. I will remember standing up on those cardboard reinforced battlements with John, looking round on a view that can't have changed much since Doune Castle was built.

Tomorrow is the last day of filming. Already an end of term atmosphere. Eric left at lunchtime with Lyn and Carey [their son] – to spend a night at Edinburgh on the way home. John will not be seen again after we've finished on the battlements. The WI hall is no longer looking like an over-stocked jumble sale – the majority of the costumes are packed away in their skips, ready to be taken back to London.

Friday, May 31st

The weather seems to have turned at last. Today is cloudy and it's been raining quite hard in the night.

The long and wordy Constitutional Peasants scene. Feel heavy, dull and uninspired – wanting above all else for it to be the end of the day. Arrive at a bleak location in the hills above Callander. Mud is being prepared.

Terry Bedford is angry because Mark has been trying to economise by buying old film-stock. Some of the film which has arrived today is six years old. Terry will not use it – in fact he threw a can into a nearby moorland stream – so we have 1,000 feet on which to do this entire scene. Very little chance of re-takes. Somehow it takes a supreme effort to get the words and the character together. We do the scene in one long master shot and, thank God, we get through it first time without a hitch. Ideally would have liked another take – just to see if any part of the performance would be better, but there is not enough time or enough film. The day gets greyer as it progresses, blending perfectly with our peasants' costumes and mirroring the generally downtrodden air.

Willy and Helen arrive midway through the afternoon. Willy is a little apprehensive of me at first, what with sores on the face, a shock of red hair, blackened teeth and rags, but he stays long enough for doughnuts and milk at tea.

I'm almost too tired to enjoy fully the elation at the end of the day, when the filming, or my part of it anyway, is finally completed. Want to leap up and down, but can't. So I just stand there looking out over the

Scottish hills, all grey and dusky and hazy as evening falls, and feel wonderfully free.

That night, back at the hotel, I had a drink with Tommy Raeburn and the other chippies and drivers – hard men of films, who nevertheless reckoned the chances of the film's success to be very good. Roy Smith, the Art Director, said he wished he had money in it.

Three large gin and tonics and a bottle of red wine floored me early on, however. As the Rosses finished serving up a special five-course meal with a jokey 'Holy Grail' menu, complete with 'Mud Sorbet à la Palin', I began to feel my legs getting wobbly and my vision beginning to swing out of control and, about 11.30, went up to bed, thirty-two days after we had first clung to the side of the Gorge of Eternal Peril in Glencoe.

Wednesday, June 5th

Today I talked to Gail at Charisma. She says that 70,000 copies of the *Live at Drury Lane* album are being pressed, tho' not at EMI – for the lady pressers there, whose unofficial censorship we have come up against before, would not consider dealing with a record containing, as Gail put it, 'three fucks and a dagger up the clitoris'.

At 4.30 we met at Henshaw's. We talked about various points, including a fund, from our film proceeds, to give most of the main members of the crew a share in the profits. This was agreed, in principle, to be a good thing.

Wednesday, June 12th, Southwold

Caught 9.30 train and breakfast to Ipswich.

Father and Mother on the platform at Darsham. At first appearance, my father, who three months ago seemed quite seriously ill, looks extremely fit and well. Very sun-tanned and, tho' a little stooped, certainly not the shuffling wreck he had been in St Audry's. His mind seems stronger. He can understand more, and his recent memory is no longer so clouded. Also his hallucinations have stopped. All this since he has been taken off the wonder drug L-Dopa.

After lunch – dressed crab and Adnams beer – I took him for a drive, which was quite successful. Again impressed by the improvement in his mental condition (the awful twist being that this improvement makes him more aware of his physical deterioration).

We visited Benacre Church, Henstead Church and then on to Wenhaston – through sunlit Suffolk lanes, with lush green countryside almost overgrowing the road on either side. Ended up at the Harbour Inn about six – the sky was a perfectly clear azure blue above the sea – Southwold looked clean and brilliant, like a newly unwrapped present.

Monday, June 17th

A damp, musty kind of morning – pools of water on the roofs and roads after the night's rain, which came down after a series of thunderstorms last night. Have just heard on LBC that the Houses of Parliament are burning – a bomb was placed in the kitchens at Westminster Hall and went off at 8.30. There have been five casualties, one serious. The fire-boat is out on the Thames and, according to the news, the fire is still spreading. This must be the biggest propaganda coup of all for the IRA (if it is them), but I think it will rebound heavily – echoes of 1940, when P'ment was last burning, etc, etc.

Occasionally, when these rather traumatic things happen, you imagine for just a moment that this is it – there'll be a national panic, a crisis after which nothing will ever be the same again! But in an instant it all passes. Thomas is at school giving flowers he's brought back from Abbotsley to Mrs McCann, with a look of great pleasure and achievement on his face, Helen is at the doctor's, having an examination for our third child, Mrs B[1] is being relentlessly importuned by William, who is trying to persuade her to stop cleaning the bathroom and buy some sweets for him, and I am about to sit down, reach for the notebook and try and think of ways to make people laugh. So life goes on, and Parliament-burning quickly assumes a perspective.

Monday, June 24th

This morning we saw a rough cut of the film – the first time I've seen the whole lot put together. In its raw state, without dubbing, sound f/x, music and any editing guidance by the two Terrys, it tends to be rather heavy in certain scenes – the Knights of Ni and the opening of Anthrax possibly – but there are set pieces like the Plague Village, the fight with the Rabbit and the Holy Hand Grenade which work very well, even at

1 Lilian Blacknell, neighbour, cleaning lady, baby-sitter and general good sort.

this stage, and the recently filmed Black Knight fight wasn't in, which I hear is also a great set piece.

The only scene which I felt was seriously deficient at this stage is the appearance of the Three-Headed Knight. It just doesn't look imposing enough, and very similar in set-up to the Knights of Ni.

Ended up at the Linguaphone Institute in Oxford Street, where I enrolled for a course of Italian lessons. Rather dog-eared surroundings, but the people there are pleasant and smile a lot and Mr C, my Italian coach, looks convincingly Italian and makes little jokes about his language – 'When you hear an Italian couple having a row, it sounds as if they are singing in an opera' – and little jokes about his own incompetence with the tape recorder – 'I am the only man to have fused a candle' and 'I pressed so many knobs, I eventually got Vatican Radio'. Anyway, he's jolly. But the course he started me on looked so unutterably dull – it was all about being a businessman and leaving briefcases at the airport and meeting secretaries and – oh! – it was so awful I told them I didn't think I could manage to summon up any enthusiasm for it. So he went away and came back with a slightly more difficult course, still heavily business-orientated, but with more general conversational words and phrases.

So I got into my little booth and played with the tape recorder. I hope I can keep this course going. It was a big psychological step to come in off hot and dusty Oxford Street and commit myself to it, but I feel that I must start now if I'm ever going to learn a new language – or at least attempt to become anything less than helpless when I travel.

Wednesday, July 3rd

A grim, grey morning with gusting winds and bursts of rain and general drizzle. Suddenly the sunny days of May and early June seem light-years away. But it's good for application. Started work at 9.15 [on new Python TV series] and by lunchtime had 'The Golden Age of Ballooning' typed and organised into a twenty-nine-page script, which could do as a half-hour on its own. Feel rather pleased, as it is almost entirely my own work.

With this satisfactory morning behind me and even a little sunshine peering through to cheer the day up, I drove over and looked through Drew Smith's[1] black and white stills from the film, and selected a batch.

1 Drew Smith was stills photographer on the *Holy Grail*.

Then up to the Angel at Highgate to meet Graham. As at the Monarch, Graham has developed an almost familial relationship with the people who run the pub, which makes for a very pleasant atmosphere and nearly always a free drink. I looked through the work on the 'Michael Ellis' script which G and I had worked on together. Some good ideas there – and it made me laugh. Also made me aware of the usefulness of co-writing, after my euphoria of the morning! There are just jokes and ideas in the Michael Ellis script which I would never have made as funny if I had been writing it on my own.

Came back to find Thomas not well and asleep under a rug on the sofa. Willy, quite disconcerted by this, was trying hard to feel ill himself, and lay, rather unconvincingly, on the other sofa, under a blanket.

I took W swimming in the end. We spent an hour there. W is a real joy to take around. He talks to everybody, especially men in showers, and gives complete strangers a running commentary on the progress of his latest wee, and how Daddy is wearing trunks, etc.

Thursday, July 11th

Writing with Graham. Started about 11.00, worked until 12.45 then off to the Angel; drank a v. good pint of ale, played a couple of games of bar billiards with Graham, talked, and tried to avoid eating until 2.30. Started work at 3.00 – Graham took a little time to get upstairs and, when he eventually joined me, he muttered happily that 'These French cleaners are so passionate'.

Graham is a very good person to write dialogue with, and has very good silly ideas, but there is a rather uncomfortably undisciplined feeling to the day's work. We manage about two hours in the morning, before he starts getting really fidgety, then two more hours in the afternoon. Whereas Terry and myself, when we have a full day's writing, put in about six and a half solid hours.

Anyway, at 5.35 I remember I have a tutorial with Mr Cammillieri and, going against the rush-hour traffic, make Highgate to Soho Square in 15 minutes. An interesting tutorial. He just spoke Italian to me, but we at least got on to interesting topics. He said he was surprised I was an actor, but not surprised I was a writer. Perché? Well, all the actors he has met are self-centred, constantly play-acting and not genuine. Feel flattered, I suppose.

Sunday, July 14th

My mother rang to say that Father has started to see visions again – this time mice, hamsters and Welsh choirs. She sounded worried enough to suggest that I should try and go up there for a day this week.

But it's a busy week ahead, as Eric is back from France today for two weeks and, by some sort of Herculean effort, we should have most of the six new TV shows mapped out by the time he goes back.

Monday, July 15th

St Swithin's Day, apparently. The weather today should hold for forty days according to the horny adage (as I'm reading *Return of the Native* by T Hardy, I'm full of horny adages). Well, this St Swithin's Day was one of the coldest, wettest and most depressing days of the summer, so things don't look too good.

Graham, looking ravaged and with a hangover you could almost touch, arrived outside Julia St at about 10.30 for a lift down to the 10.00 writing meeting at TJ's. Yesterday had been the eighth anniversary of him and David, and G had had too much. He was fragile for most of the morning and only a large amount of gin revived him at lunchtime!

The 'Ballooning' story, Mr Neutron and, read last, but appreciated most, the Michael Ellis 'Harrods Ant Counter', which I'd put together with GC, and typed up rather uncertainly on Friday, very well received, which was most encouraging.

Thursday, July 18th, Southwold

To Southwold on morning train. Father shuffles more than even a month ago, and walks all the time with shoulders bent and sagging.

I took him out to the Queen's Head at Blyford in the early evening. He grimly hung on to a half-pint of bitter, grasping the handle of the glass doggedly, refusing to let it go. He clearly has few enjoyments left, but the chiefest of them is being at home, and here lies the difficulty. How long can Mother lift him out of the bath, support his dead weight as he gets out of the car? How long can she endure five or six interruptions to her sleep each night, putting his legs back into bed, cleaning up the carpet? How much longer can she dress him and undress him? How long will her mental stamina last in the constant presence of someone who never talks to her?

At least Angela and I are now visiting her more regularly, which cheers her up, and she has extraordinary reserves somewhere which keep her going.

Tuesday, July 23rd

Dreamt that John Cleese had been offered a series of thirty shows by Jimmy Gilbert!

Worked up at Graham's. A poor day. Graham's house, expansive as it is, is unaccountably shabby. There is hardly a working-surface in the place. G in a state of high nervous tension because John [Tomiczek] is out all day, and so is David at the moment (he's working at Covent Garden dressing the Stuttgart Ballet). Meanwhile Towser the pedigree dog is playing havoc ripping the innards out of soft furnishings and has to be kept in the kitchen. Graham keeps on disappearing upstairs. A callow choral-singer from California, called Walter, who is staying at the house, wanders about.

I find myself a cup of coffee and eventually a bit of table space in the 'dining' room, which is a pleasant-sized room, with a fine wooden table, but the whole place is littered with bottles of every conceivable beverage from Kum-Kwat to strange Italian liqueurs. On the floor there are boxfuls of Foster's lager and tonics and ginger ales.

Graham eventually appeared, shaking with nervous effort, poured himself a gin and tonic and gradually subsided. But the rest of the morning was taken up with incessant calls from our publicists, to try and fix up an interview about our new LP. A good half-hour wasted. What happens when publicity takes over the thing you're trying to publicise.

Wednesday, July 24th

At 6.30 a Python business meeting at Henshaws'.

What was the meeting about? Oh, I think, what should we do with the Python fortunes when they really start coming in? A pension fund? An office in Tuscany? How to avoid paying ourselves and the taxman all the money that is going to come in. Is it? I suppose so. After all, *Python Live at Drury Lane* does sound to be the bestseller of all our albums – No. 19 next week, according to Gail at Charisma.

Then Mark talked over publicity for the film. Eric refused to become involved in most of it. A few heated words, but he would insist on this silly point of principle that no interviews ever do anyone any good, and are hateful, degrading, etc, etc.

Thursday, August 1st

Up to Graham's for our script meeting with Ian. G had prepared, or was preparing, in his usual chaotic style, a barbecue lunch to mark the occasion.

After lamb kebabs, tandooried chicken, a Foster's lager and several glasses of red wine, in a hazy August sunshine, we retired indoors to read the scripts.

Ian was drinking scotch with dedicated frequency, inveighing against Terry Gilliam for wanting assistants for his animation, against Jill Foster (his, and our, agent) for some unspecified, but clearly deeply felt reason, us for trying to get shows in that were too long, and so on and so on. We tried to discuss Neil's position with Python, but Ian leapt at Neil with an almost paranoid intensity and the last two hours of the meeting were a pointless waste of time, with Ian at his worst. No longer jolly and charming and ebullient, but confused, aggressive and quite unconstructive.

I left at 7.00 with a deep feeling of frustration that remained with me throughout the evening, despite Neil and Yvonne's excellent company at supper. I began to feel what was the point? Here was a series that only Graham was really keen to do, and yet only Terry and I were writing. Here was a series which we had, for better or worse, fought for from the BBC and, with not a few misgivings, we had asked for Ian only to direct it, and yet Ian comes back at us with a totally unrealistic 'this is my show, you do what I say' attitude. We didn't need to do it for the money – why the hell were we doing it?

With these gloomy thoughts I went to my bed at half past twelve.

Tuesday, August 6th

One of the most satisfying copies of *The Guardian* that has ever come through my letterbox swished onto the mat at 8.00 this morning, bearing front-page news of Nixon's admission that he knew about the Watergate cover-up and personally directed it within five days of the incident. As I drive down to Terry's to write, I remember the day, five and a half years ago, when TJ and I drove out along the A40 on our way to film *The Complete and Utter Histories* and despondently listened to the unbelievable news of Tricky Dicky's elevation to the Presidency. Now I listened to the equally unbelievable news that he had lied blatantly and repeatedly to his supporters, his lawyers, his 'friends', his country and the world, for two years!

Father went into hospital at St Audry's again for a two-week period. He is seeing hamsters everywhere now – they squelch under his feet as he walks in the sitting room. My mother has to carry a bag to put them in. When the doctor arrived the hamsters got up Grandfather's trousers and began to attack his privates. My father, so staid and unimaginative over most of his life, is now becoming quite Pythonic. The hamsters seem to bother more than frighten him, as do the two men who have evidently been in the garage since 1966!

Fraser and Dunlop rang with an offer of £4,000 to do a Stone's Ginger Wine commercial. One day's work. My hands went clammy, and I told Jill I'd think about it. £4,000 for a day's work is the kind of proposition that gives greed a good name.

Thursday, August 8th

For the last two days little but writing (we now have four scripts completed) and Nixon. Only this evening, two days after his self-confessed lying, does it seem that the man has finally got the message, and is probably about to become the first American President to resign in office.

A wonderful galaxy of early Nixon film – the suffocatingly schmaltzy Checkers speech, the effusive endorsements from Frank Sinatra, Gerry Ford and Eisenhower speaking of Nixon as 'a man of integrity' in 1968. But there can have been no TV spectacle as chilling as the replays of Nixon's last three Watergate addresses to the nation – where Nixon looks the world in the eye and lies.

Monday, August 12th

Stop Press: writing my diary at 11.15 when the phone rings. It's Nancy from New York, almost speechless with good news. As from October, the entire Python first series is being screened on American TV by PBS.[1] I

1 The Public Broadcasting Service (Channel 13). The only non-commercial channel on US television. It is supported by public subscription.

told Nancy it must be Gerry Ford's doing. Python, which has been going for almost as long as Richard Nixon was President, has finally broken in the States within four days of his resignation.

Sunday, September 1st, Abbotsley

In many ways these last two days have been an extension of last week's summer holiday in the Lot – totally relaxing days spent with the family, away from work and away from too many other people. Worked in the garden, had the best night's sleep for a week, and ended up today astride a tree, half-submerged in the stagnant pond, wearing only my under-pants! I was trying to salvage my appalling attempt at tree-felling, which had propelled the tree straight into the stagnant water.

My Tarzan-like activities were greeted with much mirth by Helen. Willy leant up against the wire and made up songs to sing to himself, and Thomas fussed around like an old hen worrying about me – 'Oh, do be careful, Daddy.' 'Oh, isn't Daddy strong?' 'Oh, Daddy, you're *so* nice,' and other slightly unhelpful observations.

Sunday, September 8th, Exeter

From today we start filming on the fourth Python series. Packed during the morning – took Helen and the boys out for a very pleasant goodbye lunch at Maxwells, and left with the Mini and Terry Jones, about 2.00.

Arrived at 8.30 at the White Hart Hotel in Exeter. An historic inn, with its history quite spectacularly displayed – beams, torture instruments on the walls, cannon, etc. But a fairly cosy, un-smart bar, where Ian, Eke, Graham and John and Douglas (Graham's writer friend from Cambridge)[1] and others all sat.

Thursday, September 12th, Exeter

Today the weather was grey and rather miserable and, owing to a wrongly chosen location, I stood around for two hours in full drag, false eyelashes and all, before shooting for the day was cancelled. Eric and I walked up to the castle, or what remains of it after Cromwell. The weather began to

---

1 Douglas Adams, who later wrote *The Hitchhiker's Guide to the Galaxy*, had recently been asked by Graham to help him on his solo project *Son of Dracula*.

improve and we wandered around some gardens, then, both in rather a silly mood, walked back through the town and stopped at a shop which was prominently displaying ladies' panties with little messages on the front. We went inside. A chunky, middle-aged lady assistant, looking rather like I had done an hour previously, came up to us.

'Oh, she'd love a pair of these,' she said to us.

Eric indicated me, 'No, they're for him.'

I told her I wouldn't be able to get them over my head.

'We're looking for some with the AA sign on them,' said Eric.

She took this quite seriously and helpfully said 'We *did* have some with road signs on.'

'No, it's AA ones we want,' Eric confirmed.

We later bought some dressed crab and ate it with our tea back at the hotel.

Friday, September 27th

Filming aboard HMS *Belfast* moored by the Tower of London. I was to go along there at lunchtime, meet them and prepare for quite a long sketch to be filmed on Westminster Bridge in the afternoon. The rain fell heavily and persistently all morning and I arrived at HMS *Belfast* at about 12.45. 'Oh, the BBC, yes,' said an obliging Petty Officer. 'You know where the bar is, don't you?'

Well, I found the BBC ensconced, incredibly happily, in a warm, busy bar amidships – the only oasis of light and warmth and cheerfulness on board this steel-grey hulk. Terry, with an angelic smile, recommended the rum. Ian was as red-faced as I'd ever seen him on this filming. Outside it still poured. The morning's shot had been completed, but with much laughter amongst the crew of *Belfast* – for Graham was dressed as a Captain in full drag. 'Better keep Les below decks,' and other naval banter was apparently heard.

On from *Belfast*, in heavy drizzle, to our rendezvous point in a car park beside County Hall. When we arrived it was raining heavily again and it was obvious they wouldn't be able to film for a while. However, in the car park there just happened to be an enormous marquee, with '2nd International Festival of Wine' in large letters outside. So I added four glasses of wine to my rum and lagers and, when we actually came to start filming, at about 4.00, beneath the South Bank Lion, I was in an extremely cheery state and ready for anything.

The advantages of being dressed as a policeman are that I was able to stop four lanes of traffic on Westminster Bridge at rush hour, walk across the road, hit Terry, dressed as a lady, grab his armchair and walk back across the road with the cars still respectfully at a standstill!

Disadvantages of being dressed as a PC were that, as I waited for the cue for action, I would be approached by Americans asking where they could find a restaurant where they wouldn't need to wear a tie and harassed motorists asking me where the GLC licensing department was. One old lady approached me, stared hard at my false moustache and said, 'What are you? Real or a fake?'

'Have a guess,' I said

She surveyed my loose moustache and pinned-up hair for a moment, 'You're real.'

Tuesday, October 1st

In the evening we had an investors' preview of *Monty Python and the Holy Grail* at the Hanover Grand.

Tony Stratton-Smith was there, and Ali and Brian Gibbons – the financial wizards behind Charisma. I chatted up Madeline Bell to try and get her to appear as the Ronettes in the next Python record,[1] and there were a lot of beautiful people, presumably Pink Floyd and their wives, and also Maggie Gilliam, Carol Cleveland and Helen, who had never seen the film before.

Mark had to make an announcement before the film explaining that it was not yet finally cut. But the result was even more disastrous than I'd thought. It was one of those evenings when Python flopped. There was some laughter and there was some enjoyment and there was polite applause at the end. Michael White and John Goldstone wouldn't speak to us. White walked out at the end, giving Terry G a brief and non-committal pat on the shoulder.

Undoubtedly the poor quality of the print hadn't helped. A couple of times there were booms in shot which killed the scenes after them. The soundtrack had been so realistically and thoroughly dubbed by Terry G and John Hackney that the slightly gory sequences had a sickening impact which didn't help loosen people up.

---

1 Madeline Bell, African-American soul singer who had many hits in the UK with the group Blue Mink after making a mark as a backing singer for Dusty Springfield.

I didn't, I must admit, immediately look to technical faults to explain away my acute discomfort through most of the showing. I just felt, looking at it, that there were not enough jokes there. The film was 20% too strong on authenticity and 20% too weak on jokes.

None of the investors seemed anxious to shake us by the hand or even tap us on the shoulder. Only Tony Stratton-Smith came up and was clearly distressed to see us unhappy. He tried everything to jolly us up, for which I'm eternally grateful. The room was too hot, said Tony, the drink wasn't free, the projection was terrible – which in fact it was.

Terry J clearly felt that what was wrong was there was too much animation and too noisy a soundtrack. Both faults of TG. Poor TG. He had to put up with stick from Mark and Michael White later in the evening, and has been working eighteen hours a day on the film.

Helen and I went on to a meal at Rugantinos with Eric and Lyn. Eric had walked out half-way through the viewing.

Wednesday, October 2nd

Spent a most uncomfortable day in a studio jungle at Ealing, trying to portray the almost unparodyable David Attenborough. We got the make-up on, hair pinned up, bladder stuck on and wig over that – but after nearly an hour it wasn't quite right. Then suddenly I made a face that caught Attenborough and made the whole ensemble work. I spent the rest of the day trying, with various degrees of failure, to recapture this expression.

The discomfort of the make-up was nothing, compared to the special effect required to make Attenborough sweat profusely – this consisted of pipes thrust up my trouser legs and under my armpits and connected to the water supply for the studio. Unfortunately, for some reason, the supply wasn't working and I had to stand around in the tubes, anchored to a long rubber pipe for about 30 minutes before I could be reconnected to another studio! When the shot was eventually ready, it was impossible to do a fully practical rehearsal, so I was half-way into a take of a long speech when I felt ice-cold water pouring from my armpits.

From filming, I drove straight to Regent's Park and a Python film meeting. Michael White was the surprise guest – he had come along, he said, to tell us not to be too disheartened about the film. There were things that could be done to save it. It was, in his opinion, far too bloodthirsty, far too unpleasant in its atmosphere; almost every scene, he complained, showed death, disease, dirt or destruction, and his feeling, and the feeling of many people at the showing, was one of profound depression after seeing it.

It was not easy to take the whole White approach as The Word, but several aspects of it rang true.

TG stayed quiet and didn't fight. Graham bristled at every criticism of the violence – he regards it as important, honest, etc, etc. Terry J, like a cat with his hackles up whenever Mark's around, prowled the room, arguing fiercely that it should never have been shown in its unfinished state, that the film we saw on Tuesday was a badly edited cut, full of mistakes, and that anyone who had seen the viewing a month or so ago would realise what damage had been done.

Thursday, October 3rd

A rare day of sunshine – even tho' it was cold. Drove Graham down to Motspur Park, where we were filming a cricket match. Graham still mightily depressed about the reaction to the film. He really does feel that we are in danger of being panicked into drastic alterations to what he considers is one of the best pieces of work we've ever done.

A mournful drink after lunch with Ian, Terry and Graham. Eke has gone back to Germany and Ian has reverted to the spirits, which Eke seemed successfully to divert his mind from. In the afternoon he could hardly stand up and at one point he actually fell backwards over the camera tripod.

Apart from this afternoon, Ian has been a changed man – confident, co-operative and always in control, both of us and the crew.

Saturday, October 5th

At 10.00 down to the Henshaws' for a meeting about the film with Eric, Terry G, TJ, Gra, Mark and John Hackney, the editor.

The meeting, which Terry J had wanted to make very brief (his point being that there was very little to do to the film apart from losing all the 'improvements' made over the last four weeks), lasted solidly from 10.00 until 5.00. Everybody had their say about every part of the film. Eric and Mark won a point over the Three-Headed Knight (which all the rest of us who were actually in England working on the film in the summer thought was disastrous), which is now back in for us to look at. The animation has been cut down (the first time I can remember in all Python history when we have actually chopped any of TG's stuff). Some of Neil's music was thought to be not right, so we are putting on a lot of stock music. We have lost more of the 'Ni' sequence. There was nearly deadlock over reshooting the very important opening joke with the coconuts. Mark clams up on any mention of reshooting and TJ rises accordingly.

Thursday, October 10th

The second election this year. I feel more strongly pro-Labour than I did in February. Then it was a case of voting on the single issue of stopping the country grinding to a halt as a result of E Heath's appalling mis-judgement of the 'have-nots' and their strength. Since then the record of the Labour government has been impressive. They actually have held back rising prices, they have kept mortgage rates down, they've cut VAT, they've introduced fairer legislation on the sharing of North Sea Oil rev-enues and, on the international front, they have been a strongly heard voice in Washington and in the Common Market, and they have actually produced the 'social contract', which seems more than just another eco-nomic formula for trying to save the British economy (again) – it is an attempt to use and build on a sense of corporate responsibility among the working classes, which men like Sir Keith Joseph[1] would deny they ever had.

So that's why I once again found myself in the Polling Station at Tom's school, at 9.15 on a wet October morning, voting for Jock Stallard[2] for the second time in a year.

Friday, October 11th

The Labour overall majority is three. Big gains by Scottish Nationalists. The Liberal revival failed again – their share of the vote was down – and the Tories lost about twenty seats.

1 Secretary of State for Social Services in the Heath government. Architect of free-market Conservatism.
2 MP for St Pancras North.

Monday, November 4th

As soon as we got to rehearsal today and started to read through the 'Mr Neutron' script, an almost tangible blanket of gloom fell on everyone. The script was bitty, and rather difficult to read, admittedly – it's a show where we only need ten minutes' studio – but this alone couldn't account for the unprecedentedly dolorous mood around the table. Then I tracked it down – it was emanating from Eric. Eric, who can so often be the life and soul, was very deep into one of his dark, silent moods.

Because Eric was in France for all but two weeks of the entire writing and planning stage of the series, there is very little of his contribution in the series. In a welter of bitterly delivered contradictions, he criticised us for not accepting his half-hour, and at the same time bemoaned the fact that we wrote half-hours at all. He didn't like writing stories, he liked writing revue.

At lunchtime came a fresh jolt from the BBC. In Graham's speech as the Icelandic Honey Week rep – very funny and all recorded – they wanted the lines 'Cold enough to freeze your balls off, freeze the little buggers solid in mid-air' cut from the tape, as well as one 'piss off' (we could keep the other). Jimmy had apparently said very strongly to Ian that 'if and when Python Productions made their own series they could say what they like', but for now they must accept what the BBC say. Censorship in fact. Yes, says Jimmy, it is 'censorship'. We had already burned off most of our frustrated anger at the BBC's decision to omit the word 'condom' from that show. I mean, if condom is considered a bannable word on British TV in 1974, what hope is there!

One of Jimmy's reasons for this fresh bout of anti-sexual censorship is that we are going out at 8.30 on BBC1 when the shows are repeated. So, from lunchtime today, we are faced with an important decision. Do we let the BBC change Python into a soft, inoffensive half-hour of pap, or do we fight to keep its teeth, its offensiveness, its naughtiness? Do we have to conform or disappear?

Came home to cauliflower cheese, a couple of glasses of white wine and a sit by the fire whilst I watched *Panorama* on the World Food Conference in Rome. Within the year one in five of the world's population will suffer from starvation. It's like saying they'll suffer from death.

How small and insignificant it makes the events of today seem – and yet they have left me quite drained.

Tuesday, November 5th

Tom very pleased with himself this morning as he has learnt to tie his shoelaces. He keeps tying and untying them and had to show Mr Jarvis[1] how to do it. Helen later tells me they kept on coming undone as he walked to school.

A few fireworks at the Guedallas', and quick drink, then Robert H came round for the evening.

Robert thinks we ought to stop Python whilst we're still at the top. I think 31 is a little early to quit – but a few more mornings like yesterday could change my mind.

Wednesday, November 6th

Rehearsals a lot more convivial today, but Graham is feeling very low, as in Monday's editing Terry and Ian decided that, in view of the censorship cuts demanded by the BBC, the entire Icelandic Honey Week speech from Show 2 would have to be taken out. The loss of three sentences at the BBC's behest has therefore effectively castrated a funny, absurd, harmless and well-performed little piece.

Anne Henshaw[2] came to the rehearsals to give us some money from the book (which seems set for some good sales again this Christmas – the *Papperbok* is No. 3 in the best-selling lists, below *Watership Down* and Lyall Watson's *Supernature*) and she also showed us a letter from the financial front-man at Charisma, which tried to argue that we were not owed £11,000, but nearer £6,000. This is clearly not true, so the situation there is deteriorating rapidly. Anne is going to keep plugging away at them, but it seems as though Python may find itself in the courts for the first time. What a depressing week it's turning out to be.

Friday, November 8th

Nancy rang from New York to say she was ecstatic about the critical success of the TV show in New York, and especially over a rave review to be published in the prestigious *New York Sunday Times* in a couple of days. Boston and Philadelphia have bought the show.

1 Sam Jarvis, our house-painter.
2 Anne had taken over as our manager from John Gledhill.

'Discover for the first time
the full story of my
great-grandfather, Edward
Palin, who married Brita
Gallagher, an orphan
of the Irish potato
famines of the 1840s.'
(September 30th, 1977)

'Sorted through an old
chestful of Grandfather's
papers ... In the
Shrewsbury and India
days much evidence that
he was quite a character:
"always looks as though
he has done something
wicked but never has" –
school report from
Shrewsbury.'
(April 15th, 1975)

'In 1966 my parents,
Edward "Ted" and
Mary Palin, retired to
a village just outside
Southwold in Suffolk.'

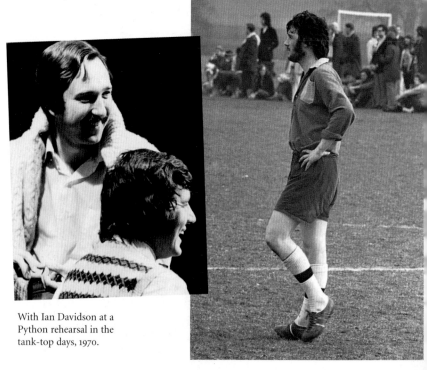

With Ian Davidson at a
Python rehearsal in the
tank-top days, 1970.

Charity football and
experimental beard, 1970.

Pythons at play,
Germany, 1971.

Filming 'Kamikaze Scotsmen' at Norwich Castle, 1971. With Eric Idle and Hazel Pethig.

With 'Auntie' Eric. 'The Cycling Tour', Python, 1972.

'Almost two years and nine months to the day since we shot our first feet of Python film, we were at Windsor to shoot what is probably our last.' With Ian MacNaughton. (April 6th, 1972)

Helen's mother and her
grandsons, Willy and
Tom, Abbotsley, 1972.

Helen's sister,
Cathy, with Tarquin
at Abbotsley.

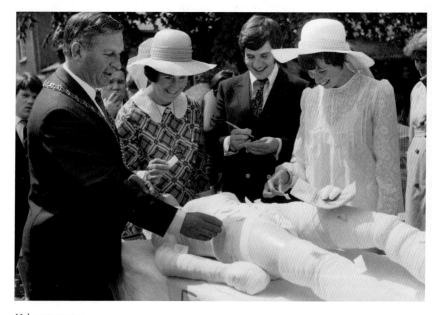

Helen attempts a
circumcision, local
fete, 1972.

Heyday of the flares.
With Tom at home, 1973.

'The longest day and my
father's three-quarter
century.' My mother
had baked him a cake
in his house colours
from Shrewsbury
School.
(June 21st, 1975)

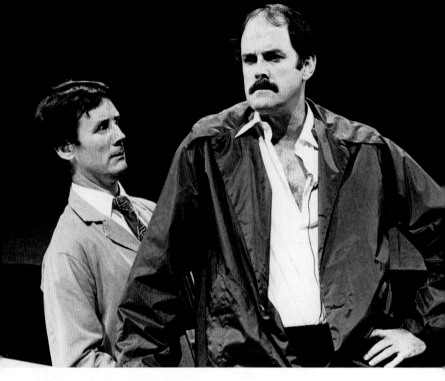

'John turned to me and said "No". The unconventional end of the 'Dead Parrot' sketch on my thirtieth birthday.
(May 5th, 1973)

'How do you know he's a producer? He's the only one who hasn't got shit all over him.'
Eric, myself (as Mud Eater) and Mark Forstater, *Holy Grail*, 1974.

'The first TV play written by Terry and myself . . . had been given a blaze of pre-publicity.'
The launch of *Secrets*.
(August 14th, 1973)

'First day of filming. Graham got vertigo ... and Eric and I and John sat around listening to stories from the mountain rescue boys about how many people perish on the mountains each year.' (*Holy Grail*, April 30th, 1974)

'How can you react without laughing to a broad Glaswegian accent saying "Of course I'm French, why do you think I am using this outrageous accent?"' (May 11th, 1974)

Graham as the lecturer,
Terry G, Terry J and
myself take up positions
for the 'Custard Pie'
sketch, 1975.

'The Surprise Pie.'
Terry and me at
Drury Lane, 1975.

Saturday, November 9th

Our fifth recording. Graham is round here in a mini-cab at 9.30, catching me with the toast and marmalade fresh in my mouth. But we are round at Eric's by ten to ten, and at the BBC 25 minutes early (a record, I think). Not a great deal of pressure this week as 19 minutes of the show are on film. So it all goes smoothly and unremarkably. For the fireside scene in which the Trapper and Captain Carpenter talk to Teddy Salad, the CIA agent disguised as a dog – John Horton and Richard had excelled themselves – Richard just working the dog with his hand right up its backside was funny enough.

At the end of the dress run-through, Jimmy Gilbert appeared, a little awkward perhaps, but clearly on placatory mission. Great show last week, he said, and apparently the viewing figures – at 5.8 million for Show 1 of the fourth series – were the best on BBC2, apart from *Call My Bluff*!! This doesn't strike me as all that wonderful.

Wednesday, November 13th

After rehearsal today Anne Henshaw came to tell us that Charisma are, in fact, broke. How serious it is we don't know – but at least they admit that we are owed £13,000 and presumably this money increases every time someone buys one of our records.

Thursday, November 14th

Simon A came round. He had been at a union meeting called to talk about the next step in his continuing war against the producer and editor of *World in Action*, who, in their bid to lure Granada reporters up to Manchester, have taken the unprecedented step of threatening to fire those who won't come. It sounds as though a fearless *World in Action* exposé of *World in Action* is required.

SA has been working for the last seven weeks gathering material for a programme on police corruption. He says the information is incredible. Corruption starts early in the Metropolitan Police, when bobbies, in order to be well considered, are judged on the number of arrests they make. According to SA's sources, it is commonplace therefore for vagrants and down-and-outs to be quite falsely charged with trying to break into cars, etc, etc. The corruption at the top is almost institutionalised. One forgets the close social connections between police and the underworld. In many cases there is a mutual respect, in some real friendship – and SA says a man like James Humphries, the recently gaoled Soho 'porn king', was a regular dinner party guest of senior policemen.

Tuesday, November 19th

A clear, sunny morning. London is drying out after a week of heavy rain. The pound at its lowest level ever yesterday, share prices down to 1958 levels, the miners' rejection of a big productivity deal, and another report from the Hudson Institute in Paris, which prophesies that Britain has had it, and in the 1980s there will be a decline in living standards, which will leave us on a level with Spain. Certainly we have already made our mark on Benidorm, so maybe UK and Spain should amalgamate and go into leisure in a big way, and leave the smooth, Tonik-suited executives of Germany and Holland to run our business for us.

Anyway, despite this gloom, life goes on, and Python flourishes. Our third show finally seems to have brought people back to the fold. Both the *Sunday Times* and *The Observer* noted this weekend that the show was back on 'cracking form' (the *Sunday Times*). We recorded our last show on Saturday – to a very receptive audience, which was most encouraging. The BBC, or rather J Gilbert on the phone to G Chapman, have confirmed that they want us to do seven more shows in the spring, and Eric was heard on Saturday night to agree to doing them – provided there are plenty of sketches and not so many storylines.

Friday, November 22nd

The depressing pattern of grey skies, rain and dark days is matched only by the news. In Tunis Arab guerrillas select an unarmed businessman from a plane they have hijacked and, merely to hurry up the business of forcing the release of six of their murdering compatriots, stand the man in the doorway of the plane and shoot him in the back. This evening there are two explosions in Birmingham pubs. Seventeen people are killed. An Irish voice gave an 11 minute warning, but so far the Provisionals have not claimed responsibility.

Saturday, November 23rd

An evening out with Nigel and Jude.[1] We met Nigel at his gallery in Sloane Gardens.

I found his current exhibition quite baffling. Why is it that modern art should make you feel so clumsy for not understanding it? It's a curious feeling of inadequacy to stand and look at a roomful of carefully-hung, expensively-lit objects, which someone considers paying nearly a thousand pounds for, and to find them as meaningful as a tin of anchovies.

But Nigel would probably counter this by saying that he has an exhibition of tins of anchovies opening only next week.

Monday, November 25th

Saw John C for the first time in many weeks – we did a couple of voice-overs together. The first in Studio G, Wardour Street, was a frightfully banal affair for Nairn Cushionfloors. An attractive lady producer, with the usual helpful and precise instructions – 'Can you read it slower, but with more pace?'

'Try the high-pitched, deep voice and don't emphasise the bit about "warm" and "springy".'

'You don't want them emphasised?'

'No, not emphasised, but just strongly delivered.' Etc, etc.

Whilst John and I were involved in this quite appallingly worthless artefact ('Never look a gift horse in the mouth, Mikey,' said John), a pillar box exploded in rush-hour Piccadilly, less than a mile away. All part of the IRA war.

Friday, November 29th

5.30: Arrive at 22 Park Square East [Michael and Anne Henshaw's home] for a Python meeting. Nothing of great interest until we start, in the absence of JC, to discuss 'Next Year'.

Eric: 'Does anyone feel like me that the TV series has been a failure?'

One can almost feel the 'Oh, no, here we go again' ripples spread

1 Nigel and Judy Greenwood. Together with elder sister Sarah, they were the three children of my father's sister. Nigel was a couple of years older than me.

round the room. So we are into the area which had surfaced briefly at the Old Oak Club at the beginning of this month and which had submerged, I hoped finally, during the last three weeks. The area of Eric's Doubt. If pushed he will say he regards the series as a near disaster, beneficial to none of us. If one counters with the fact that nearly all the major newspapers have come round to the view that Python without John was worth doing again, Eric retreats into a 'Well, if you believe the press you'll believe anything' attitude.

TG and I are both keen to do another seven. I am decided in my own mind that the last six have been good enough, and well-received enough, to try and complete a further seven – as a group, using TG and Eric more fully and TJ and MP less.

Then, after half an hour or so, Eric is suddenly agreeing, not only to the series, but to a rescheduling of dates taking us up to July. He doesn't look all that happy, but he seems to have agreed. So Python carries on. Then we elect a new Chairman by playing stone and scissors. I win, so Terry G has to be the new Chairman.

I caught up with Eric as we got outside the front door and asked him whether he was really happy about what had been decided. He feels that he no longer gets satisfaction out of Python because it is restricting. His writing and his ideas come up against the T Jones wall and he has no longer the stomach to keep fighting every inch of the way over every inch of material. Also he feels that, with John no longer there, he hasn't an ally. Having unloaded himself of this much, we say goodnight.

Saturday, November 30th

Eric comes round about 3.00. He suggests going for a walk. So, Eric and I set off for the Heath, both of us in thick coats, the watery November sun sinking splendidly as we reach the top of Parliament Hill. It's so like le Carré[1] I have to pinch myself.

Eric goes through his reasons for dissatisfaction. (I learn later from Terry G that Eric is reading Sartre at the moment – he was reading McLuhan a month ago when he was arguing that the content of Python books is quite unimportant compared to the form – and during the filming in Scotland he was reading Machiavelli. TG thinks if we can get

1 I was deep into John le Carré's *Tinker, Tailor, Soldier, Spy* and for quite a while tended to see everything through his eyes. And November is a very le-Carré-like month.

at Eric's library cards, we can get at the man!) He feels Python no longer works as a group. The formula is dull, we no longer surprise and shock, we are predictable. But he clearly misses John a great deal. None of us are as good as John or ever will be, he says.

Lynsey de Paul[1] moved today. I shall miss the slightly sexy, exotic atmosphere she gave the street, but not the drunken groups of local morons who try and sing 'No Honestly' outside her house at 11.30 at night.

Sunday, December 1st

Grey, but dry day. Two long phone calls re Python in the morning to TG and TJ. I have an instinctive warmth towards TJ – and yet TG is the only person whom I can now talk to fully and objectively about Monty P.

Mary and Edward [Helen's sister and brother-in-law] come round to supper in the evening. I have a rather good theory that in twenty-five years' time there will be far more countries (far more national divisions) in the world than now. I would like to see Estonia and Latvia as independent nations and Wales and Scotland for that matter. And I think it is going to happen – as people get less and less satisfaction from being part of a large international wodge. Look at the signs – Palestine's representative at the UN, Scottish Nationals with eleven seats in Parliament. In its nastiest form – the IRA.

Tuesday, December 3rd, Brace of Pheasant Inn, Plush, Dorset

I left for Dorset at 12.30 after booking a room in an out-of-the-way six-teenth century thatched inn (thank you, *Good Food Guide*) at Plush, a village fourteen or so miles north of Dorchester in what looked good Hardy and walking country.

My much needed spell of 'time off' had acquired a certain signifi-cance and I left unhappily. Helen upset because of the baby being due in a month or so and my going away – even tho' I know she wanted me to go. If I'd just taken off that morning it would have seemed all far less calculated.

It was a grizzly grey day as the train rattled over Egdon Heath. My

1 Lynsey de Paul. Singer, songwriter, glam rocker and, for a few years, our neighbour. She sang the British Eurovision entry in 1977.

first impression of Dorchester was of seeing schoolboys out of the corner of my eye, nudging each other and pointing at me. One followed me back from the station. So much for getting away from Monty Python. But as soon as I left Dorchester in a cab for Plush, I felt very Sherlock Holmes-ish – the night was dark, I could dimly see the outlines of hills on either side, the road wound crazily and suddenly the taxi had stopped. 'Right, this is it, sir.' Oh, yes, there was a whitewashed thatched house outside, but that was about all. The cab turned and sped off into the dark.

A snug little inn – my room is tiny and I share it with a huge chimney-breast. The pub is well unimproved. A low beamed ceiling and a single bar/dining room which makes for a cheerful communal spirit. An open fire, a landlord with a rather jolly, but loud voice, just returned from a holiday in Tenerife, where he had taken his wife to recuperate from a stroke. She was in hospital at the moment having her kneecaps removed (I couldn't work out whether this was in some way related to the holiday or not).

A rather frail, but florid-faced chap with a fine check sports coat, cavalry twills and a military moustache, came in from the night.

'Hello, Colonel,' says the barman.

'I could ring Roy Mason's bloody neck,' says the Colonel ruefully, tho' not violently, as he eases himself onto the bar stool. (Roy Mason had just announced some almost universally applauded and long-delayed cuts in our defence budget.)

That was rather the tone of the evening. A characteristic I noticed from my vantage point by the fire (where I sat with a large whisky and ice, trying to read *Tinker, Tailor, Soldier, Spy*) is that these country chaps talk only of facts – the size of an aeroplane, the hours of sunshine, the number of pigs so and so has – never feelings, nor impressions and certainly not emotions.

Wednesday, December 4th, Plush

Today I have walked nearly twenty miles over the hills and across the muddy fields of Dorset, I feel deliciously tired, I have had a long soak in a hot bath and in half an hour or so I will don my brown velvet jacket and elegantly clump downstairs for a drink, a read perhaps around the open fire, and then a meal which I know will be excellently cooked, and a bottle of rather expensive wine.

But it's all such a lovely illusion. I know that the maître d'hôtel will greet me with a booming voice when I get downstairs – and there'll be absolutely no chance of me slipping unobtrusively into a seat until everyone in the bar knows where I've been and what I'm drinking. I shall then try to read and yet find it impossible in the confined space of the bar to avoid hearing the rich country voices of the customers airing their rich country views.

Though there have been wonderful things down here – the food and the stunning sunny weather today and striding along the chalk ridges with the sun lighting the valleys – I am looking forward to being in that train pulling into Waterloo at 1.20 tomorrow. Pulling into the jostle and the bomb scares – but pulling into the richness of life which can only come when you have many people doing many different things. Down here, in the heart of an agricultural community, I feel the oppressive weight of years of tradition, convention and orderliness on the people around. I could get used to it, I suppose, but I feel this evening that I am too hopelessly and happily corrupted by the richness of London life ever to be right for Dorset, or vice-versa.

Monday, December 9th

I lit a fire at lunchtime, tho' it's not much less than 50° outside, but Willy wanted to send a letter up the chimney to Father Christmas to ask for a sweet factory.

William is sitting on the floor of my room, looking through old photos of the first four years of his life – like an old man looking back on his memories.

Nothing is expected of me for at least a week. This must be the root cause for the blissful sense of relaxed contentment I feel at the moment – though just having written that fills me with a little apprehension! A twinge of guilt.

Friday, December 20th

Lunchtime at the Angel in Highgate. The jolly lady who runs it has now given five copies of *Bert Fegg's Nasty Book* to people for presents. I had to sign one today. (Later in the afternoon, shopping at W H Smith's in Kensington High Street, I noticed that there were an awful lot of *Bert Fegg* books on the counter. Unsold or there owing to popular demand? I counted nearly fifty in a pile before I became embarrassed and moved away!)

Talked to Douglas Adams about the disappointed reactions he had had to Python series four. He thought the scripts were far better than the shows.

Saturday, December 21st

A great party at Robert Hewison's. Ten or fifteen people in his little room at Fetter Lane. Lunchtime – excellent mulled claret, no one from Python, so little shop talked. Renewed acquaintance with the Walmsleys[1] and enjoyed ourselves enormously.

Nigel told us that a man actually exists somewhere in the labyrinthine bureaucracy of the government, whose sole job it is to scrutinise every new car number to ensure that the combination of letters and numbers do not accidentally spell something rude, misleading or even ambiguous – in *any* language. Nigel, too, laughed when he first heard this, but it was put to him that maybe the government had a duty to protect spinster schoolteachers from the possibility of their driving through Czechoslovakia with 'Want a Good Time?' on their bumpers.

Wednesday, December 25th

On Christmas morning, the four of us had the house to ourselves. The boys played happily, Helen and I sat around and I read some of *A Christmas Carol*. Great stuff. After Hardy I feel myself being drawn, unprotesting, into the nineteenth century world, whose books and authors used to be forced at you from an early age, so I developed an image of Dickens, Jane Austen, George Eliot, as being heavy, worthy and boring. But now I'm acquiring an enormous taste for these same authors, and rediscovered Dickens' *Christmas Carol* (my old Birkdale school copy) with sheer joy.

---

1 Nigel Walmsley and wife Jane. Nigel was at Brasenose with me and went on to run the Post Office for a while. Jane was a journalist and TV presenter.

1975

Wednesday, January 1st

No newspapers, no letters. A bank holiday and all that that entails. All my working urges suddenly evaporate. Everything is still and quiet outside. Decide to treat it in the spirit which Heath intended this holiday when he decided on it for the first time last year. Rang Ian and Anthea [Davidson] and invited them for drinks, rang Robert for his mulled wine recipe and settled down to not working until this afternoon. But, well, one thing led to another. I should have started a play, Ian should have been writing for *The Two Ronnies*, Anthea should have been designing her summer clothes for the shop and Helen should have been having a baby, but somehow twelve and a half hours, four bottles of wine, three or four beers, several games of Scrabble and cribbage and one Indian take-away meal later, we were all still in the sitting room.

As Anthea said, this could be the year we learnt not to work too hard!

Monday, January 6th

A dull, overcast day. A gusting moderate wind sends icy draughts into my eyrie.[1] It takes most of the morning to warm the place up. My brain doesn't seem to warm up at all, and I struggle with an uninteresting idea for a play.

After lunch I take Thomas and Anthony Tackerberry to see *Dr Who and the Daleks* at the Adelphi. The kids are good company – the seriousness and lack of self-consciousness of six-year-olds makes their conversation a delight to listen to. Anthony, having told me his father was a barrister, said to me, 'I know what you are … you're a filmer.' Or the time he'd hit his head on a radiator – 'My *God* it hurt,' he said, with such feeling you almost had to wince. 'It came down my head and down my neck and onto my shirt …' adding, almost as an afterthought, 'the blood.'

Anyway, we arrived early. Parked in the now almost deserted streets

---

1 A new, half-glassed-in extension had been built on top of the house. My first custom-built work-room.

of Covent Garden. The main market buildings are fenced off. I don't know what they're doing in there, but the whole area could be allowed to become a most amenable shopping, eating, walking, living area. At the moment, in the first shock of losing the market that gave it its character and shaped its life, it is eerily quiet – only just breathing.

Wednesday, January 8th

After the excesses of rain and wind in October and November, the weather lately has settled down into a meek routine of still, lifeless, grey days. The IRA New Year truce lasts until January 16th and the total absence of any bomb attacks since the day the truce started shows how well-controlled the IRA is. The feeling in the press is that we have a bad year to come – increasing unemployment, steeply rising prices, etc, etc, but it's as if the worst is over. The nation is now entering a year bad enough to bring out all the Dunkirk spirit, whereas last year it was a year of such sudden and bewildering change that no one knew quite how to react.

Everywhere the talk is of cuts, savings and 'trimming back'. Notable exceptions, of course, being the now blue-eyed coal industry and the railways – five years ago the twin symbols of decline in a world of technological evolution.

Thursday, January 9th

Another sign of the times. The Beatles' company, Beatles Ltd, officially and finally ceased to exist today. The company, which held the Beatles group as such together in various legal obligations, has become increasingly obstructive to their various separate careers. The group haven't played together since 1969. We began when they finished.

Friday, January 10th

By one of those strange coincidences, today was the day that Python and the Beatles came together. In the last two months we've heard that George H has been using 'Lumberjack Song' from the first BBC LP as a curtain raiser to his US stage tour. So it seemed almost predictable that the two groups would be sooner or later involved in some joint venture.

Terry J, Graham and myself on behalf of Python and Neil Aspinall and Derek Taylor[1] on behalf of the Beatles, found ourselves at lunchtime today in a hastily converted office at the Apple Corp's temporary head-quarters in smart St James's, to watch the *Magical Mystery Tour* – the Beatles' TV film made in 1967. At that time I remember the film being slated by the critics and it vanished, swamped by an angry public who doubtless felt the Beatles had let them down by not subscribing to the image of success and glamour which the public had created around them. When it was suggested at a meeting late last year that we should try and put out the *Magical Mystery Tour* as a supporting film to the *Holy Grail*, there was unanimous agreement among the Python group. After several months of checking and cross-checking we finally heard last week that the four Beatles had been consulted and were happy to let the film go out. So today we saw it for the first time since 1967.

Unfortunately it was not an unjustly underrated work. There are some poor and rather messy sequences, it's very obvious when the group is miming to playback and there's a cutesie *Top of the Pops*-type look at Paul during 'Fool on the Hill', which is very tacky and dated. However, it *is* extraordinary still, it is far too impressionistic and odd to be just outdated and many sequences are very successful. It's also quite long – nearly an hour, but all in all we were pleased. It will have great curiosity value and should be complementary to the Python film, because much of it looks like familiar Python territory.

Ringo was suddenly there, talking with Graham and Terry. He was dressed like a British Rail porter, with a black serge waistcoat and black trousers. I noticed his hair was streaked silvery at the sides. He looked rather ashen-faced – the look of a man who needs a holiday.

I was given George Harrison's number by Aspinall, who said he thought George would appreciate a call – he's apparently the all-time Python fan, and it was at his mansion near Henley that they had been last night looking at the last Python TV series.

Later in the evening, fortified (why did I feel I needed fortifying?) with a couple of brandies, I phoned George Hargreaves (as Derek Taylor and Aspinall referred to him). An American girl answered – or rather a girl with an American accent. She sounded bright, but when I said I was from Monty P she positively bubbled over and went off to get GH. George and I chatted for about 20 minutes or so. He adores the shows so much – 'The only sane thing on television' – he wants to be involved in

1 Neil was the closest to a manager the Beatles had at the time; Derek was the press officer.

some kind of way with us in the States. He said he had so many ideas to talk about, but I was a little wary – especially when he told me he envisaged a Harrison-Python road show, with us doing really extraordinary things throughout the show, such as swinging out over the audience on wires, etc. Hold it George, I thought, this is hardly the way to get John Cleese back into showbusiness! But he's clearly an idealist who has warm feelings towards us and it's very flattering to hear one of one's four great heroes of the '60s say he'd 'just like to meet and drink a glass of beer with you, and tell you how much I love you'.

Monday, January 13th

Monday, 13th January was only one and a half hours old when Helen woke me lightly and said she thought we ought to go in. There was no fuss or panic, but the contractions were now at five minute intervals.

At 2.00 we drove through Camden Town and the deserted Hampstead Road in the direction of UCH, over which the GPO Tower flashed its red light, like a twentieth-century Bethlehem.

At about 2.15 I left Helen with the midwife and was shown into the waiting room. A cluster of fathers there – one in a white hospital gown smoking a cigar, who had clearly just become a father, and one other, a nervous-looking man, biting his nails and staring at the floor. The orderly switched the radio on, to loud and raucous strains of *Oliver* or *Mary Poppins*. 'Better to have this than no noise at all,' he said.

Helen began to have major contractions at about 3.00. She counted six of them and on the sixth Sister Whitbread announced that she could see some hair! Excitement – hair! We've never had a baby with hair before. Then a few more pushes. Helen managing really well. Keeping in control. I was telling Helen it had hair – dark hair – when a look of pure, spontaneous joy filled her whole face – 'It's a *girl*!' That was the best moment of all. A great moment – not seeing it was a girl, but seeing Helen's face at the exact second when she saw Rachel for the first time.

Now she was out – the usual greyish-purple colour which so frightened me when Tom was born. Sister Whitbread was cleaning out her nose. She was big, they all said. Helen could not believe it. Her enjoyment was total. It was twelve minutes past three.

Monday, January 27th

Terry Gilliam rang about 9.30 and set off a whole chain of calls which resulted in a total replanning of the year ahead.

TG had seen Ian MacNaughton at Sölden – he had driven over from Munich with Eke to ski with them for a day or two. On the slopes Ian told TG that he was highly dissatisfied with the way the BBC and Fraser and Dunlop (Ian MacN's agent as well as ours) were treating him. He has a job in Israel, which both the BBC and Jill knew about, which would prevent him from working on the Python TV show until May (i.e. until after our filming). So it appears that, if we want Ian to direct our shows, and I think everybody does, we cannot start filming until May. This would mean studio dates running into August, which I know will be unacceptable so, as TG said, the alternative is to put it all off.

I rang off and digested this new situation – and the more I thought about it, the more attractive postponement of the recordings became. TJ was keen and, when I rang Eric, he was not only keen, but as positive about Python as I've heard him in a long while.

Tuesday, February 4th

Good news from New York – Python is top of the PBS Channel 13 ratings there, beating even *Upstairs Downstairs*, which has just won an Emmy and all. Sales to other stations increase – far away places with strange-sounding names – to Pensacola, Florida, to Utica, Illinois, Syracuse, NY, Athens, Georgia and so on. It sounds as though there's been a mistake and we've sold it to Greece.

Thursday, February 6th

We have written a synopsis of the *Holy Grail* for the EMI publicity people. Eric wrote it some time ago and it is extremely funny and totally unrelated to anything that happens in the film. 'Might this not be a bad thing?' says Mark to me over the phone today. EMI are worried that Up North there are critics who often review the film entirely from the synopsis, without ever seeing it; surely therefore we should provide a straight synopsis as well. My mind boggles at asking Python to help incompetent idiots who haven't time to see the film they're talking about.

Monday, February 10th

Mark rang, as he usually does when I'm having an enjoyable evening, this time on a matter of great profundity – the invitations for the Magazine Critics' showing of the *Holy Grail*.

I am so sick of being Python odd-job man, and yet the alternative is to *not* know what's going on in your name – which is infinitely more dangerous. I think of this when Mark rings and it just keeps me from physical violence.

Saturday, February 15th, Southwold

A drizzling, grey morning. We are going to Southwold for the weekend. Manage to pack three kids, carrycot, ourselves and Tom's new bicycle in the Citroen and we arrive, after a slow run, at about 2.45. A late lunch. But at least the weather has improved – it's sunnier and colder than in London. A fresh Suffolk wind off the sea clears the nostrils and freezes the fingers. We are staying at the Swan Hotel.

Funny that, fifteen years ago, when Helen and I first met in Southwold, the Swan Hotel represented the unattainable – the comfort and sophistication which we were never likely to know. Heavy tweed suits, ladies in suede jackets moving between heavy leather armchairs and through finely carved doorways – it was a world miles away from our own.

And now we are here, part of it all, in rooms which are floodlit from outside, with wrought-iron balconies and a view out onto a square that, in scale, feels like Toy Town – a neat, little miniature, into which at any time you expect a Victorian coach and four to appear, with ladies in big bonnets and men with side whiskers.

Wednesday, February 19th

Am now reading Dorothy Wordsworth's Journals, so watch out for hypersensitive observations on the weather. If she were alive now she could totally transform the image of the Meteorological Office. Weather forecasts would become works of art.

Me, myself, personally having always rather keenly felt the changes in atmosphere and attitude which different kinds of weather create, took it as a good omen that today was a sunny, brilliantly sunny, neo-spring morning, for the first gathering of all the Pythons for six months or so.

At any rate, Eric and John were at the Henshaws' when I arrived – both tanned. Eric was back from a week in Tenerife with Barry Cryer, and John from Africa. Anne Henshaw was a good deep skiing brown. I felt like the skinny schoolboy whose mother never lets him go out. Fortunately Mark looked more sallow than usual and Graham when he arrived looked truly dreadful. Pale as if he had just come out from under a stone and hobbling with a broken bone in his foot. He'd done it on a chair. Graham seems to be going through his body breaking every bone at least once.

But there is a good feeling to the group and, when we start to talk about publicity ideas the chemistry works and ideas bubble out in a stream.

When we suggest a 'Dummy Premiere in the presence of Her Royal Highness the Dummy Princess Margaret' – with a car laid on to transport this now famous Python dummy lady to the theatre,[1] and us all lined up shaking hands, Mark says that EMI just wouldn't wear it. Terry J said 'Mark, if you don't feel that you can fight EMI for the things we want, then someone else ought to be doing the job.'

Well, at the end of the meeting, Mark is still doing the job.

This evening dinner at the Henshaws'. A famous bearded playwright is there. Yes, David Mercer himself.[2] Odd to sit opposite a man you have unflatteringly impersonated on TV. Also an American writer called Al Levinson. A sort of Earth Father figure in his fifties, solid, smiling, sensitive, dependable. He shut himself in the kitchen at one point, trying to soothe Rachel's cries on his broad shoulder.

'You're much better looking than you are on television,' he started, before I'd hardly been introduced to him. He was a great fan of the show, and I still get a kind of kick from hearing someone talk about friends in New Jersey who will never miss a Python episode.

Famous Playwright Mercer describes himself as 'a sort of rich man's Alan Bennett'. He delivers this in tones which demand a reaction so we all laugh. I even say 'very good' and retreat as though outclassed by Oscar Wilde on his best form. And then I realise that I laughed because I didn't know what he was talking about and, on reflection, I don't think anyone knew what he was talking about.

---

1 The life-size Dummy Princess Margaret had been created for the Python TV series and, rather than leave her in the props store, we used her to add a bit of class to the Drury Lane stage show, in which she occupied a box throughout the run.

2 David Mercer, author of *Morgan: a Suitable Case for Treatment*, *The Parachute*, *Let's Murder Vivaldi*, died in 1980, aged 52.

Oh, I nearly forgot the best bit of news today – a letter from Stephen Frears at the BBC, asking if I would be at all interested in taking a part in a new TV version of *Three Men in a Boat* which he is filming in the summer. He is a superb young director,[1] much involved with Alan Bennett, and I hear that Tom Stoppard is writing the adaptation. Given the new Python schedule, I could do it without unduly buggering anyone else up. Am not raising any hopes – but it is the most exciting work prospect since we first talked about Monty Python.

Thursday, February 20th

Another Python meeting. This time to discuss affairs of Python generally and to plan our future in general.

When I arrived, Eric was the only one there, stretched comfortably in a corner of the sofa, wearing what looked very much like a bovver boys outfit, with TUF boots and jeans with rolled-up bottoms.

Good news at the beginning of the meeting – Nancy rang through to say that a US record deal was signed today with Arista Records – we would get an immediate $10,000 advance on *Matching Tie* and *Live at Drury Lane*. So good work there from Nancy, who has also secured her pet consideration on a record contract – $50,000 set aside just for publicity.

It was on the subject of paying off Gledhill[2] that the meeting suddenly and abruptly took off. As I remember it, Graham was on the phone to Jimmy Gilbert to check the autumn TV recording dates, John Cleese was being unusually co-operative and had even indicated that he might consider coming on this publicity tour to the US in March, when Eric suddenly became quite animated, attacking the Terrys and anyone around for being mean with Gledhill. From here Eric went on bitterly to criticise Python for becoming nothing more than a series of meetings, calling us 'capitalists' and ending up by saying 'Why can't we get back to what we enjoyed doing? Why do we have to go through all this?' It was rich dramatic stuff.

Terry J was on his feet – 'Well, if that's how Eric feels, we might as well give up,' and he nearly left there and then. GC and JC looked at each

1 Assistant director on *Charlie Bubbles* in 1967, he had directed Albert Finney in the excellent *Gumshoe* in 1971.
2 John Gledhill had ceased to be our manager as from November 1974.

other in amazement. Only the entirely admirable Anne H managed to cool everything down by giving out cheques for £800 each from Charisma – an advance for the LP made last May!

A selection of letters are read out to the assembled gathering. From CBC Canada – 'We would like the Python group to contribute up to ten minutes of material for a special programme on European Unity. The group can decide –' the reading was interrupted here by farting noises and thumbs-down signs. On to the next.

'Dear Sirs, I am writing on behalf of the Television Department of Aberdeen University … ' An even louder barrage of farting.

'Dear Monty Python, we are a production company interested in making TV films with Python, George Harrison and Elton John …' Despite the fact that £36,000 is mentioned in the letter as a possible fee for this never-to-be-repeated offer, it is jeered raucously and I tear the letter up and scatter it over the Henshaws' sitting room. In this symbolic gesture, entirely characteristic of the general irresponsibility of the assembled Pythons, the meeting staggers to an end and we all make our several ways.

Saturday, February 22nd

I suppose this could be said to be the day on which Python finally died. Obviously only time will tell whether this is a hopelessly over-dramatic reaction – but at the time of writing it does feel as though the group has breathed its last after nearly six years of increasingly doddery life.

The conditions of its demise were quite unspectacular. We ate lunch in my sunny work-room and afterwards I took Thomas, Holly and Willy to Little Venice, where, on a housing estate bordering the M4 elevated section, I had seen a big galleon-shaped climbing frame, which I thought they would like. They clambered on it and Tom rode his bicycle round the paths with arrogant confidence. Back in time for *Dr Who*.

I noticed Eric's car outside the house and felt quite pleased. It proved that his mood on Thursday was just a mood, and things must be alright if he could come round to tea.

He'd signed me a copy of his novel *Hello Sailor* and, though he wasn't ebullient, we had a cuppa together and chatted vaguely, and I really had no idea that he had any bad news, or even news, for me. (Helen said she had known something was up as soon as he appeared on the doorstep.) Carey was bashing around. He seems to me a very lively, jolly little fellow with a lust for biscuits. Eric asked when we were going to the States and then said he wanted to talk. We went upstairs to my work-room, trying not to make the occasion seem too momentous – both deliberately playing down our behaviour!

Upstairs, in the now cold room – we didn't bother to put the fire on – Eric told me, again, but finally this time, that he couldn't go on with Python. He'd thought about it a lot over the last few weeks, the decision hadn't come lightly – but he felt that he had to get out or he would, as he put it, 'go mad'. It wasn't just Python, there had been other troubles over the last few weeks – he'd tell me about them 'over a pastis in the summer,' he smiled. He hadn't anything he was going to do – he just wanted to enjoy the experience of 'waking up in the morning, knowing I don't have to do anything'.

I must admit I had slight pinch-of-salt feelings. At my most cynical I felt here is someone who has his own novel, and another virtually commissioned, about to come out, and his own TV series too [*Rutland Weekend Television*], to add to an already short and success-ful radio series, and he is understandably anxious to shed his old Python skin. Eric the loner feels that he has taken all he can from the Python group – he's moving on, like John did. Oh, he did say in passing that if John came back to do a TV series he would come back too. But meantime, he just wanted to take it easy, write his new book, maybe work on a play.

There was nothing I could say but bully for you. I have long since got over feelings of reproach or bitterness towards Eric. Now I feel just bliss-fully liberated from a tiresome duty as one of the Python anchormen – now perhaps I can be selfish as well. The prospect is interesting.

Eric and I parted on good terms. There's no animosity – we'll see him and Lyn and Carey socially – so perhaps in a year, or even six months, we'll all be back in the fold again. But if not ... now that's a really excit-ing prospect ... if not ... this clear and rapidly cooling February evening, as Eric's Volkswagen Beetle clatters off down Oak Village – this evening could be the end of lots of things.

Monday, February 24th

To the Henshaws' for what could be yet another momentous Python meeting.

I'm the first there – Anne H hurries up the stairs with some coffee and says ruefully, 'This is going to be quite a morning, isn't it?' Graham arrives next. He takes the news of Eric's latest decision stoically to say the least. He smiles as if he knew what was going to happen and betrays no outward and visible signs of distress, anger or anxiety whatsoever – apart from taking a beer at 10.30. The two Terrys are equally resigned (TJ had felt this was an almost inevitable sequel to last Thursday's meeting anyway).

The news from America daily lends an extra air of unreality to the situation for, by all accounts, Python is catching on in the States as *the* prestige programme to watch. Nancy rings to say San Francisco has now taken the series, Yale University are doing *every*thing they can to get a print of the first Python film off Columbia, the illustrator of the *Marvel* and *Incredible Hulk* comics wants to do a Python comic. Python is set to become the latest cult amongst the AB readership group, whilst back in little old quaint, provincial London, it has finally run its course, and four of its creators are sitting around deciding who is going to do the cleaning-up before the place is finally locked up for the year – or maybe for ever.

The new book is off for the summer, the TV series is off for the autumn. Touring seems the only hope of getting us together again. But, though I am prepared to ring Geoffrey Strachan and Jimmy Gilbert and all the others whom we are constantly messing about, and tell them it's all off, I do not feel, at this stage, that we can ring Tony S-Smith and change our minds once again over the album of the film. So the four of us agree to put the album together in the next couple of weeks. Eric and John have intimated that they are available to do any voices, but the way I feel at the moment, it's a matter of pride to do it without them.

We lunch together, the four of us, united at this time like a group who have just lost a close relative, at the Villa Bianca in Hampstead. Graham apologised for being late, but he was buying Plasticine and knitting needles. A moment's incomprehension, then GC explains that you make the figures out of Plasticine and stick knitting needles in them.

As if not enough had happened today, Mark rings to say that we haven't got the Casino for our West End opening – we are back to the ABC Bloomsbury, the Scene at the Swiss Centre and the ABC Fulham Road (now four cinemas). TJ is especially furious – he feels that Python will just not work in small cinemas – it will appear to be slow-moving and unfunny – it needs big audiences. Terry speaks on this point with the conviction of an early Christian missionary.

Tuesday, February 25th

At 10.00 Graham and Douglas Adams arrive at Julia Street and, over coffee, we work out select front-of-house photos for all the cinemas (we include one of Tom standing beside a Christmas tree at home) and work out silly captions – then down to Soho to meet Jack Hogarth, head of EMI distribution, to try and put our arguments against an ABC Bloomsbury opening. The receptionist's soft instructions, the carpeted corridor, the name on the door, the secretary in the outer office, and the huge ten-foot desk which Hogarth gets up from, all work their insidious spell. They are the trappings of authority and responsibility. Abandon hope all idealists who enter here. How can you speak on equal terms to a man with forty square feet of polished wood between him and you?

Terry J took the lead, I tried to back him up, and GC said nothing. Not that there is much you can say when Terry is in the form he was today. He was away with guns blazing, and it was a joy to watch.

Hogarth was treated to a pyrotechnic display of Jonesian extrava-gance ... Did *he* know we could pack any cinema anywhere? Did *he* know people had marched in sub-zero temperatures in Toronto to get the series put back on CBC? And so on. We came out with a vague promise by Hogarth to look into it, but for the rest of the day TJ was seething, prowling dangerously like a leopard with a thorn in its bottom.

Thursday, February 27th

The Indian spring continues. As do the phone calls. It took me one and a half hours to make myself a cup of coffee this morning. Every time I got downstairs the phone rang and I had to come up again. Finally drank mid-morning coffee at 1.30!

The film and the film publicity is gathering an almost inexorable impetus. The good news is that EMI have put us into the Casino after all, and the incredible news is that they are simultaneously opening us at the ABC Bloomsbury and ABC Fulham Road. Nat Cohen of EMI now seems to be quite converted to Python and is prepared to give it the full treatment. It shows how fast things are moving – only 48 hours ago we were being told we were lucky to get a cinema like the ABC Bloomsbury at all. Now they are confident in filling 1600 places.

A half-hour call from John Goldstone. He has had a letter back from the censor. The film cannot be given an 'A' (over-fives, accompanied), unless we cut down two gory moments, and lose one 'shit', the words 'oral sex', the entire phrase 'We make castanets of your testicles' and some of King Arthur's repeated 'Jesus Christs'.

I was prepared to trade the 'shit' for the 'oral sex', otherwise we'll settle for an AA (over-fourteens). It's all too silly.

A call from Jill. She has told Jimmy Gilbert at the BBC of our decision to drop the autumn series after all. But Jill tells me that JG is interested in a Michael Palin show to fill the slots he'd reserved. I couldn't quite believe it, but, coming a week after Stephen Frears' *Three Men in a Boat* offer, it makes me feel excited and confident and quite unsure of the future. Too much is happening.

Friday, February 28th

Up to G Chapman's for record writing. A gorgeous morning in Highgate. We listen (TG, TJ, Graham, Douglas and myself) to the tapes of the film. And surprisingly involving it is too.

Plenty of ideas come out for presentation, etc, but the work fizzles to a halt at lunchtime when TG has to go off and strip wallpaper in his new house and Graham and Douglas had obviously pre-arranged a meeting in the pub.

TJ and I both sensed another day was falling apart, but the marvellously warm, almost balmy air of Highgate in this unbelievable February, helped to keep us from becoming depressed. Instead we went to the San Carlo restaurant and, over whitebait, liver and a couple of glasses of wine, we discussed some ideas for future writing projects.

I feel that TJ and I have spent over a year as caretaker to Python, and from today on, I say, over my big cigar[1] and Calvados, Terry and I are going to do our own thing again.

Or do I really mean my own thing? I must say the Stephen Frears and Jimmy Gilbert offers have boosted my confidence and my determination. But I think we both felt better as a result of lunch. TJ is going up to North Yorkshire today for a weekend break with Al, and Helen and I are going to Abbotsley.

The last few hours of the week were typical of this whole mad, frenetic week. Phone calls on every subject under the sun, including an

1 I gave up smoking in 1969, but somehow neglected to give up the occasional recreational cigar. Until later in 1975, that is, when my system rebelled against even these.

238   1975

enquiry via Jill for me to do a short film next week to publicise Mike
Oldfield's new single, 'Don Alfonso'. It's all very urgent, etc, etc. Virgin
Records sent me a copy of the disc by taxi and, around six o'clock, one
Richard Branson rang. I hadn't heard the record, but said I was too busy.

When I did hear it I realised I had made the right decision.

Saturday, March 1st, Abbotsley

Helen's sister Mary, who has exams this coming week, is using my work-
room while we're away, and she rings after lunch, while I am out
trundling Rachel round the quiet, muddy roads of Abbotsley village,
with my mind on nothing in particular, to say that a BBC Radio 4
reporter has been pestering her to find out details of the 'Python break-
up'.

Mary had given nothing away. She said she knew none of the
Pythons' whereabouts or phone numbers. The reporter, according to
Mary, said 'Oh, surely there's a phone book of his beside the phone.'

However, G Chapman had been tracked down and, at 5.30, as I
cleaned my car in the drive at Church Farm, out of the radio came the
Python theme music, which they then ran down. 'Yes, after five years,
Monty Python is no more,' etc, etc. Graham gave an excellently
controlled, sensible, low-key interview, which didn't deny the story.

Monday, March 3rd

This morning at GC's, where we are assembled to finish writing the
record of the film soundtrack, TJ was very gloomy. He felt that the
'break-up' story was not going to do us any good, and it was his fault
that it ever got out in the first place. It turns out that the story first
appeared in Saturday's *Sun*, written by Chris Greenwood under the
headline 'Python Packs It In', describing an interview 'with Python
spokesman Terry Jones'. Poor Terry knows the guy – a friend of his
brother's – and couldn't really lie … but he feels very bad about it today.

A depressing morning's work. Once again Douglas is present,
which gives me an irrationally uncomfortable feeling. Is this a Python
album or a Python-Adams album? Graham is restless and contributes
little … he has a lunchtime meeting and constant phone calls about
future plans, which distract terribly.

Tuesday, March 4th

Down to Soho for a meeting at 11.00 with Stephen Murphy, the film censor. Outside the doorway in sunlit Soho Square are gathered as evil-looking a crew as I've seen outside of *The Godfather*. Terry Jones, looking lean and impish, Gilliam in his absurdly enormous leather coat, which makes him look like a looter, Mark Forstater and John Goldstone, dark and efficient.

We marched in this formidable phalanx into S Murphy's office. It was not unlike a university don's room, there was a fine mahogany table, books around the walls and a bay window, which added a rather medi-aeval feel to the place. From up here Soho Square looked idyllic, like a sunlit university quad.

Murphy has a donnish air, he chain-smokes and has a mischievous face and a slightly uncoordinated physical presence. But he's genial and easy and a wonderful change from the executives of EMI. Of course the censor is not a government watchdog, but a man appointed by the industry to protect itself, so there wasn't a great deal of unseen pressure as there is at the BBC in these sort of discussions. Jolly Mr Murphy claims he has done a great deal for us and, if we want this 'A' certificate (in order to make more money!) we must go a little way with him. So could we lose 'oral sex', 'shit' or any of the 'Jesus Christs'? '"Oral sex" *is* a problem,' he said, very seriously.

Well we came out and, over a coffee in Compton Street, decided that we would agree on changing a couple of Arthur's angry 'Jesus Christs'! TJ eventually came up with a replacement. Arthur should say 'Stephen Murphy'!

TJ and I drive down to Thames studios at Teddington to talk to Verity Lambert, Head of Plays there. Do we want to write a TV play? Anyway, there is an offer open from Thames, which is nice.

We go and have a pint of Young's at a nearby tavern. A well-intentioned demonstration march goes by. 'Evening Classes for Richmond' is on their banners. Some of the rude labourers from the pub go to the door and shout 'Eat babies!!' Much laughter.

As the American bandwagon rolled on, there was an almost insatiable demand for Pythons to help publicise the TV series on PBS and the release of a new record album. The two Terrys, Graham and myself agreed to go over.

Friday, March 7th, Marriott Essex House Hotel, New York

We fly from a grey and drizzling London morning at 12.00 on a TWA jumbo. The plane isn't full, apart from the first class section under the bulbous nose. For us galley slaves back in 'the coach' as they coyly call it in the airline publicity, there is plenty of room to wander and stretch out. Terry J has an early burst of windowitis, and thoroughly disturbs himself as he darts from window to window, seat to seat, seeking the perfect view. The journey is inexorably and crushingly boring. Lunch nasty, brutish and short.

Since we were last in New York City, nearly two years ago, there has been the oil crisis and Watergate, the rise of unemployment, the dire situation in the US car industry and President Ford's drastic economies. But New York is as brash, as bold, as booming as ever.

Once again I was amazed, impressed, excited by the size and grace of these huge soaring steel and glass monsters on either side. Some now are in jet black colours, like huge natural outcrops of granite – not buildings at all. But clustered around the streets at the base of these huge monuments to financial freedom are many small shops and delis, which give New York its life. In a half hour on the street all the cobwebs of that long, dull flight were blown away and I experienced again the sheer delight of walking in New York.

Back to the hotel – drenched. In T Gilliam's room we launched into our first interview – with a guy called Howard Kissel from *Women's Wear Daily*. He looked just like Tiny Tim, he was easy to talk to, had a good sense of humour, and asked intelligent questions.

We walk round the corner to the Russian Tea Room. Clearly a place to be seen. Full of chic, sophisticated New Yorkers, looking over their shoulders all the time to spot the celebrities. Caroline Kennedy, daughter of JFK, was at the table next to ours. Funny that on our first day in NY in '72 Terry and I passed Ted Kennedy in the street. Maybe they just walk around all the time.

TJ flaked out, but I was so high on New York that, despite being over-full of blinis and red wine, I walked around a bit with Michael Winship of PBS. An interesting guy, he had been a member of the Washington press corps during Watergate. He said the night Nixon resigned there was a numb feeling of total paralysis, then, as the helicopter flew off from the White House lawn, a huge burst of festivities broke out. 'The King is Dead', 'Long live the King' atmosphere, he says, was incredible.

Well, this extraordinary day ended about 12.00 (4.00 a.m. British time). G Chapman, who always seems to wander into my life at the end of the day, appeared in the hotel corridor. He was shaking his head in disbelief and seemed anxious to tell me a story of his visit to the City Baths.

I sank into a fitful sleep. Make a mental note not to eat or drink ever again.

Sunday, March 9th, New York

We wandered down with our photographer towards the Park Plaza Hotel. He took a few shots of the four of us standing in front of the ponies and traps which do trips round Central Park. After only about 20 seconds of shots, one of the men sourly grunted about us losing him custom (there was no one for miles anyway) and moved his horse to the other side of the street. Then this generous spirit of animosity was carried on by another horse owner, a young long haired boy, who, somewhat to our amazement, for we had hardly been there for a minute, began to lecture us on the American way of life in general, and paying modelling fees to horse owners on Central Park in particular.

But the final straw, which caused GC and I to laugh all the way to the Plaza Hotel, was when one of the horses took a sudden and very violent lunge at Terry J. The wonderful aggrieved indignation in Terry's voice I'll remember for ever.

'He's bitten a lump out of my coat!'

Sure enough there was a chunk of fur missing from the sleeve of Terry's brand new big, brown shaggy coat.

Over to Channel 13, which is in a small, cramped, but friendly basement a couple of blocks from the UN and on the edge of the East River. In the studio is a small presentation area, in which sits Gene Shalit, a genial Harpo-Marx sort of character. Behind Gene are some thirty or forty people at desks with telephones. Throughout this evening and the next 11 evenings, the programmes of Channel 13 (which include English imports like *Upstairs Downstairs* and *The Ascent of Man*) are interspersed with jolly sales pitches from Gene in which he asks the audience to phone up and pledge money – five, ten dollars, whatever – to keep this non-commercial station going.

Gene Shalit's children are there (his daughter, who can't have been more than fifteen, leaned conspiratorially towards me and whispered softly, 'You know, Python and grass go very well together'), also a few fans (unattractive but keen) and we are all squashed in a small viewing/reception room. Periodically during the five hours we appear with Shalit – at one time answering phones, at another being interviewed.

The general chaotic business of the evening sorts itself out by around 12.00. Two Python shows have gone out on Channel 13 that evening, plus at least half an hour's screen time of ourselves. We later heard that the viewing figures for tonight were the highest Channel 13 ever had.

At the end of the evening, on air, we make a very committed statement about public subscription television and the freedom which it brings. Python, as far as we are concerned, could never have gone out in the States without public broadcasting – fortunately tonight has proved that we now have enough power to enable us to cock a mild snook at the commercial stranglehold on American TV.

Monday, March 10th, New York

A poor night's sleep. I have a nagging sore throat, aches all over and the appalling continuous hum of the air-conditioning outside my window. I feel just … just bad. But this is a promotional tour and physical weakness has no sympathetic hearing.

Today is dominated by a party, to be held at Sardi's restaurant, to launch us as new stars on Clive Davis' Arista label. Nancy has kept phoning, anxiously mentioning the party – there is talk of us changing (into what? We have one suit between us). Anyway, there is generally evident a feeling of rising excitement, as though one of the Main Reasons for our trip is to be fulfilled. We arrive at Arista's offices at 1776 Broadway (which must equal the White House, Pennsylvania Avenue, for *the* all-American address).

Well-dressed girls are at desks everywhere. We are given a beer each and the 'Clive won't be long now's' increase in frequency. At last the moment comes to go into the presence of Him. When I asked if we should kneel, they laughed, but slightly nervously.

The first thing that impressed me about the Great man of the American Recording Business was his office. He had the kind of exaggerated fifteen-foot desk which we write into sketches, and yet you could see he needed it. It was full of papers, letters ready for signing, telephones, intercoms, etc, etc. There seemed to be no acreage which was just added on for show. Around the walls were at least twenty gold discs, pictures of him with his family, citations from the Pope and an embossed certificate for outstanding services to the Jewish community in New York. Huge sofas and beautiful speakers and a washroom attached.

He was evidently concerned about spending money on this launch party without being sure of getting something out of the function – i.e. a little sketch from us, perhaps, a short appearance, a few jokes. He was clearly feeling his way with the Python group. He may be World Expert on Dylan, Sonny and Cher and Blood Sweat and Tears, but one got the feeling he was not yet certain about why he liked Python or why others liked Python. He was at the stage of simply being aware that people did like Python.

Like a fussy mother with new-born chicks, Davis ushered us into the lift. He twinkled, smiled, joked about the pouring rain in Broadway, 'We had it specially imported to make you feel at home', and got us all taxis. Then he bustled us into Sardi's, waiting until we'd all handed in our coats before leading us upstairs. Some 150 folk were assembled.

Clive said a few words, we joked a little and then the 'Thomas Hardy Novel-Writing' track was played. I had to pinch myself to believe it was all happening. Were we really in Sardi's, the renowned Broadway restaurant, with Clive Davis, the renowned record producer, surrounded by a crowd 'ooohing!' and 'aaahing' with uncertain delight as a not brilliant sketch about Thomas Hardy writing a novel was played over a hastily rigged-up record player system? No, it couldn't be true, I'd finally flipped. Then was everything afterwards untrue? Did a stout little lady with a Middle European accent keep badgering me about Swiss rights to Monty Python? Did the wife of Bill Ryan of *Esquire* magazine really claim that *Bert Fegg's Nasty Book* had made her laugh so much it had cured her back pains?

Tuesday, March 11th, New York

Another fitful night's sleep. Terry came in about 10.00 bearing a note from two Python groupies which had been slipped under his door last night. Jones and Palin Ltd were offered a good time in New York, by two fans who were hopelessly in love with us and had waited in the bar for five hours last night.

But we had no time for that sort of stuff. Oh, no, another Herculean day lay ahead. I felt better in my stomach today, and enjoyed a French lunch at a restaurant called Mont St Michel, in the quiet and civilised company of the cravatted John O'Connor of the *New York Times*.

Later, whilst lying flat out, but sleepless on my bed, the phone rang, and one of the co-authoresses of Terry's letter gave me a ring. They were downstairs. But this schedule has ruined me in more ways than one, and I mumbled excuses, saying that I was, well ... I was no fun at the moment!

Unfortunately TJ had asked his fan to ring back later and therein lies a grand tale. TJ was back in his room at 12.30 (after a Chinese meal we'd had together with Ina Lee Meibach and others at the Hunan Yin) when the phone rang and the persistent Python groupie told TJ she was in the lobby and would like to see him – but couldn't because 'they' wouldn't let her up to his room. Here TJ, sensing a cause, and especially one against Marriotts, made the wrong move of the evening and went downstairs. True enough, two armed guards stood by the lift and forbad TJ to take this lady up to his room.

I would love to have been a fly on the wall, for TJ, by his own account, went berserk. All the bitterness of the TWA food and the static which afflicted him unmercifully and the noisy air-conditioning, must have poured out at these poor heavily armed men. But they insisted that Terry must pay if they were to let the girl into the room. So they obviously weren't anti-hookers, they were perpetuating a system whereby hookers were OK if Marriotts got a rake-off. So Terry's wrath was well-directed and in the end he defied these thugs and got the girl upstairs. It was only then that he discovered that she was a heavy lady of un-outstanding features and by no means a beautiful princess rescued from the jaws of the dragon. The next morning Terry was therefore full of shame, he said, but the story is such a classic that I think it worthy of this full account.

Wednesday, March 12th, Barclay Hotel, Philadelphia

I never imagined, and certainly from hearing the opinions of Americans on the subject, I was never encouraged to imagine, that Philadelphia would be an improvement on New York. In fact it's like being released from jail. The Amtrak ride from Penn Central in New York is through some of the most dreary, miserable landscape in the world, a vast dumping ground – Manhattan's colostomy bag – but, in just the four hours we've been here, I've felt like a bird released from a cage. Now this may have something to do with the fact that my room looks out over the city and is on the twenty-first floor, rather than the dungeon in the Essex House which looked out on brick wall and more brick wall, but, for instance, I just heard a clock chiming – and I haven't heard that since I left London. There is light and space and air here. But unfortunately there is no time. We have done two newspaper interviews already in our twenty-first-floor suite and are about to go out to dinner … God! How food terrifies me now … I just can't wait to not see it. And after that there is a radio inter— I can't go on, I must go and change, my phone is being paged and my door banged on.

Thursday, March 13th, Philadelphia

The morning spent at the Philadelphia PBS TV studios. We recorded some direct, almost sincere, straight-to-camera promos, extolling the thinking man's channel. Then, from somewhere, they conjured up a rather nervously cheerful lady, who was going to interview us. She looked afraid but, on discovering we were nice lads, loosened up. Typical of the refreshingly disorganised set-up – this ten-minute chat suddenly took off when the director snapped his fingers and cried 'Hey, if you give me 15 minutes to get another camera, we could make this a 30-minute special!' And a 30-minute special it became.

Left Philly at 3.45 with fond memories. Arrived in Washington about 5.00. We have a sumptuous suite in the Watergate Complex, overlooking the Potomac. (A dirty river, a lady reporter told me – especially where it flows past the Pentagon, where it is full of used prophylactics.) I go around stuffing my case full of anything marked 'Watergate' – soap, writing paper, even, to Graham's irritation, the room service menu.

Saturday, March 15th, Dallas

We are driven into, or almost into, Dallas, to an incongruous looking fifteen-storey hotel set in the Oak Lawn area – full of attractive weather-boarded houses. We learnt later that these are the only old houses allowed to survive in this rich and developing city. My room at the Stoneleigh Park Hotel is quite stupendous. The bedroom has views on two sides and an eight-foot-wide, beautifully comfortable bed. A bathroom, generously proportioned, is attached, but the star turn is a long sitting-room – forty feet long at least – furnished in the Empire style, with elegant sofas, chaises longues, and Watteau reproductions on the wall.

Drove down to the PBS station, to find ourselves facing a barrage of microphones and reporters, who sat amongst the scenery and props, barring our way to the studio. I have never seen anything like it. Admittedly, most of the microphones belonged to young fresh-faced lads with cheap Philips cassette recorders and none of the mikes had NBC, ABC or CBS News stuck on the end, but this was the first time any of us have ever experienced this saturation coverage. Every word was recorded or written down, questions fell fast, one on top of the other, as did the answers. It could have been awful, but as it was so spontaneous it was exhilarating.

There are a great many people out here who do want to know *all* about Monty Python. It's as genuine, simple and direct as that. And, as a result, the self-consciousness I had always felt about talking about ourselves to English journalists, etc, does not apply here. One can answer directness only with directness.

After the 'press conference' we are moved through into the studio, which is packed, mostly with young people, college kids, and one or two 30–40-ish liberals. I am handed a rather fine stuffed armadillo, as a present from Dallas. This I hang on to throughout the interviews.

The next few hours are all handled very informally. We are in chairs on a podium and are chatted to at regular intervals by Ron Devillier,[1] programme director of the station. A lovely man, comfortably built, soft-voiced, bearded, about 35–40, with a lack of pretension and a great deal of knowledge and intelligence. Ron asks people, as usual, to ring in with pledges of money and buy membership of Channel 13 for a year. The phones ring behind and an army of volunteers answer them.

Graham establishes on the air that he is a supporter of gay causes – and gets a greater number of appreciative and enquiring calls from viewers than anyone else.

During the course of the evening they played no less than three Python shows. It was an orgy of Python – a total immersion in total enthusiasm, that didn't end until after 12.00. Thankfully we disengaged ourselves and, with about ten folk from the station, went to a tatty nearby clapboard house for a quite superb Mexican meal.

1 Ron was the man who broke *Monty Python's Flying Circus* on US television. Python's success began not in New York, but in Dallas.

I still had the armadillo with me when I got back to the hotel room and, later that night, frightened myself with it quite considerably when I went for a pee.

Sunday, March 16th, Navarro Hotel, New York

Ron Devillier picked us up at 12.00 and took us for a drive round Dallas. Devillier, clearly no lover of the downtown area – though he lives in Dallas – shows us the Kennedy Memorial, which it took eight years to put up. He says that now it is hard to imagine how much people in Dallas hated President Kennedy and all he stood for. After his assassination, classes of schoolkids cheered and a teacher who tried to give her class a day off in Kennedy's memory was fired.

We eventually found ourselves at the scene of the shooting. What struck me most was the eerie ordinariness of the spot. Possibly I'd expected the area to be razed to the ground, but here we were, on a cool March Sunday, standing on the most famous – the *only* famous – grassy knoll in the world, looking up at the Book Depository windows from which Oswald had fired, and across to the road, narrow by American standards, where Kennedy had been shot. The strongest impression is that Oswald must have been a genius to fire three times accurately from that angle, at a car travelling away from him down a sloping road. Second impression is that the grassy knoll, besides offering a much closer and easier view of the target, was an ideal place for an assassin to escape from. An expanse of open railway land, away from streets, cars, sightseers.

As we walked back to Ron's car and drove down towards the railway bridge, I reflected on how much more far-reaching an event had taken place here than the great and utterly anti-climactic triumph of America – the landing on the moon. The '60s and the '70s are notable for their disasters, not their triumphs.

American Airlines flight to NY. At La Guardia, as I wait for our luggage, with my armadillo's explicit and rather white rear end sticking out from under my arm, a heavily furred and expensively coiffed American lady drawls at me, 'Where d'you get that?' I explained I was given it by some friends in Texas. She obviously couldn't comprehend this ... 'Well, I'm from Texas and I wouldn't have given you a thing like *that.*'

We are spared the Essex House Hotel again and stay instead at the

Navarro, also on Central Park South. This is a smart, pleasant hotel, which is mercifully not part of a chain. A comfortable suite – this time on the 12th floor *and* overlooking Central Park.

I have a bath and, feeling greatly refreshed and looking forward to an evening with no interviews, TV phones to answer or any promotional activity of any kind, skip through the *NY Sunday Times*, and then down to the bar to meet Nancy. But the day is not to end totally pleasantly, for Nancy is suddenly recognised by Kit Lambert, manager, or ex-manager, of The Who (whose film *Tommy* opens in NY on Tuesday). He shouts, there is much embracing as of old friends, and he joins us at our table. He is quite obviously in an emotional state. Though he is clearly aware that we are all listening, he seems anxious to hire Nancy to work for him and offers her £1,000 a day. Nancy laughs it politely away and remains noncommittal. But Lambert has an even less tolerable friend, an English accountant, who laughs gratuitously and ingratiatingly at Lambert. He tries to chat up the waitress and makes a thoroughly unpleasant mess of it.

A young boy arrives, sits quietly and eyes the decaying Lambert with a mixture of disappointment and disgust. After a half-hour that seems like a lifetime, the festering and smouldering atmosphere is relieved by the arrival of a girl, who is also English and clearly has the unenviable task of fixing dinner for this frightful threesome. After an hour, they leave. I had warmed to Lambert in the meantime. At least he sounded bright – he reminded me of the hero of Lowry's *Under the Volcano*, with often flashes of a brilliant display of knowledge – of languages, literary references, etc. And so it didn't come as a great surprise to hear from Nancy that he is a brilliant failure. He is suing, or being sued by, The Who, who now clearly try and avoid him. He has a self-destructive urge, which takes the form at present of regular over-indulgence in cocaine and alcohol – and from his face (a handsome face) and general bearing, it looked sadly as though he was doing a good job of it.[1]

Monday, March 17th, New York

Back to promotion with a vengeance today.

A photographer was trying to get some zany photos. 'Could you all lie on the bed as if you're dead, please?' 'No,' was the easiest and most

1 Lambert died in 1981, aged 46.

painless reply. Once again we have to go into our spiel about not doing zany pictures. It now sounds like some sort of religious thing – like Jews not eating pork. But in the end we used the armadillo a lot and that seemed to keep him happy.

Down to the bar for lunch and a drink with Rik Hertzberg and friend from the *New Yorker*. We ate looking out over Central Park South and the very well-heeled class of persons passing by. Definitely one of the world's superior sidewalks. At one point a man came in and shook us all by the hand. I don't know who he was, but later he rang, saying he was a film producer and would like to 'talk over some ideas'. While we were thus on display, and chatting very pleasantly (Rik seems the nearest to one of us we've met), they pointed out a man who was apparently well-known in NY for star-spotting. He spends all his time outside hotels approaching people indiscriminately and asking them if they're celebrities. He then takes an autograph off them. Rik guaranteed that if any of us popped out of the elegant revolving door of the Navarro, we would be accosted instantly. We tried it with Terry Jones with total lack of success. Terry even hung around waiting to be recognised. Finally, in some disappointment, Rik buttonholed the star-spotter and said, 'Aren't you going to ask your usual question?' He viewed Terry rather sceptically and then said … 'OK, can you lend me ten bucks?'

Tuesday, March 25th

Grand Python reunion at the recording studio![1] [Neither Eric nor John had come on the US publicity tour.] All of us, except Terry Gilliam, contributing. John C had written a piece about a Professor of Logic. We recorded it first time. I think John's psychiatrist should be sent a copy. It was a funny piece, largely, but loaded with rather passionless and violent sexual references, which sounded odd, for some reason. But there was a generally convivial atmosphere – and we had an excellent lunch at Cheung-Cheung-Ki, about fifty yards down Wardour Street.

We decided that our next film would be 'Monty Python and the Life of Christ' – with Graham as Christ, and featuring exciting new characters like Ron the Baptist. We also decided with remarkably little fuss that we would all get together to do a six-week stage show in the US next spring.

---

1 André Jacquemin's new premises in Wardour Street.

Terry and I much brightened this evening, when we go to talk to Helen Dawson of *The Observer*,[1] who had just seen the film on her own. TJ had raced around that morning all in a tizzy trying to prevent her seeing it. Terry has this quite reasonable theory that comedy is best enjoyed with an audience of over 1,000, preferably packed closely together – but from this he has drawn the erroneous conclusion that no one can enjoy comedy *except* in a crowd of over 1,000. Helen Dawson turned out to have loved the film and laughed at all the right places and even at the Knights of Ni! She talked to us for a half-hour or so. She's a lively, capable little lady. Needless to say we both warmed to her! Terry confided that this time last night he had been unhappy because Sheridan Morley[2] had disliked the film. 'Great!' she said, 'If Sheridan Morley didn't like it, you're alright.' And she didn't say it with any malice.

Wednesday, March 26th

To London Weekend Studios for a Saturday morning children's show with Michael Wale and an audience of kids doing the interviews.

They showed two clips of the *Holy Grail* film and then the kids asked questions. First was 'How much do you think John Cleese was missed in the last series?' I went on about how we lacked an authority figure, etc, etc, at the end of which Terry said, 'Well, we really ought to ask you that question.' 'Oh, I didn't think it was half as good without him,' came the smart reply. The last question was from M Wale, who asked us what we thought of the Goodies. Up spoke young Jones and denounced the Goodies publicly for trivialising serious topics and having no values. The interview ended with a Geordie jug band group throwing eggs at us.

Good Friday, March 28th, Southwold

Really quite heavy snow in the village this morning. On the nine o'clock news they were talking of 'treacherous' conditions on the roads around London. But the sun came out and melted everything in a couple of hours. Helen and I left, in separate cars, at about 12.30. She to Abbotsley with the kids and me in the Mini to Southwold for a couple of days, as

1 Soon to marry John Osborne.
2 Son of actor Robert, Oxford contemporary of Terry Jones.

Mother had rung during the week to tell me that Father had had a sharp deterioration in his condition last Tuesday.

Physically, he is fast becoming a write-off and there's a temptation to think that death would be a merciful release – but when I see the twinkle in his watery eye when he struggles to make a joke, or the enjoyment he gets from buying and giving two boxes of chocolates to Mother on Easter morning, or his sad 'Come again, soon' as I leave, I find the 'merciful release' attitude dangerously simple.

Thursday, April 3rd

Today our second film opens in London. An encouragingly good notice in *The Guardian* this morning. Even though they exhorted the team to stay together, they couldn't remember our names: 'Cleese, Idle, Chapman, Graham and Jones'!

Graham and I did a voice-over for Bulmer's Cider in the morning. After the voice-over I dropped in at Anne's. It has taken her and Alison[1] a week to cope with the complications of tickets, parties, dummy Princess Margarets, etc – all the ramifications of a premiere which none of us really wanted, which EMI got cold feet about, and which Mark Forstater has washed his hands of. Anne, finger in the dyke, is single-handedly avoiding disaster tonight.

A very good Alexander Walker review in the *Evening Standard* ('The brightest British comedy in ages') and *Time Out*, who've also enjoyed it, help to cheer us all up, for these two are influential amongst our London audience. In fact there is no bad review today – but there is an unpleasant little piece in the *Daily Mail*. Not a review, but a variation on the Python split-up story, which seems as elusive as the Holy Grail to most papers.

In the foyer, the flabby head of EMI Distribution was trying to be jolly, but was obviously quite worried about the Princess Margaret dummy, which he had heard was to be around after all. He was clearly very nervous about how and where and when we were going to spring this royal embarrassment on them.

Up in the circle bar, the head-nodding, the hand-shaking, the across-room smiles had all begun. There were just so many people to talk to there. I talked to John Peel briefly and Brian McNulty, and Ron Hellard,

1 Alison Davies, Anne's assistant, another Python stalwart.

and even my wife. Ten-week old Rachel Mary lay, undisturbed by all this merrymaking, in a corner of the bar.

The film was very well received. Simon A, and André, both of whom were quite severe critics of the showings, both enjoyed the film for the first time tonight.

Afterwards, a party had been laid on in the stalls bar (this entirely due to Anne H and Terry G's initiative) for all the crew (who had not been invited to the later party at the Marquee).

I was particularly touched when Terry Bedford, who has had a good deal of praise in the reviews for his photography, said 'You were great.' I'm so used to being anonymous in Python that it's nice to know someone noticed.

From the Casino we all moved on to the Marquee Club. A party which I hadn't been looking forward to, but which turned out to be excellent, full of nice people and everyone in good spirits. The occasion had really been organised and paid for by Charisma – the company which we all love, but which doesn't actually seem too keen on paying us royalties.

Neil Innes, looking like a Belgian shopkeeper in his Sunday best, is on good form. He and I decide that the time has come to talk to our backers, and we converge on Messrs Page and Plant from Led Zeppelin, who are standing, almost shyly, together. They are great fans of the show – they liked the 'Bicycle Tour' particularly – and apparently many pop groups now carry video cassettes of Python, as an obligatory part of their equipment.

Sunday, April 6th

The popular press, *News of the World*, *Daily* and *Sunday Express*, *Daily Mail*, *The People*, *The Sun*, have given us rave reviews. The *News of the World* even said that the credits on their own were funnier than most comedy films.

Dilys Powell, in the *Sunday Times*, in a much longer review, was soft, kind and unenthusiastic, and *The Observer* joined *Sounds* and the *New Musical Express* in panning us. But I am generally surprised and greatly relieved by the reactions.

Graham rings to tell me that the *Sunday Express* is the latest paper to join in the Python-splitting activities, and that I am quoted this time as saying that John Cleese is interested only in the money, etc, etc. There is a long reply by John in which he says it is 'malicious' to suggest he's only interested in money.

I rang Connie after supper. She sounded quite emotional and said John was very upset, though mainly it seemed with the *Express* reporter who had rung and put words into his mouth, rather than with my alleged 'attacks' on him. John himself rang later and, if it's any satisfaction to the *Sunday Express*, we had the fullest and friendliest chat we've had for ages.

Friday, April 11th

An old-fashioned pub-crawl. Down to Cambridge Circus on the 24 bus, walk along Old Compton Street, past the cinema with its huge and quite grabbing adornment of posters, turn down Dean Street at 5.45 and into the York Minster. Eric, whose suggestion this little jaunt was, rolls along about 6.00, and we split a half bottle of champagne.

From the York Minster we move on up Dean Street to the Nellie Dean, where we find Tony Stratton-Smith, ebullient and highly excited by the first week's figures. *Grail* is No. 3 in London this week, and has grossed nearly £19,000.

I really must try and cut down on this wining and dining, but it's all part of the unnerving transitional world Python is in. Terry G and I admit we spend far more time than is healthy talking, analysing, discussing every aspect of the group and the group's dynamic, but, as Terry says, it's becoming like a drug. We need our daily fix of Python. I know as I sink, heavy-stomached into my bed, that Terry G will ring me over the weekend, and tell me how he thinks Eric's becoming very positive again ... and if we can only get rid of Graham ... goodnight Vienna ... At least we still laugh about it all.

One thing is different this time – whereas before Python in '69 we were only a moderately saleable commodity as a group, and quite unsaleable as individuals, now we have a high reputation and a good name as both. The film's success in the last couple of weeks has helped to prolong Python's life and greatly increase its prestige.

Wednesday, April 17th

This afternoon, I go to the BBC to see Jimmy Gilbert. I have already decided to turn down, on grounds of dangerous lack of time, JG's offer of the six now defunct Python slots next autumn. This didn't seem to deter him. He clearly just wants me to do a show – he isn't really concerned about subject matter and he has a director, Terry Hughes, who wants to work with me.

Terry Hughes, neat, almost over-amiable, smiling, regular-featured – he looks like an advert for suits – has been anxious to do a show with me for two years, and now clearly feels that he has priority over others when JG wants to get a show together around me.

Terry and I talk – me fencing a little to try and find TH's attitudes. He says he wants to do a show which is exciting and experimental. He drops his voice and says, wearily, 'Anything after two and a half years of *Two Ronnies*.'

So … OK, I say, I would be happy with JG's plan to commission one show, which will be the first of a series if it works. Whereas this sort of caution would have driven us mad in Python, or *Do Not Adjust*, now it suits me fine.

With Monty Python and the Holy Grail set to open in New York, we set off across the Atlantic for the second time in a month.

Thursday, April 24th, New York

Eric has been in NY since last Saturday, Terry G since Sunday and Terry J since Tuesday night – and today Graham and I have to leave hot and sunny London to join them. We take off around 12.30.

No one could be found to meet us, so we took a cab from Kennedy. Sadly we seem to have exchanged fine weather for foul. It was grey, glowering and raining as we joined the traffic jams on Van Wyck Expressway and East River Drive. Both of us hungry, so we revived ourselves with large and delicious club sandwiches and beers at the St Moritz Hotel. As we walked back to the Navarro, two girls, one Oriental and spotty, the other American and fat, accosted us. 'Oh, it's you … Oh! We've just been talking to the two Terrys and they were so nice, but Eric just walked past us!'

Friday, April 25th, New York

I was up at 6.00 and in the lobby of the Navarro at 6.30. Met John Goldstone and Eric I there and was driven in a huge, greedy limousine to the ABC *A.M. America* studios. We (the Pythons) were to co-host this nationally networked ABC TV morning show – and it runs for two hours.

At 7.00 the show began, hosted by a lady called Stephanie something or other, an attractive redhead, with a cool, head-of-school-like assurance, but she was playing along well with us. Eric kept holding up cards on which he'd scribbled things like 'Norman Mailer – Ring Your Mother'. Once or twice before an item of serious news – e.g. the fall of Saigon – Stephanie would ask us to refrain from being *too* silly, but generally we were allowed a loose rein.

Eric and I did the first hour of the show, then Graham added to our number and TG and TJ joined at 8.30. Terry G made a rude drawing of a man with slobbering tongue and staring, lust-filled eyes and held it alongside Stephanie's head as she signed off and, as the credits rolled, they actually exhorted us to wreck the studio.

No one seemed to feel it was incongruous that we should be part of a programme which included the latest bulletins on the end of America's longest war, or serious interviews about Reagan's chances in 1976.

We ended up in the Plaza Hotel for breakfast, and drank orange juice and champagne out of the largest, widest glasses I've ever seen. Typical of America, always confusing quantity and quality – to the eternal detriment of the latter.

At 12.00 we rolled up outside a modestly fashionable 'brownstone' with a recently restored front, on one of the streets somewhere in the East 60ths. This is the studio of Richard Avedon – by all accounts One of the World's Leading Photographers and He has chosen to photograph no less than us. Python is to be immortalised in the pages of *Vogue*.

Avedon turns out to be a slight, wiry, dark-skinned, bespectacled man, who could be between 25 and 55. Full of vitality and easy charm.

We are dazed from our efforts in NY and our early appearance on ABC and he must have found us a lifeless lot as he made us coffee. But after ten or 15 minutes of uninspired ideas, he leapt on the suggestion, made by Graham and Terry J, that we should be photographed in the nude. The idea sounded no worse and a lot better than putting on silly costumes or funny faces, so it was resolved. We would keep our shoes and socks on, though, and I would wear my hat.

Avedon – remarkably spry for one who has, by his own account, just worked a 15-hour, non-stop session – took us into his studio, a simple, square room, white-walled, about twenty feet high. Apart from camera equipment, simple lights and photos of Marilyn Monroe and a huge blow-up of A's photo of the Chicago Seven, the place was quite austere.

Soon the Python group were a little naked gaggle and Avedon was busy arranging us in a parody of the sort of beautiful person photo where all is revealed, but nothing is shown. So our little tadgers had to be carefully hidden behind the knee of the man in front, and so on, and every now and then Avedon would look through the viewfinder of his Rolleiflex and shout things like 'Balls! ... balls Graham, balls.'

After a few more exhortations like this, GC was heard to mutter, 'Are you *sure* he's the world-famous photographer?'

We dressed, muttering jokily amongst ourselves about how ashamed, how very ashamed, we were of what we had done. The elfin Avedon, busy as ever, talked to us as he scribbled some letter. I couldn't help noticing that the one he was writing began 'Dear Princess Margaret.'

As we walked out into the sunlit street, I felt slightly high and rather relieved, as though I'd been for an exotic medical check-up.

Took a few hours to myself this afternoon. I decided to take a trip out to the Statue of Liberty, as Tom had specially asked me to get some pictures of it. I travelled down by Subway, which is one of NY's finest features – like its telephones. It's noisy, dirty and literally every coach is covered in aerosol drawings – or just simply people's names (crisis of identity of many people in the States, suggested the *New York Times* reporter today – alienation of the individual, etc, etc). But these noisy, dirty Subways are faster, more frequent and more efficient than the London Underground, and I'm very endeared to their ear-shattering clatters and their functional stations thick with the smell of fresh-cooked doughnuts. It's a refreshing break from the carefully tailored world of limousines and hotel suites.

Missed the Statue of Liberty ferry, walked back up Broadway, bought two plastic statues of Laurel and Hardy in a tatty street market on Canal Street, so by the time I reached Gallagher's Bar to see Earl Wilson I was over half an hour late and it was raining.

The place was almost empty but, at a table in the corner, surrounded by photos of jockeys, horses, etc, Graham, Terry J, who had nobly sat in for me, Sue from the public relations agency and the small, neat, elderly and very bemused-looking E Wilson. He seemed to suffer from an unfortunate impediment for a reporter – he couldn't hear a word. Added to this, GC was being quite irresponsible and saying very strange things.

Sue, a PR lady and not a bright soul, just tried to look happy as he shouted for the fourth time in the ear of this hapless columnist, '*Penis!*'

From Gallagher's we took a cab to the offices of Don Rugoff and Cinema 5, the man and the outfit who are distributing our film in the US. He looks a fair shambles. Around 45-ish, thick glasses, a strong face, made permanently grumpy by his habit of pushing his chin into his neck and turning the sides of his mouth down. The rest of his body was mostly stomach, a huge pointed paunch which he pushes in front of him, like some antenna casing. Rugoff's voice, like his general physical presence, is rough and untidy. I liked him a lot.

We excused ourselves about 6.00, and walked back to our suite at the Navarro, where Nancy, or somebody, had organised a cheese and wine party for our friends. I suddenly realised I had had only two hours sleep in the last 36, and Italian white wine wasn't likely to revive me. But the party was quite well attended. All sorts of strange people began arriving, including Martin Scorsese, director of *Mean Streets* and *Alice Doesn't Live Here Any More*, the ubiquitous Jo Durden-Smith[1] and several Rolling Stone staffers. Ed Goodgold,[2] whose company is always good fun, maintains Python has done and will do a lot for the Gentiles in America, who've been until now totally swamped by Jewish comedians and Jewish comedy – Lenny Bruce, Woody Allen, Harvey Kurtzman, Mel Brooks, Carl Reiner, etc, etc.

Sunday, April 27th, New York

We were to be at Cinema II on Third Avenue at 11.00 a.m. to welcome the first crowds and to give out coconuts as people came out. The phone rang and woke me about 9.40. It was John Goldstone. Could we get down to the cinema as quickly as possible; there had been people queuing since 5.30 a.m. and Rugoff had already opened the film, with a special extra 9.30 performance. Time only for a delicious American grapefruit and a quick coffee and into the limousine.

When we reached the cinema there were, indeed, your actual crowds. People queuing right round the block. There was only one way into the cinema and that was through the main entrance – so through the crowds we went.

1 An Oxford contemporary. Like my friend Simon Albury, Jo worked on *World in Action*.
2 Rock group manager (Sha-Na-Na) and colleague of Nancy's at Buddah Records.

Once in the cinema we were taken to a kind of broom cupboard below stairs, where we felt like prisoners. There was coffee and doughnuts. Rugoff told us we couldn't go out of the theatre, or let ourselves be seen at a window (!) for fear of inciting riots on Third Avenue. 'We've only got one patrolman,' he kept muttering morosely. I think he hoped and expected that there would be riots, but we know our audience quite well – they want to be silly, they want to chat, they want to shake hands, they want you to sign the plaster on their broken arms, but generally speaking they don't want to tear us limb from limb.

But they did fill the cinema all day long and Rugoff was able to claim at the end of the day a house record take of ten and a half thousand dollars. He even had photographers taking pictures of the crowds (which he was later to use in a very good double page *Variety* ad).

Plant and Page from Led Zeppelin came to the 8.00 performance, which brightened things up a little. We greet each other like old friends now. Suddenly someone shouted 'Led Zeppelin!' as we talked and, as the chant grew, we moved discreetly away – for they *can* cause riots.

Monday, April 28th, New York

To see Clive Davis at Arista. He smiled benignly round at us all. Chided us for doing a nude spread in *Vogue*, but not *Playboy*, which is where the market is. The *Matching Tie* album has been out a week and a bit and already he's getting a good demand for it, he says. He even gets us to talk to eighteen countrywide reps, who are at this moment all connected up on a conference line. So we say 'hello' to disembodied voices in LA and Chicago and Davis encourages them to 'break records, to sell records'.

The whole tenor of our discussion today is that of an enlightened headmaster to his star pupils. He's giving us a lot of rope, but he still firmly holds the end.

To a sound studio to record some radio commercials for Don Rugoff. Terry and I manage to write and record three 30-second commercials before Rugoff finally turns up. I've noticed the look in people's eyes when he's around. He seems so harmless and yet he must have a reputation, for there is a look of anticipated fear and anxiety which flashes across people's faces in his presence. I've seen it with Sue, the PR lady, and I saw it again today in the eyes of the girl who was organising this voice-over session. Rugoff grumpily accused people of not doing their job properly. He introduced an air of tension and then accused everyone of not being relaxed. He asked me to do it more upbeat, which was completely wrong, and had to change his mind afterwards. The only light in this hour of greyness was when we played him the three commercials we'd done – and he liked them all. He actually smiled. So everyone relaxes and is happy and Rugoff wins hands down because he is a lovable bastard.

So, on to the party, held in the massage parlour of the Commodore Hotel in honour of Python. As we swept in, high in the sky with our well-nurtured popularity, the photographers looked past us to see if there was anyone famous around. It was a total, unreal, fantasy. Clive Davis ushered me over to meet Andy Warhol. I talked a while to the King of the Beautiful People. Led Zeppelin were there and Jeff Beck and Dick Cavett, but *no* Norman Mailer or John Lennon or anyone *really* interesting!

I just remember Loudon Wainwright III, to whom I was very effusive and gave my address, and the rather lovely dark eyes of one of the masseuses.

Thursday, May 8th, Southwold

A perfect May morning – a slight haze clearing away from the trees and fields in the distance. Cows munching the lush, rain-soaked grass in the sunshine. A nine-hour sleep behind me. I feel as contented as the cows.

Have promised to take Dad to Lowestoft – which we do. He needs someone around all the time, and I have to try and get to his stream of dribble before it hits the newly polished floor of a shop. A wonderful piece of Englishness – there is a new and splendid library in Lowestoft, and here my father would have been really happy. However, on approaching it, we are faced with a notice on the door: 'OPENING OF THE NEW LIBRARY ...' – encouraging so far – '... THE LIBRARY WILL BE CLOSED ALL DAY FOR THE OPENING'.

Father had given me an excellent birthday present, conceived, bought and wrapped entirely by himself. It was a big Adnams poster showing all their pubs, and we used it to find ourselves a splendid little place called the Wherry Inn at Geldeston, a little village tucked away a mile or two off the Beccles–Norwich road. A friendly pub in a friendly village; everyone stopping for a chat with each other. We were able to sit out in the sun, on our own, with beer and sandwiches, and Father could droop and dribble to his heart's content and still enjoy himself.

A trip which cheered us all up. And Father is rarely cheerful these days. I went for a walk last night with him, and he told me that he really would like to be 75, and after that he doesn't care.

Tuesday, May 13th

Eric's new show *Rutland Weekend Television* was on for the first time last night. Quite a milestone for Python – the first TV manifestation of the parting of the ways. Not a world-shattering show, but a very palatable half-hour's TV. I didn't feel that Python was being used. Of course there were ideas which Eric would not have written without the influence of five years with Python, but it was still very much his work, his show and his particular kind of humour. Bits went on beyond the cutting stage, some ideas were woolly and it lacked the solid richness of Python, but I enjoyed it and TG, who was watching with me, felt the same. A neat, nice and simple idea too – a TV station with no money. Neil Innes as great as ever, and the camerawork made it seem anything but cheap. GC rang afterwards, he didn't like it. I smell grapes.

Stephen Frears, the director of *Three Men in a Boat*, comes round to see me. He makes the distinction between Pythons and 'actors' and says that the others he will get will be actors. He ends up giving me the script to read and says he thinks of me as Harris. We chatted for an hour or so. He didn't relax me a great deal – he's rather a disconcerting guy, with big, round, slightly poppy eyes, unkempt hair and clothes and a rambling, discursive style of talking which makes it very difficult for me to tell what he's actually saying.

After I'd read it, I rang him back, as he'd asked. He was pleased that I liked the script (Stoppard – very impressive, funny and yet full of period feeling, a sympathetic adaptation of the book, full of love of the Thames Valley). But he rambled a little about getting all the three actors at once, then apportioning parts only after he'd selected all three and played around with their relative ages, physical appearances, etc, etc. So would I mind waiting for a final decision? This confused me, I must say, but all I could say was I was 100% enthusiastic and to be involved as any of the three characters would be tremendous fun. I'm not sure whether he is preparing me for the worst or not.

Helen had made a superb steak and kidney pie with a *Three Men in a Boat* design on it. We ate it with a half-bottle of Bollinger '64!! A little prematurely, perhaps.

Thursday, May 15th

Mid-afternoon and I'm rewriting the last two pages of one of our Crucible plays[1] when Tony Stratton rings. He was having dinner last night with Steve O'Rourke – Pink Floyd's manager. Floyd are very keen to get us on the bill for their prestigious open-air gig at Knebworth in July. We'd said no, but O'Rourke has made us a new offer. For five of us, a half-hour cabaret appearance, £1,000 each in notes, no questions asked, ready at the end of the show. It's like an offer from the underworld.

Cleese rang. The *Sunday Express* have apologised for the article a month or so back in which I apparently accused John of working for money only. They want to give John and me a lunch. John keen on acceptance, which I went along with against my better judgement.

Friday, May 16th

Read *Three Men in a Boat*, as I got a call asking me to go and meet Frears and Tom Stoppard for tea at the Waldorf at 5.00. On re-reading, Harris is really the part I would like (he's the funniest), though I still feel I'm physically wrong.

At the Waldorf at 5.05. Tea is taken in a tall-ceiling lounge, with steps down to a sunken dance floor. Frears and Stoppard are discreetly tucked away on a sofa in the corner. Frears, crumpled and worried-looking, Stoppard, a lean and neatly dressed contrast. Frears introduces me to Stoppard and we make small talk about sharing agents, etc. Tea is ordered. It turns out that Stoppard is very easy-going about the play. Evidently it is Frears who is going through agonies of indecision on the casting. There doesn't seem to be too much worry about myself. Stoppard is complimentary and says virtually do whichever part you like. Much discussion on whether, if I was Harris, I should eat potatoes and drink beer for a month to 'heavy' myself up. I decline a sickly cake, as one passes on a silver tray.

Stoppard a breath of fresh air after Frears' gloomy frownings. He says, when it all boils down to it, filming is about getting together a group of people you like. He quotes Evelyn Waugh, 'The Second World War wasn't bad, provided you were with nice people.'

1 Two short plays commissioned by David Leland from Terry and myself for the Sheffield Crucible's studio.

So the conversation steers away from me, without a decision, and on to who should be J – the other main part. Tim Curry of *Rocky Horror* fame is suggested as having the right public school background. Frears is worried that Tim may be enjoying life too much in Los Angeles. Robert Powell is suggested.[1] They both agree he's brilliant, but Stoppard is doubtful about his looks. 'He's a little Spanish-looking, gypsy-like for J.' So nothing is decided.

Stoppard has to go to a rehearsal of *Travesties* (yet another in his long line of award-winning plays) next door at the Aldwych. As he leaves we shake hands and he says, 'If I next see you in a striped blazer and a boater with a pillow stuffed up your trousers, I'd be very pleased.'

Saturday, May 17th

It's foul weather again. Little sympathy among the gods for Gospel Oak's Nuts in May Festival. Mary and Catherine B [Helen's sister and her daughter] lunch here and we stand in the rain in Lamble Street waiting for the procession to appear. Bedraggled but unbowed, the floats begin to turn the corner from Grafton Road. They vary from flower gardens, to pleasantly unspectacular scenes of nursing life, to a Gothic anti-eviction float from the squatters, with a huge, bloody papier-mâché axe poised above the grinning kids on top of the float. On one a girl dances like the neighbourhood Isadora, long, flowing, rather absurd movements, for she is dressed in army boots and is clearly well stoned. There is a huge carnival traffic jam in Lamble Street as they try to manoeuvre an extra-large float into Lismore Circus. I film some of it. No respite for my identity problem. I am spotted by two girls atop the Inter-Action Art Bus, who wave excitedly. One of them bends down to shout something into the cab. Within moments the loudspeaker booms out 'A big hello to Mr Eric Idle, who you can see is with us today.'

Thursday, May 22nd

Out to lunch at Gay Hussar with John Cleese and the *Sunday Express*.

The *Sunday Express* was represented by an attractive, dark-haired, heavily-pregnant lady called Olga something,[2] who turned out to be a

---

1 Popular actor – *Doomwatch, Jude the Obscure*. Chosen to play Jesus Christ in Zeffirelli's TV mini-series, *Jesus of Nazareth*.
2 Lady Olga Maitland, later a Tory MP.

writer for the Express *Diary* (no, *not* the Express *Dairy*). She tried hard to be nice and understanding, and in return we were models of public school charm and politeness. I'm glad it was just a diary story, because this sweet lady did constantly get the wrong end of the stick, and I would hate to have entrusted her with hard information. But I suppose she will be the first journalist to learn of our plans for a new film – and my part in *Three Men*.

At 6.00 at the Henshaws' for a Python meeting. All present, except Eric, who is in France. Briskly it was decided to set aside Sept/Oct period of 1976 to write a new film and May/June 1977 to film it.

Gilliam is the lone voice of bitter protest against this timetable. He rants and raves about 'leisurely lives' and clearly fears that we are signing ourselves a death warrant. The rest of us accept it. Actually I think what we have decided is quite sensible, though I feel that a year's break would have been better than eighteen months – and he's right, there's no certainty that when the next movie comes out – in New Year 1978 – Python will carry the same impetus which is filling the box offices at the moment.

My dates for *Three Men in a Boat* were confirmed today. They amount to nearly six weeks' work. The fee is a little more than half what I was offered to spend half an hour at the Knebworth concert. C'est showbiz.

Saturday, May 24th

Copy of a letter arrived in the post from Maurice Girodias, famous publisher of the Olympia Press in Paris in the 1950s – the first man to publish *Candy, Lolita, The Ginger Man* and other post-war underground classics which are now school curriculum material. He's a pioneer of total literary freedom and apparently has run into trouble over the last few years (since *Last Exit to Brooklyn*) from Sir Cyril Black.[1] He was served with writs by Sir Cyril after Girodias had, in his own words, 'published under the Ophelia Press imprint a book with the title "Sir Cyril Black", in which a particularly vicious villain carries that noble name'.

Girodias now wants us to appear as witnesses at his trial. He says 'I am sure they (MP) will not be indifferent to my plight since, after all, I have fought many battles in the past which have opened the way to the (relative) freedom of expressive opinion we are now enjoying,' and later

---

1 A Tory MP and deeply religious, pro-censorship, disciplinarian, temperance campaigner.

slightly fudges the fine moral tone by saying 'such an occasion could be turned into a rather wild occasion for both publicity and fun, rolled into one'. He even says he can apply for a postponement of the trial if we are not available. To be asked to appear at Girodias's trial has the same ring of unreality as being photographed by Richard Avedon.

What do we do? I am utterly opposed to such bigots as Sir Cyril Black; of Girodias I know nothing except his taste in literature, which roughly accords with my own. So support should be given. But three or four days in New York at the end of the week would deal my already limited writing time a severe blow. Also our appearance would be publicised in a way in which we have no control. We need to be absolutely certain ourselves about our dedication to Girodias, our knowledge of the case, and how we feel we can best help.

So I am trying to concentrate on what I do know about – my writing – through which my own views about Sir Cyril Black can, I feel, be better put over than by attending a show trial in New York.

But I feel so weak for not doing anything. I certainly feel Python's name should be linked with this very worthy cause in some way. This difficult moral problem disturbed me more than it ought as I sat on the loo reading the letter before breakfast.

Monday, May 26th

En famille, we drove up to South End Green, briefly surveyed the photo display for *Monty Python and the Holy Grail* playing at the Hampstead Classic this week, then went on to sample the delights of the Bank Holiday Fair on the Heath. Subjected ourselves to the usual gut-gripping violence on Big Wheels, Rotordyne, where you are spun round at colossal force until you stick to the wall, and Whizzers, where you're just hurled around until you feel your stomach is going to come out of the top of your head.

Thursday, May 29th

Yesterday I started on one of the 'atmosphere' pieces for the Jimmy Gilbert show. Set in a boys' school in Edwardian England. I read it to Terry this morning, who enthused greatly – but he's worried that Light Entertainment will do it badly and the 'atmosphere' which it needs may be lost. I am enjoying the writing routine again, though.

Monday, June 2nd

Referendum day is Thursday,[1] and we are alternately told that whatever we say doesn't matter a jot in the great pattern of things (James Cameron in *The Guardian* on Saturday) or that it is the most important decision we will ever make in our lives (most politicians). I am still undecided. In both cases it boils down to having confidence in Britain. Either to stay in Europe and keep up with the fast pace of material progress which undoubtedly have made France and Germany quite attractive places to live in, or to have the confidence to break from the incentive and the protection of Europe and become a one country independent free trader, as in the good old days. Neither decision, I think, involves the downfall of our nation. Once a decision is taken it will all be absorbed into the system and the country will carry on working (or not working) as it always did. For once a major politico-economic issue in Britain has not been debated on purely class lines. Tories mix with Labour, socialists with Monday Clubbers, unionists and bosses on pro and anti platforms. Only the implacable revolutionaries, who see the Common Market as a purely and quite reprehensibly capitalist device, seem to have a unity in the ranks.

I tend towards Cameron's view – though I will probably vote 'No' as a vote against the smugness and complacency of the over-subscribed 'Yes' campaign. I think Britain will survive both decisions – but it will be more exciting, I feel, to watch the consequences of a 'No' vote and, as one of society's little band of jesters, excitement helps my business.

Drove down to Terry's in a torrential storm, with cold winds whipping round the car. We worked steadily on with 'F J Tomkinson's Schooldays' – as the half-hour has now become. It needs consolidating and tightening, which we do bit by bit. As usual the last ten minutes are the most difficult.

Drove home in another storm. Watched a long TV Referendum debate. There ought to be one channel, run as a public service, which broadcasts all parliamentary proceedings, because they are quite involving and, rather than bore the pants off everyone, they may cure our national political apathy, for on major issues like this there are some very good performers about.

1 Harold Wilson's Labour government asked the question 'Do you think the UK should stay in the European Community?' Edward Heath's Tory government had taken us in on January 1st, 1973.

John Goldstone rang to say that the *Grail* has broken records on its opening in Philadelphia and Toronto and that Don Rugoff has plans to transfer it to a new cinema in NY and wants to have a death cart trundled through the streets of NY as an ad. Given Mayor Beame's reported plans to sack 67,000 city workers in order to meet huge unpaid bills, this may be a public service as well as a publicity stunt.

Thursday, June 5th

Today at 10.00 I remembered that our kitchen was to be photographed by the Royal Duke.[1] So there was hasty cleaning of the kitchen, then Helen took Rachel and William off for injections (routine NHS stuff). While she was away, I locked myself out while emptying the waste-paper basket. Managed to enlist the sporty help of Clare Latimer[2] next door, but trod in dog shit in her yard, then nearly castrated myself on our roses and fencing. She laughed and declared it was all very Monty Python. In the end I climbed over the roofs and into my room, just in time to clean the shit off my shoes and welcome the Duke of Gloucester into the kitchen.

Cast my vote in the Referendum. I voted 'Yes' because I was not in the end convinced that the retention of our full sovereignty and the total freedom to make our own decisions, which was the cornerstone of the Noes' case, was jeopardised seriously enough by entering the Market. And I feel that the grey men of Brussels are no worse than the grey men of Whitehall anyway. But I didn't decide on my vote until this morning, when I read the words of one of my favourite gurus, Keith Waterhouse.[3] He would vote 'Yes' he thought, but without great enthusiasm for the Referendum or the way its campaign has been conducted, because of the attractions of the European quality of life! And he concludes, 'I may be naïve in hoping that remaining in Europe will make us more European, but after a thousand years of insularity from which have evolved the bingo parlour, carbonised beer and *Crossroads*, I am inclined to give it a whirl.'[4]

1 The Duke of Gloucester was a partner in Hunt Thompson – for whom my brother-in-law worked as an architect. They designed a number of improvements to the house.
2 Clare Latimer, our neighbour for many years. Now a celebrated caterer and food writer.
3 *Daily Mirror* columnist, novelist and playwright – *Billy Liar, Jeffrey Bernard Is Unwell.*
4 67 per cent said yes. Of the administrative regions, the only rejections were in Shetland and the Western Isles.

Tuesday, June 10th

The hot weather continues. Spent yesterday and most of today working on the last quarter of the Palin Show script. Quite pleased with progress – at least there is now an ending.

Midway through the afternoon, drove over to TV Centre to have my hair shorn unmercifully.

With my new short back and sides, drove over to Cosprops in Regent's Park Road to try on the blazers, striped swimsuits, etc, for *Three Men*. Stephen Moore (George)[1] and Stephen Frears and I went for a drink afterwards. Moore is a delightfully easy-going, affable bloke, very good company. Frears is very endearing in his scruffy, self-deprecating way. I like them both a great deal.

Wednesday, June 11th

The first-time writer, director and all three Men in the Boat get together. The place, the airless, featureless cell of room BO 55 at the TV Centre. Present today, narrow Tom Stoppard, eyes sparkling. 'How are *you* today, Michael?' Rather quiet, frazzled, detached producer – Rosemary Hill. She looks anxious. Two large PAs – one of whom I later discover is Jack Hawkins'[2] son. The dog, Montmorency, who is at least affectionate. Stephen M and last, but not least, Tim Curry – smaller than I expected, dark/olive-skinned, curly-haired, with prominent eyes.

The read-through goes well. At the end Frears says the casting was exactly right, and one gets the feeling that all three of us fit Jerome's characters near enough to require no great feats of acting. Stoppard is pleased too. Rosemary Hill does not express an opinion, but is more concerned with the fact that it's going to be too long. Stoppard and Frears are clearly opposed to making major cuts at this point – so the discussion drags on in a rather desultory way. I don't think anything very worthy will ever be decided in BO 55.

Up to the bar, where I met Tim B-T and Graeme Garden (surrounded by beautiful women). They are on *Top of the Pops*, plugging their latest epic 'Black Pudding Bertha' tonight and Graeme has just had a son. They are quite envious about the *Three Men in a Boat* job.

1 An Old Vic, Royal Court actor, just beginning to make his name in television.
2 Jack Hawkins (1910-73), star of many of the classic movies of my childhood – *The Cruel Sea, Bridge on the River Kwai*, etc.

Thursday, June 12th, Southwold

The weather continues to be dazzling, perfect, clear hot sunshine. Up to Southwold on the 9.30 train to take my parents to see the *Holy Grail* film which starts today at Norwich. Some twenty or thirty people at the 1.40 showing. I enjoyed watching the film today more than I've ever done. It may partly have been due to the fact that I was carrying one and a half pints of Adnams, but I think it was because I was under no strain, rush or pressure, as at previous showings – premieres, etc. I was also able to crystallise and analyse my disappointments in the film – there is a patch where we really do lose touch with the audience, and that's at the end of the otherwise excellent 'Wedding' scene, through the old lady in the 'Ni' village, and the second 'Knights' which terminate in easily the most embarrassing piece of the film, when the king meets Sir Robin in the forest. But I think the parents enjoyed it, and Daddy laughed quite spontaneously a few times.

A quick trip to the cathedral, then home to Croft Cottage, where we sat in the sunshine and had a cup of tea. Daddy's chair kept tipping over and once, when he'd taken a bite of rock cake, his teeth came out firmly clamped to the rock cake.

Read Thomas Hardy's *The Trumpet-Major* as I rattled home on the 6.30 train from Darsham.

Friday, June 13th

In the afternoon I had a tetanus jab at the BBC because of the suspicious nature of the Berkshire Thames – it rather deromanticised the whole thing – then Tim, Stephen M, Stephen F and I roared up the M4 in Stephen F's very shabby Cortina, through Reading and up to Goring, where we found the thirty-foot skiff, which we will get to know rather well over the next three or four weeks. We bought some tea, and went for a trial row up the river. We fell uncannily easily into the roles. I rowed, because I like rowing and generally getting things done (being Harris), Tim, in dark reflecting glasses, languidly took the rudder, while Stephen M just generally helped.

Monday, June 16th

The first day's filming on *Three Men in a Boat*. Up at 7.00.

A brilliantly sunny morning as I drove to the BBC. It didn't stay like that and, by the time of our third or fourth shot at a boathouse at Walton, we were indoors, sheltering from the rain. But there were sufficient breaks in the showers for us to maintain a good rate of filming, despite having to get used to the boat, full of gear and Montmorency the dog. It's bad enough having to do retakes anyway, but to row yourself back for the retakes often adds insult to injury.

Stephen F comes to life and directs briskly, but not at all autocratically. We tend to cover sequences from more than one angle, and Brian Tufano, the most prestigious BBC cameraman, is painstaking over light and composition of shots.

Tom Stoppard is in attendance – very friendly – a rather languid figure in his expensive woollen jacket, loose-fitting camel-coloured slacks and Gucci bag full of scripts. He gives Tim and me a lift to one of the locations in his metallic green BMW automatic. I can't help noticing high-class jetsam in the car – an invitation from 'Mr and Mrs Kingsley Amis at home'.

I find the combination of the long hours – shooting began at 9.30 and ended at a quarter to seven – the concentration of my rusty mind on lines and performance, and the physical effort of rowing and controlling the boat, utterly exhausting.

To bed at 11.15, but woke at 3.00, and tossed and turned for an hour or so, full of depressing thoughts as to my stamina and ability to go through three weeks of this. Got up at 8.00, still feeling heavy and gloomy.

Wednesday, June 18th

Filming began at Datchet – in sunshine. Police were on hand to clear a stretch of riverside road so we could film with the houses behind. After one take they told us that one of the cars held up by the filming was the royal party on its way to Ascot!

Windsor Castle, like a huge and over-drawn backcloth for a fairy tale, lay in the sun on the left bank. We worked our way up the river, ending in a sort of surreal evening sequence in the majestic, silent serenity of Cliveden Reach. Tim, Stephen and I in our little sculling skiff, the crew on Tufano's specially designed camera boat – a simple flat-bottomed 15 feet x 6 feet rectangle with a scaffolding frame all around from which the camera hangs on a specially balanced spring (called a pantograph). It looks like a floating four-poster.

We finish filming today at about ten past eight. I drive Tim, Stephen and myself to the Swan Hotel, Streatley – our base for the rest of the film. We arrive at about 9.15. We're all rather tired and hungry after a long day.

Our first contact with the staff of this pleasantly situated riverside hotel goes something like this:

Us: 'Can we ... eat here, please?'

She   (small, bespectacled, young): 'Ooh *no*!'

Us: 'Why ... er ... why not?'

She: 'It's after quarter to nine.'

Myself (seasoned to this, so valiantly co-operative): 'Oh, I see ... and there's no chance of squeezing a meal in for us?' (We do see people eating in the dining-room.)

She: 'No.'

Us: 'A sandwich ... or just a piece of cheese?'

She: 'No.'

Us: 'Is there anywhere round here ... ?'

She   (oh how Jerome K Jerome would have laughed): 'There's a Chinese in Pangbourne.'

Us: 'Well ... we might try that.'

She: 'Oh, we do have a problem. We close the hotel at 11.30 and there are only two keys.'

Stephen and I – Tim adapting to the situation and choosing to sit out beside the river and sip white wine – make our way to a charming thatched-roof little pub up the road called the Bull. It's 10.15 – they close at 10.30. Here the conversation goes (after ordering a drink):

Us: 'Can we ... get anything to eat?'

She   (small, fat, middle-aged – what the girl at the Swan will probably turn into): 'No.'

Us: 'Is there ... ?'

She   (triumphantly indicating empty food cabinet on bar): 'Oh, no. There's nothing left now.'

We manage to order some nuts and crisps, though we are given these with heavy reluctance and much raising of eyes to heaven.

Us: 'Oh, and some pickled onions, please.'

The order arrives without pickled onions.

Us: 'Pickled onions?'

She   (after brief conversation with friend): 'No, I can't give you any.'

Us   (jaws going slack rather than tempers rising): 'What ... ?'

She: 'I can't give you any. I'm not allowed to.'

The combination of the Swan and the Bull was fairly deadly. This is Southern England with a vengeance. We feel like lepers, as we walk down the pretty, the fucking pretty little main street, clutching some of the crisps she was good enough to let us have.

Saturday, June 21st, Southwold

The longest day and my father's three-quarter century.

Present at the party were all our family, including Rachel, just five months. There was champagne on the lawn and then various pies, patés, cold meats, salads, strawberries and coffee, etc, inside. The house coped well with the numbers and the sunshine helped to bring the whole thing to life.

Father was not in bad form – he finds it difficult to get his words out, but he was aware of who everyone was and what was going on, and smiled and drank rather a lot of champagne and didn't get cross at all. It was really as successful as I ever dared hope.

Wednesday, June 25th, Streatley

Danny La Rue[1] has been in residence, or in evidence, at the Swan this week; he is Chairman of the hotel, a fact which must account for the occasional groups of middle-aged ladies who are to be found standing on the bridge and gaping down at it. Danny gravitated rather surely towards Tim, but, in the bar after the meal, he was clearly anxious to talk to any of us. He talked mainly about the wonderful tour he'd just finished and how he'd broken all box-office records at Scarborough, only two or three nights ago. He really exudes star and showbiz. His talk is self-boosting, he has a small entourage, including one very beautiful young man, who hover about him. I have occasionally seen his eyes flick around the bar with a sort of panic, when he has no one to talk to.

None of us have, of course, been anything less than charming to him, however. No one has so much as hinted that his hotel must be one of the most beautiful and worst-run in England.

---

1 Irish-born cabaret star. Brought the art of female impersonation out of the night-clubs and into the mainstream.

Friday, June 27th, Streatley

The weather looked like breaking this morning; grey clouds piled up, but no rain. Spent most of the morning reading James Cameron's *An Indian Summer*, basking in the near perfect balance of his intelligence, humour and sensitivity.

I read in the Mini parked by the side of a lane at Bushey Lock, on the Upper Reaches beyond Abingdon, where Stephen M and Harry Markham were doing a scene. Harry Markham was in Stephen F's highly praised *Sunset Across the Bay* and he's one of Stephen's favourite actors. He's only on the film one day, but he comes down with his wife, Edna – they're a very dear, down-to-earth Northern couple, a great antidote to Hampstead. I asked them about their hobby, which turns out to be walking along canals. They recently walked the Liverpool–Leeds canal.

'Oh, how lovely,' I gushed.

'Oh, bits of it are very dangerous, you know,' replies Harry very seriously.

Edna is equally serious. 'There was a gang of youths came up to us just outside Liverpool … they started fingering his windcheater …'

A pleasant lunchtime drink at the Trout at Bushey Lock – an out-of-the-way pub, with very friendly clientele. I learn a little more about Tim, who used to be rather quiet for the first few days, but has gradually opened up and become more garrulous and at times quite ebullient. He told me today that his father was a naval chaplain, who died when he was 12, and from then on he was brought up by women. There's a soft, very English quality about Tim which is quite at odds with the *Rocky Horror*/Lou Adler LP side.[1]

Tuesday, July 1st, Streatley

Stephen F doesn't really like days when there are a lot of extras. The awful depression he affects on such days, when shots take a long time to set up and then someone hasn't understood and walks slap across shot at the vital moment, is, I think, quite deep-seated.

Annie Z[2] says that Stephen totally lives the film while he's working. He's

1 Tim created the role of Frank N. Furter in *The Rocky Horror Show*.
2 Anne Zelda: actress. Stephen's girlfriend, now wife. She appears in the *Ripping Yarn* 'Murder at Moorstones Manor'.

one of life's restless pacers, she says. Some mornings he starts pacing about six o'clock.

Anyway, the first of July has a richly comic ending. 'Tucker' Leach, one of the Props boys, a cheerful stammerer, who is no intellectual giant, plays his second role of the day – as a passenger on board a steamship that nearly runs us down (again!). After complicated positions have been worked out, the shot finally gets under way. It's a good take – which actually ends on my line as the steamboat swishes past: 'I say, any chance of a tow?' No sooner have I said the line, than Tucker yells back, loud and clear and deliciously in shot, 'No way!'

Wednesday, July 2nd, Streatley

The morning's hot again, and I'm settling down to a cup of coffee and a read of the Palin Show script, before sending it off to Terry Hughes. But Stephen F finds me and, motioning vaguely to the terrace in front of the hotel, invites me to bring my coffee along and join everyone. Everyone turns out to be me and Stephen.

He tells me that, in addition to the already crowded schedule, he wants to reshoot the dead dog floating down the river sequence. It was shot in an end-of-the-week afternoon of careless abandon last Friday, and both Stephen and Brian are aware they've shot it in a dull way. An example of the difference between LE and Drama shooting. I've never, in all my experience of Python filming, both on TV and in two movies, ever been involved in a retake of a scene for purely artistic reasons.

I scribble a note off to Terry Hughes, enclosing the script.

Retake the dead dog sequence. This time it worked well – the Woolworths toy dog, which had looked rather ineffective last time, was replaced by a newly killed sheep, which gave an Oscar-winning performance.

Sunday, July 6th, Streatley

Talked to Tom Stoppard on a sunny lawn between takes. He seems to be a little preoccupied with rehearsals for *Travesties* for the US tour. Stephen M tells me that sometimes Tom's rather forthright notes to the actors have caused some of them to walk out on him. On this film he has been discreetly available – present for a few hours most days – but sometimes marooned on the wrong side of the river, as we are often rather difficult to find. He liaises with Stephen mainly and doesn't talk a great deal to us about the way things should be played. He brings his kids – his younger set of kids – out with him, and on occasions his wife, the buoyantly chatty Dr Miriam Stoppard, and at Radcote Lock the other day, he even appeared with his mother. It was rather sweet really – she sat in the limited shade of a lifebelt holder watching us sweat in the lock, with a copy of a magazine article about Tom laid open beside her.

Wednesday, July 9th, Streatley

The final day of filming. We ended, rather fittingly, with a long journey down the river in bright sunshine, from Shepperton Lock to Hampton Court. Brian T, who was in good form, kept stopping to take shots of swans, ducks, willow trees waving and other artistic items that caught his eye. As we passed Hampton Church he began murmuring about needing a shot of it, etc, and for the first time in the entire film, I thought I was aware of Stephen F curbing Brian's enthusiasm, because of lack of time. In the last two or three days word has clearly filtered through from the BBC that *Three Men in a Boat* is costing too much. Then, after we passed an island, the church reappeared with the sun behind it and framed by tall trees and Brian could control himself no longer. Stephen responded and the boats turned and stopped and the shot was taken.

Back to Hampton Court Pier and a last drink with the crew at the Mitre hotel. The last I see of Tim and Stephen Moore is on the corner of Hammersmith Broadway.

Thursday, July 10th

Wrote letters, played squash with Terry, and tried to put off the inevitable moment when I would have to re-immerse myself in the affairs of Python. I have tasted self-sufficiency for four weeks and a most agreeable taste it is.

Friday, July 11th

Our nude photo, which makes us all look rather blatantly and unsexily bare, appears as a full page spread in *Vogue*. The photo is fun, but accompanying it is the most dreadful piece of blurb about 'Monty

Python … that six-manic, smash-them, trash-them comedy commune from Britain.'

Monday, July 14th

To the BBC by 12.00 to meet Terry Hughes and so really begin the Palin Show project. Both Terry and Jimmy G have apparently liked the script. It's clearly too long, but I'm heartened and encouraged by Terry H's attitude, which is to try and do it as a 45-minute special. Jimmy G is adamant at the moment about 30 minutes.

We discuss the thorny subject of casting briefly. Terry J wants to play Tomkinson's mother, but I'm afraid that TJ in drag does have an instant link with Python and may disturb the reality which the character needs in this particular script. But major decisions are put into abeyance until we have done our rewriting.

Sunday, July 20th

Wrote to Al Levinson, the wise, likeable American I met at the Henshaws' last year. His letters still outnumber mine three to one, but I enjoy writing to him. It's being required to step back and look at yourself and your life in relation to someone 3,000 miles away, whom you have hardly met, but with whom you feel an unexplainable empathy. Ours is purely a literary relationship, a written relationship. It's different from all my other relationships. That's what makes it interesting and stimulating too, I suppose.

Tuesday, July 22nd

Terry and I worked together today on *Fegg*. It's the third successive day I've spent on new material for the book [for the upcoming American edition].

Then up to Dr Chapman's house at Southwood Lane, Highgate, for an interview with a Yugoslav journalist – for the Yugoslavs have apparently bought the *Holy Grail* film. A squat, rather scrubby-bearded man with a tape recorder was sitting on his own in what passes for Graham's sitting room. I said hello, then heard a shout of 'Get your trousers off, then', in a bad Scottish accent, from the next room. McKenna, Bernard was there, surrounded by sheaves of paper, covered in his squiggles, looking harassed, while Dr Chapman sat in his usual writing attitude – glass of gin and tonic in one hand, legs stretched out, gazing into space.

Graham looked grey – as if he had spent the last five years un-dead. Which really was nearer the truth than it seemed. Graham, having lately fallen in with Ringo Starr – for whom he and Douglas have written a TV spectacular (American) – has also drifted into the Keith Moon/Harry Nilsson orbit.[1] Now Moon is a genuine loony and drives Rolls Royces into swimming pools and leaves them there, but Nilsson, as I heard from Tim Curry, and heard again tonight from a slurred and shattered Chapman, is a man bent on self-destruction. Graham, sounding like a Sunday school child on an outing to Sodom, told me how Nilsson had had to be helped from GC's house last night utterly and totally smashed. Graham had bruises today to show for it. Nilsson drinks neat gin – a bottle in one evening – pops every pill possible, but most of the time prefers cocaine. Graham was really shocked.

We talked for an hour or so to the very affable Yugoslav, who told us that there had been many anti-Python protests in Yugoslavia, but that the show had become a rallying point.

Sunday, July 27th

I began work just after 9.00, writing up a couple of new ideas. Terry, Alison and Sally arrived about 10.00 and, whilst Helen packed and Alison and Sally took William up to Parliament Hill and Thomas watched *Thunderbirds*, Terry and I sat in the increasingly uncomfortable heat of the work-room and slogged away at *Fegg* with a ferocious concentration.

The room became hotter – outside the temperature was over 80° – and we finally emerged, like the National Union of Railwaymen after an all-day attempt to avert a strike, sweaty, crumpled but happy, at 9.30 in the evening.

We opened a bottle of champagne and celebrated wearily amongst the piles of washing, clothing, toys, cameras and books destined for Italy. For myself, it couldn't be better timing. To have worked literally to the last moment, and to be able to leave for a month in Europe, after

1 Keith Moon, drummer of The Who. Harry Nilsson, rock musician, huge fan of Python and excess generally. Died, after a heart-attack, in 1994, aged 53.

such a mind-draining concentrated spell of work, gives me that warm, satisfied feeling of all the systems being totally and fully used.

After a three-week holiday in Italy with the Davidson family, it was time for yet another trip to New York, this one occasioned by publication of the Fegg *book in the US.*

Wednesday, September 3rd

All-out onslaught on letters, etc, before leaving for NY tomorrow. The American fan mail is sometimes quite extraordinary. Less restrained than the English. I received one quite steamy letter, full of declarations of love, meant for my eyes only, which ended with the note, 'I hope you're the one I mean', and another from what must be one of the world's least-known organisations – the Michael Palin Sub-Committee of the Python Fan Club of Apartment 4c, 825 West End Ave, NY.

Thursday, September 4th, New York

To New York again. Very smooth, easy flight from sunny Heathrow at 11.00 to sunny New York at 1.30.

By 4.00 we were at the offices of Berkeley Books at 200 Madison Avenue to meet the publishers and designers of the American *Fegg* book. Ned Chase, a 50-year-old, who looks lean and well exercised, and has a Harvard correctness to his accent and general bearing (he was at Princeton, in fact) and Steve Conlon, big, white-haired, white-bearded, looking like a slim Burl Ives and using more down-to-earth Americanisms – his speech is littered with 'son of bitches' and 'get the fuck out of its' – for the publishers. And two younger men – about our age – Mike Gross and David Kaestle, who used to work as staff designers and illustrators on the *National Lampoon*.

Certainly their work is impressive – they have designed, and Mike Gross has drawn, some of the parodies of famous American artists on the *National Lampoon* Bicentennial Calendar – which is a calendar devoted entirely to disasters of one kind or another, ranging from assas-sinations and political scandals to typhoons and mass murders in the 200 years since the US was started.

They are also instantly likeable – because they like *Fegg*, I suppose –

and the combination of their obvious experience and flair and their immediate sympathy with the *Fegg* character and material made us both very pleased and the meeting quite a success.

Saturday, September 6th, West Granby, Connecticut

Left the Navarro at 8.45 for a weekend in Connecticut at the invitation of Steve Conlon.

My first glimpse of New England. It is like Sussex, only with more space. No black faces up in Northern Connecticut. Houses all of wood are rather attractive, and Steve's place is magnificent. It's a large barn, across the road from a farmhouse, white and weather-boarded, in which lives Steve's brother Henry (at weekends). Steve and his neat and organised English wife, Bet, have been converting the barn for about thirty years and it's now complete. Very fine interior, all open plan except for three guest bedrooms at one end. The original wooden beams complemented with some simple old pieces of wooden furniture, a feeling of comfort, but not luxury. Immediately in front of the barn is a spacious meadow.

So a feeling of space, quietness, and inside the barn, comfortable orderliness. An utter contrast to the throbbing, noisy heartbeats of NYC.

Later in the day two other Berkeley authors arrive. Lyn and Sheila – they wrote a best-seller some years back about research into psychic phenomena in Russia.

The pace quickened and we were joined for cocktails (their word, not mine) and dinner by a local Episcopalian minister, George, who Steve rather carefully made a point of telling us earlier was doing good work with homosexuals, and two local young men, Frank, a teacher in West Hartford – again with a very New English accent – and Charles, another youngish man, with a small moustache and a lazy left eye, who was a violinist and brother-in-law of Ted Sorensen (of Kennedy clan fame). All very jolly.

TJ was in high spirits and expansive good form. I sat beside the violinist and the Episcopalian minister, feeling rather dull. The minister talked softly about his work, describing how he counsels boys who come to see him. 'I give them the names and addresses of some gay clubs, gay discos, you know, and I tell them go on ... off you go, there's nothing wrong.'

We eat an excellent chicken casserole and a grape and cream

concoction for pudding – once again served up by Bet with a sort of clean efficiency which almost detracts from one's enjoyment.

Steve is a little shirty throughout, as the water supply appears to have run out. The fault is traced to our toilet cistern, which jammed and was left running. I think he is a little cross that the smooth running of the place, which he clearly prides himself on, should be interrupted on tonight of all nights – and I get the feeling he blames it on us.

Sunday, September 7th, West Granby, Connecticut

The sun is high and hot in a clear sky. We visit a nearby store for some last minute provisions. There is a comfortable neatness about the shop – untainted as it is by any slightly exciting food. Buy the *New York Times* and the *Hartford Courant* – both with about thirteen sections and several hundred pages – then back to the barn, where we read them lying in the sun. There's a lunch out of doors, which Bet is extremely proud of – because it is so well organised. All the cold meat and cheese is symmetrical. But in fact the lunch is very congenial and everyone seems a lot more relaxed than yesterday.

A drink in the early evening with Charles and Frank, whom we met last night. They live together in a wooden house on stilts with a fine view from the top of a hill. We drink whisky sours. Frank, whom I like a great deal, gives me a book of early Maurice Sendak drawings, not usually available. He knows Sendak apparently. However cynical one may be of this clean, bland American way of life, the people are exceptionally generous to strangers.

To bring us back to reality with a bump, we watched the first of the new Monty Python series to be shown in the States. It was the 'Scott of the Antarctic', 'Fish Licence', 'Long John Silvers v. Gynaecologists' programme. Strange how many of its items have become legendary, and yet looking at them, TJ and I were amazed and a little embarrassed at how very badly shot everything was. Ian really has improved but, judging by that show, he needed to. Was this really the greatest comedy series ever? Steve slept through it.

Monday, September 8th, New York

Steve wakes us at 6.10. We leave the barn just as it's getting light – about twenty to seven.

We arrive at Grand Central Station – in dark, dingy bowels, which make Liverpool Street look like some exquisite classical drawing room – at 10.10. Spend the morning and lunchtime and afternoon working on alterations to the *Fegg* material, in our room at the Navarro.

At 6.00 an historic moment. After three trips and at least a dozen phone calls, I meet Al Levinson, my new American friend, for only the second time. He and wife Eve come to the apartment. Al, big, bronzed, an almost olive colour; his face, I notice, like the bust of the Greek emperor I saw today in the Metropolitan Museum, fine, firm features. He looks serious underneath it all, as though the troubles of the world hung heavy on him when he stopped to think. Anyway, the great relief is I really do like him – and we get on easily, without infatuation on either side.

Nancy arrived to join us, so quite an impromptu party got under way before myself, Al and Eve left to have a look at Al's new house in Gramercy Park, which is right in the heart of nineteenth-century New York. They both clearly love it. The apartment is small, but in a four-storey brownstone which stands on its own, next to a Quaker chapel of the 1860s which has a preservation order on it.

We wound up at Nancy's drinking wine till after midnight. Met Dave Hermann, DJ of WNEW's morning show – he promised to wake me in the morning. He tells the story of how he was playing the 'Fairy Story' from the Pythons' second German show on the air and managed just in time to bleep the word 'tits'. (These progressive stations still have to be careful – after all, they're spending advertisers' money.) Then a phone call came through and Dave left the record playing only to hear, as he was winding up the phone call, 'Because she's a fucking princess.'

Tuesday, September 9th, New York

Listened to DH's early-morning programme. Sure enough, at 9.45 he told his audience that somewhere in NY MP and TJ of Monty Python were waking up. He played some music for us, which was very kind and silly.

To Sardi's restaurant, where we had a truly appalling meal, but did meet Arthur Cantor, a Broadway impresario with a fine sense of the absurdity of it all.

Cantor talks straight and doesn't try to impress. He would like to know if the Pythons are interested in a stage show in New York at the

City Center Theater for three weeks starting April 11th 1976. The theatre is owned by the City of New York, it's old and has an ornate interior and a seating capacity slightly larger than Drury Lane, though it feels equally intimate – we went to see it after our meal.

I like the theatre, I like the dates, I like the fact that the seat prices would not be as high as they would be on Broadway and I like Arthur Cantor. So I'm converted to a three-week stage show – if Python still exists!

From seeing Cantor and the theatre we go to a final meeting with Gross and Kaestle to look at the page layout. Everyone chips in with ideas and Ned and Steve discuss business, copy runs, initial prints, costings, etc, quite openly. There is no hierarchical aspect to the discussion.

Then we take Steve back to the hotel. Before we leave for the airport, we finish off our wine and beer with Ed Goodgold, Nancy Lewis and Ina Lee M and Steve, her partner.

Ed brought me a couple of cigars for the trip, which I appreciated, but eventually left in the bottom of a chest of drawers, beside a half-used box of sanitary towels left by some previous resident.

Left NY on the 10.00 BA flight.

Friday, September 12th

In the afternoon TJ and I go to the BBC for a meeting with Terry Hughes.

The *Tomkinson's Schooldays* scripts arrive with the title 'Michael Palin Special' writ large across them. But the meeting with Terry H goes well. Milton Abbas School in Dorset have given us permission to film there, and even to use the boys, provided their faces are not featured. We look through *Spotlight*. Judy Parfitt looks right to both TJ and myself as the mother, and TH says she's fun to work with, so she gets a call for the mother's part. TJ is still to play the School Bully, though TH suggests Ian Ogilvy, who strikes both of us as ideally physically right.

Tuesday, September 16th

Gilliam and Maggie round for a meal this evening – TG to tell me about his *Jabberwocky* film, which he wants me to write with him. He has an overall plan for the film now, which I like the sound of very much. In addition he has the backing of Sandy Lieberson, an American, who, with the Englishman, David Puttnam, runs Good Times Enterprises, who have a record of backing and setting up better-than-average movies.

I'm undecided about whether to work on *Jabberwocky*. I like it because it sounds like a starter and I like TG's sense of excitement about it, and I am quickly infected by his enthusiasm. I'm also very confident that anything he puts his mind to will at least not be dull – but I want to see how successful *Tomkinson's Schooldays* will be and how successful *Three Men in a Boat* will be and I want to find some project of my own.

For all these reasons I hang back.

Friday, September 19th

This evening is the first of John Cleese's solo efforts – *Fawlty Towers* – which he's been working on with Connie for over a year. Angela and Veryan and Michael and Anne Henshaw came round to have dinner and watch it with us. Helen and I were reduced to tear-streaming laughter on one or two occasions, the Henshaws less so and Angela and Veryan (probably put off by the intensity of my reaction) were quite quiet throughout. John has used a very straight and conventional Light Entertainment format in design, casting, film and general subject, but his own creation, Basil Fawlty, rises above all this to heights of manic extraordinariness. It all has the Cleese hallmark of careful, thoughtful, well-planned technical excellence and there was hardly a spare line in the piece or a moment when John wasn't going utterly spare. Anne said I was clearly enjoying it more because I knew John, but it was by any standards a really hard-working, well-realised performance. Whether he can keep it up, I don't know. It could become a bore and certainly there are as yet no reserves of warmth or sympathy in the character of Fawlty to help it along.

Thursday, September 25th

I spent the lunch hour in a recording studio doing three voice-overs for Sanderson Wallpaper. I really did it because I wanted to keep my hand in and a voice-over, however dull or badly written it may be, at least requires a bit of application and a little bit of performing. It's good practice. By the same token I've accepted an offer to appear as the guest on two editions of *Just a Minute*, a Radio 4 quiz game, next week.

Down to Regent's Park for a Python meeting.

Eric was very positive and I could scarcely believe that it was the same Eric who had berated us all for turning Python into a money-obsessed, capitalist waste of time in this same room in February last year. Eric's moods should really be ignored, but it's impossible because he nearly always has a big effect on any meeting. Today it was nice, kind, helpful, constructive Eric.

John had just returned from three days in Biarritz. He was the same as ever, unable to resist a vindictive dig at T Gilliam (on the usual lines of us 'carrying the animator' for three years). This didn't find much support amongst the gathering and squashed TG more than John intended.

Terry J had had a lunch with Michael White, who felt it would be suicidal for us not to make another film this year. Anne said that most 'advice' tended this way.

Saturday, September 27th

Thomas woke me, thankfully, at 8.30, with the news that the kitchen was leaking and it *was* late. He was absolutely right. At quarter past nine I was in mid-Weetabix when the phone rang. It was Stephen Frears – the plugs in his car were wet, could I give him a lift?

So we arrived, the director and I, at Ealing Film Studios, about ten minutes late. Renewed acquaintance with Tim and Stephen (who had done some work on the soundtrack yesterday) and the familiar, darkly sparkling features of Tom S. I was very happy to see them all again.

To work on re-recording the dialogue in lip-synch, as every soundtrack had the noise of the camera boat's engine in the background. I found it difficult at first to slip into the character of Harris, or indeed the whole tone and atmosphere of the film. I strained for the character and my voice must have come out sharp and shrill, as they kept telling me to relax. But after a rather gruelling morning, I began to settle into it and remembered Stephen's oft-repeated instructions on the filming to avoid giving Harris a funny voice! It's a rather daunting way to start the day, though, stuck out in the darkened studio with everyone else behind you in the control room, minutely examining your every word, every nuance, every inflexion.

Tim Curry left at lunchtime. He, poor bugger, has two performances of *Travesties* this afternoon.

Sunday, September 28th

A fine, fresh, sunny Sunday morning. Glad to be up and climbing into my car when everyone else was still enjoying Sunday lie-ins. Pick up Stephen F in Belsize Village. He was standing in the middle of the unusually quiet and traffic-free crossroads and scanning through the Sunday papers. Rave reviews throughout of *Daft as a Brush* – his latest film, which went out last Wednesday night. Actually, the rave reviews were reserved for his direction, 'coolness and sensitivity we have come to associate with him' and the performances by Jonathan Pryce and Lynn Redgrave.

Anyway, Stephen was clearly pleased as we enjoyed a sunny ride out to west London. He lives for films and the group of technicians – cameramen, make-up, sound, editors, etc – with whom he works are the best in the business, painstakingly collected by Stephen over the years. He seems to have life pared down to essentials. Clothes, cocktail parties, awards, purely prestige jobs don't interest him, and he doesn't let them occupy his time or divert his efforts. At the same time, he is a critic – of politics, of the establishment, of the status quo, of television, of films, without ever becoming doctrinaire or predictable.

We worked from 10.00 till 12.15 Monday morning with a couple of one hour breaks. I'd read all the Sunday papers about four times each by the time we finished. Tom S occasionally sprawled on the floor (with either a sweet or a cigarette in the mouth) writing new lines up to the very last minute. Tom is a writer I trust, too. Like Stephen he is devoted to his craft, and will never accept an easy way out – even the new lines are charged with a special interest, they're never just fillers.

We had an Indian meal at the Karachi restaurant across the road and Tom bought us champagne. I don't think he really expected us to accept it, but it set us up well for a final three hours of some very difficult dubbing, where often there was no guide track at all – and we had to work out from our rapid lip movements what on earth we were saying. But at last, just after 12.00, we finished the last of Tim's many voice-overs. It was about Harris being a Pole and Tim had got the giggles over it earlier on and been unable to do it.

Home and a bath about 1.30.

Tuesday, September 30th

To the TV Centre at 10.30 for a day of production meetings on *Tomkinson's Schooldays*.

After Judy Parfitt turned down the part, I asked Tom, Tim and Stephen at the weekend for 'Gwen Watford'-type ladies, and Stephen Moore said, 'Why don't you ask Gwen Watford …?' So today this is just what we did. I spoke to her agent, who was very approachable, and then to the great lady herself, and she was interested enough to ask for a script – so we've sent one off this evening and are just keeping fingers well crossed.

Ian Ogilvy is also on, as far as I know, so it's becoming an all-star cast – apart from myself!

Finished at the Beeb about 7.00. Had a drink at the Sun in Splendour, Notting Hill on the way back with Terry J. He is a little vague and not entirely happy about what to do next. I said I was also vague – and intentionally so, enjoying, as I am at the moment, a sort of directional limbo, trying to absorb influences from all sides, without having to commit to any long-term projects. For the first time we actually talked about whether he should go and do something on his own. I said I didn't want to drag his heels as well as my own.

Friday, October 3rd

At 5.15 arrived in taxi at the BBC's Paris studio – which is not in Paris, of course, but in Lower Regent Street – for recording of *Just a Minute*. A few people from the queue came up and asked me for an autograph – and there was my face on a display board outside. Inside, the peculiarly non-festive air which the BBC (radio especially) has made its own – everything from the colour of the walls and the design of the furniture to the doorman's uniform and the coffee-serving hatch seems designed to quell any lightness of spirit you may have.

Then I met Clement Freud. He stared at me with those saucer-shaped, heavy-lidded eyes with an expression of such straightforward distaste that for a moment I thought he had just taken cyanide. The producer, John Lloyd[1] – a ray of light in the darkness that was rapidly closing in on me – hurriedly took my arm and led me aside as if to

1 He later created *Not the Nine O'Clock News*.

explain something about Clement F. It was just that he had a 'thing' about smoking – and for some inexplicable reason I had just taken one of John L's cigarettes. Still, this blew over.

A depressingly half-full house filed quietly in and at 5.45 the contestants – three regulars, Freud, K Williams, the rather forbiddingly authoritative Peter Jones,[1] myself, not exactly in my element any more – and quiz master Nicholas Parsons were introduced to friendly applause and took our places at our desks. The three regulars have been playing the game together for five years – Williams and Freud for eight – and it shows. They are smooth and polished, they know when to ad-lib, when to bend the rules a little, and when to be cross with each other. I buzzed Clement Freud when he was at full tilt and, when asked why, I apologised and said I was testing my buzzer. That's the only time I saw him smile in my direction.

The game became easier, but I never mastered the technique of microphone-hogging which they all have perfected.

Before I knew it, two shows and about an hour and a half had passed and it was all over. I signed autographs. Peter Jones was very kind to me and complimentary, Freud I never saw again and Nicholas Parsons was the only one to come round to the pub and drink with us. Us being myself, Douglas Adams (who had recommended me to his friend, the producer) and John Lloyd. They seemed to be quite pleased with me and Peter Jones, as he left, said he would see me again on the show. I gather some guests manage it (Barry Took, Katharine Whitehorn) and some don't (Barry Cryer, Willy Rushton) and at least I wasn't considered amongst the don'ts.

From the Captain's Cabin to the Work House – the studio in Old Kent Road where we are to re-record 'Lumberjack Song'.[2] The Fred Tomlinsons have been rehearsing for an hour by the time I arrive (just after 8.00), and up in the control room are Eric and George Harrison. George grasps me in a welcoming hug and Eric pours me some Soave Bolla.

Downstairs, noisy rumblings of Fred Toms. I get down there to find them in the usual hearty good spirits – no Soave Bolla in evidence down there – just huge cans of beer and cider!

1 He later became the narrator of *The Hitchhikers Guide to the Galaxy*, something I'd inexplicably turned down.
2 George loved the song so much he offered to produce it as a Christmas single. It reached No. 51, but no higher as the Pythons refused to sing it on *Top of the Pops*.

Instead of dividing the song and introduction up into different takes, we just launch in, and soon we've done three versions straight through and my voice is getting hoarse from all the added shouting at the beginning. But one of the takes seems to please everybody.

George, Olivia, Kumar,[1] Eric and I leave in George's BMW automatic for a meal. We drive, if that's the word for George's dodgem-like opportunism, to the Pontevecchio in Brompton Road.

George's a vegetarian, but he managed to demolish some whitebait quite easily, and did not pass out when I had duck. (I noticed everyone else ate veg. dishes only.)

Saturday, October 4th

At half past four drive up to collect Eric and take him out to George's house in Henley to mix the song we recorded last night. Eric philosophical about his recent separation from Lyn. He laughed rather ruefully when he told me he'd taken Carey out to the zoo this morning – 'With all the other divorcees,' as he put it. But he cheers up when we get to Henley and in through the gates of Friar Park, the magnificent, opulent and fantastical mid-Victorian Gothic pile which George bought seven years ago with the Beatle millions. George's flag flies above its mock embrasures – it's an Indian symbolic design of the sun and the moon and bears 'om' mantra.

In the gardens there are grottoes with mock stalactites and stalagmites in mock caves and there are Japanese houses and Japanese bridges and all kinds of other ways in which an enormously rich Victorian can spend money on himself. George has endorsed it all by cleaning everything up and looking after it and generally restoring the place to its former splendours. The nuns whom he bought it from had let it rather go to seed and, according to George, had painted swimming trunks on the cherubs and cemented over the nipples on some of the statues.

It is delightful just to walk around and examine the intricate details of the carving – the recurring naughty friar's head motif – even in evidence in brass on every light switch (the face is the fitting – the switch is the friar's nose). It has none of the feel of a big draughty Victorian house, but one can't escape the feeling of George somehow cut off from everyday life by the wealth that's come his way.

1 Olivia, George's wife. Kumar was his assistant.

Maybe he feels the same way, for almost the first thing we do is to walk through the grottoes, across the lawns and down to the elaborate iron gates and into the world outside. Henley, with its narrow streets and the fine church tower standing protectively over the little town, with thickly wooded Remenham Hill looming behind.

This was the town my mother was born and brought up in – in fact, she had been to Friar Park for tea when it was owned by Sir Frank Crisp, a barrister. Strange to think of the circumstances that brought me into Friar Park sixty years after she came here for tea.

Anyway, we all walked down to the local pub – where we drank Brakspear's Henley Ales and played darts.

George was clearly anxious that we should stay the night, play snooker on his Olympic size snooker table, smoke, drink, mix the record and generally enjoy ourselves. But this was my second evening devoted to the 'Lumberjack Song' and I wanted to be back with Helen, so I reluctantly resisted most of the mind-bending delights of Friar Park and stuck to a couple of glasses of white wine.

Half-way through the evening, George went out into Henley and returned with vast amounts of vegetarian food from a new Indian takeaway that had just opened. We all ate too much – George dipping in with fingers only.

Home about 4.00. Helen not pleased, as she had really expected me a lot earlier – and I very indignantly tried to tell her how much hospitality I had had to refuse, to get back even by 4.00. Still, it's no time of night for an argument.

Wednesday, October 8th

Lunch with Gwen Watford, who has agreed to take the part, and Ian Ogilvy. Realise that there are several peaks of nervousness in one's first half-hour show, and one is meeting the other actors – especially when they are as exalted as Gwen W. Will they be right? What will be their attitude to the piece? Is it just a light diversion which they needn't bother with much? All anxieties dispelled on first meeting. Gwen I met in the make-up department, where she'd come for a wig fitting. She's charming and very approachable, and, like Ian Ogilvy, straightforward and down-to-earth.

Thursday, October 9th

Just as the week seemed to be settling down smoothly, 'Lumberjack Song' rears its ugly head again. Anne rings to say that Tony Stratton-Smith still prefers the Drury Lane 'Lumberjack' to the new version so laboriously conceived last weekend.

There is a definite split on the two versions of the 'Lumberjack'. Graham and Adams have been in after lunch (Anne said she wasn't quite sure how compos Graham was) and prefer the Drury Lane version. Terry J prefers Drury Lane. I really feel they are so different from each other in style as to be incomparable, and I feel I would hate the weekend's work just to go out the window. Eric has rung. He has 'flu and is not happy at all. He positively doesn't want Drury Lane.

Friday, October 17th, Dorchester–London train

Rattling back home after the week's filming on *Tomkinson*. Amazingly we are still able to have a meal on the train at 9.30 – a not unpleasant British Rail steak.

I think it has been the most solid week's work in my life. Since Monday morning I have been totally involved – in the setting-up and shooting, as well as the acting, of almost every shot. The feeling of responsibility tightens the concentration and, though the actual application is hard, it's the only way – especially as I feel TJ is waiting just behind me to take over. I don't mean that in any malicious sense, it's just that I fear his enthusiasm – it's the sort that is so deeply felt it keeps me on my toes, because I must keep thinking of ideas first.

At the moment, sitting back as the train roars towards London, I feel as happily and justifiably exhausted as I have done after any filming in a long while. Not only have I enjoyed the extent of my own involvement, I've enjoyed working with Terry Hughes. After the physical and mental strain of Ian Mac, Terry is more easy-going, open, adaptable, never rattled, never defensive – I suppose it stems from the fact that he has no one to fight. He is a blue-eyed boy at the BBC – director of *The Two Ronnies*, at present the No. 1 show in the ratings – whereas Ian was always at loggerheads with his employers. And Ian had six Pythons to cope with, Terry H only has two.

Tuesday, October 21st

Down to Ray Millichope's[1] at 10.30 to see the rushes. Terry H, Terry J and myself crowd around Ray's Steinbeck[2] at his new cutting rooms next door to the Nellie Dean pub in Carlisle Street. Euphoria gathers as we watch almost two hours' worth of rushes.

I feel very, very happy this afternoon as I drive back home. I think for the first time that *Tomkinson* is going to work in the area in which it is most distinctive – the area of quality, of atmosphere, of style.

Friday, October 24th

This morning we (i.e. the Pythons) are to meet Alan Freeman for an interview for some US radio programme he does. Freeman is one of those folk heroes of the sixties – *Pick of the Pops*, etc – who's still around and amazingly durable in the '70s. Graham tells me he's keen on motor bikes and leather and men.

I was twenty minutes late, but the first one there. Greeted with the same warm enthusiasm which gets Freeman so much work. His shirt is a little tightly stretched over a few folds of good living, and he seems a little hot in the face. He talks compulsively and shows me into the flat, furnished lushly with a great deal of ormolu and marble and rather fussily camp objects. A cigarette lighter is never a cigarette lighter ... it's a gun or a sea-shell. A very likeable man – who endeared himself even more to me personally by raving about the Python credits. Said he was embarrassed that he didn't know our names, but he'd rung Python Productions for photos and they said they hadn't any.

Alan F taped quite cheerfully. He asked me if I ever regretted not playing a musical instrument and I got going on that. When he wasn't asking questions, we (Terry G, Terry J, Gra and myself) fell into a rather serious vein and talked about the problems of the world, etc. Graham said contraception and the control of the population was the world's major problem. At least he's doing his bit to limit the population.

John C, not unpredictably, was absent from all the various Python functions today, but the last of his *Fawlty Towers* series had me laughing as long and as loud as anything since *Hancock and the Vikings* – which must have been 15 or 16 years ago.

1 TV editor who worked on *The Frost Reports* and the Python TV shows.
2 The most commonly used machine for editing film in the pre-digital age.

Wednesday, October 29th

Just after 9.30 this evening, when I'm getting my Chinese take-away out of the oven, and my bottle of champagne out of the fridge, prior to watching England v. Czechoslovakia all on my own, I hear the dull thud of a blast. It could be anything, but it's a measure of the times that I am certain it was a bomb. Sure enough, on the 11.30 news there are the familiar pictures of ambulance, police cordons, etc, etc. At 9.40 a bomb went off in an Italian restaurant in Mayfair. No warning – eighteen injured. But the fact that I heard the explosion in our kitchen seemed to bring the whole horror closer to me – and genuinely set me thinking as to what I would do with myself and the family if a totally indiscriminate bombing campaign (as this recent one seems to be) continued in London.

No conclusions of course. I shall carry on shopping in the West End, parking in the West End, working in the West End, eating in the West End, as everybody else will – all helpless potential victims.

Saw Stephen Frears and Annie Zelda in the Welcome Chinese earlier. *Three Men* is ready, apart from the music. Stephen quietly, with eyes slightly mischievous, murmurs, 'The word is it's good.'

Saturday, November 1st

Studio recording day for *Tomkinson's Schooldays*. I estimate this will be getting on for the seventy-fifth half-hour I've performed in and helped to write since *Do Not Adjust Your Set* began in 1967.

I feel more and more confident as the day goes on. Strangely enough both Gwen and Ian are a little less at ease. After all, neither of them have ever done a TV show to a live audience – whereas for Terry and myself this is our world, for both of them it's an unfamiliar territory. But both play well during the recording and the audience seems to receive the show with many laughs.

I am racing around changing like a mad thing, and at the end of the one and a quarter hours recording, I think I'm the least qualified person in the entire studio to judge how it went. A feeling that I cannot get rid of is that the studio scenes received less reaction than they should have done – but everyone seems happy.

Tuesday, November 4th

Reactions to Saturday night's recordings have been so far favourable. Anne H and daughter Rachel liked it very much. Robert H enjoyed it and laughed a lot, but thought I was a bit *Whacko!*[1] I've had two long chats with Simon Albury, who liked it generally, but felt that there should have been more character detail – the School Bully especially, he felt, was one-dimensional and didn't like him at all – whereas Graham Chapman (the only Python apart from TJ at the recording) thought the Bully was very good. More basically, Simon felt that I came out of it too softly, self-effacingly and passively – if the object was to make it into a Michael Palin series.

On the phone today with TJ the difficult question of *Tomkinson* and our own working relationship came up. Tony Hendra (of *National Lampoon*) had offered him a pirate film to direct. Terry was writing back to say he couldn't do it – whereas in fact he really didn't want to do it because it would mean a lot of hard work which he didn't have time for if we were working on the series.

Well, we eventually talked it out over lunch at the Brasserie du Coin in Lamb's Conduit Street. I suppose it was a little awkward, as it always has been whenever we've had to stop and examine our relationship – which has, for ten years, grown, stretched and adjusted itself by fairly effortless natural processes.

Terry said that he didn't feel particularly frustrated or unfulfilled by the imbalance of writing and performing on *Tomkinson* and he would be quite happy if that same imbalance were to occur in a future series, but what he wanted to establish was that his own ideas and suggestions were treated with equal importance – if they weren't, and if I were 'in control', then it would not be a relationship he was satisfied with. He thought it quite reasonable if I should want to be 'in control', but then it would be a Michael Palin show and not a Jones/Palin show, and, in that case, TJ would be happy to come in and edit and work on scripts after I'd written them and do some performing if needed, but in the meantime would rather get his teeth into another project of his own.

However, I value Terry and his judgement too much to just use it for a half-day every two weeks – and I know that Terry would never be

[1] A reference, I think, to the broad comedy style of Jimmy Edwards, who played the headmaster of Chiselbury School in the TV sitcom *Whack-O!* (1956–60; 1971–2). It was written by Frank Muir and Denis Norden.

happy if he didn't have the freedom to contribute and develop ideas from the start. So, though I do want to keep it the Michael Palin show, I do not want to lose Terry and so we agree that it will be an equal talents, equal involvement show.

All happy at the end of the meal – except that I can't quite see how it can be equal if I am to do the bulk of the performing.

Friday, November 7th

To Robin Powell's in the morning. Deborah cleaned my teeth out as usual with the frightful pointed, nerve-jarring steel prong, but she talks more about Python, etc, each time I go, and this time we chatted for 25 minutes and gum-gouged for only ten. She tells me Robin Powell is to be made a professor. It's all very hush-hush at the moment, but he's the first ever Professor of Periodontal Surgery. Feel quite proud to have been treated by him. Despite his gloom three or four years ago, my teeth are still not falling out.

Monday, November 10th, Southwold

Up to Southwold.

Last week Father had a fall when out walking past Bullard's Farm – and cut his head in several places. He was taken to Southwold Hospital for stitches and is being kept in there, as Dr Hopkins is worried about the state of his legs – for the fall this time was quite serious, and seemed to have no other cause than his legs giving way.

Southwold was cold and inhospitable today. In the little cottage hospital Daddy was sitting up, but his head looked in a bad way, with three quite severe lacerations and lots of minor cuts and bruises.

He seemed pleased to see me, and laughed self-deprecatingly when I mentioned his fall. But he couldn't say more than half a dozen words in the entire hour we were there. This appalling difficulty with his speech – which, as he cannot write legibly for more than half a sentence, amounts to an almost total inability to communicate – was the single most obvious indication of the deterioration of his condition since I last saw him. This Parkinson's does demean people so much. It certainly has rendered him almost helpless – and on today's standards, I can't see any likelihood of him returning to the form of his 75th birthday party.

Tuesday, November 11th

A gorgeous morning. A slight frost disappearing as the bright November sun makes the fields steam. Sharp fresh smells of the countryside.

Back to London by a quarter to twelve, time to get back home on the Broad Street line, change, grab a quick coffee and drive down to Berkeley Square to have lunch with John Cleese at Morton's. I rang John at the end of last week, as I just suddenly felt like a chat with him – warmed, as I had been, by his quite superbly funny performances in *Fawlty Towers*.

We drank a couple of whisky sours at the bar and, as so often happens to John, we're joined at the bar by a rather boring man, an architect, who was just off, as he put it, to 'Saudi'. Five years ago, if a man had said he was going to Saudi Arabia, you'd probably think he'd been in trouble with the police. Now it's where the money is – and the resource-ful Brits are engaged tooth and nail in the process of bringing back the money we're paying for the Arabs' oil.

We go up to the restaurant and, despite his having just completed a very funny, widely praised series on the awful way people can be treated in hotels and restaurants, John and I are shown to the smallest table in the room, at which John has great difficulty in actually sitting. We share a bottle of Puligny Montrachet and tuck into smoked trout and eggs Benedict, looking out over Berkeley Square.

John is still not living with Connie and sounds sad about it … my God, he's the third person I've had lunch with in five days who's sepa-rated in the last year. Otherwise a good chat – both John and I feel that everyone is better off for having less involvement with Python.

He was strongly defensive when I suggested that there was a certain resentment that he had never been present on any of the film publicity trips. 'I thought people liked going,' was John's response.

There was not much feeling of latent group responsibility in much of what he said – but we nattered on quite absorbed until nearly four o'clock. I then went down to the King's Road, and bought clothes and some very fine Victorian ceramic tiles for our new sitting room shelf.

Dark nights shopping in the King's Road made me long to be warm and indoors, so I dropped in at Nigel's studio to see him and Judy. All was quiet. Nigel says the art market in England is in a deplorable state. They sit sometimes for days with no one coming round – Nigel seems to manage to make ends meet by sales in New York. American money does have its uses.

Sunday, November 16th

A wild, black November day. Rain, strong winds and grey and gloomy light. Nancy L rings in the morning. She's in London for a week.

Nancy is with Arthur Cantor, the genial Jewish impresario who is to put on our show in NY next April. He is a very unobtrusive sort of hustler and has plenty of other things to talk about besides when, where and how much? He is very pleased with himself this evening as, in a collection of 1,000 books which he bought for £550 from the estate of another impresario, 'Binkie' Beaumont, he has discovered some little masterpieces. He showed me two postcards, hand-written by George Bernard Shaw, which he had found tucked into a book. In one of the cards – to a producer or director of *Caesar and Cleopatra* – he tells the recipient not to worry unduly about the casting of Cleopatra, as the play is Caesar's anyway.

Tuesday, November 18th

In the evening I go with Nancy to the Bruce Springsteen concert at Hammersmith Odeon. This is the first show outside the US for a 26-year-old New Jersey boy who has been hailed as the new Dylan, Lennon, Van Morrison and so on. The trouble is that the enormous reputation has been chiefly created by CBS Records and there is a certain scepticism around as to the legendariness of Springsteen. So, was this the New Messiah? Was this to be one of those concerts which fathers tell their sons about in years to come?

Of course the concert didn't start until 45 minutes after the advertised time – and we kept having wretched announcements about it being your last chance to buy cigarettes and smokes before the concert began. The air inside the Odeon was so foul and heavy that this was hardly doing anyone a favour.

Nor did Springsteen start too well. A solo with piano. His croaky, straining voice sounding as though he'd just done a six-week Gumby season, the spotlights all over the place. No, definitely no magic until the full six-piece band strolled on and everyone was riveted by the white suit and matching white trilby of the tubby, middle-aged sax player, Clarence Clemons.

The band went off at such a lick that one could sense the relief. Springsteen leapt into action – twitching and leaping and throwing himself into strange spasms as he urged the band on. The sound system failed to make head or tail of Springsteen's poetry, but the band kept the evening alive – and he did three encores.

Afterwards, a party given by CBS in the balcony bar. Talked with John Walters, a very funny man. He and Peel, whom he produces, are a formidably intelligent pair – well above the general level of Radio 4.

Final word on Springsteen from Walters – 'We came expecting the Messiah, and got Billy Graham instead.'

Wednesday, November 19th

William's five today. He is very neat and tidy with his presents, quite unlike Tom. Having taken them out of their boxes, his chief delight is to put them back in again, and then collect them all together in a cupboard.

Thursday, November 20th

A Python meeting at 22 Park Square East to discuss the New York show in April and to meet A Cantor. John C on the latest form of table-booking at select Mayfair restaurants, 'Er … excuse me, are you being bombed tonight?'

We have a lot of fun deciding on silly names for our US company, or partnership, or whatever it's called. 'Evado-Tax' is the one we all wanted, but Anne really thought there may be problems, as the company is operating on the fringes of legality! So I suggested Paymortax – and so we now have an American company called Paymortax and McWhirter!

Some time spent on the title for the American show. I'd suggested 'Monty Python v. Muhammad Ali' – with 'Muhammad Ali' in enormous letters but very obviously crossed out. John C was worried in case Muhammad Ali got more out of it than we did – and also I think he was afraid that the living legend would come along and thump us on the opening night.

Tuesday, November 25th

Terry comes up after lunch and we go over to Studio 99 in Swiss Cottage to look at the cassette recordings of Python's first ABC compilation.[1] A very cool American voice – the kind we would only use as a send-up – announces, quite seriously, that 'The Wide World of Entertainment presents the Monty Python Show'. It started well, with 'The World's Most Awful Family', which works a treat after the smooth and glossy ABC packaging of the show, but then the cuts begin. The cat-in-the-wall bell push (a big laugh in the studio) is cut, the man pouring blood all over the doctors is cut after the opening lines – before the point of the sketch has even begun. In the 'Montgolfier Brothers' the words 'naughty bits' are bleeped out!!

In fact any reference to bodily function, any slightly risqué word, anything, as Douglas Adams put it, 'to do with life', was single-mindedly expunged.

The cuts which to me seemed the most remarkable were in the 'Neutron' sketch, when I played the US Bombing Commander who had personal odour problems. The character was in, but every appearance was topped and tailed to avoid all reference to his bodily hygiene. As that was the only original and Pythonesque twist to the character, he just came out as a below-average imitation of George C Scott.

Our reaction turned from disbelief and amazement to anger and outrage and eventually resolved into a very clear and simple position.

The first step as far as we're concerned is to let as many people in America as possible know that we disassociate ourselves from the ABC sale and, better still, to let as many people as possible know the reason why. It was suggested that we use our seventeen thousand lawyers to try and put together grounds for an injunction to prevent ABC putting out the second compilation (due in December). However legally unenforceable this may be, at least it's a fair try for a story – 'Python Sues ABC' would be all we'd need.

Monday, December 8th

My wretched cold is hanging on into its second week and really bringing me down. I can't even think straight, let alone smell anything. Terry J

1 ABC, one of the big three American commercial networks, had bought Python's fourth series (without John) and reorganised it into two specials. We had been tipped off that the result was not good and that we should take a look at it.

drops in later in the afternoon. We're both very pleased with the cover of *Dr Fegg's Nasty Book of Knowledge,* which arrived from the States this morning. It's funny and, what's better, it's actually quite interesting as well. There's a lot of detail in Bruce McCall's vision of the 'Great New World of Technology' which you only see after looking at it several times.

Terry and I plunge into discussion of the future. Terry is, as he says, restive at the moment – wants to unleash his straining enthusiasm in some direction, but doesn't know where to go. The Tony Hendra pirate film, *The Legend of the Nancy Hulk,* is still on offer and could tie him up for six or seven months on a major project. I read it at Southwold over the weekend and feel Terry shouldn't do it. Although very funny in some ways – the awful pirate crew are a fine invention – it seems to me to be very second-hand Python. Its costume and period flavour lend a similarity to the *Grail* which is just not backed up by the originality of the writing.

Wednesday, December 10th

To see Dr Freudenberg – as my cold had developed into a regular and implacable headache. In the waiting room, with her little baby, was Lindy, wife of Nick Mason of the Pink Floyd. She was cross – her appointment had been at 10.30, it was now after 11.30. A nice chat. They're not sending their child, Chloe (a little younger than Willy) to Gospel Oak, partly because the classes are too big. I sympathise. She grumbled a little about the legion of financial advisers, etc, which come automatically with all the loot Floyd must be making. They're not the house in Switzerland, private jet mob, though – it's state schools and Kentish Town, and they can't stand the thought of having to leave England for tax reasons. The wealthy anti-rich.

Freudenberg says I have a touch of sinusitis and bronchitis.

Arthur Cantor rang and tried to ask Helen and me out to see the new Ben Travers farce *The Bed Before Yesterday* at the Lyric. Every date he suggested was already full. 'This is getting like the Cheese Shop,' rumbled Arthur. We settled on Monday next. For some reason he has a soft spot for me, and he asked if I would write a play for him. He was very keen and said he would commission it. He sounded as though he wanted me to sign then and there, so I retreated into the Palin shell and promised I would think about it. I really wouldn't mind writing a play –

on my own. But I immediately felt guilty about Terry and cross with myself for feeling guilty and really in quite a muddle.

In the evening we drove over to Wimbledon for a party at the house of Jacqui, David Wood's[1] new wife, next to the Crooked Billet beside Wimbledon Common.

Talked with Andrew Lloyd Webber – he of *Superstar* fame – who made a fortune from a smash hit as soon as he left Oxford.[2] A rather nervous, soft-spoken chap, he said his investment in the Python film was the only thing keeping him going at the moment – after *Jeeves*.[3] He promised to send me a review in a Toronto paper in which the reviewer raved about Python and slammed the indecency in *Jesus Christ Superstar*!

As we drove back across London from this convivial houseful, we passed the police cordons around Dorset Square and, as we waited at the traffic lights, we looked across to the anonymous first-floor flat in Balcombe Street which has suddenly become the focus of national attention. In the flat are a middle-aged couple and four Irish terrorists, one of whom may be, according to the police, the organiser behind the London bombings and shootings of the past two winters.

The flat was floodlit. Groups of police, smiling, telling jokes, stood around at the barriers. There was a Thames TV van with a camera crew on top – even location caterers. It seemed quite unreal. Surely it must be night filming? Surely it must be a scripted adventure? But I suppose in that little living room in Balcombe Street, there are five people whose lives have now been totally altered. The lights changed and off we went to our cosy, non-floodlit little home.[4]

Thursday, December 11th

School concert. Tom was the Pied Piper, with words to say and music to play. He looked lovely and full of mischievous grins at the audience. Willy was a snowflake in his first ever concert.

1 Actor, and writer of many children's shows, David had appeared in *The Oxford Line*, a revue I produced and directed for the Edinburgh Festival in 1965.
2 This was *Joseph and the Amazing Technicolor Dreamcoat*. Lloyd Webber was a small investor in *Holy Grail*.
3 *By Jeeves*, a rare Lloyd Webber/Tim Rice flop.
4 The six-day siege ended, peacefully, two days later, when the IRA gunmen gave themselves up. They were charged with ten murders and twenty bombings and jailed for life.They were released in April 1999 as part of the Good Friday Agreement.

Friday, December 12th

Anne rings in the evening. Everyone apart from Eric and Graham, who hasn't been contacted, is solidly in favour of legal action – i.e. the injunction against ABC. Ina Lee M has already spent several thousand dollars of our money to take advice as to whether or not our case is strong. She assures us that we will only have to pay $15,000 *if* the case is to be fought and, if we win and they appeal, maybe $20,000 more on the appeal. So the injunction is almost on its way and I feel it *is* worthwhile carrying it through.

In the evening Jimmy Gilbert rings. He tells me that *Tomkinson* is to be shown on BBC2 on January 7th. He calls its transmission 'a first night' – a chance for him to gauge reaction. So clearly he is not yet decided on a series.

Sunday, December 14th

Things are gathering momentum. Just after 10.00, with fresh papers to read and bacon and eggs cooking, phone rings. It is T Gilliam. He wants me to go with him to the US tomorrow to be present in New York as Python representatives during the injunction action, etc, etc. We would return Wednesday.

Monday, December 15th

Very heavy frost. Collected by large Jaguar at 9.15, full of Terry Gilliam, in his big white furry Afghan coat, which he is painting himself. From 11.00 to 4.30 sit on our British Airways jumbo jet at Heathrow gazing out at the ever-thickening fog. Feel very glad that Anne talked us into going First Class – despite our guilt feelings. Attentive waiters served champagne and, when it became obvious, round about 4.00, that there would be no flights from Heathrow today, they offered to serve those of us who wanted it a meal.

The airport was silent and visibility down to about ten yards when we left. The cab journey home took well over an hour. But Helen was glad to see me back – and we enjoyed a sort of bonus evening – an evening we weren't meant to have.

Nancy was apparently waiting with newsmen in New York – all eager for the story – whilst Gilliam and I were enjoying a rare uninterrupted natter, lasting from nine till six, aboard our fogbound restaurant at Heathrow.

Tuesday, December 16th, New York

When we arrived at Heathrow at about 11.15 it was fairly obvious that the Queen Mother herself could hardly expect to get a second look at the check-in counters. The BA Intercontinental check-in area was a mass of people, becoming more solid all the time.

In eccentric British fashion, many people were trying to be more cheerful in the face of it. One cantankerous Scotsman was the only exception to all this. He carped and grumbled loudly and consistently and wagged his finger at the BA girl when he got to the counter, telling her how she couldn't expect him to travel by her airline again – which must have been the only bit of good news for her that morning.

Anne had fortunately also booked us on TWA's 2.30 flight, so we fought our way out of the crush and across to the TWA section. It was almost deserted – and not only this, but they were duplicating their flight of yesterday, and did have two seats in First Class. So, from the totally unproductive frustration of a few minutes earlier, we suddenly found ourselves within an hour taking off for New York. A day and a half late, I suppose.

We reached New York about 3.30 their time, after a long, clear run in down the length of Long Island. A huge limousine, sent by Nancy, met us at JFK, and drew us comfortably across the 49th Street Bridge and into the Big Apple. All fine, except that TWA have lost my bag.

There is a great deal of interest and sympathy for Python's case. We make short articles on the Television pages of the *New York Times* and *New York Post*. In the *Times* we learnt for the first time that Time-Life had edited the shows in collaboration with ABC – and that several of the cuts had been made by ABC, said a spokesman, because some passages were considered 'inappropriate'.

One slightly ominous note, though – Nancy says the court hearing is on Friday – and yet we have to leave Thursday night at latest.

Wednesday morning, December 17th, New York

Up at 9.30. Walk across to the Stage Delicatessen for breakfast. Eggs, bacon, coffee, bagels, cottage cheese.

Up to Nancy's office at Buddah where we meet Rik Hertzberg – good old friend from *The New Yorker*. We have a good time and give him a lot of information, including, for the first time, copies of letters, affidavits and other court material. Rick is not just a good and sympathetic friend – he also, in his *New Yorker* piece earlier this year [welcoming the Python TV series], has the immeasurable skill of being able to quote our material and still make it sound funny.

After an hour or so with Rick, we take a cab down Broadway to Sardi's for lunch with John O'Connor – another Python sympathiser and TV critic of the *New York Times*. It's interesting how much greater access we have to TV journalists and writers in New York than in London.

From Sardi's the Dynamic Duo, the Fighters for Freedom, find themselves in a rather dingy doorway next to Cartier's shop in Fifth Avenue, waiting for an elevator up to see the lawyers whom Ina has hired to represent us in our struggle against the American Broadcasting Companies, Inc.

They're led by short, blond-haired Robert Osterberg, he must be mid-thirties. A fit, tidy, rather bland sort of man with the eyes and smile, but unfortunately nothing else, of Kirk Douglas.

He begins by saying that we really ought to be in court on Friday. He says, quite rightly, that if no Pythons are prepared to be in New York to defend their own case, that case is immeasurably weakened. And so on. He's right of course, but both Terry and I have avoided confronting the awful, stomach-gripping truth that we will actually have to defend our position in a US Federal court. Now that's almost a certainty and I have to let Helen know that I won't be back for the Gospel Oak Old Folk's Party. In addition, TWA have still not found my case, so I'm unshaven and crumpled and tired as well as shit-scared.

Thursday, December 18th, New York

Feel much calmer about the whole court bit now. Rang Helen, which was the worst thing I had to get over. It was twenty past eight here and I was in bed in the Navarro, with sunny New York outside – and Helen was in her fog-bound Gospel Oak kitchen with the kids all wanting things. There really couldn't be much contact. I just had to tell her the facts – very unsatisfactory, but now she knows, I know she'll get over it and begin to make other plans and I'm sure friends will rally round. So I feel better now. I feel ready for a fight.

We breakfast at the Grand Central Café. (Good news for Grand Central Station fans – yesterday a demolition and development plan for it was finally quashed.)

A visit to the lawyers, then all of us in a deadly accusing phalanx – Ina, Osterberg plus one, Terry G and myself – make our way over to ABC TV. A slender, not unattractive thirty-five-storey dark stone and glass block ... this is what we're taking on.

Up to the twenty-first floor.

We're at ABC today because they yesterday relented their earlier decision not to let us see the proposed December 26th compilation – and the lawyers regard this viewing today as a significant concession. ABC's point is that, if we find that the compilation we see at today's viewing is acceptable, then the whole case may be dropped.

We meet, for the first time, the highly plausible and eligible Bob Shanks, who is Head of Night Time and Early Morning Programming at ABC. Intelligent, charming and the man ultimately responsible for our being in New York today. With him is a member of their legal department – a lady in her late thirties, early forties with a long-suffering look in her eyes and a kindly, almost saintly face, as in a sixteenth-century religious painting.

At this stage it's smiles, handshakes, genial informality as far as we're concerned – but for Ina and Bob Osterberg detached cool politeness is the order of the day. At one point early on in the discussion, Bob appears quite irrationally strong with Shanks – and we feel the first hint of a fight ... the first punch thrown and missed as Osterberg raises his voice over a point and Shanks charms quietly back, 'Let's not shout at each other ... let's just talk about it in a reasonable way.'

ABC at this point present us with a list of their cuts in the three shows we are about to see. A cursory glance at the list shows that our trip to New York has not been wasted. There are thirty-two proposed cuts. Some ludicrous – 'damn' cut out twice, 'bitch' as describing a dog cut out, etc, etc.

I think that ABC were quite honestly taken aback by our reaction. I just wanted to walk out, but Osterberg advised us to see all the shows, which was obviously good sense.

Next to me on the couch as I told them that the cuts they suggested were totally unacceptable and, in our opinion, ludicrous, was a young, short-haired, conventionally handsome executive, whose eyes would not look at ours for long, and whose face was flushed with confusion. He turned out to be the head of ABC TV's Standards and Practices Department and a Vice-President of the Company.

This was the man whom ABC pay to censor their programmes – the man who had actually decided that the American public wasn't ready for 'naughty bits' – the man who had decided that Eric Idle as Brian Clough dressed as Queen Victoria was a homosexual reference and should therefore be cut. Judging by the list he had compiled one would expect him to be a sort of obsessive religious maniac. A wild eccentric who lived on top of a mountain seeking to preserve himself and his few remaining followers from the final onslaught of the people who say 'damn'.

But the deceit is that of course he was himself no more offended by these words than I am. He laughed, as they all laughed, when we talked about cutting a 'tit' here and a 'tit' there – and yet he will not permit others in his country to have the choice of laughing at those words as well. 'It's alright for us, but we've got to think about people in the South – in Baton Rouge and Iowa as well.' Then we tell him that Python has been running in Baton Rouge and Iowa for over a year on PBS, without complaint.

It all seems so pointless, in this little viewing room in a comfortable office block with a group of people playing idiotic games with each other, but then I remember the power of ABC – the ability to beam a show simultaneously into all the sets in the USA. The papers we have talked to, the radio shows we have talked to, can never hope to reach anything but a small proportion of the audience our mutilated show can reach via ABC.

Our lawyers play games – their lawyers play games. After viewing all the shows we begin sort of negotiations. This involves a worried lady lawyer for ABC asking us if we would ever consider the possibility of re-editing. Yes, we say, despite the obvious harm the 90-minute format and the commercial breaks will do, we would consider re-editing. Their ears prick up. Our re-editing would be based entirely on artistic and comedic criteria. If in the course of *our* cutting some of their censored words were lost, then fair enough.

'Are there any cuts which we propose,' she says, 'that you would agree with?' 'No,' we say, 'It's easier for us to tell you cuts on which we will *never* negotiate and you can work backwards from there.' We single eight points out of the first twelve on which we are immovable.

Much to-ing and fro-ing. The lady and the zombie reappear. Yes …

there could be some negotiation, but first can we tell them the points in the two other shows which we would be prepared to talk over. Here Osterberg starts to play the impatience game. And quite rightly. He insists, on behalf of his clients, of course, that ABC must first agree to restore all the eight cuts which we regard as non-negotiable. And here they baulk, and the lady lawyer looks more and more desperate, and the zombie walks out and leaves her to us, just as Shanks has earlier ditched him.

Osterberg orders us to put our coats on and we make our way across the heavy, soft carpet, past the clean, neat white desks, with their clean, neat white telephones, towards the elevators. The lady lawyer implores us to keep talking. 'I've been asked to settle this,' she pleads, her eyes moistening with what I would say was genuine fear – whether of us or of her superiors I don't know. Terry G and I smile sheepishly and the elevator doors close.

Over to the Stage Deli for lunch to restore our sense of proportion. Thank goodness we have each other to compare notes with. I like TG because he is very sane, very realistic, entirely down-to-earth. A couple of waitresses ask us for autographs. They'd loved the *Holy Grail*.

Back to the lawyers later. A gruelling and concentrated working-over of our testimony for two hours, followed by further rehearsals and a taste of cross-questioning.

It was decided that Nancy L should be our first witness in court, followed by myself – through whom Osterberg would bring out all the salient points of our testimony – followed by Terry G, who would weigh in with lavish doses of enthusiasm, conviction and generally play the bruised artist.

Ray, Bob Osterberg's junior, gave me some sample cross-questioning. Although I knew full well it was just a rehearsal, I couldn't help getting thoroughly riled by his techniques of incredulousness, heavy sarcasm and downright mocking misrepresentation. All – he assured me afterwards – perfectly permissible legal techniques for breaking down witnesses. All I can say is, they worked. I left the office around 11.00 feeling tired, depressed and angry. Totally evaporated was my clear-eyed crusading enthusiasm of yesterday. I realised now that it was to be a sordid struggle played on their terms, not ours.

Friday, December 19th, New York

Woke about 6.00 this morning. Felt well rested and, after a pee, turned over to go to sleep again when it hit me – with a sudden heart-thumping, palm-sweating realisation. In three and a half hours I would be reliving the horrors of the evening before – only this time in court and for real. Across the suite, in the other bedroom, TG had woken at about the same time.

I lay there and tried to accept the extraordinary day ahead philosophically. There was no alternative – we were doing the only right thing. We weren't having to lie or defend a dishonourable course of action. We just had to remember the purity of our initial indignation and it would all turn out fine – and anyway, by this evening we'd be on a plane back to London.

And yet my mind kept racing over possible fresh arguments, trying to turn and hone fine new phrases – only to suddenly discover weaknesses in my recollection. Surely lawyers didn't go through this every morning before an important case – they'd go mad.

As I was shaving – my case having been finally delivered to me by TWA in the early hours of Thursday morning – TG appeared, with a towel wrapped round him. He paced the room restlessly, looking quite idiotic in his towel and saying, 'I've got it … the *real* point is …' Then his eyes would take on a Martin Luther King-like intensity and I would hear phrases like, 'If just one. Just show me one person whose opinion of Python has suffered as a result of ABC … just one … and that is enough for me.' This was Gilliam's new line. He seemed on good form, but he and I nevertheless took a good shot of Bourbon before leaving the suite.

I try hard to keep a hold on reality, but it's difficult as TG and I and Nancy, with our entourage of lawyers, mount the steps of the vast twenty-storey tower of the US Federal Court House in Foley Square.

At first glance the courtroom was softer, warmer and far less intimidating than I expected. As plaintiffs in the case, we were allowed to sit with our lawyers at a vast and solid table in the front of the court, with the judge's box raised about four or five feet above us, and between him and us the enclosure for the clerks of the court and the court recorders. On our left the jury box, empty of course. Behind the jury box a line of tall windows brightened the court. Immediately behind us the ABC lawyers' table and then, at the back, about a dozen rows of wooden benches for spectators.

The hearing began with the entry of the judge behind a clerk of the court, who was not the old and wrinkled be-robed gent I had expected, but a young, casually dressed, Brooklyn-accented, probably Jewish, 20–25-year-old girl. She looked like the archetypal Python fan, and it's some indication of how surprisingly and pleasantly informal it all was, that I very nearly corpsed when she stood and made some odd opening ritual about 'Hear ye … Hear ye … Yeah verily …' and other strange nonsense. I was reminded perversely of *The Exorcist*, in which another perfectly ordinary all-American girl is made to say strange things and speak with strange voices.

The judge, Morris Lasker, was not robed either. I wondered whether or not he had seen the Python show which went out in New York on PBS last night, which contained a sketch about a judges' beauty contest!

Nancy testified first – speaking softly and looking composed, but endearingly vulnerable. The judge was correspondingly gentle with her. He was a honey-voiced, sensible, straightforward sort of fellow, anxious it seemed to avoid long legal discussions. As he said, he had read and studied the legal side of the case – today he wanted to hear witnesses. After Nancy, there was a short break for no apparent reason, then I gave testimony.

It was quite comfortable in the witness box – there was a chair, which I hadn't expected, and I was on the same level as the judge, which helped to put me at ease. As with Nancy, he was kindly throughout my evidence and cross-examination, repeatedly overruling ABC lawyer Clarence Fried's objections. I was not grilled particularly hard by Mr Fried. He had a face like an old, wrinkled prune, and kept pursing his lips in a sort of twitch. He wasn't anywhere near as aggressive or sardonic or incredulous as I had anticipated from the cross-questioning rehearsal last night.

The most difficult bit was having to describe sketches to the court which had been cut and make them sound funny.

One of the ABC-mutilated sketches which I had to describe to the court actually involved a fictional courtroom, in which an army deserter is being tried before a judge who is constantly interrupting with highly detailed queries. At one point the judge is particularly persistent about a pair of 'special' gaiters worn by the deserter.

What made the gaiters 'special' asks the judge?

'They were given him as a token of thanks by the regiment,' replies the prosecutor.

The judge asks why.

'Because, m'lud, he made them happy. In little ways.'

'In which little ways did he make them happy?' persists the judge.

At this point a bizarre situation became truly surreal as the prosecutor in the real court interrupted me and addressed the judge, in the real court. The following exchange is from the official transcripts:

'Mr Fried: Your honor, this is very amusing and interesting, but I think it is off the track.

'The Court [Judge Lasker]: Mr Palin is trying to tell me what the original was like so he can tell me what the effect of the excision will be. Overruled. Go ahead. I am not sitting here just because I am amused, although I am amused.'

Terry Gilliam testified after me. From where I was he sounded very straight, honest and direct. A real all-American boy.

Then, despite attempts from ABC's lawyer to put it off, the really damning evidence was produced. A colour TV was wheeled in and the judge, and as many as could squeeze in around him, took their places in the jury box to watch two tapes. The first was Show 3 of the fourth series of Monty Python – as it was shown on the BBC. A good show, with the 'Court Martial', 'Gorn' and 'RAF Banter' sketches in it. It went down well. The court recorder chuckled a great deal, as did the judge and the people operating the TV recorder. Definitely a success. Then was shown the ABC version of the same show.

The ABC version contained long gaps of blank screen where the commercials would go. Three such major breaks in the course of half an hour. The effect on the audience was obvious. It was the end of a very good morning for us.

After lunch Fried began to call his witnesses. A Mr Burns of ABC's Contracts Department spoke laboriously and with infinite, finely tuned dullness about the possible loss of money caused if the show was cancelled.

Shanks was next. He turned on a bravura display of ingratiating smugness. Oh, he'd been a writer in his time, he grinned. He knew the problems ... goddammit, he wouldn't like to lose a line of his own material ... but ... (Could this be the same man who was quite prepared to authorise the excision of 22 minutes out of 90 minutes of Python material? Talk of not wanting to lose a line – we were losing one line in every four!)

Fried bored the pants off everyone with heavy-jowled witnesses from Time-Life who all looked as if they were concealing mass-murders.

But a jarring note was struck at the end of the day when a lady at ABC testified that Ina Lee Meibach had rung her on December 10th and had told her that we were not only going to sue ABC, but we were going to drag their names through the mud and squeeze every last ounce of publicity from their predicament. For the first time in the entire proceedings we suddenly felt bad. We were found to be using distasteful, though doubtless common, tactics, and I think it reflects a serious weakness on Ina's part. She is sometimes *too* tough – she takes firmness to the point of vindictiveness.

At 5.00, as it darkened out in Foley Square, the judge finally withdrew. He re-appeared a half-hour or so later and delivered an impressively fluent summing-up which began by raising our hopes at the plaintiffs' table.

He found that ABC's cuts were very major and destroyed an important element of Python's appeal. He found our material was irreparably damaged. My heart leapt. 'But,' he went on to say that he could not grant the injunction for two reasons. One was that the BBC owned the copyright of the tapes sold to ABC, so the BBC should really have been in court too. He was disturbed by the delay in our proceeding against ABC, and had to take into account the amount of damage to ABC by our proceeding against them less than one week from the transmission date. So ... ABC were off the hook. We'd tilted at windmills and lost.

'But ...' Lasker, with a fine sense of timing, had one more twist for us ... because of the nature of the damage to us, he would look very favourably on any disclaimer the Pythons would like to put in front of the show when it went out on December 26th. There he finished – and our hopes were raised again. A disclaimer could be as strong and effective as a total ban on the show. Everyone would see us blame ABC openly.

Typical of ABC's extraordinary lack of understanding was that, following this verdict, they approached Terry G and suggested we work out a jokey little disclaimer together!

Out in Foley Square about 6.15. The cold, sub-zero wind whipping around us as we search for a subway entrance. A dark-coated, pipe-smoking figure, head bent down against the wind, crosses the square towards us. It's none other than Judge Lasker. He shows we three frozen plaintiffs the subway and walks down there with us. Alas we have no tokens for the barrier. The judge scrabbles around in his pockets, but can only find two to give us. Give me the money, he suggests, and he'll go through the barrier, buy us some tokens from the kiosk on the other side and hand them through to us.

We travelled, strap-hanging, with the judge, up to Grand Central Station. The nearest he got to talking about the case was when Terry G voiced his worries that the existence and the modus vivendi of the Standards and Practices Department of ABC was never questioned, and surely should have been. Yes, said Lasker, he too was worried about the Standards and Practices Department.

He merged into the crowds at Grand Central and we made our way back to the Navarro, packed our bags and, leaving Nancy and Kay-Gee-Bee Music with the bill, stretched out in an enormous limousine which bore us from the rather pretty Christmas atmosphere of New York away out to JFK yet again.

All usual flights to London until next week being booked, we found ourselves on Air Iran's flight to Tehran via Heathrow. So new was the flight that apparently the booking clerks at JFK didn't even know it stopped at London.

Saturday, December 20th

Woke uncomfortably with the dawn. Feeling dirty, crumpled and dreadfully tired – as only those who fly the Atlantic overnight *can* feel. The plane started to drip on Terry G ... but the hostesses were cheerfully dismissive of his complaints.

I have to wait for at least an hour at Christmas-crowded Heathrow before ascertaining that my case is definitely on its way to Tehran.

Monday, December 22nd

Further news of Python's ever-increasing international status – some fine reviews for *Holy Grail* in France. 'Mieux que Mel Brooks' – that sort of thing – and the film has apparently opened at a fourth cinema in Paris.

Wednesday, December 24th, Abbotsley

The harsh realities of the world away from the cosy log fires of Church Farm impinged deadeningly and depressingly. Terry Gilliam rang to say that, after Judge Lasker had accepted, with minor alterations, our disclaimer for the front of ABC's Boxing Day Special, ABC had appealed, on Monday afternoon, to three other judges, who had overruled his decision. All that will appear are the words 'Edited for television by ABC'.[1]

So, in terms of actual tangible legal rewards for our week in New York and the $15,000 of Python money spent on the case, we were left with very little. I wait to see evidence of the non-legal rewards, in terms of press coverage, etc, etc, before totally writing off our trip, but today's news was a pretty nasty Christmas present. But at least my bag arrived, having reached Abbotsley via Tehran.

Wednesday, December 31st

Almost the last event of 1975 is also one of the most important – the showing on BBC2 of *Three Men in a Boat*. We have quite a houseful here by 7.50 when it begins. Catherine Burd is watching with Tom and Willy (who are allowed to stay up) and Jeremy and Alex [neighbours] with their children, both a long way from the sitting still and shutting up age, are here as well. So quite a crowd, and it's rather difficult to judge the piece – especially as Stephen has opted for a very gently paced, softly played treatment – which seems to be at least ten decibels quieter than any other TV shows. I keep turning the sound up and sitting nearer, but it's very difficult not to be distracted and I really don't feel I've seen it in the best circumstances when it draws to its languid conclusion at 8.55.

1 We had wanted: 'The members of Monty Python wish to dissociate themselves from this programme, which is a compilation of their shows edited by ABC without their approval.'

1976

Friday, January 2nd

Up at 9.00 to gather all the papers. The *Daily Telegraph* calls *Three Men* 'as near to television perfection as makes very little matter'. A rave, no less. But, as I had expected, reviews were mixed and there was a very extensive and less friendly review in *The Times* by Michael Ratcliffe. Large photo above it and ominous heading 'Playing A Very Straight Bat'. Criticism of the lack of humour was the key note – Frears accused of being unable to 'find a comic style faithful to both writers' – Jerome K Jerome and T Stoppard, I presume. A pity that the *Times* review will be the one my friends will see. The *Daily Tel* may be a blue-rinse rag politically, but they do have extremely perceptive TV critics! No other reviews.

A very cordial Python meeting at Park Square East to discuss the content of our stage show in New York. Once again proved that Python works well as a group when discussing the creation of sketches and jokes – the reason, after all, why we originally got together. Python group at its worst discussing business, contracts, hiring and firing personnel, and other areas which we are better at making fun of than taking seriously.

Today, 'Blackmail' was added to the list, John having said that, although he may be sounding rather selfish, he wanted to cut down the number of sketches he appeared in, and he felt that I was very light in number of appearances. So 'Michael Miles' out and 'Blackmail' in. Graham protested briefly, but the general consensus was that 'Cocktail Bar' should go, along with the 'Bruces' and the 'Pepperpots' in a big purge of the generally accepted weak middle of the first half. In went 'Salvation Fuzz' (entirely new to stage), 'Crunchy Frog' (ditto) – with Graham taking John's role as Inspector Praline – and an amalgamation of court sketches to replace 'Silly Elections' as a closer.

Judging by today's meeting, it really seems that Python has emerged remarkably healthily from the mire of the last two years. There's a much friendlier, looser, more open feeling amongst the members of the group now. I wonder if it will weather the month's hard work on the New York stage show, and if it will produce an equally friendly and relaxed working atmosphere for September and October, when we get together to write the third Python film.

Strong, violent, gusting gales tonight. Up to 105mph in Cambridgeshire and many people killed (twenty-four).

Saturday, January 3rd

A busy, socialising weekend. Liz Garden rang on Saturday morning to ask if they could come over and fly Sally's new kite on Parliament Hill. I warned her about me and kites – that the two should never meet – but, despite warnings, Graeme, Sally, Tom, Willy and I braved a finger-numbing wind on the lower slopes of Parliament Hill. Bill Oddie had given Sally the kite, as he is now apparently a very serious kiter – a 'Formula One' kite flyer, as Graeme calls him.

True to form, I rip part of the thin cellophane fabric before the kite's even been flown. Several desperate attempts to get it in the air – it twists, wheels, turns like a bucking stallion at a rodeo, before plunging, inevitably, into the ground. After half an hour, when we think we have at last mastered the ballistics problem, Willy treads well-intentionally on one of the struts and the kite is finally written off.

Off to Le Routier at Camden Lock for lunch.

Very different from our local Queen's Crescent Market – the stall-holders are your traditional cockneys there – here at Camden Lock the stalls are run by the New Wave of stallholders – young, middle-class, usually feminine, emphasis on the arts and crafts and inter-stall talk about recent Fassbinder movies. Also appalling tat – they will clearly sell anything – as evidenced by several copies of the 1971 AA Book.

Sunday, January 4th

A couple of reviews in the Sundays. Philip Purser very favourable in the *Sunday Telegraph* – 'the languid trio was beautifully cast' – while Peter Lennon in the *Sunday Times* gave a brief and rather churlish dismissal of the whole piece, saying that Frears allowed his actors to settle 'for a relentlessly arch air which quickly grew tedious' and the Three Men 'suffered from an inability to sound at ease delivering lines which read agreeably enough in quaint, old-fashioned essay, but needed more drastic transformation by Tom Stoppard to work as dia-logue'. So raps on the knuckles all round. Against all my better feel-ings I was goaded into a short burst of bitter anger by the *Sunday Times* review. But it passed and rational thought returned.

Took boys to swim at the Holiday Inn for an hour, then Terry with Alison and Sally arrived bringing their Christmas presents. They gave Tom and Willy a steamroller, a beautiful, solid, working model, complete with whistle which blows a column of steam up your nostrils if you're not careful. Terry and I then drove out to Acton to play in a charity football match.

A rather forlorn, rain-soaked notice tied to the railings, which read 'Big Charity Match: All Stars XI v Happy Wanderers'.

A very strange afternoon altogether. I scored an own goal (though we won in the end). TJ scored his first goal since he was ten, there was an apparently total absence of any paying spectators, the changing room was minute and the beer was Watney's Red Barrel. Oh, the glamorous life of an All Star!

Wednesday, January 7th

Very warm again. Temps over 50. Sitting up in my room as I have done, with great pleasure, for the last three mornings. The boys went back to school on Monday and I embarked on a vast pile of letters – mostly from America. In two days I wrote about twenty-three replies to fan letters (*not* the very naughty ones!) plus a four-page New Year missive to Alfred Lord Levinson.

Today is *Tomkinson* day. To Terry J's to watch the show. Also there are Eric, Terry Gilliam, Chuck A,[1] Nigel and Dizzy.[2] The show looks fine. The reaction within the group of us was very, very good. Terry G ... 'Ah, well ... you've got no problems with that.' Chuck chuckled throughout. Eric was highly enthusiastic. Terry Hughes rang to tell me that Ronnie Barker had called him as soon as it finished to say how much he liked it.

When we got home later my head and stomach were suffering from excitement, relief, tacos and too much cheap Spanish wine. Kitty, our baby-sitter, had a list of calls which she'd rather nicely headed 'People who enjoyed *Tomkinson's Schooldays*'. Graham C rang to say how much better it was than he remembered it. Went to bed feeling rather ill.

---

1 Charles Alverson, American thriller-writer friend of TG.
2 Terry's brother and sister-in-law.

Thursday, January 8th

Gradually dawns on me during the day that *Tomkinson* has been something of a success. But for all the right reasons – nearly everyone who has liked it has mentioned its quality. Fresh, different, etc, etc. A meaty and handsome review in *The Times* by Alan Coren makes my day. Met Denis Norden in a shop, and he grasped my hand and told me he hadn't laughed so much since before Christmas!

Finally, as the shadows were lengthening over Gospel Oak, Jimmy Gilbert rang to give the official BBC verdict. He wants me to go in next Monday and talk about more shows.

I'm as pleased for Terry Hughes as I am for anyone. He worked the BBC system superbly – got us everything we wanted. He was always in sympathy with the script and its intentions and had an instructive and highly accurate sense of where it worked and didn't work.

Monday, January 12th

The continuing backwash of enthusiasm for *Tomkinson's Schooldays* has helped enormously – our reception by Jimmy at lunch in his office was tinged with more than just his usual cordiality – there was an undeniable air of self-congratulation which resulted in broader smiles, firmer handshakes and a generally more relaxed feeling. Only on a couple of occasions after Python's success did I ever feel this warm glow of unstinted BBC approval and even then it seemed qualified because of our naughty, enfant terrible reputation.

Then there's the question of front money from America. Jim clearly regards himself as something of a transatlantic supersalesman, and is working hard on Time-Life (whom Gilliam and I dragged into court less than a month ago!) to buy a series based on the successful *Tomkinson*, and therefore put up front money so that the BBC can afford our expensive services.

Out of all this we won several points. In the end Jimmy agreed that Terry Hughes should direct them all, he also agreed (a momentous point of principle here) that we could, if we needed to, do entire shows *on film*. I never thought I would live to hear a BBC Head of Comedy make such an heretical suggestion. In return for all this, Terry and I will supply the BBC with thirteen *Tomkinson*-style shows by mid-summer 1978.

Thursday, January 15th

About 1.00 Terry and I drove out to Beaconsfield in Bucks to talk about ourselves to the National Film School (Brian Winston, ex-Oxford and *World in Action*, having hustled us into it quite successfully).

It has the run-down air of a half-deserted RAF camp. There are suggestions of over-grown roads and pathways – the buildings are stark, functional and presumably cheap brick and concrete constructions without any refinements. It used to be the Crown Film Unit Studios, where 'chin-up' patriotic films were made to boost the nation's morale in wartime. Ironic, really, because it wouldn't do the nation's morale a lot of good to see it now.

Terry and I are there as part of a week's seminar on comedy. Winston told us afterwards, rather glumly, that there wasn't really anyone there who wanted to, or could, make comedy films. They were all too serious. We talked for almost two hours to about twenty students. They had watched *Tomkinson's Schooldays* in the morning and discussed it in terms of social relevance, criticism of authority, etc. I think they were a little disappointed when I told them that the choice of public school for the story was made simply because its absurd rituals and closed formal world were a very good area for jokes. Even Brian Winston, who was trying hard to defuse any pretentiousness, still referred to the nailing-to-the-wall joke as the 'crucifixion' sequence.

Friday, January 16th

Anne had had quite a traumatic meeting this afternoon with Arthur Cantor (who is over in England for two weeks) and Jim Beach[1] to try and finalise the Live Show deal for New York. The outcome was that Cantor has at last backed out. Cantor is a cautious, kindly theatre producer who likes to get to know the people he's working with and is temperamentally quite unsuited to the world of big advances, limousines, $75,000-worth of publicity – mostly to be spent on 'Sold Out' kind of advertising, and general image-building, which Nancy and Ina's people have been insisting on. Ina's office lose yet more popularity points by having apparently on our behalf been thoroughly unpleasant to A Cantor – who may be a little over-cautious and vacillating, but is a decent man.

1 Our legal adviser at the time. Later manager of Queen.

So now Anne is having to fix up Allen Tinkley [another American producer] and yet another rather shoddy chapter in Python's American adventure is closed.

Saturday, January 17th

Took the boys out in the morning to a Journey Through Space exhibition at the Geological Museum in South Ken.

Afterwards Tom and Willy pressed buttons in the How the Earth Began exhibition and we watched a film of a volcanic eruption, with a truly fantastic shot of a wall of lava just slowly enveloping a country road. Even better than the Goodies.

Late afternoon, and T Gilliam comes round. He now has a typed script of his *Jabberwocky* film, which runs at two and a half hours! He has seen *Jaws!* and was impressed – he's decided to try and make the threat of the Jabberwocky as frightening as the threat of the shark.

Wednesday, January 21st

I sat and dug deeper into *Something Happened* after supper. Joseph Heller is another important and original American humorist, but *Something Happened* doesn't make you laugh like *Catch-22*. It's a bleak account of modern American materialistic man and the extraordinarily bad state of his personal relationships and his ability to communicate. The portrait of Slocum, surrounded by family and friends, is nevertheless of a man as apart from his fellow beings as Meursault in Camus' *L'Étranger*. But Heller has a good, perceptive eye, and the joy of the work comes from catching a glimpse of yourself in a mirror – a moment of recognition of yourself – and of yourself in relation to other people.

Finally, watched *The Glittering Prizes* – a 'major new drama series' as the BBC call it. Scripts by Frederic Raphael (who wrote *Darling, Nothing But the Best* etc), six 80-minute plays about a group of Cambridge students of the early '50s. I rather admired this first one – 'liked' isn't quite the word – it was cleverly, neatly written, it bore all the trademarks of the Cambridge urbanity, wit, worldliness, which Oxford never seemed to quite share – certainly *I* didn't (perhaps that's what I'm saying).

Thursday, January 22nd

Tomorrow I must be on the ball, for even more important discussions, this time about the professional future, must be raised with Terry as a result of a couple of calls from Jimmy Gilbert who has once again emphasised that he would like the *Tomkinson* series to be a Michael Palin series, written by Michael Palin and Terry Jones and starring Michael Palin.

Friday, January 23rd

Today, upstairs in Terry's work-room, I told him of Jimmy's attitude. TJ looked hurt – but there was a good, healthy fighting spirit there too. TJ feels that *Tomkinson* may well have been originally my project, but it worked as a team project and Terry is now very angry that the BBC want to break the team by institutionalising a hierarchy into our working relationship – i.e. The Michael Palin Show.

We talked ourselves round in circles. I couldn't honestly say that I was prepared for TJ to take an entirely equal part in the acting, because this would involve me in a tussle with Jimmy over something I didn't feel was in my own best interests. We break off for lunch with Jill Foster at Salami's in Fulham Road.

It certainly seems that 1976 is all-change year. After almost ten years together, Terry and I are exploring and altering our relationship and Jill Foster and Fraser and Dunlop are doing the same. In short, Jill is leaving. She felt stifled at F & D, so now she wants to set up on her own.

We think we'll stay with Jill, despite the various problems that have cropped up over our Python activities. She's a good agent for us in many ways – a good talker, not renowned as vicious or hard in the business, but always seems to deliver an efficient, worthy, if not startling, deal.

After lunch we drive down to Terry's, talking again about the series. A peripatetic day, in fact, both literally and metaphorically. We decide to meet Jimmy together, but he can't make it until Monday. So I leave about 5.00 – with Terry still reeling slightly under a blow, which he hadn't after all expected. It's a rotten situation and rotten to see someone you like and whose friendship is so valuable being given a hard time. But it's all got to be said and to be gone through.

Monday, January 26th

Another meeting about the Jones/Palin relationship. This time at the BBC. Meet TJ for a coffee first and he, as I had expected, had taken stock of the situation over the weekend and come to an optimistic conclusion. He would write the series with me and then go off and make a film for children (a project he's had his thoughts on before) whilst I was filming. He seemed very happy.

However, once in Jimmy's office, TJ took a rather less accommodating line (quite rightly for, as he said afterwards, there was no point in the meeting if he didn't try to change JG's mind with a forceful view of his own).

I didn't do a lot of talking – I let Terry say all he wanted to say and Jimmy say what he wanted to say. JG was excellent I thought. He held to his position, but was sympathetic to all Terry said so, at the end of one and a half hour's meeting we were all still friends – and Jimmy adjourned us for a week to think about it. TJ did seem to be less angry than impatient with Jimmy and we went off for a lunch at Tethers.

I'm trying to avoid an utterly basic dissection of our relationship, because I think it's a relationship that obeys no strict rules, it works without introspection – it's an extrovert relationship based on writing and often performing jokes together. It's instinctive and I don't want to damage it by over-examination. I want (for such is my half-cowardly nature!) to solve this re-adjustment crisis without tears.

Tuesday, January 27th

Spoke to Terry, mid-morning. Rather than pursuing the Children's Film Foundation, TJ has instead revived that most hardy perennial – the *Fegg* film. He has rung John Goldstone, who reckons that 'The Nastiest Film in the World' has distinct possibilities!

Wednesday, January 28th

Another gorgeous day of clear, crisp, sharp sunshine. Terry comes up to Julia Street to talk about the *Fegg* film. We have some nice ideas – Fegg is a brooding and malevolent influence who lives in a corrugated iron extension up against a Gothic castle, near to the world's prettiest village, where everyone is terribly nice to each other. But the presence of Fegg (whom we see in a sinister, opening build-up sequence letting the air out of someone's tyres) is too much for them. They advertise for a hero. Scene cuts to a Hostel for Heroes, where unemployed heroes sit around in a sort of collegey atmosphere – occasionally getting jobs.

At the end of our day on *Fegg* – and with a possible commitment to writing on *Fegg* until we go to the US – I suddenly feel a touch of panic. Helen, with her usual down-to-earth perspicacity, provoked it by her reaction to the news of the *Fegg* film. I know she's right – I am taking on too much. The *Fegg* film is going to take time and ideas away from what should really be my primary project of the next two years – the BBC series of thirteen. Helen forces me to confront the fact that I am in danger of losing what I am trying to save.

Thursday, January 29th

Very cold again, but sunny. Reading the papers, hearing the news (imperfect form of information though that is), I get the feeling that there is an air of optimism about, a general air of improvement in the state of the country, which has been so battered over the last few years.

The Balcombe Street siege has, touch wood, marked the end of a couple of years of IRA terror, but it was the way in which the siege ended – peacefully, almost sensibly – and the way in which Jenkins[1] and the government refused to restore hanging in response to the primitive blood lust emotions of probably the majority of the country – that was the most hopeful outcome of the whole affair.

I rang Terry towards the end of the morning. He, too, had been worried when faced with actually writing the *Fegg* film, together with all our other commitments. But, later in the call, as we meandered around the area of commitments and involvements, Terry asked again the very basic question – 'Sod Jimmy Gilbert, Mike … what do *you* actually want the series to be?'

The almost continuous reflections on this subject over the last couple of weeks, the gut feeling that anything less than the independence I felt on *Tomkinson*, made me feel somehow, somewhere, dissatisfied, really gave me only one possible answer … 'Yes … I think I *do* want it to be the Michael Palin Show.'

1 Roy Jenkins. Labour government's Home Secretary.

Once I said this – and I had never said it with quite such conviction before – the debate and discussion was as good as ended. Terry accepted that – reluctantly, obviously, but quite generously and with relief that we were being honest with each other. God knows how it will turn out from here on, but the crucial question has been answered. Yes, I *do* want my independence, yes I *do* want the responsibility to be ultimately mine.

Fegg, we decide to shelve for a while. A well-intentioned attempt to please everybody, a project which I am genuinely enthusiastic about, but, thank goodness, this morning realism has prevailed all round.

Friday, January 30th

January draws to a close in bitter cold. Last weekend there was some snow – which was preferable to the bitter, ear-aching, sub-zero winds which blow around London today. But it's sunny again this morning. I have a meeting at the BBC with Jimmy G and Terry Hughes. Bill Cotton flits through, shakes my hand and says how pleased he was with the reaction to *Tomkinson*. The official warmth of the BBC's approval wafts around. I fear and mistrust it. Self-doubt and official disapproval are better for you.

We talk about money. Jimmy would like £4,000 per show guaranteed front money from the US. *Tomkinson*, according to computer forecasts (the BBC have a computer!), will cost £34,000 per episode in 1977, about double the average LE sit-com episode.

Thursday, February 5th

A Grammy Award Nomination arrives in the post from LA. *Matching Tie and Handkerchief* has been nominated for Best Comedy Album of the Year. The Americans are very good at the Awards business – the Grammy nomination is impressively announced all over the envelope (postmen and friends please note). The awarding body is the extraordinarily impressive National Academy of Recording Arts and Sciences and the letter, when opened, brings tears of joy and emotion. 'We extend our sincere congratulations to you for this honor bestowed upon you by the Recording Academy's voting members who are your fellow creators and craftsmen.' I could almost hear soaring strings and stirring brass play as I read these words. It's exactly the sort of pomposity that Python's LPs attempt to deflate, but it was still a Truly Wonderful Letter to Receive.

By February 13th we have to decide how we are going ahead on the ABC case. Osterberg is keen to fight on; feels that Lasker's summing-up was 'transparent', and that his decision would be reversed by the Court of Appeals. However, O has given us no indication as to how this would be achieved and on what grounds Lasker was 'transparent'. In view of the costs involved, and the fact that no one really has the time to single-mindedly pursue the case, I reluctantly tell Anne that I feel we should pay Osterberg's $15,000 and forget it.

Wednesday, February 11th, Southwold

Arrived at Darsham at 11.30 – from the train I could see Father hunched up in the car – it's not so easy for him to come on to the platform, especially on a wet, cold morning like this.

His speech is a little better, but he has great difficulty eating. The latest refinement is for him to use his teeth as and when required. He has them beside him in a plastic container and puts them in if there is some particularly tough piece of food to cope with.

The wind increases during the day, until by night-time it's nearly gale-force. It's the kind of weather which emphasises the bleak aspect of the east coast. But it's cosy enough inside Croft Cottage – with the fire and my appearance on *Just a Minute* to listen to on a crackly radio.

This morning an IRA man, Frank Stagg, starved to death at the end of a hunger strike in Wakefield. The IRA have sworn to 'avenge' his death and made various threats about England 'paying for it' ... which everyone knows they can carry out. An atrocity isn't far off, I feel.

Friday, February 13th, Southwold

Woken by Father drawing the curtains at 8.30.

Glad to stay in, as the gales roared out of grey skies all day long. Managed an hour or so's work on a whodunnit – for the *Ripping Yarns*.[1]

1 The name came from a suggestion by Terry's brother, Nigel, who'd spotted a book on one of Terry's shelves with a similar style of schoolboy tales.

Train back to London at 6.30. Leaving them both with a certain amount of optimism for once. Clearly, Father is at his happiest at home and the fact that a nurse now baths him once a week and he goes to Blythburgh Hospital for therapy, etc, twice a week, has lightened the load on my mother a little.

In the station buffet at Ipswich the newspaper seller has a rumour for us – a bomb at Piccadilly Circus. When I finally get back to an eerily quiet London, I hear that the bomb was at Oxford Circus and didn't go off. But it was twenty pounds-worth of TNT in the main concourse on the Underground. It could have been the bloodiest explosion yet.

Saturday, February 14th

A sunny morning. We pack the car for a weekend at Abbotsley. The sun brings people out as if it's a holiday. Thomas gets a Valentine from Holly – which he can't stop talking about – and Holly, of course, doesn't want him to know it's from her. All I get is a bill from the dentist.

Vivid impressions of South East Asia in Paul Theroux's *The Great Railway Bazaar* – a book which has stirred up so many of my travelling impulses.

Monday, February 16th

Worked all day adapting the Fegg book's 'Across the Andes by Frog' for one of the *Ripping Yarns*. Terry rang in the morning. He sounded very down – he was getting yearnings to make films, programmes, to make something – and saw the year ahead passing without achieving this.

However, he had cheered up considerably by the late afternoon and we played squash – quite hard games – and afterwards drank beer and chatted about life, art and other Hampsteadisms up at the Flask. It was nearly eight o'clock when he dropped me back home. Out to dinner with Robert H.

Bomb-scare talk with the cab driver. So far no deaths or dangerous explosions since Stagg's death, but the cabman tells me that Warren Street Underground has been cleared and that there's a road block at Notting Hill Gate. Pick up Robert and on to Odin's – which has been boarded up outside like a wartime restaurant. There is a man standing outside who checks your name on the reservation list and only one small rectangle of glass on the door has been left uncovered. I suppose the more expensive the restaurant the heavier the bomb-proofing – there was nothing at all over the extensive glass frontage of the Italian caff on the corner opposite.

Home about 12.15, feeling a bit swivel-headed – and remembering that we drank a whole bottle of champagne as well. What swells we've become in the thirteen years we've known each other. The potential was always there, I suppose – but the money never was!

Tuesday, February 17th

Afternoon visit to a showbiz, sorry, *the* showbiz throat specialist. Jill F had suggested I go and see him before taking any voice projection lessons, just to check that there was no damage to my vocal cords, etc, since previous screamings.

His surgery is in Wimpole Street, where illness and privilege combine to create a pleasantly elegant part of the world. The ceilings were high, the hallway opened out into a sort of circular covered atrium with heavily impressive, brass-handled doors leading off on all sides – like a dream where you have to choose between six identical doors. They apologised for their heating having gone off.

Mr Musgrove was at his desk in the far corner of a huge room. I noticed a leather armchair, but that's about all. He wore a reflector plate on his head, talked beautifully and, from where I was sitting, he could have been Kenneth More playing the role. He sat me down on a swivel chair beside a table full of instruments, which looked like a still life from a book of Edwardian medical studies.

Holding my tongue and nearly bringing me to the point of vomiting, he investigated my vocal cords, occasionally sterilising his mirror in a small gas flame.

But he was efficient, convincing and reassuring. No sinus problems and, he was glad to say, my vocal cords were in good shape – no trace of damage. Prescribed some nose drops for me to take only if things got really bad. He told me he'd treated Julie Andrews every day for six months when she was shooting *Sound of Music*. 'Oh, yes … we got her through,' he said. Suddenly I felt my problem was really quite insignificant – which I'm sure is the best way I should feel about it. I paid him £10 thankfully.

Thursday, February 19th

Down to Wimpole Street (for the second time in a week) for a medical examination for insurance for the City Center Show. After having my throat, eyes, balls, back, thighs, glands and penis examined (in a way which made me feel more like a racehorse being checked for doping), I took myself off to South Kensington to Willy Rushton's apartment in Old Brompton Road. It looks out over one of the busiest, most cosmopolitan, open-all-night stretches of London, just by South Ken tube. WR describes it as rather like a 'cold Tangier'.

Ian Davidson, Terry J, Willy and myself are performing 'Custard Pie'[1] at a charity show at the Old Vic on Sunday night in memory of an actor called James Mellor, whom, it transpired as we sat around the table at Willy's, none of us actually knew. Willy R does rather a lot of these good causes (shows for Angola, Chile, refugees, etc) and we fantasised on the idea of professional charity performers having a 'Chile show' that 'might run' and 'a week on Namibia in June', etc, etc.

Willy knocked back two and a half pints very swiftly and, about 9.00, we made our separate ways, to meet again at the Old Vic on Sunday. 'I'm never quite sure where the Old Vic is,' says Willy, in his famous crusty-colonel voice, which, as far as I can gather, is his actual voice. I like him. He makes you laugh, and enjoys being made to laugh himself.

Sunday, February 22nd

At the Old Vic, Albert Finney is on the stage sorting out the acts.

We run through 'Custard Pie', then hang around in the not altogether convivial atmosphere of dozens of well-known faces. Jimmy Villiers, Mike Jayston (they are familiar via the footy matches), John Le Mesurier, Julian Holloway, Barry Rutter, Glenda Jackson, Gaye Brown, George Sewell, Joss Ackland, Ron Pickup, Bernard Cribbins (lovely feller) etc, etc. Everyone being a wee bit defensive, so am quite glad when we four dilettante comedy artists, who find ourselves at the end of a bill lasting at least three hours, leave the claustrophobic clutches of the Old Vic and end up across the road in the George Inn, London's last galleried pub. Inside, on uncarpeted floors, with black beams and yellow-

---

1 A deadpan lecture about slapstick, with demonstrations, originally written by Terry J, myself and Robert Hewison for an Oxford Revue in 1963.

ing walls and benches and tables, we find the perfect place to while away a couple of hours. We drink a few pints and swap stories of old cabarets.

Back at the theatre we stand in the bar and watch the performance on closed circuit TV. It's 10.00 and they are still doing the second act – we are at the end of the third.

Willy R was now on the double scotches and philosophising about this being the ideal way to go to the theatre. Sitting in the bar watching it all on TV – perhaps all the theatres in London should be wired up so, drink in hand, you could switch over to the Wyndhams when you got bored with Ibsen at the National.

We went on eventually and did our bit. Albert Finney was drinking champagne and swaying about a little as he introduced us. We proceeded to do less than the best version of 'Custard Pie', but no one cared by then.

Tuesday, February 24th

Worked a near four-hour stint this morning on the 'Mystery at Moorstones Manor' whodunnit story. Useful reading it to the Herberts on Saturday night last, their reaction helped me to sort out a new sense of direction for the sketch – which is nearing an ending – as TJ arrives up here about 1.30.

We chat, Terry had a bad week for writing last week – he was buying cars for Nigel, etc, and lost all the afternoons. My strategy of fairly disciplined writing and trying hard not to get involved in side work has paid off with the whodunnit, which TJ liked a lot and he's taken it away now to think of an ending.

Wednesday, February 25th

Work on the 'Curse of the Claw' – a story begun by Terry and featuring the wonderfully scabrous Uncle Jack, the boy/narrator's hero who has all the diseases known to man, at the same time.

Both Terry Hughes and Jimmy G were on the phone today to firm up arrangements for the twelve *Ripping Yarns*. Python film writing is now almost certainly shifted to November/December this year, leaving September/October free to film two *Ripping Yarns*.

Then comes the problem of the day – a bulky script bound in livid purple and called *Jabberwocky*, which was dropped in by T Gilliam yesterday for me to read. He wants me to play the part of Dennis, the peasant, one of only two central figures in the script. It sounds something I would like to be involved in, but will require a two-month commitment in the middle of the year.

Talking to Jill F on these matters, she tells me that she had been asked about my availability for a new Tom Stoppard play at the Open Space. Job of jobs! Delight of delights! But unfortunately it's in April and I'll be treading the boards on Broadway. Well, *near* Broadway.

Friday, February 27th

I work through until 5.00. Steady and pleasing progress on 'Across the Andes by Frog', one of three storylines which are already in sight of an ending.

The last two weeks' work have been very prolific and satisfying, with only a couple of days when I chased a red herring and got stuck up a gum tree in a cul-de-sac, and very little dull stuff. Most of the writing has been a pleasure to read the next morning, which is the best test of quality. I enjoy the writing, I enjoy my house, my family and, more than anything I enjoy the feeling of seeing each day used to the full actually to produce something. The end.

Monday, March 1st

A cloudless, blue-sky day. London sparkles, everyone and everything looks better for this dose of reviving spring sunshine. To the Aldwych Theatre for the first of my lessons with Cicely Berry – premier voice-training lady of British Theatre (so everybody says).

She concentrates on transferring my breathing from the top of the rib-cage to the stomach. Once, and she says it will take time, but once I can feel myself breathing out of my stomach, then the tensing of shoulder and back muscles will not affect my voice production, as happens now. Read out Dylan Thomas poem and tried the new breathing techniques. I see her again on Friday.

Call from TG. He says that Sandy Lieberson, producer of *Jabberwocky*, is now going off the idea of Michael Crawford and is almost persuaded to employ me. Apparently the condition he made today is that J Cleese should be in it as well. TG rang John and offered him a couple of days' work in August. John apparently accepted without wanting to see the script.

Wednesday, March 3rd

Writing at home during the day. Terry is scribbling down in Camberwell. In the evening a meeting with Michael and Anne Henshaw re what to do with the Palin millions.

As I sit, like a spectator at a game of tennis, watching Michael and Anne lob and volley tax avoidance chat, very little of which I begin to understand, I feel that same surge of panic in my ignorance as when I was taught maths at school, and as the problem, equation, or whatever was remorselessly expounded, I found myself nodding helplessly along with the rest of the class, knowing full well I didn't know what was being talked about, but realising that if I asked I would still panic again when it was explained. I sometimes think the Inland Revenue are doing me a favour – it would be the simplest thing to let them do all the sums and take the money and pat me on the head and leave me to the rather modest way of life which is the despair of a true accountant.

Thursday, March 4th

TG rang this evening. Evidently, after some hassles with 'them' – i.e. the producers – he has finally persuaded them that I should play Dennis the Peasant in *Jabberwocky*. So, contracts permitting (and I'd do it for no money anyway), I shall be filming from July 27th to the end of September, and straightaway after that filming two *Yarns*.

Drove down to Terry J's for a couple of hours of reading new material. London splendid in the hazy sunshine.

'Across the Andes by Frog' and 'Mystery at Moorstones Manor' are virtually complete and over the last couple of days I've made some headway elaborating on TJ's very funny start to 'The Wolf of the Sea'.

A couple of bomb explosions as we're eating our supper. That makes three today, but no one hurt in any of them.

Start to read *Jabberwocky* again – realise that I get peed on twice by page fifty!

Friday, March 5th

To the Aldwych Theatre for another session with Cicely B. Cicely as usual exuding her air of comfortable friendliness. She's the kind of person you meet once and would tell everything to.

Another very satisfactory hour's session on the voice. I do think I know and can actually now put into practice the main part of her advice, which is that we should breathe up from our stomachs, which is, after all, the centre of the body, and try and forget chest and shoulders. I try Gumby at full stretch a few times. Cicely cowers away.

Tuesday, March 16th

Harold Wilson is resigning. Quite a bombshell, for there were none of the usual press leaks. But he has just 'celebrated' (as they say), his 60th birthday, which is a very statesmanlike thing to do, and Harold, of all recent Western politicians, from Kennedy and Johnson through Brandt and Nixon and Maudling and Thorpe, is still clean – so presumably he's getting out while the going's good. Still, he's been PM for nine years and was becoming as secure a British institution as the Queen or Bovril.

Terry G rings, distraught. The Neal's Yard property is in jeopardy[1] – evidently the owner, who had constantly reassured TG it was his, now says he has another buyer. TG very worried, as he has bought the film equipment and needs to set it up somewhere before April 5th – end of tax year!

In late afternoon, down to Covent Garden with TG to look at premises. It's exciting down there – a lot of well-designed shop-fronts, and well-renovated, sturdy old buildings. Art designers, film and recording studios, craft shops and ballet centres are moving into old banana warehouses and there's a good healthy feeling of an area coming to life again. Neal's Yard premises look perfect for us. I hope we don't lose them.

Monday, March 22nd

Arrived at Anne's about 10.00 for the first read-through of material for an ambitious charity show in aid of Amnesty International. As I'm parking outside Park Square East, I nearly run over Jonathan Miller – who is to produce the Amnesty show – loping towards Anne's door. His curly hair is unbrushed, his clothes are an unremarkable heap of brown, and his eyes look a little red. He greets me very cheerfully.

1 Encouraged by Terry Gilliam and Julian Doyle, I was about to become part-owner of a property at 14/15 Neal's Yard, in Covent Garden, which we hoped would become a production base for Python and individual work. André Jacquemin's sound studio, in which I already had a financial interest, would be an important part of the mix.

As we go upstairs, I catch sight of a gun mike pointing in our direction and a blinding early morning sun shining directly at us suffuses the scene with a Gala Premiere-like quality. The mike and the camera belong to the Roger Graef team, a 'specialist' documentary group, whose typical product is the long, minutely observed documentary of people at work. Evidently they are going to trace the whole process of putting on the Amnesty show. They try to work as unobtrusively as possible. They don't use any artificial light and Chas Stewart, the cameraman, usually crushes himself discreetly, if uncomfortably, into a corner of the room. Only the flick of the gun mike is impossible to ignore.

Jonathan Miller is disarming and jokey, and not at all daunting, as I think I had expected. He certainly has a very encouraging attitude to the Amnesty show. Organise it, direct it, by all means, but let's keep the feeling of a spontaneous, anything-might-happen evening.

After a half hour's discussion and coffee – when it was agreed that Peter Cook should take over Eric's role as the condemned man in the 'Court Sketch' and that Terry J should be transferred to a Cook, Bennett, Miller sketch, in lieu of Dudley Moore who is in the US – Miller left, but with a very good parting shot. He gazed out of the windows into Regent's Park and murmured nostalgically, 'I used to play in those gardens when I was three. I remember a girl of eight asked me to show her my cock … It's never happened since,' he concluded, rather sadly.

R Graef is a very bright, approachable and likeable man. He shares the view of the *Weekend World* team that news presentation is, generally speaking, dead and flat and goes on to say he feels TV as a whole fails to involve its audience. His prolonged documentaries are an attempt to involve the TV viewer, without the smooth, glossy aids of well-worked storylines, and rather by presenting real people 'warts and all'. His technique begs a lot of questions, but it's refreshing to talk to someone who feels that something *can* be achieved on TV and is not for ever shaking his head sadly and saying 'Well of course, it would be lovely to do this, but …'

After lunch Terry and I play squash. Not a bad game, considering we both had curry behind us. Terry has a theory this is why Pakistanis make such formidable squash opponents.

Tuesday, March 23rd

At 12.00, via the bank to Anne's to drop off visa forms plus ghastly photo of Helen for States. Then to Fetter Lane for an extremely civilised hour of culture with Robert. We had lunch (white wine, smoked ham, Camembert and granary bread and salad) and I looked over Chris Orr's Ruskin etchings,[1] which will be the basis of the book I'm funding. I like them very much. Quite different from what I had expected, they are full of references to Ruskin's (Chris Orr's) sexual repression and fantasies. This theme gives the etchings a clear unity, but within that there is a wealth of detail and some very successful theatrical effects in the etchings themselves.

To Liverpool Street to meet my mother off the Ipswich train. Bring her back home for a cup of coffee and a quick glimpse of her youngest granddaughter. Father is in Southwold Cottage Hospital for two weeks. He's resigned to it, but not happy about it, but Mother really does need the breaks if she's to survive.

From here I take her down to Angela's, where she's to spend the next couple of days. As I leave Angela tells me that she is really feeling awful – she's in the grip of a repetition of the depression which hit her over ten years ago. She's on pills and anti-depressants, but these seem to do nothing for her confidence, though they may overcome the symptoms for a while.

She warned me that Ma would have to hear about it all and, as she put it, I would 'have to pick up the pieces' when Ma came over to stay with us on Thursday. I walked back to the car feeling almost as Angela was – on the point of tears. I feel so helpless.

Friday, March 26th

At the Tate Gallery for the Constable exhibition. It really was packed and, not having the time or the inclination to join the line of people two or three thick slowly moving round the 300-odd works in the exhibition – like a crowd lining up to pay their last respects to a dead monarch – Granny and I weaved in and out, wherever there was a gap. Once again, with pictures like the Haywain, seeing the original makes one aware of what a gross disservice to the painter are reproductions – and especially with a popular and acceptable painter like C, whose paintings are on matchboxes, chocolate boxes and soap boxes ad nauseam. There is so much delicacy of detail in the Haywain that these reproductions miss

1 The artist Chris Orr was introduced to me by Robert, who was a big fan of both Chris Orr and John Ruskin.

totally and it's really a far better painting than its clichéd popularity led me to think.

I go and do some shopping in Long Acre and Piccadilly – a gorgeously rich blue sky, Londoners on their way home blinking in the bright sunlight, buildings picked out in sharp definition by the evening sun. I could have enjoyed London for another couple of hours, as it emptied for the weekend, but I had to get home.

To bed late again. Can't bear to think of what there is to do before we fly off to New York now – only just over a week away!

Sunday, March 28th

Spend the morning at a rehearsal for 'Poke in the Eye'.[1]

Jonathan Miller took the part of the director. Rather well, I thought. He made intelligent suggestions, managed to avoid sounding bossy, kept the work-rate going steadily, and didn't at all justify John Cleese's early grumpiness. 'I wrote a film for Video Arts yesterday about how to chair a meeting, and one of the most vital things is for the chairman to have done his homework,' said Cleese icily.

All in all a very jolly morning – when people started going through their pieces it was like an old folk's nostalgia evening. Alan Bennett did his 'Norwich' telegram piece, Eleanor Bron some witty Michael Frayn material – performed with her stunning, but sometimes quite alarming sense of realism. John Bird arrived, looking windswept and awry, as if just woken from a very long sleep, just in time to rehearse his Idi Amin speech.

By way of a complete contrast Barry Humphries swanned elegantly in, fedora at a rakish angle, smart herringbone suit on and giving off a delicately perfumed fragrance. He was off to a dinner engagement so couldn't stay long.

Roger Graef and team filmed away, drawn to Jonathan M, as far as one could tell, like moths round a flame. The more I see of them at work, the more dangerous I think it is for them to give the impression in their programmes that they are following and revealing everything important as it happens. Their own selectivity dictates the programme.

Robert H round in the evening. We finalise details about Chris Orr's Ruskin book, which is to be a Signford[2] publication. They'll print 1,500 copies and I'll put in £1,500.

1 *A Poke in the Eye with a Sharp Stick* was the title of the Amnesty extravaganza.
2 Signford was an off-the-shelf company and my first, and last, publishing enterprise.

Monday, March 29th

Lunch with Terry H at the Arlecchino in Notting Hill Gate to discuss script of 'Moorstones' and 'Andes by Frog'. Terry J also there.

Terry J talks of what a wonderful unit Python was together, how we functioned best then. I feel I'm functioning best *now* – with my hard-won independence. It's not selfishness or conceit, it's just to do with avoiding the wear and tear on the nervous system.

Shopping in the King's Road all afternoon, then dropped in to see Nigel [Greenwood] at the gallery. He was in, the gallery was empty. It was six o'clock, so it gave him an excuse to bring out the scotch. We drank and chatted for an hour. I told him about Robert and the Ruskin book. He was interested to know who was publishing, as he himself publishes books. He's just spent thousands on a Gilbert and George[1] book which the printers have heavily fucked up.

He said that, although the gallery has a very experimental attitude and is known for showing the most unconventional and outrageous works, the artists he shows don't like the gallery world … Nigel a bit resigned, but rather rueful about this.

Wednesday, March 31st

The Amnesty bandwagon gathers momentum today – a second and final rehearsal on stage at Her Majesty's, with Roger Graef and team poking about. I notice them filming, at great length, a conversation between Cleese and Peter Cook on the stage, and it occurs to me that, as the cameraman himself is small (or average) compared to them, he's probably much happier filming tall people. I asked Graef whether I would be a better bet for tele-verité if I were six inches taller … 'Oh, yes, undoubtedly,' he assured me. 'They can get lovely angles if you're tall – shots against the sky, or, in this case, against the spotlights.' Yesterday they'd been filming the Goodies at rehearsal and the cameraman had found Bill Oddie quite a problem.

Peter Cook – who apologised for his slightly glazed state, saying he was recovering from a long night spent with John Fortune discussing Lenny Bruce's drug problem – steadfastly refuses to learn the words of

---

1 Artists who called themselves 'living sculptures'. They were just beginning to make a wider name for themselves.

the Condemned Man in our 'Court Sketch'. He does ad-lib very well, but it gives Terry J a few hairy moments.

At about 12.30, more press photos outside. For some reason a *Daily Mirror* photographer issues us all with pickaxes – no one knows why until we see the photo in the *Mirror* on April 1st with the caption 'Pick of the Jokers'. No wonder the *Mirror* are losing their circulation battle.

Thursday, April 1st

At the theatre the last of the bare-breasted *Ipi-Tombi* dancers[1] are leaving (in sensible Jaeger sweaters and two-piece suits!). Neil's band Fatso are heaving in their equipment. Outside in King Chas II Street the Manor Mobile Recording Studios are parked with cables and wires running into the stage door.

People milling around. We're all in one dressing room – Cook, Bird, Jones, Gilliam, Cleese, (not Bron), Bennett – all of us plus Roger Graef's camera and mike, which searches around picking up snatches of conversation here and there. Brief 'Lumberjack Song' rehearsal. A book is opened at P Cook's instigation on the length of the show.

Curtain up at 11.35. Jonathan and I walk out. Me sweeping the stage, him directing me. Then into 'Pet Shop' and we're away. First half runs till 1.00. JM does some ruthless cutting of the second half. Eleanor and Johnny Lynn[2] fed up their bits have been excised, but so has 'Crunchy Frog'.

Roar of recognition and applause (still!) on things like 'Argument', 'Lumberjack' and 'Pet Shop'. End with making a balls-up of 'Lumberjack Song'. I start too early, try again – too flat – try again and we get through it.

Many curtain calls at the end, though – they really enjoyed it. It's 2.15 and Roger Graef is filming 'after the show' atmos. Feel tired, depressed, just want a scotch.

Saturday, April 3rd

Probably the best night of all tonight, though 'Argument' is cut for time and Graham is boisterously drunk. Alan Bennett feigns mock-horror in

---

1 *Ipi Tombi*, a South African musical about a boy looking for work in the mines of Johannesburg. It was said to be the first musical performed by nude actors in London.
2 Jonathan Lynn, film director. Creator and co-author of *Yes Minister*. Cambridge contemporary of Eric Idle, whom he later directed in *Nuns on the Run*.

the dressing room as Graham, at his most baroque, is fondling Terry J as he changes. 'Oh dear,' says Alan to Jonathan, shaking his head with a worried frown, 'We *never* used to do that sort of thing. We never used to touch each other.'

Graham and Peter make a strange pair – both with inflated eyes and a sort of boozy calm which can and does easily flare up. Graham's bête noire tonight, and not for the first time, is Bill Oddie. Tonight is the only night the Goodies appear. They are in a different world from everyone else in the show, with their 'Funky Gibbon' pop numbers, complete with dance movements – a rather gluey, trad. middle-of-the-road *Top of the Pops* appearance.

John Bird has useful suggestion for 'Court Sketch', which I worked on hard tonight. He says I'm doing my Prosecutor in the same way as Cleese (i.e. starting with outrage and working up from there) and I should play it differently. Good thinking.

We may have made £15,000 or £16,000 for Amnesty from the three nights.

Sunday, April 4th

A winding-down day. No need to prepare for America until tomorrow. So just enjoy, for once, the laziness of Sunday. Up at 9.15 – no adverse effects from Amnesty show – brain damage, throat damage, hangover, etc. Feel in good shape. Buy croissants and papers up at South End Green.

Spend a couple of hours in the evening working my way through the entire American show, trying to look carefully at characters, possible rewrites for US audiences, dangerously difficult English regional accents, etc, etc. I feel it's very important to sit quietly and work out one's own problems before we reach New York. After tonight's session, I feel I know the show much better and, if we suddenly had to put it on tomorrow, we could.

Tuesday, April 6th, New York

Sunshine in New York and a freshness in the air – a perfect spring afternoon. First sight of our home for the next four weeks, our very own brownstone in East 49th Street between Second and Third Avenues.[1] No.

---

1 I shared the house with Terry J – and, later, our families.

242, once home (still sometimes the home, I presume) of a writer, Garson Kanin,[1] and his actress wife Ruth Gordon. A feeling of euphoria swept over me as I explored its four floors – none of which had a room, a picture, a piece of furniture, an ornament, an element of any kind which wasn't pleasing without being pretentious. There were no disappointments – no dingy back rooms or peeling wallpapers or Formica partitions – and, at the same time, no forbidding luxuries. Though it's clearly the home of wealthy, or once-wealthy collectors and high-livers, it has a comfortable, warm friendliness about it.

As if the house itself (complete with library) wasn't a joy in itself, it backs on to a Spanish-style pattern of gardens, known as Turtle Bay Gardens. Courtyards with trees and flowering shrubs and daffodils and a fountain – again, like the house, cosy, comfortable, peaceful in the heart of a city which is unceasingly noisy.

I bounded around the house, probably boring TJ stiff with constant and repetitious enthusiasm.

Wednesday, April 7th, New York

Woke about 4.00, feeling distinctly unsleepy.

The incessant hum of New York begins to build up to what is, by Oak Village standards, an early-morning roar. It's almost like a magnet, drawing you up and out, defying you to stay in your bed, defying you not to get involved.

Later in the morning a huge black limousine swishes up outside and drives Terry J and myself plus Carol and Terry G to the helipad on the East River, whence we are to be airlifted over the steel mills and scrap yards of the Garden State. In about 40 minutes Philadelphia can be glimpsed on the horizon straight ahead – a cluster of tower blocks and skyscrapers rising skywards like a petrified explosion.

We land on the roof of a bank, and are whisked downstairs and across the road to the Westinghouse TV Studios where the Mike Douglas Show is recorded. We're told it's the biggest regular single TV audience in the world – 40 million watch each show.

He showed two good clips from the TV Pythons and the Black Knight fight in its entirety from the film. The Black Knight fight

2 Garson Kanin (1912–99), New York-based actor, writer, director and author of very readable Hollywood novel *Moviola*.

contrasted nicely with the clean teeth and the 'He-Tan' make-up of all the guests. There was Ron Vereen, who didn't need He-Tan as he was black, but wore a very well-tailored Savile Row suit and kept smiling. And there was Gabriel Kaplan, a TV comic who kept smiling and another TV actor called David Soul, who was very blond and slightly embarrassed when Terry J sat on his knee after we'd all been introduced. But I did get to meet one of the folk-heroes of my youth – in fact I sat next to him and smiled along with him for all the forty million viewers to see – Neil Sedaka, writer and singer of great hits of my teenage years, made-up lavishly, like a badly restored painting. 'You guys are just crazy,' he cooed.

Thursday, April 8th, New York

This time I must have woken even earlier – 3.30 or so. I tend to wake up with that momentary flash of terror, as if something really nasty is going to happen today. I chase the feeling away quickly enough, but I suppose it will continue to be there until the show has opened, settled into a routine and the pressure on us to be brilliant and successful is relaxed.

About 8.00 get up, do a half hour of voice exercises, soak in the bath and read a little Pirsig,[1] which concentrates the mind wonderfully. Coffee for breakfast downstairs, then a 25 minute walk across town to our rehearsal room near Broadway. Big, functional, mirrored rehearsal room.

Bad news of the day is that Eric has been ill in bed since yesterday and may have a mono-something or other – a liver problem – and be bad enough for us at least to discuss an alternative show if he couldn't make it.

The rehearsal is quite gruelling and, around 1.00, a rather aged and slow camera crew arrive with a pleasant, dumpy compere to film us rehearsing for use on a news/current affairs show later this evening. They are certainly no Roger Graefs, and the result is an extra hour of rehearsal, until after 2.00. Everyone is a little short-tempered and, when the interviewer finally interviews each one of us and says he wants us to be as loony and silly as we want, the numbing feeling of being rats in a cage comes over me again. We manage some facetiousness and paltry slapstick.

1 *Zen and the Art of Motorcycle Maintenance* by Robert Pirsig.

Terry and I have an evening appointment with the singular Mr Conlon, our publisher. He meets us in the lobby of the Yale Club, on Park and Vanderbilt. Classical columns, and old group photographs. We are both given ties to wear and copies of *Dr Fegg's Nasty Book of Knowledge* – our first sight of the completed new American version of *Fegg*. Both of us are very pleased with the look of it. Steve is full of disparaging banter. It's cost them far more than they'll ever get back, he says. The recent batch of alterations finally broke the chances of economic success and anyway the book is stuck at the printers in Wisconsin because of stroppy truckers. 'Goddamn truckers rule this goddamn country,' he grunts sourly, then breaks into a broad grin and introduces us eagerly to a man called Marvin Goldwater, who is president of 'Beards of America' and cousin of Barry, the Vietnam Hawk himself.

Saturday, April 10th, New York

Beginning, slowly, to relax into New York pattern of life.

A lunch in our garden in the sun with Neil and Yvonne, Miles and Luke[1] and Al Levinson – looking tanned (from Jamaica), curly-haired and broad-shouldered. As he quotes someone in one of his poems as saying on first meeting him: 'I cannot imagine you indoors'. Al brought, apart from jokes and good company, a bit of New York intellectual class and a bottle of scotch for the house.

At 2.00 the others (bar Eric) begin to arrive and we have a very good three hour rehearsal upstairs at 242. Al remarked on how well we mixed and how there was no apparent leader.

Nancy arrived and she and I went round to Stephen Sondheim's house, next door but one. SS's housekeeper, Louis, apparently organises cleaners, etc, for 242. The Sondheim house is decorated in a more modern and much more opulent style than 242 – yet with carefully restrained taste. Full of remarkable surprises, too. One room full of antique nineteenth and twentieth century games – early skittle alleys, very old pinball machines.

Louis – Spanish, I should think, small, chunky, camp, with a ready smile and friendly open manner. Very excited to meet a Python. He shows me a copy of *New Yorker* for the week, which contains a long article by Hertzberg about the court case in December. A long and very

1 Yvonne Innes, Neil's wife. Their boys, Miles and Luke, and ours had become firm friends.

accurate article with quotes from Gilliam and myself – 'Michael Palin, charming and boyish'!

On the way downstairs I meet the distinguished Mr Sondheim. He shakes hands briefly, distractedly, as he flits from one room into another with a grand piano in it.

Tuesday, April 13th, New York

Lunch at Ina's office, where a Python business meeting has been called to discuss offers of a TV special to be made of the show. Terry J is, as usual, the chief originator of doubt about the project. He wants a Roger Graef-style film of the stage show, whereas Ina thinks we can only sell a TV special of the show, to be made after the end of the run at the Ed Sullivan Theater. TJ and TG against, John keen to earn the extra £3,000 we're promised for doing it. I urge that we examine more carefully what is involved in moving the show to another theatre and preparing it for TV. It's all being sold to us as a two day extension – I think we'll be here an extra week!

Really I couldn't care less. Here we are all being encouraged to be very greedy and complicate our lives further, when we have a theatre opening down the road in a day and a half and we haven't even been on the stage.

Two incidents at the end of this unsatisfactory meeting. John, who has been lying on the floor to 'relax his shoulders', gets up and, as he does so, dislodges a huge picture on the wall, which crashes down on his foot, eliciting Fawlty-like shrieks of pain and explosive anger. I think he really did shake his fist at it. Then we find he actually has sliced a bit of flesh off his heel and he is sat down and a doctor called. It's his 'Silly Walks' foot too.

Wednesday, April 14th, New York

One of those totally gruelling days that only happen in the theatre and, if they didn't have to happen, the theatre would invent them.

Breakfast of fresh orange juice, grapefruit and scrambled eggs and bacon at Francine's – a coffee shop across the street from the stage door. Eric came in – he's all right.

10.00 into the theatre, past the small knot of girls who seem to have already taken up permanent residence there. An a.m. technical stagger-through, topping and tailing.

In the afternoon, a dress rehearsal. Our first and only, despite Hazel's usual protestations. I seem to have the most changes, seventeen or eighteen. Gloria, my dresser, a Patricia Neal look-alike, looks worried, but I'm told she's 100% reliable. One thing that irritates me about the afternoon run, which is so important to us, is that we have not been warned – or I have not been warned – that the press has been allowed in.

I felt even more cross by the little production chat we had at 6.00. No one smiled. Anne frowned, Allen Tinkley [our producer] frowned, they all seemed to be deeply gloomy and I just wanted to get away from them all and do the show.

At 8.00, almost punctually, the curtain rose to prolonged applause and cheers.

The whole show went predictably well, with very few problems and the usual reaction of ecstatic recognition of sketches. The only trouble spot was the 'Court Sketch', which was running 15 minutes and failed to work at any stage and 'The Death of Mary Queen of Scots' which was too long.

Afterwards I felt hugely relieved. My voice had survived four run-throughs in two days, which it would never have done before Cicely Berry, and the reaction to the show was as good as it had ever been. I think we're in for an enjoyable run.

Charisma gave us an after-show party at Orsons. That's where the voices really become strained – not during the shows! Tomorrow the family arrives.

Thursday, April 15th, New York

A complete change in the weather today. The temperature has hurtled up into the 70s and is heading for the 80s and the cool crispness that has made New York so acceptable this past week has been replaced by a clammy balminess.

A limousine picks us up at the Navarro and takes TJ and me out to Kennedy Airport to meet the families. Small blond heads are glimpsed through the customs shed door at around 1.00 and soon we're all packed in the limousine heading into NY over the Triborough Bridge.

A couple of hours settling in at 242. The house is not a perfect house for kids, and I'm suddenly aware of the enormous numbers of stairs. Terry and I get very hot and bothered moving the two enormous cots we've rented for Rachel and Sally. We keep knocking Noël Coward's painting off the wall as we struggle to get them up two or three flights.

In late afternoon TJ and I have to go to a reception being given by the BBC. A couple of gin and tonics, and the good news that we have a rave review from Clive Barnes of the *NY Times*. The review, out tomorrow, was circulating the party, as was its author – small, owl-like doyen of NY theatre critics – Clive B himself. I was introduced to him by Nancy. He said how much he'd enjoyed it, I went over some of the things that had gone wrong – e.g. the till not working in 'Blackmail' – he said that sort of thing made the show even more fun, and excused himself, but he had to dash off and see a play in New Haven.

After tonight's show another party – this time quite a cheery affair thrown by Arista in the New York Experience – an exhibition in the bowels of the Rockefeller Center.

At the party – Clive Davis, of course, with photographers in careful attendance. Talking with Clive is like going into one of those photo booths on stations. The lights start popping and, before you know it, 600 pictures of you and Clive happy have been taken. But Clive doesn't embrace you for no reason – throughout the session he's working on me to agree to extending our visit by taking the show on to LA until the end of May. It'll sell so many records if we do go to the West Coast.

Meet John Cale, another complete Python fan. A breathless PR lady rushes up and asks me to come and have my photo taken with Leonard Bernstein. This means being pulled through the crowds of ordinary plebs and being held in position, like a greyhound in a stall, whilst Lenny finishes talking to someone else. Then, after a while, Lenny turns, shakes my hand. He's smaller than I expected; short and dynamic. The flashbulbs go crazy. Lenny introduces me to Adolph Green, another songwriter, who is nice and quiet and amiable. As I talk to Lenny I'm actually being pulled to one side by this wretched PR lady so that I don't spoil the shot by obscuring his face from the cameras. He goes on about how he and his kids adore the show. Later he asks John and Eric to do bits of sketches and Eric replies by demanding that Bernstein sing a bit of Beethoven.

Clearly the little fellow loves the publicity and plays up to it – sending it up rotten, but playing along nevertheless, and, always behind and around, the acolytes, the standers and watchers.

It's the NY treatment, and it goes on till two or three – I forget which – when the waiting limousine whisks us back, exhausted, to 242.

Friday, April 16th, New York

A night to remember. For its sheer awfulness. The children up and about even before dawn, myself trying desperately to catch up on much-needed sleep and poor Helen, up and down calming or quieting the kids, then back to a bed which she found terribly uncomfortable. I had been aware that it was a hard bed, but had put my lack of sleep down to nervous energy rather than discomfort. Now Helen's misery made me feel just how hard the bed is. I can't sleep, she can't sleep, the children can't sleep.

I ring home, to be congratulated by my mother on our tenth wedding anniversary, which I'd totally forgotten.

Try to buy a mattress for the bed – very difficult on Good Friday. Finally track down a foam rubber store and, with the help of a huge Cadillac limousine, provided by Nancy, I'm able to buy and bring back a 6' x 6'6" piece of foam rubber before the shop closes at 2.00. Many strange looks as the impressive limousine purrs uptown with a huge ball of foam rubber taking up the entire back seat.

In the afternoon everything improves. The new mattress is a winner (the best $43-worth I've ever spent). The evening show receives the best reaction yet – a truly thunderous ovation.

Saturday, April 17th, New York

Two shows tonight: 6.00 and 9.30.

At the theatre Neil tells me that their flat has been burgled. He's now about the fourth or fifth of the Python group to have lost money or had it stolen since we arrived in NY. Charles K,[1] Mollie[2] and Carol have all had money taken and, in a strangely un-detailed episode, I gather that John C was rolled by a couple of hookers!

At the first show someone is letting off firecrackers very irritatingly. It comes to a head in 'Argument', in which a crack completely obscures a line and Graham leaps in, doing his favourite bit, shouting – or rather, yelling – at hecklers. As he's just done the Man Who Gives Abuse, it all fits in very neatly. The offender is seen to be removed forcibly from the

---

1 Charles Knode, tall, droll, costume designer friend of Hazel's. After the flying saucer sequence in *Life of Brian* he utters the immortal words 'You jammy bastard!'
2 Mollie Kirkland, stage manager.

theatre by Jim Beach. G's volley of abuse follows him right up the aisle. The sketch goes swimmingly after that.

Sunday, April 18th, New York

Well here we are, about to play two shows at the end of one of our hardest weeks ever, and the temperature hits 96° – the highest April temperature recorded in New York.

Crowds outside stage door now number forty or fifty. Much screaming and autograph signing. Nothing like this in London. It's quite nice for a while. Am given two beautiful Gumbys – one made in plaster, and another elaborately and painstakingly embroidered – plus flowers, etc. TJ is given a flower for every performance by one fan.

Tuesday, April 20th, New York

An incipient sore throat. It worsened, perversely, on the day off, probably as a result of heat and dust and tiredness. Today's schedule gives it no chance.

At 10.10 we all leave the house to go to a Warner Books 'Literary Reception' at the Bronx Zoo. A good chance to mix business and pleasure. Due to a mix-up with the limousines, we do not arrive at our destination for an hour and 20 minutes. It's free day at the zoo and the place is packed. Our limo noses its way through the crowds to the back of the reptile house. Unbeknown to us, Warner Books have laid on a stunt. We are to present a python to the zoo, and this involves us in having to hold the thing whilst press and TV take their photos.

An unpleasant little episode. Eric refuses to join in. The press and photographers are singularly objectionable and the python is getting very hot and disturbed. It's about eighteen feet long and, after a while, its huge body begins to writhe slowly in discomfort. The idiotic pictures go on and on … 'Would you stand here by its face, please?' 'Come on, someone tell a joke …' 'You're Pythons – do something funny for me.'

We have to hold up a copy of our book by the python's head. All of us, including the snake, are getting hotter and crosser. Finally I can't take any more of these asinine remarks from the cameramen and I walk away, muttering angrily. Most unpleasant.

At the show tonight George Harrison, looking tired and ill and with short hair, fulfils what he calls a lifetime's ambition and comes on as one of the Mountie chorus in the 'Lumberjack Song'. He's very modest about it, wears his hat pulled well down and refuses to appear in the curtain call. He's now off on holiday to the Virgin Islands. He needs it.

Thursday, April 22nd, New York

Suddenly we're half-way through.

After the show, who should come round but Ruth Gordon and Garson Kanin, owners of 242. My heart missed a couple of beats as it was only today that Sally Jones[1] had painted a mural over one of their walls. But they were a charming, disarming pair. She, who must be 80, full of life – a real sparkle in her eyes. Did she enjoy doing *Where's Poppa?* (one of my favourite comedies), I asked cautiously. No, hated it, she replied, quickly and convincingly – then, with a broad grin, accepted the compliment and eulogised over the film with me.

They had both loved the show and Kanin commented on how surprised he'd been by the mixture of people in the audience – young, middle-aged, old, smart Broadway pros, scruffy college kids and boys and girls with their parents. 'Just one thing,' said Ruth G, as they left, 'When you write another Python movie, make sure there's a part for me in it.' I will, too.

Friday, April 23rd, New York

Up at 10.30 after good sleep. Breakfast at coffee shop. Oh, the fresh orange juice! Nancy rings about 11.00. Familiar tale – could I go to an important ABC radio interview with Gilliam this afternoon? Eric won't, John has a 'prior commitment'. Either I refuse and Nancy breaks down – she sounds very weak, having been up all night on the LP – or I accept the emotional blackmail. I feel good this morning – New York's sunny. A perfect day. Yes, I'll do it.

On the way out my one and only encounter with our legendary neighbour – Kate Hepburn. She's at the wheel of an unpretentious green car, she wears a headscarf which carefully covers most of her face. Low, gravelly voice offers Tom and Willy the use of her fountain to paddle in.

---

1 Terry's daughter. She was three at the time, and is still an artist!

John is, on a good night, one of the world's greatest corpsers.' And I am not far behind. 'Silly Walks' at Drury Lane, 1975.

Passport photo, 1975: big collars and mad, staring eyes. Why did anyone allow me in their country?

On Central Park South, first New York publicity trip, March 1975. I am reading from the guidebook, which always used to annoy Graham.

Terry, Ma, Jeremy
Herbert, Al and me,
Camberwell.

Helen, Rachel, Will
and Tom with friends
Diana and Sean
Duncan on their boat,
Pilcomayo, on the
River Dee, 1975.

Fans in America, 1975.
Graham lights up
behind me.

Python publicity
photo with Neil Innes
selflessly standing in
for Terry Jones.

Summer of '75,
Three Men in a Boat.
Stephen Moore,
me, Tim Curry and
Montmorency the dog.

Prelude to disaster. The
photograph sequence
(followed by the boat
getting trapped in the
lock gate). *Three Men
in a Boat*, June 1975.

With Ma and sister
Angela at Dulwich.

Next generation. Miles
Innes and Tom Palin
became good friends
during *Live at City
Center*, New York, 1976.

Rachel, Helen and the
back garden, Gospel
Oak, London, 1976.

'Peter Cook, who apologised for his slightly glazed state saying he was recovering from a long night . . . discussing Lenny Bruce's drug problem – steadfastly refuses to learn the words of the Condemned Man in our "Court Sketch".' Amnesty show at Her Majesty's. (March 31st, 1976)

My vocal nemesis, 'Gumby Flower Arranging' at full blast. City Center, New York, 1976.

'You're Pythons. Do something funny for me.' An unpleasant little episode at the Bronx Zoo, New York. (April 20th, 1976)

Photos by Bill Meng, NYZS

. . . *Monty Python's Flying Circus at the Zoo. On an awfully sunny Tuesday in April, six, er . . . rather five British Pythons—Terry Jones, Michael Palin, Graham Chapman, Terry Gilliam, and Neil Innis—presented a python (named Monty, of course) to General Director William G. Conway and the Reptile House keepers. (Another member of the Python group, Eric Idle, is afraid of snakes and would not take part in the official presentation. Phoo!) The snake—a real Burmese python about fourteen feet long—was donated to the Bronx Zoo by Warner Books to commemorate the 100,000th sale of Monty Python's Big Red Book (which is really blue and very silly).*

August/September   N3

'Really quite enjoy flashing a naughty part of the body in a public place – and getting paid rather than arrested for it.' *Jabberwocky* filming at Chepstow Castle. (September 16th, 1976)

'I like my gear. At least it's going to be a deal more comfortable than the armour of *Holy Grail*.' As Dennis Cooper in *Jabberwocky*. (July 14th, 1976)

Helen and our friend
Ranji, Amsterdam, 1971.

Perks of being a
director of Shepperton
studios; submarine
cannon from the film
*The Land That Time
Forgot* is saved from
the rubbish tip and
ends up in my back
garden, 1978.

I introduce the boys. 'Oh, *I* know Tom and Willy, I've seen them out in the garden.'

From ABC and the crowds in sunny Sixth Avenue, I meet Helen and the boys and we take a cab down to Battery Park and out to the Statue of Liberty. A great success. The weather sunny and clear. Fine views of Manhattan skyline and climbing inside Liberty's 'skirt' appealed to the boys' imagination. 'We'll soon be at the underpants,' says Willy – as the three of us toil towards the crown.

Sunday, April 25th, New York

The boys come to see the matinee this afternoon. Favourite moment – Gilliam's exploding stomach!

During the second show a two-foot-long prick is thrown on stage. Eric – 'One of these little American penises.'

Wednesday, April 28th, New York

The boys, dressed in their new Spiderman outfits (bought yesterday), escorted me across Second Avenue to the coffee shop. At 11.00 all the Pythons, bar Terry Gilliam who is giving a court deposition, arrive at 242 for the first meeting/discussion about the next Python movie. It's a pleasant day. Sunny and warm. Resist temptation to work out in the gardens and use Ruth and Garson's living room, where, beneath the Grandma Moses hanging above the fireplace, we have the first positive thoughts about a new movie.

Are we or are we not going to do a life of Christ? All feel that we cannot just take the Bible story and parody or Pythonise every well-known event. We have to have a more subtle approach and, in a sense, a more serious approach. We have to be sure of our own attitudes towards Christ, the Scriptures, beliefs in general, and not just skate through being silly.

John provides a key thought with a suggested title – 'The Gospel According to St Brian' – and from that stem many improvised ideas about this character who was contemporary with Jesus – a sort of stock Python bank clerk, or tax official, who records everything, but is always too late – things have always happened when he eventually comes on the scene. He's a bit of a fixer too and typical of St Brian is the scene where he's on the beach, arranging cheap rentals for a fishing boat, whilst, in the back of shot, behind him, Christ walks across frame on the water. St Brian turns, but it's too late.

So at the meeting, which breaks up around 1.00, we seem to have quite unanimously cheerfully agreed to do a film, and a Bible story film, and have had enough initial ideas to fill all of us with a sort of enthusiasm which has been missing in Python for at least a couple of years.

Tonight Harry Nilsson joins me on stage for the 'Lumberjack Song'. He is coked to the eyeballs and full of booze too, but grins benignly and seems to be enjoying himself, when, at the last curtain call, I see him suddenly lurch forward towards the edge of the stage, presumably to fraternise with the cheering audience. As he goes forward, the curtain starts to fall and, before I can pull him back, Harry keels over into the front row and lies helplessly astride the wooden edge of the orchestra pit. The curtain descends, leaving me with this bizarre vision of a drunken Mountie lying on top of the audience!

Thursday, April 29th, New York

Nancy rings at 10.30. A CBS film crew want an interview, walking in the park or something, this lunchtime. Should help to sell a few seats for the weekend. It's important, of course.

Today Helen and the kids are going back home and here am I, with pathetic lack of resistance, sucked into the publicity machine.

A less productive film meeting at 242 this morning, although we take the Bible story into wider areas, Rome perhaps or even the present day. A silly World War I opening is suggested, which starts with a congregation of English soldiers singing in some chapel. A moving scene. Except in one row at the back there are four Germans singing. Nobody likes to look at them directly, but heads begin to turn.

When I get home, Helen is in the throes of packing.

Took a cab across town and picked up the boys from Yvonne. They'd been up the Empire State Building and had more pressies in their hot little hands. Back to 242 with them. Give Helen a goodbye peck, grab my thermos of tea, which I've been taking into the theatre for the vocal cords. So off I go, clutching my thermos like a miner going off t' pit.

Sunday, May 2nd, New York

Woke with the nightmarish realisation that I had no voice at all. I croak, ooh and aah and try a few of the exercises, but realise with a flush of horror that my voice has disappeared – more suddenly and severely than I ever remember. My reactions – it's about 11.00 and I've slept a good nine hours – vary from urgent panic to reluctant acceptance and then to cautious optimism. I have often heard of doctors who deal with this sort of vocal paralysis with one squirt or one jab. So, I try to ring Nancy. She's not there. So I try to ring doctors myself. This isn't much fun as I have to croak gutturally into the phone and it's difficult to make them hear. Dr Lustgarten, the Park Avenue specialist, is away. His partner, Dr Briggs, will ring me back. Dr Briggs doesn't ring me back. I have a bath.

My predicament seems like a particularly vicious stroke of fate. Only two shows to go, and, instead of recovering and consolidating during the night and day (as it has done throughout the run), the voice has perversely decided to vanish today, leaving me the last two shows – the two fun shows, when everyone will be happy and jolly and enjoying themselves – as millstones.

I try a contact of Dr Lustgarten's. He's also away, but a Dr Ryan rings me back. Dr Ryan has not got the expected message of hope – all he can suggest is that I buy 'Afrin' nasal decongestant and try and squirt it on my vocal cords. This doesn't sound like the miracle cure I've heard so much about, but I'll give it a try.

Out around midday. It's a warm, sunny Sunday morning. Walk along Second Avenue to try and find a pharmacy with the miracle 'Afrin'.

Police everywhere. A buzzing feeling of something being about to happen takes my mind off my own predicament. Turns out there's to be an enormous 'Free Soviet Jewry' march on the United Nations, only about half a mile away from our house. Find 'Afrin'; head home as the police take up their positions in serried ranks along Second Avenue.

Absolutely no effect. Depression and gloom close in again. Buy a huge copy of the *New York Times*; and decide to sit out in Turtle Bay Gardens in the sun with a beer and hope that rest will somehow save the remnants of the voice.

It's 2.00 and time to go to the theatre. Once there, I decide to try everything and see. Funnily enough, Gumby is the easiest. The grunting can be easily brought up from the depths of the stomach in the proper way – it's things like upper-register incredulity and emphasis in 'Travel Agent Sketch', for instance, which prove most difficult.

At half-time in the first show Dr Briggs arrives. Smooth, receding hair neatly brushed back with a precision only doctors seem to achieve. He has his daughter with him and seems more anxious to get my autograph than to treat the voice. He whizzes me upstairs, whilst they hold the curtain, and gives me a Cortisone jab in the arm and sprays my throat with Novocaine. The spray is re-applied midway in the second half. My voice is now a rather sinister manufactured thing, like Frankenstein's monster. At the end of the first show I'm supposed to rest it, but instead there's a birthday party organised for me by Loretta and Laura, two fans who've been outside for every single show. They've made me a cake, given me a present of two T-shirts and other presents for the kids and even bought me a bottle of Great Western New York State Champagne. Everyone sings 'Happy Birthday' to me in a hoarse whisper.

Clearly Dr Briggs' much-vaunted Cortisone treatment hasn't worked by the second house, despite his confidence – 'I got Robert Eddison on to play Lear and his voice was far worse.' I suppose there are better people than Dr Briggs, but I was paying the penalty of losing my voice in New York on a Sunday. No one was there. Before the 7.30 show another doctor, this time with halitosis, appeared, and, before he looked down my throat, asked me who was going to pay him the $40. Then he treated me utterly ineffectually and went away.

Neil, meanwhile, kept offering me large swigs of scotch as 'the only cure'. He was right. I drank enough not to care, and managed to survive the last show. As the audience knew my voice had gone, they were very sympathetic and we made some capital out of it. But there is still something terrifying about going on stage in front of 2,000 people and not knowing if you will be able to speak.

Monday, May 3rd, New York

A record-signing had been laid on at Sam Goody's Store from 12.00–2.00. A limousine with all the others in was supposed to pick us up at 12.00. It didn't arrive. It was getting rather cold suddenly and we were all in summer gear, feeling like Indians in Aberdeen, pathetically trying to ring Nancy. No luck.

At 12.10 we set off for the record-signing – and then realise we don't know where the store is, so we stop and ask a pretzel seller. All at once we're there. Through the traffic, on the opposite side of the road, a queue half a block long. And they're waiting for us. With an increased confidence in our stride we cross the road. A few screams and shouts and we're into the store. The entire basement is full of Python records. The album *Live at City Center* has been marketed in only ten days since the master was cut. There they are. Racks of them. And it's playing in the store as well.

8.30: Limousine arrives, pack the cases and the best journey of all begins – out to Kennedy, with Alan Price's 'O Lucky Man' score playing on the cassette, with a kind of appropriateness. I had seen the hard side of New York today, the constant pressure to say something, to stand up in case people don't recognise you. That's the trouble with the city, that's why it's unrelaxing – because of the fear that if you sit down and relax for half an hour everyone will forget who you are.

Monday, May 10th

Last twelve months have been the driest since records began in 1727. Drought conditions near in some parts of the country. Cathy Gib took it all very seriously and was going around putting bricks in the cisterns.

TG and Maggie come round in the evening – talk of *Jabberwocky*. It may now be largely shot in Chepstow and Pembroke Castles and far less in Shepperton Studios than originally expected. I approve. Arthur Lowe wants to be in it, but Iain Cuthbertson has said no.

Monday, May 17th

Began a *Ripping Yarn* script about a Northern family, but was only able to work on it for about an hour, then a series of prolonged phone calls.

With Helen to the Academy, where we saw *Spirit of the Beehive*, a beautifully photographed, unpretentious, unspectacular, gentle Spanish film by Victor Erice. Delightful and satisfying. And afterwards Piero kept his restaurant upstairs specially open for the two of us (even the guitarist came back and played for ten minutes!) – superb meal. Piero has achieved a consistent excellence at the Pavilion, which has never let us down.[1]

1 Despite Piero's death and the disappearance from Oxford Street of the Academy Cinema, the Pavilion, now run by his friend Vasco and his son, remains our family's favourite. It has moved to Poland Street.

Wednesday, May 19th

The weather's cooled down perceptibly. Writing easier and actually I make a good start on a First World War *Ripping Yarn* set in a prison camp.

Down to 14 Neal's Yard, which is, since last Monday, the leasehold property of Messrs Palin, Doyle and Gilliam. We discuss how the buildings will be used. André and the studio are settled and it's looking good. He could have builders in on Monday.

Home around 8.00. Watched Liverpool win UEFA Cup Final at Bruges.

Thursday, May 20th, Sheffield

Caught 13.05 from King's Cross for the opening night of *Their Finest Hours*.[1] Arrive at the Crucible about 7.15. Jill Foster is there and we meet Norman Yardley and his wife as well. Yardley, a childhood cricketing hero,[2] is gentle and genial and his wife, a bright attractive lady, is nice to us as well.

As soon as *Underwood* starts I know we'll be alright – the audience warm instantly to the situation, the cast play it impeccably, the pace sustains and so do the laughs, coming with a volume and consistency which I just didn't expect. The whole of *Underwood* works like a gem, including the ending, when an entire cricket team walks through and the mother rises up to the strains of the 'Hallelujah Chorus'. Came out feeling almost tearful with emotion and gratitude to David Leland and the cast.

Buchanan was slower, but the effect of the boxed-in cast worked superbly. Clarity a problem, but much, much better performance from Philip Jackson as the Italian – he was splendid – and Julian Hough hardly missed a laugh as the Frenchman. Again the audience reaction sustained well, apart from a morose, fidgety lady, who finally left halfway through *Buchanan* and was, I heard later, the *Guardian* critic!

---

1 Our one-act plays. *Underwood's Finest Hour* is set in a labour room with a mother straining to give birth and a doctor straining to listen to a particularly exciting Test Match. *Buchanan's Finest Hour* is about a marketing idea gone awry. The cast, including the Pope, are trapped inside a packing crate throughout.
2 Norman Yardley, Yorkshire and England Captain. Cricketer of the Year 1948.

Friday, May 21st, Sheffield

Woke up in the small hours with a dream of awful reviews. Terry had had exactly the same dream!

At 7.30 a knock on the door – a cup of tea, *The Times* and the *Morning Telegraph*. Nothing in *The Times*, but I hardly expected it – but Paul Allen in the *Morning Telegraph* gives us a useful and quite charitable review. He was impressed with the experiment with the boxes, and also said there were 'breathtakingly funny moments'. Read it again while shaving. Fourteen years since I last searched the Sheffield papers for the theatre reviews![1]

Outside my window it's a bright, sunny morning. Directly below me the forlorn and deserted platforms of Victoria Station, once the starting place for Sheffield's own prestige express – the Master Cutler. Now it's boarded up and even the track has been taken out on Platform One. Allow 30 seconds for bout of railway nostalgia.

Downstairs to meet Jill and very crumpled Terry – I tell him to go back to his room and get up again. Despite a lot of discussion on how much better it is to go back to London early and not lose another *Ripping Yarn* writing day, TJ remains unhappy about not talking to the cast – even though David isn't planning to meet them until this afternoon. Even after we've left Sheffield on the 8.30, ordered breakfast and settled down, Terry is still itchy with indecision and at Chesterfield, our first stop, he suddenly grabs his bag and, with a muttered 'I'm going back', he disappears off the train.

The bemused restaurant attendant has just cleared away Terry's breakfast things when he reappears. 'It's 55 minutes until the next train back,' he says resignedly, and sits down and comes back to London.

A bad review in *The Guardian*, coldly and heavily giving away the plot and all the surprises (such as they are) of *Buchanan* and saying that if *Their Finest Hours* could have been *Their Finest Minutes* it would have got a few more laughs.

Strangely enough, no sooner am I back in London and at my desk than Bob Scott rang from the Exchange Theatre, Manchester, to ask me to do an 'evening' up there later in the year. He knew the *Guardian*

---

1 During my 'gap' year in 1962, I joined a local amateur dramatic society – the Brightside and Carbrook Co-Operative Players. Won Best Perf. (Gentleman) at Co-Op (N.E. Section) Drama Festival in Leeds in 1962.

reviewer and confirmed she was a sad lady, who even found Strindberg light.

Good news from David Leland later in the day, telling us the Crucible want to extend its run beyond June 5th.

T Gilliam drops in to say John Bird has plumped for the part of Reek in *Jabberwocky*, and Harry H Corbett for the Squire. Both pleased me – they sound very right. John C has now definitely backed out, but apparently rang Terry G and was very contrite and even offered to come and talk about the script with him.

Finally got down to reading some more of Al Levinson's long, unpublished novel, *Millwork*. Like most books it repays a longer session rather than three pages at a time before falling asleep. Am getting quite involved.

Saturday, May 22nd

Lunch down at Dulwich. Angela looking well and tanned. She plays tennis very regularly now (to keep her from sitting in the house brooding, she says). Much more positive, or certainly less negative, than when I last saw her. Veryan is away walking the Ridgeway.

Jeremy hovers, trying, whenever he can, to get in a plea for his latest passion – owning a moped. He's not allowed to ride one for a couple of months, but apparently most of his friends at Alleyn's School have them. He shows me his electric guitar. Looks fine, but he's trying to play the Led Zeppelin songbook, before he's learnt basic rock 'n' roll. I can understand how his few oft-repeated heavy rock chords can send Angela batty.

I feel sorry for Angela, suddenly confronted with Jeremy's emerging independence. Just how long should he stay out at the pub listening to Meal Ticket tonight? Either she's cautious or she's taking a risk. No solution. I suppose we've got it coming.

A pleasant wander around Crystal Palace Park with the kids. Lots to see and do. The prehistoric monsters on the islands are still one of the sights of London; there's a little zoo where goats and sheep wander around 'mingling' with the crowds. Rachel loved them – and wandered around in primal innocence tapping rams on their bottoms and laughing.

Sunday, May 23rd

Sunny and dry again. After morning's swim at Holiday Inn and completion of a letter to Al L, we drive over to the Davidsons' for lunch.

Ian tells a good Barry Humphries tale[1] – apparently Barry was in full swing as Edna in his show at the Apollo, when a man in the front row, ever so discreetly, ever so carefully, left for a pee. But he couldn't really escape Edna's eye and Edna remarked on his absence and talked to his wife for a while about his waterworks. Having found out the man's name, Edna and the audience plotted a little surprise for him. So when he duly reappeared from the gents and made for his seat, once again stealthily and soundlessly, without disturbing a soul, Edna gave a cue and, as he was half-way down the gangway, the entire theatre chanted 'Hello Colin!'

Wednesday, May 26th

Drive down to Terry's in late morning for a combined session on *Ripping Yarns*. Don't really get down to work until after lunch. TJ has made a very funny start on an episode centring round a vicar and an adoring women's club who all want to marry him. Nicely written nineteenth century polite language. We chat about it and decide it could make a half hour of the *Tenant of Wildfell Hall, Wuthering Heights*, Brontë/Austen/Eliot style. Lots of repression and social restrictions and smouldering passions and breaking hearts.

I read 'Escape from Stalag Luft 112B', which I've been working on these past seven days. Despite one or two blockages, it wrote itself fairly easily and Terry was very pleased. He thinks it's nearly half an hour already. Within a few minutes of talking about it Terry came out with a very clear and funny ending, so I don't think we were over-optimistic in thinking that we have another *Ripping Yarn* as good as finished and a strong idea for a fifth script. I took the vicar and left TJ with the escape.

Tuesday, June 1st

I find myself at the door of the Hampstead Theatre Club. This highly respected little theatre still has the air of a gypsy caravan in a bombed site.

1 Ian collaborated on material for Barry Humphries' stage show.

Meet David Aukin at the door of the caravan. He looks thinner, otherwise the same as when he and Rudman were carrying off the glittering prizes on the Oxford stage in '62/'63. Mike Rudman joins us. He has that slight edge of American forthrightness, or aggression, or perhaps directness, which always makes me a little uncomfortable. I reach quickly for my English defence – and make a few jokes.

My task is to deliver the scripts of *Finest Hours* to him, in the hope that he will be able to go and see the plays and maybe bring them back to the Theatre Club. For some reason I am still a little uneasy as I push them – for I feel that they're lightweight.

Off about 7.00 to drive down to Whitechapel Galleries, where Chris Orr is having his first complete exhibition and his first exhibition in London.

After a few attempts, find the Whitechapel Galleries – they're well off the beaten artistic track, in the Jewish East End a few doors down from Blooms Deli, which makes me agreeably nostalgic for New York, and facing out over the bewildering, traffic-filled wilderness of the new, improved, enlarged Aldgate roundabout for cars and not people.

Chris Orr is very helpful and shows me round his stuff. Find a mutual admiration for the work of Pont, the 1930s cartoonist, whose gentle, satirical studies like 'The British Character' come to mind when you look at some of Chris's finely drawn pictures.

Robert shows me the 'rushes' of the first Signford production *Chris Orr's John Ruskin*, which is out in a couple of weeks, but later he tells me of a much more interesting proposition involving buying a fifteenth-century barn, owned by New College, Oxford. It could, R thinks, be bought for a song, and both Helen and I liked the adventure of working (Harold and Vita-like!) on an old, historic hulk and literally shaping the interior ourselves.

Wednesday, June 2nd

Have to buy the *Mirror* today as the first page trails a picture of John and Connie and the heading 'When Love Turns Sour at Fawlty Towers'. Inside, disappointingly accurate account of J and C's new living arrangements, whereby they share the house, but not the bed.

The boiled egg is scarcely dry upon my lips, when a man from the *Evening News* rings asking for JC's phone number. I decline to give it as politely as possible – but nearly spill the beans about the time John ... later, later.

Wednesday, June 9th

Terry rings. Mike Rudman of the Hampstead Theatre Club has read *Their Finest Hours*. He loved *Underwood* and disliked *Buchanan*. *Underwood* he wants to bring down and put on, and tentatively asked if we would be prepared to accept a commission to write another one to go with it! Back to square one.

Dave Yallop, friend of Graham's, and one of the few men I've seen tell Frost to shut up and sit down (when Dave was floor managing *Frost on Sunday*), wants to write a documentary about Python's court experiences in the US. Dave has good credentials – he wrote a respected and hard-hitting documentary on the Craig-Bentley case, and he's approaching the US case from the anti-censorship angle, which could and should be aired. It appears that Rik Hertzberg's prestigious *New Yorker* piece has started a few balls rolling since it was reprinted in the *Sunday Times*.

G Chapman, whom I also spoke to, is well set in his new career of film producer (on *The Odd Job*). Only yesterday he'd tried to get hold of Jack Lemmon, through his agent, a Mr De Witt – only to be told by a secretary that he couldn't speak to Mr De Witt, as he'd just died!

Thursday, June 10th

Work on a possible new *Ripping Yarn* – 'The Wreck of the Harvey Goldsmith', just because I like the title.

Squash with Richard[1] in the afternoon and Ian and Anthea D and Michael and Anne Henshaw to supper. We watch Monty Python Series Four repeats. It's 'Golden Age of Ballooning', a very rich show and I still can't quite figure out people's disappointed reaction to it when it first went out. Interesting to note in *Stage* today that after its second programme, Python was rated by Jictar[2] No. 2= in the London area and 5 in the south (both times above *Porridge*). In the rest of the country, nowhere.

---

1 Richard Guedalla, a neighbour.
2 Joint Industry Committee for Television Advertising Research.

Sunday, June 13th

Finish the day, and Al Levinson's *Millwork*, sitting outside my room in the gathering dusk with a glass of scotch. I liked the novel in the end, after a sticky start. It's warm and friendly and sympathetic and generally full of Al's humanity. Must write my review to him tomorrow.

Tuesday, June 15th

At five o'clock this evening to Neal's Yard. Four or five builders working in André's studio; they glower at me rather resentfully as I wander in, looking as if I owned the place, which of course I do. Terry Gilliam has summonsed me to my first piece of work on *Jabberwocky* – to do a scene with an American girl, Deborah Fallender, whom TG wants to screen test as the Princess.[1]

Upstairs, in Terry's part of 14/15 Neal's Yard, Julian has set up the camera. Terry Bedford, his small frame bulging a little in places, indicating incipient symptoms of the good life, which he must be enjoying as a highly paid member of the world of commercials, has already stuck a pair of tights over the lens to achieve his award-winning soft-lighting effect.

Deborah is very nervous, but quite sweet, and with a good sense of humour. We do the scene two or three times – unfortunately it reminds me so forcibly of the Castle Anthrax scene that I can't tell how good or bad it is.

To meal at the Siciliano with the Walmsleys and Simon A. Jane W very fed up that 'Kojak' – Telly Savalas – has today won a libel suit of £34,000 damages at the Old Bailey. He sent each member of the jury a signed photo of himself with 'Thank You' written on. Now, as taxi drivers say, there must be a sketch there. Jane W has interviewed the said Savalas, didn't like his pushy arrogance one bit, and finds it easy to believe the libel.

Thursday, June 17th

At 11.30 have to drive over to the Beeb to meet Fred Knapman, senior designer at the BBC, who's going to show me a possible Peruvian village set for 'Across the Andes by Frog', out at Pinewood.

1 She got the job.

The set, on a back lot, is in quite a run-down state (T Hughes tells me it was made for Dirk Bogarde's *Singer Not the Song*), but for that reason rather good for our purposes.

They are preparing for a new James Bond film at Pinewood – starting shooting in August – and a 300-foot-long, 40-foot-high steel-frame building is being erected there for one set-up! I feel very cheap, grubbing around the decaying back lot!

Down to Regent's Park for a Python Annual General Meeting. We have three companies – Python Productions Ltd, Python (Monty) Pictures Ltd and Kay-Gee-Bee Music Ltd. We manage to go through the official convening and closing procedure of all three companies in four minutes!

Terry J models the Python T-shirt, which is approved, with a few design alterations.

Finally we agree to spend £30,000 on acquiring full rights from Bavaria TV to the two German specials.

Taxi back with Dr Chapman, who has had a very tiring week film producing – and finds the whole thing much harder than he expected. Apparently Peter Sellers is very anxious to do the odd job – and is muscling in through his agent – whereas Graham wants Peter O'Toole in it, but O'Toole is less 'bankable' than Sellers.

Monday, June 21st, Southwold

My father's 76th birthday. I decide to go up to Southwold for the day, which is a pleasant way of giving him a present and marking the occasion, even though I suppose I should be writing away in London.

He's watching the Test Match on TV when I arrive at Croft Cottage. I take him cards from us all and a collection of reminiscences from a BBC Radio series about the British in India from 1900 on, which I hope will find an echo amongst his own memories of India, which seem to become more vivid the older he gets.

A bottle of champagne for lunch and a little stroll outside on the lawn, where a year ago we were drinking and eating with quite a crowd as we celebrated his 75th. Today just me and Mother, but he has had a letter from Angela and Aunt K [his sister].

Head down over lunch – he must concentrate all his energies on getting the food into his mouth, and cannot talk. Even after lunch, when there is discussion as to what to do in the afternoon, he cannot manage to make the word, so he writes down 'Rhododendrons'.

I take him for a drive to see the rhododendrons, which flank the road near Henham in lush profusion at this time of year. Sadly they've been heavily trimmed back and there's little to see, but he's enjoyed the ride in the car and didn't seem to want to do anything more ambitious.

Read Pirsig's *Zen and the Art* on the train back and found the simplicity and effectiveness of some of his words of wisdom revelatory. A sort of enlightened calm had taken hold of me by the time I got home. I really was reacting to things in a quite different way. Books affect me a little like that anyway, but this more so than any I have read.

Though on this tranquil summer's evening his theory of quality as reality may induce fine thoughts and comfort, it's going to be difficult when the radios start playing on the building sites and the ads blare out of my car radio and the phone starts ringing.

Wednesday, June 23rd

Drive into London to watch a two-hour showing of the Amnesty documentary shot by Roger Graef at the end of April. Jonathan Miller and I are about the only participants there.

It's a fascinating start – all the little glimpses of rehearsals in progress. The Goodies stand out like a sore thumb when rehearsing 'Funky Gibbon', but come out as nice, human chaps when they sit around talking, and Alan Bennett's asides and revelations on his Fringe colleagues are sweetly, disarmingly, catty. Talking to TJ about Python, he ends up rather sadly, 'Well, if you ever want another member for the group …'

Am struck by how relaxed and worldly-wise the *Beyond the Fringe* team are. Beside them, not that the film makes comparisons, the Pythons seem jolly but sort of more businesslike, less rambling and discursive. Maybe in ten years' time we'll have aged and mellowed in the same rather comforting way.

Thursday, June 24th

I enjoy a rare day with no need to go out – not even a game of squash. And I find myself with time on my hands. I read Sylvia Plath's *Letters* at lunch and outside in the evening. Rather brittle, full of sudden ups and sudden downs. Plathitudes. Life/Man/Work is one day marvellous, brilliantly handsome, ecstatic, unbearably wonderful, and the next depressing, frightful – a great monster of awfulness. She expresses herself so articulately, but her underlying wide-eyed attitudes are the same as any awkward teenager's.

A hot evening – doors and windows open all over Gospel Oak.

Thursday, July 1st

So far an excellent week for writing. On Tuesday I worked an almost unbroken seven-and-a-half-hour-stint typing, correcting, revising, sharpening and generally putting together the northern tale ('The Testing of Eric Olthwaite').

Talk to Gilliam at Neal's Yard late Tuesday, where I'm having a fitting for the Dennis costume. He's slightly worried, and so am I, that various actors are very keen to get in ideas of their own – which don't exactly fit in with the spirit of the movie. Harry H Corbett wants his codpiece to be gradually enlarged throughout the film. Max Wall suggests putting small rubber balls in the end of the fingers of his gloves, so when he takes them off they bounce.

Down to Terry's, revelling in the Mini sunroof, where we work on with 'Curse of the Claw'.

The writing seems to come easily and the plot and story falls into place so well that by 4.00 we have completed a sixth *Ripping Yarn*! The third since we began writing again after New York – so that's three half-hours in five weeks.

So I left TJ at 4.30; we don't in fact need to write any more scripts until next year – and July will see us, for the first time, largely going our separate ways. And yet during this last spell of writing I've felt closer to TJ than at any time since before the *Grail*. I feel happy that the demarcation problems following on from *Tomkinson* have not, in any way, appeared to lessen our writing strength, or weaken our writing relationship. We've adjusted (or is it just me?) to our new work relationship and actually improved our personal relationship (or is it just me?).

From TJ's to Anne's. Whilst I'm there a phone call to say that the appeal judges in the US have just laid down a twenty-page judgement on the Python v ABC case, which is unequivocally favourable to Python. This sounds better news than we ever hoped for.

Saturday, July 3rd

Woke this morning determined to drink only moderately today. Failed hopelessly. No sooner had last night's mixture of lager and cider seeped through my system than it was being quietly worked on by some very more-ish sangria at the Denselows.[1] Helen and I and Rachel were round there for a lunch party, which turned into a very late barbecue.

An interesting split of guests between a large group of peaceful, rather bucolic folk, who turned out to live in a commune in Haverstock Hill. They sat indoors most of the time, whilst out in the blazing heat – near the drinks – were Robin's media friends from *Panorama*, Bush House, *The Guardian*, etc.

The communites were amicable, but tended to talk about 'cosmic awareness' and 'waves of communication responses'. I find unless you know a little of their terms of reference, it's hard to climb aboard their thoughts. But a man called Ian, who was a sort of translator-figure for them, was very chatty and asked us along any time. He said he was in charge of security.

Tuesday, July 6th

Off to some bookshops and then over to Professor Dr Powell for what turns out to be quite a tough piece of surgery on my back left lower teeth, which have been giving me trouble over the last two months. Powell digs deep and furiously. It's the first surgery since 1972 and he certainly is thorough over it. It's stitched and I experience with a stirring of nostalgia the taste of the dressing over my gums.

I drive from Powell's over to Shepherd's Bush. Join about fifty others in the tiny Bush Theatre to see *Blood Sports* by David Edgar.

I only stay for the first hour – but saw an actor, Simon Callow, who I think would be excellent for RSM in 'Across the Andes' – because I know the injections are about to wear off and the tooth (or what's left of it) will start hurting. 'Bone just melts away in your mouth,' was one of the encouraging things Powell had said as he levered and drilled and scraped away at my jaw.

Well, it did begin to hurt. Hardly slept at all. I listened to two sides of

1 Robin Denselow, *Guardian* music journalist, BBC documentary maker and reporter. Lived a few doors down from us with his first wife Bambi.

a Lenny Bruce LP. I sat outside in the garden with a glass of Laphroaig at 3.00. I read the local paper cover to cover at 4 a.m. I was up at my desk at 6.00 – and finally fell into a deep sleep at around 6.30 in the morning.

Friday, July 9th

Anne brings me a copy of the Federal Court of Appeals Judgement in the Python v ABC case. The Judgement was dated June 30th 1976 and is very strongly favourable to Python – they recommend that the injunction should be upheld. So Terry's and my trip, in that cold and bleak December (which seems light years away now) was worthwhile after all.

The Judgement indicates that, in the judges' opinion, Python would have a substantial chance of a favourable verdict in the courts and damages and all else that could follow.

I personally am against a big damages award – it may be the way lawyers play it, but I think that the popular image of Python winning $1 million would erase in people's minds some of the reasons why we won it. But I think we should have a strong bargaining counter in any attempt to recover our costs. We shall see.

Monday, July 12th

Hard look at *Jabberwocky* script this morning. It's all held together by a manic intensity of vision and atmosphere, and if this intensity can be sustained in the characterisations as well, the film will be, well, certainly not dull. The writing in certain individual scenes is sometimes flat, sometimes conventional and occasionally gives the impression of being rushed – but I think a careful look at the script before each day's shooting will tighten up dialogue, which, by comparison to some of the *Holy Grail* scenes – the death cart, the philosophical peasants – is sparse in comic impact.

But the shape of the film is good, and it's just up to Terry G to try and achieve the Herculean task of recapturing his animation style in a live action movie – and for £400,000.

Wednesday, July 14th

Posted off the *Esquire* article about Python's New York adventures to Lee Eisenberg, plus long missive to Eric in France.

At ten down to Fitzroy Square for a read-through with some of the *Jabberwocky* principals. Max Wall and John Le Mesurier speak softly together in one corner. Old Acting Hands, both of whom have been through long spells of rejection and have come out wise, kindly, but above all unhurried. Then there are the Actors – Derek Francis, the Bishop, Peter Cellier as the Leading Merchant – working actors, not stars, not personalities, their personalities are their parts and they click into theatrical speech and gesture from the first read-through.

My friend for the morning is John Bird, amiable and sharp as ever. He's playing the Herald, and is not particularly happy with it. 'I do hate shouting,' he mutters sadly.

He and I are joined after half an hour by John Gorman, so there are now three of us in the Brash Young Men of Revue corner. Gorman's down from his Old Bakery in Suffolk. Slightly subdued – which means quite over the top by anyone else's standards. Covered in strange badges – including one for 'The Womble Bashers', which I like.

John Le Mes is marvellous, his pained double-takes are a joy to watch. Max has difficulty finding his lines, but as they mainly consist of 'Er … Oh …' it doesn't really matter. The Actors Act and John G and Bird make people laugh.

At lunchtime costume fitting session. I like my gear. At least it's going to be a deal more comfortable than the armour of *Holy Grail*.

A drink with Terry G, Max W and Bird. Max tells long, rambling, discursive tales – very funny if you've got an afternoon to spare. He drinks pints of Guinness in the pub at Seven Dials – but he drinks them slowly. He's also deaf in one ear and most of what Bird says in his low murmur (which is almost incomprehensible anyway) is totally lost on Max. But always those kind, wise, soft eyes and slow smile.

Back home via Dodo in Westbourne Grove, where I buy Graham and David a huge basket of plastic fruit for their tenth anniversary party tonight.

Off to the theatre at eight to see *Funny Peculiar* by Mike Stott. Only ten years ago you couldn't carry a plank across the stage without the Lord Chamberlain's permission – and now here's a comfortable, rather staid, London theatre audience, watching two women quite explicitly sucking off a man as he lies in his hospital bed. Funny and liberating, but deeply shocking to a man used to writing for television!

Off up to G Chapman's party. Sangria, champagne and good nosh. The house was cleaner and tidier than I'd ever seen it. The gathering was smallish and quite organised – the garden floodlit by Strand Electrics. Graham, on very good behaviour, wandered through in white suit looking like a benevolent tropical planter at a festivity for his employees. Peter Cook was soberish too.

Alison (still great with child) and Terry, Neil and Yvonne, Barry Cryer, Jo Kendall,[1] David Yallop are all there. But we're all getting older and staider, I thought, until Graham, Bernard McK and Dave Yallop gave their rendition of 'Without You' to a bemused audience. They stand in Gumby-like rigidity and yell the chorus to this lovely song at a hideous, horrendously loud pitch – and with trousers down for the second chorus.

Back home around 1.15.

Friday, July 16th

After lunch walked round balmy, humid London – to the studio, to the *Jabberwocky* office. To Great Titchfield Street to meet Warren Mitchell and read through my part with him. A tough little guy – close cropped hair, a tight, intense way of talking … but busy and extrovert in his command of a conversation.

Talk for a while about how bad actors are at dealing with praise. Warren said he approached Paul Scofield once and told him how marvellous he'd been in something, and, as Warren described it, 'the poor guy didn't know where to put himself'.

A bit of a read through. Warren tries his funny teeth he's brought along. Eventually fall to chortling over *Till Death*. Warren says he was third choice for Alf Garnett. First choice was Leo McKern! Problems of success of *Till Death* – who created Alf Garnett? Was it [writer] Johnny Speight or Warren? Clearly they both think they own more of Alf than the other thinks they deserve. God, if Python split over who created what, it could be the court case of the century!

'Silly old moo' – the famous phrase, Warren says, wasn't scripted. It came out during a rehearsal when he forgot the line 'Silly old mare'.

---

1 A Cambridge contemporary of John and Graham, Jo was in the cast of *Cambridge Circus* with them and later in *At Last the 1948 Show*.

Monday, July 19th

To Southwold for last visit before *Jabberwocky/Ripping Yarns* filming begins. Notice today how frail Ma is becoming, at the same time as Dad's muscular mobility is worsening.

There are no solutions to the problem which can give anyone any pleasure. The wretched twin attacks of Parkinson's and hardening of the arteries are destroying Father physically and the permanent hospitalisation which looms, now I would think, within the year, will destroy him mentally.

It rains hard as the train pulls into Liverpool Street at nine. Clatter home on the Broad Street Line. Comforting melancholy.

Wednesday, July 21st

Rehearsals with Harry H Corbett (a good actor, but oddly unsure of himself – he wears a suit and he mumbles rather self-deprecatingly that he feels it's important to look smart on the first day of a job! And I think he meant it.). But we get on well, and the scenes together will be funny. The same with Paul Curran, who plays my father. A Scot, friend of Jimmy Gilbert and Ian MacNaughton, from the seemingly inexhaustible supply of actors spewed out by Glasgow Citizens' Theatre.

Take Tom swimming after game of squash with Richard. In the evening Simon A rings and asks me to go and see *Hester Street* (written and directed by Joan Micklin Silver) with him. A delightful film – unpretentious and wholly successful. 10/10.

Back from this sensitive, sensible look at early Jewish immigrants struggling to settle in New York in 1896 to a phone call from Michael Henshaw to tell me that a meeting of lawyers and accountants representing all the Pythons have decided (not even recommended) that the next Python film should be written abroad. Oh ... and that they had projected its profit at £1 million.

Talk into Thursday with Simon A over the question of lifestyles and the way money isolates you from people. Simon quotes the case of a house in Mill Hill which he went to at the weekend, where there is opulence on a scale which stunned even Simon. It's the home of a man who just does deals. He benefits no one but himself, is surrounded by non-friends and basks unhappily in wealth that could rehouse half Camden's waiting list in a week.

Contrast with Clive Hollick, Simon's City friend[1] – head of Vavasseur and Shepperton Studios, etc, and a committed socialist who feels the City is hopelessly corrupt, but is trying to change it from within. He won't take any more than his £15,000 salary and refuses all expense account perks. A man to watch.

Monday, July 26th

Letter from *Esquire* (Lee Eisenberg) to say they like the article,[2] will print it almost uncut and have offered me $1,500 payment! Which, given the present dilapidated state of sterling, is nearly £800.

Jill rings, hardly able to contain her excitement. They want me for two days, to advertise Mattessons' sausages, and will pay £10,000 and may go higher! Jill is obviously keen for me to accept (it will mean £1,000 to her, after all), but I can't – and in a sense the enormity of the money offered (almost double my entire writing fee for thirteen *Ripping Yarns*!) makes my refusal easier. Jill clearly thinks I'm bonkers, but we decide to elbow any further commercial offers – and there have been a spate of them in the last few months – until March next year.

Filming on *Jabberwocky* began this morning at Shepperton, but I'm not required until Wednesday and have no words until Friday.

Wednesday, July 28th

A leisurely start to *Jabberwocky*. I'm not called until 10.30. No cars available on this picture, so I drive over to Shepperton myself to see how long it takes. Miss the turning off the M3 and career on for a further twelve miles before I can turn and roar back again. At the gates of Shepperton a uniformed gateman has no idea where *Jabberwocky* is being shot and directs me to a back lot where there is nobody to be seen. So my carefully nurtured calm is ruffled a little.

Eventually sniff out the studio where they're filming the crumbling court of King Bruno. The entire set is thick with dust and debris. The normally searingly bright studio lights are veiled with black drapes, giving the set a dim, sepulchral, twilight appearance. Pigeons cluck at

1 Clive, later Lord Hollick, and Simon Albury were friends from Nottingham University.
2 About Python in New York.

the top of the throne, rubble is dropped during the takes, whenever John Bird as the Herald bangs his staff.

In the middle of this murk, little figures, dwarfed by the height of the set, move around. Two cameras are in use. TG looks thin, but excited. He directs softly, padding around the camera, letting the First Assistant do all the shouting. They're a half-day behind already and the producers are looking around with fixed grins. Terry agrees it's like the first week of the *Grail* – an immediate artistic/economic gap.

Max looks wonderful as a little, wizened king. He's taken his teeth out and hasn't shaved. He is the personification of death warmed up. John Le Mes in his severe black skull cap looks more sinister than I've ever seen him. It's a magnificent fusion of imaginative costumes (Hazel and Charles), imaginative sets (Roy Smith), and imaginative make-up (Maggie).

Terry says that Milly Burns and Bill Harman have done a jackdaw job all over Shepperton, pinching bits of other sets. They've just finished a German co-production of Mozart's *Figaro*, from which quite a few props/sets will recur in *Jabberwocky*!

I wait until 3.30 to play a short and rough scene with Bernard Bresslaw and Bryan Pringle. TG says it looked terrifying. We do an impromptu fight – none of us knowing quite what's going on – but there's a rush to get Bernard B off to Bournemouth, where he's doing a summer show on the pier.

Friday, July 30th

Up at seven. The first taste of the real joys of filming. As Eric puts it in his letter from France which arrived today ... 'Up early to be carried around by talkative drivers to wrong locations in time to get into the wrong costume and be ready to wait for five or six hours for a couple of seconds' appearance on celluloid.'

It's not as much fun as that yet.

On set by 8.30, rehearsing a long scene in the Queen's Haemorrhoids with Bernard Bresslaw and Harry H Corbett, both of whom get to fling my (only eleven stone two by our scales this morning) body around. Bernard is kind, friendly, soft and cheerful as ever and I learn to my amazement that he's breaking at ten to go to his brother's funeral.

Harry and I are quite soon into the turkey-eating scene and Terry G says that this is the fastest they've worked all week. Yesterday had been particularly frustrating. He had spent 45 minutes with Peter Cellier, who plays the Merchant, trying to overcome his reluctance to pick his nose on screen.

A long day. One hour's lunch break – I eat with Harry H in the grim canteen. (Like much of Shepperton Studio Centre, it bears all the tacky indications of an enterprise on its last legs, which was being dismantled by the broker's men as a reprieve came through.)

Harry doesn't enjoy film acting. He finds the dehumanisation of the actor on a film set troubles him. I noticed today that even an actor of his experience seems to harden and tense up on the take – losing a little of the fun he's had on rehearsal.

On set from 8.30 until a quarter to seven in the evening – then gratefully and happily into a hot bath to clean off the sweat and grime of the day's work. This kind of manual acting takes it out of you.

Monday, August 2nd

Out on the *Oliver* lot[1] for most of the day, doing stunt work rather than acting. Much lying face-down in the dirt (peat and hay mixture) with Bernard Bresslaw, who is in fine form.

Encouraging viewing of Friday's rushes. The painstakingly lit sequences are not as good as the hastily grabbed, hand-held shots of me trying to distract Bernard's attention in the pub. This sequence was fresh, fast and – to prove the point – got consistent laughs at rushes.

I learn from the rushes that I must keep my performance up – the naturalistic way of playing (Frears' influence here) is not sufficient – a touch of silliness is required.

Tuesday, August 3rd

Cope with letters in the morning, phone calls, and eventually at lunchtime sign *Jabberwocky* contract (£6,000 due by end of filming, £1,500 deferred and 2½% of producer's gross). A motorcycle messenger in big boots and a rubber suit witnesses this impressive document.

Robert's for a glass of BBC Chablis at 6.30. He's been chairing a discussion programme for the Beeb Foreign Service on philosophy – Stuart

1 The set had been built in the mid-sixties for the hugely successful musical, *Oliver* by Lionel Bart. Directed by Carol Reed (*The Third Man*).

Hampshire and Ben Whitaker amongst the participants. Robert jokes about it, but I'm quite impressed. We walk from Robert's, through the Dickensian back alleys north of Fleet Street, skirting round the Inns of Court and across Waterloo Bridge to the concrete cultural wilderness of the South Bank.

At the National Theatre (the first time I've been inside it) I long for that hustle and bustle you get in St Martin's Lane and Shaftesbury Avenue. Here the audience is entirely made up of respectable bourgeois folk like ourselves. No coach tours here, no stout elderly ladies out for a giggle or a treat. Just a flood of serious, trendy, culturally aware, white wine bibbers like myself.

It's comfortable inside the Lyttelton Theatre, and the sight lines and acoustics require no effort or strain as in many other London theatres. The play *Weapons of Happiness* by Howard Brenton is not, as they say, 'my cup of tea'. It belongs to the belligerent, strident, didactic school of theatre, in which dialogue is sacrificed to monologues, characters depressingly clichéd, angry cockney workers, champagne drinking employers, etc. Occasionally some pleasing and quite moving writing, but as a whole I disliked it, as I felt most of the audience did.

We eat at the Neal Street Restaurant. David Hockney posters on the wall and David Hockney himself at a table.

Walk back to Fetter Lane discussing possibilities for a new Orr/Hewison/Signford book – a catalogue of 'All The Things You Ever Wanted'. Busy, by the light of the *Daily Mirror* building, discussing and enthusing over who would contribute to it, when we discover it's a quarter to two.

Thursday, August 5th

Cast of many at Shepperton today for the flagellants' procession. Graham Crowden is the leader of the fanatics. He's a splendid figure, but has trouble remembering his many and strange words. Hugely impressive takes of him and his crowd of grotty followers streaming up the mediaeval streets keep ending with Graham, white beard flowing and hand up-raised like Ivan the Terrible, coming to a sort of paralysed halt with a heartfelt 'Oh, fuck!'

Lunch with Christopher Logue. A nice, gentle chap, he's playing a flagellant with heart-warming enthusiasm and enjoyment. I ask him about the *Private Eye*/Goldsmith case soon to come into court. He says

Goldsmith is a nasty piece of work, but there is one, though only one, untruth in all *Private Eye*'s allegations – when he was said to have attended a meeting he didn't in fact attend.

Michael White is down today. Michael looks around at TG's carefully chosen extras and declares that this must be the ugliest film ever made.

It's a long day and the shocking canteen food doesn't raise any spirits. The chicken at supper tastes, as Crowden puts it, as though it had done panto for two years at Ashton-under-Lyne.

We night shoot until 12.30 a.m. (the extra half-hour will cost thousands as the unions can claim for an entire extra day) catapulting a blazing fanatic over the walls of the castle. The effect works superbly and everyone trails back to the dressing rooms.

Home and to bed by two. A nineteen-hour day, I reckon.

Friday, August 6th

Only the jolly, down-to-earth good humour of Bryan Pringle and the unquenchable cheerfulness of Bernard Bresslaw make this long day of waiting bearable. Finally, having been on set since eleven, am used at five for a 30-second take. It's the getting dirty and the cleaning up – a process lasting an hour at least – which is the most wearing and when I get home at 8.30 I'm in the mood for a good meal and a chat.

Ring Simon Albury and we go to Au Bois St Jean. Simon very interested in Shepperton – my remarks about food, etc, have led, I'm told, to speedy action from Mr Hollick! SA says he may be asked to run the place (i.e. Shepperton), but says it's all very vague.

Saturday, August 7th

The alarm shrills into my hangover at seven. God – only five hours' sleep behind me and I have to curse my enthusiasm in arranging a horse-riding lesson at Luton at nine this morning!

In my still-hungover state, I'm fairly relaxed and once I've got used to the size of the horse and the unexpectedly long distance from the ground, I get on well. The horse is used to it – it was under Glenda Jackson on *Elizabeth R*! Also ride a mule and a donkey, which cleverly made straight for a metal-roofed cow shed and nearly scalped me.

Tuesday, August 10th

Rushes at lunchtime today were very encouraging. Yesterday we had shot the Knight and Dennis departing the city and Dennis arriving back. For once everybody seemed pleased.

The donkey behaved marvellously this morning and manoeuvred the cheering crowds with great confidence. Better than yesterday when I had to sit on boxes and rock gently, to give the impression I was on a donkey.

Max Wall, as the King, looks quite marvellous and he and John Le Mes have developed this sad, forgetful, melancholic, vaguely homosexual double-act which suits the crumbling kingdom perfectly.

Max has a wonderful drawing power. He sits there, curled up like a caterpillar in his vast robes, never complaining about any discomfort, and people are attracted to him like a magnet – especially a willowy young lady photographer from *Celebrity* magazine, who sits beside him adoringly. Max enjoys this. His conversation is slow, measured, nostalgic, gentle and wise.

Wednesday, August 11th

In to Shepperton by two. It's the scene with the Princess and me driving away after we've been married. The Princess makes my nose run every time she kisses me. Gilliam instructs 'No French kissing … I don't want to see any tongue work there.'

Drive into Soho to see Herzog's *The Enigma of Kaspar Hauser* – a beautiful, careful, memorable little movie. The subject of the 'noble savage' suddenly faced with the world seems to lend itself to film – Truffaut's *L'Enfant Sauvage* was another excellent and intelligent movie on this theme.

Ate a curry at the Gaylord to try and chase away my cold.

Sunday, August 15th

Terry Gilliam and the script appear to be losing the battle for survival at the expense of Terry Bedford and the technicians, who have, fairly ruthlessly, dictated the pace of the shooting so far. Every day now, as the confidence of the camera and lighting department grows, the shooting schedule falls further and further behind.

Rumour has it that the Rolling Stones are rehearsing here this week – across on Stage A. Will wait to hear more. Last week I got a letter from an hotel on the Cap D'Antibes, written by Ronnie Wood (whom Eric has been gallivanting around with this summer) saying that Eric was too busy to write, but he'd asked Mr Wood to write and tell me that if my letters didn't become more interesting he'd have to write to one of the Goodies.

Thursday, August 19th

The day drags on – the unions are asked to work until eight. Much muttering and sounding. They seem to agree, but no one can have asked the electricians, who, at seven, pull the plugs out and that's it for the day.

Home to see the last hour of *Sunset Across the Bay* – Frears/Bennett/ Tufano teleplay. Wish I'd seen the lot. Terrific playing from Harry Markham.

How I would love to work on something with Alan Bennett – I really admire and enjoy his writing and performing. It's spare and honest. His world and his characters unglamorous, but delicately drawn and wonderfully believable. He portrays lack of confidence with confident assurance. A craftsman too – he works with care and deliberation on the simplest of lines and his scripts are like softer and gentler Pinter – with the same good ear that Pinter has for human small talk.

Friday, August 20th

Eric rings and comes round for lunch – or with lunch, I should say. Bearded, tanned, in a white cotton boiler suit and a gorgeous perfume. Helen is rather rude about Eric's smell and says it stinks the kitchen out. Eric is very patient with her! We open a bottle of Jules Laurier sparkling blanc de blancs and eat up kipper pâté, cold beef and salads which Eric has brought from Au Bois St Jean. Spend afternoon chatting outside.

Eric tells me about his summer with the Rolling Stones, or Ronnie Wood, mainly. He likes Ronnie – he's good company and a laugh – but is more guarded about Jagger (very sharp business mind) and Keith (pleasant, but so doped-up Eric reckons he has only a year to live).

Eric is going over to New York in early October to appear on and co-host *Saturday Night Live* – the Chevy Chase late-night programme that's swept the US and which Pythons have, as a group, quite regularly turned down.

As Helen says, Eric 'doesn't lack confidence', but I feel that he's still lacking something. He is very anxious to get back to Python writing and performing, as if he feels that the fast France/New York world which he's recently joined and in which friendship tends to be based on how many LPs you've had in the charts, does not offer the feet-on-the-ground atmosphere of the Python group.

But, as always, EI is entertaining and amusing and it's a lovely way to lose an afternoon off!

Saturday, August 21st

In the evening Helen's cooking again, this time for Terry G and Maggie. They arrive – TG looking unusually gaunt and unshaven, pale-faced and completely without his little bulging stomach. He has some quite impressive news. Apparently Terry Bedford is no longer on the picture.

Yesterday, while I had been pleasantly reminiscing in the sunshine with Eric and sparkling white, Gilliam and Terry B had almost come to blows on the set, after a morning when only two shots had been done. A shouting match had developed and, whilst Max Wall sat patiently in a pool of water (for it was the scene in which John Le Mes wakes him up by throwing a pail of water over him), Terry B had walked off.

The producers rallied (Goldstone being especially calm and level-headed, according to TG) and began the search for an alternative cameraman. Sandy rang Nic Roeg, who was quite prepared to do it himself, but couldn't, so suggested young whizz-kid Tony Richmond. Richmond couldn't take over for a week, but suggested John Wilcox. John Wilcox, a veteran of 60, was checked out and found to have the highest recommendations.

So tonight we have a new cameraman. To me it seems indecently sudden, but on this film, as it is totally his brainchild, TG must be the boss. He's a thick-skinned fellow and very harsh words must have been spoken to wound him like this.

We talked a little about Python and the next movie. TG said he reckoned the film was TJ's to direct – he'd far rather be directing another film of his own. He has an idea for using the Port Talbot industrial complex as the basis for a science fiction film which, as he says, he'll 'write with *anyone*'.

Monday, August 23rd

Terry Bedford is still the cameraman. Julian [Doyle, editor] tells me that he rang around on Sunday and placated everyone and told them that the good of the film was the co-operation of all the elements in it. Julian persuaded Terry B to ring Gilliam – because he knew Gilliam wouldn't ring Terry B.

It's hot, hot, hot still. The Prime Minister's having an emergency Cabinet meeting about the drought.

Tuesday, August 24th

Chasing up and down corridors. A bit of sub-Errol Flynn work. Anti-swashbuckling. To be actually living these childhood dreams and fantasies – and getting paid handsomely for them – I have to pinch myself mentally to be sure it's happening. Fifteen years ago Graham [Stuart-Harris] and I were lapping up all the films, good or bad, that hit Sheffield, and now here I am making the bloody things.

Eric (complete with specially printed T-shirt '*Jabberwocky* – The New Python Movie') and Susie the wet-lipped Aussie model, came to see us on set. Eric brought me a signed advance copy of the book which he says has already had massive re-orders, *The Rutland Dirty Weekend Book* (containing three pages by M Palin!), to be released next month. It's a lavish production job – a combination of the Goodies and Python book designs over the last four years, but fused and improved.

I feel that it pre-empts more Python books – a particular area of comic book design has been capped by the *Rutland* book – and if the Python 'periodical' which is being heavily sold to us by Eric, is to be the work of these same designers, I fear it will look unoriginal – and that Python, far from creating a bandwagon, will appear to be climbing on one.

Sit in the sun and read more of *The Final Days*,[1] chase up a few more corridors.

---

1 Woodward and Bernstein's book on Nixon. Famous for Deep Throat's disclosures about the Watergate break-in.

Thursday, August 26th

At the location by eight and on my donkey to take advantage of early-morning shafts of sunlight through the pine trees.

After about 10.30, the sandy hollow, a dry dust bowl at the bottom of it and ringed picturesquely by pine trees, becomes like some gladiatorial arena. The school kids and the various hangers-on of the film unit – press, producers' friends, etc – sit up in the shade of the trees, looking down on the little group around the camera who work away, exposed in the sandy arena to the increasingly hot sun. Every now and then actors troop back after their takes to rest in the shade, or a clapper boy or production assistant walks down with cold drinks.

Warren Mitchell loses his temper briefly, but ill-advisedly, with John, one of the hard-working props boys, who accidentally treads on Warren's hand. A ripple of tension. Warren is a hard worker and an extrovert. He leads a full and busy life and talks about it a great deal.

But it's a long, hot day and we're still shooting at seven in the evening, when I lose my temper during a shot in which I have to run away from camera carrying a large, unwieldy pack. I do all that's required, but behind me I can hear someone yelling and shrieking. I can't think what I'm doing wrong and I can't hear what it is they're shouting. Finally turn and stop and bitterly throw my pack down. The crew are grinning back there in the distance, but I still don't know what the hell I was being shouted at for. It turned out it was only TG doing some off-camera atmosphere noises. He did that this morning, when he was trying to help my reactions by giving me an off-camera impression of raping and pillaging. The result was so extraordinary I just broke up.

Home about 8.30. Wash away the day's grot. Then Helen, in keeping with the drought spirit that has gripped the land, waters the flowers with my bathwater.

Long phone call home to find out the latest on Father, who yesterday fell quite severely. The doctor says it's time for him to go into hospital permanently, but a geriatric specialist visited him today and pronounced him much fitter than he'd expected. The specialist says my ma should not do so much for him – and should let him spend all day dressing if he needs to. Mother needed calming down after this theoretically very humane, but practically rather callous verdict.

Friday, August 27th

Feel confident and eager to work on these opening scenes. Presence of Paul Curran, who's playing my father, increases this spirit of enjoyment. We complete our early part of the scene quickly, then Warren appears and we work on the main body of the scene. It goes well and feels lively. Warren says he enjoys working with Paul and myself – I think because we adapt to his rather naturalistic way of playing. He says he throws some actors who complain that their sense of 'timing' – W makes it sound like a dirty word – goes if there is any improvisation at all.

But the irrepressible Mitchell ego, which has been bristling over the last couple of days, suddenly and quite abruptly bursts out. A BBC *Film '76* camera crew hover and start to film us rehearsing.

Warren: 'Who are these people?'

Mumbled lack of response from everyone.

Warren, louder: 'No, come on, who *are* these people? What are they doing?'

By now he's got the embarrassed attention of most of the unit. He refuses to be filmed rehearsing. He, quite reasonably, if rather loudly, points out that no one asked him if he would mind. Barry Norman[1] is seen scowling in the background and after a hurried discussion they very huffily leave.

Wednesday, September 1st

An incident at Shepperton. I'm being made-up when I hear raised voices in the corridor outside. One of the extras, a short, stocky, barrel-chested man with a nose spread all over his face, is shouting loudly and angrily at Maggie Gilliam. But the shouting is of a particularly vicious, abusive and violent kind. He sounds more than just angry, he sounds dangerous. I intervened and he turns on me. I could see his eyes blazing – he shouted at me to keep out of it. Who did I think I was? Sir fucking Galahad? (Wrong film, but nearly ...)

He was shaking with a barely repressed threat of physical violence, so I found Peter, the second assistant director, and told him to get the man out. He'd reduced Maggie to tears (not an easy task) and I said that I

---

1 TV presenter and journalist. Originally asked to front *Film '73* for a few weeks, he made it his own private domain until *Film '98*.

would refuse to go on the set with him. Peter went upstairs and later the extra left.

It turned out that he was no ordinary extra, but a mate of Peter's who had been Frank Sinatra's bodyguard and was no more or less than an East End villain. It's terrifying the feeling of violence which one man can give off and all because he thought Maggie might clip his moustache! The incident left everyone involved rather shaky.

Work late again. I'm in the coracle at half past six. Then goodbye to Shepperton – this tatty, crumbling world which I've grown rather fond of. I'm pulled across the lake for the last time – across the same waters Huston used in *The African Queen*, and the same waters George Sanders must have got to know in *Sanders of the River*. (Did they have to keep stopping for planes landing at London Airport in those days?)

Tomorrow Wales.

Tuesday, September 7th, Pembroke

Bright and sunny as we film in the castle. Harry H and I have two or three scenes together.

Max Wall arrives tonight. We all eat together. Harry H expresses his admiration for Laurence Olivier – Max his for Enoch Powell.

Wednesday, September 8th, Old King's Arms Hotel, Pembroke

Work until twelve – chasing turnips round the keep – then I'm finished for a while as they start to shoot the joust.

Later in the afternoon a long, rambling chat with Max. I warm to him and the strange Joan Lee, daughter of Stan Lee of Marvel Comics fame, who drapes herself around him. Max listens courteously, talks effortlessly, humorously and intelligently – but he wanders occasionally into obscene asides, or stops and marvels at a word he's said, or suddenly laughs. He's such an original – conversations with him are like setting out on a voyage without a map. I think he sat all afternoon in the bar with his Guinness and Joan.

Thursday, September 9th, Pembroke

Breakfast with Dave Prowse. His enormous shoulders look as though he has full armour on under his shirt. He's back to London after this to go back to his lucrative body-building salons at the Dorchester, etc. A nice, amiable, soft, but deep-spoken giant. A man who used to be almost a cripple – he grew so fast – but overcame it spectacularly to become one of the leading body-builders/muscle-toners, etc. He took two stone off Edward Heath and says he gets a lot of politicians at his gym. Dave is to be the figurehead of an £800,000 campaign to teach kids the Green Cross Code [and later became Darth Vader in *Star Wars*].

Write p.c.s in the room. Terry Hughes phones with a lovely, heart-lifting piece of news. Iain Cuthbertson wants to play the Scottish doctor in 'Murder at Moorstones'. This is marvellous. It was a complete stab in the dark – all I wanted was an Iain C type, and never expected that an actor with a TV series of his own [*Sutherland's Law*, 1973–76] would be at all interested in this small and rather silly role. But he's read the script, loves it, and is very pleased that the piece is to be staffed by actors rather than just comics.

No chance of Simon Callow for RSM in 'Andes' – he wanted to, but is totally committed to Joint Stock Theatre Co. But Terry, now in his second week as Assistant Head of LE Variety at the Beeb, is confident of Isabel Dean as the mother in 'Moorstones' (I don't know her, but everyone says she's great), Frank Middlemass as the father, and Bob Hoskins for the RSM in 'Andes'.

After lunch up to the castle. The fierce cold wind is lessening, but everyone looks huddled and besieged. The tents won't stay up. The horses are more frightened than ever. The peat that's been spread around the lists is blowing in people's eyes. The good extras of Pembroke, on their pathetic £5 a day, are working hard and remarkably cheerfully. But I hear that their lunch was actually cut down today, presumably to save money, which is scandalous and, as Elaine[1] pointed out, unpleasantly ironic in a film which had more than a bit to say about the oppression of the peasants!

There is much discontent amongst the crew – meetings in small groups are constantly being held – and it centres over daily food allowances, which most of the crew feel at £3.50 are mean and unrealistic. Sandy, who looks hunted as anybody approaches, but at least is always available, has made a £4 offer. This has been refused.

I don't know where they go from here, but as long as people know

---

1 Elaine Carew, worked closely with Maggie Weston on make-up for Python and Gilliam films.

that Sandy is getting 15% of the film, and as long as the rushes continue to be as encouraging as they are, the producers are in a losing position. If the film looked bad, and Sandy was manifestly broke, it could be different – but the hard-worked crew are not in a mood to be charitable.

Friday, September 10th, Pembroke

Waiting again. Breakfast with Max at half past nine. Read *The Guardian*, which has only been printed in London once this week. Realise how poor a substitute is the dry, in content, style and format, old *Times*. Can't bring myself to buy the *Telegraph* instead – with its right-wing scare stories – especially as it's a lot better in amount of news, presentation and general interest than *The Times* and I might begin to like it.

Rushes of the knights playing hide and seek are very funny. Terry, as usual now, seems more inclined to bemoan than praise what's going on. The processes of dealing with the people involved in keeping the film going, with all their different egos and personal ambitions, Terry cannot deal with; people get him down daily.

But all this doesn't matter too much, because Terry's greatest con-tribution – his visual sense – is working well. He still niggles a little at the praise that Simon and Terry B get for shots – which praise, he says, is as much for Hazel's costumes, Maggie's make-up, Milly's designs and hell! says Terry, I choose the shot.

Saturday, September 11th, Pembroke

More familiar British weather is returning. Though it dawned blue and cloudless, stormy wind and rain spread throughout the day, buffeting the castle yet again. Tents blew down, the crowd huddled into any avail-able Norman-arched doorway in the castle walls between shots. With cameras wrapped in polythene bags and in between vicious cold squalls of rain that turned umbrellas inside out, the joust scene gradually progressed.

It was 7.30 in the evening when Bill Weston's last and most spectacu-lar stunt ended the miserable day and ended our filming in Pembrokeshire. He was pulled backwards off his horse by Derek Bottell – the 'jerk-off' specialist!

The crowd, who had stoically defied the weather – and were really in a state of high excitement which had carried them through it all – swarmed off through the Barbican gateway and across the road to the pub. Here Terry Gilliam bought them drinks for two hours – and later that evening he appeared at the Old King's Arms, shaven for the first time in a week, and rosy-cheeked, his eyes tired, but glazed, in a very happy, silly mood.

In the bar until late. I think Max has finally tired of the attentions of his chief acolyte – he muttered something uncharacteristically uncharitable about her being the sort of person who might turn him homosexual!

Sunday, September 12th, Chepstow

Wake at nine, surprisingly clear-headed. It's a grey day. Winter's in the air suddenly. Buy papers, breakfast, pay fond farewells to the Old King's Arms, Pembroke. A nice town, a marvellous hotel. Up at the castle the last windswept remains of the pavilion and lists are being packed.

Go for a three-hour walk by the sea, along Stackpole Quay to Freshwater Bay East Coast Path. A few hours of solitariness, a rather vital release from the gregariousness of filming. A quick look at Castle Carew – a splendid Gothic ruin, full of different architectural styles, deserted great halls and ivy-covered walls, with crows nesting.

Depressing arrival at the Two Rivers Hotel, Chepstow. It almost certainly had to be an anti-climax after the Old King's Arms, but I did not expect the belligerent sullenness of the receptionist, nor the total tackiness of all the decoration. A 'Fresh-Aire' machine in the corridor near my room gurgles dyspeptically and discharges a foul and sickly sweet-smelling gas up the passage.

The evening cheers up with the arrival of Neil I. At the Two Fingers Hotel (as we've decided to rechristen it), we end up round a table in the restaurant with Max, Joan Lee, Johnny Cole the props man and wife, making up limericks.

Thursday, September 16th, Chepstow Castle

A moment of quite stimulating liberation when I am required to drop my trousers in a shot and reveal my un-knickered bum to all and sundry. As we're outside the main gates to the castle, quite a little crowd has gathered to watch the filming – about fifty or sixty in addition to the fifty extras in the scene.

Realise I feel less embarrassed than they do, and really quite enjoy the experience of flashing a naughty part of the body in a public place – and getting paid, rather than arrested for it. Can see the exhilaration of 'streaking' – a sort of heady feeling of freedom comes over me as I point my bum for the third time at a twin-set and pearl-bedecked lady standing not ten yards away!

Saturday, September 18th, Chepstow Castle

Yesterday was the last day of principal photography – contracts for most of the crew ended at 5.30 on Friday evening. But everyone is aware of how incomplete the film is – it's more than days, it's at least two weeks away from completion. So today work goes on, but without Terry Bedford, Jenny, Simon, Mick the Loader and other familiar faces.

I miss them, though I know Terry G and Julian don't. They've been longing for this day. Longing to be rid of 'The Circus' as they call them.

Roger Pratt[1] is still there – doughty, reliable, straight and reassuring (not a 'Circus' man, I'm told). Julian and Terry G do most everything else, leaping around with the unbounded delight of those from whom a great weight has been lifted.

Terry operates like he so much wanted to do. Julian can organise in his direct and unsophisticated way, which never worked with a full crew.

I feel at last drained and physically exhausted. I want to go home. Just for a couple of days, that's all I need. Away from dirt, discomfort, cameras and castles. I want to stop being stared at for a day or two.

I begin to harbour murderous thoughts towards the vacuous tourists who cling to the unit like leeches, ordering their spotty, whiny little kids to stand beside me and have their photo taken. 'Could you sign these for two little girls who are friends of the lady who works Thursdays only in the shop next to the one I work in?' 'When are you doing more Pythons?' 'What is this?' 'Who are you?' It's all becoming a big nightmare from which I want to wake up and scream 'Fuck off!' from the battlements of Chepstow Castle.

At a quarter to six I run up the stairs as Gilliam films me, for the last time. It's over. Throw my potato the length of the Outer Bailey – and by 6.30 I'm heading for London in my Mini, with a huge and generous

---

1 Focus puller. Worked as lighting cameraman with Terry Gilliam (*Brazil*, *The Fisher King*, *Twelve Monkeys*) and has since shot two of the Harry Potter films.

sunset behind me – a final farewell from Wales, for which, despite today, I shall only have the happiest of memories.

Home around 8.30 (praise the M4). Willie, naked, runs down the stairs to open the door for me. Cuddles all round. Even Rachel hasn't gone to sleep and she welcomes me with a soft, broad grin which warms me no end.

Tuesday, September 21st

All day at the BBC working on pre-production for *Ripping Yarns*.

Casting continues to provide surprises. Denholm Elliott has agreed to play Gregory in 'Andes'. Terry H keeps telling me not to underestimate the scripts when I show stunned incredulity at the involvement of an actor of D Elliott's legendarity.

Wednesday, September 22nd

Pouring rain (still rare enough to be remarkable) as I drive out to Shepperton, after a BBC wig and costume fitting, to see the final Welsh rushes and an assembly of the film so far.

The opening castle stuff works surprisingly badly – even Max doesn't come across as positively as he should – and the chiaroscuro lighting effects, and some quite wretched minor performances, make the whole thing irritatingly difficult to follow. Moment of depression – it's misfired. But it perks up and lightens and brightens and, by the end (when the editor has skilfully put on some wedding music), the film, despite its 'Scene Missing' caption cards and its lack of effects, has grabbed people enough to elicit spontaneous applause. John G and Sandy are very happy. Happier than I ever saw producers on the *Grail*.

I'm happy too. Deep down, and confiding this only to the diary, I'm pretty pleased with myself – like I never was on *Grail*. There are only a few moments where I let my performance slip. I was trying hard on *Jabberwocky* to make up for what I felt were unrelaxed performances on the *Grail*. God, it's been a long time since I've really enjoyed my performance.

Friday, September 24th, Southwold

Up to Southwold – left London in pouring rain.

Saw Father in hospital. Sitting hunched, huddled and silent with three others. He's draped in a cellophane sheet under his dressing gown like a chicken in a supermarket. He seems pleased to see me and gets a few words out in the 45 minutes we're there – something about having a picture of myself (walking) in my old school tie. The sooner he gets out of Southwold and to Blythburgh, where he will be made to walk and work a lot more, the better.

At present he's not steady enough to be at home – so sits in this strange silent world, of grunts and occasional indecipherable ramblings from the other patients – one of whom, Percy, tries to push himself out of his chair and, as he does so, pees all over the floor. Silence. No nurses rushing to him, he cheerfully sits down again.

Monday, September 27th

This morning back at familiar Shepperton. A short scene with Harry H (full of doubts again, but I've grown very fond of this strange, self-critical, introspective extrovert). Then a strange and uncomfortable series of shots of me being flung around on the end of Bernard Bresslaw's legs and picked up and hurled out of the Queen's Haemorrhoids – a harness of quite unbelievable awkwardness for this shot – and finally into the rain-soaked woods in the back lot for a scene of wood-gathering, when I'm surprised by Terry Gilliam (playing Patsy from the *Holy Grail* again). Much crouching and being savagely attacked.

Terry is very sick today and keeps having to retreat to the bushes to throw up. But he battles bravely on. How he will shape up to the week, I don't know. It's going to be hard and they're already behind. I must finish Sunday – I start *Ripping Yarns* on Monday – but it'll be a hell of a push.

Tuesday, September 28th

No Jabberwocking for me today, but my last day off, apart from Sundays, until late October. Letters, visit Anne Henshaw. She has her head down in the labyrinthine affairs of Python as usual. She reports that the sooner we start writing the Python film the better for some in the group – she says Graham especially seems to be at a loose end and drinking more, with several of his projects, TV series and his film of Bernard McKenna's script, having collapsed.

Shopping in the King's Road – have to give brief run-down on Python plans in almost every shop – the assistants all seem to recognise me and want to talk.

To BBC to meet Don Henderson – T Hughes' selection for the RSM in 'Across the Andes'. I'm in trepidation for this is a major role and I don't even know the guy.

Fears allayed – he looks good – with a rather fierce, red face and a good sense of humour. He's easy company and seems to understand the role well. Still no Dora – as Michele Dotrice turned down the role (the first artist to turn down a *Ripping Yarns* role this time around!).

Out to dinner in the evening with Robin S-H and Barbara.[1] By a strange stroke of coincidence a Peruvian is present. I tell him about 'Across the Andes by Frog' – and to my amazement he tells me that the biggest frogs in the world live in Lake Titicaca, Peru, and that the frog is a common motif in old Peruvian carvings!

Thursday, September 30th

At Shepperton – on waste ground behind the *Oliver* set – our little unit struggles through the day. Terry G is even more terrier-like than usual – leaping around with the camera, building sets and taking time off only to curse some particular piece of inefficiency.

I just grin and bear it. Much walking with banner and pack after a morning spent under the belly of a horse being prodded by bandits.

Away on H Stage they are on the first day of shooting *Julia*.[2] There are 300 extras in beautiful '20s costumes and a huge ocean liner set to go with it. Meanwhile, on the rubbish tip, *Jabberwocky* works on!

Monday, October 4th

Slept well, and was at Pinewood for the first day of 'Across the Andes' shoot, feeling quite fresh. In the village our cameraman Peter Hall was directing a lighting rig the size and scale of which made *Jabberwocky* look like home movies, a track was being laid, flags being nailed up, statues erected. A feature film atmosphere of bustle and preparation.

---

1 Robin, younger brother of my childhood friend Graham Stuart-Harris. A doctor. Married Barbara, a New Zealander.
2 Fred Zinnemann's film about Lillian Hellman, starring Vanessa Redgrave.

Terry H and I stood in the square – me in my Snetterton shorts and helmet – and surveyed it. Terry must have read my thoughts. 'D'you ever feel responsible for all this?' he asked with a half-smile.

Denholm seemed to relish his part as the seedy Vice-Consul. An actor of enormous experience – he was one of my childhood heroes in *The Cruel Sea* – and greatly respected and in constant demand. But here he was doing his first part after three months off in Spain, and he'd chosen to do a *Ripping Yarn* because he loved the script and because, as he explained in his effortlessly classic English upper-class accent, it was nice to do some comedy. He'd been offered some life of Marx thing, he told me with an unhappy frown, and was soon off to do 'some bloody Brecht' for the BBC, which didn't seem to make him much happier either.[1]

Friday, October 8th

Before night filming, Jimmy Gilbert drops in to see Terry H and me. He's read 'The Testing of Eric O' and is very enthusiastic. According to TH, Jimmy is treating the *Ripping Yarns* as one of his major projects – which is exhilarating and frightening at the same time. Each episode is costing twice as much as each episode of Python. All the more reason why they *must* work so well. There can be no excuses.

A long, but mercifully warm and dry night at Pinewood. We get through a great deal, but Don Henderson and I are still quelling a frog riot at three in the morning. Home by five.

Monday, October 11th, King's House Hotel, Glencoe

Marvellous journey from London, ending up on the West Highland Line – pulling past Loch Lomond and into ever higher remoteness. It's very wet. Streams are pouring off the slopes like water off the back of a newly emerged whale.

Our little band – some fifteen strong – disembarks from the Euston sleeper at Bridge of Orchy Station – so small that it takes one or two tries before the driver can get our carriage parallel with the platform.

To the King's House Hotel – haunt of previous Python filmings.

---

1 Denholm caused consternation by enquiring, very politely, if it might not be too much trouble to make his call a little later in future. 'Only I do like a fuck in the morning.'

Misty cloud swirls across the tops of the mountains. Have learnt from past experience that it's no good belting all over the Highlands for just the right mountain. Some of the best are right by the hotel and, because of the enormous benefits of being near our base, we decide to locate Snetterton's camp about 300 yards from the hotel with the dark, stony, fierce pyramid of Buachaille Etive Mor as our El Misti.

Monday, October 18th

Lunch with Clive Hollick (and Simon A) at his invitation. Clive, whose group, Mills and Allen, own Shepperton Studios, wants me to join the board of Shepperton as a non-executive adviser – representing the users of Shepperton from the artistic side.

He has plans to brighten Shepperton's image and make it into the most exciting studio to work in in London. Pin-tables and neon lights announcing who's in today, may be going a bit far – but a bit of show-manship will not be a bad thing for the film industry, which needs any boost of confidence it can get. As I prefer Shepperton to the more oppressive, institutionalised atmosphere of Pinewood, I feel quite amenable.

Monday, October 25th

Woke – in advance of the alarm – at about seven. A dull, heavy, unin-spired feeling. One thing I know for sure – I don't want to work today, or for a long time. But I have two weeks of filming ahead, in which another *Ripping Yarn*, 'Murder at Moorstones Manor', is to be put down. The script has been acclaimed and yet I feel as if it's the first day of a winter term at school.

A great deal of dialogue to do today, which took me a couple of hours of concentration to get under my belt last night. It takes me a little over 45 minutes of not difficult driving out along the A40 to get to Harefield Grove, a once-stately home near Rickmansworth.

Isabel Dean, who plays the key figure of the mother, is gloomy fol-lowing the West End opening of *Dear Daddy*.[1] She looks perfect for the part, but seems a little strained and tired and has trouble with her words.

1 Written by Denis Cannan, it ran eight months at the Ambassadors. Isabel left the cast before the end of the run.

Friday, October 29th

Out to Harefield again. I enjoy these early morning drives now – I happily let Capital Radio, with its inane links and good music, flow over me. It's a relaxing 45 minutes. There's now much to look forward to – the week has steadily improved. I seem to have survived a peak of tiredness, which was at its worst on Tuesday morning, but has since receded.

Terry H shows no signs of anything other than totally enjoying himself. Isabel worries on, but could be giving a perfect performance – I'm just not sure until we see it. She's a much more jolly, funny person than her somewhat anxious exterior might indicate – and is gratifyingly happy to be doing this during the day alongside *Dear Daddy* in the West End – the play and cast of which she can't stand.

Wednesday, November 3rd

Evening meal in Chelsea with Iradj B[1] and Frank and Franny Reiss.[2] Iradj has been selected (by the Shah himself) to start a publishing industry in Iran. No books are made or printed there as yet, so Iradj (and Time-Life whom he works for) would be starting literally from scratch.

I would think it a dangerous job – how much freedom will he have to publish what he wants? But Iradj is a pragmatist, he'll end up on his feet. One of his problems is an illiteracy rate of 50%, but he maintains there's a functional illiteracy rate of 75% (people who can read nothing more than simple signs, instructions, etc).

He hadn't changed from the slightly patronising, but totally engaging, aristocratic Persian layabout he was when I shared a room with him in Germany for ten weeks in the summer of '63. I feel Iradj is one of those people who is now as old as he will ever get. Also one of those people who will keep recurring at odd intervals and in odd places throughout one's life.

1 Iradj Bagherzade inveigled me into an unsuccessful attempt to sell encyclopaedias to American servicemen in Germany during my first summer at Oxford. I sold four sets in ten weeks, one to a family who defected to the Soviet Union.
2 Friends from Oxford days.

Monday, November 8th

Half a year and a few days after we last played *Python Live at City Center* in New York, the Pythons reassemble at 22 Park Square East for the first day of a two-month writing period on our new film. A fine, sunny day, a good day to take resolutions and make plans.

John suggests straightaway that at some point during this writing period we all go abroad to the sun for a week or ten days (to 'really break the back of the film'). This is shelved. As Terry J says, 'Let's all see if we like each other at the end of the day.' But we make plans for the next year – writing until Christmas, rewriting throughout March and filming delayed until September/October 1977. There follows some good chat and exchange of ideas about the story and how to treat it. JC now thinks the film should be called 'Monty Python's Life of Christ'.

At lunchtime, TG leaves to complete filming of the *Jabberwocky* monster in Pembroke. We all go off to Auntie's restaurant. A bottle of champagne (that's all) among us to celebrate the reunion. They all want to know about *Jabberwocky*. The worse news the better, I sense! John's passed his driving test and now has a car of his own – 'A very *old* Rolls-Royce,' he tells me, unable to stifle a trace of embarrassment.

Wednesday, November 10th

Writing with Terry – some hopeful starts, but nothing great as yet, the most promising being a piece Terry has begun about the Three Wise Men, confused over which star they're following and being constantly mistaken for the wrong sort of astrologers and having to tell people about their star sign. In the classic Python mould of the humour of frustration; irritation at constantly being diverted by trivia.

Friday, November 12th

Python meeting at Park Square East at ten. All there except TG. Anne sits in (having asked if we didn't mind). All rather institutional. It falls to Palin to start the ball rolling and read the first new, all-Python material since we wrote the *Holy Grail*.

Enough good material from everybody to suggest things haven't changed. In fact, in John and Graham's case, I think they've improved.

They wrote the stoning section and an ex-leper and psychopath section – both of which were back on their best form. Very funny.

Anne supplies lunch – prawns and smoked salmon and no booze, except for GC who seems to find a G and T from somewhere. He is on fine form and really elated by his writing week with John. By contrast, I feel our week has not produced strong material. I'm suffering from slight, post-filming loss of energy. Terry J is too preoccupied with domestic and philanthropic problems.

Sunday, November 14th

Today I am going with TJ to the BBC to see a rough cut of 'Across the Andes'.

It didn't strike me as as funny as it should be, but he liked a lot of the shooting and the acting. Terry J's main worry was my part. I think I'm not at my best with sub-Cleesian public school aggressives – and Snetterton is a middle-man figure, not extraordinary in himself. TJ feels that the prominence of Snetterton should be built up more – putting him squarely and confidently as the centrepiece of the film. Then at least he would become less of an irritating attempt at someone being irritating.

Wednesday, November 17th

Film writing with Terry. He's still not producing much – what with helping his brother Nigel move, etc – but today we have a good read-through and work on with the Three Wise Men. Squash together at five. Two games all.

Drive over to Kingston for dinner with Nigel Pegram and April O.[1]

Nigel as dapperly charming as ever; someone it's very difficult not to like. April was telling me quite extraordinarily Pythonesque stories of her neighbours. She has a woman who came in and asked April if she would go and sniff her house! She meant it literally too – she was worried about some smell in the house and people were coming round. Also of a neighbour who knows King Olaf of Norway, who is apparently

1 Nigel was one of the cast of the Oxford Revue at the Edinburgh Festival in 1964, with Terry Jones, Annabel Leventon, Doug Fisher and myself. He married the actress April Olrich.

a compulsive farter. This is well known and hosts are now prepared for it and cover up for him in all kinds of ingenious ways.

Thursday, November 18th

A writing meeting of all the team this afternoon. John and Graham had written little and were not as pleased with themselves as before. Eric had done more thinking than writing – whereas Palin and Jones had produced a mighty wodge of at least 25 minutes of material. So reading was not made easier by the fact that there was a total imbalance of contributors. Fortunately Terry Gilliam had taken time off from editing at Shepperton to be at the meeting and his generous and noisy laughter helped a great deal and, by the end, we'd acquitted ourselves quite respectably.

The sketches, or fragments, which work least well at the moment are those which deal *directly* with the events or characters described in the Gospels. I wrote a sketch about Lazarus going to the doctors with 'post-death depression', which, as I read it, sounded as pat and neat and predictable as a bad university revue sketch. The same fate befell John and G's sketch about Joseph trying to tell his mates how his son Jesus was conceived. The way the material is developing it looks as though the peripheral world is the most rewarding, with Jesus unseen and largely unheard, though occasionally in the background.

John and Graham are troubled by the lack of a storyline. At the moment, after only about seven or eight days' writing, I feel it's the least of our worries and that we should carry on writing and stockpiling funny material to be fitted into a storyline later. 'But we only have another thirty-two and a half days' writing, little plum,' says John, consulting his diary.

Friday, November 19th

In the same week as I describe in *Melody Maker* the pain and joys of filming *Jabberwocky* on a rubbish tip at Shepperton, I find myself filming *Jabberwocky* on a rubbish tip at … Shepperton.

Nearly four months after my first shot, I'm being made up as Dennis again, with the blood, the dirt and the fringe – only this time we can't afford a make-up girl on set, so I have to go up to South Hill Park to see Maggie, who makes me up before breakfast.

At Shepperton we find a haggard and unshaven cameraman – played by Julian Doyle. The three of us make our way to the rubbish tip. Julian, by this time, has found some ends of film to use up. We retrieve a chair from the tip, which Terry G stands on. I climb under my shield and drag myself across the dirt patch while Julian squirts smoke around us. A lonely, surreal little scene, which *Film '76* should have captured.

Sunday, November 21st

A new thing in Hampstead trendiness, a croissant delivery service. A long-haired young man with brightly-painted Citroen Dyane out in Oak Village at nine o'clock, distributing croissants to the discerning – like a sort of super-sophisticated Meals on Wheels.

Take Tom and Willy swimming at midday, then over to Carlton Hill, St John's Wood, where I've been summoned to meet Ronnie Wood – once of the Faces, now of the Stones and, perhaps, apart from Paul Simon, the closest and most genuine of Eric's friends in the pop aristocracy.

Whilst Tom and Willy play records on the juke-box in Eric's kitchen and generally complain about being there at all, I explore the house. Rather like a seaside farce, there's a lady called Charlotte in the sauna, and on the top floor, next to Eric's work-room, with its 'Bible' commentaries on the desk, an Australian girl called Shirley is staying.

'Woody' arrives in a chauffeur-driven Mercedes, neatly dressed, dark-haired and with such a tan it looks like make-up, but of course it isn't, he lives in Malibu. I thank him for his letters and assorted scribbles during the summer. Eric opens a bottle of Dom Perignon (a gift from Dark Horse Records for writing and directing a couple of promo films for George's album *33 ⅓* in the summer) then we walk in the crisp November sunshine round to the Clifton Arms. It's full of people and smoke and Woody solicitously finds a kids' room at the back. He's a nice, unaffected, friendly man – very warm.

He describes Stones business meetings – they have even more than Python – with Keith Richards, who sounds *very* eccentric, lying prostrate and apparently dead for much of the meeting, apart from the occasional devastating one-liner. Charlie Watts remains very silent until suddenly, out of the blue, coming up with an idea about plastic record covers.

His position as a relatively new member of the Stones is considered differently by the Stones and their 'businessmen'. As he puts it, the band are all very democratic, split everything equally, 'but as soon as the businessmen come in it all changes'.

In the early evening Al Levinson comes round, in a mellow haze of cigar smoke. It seems that my favourable comments on *Millwork* really encouraged him and he's now writing fast and furiously on a new 'Fish'[1] novel, 'Fish Full Circle'.

Wednesday, November 24th

A good, workmanlike Python meeting. John and G have a good idea for a *Brian* storyline and their two new pieces, though short, are not just on the point, but very funny – writing 'Go Home Romans' on the wall is going to be a little classic. I wish I'd thought of such a neat idea.

From 22 Park Square East we all (except Gilliam) pile into John's Rolls and purr down to Audley St, Mayfair, for a viewing of selected Biblical epics, which we feel we ought to see. We nearly run over Elton John in North Audley Street and muse on what a strange headline it would make – 'Elton Run Over by Pythons'.

The viewing theatre at Hemdale is very comfortable, which is just as well as the films – *Barabbas, King of Kings, The Greatest Story Ever Told* and *Ben Hur* (we see bits of each) – are extremely heavy and turgid. Best performances and best writing always centre on the baddies – Herod, Pilate, etc – and the nearer you get to Jesus the more oppressive becomes the cloying tone of reverence. Everyone talks slower and slower and Jesus generally comes out of it all as the world's dullest man, with about as much charisma as a bollard.

We had a few good ideas during the viewing (midst much silly giggling and laughter). I suggested we should have four Wise Men – the fourth one being continually shut up by the others, who always refer to themselves as the Three Wise Men. '*Four*'. 'Ssh!'

Tuesday, November 30th, Southwold

Depressing visit to the hospital in Southwold. Daddy looking thinner than before. His staring, largely immovable eyes register my appearance briefly, but cannot manage much more. His speech in fits and starts.

1 As Updike had his Rabbit, Al had his Fish – Leo Fish, his alter ego and central character of all his novels.

Sometimes he doesn't make sense at all. Much talk of ties and headmasters.

Look out towards the church, the beautiful Southwold Church he loved so much and the grey November afternoon closing around it. A pretty melancholy realisation that my father will never be at home again.

It was ten years ago to the day that they moved to Southwold from Sheffield. Then he was full of hope and excitement and relief that a drab and unhappy salaried life was past, and he was back where he always wanted to be, amongst old churches, choirs and organ music.

Thursday, December 2nd, Oxford

Arrive at Oxford to speak in a debate only to find there is a strike of hotel workers at the Randolph so, rather than cross the picket lines, I make for the nearest hostelry in Broad Street and sort out the seven or so foolscap pages of my speech into some order, over a pint of Burton Ale.

The debate starts at 8.15 with the usual nonsense about elections and re-elections, spiced up a bit this year by the hawk-nosed grace of Benazir Bhutto – daughter of Pakistan's Premier and next year's President. She looks incongruous amongst the Tory rowdies who make up the Union establishment and bay most unpleasantly at some poor man who stands up to protest against 'the scandal and malpractice within this Union'. I long to hear what the scandal is, but the hounds of reaction stalk him out of the hall. I feel embarrassed being in my DJ up at the front with these idiots.

About ten, I'm eventually called upon to speak. A warm and rather surprising round of applause. The speech goes well. Some good laughs and for some reason, after a bad joke half-way through, I pour the water glass provided over my head. Even bigger laughs, but it makes the ink on my script run and the pages stick together and the last part of the speech is less successful.

The whole thing ends, much to my relief, about 11.30. Talk to three or four undergraduates who are trying to set up a magazine called 'Passing Wind' in Oxford next year. They all seem rather earnest and sit me down in a big armchair and treat me far too like a guru. I hope they aren't short on humour. One of their interview questions was (quite seriously) whether there was any relationship between Neil Innes and Eric Idle.

Monday, December 6th

Clive Hollick rings in the evening to say that Shepperton Studios *did* make a profit last year (£40,000) and have clinched the *Superman* deal. They want the stages for fifty-two weeks next year. Marlon Brando and Gene Hackman will be there, so it seems a good time to accept their offer of a directorship.

Wednesday, December 8th

A Python writing meeting in the afternoon. Quite substantial chunks of material from everyone, including a neat and funny bit by Eric with a magnificent creation – a Jewish Hitler called Otto the Nazarene, who wants more Lebensraum for the Jews.

Is it paranoia, or did I detect a sort of wariness of Palin/Jones material? Our stuff was received well, but both John and Eric unable to accept anything without qualifying their approval – and there also seemed to be a marked resistance to reading all our material.

I think this is partly the fault of late meetings. Two-thirty is not the time when everyone is freshest, and by 4.30 Graham was probably right when he said he felt we were 'sated'. But I don't approve at all of stifling Python at source. We always used to give everything anyone wanted to read a hearing, then throw it away.

Thursday, December 9th

Willy's school concert. Willy plays a tree – one of the leading trees, I hasten to add. Quite a difference from the frightened little snowflake a year ago, who could hardly leave go of his teacher's hand. This time he sang lustily. I noticed he was quite tall – and towered over Bonnie Oddie, who was next to him.

Sunday, December 12th

Round at Eric's in Carlton Hill by 2.30 to say hello/goodbye at his party. Oysters and black velvet in the kitchen, plus strangely and brightly attired young folk and reassuringly stocky, functional frame of Derek Birdsall.[1]

1 Designer of the first Python book.

Everyone seems to have seen the clip of me and Terry G on *Film '76*, which shows that these casual little interviews are worth doing well.

On one end of the talent-packed sofa is Jagger. He's smiling in a rather far-off way, but much chattier than when I last met him. He's 33 as well – like George and Eric. We talk of old record albums. I really never listen to the LPs we've made, I say, and I don't know what's on them. Mick agrees. He apparently never can stand listening to an album after he's been through the grind of making it.

Brief chat with EI, who seems concerned that Terry J should not have too much control of the next Python movie. He does blow hot and cold. It was only a few months ago that Eric wanted TJ to direct his TV series! But now he feels that TJ's problem is that he doesn't appreciate compromise.

Our chat was inconclusive, but I can see that the direction of the film will be a difficult issue looming up.

Tuesday, December 14th

Last night T Gilliam rang to tell me that my impending appointment at Shepperton is causing quite a stir. TG was talking yesterday with Graham Ford, the general manager, who said that more has got done in the last two weeks than in the last two years. The reason is that the three other directors are quite rattled at the thought of someone who knows the remotest thing about films being appointed to the board. TG says I might save the British Film Industry after all!

To 22 Park Square East for an all-day Python session.

Quite a successful meeting. John reckons we have about 40 per cent good material – good meaning strong. I think I'd put it a little higher, though not much. Today we decide on a public school opening – details of which are improvised at the meeting – and also the rough pattern of Brian's life – a bastard with a Roman father, toys with joining various Messiahs, is disillusioned, joins, or dabbles, with the resistance, is caught, escapes from the Romans, disguises himself as a prophet and gains a large and devoted following which he also tries to escape from. John and Graham seem to be keen on using my 'Martyrdom of St Brian' (the soft and luxurious martyrdom) as an ending … but it's on endings we're weakest.

Thursday, December 16th

Almost a year since we went over to defend our reputation in the US Federal Court, we have heard the terms on which ABC are prepared to settle the case, following the successful hearing of our appeal in June. ABC are prepared to pay our legal costs up to $35,000 and are undertaking not to edit any shows without our co-operation and approval. We have established that, should we refuse to edit, the shows cannot go out. From the BBC and Time-Life we have won deadlines within the next five years when the ownership of all the tapes will revert to us.

This was neat justice. The BBC had allowed ABC to make cuts without bothering to consult the Pythons because they didn't consider the American market anywhere near as important as the UK market. So, after US Federal Court judges had deemed this breach of copyright, the BBC were prepared to give us back the rights to all our tapes, so long as they hung on to those for UK TV.

Not only did they still fail to appreciate the growing strength of Python in America, they also failed to predict the burgeoning growth of video and other ancillary rights. Thanks to the BBC's dumbness, sorry, generosity, we were able to negotiate all these valuable rights for ourselves, and the licence payers missed out on quite a few bob.

Sunday, December 19th

In the evening to TV Centre for the BBC Light Entertainment party. Helen looking very impressive in a flowing, sort of crêpey black dress with a halter neck and embroidered borders which we'd bought together up Hampstead. Me, almost conforming to the intolerable black-tie stuffiness, but in the end the size of my black bow tie – acquired hastily in St John's Wood for the debate in Oxford – brought such instant laughter from Helen that I was forced to abandon it in favour of an ordinary dark blue tie and black velvet suit.

Everything in full swing when we arrived, but as I hadn't been there since the 1973 LE party, we went in the wrong entrance and found ourselves in a small ante-room, empty save for Jimmy Savile, crouched over a large plate of food. A cheery exchange and we walk through to find a throng of people we once saw so much. Tim Brooke-Taylor and I commiserate over our eternal branding together in John's mind as 'nice' people. Bill Oddie, small, dark and glowering. 'I don't know why I come here,' he says. Yet he always does.

Tuesday, December 21st

Another very dark day – it's been like this now for a week. Real Day of Judgement conditions. To Park Square East for a final Python reading meeting.

High standard from John and Graham, Eric average and Terry's and my first offering frankly bad. A poor rewrite of a poorly written original is never going to stand much chance before this audience – and it bombs embarrassingly.

A second very encouraging piece from John and Graham – about the crowd outside Brian's home being talked to sharply by Brian's mother.

My personal gloom finally lifted by the reading of our piece about Brian and Ben in the prison and the Centurion who can't pronounce his 'r's. This five- or six-minute piece, read right at the end of the meeting, with both GC and JC poised to leave, really brings the house down. It could be pre-breaking-up hysteria, but it's a good note to end this six-week writing stint.

John Goldstone rings to say the censor has seen *Jabberwocky* and, subject to the removal of one 'bugger', given it an 'A' certificate.

Wednesday, December 22nd

To the Coronet Viewing Theatre in Wardour Street to see the two Python German TV shows in order that we may finally decide whether to buy them for Python Productions or not.

The first German show, in German, is, apart from 'Silly Olympics' and 'Little Red Riding Hood' and one or two bits of animation, fairly difficult to follow and looks a little rough, whereas the second looks smooth, polished and expensive. John is anti buying them and Eric very pro.

In the end I side with Eric. The money we use to buy the shows would otherwise be taxed very heavily and I feel that it is a good principle for us to buy the world rights to our work wherever they become available. John keeps saying 'My mother's in London', but he agrees before leaving to the purchase of the shows (cost around £42,000, largely owing to the strength of the Mark and weakness of the pound). Eric agrees to undertake their re-editing.

So Python finally breaks up for Christmas and for me a huge pile of work, stretching unbroken from October '75, which I once thought insurmountable, is over. Six weeks of comparative freedom from schedules stretch ahead.

Soho is packed with pre-Christmas shoppers and *King Kong* posters are going up outside the Casino in preparation for the biggest ever simultaneous world-wide opening, as I walk back to my car.[1]

Thursday, December 23rd

To Southwold on the 9.30 from Liverpool Street.

Ma and I drive over to Blythburgh Hospital to which Father has recently been moved.

Surprised at the number of people packed into the ward – twenty-two I later discovered – but as he is wheeled by a cheerful Pakistani nurse – a young man with a ready smile and an apparently total resistance to the rather depressing conditions around him – I notice how small he appears, almost shrivelled in his chair. He reacts to seeing me, with a half-smile of pleasure, but after five minutes of talking his eyes wander and he appears to switch off.

Whilst we were having lunch at Croft Cottage, we heard, via various phone calls, that Aunt Katherine[2] had died of a heart attack in the night. This was totally unexpected. Aunt K was always the most vigorous and vital life force – loving her work, although she always seemed to have too much – whereas Uncle Hilary, her husband, has been very ill, with an apparently uncurable long-term depression, and has been suicidal over the past month.

Still, we had to tell Father about the death of his only sibling. I wondered how he'd react. For a moment it looked as though he would completely break down. His mouth hung open and seemed about to form a word, but couldn't. His brow contracted, his eyes took on a stare of what looked like disbelief and began to fill with water. It's difficult to tell the extent of his feelings behind the mask of Parkinsons. Was it utter desolation for a moment, or what … ?

1 This version, directed by John Guillermin, starred Jeff Bridges and Jessica Lange.
2 Katherine Greenwood, née Palin, my father's younger sister.

A few minutes later, unable to get anything more than three or four rushed words out of him, we left. The cheerful Pakistani seemed very ready to talk to us about him and I also briefly met the physiotherapist who says he can only just stand up and cannot walk at all yet. Is this the result of being stuck in hospital for the last three months? Could we have done more to keep him mobile?

All imponderables. On the debit side of Blythburgh are the feeling of crowding, the TV room full of stale smoke because no one can replace the air extractor, and the constant presence of old men coughing – great chest-ripping, rheumy roars rattling their ribs, a truly awful sound. On the credit side, the enthusiasm and spirit of the staff, which counts for a lot. It's busy, too – Christmas trees, trolleys with various goodies on are wheeled through the wards by middle-class, middle-aged social workers with tweedy skirts.

On the whole I feel the credits outweigh the debits, but there's no escaping the wretchedness of his condition.

Saturday, December 25th

The weather's good – cold enough for fires and other housebound comforts, but bright and sunny too. And silence over Gospel Oak – only the sound of a dog barking – the rush and bustle of London is off the streets and indoors.

After breakfast helped prepare tables and things. Helen had polished all the family silver, which glistened on the white tablecloth in spectacular fashion.

The only really new departure from the traditional family Christmas was taking Tom, Willy and Catherine to the Holiday Inn for a pre-lunch swim. We were about the only people there. Great spirit of Christmas – the attendants threw each other in fully clothed whilst Tom and Willy and Cath watched open-mouthed.

All went well, despite Mary and Ed forgetting the Christmas pud and Ed uncharacteristically dropping it on the floor when he went back for it.

Everyone went home about eleven. I think I've learnt to handle these family Christmases a bit better. I feel tired, but not heavy, fat or blotto with it. Sit and appreciate the tiredness over a film in the excellent BBC 'Christmas with Cagney' selection. I find Cagney quite mesmeric.

Thursday, December 30th

Trying to write a *Jabberwocky* trailer whilst Rachel sits on one knee playing with the telephone – 'Hello Granny,' ad nauseam. In the middle of all this, the Health Visitor arrives – an unexpected bonus, as she looks after Rachel for a quarter of an hour, whilst seeing if she can walk and talk properly.

Drive out to Shepperton to meet Graham Ford, general manager of the studios. I had arranged to meet him on my own initiative, just to get a little background on how Shepperton works from the man on the shop floor, as it were, rather than the directors, of whom I am now officially one.

Ford is young (around my age), thinning hair, waistcoat stretched over an incipient paunch, looks like the young manager of a prosperous record store. Smart office – the only part of the Shepperton complex that looks at all dynamic.

Over lunch he elaborates on the rumour I've heard that he doesn't get on with Clive [Hollick]. In fact, he likes Clive personally, but makes the very good point that Clive is a director of several companies, not just Shepperton, and Ford feels that Shepperton is just a name on a list. Though from my talks with Clive I feel he is in sympathy with Ford's desire to brighten up Shepperton, I quite appreciate that his decisions take a long time to come through.

I come away feeling that, as a director without sixteen other directorships, I could be the one who cares most and most directly about Shepperton. We agree to meet and chat regularly.

1977

1977 began with a new departure for the Palin family, a winter sun holiday. We spent two weeks on the West Indian island of Tobago. Helen learnt to stay up on one water-ski and the children loved being by the beach, but according to my entry of January 15th I had mixed feelings about it.

'Seldom have I enjoyed a holiday as much and wanted to get home as much,' I wrote. 'I have a feeling my brain could atrophy in this alluringly beautiful part of the Caribbean.' Once home, and back in my hair shirt, I worked on an article about the holiday for Lee Eisenberg of Esquire, and took it personally to him in New York, only to find he'd resigned from the magazine.

Meanwhile my father's condition had deteriorated and he was now permanently in bed at Blythburgh Hospital, just outside Southwold. His previous accommodation, St Audry's at Bury St Edmunds, had been built as a lunatic asylum, this one as a workhouse.

Monday, January 31st, Southwold

Even the old workhouse at Blythburgh looks like a French chateau in the crisp sunny beauty of this winter's afternoon. Father is lying in bed, with the iron side up, like a cot, his glasses off, his face so thin, his eyes shut and mouth open. He looks more like a corpse.

For a while he seems bewildered, his eyes stare, as he's probably just woken up. Then he sees us and his look softens a bit. Colour returns to his face, and he manages to get more words out than usual, though hardly any complete sentences, so you don't really know what he's saying.

Much entertainment from the rest of the ward, though. One rugged-looking old man with large, piercing eyes, beckoned urgently towards us. When Ma went over to speak to him, he fixed her with a very serious gaze and asked her if she was wanted by the police.

At the next door bed, from behind the curtains, meanwhile, repeated BBC radio acting cries of 'Gawd! Oh my gawd! Oh gawd! Gawd! Gawd! Oh bloody gawd!' I was told that this stream of half-hearted, and yet strangely heart-felt cries is a common sound in the ward.

When I first came here to see Dad, it was an unfamiliar world, from which I rather shrank back. The sight and sound of twenty old men in one room takes a little getting used to. Now I feel much easier and happier there. The nurses are not only dedicated, but, I think, cheerful and sensible.

Back to Croft Cottage for local fish (delicious) and a bottle of Alsace and a game of Scrabble and to bed with Doctorow's *Ragtime*. In the company of Houdini, Evelyn Nesbit and Commander Peary of the US Navy, January dwindled.

Tuesday, February 1st, Southwold

After lunch, drove over to Blythburgh to see Dad. He was in his chair today, dressed and looking much improved. His lack of speech is still the greatest drawback, but he responded with pleasure to seeing us. He seems to drift off, though – as if his concentration easily goes, and he sometimes stares fixedly at some point, as if seeing something we haven't. His fingers pick at surfaces and edges – whether it's the corner of the sheet on his bed, or the wooden rim of his table.

But he'd fed himself lunch, and they were pleased. I hope he has more days like today – and that he doesn't linger and waste away to his death.

Wednesday, February 2nd

Am going to try to keep to a routine of an hour's work before breakfast. Managed to wake up at ten to eight today, so did 40 minutes. Worked on Shepperton business.

John Goldstone rings and, in his dangerously persuasive way, makes me agree to meet Don Rugoff, American distributor, for a chat about advertising slogans for *Jabberwocky*. So I find myself at the Connaught Hotel at ten to six, heavily wrapped up, blowing my nose every four minutes and reading the *Evening Standard*. Don doesn't arrive until about 6.15. He seems more like a gargoyle every time I see him. With him is his glamorous assistant, Susan, who doesn't seem entirely at ease, but then who would be, having to accompany Don all day.

Up to Don's room, or rooms. (I like the Connaught. It's small, intimate and Edwardian – much less dauntingly impressive than I expected.) We drink flat Perrier and Don reels out a list of slogans he's thought of. It's back to square one – and I feel depressed and trapped having to re-explain basic principles about avoiding the comparison with *Holy Grail*, etc, etc.

But Don has a technique, unsophisticated though it may be, of acquiring co-operation and, as the evening rolls on, we begin to warm to the spirit of the whole silly operation, and run up quite a list of ad-lines. I really liked Don's 'At last! A film for the squeamish!'

Before I leave, just after eight, he's not only wheedled a whole new crop of ad-lines from me, but also several trailer ideas. Don cleverly flatters me – 'Oh, wonderful, that's wonderful' – thanks me profusely and effusively and shuffles me out into the passage.

Home, very hungry, by nine. It's been like a session with a mad psychiatrist.

Thursday, February 3rd

Arrive BBC about a quarter to two. Terry Hughes and I lunch in the canteen. I am to meet Jimmy G at 2.30 to discuss the situation. I just learned yesterday from TH – that the BBC will not release him for the filming of the next three *Ripping Yarns*.

I had an inkling when he was made Assistant Head of LE Variety last year that this would come. TH has repeatedly said he regarded these shows as the most important and satisfying things he's done. But he seems to have yielded to the blandishments of high office and, as Bill Cotton sounds to be about to leave Light Entertainment for higher things, I understand their cultivation of the Golden Boy.[1] He will remain executive producer, however, and Jim Franklin will direct. Luckily I like Jim and find him unassuming, efficient and very down to earth. But I slightly resent the fact that I wasn't consulted at all, until a fait accompli had been prepared.

Jimmy Gilbert tells me the BBC wiped the tapes of the first two Python series! But he is trying to find film copies from all over the world to get together the three early Pythons they're planning to show in April/May.[2]

---

1 Terry was duly promoted to Head of Variety at the BBC, and no longer allowed to direct individual shows. Two years later he was seduced away to America by EMI, where, among other things, the golden boy made a name for himself directing *The Golden Girls*.
2 I'm not sure of the provenance of this scare story, but Terry Jones remembers being alerted by a BBC editor, Howard Dell, that plans were afoot to wipe the series in the early '70s. Terry J had them recorded onto Philips VCR tapes and stored them at his house. For a long time, he thought the only copies of Python TV shows were in his cellar!

Tuesday, February 8th

Finished, at last, a six-month-old pile of fan letters. Mostly from Japan, beautifully written, generally on very delicate paper, and nearly always beginning 'I am a schoolgirl of 14', as if to add a frisson of danger for the reader. The language is fine too. Python is translated as 'Gay Boys' Dragon Show' on Japanese TV, and one of the letters eulogises 'Upper Class Twit of the Year', but calls it, splendidly "The Aristocratic Deciding Foolish No. 1 Guy'. American letters, too, but coarser and more violent generally, shouting at me off the page.

In the evening Helen makes a delicious, non-meaty repast for David and Stephanie Leland, who bring Chloe with them to sleep here.

David is in the process of leaving his agent. As he says, you 'fire' solicitors, and you 'change' accountants and you 'leave' wives and agents. That's what makes it difficult.

He wants to do a season of three or four new plays in repertory at the Crucible next autumn. He wants to remove the 'new play' from its neat little slot amongst all the trad classical revivals and generally show that the theatre and that playwrights are very much alive and modern in their outlook and topics.

I suggest that the only way really to ensure that a provincial theatre receives the credit and attention it deserves for pioneering new plays is to have a clause in the contract which says the play cannot be shown in London for a period of, say, eighteen months from its out of town opening. Then get Tom Stoppard, or some other London darling, to write a masterpiece, and for eighteen months the provincial theatres might be full of coachloads from Hampstead and Kensington.

Sunday, February 13th

Our croissants, duly delivered, slipped down a treat and, after breakfast and a quick check to see that Sheffield United had resumed their slide down the Second Division, I took all three children to the Holiday Inn for a swim.

Rachel 'helps' us all get dressed. She likes these sort of activities and supervises most efficiently – wandering up with various pieces of clothing which, if you are not exactly ready, she will drop in a puddle on the floor.

Monday, February 14th

It's another splendid morning and I go down to Camberwell on the bus. It's good to be able to pace one's life, so that if I want to take an extra 30 minutes to get to Terry's by bus I can. The walk at the other end is a slog, but on a day like this it's all justified by the feeling of busy, buzzing London life all around. Faces in the sunshine. The river sparkling as we ride over Westminster Bridge.

Terry suggests a beer for lunch and we have a couple of pints at a rather unpleasantly refurbished Young's pub beside Peckham Common. Sitting next to us are a very odd middle-aged couple, a little tipsy. They have two Pekinese dogs which they treat with affected bantering politeness. The woman licked pieces of chocolate before giving them to the dog and the man accused Terry of coming from Wrexham.

Wednesday, February 16th

To the BBC. Meet Jim Franklin and his PA Eddie Stuart. Jim Franklin, straight, direct, likeable, a special effects boffin, who lovingly describes how he yesterday shot John Cleese being run over by a bus with a flowerpot on his head for a Diana Rigg show.

We talk over attitudes to the shows. Should we have an audience on? Jimmy Gilbert pops his head round the door to say he wants to show it to an audience. When we ask why, he says 'Because it's funny.'

'Well, then it doesn't need an audience to tell people that,' I counter.

'I've heard that before,' says Jimmy.

I wouldn't worry, but he has an infuriating habit of being right.

Thursday, February 17th

Down to Camberwell on the bus again. An hour and a quarter door to door. Normal car journey: 35 minutes. Read *Memoirs of George Sherston* – a world away from Walworth Road in the drizzle. But then not as far away as one might think, for Sassoon is always detaching himself from the stereotyped county hunting image. He's interested in people, really. And there's a lot of them in the Walworth Road today.

A solid work day at Terry's. By the time I left at five, 'Eric Olthwaite' felt in much tighter shape.

In to London to the studio, passing through Covent Garden on the way. Studios, galleries and smart new restaurants are sprouting daily now. The rush is on to be in the new trendy quarter of London, now that threats of large-scale demolition and 'development' seem to have receded. Once again feel that going in with Terry G on Neal's Yard was one of the best things that could have happened to a lad with £70,000 to spend.

Drop in at Penhaligon's to buy some of their aftershaves, which brighten up my mornings immeasurably. Talk with Sheila Pickles,[1] who I think at first thought I was something the cat had brought in. I had on my Kickers with holes in, my jeans with holes in and my Fiorucci anorak with the hood up. And her shop is very smart.

Sheila promised to publicise my studio to her well-connected film friends. Zeffirelli apparently is working on the *Life of Christ* at such a slow rate that Python could still pip him to the post. He has to make it in different lengths for different countries. Six one-hour episodes for Italy, three two-hour episodes for the US, two three-hour episodes for the UK. It's a bit like ordering meat.

Saturday, February 19th, Abbotsley

After a bath, in which I read a fascinating chapter from *Plain Tales from the Raj* – a book of reminiscences about the British in India [by Charles Allen] – and concluded that we must write a colonial *Ripping Yarn* next year, walked to Highgate West Hill and caught a 214 bus to King's Cross and then the 9.30 Cambridge train and reached St Neots at a quarter to eleven.

On the journey read a synopsis sent to me in the post today by Christopher Matthew's agent with a letter beginning 'Over lunch with John Cleese, Christopher Matthew said how very much he would like to turn his *Sunday Times* column – "Diary of a Somebody" – into a television series. John's instant reaction was that you were absolutely the right person for it.'

Actually I like the columns – a modern *Diary of a Nobody*. They're very well written and he can turn a humorous phrase, but, even if I did have time, I reflected, as the train chattered through the industrial estates of Stevenage and Biggleswade, that I didn't really want to do

1 I had met Sheila through mutual friends – Ian and Anthea Davidson. She started the Penhaligon's perfume business.

comedy all my life. A commitment to this would be a commitment to light, rather parochial comedy for another two or three years, and then I'll be nearly 40 and too old for the Robert de Niro roles I subconsciously yearn for.

Monday, February 21st

Woke feeling gratefully fresh, after a long, deep sleep. Another day of fairly continuous rain showers. Terry came up here to write.

At two we went up to Hampstead for a pizza and saw the Goodies, Tim, Graham and Bill, all in almost identical blue anoraks walking up Flask Walk ahead of us. Enjoyed ourselves immensely, shouting loud and coarsely after them – 'Goodies!' 'Eric Cleese!' 'Do us your silly walk!' 'Where's your bicycle?' and watching them deliberately not turn around or quicken their pace in the face of this volley. Even at the top of the hill, when we were almost beside them, they only looked round very furtively and then away again. Finally Bill did an enormous double-take.

Friday, February 25th

More writing on 'The Curse of the Claw'. Helen leaves for Amsterdam at a quarter to four [to visit her friend Ranji]. The kids are all very good, though boisterous (Tom has his friend Jud for tea). But I get them all out of the way by 8.15.

Monday, February 28th

The weekend with the children was very successful, but rushed, of course. To the Columbia Theatre for the children's 'trial' preview of *Jabberwocky*. I took Tom and Willy, Nicky[1] and Catherine Burd.[2]

It still strikes me as a very good film overall, but the high spots – jousts, monster and black knight fights – are so good that I couldn't help noticing points where the flow of the film – the headlong, extrovert flow – gets snagged up in little scenes which don't have the vitality of the rest. But the children enjoyed it. For Thomas it was the best film he'd ever seen, much better than *At the Earth's Core* or *Island at the Top of the World*!

1 Nick Gordon, a friend of William's, and now a director of commercials and pop videos.
2 Helen's niece.

Saw Terry G afterwards. He'd been at the back, taking, as they say in the States, an 'overview'. He had just returned from a crash course in US film distribution. Apparently, after a week of showings and discussions and soundings, Rugoff's now convinced *Jabberwocky* could be a big one, and is talking of ordering 1,000 prints.

Terry said the energy of this apparently sloth-like man is incredible. They never finished a meal and, when Terry suggested that the reactions to the film were so far all from sophisticated New York audiences, Don Rugoff nearly flew him off to Austin Texas on the spot. But Terry and John looked very happy, both with the States and with the enthusiastic reaction from the kids today.

To Mary and Edward's for a very pleasant, effortless Sunday lunch, then Willy is off to another party. The Willy phenomenon has to be seen to be believed. No sooner had the door opened at the house of the party than William was grabbed by two or three girls, and soon a whole crowd of them had gathered around him chanting 'It's William! It's William!' and he was borne away into the party by the adoring mob.

Friday, March 4th

Python reassembles. The meeting is at 2 Park Square West, the first time we have met in the Henshaws' sumptuous and very well-appointed new house [on the opposite side of Regent's Park from their previous one]. It gleams and glistens and the front door is being painted as I arrive.

Eric is there (as usual) already, John arrives shortly after me, then Terry J, and we have to wait for an hour before Graham joins us. We've put a rather hard wooden chair out for him with the words 'Latecomer's Chair' written on it, and 'Dr Chapman' written across the back.

But the general tone of the meeting was of optimistic good humour, stretched almost to the point of hysteria. It was almost impossible *not* to get a laugh. We talked for two to three hours about the script and very silly ideas like a stuffed Pontius Pilate came up. I was in tears on several occasions.

Eric suggests we do our next Python stage show on ice, but don't learn how to skate.

Towards the end of the meeting, Eric asks me if I would be interested in writing for a George Harrison TV special in the States. I say no on grounds of time. Eric, too, doesn't think he can do it as he appears to have lined up an £800,000-budget film for NBC on the Rutles (Eric's and Neil's pop group parallel of the Beatles). Clearly he commands enormous respect from NBC, who are letting him direct the thing as well.

Sunday, March 6th

Read Hunter Davies' article on JC over my croissants. Not a bad article, some nice observations, but Python gets short shrift, and Graham even shorter. Connie, on the other hand, is effusively praised, and I get pulled in too – 'She's enormously fertile with funny ideas. Only Michael Palin compares with her for funny ideas.' An unexpected acknowledgement which was nice of him and quite makes my Sunday.

I thought his mother came off best out of the article. She had some very humorous quotes, if unintentionally so. 'I know John goes on about us never allowing him a bike. But he didn't need one. The school was opposite our house anyway.'

Swimming with Tom and Willy at Holiday Inn. Willy to a party. Another girl, another Valentino entrance. William starts being silly/funny before he arrives. He does it, he says, to cheer them all up.

Helen and I and Rachel cap a very Londony weekend by walking up and around the roads of Parliament Hill neighbourhood, with half an eye for houses.

Decide when we get home that we're very lucky to be in a house with such character. The late-Victorianness of North Mansfield Road, Parliament Hill, even when restored and cleaned, leaves a depressingly claustrophobic feeling. I was very glad to be back in our mid-Victorian shoe box.

To dinner with Peter Luff and Carolyn.[1] Peter had been with Tom Stoppard to visit Amnesty cases in Russia. He gave me a lovely box full of about twenty boxes of matches, all with rather nice Pushkin drawings on them. Each box had been thoroughly searched by the Russians before they left the country.

Parts of Moscow and most of Leningrad are very beautiful, he said, but Russian official behaviour sounds pretty wretched. Notebooks confiscated. Tom Stoppard had apparently yelled at them as they took his notebook away 'If you publish that, I'll sue!' It was returned, copied presumably.

1 Peter was behind the Amnesty charity show in 1976.

Peter doesn't think the Soviet Union will ever work – there are too many forces of nationalism, etc, within it. At present he says there is a repressive regime, reacting to the liberalisation under Khrushchev with surprising force.

An interesting evening.

Monday, March 7th

Down to 2 Park Square West. We're all there, TG included, for chats about 'Life of Christ'. John a little embarrassed when Terry J comes in asking 'Who were the two, then?' – referring to John's rather bald statement in the *Sunday Times* article that towards the end of Python there were 'two people' he couldn't get on with. But he skated over all that successfully and avoided having to say.

A good ideas session. We talked until four. Cleaned up the ending a good deal. The Centurion who can't pwonounce his 'r's has become quite a leading figure now – in fact he's probably Pontius Pilate.

At lunch we all split for an hour. Anne had made sandwiches. I felt bad at ignoring them, so Eric and I packed a bag of sandwiches and Perrier water and walked into Regent's Park, sat and ate our lunch in the rose garden. Rather sweet.

Eric tells me he's becoming vegetarian. Presumably under the influence of George H.

Tuesday, March 8th

To Buchanan House, Holborn, to meet the Shepperton Studios Board. First of all we had lunch – pâté, beef, cheese and no wine – and I met fellow director Charles Gregson, ebullient, talking in that enthusiastic upper-class rush. His hair was longer and he was much younger than I expected. Rather schoolboyish in fact. He's the Managing Director. Burrows is the Financial Director, older, quieter, rather neat and shy. Fawcett, the Company Secretary, is the only man from Mars. He talks in a delicious, rich, aristocratic rumble, which he uses tantalisingly rarely. He wears a perfectly tailored pin-striped suit and an elegant pastel shirt with white collar. Have a feeling he is either less or more intelligent than he appears. Probably less.

Clive [Hollick] displays the sort of sharpness, easy intelligence and businesslike charm which must have put him where he is. He handles the Chairman's job as if he'd been used to running things all his life – but at the same time creates a good, participatory working atmosphere.

The board meeting begins with financial reports. Then our debtors are discussed – *Lisztomania*, Ken Russell's last great folly, a monumental flop, is top of the list.

Brando is expected on March 21st. Discussion as to what we should lay on for him. Charles Gregson suggests, rather pathetically, putting flowers in his room. I suggest a couple of bottles of champagne might be more realistic.

The only real excitement of the meeting is discussion of the highly confidential Ramport negotiations. Ramport are the production company of The Who, who already have an almost permanent base in one of the Shepperton studios. They want a 999-year lease on an area of property within the Shepperton complex, including the old house, the lawn in front, some office buildings and J and K Studios (both small).

The asking price is nearly half a million pounds, which would, at a stroke, clear Shepperton's debt, pay for major improvements to the heating system and generally set the place up on a very sound financial basis. Against it are the usual arguments over losing any part of a film studio. Allegations of asset-stripping will be revived.

Thursday, March 10th

March has been delightful so far. Helen drops me in Regent's Park and I walk across this beautiful expanse, flanked on one side by Nash terraces and the other by the copper dome of the new mosque.

Eric very positive and clearly the one who's done the most work on our two 'separate' days since Monday. He has worked out a putative running order which is a good basis for discussion. By twelve we are all there, including Gilliam, who has been at the final dub for *Jabberwocky*.

High point of the day is writing an extremely sick piece for use at charity shows (which we are all rather tired of being involved in). A speech about the 'so-called handicapped' who get so much attention anyway, and why should not the carrot of financial reward be dangled before those who are, by no fault of their own, normal, etc, etc. I don't know who'll be brave/foolhardy enough to do it. At the Albert Hall.

We decide to send a very lushly packed gift box of sexual aids for

Ina's wedding present and a golden foot for Robert Osterberg[1] is to be inscribed 'To Our Dear Friend Roy Ostrichberger, From Monty Python – In Lieu of Fee'. I'm against 'In Lieu of Fee', but was out-voted.

Friday, March 11th

Decide not to send a gift pack of sexual aids to Ina for her wedding present. Still, it was funny at the time.

Down to Gerry Donovan, my first London National Health dentist. Half of the bridge Gerry put in has just come adrift.

Home by public transport. It takes me an hour, including a 20-minute wait at a bus stop for buses advertised as every six to eight minutes. As I wait I become aware of how important time has become to me now. To stand at a bus stop for 20 minutes staring into space seems a crime.

It does rather throw my working day, but I manage to write some more of the 'Twibune'. Helen suggests he should have a friend, so I write in Biggus Dickus, who thpeakth with a lithp.

Wednesday, March 16th

In the post, an invitation to the preview/premiere of *Jabberwocky*. I notice they've spelt my name wrong on the film credits – '*Michel* (sic) Palin'.

Slowly begin to overcome some indefinable resistance to writing any new material for the 'Bible' story, and by mid-afternoon I'm beginning to gather momentum. Complete a new 'Headmaster' piece for the opening, then literally race along with an ending montage, pre-crucifix-ion. The ideas suddenly seem to be released.

I work, with no interruption, until nearly six. Outside it's pouring. Feel very pleased with the day's work. I suppose I needed a day on my own at my own pace.

Completed my will. Put the envelope in the post, but cannot kill myself yet, as it was only a draft will.

1 Ina and Robert were the driving forces behind Python's action against ABC.

Thursday, March 17th

Across sunny London to the Columbia Theatre, where the *Jabberwocky* magazine-writers' preview is just finishing.

I am warned that there are men from the *Sunday Mirror* here, who have not bothered to see the film. They stand, like Tweedledum and Tweedledee, grinning ingratiatingly and nosing out any sensation there is to be had like pigs searching for truffles. I find myself talking to one of them, in the event of Columbia-Warner bringing no one else for me to talk to, about Python and then about the new Python film. The notebook suddenly slides out and I realise that he is onto a 'story' – a 'Python to send up Bible story' story. So I remember why I'm here and move away from that one.

Peter Noble waddles by, fondling my arm like an overfed but harmless Roman patrician and lining me up for a snap of him talking to me, for his newspaper, *Screen International*. Then he waddles off.

Max W is there. Seemingly unchanged by his bad reviews for Malvolio at Greenwich and as endearingly chatty and jokey as ever. The world could be ending outside, but Max would keep up his gentle monologue. He has never, as long as I've ever been with him, showed any trace of alarm, or sudden reaction of any kind. He paces himself beautifully and I found talking to him was like finding the eye in the centre of the hurricane.

I found amongst the gathering a qualified enthusiasm. Words like 'smash hit' and 'success' were not on everybody's lips.

Friday, March 18th

Difficult, but finally constructive Python meeting at 2 Park Square West. We assembled at 10.15, but Eric looked unwell, and John did not arrive until ten to eleven.

So neither of those two seemed in the best of moods, and Terry's suggestion that the 'Healed Loony' sketch should open the main bulk of the film (after the 'Nativity') was very sulkily received by John and Eric. The rest of us, including Graham, all remembered liking it and still liked it, but John claims he didn't and Eric doesn't think it's funny enough to start a film with.[1] Terry looks terribly hurt and deflated and

---

1 It never did get into the film, but is reproduced in the *Life of Brian* book, along with the 'Headmaster' and other plucky failures.

says things like it was putting this sketch first that suddenly restored his enthusiasm for the film. But Terry's enthusiasm can work two ways, and it was clearly only hardening John and Eric's attitude today.

Well, fortunately for the meeting, the script and all concerned, we soon got out of this area and began to make some rapid progress with the end, which is now to culminate in a huge crucifixion musical number.

It's interesting to know how people would react. We have de-Jesused the crucifixion, by keeping him out of it (although there were lovely fantasies of him saying to others in the crucifixion procession, 'Oh, do come on, take it seriously'). Instead we have about 150 assorted crooks being led out for crucifixion – which was, after all, a common enough event at that time. But the crucifixion has become such a symbol that it must be one of the areas most sensitive to the taint of historical truth.

Monday, March 21st

Phone call from John Goldstone – the IBA [Independent Broadcasting Authority], or powers that be, have heard our *Jabberwocky* radio commercials and will not let us say 'warm, brown heaps', mention the Queen, name roads (e.g. M40, A4), say 'here is a flash', dub on screams or sirens, and we can't say the word 'motions' in an ad in which a little boy is saying that he was on his way to school 'when a huge, fire-breathing monster ate the entire school buildings, including the toilet. The headmaster says the buildings may reappear in his motions, but until then we've got the day off.' To think that someone is drawing a salary for preventing people hearing the word 'motions'.

Wednesday, March 23rd

Do not wake until eight, despite reasonably early night. The hour before breakfast doesn't seem to be falling naturally into my schedule. Both body and mind, but in that order, seem to be rebelling. But I just don't feel I can do all the work that I've let myself in for at the moment without that extra hour.

The Python meeting is very constructive. Eric, who hadn't written much apart from a song, which wasn't that special, was nevertheless on good analytical form, putting his finger time and time again on what was right and wrong with the more sizeable contributions from John C and Graham, and Terry and myself. But we had supplied some good ideas, especially for the end, and the morale of the meeting was high.

We decided that John Goldstone should produce it, and the shooting dates would be January/February/March 1978, abroad. Cleese is anxious to take a tax year out of England and does not want to work here after April 6th 1978. He'll be doing this plus a series of seven *Fawlty Towers* before then. We have given ourselves a three-week writing session in July and a final session in October. We didn't discuss director – I feel that Terry J will do it, unless anyone feels strongly enough against.

Terry J suggests a press ban on discussion of the film. We agree to keep it a secret. John and Eric particularly vociferous about press on set. They just get in the way and do no good. Eric very positive on no deals with censors or producers over language or taste. We and we alone must decide what the final form of the film is to be.

With a great show of solidarity, we adjourned to Odin's restaurant for lunch. The only other diner anywhere near our noisy table was Harold Pinter, dining alone and darkly debonair in a corner, shaking me for an instant with immediate recall of him sitting in a restaurant in *The Servant*. Rather comforting to sit beside Harold Pinter after a long writing session.

Back home. Unsatisfactory attempt to take Tom, Willy, Jake and Rachel swimming. Pool closed. Marine Ices (our second choice) closed. Ended up at 32 Flavours in Hampstead though even there sixteen flavours were off!

Heard from John Goldstone that after Sandy Lieberson had personally canvassed the Managing Director of Capital Radio, he had withdrawn a number of objections to our commercials, but we were still not allowed to call a commercial a commercial, we can't mention 'motions', and 'large, warm, brown heaps' can only be 'large heaps'.

Sunday, March 27th

We drove up to Abbotsley yesterday morning.

Today it rained incessantly, though never very heavily. But icy-cold north winds kept us indoors for most of the time.

In the early evening the steady rain gave way to showers – some of hail and snow – and dramatic skies – huge, black clouds against white, sun-filled patches. Took William out up the road and he learnt to ride his bike. A snowstorm swirled around us as we came back – Willy's cycling career heralded with a virtuoso display of weather.

Back to London by nine.

By this time next week I will at least have *Jabberwocky* opening behind me, and we'll have finished the first real draft of the *Life of Brian*, as Eric suggested calling it on Friday.

Monday, March 28th

At 7.30 took seats in the Columbia [for the *Jabberwocky* premiere] (in a row with Terry J and Al and Terry G and Maggie). The theatre was full – caught sight of Ian Ogilvy, Ned Sherrin and other premiere luminaries. Unfortunately there seemed to be no representatives of yer average viewing public, and their absence was all too apparent as the film got under way.

It was hard work, sitting there watching yourself on screen messing around in the Middle Ages, and experiencing the almost tangible sensation of mild audience enthusiasm. Laughs – real laughs – seemed to come reluctantly, but when they did I breathed easily before going back into a sort of dry-mouthed muscular strait-jacket which tightens whenever I'm watching myself.

Eventually the quest and the undeniably effective monster fight won them over – and the applause at the end was not just sycophantic – but it was a tough viewing. I could hardly believe it was the same film I'd seen with the children two weeks before. Then there was a real sense of excitement and enjoyment and involvement. Tonight I felt that no one quite knew how to react.

One or two handshakes. We were all promptly cleared out of the foyers by a zealous theatre attendant and Helen and I gave Neil Innes and Yvonne – our good friends of these occasions – a lift down to the London Dungeon where the *Jabberwocky* is now permanently on display.

Wine and much chatter in the cold and semi-darkness. There seemed to be equivocal feelings about the movie itself. Some unreservedly loving it, others, like Eric Idle, now hardening into strong opposition to it. (Graham Chapman left half-way through! John C rang at the last minute to say he couldn't make it!)

One strange looming man shook my hand warmly and advised me that I was 'about to make the quantum leap. Men in America will see this and within two years you'll be an international star.'

Tuesday, March 29th

Woke early – about sevenish – heart thumping like a tugboat engine, head aching. The sort of feeling which resolves me never to touch alcohol again.

To Park Square West for a Python writing meeting. A very good session. Our rather hastily written and assembled ending up to the crucifixion reduces people to crawling the floor with laughter. Simple expedients like funny voices finally triumphing over careful intellectual comment.

So all immensely cheered. The film now has an ending – which is something the *Grail* never had – and we seem to have successfully tackled the difficult area of the crucifixion – by treating it all with historical unemotionalism.

In the evening revel in the beauty of Ken Loach's *Price of Coal*. Script, camerawork, direction, acting – everything combines to warm and comfort with its rightness and honesty. No artifice evident – a straightforward, highly competent piece of filmmaking. The best view of Yorkshire since *Kes*. It made me feel homesick – and said in fewer, funnier words than any polemical film, that working class life isn't just noble or fine or any of those overblown words used by the non-working class – it's a good life. Very funny, and it had all the production qualities I would like to achieve in *Ripping Yarns*.

Wednesday, March 30th

Morning writing session on Python. Though we work far fewer hours together now, the sessions are becoming more efficient.

Problems once so complex are being solved with a natural ease and unanimity which seemed impossible a year ago. Terry J will almost certainly direct. Gilliam may be in control of design. There is no room as yet for animation.

Thursday, March 31st

My bottom thrusts itself at me from *The Guardian* accompanied by a review from Derek Malcolm which begins 'I like *Jabberwocky*'. He goes on at some length and it is a very complimentary, but not uncritical review. An enormous encouragement.

Time Out dismisses the film as a straining attempt to make people laugh, which doesn't ultimately succeed. It seems to me there are two sorts of critics – one lot would prefer to like the things they review, the others prefer to dislike the things they review.

Friday, April 1st

All Fools' Day. Begins badly. Mercifully brief, but poor reviews of *Jabberwocky* in *The Times* and the *Telegraph* and the *Mirror*, which calls it tedious. Doldrums for a while.

At two drive over to Notting Hill Gate to J Cleese's rather sweet little cottage at the back of the Notting Hill Gaumont.

Much appreciation of a very good *Guardian* April Fool – a seven-page report on a totally fictitious island in the Indian Ocean called San Seriffe. Very well done – complete with photos and adverts and always just on the right side of probability. Eric suggests we send them one of our golden feet (originally made as a present for our US lawyer, Bob Osterberg). Anne is contacted and we send the foot to *The Guardian* 'for services to San Seriffe' on paper headed 'Python Productions Ltd, Evado Tax House, San Seriffe'.

(It's not the first time this week that Python has been moved to feats of appreciation by the newspapers. A *Guardian* report on Monday that *Gay News* are short of £12,000 funds to help them fight the blasphemous libel case brought against them by M Whitehouse for publishing a poem which suggested that Christ received some sexual favours while on the cross, moved us to send £500 as a Python contribution to the mag.)

Sunday, April 3rd

For about the fourth day running I have to buy every morning newspaper as *Jabberwocky* breaks over London. After Friday's setbacks, I'm prepared for everything or anything.

Relief comes in grand style. Alan Brien leads his *Sunday Times* 'Cinema' column with a long, funny, appreciative review, and we get the photo too. Marvellous – the best review so far. We also get the photo in *The Observer*, which turns in a long *Time Out*-ish review, quoting many of the funnier ideas of the film, calling me well-cast, but wasted, and lauding Max Wall, but ending by calling the film 'forgettable', which seems an odd adjective to use at the end of a long and detailed review.

But the *Sunday Telegraph* is unequivocally favourable, as are the *Sunday Express* and the *News of the World* ('loveable lunacy'!). So I settle down to my croissants reassured and revived.

Monday, April 4th

Spend the morning mugging up on latest financial reports, etc, etc, in preparation for a board meeting. Drove out to Shepperton – approved of the big new sign outside. Air of great activity about the place. Passed Brando's caravan and drove on round to Graham Ford's office.

Cheerful chat about *Jabberwocky*. Both Graham and his wife/secretary very enthusiastic but, as no one had turned up after 20 minutes, I ventured to ask how things were with *Superman*. Then Ford quite casually dropped his bombshell. *Superman* is leaving Shepperton in a couple of months to complete at Pinewood. Ford blathers chirpily about some financial deal which *Superman*'s producers must have made with Pinewood and quite steadfastly refuses to get angry, anxious or even excited about the whole matter.

With this shadow hanging over us, we walk over to the restaurant. At a table are Richard Donner, tall, bespectacled, with a greying mop-head of hair and an intelligent face – director of *Superman* (and *The Omen*) – Ilya and Alex Salkind, the producers. At another table is a quiet, regular-faced young man with a college boy look and a battered old sweater with a huge hole in it. This is Superman (Christopher Reeve). A man keeps looking over towards us rather nervously – as well he might. He's the English producer, who got the production into Shepperton.

Clive H and Chas Gregson arrive, with them is Clancy Sigal, an American writer now working in England, who's come to do an article on Shepperton and *Superman*. Oh the ironies of the day!

Clive has been to see the Salkinds, and his account of the meeting tends to Ford's theory that the Salkinds have done some deal with Pinewood (which is empty, and yet fully union staffed). *Superman* has moved studios already – from Cinecitta, Bray and now Shepperton – it is running behind schedule and Pinewood is owned by Rank, who also own one of the two main distribution networks in the UK.

Salkind says Shepperton has no major shortcomings itself. The inefficiencies here, he said to Clive, were like a splinter in the toe – a source of irritation, not enough to stop you walking. He (Salkind) doesn't seem angry at Shepperton, or want to make any big publicity point about moving. Clive reckons £190,000 is owed to us by *Superman*. Brando and Hackman *have* to be filmed here, because of their limited availability, so we appear at the moment to be in quite a strong position.

Wednesday, April 6th

Five past twelve – settling in bed with Siegfried Sassoon and the Somme Offensive, when the phone rings. It's John Goldstone. Rugoff wants to open *Jabberwocky* at Cinema One in New York on Friday, April 15th – a week earlier than he had planned. I tell him that I can't really go until Wednesday of next week – Easter, with trips to Abbotsley and Southwold, being almost upon us, and a day looking at locations on Salisbury Plain planned for next Tuesday. John will transmit this news to Rugoff.

Back to the Somme.

Tuesday, April 12th

Wig fitting with Jean Speak at ten. Then along to Jim F's office. The buyer, John Stevens, is there, with a catalogue of cars for the 'Olthwaite' episode. We have blithely written in police cars for a chase (dated 1934), but find that they didn't have police cars until 1938. This does seem to have given robbers an unfair advantage, but Jim says robbers couldn't afford cars either.

Drive down to Salisbury Plain to look at the locations they've chosen for 'Escape from Stalag Luft 112B'.

Spend an afternoon in huts, built during the First War, which are still used during training exercises. They are Spartan and the attempts to brighten them up are very tacky, and only emphasise the gloomy temporariness of the camps themselves, which cling unconvincingly to the Plain in the teeth of vicious winds. It's so remote and exposed up there that one could almost be in Labrador rather than one and a half hour's drive from London.

Drive back along the M4, arriving at the Centre about 7.30. Taxi home, where I arrive, feeling well and truly flattened, to a volley of phone calls and phone messages which have accumulated over the weekend and in anticipation of my departure for New York tomorrow.

A little clump of unkind press cuttings about *Jabberwocky* don't raise my spirits. John Goldstone sounds cheerful over the phone. After a poor weekend, *Jabberwocky* attendances are up again, and it's doing remarkable business in Bromley!

Wednesday, April 13th, New York

The *New York Times* has a total Python-style ad. 'Michael Palin and Terry Gilliam will be giving away 1,000 potatoes at Cinema One on Friday.' The motif for the ad is a cowering Dennis figure with a sword and Don is using, to my distress, slogans such as 'Makes King Kong Look Like an Ape', which came up at the Connaught meeting in February and was, I had hoped, firmly rejected.

Terry G has a bagful of books of illustrations by Doré and others, and he is going to redesign the poster yet again.

Biggest problem of the day is the rating. After viewing the film the authorities have given it an R (Restricted) rating – which means anyone under 18 has to be accompanied. Python was PG – a wider certificate and the one we really want. They say that we can have a PG if we trim the shots of the steaming three-quarters-eaten bodies of the two Terrys and cut the shot of Dennis being peed on as he wakes up.

Terry refuses to make the cuts.

Friday, April 15th, New York

The afternoon audiences have been depressing, but the 700-seat cinema builds up to over half full for the evening shows.

At ten o'clock the next morning's papers arrive. Don and his producers pounce eagerly on the *New York Times*, searching for the word of Vincent Canby. Exactly the same feeling as on the *Grail* opening in this same cinema two years ago.

Except that the review is better. It's longer than the *Grail*, it's headlined '*Jabberwocky*: Monster With Heart', it's the top film previewed, and there's a photo too. The review is a joy, better than anything so far in the UK or US. Vincent clearly loves *Jabberwocky* and went to some lengths to say so. Not a harsh word or a qualification – 24-carat gold praise.

Don and the executives of Cinema-5 (who suddenly materialise from the foyer) are overjoyed and read and re-read the paper like men who've just won the Pools. So it is a good picture after all, they seem to be saying.

Saturday, April 16th, New York

To breakfast with Terry. Bought *New York Post*, which slams the film most violently. '*Jabberwocky*: Read Meaningless' is the headline – and the reviewer hates the film as violently as Canby likes it. His only non-violent comment is that I was 'amusing but misused', the rest is hatred.

Terry G, I'm glad to say, laughs, and indeed the intensity of the man's dislike would make grand reading next to Canby's panegyric. If they're both talking about the same film, it would make me curious to see it!

Back to my room for an interview with college kids from Princeton for a syndicated radio programme called *Focus on Youth*. A grim, two-hour ordeal by pretension.

After a quick shopping spree in FAO Schwarz (a magic set for Willy, a bowling game for Tom and a wooden scooter and painted bricks for Rachel), and a hasty snack at the Plaza, we are just in time for the end of the first Saturday performance at the cinema.

Not a bad crowd, but they certainly don't fill the place. A one-legged man approached me as I was about to cross Fifth Avenue. 'Hi Mike,' he shouts, 'How's this for a silly walk!'

Sunday, April 17th

Arrive at Heathrow at a quarter to eleven at night.

Make for the taxis and home at last. No taxis – just another long queue. Resign myself to a late arrival home and decide to take the airport bus. But this only goes to Victoria, and can't leave until it's absolutely full. We are forced to wait for nearly half an hour.

The bus rattles down to Victoria. It's all rather embarrassing and dis-heartening to realise that for most of the passengers (American tourists) this is their first impression of England. Even more disheartening is to be dumped at the Victoria terminal, which has no facilities and, today, no taxis.

Wander up Buckingham Palace Road with the handle of my FAO Schwarz bag now cutting into my fingers. At last find a cab, but he refuses to take me to Hampstead, saying it's too far away.

Almost going spare, I suddenly glimpse an N90 bus with the magic words 'Camden Town' on its destination board, stopped at some traffic lights. I race towards it, and leap on with the same feelings of gratitude and relief that someone lost in the desert would show towards a water hole.

But the conductor, a crusty, near-retirement veteran, was clearly not going to have weary travellers thankfully boarding his bus at half past midnight.

'Where are you going?' he demands.

'I'll go anywhere you're going,' I reply, still full of happy relief and not yet aware that the man has no sense of humour. This doesn't go down at all well.

'You tell me where you're going and I'll tell you where I'm going,' he snaps.

We settle on Camden Town.

The bus trundles on through Pimlico. My breath is coming back and I'm beginning to recover from the last two hours, when an unfriendly voice cuts through my grateful reverie.

'You'll have to move that, you know.'

It's the conductor indicating my FAO Schwarz bag, once the pride of Fifth Avenue, now the target for abuse on the N90. 'Yes, alright … I will move it, but just for a moment let me get my breath back.'

This perfectly reasonable request makes his face twitch and his eyes dart angrily from side to side, but what finally makes this kind and long-suffering man explode is when I ask him to 'Cool down'. He moves quickly into a fury, tapping his badge and screaming that this is his bus and no one is going to ask him to cool down.

Well, I reckon if it's this bad at this stage of the journey, by the time we reach Camden Town one of us will have died of a heart attack, so I pick my cases up and get off.

Once I'm off the bus and waiting for the lights to change, he changes his tune completely. 'I was only doing it for your own good,' he cries. And 'You'll never get another one, you know.'

As the N90 finally disappears, leaving me laden down in a dimly lit, anonymous Pimlico Street, at a quarter to one in the morning, shouting 'Keep Smiling!' at the top of my voice, I find it rather pleasing to think that 24 hours ago I was the star of a New York film premiere.

Eventually find a cab who has no moral, ethnic, financial or personal reasons for not taking me to Oak Village, and I finally arrive home at 1.30, it having taken me nearly half the time to get from Heathrow to Oak Village as it took me to get from New York to London.

Thursday, April 21st

Wig-fitted by an excited Scotsman at Wig Specialities, who greeted me with a little clap of the hands, 'I've seen your bottom simply everywhere.' (I suppose *Jabberwocky* has made modesty in my case rather superfluous.)

A tall, gangly lady, with attractive bony knees rather like Helen's, was also being wig-fitted. It turned out she was Fiona Richmond, star of most of Paul Raymond's sex shows – like *Pyjama Tops* and *Let's Get Laid*. The little Scotsman couldn't control himself after she'd gone. 'Well I never,' he said. 'Two of the country's top sex symbols in here together!'

I've taken the rest of today off to escort my Ma to *Jabberwocky*. She arrives at Liverpool Street on the 11.30.

To Old Compton Street for tea at Patisserie Valerie, then to the 5.40 showing of *Jabberwocky* at the Columbia. It's only about 150 souls full, but the audience does seem to enjoy it and only three people (young, rather attractive girls) walk out. I try to hide myself in my coat, but am spotted by the usherettes, who are frightfully excited, and rush up, saying very nice things about me.

My mother seemed to enjoy it a lot, and I felt that same feeling of enjoyment which I had when I first saw it put together. There are faults, but at least Terry has made a film which, for most of its length, involves, amuses and entertains an audience – with striking and original images and a brilliantly effective evocation of the crumbling mediaeval world. The modern allusions seem to be the ones which sit most uneasily within it. But I felt again what a good piece of work it is.

Saturday, April 23rd

Woken at 7.15 by Tom telling me the phone was ringing. It's Granny. Father is not expected to live much beyond lunchtime. She is just off to the hospital. I promise to get up there as soon as I can. Feel dreadfully bleary and tired. Tell the children. Willy says, quite seriously, that he hopes Rachel (who's got a slight cold) won't be dead by lunchtime too.

Ring Angela. By a quarter to nine Veryan has brought her round and I have woken up sufficiently to drive us both up to Blythburgh. It's a sunny day, which helps to keep the gloom from settling too heavily. Angela natters on compulsively about her job – her social welfare work in Croydon sounds far more harrowing than anything we are experiencing today.

Arrive at Blythburgh Hospital just after eleven. As we walk from the car, neither of us, or certainly I myself, have any real idea of what to expect. I have never been near anyone dying before.

Daddy is breathing heavily and noisily on his back in bed, eyes almost closed, one half-open, glazed and unseeing. His skin is pale and parchment-like and drawn tight over the bones of his face. Mother sits at the bedside, hardly racked with grief. Indeed she greets us very matter of factly, as if we'd just arrived at a coffee morning.

A marvellously sane and intelligent middle-aged lady doctor takes us into her room after examining him and tells us that he has pneumonia on the top of one of his lungs and is not likely to survive. She has brought us in here, she says, because, although he is unconscious to all intents and purposes, one never can be sure about the sense of hearing. This worries me a little, as I had, when I arrived, rather loudly queried whether it was terminal.

The doctor, grasping my mother's hand in a firm, comforting, but unsentimental clasp of reassurance, cannot give us any real estimate of how long Dad will live. His unconsciousness means that the heart has the minimum of work to do and he could survive for anything from an hour to two or three days. She suggests, very tactfully, that there is little to be gained from us all clustering around the body waiting for him to die, so on her advice I take Ma (who has been at his bedside for five hours) back to Reydon, where we do a bit of shopping and have some lunch.

We return to the hospital just after two. His condition is the same. I wait beside the bed, and after a while find myself becoming quite accustomed to the rattling gurgle of deeply drawn breaths which had so unnerved me when I first saw him.

As we really don't know how long he will survive, it's decided that I shall go back to London and Angela will stay with Mother, at least until Monday. Tomorrow I have to travel to Durham and on Monday morning the first of the last three *Ripping Yarns* begins filming.

On the way back I stop at the hospital. Father has been moved up to one end of the ward. He's breathing as heavily and noisily as before. The nurses still wash him and turn him regularly. He lies in a clean and comfortable bed. In the background the news and the football results. What a ritual *Sports Report* always used to be on a Saturday. At about 6.25 I leave.

I'm 33 and he's 77 when I last see him, an emaciated, gravel-breathed shadow of the father I knew.

Say goodbye to the nurses, knowing I won't see them again. One of them says he'd really grown to like my dad, which is nice, because it didn't happen that way often during his life.

Into the car and down the A12 to London. Beyond Ipswich, a colossal rainstorm. I must have been passing Colchester when Father died – at 7.25. Mother and Angela were almost at Blythburgh, slowed down by the heavy rain. He was dead by the time they got there.

Sunday, April 24th, Durham

Preparations for departure. Packing cases, writing last-minute letters, regretting lack of time and feeling of unpreparedness for the weeks to come.

Swimming – always good for calming the troubled breast, then a roast beef lunch, and am driven down to catch the three o'clock train at King's Cross.

Settle into the seat, armed with unlearnt script and the Sunday papers, and it's only as we pull out of King's Cross and are rumbling through Hertfordshire that the pressure of events in the last few days hits me with a wave of depression. Fortunately I only feel such depression very rarely, but it intensifies as the train nears familiar stations like Sandy and familiar views like the fields beyond St Neots. I miss home and family. I feel unutterably sad that I am going away to the grey north having seen so little of them for the last two weeks. I feel, too, the sadness at my father's death which eluded me yesterday.

It's a feeling of loneliness. A feeling that I am speeding away from the familiar world, which for some reason I need at the moment, to an unfamiliar world of new faces, new people, new work. And the skies turn greyer too. Increasing the melancholy.

Fortunately this despondency does not last even the length of the journey and I'm a little more phlegmatic about things as the train edges round the curving viaduct with the splendid mass of Durham Cathedral looming across the River Wear.

To the County Hotel – an old, probably Georgian building, which has been expanded, in the process becoming rather airport loungefied. Met by Eddie S, Liz.[1] Aware of the slight awkwardness with which they bring up the subject of Father's death. No mention of death, just 'Sorry about your news'. They're kind people, though, very straightforward.

---

1 Eddie Stuart and Liz Cranston – members of the production team.

Decide not to eat that night, still feeling metabolically maladjusted. A few drinks in the hotel bar with a smattering of wardrobe and props boys. Put on as cheerful a face as possible.

Friday, April 29th, Durham

Tonight Jim [Franklin, the director] has laid a car on for me to return to London, for tomorrow is Father's funeral, and we film again on Sunday.[1] Say my goodbyes to all, including Ken Colley, who, I'm pleased to say, has turned out to be a stroke of genius choice for the part of the Robber. He's not only a very good, no-nonsense actor, he's also very good company.

Saturday, April 30th, Southwold

We troop off to the church, taking Mrs Pratt[2] with us, in time for the service at two. Father had been cremated at Gorleston during the week, and so it's more of a memorial service than a cremation. There is a representative of the Funeral Directors – heavy dark coat matching his eyebrows, despite the warm afternoon. Then there is the vicar, muted, grave and cold.

Quite a small congregation – thirty or forty at most. Father's ashes are in a small wooden box at the end of the aisle. I am quite severely nervous for the first part of the service – 'The Lord's My Shepherd' – as I am to read the lesson, a heavy piece of Revelations. But that goes well, as does the service, and even the vicar's little address (about my father being a man of patience, bearing with extreme tolerance and fortitude the slings and arrows. I suppose in a sense he was patient – for a man carrying a severe stammer for much of his life. I just remember so many moments of *im*patience and *in*tolerance).

At the end we process out behind the box of ashes and into the churchyard. The solemnity and dignity of the occasion is somehow less easy to maintain the further we process from the organ and the hymn singers, and I find that we are wending our way in a direct line towards the Southwold Cottage Hospital where I have an awful feeling that Father's spirit was finally broken last autumn.

His ashes are lowered in – 'Dust to dust', etc, etc – and the ceremony is over. Shake the vicar's hand and receive in exchange a bland smile.

1 On 'The Test of Eric Olthwaite'.
2 Lily Pratt, my mother's neighbour.

Still, Father would have loved the church today, filled with sunlight, the mediaeval pews and the fine old screen which has witnessed funeral services for 500 years.

Back to Croft Cottage for tea. No tears, except from Camilla, a little, and Angela, a sniffle. Mother quite composed about the whole thing. Tea turns into a jolly family reunion in the best tradition of funeral teas, and we leave for London at about five.

Thursday, May 5th, Tow Law and Durham

Birthday on location again. Thirty-four, and I feel it.

Out in the bus to Tow Law. This is an exposed and underprivileged sort of town. A long line of small houses and not much more. No green, no parks, no opulent houses or even well-off areas – just the skeleton of a town custom-built for mining, in the days when there was something to mine. A cold wind whips through the grid-frame streets and all in all it's a depressing place to spend a birthday.

I organise free drinks at lunchtime for the crew and all at the Tow Law Hotel. A blind pianist plays 'Happy Birthday', with lush holiday camp trills thrown in, on an organ. I am presented with a shovel, signed by all the crew, which is very touching. I'm also given a birthday cake with one candle. But it's a celebration only just on this side of tragic. The place, the town, the hotel are all grim.

Friday, May 6th, Durham

We were supposed to return home yesterday, but the bad weather on Tuesday put us a day behind.

Somewhere away to our north-east, ten or fifteen miles, President Carter is pressing the flesh in Newcastle. The Tories have swept Labour under the carpet in the local government elections – Wearside and Durham County are amongst a tiny handful of councils where Labour has held on. I fear for Helen's Ma, so vociferous is the reaction against the government, Labour and their sympathisers.

At the very moment that Peter has set up a skyline shot with a colliery wheel in the background, Eddie Stuart appears over the hill with a man in a suit and helmet who looks very unhappy. This turns out to be the colliery manager, who is concerned, as it turns out, about the image of the National Coal Board.

With much palaver and banging of helmets and raising of spectacles, the manager pronounces that we can film on, provided we go easy on shots of the slag heaps.

We then move on to a windswept line of stone-built houses with a rather dark and moody back alley running alongside them. A lady berates us for filming the alley, calling it a disgrace, and bemoaning the fact that her husband's wheelchair gets stuck along it in bad weather. At another house, a family who've just returned from two weeks' holiday in Spain. It seems the days when you could point to a street and sum up its character straightaway are gone.

Saturday, May 14th, Abbotsley

Drove up to Abbotsley for two-day break from city and work. Long bicycle ride with Tom and Willy – the older they get the more we can do together. We cycled all the way to Waresley, where we met a dog which followed us all the way back. In the end Helen and I had to drive it back in the car. Tom collected a hoard of spent cartridges from roadside shoots along the Tetworth Hall Estate. Very happy day and fine May sunset.

Sunday, May 15th, Abbotsley

Worked hard in the morning, mowing and clearing the grass and weeds which have grown in lush profusion this year after the wettest winter for 100 years.

Roast beef lunch. Helen's Ma, who lost her seat in the council elections of May 5th, is just beginning to feel the effects. She will no longer be on the Education Committee – the Conservatives are going to run it under their own tight political control, and her work will be cut down enormously. For someone who worked so hard and so thoroughly for the local people it's a tragedy that national politics should retire her prematurely. But the Tories were returned up and down the land regardless of their quality. At Eynesbury, near St Neots, a man got in who couldn't even pronounce the name of the town.

She has a mound of letters from all sorts of people, from Lord Hemingford to the Headmaster of Kimbolton and the Cambridge Borough Architect, to say how much she will be missed.

To London this evening – I must prepare for another *Ripping Yarn* tomorrow. Long learning session.

Friday, May 20th

A mixed week of filming [on 'Escape from Stalag 112B'] draws to a close in perfect sunny weather. We are on schedule and generally all has gone well. But mid-week I had some worries about performances. Roy Kinnear,[1] on his first day, seemed a little too stock – relying too much on the well-loved Kinnearish fat-man grimaces, than on his natural skill as an actor. But he began to improve and enjoy the part in a more original way as the week went on.

Marvellous props, such as the glider made out of toilet rolls.

The First World War cricket match created a totally believable atmosphere out there with the German watchtowers and the barbed wire surrounding the pitch. The more or less continuous thudding of guns in the distance (for we are in the middle of a tank-training area) helps too and puts me in mind of Sassoon's descriptions of being behind the lines in France during the First War.

Monday, May 23rd

Helen rang me in Salisbury. We are going ahead with plans to purchase No. 2, the house next door but one. Helen got frightened by the sound of prospective buyers just the other side of our wall, and she, Edward[2] and others, seem to feel it's a good thing to buy the property and enlarge our garden – give the kids a plentiful playroom, a permanent spare room etc.

Friday, May 27th

I have been filming, I suppose, daily for the past five weeks and maybe a cumulative tiredness is creeping up on me, but Wednesday and Thursday this week were days I had to drag myself through, force myself, like a runner at the end of a long race, to keep up the enthusiasm, the involvement and the energy that these films *must* have, when my body and mind are about to stage a mutiny.

1 Kinnear made his name on the satire show *That Was The Week That Was* (1962). Constantly in demand as a character actor, he died from a fall from his horse whilst filming *The Return of the Musketeers* in 1988.
2 Edward Burd, my brother-in-law, was an architect.

Saturday, May 28th

The hot weather continues. After breakfast, go round to see Mr and Mrs Pym, whose house we are hoping to buy. (Helen has been working hard on it all week and yesterday we made our offer, but I wanted to check with them.) 'Oh, yes,' says Mrs Pym, dismissing the subject as though it had all been settled and bustling me out into the back garden to ask how much we would give her for her rotary clothes drier. 'It cost £8, and he made a stand for it,' she reassures me, pointing at a concrete lump into which it has been sunk. Anyway, she seems far more interested in getting rid of the rotary drier, so I agree to buy it for £18,754 – with the house thrown in.

The Pyms have been there twenty-five years. They're a quiet, self-contained, working class couple. He's a dustman. She has that Welsh darting quickness and busyness.

Good news, or nice news – *Jabberwocky* has been selected as the British entry for the Berlin Film Festival, so it's brush up on the German and off to Berlin for TG and me at the beginning of July. It's still being held in at Cinema One in New York. Don Rugoff is forever devising new campaigns, hoping that kids will flock in during the long school holidays and save the picture.

Monday, May 30th

To the BBC at ten o'clock for a sort of review of the situation so far with Jim F. I think they are running into heavy production problems with 'The Curse of the Claw', one of which is casting the very difficult Chief Petty Officer part. Gwen Taylor, whom Eric recommended to me as being 'a female Michael Palin', now can't do it (because of the new dates), nor can Penny Wilton, our second choice.

Tuesday, May 31st

We talk to and read through with four girls from four until about half past five. Eventually select Judy Loe.[1] She's a straightforward, jolly, easy-going lady and straightaway understood and appreciated the part.

Up to Terry Hughes' office for a glass of wine – Jimmy Gilbert, now

1 Married to Richard Beckinsale. Mother of Kate.

Head of Light Entertainment, and Bill Cotton, new Controller of BBC1, there. Very matey and jolly and we talk about my house-buying as if we were old friends at the pub. Continually amazed at the change in their attitude (or is it the change in mine?) since Python!

But they have shown great confidence in the *Ripping Yarns*. I hope they will be as good as everyone thinks they're going to be.

Friday, June 3rd

A hot day. Into Soho to see what Ray [Millichope, the editor] has done to the still unsatisfactory 'Moorstones' and 'Andes'.

Difficult to work up in Wardour Street as groups of chanting, singing, shouting Scottish football fans are roaming the West End, waiting for the pubs to open. As I drive from Soho down through St Martin's Lane and Trafalgar Square (where one of them is later killed jumping into a fountain), I see the Scots everywhere. In high spirits – the weather, the booze and the anticipation of rubbing England's nose in the turf – they have taken over Trafalgar Square from the American tourists and they have easily upstaged the colourless pink and washed-out turquoise of the Jubilee decorations.

Lunch with Jill Foster in the King's Road. The subject of Graham C comes up. I mention how cowardly I am about confronting him with direct criticism of his wasteful lifestyle. Jill says she took him out to lunch the other day and told him he was a boozy old wastrel who was destroying himself and his chances of work. GC took a gin and tonic off her and agreed.

In the early evening, swimming with the kids at the Holiday Inn, where there are three or four men of ruddy body and glazed eye hurling themselves at the water with vicious smacks. It turns out – yes – they're Scottish football supporters. I sign an autograph for them. They can't believe that at the hotel in one day they've seen Kevin Keegan, John Conteh and now a real live Monty Python.

Tuesday, June 7th, Jubilee Day, Abbotsley

Rather grey to start with, but the rain held off. Church Farm decked out with streams of coloured flags. In the afternoon went to Abbotsley Village Sports in the field at the back of the Eight Bells pub. Helen and I came second in the wheelbarrow race and I entered for the obstacle race

– two heats – and though I came third overall, I was nearly dead after crawling under nets, etc.

Later in the evening, as it got dark, we returned to the sports field for the village firework display, having just watched the royal bonfire being lit at Windsor Castle – a dramatic sight – huge flames and great surging crowds of people. Abbotsley firework display upstaged by more expensive pyrotechnics which burst in the air above St Neots, a few miles away.

Wednesday, June 8th

Pleasant drive up into Lincolnshire.[1] Sun is out when I arrive in Rippingale, a small village between Bourne and Sleaford, lying in unexpectedly attractive country – more wooded and gently hilly than the bleak, flat Fenland just to the east. The villages are full of fine stone houses, like the Cotswolds.

The house itself is a stone-built Georgian rectory, of simple, unadorned design, with additions in red brick. It is in quite a poor state indoors and Uncle Jack's[2] bedroom needs absolutely nothing doing to it – the walls are damp, mildewed and peeling – just perfect.

Drive into Peterborough – about half an hour down the A15. An extraordinary city. A fine and impressive cathedral and all around it lines of insubstantial brick terraces, reaching right into the city centre. There is hardly anyone about – even at 5.30. Then I realise, of course, Peterborough – or Greater Peterborough as it now calls itself – has expanded along the American pattern – from the suburbs outwards. No-one really needs the centre of Peterborough any more.

Saturday, June 11th

After a great deal of heart-searching over the last few weeks, I finally sat down to write to Hamish MacInnes,[3] and excuse myself from his Yeti expedition.

1 For 'Curse of the Claw' filming.
2 Uncle Jack was a character who had all the world's diseases, at the same time.
3 An experienced climber who lived in Glencoe and who had helped us on *Monty Python and the Holy Grail* by throwing dummy bodies into the Gorge of Eternal Peril. Unfortunately he was head of Mountain Rescue at the time.

In recent weeks I had received the latest newsletters on the expedition from Hamish, which contained a rather worrying mixture of uncertainty over finance and jolly, harrowing asides like 'We will have to move fast to get out of this valley, where some years ago a Tibetan expedition were trapped and actually ate their boots before being discovered ... dead.'

Despite the obvious pleasures of a trip to unknown lands in the company of top climbing folk like Hamish and Joe Brown, I have been so infrequently at home over the last year, what with *Jabberwocky* (ten weeks) and *Ripping Yarns* (seven weeks) and a week and a half in New York, that I feel I can't commit myself to two months in the Himalayas only a month or so before we plan to shoot *Life of Brian* in North Africa. But it goes against instincts I've had since early childhood to opt out of an expedition to an almost unknown part of the world.

Saturday, June 18th

Playing charity football this afternoon at Wembley Stadium. Cavernous rooms and passageways round the back.

Finally discovered our dressing room. Teddy Warrick[1] there, small and beaming, and most of the Radio One side with him – Peel, Gambaccini, Kid Jensen and Paul Burnett. Quiet, rather subdued atmosphere. Ed Stewart arrives and starts to organise everyone in a very loud voice.

On our side only Paul Nicholas here at the moment. Another quiet lad – I like him. Alan Price arrives, then Graham Chapman and John Tomiczek. John will play in goal for us and I suggest Graham, in his strange Trilby hat, should be team psychiatrist. A sort of cheer goes up as Tommy Steele arrives, bubbling, flashing a lovely white Cockney grin of the type usually described as 'infectious'. He is tacitly assumed to be senior 'celebrity', and takes over captaincy of our side.

We are given free bags and kit by some sports company, which is a nice bonus. The CID appear in the dressing room – apparently to offer us some sort of protection – and say they will guard the dressing room until we get back – if we get back. We sign programmes for them.

Gambaccini claims he didn't sleep at all last night. He can't cope with

---

1 Enormously experienced and much-liked Radio 1 producer. In 1965 he got me some work as a DJ on a programme called *Playtime*.

it all, he says. 'Three times I've played football, and already I'm at Wembley!'

Alan Price finishes a last cigarette and stubs it beneath his boot as we move off up the tunnel. The noise grows, heads turn – heads of officials, policemen, commissionaires – the flotsam and jetsam of officialdom who are allowed to hang around at the very cervix of Wembley. Ahead is the pitch, above us a net to protect players from missiles.

And suddenly we're walking out. I want to freeze the moment, savour it like the finest wine. All I'm aware of is empty terraces.

There are, in fact, 55,000 people here for the Schoolboy International which follows our game – but at Wembley that still leaves bald patches – bald patches mirrored in the sacred turf itself, ripped up by the Scottish fans a couple of weeks ago and still not all replaced.

As we kick around they announce our names, and cheers rise. Biggest for Ed Stewart (good at projecting his personality), softest for John Peel (the brightest of the lot of them).

The game (the width, not the length of the pitch) is a kick and run affair – with Tommy Steele vainly trying to organise a team of six people, all of whom want only one thing, to score at Wembley. Ed Stewart plays a miraculous blinder in goal for Radio One, and it's even scores at half-time.

In the second half I hit the crossbar and completely miss another, and John Peel scores the winner for Radio One. As Teddy Warrick put it, the best team lost, which is, along with a car sticker for Wembley Stadium Main Car Park, a free kit-bag and a No. 4 blue shirt, my only consolation.

Friday, July 1st, Berlin

Meet up at London Airport with Sir John Terry of the NFFC[1] – big and benign, like Father Christmas – John Goldstone, grinning bearishly through a beard which threatens to overrun his face, and Terry Gilliam.

I find myself sat next to a short-haired, fortyish Englishman, who talks compulsively. It turns out he's with the British Forces in Berlin, and is scared stiff of flying. He has his air-sickness bag ready, grasps the edge of the seat with hands continually clenching and unclenching. He's a crack shot and trains people in rifle use.

1 National Film Finance Corporation.

Meet Michael White in the lobby of the Kempinski Hotel. He's in a crumpled white suit and has just flown in from Paris after an all-night party given by Yves St Laurent.

The bad news of the day is that *Jabberwocky* is now *out* of competition as we have been naughty and broken the rules by opening the film in Paris before the festival. It takes some of the edge off our jaunt to know that, however well received, we can't win any Golden Bears. 'Just as well,' says Goldstone, not very convincingly. 'These sort of awards can put audiences off, you know.'

Saturday, July 2nd, Berlin

In the afternoon, after a typical German lunch, served by a large, perspiring waiter, M White hires a BMW and we all squash in and go across to East Berlin. What a change from 1972.[1] The Alexanderplatz looks cleaner, brighter, more colourful than before. The bombed and shot-up churches are being restored. Altogether a much more Western look to the place. But the coffee is terrible and the cakes are hard and it still takes half an hour to cross through the wall.

Find a wonderfully seedy hotel just beside the wall at Brandenburg Gate, Hotel Adlon. It used to be right next to Hitler's bunker, which Whitey tells me the East Germans are excavating. Tea at the Orangerie in the Charlottenburg.

Alan Brien[2] sees me reading Nabokov's *Despair* and tells me that he is mentioned in *Ada* after conducting some correspondence with Nabokov about skin disease. (Nabokov, one of my literary heroes, died last week.)

In the Kempinski, like in some grotesque dream, tarted-up, over-beautified fat ladies and heavily-sweating men gather for the Film Festival Ball, which seems to be remarkable for having nobody recognisable present.

We Brits can't get in anyway, but stay on the outside, make guerrilla raids on the rather good food and buy ourselves a couple of bottles of sparkling. M White observes that this is why Hollywood stars never leave Hollywood.

1 My only previous visit to Berlin, with Robert Hewison.
2 Author, journalist, and, at the time, film critic of the *Sunday Times*.

Sunday, July 3rd, Berlin

Kill time until three o'clock, and the first showing of *Jabberwocky*. A half-full house. Perhaps a little more. Good laughs. At the end Gilliam and I have to come through the curtains and make a brief appearance. Applause. It's not too embarrassing. The worst is yet to come.

We are shown into a back room of the Cinema Am Zoo, where two long tables are pushed together and rigged with chunky, old-fashioned mikes. A few scruffy-looking people with notepads sit around.

Wolf Donner, the organiser of the festival, is a pleasant, open-faced man with a firm, friendly handshake, who says he enjoyed the film. Questions are vague or just downright dull. Someone persistently asked us for details of the jokes we *rejected* from the film. A Turkish journalist wants to know what the monster represents in British politics today. He seems very happy when I suggest it is the rise of fascism.

John Terry gives a short, obviously well-prepared speech about *Jabberwocky* being a British film, part-financed by the British government. But there are long silences, probably because the whole electronic system of mikes and simultaneous translation may be OK for the United Nations, but is utterly dampening in a roomful of twenty people. The whole miserable charade lasts about three-quarters of an hour.

Monday, July 4th

In keeping with our way of meeting all the interesting film people on the last day of the festival, we find ourselves in a car with Barbara Stone, an American who now lives in London and with her husband runs a small film distribution network and a cinema – the Gate at Notting Hill. They are one of several new distributors who are doing very well in London, feeding quality (mainly foreign) films to the eager London sophisticates (or just, let's face it, people who enjoy a good intelligent movie). They're making money now, and are directly able to help directors (such as Derek Jarman, who made *Sebastiane*). A good sign – nice to meet someone who is optimistic about the cinema in Britain. A Londonophile too – she says they couldn't start and run a similar cinema in the States.

In the evening, despite terminal drowsiness, I have to read the Python film script, which I haven't touched for three months, and have intelligent comments on it ready for our meeting tomorrow.

Tuesday, July 5th

Eric is the first person I see. He was in hospital a week ago, being fed intra-venously and with pipes through the nose to drain his stomach. Apparently there was a complication after his appendix removal, and he was back in the highly expensive Wellington Hospital for Arabs (as Graham said, when he visited him, Eric appeared to be 'the only Caucasian in the place'). So Eric is thin as a stick, long-haired and bearded. He thanks me for the pile of books I sent him. I apologised for not having had time to visit him, but I sent him an Intellectuals Get-U-Well Reading Pack, which included a potted biography of Debbie Reynolds.

According to Terry's report (he and TG went location-hunting in mid-June), Tunisia sounds the easiest of the Mediterranean countries to film in. They are well organised, there are good sites and comfortable hotels and the film entrepreneur is the nephew of the President – so no problems stopping the traffic!

But Terry J is not entirely happy with Tunisia – he is worried that we will merely be duplicating all the locations Zeffirelli used, and that it doesn't really look like the Holy Land. John Cleese had had a letter from Israeli Films, trying to persuade us to film there. Terry J wants to look at Jordan. Gilliam says the best hilly city streets are not in Tunisia but in Fez in Morocco, so no solutions are obvious.

A lunch break. John, Terry G and I go and lie in Regent's Park in the sunshine, whilst Terry J has to organise one of his many philanthropic projects (*Vole*, Kington Brewery, etc)[1] with Anne. John gets on to a well-worn theme – money. He makes no bones about it, says he, this film must make him a great deal of money. Apparently nothing else does apart from commercials. Coming from a man whom I saw having diffi-culty parking his Rolls-Royce this morning, that does sound a little un-sad, but it's a jolly chat and indicative of a generally more relaxed, easy feeling amongst us.

This evening, a civilised and funny and enjoyable evening with Simon Albury and Derek Taylor[2] and wife. We go to Langan's Brasserie,

1 *The Vole* was an environmental magazine edited by Richard Boston. The Penrhos Brewery, near Kington, Herefordshire, was a real ale venture run by Martin Griffiths. Terry was fairy godfather to both.
2 Derek Taylor, a journalist from Hoylake in the Wirral who became the Beatles' press officer. He had a terrific, very English sense of humour and wrote memoirs such as *As Time Goes By* and *Fifty Years Adrift*.

passing on our way the Berkeley Square Jubilee Party – £25 entrance tickets, of course. Packed densely inside the railings, men with no chins mingled with ladies with large teeth. Protruding jaws spread wide into baying laughs and huge noses assailed with the bouquet of champagne. All in all it looked like a gigantic zoo exhibit – 'The Upper Classes – British – circa 1970s'.

But Langan's is, of course, posh and moneyed and quite obviously aimed at those with enough money to pay for style rather than essentials. Derek is the ideal company to enjoy such a place with. He's sensible and sensitive and articulate and enjoys laughing a lot. They have legions of children – one of whom is into punk rock at the moment.

Sadly, Derek is away to Los Angeles to live for a few years – accepting promotion to Vice-President of Warner Brothers Records. I hope he doesn't stay away for long – England needs people like him. His wife Joan is jolly and down to earth and they both know a lot of famous people (via the Beatles) and yet can enjoy jokes about people knowing famous people. They know what's bullshit and what isn't. A rare quality in the frenetic music biz.

Sunday, July 10th

Al and Eve Levinson are in London at the moment. I saw them last week, when Al proudly thrust his latest Fish novel/autobiography upon me. It's longer than *Millwork* (my favourite) or *Shipping Out* (naval larks) and has an awful pun for a title – *Rue Britannia*.

Through Eve I have made the acquaintance of Arnold Wesker.[1] I took Eve up to Wesker's in Highgate (within spitting distance of G Chapman's). Eve persuaded me to go in and say hello, and Arnold's wife got very excited and said that their daughters had been dying to meet me. In the sitting room were gathered lots of young teenage kids – mostly Weskers – and a brace of Americans, including a professor from the University of Wisconsin who is doing a paper on Arnold. Arnold stands, stockily built, but in good trim, shirt open three or four buttons revealing hirsute chest, an easy manner, but on his toes like a boxer.

Then the boyfriend of the daughter, who is an enormous fan, arrived and she introduced him to the professors, playwrights and unpublished

1 Playwright, best known for *Chicken Soup with Barley*, *The Kitchen* and *Chips with Everything*.

novelists' wives, but missed me out. She made up for it by saying she was leaving me to last – which she did – and with a flourish said – 'and *this* … is Terry Gilliam!'

Wednesday, July 13th

Wake heavy-headed after late night with the author of *Rue Britannia* and his wife. They dropped in last night from the theatre and much vodka (Eve) and brandy (Al) was drunk and Helen and I struggled to stay awake and reconcile our gentle domestic mood of approaching somnolence with Al and Eve's holidaymakers' energy.

I seem to remember a lot of laughter – and Eve looking very sour as I played Elgar. 'What *is* this … ?' she demanded in tones which only a true Brooklyner could affect. I changed it for reggae and Al and Eve danced to Bob Marley.

Some last-minute script work on *Brian*, then drive down to Park Square West for a group meeting. The changes and rewrites to the script are amicably accepted, but we have to agree today on some casting for Friday's read-through. This casting, whilst it need not be binding for the film, could, as Eric put it, 'stick', so we have to make fairly far-reaching decisions between 12.45 and 1.30, when John has to leave.

Eric tells John (Graham being out of the room) that he, the two Terrys and myself, are of the opinion that John would be wasted as Brian and that Graham might be the best for it – he's Roman-looking, which helps, and was quite good as the central figure in *Grail* – Graham looks good and is watchable.

John erupted at this – far more vehemently than I would have expected. Casting a quick eye at the door in case GC should reappear, he hissed agitatedly that it would be a disaster – take it from John, he'd been working with him recently and he (GC) couldn't even find his place in the script.

Then Graham reappeared and, despite John's outburst, it was suggested to him that he play Brian. Graham mumbled woollily and we went on to cast the rest – as John had to go. I was given Pilate, Ben, the Ex-Leper and the follower Francis, as well as Nisus Wettus – the centurion in charge of the crucifixion. Feel liberated from Dennis/*Ripping Yarn* juve leads at last, and into some genuinely absurd parts.

Dash off to Willy's school concert at two. Willy, looking rather bewildered, is third child along in the Monster – the Marvellous Monster from Mars. He was very proud to be chosen for the Monster – they took six children from the whole of the infants – noted for their 'patience', Willy said. Patience was also a necessity for the audience.

In the evening to Anne and Michael Henshaw – socialising this time. In the same room where eight hours before we had been casting *Life of Brian* were now assembled myself and Helen, Anne and Michael, Al and Eve and a very bouncy director called Richard Loncraine (who is, apart from Python, Anne H's only other client). Immediately friendly and jokey, he's the sort of person you feel after ten minutes you've known for years. Or else, I suppose, he drives you mad.

Friday, July 15th

Drive over to Primrose Hill for *Life of Brian* recorded script read-through at Sound Developments. A pleasantly warm July morning. Tuck the Mini into a parking space as Cleese's Rolls glides by.

Talk to John on the way in. I had misjudged exactly how much he *wanted* to play the rather dull central role of Brian. John wants to do a lead, he told me. He wants to have a go at being a Dennis, because he says it gives him more chance to work closely with the director, to be bound up in the making of the film much more intimately than he was on the *Holy Grail*.

The recording starts well – the studio is spacious and cool and the engineer unfussy. Al Levinson is there to read the voice of Christ! We make Al religious adviser to the film. When asked what advice he's given, Al will say he told us not to do it.

But as the day wears on it's clear that Graham is once again being his own worst enemy. He arrived at ten quite 'relaxed', and has drunk gin throughout the morning. Everyone else is on the ball, but Graham can never find where we are in the script, and we keep constantly having to stop, re-take and wait for him. Occasional glimpses of how well he could do Brian, but on the whole his performance bears out every point John ever made.

Saturday, July 16th

Launch day for Penrhos Brewery. At Hereford Station by one. A minibus drives us to Penrhos Court, where a wonderfully laid out array of cold pies, tarts, a cooked ham and salads various is prepared in the restaurant.

The beer is tasted and found to be good. Jones' First Ale it's called – and at a specific gravity of 1050 it's about as devastating as Abbot Ale. But the weather has decided to be kind to us and the collection of buildings that is Penrhos Court – basically a fine, but rundown sixteenth-century manor house with outbuildings housing the brewery, restaurant and Martin Griffiths' office and living accommodation – look well in the sunshine and provide a very amenable background to the serious beer-drinking.

After lunch and beer we are organised into a game of rounders in a nearby field, which affords a most beautiful view of rolling Border country – gentle hills, wooded and cultivated, with the town of Kington nestling amongst them and providing that ideal blend of nature and man which makes poets cream their notebooks.

A jolly game – or games – of rounders. Most people play, but Richard Boston reclines on bales of straw and watches and Mike Oldfield, who lives nearby, spends the afternoon taking photographs of his girlfriend. She has dark hair in ringlets and both his behaviour and his preoccupation with her seem a little narcissistic to a jolly rounders-playing fellow like me. I suffer heavy flatulence as a result of Terry's ale.

In the evening a gorgeous sunset completes the idyllic picture of hills, fields and woods in this Rupert Land.

Monday, July 18th

To Sound Developments at nine to listen, with the rest of the Pythons (bar Eric), to the tape.

We decide to simplify the central section with the raid on Pilate's palace, and cut down on the number of characters – amalgamating a lot of them – and also to shorten the end sequences. General feeling that the first third of the picture is fine.

We split up – Graham and I to write together on the middle section, because John wants to work on the end with either Terry or myself. Given GC's behaviour on Friday at the reading, I don't particularly relish a day's writing with him. I would really rather work on my own.

By chance Barry Cryer rings during supper this evening. He is disenchanted with the Chapman situation, and says he doesn't feel at home or comfortable in the house at Southwood Lane any more. Sad, for Barry was a very loyal and sensible friend of Graham's.

Tuesday, July 19th

To Graham's at eleven. A very good day's work. We complete the re-think of the whole central section and work well together on new scenes and new dialogue during our five hours writing together. The Doctor has about six gin and tonics, and when I leave at four he seems on the verge of incapability – evenings can't be much fun.

But until four we find a very easy-going, productive way of working – mainly because we have something to work on, and I am quite disciplined about what we have to do. Occasionally the phone rings and Graham becomes a producer. He seems to find this a nerve-racking business. He puts the phone down, tells me they've got another £750,000, and then has to have a large gin and tonic to calm himself down.

Friday, July 22nd

Meet Geoffrey Strachan and the marketing man at Methuen to discuss ideas for promoting the new book of the *Holy Grail*.

We meet at Odin's. I suggest we should publish our own top ten list of bestsellers in every ad, and make up specious names like 'The Shell Guide to Dead Animals on the Motorway', or else we should do a series of direct appeals to the buying public, of an abject and grovelling tone, mentioning wives, families to support … 'living in the manner to which we've become accustomed', etc, etc.

Geoffrey seems highly pleased and we part and walk over to Park Square West for a final Python meeting. Because we only have a little over an hour to make decisions, we work well and extraordinarily productively. No writing again until January – when we shall spend two or three weeks writing and rehearsing. The West Indies is mentioned, Eric favours Barbados.

Tuesday, July 26th

On a hot afternoon go all the way to Sun Alliance in Chancery Lane, only to be told that they wouldn't insure my new house because of my profession. 'Actors … and writers … well, you know.'

I didn't know, nor did I try to find out, but I couldn't help feeling something of a reject from society as I walked out again into Chancery

Lane. But my solicitor cheerfully informs me that several big companies, including Eagle Star, won't touch actors. The happy and slightly absurd ending to this story is that I finally find a willing insurer in the National Farmers' Union at Huntingdon.

Friday, July 29th

Today we dub 'Stalag Luft 112B' at the Centre. There are twenty-two music cues, however, so it's not easy.

The Goodies are in the bar at lunchtime. Tim has been in Australia (Perth) for two months doing a long part in a stage play, just to see, as he put it, 'if I could make people laugh again'.

The talk is of the two scripts for the new Goodies series which the BBC have rejected. One, Jim told me, was the first the BBC had rejected, and it was because it wasn't funny. Bill, on the other hand, said it was about punk rock and the BBC couldn't stomach it. Jimmy Gilbert came under attack for his pusillanimity – and apparently Tim had been the most aggressive of the lot with him. Times change. John C used to describe Tim as the only man who could get Hitler and Churchill to come to tea together.

Monday, August 22nd

Jill Foster rang to say that Python had been approached to appear in the Royal Variety Performance this year. She said that when the gnarled old showbiz pro who puts the show together rang her, he had been rendered practically speechless by the fact that she said she'd ask us and see, but there wasn't a great chance we'd do it.[1]

Mother very excited when I told her. I saw Tim Brooke-T and Bill at the Holiday Inn. The Goodies haven't been asked, Tim admitted. I told him to wait a week! Tim did it once with Marty Feldman, and he strongly advised me against it. The audience was made up of the rich and ruthless of British showbiz – the sort of men who, as Tim put it, 'make chorus girls cry'.

1 She was right.

Thursday, August 25th

A phone call from Tariq Ali, of all people, who wants me to write an appreciation of Groucho Marx, who died this week aged 86, for *Socialist Challenge*. Decline on the grounds that I don't know enough about him, and suggest Ian Davidson. But Tariq doesn't sound very interested – they're really only after big names, these socialists.

Saturday, August 27th

A fine morning for Clive Hollick's wedding party at Shepperton. We all drive over there in our Saturday best. The Old House is a perfect location. Tables have been set out on the verandah and the rich green lawn (well watered this year) stretches away, dominated by the great cedar tree. A band from Ronnie Scott's plays, there's sparkling wine and a buffet. Croquet and cricket on the lawn.

Don't know many people, but Simon A is best man, resplendent in white suit and hat, dark blue shirt, blue tie and shoes. Looking like the Young Burl Ives. A best woman there as well, as it is a very egalitarian occasion. Simon tells some of Ronnie Scott's old jokes, but they are rather borne away on the wind.

The Old House really is a remarkable relic of the days when film moguls built themselves headquarters which were as extravagantly theatrical as the films they made. As I wandered through it, marvelling at the richness of art nouveau plasterwork and fine stained glass windows, I felt a definite twinge of remorse that I was one of the four people who confirmed the decision to lease it off for 999 years to Ramport Ltd. Still, I rationalised through my glass of Veuve de Vernay, they will have much more money to look after it than we will.

Sunday, August 28th

Down to Dean Street in Soho for my postponed day on Eric's *Rutles* film *All You Need is Cash*. They're not ready, so I wander into Soho Square, which is a peaceful refuge and very quiet today without cars or bustle. A few tramps sitting or lying on the benches.

We end up shooting in Golden Square, near Piccadilly. I'm playing the part of Eric Manchester (Derek Taylor), who is being interviewed and giving confident denials about the 'petty pilfering' at Rutle Corps –

whilst behind him the entire building is being emptied. George Harrison – complete with grey wig – interviews me. Later Ronnie Wood turns up to be a Hell's Angel.

It all seems very pleasantly disorganised. The cameraman/director Gary is American. He shoots everything hand-held. It's a totally different world from the careful, painstaking preparations of Hall and Franklin on *Ripping Yarns*.

A lunchtime drink in a quiet, uncluttered pub in Poland Street with Neil I, Eric, Ronnie Wood and George H. But only minutes after saying how nice it is to be in Soho on a Sunday, we're kicked out as it's two and drinking-up time. England, oh England, you perverse and silly land.

Back home for a wash and then out to Richmond at the invitation of Ron Wood. He lives in one of the prime sites in all London. On top of Richmond Hill, with a view over the Thames as it curves round and away into the trees.

Ron is living with wife Chrissie and Jess, their son, in the cottage down the hill from the main house. It's a pretty little cottage, not too vast, and makes a change from the usual cavernous rooms and feeling of aimless spaciousness which pop stars with lots of money usually seem to live in.

He plays a tape of their most recent concert – at a small club in Tokyo, the same club where Margaret Trudeau's[1] friendship with the Stones was first noticed by the press. They played the club unannounced – everyone had come to hear a popular local band.

Anyway, after watching the sun swell and turn from yellow through orange to crimson before sinking triumphantly below the western horizon, we walked down to the cottage and drank wine and Chrissie Wood showed me round the big house and we looked out at a truly stunning view – the Thames in its valley under a full moon. The river was silver, the trees that crowded protectively to its banks were opaque, mysterious. London in 1977, and yet that view cannot have changed for hundreds of years.

On a less romantic note, she showed me the splintered door frame which was nearly ripped from the wall when fifteen policemen burst in to search her bedroom for drugs.

1 Wife of Pierre Trudeau, Prime Minister of Canada 1968–79. She memorably said 'I want to be more than a rose in my husband's lapel.'

Monday, August 29th

Watch repeat of *Three Men in a Boat*. It's a beautifully and confidently created world. As Eric said when he rang me later, 'Everything else seems like television.' But I felt that it was a little too meditative, a little distanced, at times – if Frears had gone just a bit closer to the characters he might have given some substance to their strange friendship. Impressive, though.

Friday, September 2nd

A Python meeting at eleven to discuss what needs to be rewritten, if anything, on the *Brian* film script. Because the retyped version only became available yesterday, no one's had much chance to read it, so we fall to talking of dates, budgets, etc.

John and Eric have very little use, at the moment, for England. John says he's made a resolution to stay away from England during January, February and March because the weather's so awful. Eric, having nearly completed the Rutles, will be relaxing and recuperating for several months in the Caribbean.

Tunisia is decided upon for all the filming, so we set aside ten weeks – starting on April 10th (the nearest date after the end of this financial year). John wants to take a masseur, and thinks the whole unit could avail themselves of his services. Eric wants to have a chef specially for ourselves. John suggests only a five-day week (which I heartily agree with). Eric wants First Class travel everywhere, and so on.

Terry G is in France (just as well, for he would be unable to watch this spectacle without making a bit of noise!) and Terry J is very quiet.

I put my foot down over writing abroad in January *and* March as preparation for the film. My life is here in London, with my family. I love travel, but I love them more. However we agree to meet and write and read and rehearse in the West Indies in January. Even writing this shocks me with its self-indulgence. Is this really the best way to spend our money?

We part on good terms – the great thing about arguments over style is that they never really scratch the surface of our personal relations. We all know we need each other and we all agree to differ. But at least we vetoed a special chef for the actors – on the grounds that there should be good food for everybody.

So Python winds down until January 1978 in the West Indies. 'See you next term,' shouts Eric, as I disappear into the rain.

Monday, September 5th

To the BBC to look at 'Moorstones' and 'Andes', which are being previewed prior to tonight's showing to an audience.

Horrified to find – not one minute into 'Andes' – that between them Hughes and Millichope have failed to leave sufficient background for the opening titles. Some ten seconds are missing. I really can't believe that, after nearly a year, these shows are still not complete.

Fortunately Alan Bell, a PA who is in nominal charge of this evening's audience recording, and Jim Franklin, who fortuitously pops in to see the preview, tackle the situation very coolly and we resign ourselves to some hasty editing before this evening.

To the Television Theatre in Shepherd's Bush to check on the night's recording. The audience watch the show on an Eidophor screen in black and white and on monitors above their heads in colour. Terry and I do a silly warm up and we kick off with 'Across the Andes by Frog'. Not a great deal of laughter and, when it does come, it grates horribly against the laid-back atmosphere of the piece.

At the end, when I ask the audience how many would rather see these shows with the help of recorded laughter, or without, the withouts are in a three to one majority.

Tuesday, September 6th

Much telephonic activity over the shows. Go to the BBC at lunchtime to watch a playback, which just confirms my feelings last night. 'Andes' is clearly wrong with an audience. As Anne Henshaw said, it's a very personal sort of show – one doesn't want other people's interpretations imposed.

Wednesday, September 7th, Southwold

Drinking fourth coffee of the morning, on arrival at Southwold, when the phone rings. It's Jimmy Gilbert. He's seen the playback of 'Moorstones' and thinks that the audience reaction is so good that it would be a waste not to use it. Quotes Aubrey Singer, the head of BBC2, who has told Jimmy that they have had a 100% failure rate on BBC2 on comedy shows with no laughter.

Mother seems well. She worries more as she gets older, but seems to have many more regular friends than when Dad was alive. Her chief worry is whether to move into the centre of Southwold or not and the feeling of isolation out at Reydon.

Monday, September 12th

It gave me real pleasure to visit Neal's Yard today. The sun was shining, there was a crisp and clear September freshness in the air. The builders were at work completing the restaurant on one side of the Neal's Yard triangle, and the wholefood store was busy sorting sacks of brown rice on the other. A bustle of activity, of which Redwood is a part.

Next door to Redwood is ALS – Associated London Scripts – a rather chic reception area leading to agents for Denis Norden and many others. And at almost the apex of the triangle, the rich mix is completed by White's the Armourers!

André [Jacquemin] and I listened to his compilation so far of the new Python album material. It sounds rather good – tightly packed Python gems. After discussion of the contents, I leave André to finish putting it all together – he'll drop a cassette in to me at home and we can edit further after that.

Up to sunny Belsize Park for a very hard game of squash with Terry, followed by a trip to the Flask.

Al Alvarez is in the Flask. Terry offers the literary lion the first edition of *The Vole*. Alvarez' eyes don't exactly light up. 'Oh yes … it's Richard Boston's thing, isn't it?' Terry, glad at least of some positive reaction, affirms. '… He's such a tit, isn't he?' muses the poetry critic of *The Observer* as he flicks through.

Alvarez seems very cynical about the readership – 'city countrymen' he calls them, uncharitably. But I know what he means, in a way.

Tuesday, September 13th, San Sebastian

To San Sebastian today for the 25th SS Film Festival – in which *Jabberwocky* rears its beautifully shot head in the 'New Creators' section. ('New Creators' sounds like some awful Biblical quiz game in which contestants have seven days to … etc, etc.)

Wednesday, September 14th, San Sebastian

As I soaked in my bath this morning, reading with admiration Kingsley Amis' *Ending Up*, I had a flash of inspiration. For my next project I would try and write a novel. A book. On my own. Cheered with relief and excitement at this simple solution.

After a breakfast of eggs, bacon, croissant and coffee, Terry, Hilary[1] and I drove to the eastern part of town, where we eventually found the Savoy Cinema, in an unremarkable street of shops and houses and garages. I really couldn't imagine *who* would come out to see a film here at what is, for the Spanish, almost crack of dawn. But amazingly some forty or fifty Spaniards – definitely *non*-press and non-film people, some of them students, some looking like lorry drivers – arrive in this improbable street at breakfast time to watch *Jabberwocky*.

At least they're rewarded with a very good print, but there are no subtitles. It must be totally mystifying to them.

We went into a coffee bar next to the cinema. Met a young, curly-haired English producer, who was showing a rather remarkable film (after ours) at the Savoy at twelve. It was a documentary account of how a small village-full of Portuguese peasants coped with an almost overnight transition from being vassals of a feudal baron to free men, during the liberation period of the early 1970s.

Tremendous feeling of history in the making. What power to the people means. A fascinating document, with an almost Pythonic, but true, scene, where an old worker has to be persuaded to give his spade to the cooperative. He clearly doesn't understand the principle. 'If I give you my spade,' he says grimly, tightening his grip on it, 'you'll want everything else – my clothes – I'll be naked …' The peasant organiser has to explain there and then the principles of socialism at their most basic.

Terry G and I and Peter Willetts, the director, sat and watched it for over two hours. I'd hardly noticed that I'd spent over five hours in the Savoy, San Sebastian, and it was only lunchtime.

Willetts doesn't see much chance of the big companies buying his film and I can see why not. It's like Al Levinson's books – honest, straight and with plenty of detail and interest, but very little commercial angle, very little to hit an audience with and make a reader/viewer see this film as opposed to 101 others.

---

1 Hilary Sandison, responsible for overseas sales of *Jabberwocky*.

Friday, September 16th

I am still resolved to begin the novel. Today I 'firmed up' my decision by ringing Jill F and asking her to keep me up to the mark.

I reckon I will allow myself three months – up till Christmas Day – to finish the work, and by that time there should be enough to tell me whether I can do it or not. Jill reckons I should aim to complete roughly 60,000 words by the end of November – just over two months – and leave December for edits or rewrites.

Monday, September 19th

A bad week for starting novels. Typewriter isn't working properly and meetings every day for the next three days.

Today is the Shepperton board meeting. Drive down there for one o'clock. Remember that rather sickening day half a year ago when I stood, as now, in the outer room of Graham Ford's office, only to hear that *Superman* had decided to go, and there was nothing else around.

Today it was different. A picture, *Dominique*,[1] is starting a six-week shoot at the studio today and, even as I was staring at a *Jabberwocky* publicity photo of my bum pinned on the board with the words 'One of our directors at work' written in underneath, the door to Ford's office opened and three men appeared. We all shook hands and nodded and with great relief I noted that they were bringing a picture in rather than taking it out. They were the advance guard for the new Pink Panther movie.

A third picture, *Force 10 from Navarone*, is almost certainly coming in to use H Stage (as *Star Wars* did), which, since its condemnation and sale to the council, is suddenly in demand [largely for its hangar-like size].

The bad news is still from *Superman*. Some £30,000 is owed altogether, which is not so serious. What *is* serious is a £150,000 deferment which, if they don't pay, could hit us rather hard. They are being chased.

We look around the newly painted and refurbished dressing rooms and the editing room block. All look satisfactory. Good colour schemes and the rooms are inexpensively smart. But the big new heating programme (being financed by the Ramport deal) is not yet completed and today heating is off in much of the site.

1 Thriller, directed by Michael Anderson, starring Cliff Robertson and Jean Simmons.

But generally speaking an optimistic day and, walking down to the river at the end of the afternoon and looking out over the brackish pond where the Fishfinger family in *Jabberwocky* had their home, I couldn't help feeling a deep, sentimental regard for Shepperton – not the sort of feelings one usually associates with a business – more like an old school or college!

Wednesday, September 21st

Today is Redwood/Signford day. Down to the studio for one o'clock and lunch with André, Bob Salmon,[1] Anne Henshaw (who Gilliam told me on Monday had split up with Michael, though I've heard no more) and Grace Henderson. A Kiplingesque name for a Kiplingesque lady, an oriental auditor, who effortlessly bandies international financial chit-chat with a beautiful eastern smile and an intimate knowledge of the English tax system.

We eat at Mon Plaisir in Monmouth Street, an unpretentious, small, cheerful, good quality French restaurant only yards from the studio.

Waiter in mid-service recognises me from 'le moyen age' – *Jabberwocky*. He says 'Many people in Paris like what you do.' I return the compliment.

See Terry G in the evening. He is very enthusiastic about the cover design (the self-forming box) for the new 'Best Of' album, which TG wants to call *Monty Python's Instant Record Collection*. He wants material for the cover – blurb of any kind and lots of false titles for LPs, so the novel is put off for another day.

Friday, September 23rd

Squash with Terry Jones at five. Beaten again, I'm afraid. Then up to the Flask for a drink. Tell Terry J that I shall be writing the novel (hereinafter called 'the work') until Christmas. He doesn't sound disappointed. Says that it will suit him, as he has further work to do on Chaucer, now his book has found a publisher. He's just finished a translation of 'The Prologue', which TJ says he's more excited about than the book.

Off to Abbotsley tomorrow for a quick burst of countryside, then back to London and the novel on Monday. A strange feeling – not

1 André's accountant, with a share, like me, in Redwood Studios, André's company.

knowing quite what will come out. I keep wanting to start – waking up in bed and composing cracking first six lines, then controlling myself.

Will I be able to keep the diary up? Will I choke on a surfeit of writing? Will the malfunctioning, non-reversing ribbon on my typewriter cut short a promising career? Watch these spaces …

Monday, September 26th

After writing a few letters between eight and breakfast time, I started on the work at 9.30.

The omens were good. The sun was shining, God was in his heaven and all was well. Slogged through ten lines – without an idea in my head, but used an opening I had thought of a week ago. A man wakes up in a strange room, a strange bed, almost in limbo, and has to reconstruct his life from there.

Over to Shepherd's Bush for the showing of three *Ripping Yarns* to an audience. John Jarvis in a panic in his editing rooms because tomorrow's showprint of 'Olthwaite' has arrived scratched in one place. He's spent the afternoon re-dubbing 'Claw' because he felt the early lightning flashes weren't right. Such dedication.

A full house – over 300 people tonight – and a good and warm and responsive audience. I suppose that the *Radio Times* publicity and the start of the series last week has helped. All three films go well – I watch them much more easily than the last two – but 'Curse of the Claw' goes best of all and seems by all accounts a winner.

Tuesday, September 27th

As I was leaving home, a black Rover drove slowly up Oak Village. Inside was the Lord President of the Council of Great Britain – Michael Foot – and a doubtless well-meaning, but obviously harassed lady driver who was lost.[1] Foot had put down his *Guardian* and was looking around in some bewilderment. Their progress up Elaine Grove was brought to a smart halt by our neighbour Philip Clough doing a three-point turn in front of them.

Late as I was, I had to run back in and tell Helen there was a Cabinet Minister stuck in our street.

1 Not far from home. Foot lived only half a mile away up in Hampstead.

At the Beeb, watched 'Olthwaite' with Terry J, who arrived hotfoot and with a hangover. The laughter/no laughter debate began again as we were dubbing, but I tend now very strongly towards using it, so does Jimmy G. We compromised by dubbing it carefully – no words were lost, any titters or coughs were expunged and we only used it lavishly in scenes where it came lavishly.

There is an extraordinary feeling of optimism in the Beeb over the *Ripping Yarns* – despite the fact that no new ones have gone out. The top brass simply love them, and silvery-haired Mr Scott the Controller[1] came up and shook my hand and said how much he'd enjoyed 'Tomkinson' the second time.

Back home. Watch 'Olthwaite' with Robert H, Helen and the boys. All enjoy it unreservedly. I must say I felt chuffed as I watched it. It's so rich – almost too rich for telly – you have to concentrate on it hard or you miss lines, characters, beautiful shots. Whatever the press say, I feel that of all the things I've ever done, I find 'Olthwaite' and 'Claw' the most satisfying.

Friday, September 30th

At Darsham by 11.30. Am cutting back a profuse cotoneaster hedge when an 1100 eases its way into the drive before the garage, bearing Joyce Ashmore, a cousin of my father's, and holder of many of the family records.

A very capable lady with a brisk and confident well-bred manner. She has a rather heavy jaw, but seems exceedingly well and lively. She is down to earth and unsentimental about the family, but interested in and interesting about stories of the Palins.

Discover for the first time the full story of my great-grandfather, Edward Palin, who married Brita Gallagher. Evidently Brita was an orphan of the Irish potato famine of the 1840s, sent on what were called 'coffin ships' to America by some philanthropic organisation rather like those who nowadays bring war babies out of Vietnam. Brita arrived in America with only a label on her dress with her name on.

She was lucky enough to be looked after by a rich American spinster – Caroline Watson. She brought her up to be a well-dressed, well-educated young lady and in 1861 Brita and Miss Watson went to Europe.

1 Robin Scott, then Controller, BBC2.

Whilst at an hotel in Switzerland they met an English don from Oxford (Edward Palin), who was climbing in the Alps. Edward Palin describes their meeting rather touchingly in a diary he kept of his stay in Switzerland. Unfortunately Brita (or Beda, as he calls her), was only 19 and he 36 … 'otherwise I don't know what might have been'.

But he must have seen her again, for in 1867 they were married in Paris. Edward P had to give up a Fellowship at St John's, Oxford (dons weren't allowed to marry then). The college, who obviously regarded him highly, found him a living at Linton in Gloucestershire, where he spent the rest of his life with Brita, and their seven children, the eldest of whom was my grandfather.

But what rankled with Joyce Ashmore (granddaughter of Edward Palin) is that, when Caroline Watson was on the point of death at Linton, some years later, and wanted to change her will in favour of the Palins, my great-grandfather would not let the necessary lawyers make the change as he didn't want Miss Watson's last hours sullied by their attentions. So … the Palins missed being very rich!

Friday, October 7th

End of second week's writing. Seven thousand words for the week – 1,000 short of target. Have given them to Helen to read, and she has a useful and helpful reaction.

She liked the first character, Avery, who begins the novel waking in a strange bed, but found the introduction of the second Avery brother was a disappointment, just as the first one was becoming interesting. The third brother – the radio interviewer – she just didn't like.

Good advice, but goodbye 5,000 words.

Wednesday, October 12th

A letter from Al Lev to tell me in desperation of Eve's latest and most serious suicide attempt. He only just saved her. She'd locked the door and taken pills.

At work at 9.30, but spend first half of the morning writing a letter to Eve – a much tougher proposition than the novel. But start by twelve, having responded to Al's obvious plea for help.

Various phone calls during the day bring messages of good cheer. Terry Hughes rings to apprise me of 'near-ecstatic' reaction to

'Moorstones' at the Heads of Department meeting this morning. Terry Gilliam reports a fantastic reaction to *Jabberwocky* at the Cairo Film Festival. An audience of 800 gave the film a standing ovation! Once again the virtues of not understanding the story become apparent!

The Guardian didn't like 'Moorstones', but a review in the *Daily Mail* calls the series 'intelligent at the core'.

Monday, October 17th

Dr Chapman on the phone for the first time in many weeks. To say how worried he is about the content of the 'Instant Record Collection'. I grit my teeth, for it is a little late in the day for fellow Pythons to start showing interest in a record they all seemed fairly apathetic towards two months ago. I was left to put it together, and it was mastered last week.

But, as I haven't seen the Doctor for a while, I'm quite happy to go round and talk over the record with him, as requested, later this afternoon.

Graham, gin and tonic in hand, looks well scrubbed and far more normal than usual. His hair is brushed, not forward, but to the side, such as I haven't seen all the time I've known him.

GC definitely gives the impression of someone anxious to convey seriousness of purpose. The very summons itself is for business – but that crumples quickly and I am able quite easily to talk him out of most of his peripheral worries. GC just seems pleased to have a fellow Python to chat to.

His film, *The Odd Job*, has still got money problems, and the revised shoot is now February/March 1978. If GC is also going to play Brian in April/June '78, he is cutting it a bit fine. I think the prospect of this mammoth thespian effort is what is behind this latest attempt of his to find a level of non-drunken respectability and to restore a little of his natural seriousness to his affairs. I hope upon hope he succeeds, for I am fond of him – and the old Chapman warmth came through today despite his underlying anxieties.

As I left he told me that he was thinking of taking the whole of December off, to go away somewhere and prepare – maybe on his own. Just walking round the Highlands on his own. Brave words. But Keith Moon was coming round in a half-hour, and I notice that Graham now helps himself to gin from a bar-style dispenser – so I don't think all that much has changed.

Friday, October 21st

Four thousand words this week. I'm as bad as Leyland Cars in the constant failure to reach my production target.

Jim F tells me that Spear and Jackson[1] are suing the BBC for libel in the 'Eric Olthwaite' Yarn!! What's more, it sounds as though the cowardly Beeb are settling out of court.

Monday, October 24th

A letter from Eve Levinson. Evidently my spontaneous response to the news of her suicide attempt had contained the right things – and she touchingly said that I had said things that other, closer friends of hers found themselves 'unable to say'. I'm glad the strength of my feelings worked, expressed as rudely as they were.

Arrived at Shepperton at 9.25 for a 9.30 Annual General Meeting in the wonderful, mirror-panelled boardroom of the Old House.

I was re-elected, Clive signed various bits of paper, and we talked for a while about Shepperton and memories of the men associated with the place – especially, of course, Alexander Korda. This is the 43rd Annual General Meeting, so the place must have been going since at least 1933.

Much talk over catering. At last this has become the main problem we have to face, and Paul Olliver, the tubby troubleshooter from Vavasseur, who has been given the job of investigating the frightfulness of the catering arrangements, has now expressed a wish to run them himself!

Paul Olliver and I are booked to visit Pinewood for lunch and a look around, as I have often felt that we should know more about the opposition.

We are not offered lunch – it now being 1.30 – and are taken round by a late-middle-aged gent, who personifies all that is wrong with Pinewood. He's getting on, is rather shabby, and yet talks to us from Olympian heights about Pinewood being the greatest studio in the world, blah, blah, blah.

Pinewood seems to have set its face into the past, favouring the

1 A Sheffield firm which made, among other things, shovels. My reference to Eric Olthwaite's 'Spear and Jackson No. 3 with a reinforced brass handle' was meant fondly, but clearly not taken that way by the manufacturer.

traditional and the conventional. It remains Britain's biggest studio, but not its brightest. Shepperton, with its mix of commercials, pop group influence and movies, feels much more fresh, alive and relevant to the '70s.

Tuesday, October 25th

Mostly business, and have no time to write any of the novel. Instead, spend an hour reading what I have so far. It's patchy. Some sections I am pleased with, but at the moment it's like an inconsistent car engine – good in some gears, jerky in others and not, as yet, getting me anywhere.

Up to Elstree by 12.30 for the second visit to our Shepperton competitors in two days. John Skinner, our contact, is much less concerned than the Pinewood mogul with trying to pretend that everything in the garden is lovely. A realist, not a bullshitter.

Elstree, of all the major studios, was the one which committed itself most of all to TV series in the '50s and '60s. Now the only TV series made in this four-wall studio is *The Saint*, and at the moment it's empty of movies – though waiting for the prestigious new Stanley Kubrick – *The Shining* – to come in.

It's part of the magical nature of film studios that you should have such wonderful incongruities, like the front of the hotel which will be used for *The Shining*, rearing up sixty feet or so, but only a couple of hundred yards from Elstree High Street. *Moby Dick* was filmed 200 yards from the Elstree branch of Woolworths!

Drive back in the sunshine past the huge bulk of the old MGM Borehamwood Studios – chief victim of the '70s slump, now a cold-storage firm.

Wednesday, October 26th

Terry J rang about 'Curse of the Claw', last of the series. Good reactions from him and those who saw it with him. But I had to tell him that I wasn't feeling too excited about the general reaction. I think Clive James was not far wrong when he said the series 'half worked'. In defence, I'd say that it was a pioneer in many ways, and suffered from being formularised or categorised. It was a series, and yet not a series, comedy and yet not comedy.

TJ thinks that it was difficult for people to get their teeth into – there was no continuity to each show apart from opening titles and my own presence, in many different disguises. TJ also felt that I had wasted myself by playing too many dull, central roles.

Sunday, October 30th

I leave home with T Gilliam, Maggie and Amy [TG's daughter] to go down to lunch at Terry Jones' before going on to play charity football at Dulwich Hamlet. At lunch Allen Tinkley and wife Diana – who had put on Python in New York. Allen is interested in the new Python movie and has money available from Blake Edwards – whose wife Julie Andrews is, believe it or not a Python freak (she wanted us to co-star with her at the Palladium earlier this year!).

Our team is quite impressive. Peter Purves, of *Blue Peter*, is in goal and myself, Terry J, Terry G, John Cleese and Graham Chapman – who, as a new variation to his silly behaviour, actually got changed this time, but was substituted as soon as he came out, being carried off on a stretcher before the ball was kicked.

Home by seven. In my work-room this evening must reluctantly write '0' against words target for this last week.

Tuesday, November 1st

Nearly 2,000 words on the typewriter. At ten to four we have a three-hour power-cut. Willy brings me up a candle and I carry on writing in very Dickensian spirit. The children all love the blackout and there are groans of disappointment when the lights come on again.

Saturday, November 12th, Oxford

A letter from Eve Levinson. She's home and much on the mend, but now a cloud approaches. Some of the admin of her school are trying to take her job away – presumably people who try and kill themselves are unreliable. This sounds hard – but Eve does discuss the possibilities of life without the job. I think she only teaches now for the money.

Helen's mother rings to say that in last night's wild winds one of the trees in the garden was uprooted. H decides to take the children up to Abbotsley for the day to see the devastation and help her mother clear up. I stay here to prepare a chat for Brasenose tonight.

I leave for Oxford at four, having read my novel and done one hour's prep on the talk. A very wild sky – some sunshine and blue patches, blotted out by a huge jet-black cloud. Rain, high wind. But it passes over me and by the time I reach Oxford it's damp, cold and blustery, but the force of the storm has lessened.

To BNC[1] at seven. Am met by at least six rather nervous members of the 'Events Committee' in the lodge. Am taken to a room in the Principal's lodgings for sherry, and meet four other members of the committee – two women, for Brasenose is now co-ed. Sherry is drunk, but the undergraduates don't talk amongst themselves – they sit, awkwardly, and wait for me to speak.

It is a peculiar feeling to know that you are an impressive, important, well-known figure – when inside you are probably as nervous as all the faces turned towards you. A funny little unnecessary barrier exists now – which wouldn't be there if I hadn't done Python. I try to muck in and defuse the reverence as quickly as possible. Only then will I feel less of a fraud.

The JCR at Brasenose is absolutely packed, which is rather flattering. They say they've never seen as many people. Try to think back to the very few occasions in my own time when I went to hear a visiting celebrity. I remember the Union bursting at the seams for James Baldwin, but that's about all. They are literally all around me – and it makes for a good atmosphere.

In fact the whole talk works like good cabaret. They're warm and generous with laughter (especially when I read 'Fegg' extracts and mention the Goodies) and I must confess that all my latent theatricality was released and I milked them rotten. Talked and answered questions for nearly two hours – until it got too hot – then signed autographs and was treated to drinks down in the Buttery.

Sunday, November 13th

Today, helped no doubt by the hard, bright freshness of a cool, sunny November morning, I have a feeling of completeness. The world makes sense this Sunday morning. Even the weather seems to be resting, peaceful and mellowed after the angry squalls of the last two days.

There's a smell of beef and Yorkshire pudding and from where I

1 Brasenose College, my alma mater 1962–5.

write I can see the chimney letting out wisps of smoke from the fire in the sitting room.

Yesterday I read through the novel so far and was greatly heartened. I saw much that worked and I also saw clearly what didn't work. I can see the way ahead and I can't wait to get going again tomorrow.

I just feel very happy and very content at this moment. Nothing is expected of me today except to be here at home. I am perfectly well aware that around the borders of my life are problems, difficulties, painful decisions, even human tragedies demanding my involvement. I know I cannot live in a continual vacuum of happiness – but a day like today restores energies, tops up batteries, rebuilds whatever faith one has.

Today there is nothing more I want than what I have.

Monday, November 14th

T Gilliam rang with the offer of a ticket to Bertolucci's *1900*. It's an all-day job, lasting over four hours with lunch in between.

In the foyer of the NFT I see a sprinkling of critics, including Dilys Powell and John Coleman of the *New Statesman*, who gives me a cheery greeting. In the gents someone of familiar face introduces himself – it's Jonathan Pryce, whom I last met in a playground in North Kensington, where he was filming for Stephen Frears. A nice, rather gentle man, about our age. All three of us (he and I and TG) walk over to the Old Vic for lunch.

Down in the basement they have a thriving little serve-yourself restaurant with lovingly home-made pies, treacle tarts, salads and a fine selection of white wines. A mixture of folk, too – at one table a clutch of Britain's top actors – Dorothy Tutin, Derek Jacobi, Alec McCowen, all presumably rehearsing at the National – at the end of our table a couple of businessmen.

Back to the NFT for Part II of *1900*, which lasts from 2.30 until just after 4.30. As always with Bertolucci, the images in the film are clear, cool, sharp and confident – the pictures absolutely breathtakingly beautiful. But that aside, and taking into account some perfectly shot, written and acted moments, I found the whole one big soap opera – complete with unremittingly villainous villains and unremittingly decent good guys (the peasants).

I felt it was a commercial film – despite its four-hour length. Why else import Burt Lancaster, Sterling Hayden and Robert De Niro into an otherwise convincing north Italian village, filled with real Italian peasants, and dub on a soundtrack that turns it into *Peyton Place*?

Tuesday, November 15th

Up at eight. Work on Shepperton papers in preparation for a meeting with Clive at lunch. Long chat with Graham Ford on the phone – all well, except when I mention my idea of asking Barry Norman's *Film '77* bunch if they want to do 'A Day in the Life of a British Studio' (i.e. Shepperton).

Ford doesn't like Barry Norman, for the same reasons, I think, that Peter Noble doesn't – they find him too critical of the industry. I think this is his greatest quality – and a vital antidote to the 'everything in the garden's lovely' attitude of Noble. But he conceded that it is a good idea, but maybe next March when we're all smart and the new signs are up.

He completely missed my point that when we need them is now – so that we don't have to pull any wool over anyone's eyes. We have a full and thriving studio, which is good, but we also have the problems of a studio trying to heave itself out of a depression which was, four years ago, almost fatal. This is the first time I've felt seriously at odds with the competent G Ford. I was disappointed at his lack of imagination.

Wednesday, November 16th

The weather has settled down, after the frantic activity of the last week it's raw, cold and dry. The gales seem to have blown themselves out.

There's been a flurry of activity this week from Jimmy, Jim Franklin and others to try and 'firm up' *Ripping Yarns* or 'Palins', as Jimmy insists on calling them and, after their offers today, the nearest thing I have to a future now looks like stretching until the end of 1979 at least.

Friday, November 18th

My hopes of going into writing retreat at Charney Manor – beautiful house, Quaker-run, therefore lots of peace – are dashed. It's full.[1] After much phoning, end up at the Bell Inn, Charlbury.

1 With everything else to do, I'd fallen so far behind with the novel, that escaping London seemed the only way to finish it.

A two-hour Shepperton board meeting. I suggest that *Film '77* be approached. Clive *very* enthusiastic and the board authorises me to get in touch.

Saturday, November 19th

Fine, fresh, very cold day for William's seventh birthday. Tremendously excited (both Willy and Tom). William is up from a quarter to seven until midday before he even realises he's only got pyjamas on.

At two I drive up to Hampstead to open the Red Cross Bazaar (in lieu of Terry J, who's in Tunisia). A crowd (small) of mostly old ladies, who wouldn't know me from Adam, huddle against the cold, outside the locked door. 'Let us in,' they beseech me. But the Red Cross won't open their doors until two, so the queue shivers. It's all rather pitiful.

I give a short opening exhortation, then everyone gets stuck in at the bargains. At a quarter to three I run an auction, and by three I'm out – profusely thanked and presented with a gun (toy) to take to William for his birthday. I can hardly say 'a gift from the Red Cross' as I give him this device for blowing people's heads off.

Willy's birthday party is more an exercise in crowd control – nine highly excited nippers, apart from Willy, storm the house and hold us besieged for two hours. William very cleverly avoids most of the shindig – and tucks himself away upstairs to lay out his pressies.

As quickly as they have come, they're gone. The hurricane has passed through and Helen and I slowly pick up the pieces.

Sunday, November 20th

Chop wood for the fire and clear up in preparation for lunch party. Ron Devillier, of Dallas, Texas, the man who finally got Monty Python onto American TV, is in town, got in touch, and I've invited him for lunch with Mary, Ed and Catherine.

Ron is now the buyer for the entire PBS network and is based in Washington. Big, bearlike, bearded, with a wide, generous, easily smiling face, Ron is immensely and immediately likeable. Though he does wield power and influence, he still comes across as an almost boyish enthusiast.

Over lunch he tells the true story of Python in the US. In 1972 Ron was in New York. 'It was raining, and I had nothing to do,' was how he started the tale. So Ron rang Wyn Godley of Time-Life Sales and asked if there was anything at all left for Ron to view. Wyn looked at his lists and said there was a BBC comedy show called Monty Python, but everyone who'd seen it had rejected it. Ron was a little intrigued, and it was a filthy day, so he went over to see it.

It was Monty Python's 'Montreux' episode. Ron liked it. Took a copy back to Dallas, looked again and rang Wyn back to ask if there were any more. Wyn returned to the files and found that there were thirteen tapes available. 'Send 'em all,' asked Ron, at which Time-Life nearly fell off their seats. But thirteen tapes were duly despatched to Ron's station in Dallas.

One day, coming in to the office at six, Ron sat down and viewed all the tapes, finishing at seven that evening. Ron fell in love with them. His only problem then, he said, was to avoid racing to the phone or in 'any way letting Time-Life know that I thought they were the greatest things I'd ever seen'.

In the end he controlled his enthusiasm, but still found Time-Life asking $500 each for the right to two showings of each programme. Ron, alone, consulting nobody, wrote out the $6,500 cheque one evening. That was his act of faith – for $6,500 is a great deal to a small station.

But the fairytale ending is that the shows were such an immediate success in Dallas that, on the first night an uncut Python show was aired in the US,. Ron received more pledges of money to the station than the $6,500 he'd paid for the entire series.

New York got wind of this success and for once the smart East Coast found itself having to follow Texas, but NY paid $2,000 per show. The rest, as they say, is history. One hundred and forty-two stations since bought Python, and Ron is in no doubt that it revolutionised American TV thinking.

Last week Ron saw three of the *Ripping Yarns* ('Olthwaite', 'Tomkinson' and 'Stalag') and says he is quite sure they will go in the States. After our Sunday lunch we walk up Parliament Hill and down to Highgate Ponds and Ron asks how the *Ripping Yarns* are financed and whether or not there is any way in which PBS can invest in them at this stage.

Usually these negotiations are conducted through dozens of inter-mediaries – Time-Life, BBC Enterprises, etc – and this is why it's such a breakthrough to talk directly to Ron – the buyer – and it must be the first time such a deal has been discussed directly between American finance and the creator of the programmes. So who knows, it may turn out to have been a very profitable walk on the Heath!

Monday, November 21st, Charlbury

Arrive at 3.15. The hotel is unpretentious. My room is spacious, with a low ceiling and two exposed beams – original, I expect, and that means 1700, when the Bell was built. The wallpaper is bright and tasteful – of the pastoral variety. There are two brass bedsteads and a fine bay over-looking the main street. The table is of the right height and reasonably solid, so I set my typewriter up in the bay. By the time I'm ready to write, it's getting dark. A quarter to four, the worst time to begin. It's hard to concentrate, to shut out all the new sensations of this place, but I persevere, hoping I'm not disturbing anyone with my tapping, and by half past six have added 1,000 words to the morning's total.

Take a walk around Charlbury – deserted and bitterly cold. My ears ache in the wind. Glad to get back to the warm, cosy hotel. Ring home. Have a Glenmorangie in the bar and a good meal of haddock in a pastie and pheasant and cheese.

The ambience of the hotel is restful, pleasant and unhurried.

Asleep by 11.30.

Tuesday, November 22nd, Charlbury

Up a little after eight o'clock. A thoroughly refreshing eight hour kip behind me. Pull back the heavy salmon-pink curtains in my little bay and am confronted with clear blue skies and a sun shining brightly on the grey stone cottages across the street.

Bath and breakfast (the breakfast menu is dangerously appetising, and bigger than the dinner menu in the evening). Choose smoked haddock and half a grapefruit. Then a short walk down by the church and back to the Bell to begin work.

Start slowly – still the unfamiliar distractions, which I hope I will get used to – cleaning ladies talking noisily just outside the door, the bus which stops almost outside my window – the everyday life of Charlbury. But I don't think I would have found a place with much *less* everyday life, and the hotel grows more congenial every extra hour I spend here. Coffee is brought to me, unbidden, at eleven.

I drive into Burford for an hour's lunch break. Go to a quiet

Wadworths pub, where I am recognised and get a free half of bitter in exchange for some signatures.

Back to the Bell. Put my typewriter down, as it were, at 6.30. A thoroughly satisfactory eight-hour writing day. Four thousand words completed (half a normal week's target in one day). Greatly enthused, I take a walk in the bleak and chilly darkness down to the bridge to look at the Evenlode.

Thursday, November 24th, Charlbury

Discovery, at lunchtime, of the thatched village of Great Tew, tucked away in the steep fold of a valley, about ten miles north of here. Complete with tiny, mullioned-windowed village pub, the Falkland Arms. A front room, with a roaring fire. A crusty old gent, a real relic of the past, held forth, and in the middle of all this – as if I hadn't had a surfeit of images of traditional English life – it began to snow.

An icy cold afternoon, though, which made my warm bay window vantage point in the Bell all the more attractive. It must have soothed my mind into a productive state, for today I became deeply absorbed in a confrontation of Avery with Annie and Sarah – really absorbed – and I finished just before seven with 5,000 words done – 15,000 since I have been at the hotel.

Friday, November 25th, Charlbury

I lunched in the bar of the Bell for the first time – an agreeable stone-flagged floor, beams and a big open fireplace. It pleased me to think that nearly a third (for that is the extent of my achievement this week) of the book was written directly above this room.

Wednesday, November 30th

Just after three o'clock, the novel comes quietly to a halt. It's finished and quite acceptably so.

I christen the book 'A Bit of a Break', but I don't know if that will stick.

Thursday, December 1st

Began reading the novel through a little before ten and finished at a quarter to seven in the evening. I reckon about eight hours' solid reading. I made notes – generally about passages which were too dense, complicated or repetitive. What the book needs, basically, is clarification. The beginning is quite jolly, the middle is soggy and tends to lose its way, and the end moves fast to quite a neat conclusion.

Friday, December 2nd

Finished the novel just in time, for this morning we have the first meeting of the Pythons to begin the lead-up to the movie which starts, all being well, in April.

John Goldstone addresses us first. John, now firmly established as producer of the next movie, wishes us to help him out in raising the loot. So far the four million dollars has not been forthcoming. John virtually rules out private investors, and Michael White says there is no way he can lay his hands on the money we require – about eight times as much as we were asking for on the *Holy Grail*. So we are looking for a friendly American major to finance the film and take distribution, etc, etc.

John G says Warner's have all read it and loved it (which I can't believe), but a bit of Python flag waving would not go amiss. To this end he suggests an interview with *Variety*, *Hollywood Reporter* and other magazines which land softly on air-conditioned office desks in Burbank.

Eric is appalled by the idea. (I'll grant Eric that – his attitude to the press is one of the few that has remained consistent over the last five years!) He suggests putting an ad in *Variety* aimed at showing American producers what an extraordinary world-wide force Python is. John suggests a byline – 'You were late for World War One, late for World War Two … Don't be late for …'

The next leading question is where we should rewrite in January. For Eric and John, writing in England is out of the question. John likes to edge all his comments with a geriatric appeal – 'I don't know about you others, but I'm nearly 40 and I need more … (money, sunshine, sleep, reading, etc, etc)'.

Eric suggests Barbados – which sounds lovely – but both the Terrys look miserable. Graham, as usual, says nothing. I question whether we would actually do any work in Barbados. It's a long way to go to do a little. This consideration doesn't seem to weigh heavily on John or Eric, nor does Terry's appeal for more time at home – 'Bring the family,' orders Eric, and Terry rather meekly accepts. It was decided in JC and EI's favour, as you might expect.

We then went on to order a bollocking for Methuen for their pusillanimous handling of *Monty Python and the Holy Grail* (book), but the cover of the *Instant Record Collection* was greatly approved of. Thank you, Terry Gilliam (though I don't think anyone got around to saying that).

The *Penguin Dictionary of Modern Quotations* have been on to us – they would like to include some Python lines in their new edition. This iconolatry is greeted with such suggestions as 'That is my theory and what it is too', 'What's ten quid to the bloody Midland Bank', and 'His hobbies are strangling animals, golf and masturbating'.

Wednesday, December 7th, Sheffield

To Gospel Oak School at 2.30 for William's Christmas Concert. This year he's a Roman centurion. Less lively and spontaneous than shows in the past – the heavy hand of religion?

To St Pancras and the Sheffield train. Meet up with Terry J – we're off to spend an evening at the Crucible Studio, where David Leland's Season of New Plays is in its last week. Sit on the spindly plastic seats in the buffet car, which would appear to be deliberately designed to stop people idling their time away in the buffet for reasons of comfort. But, warming ourselves with scotches, TJ and I manage to last the whole two and a half hour journey on these nasty little things.

Chat about Python. TJ is fond of pointing out that we have all become harder, tougher individuals as a result of Python – though I think he regrets the loss of the team spirit. He thinks he's softened. He no longer holds views – or perhaps he no longer propagates views – with the same intensity. He's determined to play the film easily.

See two plays. The second, an Irish play called *Says I, Says He*, by one Ron Hutchinson, excellently performed. I am very receptive to a bit of the Irish – the prose is full, flowery and flowing and the language constantly rich. Makes English seem very dry. It's about gunmen in the end, of course. The wastefulness of the Irish is utterly depressing. At least they go down talking well.

After the plays, a kebab and retsina and several jugs of red wine with David and a director from the Royal Court called Stuart Burge, and a lady from a theatre in Amsterdam which specialises in putting on new foreign plays. NB – where is somewhere like that in London?

Thursday, December 8th

Back to London on the Master Cutler – 7.20 from the Midland station. Meet Stuart Burge and friend and join them at breakfast.

He is late fifties, of the old establishment who were once angry young men. Tells a good story of how he brought over a young Greenwich Village folk singer for a BBC TV play many years ago. The guy was obviously high when it came to the read-through at some North Acton boys' club – though at that time people didn't really understand non-alcoholic highs. Anyway, the folk singer was Bob Dylan and he sang 'Blowing in the Wind' in this BBC play, for probably the first time ever outside of the Village. The BBC have since destroyed this momentous tape.

This evening to Gospel Oak again for Tom's concert. A very loose adaptation of 'Cinderella', complete with skateboard sequence. Tom amazed me with the supreme confidence of his performances – whether in the chorus singing 'Consider Yourself' with real enjoyment and wholehearted participation, or giving a very passable impression of Elvis in a pop group, or his tour de force – a rather arch version of 'You Are My Sunshine' – he was certainly not the retiring Tom I expected to see.

Afterwards so many people came up – sharing my astonishment, but saying how good he was – that I felt very proud, and happy for Tom, too. He likes acting, he says now. If he ever does tread the boards, I think his career will date from December 8th 1977!

Friday, December 9th

Sunny, but still very cold. The novel lies at one end of the desk, untouched. A piece of good news – Redwood has won two awards at the *Campaign Magazine* Radio Commercials do last night. Only Molinaire, among London studios, took more awards. André deservedly chuffed. It sets a very effective seal on a first year's operation that's not even finished yet.

Thursday, December 15th

Drive down to Clerkenwell Green to talk with Chris Orr over future Orr/Signford plans. Clerkenwell Green is a rather attractive little backwater, as is much of the area around St Bart's Hospital and Smithfield Market – many old buildings remain and comprehensive redevelopment further east and north and the office block building boom which transformed the Liverpool Street area, have left the Green relatively untouched. In one of these graceful old terraced houses Chris Orr has his lithographic printing press – he does his engraving work down at Wapping.

One thing I'm beginning to learn from Chris is the complicated technical side of his work. The materials he works with – inks, plates, acids, zinc and special Bavarian stone tablets for the lithographic reproduction – are complex and make the process of a Chris Orr picture as involving as the picture itself.

Before I left I tried to hint that the Chris Orr I liked should be brought clear of the self-appreciative, incestuous world of the art galleries, and tried against stiffer opposition in the bookshops. Also mentioned my feeling that he should consider an animated film sometime. But although he thoroughly agreed, I felt as I said goodbye and walked down the short flight of steps into Clerkenwell Close and along towards the Wren church next door, that I was saying goodbye to Moley – someone who didn't really want the big wide world to disturb him. And I felt sympathetic towards him and worried that I had been talking like a Light Entertainment department.

We all assemble at Eric's house in Carlton Hill to look at tapes of various ladies we're considering for the Judith part.

The Judy Loe extract – the cabin scene from 'Curse of the Claw' – goes down well, John falling about especially loudly, which was gratifying. Gilda Radner from *Saturday Night Live* is seen, but an American Jewish Judith doesn't seem to attract a great deal of support. Penny Wilton's *Norman Conquests* performance goes down well, but Kika Markham is given short shrift by the Cambridge lads, who rule out her Workers Revolutionary Party involvement as being too frightful to work with.[1]

The final list is Judy Loe, Penelope Wilton, Maureen Lipman, Diana

1 Recently founded Trotskyite group led by Gerry Healey. Corin and Vanessa Redgrave were loyal supporters and attracted other actors to the cause. Kika later married Corin Redgrave.

Quick and Gwen Taylor – and we decide to arrange a read-through with them all as soon as possible.

Saw a glimpse of *All You Need is Cash*. It was impressive – well paced and well shot and with some very funny performances by such as Neil Innes. John needed persuading that Neil could act. The rest of us are unanimously pro-Neil for the film, but there are quite strong differences of opinion as to who and how many we need for the supporting repertory cast in Tunisia. Good company is considered by all to be a major requirement, and some of the names bandied are Roger McGough, Ken Colley and Terry Bayler (from *All You Need is Cash*).

All in all the group seems very charitable and well disposed this afternoon – except to WRP members. We break around five. Eric to return to Barbados, where we shall join him on January 7th.

Friday, December 16th

The days become slighter and slighter as Christmas nears. The cold weather has been replaced by mild, grey, greasy weather, which makes the city feel like a used handkerchief. I finally complete the prolonged job of editing the newly typed *Yarns* and take them in to Geoffrey [Strachan].

Then back up to Hampstead for a squash game with TJ. On the way up to the Flask for a drink afterwards I buy the *Melody Maker*, which contains something of a landmark in Python history – the most comprehensive, overt piece of mud-slinging yet seen in public from one of the group.

Under the heading 'Siphon the Python' is a rambling tirade from a 'tired and emotional' G Chapman. Wild, angry and drunk, Graham at last says what he feels about the *Ripping Yarns* and the various Pythons. I think it's a sad comment on our collective relationship when we can tell the papers things we haven't dared tell each other. I must admit, though, I laughed greatly when I read it – at GC's drunken audacity, which makes for brighter reading matter than most of our interviews, and just goes to show what weird and wonderful rubbish sells papers.

Gilliam, needless to say, was on the phone within hours of publication of the interview. He was jolly, but not pleased.

Oh, well, GC once again spices our life up – it's a pity he had to spice it up with such misanthropic stuff.

Saturday, December 17th

Christmas starts here – well, this weekend, anyway – with two traditional entertainments: the Robert Hewison Saturday mulled-wine party (or how many guests can he fit into 82 Fetter Lane this year?) and the BBC LE party, with its history of tortured heart-searchings as to whether to go or not to go.

Robert's do is pleasant. Chat with his editor at Weidenfeld[1] – a young, attractive lady to whom I am ridiculously coy about my novel. I should either not mention it at all, or be prepared to brag a little about it.

Simon arrives back with the boys, whom he has just taken, as a Christmas present, to see the Circus World Championships at Clapham Common. Then T Gilliam arrives – the irritation of Chapman's insults mollified a little by reported good business and reviews for *Jabberwocky* in West Germany this last week, a place in Alexander Walker's best films of the year round-up, and an award from *Films and Filming* for being the Best British Film of 1977.

Sunday, December 18th

To the BBC party in the evening.

The usual lot. Val Doonican and Eric Sykes seem to be still fans – Doonican is especially enthusiastic and towards the end of the evening even Eric Morecambe grasps my hand warmly – 'Great fan,' he says … 'Great fan.'

Talk to Richard Beckinsale and Judy Loe, who, with me, Ian Davidson and the Goodies, seem to represent the 'younger generation' in a sea of old and well-established faces.

Aubrey Singer, recently transferred to Head of BBC Radio, warns me against a precipitous sale to PBS in the States – 'The big networks *do* pay a great deal more,' he cautioned. Does he know nothing of Python's struggle against the eunuchs?

1 Robert's book *Under Siege, Literary Life in London* 1939–1945 had been published earlier in the year. Harold Pinter called it 'a vivid, highly readable, important book'.

Tuesday, December 20th

To BAFTA's luxurious preview theatre in Piccadilly at 10.30 for a screening of the latest Mark Shivas/Richard Broke TV film, an adaptation by John Prebble of *The Three Hostages* by John Buchan.

Whereas Scott Fitzgerald's adult view of the 1920s survives, Buchan's eternal school prefects don't. The sheer mechanics of this dastardly plot, with Hannay being constantly hypnotised and men in turbans flashing orientally sinister looks, make it very, very hard for an audience to take seriously. Afterwards Shivas, looking moderately happy, did confess that there were 'a few more laughs than I'd expected'.

Ended up drinking with Malcolm McDowell. We talked about the state of British films. McDowell dislikes the Lew Grade blockbusters that are taking over the industry and feels that there aren't any films any more which are trying to say anything. He uses Lindsay Anderson's *O Lucky Man!* as an example of a film which tried to criticise and stir up a few passions, but which was crucified by the critics. A serious chap. I like his restlessness, though. He is well-established, but anti-establishment. A useful combination.

To John Goldstone's party in D'Arblay Street. There meet Graham, whom I roundly and cheerfully take to task over the *Melody Maker* article. GC retreats in disarray, blaming the press for quoting 'only the bad bits'.

Sandy Lieberson is there – he tells me he's nominated me for the Best Newcomer Award at BAFTA!

Wednesday, December 21st

Took Thomas, William and Holly over to Shepperton. We watched them building and rigging *Force 10 from Navarone*. Twenty-two years after my heart swelled to the 'Dambusters' March', they're still building Lancaster bombers at Shepperton!

The sun came out as we wandered through the crumbling *Oliver* set and nosed around on the back lot, where odd pieces of filmic flotsam and jetsam lay about – giant rubber mushrooms and a ten-foot-high birthday cake complete with icing.

Read through the film script this evening in preparation for the Judith auditions. Embarrassed at how slight a part it is.

Thursday, December 22nd

The auditions were pleasant, easy and pre-Christmassy. Maureen Lipman, surprisingly, seemed to find it hard to become a character, but she's nice and fun and probably would, with work, have been right. Then Diana Quick, exuding confidence, swept the place with a devastatingly assertive, aggressive reading of Judith, which confirmed Terry J's suspicion that Diana, just being Diana, was the sort of character Judith should be. Judy Loe was not as forceful, and a little pantomimey.

As John C put it afterwards, he rated both Judy and Maureen as lovely, easy, friendly people whom we'd obviously have no trouble in fitting in with, and vice versa, but Diana Quick clearly gave Judith a new dimension of aggression and single-mindedness, which brought the limpid part to life. So Quick will be asked to do Judith. If she does it, she and I will be renewing a working relationship that started at the Oxford Revue of '65.

Thursday, December 29th

Despite the long holiday period, dubbed 'The Twelve Days Off Christmas' in the *Evening Standard* of a couple of days ago, I'm at work today, quite gratefully, going through the text of the *Ripping Yarns* with Geoffrey down at Methuen.

Home and Helen says to me, rather gravely, 'Well … Graham Chapman …' My first instinct is to ask if he's dead, but he's not, of course, although he is in hospital, having collapsed at home after four days off the bottle altogether. He rings me later, and sounds small, weak and very old. He confirmed the story that he had been trying to give up – had three days of withdrawal symptoms, seemed to be coping when suddenly today he collapsed. He added that it was remorse for the nasty things he's been quoted as saying in newspaper reviews recently about all the rest of us – but particularly about John C in yesterday's *Daily Mirror* – that shocked him into giving up.

'… I tell you one thing, Mikey, I'm never going to drink strong drink again' (and he sounded as if he meant it).

Saturday, December 31st

Late morning start on a trip with Helen, Rachel and all to the Science Museum, where there is a space exhibition. A chance to see the actual

Apollo 10 capsule – its base charred and huge chunks burnt out of it during re-entry.

How long ago all the space missions seem now. The special thermal clothing and the poo-poo disposal bags worn by the astronauts don't look a lot different from Elizabeth I's underwear in their solemn display cases.

As the days go by I grow more and more proud of myself in actually completing the novel – as well as three TV films and a Python film script this past year. But the pressure has been there. I feel it now in bursts of tension when I find it very, very hard to relax. It's not so much the work itself, but the fact that, as each year goes by, I find myself becoming a more powerful figure – a lot more people depend on me than just the wife and kids.

1978

Sunday, January 1st

John rings. He's been away in the country for the weekend. Has just returned to find a message that Graham has had a nervous breakdown. John admits that at first he saw it as just another Chapman wheeze to avoid the stick which would inevitably fly in Barbados over his newspaper interviews. Not far off the truth, John.

Tuesday, January 3rd

In the afternoon I took Willy to see the latest James Bond movie – *The Spy Who Loved Me*. I thought it most unpleasant. No attempt was made in the imbecile script to create any characters, it was wooden puppets saying wooden lines. The action sequences, of course, were brilliant, but then we all know Britain leads the world in aimless explosions. Otherwise I think it's the sort of mindless garbage Britain has no reason to be proud of. The American-inspired and scripted *Star Wars* was a far, far better adventure.

But I enjoyed being out with William. He's good fun. They all are. And they are at the stage when they respond with an infectious over-enthusiasm to everything new. Willy is absolutely *dying* to go to America. He says he wants to live there now.

Dropped in to see Graham in Southwood Lane. He came out of hospital yesterday and is not supposed to drink ever again. He looked sallow and tense. It's going to be a great struggle for him. Barry Cryer was there too. We sat and sipped tea and Barry and I joked rather forcibly. It seemed the only thing to do at the time.

If the next few entries sound a little different in tone – a little forced, a little self-conscious – it's probably because they were deliberately written for publication. As a way of garnering material for the book of the Life of Brian, *it was agreed that all of us would keep a daily diary of our time in Barbados. The six different accounts of the same working holiday would then be interestingly compared and contrasted. In the end, however, only Terry Jones and myself (both diarists already) played the game.*

Saturday, January 7th, Barbados

On the flight out, a sensational game of Scrabble with Dr Chapman.

Graham, after some deliberation, led off with the word 'fep'. I didn't challenge it immediately, thinking either that it was possibly the prelude to a longer word – feppicle, fepid, fepidicular – or perhaps a medical term which it would betray appalling ignorance to challenge. But it was Graham who looked most puzzled by it and after a while replaced the 'p' with a 'w'.

The game then surged on by 'ys' and 'ands' until Graham selflessly dropped his letters. All were retrieved, apart from the 'z', which is wedged for eternity between the seats of the upstairs lounge of a jumbo jet. Stewards and stewardesses with torches and screwdrivers tried to help out, and to anyone who came up the stairs for a quiet read and saw a large group of people clustered on the floor around a seat which had been entirely removed from its base, we smiled and assured them we were just playing Scrabble.

We reached Barbados an hour before sunset – a little after half past five their time. Drove along lanes with sugar cane plantations on either side and neat, white signposts with names on long arms.

Our way wound up the west coast of the island and from Bridgetown north it was a dense collection of hotels, shops, clubs, some discreetly set away behind shrubberies and palm groves.

Down one such turning is Heron Bay, built by Sir Ronald Tree. Our first sight of our home for the next two weeks is a sensational surprise. Its scale is breathtaking – wrought iron gates, marble floors, piano nobiles – the full Palladian bit. All built in 1947.

Through the hall, a table is set for dinner beneath an enormous hanging lantern. Mighty columns thirty feet high rise above us and balustraded staircases lead up to the piano nobile. On either side of the main house run two colonnades, off which are our bedrooms. All furnished and decorated tastefully and individually. In the centre of the courtyard are three huge spreading trees which cover the whole area in lush greenery.

John spreads himself across a huge, soft, cushion-filled sofa and declares 'This is what my whole life has been leading up to.'

We are greeted by servants, one an old, leathery-faced Barbadian who is introduced to us as 'Brown', but the two Terrys prefer to call him 'Mr' Brown, which is probably a terrible insult.

Churchill has stayed here and there's a photo of Eden and signed photos of impressive looking men in medals and uniforms. Perhaps a Richard Avedon photo of the five nude Pythons would look a little out of place among such company.

Whilst John, Eric, Terry J and myself are lying disbelievingly amongst fine things and wondering whether to set up a preparatory school here (John wants to be maths master), Terry Gilliam (whom we have designated as sports master) is eating the local apples. They're very small, they fall with sharp little whacks from the spreading trees in the courtyard, and they are, we've just been warned, poisonous.

Whether Terry will snuff it before the night's out, we're not sure, but arrangements have been made for the redistribution of his fees for the film, and anyway it's probably God's way of punishing him for having forgotten to bring his script.

Terry J and I bathe. It's very dark and there are warnings of sea urchins. Terry is very worried about the sea and thinks big fish will eat him or perhaps even a lot of little ones will gang up.

He's brought *Wild Wales* with him to read. It's difficult to believe in Llangollen and Aberdovey when you're in a place like this.

Dinner is held up for a few minutes as we await the arrival of the guests for the evening, Mr Jagger and friend and his friend Mr Rudge and his wife. When they arrive we descend elegantly to the table – also designed to match the local limestone material from which the house is built. I don't think I've ever had my dinner off a table made entirely of limestone.

A jolly evening developed – the epically proportioned piano nobile (you couldn't really call it a sitting room) was soon filled with a rather rude game of charades. Mick's graphic mime of the Sex Pistols will stay in the memory particularly.

I think dawn would have been breaking in England when we finally separated to our various tasteful bedrooms.

And Gilliam was still not dead.

Sunday, January 8th, Barbados

The sea and the beach are so clean here – and at half past seven everything shines with a sparkling brightness as if it was the first day after the Creation. I walk up the beach. Meet a man who has a four-month-old pet sea turtle which he keeps in a basin and feeds on pilchards. I think he said pilchards, but I may be doing a Graham on this one. (I told Graham that we had ended up the evening at the Pink Cottage. '*Pig* Cottage?' he asked incredulously.)

I swam – the water was clear and clean. Cleese was the only other one who was up. He'd swum at 9.15, and was now sitting at the massive stone table, looking like Christ at the Last Supper before the rest of the guests arrived.

I tried water-skiing for the first time. No one was watching here so I decided to try it. It was third time lucky – on the third start I pulled up cleanly and stayed up and was very pleased with myself.

Graham is stoutly and very worthily maintaining his non-drinking, helped by a pill called Heminevrin. Talking with Eric and Graham in the front row of the stalls at sunset – when the sky and the bay go through so many rich colour changes in half an hour – Graham suddenly asks me the date. When I tell him it's the 8th he murmurs with ruminative interest … 'Mm … It's my birthday.' So we toast GC's 37 years in fruit juice.

Monday, January 9th, Barbados

'Had egg for breakfast' takes on a new significance here. I've rarely had an egg for breakfast beneath soaring columns and beside balustraded stone staircases, and the fact that this is a fifty-yard sprint from the clear blue waters of the Caribbean only adds to the unbelievability. Mind you, the Squirrel marmalade tastes as alarming as it sounds.

We fairly roar through the script and there's a very productive feeling that at this stage anything is worthy of discussion. We are not under pressure, everyone is warm, comfortable, happy, looking forward to a swim and sunbathe, and therefore amazingly tolerant of any ideas, however devious, deadly or heretical. The script is being turned upside down and inside out.

More work in the afternoon, but we break after one and a half hours to take in the sunset. I go for another water-ski – this time with TG, who is quite impressive, considering he hasn't done it for ten years (water-skiing, I mean).

I think I could cross my heart and say that we did work hard today, with Anthony Eden surveying us urbanely from his signed photograph.

Tuesday, January 17th, Barbados

Tonight the first clouds of discontent appeared on the otherwise clear horizons of a perfect ten days.

Towards the end of last week we began to summarise what we had achieved and this meant going back over well-trodden ground. Ideas, lines and jokes lost their originality and spontaneity and false trails were too laboriously followed. The lightness of touch was lost and the work became harder. But we kept at it successfully, and over the weekend reached the stage where we were to split into separate writing units and begin to actually rewrite along the lines of the five days' discussion.

This morning we had a read-through of everyone's rewrites. Terry and I may have had the easiest part of the script, but our work was mostly accepted and approved. John and Graham had worked on the second section, which was stretched out painfully in certain areas – Eric reckoned 25% of it was superfluous. John took this well. He has remarked in several beachside chats last week on how unselfish we all are with our material.

Keith Moon, who arrived here last night – with a formidable effect – hove to, walking up the beach from the Colony Club and bearing a bottle of champagne. He generously splashed this around and we all got very sandy and talked of Shepperton and Malibu. Keith is planning to have a suite built for himself in the Old House at Shepperton. He has positive ideas about the place – including a cricket pitch on the lawn. 'And football for the roadies,' he adds.

He's lived out of England for three years and has saved a large chunk of tax-free money as a result. He bought a house in Malibu Beach, for $325,000, and since then a law has been passed banning sale of any more building land in this sought-after piece of California. All of which is great for Moonie, who is hoping to get one million for his house. It's next door to Steve McQueen and Herb Alpert. Judging from Keith's stories Mr McQueen at least will be glad to get rid of him – Keith woke the McQueen household up at four a.m. on his last birthday, trying to score coke from McQueen junior and barking at their dog.

After this jolly beach banter Terry and I set to work rewriting some of this morning's rewrites. JC and Graham were doing the same, but when I went out into the garden where they were working there was no sign of Graham – just a very aggravated JC, who muttered angrily that he had to spend three-quarters of the time explaining the plot to Graham and that he was absolutely no help at all.

Graham has just knocked on my door, as I write this, to say that Des O'Connor is coming to dinner. We have decided to try and invite someone every evening. We have scoured the island for Harry Secombe, only to hear that he's left. Marty Feldman cannot be traced, though he's supposed to be here, as is Michael Caine. Maybe Des can throw some light on this tonight.

Des excels at charades and Keith and Graham do a very good double act and it's after one before I'm off towards bed.

And even then, a rather maudlin Keith M appears in my room and I offer him some Glenlivet and he talks morosely and not immodestly about his 'talent' and how important the *Odd Job* film[1] is, as if wanting some reassurance. He's been a hit with all of us – less destructive, more gently jolly and humorous than I'd anticipated.

He takes himself and his wondrous Turnbull and Asser gold-trimmed dressing gown off along the beach to the Colony Club. It's nearly two o'clock.

Wednesday, January 18th, Barbados

Terry J is the only other one who takes any pre-breakfast exercise. He ran with me one day, but now only swims. We compare notes about the sea-lice content of the Caribbean. These invisible creatures are felt, usually in the mornings, as very minor electric shocks along the arms and legs.

I've been reading a little about the instigator of this 1947 classical gem – Sir Ronald Tree. Mr Tull[2] obviously admired and respected Tree a great deal. He has lent me his own, well-thumbed copy of Tree's book *When the Moon is High.*

Tree bought Ditchley Park, a 1720 Gibbs house near Charlbury in Oxfordshire (there's a neat tie-up with eight weeks ago). In the early years of the war, Churchill's house at Chequers was considered to be at risk from enemy bombing on well-lit, cloudless nights. On these occasions Churchill asked if he could spend his weekends at Ditchley Park. 'When the moon was high.'

1 Written by Graham Chapman, it was to be made later in the year. He wanted Moon to star in it.
2 Who looks after the house with Brown.

Tree's finest work, apart from hosting Winston, Eden, General Sikorski and others, was to exert as much pressure as he could to bring America into the war. He tells in his book of meeting leading American businessmen who, in 1941, were predicting a defeat for England – and the Chairman of Sears Roebuck at the time told him it would be a good thing anyway, Britain had become degenerate and Europe badly needed German leadership.

The servants here were very fond of Sir Ronald, and I think his death two years ago has left a vacuum which has not been filled. There is no one of his stature for them to serve loyally and I think that the Pythons, sauntering around in *Muppet Show* T-shirts and torn off denim shorts, are really no substitute for the elegance of the Trees.

Graham seems to me to be the one who would fit best into that world. He always looks a little smarter than the rest of us, and his pipe adds a definite air of distinction. He's also a fully qualified eccentric, and I think in twenty or thirty years he will be a well-matured loony, in the best traditions of the English privileged classes. During this afternoon's session he fills up the teapot with hot coffee.

Apart from a break for lunch today we work assembling the script from 9.45 until 1.00 and 3.30 until 7.30.

And suddenly it's there and ready.

There is now casting, reading-through and minor line rewrites left. John suggests a light day tomorrow, and nobody really argues. We're all feeling rather pleased with ourselves.

Celebrity note: the Michael Caine/Marty Feldman rumours have taken a bizarre twist. It appears that neither Marty nor Michael Caine are on the island, but Marti Caine[1] is.

Thursday, January 19th, Barbados

At breakfast today, TJ, John and I compare notes of books we're reading. It turns out that all of us are reading books which irritate us. John is reading *Twelfth Night* and it's driving him potty.

His indignation over Shakespeare is intense – even at this time of the morning. He claims that Shakespeare's jokes wouldn't even get on a BBC

---

1 Sheffield-born comedienne (1945–95) with her own show on BBC. She had plastic surgery to make her nose smaller. 'The old one kept knocking people off bicycles,' Mark Lewisohn's *Guide to TV Comedy* quotes her as saying.

radio show these days. Terry J, no great supporter of Shakespeare, demurred here, feeling that this was just too harsh a judgement on anybody (apart from BBC Radio, presumably). But John will not be moved from his growing conviction that much of Shakespeare is second-rate and panto, and he wanders off in his *Muppet* T-shirt shouting 'Zounds!' and 'Forsooth!', much to the amazement of the local labour force who appear in the morning to rake the grass.

Terry J is reading *Watership Down*, which he doesn't look to be much enjoying. He says he doesn't think he'd like Richard Adams and finds it all very old-school, reds under the bed and unsatisfactory politically.[1]

Time passes strangely here. I feel as though these days have been weeks. There's an all-embracing benevolence in the climate which means that at any time of day or night there is the same balmy, soft warmth. It's difficult to punctuate time. And unnecessary, I suppose.

Friday, January 20th, Barbados

Why do things always happen to Graham? Today at breakfast he was spreading soft butter on a little piece of toast, and yet broke his knife. Extraordinary.

Casting completed this morning. Most of the main parts re-affirmed. Brian is Graham (unchallenged), Terry J Mandy (John being the only other one in the running, but it was felt that a motherly rat-bag was needed, and TJ's women are more motherly than JC's long, thin, strange ones), Eric Otto, me Pilate, and so on.

TJ feels that the Pythons should play as many parts as possible. John C feels we should be able to afford to take really good actors to play supporting parts, but the general consensus is that our rep company should avoid actors, and be composed of people who can act but will, more importantly, be good companions over ten weeks in Tunisia. John C suggests Ian Davidson (carried nem con) and Neil and Bernard McKenna go on to the list.

Today is our first cloudy day, which means that there are only eight hours' sunshine, instead of ten. There are rumours of apocalyptic storms and floods and snow in England, and Margate Pier has been washed away.

A bad afternoon for morale. Can only keep up on one ski for about

1 I think I was battling with *Daniel Martin* by John Fowles.

100 yards, whereas TJ, who began water-skiing a day after me, is now almost better on one than two.

Saturday, January 21st, Barbados

Paradise was soured a little by some strange texture to the orange juice. Graham later described it as 'Brown's revenge', which I'm sure is not entirely unlikely. Brown can be very smiley and jokey and his face like an old Brazil nut can crack very easily into a grin, but at the same time he can put over the impression of glowering resentment as well as anyone I know. I think he likes us, but is disappointed in our style.

We are about as well dressed as shipwrecked mariners. We have tolerated a situation where Brown and Tull are the only ones who dress for dinner. In addition, we are guilty, I fear, of being too apologetic, too accessible, too informal.

I have noticed a misogynistic streak in Brown, too. Tania[1] tells me today that every time he brings round the salad bowl he bangs her on the side of the head, ever so slightly, but quite deliberately.

The sunset was ten out of ten today – as if laying on some special final perfect treat for us to remember the island by. Eric, in his long Messianic white robe, strummed his guitar beside a beach fire, with a full moon shining over the Caribbean.

Tuesday, January 24th

More sombre weather. Set about organising our *Ripping Yarn* book-cover photo-call for tomorrow. Milton Abbas School have finally indicated their disapproval of 'Tomkinson' and will not let us film there again, so it has to be Hampstead Heath.

Thursday, January 26th

The rain is back. Find myself unable to settle to very much. Post-Barbadian lethargy. Feel sleepy and incapable of dynamic thought or action.

---

1 Tania Kosevich became Mrs Idle in 1981.

Monday, January 30th

Gather at 12.30 at 2 Park Square West. Summonsed by John Goldstone, who has news for us. Only three Pythons – myself, GC and TJ – left in the country.

John G settles us down and goes into quite a performance. Refuses to let on whether it's good news or bad. After a lot of long looks and glum expressions, he produces papers which he hands to all of us. Set out in the type-written sheets are the terms of an anonymous offer which looks to provide us with what we were asking for: £1,240,000, which covers our budgeted below the line costs, and £512,000 (less than the £600,000 we asked for) for above the line. Artistic controls are not required and the terms of finance are 50% of the profit.

So far so good. John, warming to his theme, gives an impish smile and is very coy about revealing who it's from. 'The National Front?' I asked him. John grins and produces another piece of paper headed with the dread name EMI. So EMI are back. EMI, who turned down the *Holy Grail* – then later picked it up for distribution and produced a pusillanimous campaign which rejected nearly all our ideas.

Now, three years later, we have a memo which reads 'The board have already said it would be scandalous if EMI did not support its own major talent [i.e. Python] and let it go to an American major.' Ho! Ho!

For the volte face we have to thank the new brooms of Michael Deeley and Barry Spikings, who used to run British Lion, and have now been brought in to zip up EMI's film production. They already have a De Niro film – *The Deer-hunter* – and a Kristofferson picture – *Convoy* – in production. All this happened in the last week.

JG is very happy and recommends acceptance. It certainly brightens the drab day. And makes the new film a reality suddenly.

In the evening Nancy L rang. *Saturday Night Live*[1] definitely want me to be a guest host sometime during the next full year's schedule.

Tuesday, January 31st

January washes itself away. Brighten a drab day with lunch at Bianchi's in Frith Street with Julia Nash, an editor at Heinemann. We talk over Al's

1 This 90-minute, topical, comedy-variety series began in October 1975. It became an American institution and was recently renewed by NBC until 2012.

Rue Britannia, which she read. Although she didn't feel it had enough story development to make it a commercial proposition, she said it was good to read a manuscript by someone who could write. Nine out of ten unsolicited manuscripts are frightful, she says – and she's not a tough or vindictive lady.

But sadly I agree with her assessment of Al's commercial potential. His writing is solid, dependable, honest, sometimes poetic, but his sense of story and incident and development of plot is very low-key. As Julia said, she became involved in the set-ups, then nothing happened.

Afterwards across Compton Street to Bifulco, to buy sausages for supper tonight. Then to see Gerry Donovan in Harley Street.

Gerry has been in touch with Kieser.[1] He is proposing to take out three of the more precarious teeth on my upper jaw and replace them with an acrylic denture plate. Dentures are essentially jokey – and I view the prospect of them with mixed feelings. Actually, I think I might quite enjoy the notoriety they will bring to my mouth. And of course I'll be all ready for playing prisoners and old men in the new Python film.

Wednesday, February 1st

Just as I am recovering a little after last week's lethargy, comes a considerable blow to the pride. Last week, whilst rooting out my piles of letters and scripts in an effort to clear the desk, I came across 'Arrochense Los Cinturones', the article I wrote after Tobago, and which foundered in New York a year ago when Lee Eisenberg left *Esquire*. It didn't look bad in parts, a little long, so I trimmed, chopped, and with a swallowing of pride and an apologetic covering letter sent it off to nice Mr Alan Coren, editor at *Punch*.

Today it arrived back rejected, politely but firmly. 'Sending back a Michael Palin piece could well be the sort of action that would cause posterity to desecrate my grave.' But his reasons for rejection were very sound, absolutely correct and put me well in my place.

But I determined that in order to salvage my pride, I would write another article and send it off by return. It was to be about a man whose articles are constantly rejected.

Simon Albury came round and read both the new piece and Tobago,

---

1 Bernard Kieser, a South African, had taken over the unenviable task of looking after my mouth after Robin Powell's return to Australia.

and, good friend that he is, gave them considerable thought, and finally confirmed my own suspicions that both misfired. His comments made me aware that I had fallen into the 'Humorous Article' trap. It's not me, he said, it's not the way I talk or the way I express myself – it's an affected style. I feel a little better after our long chat and resolve not to waste any more time on the matter tomorrow.

Friday, February 3rd

Sit up in my room full of the joys of life and write a long letter to Al L, detailing my slow recovery from West Indian culture lag. I'm thirsty again for books, films, magazines, the lot, and am currently reading Harold Nicolson's 1945-62 letters in a curious tandem with John Dean's *Blind Ambition*.[1] Two very different descriptions of the same subject – power. It does strange things to people. You can't carry a comparison between Winston Churchill and Gordon Liddy too far, but the fact you can start at all is food for thought. I mean, both did very odd things in the name of power and both were rather aggressive, pugnacious men, concerned with the problems of leadership.

Interesting Nicolson observation that the Tory Party really were embarrassed by Winston's presence after the defeat in '45. The problems of living with a living legend!

A lovely morning to myself, followed by a meeting in the Nag's Head, Hampstead, with Gwen Taylor – who seems to be on for our leading rep lady in Tunisia. [We were still searching for someone to play Brian's girlfriend, Judith.] Unassuming, straightforward and likeable – a good addition to the cast.

Drive from Hampstead out to Shepperton for a special viewing of *Dominique*, which has been laid on for the Shepperton staff, wives and families.

At the end Charles Gregson says, with his effervescent cheeriness, 'Not bad for one million two.' I thought it was very bad for that.

Monday, February 6th

Must begin work today on this year's *Yarns* – as much as possible to be written in the two months before we leave for Tunisia.

---

1 Insider's account of the Watergate scandal, by Nixon's White House lawyer.

The great imponderable is TJ's time. He valiantly underestimates the extent of his directing involvement on the new film – he was going to run the shot-list off in a couple of days, it'll now take a couple of weeks. So I am preparing for the worst – which is to write the stories myself and rely on Terry for heavy checking. That way it won't be a brake on the work and it will be a great bonus if he can find a clear week away from the film.

Having decided this, also decided to try and continue my last year's effort to work before breakfast.

To be honest there was little enthusiasm for the work. In the back of my mind lies a distinct reluctance to work on more films for the BBC. Is my reluctance something to do with the bland reaction to the *Yarns*? Is it that the *Yarns* form looks dull compared to the new film, which will take up much of the year?

It's all those things, plus an unresolved yearning to do something a little more serious – or a new direction at least. It could be the novel … it could be a film. The more involved I become with the film world (via Shepperton) the more tempted I am by its freedom. I don't want to get stifled by BBC thinking.

Well, all this jumble of vague hopes and dissatisfactions was holding back my progress this morning. I wrote, but wrote mechanically – the sheer joie-de-vivre of embarking on a new series was sadly lacking. I wish I knew what I really wanted to do.

Tuesday, February 7th

Down to Soho to meet David Dodd[1] at the Falcon pub on the corner of Lisle and Wardour Streets. David says he knew of it before – his father, who was Inspector of Police eventually, was in the 1930s a London copper in the days when Soho really lived up to its naughty image. Vice rings abounded and the Falcon was a meeting place for pimps and peddlers. Mr Dodd, Constable Dodd, used to sit in the corner behind his *Sporting Chronicle* and smoke a pipe and clock his suspects as they came in.

David claims he only knows one man in Guyana who is faithful to his wife. Everybody else, from the PM downwards, is balling on the side. Only the men, it seems; the women marry and stay at home – their side

1 A friend from Oxford who was working at the time at Georgetown University in Guyana.

of the marital contract honoured – but the men are at it like rabbits, all over the Caribbean.

David said he had given words of caution to Judith Hart, the Minister for Overseas Development, who had recently been in Guyana and had addressed a meeting of Guyanese with statesmanlike words about nurturing democracy, guarding the fragile plant which is growing here, etc, etc. David said all this meant nothing – but the £10 million aid cheque she was in Guyana to sign did.

Hearing David I can't help but feel that ideals wither and die in the Tropics. Our culture, our western culture, especially the Protestant form, becomes irrelevant in the heat.

Thursday, February 9th

Gerry Donovan pulls out three of my upper teeth.[1] All very neat and quick (G Donovan goes up in my estimation for turning out to be a fan of *Stay Hungry*[2] – my favourite movie of 1977).

Saturday, February 11th

Take Tom, Willy and Louise Guedalla to see Chinese New Year decorations and we eat an excellent meal at the Dumpling Inn in Soho. Louise tells me that, according to her mother, 'some of the nastiest people in the world live in Soho'. I must say, such was the ignorance about the place when I was young, that my parents would probably see me as little more than a child pornographer for taking three children to Saturday lunch in Gerrard Street. Now, of course, it's full of very well-turned-out Chinese entrepreneurs and sleek Euro-tourists.

Tuesday, February 14th

Write a lyric for the Shirley Bassey-style *Brian* song which I want André and Dave to have a go at – just to see whether it works. They have a choir at their disposal for a session, and actually asked me if I had anything I wanted them to do. Should be interesting.

---

1 Gerry, an Australian, had been recommended to me by Eric Idle's mother-in-law, Madge Ryan. Apart from installing false teeth, he also wrote the B-side of Eartha Kitt's 'An Englishman Needs Time'.
2 Bob Rafelson film starring Jeff Bridges and Sally Field.

Worlds collide, restoration drama meets John Belushi, *Saturday Night Live*, April 8th, 1978.

'The Chilites dance routine does not please Lorne and is cut just before dress rehearsal. "You'll thank me in years to come," says Lorne. I'm thanking him now.' Garrett Morris (left), Bill Murray, myself and Dan Aykroyd. (April 8th, 1978)

'An awful, monumentally awful moment.' Dancing with live cats down my trousers, *Saturday Night Live*, New York. (April 8th, 1978)

Eric and Carey,
me and Rachel, *Life
of Brian*, Tunisia, 1978.

Holidays at Roques.
Helen and me, Tom,
Anthea, Ian Davidson
and Edward Burd.

'Tom decided he would
like to appear in the
afternoon's filming . . .
It was one of the less
comfortable scenes but
graced by the presence
of the visiting George
Harrison. So at least he
can say he was in a
scene with Pythons and
Beatles.'
(*The Life of Brian*,
October 22nd, 1978)

Happy family. The
Coach House, Sag
Harbor, NY, 1979.

'1979 comes in cold.
Very cold.' On the
pond at Abbotsley.

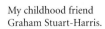

My childhood friend
Graham Stuart-Harris.

'I have to open a fete at
William Ellis School
... I smile and sparkle
and fail to hit anything
with seven balls.'
(May 19th, 1979)

Mary and Edward
Burd, Roques.

Saturday Night Live.
Lorne Michaels
hypnotises me before
the show.

'Mikoto comes to cook us a Japanese meal. The preparation is a painstaking and delicate business – as indeed is communication with Mikoto.'
(June 12th, 1979)

Al Levinson, my American friend, with Rachel, Sag Harbor, NY, July, 1979.

'They gave us grapefruit segments, beef in a brown and unexciting sauce ... and a trifle which looked like the remains of an unsuccessful heart-swap operation.' With Donald Carroll (left), Jilly Cooper, Steve Race and Katharine Whitehorn at a *Yorkshire Post* literary lunch.
(October 25th, 1979)

Gospel Oak, 1979,
with Will, Rachel
and Tom.

Yield to Willy's insistence and take all three kids round Madame Tussaud's. A really basic misconception about Tussaud's is that you will see famous people looking utterly life-like. Well, the figures, with their waxy pallor and their disturbingly piercing glass eyes look uncannily death-like. Many of them – Prince Charles and Paul McCartney to name a couple – are grotesquely bad, and I'm surprised the royal family haven't been down there to kick a few heads.

Wednesday, February 15th

Spent half the morning on a play idea. It's very neat – a day in the life of a BBC film unit, but also a day in the life of the beautiful mediaeval church where they are filming. Lots of possibilities for characters – from the Greek chorus of sparks through to the murky romantic involvements of PAs and make-up artists, to the power struggles of the director and cameraman, and with the infinite possibilities of the arrival of the Orson Welles figure who is to present the programme. He stirs up and rearranges all the internal relationships and is the deus ex machina who tips the whole thing into a climax of literally Gothic horror, as he orders parts of the church removed and sawn down – better to accommodate the cameras. Anyway, I made a start this morning.

TJ arrived midday for a session on the *Yarns*. Needless to say it was Python film business which dominated.

We spent a couple of hours on a rewrite for the second Pilate and Brian scene, which benefited, I think, but I'm always wary of duty rewrites – alterations resulting from irritation with other alterations. I tend to think that a lot of final details are best sorted out when we rehearse together.

Sunday, February 19th, Brighton

Have to be in Brighton this evening for a banquet at the Old Ship Hotel laid on by BBC Enterprises in order to launch a week's selling of their progs – *Ripping Yarns* being one they are specially anxious to push (presumably because they cost so much).

Read in an old copy of *The Times*, on which I was cleaning my shoes, that there are 450 bookshops in the whole of the United Kingdom – whilst, in Europe, Berlin alone has 263 bookshops and Munich 244.

Train down from Victoria. A dirty Sunday train – quite an

embarrassment as I hear guttural continental voices in the compartment next door.

A tiny, mean, British measure of scotch in the 'Regency Room', which confirms my suspicions that this hotel may once have seen stylish days, but has now fallen on plastic times. Meet a cheerful Finn and a very anglicised Dane, who wants me to go to Copenhagen in October and talk about *Ripping Yarns* (he seems decided to buy them, which is nice).

Then we're all ushered into a long room, overlooked by a balcony on which Paganini was supposed to have played in 1831. An average meal, but a jolly table with a well-preserved Swedish lady with a Mai Zetterling mixture of brains, looks and years, and my kind Danish friend. Frightfully uninspired speeches. Alan Bates, Billie Whitelaw and myself and others have to stand and be acknowledged.

After the meal, Terry Nation (creator of Daleks and presently writer of *Blake's 7*) seeks me out and lavishes praise on the *Yarns* – but especially on 'Olthwaite', which he can hardly stop talking about. He brushes aside my return of the compliment and raves on. Fall in with two very jokey Irishmen from RTE, one of whom has a twitch which causes his right hand to shoot out towards the bar after every third sentence.

Monday, February 20th

All is calm and quiet here. The two Terrys, Goldstone and others are in Tunisia on a week's recce. The boys, and Rachel, have gone back to school after half-term. It's very cold outside. I have no games of squash planned and no meetings. An ideal set of conditions for writing. And yet, once again, it does not come.

I realise that I am severely short of motivation. Apart from the odd manic enthusiasts – like Terry Nation and Mel Calman[1] – most of the rest of my friends have found the *Yarns* flawed in some way or other. Whatever the reason, the *Yarns* have, I feel, been un-rated rather than underrated. I know the BAFTA nominations are now complete, and I have heard nothing from anyone in the know – which gives me the sinking feeling that the *Yarns*, quite aside from being wiped off the board by the Muppets, may not even be nominated.

To cheer myself up I go down to Thumb Gallery for a private view.

---

1 Cartoonist and good friend. Never have I laughed so much with someone so morose. He died in 1994.

Robert H and Chris Orr are there. Robert is as up as I am down. He's doing a Ruskin film with Les Megahey (ex-Oxon) for *Omnibus*.

A girl comes up and asks me if I'm Kenny Everett. When I tell her I'm Michael Palin she says 'Oh, yes, I *meant* to say that.' Such is fame.

Wednesday, February 22nd

Spend most of the afternoon in the Owl Bookshop, Kentish Town, rather frustratingly trying to spend a book token. The trouble is I want to read everything. Come out with several books for the kids – including T H White's *The Sword in the Stone* and a 'Biggles' comic book for Tom. For myself, three novels by 'Britain's most underrated twentieth century novelist' – Henry Green – plus Kingsley Amis' latest, *The Alteration*. My reading veering towards novels once again, having completed the sorry, but compelling, story of John Dean.

Discovered the joys of T H White whilst reading to Willy tonight. Such richness – such a delightful and intelligent and satisfying mixture of humour, excitement and interest. Smashing.

Thursday, February 23rd, Southwold

Yarns stop for two more days, as I take a 48-hour trip to Southwold.

On the train a silvery-haired and dapper gent opposite introduces himself to me. His name's Whinfrey and I've met him several times at *Punch* lunches. He's the business manager of *Punch*. Will I be writing an article for them again soon? I say I have and it was rejected. He laughs uncertainly and goes on as if I hadn't said anything.

Walk with sprightly Ma along the front. The sea in heavy swell and the familiar Promenade littered with the remains of beach huts wrecked in the January storms. The 'Bide-A-Wees' and 'Little Huts' and 'Rocamars' twisted and smashed.

Saturday, February 25th

Work days slip away. Another week has gone by – and only one day's work on the *Yarn*. Still, I'm very happy and beginning to feel a cautious return of the writing urge.

Tom, Willy and I lunch at Nontas Greek in Camden Town, the idea being to try them on a lot of different countries' cooking. Willy wants to go and eat Turkish because he's heard that you can burp after the meal.

Sunday, February 26th

André J brings round the tape of the Shirley Bassey-type *Brian* song that they've put together. It sounds stupendous. Massive brass backing and a great female voice. All done by three people and a lot of mixing.

Back home, ring Graham to wish him well for the start of *Odd Job* filming – at Shepperton tomorrow. His new director, Peter Medak, seems to have won the casting battles hands down. Keith Moon is out and not because he was too busy with The Who – this was the official reason given to the press because Medak and others didn't want him. Replaced by David Jason. GC has brought Diana Quick in to play his wife. She signed up only last Friday. I wished GC well, and told him to make sure he was still in it!

Monday, February 27th

To Gerry Donovan's for a first glimpse of my false teeth. Try not to read too much psychological significance into this, but I never imagined I would be wearing false teeth at the age of 34. This is ridiculous, of course, for I've had bridges fitted for two years, but false teeth to me are things you take in and out and leave in a bowl of water beside the bed at night – they are like mothers-in-law and big tits, a traditional joke area. Now I have them – a little pink band to go across the roof of my mouth, a little dental chum to lie beside me at night. I feel a little – uncool, man.

To Anne's for a meeting. Played the Bassey *Brian*. Good reaction, especially from JC. All full of admiration for André's arrangement, though not for my lyric particularly. I agree.

Tuesday, February 28th

J Cleese has asked Helen and me out to dinner this evening. We called round at his still-scaffolded Ladbroke Road house, recently acquired from Bryan Ferry, the singer and generally chic society figure. Huge rooms, and lots of them, and only John there, wandering through it, rather lost.

We eat at a rather tasteful little restaurant – a bit elaborately frilly and soft-furnished – called Pomme D'Amour in Bayswater Road. Pleasant, easy chat with just the three of us – about books, Alexander Technique (JC's been at it for three years) and JC's desire to do a *That Was The Week That Was*-style show – mainly I think because he feels that the people who need the boot in now are not the old hags of the Macmillan right-wing establishment, but the new and humourless tyrants of the left.

Wednesday, March 1st

Am finishing typing a *Telegraph* 'Opinion' piece, when a grave S Albury enters the writing sanctum. He's been talking to Barry Spikings, who's been talking to Lord Delfont, who has stopped the EMI/Python deal because he was so outraged by the script.

My immediate reaction is a surge of relief, spreading to all parts of the body. Breathing space to write the *Yarns*, confirmation of fears that I had pushed back into my subconscious that EMI would 'find us out' at some stage and get cold feet. But I'll believe it when I hear it and am not going to race to the telephone.

Instead I pour myself a glass of wine and go off with Simon and [his wife] Phillida to see *Smile Orange* – a sort of black *Fawlty Towers* with a hint of *MASH* and with as much humour and far more endearing characters than either of them.

Thursday, March 2nd

It's pouring solidly at 9.30 and Helen and I are eating rather cosily and discursively in the kitchen, when John Goldstone calls. The facts are correct. Michael Carreras[1] showed the script to Delfont, who vetoed it. Spikings, however, has undertaken to provide us with £50,000 to keep our production team together whilst we find new backing.

Friday, March 3rd

Evidently none of the Pythons is distraught over the collapse of the EMI offer. Terry J greatly relieved that Python still has its powers of aggravation. EMI are the black-tie gala luncheon, awards dinners establishment

1 Film producer, specialising in Hammer horror films, and at the time working for EMI.

– the Grades and the Delfonts of this world – and no territory is less familiar or acceptable to us than this chummy world of showbiz conformists.

This morning's newspapers, by coincidence, show that EMI's half-yearly profits have slumped and yesterday £19 million were wiped off the value of their shares.

Just before lunch my ragged morning is brightened by a phone call from Terry Hughes, who informs me, joyfully, that *Ripping Yarns* has not been forgotten. It's won the Press Guild Critics' Award for Best Comedy Series of the Year. This boost, coming together with the news of the dates of repeats and with the extension of writing caused by the post-ponement of Python, revives the *Yarns*, which a week ago I felt were in danger of foundering under my lack of enthusiasm. Now, with such a confirmation of appreciation, shall begin an assault on them with renewed spirit.

Monday, March 6th

In to work-room by 7.20. After breakfast JC rings with comments on the rewritten *Brian* ending. Generally he finds it an acceptable and much improved replacement, but there are one or two points – like the stam-mering Gaoler – which he has always disliked, and when he turns the full beam of his intellectual logical judgement upon what strikes us as spontaneously funny, it does wither the material. I predict a stubborn confrontation on that scene. But all else constructive.

I now favour a clear decision to avoid the summer and begin *Brian* in autumn, but there are difficulties – costumes are hired, sets in Tunisia are apparently not available in the autumn, etc, etc. Meanwhile, wigs are measured, scripts are rewritten and costumes continue being sewn.

Wednesday, March 8th

Gilliam rings for half an hour, proposing a new course of action on the movie – i.e. to cut our budget to a reasonable size by abandoning plans to film in Tunisia, using Britain and finding unusual locations and using a stylised design treatment. The talk turns to castles and salt mines in Wales. 'Jesus of Shepperton', I call this plan.

Thursday, March 9th

Nancy rings in the evening. Evidently it's the first day of spring in New York and she's in very high spirits. Once again she puts a little pressure on to get me to do *Saturday Night Live*. Once again I resist, but then Helen shouts from the kitchen that we need the money. On reflection I certainly could do with a break. Promise to ring Nancy after next week's movie decisions.

The Delfont story is out. A restrained piece in the *Evening Standard* which could help us.

Friday, March 10th

Eric rings – normal waking hours for him, late for me – at half-past eleven. Mainly to let me know how well *Rutles* is going to do in the States. He urges me to get over there and, via *Saturday Night Live*, try and emulate this success. 'Stop piddling around with the BBC, Mike … get over there … it's the next step,' and this sort of talk.

The trouble is that I know that the American 'success', in our line of work almost certainly involves a constant compromise with quality and with personal, individual control. If we accept their terms from the start, we will never produce something which, like Python, was truly our own.

Still, I must admit Eric plays the American game well. He has flair, intelligence, skill and style – and is shamelessly good at using them. But I fear he is in danger of becoming the victim of his own image – of believing that the shimmering reflection is the reality.

Sunday, March 12th

In the evening drinks with our next-door neighbours, who are leaving to work in Brunei for ten years. He's a lawyer, middle-aged and, having missed great attainment, is left with something of a chip on the shoulder – elegantly carried, though. I think Brunei will suit him. He says it is almost fanatically Anglophile – which will make a change from Kentish Town.

Monday, March 13th

At 9.30 Python, less Graham, assembles to contemplate the wreckage of the EMI deal. Surprisingly little vindictive comment or post-mortem gloom – though we all feel that EMI should be pressed as hard as is legally possible to provide some recompense for pulling out of a deal after hands were shaken and firm commitments given verbally and literally.

Meanwhile all potential money sources are to be tapped – and Eric suggests that he and J Goldstone go to New York together and try to rifle the pockets of heavily solvent record companies. Anne is to investigate the legal and commercial likelihood of raising the money by shares from the public (fans, etc). Meanwhile Python (Monty) Pictures is left with a near £70,000 bill to pay for work on *Brian* so far. It looks as though all our income through Python will have to stay there for at least six months. Times look hard again.

Tuesday, March 14th

Nancy had rung several times to try and force me into a decision on *Saturday Night Live*. Finally I agreed to host the April 8th show. Nancy sounded overjoyed.

At half past ten drove round to Eric's to watch a couple of *Saturday Night* tapes and talk to him about his experiences of the show. He didn't make a great deal of sense. 'They love Python, be yourself. Enjoy being King of New York for a week.'

Wednesday, March 15th

Lay in bed around eight and decided that if this was to be a fragmented 'sorting-out' week, I should try and clear the decks of tasks and duties which lie in the back of my mind – such as visiting Shepperton.

The place is overflowing with work. Portakabins are being hired to accommodate everyone – it looks like a Yukon town at the height of the gold rush. *Odd Job* and *Pink Panther* are shooting. *Alien*, needing three stages, is building. *Thief of Baghdad* is in pre-production too.

Chat to Ford for a while, then walk over to the canteen. It causes me great personal distress that in my year on the board of directors I've been unable to make any discernible improvement in the catering at the studio. It sounds a small point, but the service and the surroundings are appalling by any standards, and this can only reflect badly on Shepperton's reputation. I have pushed and pushed for some improvements, but, although everybody agrees the situation is grim, nothing seems to get done.

The catering manager reigns supreme, reaping the benefits of this Shepperton boom which he did nothing to create. When I finally reached the dining room I found I had walked into a hornet's nest. I was greeted with shouts, not altogether of a friendly nature, from a long table consisting of Graham Chapman, David Jason, Bernard McKenna, Diana Quick and a very doleful looking man who was introduced to me as the *Odd Job* publicity man. They had been waiting for half an hour for their food to arrive, and had to be back in the studio, on the floor, in another 20 minutes. I felt rather like Lee J Cobb confronting the mob in *On the Waterfront*. They were right and all I represented was the inadequate Shepperton organisation.

Walked back with Graham C, who was fed and placated by that time. He looks tired, but that's to be expected. He's full of optimism about the rushes and, I gather from talking to people on the set, is doing well in his first sober acting role – probably in fifteen years.

As I got home, Terry J rang. I'd still not recovered from trouble-shooting at Shepperton and had had nothing to eat all day, so was not at my best when Terry asked if we could talk about acting in the three *Ripping Yarns* which we are about to write. Arranged to meet him for lunch tomorrow.

Then all the world and his dog either rang or turned up. Terry Gilliam and I had a long chat. I feel that he must get on with his next movie, because I think he's the only person I know who could make a better movie than *Close Encounters*.

Thursday, March 16th

Must spend some time this week reappraising the financial situation. The hopes raised and dashed by EMI leave me with a financial squeeze on. Might have to turn to commercials. The trouble is I have to spend another £10,000 on Redwood's new mixer very soon and £10,000 at least on our second house and the Python cash has stopped coming in.

To Pizza Express in Hampstead, where almost two years ago Terry and I were going through the difficult motions of rethinking our working relationship. The problem had to be faced again today, but was settled instantly and amicably. Since yesterday evening I had had enough time to decide that I must, as before, follow my instincts – and I told Terry, accordingly, that I felt it better not to change the structure of the *Yarns* at this stage. TJ, I think, was sad in one way, but much more relieved in another – and he says he can now plan to think of other projects whilst I'm away filming.

Friday, March 17th

In the evening we go to dinner with Anne Henshaw.[1] Meet there Basil Bunting, a 78-year-old with twinkling, kindly eyes and a well-worn beard. He's evidently a poet and writer, in London for the publication of a new collection by Oxford University Press.

In the Second World War he was in military intelligence and travelled a lot – in Persia, North Africa and the Russian borders. Most of his work consisted of 'getting people drunk'. He used to give scotch whisky to Russians, whilst he himself drank scotch-looking cold tea. A marvellous man, with such richness of experience.

Some things he wouldn't tell me, claiming they were still classified under the Official Secrets Act, but he was closely involved in diplomatic activity at the end of the Second War, when he wrote very strong recommendations to President Truman – 'not a very intelligent man … but …' – concerning the Russian threat to the West – in purely military terms. He thinks that much of his information formed the basis of Churchill's 'Iron Curtain' speech in Fulton, Missouri – and he says that's the only period of his life when he felt his actions could in any way have affected the course of world events. He reckons that the war could have been over three or four weeks earlier if the Allies hadn't agreed to stop their advance in order to let the Russians take Berlin.

Fascinating.

Sunday, March 26th

Anne rings on Easter morning, no less – with a problem I could well do without. Eric is back, full of *Rutles* success in the US. He's probably going to edit *All You Need is Cash* film into a 70-minute version for the cinema, and is strongly urging us to put his 40-minute compilation of the Python Bavaria material out, as a second feature. It would keep Python's name in the American eye whilst we are refinancing *Brian* and would, given the success of *Rutles*, be a sure money-earner.

---

1 By now separated from her husband Michael.

Apparently the two Terrys and John will hardly consider the idea at all.

Monday, March 27th

Watch the tape of the *Rutles* film, which went out earlier in the evening. A smoothly made piece. Elaborate, ingenious, fun. It's interesting to compare what two Pythons have done with half a million and three-quarters of a million pounds respectively – Gilliam created *Jabberwocky* and Eric imitated the Beatles.

Wednesday, March 29th

Ring Neil I and congratulate him on *Rutles* – his music and performance both eminent. Then I ring Eric and get Tania, who is cheerful, but suggests that Eric is not in an expansive or chatty mood – and it's his birthday.

Decide to forsake my evening of work at home and go round to cheer him up. Take a couple of bottles of champagne and an old book on cricket (complete with the tantalising chapter – 'Making a Young Wicket-Keeper').

We all ended up having a good drink, chat and so on. Eric was rather low earlier, I think because he felt he had tried to do something with the German film and been sat on by the rest of us without even a chance to explain it at a meeting. But I didn't really need to tell him how jealous the Pythons are of each other's material. How ruthlessly and subjectively biased they are against anything which any individual in the group tries to do – and that's probably at the root of their/our unwillingness to throw 40 minutes of Python in with the *Rutles*. I personally think Eric was a little slow not to anticipate this reaction, but then he's not really living in the real world at the moment.

Phone calls from the States pour in for him.

Thursday, March 30th

The next two days I must pack in nine hundred and one things before leaving for the US Saturday morning. Nancy has booked me on Concorde – so I will arrive in NYC two hours earlier than I left London. I don't really approve – but it's got to be worth the experience. Once.

Drive down through sunny London to collect our Broadcasting Press Guild Award. The new Press Centre in Shoe Lane is depressingly smart – and several of the journalists there complain about this shiny-smooth monster which has replaced the smoky dens where journalists used to meet.

A rather small and touchingly simple ceremony. Present are Tom Stoppard and Peter Barkworth – collecting awards for *Professional Foul.*

Talked to Peter Barkworth. He remembered my sister Angela from the days they worked together in Sheffield.[1] 'Trim girl ...' He's also a diarist and writes for an hour every morning. Of *Professional Foul,* in which he was first-rate, he said 'I was so depressed – I woke up one morning and said "It's not me ... I can't do it ... I'll never be a Stoppard actor".' He talks in a clipped, but unselfconsciously theatrical style. Like Noël Coward without the 'my dears'. A very likeable man.

Derek Jacobi was there to collect an award for *I Claudius.* He left early for *Henry IV* rehearsals. 'I must dash off and be deposed,' quipped he.

Saturday, April 1st, New York

Concorde check-in smooth, no waiting, your very own special escalator and colour scheme, whilst the boarding room – normally that feature-less little box where passengers gather and gaze silently past each other, very often in a state of delay – is, for Concorde, a well-equipped lounge, with phones. Glasses of champagne have to be warded off, so liberal are they with the freebies on this hugely expensive flight. (Concorde return to NYC – £920. Freddie Laker Skytrain return to NYC – around £90.)

Word comes through that Concorde will leave late as the automatically extending jetty has stuck, four feet from the aeroplane. They apologise for the delay, but when we do board we will board up a mobile ramp, which will be drawn up to the catering hatch entrance.

It transpires that Concorde is too high for the ramp, and the only way to lower it is to fill the nose – the famous Concorde droop-snout – with as many British Airways employees as possible. This wonderfully manic piece of improvisation still doesn't quite work, for as I'm half-way up the ramp, about to make my inelegant way into this beautiful, pencil-slim plane through the catering door, we are all shooed back – as the plane (by now filled up with many passengers)

1 She was an assistant stage manager at the Sheffield Playhouse for a time.

had sunk below the top of the steps. It was nearly midday when the last of us completed this ignominious boarding. Before take-off the captain, clearly very grumpy, urged us to write to British Airports Authority and complain!

Due to a combination of the free champagne and mean toilet space, several passengers, myself included, are queuing for a pee when the sound barrier is finally breached. Fifty-eight thousand feet and the digital counter hovering at 1.99 – with free Dom Perignon and a five-course meal to look forward to – is as heady and exhilarating a feeling as I've experienced.

The American coastline arrives with the last sips of Napoleon brandy, and we are down at Kennedy by 9.50 US time, having left Heathrow just after midday.

I ring Al and Eve and am soon in a cab round to their small, welcoming little flat in Gramercy Park. I think I'm still suffering a post-Concorde high and gabble on unrestrainedly.

Sunday, April 2nd, New York

Nancy and I go over to an ABC TV studio at the Elysee Theater, off Seventh Avenue – within spitting distance of City Center – where I am to make a brief appearance in a show being recorded for one of the several new cable TV outfits springing up. It's called Home Box Office, and the show is a special featuring comedy teams, or partnerships. They're showing a Python clip and want me to introduce it.

I suddenly find myself on the bill alongside hosts Rowan and Martin and such great and famous names as Sid Caesar – whose *Show of Shows* was one of the most influential American comedy programmes of all time. Meeting this rather shy, thin, drawn man who appears not to have aged, I think I probably poleaxed him with my effusiveness.

Rowan and Martin and everyone there seem very honoured to have me around. Dan Rowan – very smooth, on and off the camera – remembered his favourite Python line – the line in the 'Proust Competition' about giving the prize to the girl with the biggest tits.

Throughout the evening, the staff are overbearingly and unreasonably bossy. I am required to be at the ready, dressed and in the wings half an hour before the recording starts and once the recording does start I am to wait in the wings – not in my dressing room – despite the fact that I am not on for two hours.

The audience assembles, the live band starts to play and suddenly I'm part of an evening of American music hall, exchanging nervous back-stage pleasantries with the likes of The Flying Volantes.

In a makeshift dressing room, Senor Wences, a small, lined, balding little man, who was busy making up his left hand in preparation for his celebrated – and brilliant – ventriloquist act.

I was, apart from The Flying Volantes, easily the youngest person in the show – and I was, after much draughty waiting, finally announced by Dan Rowan, and ran out to spontaneous applause – cued up on the 'applause' signs which flashed above the audience.

My little piece went well, but not as surely and confidently as at the run-through. They didn't have the Python film clip ('Soft Fruit') to show, so I was left with some egg on my face after the announcement. All I could think of to do was eat the postcard which I was using as a prop. This at least had the effect of corpsing Rowan and Martin as they walked on later.

As it transpired, the evening belonged to the Ritz Brothers, two sharp old men who I'm afraid I had to admit I'd never heard of, but who evidently were legends in American showbiz for 50 years. Films, theatre … etc … they danced nostalgically and everyone loved them.

So, in the final line-up, as the audience were herded into endless applause, I found myself in the same jeans I'd worn since yesterday morning, shaking hands with these great men of American showbiz as this special drew to a close.

I was taken round, with Nancy and the others, to Charley O's, where a sumptuous cold buffet had been laid on for all concerned with the show. The producer's son was a frightful pest. He buzzed around the table constantly making alternately fawning and facetious Pythonic references. 'I mean, wow – oh, I get to shake the hand of Michael Palin, *the* Michael Palin …' And so on and so on and so on. Ed Goodgold, who I was talking with, finally lost patience with the boy. He called him over.

'Hey,' says Ed, 'are you Jewish?'

'Half,' returns the gawky acolyte quickly.

'Well, it's your worse half.'

Monday, April 3rd, New York

At five over to NBC – in the RCA building at 30 Rockefeller Plaza. One of the old-fashioned skyscrapers, soaring sixty or seventy storeys above the skating rink in the Plaza, with the flags billowing all around it.

The décor of the foyer is New Deal Inspirational. 'Wisdom and Knowledge Shall be the Stability of Thy Times' is picked out in bold relief above the doors, whilst inside murals – in oils and what looks like gold stucco – mix airliners with naked maidens.

A bewildering variety of lifts, from which I was eventually spilled out at the seventeenth floor.

Magnificent views – the Empire State Building dominating to the south-east and, to the north-east, the twin gothic spires of St Patrick's cathedral on Fifth Avenue, guarded by sweeping skyscraper blocks on all sides. A classic New York panorama.

Lorne Michaels was not in his office when I arrived. I got to know the room a little first. It was small and individually furnished – not at all like the usual American executive office, more like a rather trendy Oxford don's room. Along one wall were framed mementoes of *Saturday Night Live* – the show Lorne created and has guided through three years and eighty-seven shows. Pictures of the cast meeting President Ford, numerous jokily inscribed photos from Chevy Chase,[1] letters from the White House, Emmy awards. On the facing wall, two wood-framed cabinets full of video cassettes of the shows labelled according to their host – 'Steve Martin', 'Anthony Perkins', 'Lily Tomlin', 'Richard Pryor', 'Eric Idle', 'OJ Simpson', 'Kris Kristofferson', 'Paul Simon', 'Art Garfunkel' and so on.

Lorne ambled in. Small, unremarkably dressed, with a bright, intelligent face and disproportionately large head. An attractive, easy confidence as he shook hands. A lack of calculated effusiveness, but no lack of warmth in the welcome. I knew I was going to get along with him and felt suitably relieved.

I felt like a new boy at school with Nancy Lewis chaperoning me, and the sensation increased as Lorne took me around the offices and then down to Studio 8H, the legendary RCA studio where Toscanini recorded. Showing me the studio was a shrewd move, which I appreciated later, for from Thursday lunchtime until one o'clock Sunday morning it was home – the hub, centre and focus of the colossal outpouring of nervous energy that creates *Saturday Night Live*.

There are about fifteen writers who assemble in Lorne's office, five or

---

1 Catch phrase, 'I'm Chevy Chase and you're not,' he originally joined as a writer, became the star and left after one year to be replaced by Bill Murray.

six of them women. All, bar one – a venerable, white-haired father-figure[1] – look younger than me. Mainly scruffy. A rather earnest, college boy look about them.

The meeting is a curiously stilted affair. Lorne presides gently, analyses the ideas that come up and shows encouragement for the good and half-good, and firm but diplomatic discouragement for the bad. But no one sounds energetic. No ideas are put forward with great conviction. It's as though this first meeting is part of a formula which has to be gone through – the real ideas will form tomorrow.

Lorne invites me to a party to be thrown at the fashionable disco, Studio 54, by Truman Capote and Andy Warhol.

Outside huge arc lamps are directed at the entrance to the club. A crowd, probably hired by Warhol and Capote along with the lamps, clusters around the entrance and I'm ushered quickly through the ropes and into the club.

There's a broad passageway in, and cameras are pointing at us as we go down it. 'Smile,' somebody says. As we push in through double doors, I catch sight of the black-cloaked figure of T. Capote. In the bright light he looks like a mole or a badger, appearing briefly, immaculately ... then gone. Inside, the club is like any other heaving mass of bodies. Strobing lights, helpful darkness for those who want it – strategic pools of bright light for those who want it.

Almost immediately brush up against Mick J and Jerry. Jagger is at his most inelegantly slurry, and warns me against the poofs here. He greets me with congratulations on the film, which I dopily don't comprehend. He is referring, of course, to the *Rutles* film. I compliment him on his performance – and he is lost, borne away on the crowd.

The party was ostensibly to watch the 50th Academy Awards Ceremony live from LA and at the same time show off Polaroid's video-beam technique – by which a TV picture can be projected by means of three light sources onto a flat screen. The lights and cameras on the way in were to demonstrate the new instant film techniques. So we were all being used in a way – either for Capote and Warhol's ego, or simply Polaroid's salesmanship.

A glorious mixture of people. On one journey through the crowd I passed Dick Martin and Salvador Dali (not together). The model girl,

1 Herb Sargent, the head writer, brother of Alvin, the screenwriter (*Ordinary People, Spider-Man*, etc).

Brooke Shields, who plays the twelve-year-old whore in Louis Malle's shortly to open *Pretty Baby* was sitting beside us.

They bayed at the Academy Awards, especially when Vanessa Redgrave gave her short and rather mistimed speech about anti-semitism and fascism and they roared with exultation at the three awards for *Annie Hall.* It was quite exciting in a wasteful way – for in the end the home crowd won. The starched and trim bronzinos of the West Coast, with their showbiz smiles and oozing wealth, were routed by the forces of the East Coast – by the critical, introspective, tasteful Mr Woody Allen. Woody, who was not even at the Hollywood awards, but was playing clarinet in Michael's Pub in Greenwich Village. As Lorne said, 'Woody always has taste, and not being at the awards demonstrates taste at its highest.'

After the awards everyone headed either to the bar or to dance – ignoring glasses on the dance floor, which were smashed and trodden underfoot. At the bar the epicene bar boys held court. They pulled off their tight black T-shirts and swayed and swished and showed off. It was hard and aggressive and not at all friendly. The place was filling up and there was a growing compulsion to decadence – as if it was expected of the audience here to be outrageous, egomanic, wild and uncontrolled. I found it horribly depressing – almost a nightmare, and was relieved when we left just before one.

Tuesday, April 4th, New York

Woke, frightened, after about two and a half hours' solid sleep. Lay there – aware I had been losing sleep at the rate of four hours a night over the last five days and wondering how it would affect the rest of the week.

At five in the afternoon round to NBC, to the well-worn sprawl of offices – like a very liberal arts college, with Professor Michaels presiding. Unlike England, where writing is largely a domestic industry, here in the States they assemble in a suite of offices and start to tap out ideas.

Around ten, Lorne and Jean Doumanian – the assistant producer – wander down and across Broadway to eat at Wally's. Another unpretentious restaurant, which seems to be Italian despite the name. We join a table of Lorne's friends (he seems to have friends everywhere he goes), comprising Paul Simon, Shelley Duvall,[1] David Geffen,[2] Diana Ross, her

1 Actress girlfriend of Paul Simon. Favourite of Robert Altman's. About to start filming on Kubrick's *The Shining* with Jack Nicholson.
2 Agent, record producer, co-founder of Dreamworks in 1994.

escort – a handsome, but taciturn young Nordic chap – and a lady called Diana Von Furstenberg,[1] who's just seen and 'adored' *Pretty Baby*. She looks like Cher's grandmother, but is clearly something of a NY society lady.

The talk turns to the Oscars. Paul and Shelley were in *Annie Hall*, so are obviously pleased. There is much talk of John Travolta, the newest and most instant Hollywood star on the strength of one movie – *Saturday Night Fever*. All except Paul Simon are unqualified in their praise of him – or rather of what he represents – instant, assured, powerful glamour. Lorne, who talks easily, volubly, and on the whole wisely, reckons *Saturday Night Fever* is the movie of the '70s – the same way as *Easy Rider* was the movie of the '60s. Some truth. Paul S bemoans the passing of the '60s. He regards the '70s as dull and derivative – in the '60s everything was fresher. I agree with him that issues seemed clearer, sharper then.

Wednesday, April 5th, New York

The phone wakens me at ten past eight. 'Where's Eric Idle?' enquires a girlish voice – and it's some while before I can assure her that I don't know. 'Did I wake you?' the voice turns on me provocatively. 'Yes …' 'Well, I hope you can go back to sleep, because I *never* can after I wake up …' I put the phone down. Aw hell, four hours.

Over to the restaurant somewhat heavily named 'Sea-Food of the Aegean', where we are dining with Bob Osterberg and Ray Brodie – our lawyers in the Python versus ABC case. Osterberg is straight, Ray Brodie the gushing enthusiast. Very good to see them and pay back some of our thanks.

Then half an hour of still pictures for continuity on the show and at 3.15 ready for the read-through. This takes place in the Green Room on the ninth floor (this is to become one of the landmarks of the building over the next few days). Bowls of salad, coffee and beers are provided and the room is crammed with twenty or thirty people.

My feelings after the read-through were that I was reading an awful lot of narrator/link man parts and would have preferred to have done more characters.

The writers sensed and appreciated this and went off to rewrite,

1 She was known as New York's Fashion Queen.

whilst myself, Dan Aykroyd, Bill Murray[1] – grim-faced and unshaven
– and Garrett Morris – the neat, chirpy black member of the cast –
began first rehearsal for our Chilites dance routine. Sometimes I find
it hard to figure out quite how Lorne's mind works. He loves the
Chilites' song 'Have You Seen Her' – a hit of eight years ago – and
wants to see it on the show. However, since that time two of the
Chilites have been imprisoned and one is dead. Lorne still has the
lead singer – Eugene Record – and hopes that the rest of us, in Afro
wigs, will be able to recreate the Chilites behind him. I'm sceptical,
dear diary.

Decline Lorne's invitation to dine with Paul at Wally's and am just
heading east to the Essex House when Laraine[2] and a group of the
writers ask me to eat with them. Well, I am hungry, and it's good to
take any opportunity to get to know them better, so I find myself up
on W91st at Marvin Gardens – huge but cheap plate of turkey salad
and a couple of bottles of wine with Laraine, Bill Murray, Al Franken,[3]
Brian Doyle-Murray[4] and others.

In the cab on the way back Al F says how easy people are finding it
with me – which I take as a compliment – and fall into bed, tired but
grateful, just after one.

Thursday, April 6th, New York

To NBC and Studio 8H, for the first day of 'blocking' the sketches.

I have to do a series of visual promos between four o'clock and five
o'clock, which go smoothly and in their small way give the studio crew
confidence in me. We work on with blocking, rehearsing our Chilites
number, which is fast becoming my bête noire of the week – it's
musically quite complicated.

That night I eat with Lorne at Charly O's. He's inquisitive, but not
prying. We talk about marriages, kids, relationships. His marriage (to
one of the present writers) lasted ten years. He thinks kids would have

---

1 Bill Murray had joined the cast three months earlier.
2 Laraine Newman was one of the regular cast, who called themselves The Not Ready For
Prime Time Players.
3 Al was also in *All You Need is Cash*, and now he has since made a lucrative career out of
protest. He has his own show on TV and wrote the bestseller *Lies and the Lying Liars Who
Tell Them*.
4 Writer and cast member, brother of Bill Murray.

saved it. He's a Canadian, won his spurs with CBC, trained for the law, but never practised, wrote for the 'Laugh-In', etc. He's a very effective, rather stylish leader of men and, though his own ego is clearly a thing of pleasure to him, he does give as well as take. I like him more and more.

It's at two in the morning that myself, Lorne, writers Al Franken and Tom Davis, stumble eventually onto what is to become the shape of the opening monologue – my own proving-piece. I am to play my manager and come on and apologise for Michael not having arrived.

The ideas fall thick and fast and I suggest that the manager should talk about his other acts, and then possibly end on an act of his own. This fits neatly in with an idea of James Downey, one of the young, new writers, who said he's always wanted to see someone dancing with ferrets down their trousers. I adapt this to dancing to 'The White Cliffs of Dover' whilst putting sea-food salad and two cats down my trousers. Great is the nocturnal hilarity. I just hope it wears well in the morning.

Friday, April 7th, New York

There is a lift operator at Nancy Lewis's apartment building on Central Park South who is genuinely, creatively loopy. The last time I saw him he told me in some detail, with a perfectly straight face, that he is currently making replicas of New York public buildings out of false teeth. 'I have a lot of dentists in this block, you see.'

Now I understand why Python can be so successful in the US. And it is prestigious. It is repeated endlessly – currently on Mondays on Channel 13 in New York and five nights a week in Los Angeles, five nights a week in New Orleans, plus numerous other regional showings one hears of, in Pennsylvania and North Carolina, etc, etc.

Such is the respect for Python, that Lorne confided to me today that he felt it has adversely affected some of the writing on this week's show. Some of the newer writers, he feels, have become self-conscious and forsaken their own style and their own instincts in favour of attempts to supply me with Pythonic material.

There is one sketch in particular, which has changed from a lecture on drama and a 'What's wrong with this scene from Chekhov?' idea to a fully fledged RADA-trained actor escaping from chains, locks, padlocks and a trunk whilst performing *The Seagull*. All this grew from an observation of mine that the narrator needed brightening up and couldn't one possibly begin by, say, breaking out of a trunk, before going into a perfectly straight introduction?

Finish blocking around nine. But then there's wardrobe fittings and yet another dance rehearsal – and it's nearly eleven by the time I'm relaxing in Lorne's office. Lorne is staring up at the order of sketches pinned on cards to one wall of his office – 'Holmes', 'What's Wrong?', 'Nerds', 'Cold Opening', etc, etc. And when we leave for a meal half an hour later writers are still writing in smoky offices.

Dan Aykroyd (Watson), Bill Murray and myself (Holmes) watch an old Basil Rathbone movie in order to check on our voices and performances for tomorrow's sketch. Then Lorne and I go up to the Japanese restaurant.

Lorne says he wants to tell me – before tomorrow night so anything said will not be affected by the show – that he would like to work with me again. Ideally he would like to set up a Michael Palin show, which would be financed by NBC, but co-produced by Lorne and myself, so that we would retain overseas rights. Like the *Rutles*, in fact.

All this profession of confidence sweeps over me, but almost fails to make contact in reality. I can't really believe it can be as easy as this. Am I really being offered *at least* one 90-minute show of my own on NBC? I think that my failure to connect must come across as either diffidence or supreme confidence.

Saturday, April 8th, New York

Shave, select clothes that will be seen across the nation tonight – and I think that's probably the last time today that I consciously stop and think about the awesome accessibility of TV. The number of homes all over America who will be looking at me, tonight, in these jeans I'm just hauling myself into. The number of friends whom I may never see again, who will see me, after their dinner party, or as they row, or because they can't sleep. The number of film stars I idolise, sports heroes, ex-Presidents of the World Bank, Watergate conspirators (Dean), authors I'm reading at the moment (Bellow), boxers, test pilots, Mick Jaggers, Senators, Congressmen, criminals, who may be looking at this shirt, or these white sneakers, before this day is out, is a thought too colossal to comprehend.

So I don't. I get going. My philosophy of the day is that this is a cabaret. And the words are all on cards.

To the studio around lunchtime. Almost the first person I see is John Belushi – he is a regular member of the team and probably the best-known now Chevy Chase has left. He has flown in overnight from LA, where he has been working on a movie, and he returns tomorrow.

The Chilites dance routine does not please Lorne and is cut just before the dress rehearsal. 'You'll thank me in years to come,' says Lorne. I'm thanking him now.

My main worry centres around a Sherlock Holmes sketch which is not just a rather long one joke item, but which requires a certain amount of playing and elaborate use of cue-cards. I find it hard and unrewarding work. Lorne said yesterday that it's a sketch which will not work until the show. Brave words.

We still have sketches unblocked when the audience come in for a full-house dress rehearsal at 7.30. For the first time today I feel nervous.

At eight we roll – the cold opening – an encouragingly funny retrospective look at the Academy Awards with Vanessa Redgrave (Jane Curtin) introducing a splendid Yasser Arafat from Belushi. Then titles – my name in lights on an electric billboard in Times Square (oh, Lorne the showman), the cast and then the rich, trusty tones of announcer Don Pardo – 'Your host for tonight … Michael Palin.'

This is the moment of truth. For the next five or six minutes it's just me. The monologue goes averagely. The show speeds on – no major boobs, but a poor audience. However, I appreciated the psychological boost of a full-audience dress rehearsal. Most of the terrors are gone now. From now on there's no time to think.

First there is a meeting of technical staff in Lorne's office. Briskly, but unhastily, Lorne runs through the show. Two sketches disappear altogether. 'Holmes' is still there and didn't go too well at dress. Lorne remains confident. Writers are sent scurrying off to rewrite material. By 10.15 a smart, new, typed running order is issued. Decisions on material that have taken three days of the week are reversed or replaced by other decisions in the space of 30 minutes.

Then to the dressing room – and Nancy and Al Lev and telegrams from Terry and Eric – 'Please Stay In America' – and into the wonderful, baggy, shiny grey suit with the specially protective cat lining in front. It could be a Python recording. I feel strangely and completely at home as 11.30 nears.

I'm moved into position by Joe Dicso, the dependable, refreshingly un-camp floor manager, and at 11.30 we're off. The cold opening, the big build-up – 'And now your host …' – and out I go – into America.

A warm reception, the monologue intrigues them, but I can't wait to get to the dance with the cats and sea-food salad. All is going well, but the cats have stage fright and, as I gyrate and at the same time try and coax these pussies into my trousers, I become aware of a frightful smell, and a warm, brown mess all down my arm. Even as I am grinning man-ically and pushing it down, the cat is shitting more violently. I can't hear the audience reaction above the band, but I know that the worst is happening. This is going to be tele-embarrassment on a monumental scale.

The offending cat leapt away, and I was left stroking the other one's little marmalade head as it peeked out of my trousers. I caught sight of myself on the monitor and it looked nightmarishly obscene. But the red light of the camera shone unblinkingly at me – revealing to the entire US a man who looked as if he was masturbating with an arm covered in shit. Awful. An awful, monumentally awful, moment.

No time after it to stop, think, question – I had to run into a one-minute costume change (the show could never work without commer-cial breaks) to become an RC priest in a confessional. I reached the confessional with five seconds to spare, slid back the partition and sud-denly realised my arm was still stained with cat nerves. In a split second I changed arms – which must have greatly thrown the director – and the stink in the cramped little confessional grew by the minute.

Even after the confessional there was no time for the scrub I needed, for I had to be raced the length of the studio, tearing off my soutane as I rocketed through the audience, in order to make a change into a Very Famous Actor. This time I was locked in a trunk with my smell.

Half an hour of high-pressure insanity had gone by before I was able to stop and think and gauge reactions to the hideous occurrences during the opening monologue. Lorne, who was on the floor throughout the taping, was the first to try and convince me that the opening had been hilarious – and I realised that nobody knew the hell of embarrassment I'd been through. After all, you can't smell on TV and the camera was never close on my arm – and anyway, it all looked like sea-food salad. No … it was great, they all said.

The 'Holmes' sketch came to life – or as much life as it'll ever come to – which was especially rewarding as we approached one o'clock. Lorne was cutting and changing and reshaping even as we were on the air, and we lost a sketch before one, and the farewells and thank yous and it was all over.

Nancy had a huge magnum of champagne ready, but I hardly had time to drink any. Many congratulations, but I think mainly just the joy of relief – of having done it. Completed this 'dangerous' show, as Lorne called it. 'Come and meet a fan', I was asked, and rushed from my champagne, which everyone else was drinking anyway, to meet a scrawny, freckled youth in loose clothes, who was introduced as Jeff Carter, the President's son.

Up to Lorne's office to see the tape. It did look monstrously funny. Bill Murray thought it was the best show this year. Everyone very happy.

Sunday, April 9th, New York

Woke just before seven. Head and senses centrifugal. My condition brings to mind Yeats – 'Things fall apart the centre cannot hold'. Shower, Alka-Seltzer, and I sleep again until ten. Amazing how resilient is the human system.

There are two fans outside my room. Yesterday one of them tried to reach me posing as an NBC cameraman. Now, as I first venture out, they're there. A big fellow and a girl. Unattractive, damp-handed. They look frightened. In the lobby a tall, elegant girl with dark glasses approaches and hands me a picture she's drawn of myself and Rachel (taken from a photo in a Central Park playground nearly two years ago).

Around five, people start arriving for a small party which I felt I should give for production team and cast. Partly because my suite needs filling up. Now they arrive, I'm feeling low on energy and would really rather be sitting in an aeroplane. But the place fills up. Nancy has brought wine, Laraine N brings hot bagels and cream cheese, and I try to make the superhuman effort to bring together the disparate elements of my own friends, who have only me in common, and the *Saturday Night Live* folk, who have each other in common.

John Belushi has flown back to complete his movie, but his wife is at the party, and Dan, Bill, Laraine and Gilda and a lot of the writers turn up. Many of them bringing presents. Tom Schiller (he who was wont to tap on my dressing room door and shout '258 minutes please, Mr Palin!') has brought me *Saturday Night and Sunday Morning*.

The cast end up smoking in the bedroom and watching a TV programme on airline hijacks. Ed Goodgold was not impressed by last night. His angle seemed to be that I was too good for the show and shouldn't soil my hands. I like Ed, but sometimes I think he's away in a too-private world. When I spoke to Lorne on the phone he said he had heard good reactions. Paul S had rung especially to say he liked it.

The Essex House party is still in uproarious form as I leave for the plane. Dan, Bill and I perform our Chilites routine and I am given a send-off at the lift, at the front desk and at the limousine.

At the airport the check-in girl complimented me on the show, as did a couple of passengers.

Unspeakable joy of sinking into an aircraft seat and being served champagne and a meal as I let my mind drift happily over the extraordinary week. Next to me a burly young man reads *Chocolate Production and Use*. Very seriously.

Thursday, April 13th

General resurgence of fortunes continues. Anne rings with positive news on John Goldstone's meetings with Denis O'Brien,[1] our latest, and probably last, hope for *Brian* backing. Apparently O'Brien has okayed the budget, but is negotiating over above the line costs. So *Brian* is on the way to a resurrection.

Cleese rings, no, sorry, Cleese's secretary rings to ask me if I would like to go with him to see Alan Bennett's play *The Old Country* tonight. I accept (in the absence of my secretary!).

Terry Hughes is going to speak directly to Bryon Parkin, head of BBC Enterprises, over the *Ripping Yarns* and Lorne. Great excitement, atmosphere of things happening. Probably quite illusory.

I fall asleep easily these days – the legacy of New York. I reckon I still have ten hours' sleep at least to catch up. Managed to stay awake for most of *The Old Country*, but neither John nor I rated it very highly. Full of surface wit, some elegant lines and well-turned phrases, and many funny moments, but, with the exception of Guinness, it was woodenly played by a cast which seemed to have less energy than the audience. This had the effect of leaving the mellifluous and gently confident Guinness high and dry, giving a Great Performance.

We walked across Shaftesbury Avenue and into Gerrard Street. The

1 American merchant banker introduced to us by George Harrison. He'd been Peter Sellers' financial adviser.

warm, bright lights and hanging cooked ducks in the windows brightened us against the unseasonable cold. Ate at a Szechuan restaurant.

We talked about America. When I described to him the day of recording, John grimaced and said he could feel his stomach tightening even as I spoke. I told him he ought to be out doing a decent movie part. He's always landed with poor roles in movies which doubtless make him money, but end up either getting cut or making no impact at all.

John is defensive – he's happy at the moment, writing new *Fawlty Towers* with Connie, though he says each script takes a month's hard work, but he gets a great deal of satisfaction from them. He makes money from 'hack work', as he calls it. Easy-money training films for Video Arts, commercials, films in which he has little involvement.

So John has polarised his life into earning (routine, no great pleasure) and non-earning (creative and artistically satisfying). A dangerous set-up, I would say. I believe the only sane and satisfying way to live is to fuse the two and avoid, wherever possible, cheapening yourself for money. In that way talent gets eradicated.

Tuesday, April 18th

Jill Foster rings to say that the Pascall Bon-Bon commercial may be on next Thursday.

In a weak moment in darkest March, when it looked as though we would be begging on the streets this summer, I came as near to agreeing to consider doing a commercial as I have done for years. My present confusion is the result. But they still haven't let me see a script.

Wednesday, April 19th

Arrival of the Pascall Bon-Bon script over breakfast. I read it and straightaway felt slightly nauseous. Jill had mentioned a figure exceeding £20,000 for this commercial, or possibly two, and what I had just read was a 30-second piece of trivia – worthless, unoriginal and banal. It looked as though it had been written in four minutes after a drunken lunch. Yet again my mind boggles at the huge discrepancy between money and talent.

I could so easily pick up the phone to Jill and say yes. Yes, I will ignore all my creative and artistic instincts, I will get an injection from the doctor on the morning of the commercial which will render me intellectually numb for the period of a day – at the end of which I will have done the horrendous deed, and be thousands of pounds better off.

Quite a temptation. But I realise that if I did this script I would be committing a crime against all the principles that concern me – honesty, value, integrity – all would be totally compromised. Helen reads the script and agrees. So I have to phone Jill and withdraw my toe from the seductive waters of advertising yet again.

Fortunately Jill has seen a script and is equally unimpressed, so the problem of hurting her doesn't arise. She phones the agency. An hour later the director calls back and asks if I would still be interested if the script were entirely rewritten.

Friday, April 21st

In the afternoon drive down to Anne's for a meeting with John Goldstone and the Pythons to discuss the new *Brian* deal.

This has been put together by Denis O'Brien and his company, EuroAtlantic. He will collect £400,000 from four rich folk and then borrow the rest, on their behalf, from the bank. The £2 million borrowed can then be written off against taxes.

Nearly everything we asked for is granted – and they seem less worried about controls than EMI. They *do* want to work closely with John on all distribution deals and we are being asked to put up £200,000 of our (and John Goldstone's) fees to cover the completion guarantee and £177,856 of our fees for the contingency money.

If we are all good boys and the weather's nice and there are no revolutions, we will make more money upfront than the EMI deal. But if we overrun or overspend then, by the terms of this deal, Python stands to be hit harder.

We talk on for two hours. Eric is aggressive – sometimes quite outrageously awkward over small points – but it's very good to have someone in the group stirring it up, when the rest of us are really happy to accept this stroke of good fortune.

Wednesday, May 3rd

The BBC ring to say that they cannot get the 'resources' for two *Ripping Yarns* this summer, and can record only one in July and the other two will have to wait until March/April 1979. Once more I feel the dead weight of BBC bureaucracy and mentally resolve to do without them for a while. Maybe I will use July/August to prepare a special for NBC. That is, if Lorne's still keen.

Friday, May 5th

Half-way to seventy today.

We signed the contract with EuroAtlantic, which gives us £2 million to make the next Python movie.

When Anne asked if there were any points in the contract we wished to discuss, there were unanimous shouts of 'Get on with it!' and 'Give us the money', so the signing went ahead with due irreverence for this vast sum we are acquiring. A magnum of champagne was opened and Anne produced a birthday cake for me, so everyone had to sing 'Happy Birthday'.

At this point Oscar Beuselinck,[1] the lawyer we have approached to help us on the Bernie [Delfont] front, arrives in the champagne and chocolate cake-stained salon. He sits himself down comfortably and confidently – a marked contrast to most people's behaviour when first confronted by the massed Pythons – as if preparing for a performance.

Oscar, who is only slightly less obsessed with being Jewish than Edwin Goodgold, clearly relishes the case. In his opinion, Bernie can't take the Otto bit about Jews putting people into 'little camps' – too near the truth about the West Bank, etc.

The upshot of Oscar's jolly visit is that we are, on his advice, going ahead with plans to sue Delfont for the money we had to pay out, and for loss of earnings due to rearrangement of our activities – on the basis that there was an oral contract, and with the moral point that we should do everything legally possible to react against this blatant act of personal censorship as being detrimental to us, good business and the British film industry … Amen.

Python has always enjoyed a fight – and with the heads of ABC and Time-Life on a charger already, we're now spoiling for action nearer home.

---

1 Much-sought-after entertainment lawyer. Known for ringing up his opponent and saying 'I'm Oscar, what's your best point?'

Saturday, May 6th

Pull myself from slumber by nine and wake myself up by driving down to Old Compton Street for croissants and newspapers.

Time to clear up and clean up before Danny Aykroyd, Rosie Shuster and friend Margot Kidder drop in … 'What a well-vacuumed house,' Danny comments. Danny and Rosie have come over on Laker's Skytrain, and say it's grim but cheap.

Margot Kidder is playing Lois Lane in the *Superman* movie (which is still shooting, over a year after they pulled out of Shepperton).

Apparently most of her work involves hanging in harness alongside Christopher Reeve whilst people do strange things to them. They have to fight an eagle on the top of the Empire State Building. The first 'eagle' they got was from Taiwan and looked so un-eagle-like, with a funny red crop on its head, that it was sent home and it was decided instead to use large falcons. The falcons would only fly after chicken bones, so Margot and *Superman* were suspended, with wind machine blowing them, between one man hurling falcons towards another man holding chicken legs.

As Superman perspired heavily, leaving tell-tale patches around the armpits of his costume, one member of the crew was standing by to blow-dry his armpits.

The length and design of Superman's cock was the subject of much controversy, which culminated in Superman appearing at a photo-session with a large metal dong down his tights. Margot said she got so fed up with this thing digging into her leg that she took to flicking it with her fingernail, causing a light but noticeable metallic ting every time she touched his shorts.

The Salkinds are not the most conventional businessmen, she readily admits, but she thinks the movie will be great and confirms the rumour I heard at the Shepperton board meeting that it will be premiered at the White House.

Monday, May 8th

To Devonshire Place to face Dr Kieser and the dreaded world of gingivectomy.

Debbie is there and bucks me up in the waiting room with enthusiastic words about the *Ripping Yarns* – had I seen Celia Brayfield's piece in the *Standard* last Friday saying that the *Yarns* were the only things worth staying in for on Friday evenings … ? These crumbs of comfort are gobbled up eagerly.

The surgery, which involves one half of my mouth, top and bottom, begins just after six and goes on for two hours, almost without a break. Kieser is thorough, but much more gentle than Robin Powell, constantly congratulating me on being a model patient and doing everything to make sure I'm as comfortable as it's possible to be with someone slicing into your gums and scraping away at the exposed bone.

I'm stitched up and sent away with a reassuring collection of mouthwashes, extra-strong aspirin, should I need it, swabs, should bleeding recur … and the plaudits of the cheery, extrovert South African ringing in my ears.

Thursday, May 18th

Just like the old days. Up at 7.45 for an hour's work, then down to Terry's around ten for a day's writing that lasts until seven. With a great effort of concentration we have completed a typescript of the 'Potter of the Punjab' tale, now called 'Roy of the Raj'. It will go to the BBC tomorrow and I have a feeling that we shall be filming it in July.

Saturday, May 20th

Wonderful start to the day – a letter from Spike Milligan saying simply '*Ripping Yarns* are super – more please.' What an accolade. For me it's like Pelé telling you you're a good footballer.

Gilliam and Terry J dropped in – though at different times. TG has finished his film script, he says. I asked what he was going to do now. 'Write it,' quipped the paranoid animator.

Sunday, May 21st

To a lunch party at Tom Stoppard's in Iver Heath.

It's a marquee do – with lots of noise and clinking of opinions.

Miriam greets us effusively. Her two – or two of her several children – are great *Ripping Yarn* fans. I'm getting worried by all these children who love it – not by them, but by the lack of corresponding enthusiasm amongst grown men and women. Tom asks what it's like to be everybody's favourite children's programme.

Talk to Prunella Scales and husband Tim West. Pru says she was not really happy doing the first series of *Fawlty Towers* – she was so concerned with getting it right and lacked confidence in her part. But I think this is a touch of theatrical modesty.

Clive James, looking very pallid – as if trying deliberately to throw off the bronzed Aussie image – heaves over to our table, plonks himself down beside Prunella and declares 'I'm Clive James, I've come to lionise you.'

After finishing with Prunella, he turns to lionise me. Says he liked 'Stalag Luft' and had not seen it the first time round, when he first wrote his *Ripping Yarns* review in *The Observer*. He would have re-reviewed it, but ... He said two revealing things. One being that the arts pages of most Sunday papers go to press on Friday afternoon – so programmes on Friday night (on which the *RY* repeats currently are) stand less chance of review than almost any other slot in the week.

I asked him why comedy got such short shrift in TV columns – and why Alan Coren should be so dismissive of *Ripping Yarns* after raving about *Tomkinson*. James put it down to jealousy. 'We all want to be doing your job,' he says. 'We can write and talk, but we're frustrated because we can't perform.' Interesting.

I take the plunge and ask Stephen Frears if he would be at all interested in directing a comedy special for NBC with me. To my intense enjoyment he says yes ... and I think the idea appeals to him.

Monday, May 22nd

With Spike's card facing me at my writing desk, and Stephen Frears' interest in the NBC special, I start this week with a stirring sense of optimism. So much could go wrong – the NBC special is still not a firm offer – but so much could, if it goes right, be some of the most exciting work I've done.

Today, after checking out my body – Alexander class at 8.50 – and my teeth at 11.30 – I drive over to the BBC to hear the verdict on our *Yarn* for July. Fairly predictably, 'Roger of the Raj' (as it's now known) is the one they're keen on. John Howard Davies, now Head of Comedy, doesn't like the 'child-molester' references, I hear.

Talk over the script with Jim F and the various points of rewriting to be done. It's a big cast, and I find myself stuck with Roger ... another juve lead!

Wednesday, May 24th

In to the BBC at 2.30 to help Jim audition young lads for the part of Roger as a young boy. One had a black eye, the other a sore throat and a magnificently irretractable Cockney accent, and only one was any good at all …

Then more casting chat with Jim, mainly involving desultory turning of *Spotlight* pages. I want to aim high and suggest we try for someone like Ralph Richardson for the father. BBC Artists' Bookings are amazingly unimaginative as usual, and say Ralph Richardson will cost £1,000. The booker said, 'You know, he's almost ga-ga.' Anyone who can command £1,000 for a half-hour can't be entirely ga-ga.

Sir Michael Redgrave, another possible, is £200 cheaper than Sir Ralph, but Peter Lovell, the PA, said that when Sir Michael was doing a one-liner on Morecambe and Wise, he took eight takes to get it right. And there's a suggestion that he's 'not awfully well'. I stall Jim into letting me make my own enquiries. Refuse to be put off by BBC Artists' Bookings.

Back home, ring Tom Stoppard to check out Sir Ralph. Tom doesn't know him, but will ring Michael Codron, who put on Sir Ralph's last play, and test the water for me. So hopes are still high.

Thursday, May 25th

John Howard D is persisting in his objections to the words 'child molester' in the 'Roger of the Raj' script. Jim says I'll have to go and see him tomorrow. Also every avenue of exploration into the Sir Ralph situation seems fraught with money and Jim sounds as if he would rather drop the whole approach. Shall have to try and rally the troops tomorrow.

Friday, May 26th

Hot again. Into the sizzling silly season for the newspapers. The *Mirror* is pulling every stop out – even the weather – to try and boost Callaghan and the government before the election (not yet announced, but everyone thinks it's October). Callaghan is personally very popular at the moment and Thatcher is not. I think anyone with any information of substance must realise that Jim's good news basket is a very small one and all the signs are that the present drop in inflation (now down to 7.8%) and unemployment figures cannot be maintained.

Still, I'm better disposed to letting the present Labour government run my country for me than any other group – apart, perhaps, from Pan's People – and I feel better governed (in a moral, rather than material sense) than at any time for many years.

Over to the BBC. At least JHD doesn't attempt the economic argument to convince me why 'child molester' should be omitted. He tries hoary old chestnuts like 'What happens if a child is attacked that evening?' He tries the power approach, '*I* really can't let this sort of thing go out.' I absorb everything cheerfully and can only plead that every line is part of the creation of a vital character and is used in innocent reflectiveness for the purposes of getting a laugh. Which it will get. JHD cannot pull experience on me either. We are almost the same age. So he capitulates with, I think, mock-crossness, and I think he's not so bad after all. He's just frighteningly competitive, that's all.

Monday, May 29th

A thoroughly pleasant, though I suppose at times awkward, canal trip on Chris Orr's converted ice-breaker 'Scott'. The 'voyage' had been arranged by Robert, in order to get Chris and I talking about 'Arthur', his latest project, a story with lithograph illustrations. Chris needs up to £5,000 to get the project under way. The Arts Council and the Fraser Gallery have been approached – unsuccessfully.

I've read the book over the last week and am very disappointed. I found it loose, undisciplined – in short a mess of good ideas, bad ideas, in about 40–60 proportion. Am I getting old? Why do I feel exasperation with this 'experimental' style? If only Chris would pare it down to essentials – but I fear that the very diffusion of style is what's important to him.

Tuesday, June 6th

Ring Laurence Evans, Sir Ralph R's agent one last time. A lady assures me that he has all the details and has been trying to get in touch with Sir Ralph. This game has gone on for well over a week, and I still haven't even spoken to Laurence Evans.

I ring Lindsay Anderson. Lindsay is at his most charming and cheerful and, fortunately, helpful. He is interested to hear of my lack of success with Richardson's agents. 'They're shits,' he says, with feeling, 'and I should know – they're my agents as well.' He himself will ring Sir Ralph (an old friend) and mention my interest.

A little breakthrough. Lindsay calls back. He's spoken to Sir Ralph, who sounds to be available, and he has asked me to drop a script at Sir Ralph's house in Regent's Park.

Lindsay suggests that I give Sir Ralph a ring before dropping round – 'His wife will probably answer, but if you can get through her you're alright' – so I'm relieved but momentarily shaken to hear the familiar voice of Sir Ralph himself at the other end of the line. Would he mind if I brought him a script … ? 'No … no … by all means. I have my plaque up … "Actor available, no waiting …"' the great man assures me genially. 'I'll read it … Put your phone number on the bottom and I'll give you a ring.'

It's not often one speaks to a Living Legend – there aren't many left – and it takes me a while to come down from a slightly sweaty tremble of excitement. But in a cooler, more rational moment I remember what Lindsay had said – don't be apologetic, if you've got a good script, an actor will jump at it.

So, armed with a good script, and William, who's come along for the ride, I make my way to No. 1 Cumberland Terrace, the residence of Sir Ralph and Lady Richardson. It's on the end of one of Nash's impressive, classical terraces – full of ambassadors and burglar alarms. Lady Richardson answers the door and I hand her the script. Exchange of charming smiles and the door shuts.

Wednesday, June 7th

A crisp and efficient two-hour production meeting at the BBC. After we've been through the show and Jim is politely grumbling about the BBC, Sir Ralph phones and asks for me.

His voice has a chuckle in it. 'Yes … Yes …' says the Great Man. 'He's rather a nice old chap isn't he … rather charming …' He chuckles again. It's as if he's talking about himself, but I realise he's communicating cautious approval, enjoyment even, of the character of Lord Bartlesham. I mutter something solidly flattering (to both myself and Sir Ralph) about the character working on two or three different levels and that's why we need the best player we can get. He mutters and grunts and makes noises of distinct pleasure, but then says he's off to watch the Derby and we'd better ring his agent, who will be expecting a call. 'You see, I'd like to take my wife with me.' He promises to read the script again tonight and asks who will be Lady B. With that, our goodbyes.

It's not a great surprise when Jim rings a few hours later to say that despite the BBC stretching all its resources (!!) Laurence Evans has turned down the offer, explaining that, 'He likes a bit of luxury, you know.'

Thursday, June 8th

A patchy day of sun and cloud. Patchy in achievement too. John Le Mesurier evidently likes the 'Roger of the Raj' script so much that he's very happy to do a small part (Runciman). This encourages me, because I know he will be brilliant.

More encouragingly, I find that 'The Wreck of the Harvey Goldsmith' looks in good shape – an abundance of funny material (but an expensive show) and I start a new tale, 'Dracula at St Dominic's'.

TJ tells me Diana Quick can't do Judith in the *Life of Brian*, as she is committed to the RSC in the autumn. We are seeing a girl called Sue Jones-Davis tomorrow morning.

Friday, June 9th

Regent's Park bathed in sunshine as I drive down to Park Square West for the Python meeting. Terry J and John Goldstone are present. Eric didn't think it was worth coming. John is out of the country, evidently playing cricket in Corfu! Gilliam is still in France.

So TJ, myself and a very much slimmed-down Dr Chapman, meet Sue Jones-Davies. A tiny, boyish little Welsh lady with an upturned nose. Dressed in jeans and shirt – no frills. She reads Judith in a delightful Welsh accent. She's quite a tough and sparky little girl, and has a strong, open face, which should come across well in all the Judith v Brian close-ups. Not a versatile comedy lady like Gwen Taylor, but a good Judith we all think.

John Le Mesurier's agent rings to say he wants his full *Dad's Army* fee for playing the one-day cameo in 'Roger'. Jim will sort this out, though he's puzzled and rather cross about it.

Wednesday, June 14th

Have been reading extracts from Virginia Woolf's *A Writer's Diary*. How hard she worked at writing. What impossibly high standards she always seemed to set herself.

Sylvia Plath – another lady whose depth of perception and whose shining intelligence seemed to render her always more vulnerable than secure – expressed this in *The Bell-Jar*: 'I feel like a race horse in a world without race tracks.' In *Christopher and His Kind*, Isherwood expresses a less fraught attitude: 'Christopher said to himself that only those who are capable of silliness can be called truly intelligent.'

I'm with Isherwood.

Friday, June 16th

Complete a reading of the *Brian* script this morning, then drive down to Park Square West.

Keith Moon is unanimously voted into the rep company. John Young, the Historian in *Grail*, is unanimously voted in as Matthias, the largest single non-Python role in the movie. We can't agree yet on a Judith.

Eric's two songs – 'Otto' and the 'Look on the Bright Side' crucifixion song – are rather coolly received before lunch.

My suggestion of Ken Colley as Jesus is accepted nem con – thus solving quite a long-term problem. And the title is to be *Monty Python's Life of Brian* – not 'Brian of Nazareth' as GC and I liked, or 'Monty Python's Brian', as TJ suggested.

Thursday, June 22nd

Down to Donovan at lunchtime to surrender my false teeth, which will be 'reworked and reordered' for me to collect them tomorrow. Toothless, out into chill London.

Drive to a reception at the National Book League (again), this time for contributors to *The Writers' Book of Recipes*, which I had evidently replied to about fifteen months ago. At the cocktail party my letter is included in a hastily assembled display case – right next to one from Jan Morris.

I sauntered over and was, hopefully rather discreetly, glancing over my letter of 16th March '77, when a soft, rather deep, voice charmingly insinuated on my private gloat. Looked up to find myself confronted by a large lady with rather dry and unkempt wispy grey hair, which sat unsatisfactorily on a bold, square head. Kind, warm eyes, a generous mouth. An interesting, but rather disturbing face – fine and strong in the features, but messy in detail.

This was Jan Morris, who, as James Morris, wrote one of the travel books which most affected me – in fact one of my favourite books of all – that on Venice.

Jan said how much she'd enjoyed 'Across the Andes by Frog' – especially remarking on the way development heaped on development. I in turn gave a quick rave about Venice – the book.

Had this comfortable, tweedy lady really climbed the Himalayas as a man *and* written for *Rolling Stone* as a woman? This encounter was the high point of the cocktail party for *Recipes*, which seemed ironic as I had no teeth in.

Saturday, June 24th

TG drops by for some more chit-chat. He's more worried than ever about the words – the dialogue in his films, which he's always had an inferiority complex about – and is thinking of trying to make his new film tell its own story – like his animations – and be less 'written'. His dream sequence ideas sound great – especially the brick skyscrapers with no windows.

Wednesday, June 28th

Lorne Michaels called from the Savoy mid-afternoon. He'd arrived from New York just before lunch. Now recovered, he was making arrangements to meet. I would have liked to talk privately, but there were various people who wanted to have dinner with him, so we agreed to meet up at the Savoy around nine.

To the Savoy, where I find Lorne in a comfortable, but a little colourless suite with an impressive panoramic bay window view of Waterloo Bridge, the Thames, St Paul's and the City.

He thinks that I should consider spending six to eight weeks in the US each year and bring family, etc. This is the difficult area in our plans. It's one thing to do a special with freedom and money, but this freedom is going to be compromised in many little ways – and I fear the American exposure bit is one of them.

Thursday, June 29th

It's raining heavily as I set off for the Arlecchino restaurant in Notting Hill to meet Terry Hughes and Lorne Michaels for lunch. Lorne hasn't slept all night – but looks exactly as he always does and he talks rather more than usual, relishing a new audience. He drinks coffee, but little else.

Almost on cue, an American girl and her friend come across the restaurant and tell me how much they loved 'Across the Andes by Frog' – and with Terry there too. What timing.

About 3.30 we cram into my Mini and drive through the rain to the TV Centre. In Terry's office Lorne produces a tape of a Steve Martin *Saturday Night* show, which he's putting in for an award. Terry H disappears, and some time later, when we've finally got the BBC machine to work (this takes four or five people, secretaries, window cleaners, etc), Terry emerges from Jimmy Gilbert's office and, in an urgent whispered aside, tells us that Bruce Forsyth has just signed for ITV, and that Jimmy is in a state of utter confusion and trying to write a press release.

Eventually Lorne and I leave. I can't help finding it remarkable that, even with the Forsyth saga going on, the head of BBC Light Entertainment doesn't have time even to shake hands with one of the US's top LE producers – or top producers, period.

To the house Shelley Duvall has rented in Avenue Road, while she's working on *The Shining*. It's furnished like a luxury penthouse in a bad English 'B' movie, and I find myself feeling little envy for the sort of life which results in having to live for six months in such colourless, characterless transitory surroundings. Shelley says the ambassador for Ceylon lives next door, so she's alright for tea.

Shelley I like more and more. She's humorous, silly almost, direct and accessible and defiantly un-glamorous – and she loved 'Escape From Stalag Luft 112B' and my *Saturday Night* show!

Friday, June 30th

Drive to Shepperton for lunch with Graham Ford and Paul Olliver. The catering manager, whose guts I'm after at every board meeting, is most obsequious – offers me cod 'fresh caught from Grimsby' and whispers loudly how very much he enjoyed the *Ripping Yarns.*

Saturday, July 1st

A Python read-through at Anne's. We begin by trying to do the quiz in the 'Complete Monty Python' fan book. The questions are incredibly hard, and the entire team scores only 60% – on our own material!

Read-through a little stilted to start with. Graham has a long list of suggestions and each scene is rather heavily post-mortemed. Then we suddenly find three hours have gone by and Terry J hurries us all through. The state of the script isn't bad, but doubts are voiced about Judith's role (by Terry G) and Brian's. The usual arguments that they're rather dull parts – and as soon as we start to work on the Brian/Judith relationship we lose the comedy.

Indecision still over the casting of Judith. Gwen is good, but I feel Judith needs to be tougher, stronger, more dangerous than Gwen could ever be. We need a stroppy feminist with a sense of humour to play the role.[1]

Tuesday, July 4th, The Bull Inn, Bethersden, Kent

'Roger of the Raj' shoot begins. Meet Richard Vernon and Joan Sanderson at breakfast as well as Jim and co.

Richard and Joan haven't rehearsed together and it's only when we're in and sitting round the dining room table in this beautifully furnished Elizabethan manor house, with the sparks rigging the lights, that they have a chance to play the scene together. Joan tends to overplay, Richard to underplay, but they are both very willing listeners and extremely gentle, approachable folk.

Happy to be working again with this tight, efficient little unit and with the increasing feeling that the series now has acquired a much greater prestige than I thought (Joan Sanderson was telling me of its high reputation among 'the profession'), I feel as easy, confident, optimistic and relaxed as I can ever remember on filming.

1 After a few more auditions Sue Jones-Davies was confirmed in the role, and was brilliant.

Friday, July 7th, Bethersden

The pattern of filming now well established. Up at a quarter to eight, down to breakfast (coffee and grapefruit juice only) at eight o'clock. Various ablutions and bodily functions, then a ten-minute drive through Kentish fields to High Halden and down the long avenue of trees that leads to Harbourne Hall.

Here we have ensconced ourselves comfortably. The BBC has taken over, installing wires and cables and new shutters and blinds on the windows and palm trees and Edwardian lamps and cane tables and chairs. This is India for two weeks.

Today is the Regimental Dinner, for which several actors, including John Le Mesurier, have been imported, and the dark back room in the servants' quarters which houses Make-up and Wardrobe is overflowing.

John Le Mes, it transpires, is a great friend of Derek Taylor's, and Derek, who was taking a short break over here from his irksome life in Warner Bros, LA, had reassured John Le Mes that he was a great fan of the *Yarns*. So maybe Derek was instrumental in securing John.

The scene works marvellously. All the performances are strong and first rehearsal brings the house down. Of course the volume of laughter never greets the scene again, as we plod through it during the day, but the actors work hard to keep the freshness, despite all the technical delays and waits.

John Le Mes wears his slippers for the last shot. He doesn't drink any more now – after a bout of hepatitis – but chain-smokes instead. He looks physically frail, but his eyes are sharp, bright, lively and humorous.

Monday, July 10th, Bethersden

The last of our day shoots. From tomorrow until the end of the week we work all through the night.

Catch up a little today. But I feel that some of the ensemble work between Roger Brierley, Richard Vernon and Joan S lacks something – some spark. It's almost as though they're finding it too easy. So I'm up and jumping around and giving hints and encouragements whenever I can.

Jim is very good here and lets me work with the actors as much as I like. But I have the first feelings of irritation that the camera and lighting have once again set the pace, so that the actors tend to be forgotten –

expected to just turn on the right performance after waiting an hour for a shot to be lit. The priorities are becoming muddled. The show ultimately stands or falls on how good the actors are – and they need as much work as the lights.

Wednesday, July 12th, The Brecknock Arms, Bells Yew Green, East Sussex

I'm sitting alone in the small back garden of this unassuming little pub. There is no muzak, there are no coloured lights, or chairs and tables crafted crudely to the shape of bent tree bark. Just an iron table and comfortable but inelegant iron chairs, slatted with wood. And a pint of Harvey's best Sussex bitter, brewed in Lewes and looking very friendly with the sun shining through it. A blackbird or a song thrush, something very melodious, trills in the tree above me. Peace and solitude.

Last night's filming was hard work. Neighbours complained about rifle fire in the middle of the night and threatened us with an injunction (they know their rights down here) and this was even *before* Joan Sanderson opened up with her 1914 Lewis machine gun – the crack echoing around the whole of Kent, so it seemed, to such an extent that after the third or fourth round there was an impassioned cry from the black depths of the woodland – 'Shut up!' We finished at ten past four this morning.

Friday, July 14th

The final day of shooting on 'Roger'.

Back to Harbourne Hall for the last time. The Major and his wife appeared every now and then – the Major ruddy-faced, obviously enjoys a drink. I became aware, talking to him, of the pathos of their situation – both married for the second time – the children belong to Mrs F, not him – 'So we don't always see eye to eye.' He was in tanks at Alamein, the kids are on motorbikes in Tenterden. He looks blearily round at the huge, red bulk of the unattractive house behind him – 'It's always been a happy home.' He repeats this sadly, shaking his head. It's very moving.

At dawn we're gone, packed up, the cables stowed away and the house returns to normal. On Wednesday this 'happy home' is up for sale by auction. Major F talks of a bungalow in Bethersden they've got an eye on.

Wednesday, July 19th

Python medical today. More thorough than usual. Begins with a chest X-ray, then a visit to Dr Ronald Wilkinson, who holds my testicles and asks me to leave my urine in his bathroom. A girl takes a sample of my blood and a man sticks electrodes all over me for an electro-cardiograph test. Wilkinson reassures me that this all means I'm a much bigger property than when he last held my testicles.

The ECG man purred happily as he unravelled my reading. 'A very nice heart,' he pronounced.

Thursday, July 27th

Off to Ealing full of anticipation. My first look at the two weeks of pictures from 'Roger'. Instant disappointment on almost every front, except the look of it – costumes, colour, design, the house, etc. The performances of Lord and Lady B only adequate, the whole tale seems flatly paced and humourlessly edited. My role as Roger is another of those irritating, ingenuous younger sons which are in danger of becoming a real bore.

Even the regimental scene, a sure-fire winner, seems to be misfiring. There's a great deal of re-editing to do, and the first task is to establish a rapport with Dan Rae, the editor. He's tall and taciturn and rather likeable, but he begins by appearing to resent my suggestions.

This turns out to be defensiveness on both our parts. As we go systematically through the film (Jim F is away on holiday, so I have a free hand), both of us ease up. I realise that it was a shock to all my carefully nurtured pre-conceptions of the piece to see it for the first time through [cameraman] Reg Pope's and Jim Franklin's eyes, and Dan Rae has realised I am neither an unnaturally lugubrious old bugger, nor a stroppy writer who can't stand to see any editor touch his work. We carry on after lunch and when I leave at four Dan reckons he has four more days to do on tightens, corrections, re-positioning and finding new shots. Fingers crossed it will work then.

Friday, July 28th

First progress of any sort on the NBC special. Work on outlines for a new Robin Hood tale – the story of an insecure, nightmare-ridden, ex-hero, trying to live with his legendariness. At least there's a character there I'd like to play.

But writing up in my room today is like resting on an anthill. The children, plus friends, are all at home, there are four builders in No. 2 and, after lunch, Helen trying to grab some of the hot sunshine out on my balcony. I like my house and my family, but today the attractions of a quiet hotel room with just a bed and a typewriter flashed briefly, but poignantly across my mind.

Off to play squash with Terry and try to rid myself of this inability to produce brilliance. The game revives me.

Afterwards we pay a visit to Michael Henshaw.[1] Michael is anxious to talk over a tax-avoidance scheme to deal with the estimated £82,000 in foreign-earned money which we should be receiving as our full share of the performance fee on *Brian*.

An endearingly frank middle-aged man with greying hair and a lisp explains the scheme. It would involve Terry and me becoming a partnership, based on the island of Guernsey, with the aid of a Guernsey partner whom this man would find for us.

He was disarmingly open in acknowledging that there were risks. 'The worst that can happen is that after six years you may have to pay it all back,' he told us. 'What if it's all been spent on the houses and swimming pools it will enable us to have?' asked I. His reply was equally cheerful. 'You can always go bankrupt.'

A hot evening, but two pairs of cold feet as we left Michael's.

Friday, August 4th

To Dog's Ear Studio in Wapping, where Chris Orr was having an open day party to celebrate the completion of printing of the *Arthur* lithographs.[2]

London Docklands is a weird and wonderful place – a desert of empty warehouses and forlorn cranes frozen for ever in semi-tumescence. Dog's Ear is on the third floor of one of these warehouses. Dark and solid buildings where your footsteps echo from stout stone floors and ring through empty stairwells. Then the delight of the studio

1 Despite his separation from Anne, he was still, officially, the accountant for Terry and myself.
2 I'd decided, despite my earlier reservations, to publish *Arthur* through Signford Ltd.

itself – a long thin room of quite unusual scale, almost seventy yards long.

Chris is at the end of the room, setting bottles of wine out on a white-clothed table, and, as I walk down the room to him, my customary sense of proportion and perspective is quite thrown. I never normally spend this amount of time crossing a room.

At the far end and beyond the table is the wide river access and, three floors below, with no walkway or garden or patio to interrupt access, is the green-brown slosh of the Thames. A stunning location – and a more dramatic London setting for a studio it would be hard to imagine. I feel that the docks are, must surely be, about to undergo a renaissance. Already hotels are creeping down from Tower Bridge, and these strong, spacious warehouse buildings with the immeasurable asset of direct river access, will, in ten or twenty years, be full and busy again.

To add to the pleasure of the place there was also the satisfaction of seeing the fruits of Chris and friends' careful craftsmanship in the production of the lithographs. The end results were sharper, clearer and had much more impact on me than the original proofs.

Drove to the Savoy and there met Lorne (discreetly behind shades).

Lorne, en passant, muses on what it would be like if J Cleese and I were to do a show together ... Now that would be a world-beater, he says, ever so gently.

Tuesday, August 8th

Out to dinner this evening with Anne Beatts – a *Saturday Night Live* writer who is over here – and Shelley Duvall, with whom she's staying. Helen came along too, reluctantly at first, for this was to be a rare evening at home. Shelley is good company, though, tells a good tale and has an effortlessly appealing warmth which wins over one's confidence easily. She's very sharp and intelligent – except for buying a very small and cross dog, which leaves little pools all over the carpet.

She's just had sixteen days off from *The Shining*, whilst Jack Nicholson's back recovered, but is now back on the 8.15 to 8 routine at Elstree. She very much wants to borrow my tape of 'Eric Olthwaite', which she raves about, to show Jack and Stanley. Now there's a thought.

Wednesday, August 9th

What a silly business I'm in. In what other walk of life would a 35-year-old company director be signing his tax return for the year whilst dressed as a Jewish shepherd? This was my first full fitting of the costumes for *Brian* – the project which will affect my tax bill more than anything else in the next couple of years.

Friday, August 18th

At the TV Centre for the dub of 'Roger of the Raj'.

A depressing day. The show still lacks the humour of 'Tomkinson' or the impact of 'Olthwaite', or the good old reassuringly familiar territory of 'Murder at Moorstones'. 'Roger' is quite an ambitious little script and needs to be very tight to work. It still is loose and lazy in vital areas – the acting, some of the lighting and the serious dearth of close-ups, which could have been used to great effect.

So today needed patience, time and tolerance. None of these seemed to be forthcoming from the dubbing editor. He was brisk, rather curt, and gave the whole session an unenjoyable and uncreative tension.

But the faster and less patient he became, the more I dug my heels in, voicing every suggestion and every tiny idea. Then at eight in the evening – after nearly ten hours' solid dubbing – it became obvious we'd need more time and, as the show wasn't due to go out until probably 1980, it seemed that such a thing wouldn't be out of the question! The editor suddenly brightened, admitted he was tired, and made various constructive suggestions that we should all have talked over at ten this morning when we started.

As had now become an almost annual event, we escaped for a few days to Mary and Edward's rural retreat in the Lot Valley.

Wednesday, August 30th, France

Woke at a quarter to eight and creaked my way downstairs as noiselessly as possible and pulled open the big, old, well-weathered wooden front door of the house.

The grass and the surrounding fields were in shade, as the sun does not mount the trees on the hill behind until nearly ten o'clock at this time of year. But it was dry, as it has been every day, and crisply cool. Not a breath of wind stirs the trees. The only sound is a distant dog barking and a very cod cock crowing. Everything feels fresh, clean and renewed.

Monsieur Crapaud, as we have christened the warty-backed toad who lives down in the bathroom, is easing his way around the shower floor – and we gaze at each other for a moment as I sit on the lavatory. Then he makes his stretched, rubbery way towards the door, where he hangs a sharp right turn and crawls under the washing machine.

Then into my white shorts, socks, gym shoes and 'Central Park' T-shirt from Macy's and begin my last pre-breakfast run. Up through the woods – an uphill start and very vicious – through gorse bushes on the path with freshly spun spiders' webs catching at my face. But the nearer I get to the top of the hill, the nearer I get to the sun and to the open ground.

Finally out of the gloom of oak and sweet chestnut saplings, beneath tall pines and into a sun-filled field of maize in hard red earth. Three times round this uneven rustic race-track (with three sprints), then down the far side of the hill and across a ridge covered in blue anemones, with copses and small, irregularly shaped, irregularly stocked fields of maize and vines and weeds and pasture, where sheep with bells graze on either side. And hillsides empty of buildings stretch away to the north-east and south-west, their colours softened by the subtle haze of morning sunshine.

I drank it all in today – my last run through this Elysian countryside for a year or more.

We've been in France for eight and a half days. The weather so warm, dry and settled that I estimate we spent 16 hours every day in the open air. They were commonplace and unremarkable holiday days. I wrote nothing and revelled in the complete lack of any vital tasks apart from those involved with day-to-day living.

Back home, it's very cold and there's a letter awaiting from Bryon Parkin[1] – the carbon of a letter to Lorne confirming that there is no way two of the *Ripping Yarns* can be sold to NBC for a special, as the contract with PBS has gone ahead.

---

1 Head of BBC Enterprises – sales arm of the BBC.

Thursday, August 31st

Down to 2 PSW for all-day session of rehearsal. Feel drained physically by five, when we break.

In the evening I try to rally my flagging resources to write letters, etc, and to think sensibly about the consequences of Bryon Parkin's letter about the *Yarns*. Lorne rings – he's equally depressed at the news, will call again in a week's time … We confirm once again the 'intent to work together'. Though when I stop and think about it, I've altered my perspective slightly after the stay in France. My scheme to retire at 40 and write and travel (write travel books – but decent, original, bright, funny ones) has been thrust well to the fore, the BBC has gone right to the bottom of the list and Python and Lorne float somewhere in between.

Saturday, September 2nd

I take William down to Covent Garden, where they're holding a two-day street festival. A genial, scruffy bunch of folk selling a lot of wholemeal bread and entertaining noisily and a little desperately in the shadow of the two big new office blocks that are rising up around them – showing that money, not good intentions, is still boss in Covent Garden, as in any other part of London.

But for the moment what's left of the Alternative Society is all here today, and I even catch a nostalgic whiff of grass – a smell of ten years ago, when people like this had never really been seen on the streets of London before. The middle classes letting their hair down and coping, in one way, with all the guilt their parents left them.

Thursday, September 7th

To Redwood by eleven to record a radio commercial – the first I've done for a couple of years. It was an anti-smoking radio commercial made (on a pittance, of course) for the Scottish Health Council. I had asked Charles McKeown[1] to come along and do it with me. Tony Herz of Radio Operators had written and was producing it. It's one of several in the campaign, part of an impossibly uphill struggle to try and make non-smoking as glamorous as smoking appears to be.

1 A versatile actor and writer who I'd met through David Leland. He appeared regularly in *Ripping Yarns*, as well as in a variety of roles in *Life of Brian*.

From Redwood down through Covent Garden and along Fleet Street to the offices of Methuen.

I talked myself rather rapidly into a one week book-signing, radio and TV promo-tour at the end of November. Suggested that we had a theme for the tour that was pertinent to the book – something like an expedition. This was eagerly taken up by Jan Hopcraft [the publicity manager], and hardened into Round Britain By Frog – the Palin/Jones expedition to British bookshops 1978. I hope this won't sound too wet by November. But I made them promise to avoid extreme efforts at wackiness.

Saw some proofs of the book (artwork included) – enough to give me encouragement that at least we will be publicising and signing a well-made article. Will anybody come along, though? Nightmare vision of sitting in bookshops waiting for someone, having to resort to low methods of accosting passers-by.

To Robin Simmons for a quick Alexander reminder. Already feel myself tending to stiffen up in anticipation of the excitement of Tunisia, so must remember what I've learnt.

Sunday, September 10th

As a result of having time last week to plan for Le Grand Depart, this morning's leave-taking is easier, emotionally and physically, than some I can remember.

It's almost a psychic phenomenon, my departures, for some sixth sense seems to inform the 'villagers' that something is about to happen and, as I try discreetly to slip away, doors open and cars drive up and the place is soon like a stadium. Today they weren't let down. An enormous American limousine, of the low, interminably long, black New York variety, swung into the village, and out stepped Dr Chapman in immaculate light grey suit, and matching it, and creating the final and complete effect of flamboyant elegance – nay, even stardom – was a light grey fedora. Never, outside of a sketch, have I seen the Doctor looking quite as dashing.

My last memory of the children is of Tom, Willy, Rachel (in Helen's arms), Holly, Catherine, Louise and Helen Guedalla forming a tableau in the back window of the Cadillac. It felt like an archetypal image of the native son off to the big city to find fame and fortune. Except he wouldn't have left in a Cadillac.

We went on to Eric's, and I realised that these vast cars are designed to make the occupants look important, rather than to take on goods and chattels. So, despite being twice as long as any other non-goods vehicle on the road, we still had to go through a minor comedy routine with the cases.

Graham had by this time taken his hat off, and looked less jaunty. Through growing clouds of pipe smoke he told me, a little apologetically, that he'd only bought the suit because he was going to take a tax year out of the country (and this was the first day).

Eric has equally positively decided to move out of London, though only as far as the outer commuter countryside – Oxfordshire, possibly – 'to be near George [Harrison] and near London'. He talks of the country wistfully now, as if drawn to it as the next inevitable step in his development.

I had nothing to equal such hefty decisions.

Graham and I talked of Keith Moon, who was to have been in the movie and flying out soon to join us, but who died some time on Thursday night, after a party. Graham, whose abstention from alcohol has increased his appeal a hundred per cent – he now sounds like, as well as looks like a very wise old owl – told me that Keith was trying to cut down his Rabelaisian appetite for booze, and had some pills called Heminevrin to help out, but these should be taken under carefully controlled conditions and never with alcohol – for they act to increase the strength of anything you *do* drink.

So Keith had just gone too far and, although his whole life was lived constantly up to the limits, this time, like an adventurous schoolboy on a frozen pond, he'd stepped a little too far out. What a waste. But GC reckons both Peter Cook and Ringo S are also in trouble with booze.

A long taxi drive from Tunis to Monastir as night fell. Impressions of aridity, emptiness, scrubland stretching away on either side of the road. A camel train tottering, or rather swaying, in that peculiarly restful camel motion, along a dried up river bed.

The villages we pass through are reminiscent of Ireland or Cyprus – not neat and tidy Best Kept Village candidates as in France, Germany or Britain, but collections of houses built as basically as possible to provide shelter for men, women, children and their animals. No time or money for grass verges or floral clocks here.

To the Hotel Meridien by eight. It's large, new and comfortable – as different from those villages as England is from the moon. An international standard of comfort and atmosphere, protecting the Overdeveloped from the Underdeveloped.

The bed is comfortable and the room has no fewer than three balconies with views out over the sea – which sounds near. Unpack and drift off to sleep about two o'clock. Almost my last memory is of Rachel sitting in my bed this morning and asking 'Where are you going today, Daddy?'

'Africa, darling.'

Monday, September 11th, Hotel Meridien, Monastir, Tunisia

Looking through the script, it strikes me, not for the first time, that the schedule is very full indeed. A long and ambitious film to be squeezed into the eight-week shoot we have planned. Can't help but feel that some scenes will be trimmed or cut altogether.

Lunch on the terrace of the Sidi Mansour Hotel, where TJ, TG and most of the crew are staying. Terry J was struck down by some metabolic demon in the night and is still in a very delicate state. The art director, Roger Christian, is in bed with sunstroke, and Doctor Chapman, with his napkin draped over his head as an improvised sunshield, has already been called upon to dispense from the apothecary's treasure trove he brought out with him yesterday.

Graham claims to have seen a hoarding advertising a film about my old school called 'The 12 Salopians'. It turns out to be *Les Douze Salopes, The Dirty Dozen*.[1]

In the afternoon we walk around the Ribat – the old fort of Monastir, now a public monument. It's built of very light, almost golden, local sandstone, and the innumerable dark passageways and steep stone stairs leading to doorways and more stairs and passages is reminiscent of Doune Castle. Terry J shows us as many of the locations as he can before his bowels seize up again and he is rushed away by Graham.

To the Café de la Plage at Coq Égyptien – known to all as the Coq. This is local, not international, and lacks air-conditioning and imitation leather carte des vins and other trappings of international hotel life.

---

1 Gung-ho US war film of 1967, directed by Robert Aldrich and starring Lee Marvin and Charles Bronson. It was marketed with the tag-line, 'Train Them! Excite Them! Arm Them! ... Then Turn Them Loose on the Nazis.'

Instead it has peeling, pink-painted walls, decorated with rather shrine-like devotional pictures.

Fish were brought round on a tray and we selected those we wanted. As usual with any group of eight foreigners in an ethnic stronghold like the Coq, we probably made the waiter's life unbearably complicated, but he was tolerant about the whole thing.

Wednesday, September 13th, Monastir

The Meridien has an atmosphere of almost eerie spaciousness. Lights are lit around empty swimming pools. Wide new tiled corridors, discreetly lit and elegantly dotted with well-chosen chairs and sofas, lead into empty hallways where immaculately turned-out staff can be found at doors and behind desks. It's a perfect relaxation from the Sidi Mansour, though, and I enjoy an hour's guilt-free read of a Kingsley Amis (*The Green Man*).

A phone call from John Goldstone and Terry J to see if I could exert pressure on John to agree to shooting the stoning sequence on Saturday. Tim Hampton had suggested we start two days early as all the crew were here and ready to go, and it would give us an invaluable extra day in the packed schedule.

John stuck to an awkward stance – that we could indeed do the day, but he wasn't going to endanger a 'major' comedy scene like the stoning on a first day. Some sense there. But, as we rehearsed it today, it seemed not only easier to shoot than perhaps we'd feared but, even at this stage, very funny. I don't think delay will help it. Anyway, I told Goldstone to ring John himself.

At dinner John told me of the call and expounded what he called The Cleese Theory of Convenience. I think, roughly précised, it means that everyone will do only what's most convenient for them – and if you want things done your way you must not appear too agreeable or easy to please, or you will be the victim of other people's desire for convenience.

John and I consumed a bottle and a half of a fine, big Tunisian red wine, then back in John's room – seemingly full of underpants and duty-free bottles of spirits – we took a slightly woozy, but thorough, look at the Pilate scenes.

Thursday, September 14th, Monastir

Woken at 8.15 by Terry Gilliam who, with a construction team waiting, was anxious to have the latest on whether JC was prepared to do the stoning scene – for stones and rocks have to be made today. Able to reassure him that John was only pursuing the Cleese Theory of Convenience.

After rehearsals we go up to the Ribat for a photo-call for a *Variety* ad to herald the start of shooting. Nostalgia time. John was dressed in his Pacamac as Praline,[1] complete with dead parrot. Terry had drag on and a huge lipstick smudge across his lower face. Graham C was in his Colonel's outfit – which hangs off him now he's lost weight! Eric was in spangly jacket and I was in knotted handkerchief. And here we were photographed against mosques and palm trees. The past catching up with the present.

Saturday, September 16th, Monastir

The first day of filming.

Woke early, listening for JC rising early in the room above. He was called for seven, after a decision reached last week that we should start early and have as much time off as possible in the heat of the middle of the day. We have to finish before six, when we lose the light.

Went for a swim in the hotel pool – which was cool and invigorating – and shaved close (I have to play a woman today) with great care, packed an (Indian) bag full of script, towel, swimming trunks, black notebook and 1930 Macmillan edition of Hardy's *Tess of the D'Urbervilles* (part of my cultural survival kit) and drove in my little grey Renault 5 along the road across the salt flats, past Monastir Airport, past Bourguiba's summer palace, through the plywood triumphal arches, taking great care to avoid bicycles, wandering old men and dozens of women, bottle-shaped in their white chadors. Finally turned sharply left in the direction of the bright, white, elegantly simple and unadorned lines of the Ribat – and its false sister building (built by Zeffirelli for *Jesus of Nazareth*), which stands rather impertinently beside it.

A take has just begun, and John Young, dressed in loin cloth, is being

---

1 Mr Praline was the name John gave to his man in the plastic mac.

dragged to the stoning yard beneath the outer walls of the Ribat by a wonderfully dressed, swirling crowd. It's an impressive, exciting, authentic Biblical crowd – and more than anything today gave me a sharp boost of confidence. This film really could be impressive.

A crowd of ladies in beards has been assembled from a nucleus of our rep company, Tunisian actresses, Tunisian non-actresses and several people from Manchester who are on holiday.

John C is a little stiff in his early performances, but loosens up as he realises it's going to be rather good. John Young is wonderful. As JC says, though, at the end of the day, considering this is the first day of principal photography on a 'major motion picture', there's no sense of occasion, we just get on with it. Terry J hops about in a businesslike way, and doesn't exude any of the egomania of the Great Director. Peter Biziou[1] and John Stanier (camera operator on *Midnight Express*) are equally efficient and unflamboyant.

Then later in the afternoon the camera breaks down. Could this become a traditional feature of Python first days?

I change and, while a huge stone is being dropped on John Cleese, go into the Ribat and work over my words for the Pilate scene on Wednesday. Then I sit in the rather calming air-conditioned comfort of the caravan and learn some of the Shepherds scene.

In the evening back to the Meridien to change, then out to eat at the Coq with Terry J, Peter and Cristina [Peter's partner] and Gwen [Taylor] and Andrew McLachlan.[2] Drink rather a lot of wine and end up plunging into the sea starkers at midnight. A small but lecherous crowd of Tunisians gathers to watch and, as we walk away, a young boy offers us 40 dinars for an English girl who happens to be the girlfriend of Garth Marshall, our sound recordist. Then later offers me the services of a young man 'only just down the road'.

Sunday, September 17th, Monastir

Breakfast out on my balcony. Early light cloud disperses by mid-morning. Write various postcards and ring Helen and talk to the kids. Of course I miss them, but because of the holiday in France and the fact that this was all planned so long ago, I think we're all adjusted to being

1 Director of Photography – also for, among others, *Bugsy Malone*, *Mississippi Burning* and *The Truman Show*.
2 Friend of Terry J's from Oxford and another of our rep. company.

apart, so it's just good to hear them – not at all painful – apart from Willy, whose chief topic of conversation is that he's just been hit on the head by Rachel.

A walk up the beach and a swim before lunch. Then afterwards feet up and an hour's read of *Tess of the D'Urbervilles*. Hardy travels well. His stories especially suit Tunisia, a country with still much of the slow pace and time for social intercourse that Hardy regretfully saw passing in Dorset.

In the evening, two friends of Eric and Tania – Anjelica Huston and Nona Summers – arrived from London, bringing Sunday papers, which we grabbed from them avidly. Wine up on the balcony in Eric's suite and briks (local speciality – a crispy pancake enclosing usually egg and tuna – a sort of Tunisian equivalent of the hamburger).

Monday, September 18th, Monastir

Woke early – around seven – but snoozed fitfully until 8.30, having, in wonderful solitude, read *Tess*, and tried some Pilate oratory for Wednesday. I can really bellow here, and am happily screaming something like 'This man wanks as high as any in Wome', when, out of the emptiness, a young Arab on a bicycle appears. He cycles, slowly, warily, past me for a moment, then, after he's put in a suitable distance, he takes one last look and cycles off like a man possessed.

Enthusiastically closing the day with some press-ups, feel a muscle go in my back. Curse my luck.

Tuesday, September 19th, Monastir

Called today to be Francis crawling through tunnels on the way to capture Pilate's wife, but late enough for me to have a swim, breakfast and a read before going in. My pulled muscle, or whatever, was still painful enough in the night to jolt me awake two or three times, but seems no worse this morning.

What finally cures my back is two or three hours of very uncomfortable work in the tunnels.

We filmed on until seven, when the last platoon of Roman soldiers had tramped over our heads. Back at the hotel Graham gave me some back rub – but it all feels much better after the mini outward-bound course.

Graham is rapidly becoming a saint. He's been treating so many people in the unit – and now he's stopped drinking he has time to do his medical work properly, and the ability to do it without shaking or dropping whatever he's about to stick in you. In the evenings Graham does his rounds, with pills and rubs and words of reassurance.

Apart from his medical activities, he's sharp on his words and, from being a rather disconcerting influence on previous Python epics, he's now become a model of co-operation and efficiency, and his avuncular presence is calm and reassuring. In fact John today suggested that Graham was reminding him more and more of a vicar.

Wednesday, September 20th, Monastir

Up at six, and on the road to Monastir by six-thirty. My first really testing day – the Pilate Forum speech.

I know that I have to beware of factors such as being overawed by the scale and size of this particular movie. I have to try and forget previous successes or failures. I have to feel light and bright and free of any diversionary anxieties.

Well today, as I drive across the salt and mud flats, with the sun low above the eastern horizon, casting a bright golden glow hard into my eyes, I feel good and prepared and just downright happy to be performing again. So the morning goes well, except that it is possibly the hottest, least windy day yet and out on our rostrum it becomes almost unbearable.

But we cover everything bar John's close-ups, then bring in the Tunisian crowd, whom we have heard outside the walls of the Ribat learning to shout 'We want Wodewick!'

They are marvellous and it's a tremendous confidence boost for the rest of the filming, for at one time the difficulties of teaching Python techniques to a crowd of Tunisians seemed almost insuperable. However, today, Terry J has this mixed bunch of Arab students, peasants, grandmothers, mothers with babes in arms, old men with missing noses, middle-aged men with almost leprous skin, lying on their backs and waggling their feet in the air. They find no trouble in jeering at the posturings of the Roman Empire, and seem to enjoy it immensely.

I talked yesterday with Mahomet, who is one of our Tunisian extras, and was one of the raiders in the tunnel. He belongs to a theatre group in Mahdia, and much of their work is critical of the status quo in

Tunisia. 'Anti-Bourguiba?' I asked. He shushed me quickly. 'You can end up in prison saying things like that.'

Mahomet is a Tunisian nationalist of a different sort from Habib Bourguiba, whose likeness adorns the road into the town in twenty-foot-high posters. Mahomet wants Tunisia to be independent on its own terms and by virtue of its own resources. He's not a pan-Arab, and he certainly does not approve of independence based on dependence on America, Europe or Russia.

We took a late lunch – I managed a swim at the Sidi Mansour pool – and were back at three for more crowd reactions. Terry J won them over with a masterly display of co-suffering. He ran and jumped and grinned and lay on his back for them, and I could feel a great Celtic–Tunisian bond being formed.

In an excess of zeal tonight I crack the top of my dental plate whilst cleaning it.

Thursday, September 21st, Monastir

Back on our imperial rostrum again this morning.

One of the great delights is playing with John on his close-ups. John is, on a good night, one of the world's great corpsers, and today I have the rare luxury of being able to try and corpse him absolutely legitimately. On one take he is unable to speak for almost half a minute.

Drive back with JC. We take a bedtime Armagnac in my room and I bore him with a monologue about my novel. JC doesn't think he could write one. His mind tends to the factual and informative, he says – he feels he can't reproduce or create atmosphere.

Friday, September 22nd, Monastir

At the location by eight to provide off-camera lines for the crowd at Mandy's house, which is located in a busy corner of the Ribat, dressed to give the feeling of a Jerusalem tenement block of AD33. Lots of Gilliam detail. Full of Arabs, it really looks amazingly good.

Graham gives us a few full-frontals early on. He does pose rather well – probably an unconscious result of many years' absorption in gay mags.

As well as our ever-enthusiastic crowd of Arabs, we also have some English tourists, rounded up from nearby hotels and referred to by various collective nouns – the 'Clarksons', the 'Cosmos'.

I was asking our patient, hard-working Arab assistant director, who has the unenviable task of explaining Terry's instructions, how the locals were assembled. Apparently some are students and others just villagers, recruited after a tour of the surrounding areas in which the assistant director, as he told me, 'explained Python to them'. That must be worth some sort of award.

Terry J's method of teaching an Arab crowd to speak English is quite a phenomenon … He was pressed for time, admittedly, but the Jones technique went something like this …

'Let's try it then … "We are all individuals".'

The good-natured, completely baffled Arabs mimic Terry as best they can.

Terry: 'Good …! Good … you've nearly got it … Once more, "We are all individuals".'

Arab noise.

Terry: 'Very good! Now let's try "Yes, we must decide everything for ourselves".'

Economic note: the Arab extras get 3 dinars per day (£3.50), plus a loaf of bread and a tin of sardines at lunchtime. We are getting about a thousand pounds per filming day, plus accommodation at a first class hotel and a lunch from the Italian caterers which will be a choice of spaghetti, ravioli, steak, veal, omelette, salad and fresh fruit. At the Hotel Meridien, pride of Air France's new hotels, the Arab who comes to turn my bed back in the evening gets one dinar 500 millimes per day.

Avoid an invitation to a spaghetti party this evening – Signor Memmo, the caterer, is challenging Achmed, our Arab production head, to a spaghetti-making contest. My voice is strained after two days as Pilate and today's efforts, so I will rest it before the Ex-Leper tomorrow.

Eat in the gloomy Meridien restaurant. But food good, and fall to talking with John about relationships. John has been going to therapy groups for two or three years. Says he finds most of those present are Jewish couples. He seems to be very conscious of the fact that his mother gave him very little affection. He was always close to his father.

However, he has a very good relationship with the head waiter. I found that the reason was that John had given him ten Mogadon, as the man hadn't slept properly for a month. Now he's eating out of JC's hand.

Saturday, September 23rd, Monastir

At the make-up house at seven to prepare for the Ex-Leper. He's supposed to look golden, tanned, muscular and fit, and I must say, as a
result of my recent sun-bathing, plenty of swimming and running
through French woods and along Tunisian beaches, I don't look too bad.
Certainly in better shape than for a while, and mentally congratulating
myself for having coped with the food over these first two weeks
without any recourse to pills, potions or other medicaments. This seems
to be an increasingly rare thing on the unit.

On the set, I realise how much of an ivory tower I am in at the
Meridien – and such detachment surely does not behove a diarist. I
missed, for instance, the scenes after Pilate's filming. Apparently there
were near riots as people struggled to make sure they got their 3 dinars.
On Friday morning Terry J's car was chased by hopeful extras as he left
the hotel.

Also I missed (thankfully) the sparks' excesses at the spaghetti party,
when a specially prepared giant cake was thrown at the wall. They can't
stand any form of lack of excess.

This evening we are invited to a cocktail do by the Tunisian Minister
of Tourism. Drive round to the Skanes Palace Hotel at 7.30. Cosier decor
than the Meridien, but still in the International Modern Airport style.
First thing I see is one of the chippies with a sticker across his forehead
and the word 'English' on it, looking dangerously provocative, but it all
passes off without incident.

Monday, September 25th, Monastir

Up at 7.30. Swim, breakfast in room. See John C leaving. He says, ominously, that although he's not in today's scenes, he is going to 'help out'
behind camera. John Goldstone is worried about TJ's unshakeable commitment to full-frontals in the Mandy/Brian bedroom scene. Says he's
talked to John about it. So that's why John's gone in.

Arrive on set to find a harassed Terry J. He's not pleased at John's
interference today – words have been changed at the last minute. By the
pool at the Sidi M, over lunch, TJ, GC both feel very tensed up by John's
presence 'behind the camera'. The first sign of any serious split in the
Python ranks.

There's little danger from Eric, who keeps himself very much to himself and will not get into costume unless he's absolutely certain that he will be seen. The lengths to which he has to go to preserve this elusiveness would seem to me hardly worth the strain.

I actually enjoy a fairly unrewarding afternoon as a revolutionary creeping up smoky passages – and have pleasant chats with Bernard [McKenna] and Andrew and others. We shoot till six in conditions of increasing discomfort.

Tuesday, September 26th, Monastir

Long, complicated, but unusually vivid dreams these nights. Last night I was in a jumbo jet flying from Australia to London, in which there were rooms, pillared, columned and lavishly spacious – rather like those of Heron Bay. I wasn't feeling well, and Graham diagnosed measles. I remember thinking it could be a three- or four-week break in the schedule – but Graham said he'd give me some special stuff, which, provided I kept out of everyone's way for a few days, would put me right. I was then confined to the bulbous interior of a cargo aircraft's nose, surrounded by blocks of ice.

Was promised a day off today and, after a swim, settle to a longer than usual breakfast in my room of two very tastily fried eggs, fruit juice, croissant and coffee. Talk briefly to the dear, dark-eyed lady at reception, who always replies to one's 'Thank you' with a disturbingly cheery 'Never mind'.

Then I'm called in and sit in the caravan in a full beard and wig make-up until lunch, when, still not used, I strip it all off and take to the pool, where GC is relaxing after his usual busy morning. Medical work is running acting very close as Graham's chief activity these days – even at the poolside today he was approached by the stills photographer's wife with a raging sore throat, Terry J with a sore throat and Peter Biziou on behalf of Cristina, who is ill in bed.

This afternoon hang around, but am still not used. However, finish *Tess of the D'Urbervilles* and begin *Vile Bodies* before a rather cool and buffeting wind drives me off the poolside and down to the bar of the Sidi.

For the first time since our arrival, found myself drinking out of sheer laziness and, as more and more people wandered into the bar, I could hardly be bothered to get out of the way of about four beers and, two hours later, a group of us spilled over to the Coq for briks and things.

Today has shown signs of strain in the unit. Terry G is worried that TJ is driving everyone along at such a frenetic pace that he isn't leaving enough time to get the best shots. Gilliam is especially irked that the elaborately splendid detail of his market place is not being seen. He keeps muttering that this might as well have been done at Shepperton for two million less.

Thursday, September 28th, Monastir

Boring Prophet morning for me. Quite exhilarating as had to ad-lib most of the dull, droning speech. We did four or five takes and I tried to, or rather felt compelled to, make it a little different each time. Terry G spends most of the day coated in mud and does another of his extraordinary and grotesque gargoylical performances – this time as a Blood and Thunder Prophet.

I'm through by three and, feeling oppressed by the layers of dirt – mainly fuller's earth and the less wholesome aerosol spray – which attend nearly all my characters, I soak some of it off in the sea. A fresh north-west wind has blown everyone off the beaches and left empty deck chairs whose canvases now flap and slap violently in the wind, as if repelling unseen occupants.

Tonight at rushes (one and a half hours' worth) my chief worry is the Ex-Leper. The dancing, prancing, gum-chewing character seems to go down well enough, but he looks like a cross between Tarzan and Geronimo – and somehow this detracts from the impact of the scene. As TJ says, he's the only character so far who has looked out of period. The Terrys agree, and a reshoot of this end part of the scene is scheduled for tomorrow.

Dinner at the Sidi Mansour with the British Ambassador and his wife. A special menu, fresh flowers, champagne and lines of various shaped glasses adorn the table. No ethnic music, fortunately.

Sit next to Mrs Ambassador. A plummy-voiced, not unattractive lady a hand taller than her husband. She speaks with lazy confidence and I marvel at how very British she is – she manages to sound and look more like a bishop's wife on a four-day visit to Tunisia, than someone who's been here a year. Not a trace of tan, or any real enthusiasm for things Tunisian.

She was not unkind, but the very nature of her language and way of expressing herself produced some treasured lines ... 'Do you know, our gardeners, every night, whenever they go home ...' I wait with bated breath for the revelation, '... always take a little bunch of weeds with them.' She was referring to the Tunisian habit of not wasting anything. She was also good on not 'spoiling the local people'. Her example was not giving them the best Fortnum and Mason tea, 'which they probably wouldn't like anyway'.

Friday, September 29th, Monastir

A hard last day of the week. Into the small Ribat today, where a hypocaust has been constructed which is even harder to walk through than the tunnel. It's very hot, too, and besides being encumbered with extraordinarily clumsy props, there's an almost stifling smell of incense[1] inside the tunnels.

A BBC film unit arrive to shoot us. They look a sad little group – white and flabby and rather down at heel. Makes me aware how well we all must look after three weeks of sunshine out here.

Swim in the sea at lunchtime. Re-do the Ex-Leper ending afterwards. All sorts of things go wrong – a plane flies over, the BBC camera crew get in shot, the Ribat lavatory attendant gets in shot, an extra called Mahomet wanders in and out of shot at unpredictable moments, as no one takes the trouble really to explain things to him.

Terry G keeps strewing the ground where I'm standing for the Ex-Leper with scatterings of sheep's legs, squashed water melons and foul-smelling water around which the flies gather.

Then back to crouch in the tunnel again as Francis. John Stanier, the operator, says it isn't nearly as bad as filming forty feet down in a water-filled sewer in *Midnight Express*. This cheers me a little. It's now after seven and darkness has fallen on the Ribat. Final massive shot of the wall being cleaned at night. Comradeliness of night-shooting compensates for feeling of discomfort caused by dirt, very uncomfortable gear and cold wind.

Sunday, October 1st, Monastir

Beside the sea an Arab boy is striking a recalcitrant camel with a stick. Big, swinging blows directed at the head. Have noticed before that there

---

1 At this time, church incense smoke was regularly used by directors to create a diffused light. Later it was proved to be dangerous to health.

are some quite vicious camel and donkey punishers plying the Corniche. Tania once saw an elderly man striking an even more elderly and wretched horse with such force that it fell on to its side, whereupon he began to kick it. Tania (ex of Bronx Zoo, and as fine an example of how to treat God's creatures well as you could wish to find) ran up and remonstrated with him.

The hotel is quiet. Tim Hampton [our line producer] arrives at five to eleven with his four-year-old son Piers to play tennis with me in the Python competition.

Our tennis match, on a rough-textured, dusty court, surrounded by palms and reminiscent of Barbados, lasted for nearly one and a half hours in punishing heat. Neither of us could serve very well, but we played comfortable, if unexciting rallies – and took almost every game to deuce. Tim, an awfully pleasant and well-mannered chap, was a gallant loser – and I a winner only by consistent mediocrity and once holding my serve.

Woken at a quarter to one by flashes. A violent storm passes down the coast. Almost continuous blue, yellow flashes and hotel-splitting cracks of thunder. And torrents of rain.

Monday, October 2nd, Monastir

Wake at six. Today we're at Sousse, filming outside the city walls, where Zeffirelli filmed his crucifixion scenes. The day doesn't look promising. Though it's not actually raining, the countryside is waterlogged and the sky much cloudier than usual. It's cooler too.

The opening shot (of Mandy and Brian) seems to take forever, and I sit around, half-naked, made up as the Ex-Leper. I've even been evicted from my caravan, which is being used as a make-up base for extra lepers. An hour and a half before I'm used – leaping up, bronzed and fit, from a crowd of lepers at the city gates. Eric is quite impressed by my Steve Reeves-ish torso.

No sooner is the leper shot done, than the heavens open and a steady, unspectacular rainfall begins. The clouds merge into a single leaden sky, and Sousse, and its ancient and impressive castle walls, becomes Yorkshire or Scotland or Dartmoor.

I share Eric's caravan. Gwen, Eric and I natter. Eric takes a cluster of health pills – a small handful from a little pill box with compartments. Discover Gwen has three names – Allsop, Blount and Taylor. The first her real one, the second her married name, the third her adopted stage name. She worked in a bank for eight years before going to Stratford East Drama School, married a toolmaker called Fred Blount, who had a habit of obsessive hand-washing, and whom she divorced partly for this reason.

Eric told of his father, who was killed in the war when Eric was two. He was an RAF gunner – killed in a car accident whilst on Christmas leave. Which was why Christmas was never a very happy time at the Idles'.

Jonathan Benson (our genial, well-bred assistant director, who is writing a screenplay about the Lord Lucan affair) chimed in here, without a trace of anger or even malice, 'I went to the pictures the night my old man died. He was a judge. We were glad to get rid of him ...'

John Cleese was judging a flower show near Weston-super-Mare as his father was dying. He didn't know whether to cancel or not – and felt he couldn't let them down.

Tuesday, October 3rd, Monastir

The schedule has been rearranged and much of my heaviest work will now be when Helen and the children are here. The weather seems to be more settled this morning, but it rained again in the night.

After rushes last night I sat up talking with Anjelica Huston who told me of their experiences down in the desert. It sounds depressing – things you don't expect, like the oases, which look beautiful, but on closer inspection are littered with plastic detritus and cotton wool swabs. And flies which cluster at nose and mouth and every other orifice within a matter of seconds.

We talked over Armagnac for a couple of hours. She's one of those people I feel instantly at ease with. She's articulate, but has a certain quality of apologetic nervousness.

She talked about her dad, John Huston, and the childhood in Ireland – which sounded almost perfect – not only comfort and space and horses to ride, but also a steady stream of visitors like Brando and William Wyler and Katharine Hepburn – many of whom used her to get through to her father.

Then father and mother split and she didn't see a lot of him and, for a while, was 'kind of scared of him'. Now he's living in Mexico, still making plans for movies, though he's had a serious operation. He acts, but has great contempt for actor's bullshit. He likes Jack [Nicholson], she said with a smile, and would quite like her to marry him … She laughed, as if appreciating the thought, but having no intention of acting on it.

Then there was more lightning to entertain us and more Armagnac and I began to talk about Python. Then she suddenly got up and said she ought to go – and we exchanged a polite kiss – the Armagnac had not altogether overcome a hint of attractive awkwardness in her as we said goodbye.

First thing this morning, the BBC filmed Eric, John and myself getting ready. John shows them his hair transplant and I show them how my dentures no longer seem to fit.

Then a rather jolly day inside Matthias' room as plotting revolutionaries. Everyone on good form and much improvised joking. At lunchtime a meeting with John G and Anne H.

The subject of EMI's settlement came up. They are talking of offering us something by way of recompense but would probably insist on a secrecy clause. John C resisted this idea for a bit, but when told that the alternative was a possible two-year wait for a court hearing, he agreed quite sharply.

Drove back to the hotel with JC. I took him a silly route through the car park which he enjoyed so much I had to drive him round again – in and out of narrow gaps, tightly round trees, almost on two wheels. He really enjoyed it and seemed genuinely impressed that I could drive like that! I know John can only drive automatics, but I didn't know he couldn't go round corners.

No rushes tonight as the projector has broken down, so avoid the rather cloying atmosphere of the unit-filled bar at the Sidi and go out to the Coq with the two Terrys and Anne and Rachel Henshaw.

The quiet shattered by the arrival of Spike Milligan! Spike is staying at the Skanes Palace for a two-week holiday, revisiting Second World War battlefields.

Relaxed a little by the wine, he starts to treat the assembled throng – Chris Langham,[1] Carol Cleveland, Andrew McLachlan, Anne H, Rachel and myself – to Milligan's potted précis of 'Tomkinson's Schooldays' (he's another fan of the school leopard line – which must be one of the most enduring last-minute ad-libs I ever came up with!), and the

---

1 Chris Langham, another of our rep. company and partner of Sue Jones-Davies who played Judith.

Yorkshire tale, and then 'Parrot Sketch' (the Norwegian Blue becomes the Arctic Grey, as Spike tells it).

Wednesday, October 4th, Monastir

A long and arduous morning in Matthias' house. John Stanier is strapped into his Steadicam harness, which makes him look like a walking dentist's console.

John C takes Reg at a frenetic pitch, which loses all the nuances that had us rolling about in rehearsal. John becomes hot, tired and rather touchy as he tries to relax into the performance.

We slog on for three hours solid. There are no tea breaks as such out here, but Cristina and other unit ladies regularly do the rounds of crew and actors with water, Coca-Colas, coffees, etc, rather like the WVS or Meals on Wheels. By lunchtime it's finished and John stays on to do the Centurion and Matthias in the afternoon.

Helen rang later, but the line can be so indistinct I really can't wait to see her and talk without crackles.

Thursday, October 5th

A rather touching reminder from Kim H Johnson[1] in my pigeonhole at the hotel this morning – a card showing the Ribat and reminding us it's nine years to the day when the first Python show was transmitted.

Out to the location in Sousse. Clouds hamper progress today. On the slopes outside the impressive city walls, a huge, nude statue of me as Pilate is hauled towards the city on an oxen-drawn cart.

Almost every hour, on the hour, one of the donkeys has sexual intercourse – which entertains the unit, extras and citizens of Sousse marvellously.

At one point I find myself standing beside the lady donkey with Eric. 'How many times do you think she's been banged today?' I asked …

'Including the crew?' says EI. The wag.

The BBC crew are still at work. They do seem to favour John, and John, who's been strangely ill at ease performing, laps it up and is constantly to be found giving interviews behind caravans.

---

1 Python super-fan from Chicago, who had been given various parts in the movie. He later wrote one of the first histories of Python.

Spike Milligan turns up to do a part. He over-plays thoroughly and becomes very testy when asked to wait for the clouds to pass for a retake. Mind you, I rather feel for anyone who arrives to help out and is asked to do a role which involves saying 'Let us pray' before being trampled by 300 Tunisian extras.

Sunday, October 8th, Monastir

Take a long walk up the beach and, feeling well fatigued, get back to my room and enjoy the incomparable sensation of being quite mentally adjusted to doing nothing more than putting my feet up and steeping myself in Paul Scott's *The Raj Quartet*.

The phone rings. It's JC. 'Have you got a couple of minutes, Mikey … ?'

So I find myself spending the next hour or so rewriting the legendary, oft-written Scene 62 again.[1] Actually it turns out rather well, and we make each other laugh – and it is a lot better than what was there before.

John and I eat together at the Skanes Palace (international wine list and waiter syndrome) with John's secretary, Joan Pakenham-Walsh. Joan's cheery, extrovert company together with two bottles of very good red wine make for a happy evening.

Spike Milligan, white suit matching his fine, close-cropped white beard, wanders rather morosely into the dining room to ask us if Eric is usually more than five minutes late picking people up. He's evidently eating out with them.

John is rather short-tempered about Spike. His self-righteousness is what irks JC. The self-righteousness of a man who one day is protesting against the killing of eels in biological experiments, and the next moment is shooting air gun pellets at kids who climb into his garden.

Monday, October 9th, Monastir

Start of week four. The nineteenth day of filming. We'd have shot almost two *Ripping Yarns* by now.

At the make-up house by 7.30. Tunisians, eager for work, cluster

1 In Mandy's kitchen, in which Judith tells the revolutionaries to stop talking and do something about it.

round the wrought iron gates of the two-storey villa lent to us as a wardrobe and make-up base. I have to shoulder my way through. They stare at me, unblinking stares.

Emerge three-quarters of an hour later as Pontius Pilate, in short grey wig and long white under-toga and, thus attired, pile into my Renault, under the half-smiling gaze of a beautiful dark-haired, dark-eyed little boy working with his father, who is building a wall from a dusty pile of rubble.

A delay for lighting, then a very gruelling day shooting the first Pilate scene. The need to keep the vital giggling ingredient fresh and spontaneous made it a little bit harder to play than an ordinary scene with set words and reactions. The success of this scene will depend on the genuineness of the guard's reaction to Pilate. It can't all be acted, it must be felt.

So I have to do a great deal of ad-libbing at the end of the scene – and by the end of the day I must have thought up over twenty new names for Biggus Dickus' wife – ranging from the appallingly facetious Incontinentia Buttox to the occasional piece of inspiration which resulted in breakdown from the guards. Bernard McKenna in particular did the nose trick spectacularly – once right down my toga.

Tuesday, October 10th, Monastir

My two busiest days of filming are complete now – and so is Pilate, my hardest part. So I feel pleased. I think I managed to keep on top of it in quite trying circumstances – endless retakes for noises off, lighting, curtains flapping, Graham's hat, etc. Last thing I remember: JC on Jonathan Benson, the assistant director, after one of his barked instructions for silence, or 'skirt' in Arabic: 'That's what a sergeant major would sound like if he'd been to Eton.'

Wednesday, October 11th, Monastir

The rushes include a liberal amount of copulating donkeys and some good stuff at the gates of Sousse. But I find myself becoming very angry now whenever I see John wearing his tiny beard and moustache make-up – which was designed for him when he complained about the discomfort of full beards. So the rest of the crowd look wonderful – absolutely convincing Biblical figures – and there, looming large on left of frame, is John looking like a sort of fourth-rate Turkish illusionist advertising on the back of *Stage*.

Dine with Eric, Elaine [Carew], Tania and Spike Milligan and his lady Shelagh. They hold hands lovingly. Eric is nodding off towards the end of the meal. A huge and tasty fish couscous is specially prepared and served up for us in a big china bowl – they do take trouble.

Spike relaxes quite quickly and becomes genial, slightly nostalgic and almost expansive. Notice that his eyes have a great expressive sadness in them. He could be a very moving tragic actor.

Some nice silly ideas come up – such as a trick bow tie which stays still whilst the entire body revolves – and Spike is genuinely touched when I remember sketches and ideas from Q5 and his other shows. He too is generous in his appreciation – in particular he compliments me on my pet-shop owner. Spike says he tends to identify with the fall guy or feed man in a sketch.

Thursday, October 12th, Monastir

Down in the lobby when a travel-stained bus pulls into the almost deserted car park and disgorges three Palin children, one wife, Chris Miller [Eric's PA], Eric's son Carey (almost indistinguishable from William).

Their arrival virtually doubles the occupancy rate of the entire Meridien and for a couple of hours the lobby and lifts are full of restlessly energetic English nippers bringing more life to the place than I've detected in five weeks.

Friday, October 13th, Monastir

A grey, overcast ride in at a quarter to seven for a one and a half hour make-up session in preparation for Ben's cell.

About 7.15 on this cold and unfriendly morning the heavens open and Elaine's whitening of my body seems awfully symbolic. The rain is relentless; there's no break in the clouds. Spirits sink. After three-quarters of an hour of make-up the decision is taken to abandon Ben for the day and to go into Matthias' House for our weather cover scene.

Feeling suitably Friday thirteenth-ish, I trudge through the rain to the Sidi M, and wash all the grease off in Elaine's bath. A good part of my gloom is disappointment at the thought of the family all waking to streaming rain and grey skies on their first morning in Tunisia.

Change into Francis and drive myself up to the Ribat. It's a quarter to nine, the rain is heavier than ever, and the place is almost deserted. Rush into the nearest caravan, which happens to be Eric's. Eric and I watch the rain soaking the scaffolding and threadbare plaster walls of what remains of Zeffirelli's temple.

'This is filming,' Eric says, with a certain air of satisfaction.

At rushes this evening, I watch my endless takes of the first Pilate scene. Have never seen myself working so hard. Take after take – with instructions thrown out from behind the camera during the scene, making me seem like the dog at a sheep dog trial.

Monday, October 16th, Monastir

Up early (after three sessions on the loo during an eight-hour night). This time the weather looks more settled and the Ben cell scene goes ahead. Aided by a bicycle saddle and two wooden pegs for my feet, I'm able to hang from real iron handcuffs, ten feet up a wall.

The first take sounds tight and unfunny and this, allied to the discomfort of doing it, makes me feel rather depressed. But the problem is that my movements are so restricted if my arms are *directly* above my head, that I'm mainly concerned with surviving rather than performing.

Anyway, the camera breaks down at this point, so we have pause for consideration. Decide to lower the manacles. This makes a tremendous difference and, though it's never very easy, I manage several takes full of the sarcastic vehemence that makes Ben funny.

The children and Helen come to the location for lunch. Rachel is quite frightened by my appearance and will not come near me.

Tuesday, October 17th, Monastir

I'm off by 3.15 in the afternoon and back to the Meridien for a swim, a run up the beach, a brief lie in the sun, a look at the *Sunday Express* for news of the Sheffields (both uninspiring draws) and a chance to see Rachel leaping into the pool – this time with no arm-bands – and swimming along under the water. So she becomes the youngest of all the Palins to learn to swim. She's on marvellous form here now.

Sunday, October 22nd, Monastir

Hotel Meridien, twenty to five in the afternoon. It's a sombre Sunday – heavy grey clouds have built up since this morning, locking in most of the sky.

Elgar plays on the tape recorder. *Enigma Variations.* The suite is painfully quiet now Helen and the children have gone. It's back to being my comfortable cell.

The presence of Helen and the children had set a very different pace to this last week. The children swam as much as possible, Helen took Connie Booth to Sousse and was very proud of her achievement in getting her to haggle. Helen definitely was cut out for the cut and thrust of Tunisian market techniques. One man wanted to come back to the hotel with her, until he discovered she had three children – then he said he wouldn't come after all.

On Saturday, after they'd all come in for a taste of Signor Memmo's lunches, Tom decided he would like to appear in the afternoon's filming, so he was supplied with a long robe and turban and looked very handsome. He was the only one of the Python children to have a go, but was very proud of himself. The room was packed and it was definitely one of the less comfortable scenes, but graced by the presence of the visiting George Harrison, who took the part of Mr Papadopolous, the impresario in charge of the Mount.

At least Tom could say he'd been in a scene with Beatles and Pythons.

Couldn't really face the empty rooms of the suite – with traces of breakfast and freshly crumpled beds – so I walked along the beach, then played my tennis match with John C. Playing solidly rather than cleverly I rattled him enough to take the first set 6–2. Great elation. But I relaxed and the wind began to strengthen (favouring the technically proficient player who could control his shots), John recovered his confidence and began to play me solidly, if not spectacularly, off the court.

Then Terry J dropped by – we drank a beer each then went into Sousse for Sunday lunch at the Lido. As cheerful and restorative to the spirits as ever. Body and soul brought together with grilled prawns and sole and perch and goat's cheese, washed down with Tunisia's best white wine – Domaine de Karim. We sat next to two Tunisian couples who work on the film, who insisted on sharing various of their dishes with us, giving us a taste of harrissa (the hot sauce), pomegranate, and showing us how to eat dates with butter.

After a leisurely lunch, we walked out onto the quay where two or three Russian cargo boats were unloading (Sunday being a half working day here), feeling all was very well with the world. Walked up through the narrow streets of the souk – the smell of leather mingling with the sweet aroma of the many confectionery stalls. Watched a cow's head being skinned and cut up in a butcher's – you'd never see that in England – past kids playing football (very well) and men hammering patterns onto brass plates for the tourists. Took mint tea in a café, then back to the docks. Decide that I feel safer in cities with the sea on one side ...

I've just placed a call to London to see if they've arrived. Six thirty-five, they have ... It's raining in London. Feel a bond with them as I listen to the angry windswept sea in the darkness outside.

Monday, October 23rd, Monastir

Walking on the beach after breakfast I frame an idea for a *Ripping Yarn* – 'Golden Gordon', a soccer tale. It feels good, as the surge to write returns after all these weeks. I sit at a table in the sunshine and scribble away for a couple of hours. Then, having reached an impasse, lie in the sun by the pool and read through 'Whinfrey' to get a timing on it.

Eric and Tania – buoyant – join me and we have lunch together. Eric reads in the *Daily Express* that Nelson's last words were in fact 'Don't throw me overboard, Hardy.'

In the afternoon I run along the beach, then write a couple of letters to Al L and my ma – and by a quarter to six it's dark.

Eric, Tania, Charles McK, Terry J, Andrew M, Bernard and the Hamptons fill a table at the Café de la Plage et Coq. There is much singing of old English music hall numbers and First World War songs – at full voice, utterly drowning anyone else in the restaurant. A fine display of selfish and high-spirited behaviour. A release of a lot of tensions. The Coq treat us to a very tasty eau de vie-like liqueur and we toast the World's Greatest, Most Long-Suffering and Least Flappable Waiter – Ali – with a rising chorus of 'Ali, Ali, pride of our Sally'.

Tuesday, October 24th, Monastir

Farewell to Monastir.

I'm going to miss the place. I've shared a lot of experiences with the

Hotel Meridien. The intense feelings of preparation for the movie and the five weeks of performing – with all the various degrees of tension, stress and strain which the peace of the Meridien has helped to smooth and minimise. In all its grand emptiness, it's like leaving an old family home. The staff probably account for these feelings of sadness at departure. They have been universally friendly and good-natured. Yes, I shall miss them.

Gabès a nice, muddled town, at first glance, and the Hotel L'Oasis is down by the beach. The decoration is Russian twentieth century luxurious, but the two rooms I have (and two bathrooms) are pleasantly proportioned and have vaulted, white-painted ceilings.

Ate at the Ex-Franco Arabe Café de L'Oasis, to give it its full title, with John C and friend Charlotte. It turned out that most of the crew were in there, as well as dozens of locals, so we took an age to get served – despite JC breaking a plate on the floor to attract the waiter's attention.

Sunday, October 29th, Hotel L'Oasis, Gabès

Toy with the idea of treating Gabès as a series of abstract impressions – 'Sea, smell of seaweed, spreading sands … hotel continuously alive with jarring sound of chairs on marble floors, tiredness, tat, two toilets, infinitely slow emptying baths, locals quick to laugh and equally quick to take offence – '.

Long to return to England and really concentrate on writing. Urge to work carefully and thoroughly on a second novel grows daily. Together with a curiosity about Jill's reaction to my first one – and a growing frustration with the tedium of film-acting.

Friday's filming of the Sermon on the Mount was difficult – mainly because we had a crowd of 600 local extras. Prouder, more independent, less malleable folk than up in Monastir.

Ken Colley performed marvellously as Jesus – using a modern translation of the Beatitudes, which we'd decided on in preference to the St James version, because it felt less like a set up for a joke, and more of an attempt to portray Jesus as honestly as possible.

After the early takes, stunning in their recreation of the image of the Bible story, the extras started getting restless. It turned out that many of them had left their homes at 2.30 in the morning and had had neither food nor water since then.

At one point the crowd thought they were finished, and streamed from the Mount down towards the coaches, whilst Hammeda, one of our Tunisian assistants, pursued them screaming and shouting. The womenfolk had to be taken back early, because if they arrived back after sunset there would be hell to pay from the male villagers. All very different from the jolly, co-operative crowd who rolled on their backs at Monastir.

So to this Sunday. I sit listening to my latest favourite tape – Kate and Annie McGarrigle's 'Dancers with Bruised Knees' – sipping a Glenlivet from the litre bottle which Helen brought two and a half weeks ago and which is half gone, and looking out onto the darkening sky and sea.

This morning I looked through an assembly of the film – from Pilate's forum up to the crucifixions – and was greatly encouraged.

I'm not quite sure that I'd go along with TJ, who last night ventured to me that it was going to be 'a masterpiece', but, having seen the stuff this morning, I feel closer to his judgement than to Terry Gilliam, who spread gloom and despondency over me on Friday morning, as we motored out to Matmata, with his analysis of shortcomings and missed opportunities.

But more of this later. Night has fallen on the end of our seventh week in Tunisia. I feel optimistic about the film tonight and less depressed at the thought of being trapped here for two more weeks. All I have to decide now is which of my two baths to use …

Tuesday, October 31st, Gabès

The violence of the downpour is increasing as I listen. The prospect of an enforced day off tomorrow looks ominously likely.

Yesterday morning I was hauled up on the cross. It wasn't an unpleasant sensation, but I was stretched out for half an hour or so whilst various takes of Big Nose were done and, as I write, I've numbed a nerve in my left arm and lost some control of my muscles, so the arm keeps rising involuntarily – rather like Peter Sellers' rogue limb in *Dr Strangelove*.

Thursday, November 2nd, Gabès

Wake to sunshine. Give Cleese a lift out to the location. Have to wait five minutes at a shop whilst he buys honey and almonds for his breakfast.

John is sharing a caravan with TJ and me at the moment, so that make-up can have extra space. As a result I have Cleese, who has a cold, and his girlfriend, Charlotte, who arrives around lunchtime and smokes.

Today we spend most of our time and effort on the final song, which twenty-four crucifees sing as the climax of the film.

I'm in one of the front-row crosses. There's a slightly heady feeling – a tiny rush of vertigo as I clamber up onto the racing bicycle saddle (which protrudes absurdly anachronistically from an otherwise convincing cross). There's a certain sense of camaraderie amongst us all as we clip our nails over the top of our hands and push aching arms through the ropes.

Among the few compensations is a wonderful view over the hills of Matmata.

Saturday, November 4th, Gabès

Wake up to grey skies again. The weather is being really unkind these days.

Drive out to the location at Matmata with sinking spirits. Prospects for a return to England on the 13th look in jeopardy as the rain comes down and we wait for half an hour as the water pours across the road so fast no one dares venture across. One loony tries to get across in a Peugeot taxi, skids in the mud and bounces off one of our Renault 5s.

Sitting in one of the caravans waiting for us to be called, the talk turns to discussion of tomorrow's rest day. Roy Rodhouse, chief electrician, maintains this film has been a doddle – and anyone who's feeling the pressure ought to try 'a day or two with bloody David Lean – then they'll know what slave-driving is'.

Charles Knode reckons it's been the hardest picture he's worked on – mainly because he feels his work isn't used. For instance this week he's been up early to dress seventy-five extras each day, and the most they've eventually used is six of them.

There's no consensus of discontent, but from the attitudes of everyone I reckon the most disruptive element in any operation like this is lack of diplomacy – and that means regular attention to every department to make sure they're given time to air their grievances and lashings of appreciation. In a big unit like this there doesn't seem to be time to look after everyone like that.

Monday, November 6th, Gabès

Out to Matmata for the last time. Still cloudy, but dry. Much running about, sometimes carrying Terry aloft, sometimes followed by 150 Arabs.

One long chasing shot has to be done all over again after one extra, wearing leather shoes, Terylene socks and smoking a cigarette, stops and looks straight into the lens, before being attacked with angry howls by Habib, Hammeda and the massed Anglo-Tunisian assistant directors.

Friday, November 10th, Carthage

Carthage is a comfy, bourgeois suburb – the Beverly Hills of Tunisia – and there is no centre of the old town and precious little on display to show for the years when people from this shore dominated the Mediterranean. The Roman Empire has been put away, as it were, and the Punic is under the ground.

John dropped in for breakfast. We looked through Three Wise Men together – the steady, unrelenting rain gave us the thought of doing a play about an English holiday called 'It's Clearing Up'.

John Goldstone and Tim are of the opinion that we should aim to leave on Monday whatever happens – and that the amphitheatre close-ups and the Three Wise Men can be shot in London. The weather forecast offers no cause for hope.

At three we travel down to the location beside the sea, where amidst the bulky ruins of a Roman baths we are to shoot the Three Wise Men.

The roof of the stable drips occasionally as a welcome reminder that it *could* have been raining on Jesus' birthday. The costumes are excruciatingly hard to bear. My headdress is like having a sixty-pound haversack on one's skull, and both Graham and I have immense trouble with long, swirling trains – as we make an impressive exit, Graham's train catches on the door, rips down the middle and pulls the door off its hinges.

Saturday, November 11th, Carthage

At the amphitheatre at eight.

The consistent sunshine keeps us moving steadily forward, and my last shot of the movie (witnessed by the British Ambassador, who appears mid-afternoon in the ruins of Carthage and is observed by T

Gilliam tapping tentatively on solid rock to ascertain whether it's false or not) is myself as one of the Revs 'flitting' through the streets. Then John, Eric and myself are finished.

Succumb to the temptation of the cool, calm sea and take what is probably my last Tunisian dip. A chill, fresh edge to the water – not a day for drying out on the beach. Instead back into my chalet for a long, lingering hot bath.

November's connotations seem the same whether in foggy England or sunny North Africa – warm fires, warm baths, protection and shelter are the order of the month.

A fine sunset – a great final curtain. Dinner at the Gulf restaurant with TJ, after rushes. He's pushed through thirty-six shots today and only the wide-shots of the amphitheatre, with Neil running away from the giant gladiator, remain to be done.

Sunday, November 12th, Carthage

I left the chalet at a quarter to seven.

Eric is outside already, standing on the sea-shore, looking towards the sunrise. A canopy of small, white, grey-edged flecks of cloud dot the sky, changing from rich red to deep gold as the sun slowly rises.

Bernard McK leapt out of his chalet and intercepted me with the joyful news that he had been writing his *Robin's Nest*[1] episode since three o'clock in the morning and the end was in sight!

Left the cheery Bernard and reflective Eric and climbed up the path, past good, fresh smells of early morning – pine and grass and the hint of soft, sweet scents from bougainvillea and camellia.

Back in London by twelve, but Helen was over at Mary and Ed's with the children for lunch. Drove over there in the Citroen, and had not gone one mile before I was hit a glancing blow on the back wing from a careering Triumph Herald. I could hardly believe it. After nine weeks' driving in Tunisia without a scratch (despite all TJ's warnings about manic Arab drivers) I return to Kentish Town and wham! The driver, a dapper young man with untrustworthy eyes, actually tried to make a fight of it, accusing me (who had been stationary at a junction) of taking up too much road. I refused to argue, but I was shaking with anger by the time I eventually reached my family.

---

1 *Robin's Nest*, starring Richard O'Sullivan, was a big ITV comedy hit.

Tom played me in with a clarinet fanfare. Rachel was shy at first and pretended not to notice and Willy bounded up and nearly bent me double.

Later in the day the man who had thudded into the back of my car appeared contritely at our door to apologise and admit full responsibility! He turned out to be a very frightened, newly qualified young barrister. His girlfriend had recognised me and given him a frightfully guilty conscience all afternoon. He had finally found my address by ringing up a couple of policeman 'friends' who gave him information from the police computer!

Monday, November 13th

Start to dig through the oceans of mail and assorted papers. Appeals from Birkdale Preparatory School, Shrewsbury School, the ETC [Experimental Theatre Club] at Oxford – my past seems to have run out of money.

Otherwise there are those who want a name to boost appeals or appear at concerts – a concert for racial equality in Oldham, Fair Play for Children in Kentish Town, The Association of Boys' Clubs, Sheffield University Medical Society, The Dog-Lovers' Club of Northern Kent. One-Parent Families want me to do a Christmas show.

In the evening watch the third of the Monty Python repeats. Shows as old as this diary. Capering around as Cardinal Ximenez in the 'Spanish Inquisition'.

Tuesday, November 14th

Confirmation of my suspicions that the BBC will not commission any more *Yarns* after April, on grounds of cost. Jill quotes a letter from John Howard Davies saying that the shows 'though prestigious', are 'beyond the BBC's resources'.

I am greatly relieved by the news, for the go-ahead on three more would have stretched my/our ideas, would have filled up next year – which is now left tantalisingly clear for any involvement with Lorne M.

Mind you, you could say they let us go without much of a struggle.

Friday, November 17th

One of the odd things about the Tunisian trip is that it's very easy to believe it didn't happen. It's as though I've been in a time-warp, and I feel as if there has been absolute continuation of my time in England, and that this is mid-September. The Tunisian episode is like the hour a drunk cannot account for.

I suppose this is partly because of today's summery sunshine, which matches September quite well, if you don't look at the trees, but mainly because my life in Tunisia was such a neat and self-contained entity. It was nine weeks of creating fantasy – and it's easy now to see it all as a fantasy anyway. A complete break, in dress, food, habits, climate and surroundings, held together by a story set 2,000 years ago.

Monday, November 20th

To the Hemdale Preview Theatre in Audley Square at four to see the assembly of all the *Brian* material. Apart from the Python team – all looking a lot more like pale-faced Englishmen after a week of British November – Tim Hampton and John Goldstone, Anne Henshaw, George Harrison and Denis O'Brien were there.

After cups of tea and a 15-minute wait for Dr Chapman, the film starts. The whole preparatory assembly runs two hours and eight minutes.

General consensus is that it's a most encouraging viewing. Some scenes provoked gales of laughter – including the latter half of Ben and Pilate's audience chamber, the Hermit's hole, Brian's bedroom when the crowd arrive, and the Centurion and Matthias at the door of Matthias' house (the searching). There was a consistent level of interest and no embarrassments, though I confess to finding Otto dangerously like a cameo sketch.

The raid on Pilate's palace could be cut down too, by five or six minutes.

Round to Langan's for a drink, then John Cleese, Anne, John G, myself and Gilliam stay for a meal. We discuss Richard Ingrams (briefly) and his pairing of *Citizen Kane* and Monty Python in his *Spectator* TV column last week. He was talking about over-estimated phenomena and thought *Citizen Kane* quite useless and Python, now he had finally seen it, junk. Quite a refreshing bucket of water after the almost unqualified critical praise which Python has had to endure these last few years.

Tuesday, November 21st

Late in the afternoon, to Robert Maas[1] to hear the latest on the Signford tax saga, which broke last August with the issuing of precepts. Maas, admirably downbeat in style, told me that Signford's status with the tax authorities was still not settled.

If Maas succeeds in persuading the Inspector of Taxes that Signford was not set up with intent to trick or defraud, and that the time gap between the setting up of the company and the performance of the services from which the company derived most of its income was permissible and done in good faith, then Signford will have succeeded.

If not, there could be a bill of £26,000 to pay straightaway, in addition to a personal tax bill up to the end of August '78 of between £15,000 and £20,000.

But Maas is competent and efficient and very sharp, so I have some hope. At the very worst I still have two cars and two houses and the best-equipped 8-track recording studio in London to show for nine years of Python!

Thursday, November 23rd

Up to Suffolk. The peace and pause for reflection worked almost immediately. As the Ipswich–Darsham train swayed up from Wickham Market to Saxmundham, with still green fields and rapidly emptying oaks and ashes and elms on either side, I suddenly felt very clear about the next year. I would complete the *Yarns* in March and April, then work from May 5th (a symbolic starting date: 36th birthday) until December 31st on a new novel.

The prospect brightened me, as we passed through Saxmundham and alongside dark, rich, fresh-ploughed fields south of Darsham. By the time I reached Darsham and saw the smiling, diminutive, almost gnomic little figure of my Ma, I knew it was the right decision.

Saturday, November 25th

Embark for George Harrison's in the Mini.

Arrive at Friar Park as the sun has just set. It must be two years since I

1 My new accountant.

came here with Eric to complete the mixing of 'Lumberjack Song' (or was it three?). There's a blazing log fire in the galleried hall and George has just come in from planting bulbs in the garden. He seems very relaxed and settled into the role of a country squire – his face has fleshed out a little, he looks less frail and tortured.

We have tea and talk about the house and Sir Frank Crisp, the eccentric lawyer who built it.[1] And died penniless as a result. My mother remembers Sir Frank hiding behind bushes in the garden and jumping out on her and her sister when they visited the place as little girls.[2]

Saw George's four-month-old boy, Dhani, then his other recent enthusiasm, his book. Called *I Me Mine*, it's an expensively leather-bound collection of his songs with his own hand-written notes and corrections.

We find out that George is just older than me. He was born February 1943. He is quite struck by this and, as a memento of him being just older, gives me one of the glass eyes made for his Madame Tussaud's dummy!

Derek Taylor and Joan arrive later and we eat a superb Indian meal cooked by Kumar. Quite delicious and delicate.

Derek tells of the horrors of LA that have driven him back to England – to a farmhouse in Suffolk. So humourless and depressing were his colleagues in Warner Records, that Derek took great pleasure in puzzling them by eccentric behaviour. He would insist on playing Hollywood record moguls a tape of Violet Bonham-Carter[3] being interviewed. They sat there polite but utterly bewildered. 'Twenty minutes' peace,' Derek recalled with feeling.

Monday, November 27th

Taxi arrives when I'm half-dressed, just before eight. Half a cup of tea, then leave for the BBC at 8.15. To Studio 4A at Broadcasting House for *Start the Week*, with Richard Baker – a jolly, harmless, middle-of-the-road therefore well-liked chat show, which goes out live.

RB frightens me with quick asides like 'We'll be talking travel ... oh,

---

1 Crisp (1843–1919) bought Friar Park in 1895. He, like George, was a keen horticulturalist. Unlike George, he was a fully paid up member of the Royal Microscopical Society.
2 My mother was born and brought up on Hernes Estate, which borders Friar Park.
3 Extremely English upper-class daughter of former Prime Minister, H. H. Asquith; leading figure in Liberal politics.

and bicycles ... so if you'll get some travel and bicycling stories together ... Right, we're on air.'

Not as hair-raising as I thought. I manage to hold my own, though Sandra Harris, who interviews me, is another of those people who feel the need to describe me as a 'nice middle-class boy'.

Drive over to Gough Square. It's nearly half past three and the shafts of sunshine are few as the buildings of London block out the low November sunshine. The city seems all in shadow. I tape a pre-recorded interview for London Broadcasting. Catch a glimpse of a visitors' book which is lying open – the last name is M Thatcher, H of C. Think of writing G Rarf, London Zoo, but refrain.

Before Christmas the Ripping Yarns *book was published and my signing tour began, as they still do now, in Scotland.*

Tuesday, November 28th, Stirling

Leave King's Cross at 11.55 on the Aberdonian.

Arrive in Stirling at a quarter to seven. Met by student organisers who say they have had to move the audience to a larger lecture theatre. I'm told the Literary Society (whom I am addressing) usually expect 80 or 90 for a visiting speaker, but 250 have turned up.

Give my talk eventually to a full house, ranged in front of and above me along steeply-banked rows of desks. Analysis of my method of writing doesn't go down well, but any jokes or sketches are rapturously received.

Wednesday, November 29th, Stirling

Up at a quarter to nine. Comfortable night in excellent, clean and well-equipped hotel. Breakfast alone with a *Scotsman* (the newspaper). Then walk down to Allanwater, away from the main road and along a path which follows the river. The air is clean, fresh and cold. It's marvellous to be in Scotland. I relish the short walk inordinately, gratefully drinking in the air and the sight of a quiet, full river flanked by bare-branched beech trees.

I still am affected by a post-Tunisian euphoria. A delight in being wherever I am, provided it's not Tunisia.

To Grant's Bookshop in Stirling for my first signing session.

Despite a big window display, the attendance at the signing session is not good. I console myself with the fact that thirty books were signed after last night's talk and publication isn't really till tomorrow. But I sit at my table with embarrassingly large piles of books beside me and sign less than twenty in one-and-a-half hours. At one point an irate lady who obviously thinks I work here, comes across and complains that a book about angling she bought for her nephew has two pages stuck together.

John Lennie, the Methuen rep for Scotland, drives me to Edinburgh.

Terry J arrives. He and I go for a nostalgic walk up to the Royal Mile. We nose around the Cranston Street Hall in the traditional manner. TJ remembers the thrill of seeing the feet of a forming queue through a small window down in the toilets ... That was fifteen years ago.[1]

We find ourselves in a wonderful, small, grubby, friendly bar in Young Street – the Oxford Bar. This is the glorious opposite of all the carpeted 'lounges' where drinks are now taken. It's small and gossipy and quite uncompromising with regard to comfort and décor ... definitely a new 'must' when visiting Edinburgh.

Thursday, November 30th, Caledonian Hotel, Edinburgh

Publication day for *Ripping Yarns* and St Andrew's Day for Scottish people. Terry and I are hurrying along Queen Street. It's a quarter past seven and still dark.

Arrive five minutes late for live interviews.

We're out by 8.30. Time for an appalling breakfast at the otherwise splendid Caledonian, then we're running along the gracious streets – this time to Radio Forth, where we record a one-hour chat programme with a man called Clark Tate. The chat is easy and comfortable and the time passes fast.

By grubby train to Glasgow. Through countryside thick with snow.

From Radio Clyde to Grant's Bookshop. Heads turn as we enter. People look up uncertainly from their books. Bookshops are rather like churches – any incipiently flamboyant behaviour is rather discouraged.

---

1 The Cranston Street Hall, then head office of the Edinburgh Parks and Burials Department, was where he and I first performed together at the Festival in 1964. It was the first time in my life that I had the slightest intimation that there might be a living from comedy.

We settle down at our table and sign for an hour. Sixty books here, they reckon. Good reactions from people to the book and the series. Many want to know when there will be more …

A group of students attach themselves to us, one of them carrying the frog box[1] to the Albany. One of them makes a perceptive remark when he observes 'You're just kids really …'

Wednesday, December 6th

At six o'clock I go down to John Goldstone's office in D'Arblay Street. He has a two-page ad for *Variety* to announce the completion of filming. John takes all this side of the publicity very seriously. It's odd, such a quiet man setting such store by making a noise, but I'm assured it's essential with million dollar epics. *Superman*, I notice, has a ten-page ad in the latest *Variety*!

We both walk over to the Sapphire Theatre for the (much discussed and, for TJ, slightly feared) viewing of Julian Doyle's *Life of Brian*![2]

The film ran two hours and the reaction was very encouraging. The laughter (in scenes like Pilate's first audience chamber and the Gaolers in the cell) was long and loud. The song at the end worked and there was plenty of quite unequivocal applause.

Julian has done a good job and provided TJ with a well-shaped, well-structured cut on which he can work to lighten up all the details. It was a very good reaction tonight and the film can only get better.

Friday, December 8th

Collected Rachel from school at twelve and she and I walked into Kentish Town to have lunch at a new McDonald's there. Instead of seats they have perches – sloping plastic padded shelves which give you the feeling that they are trying to tip everyone out of the restaurant. Not entirely untrue, either – they're obviously designed to discourage quiet sitting and reflection and increase cash-flow.

Schoolkids hiss 'Who is he?' amongst themselves after a couple of the staff have asked me to sign autographs. I maintain a stoic display of unconcern and attend to Rachel – who is a lovely companion.

1 The box, as used in 'Across the Andes by Frog', was one of the props to enliven our book-signing tour.
2 Julian had assembled an early working cut of the film, more or less on his own.

A thought struck me as I left – the bags in which you are given food at McDonald's are almost identical in texture, shape and size with the vomit bags tucked in the seat pockets of aircraft.

After a couple of hours of profitable writing on 'Whinfrey's Last Case', drove down to St Pancras and took the 4.16 to Sheffield. Was able to work on the train. Took a taxi up to the Cutlers' Hall, where the Medical Society of Sheffield University were holding their 150th Annual Ball.

I speak for 20 minutes or so and despite, or perhaps because of, there being five speeches before me, mine is well received.

Afterwards I'm presented with a special brick and sign endless auto-graphs. I have to stay and judge the cabaret acts, which is an impossible task as I can't hear or see anything. About 12.30 they're mercifully over and I make my judgement and present the winner with his trophy – a stainless steel bedpan with a plastic turd in it.

To think our life is in their hands.

Monday, December 11th

Visit the Royal Geographical Society, of which, thanks to Peter Luff,[1] I am now a Fellow. Complete peace and quiet, in a very avant-garde house, built in 1874 by Norman Shaw facing Hyde Park.

To me, the place was like Nirvana – for my earliest ambition, which endured for many years, was to be an explorer. And here I was, Fellow of a society set up in 1830, which has on display Charles Darwin's application for membership dated 1838.

Tuesday, December 12th

Down to Neal's Yard. Hive of activity. Val Charlton[2] and Terry Gilliam are making Martians upstairs for the interior of the Flying Saucer in *Brian*, next door Terry J is editing and in the studio André has put together a demo of the new *Brian* song.

Walk through rainwashed Leicester Square. Pick up tickets for the *Superman* film on Saturday and Dame Edna's new show, which opens tomorrow night.

1 Producer of the early Amnesty shows.
2 Modelmaker and partner of Julian Doyle.

Home to work on the *Yarn* with TJ.

Then Chris Orr arrives and I'm discussing with him the arrangements for further work on his 'Arthur' book (the revised, shorter version of which I like very much), when Roger Wilmut, a BBC sound engineer who's doing a book on the Oxbridge revue and comedy Mafia, arrives.

Juggle all these people around and cope with a constant barrage of phone calls and am finally left talking to Wilmut about How It All Began. I've never felt less like talking about How It All Began – the whole madhouse here is more indicative of How It All Will End.

Sunday, December 17th

Ian and Anthea and Clemency and growing, toddling Grace,[1] come round for roast lamb and apple crumble lunch. In the interval of one Barry Humphries show last week, Ian was up in the bar and overheard snippets of conversation between two people. One was accusing the other of 'sighing'. 'I wasn't sighing.' 'Yes you were, you were sitting there sighing all through it.' The other then produced the sharp rejoinder 'Don't be so combative.' Ian noted the whole exchange and, when he went back to Barry's dressing room, told him of it.

He couldn't believe his ears when, half-way through Edna's monologue to a packed 1,500-strong house, Edna told of how she couldn't take Norm to the theatre because he'd just sit there and sigh, and eventually become very 'combative'. Afterwards Barry said he'd slipped it in because of his enjoyment of the effect it would have on just two people. As Barry put it, it would make, for them, a truly 'uncanny' night in the theatre.

Wednesday, December 20th

Morose, east wind weather. Grey and with drizzle just this side of snow.

A power-cut yesterday blacked out the whole of France (bar Alsace).

London is full of queues at petrol stations because of rumours that there will be a tanker drivers' go-slow in January. All in all it's siege conditions again ...

As the days get shorter and colder and darker a sort of pessimistic gloom descends. The next three months are low points for everybody,

1 The expanding Davidson family.

when our technology can't quite cope and our 'civilised society' shows alarming cracks.

I cheer myself up writing copy for J Goldstone's *Variety* ads for *Brian*. Re-read the 'Whinfrey' script and tighten. It looks good, but I wish the uncertainty over the rest of the *Yarns* and the director could be sorted out, for I feel like writing now and yet if it's to be top priority I need to know *who's* doing them and when.

Thursday, December 21st

Goldstone rings. He's very pleased with the *Variety* ad copy – it's going into early Jan or mid-Jan issue. His plan is to create as much of a stir as possible inside the US before showing the assembly to distributors in late January. It's essential to arrange a US distribution deal at least six or seven months in advance in order to have any chance of booking up cinemas.

He has a strange snippet of info – the film about Hitler called *Hitler – A Career* is attracting so many National Front supporters in the West End that they're thinking of taking it off. First time I've ever heard of a film being taken off for being too popular.

By two this afternoon it's almost dark. The sky is low and leaden grey and there's rain and sleet and a chill wind. The sort of day which sends wise men to the travel agents.

Tuesday, December 26th

A return to the greyness – and not just outside, where a blanket of slow-spattering rain covered London. At about ten Overseas Telegrams rang – news from New York. 'Not too good, I'm afraid,' said the faceless man at the other end. 'Eve died on Christmas Day,' he reads.

The outcome, which Al feared for a long time, but which he only resigned himself to in a letter to me last September, of Eve's recent severe depressive bouts (twice hospitalised) has finally come to pass.

At midday in NYC, I rang Al. Spoke to his son, John, who sounded tight and tense, but said it would mean a lot to Al that I rang. An hour later I spoke to Al himself. His voice cracked as soon as he spoke, though he said he'd been trying to keep himself together. Eve had committed suicide – no details – but John was asleep and Al had gone out for a walk. He returned to find an ambulance waiting there.

Now Al wanted to get away for a while. The apartment, which Eve found, Sag Harbor, which she adored, all were now an intolerable sorrow. The only thing that could in any way lighten the pain was that he had seen it coming. It was almost inevitable. As I said to Al, Eve had a terminal illness.

Friday, December 29th

The toyshop in Malden Road opens for the first time since the holiday, and is visited largely by parents returning malfunctioning goods. Kindly, middle-aged women with headscarves can be heard at the counter asking for advice ... 'I pressed the auto-destruct and the bit came off ...' or 'Every time it goes round a corner all the missiles fall out.'

I take Willy's Scalextric controls, which have been such a headache over the last few days. It turns out I've got a new model on which the controls have been improved. He gives me some old ones, and the whole thing works perfectly.

I then drive down to Dulwich, collect Granny for the day and drop in our Christmas presents to the Joneses. (They took Terry's father and Norah, his new wife, to see TJ editing. They showed Norah some of the film, and according to Alison she was most offended! But then she's from Welsh Fundamentalist stock and it's as likely that a Welsh Fundamentalist will laugh at people cracking jokes on the cross as it is that Snowdon's made of pâté.)

Over lunch at the Barque and Bite I try to allay my mother's fears about the film – aroused by the indexing of our film on totally specious grounds by the Festival of Light.[1] I hope she doesn't feel she's in for a rough year. Despite being a regular *Telegraph* reader, she's still tough and bright and with a mind of her own, so I'm not too worried.

Sunday, December 31st

Helen and I were watching *Top Hat* last night before a blazing coal fire and Helen was forever parting the curtains and looking out in glee as the powdery snow, driven by a sharp, south-easterly wind, covered Oak Village.

As we drive down to Dulwich I listen to the car radio and hear tales

1 A Christian pressure group.

of horror from all over the UK. Edinburgh is almost cut off from the rest of Scotland (a fact which the weather only confirms!) and Scotland is almost cut off from the rest of the UK. The police are advising only 'essential' journeys.

The result is a wondrously empty London. Even the streets of the West End are white with caked snow.

More bad Christmas news – this time that Veryan's mother died in a fire at her home early this morning. But Angela and Veryan want our visit to carry on as normal, and possible gloom is dispelled by pre-lunch cocktails with two neighbours and their three daughters, who bring with them a game called Twister, which involves participants in a grapple on the floor and, in the immortal words of Eric's joke salesman, 'Breaks the ice at parties'.

Driving back across Westminster Bridge at a safe and stately pace just before seven, with the Houses of Parliament floodlit and the bridge still uncleared of snow.

Al Levinson rings to wish me a Happy New Year. There was a memorial service for Eve yesterday and 150 people turned up. Which is very heartening, but only seems to emphasise the crippling irrationality of the condition that destroyed her. She was loved and she will be missed.

1978 passes – perhaps the swankiest year yet for me, what with two-week writing sessions in Barbadian luxury and elegance, a Concorde flight to the US, a week in New York with my own personal limousine (which I never used), and nine weeks of star treatment in Tunisia.

I feel that in the last year my work rate has slackened, but the slack has been largely taken up by increasingly complex business arrangements, more meetings and by a slowly, inexorably increasing number of memberships, demands for money, speeches or introductions to rag magazines – all the impedimenta of notoriety.

Next year we will have to live with the impact of the film. I know that, although now it seems that we just had a great deal of fun, both writing and performing, there is going to be something of a sensation when the subject matter is finally revealed.

1979

Monday, January 1st

1979 comes in cold. Very cold. Minus 7° centigrade.

Walk across the crackling snow to a party at neighbours. He's in advertising and has gathered a collection of 'hangover killers' from an article in *The Guardian*, which he's displayed like some alcoholic's stall at a Bring and Buy. Each with instructions. So you can have Fernet Branca, Bovril and vodka – known as a Russian Bison – Prairie Oysters – raw eggs are laid on – and a drink which Kingsley Amis christened 'The Final Solution': one spoonful of ground coffee, one spoonful of sugar wrapped in a slice of lemon, sucked and, in mid-mastication, swept through with a tumblerful of brandy. I tried it and I think I blame it for a consequent feeling of elation and a loss of all sense of time.

After a Final Solution and a couple of Buck's Fizzes, we slithered across to the Guedallas for lunch. Present were the Maliks, the Taylors. (Mary, very jolly, told us the latest Jeremy Thorpe stories. What's the similarity between Jeremy Thorpe and William the Conqueror? They're both fucking Normans.)[1]

Thursday, January 4th

Jimmy Gilbert rings to tell me his suggestion for the new director for the *Yarns*. Turns out it's Alan J W Bell[2] – the PA who should have been a director, who came in to help out with *Yarns* when we were arranging audience screenings. I'd forgotten about him – but he fits the bill rather well. He knows the *Yarns*, I know him, he's keen on film and, not identified with any particular programme so far, he could be very keen to make his mark.

Lunch at the San Carlo in Highgate to meet 'fellow speakers' at the Barclays Bank Northern Managers' binge next Thursday week. I'm doing it because the Highgate manager, Brian Kemp, is one of the organisers and is a bright, humorous, intelligent sort of bloke – met through Graham Chapman.

1 See footnote, page 623.
2 Later to direct the *Last of the Summer Wine* series.

Graeme Garden, who's also speaking, is there, which avoids the conversation becoming utterly stodgy. The other bank representatives look very English macho, rugby club rednecks, and not really the sort of people I would spend more than 12 minutes with if possible. My heart sinks as Brian (whose wife is, rather neatly, called Judith) tells me that there will only be two or three women there so we can be as filthy as we like.

Graeme is going back to theatre acting in the next couple of weeks. He's going to do Charles Dyer's *Rattle of a Simple Man* for Johnny Lynn and the Cambridge Theatre Company. He's only going on tour though. He hated the West End run of *Unvarnished Truth* and claims that the provinces provide much more enthusiastic audiences.

Saturday, January 6th

A party at Anne Henshaw's.

Talk to Richard Loncraine,[1] who says the BBC never asked him about directing the *Yarns*, and he would now almost certainly have been available.

Loncraine says he would have liked to have worked on the *Yarns*, which, he said with characteristic directness, always scored eight out of ten with him. He felt they all peaked at a certain point and the endings were a little disappointing. I agree. I don't think Terry and I ever quite got the measure of the 30-minute format. We always had too much to cram in.

Monday, January 8th

Alison[2] finishes typing 'Whinfrey's Last Case' and I collect it at lunchtime. Most garages are closed and the roads probably full of cars, like me, wasting petrol looking for a garage that's open. Plenty of petrol in Bantry Bay, however, where an unloading tanker blew up killing fifty people.

At four, in to the BBC to take the script and meet the new director and executive producer.

1 One of Anne's other clients. Successful commercials director who started Loncraine-Broxton, a novelty toy company. I'd suggested him to the BBC for the *Yarns*. We eventually worked together on *The Missionary* in 1982.
2 Alison Davies, our PA at Anne's office.

The talk is all positive. They are expecting a second script by January 17th and hardly a word is written yet. But at the same time they seem curiously uncertain as to their intentions. When I ask them what they'll do with these three *Yarns* it's as if they've never thought about it before.

Tuesday, January 9th

Write in the afternoon. Pleased to be away from 'Whinfrey' and on to something with a little more soul – and a good part for yours truly – namely the 'Golden Gordon' northern football saga. I do hope it works. I will dedicate it to the Meridien Hotel, Monastir, if it does – for that's where it began.

In the evening Willy and I join another 37,985 people at a chilly Highbury Stadium to watch the replay of Arsenal v Wednesday's Cup Tie. High up in the stands we get a good clear view and for once Sheffield give their supporters plenty to be proud of. They tackle fast and accurately, mark, move and even shoot much more tightly and efficiently than Arsenal. And just before half-time they score.

Willy and I drink our Thermosful of hot chocolate at half-time, well pleased. Wednesday even manage to hold out in the second half. We cannot bear to look at the clock. Terrific excitement – as gripping as any theatrical event I've ever seen. With four minutes to go, Arsenal hustle an equaliser. Everyone around us is up on their feet. But Wednesday survive what should have been Arsenal's surge of confidence until the end, and also through 30 minutes of extra time. So, still 1-1 and another replay in sight.

Willy and I feel like kings as we join the sea of people flooding down the neat residential streets, away from the ground. Passing groups of 10- to 18-year-olds waiting for 'Old Bill' to go so they can have a fight with Wednesday's equally pugnacious 10- to 18-year-olds.

Wednesday, January 10th

An unexpected boost, when Alan Bell rings to tell me how much he likes 'Whinfrey's Last Case'. Syd Lotterby, the executive producer,[1] finds the

---

1 Legendary BBC comedy producer and director (*Porridge, Butterflies, Last of the Summer Wine*). John and Graham particularly liked the sound of his name, and I seem to remember a sketch on *At Last the 1948 Show* in which every character was called Sydney Lotterby.

script funny and the only criticism is from Jimmy Gilbert about the 'non-ending'.

I take a pinch of salt and breathe a sigh of relief. Now we can go ahead. The work will be hard – the two new *Yarns* will have to be filmed back-to-back throughout March.

Thursday, January 11th

Round to a buffet supper at J Cleese's. John, who starts next week on a set of six new *Fawlty Towers*, saw the *Brian* film tonight at a showing laid on for him at the Audley Square Theatre. He'd asked me over to gauge reactions from his friends, most of whom had been in the audience.

Ronnie Eyre, a theatre director who recently completed an epic series on world religions called *The Long Search*, thought the film funny and important. He felt the script was at most points saying things and making thought-provoking observations – only occasionally, as in the Pilate's Wife raid scene, did it become one-dimensional.

Michael Rudman, looking, if possible, younger than when he was at Oxford fifteen years ago, said he only saw five films a year, but felt that this was going to be a big success. Jim Beach was greatly impressed – especially with Pilate – and I received many flattering remarks about my various hammy performances. Humphrey Barclay was full of praise and Michael Peacock,[1] who didn't like the haggling sequence because of its lack of urgency and wasn't keen on Otto, thought both script and performance were on the whole stronger than the *Grail*. He also thought Terry's direction was better than the *Grail*.

Saturday, January 13th

Terry J rang from a dubbing theatre at half past nine and, as in a call yesterday, referred to his paranoiac feeling of being 'ganged up' on by Julian and others at Neal's Yard during the editing. Terry G and Julian had sat together at the viewing and at a meeting afterwards Terry G had demolished all of the work Terry J had done.

Purposely try to avoid taking sides with either Terry. It won't help. Terry J must just be allowed to work as uninterruptedly as possible in

---

1 Along with John Cleese, he was one of the founders of Video Arts, who, very successfully, made training films for industry, many of them written by and starring Cleese.

order to make the film ready for the January 19th viewing. In a way TJ's call was a cry for help and support and I said I was prepared to go in and look at any edited film if it will help to get things ready any faster – but if it's merely to help TJ make a point, I said I felt that may be a waste of time at this stage.

Rachel's birthday party got under way at 3.30. Six or seven children. Alison brought Sally. They are at the age when a party is still very exciting and quite a new experience. Willy helped to entertain them – playing monsters in a very avuncular fashion. At one point I saw him leading them all upstairs for a puppet show. But within five minutes they were down again, leaving Willy sadly reflecting that only Sally Jones had really wanted to watch.

Wednesday, January 17th

J Goldstone tells me that the Warner Brothers chief – John Calley – is very enthusiastic about the movie, thinks it could be one of the greatest comedies ever, but the only part they all seemed to find offensive was Graham's brief protestation, after his mother tells him he's the illegitimate son of a Roman, that he's a 'Hebe, a Kike, a Hooknose, a Yid, a Red Sea Pedestrian and proud of it!' Memorable words, written almost a year ago to the day by TJ and myself in Barbados, and now the only section of this deeply controversial film which offends every member of Warner Brothers' Board of Directors!

It's still sleeting as I drive out to the BBC. The dull, harsh, uncomfortable weather seems to reflect the spirit of the times. More people are on strike at the moment than at any time since February 1974, when Heath confronted the miners and the country was put on a three day week.

I still regard the strikes and the disruptions that seem to hit British industry so severely every now and then as a healthy sign. A sign that there are people out there, amongst the computers and the rationalisations, concerned to defend their quality of life by shouting out in indignation rather than submitting Claim Form No. 478B to be heard at the Arbitration Committee's Headquarters by some faceless civil servant in eight months' time.

But there are still plenty of instances of the most wasteful and debilitating lack of personal trust and co-operation. The rail strikes this week seem to be a prime example. The two rail unions, ASLEF and the NUR, hate each other, with the result that, whilst many of the country's road hauliers are on strike, the railways, far from benefiting and offering an uninterrupted service in these cold, grey days – which would win them enormous goodwill – are going on strike too.

But amidst all this gloom there is a golden ring of light – the heroic, titanic struggle between Arsenal and Sheffield Wednesday in the third round of the FA Cup.

Tonight they face each other for the fourth time to try and break the deadlock. We have the radio on in the kitchen but I can hardly bear to listen. One-nil to Wednesday – heart surges. Arsenal miss a penalty – heart practically bursts. Then a minute later Arsenal equalise – numbness. Then Arsenal draw ahead – feeling of resignation, pulse rate almost down to normal. Then Wednesday equalise two minutes from the end! Extra time again. Over seven hours of football and still tied. Then an extra goal apiece in extra time. Another heroic evening. And they play again – in Leicester next Monday.[1]

Friday, January 19th

Brian screening. Terry Hughes, Michael White, George H, Jill Foster. John Goldstone issues us with clipboards and little torches to make notes. Just before time, Graham and Eric – our foreign exiles – arrive.

The showing does not go that well. Long periods of audience silence. But afterwards we all meet (mafia-like) in a private room above the Trattoria Terrazza. General feelings are that the movie works 75%. Disagreement on cuts, however. TJ wants to lose stoning. Eric feels that the Ex-Leper should go before the stoning. All are agreed to cut Haggling and most of the raid. I suggest cutting Mandy's last speech. TJ agrees. Eric is worried about Otto – we all feel that it half works. There are many instances of jokes half working, which disappoints me.

It's a good, workmanlike session, though people about to make earth-shattering points about the movie tend to be interrupted by waiters asking whether they'd like some aubergines.

---

1 Some readers of the diary may find it confusing that I appear to support both Sheffield football teams (a crime punishable by disembowelment in Sheffield itself). Living in London I'm always glad to hear of any Sheffield success. When I lived in Sheffield I was always a United fan, so that's what I've had to settle for.

My first appearance on Saturday Night Live *had gone well enough for me to be courted again. I was scheduled to guest host at the end of January and quite an adventure ensued.*

Saturday, January 20th

Managed to cope with a packed couple of days on Thursday and Friday, in order to make the 11.15 Concorde to NY this morning for my second guest hosting of *Saturday Night Live*.

About 40 minutes outside London, with the first cocktails flowing and freeing the traveller's brain from the numbing buzz of a hundred other conversations, the pilot's voice comes over the PA and, in bold, almost reassuring tones, advises us that there is 'bad news'. Momentarily visions of the worst sort flash through my mind, but the facts are quite mundane. There is a malfunction with the cooling system in one of the engines and 'transonic' flight will not be possible. We have to return to London.

So I find myself back in the lounge.

As the delay in repairing our aircraft grows longer (the airline even has a term for it – 'creeping delay'), I'm stuck for two more hours with a roomful of over-achievers. And no brunch.

Sunday, January 21st, The Hospitality Inn, Enfield, Connecticut

8.00 A. M.   Outside my room drizzle falls out of grey skies onto snow. Thin, spiky bare birch woods away to my right. Below me a man is clearing his car window of three inches of snow – the result of the storm that eventually ensured our progress across the Atlantic was nearer 22 hours than the three and a half Concorde proudly boasts.

I kept a note of the lost day – January 20th – which surely will go down in the annals of supersonic flight.

12.15–   We wait in the departure lounge for five and a half hours
5.45 P.M.   whilst a new part is found for the aircraft. By then it's too late for the old crew to work, so a new crew has to be found.

5.50 P.M.   BA 171 starts take-off six and a half hours behind schedule. Take-off aborted as anti-skid warning light fails to function. We taxi back to ramp.

5.50–   Two hours' wait in the aircraft (more champagne) for new
8.00 P.M.   part to be installed and fuel tank topped up – 'Only three

tons,' says the captain cheerfully, though this may be a reference to the Dom Perignon.

8.00 P.M.	Successful take-off from Heathrow eight and a half hours late.
12.00 A.M.	Land at Bradley Field Airport, Connecticut, as there is congestion at JFK due to a snowstorm and Concorde, with its gargantuan fuel appetite and lack of big enough tanks, cannot afford to go in the stack.
1.30 A.M.	We leave the aircraft in a swirling snowstorm and wait in a baggage collection area (we cannot go through into the restaurant or even to the toilets because we have no immigration or customs men to clear us).
12.00– *1.30 A.M.*	We wait as the decision is taken to put 82,000 gallons more fuel into the aircraft.
1.30– *2.45 A.M.*	Wait in limbo at Bradley Field International, an airport that seems to be run entirely by students between the ages of 18 and 21.
2.45 A.M.	Board Concorde for the third time today. This time with a film crew to capture our every indignity.
4.00 A.M.	Pilot decides not to take BA 171 into JFK tonight owing to bad weather.
5.00 A.M.	We disembark for the third and final time.
5.45 A.M.	As we wait in the no-man's-land – now into our nineteenth hour in airports – news that the doors of the luggage bay are iced up.
6.00 A.M.	Our baggage is retrieved.
6.10 A.M.	Board our coach.
7.10 A.M.	Our coach arrives at Hospitality Inn, Enfield.
8.30 A.M.	Bed.

Still some doubt as to whether JFK or La Guardia are open. The remnants of flight BA 171 are now splitting into smaller groups to find their way to their final destination.

At ten, four of us – Pat, a stocky, young paper salesman, Nancy, a slim, wide-eyed New York model, and the white-haired, ruddy-faced, cherubic director of a Minneapolis-based agricultural foodstuffs corporation – set off, crammed tight into a yellow cab.

Even the cab drive is something of an ordeal. The driver is

short, squat, off-hand and incompetent. At one point, on the outskirts of Hartford, we find a road blocked by flooding and have to turn back.

An uncomfortable hour brings us to Hartford Station. An almost empty, long booking hall, of a vaguely classical design. It's shabby and run down. The poor relation of US transport – the railroad. But, full of hope, we board the 11.30 for New York via New Haven.

On the outskirts of New Haven, the line is submerged for about half a mile and we move slowly through the water, to arrive at New Haven ten minutes late, at 12.35. Another transfer of heavy bags and baggages to the New Haven–Penn Station train.

The station at New Haven is still well below the standards of British counterparts, but the Amtrak 'Parlor' Car – a First Class service – is comfortable, with modern, expansive armchair seats and a bar which serves food and drinks. My spirits rise.

However, the train does not move and the Awful Rumours begin. There is a derailment on a flooded line, further up the track, a power sub-station in the Bronx is out of action due to flooding, so none of the electric locomotives can function.

At one point the Parlor Car empties as we are advised that another train will be leaving for NY before us. This proves to be a false alarm, and everyone reboards. But fifteen minutes later, as I am about to settle down to a cool glass of Inglenook Californian Chablis, the word comes again that a train will definitely be leaving for Grand Central Station right away on Track 6. So everyone, apart from one man who remains because he can't bear the thought of standing all the way to New York (Wise and Shrewd Traveller) makes their way once more up the long platform, down the subway and up to the Connecticut Railway platform.

There's still a ten-minute wait, but the good news is that we do have the satisfaction of being the first train to leave New Haven since early morning. The bad news is we're squashed into a crowded open coach without lights or heating. There are gloomy predictions that the ride could take up to two hours.

In the end it takes over five hours. During that time we spend nearly an hour in darkness, with no fresh air, at a standstill somewhere in the outer suburbs of New York. The compartments have become fuller and fuller, and we have even suffered the indignity of seeing the Amtrak train – with my freshly opened half-bottle of Inglenook undrunk beside a broad and empty armchair – hurtle past us two hours before our arrival.

What makes it worse is that the train is full of Python devotees, who cannot believe that this crumpled ruin, with a once-fresh Concorde label on his bag, is to be the host of their favourite TV programme of the week.

Finally we reach Grand Central Station – it feels like rounding Cape Horn – but there is one final twist. Before we all split up we find that one of the cases we have been dragging around for the last nine and a half hours does not belong to any of the four of us. And it's the heaviest.

Wednesday, January 24th, New York

The read-through slowly fills up. There are thirty or forty people packed in the room to get the first inkling of what the show may be like. Belushi, as crumpled and unkempt as Aykroyd, is given 'Happy Birthday'. He's 30 today – and has a No. 1 film – *Animal House* – and No. 1 record to celebrate it. He's a big, fat boy made good. He eats like a Bunter and grunts and sniffs and emits continuous breathy groans.

The material is plentiful – the result of a three-week lay-off for the writers. There is one quiz game – 'Name the Bats' – written by Brian McConachie, which has one of the best receptions of any sketch at a first reading that I've ever heard. Myself, Belushi and Gilda can hardly read it. An absolute winner. A masterpiece of absurdity.

At the end of a read that lasts over two hours, Lorne declares that he thinks this is some of the best material he's heard for a show, and hastens to add that he never says things like this on a Wednesday. So everyone goes away pleased, apart from the few whose material died, and possibly Laraine and Jane[1] and Gilda, who never have enough material to suit their talents.

Thursday, January 25th, New York

Spend the morning working on the monologue and take it in with me to NBC at a quarter to one.

Bill Murray drops by the dressing room. He's making a movie (his second since I last told him he should be doing at least as many as

---

1 Jane Curtin – original cast member and very funny lady. Later starred in *Kate & Allie* and *Third Rock From the Sun*.

Danny and John), in which he plays Hunter S. Thompson, with Peter Boyle as Thompson's lawyer, who hasn't been seen for five or six years. They were the narrators of *Fear and Loathing in Las Vegas* – a twentieth-century masterpiece.

He knows Hunter quite well now. A dangerous man, says Bill, in the sense that he loves to live on the brink of excitement and the limits of human stamina and ingenuity. His wit and humour works even better, Bill maintains, because one's response to it is in part sheer relief that he's still alive.

Friday, January 26th, New York

Sleep until 8.30 – an eight and a half hour stretch or more, punctuated only by an early morning alarm call which wrenches me awake at six. It's for a Mr Malone. Wrong number, I protest. 'You sure you don't have a Mr Malone with you?' Her tone is such that I have for a moment to think very clearly as to whether I might have a Mr Malone with me after all.

To NBC at two.

Reading the sketches there are some real gems – including a long 'What If Superman Had Been a German', in which I play Hitler.

We start blocking about three and make slow progress until eleven when we have to stop, with one and a half sketches still untouched. One encouraging thing is that from all around I'm picking up good word, not only on this show, but on the last we did together. Bill Murray, over an hour's supper break at Charley O's, still reckons it was the most consistently funny show they did last year.

Bill is very flattering in his serious, downbeat way, which makes cynical Englishmen, unused to accepting praise, worry a little in case they're being sent up. Still, he's very surprised that I have had no outside offers after *SNL* – he thinks I would be a cert for American movies!

I must say, one feels a very poor cousin hearing of all the movies these people are doing. Belushi and Dan A are both in Spielberg's *1941* and return to LA Sunday to continue shooting.

Saturday, January 27th, New York

Walk down to NBC with Nancy. She tells me Eric has arrived on this morning's Concorde. I find I now wince involuntarily whenever I hear that name (Concorde, not Eric).

My major problem of the afternoon is that the much improved and carefully honed monologue, in which I refer casually to a lack of proper socks (when everything else is perfect) and gradually build it into an obsession, just isn't working. It raises hardly a laugh (except from Bill Murray – my greatest fan!) and I return to the dressing room in a state of some despondency. How I could do with the security of the cat routine now!

After the meal break, and as the audience are beginning to file in for the dress rehearsal, I tell Lorne that I feel that a possible salvation for the monologue would be to lose the cards and do it ad-lib. Lorne agrees and I wait for the start of the dress rehearsal with added adrenaline output – knowing that I have to make up four or five minutes of spiel.

The monologue founders at dress rehearsal. I stumble on painfully. The whole of the rest of the show seems to sag too.

Various suggestions for cut-down monologues. Lorne says it may be best to be straight, sincere, say we have a fantastically full show and get off after 30 seconds. But someone – I think it may be director Davy Wilson, with his solid, dependable good humour – decides me to go with it.

11.30 – again the wait backstage, the very successful Carter cold opening, then the music builds and Don Pardo's classic American announcer's voice builds with stomach wrenching speed up to the climax – 'Michael Palin!' And out I come. And I know I'll survive. They're listening and I sense they're not embarrassed. In fact it begins to get a few laughs, I enjoy playing it, and it comes to an end with applause I'm very happy with. Not a great monologue – for it was always a slight idea – but I feel immeasurably happier throughout the show because it had worked – I had saved it.

The show, predictably perhaps, really takes off. Sketches, cut only within the last half-hour, work better than ever, performances are all tweaked up, the live magic works and even during the show, but certainly by the end, word gets around that it's a good one.

It's a nice, silly time of one's life, this hour or so after hosting a successful show. For a while you're King of the Castle.

The air of unreality continues at the after-show party at 1 Fifth Avenue, when half-way through our meal a waiter arrives, announces a telephone call for me and leads me off through the kitchens to the back of the restaurant where stand huge, evil-looking basins full of clogged washing-up. I'm told that one of the washing-up staff has always wanted to meet me, and was shown the man, who rather sheepishly turns round and breaks into a grin. It's Alan Bennett, a friend of the restaurant owner, hands in the sink. He immediately goes into profuse self-deprecation, saying what a fool he's felt waiting for me for an hour!

Eventually he comes to the table and I ask if he's going back to London for the press showing of the last of his Frears/London Weekend plays. Alan doesn't think he is. He likes New York. Stephen wants him to write a play about it, but he just enjoys being here and can't put his mind to work.

Monday, January 29th, New York

Lunch, organised by PBS, with TV critic Marvin Kitman, an eager, talkative, spongy-faced character, who's full of bounce and one feels is used to sharp, quick one-liners, which I can never supply very well. But we had a good talk. He noticed a difference between my two shows. In the first one my own contribution resulted, he felt, in two pieces which broke new ground for the show – one was the cats down the trousers, and the other was the escape from the box during *The Seagull*.

This time, he felt, the show was within itself and lacked a unique edge. Which I had to agree with. I should have registered my feelings more strongly to Lorne perhaps, but I did want to play a character – or at least do something original enough to top the cats.

Kitman told me of George Carlin, American comic, who once did a spot like that on a show and simply came out, said nothing for four minutes, then walked off again. And it worked!

Friday, February 2nd

To Neal's Yard this morning. Pick my way through piles of uncollected garbage piled up in the passageway from Monmouth Street. At least we've had heat and light, but we don't have any dustmen at the moment.

At six I'm in De Lane Lea's basement for a preview of *Brian*.

The audience is three or four times the size of the last showing I attended, the night before I left for New York. And, although the film is shorter, with Shepherds and a large part of the raid removed, I think it's the size of the audience that makes all the difference. They are much noisier in their appreciation and the end section goes particularly well.

I end up in the Carlisle Arms with Anne H, John G and Terry G and

Julian. Julian is finding it almost impossible to spend any time on his own fine-cutting the movie without constant interruptions from Terry, over small points which Julian now regards as of secondary importance to getting the movie completed on time.

I am appealed to, almost as if they'd tried everything else, to talk to Terry and impress upon him the need to keep away from Julian for the next few days.

Saturday, February 3rd

A clear, bright, sunny morning. My first weekend with the children since Rachel's fourth birthday on the 13th but I have to spend today at Neal's Yard, trying to patch up the wretched PR problems between editor and director. Gilliam arrives on his bicycle with a list of points on the film – 'A Few Hopefully Helpful Hints in the Pursuit of Perfection', which I take down with me.

I get to the editing rooms by 10.15. Terry is already there and Julian has been in since six!

Terry, Julian and myself sit and work amiably and constructively through the entire film, raising all the points from yesterday's viewing. Terry G's as well. TJ is amenable to most of the suggestions and some good cuts are agreed on.

Drive TJ back up to Hampstead at four and as we go he tells me of the difficulties of working with Julian. Terry acknowledges in one breath that Julian is an excellent editor, but at the same time bitterly accuses him of not taking a blind bit of notice of any of TJ's suggestions. I urge TJ to take a breather from the film – at least for twenty-four hours. He looks as baggy-eyed as Julian is red-eyed.

Tuesday, February 6th

Completed a rewrite on the end of 'Whinfrey' this morning.

Drive into Soho for one o'clock viewing of *Brian* – mainly for Eric who arrived back from LA last night. He has to leave the country again on Friday – for tax reasons. The showing is a good one and confirms my feeling after last Friday that the movie is consistently funnier than the *Grail*, but without the high points of visual and verbal felicity such as Trojan Rabbit and Black Knight fights.

Sandy Lieberson is at the viewing. He warns us that it will be 'X' rated because of the full-frontal nudity and that's about all. I feel we must not compromise on the 'full-frontal' (what an absurd phrase anyway). It's a very funny scene, and Graham's reaction as he appears stark naked at the window, only to find 500 'followers' waiting to worship him, is one of the biggest and best laughs of the film.

Eric looks unhappy. He feels both Haggling and Ex-Leper should go. He is dissuaded from this, at least until they're dubbed – the general feeling being voiced by Julian, who claims that they are both scenes which people listen to and appreciate rather than roar with laughter at.

Clash over 'Brian of Nazareth' *Life of Brian* title suggestions. Eric says everyone in America he's talked to will be very disappointed if it's not 'Nazareth'. TJ and I maintain it's inviting a misleading comparison with *Jesus of Nazareth*. Eric says we could lose a million dollars or so with a flat title like *Life of Brian*. Eric's sharpness makes me sharp in return. A pity, because we need to listen to each other a bit more.

David Leland and Stephanie come round to dinner this evening. We have a chat over the 'Northern Yarn' ('Golden Gordon') and he gives me a lot of useful casting suggestions for the small but vital parts in it. I persuade – not that it takes much doing – David himself to play the Football Manager. He rather likes the idea of wearing long shorts and old-fashioned boots with the huge toe-caps that curl round like Arab slippers.

Saturday, February 10th

Drive to Soho to get *Variety* and croissants. The piles of uncollected rubbish are now being blown apart by the wind and central Soho looks like a tip from which buildings emerge.

Gilliam tells of the latest *Brian* saga. Paramount Pictures are now the most likely distributor, and to further the deal Julian was to be sent over to Hollywood with the cutting copy of the film to show them the latest progress. All was well until it was discovered that Julian, in filling out his visa application form, had felt bound to note that he was a communist. America will not let in communists, so there was great commotion. However, after application to some special US department at Frankfurt, Julian was given permission to go. So the self-confessed communist travelled First Class in a Jumbo and will be staying at the Beverly Wilshire.

TG and I consoled ourselves with a *Variety* clipping which shows that *Jabberwocky* has out-earned *Rocky* and *Looking for Mr Goodbar*, in Spain!

Wednesday, February 14th

Terry tells me the latest on the American viewing of *Brian*, which Graham rang him so gloomily about at the weekend. It transpires that Graham had attended, not *the* viewing in LA, but a later, less well-attended overflow viewing. He had arrived late and the sound had been very bad. But GC still feels that 'an alien force' (his words) has been at work on the editing and he is flying back to England at the weekend with his thoughts and criticisms.

I don't think anyone is going to listen very sympathetically. John C thinks that Graham is being an old woman and anyway he's too busy putting *Fawlty Towers* together to attend any meetings. T Gilliam will not, on principle, attend any meetings unless we're all there. So the prospects for Chapman's Flying Visit don't look too hopeful.

A meeting at the Lamb with John Gorman and Chris Tarrant to discuss what TJ and I are expected to do on the ATV Saturday morning program *Tiswas*, which we are guesting on in a couple of days. Everything's left delightfully vague, but they're expecting two or three sketches from us, so it won't be a complete doddle.

Take Helen to the ICA to see Victoria Wood's play *Talent*, which was originally directed by David Leland for the Crucible – and two or three of the actors in it have been highly recommended by David for parts in the *Yarns*. I'm impressed by the cast, but also by the earthy, untheatrical directness of the play. It's not profound, but a very funny, well-observed slice of life ...

And obviously a cult success – Michael Codron and Humphrey Barclay are in a packed audience of 200 or so. Talk to Humphrey afterwards. He tells me he lives at the bottom of Derek Jacobi's garden, and gives a naughty smile.

Saturday, February 17th

Coffee at the Monmouth Coffee House, then across to the Bijou Theatre for another viewing of *Brian*. Sit next to Graham, who looks trim and healthy. Altogether a new, meek Graham. Then I remember he has got us here for a viewing no one particularly wants (and John Cleese and Terry Gilliam have refused to attend anyway).

Afterwards, at a meeting at John Goldstone's office, Eric, Terry J, myself and Graham have a rather efficient, direct and radical appraisal of the movie. I now feel that the Ex-Leper sketch, funny though it ought to be, isn't getting the right reaction, and is structurally holding up progress of the story at that early stage in the movie. Eric has always felt that and he feels Otto should go for the same reason. There is still a split on the title of the movie, however, between *Life of Brian* (John, Terry J and myself) and 'Brian of Nazareth' (the others).

Graham's fears about the pace of the film, of the 'alien force' in the editing, are all rather predictably more bark than bite and, apart from a couple of fairly tiny points, he makes no fight over the present look of the movie. If I were really uncharitable, I might think that this whole 'Graham Is Unhappy With The Film' scare of the past week was GC's way of getting a free ticket over to the UK to see his home again. But I'm not uncharitable.

Monday, February 19th, Penzance

Woke, seconds before production assistant John Adams' alarm shattered the peace of the Longboat Hotel at six. Easily caught the 6.31, and I was almost sorry to leave the attractive, atmospheric chunkiness of Penzance Station, after a whirlwind scouting of locations for 'Whinfrey'.

At Plymouth, two hours later, the train filled to the brim with eager south-western businessmen. We ate breakfast and I read the treatment of Terry Gilliam's new film, *Brazil*.

Marvellous effects and stupendous graphic ideas in TG's story – but with such stunning sets and surroundings the story needs to be very straight and simple or utterly fantastic. It isn't comfortably either.

Arrive at Paddington at half past twelve. No let-up for location hunters and Alan [our director] insists that we take a cab over to the Turf Club to see one of our London locations for 'Whinfrey'.

The club is in Carlton House Terrace and we meet our designer, Gerry Scott,[1] outside. The suave and elegantly pin-striped club secretary is thrown into frightful confusion by our arrival. He looks us up and down and then very reluctantly lets us in.

We have broken all the rules – especially bringing Gerry, quite

---

1 Production designer on 'Whinfrey's Last Case' and 'Golden Gordon', she went onwards and upwards to design some of the BBC's great period dramas, including *Pride and Prejudice*, *Clarissa* and *The Way We Live Now*.

manifestly a female, into these hallowed quarters – but there has been no revolution or mass resignations, so he's happy. I think he quite enjoys the frisson of naughtiness which letting us in involves. When it boils down to it, there are not many places we have visited whose head isn't turned by the BBC's name and the BBC's money.

Monday, February 26th, Southwold

My long-delayed visit to Southwold.

The weather continues fine, clear and sunny – the countryside up in East Anglia emerging from its most severe winter since 1947. Mother has survived the worst that this harsh winter can bring – and on her own as well. She looks a good colour and seems very bright and vigorous.

After lunch, a walk on the front to survey the damage of the gales – breakwaters smashed like matchsticks and the pier, landmark of my courting days with Helen, lies truncated, a mass of bent and twisted metal curving up from the sea.

Watch a marvellously constructed, very funny *Fawlty Towers*. It's so good it makes me want to give up!

In bed by eleven.

Tuesday, February 27th, Southwold

After breakfast, I work for a couple of hours, bringing the diary up to date and rewriting (again) D Leland's speech as the Football Manager. I think it should be a nervous breakdown, Alan Bell doesn't. Difficult to decide, but I think I must follow my own instinct. Dictate new nervous breakdown speech to the office over the phone.

Ring JC on impulse and congratulate him on last night's disgustingly funny *Fawlty*. JC worried that three jokes out of the still to be broadcast *Fawltys* have appeared in films he's seen over the last couple of weeks. Particularly worried that a scene of Fawlty talking to a dead body, which he wrote a year ago, has just cropped up in Altman's *A Wedding*.

He is very anxious to be in one of the next two *Yarns*. He says he will do anything silly for expenses only – provided 65% of his body is in shot.

Friday, March 2nd

Woke early – rewriting my words for the day over in my mind. The excitement and peculiar nervous tension involved in the first day of any new acting project does not lessen as the time goes on. Instead one grows to learn to accept it and how to deal with it, but it's still there. Tight stomach and loose bowels.

Today is the first day on the first of the two remaining *Yarns* – with a predominantly new crew and with scripts patched and sewn together more rapidly than the others.

Helen dropped me off at Russell Square, after I'd taken Rachel to playschool, and we set to on the single-shot, virtually one-take sequence in which the Orson Welles Introducer is consistently interrupted by everyday life when attempting to introduce a film in the centre of London.

Of course life imitated art. At one point a van drew up exactly where our van was due to draw up – and Alan exactly re-enacted the script when he dashed across the road and shouted at the van driver to move on. At times it seemed quite farcical – a man detailed to stop any traffic impeding the progress of our van ended up stopping our van as well.

Then an hour and a half with an affable, weather-beaten jack-of-all-trades called Reg Potterton, who interviews me for a Python *Playboy* interview. I like him, but an accident-prone day continues when he finds that he's recorded my interview over Terry Jones's!

Finally back home at six. Plenty of letters and phone calls and words to learn for a more gruelling filming day tomorrow – when we start at 8.30, on interior scenes, with actors I don't really know. A baptism of fire for all of us.

Saturday, March 3rd

The first problem of the day is to sort the set out – make suggestions about the look of the office without hurting the designer's feelings too much. There isn't much to do – a few adjustments – replacements of old maps for the recent ones of Europe which the props buyer has inexplicably provided with a great lack of historical sense.

More formidable a task is to tone down the performance of two of the actors – Jack May and Gerald Sim – who are delivering caricatures.

I watch the scene play through, rather anxiously, and constantly have to step in to adjust the actors' performances. I've given up doing this through the director as it just wastes time, and Alan seems very happy for me to talk to them whenever I want.

We complete the scene in mid-afternoon, but the weather is grey and dull beyond the windows and we shall not get the full value of our priceless, unchanged London skyline in the background.

Sunday, March 4th

Quick Sunday lunch, then on to a packed Penzance-via-Bristol train at Paddington. Work on the script – incorporating adjustments suggested by Terry at our meeting on Friday lunchtime.

Maria Aitken[1] and Edward Hardwicke (Otway and Girton) are the only other members of the unit on the train, which reaches Penzance a little after a quarter past nine. The Queen's Hotel, predictably and with some relish, greet us with the news that we can't eat there.

Maria is very complimentary about the script and says her husband (Nigel Davenport) laughed aloud whilst reading it, which is, she tells me, a rare thing. All this helps as I feel rather defensive about 'Whinfrey'.

Monday, March 5th, Penzance

Our luck is in. Awake to fine, almost cloudless skies. The location – around Cape Cornwall – is superb, and can be seen and used today to real advantage. An excellent first day – spent clambering up precipitous cliff sides and in and out of caves wearing dressing gown and pyjamas. Weather remains immaculate, though the wind is so strong I have to have my trilby hat stuck onto my head with double-sided tape.

Wednesday, March 7th, Penzance

The gods are with us. The sea on this side of the peninsula is millpond calm, Penzance quiet and settled once again in its own particular brand of out-of-season silence.

By a combination of eliminating our second cliff location today, good weather, and pushing a reluctant cameraman into an hour's extra

---

1 Maria later played John C's wife in *A Fish Called Wanda*.

shooting, we catch up all we lost yesterday. The sun is bright again – and the cliffs are well displayed. The wind has shifted to the north and is obligingly whipping up the sea below us and crashing it against the cliffs to spectacular effect.

Sunday, March 11th

Eric writes from the Chateau Marmont, thanking me for the *Life of Brian* book material and brimming over with facts and figures about the vast numbers of copies we'll be selling of this book we know nothing about. He's also floating the idea of an LA stage show in September.

Monday, March 12th

Supposedly a day off before completing 'Whinfrey' on the Ealing stages, but the continued strike of riggers and drivers has changed all that. At the moment we can do no more filming until the dispute is settled – and I hear that the last *Fawlty Towers* episode has been cancelled altogether.

Graham Chapman rings from LA. Mainly to voice anxiety over a page of the book he has seen, which, he says, reads like the story of how Eric Idle put the *Life of Brian* together. GC is much concerned with this interpretation of Python history – probably because he's not mentioned at all – but it does increase my own concern that this book is becoming Eric's fait accompli, and we simply must see what is and isn't in it.

Wednesday, March 14th

Cold and wet. North-easterly winds roll the clouds across and I'm glad we're not down in Devon trying to pick up shots. In fact the *Yarns* remain immobilised. Word is that the terms on which the BBC will climb down over the strike are settled, but the strikers have to meet and are unlikely to start the transport moving again until tomorrow morning. So two more unexpected days of peace lie ahead.

One of the many tests of my resolve to write a book this year – when Frank Dunlop rings and asks me if I would like to play in a new West End production of *Rookery Nook*. Ben Travers revivals are all the thing now, and Dunlop, who sounds straightforward, friendly and totally without bullshit, reckons *Rookery Nook* is his best.

I'm so looking forward to writing that it would take something very important to sway me. Farce in the West End would be delightful, but I don't think I really want to make my mark as an actor of farce. Still, can't put the phone down without pangs of regret.

To dinner with the Davidsons. Sheila Pickles is there. Much talk of LA, from which she has just returned. She stayed with Zeffirelli, who is reported to be very cross with the Tunisians for letting Pythons use his sets, and has threatened to decline Bourguiba's offer to make him Minister of Culture!

Sunday, March 18th, Black Horse Hotel, Skipton

Drive to the hotel in Skipton where I'll be staying for most of 'Golden Gordon'. A short back and sides to turn me into Gordon Ottershaw. A drink and a meal at the hotel – cooked by a chef who has seen the *Holy Grail* five times and who approached me, with trembling hands, clutching one of our LPs and five or six of our cassettes for signing. He and his wife will look after us well, I think …

Then to the elegant, tasteful portals of Kildwick Hall, by whose mighty fireplaces Laurence Olivier stood in the film *Wuthering Heights*, and on whose frieze mouldings are the letters W and C – C signifying the Currer family, friends of Charlotte Brontë, and from whom she took her pen name Currer Bell.

Sitting amidst this unretouched history, knocking back scotches in fairly rapid succession, is Bill Fraser, with whom I play the Foggen (scrap merchant) scene tomorrow, and a rather narrow-faced ex-tax inspector, who appears to be the hotel's only other resident.

Bill F looks older, rounder and a little smaller than I remember him.[1] But he is 71 and he has this day completed recording of the Trevor Griffiths' play *Comedians* for the BBC. He finished at 5.30 and was driven straight up here. So no wonder he's winding down.

A joke for bedtime – clamber into my pyjamas, only to find they're Thomas's. I laugh out loud and feel very silly with the little jacket half on before I realise.

---

1 He starred in *The Army Game* and *Bootsie and Snudge*, two of the few television programmes which united my father and myself in helpless laughter.

Monday, March 19th, Skipton

Today the last of the *Ripping Yarns* gets underway. I've no regrets that it is the last one, and yet I'm looking forward to putting it together almost more than any of them.

Bill is quieter this morning – and a little crustier – but he's good on his lines and turns in an effective performance, though not quite as dominating as I'd hoped. But by half past six we have four and a half to five minutes in the can.

Dickie Betts, the lighting gaffer, specially made a point of coming up to me and saying what a good piece of writing the scene was. This I take as a very high compliment, and I hope it will bode well for the rest of the filming.

For myself I found the day hard work and I was very happy to have cleared my own private hurdle – the rattling-off of two complete football teams, both with slightly different players' names. In a strange way the last week's enforced lay-off made it harder to start again. Still, now the wheels are turning once more and Gordon Ottershaw is beginning to come to life.[1]

Bad news at the end of the day – Richard Beckinsale has died: a heart attack at 31. Salutary perhaps. He had been working incredibly hard over the last two or three years, and especially recently. Didn't know him really, but Judy Loe, his missus, was in 'Claw' and a lovely person to work with.

Meal at Kildwick with a relaxing Bill. He's been very professional all day, not touching a drop, but he's now downing scotches with indecent haste and being charming and cantankerous.

Talks wryly of working at the RSC with Trevor Nunn. 'Well, we didn't really see eye to eye … you know, we'd all be in rehearsal and asked to think ourselves into being someone else, and they'd all crouch down on the stage and I'd go off in a corner and if anyone came along and asked what I was I'd say "A piece of shit" and they'd leave me alone.'

---

1 Gordon Ottershaw was the super-fan who smashed up his living-room every time the team lost. Which was most weeks.

Tuesday, March 20th, Skipton

In the evening we shoot some 24 carat gold exteriors at Kildwick Hall.
The fine Jacobean façade illuminated by one single 250 amp arc light on
a 120 foot hoist. Dickie Betts is in his element, strutting squat and small,
with his Alaskan trapper's fur hat on and talking into his radio – 'Bring
the moon round, Ron,' and other classics.

Friday, March 23rd, Skipton

A real bonus – a heaven-sent reward for our dogged perseverance. Sun
shone all day and we moved to the football pitch at Saltaire to shoot
arrivals of Bill Fraser (who'd patiently waited in solitary splendour at
Kildwick for two or three days, waiting for the weather to clear) and
Teddy Turner (a marvellous piece of casting by Syd Lotterby).

Then it was over to David Leland and his group of footballers – all cast
at David's suggestion, and mostly from 'Talent'. David was excellent – efficient and very funny. The whole scene played beautifully and David did his
long speech in one take. The crew and onlookers applauded as he raced off
into the distance with his trousers down. Four and a half minutes in the
can in a couple of hours. A reviving and morale-boosting day.

Sunday, March 25th, Skipton

Today the rain comes – and today is our only day off. Breakfast, buy *The
Observer*, read hardly any of it, and retire to my low-ceilinged room
looking out over the High Street to read through page proofs of the
Brian book, which Eric has sent over.

Vaguely unsettled by the balance/bias of the book. Tendency to hagi-
olatry of Python – as well as an overbalance into the more specific, less
subtle, Biblical parodies. Not a book I feel warm to so far.

No chance of working above the noisy bar of the Black Horse, so I
drove on to a pub called the Cross Keys at West Marton, which sells
Theakston's beer on draught. Bought a pint, found a table and settled to
write some material for the Python book. But trying to be as anonymous as possible doesn't really work. People kept coming up with lines
like 'Excuse me, but we've got a bet on – are you Eric Idle?' One kind
lady bought me a beer – she had watched and enjoyed all the *Yarns*,
especially 'Eric Olthwaite'.

To bed unusually early – about 11.15 – after watching heroes of mine, the Joint Stock Theatre Co, made to look pompous and very pretentious in a TV documentary. God save us from TV arts documentaries. Oh, and help *Ripping Yarns* with the weather next week ...

Tuesday, March 27th, Skipton

Our second attempt at the football match is rained off after two shots. Two to three thousand pounds in cancelled fees, etc. Gwen Taylor summoned from her day off, etc, to go back to shoot interiors at Brontë Street.

This evening eat at Oats with Gwen and Syd Lotterby – Syd's status enhanced by his collection of a BAFTA award for Best Comedy Series last week – *Going Straight* – Barker, Clement/La Frenais. We will need to use all this status too, as the 'Gordon' costs look like escalating almost to 'Whinfrey'-ish heights.

Leave at ten to collect John Cleese from the 10.20 train at Skipton. Arrive at my car to find fans clustering around. 'Oh, sign this.' 'I can't, I have to meet a train.' Visions of Cleese standing on a cheerless station whilst I sign autographs causes me to be uncharacteristically abrupt with the fans. 'Well, give us a kiss then,' they say, as I slam the car door and search frantically for keys. Then I hear one say 'John Cleese is in there, you know' and point to the hotel I've just come out of.

Out of the car, across to the Black Horse – the downstairs bar, full of young and younger folk, is buzzing with excitement. I push through people looking for the normally unmissable Cleese. Everyone grins – they think it's a Python sketch. I'm directed upstairs, where more excited fans are clustered. It's like a scene out of the *Life of Brian*.

Finally track him down in Ron, the manager's, sitting room. He had reached Leeds by train, then been given a lift to Ilkley, and had taxied on from there to Skipton. Ron, the manager, a rather overweight, round-shouldered fellow with a thick head of red hair that I'm told is not his own, became conspiratorial and told me which button to press on the telephone in order to summon him, and at a moment's notice he would smuggle us out via a special back route.

So a few minutes later buttons were pressed, back stairways descended, back doors opened and John and I walked out into Skipton High Street, feeling like newly released prisoners.

Drove JC over to Kildwick Hall, where the Davises[1] greeted us and Hassan, the Moroccan waiter, hovered, mouth half-open, waiting to be introduced – a perfect echo of Manuel. After a few minutes the temporary excitement subsided and John and I talked for an hour or so.

At one in the morning, I drive back into Skipton, only to find the door of the Black Horse firmly bolted. Knocking won't raise anyone, no windows are open and they don't answer the phone.

Drive back to Kildwick and put up for the night there in conditions of extreme comfort – yet I have to sleep in my shirt and they don't supply toothbrushes.

Wednesday, March 28th, Skipton

Wake early as usual. So many thoughts streaming through my head. Filming a *Yarn* requires not just enthusiasm but stamina. Feel like a coachman controlling fiercely energetic horses, straining to go forward – a crew of fifty or sixty, extras, actors like Bill F, John C, David Leland and Gwen – lots of egos to be harnessed then turned in the right direction. And the weight of it all ultimately devolves on me – I'm the one holding all the pieces together. Only three or four more days to hang on.

It's very jolly working with John at Brontë Street. He looks fine in 1930s gear and wide felt hat. A good-humoured, happy atmosphere. Smash up Brontë Street and by six we are finished there.

Sunday, April 1st

Back home for a while now. Work out that I've been away four of the last nine months.

Today we meet with Denis O'Brien. Eric brings the mock-up of the book, which looks wonderful and allays most of my fears. Everybody approves. Denis O'Brien then fills us in on distribution information. Paramount, MGM, Twentieth Century Fox and Universal have all turned the film down. Paramount after being incredibly keen, until one powerful man on the board said no. Paramount and Universal both took offence at the unsympathetic Jews in the film (e.g. Otto, etc).

Warner Brothers – or rather John Calley, one of their top men – are keen and Denis and George are happy to go with Calley although he is

1 Owners of the hotel.

not offering them an enormous advance, or indeed any advance at all. But they like him. In passing Denis tells us that in fact there is more of his personal money at stake in this movie than George's – but then he smiles when we become solicitous and says 'Well, if it bombs, it's just a couple of houses.' I must say he's the nicest rich man I know.

We talk about the stage show. Eric is like the Top Scholar of the Year at the Dale Carnegie School of Positive Thinking. A powerhouse of ideas, projects, facts – all very impressive.

He sees the stage show in LA as a glorious celebration of Python – and Denis comes in with fervent enthusiasm. It'll be a sell-out, at whatever price, at whatever place. It's all rather like a revivalist meeting. America the Promised Land, wrapped up in contracts and million dollar bills and stuffed down the throats of the recalcitrant, thankless English members of the group.

John C is most vocal in resisting the idea of an expensive, big theatre show. He wants to do it well in a smaller place. But I'm afraid Eric is right – we *could* fill the Hollywood Bowl.

Monday, April 2nd

Back to the Bijou Theatre for another viewing, with some of yesterday's adjustments made. A tiny audience, but I enjoyed the showing much better. 'Ben's Cell' scene is a strange phenomenon. It appears to be very delicately balanced at the opening. If it starts well, then there is great laughter all through, but if something goes wrong at the beginning (God knows why), it can go in silence.

Peter Cook, with frizzed and hennaed hair, is amongst the audience. He seems to enjoy it. It must hurt, because he is so funny himself and yet has had so little success (apart from Derek and Clive records) in the last few years.

Tuesday, April 3rd

At the end of the day I have another Python session. This time to cover as much general ground as we can before Graham returns to Los Angeles tomorrow.

I get to 2 Park Square West by 6.30. They're just discussing the day's film viewing. 'Leper' is back in. It just hadn't worked without it. 'Otto' see-saws between condemnation and popularity. At the moment it's in favour. When discussion comes round to appropriately silly music to be played behind JC's dance, Graham suggests bagpipes and I suggest the bagpipes play 'Hava Nagila'.

The meeting now rattles on with decisions coming thick and fast. I agree to supervise the making of the soundtrack album, JC will put together a short to go out with *Brian*. Eric is keen to go into the merchandising, but his visionary commercial delights appeal not at all to JC, and to a lesser extent TJ, and I must admit I myself baulk at the idea of Python 10 Year mugs, which have the Queen's face crossed out on them.

One good and promising idea of his, though, is that Python set up its own label for the world-wide marketing of Python video cassettes – and also Python-related video cassettes, such as *Yarns*, *Rutland Weekend* and *Fawlty Towers*.

To round off the evening, Iain Johnstone brings his Python documentary (shot in Tunisia) to show us. It's ten o'clock and we're tired, but a little high on all our discussions and decisions and dreams of the future, and Iain's film goes down a treat. It manages to make every one of us look articulate and quite amusing, but wittily avoids being pretentious itself or allowing us to be pretentious.

An odd therapy to all sit round and hear ourselves saying things about each other on screen which we'd never say directly!

Wednesday, April 4th

In the evening (free of Python meetings for once), to dinner with J Cleese. Ronnie Eyre present with JC's psychiatrist's wife, and Christopher Falkus of Weidenfeld's plus wife. Superb meal of asparagus mousse and Jerusalem artichoke salad and roast beef with magnificent trimmings.

Ronnie Eyre, blunt, sane, humorous and down to earth. An effective debunker of pretension and a man whose combination of sharp intelligence, honesty and lack of deviousness makes him a joy to listen and talk to. He says that every religious group was in part offended by his TV programme *The Long Search*, except for the Moslems, who took it rather well.

I end up chatting to him about the *Brian* movie. He's not surprised to hear that the Festival of Light are almost daily ringing the censor's office. He could be a great ally if it ever came to public debate.

Monday, April 9th

Am up in my work-room by seven to look through the *Brian* book proofs and try to unblock some of the problem areas. Terry G is unhappy with the cover and wants me to try and bend Basil Pao's[1] ear on this, but TG is away in Cornwall having a week's break with Maggie. Cleese is in Jamaica, Eric seems to have washed his hands of the book now and is in Nice, and GC's in Los Angeles. So changes, if any, and improvements, are down to what I can think up and work out with Basil between now and lunchtime – when I have to take myself off to Devon for a day's 'Whinfrey' shooting.

Fortunately I'm feeling in quite a relaxed and creative mood and have written enough by the time Basil arrives at midday to satisfy me on several of the more problematical areas of the book. Basil, in turn, seems to be enjoying the book a little more now, after what sounds like an horrendous working experience in LA. I'm glad that Basil agrees with me on the changes – which will involve a week's more work, but which should still enable him to make the deadlines.

He and I leave in a cab at half past one. I to Paddington, Basil to go to the British Museum. Both of us, I think, rather pleased with ourselves.

Tuesday, April 10th

Drive out to Staverton Station. Heavy rain, maybe, but conditions exactly match those of March 10th (a month ago precisely), when we were last here. The shot in the train goes well. Smoking a cigar, leaning back on a soft, plush seat in a railway carriage made for Queen Victoria whilst being paid, filmed and drawn through pretty Devon villages by a steam engine is one of the perks of the job, I must say.

Back to London by half past ten.

Wednesday, April 11th

At 7.30 down to Soho for a viewing of *Brian* (this must be around the twentieth public viewing). Terry J, with a heavy cold and semi-flu, and I are the only Pythons. But, in a small audience, Barry Took (whom it's

1 Basil Pao, then working for Warner Bros in LA, designed the book. Now a writer and stills photographer, he has worked with me on six of my BBC travel shows and books.

reassuring to see, considering his part in the birth of Python) and Yves de Goldschmidt, our natty, suave, French distributor, who greets me very warmly with the news that *Grail* is still running in Paris.

'Otto' has been cut entirely from the movie for this showing. An enormous improvement. Tightens the impact of the film, confines it beneficially to the major characters without going off into extraneous areas.

Barry liked it and Goldschmidt says afterwards that he reckons it a much more intelligent film than the *Grail* – but posing many and greater problems for a translator.

Out to London Airport, which is delightfully empty, and meet Al Lev off the New York flight. I've taken along a couple of bottles of Penrhos porter, which we crack sitting in the Mini in Car Park 3.

Thursday, April 12th

To Robert Maas [accountant] for a meeting at two o'clock. Oxford Street and the main West End roads swollen with people. Pre-Easter influx I suppose.

Walk through Soho. Despite the crowds, I love its grotty eccentricity – the sex shops next door to the Chinese restaurants, the boiled duck looking very similar to the artistes on display in the strip clubs.

John Goldstone says the censor has been along to see *Brian* and reckons it would be an AA, and he liked it, but he is concerned about licensing a movie against which there could be legal proceedings. He is sure that the Festival of Light will try and use the blasphemy law (upheld in the *Gay News* case) to try and stop the film. Lord Justice Scarman's judgement in the *Gay News* case[1] gives them a ridiculously wide area to play with. JG wants to be sure of the church's attitude and so does the censor.

Friday, April 13th

Nancy rings from NYC. Apart from wanting me to do another *Saturday Night Live* stint on May 12th, she says that the *Yarns* are due to air on May 6th. Following an interview with me which appeared in *Publishers'*

---

1 Scarman upheld the ruling under the Blasphemy Act of 1697 that *Gay News* had offended by claiming that Christ was homosexual.

Weekly in the US, the op-ed page of the *New York Times* wants me to write a 750-word piece on the state of the English and the elections in particular. A nice little project to take on.

Tuesday, April 17th

I took Anne Henshaw, Jonathan,[1] Al Levinson and Helen to Leith's Restaurant for our thirteenth anniversary meal. With wine from vines just starting to bud when we got married at Abbotsley in April 1966 – and very good food – it set me back £132, but was very jolly. Al in good form, and he and I got the giggles over Dusty Wesker's[2] quite serious offer to Al of 'unattached Canadian girls'. We laughed long and loud over our Calvados.

I think these two weeks will help Al's rehabilitation no end. He has a naturally warm and sunny side and this warm and sunny Easter is bringing him out of a dark and gloomy winter shell.

Anyway, we left Leith's in high spirits. Would say Helen and I are as together as we've ever been. (This could be the beginning of the end – ed.)

Friday, April 20th

After some early work on letters, etc, I took Thomas and Louise over to Shepperton Studios.

Alexander Korda[3] would turn in his grave if he could see the first sight that greeted me as I turned into the front gate of the studio – half the lawn outside the big house has been torn up and the cedar tree – symbol of the comfort, space and style of Shepperton – now ringed by a preserving fence and standing forlornly marooned as the builders hustle around it.

Inside the studios, on the other hand, Korda would feel quite at home. Every available piece of space is being utilised.

We watched the *Titanic* being sunk on H Stage, which had been flooded all over to a depth of five feet with one and a quarter million gallons of water – direct from the nearby reservoir. Polystyrene ice

1 Jonathan James, her new partner, whom she later married.
2 Arnold Wesker's wife.
3 Hungarian-born film producer who founded Shepperton in the 1930s.

floated on freshwater sea, ruffled occasionally by wave machines. Props boys and chippies in rubber diving suits busied around in the water, and dozens of extras looked convincingly tired and cold as they waited in the lifeboats for something to happen.

Then we were shown a wonderfully elaborate space set for *Saturn Three*, and Louise sat in Farrah Fawcett Major's chair.

The movies being made here are now American or Lew Grade[1]-financed blockbusters – there's nothing small about them – and the telegrams pinned to the *SOS Titanic* noticeboard in the production office chilled me to the marrow. They were from Hollywood and ran on the lines of: 'Have just seen the 15-minute assembly. I was moved, awed and excited by the tremendous brilliance of the material. You are creating a true masterpiece …' etc, etc. The schmaltz and sincerity dripped onto the floor like cream from an over-filled cake.[2]

Saturday, April 21st

Talk with TJ on the phone. Last Wednesday night he was attacked by an old gent in Soho who asked him where Charing Cross Station was. When he told him, the old man called our director 'a lying bastard' and belaboured him with his stick. TJ's head was cut and bleeding. A 'passer-by', who TJ thinks may have been a plainclothes man from the Metropolitan force, leapt on the old bloke and hauled him off to the nick. Apparently he had just attacked someone else further up the street.

Sunday, April 22nd

Long sleep. Rise just before ten. But a long recuperative day is not on the cards. TJ rings to ask me if I could spare time today to have another look at the 'Ben's Cell' scene. Although I bridle at the idea of endless re-editing, I think this is useful. There is something about 'Ben' which seems to hold it back from being as funny as it should and could be.

Collect Al L from Jack Cooper's house in Hampstead.[3] Jack, as I am

---

1 Lew Grade and his brothers Bernard Delfont (who abandoned *Life of Brian*) and Leslie Grade pretty much ran popular entertainment at the time.
2 A year later Lew Grade went on to make *Raise the Titanic*, which was such a flop that he famously said it would have been cheaper to lower the Atlantic.
3 Jack and Liz Cooper were famous Hampstead figures. Jack, who knew Al before I did, looked like the Laughing Cavalier.

discovering rapidly, is the Very Life Force itself. Last night he was grinding Al through a guided tour of six or seven malt whiskies. By Al's account Jack went to bed quite blotto, but was up at seven for three hours' birdwatching on the Heath. He spotted a Greater Crested Grebe and was delighted. This afternoon he's taking us to Lord's – he's a member of the MCC, of course.

I take Al home to unload, then we go on to Covent Garden. It's lovely and quiet around the Garden this Sunday morning – a good time to show it off. Al is impressed. We choose new takes of 'Ben', which improve the scene, I think.

Monday, April 23rd

Builders, phone calls, electrician. One of those all too frequently frenetic days at No. 4. I race around the house like a mad scientist trying to prevent the destruction of the world. Al, over in No. 2, gets some writing done. Unblocks that creative side which he has kept tight closed since Eve's death. So he's in good form.

At lunchtime, after I've taken Rachel up to the swings, a lead-grey sky suddenly opens up. Hailstones, leaky kitchen – the works.

J Goldstone tells me that EMI are re-releasing *Holy Grail* on a nationwide basis with *Blazing Saddles*. Fifty-fifty at the box office, and the whole double-bill could be worth £400,000. So EMI are backing Python after all.

Tuesday, April 24th

Work on my *New York Times* article on the election. It gradually comes together during a spotty morning's work. It's not easy to cut oneself off and concentrate during school hols.

Nancy sends me a telegram telling me that, with my Concorde track record, I should embark on a boat for NYC now to arrive in time for *Saturday Night Live* on May 12th. So they do want me. I accept the news with a few misgivings. Something deep down says don't do it.

Thursday, April 26th, Southwold

Buckle down to another journalistic task – this time 750 words for *Variety* – they want a Python piece to go in their Cannes Film Festival issue. Write it between nine and eleven. It comes easily, whereas the *NYT* article kept trapping me, by its status and 'importance', into trying to be heavy and significant.

I had spent an hour in bed this morning contemplating my *SNL* appearance, and had decided that I should begin my novel on May 5th as planned, and that *SNL* would not be progress forward, but a repetition of something I'd done as best I could anyway.

Armed with all these and other supportive arguments, I rang Nancy this evening to ask her to get me released from the show. There was a long and pregnant silence and Nancy finally desperately told me that she couldn't get in touch with them. Lorne and Jean and everyone had settled everything then left for European holidays.

Funnily enough, Nancy's decisiveness must have struck on some equally deep desire of mine to go to New York. I suddenly thought, well, if I have to do it, I'll do it and be positive about it. Armed with this new frame of mind, I don't feel nearly as bad about my volte-face! My 'conversion' was helped by a talk with Howard Goldberg of the *NYT* who was very happy with the article and is leading the op-ed page with it tomorrow – Friday 27th.

Friday, April 27th

Joe McGrath phones early, as I'm typing up the *Variety* piece. He's hustling me to do a commercial. Uses many techniques when I say no – 'They wanted either you or Peter Sellers or Stanley Baxter. I wanted you.' Etc, etc. Eric has recently done one for their company … But I stand firm and he uses his last card, which is loot. He'll still, if I don't mind, get the agency to ring my agent. What persistence.

Meal at Anne Henshaw's. She's 38 today.

Home to find Kelly, our baby-sitter, has been rung by John Cleese, who was stuck in Hull without a *Good Food Guide*! Kelly had to look through and find him somewhere. No luck!

Saturday, May 5th

Rachel is the first one to remember my 36th birthday. Shyly she potters into our bedroom around eight. Helen gives me the new Joseph Heller book, *Good as Gold*, as well as 'The Book of Lists' and a hammer.

Simon Albury arrives with a cake and forty candles just in case. SA announces his intention of trying Gestalt therapy – just once. Then Terry Gilliam arrives and I have an impromptu birthday party. Simon A is busily trying to sell Gilliam his idea for a 'Gilliam World' park – like Disneyworld, only nastier.

I leave for New York tomorrow for yet another *SNL* – and rather wearily start packing just before midnight.

Thursday, May 10th, New York

Down to NBC Studios. Reassuring old 8H. Big, clumsy and un-modern – it's a joy in the middle of all these glass and steel air-conditioned silences. NBC is going through rough times in the ratings war, but this is considered to be a 'good' process, which will lay bare the waste and reveal it as the only network with some soul and independence.

Tape, and write, my promotional announcements. I never enjoy being stuck up there in a vast empty studio at midday, having to say *Saturday Night Live* very fast many times. It's the selling bit of the week.

They're finished by two and suddenly I feel a surge of well-being and in a buoyant mood I begin to write the sort of monologue I wanted to write last January, and for most of this week, but couldn't. Now a nice fantasy forms itself, with good jokes and one liners – more like the Oxford or Cambridge Union speeches.

Belushi, big and panting like a steam engine at a station, sprawls round my dressing room. We talk about groupies. Belushi blows, wheezes, scratches his crotch and confides that 'I'm only fucking my wife now'. I concur and we agree only to fuck each other's wives.

The work in progress on the monologue is brought to a temporary halt by more media exposure. I'm driven over to some studio some-where for a show hosted by an actor called Robert Klein – a brisk, dark, intense-looking man who has just picked up a Tony nomination. He's talking to three guests on his one and a half hour (with commercials) show: Jerry Garcia of a seminal and long-lasting West Coast group called the Grateful Dead, Clive Davis of Arista and myself. There is an audience of forty or fifty kids packed in a small studio, in which the air conditioning has failed.

Jerry Garcia is big, bearded and looks and sounds deep and rich. He freely bandies words like extrapolate and seems to need no help so I slope off to a small back studio and continue to scribble the monologue.

I do a 20-minute chat with Klein. He's easy, informed and intelligent with a good sense of humour. One of the two or three best people who've ever interviewed me on Python matters.[1]

Saturday, May 12th, New York

Sleep well. I don't suffer from nerves on account of the show quite so much now. I think my experience with the monologue last January at least convinced me that even if the worst happened there would always somehow be a show. Breakfasted – for the first time this week – on the full works – eggs and bacon, etc.

At dress rehearsal the show is well over half an hour too long and feels heavy and much more hit and miss than my previous two shows. With less than an hour to go before air, Lorne begins his selection process. Two or three sketches are cut (one, a Nerds piece about Mr Brighton arriving with a Pakistani wife, I had never liked) and cuts are made within a long pirate spoof, 'Miles Cowperthwaite'.

I do not react well when Lorne sends Al Franken down to my dressing room to cut the monologue. Lorne's touch, however positive, is nearly always delicate, and to send poor Al down with 55 minutes left before I have to go on – and to have him put his pencil through whole chunks of what I spent most of the later part of the week writing, is a most uncharacteristic and tactless move.

At 11.35, after Belushi's cold opening, as I wait behind the tacked-up scenery flats, only a half-inch of plywood separating me from the Great American Public, Lorne threads his way through the old scenery and counsels me to take it easy. 'Look them in the eyes – they'll like you because you're nice.'

The monologue starts well, but half-way through some part of my brain closes off and I'm not wholly riveted to the task of communicating my jokes to the Great American Public. Instead a voice in my head queries the importance, or indeed the necessity, of what I'm doing and why I'm standing here, and suddenly I'm conscious of the silence between the laughs, rather than the laughs themselves.

But the rest of the show swings along merrily. The miracle happens again. Lorne and others are complimentary about the monologue, and I cheer up considerably.

1 Klein later interviewed all the Pythons (bar Graham who was represented by an urn containing his ashes) on stage at the Aspen Comedy Festival in March 1998.

When we get to the goodnights, James Taylor, the week's musical guest, and Billy Murray hoist me on to their shoulders. As one of the stagehands told me later, 'It's not every host they put on their backs.'

3.30 a.m: to Danny's Bar – more drinking, dancing and, as dawn breaks outside, Belushi and two others start playing live. Strong, fine, noisy music. People have to spill out of the tiny bar onto the street to talk. It's six or six thirty – a remarkable sight. The tatty bar in a storehouse and factory area, with a line of limousines waiting outside in the odd white light of a New York dawn.

Thursday, May 17th

Back to my writing room for the first time in two weeks. At the desk by a quarter to eight. And then three hours after breakfast. The novel turns into a play – which seems to rattle very easily off the typewriter – so I will blow with this wind for a while.

Saturday, May 19th

In the p.m. I have to open a fete at William Ellis School. Usually try to avoid public appearances in the local area – once you start they all want you – and anyway, the less conspicuous I am around here, the more comfortable life is. But W Ellis is the most likely school for Tom and William to go to, so I'm interested to see it. It's on the edge of the Heath, was a boys-only grammar school, now a voluntary aid school within the comprehensive system (though still boys-only).

We are collected, en famille, by a car at a quarter to two and don't get home until after five. I give a short opening speech, then have to walk around like the Duke of Edinburgh, with various members of the 'committee' at a discreet distance behind me, whilst I smile and sparkle and fail to hit anything with seven balls on the smash the crockery stall!

Tea with the headmaster in the middle of all this. He's a short, unflashy, rather serious man, who I'm sure does his job well. I think there'll not be much problem getting the boys in. He practically kidnapped them on the spot.

Sunday, May 27th

Take Ma to see the Tate extension. Enjoy the Rothko room this time. After a bit Ma, who has been patient, says rather touchingly 'Before we leave, we will go and see some nice pictures, won't we?'

Home for Sunday lunch, then a trip to the zoo between showers (all except Willy, who won't come because it's cruel).

To help convince Warner Bros that they were doing the right thing in backing Brian, Denis O'Brien corralled most of the Pythons into a marketing trip to Los Angeles.

Friday, June 1st

Taxi collects me soon after ten. Another Oak Village send-off, as the children cluster out in the street to wave and Tom announces to Mrs B and any others who may be around that Daddy is going to Hollywood!

The plane takes off an hour late – they've had to change aircraft as the first one was faulty – and we head off on a route I'm not accustomed to – straight up England, past Gospel Oak. Soon after which the pilot makes the momentous announcement that we are flying over Sheffield. He must have relatives there.

At LA Airport meet Graham and Bernard McKenna. Graham is at the wheel of a long, grey Cadillac, which is in itself an astonishing sight – I've never seen GC behind the wheel of a car in my life. But here he is, with his leased Cadillac, heading us through heavy traffic – eight lanes of cars on either side of the freeway making rather a mockery of the hair-tearings over the world fuel shortage.

The weather is dull and cool as we pull up to GC's bungalow in Brentwood – a most salubrious-looking area of extensive houses and gardens. He pays $3,000 a month for this pleasant abode and, sitting out in the garden, sipping a Perrier and watching humming birds darting about and pointing their long noses into hibiscus and honeysuckle, it looks almost worth it.

Graham drives us back to the crumbling Chateau Marmont. It's quite a reasonable time in LA – before midnight. But it's dawn in England as I nod off over Evelyn Waugh's diaries.

Saturday, June 2nd, Chateau Marmont, Los Angeles

No one seems to have slept very well. Potter in my room until mid-morning, then go with a group of us to the Egyptian Theater, Hollywood Boulevard, to see *Alien* – the Shepperton-shot, British-directed, space monster movie that is the latest to do record-breaking business in this film-hungry country.

The Egyptian Theater is a wonderful piece of extravagant decoration in itself – a lot brighter and more cheerful than the movie, which is very well directed and very creepy, up to a point, and loses its way in the last half-hour, by which time all the best shocks have happened.

Out into Hollywood Boulevard. There is nothing of the breathtaking beauty of New York about this city. Low, flat, sprawling and laid-back – like a patient on a psychiatrist's couch.

As Basil the elegant Pao says, people come out here to Hollywood and lease a lifestyle. Here the problem is not how to cope with the difficulties of living, it's how to cope with the ease of living.

A meeting at 5.30. People wander in about six. Graham arrives in dark suit and tie, in extraordinarily voluble form. It gradually dawns on the assembled gathering that he is 'speeding'. Whatever he has taken has turned him into a parody of Ian MacNaughton agreeing and disagreeing without discrimination or information, but with enormous enthusiasm. It's an extraordinary phenomenon and renders the meeting quite useless.

Two limousines arrive to take us to the Bruin Theater in Westwood where *Brian* is to be 'sneak previewed'. At the theatre we find a full house and 1,000 people turned away. Meet the Warner's executives who are, understandably, grinning pleasurably.

John Calley, our greatest supporter and second in command at Warner's, turns out to be a very soft-spoken, pleasant-faced, tweed-jacketed 45–50-year-old, more like an English public school headmaster than a Hollywood mogul. In fact, none of the people I'm introduced to from Warner's are in the least bit mogulish. Not a cigar in sight in the foyer and jeans and soft jackets are the order of the night.

Mike Medavoy – head of Orion Pictures, a chunky redhead with compellingly smiling eyes – takes Terry J out to look at the line (or queue, as we would say in the UK), stretching round the building.

Eric and Graham, meanwhile, are lurking in their limousine, waiting not to get mobbed. They eventually rush out of the limousine, heads down, and race for the door across a, by now, virtually deserted sidewalk.

But inside the theatre are sights and sounds to glad our hearts. A full house – 800 strong – and a tremendous air of anticipation. Cheers and applause as the lights eventually dim.

It's a marvellous showing. Great laughs and applause on a scale we have not yet seen for *Brian*. At the end Eric leads the rush out – and gets into the wrong limousine – whilst Terry and I stand on the sidewalk and talk to one or two of the audience and those waiting – who are not of the tear-your-clothes-off fan type and want to talk quite unsensationally about the movie.

Back at the Marmont for a party (with Thai food) in Basil's room, it's clear that the viewing was a good one. A few people at the party. Harry Nilsson, looking very white and unhealthy by any standards, especially LA, is a father today.

Later in the evening TJ gets woken in his room by a present from Harry in the shape of a Los Angeles naughty lady.

Sunday, June 3rd, Los Angeles

Out to Graham's long, low Brentwood residence. Still cloudy and overcast. A meeting arranged for 11.30, but no one seems to want to get down to anything, application seeming a bit of a crime in this balmy, West Coast atmosphere.

Denis O'Brien, benign as ever, arrives with some lunch – and can hardly contain his excitement over last night. He returns to it with awe and wonder, and even he, who is one of the most level-headed men I've met, comes out with such assurances as 'You know, none of your careers will be the same after last night … the way they were talking in that foyer …'

Eventually we start the meeting and become a little more down to earth discussing what is still wrong with the movie. Warner's are worried about the stretch from 'Leper' to 'Ben'. There is nothing but agreement for the 'Otto' cut. Graham is down from yesterday and more gently avuncular.

We discuss our attitude to censorship, on which there is total agreement within the group that we do not and will not change anything because we're told to, unless we happen to agree that it isn't funny anyway. We're all happy to go to court in defence of the movie.

The day drags on into a party, which Graham has arranged for us. None of us is on best partying form. Timothy Leary, he of the drug culture, is there smiling and laughing and seeming very jolly – and again looking like a public school master. A marvellous advert for drug use.

Monday, June 4th, Los Angeles

I slept until four, then woke and stayed awake on a hard bed, streams of thoughts going through my mind – what to do with the *Ripping Yarns*, *Saturday Night Live*, what to say to Warner's today ... Then the birds started. It's like sleeping in an aviary. Gorgeous trilling sounds, dozens of different voices – including one bird with a broad American accent calling 'Dor*een*! Dor*een*! Dor*een*!'

Well, it's 8.35, I'm washed, dressed, bathed and going to meet John, Terrys J and G and Anne for breakfast at Schwab's.

At the moment I feel as though I'm stuck fast in some awful enervating dream. Being slowly flattened by the insidious luxury of Hollywood life – and ready for some enormous creature to come and remove my brain and other vital organs. I must get home. It's dreadful here. To add injury to insult my room smells of gas and I've been bitten quite severely by some maliciously hungry LA flea.

We drive out to Burbank Studios to talk to a small contingent (eight or nine) of Warner Bros marketing people. They are all now solidly behind the movie and have decided to give it the treatment.

Some of us, TJ especially, are concerned over the American fundamentalist Baptist backlash – after all, George Harrison, as producer, has already had letters threatening never to buy his records again – but Warner's dismiss all this.

GC comes up with an excellent idea for Python movie No. 4 – 'Monty Python's World War II'. I think it could be a marvellous format for more of a sketch-type film – which everyone seems to want.

So Hollywood can be creative.

A bright end to a day that started for me in quite considerable gloom.

Tuesday, June 5th, Los Angeles

No further bites tonight and a much better sleep.

At Burbank we go first to Warner Records – a lovely, entirely wood and glass-framed low, long building.

Their marketing strategy, developed since we met yesterday, is to concentrate us all in New York for nine days – with all the press coming in from across the US to see the movie (which will have been running in NYC for two or three weeks) and climaxing with a big party.

But all their ideas and enthusiasms fuse into one great howl of approval when Eric suggests using Jeanette Charles (the Queen's double) to spearhead a Royal 10th Anniversary of Python celebration in New York. They all absolutely love this, but, I must admit, using J Charles fills me with little enthusiasm. Eric's used her on *Saturday Night Live*, and she is a rather easy, tacky option for us. Still, if handled quite straight it could be fun.

Back to Warner Records' wooden shack for chats with Denis in an office walled with G Harrison's gold discs. I remember, as I admire again this pleasant working environment, that this is the place which drove Derek Taylor back to England on the verge of madness.

Business chat with Denis – merchandising and the like, then out to the airport with a rather unpleasant cab driver, who admits to his dislike of black people. 'They're bad drivers and bad people and that's that.' He looks Mexican and drives appallingly.

Must get back to the novel. Eric says he's writing a play which has turned into a novel, whereas I have a novel which has turned into a play.

Friday, June 8th

The idea of a full-length *Ripping Yarn* movie, based on the existing films, is crystallising in my mind. Must draft a letter to John Howard Davies and to Bryon Parkin at BBC Enterprises.

In the evening go with Helen and Willy to see Tom play recorder in the Gospel Oak concert. Large orchestra and choir; audience crammed in at the back. Fair share of laughs – someone sick at the back of the orchestra just after a child had announced that she would play 'Variations on Theme of a Lark Song'. 'Hava Nagila' by the massed violins and recorders was wonderfully silly and reminded me to make sure that Python's bagpipe version of the same song should not go unnoticed.

Tuesday, June 12th

The '£1 a gallon petrol' having arrived, I decide to walk Rachel to playgroup for ecological reasons. So she and I, hand in hand, trip lightly through the dirt and dog shit down Grafton Road, dodge the lorries turning fiercely and uncompromisingly out of the Building Depot and into the little oasis of tiny people – the Camden Playgroup.

In the evening Mikoto, Helen's Japanese badminton friend, comes to cook us a Japanese meal. The preparation is a painstaking and delicate business – as indeed is communication with Mikoto. The food – tempura I think they're called – vegetables in batter – is quite delicious. We drink sake with it. The kids rave.

I end up eating too much. The food, the sake and the strain of four hours with someone who doesn't speak your language or you his, is perhaps to blame for a colossal drowsiness which numbs my senses about midnight.

Stay awake long enough to see that I and other rich folk are the chief beneficiaries of the first Thatcher–Howe Tory Budget. The top rate of tax is down from 83 to 60%, dividend restraint is lifted, tax thresholds are all lifted. In short, I'm probably £10,000 a year better off after today. There is some inescapable lack of social justice in all this. But it doesn't keep me awake.

Thursday, June 14th

Another viewing of *Brian*. Small audience at the Bijou Theatre – all Pythons there, bar Graham. John Mortimer[1] and Oscar Beuselinck represent the law – Mortimer is to give us his opinion afterwards.

He's a nice, friendly, disarming man, with small, but not at all humourless, eyes, and a ready smile. He's clearly chuffed to be amongst such humorous company. He loves the film and reckons that we are quite safe. The chances of a jury convicting Python of blasphemy on the basis of this film are very remote, he believes – but not impossible. However, should an action be brought, Mortimer thinks it would take at least a year to come to court, by which time we'll have hopefully made our money and our point.

Friday, June 15th

Slow journey over to Chelsea, where I arrive 25 minutes late at chic French seafood restaurant Le Souquet, for lunch with Iain Johnstone,

---

1 Barrister, playwright, novelist, creator of *Rumpole*.

producer of *The Pythons*,[1] who has a proposition for me. It turns out to be the offer of host on a new BBC2 chat show which Iain is hoping to produce from October onwards for thirteen to twenty-six weeks.

My first reaction is fear – how could I cope with this world of wit and repartee? Iain tries to assuage my doubts by telling me that Brian Wenham, head of BBC2, and other BBC luminaries were all very pleased that he'd suggested my name. So I feel a bit wanted, I suppose, but still doubtful. Iain talks of it bringing me 'real fame'. But I think if I have to have 'real fame', I would rather it came from acting or writing, rather than hosting a chat show.

Saturday, June 16th

Spend the morning buying bikes – one each for Tom and Willy, who are now thoroughly enjoying cycling round Gospel Oak, and one for Helen and myself to use as a family workhorse. Equipped like a tank, with voluminous wicker basket on the front and a child seat for Rachel on the back.

In the evening to a party at Eric's – given by Chris Miller[2] (Eric having returned to France) for Carrie Fisher (the heroine of *Star Wars*), who is renting EI's house whilst she works on a *Star Wars* sequel at Elstree.

Carrie looking very small and delicate, her soft, pale skin a refreshing change from the butch aerosol-spray health look of most Los Angeleans. She doesn't know anyone, but is straight and funny at the same time, and we have a mutual line of chat – both belonging to the select band of *Saturday Night Live* hosts. She is currently 'going with' Paul Simon, so sees a great deal of Lorne. Lorne the Great Catalyst – whose name is the criterion for meeting sympathetic people.

The two heroes of *Star Wars* are also there – Mark Hamill (Luke Skywalker) and Harrison Ford.

Hamill is chirpy and is dressed like a delivery boy. Harrison Ford looks young and alienated. He would look over his glasses at us if he had any. As it is he moves broodingly around – like a famous man might do if he knew how famous he is.

---

1 A documentary, made for BBC1 to mark the tenth anniversary of Python's birth.
2 Chris looked after the house while Eric was away.

Monday, June 18th

Collect Rachel from school on the new bike. She laughs and giggles all the way home as we cycle over the bumpy, pitted roads beside the garment factories and under the railway. Definitely a successful purchase.

In the mid-afternoon, Cleese comes round with a small, slim, handsome, trim-faced girlfriend called Suzanne.

We sit in the garden and John eats fruit and talks me into doing a few sketches for the Amnesty shows next week. Nothing terribly exciting. 'Custard Pie Lecture' again. 'Cheese Shop' to look forward to.[1]

Sunday, June 24th

Midsummer's Day. To Her Majesty's Theatre for rehearsal of the second Amnesty Show [*The Secret Policeman's Ball*]. John being very serious and efficient as director. Like a character in a sketch who one expects to suddenly crack into uncontrollable comic spasms – but it never happens.

Meet Rowan Atkinson and Buckman and Beetles[2] for the first time. I suppose we (i.e. the Pythons) are the senior team now – the 'famous ones'. But Eleanor and Pete Cook are there – comforting figures from *our* past.

Helen applies coat after coat of bronzing cream to recreate Tunisian tan on my white body ahead of a *Brian* reshoot tomorrow.

Monday, June 25th

Drive out to Shepperton soon after eight to shoot a new opening to the much-filmed 'Ex-Leper' sequence – a last ditch attempt to try and salvage a piece which everyone (with the possible exception of Eric) thinks ought to be in, but are not quite happy with.

It's over seven months since we last shot 'Ex-Leper' – I've put on a few pounds, but make-up does a pretty good job (Elaine and Maggie).

---

1 One of my favourite sketches with John. I don't think once, either on television or on stage, was I ever able to get through it with a straight face.
2 Rob Buckman and Chris Beetles carried on the tradition of doctor/comedians (Jonathan Miller, Graham Chapman, Graeme Garden) with *The Pink Medicine Show* in 1978. Buckman remains a doctor, Beetles runs an art gallery.

Shepperton depresses and embarrasses me – the dressing rooms are uncleaned, the place looks shabbier and more down-trodden than ever. The canteen, now partitioned off with hideous paint and a huge, unsightly, unfriendly expanse of plastic sheeting, is unspeakably grim.

We shoot at the main gate of the old *Oliver* set – in itself a sad and crumbling place, with memories, for me, of *Jabberwocky*. The shooting, between showers and aeroplanes, goes along well and we even do some hand-held dialogue shots.

At one point, a strange occurrence. The catering manager shuffles up to me and asks if he might have a word. Is this the moment of truth, when he will at last confess to the appalling service he has inflicted on Shepperton these last few years? Not a bit of it. He tells me he is going to Los Angeles with a film script *he has written* and slips an envelope containing said script into my Ex-Leper's palm, for my perusal – and could I give a copy to Mr Galsworthy (John Goldstone). Game, set and match to him.

Afterwards, over a drink and a very acceptable sandwich in the 'executive' canteen, I talked to David Munro[1] and was astounded to be told by him that he resigned five weeks before, and is only staying on for another month.

On the way home I drop in at Cleese's mighty ex-Bryan Ferryish pile in Ladbroke Road and we rehearse 'Cheese Shop' together. I notice John has all the books I see reviewed, covet and never buy, in his shelves, in pristine condition. 'For my retirement,' John tells me.

Wednesday, June 27th

First night of *The Secret Policeman's Ball*. The shows have all been sold out since Monday and they've been selling standing tickets.

A motley crowd assembles at Her Majesty's about 10.30. The pattern of the evening is set by the first sketch, an E L Wisty piece involving Cook and Cleese and a park bench, which is down on the running order as three minutes, but by the time John C has finished corpsing and Peter ad-libbing, is well past nine.

We take a book on the time of final curtain (curtain up being 11.15). I plump for 1.53 and am nearly an hour out. By the time we pull sweaters up over our heads for Peter Cook's *Beyond the Fringe* 'End of the World Sketch', it's just passing 2.30 – we finally take our bows at 2.35.

1 The successor to Graham Ford as manager of Shepperton.

Saturday, June 30th

Drive over to Anne Henshaw's for a meeting with Denis O'Brien, only to find that the meeting is at Denis's place in Cadogan Square. Dense traffic down Piccadilly, the carbon monoxide fumes filling my lungs as bitter anger fills my rapidly wearying brain.

Finally reach Denis's. John C, Terry G and Terry J – the 'Home' Pythons – are all there. John G and Anne as well. They've been waiting for me. For once I cannot raise a smile in acknowledgement of the usual abuse which any late Python arrival has to endure.

Then Denis pitches in. He's never aggressive, never boorishly arrogant, but by God he's persistent. He would like to take on Python and any individuals in Python. He claims that his organisation (EuroAtlantic) will be able to minimise our UK tax liability on the money we earn from *Brian* – which could be substantial.

So, after very little hard talking, Denis has managed to persuade the four of us that we should let him 'structure' our earnings from *Brian* right away. I suppose this is the thin end of the wedge and I expect that Denis and EuroAtlantic are with Python to stay.

Drive back across London. The parks look green and pleasant, and the Gay Pride March, which caused the traffic build-up which nearly resulted in my death from carbon monoxide poisoning four hours earlier, has dispersed.

Can't get in till late at Her Majesty's as *Ain't Misbehavin'* has come down late. A relaxed show – usual, very warm, very appreciative audience.

Mike Brearley[1] beats up Terry J in the 'Celebrity Sketch' rather well, and Peter Cook's judge's summing-up of the Thorpe court case, which he wrote yesterday, is the small triumph it deserves.[2] Sad it is for the country that political satire, or just satire of important people, has been so effectively stamped out of the media in the last ten years. Good for P Cook.

A huge crush of folk in the stalls bar for a party afterwards.

Home by four. Dawn is breaking over Gospel Oak. Richly satisfying 'after the ball' feeling …

1 Captain of the England cricket team that won the Ashes in 1981. Now a psychoanalyst.
2 Jeremy Thorpe, the Liberal leader, had just been acquitted on charges of involvement in the attempted murder of his gay lover, Norman Scott. The judge's summary was seen by many to be blatantly biased in Thorpe's favour.

Monday, July 2nd

Ate lunch at an empty but excellent Indian restaurant in Berwick Street with Clive Hollick and put to him as clearly and forcibly as I could the extent of my dissatisfaction with Shepperton's progress over the last year. He would not at first accept that things were as serious as I made out – as indeed they are not from the point of view of the balance sheet – but I was talking about the guts and soul and down-to-earth human appeal of the studio, which has suffered disastrously.

He began to take this in, I think, and I persuaded him that things were urgent enough for us to pay a visit within the next week to the studios, as a Board, and inspect it, and I think I dissuaded him from accepting Charles Gregson's recommendation that we should not employ a replacement for Munro, but busk along with two girls. This was contrary to all I felt was needed.

Shepperton needs someone with a spark of fight in them – someone who will be fiercely proud of the studio, who will not be intimidated, who will not be a forelock-tugger to the Board. Ideal sort of man would be Simon Albury, I suggest, almost flippantly, but the more we think about it, the more of a possibility it becomes.

Back into London for some dubbing and post-synching on *Brian*. The new work on the 'Leper' last week does seem to make the speech clearer, but I see-saw on the effectiveness of the sketch. Terry J is the greatest champion of the 'Leper' at the moment. I think Denis O'B would rather see it out. (Have noticed his artistic and creative participation increasing slowly but surely as he and we have got to know each other better.) I dub George Harrison's voice on – another to add to my collection.

Wednesday, July 4th

To the Camden Swimming Gala at Swiss Cottage Baths. Tom P wins the third-year crawl against six other schools, makes up ground in the relay and helps Gospel Oak to the overall and the boys' trophy – and they only just missed a clean sweep in the girls'. A terrific occasion. I feel wonderfully proud. Tom does not brag or boast and is quietly over the moon.

Thursday, July 5th

To John's for a writing session and discussion on film posters and publicity generally in preparation for the Warner launch. JC says he'll chair the meeting, as he's written a film on how to chair meetings – he means it half in fun, but mostly seriously.

Eric is in France and has sent a letter with suggestions. GC is in Los Angeles and has sent a request for another loan from Python. TJ bears gloomy news about our post-*Grail* tax situation. The authorities are getting tougher and could interpret our tax position in such a way that we fork out at least £60,000 of our *Grail* earnings to the government.

But it's a sunny day and we are brought cups of coffee by John's lady retainers and we spread out over his huge dining table (originally in Holloway prison) and churn out the sort of easy drivel which gives much pleasure and does not have to follow plot, story or character. JC works upstairs, writing heavily sardonic biographies of us all, and TG looks through photos.

I read out a long and inaccurate synopsis of the film which brought tears to assembled eyes (there is no better moment in one's creative life than hysterics at a first read!).

Wednesday, July 11th

I go to Neal's Yard and yet my heart is not really on the [*Life of Brian* soundtrack] album – it's somewhere else, with the children in the sun. I find myself gazing at pictures of the countryside, looking at maps, reading novels – all the paraphernalia of getting away seems much more important than the paraphernalia of getting on.

In the back of my mind plans turn towards all the things I want to do, but keep postponing – learning Italian again, going on walking weekends with the boys, travelling to India – getting out on a limb again, taking a few risks, facing a few unknowns.

A new kind of summer holiday for the Palins this year. Instead of Europe, we stayed for almost a month at Al Levinson's house in the old whaling port of Sag Harbor on Long Island.

Sunday, July 29th, Sag Harbor

Here in the middle of this cosy, little New England town (they all call it a village, but it's Southwold size), I have, for almost the first time in a week, a few moments free of my family and Al, who is taking the boys for a swim, and my first urge is to get to the diary.

In the mornings I rise good and early and each new day is greeted with elation – a run through sweet-smelling gardens and woods – breakfast is jolly, and our mornings, spent on the beach at Bridgehampton – a huge, broad, clean sweep of sand with a big clear sea and Atlantic rollers to add to the entertainment – are unequivocally fine – cool in the water, hot in the sunshine, full of invigorating physical activity.

The holiday so far has been a helter-skelter of happiness and frustration. Great ups and downs of pleasure and irritation. I'm afraid that I cannot get France or Italy out of my mind and keep making unfair comparisons between their sophistication and the naïvety of America.

Sag Harbor *is* a beautiful little town, with delightful clapboard houses, all comparatively well-kept, all architecturally consistent, nothing new and horrendous. It's attractive to walk around, full of trees and the scent of flowers and yet … and yet … What is it? What is this gloss with which the American Way of Life coats everything? Is it trying too hard to impress?

Is it that the freshness of America has been near-suffocated by the materialism of the place – by the vast wealth of the country, which pours forth a million products, where a thousand would do?

Standards of food and television are appallingly low, and yet there are lots of both. Yet the standards of kindliness and consideration amongst the people are high – though they are sometimes made fools of by their over-sufficiency. See the size of so many over-fed citizens of all ages. Human incarnations of the economy of waste.

Tuesday, July 31st, Sag Harbor

At about six – when my resources were not at their best after a long, hot, tiring day – the phone rang. It was Anne H, from London, ringing to say that Warner's go to press on the posters in two hours.

They have finally rejected our unanimous Python ad-line 'He Wasn't the Messiah, He Was a Very Naughty Boy', and have suggested three alternatives – all of which are dreadful and tend to accentuate the 'outrageousness' of the movie.

Wednesday, August 1st, Sag Harbor

Al's 'guru', the poet and writer Norman Rosten, has arrived. Like Jack Cooper, he is the sort of charming, slightly roguish, loquacious, salt-of-the-earth character that Al seems to attract to him. One of the Brooklyn writers' group that included Mailer, Arthur Miller, James Jones, Joe Heller – a real group of literary giants.

Rosten is respected, but never achieved world status. He wrote a nice little book on Marilyn and he reminisces easily and unselfconsciously about her. His friend was Arthur Miller, and he remembers Miller going to meet Marilyn at the penthouse in the Barbizon Plaza. 'He was scared stiff ... I mean, Arthur was a good Jewish boy ... he asked me to go up with him because he was literally afraid of going up there on his own.'

Rosten is wonderfully dry and self-deprecating and wittily observant. Marilyn really wanted to be a housewife, and she ended up with Miller and Di Maggio, both 'very religious men' – Rosten called them the two high priests, Jewish and Catholic, presumably to stress the irony of their association with a lady of such profane associations.

Rosten talks of Nixon's revival – of his threatened return to active life and New York. R reckons Nixon one of the two 'diabolic' forces in America. I can't remember the other one. Norman advises me to read De Tocqueville's observations on America as providing some of the best insights on the US, albeit 140 years ago.

Thursday, August 2nd, Sag Harbor

Up at half past seven. Run along the quieter roads, full of a wonderful mixture of scents – musty, sweet, poignant, sharp – rising from the woods and gardens. It's a very sticky, close morning again.

Rachel and I saw a middle-aged man wearing a T-shirt: 'More people died in Ted Kennedy's car than at 3 Mile Island'.

Thursday, August 9th, Sag Harbor

Cooler, clearer sunshine on the way.

Am dripping with sweat on the patio after my fourth run this week when the phone rings. It's Denis O'Brien, to apologise for his sudden indisposition and to renew the invitation to Fisher's Island. Although he has fathers, mothers, children and hordes of relatives arriving and departing, he says we *must* come. 'We'll try and break house records,' he promises cheerfully.

I take a call from Nancy. She has some request for the two Terrys and myself to go to Toronto during our film publicity in September. This 'publicity binge' rears menacingly close. God, it's then I shall miss these superb, drifting, timeless, sunny days. This Thursday is near-perfect – sunlight bright, sky royal blue, all the countryside lit as if God was showing round prospective buyers.

Friday, August 10th, Sag Harbor

Shopped for presents, then took an early lunch and drove in search of Easthampton Airport. At the airport we waited for a single-engined Piper Cherokee Six to float in like a butterfly over the low surrounding woodland and taxi up to the little suburban bungalow with sun-deck, which served as the airport office building, refreshment room and control tower. This was our Yankee Airways flight to Fisher's Island.

The entire Palin family filled the little plane, with one spare seat for the pilot. Weather was good and we turned north and then east in a circle to avoid some restricted area over Plum Island where 'they do experiments on animals' (said the otherwise taciturn pilot, darkly), then within 20 minutes we were turning over Fisher's Island and down onto an overgrown strip surrounded by what looked like a scrap yard.

Brian, Denis's 'man', who is from Huddersfield (with a Yorkshire accent tempered weirdly by fifteen years in Vancouver), meets us and drives us the length of the island (about six miles) to what he calls 'The Castle', but Denis calls 'The Farm'. This confusion is understandable, the house on the point is a hybrid of Scottish baronial and French fortified farmhouse. Built in the middle of the Depression (1930) by a man called Simmons – a bed magnate! – who spent money on a grand scale.

We sat after dinner in the long, dark room, and Denis turned the lights so low that at one point (his wife) Inge thought Helen had gone to bed, although she was in fact sitting in a chair opposite.

We went up to our brass four-poster bed soon after ten. Rachel's rubber lilo kept deflating and we had to improvise a bed for her. Eventually, and slowly, I drifted off to sleep, surrounded by a cacophony of nocturnal seagulls and buoys making a variety of doom-laden, bell-tolling rings out on the Sound.

Saturday, August 11th, White Caps, Fisher's Island

After breakfast, Denis and I adjourn to the long room, sinking into their comfortable sofas and looking out towards the not-too-distant Connecticut shore and the bevy of fishing boats come to snatch bluefish from the rich waters off the headland. Denis and I talk about his taking over my financial affairs – everything will be looked after from holidays to contracts, all of which will be personally negotiated by Denis himself. He wants to give us 'flexibility' – that is to take all possible measures to ensure that we control as closely as possible the commercial exploitation of all our work.

After a good talk, Denis suggests that he and I go over to see John Calley, who lives mid-way down the island.

John Calley, friend to the talented (viz Kubrick, Lorne Michaels), genial face full of neatly cropped beard and big, black-rimmed spectacles, is wearing a colourful, light wool topcoat over a *Superman* T-shirt and green striped slacks with shoes and no socks.

He takes us through endless sitting rooms and libraries until we settle on a room to sit in – the size of the coach house where eight of us are living at Sag Harbor! It turns out that he is only on Fisher's Island for a month of the year. Denis confirms that the summer population may be 3,000, but in winter it shrinks to 300 all-year residents.

Denis goes to phone the airline, leaving me with Calley. Decide to go in at the deep end and ask him if he will look at the three new *Ripping Yarn* films I've brought over and advise on whether they may be combined as a theatrical movie in the US.

As soon as we start talking 'business', I find myself talking easily and constructively to him, rather as I can with Lorne. Calley does not react in any stereotyped Hollywood way – he muses, reflects and suggests, gently and amusingly, not playing the mogul. I felt contact being made on a sensible and sensitive level and I will be very interested to hear his reaction to the *Yarns*, which he promises to view next week.

From Calley's we drive in the Black Bronco down the road (mostly unmade, with occasional strips of tarmac) back to White Caps. The weather is holding firm, but overcast – the flights are going. The Palins are lifted off Fisher's Island in two planes – Helen, Willy and Rachel first, then myself and Tom a few minutes later.

A useful visit, but I'm glad to be back in the cosy, crowded warmth of Sag Harbor and the coach house. I still feel uncomfortable and a little uneasy in enormous houses. For me they are still like living in museums. It sets me to thinking about our little home and 'living in the community' – as Al puts it.

Enough philosophising. This short trip and the talks of August 10th/11th with Denis and Calley could alter all our circumstances within a year. We may just have to spend, throw away or give away an awful lot of money – being accepted on Fisher's Island seems to mean that.

Sunday, August 12th, Sag Harbor

It sounds to be raining every time I wake in the night and there's a strong wind too. All rather cosy inside our house.

Al comes in at ten – I'm just looking at the first Python poster of the *Brian* campaign, which appears this morning in the *New York Times*. Al looks worried and says a 'North-Easter' has set in and high wind and rain could persist all day. Temperatures must have dropped almost 30 degrees over the weekend and I roll on my sweater for the first time.

It's the day, suddenly, amazingly, for a log fire. And where else but America would you *buy* a log at the local delicatessen. Smoked salmon and a log, please. It comes ready-wrapped with instructions on how to unwrap and light it. Extremely – dare I say – sensible and a Godsend on a rip-roaring wet day when you have no other dry wood to burn. So, what with our instant log fire, our resident screaming wind and lashing rain, we settle into our (now) traditional lox, bagels and champagne Sunday lunch, which the last two weeks have been eaten sweatily, in shorts, trying to avoid the heavy, omnipresent heat.

Monday, August 13th

Try to make farewells as quick and impermanent as possible, for I know Al will miss all the life at the coach house.

This has been a great children's holiday, and they have been generally easy company too. Though perhaps my list of books read – one Anthony Powell, ninety pages of a Steinbeck, fifty pages of a Levinson work in progress – testifies to the way they dominated the holiday. I feel good, though, and I am looking forward to home and writing.

The New York–London flight passes unmemorably. It's efficient and notable only for the sight of very high seas and white caps and breaking waves on the approach to Cornwall. I've never seen the sea in such turmoil.

Tuesday, August 14th

Within a quarter hour of arrival at Gospel Oak, the phone contacts begin. A series of quite important calls. Bryon Parkin from BBC Enterprises calls to say that 'his colleagues' at TV Centre have assured me that there would be insurmountable problems from unions in the way of a theatrical release for the *Ripping Yarns*.

What a complete Beeb man is Parkin. He seems to have about as much drive as Rachel's tricycle and has consistently failed to come up with the goods on anything I've asked him.

Alan Bell calls to confirm dates for the three new *Yarns* – beginning Monday, September 24th at 9.25. He tells me that John H-D has viewed the three shows and recommended laugh tracks on them all. Alan Bell softens this other bit of BBC recalcitrance by saying that he, too, watching them on TV, felt the audience helped. Back to square one there. But, again, I don't feel angry or even disappointed. The holiday helped.

Terry Gilliam tells me that Eric was so unhappy with the Python soundtrack album André and I had produced, that he is working on a replacement. The objection was, I'm told, basically to the live album, audience idea. I feel not bitter, but just frustrated. I was never wholly keen on the live album, Eric was away and quite inaccessible for quick decisions and Warner's wanted the album quick. So my work was wasted. I'm quite glad it at least stirred other Pythons into some sort of action, and I shall send back £1,000 of the £1,500 fee I took for my work on it. An episode in my creative career that I shall happily forget.

Thursday, August 16th

The jet-lagged Palin household (still living in US time) finally rose around ten. I see from the paper that the white-capped waves which I noticed on the approaches to Cornwall on Tuesday morning have so far claimed seventeen lives. As we sat rather comfortably in our First Class lounge, dabbing

Cooper's Oxford on dull croissants, the yachtsmen in the Fastnet Race were directly below us, fighting huge storms, forty-foot waves and the worst conditions the race has ever run into.

My cold is still heavy, but after a morning's work on letters and phone calls I drive down in sunshine and scudding cloud to Neal's Yard.

Eric arrives heavily bearded. His land in the Var has been razed to the ground by a forest fire, poor bugger. Graham is here too, and Terry G. We listen to the 'new' album – which is the stereo soundtrack *without* laughs, which evidently all the Pythons prefer. I must say the selection sounds lifeless, but Eric and Graham's ad-libbed links are funny.

At the end, all present OK the new album, but without enthusiasm. André does not look happy at the prospect of working for two more days – and probably nights – to complete this one. Eric and Graham will have to supervise the work. I refuse.

Friday, August 17th

Opening day for *Brian* in New York and Los Angeles. It seems difficult to grasp that we will actually be starting to get our money back, as from this evening.

Terry J rang from New York to say that there was a queue of *one* at the Cinema One at first light this morning – and he had a copy of the *Ripping Yarns* book.

But Canby's review in the *New York Times* was a rave and that the 'Post' and 'News' too were good. So far a clean sweep of reviews.

Saturday, August 18th

At lunchtime I cycle up to the Freemasons for a drink with GC, John Tomiczek and Bernard McKenna.

They all came down to inspect No. 2. Graham quietly pottering and muttering about all the bills he still has to face from *Odd Job*. Still, he's driving a hired Mercedes, which EuroAtlantic found for him, and seems well, though a little quiet since he gave up the booze. Bernard as big and warm as ever. A lovely man. Rachel takes to him immediately.

I take the boys to St Martin's Lane Odeon to see *The Spaceman and King Arthur* – jolly tiring Disney wholesomeness sticks in the gut of a true cynic, but by the end its sort of charm won even me over. John Le Mesurier playing an exact replica of his *Jabberwocky* role – standing just behind the king and getting wonderful laughs from beautifully thrown asides.

Sunday, August 19th

A call from Denis on Fisher's Island to tell me that the audiences are rolling into *Brian*. Warner's hoped for an $8,000 take at Cinema One on opening day and took $13,000. In Los Angeles all the movie houses showing *Brian* are good. In the Python stronghold of Orange County, one movie theatre took as much on opening day as it did in a week of *Grail*.

Wednesday, August 22nd

I have endeavoured, to help Anne and everyone else, to try and bring the five Pythons present in the UK together for a chat. After many time-consuming phone calls, a meal is arranged for tonight.

At L'Etoile by 8.30. When I arrive Cleese is waiting.

JC and I talked of future plans. Once again, as so often in the last few months, I caught the feeling that Python had come full circle. After ten years, climaxed by what sounds to be a successful opening of *Brian* in the US, John is telling me how he would like to work together on something. A real April '69 conversation between us. It's nice to feel, as John says, that we do work well off each other. No conclusions were reached when Graham, then Eric and TG finally arrived.

JC made the point that in the next Python film we should perhaps stick less to our rigid writing combinations and write with more fluidity. He thought this would help Eric, who always wrote by himself. 'I like writing by myself,' Eric countered, rather defensively.

I said I would rather not work on a new Python script for a full year, JC having proposed that we should all 'go somewhere very nice and just talk for two or three weeks about the subject'. I was called selfish by Eric. JC accused him of bullying. TG came in, as he said, to 'bale me out', by stating that he was not interested in working on another Python movie until he had completed something of his own. Graham said nothing.

But there is remarkable agreement thus far on the main points – that we should do another movie, that it should be completed within three to three and a half years from now, and that World War II is a good area to start thinking in.

Thursday, August 23rd

Drive out to Shepperton for a board meeting.

An efficient meeting, followed by a walk around the site. There have been radical improvements in almost every area which so depressed me six weeks ago. The canteen is cleaner and better equipped, the toilets cleaned, the on-site mess has been drastically reduced and, with the smart new gatehouse and opening of 'Studios Road' as a symbol of this regeneration, the place is suddenly well on the way to looking an attractive and exciting place to work.

Great news that we will probably be able to rent 'H' Stage back, for a very reasonable fee of £92,000 for five years, from the council – impoverished by Thatcher's local spending cuts. At present a *Flash Gordon* forest set, full of swirling tendrils and rubber lianas, fills the place, at a cost of over $1 million in construction fees.

Friday, August 24th

T Gilliam arrives. He's been writing *Brazil* with Alverson[1] all week. He looks a bit unwell. I think he feels their writing combination is not working as well as it should. He's also in the middle of a debilitating hassle with Warner's over the poster. They are determined to use their own wacky in-house ads that they first showed us in LA in June, and which we all immediately and instinctively disliked. But TG and Basil have been unable to produce our own strong alternative. Basil has now given up and Denis O'B, who really doesn't know quite why we're making a fuss over the Warner's poster, is trying to heal the gap.

Saturday, August 25th

Get up a little earlier than I should to buy *Variety*. *Brian* is 'Big 65G' in New York. There is a full-page ad extolling our opening grosses and an editorial piece headed 'Is Holy Screed Fair Game For Hokum?' – which is a fine example of the mid-twentieth century *Variety* style, and to which the answer is – all together now – if it makes money, yes!

I think that Python has actually stolen a march on the critics with this one. As one admitted, he really didn't know how to begin a critical

---

1 Charles Alverson, American thriller writer, and friend of TG, Terry J and myself.

assessment of the movie. Similarly, trade press, though obviously liking the movie, are still a little wary – like children in a playground who've just found a huge, unopened box of chocolate and aren't quite sure how much to enjoy it.

Monday, August 27th

Just musing with Helen over our supper that we have not had one phone call all day, when the instrument of terror tinkles. It's Anne to say that some Jewish groups in the US are offended by *Brian* and are counselling their followers not to see the movie.

There are worse things going on in the world. Today the Provisional IRA took 'credit' for blowing up Lord Mountbatten's yacht, killing Mountbatten, his fourteen-year-old grandson and another young boy, and wounding four others. Two hours later they killed fourteen soldiers in an ambush.

The Mountbatten thing makes me feel almost physically sick.

Saturday, September 1st

The hot, dry weather continues.

Helen tidies the house like a maniac as soon as she hears Uncle David[1] is coming, and it gleams and sparkles by the time the Vice-Chancellor of Loughborough arrives.

A lunch for ten, then we sit around for a while. I do not bring out the copy of *Variety* I bought this morning, which has one entire page devoted to the condemnations of various religious groups. 'Catholic Org Rap Orion For Brian', 'Rabbinical Alliance Pours On Condemnation of *Life of Brian*', 'Lutheran Broadcast Slam at *Life of Brian* – Crude, Rude'. It looks as though we may become a major force for ecumenical harmony.

The next page shows that there are as many of open mind as there are of closed – we are the 21st top-grossing movie, despite playing at only three sites.

Uncle David has a habit of pointing to various domestic improvements we've had done at great expense and enquiring heartily 'You've

---

1 David Collett was Helen's uncle. When I first set eyes on her, in Southwold in 1959, she was last in a column of sisters and cousins being led out behind Uncle David for an early-morning dip in the North Sea. Something about her obvious reluctance appealed to me.

made this, have you, Michael?' I plead incompetence and feel very much the flaccid aesthete in his company.

Monday, September 3rd

Up at seven and out and running down Oak Village by ten past.[1] A quiet, windless morning with much cloud. Straight up to the crest of Parliament Hill, then through beech and oak woods to Kenwood. A half dozen other runners and as many people again walking their dogs.

I do feel much better prepared for the day. This should be the start of the 'new work' season.

Wednesday, September 5th

Attack Parliament Hill in the gleaming early morning sunlight, a haze of warmth to come, through which trees and spires can be glimpsed from across broad fields. The very best morning so far – the freshness of the air and the shafts of sunlight piercing the dark ceiling of oaks and beeches are quite dazzling.

Mind you, I can only move with difficulty for the rest of the day.

George Harrison calls. He has just come back from appearing in court in his continuous saga of the fight for Allen Klein's Beatle money. He said he was very nervous before taking the stand (he went to the lavatory three times before he even left for the court-house). He went to see *Brian* – found a one-third black audience and a row of orthodox Jews – all enjoying it.

But he does tell me of an exquisite piece of justice. Whom should George find himself in the first class lounge at Kennedy with, but Bernard Delfont – the man who turned down *Life of Brian*. George was not backward in going forward and in an informal way enquired whether or not Bernie was acquainted with the fact that Python had taken $1 million already. George thanked him profusely. A heartfelt thanks – echoed by us all.

With Brian *storming the US box office, Denis was increasingly keen to fly the Pythons to America to discuss our future together.*

1 After regular running at Sag Harbor I decided to make it part of my regime in London.

Thursday, September 6th

Up to 80 today as the hot weather continues. A poem from Norman Rosten – 'Good news, about spokesmen for Catholics and Jews' – inspired by the ecumenical outcry.

Denis O'Brien calls. He is assiduous in his efforts to make us all want to come over next week and anxious to assure me, whom I think he sees as chief opposition, that it will be worthwhile.

This evening all the Pythons meet at Anne's to discuss it. As we sit around, it's John who asks 'Isn't there someone missing?' We all agree that we have this sensation whenever the Python group assembles nowadays. The unknown Python. The present 'seventh' Python (taking over from Neil Innes) arrives a moment or two later in the person of George Harrison.

To Odin's for a nice meal and too much wine. Eric, over a glass of champagne, checks round the table, revealing that three Pythons are broke – himself, GC and TJ – and three aren't. George tells tales of the Beatles – of the hugely dominant Yoko who has reduced J Lennon to a housewife, of George's liking for Paul and his 'ego', and Ringo who's ... 'You know, very simple'. Other little glimpses into the lives of the rich and famous – like the fact that George admits (with a smile acknowledging the absurdity) that he doesn't buy clothes any more. Clothes come to him.

And, having once again outlasted all other diners, we meander back to Park Square West. It's a full moon and the entire kerb is taken up with Python cars – George's little black Porsche, John's dirty Rolls, my Mini, Terry J's yellow Volkswagen Polo, Gilliam's mighty yellow Volkswagen tank and G Chapman's rented Mercedes.

Loud farewells, door slams, car tyres reversing on the road and the Python fleet heads off in the moonlight to find a way out of Regent's Park.

Wednesday, September 12th, Plaza Hotel, New York

Fixx would have been proud of me.[1] Knowing from previous experience that I would not sleep much after six this morning and spurred on by

---

1 James E Fixx wrote the influential *Complete Book of Running* (1977), which used to inspire me whenever I felt like giving up. The author, rather unfortunately, died of a heart attack in 1984, whilst out running.

the gradually expanding pink-gold rim around Central Park, promising another clear, hot day, I did my ten minutes' warm-up and forsook the thickpile carpets and the marble halls of the Plaza for the worn and scruffy herbiage of Central Park.

It was worth the effort, for I ran well and easily and enjoyed passing the Guggenheim and the Frick and the Met before most New Yorkers were up. But as the time neared seven joggers poured in from all the entries and exits. Very different to the solitude of the Heath.

Rang Al in Sag Harbor – a bleary, but heroic voice. He has Terry's two French lady friends staying with him,[1] and has fallen passionately in love with one of them. As Al says, 'As soon as she slipped her top off when we went bathing in the ocean, I knew she was the girl for me!' So, stirrings at Sag.

Denis O'B, eyes sparkling like a child with a new toy, buttonholes each of us with the good news that 600 cinemas throughout the US will be taking *Brian* by early October and, because of the performance and reputation of the movie so far, Warner's have been able to do deals split 90–10 with the exhibitors (90 to Warner's, 10 to the exhibitors). The *Grail*'s deals were 50–50 usually.

Thursday, September 13th, New York

Another early-morning run. It's becoming addictive. Up to 96th Street and back by 7.35. The good weather goes on.

To the Navarro for an interview (me and TG) for *Chapter One*, a publishing magazine. Then at twelve I stand in for Eric in an interview for the *Washington Post* book column.

We chat for a half-hour, but I take a while to settle, having been far more rattled than I should have been by EI's outburst over our Tom Snyder *Tomorrow* show interview. Eric, who has become far more obsessed with the interviews than I would have expected from such a press-hater (he's already looked at our *Good Morning America* on tape twice), berates me for mentioning the *Gay News* blasphemy case and the Jorgen Therson *Sex Life of Christ* in the same breath as *Brian*.

The Snyder interview was not just about *Brian* – that got good plugs – it was also about censorship, and that's why I instanced the two cases.

---

1 One had been an au pair at the Joneses' in London. They were on a budget trip to the US so Terry had asked Al if he could put them up.

It's a one o'clock in the morning show, it was a relief to be able to talk about our concerns in some detail – and it now turns out that Eric is in favour of censorship – at least in interviews, which I can't accept.

Back to the Navarro – this in itself quite an exciting little trip, as The Who's fans are thick outside the hotel, and word has gotten around that Pythons *and* George Harrison are also in there. George walks with practised skill, firmly ahead and steadfastly refusing to even see anybody. 'Pretend they're invisible, it's the only way.'

At Terry Gilliam's apartment, with fine views of the New York canyons below, a party develops. Eric is by now utterly mellow and a quite changed man. He apologises for this morning's episode and says he has since rung a friend in LA, who thought the *Tomorrow* interview was very good.

A photographer from the *Post* has now joined Cindy Stivers, the *Post* reporter. We pose for photographs outside the restaurant – all lying slumped on the pavement with empty gin bottles. Will we regret it in the morning?

Friday, September 14th, New York

This morning I passed a paper on the newsstand called *Home Reporter*, with a banner front page: 'Clergy Ban Python Film'. Inside a massively misinformed report of the movie (Brian is Christ, of course), being banned in England and how a new group calling themselves Citizens Against Blasphemy are planning a demonstration on Sunday to try and get the film taken off here. Also notice that the *New York Post* carries a spread of drunken Pythons lying on the sidewalk outside a New York restaurant.

Finish reading TG's *Brazil* script. Rather dull characters complicate an otherwise quite striking visual feel. Later in the evening, when we are all taken to Elaine's by Denis and George, TG and I talk about it. He's near desperation on the script – knows what needs to be done, but can't do it himself.

Champagne in my suite with Al Levinson and Claudie, the French lady to whom he has lost his heart. She is indeed lovely – slim, long dark hair framing a small face with lively eyes. She is obviously quite taken aback by the champagne and Plaza style – and when George H comes down to join us for a drink, her smashing eyes widen to 70 mill. George, so nice and so straight, disarms her.

He brings a tape of some Hoagy Carmichael[1] songs – one of which he's thinking of recording – whilst the remains of Hurricane Frederick finally reach Manhattan with a brief but impressive display of lightning and sheeting rain outside.

Sunday, September 16th

By limousine to the 59th Street helicopter terminal, where the Warner Bros chopper awaits to take us to Fisher's Island.

As we whirl up over the East River and over La Guardia Airport, read the visitors' book. It's headed by Frank and Barbara Sinatra.

Below, a perfect day. Hundreds of yachts fill Long Island Sound and we keep at a 120-mph speed and a height of 2,000 feet and maintain course up the mainland shoreline, with a clear view of the Good Life of America below us. Sailing boats, swimming pools, houses on the water – a huge, middle-class commuter belt stretches, unbroken by farmland or parkland, right up the NY and Connecticut coast as far as New London, where we turn and head across the untroubled blue waters to Fisher's Island.

Up the length of the island, swing round over the point and then down onto the gravel pathway right outside Denis' front door.

In the evening, after dinner, George and Eric bring guitars out, and we sing the oldies – including many Beatles songs which George can't remember.

Monday, September 17th, White Caps, Fisher's Island

A leisurely breakfast – banana bread and corn bread and nut, honey and cream spreads, and good, fresh fruit and tasty coffee – discreetly provided by the two girls in the kitchen.

Then to business. Denis had softened us up the night before, when we had a pre-meeting meeting to discuss agendas, etc, so it was no surprise to us when he began his pitch this morning by strongly advising a sooner-rather-than-later schedule on the new movie. The argument being that he would like to strike while *Brian* is hot and likely to get hotter with the 600-cinema release this coming Thursday.

1 Hoagland Carmichael (1899–1981) was a jazz musician and composer who wrote some all-time classics such as 'Georgia on My Mind' and 'Up a Lazy River'.

Warner's want a deal, and Paramount too. Denis reckons at the moment he can, with a few trimmings, go to Warner's and get a percentage of gross deal. Something like 10 or 15% of gross – which means 10 or 15 cents of every dollar paid at the box-office. (Usually this would be a percentage of distributor's gross.) He would like to try and prise *Grail* away from Cinema 5 and give it to Warner's together with our German film as a double-bill pot-boiler for next summer.

Enthused by Denis' evangelical approach, and in good spirits because of *Brian*'s success here, there is little opposition to a tighter schedule to the new movie than that discussed at L'Etoile in mid-August. In fact, by the end of the morning session we have agreed to a delivery date for the finished movie in November 1981. Shooting would be in March/April 1981.

Before lunch we held a Monty Python Walking on the Water competition in the swimming pool. I got slightly further than Terry.

Tuesday, September 18th, Fisher's Island

After breakfast we spread out on Denis' impeccably well-chosen sofas and armchairs and begin our first group session on the fourth film.

It's rather a desultory affair.

I think that JC brings up the same sequence that he did when we first began *Brian*. In which a spacecraft with alien beings looking just like us lands. The beings emerge, give a stirring message of hope to the world, turn to re-enter their ship and find they've locked themselves out.

Other suggestions are a sci-fi movie of a vision of the future where everything's almost exactly the same. Or a state of war – but a war which is always in the background. Or a vision of hell, or Monty Python's 'Utopia'.

Denis, walking by the pool, looks anxiously at us for signs of A Great Breakthrough or A Hugely Commercial Idea, or at the very least some outward and visible sign that genius has been at work.

After lunch we desert the sun reluctantly and listen to Denis describing the 'structuring' of our future earnings.

In a scenario which is more like what one reads in the back of *Private Eye*, Denis tells us of the bizarre odyssey that some of our earnings will make, via Holland, Panama and Switzerland. Denis speaks of all this with the zeal of a fiendishly clever scientist who cannot help but be light years ahead of governments and bureaucracy and officialdom.

Not that Denis is sensational as he tells us of this wonderland of vastly increased wealth. He is dependable Denis – with his reassuring eyes, balding, domed head and affectionate bear-like presence. But occasionally John and I have to laugh when he strays into the satirisable. He talks of a company called Ganga Distributors: 'An old-established company – a company which we have representatives with … and … and I would gladly let the world know that.'

When we re-emerge into the dwindling sunlight around the pool at 5.30 this afternoon, we have all become accomplices in something most of us don't understand.

Terry J and I bathe in a brisk, bracing, choppy sea below Henry Luce's house. There's a fine sunset.

Drinks are a little quieter. After dinner there is Calvados, but no sing-a-long. Terry J becomes voluble over politics, over progress and the lack of it since the fourteenth century, and Denis joins the rest of us, until he receives a quite gratuitously shrill attack from TJ during the 'debate'. Denis' eyes momentarily widened, as if to say 'Is he often like this?'

Wednesday, September 19th, Fisher's Island

Last run. This time 45 minutes non-stop with sprints. The island seems empty. I frighten hen pheasants, rabbits, crows and water rats as I pad by. The sun warms me and when I get back to White Caps there's only Brian, the major-domo, around. Bathe, then luxuriate in the jacuzzi.

As if a symbol of our new life under O'Brien, we leave the States majestically. Fresh and tingling from the massage pool, we're served fresh fruit and coffee breakfast, then a helicopter lifts us off from outside the front door, heads us over Long Island, passing over and around Sag in which I was running a little over a month ago, along the sun-filled shoreline into JFK, where a coach transfers us to the Concorde lounge, then across to darkening London in three hours, sixteen minutes.

Sunday, September 23rd

Terry G comes round in the evening and gives me the first 'unofficial' inkling of *Brian*'s progress in the States. Apparently one and a half million dollars were taken in the first couple of days (Thursday/Friday) and Warner's are now looking beyond a $25 million gross.

Rain comes down from heavy, darkening skies as I sit in my work-room talking with TG about his future plans – *Brazil* or *Theseus*.

Apparently John Calley liked *Jabberwocky*. TG is caught. He has stated that he will and must do his own movie in the next two years. He only wants to do animation and a bit of performing for Python. Can he do both and resist Eric's suggestion that he alone should direct Python 4?

Tuesday, September 25th

Yesterday morning I began my new 'finish the play' schedule. Up in my work-room by nine o'clock. Unplug the phone and concentrate solely on the play until one.

Good progress yesterday and today. It's taking a more serious turn, which I'm happy with.

Wednesday, September 26th

Morning's work curtailed in order to get to Shepperton for a board meeting. Arrive there soon after 1.30. All sorts of men in green tights with leafy costumes and panto-style helmets wandering about. A group of dwarfs, smoking. Charles Gregson is about the first person I see in modern dress. *Flash Gordon* is filming crowd scenes today.

I am extremely happy that we choose Hall Ellison as the best of the three catering bids. They are independent. The other two are sub-sidiaries, of Trust House Forte in one case, and Grand Met in the other.

Both THF and Grand Met emphasise economy, cost-effectiveness and profit maximisation and hardly mention food at all. Hall Ellison propose to pay their chef a weekly salary of £115.00 and their manager £120.00. THF would pay the chef £75.00 and the manager £134.00.

To Methuen for a preliminary meeting on the launch of *Monty Python's Scrap Book* on November 15th. So good to be amongst publishers who actually sell books. I feel very well-disposed towards Geoffrey, Jan H and David Ross. They've stood by us well. Geoffrey gives TJ and me a copy each of a new edition of Noël Coward's plays, because one of the plays in the collection was said to have had its first performance at Oflag VIIB and lists the POWs who made up the cast.

Thursday, September 27th

Talk to Denis O'B after breakfast. He says he's almost 'too embarrassed' to talk about *Brian* figures, but on the first three days of our 'break' in the US (this is film-man's jargon for first nationwide exposure), we have broken nine house records and done 250% better business than Warner's next best this summer – *The In-Laws*. He confirms the figure of one and a half million dollars taken in the first three days in 120 cinemas.

Work on with the play – keeping my feet on the ground until 2.30-ish.

At four down to Donovan's for a check-up and I record him doing a radio commercial for *Brian* – 'Hello, I'm Michael Palin's dentist' – to the effect that Michael requires all the money he can get to pay for expensive dental treatment. This is an extension of the 'interviews with our mothers' idea, which has produced at least one gem – from John's mother, in which she shows immaculate comic timing in pleading for money to keep her in her old age.

Friday, September 28th

Variety calls *Brian* variously 'Swell', 'Fat', 'Potent', 'Brawny', 'Loud', 'Smash', 'Booming' and 'Hot' – and it looks like the biggest-grossing film in the US this last week in September.

Visit EuroAtlantic in mid-afternoon. I meet Mark de Vere Nicholl, Philip McDanell (frighteningly young, like an elder brother of Tom) and others of benign Denis's rather Kensingtonian staff. The offices and the building in Cadogan Square are clean-limbed, neat, elegant and cool without forcing any effect of dynamism or modernity.

Denis talks first of *Jabberwocky*, which both he and Calley feel is a small masterpiece. Denis feels bound to ask me why Terry G, after proving his directorial ability so clearly in *Jabberwocky*, didn't get to handle *Life of Brian*. So I try to fill him in on a little Python folklore.

From Denis' I drive to Shepherd's Bush to John Jarvis' cutting rooms, where JC is on the final stages of preparation of the Pythonised travelogue[1] which will make up the complete all-Python bill when the *Life of Brian* opens in London.

---

1 It was a traditional, bland piece about Venice, made special by John's commentary – 'gondolas, everywhere fucking gondolas'.

John is in his element with the slowly building rant, which he can take to hysteria and beyond like no one else I know. Suggest a couple of cuts which he seems happy with.

Wednesday, October 3rd

Python's *Life of Brian* has made No. 1 on the latest *Variety* chart. One year to the day since we were packed in a tiny upper room of the Ribat in Monastir, ours is the film most people in America want to see.

Maybe subconsciously this reassuring state of affairs propels me to the end of the second act of my play.

Thursday, October 4th

Out in the evening with Denis O'B, Inge and John Calley, who is in town for a couple of days.

Calley asked a few leading questions of the 'what next for you?' variety as we ate in the cosily sumptuous surroundings of Walton's restaurant. Denis steered him towards the 'Roger of the Raj' *Ripping Yarn* and I told Calley of my fondness for Indian subjects – and the British in India – eccentricity developing there quite splendidly. He seemed very keen for me to do a *Ripping Yarn* movie, which was nice.

But he was tired and popped into his waiting Rolls after the meal.

Friday, October 5th

Talked to Denis in the morning. He said that John Calley had called him before leaving Heathrow to tell me or any other Python that any recce to India would be paid for by Warner Brothers.

Saturday, October 6th

Drop in on George at Friar Park. He's about to have his breakfast (onions, egg and peppers (green)). I apologise for arriving too early, but George (half-way into a new beard) assures me that he's been up a while, and out planting his fritillaries.

He takes the gardening very seriously and has a bulb catalogue, which he refers to now and then in between telling me of the $200 million suit the Beatles are bringing against the management of *Beatlemania,* a live show in the US using their look-alikes.

He hasn't heard that *Brian* is No. 1, but is greatly chuffed at the news and shakes my hand.

'Now you can all have one of these,' says George, nodding round at Friar Park.

'The trouble is,' I have to say, 'I'm really happy where I am.'

'Nonsense, Palin,' replies the Quiet One, 'you'll have a mansion and like it!'

I enjoy George's company and I think he mine. Despite all his trappings he's a down-to-earth, easy-to-please character.

Have promised to take Tom and some friends on a pre-eleventh-birthday treat. We drive down to South Ken and visit the Science, Geology and Natural History Museum (which has a worthy ecology exhibition) and then to Wolfe's in Park Lane for highly expensive hamburgers. The children delight in telling me in large stage whispers how pricey everything is … 'Cor! Coca-Cola 50p!' 'You can get a can in the shops …' and so on. It's like the Young Consumers' Club.

Sunday, October 7th

Into the sixth week of dry, warm and sunny weather. I am much lifted by the Sunday press previews of the new *Ripping Yarns.* All papers carry extensive details and are uniformly glad to see the series back. 'Topping treat of the season so far' says Purser, and *The Observer* are very nice. All helps to counter *Time Out*'s 'return of this desperately disappointing series'.

Feel tired, but rally to take the family down to Dulwich. Family lunch with all the Herberts (Jeremy just about to go up to York University for first term). Conker hunting along past Dulwich Picture Gallery in the afternoon.

Monday, October 8th

Begin work on the third act of the play. I feel committed to it now and am writing eagerly and easily – as if I'm now warmed-up, loosened up to the task and the end is in sight. I think I might actually make the self-imposed deadline of the end of October.

Over to Cadogan Square to talk to Denis O'B. He is off to the US on

Wednesday to begin negotiations with Warner's for the next Python movie. He wants 15% of the gross for the Pythons. Unheard of.

This afternoon in Denis' small, rather endearingly cramped upper-room office, with bottles of Penrhos Porter on the table, we talk about Redwood and the future. Denis is hard. He says that he wouldn't really mind if everyone involved with the studio left tomorrow – he could put people in to run it. He wants to protect and to use my £80,000 involvement in the studio to give me control and a steady profit – and to stop the rather generous but disorganised drift in the running of Redwood's affairs.

All good sound business sense, but I have to fight hard for the consideration of the personal side and the relationships and obligations I feel I have with André, which cannot be easily commercially quantified.

I drive home feeling a little oppressed, knowing that all this will not be easy and feeling that Denis is being more destructive than constructive and is in danger of putting the whole spirit of Redwood and Neal's Yard – the fun and the enjoyment – in jeopardy.

Tuesday, October 9th

To lunch at the Trattoria San Angelo in Albemarle Street with Aidan Chambers, who wants me to write a children's book for Macmillan.

He brightens my day considerably. We are both northerners; he has a very blunt and untwee attitude to children's books. He's always fighting publishers for the right to be as open as possible with kids and to avoid either patronising or pretentious writing. I agree, for a tiny sum, to write one of the three new books for 8–11-year-olds. He's trying to get Joyce Grenfell to do the other one.

Denis calls with another incredible piece of news. Before leaving for the US he was collating all the info on *Jabberwocky*, saw the agreement with me and was shocked. He could not believe that I was only getting 1½% and told John Goldstone that he would not dream of speaking to Warner's on *Jabberwocky*'s behalf unless the percentages for me and TG were greatly improved. Within a couple of hours Denis had upped my percentage from 1½ to eight!

Wednesday, October 10th

More extensive coverage of tonight's *Ripping Yarn* first episode. I really couldn't have believed when I came back from Sag Harbor in mid-

August to find that all the ITV channels had been off the air for over a week, that they would still have found no solution by mid-October. So 'Whinfrey's Last Case' rivals only *Sportsnight* – boxing – for the TV viewers' attention tonight. And it follows twenty-five minutes of *MASH*, which is the most successful (*only* successful) US comedy import.

Watch 'Whinfrey' with Nicky[1] and Helen. Do not enjoy it at all, but then I never do when watching coldly at home – and especially not after two big-screen showings at BAFTA with laughter and great appreciation. The selective replaying of the audience track is neither honest nor successful.

Thursday, October 11th

It's a warm and benign morning – and sunshine rather appropriately streams in the window of All Hallows open-plan church, into which Helen and I troop at a quarter to eleven for the Gospel Oak School Harvest Festival Service. As we leave, the vicar beams at me: 'If they're all as good as last night, I shall cancel my engagements *every* Wednesday.'

Terry J rings to say that the show was approved of very much in Camberwell. So the day is bright.

Drive to Notting Hill to buy a birthday present for Helen. Wander about. To BAFTA by 2.30 to do an interview with Ivan Waterman of the *News of the World*. I'm thankful of being warned by Maggie Forwood of the *Sun* on Tuesday that Waterman was 'very keen' and always muttering 'must make it dirtier ...' He seems to be quite bright.

But I have to guffaw when, at about ten past three, as burly BAFTA ladies are hoovering under our feet he asks 'And finally, sex?'

At nine the phone rings. It's Al from Sag Harbor. He's decided to marry Claudie. He wants me to investigate the possibility of a register office wedding in Hampstead in mid-November. He would like a gathering of 'just a very few people' and he and Claudie want to come and stay at No. 2 for a while after the wedding. 'We're a couple of old romantics, Mike. She's rung her sister, and I've rung you. You're the second to know.'

I am unaccountably depressed by the news. Why he should feel he has to marry her, I cannot totally understand. Lovely girl though she seemed. It's Al's huge, warm, lovely, romantic soul welling out of him

---

1 Nicky Boult, Helen's niece and a newly qualified teacher, who was staying with us.

with happiness. And as such I don't think he is in a fit state to decide on marriage. He is not yet back in life. He may think he is, but his affair with Claudie is still too much like a dream, I fear, for the reality to be anything other than anti-climax. I would rather big A had got back into the mainstream of life – a job, an interest, a project that brought him back amongst people – than pursuing so single-mindedly a relationship which can only isolate him further.

I may be wrong in all this.[1]

Friday, October 12th

Up at seven to prepare for departure to Gordonstoun to address the sixth form and the Preparatory School before this day is out.[2]

In the queue for the Inverness flight, meet Les Megahey.[2] He's off to the Highlands to do a week's research for a film on Landseer. He's second in command to H Burton at BBC Music and Arts. Later on the plane – a reassuringly plodding Viscount crossing the country at 320mph – he mentions that if TJ and I, or either one of us, have any ideas for films we might like to do, he does control twenty of them a year, and has a very good relationship with crews and technicians.

On arrival at Gordonstoun, was taken on a tour of the school site by Graham Broad – the brother of David, my classmate at Shrewsbury in 1960–61. He walked me up the Silent Walk – a mile-long stretch of isolated school site, where boys have to walk in silence as a punishment. Graham assured me, quite seriously I think, that it was alright for *us* to talk. The trouble is anything he said on the Silent Walk was drowned out by the screaming roar of Nimrod and Jaguar fighters, taking off in pairs from RAF Lossiemouth – about three-quarters of a mile away!

Tea with the headmaster. A young, bright, effective-looking man, four years my junior. G Broad seems very scared of him. Two sixth-form girls and two sixth-form boys – one with hairy legs protruding from shorts – are also present. A cake is passed around. I feel I must consume my slice. It's given in that sort of spirit. Everyone dutifully eats their slice.

At 6.30, as dusk is falling, I leave Gordonstoun and, with the 16-year-

1 And I was. They lived together very happily until Al's death in 1989, and had a daughter, Gwenola.
2 Friend and fellow thespian at Oxford.

old daughter of the prep school headmaster as my guide, drive over to Aberlour House – the prep school of Gordonstoun.

I arrive just as the smallest boys (many of them, inexplicably, blond, blue-eyed and yet from Peru) are squatting on the floor engaged in some ritual prior to being packed off to bed.

The headmaster was a quite different character to the steely Mr Mavor of Gordonstoun. Tall, rambling, with that air of slightly disreputable elegance which speaks of nights, rather than days, well spent. Even the name, Toby Coghill, is straight out of le Carré.

Soon after arriving I'm taken in to talk to a roomful of about fifty boys and girls. They're all so young – most of them younger than my eldest son – and only a very few put their hand up when I ask who's heard of *Ripping Yarns*. But it makes for an easy, jolly, relaxed talk. They're fascinated by how we nailed the boys to the wall in 'Tomkinson'. 'First we select three really naughty boys,' I began, and they all titter.

Saturday, October 13th, Gordonstoun School

Dozed until 8.15, when Mrs M left a cup of tea and orange juice outside my room.

Thumbed through a book on Gordonstoun School as I sipped tea. Influence of Plato's *Republic* on Kurt Hahn's original philosophy of the school – preserved in the houses, where housemasters are Guardians and heads of house Helpers. But what stuck most in my mind was the reason why one of the Gordon family built the fine stone dovecote in the grounds mid-way through the nineteenth century. It turns out that there is a highly improbable Scottish saying 'A new doe'cot means a death i' the family'. He hated his wife, and built four of them.

Aberdeen by 11.30. Checked car in, walked through drizzle around grey granite squares. A man nearly scared me to death with a bellow of greeting –'You're my *hero!*' Neither of us had pencil and paper for autograph, so I gave him my Municipal Arts Society of New York membership card.

Thursday, October 18th

Speak to both Jack and Liz Cooper, who are as concerned as I am by our mutual friend Levinson's precipitate leap into wedlock. Jack wrote him quite bluntly advising that they think a lot more carefully – and just live together. What a fine reversal of the traditional social and moral position – advising someone not to marry but to live together. But, as Jack says, 'We're in this together.'

As I'm sitting trying to look at a rather good TV play by Stephen Lowe, there is a knock on the door and a man from the flats behind our house comes round to see if his escaped owl has taken refuge in our garden. We can't find it, and he's rather in despair because it's one of a breeding pair. Nice to meet an owl enthusiast.

Tuesday, October 23rd

T Gilliam is round to borrow a bicycle pump. We end up talking for an hour. Last night TG saw Denis, freshly returned from LA, but found him strangely low. None of the deals he'd gone to the States to make had been made – the main reason being a 30–35% dive in *Brian* business on the very weekend Denis arrived in the US. So Warner's were not falling over themselves to sign on any of Denis' dotted lines. He's chatting up Paramount now.

I gather we are now banned in South Carolina – the first *state* to prohibit *Brian* – thanks to the activities of that great fighter for human rights, Governor Strom Thurmond. Someone told me of a news item about a cinema in Oklahoma being sued for showing the movie.

So the backlash has finally hit and Denis is now trimming his estimates about the gross. No longer are we on the upward spiral towards 40 million and beyond; he now seems to be happy to settle for a total of 24 or 25 mill, across the US, which would leave a distributor's gross of 15 mill. Still way above anything the *Grail* did, but nevertheless bigotry, prejudice and intolerance – or pure and untarnished ideals – have at last shown there is a limit to *Brian*'s heady progress. The Promised Land of the dollar millionaires is way beyond us after all. Actually both TG and I breathed a sigh of relief.

Wednesday, October 24th

ITV returns, the weather changes, grows colder and wetter. The *Ripping Yarns*, which have been so well received and have seemed to highlight the sunny, gentle, equable days of early October, end tonight.

The news of *Brian* seems to set the heady, warm, jacuzzi-lounging, golf course running days in the sun at Fisher's Island firmly in perspective. Then Python and *Brian* were unbeatable, set to be the biggest, and Denis was making plans accordingly. Now the brakes are on.

Even Shepperton suddenly faces an end to the volume of activity which has kept the place full for eighteen months. After *Flash Gordon* there is not a single movie lined up. Elstree and Pinewood also reflect this lack of activity. The BBC's plans to hire Shepperton to make films for a year (which would have been excellent for the studios) have been shelved owing to lack of money and union co-operation. The 1980s look bleak – here, as elsewhere.

Owing to my cold, I've put off a proposed curry evening with TJ and Alison at Veeraswamy's to celebrate 'Roger of the Raj' and the end of the *Yarns*.

So happily watch at home, with Helen and a half bottle of champagne – and thoroughly enjoy it. 'Roger of the Raj' is now, in my book, quite restored to top status. It's been a long process of rehabilitation after the depths of gloom into which I unaccountably sank over it last summer. It's now up there with 'Tomkinson' and 'Olthwaite' as one of my three greats.

T Gilliam, who is very restless at the moment since 'Brazil' has not been accepted unequivocally by anybody, was round again this morning, bubbling over with a mixture of excitement and embarrassment. He has a new plan for a subtle sort of Gilliam/Palin link-up. I will write my children's book for Macmillan and he will film it! Simple – except that I'm writing a book, not a film script, and I won't be putting thoughts to paper until January.

TG is only slightly daunted by this. He still thinks that for the two of us to collaborate on a children's film – me the basic script and characters, TG with the visual fireworks – would be an unbeatable combination and manage to solve the problem of his almost all-consuming urge to do his own movie in the next two years. Otherwise, he says, he will go mad.

Thursday, October 25th

Taxi takes me to King's Cross to catch the 7.45 to Leeds. Dawn only marginally lighter than the pitch darkness of an hour ago has rather resentfully broken as we move out of the station, as if God didn't really want today to happen.

The restaurant car is packed. I sit with David Ross, whom I like more and more each time I see him. Droll Scottish humour. Breakfast as we nip along across a flat landscape, dimly lit by a sullen sky, to whatever awaits us at the *Yorkshire Post* literary lunch.

To the Queen's Hotel. Only Steve Race, a fellow speaker, in evidence. A soft-spoken, humorous man, much concerned with being polite – in the best way. I liked him and had to tell him that he was one of my earliest television heroes. He and Hank on *Whirligig*.[1] It was satisfying to share pure nostalgia with the man responsible for it.

Into a sort of large public ballroom with windows boarded up. A sea of faces at long tables – maybe 400 people out there. About 10% were what one might call 'young people' – under 35. But mostly they were middle-aged, generally female, wearing hats and there to be seen to be there, without exuding any obvious signs of literary curiosity.

They gave us grapefruit segments, beef in a brown and unexciting sauce, good Brussels sprouts and a trifle which looked like the remains of an unsuccessful heart-swap operation.

Donald Carroll, an American, spoke first. He mumbled, was a little pissed and his confidence dried up in the face of this monstrous regiment of women. Jilly Cooper, nervous, but attractive because of this, showed that it *was* possible to make them laugh, particularly if you quoted someone else. I spoke third and delivered a bit of half-farce, half-fantasy which I thought deserved a lot better than it got. There were many laughs, but it was impossible to get this audience to just enjoy itself – presuming, that is, that many of them would know how to go about enjoying themselves in the first place.

Katharine Whitehorn spoke with the cool, poised, assurance of one who knows exactly where her appeal lies. Quite shamelessly disdainful and Hampsteadian, and she has the profile of a rather beautiful cow. Steve Race was nice and clean and funny.

Afterwards we signed. An embarrassing moment, this, if you're not a favoured author. Donald Carroll had not a single taker. I can quite understand how, on the train back, he could refer to today as 'the worst day of my life'.

---

1 A fortnightly children's show in the 1950s, probably my first favourite programme. Hank the Cowboy was a ventriloquist's dummy and Steve Race accompanied his adventures on the piano.

Friday, October 26th

Anne H has asked to have a meeting with me. She doesn't look cheerful and what she has to say is disturbing. Her 'relationship' with Denis has crumbled to nothing. After various attempts to acquire information (on our behalf) about matters such as copyright of Python material – songs, etc – Denis became very sharp with her and they haven't spoken for two weeks.

I had fears that this transition would not be easy, but I am a little worried by the uncompromising toughness that Denis is showing to those who are our friends and those whose value and service to us is proven – Anne and André, to name but two.

Monday, October 29th

The weekend at Abbotsley unblocked the system most successfully. Worked in the garden picking apples on Saturday and quite heavy work clearing the banks of the pond on Sunday. But my cold lingers on and I feel uncertain about my *Desert Island Discs* recording. I know it's daft to worry, but once you have agreed to do the show you're committed to a half-hour's fairly intensive study of yourself and your taste, so it's worth working on it.

I spend much of this morning, then, thumbing through my record collection and redigesting ideas for my eight records. Eventually come up with a pleasingly Catholic selection: Ellington, Elvis, Elgar, the Beatles, 'Lullaby of Broadway', a song from *Oh What a Lovely War*, some brass band and a *Goon Show*. And, after many second thoughts, plumped for Thackeray's *Vanity Fair* as my book, even though I haven't yet read it, so impressed and cheered am I by the first forty pages!

Armed with these decisions, I took a run on the Heath, greatly enjoyable because of the sunshine, and, after a bath, took a cab down to the Garrick Club to meet Roy Plomley for lunch.

Lovely, rather dusty atmosphere, with fine rooms and above adequate menu. Smoked eels, very tasty and uncluttered kidneys and bacon, a rather average cheeseboard and good house wine. Plomley keeps referring to the club as 'we'. I think he's a bit of a snob and not frightfully exciting company. I feel tired and find the effort of making conversation harder than usual.

Considering he does fifty-two programmes a year and has done for the last twelve years, it's not surprising, though a little disappointing, that once on air Plomley clicks into a routine. He doesn't listen all the time and, having confessed he has only seen two Python shows and no *Ripping Yarns*, there is little chance of a similarity of interests. So it's a touch formal, but he seems very happy.

Taxi home and within an hour leave with Helen for a party at the ICA and a showing of *Brian* for the crew. About 300 people there – all the old faces of those who were either hoisting me up on crosses, or making the crosses, or filming me being hoisted up, one year ago today.

Afterwards a drink and eats. Much good-mouthing of *Ripping Yarns* – Chris Miller says that John Osborne raves about me and the *Yarns*.

And Helen enjoyed much of the movie. Very praiseworthy of GC's central performance.

Wednesday, October 31st

To an Oak Village Residents' Association meeting.

The chairperson took me aside at the start of the meeting, before I went in, to warn me about certain 'activists' on the Association and their dangerous work. Armed with these fears, and ever watchful, I approached the hall to find about six people sitting there. None of them really seemed to fit the bill as 'activists'.

Anyway, I spoke up, rather insistently, about the appalling state of Lismore Circus and have undertaken to gather signatures about it. I was almost voted on the committee at one point, when Bruce Robertson proposed me, amidst uproar, after one lady had questioned the necessity for a committee at all and the chairperson had been accused of 'intolerable restriction of debate'.

All excellent entertainment. I made a good friend out of the admirable Bruce Robertson, and I've also lumbered myself with the job of organising next summer's street party.

Thursday, November 1st

A large Jaguar picks me up after lunch and takes me down to a BBC interview at Broadcasting House, this time with Gerald Priestland for the networked *Today* programme. John C is also on with me.

Priestland is enormous – he's actually *taller* than John, but amiable and donnish. They play back his review of the film, which swings from great praise –'very funny … Pythons at their best' – to a note of distinct criticism for our handling of the 'Crucifixion' sequences – or for the 'Crucifixion' sequence period. He equates it with 'whistling at Auschwitz' and to him it appears that we are condoning suffering.

JC answers smoothly, as if he's rehearsed. I become a little tongue-tied faced with Priestland's penetrating stare and huge bulk – and the always disconcerting sight of soundless technicians behind the control room glass, gazing impassively at me as if I were a goldfish gasping for breath.

But the interview seems to pass off well. Priestland is not huffy or offended, and we part good friends. 'Here's a sex manual for you, Michael,' he jokes at one point, handing me a paperback by some theologian, titled *The Orthodox Way*.

Friday, November 2nd

Am working on the play in the solitude of No. 2 when Mrs B buzzes on the intercom, which she really can't figure out very well, so I have to leave the brief progress I've made on the work anyway and cross over into No. 4. Here I find Mrs B talking to Spike Milligan on the telephone.

Poor Spike, who tried to phone after 'Roger', but Jill Foster Ltd would not give him my phone number, is now being given the cold shoulder by Mrs B, who, quite rightly, is trying to respect my privacy – as instructed. I apologise profusely to the great man, who tells me rather pitifully that he had only wanted to say how bloody marvellous 'Roger of the Raj' was, whilst his enthusiasm was white-hot. Now, as he says, it's two weeks later and he thinks it's bloody awful!

To hear Spike thus praise the show and tell me that there are only two people who make him laugh these days – myself and John Antrobus – is wondrous music to the ear. Only on Monday was I telling the listening millions on *Desert Island Discs* of how I used to race home from school, running two miles if there was no bus, pushing myself to the limits of physical endurance, just to get back in time to hear *The Goons*. Now, twenty-four years later, the creator of Eccles, Moriarty and Henry Crun is asking me to dinner.

This was worth interrupting a morning of interruptions for. Already, over breakfast, I was forced to read TG's latest treatment for a new TG movie – this time just for kids.

I was still reading his synopsis on the lavatory at 9.30 when he called to hear what I thought. As I saw it, there were two courses of action open to me in the face of the Gilliam treatment. One was to agree, and the other was to agree instantly. After a half-hour's chat I threw in my lot – cautiously – with what I feel is a much stronger movie for TG than *Brazil*.[1]

Tuesday, November 6th

Work on the play rewrites. Alternate feelings of elation and despair about its contents. Run on the Heath in light drizzle.

Drove over to JC's for co-interview with a lady from LBC. JC expressed disillusion with the Labour Party – for whom both he and the lady once used to work. Inability to deliver is, JC feels, their main drawback.

Out in the evening to dinner with Spike, at his request, with Terry and Al as well. Everyone, apart from Helen and myself, seemed to be ill.

Spike quite subdued, but the kind, gentle and generous side of his nature was well to the fore. Shelagh said he's very vulnerable and easily hurt and a meal like this boosts his confidence. They recently had dinner with Graham, who didn't say anything. I rather enjoyed myself and was quite loud and ebullient.

Wednesday, November 7th

Heard from TG that Denis has told him to start work on his kids' film – the money will be there! So within two weeks TG has written a synopsis from nowhere, sort of persuaded me into co-writing and has finance for an April/May shoot! He says as soon as he heard the news he went home and panicked.

Helen goes out to badminton, I put the children to bed and placate my mother, who is literally counting the hours until *Brian* is unleashed on the British public. She really does fear public outcry, picketings and general national anger and whatever I say can't really calm her. I was able to tell her that the Festival of Light are now taking a much saner view of the movie and come to the conclusion that 'it is extremely unlikely that the film would sustain a successful prosecution in English law'.

1 Its working title was *Time Bandits*.

Really I feel just very tired. Tired of talking, tired of endlessly having to justify the film – to defend it against a controversy that will probably never happen. At least opening day is now less than twenty-four hours away.

Friday, November 9th

I go for a run across the Heath. Tonight is our confrontation with Muggeridge and the Bishop of Southwark [on BBC2's *Friday Night, Saturday Morning*] and, as I squelch through the now leafless beech-woods and around West Meadow, with Kenwood House a glittering white symbol of order and reason in the background, I sort out my thoughts about *Brian*, and the points that the movie tried to make seem to be all to do with power – its use and abuse by an establishment.

As I work in the afternoon on committing to paper some of my morning's thoughts, I find myself just about to close on the knotty question of whether or not I believe in God. In fact I am about to type 'I do not believe in God', when the sky goes black as ink, there is a thunderclap and a huge crash of thunder and a downpour of epic proportions. I never do complete the sentence.

Look for the last time at my notes and drive down through Aldwych and across Waterloo Bridge to the Greenwood Theatre. Over drinks we meet Tim Rice, the presenter – tall, open, unassuming and quite obviously a sensible and sympathetic fellow – then little gnomic Muggeridge – great smile and sparkling eyes – and Mervyn Stockwood, the Bishop of Southwark – big, impressive, avuncular, cradling the second of his whiskies and complaining gently that he'd been told the wrong time of the film and had missed 'some of it'. But his chaplain had told him all about it, he assured me. I found him quite amenable.

JC was, and always is, nervous at first and had asked Tim Rice to direct his early questions at me! As I found Tim so easy to talk with this was quite an easy task and I felt that I was being as fluent and as relaxed as I'd ever been. We must have talked for ten to fifteen minutes, getting a few laughs, making very clearly the point about Brian not being Jesus and the film not being about Jesus, and I think keeping the audience amused.

Then Stockwood and Muggeridge joined us and were asked for their opinion of the film. From the moment that Stockwood, resplendent in his purple bishop's cassock, handsome grey hair, fingering his spectacles and his cross with great dexterity, began to speak, I realised his tack. He began, with notes carefully hidden in his crotch, tucked down well out of camera range, to give a short sermon, addressed not to John or myself but to the audience.

In the first three or four minutes he had brought in Ceauçescu and Mao Tse-tung and not begun to make one point about the film. Then he began to turn to the movie. He accused us of making a mockery of the work of Mother Teresa (a recent Nobel prize-winner), of being undergraduate and mentally unstable. He made these remarks with all the smug and patronising paraphernalia of the gallery-player, who believes that the audience will see he is right, because he is a bishop and we're not.

'If there'd been no Jesus, this film would not have been made,' crowed Stockwood. I wanted to say 'If there had been no Jesus, we wouldn't have needed to make the film.'

Muggeridge, in his odd, obsessive way, accused us of denigrating the one man responsible for all the first works of art ever and made other thoroughly irresponsible digs. Vainly did John try and remind him that there were *other* religions in the world, that there *was* a civilisation before Jesus, that there have been artists who have *not* painted the Crucifixion or written about the Incarnation, and the world's religions have never been above a bit of torture if it suited them.

No, Malcolm was gone, set on a bizarre course, armed with his own navigational guides, and nothing we could do could prevent him going straight for the rocks. But the Bishop was meanwhile throwing himself off the cliffs. Outrageously dismissing any points we made as 'rubbish' or 'unworthy of an educated man', he posed and preened and pontificated. And he ended the long 'discussion' by saying he hoped we would get our thirty pieces of silver.

In the hospitality room we were surrounded like heroes returning from a war. I was introduced to Raymond Johnston of the Festival of Light – always our most arch-enemies.[1] Instead I found myself confronted with a thin, rather nervous man, a committed Christian, who had been embarrassed at the display of the Bishop. He (Johnston) *had* seen the film. He had found it quite clear that Brian and Jesus were separate people. He had many differences of opinion with us, but he

---

1 They had called for the film to be banned. 'Though not in itself blasphemous, it will tend to discredit the New Testament story of Jesus in confused semi-Pagan minds.'

thought the film not malicious, not harmful and, furthermore, he saw and appreciated that we were making very valid points about the organised religions which told you what to think, in the same way that Stockwood tonight had used the cheapest and most dishonest methods to tell people what to think.

Later I watched it go out and fortunately the Bishop's 'performance' came over as badly on air as it did in the studio. TG rang as the last words of the interview faded and ranted with anger for a full half-hour. He thought that the programme was Python's finest hour since the ABC trial.

Saturday, November 10th

I had only just got up this morning when my mother rang – quite incensed by the behaviour of Stockwood last night. At last I feel she realises what *Brian* is saying and perhaps feels that we *do* have a point, that religion *can* be criticised without malice or spite. She saw the Bishop as an Inquisitor – smug, fat and well-fed. Angela was with her, fortunately, and I think they both went to bed quite disturbed.

Sunday, November 11th

The Sunday reviews – the last main batch, thank God – are very favourable. *The Observer* is a rave, as are most of the popular papers (from whom I expected more disapproval). Once again the *Telegraph* shrinks from enthusiasm – as if unwilling to endorse us, which I regard as a sign that we may have hit the Establishment quite hard on the nose. But they positively state that the film will not harm anyone, and there should be no 'shades of the Ayatollah' over *Brian*.

Monday, November 12th

Final work through the play. Though I have misgivings about the ending, I deem it typeable – and Monday, November 12th goes down as the finish date of 'The Weekend'. (I've gone for the simple title – either this or a totally silly one; had toyed with '4 Letters Beginning With H'.)

Tuesday, November 13th

Thankfully it's a good day. Bright, dry and clear. To Heathrow to meet Al and Claudie off the 9.10 Pan Am from New York and Detroit. Then bring them back to Hampstead and the delightful Willow Hotel in Willow Road, which Jack Cooper has found for them. It's wonderfully decorated with lacquered wood, pot plants, bamboo blinds à la Somerset Maugham, and a big, brass bed for the newly-weds on their 'lune de miel'.

Wednesday, November 14th

Letter in *The Guardian* from the Vicar of Hampstead, very critical of Stockwood and Muggeridge, thinks that the church needs its pretensions pricking by such as Cleese and myself.

To Pizza Express in Hampstead for lunch with T Gilliam. TG has expanded his film well and wants to hear my views on the various episodes and once again to confirm my availability to write some material. I hope I will not regret saying yes.

Denis O'B rings to say that the first-week take at the Plaza is £40,000. 'Forty thousand *pounds!*' Denis incredulates in tones of almost religious fervency. It is impressive and has beaten the previous highest-ever take at the Plaza (which was for *Jaws*) by £8,000, with seven fewer performances. So all the publicity has had maximum effect.

Monday, November 19th

Started work on the new Python movie. A bright, crisp morning. Cycled to the meeting at 2 Park Square West and arrived about tennish.

Then a general chat about the world. The Anthony Blunt spy story[1] is top news at the moment. America is about to indulge in its own maudlin fascination with power and privilege now that Ted Kennedy is running officially for President. We in beleaguered England, continually battered by stories of our imminent economic collapse, at least have one of our own scandals to keep us happy.

1 Blunt, son of a bishop, Professor of Art History at London University, Surveyor of the Queen's Pictures, had been found to be spying for the Soviets for many years. Though he had been unmasked in 1963, he had been allowed to retain all his posts to avoid scandal tainting the Royal Family.

Have we not become as established as the Establishment we seek to kick? Are we not really licensed satirists? Keepers of the Queen's Silly Things, enjoying the same privileges as the Keeper of the Queen's Pictures who has been revealed to have been a very naughty boy – but will be given the full protection of a Cambridge man in an English Establishment that is still Oxbridge-controlled?

JC thinks war is a limiting subject. EI and myself both see it in wider terms. The talk then shifts, or is shifted, by TJ who is lobbying indefatigably for World War III, to a science fiction world of the future. Where very little has changed. Possibly a benevolent and very well-meaning society in which everything is attended to, but it is quite unworkable. Enormous queues to complain everywhere. Everyone born into this society, I suggest, is handed a raffle ticket on birth which gives him or her the chance of being PM eventually.

Some good chat – generally concerned with revealing the idiocy of many of our rules and regulations, hardly a new area, but there is a certain satisfaction in the combined strength of all our input.

We walk in the park, then lunch at our 'regular' round table by the window at Odin's. Over Primeur, Muscadet, walnut and lettuce salads and liver, we become very happy and it's decided that we shall not shackle ourselves with too much discussion – we shall go away for a couple of days and write *any*thing. We pledge ourselves, like the Three Musketeers, that we will do all in our power to bring about a silly film. JC warns, splendidly, that 'We'll show them how silly a film can be.'

Wednesday, November 21st

At 3.30 to the Mornington Foot Clinic to have my corn attended to by Mr Owen. A small, distinguished, elderly man working in a small, undistinguished, elderly room. But he's quite a character. Prophesying doom and the collapse of the world (at the hands of KGB-inspired anti-American Muslim rioters), as he slices into my corn and cauterises it most expertly.

Actually there does seem some cause for his concern as we approach 1980. Read in the paper today that armed men are holding hostages in Mecca – the most holy mosque in the whole Muslim religion 'violated'. And the Ayatollah Khomeini still holds American hostages in Iran. All rather worrying. But my foot feels better!

Thursday, November 22nd

Drive down to TJ's, stopping off at Henry Sotheran in Sackville Street – my favourite London bookshop – to buy a birthday present for T Gilliam, who is 39 today. At Terry's it's like old times, writing together up in his top room as darkness falls. TJ has written a classic piece about soldiers presenting their officer with a clock under fire. Really funny. We complete that and by 5.45 find ourselves with a large output – maybe 20 or 25 minutes, for the meeting tomorrow.

Up to T Gilliam's for his 'surprise' birthday party, which isn't really a surprise. Chris Miller is there and Elaine Carew and Richard Broke.[1] Richard tells me that at the BBC Programme Review Board after the *Friday Night, Saturday Morning* epic the Head of Religious Broadcasting, Colin Morris, castigated the BBC for presenting two such 'serious and brilliant' performers as JC and myself with such 'geriatric' opposition!

Friday, November 23rd

Up at 8.10. Leave the house at 9.15 to drive to JC's for writing session.

A very angry, abusive letter to *The Times* from a man called Allott in Finchley, who clearly doesn't like the *Life of Brian*, but admits he hasn't seen it. It is proposed to send a Python reply to *The Times* saying 'We haven't seen Mr Allott, but we don't like him.'

Finally we start to read the first sketches of the new movie. Eric has a couple of quite tart monologues, then I read the first of our two block-busters. It's received with much nodding and the '*Some* good bits' line. JC reads a long and rambling and not awfully funny piece about Kashmir and sex and male brothels, which doesn't go down very well. It's our second effort (mainly TJ's), including the clock presentation, which is the one big hit of the session.

Sunday, November 25th

This is the day I *should* be looking forward to but am not. I have to give a party for Al and Claudie – or rather I want to give a party for Al and Claudie – but, as it turns out, I've rarely felt more in need of a Day of Rest.

1 He and fellow-producer Mark Shivas had produced *Secrets* by Terry and myself in 1973.

Al is very morose, though tries his best. He has done little on his trip but stay in or on bed at the Willow Hotel and lately make several frustrating trips to the US Embassy, to find that he has serious problems with Claudie's visa – if she tries to enter the US as Al's wife. Al really should have checked all this out before he left, but that's Al – we love him for his romantic enthusiasm, not for his practical knowledge of the immigration system of the US. But he is down in the dumps.

Fortunately the combination of the champagne and Gilliam and Simon A and the Coopers all get to work on him. We have a little speech from yours truly and Willy presents Al and Claudie with portraits of them!

My mother survives, indeed flourishes, on all of this. The fire crackles. Clare [from next door] makes a superb theatrical presentation of two dressed salmon. The French contingent smoke themselves silly and a good time is had by all.

Al and Claudie are the last to leave. Al, with a few nips of Laphroaig and a good chat under his belt, steps out into the wet streets at seven.

Take my mother to see *Life of Brian*. The Plaza is packed. A sell-out. I think she enjoyed it, except for a few qualifications about the 'Crucifixion' ending. But the fact she's awake at all at the end of a day like this, says a lot for her strength and stamina. Remain virtually incognito and afterwards we slope off to the Dean Street Pizza Express.

Tuesday, November 27th

A grey, unprepossessing day. Damp and quite warm. Take Al and Claudie out to Heathrow to catch the two o'clock Pan Am return to NYC. Al, leathery tough though he may look, is a softie at heart, and confesses that he is very frightened of what might happen when they arrive at NYC immigration. But I try to cheer him up and give him and Claudie a small book of Bewick's woodcuts with careful and finely drawn vignettes of an idyllic and calm rural world – long before US immigration regulations and Kennedy Airport.

I hear Mervyn Stockwood announced his resignation today. I also hear that he has cancer and drinks heavily to douse the pain.

Wednesday, November 28th

As November, and our two-week Python writing period, draws to a close, I find myself fighting for time. Suddenly everyone wants me for something or other. Quite apart from TG's film looming, I'm also contacted by a BBC Manchester TV features producer, who wants me to do a programme on railways for him; four or five managements have written expressing interest in my play.

Mel Calman is almost daily in touch, like a sheepdog trying gently to bring me into the fold of his new humour mag. I have a book review for *New Yorker* magazine, which I must do by December 1st and today I have to present the *Melody Maker* pop awards at lunchtime and talk to Hunter Davies for a piece in the *Sunday Times*.

A hired car smoothes me down to the Waldorf Hotel in the Aldwych, where I spend the next three hours, drinking and talking and only for about twenty minutes mounting a stage and presenting eighteen or twenty 'trophies' to the *MM* readers' favourites.

Met Bob Geldof of the Boomtown Rats – the current articulate pop idol, just down from a tour of Scotland. He was unshaven, slouched and wore a loose-fitting yellow velour suit that looked as though it had been slept in since Carlisle. An anti-hero for the times. Nothing spruce, no bright eyes, needed here. He's a very rude man and shows his bottom at the coach window to passing old ladies. I liked him a lot.

Friday, November 30th

Collect Terry and Maggie and we drive out in the Citroen to George H's for a Python dinner. George scuttles around putting records on the juke-box, playing silly pieces on the piano and generally trying to make everyone feel at home – whereas all the guests are of good bourgeois stock and far more ill at ease with George's unpredictable caperings than with standing sipping champagne and making polite conversation.

Cleese and I decide that the house would make a superb set, for a period film. We agree to write a farce together set in Friar Park. 'Ripping Towers' suggests JC's blonde and lovely girlfriend (whom I've not seen before).

The table in the dining room is set splendidly. Table seating has been worked out by Olivia, who clutches a piece of paper as nervously as George earlier pottered with the juke-box. I end up sitting next to George, with Joan and Derek [Taylor] and Eric up our end. Excellent food, especially the salmon, and 1966 claret which was virtually on tap.

George confesses to feeling uncomfortable with a 'posh' evening like this, which I find reassuring – all the glitter and glamour that money can buy, all the success and adulation, has only affected our George very superficially.

Monday, December 3rd

To JC's, via the bank. Coffee, a chat. JC very indignant over decision of Southend and Harrogate councils to ban *Brian* from their towns. It's suggested we take big ads with all the good reviews and paste them up on hoardings in the aforementioned towns with big stickers like 'Banned In Southend' across them.

Then to reading of material. JC and GC, some very funny material (at last) of the British Raj sort. Gilliam has a wonderful idea for a cartoon in which the town fights the countryside – and one marvellous idea of Central Park in NYC spilling its banks and flooding the city with green.

All in all we have about 30 minutes of a very good TV show to show for our two weeks on the film. But morale is high – we seem to be getting on together well. TJ harries and hurries, but the rest of us seem moderately un-panicked.

An over-sybaritic lunch at the Pomme D'Amour in Holland Park rather flatters us. TJ suggests Benn is one of the best politicians around, which makes JC twitch uncontrollably. 'Why is John so afraid to be left-wing?' pleads TJ, ingeniously.

Tuesday, December 4th

I have been offered a one-hour documentary on a railway journey through England after a mention of my railway enthusiasms on *Personal Call*[1] and I've had a letter from Weidenfeld and Nicolson who want to read my novel after a chat with Hunter Davies!

Wednesday, December 5th

Work at Ladbroke Grove. John is half in pyjamas, half in clothes and dressing gown. He says he's not very well, but we sit in his kitchen and a list is made up of the first two weeks' certs. Kashmir and army are strong, but there is no coherent theme yet.

---

1 A radio phone-in, chaired, as I remember, by Simon Bates.

We break up soon after four after John threatens to call the police to have us removed.

To the school carol concert at All Hallows Church. Willy is the percussionist and Tom and Holly are the two clarinettists. Tom sits so straight and blows so hard it brings tears to my eyes. Sing 'Once in Royal David's City' lustily.

Thursday, December 6th

Another grey, unreal awakening. It's ten past eight and feels like the middle of the night. Complete the Oxford Union speech on the motion 'That civilisation ends at Watford'. I'm quite pleased with it.

Sit in a half-mile-long, three-lane jam from White City to Acton. Little to do but sort out the cassettes in the glove compartment, listen to tapes and buy an evening paper, from kids who walk amongst the stationary, helpless cars selling *Standards* with the headline 'Garages Running Dry'. Yes, there's another dispute featuring the country's top blackmailers – the poor, oppressed tanker drivers, who realise the enormous power they hold and are putting the screws on for the second Christmas running.

Decide to call in at Stanton St John as I'm early and, if I've learnt one thing from regular debating at Oxford and Cambridge it's to avoid the pre-match meal. So I find myself stumbling, in the dense and unaccustomed darkness, up the driveway of Robert H's little cottage. I see a light is on and, sure enough, Robert is inside, with a bottle of wine warming on the mantelpiece, a small wood fire, Radio Three simmering away with some piano concerto, going about his business of being a writer.

I do like and admire Robert's self-contained world. I couldn't honestly see myself sitting alone in a cold Oxfordshire cottage, without carpets, midst a slight smell of damp, working. It seems so cut off. Cut off from my sort of life, I suppose.

We talk over his proposal to write an official Python biography, which was turned down by the chaps – for the moment anyway. I don't think people could face any more interviews about the past. But I will press for Robert to be made chronicler of the *Brian* struggle. I think there is a useful book to be done on the whole controversy and its various manifestations.[1]

1 This was eventually commissioned by Geoffrey Strachan at Methuen and came out as *Monty Python: The Case Against* in 1981. It is the first, best and last word on the history of Python's run-ins with the censor.

Arrive at the Union at 8.10. The usual collection of rather smug, self-important little poseurs and meek women with them who look much more interesting.

I rise to speak at 10.35 – having sat for two and a quarter hours on the hard bench. Peter Sissons of ITN sat next to me and I whispered to him as ten o'clock struck that this is the moment when I always decide never to do another debate.

Walk round the Radcliffe Square for old times' sake.

Home by five past one. Read *Decline and Fall*. Asleep by two.

Saturday, December 8th

Drive up to a party in Hampstead at half past nine.

I get talking to a lady – a forceful, well-preserved middle-aged lady (who might have been Mrs Foot) – who knew all about the Gospel Oak Redevelopment Scheme. I asked her if it was just a combination of a genuine desire to house as many people as possible as decently as possible, as quickly as possible, and to do this according to new Corbusier-esque principles which the architects had eagerly espoused.

She said that the scheme was a result of these two 'forces', but added, most positively, a third – corruption. T Dan Smith of Newcastle was just unlucky to be caught out, she reckoned – the corruption in awarding of contracts in schemes was widespread throughout Britain, and Bruno Schlaffenberg – the planner of Gospel Oak, who once said 'Ze English must learn to live in flats' – was not immune.

Later in the evening I was introduced to James Cameron, one of my great living heroes. He has only been out of a long hospital spell for three days. Like Michael Foot, he seems to be cracking up physically, but on great form mentally. He tried to write in hospital, but reckoned it was impossible – 'Every ten minutes people are coming to stick something up your bum.'

We talked of Malcolm Muggeridge, and Cameron, with his peculiar, hissing, rather blurred delivery (caused, I'm told, by having to work hard to keep his teeth in), said he hadn't seen the interview but 'One must remember that Malcolm was, for many years, a promiscuous, drunken bum.' He said this cheerfully, with no malice.

I was able to express my admiration for the man and his work. He brushed the compliment aside – '... Well, ten years ago *perhaps*.'

Monday, December 10th

A run is a must today. Rewarded with warm, refreshing sunshine. To lunch at the Barque and Bite with Ken Stephinson, BBC Manchester producer who wants me to do the *Great Railway Journey* with him.

I like Stephinson immediately. He's easy company and straightforward. He knows what he wants – he wants to make this journey the best of the lot (and there are others written and presented by such luminaries as Ludovic Kennedy, Julian Pettifer, Michael Frayn and so on). He has ambitious plans for shooting – and clearly loves film and filming. It seems hardly likely to be *un*pleasant work, but whereas he says all the other presenters are on twelve-week contracts, he would be happy to adapt as much as he could to my needs.

Thursday, December 13th

Work on Gilliam film until midday then down to Covent Garden – to be bought yet another lunch. This time at Poons, by Peter Luff.

Peter, eager and enthusiastic as ever, had sent me some ideas he's been mulling over for a TV series on Values – contrasting the unity of tribal values in the primitive tribes he and his organisation, Survival, are trying to protect, and the complex structure of values based on a split between the intuitive and the empirical which characterises our own society. Good basic questions are asked. I have to be strict with myself and express great interest but, looking at my diary, appear to have no time for any major involvement for one and a half to two years. Peter says he's rather glad he doesn't find himself in that position.

Friday, December 14th

Determined to produce a sizeable slice of *Time Bandits* script for TG to read later today, I worked hard on 'Napoleon' and 'Robin Hood' scenes throughout the morning. The still clear skies lured me out on a run, instead of lunch, then, after a bath, I committed a rather rushed song called 'I Was Born Sir Keith Joseph's Double' to tape as my only contribution to this afternoon's 'Python Sings' record meeting.

Round to E Idle's in Carlton Hill at 2.30. Terry J had written ten songs or fragments of songs. All rather sweet – sung into his pocket tape-recorder in Terry's delightfully doleful voice, which wanders occasionally into areas of deep tunelessness.

Take Willy and Tom to the school. The concert is not quite as enjoyable as previous years'. W plays Sir Lancelot and it's rather touching watching him mouth the other actors' lines before he speaks. Tom is 'Sloth', one of the Seven Deadly Sins, but they have to sing some endlessly tedious sub-Elgarish song by Malcolm Arnold. Needless to say the audience is ecstatic.

Sunday, December 16th

On our own until midday, when TG comes by with David Rappaport, who we both hope will be the leader, Randall, of the dwarf bandits. He must be in his thirties and is about the same height as Rachel.

He is wonderful company – articulate, bright, extrovert, immediately easy and likeable. He's grumbling about his part in *Cinderella* in Newcastle – everyone takes the panto so seriously (in the cast, that is), that he feels that his and Sylvester McCoy's anarchic, spontaneous, disciplined lack of discipline is not being sufficiently used.

He eagerly accepts an invitation to lunch and has a rather chaotic Sunday repast with us. Then I take him up to TG's again. I'm very encouraged, meeting him, that he will be our man.

Wednesday, December 19th

No business lunch today – in fact after this afternoon business at Palin Ltd will be closing down for nearly two weeks, until the 1970s have been tidied away and January – which is nose to the grindstone month – heralds in nose to the grindstone year.

Run in celebration across the Heath. The balmy westerlies, which somehow skewed round warm air destined for the Med onto the Heath in early December have been replaced by biting, piercing easterlies, which will have Londoners filling the pubs and wine bars and reaching for the second bottle of ginger wine if they continue over Christmas.

Thursday, December 20th

First really cold morning for a while. The Mini won't start, which makes me want to kick it, but the Simca, the French alternative, purrs instantly into action.

Take Tom, Willy and Tom's friend Glen to a lecture by David Fanshawe at the Royal Geographical Society at 2.30. They're televising the lecture and the first person I recognise is the burly, barrel-like, uncompromising figure of Ted, the lighting rigger who I remember most from the night-shoot party in Kent on 'Roger of the Raj'. 'You must be a millionaire by now Mike,' he says cheerily. I laugh. But I know he's keenly aware of the fact that I might be.

Lord Hunt introduces the lecture. Fanshawe is quite a jolly character. Typical British explorer type and it's good to see they're still making them. 'This is the hut where I recorded this priceless music, the chap outside's got leprosy – you can see that there.'

But always unexpected touches – he shows us the simple rush mat he always sleeps on, saying that the mat is all he needs, that and four sleeping pills. He then gets the kids to hold up the box of Mogadon as evidence of the sort of thing the modern explorer carries.

He's keen, enthusiastic about life, music, the world – his motto is 'Every day is a day of praise and history'. He records African tribal music and harmonises it with Western choirs into a mass he calls African Sanctus – and it is exciting, stirring, powerful music.

Friday, December 21st

Drive up to Southwold to collect Ma. An unexpected white Christmas scene at Reydon. A shower of snow followed by sharp, bright sunshine makes the countryside look beautiful. But on the way back a storm replaces the showers and it's hard going on the A12. No one is gritting or clearing the snow and sometimes I feel as though I'm going into a black hole as I push on past the massive, terrifying, hurtling bulk of forty-ton super-trucks, hurling mud and slush at the windscreen.

Sunday, December 23rd

Deep in the murky depths of pre-Christmas. Flat skies. Chill, damp, grimy weather. The newspapers forecast a white Christmas for the south

of England. The colour supplements are flaccid and empty – all advertising budgets spent. The recession is just around the corner, but seems
to be being staved off for the moment. *Brian* is top film in London yet
again and the *Life of Brian* book is up to No. 3.

Next door to an excellent little party at Clare's. Oak Villagers do give
good parties and it's marvellous not to have to drive. Hugh Latimer,
Clare's father, a wonderful, extrovert theatrical, tells me a story of how
Yvonne Arnaud had once had 'too many greens' at lunch and in the
matinee farted so severely that the curtain had to be brought down
early.

Thursday, December 27th

Rain throughout the day. Great weather to be indoors before a roaring
fire.

Helen's mother reminisced over supper about H's eccentric relations, including Norah Gibbins who, among other things, tried to raise
money for orphaned German boys during the First War and slept
outside all year round in her garden at Seaford, under a cover of parachute silk. I must say Rachel has inherited the genes of a remarkably
strong set of maternal grandparents.

Sunday, December 30th

A cold, dry day. Light the fire in the morning and sit beside it with Ma,
reading Sunday papers.

Decade spotters seem to be rather disappointed with the 1970s. The
decade of selfishness, narcissism, introversion, etc, etc. I suppose for me
it's been a 'decade' of general upward progress – in status, work, earnings, freedom and enjoyment of life. Personally I'm well pleased. The
1980s will be interesting. Python has established itself and we are now in
an almost unassailable position of respect and comfortable living – and
we now have to face up to the prospect of what the hell we do with this
respect, freedom and comfort. They're not always the bedfellows of
creativity.

In a sense I feel my big creative push has been and gone – and yet I'm
writing as fluently as ever and taking on as much work as in those heady
days between '68 and '75 when we did *everything*. Will the next direction
be into more personal, solitary writing, using Python still as a base? Will

Python wither and die of natural causes? John will be 50 in ten years' time. But then Spike Milligan is well past 50 and still being very silly.

This extraordinarily pleasant, settled interlude beside the fire lasts only an hour or less and then I'm walking up to a party at Jack and Liz Cooper's. Full of Hampstead folk.

Met portly Ian Aitken – *Guardian* political correspondent – who's lost his eye. 'I think the cleaner must have put it somewhere.' He has a host of wonderful false-eye stories – including the time when he was bathing off Guadeloupe (covering a summit meeting of Callaghan, Giscard and Carter) and his eye fell out whilst diving. Two or three days later an American walks into the press centre and shouts 'Hey, anyone here lost an eye?' He had found it whilst swimming.

Monday, December 31st

Last day of the 1970s. Clear, dry, fine, cold. Up in time to read work so far on the Gilliam film before taking Granny to Broad Street on the Gospel Oak line to catch the 11.30 to Suffolk. On the way back to Hampstead Heath a magnificently cheery black ticket-collector waived my offer of the extra 16p for my ticket with great bonhomie. 'Happy New Year,' he shouted. It was like the end of *A Christmas Carol*!

Friends come round in the evening and we eat Chinese take-away and play games and half watch a poor compilation of the 1970s from BBC TV. As midnight strikes and the first chimes of the 1980s are met by the obligatory cheers of well-oiled Scotsmen on the box, we take photos of ourselves in celebration and agree that whatever happens – barring the work of the Grim Reaper, of course – we will look at these pics together on December 31st 1989!

Index

Read on for an exclusive extract from Michael Palin's
Travelling to Work: Diaries 1988–1998

1988

Wednesday, September 28th: Espresso Egitto *on the Adriatic*

I've just got up, washed two pairs of socks and pants and considered what to wear for the day. As we have shots that are continuity with last night, I have to settle for the trousers I've worn since leaving London on Sunday morning and my second shirt of the voyage.

The sea is calm, my cabin, which is one of the more comfortable, has two beds alongside each other and a shower and loo. A porthole looks onto the deck and a lifeboat hangs above.

The journey has been fast and furious until now. Yesterday we were up and filming at first light in Venice – we left the city yesterday evening.

I still find the nights a problem. Last night I slept six hours, but that was with the help of a pill which I took in a panic about two. I swear not to take them again except in extremis. They do so little anyway.

Occasionally the realisation that this whole project is supported on my shoulders and demands not just my survival but my wit, energy, exuberance and enthusiasm quite terrifies me. It is going to be a supreme test, and now, only onto my fourth day and feeling low on all levels, I just can't contemplate the same continuing for two and a half more months.

But I'm determined to pull this off. Failure is unthinkable.

Thursday, September 29th

It's nearly one o'clock and clear skies outside over the Saronian Gulf. We've just completed the quite dramatic navigational feat of the passage of the Corinth Canal – a man-made gorge it took us an hour to pass through.

Feel in good spirits today after a long sleep.

Phone Helen after breakfast and, despite the crew crouching and filming every word, it is one of our better phone calls and Helen sounds clear and very pleased to hear me – and surprised too. I don't think she'd expected a call from the ship. These boat journeys will, I think, be a necessary interlude between periods of intense rush and activity.

The crew of the boat are treating us nobly, though I suspect they could turn ugly if they're not enjoying themselves. Today I got up in my *Adriatica* T-shirt, which pleased them – I was promptly given a sailor's hat.

It's hot outside now – the scrub-covered mountains of Greece are all around. Glad of the air-conditioning on the *Egitto*.

Friday, September 30th

This boat trip has been restorative. I'm eager and receptive to places – especially glad I stirred myself from bed this morning to run into Heraklion. I don't suffer, as yet, from seasickness or homesickness.

Fears about my adequacy for the journey persist. I don't think now that I shan't make it, as I did that gloomy first morning on the *Egitto* – my worries now are what I shall make out of it.

My style is friendly, humorous and laid-back. It isn't best suited for revealing things about people – whose right to privacy I respect, as I would want them to respect mine. How much of the time should I be acting?

Saturday, October 1st

Slept fitfully until finally rising at 6.20 to watch us approach Alexandria.

A thorough break with Europe, which I suppose could have been disturbing, but which I find exhilarating and energising. So the day dazzles and everything, all the hard work and the rushing around from location to location and city to city, encourages and stimulates me.

All we need at the end of our first week is sleep. We've filmed well and interestingly on the whole – though it *is* hard to get people on camera to be as easygoing and informative and anecdotal as they are off.

Sunday, October 2nd: Cairo

Sour taste of tourism at the Pyramids, and back to film two interviews in the bar of the Windsor[1] (where many stars of Egyptian theatre and opera gather!). Conscious of asking easy questions, not probing enough, being almost too respectful. Always after the interview I think of the one question I should have asked.

Monday, October 3rd: Suez

Seven o'clock at the Red Sea Hotel – the silence outside on the straight, empty avenues is quite a shock after Cairo. So is the hot water, even though it's only a shower – no bath since Venice. The room is quite characterless and depressing, as is Suez. Can't wait to get on a boat tomorrow and get moving.

This morning we completed various shots in and around the hotel and I didn't have to go out. As in New York City, one has to be fit and strong to go out into the streets of Cairo, and a two-hour lay-off in the morning to write cards and ring the office was much needed and appreciated. *Wanda* is over 50 million in the States now. [The film *A Fish Called Wanda* had been released in the USA on July 15th.] Terry J starts *Erik the Viking* in Malta on the 19th.

The journey by taxi to Suez was pretty grim. The heat, dust, traffic and fumes of Cairo for the first half-hour were as uncomfortable as anything I've experienced so far on the trip. Once out of Cairo we were in desert – relics of war, barracks and endless rubbish tips.

The hotel is dry and we're all meeting at 7.30 to seek out a place for beer.

Wednesday, October 5th: Aboard the Saudi Moon 2, on the Red Sea

As of today the journey has become quite an adventure. Information reaching us from Jeddah indicates that all our options must be reconsidered. I might have to drive across Arabia – but our visas, we think, confine us to Jeddah. I may be dropped from a container boat to go

---

1 The Windsor Hotel. Eccentric city-centre hotel. The air-con unit was noisier than the traffic outside. 'I now know why they laughed at me when I'd asked for a quiet room' (*Around the World in Eighty Days*).

ashore at Muscat, or we may be in Jeddah for four or five days, losing precious time.

The Arab world was always to be the most difficult, Clem Vallance had warned. Even he is now lost for answers. So we move on a rolling sea towards Jeddah and uncertainty on a considerable scale. It will be very hot, we shall have our patience tested to the limits, and we shall have to work a hard and long day.

What's more, we have been eleven travelling and filming days in succession and a day off would be an orgasmic pleasure. None beckons. Add to this poor food on the boat and a delicate situation in my stomach. Still, thanks to Allah – *Insh-Allah*! – it'll be the longest time I've been without alcohol for decades!

Out on deck as I write (ten p.m.) are sleeping, like corpses, hundreds of Egyptian workers, many of whom are leaving everything behind for a year or more.

Friday, October 7th: Red Sea Palace Hotel, Jeddah, Saudi Arabia

Day 13, country number 9. Outside my fourth-floor windows to the left it is a modern cityscape that looks back at me, dual carriageways, roundabouts, traffic moving in plenty of space, tall, featureless concrete high-rise clusters. Move a little to my left, say, to pick up an apple from the complimentary basket, and I look down on a beleaguered, ill-kempt quarter of older houses, four storeys at most with balconies of wood and screens and carved details about the windows.

First thing to be said about Jeddah is that it has been a rest and renewal stop. Our arrival on an uncluttered dockside, even our efficient clearance through customs, thanks to Ahmed and the presence of young Nick from the embassy in Riyadh, was much less of a strain than doing anything in Egypt.

The hotel – affluent, international, but really conforming to American standards of comfort and service – may be nothing to do with the real Saudi Arabia, but it has provided hot water and a bath and space and service and laundry and room to move and gather wits.